W9-CPO-797

FICTION CATALOG

FIFTEENTH EDITION

STANDARD CATALOG SERIES

JOHN GREENFIELDT, GENERAL EDITOR

CHILDREN'S CATALOG

FICTION CATALOG

MIDDLE AND JUNIOR HIGH SCHOOL LIBRARY CATALOG

PUBLIC LIBRARY CATALOG

SENIOR HIGH SCHOOL LIBRARY CATALOG

FICTION CATALOG

FIFTEENTH EDITION

EDITED BY

JOHN GREENFIELDT

NEW YORK AND DUBLIN
THE H. W. WILSON COMPANY
2006

Printed in the United States of America

ISBN 0-8242-1055-7

Library of Congress Cataloging-in-Publication Data

Fiction catalog.— 15th ed. / edited by John Greenfieldt.
p. cm. — (Standard catalog series)
Includes index.
Kept up to date between editions by annual supplements.
ISBN 0-8242-1055-7 (alk. paper)
1. Fiction—Indexes. 2. Best books—United States.
I. Greenfieldt, John. II. Series.
Z5916.F5 2006
[PN3451]
016.80883—dc22

2006000549

CONTENTS

PREFACE

Fiction Catalog is a selective list of classic and contemporary works of adult fiction either written in or translated into English. This fifteenth edition includes 8,000 titles and 800 analytical entries for novelettes and novels contained in composite works. This is an increase of nearly 3,000 titles over the fourteenth edition. This edition of the Catalog will be updated by three annual supplements, containing approximately 2,000 new titles over the next four years.

Scope and Coverage

Books listed are both hardcover and paperback editions that were published in the United States, or published in Canada or the United Kingdom and distributed in the United States. Out-of-print titles have been included in the belief that good fiction is not obsolete simply because it happens to go out of print. Information about an out-of-print title that is reissued between editions of the Catalog will be included in a supplement.

Fiction Catalog is a guide only to works of fiction. Users who seek literary criticism, literary history, biographies of authors, and books on the writing of fiction are referred to *Fiction Catalog*'s companion publication, *Public Library Catalog: Guide to Reference Books and Adult Nonfiction.*

Preparation

The titles in this volume have been selected with the assistance of experienced librarians from public library systems in various geographical areas. Since the voting represents the collective opinion of a number of librarians in most cases, the consensus is relatively broad-based. The choices reflect both a librarian's evaluation of a book and readers' interest in the title.

Organization

The Catalog consists of two parts. The first part lists works alphabetically by author. Following the bibliographic information are notes about related works, a descriptive summary for novels and a contents note for story collections, and, in most cases, an evaluative comment from a quoted source. Subject tracings are not given under entries in Part I.

The second part of the Catalog is a Title and Subject Index. Access is provided by subject or theme, and by genre, form, and literary technique. This access is one of the Catalog's most important features and is especially valued by readers' advisors.

More detailed information about the arrangement and content of the Catalog will be found in the Directions for Use.

Acknowledgments

The H. W. Wilson Company thanks those publishers who supplied copies of their books and information about editions and prices. The Company is especially indebted to the following librarians, who were instrumental in the selection of titles for this Catalog, in many cases with the participation of their colleagues:

Beth Andersen
Reference Librarian
Ann Arbor District Library
Ann Arbor, MI

Jennifer Baker
Fiction and Readers' Advisory Librarian
Seattle Public Library
Seattle, WA

Beth Curran
Fiction Department
Providence Public Library
Providence, RI

Megan McArdle
Director of Collection Development
Chicago Public Library
Chicago, IL

Kaite Mediatore
Readers' Services Librarian
Kansas City, Kansas, Public Library
Kansas City, KS

Richard Oloizia
Assistant Manager
Fiction Department
Enoch Pratt Free Library
Baltimore, MD

Nancy Pearl
Writer & Consultant
Seattle, WA

Don Wentworth
Senior Staff Librarian
Reference Services Department
Carnegie Library of Pittsburgh
Pittsburgh, PA

DIRECTIONS FOR USE

Fiction Catalog is arranged in two parts as follows:

Part I lists works of fiction in alphabetical order by the last name of the author or by title, if it is the main entry. The following bibliographical information is provided: author, title, publisher, date of publication, paging, illustration note, price, out-of-print status, reprint publication data, ISBN designation, and, when available, Library of Congress control number. Notes regarding sequels, publication history, and contents of story collections are also supplied. A descriptive summary and, in most instances, an excerpt from a reviewing source conclude the entry. References are made from variant forms of authors' names, from names of joint authors, and from names of editors or compilers of short story collections. Analytical entries, which are identified by the word *"In,"* are made for parts of composite works. Analytical entries heighten the usefulness of the Catalog by expanding access to the library's collections.

Part II is a Title and Subject Index. Each book is listed under title, which is followed by the name of the author under which the entry for the book will be found in Part I. Books are also listed under their main subjects or themes, as well as under headings for genre, form, or literary technique, if appropriate. Among specific headings are those for persons, places, events, historical periods, lifestyles, and legendary characters. Subject headings and subject cross references are printed in capital letters.

FICTION CATALOG

FIFTEENTH EDITION

200 years of great American short stories; edited by Martha Foley. Houghton Mifflin 1975 968p o.p.

Contents: A pretty story, by F. Hopkinson; Rip Van Winkle, by W. Irving; Peter Rugg, the missing man, by W. Austin; The grey champion, by N. Hawthorne; The big bear of Arkansas, by T. B. Thorpe; The cask of Amontillado, by E. A. Poe; Bartleby the scrivener, by H. Melville; Tennessee's partner, by B. Harte; Captain Kidd's money, by H. B. Stowe; Marjorie Daw, by T. B. Aldrich; The lady or the tiger, by F. Stockton; Over on the T'other Mounting, by C. E. Craddock; The revolt of mother, by M. W. Freeman; One of the missing, by A. Bierce; The return of a private, by H. Garland; The real thing, by H. James; The courting of Sister Wisby, by S. O. Jewett; The open boat, by S. L. Crane; The man that corrupted Hadleyburg, by S. L. Clemens; The furnished room, by O. Henry; To build a fire, by J. London; The strength of God, by S. Anderson; The teacher, by S. Anderson; The diamond as big as the Ritz, by F. S. Fitzgerald; Haircut, by R. Lardner; Double birthday, by W. Cather; Spring evening, by J. T. Farrell; Masses of men, by E. Caldwell; The gilded six-bits, by Z. N. Hurston; Silent snow, secret snow, by C. Aiken; An odor of verbena, by W. Faulkner; The daring young man on the flying trapeze, by W. Saroyan; The snows of Kilimanjaro, by E. Hemingway; A tooth for Paul Revere, by S. V. Benét; Noon wine, by K. A. Porter; The leader of the people, by J. Steinbeck; Lily Daw and the three ladies, by E. Welty; Fire and cloud, by R. Wright; The patterns of love, by W. Maxwell; The ballad of the sad café, by C. McCullers; Cass Mastern's wedding ring, by R. P. Warren; The wedding: Beacon Hill, by J. Stafford; Rain in the heart, by P. Taylor; Gunners' passage, by I. Shaw; The lottery, by S. Jackson; February 1999: Ylla, by R. Bradbury; The country husband, by J. Cheever; A good man is hard to find, by F. O'Connor; The Mexican girl, by J. Kerouac; The Pedersen kid, by W. H. Gass; Seven say you can hear corn grow, by K. Boyle; Where are you going, where have you been? by J. C. Oates; Tell me how long the train's been gone, by J. Baldwin; Son, by J. Updike; Yellow woman, by L. Silko

999: new stories of horror and suspense; edited by Al Sarrantonio. Avon Bks. 1999 666p o.p.

ISBN 0-380-97740-0 LC 99-20895

"From Kim Newman's grotesque tale of zombies in Communist Russia ('Amerikanski Dead at the Moscow Morgue') to 'Darkness,' an eerie new short novel by William Peter Blatty, the 29 tales of horror and suspense that make up this end-of-the-millennium collection illustrate a broad spectrum of new and veteran talent. Including contributions from Stephen King, F. Paul Wilson, Neil Gaiman, Nancy A. Collins, this volume belongs in most libraries." Libr J

A

Abani, Christopher

GraceLand. Farrar, Straus, and Giroux 2004 321p $24

ISBN 0-374-16589-0 LC 2003-12705

"The city of Lagos, Nigeria, provides the backdrop to the story of Elvis, a teenage Elvis impersonator hoping to make his way out of the ghetto. Broke, beset by floods, and beatings by his alcoholic father, and with no job opportunities in sight, Elvis is tempted by a life of crime. Thus begins his odyssey into the dangerous underworld of Lagos, guided by his friend Redemption and accompanied by a . . . hybrid of voices including The King of Beggars, Sunday, Innocent and Comfort." Publisher's note

"This book works brilliantly in two ways. As a convincing and unpatronizing record of life in a poor Nigerian slum, and as a frighteningly honest insight into a world skewed by casual violence, it's wonderful." N Y Times Book Rev

Abe, Kōbō, 1924-1993

The woman in the dunes; translated from the Japanese by E. Dale Saunders; with drawings by Machi Abé. Knopf 1964 239p il o.p.

Original Japanese edition, 1962

The protagonist of this novel "is Niki Jumpei, an amateur entomologist who, on a weekend trip from the city, discovers a bizarre village in the dunes where residents live in deep sand pits. Imprisoned with a widow in one of the pits, he must shovel the omnipresent sand that threatens to bury the community. The novel relates Niki's attempts to escape the pit, his relationship with the woman, and his gradual acceptance of a new identity." Merriam-Webster's Ency of Lit

Abel, Kenneth

The burying field. Putnam 2002 291p o.p.

ISBN 0-399-14796-9 LC 2001-48848

Danny Chaisson "just can't seem to outrun his past as bagman to a Louisiana state politician. Years after he cleaned the stacks of cash from his safe and started to earn a precarious living as a lawyer for small-time collection agencies and sometime criminal cases, Chaisson still finds himself pursued by New Orleans highfliers convinced he has connections. This time, his ex-wife, a

Abel, Kenneth—*Continued*

lawyer, links Chaisson to a leading real-estate developer with a problem. . . . A mystery that manages to be both reflective and fast moving." Booklist

Cold steel rain. Putnam 2000 386p o.p.
ISBN 0-399-14662-8 LC 00-35247

"Danny Chaisson resigned from his job as assistant district attorney three years ago to work as a bagman for New Orleans political boss and state senator Jimmy Boudrieux. Danny is resigned to his fate—his old man worked for Boudrieux, too—but then he inadvertently witnesses the murder of a gun runner by Boudrieux's henchmen. Tying up loose ends, Boudrieux puts out a contract on Danny." Booklist

"The New Orleans setting is well integrated into the story; the weather descriptions, the slowness of people's daily activities and the duplicity of many of the characters' actions combine to create a dense miasma of sleaziness." Publ Wkly

Ablow, Keith R.

Compulsion; {by} Keith Ablow. St. Martin's Press 2002 321p o.p.
ISBN 0-312-26641-3 LC 2001-58861

"Battle-scarred Boston forensic psychiatrist Frank Clevenger is reluctantly drawn into the Nantucket murder case of five-month-old twin Brooke Bishop. All evidence points to the younger of the victim's two adopted Russian-born brothers, 16-year-old problem child Billy." Publ Wkly

"Clevenger does not spout jargon, and if you can get past the unnerving glibness, he comes across with fascinating clinical insights into murderers and other psychos." N Y Times Book Rev

Abraham, Pearl, 1960-

The romance reader. Riverhead Bks. 1995 296p o.p.
LC 95-964

"Rachel, romance reader and the oldest of seven children is only 12 as the novel opens and grows into a 19-year-old married woman in the course of . . . [this] novel. This surreptitious reader of romance novels breaks the rules of her Hasidic parents with her visits to libraries and growing independence of mind. Rachel and her sister take advantage of their mother's visit to Israel to take lifesaving lessons and apply for jobs at a private pool. These adventures leave Rachel totally unsuited to the conventional arranged marriage she finds herself in near the novel's end." Booklist

"Abraham's intense, sensitive prose and her ability to create vivid scenes and memorable characters augment this authentic, often disturbing, look at Hasidic home life and beliefs." Publ Wkly

Abrahams, Peter, 1947-

Crying wolf. Ballantine Bks. 2000 330p $25
ISBN 0-345-42385-2 LC 99-41500

"College is an expansive experience for Nat, a small-town boy from Colorado, not just because he's enrolled at prestigious Inverness College in New England but also because he meets wealthy, beautiful twins, Grace and Izzie. . . . When Nat's mother loses her job, he faces the threat of leaving Inverness and losing Izzie. The twins devise a fake kidnapping plot, a 'victimless' crime with one of them as the kidnapping subject, to get the money from an indifferent father. . . . Abrahams ably builds suspense in this novel about secret lives, madness, and mistrust." Booklist

The fan. Warner Bks. 1995 338p o.p.
LC 94-28962

"From the day Gil Renard's father died outside the ball field where his son was pitching a critical Little League game, Gil has been rabid about baseball. His favorite player is Bobby Rayburn, centerfielder for the Sox (of an unnamed city) who is himself obsessed—with pulling out of a hitting slump. In alternating chapters filled with telling details, Abrahams gradually reveals these men's diverse frustrations, then dramatically brings them together with a violent act of Gil's that relates to his other fixation: a knowledge of fine knives and knifemaking also 'inherited' from his father. . . . His eventual slide into madness is frighteningly depicted in this finely crafted, edge-of-the-seat thriller." Publ Wkly

Hard rain. Dutton 1988 374p o.p.
LC 87-18947

"A sinister deal struck at the Woodstock festival in 1969 sends a poor young man to Vietnam in the place of a rich young man, who finds a new life in California. Nearly 20 years later, the now-divorced man and his daughter have disappeared, and Jessie Shapiro, the child's mother, begins a cross-country hunt. Jessie's search ends in Vermont, the home of her husband's family and the location of a commune in which he once lived. Jessie also finds the home of the man who took her husband's place, thought to be killed in action but now returned." Booklist

"Jessie is an appealingly ordinary heroine, a resilient working mother. And each of the characters she encounters on her descent into a violent world of personal and political deception is vividly drawn. 'Hard Rain,' which takes its title from a Bob Dylan song, is infused with a knowing, affectionate feeling for the pop culture of the 1960's." N Y Times Book Rev

A perfect crime. Ballantine Bks. 1998 322p o.p.
ISBN 0-345-42384-4 LC 98-22714

"The discovery of an adulterous affair leads a brilliant but unstable man to plot the perfect murder. Francie and Ned, both married to others, meet illicitly at a cabin in the New Hampshire woods. Francie decides to end the affair when she discovers that her new tennis partner is Ned's wife, who suspects Ned of being unfaithful but is unaware of Francie's involvement. Francie's husband, Roger, suspects, too—and plots a deadly trap for the lovers at their remote hideaway." Libr J

"Each stage of this perverse puzzle has been constructed with deadly artistry, but nothing is sweeter than the moment of pure chaos when it all flies apart." N Y Times Book Rev

Their wildest dreams. Ballantine Bks. 2003 291p $24.95
ISBN 0-345-43939-2 LC 2002-43655

"Nicholas is slowly losing his zest for writing as the sales of his last crime novel plummet. . . . To spice up his life, Nick heads to a small town on the Mexican border, where he stumbles into a strip club patronized by

Abrahams, Peter, 1947-—*Continued*

Clay, a crooked detective. Stripping for the house is Mackey, who has troubles of her own. Stuck with an IRS bill from her ex-husband, she scrubs toilets and bares almost all to pay the mortgage. To top it off, she is raising her teenage daughter alone. When Mackey meets Nick, their lives are never the same again." Libr J

"The author's up-to-the-minute pop-culture references lend an easygoing immediacy, and his wry humor is spot on." Publ Wkly

Abu-Jaber, Diana

Crescent. Norton 2003 349p $24.95
ISBN 0-393-05747-X LC 2002-152907

"Sirine's now-deceased missionary parents were Iraqi and American; she's been raised since she was nine by her beloved Iraqi uncle. Her world is his house, the cafe where she is chef, and the air of Los Angeles. She's nearly 40, and inside her pale skin and green eyes she feels the rhythms of her uncle's Arabic stories and the scent of Eastern spices. Hanif ('Han'), a professor of Arabic literature at the local university comes to the cafe for the tastes of home, and he and Sirine fall into an affair of wild, sweet tenderness. . . . Abu-Jaber's language is miraculous, whether describing the texture of Han's skin or Sirine's way with an onion. It is not possible to stop reading." Booklist

Achebe, Chinua, 1930-

Things fall apart. Astor-Honor 1959 215p $15.95
ISBN 0-8392-1113-9

First published 1958 in the United Kingdom; first United States edition published by McDowell, Obolensky

"The novel chronicles the life of Okonkwo, the leader of an Igbo (Ibo) community, from the events leading up to his banishment from the community for accidentally killing a clansman, through the seven years of his exile, to his return. The novel addresses the problem of the intrusion in the 1890s of white missionaries and colonial government into tribal Igbo society. It describes the simultaneous disintegration of its protagonist Okonkwo and of his village. The novel was praised for its intelligent and realistic treatment of tribal beliefs and of psychological disintegration coincident with social unraveling." Merriam-Webster's Ency of Lit

Ackroyd, Peter

The Clerkenwell tales; Peter Ackroyd. 1st U.S. ed. Nan A. Talese 2004 213p $24.95
ISBN 0-385-51121-3 LC 2004-41211

This novel is set in medieval London. "A group of heretics called the 'predestined men' are staging arson attacks on churches to fulfil an obscure prophecy and thus, they hope, to bring about the Second Coming. But the ringleader, a renegade friar, is really working for an atheist secret society known as Dominus, which has 'the sole purpose of dethroning Richard II'. The highly placed members of Dominus are fed up with Richard's confiscatory taxes. The idea is that the rabble will be outraged by the church-burning business and the king will look 'weak and foolish' for not putting a stop to it." New Statesman (Engl)

"Of special interest to these medieval characters is the tension between predestination and free will. New ideas about God and man, combined with the Church's crumbling doctrinal control, were leading more and more people to ask troubling, radical questions. . . . In Ackroyd's dramatization, all these arcane theological and political issues come bracingly alive as the plot turns and twists through a murky world of betrayal and fanaticism." Christ Sci Monit (Eastern Ed)

The last testament of Oscar Wilde; Peter Ackroyd. Harper & Row 1983 185p o.p.
ISBN 0-06-015187-0 LC 83-45749

This novel, "a fictional memoir told in Wilde's own extravagant voice is a brilliant parody." Oxford Companion to 20th -century Lit in Engl

The trial of Elizabeth Cree; a novel of the Limehouse murders. Talese 1995 261p o.p.
ISBN 0-385-47707-4 LC 94-37348

First published 1994 in the United Kingdom with title: Dan Leno and the Limehouse Golem

"Well-known but incidental Victorian 'characters'—Karl Marx and the novelist George Gissing—converge in this mystery/anti-suspense fiction about a former music-hall actress, Elizabeth Cree, and her husband, an apparent serial killer. Chapters of Mr. Cree's diary alternate with transcripts of Mrs. Cree's trial for his murder and sections of third-person narrative." New Yorker

"Mr. Ackroyd's methods are both subtle and outrageous. Everything and everyone in this novel is so intimately connected that one reads with a sense of the world becoming progressively smaller and tighter; a kind of anguished claustrophobia sets in. The tone is agitated and compelling, by turns macabre and inventive." N Y Times Book Rev

Adam, Christina

Love and country. Little, Brown 2003 276p $23.95
ISBN 0-316-73500-0 LC 2003-40148

"In a small Idaho town, new arrival Kenny Swanson is still off-balance from his parents' divorce. A high-school freshmen, he is not allowed to pursue his passion for bronc riding because his mother, Lenna, can't afford insurance. Lenna fears her life is becoming the stuff of country songs and struggles to balance her mothering instinct with her own need for love. On the other side of the tracks, Cynthia Dustin, a highschool senior and an aspiring pianist, has yet to find a single foothold in her relationship with her hard-edged father. Linking them all is Roddy Moyers, a handsome, free-spirited rodeo hero." Booklist

"Adam's loving portrayal of Idaho ranch country . . . and her strong supporting cast of hardscrabble cowboys and local eccentrics gives depth and texture to her tale." Publ Wkly

Adams, Alice, 1926-1999

After the war; a novel. Knopf 2000 305p $25
ISBN 0-375-40683-2 LC 99-47104

Adams' final novel, set in 1940s North Carolina, "picks up where her previous book, 'A Southern Exposure,' left off. Cynthia Baird, a transplanted Yankee, is

Adams, Alice, 1926-1999—*Continued*
floating from one affair to another while her husband, Harry, is off fighting in Europe; her housekeeper, Odessa, the moral center of this particular universe, keeps turning out her ham biscuits; the local girls, including Melanctha Byrd, who is heading North to Radcliffe . . . are growing sly and eager to leave town. There are so many subplots—about race relations, sex, politics, and adolescence—that it's as if Adams wanted both to capture an era entirely and to make things, this once, come out right. The result is lovely, tender, and a little hokey, like that moment just before the birthday candles are blown out." New Yorker

After you've gone; stories. Knopf 1989 229p o.p.
LC 89-45283

Contents: After you've gone; 1940: fall; The end of the world; Child's play; Fog; Lost cat; Tide pools; Favors; Ocracoke Island; On the road; A sixties romance; What to wear; Traveling together; Your doctor loves you

"Alice Adams writes fiction in an elegant, fluid style. And even though her literary inclination is to investigate those recesses of the soul where less than noble motives reside, she ultimately brings to the fore the strengths of character that enable people to overcome their darker impulses." Booklist

Almost perfect. Knopf 1993 243p o.p.
LC 92-54797

"To talented but insecure journalist Stella Blake, her intense affair with charismatic advertising entrepreneur Richard Fallon is 'almost perfect.' Richard is startlingly handsome, likes to cook, always brings flowers. Soon, however, it becomes obvious that he is unstable: he drinks too much and flies into rages. Accustomed to disparaging herself as small, dark and dowdy, Stella is astonished that gorgeous Richard is in her bed, and even as her disquietude increases she is helpless to restrain her love." Publ Wkly

"Although the novel is filled with details about San Francisco's social hierarchies (the privileged as well as the working class, the straight and the gay), 'Almost Perfect' is much more than a comedy of manners. Ms. Adams deftly shows how social and business pressures affect her characters and, in the case of Richard Fallon, exacerbate his decline as he plunges into a series of dangerous and destructive acts." N Y Times Book Rev

Beautiful girl; stories. Knopf 1979 c1978 242p o.p.
LC 78-54932

Contents: Verlie I say unto you; Are you in love; Alternatives; Winter rain; Gift of grass; Ripped off; The swastika on our door; A jealous husband; Flights; Beautiful girl; Home is where; A pale and perfectly oval moon; Attrition; Roses, rhododendron; What should I have done?; For good

"Love and its loss is a unifying theme in these 16 stories. . . . Set primarily in sharply recalled San Francisco and North Carolina scenes, these stories are written on a plane under the skin and close to the nerve, in spare, polished prose. Special and fine." Libr J

Caroline's daughters. Knopf 1991 307p o.p.
LC 90-52908

This novel, set in San Francisco, depicts the lives of Caroline Carter's five daughters. "Sage, 41, is a ceramist who initially has more luck in attracting unfaithful men than in becoming a successful artist. At 35, Liza is the most dependable and dreams of being a writer instead of fulfilling the desires of her children and sexually demanding husband. Fiona, 33, is a wealthy, hedonistic restaurateur who falls victim to one of Sage's ex-lovers. A . . . 31-year-old lawyer, Jill satisfies her fantasies by indulging in a scandalous pastime. Portia, 25, . . . drifts from housesitting to gardening and writing poems." Libr J

"If this cast of characters and their convoluted scripts sound overwhelming, they may well have been in the hands of a less skillful writer. Alice Adams knows exactly where she is going, and why. She delivers a fluid, meaty, sexy and rewarding novel. . . . And let us not forget one of the stars of Caroline's Daughters: the setting." Women's Rev Books

Medicine men; a novel. Knopf 1997 239p $23
ISBN 0-679-45440-3 LC 96-42001

"When young widow Molly Bonner complains of headaches and fatigue, her symptoms are dismissed by several doctors, and the rare, golf ball-sized malignant tumor in her sinuses is discovered belatedly. In addition to the phalanx of cold, grossly insensitive and obtuse physicians with whom she comes in contact, Molly is also plagued by Dr. Mark Jacobs, a widower who wants to marry her." Publ Wkly

"In Adams' skilled hands, this 'medical' novel transcends any of the genre's stock characters and hackneyed situations to become a trenchant psychological exploration of physical and emotional pain and recovery." Booklist

A southern exposure; a novel. Knopf 1996 305p o.p.
ISBN 0-679-44452-1 LC 95-16109

This novel takes place "during the Great Depression. Harry and Cynthia Baird and their daughter, Abigail, run from their New England roots to Pinehill, North Carolina, hoping to escape from debt, social obligations, and boredom. Instead, they stumble into a small-town soap opera with its own rules of conduct they struggle to understand. The mystery of the Southern way of life unravels as they settle into its rhythms." Libr J

"Though this plot teeters on the edge of soap opera, it never slips into the slush, thanks in part to the sobering imminence of war, which casts an air of gravity over all these amorous proceedings. Ms. Adams's breezy, wistful lyricism perfectly captures this lovely place and golden time, just before things got so damn serious forever." NY Times Book Rev

The stories of Alice Adams. Knopf 2002 622p $30
ISBN 0-375-41285-9 LC 2002-70940

Contents: Verlie I say unto you; Winter rain; Ripped off; The swastika on our door; Flights; Beautiful girl; Home is where; A pale and perfectly oval moon; Roses, rhododendron; For good; Snow; Greyhound people; By the sea; An unscheduled stop; The girl across the room; Lost luggage; Berkeley house; Legends; At the beach; Truth or consequences; To see you again; Alaska; Return trips; La señora; New best friends; A public pool; Waiting for Stella; Barcelona; Separate planes; Molly's dog; Mexican dust; Elizabeth; Sintra; My first and only house; 1940: fall; The end of the world; Fog; Tide pools; Favors; Ocracoke Island; Your doctor loves you; After

Adams, Alice, 1926-1999—*Continued*
you've gone; His women; The haunted beach; Great sex; Raccoons; Old love affairs; A very nice dog; The visit; The last lovely city; The islands; The drinking club; Earthquake damage

"Taken together, these stories betray the changing mores of the past half-century; taken in sequence, they trace the changes in the American short story over the past 40 years, some of those changes wrought by Adams herself." Publ Wkly

Superior women. Knopf 1984 367p o.p.
LC 84-47507

The author "follows the lives of five women, from their first meeting during Radcliffe freshman orientation week in 1943, through their college years, and on to the rest of their lives up to 1983." Booklist

"The present-tense vignettes which make up the novel—told from the perspective of now one, now another of the friends—allow the author to develop her characters with the necessary mixture of irony and complicity." Libr J

Adams, Douglas, 1952-2001

Dirk Gently's holistic detective agency. Simon & Schuster 1987 247p $14.95
ISBN 0-671-62582-9 LC 87-9464

"Is the book about the Electric Monk on a faraway planet; or Reg, the Regius Professor of Chronology; or perhaps Richard, the befuddled computer whiz? Then, of course, there's detective Dirk Gently, a weasly sort, who is more interested in telekinesis than in tailing suspects. That Adams manages to bring together his various scenarios and round up his wandering characters shows his skill as a writer. His insightful commentary on the human condition is the hot fudge on this literary banana split." Booklist

The Hitchhiker's Guide to the Galaxy. Harmony Bks. 1980 215p o.p.
ISBN 0-517-54209-9 LC 80-14572

"Based on a BBC radio series, . . . this is the episodic story of Arthur Dent, a contemporary Englishman who discovers first that his unpretentious house is about to be demolished to make way for a bypass, and second that a good friend is actually an alien galactic hitchhiker who announces that Earth itself will soon be demolished to make way for an intergalactic speedway. A suitably bewildered Dent soon finds himself hitching . . . rides throughout space, aided by a . . . reference book, The Hitchhiker's Guide to the Galaxy, a compendium of 'facts,' philosophies, and wild advice." Libr J

Followed by The restaurant at the end of the universe

Life, the universe, and everything. Harmony Bks. 1982 227p o.p.
LC 82-15470

Third volume in The hitchhiker's series

In this volume, "Arthur finds himself in a cave on prehistoric earth, awaiting the arrival of his extraterrestrial friend Ford Perfect so that they may resume their travels in time and space. Their mission: to save the universe from a cataclysm." Booklist

"Arthur Dent and his motley crew do tie up most of the loose ends and manage to prevent the destruction of the universe, but the first two novels . . . 'must' be read to understand the situation, and even then it's confusing." Libr J

Followed by So long, and thanks for all the fish

The long dark tea-time of the soul. Simon & Schuster 1988 319p $17.95
ISBN 0-671-62583-7

"An explosion at London's Heathrow Airport, where Kate Schechter is about to board a jet en route to Oslo, lands her instead in a weird nursing home. She befriends another casualty of the explosion . . . and learns that he is Thor, the God of Thunder, come down from Valhalla to cope with a scandal involving his father Odin, who has sold his immortal soul to a couple of human shills. Meanwhile, sleuth Dirk Gently . . . is investigating the perfidious pair—a lawyer and an advertiser—to whom Odin is in thrall. The plot's ramifications are marvelous, bloody and irresistable." Publ Wkly

Mostly harmless. Harmony Bks. 1992 277p o.p.
ISBN 0-517-57740-2 LC 92-25457

"A Grebulon reconnaissance ship with faulty programming, a news reporter suffering from a bad case of missed opportunities, a fugitive from the new 'improved' offices of the Hitchhiker's Guide to the Galaxy, and a hitchhiker lost in a parallel universe come together in grand style in the fifth installment of Adams's best-selling 'trilogy.'" Libr J

The restaurant at the end of the universe. Harmony Bks. 1981 c1980 250p o.p.
ISBN 0-517-54535-7 LC 81-6563

Second volume in The hitchhiker's series

First published 1980 in the United Kingdom

"Poor uprooted Arthur Dent finds himself swept along in the wake of Zaphod Beeblebrox, former President of the Galaxy, as Zaphod searches for the man who rules the Universe. They and their companions tumble from one scrape into another, with the erratic aid of Zaphod's dead great-grandfather and Marvin, their perpetually depressed robot. Adams's lively sense of the ridiculous has concocted many hilarious episodes, though the inspired lunacy of the first book has become rather uneven here. Still, this is one of the best pieces of sf humor available." Libr J

Followed by Life, the universe, and everything

So long, and thanks for all the fish. Harmony Bks. 1985 204p o.p.
LC 84-19350

Fourth volume in The hitchhiker's series

Arthur Dent "returns to a supposedly destroyed Earth to build a hyperspace bypass. The night of his return, Arthur falls in love with a sedated girl (her brother says she's 'barking mad'), only to lose her, then accidentally find her twice more. She is Fenchurch, the girl who in . . . 'Guide' . . . discovered the secret of Earth's potential happiness moments before it was demolished. Her 'madness' stems from the time when Earth should have been destroyed, and wasn't, but when all the dolphins disappeared. . . . The humor is still off-the-wall, but less forced and more gentle than the other books. . . . The series seems to be winding down, but it is still an addictive commodity to its fans." SLJ

Followed by Mostly harmless

Adams, Henry, 1838-1918

Democracy; an American novel; introduction by Arthur Schlesinger, Jr. Modern Library 2003 xx, 209p pa $12.95

ISBN 0-375-76058-X LC 2002-19645

First published anonymously 1880

"A social and political satire based on the corruption of the second Grant administration, the book includes characters modeled on President Hayes and James G. Blaine. A charming and intelligent young widow, Madeleine Lee, moves to Washington 'to touch with her own hands the massive machinery of society.' She finally rejects an offer of marriage from a senator who has compromised his moral integrity for political advantage." Reader's Ency. 3d edition

Adams, Lorraine

Harbor. Knopf 2004 291p $23.95

ISBN 1-4000-4233-X LC 2004-40916

This novel "tells the story of Aziz Arkoun, a twenty-four-year-old Arab Muslim from Algeria who enters America illegally by hiding for fifty-two days in the hold of a tanker and swimming into Boston Harbor. Aziz falls in with a group of young Algerians in East Boston, including Rafik, a childhood friend who is now a petty criminal. Hopes for prosperity and safety are dashed: Aziz takes low-paying jobs, is beset by chaotic living arrangements, and, after stumbling across some suspicious secret dealings of Rafik's, gets caught up in the F.B.I. investigation of an international terrorist cell. Though the premise of the novel may seem too topical for its own good, Adams displays a gift for detail and character that takes us fully inside the complex systems of survival, kinship, and religious ideology which form Aziz's world." New Yorker

Adams, Richard, 1920-

Tales from Watership Down. Knopf 1996 267p o.p.

ISBN 0-679-45125-0 LC 96-17047

Includes the following stories: The sense of smell; The story of the three cows; The story of King Fur-Rocious; The fox in the water; The hole in the sky; The rabbit's ghost story; Speedwell's story; The story of the comical field; The story of the great marsh; The story of the terrible hay-making; El-ahrairah and the lendri; The secret river; The new Warren; Flyairth; Flyairth's departure; Hyzenthlay in action; Sandwort; Stonecrop; Campion

In this sequel to Watership Down "Adams looks in on the lives of the Watership warren a few months after the climactic battle with the evil rabbit General Woundwort that concluded the first book. More a loose collection of short stories than an epic narrative, 'Tales From Watership Down' is divided into three sections. The first two focus primarily on the rabbits' leisure-time retelling of the various mythic exploits of their folk-hero, El-ahrairah, and his faithful sidekick, Rabscuttle. The third section returns to the present-day doings of Hazel and his companions." N Y Times Book Rev

Watership Down. Scribner Classics 1974 c1972 429p o.p.

ISBN 0-684-83605-4

First published 1972 in the United Kingdom; first United States edition 1974 by Macmillian

"Faced with the annihilation of its warren, a small group of male rabbits sets out across the English downs in search of a new home. Internal struggles for power surface in this intricately woven, realistically told adult adventure when the protagonists must coordinate tactics in order to defeat an enemy rabbit fortress. It is clear that the author has done research on rabbit behavior, for this tale is truly authentic." Shapiro. Fic for Youth. 3d edition

Adams, Sheila Kay

My old true love; a novel; by Sheila Kay Adams. 1st ed. Algonquin Books of Chapel Hill 2004 289p $23.95

ISBN 1-565-12407-3 LC 2003-70809

"Hackley and Larkin are rivalrous cousins raised as brothers in the North Carolina mountains and bred on the songs of their ancestors. Predictably, they both fall for Mary, a singular Appalachian beauty. Hackley soon wins her affections and marries, only to be whisked away by the Confederate draft. Left in Larkin's care, Mary swoons for the other cousin, inviting tragedy into their country lives." Publ Wkly

"Paying keen attention to the nuances of relationships between individuals as well as between people and their geographical and temporal contexts, Sheila Kay Adams writes a uniquely private and complex Civil War novel. Adams elegantly interweaves folk songs and nature into her narrative in ways that never stray from her purpose, which is to tell a family's story." Hist Fic Rev

Adler, Elizabeth

All or nothing. Delacorte Press 1999 327p o.p.

ISBN 0-385-33380-3 LC 99-31965

This suspense novel features retired New Orleans homicide detective, now Hollywood Hills private investigator Al Giraud and his partner, law professor and ex-DA Marla Cwitowitz. The wife of electronics executive Steve Mallard hires the duo when her husband becomes the prime suspect in the disappearance of realtor Laurie Martin

Fortune is a woman. Delacorte Press 1992 433p o.p.

LC 91-24977

"Francie Harrison is the poor little rich girl with a misogynistic father in turn-of-the-century San Francisco. She escapes the doll's world he plans for her and finds love, only to have it disintegrate in the earthquake of 1906. Amidst the destruction, she meets Lai Tsin, an illegal Chinese immigrant, and the strong Yorkshirewoman Annie Aysgarth, who, together, help her build a world for herself. All three profit from the alliance and emerge on top of the business world, rich in friendship as well as treasure. . . . Writing and characterization are tight, depictions of Nob Hill and Oriental influence ring true, and pacing is superb." Booklist

In a heartbeat. Delacorte Press 2000 296p $24.95

ISBN 0-385-33383-8 LC 00-31647

"Millionaire Ed Vincent is nearly killed by four bullets to the chest. As Vincent's lover, Zelda Merrydew, helps a charming homicide detective investigate the attempted

Adler, Elizabeth—*Continued*

murder, she uncovers things about the man she loves that he'd rather she didn't know. . . . Vincent is an immensely sympathetic character, and he turns this otherwise typical novel of buried secrets into something special." Booklist

Now or never. Delacorte Press 1997 346p o.p.
LC 96-24146

"A serial killer is stalking young women in Boston, and the police are at a loss for clues. The best they've come up with so far are a composite drawing of the killer and some educated hunches. Totally frustrated, Detective Harry Jordan turns to Mallory Malone, the beautiful star of a prime-time investigative TV show, in hopes of obtaining some air time from her for the case." Libr J

"Predictably, romantic sparks fly, but there's something mysterious about the beautiful Mallory. Eventually Harry pries his lover's deepest secrets out of her and finds she may hold the clue to the murderer's identity. Nerve-jangling suspense, steamy sex, glamorous characters, and graphic descriptions of the victims' last moments will grab readers' attention." Booklist

Agee, James, 1909-1955

A death in the family. McDowell, Obolensky 1957 339p o.p.

"Six-year-old Rufus Follet, his younger sister Catherine, his mother, and various relatives all react differently to the unexpected announcement that Rufus's father has been fatally injured in an automobile accident. The poignancy of sorrow, the strength of personal beliefs, and the comforting love and support of a family are all elements of this compassionate novel." Shapiro. Fic for Youth. 3d edition

also in Agee, J. Let us now praise famous men; A death in the family, and shorter fiction

Let us now praise famous men; A death in the family, and shorter fiction; . Library of America 2005 818p il $35

ISBN 1-931082-81-2 LC 2005-45098

Contents: Let us now praise famous men; The morning watch; A death in the family; Stories: Death in the desert; They that sow in sorrow shall reap; A mother's tale

Let us now praise famous men (1941) is a journalistic collaboration with photographer Walker Evans that depicts the lives of Alabama sharecroppers. A death in the family is entered separately. The morning watch (1951) is an autobiographical novella where a twelve-year-old school boy in Tennessee wrestles with religious issues. Several short stories are also included.

The morning watch

In Agee, J. Let us now praise famous men; A death in the family, and shorter fiction

Agnon, Shmuel Yosef, 1888-1970

Only yesterday; [by] S.Y. Agnon; translated by Barbara Harshav. Princeton Univ. Press 2000 652p o.p.

ISBN 0-691-00972-4 LC 00-21147

In this "novel, first published in 1945 and now translated into English for the first time, Agnon paints the panorama of the second Aliya, or immigration, of Jews to Palestine, which occurred between the turn of the century and WWI. Isaac Kumer is a young, fervent but feckless young Zionist in the Austrian province of Galicia, whose disappointed father gives him the money to emigrate to Israel. Once Isaac reaches the Land, he becomes a housepainter. . . . In Jaffa, Isaac tastes his first experience of love with Sonya, a modern woman, but in Jerusalem he meets Shifra, the daughter of a strict religionist, and he is torn between the two. . . . Impulsively, Isaac one day paints 'Crazy Dog' on the back of a friendly stray. The scruffy canine then wanders around Jerusalem, causing the population to panic. This fantastical subplot 'dogs' Isaac's stay in Jerusalem and is interwoven with his fate and that of Shifra's father." Publ Wkly

"Though Agnon would go on to write much of compelling interest during his remaining 25 years, this would be his masterpiece-a novel that deserves comparison with Kafka's The Trial, Mann's The Magic Mountain and Hermann Broch's The Sleepwalkers as a deployment of the resources of fiction for plumbing those abysses of cultural and personal crisis that haunted so many imaginations in the modernist period. Its appearance in English now, delayed for half a century by the formidable difficulties of translating its Hebrew, makes available to American readers a work of powerful, and eccentric, originality." Los Angeles Times Book Rev

Aiken, Conrad, 1889-1973

The collected novels of Conrad Aiken; Blue voyage, Great circle, King Coffin, A heart for the gods of Mexico [and] Conversation; introduction by R. P. Blackmur. Holt, Rinehart & Winston 1964 575p o.p.

Blue voyage, published 1927, describes the people and incidents of a transatlantic voyage, written mostly in stream-of-consciousness style. Great circle, published 1933, is a psychological novel also written in stream-of-consciousness style in which the central character, fighting alcoholism, fears his wife is untrue to him and his best friend has betrayed him. King Coffin, published 1935, is a psychological horror story which follows the twisted thinking of an intellectual mind rapidly going insane, as he broods over the idea of a perfect crime, the unmotivated murder of a stranger. A heart for the gods of Mexico, written 1939, a portrayal of Malcolm Lowry, takes a woman and two men on a mortal journey across a changing American landscape into a heightened awareness of life and finality. Conversation, published 1940, probes the conflict between art and human relationships in a domestic crisis between man and wife

Aird, Catherine

After effects. St. Martin's Press 1996 215p o.p.
LC 96-3514

In this "Detective Inspector Sloan procedural, Sloan investigates the deaths of an elderly woman who took part in a drug test and the unexpected suicide of a doctor connected with the test. Quality writing from a practiced hand." Libr J

Akst, Daniel

The Webster chronicle; a novel. Putnam 2001 311p $24.95
ISBN 0-399-14812-4 LC 2001-25679
Protagonist Terry Mathers "struggles with the declining financial stability of the small-town newspaper he co-owns and edits, his failing marriage, and his long-suffering relationship with his successful television journalist father. While he fights his own demons, he must objectively cover crucial matters in the village of Webster—including the threatened takeover of a local department store by a big chain and allegations of sexual abuse and Satanism at the local preschool." Libr J
"Akst vividly illustrates the rocky road from ethical journalism to tabloid sensationalism." Booklist

Akunin, Boris, 1956-

Murder on the Leviathan; a novel; translated by Andrew Bromfield. Random House 2004 223p il $21.95
ISBN 1-400-06051-6 LC 2003-70379
Original Russian edition, 2000
"In 1878, a horrible murder shakes Paris; Lord Littleby's skull has been cracked open, a precious statue is missing, and seven servants and two children in the household lie supine, dispatched by poison. Blustery 'Papa' Gauche deduces that the killer will board the Leviathan, a luxurious cruise ship making its maiden voyage to India, and he arranges passage. In short order, he collects suspect passengers in a salon and attempts to entrap them, only to be quietly shown up by a young Russian diplomat named Erast Fandorin." Libr J
"Snappishly witty in Andrew Bromfield's crisp translation, Akunin's dry observations on the moral poverty of the upper classes are drolly set off by his lush descriptions of the material luxuries by which they measure the value of life itself." N Y Times Book Rev

Alai, 1959-

Red poppies; translated from the Chinese by Howard Goldblatt and Sylvia Li-chun Lin. Houghton Mifflin 2002 433p $24
ISBN 0-618-11964-7 LC 2001-39530
Original Chinese edition, 2000
"The story involves a Tibetan chieftain, his two sons, and a first-time crop of opium poppies that not only brings the family unprecedented wealth but also destroys the balance of power among neighboring fiefdoms and leaves them open to the machinations of the Chinese. The older son cares only for warfare and carousing. The younger son, considered an idiot, narrates, and it soon becomes clear that one man's idiot is another man's visionary." Booklist

Albahari, David, 1948-

Götz and Meyer; translated from the Serbian by Ellen Elias-Bursac. Harcourt 2005 168p $23
ISBN 0-15-101141-9 LC 2005-40359
Original Serbian edition, 1998; this translation first published 2004 in the United Kingdom
This "novel draws on a wealth of archival materials, maps, and Nazi bureaucratic records about the concentration camp at the Belgrade Fairgrounds, from where, over five months in 1942, 5,000 Jews were loaded into a truck and gassed. A Serbian Jewish college professor looks back now and obsessively imagines himself as perpetrator, victim, and bystander. Who were the two drivers who connected the exhaust pipe each time so that the fumes killed the passengers? How did it become just a routine job? Who buried the heaped corpses? What if one kid tried to resist? How could Belgrade citizens not know? There are no chapters or even paragraphs, but the spacious text is simple and eloquent, and readers will be drawn into the professor's obsessive first-person narrative in which the horror is in the facts of bureaucratic efficiency and the unimaginable evil in ordinary life." Booklist

Albert, Susan Wittig

Chile death; a China Bayles mystery. Berkley Prime Crime 1998 306p o.p.
ISBN 0-425-16539-6 LC 98-13766
"Texas Ranger Mike McQuaid is recovering from a paralyzing gunshot wound in a Pecan Springs nursing home, with the help of his lover, China Bayles, amateur sleuth and owner of the herb shop Thyme and Seasons. Roadblocks on the way to McQuaid's recovery include a series of robberies, mischief with wills, and the chilling death of a local lothario during the Pecan Springs chili cook-off." Booklist

Lavender lies; a China Bayles mystery. Berkley Prime Crime 1999 306p o.p.
ISBN 0-425-17032-2 LC 99-33252
"Just before herbalist China Bayles' and police chief Mike McQuaid's wedding in Pecan Springs, Texas, the town is rocked by the murder of a greedy developer. China and McQuaid bring their unique skills to the task of finding the murderer before the case preempts their wedding." Booklist

Love lies bleeding; a China Bayles mystery. Berkley Prime Crime 1997 308p o.p.
ISBN 0-425-15969-8 LC 96-53666
"Pecan Springs, Texas, is all shook up over the apparent suicide of Texas Ranger Roy Adcock. But there are a few murmurs that Adcock's death was murder and that it had to do with drugs and corruption. China's old lawyer friend, Justine, wants China to investigate, but China's herb shop, garden, and proposed tearoom are keeping her plenty busy, plus she's mildly disconcerted at her lover McQuaid's unexplained absences. But when China finds that McQuaid and his attractive research assistant know more about Adcock's death than is good for them, she is pulled into the case." Booklist

Rosemary remembered; a China Bayles mystery. Berkley Prime Crime 1995 296p o.p.
ISBN 0-425-14937-4 LC 95-15062
In this mystery China Bayles "discovers a dead woman—who resembles herself—in a pick-up truck. China interrupts her herb-shop business to investigate the woman's past and uncovers a small host of likely suspects. The best of small-town Texas." Libr J

Rueful death; a China Bayles mystery. Berkley 1996 305p o.p.
ISBN 0-425-15469-6 LC 95-26165

Albert, Susan Wittig—*Continued*

"A Berkley Prime Crime book"

Sleuth China Bayles, "is vexed by troubles at a Texas convent where the mother superior has just died." Libr J

"When China realizes that one of the sisters may be the perpetrator, things get quite uncomfortable. A well-plotted mystery with strong characters and a wonderfully realized setting." Booklist

Alcott, Louisa May, 1832-1888

The abbott's ghost

In Alcott, L. M. Behind a mask: the unknown thrillers of Louisa May Alcott p209-77

Behind a mask [novelette]

In Alcott, L. M. Behind a mask: the unknown thrillers of Louisa May Alcott p1-104

Behind a mask: the unknown thrillers of Louisa May Alcott; edited and with an introduction and afterword by Madeleine Stern. Morrow 1995 xxxiii, 281p o.p.

ISBN 0-688-00338-9

A reissue with a new afterword of the title first published 1975

A collection of four novelettes which originally appeared in periodicals. Behind a mask (1866) and The abbot's ghost (1867) were published under the pseudonym A. M. Barnard. The first is about an actress who masquerades as a governess and deliberately arouses the passions of the male members of an aristocratic family in order to secure a wealthy titled husband while humbling the proud family. The second, set during a Christmas gathering in a haunted English mansion, brings out the loves, hates, jealousies, friendships and guilty secrets of those present. Pauline's passion and punishment (1862), published anonymously, concerns a woman scorned by her lover who becomes obsessed with revenge. The mysterious key and what it opened (1867) involves the revelation of accidental bigamy. A blind girl who seeks her rightful inheritance surrenders it to her half sister and stepmother after the young man who aided her falls in love with her half sister

"The stories are full of the clichés of 19th-Century melodrama but are told with verve and include some engaging liberated women characters. And, surprisingly, evil isn't invariably punished. Essential for students of Alcott because these are precisely the kinds of stories Jo March of 'Little Women' was writing to support herself." Libr J

The inheritance; with an afterword by the editors, Joel Myerson and Daniel Shealy. Dutton 1997 188p o.p.

ISBN 0-526-45756-9 LC 96-29731

"Alcott's first novel, written at age 17 and discovered in 1988, is a . . . rags-to-riches ramble in the life of orphan Edith Adelon, who is taken in by Lord and Lady Hamilton to serve as a companion to their young daughter, Amy. When Lord Hamilton dies, Edith is treated as a servant in the household—until she saves Amy's life." SLJ

This work "proves that years before Alcott invented the young adult novel, she could already give voice to the preoccupations and fantasies of the 'little women' who would become her most enduring subjects." Publ Wkly

Jo's boys

In Alcott, L. M. Little women; Little men; Jo's boys

Little men

In Alcott, L. M. Little women; Little men; Jo's boys

Little women

In Alcott, L. M. Little women; Little men; Jo's boys

Little women; Little men; Jo's boys; [Elaine Showalter, editor] Library of America, Distributed to the trade in the U.S. by Penguin Putnam 2005 1092p il (The library of America) $40

ISBN 1-931082-73-1 LC 2004-48828

Contents: Little women; Little men; Jo's boys

"Little Women (1868-69), set in New England during the Civil War, introduces the charming, unforgettable March sisters Meg, Jo, Amy, and Beth as they begin to make their way into the world. Little Men (1871) follows the intellectual tomboy Jo, now married, into adulthood, as she finds herself the caretaker of a houseful of rambunctious children at Plumfield school. Jo's Boys (1886) returns to Plumfield a decade later. Now grown, Jo's children recount adventures of their own." Publisher's note

The mysterious key and what it opened

In Alcott, L. M. Behind a mask: the unknown thrillers of Louisa May Alcott p153-208

Pauline's passion and punishment

In Alcott, L. M. Behind a mask: the unknown thrillers of Louisa May Alcott p105-52

Aldiss, Brian Wilson, 1925-

Helliconia spring; [by] Brian W. Aldiss. Atheneum Pubs. 1982 361p o.p.

LC 81-66036

"In this first of a trilogy, Aldiss presents Helliconia, a dual-star system planet that is beginning to thaw from its centuries-long winter. Humans, humanoid protognostics, and the animal-like phagors contend for its sparse resources, and Aldiss relates episodes from the lives of several of the inhabitants." Libr J

"Aldiss has not only written a science fiction novel about another world, he has created another universe complete with it's own language and flavor, peopled with colorful characters (both human and otherwise) who engage sympathy and interest." Best Sellers

Followed by Helliconia summer

Helliconia summer; [by] Brian W. Aldiss. Atheneum Pubs. 1983 398p o.p.

LC 83-45062

"In this second novel in Aldiss's trilogy, the planet Helliconia . . . is presented as an epic miniature of humanity's loftiest aspirations and basest shortcomings. The action takes place on two levels, represented by the geometrical symbol of the planet's supreme god Akhanaba.

Aldiss, Brian Wilson, 1925-—*Continued*

Some events proceed along the inner rim, driven by incessant racial wars between the cohabitant Helliconian humans and the 'ahuman' Phagors. Along the outermost rim are the concerns of the king of Borlien . . . and the nefarious intrigues of court hangers-on ranging from chancellors to child prostitutes." Publ Wkly

Followed by Helliconia winter

Helliconia winter. Atheneum Pubs. 1985 281p o.p.

LC 84-45607

In this concluding volume of the "trilogy, the planet Helliconia begins its descent into a winter that will last for centuries. Nonhuman phagors, better suited to the changing climate, begin to reclaim their ancient lands, and the plague they bring panics the Oligarchy into ever more repressive measures to stave off a new dark age. As young Luterin Shokerandit learns, however, such civilized willfulness only subverts the grand, interdependent cycles of the natural world." Publ Wkly

"This conclusion to the Helliconia trilogy ranks as a landmark of fictional world-building." Libr J

Aldrich, Bess Streeter, 1881-1954

A lantern in her hand. Appleton, D. & Co. 1928 306p o.p.

"The story of a pioneer woman who, as a bride, followed the covered-wagon trail to the Nebraska prairies and lived there the rest of her eighty years. A devoted wife and mother, Abbie Deal brought a large and united family through poverty and hardship. Denying herself that the children might have the advantages her talented youth had coveted, she went through life with 'courage her lode-star and love her guide, a song upon her lips and a lantern in her hand.'" Open Shelf

Followed by A white bird flying (1931)

Aleichem, Shalom *See* Sholem Aleichem, 1859-1916

Aleichem, Sholem *See* Sholem Aleichem, 1859-1916

Alexander, Alma

The secrets of Jin-Shei; a novel. HarperSanFrancisco 2004 503p $24.95

ISBN 0-06-056341-9 LC 2004-47287

This "fantasy explores the meaning of friendship and loyalty among eight young women-sisters of the heart-in a mythical Chinese realm. Ever since the dawn of time, mothers have passed on to their daughters a special language (jin-ashu) and the existence of special friendships (jin-shei) that cross boundaries of class and heritage. Accepting someone's offer of jin-shei brings both benefits and responsibilities, and Alexander's characters find their lives both complicated and enriched by these friendships." Booklist

Alexander, Bruce, 1932-2003

Smuggler's moon. Putnam 2001 274p o.p.

ISBN 0-399-14778-0 LC 2001-19726

Jeremy Proctor "has seen a good deal of the hurly-burly of 18th-century London street life in the four years since he became the ward of Sir John Fielding, the blind magistrate of the Bow Street Court. Now, in his most dangerous adventure to date, the naive apprentice gets his big chance to play the hero. 'What a grand thing it would be to live one's life by the sea,' Jeremy says upon his first glimpse of Deal, a picturesque (and suspiciously prosperous) fishing village on the coast of Kent. As he soon learns, Deal is the center of 'the owling trade,' as the 'raw and boisterous men' who rule the roost here refer to their thriving smuggling industry." N Y Times Book Rev

"The author deftly captures the flavor of the period without overdoing the archaic language." Publ Wkly

Alexie, Sherman, 1966-

Indian killer. Atlantic Monthly Press 1996 420p o.p.

LC 96-27996

"Bodies in trendy Seattle have been turning up scalped and decorated with owl feathers, prompting anti-Indian rhetoric from a vitriolic shock jock and leading to a spate of street violence, white against Indian and Indian against white. The killer, John Smith, is an Indian without a tribe. Adopted by a white couple, John quickly slips into a delusional fantasy life in which he dreams of righting all the wrongs inflicted on Native Americans." Booklist

"Sherman Alexie is too good a writer, too devoted to the complexities of a story, to settle for a diatribe. His vigorous prose, his haunted, surprising characters and his meditative exploration of the sources of human identity transform into a resonant tragedy what might have been a melodrama in less assured hands." N Y Times Book Rev

Reservation blues. Atlantic Monthly Press 1995 306p o.p.

LC 94-46132

This novel relates the "whimsical tale of Coyote Springs, an all Indian-Catholic 'four-and-a-half chord' rock band formed after a chance encounter with none other than the legendary—and long dead—Delta bluesman Robert Johnson, who happens onto the Spokane Indian Reservation looking for the woman in his dreams to save him from the mysterious 'Gentleman' on his trail." Libr J

"Hilarious but poignant, filled with enchantments yet dead-on accurate with regard to modern Indian life, this tour de force will leave readers wondering if Alexie himself hasn't made a deal with the Gentleman in order to do everything so well." Publ Wkly

Ten little Indians; stories. Grove Press 2003 243p $24

ISBN 0-8021-1744-9 LC 2003-44832

"These short stories feature Spokane Indians from many urban walks of life. Alexie's characters include a student, a lawyer, a basketball player, and a feminist mother; their stories might be angry, tragic, humorous, or ironic—but they are all believable, and irresistibly engaging." SLJ

The toughest Indian in the world. Atlantic Monthly Press 2000 238p o.p.

ISBN 0-87113-801-8 LC 99-86360

Alexie, Sherman, 1966-—*Continued*

Contents: Assimilation; The toughest Indian in the world; Class; South by Southwest; The sin eaters; Indian country; Saint Junior; Dear John Wayne; One good man

The author "is a clever satirist. He won't hesitate to attack racist idiocy and historical injustice. He's good at turning a plot in unexpected directions and making a sequence of events surprising. The stories in this collection are all designed to shock and usually revolve around an action a character perceives as transgressive." N Y Times Book Rev

Alfred Hitchcock presents: Stories not for the nervous. Random House 1965 363p o.p.

Short stories included are: To the future, by R. Bradbury; Rivers of riches, by G. Kersh; Levitation, by J. P. Brennan; Miss Winters and the wind, by C. N. Govan: View from the terrace, by M. Marmar; The man with copper fingers, by D. L. Sayers; The twenty friends of William Shaw, by R. E. Banks; The other hangman, by C. Dickson; Don't look behind you, by F. Brown; No bath for the Browns, by M. Bennet; The uninvited, by M. Gilbert; Dune roller, by J. May; Something short of murder, by H. Slesar; The golden girl, by E. Peters; The boy who predicted earthquakes, by M. St. Clair; Walking alone, by M. A. deFord; For all the rude people, by J. Ritchie; The dog died first, by B. Fischer; Room with a view, by H. Dresner; Lemmings, by R. Matheson; White goddess, by I. Seabright; The substance of martyrs, by W. Sambrot; Call for help, by R. Arthur

Algren, Nelson, 1909-1981

The man with the golden arm; a novel. Doubleday 1949 343p o.p.

"Set in the slums of Chicago, the novel, which won a National Book Award in 1950, tells the story of Frankie Machine (Francis Majcinek) who is said to have a 'golden arm' because of his sure touch with pool cues, dice, his drumsticks, his heroin needle, and his deck of cards. Unable to free himself from his slum environment, Frankie is finally driven to suicide." Reader's Ency. 4th edition

A walk on the wild side. Farrar, Straus & Cudahy 1956 346p o.p.

A novel about the residents of a slum street in New Orleans during the early years of the Depression

"Algren's vivid writing gives this degenerate cast the power to shock or appall, and if a glimmer of compassion leaks through occasionally it is slapped down before it gets out of hand." Libr J

Ali, Monica

Brick lane; a novel. Scribner 2003 369p $25

ISBN 0-7432-4330-7 LC 2003-42795

"Nazeen, a young Bangladeshi woman, moves to London's Bangla Town (around the street of the title) in the mid-nineteen eighties after an arranged marriage with an older man. Seen through Nazeen's eyes, England is at first utterly baffling, but over the seventeen years of the narrative (which takes us into the post-September 11th era), she gradually finds her way, bringing up two daughters and eventually starting an all-female tailoring business. . . . In Ali's subtle narration, Nazeen's mixture of traditionalism, and adaptability, of acceptence and restlessness, emerges as a quiet strength." New Yorker

Alison, Jane

The marriage of the sea. Farrar, Straus & Giroux 2003 262p $24

ISBN 0-374-19941-8 LC 2002-33887

"The fulcrum of this novel is Oswaldo, a frail, elderly, and very rich Venetian. He funds a foundation that gives grants to artists. One recipient, Anton, a struggling architect nearing 40, reluctantly leaves his wife in New Orleans and goes to Venice on a grant to teach architecture. In Manhattan, artist Lach abandons his lover, Vera, and flees to Venice for a romantic rendezvous. But Vera has won a prize from Oswaldo's foundation, so she also embarks for Italy. Meanwhile, Max quits London for New Orleans, ostensibly to accept a chair in the History of Food, but primarily to woo Lucinde, an events planner. As soon as Max arrives, however, Lucinde flies to Venice to stay with Oswaldo, an old mentor of hers." Publ Wkly

The author "wonderfully captures the romantically stymied antics of smart people who lack the emotional grit needed to figure out the relationship they are in before drifting on to the next." Libr J

Natives and exotics; Jane Alison. Harcourt 2005 238p $23

ISBN 0-15-101201-6 LC 2004-23118

"Transplanted halfway around the globe in 1970, nine-year-old Alice, the unrooted child of diplomats, is ravished by the beauty of Ecuador, a country her parents are helping to despoil. Forty years earlier, her grandmother Violet, a newlywed making a home in the wilds of Australia, confronts troubling traces of her country's past. In early nineteenth-century Scotland, Violet's great-great-grandfather George flees the violence of the Clearances for the Portuguese Azores, unaware that he will have a hand in destroying the unearthly paradise he finds there and be forced to flee again." Publisher's note

"As 'Natives and Exotics' works its earnest, somewhat overdetermined way from Alice to Violet to George, it becomes more a novel of scenes than of story. There is Alice as a 9-year-old living in Ecuador as that country tries to stand up to the neighborhood bully, the United States. There is Violet, pawing at the untamed ground of the Australian wilderness, which may never yield to her as a home. And there is George, Alison's most fully imagined character, a mute and a misfit who somehow manages to find his way into the world of people and progeny. Though it's never clear how this happens—George is still a primitive when he flees the tropics—the result is a kind of family album where, finally, no one is out of place." N Y Times Book Rev

Allan, John B.

For works written by this author under other names see Stark, Richard; Westlake, Donald E.

Allen, Henry W., 1912-1991

For works by this author under other names see Henry, Will, 1912-1991

Allen, Hervey, 1889-1949

Anthony Adverse; decorations by Allan McNab. Farrar & Rinehart 1933 1224p il o.p.

"This vast romantic novel recounts the story of Anthony—born in 1775, illegitimate, orphaned, left to die in a Catholic convent, educated by the Church, and apprenticed to a wealthy Italian merchant whose heir he became. His business interests were world wide; in early manhood a slave trader, he was later connected with the financial interests of Napolean in France, England, Spain, and the new world. Anthony carried with him through life his one link to the past, a beautiful small figure of the Madonna that identified him to others though he himself never learned his identity." Booklist

"Only a scholar could have assembled the enormous knowledge that has gone into the book and only a poet and a critic could have caught so acutely the implications of that knowledge as idea and emotion in human beings. The triumph of the book, however, is that this wealth of fact and feeling is fused by the gusto of the true storyteller." N Y Her Trib Books

Allende, Isabel

Daughter of fortune; a novel; translated from the Spanish by Margaret Sayers Peden. HarperCollins Pubs. 1999 399p $26; pa $14

ISBN 0-06-019491-X; 0-06-093275-9 (pa) LC 99-26021

Original Spanish edition, 1999

A "historical novel flavored by four cultures—English, Chilean, Chinese and American—and set during the 1849 California Gold Rush. The . . . tale begins in Valparaiso, Chile, with young Eliza Sommers, who was left as a baby on the doorstep of wealthy British importers Miss Rose Sommers and her prim brother, Jeremy. Now a 16 year-old, and newly pregnant, Eliza decides to follow her lover, fiery clerk Joaquin Andieta, when he leaves for California to make his fortune in the gold rush. Enlisting the unlikely aid of Tao Chi'en, a Chinese shipboard cook, she stows away on a ship bound for San Francisco." Publ Wkly

"This novel has pretensions, but they are overridden by Allende's riproaring girl's adventure story. . . . Throughout it all, Allende projects a woman's point of view with confidence, control and an expansive definition of romance as a fact of life." Time

Eva Luna; translated by Margaret Sayers Peden. Knopf 1988 271p o.p.

LC 88-45272

Original Spanish edition, 1987

This novel "gives us successive episodes in Eva's life, from illegitimate birth and orphanhood through drifting adolescence to relative stability and success, but also recounts in parallel the biography of Rolf Carle, from his wartime childhood in Austria to his emigration to Latin America, subsequent fame as a controversial documentary film-maker, and finally his encounter and love affair with Eva herself. A third narrative strand deals with the fortunes of Huberto Naranjo . . . guerrilla fighter and [Eva's] transient lover." Times Lit Suppl

The author "has a delicious humor that often punctuates her multifaceted story. She succeeds, too, in introducing us to an ensemble of characters who are offbeat, alien to our ken, but who become part of our sensibilities." West Coast Rev Books

The house of the spirits; translated from the Spanish by Magda Bogin. Knopf 1985 368p $29.95

ISBN 0-394-53907-9 LC 84-48516

Original Spanish edition, 1982

This novel "tells the story of the Trueba family, with its deep loves and hates, following them from the turn of the century to the violent days of the overthrow of the Salvador Allende government in 1973." Christ Sci Monit

"The style is superbly controlled (and/or the translation is marvelously sensitive), balancing detail rich in associations with a deadpan humor that completely demystifies things that would be otherwise inexplicable. In other words, sentimentality never intrudes on the emotions you develop for these hopelessly well-meaning people and their equally errant children." Best Sellers

The infinite plan; a novel; translated from the Spanish by Margaret Sayers Peden. HarperCollins Pubs. 1993 380p o.p.

LC 92-54741

Original Spanish edition, 1991

This is the "story of Gregory Reeves's journey from childhood to middle age and long sought peace and happiness. Gregory's journey is marked by the contending philosophies of his mother's Bahai faith, his father's personally revealed, metaphysical explanation of the universe called 'The Infinite Plan' (the selling of which provides the family's income), and the traditional Catholicism and sense of nostalgia that permeate the Latin barrio where Gregory lives as a child." Libr J

"Allende's intensely imagined prose has clarity and dimension; she describes the exotic and the mundane with equal skill." Publ Wkly

Of love and shadows; translated from the Spanish by Margaret Sayers Peden. Knopf 1987 274p o.p.

LC 86-46164

Original Spanish edition, 1984

"A journalist and a photographer have teamed up to report on a young girl who seems to be inflicted with mystical trances, but their story unexpectedly takes a sinister turn when the girl is seized by the military police. The search for the girl leads the two reporters to a secret mass grave in the countryside that documents a reign of terror; the grave's discovery leads in turn to a government plot for deadly revenge." Booklist

"Ms. Allende skillfully evokes both the terrors of daily life under military rule and the subtler forms of resistance in the hidden corners and 'shadows' of her title, particularly in the churches or in simple unsung acts of solidarity. At the same time the author ably captures the voices of the regime's apologists—the complex lies and clichés of its proud male foot soldiers and the pat false phrases of its rich lady cheerleaders." N Y Times Book Rev

Portrait in sepia; translated from the Spanish by Margaret Sayers Peden. HarperCollins Pubs. 2001 304p o.p.

ISBN 0-06-621161-1 LC 00-54127

Sequel to Daughter of fortune

Original Spanish edition, 2000

The narrator of this novel "is a photographer named Aurora del Valle, who tells the story of her life as she

Allende, Isabel—*Continued*

reconstructs it with the help of old pictures and family gossip. She learns that her mother died during childbirth and that she was only 5 when sent to live with her paternal grandmother, one of many bigger-than-life women who would instill a sense of independence in her despite the inchoate feminism of 19th-century South America." N Y Times Book Rev

"Through Aurora, Allende exercises her supreme storytelling abilities, of which strong, passionate characters are paramount." Publ Wkly

The stories of Eva Luna; translated from the Spanish by Margaret Sayers Peden. Atheneum Pubs. 1991 330p o.p.

LC 90-39615

Contents: Two words; Wicked girl; Clarisa; Toad's mouth; The gold of Tomás Vargas; If you touched my heart; Gift for a sweetheart; Tosca; Walimai; Ester Lucero; Simple Maria; Our secret; The Little Heidelberg; The judge's wife; The road north; The schoolteacher's guest; The proper respect; Interminable life; A discreet miracle; Revenge; Letters of betrayed love; Phantom palace; And of clay are we created

"The title character of Allende's *Eva Luna* returns to frame this collection of stories in a Scheherazade-like fashion. . . . Allende covers familiar territory: social warfare between the rich and the poor, sexual battles between men and women, the dissolution of corrupt politicians and macho military leaders, all set within the landscape of contemporary South America." Booklist

Zorro; a novel; translated from the Spanish by Margaret Sayers Peden. HarperCollins Publishers 2005 390p maps $25.95

ISBN 0-06-077897-0 LC 2005-46389

"Born to an aristocratic Spanish father and a tamed Shoshone warrior in 18th-century California, Diego de la Vega learns the lessons of injustice early. His mother's Indian blood and the violence perpetrated against the Native Americans by European settlers ignite a slow-burning fire in Diego. When Diego is sent to Barcelona with his 'milk' brother Bernardo to be educated in the ways of his forebears, he studies with a fencing master and joins an underground resistance group, where Zorro the romantic revolutionary is truly forged." Libr J

"The odd but fruitful pairing of this rather serious novelist with the popular Latino hero, originally created in 1919 by the pulp writer Johnston McCulley, was the brainchild of the family that has owned the Zorro license for several generations and felt the masked adventurer was in need of 'quality lit' treatment. . . . [Allende] turns out to be perfectly suited to this material." New Leader

Allingham, Margery, 1904-1966

Crime and Mr. Campion. Doubleday 1959 575p o.p.

"Published for the Crime Club"

An omnibus volume containing the complete texts of three mystery novels all starring the British detective Albert Campion. Death of a ghost (1934) is based on art forgery, Flowers for the judge (1936) is about the murder of a publisher and Dancers in mourning (1937) concerns a group of theatrical characters

Dancers in mourning
In Allingham, M. Crime and Mr. Campion p363-575

Death of a ghost
In Allingham, M. Crime and Mr. Campion p7-175

The fashion in shrouds
In Allingham, M. Three cases for Mr. Campion p9-255

Flowers for the judge
In Allingham, M. Crime and Mr. Campion p177-362

The Gyrth chalice mystery
In Allingham, M. Three cases for Mr. Campion p421-604

Three cases for Mr. Campion. Doubleday 1961 604p o.p.

"Published for the Crime Club"

"The Gyrth chalice mystery" unravels Mr. Campion's solution to the secret in the locked room of Gyrth Tower; "The fashion in shrouds" involves the theft of dress designs, sixty cages of canaries, and blackmail, as Albert Campion investigates a three-year-old murder; "Traitor's purse" finds Albert Campion, an amnesia victim haunted by an urgency to do something of immense consequence before time runs out

Traitor's purse
In Allingham, M. Three cases for Mr. Campion p257-420

Allison, Dorothy, 1949-

Bastard out of Carolina. Dutton 1992 309p o.p.

ISBN 0-525-93425-1 LC 91-34607

"Set in the rural South, this tale centers around the Boatwright family, a proud and closeknit clan known for their drinking, fighting, and womanizing. Nicknamed Bone by her Uncle Earle, Ruth Anne is the bastard child of Anney Boatwright, who has fought tirelessly to legitimize her child. When she marries Glen, a man from a good family, it appears that her prayers have been answered. However, Anney suffers a miscarriage and Glen begins drifting. He develops a contentious relationship with Bone and then begins taking sexual liberties with her. . . . Unaware of her husband's abusive behavior, Anney stands by her man. Eventually, a violent encounter wrests Bone away from her stepfather." Libr J

Alther, Lisa

Kinflicks; a novel. Knopf 1976 c1975 503p o.p.

"Virginia Babcock Bliss, having been discovered in a compromising position with a hippie draft deserter, is thrown out of the house by her husband. She returns to her home town in Tennessee to find her mother dying in a hospital bed. . . . [A series of flashbacks reveals Ginny's development from] an impressionable young woman [who] moves from cheerleader through girl of a motorcycle hood, prim collegian, antiwar lesbian, organic farmer, and model housewife to emerge in her present predicament." Libr J

Alther, Lisa—*Continued*

"An ambitious, funny, lucid, and unfailingly honest first novel. . . . While a number of excellent writers have covered various parts of the turf covered here . . . no other writer has yet synthesized this material as well as Miss Alther has." New Yorker

Alvarez, Julia, 1950-

How the García girls lost their accents. Algonquin Bks. 1991 290p $18.95

ISBN 0-945575-57-2 LC 90-48575

This novel "tells the story (in reverse chronological order) of four sisters and their family, as they become Americanized after fleeing the Dominican Republic in the 1960s. A family of privilege in the police state they leave, the Garcias experience understandable readjustment problems in the United States, particularly old world patriarch Papi. The sisters fare better but grow up conscious, like all immigrants, of living in two worlds." Libr J

"This is an account of parallel odysseys, as each of the four daughters adapts in her own way, and a large part of Alvarez's accomplishment is the complexity with which these vivid characters are rendered." Publ Wkly

In the name of Salomé; a novel. Algonquin Bks. 2000 357p $23.95

ISBN 1-56512-276-3 LC 00-25818

"When Camila was three, her mother, Salome Urena, the Dominican Republic's 'National Poetess,' died. For years, the youngster wrestled with the loss, holding fast to the dream that her mother would someday reappear, a mysterious, larger-than-life stranger. . . . As Salome's story intertwines with Camila's, we are made privy to politics both personal and international." Libr J

"This is Alvarez's most ambitious work to date. In fact, her subject—the mingling of historical and personal destinies—is so rich that she can't quite do it justice. . . . And yet, despite its precious, contrived moments, the book delivers a strong sense of who these people were." N Y Times Book Rev

In the time of the butterflies; a novel. Algonquin Bks. 1994 325p $21.95

ISBN 1-56512-038-8 LC 94-15004

This novel is "based on the lives of the four Mirabel sisters (code name: 'Mariposas,' that is, butterflies), three of whom were martyred in 1960 during the liberation of the Dominican Republic from the dictator Trujillo. Through the surviving sister, Dedé, as well as memories of Minerva, Patria, and Maria Teresa, we discover the compelling forces behind each sister's role in the struggle for freedom." Libr J

"Alvarez captures the terrorized atmosphere of a police state, in which people live under the sword of terrible fear and atrocities cannot be acknowledged. As the sisters' energetic fervor turns to anguish, Alvarez conveys their courage and their desperation, and the full import of their tragedy." Publ Wkly

Yo!. Algonquin Bks. 1997 309p $18.95

ISBN 1-56512-157-0 LC 96-24611

Sequel to How the Garcia girls lost their accents

"Yolanda Garcia's mother and sisters are furious at her for having plagiarized their lives in her all-too-celebrated novel. The balance of *this* novel is a rebuttal of sorts, narrated by her defenders. For everyone else who has come into contact with Yo and her storytelling prowess—from her repressed professor to her downtrodden landlady—life has changed for the better. These high-spirited accounts indulge the pleasing fantasy that we are the heroes not only of our own lives but of everyone else's as well." New Yorker

Amado, Jorge, 1912-2001

Dona Flor and her two husbands; a moral and amorous tale; translated from the Portuguese by Harriet de Onís. Knopf 1969 553p o.p.

Original Portuguese edition published 1966 in Brazil

"Dona Flor has such a harridan of a mother (Dona Rozilda) that you would like her to have her cake and eat it, too, and she very nearly does. Dona Flor's first husband, Vadinho, is a scamp, a prevaricator, and a 'shameless lover.' On Carnival Sunday, at the height of the gaiety, filled with rum, he drops dead. Dona Flor is desolate but cuts a handsome figure as a widow. She lives through the wake (a gem of a scene) and her mourning quite well, with memories and her cooking school to sustain her. Then suitors appear. None appeal but Dr. Teodoro Madureira, pharmacist and bassoonist, a pillar of propriety. Dona Rozilda is ecstatic, but the well-rounded Dona Flor has her troubles, for alas, Dr. Teodoro is no lover. Dreams haunt her and strange things begin to happen. Thanks to a Yoruba charm, Vadinho returns to ravish our bewildered heroine, and then the fun begins. Bahia in Brazil is the setting for this delectable rum cake of a novel." Publ Wkly

Gabriela, clove and cinnamon; translated from the Portuguese by James L. Taylor and William L. Grossman. Knopf 1962 425p o.p.

Original Portuguese edition published 1958 in Brazil

"Ilhéus, a Brazilian town near Bahia, is fortunate in the wealth it is realizing from its cacao crop. Money flows freely and is spent in cabarets, in bordellos, and on gambling during the period 1925-1926. . . . The removal of a sand bar blocking the harbor is the basis of this fascinating portrait of politics in a provincial Brazilian town. Amado also tells the love story of Nacib, the Arab owner of the most popular café in town, and Gabriela, a child of nature. Amoral rather than immoral, with skin the color of cinnamon and smelling of cloves, Gabriela gives her love readily and freely. Her skillful cooking makes her more valuable to Nacib as a mistress than as a wife. The atmosphere of this entertaining novel is lusty, sensual, and humorous." Shapiro. Fic for Youth. 3d edition

Showdown; translated by Gregory Rabassa. Bantam Bks. 1988 422p o.p.

ISBN 0-553-05174-1 LC 87-47789

Original Portuguese edition published in Brazil

This novel is about a Bahia settlement in Brazil "at the turn of the century. It tells the story of the settlers who later became Brazil's proletariat: gunslingers, landless farmworkers, prostitutes, peddlers and cowboys, many of them the children of slaves. The characters endure the archetypal troubles of frontier life (an invasion by bandits, a catastrophic flood, a plague) and find joy where they can, in sex, romance, folk rituals and celebrations. The book ends with their defeat at the hands of an unscrupulous and decadent urbanite." Nation

"No doubt 'Showdown' would make a compelling

Amado, Jorge, 1912-2001—*Continued*
movie, but it is essentially a verbal performance. . . . Mr. Amado grounds even the most minor character-drawing in anecdotal devotion to detail." N Y Times Book Rev

American West: twenty new stories from the Western Writers of America; edited with an introduction by Loren D. Estleman. Forge 2001 367p $25.95

ISBN 0-312-87317-4 LC 00-48446

"A Tom Doherty Associates book"

This collection of stories about the West includes works by Don Coldsmith, Jory Sherman, Elmer Kelton, Richard S. Wheeler, Johnny D. Boggs, and Max Evans

"Uniformly fine writing makes this a welcome addition to any western collection." Booklist

Ames, Jonathan

Wake up, sir!; a novel. Scribner 2004 334p $23

ISBN 0-7432-3004-3 LC 2003-70357

"Alan Blair is a ne'er-do-well New Jerseyite who has failed to follow his first novel, 'I Pity I,' published seven years ago, with a second. At thirty, he's alcoholic, afraid of confronting the bellicose uncle with whom he lives, and would be penniless but for an accident settlement. His most treasured possessions are a collection of dubious sports coats and a valet, who just happens to be named Jeeves. As you'd expect, Jeeves is circumspect, judicious, and ready at hand; what he may not be is real. Ames's inventive romp follows its hero into very un-Wodehousian territory—an artists' colony in upstate New York (based, in withering detail, on Yaddo), where the action revolves around art, sex, and larceny." New Yorker

Amidon, Stephen

Human capital. Farrar, Straus and Giroux 2004 375p $25

ISBN 0-374-17350-8 LC 2004-43985

"It's the spring of 2001, and Drew Hagel has spent the last decade watching things slip away-his first marriage, his real estate brokerage, his beloved daughter, Shannon, now a distant and mysterious high school senior. He is in danger of losing his place in the affluent suburb that his father once ruled. And then an unexpected friendship with Quint Manning, the manager of a secretive hedge fund, opens to Drew the prospect of vast, frictionless wealth." Publisher's note

"It's all sounds a bit like Peyton Place, but Amidon's intentions are far more serious. Writing with a sociologist's insight, he crafts a sharp page-turner mined with moments of dark satire. Amidon's previous novels had moments of profundity, but this exceptional novel delves deeper and more passionately into the fractured lives of people whose lives revolve around money." Publ Wkly

The new city; a novel. Doubleday 2000 445p il $24.95

ISBN 0-385-49762-8 LC 99-25619

"Austin Swope is an ambitious white lawyer; Earl Wooten is an accomplished black builder. In the late nineteen-sixties, they are hired to jointly create and manage Newton, a utopian, mixed-race development on the outskirts of Washington. The two men rapidly become friends, raising their sons, Teddy and Joel, almost as brothers. By 1973, however, the dream is tarnishing: sales are down, teen-age crime and racial tensions are on the rise, and Swope learns that Wooten may be up for the job he considers rightfully his." New Yorker

Amidon's "well-developed characters are human and deeply flawed; his novel stands as a modern allegory on race relations, suburban living, and social engineering." Libr J

Amis, Kingsley, 1922-1995

The Green Man. Harcourt, Brace & World 1970 c1969 252p o.p.

First published 1969 in the United Kingdom

The Green Man is a pub. "It is also a very nasty thing conjured up by the resident ghost, a 17th-century diabolist parson, handily capable of destroying his enemies at a distance. . . . Maurice Allington, owner of The Green Man and narrator [of the story], neglects his daughter, ignores his second wife and despises his mistress—although he spends what energy he can spare from drinking and ghost-hunting in trying to get the ignored and despised into bed with him at the same time." New Statesman (1913)

"The dialogue is filled with humor and a chilling strangeness. Indeed, the success of this short novel depends very much upon the balance that Amis maintains between laughter and fear." N Y Times Book Rev

Lucky Jim; a novel. Doubleday 1954 c1953 256p o.p.

First published 1953 in the United Kingdom

"The title is ironic, since the story is about the comic misfortunes of Jim Dixon, a young lower-middle-class instructor at an English university. The book satirizes the academic 'racket' and cultural pretensions." Reader's Ency. 4th edition

The old devils; a novel. Summit Bks. 1987 294p o.p.

LC 86-23084

"Set in South Wales, [this novel] opens as three couples at the beginning of their 'golden years' . . . find their lives turned upside down by the return, after thirty years, of successful poet Alun Weaver, and his stunning wife Rhiannon. Alun (born Alan) . . . has made a career for himself by talking about 'all things Welsh' on the television." Publisher's note

"The Old Devils has a tough honest crust and scuttling sideways humor. Nowhere in it does Amis attempt shapely sentences or lyrical, dying falls. His is an aesthetic of the anti-beautiful. The book's astringency feels just right." New Repub

The Russian girl. Viking 1994 c1992 296p o.p.

First published 1992 in the United Kingdom

"Dr. Richard Vaisey is an esteemed scholar at the London Institute of Slavonic Studies whose wife, Cordelia, has perfected the art of manipulation. When Anna Danilova, an obscure Russian poet, asks his help in freeing her brother from a Russian jail by making her 'famous'

Amis, Kingsley, 1922-1995—*Continued*
and thus calling world attention to the brother's plight, Richard finds himself torn between his growing passion for her and his outright dislike of her poetry. Realizing what is going on between her husband and 'the Russian girl,' Cordelia, plots revenge." Libr J

"What makes 'The Russian Girl' such a jolly good read is precisely [its] scathing level of insight, to say nothing of Amis's dazzling virtuosity with the old bons mots. They litter the floor. He also manages to be very, very funny, even when he's being very, very serious." NY Times Book Rev

Amis, Martin

The information. Harmony Bks. 1995 374p o.p.
ISBN 0-517-58516-2 LC 94-44512

Set in contemporary London, this novel recounts the rivalry between two writers named Richard Tull and Gwyn Barry. "Tull, a fortyish book reviewer and failed novelist, is driven to distraction by the effortless and unmerited success of fellow Oxonian Barry. While Barry's simpleminded novels become overnight best sellers, Tull's dense experimental manuscripts send a succession of literary agents to the hospital with migraine. Tull finally decides it's payback time, and this novel chronicles his . . . attempts to annihilate his friend." Libr J

"Mr. Amis, the prince of hip, is in top form; his humor is more daring than ever, and his mastery of phrase and metaphor makes his gorgeous, dark invention crackle. He is also smart about being smart: at just the right moments he sinks the blade of his satire into himself." N Y Times Book Rev

London fields. Harmony Bks. 1989 470p o.p.
LC 89-49558

This novel, set in 1999 London, follows the exploits of Nicola Six, who has the "knack of knowing what will happen next, and what is going to happen on the morning of November the Sixth—her thirty-fifth birthday—is her own murder. One day she walks into a pub where the palely loitering aristocrat Guy Clinch and the [drunken] tabloid dartsman Keith Talent are separately drinking (as is our narrator, a terminally ill American) and recognizes her future murderer. For the rest of the book she manipulates Guy (through a parody of love) and Keith (through a parody of sex) to bring about the end she requires." Times Lit Suppl

"Amis's technical virtuosity is extraordinary. . . . [This is] the most intellectually interesting fiction of the year, and a work beyond the reach of any British contemporary. Amis's figures, like those of Dickens, are caricatures that have their own gigantic reality." London Rev Books

Night train; a novel. Harmony Bks. 1997 175p o.p.
ISBN 0-609-60128-8 LC 97-28163

This novel is set in an unnamed American city. It is narrated by a "female cop, Mike Hoolihan, who investigates the apparent suicide of Jennifer Rockwell, a golden girl who happens to be Mike's friend. Jennifer's father, Mike's longtime colleague and mentor, hopes Mike will prove that the suicide was really murder, but the deeper she probes, the more murky matters become." Booklist

This is the "first book Mr. Amis has written in an exclusively American voice. Though the accent wavers unavoidably at times, the prose itself is as mean and controlled as Mr. Amis at his considerable best." Economist

Time's arrow; or, The nature of the offense. Harmony Bks. 1991 168p o.p.
LC 91-4144

This novel "shoots us into the past as it reveals the true identity of a man called Tod Friendly. As Tod lies in a hospital bed, his consciousness distances itself from the present and assesses his life in reverse, like a film run backwards. Every action is reversed and every conversation inverted. This voice, this estranged soul, watches Tod create food and beverages at meals, get paid for bringing items into stores, and grow younger. As his American identity is stripped away, his hideous past as a German doctor and executioner at a Nazi extermination camp is revealed." Booklist

"With Time's Arrow, Amis takes another look at our diseased world. This time he pares the story down to essentials. Though his writing is as fizzy as ever, it doesn't call attention to itself. His artfully contrived structure serves a purpose: to present the horror in a way so unfamiliar it can't be anesthetized." Voice Lit Suppl

Ammaniti, Niccolò, 1966-

I'm not scared; translated from the Italian by Jonathan Hunt. Canongate 2003 200p $23
ISBN 1-84195-297-4

"During a piercingly hot summer, a few kilometres from a bone-dry hamlet in rural Tuscany, a shy, nervy, nine-year-old boy called Michele explores a derelict house and discovers, under moldering leaves, a horrifying secret. The novel is saved from sensationalism by Ammaniti's almost cinematic ability to conjure detail." New Yorker

Anatoli, A., 1929-1979

Babi Yar; a document in the form of a novel; [by] A. Anatoli (Kuznetsov). Translated by David Floyd. Farrar, Straus & Giroux 1970 477p o.p.

Original Russian edition published 1966 in censored form under author's former name A. Kuznetsov; English translation by Jacob Guralsky of this version published 1967 by Dial Press

A documentary novel about the period from 1941 to 1943 in which the Germans systematically murdered some 2,000,000 people, including 50,000 Jews, at the ravine on the outskirts of Kiev known as Babi Yar. The author, who was twelve years old at the time, based his work on interviews, newspaper clippings, diaries and other documents

Andersen Nexø, Martin, 1869-1954

Pelle the conqueror: v1 Childhood; translated from the Danish by Steven T. Murray; edited and with an afterword by Tiina Nunnally. Fjord Press 1989 244p o.p.
LC 89-7837

"The first of a four-volume Danish classic follows the fortunes of Lasse Karlsson, an impoverished, aging Swede, and his young son, Pelle. Attracted by legendary prosperity . . . they migrate to Denmark in the late 19th

Andersen Nexø, Martin, 1869-1954—*Continued*

century." Publ Wkly

"Andersen Nexo, who was born in the slums of Copenhagen, ultimately developed Pelle into a proletarian epic hero. In this first, largely autobiographical volume, however, there's scant evidence of his strict social realism. Rather, Andersen Nexo's robust sense of life, his convincing evocation of childhood, his moral vision—and, above all, his brave young hero—make this novel generous and grand." N Y Times Book Rev

Pelle the conqueror: v2 Apprenticeship; translated from the Danish by Steven T. Murray & Tiina Nunnally; with an afterword by Niels Ingwersen. Fjord Press 1991 224p o.p.

In this volume "Pelle begins the journey the European proletariat undertook when the modern capitalistic society was formed; he goes from rural misery and poverty to the same or worse in an urban setting. As a shoemaker's apprentice in the nearest town, he retains some ties with the past but grows into adolescence in a milieu of different values and new people, establishing solidarity with the poorest. . . . With his faults and virtues, endurance and optimism, Pelle is one of literature's most charming heroes." Libr J

Anderson, Alison

Darwin's wink; a novel of nature and love; by Alison Anderson. 1st ed. Thomas Dunne Books\St. Martin's Press 2004 288p $23.95

ISBN 0-312-33199-1 LC 2004-17763

"Christian, a disenchanted, 30-something Swiss man haunted by his experiences as a Red Cross worker in Bosnia, comes to Egret Island, . . . off the coast of Mauritius, to work for Fran, a middle-aged, outwardly brusque American naturalist seeking to restore the island to its original, untouched state and the endangered mourner-bird to its previous strength. Like Christian, who left behind a pregnant lover, Fran has also loved and lost; she tries to confine herself to a cerebral approach to work and life, blunting her sexual frissons and painful flashbacks through Darwinian logic. . . . Readers will find the plot distantly secondary to the novel's rich emotional palette, as Anderson captures the expansive beauty of Mauritius and the nuances of human character with languid, sensual and occasionally violet prose." Publ Wkly

Anderson, Kevin J., 1962-

(jt. auth) Herbert, B. Dune: House Atreides

(jt. auth) Herbert, B. Dune: House Corrino

(jt. auth) Herbert, B. Dune: House Harkonnen

(jt. auth) Herbert, B. Dune: The Butlerian jihad

Anderson, Poul, 1926-2001

Genesis. TOR Bks. 2000 253p o.p.

ISBN 0-312-86707-7 LC 99-58829

"A Tom Doherty Associates book"

"Christian Brannock agrees to have his personality uploaded into a computer so that his mind can explore the stars long after the death of his body. When his billion-year journey brings him back to an Earth that has undergone many cosmic changes, Brannock encounters another uploaded personality who restores to him the wonder of being 'human.' The lyrical approach of this sf master to the meaning of human existence gives his latest effort a surreal, allegorical feel." Libr J

Goat song

In The Hugo winners p330-64

Going for infinity; a literary journey. TOR Bks. 2002 416p $25.95

ISBN 0-7653-0359-0 LC 2001-58351

"A Tom Doherty Associates book"

Contents: Gypsy; Sam Hall; Death and the knight; Journeys end; The horn of time the hunter; The master key; The problem of pain; Quest; Windmill; Three hearts and three lions; Epilogue; Dead phone; Goat song; Kyrie; A midsummers tempest; The shrine for lost children; The queen of aiar and darkness

The late author provides a "sampling of his work originally published between 1950 and 1999. Anderson provided lively interstitial commentary, which is especially helpful in setting the context for excerpts from novels or tales from series that assume familiarity with a shared background." N Y Times Book Rev

Harvest of stars. TOR Bks. 1993 395p o.p.

LC 93-15627

"A Tom Doherty Associates book"

"A future North America is dominated by the Avantist police state, while space is ruled by the vast Fireball corporation. Founded by entrepreneur Anson Guthrie, Fireball is devoted to a nearly libertarian ideal of individual freedom and laissez-faire economics, the antithesis of the Avantist policy. The original Guthrie is long dead, but his mind, downloaded into a computer, lives on to direct Fireball. When the Avantists capture a second copy of Guthrie . . . they have the power to destroy Fireball." Publ Wkly

"Sweeping, fast-paced, intricate, provocative, Anderson's latest will appeal to older, more sophisticated sf fans." Booklist

Harvest the fire. TOR Bks. 1995 190p $18.95

ISBN 0-312-85943-0 LC 95-30304

"A Tom Doherty Associates book"

Third title in the author's future history series. Previous titles: Harvest of stars and The stars are also fire, entered in 1994 and 1995 supplements, respectively

"In the far future, a poet and a revolutionary find themselves in the midst of a conspiracy to liberate the human spirit from the benevolent but stifling patronage of the machine intelligence: Teramind. . . . Deceptive in its brevity and simplicity, this gemlike story of passion and the poetic soul belongs in most sf collections." Libr J

Hunter's moon

In The Hugo winners p510-50

The longest voyage

In The Hugo winners p279-310

Mother of kings. TOR Bks. 2001 444p $27.95

ISBN 0-312-87448-0

"As the daughter of a Norse chieftain, Gunhild sets her ambitions high—to learn the ways of shamanic magic and to wed Eirik Blood-Ax and lead him to the throne of a newly united Norway. . . . [Anderson] adds an ele-

Anderson, Poul, 1926-2001—*Continued*
ment of myth and pagan magic to a true story set in the tenth century, as the advent of Christianity in Scandinavia spells the end of a violent and heroic way of life. Fans of historical fantasy and Norse mythology should appreciate this well-crafted tale of epic adventure." Libr J

Operation Chaos. Doubleday 1971 232p o.p.
"Doubleday science fiction"
"This is a fast-moving science fantasy, set in a 'world of if' where magic has been scientifically developed along with laws of physical science. Steve Matuchek is a werewolf using his talent for army intelligence in a strange World War II, and Ginny Graylock is a witch he meets on a commando raid. The four sections of the novel carry them forward to a present in which the cold war is a struggle directly with hell, and irresponsible use of magic by student protestors threatens to turn chaos loose in the world. The story is well developed within its postulates, and has as much hard-boiled physical action as wand-waving." Libr J
Followed by Operation Luna

Operation Luna. TOR Bks. 1999 316p $22.95
ISBN 0-312-86706-9 LC 99-24483
In this sequel to Operation Chaos "licensed witch Ginny Greylock and her werewolf husband, Steven Matuchek, seek to discover the reasons behind the catastrophic failure of NASA (National Astral Spellcraft Administration) to launch a spaceship to the moon. Tongue-in-cheek humor overlays this lighthearted cross-genre tale of science and mysticism." Libr J

Orion shall rise. Timescape Bks. 1983 463p o.p.
LC 82-19338
"How would earth's reemerging societies change, adapt and interact many generations after a nuclear armageddon? In his conception of how earthly society might evolve, Poul Anderson presents a heterogeneous world, some cultures far more advanced than ours and some a hundred years behind. The Maurai, a people seen in previous Anderson novels, are the stewards of a large part of earth, and their rules and regulations serve to conserve scarce energy, inhibit pollution and preserve the ecosystem. This control is insulting to the Norrmen, who wish to elevate their quality of life and status through nuclear technology, forbidden by the Maurai. . . . [A coup among the sky-based] Aerogens, protectors of a large domain which was once Europe . . . delivers the novel's hero, Talence Iern Ferlay, to the ground, where he quickly becomes involved with the Norrmen and Maurai." Best Sellers

The Queen of Air and Darkness
In The Hugo winners p143-90

The Saturn game
In The Hugo winners p269-325

The sharing of flesh
In The Hugo winners p558-94

The stars are also fire. TOR Bks. 1994 413p $22.95
ISBN 0-312-85534-6 LC 94-7020
"A Tom Doherty Associates book"
Sequel to Harvest of stars, entered in 1994 supplement
"As human governments labor to construct a habitat in space that will enable Earth's population to exploit the mineral resources of its moon, a small group of Lunarians, genetically altered for survival in low gravity, search the past to find a way to preserve their way of life and their independence. Spanning 500 years, Anderson's latest novel offers a tale of dynastic intrigue and high adventure as two distinct visions of human destiny struggle for ascendancy. Combining complex, believable characters with a skillfully orchestrated plot, the author . . . continues to demonstrate his storytelling excellence." Libr J

War of the Gods. TOR Bks. 1997 304p o.p.
ISBN 0-312-86315-2 LC 97-19383
"In this historical fantasy about the little-known Viking king Hadding, Anderson . . . fleshes out extant Norse literature to create an epic tale of a young man raised in secret by giants after his parents are killed. The heir to the Danish throne grows up and gathers armies to support his effort to reclaim his kingdom." Libr J
"Anderson writes with a spare style, often relying on the alliterative, rhythmic prose of Scandinavian folklore, giving this epic tale an original spirit and tone. Readers bored with Tolkien-clone fantasies will be enthralled by the intricately detailed world and characters Anderson brings to life here." Publ Wkly

Anderson, Sherwood, 1876-1941

Poor white; a novel. Huebsch, B.W. 1920 371p o.p.
This novel "describes the changes occurring in a Midwestern town when industrialism replaces the old agrarian, craft-centered society. The town itself is the protagonist of the early part of the book, and Anderson successfully depicts its shabbiness, isolation, and sterility. Hugh McVey, the central character, is an introverted inventor who does not become aware until it is too late that his own genius contributes to the corruption of his environment." Reader's Ency

Short stories; edited and with an introduction by Maxwell Geismar. Hill & Wang 1962 289p o.p.
"American century series"
Contents: The dumb man; I want to know why; The other woman; The egg; The man in the brown coat; Brothers; I'm a fool; The triumph of a modern; The man who became a woman; Milk bottles; The sad horn blowers; Death in the woods; There she is—she is taking her bath; The lost novel; Like a queen; In a strange town; These mountaineers; A meeting south; Brother death; The corn planting; Nobody laughed; A part of earth; Morning roll call; The yellow gown; Daughters; White spot; A walk in the moonlight; His chest of drawers; Not sixteen

Tar: a midwest childhood. Boni & Liveright 1926 346p o.p.
Tar is one of the many children born to Dick and Mary Moorehead. Dick is a garrulous, idle, affable fellow, and his wife a darkly beautiful woman, silent but not taciturn. Tar has something of both parents. The story begins when Tar is about four and continues up to early adolescence, describing the incidents in small town

Anderson, Sherwood, 1876-1941—*Continued*
life in 19th century Ohio that brought his consciousness to a new focus and marked a new stage in his development

"Unforgettable, and so tenderly told! A childhood well remembered—and yet, one feels the book is not remembrance, but imagination." Boston Transcr

Winesburg, Ohio. Modern Lib. 1995 231p o.p.
ISBN 0-679-60146-5 LC 94-23229
A reissue of the title first published 1919 by B.W. Huebsch

"A series of twenty-three vignettes, *Winesburg, Ohio* is a character study of a small town. It highlights individual residents and scrutinizes who they are and why this reality often conflicts with their dreams. The short stories are linked through George Willard, a young newspaper reporter who is disenchanted with the narrow-mindedness of small towns." Shapiro. Fic for Youth. 3d edition

Anderson-Dargatz, Gail, 1963-

A recipe for bees. Harmony Bks. 2000 305p o.p.
ISBN 0-609-60451-1 LC 99-25269
First published 1999 in the United Kingdom

"Having lost her mother at 14, Augusta was no stranger to hardship when she married at 18. Still, life with the much-older Karl and his miserly father on a remote {Canadian} farm that had not seen a woman's touch in decades was initially almost too much to bear. But, finally, after she had found tenderness with another man and borne his child, Augusta was able to lure Karl from his father to a farm of their own. There, Augusta started keeping bees to earn a little extra money and began to find some sweetness in her marriage." Libr J

"Augusta is a headstrong heroine with prismatic perspectives; her long, never-dull life as told by the gifted Anderson-Dargatz is both charming and impressive in its quiet, cumulative power." Publ Wkly

Andrews, Cecily Isabel Fairfield *See* West, Dame Rebecca, 1892-1983

Andrews, Colin *See* Wilson, F. Paul (Francis Paul)

Andrews, Mary Kay, 1954-

Every crooked nanny. HarperCollins Pubs. 1992 286p o.p.
LC 91-58359
This novel introduces "J. Callahan Garrity, a former cop and failed gumshoe who now runs a cleaning service in Atlanta, Ga. While cleaning the home of snooty society lady Lilah Rose Beemish, Callahan is hired to trace Kristee, the family's Mormon nanny, who has absconded with furs, jewels and, Callahan learns, incriminating business secrets gleaned from Lilah's husband Bo during their affair." Publ Wkly

"This quick-paced thriller provides an intriguing introduction to a delightfully down-to-earth sleuth." Booklist

Irish eyes; a Callahan Garrity mystery. HarperCollins Pubs. 2000 296p $24
ISBN 0-06-019421-9 LC 99-55680

"Former Atlanta cop Garrity returns to crime solving when her ex-partner, Bucky Deavers, is shot on the way home from a party he finagled her into attending at the Shamrock Society. With the help of the eccentric staff of her housecleaning business, Garrity vows to get to the bottom of the shooting. This is an entertaining, suspenseful romp." Booklist

Andrézel, Pierre, 1885-1962

For works written by this author under other names see Dinesen, Isak, 1885-1962

Andrić, Ivo, 1892-1975

The bridge on the Drina; translated from the Serbo-Croat by Lovett F. Edwards. Macmillan 1959 314p o.p.
The first volume of the Bosnian trilogy; other titles are: Bosnian chronicle (1963) and The woman from Sarajevo (1965)
Original Serbo-Croatian edition, 1945

"This long narrative relates in a series of episodes the history of a bridge near the Bosnian town of Višegrad. That history covers three and a half centuries, through much of which the Bosnians lived under Turkish overlords. This is probably the most important of Andric's several novels about his native Bosnia." Reader's Ency. 4th edition

Angell, Roger

(ed) Nothing but you. See Nothing but you

Ansa, Tina McElroy, 1949-

The hand I fan with. Doubleday 1996 462p o.p.
LC 96-6256
Sequel to Baby in the family (1989)

This novel is set in Mulberry, a small central Georgia town, where Lena McPherson, "a single, 40-ish African American, is regarded with awe. Vested with psychic powers as a result of being born with a caul, Lena enjoys 'an abundance of blessings' (good real estate investments, a beautiful house, prestige cars, designer clothes). . . . Within days of conducting a ritual to bring a man into her life, Lena is knocked down by an invisible force while inspecting one of her properties." Publ Wkly

"Ansa writes believably of the spirit world; on the other hand, her inventories of Lena's many material possessions can be overlong and jarring. Yet a strong sense of place and an engagingly eccentric cast of characters keep the narrative moving—and ultimately bring Lena's two worlds together." N Y Times Book Rev

You know better; a novel. Morrow 2002 322p o.p.
ISBN 0-06-019779-X LC 2002-22252
This novel focuses "on three generations of troubled women in a small Georgia town. . . . LaShawndra, an 18-year-old 'coochie' who engages in indiscriminate sex and whose greatest aspiration is to dance in a music video, has disappeared. Her mother, Sandra, is too busy with her real estate career, her new romance with a pastor and youth-enhancing beauty treatments to look for LaShawndra. So it falls to the girl's grandmother, Lily, a respected pillar of the community, to perform the

Ansa, Tina McElroy, 1949-—*Continued*

search. The book is a first-person triptych, the three Pines women taking turns from oldest to youngest in detailing how they arrived at this latest crisis point—and each has a different spirit guide to help her out." Publ Wkly

Ansay, A. Manette, 1964-

Midnight champagne; a novel. Morrow 1999 225p o.p.

ISBN 0-688-15244-9 LC 99-11467

"A snowbound wedding at a brothel turned resort in Wisconsin is the setting for this hectic, entertaining tale about love and compromise. Can arty, beleaguered April find happiness with Caleb, the earnest son of a fundamentalist minister? Ansay creates a zany tribunal from the guest list—spurned aunts, awkward teen-agers, a grandmother who searches for lucky pennies as if her life depended on it—and by the novel's end the answer is that everyone, including the reader, hopes so." New Yorker

River angel. Morrow 1998 243p o.p.

ISBN 0-688-15243-0 LC 97-31006

"A rural legend—of an angel watching over a river—provides the framework for this . . . novel about faith and its power to transform individuals and a community. When odd, overweight Gabriel Carpenter comes to Ambient, Wisconsin, he's taunted by other children and instantly disliked by his fifth-grade teacher. One night, teenagers, drinking and up to no good, take Gabriel to the bridge, where he somehow jumps, slips, or is pushed into the river; then his body is found, warm and fragrant, lying in a distant barn, presumably delivered there by the river angel. The legend is reborn, the barn becomes a shrine, and a small town struggling with progress is given new life." Booklist

"With 'River Angel,' A. Manette Ansay has moved beyond her prior mastery of the family scene to a lucid, eloquent representation of the commingled and conflicting lives of a town." N Y Times Book Rev

Anshaw, Carol

Lucky in the corner. Houghton Mifflin 2002 245p $23

ISBN 0-395-94040-0 LC 2001-51891

"Nora and her teenage daughter, Fern, have a typically contentious relationship. They share a house with Nora's partner, Jeanne, and their dog, Lucky, and is purring along until Nora makes a bad decision that results in a painful disruption of their family life. Fern, wise beyond her years, emerges as the real caregiver, checking in with her depressive boyfriend, rescuing her best friend from becoming a child abuser, and ultimately even putting her battles with her mother on hold long enough to help Nora recover her footing in life." Libr J

Anthony, Evelyn, 1928-

Anne Boleyn. Crowell 1957 310p o.p.

Historical novel, based on the life of Anne Boleyn, the second of the wives of Henry VIII of England. The period covered is from 1526 when Henry met Anne in the garden of her father's castle, to the day of her death on Tower Green in 1536

The author "emphasizes Anne's ambition and her vindictiveness so that Anne is not an especially attractive heroine until she gains the reader's sympathies toward the end of the book. . . . A good, straightforward, but not unusual historical novel." Publ Wkly

The Cardinal and the Queen. Coward-McCann 1968 221p o.p.

Set against the intrigue-ridden glitter of Louis XIII's court, this is the story of the proud, beautiful Anne of Austria, her humiliating marriage to the listless Louis and her passionate affair with Cardinal Richelieu, the King's minister

"The Louvre, Luxembourg Palace, and other royal buildings of seventeenth-century Paris provide much of the authentic background for this historical novel." Booklist

The house of Vandekar. Putnam 1988 288p o.p.

LC 88-11555

"Ashdown, house of the Vandekars, is the stateliest of English homes, its verdant lawns and magnificent facades making it a legend of elegant refinement. But within its vaulting walls, Ashdown reveals its darker aspects: buried desires, deceit, and tortured expiation, played out by three generations of women and the men they love too much." Publisher's note

"Anthony renders her characters' soured romances and dramatic confrontations with compelling realism." Publ Wkly

The Janus imperative. Coward, McCann & Geoghegan 1980 275p o.p.

LC 79-20768

"Political journalist Max Steiner is interviewing a German politician in Paris when the man is assassinated. His dying word is 'Janus.' As a Hitler Youth 25 years earlier, Steiner had heard another dying man utter the same word in Hitler's Berlin bunker in 1945. He persuades his boss to let him do an in-depth story on the assassination and hurries to Germany to dig into Bunker archives for connections between the two Januses. But as he starts interviewing survivors, a terrorist group is proceeding to murder the same survivors. German intelligence and the CIA become involved, and Steiner's quest ends in a convent in Munich, where some unholy violence takes place." Publ Wkly

This novel has "strong, believable characters, clear prose and good description." West Coast Rev Books

The tamarind seed; a novel. Coward, McCann & Geoghegan 1971 246p o.p.

"Judith Farrow, an attractive young British widow, trying to get over an unfortunate love affair in the Caribbean, meets Feodor Sverdlow, a high-ranking Russian intelligence agent. The pair's quite inadvertent meeting and few days' companionship turns into a 'cause cél ebre' that rocks Moscow, London, and Washington." Publ Wkly

Anthony, Piers

And eternity. Morrow 1990 369p (Incarnations of immortality, bk7) o.p.

LC 89-3418

"Three women (two ghosts and one mortal teenager) join together in a quest that leads them, ultimately, to a replacement for the Incarnation of God, who actually is

Anthony, Piers—*Continued*
offstage for the duration of the story. . . . In part, Anthony is using the novel as a platform to speak out on the state of the world—pollution, overpopulation, war, etc.—and about the concepts of good and evil." Booklist

"This grand finale to one of the author's most popular series showcases Anthony's multiple strengths: high humor, appealing characters, serious themes, and a surprising—although, in hindsight, inevitable—conclusion." Libr J

Bearing an hourglass. Ballantine Bks. 1984 293p (Incarnations of immortality, bk2) o.p.
LC 84-3083

"A Del Rey book"

In the second volume of the Incarnations of immortality series, "a grief-stricken Norton assumes the position of the Incarnation of Time but discovers that such a role involves an increasingly deadly duel with Satan." Booklist

"Amid weighty and often convoluted speculations about the nature of good and evil, time and space, and magic and science, Anthony's irrepressible humor asserts itself in unexpected ways." Libr J

Followed by With a tangled skein

Being a green mother. Ballantine Bks. 1987 313p (Incarnations of immortality, bk5) o.p.
LC 87-47742

"A Del Rey book"

In book five of the series "a young girl's lifelong pursuit of the 'Llano'—the elusive Song of Nature—leads her to her destiny as the Incarnation of Nature and tricks her into a bargain with the Incarnation of Evil to halt the world's destruction." Libr J

Followed by For love of evil

Blue Adept. Ballantine Bks. 1981 327p il o.p.
LC 80-21754

"A Del Rey book"

In this second book in the Apprentice Adept series "our hero, Stile, is living in both worlds, striving to rise from serf to citizen in one by winning the all-encompassing Game, while he struggles to become a master of magic in the other—through the new Blue Adept. . . . [He] fights a dragon, wins a magic flute, competes in the unicorn olympics and, with the help of his beautiful robot guardian, Sheen, survives in Proton to progress to the Game finals." Publ Wkly

"Although the alteration of fantasy and sf chapters is rather gimmicky, the story maintains its exciting pace with many unexpected twists, and Anthony's humorous touches continue to delight the reader." Libr J

Followed by Juxtaposition

Chaos mode. Putnam 1993 300p o.p.
LC 93-3690

"An Ace/Putnam book"

In this third title in the Mode series "Colene has discovered travel on the Virtual Mode, a buffer zone that connects Earth with thousands of alternate realities. With three companions—Darius, Nona and the telepathic horse Seqiro—she meets Burgess, a tentacled being from a world whose evolutionary development differs dramatically from that of Earth. Anthony effectively conveys Burgess's radical otherness through the creature's community-oriented vocabulary." Publ Wkly

Currant events; Piers Anthony. 1st Tor ed. Tor Books 2004 336p map $24.95
ISBN 0-7653-0407-4 LC 2004-48039

"A Tom Doherty Associates book"

"Clio, the muse of history, has a problem connected with the twenty-eighth chronicle of Xanth. When she sits down to write it, she discovers that it has already been written—and unintelligibly. So the scholarly lady must repair to the real Xanth, where she is sent by the Good Magician Humfrey on a quest to save two pocket-sized dragons, Drew and Drusie, who are essential to the environment of Xanth. . . . The puns for which the Xanthian corpus is famous are as numerous and outrageous as ever." Booklist

The Dastard. TOR Bks. 2000 303p o.p.
ISBN 0-312-86900-2 LC 00-31679

"A Tom Doherty Associates book"

Another adventure set in the land of Xanth. "Many familiar characters make their appearance in this slowly unwinding yarn about the eponymous boy, self-named for his dastardly deeds, who undoes history in order to ruin the happiness of everyone he meets, and about the triplet princesses—Melody, Harmony and Rhythm—who are in the conspiracy to stop him." Publ Wkly

This installment "includes the author's usual array of puns and assorted verbal gags as well as an earnest tale about the heart's ability to transform evil into good." Libr J

DoOon mode. TOR Bks. 2001 368p o.p.
ISBN 0-312-87463-4 LC 00-48834

"A Tom Doherty Associates book"

In this novel "a trio of cat-based androids from DoOon Mode accepts a challenge posed by the evil Emperor Ddwng to find clinically depressed, suicidal 14-year-old Colene and her loving, stable husband, Darius, to force them to hand over the powerful Chip. With the Chip, Ddwng will be able to travel the multiverse—and raid it ruthlessly for supplies and genetic material." Publ Wkly

"Anthony delivers a parable that uses high-tech trappings to conceptualize the struggle between good and evil." Libr J

For love of evil. Morrow 1988 383p (Incarnations of immortality, bk6) o.p.
LC 88-2975

"Fleeing persecution by the Church, a young sorcerer in medieval France seeks refuge among the Franciscans, dedicating his life to the triumph of good over evil until a strange twist of fate forces him to assume the role of his greatest enemy and take his place among the immortal Incarnations. . . . Anthony tackles sensitive moral issues with his customary high spirits." Libr J

Followed by And eternity

Fractal mode. Putnam 1992 302p (Mode) o.p.
LC 91-11745

"An Ace/Putnam book"

In this second volume in the Mode series Colene and "her traveling companions continue their trek across the dimensions of reality, they encounter a fractal world where a young woman struggles to change her oppressive society. . . . The author's protagonists are as ingenuous as ever, infusing his story with an innocence that wavers between charming and cloying. His enthusiasm for new ideas, however, is infectious, and his imagination shows no signs of wear." Libr J

Followed by Chaos mode

Anthony, Piers—*Continued*

Hope of earth. TOR Bks. 1997 416p il (Geodyssey, v3) o.p.
ISBN 0-312-86340-3 LC 96-53954
"A Tom Doherty Associates book"
The third volume of "Anthony's geodyssey series explores what makes humans human via several characters living in various places and times throughout the world's history. Based on meticulous historical research, the book paints a vivid portrait of humanity and its hell-bent rush to destruction from disease." Libr J

Isle of woman. TOR Bks. 1993 448p (Geodyssey, vl) o.p.
LC 93-25511
"A Tom Doherty Associates book"
In this first volume of the author's Geodyssey series "an archetypal man and woman, joined by their unfulfilled destiny, provide the link in a series of vignettes that explore the panorama of human history. . . . [This] novel is, on one level, a story of reincarnation, as the couple known as Blaze and Ember seek each other through the centuries. On a deeper level, the author identifies those human instincts that at one time guaranteed the species' survival but that now harbor the seeds of its self-destruction. . . . Well conceived and written from the heart." Libr J
Followed by Shame of man

Juxtaposition. Ballantine Bks. 1982 358p il o.p.
LC 81-69507
"A Del Rey book"
In the third book in the Apprentice Adept series, the hero "Stile achieves his long-sought goal of pluto-cratic Citizen status on the science-based planet Proton while further exploring the parallel magic-based world of Phaze, where he is the Blue Adept. Now, however, the overlapping worlds are drawing apart and unless Stile can overcome the opposition of most of Proton's Citizens and Phaze's Adepts to correct an imbalance between them, both worlds could be destroyed. Should he succeed, he will face the ultimate dilemma of which world to live in permanently. Fans of this series will find all the action and incidents they've come to expect. . . . Moving events along a breakneck pace, Anthony efficiently clears up the mysteries of Stile's life, ties up all the loose ends and provides a happy ending. Like the first two books, this is a diverting lightweight science-fantasy adventure." Publ Wkly
Followed by Out of Phaze

Muse of art. TOR Bks. 1999 445p map (Geodyssey, v4) o.p.
ISBN 0-312-86896-0 LC 99-12905
"A Tom Doherty Associates book"
Sequel to Hope of earth
"This fourth volume of the Geodyssey series examines the role of art in society, with art defined broadly to include storytelling and ritual as well as the plastic arts. It features the bright, difficult, and so aptly named Melee, the inarticulate but still eloquent Dillon, the crippled Od, and the wise Bata struggling with the various motivations for making art: love, spirituality, even greed. While the book ranges from prehistory to Olmec Mexico and Augustan England to posthistory after an awesomely destructive Third World War, Anthony's message remains hopeful." Booklist

On a pale horse. Ballantine Bks. 1983 249p (Incarnations of immortality, bk1) o.p.
LC 83-6043
"A Del Rey book"
In this first volume of the Incarnations of immortality series "a young man named Zane tries to commit suicide and winds up killing Death instead, whereupon he has to take on the job himself. Zane subsequently learns the responsibilities of his position and deals with an array of logical complexities." Booklist
Followed by Bearing an hourglass

Out of Phaze. Putnam 1987 288p (Apprentice Adept) o.p.
LC 86-25448
"An Ace/Putnam book"
This is the fourth installment in the author's Apprentice Adept series
"The sister worlds of magic-based Phaze and science-based Proton intersect as a magician's son and a self-willed machine transfer minds, becoming stranded in each other's potentially hostile world. . . . [This is] a tale of adventure and intrigue featuring unicorns, evil wizards, extraterrestrials, and political tyrants, as well as two engagingly naive protagonists." Libr J
Followed by Robot Adept

Phaze doubt. Putnam 1990 303p o.p.
LC 89-24249
"An Ace/Putnam book"
In the concluding volume of the Apprentice Adept series "the spacefaring Hectare have conquered the planet and captured its leading citizens. The only Adept left is Nepe/Flach, the grandchild of Stile and Blue. Following obscure clues from the Oracle, Nepe/Flach must logically entice a Hectarian spy into switching sides and helping the loyal underground." Publ Wkly

Robot Adept. Putnam 1988 286p (Apprentice Adept) o.p.
LC 87-19148
"An Ace/Putnam book"
In the fifth installment in the author's Apprentice Adept series "two pairs of star-crossed lovers hold the fates of magic-based Phaze and its sister-world Proton in their hands as Adverse Adepts and Contrary Citizens plot to gain control of an all-knowing computer and its magical analog. Fans of games, logic problems, and mental conundrums will appreciate the plot permutations that highlight the adventures of four feisty heroes." Libr J
Followed by Unicorn point

Shame of man. TOR Bks. 1994 380p (Geodyssey, v2) o.p.
LC 94-21747
"A Tom Doherty Associates book"
In this second volume of the Geodyssey series Anthony "weaves strands that stretch across all human time into tales that exemplify the changes wrought by evolution and cultural development. The characters in any one chapter are reincarnated in the next, so that the main character here, originally prehuman Hu, becomes Hue and Hugh and Hu'o and Huu as time and change march on." Booklist
Followed by Hope of earth

Anthony, Piers—*Continued*

Split infinity. Ballantine Bks. 1980 372p il o.p.
LC 79-20282

"A Del Rey book"

In this first volume of the author's Apprentice Adept series "Stile, the principal character . . . takes his turns between two parallel worlds. His home world of Proton is a strictly regulated mechanized society where wealthy Citizens own serfs who work and compete for them in the Games. These Games are a central feature of the novel and range from tiddlywinks to marathon racing. The fantasy land of Phaze is an organic world into which he escapes to avoid a mysterious killer. There he meets a unicorn, . . . who changes into a woman, and a man who changes into a werewolf, among others. Here he discovers that he can cast magic spells and sets out to find his alter ego." Voice Youth Advocates

Followed by Blue Adept

Unicorn point. Putnam 1989 303p (Apprentice Adept) o.p.
LC 88-18478

"An Ace/Putnam book"

The sixth volume in the author's Apprentice Adept series witnesses "the parallel wars of wits and politics on the magical world of Phaze and its technological sister-world Proton take a bizarre twist as the children of the Robot Adept Mach and his Phaze-born counterpart Bane play hide-and-seek for keeps to foil the plans of the Contrary Citizens of Proton and the Adverse Adepts of Phaze." Libr J

Followed by Phaze doubt

Virtual mode. Putnam 1991 304p (Mode) o.p.
LC 90-42919

"An Ace/Putnam book"

In this first volume of the author's Mode series "Darius, a Cyng of Hlahtar, had traveled to earth in order to meet his true love, a suicidal teen named Colene, and bring her back to his universe. But in proving to her that other worlds exist, Darius uses up the power of the artifact that would have permitted them to travel, and they must try a slower, more dangerous method: the creation of a four-dimensional universe." Publ Wkly

"Anthony's 'realism' manages to avoid sleaze, and the lighter parts of the narrative, while indeed light, are seldom frivolous. In addition, Anthony's pacing and world building are up to standard." Booklist

Followed by Fractal mode

Wielding a red sword. Ballantine Bks. 1986 297p (Incarnations of immortality, bk4) o.p.
LC 86-7900

"A Del Rey book"

"The fourth book in Anthony's . . . Incarnations of Immortality series describes the recruitment of an Indian prince to become the latest Incarnation of War—serving alongside Death, Time, Nature and others. Mym reluctantly accepts the office as a way to cut through the tangled political web that has produced famine in his homeland and trampled on his private life. As hard as Mym works to keep earthly peace, however, Satan is ahead of him with snares and lures that lead to hell." Publ Wkly

"Anthony is not quite as comfortable with the Indian background or the action scenes as one would wish. Otherwise, this book contains about the best prose and characterization the author has yet produced in a major work." Booklist

Followed by Being a green mother

The willing spirit; {by} Piers Anthony and Alfred Tella. TOR Bks. 1997 287p o.p.
ISBN 0-312-86266-0 LC 96-29211

"A Tom Doherty Associates book"

"Mohini, the beautiful goddess of love, and the god Ravana, ugly and cruel and lustful, gamble over the fate of a human named Hari. If Hari, with Mohini's help, can seduce (or be seduced by) seven women before Ravana can get him killed, Mohini will win a century of peace from Ravana; if not, she'll owe the dark god 'a century of erotic frenzy.'" Publ Wkly

"An unusual plot, skillfully rendered." Libr J

With a tangled skein. Ballantine Bks. 1985 280p (Incarnations of immortality, bk3) o.p.
LC 85-6179

"A Del Rey book"

In this third volume in the Incarnations of immortality series "the beautiful Irish lass Niobe takes on the duties of one of the three Fates—Clotho, spinner of the thread of life—in order to avenge her dead lover. She finds, however, that she has only begun a duel with the Devil." Booklist

"Much of the fascination of Anthony's book lies in the idea of the Incarnations and their relationship to the world. His universe is meticulously worked out, and the rules are consistently applied. Clotho emerges as a genuinely real and sympathetic woman, and Satan proves to be a compelling deceiver. The story is gripping, and the question of Fate's role in the life of humanity gives the novel an added depth of meaning and interest." Best Sellers

Followed by Wielding a red sword

Xone of contention. TOR Bks. 1999 304p o.p.
ISBN 0-312-86691-7 LC 99-22200

"A Tom Doherty Associates book"

"Edsel and Pia travel from Mundane to magical pun-filled Xanth by way of the 0-XOne—a PC with Magic Mesh access. Because theirs is a virtual visit, Edsel's and Pia's bodies are vacated in Mundane until Chlorine and Nimby (Xanth folks) take them over. . . . The intentionally outrageous plot is inevitably loaded with puns that range from hokey to hilarious." Voice Youth Advocates

Yon ill wind. TOR Bks. 1996 320p o.p.
ISBN 0-312-86227-X LC 96-16216

"A Tom Doherty Associates book"

In this title set in the magical land of Xanth "the plot follows the Demon X(A/N)th as he tries to win a wager with his fellow demons by assuming the form of one of the creatures of the realm he rules. He becomes a Nimby (Not In My Neighborhood), a creature with the body of a dragon and the head of an ass, who must wring a tear from the first person he meets. Further complications ensue when a human family from Mundania (i.e. Florida) is blown into Xanth while traveling through a hurricane in their RV." Voice Youth Advocates

Zombie lover. TOR Bks. 1998 303p o.p.
ISBN 0-312-86690-9 LC 98-23526

"A Tom Doherty Associates book"

In this installment in the Xanth series, "a gorgeous black girl named Brianna finds herself lusted after by

Anthony, Piers—*Continued*

Xeth, king of the Zombies. Being inclined, even grimly determined, to decline his attentions, she thereupon must flee to the Isle of Women." Booklist

This fantasy provides "outrageous puns and offbeat humor as well as the author's customary commentary on moral and social issues." Libr J

Antunes, António Lobo, 1942-

The inquisitors' manual; translated by Richard Zenith. Grove Press 2003 435p $25

ISBN 0-8021-1732-5 LC 2002-33858

Original Portuguese edition, 1997

"Antonio de Oliveira Salazar is not the best known of 20th-century dictators, but he was as cruel and ruthless as any of them in his rule over Portugal from 1932 to 1968 . . . . [The author] recreates the harrowing story of Salazar's regime, building gradually from the petty problems and thoughts of a host of characters, related in stream of consciousness, to blunt exposition of the inhuman inner workings and brutal violence of authoritarianism." Publ Wkly

"Lobo Antunes, one of the most skillfull psychological portraitists writing anywhere, renders the turpitude of an entire society through an impasto of intensely individual voices." New Yorker

The return of the caravels; a novel; translated from the Portuguese by Gregory Rabassa. Grove Press 2002 210p $24

ISBN 0-8021-1708-2 LC 2001-51236

Original Portuguese edition 1988

The author "follows half a dozen characters through the breakup of Portugal's colonial dominion in the 1970s while occasionally backtracking to the 16th century to trace the effects of Vasco da Gama's journeys." Publ Wkly

"Antunes has to fight to stop himself from being swept away by the almost appalling energy of his language. You sense that rather than struggling for the next phrase, his art lies in containing words without taming them. Line by line, you get exact physical detail. Antunes makes you see. He's also obsessive, repetitive, entirely preoccupied by memory." N Y Times Book Rev

Appelfeld, Aharon *See* Appelfeld, Aron

Appelfeld, Aron

Badenheim 1939; [by] Aharon Appelfeld; translated by Dalya Bilu. Godine 1980 148p o.p.

LC 80-66192

Originally published in Hebrew

"Year after year the regular summer guests, most of them comfortably wealthy middle-class Jews, come to the little resort town Badenheim near Vienna to be entertained, to eat strawberry tarts, to find love. Even in 1939, with the Nazis firmly ensconced in Vienna, no one is allowed to worry, and the few who do are declared mad. In the end, Badenheim is closed off; all its people—guests, musicians, pastry chefs, even the dogs and goldfish of the town—are packed into cattle cars. Still the people delude themselves into thinking that they are going 'home,' back to their origins in Poland, and anyone who doubts this is argued down. The novel ends with the closing of the cattle cars' sliding doors." Libr J

"The most shocking thing about this novel is not its satirical humor, but its charm. Appelfeld manages to treat his appalling theme with grace." N Y Rev Books

The conversion; translated from the Hebrew by Jeffrey M. Green. Schocken Bks. 1998 228p o.p.

ISBN 0-8052-4153-1 LC 98-18169

Original Hebrew edition, 1991

"Some time before WWII, Karl Hübner, petty municipal bureaucrat in a provincial Austrian town, converts from Judaism to Christianity to advance his career. . . . Although the Holocaust is never mentioned (nor are years and dates), it is ever-present—and directly prefigured in the tragic finale, when Karl and his former housemaid, Gloria, an observant Jew with whom he is reunited and falls in love, are murdered by anti-Semitic peasants." Publ Wkly

This "is at once a historical novel about the Austrian past and an allegorical analysis of the significance of religious identity, addressing issues that Appelfeld sees as still relevant at the end of the 20th century." N Y Times Book Rev

Katerina; a novel; [by] Aharon Appelfeld; translated by Jeffrey M. Green. Random House 1992 212p o.p.

LC 91-50975

Original Hebrew edition, 1989

This is the "story of Katerina, a Polish housekeeper who works for a succession of Jewish families in the years before WW II. Raised in a culture permeated with virulent anti-Semitism, she must constantly try to overcome the prejudice instilled by her bitter mother, who beat her, and her callous father, who attempted to rape her. One by one, Jewish people who are good to Katerina die: an employer murdered by thugs on Passover; a moody, perfectionistic female pianist. Then her own baby, whom she has raised as a Jew, is snatched from her arms and killed. For knifing her son's murderer, Katerina spends more than 40 years in prison. Other inmates cheer as freight trains take Jews to concentration camps. Released from prison, Katerina lives in a hut on her deceased family's deserted farm and, at age 79, narrates her life story." Publ Wkly

Archer, Jeffrey, 1940-

As the crow flies. HarperCollins Pubs. 1991 617p o.p.

LC 90-56105

This novel "tells the story of a poor barrow boy or street peddler, Charlie Trumper, born in the year 1900 in the slums of London's Whitechapel district. Charlie . . . rises to become the founder of Britain's first and most prestigious department store, [and] a member of the peerage." N Y Times Book Rev

This novel has the "usual Archer signature: fast-moving plot, romance, high finance, and good natured mockery of Britain. It uses the conventions of the classic revenge tale, featuring a feud that continues through two generations and the stock characters of the genre: the resourceful hero, the clever childhood sweetheart, the bastard son, the nefarious mother. . . . Archer knows what fast-reading light fiction is all about and dishes it up with panache." Quill Quire

Archer, Jeffrey, 1940-—*Continued*

The collected short stories. HarperCollins Pubs. 1998 599p o.p.

LC 98-17260

Contents: Never stop on the motorway; Old love; Shoeshine boy; Cheap at half the price; Broken routine; An eye for an eye; The luncheon; The coup; The perfect murder; You'll never live to regret it; The first miracle; The loophole; The Hungarian professor; The steal; Christina Rosenthal; Colonel Bullfrog; Do not pass go; Chunnel vision; Dougie Mortimer's right arm; Clean sweep Ignatius; Not for sale; One-night stand; A chapter of accidents; Checkmate; The century; Just good friends; Henry's hiccup; A matter of principle; Trial and error; The perfect gentleman; À la carte; The Chinese statue; The wine taster; Tinco Danaos . . .; Not the real thing; One man's meat . . .

The eleventh commandment. HarperCollins Pubs. 1998 359p o.p.

LC 98-3670

"The story begins with the assassination of a Colombian presidential candidate by one Connor Fitzgerald, considered to be a professional's professional. Fitzgerald is a CIA operative, and the dead candidate was the boss of a cocaine cartel. Fitzgerald is sent to Russia to do a number on the Communist Party leader who is running for president there. But Fitzgerald is arrested and thrown into an escape-proof prison. . . . It's a classic CIA sting, but with a difference—this time it is one of their own they leave languishing in a foreign jail. What keeps the suspense going is the fact that the U.S. president and the CIA director are vying for ultimate power, and if the president loses, it's good-bye Fitz." Booklist

First among equals. Linden Press/Simon & Schuster 1984 415p o.p.

LC 84-11267

"Despite radically different family backgrounds and political beliefs, Charles Hampton, Simon Kerslake, and Raymond Gould all share a fiercely held ambition: to be prime minister of England. Hampton, the aristocrat, employs deceit and petty trickery to gain position in Tory leadership; party archrival Kerslake suffers near financial ruin in the aftermath of an ill-chosen investment; and Gould, the intellectual Labourite, risks scandal with his romantic entanglements." Booklist

"Covering their careers from 1964 into the future to 1991, the author manages the labyrinthine British parliamentary system with an adroit hand and generates real suspense in the race. For there can be only one winner, and even in the striving each man pays a price. Fastpaced and satisfying." Libr J

The fourth estate. HarperCollins Pubs. 1996 549p o.p.

LC 96-18978

This novel "explores the lives and careers of Richard Armstrong and Keith Townsend—incredibly rich, incredibly ruthless and the biggest newspaper barons in the world. Armstrong, born an impoverish Jew in Eastern Europe, rises to power through cunning, deceit and cruelty; Townsend, born a privileged Australian, expands his father's media empire by lying, scheming, and back stabbing. . . . While 'The Fourth Estate' describes in excruciating detail the processes by which both men go about snapping up newspapers, the account of both men's childhoods are interesting, as are some of the scenes of their head-to-head competition." N Y Times Book Rev

Honor among thieves. HarperCollins Pubs. 1993 381p o.p.

LC 92-56224

In this suspense novel about Saddam Hussein's attempt to steal the Declaration of Independence "Hamid Al Obaydi, Hussein's conniving . . . Ambassador to the United Nations, hires Antonio Cavalli, the ineffably suave son of a New York Mafia lawyer, to pinch the parchment. Among the eager participants Cavalli recruits are an actor who can mimic President Clinton's voice, a besotted Irish forger, a Hollywood film director convicted of statutory rape and a corrupt Presidential adviser." N Y Times Book Rev

The "deficit in verisimilitude doesn't detract too much from the novel's entertainment value, . . . and some will be amused that Archer himself good-naturedly joins in the criticsm." Publ Wkly

Kane & Abel. Simon & Schuster 1980 c1979 540p o.p.

LC 79-23311

First published 1979 in the United Kingdom

A "novel about obsession and ambition. William Kane is the scion of a wealthy Boston family; Abel Rosnovski is the illegitimate son of a Polish baron. Both men are born on the same day in 1906; both are extremely ambitious and intelligent; and both go on—through very different means—to amass great wealth, prestige and power. This book traces their 60-year rise to the top and the terrible feud that arises between them." West Coast Rev Books

"This is a novel of plot. It entertains, as it was meant to do. . . . It has adventure, war, suspense, surprise, sex, thwarted young love, and conflict. If things are manipulated a bit, who cares?" Best Sellers

Followed by The prodigal daughter

A matter of honor. Linden Press 1986 399p o.p. ISBN 0-671-62434-2 LC 86-7405

"Adam Scott is left a most unorthodox bequest in his father's will that takes him on a terrifying chase across Europe pursuing a priceless icon and being pursued by Soviet, American, and British intelligence forces. Archer cagily impels his well-crafted characters straight into action, then ever so slowly fills in all the dimensions of the struggle in which they are engaged. . . . Scott's steely determination to uphold his family's honor holds the reader's interest, and his skill at eluding the enemy culminates in a master stratagem that gives the story its final twist. A fast-paced and exciting, though corpse-riddled, thriller." Booklist

Not a penny more, not a penny less. Doubleday 1976 230p o.p.

"Harvey Metcalfe, an American entrepreneur with a continuous string of shady deals to his credit, pulls his latest one on an assortment of three Englishmen and one American. These four purchase large numbers of shares of stock in Discovery Oil, a bogus company Metcalfe has established. Metcalfe makes a killing, and the four lose a total of a million dollars in the process. . . . One of the four, Stephen Bradley, an American mathematician, decides to contact the others and arrange a counter-

Archer, Jeffrey, 1940-—*Continued*

swindle. They meet and agree to his plans." Best Sellers

"A jolly good British crime caper, marvelously well plotted, with just the right amounts of romance, wit and savoir-faire, this is fun all the way. Not the least of that fun comes from the knowledge that when the author was a young M.P. he himself was swindled out of a bundle in a trick scheme not unlike the one to which his four stalwart heroes fall victim here." Publ Wkly

The prodigal daughter. Linden Press/Simon & Schuster 1982 464p o.p.

LC 82-15310

"Archer continues the family saga begun in 'Kane & Abel'. The prodigal daughter is Abel's only child and pride of his life. She meets and marries her father's arch-enemy's only son. This naturally causes a break with both families. However, through her tremendous drive for success, hard work, and good business insight she succeeds in establishing a boutique chain, then reconciled with her father, she heads the hotel empire he started. Later she enters politics, where her honesty and drive lead her eventually to the U.S. presidency." Libr J

Arkin, Frieda

Hedwig and Berti; Frieda Arkin. Thomas Dunne Books 2005 258p $23.95

ISBN 0-312-33354-4 LC 2004-56107

This novel depicts the "unlikely marriage of a grandly Teutonic woman, Hedwig Kessler and her diminutive cousin Berti, two upper-class German Jews forced to leave their homeland during the rise of the Nazis. They flee to London, then to New York City, and from there, finally, to a university town in Kansas. In London, Hedwig gives birth to a daughter whose broodingly dark construction and immense genius for the piano point back in time to the tragedy of her bloodline." N Y Times Book Rev

"While the story starts slowly—not much happens until Gerda is old enough to talk—the book is infused with the keen ache of loss, the constant bewilderment and defensiveness of the immigrant and the queer charm of odd couple Hedwig and Berti, by turns furiously miserable and delightfully absurd." Publ Wkly

Armitage, G. E. *See* Edric, Robert, 1956-

Arnow, Harriette Louisa Simpson, 1908-1986

The dollmaker; [by] Harriette Simpson Arnow. Macmillan 1954 549p o.p.

"Gertie Nevels, a courageous and unselfish Kentucky countrywoman who has a talent amounting to a passion for whittling small objects out of wood, is forced by the war to leave the happy, although poverty-stricken, community where she has spent her life and go to Detroit, where her husband has found work in a factory. The meanness, squalor, and lack of privacy of her new surroundings, and the debasing effect of the city on her husband and on some of their children, oppress her, but she maintains her integrity and her fatih in her fellow human beings." New Yorker

"It is hard to believe that anyone who opens its pages will soon forget [Gertie] and her sufferings as traced in Harriette Arnow's long, heavily packed masterwork." NY Times Book Rev

Arouet, François Marie *See* Voltaire, 1694-1778

The **Art** of the story; an international anthology of contemporary short stories; edited by Daniel Halpern. Viking 1999 667p o.p.

ISBN 0-670-88761-7 LC 99-13816

Contents: A gift from somewhere, by A. A. Aidoo; The keeper of the virgins, by H. Al-Shaykh; Amor divino, by J. Alvarez; The immortals, by M. Amis; The glass tower, by R. Arenas; Wilderness tips, by M. Atwood; Gorilla, my love, by T. C. Bambara; My mother's memoirs, my father's lie, and other true stories, by R. Banks; G-string, by N. Barker; Evermore, by J. Barnes; Aren't you happy for me? by R. Bausch; In Amalfi, by A. Beattie; Rara avis, by T. C. Boyle; Mr. Green, by R. O. Butler; The fat man in history, by P. Carey; The courtship of Mr. Lyon, by A. Carter; Are these actual miles? by R. Carver; The old man slave and the mastiff, by P. Chamoiseau; Dharma, by V. Chandra; Never marry a Mexican, by S. Cisneros; The prospect from the silver hills, by J. Crace; Night women, by E. Danticat; The house behind, by L. Davis; All because of the mistake, by D. del Giudice; Ysrael, by J. Diaz; Betrayal, by P. Duncker; Reflections of spring, by Thu Huong Duong; The girl who left her sock on the floor, by D. Eisenberg; The twenty-seventh man, N. Englander; The parakeet, by V. Erofeyev; Roberto narrates, by P. Esterházy; My father, the Englishman, and I, by N. Farah; Optimists, by R. Ford; The story of the lizard who had the habit of dining on his wives, by E. Galeano; The Hammam, by H. Guibert; Escort, by A. Gurnah; Midnight and I'm not famous yet, by B. Hannah; Portrait of the avant-garde, by P. Høeg; Moving house, by P. Huelle; A family supper, by K. Ishiguro; Encounter, by R. Jacobsen; The first day, by E. P. Jones; Remember young Cecil, by J. Kelman; Intimacy, by H. Kureishi; The stump-grubber, by T. Lindgren; Wish, by B. A. Mason; Everything in this country must, by C. McCann; Pornography, by I. McEwan; Behind the blue curtain, by S. Millhauser; Willing, by L. Moore; The lifeguard, by M. Morris; The canebrake, by M. Mrabet; The management of grief, by B. Mukherjee; Muradhan and Selvihan; or, the tale of the crystal kiosk, by M. Mungan; The elephant vanishes, by H. Murakami; Mark of Satan, by J. C. Oates; In the shadow of war, by B. Okri; Where the Jackals howl, by A. Oz; The life and adventures of Shed Number XII, by V. Pelevin; Talking dog, by F. Prose; The free radio, by S. Rushdie; Africa kills her sun, by K. Saro-Wiwa; The ring, by I. Schulze; Learning to swim, by G. Swift; A riddle, by A. Tabucchi; Minutes of glory, by Ngugi wa Thiong'o; On the golden porch, by T. Tolstaya; John-Jin, by R. Tremain; Who, me a bum? by L. Valenzuela; Cinnamon skin, by E. White; You can't get lost in Cape Town, by Z. Wicomb; Doc's story, by J. E. Wideman; The farm, by J. Williams; Dirt angel, by J. Wilmot; The green man, by J. Winterson; The night in question, by T. Wolff; The child who raised poisonous snakes, by Ts'an-hsüeh; Helix, by B. Yoshimoto

Asch, Sholem, 1880-1957

The Apostle; translated by Maurice Samuel. Putnam 1943 804p o.p.

"Around the life of St. Paul the author has built a picture of the early spread of Christianity. The novel opens soon after the crucifixion when Paul with others in Jerusalem became aware of the disciples' preachings, and it follows Paul to his death. Religious and social conditions important in the development of Christianity are portrayed, but Paul's work is always the dominant theme." Booklist

In "'The Apostle,' Sholem Asch has written a book which should stand beside 'The Nazarene.' Its erudition, its essential reverence for the two faiths concerned, its scholarly and dramatic portrayal of the Jew who spread the gospel to the gentiles will call forth the respect of every civilized and intelligent reader." N Y Her Trib Books

Mary; translated by Leo Steinberg. Putnam 1949 436p o.p.

This follows the story of the Virgin Mary and her Son from Mary's marriage to Joseph to the Crucifixion and Resurrection

"With the addition of little not inherent in Biblical records, a unique mother-son relationship becomes the basis for a novel of great beauty. From the time when Mary the pure in heart hears heavenly voices proclaiming her as mother of the long promised Messiah, until years later when she beholds Jesus triumphant over death, she experiences all possible maternal pride, humility, anguish. Her early married years comprise most of the book; Jesus' increasing social consciousness, his visions of destiny, and Mary's perplexed awareness are vividly pictured against the background of a devout Jewish home." Libr J

Moses; translated by Maurice Samuel. Putnam 1951 505p o.p.

This novel depicts the life of Moses and the Exodus of the Jews from Egypt and their wanderings and sufferings before reaching the Promised Land

"With the deft craftsmanship of a master, Sholem Asch has recaptured the magnificence of Moses and the heroic moment of his epiphany on the pages of Hebrew history. He has assembled . . . facts in the life of the chosen leader of a chosen people, the Orientalia, Scripture, law, customs, traditions, and having assimilated them, he has reassembled them creatively to call to life out of the dusty tomes of the library, a titanic personage, an elect yet human people, an outstanding epoch in the history of man. Here is the historical novel at its literary best." Best Sellers

The Nazarene; translated by Maurice Samuel. Putnam 1939 698p o.p.

A novel based on the life of Christ told from three different points of view. First there is the narrative as a modern Polish Jewish scholar hears it from lips of one who claims to be the reincarnation of the Roman military governor of Jerusalem. Then there is the 'fifth gospel' written by Judas Iscariot, and finally there is the story as the young Jew remembers it when he realizes that he himself is the reincarnation of a disciple of the Pharisee, Rabbi Nicodemon

"Judged purely as a novel, The Nazarene is a superb achievement. Even on the factual side, a work such as Papini's Life is thin beside it. This is because Mr. Asch has taken an infinite amount of trouble to build up an historical background against which the figure of Jesus may move authentically, with that sense of reality which we should expect of fiction as of life." Atlantic

The prophet; translated by Arthur Saul Super. Putnam 1955 343p o.p.

This volume tells of the second Isaiah, or Deutero-Isaiah, who supposedly lived during the conquest of Babylon by Cyrus the Persian in the fifth century B.C. At the close of the book the first of the Israelites are about to set out for their homeland

"The story unfolds against a lush . . . background of pagan life in Babylon. All the same, it remains high level fiction of biblical background, about one of the strangest but most inspired of the great prophets of Israel, in her time of troubles." Chicago Sunday Trib

Asher, Neal L.

The skinner; [by] Neal Asher. TOR Bks. 2004 c2002 1v 473p $26.95

ISBN 0-7653-0737-5 LC 2004-274424

"On the planet Spatterjay arrive three travelers: Janer, acting as the eyes of the hornet Hive mind, on a mission not yet revealed to him; Erlin, searching for Ambel the ancient sea captain who can teach her how to live; and Sable Keech, on a vendetta he cannot abandon, though he himself has been dead for 700 years. This remote world is mostly ocean, and it is a rare visitor who ventures beyond the safety of the island dome. Outside it, only the native Hoopers dare risk the voracious appetites of the planet's wildlife." Publisher's note

"Asher displays great virtuosity in dramatizing Spatterjay's eat-and-be-eaten ecosystem. . . . Episodes of horrific violence alternate with surprisingly lucid conversations that touch on issues like the psychology of revenge in the aftermath of a holocaust. Asher keeps raising the stakes so that despite the repetitive nature of the violence, it never becomes merely formulaic. You may not relish your stay on Spatterjay. But you won't easily forget it." N Y Times Book Rev

Asimov, Isaac, 1920-1992

The best science fiction of Isaac Asimov. Doubleday 1986 320p o.p.

LC 85-31200

Includes the following stories: All the troubles of the world; A loint of paw; The dead past; Death of a Foy; Dreaming is a private thing; Dreamworld; Eyes do more than see; The feeling of power; Flies; Found; Franchise; The fun they had; How it happened; I'm in Marsport without Hilda; The immortal bard; It's such a beautiful day; Jokester; The last answer; The last question; My son, the physicist; Obituary; Spell my name with an S; Strikebreaker; Sure thing; The ugly little boy; Unto the fourth generation

This collection contains "28 pieces, including two comic poems . . . and six short-shorts. . . . These selections date mostly from the '50s, the period in which Asimov [was] beginning to explore a variety of ideas and story types." Publ Wkly

The Bicentennial Man

In The Hugo winners p259-99

In Asimov, I. The complete robot

Asimov, Isaac, 1920-1992—*Continued*
In Asimov, I. The complete stories

The caves of steel
In Asimov, I. The rest of the robots p165-362

The complete robot. Doubleday 1982 557p o.p.
LC 81-43134

Contents: A boy's best friend; Sally; Someday; Point of view; Think; True love; Robot AL-76 goes astray; Victory unintentional; Stranger in paradise; Light verse; Segregationist; Robbie; Let's get together; Mirror image; The tercentenary incident; First law; Runaround; Reason; Catch that rabbit; Liar; Satisfaction guaranteed; Lenny; Galley slave; Little lost robot; Risk, Escape; Evidence; The evitable conflict; Feminine intuition; . . . That thou art mindful of him; The Bicentennial Man [novelette]

"This massive volume contains 31 of Asimov's robot stories, from 'Robbie' of 1940 to the Hugo and Nebula award-winning 'Bicentennial Man' of 1976. It is far and away the best available single presentation of Asimov's concepts of the robot, which have influenced not only science fiction but to some extent actual thinking about industrial robots." Booklist

The complete stories. Doubleday 1990-1992 2v v1 pa $19.95
ISBN 0-385-41627-X (v1 pa) LC 90-3136

"A Foundation book"

This set contains all of Asimov's science fiction stories including the "collections 'Earth Is Room Enough' and 'Nine Tomorrows' from the 1950s as well as . . . 'Nightfall and Other Stories.'" SLJ

Fantastic voyage; a novel; based on the screenplay by Otto Klement and Joy Lewis Bixby. Houghton Mifflin 1966 239p o.p.

"Five people are sent on a rescue mission in a submarine, but this is no ordinary submarine moving through an ordinary sea. The people and the submarine are miniaturized. They are moving through a man's blood vessels to reach and break up a blood clot in his brain. The miniaturization will not last—they have only 60 minutes to do the job and leave the man's body, before they return to ordinary size." Publ Wkly

Forward the Foundation. Doubleday 1993 415p o.p.
LC 92-46655

"A Foundation book"

This volume and Prelude to Foundation predate the other Foundation novels in terms of internal chronology

"As a galactic empire struggles to hold onto the million worlds it purports to rule, one man conceives of an idea that will preserve human knowledge during the dark ages that will follow the empire's inevitable fall. The man is Hari Seldon. His idea: psychohistory." Libr J

Although "Asimov leans rather heavily on dialogue to carry the story, we are privileged to learn something more of Seldon, whom Asimov regards as his alter ego—intellectually vigorous, witty, vulnerable, and deeply concerned about the fate of his fallible species." Christ Sci Monit

Foundation. Gnome Press 1951 255p o.p.

"A story of a Galactic Empire of the future, and its successor in the government of the Milky Way." Publ Wkly

Followed by Foundation and empire

Foundation and earth. Doubleday 1986 356p o.p.
LC 86-2130

In the fifth novel of the Foundation series "Golan Trevize rejects the vaunted Selden Plan of Foundation and Empire in favor of a bold experiment in galactic unity. To ferret out the reason for his instinctive decision, Trevize embarks on a journey through uncharted space in search of a legendary planet known as Earth. Asimov's latest entry in his epic series features his usual cast of intelligent, likeable characters and just enough action to give substance to this novel of lucid speculations." Libr J

Foundation and empire. Gnome Press 1952 247p o.p.

In this second volume of the Foundation series "two groups struggle for control of the world's destiny in a future time when mankind has settled in the Milky Way. Then a mutant appears bringing with him a new threat for everyone." Chicago Public Libr

Followed by Second Foundation

Foundation's edge. Doubleday 1982 366p o.p.

The fourth novel in the Foundation series "shows us the Seldon Plan at midpoint and still surprisingly on target in spite of the passage of time and unforeseen events. The focus has narrowed to power struggles between the Foundations, both wishing to be the controlling element in the planned Second Galactic Empire, quite unlike Seldon's idealistic vision. And new players have been introduced into the game." Libr J

Followed by Foundation and earth

The gods themselves. Doubleday 1972 288p o.p.

"A three-level tale of the 21st century. The first level is told from the point of view of the Earth Scientists who are receiving mysterious messages from the para-Universe that matches Earth's in some unfathomable realm of time and space. The messages have to do with the Electron Pump that transfers matter back and forth between the two Universes. The second level of the story is told from viewpoints of the nonhumans in the 'other' Universe, where the messages are coming from. The third level is many years later at a time when scientists on a moon colony are grappling with the problems of the two Universes." Publ Wkly

"Imagination is the fount of Isaac Asimov's mastery. The suspense he generates . . . is low-key and subtle, and he has a gifted knack for making wild and indescribable superbeings (for he never quite describes them) seem lifelike, though scarcely human." Best Sellers

I, robot. Gnome Press 1950 253p $24; pa $7.99 o.p.
ISBN 0-553-80370-0; 0-553-29438-5 (pa)

"These loosely connected stories cover the career of Dr. Susan Calvin and United States Robots, the industry that she heads, from the time of the public's early distrust of these robots to its later dependency on them. This collection is an important introduction to a theme often found in science fiction: the encroachment of technology on our lives." Shapiro. Fic for Youth. 3d edition

The naked sun
In Asimov, I. The rest of the robots

Asimov, Isaac, 1920-1992—*Continued*

Nemesis. Doubleday 1989 364p o.p.
LC 89-32938

"A Foundation book"

"Using a primitive interstellar drive, an orbital colony reaches a newly discovered nearby star, only to find that it is on a collision course with the Solar System. The leader of the colony, determined to create a utopia, is opposed to doing anything to warn Earth, which, having discovered its own peril, is racing to build a much-improved starship. The scientific problems and characters are both well developed, and the pace is brisk throughout." Booklist

Nightfall; [by] Isaac Asimov and Robert Silverberg. Doubleday 1990 339p o.p.
LC 90-32469

"A Foundation book"

"Science and religion form an uneasy and fractious alliance on the planet Kalgash when a group of astronomers and a cult of religious fanatics predict the inevitable coming of darkness to a world that has never known night. Based on Asimov's short story 'Nightfall,' this joint venture by two of sf's most revered veterans focuses less on characterization than on the exploration of the human psyche's ability to cope with the imminent destruction of civilization." Libr J

Prelude to Foundation. Doubleday 1988 403p o.p.
LC 87-33086

"A Foundation book"

This novel and Forward the Foundation are set chronologically prior to other volumes in the Foundation series

"On Trantor, capital world of the Empire, the 32-year-old Seldon, a mathematician of promise who knows nothing of history or politics, attracts the unwelcome attention of the Imperial Government with his speculations about the predictive power of his equations. Before the Imperials can turn the new tool of psychohistory to their own purposes, a journalist named Chetter Hummin helps Seldon disappear into the cultural maze of Trantor—an experience that provides the naïve academic with an education in human diversity and duplicity." N Y Times Book Rev

This "is vintage Asimov, a novel that places ideas ahead of all its other elements but doesn't stint on characterization or entertaining plot lines. It also contains a fair number of mysteries, and . . . all of this is handled in a simple, direct style that never gets between the reader and the story." West Coast Rev Books

The rest of the robots. Doubleday 1964 556p o.p.

"Doubleday science fiction"

Short stories included are: Robot A1-76 goes astray; Victory unintentional; First Law; Let's get together; Satisfaction guaranteed; Risk; Lenny; Galley slave

The return of the Black Widowers; foreword by Harlan Ellison; edited by Charles Ardai. Carroll & Graf Publishers 2003 335p $24

ISBN 0-7867-1248-1 LC 2004-297972

"An Otto Penzler book"

Contents: The acquisitive chuckle; Ph as in phony; Early Sunday morning; The obvious factor; The iron gem; To the barest; Sixty million trillion combinations; The redhead; The wrong house; Triple devil; The men who read Isaac Asimov / by William Brittain; Northwestward; Yes, but why?; Lost in a space warp; Police at the door; The haunted cabin; The guest's guest; The woman in the bar; The last story / by Charles Ardai; Afterword: Birth of the Black Widowers

This is a "collection of the late Asimov's Black Widower stories, one of the incredibly prolific author's relatively rare ventures into the mystery genre. . . . For fans of puzzle mysteries, this one's a gem, from a kinder, gentler era." Booklist

Robot visions; illustrations by Ralph McQuarrie. New Am. Lib. 1990 482p il o.p.
LC 90-60121

"A Byron Priess Visual Publications, Inc. book. A ROC book"

Stories included are: Robot visions; Too bad!; Robbie; Reason; Liar!; Runaround; Evidence; Little lost robot; The evitable conflict; Feminine intuition; The Bicentennial Man; Someday; Think!; Segregationist; Mirror image; Lenny; Galley slave; Christmas without Rodney

Robots and empire. Doubleday 1985 383p o.p.

This "novel opens nearly two centuries after the close of . . . 'Robots of Dawn'. Earth has resumed interstellar colonization on a grand scale, and the Settler worlds are increasingly seen by the roboticized Spacer societies as a deadly threat. Gladia, heroine of 'Robots of Dawn,' must leave Aurora and travel the Galaxy with a descendant of Elijah Baley and the two robots Giskard and R. Daneel Olivaw in order to defeat a plot against Earth." Booklist

This novel "provides a link between Mr. Asimov's well-known Robot stories and his even better-known stories about the fall of the Galactic Empire and the rise of the Foundations that vie for dominance in the Post-Imperial galaxy. . . . Not only has Mr. Asimov once again turned an ethical dilemma into the basis of an exciting novel of suspense, but he has included within the body of the text all the information that readers unfamiliar with his previous books must know in order to follow the action and to appreciate the dilemma." NY Times Book Rev

The robots of dawn. Doubleday 1983 419p o.p.

Another of the author's novels featuring Interstellar police detective Elijah Baley, who is "coerced into solving a crime on alien territory that no one else has been able to crack. Here he takes on not only an unusual case but also a politically charged, hostile environment. However, Baley is by no means a superhero. Asimov has created an ordinary man with middle-class aspirations and mundane concerns. His foibles contrast with the flawless behavior of the numerous robots in the story." SLJ

The author's "narrative technique is more dependent than ever on dialogue, but his plotting is as ingenious as always. The mystery unravels with the polished, logical precision of a robot's program; but even with all the clues at hand, few will beat Baley, and Asimov, to the punch." Publ Wkly

Second Foundation. Gnome Press 1953 210p o.p.

Third book of the Foundation series about the efforts of a group of scientists who are trying to subdue the chaos and conflict of the galactic world. The story centers

Asimov, Isaac, 1920-1992—*Continued*
on fourteen-year-old Arkady Darrell's search for this secret group
Followed by Foundation's edge

Atherton, Nancy

Aunt Dimity, detective. Viking 2001 229p o.p.
ISBN 0-670-03021-X LC 2001-26322
"American born Lori, her attorney husband, Bill, and their adorable twin sons live near Finch, in a Cotswold cottage left by her mother's friend, Dimity, who offers Lori advice from beyond in the form of ghost writing in a blue leather journal. When Lori and her family return from a three-month visit to the States, she finds the town atwitter over the death of Prunella 'Pruneface' Hooper. . . . Bill conveniently stays in London while Lori gets to the bottom of things, which include the local Wicca, the ninetysomething Pym sisters, an old heartbreak from World War II, and assorted characters from central casting, British charm division." Booklist

Aunt Dimity digs in. Viking 1998 275p o.p.
ISBN 0-670-87061-7 LC 97-34633
"Living in the cottage left to Lori by her mother's close friend, Dimity Westwood, Lori is thankful for the arrival of the local and unmarried Francesca Sciaparelli to aid with the double joys of motherhood. In this corpseless tale, the mystery concerns a document stolen from the vicarage. . . . Asked to resolve the dilemma, Lori, a rare book expert, is aided by Aunt Dimity who communicates with her ghostly handwriting in a special blue journal." Publ Wkly

Atkins, Jack *See* Harris, Mark, 1922-

Atkinson, Kate

Case histories; a novel. Little, Brown 2004 312p $23.95
ISBN 0-316-74040-3 (Little, Brown); 0-385-60799-7 (Doubleday) LC 2004-2379
"Cambridge P.I. and Francophile Jackson Brodie serves as the link among three interwoven tales. Red herrings abound as Jackson plows through the sad cases of a missing toddler, a young woman brutally killed while temping at her father's law firm, and an overwrought mother driven to ax murder." Libr J
"The novel is packed with women whose appetites are large, and Atkinson's prose is correspondingly loose and louche: no single point of view predominates, and everyone's thoughts effortlessly rollick along." N Y Times Book Rev

Emotionally weird; a novel. Picador 2000 343p o.p.
ISBN 0-312-20324-1 LC 2001-269169
"It is 1972, and 20-year-old Effie and her 37-year-old mother, Nora, are holed up in the family cottage on a forsaken Scottish island, where they tell each other the secret details of their lives, sometimes truthfully, sometimes not. Effie's narration concerns her and her slovenly, oddball University of Dundee classmates. . . . Nora is equally cagey about her own story, which ultimately reveals the identity of Effie's father." Libr J
"Effie's story, which unfolds in a digressive, Tristram Shandy sort of way, perfectly exemplifies what Aquarian Age college life was like if you were bright, alienated, and addicted to novels." New Yorker

Human croquet; a novel. Picador 1997 349p o.p.
ISBN 0-312-15550-6 LC 97-802
"Young Isobel and her brother, Charles, are abandoned by their parents to the loveless care of a sour aunt, stern grandmother, and evil school master. They spend seven years yearning for the truth about their parents' disappearance and for their mother's return. It is their father, however, who returns—with a new young wife. The home of the protagonists is built on a site where, in the late 16th century, parallel events took place, and the novel warps and wends from past to present to future." Libr J
"Human Croquet is peppered with snatches of hilarious nonsensical suburban dialogue; big, exuberant exclamations; savvy rhetorical questions and a knuckle crackingly morbid sense of humor. . . . The narrator's youthful cynicism does not descend into mannerism. Atkinson shows that it is the logical outcome of cruelty and trauma." New Statesman (1913)

Not the end of the world; stories. Little, Brown 2002 244p il $23.95
ISBN 0-316-61430-0 LC 2003-40117
Contents: Charlene and Trudi go shopping; Tunnel of fish; Transparent fiction; Dissonance; Sheer big waste of love; Unseen translation; Evil dopplegangers; The cat lover; The bodies vest; Temporal anomaly; Wedding favors; Pleasureland
"While not as intense or unified as Atkinson's full-length work, this is a sharp and wholly original collection." Publ Wkly

Attebery, Brian, 1951-

(ed) The Norton book of science fiction. See The Norton book of science fiction

Atwood, Margaret, 1939-

Alias Grace. Talese 1996 468p il o.p.
LC 96-21689
This "novel is based on the case of Grace Marks, who in 1843 was sentenced to life imprisonment for her role in the murders of her employer and his mistress. In this fictional rendition, three men try to spring the beautiful alleged murderess from prison, by way of religion, pre-Freudian analysis, and chicanery." New Yorker
"Always a powerful writer, Atwood outdoes herself with compelling prose, expert control of the material, and fine attention to historical detail." Libr J

The blind assassin. Talese 2000 521p $26
ISBN 0-385-47572-1 LC 99-462109
"Dying octogenarian Iris Chasen's narration of the past carefully unravels a haunting story of tragedy, corruption, and cruel manipulation. Iris and her younger sister, Laura, are born into the privileged Canadian world of Port Ticonderoga in the early part of the 20th century. At 18, Iris is the marital pawn in a business deal between her financially desperate father and the ruthless, much-older industrialist Richard Griffen. When the father dies, the rebellious Laura is forced to move into Richard's controlling household, accelerating the tangled mess of relentless tragedy. At this point, Atwood . . . overlays a

Atwood, Margaret, 1939-—*Continued*

second story, an sf novel-within-a-novel, credited to Laura Chasen, that features nameless lovers trysting in squalor." Libr J

"Within the novel, stories produce anguish and arousal, charges and vindications, guilt and vengeance. For readers of the novel, all this may foster something like delight, although the fictional universe is hardly a pleasant one." Women's Rev Books

Bluebeard's egg and other stories. Houghton Mifflin 1986 281p o.p.

LC 86-10336

Contents: Significant moments in the life of my mother; Hurricane Hazel; Loulou; Uglypuss; Two stories about Emma; Bluebeard's egg; Spring song of the frogs; Scarlet ibis; The salt garden; In search of the rattlesnake plantain; The sunrise; Unearthing suite

"As Atwood's attitude ranges from the hilarious to the shocking, the reader is introduced to a series of relationships—husband and wife, parent and child, man and woman—in which the characters' inner and outer worlds are beautifully probed, expressed in the author's understated style." Booklist

Bodily harm. Simon & Schuster 1982 266p o.p.

LC 81-18370

"Renata (Rennie) Wilford, an attractive middle-aged woman journalist, author of fashion, travel and trivia articles for various Toronto 'lifestyle' magazines, abruptly loses part of a breast to cancer, breaks-up with her lover, and goes on a working holiday to a remote Caribbean island in the hope of restoring the 'normal' to her life." Can Forum

"Though this story gets off to a slow start, there is nothing gratuitous here. Margaret Atwood has . . . created a sophisticated, superbly orchestrated allegorical novel. Her characteristically introspective style is greatly enhanced by an unusually cohesive plot and a political theme that manages to steer clear of didacticism. Bodily Harm is Atwood's richest, most fully realized work to date." Saturday Rev

Cat's eye. Doubleday 1989 c1988 446p o.p.

LC 88-24345

First published 1988 in Canada

Elaine Risley, the narrator of this novel, "is a Canadian painter of some renown who, at 50, has returned to her childhood city of Toronto for a retrospective of her work. The dull, provincial city of her youth has become world class in the intervening years . . . but in the week she is there her interest in the city's new galleries and restaurants and shops and, in many ways, in the retrospective itself, is only glancing. Her focus, and the novel's, is all on the past." N Y Times Book Rev

"Atwood's achievement is the decoding of childhood's secrets, and the creation of a flawed and haunting work of art." Time

Dancing girls and other stories. Simon & Schuster 1982 c1977 240p o.p.

LC 82-10308

First published 1977 in Canada

Contents: The man from Mars; Betty; Polarities; Under glass; The grave of the famous poet; Hair jewellery; When it happens; A travel piece; The resplendent Quetzal; Training; Lives of the poets; Dancing girls; The sin eater; Giving birth

"All the pieces in this collection offer solid, easily graspable plots, mostly about love relationships. Atwood maintains a steady, low-key pace throughout. No story shines above the rest; all are of high quality and should be attractive even to readers not ordinarily comfortable with the short-story genre." Booklist

The handmaid's tale. Houghton Mifflin 1986 311p o.p.

ISBN 0-395-40425-8

"The time is the near future, the place is the Republic of Gilead—formerly known as the United States. A coup d'etat by religious fundamentalists has left the President and Congress dead, The Constitution suspended, and the borders sealed. . . . Atwood's storyteller, a 33-year-old woman known only as Offred, serves as a handmaid to one of the ruling Commanders of the Faithful, Fred, from whom she takes her name. . . . Her sole function . . . is to carry out a . . . version of Old Testament lore and bear a child for the aging Commander, with the collusion of his barren wife." Christ Sci Monit

"A gripping suspense tale, The Handmaid's Tale is an allegory of what results from a politics based on misogyny, racism, and anti-Semitism." Ms

Lady Oracle. Simon & Schuster 1976 345p o.p.

"The heroine, after her staged death by drowning, hides out alone in Rome. A miserable bundle of low self-esteem, she reviews her life to that point. Her several selves—former fat girl, present thin one, secret author of gothic novels, wife of one man, lover of another—each nurtured privately, are jostling for open exposure." Booklist

"The novel ends on an ambiguously affirmative note, as Atwood undercuts the terror she has wrought, suggesting that the dark fears we hold are perhaps less painful than we imagine: the gothic fiend reaching out for our throats is only a curious reporter hunting for a story. The novel thus tests the conventions by which we order reality. Atwood's versatility and maturity show in this novel, which confirms once again the excellence of her craftsmanship." Choice

Life before man. Simon & Schuster 1980 317p o.p.

LC 79-20281

This novel set in Toronto in the mid-1970's is "about the entangled relationship of three characters: Elizabeth, aggressive and intimidating, mourning the suicide of her lover; Nate, her husband, helpless within and without the marriage, and Lesje, whose work with fossils at the museum is more absorbing and safer than the present, than her affair with Nate." Libr J

This "is a powerful, introspective view of contemporary marriage and the changing roles of the sexes. . . . [This novel] returns to the survival and identity theme of Atwood's early thematic guide to Canadian literature, but at a level that transcends the national. With men and mores rooted in the prehistoric past, Atwood forces us to confront a harrowing present that anticipates an ecologically and culturally doomed future." Choice

Oryx and Crake; novel. Talese 2003 376p $26

ISBN 0-385-50385-7 LC 2002-73290

"Having once led a life of comfort and self-indulgence, Jimmy, now known as Snowman, has survived an ecological disaster that has destroyed the world as we know

Atwood, Margaret, 1939-—*Continued*

it. As he struggles to function without everythinghe once knew, including time, Snowman reflects on the past, on his relationships with two characters named Oryx and Crake, and on the role of each individual in the destruction of the natural world." Libr J

"Rigorous in its chilling insights and riveting in its fast-paced 'what if' dramatization, Atwood's superb novel is as brillantly provocative as it is profoundly engaging." Booklist

The robber bride. Talese 1993 466p o.p.
LC 93-24267

This novel "opens on Tuesday, October 23, 1990. . . . Three middle-aged Toronto women—Tony, a military historian; Charis, a flower child; and Roz, an entrepreneur—who have been friends since university, are meeting for lunch in a trendy Queen Street restaurant called The Toxique. The seemingly disparate trio are bonded by their mutual hatred and fear of a fourth classmate, the evil marauder Zenia, who has the power to bridge their defences, steal their lovers, and even to come back from the dead." Quill Quire

"The amoral, spiteful, ruthlessly self-interested Zenia is almost too bad to be true, but she represents all the impulses that Tony, Roz and Charis have repudiated or suppressed. Good women, in Ms. Atwood's view are their own enemies, and whether one agrees with her opinion or not, she has written a brilliantly intelligent novel to support it." Atl Mon

Surfacing. Simon & Schuster 1973 c1972 224p o.p.

"The heroine, her lover, Joe and a married couple, David and Anna, travel from the city towards her family cabin on a remote Quebec lake. Their mission is to investigate the disappearance of the heroine's father. . . . When the father remains lost and they decide to stay on at the lake for a week, the underlying strains of their relationships begin to take effect." N Y Times Book Rev

The author's "frightened and deadened characters are in fact, extremely interesting. Foolish victims, empty of creative introspection, victimizing and dehumanizing one another, they are the same people who glibly promote new game plans for sex, education, love and war in the mass of semi-erudite words that pour daily from the media. Atwood reveals them with skill and wit." Can Forum

Wilderness tips. Doubleday 1991 227p o.p.
LC 91-17086

Stories included are: True trash; Hairball; Isis in darkness; The bog man; Death by landscape; Uncles; The age of lead; Weight; Wilderness tips; Hack Wednesday

This is a collection of stories "portraying aspects of contemporary Canadian life, which move forward in time, from the first story set in the '50s to the last set in the present, and shift back and forth in space from urban to wilderness scenes." Can Forum

Aubert, Rosemary, 1946-

The ferryman will be there; an Ellis Portal mystery. Bridge Works 2001 258p $22.95
ISBN 1-882593-44-8 LC 00-52900

"Middle-aged detective Ellis Portal, a former judge who fell from grace through drink and drugs, wound up homeless on the streets and re-ascended to the edge of respectability, helps his friend, Det. Sgt. Matt West, to locate a young woman, Carrie Simm. Her father, a Toronto movie producer, was murdered in front of her, in full view of hundreds of people, at a film premiere. Possibly fearing for her own life, Carrie disappeared." Publ Wkly

"Portal's indomitable integrity and checkered past make his ministrations to the troubled girls utterly believable and moving. This is quickly becoming a very special series." Booklist

Auchincloss, Louis

The anniversary and other stories. Houghton Mifflin 1999 192p o.p.
ISBN 0-395-97074-1 LC 99-18697

Contents: DeCicco v. Schweizer; The interlude; The anniversary; Man of the Renaissance; The last of the great courtesans; The Devil and Guy Lansing; The facts of fiction; The Virginia redbird; The veterans

The book class. Houghton Mifflin 1984 212p o.p.
LC 84-522

"In 1908 a group of Park Avenue debutantes begins to meet once a month to discuss books, past and present. 'The Book Class' endures for 64 years, creating a lasting and telling impression on the son of one of its members, the novel's narrator, Christopher Gates. These pampered and seemingly fragile women, whose lives are filled with great passion, disappointment, and tragedy, exude an aura of power and mystery which fascinates Gates and which he probes throughout his life." Libr J

"Auchincloss may work on a small canvas, but no one excels his finely etched portraits of sophisticates of good breeding and inherited wealth." Publ Wkly

The collected stories of Louis Auchincloss. Houghton Mifflin 1994 465p o.p.
LC 94-14364

Contents: Maud; Greg's peg; The colonel's foundation; The mavericks; The single reader; Billy and the gargoyles; The gemlike flame; The money juggler; The Wagnerians; The prince and the pauper; The prison window; The novelist of manners; In the beauty of the lilies Christ was born across the sea; The Fabbri tape; Portrait of the artist by another; The reckoning; Ares; The stoic; They that have power to hurt

East Side story; a novel; Louis Auchincloss. Houghton Mifflin 2004 257p $24
ISBN 0-618-45244-3 LC 2004-47499

This novel traces "traces the history of a wealthy New York family, the Carnochans, from their beginnings in this country before the Civil War to the present. The family line begins honorably enough with its founder, David, immigrating to America from Scotland and earning a fortune manufacturing thread. Subsequent generations, however, make carefully calculated but ultimately ruinous choices in the name of self-interest. Love is the greatest casualty, defeated again and again by pretension, ambition, and cowardice. Auchincloss's characters are extraordinarily self-aware and articulate, but it does them little good. Most expend all their cleverness simply trying to convince themselves that they are happy. A disturbing and powerfully realized novel." Libr J

The epicurean
In Auchincloss, L. Three lives

Auchincloss, Louis—*Continued*

Her infinite variety. Houghton Mifflin 2000 224p $25

ISBN 0-618-02191-4 LC 99-47302

This novel "relates how a Depression-era Vassar graduate named Clara Longcope—the shrewd and beautiful daughter of a Yale professor—charms and manipulates her way to the pinnacle of New York society." N Y Times Book Rev

"An astute and witty novel about a woman who disdains the old values of money and class in favor of a feminine meritocracy in the world of business." Publ Wkly

Honorable men. Houghton Mifflin 1985 278p o.p.

LC 85-5257

"'Chip' Benedict, Yale '38, married Alida, the debutante of her year, and they had the mandatory two children. But trust funds and connections do not fend off life and the world. When we meet Chip, Alida has decided to leave him; his daughter, a physician, is a lesbian and an anti-war activist; his son evaded the Vietnam draft by fleeing to Sweden; and Chip himself is now a special assistant to the Secretary of State. Vietnam disturbs him and he suffers a troubled conscience over the 'multitudinous sins' of his earlier life." Publ Wkly

"Auchincloss knows his period and social circle well, and he has put that knowledge to good use here with a perceptive character study of a troubled power broker and the private toll he must pay for success." Booklist

The realist

In Auchincloss, L. Three lives

The Rector of Justin. Houghton Mifflin 1964 341p o.p.

The rector of a New England Episcopal private school, eighty-year-old Dr. Frank Prescott, is seen through the eyes of both admirers and detractors. The principal narrator is Brian Aspinwall, a shy young English master. Others include former students, Prescott's youngest daughter, Cordelia, and his oldest friend, Horace Havistock

"This is not only a passionately interesting, but a spiritually important study of the American character. . . . If Mr. Auchincloss had confined his portrait of Dr. Prescott to the gentle brush strokes of Brian Aspinwall . . . we would never have had the blazing totality of the man that emerges from this book. . . . In revealing both the best and the worst of Dr. Francis Prescott, he has created as inspiring a character as any reader could want." N Y Times Book Rev

The stoic

In Auchincloss, L. Three lives

Three lives. Houghton Mifflin 1993 213p o.p.

LC 92-27588

This book contains three novellas about the lives of "three New Yorkers born to wealth around the turn of the century. 'The Epicurean' is Nat Chisolm, whose life is a constant pursuit of the next pleasureful challenge in sport, art, love, or war. 'The Realist' is Alida Vermeule, an intelligent woman who finds a way to exercise power despite early twentieth-century restrictions upon her gender. 'The Stoic' is principled, austere, and virginal investment banker George Manville, who manages to attain everything that most satisfies him, including an heir, despite—or because of—the follies and emotional indulgences of those around him. Each novella is as fine an example of the literature of manners as you're likely to find." Booklist

Auel, Jean M.

The Clan of the Cave Bear; a novel. Crown 1980 468p (Earth's children) o.p.

ISBN 0-517-18918-6 LC 80-14581

"Young Cro-Magnon orphan Ayla is adopted into the Neanderthal Clan of the Cave Bear and grows up mothered by medicine woman Iza and protected by magician Creb. However, her different characteristics and abilities bring her into conflict with the clan time and again. Broud, clan-leader's son, is her chief adversary: to him Ayla is an intolerable threat to tradition who must be subdued or die." Libr J

"It's subject matter, its vast research . . . make this fictional excursion into prehistory a thing of wonder. But it's an enjoyable story, too, though leisurely and not notable for the quality of its prose. . . . The depiction of how the cave-dwelling Neanderthals lived—how they performed their totemistic rituals, gathered medicinal plants, slew mammoths and other animals—is solid, convincing and sometimes exciting." Publ Wkly

Followed by The Valley of Horses

The Mammoth Hunters. Crown 1985 645p (Earth's children) o.p.

ISBN 0-517-55627-8 LC 85-17503

Sequel to The Valley of Horses

This novel "tells of Ayla and Jondalar's meeting the Mamutoi of the Lion Camp, a hunting people with whom they are invited to dwell. Living for the first time among a group of people like herself brings Ayla many new experiences. She is attracted to the Negroid artist, Ranec, which arouses Jondalar's jealousy. She enjoys the friendship of Deegie, a woman of her own age with whom she shares interests. She evokes both the adulation and resentment of Lion Camp members when her talents for healing and animal training are demonstrated." Best Sellers

"The story is lyric rather than dramatic, and Ayla and her lovers are projections of a romantic rather than a historical imagination, but readers caught up in the charm of Auel's story probably won't care." Publ Wkly

Followed by The plains of passage

The plains of passage. Crown 1990 760p (Earth's children) o.p.

ISBN 0-517-58049-7 LC 90-38330

Sequel to The Mammoth Hunters

"Ayla and Jondalar begin the long journey back to Jondalar's people, the Zeladonii. Along the way, they meet different groups of people, including members of another clan, and discover the true depths of their love for each other. More than just another adventure storyteller, Auel continues to offer a wealth of information about the prehistoric world. Her detailed descriptions of animal and plant life, of tools and tool-making, and of the general life-styles of prehistoric societies provide a relaxed pacing that not only mirrors Ayla's and Jondalar's journey but makes important anthropological information accessible to the general public." Booklist

Auel, Jean M.—*Continued*

The shelters of stone. Crown 2002 753p (Earth's children) $28.95

ISBN 0-609-61059-7 LC 2002-995

Sequel to: The plains of passage

In this fifth book in the series, "beautiful Ayla and her tall, gorgeous Cro-Magnon lover, Jondalar, arrive in Jondalar's Zelandonii homeland, to live with his clan in vast caves of what today is France. Travelling with a pet wolf and two horses, able to speak the strange languages of the 'flatheads,' Ayla is once again an exotic outsider. Pregnant with Jondalar's child and as zealous in her desire to help as she is resourceful and creative as a medicine woman, Ayla soon wins the respect of the people she wishes to join." Publ Wkly

The Valley of Horses; a novel. Crown 1982 502p (Earth's children) o.p.

ISBN 0-517-54489-X LC 82-5123

This sequel to The Clan of the Cave Bear "recounts Ayla's three years of solitude in a cave after being pronounced 'dead' by the Neanderthal clan who had raised the Cro-Magnon girl as their own. Her story alternates with that of Jondalar, a handsome young man of immense sex appeal who is journeying with his brother because he can't seem to find himself. After {various} . . . adventures, the brother is killed by Ayla's pet lion, and she brings the wounded Jondalar back to nurse him to health. Ultimately . . . they fall in love. . . . The book ends with their meeting more of their kind while out of their cave." Voice Youth Advocates

Followed by The Mammoth Hunters

August, David

(jt. auth) Lutz, J. Final seconds

Austen, Jane, 1775-1817

The complete novels of Jane Austen. Modern Lib. 1983 1364p o.p.

ISBN 0-394-60436-9 LC 83-5473

First Modern Library edition, 1933

Contents: Sense and sensibility; Pride and prejudice; Mansfield Park; Emma; Northanger Abbey; Persuasion

Emma; with an introduction by Marilyn Butler. Knopf 1991 xlvii, 498p $19

ISBN 0-679-40581-X LC 91-52988

"Everyman's library"

First published 1815

"Emma is a pretty girl of sterling character and more will than she can properly manage. She thinks she knows what is best for everybody, and is a prey to many deceptions. She is imposed upon, and imposes upon herself; it is a long while before she sees things as they are, and recognizes where her own happiness lies. Her hero is one of Jane's sober, clear-eyed, and perfect men. The Fairfax and Churchill subplot furnishes a comedy of dissimulation contrasting didactically with Emma's honesty. A formidable snob and vulgarian, Mrs. Elton, and a good-natured bore, Miss Bates, who would be insufferable outside these pages, are among the more laughable characters." Baker. Guide to the Best Fic

also in Austen, J. The complete novels of Jane Austen

Mansfield Park; with an introduction by Peter Conrad. Alfred A. Knopf 1992 xxxvii, 488p $21

ISBN 0-679-41269-7 LC 91-58689

"Everyman's library"

First published 1814

"Presents a household of young people in love with the right or the wrong person. Thru the device of marrying off three sisters into different ranks, upper middle-class distinctions come in for amusing comparisons." Lenrow. Reader's Guide to Prose Fic

"Her most considerable piece of work, not in mere dimensions, but in the mastery of a difficult problem. . . . In truth, nowhere is the difference between true comedy and satire better exemplified." Baker. Guide to the Best Fic

also in Austen, J. The complete novels of Jane Austen

Northanger Abbey. o.p.

First published 1818

"The heroine is a girl in the first innocent bloom of youth, whose entry into life is attended by the collapse of many illusions." Lenrow. Reader's Guide to Prose Fic

"Though not published until 1818, this was written 1798-9 and entitled 'Susan', revised in 1803 and sold for publication; it may perhaps have been rewritten or touched up later, before it appeared posthumously. Begun as a parody of sentimentalism and the romantics, it developed into the genre which was to be peculiarly Jane Austen's—the portrayal in sober and faithful tints of the quiet middle-class life she knew; the satire restrained, the comedy all-pervasive." Baker. Guide to the Best Fic

also in Austen, J. The complete novels of Jane Austen

Persuasion. Alfred A. Knopf 1992 xxxvii, 260p $18

ISBN 0-679-40986-6 LC 91-53181

"Everyman's library"

First published 1818

"The heroine, Anne Elliott, and her lover, Captain Wentworth, had been engaged eight years before the story opens but Anne had broken the engagement in deference to family and friends. Upon his return he finds her 'wretchedly altered,' but after numerous obstacles have been overcome, the lovers are happily united." Gerwig. Handb for Readers and Writers

also in Austen, J. The complete novels of Jane Austen

Pride and prejudice; introduction by Anna Quindlen. Modern Library 1995 281p $14.95

ISBN 0-679-60168-6 LC 95-6310

First published 1813

"Concerned mainly with the conflict between the prejudice of a young lady and the well-founded though misinterpreted pride of the aristocratic hero. The heroine's father and mother cope in very different ways with the problem of marrying off five daughters." Good Read

"The characters are drawn with humor, delicacy, and the intimate knowledge of men and women that Miss Austen always shows." Keller. Reader's Dig of Books

also in Austen, J. The complete novels of Jane Austen

Austen, Jane, 1775-1817—*Continued*

Sense and sensibility; with an introduction by Peter Conrad. Knopf 1992 xxxix, 367p $16

ISBN 0-679-40987-4 LC 91-53182

"Everyman's library"

First published 1811

A story "in which two sisters, Elinor and Marianne Dashwood represent 'sense' and 'sensibility' respectively. Each is deserted by the young man from whom she has been led to expect an offer of matrimony. Elinor bears her deep disappointment with dignity and restraint while Marianne violently expresses her grief." Reader's Ency. 4th edition

"A study of character and manners in a very delicate, precise, miniature style; the characters just everyday people, drawn as they are without exaggeration; the minute differences of human nature delicately penciled; the satire directed against mere commonplace foolishness, conceit, and vulgarity, rather than vice or eccentricity. In truth, the social failings and personal foibles are self-revealed rather than satirized and make spontaneous comedy." Baker. Guide to the Best Fic

also in Austen, J. The complete novels of Jane Austen

An unequal marriage; or, Pride and prejudice twenty years later. St. Martin's Press 1994 186p o.p.

LC 94-26108

"In this sequel-to-the-sequel, [Elizabeth and Darcy] experience the mixed blessings children can bring. At 17, Miranda is lovely, competent, and her father's pride and joy, but heir-apparent Edward, a student at Eton, has long been a problem. As guests gather for the wedding of close friend Colonel Fitzwilliam, reports come that Edward has fallen under bad influences in London and gambled away part of the family estate. Cold disciplinarian Darcy acts, while compassionate chatelaine Elizabeth is distraught and susceptible to the admiring glances of handsome Mr. Gresham." Libr J

Auster, Paul, 1947-

The book of illusions; a novel. Holt & Co. 2002 321p $24

ISBN 0-8050-5408-1 LC 2002-17218

"David Zimmer, an English professor in Vermont, is trying to rebuild his life—after his family perishes in an airplane crash—by researching the work of Hector Mann, a minor figure from the era of silent movies. . . . Mann disappeared at the height of his career in 1929, but when Zimmer's book about him is published in the 1980s, it elicits a mysterious invitation: would Zimmer like to meet Mann, who is alive and has been working in secret as actor/director Hector Spelling?" Publ Wkly

"Auster limns Mann's many-layered cinematic and earthly worlds in mesmerizing and voluptuous detail within an artful, poignantly metaphysical, and delectably Hitchcockian tale of mayhem, murder, and myriad illusions within illusions." Booklist

In the country of last things. Viking 1987 188p o.p.

LC 86-40257

"Imagine an American city in the near future, populated almost wholly by street dwellers, squatters in ruined buildings, scavengers for subsistence. Suicide clubs offer interesting ways to die, for a fee, but the rich have fled with their jewels, and those who are left survive on what little cash trade-in centers will give them for the day's pickings. This . . . dreamlike fable about a peculiarly recognizable society, now in the throes of entropy, focuses on the plight of a young woman, Anna Blume." Publ Wkly

This novel "is distinguished by an uncanny grasp of the day-to-day realities of homelessness. This is a scary but highly relevant book." Libr J

Leviathan. Viking 1992 275p o.p.

LC 92-1282

The chief protagonist in this story "is a novelist-journalist named Benjamin Sachs who impressed just about 'everyone' as brilliant, witty, and talented. At the beginning of the novel he is blown to scraps while attempting to manufacture a bomb by the side of a snowy winter road in Wisconsin. How he came to this abrupt, untimely end is the ostensible topic being investigated by the imaginary author of the present novel, one Peter Aaron, who had known Sachs intimately for some fifteen years." N Y Rev Books

"Mr. Auster may write about coincidence, but there is nothing coincidental about his prose, in which seemingly straightforward information has an allegorical dimension. . . . Thus in the literary looking glass of 'Leviathan,' in which things are not always what they seem, our pleasure in reading the story is enhanced by the challenge of making other connections." N Y Times Book Rev

Oracle night. Holt 2003 243p $23

ISBN 0-8050-7320-5

"One morning in September 1982, a struggling novelist recovering from a near-fatal illness purchases, on impulse, a blue notebook from a new store in his Brooklyn neighborhood. . . . Reflecting on a past conversation and armed with his new notebook, Sidney Orr is compelled to write about a man who walks away from his comfortable, staid life after a brush with death. . . . Orr's description of his fictional project takes over for a while, but through a framing narrative and a series of long, occasionally digressive footnotes, he teasingly reveals himself, his lovely wife, Grace, and their mutual friend, the famous novelist John Trause. While Orr's hero finds himself locked in a bomb shelter, Grace begins behaving strangely, the stationery shop is shuttered, John's drug-addicted son looms menacingly in the background and the blue notebook exerts a troubling power." Publ Wkly

"A novelist writing about a novelist writing about an editor reading a novel: these Russian dolls might come across as merely cute, were it not for the fact that the lucid Mr Auster is a natural storyteller, with a seemingly inexhaustible trove of yarns at his disposal. All of the stories within stories are compelling in their own right." Economist

Timbuktu; a novel. Holt & Co. 1999 181p o.p.

ISBN 0-8050-5407-3 LC 98-46742

"A forbearing mutt spends the first half of this compact story by his dying mentor—a schizophrenic, often homeless would-be poet—and the second looking for a new love and keeper." New Yorker

"Auster handles the language better than almost anyone else writing today, . . . the first chapter of Timbuktu is one of the finest and most polished to have appeared in any recent novel." Natl Rev

Axton, David, 1945-

For works written by this author under other names see Koontz, Dean R. (Dean Ray), 1945-

B

Babel´, I. (Isaac), 1894-1940

The collected stories; edited and translated by Walter Morison; with an introduction by Lionel Trilling. Criterion Bks. 1955 381p o.p.

"The text of this volume follows that of the 1934 Russian edition of Babel's stories, which included 'Red Cavalry' [first published in the United States 1929 by Knopf], 'Tales of Odessa,' and all but the last five of the group called 'Stories.'" Translator's note

Contents: Crossing into Poland; The church at Novograd; A letter; The Remount Officer; Pan Apolek; Italian sunshine; Gedali; My first goose; The Rabbi; The road to Brody; Discourse on the "Tachanka"; The death of Dolgushov; The Brigade Commander; Sandy the Christ; The life and adventures of Matthew Pavlichenko; The cemetery at Kozin; Prishchepa's vengeance; The story of a horse; Konkin's prisoner; Berestechko; Salt; Evening; Afonka Bida; In St. Valentine's Church; Squadron Commander Trunov; Two Ivans; The story of a horse, continued; The widow; Zamoste; Treason; Chesniki; After the battle; The song; The Rabbi's son; Argamak; The King; How it was done in Odessa; The father; Lyubka the Cossack; The sin of Jesus; The story of my dovecot; First love; The end of St. Hypatius; With Old Man Makhno; You were too trusting, Captain; Karl-Yankel; In the basement; Awakening; The S. S. "Cow-Wheat"; Guy de Maupassant; Oil; Dante Street; The end of the old folks' home; Through the fanlight; The kiss; Line and color; Di Grasso

The complete works of Isaac Babel; edited by Nathalie Babel; translated with notes by Peter Constantine; introduction by Cynthia Ozick. Norton 2001 1072p il maps $39.95

ISBN 0-393-04846-2 LC 2001-44036

Contains the following short stories: Old Shloyme; At grandmother's; Elya Isaakovich and Margarita Prokofievna; Mama, Rimma, and Alla; The public library; Nine; Odessa; The aroma of Odessa; Inspiration; Doudou; Shabos-Nakhamu; On the field of honor; Thedeserter; Papa Marescot's family; The Quaker; The sin of Jesus; An evening with the empress; Chink; A tale about a woman; The bathroom window; Bagrat-Ogly and the eyes of his bull; Line and color; You missed the boat, captain!; The end of St. Hypatius; The king; Justice in parentheses; How things were done in Odessa; Lyubka the Cossack; The father; Froim Grach; The end of the almshouse; Sunset; Crossing the river Zbrucz; The church in Novograd; A letter; The reserve cavalry commander; Pan Apolek; Italian sun; Gedali; My first goose; The rabbi; The road to Brody; The Tachanka theory; Dolgushov's death; The commander of the Second Brigade; Sashka Christ; The life of Matvey Rodionovich Pavlichenko; The cemetery in Kozin; Prishchepa; The story of a horse; Konkin; Berestechko; Salt; Evening; Afonka Bida; At Saint Valentine's; Squadron commander Trunov; Ivan and Ivan; The continuation of the story of a horse; The widow; Zamosc; Treason; Czesniki; After the battle; The song; The rabbi's son; Makhno's boys; A hardworking woman; Grishchuk; Argamak; The kiss; And then there were nine; And then there were ten; A letter to the editor; The story of my dovecote; First love; Karl-Yankel; The awakening; In the basement; Gapa Guzhva; Kolyvushka; The road; The Ivan and Maria; Guy de Maupassant; Petroleum; Dante Street; Di Grasso; Sulak; The trial; My first fee; Roaming stars: a movie tale; A story; Information; Three in the afternoon; The Jewess

In addition to the stories this volume contains sketches, journalistic pieces, a diary, plays, and screenplays

"Few writers possess Babel's level of genius and temerity, and this first complete collection should acquaint more readers with his unjustly neglected work." Publ Wkly

Red cavalry

In Babel´, I. The collected stories p41-200

Babel´, Isaac *See* Babel´, I. (Isaac), 1894-1940

Babson, Marian

Canapes for the kitties. St. Martin's Press 1997 220p o.p.

ISBN 0-312-16929-9 LC 97-16232

"A Thomas Dunne book"

"When Lorinda Lucas, a well-known mystery writer in Brimful Coffers, kills off her popular fictional heroines, neighboring writers rebel. Old and new resentments (that even involve local cats Had-I, But-Known, and Roscoe) lead to murder." Libr J

Babson's "lighthearted good humor and skewed view of the world enliven every page of this charming morsel of a mystery." Publ Wkly

The company of cats. St. Martin's Press 1999 183p o.p.

ISBN 0-312-19924-4 LC 98-52967

"A Thomas Dunne book"

"Annabel Hinchby-Smythe, who feeds gossip tidbits to a tabloid, agrees to redecorate billionaire Arthur Arbuthnot's flat. When he is murdered, his faithful feline companion, Sally, suddenly is in danger. Annabel kidnaps Sally to protect her, and the fun begins. Readers who love cats will enjoy the Annabel/Sally relationship." Booklist

Murder at the cat show. St. Martin's Press 1989 192p o.p.

LC 89-30162

"Doug Perkins describes the larky and suspenseful action at the cat show that he and his partner, Gerry Tate, have been hired to publicize. Their efforts are hardly needed, since media people swarm about the exhibit, but then famous Hugo Verrier's golden cat statue goes missing and show-organizer Mrs. Chesne-Malvern is killed." Publ Wkly

"A very lighthearted and pleasurable mystery, filled with cat-loving eccentrics and disdainful felines." Booklist

Baca, Jimmy Santiago

The importance of a piece of paper. Grove Press 2004 225p $22

ISBN 0-8021-1765-1 LC 2003-57089

Contents: Matilda's garden; The three sons of Julia; The importance of a piece of paper; The Valentine's Day card; Enemies; Mother's ashes; Bull's blood; Runaway

"The rural Southwest landscape of Baca's short stories is inhabited by outsiders: drug addicts and convicts, absentee mothers and runaways. Baca's first collection of fiction . . . paints a picture of Chicano life that is at once cruel and sweetly redemptive." Publ Wkly

Bachman, Richard *See* King, Stephen, 1947-

Bacon, Charlotte

There is room for you; Charlotte Bacon. 1st ed. Farrar, Straus and Giroux 2004 276p $24

ISBN 0-374-28185-8 LC 2003-59579

"Already grieving over the loss of her father, thirty-something Anna Singer finds herself even more alone when her husband runs off with a younger woman. Feeling adrift, she embarks on a trip to India, where her English mother, Rose, spent her youth and about which she wrote a memoir addressed to her daughter. The narrative shifts between Anna's trip in 1992 and her mother's reminiscences, interweaving their stories and exploring family connections and sorrows." Libr J

"Rose's memories bring to Bacon's novel an intensity that Anna's travel-writing persona only sporadically achieves. As she uncovers Rose's past and stumbles upon its best-kept secrets, Anna's pronouncements on her American life and Indian experience gain coherence." Washington Post

Badami, Anita Rau

Tamarind woman. Algonquin Bks. 2002 266p $23.95

ISBN 1-56512-335-2 LC 2001-58970

First published 1996 in Canada with title: Tamarind mem

This "novel explores the relationship of a mother and daughter, Saroja and Kamini. In the first half, Kamini comes of age among postcolonial India's railway colonies. Her father is often away, charting new frontiers for railway expansion, and she is left home with her mother and sister. She eventually leaves for Canada, where she remains wistful for the smells and sounds of India. . . . Saroja then speaks, telling her story of longing for a life independent of the demands of a husband and family" Booklist

"Badami writes graceful, evocative prose and plays complex variations on her themes." Publ Wkly

Bahal, Aniruddha, 1967-

Bunker 13. Farrar, Straus & Giroux 2003 345p $24

ISBN 0-374-11730-6 LC 2002-192521

This novel's "protagonist, MM, is a tough-as-nails ex-army officer turned investigative journalist with a penchant for risk, drugs and rough sex. Covering the army, MM learns that a small band of corrupt officer s in Kashmir are engaged in smuggling drugs and weapons, and he soon becomes involved in an intricate web of guerrilla fighting, espionage, Russian mobsters and nuclear missles." Publ Wkly

"The story proceeds with tremendous energy and in a whirl of gaudy literary effects from Delhi to Kashmir to Moscow and back again." N Y Times Book Rev

Bahr, Howard, 1946-

The year of Jubilo; a novel of the Civil War. Holt & Co. 2000 376p o.p.

ISBN 0-8050-5972-5 LC 99-88634

A tale set in the aftermath of the Civil War. "Shamed by his girlfriend, Morgan Rhea, and her father into signing up with the Confederate army, former Cumberland, Miss., English teacher Gawain Harper is on his way back to the civilian life he abruptly left three years before. Taking up with another returning soldier, Harry Stribling, an enigmatic fellow Southerner who fancies himself a philosopher, 40-year-old Gawain confronts the dispiriting realities of change." Publ Wkly

"Along with the sweeping, cinematic story of rebellion, loyalty, revenge and reawakened romance, Bahr's evocation of place and time is the most enduring achievement of the novel." N Y Times Book Rev

Bail, Murray, 1941-

Eucalyptus; a novel. Farrar, Straus & Giroux 1998 255p o.p.

ISBN 0-374-14857-0 LC 98-5880

"In this contemporary Australian fairy tale, a widower named Holland acquires a sprawling property in New South Wales and plants it with hundreds of varieties of eucalyptus . . . when it is time for his daughter, Ellen, to wed, he offers her hand to the suitor who can name each specimen on his estate. In the meantime, Ellen encounters a handsome stranger under a coolabah who courts her with stories that prove to be less random than they appear. The novel's categorizations and mysteries become a playful inquiry into the nature of storytelling, with an unpredictable conclusion." New Yorker

Bailey, Charles W. (Charles Waldo), 1929-

(jt. auth) Knebel, F. Seven days in May

Bailey, Paul

Uncle Rudolf; Paul Bailey. 1st U.S. ed. St. Martin's Press 2004 c2002 183p $21.95

ISBN 0-312-31834-0 LC 2003-58773

The "tale of a young boy's escape from fascist Romania in the late 1930s to England. Now 70, Andrew is writing his memoirs about life in his adopted country with Uncle Rudolf, an internationally acclaimed operetta tenor. This contemplative, retrospective focus heightens the emotional weight of the events he recounts and gives power to this novel of exile and loss. Andrew had spent years wondering about his parents–until he learns that his mother was murdered by fascist thugs and that his father committed suicide soon after. He struggles his whole life with guilt about having left them for a life of luxury with his generous, outrageous, internationally beloved uncle. Bailey explores these emotions with considerable skill and sympathy and brings the historical milieu convincingly to life." Libr J

Bainbridge, Beryl, 1933-

According to Queeney. Carroll & Graf Pubs. 2001 216p $22
ISBN 0-7867-0773-9 LC 2001-35948
"Recalling the world of Georgian England, Bainbridge explores the complex relationship between Samuel Johnson and his patroness, Mrs. Thrale. Meeting at a dinner party, the two strike a lasting friendship. . . . Witness to it all is Thrale's oldest daughter, Queeney. Preternaturally intelligent, Queeney absorbs the events around her and later seeks to forget them in the letters to a Johnson biographer that frame the novel." Booklist
"The tension between the bizarre manners of the day and the unexpressed passions burning within is beautifully caught, and Queeney's skeptical commentary lends just the right distance." Publ Wkly

The birthday boys. Carroll & Graf Pubs. 1994 c1991 189p o.p.
ISBN 0-7867-0071-8 LC 94-1264
First published 1991 in the United Kingdom
"The story of Capt. Robert Scott's second expedition is narrated by Scott himself and the four men who perished along with him in the frigid weather and miserable conditions of Antarctica. Beginning with their June 1910 departure from Cardiff on the 'Terra Nova,' and ending with the terrible journey by sled back to the ship in March 1912, the five men consecutively recount their journey through an emotional as well as physical landscape." Libr J
"These five monologues, which contain some of the most convincing and slyly revealing first-person narrative I've ever read, span a remarkable range of voices and dispositions, but what they share is a mesmerizing readability. . . . They present us with a microcosmic society of flawed individuals, pushed and pulled even in a frozen wilderness by the subtle dictates of class, personality and ambition." N Y Times Book Rev

Every man for himself. Carroll & Graf Pubs. 1996 224p o.p.
LC 96-32518
This novel "takes place on the ill-fated Titanic. The story is narrated by Morgan, a young American, and follows the events between boarding and rescue by the Carpathia." Libr J
"Bainbridge hits a tremendous pace as her story reaches its climax. In a remarkably concise book, shot through with laconic wit, she establishes complex characters who engage first the reader's curiosity, then affection. The elegiac theme extends far beyond the historical event." New Statesman (1913)

Master Georgie; a novel. Carroll & Graf Pubs. 1998 190p o.p.
ISBN 0-7867-0563-9 LC 98-43228
This "novel spans eight years in the life of one George Hardy, a beamish boy who meets his end tending Crimean War dead. His story is told by a motley trio: Myrtle, a foundling who attaches herself to George with ferocity; Pompey, a street urchin who arrives on the scene pushing a Punch and Judy carriage; and Dr. Potter, a barmy evolutionist besotted with George's sister. By weaving together their surprising tales, Bainbridge, skillful as a spider, delineates the traps laid for the soul by the human heart." New Yorker

Baker, Dorothy, 1907-1968

Young man with a horn. Houghton Mifflin 1938 243p o.p.
"Rick Martin is not interested in school but is intrigued by music. Learning how to play the jazz trumpet from black musicians, Rick becomes a genius in the art of 'swing' and quickly rises to fame in the Phil Morrison orchestra. The inability to cope with success, as well as a bad marriage and gin, lead to his fatal end." Shapiro. Fic for Youth. 3d edition

Baker, Kage

The anvil of the world. TOR Bks. 2003 350p $25.95
ISBN 0-7653-0818-5 LC 2003-42649
"A Tom Doherty Associates book."
"Smith agrees to lead a small caravan from desert-bound Troon to Salesh by the sea and, although inexperienced as well as incognito, gets most clients and cargo safely across the intervening, bandit-and-demon-infested wasteland. . . . Imagine an Errol Flynn classic ebulliently re-imagined by Monty Python director Terry Gilliam: that's this wacky romp whose pace never flags." Booklist

The graveyard game. Harcourt 2000 298p o.p.
ISBN 0-15-100449-8 LC 00-27790
"When the cyborg known as Mendoza disappears out of grief for her murdered lover, fellow operatives Joseph and Lewis begin a search through time for her and discover some unpleasant secrets about their employer–Dr. Zeus Incorporated, otherwise known as The Company. . . . [This installment] spans centuries and includes stops in late 20th-century Hollywood and early 21st-century London, among other times and places." Libr J

In the garden of Iden; a novel of the company. Harcourt Brace & Co. 1998 329p o.p.
ISBN 0-15-100299-1 LC 97-23284
"The initial assignment for 18-year-old Mendoza, transformed into an immortal cyborg by the 24th-century Company, is to retrieve from Renaissance England an endangered plant that cures cancer. Posing as a Spanish lady accompanying her doctor father, she falls in love with the mortal Nicholas Harpole, secretary to the owner of Iden Hall and its exotic gardens. Amidst the raging Catholic/Protestant powerplays revolving around the English throne and the fervent religious bloodlust of common folk, Mendoza is torn between her task and her love. Baker's story comments powerfully on religious hypocrisy and xenophobia." Libr J

The life of the world to come; Kage Baker. 1st ed. TOR Books 2004 334p $25.95
ISBN 0-7653-1132-1 LC 2004-49574
"Cyborg biologist Mendoza has been exiled to the extremely distant past to live her immortal span farming maize and lettuce for wealthy tourists of the twenty-fourth century. She occasionally reminisces about the man she loved in, first, the sixteenth, and then, the nineteenth century. Then, one day, he crash-lands in her cornfield. It isn't precisely he, of course, but someone from the same Company project named Alec Checkerfield. . . Most of the story is his, from childhood spent on a sailing ship to his youth and education in London to growing wealth and power. As he discovers

Baker, Kage—*Continued*

ever more about his parentage and the power of Dr. Zeus, Inc., to manipulate people and the world, he determines to bring the Company down. Mendoza provides him the key tidbit that, after 2355, Dr. Zeus' knowledge is blank. That time will be Alec's window of opportunity. Alec is quite a character, especially for the sedate twenty-fourth century, and in Baker's skillful hands, his story is well told and engrossing." Booklist

Mendoza in Hollywood; a novel of the company. Harcourt 2000 334p o.p.

ISBN 0-15-100448-X LC 99-14949

"Assigned, along with other time-traveling members of the Company, to Cahuenga Pass, CA, in 1862, Mendoza discovers firsthand the dangers and pleasures of living in the American West during the Civil War. Haunted by dreams of a long-lost lover and pursued by his ghost, Mendoza struggles to come to terms with her personal past while fulfilling her duties to the future–with mixed results. Baker's latest tale of the wisecracking cyborg mercenaries from the 24th century combines historical detail and fast-paced action with a good dose of ironic wit and a dollop of bittersweet romance." Libr J

Mother Aegypt and other stories. Night Shade Books 2004 249p $27

ISBN 1-892389-75-4

Contenets: Leaving his cares behind; The Briscian saint; Desolation Rose; Miss Yahoo has her say; What the tiger told her; Nightmare Mountain; Merry Christmas from Navarro Lodge, 1928; Her father's eyes; Two old men; The summer people; How they tried to talk Indian Tony down; Pueblo, Colorado has the answers; Mother Aegypt

"Told with splendid clarity, the 13 tales in this collection . . . are deceptively simple and seem, at first, to be comfortably folkloric. Each then takes a distinctive turn, often an O. Henry twist, and becomes indelibly the author's own." Publ Wkly

Sky coyote; a novel of the company. Harcourt Brace & Co. 1999 310p o.p.

ISBN 0-15-100354-8 LC 98-16833

"Fresh from a cushy R&R after a supervisory stint in the Inquisition, time-hopping cyborg Facilitator Joseph jaunts to 16th-century Alta California. There, cybernetically outfitted with fur and paws, he apotheosizes to the cannily entrepreneurial Chumash Indian tribe so he can collect them and their entire biosystem for Company studies in the remote future." Publ Wkly

The author "blends accurate historical research and arch comedy to produce an entertaining tale of time travel and mythic adventure." Libr J

Baker, Kevin, 1958-

Dreamland. HarperCollins Pubs. 1999 519p o.p.

ISBN 0-06-019309-3 LC 98-39205

"Narrated by a diverse group of characters—two Jewish gangsters, a seamstress, a whore, a Tammany Hall politician, Sigmund Freud, a dwarf from Coney Island—the novel looks at the ways we see ourselves, often distorted as if through a funhouse mirror. Events like a garment workers' strike, the gangland murder of a talkative gambler, and the fire that burned Coney Island's Dreamland swirl together in this larger-than-life story of people trying to understand themselves in a New York that seems out of control." Libr J

The novel "teems with violence, humor, information and hustle. 'Dreamland' is historical fiction at its most entertaining and, in a number of spots, most high-handed." N Y Times Book Rev

Paradise Alley; a novel. HarperCollins Pubs. 2002 676p o.p.

ISBN 0-06-019582-7 LC 2002-276256

This novel, set in New York City, "focuses on the Draft Riots of 1863, when rampaging Irish immigrants literally burned the city. To tell the story of those three fateful days in July, Baker employs multiple narrators: Herbert Robinson, a reporter for the Tribune, and Maddy, his Irish mistress, Billie Dove, an escaped slave, and his wife, Ruth, an Irishwoman who survived the potato famine; and Johnny Dolan, a murderous Irish thug, his upwardly mobile sister Deidre, and her husband, Tom O'Kane, now serving in the Union army." Libr J

"Baker interwines love, violence, history, adventure and social commentary to give readers an invigorating, heartbreaking tale of the immigrant experience." Publ Wkly

Bakker, Robert T.

Raptor Red. Bantam Bks. 1995 246p il o.p.

LC 95-17907

This novel "tells the story of Raptor Red, a giant carnivore of the Early Cretaceous period. Having lost her mate in a botched hunting attack, Red (so-named because of the red stripe on her snout distinguishing her from other raptor species) joins forces with her sister and her sister's three chicks to survive in a world of hostile natural forces." Libr J

"Even lacking much polish as a stylist, Mr. Bakker very nearly succeeds in bringing off the illusion that we are seeing the world as Raptor Red might have, an ambitious feat for any writer and one that is undeniably very satisfying to the adolescent dino-fan in all of us." N Y Times Book Rev

Bakopoulos, Dean

Please don't come back from the moon; Dean Bakopoulos. Harcourt 2005 273p $23

ISBN 0-15-101135-4 LC 2004-11237

"During the summer of 1991, when times were tough, the men of blue-collar Maple Rock outside Detroit disappeared one by one, with one of them leaving a note saying he was going to the moon. The women rage and weep, then start new lives—finding jobs, remarrying, moving to nicer suburbs. But the fatherless sons, among them 16-year-old Mikey Smolij, flounder for years. After an initial period of freedom and licentiousness, during which they take over the local tavern and serve as studs for older women, these teenage boys live with doubt about whether whatever caused their fathers' disappearances might get them too." Booklist

"By deftly welding magic realism with social satire, Bakopoulos captures the dark side of the working-class dream." N Y Times Book Rev

Baldacci, David

Absolute power. Warner Bks. 1996 469p o.p.
LC 95-22956

"The action begins when a grizzled professional cat burglar gets trapped inside the bedroom closet of one of the world's richest men, only to witness, through a one-way mirror, two Secret Service agents kill the billionaire's trampy young wife as she tries to fight off the drunken sexual advances of the nation's chief executive. Running for his life, but not before he picks up a blood-stained letter opener that puts the president at the scene of the crime, the burglar becomes the target of a clandestine manhunt orchestrated by leading members of the executive branch. Meanwhile, Jack Graham, once a public defender and now a high-powered corporate attorney, gets drawn into the case." Publ Wkly

Saving Faith. Warner Bks. 1999 451p $32
ISBN 0-446-52577-4 LC 99-66599

In this thriller "a renegade CIA faction attempts to reassert the agency's primacy over the FBI by manipulating members of Congress who fund both outfits. To do so, the CIA conspirators aim to take over a bribery scheme they've discovered. The scam was concocted by legendary lobbyist Danny Buchanan, who has been greasing the palms of lawmakers to gain their support of bills aiding the poor and hungry overseas. The spooks plan to assassinate Buchanan and his protégé, the lovely Faith Lockhart, and force the legislators, under threat of exposure, to support the CIA over the FBI." Publ Wkly

"Yes, the plot is too busy and more than a little improbable, but Baldacci makes it work with solid suspense, pithy dialogue, and plenty of hot but tender sex scenes." Booklist

The simple truth. Warner Bks. 1998 470p o.p.
ISBN 0-446-52332-1 LC 98-22548

In this legal thriller "the principals are Rufus Harms, a slow-witted black giant who, after decades in a military prison, realizes that, for reasons revealed only at the novel's end, he is morally innocent of the murder for which he's doing time; John Fiske, a cop-turned-lawyer who's drawn into Harms's quest for justice after his younger brother, a Supreme Court clerk interested in Harms's case, is murdered; and Sara Evans, another Supreme Court clerk who joins forces—and beds—with Fiske." Publ Wkly

"The crime being covered up is stale beer compared to the Supreme Court setting, but as with a scenic drive, the destination of a Baldacci cliff-hanger is less important than the route taken." Booklist

Total control. Warner Bks. 1997 520p o.p.
LC 96-32869

"Sidney Archer is devastated when she hears that the plane carrying her husband to Los Angeles has crashed. But her nightmare begins when she learns he'd traded identities and flown to Seattle instead. Evidence suggests that Jason Archer was selling corporate secrets to a high-tech rival. Soon Sidney herself is caught in a web of intrigue as wealthy men vie for more power and money." Libr J

The winner. Warner Bks. 1997 513p $32
ISBN 0-446-52259-7 LC 97-34569

In this suspense tale "the national lottery has been fixed 12 times by a man who demands access to his handpicked winners' windfalls and who now, to protect his secret, aims to kill the last—and lovable—illicit winner, LuAnn Tyler. To save her baby girl from a hard-scrabble life, bright, beautiful and dirt poor LuAnn accepts the offer of the mystery man known as Jackson to reap nearly $100 million in a forthcoming drawing." Publ Wkly

"A spunky heroine unafraid to go gun-to-gun with her evil antagonist, LuAnn Tyler earns the riveting attention of fans of Baldacci's pedal-to-the-metal plotting. This is undemanding fun." Booklist

Wish you well. Warner Bks. 2000 401p $24.95
ISBN 0-446-52716-5 LC 00-42348

"Adolescent Louisa May Cardinal, called Lou, is living with her mother, father, and brother, Oz outside New York City in 1940. An automobile accident results in her father's death, her mother's withdrawal into a catatonic state, and Lou and her brother's move to rural Virginia to live with their paternal great-grandmother. . . . Then a crisis arises seemingly out of nowhere. The local coal-and-gas company comes sniffing around their great-grandmother's property, conniving to seize it." Booklist

"What the novel offers above all is bone-deep emotional truth, as its myriad characters . . . grapple not just with issues of life and death but with the sufferings and joys of daily existence in a setting detailed with finely attuned attention and a warm sense of wonder." Publ Wkly

Baldick, Chris

(ed) The Oxford book of gothic tales. See The Oxford book of gothic tales

Baldwin, Alex

For works written by this author under other names see Griffin, W. E. B.

Baldwin, James, 1924-1987

Another country. Dial Press (NY) 1962 436p o.p.

This novel is set in "New York City and focuses mainly on Harlem society. The death—perhaps suicide—of the main character, Rufus Scott, is representative of the treatment individuals receive in an environment which is essentially hostile and which erects barriers to their desire for love." Camb Guide to Lit in Engl

also in Baldwin, J. Early novels and stories

Early novels and stories. Library of Am. 1998 970p $35
ISBN 1-88301-151-5 LC 97-23028

Contents: Go tell it on the mountain; Giovanni's room; Another country; Going to meet the man

Giovanni's room; a novel. Dial Press (NY) 1956 248p o.p.

"We meet the narrator, known to us only as David, in the south of France, but most of the story is laid in Paris. It develops as the story of a young American involved both with a woman and with another man, the man being the Giovanni of the title. When a choice has to be made,

Baldwin, James, 1924-1987—*Continued*

David chooses the woman, Hella." N Y Times Book Rev

"Mr. Baldwin has taken a very special theme and treated it with great artistry and restraint." Saturday Rev

also in Baldwin, J. Early novels and stories

Go tell it on the mountain. Knopf 1953 303p $15.95; pa $6.99

ISBN 0-679-60154-6; 0-440-33007-6 (pa)

This novel is an "autobiographical story of a Harlem child's relationship with his father against the background of his being saved in the pentecostal church." Benet's Reader's Ency of Am Lit

also in Baldwin, J. Early novels and stories

Going to meet the man. Dial Press (NY) 1965 249p o.p.

Contents: The rockpile; The outing; The man child; Previous condition; Sonny's blues; This morning, this evening, so soon; Come out the wilderness; Going to meet the man

also in Baldwin, J. Early novels and stories

If Beale Street could talk. Dial Press (NY) 1974 197p o.p.

"Tish, aged 19, and Fonny, 22 years old, are in love and pledged to marry, a decision hastened by Tish's unexpected pregnancy. Fonny is falsely accused of raping a Puerto Rican woman and is sent to prison. The families of the desperate couple search frantically for evidence that will prove his innocence in order to reunite the lovers and provide a safe haven for the expected child. There is some explicit sex but it is not treated in a sensational manner, nor is the use of street language gratuitous." Shapiro. Fic for Youth. 3d edition

Just above my head. Dial Press (NY) 1979 597p o.p.

"Two years after the death of his younger brother Arthur, Hall Montana is finally able to 'stammer out' the story of Arthur's career as a gospel and soul singer, his homosexual love affairs, and his inglorious death in the men's room of a London pub. He also comes to terms with his own more conventional adventures in love." Libr J

Tell me how long the train's been gone; a novel. Dial Press (NY) 1968 484p o.p.

Leo Proudhammer, a successful black "actor has a serious heart attack on stage. Barbara King, his leading lady . . . and in a strange way his inamorata, stays by his side. In a series of flashbacks . . . Leo relives his past from his Harlem boyhood on. Although he learned early to hate 'the man,' Leo's own betrayal as a man and as a human being is not limited to the white man's corruption. It encompasses his painful relationship with his brother, who lures him into homosexuality. Paralleling this story is the tale of Leo's career. The third thread is his bisexual private life in which the two main figures are white Barbara, his true but unattainable love, and black Christopher, worshipful and available." Publ Wkly

Baldwin, Margaret *See* Weis, Margaret, 1948-

Ball, John Dudley, 1911-1988

In the heat of the night; by John Ball. Harper & Row 1965 184p o.p.

"Virgil Tibbs is found with a full wallet in the waiting room of a railroad station in Wells, a small town in the Carolinas. Because he is black he becomes the prime suspect for the murder of the town's musical director. The local police chief learns that Tibbs is a homicide expert from the Pasadena police department and enlists his assistance. Tibbs solves the crime, despite the bigotry to which he is exposed." Shapiro. Fic for Youth. 2d edition

Ball, Margaret

(jt. auth) McCaffrey, A. Acorna

(jt. auth) McCaffrey, A. Acorna's quest

Ballard, J. G., 1930-

The best short stories of J. G. Ballard. Holt, Rinehart & Winston 1978 302p o.p.

LC 77-28234

Contents: The concentration city; Manhole; Chronopolis; The voices of time; Deep end; The overloaded man; Billenium; The garden of time; Thirteen for Centaurus; The subliminal man; The cage of sand; End game; The drowned giant; The terminal beach; The cloud-sculptors of Coral D; The assassination of John Fitzgerald Kennedy considered as a downhill motor race; The atrocity exhibition; Plan for the assassination of Jacqueline Kennedy; Why I want to fuck Ronald Reagan

The day of creation. Farrar, Straus & Giroux 1988 254p o.p.

ISBN 0-374-13527-4 LC 87-37525

First published 1987 in the United Kingdom

The narrator of this novel, Dr. Mallory, "is a physician with the World Health Organization, working in a mythical central African country, who launches what appears to be a vain search for water to forestall the desertification of the region. He accidentally releases the flow-and in fact thinks he is the creator-of a new river. . . . {He later} embarks on a dangerous journey to find its source and destroy it." Books Can

"Had Conrad been more inclined to fantasy, or less to fact and discipline, this is a novel he might have written. A blend of animated reverie, myth and adventure story, The Day of Creation imprints itself on the mind by its acid sweetness." Times Lit Suppl

Empire of the Sun; a novel. Simon & Schuster 1984 279p o.p.

LC 84-10630

"The day after Pearl Harbor, Shanghai is captured by the Japanese, and 11-year-old Jim is separated from his parents and spends some months living on his own. Then he is captured and interned in a Japanese prison camp with other civilians. The story of the next four years is one of struggling to stay alive by any means possible." Libr J

"This novel is much more than the gritty story of a child's miraculous survival in the grimly familiar setting of World War II's concentration camps. There is no nostalgia for a good war here, no sentimentality for the human spirit at extremes. Mr. Ballard is more ambitious than romance usually allows. He aims to render a vision

Ballard, J. G., 1930—*Continued*
of the apocalypse, and succeeds so well that it can hurt to dwell upon his images." N Y Times Book Rev

Followed by The kindness of women (1991)

The kindness of women. Farrar, Straus & Giroux 1991 343p o.p.
LC 91-73730

This sequel to Empire of the Sun "begins again with a boy's traumatic experiences in Japanese-occupied Shanghai and ends some 40 years later with his viewing a film based on his novel about those experiences. Before this 'last act in a profound catharsis,' however, the narrator Jim stumbles through medical study at Cambridge, trains briefly as an RAF pilot in Canada, marries, and suffers domestic tragedy." Libr J

"For a writer whose inventiveness is so firmly anchored in 20th century-icons . . . Ballard remains firmly ambivalent about our image-led culture. His whole work is a celebration and an excoriation of 'the media landscape' and [this book] comes face to face with the contradictions." New Statesman Soc

Rushing to paradise. Picador 1995 238p o.p.
ISBN 0-312-13164-X LC 95-5217

First published 1994 in the United Kingdom

In this novel, "Barbara Rafferty heads an ecological mission to the Pacific island of St.Esprit, an albatross breeding ground and the prospective site for the French military's nuclear weapons testing program. Her teenage assistant, Neil Dempsey, is shot in the foot by a French soldier, and the ensuing publicity attracts the largess of a billionaire, who provides them with the means to return to the island and set up a sanctuary for endangered species. As the news media's fascination with the project tails off, Dr. Barbara . . . decides that the community of St.Esprit is an ideal place in which to start a wildly feminist eugenics project, using Neil as a stud to impregnate the women and producing, in the end, an all-female (save for one healthy male) population." N Y Times Book Rev

Ballard's prose-style is "fluid. His dialogue, generally speaking, is less sparkling than the commentary. Too many ellipses . . . lead us unknowingly into the symbolic selva oscura, but his ear for the descriptive cadence is unerringly acute." Times Lit Suppl

Super-Cannes. Picador 2002 c2001 391p $25
ISBN 0-312-28419-5 LC 2001-133035

First published 2001 in the United Kingdom

The action of this novel is set in a French "multinational business park called Eden-Olympia. The narrator, Paul Sinclair, and his wife, Jane, move there because she's taken a job as a doctor in residence at the park's private clinic. He is a publisher of aviation journals, recovering from injuries sustained in a minor plane crash. . . . The mystery at the heart of Eden-Olympia, . . . is that the well-ordered executives from the multinationals revitalize themselves by committing violent crimes." N Y Times Book Rev

"Ballard's dystopian vision, frightening and provocative, vividly depicts a postindustrial society in which psychopathy isn't just the norm. It is a driving force." Booklist

Balzac, Honoré de, 1799-1850

At the sign of the Cat and Racket
In Balzac, H. d. The short novels of Balzac

Colonel Chabert
In Balzac, H. d. The short novels of Balzac

A commission in lunacy
In Balzac, H. d. The short novels of Balzac

The country doctor. o.p.

Original French edition, 1833. Part of the series: Scenes of provincial life

The device with which this character study is held together concerns the visit of Pierre Joseph Genastas, an ex-soldier, who is searching for the saintly doctor Benassis. "A minute description of country life in the hilly region about Grenoble; the agricultural doings, the wretchedness of the peasantry, and M. Benassis' persevering attempts to ameliorate their condition, furnish a good example of Balzac's indefatigable realism. In this practical philanthropist, the reformed sinner who becomes a public benefactor, an ideal figure is created, a great soul, unselfish, full of love for man, unconquerably patient." Baker. Guide to the Best Fic

Cousin Bette; translated from the French by James Waring. Knopf 1991 xliii, 484p o.p.
ISBN 0-679-40671-9 LC 91-52964

"Everyman's library"

Original French edition, 1846. Part of the series: Scenes of Parisian life

"This powerful story is a vivid picture of the tastes and vices of Parisian life in the middle of last century. Lisbeth Fischer, commonly called Cousin Bette, is an eccentric poor relation, a worker in gold and silver lace. The keynote of her character is jealousy, the special object of it her beautiful and nobel-minded cousin Adeline, wife of Baron Hector Hulot. The chief interest of the story lies in the development of her character, of that of the unscrupulous beauty Madame Marneffe, and the base and empty voluptuary Hulot. . . . Gloomy and despairing . . . [it is] yet terribly powerful." Keller. Reader's Dig of Books

Cousin Pons. o.p.

Original French edition, 1847. Part of the series: Scenes of Parisian life

"Exposes the selfishness, vanity, and corruption of Parisian life with . . . relentless realism, in the lower social world of the minor theatres, lodginghouse keepers, curiosity shops, poor artists and bohemians. Over against this sordid section of society is set the friendship of two old musicians, the sentimental Schmucke and Cousin Pons. . . . Pons is a virtuoso who, in spite of poverty, has collected a treasury of beautiful things." Baker. Guide to the Best Fic

Droll stories; edited by Ernest Boyd; illustrated by Ralph Barton. Garden City Pub. Co. 1935 c1928 2v in 1 o.p.

The stories were written between 1832-1833. First published 1928 in a limited edition by Boni & Liveright

Contents: Fair Imperia; Venial sin; King's sweetheart; Devil's heir; Merry jests of King Louis the Eleventh; High constable's wife; Maid of Thilouse; Brother-in-arms; Vicar of Azayle-Rideau; Reproach; Three clerks of St. Nicholas; Continence of King Francis the First; Merry tattle of the nuns of Poissy; How the Chateau d'Azay came to be built; False courtesan; Danger of being too innocent; Dear night of love; Sermon of the merry vicar

Balzac, Honoré de, 1799-1850—*Continued*
of Meudon; Succubus; Despair in love; Perseverance in love; Concerning a provost who did not recognize things; About the Monk Amador, who was a glorious Abbot of Turpenay; Bertha the penitent; How the pretty maid of Portillon convinced her judge; In which it is demonstrated that fortune is always feminine; Concerning a poor man who was called Le Vieux par-Chemins; Odd sayings of three pilgrims; Innocence; Fair Imperia married

Eugénie Grandet; translated from the French by Ellen Marriage. Knopf 1992 237p o.p.
ISBN 0-679-41716-8 LC 92-52896
"Everyman's library"
First appeared 1833. Part of the series: Scenes of provincial life
"Grandet, a rich miser has an only child, Eugénie. She falls in love with her charming but spoiled young cousin Charles. When she learns he is financially ruined, she lends him her savings. But her father will never consent to her marrying a bankrupt's son. Charles goes to the West Indies, secretly engaged to marry Eugénie on his return. Years go by, Grandet dies and Eugénie becomes an heiress. But Charles, ignorant of her wealth, writes her to ask for his freedom: he wants to marry a rich girl. Eugénie releases him, pays his father's debts, and marries without love an old friend of the family." Haydn. Thesaurus of Book Dig

Gobseck
In Balzac, H. d. The short novels of Balzac

Juana
In Balzac, H. d. The short novels of Balzac

Lost illusions; translated by Kathleen Raine. Modern Lib. 1997 699p o.p.
ISBN 0-679-60264-X LC 97-2727
Original French version written in three parts 1837-1843. This translation first published 1951 in the United Kingdom. Part of the series: Scenes of provincial life
"Lucien de Rubempré, a weak and dandified young author, is the central figure throughout. After scandalizing the people of Angouleme by his platonic relations with a great lady, he goes to Paris as her protégé. full of confidence about the sensation he is to make. His disillusionment begins without delay. First taken up by the Cénacle, a coterie of literary men, he is soon dropped by them, and enters upon journalism. Parisian journalism is abominably corrupt, and Lucien, after a meteoric career, goes back to his native city, ruined in money, morals, and health. His calamities also involve his blameless relatives, the young married people. Eve and David, two quiet and industrious tradespeople, a model of conjugal fidelity." Baker's Best

Louis Lambert
In Balzac, H. d. The short novels of Balzac

Maitre Cornélius
In Balzac, H. d. The short novels of Balzac

Paz
In Balzac, H. d. The short novels of Balzac

Père Goriot (Old Goriot); a new translation: responses, contemporaries and other novelists, twentieth-century criticism; translated by Burton Raffel; edited by Peter Brooks. W.W. Norton & Co. 1998 370p map pa $11.25
ISBN 0-393-97166-X LC 97-19938
Original French edition, 1835. Part of the series: Scenes of Parisian life
"Goriot, a retired manufacturer of vermicelli, is a good man and a weak father. He has given away his money in order to ensure the marriage of his two daughters, Anastasie and Delphine. Because of his love for them, he has to accept all kinds of humiliations from his sons-in-law, one a 'gentilhomme,' M. de Restaud, and the other a financier, M. de Nucingen. Both young women are ungrateful. They gradually abandon him. He dies without seeing them at his bedside, cared for only by young Rastignac, a law student who lives at the same boarding house, the pension Vauquer." Haydn. Thesaurus of Book Dig

The secrets of the Princess de Cadignan
In Balzac, H. d. The short novels of Balzac

The short novels of Balzac; with an introduction by Jules Romains. Dial Press 1948 503p o.p.
"Permanent library series"
Contents: Gobseck; At the sign of the Cat and Racket; Maitre Cornélius; Colonel Chabert; The vicar of Tours; Louis Lambert; Juana; A commission in lunacy; The secrets of the Princess de Cadignan; Paz

The vicar of tours
In Balzac, H. d. The short novels of Balzac

Bambara, Toni Cade

Gorilla, my love. Random House 1972 177p o.p.
Contents: My man Bovanne; Gorilla, my love; Raymond's run; The hammer man; Mississippi Ham Rider; Happy birthday; Playin with Punjab; Talkin bout Sonny; The lesson; The survivor; Sweet town; Blues ain't no mockin bird; Basement; Maggie of the green bottles; The Johnson girls

The salt eaters. Random House 1980 295p o.p.
LC 79-4806
"Velma Henry has tried suicide and survived and now sits on a stool in the Southwest Community Infirmary in Clayborne (a Southern city) listening to faith healer Minnie Ransom ask a hard question about what she wants. Fitfully she asks herself some questions, too, and in the process remembers what happened, fingers the past, absents herself from her own healing to recollect other times, other places, other folks, as she mentally travels abroad in Clayborne in search of answers." Publ Wkly
This novel "with its beautiful, difficult prose, is a work at once intensely personal and political that will assure Bambara's place in black American fiction." Libr J

Those bones are not my child. Pantheon Bks. 1999 676p o.p.
ISBN 0-679-44261-8 LC 99-21534

Bambara, Toni Cade—*Continued*

This novel is based on the real-life killings of black children in Atlanta, Georgia, in the early 1980s. "White police suspected parents; African Americans saw the hand of the Ku Klux Klan; others believed that a child pornography ring was responsible." Time

"The anger and desperation of the parents is portrayed so vividly that their search for the truth becomes the reader's. Bambara's final work is an honest and passionate tour de force." Libr J

Bank, Melissa

The girls' guide to hunting and fishing. Viking 1999 288p $23.95

ISBN 0-670-88300-X LC 98-48590

This novel traces the love life of its central character, Jane, "episodically from the time she is 14 through her 20s and 30s as she orbits Manhattan's publishing world." Time

"Often funny, poignant, and well sprinkled with razor-sharp wit, Jane's search for love (usually in all the wrong places) is going to be familiar to many." Booklist

Banks, Iain

Look to windward; {by} Iain M. Banks. Pocket Bks. 2001 369p o.p.

ISBN 0-7434-2191-4 LC 2001-21833

First published 2000 in the United Kingdom

"When the 800-year-old light of a distant space battle reaches the Masaq'Orbital, an emissary from Chel arrives on a mission hidden even to himself. Only Ziller, a Chelgrian composer, can unlock a secret that could save or destroy an entire world." Libr J

"Although things start a bit slowly, Banks's fine prose, complex plotting and well-rounded characters will eventually win over even the most discerning readers, and all will find themselves fully rewarded when the novel reaches its powerful conclusion." Publ Wkly

Banks, Oliver T.

The Caravaggio obsession; a novel; by Oliver Banks. Little, Brown 1984 230p o.p.

LC 83-17497

"When a friend in the art auction business is killed in New York, Amos [Hatcher] tracks art and murder to Rome. There he is thwarted by the police and threatened by quasi-radical thugs. Amos soon realizes that his friend's murderer, the ringleader of the robberies, is obsessed with that earlier dark genius, the painter Caravaggio. Banks crams his story with history and lore in ways that are essential to the plot and fascinating to even the most culture-resistant reader. The spirit of Caravaggio and the desperate, beautiful city of Rome haunt this superlative thriller." Wilson Libr Bull

The Rembrandt panel; a novel; by Oliver Banks. Little, Brown 1980 268p o.p.

LC 80-11964

"Art investigator Amos Hatcher turns up in Boston after two murders that just don't make sense. One victim is a 'runner,' a man who leads a shoestring life and occasionally is able to provide dealers with minor finds. The other is Samuel Weinstock, a pleasant, principled Charles Street gallery owner who prides himself on his integrity and his careful scholarship. Hatcher, with Weinstock's assistant Sheila Woods, aided and abetted by two canny and amusing Boston homicide detectives, discovers there's much to meet the sophisticated eye in the case. The plot turns on a long-missing Rembrandt portrait and also involves a priceless Greek vase. Museums, dealers, scholars, all have intricate parts to play." Publ Wkly

Banks, Russell, 1940-

Affliction. Harper & Row 1989 355p o.p.

LC 89-45075

"Wade Whitehouse is a small-town policeman in his early forties made crazy-desperate by a life of chronic failure and intractably self-destructive behavior. Like his father, he's moody, abusive, and a mean drunk. Wade's got a good heart, and he'd like to change his ways, but his desire to reform is thwarted by his baser male instincts. Things just keep getting worse until he finally can't take it anymore, whereupon he snaps and literally runs amok in a mad and murderous rage of Oedipal annihilation before vanishing, ghostlike, into the snow-covered New Hampshire countryside. Wade's tragic saga is related by his younger brother, Rolfe, a bookish history teacher who suppresses his own self-destructive tendencies by submerging himself in scholarly pursuits." Booklist

This novel is "psychological portraiture of a high order, and like all profound portraits it finds in its subject astonishing contradictions." N Y Times Book Rev

The angel on the roof; the stories of Russell Banks. HarperCollins Pubs. 2000 506p o.p.

ISBN 0-06-017396-3 LC 99-57738

Contents: Djinn; Defenseman; The caul; The fisherman; Firewood; Quality time; The lie; Indisposed; The child screams and looks back at you; Sarah Cole: a type of love story; Assisted living; The neighbor; The rise of the middle class; The burden; Mistake; Plains of Abraham; Theory of flight; Comfort; Success story; Cowcow; With Ché in New Hampshire; Dis bwoy, him gwan; The fish; The Moor; Searching for survivors; Black man and white woman in dark green rowboat; Xmas; The guinea pig lady; Queen for a day; The visit; Lobster night

"At his best, Banks writes with an agonized clarity that seems to spring from temperamental reticence, as if he were being pulled, against his will, back to his origins and to his entwined themes, the mutual betrayals committed against each other by parents and children, men and women, blacks and whites." N Y Times Book Rev

Cloudsplitter; a novel. HarperCollins Pubs. 1998 758p o.p.

LC 97-22163

In 1859, five insurrectionists escaped Harpers Ferry, "including Brown's son Owen. In 'Cloudsplitter' Owen decides to tell his tale. He has fled . . . to a California mountaintop, there to remain in seclusion until the end of the century, when one Miss Mayo requests an audience for a biography of John Brown she's researching. Owen responds with this book, a very long suicide note addressed to her but, as he explains, also to his father, his brothers, and others among the already dead. It is Owen's brief for Purgatory, where he expects to meet all

Banks, Russell, 1940-—*Continued*
those who devoted their lives to John Brown." New Yorker

"To rise above period costume and stately diction, a historical novel must have a saving tincture of anachronism, a point of forced contact with the unfinished business of the present. Cloudsplitter, is brought alive by Owen's ambivalent, recognizably modern consciousness." Nation

Continental drift. Harper & Row 1985 366p o.p.
LC 84-48137

"The novel charts, in alternating chapters, the eventually intersecting paths of two people desperately on the move: Bob Dubois, a 30-year-old native of Catamount, N.H., who decides one cold December night in the late 1970's that he wants something better than the life he has had so far and takes off with his wife and two daughters for Florida—and Vanise Dorsinville, a Haitian woman living in a tiny cabin in the hill country near Port-de-Paix, who leaves the poverty and bitter hopelessness of her island life for the bright promise of America." N Y Times Book Rev

"There are raw edges to Bank's novel, and a numbing insistence on the powerlessness of its characters, but there's no denying its almost frightening intensity." Libr J

The darling. HarperCollins 2004 392p $25.95
ISBN 0-06-019735-8 LC 2004-47431

"Over a decade after leaving her three sons behind in Liberia, Hannah Musgrave realizes she has to leave her farm in the Adirondacks and find out what has happened to them and the chimpanzees for whom she created a sanctuary. {This} is the story of her return to the wreckage of west Africa and the story of her past, from her middle-class American upbringing to her years in the Weather Underground." Publisher's note

"'The Darling' has large ambitions and themes: politics, violence, class, race, sexuality, even the bonds and the boundaries between species. If it offers no definitive conclusions, why should it? The business of serious fiction is to set forth the complications, not to lay down the law." Newsweek

Rule of the bone; a novel. HarperCollins Pubs. 1995 390p o.p.
LC 95-11701

The protagonist of this novel, fourteen-year-old Bone, "has a disturbed stepfather, a long-suffering mother, and a long-gone father. The first half of the book chronicles his willing but innocent drift into criminality. His life takes a turn for the better when he moves into an abandoned school bus with a Jamaican mystic. He travels to Jamaica with 'I-man,' and there he finds his self-centered druggie father, turns 15, is sexually initiated, and loses I-man in a violent drug deal." SLJ

"Intoxicating and unsparing, 'Rule of the Bone' is a romance for a world fast running out of room for childhood." N Y Times Book Rev

The sweet hereafter. HarperCollins Pubs. 1991 257p o.p.
LC 90-56404

In this novel the story "is told by four people: Dolores Driscoll, a school-bus driver in a small town; Billy Ansel, father of two of the children on the bus; Mitchell Stephens, a lawyer; and Nichole Burnell, a student. In the accident on which the story is centered, Ansel loses his children and Nichole is paralyzed. Dolores survives the accident—the plunge of the bus through the guardrail and into the water-filled quarry—and then tries to survive survival. Mitchell Stephens becomes the attorney for the group of parents who mount a lawsuit." Christ Sci Monit

"Banks handles his dark theme with judicious restraint, empathy and compassion." Publ Wkly

Bannister, Jo

No birds sing. St. Martin's Press 1996 297p $21.95
ISBN 0-312-14382-6 LC 96-7296

This procedural "about the Castlemere, England, police department boasts a wonderful cast of multidimensional characters: Detective Superintendent Frank Shapiro, Detective Inspector Liz Graham, and the department's wild Irishman, Detective Sergeant Cal Donovan. In this . . . installment in the series, Castlemere is hit by a smash-and-grab gang, train hijackers, and a rapist. Watching Bannister weave these disparate elements together to produce another gripping tale is half the fun." Booklist

True witness. St. Martin's Minotaur 2002 263p $23.95
ISBN 0-312-30817-5 LC 2002-24508

"Quiet, unassuming, and harmless Daniel Hood . . . witnesses a brutal murder and then tries unsuccessfully to help police. The detective in charge, however, has his own agenda: this murder has strong connections to three ten-year-old rape/murders, and he thinks that he knows the culprit. Locals scapegoat Daniel for not identifying the bad guy until his friend Brodie—who finds things for people—acts on her own theory. This well-done British police procedural features psychological interaction, small-town insecurities, and parental fears." Libr J

Bannister, Patricia V. *See* Veryan, Patricia, 1923-

Banville, John

Athena; a novel. Knopf 1995 232p o.p.
ISBN 0-679-40521-6 LC 95-14452

"Art historian Morrow is hired by smalltime crook Morden to authenticate and catalog a cache of eight paintings stored in a decrepit house. . . . Morrow's brief glimpse through a crumbling wall of a woman's leg in stockings and black high heels is the beginning of his increasingly destructive sexual obsession with the woman, identified only as A." Libr J

"Banville's art eschews the vulgar artificiality of life in favour of the stylish artificiality of art itself. He paints a painted world. Characters are caricatures, images are ice-bright hypermetaphors, narrative knows it is so." New Statesman & Society

The book of evidence. HarperCollins Pubs. 1990 219p o.p.
LC 89-10985

First published 1989 in the United Kingdom

"Freddie Montgomery is a schizophrenic 38-year-old ex-scientist. . . . After study in America, Freddie returns to Ireland to find that his disowning mother has sold

Banville, John—*Continued*
what he believes is part of his inheritance from his late father, some paintings that include an Old Dutch master of a woman he thinks regards him with caring, benevolent authority. As he steals it, he murders a maid who catches him in the act. His lawyer advises him to plead manslaughter to quash evidence. Instead . . . Freddie writes the 'book of evidence' that we read." Libr J

"This novel, the inventive testimony of a murderer more interested in making an impression than escaping conviction, is . . . hauntingly beautiful and original. . . . Mr. Banville shows his uncanny ability to make everything he describes seem new and rare, yet instantly recognisable." Economist

Eclipse; a novel. Knopf 2001 211p $23
ISBN 0-375-41129-1 LC 00-62014

"The novel tells the story of Alex Cleave, a successful middle-aged stage actor. . . . One day, seemingly without cause, he leaves the stage in mid-performance and retreats to his abandoned childhood home 'to cease performing and merely be'. . . . Abandoning his uncomprehending wife, Lydia, Alex enters a house that appears to be empty, but proves to be cluttered with ghosts from his past, premonitions of the future, and a couple of flesh-and-blood intruders who inveigle their way into Alex's present." Economist

"Banville's writing is richly descriptive and full of original images. . . . Eclipse is essentially a reflective work. The actual narrative is Cleave's interior journey, not the rather banal series of lived events, and for this reason the magnificent atmospherics, in a way, are the story." New Leader

Ghosts. Knopf 1993 244p o.p.
ISBN 0-679-40519-4 LC 93-2948

This novel "begins when the shipwrecked occupants of a pleasure boat make their way to a big beach house for comfort, food, and rest: . . . the beautiful Flora; the three ungainly children, Hatch, Pound, and Alice; the cynical photographer, Sophie; dapper old Croke, in his panama and striped blazer; and sleazy, leering Felix. The group is watched and awaited by the house's occupants: Professor Kreutznaer, interrupted in his life's work, studying and writing about the artist Vaublin; his aide—both cook and typist—the dreamer Licht; and the book's narrator, an ex-con who came to the island for solitude and the opportunity to work with the professor on his book." Booklist

"Larded with veiled references to Wittgenstein and Frankenstein, to Nietzsche, Goethe and Shakespeare, to Beckett and, indeed, to Banville, it sometimes seems a little like a crossword puzzle with unnumbered lights. But if it doesn't yield up everything on a first reading, Ghosts has a melancholy power that will draw the reader back for further bids to plumb its mysteries." New Statesman & Society

The sea. Knopf 2005 195p $23
ISBN 0-307-26311-8 LC 2005-50418

"When Max Morden returns to the coastal town where he spent a holiday in his youth he is both escaping from a recent loss and confronting a distant trauma. The Grace family appear that long ago summer as if from another world. Drawn to the Grace twins, Chloe and Myles, Max soon finds himself entangled in their lives, which are as seductive as they are unsettling. What ensues will haunt him for the rest of his years and shape everything that is to follow." Publisher's note

"What's strangest about 'The Sea' is that the novel somehow becomes simpler and clearer as it gets more selfconscious: a consequence, I suppose, of its author dropping the pretense of being one kind of writer and giving in to his authentic and much more complicated creative nature. This misshapen but affecting novel turns out to be about something even more familiar than the loss of innocence: it's about grief, the misery and confusion the narrator feels on losing his wife." N Y Times Book Rev

The untouchable. Knopf 1997 367p o.p.
ISBN 0-679-45108-0 LC 96-49637

"Victor Maskell, nearing the end of his life, has been revealed as a former Soviet spy. This tabloid outing is so distasteful to Victor—son of a bishop, author of an influential monograph on Poussin, part of a rarefied gay Cambridge clique, confidant to H.M. the King—that you can almost hear his bones creak as he stoops to answer the ruinous allegations. Victor's apologia is stunningly unapologetic: his 'Bolshie' youth, grim marrriage, and hushed assignations (both sexual and strategic) roll by with a dreamy kind of stoicism that the author renders with characteristic virtuosity." New Yorker

Bao Ninh, 1952-

The sorrow of war; a novel of North Vietnam; translated from the Vietnamese by Phan Thanh Hao; edited by Frank Palmos. Scribner 1995 233p o.p.
LC 94-22390

Original Vietnamese edition, 1991

This novel is based on the experiences of a North Vietnamese soldier who fought in the South for over ten years. "The tale is told in a series of flashbacks by the novel's hero, Kien, who is writing his story as an act of therapy in the late 1980s. As a young man, Kien had been led to believe that a patriotic war was being waged as an example to future generations. He gradually comes to believe that the three golden rules of preparedness he had learnt at school were empty sloganeering. To the common soldier in this story, the realities of war are a frenzied, dehumanising aggression, and the creation of an unnatural thirst for killing and wanton cruelty." Economist

"The word classic is bandied about with ridiculous laxity, but in this case it is hard not to fall back on it. Nothing else really fits the elemental simplicity of theme and treatment: love, war, death, disillusionment, betrayal." New Statesman (1913)

Barbash, Thomas *See* Barbash, Tom

Barbash, Tom

The last good chance; a novel. Picador USA 2002 440p $24
ISBN 0-312-28796-8 LC 2002-25847

"Steven Turner is a young journalist exiled at a paper in Lakeland, a decaying port town in rural upstate New York. His best friend, Jack Lambeau, is the Lakeland town planner. An ambitious Ivy League graduate, Lambeau had had difficulty advancing his experimental

Barbash, Tom—*Continued*
urban planning ideas in New York City. When Lakeland's mayor, William Hickey, promised him carte blanche for his New Urbanist—style visions, Lambeau agreed to return to his hometown. With evangelical fervor, he tries to revive Lakeland through a glittering lakefront development project. What he doesn't know, and what the mayor does, is that there are tubs of toxic materials illegally dumped under the lakefront. . . .This is a taut, intricate vision of ambition, corruption and love in the postindustrial era." Publ Wkly

Barfoot, Joan

Critical injuries. Counterpoint 2002 336p $25
ISBN 1-58243-208-2 LC 2002-23845
"At 49 Isla revels in her second marriage and loves her advertising career, a happy life forever changed when she walks in on a robbery and the startled gunman, 17-year-old Roddy, shoots. . . . As Isla lies frozen in a hospital bed and Roddy emotionally freezes everyone out as he lies hopeless in jail, their thoughts are remarkably similar as they revisit the people and events that shaped their lives and worry about each other." Booklist

Barker, Clive

Babel's children
In Barker, C. In the flesh

The books of blood. Pantheon Bks. 1988 c1984 462p o.p.
LC 88-2404
"An Ace/Putnam book"
Omnibus edition of volumes 1-3 of Books of blood originally published 1984 in the United Kingdom; 1986 in paperback in the United States. Volumes 4 and 5 of Books of blood published with title: The inhuman condition and In the flesh
Contents: Volume one: The Book of Blood; The midnight meat train; The Yattering and Jack; Pig blood blues; Sex, death and starshine; In the hills, the cities
Volume two: Dread; Hell's event; Jacqueline Ess: her will and testament; The skins of the fathers; New murders in the Rue Morgue
Volume three: Son of celluloid; Rawhead Rex; Confessions of a (pornographer's) shroud; Scape-goats; Human remains; The Book of Blood (a postscript): on Jerusalem Street

Cabal. Putnam 1988 377p o.p.
LC 88-23308
The title novella "tells the story of Boone, a troubled young man who has never found his place in the world most people think of as 'real.' After spending years in therapy, and coming to believe that he is finally getting well, Boone's therapist convinces him he has been committing hideous murders, without any recollection of the crimes. Shocked by Dr. Decker's revelations, and desperate to find a place to hide, Boone takes refuge in Midian, an underground community whose inhabitants are no longer—and perhaps never were—human. . . . Of the four short stories which accompany the novel—'The Life of Death,' 'How Spoilers Bleed,' 'Twilight at the Towers' and 'The Last Illusion'— 'How Spoilers Bleed' is the most unsettling. . . . The muscularity of Barker's writing and his ability to pull you into his stories combine to make all of the stories in this book fiendishly effective." West Coast Rev Books

Cabal [novelette]
In Barker, C. Cabal

Coldheart Canyon. HarperCollins Pubs. 2001 676p o.p.
ISBN 0-06-018297-0 LC 2001-279145
Years ago, many film stars and "their colleagues were drawn by the beautiful, rapacious film star Katya Lupi to her magnificent home in Los Angeles's Coldheart Canyon. What kept them at the house, even after death, is the incredible room in its lowest story. Assembled from thousands of painted tiles, that room—brought to California in the 1920s from an ancient monastery in Romania—is literally alive with evil. . . . The room's powers bestow timeless youth on some, including Katya, but give rise to monstrous entities as well. In the present day, into this horrific place enter several modern sorts, most notably A-list film hero Todd Pickett and a dowdy woman, head of Todd's fan club, whose courage and good sense mark her as the novel's hero." Publ Wkly

The damnation game. Putnam 1987 c1985 379p o.p.
LC 86-26478
"An Ace/Putnam book"
First published 1985 in the United Kingdom
"Set in modern Britain, the story thrusts a flawed 'innocent'—parolee Marty Strauss—into an epic conflict between wealthy Joseph Whitehead and Mamoulian the Cardplayer, a centuries-old creature with whom Whitehead had struck a bargain to obtain his wealth and power. Whitehead reneges, and the resulting struggle is played out primarily on his fortress-like estate. Barker's excellent writing makes the graphic, grotesque imagery endemic to current horror fiction very effective." Libr J

Everville; the second book of the art. HarperCollins Pubs. 1994 697p o.p.
ISBN 0-06-017716-0 LC 94-27296
This second volume in a projected trilogy is about "several overlapping searches all taking place in and between the parallel worlds of the Cosm (i.e., reality as we know it) and the land that is bordered by a sea called the Quiddity. That body of water lies right on the other side of a door between worlds situated on a mountain above Everville, Oregon. Opened during the nineteenth century, the portal has never quite shut; indeed, malevolent forces on the other side will soon come pouring through to wreak havoc but will also afford the opportunity for several otherworld exiles to go home." Booklist
"At times profoundly moving as flawed heroes and heroines martyr themselves to love or goodness, this novel confirms the author's position not only as one of horror's most potent and fertile minds but also as one of modern fiction's premier metaphysicians." Publ Wkly

The forbidden
In Barker, C. In the flesh

Galilee; a romance. HarperCollins Pubs. 1998 582p o.p.
LC 98-165556
"The Barbarossas may be divinities, but their lives have been entangled with the all-too-human Gearys since the Civil War. It hasn't been a pretty collusion. Now,

Barker, Clive—*Continued*
when it appears that both families are on the verge of splintering out of existence, Edward Barbarossa is enticed into writing the story of both clans, focusing on Galilee Barbarossa, the prodigal son." Libr J

"The novel's scale is smaller than that of previous Barker efforts—missing are the titanic battles of form vs. chaos, good vs. evil, the riot of wonders and terrors. But it's less cluttered, too, despite abundant inspiration and invention and satisfying smatterings of Barker-brand sex, scatology and violence. Above all, there is a new richness of character, of its warpings and transfigurations by hatred and love, blood legacy and death." Publ Wkly

The great and secret show; the first book of the art. Harper & Row 1989 550p o.p.
ISBN 0-06-016276-7 LC 89-45787

"Nebraska postal clerk Randolph Jaffe works in the Dead Letter Room, opening and inspecting loads of undeliverable U.S. mail. Soon, through a series of cryptic dead letters, he taps into an ethereal network of mysterious revelations which provides access to enormous power channels. . . . [A] battle of light forces versus dark forces commences, with greedy Jaffe heading the latter, and mad yet philanthropic scientist Richard Fletcher representing the former." Libr J

"Like most fantasy novelists, Barker does not feel compelled to be logical or consistent: the dreamlike narrative has a kitchen-sink inclusiveness and cheats the rationalist in that characters turn out in mid-action to be someone else entirely, cunningly disguised. But the images are vivid, the asides incisive and the prose elegant in this joyride of a story." Time

Followed by Everville

Imajica. HarperCollins Pubs. 1991 824p o.p.
LC 90-56405

This fantasy "begins when a rich gent hires a peculiar assassin to off his estranged wife, the tome's female protagonist, whom he'd . . . stolen a while back from the professional art forger who's the male protagonist. The attempt fails but starts the romance's personae plunging back and forth between 'Dominions,' of which there are at least five, the Earth upon which we all dwell being the fifth and seemingly least developed of the lot." Booklist

"Barker's prodigious imagination delivers magicians, doppelgängers, Boschean creatures of staggeringly various descriptions and a pantheon of gods and goddesses seduced by power and redeemed by love in a story of violence, occasional unconventional eroticism and mesmerizing invention." Publ Wkly

In the flesh. Poseidon Press 1987 c1986 221p o.p.
LC 86-20450

First published 1985 in the United Kingdom with title: Books of blood v5

This collection contains four novellas. "The title story, the longest in the book, is an absolute knockout, a nightmarish tale of a convict who seeks out, and finds, his long-dead, murderous grandfather. The evocation of the city of the murdered dead is haunting. 'The Forbidden' seems to be an attempt to write in the manner of Ramsey Campbell, and the narrative succeeds at that, and on its own terms. 'The Madonna' is a turgid and somewhat confused horror story, and 'Babel's Children' is an interesting, offbeat thriller of political conspiracy, madness and magic." Publ Wkly

In the flesh [novelette]
In Barker, C. In the flesh

The inhuman condition; tales of terror. Poseidon Press 1986 220p o.p.
LC 86-5086

First published 1985 in the United Kingdom with title: Books of blood v4

Contents: The inhuman condition; The body politics; Revelations; Down, Satan; The age of desire

This collection "combines subtle wit with an original style that ignites the very explosive power of horror-fiction." West Coast Rev Books

The Madonna
In Barker, C. In the flesh

Sacrament. HarperCollins Pubs. 1996 447p o.p.
LC 96-164648

"Brilliant, gay wildlife photographer Will has spent his career chronicling death—something he doesn't dwell on until an accident sends him into a coma. During his physical stasis, Will's mind explores the past, and he relives his life-altering meeting with the inhuman Joseph Steep. Steep taught Will the pleasures of causing death. Will lives Steep's memories and sees things that weren't intended to be remembered, which shapes the next 30 years of his life. But the eyes of an adult see differently from those of a child. Will awakens to new purpose: to uncover or perhaps recover a powerful artifact." Libr J

"Even in this fractured tale, Barker presents an astonishing array of ideas, visions and epiphanies; but they're seen as if through a glass beveled and crazed." Publ Wkly

Weaveworld. Poseidon Press 1987 584p o.p.
LC 87-18602

This fantasy concerns "the Fugue, a magical land inhabited by descendants of supernatural beings who once shared the earth with humans. The Fugue has been woven into a carpet for protection against those who would destroy it; the death of its guardian occasions a battle between good and particularly repulsive evil forces for control of the Fugue." Libr J

Barker "creates a fantastic romance of magic and promise that is at once popular fiction and utopian conjuring. . . . There is great wit in the struggle that ensues, and keen attention to the facts of poverty and exile." NY Times Book Rev

Barker, Nicola, 1966-

Behindlings; a novel. Ecco Press 2002 535p $27.95
ISBN 0-06-018569-4 LC 2002-69731

In this novel, "a wily practical joker named Wesley is continually glancing behind him. The creator of the Loiter, a nationwide treasure hunt devised for a confectionary company, he is followed by a motley collection of fans as he tramps around Great Britain. The Behindlings, as Wesley calls them, spend the book debating elaborate riddles, found in candy-bar wrappers, that lead them to Canvey Island, a dreary spot in the Thames estuary. Barker is a talented writer whose verbal acuity can be exhilarating." New Yorker

Barker, Pat, 1943-

Another world. Farrar, Straus & Giroux 1999 c1998 277p $24

ISBN 0-374-10525-1 LC 99-230285

First published 1998 in the United Kingdom

"Geordie, a WWI veteran, is over 100, but is hanging on to life with the same stubborness and iconoclasm that have seen him through the entire 20th century. His grandson, Nick, living in grim, contemporary Newcastle-on-Tyne, is struggling with his own life as he monitors Geordie's last days. Nick's teenage daughter from a previous marriage, Miranda, has come to stay; his new wife, Fran, with her own kid, Gareth, a computer games freak, has two-year old Jasper to contend with and another baby on the way. Now it seems that their new house may be haunted by the kind of malign domestic spirit at large among Nick's little family." Publ Wkly

This novel "demonstrates the extraordinary immediacy and vigor of expression we have come to expect from Barker." N Y Times Book Rev

Border crossing. Farrar, Straus & Giroux 2001 215p o.p.

ISBN 0-374-18115-2 LC 00-52745

"When Tom Seymour, a psychiatrist in Newcastle, rescues a suicidal young man from the river behind his house, he doesn't recognize the mud-smeared face; after all, when Tom's testimony helped convict Danny Miller for the murder of an elderly woman, thirteen years earlier, the boy was only ten years old. Now Danny is free again—living under an assumed name, hunted by the press, anxious to make sense of his past—and he turns to his former enemy for help. But was their reunion really a coincidence? One is unsure whether or not Barker's latest novel is a thriller until its final pages—a knife-edge ambiguity underscores the author's impatience with platitudes about good and evil." New Yorker

Double vision. Farrar, Straus & Giroux 2003 258p $23

ISBN 0-374-20905-7 LC 2003-54736

"Kate Frobisher, a sculptor working on a monumental figure of Jesus, is recovering from a car accident and grieving for her husband, Ben, a war photographer killed in Afghanistan. Stephen Sharkey, a journalist (and friend of Ben's) suffering from post-traumatic stress syndrome after covering Bosnia, Rwanda and other conflicts, has left London and a failed marriage to write a book about 'the way wars are represented.' An ensemble cast gathers around these two haunted figures: Stephen's brother Robert and his family; Alec Braithewaite, the friendly vicar, and his Cambridge-bound daughter Justine; and Peter Wingrave, Kate's studio assistant and Justine's ex." Publ Wkly

Barker "writes superbly, with economy and a lovely talent for darting images. The subject matter is dark, and much is left unsaid, but the reader is drawn on, from page to page." Economist

The eye in the door. Dutton 1994 c1993 280p o.p.

LC 93-43833

First published 1993 in the United Kingdom

"Revisiting World War I England to explore war and its effects on individuals and society, Barker brings back characters . . . from *Regeneration*, including bisexual war hero Billy Prior and psychiatrist William Rivers. In 1918, the war was not going well for the Allies, and hysteria took root—the targets being pacifists and homosexuals, who were allegedly open to blackmail. Prior has connections to a group of pacifists who are being persecuted, and he also suffers from psychological episodes in which his personality alters dramatically. Dr. Rivers treats both Prior and other homosexuals on 'The 47,000,' a list of all purported gays in Britain." Libr J

This work "succeeds as both historical fiction and as sequel. Its research and speculation combine to produce a kind of educated imagination that is persuasive and illuminating about this particular place and time. . . . The novel's greatest success, however, has to do with the insight it provides into its central doctor-patient relationships." N Y Times Book Rev

Followed by The ghost road

The ghost road. Dutton 1996 c1995 278p o.p.

LC 95-46863

"A William Abrahams book"

First published 1995 in the United Kingdom

This novel's main protagonists "are Dr. William H. Rivers, the English psychologist who treated the poets Siegfried Sassoon and Wilfred Owen, among others, for shell shock, and the fictional Billy Prior, a former 'cured' patient who insists on returning to the front in France even though the war is winding down to its bloody finale. In the late summer of 1918, ghosts—of the dead and of the soon-to-be-dead—roam the land. . . . Rivers, facing the moral dilemma of healing men so that they might be killed, recalls an anthropological trip he made to a Melanesian tribe whose head-hunting practices were banned by the British." Libr J

"The Ghost Road is a startlingly good novel in its own right. With the other two volumes of the trilogy, it forms one of the richest and most rewarding works of fiction of recent times. Intricately plotted, beautifully written, skillfully assembled, tender, horrifying and funny, it lives on in the imagination, like the war it so imaginatively and so intelligently explores." Times Lit Suppl

Regeneration. Dutton 1992 c1991 251p o.p.

LC 91-41264

"A William Abrahams book"

First published 1991 in the United Kingdom

This novel "blends fact and fiction in relating a pivotal incident in the tragic life of noted English poet Siegfried Sassoon. In 1917, Sassoon, an army officer who had been decorated for his gallantry, was sent to a military sanitarium at Craiglockhart, diagnosed as suffering from shell shock. In fact, he had been assigned to the hospital less for medical reasons than political ones. No longer believing in the government's vaguely stated war aims and haunted by memories of the victims of the carnage he experienced, he had issued a declaration condemning the war. Only the intervention of his friend, poet Robert Graves, prevented a court-martial." Publ Wkly

"'Regeneration' is an antiwar war novel, in a tradition that is by now an established one, though it tells a part of the whole story of war that is not often told—how war may batter and break men's minds—and so makes the madness of war more than a metaphor, and more awful." N Y Times Book Rev

Followed by The eye in the door

Barnard, Judith

For works written by this author in collaboration with Michael Fain see Michael, Judith

Barnard, Robert

The bad samaritan; a novel of suspense featuring Charlie Peace. Scribner 1995 233p o.p.
LC 95-16383

When Detective Constable Charlie Peace and his boss "Mike Oddie investigate the unsurprising murder of the village parish Lothario, they question Rosemary Sheffield, the vicar's wife. Rosemary, who has recently 'lost' her faith and been accused of immoral behavior with a Yugoslavian refugee, makes a perfect suspect." Libr J

"The author is at the top of his form. . . . On the surface, St. Saviour's parish is a close-knit, respectable, and ever-so-middle-class church community. When Barnard finishes with this small English village, everyone learns a hard lession in hypocrisy. He strips the veneer of respectability from a number of its prominent citizens." Christ Sci Monit

The bones in the attic. Scribner 2002 267p o.p.
ISBN 0-684-87379-6 LC 2001-49569

First published 2001 in the United Kingdom

In this mystery, "former soccer star Matt Harper, now a television and radio personality, is the new owner of Elderholm, one of a small street of sturdy old houses in Leeds. As he and his remodeling contractor take a look around the attic, they come upon the skelton of a toddler-sized child. The deeper Matt and Det. Sgt. Charlie Peace probe, the more certain they become that the child met its tragic death in 1969, the same fateful summer Matt has spent in this very community." Publ Wkly

The case of the missing Brontë. Scribner 1983 182p o.p.
LC 83-3328

Scotland yard's Perry Trethowan "is relaxing in a village pub with his wife when he meets Edith Wing, a retired schoolteacher. When she shows them a large piece of yellowing paper covered with tiny writing and confides that she has 200 similar pages at home, inherited from a cousin whose family connections with the Brontes go back five generations, it seems apparent that she is in possesion of an invaluable, previously unknown Emily Bronte manuscript. When Perry suggests that she seek expert advice on the manuscript's authenticity from a local professor, he doesn't suspect that he is very nearly sending Edith to her death." Publisher's note

The corpse at the Haworth Tandoori. Scribner 1999 283p o.p.
ISBN 0-684-85532-1 LC 98-39263

First published 1998 in the United Kingdom

"The body of a young man has been found in the trunk of a car parked at the Haworth Tandoori restaurant in the town of Haworth in Yorkshire. Detective Constable Charlie Peace's investigation takes him to the neighboring community of Ashworth." Booklist

Corpse in a gilded cage. Scribner 1984 211p o.p.
LC 84-10703

"The death of a distant cousin catapults happy, middle-class Perce and Elsie Spender into the British aristocracy: they become the twelfth earl and countess of Ellesmere and owners of that forbidding Jacobean manse, Chetton Hall. The Spenders want to spend their fortune elsewhere, but their ill-assorted offspring . . . are dazzled by the prospect of living like lords. The family assembles for the earl's sixtieth birthday, tensions become exacerbated, and a body is found under one of the estate's Bernini statues." Booklist

"A delightful romp through the British class system." Publ Wkly

A cry from the dark; Robert Barnard. 1st Scribner ed. Scribner 2004 277p $24
ISBN 0-7432-5345-0 LC 2003-190056

First published 2003 in the United Kingdom

"Well-respected London writer Bettina Whitelaw is a tough old lady in her eighties. Her story spirals from the present, where her agent and everyone else want to know if she is writing her memoirs, to the past, when, growing up in Bundaroo, Australia, she knew she was too smart to stay there. Why Bettina left Bundaroo sooner than she intended unfolds like an origami puzzle. Along the way, we meet her brother; the child she had but didn't raise, a woman now in her fifties; and Hughie, who came to Bundaroo and also left but remained close to Bettina (after a fashion) over the decades. There's real intelligence in the unfolding, which begins with a breakin at Bettina's flat and ends with a murder. Barnard has created a perfectly credible older woman who has been shaped but not crushed by the secrets in her life." Booklist

Death and the chaste apprentice. Scribner 1989 211p o.p.
LC 89-4205

This mystery takes place at "the Saracen's Head outside London where performers have gathered since medieval days to re-create, fittingly, Elizabethan entertainments. Under the new management of Des Capper, a 'loathsome know-all,' the inn becomes a crime scene when he is murdered and all present, save one, had cause to kill the bounder." Publ Wkly

Death by sheer torture. Scribner 1982 c1981 186p o.p.
LC 81-14569

First published 1981 in the United Kingdom with title: Sheer torture

The novel "tells of the odd death of a wacky old gentleman in a dingy castle in England: the fellow met his untimely death wearing gauzy spangled tights in a self-manufactured torture machine he had read about in a book on the Spanish Inquisition. . . . On this particular day someone had cut the cable, and the machine and its screwball master plummeted to the floor with fatal consequences. It was murder, all right, and onto the scene came the local detective, [Perry Trethowan] no other than the estranged son of the victim." Best Sellers

"A good, satisfying whodunit made absolutely delicious by the crazed egotists." Publ Wkly

Death of a literary widow. Scribner 1980 c1979 192p o.p.
LC 80-13128

First published 1979 in the United Kingdom with title: Posthumous papers

"Two elderly women, Viola and Hilda, live in the same house, avoiding each other like the plague. Both

Barnard, Robert—*Continued*
have been married to the same man, the late writer Walter Mackin, who is the object of a sudden, intense renewal of interest—articles are written about him, his books are reissued. The great concern of the two wives is who will profit from Mackin's posthumous reputation. One of the old ladies dies in a fire, leaving everyone wondering whether she went out in an accidental blaze or as the result of someone's murderous rage." Booklist

Death of a salesperson, and other untimely exits. Scribner 1989 200p o.p.
LC 89-6264
Contents: The woman in the wardrobe; A business partnership; Little terror; Breakfast television; What's in a name?; Sisters; The injured party; Just another kidnap; Blown up; A process of rehabilitation; Holy living and holy dying; The Oxford way of death; Daylight robbery; Happy release; Death of a salesperson; My last girlfriend

A fatal attachment. Scribner 1992 281p o.p.
ISBN 0-684-19412-0 LC 92-10431
"An aloof but admired celebrity in her Yorkshire village, Lydia indulges her fantasies by writing popular biographies of historical swashbucklers like Lord Byron and T. E. Lawrence, and by mooning over a dashing explorer she almost married. But when she begins to instill her reckless notions in two impressionable brothers from the village, someone among Lydia's many past conquests gets a mind to strangle her. Two well-matched police detectives handle the murder investigation." N Y Times Book Rev
"The book's pleasure comes from Barnard's easy use of police procedures, his subtle characterization and his eye for village color. Lydia is a delicious monster, and the ambiguous ending delivers an extra kick." Publ Wkly

Fête fatale. Scribner 1985 183p o.p.
LC 85-14583
Published in the United Kingdom with title: Disposal of the living
"The village of Hexton-on-Weir is run by its women, and a nasty lot they are, barely excepting the narrator-wife of the murdered man, whose tongue can be as acid as those of her enemies. An unlikely murder weapon and a forced ending mar only slightly the pleasure of Barnard's gifts for characterization and local color." Barzun. Cat of Crime. Rev and enl edition

The graveyard position. Scribner 2005 277p $25
ISBN 0-7432-5346-9 LC 2004-59131
First published 2004 in the United Kingdom
In this Charlie Peace mystery, "spiritualist Clarissa Cantelo's death reunites her surviving family members, an eccentric clan guarding some dark secrets. . . . When Clarissa's nephew and heir, lawyer Merlyn Docherty, who's been living in Brussels, resurfaces after two decades, his relatives challenge his claim; everyone thought he was long dead. Motivated by self-preservation to probe the Cantelo family's twisted dynamics and complex alliances, Merlyn slowly pieces together a pattern that hints at conspiracies and sexual deviancy. . . . Fans of classic murder puzzles will be delighted by the careful hiding of clues in plain sight." Publ Wkly

A hovering of vultures. Scribner 1993 231p o.p.
ISBN 0-684-19625-5 LC 93-19371
"Detective Charlie Peace travels to rural Yorkshire to attend a weekend gathering of devotees of brother-sister writers Joshua and Susannah Sneddon, who in 1932 died in a murder-suicide incident. There's something odd about this convocation, and as we try to figure out why Detective Peace is in attendance in the first place, we observe him persevering in attempting to learn who murdered the organizer of the literary weekend." Booklist
"While skewering literary pretensions, Barnard . . . writes a tale that is both cozily down-home and wittily urbane." Publ Wkly

The masters of the house; a novel of suspense. Scribner 1994 214p o.p.
ISBN 0-684-19728-6 LC 94-5853
"Thirteen-year-old Matthew Heenan and his 12-year-old sister Annie assume control of their shattered household when their mother dies in childbirth and their unemployed father has a breakdown. Annie, who is the managing type, runs the house and takes care of the younger children. It falls to Matthew . . . to hide their father's catatonic state from the neighbors—and to solve the murder of Mr. Heenan's girlfriend, whose body the children bury in a nearby field." N Y Times Book Rev

The mistress of Alderley. Scribner 2003 281p $24
ISBN 0-7432-3688-2 LC 2002-30461
"Caroline Fawley, the weekend mistress of a married tycoon named Marius Fleetwood, glories in her unorthodox status. She lives on a gracious Yorkshire estate, accepted by all the nice people in the village. Her younger children get on swimmingly with her lover's son, and everyone admires her grown daughter, who is poised to make a brillant debut as an opera singer. It's all so very civilized—until Marius is murdered and these perfectly lovely people turn perfectly hateful." N Y Times Book Rev

A murder in Mayfair. Scribner 2000 270p o.p.
ISBN 0-684-86445-2 LC 99-46962
"When Colin Pinnock becomes a junior minister in the new Labor government, he is full of promise and resolve, until a curt message on a grubby postcard—'Who do you think you are?'—challenges all his assumptions about himself. . . . Barnard is meticulous about building up the suspense as Colin is hounded by the faceless fury bent on ending, or at least ruining, his blameless life. But there's more nasty fun in reading the story as the revenge of the ousted Tories on the cheeky whippersnappers who think they can keep their integrity, not to mention their sanity, once they start playing politics for real." N Y Times Book Rev

No place of safety. Scribner 1998 186p o.p.
ISBN 0-684-84503-2 LC 97-32909
First published 1997 in the United Kingdom
"Chief Inspector Mike Oddie and partner Charlie Peace investigate the murder of a homeless-shelter owner in northern England. Two runaway teens seem to hold the key." Libr J
"With characteristically clever twists and without a single cookie-cutter character, Barnard delivers accomplished entertainment." Publ Wkly

Barnard, Robert—*Continued*

Out of the blackout. Scribner 1985 c1984 o.p.
LC 85-1694

"An unusual piece of detection in that the central character is searching for himself—who was he before he was taken, with other children, to foster homes in the country during the London blitz? Though the tale is not wholeheartedly crime fiction, a murder is discovered and its ramifications elucidated by the self-searching hero." Barzun. Cat of Crime. Rev and enl edition

A scandal in Belgravia. Scribner 1991 245p o.p.
LC 91-8603

"While writing his memoirs, ex-cabinet minister Peter Proctor questions the 35-year-old unsolved murder of Timothy Wycliffe, his good friend and colleague in the Foreign Office. Soon diverted by fond memories of this engaging and fully alive fellow—who happened to be gay—he researches the murder, questions Timothy's friends, family, and lovers, finally reconstructs the murder, and confronts the murderer." Libr J

"Mr. Barnard never loses control of his polished form, even as he does his pretty hatchet job on the last half-century of Conservative Party politics in England." NY Times Book Rev

The skeleton in the grass. Scribner 1988 c1987 199p o.p.
LC 88-3075

First published 1987 in the United Kingdom

"Young Sarah Causeley has signed on as governess to the Hallams, a family of intellectual and political renown, whose seat is a big country house in Oxfordshire. But the Hallams are of a pacifist persuasion, a position that, given the tenor of the times—the rise of fascism in Germany and the outbreak of civil war in Spain—makes them not too popular with many of the people in their environs. In fact, their unpopularity leads to murder." Booklist

Unholy dying. Scribner 2001 281p o.p.
ISBN 0-7432-0149-3 LC 00-47101

First published 2000 in the United Kingdom

This mystery "follows a small-town scandal concerning rumors of unbecoming conduct by the local parish priest. . . . When Cosmo Horrocks, reporter at the *West Yorkshire Chronicle*, relates the rumors, the scandal grows exponentially, which may have something to do with the subsequent murder of the unfortunate Cosmo. Inspector Mike Oddie and Sergeant Charlie Peace are called in to find the killer; readers can count on being surprised by the results of their investigation. An outstanding village mystery in the grand tradition." Booklist

Barnes, Djuna, 1892-1982

Nightwood. Modern Lib. 2000 c1937 xxxii, 169p o.p.
ISBN 0-679-64024-X LC 99-56308

First published 1936 in the United Kingdom; first United States edition 1937 by Harcourt, Brace

"An account of the tangled sexual and psychological relationships between various expatriates in Paris and Berlin. Narrated in part through an alcoholic haze of stream of consciousness, it owes its reputation as an avant-garde work partially to its frank treatment of lesbianism." Benet's Reader's Ency of Am Lit

Barnes, John, 1957-

The merchants of souls. TOR Bks. 2001 398p $25.95
ISBN 0-312-89076-1 LC 2001-42323

"A Tom Doherty Associates book"

"When the pleasure-seeking inhabitants of Earth attempt to download recordings of the personalities of deceased individuals for recreational purposes, the Office of Special Projects enlists its best agents, Giraut and Margaret Leones, to stop the process. Recently divorced and unsure of their relationship, they find themselves at the center of a controversial web of political and galactic intrigue that threatens the future of humanity throughout the universe." Libr J

The sky so big and black. TOR Bks. 2002 315p $24.95
ISBN 0-7653-0303-5 LC 2002-22307

"A Tom Doherty Associates book"

As Terpsichore (Teri) Murray and her eco-prospector father "escort a group of students from Mars's highlands to their school in Wells City, a catastrophic solar phenomenon occurs, decimating many of the human colonies and disrupting communication planet-wide. Left to her own devices to rescue herself and the survivors in her group, Teri is forced to compromise her principles and make an alliance with a force that could mean the end of Martian independence." Libr J

"As always, Barnes's character are beautifully natural. His sense of how the conditions of a place can create a culture and individual sensibilities is outstanding, and here he even allows his slang to evolve." Publ Wkly

Barnes, Julian

England, England. Knopf 1999 c1998 275p o.p.
ISBN 0-375-40582-8 LC 98-46170

First published 1998 in the United Kingdom

"This tale of a theme-park England created on the Isle of Wight by a hateful entrepreneur—complete with fake Stonehenge and half-size Buckingam Palace—does not disappoint. But it is deepened by the story of Martha Cochrane, an overachiever employed to be the project's official naysayer. Both personally and professionally, Martha is devoted to searching for the authentic: for the missing jigsaw piece that disappeared in her father's pocket when he abandoned her family; for the missing piece in her love for a shy fellow-executive; and for the missing ingredient in success. Her meditations are worth any number of clever entertainments." New Yorker

Flaubert's parrot. Knopf 1985 190p o.p.
LC 84-48550

"Geoffrey Braithwaite, widower and retired physician, devotes his final years to a manic examination of literary 'factoids' (to borrow Mailer's term) concerning his favorite author [Gustave Flaubert]. Is Félicité's parrot, immortalized in Un Coeur Simple, the stuffed bird on display at the Hôtel-Dieu, or the one at Crosset? Or is it one of several others stored in the attic of the Museum of Natural History in Rouen? Braithwaite ridicules scholars who pounce upon inconsistencies . . . but is caught up in the game himself." Libr J

"A minor classic, and one of the best criticism novels ever, because its critic/narrator has some dignity, because his choice of subject makes emotional sense and because

Barnes, Julian—*Continued*
the book has a lively, questioning spirit. . . . [Barnes has] written a modernist text with a nineteenth-century heart, a French novel with English lucidity and tact." Nation

A history of the world in 10½ chapters. Knopf 1989 307p o.p.
LC 89-45266
"A revisionist view of Noah's Ark, told by the stowaway woodworm. A chilling account of terrorists hijacking a cruise ship. A court case in 16th-century France in which the woodworm stands accused. A desperate woman's attempt to escape radioactive fallout on a raft. An acute analysis of Géricault's 'Scene of Shipwreck.' The search of a 19th-century Englishwoman and of a contemporary American astronaut for Noah's Ark. An actor's increasingly desperate letters to his silent lover. A thoughtful meditation on the novelist's responsibility regarding love. These and other stories make up Barnes's . . . retelling of the history of the world." Libr J
This book "shapes up not only as Barnes's funniest novel but also his most richly cargoed and imaginatively designed. . . . As satirist and story-teller he has few equals at present." New Statesman Soc

The lemon table; Julian Barnes. Knopf 2004 241p $22.95
ISBN 1-4000-4214-3 LC 2003-60481
Contents: A short history of hairdressing; The story of Mat Israelson; The things you know; Hygiene; The revival; Vigilance; Bark; Knowing French; Appetite; The fruit cage; The silence
"The best of these tales are beautifully wrought elegies for lost youth, lost promises and lost loves. They are stories that reveal an emotional depth new to the writings of the usually cerebral Mr. Barnes." N Y Times (Late N Y Ed)

Love, etc. Knopf 2001 227p $23
ISBN 0-375-41161-5 LC 00-62013
Sequel to Talking it over (1991)
First published 2000 in the United Kingdom
"Straight, rather stuffy organic-food kingpin Stuart; his former best friend, the ebulliently witty layabout Oliver; and Gillian, whom Oliver stole from Stuart, address the reader in turns about just what happened. . . . There's no doubt that in most ways Stuart deserves Gillian more than Oliver does, and the latter's attraction for her seems odd. On the other hand, Oliver is, unexpectedly, quite a good father, and there are hints of obtuseness and brutality about Stuart's bluff self-satisfaction. Poor Gillian, whose French-born mother also comments on the proceedings from a cynical distance, seems quite unable to decide between the two men when Stuart forcibly reenters her life." Publ Wkly
"First, we are flattered by the intimacy of the characters' confessions; then we become fascinated by the little deceptions that they practice on themselves and one another. By the time we realize that we ourselves may have been deceived—well, we're done for." New Yorker

Barnes, Linda

The big dig. St. Martin's Minotaur 2002 275p o.p.
ISBN 0-312-28270-2 LC 2002-68353
In this mystery Boston private investigator Carlotta Carlyle is sent "undercover as a secretary on a construction site where rumors are flying about equipment walking off the site and excavated tunnel dirt being spirited away. It seems like penny-ante stuff to Carlyle, until a construction worker is killed and the contractor's wife goes a little crazy." NY Times Book Rev
"The many plot threads are abruptly but satisfyingly tied up with writing that's vivid, economical and fun." Publ Wkly

Cold case. Delacorte Press 1997 385p o.p.
LC 96-38216
"Adam Mayhew shows up on PI Carlyle's Cambridge, Mass., doorstep with the first chapter of a manuscript that he says could only have been penned by Thea Janis, who disappeared so long ago. When her clothes were later found on a beach, Thea Janis was presumed to be a suicide. But Mayhew, a relative of the author, insists that the manuscript—which makes reference to the fall of the Berlin Wall—proves she is alive and writing. Carlyle's task is to find the writer." Publ Wkly
"Carlotta isn't as smooth an operator as some of her colleagues . . . but her gung-ho technique works for her and it's easy to get caught up in her enthusiasm." N Y Times Book Rev

Coyote; a Carlotta Carlyle mystery. Delacorte Press 1990 257p o.p.
LC 90-34505
"Boston private investigator/part-time cabbie Carlotta Carlyle's search for a frightened woman's green card involves her in an underground world of illegal immigration, labor exploitation, and gruesome mutilation murder." Libr J
"Carlotta is at her best when she focuses on the personal plight of the individuals who make up the nameless legion of potential deportees. While discovering the truth about them, she convincingly provides wisdom and comfort to the child she adores." Publ Wkly

Deep pockets; Linda Barnes. 1st ed. St. Martin's Minotaur 2004 310p $24.95
ISBN 0-312-28271-0 LC 2003-61006
"African-American Harvard professor Wilson Chaney asks Boston PI Carlotta for help because someone is blackmailing him over his affair with Delani Brinkman, a seductive Harvard rowing star. When Delani turns up dead in a boathouse on the Charles, incinerated on a gasoline-soaked futon, a note left by the victim suggests suicide. . . . When Delani's ex-con boyfriend is killed by a hit-run driver on a dark city street, suspicion points back to the urbane Professor Chaney—or does it? Almost every character carries a secret, including Carlotta, who's gingerly resuming her romance with a charming Mafioso. If a couple of red herrings aren't fully explained, Barnes makes superb use of town-gown tensions and the contrasting worlds of Harvard bureaucrats, blue-collar cons, the Brattle Street swells and more." Publ Wkly

Flashpoint; a Carlotta Carlyle mystery. Hyperion 1999 276p o.p.
ISBN 0-7868-6317-X LC 98-56063
Home health aide Gwen Taymore hires Boston PI Carlotta Carlyle "to provide security advice to Valentine Phipps, an old lady struggling to keep her rent controlled apartment, Carlotta agrees, as much out of civic duty as

Barnes, Linda—*Continued*

out of a desire for a paycheck. But Mrs. Phipps's sudden death, which may have been murder, casts suspicion on elusive Gwen, as well as on the building's possibly mob-connected landlord." Publ Wkly

"Unlike most mysteries, once the antagonist is uncovered, Barnes proceeds to write a smart finish." Libr J

Hardware. Delacorte Press 1995 338p o.p.
ISBN 0-385-30613-X LC 94-28706

Carlotta Carlyle "is almost a casualty on the information superhighway when she and her sometimes boyfriend Sam Gianelli are on the receiving end of a driveby shooting following the purchase of her first computer. More than modems and communications software fill her mind after Gloria, the dispatcher for the cab company where Carlotta moonlights, and Sam are injured in a bombing that is seemingly part of a campaign against independent cabbies. Carlotta's . . . determination to find the bomber places her in potential danger from the Mob." SLJ

"The puzzle works well, but mainly it's Carlotta and her interactions with the well-drawn folks around her that make Barnes's story hum." Publ Wkly

The snake tattoo. St. Martin's Press 1989 290p o.p.
LC 88-30525

Private eye Carlotta Carlyle "is faced with two equally difficult cases: finding a missing teenage girl, who seems to have traded posh suburbia for the moral sewer of Boston's Combat Zone, and helping Beantown cop and longtime friend Mooney, who stands accused of assaulting a supposedly unarmed man in a bar fight." Booklist

"Bright, witty, and a touch sarcastic." Libr J

Snapshot; a Carlotta Carlyle novel. Delacorte Press 1993 325p o.p.
LC 92-41734

"Carlotta Carlyle, Boston's snappy, redheaded PI, investigates the suspicious death of a woman's daughter after receiving a series of snapshots in the mail. Carlyle also attempts to locate the biological father of her own 'little sister' Paolina. Both cases ultimately involve drugs and conspiracy." Libr J

"Carlotta uses determination, feistiness, and intelligence to outwit the bad guys and solve the crime. . . . The action is gripping, and there are enough surprises to keep readers interested." Booklist

Steel guitar. Delacorte Press 1991 257p o.p.
LC 91-14529

After Boston PI Carlotta Carlyle "saves old friend, now blues star, Dee Willis from publicity and prosecution in a dangerous park incident, Dee hires her to find their long-ago mutual heartthrob Davey Dunrobie. Davey claims that Dee has plagiarized several of his songs. When Dee discovers a murdered band member in her bed, she realizes Davey means business. Carlotta—tall, vivacious, sensitive—unravels all the knots with breathtaking verve." Libr J

A trouble of fools. St. Martin's Press 1987 208p o.p.
LC 87-16147

"While looking for a missing cab driver, [Carlotta Carlyle] stumbles upon some strange goings on at the taxi company. From the trashing of her client's house to a strange scam involving large sums of money, Carlyle moves through Boston until the threatening violence explodes when least expected." Libr J

Barnes, Steven

(jt. auth) Niven, L. Saturn's race

Barr, Nevada

Blind descent. Putnam 1998 341p o.p.
ISBN 0-399-14371-8 LC 97-34083

"National Park Service (NPS) ranger Anna Pigeon . . . is called to the Carlsbad Caverns in New Mexico, where good NPS friend Frieda Dierkz has been seriously injured during a subterranean exploration. Frieda dies during the rescue attempt, but not before whispering to Anna that she knows things she shouldn't and someone wants her dead." Libr J

"Barr's descriptions of this Stygian underworld—so beautiful, so mysterious and so treacherous—have a stunning visceral quality, largely because of her heroine's affinity with the natural world." N Y Times Book Rev

Blood lure. Putnam 2001 320p o.p.
ISBN 0-399-14702-0 LC 00-55352

"On a training assignment to study grizzly bears in the Waterton-Glacier National Peace Park, near the Montana-Canada border, park ranger Anna Pigeon hikes into the mountains with researcher Joan Rand and an Earthwatch volunteer, Rory Van Slyke. But Anna's joy at returning to the wilderness quickly turns to terror when their camp is ravaged in the middle of the night by a grizzly. Rory disappears, and in the morning the faceless corpse of a female camper is discovered." Libr J

"The author's masterful descriptions of the natural world immeasurably enhance an exciting, suspenseful story." Publ Wkly

Endangered species. Putnam 1997 306p o.p.
ISBN 0-399-14246-0 LC 96-42516

"Sent to isolated Cumberland Island National Seashore off the coast of Georgia on summer fire patrol, Anna [Pigeon] is bored despite the natural beauty of the area. Then the seashore's local ranger and his pilot are killed when their small plane crashes on the island. When Anna and her crew investigate, they find the plane was sabotaged. Anna develops a list of possible suspects, including some of her own crew." Booklist

"A refreshing change from the brash, wisecracking order of female PIs, Barr's thoughtful and sensitive heroine . . . rings true on every page." Publ Wkly

Firestorm. Putnam 1996 307p o.p.
ISBN 0-399-14126-X LC 95-38311

"Far from her base park of Mesa Verde, Anna Pigeon volunteers as a medic at a spike camp of firefighters battling the Jackknife blaze in Northern California. With the fire diminishing, the last crew is called back, but Anna, her co-medic, their litter-bound patient, and other firefighters are unexpectedly trapped in a firestorm. When the fire blazes past on its destructive trail, Anna discovers a dead firefighter in his shelter, killed by a knife." SLJ

"The striking visceral quality of Ms. Barr's action scenes is all the more remarkable because she writes with such a cool, steady hand about the violence of nature and the cruelty of man." N Y Times Book Rev

Barr, Nevada—*Continued*

Flashback. Putnam 2003 387p il $24.95

ISBN 0-399-14975-9 LC 2002-68264

This Anna Pigeon mystery is "set in little-known Dry Tortugas National Park, 70 miles off Key West in the Gulf of Mexico. Anna takes up her post on Garden Key, home to Fort Jefferson, a notorious Union prison during the Civil War, after fleeing a marriage proposal from just-divorced Sheriff Paul Davidson. As she goes about her duties, Anna quickly becomes ensnared in one life-threatening situation after another." Publ Wkly

"Barr's technique of flashing between the past and present in intervening chapters works magically, weaving the two together into an exciting climax." Booklist

High country; Nevada Barr. 1st ed. Putnam 2004 323p $24.95

ISBN 0-399-15144-3 LC 2003-47243

This mystery finds Ranger Anna Pigeon "undercover as a waitress at the famous Ahwahnee Hotel in Yosemite National Park. Four seasonal workers have been missing for two weeks, and not even a professional rescue team can scrounge up a clue. Are they AWOL, or is it foul play? Anna waits tables, plays mom to a couple of twentysomething roommates, takes flak from the dining room manager, and deals with bullies before striking out on her own to figure out what has happened. The gossip among hotel staff and visitors is that there's a gold mine in the Sierra Mountains. Barr's even pace and deft characterizations will please series fans while winning her new readers." Libr J

Hunting season. Putnam 2002 322p il o.p.

ISBN 0-399-14846-9 LC 2001-48386

In this adventure, "District Ranger Anna Pigeon investigates a murder at an old inn on Mississippi's Natchez Trace Parkway. After the discovery of the corpse—naked and marked in such a way as to suggest an S & M ritual—interrupts Anna's brunch with her new romantic interest, local sheriff Paul Davidson, the intrepid ranger finds herself forced to untangle a poaching plot with roots deep in Mississippi history." Booklist

Ill wind. Putnam 1995 309p o.p.

LC 94-33370

In this mystery Anna Pigeon "leaves cold, damp Lake Superior for the dry heat of Mesa Verde National Park. In a land filled with unanswered questions about the Anasazi, she raises even more following the death of fellow ranger Stacy Meyers, found lying on the sandy floor of a ceremonial Indian kiva. After a young tourist dies, rumors attribute the two deaths to spirits." SLJ

This novel is as "much a personal journey of self-discovery as it is a mystery. Anna is a flawed but admirable woman struggling daily to determine her values and her value in a harsh world. An outstanding novel." Booklist

Liberty falling. Putnam 1999 321p o.p.

ISBN 0-399-14459-5 LC 98-37343

In this episode Anna Pigeon "confronts the wilds of New York City. In between hospital visits to her critically ill older sister, Anna flees crowded Manhattan for Liberty Island, where she's staying with a fellow ranger, and Ellis Island. However, several mysterious incidents—the fatal fall of a teenager from the pedestal of the Statue of Liberty, the apparent suicide of a policeman accused of pushing the 14-year old girl, a series of physical attacks on Anna—compels her to find answers." Libr J

Barrett, Andrea

Servants of the map; stories. Norton 2002 270p o.p.

ISBN 0-393-04348-7 LC 2001-44209

Contents: Servants of the map; The forest; Theories of rain; Two rivers, The mysteries of ubiquitin; The cure

"The six stories that make up this collection turn out to be connected, but you won't know exactly how until you read the last one. . . . Like fossil-hunters, most of Barrett's characters are looking for a way to piece together fragments of the past; when, in the last story, a cherished belonging of one character shows up in the life of another, we feel rescued and redeemed." New Yorker

Ship fever and other stories. Norton 1996 254p $21

ISBN 0-393-03853-X LC 95-14562

Contents: The behavior of the hawkweeds; The English pupil; The littoral zone; Rare bird; Soroche; Birds with no feet; The Marburg sisters; Ship fever

Barrett "tells her stories through alternating voices, diaries, letters—whatever seems to hint at the most promising results. Seen against a larger fictional landscape overpopulated with the sensational and affectless, her work stands out for its sheer intelligence, its painstaking attempt to discern and describe the world's configuration." N Y Times Book Rev

The voyage of the Narwhal; a novel. Norton 1998 399p o.p.

ISBN 0-393-04632-X LC 98-11246

"Erasmus Wells is already a broken man when he leaves Philadelphia, in 1855, on an Arctic expedition with his future brother-in-law, Zeke. Zeke proceeds to recapitulate Erasmus's traumas, stealing the quiet naturalist's work for his own glory and insuring that people think the worst of him." New Yorker

"Barrett's marvelous achievement is to have reimagined so graphically that cusp of time when Victorian certainty began to question whether it could encompass the world with its outward-bound enthusiasms alone." N Y Times Book Rev

Barrett, William E.

The lilies of the field; drawings by Burt Silverman. Doubleday 1962 92p o.p.

"Homer Smith is an amiable Southern black man. Driving through the Southwest after getting out of the Army, he stops to help four German refugee nuns build a church. After teaching them English and survival skills, he disappears, leaving behind the legend of his faithful help." Shapiro. Fic for Youth. 3d edition

Barron, Stephanie

See also Mathews, Francine

Barry, Max

Jennifer Government; a novel. Doubleday 2003 321p $19.95

ISBN 0-385-50759-3 LC 2002-19436

"Free enterprise runs amok in Barry's satirical near-future nightmare: the American government has been privatized and now runs most of the world, including

Barry, Max—*Continued*
'the Australian territories of the U.S.A.,' where the book is set. American corporations sponsor everything from schools to their employee's identities, and literally go to war with one another. By taking a drink at the wrong water cooler, Hack Nike, a merchandising officer at the athletic shoe company whose name he bears, is coerced into a nefarious marketing plot to raise demand for Nike's new $2,500 sneakers by shooting teenagers." Publ Wkly

"Though pensive readers may extract political commentary from it, Barry's latest novel has more value as entertainment. A refreshingly creative and unique read." Booklist

Barry, Sebastian

Annie Dunne. Viking 2002 228p o.p.
ISBN 0-670-03112-7 LC 2002-20675
This story is "narrated by the eponymous Annie Dunne, who, in her 60s, has come to live with her cousin Sarah on an impoverished farm in Kelsha, County Wicklow. Plain and poor, and afflicted with a humpback since a childhood attack of polio, Annie is grateful to Sarah for taking her in. She loves the farm and attacks the backbreaking daily chores with fierce ardor. But when a scheming handyman on a neighboring farm begins to court Sarah, Annie sees her livelihood threatened and fights back with the only weapons in her arsenal; bitterness and rage." Publ Wkly

"Barry is also a playwright, and his dialogue is clear and musical. But it's Annie's passionate observations and shifting moods—rendered in dense prose that's close to poetry—that fuel this fine novel." N Y Times Book Rev

Bart, André Schwarz- *See* Schwarz-Bart, André, 1928-

Barth, John

Bellerophoniad
In Barth, J. Chimera p135-308

Chimera. Random House 1972 308p o.p.
Contents: Dunyazadiad; Perseid; Bellerophoniad
"Barth's three interlocked novellas are based on the stories of Scheherazade, Perseus, and Bellerophon, combined in a way that suggests an attempt to present the artist as mythic hero." Atlantic

"The protagonists of these witty confessions are walking psyches, at war with ultimate ambivalence. (Far from clarifying what is ambiguous, Barth deepens it—by retelling familiar stories, deploying their unsettled alternatives so as to virtually insist on their unreality). . . . [He] employs literary devices that multiply confusion [including] . . . the removal of all barriers posed by time and history." Libr J

Coming soon!!!; a narrative. Houghton Mifflin 2001 396p $26
ISBN 0-618-13165-5 LC 2001-24988
This novel "chronicles the encounter—part seduction, part duel, part vaudeville routine—between an unnamed 'novelist emeritus' in search of a 'circle-closing, desiècle-finning, last-hurrah novel-notion' and Johns Hopkins Johnson, known as Hop, a 'novelist aspirant' with an unusual idea for a competition-cum-collaboration." N Y Times Book Rev

"Employing his signature wordplay and liberally salting his gleefully postmodern narrative with paeans to sailing, the Maryland coast, sex, and marriage, Barth, witty, wily, and a tad sentimental, muses over the creative process, the thin line between fact and fiction, growing old, and the tenuous survival of literature and theater in the digital age." Booklist

Dunyazadiad
In Barth, J. Chimera p1-56

The end of the road. Doubleday 1958 230p o.p.
"In the story, at once comic, tragic and satirical, Barth made a frontal attack on the excesses of Sartrean existentialism and existential philosophy popular in the 1950's. The hero is Jacob Horner, a Kafkaesque character, whose quack therapist advises him to teach prescriptive grammar as an antidote to his fits of manic depression. Horner takes a job at a small teachers' college in Maryland and meets Joe Morgan, history teacher and Boy Scout troop leader, and his wife, Rennie. Joe and Rennie believe in the perfect existential love relationship, involving endless intellectual probing and analysis." Publ Wkly

"The plot sounds absurd, but beneath the comic surface, questions are being raised regarding choice and meaning in life." Libr J

The floating opera. Appleton-Century-Crofts 1956 280p o.p.
"A 50-year-old bachelor relives the day 10 years before when he decided to commit suicide. He had changed his mind (in true existentialist fashion) only because suicide, just like every other action in his life, would have been without meaning. In retracing the day he fills in the main events of his life as child, student, and lawyer in a sleepy backwater Maryland town." Libr J

"Just as Voltaire's Candide decides to contentedly cultivate his garden after a disillusioning journey, so does Barth's Todd come to terms with life by discovering in time that it is best to choose among the relative values that life offers rather than cynically rejecting all values by way of suicide." N Y Times Book Rev

Giles goat-boy; or, The revised new syllabus. Doubleday 1966 xxxi, 710p o.p.
"The novel's protagonist, Billy Bockfuss (also called George Giles, the goat-boy), was raised with herds of goats on a university farm after being found as a baby in the bowels of the giant West Campus Automatic Computer (WESCAC). The WESCAC plans to create a being called GILES (Grand-Tutorial Ideal, Laboratory Eugenical Specimen) that would possess superhuman abilities. Billy's foster father, who tends the herd, suspects Billy of being GILES but tries to groom him to be humanity's savior and to stop WESCAC's domination over humans." Merriam-Webster's Ency of Lit

The last voyage of somebody the sailor. Little, Brown 1991 573p o.p.
LC 90-44991
"Simon Behler—or Baylor, as he refers to himself in his countless best-selling books of New Journalism—falls overboard during a cruise retracing the legendary voyages of Sindbad the Sailor and is pulled from the water by contemporaries of the real Sindbad. Trapped in the distant past but never at a loss for words, Behler—or

Barth, John—*Continued*
Bey el-Loor, as he is now known—amuses his new friends with his exotic tales: boyhood on Maryland's Eastern Shore, first love, early literary success, marriage, and divorce." Libr J

"If the setting is sober, the narrator is not. This is John Barth, . . . after all, and his hero is variously exuberant, obnoxious, funny, self-conscious, and, not sober at all, but thoroughly intoxicated with sex, love, and story telling, especially with their commingling." Commonweal

Lost in the funhouse; fiction for print, tape, live voice. Doubleday 1968 201p o.p.

Contents: Frame-tale; Night-sea journey; Ambrose, his mark; Autobiography; Water-message; Petition; Lost in the funhouse; Echo; Two meditations; Title; Glossolalia; Life-story; Menelaiad; Anonymiad

"The book's creator-heroes are a small boy, a goatherd minstrel banished from the court of Clytemnestra, and the author-figure himself. Their lives are seen as a giddily terrifying tour of a Funhouse, an isolated exile on an island, and a long meaningless swim in a vast 'night-sea.'" Newsweek

On with the story; stories. Little, Brown 1996 257p o.p.

LC 95-45790

Contents: The end: an introduction; Ad infinitum: a short story; And then one day . . .; Preparing for the storm; On with the story; Love explained; "Waves" by Amien Richard; Stories of our lives; Closing out the visit; Good-bye to the fruits; Ever after; Countdown: once upon a time

"The collection's title is apt: many of the stories thematically address narrative conventions of beginning, middle, end, and delays therein. . . . Woven with Barth's characteristic wit, these stories will probably sharpen the reader's awareness of some realist fictional convictions and some postmodern alternatives to these." Booklist

Perseid

In Barth, J. Chimera p57-134

The sot-weed factor. Doubleday 1967 806p o.p.

Picaresque novel "originally published in 1960 and revised in 1967. A parody of the historical novel, it is based on and takes its title from a satirical poem published in 1708 by Ebenezer Cooke, who is the protagonist of Barth's work. The novel's black humor is derived from its purposeful misuse of conventional litarary devices." Merriam-Webster's Ency of Lit

The Tidewater tales; a novel. Putnam 1987 655p o.p.

LC 86-25486

"Peter Sagamore, novelist, has come down with a bad case of minimalism. Ruthless self-editing leaves him with works only a few words in length, and no readers. His wife is a 'maximalist' oral historian with an MLS. In June 1980 they spend two weeks sailing around Chesapeake Bay in their boat *Story*, telling stories." Libr J

"What is moving about 'The Tidewater Tales' is its frequent and frequently incidental richness as a love story—marital, filial, domestic—and also its love of a place, of a country, even as place and country are scarred by human depredations. Whether the novel's ending—or its various coves and shallows sailed into along the way—give us something more rich and strange than a funhouse may be left to the reader." N Y Times Book Rev

Barthelme, Donald

Sixty stories. Putnam 1981 457p o.p.

LC 81-8646

Contents: Margins; A shower of gold; Me and Miss Mandible; For I'm the boy; Will you tell me; The balloon; The President; Game; Alice; Robert Kennedy saved from drowning; Report; The dolt; See the moon; The Indian uprising; Views of my father weeping; Paraguay; On angels; The Phantom of the Opera's friend; City life; Kierkegaard unfair to Schlegel; The falling dog; The Policemen's Ball; The glass mountain; Critique de la vie quotidienne; The sandman; Träumerei; The rise of capitalism; A city of churches; Daumier; The party; Eugénie Grandet; Nothing: a preliminary account; A manual for sons; At the end of the mechanical age; Rebecca; The captured woman; I bought a little city; The sergeant; The school; The great hug; Our work and why we do it; The crisis; Cortés and Montezuma; The new music; The zombies; The king of jazz; Morning; The death of Edward Lear; The abduction from the Seraglio; On the steps of the conservatory; The leap; Aria; The emerald; How I write my songs; The farewell; The emperor; Thailand; Heroes; Bishop; Grandmother's house

Barthelme, Frederick

Bob the gambler. Houghton Mifflin 1997 213p o.p.

ISBN 0-395-80977-0 LC 97-4363

This is the story of a "fortyish Biloxi couple who gamble themselves into near-poverty. . . . Ray Kaiser is an architect whose career couldn't withstand the onslaught of talent brought in to design the casinos that line Biloxi's waterfront. When Jewel, Ray's wife, suggests they visit one of these new casinos, the floodgates to financial ruin are opened. Pastime soon turns to addiction, with Ray losing $35,000 in one frenzied night and, ultimately, their middle-class lifestyle." Libr J

"Paradise, as it happens, is the name of the local casino. The irony in this is obvious enough, but it is Barthelme's peculiar post-modern gift to be able to invert the easy ironies of contemporary life and reveal the truths beneath them." N Y Times Book Rev

The brothers; a novel. Viking 1993 262p o.p.

ISBN 0-670-83242-1 LC 93-6728

"Shortly before his 44th birthday, recently divorced Del Tribute relocates to Biloxi, where his brother Bud lives. But Bud is on the road to Hollywood, where he seeks revitalization and success, and Del finds himself sharing a house with his attractive sisterin-law Margaret. Their mutual affection rapidly goes beyond acceptable bounds, creating guilt, awkwardness and confusion upon Bud's return. While Del begins a new life that soon includes Jen, a sexy young true-crime buff, Bud and Margaret try to repair their marriage, and all four grapple with their changing relationships." Publ Wkly

"This is a deceptively lighthearted trompe-l'oeil whose glossy surface suddenly shifts to reveal an abyss of surburban despair." Libr J

Elroy Nights. Counterpoint 2003 228p $24

ISBN 1-582-43128-0 LC 2003-7830

Barthelme, Frederick—*Continued*

"Elroy Nights is a 50-something art professor at a small, third-rate Mississippi university. Amicably separated from his wife, Clare, he fills his otherwise solitary life with occasional visits or dinner at Clare's when her grown daughter Winter is there. When Winter brings home Freddie, a free spirit of a girl who will be Elroy's student in the coming term, Elroy is instantly smitten. But the affair into which they casually fall leads to tragedy for their friends and near disaster for them." Publ Wkly

"Barthelme's world is vague and unclear. Conversations dead-end, spousal jabs go unanswered, Elroy and Freddie's relationship never evolves into anything defined. Still, currents of hope run through 'Elroy Nights.' Elroy and Clare's relationship contains remarkable moments of kindness-not in showy grand scenes but in small gestures, in bitten tongues, in the silent lowering of expectations." N Y Times Book Rev

The law of averages; new & selected stories. Counterpoint 2000 364p o.p.

ISBN 1-58243-115-9 LC 00-55516

Contents: Shopgirls; Pool lights; Domestic; Grapette; Violet; Instructor; Export; Pupil; Driver; Reset; Chroma; Cooker; Law of averages; War with Japan; With Ray & Judy; Margaret & Bud; Retreat; Spots; Travel & leisure; Tiny ape; The great pyramids; Bag boy; Larroquette; Galveston; Harmonic; Red Arrow; The autobiography of Riva Jay; From Mars; Elroy Nights

"This collection of 29 stories, including several new ones and spanning 20 years of the author's career, exhibits Barthelme's power as a miniaturist, expertly finding drama and meaning in those fleeting, significant moments when the raised voice or the irreparable breach are avoided." Publ Wkly

Painted desert; a novel. Viking 1995 243p o.p.

ISBN 0-670-86469-2 LC 95-6769

Sequel to The brothers

"Televised spectacles of mayhem in Southwestern California propel Del and his girlfriend, Jen, a 'cybermuckraker,' on a cross-country anti-pilgrimage toward-maybe-Los Angeles. Jen's dad and her 'nonharmonious' friend Penny join them for the air-cooled ride through the Southwest, where the four unsuspectingly drive past their tight cynicism into the open spaces of ironic wonderment. Laced with sharp dialogue and wit, this novel suggests that we are what we witness, whether it's the gypsum hills of White Sands or the slaying of a stranger a thousand miles away." New Yorker

Basch, Rachel

The passion of Reverend Nash. Norton 2003 330p $23.95

ISBN 0-393-05768-2 LC 2003-1045

This novel revolves around 'Rev. Jordanna Nash, the new minister at Hutchinson Congregational Church. Jordanna has the support of her sister, who helped her get the job, and her dynamic personality and massive presence-she's over six feet tall-to win over her congregation. But just as things seem to be going well, her professional and personal lives begin to unravel." Libr J

"Only after humbly assessing and forgiving her own shortcomings is Jordanna able to figuratively rise again in this uplifting-but never saccharine-tale of faith, doubt, and redemption." Booklist

Bass, Cynthia

Maiden voyage. Villard Bks. 1996 257p o.p.

ISBN 0-679-43034-2 LC 95-47379

"Sumner Jordan, 13, is a first-class passenger on the ill-fated *Titanic*. He comes from a Bostonian family famous for its involvement in the causes of antislavery and women's suffrage. Sent to visit his expatriot bohemian father in London, Sumner has a coming-of-age experience upon meeting beautiful, mature Ivy Earnshaw and, once aboard the ship, debonair Pierce Andrews." SLJ

"The lifeboat scenes are top-notch, as is the depicted aftermath of survivors' guilt. . . . Bass expertly conveys the peculiarly self-conscious isolation of a child possessed of an adult intelligence; as Sumner grapples with issues of heroism and justice in the face of trauma, she gracefully blends the coming-of-age tale of one boy with that of an entire society." Publ Wkly

Bass, Rick, 1958-

The hermit's story; stories. Houghton Mifflin 2002 179p $23

ISBN 0-618-13932-X LC 2001-51616

Contents: The hermit's story; Swans; The prisoners; The fireman; The cave; President's Day; Real town; Eating; The distance; Two deer

"Beautiful in their magical imagery, dramatic in their situations, and exquisitely poignant in their insights, these stories of awe and loss are quite astonishing in their mythic use of place and the elements of earth, air, fire, and water." Booklist

Bassani, Giorgio, 1916-2000

The garden of the Finzi-Continis. Atheneum Pubs. 1965 293p o.p.

Original Italian edition, 1962

"The Finzi-Continis, a wealthy Jewish Italian family, lived in a beautiful and seemingly secure environment and enjoyed intellectual pursuits. The narrator remembers the family, his unrequited love for the beautiful but cold Micol, and his friendship with her brother, Albert. The novel describes the assimilation of Jews into Italian society and then the changes effected when fascism overtakes Italy and anti-Semitism destroys the family." Shapiro. Fic for Youth. 3d edition

Bastable, Bernard

See also Barnard, Robert

Bates, H. E. (Herbert Ernest), 1905-1974

Fair stood the wind for France. Little, Brown 1944 270p o.p.

"An Atlantic Monthly Press book"

A British bomber, returning from a mission over Italy, crashed in occupied France. The members of the crew managed to escape via the underground route, all but the pilot who was too ill. He was cared for by a family of French peasants, whose innate goodness made such an impression on him that when he finally left France he

Bates, H. E. (Herbert Ernest), 1905-1974—*Continued*

took with him the daughter of the family, as his wife

"An almost unbearable suspense, the romance of the two young people and a true portrait of the little people of France, defenseless but possessed of an enduring power, all these go to make an unforgettable story, beautifully told." Bookmark

Bates, Herbert Ernest *See* Bates, H. E. (Herbert Ernest), 1905-1974

Battle, Lois

Bed & breakfast. Viking 1996 372p o.p.

LC 96-17258

"Josie Tatternall, the septuagenarian widow of an unfaithful martinet of an army officer and owner of a bed and breakfast in upscale Beaufort, S.C., is determined that all three of her daughters will be reunited for the upcoming Christmas holidays. That will be no easy task after years of real and imagined affronts among the siblings and their mother." Publ Wkly

"The story introduces a cast of memorable characters, primarily Josie herself, who fully reminds us that life, love, and growth are not limited to any particular age." Libr J

The Florabama Ladies' Auxiliary & Sewing Circle. Viking 2001 358p o.p.

ISBN 0-670-89469-9 LC 00-47740

"Bonnie Duke Cullman, a displaced, wealthy, Atlanta housewife and socialite, is forced to find work after her husband declares bankruptcy and leaves her for a younger woman. Her best friend and her father conspire to get Bonnie a job teaching at a junior college in southern Alabama, where she will coordinate the program for displaced homemakers. On the same day that Bonnie leaves Atlanta for Florabama, the local lingerie factory closes, displacing the women who will become Bonnie's students." Libr J

"At times the novel feels like a stage set hammered together to support its pro-education message, but it compensates with likable characters and a core of compassion and independence." Publ Wkly

Southern women. St. Martin's Press 1984 404p o.p.

LC 83-22999

This novel "depicts three generations of Southern women represented by the female line of a prominent Savannah family. Eunnonia Grace Hampton, known as Nonnie, is matriarch of the clan; over 70 when widowhood permits her her first real independence. . . . Lucille Hampton Simpkins, her youngest daughter, has devoted her life to cultivating those traditional feminine charms that only fleetingly satisfy her vanity and leave her vulnerable at 50 to a consummate roué. Lucille's daughter, Cordy, 30, wants more from life than her marital bed can provide, and has become a romance novelist. The book begins when Cordy, after leaving Chicago and her husband, returns home to Savannah." N Y Times Book Rev

"The author's characters are the type that readers of light fiction enjoy: they possess ordinary urges and desires overlaid with tinges of nobility, tragedy, and/or glamour. The plot unravels quickly but logically, with no artificial twists and turns." Booklist

Storyville. Viking 1993 435p o.p.

LC 92-50347

"Kate is an innocent country girl who is seduced by a rake and abandoned, with little recourse but to become a woman 'in the life.' Beautiful and appealing, she snares the heart of young Lawrence Randsome, scion of an old, distinguished New Orleans family. Meanwhile, his mother, transplanted Boston blueblood, bluestocking and suffragette Julia Randsome, has discovered that her husband Charles owns whorehouses in the District, and their marriage is damaged by her bitterness and lack of trust. Eventually, tragedy adds another dimension to their domestic squabbling; then Julia befriends the luckless Kate and comes into her own as an activist for women's rights." Publ Wkly

"Battle has great command of her complex plot and its contentious historical context and conflicting passions. As she sets the steamy, jazzy ambience of New Orleans against the chilly propriety of Boston, the self-sacrificing dutifulness of Julia against the glamorous pragmatism of Kate, she gives form to the divided heart of womanhood." Booklist

War brides. St. Martin's Press 1982 359p o.p.

LC 81-16732

This novel "traces the experience of three Australian war brides who come to post-WWII America to begin life with the husbands they have scarcely had time to get to know. . . . [The author writes] of the different ways each of her heroines adjusts to the challenges of an unfamiliar country. . . . Friends on board ship, they keep in touch over the years, and several twists of fate bring them into occasional direct contact with each other." Publ Wkly

"The book has a well-rounded cast, predictable plot, and adequate writing." Libr J

Bausch, Richard, 1945-

Hello to the cannibals; a novel. HarperCollins Pubs. 2002 661p $27.95

ISBN 0-06-019295-X LC 2002-23270

"Lily, a precocious late twentieth-century American, becomes fascinated with Mary Kingsley, the nineteenth-century British explorer, pioneering social anthropologist, and writer, after seeing her photograph in a book. A moody college drop-out, Lily marries an irredeemably unhappy man, and, already pregnant, moves into his mother's tragically dysfunctional Mississippi household, where she finds refuge in writing a play about Kingsley." Booklist

"The novel is ambitious not only in its historical and geographical sweep but also in its author's choice to confine himself, with admirableconviction and credibility, to the consciousness of two women." NY Times Book Rev

In the night season; a novel. HarperFlamingo 1998 326p o.p.

ISBN 0-06-018735-2 LC 97-43690

"When black TV repairman Edward Bishop and widowed, white schoolteacher Nora Michaelson start getting hate mail from a mysterious group of white supremacists, both friends wonder whether Edward should stop dropping by in the afternoons to look after Nora's 11-year-old son. But neither Edward nor Nora—nor kindly local investigator Philip Shaw—can predict the terror that is about to visit their small Virginia town when two hood-

Bausch, Richard, 1945-—*Continued*

lums break into Edward's house to interrogate him about the late Jack Michaelson's shady business dealings. . . . If the novel has a flaw, it is Bausch's humaneness: he goes to what may be unprofitable lengths to make his villains interesting people." Publ Wkly

Rare & endangered species: a novella & stories. Houghton Mifflin 1994 257p o.p.
LC 94-9528

Contents: Aren't you happy for me?; Weather; High-heeled shoe; Tandolfo the great; Evening; Billboard; The person I have mostly become; The natural effects of divorce; Rare & endangered species {novella}

"Most of the stories examine relationships that cross generations, mainly between grown children and their parents. . . . Death, birth, the arcing of love—this is Bausch territory, mapped with a fine, unwavering hand." Publ Wkly

Rebel powers. Houghton Mifflin 1993 390p o.p.
ISBN 0-395-59508-8 LC 93-9194

"Thomas Boudreaux, divorced proprietor of a used-book store in Virginia, writes about his family in 1967, when he was 17 and his father Daniel, an Air Force career man and Vietnam hero, was caught stealing a typewriter from his Maryland base and sentenced to two years of hard labor in Wilson Creek, Wyo. Daniel's surprising act and rapid conviction pitch his family—his wife Connie, Thomas and eight-year-old Lisa—into nearly overwhelming uncertainty. After they move off the base and into a new town, Connie decides that they must go to Wilson Creek. On the train ride across country, they are befriended by young Penny Holt. Thomas's initial interest in Penny becomes obsessive after she moves into their Wilson Creek boarding house, where she will play a central role in the family's drama." Publ Wkly

"The key to the novel's credibility is the unretouched quality of its portraiture. Its characters live in a carefully chronicled American moment when threatening new ideas are beginning to rub up against weighty old certainties." N Y Times Book Rev

Someone to watch over me; stories. HarperFlamingo 1999 214p o.p.
ISBN 0-06-017333-5 LC 98-50193

Contents: Riches; Not quite final; Self knowledge; Glass meadow; Par; Someone to watch over me; Valor; The voices from the other room; Fatality; Two altercations; 1951; Nobody in Hollywood

"All 12 stories here are full of domesticity, danger and people who sense disaster but, in a kind of dream-state impotence, can shout no warning." Publ Wkly

The stories of Richard Bausch. HarperCollins 2003 651p $29.95
ISBN 0-06-019649-1 LC 2003-42318

Contents: Nobody in Hollywood; Valor; Riches; Self knowledge; Glass meadow; Par; Someone to watch over me; Fatality; The voices from the other room; Two altercaations; 1951; The man who knew Belle Starr; What feels like the world; Ancient history; Contrition; Police dreams; Wise men at their end; Wedlock; Old West; Design; The fireman's wife; Consolation; The brace; The eyes of love; Luck; Equity; Letter to the lady of the house; Aren't you happy for me?; Not quite final; Weather; High-heeled shoe; Tandolfo the Great; Evening; Billboard; The person I have mostly become; 1-900; "My mistress' eyes are nothing like the sun"; The weight; Accuracy: Unjust: Guatemala; The last day of summer

"Failure and its exactions this is Bausch's big subject. These 42 stories test the play of hope and disappointment in the lives of spouses and lovers, of parents and children and siblings. And while Bausch does in several instances write with insight and authority from a woman's perspective, it is the sons, fathers and husbands in their daily trials that he registers most memorably. Indeed, so alive are these characters, with their credible flaws, their complaints and loud excitements, that closing the book feels like pushing the door shut on some clamorous party." N Y Times Book Rev

Violence. Houghton Mifflin 1992 293p o.p.
LC 91-31419

"Expecting their first child, moody, impatient Charles Connolly and his somewhat dismayed young wife Carol travel to Chicago to celebrate Christmas with Charles's mother. During this visit, Charles is temporarily held hostage with a group of customers in a convenience store—an incident that ends in bloodshed. This random act of violence shatters the couple's marriage and leaves Charles paralyzed by guilt and fear." Libr J

"For both Charles and the reader, the public tragedy becomes the catalyst that produces a painful awareness of a darker, less immediately visible brutality. Thus Mr. Bausch follows the twists and turns of Charles's psychological journey to the novel's difficult, revelatory and finally transfiguring conclusion." N Y Times Book Rev

Bausch, Robert, 1945-

The Gypsy Man. Harcourt 2002 495p $31
ISBN 0-15-100172-3 LC 2002-5649

"It's 1959 in the mountaintop town of Crawford, VA, and people are still reeling from the disappearance of a black boy, Terry Landon, and the accidental murder of a black girl by John Bone six years earlier. Penny Bone, who thinks of her husband as dead during his 20-year jail term at his insistence, fears for the safety of her daughter when an old neighbor notices signs of the return of the Gypsy Man, a feared local legend believed to kill children." Libr J

"There are a couple of plot points that strain credulity . . . but by the time Bausch has assembled the chief characters on the mountaintop, it's clear that he knows how to set up a gripping showdown." N Y Times Book Rev

Bawden, Nina, 1925-

Family money. St. Martin's Press 1991 250p o.p.
LC 91-21186

This is the "story of a woman attempting to come to grips with old age. When sixtyish widow Fanny Pye is mugged after witnessing a street crime, she finds her loss of memory a frightening portent of things to come. No one will take her seriously; her fears that she may have recognized her mugger are treated as irrational. In effect, friends and family have 'just lumped her into a sack labelled OLD WOMEN,' but Fanny fights back." Libr J

"Sharply observed and drawn with precision, Fanny's troubles and their eventual resolution make a compelling read." Publ Wkly

Baxter, Charles

The feast of love. Pantheon Bks. 2000 308p o.p.
ISBN 0-375-41019-8 LC 99-53088

"An insomniac Mid-western novelist named Charlie Baxter becomes the unwitting audience of a neighbor's midnight confession, and is drawn into a tale of love in its manifold guises—confused, ecstatic, unrequited. We hear the story of Kathryn, who left her husband for the female shortstop of a local softball team; of Diana, a capricious lawyer who doesn't want anyone to want her too much; and of Chloé, a pierced teenager with a strong sense of justice and a doomed passion for a former drug addict. Baxter's novel is a modern Symposium, unexpectedly hilarious in its attempt to get at the evasive truths of love; unlike Plato's treatise, though, its strength lies in its recognition that such truths aren't universal." New Yorker

Saul and Patsy. Pantheon Bks. 2003 317p $24
ISBN 0-375-41029-5 LC 2003-42027

"Young-marrieds Saul and Patsy move to Five Oaks from Evanston, Ill., when Saul is hired to teach at the local high school. They rent a farmhouse, where they make love in every room and even in the backyard, settling into the rhythms of domestic life. Patsy, a former modern dancer who finds work as a bank teller, gives birth to a daughter, and with infinite patience tolerates her 'professional worrier' of a husband. The narrative is dense with quotidian detail, precisely charted shifts of consciousness and pitch-perfect moments of emotional truth." Publ Wkly

"Baxter's prose is succulent, his characters magnetic, his humor incisive, his decipherment of the human psyche felicitous, and his command of the storyteller's magic absolute." Booklist

Baxter, Stephen

Evolution; a novel. Del Rey/Ballantine Bks. 2003 578p $25.95
ISBN 0-345-45782-X LC 2002-31422

"As a group scientists gathers in the South Pacific for a conference to save the human race from extinction, their actions represent the culmination of millions of years of struggle by their primate ancestors to survive in an ever-changing world. . . . [Baxter] uses a modern-day story as a frame within which he relates a series of vignettes tracing the history of the evolution of intelligent life on Earth, from its mammalian beginnings in the Cretaceous era to the present. Spanning more than 165 million years and encompassing the entire planet, Baxter's ambitious saga provides both an exercise in painless paleontology and superb storytelling." Libr J

Bayley, Iris *See* Murdoch, Iris

Beach, Edward Latimer, 1918-2002

Run silent, run deep; [by] Edward L. Beach. Holt & Co. 1955 364p o.p.

"Commander Beach has taken the exciting material of a submarine war patrol in the Pacific in World War II and woven it into a novel. The author speaks and sees through the eyes of the book's central character, an Annapolis two-and-a-half striper with his first fleet submarine command, the Walrus." N Y Trib Books

"If ever a book has the ring of reality, this is it. From the moment the reader steps aboard a training boat in New London, Conn., to the time when the submarine Walrus dives deeply to avoid the depth charges of the enemy's destroyers, there is awe and respect for the author who created them." N Y Times Book Rev

Beagle, Peter S.

A fine and private place; a novel. Viking 1960 272p o.p.

"Mr. Rebeck has lived in a cemetery for 19 years and can talk to ghosts. He has been supplied with food by a cranky and hilariously funny raven who scavenges the city not only for food but for information of the world outside, so that Mr. Rebeck can remain cloistered. A living companion enters his life when Mrs. Kapper, a Bronx widow, begins to make regular visits to the grave of her deceased husband. Rebeck becomes involved also in the growing relationship between two ghosts, a young professor and a bookstore clerk, neither of whom was honest with himself or herself or others until death allowed them that freedom. This fantasy, rich with characters and situations, takes a less grim look at death than we usually encounter." Shapiro. Fic for Youth. 3d edition

The innkeeper's song; a novel. Roc 1993 346p o.p.
LC 93-3800

"Three powerful women (each with her own secret past), a stable boy, a weaver's son, and an innkeeper set in motion a series of events that bring each of them face to face with the forces of magic and the workings of fate." Libr J

"In elegant yet simple prose Beagle illuminates the shifting relationships among the various major and minor players . . . who people this affecting tale." Publ Wkly

The last unicorn. Viking 1968 218p o.p.

"A beautiful and previously happy unicorn learns she may be the last unicorn left on earth. Wanting not to believe it, she sets off in quest of her fellows. In the course of her journey, she meets a carnival magician of little ability, has encounters with a Robin Hood-like band, a king presiding over a hate-filled and miserable land, with the aid of the mysterious Red Bull, and a glamorous, if previously ineffectual prince." Publ Wkly

"Beagle is a true magician with words, a master of prose and a deft practitioner in verse. He has been compared, not unreasonably, with Lewis Carroll and J. R. R. Tolkien, but he stands squarely and triumphantly on his own feet." Saturday Rev

The unicorn sonata; illustrations by Robert Rodriguez. Turner Pub. (Atlanta) 1996 154p il o.p.
LC 96-16007

"Josephine 'Joey' Rivera, a 13-year-old girl in suburban Los Angeles, visits her grandmother every weekend, does poorly in school, and helps clean up a music store in exchange for lessons. After a strange young man comes into the store to sell his horn, Joey hears his beautiful music late at night and, following the sound, crosses the Border into the magical world of Shei'rah. The unicorns are going blind, and Joey and her grandmother vow to help." Libr J

"The story is slight, but the characterizations are grand,

Beagle, Peter S.—*Continued*
enhanced by graceful prose laced with exquisite detail, and through both literary creativity and folkloric expertise where unicorns are concerned." Publ Wkly

Bear, Greg, 1951-

Anvil of stars. Warner Bks. 1992 434p o.p.
LC 91-50411

Sequel to The forge of God

"One alien culture has destroyed Earth; another, called the Benefactors, has offered the survivors a chance for revenge by building a spaceship for a group of young volunteers whose goal is the extermination of their enemy." Libr J

"Bear is superlatively competent in the English language and a master of both technical wizardry and powerful scenes. Throughout the book, he addresses the question of an ethical basis for genocide, leaving the matter sufficiently open to make one wonder whether the story is yet completed." Booklist

Blood music
In Bear, G. The collected stories of Greg Bear

The collected stories of Greg Bear. TOR Bks. 2002 653p o.p.
ISBN 0-7653-0160-1 LC 2002-20466

"A Tom Doherty Associates book"

Contents: Blood music [novelette]; Sisters; A Martian Ricorso; Schrodinger's plague; Heads; The wind from a burning woman; The venging; Perihesperon; Scattershot; Plague of conscience; The white horse child; Dead run; Petra; Webster; Through road, no whither; Tangents; The visitation; Richie by the sea; Sleepside story; Judgment engine; The fall of the house of Escher; The way of all ghosts; MDIO ecosystes increase knowledge of DNA languages (2215 C.E.); Hardfought

In addition to Blood music (1985), a novelette where a genetic engineer injects himself with experimental intelligent microorganisms with disasterous results, this "volume subsumes Bear's earlier collections, The wind from a burning woman (1983) and Tangents (1989), while also including more recent work." Anatomy of Wonder 5

Darwin's radio. Ballantine Pub. Group 1999 430p $24
ISBN 0-345-42333-X LC 99-21833

"The discovery of a sexually transmitted retrovirus heralds a breakthrough in the understanding of the human genotype while spelling potential disaster for the human race—and the beginning of a new phase in evolution. As scientists and researchers wage a desperate battle to unlock the secrets of the virus known as SHEVA, a few farsighted individuals attempt to cope with the possibility that something entirely new might replace humankind in the evolutionary pattern. . . . Filled with the author's lucid intelligence, this compelling novel should appeal to fans of science mystery as well as to hard-core sf readers." Libr J

Dead lines. Ballantine Books 2004 246p $24.95
ISBN 0-345-44837-8 LC 2004-556051

This novel "envisions what might happen should a new technology open the floodgates on another dimension. In the near future, the technology in question is the 'trans,' a sort of souped-up cell phone with near-infinite bandwidth and perfect reception anywhere in the world. Peter Russell is a washed-up director of soft porn, living on handouts and reeling from the death of his closest friend, when the device's manufacturers offer him a chance to revamp his career and film their promotional videos. One of the assignment's perks is, of course, a batch of free trans phones—a blessing that may actually harbor a curse. For Peter begins to unravel and to see ghostly simulacra of both the living and the dead." Booklist

"Bear has managed to imbue the sunny Californian clime with all the dank existential misery of the creepiest British graveyard." Washington Post Book World

Dinosaur summer. Aspect 1998 325p il o.p.
ISBN 0-446-52098-5 LC 97-12318

In this adventure Bear "looks backward for some old-fashioned SF with a modernist spin. . . . His premise is strong: in 1947, an American expedition travels to the Venezuelan plateau explored by Conan Doyle's Professor Challenger in order to return to their natural habitat the handful of dinosaurs surviving from among the many taken long ago from the plateau for human amusement. The spin comes not only from Bear's mixing of science fact and fiction but also from his blend of fictional principals with real-life ones. Focal character Peter Belzoni is made up, though his 15-year-old mind and heart seem real enough and give the book a warm YA feel and an effective coming-of-age turn." Publ Wkly

The forge of God. TOR Bks. 1987 474p o.p.
LC 87-50482

"Three geologists discover an alien artifact in Death Valley and set off a chain of events leading to the discovery that Earth is about to be invaded by two alien races. One race sends out planet-wrecking machines; . . . the other is trying to enlist the survivors of humanity in tracking down and destroying the planet wreckers. The battle over Earth is seen through the eyes of a large cast of well-drawn characters, crowned by a climax of enormous power." Booklist

Followed by Anvil of stars

Foundation and chaos. HarperPrism 1998 342p (Second Foundation trilogy) o.p.
ISBN 0-06-105242-6 LC 97-47274

This second title in the Second Foundation Trilogy, a prequel to Asimov's classic series, follows "an aging but still committed Seldon, a man who has guided his daring project almost to completion, but who now finds himself on trial for treason against the Galactic Empire. Complex political intrigue swirls around Trantor, the capital of the Empire, as a variety of human and robotic factions fight for their own particular versions of the future." Publ Wkly

Beaton, M. C.

Agatha Raisin and the day the floods came. St. Martin's Minotaur 2002 213p o.p.
ISBN 0-312-20767-0 LC 2002-17141

Beaton, M. C.—*Continued*

"Agatha's latest adventures begin when her husband runs off to join a monastery in France. Agatha seeks solace in a island vacation. During her getaway, she notices a newlywed couple; within days, the groom drowns the bride. On her return home, during a dramatic flash flood, Agatha sees another dead bride, wearing a white gown and clutching a bridal bouquet, sweeping past on the river. Agatha swings into action, pestering the locals and enlishing the aid of her new neighbor, a mystery writer. Very improbable detective work, but a satisfying read nonetheless for cozy lovers." Booklist

Agatha Raisin and the fairies of Fryfam. St. Martin's Press 2000 197p o.p.

ISBN 0-312-20496-5 LC 00-24300

Agatha Raisin "has been spurned by the love of her life, her Cotswolds neighbor James Lacey, which has a lot to do with her removing herself and her two cats, Hodge and Boswell, to the village of Fryfam. There she meets the members of the Fryfam's Women's group, to whom she explains her presence by saying she's writing a crime novel, *Death at the Manor*—an unfortunate fib as the village squire, Tolly Trumpington-James, is soon murdered at his manor house. Aided by suave friend Sir Charles Fraith, Agatha sets about prying into the lives of the locals to discover who wanted the squire dead." Publ Wkly

Agatha Raisin and the quiche of death. St. Martin's Press 1992 201p o.p.

LC 92-28381

"Bored with her early retirement and still on the lookout for romance wherever she can find it, Spunky Agatha Raisin, former owner of a London public-relations firm, welcomes the arrival of veterinarian Paul Bladen to her quiet Cotswold village. When the new vet, whose charming con-man exterior conceals a hatred of dogs and cats, dies from an injection from his own hypodermic syringe, Agatha and her neighbor James Lacey decide that Bladen has been murdered—and line up an extended list of possible suspects." Booklist

Agatha Raisin and the witch of Wyckhadden. St. Martin's Press 1999 196p o.p.

ISBN 0-312-20494-9 LC 99-15884

"Agatha Raisin, her hair falling out after an incident with a hairdresser-cum-murderess travels to an old-fashioned hotel in order to repair the damage. Unhappy about the slow results and prompted by the elderly residents of the resort, she consults the local witch for help. Agatha purchases a hair tonic and is soon sprouting hairs but unfortunately the witch is murdered and Agatha is determined to solve the mystery." Publisher's note

Agatha Raisin and the wizard of Evesham. St. Martin's Press 1999 196p o.p.

ISBN 0-312-19822-1 LC 98-50566

"While her neighbor and sometime love interest James Lacey gallivants on the continent, Agatha . . . grows bored in the English village of Carsely. After witnessing the fearful reactions of several women to her choice of a talented and charismatic new hairdresser in nearby Evesham, she's ready to attach some nefarious plot to the man. With the help of friend Sir Charles, she begins nosing about. . . . Another delightful cozy featuring Cotswolds surroundings, a bit of history, and buoyant characters." Libr J

Death of a celebrity. Warner Bks. 2002 259p o.p.

ISBN 0-89296-676-9 LC 2001-32679

Constable Hamish MacBeth "has theories about who murdered nosy BBC television reporter Crystal French. Although ordered to drop the case, he can't help but see clues—in the local astrology column and elsewhere." Libr J

Death of a dentist. Mysterious Press 1997 200p o.p.

LC 96-42016

"Desperate for relief, Scottish constable Hamish Macbeth takes his toothache to a nearby dentist with a lousy reputation. Unfortunately, he discovers the man dead of nicotine poisoning. As he investigates, Hamish finds that the victim had many enemies, including his own wife." Libr J

"Beaton lavishes so much affection on her laconic copper that it's well nigh impossible not to fall for ace moocher Hamish, with his quick mind, deceptively simple manner and accursed luck with the fairer sex." Publ Wkly

Death of a dustman. Mysterious Press 2001 215p o.p.

ISBN 0-89296-631-9 LC 00-61666

"When, in an effort to gain publicity for the local community and herself, bullying Strathbane Council member Freda Fleming gets drunken Lochdubh dustman Fergus Macleod promoted to 'environmental officer,' Fergus can't believe his luck. Alas, he doesn't have much time to strut his new military-style uniform . . . because someone bashes the back of his head in and dumps his body in a rubbish bin. Enter policeman Hamish Macbeth, who soon discovers that Fergus had a second career as a blackmailer." (Publ Wkly) "Although Beaton takes a stern view of petty despots like Freda and Fergus, she couldn't be kinder to the eccentric villagers who live by their own clannish rule." NY Times Book Rev

Death of a hussy. St. Martin's Press 1990 164p o.p.

LC 90-36883

"The Scottish village of Lochdubh has a problem: the beloved police constable, Hamish Macbeth has been transferred to Strathbane because of a dearth of local crime. In a successful bid to get him back, the villagers, led by newcomer Maggie Baird, organize a crime wave. On his return Hamish is confronted with a possible murder." Publ Wkly

"Maggie is a devil, all right, but splendid fun as a character. And the mischief she makes in Lochdubh is resolved by Hamish in an easygoing Highland fashion that is no less canny for being so droll." N Y Times Book Rev

Death of a macho man. Mysterious Press 1996 216p o.p.

LC 96-7268

"Scottish constable Hamish MacBeth, finding his reputation on the line, agrees to a public fight with a tattooed stranger who claims to be a professional wrestler. When someone prevents the match by murdering the stranger, suspicion falls on Hamish, who then investigates." Libr J

"Befuddled, earnest and utterly endearing, Hamish makes his triumphs sweetly satisfying." Publ Wkly

Beaton, M. C.—*Continued*

Death of a nag. Mysterious Press 1995 216p o.p.
ISBN 0-89296-530-4 LC 95-10292
Hamish Macbeth "and the ravishing Priscilla Halburton-Smythe have ended their long engagement, and the townsfolk blame Hamish. To escape Lochdubh's wagging tongues, Hamish embarks on a short vacation at Friendly House, a bed-and-breakfast in the seaside resort of Skag. But instead of the relaxation and solitude he sought, Hamish finds he's involved in yet another murder case. . . . A fine, well-told police procedural with plenty of human interest." Booklist

Death of a poison pen; M.C. Beaton. Mysterious Press 2004 244p $23.95
ISBN 0-89296-788-9 LC 2002-44429
"Lochdubh's Constable Hamish Macbeth . . . unwillingly becomes a romantic interest to several women. After a poison-pen letter accuses Macbeth of having an affair with the minister's wife, the postmistress is discovered suspiciously dead near another such letter. A third woman offers her sleuthing 'skills.' Cool fun." Libr J

Death of a village; a Hamish Macbeth mystery. Mysterious Press 2003 245p
ISBN 0-89296-677-7 LC 2002-75360
"Macbeth knows something is amiss in the village of Stoyre, because the residents have become even more religious and closemouthed than usual. Discovering and rooting out the cause will cost him dearly. All Macbeth's talents are on display as he performs a heroic rescue, outwits some crooks and meets violence with violence. For all his nonchalance, the laconic Macbeth does his best to protect his people and preserve his way of life among them." Publ Wkly

Death of an addict. Mysterious Press 1999 215p o.p.
ISBN 0-89296-675-0 LC 98-37555
"When Parry McSporran rents his vacation chalet to recovering drug addict Tommy Jarret, he has no idea of the trouble to come. Not long after Tommy declares he'll never touch drugs again, he's found dead of a heroin overdose. The Strathbane police claim Tommy's death was a sad but predictable tragedy. But stubborn, redheaded police constable Hamish Macbeth isn't so sure." Booklist

Beattie, Ann

Another you. Knopf 1995 323p o.p.
ISBN 0-679-40078-8 LC 95-2667
This novel depicts "the confused world of college professor Marshall Lockheed and his wife, Sonja. As Marshall ponders whether to tell Sonja about his complicated infatuation with a student, Sonja ponders the pros and cons of revealing her brief affair with her boss. Meanwhile, repercussions from their rather unexceptional indiscretions are about to plunge both Lockheeds into . . . unusual territory." Libr J
"As truth proves to be more elusive than a subatomic particle, Beattie's addled but resilient characters cling to love and strive for compassion, if not comprehension. This is a powerfully composed work of great wit, subtlety, literary finesse, and insight." Booklist

The burning house; short stories. Random House 1982 256p o.p.
LC 82-5292
Contents: Learning to fall; Jacklighting; Girl talk; The Cinderella waltz; Playback; Winter: 1978; Gravity; Sunshine and shadow; Desire; Happy; Waiting; Afloat; Running dreams; Like glass; Greenwich time; The burning house
These "are marvelously written, moving tales, poignant in that they reveal so much about the way we live now, the way we feel now. . . . Beattie's world is grisaille, sharply observed, carefully shaded with nuances of feeling made tangible and almost surreal by brilliant, seemingly offhand, perfectly chosen significant detail. Beattie's fictions are stunning." Publ Wkly

Chilly scenes of winter. Doubleday 1976 280p o.p.
Charles, the protagonist "loves Laura and is waiting for her, as he must; she is married, not well, and he can only wait for her to return to him, if she will. Waiting, he turns 27, works at the dull job he can't afford to leave, endures his grotesquely crazy mother and his well-meaning but stupid stepfather and kills time with his old buddy Sam." N Y Times Book Rev
"Beattie has an instinct for the grotesque that verges on the edge of real wit and pain. She is obviously a first-rate craftswoman with an eye for idiosyncratic detail." Saturday Rev

The doctor's house. Scribner 2002 279 $24
ISBN 0-7432-1264-9
This novel "explores the fraught relationshp between a reclusive 40-ish woman named Nina, a freelance copy editor in Cambridge, Mass., and her slightly older brother, Andrew. At issue is Andrew's flagrant womanizing—specifically, his habit of looking up women he knew long ago, in high school, and having affairs with them. . . Beattie gives us a triptych of first-person narratives, Nina first and Andrew last, with a middle section narrated by their alcoholic mother, all delving into their messy family past." N Y Times Book Rev

Falling in place. Random House 1980 342p o.p.
LC 79-3880
This novel is set "in the summer of 1979. Skylab is falling, 'Norma Rae' is showing. . . . John Knapp, a 40-year-old ad-man with three whiny children and a glum wife in Connecticut, is having an affair with 25-year-old Nina. . . . The Knapps' threadbare suburban marriage . . . has worn down to numb, toneless bickering. Nina's affair with John is her best hope of extricating herself from a floating circle of drug-dazed friends from her college days." Newsweek
"Describes with light irony the dilemmas of failed marriages, fragile affairs, sibling rivalry, and the petulance and irresponsibility of spoiled children. Beattie captures the petty conflicts, studied egoism, and pathetic mistakes and misdirections that characterize the Knapp family and those who surround them (friends, lovers, teachers, neighbors). 'Falling in place' is a casual, witty depiction of the broken American dream—the sterility of a middle-class family without purpose or direction." Choice

Follies; new stories. Scribner 2005 305p $25
ISBN 0-743-26961-6 LC 2004-65087

Beattie, Ann—*Continued*

Contents: Fléchette follies; Find and replace; Duchais; Tending something; Apology for a journey not taken:how to write a story; Mostre; The garden game; The rabit hole as likely explanation; Just going out; The last odd day in L. A.

"The tales in this volume showcase a newly flexible voice that accommodates both the author's patented gift for social observation and her more recent interest in her characters' inner lives, a voice that allows her to move fluently back and forth in time, back and forth from memory to rumination." N Y Times (Late N Y Ed)

Love always; a novel. Random House 1985 247p o.p.

LC 84-45749

"A Vermont-based magazine devoted to the last remaining vestiges of the counterculture harbors a number of people who have turned on and dropped out but still haven't quite mellowed out. Beattie observes these characters over the length of a summer as they sort through their myriad distractions and cope with the stresses of an overprivileged country life-style." Booklist

"The story seems to advance aimlessly, as an offbeat cast of characters . . . moves in and out of the action, humorously converging by chance or coincidence. A funny satire of contemporary media culture and its confusion between reality and invention, and a sad story of disaffected lives." Libr J

My life, starring Dara Falcon. Knopf 1997 307p o.p.

ISBN 0-679-45502-7 LC 96-36679

"Raised after her parents' death by an unloving maiden aunt, young Jean Warner has struggled to leave the loneliness of her childhood behind: she dropped out of college, rushed into marriage and lost herself as best she could in the bosom of her husband's large, close-knit New Hampshire family. But when she falls under the spell of Darcy Fisher, aka Dara Falcon, a seductive aspiring actress with a mysterious past, Jean's marriage begins to reveal its flaws, and Jean is forced to taste the bitterness that permeates her new family's claustrophobic self-involvement." Publ Wkly

"Dara is a fascinating character, and though she finally gets on the reader's nerves, Beattie has crafted a fine study of obsessive relationships with her usual aplomb." Libr J

Park City: new and selected stories. Knopf 1998 477p o.p.

ISBN 0-679-45506-X LC 97-49470

Contents: Cosmos; Second question; Going home with Uccello; The siamese twins go snorkeling; Zalla; Ed and Dave visit the city; The four-night fight; Park City; Vermont; Wolf dreams; Dwarf house; Snakes' shoes; Secrets and surprises; Weekend; A vintage Thunderbird; Shifting; The lawn party; Colorado; Learning to fall; The Cinderella waltz; Jacklighting; Waiting; Desire; Greenwich time; The burning house; Janus; In the white night; Heaven on a summer night; Summer people; Skeletons; Where you'll find me; The working girl; In Amalfi; What was mine; Windy day at the reservoir; Imagine a day at the end of your life

Perfect recall; new stories. Scribner 2001 347p $25

ISBN 0-7432-1169-3 LC 00-50465

Contents: Hurricane Carleyville; The big-breasted pilgrim; Mermaids; Cat people; The women of this world; The infamous fall of Howell the clown; See the pyramids; In irons; Coydog; Perfect recall; The famous poet, Amid Bougainvillea

"Beattie still captures the zeitgeist like no one else, effortlessly—or so it seems—revealing the sudden intimacies and sweet ironies of a crowded, improbable world." Publ Wkly

Picturing Will. Random House 1989 230p o.p.

ISBN 0-394-56987-3 LC 89-42781

"Aspiring photographer Jody, abandoned by husband Wayne—now on his third wife—is deeply devoted to her young son Will but hesitant to commit to lover Mel. Still, she visits Mel in faraway New York City, where Mel's friend, gallery owner Haverford (whose name she can recall only as Haveabud), takes a shine to her work—or to her. When Mel takes Will to visit his father in Florida, Haveabud goes along for the ride, bringing Spencer, a former protegé's son. . . . Meanwhile Wayne demonstrates his continued instability by cheating flagrantly on his new wife, Corky." Libr J

Beattie "has almost as many narrative voices as characters in this book, yet the result is never confusing. . . . 'Picturing Will' would be admirable for its technique alone; what makes it Beattie's best novel is her new and fearless way with emotional complexity." Newsweek

Where you'll find me and other stories. Linden Press/Simon & Schuster 1986 191p o.p.

LC 86-7396

Contents: In the white night; Snow; Skeletons; The big outside world; Coney Island; When can I see you again?; Lofty; High School; Janus; Spiritus; Times; Summer people; Cards; Heaven on a summer night; Where you'll find me

"At the risk of repeating herself thematically and stylistically . . . Beattie sticks to her succinct depictions of middle-class, early middle-age lives." Booklist

Beauvoir, Simone de, 1908-1986

The age of discretion

In Beauvoir, S. d. The woman destroyed p9-85

The mandarins; a novel. World Pub. 1956 610p o.p.

Original French edition, 1954

This "semiautobiographical novel addressed the attempts of post-World War II leftist intellectuals to abandon their elite, 'mandarin' status and to engage in political activism. The characters of psychologist Anne Dubreuilh and her husband Robert were roughly based on de Beauvoir and her lifelong associate Jean-Paul Sartre; de Beauvoir's account of Anne's affair with the American Lewis Brogan was a thinly veiled account of her own relationship with novelist Nelson Algren." Merriam-Webster's Ency of Lit

The monologue

In Beauvoir, S. d. The woman destroyed p87-120

Beauvoir, Simone de, 1908-1986—*Continued*

The woman destroyed; translated by Patrick O'Brian. Putnam 1969 254p o.p.

Original French edition, 1967

"The title story describes the heartjolting experience of a betrayed wife, and her gradual descent into the abyss of absolute estrangement from her husband. In a grimly revealing 'Monologue,' about another lady in deep distress, Mme. de Beauvoir permits her to speak for herself in a shattering rage against the world that has cast her out for her crimes against it. The third story, 'Age of Discretion,' has overtones of autobiography as it takes the reader on a voyage of discovery between the heroine, a writer, and her scientist husband, as they come to share, at last, the bitter knowledge of their son's reputation." Publ Wkly

The woman destroyed [novelette]
In Beauvoir, S. d. The woman destroyed p121-254

Beckett, Samuel, 1906-1989

Malone dies
In Beckett, S. Molloy, Malone dies, The unnamable

Molloy
In Beckett, S. Molloy, Malone dies, The unnamable

Molloy, Malone dies, The unnamable; with an introduction by Gabriel Josipovici. Knopf 1997 xliii, 476p $22

ISBN 0-375-40070-2 LC 98-119494

"Everyman's library"

A reissue of the title first published 1959 by Grove Press; Original French editions of Molloy and Malone dies published 1951; The unnamable, 1953. These translations published separately 1955, 1956 and 1958, respectively

The trilogy "is concerned with the search for identity, for the true self which can rest from self-caricature; and as a parallel it is concerned with the true silence which is the end of speech. Molloy, Malone and their final unnamable incarnation are paradigms of humanity in general and of the artist in particular. . . . The trilogy seen as a whole composes one of the most remarkable, most original and most haunting prose-works of the century." Times Lit Suppl

Murphy. Grove Press 1957 282p o.p.

First published 1938 in the United Kingdom

"The story concerns an Irishman in London who yearns to do nothing more than sit in his rocking chair and daydream. Murphy attempts to avoid all action; he escapes from a girl he is about to marry, takes up with a kind prostitute, and finds a job as a nurse in a mental institution, where he plays nonconfrontational chess. His disengagement from the world is shattered when his fiancée, with a detective and two new lovers in tow, discovers him. He is killed when someone accidentally turns on the gas in his apartment." Merriam-Webster's Ency of Lit

The unnamable
In Beckett, S. Molloy, Malone dies, The unnamable

Begley, Louis

Schmidt delivered. Knopf 2000 292p o.p.

ISBN 0-375-41088-0 LC 00-41241

"Albert Schmidt is a retired lawyer who torments his only daughter with ingeniously manipulative trust arrangements, then wonders why she doesn't visit him in the Hamptons home he shares with Carrie, a Puerto Rican trophy waitress. This time out, everyone's after either cash or Carrie, and Schmidt's foils include a meddlesome billionaire, an ambitious masseur, and a motormouth handyman. Once again, Begley, with his impeccable ear for Episcopalianisms and his gift for humiliating sexual entanglements, engineers an improbably cozy ending—even though it isn't exactly clear who is ending up with what." New Yorker

Belfer, Lauren

City of light. Dial Press (NY) 1999 518p o.p.

ISBN 0-385-33401-X LC 98-52917

This novel is set in Buffalo, New York, in 1901, where a Pan-American Exposition is being planned and Niagara Falls is about to be transformed into a hydroelectric power station. Narrator Louisa Barrett, headmistress of a girls' school, is worried about her nine-year-old goddaughter Grace Sinclair, who has been troubled since her mother died. Grace's father Tom is in charge of the power station, where a mysterious death occurs, and Louisa decides to investigate

"The book is part mystery and part historical melodrama, fluently mixing fact and fiction, with the sort of Victorian plot devices that guarantee a straight-through, sleepless read." Time

Bell, Acton *See* Brontë, Anne, 1820-1849

Bell, Christine, 1951-

The Perez family. Norton 1990 256p o.p.

LC 89-25569

This is a "novel about a Cuban ex-prisoner's arrival in America in the Mariel boatlift. . . . Juan Raul Perez was imprisoned 20 years ago for his political views in his native Cuba, while his wife and young daughter fled to Miami. Few letters have gotten through in the ensuing 20 years, and Juan doesn't know what to expect when he finds them again. But before the reunion, Juan must survive the dizzy world of refugee relocation." Libr J

"Christine Bell is much more than a lighthearted comic novelist. She's one of those writers like Flannery O'Connor or Isak Dinesen: she doesn't so much write stories as spin tales. . . . What may have seemed cartoonish in the middle of the book, you now realize, was mythic, archetypal. What you have been reading turns out to be a profound little parable about the redemptive power of love." N Y Times Book Rev

Bell, Currer *See* Brontë, Charlotte, 1816-1855

Bell, Ellis *See* Brontë, Emily, 1818-1848

Bell, Madison Smartt

All souls' rising. Pantheon Bks. 1995 530p o.p.

ISBN 0-679-43989-7 LC 95-12339

Bell, Madison Smartt—*Continued*

"Set during the struggle for Haiti's independence in the late 1700s, this intensely imagined epic novel of racial hatred and bloody upheaval illuminates the enmities among the astonishingly complex ethnic populations of the Caribbean island. Bell evokes a society caught in the crucible of violence with superb characterizations, ranging from the arrogant *grand blanc* plantation owners to the black slaves—including Toussaint L'Ouverture, the leader of the black revolt." Publ Wkly

Anything goes. Pantheon Bks. 2002 306p o.p.
ISBN 0-375-42125-4 LC 2001-55449

A novel narrated by "Jesse Melungeon, a 20-year-old traveling with a bar band across the South. . . . Jesse's band is verging on decline until Estelle, a salty girl with a strong voice, transforms its image." Publ Wkly

"Bell, keenly sensitive to race matters, excels at group dynamics and possesses a fluent sense of place, strengths he draws on to create compelling scenes of strife, revelation, resolve, and redemption set in various evocative locales all up and down the East Coast from Key West to Vermont." Booklist

Master of the crossroads. Pantheon Bks. 2000 732p o.p.
ISBN 0-375-42056-8 LC 00-29835

"The second installment in Bell's trilogy on the Haitian slave revolt of the 1790s (following All Souls' Rising) picks up the story in 1794, three years into the conflict. Toussaint Louverture, an itinerant herb doctor, has quickly risen through the ranks of the black militia to become supreme military commander of the island. Toussaint is a brilliant tactician who practices a form of horse-mounted blitzkrieg, racing his cavalry along narrow mountain trails in the dead of night to take the enemy by surprise. He is also an astute politician who shrewdly plays Haiti's numerous factions against one another to his own advantage. But the real key to Toussaint's power, according to Bell, is his mastery of the language of his oppressors." Libr J

"This meticulously researched novel . . . has the feel of a tableau by Delacroix: a gorgeous swirl of individual and collective fervor." New Yorker

The stone that the builder refused. Pantheon Books 2004 747p $29.95
ISBN 0-375-42282-X LC 2004-40027

This is the concluding volume of the author's Toussaint Louverture trilogy. This "installment centers on Toussaint's last two years, in which Haiti's war-ravaged economy begins to rebound and a constitution is drafted and sent to France for ratification, only to raise Napoleon's ire. France then reinvaded Haiti, which led to Toussaint's capture and death in prison in 1803. Ultimately, Haitian independence did prevail, though the path was not always smooth. As in the earlier two acclaimed novels, Bell crafts his characters and prose artfully, and the reader is immersed in the book's times and setting." Libr J

Ten Indians. Pantheon Bks. 1996 264p o.p.
LC 96-14357

The protagonist of this novel is "Mike Devlin, a middle-aged white child-therapist who, for somewhat murky reasons, decides to open a Tae Kwon Do school in the black projects of inner-city Baltimore. Unbeknownst to him, Devlin's school attracts members of two drug gangs increasingly caught up in a murderous rivalry. Meanwhile, the singularly oblivious Devlin lets his daughter, Michelle, come down to the projects to train; she soon launches an affair with the leader of one of the gangs." Publ Wkly

The novel, "told partly from Devlin's viewpoint and partly, in convincing street language, from that of the drug dealers and their women, is spare and cinematic. Devlin, far out on a lonely voyage, saves his honor. Saves his daughter too. But it is the neighborhood that wins. Good ending, good novel." Time

Bellow, Saul, 1915-2005

The actual. Viking 1997 103p o.p.
LC 96-51173

"Harry Trellman has been drawn back to his hometown of Chicago after a lucrative business career has propelled him to such locales as Guatemala and Burma. By chance, Harry meets mega-elderly and mega-rich businessman Sigmund Adletsky, who immediately perceives Harry's ability to discern human nature and enlists him as part of his 'brain trust.' This business with the old geezer brings Harry into contact with Amy Wustrin, a woman Harry loved many, many years ago and whom he has never forgotten: thus the emotional tug that drew him back to Chicago in the first place." Booklist

"Bellow is a conservative in the best sense: he calls his readers constantly back to what they can't help but believe, at the same time insisting, as Trellman puts it, on a common recognition 'that the powers of our human genius are present where one least expects them.' As usual in Bellow's more recent fiction, plot is secondary here. So is character, for the hero of this small love-story is character itself." Publ Wkly

The adventures of Augie March; with an introduction by Martin Amis. Knopf 1995 xxxvii, 616p o.p.
ISBN 0-679-44460-2
"Everyman's library"

A reissue of the title first published 1953 by Viking

"It is a picaresque story of a poor Jewish youth from Chicago, his progress, sometimes highly comic, through the world of the 20th century, and his attempts to make sense of it." Merriam-Webster's Ency of Lit

also in Bellow, S. Novels, 1944-1953

The Bellarosa connection. Penguin Bks. 1989 102p o.p.
ISBN 0-14-012686-4 LC 89-32936

"This is the story of clubfooted, multilingual Harry Fonstein, a lucky refugee from Holocaust Europe, and his grandly obese wife, Sorella. Arrested in Mussolini's Rome, Harry was imprisoned and awaiting deportation when his escape was arranged by an underground group, bankrolled by Broadway bigshot Billy Rose. Harry wants personally to thank Rose, but all his efforts are rebuffed. Finally, Sorella confronts Rose in Jerusalem, ready to blackmail him into meeting with Harry." Libr J

"The end of 'The Bellarosa Connection' is abrupt, matter-of-fact, almost offbeat. It is a conclusion, perhaps, in which nothing is concluded, . . . but it is appropriate to the overall pitch and voice of this cannily resourceful entertainment." N Y Times Book Rev

also in Bellow, S. Collected stories

Bellow, Saul, 1915-2005—*Continued*

Collected stories; preface by Janis Bellow; introduction by James Wood. Viking 2001 442p o.p.
ISBN 0-670-89486-9 LC 2001-17595

This volume contains three novellas: A theft, The Bellarosa connection, and What kind of day did you have? and The following short stories: By the St. Lawrence; A silver dish; The old system; Looking for Mr. Green; Cousins; Zethland: by a character witness; Leaving the yellow house; Mosby's memoirs; Him with his foot in his mouth; and Something to remember me by

"Bellow likes to take a man at 'the top of his field' and, from that perspective, survey the discontents of civilization. Some-like Victor Wulpy in 'What Kind of Day Did You Have?'—refuse to retire and take mistresses in their mid-70s. . . . In 'A Theft,' Clare Velde, who has successfully formed her own journalism agency, still defines herself interms of her husbands. . . . The crowning jewel here is 'The Bellarosa Connection,' in which the unnamed narrator is a retired Philadelphia memory expert who reflects on his friendship with a man still obsessed with his escape from WWII Europe and the legendary showbiz promoter who helped him. Bellow's stories spread rather than march in straight lines, like memory itself, giving a kinesthetic sense of a stained, bamboozled and fundamentally comic culture." Publ Wkly

Dangling man. Vanguard Press 1944 191p o.p.

This story purports to be the journal of a young man living in Chicago, who gives up his job, expecting to be inducted into the army. Owing to technicalities Joseph is left dangling for almost a year. His journal explains his psychological reactions to idleness, how he passes his time, his growing unrest, and finally the relief when the call comes

"The book is an excellent document on the experience of the non-combatant in time of war. It is well written and never dull—in spite of the dismalness of the Chicago background and the undramatic character of the subject. It is also one of the most honest pieces of testimony on the psychology of a whole generation who have grown up during the depression and the war." New Yorker

also in Bellow, S. Novels, 1944-1953

The dean's December; a novel. Harper & Row 1982 312p o.p.
LC 80-8705

This is a "'tale of two cities', both seen through the eyes of Albert Corde, who visits Bucharest to see his dying mother-in-law, where he reflects on the contrasts between the violence and corruption of Chicago and the bureaucratic chill of Eastern Europe; the novel has, like much of Bellow's work, a strongly apocalyptic note." Oxford Companion to Engl Lit

Henderson the rain king; a novel. Viking 1959 341p o.p.

This novel, "designed on a grand and mythic scale, records American millionaire Gene Henderson's quest for revelation and spiritual power in Africa, where he becomes rainmaker and heir to a kingdom." Oxford Companion to Engl Lit

also in Bellow, S. The portable Saul Bellow

Herzog. Viking 1964 341p o.p.

"Beleaguered by the intensity of his introspection, Herzog worries over his life: an intellectual stumped in the middle of his second book—tellingly, an inquiry into Romanticism—a husband brooding over his second failed marriage, and above all a man trying to think his way into clarity, all the while wryly aware that he is the creator of his own paralysis. The epitome of this condition is the spate of letters that Herzog writes—to the living and the dead, to the famous and to his own circle of friends and enemies—but never sends. The letters document Herzog's detailed, vivid, and anxious apprehensions of contemporary American life in Chicago, in New York, and in the more pastoral setting of his retreat in the Berkshires. They also serve as a wonderfully colloquial venue for his irreverent, chatty, but also profound reflections on the fate of the individual in modern society." Benet's Reader's Ency of Am Lit

Him with his foot in his mouth and other stories. Harper & Row 1984 294p o.p.
ISBN 0-06-015179-X LC 83-48322

Contents: Him with his foot in his mouth; What kind of day did you have? {novella}; Zetland: by a character witness; A silver dish; Cousins

"Love totally eludes Katrina Goliger in 'What Kind of Day Did You Have?' The banal title of the story becomes increasingly ironic as Katrina's predicament unfolds. Freshly divorced, under scrutiny by her husband as he waits for an excuse to seize his two daughters, Katrina pursues an affair with a dying intellectual named Victor Wulpy." Best Sellers

"An impressive collection: Bellow's lush, intellectual fiction vigorously confronts ideas and connects individual experience to a broad scheme of life and art and thought." Libr J

Humboldt's gift. Viking 1975 487p o.p.

"The story of Charlie Citrine, a successful writer and academic plagued by women, lawsuits, and mafiosi, whose present career is interwoven with memories of the early success, failing powers, and squalid death of his friend Von Humboldt Fleischer, whose poetic destiny he fears he may inherit, together with his manuscripts." Oxford Companion to Engl Lit

More die of heartbreak. Morrow 1987 335p o.p.
LC 87-5770

"The novel is narrated by Ken Trachtenberg, a Paris-born and -educated 35-year-old professor of Russian. . . . The main character, Ken's uncle Benn Crader, is a world-famous botanist. After experiencing numerous sexual miseries during his 15 years as a widower, Benn marries a wealthy and beautiful young woman, Matilda Layamon. Between marriages, Benn had been swindled by his uncle, Harold Vilitzer, a crooked political boss. . . . Matilda's father, Dr. Layamon, plans to use Benn to recover a few million from Vilitzer, so that his daughter can live luxuriously and entertain lavishly." Natl Rev

"Bellow has always been as enthralled by crooks as by the higher realms of thought. His prose mixes soaring meditation with streetsmart wisecracks. The farcical collisions of ill-prepared idealists with hard-as-nails swindlers and connivers give 'More Die of Heartbreak' its juicy vivacity." Newsweek

Bellow, Saul, 1915-2005—*Continued*

Mr. Sammler's planet. Viking 1970 313p o.p.

"Artur Sammler, in his seventies and an escapee from the horrors of Nazi atrocities and the memory of having had to dig himself out of his own grave, theorizes about the possibility of finding a similar escape from the assaults of life in New York City, its muggings, crime, dirt, noise. Living with his bizarre daughter, Shula, also saved from death in Europe but somewhat deranged, perhaps the result of traumas suffered, is not possible, and living with his niece Margotte also has its drawbacks. The most important person to Sammler is his nephew Elya, by whose generosity Sammler and Shula are able to exist. But Elya's escape from the horrors of his own life—his son Wallace's irresponsible behavior and his daughter Angela's sexually promiscuous behavior—is by way of death. For our desire to find relief from the outrages of life in this decade, Bellow has made a metaphor of man's desire to go to the moon." Shapiro. Fic for Youth. 3d edition

Novels, 1944-1953. Library of America, Distributed to the trade in the U.S. by Penguin Putnam 2003 1029p $35

ISBN 1-931082-38-3 LC 2003-40144

Contents: Dangling man; The victim; The adventures of Augie March

Dangling man and The adventures of Augie March are entered separately. The victim (1947) tells the story of Asa Leventhal, who once held a position on a New York trade journal, and had won a certain security, but a few sultry weeks while his wife was away almost wrecked him. The remembrance of his insane mother, and the constant harrying of a Gentile friend, who insisted that Asa had ruined his career, brings him to the verge of insanity.

The portable Saul Bellow; with critical introduction by Gabriel Josipovici; compiled under the supervision of the author by Edith Tarcov. Viking 1974 xlvii, 654p o.p.

"Viking portable library"

Contains the complete novels: Seize the day and Henderson the rain king; excerpts from: The adventures of Augie March, Herzog, and Mr. Sammler's planet; and three short stories: Leaving the yellow house, Mosby's memoirs, and The old system

Ravelstein. Viking 2000 233p o.p.

ISBN 0-670-84134-X LC 99-56336

"Ravelstein is a brilliant albeit eccentric professor of political philosophy, many of whose acolytes have become the movers and shakers of today's world. He has always lived life to the fullest, even when he couldn't afford to—a point that becomes moot when he publishes, at best friend Chick's suggestion, a best-selling book outlining his ideas. When he is diagnosed with AIDS (he is, as Chick says, homosexual but not 'gay'), Ravelstein convinces Chick, a well-known writer in his own right, to become his Boswell." Libr J

This "might, like the author's earlier works, be called a novel of ideas, but that is too bloodless a description of Bellow's signature accomplishment. . . . [It] brims with life, thanks to Chick's that is Bellow's comic observations on the passing scene." Time

Seize the day; with three short stories and a one-act play. Viking 1956 211p o.p.

Anthology composed of one novella: Seize the day; three short stories: A father-to-be, Looking for Mr. Green, and The Gonzaga manuscripts; and a one-act play: The wrecker

"Seize the Day gives contemporary literature a story which will be explained, expounded, and argued, but about which a final reckoning can be made only after it ripples out in the imagination of the generations of readers to come. I suspect that it is one of the central stories of our day." Nation

Seize the day [novelette]
In Bellow, S. The portable Saul Bellow
In Bellow, S. Seize the day

A theft
In Bellow, S. Collected stories

The victim
In Bellow, S. Novels, 1944-1953

What kind of day did you have?
In Bellow, S. Collected stories
In Bellow, S. Him with his foot in his mouth and other stories p61-163

Bellows, Nathaniel

On this day; a novel. HarperCollins Pubs. 2003 265p $24.95

ISBN 0-06-051211-3 LC 2002-27272

"Narrator Warren is 18 and his sister Joan is 20 when their father dies of cancer and their mother falls apart and eventually commits suicide. Soon afterward, their father's business partner seizes the opportunity to take over their nursery business and cut Joan and Warren off. Focusing on small family moments, the eloquent yet down-to-earth narrative balances gut-wrenching scenes of grief with some funny, ironic passages." Publ Wkly

Benchley, Peter

Jaws. Doubleday 1974 311p o.p.

This is a "story about what happens when a great white shark terrorizes a small Long Island town. . . . A woman swimmer is devoured by the shark, and Police Chief Martin Brody insists on closing the beaches. But he's overruled by the town fathers who remind him that the community is dependent on summer visitors for economic survival. Two deaths later, the news can no longer be suppressed and Brody, an oceanographer and a fisherman go after the monster in an exciting chase." Publ Wkly

Benedict, Elizabeth

Almost. Houghton Mifflin 2001 258p $24

ISBN 0-618-14332-7 LC 2001-24528

"With divorce in mind, Sophy Chase leaves her husband, Will, on the Massachusetts island of Swansea. She heads to New York City to pursue her writing career and a passionate but superficial relationship with her lover, Daniel. Since neither is free to move the relationship forward, it remains unsatisfactory for both. A call from the

Benedict, Elizabeth—*Continued*
Massachusetts State Police sends Sophy hurrying back to Swansea to bury the man she just left." Libr J

"Sophy is an intriguing creation: smart, loving, combative, self-loathing. Almost has a harried plot. Still, the book is funny, harrowing and just a little messy. I don't know what to compare it to—except life." Newsweek

Benét, Stephen Vincent, 1898-1943

The Devil and Daniel Webster; illustrated by Harold Denison. Farrar & Rinehart 1937 61p il o.p.

"Jabez Stone, a New Hampshire farmer, receives a decade of material wealth in return for selling his soul to the Devil—Mr. Scratch. When the Devil comes to claim Stone's soul, the farmer has the statesman and orator Daniel Webster argue his case at midnight before a jury of historic American villains." Merriam-Webster's Ency of Lit

Benford, Gregory, 1941-

Eater; a novel. Avon Eos 2000 335p $24
ISBN 0-380-97436-3 LC 99-57969

"Benjamin Knowlton probes the extreme outer limits of our knowledge of the universe. Meanwhile, his wife, Channing, is dying of cancer. His attention, however, like that of a great many others, swiftly turns to a newly detected mobile black hole beyond the orbit of Pluto and apparently headed for Earth. As it approaches, evidence mounts that it is a sapient entity, perhaps possessing previously unimagined knowledge. But it also tends to destroy everything in its path." Booklist

"Full of astronomical pyrotechnics and the kind of intellectual verbal fencing that seems to go along with creative scientific thinking, Benford's latest should delight any serious reader of SF." Publ Wkly

Foundation's fear. HarperPrism 1997 425p (Second Foundation trilogy) o.p.
LC 96-45296

"Set thousands of years in the future, this novel begins the Second Foundation Trilogy, a prequel to Isaac Asimov's famous original." Publ Wkly

"Mr. Benford picks up the story as Seldon is about to become First Minister to Emperor Cleon I, who rules the 25 million inhabited planets of the galaxy from the imperial capital of Trantor. I have no idea whether anyone unfamiliar with the original Foundation series—which spells out what happened to Seldon and his predictions—will be able to make sense of 'Foundation's Fear.' But for the legions of readers who have long been tantalized by Asimov's cryptic references to psychohistory, Mr. Benford provides some fascinating insights into its development." N Y Times Book Rev

Followed by Foundation and chaos, by Greg Bear

Timescape. Simon & Schuster 1980 412p o.p.

"As the world lurches toward disaster, scientists in 1998 try to transmit a warning message to 1962 by means of tachyons. Their story is told in parallel with that of the scientists trying to decode the transmission, and the two plots converge on the possibility of paradox. Unusual for the realism of its depiction of scientists at work; admirably serious in handling the implications of its theme." Anatomy of Wonder 4

(jt. auth) Clarke, A. C. Beyond the fall of night

Benioff, David

When the nines roll over and other stories; David Benioff. Viking 2004 223p $23.95
ISBN 0-670-03339-1 LC 2004-49613

Contents: When the nines roll over; The Devil comes to Orekovo; Zoanthropy; Barefoot girl in clover; De composition; Garden of no; Neversink; Merde for luck

"Benioff is a storyteller in the old style: He creates an interesting premise, then steps aside to let it play out. There's a reason this kind of writing has lasted for ages; simply put, it's fun to read. The successful stories in When The Nines Roll Over are so thoroughly enjoyable that you may not reflect on their acute perceptions until you've put the book down for a while." Washington Post Book World

Benjamin, Paul *See* Auster, Paul, 1947-

Benson, Ann

The plague tales. Delacorte Press 1997 474p o.p.
ISBN 0-385-31651-8 LC 96-47246

The author alternates "between the stories of Alejandro Canches, a 14th-century Jewish physician, and Janie Crowe, a government-designated archaeologist in the 21st century. The heroic Alejandro battles the bubonic plague and sets in motion a tragic turn of events. Janie, an embittered former surgeon struggling in her new career, is still grieving over the loss of her family during one of the catastrophic sicknesses that besiege the time she lives in. Particularly horrifying are the descriptions of how contagion is fought during Janie's time; one or two methods will undoubtedly make readers wince. The two plotlines dovetail neatly and boil to a twisted, satisfying conclusion." Libr J

Benson, E. F. (Edward Frederic), 1867-1940

Lucia in London
In Benson, E. F. Make way for Lucia p179-358

Make way for Lucia. Harper & Row 1986 c1977 1119p o.p.
LC 86-45639

A reissue of the omnibus edition of six novels and one short story published 1977 by Crowell

These novels were originally published in the United States by George H. Doran Company and Doubleday, Doran & Company

Contents: Queen Lucia (1920); Lucia in London (1928); Miss Mapp (1923); The male impersonator (1929); Mapp and Lucia (1931); The worshipful Lucia (1935) [published in England with title: Lucia's progress]; Trouble with Lucia (1939)

The male impersonator
In Benson, E. F. Make way for Lucia p535-48

Mapp and Lucia
In Benson, E. F. Make way for Lucia p549-762

Benson, E. F. (Edward Frederic), 1867-1940— *Continued*

Miss Mapp
In Benson, E. F. Make way for Lucia p359-534

Queen Lucia
In Benson, E. F. Make way for Lucia p1-178

Trouble for Lucia
In Benson, E. F. Make way for Lucia p941-1119

The worshipful Lucia
In Benson, E. F. Make way for Lucia p763-940

Benson, Edward Frederic *See* Benson, E. F. (Edward Frederic), 1867-1940

Berberian, Viken

The cyclist; a novel. Simon & Schuster 2002 189p $21
ISBN 0-7432-2283-0 LC 2001-49339

"A terrorist prepares to attack a Beirut hotel in Berberian's first novel, a . . . character study that begins with the anonymous narrator laid up in a hospital after being clocked by a Mercedes while riding his bike. As his girlfriend, Ghaemi Basmati, helps nurse him back to health, he ponders the ultimate ride he will soon take to a seaside hotel with a backpack full of plastic explosives." Publ Wkly

"The complexity of the protagonist's personality is at times troubling; he can speak with such passion and longing for a plate of baba ghannooj or a ripe pomegranate, yet with only coldness and detachment when desccribing the violence and death he is soon to rain down on the unsuspecting." SLJ

Berg, Elizabeth, 1948-

The art of mending; a novel; Elizabeth Berg. 1st ed. Random House 2004 236p $24.95
ISBN 1-400-06159-8 LC 2003-66726

"At her annual family reunion, Laura Bartone, a 50-something 'quilt artist,' is forced to confront the secrets that have long haunted her family. Her emotionally unstable sister, Caroline, tells Laura and their brother, Steve, that their mother abused her as a child. As Laura and Steve-whose own childhoods were reasonably happy-struggle to make sense of Caroline's accusations and wonder how they could've been oblivious to or complicit in what happened, their father dies. This could be the stuff of melodrama, but Berg generally manages to avoid it. Her prose is often luminous and buoyant, and her insights can be penetrating." Publ Wkly

Never change. Pocket Bks. 2001 214p o.p.
ISBN 0-7434-1132-3 LC 00-69874

"Fifty-one-year-old Myra Lipinsky is the classic @old maid'; she has always considered herself unattractive and wallows in self-pity over her lack of a husband or children. Myra's job as a home-care nurse, which she loves, brings her into contact with many different people and gives her a sense of strength and importance. When Myra's high school crush Chip Reardon is assigned as her new patient, she longs for him as she did years ago. Chip is dying from a brain tumor and has chosen not to seek further treatment, letting nature take its course. Chip and Myra become lovers at a crucial time in both of their lives." Libr J

"In an inspiring, well-deserved denouement, Chip's inevitable death forces Myra to embrace the world in all its bittersweet complexity." Publ Wkly

Open house; a novel. Random House 2000 241p o.p.
ISBN 0-375-50603-9 LC 99-54258

"Samantha is in her mid-30's, happily married for many years to David, and the mother of an 11-year-old son named Travis, when divorce fractures her world. Reeling with misery and disbelief, she sets out to remake herself and her life." N Y Times Book Rev

Berg "refreshes a well-worn plot with knowing domestic detail, an understanding of familiar—sometimes conflicting—female emotions and an infectious sentimental optimism." Publ Wkly

Ordinary life; stories. Random House 2002 192p o.p.
ISBN 0-679-43746-0 LC 2001-41754

Contents: Ordinary life: a love story; Departure from normal; Things we used to believe; Caretaking; Sweet refuge; Take this quiz; Martin's letter to Nan; What stays; White dwarf; Matchmaker; One time at Christmas, in my sister's bedroom; Regrets only; Thief; Today's special

"While the men and women who populate the stories typify the monolithic entities of the fabled battle of the sexes . . . Berg's gentle probing of everyday events offers insight into turning points of life that may not set off fireworks but are nevertheless indelible." Publ Wkly

The pull of the moon. Random House 1996 193p o.p.
LC 95-41934

"Nan turns 50 and hits the road, leaving behind her husband of 25 years and a daughter bound for college. At midlife, she is deeply unsatisfied with the way things are going. Alternating between diary entries and letters sent to her husband, Nan reveals her fear of aging and her encounters with people on the road. . . . [The author] nimbly avoids all the obvious clichés of an all-too-familiar theme as she drives her narrative home with direct, heartfelt language." Booklist

Range of motion. Random House 1995 217p o.p.
LC 95-3299

"The first-person narrative describes an ordinary woman caught up in unusual circumstances. Lainey is a wife/mother/office worker whose life is suddenly changed when her husband is sent into a coma by a freak accident. The only one who believes that he will one day wake up, she visits him daily, bringing him stimulus from everyday life in an attempt to reach him. . . . Lainey is sustained through her ordeal by the support of two special women: Alice, who lives next door, and Evie, the ghost of the woman who lived in Lainey's house in the Forties." Libr J

"Normal life is contorted and magnified through trage-

Berg, Elizabeth, 1948-—*Continued*
dy here; while readers will wish to rush through the narrative to discover the emotionally resonant ending, they should instead savor Lainey's present-tense narration, so palpably full of loneliness and faith." Publ Wkly

What we keep; a novel. Random House 1998 272p o.p.
ISBN 0-375-50099-5 LC 97-42070
As the novel "opens, Ginny is flying to California to join her sister in a meeting with their mother, whom neither daughter has seen for 35 years. Ginny uses her travel time to reflect upon her memories of the summer when her mother withdrew from the family and became an outsider in her daughters' lives. Berg's precise, evocative descriptions create vivid images of Ginny's physical world, while Berg's understanding and perception are an eloquent testimony to Ginny's emotional turmoil." Libr J

Bergen, David

See the child; a novel. Simon & Schuster 2002 c1999 234p $23
ISBN 0-7432-2925-8 LC 2001-57571
First published 1999 in Canada
"Paul Unger, a prosperous middle-aged man living in a small town in Manitoba, wakes up one night to the news that his alienated teenage son, Stephen, is dead. Paul's resulting spiral of depression tears apart his marriage and drives him to isolate himself on his farm, where he throws himself into bee husbandry. When Nicole, Stephen's sluttish girlfriend, comes back to town with a child, Paul cleaves to them with a fierce intensity. . . . Bergen writes with a precision that reveals every detail, every action, carefully depicting Paul's emotional vulnerability and his need to determine how much he is responsible for his son's death and the fate of his grandson." Publ Wkly

Berger, Thomas, 1924-

Adventures of the artificial woman; a novel. Simon & Schuster 2004 198p $20
ISBN 0-7432-5740-5
"Ellery Pierce, an expert at animatronics, has decided to forgo the usual pitfalls of human companionship by creating his ideal woman from scratch. This Frankenstein is named Phyllis, and soon she decides to strike out on her own for a career in show business. Phyllis works her way up the seedy ladder of the sex industry and eventually becomes a successful action movie star. Ellery, however, pines for the robot he let get away, and as Phyllis's career begins to slide into oblivion, the two rejoin to take her vocation in a political direction." Libr J
"Berger skewers modern foibles from reality and daytime television to the cult of celebrity and presidents with voracious sexual appetites. But the brilliance of Berger's critique is in its levity, and his fanciful plot will keep readers laughing throughout." Publ Wkly

Arthur Rex. Delacorte Press/Seymour Lawrence 1978 499p o.p.
LC 78-7241
A "modernization of Malory's 'Morte d'Arthur.' The setting remains ancient Britain, but King Arthur, Merlin, Launcelot, and the knights of the Round Table suffer from 20th-Century maladies; Guinevere and other fair ladies are liberated. Sex and introspection abound. Embellishing the basic tale, Berger adds seriocomic twists, fantasies, and exaggerations." Libr J
This is a "splendid, satiric retelling of the legend of Camelot. . . . The curious truth is that Mr. Berger's revisions are most authentic, most profound, when the admixture of parody is strongest. At those times—a good three-fourths of the book—he is never merely a parodist after all, but also a compelling yarnspinner in his own right." N Y Times Book Rev

Being invisible; a novel. Little, Brown 1987 262p o.p.
LC 86-20897
"Things are not going well for Fred Wagner, a typical Berger victim. His wife has left him, his job as a catalog copywriter is becoming increasingly unsatisfying, and his novel, after six years, has not progressed beyond the opening pages. Wagner discovers, however, that he does have a talent—he can make himself invisible—and the novel recounts his struggle to make the best of this unique gift. But surprisingly, Wagner finds that whether he is trying to bypass a long line, steal from a bank, or avoid his co-workers, invisibility has its drawbacks; rather than improving his situation, each invisible adventure leads to a further mishap." Libr J
"There is much in 'Being Invisible' to celebrate—the pleasures of invention, humor, surprise, of Mr. Berger's enraged, unforgiving view. That so much of his vision seems neither freakish nor admonitory but rather, oddly tonic, says something about the era in which we live. . . . It is a sign of the times that we feel such affection for Thomas Berger's dogged, cranky courage, and for the denizens of his unwelcoming and chaotic corner of the fictional world." N Y Times Book Rev

Best friends; a novel. Simon & Schuster 2003 209p $24
ISBN 0-7432-4183-5 LC 2002-42617
"Roy Courtright is a bit of an ascetic, a wealthy vintage auto dealer who stays fit, and something of a womanizer, although more romantic than rake. Sam Grandy is a vastly overweight spendthrift with a sleek banker wife named Kristin. Their lifelong friendship is tested when Sam's heart attack throws together Roy and Kristin, who asks Roy to stop bailing out Sam (he now wants $50,000). The relationship between this formerly standoffish pair heats up, and Sam's games and tricks cause the situation to deteriorate further." Libr J
"The motor of the novel's intellectual ingenuity, its comedy and its considerable suspense is the transformation of the indicative into the conditional. Three-way betrayal is not only the plot but a theme inherent in the title." N Y Times Book Rev

Crazy in Berlin. Scribner 1958 438p o.p.
"Because of his German background, Reinhart, an American G.I. stationed in Berlin at the conclusion of W.W. II, has strong guilt feelings about the treatment of Jews in Nazi Germany. His guilt is intensified by his relationships with German-Jewish civilians, with Lt. Schild, a Jewish-American Communist agent, and with Schatzi, a black marketeer, Communist courier, and former follower of Ernst Rohm." Libr J
"A story that boasts a memorable gallery of German, Russian, and American characters. Speech and scene are

Berger, Thomas, 1924-—*Continued*
reproduced with deft precision as are the intellectual and emotional intricacies of personal relationships." Booklist
Followed by Reinhart in love

Little Big Man. Dial Press (NY) 1979 1964 xxii, 440p o.p.

"The author purports to write the story of Jack Crabb, adopted Cheyenne, gunfighter, buffalo hunter, and survivor of Custer's last stand, whom he has located at the Marville Center for Senior Citizens. In the few months before his death at the self-professed age of 111, Crabb recounts *his* version of life in the Old West." Shapiro. Fic for Youth. 3d edition

Followed by The return of Little Big Man (1999)

Neighbors. Delacorte Press/Seymour Lawrence 1980 275p o.p.

LC 79-20307

"The new neighbors drop in for a drink and chaos breaks loose, as Berger records the nightmarish distractions of a day and night among the American middle class. Existential reverses skewer the suburban lifestyle of the bourgeoisie and unleash unkempt fantasies on manicured lawns as a man's mind, life, and home are boldly and cunningly invaded and violated." Booklist

Berger "quickly conditions the reader to expect the unexpected but manages to be consistently surprising nevertheless, introducing new twists and outrages that not even the most warped spectator could have foreseen. The novel adopts a formal, almost fussy style to convey lunacy, as if Berger were describing low deeds to a maiden aunt. . . . [The book] is not at all interested in being socially redeeming, and those who read books to gain warm feelings or philosophic nuggets will come away from this one empty-handed and probably angry. . . .What Berger has produced is a tour de force." Time

Reinhart in love. Scribner 1962 438p o.p.

Sequel to Crazy in Berlin

This novel begins with "Reinhart's discharge from the Army. He goes to the home of his parents in Ohio, eventually gets a job of sorts, and meets and marries a girl; but while he is following this commonplace course, all sorts of extraordinary things happen to him." Saturday Rev

"A comic novel. . . . In richness of funny language, freakishness of situation, eccentricities of character, reckless sweep of narrative, all combined, there probably will not be another like it for five years, perhaps ever." Chicago Sunday Trib

Followed by Vital parts

Reinhart's women; a novel. Delacorte Press/Seymour Lawrence 1981 295p o.p.

LC 81-3271

"This is not the Carlo Reinhart of Crazy in Berlin . . . Reinhart in Love . . . and Vital Parts. He has been divorced from the vituperous Genevieve—his wife of 22 years—for a decade. His son Blaine, a mulish, asexual hippie ten years ago, is now a three-piece materialist; a blubbery, myopic Daughter Winona has been transformed into an anorectic fashion model. . . . Reinhart is 'housefather' in Winona's luxury apartment. . . . Hired by high-powered Grace Greenwood to demonstrate gourmet-food preparation in supermarkets, he is shocked to discover that the executive gorgon is Winona's lesbian lover. Blaine's wife has an erotic nervous breakdown in Reinhart's bedroom. Genevieve returns to stage a breakdown of her own. Helen Clayton, his supermarket assistant, bolsters Reinhart's flagging sexuality with motel trysts. A neighbor, Edie Mulhouse, as big as the hero himself, writes manic mash notes." Time

"Although the hilarity is occasionally forced, this uniquely happy novel is certainly worth reading for all it attempts to cover and mostly for sheer manic fun." Libr J

The return of Little Big Man. Little, Brown 1999 432p o.p.

ISBN 0-316-09844-2 LC 98-26862

Sequel to Little Big Man

Jack Crabb "tells of his further adventures as a disastrous bodyguard to Wild Bill Hickock, a barkeep in violent Dodge City, and a Cheyenne interpreter in a mission school. He goes to Tombstone with Bat Masterson and to Europe with Buffalo Bill Cody . . . and sees the tragic killing of Sitting Bull." Libr J

"Mr. Berger's knowledge of frontier history is formidable. His ability to convert it into intriguing fiction derives from the narrator he has invented. Jack is a relative of Huckleberry Finn—an intelligent observer whose lack of formal education leaves his mind unhampered by sentimental clichés and conventional assumptions." Atl Mon

Sneaky people; a novel. Simon & Schuster 1975 315p o.p.

"The time is the 1930's; the setting, a grimly shabby Midwestern town. When used-car impressario Buddy Sandifer plans to have his wife murdered and wed his waitress mistress, he initiates an endearing concatenation of elaborate, mutually cancelling ruses. The designated murderer has plans of his own; the victim-to-be lives a secret life far from what Buddy imagines as sexless stodginess." Libr J

Berger's "style, always good, improves with each novel, refined here to deft economical strokes that describe a person, a time, or even a culture in a few lines, to dialogue that implies a perfect ear. . . . This [is a] marvelously funny and touching story. . . . It depicts anarchic American individuals in a particular time but for all time. Berger may be our best living novelist." Choice

Suspects; a novel. Morrow 1996 294p o.p.

LC 95-42513

"The gruesome murder of a mother and her young daughter provides the backdrop to an investigation featuring a grizzled, semi-alcoholic veteran detective; his younger partner; and an odd assortment of suspects, including a strangely cold husband; a down-and-out, antisocial brother-in-law; and a plumber whose curiosity gets him into trouble." Libr J

"That 'Suspects' involves a murder in which the victims' throats are slashed, features a suspect with a very shaky alibi and is merciless in its portrayal of an incompetent police force and an exploitative press cannot be an accident: the plot has O. J. Simpson written all over it. What makes the book so unusual is that Mr. Berger has taken a bizarre murder case and used it as a springboard to something even more bizarre. . . . An engrossing, often hilarious offering from one of our most persistently strange writers." N Y Times Book Rev

Berger, Thomas, 1924-*—Continued*

Vital parts; a novel. Baron, R.W. 1970 432p o.p.

Sequel to Reinhart in love

"Down on his luck, over forty, Carl Reinhart is despised by his hippie son, rejected by his wife, and admired only by his overweight, excessively sensitive, teenage daughter. Anxious to escape domestic problems Reinhart becomes involved with his friend Bob Sweet in a cryogenic experiment, a plan to freeze a person who has died in the hope that a cure for his fatal disease is discovered in the future. The people Reinhart meets in the course of a discursive novel embody most of the anxieties of Middle Western small town life." Booklist

"As Reinhart is pushed further and further into the absurdities he prides himself so successfully on avoiding, the promise of the brilliant opening scenes is not only confirmed but fulfilled by the double takes in plotting and narrative surface." Harpers

Followed by Reinhart's women

Berne, Suzanne, 1961-

A perfect arrangement; a novel. Algonquin Bks. 2001 301p $23.95

ISBN 1-56512-261-5 LC 00-69451

"A Shannon Ravenel book"

A domestic novel set in the small New England town of New Aylesbury. "Mirella and Howard Cook-Goldman are fortunate to have found Randi Grill, who seems like the perfect nanny. Not only does she take care of their two children but she also cooks, cleans, and sews. Yet something is wrong with the flawless Midwesterner and her charges." Libr J

The author provides a "probing, intelligent exploration of a contemporary family with a strong sense of entitlement, whose future turns out to be anything but certain." N Y Times Book Rev

Bernhard, Thomas, 1931-1989

Amras

In Bernhard, T. Three novellas

Extinction; a novel; translated from the German by David McLintock. Knopf 1995 325p o.p.

ISBN 0-394-57253-X LC 94-42886

This novel was originally "published in German in 1986, three years before [Bernhard's] death. It takes the form of an extended monologue, the narrator and central character [Murau] being a figure obsessively critical of Austria. The younger son of a landed family in Upper Austria, he has for a number of years worked in Rome teaching German literature to a young Italian, whom he has, he believes, instructed in anarchy. The sudden death of his parents and elder brother in a car accident leaves him unexpectedly the heir to [Wolfsegg], the large family estate, and prompts him to come to terms with his uneasy relationship not only with his family but also with his Austrian roots." N Y Times Book Rev

"The uncompromising nature of Bernhard's art-at its finest in Extinction-gives it greatness, authority and a bewildering nihilism. He is too intelligent not to see round himself, so that the narrator's family and friends come through as moving portraits, for all his determination to preserve them in his loathing." New Statesman & Society

The loser; translated from the German by Jack Dawson; afterword by Mark M. Anderson. Knopf 1991 189p o.p.

ISBN 0-394-57239-4 LC 90-45942

Original German edition, 1983

This is an "account of an imagined relationship among three men who meet in 1953 to study with Vladimir Horowitz. In the face of Glenn Gould's incomparable genius as a piano virtuoso, his two fellow students renounce their musical ambition, but in very different ways." Midwest Book Rev

"Dawson's translation is superb. . . . The Loser is undoubtedly one of the most fascinating works of contemporary Austrian literature, and given its extraordinary meditations on art, the artist, and the reception of the creative process, it is a work that should find international readership." American Book Rev

Playing Watten

In Bernhard, T. Three novellas

Three novellas; translated by Peter Jansen and Kenneth J. Northcott; with a foreword by Brian Evenson. University of Chicago Press 2003 174p $25

ISBN 0-226-04432-7 LC 2002-45580

Amras "tells the story of two brothers, one epileptic, who have survived a family suicide pact and are now living in a ruined tower. . . . In Watten, the narrator, a doctor who lost his practice due to morphine abuse, describes a visit paid him by a truck driver who wanted the doctor to return to his habit of playing a game of cards (watten) every Wednesday. . . . Walking records the conversations of the narrator and his friend Oehler while they walk, discussing anything that comes to mind but always circling back to their mutual friend Karrer, who has gone irrevocably mad." Publisher's note

"One should commend the translators and the publisher for bringing these bizarre, irritating and very funny stories into English at a time when commercial presses shy away from 'difficult' work in translation. . . . In a world of profit-driven literary publishing, we need unconventional, strange writers like Bernhard, who refused to toe the line. Perhaps, as he maintained, everything that is said really is a quotation. But then nobody sounds quite like Bernhard." Nation

Walking

In Bernhard, T. Three novellas

Wittgenstein's nephew; a friendship; translated from the German by David McLintock. Knopf 1989 99p o.p.

ISBN 0-394-56376-X LC 88-45317

Original German edition, 1982

This novel "documents the author's friendship with Paul Wittgenstein, nephew to Ludwig and a philosopher in his own right. The novel is part autobiography and part retrospective recreation of the eccentric Paul's life." Libr J

"The narrator muses on genius, sickness, madness, and death in the world and wonders why Wittgenstein succumbs while he survives. The translation is excellent." Choice

Bernhard, Thomas, 1931-1989—*Continued*

Woodcutters; translated from the German by David McLintock. Knopf 1987 {i.e. 1988} 181p o.p.

ISBN 0-394-55152-4 LC 87-45123

Original German edition, 1984

A "tour de force in which the narrator, during the course of a Viennese dinner party, relives nonstop 20 years of his life. As he whines about the bourgeois rituals he is forced to observe at his hosts' table, he also exposes the past. The dark revelations in the story revolve around the recent suicide of a mutual friend and how this woman's death has affected the people at the dinner party. The world of the artist also comes alive in the book as the narrator/writer discourses wittily and ruthlessly on the multiple forms of aesthetic hypocrisy on display around the table." Booklist

"Mr. Bernhard's portrait of a society in dissolution has a Scandinavian darkness reminiscent of Ibsen and Strindberg, but it is filtered through a minimalist prose of obsessive repetition and ever so slight modulations." N Y Times Book Rev

Bernhardt, William, 1960-

Criminal intent. Ballantine Bks. 2002 358p o.p.

ISBN 0-345-44173-7 LC 2002-66500

In this thriller Ben Kincaid defends "an Episcopalian priest on a charge of homicide; the prosecution's theory is that this man of the cloth murdered an associate because she was among a group of parishioners who wanted him replaced because he permitted gay and lesbian groups to hold meetings at the church." Booklist

Cruel justice. Ballantine Bks. 1996 374p o.p.

LC 95-14697

"Tulsa defense lawyer Ben Kincaid finds himself with a hopeless case. His client is a mentally challenged, confessed killer. Moreover, there's a serial killer on the loose in the city, Ben's sister hands him a baby and disappears, and his mother comes to town. Ben and his helpers scramble against the clock to develop a defense for his client." Libr J

"Twists and turns and several subplots only add to the deliciousness of the complicated story line as Kincaid unearths connections between Tulsa's upper crust and the city's drug-dealing underworld. . . . Wonderfully diverting reading." Booklist

Dark justice. Ballantine Pub. Group 1999 389p o.p.

ISBN 0-345-40738-5 LC 98-28182

On a book-signing tour in Washington State attorney Ben Kincaid "inadvertently gets involved in a group called Green Rage, a conservationist organization wrestling with the local logging industry in a life-or-death struggle. One of the members of the group has been charged with a horrible murder—and who is the alleged perp? None other than [a] man Ben defended six years ago. To defend him again, Ben has to go up against prosecutor Granville 'Granny' Adams, who, despite her moniker, is attractive and tough as nails. She is bound and determined to win this case. In the meantime, subplots swirl and crash around Ben's feet, but these only serve to enrich the entertainment value of this wonderfully riveting read." Booklist

Final round. Ballantine Bks. 2002 246p o.p.

ISBN 0-345-44962-2 LC 2001-43389

"Conner Cross, long on promise and short on seriousness, barely makes the cut to compete in the notoriously stuffy Augusta National tournament. His boyhood friend John, a superior golfer, has helped him get this far, so when he finds John's body in a sand trap, he takes it personally—especially since Conner's nine iron was the murder weapon, making him the prime suspect." Libr J

(ed) Legal briefs. See Legal briefs

Murder one. Ballantine Bks. 2001 319p il o.p.

ISBN 0-345-42814-5

"Beloved veteran Tulsa police sergeant Joe McNaughton has been murdered in a particularly sadistic manner and put on public display. The suspect is 19-year-old stripper Keri Dalcanton, who had been having an affair with the married cop. Underpaid, underappreciated Ben Kincaid, a champion of underdogs, gets Keri off on a technicality, which triggers a police vendetta. . . . This fast-paced thriller pitting cops against lawyers and courts has enough surprising plot twists to maintain suspense to the very end." Booklist

Silent justice. Ballantine Bks. 2000 391p o.p.

ISBN 0-345-42812-9 LC 99-53224

In this legal thriller Tulsa attorney Ben Kincaid represents a "group of suburban families whose children have died of leukemia, apparently from drinking well water polluted by toxic waste from the greedy Blaylock Industrial Machinery Corporation. Blaylock is predictably represented by an unscrupulous, high-powered attorney who knows all about his client's culpability, but chooses to rely on his personal relationship with a corrupt judge to derail justice. . . .The counterplot involves an intrepid serial killer who is systematically torturing and murdering people who serve many different functions at the Blaylock plant." Publ Wkly

Bernhardt "keeps his readers coming back for more while also enlightening them about the relationship between big business and the legal system." Libr J

Bernstein, Michael André

Conspirators. Farrar, Straus, and Giroux 2004 506p $25

ISBN 0-374-23754-9 LC 2003-12713

"Bernstein's first novel takes place just before the First World War, on the eastern frontier of the Austro-Hungarian Empire. Economic hardship and antiSemitism have provoked unrest in the Jewish population, and Count-Governor Wiladowski, terrified of assassination, hires Jakob Tausk, an ex-rabbinical student, as a spy to protect him. Unbeknownst to him, Tausk is approached by a wealthy Jewish financier who has discovered that his only son is conspiring against the regime, and who worries about the radical influence of a mysterious rabbi with Messianic leanings. It's perhaps inevitable that an epic conceived in such grandly old-fashioned terms contains some characters and scenes that seem well worn. But, as events rush toward a bloody resolution, Bernstein maintains firm control of his plot, and painstakingly recreates the historical landscape in which an often reluctant Tausk undertakes his counterrevolutionary mission." New Yorker

Berry, Wendell, 1934-

Fidelity; five stories. Pantheon Bks. 1992 201p o.p.

LC 92-7139

Contents: Pray without ceasing; A jonquil for Mary Penn; Making it home; Fidelity; Are you all right?

"In these five interrelated stories, Berry focuses once again on the fictional town of Port William and on characters like Andrew Catlett, the central figure of his novel *The Remembering*. . . . Berry's tales are usually engaging and display a quiet but powerful dignity." Libr J

Jayber Crow; a novel. Counterpoint 2000 363p o.p.

ISBN 1-58243-029-2 LC 00-35889

"Orphaned at 4 by the flu epidemic of 1918, and again at 10, when age claims the elderly relatives who took him in, Jonah 'Jayber' Crow finds a valued place as a humble barber in a Kentucky river township. He finds love, too, though he never speaks of it." Booklist

"The richly portrayed community unfolds delicately and surely, with the human dramas of its inhabitants revealed from Jayber's perspective. A moving, lyrical work on a small canvas." Libr J

That distant land; the collected stories of Wendell Berry. Shoemaker & Hoard 2004 440p $26

ISBN 1-593-76027-2 LC 2003-25213

Contents: The hurt man; Don't send a boy to do a man's work; A consent; Pray without ceasing; Watch with me; A half-pint of Old Darling; The lost bet; Thicker than liquor; Nearly to the fair; The solemn boy; A jonquil for Mary Penn; Turn back the bed; Making it home; Where did they go?; The discovery of Kentucky; It wasn't me; The boundary; That distant land; A friend of mine; The wild birds; Are you all right?; Fidelity; The inheritors

"Set in a small Kentucky farming village, this collection of Berry's Port William stories illuminates the evolution of rural American life over the course of the 20th century. In 23 stories, Berry chronicles Port William from the 1880s to the 1980s, evoking the connectedness of the small town's denizens to each other and to the land." Publ Wkly

Best American mystery stories [date]; Otto Penzler, series editor. Houghton Mifflin

ISSN 1094-8384

Annual. First published 1997. Editors vary

An annual volume of mystery stories culled from a variety of magazines, collections, and anthologies. Loren D. Estleman, Lawrence Block, Barbara D'Amato, Joyce Carol Oates, Bill Pronzini, and Hannah Tinti are among the authors represented

The **Best** American mystery stories of the century; Tony Hillerman, editor; Otto Penzler, series editor; with an introduction by Tony Hillerman. Houghton Mifflin 2000 813p $28

ISBN 0-618-01267-2

"Dating from 1904 to the present, these stories provide a rough chronology of 20th-century crime fiction. . . . All the great writers of the genre are here—Raymond Chandler, Ellery Queen, Sue Grafton, etc.—but so are writers not normally associated with crime fiction, e.g., Flannery O'Connor, John Steinbeck, and Harlan Ellison." Libr J

"This anthology is a cornerstone volume for any mystery library." Publ Wkly

The **Best** American short stories; selected from U.S. and Canadian magazines. Houghton Mifflin

ISSN 0067-6233

This annual series began in 1915 under the editorship of Edward J. O'Brien with title: Best short stories. Editors vary

An annual anthology of stories by American and Canadian writers culled from a variety of magazines. Authors represented include: Raymond Carver, Alice Munro, Tobias Wolff, John Updike, Rick Bass, and Jamaica Kincaid

The **Best** American short stories of the eighties; selected and with an introduction by Shannon Ravenel. Houghton Mifflin 1990 393p o.p.

LC 90-30071

Contents: The old forest, by P. Taylor; The emerald, by D. Barthelme; The shawl, by C. Ozick; A working day, by R. Coover; Cathedral, by R. Carver; Exchange value, by C. Johnson; Deaths of distant friends, by J. Updike; Sur, by U. K. Le Guin; Nairobi, by J. C. Oates; In the red room, by P. Bowles; Sarah Cole: a type of love story, by R. Banks; Fellow-creatures, by W. Morris; Gryphon, by C. Baxter; Health, by J. Williams; The way we live now, by S. Sontag; The things they carried, by T. O'Brien; Dédé, by M. Gallant; Helping, by R. Stone; The management of grief, by B. Mukherjee; Meneseteung, by A. Munro

The **Best** from Fantasy & Science Fiction; 1st-20th, 22nd-24th series. Doubleday 1952-1982 23v o.p.

24th series published by Scribner. No volume bearing 21st series designation published; Special 25th anniversary volume published instead

Collection culled from a journal, founded in 1949, that "continues to publish an unusual number of first stories and award winners, to discover new, literary writers, to maintain a circulation of about half to two-thirds that of the most popular magazines, and to remain the most consistently reliable magazine in the field." New Ency of Sci Fic

The **Best** from Fantasy & Science Fiction: a 40th anniversary anthology; edited by Edward L. Ferman. St. Martin's Press 1989 376p o.p.

LC 89-215473

Contents: The cat hotel, by F. Leiber; Slow birds, by I. Watson; Judgment call, by J. Kessel; The aliens who knew, I mean, everything, by G. A. Effinger; The God machine, by D. Knight; Understanding human behavior, by T. M. Disch; A rarebit of magic, by J. Morressy; In

The Best from Fantasy & Science Fiction: a 40th anniversary anthology—*Continued*
midst of life, by J. Tiptree; Surviving, by J. Moffett; Cage 37, by W. Wightman; While you're up, by A. Davidson; Eidolons, by H. Ellison; Face value, by K. J. Fowler; Buffalo gals, won't you come out tonight, by U. K. Le Guin; The boy who plaited manes, by N. Springer; Out of all them bright stars, by N. Kress; Salvador, by L. Shepard; State of the art, by R. C. Wilson; Black air, by K. S. Robinson; Uncle Tuggs, by M. Shea

The **Best** from Fantasy & Science Fiction: a 45th anniversary anthology; edited by Kristine Kathryn Rusch and Edward L. Ferman. St Martin's Press 1994 350p o.p.
LC 94-20632

Contents: Kirinyaga, by M. Resnick; Touched, by D. Bailey; Mom's little friends, by R. Vukcevich; Cast on a distant shore, by R. Garcia y Robertson; Graves, by J. Haldeman; The dark, by K. J. Fowler; Willie, by M. E. Robins; The last feast of Harlequin, by T. Ligotti; Coffins, by R. Reed; The resurrection of Alonso Quijana, by M. Donnelly; Steel dogs, by R. Aldridge; Abe Lincoln in McDonald's, by J. Morrow; On death and the deuce, by R. Bowes; The honeycrafters, by C. I. Gilman; Ma qui, by A. Brennert; Next, by T. Bisson; The friendship light, by G. Wolfe; Susan, by H. Ellison; Guide dog, by M. Conner

The **Best** from fantasy & science fiction: the fiftieth anniversary anthology; edited by Edward L. Ferman and Gordon Van Gelder. Doherty Assocs. 1999 381p $24.95
ISBN 0-312-86973-8 LC 99-40560

"A TOR book"
"This anthology includes 22 stories published . . . between 1993 and 1998. . . . Their authors include such luminaries as Ursula Le Guin, Gene Wolfe, and Ray Bradbury, and the distinguished if less conspicuous likes of Paul Di Filippo, Terry Bisson, and Esther Friesner." Booklist

The **Best** from Fantasy and Science Fiction: a special 25th anniversary anthology; edited by Edward L. Ferman. Doubleday 1974 326p o.p.

"Doubleday science fiction"
Stories included are: When you care, when you love, by T. Sturgeon; To the Chicago abyss, by R. Bradbury; The key, by I. Asimov; Ship of shadows, by F. Leiber; The Queen of Air and Darkness, by P. Anderson; Midsummer century, by J. Blish

The **Best** horror from Fantasy tales; edited by Stephen Jones and David Sutton. Carroll & Graf Pubs. 1990 264p il o.p.
LC 89-78358

Contents: The forbidden, by C. Barker; Dreams may come, by H. W. Munn; The dark country, by D. Etchison; Dead to the world, by A. Ashley; The generation waltz, by C. L. Grant; Don't open that door, by F. Garfield; The frolic, by T. Ligotti; The sorcerer's jewel, by R. Bloch; The strange years, by B. Lumley; Red, by R. C. Matheson; Ever the faith endures, by M. W. Wellman; Extension 201, by C. Simsa; The last wolf, by K. E. Wagner; Tongue in cheek, by M. Grace; In the X-ray, by F. Leiber; The bad people, by S. R. Tem; A place of no return, by H. B. Cave; The terminus, by K. Newman; The green man, by K. Jones; The voice of the beach, by R. Campbell

The **Best** horror stories from the Magazine of fantasy and science fiction; edited by Edward L. Ferman and Anne Jordan. St. Martin's Press 1988 403p $22.95; pa $14.95
ISBN 0-312-01894-0; 0-312-01736-7 (pa)
LC 88-1987

Among the authors represented are "Brian W. Aldiss, Edgar Pangborn, Ron Goulart, Lisa Tuttle, Pamela Sargent . . . Manly Wade Wellman, Robert Bloch, Richard Matheson, Charles Beaumont . . . Robert Aickman and Charles L. Grant." Booklist

The **Best** of Sisters in crime; edited by Marilyn Wallace. Berkley Prime Crime 1997 319p o.p.
ISBN 0-425-16060-2 LC 97-14219

Contents: Afraid all the time, by N. Pickard; All the lonely people, by M. Muller; Blood types, by J. Smith; Hog heaven, by G. Roberts; The celestial buffet, by S. Dunlap; Too much to bare, by J. Hess; A poison that leaves no trace, by S. Grafton; The evidence exposed, by E. George; Upstaging murder, by C. G. Hart; Voices in the coalbin, M. H. Clark; The high cost of living, by D. Cannell; Say you're sorry, by S. Shankman; A tale of two pretties, by M. Wallace; The maltese cat, by S. Paretsky; Nine sons, by W. Hornsby; Lieutenant Harald and the impossible gun, by M. Maron; A predatory woman, by S. McCrumb; Life, for short, by C. Wheat; Extenuating circumstances, by J. C. Oates; One hit wonder, by G. Kraft; Cold turkey, by D. M. Davidson

Best of the Best American short stories, 1915-1950; edited by Martha Foley. Houghton Mifflin 1952 369p o.p.

Contents: How the Devil came down Division Street, by N. Algren; I'm a fool, by S. Anderson; The blue sash, by W. Beck; Nothing ever breaks except the heart, by K. Boyle; Horse thief, by E. Caldwell; Sex education, by D. Canfield; The enormous radio, by J. Cheever; The wind and the snow of winter, by W. V. Clark; Boys will be boys, by I. S. Cobb; Christ in concrete, by P. Di Donato; Hand upon the waters, by W. Faulkner; My old man, by E. Hemingway; The peach stone, by P. Horgan; Haircut, by R. Lardner; Man on a road, by A. Maltz; Prince of darkness, by J. F. Powers; Resurrection of a life, by W. Saroyan; Search through the streets of the city, by I. Shaw; The interior castle, by J. Stafford; How beautiful with shoes, by W. D. Steele; The women on the wall, by

Best of the Best American short stories, 1915-1950—*Continued*

W. Stegner; Dawn of remembered spring, by J. Stuart; A wife of Nashville, by P. Taylor; The catbird seat, by J. Thurber; A curtain of green, by E. Welty

The **Best** of the Nebulas; edited by Ben Bova. Doherty Assocs. 1989 593p o.p.

LC 88-38541

"A TOR book"

This volume includes the following novellas: He who shapes, by R. Zelazny; Behold the man, by M. Moorcock; Dragonrider, by A. McCaffrey; A boy and his dog, by H. Ellison; Houston, Houston, do you read? by J. Tiptree; The persistence of vision, by J. Varley. Novelettes included are: The doors of his face, the lamps of his mouth, by R. Zelazny; Gonna roll the bones, by F. Lieber; Time considered as a helix of semi-precious stones, by S. R. Delany; Slow sculpture, by T. Sturgeon; Of mist, and grass, and sand, by V. N. McIntyre; and Sandkings, by G. R. R. Martin. Short stories included are: "Repent, Harlequin!" said the Ticktockman, by H. Ellison; Aye, and Gomorrah . . . by S. R. Delany; Passengers, by R. Silverberg; When it changed, by J. Russ; Love is the plan the plan is death, by J. Tiptree; The day before the revolution, by U. K. Le Guin; Catch that zeppelin! by F. Leiber; The grotto of the dancing deer, by C. D. Simak; and Jeffty is five, by H. Ellison

Betts, Doris, 1932-

Souls raised from the dead; a novel. Knopf 1994 339p o.p.

ISBN 0-679-42621-3 LC 93-30900

"Still clearing the emotional debris left after his selfish, narcissistic wife, Christine, decamped three years earlier, North Carolina state trooper Frank Thompson is lovingly raising their 12-year-old daughter, Mary Grace. Mary is a typical adolescent, masking her insecurities with a nonchalant air. When she becomes obsessed with horses, Frank begins a romance with her young riding instructor, but the balance of all their lives goes askew when Mary develops kidney disease." Publ Wkly

"Mary's life and death are superbly and unsentimentally accomplished. . . . Yet none of this should sound grim, only appropriately sad, because Ms. Betts seems to be possessed of high spirits and a generous wisdom. And that is what buoys up her characters and makes a lot of the proceedings very funny even as her people struggle with their anger and bewilderment." N Y Times Book Rev

Beyle, Marie Henri *See* Stendhal, 1783-1842

Bezmozgis, David

Natasha and other stories; David Bezmozgis. 1st ed. Farrar, Straus and Giroux 2004 147p $18

ISBN 0-374-28141-6 LC 2003-21582

Contents: Tapka; Roman Berman, massage therapist; The second strongest man; An animal to the memory; Natasha; Choynski

"Bezmozgis's stunning debut collection centers on the Berman family, Latvian Jews who have immigrated to Toronto to escape stagnant Brezhnev-era Soviet life. . . . Taken alone, these stories are charming and pitch-perfect; together, they add up to something like life itself: funny, heartbreaking, terrible, true." Libr J

Bialosky, Jill

House under snow. Harcourt 2002 242p $24

ISBN 0-15-100685-7 LC 2001-7435

This "is the story of a mother with three young daughters, devastated by the accidental death of her husband and the toll it takes on all their lives. Hardest hit is the mother, insecure but sexually enticing Lilly Crane, whose dreamy self-regard quickly turns rancid. She spends hours primping for new boyfriends, enters into a hasty and doomed second marriage and gradually, as her romantic disaters accumulate, withdraws into sleep and forgetfulness. It is a terrifying portrait, drawn with a fierce mix of love, regret and open-eyed candor." Publ Wkly

Bierce, Ambrose, 1842-1914?

The complete short stories of Ambrose Bierce; compiled with commentary by Ernest Jerome Hopkins. Doubleday 1970 496p o.p.

Contents: Haita the shepherd; The secret of Macarger's Gulch; The eyes of the panther; The stranger; An inhabitant of Carcosa; The applicant; The death of Halpin Frayser; A watcher by the dead; The man and the snake; John Mortonson's funeral; Moxon's master; The damned thing; The realm of the unreal; A fruitless assignment; A vine on a house; The haunted valley; One of twins; Present at a hanging; A wireless message; The moonlit road; An arrest; A jug of sirup; The Isle of Pines; At old Man Eckert's; The Spook House; The middle toe of the right foot; The thing at Nolan; The difficulty of crossing a field; An unfinished race; Charles Ashmore's trial; Staley Fleming's hallucination; The night-doings at "Deadmans"; A baby tramp; A psychological shipwreck; A cold greeting; Beyond the wall; John Bartine's watch; The man out of the nose; An adventure at Brownville; The suitable surroundings; The boarded window; A lady from Redhorse; The famous Gilson bequest; A holy terror; A diagnosis of death; One of the missing; A baffled ambuscade; The affair at Coulter's Notch; A son of the gods; One kind of officer; A tough tussle; An occurrence at Owl Creek Bridge; Chickamauga; The coup de grâce; One officer, one man; The story of a conscience; Parker Adderson, philosopher; An affair of outposts; Jupiter Doke; Brigadier-General; A horseman in the sky; The mockingbird; George Thurston; Killed at Resaca; Three and one are one; Two military executions; The Major's tale; A resumed identity; A man with two lives; The other lodgers; A bivouac of the dead; An imperfect conflagration; A bottomless grave; The City of the Gone Away; Curried cow; A revolt of the Gods; Oil of dog; The widower Turnmore; The baptism of Dobsho; The race at Left Bower; The failure of Hope & Wandel; A providential intimation; Mr. Swiddler's flip-flap; The little story; My favorite murder; The hypnotist; Mr. Masthead, journalist; Why I am not editing "The Stinger"; Corrupting the press; "The bubble reputation"; A shipwreckollection; The captain of the "Camel"; The man overboard; A cargo of cat

Biguenet, John

Oyster. Ecco Press 2002 291p $23.95
ISBN 0-06-019836-2 LC 2001-50170

This "novel, set in Louisiana in 1957, opens with a set of shocking murders. The Petitjeans and the Bruneaus have always been at odds, competitors in the cutthroat oyster trade. To stay in business, Felix Petitjean has borrowed money from Horse Bruneau, putting both his house and boat on the line. When Felix is unable to pay back his debt, Horse suggests an alternative: that Felix give Horse his daughter, Therese, in marriage." Booklist

"Biguenet's gritty, violent and sometimes melodramatic first novel . . . catches the scents and sounds of the bayou, and his characters bristle with a dark intensity." N Y Times Book Rev

Binchy, Maeve

Circle of friends. Delacorte Press 1991 c1990 565p o.p.
LC 90-3944

First published 1990 in the United Kingdom

The author "explores the intertwining bonds of three women as they travel from a small Irish village to university life in Dublin." Libr J

"There is nothing fancy about 'Circle of Friends.' There is no torrid sex, no profound philosophy. There are no stunning metaphors. There is just a wonderfully absorbing story about people worth caring about. And that is a rare pleasure." N Y Times Book Rev

The copper beech. Delacorte Press 1992 345p o.p.
LC 92-18601

"The eponymous copper beech is a huge tree that shades the tiny schoolhouse in the [Irish] village of Shancarrig. For generations, graduating pupils have carved their initials on the massive trunk, and the book examines what has become of some of them. Though each of the 10 chapters offers the perspective of a single character, Binchy adroitly indicates the ways in which their lives intersect. . . . The result is a charming and compelling series of interlocking stories about ordinary people who are given dimension through Binchy's empathetic insight. While this book is more fragmentary in structure than some of her previous novels, it should leave Binchy's fans wholly satisfied." Publ Wkly

Dublin 4
In Binchy, M. The lilac bus: stories p165-327

Echoes. Viking 1986 c1985 477p o.p.
LC 85-40571

First published 1985 in the United Kingdom

"Clare O'Brien, the brilliant, ambitious daughter of an impoverished shopkeeper, attempts to transcend the rigid social strictures that govern her small Irish seaside community by earning a college degree and marrying David Power, the well-to-do son of the local doctor. Unfortunately, the class-conscious residents of Castlebay make it virtually impossible for David and Clare to bridge peacefully the wide cultural gulf that separates them." Booklist

"Sharply drawn, memorable characters and a convincing picture of a small Irish community bring freshness and zest to a familiar tale." Publ Wkly

Evening class. Delacorte Press 1997 420p o.p.
ISBN 0-385-31807-3 LC 96-34069

In this novel a group of working-class Dubliners enroll in an "evening class in Italian at the local school. Each has a particular reason for this farfetched idea—and most of them have to do with love. But the real inspiration comes from Aidan Dunne, a Latin teacher who organized the class after failing to become head of the school, and Nora O'Donoghue, known as Signora, a quiet Irishwoman who has just returned home after 26 years in Sicily. The action is seen from the viewpoints of eight characters and, after some ups and downs, each of their stories, like the book as a whole, has a satisfyingly happy ending." N Y Times Book Rev

Firefly summer. Delacorte Press 1988 601p o.p.
LC 88-5412

"When American millionaire Patrick O'Neill returns to his ancestral home in Ireland, his intent is to bring prosperity to Montfern in the form of a luxury hotel built from the ruins of an old estate. Instead, the villagers see their lifestyles irrevocably changed and the town's inner harmonies disrupted in the four years it takes to build O'Neill's hotel." Libr J

"The careful examination of life and culture in a small Irish town during the 1960s will appeal to many readers." Booklist

The glass lake. Delacorte Press 1995 584p o.p.
ISBN 0-385-31354-3 LC 94-36104

First published 1994 in the United Kingdom

This novel "focuses on the inhabitants of a small town in Ireland. Helen, wife and mother of the McMahon household, is presumed to have drowned in a nearby lake. Actually, she shook off her dull, staid life and fled to London with her lover. Successful at business, she yearns for some communication with her now teenaged daughter, Kit. She begins a casual correspondence with Kit under the guise of being an old friend of her mother." Libr J

"If some aspects of the plot are contrived and the narrative overtold, the richness of Binchy's characters makes these drawbacks easy to forgive. A weeper of an ending brings this compelling saga to an unforgettable climax." Publ Wkly

Light a penny candle. Viking 1983 c1982 542p o.p.
LC 82-19132

First published 1982 in the United Kingdom

"Evacuated from London during the Blitz, 10-year-old Elizabeth White is sent to live with her mother's former schoolmate in Ireland. Elizabeth and Aisling, the 10-year-old O'Connor daughter, become close friends immediately; a friendship that lasts. In the end, as young widows, they realize that their friendship has been the sustaining force in their lives and will continue to strengthen them for whatever the future may hold." SLJ

The maturing of the two women "often carried out in each other's company, make[s] touching reading for those who enjoy expansive but not complex plots in which one can linger for many hours of entertainment. Binchy's characters are *not* constructed with hidden dimensions, yet they are easy to identify with and care about." Booklist

The lilac bus
In Binchy, M. The lilac bus: stories p1-163

Binchy, Maeve—*Continued*

The lilac bus: stories. Delacorte Press 1991 327p o.p.
LC 91-13765

This volume contains two collections: The lilac bus and Dublin 4, first published in Ireland in 1984 and 1982 respectively

Contents: The lilac bus: Nancy; Dee; Mikey; Judy; Kev; Rupert; Celia; Tom

Dublin 4: Dinner in Donnybrook; Flat in Ringsend; Decision in Belfield; Murmurs in Montrose

"'The Lilac Bus' consists of eight connected stories, each one a revealing portrait of a Dublin worker who goes home to the outlying town of Rathdoon each weekend in Tom Fitzgerald's minibus. . . . The more fully realized stories in *Dublin 4* have only their Dublin setting in common. . . . While not as completely satisfying as Binchy novels . . . this is an absorbing, entertaining read with characters to care about." Libr J

Quentins. Dutton 2002 359p $25.95
ISBN 0-525-94682-9 LC 2002-73302

"The novel primarily chronicles Ella Brady and her involvement with Dublin's finest restaurant, Quentins. Ella wants to make a documentary film about Quentins that will capture the dramas revolving around restaurant life. The film's financial backer, Derry King, becomes Ella's suitor after she has a terrible experience with a married, thieving investment advisor." Libr J

Fans of "Binchy will be grateful that the basic formula is still intact—decent people pulling through hard times—and that some favorite characters from previous novels reappear: Cathy Scarlet from Scarlet Feather, Nora from Evening Class, Ria from Tara Road and others." Publ Wkly

The return journey. Delacorte Press 1998 214p o.p.
ISBN 0-385-31506-6 LC 97-52624

Contents: The return journey; The wrong suitcase; Miss Vogel's vacation; The home sitter; Package tour; The apprenticeship; The business trip; The crossing; The women in hats; Excitement; Holiday weather; Victor and St. Valentine; Cross lines; A holiday with your father

Most of the stories in this collection "feature characters who are indeed on a journey somewhere, though the journey isn't just a matter of getting from one place to another." Libr J

Scarlet Feather. Dutton 2001 538p $25.95
ISBN 0-525-94593-8 LC 00-59624

"Set in contemporary Ireland over a period of one year . . . [this] tale focuses on Cathy Scarlet and Tom Feather, cooking school chums who achieve their dream of opening a posh catering business, Scarlet Feather, in Dublin. Professionally, they're off to a good start; personally, their lives are falling apart." Publ Wkly

The novel culminates in the "much-anticipated wedding of Cathy's sister, who returns, American in-laws in tow, in search of an 'authentic' Irish wedding. Interwoven into the dialogue-driven plot are some far from traditional themes, ranging from homelessness to women's right to abortion. Yet despite the contemporary backdrop, traditional themes prevail; Binchy neatly demonstrates that love, not money, is ultimately what binds a family." N Y Times Book Rev

Silver wedding. Delacorte Press 1989 306p o.p.
LC 89-1276

The author "uses the story-within-a-story device to introduce the long-absent, oddball friends and relatives who will reunite at Deirdre and Desmond Doyle's silver anniversary in the couple's suburban London home. Among these are the Doyles' three grown children—a failed Irish nun, the much-put-upon eldest daughter, and the prodigal sheepherder son—the snooty yet tragically unmarried maid of honor, and the corporately well-positioned best man (who happens to be both Desmond's friend and nemesis). As celebratory preparations begin, the skeletons in this dysfunctional network are unearthed." Booklist

"An elegant literary construction, a comedy of manners as well as a soap opera. Each chapter has its own story, yet each story connects with all the others to produce a satisfying whole. Add to this a sly, understated tone and you have a book that's an effortless pleasure to read." NY Times Book Rev

Tara Road. Delacorte Press 1999 656p o.p.
ISBN 0-385-33395-1 LC 98-33768

"Dubliner Ria Lynch, cheerily domestic wife and mother, suffers from a series of betrayals dealt by her charming husband. Meanwhile, in Connecticut, Marilyn Vine's grief for her dead son transforms her into a cold, unloving person. These two strangers seize an opportunity to swap homes for a summer, each crossing an ocean to look for a way to begin again. As the two very different women inherit each other's neighbors, families, and lifestyles, they discover their strengths and their futures." Libr J

"The pleasures Binchy offers readers are her lively depiction of social connections, feuds and friendships; secrets, lies, alliances, in short, the thicket of Irish everyday life." Publ Wkly

This year it will be different and other stories; a Christmas treasury. Delacorte Press 1996 210p o.p.
ISBN 0-385-31503-1 LC 96-5386

Includes the following stories: The first step of Christmas; The ten snaps of Christmas; Miss Martin's wish; The hard core; Christmas timing; The civilized Christmas; Pulling together; A hundred milligrams; The Christmas baramundi; This year it will be different; Season of fuss; "A typical Irish Christmas . . ."; Traveling hopefully; What is happiness?; The best inn in town

Bing, Stanley

You look nice today; a novel. Bloomsbury Press 2003 291p $24.95
ISBN 1-58234-280-6 LC 2003-60092

This "novel concerns one Robert (Harb) Harbert, who seems too human to last at the Global Fiduciary Trust Company. . . . In fact, Harb's undoing is his compassion for his secretary, an apparently vulnerable creature named CarolAnne. She repays his cloying kindnesses (generous raises, a car, an apartment) with a harassment suit." New Yorker

"The density of detail makes for slow going early in the novel, but the account of the civil trial that follows is a riveting and often hilarious account of CaroleAnne's fabrications and the corporate legal response." Publ Wkly

Bird, Sarah

The Yokota Officers Club; a novel. Knopf 2001 367p o.p.

ISBN 0-375-41214-X LC 2001-89763

Set in the late 1960s, this novel "is narrated by 18-year-old Bernie, the eldest of six children in the peripatetic Root family. After her freshman year in college, Bernie joins her nomadic kin at their current home, an Okinawan air force base. They have changed: her younger sister, Kit, is out of control and 'now being played by Lolita'; her once glamorous mother, Moe, is overweight and depressed; her father, who was a heroic and swaggering fighter pilot, has become a distant, self-loathing 'ground pounder.' And Bernie can't stop thinking of Fumiko, the family's former maidservant, whom no one is allowed to mention." Publ Wkly

The author "nails the voice of Bernie in a delicate balance of confused, shy child vs. the bright emerging woman she has become. Bird's masterly use of the tricky technique of children revealing adult subtleties is breathtaking." Libr J

Birdwell, Cleo *See* DeLillo, Don

Birmingham, Stephen

The Auerbach will. Little, Brown 1983 430p o.p.

LC 83-9413

"Saga of a mail-order-house family dynasty. The central character is Essie, a Lower East Side Jewish immigrant, who falls in love with Jake Auerbach, the 'renegade' son in a prominent New York mercantile family. Sent off to Chicago after a disapproved-of marriage, Jake founds the nation's first mail-order business under two Christian names (Sears & Roebuck come to mind from beginning to end, though without substantiation). The business flourishes; Jake and Essie—she now a society figure—are restored to familiar respectability but suffer the disenchantments of fading love, mutual infidelities, unhappy children, blackmail, and hollow glory." Booklist

"Birmingham's deft handling of the fabric of family life and shifting patterns of deception, betrayal and tragedy produces a dramatic narrative. Essie is a wonderfully sympathetic figure, and Birmingham moves her gracefully through her bitter-sweet years from determined young girl to passionate woman to sophisticated grande dame." Publ Wkly

Carriage trade. Bantam Bks. 1993 469p o.p.

LC 92-39567

This "novel tells the tale of one Silas Tarkington, founder of an exclusive Manhattan department store. . . . Tarkington is actually Solomon Tarcher, a Jew from the Lower East Side who once served time for larceny. While retailing was in his blood—Tarkington's grandmother and mother created a successful millinery business back when women wore hats—his brilliant and calculating career was engineered by a nasty shyster named Moe Minskoff. We learn all the dirty secrets of Tarkington's messy life in flashbacks as his spunky daughter, fiesty mother, stunning and resilient wife, and current mistress try to fathom the chaos of the store's financial straits after Tarkington's suspicious death. . . . Birmingham's casting of women as the heroes in this mercantile thriller cum murder mystery is a nice touch." Booklist

The LeBaron secret. Little, Brown 1986 403p o.p.

LC 85-18208

"From her white mansion overlooking San Francisco's Golden Gate Bridge, the widowed Sari LeBaron rules her family-owned wine company, as well as her three grown children, with the assurance of a despot. But in an age of corporate takeovers her matriarchal tenure is far from secure, and Sari's son Eric soon hatches a plot with his oil-rich father-in-law and with his aunt Joanna LeBaron, a New York advertising executive affectionately known as the 'Medea of Medialand,' to wrest away control of the company." N Y Times Book Rev

"The author so skillfully weaves together the many strands of this trite tale that readers will be stunned by the novel's tragic conclusion. Good popular entertainment for the family-saga set." Booklist

Bissell, Tom

God lives in St. Petersburg; and other stories. Pantheon Books 2005 212p $20

ISBN 0-375-42264-1 LC 2004-52232

Contents: Death defier; Aral; Expensive trips to nowhere; The ambassador's son; God lives in St. Petersburg; Animals in our lives

The author "has a predilection for school-of-Eggers deadpan irony and pop culture references, but if his knowingness sometimes grates, his witticisms are rarely gratuitous; the conflation of American consumerism with the barrenness of the Central Asian landscape gives these stories a striking immediacy. . . . Bissell never flinches as he looks straight into the starved hearts of his characters. In these chilling stories of a region ravaged by war, exile and neglect, desperation drives men and women to do the otherwise unthinkable, and no one is quite forgiven for their transgressions." Publ Wkly

Black, Cara

Murder in the Sentier. Soho Press 2002 322p $24

ISBN 1-56947-278-5 LC 2002-17566

In this mystery, sleuth Aimee Leduc scours Paris' Second Arrondissement "in pursuit of a tip to the whereabouts of her American mother, a political fugitive since the early 1970's for her anarchist activities with a group very much like the Baader-Meinhof gang. The plot that has Aimee pounding the cobblestones of this quaint quarter is a circular affair that entails much chasing after aging urban guerrillas who tend to be incoherent, hostile or dead when found. . . . But if it lacks design, the story provides a street map to this idiosyncratic area." N Y Times Book Rev

Black, Mansell, 1920-1995

For works written by this author under other names see Hall, Adam, 1920-1995

Black, Veronica, 1935-

A vow of sanctity. St. Martin's Press 1993 192p o.p.

ISBN 0-312-09408-6 LC 93-13349

Black, Veronica, 1935-—*Continued*

Sister Joan, "loyal to her order but not exactly bowed down, spends a month-long retreat in a cave overlooking a remote Scottish loch. Despite her physical isolation and her resolve not to meddle in local affairs, she becomes involved in a six-year-old case of adultery, disappearance, and death that brings her into close contact with ancient antipapist prejudice. In this solid work, location permits vicarious experience from a traditional plot." Libr J

Blackmore, R. D. (Richard Doddridge), 1825-1900

Lorna Doone; a romance of Exmoor. o.p.

First published 1869

A romantic love-story of Exmoor and the North Devon Coast of England, telling of the outlaw Doones, the maid brought up in the midst of them, and plain John Ridd's herculean power and his service to James II during Monmouth's Rebellion

"The scenic descriptions of the lovely region befits the tale, and many local worthies have their lineaments preserved here. Though 'Lorna Doone' made little stir at the time of its appearance, it has had innumerable imitations since, and it initiated a return to . . . romanticism in historical fiction." Baker. Guide to the Best Fic

Blackmore, Richard Doddridge *See* Blackmore, R. D. (Richard Doddridge), 1825-1900

Blair, Eric *See* Orwell, George, 1903-1950

Blaisdell, Anne, 1921-

For works written by this author under other names see Shannon, Dell, 1921-

Blake, James Carlos

Handsome Harry, or, The gangster's true confessions; a novel; James Carlos Blake. 1st ed. W. Morrow 2004 304p $24.95

ISBN 0-06-055478-9 LC 2003-53991

This novel "shares the plainspoken death-row recollections of 'Handsome' Harry Pierpont, ruthless gangster and de facto leader of the Terror Gang, better known by the name of its most flamboyant member, John Dillinger." Libr J

"Taken simply as a breezy, blood-soaked tip of the fedora to simpler times, the novel cooks harder than sly narrator Pierpont does when he meets his inevitable appointment with Old Sparky after a four-month spree that left the Midwest agog. Ably squeezing the last drop of juice from a familiar outlaw narrative, Blake brings this gin-soaked era roaring back to life." Booklist

Under the skin; a novel. Morrow 2003 292p $25.95

ISBN 0-380-97751-6 LC 2002-23892

"Set in Galveston, with forays into west Texas and Mexico during Prohibition, this is the story of Jimmy Youngblood, bastard son of a Pancho Villa lieutenant, who grows up to be bodyguard and hit man for Galveston gangsters Rose and Sam Maceo. . . .A love affair with the young wife of an elderly Mexican warlord adds still other dimensions to this tough and tender story of lawlessness and retribution, exposing the human frailties of the hardest of criminals." Libr J

A world of thieves. HarperCollins Pubs. 2001 295p $25.95

ISBN 0-380-97750-8 LC 2001-24566

This novel is "set in Prohibition-era Louisiana and Texas. Sonny LaSalle, the tragic hero, is orphaned at age 18 and decides to take up with his two beloved uncles, lifelong criminals. After a bank robbery gone wrong, he lands in jail, where he accidentally kills a policeman who is the son of a very influential, very frightening man. Sonny is sentenced to 30 years at the Angola penitentiary but soon escapes with his uncles' help. They head to the oil boomtowns of west Texas, accompanied by long-suffering girlfriends and pursued by the revenge-hungry father." Booklist

"This is an entertaining novel full of outsized characters and as much humor as brutality." Publ Wkly

Blake, Michael, 1943-

Marching to Valhalla; a novel of Custer's last days. Villard Bks. 1996 288p o.p.

ISBN 0-679-44864-0 LC 96-218924

This novel is "cast in the form of a journal Custer supposedly kept during the last weeks of his life. In it, he recalls scenes from his days as a cadet at West Point, the battles he fought as the youngest federal general in the Civil War, his courtship of and marriage to Elizabeth Bacon, his first campaign against the plains Indians and his subsequent court martial, and his destruction of a Cheyenne village beside the Washita River." Libr J

"Though revisionist in its sympathy for Custer, the narrative seems rigorously authentic in its period detail, down to the flowery nature of Custer's prose." Publ Wkly

Blake, Patricia, 1927-

For works written by this author under other names see Egleton, Clive, 1927-

Blanchard, Alice

The breathtaker. Warner Bks. 2003 391p $24.95

ISBN 0-446-53139-1 LC 2003-45059

"Promise, Oklahoma, may not be much, but it is ground zero for storm chasers, an eccentric mix of meteorologists, amateur scientists, and plain-old crazies who stalk tornadoes like kids stalk ice-cream trucks. Police chief Charlie Grover is assessing the damage from a recent storm when he discovers the Pepper family. Husband, wife, and teenage daughter all killed—presumbly storm victims, but Grover suspects a serial killer among the storm chasers." Booklist

"Blanchard makes a bold move by linking her villain to tornadoes—each such powerful forces of destruction and chaos—and while it's a little far-fetched, it pays off in this dark depiction of environmental and human turmoil." Publ Wkly

Blanchard, Keith

The deed; a novel. Simon & Schuster 2003 304p $23

ISBN 0-7432-2387-X LC 2002-29435

Blanchard, Keith—*Continued*

"A missing 17th-century deed to the island of Manhattan has a young advertising executive, a petty law student and a couple of mobsters in a tailspin in Blanchard's . . . novel." Publ Wkly

"There is a winning sentimentality and a lot of fun to be found in Blanchard's urban fantasy." N Y Times Book Rev

Bland, Eleanor Taylor

See no evil; a Marti MacAlister mystery. St. Martin's Press 1998 274p o.p.

ISBN 0-312-16910-8 LC 97-39642

"Detective Marti MacAlister, of the Lincoln Prairie police department, wonders how she and her partner will find the murderer of a young woman who 'fell' to her death on the rocky shores of Lake Michigan. A homeless black man has not seen his best friend in days and wonders what has happened. And a crafty stalker wonders how best to massacre Marti, her kids, and her housemates." Libr J

"Bland tightens the suspense with realistic details and subplot twists before wrapping the narrative up in a satisfying solution." Publ Wkly

Tell no tales. St. Martin's Press 1999 264p o.p.

ISBN 0-312-20067-6 LC 98-46974

"African American police detective Marti MacAlister . . . and partner Vik juggle two murder cases and troubles at home. Marti, married at last, faces stepfamily problems, while Vik must reconcile himself to his wife's medical diagnosis." Libr J

Blasco Ibáñez, Vicente, 1867-1928

Blood and sand; a novel; translated from the Spanish by Mrs. W. A. Gillespie. Dutton 1919 356p o.p.

Original Spanish edition, 1908

This is a novel of the Spanish bull ring. No detail of the professional career of Juan Gallardo, who has risen from the lowest ranks of poverty to unprecedented heights of riches and popular favor, is spared. His vanities, his superstitions, his sufferings from fear, his daring attacks, the technique of his killings, his wounds and recoveries, and the final accident that brings his death, as well as the tortures of the beasts and the joyous delight of the populace in this national sport, are related

The four horsemen of the Apocalypse. o.p.

Original Spanish edition, 1916; first United States edition published 1918 by Dutton

"An interpretation of German and French psychology [during World War I] through the reactions of the two branches of a wealthy Argentinian family, who settle respectively in France and Germany before the war. A powerful and well-written novel, giving detailed pictures of French mobilization, the German occupation of Northern France, trench fighting, etc., and enlarging on contrasting views of humanity, liberty, culture and international relations. . . . [The] 'four horsemen' are War, Pestilence, Famine and Death." Cleveland Public Libr

Blatty, William Peter

Elsewhere

In 999: new stories of horror and suspense p561-664

The exorcist. Harper & Row 1971 340p o.p.

Set in Georgetown, "the central figure is Regan MacNeil . . . the sweet 'normal' eleven-year-old daughter of a famous actress, Chris MacNeil. . . . Overnight, Regan turns from that normal little girl into a grotesque, unrecognizable monster, possessed by a demonic force that has locked her in a life-and-death struggle. Her weird and ugly behavior baffles the best medical experts. . . . [Chris] turns to the Jesuits. Perhaps exorcism will succeed where science has failed. Father Damien Karras, who is a trained psychiatrist, is skeptical, despite his deep knowledge of Satanism and possession. That is, until the last resort is the Church ritual." Saturday Rev

"Blatty has done his homework. He discourses, a bit bookishly, on the history of possession and the relation of autosuggestion to masked guilt. . . . Blatty maintains headlong thrust, slowly increasing Regan's agony until the reader winces; no more, a part of us says, but of course we want more because Blatty handles the horror so well." Newsweek

Bleeck, Oliver *See* Thomas, Ross, 1926-1995

Blevins, Meredith

The hummingbird wizard. Forge 2003 400p $24.95

ISBN 0-7653-0769-3 LC 2003-46849

"A Tom Doherty Associates book"

"Ever since she lost her husband in a motorcycle accident, Annie Szabo has tried to steer clear of his unconventional Gypsy family—especially Mina, her disapproving mother-in-law, who also happens to be a fortune-teller, and the alcoholic, free-wheeling sister-in-law who has botched her marriage to Jerry, Annie's oldest friend. When Jerry dies under suspicious circumstances, Annie joins Mina in tracking down a murderer. . . .Blevins flavors her lively prose with frequent humor and unexpected twists." Libr J

Blevins, Winfred

Stone song; a novel of the life of Crazy Horse; {by} Win Blevins. Forge 1995 400p o.p.

LC 95-6934

"A Tom Doherty Associates book"

A "biographical novel of the Sioux leader in command at the Battle of Little Big Horn. The author . . . evokes the mystical experiences that motivated the somber Crazy Horse from early childhood, depicting incidents from his subject's adult life that include a failed romance, successful military campaigns, and his final surrender to the U.S. Army in 1877." Libr J

"A deeply thoughtful and persuasive tribute, Blevins's novel offers the compelling story of a man destined for triumph and betrayal, but ultimately for glory." Publ Wkly

Blixen, Karen, 1885-1962

For works written by this author under other names see Dinesen, Isak, 1885-1962

Block, Lawrence, 1938-

All the flowers are dying; Lawrence Block. 1st ed. Morrow 2005 288p $24.95

ISBN 0-06-019831-1 LC 2004-53643

"In a Virginia prison, a man awaits execution for the torture and murder of three young boys, a crime he denies to the very end. After the execution, one of the witnesses—the sole person who knows the truth—heads back to Manhattan to attend to unfinished business. Meanwhile, ex-cop and investigator Matthew Scudder is semiretired, content with the fact that his toughest battles are now with his own sobriety. But the killing of his wife's best friend, along with a series of seemingly random murders, leads Scudder head-on into a confrontation with a killer he ran out of town years earlier." Libr J

"Although Scudder's hunt for the killer turns into a companionable tour of colorful neighborhoods, his thoughts on the city run deep and reflect real feelings about its humanity." N Y Times Book Rev

The burglar in the closet. Random House 1978 166p o.p.

A New York dentist has set Bernie Rhodenbarr "up to rob his estranged wife, which he does. Embarrassingly, he gets interrupted and locked in a closet while the woman is stabbed to death and the boodle is stolen. In a temper, the burglar investigates, as does a corrupt policeman who wants half the take. Things are sorted out when a suitcase full of counterfeit money turns up and a couple of suspects conveniently die. Amusing and very easy to read." Libr J

The burglar in the library; a Bernie Rhodenbarr mystery. Dutton 1997 342p o.p.

ISBN 0-525-94301-3 LC 96-37537

"Panting after a copy of 'The Big Sleep' inscribed by Raymond Chandler for Dashiell Hammett ('the ultimate association copy in American crime fiction'), Bernie drags Carolyn to an inn, 'a genuine English country house' in the Berkshires, so he can relieve the unsuspecting owners of this treasure. But before he can pull the heist, the inn is snowbound, the phone lines are cut, the bridge is down and Bernie's ex-girlfriend shows up with her new husband. What next? A body in the library? Yes, and, even better, the drollest sendup of a murder-in-a-teacup mystery that you will ever hope to beg, borrow—or steal." N Y Times Book Rev

The burglar in the rye; a Bernie Rhodenbarr mystery. Dutton 1999 280p $23.95

ISBN 0-525-94500-8 LC 98-51326

Burglar/bookstore owner Rhodenbarr "has been hired by Alice Cottrell, the former teenage lover of reclusive author Gulliver Fairborn, to steal Fairborn's letters before his former literary agent Anthea Landau can auction them. Slipping into Landau's room at the Paddington Hotel, Bernie discovers the letters gone and Landau murdered. As usual, Bernie is considered a prime suspect by the police and must prove his innocence with the aid of dog washer and lesbian buddy Carolyn Kaiser." Libr J

The burglar on the prowl. William Morrow 2004 293p o.p.

ISBN 0-06-019830-3 LC 2003-55848

"After a friend asks Bernie [Rhodenbarr] to burglarize the house of a prominent plastic surgeon, in revenge for the doctor's stealing the friend's mistress, Bernie becomes entangled in a labyrinthine plot involving a serial date rapist, Latvian patriots, a linguistics professor, assorted gangsters, and a seemingly ordinary copy of Joseph Conrad's The Secret Agent." Libr J

The burglar who liked to quote Kipling. Random House 1979 196p o.p.

"Suave Manhattan cracksman Bernie Rhodenbarr, framed for murder after his latest escapade, gets help from Carolyn Kaiser, a lesbian friend and neighbor. She lets Bernie hide out in her apartment where they work undercover to solve the crime resulting from his heist of a reportedly priceless book by Kipling. J. Rudyard Whelkin has hired Bernie to steal the book from Jessie Arkwright and the thief finds that others . . . also want the volume." Publ Wkly

"Block writes with considerable wit and verve and constantly pulls the rug out from reader expectations. . . . [He] paints a crooked world where the thief is refreshingly straightforward." Booklist

The burglar who painted like Mondrian. Random House 1983 253p o.p.

LC 83-45269

Mystery revolving around Bernie Rhodenbarr's "desperate efforts to clear himself of one caper he did *not* commit. . . . While attempting to reveal how he's been framed, Bernie Rhodenbarr must conceal another crime, rescue a friend's kidnapped cat, form a liaison with a mysterious female, and juggle an increasingly number of framed and unframed paintings 'by' Mondrian. A fast-paced farce with gustsy characters and a well-drawn New York City scene." Libr J

The burglar who studied Spinoza. Random House 1980 213p o.p.

LC 80-5288

Bernie Rhodenbarr "runs a used-book store in Greenwich Village. The store loses money, but that's cool, because Bernie steals things like rare coins. He loves being a burglar. He has two partners in crime. One is a lesbian who shampoos poodles. The other is a cop who insists on a commission. The particular coin that Bernie steals, a Liberty-head 1913 V-nickel, shouldn't have been where it was in the first place. Unfortunately, there seems to have been a burglary in the house before Bernie got there, and a murder after he left." Books of the Times

The burglar who traded Ted Williams; a Bernie Rhodenbarr mystery. Dutton 1994 258p o.p.

LC 93-40191

"Rare books dealer-cum-thief Bernie Rhodenbarr decides to pull off one last job and ends up suspected of murder." Libr J

"Notwithstanding his elastic ethics and shady line of work, Bernie is incorrigibly adorable. Although he inhabits the same mean streets of Manhattan as Matt Scudder, the brooding private eye who is Mr. Block's most celebrated hero, Bernie has a whimsical sense of humor that shields him from the achy-breaky *Weltschmerz* of his hard-boiled literary sibling." N Y Times Book Rev

The collected mystery stories. Orion; distributed by Trafalgar Sq. 2000 754p $35

ISBN 0-75282-544-5

Block, Lawrence, 1938-—*Continued*

In addition to the collections Sometimes they bite (1983), Like a lamb to slaughter (1984) and Some days you get the bear (1993) this volume includes stories featuring series characters Matthew Scudder, Bernie Rhodenbarr, Chip Harrison, Martin Ehrengraf and Keller

"This omnibus collection offers an impressive testament to a modern master of crime fiction whose talent shines just as brightly in the short form as it does in the novel." Booklist

A dance at the slaughterhouse; a Matthew Scudder novel. Morrow 1991 309p o.p.

LC 91-7876

"Unlicensed New York investigator and series protagonist Matthew Scudder seeks to determine if a cable television producer raped and murdered his own wealthy wife. At the same time, Scudder hunts for a brutal man who makes video 'snuff' tapes involving teenage boys and a leather-dressed woman. The two cases merge . . . as Scudder enlists the aid of his motley assortment of interesting friends." Libr J

"The world of Lawrence Block's maverick PI Matt Scudder is a dark one. . . . The conclusion is a bloody, yet satisfying, one, with Matt teetering on the up side of the down side. Strong stuff from a real pro." Booklist

The devil knows you're dead; a Matthew Scudder novel. Morrow 1993 316p o.p.

LC 93-411

New York P.I. Matt Scudder "has a true friend in Mick Ballou, a sidekick in street urchin T.J., and a lover in former hooker Elaine. Hired by the brother of a mentally handicapped vet accused of the murder of attorney Glenn Holtzmann, Scudder finds that the victim was both less and more than he appeared to be." Booklist

"Scudder is burdened by a load of personal baggage, including romantic attachments to three women and regular attendance at A.A. meetings, that inhibits the action and stifles its sense of urgency. But when this droll, streetwise sleuth quits staring out the window at the rain and starts prowling his neighborhood haunts in Hell's Kitchen, he is just about the best there is." NY Times Book Rev

Eight million ways to die. Arbor House 1982 319p o.p.

LC 81-71698

This "novel is both a rousing private-eye story and an extended meditation on the whimsical ways of death—through freak accident, premeditated murder, and self-destruction. Private eye Matthew Scudder solves murders while he battles his own alcoholism. . . . In [this] tale, a 23-year old prostitute, Kim Dakkinen, wants out of 'the life' and asks Scudder to speak to her pimp, Chance. Scudder does, and a few days later Kim is found stabbed to death. Chance does the unexpected by hiring Scudder to find Kim's murderer, and while Scudder investigates, another one of Chance's prostitutes commits suicide; then another slashing occurs. A magnificently plotted, sensitive portrayal of two kinds of death—the kind that comes as an intruder and the kind that comes as an invited guest." Booklist

Even the wicked; a Matthew Scudder novel. Morrow 1997 328p o.p.

ISBN 0-688-14181-1 LC 96-23013

In this mystery, "Manhattan private detective Matt Scudder is working on two seemingly impossible cases. One is the city's newest serial killer, the Will of the People. Will bumps off high-profile hairballs—a child murderer freed on a technicality, a rabid anti-abortion crusader whose efforts have led to the murders of abortion clinic doctors, and a fanatical black racist. Matt's other case is the apparently senseless and motiveless murder of an AIDS sufferer who is shot while sitting on a park bench." Booklist

"As usual, Block's ingenuity in finding new motives for crime is endless, his narration polished, his entertainment value high." Publ Wkly

Everybody dies; a Matthew Scudder novel. Morrow 1998 292p $25

ISBN 0-688-14182-X LC 98-10529

"When his best friend, an Irish gangster, finds himself the target of an unknown assassin, Scudder begins asking questions and soon joins the hit list as bodies begin to turn up." Libr J

"Scudder keeps saying that this is Mick's story, and in the sense that his colorful and complicated rogue is responsible for all the trouble (and much of the grand dialogue), it is. But it is Scudder who ponders the metaphysics, striking the tone of loss, resignation and acceptance that makes this one of the most harrowing yet most rewarding chapters in the education of a hero." N Y Times Book Rev

Hit list. Morrow 2000 296p $25

ISBN 0-06-019833-8 LC 2001-274973

"Keller seems the archetypal contemporary urban man. He lives a mostly solitary and quotidian existence on Manhattan's East Side. . . . Occasionally, he visits Dot in White Plains, then goes to Louisville or Muscatine, Iowa, to murder a stranger. Keller is a contract killer, and Dot is his 'broker.' Here Keller realizes that someone is stalking him; he and Dot examine it from every angle and conclude that another hit man is pulling a Microsoft—trying to eliminate the competition." Booklist

Hit man. Morrow 1998 259p o.p.

ISBN 0-688-14179-X LC 97-34305

This novel about professional killer Keller is comprised of a series of short stories. "Each story, or 'chapter,' as designated here, presents Keller with an unusual challenge (conflicting assignments, an impregnable target, a catastrophic piece of misdirection), along with a fresh wave of existential angst. . . . Accepting his fate, he hauls himself across the country, eating at cheerless dives and drinking alone while fantasizing about retiring, or at least taking up a hobby." N Y Times Book Rev

Hope to die; a Matthew Scudder novel. Morrow 2001 320p o.p.

ISBN 0-06-019832-X LC 2001-30454

Sixty-two-year-old Matt Scudder "smells something fishy when a couple in his affluent neighborhood are murdered during a routine brownstone burglary. Exercising more imagination and analytic thought than is his wont, the mellowed hero eschews violent encounters for a brainier attack on this puzzler. In other words, a lot of walking and talking—only in more upscale parts of town. The shaggy-dog style pays off in heavily ironic sitdowns with Manhattan shrinks, Brooklyn homesteaders and sundry professional associates who share Scudder's wry sense of humor." N Y Times Book Rev

Block, Lawrence, 1938-*—Continued*

Like a lamb to slaughter
In Block, L. The collected mystery stories p275-390

A long line of dead men; a Matthew Scudder novel. Morrow 1994 285p o.p.
ISBN 0-688-12193-4 LC 94-5720
"Scudder is summoned to investigate the curious run of deaths that seem to be afflicting the members of a private club. Not just any private club, mind you, but one whose raison d'être, in a sense, is death. Thirty men gather once a year to celebrate, well . . . not having died yet. When they do die, eventually, the last survivor appoints 30 new members to keep the flame burning. The current batch, though, are dropping at an abnormally fast pace. Enter Scudder. Block takes this absolutely wonderful premise and makes the most of it. Like all the best hard-boiled writers in the post-Chandler era, Block knows that character and ambience are the heart and soul of crime fiction, but unlike so many of his brethren, he also maintains a healthy respect for plot." Booklist

(ed) Master's choice [v1]-2: mystery stories by today's top writers and the masters who inspired them. See Master's choice [v1]-2: mystery stories by today's top writers and the masters who inspired them

Out on the cutting edge; a Matt Scudder mystery. Morrow 1989 260p o.p.
LC 89-32420
This Matt Scudder "case, tracking down a missing girl from Indiana, has the PI in and out of several of New York's sleaziest drinking joints. While looking for the girl, Scudder is befriended by another recovering alcoholic, who promptly dies, taking a terrible secret with him to the grave. Matters are further complicated when Scudder finds himself falling in love with the attractive super at the building where the dead man lived." Booklist
"In this riveting mystery, Block's artistry creates a full complement of fully realized characters, each a real person regardless of his or her perhaps tenuous connection to the plot." Publ Wkly

The sins of the fathers; a Matthew Scudder novel; introduction by Stephen King. Dark Harvest 1992 179p o.p.
First published 1976 in paperback
This novel introduced the then-hard-drinking ex-cop Matt Scudder. "The father of murdered Wendy Hanniford comes to Scudder to try to find out more about his errant daughter—not to find her killer, who was apparently her living partner, a brittle young man who was found in the street raving and covered with her blood and who killed himself shortly after he was arrested. In his dour, methodical, oddly empathetic way, Scudder finds out a great deal, altering several lives in the process. . . . This is a fine opportunity to get in on the start of what has become one of the most rewarding PI series currently in progress." Publ Wkly

Small town. Morrow 2003 448p $24.95
ISBN 0-06-001190-4 LC 2002-31536
The novel's "cast includes a novelist whose next book becomes a hot property after police suspect him of murdering a real-estate agent, a beautiful folk-art dealer whose string of sexual adventures are triggered by the killing, a gay housecleaner who keeps finding his clients dead, and a serial killer who lost his family in the collapse of the World Trade Center." Libr J
"This is a novel at once profoundly disturbing, graphically erotic, satiric, and above all, entertaining." Booklist

Some days you get the bear
In Block, L. The collected mystery stories p443-568

Sometimes they bite
In Block, L. The collected mystery stories p43-175

Tanner on ice. Dutton 1998 248p o.p.
LC 97-32588
"Having been in a cryogenic deep freeze in a New Jersey basement for the past 25 years, the newly thawed and well-preserved Tanner (he's 64 but looks 39) discovers that Richard Nixon is no longer president and that his foster daughter Minna, the 11-year-old claimant to the Lithuanian throne, is now a sexy young woman. He also receives another covert assignment, to destabilize the government of Myanmar." Libr J
"Even when the fantasy wears thin and the scenery looks like cheesy pasteboard, Block's inventive wit still delights. The whole thing is silly, but yes, it is fun." NY Times Book Rev

A ticket to the boneyard; a Matthew Scudder novel. Morrow 1990 302p o.p.
LC 90-5710
"This time, former cop, recovering alcoholic, and dick-without-a-license Matthew Scudder is his own case. Twelve years past, in order to protect himself and a hooker friend, Scudder framed a man, James Leo Motley, who had it coming. Motley's out of prison now, and guess what? He hasn't mellowed." Booklist
The author "has a fine nose for the pungencies of New York's after-dark street life, and he gives his hero wonderful opportunities to swap syllables with the city's most articulate riffraff. This is primo stuff, and Scudder doesn't get any sharper than when he's interviewing transvestite hookers, desk clerks in fleabag hotels and bouncers in gay leather bars." N Y Times Book Rev

A walk among the tombstones; a Matthew Scudder mystery. Morrow 1992 318p o.p.
LC 91-41334
In this novel Scudder gets involved in assisting "high-level drug dealers whose family members are being kidnapped for ransom and returned in shopping bags. Scudder, who once carried a police detective's gold shield before falling victim to alcoholism, divides his time between AA meetings and stalking the stalkers through all means fair and foul." Booklist

When the sacred ginmill closes. Arbor House 1986 239p o.p.
LC 85-18682
In this novel "Scudder solves a New York City bar holdup by prying into the underworld of the city's taverns. Scudder deals with the IRA, murder, and the 'Westies,' a mob of toughs from the west of Ireland that has ruled Hell's Kitchen since the Great Potato Famine." Booklist

Block, Lawrence, 1938-—*Continued*

"The writing is realistic in the best sense of the word. There are no artificial heroics, forced lines of dialogue or false moves. Mr. Block knows his New York and the way people speak." N Y Times Book Rev

Blunt, Giles

The delicate storm. Putnam 2003 301p o.p.

ISBN 0-399-14865-5 LC 2002-36817

"A Marian Wood book"

"The freakish weather casts a spooky fog around Algonquin Bay, melts the ice on Lake Nipissing and rouses hibernating bears from their caves. When human body parts are found in the woods, Detective John Cardinal and his partner, Lise Delorme, are quick to recognize them as the leftover meal of hungry bears. But their macabre case turns uglier once the Canadian Security Intelligence Service. . .steps in and tries to pass the victim off as an anonymous American tourist." N Y Times Book Rev

"In a genre where writers often compete to create vile, loathsome villains perpetrating outrageous crimes, Blunt stands as a master craftsman who shows us not only darkness, but also decency." Publ Wkly

Bock, Dennis

The ash garden; a novel. Knopf 2001 281p $23

ISBN 0-375-41302-2 LC 2001-29872

This "novel considers the legacy of the bombing of Hiroshima through the lives of Emiko, a young Hiroshima native who lost part of her face in the attack and is now a documentary filmmaker, and Anton, a German physicist who worked in Los Alamos and now lives in Canada with his wife, an Austrian refugee from World War II." Booklist

"Bock's writing is both dense and immensely readable, as engaging when it focuses on life's minutiae as when it explores life's catastrophes. The Ash Garden is difficult to forget and it rewards repeated readings in a way that few novels can." Quill Quire

Bohjalian, Christopher A., 1960-

The buffalo soldier; a novel; by Chris Bohjalian. Crown 2002 404p $25

ISBN 0-609-60833-9 LC 2001-49042

"Several years after the devastating loss of their nine-year-old twin daughters in a flood, Vermont residents Laura and Terry Sheldon decide to adopt a child. When a state agency grants them a taciturn 10-year-old African-American boy on a foster parent trial basis, they acquiesce, albeit with some reluctance." Publ Wkly

"Bohjalian's characters combat their moral and racial confusion with a healthy application of ordinary love and good will, though their basic goodness often makes them feel less complex than the plot itself." N Y Times Book Rev

Midwives; a novel. Harmony Bks. 1997 312p o.p.

ISBN 0-517-70396-3 LC 96-22953

This novel is "set in northern Vermont. Now grown, narrator Connie recalls her 13th year, when her mother, Sibyl, a midwife, assists in a home delivery that goes bad: the birthing mother expires during delivery, and Sibyl performs a Cesarean to save the baby. Witnesses dispute whether the mother was really dead. The book chronicles Sibyl's trial, which pits midwifery against the medical community in the small Vermont town." Libr J

"Readers will find themselves mesmerized by the irresistible momentum of the narrative and by Bohjalian's graceful and lucid, irony-laced prose. . . . With acutely sensitive character delineation, he manages to present all the participants in this drama, from the family members to the grieving widower, as complex, fully realized individuals." Publ Wkly

Bolaño, Roberto, 1953-

By night in Chile; translated from the Spanish by Chris Andrews. New Directions 2004 130p pa $13.95

ISBN 0-81121-547-4 (pa)

Original Spanish edition, 2000

"During the course of a single night, Father Sebastian Urrutia Lacroix, a Chilean priest who is a member of Opus Dei, a literary critic and a mediocre poet, relives some of the crucial events of his life. He believes he is dying, and in his feverish delirium various characters, both real and imaginary, appear to him as icy monsters, as if in sequences from a horror film. Among them are the great poet Pablo Neruda, the German novelist Ernst Junger, and General Augusto Pinochet whom Father Lacroix instructs in Marxist doctrine as well as various members of the Chilean intelligentsia whose lives, during a period of political turbulence, have touched his own." Publisher's note

"Postwar Chilean politics and literature infuse this densely learned, richly evocative novel. In Chris Andrews's lucid translation, Bolano's febrile narrative tack and occasional surreal touches bring to mind the classics of Latin American magic realism; his cerebral protagonist and nonfiction borrowings are reminiscent of Thomas Bernhard and W. G. Sebald." N Y Times Book Rev

Distant star; translated from the Spanish by Chris Andrews. New Directions 2004 149p pa $14.95

ISBN 0-8112-1586-5 LC 2004-19033

Original Spanish edition, 1996

"'The melancholy folklore of exile' pervades this novel, which describes the divergent paths of three young Chilean poets around the time of Pinochet's coup. At university, the unnamed narrator and his friend are fascinated by a mysterious new member of their poetry workshop. Alberto Ruiz-Tagle is 'serious, well mannered, a clear thinker,' but his poems seem false, as if his true work were yet to be revealed. It becomes apparent that this is literally the case when Allende's government falls: as an Air Force officer for the new regime, he becomes famous for writing nationalist slogans in the sky. (The left-wing narrator, now in jail, reads them from his prison yard.) Bolano's spare prose lends his narrator's account a chilly precision—as if the detachment of his former classmate had become his country's, and his own." New Yorker

Böll, Heinrich, 1917-1985

And where were you, Adam?
In Böll, H. The stories of Heinrich Böll p34-152

Billiards at half-past nine; translated from the German. McGraw-Hill 1962 280p o.p.

Original German edition, 1959

"The novel examines the lives of three generations of architects and their responses to the Nazi regime and its aftermath. The present-day action takes place on the 80th birthday of patriarch Heinrich Fähmel, who built St. Anthony's Abbey. At the end of World War II, his son Robert destroyed the abbey to protest the church's complicity with the Nazis; Robert's son, Joseph, is serving his apprenticeship by helping to restore St. Anthony's. All three characters confront their relationship to building and destruction, as well as their personal and historical past. By the novel's end, the three are reconciled and share a birthday cake in the shape of the abbey." Merriam-Webster's Ency of Lit

The clown; translated from the German by Leila Vennewitz. McGraw-Hill 1965 247p o.p.

Original German edition, 1963

This novel revolves around the loss of meaning in the life of Hans Schnier, a twenty-seven-year-old clown and mime who returns home to Bonn after a disastrous performance tour. Flashbacks reconstruct Schnier's life in Hitler's Germany and his bitter experiences of the postwar period

"What Schnier (and the author) seem to be asking is: How can an honest man profess Christianity when Christian culture in the West failed to stop the rise of Nazism . . . and when the Church thrives in a society that worships nothing but the values of the marketplace? Hard questions but embodied in a bitter and brilliant book." NY Times Book Rev

Group portrait with lady; translated from the German by Leila Vennewitz. McGraw-Hill 1973 405p o.p.

Original German edition, 1971

"A sweeping portrayal of German life from World War I until the early 1970s. . . . The story's anonymous narrator gradually reveals the life—past and present—of Leni Pfeiffer, a war widow who, with her neighbors, is fighting the demolition of the Cologne apartment building in which they reside. Leni and her illegitimate son Lev become the nexus of Cologne's counterculture; they spurn the prevailing work ethic and assail the dehumanization of life under capitalism. In a larger sense, the work attempts both a reconciliation with the past and a condemnation of the pursuit of affluence in present-day Germany." Merriam-Webster's Ency of Lit

The lost honor of Katharina Blum; or, How violence develops and where it can lead; translated from the German by Leila Vennewitz. McGraw-Hill 1975 140p o.p.

Original German edition, 1974

"The novel condemned as irresponsible the coverage of the trial of the Baader-Meinhof group, a German terrorist organization, by the tabloid newspaper *Bild-Zeitung* and rebuked official government attacks on individual civil liberties. Katharina's ordered life falls into ruins after the *News*, a sensationalist local tabloid, falsely accuses her lover of a single night of terrorism and then names Katharina as his accomplice. Hounded by the press and the police, she shoots and kills the journalist who has tried to exploit her sexually and who has written the lies that have destroyed her life." Merriam-Webster's Ency of Lit

The mad dog: stories; translated by Breon Mitchell. St. Martin's Press 1997 164p o.p.

ISBN 0-312-16757-1 LC 97-16104

Contents: The fugitive; Youth on fire; Trapped in Paris; The mad dog; The rendezvous; The tribe of Esau; The tale of Berkovo Bridge; The dead no longer obey; America; Paradise lost

"Written at the height of the Nazi atrocities, [these stories] reflect Böll's fury and anguish over the weakness and hypocrisy of the church on the one hand, and the essentiality of faith on the other, as well as his sharp perception of the terrible power of corrupted institutions, especially the military. His young heroes, and, in the case of the title story, antihero, are alone in a world gone mad, searching for mercy, even love, in the devastation and spiritual chaos of war. Böll's vital renderings of the dangers of political extremism and systematic hatred are antidotes to complacency and should be experienced again and again." Booklist

The silent angel; translated by Breon Mitchell. St. Martin's Press 1994 182p o.p.

LC 94-2052

Written in 1950; first German edition, 1992

"Amid the charred rubble of Germany just days after World War II ends, cynical, numbed soldier Hans Schnitzler returns to Cologne under an alias to deliver a dead soldier's will to the widow, Elisabeth Gompertz. Hans was supposed to be shot as a deserter, but military court stenographer Willy Gompertz switched jackets with him and was killed instead. So begins what was Nobel-winner Böll's first novel." Publ Wkly

"While the bleakness Böll portrays might have made German publishers wary in 1950, the artistry of his portrayal makes 'The Silent Angel' a rich novel, one still pertinent to our own hunger for the bread of meaning amid the rubble of history. Heinrich Böll's gift to us is the skill with which he captures its first pangs." NY Times Book Rev

A soldier's legacy
In Böll, H. The stories of Heinrich Böll p316-81

The stories of Heinrich Böll; translated from the German by Leila Vennewitz. Knopf 1986 685p o.p.

LC 85-40392

This collection contains the war novel A soldier's legacy (1985), and the following novellas: And where were you, Adam?; The train was on time; When the war broke out, and When the war was over. Short stories included are: Breaking the news; My pal with the long hair; The man with the knives; Reunion on the avenue; Broommakers; My expensive leg; Children are civilians too; At the bridge; In the darkness; Candles for the Madonna; Across the bridge; That time we were in Odessa; Stranger, bear word to the Spartans we . . .; Drinking in Petöcki; What a racket; Parting; Between trains in X; Re-

Böll, Heinrich, 1917-1985—*Continued*

union with Drüng; The ration runners; Lohengrin's death; Business is business; On the hook; My sad face; Adventures of a haversack; Black sheep; My Uncle Fred; Christmas not just once a year; The Balek scales; The postcard; Recollections of a young king; The death of Elsa Baskoleit; A peach tree in his garden stands; Pale Anna; This is Tibten; Daniel the Just; In search of the reader; The tidings of Bethlehem; And there was the evening and the morning . . .; The taste of bread; Murke's collected silences; Monologue of a waiter; Like a bad dream; A case for Kop; Undine's mighty father; In the valley of the thundering hoofs; The thrower-away; Unexpected guest; No tears for Schmeck; Anecdote concerning the lowering of productivity; He came as a beer-truck driver; The Staech affair; Till death us do part; On being courteous when compelled to break the law; Too many trips to Heidelberg; My father's cough; Rendezvous with Margret; Nostalgia; In which language is one called Schneckenröder?

"From World War II experiences as a young man to the characteristic political utterances of his later years, these stories span the late German writer's entire career. Böll's questioning confrontations with life mine the modern European intellect with uncommon distinction, whether in battle-torn settings or in postwar Germany, recovering materially if not spiritually from the experience of war." Booklist

The train was on time
In Böll, H. The stories of Heinrich Böll p165-250

When the war broke out
In Böll, H. The stories of Heinrich Böll p568-81

When the war was over
In Böll, H. The stories of Heinrich Böll p582-96

Bond, Larry

Day of wrath. Warner Bks. 1998 481p o.p.
ISBN 0-446-51677-5 LC 97-32317

This suspense novel "begins when FBI agent Helen Gray and U.S. Army colonel Peter Thorn arrive in Russia to investigate the mysterious crash of a Russian cargo plane that happened to be carrying a team of American arms inspectors. The local authorities try to make the crash look like an accident, but their thinly veiled attempts at deception fail to convince Gray and Thorn, who quickly find evidence of a hidden shipment of nuclear missiles and embark on a hunt that takes the duo across Europe, where they are betrayed by a high-level FBI mole, and eventually leads them home—to Washington, D.C., where a corrupt Arab prince is masterminding plans for a lethal warhead launch." Publ Wkly

Bond, Michael, 1926-

Monsieur Pamplemousse. Beaufort Bks. 1985 191p o.p.
LC 84-24444

First published 1983 in the United Kingdom

Pamplemousse is a "gastronomic detective, an undercover critic for a prestigious Gallic dining guide. With his faithful bloodhound, Pommes Frites, Pamplemousse—a former inspector with the Sureté—investigates the cuisine of his favorite hotel-restaurant, La Langoustine. There, misfortune strikes: the specialty of the house is served to him with a man's head inside. . . . Mystery takes a back seat to fine food and hilarious characters in this ribald, side-splitting farce." Publ Wkly

Monsieur Pamplemousse rests his case. Fawcett Columbine 1991 199p o.p.
LC 91-70650

"M. Pamplemousse, retired from the Sûreté, is representing *Le Guide* magazine in Vichy, where six celebrated American mystery writers are recreating a gourmet feast supposedly once hosted by Alexandre Dumas. The Inspector arrives at the dinner as instructed, costumed as D'Artagnan and riding a horse—a wickedly unreliable horse. All too soon he finds himself thrown into a rural ditch, arrested and handcuffed, pursued on foot over the fields, locked in a country brothel (and rescued by his dog Pommes Frites), tucked in a hotel bed with a ravishing American gourmet-magazine publisher. . . . At the same time he's coping with two fake murders and one genuine one." Publ Wkly

Bonner, Cindy, 1953-

Lily; a novel. Algonquin Bks. 1992 336p o.p.
ISBN 0-945575-95-5 LC 91-40237

"Lily DeLony, is 15, hardworking, and dutiful, having taken over the responsibilities of caring for her family after her mother's death. Life on the DeLonys' Texas farm in the 1880s is demanding, and her papa is a stern, humorless man. Lily has just blossomed into young womanhood, and the son of the only well-to-do family in the area has asked her to the church fair, but her heart has already been snared by Marion, the youngest of the notorious Beatty gang. Although Marion, nicknamed Shot, shares his brothers' outlaw life, he's sharp-witted, affectionate, and not without morals. Their attraction is as unavoidable as gravity." Booklist

"A fine first novel, making the timeworn theme of a responsible young girl's falling in love with an ne'er-do-well rascal new and fresh. . . . The book's strongest assets are its verisimilitude, fortified by the wonderful use of the vernacular, and the pure, simple clarity of the writing." Libr J

Followed by Looking after Lily

Looking after Lily. Algonquin Bks. 1994 326p o.p.
LC 93-33730

As this sequel "begins, Lily's husband, Marion ('Shot') Beatty, has been sentenced to two years in jail just as his one surviving brother, Haywood, is being released. Shot begs Haywood to take care of Lily, who is pregnant and has nowhere to go. Haywood is appalled. A loner with a taste for whiskey, gambling, and whoring, he wants nothing to do with a pregnant sister-in-law. But gradually, after a series of disastrous misadventures and the near-disastrous birth of his niece, Emmaline Eliza, Haywood begins to grow into his role of guardian. The trouble is, he also falls in love with Lily. As these two tough, laconic, brave, and, yes, noble individuals struggle with the conundrums of passion and the demanding work of pre-industrial daily life, Bonner does more than hold us rapt with her storytelling skills; she also reveals the

Bonner, Cindy, 1953—*Continued*

transforming power of love." Booklist

Other titles in the author's series about members of the DeLony family: The passion of Dellie O'Barr (1996) and Right from wrong (1999)

Borchardt, Alice

The silver wolf. Ballantine Bks. 1998 451p o.p.
ISBN 0-345-42360-7 LC 98-4802

"A Del Rey book"

"As Charlemagne consolidates his empire through a combination of wars and strategic marriages, a young girl who possesses the power to transform herself into a silver wolf becomes a reluctant pawn in a game of politics and survival. Against the decadent and barbaric backdrop of Rome in the Dark Ages, the author . . . spins a love-story tinged with the supernatural. Borchardt's sensual prose and period detail provide a lush setting for her tale of a woman struggling to reconcile her human and wolf natures." Libr J

Borges, Jorge Luis, 1899-1986

The book of sand; translated by Norman Thomas di Giovanni. Dutton 1977 125p o.p.
LC 77-8418

Original Spanish edition, 1975

Contents: The other; Ulrike; The Congress; There are more things; The Sect of the Thirty; The night of the gifts; The mirror and the mask; Undr; Utopia of a tired man; The bribe; Avelino Arredondo; The disk; The book of sand

"Borges' short stories combine intriguing ideas with smooth technique. Among these 13, for example, is one in which, at 70, he meets his 20-year-old self on a park bench and discovers they have few points of agreement. In another, a mendicant sells him a book with an infinite number of pages whose beginning and end cannot be located. Like a sleight-of-hand artist, Borges delights in presenting the impossible as fact. Some of these fictions reflect his Argentinian background, others his Norse scholarship." Booklist

Collected fictions; translated by Andrew Hurley. Viking 1998 565p o.p.
ISBN 0-670-84970-7 LC 98-21217

This is a collection of all the stories written by Borges over a 50-year period

"A Borges invention . . . always takes the reader on a roller-coaster ride into some previously unsuspected dimension. This collection of the great magician's work is a new translation and includes one piece never before put into English." Atl Mon

Ficciones; edited and with an introduction by Anthony Kerrigan. Grove Press 1962 174p o.p.

Original Spanish edition, 1944

Contents: Tlön, Uqbar, Orbis Tertius; The approach to al-Mu'tasim; Pierre Menard, author of Don Quixote; The circular ruins; The Babylon lottery; An examination of the work of Herbert Quain; The Library of Babel; The garden of forking paths; Funes, the memorious; The form of the sword; Theme of the traitor and the hero; Death and the compass; The secret miracle; Three versions of Judas; The end; The sect of the Phoenix; The South

Borland, Hal, 1900-1978

When the legends die. Lippincott 1963 288p pa $6.50 o.p.
ISBN 0-553-25738-2

"Thomas Black Bull, a Ute Indian, is being reared in the traditional Native American way when his parents are forced to flee from the world of the white man. After the death of his parents Tom is returned to the white world, where he suffers the disintegration of his native heritage and traditions as he experiences school, sheep herding, and rodeo life. Following a serious accident at a rodeo he returns to the mountains and is drawn back into his past." Shapiro. Fic for Youth 3rd edition

Bosse, Malcolm J., 1934-2002

Fire in heaven; a novel. Simon & Schuster 1985 654p o.p.
LC 85-14347

Sequel to The warlord

"Vera Rogacheva Embree, former mistress of the infamous warlord General Tang, has made successful life in Bangkok as an antiques importer. Her daughter by General Tang, Sonia, is coming of age and is beginning to question not only her Russian-Chinese ancestry but also her place in Thai society. When Sonia takes up with a young member of the Communist party, Vera recognizes her own misguided idealism and tries to stop her daughter from making a terrible mistake. Sonia, however, already is drawn deeply into a romanticized view of Communist ideology. Vera counts on one last person to save her daughter—Phil Embree, Vera's American husband, who has returned from a two-year sojourn in India." Booklist

The author "has written a story of impressive richness and intensity that not only depicts with an expert's understanding an Asia caught in convulsive change, but does so through the private dramas of a half-dozen characters who are not easy to forget." Publ Wkly

The vast memory of love. Ticknor & Fields 1992 482p il o.p.
LC 92-7590

This historical novel is "set in London in 1753. Journal entries purporting to be Henry Fielding's are interspersed with the tribulations of Ned Carleton. A servant who is no longer able to find a job because of an injured hand, Carleton takes to stealing to support himself. Another linked storyline deals with a group of noblemen [including the Earl of Sandwich] who practice Satanism and pay local girls for their favors. One of the girls is detained for a month and is put on trial when lies about her captivity are exposed. Teeming with activity, the book examines the London lower classes, the causes of crime, the foibles and cruelties of the nobility, the operations of the Bow Street Runners, and the justice system." Libr J

"This is a triumph of fast-paced storytelling as well as a thoughtful commentary on the hypocrisies of high society and the degraded lives of the poor." Publ Wkly

The warlord. Simon & Schuster 1983 717p o.p.

"In the violent, disorganized China of 1927 four people are thrown together. Tang Shan-teh, a successful general, desires unity and modernization but respects and preserves the old values of Confucianism and tradition; Vera Rogacheeva is a sometime prostitute, a White Russian

Bosse, Malcolm J., 1934-2002—*Continued*

refugee; Erich Luckner sells German guns to bandits and warlords; and Philip Embree is an American missionary who has gone native to the point of enlisting in Tang's army as an axeman." Libr J

"This book is a must for the student of China as well as those interested in human nature. It is a complicated story and cannot be skimmed or read between loads at the laundromat. This story is for those who enjoy 'hunkering down' in the sun and traveling to exotic places, where they must deal with contradictions, love and hate, peace and violence, confusions, and Marxist loyalty, and ultimately betrayal." Best Sellers

Followed by Fire in heaven

Boswell, Robert, 1953-

Century's son. Knopf 2002 307p $24

ISBN 0-375-41237-9 LC 2001-38101

"Morgan, whose first name has fallen away 'from disuse,' was once a fearless labor organizer for his fellow sanitation workers; it was his uncompromising idealism that led Zhenya, his college-professor wife, to fall in love with him. But, ten years later, Morgan has abandoned his activism; he spends his days collecting garbage and contemplating his decline, which began when his son hanged himself, at the age of twelve. As if the Morgan marriage didn't have enough to deal with, Zhenya's father, the famous Russian writer Peter Ivanovich Kamenev, is coming to visit. . . . A moving portrait of a family both torn apart and united by grief." New Yorker

Boulle, Pierre, 1912-1994

The bridge over the River Kwai; translated by Xan Fielding. Vanguard Press 1954 224p o.p.

Original French edition, 1952

"In 1942 the Japanese military under the command of Col. Saito orders its British prisoners of war to construct a bridge over the 400-foot-wide River Kwai in the Siamese jungle. Complications arise when prisoner Col. Nicholson insists that officers not be treated like regular lower-class soldiers. Medical officer Clipton is much more humane, and this difference brings the two fellow prisoners into frequent conflict. When the bridge is finally completed, a British demolition team prepares to destroy it." Shapiro. Fic for Youth. 3d edition

Planet of the Apes; translated by Xan Fielding. Vanguard Press 1963 246p o.p.

Published in the United Kingdom with title: Monkey planet

"Ulysse Mérou writes of his experiences on an unusual planet where the roles of humans and apes are reversed. Gorillas wear clothing and run businesses, while humans are caged in zoos and are the subjects of scientific experiments. In the year 2500 a vacationing couple cruising through space spot a bottle-encased message, retrieve it, and soon become absorbed in Mérou's tale." Shapiro. Fic for Youth. 3d edition

"In this Swiftian fable Boulle gives full play to his not inconsiderable gift for irony and satire." Libr J

Bova, Ben, 1932-

(ed) The Best of the Nebulas. See The Best of the Nebulas

Death dream. Bantam Bks. 1994 497p o.p.

LC 93-46463

"Dan Santorini moves his family to Florida for a job with a young company working to create virtual reality games. At first, Dan is delighted to be reunited with his brilliant and eccentric former partner, Jase Lowrey. Yet Dan finds Jase uncomfortably manic, and Jase's playful barbs have a new, cruel sting. After Dan's company provides virtual reality teaching chambers to his daughter's school, his wife begins to observe a sinister effect on their daughter. Dan ignores his unease with his new company—and even his daughter's fainting spells—until two people die in a fighter pilot simulation he developed with Jase in their previous collaboration. Bova's suspenseful plot, which revolves around the use of completely interactive virtual reality for full-scale baseball games, moonwalks, and magical journeys, considers what happens when the methods used to enhance the realism become dangerous and the realism becomes too real." Libr J

Jupiter. TOR Bks. 2001 368p o.p.

ISBN 0-312-87217-8 LC 00-48021

"A Tom Doherty Associates book"

"Assigned by the New Morality, Earth's conservative ruling coalition, to act as its agent at a research station in orbit around the planet Jupiter, astrophysicist Grant Archer finds himself torn between his faith in God and his loyalty to science. . . . {This is a} first-rate adventure that combines hard science with human drama to create a challenging and compelling tale of courage and conviction." Libr J

Mars. Bantam Bks. 1992 502p o.p.

LC 91-29466

"A Native American geologist finds himself the center of political controversy as he becomes one of the first humans to set foot on the red planet. Bova's imaginary chronicle of the first human mission to Mars offers a field day for science buffs as his characters experience the challenges of exploring Earth's nearest neighbor." Libr J

Followed by Return to Mars

Orion among the stars. TOR Bks. 1995 320p o.p.

ISBN 0-312-85637-7 LC 95-14718

"A Tom Doherty Associates book"

In this episode "Orion finds himself in the future in a far distant region of the Galaxy battling simply for survival with his human clone soldiers. But he discovers that this time the human and alien soldiers are simply pawns of the gods who are fighting amongst themselves for the very survival of the Galaxy. . . . One of the best SF military series around. Lots of action but also well written." Voice Youth Advocates

Orion and the conqueror. TOR Bks. 1994 350p o.p.

LC 93-42545

"A Tom Doherty Associates book"

In this episode of the fantasy series "Orion's mission is to see that Alexandros, son of Philip of Macedonia, becomes king and later conquers the world as Alexander the Great. Orion finds himself serving King Philip as a palace guard. His respect for Philip and his duty to protect his life comes in direct conflict with the creator's

Bova, Ben, 1932-—*Continued*
desire to see Philip die from an assassin's hand as Alexandros stands ready to take over. Anya is the goddess who takes on human form because of her love for Orion and his great love for her." Voice Youth Advocates

"The sounds, the scents and the sensibility of the ancient world permeate this well-wrought adventure." Publ Wkly

Orion in the dying time. Doherty Assocs. 1990 356p o.p.
LC 90-208344

"A TOR book"

Previous titles in series Orion (1984) and Vengeance of Orion (1988)

A fantasy "about the hunter Orion, endowed by the Creators with superhuman powers. The Creators are the godlike beings into which mankind has evolved 50,000 years from now. Determined to ensure that the continuum does not veer from the path that led to their existence, they send Orion back to the nexus points in history to hunt down their enemies." Publ Wkly

The precipice. TOR Bks. 2001 349p (Asteroid wars, bk1) o.p.
ISBN 0-312-84876-5 LC 2001-34768

"A Tom Doherty Associates book"

"The greenhouse effect has caused catastrophic changes to Earth's atmosphere, guaranteeing economic, social, and enviromental collapse in the near future. When Dan Randolph and Martin Humphries enter a business partnership to seek new resources in the Asteroid Belt as the only means of saving the planet, only one of them has Earth's best interests in mind." Libr J

"This novel should appeal to Bova's regular audience, a mixture of traditional hard SF fans, space enthusiasts and libertarians." Publ Wkly

Return to Mars. Avon Bks. 1999 403p o.p.
ISBN 0-380-97640-4 LC 99-21635

Sequel to Mars

"Determined to prove that his sighting of a pueblo-like cliff dwelling on Mars was not a delusion born of false hopes, Navaho geologist Jamie Waterman returns to the Red Planet as part of a controversial second mission to exploit the resources of the solar system. Strained relations among the crew lead to the growing suspicion of a saboteur in their midst as Waterman sees his dreams fade in the face of political short-sightedness and human greed." Libr J

"Where Bova shines is in making science not only comprehensible but entertaining." N Y Times Book Rev

Saturn. TOR Bks. 2003 412p $24.95
ISBN 0-312-87218-6 LC 2003-40216

"A Tom Doherty Associates book"

"When Earth's leadership decides to 'encourage' its dissidents to leave the planet aboard an interstellar habitat destined for Saturn, Susan Lane joins the expedition, eager to begin a new life. Attracted to Malcolm Eberly, the charismatic director of the habitat, Susan (now calling herself Holly) dedicates herself to the task of helping Malcolm organize life aboard the habitat, remaining blissfully unaware of the sinister politics going on among the habitat's leaders and blinding herself to Malcolm's real agenda." Libr J

"Bova is definitely the man to do justice to the astronomical marvels of the Saturnian system with its enormous potential as a second home for humanity, especially in the complex environments of its moons. Loud, prolonged applause, then, for the strengths of this book." Booklist

Venus. TOR Bks. 2000 302p o.p.
ISBN 0-312-87216-X LC 99-462304

"A Tom Doherty Associates book"

"Van Humphries is the sickly and despised second son of a billionaire whose elder and favorite son died in the first attempt to land a man on Venus. In competition with another expedition, undertaken by his late mother's first husband, he sets out to recover his brother's body." Booklist

"When Venus turns out to be even more dangerous than advertised, the relationship between the rivals surprisingly moves to center stage. To survive the physical challenges of Venus, both Van and Lars must let go of the past, and Bova proves himself equal to the task of showing how adversity can temper character in unforeseen ways." N Y Times Book Rev

Bowen, Elizabeth, 1899-1973

The collected stories of Elizabeth Bowen. Knopf 1981 784p o.p.
ISBN 0-394-51666-4 LC 80-8729

First published 1980 in the United Kingdom

Contents: Breakfast; Daffodils; The return; The confidante; Requiescat; All Saints; The new house; Lunch; The lover; Mrs. Windermere; The shadowy third; The evil that men do—; Sunday evening; Coming home; Ann Lee's; The parrot; The visitor; The Contessina; Human habitation; The secession; Making arrangements; The storm; Charity; The back drawing-room; Recent photograph; Joining Charles; The jungle; Shoes: an international episode; The dancing-mistress; Aunt Tatty; Dead Mabelle; The working party; Foothold; The cassowary; Telling; Mrs. Moysey; The Tommy Crans; The good girl; The cat jumps; The last night in the old home; The disinherited; Maria; Her table spread; The little girl's room; Firelight in the flat; The man of the family; The needle case; The apple tree; Reduced; Tears, idle tears; A walk in the woods; A love story; Look at all those roses; Attractive modern homes; The Easter egg party; Love; No. 16; A queer heart; The girl with the stoop; Unwelcome idea; Oh, Madam. . .; Summer afternoon; The inherited clock; The cheery soul; Songs my father sang me; The demon lover; Careless talk; The happy autumn fields; Ivy gripped the steps; Pink May; Green holly; Mysterious Kôr; The Dolt's tale; I hear you say so; Gone away; Hand in glove; A day in the dark

The death of the heart. Knopf 1939 418p o.p.

"The novel is set chiefly in London in the period between the World Wars. Sixteen-year-old orphan Portia Quayne goes to live with her half brother Thomas and his wife Anna, both of whom are portrayed as urbane and empty. Bored and lonely, Portia falls in love with Eddie, one of Anna's friends; he does not return her love. Weeks later, Portia learns that Anna has been reading her diary. Thoroughly humiliated, Portia preposterously proposes marriage to a kindly family friend, who refuses her and encourages her to return to Thomas and Anna. In the end, Anna and Portia come to terms with

Bowen, Elizabeth, 1899-1973—*Continued*
each other, and Anna finally sympathizes with Portia's 'frantic desire to be handled with feeling.'" Merriam-Webster's Ency of Lit

Eva Trout. Knopf 1968 302p o.p.
In the novel "we see Eva Trout in aching clarity, a big, graceless girl, unloved, unsure, whose relentless pursuit of 'becoming' makes shambles of the lives she touches. To her homosexual guardian, Constantine, she is an awkward burden to maintain until she comes of age; to Henry, the youngest son of a neighboring vicar, she is 'Pippa Passes' in reverse, leaving 'lust and villainy' in her wake; to her former school teacher she is the ruin and salvation of a marriage; and to the deafmute child, Jeremy, she adopts, she becomes the world he cannot gain and so destroys." Libr J
"There is something about Eva that suggests one of Henry Moore's monumental women, a hugeness, a strength (like a 'dedicated discus thrower'), and a rooted stability combined with the instinctive wisdom of an E. M. Forster character." Christ Sci Monit

The heat of the day. Knopf 1949 c1948 372p o.p.
Essentially this novel presents character studies of Stella Rodney, and the two men who loved her. The background is London after Dunkirk, a London of blitzes and buzz bombs; and peaceful Ireland. The two men are Robert Kelway, Stella's lover, and the mysterious Harrison, who betrays Kelway's secret in order to gain Stella for himself
"Miss Bowen's novel expertly flicks the rawness of several unsolved queries concerning loyalty and love and ponders the degree to which human beings are strangers to each other. More densely written than her earlier work, this study of behavior is a soberly shocking, compassionate baring of the confused and vulnerable human heart." N Y Her Trib Books

Bowen, Peter, 1945-

Badlands. St. Martin's Minotaur 2003 250p $23.95
ISBN 0-312-26252-3 LC 2002-37196
Montana sheriff Gabriel Du Pré's "suspicions are aroused when the Host of Yahweh immediately destroys the ranch buildings, sells the livestock and erects a makeshift metal chapel for secret rites. Soon, reportsof mass murders and suicides bring in cautious FBI agents ever mindful of the Waco debacle. Du Pré's blunt speech and sometimes opaque thought patterns can be hard to follow, but his pursuits of wrongdoers over cliffs, canyons and arid river beds are truly riveting." Publ Wkly

Bowen-Judd, Sara Hutton *See* Woods, Sara

Bowles, Paul, 1910-1999

Collected stories & later writings. Library of America, Distributed to the trade in the U.S. by Penguin Putnam 2002 1062p $40
ISBN 1-931082-20-0 LC 2002-19452
Fifty-two of the short stories in this volume have appeared in the five books: The delicate prey (1950); A hundred camels in the courtyard (1962); The time of friendship (1967); Things gone and things still here (1977); and Midnight mass (1981). Six selected later stories are also included. Up above the world (1966) is a novella where an American couple visiting Central America have a frightening experience with an apparently wealthy local couple. Their heads are green and their hands are blue (1963) is a collection of travel essays.
Contents: The delicate prey and other stories; A hundred camels in the courtyard; New stories from The time of friendship; Things gone and things still here; Midnight mass; Selected later stories; Their heads are green and their hands are blue; Up above the world

Collected stories, 1939-1976; introduction by Gore Vidal. Black Sparrow Press 1980 c1979 417p o.p.
ISBN 0-87685-397-1 LC 79-4569
The thirty-nine stories in this volume have appeared in the three books: The delicate prey (1950); The time of friendship (1967); and Things gone and things still here (1977)
Contents: Tea on the mountain; The scorpion; By the water; A distant episode; The echo; Call at Corazón; Under the sky; Pages from Cold Point; How many midnights; The circular valley; At Paso Rojo; Pastor Dowe at Tacaté; You are not I; The delicate prey; Señor Ong and Señor Ha; A thousand days for Mokhtar; The fourth day out from Santa Cruz; Doña Faustina; The hours after noon; The successor; If I should open my mouth; The frozen fields; Tapiama; The hyena; A friend of the world; The story of Lahcen and Idir; He of the Assembly; The wind at Beni Midar; The time of friendship; The garden; Afternoon with Antaeus Mejdoub; The fqih; The waters of Izli; Reminders of Bouselhamj; You have left your lotus pods on the bus; Istikhara, Anaya, Medagan and the Medaganat; Things gone and things still here; Allal
"At the top of his art Bowles is an anima; to inhabit this book is to experience pain and immensity." Time

The delicate prey and other stories
In Bowles, P. Collected stories & later writings

A hundred camels in the courtyard
In Bowles, P. Collected stories & later writings

Let it come down
In Bowles, P. The sheltering sky; Let it come down; The spider's house

Midnight mass
In Bowles, P. Collected stories & later writings

The sheltering sky. New Directions 1949 318p o.p.
"Port and Kit Moresby, an American couple of independent means, have been traveling aimlessly for 12 years. By the time they reach Morocco they have become disaffected and alienated. They take up with a series of unreliable, rootless wanderers. On a trip to the interior Port contracts typhoid fever—out of apathy he has neglected to be vaccinated—and dies. Kit has an affair with an Arab and joins his household, but their relationship soon falls apart. Kit is found and returned to Oran.

Bowles, Paul, 1910-1999—*Continued*

She is teetering on the brink of insanity and finds an opportunity to disappear into the crowded bazaar." Merriam-Webster's Ency of Lit

also in Bowles, P. The sheltering sky; Let it come down; The spider's house

The sheltering sky; Let it come down; The spider's house; Let it come down ; The spider's house; Paul Bowles. Library of America, Distributed to the trade in the U.S. by Penguin Putnam 2002 938p (Library of America) $35

ISBN 1-931082-19-7 LC 2002-19453

Contents: The sheltering sky; Let it come down; The spider's house

The sheltering sky is entered separately. "In Let It Come Down (1952), Bowles plots the doomed trajectory of Nelson Dyar, a New York bank teller who comes to Tangier in search of a different life and ends up giving in to his darkest impulses. . . . The Spider's House (1955) . . . is set against the end of French rule in Morocco. Its characters—ranging from a Moroccan boy gifted with spiritual healing power to an American writer who regrets the passing of traditional ways—are caught up in the clash between colonial and nationalist factions, and are forced to confront cultural gulfs widened by political violence." Publisher's note

The spider's house

In Bowles, P. The sheltering sky; Let it come down; The spider's house

The stories of Paul Bowles; introduction by Robert Stone. Ecco Press 2001 657p $39.95

ISBN 0-06-621273-1 LC 2001-51231

Contents: By the water; The echo; A distant episode; Call at Corazón; The scorpion; Under the sky; At Paso Rojo; You are not I; Pages from Cold Point; Pastor Dowe at Tacaté; Tea on the mountain; How many midnights; The circular valley; The delicate prey; Señor Ong and Señor Ha; The fourth day out from Santa Cruz; Doña Faustina; The successor; If I should open my mouth; The hours after noon; The frozen fields; Tapiama; A thousand days for Mokhtar; The story of Lahcen and Idir; He of the assembly; A friend of the world; The hyena; The wind at Beni Midar; The garden; The time of friendship; Afternoon with Antaeus; Mejdoub; The fqih; Reminders of Bouselham; Istikhara, Anaya, Medagan and the Medaganat; Things gone and things still here; Midnight mass; Here to learn; The eye; The waters of Izli; You have left your lotus pods on the bus; Allal; The dismissal; Madame and Ahmed; Kitty; The husband; At the Krungthep plaza; Bouayad and the money; The little house; The empty amulet; Rumor and a ladder; In the red room; Massachusetts 1932; Tangier 1975; Julian Vreden; Hugh Harper; Unwelcome words; New York 1965; An inopportune visit; In absentia; Dinner at Sir Nigel's; Too far from home

"Earthy, violent and comfortable with corruption, these deeply affecting stories are distinguished by their lyrical rhythms and meticulous regard for language." Publ Wkly

Things gone and things still here

In Bowles, P. Collected stories & later writings

Up above the world

In Bowles, P. Collected stories & later writings

Box, C. J.

Savage run. Putnam 2002 272p o.p.

ISBN 0-399-14887-6 LC 2001-57872

"Two creepy, coldhearted guys carry out orders from an unseen other as they murder a famous environmental activist, a noted environmental writer, and the country's most powerful 'green' congressman. Called in after the first murder (by explosion), which also killed several animals in his part of the Wyoming wilderness, game warden Joe Pickett begins to suspect a broader conspiracy. With a few clues from his part-time librarian wife, Pickett moves the investigation forward." Libr J

"The 'outdoor mystery' was a thriving subgenre before Box arrived on the scene, but he has taken it to new levels of substance and style." Booklist

Winterkill; a novel. Putnam 2003 372p $23.95

ISBN 0-399-15045-5 LC 2002-37120

As the story begins, "Joe Pickett, game warden of Wyoming's Twelve Sleep County, is caught in a mountain blizzard with a dead body beside him in his pick-up truck. The body belongs to a much-hated federal bureaucrat, who may have been killed by a group of survivalists calling themselves the Sovereigns. . . .Box handles this controversial material superbly, showing vividly how government rigidity causes human tragedy in the name of patriotism. Pickett remains an utterly sympathetic, Gary Cooperish hero, but as the series developes he has begun to darken to darken noticeably." Booklist

Boyd, William, 1952-

Any human heart; a novel. Knopf 2003 498p $26

ISBN 0-375-41493-2 LC 2002-27451

"At 17, Logan Mountstuart starts a journal. He faithfully keeps it, except when he can't bear to, until his death at 85. It records, mostly at a cool panoramic distance but with plunges into close-up shattering, his life as a minor British writer, art dealer, spy, chance aquaintance of dozens of the famous, repeatedly ill-fated husband and lover, and broken-compass navigator through the mild pleasures and harsh poisons of English life over most of the 20th century." N Y Times Book Rev

"This flawed yet immensely appealing protagonist is one of Boyd's most distinctive creations, and his voice—articulate, introspective, urbane, stoically philosophical in the face of countless disappointments—engages the readers empathy." Publ Wkly

Armadillo; a novel. Knopf 1998 337p o.p.

ISBN 0-375-40223-3 LC 98-14578

"Lorimer Black is a brilliant and impeccably dressed insurance adjuster who travels across London with a briefcase full of cash, detecting and settling fraudulent claims. Black is something of a fraud himself—that's why he's so good at his job. Although he seems to be the quintessential Brit, he has a hard time pronouncing British names. . . . He is the armadillo of the title, and his carefully chosen wardrobe serves as his armor. With this level of deception, reality is a waking nightmare, and

Boyd, William, 1952-—*Continued*

Black is currently undergoing therapy for insomnia at the Institute of Lucid Dreams." Libr J

The novel "is full of loose ends, unsolved mysteries and red herrings. But it is also charming, unsettling and sneakily, serendipitously profound." N Y Times Book Rev

The blue afternoon; a novel. Knopf 1995 367p o.p.

ISBN 0-679-43295-7 LC 94-26091

First published 1993 in the United Kingdom

"A woman architect in Los Angeles in the 1930s is approached by an elderly man who claims to be her father. Although skeptical, she allows him to convince her to accompany him to Lisbon to search for the lost love of his life. On the trans-Atlantic voyage, he tells her a strange tale of love, murder, honor, and aspiration in the midst of the Philippine insurrection against the U.S." Booklist

"The Blue Afternoon beguilingly balances the elements of love story, murder, mystery, political thriller and historical romance. The contest between progress and barbarism, between muffled Realpolitik and allegedly private concerns, is set up in such a way . . . as to return the reader from the general to the particular, to the peremptory intrusion of mere happenstance and grim conspiracy of which the book is made." Times Lit Suppl

Brazzaville Beach; a novel. Morrow 1990 316p o.p.

LC 90-47371

"Hope Clearwater lives alone in a beach house in an unnamed African country, trying to patch together her shattered life. An ecologist, she had come to Africa to participate in primate research and to heal the deep wounds of her marriage to a brilliant English mathematician; but she soon found herself plunged into another crisis, one that threatened not only her career but also her life." Libr J

"As befits a protagonist telling her own story, Hope often doesn't know where she's going until she gets there, but Boyd's skill in developing her character overrides some slight confusion about the more picaresque aspects of her adventure." Publ Wkly

Boyer, Richard *See* Boyer, Rick

Boyer, Rick

The Daisy Ducks; a Doc Adams suspense novel. Houghton Mifflin 1986 276p o.p.

LC 86-3016

In this novel dentist-cum-detective Doc Adams' "soldier-for-hire pal Liantis Roantis . . . gives the adventurous surgeon a reason to take a brief hiatus from impacted wisdom teeth. Roantis needs Doc's help in finding a Vietnam buddy who has become a fanatic survivalist and is ensconced in the North Carolina mountains preparing for Armageddon. Amid the action, Boyer effectively ponders the not-so-romantic reality of life on the edge versus the sometimes somnambulant comforts of home." Booklist

"If you like action-suspense novels, Doc Adams could become addictive. Boyer's smooth style creates a character with charisma and a story that moves like a freight train at full throttle—powerfully swift." Best Sellers

Boyle, Kay, 1902-1992

Fifty stories. Doubleday 1980 648p o.p.

LC 78-22151

Contents: Episode in the life of an ancestor; Wedding day; Rest cure; Ben; Kroy Wen; Black boy; Friend of the family; White as snow; Keep your pity; Security; Dear Mr. Walrus; Rondo at Carraroe; Natives don't cry; Maiden, maiden; The white horses of Vienna; Count Lothar's heart; Major Alshuster; How Bridie's girl was won; The herring piece; Your body is a jewel box; Major engagement in Paris; Effigy of war; Diplomat's wife; Men; They weren't going to die; Defeat; Let there be honour; This they took with them; Their name is macaroni; French harvest; Fire in the vineyards; Hotel behind the lines; Summer evening; The criminal; Fife's house; The lovers of gain; Army of occupation; Cabaret; The kill; A disgrace to the family; The lost; Adam's death; Aufwiedersehen Abend; A puzzled race; The canals of Mars; The loneliest man in the U.S. Army; Winter night; Evening at home; The ballet of Central Park; Seven say you can hear corn grow

This "omnibus includes 29 of the pieces collected in 'Thirty Stories' (published in 1946) and 21 later stories. Featuring a wide range of settings, the stories are populated by both Americans and Europeans, many of whom are affected personally by the hostilities of World War II and its difficult aftermath." Booklist

Boyle, T. Coraghessan

After the plague; stories. Viking 2001 303p o.p.

ISBN 0-670-03005-8 LC 2001-26585

Contents: Termination dust; She wasn't soft; Killing babies; Captured by the Indians; Achates McNeil; Mexico; The love of my life; Rust; Peep Hall; Going down; Friendly skies; The black and white sisters; Death of the cool; My widow; The underground gardens; After the plague

"This collection is uproarious and unforgiving: 'She Wasn't Soft,' the title of one story, says it all. If Boyle finds dark humor in the lives of peeping toms, he also writes with tenderness about a widow waiting 'for something she can't name.'" New Yorker

Drop City. Viking 2003 443p $25.95

ISBN 0-670-03172-0 LC 2002-66371

"After riding cross-country together, Star and Ronnie join Norm Sender's California commune and quickly move in different directions. Ronnie attempts to take as many drugs and make it with as many women as possible, while Star gets involved with the draft-dodging Marco. Meanwhile, Norm finds out that the board of health is going to condemn the buildings and, in a classic evocation of 1960s romanticism and naiveté, informs the group that they are moving to his uncle's cabin in Alaska." Libr J

"But for all its glorious physicality and riveting action, this is a frank and penetrating critique of a naiive but courageous time, a stinging indictment of machismo and a paean to womanhood and an unabashed celebration of true love and liberty." Booklist

East is East; a novel. Viking 1990 364p o.p.

LC 89-40804

In this novel Hiro Tanaka, "a young Japanese seaman, jumps ship off the coast of Georgia and, through a series of mishaps and cultural misunderstandings, finds himself

Boyle, T. Coraghessan—*Continued*
hiding out in an artists' colony from the police and immigration officials." N Y Times Book Rev

"At its best [this book] is an exuberant combination of proficient adventure writing and burlesque. It is a tall tale—or more accurately, a spoof of a tall tale. Boyle has great fun parodying Hemingway, Faulkner and even Melville. . . . Boyle commands a quirky, ferociously energetic prose that seems to owe nothing to anyone writing today." New Leader

A friend of the earth. Viking 2000 271p o.p.
ISBN 0-670-89177-0 LC 99-462217

This book follows the "life of Ty Tierwater, a California mall manager gone rabid eco-terrorist. The novel alternates between tales of Ty's nights as a saboteur in 1989 to his work as the zoo keeper for a rock star in 2025." Christ Sci Monit

Boyle "allows for a hint of redemption in the end, but his depiction of the cruel fate of humankind—the fate of monkey wrenchers, lumber companies, the not-quite-engaged and the engaged, too—is as unflinching as it is satirical." Publ Wkly

The inner circle. Viking 2004 418p $25.95
ISBN 0-670-03344-8 LC 2003-69462

"A novel about America's premier sex researcher Alfred C. Kinsey. The story is told by John Milk, Kinsey's first hire, on the day of Kinsey's funeral. Milk was first introduced to Professor Kinsey ('Prok,' to his friends) as a student in his marriage class (basically a crash course on sex with graphic slide shows). At the end of the semester, Prok appeals to his students to share their sex histories . . . . Soon after, Prok takes on Milk as his associate, training him to conduct interviews on his own. Thus, the field of sexology has begun, and the novel is propelled forward from there. . . . This novel considers the conflict between our animal instincts and our human emotions, raising questions about the relationships among sex, marriage, love, and jealousy, and is at once titillating and maddening." Libr J

Riven Rock. Viking 1998 466p o.p.
ISBN 0-670-87881-2 LC 97-34632

"When Stanley McCormick, the brilliant but highly strung son of the inventor of the Reaper, marries Boston socialite and MIT graduate Katherine Dexter, the papers call it the wedding of the century. But the marriage is never consummated, and after a disastrous honeymoon, a catatonic Stanley is moved to Riven Rock, a prisonlike mission in Santa Barbara. Diagnosed as a schizophrenic sex maniac, Stanley is to be kept entirely separate from women, including Katherine, who may speak to him only by telephone. Katherine goes on to become a major figure in the burgeoning suffrage movement . . . but she never divorces her husband or gives up hoping for a cure." Libr J

"One can admire the way in which Boyle keeps within the confines of the restricted mind-set of pre-World War II America. The book is filled with good writing and richly observed scenes; it has humanity and humor in abundance." N Y Times Book Rev

Road to Wellville; a novel. Viking 1993 476p il o.p.
LC 92-50731

This social satire provides a portrait of 1907 Battle Creek, Michigan "from three perspectives. The first and most central is that of Dr. Kellogg himself, high priest of a sanitarium where the rich and powerful go to be cured of physical and spiritual 'autointoxication' brought about by meat eating and sexual activity. Possessed of a Napoleon complex and an abiding hatred of Post, he is saluted around the clinic as 'the Chief.' The second is that of Will Lightbody, a patient at the clinic who has trouble getting the Kellogg religion. The third viewpoint is that of Charlie Ossining, a shady businessman who tries to get a piece of the breakfast-cereal action a little too late." Booklist

The author "evokes the world of the senses with remarkable skill. As always, his prose is a marvel, enjoyable from beginning to end, alive with astute observations, sharp intelligence and subtle musicality. Possibly as an effect of his highly developed style, Mr. Boyle's vision has been one of the most distinctive and original of his generation." N Y Times Book Rev

T.C. Boyle stories; the collected stories of T. Coraghessan Boyle. Viking 1998 691p o.p.
ISBN 0-670-87960-6 LC 98-39739

Contents: Modern love; Ike and Nina; Sorry fugu; Without a hero; Heart of a champion; Carnal knowledge; Acts of God; Hopes rise; Descent of man; Caviar; All shook up; I dated Jane Austen; Caye; Little fur people; John Barleycorn lives; The hat; Whales weep; A women's restaurant; Thawing out; Back in the Eocene; Sitting on top of the world; If the river was whiskey; Juliana cloth; Big game; Greasy Lake; Peace of mind; King bee; Sinking house; The Devil and Irv Cherniske; The human fly; On for the long haul; The 100 faces of death, volume IV; Little America; Stones in my passway, hellhound on my trail; Green hell; Me cago en la Leche (Robert Jordan in Nicaragua); The ape lady in retirement; De rerum natura; The extinction tales; The fog man; Drowning; Rara Avis; The overcoat II; Mexico; Beat; Hard sell; The miracle at Ballinspittle; Top of the food chain; The Hector Quesadilla story; We are Norsemen; The champ; Bloodfall; Rupert Beersley and the Beggar Master of Sivani-Hoota; The New Moon Party; The second swimming; Dada; Two ships; The little chill; A bird in hand; The Arctic explorer; Rapture of the deep; The big garage; Zapatos; Respect; Filthy with things

The tortilla curtain. Viking 1995 355p o.p.
LC 95-1970

"The lives of two couples living in Topanga Canyon (Los Angeles) intersect when Delaney Mossbacher slams his car into Cándido Rincón. But the couples couldn't be more disparate: Delaney is a nature writer ('Pilgrim at Topanga Canyon') whose wife, Kyra, is a successful realtor; the Rincóns are illegal aliens camping out, looking for any work at all, and América [is] pregnant." Libr J

"What Boyle does, and does well, is lay on the line our national cult of hypocrisy. Comically and painfully he details the snug wastefulness of the haves and the vile misery of the have-nots. . . . Americans of every stripe will find themselves rooting for Cándido and América, right up to the riproaring *deus ex machina* ending that screams out that we are all in this together." Nation

Water music; a novel. Little, Brown 1981 437p o.p.
LC 81-12423

"An Atlantic Monthly Press book"

A "novel with two protagonists, the book chronicles the fictionalized misadventures of Mungo Park—an actu-

Boyle, T. Coraghessan—*Continued*

al Scottish explorer (1771-1806)—and his counterpart Ned Rise, a London scalawag. They team up in Africa, where they attempt to chart the course of the Niger River, experiencing every conceivable comic mishap and catastrophe." Choice

The author "bases his first novel in historical fact, but brings his story to life with an innovative wit and bawdiness reminiscent of 'Tom Jones'. He peoples the novel with a colorful cast, involves them in the mishaps of daily life, and places everything within a specific historical framework. . . . A very funny and well-written literary work." Booklist

World's end; a novel. Viking 1987 456p o.p.

LC 87-40023

"The sins of the fathers—along with physical afflictions and other worries—are visited on their children as one generation relives in contemporary terms the experiences of the past. Boyle's novel—partly a historical tale and partly a modern-day re-creation of the same story—switches from past to near present and mixes seventeenth-century Dutch settlers and their landlords with hippie motorcyclists and Indians intent on reclaiming their territory in the Hudson River valley." Booklist

"The themes Mr. Boyle develops as his story shuttles between epochs make us grasp in new terms their connection with the American social and political experiment. His mastery of history is the secret of the accomplishment here. Mr. Boyle has lost none of the qualities that marked him a wit writer before, but now he has challenged his own disengagement; passion, need and belief breathe with striking force and freedom through this smashing good novel." N Y Times Book Rev

Boz *See* Dickens, Charles, 1812-1870

Bozai, Ágota, 1965-

To err is divine; English version by David Kramer. Counterpoint 2004 244p

ISBN 1-582-43277-5 LC 2003-25393

Original German edition, 1999

"October 29, just a few days before All Saint's Day, begins normally for schoolteacher Anna Levay-until she steps out of her bath, looks in her mirror, and sees a halo around her head. Not a believer, Anna is unable to get rid of her holy burden and becomes a reluctant and often accidental miracle worker who causes fish to jump out of a lake, makes spent flowers rebloom, and even turns tap water into wine. But when a greedy doctor discovers her unearthly gift for healing the sick, he is determined to exploit her heaven-sent touch to revive the town's flagging tourist trade. . . . Bozai displays a divine touch for sly, subversive, ironic, and thoroughly delightful social comedy." Libr J

Bradbury, Malcolm, 1932-2000

Doctor Criminale. Viking 1992 344p o.p.

ISBN 0-670-84677-5 LC 92-53782

"When his London newspaper suddenly folds, young, likeable writer Francis Jay finds a job researching the life of world-renowned Hungarian philosopher Bazlo Criminale for a possible BBC program. The quest for the enigmatic Criminale–an Eastern European intellectual who has been given the extraordinary freedom to travel and publish abroad-takes Jay on an illuminating . . . romp through Budapest, Vienna, Italy, and Switzerland." Libr J

This novel "skillfully glazes big issues with a light-hearted, spy-novel frosting, and to this extent the book is reminiscent of Graham Greene's easygoing 'entertainments.'" Christ Sci Monit

To the Hermitage. Overlook Press 2001 498p $27.95

ISBN 1-58567-131-2 LC 00-50147

A "dual narrative that compares Denis Diderot's *Age of Reason* to the postmodern 1990s. The first story follows the French encyclopedist as he travels from Paris to Catherine the Great's court in St. Petersburg. The acquisitive Catherine has just purchased Diderot's personal library. Now she wants to hire him as her librarian. In the second narrative, a British novelist attends an international Diderot conference held in St. Petersburg in 1993, just as the military coup against Boris Yeltsin is unfolding. When an American deconstructionist in a baseball cap refutes the very notion of an Age of Reason, the conference collapses into drunken anarchy." Libr J

"The book is overextended, but it is also lively, thought provoking and, in its portrait of contemporary Russia, vividly chilling. For patient readers of a scholarly inclination and with a liking for the stranger corners of history, this will be a treat." Publ Wkly

Bradbury, Ray, 1920-

Bradbury stories; 100 of his most celebrated tales. Morrow 2003 893p $29.95

ISBN 0-06-054242-X LC 2003-42189

Partial contents: The whole town's sleeping; The rocket; Season of disbelief; And the rock cried out; The drummer boy of Shiloh; The beggar on O'Connell Bridge; The flying machine; Heavy-set; The first night of Lent; Lafayette, farewell; Remember Sascha?; Junior; That woman on the lawn; February 1999: Ylla; Banshee; One for his lordship, and one for the road!; The Laurel and Hardy love affair; Unterderseaboat doktor; Another fine mess; The dwarf; A wild night in Galway; The wind; No news, or what killed the dog?; A little journey; Any friend of Nicholas Nickleby's is a friend of mine; The garbage collector; The visitor; The man; Henry the ninth; The messiah; Bang! you're dead!; Darling Adolf; The beautiful shave; Colonel Stonesteel's genuine homemade truly Egyptian mummy; I see you never; The exiles; At midnight, in the month of June; The witch door; The watchers; 2004-05: the naming of names; Hopscotch; The illustrated man; The dead man; June 2001: and the moon be still as bright; The burning man; G.B.S.—Mark V; A blade of grass; The sound of summer running; And the sailor, home from the sea; The lonely ones; The Finnegan; On the Orient, North; The smiling people

"This massive retrospective of self-selected Bradbury stories offers a compendium of his eccentrics, misfits, losers, and small-town dreamers, who typically inhabit an uncanny setting or confront a strange, unsettling situation." Libr J

Dandelion wine; a novel. Knopf 1975 269p o.p.

ISBN 0-394-49605-1

Bradbury, Ray, 1920—*Continued*

A reissue, with a new introduction by the author, of the title first published 1957 by Doubleday

A novel about one summer in the life of a twelve-year-old boy, Douglas Spaulding: the summer of 1928. The place is Green Town, Illinois, and Doug and his brother Tom wander in and out among their elders, living and dreaming, sometimes aware of things, again just having a wonderful time. Doug's big discovery that summer was that he was alive

"The writing is beautiful and the characters are wonderful living people. A rare reading experience—highly recommended to all libraries." Libr J

Fahrenheit 451. 40th anniversary ed. Simon & Schuster 1993 190p o.p.

ISBN 0-671-87036-X LC 93-10885

First published 1953 in paperback by Ballantine Bks. This edition includes a foreword by Ray Bradbury

The title story, a novelette, tells about a bookburner official in a future fascist state. The other stories are: The playground; And the rock cried out

Fahrenheit 451 [novelette]

In Bradbury, R. Fahrenheit 451 p19-150

The golden apples of the sun; drawings by Joe Mugnaini. Doubleday 1953 250p il o.p.

Contents: Fog horn; The pedestrian; April witch; The wilderness; Fruit at the bottom of the bowl; Invisible boy; Flying machine; The murderer; Golden kite, the silver wind; I see you never; Embroidery; Big black and white game; Sound of thunder; Great wide world over there; Powerhouse; En la noche; Sun and shadow; The meadow; Garbage collector; Great fire; Hail and farewell; The golden apples of the sun

A graveyard for lunatics; another tale of two cities. Knopf 1990 285p o.p.

LC 89-43387

This novel is set in Hollywood in 1954. The narrator is hired to write a horror movie. "A boyhood friend has been signed to create the most dreadful monster in film history. Searching for inspiration, the buddies visit a cemetery across the street from Maximus Films. Abruptly, the body of a long-buried mogul passes in review. Is it an apparition? What about the hideous beast that begins to haunt the Brown Derby restaurant? And the performer who has played Jesus Christ in movies for 25 years: Is he an actor or an authentic Saviour? Are they all characters in someone else's movie?" Time

"For anyone who grew up on Bradbury's stories, this Baedeker to the fantasies of his own youth is like camping out with Santa Claus. Never mind that you can forecast the ending a mile off, or that the narrator's voice is too often adolescently shrill. Out of a lot of wire and paste and cardboard, Bradbury has convincingly conjured a lost world, 'lovelier than tonight or all the nights to come.'" Newsweek

Green shadows, white whale; a novel; with drawings by Edward Sorel. Knopf 1992 271p il o.p.

LC 91-58552

"This is Bradbury's comic account of his trip to Ireland to write the screenplay for Huston's adaptation of *Moby-Dick*. The movie itself is merely a background constant that anchors this series of . . . vignettes and anecdotes. Bradbury describes his awed dealings with the erratic, eccentric and impulsive director, and his delight upon being accepted among the regulars at an atmospheric pub called Heeber Finn's. It's a great place to hoist a wee drop and listen to stories told in the best Irish brogue." Publ Wkly

"High jinks follow high jinks, some of them quite funny, others just too Irish for words. It's as rewarding when dipped into randomly as when plowed straight through." Booklist

I sing the Body Electric! stories. Knopf 1969 305p o.p.

"Whatever the premise, the author retains an enthusiasm for both the natural world and the supernatural that sends a tingle of excitement through even the flimsiest conceit." N Y Times Book Rev

The illustrated man. Doubleday 1951 251p o.p.

In this work "the stories are given a linking framework; they are all seen as magical tattoos becoming living stories, springing from the body of the protagonist." Sci Fic Ency

The Martian chronicles. Avon Books 1997 268p $15.95

ISBN 0-380-97383-9 LC 96-95071

First published 1950 by Doubleday

This book's "closely interwoven short stories, linked by recurrent images and themes, tell of the repeated attempts by humans to colonize Mars, of the way they bring their old prejudices with them, and of the repeated, ambiguous meetings with the shape-changing Martians." Sci Fic Ency

Quicker than the eye. Avon Bks. 1996 261p o.p.

ISBN 0-380-97380-4 LC 96-20481

Contents: Unterderseaboat doktor; Zaharoff/Richter Mark V; Remember Sascha?; Another fine mess; The electrocution; Hopscotch; The Finnegan; That woman on the lawn; The very gentle murders; Quicker than the eye; Dorian in excelsus; No news, or what killed the dog?; The witch doctor; The ghost in the machine; At the end of the ninth year; Bug; Once more, legato; Exchange; Free dirt; Last rites; The other highway

Something wicked this way comes. Avon Bks. 1999 293p $15.95

ISBN 0-380-97727-3

A reissue of the title first published 1962 by Simon and Schuster

"We read here of the loss of innocence, the recognition of evil, the bond between generations, and the purely fantastic. These forces enter Green Town, Illinois, on the wheels of Cooger and Dark's Pandemonium Shadow Show. Will Halloway and Jim Nightshade, two 13-year-olds, explore the sinister carnival for excitement, which becomes desperation as the forces of the dark threaten to engulf-them. Bradbury's gentle humanism and lyric style serve this fantasy well." Shapiro. Fic for Youth. 3d edition

The stories of Ray Bradbury; with an introduction by the author. Knopf 1980 xx, 884p $40

ISBN 0-394-51335-5 LC 80-7655

Bradbury, Ray, 1920-—*Continued*

This is a collection of 100 of the author's short stories. There are Martian stories, stories of a midwestern childhood, Irish stories and stories from Mexico

"Bradbury has a distinctive voice, and with it he sings to us of magic, nostalgia, beauty, terror, tenderness, innocence, loss, love and wisdom. Here is a specifically American vision of wonder which will someday tell our descendants a great deal about this time and place and about the lives we lived in our imaginations." Publ Wkly

Bradford, Barbara Taylor, 1933-

Hold the dream; the sequel to A woman of substance. Doubleday 1985 632p o.p.

LC 84-25993

This novel "revolves around Emma's abdication of power over her far-flung business enterprises in favor of her grandchildren, particularly her favorite and heir, Paula McGill Fairley. As she struggles to keep the vast Harte empire running smoothly, Paula must deal not only with business crises, but with family and personal problems as well, particularly her disintegrating marriage." Libr J

"Bradford is a talented writer who can make even the most contrived situations seem credible, and the novel's only drawback is its overly long passages and slow pace. But even this flaw will appeal to readers who enjoy luxuriating in good escapist fiction." Booklist

Followed by To be the best (1988)

Power of a woman. HarperCollins Pubs. 1997 335p o.p.

At 47, Stephanie "Stevie" Jardine "is at the apex of her career and life, running the American branch of Jardine's, the prestigious Crown Jewellers of London. Finally at terms with her long widowhood, Stevie now draws emotional strength and contentment from her work and family. Then an unexpected act of violence committed by a stranger on the other side of the world plunges Stevie into turmoil and despair. In order to save her injured daughter's life and ensure her future, Stevie must go back to her past and confront a devastating relationship." Publisher's note

A sudden change of heart. Doubleday 1999 352p $24

ISBN 0-385-49274-X LC 99-196376

This novel features "Laura Valiant, a New York art dealer who specializes in impressionist and post-impressionist works. Laura has what she thinks is a storybook marriage, and her closest childhood friend, Claire Benson, now publisher and editor-in-chief of a French interior design and art magazine, offers contrast as a bitter, divorced woman who dotes on her teenage daughter. Bradford's exploration of the relationship between the two women depicts a series of heartbreaks and scandals." Publ Wkly

Three weeks in Paris. Doubleday 2002 323p $24.95

ISBN 0-385-50141-2

This novel "examines the lives of four women, alumni of an exclusive arts school in Paris, who must confront their stormy pasts when they are invited to attend a special birthday party. Anya Sedgwick, the indomitable doyenne of the school, wants her four favorite pupils to repair their destroyed friendship and help celebrate her 85th birthday." Publ Wkly

"The feud that separated them turns out to be a trivial, but watching each woman sort out her love life and find happiness is certainly entertaining." Booklist

The triumph of Katie Byrne. Doubleday 2001 338p o.p.

ISBN 0-385-50140-4 LC 00-65677

This "romantic-suspense tale stars Katie Byrne, a struggling actress who remains haunted by a horrific attack that took place when she was 17. The awful crime, which took the life of her best friend and left another friend lingering in a coma, was never solved by police, and Katie, even 10 years after the event, is obsessed by the idea that the murderer is stalking her, hoping to finish the job. Until the crime is solved, Katie will never be free to pursue romance and her promising acting career." Booklist

Voice of the heart. Doubleday 1983 732p o.p.

LC 81-47863

"The story of a world-famous movie star and stage actress who returns to New York to seek out six people who years earlier had suffered hurt, pain, and humiliation at her hands. Curiosity makes them decide to see her and thus reopen the old wounds of their past." Publisher's note

"This is a well-written 'woman's novel,' although it tends to drag and the plot is rather formulaic. There are some lively plot twists and a certain mystery about the book that will keep readers glued to it." Libr J

Where you belong. Doubleday 2000 356p $24.95

ISBN 0-385-49275-8 LC 99-88133

"War photographer Val Denning loses colleague and lover Tony to a bullet while in war-torn Kosovo. This sends her into a personal crisis, causing her to wrestle with the meaning of family, love, honor, and her place in the world. Bradford's jet-set backgrounds of Paris, London, New York, and the south of France never disappoint." Libr J

A woman of substance. Doubleday 1979 755p o.p.

LC 77-9231

"A poor Yorkshire girl rises from the servant class to found a department store and eventually head an important business dynasty. As the aged Emma recalls how she has sacrificed love and happiness for success and power, she repudiates the past for the simpler and more enduring pleasures of life." Booklist

"It's a life worth the telling, and Ms. Bradford has told it well, sparing no detail. She writes competently, if not extraordinarily, against an accurate and well drawn historical background." West Coast Rev Books

Followed by Hold the dream

Bradford, Richard, 1932-2002

Red sky at morning; a novel. Lippincott 1968 256p o.p.

"Joshua Arnold and his mother move to their summer home in Corazon Sagrado, New Mexico, when the father joins the Navy during World War II. Josh copes with the Mexican and Anglo customs and is concerned with his

Bradford, Richard, 1932-2002—*Continued*
mother's drinking. When his father dies in the war, he takes responsibility for his mother, his own life, and his father's business." Shapiro. Fic for Youth. 3d edition

Bradley, Marion Zimmer

The best of Marion Zimmer Bradley; edited by Martin H. Greenberg. Academy Chicago 1985 367p o.p.

LC 85-18517

Contents: Centaurus changeling; The climbing wave; Exiles of tomorrow; Death between the stars; Bird of prey; The wind people; The wild one; Treason of the blood; The jewel of Arwen; The day of the butterflies; Hero's moon; The engine; The secret of the Blue Star; To keep the oath; Elbow room; Blood will tell

Black Trillium; {by} Marion Zimmer Bradley, Julian May, and Andre Norton. Doubleday 1990 409p (Trillium) o.p.

LC 89-71544

"A Foundation book"

"Three princesses, Haramis, Anigel, and Kadiya, are the living petals of the Black Trillium, an ancient flower that is the symbol of the kingdom of Ruwenda. At birth they are given magic amulets by the White Lady and warned of a fearsome destiny. Seventeen years later, both the king and the queen are brutally murdered, and the three princesses, trying to escape, are scattered. One by one, they reach the White Lady and are sent on a quest for a talisman to defeat the evil sorcerer who has taken over their kingdom." Booklist

Darkover landfall. DAW Books 1972 160p o.p.
ISBN 0-886-77234-6

A Terran spaceship crashes on planet Darkover and decides to build an Earth-like colony there, only to discover that they are not alone.

Exile's song; a novel of Darkover. DAW Bks. 1996 435p o.p.

LC 96-194020

"Musicologist Margaret Alton and her mentor Ivor Davidson travel to Darkover, the planet of her birth, to collect folk songs. When Ivor dies suddenly, Margaret finds family she has never known and suffers a painful illness that awakens latent mental powers. During this journey of self-discovery, she fights for her autonomy but is drawn to remain on Darkover as a member of a powerful family." Libr J

This "entry in Bradley's venerable series is an almost unalloyed pleasure from beginning to end and one of the few . . . Darkover novels that someone unfamiliar with the series can pick up and get into immediately." Publ Wkly

Followed by The shadow matrix

The firebrand; a novel. Simon & Schuster 1987 608p o.p.

LC 87-17283

"Recounts the story of the Trojan War through the eyes of Kassandra, a princess of Troy blessed with 'the sight' yet doomed by a vengeful god to be thought mad in her prophecies of destruction. . . . As a priestess of Apollo who rode with the Amazons in the waning days of their rule, Bradley's Kassandra is caught between the whims of warring gods and greedy mortals, forced to bear witness to the awful destinies of those she loves, but unable to change the course of any life, including her own. Although these mythic figures stumble through some petty, rather too modern dialogue, the dust of the war fairly rises off the page as Bradley animates this rich history and vivifies the conflicts between a culture that reveres the strength of women and one that makes them mere consorts of powerful men." Publ Wkly

The forest house. Viking 1994 416p o.p.

LC 93-33686

"The forbidden love of a druid priestess and a Roman soldier mirrors the clash of cultures in Roman Britain. . . . The novel evokes an age when three major religions maintained an uneasy coexistence on the island of Britain. Eilan, a daughter of goddess-worshiping druids, and Gaius Marcellius, a half-British Roman, live for the coming of a legendary future king to unite the warring islanders. Bradley envisions the 'old religion' as a refreshing blend of classic and revisionist concepts, adding a distinct flavor to her seamless weave of history and myth." Libr J

The house between the worlds. Doubleday 1980 244p o.p.

LC 79-7800

"An experimental ESP-enhancing drug sends Cameron Fenton's astral body into a parallel world while his physical self stays behind in a coma. The world he visits as a ghost-like 'tweenman' is the home of the Alfar, beautiful, magical people reminiscent of Tolkien's elves. They are mortally threatened by the noisome, goblin-like Ironfolk, invaders from yet another world. Fenton wants to help the Alfar, but his only hope is to find the Worldhouse, a 'physical' gateway between the worlds, and the Worldhouse may not want to be found." Publ Wkly

"This is an excellent book, with all the virtues readers have come to expect from Bradley: literate writing; excellent characterization; sound, logical plotting; and broad humanistic sympathies." Booklist

Lady of Avalon. Viking; distributed by Penguin Putnam 1997 460p $24.95
ISBN 0-670-85783-1 LC 96-51175

This novel traces the High Priestess of Avalon and the sacrificial Sacred King through three cycles of reincarnation and mythic destiny. . . . A pillar of the fantasy field, Bradley here combines romance, rich historical detail, magical dazzlements, grand adventure and feminist sentiments into the kind of novel her fans have been yearning for." Publ Wkly

Lady of the Trillium. Bantam Bks. 1995 291p o.p.

LC 94-37056

"When the aging princess Haramis, Archmage of Ruwenda and protector of its lands, senses her impending death, she settles upon young Princess Mikayla as her successor—heedless of the fact that her plans ignore Mikayla's own desires. Set against the background created in *Black Trillium*, Bradley's . . . novel focuses not on the clichéd battle between good and evil but rather on the more subtle war of the misunderstanding and intolerance found between old and young." Libr J

Bradley, Marion Zimmer—*Continued*

The mists of Avalon. Knopf 1982 876p o.p.
LC 82-47810

This "retelling of the Arthurian legend is dominated by the character of Morgan le Fay (here called Morgaine), the powerful sorceress who symbolizes the historical clash betweeen Christianity and the early pagan religions of the British Isles." Publ Wkly

The author "deserves high praise for her work since this great and sweeping book successfully ties together legend and lore." Best Sellers

Priestess of Avalon; {by} Marion Zimmer Bradley and Diana L. Paxson. Viking 2001 394p o.p.
ISBN 0-670-91023-6 LC 00-51254

First published 2000 in the United Kingdom

In this prequel to The mists of Avalon "10-year-old Eilan, whose greatest wish is to serve as priestess for her goddess, is brought to Avalon for training. From a prophetic vision, she knows she is destined to love one man and to bear his son. When the man of her vision, a young Roman soldier, comes to Avalon, Eilan is compelled to follow her heart, which means defying her high priestess, the Lady of Avalon." Booklist

"Bradley creates a powerful tale of magic and faith that enlarges upon pagan and Christian traditions to express a deeper truth. Though Bradley died before she finished the novel, veteran fantasy author Paxson brings to completion this last work of a master of the genre." Libr J

The shadow matrix; a novel of Darkover. DAW Bks. 1997 512p $22.95
ISBN 0-88677-743-7 LC 97-229068

In this sequel to Exile's song, "Margaret Alton returns to Darkover to learn to control her newly discovered combined powers, including the shadow matrix on her hand." Libr J

"Bradley's saga is clearly showing some signs of age, but Darkover remains a monumental achievement." Booklist

Traitor's sun; a novel of Darkover. New Am. Lib. 1999 483p o.p.
ISBN 0-88677-810-7 LC 99-215583

"Senator Hermes-Gabriel Aldaran receives a telepathic wake-up call to return home to Darkover before the rapacious Expansionists in the Terran Federation destroy what few personal freedoms are left to their citizenry. Arriving planetside with his children and his wife, Katherine—who has been kept ignorant of his psychic gifts—Herm finds life on Darkover more difficult than anticipated." Publ Wkly

"Bradley's consummate skill at presenting complex political intrigue side-by-side with acute personal drama makes her Darkover series both involving and intricate." Libr J

Bradshaw, Gillian, 1956-

The bearkeeper's daughter. Houghton Mifflin 1987 310p o.p.
LC 87-2924

"To the recorded facts about Justinian I and his empress Theodora, Bradshaw adds an illegitimate son born to Theodora. John arrives from Arabia seeking the truth of statements his father made on his deathbed. Afraid to acknowledge him, Theodora finds a place for John as secretary to the palace chamberlain. Later, he becomes involved in court intrigue, riots, and war in Thrace." Libr J

"This is a deftly plotted and inviting story that will entertain romantics as well as history buffs." West Coast Rev Books

The wolf hunt. Forge 2001 380p o.p.
ISBN 0-312-87332-8 LC 2001-33825

"A Tom Doherty Associates book"

"Marie Penthièvre, a young and spirited noblewoman, is kidnapped from a convent in Normandy by enemies of her father. Escaping into the wild forest of Brocéliande, she is rescued by the renowned knight Tiarnán of Talensac. He escorts her to the duke of Brittany, who encourages her to marry one of his knights. Marie's romantic dreams of wedding Tiarnán are dashed when he marries someone else, but when he disappears soon after his wedding, Marie determines to discover the truth and preserve Tiarnán's reputation as an honorable warrior." Libr J

"Meticulously researched and hauntingly atmospheric historical fiction." Booklist

Bradshaw-Isherwood, Christopher William *See* Isherwood, Christopher, 1904-1986

Brady, James, 1928-

Warning of war; a novel of the North China Marines. Thomas Dunne Bks. 2002 341p $24.95
ISBN 0-312-28018-1 LC 2001-54806

"On the eve of Pearl Harbor, a thousand U.S. Marines maintain a shaky truce in an isolated region of northern China. After Pearl Harbor, the Marines are cut off and at the mercy of advancing Japanese forces, led by a fanatical officer. Thus begins a riveting rescue story as an equally relentless Marine captain strives to save his comrades." Booklist

Brady, William S., 1938-

For works written by this author under other names see Harvey, John, 1938-

Braff, Joshua

The unthinkable thoughts of Jacob Green; a novel; by Joshua Braff. 1st ed. Algonquin Books of Chapel Hill 2004 259p $22.95
ISBN 1-565-12420-0 LC 2004-46260

"Like a child, Jacob Green's father, Abram, wants what he wants when he wants it and will throw a temper tantrum if he doesn't get it. What Abram wants most of all is the perfect suburban Jewish family-perfectly intelligent, perfectly religious, and perfect at obeying thy father. Braff's rich, moving, and very funny first novel begins with a 1977 housewarming party at which Abram dramatically introduces each member of his family while the four children and their mother seethe with resentment at being paraded as testaments to Abram's greatness. Jacob's present-tense, first-person narration keeps the pace quick, and the exquisite plotting ensures that Jacob's growing emotional turmoil is paralleled by metaphorically resonant real-life events." Booklist

Bragg, Melvyn, 1939-

Crossing the lines; a novel; by Melvyn Bragg. 1st U.S. ed. Arcade Pub 2005 c2003 490p $26

ISBN 1-559-70738-0 LC 2004-23456

First published 2003 in the United Kingdom

This concluding volume in the author's trilogy about post-World War II England "picks up in the mid-1950s as young Joe Richardson becomes the first in the Northumbrian village of Wigton to attend Oxford. His parents, having weathered the storms of war, are approaching middle age and watch young Joe on the threshold of this great adventure with pride and affection. However, Joe is torn between his love of learning and his love for his teenage sweetheart, Rachel. He relishes his time with his learned tutors and the camaraderie with his fellow undergraduates but rushes back to Wigton and Rachel every chance he gets. Meanwhile, Rachel has left school and is cycling through jobs in a local bank, her life gradually steering away from Joe." Libr J

"As in The Soldier's Return and A Son of War, Bragg's prose is straightforward and unadorned, allowing only the occasional literary flourish, with a tendency toward understatement that is as precise as it is convincing. Devoted Anglophiles in particular will find much to appreciate in this unhurried examination of postwar English life." Publ Wkly

The soldier's return. Arcade Pub. 2002 384p $25.95

ISBN 1-55970-639-2 LC 2002-21558

First published 1999 in the United Kingdom

"In 1946, Englishman Sam Richardson returns to his wife and young son after fighting the the 'Forgotten War' in Burma. Like so many who fought beside him and lived to return, Sam feels suffocated by life in tiny rural Wigton. The men who were left behind ask too many painful questions, and nightmares rob Sam of sleep. Work is scarce and demeaning, and rebuilding his life with his wife, Ellen, and young son, Joe, is fraught with awkwardness, misunderstanding, and frustration." Libr J

"Bragg weaves a powerful, deeply moving story of a family and a society torn apart by war. His straightforward prose and the measured pace of his writing allow readers to savor every nuance of life in a small town in postwar England, and the depth and reality of his characters and his ability to bring the horrors of war alive are nothing short of brilliant." Booklist

A son of war; a novel. Arcade Pub. 2003 426p $25.95

ISBN 1-559-70686-4 LC 2002-44058

This sequel to A soldier's return "finds Sam and Ellen Richardson and their son, Joe, still in the dreary slums of Wigton, waiting for their chance for a new council house in a developing outskirt. Times are tough, and they are barely scraping by." Libr J

"A hauntingly evocative slice of postwar life." Booklist

Bram, Christopher, 1952-

Lives of the circus animals; a novel. HarperCollins Pubs. 2003 341p $24.95

ISBN 0-06-054253-5 LC 2002-192195

"Henry Lewse is a British actor starring in a Broadway musical. Jessie Doyle is his much-needed personal assistant. Her brother, Caleb, is a playwright whose latest play was shredded by theater critic Kenneth Prager. Frank, Jessie's new boyfriend, is directing a reality play in Apartment 2B. Toby, Caleb's former lover, is trying hard to break into show biz." Libr J

"Bram has a sophisticated understanding of celebrity and the intersection of gay and straight worlds. His savvy—and his easy familiarity with the New York theater scene—gives edge and nuance to this witty entertainment." Publ Wkly

Brand, Max, 1892-1944

Beyond the outposts. Five Star 1997 254p o.p.

ISBN 0-7862-0745-0 LC 97-9308

"Five Star standard print western series"

Earlier version of this story was serialized in 1925 in Western Story magazine

This western adventure follows the "journeys of young Lew Dorset as he searches for his father, an escaped convict. His skill with firearms gets him a job as a hunter with a trader's freight train heading onto the prairies to barter with the Indians. There he meets young Chuck Morris, and together they take on a Cheyenne attack party. Finding shelter in a Sioux village, they absorb the native culture. . . . Lew goes on to play a decisive role in a battle between the Sioux and Pawnee, but returns to find that Chuck has deserted his wife and son. His attempts to reconcile them culminate in great danger and, ultimately, a threat to his life." Publisher's note

Chinook; a north-western story. Five Star 1998 271p o.p.

ISBN 0-7862-1155-5 LC 98-22718

"Five Star standard print western series"

"Joe Harney heads to Alaska during the great gold rush of 1898 and finds himself impressed by a great wolf dog owned by Andrew Steen, a crusty, bad-tempered loner. When Harney saves Steen's life, Steen grudgingly agrees that they can travel overland together. On that harsh journey, they meet Kate Winslow and learn that she's headed for Circle City to meet up with a man who wants her dead. This is a tale of the tough and often ruthless folks who risked their lives to get to the frozen north and, with any luck, to find their fortune." Publisher's note

The collected stories of Max Brand; edited, with story prefaces, by Robert and Jane Easton; introduction by William Bloodworth. centennial ed. University of Neb. Press 1994 xx, 342p $40

ISBN 0-8032-1244-5 LC 93-43938

Contents: John Ovington returns; Above the law; The wedding guest; A special occasion; Outcast breed; The sun stood still; The strange villa; The claws of the tigress; Internes can't take money; Fixed; Wine on the desert; Virginia creeper; Pringle's luck; The silent witness; Miniature; Our daily bread; Honor bright; The king

Dark Rosaleen
In Brand, M. Max Brand's best western stories

Dust across the range
In Brand, M. Max Brand's best western stories

Brand, Max, 1892-1944—*Continued*

Fugitives' fire. Putnam 1991 184p o.p.
LC 90-8478

This novel originally appeared 1928 in Western story magazine as two novelettes: Prairie pawn and Fugitive's fire

This novel features fugitive plainsman Paul Torridon. "A prisoner of the mighty Cheyenne Nation, young Torridon lives in pampered misery. The Cheyenne, who call him 'White Thunder,' are convinced of his supernatural talents and expect him to deliver good luck in battle and rain in drought. He is richly rewarded for his 'mystical favors,' but he dreads the day his good luck and horse sense will fail, revealing him as only too mortal—and losing him his scalp in the bargain." Publisher's note

The gentle desperado. Dodd, Mead 1985 195p o.p.
LC 85-10321

"Silver star westerns"

This novel is comprised of three stories originally published in Western Story Magazine under the pseudonym, George Owen Baxter

"Robert Fernald was a deadly fighter, but he didn't really believe it, not even when he outgunned his opponents. To his enemies, he looked like a kid, too mild-mannered to be a threat. But then he went after Tom Gill and his men who were preying on the Larkin ranch, forcing handsome young Beatrice Larkin into bankruptcy. Everyone said it would take an army to stop the rustlers from driving the stolen cattle through the mountain passes—until Fernald faced tough Tom Gill himself in a showdown." Publisher's note

In the hills of Monterey; a western story. Five Star 1998 239p o.p.
ISBN 0-7862-0988-7 LC 97-38421

"Five Star standard print western series"

"The wealthiest landowner in the province of Spanish-controlled Alta California has sent away to Spain for a suitable bridegroom for his beautiful daughter, Ortiza Tarabal. Francisco Valdez arrives with his slave, an Englishman known as El Rojo, a courageous man who has made some enemies among the ruling class, but has the devotion of the Indians. El Rojo also has the very dangerous love of Ortiza Tarabal, despite her betrothal to Francisco Valdez and the wrath of her father." Publisher's note

Max Brand's best western stories; edited with a biographical introduction by William F. Nolan. Dodd, Mead 1981-1987 3v o.p.
LC 81-3204

Contents v1 Wine on the desert; Virginia creeper; Macdonald's dream; Partners; Dust across the range [novelette]; The bells of San Carlos

v2 Outcasts [novelette]; The fear of Morgon the Fearless; Dark Rosaleen [novelette]; Cayenne Charlie; The golden day

v3 Reata's peril trek; Crazy rhythm; Dust storm; A lucky dog; The third bullet; Half a partner; The sun stood still

Outcasts
In Brand, M. Max Brand's best western stories

Sheriff Larrabee's prisoner
In Brand, M. Stolen gold: a western trio

A shower of silver
In Brand, M. Stolen gold: a western trio

The Stingaree. Dodd, Mead 1968 c1930 216p o.p.

"Silver star westerns"

"Jimmy Green is a wild, half-Indian, half-civilized, thirteen-year-old who is undisputed king of the small village of Fort Anxious. One day, a tramp wanders into the village, and ultimately into the life of Jimmy, changing it from the complacent existence of a boy into the desperate flight of a fugitive. The stranger, also known as the Stingaree, has come from Alabama to revenge the death of his partner by the leading citizen of Fort Anxious. Although he succeeds in forcing the man to confess, he is thwarted by the police in his attempt to kill Stanley Parker. The Stingaree, along with Jimmy Green, an Indian companion, and a wild dog is forced to flee into the wilderness, beginning one of the best chase episodes." Libr J

Stolen gold
In Brand, M. Stolen gold: a western trio

Stolen gold: a western trio. Five Star 1999 255p o.p.
ISBN 0-7862-1333-7 LC 98-52067

"Five Star standard print western series"

"The three short novels collected here were all published in pulp magazines during the 1920s. . . . In the title piece, former convict Reata is duped into abandoning his hard-won domestic bliss to search for treasure. The second tale finds a drifter accused of murder. His only hope for justice is the daughter of the sheriff who captured him. The third tale features a good samaritan drawn into a web of duplicity when he tries to help a newlywed whose husband is suddenly seized by a local lawman." Booklist

The survival of Juan Oro. Five Star 1999 259p o.p.
ISBN 0-7862-1325-6 LC 98-42372

"Five Star standard print western series"

This tale "was born as a magazine serial in 1925. Now published in book form with the author's original material restored, the story tells of Juan Oro, who, raised by Yaquis and captured by the forces of Don José Fontana, is apprenticed to outlaw Matias Bordi after promising to murder Bordi once he has learned the ways of a killer. But Juan's feelings for Bordi are such that he cannot keep his promise. . . . Mainstream western fare from a master of the genre." Booklist

Brandon, Jay

Local rules. Pocket Bks. 1995 290p o.p.
LC 94-20033

"An overeager sheriff's deputy sparks the quirk of fate that finds Jordan Marshall, former prosecuting attorney in San Antonio, acting as defense for a young man accused of murder in a tiny Texas town. . . . What should have been a five-minute pro forma exercise takes on life-changing importance as Marshall, convinced that justice is being ill-served in the case, uncovers another murder and turns up a big-city number of small-town secrets." Publ Wkly

Brandon, Jay—*Continued*

Rules of evidence. Pocket Bks. 1992 294p o.p.
LC 91-27380

"Mike Stennett is a grungy undercover cop who works the predominantly black and Latino sections of San Antonio, Texas. His arrests are often brutal and tend to be made on black suspects. He's a career cop, dedicated to the job, with little chance of promotion, no partner, and few friends inside or outside the force. When he is suspended with pay after the beating death of a black derelict, Stennett chooses Boudro, a black lawyer, to represent him. Boudro has tangled with Stennett before, and he's not inclined to trust him much. But the case evolves in strange ways." Booklist

"Brandon develops an interesting contrast between Stennett, the unsavory but devoted cop, and Raymond, the skillful and competitive attorney; each considers himself rightful protector of the crime-ridden East Side where both grew up." Publ Wkly

Braun, Lilian Jackson

The cat who ate Danish modern. Dutton 1967 192p o.p.

The "adventure of Koko, The Siamese, and his Watson, Jim Qwilleran. The 'Daily Fluxion' assigns Jim to mastermind a new Sunday supplement called, of all things, 'Gracious Abodes.' But the shocking consequences of the first few issues makes Jim realize that he is back in his own field, crime reporting, and that only Koko can help with the answers." Libr J

"The mystery is mild, the satire on interior decorating fads and fancies amusing, and the Siamese cat who helps play detective delightful." Publ Wkly

The cat who blew the whistle. Putnam 1994 240p o.p.
LC 94-28462

"When the discovery of embezzlement at the Lumbertown Credit Union in Sawdust City (aka Mudville, population 5,000) coincides with the disappearance of its wealthy president, who is also a model railroad buff and owner of a salvaged and restored steam locomotive, Moose County's best-known philanthropist, columnist, and amateur detective, Jim Qwilleran, decides to investigate the mystery—with the help of his two Siamese sleuths, Koko and Yum Yum. . . . The author provides enough background information to make new readers feel at home, and devotees of the series will applaud the added interest of railroading language and lore." Booklist

The cat who brought down the house. Putnam 2003 228p
ISBN 0-399-14942-2 LC 2002-68138

"Thelma Thackery, in her 80s, comes back to Pickax after a long Hollywood career in food. She's turning the old opera house into a revival movie theater, sparks a few other local delights, but can't seem to get her ne'erdowell nephew to do well at all. Qwill plugs away at old lies and a death in Thelma's family. We learn stuff through his newspaper column and his journal entries, and through the responses of his Siamese cat, KoKo. All the murders are offstage: the fun part is in food, clothing, and the quotidian joys of small-town life." Booklist

The cat who came to breakfast. Putnam 1994 254p o.p.
LC 93-34059

"Pickax City's Jim Qwilleran and his intuitive Siamese cats, Yum Yum and Koko, investigate odd accidents plaguing a glitzy resort recently built on a nearby island in Moose County. . . . After an episode of food poisoning and an accidental drowning at the resort hotel, the owners of the Domino Inn, an already established bed-and-breakfast, ask Qwill to find out whether disgruntled locals are trying to discourage tourism." Publ Wkly

The cat who lived high. Putnam 1990 239p o.p.
LC 90-34526

"Jim Qwilleran and his Siamese sleuth Koko investigate the recent death of an art dealer, a former tenant in a once elite apartment building now seemingly destined for the wrecker's ball." Booklist

"Full of colorful, eccentric characters, small-town attitudes, and sprightly fun for cat enthusiasts, this should appeal to most mystery readers." Libr J

The cat who robbed a bank. Putnam 1999 242p $23.95
ISBN 0-399-14570-2 LC 99-32581

With the help of his Siamese cats Koko and Yum Yum "newspaper columnist Jim Qwilleran investigates the murder of a visiting jeweler, one of the first guests to stay at Pickax's remodeled hotel." Libr J

"While her plots may not be complex, Braun is hardly a lightweight writer. Her descriptive powers are excellent, and she is one of the very few mystery writers to master the art of characterizing cats without relying solely on corny, cutesy feline antics." Booklist

The cat who said cheese. Putnam 1996 245p o.p.
ISBN 0-399-14075-1 LC 95-24475

"The year-round residents of Moose County, 400 miles north of everywhere, are enlivening the postsummer doldrums with plans for a fall Great Food Explo—and with gossip about a mystery woman registered at the Pickax City Hotel. Philanthropist/journalist/amateur detective Jim 'Quill' Qwilleran, with his two Siamese gourmand/sleuth cats Koko and Yum Yum, becomes involved not only in the cheese-tasting part (20 different varieties) but also in solving a bombing at the hotel and subsequent murder of one of the witnesses." Booklist

The cat who sang for the birds. Putnam 1998 244p o.p.
ISBN 0-399-14333-5 LC 97-19094

In this mystery featuring Jim Qwilleran and his sleuthing Siamese cats, "the crime—involving fraud, bribery, and arson—centers on the murders of a 93-year-old woman and a young butterfly painter. Equally important to the story and to reader enjoyment are an adult spelling bee (developed and promoted as a baseball game complete with competing teams and pinch spellers), the painting of librarian Polly Duncan's portrait, and Qwill's brief experience with lepidopterology." Booklist

The cat who saw stars. Putnam 1999 227p $22.95
ISBN 0-399-14431-5 LC 98-24328

In this mystery Jim Qwilleran "is fighting rumors that aliens are visiting Moose County while feisty feline Koko keeps gazing at the stars." Libr J

Braun, Lilian Jackson—*Continued*

The cat who smelled a rat. Putnam 2001 229p o.p.
ISBN 0-399-14665-2 LC 00-34198
"Jim 'Qwill' Qwilleran is still enjoying life in the small town of Pickax in Moose County. . . . Having moved into his winter residence, a condominium near his ladylove, head librarian Polly, the wealthy Qwill and his Siamese cats, Koko and Yum Yum, are awaiting the 'Big One'—the first blizzard of the season. A drought has caused a series of fires in the abandoned mine shafts around Pickax-or is it arson? When a member of the citizens' firewatch patrol is killed, a sinister plot unfolds." Booklist

The cat who sniffed glue. Putnam 1988 207p o.p.
LC 88-4146
"Residing now with Jim Qwilleran, in Pickax City, Moose County, in the apartment above the carriage house of the Klingenschoen estate, the cats [Koko and Yum Yum] live the life of Riley; it doesn't hurt that the local chief of police believes they can solve crimes. And there is quite a crime: Harley and Belle Fitch, son and daughter-in-law of the owner of the town bank, are murdered. Qwilleran, with his journalist's itch, cannot help but speculate on what might have happened and snoops around in his polite and persistent way. Although Braun uses standard plot conventions, her setting, characters, and sense of the absurd guarantee a thoroughly enjoyable read." Booklist

The cat who tailed a thief. Putnam 1997 244p o.p.
ISBN 0-399-14210-X LC 96-9662
"Winter in Moose County, 400 miles north of everywhere, begins with a disagreement between the local weatherman, who predicts a normal arctic winter, and the fuzzy caterpillar, whose behavior forecasts abnormally mild conditions. . . . The residents of Pickax are even more concerned, however, with a series of petty larcenies and the Pleasant Street historic houses restoration project. It's up to the town's leading citizen—semiretired journalist/philanthropist Jim Qwilleran, assisted by his Siamese sleuths Koko and Yum Yum, to discover the connection between these events and two murders committed Down Below. . . . As always, literate and entertaining." Booklist

The cat who went underground. Putnam 1989 223p o.p.
LC 88-32185
"Koko and Yum Yum . . . lead their guardian, Jim ('Qwill') Qwilleran, on a subterranean chase for a psychotic plumber. When Qwill decides to spend a restful summer at his cabin in Mooseville, he does not anticipate endless home-repair crises. But he is genuinely astonished when Koko reveals why the carpenter never finished the room addition." Booklist
"Qwill's saving grace is that he is properly humble before the superior intelligence of his pets, while the author is shrewd enough to balance the cats' amazing antics with many amusing character studies of the Mooseville natives." N Y Times Book Rev

Brautigan, Richard

An unfortunate woman; a journey. St. Martin's Press 2000 110p o.p.
ISBN 0-312-26243-4 LC 00-24760
An autobiographical novelette in journal form. "The episodic entries, dating from January to June of 1982, at first seem whimsically random, as the narrator recounts a peripatetic six months wandering among Montana, Berkeley, Hawaii, San Francisco, Buffalo, the Midwest, Alaska, Canada and points in between, but soon it's obvious that a preoccupation with death is the dominant theme. . . . Brautigan maintains his ironic humor and his ability to write clear, often crystalline prose, though at time his mannerisms . . . become irritating. Yet the reader cannot help being moved by this candid cri de coeur of a soul in anguish." Publ Wkly

Brenna, Duff

The altar of the body; a novel. Picador 2001 327p $24
ISBN 0-312-26865-3 LC 2001-31946
This "novel tracks the intersection of four desperate souls. George McLeod is a middle-aged loner who reads Emerson and has embraced solitude since his mother's death. 'Too much emotion is unbearable for me,' he confesses. The arrival of his long-lost cousin, Mike Routelli (who's reinvented himself as Buck Root, an egomaniacal bodybuilder) puts an end to George's monklike existence. He finds himself falling for Buck's girlfriend, Joy, and coming to care about Joy's mother, Livia, who suffers from Alzheimer's." N Y Times Book Rev
Brenna "perfectly captures Minnesota dialect, and Livia's senile-to-lucid babbling is spot-on. While his characters are often sexist, their situations painful and their choices self-destructive, Brenna never allows their easily caricatured gestures to overwhelm their considerable natural dignity." Publ Wkly

Breslin, Jimmy

The gang that couldn't shoot straight. Viking 1969 249p o.p.
"The only trouble with the Palumbo Mafia 'Family' of Brooklyn is that it isn't very well organized. Kid Sally Palumbo is trying to take over from the big Mafia boss, Baccala. Baccala has his wife start his car for him every morning in case explosives are wired in. Big Mama Palumbo's watchword is 'be sure to steal-a da license plates.' Into this happy milieu wanders Mario, imported from Italy to ride in a six-day bike race that flopped. A natural-born con man himself, Mario has a brief love affair with young Angela Palumbo, and acts as finger-man for the gang in the big attempt to wipe out Baccala." Publ Wkly
"By no means a great work, this is still a strong indictment of American society—police, politicians, criminals, and the 'silent'—that deserves to offend more than Sicilians." Choice

I don't want to go to jail. Little, Brown 2001 306p $24.95
ISBN 0-316-11845-1 LC 00-58880
"Fausti 'The Fist' Dellacava is a gangster's gangster, an old school tough guy and a tyrant who uses his Mafia power to indulge a variety of whims. . . . But his neph-

Breslin, Jimmy—*Continued*

ew and namesake is cut from a different cloth: when the younger Fausti decides that the threat of jail is a steep price to pay for a mobster's life of leisure, he tries his luck in the real world with decidedly mixed results. The bulk of the novel tracks the Fist's decline and demise in parallel with his nephew's efforts to establish himself beyond the Mob—but the book's real raison d'être is to give the audacious Breslin an opportunity to tell nonstop stories about the Mafia." Publ Wkly

Table money. Ticknor & Fields 1986 435p o.p.
LC 85-28880

This "saga concerning the Morrisons of Queens, New York—from their late-nineteenth-century arrival in the U.S. to the present day—is painfully stereotypical in its depiction of the men (a long line of hard-drinking, male chauvinistic, and irresponsible tunnel workers) and their beleaguered, long-suffering women. Generation after generation repeats the same mistakes—dying too soon from alcoholism, giving birth too early in life—and even when Owen Morrison, the latter-day lad whose story takes up most of the book, wins the Congressional medal of honor in Vietnam, he finds that his hero's badge is virtually worthless on the gray borough streets and in the perilous tunnel that epitomizes his clan's plight." Booklist

Brett, Simon, 1945-

The body on the beach; a Fethering mystery. Berkley Prime Crime 2000 312p o.p.
ISBN 0-425-17500-6 LC 99-45794

This mystery, set in the English seaside village of Fethering, features "Carole Seddon, a former civil servant with the Home Office whose anticipation of a quiet and sensible retirement is shattered when she goes walking on the beach and finds the body of a stranger. Even more disconcerting, the body disappears after she reports it to the police. Only her new neighbor, a blowsy bohemian who calls herself Jude, believes in Carole, and promptly persuades her to join forces in an undercover investigation." N Y Times Book Rev

"Brett is a master at subtle characterization, superb setting, and plotting in which his characters solve themselves in the process of solving murders." Booklist

Dead room farce. St. Martin's Press 1998 207p o.p.
ISBN 0-312-19251-7 LC 98-8376

In this adventure Charles Paris "lands a real job touring the provinces in a cheesy bedroom comedy bound for the West End. If only he didn't feel compelled to play his philanderer's role off stage as well as on. Charles's peccadilloes catch up with him during a two-week engagement in Bath, when his romantic entanglements unravel and a drinking pal is murdered." N Y Times Book Rev

The dead side of the mike. Scribner 1980 176p o.p.
LC 80-18269

"Murder at the BBC. Andrea Gower, a lower-level studio manager, is found dead in a BBC taping room, her wrists neatly slashed. The police suspect suicide, but sometime actor-sometime sleuth Charles Paris, who happens to be on the scene, is nagged by a belief that Andrea was slain." Booklist

Death on the Downs. Berkley Prime Crime 2001 293p o.p.
ISBN 0-425-17953-2 LC 00-54374

In this Fethering mystery a walk has Carole Seddon "seeking shelter in a derelict barn during a downpour; she stumbles over a fertilizer bag from which protrudes the ball-joint of a human femur. Body in place, sleuth with time to detect, and Brett is off again on a marvelous send-up of contemporary British society. . . . In addition, Seddon is a fascinating psychological study." Booklist

Mrs. Pargeter's package. Scribner 1991 224p o.p.
LC 90-27463

First published 1990 in the United Kingdom

"On a tour of Greece, the mature and spirited Melita Pargeter . . . takes on a case more substantial than her earlier challenges. When she agreed to join recently widowed Joyce Dover on holiday, Melita knew she was apt to encounter the moodiness of the freshly bereaved. But Joyce appears to be importing a bottle of the Greek liqueur ouzo *from* England, and talks about her husband controlling her from the grave. When she is found dead, an apparent suicide, Melita has even more on her hands than she bargained for." Publ Wkly

"Avoiding the treacly simpering typical of so many British cozy mysteries, Brett keeps us chuckling with a steady stream of dryly noted cultural tidbits, while still supplying a wide-ranging plot that hangs together elegantly." Booklist

Mrs. Pargeter's plot; a Mrs. Pargeter mystery. Scribner 1998 249p o.p.
ISBN 0-684-83714-5 LC 97-24625

First published 1996 in the United Kingdom

"The wealthy widow of a master criminal revered by his former associates in the London underworld, . . . Mrs. Pargeter has a lot of muscle with guys like Truffler Mason and Hedgeclipper Clinton, who rush to her aid when a body is discovered in the wine cellar of her new home and the police cart off her contractor, Concrete Jacket. The setup is sweet and you couldn't hope to meet a more amiable bunch of crooks, even when they become hopelessly entangled in a plot that is at times too whimsical for its own good." N Y Times Book Rev

Mrs. Pargeter's point of honour. Scribner 1999 265p o.p.
ISBN 0-684-86295-6 LC 99-32485

First published 1998 in the United Kingdom

"Elderly Veronica Chastaigne enlists Mrs. Pargeter to oversee the secret return of her late husband's collection of 'hot' paintings to their rightful owners. To do so, Mrs. Pargeter assembles a team of her own late husband's old 'associates,' including private detective Truffler Mason and interior designer Denzil Price. But when Mrs. Pargeter's team go to pick up the paintings, they discover that someone has already scooped up the stolen collection of Old Masters. A merry chase is on, as Mrs. Pargeter and company seek to reclaim the paintings." Publ Wkly

Brett, Simon, 1945-—*Continued*

Mrs. Pargeter's pound of flesh; a Mrs. Pargeter mystery. Scribner 1993 c1992 207p o.p.
LC 92-30969

First published 1992 in the United Kingdom

Mrs. Melita Pargeter, "widow of a talented and much-loved ex-con takes the waters at a health spa in order to help a friend. Melita starts snooping, however, when she spies men removing a body in the dead of the night. Still using the services of her late husband's criminal cronies, Melita courts disaster as she nears the truth." Libr J

"Most of Mr. Brett's humor is of the all-in-good-fun variety, which invites the reader to indulge the stout-hearted Mrs. Pargeter and her merry band of lovable crooks and con men in another jolly series romp." NY Times Book Rev

Murder in the museum; a Fethering mystery. Berkley Prime Crime 2003 341p $22.95
ISBN 0-425-19043-9 LC 2003-45329

In this episode "Carole Seddon finds herself a member of the Bracketts Trust, which is responsible for the upkeep of Bracketts, former home of West Sussex litterateur Esmond Chadleigh. Tension arises between the Trust's new director, Gina Locke, who represents the new world of 'management structures,' and former trustee Sheila Cartwright, who's from the old school volunteers. While they wrangle over Bracket's future, a skeleton turns up in the garden." Publ Wkly

"Another marvelous mix of social satire and traditional cozy." Booklist

Murder unprompted; a Charles Paris novel. Scribner 1982 160p o.p.
LC 82-5578

"Here Paris is less drunk than usual, which enables us to believe that he can think as shrewdly as he does. And the situation is delightful: he gets at last a chance to act in a play that may move to a big West End theater if all goes well in the tryouts. The interplay among the cast is splendid, funny, and also touching. Murder in full view, on the first night, might bring good publicity, but other troubles develop—the whole mess handled in masterly fashion." Barzun. Cat of Crime. Rev and enl edition

A reconstructed corpse; a Charles Paris mystery. Scribner 1994 c1993 189p o.p.
ISBN 0-684-19700-6 LC 93-50797

First published 1993 in the United Kingdom

Charles Paris' "agent has just called with some exciting news: Charles' uncanny resemblance to Brighton property developer Martin Earnshaw, who has mysteriously disappeared after leaving home to visit the local pub, has landed Charles a job reconstructing Earnshaw's 'last moments' on the television program *Public Enemies*. As usual, Charles can't stop getting involved in a bit of amateur detecting." Booklist

"Charles's self-loathing has deepened and Mr. Brett's satirical edge has sharpened in this witty but hardly frivolous series. Here the author takes his best jabs at the corrosive power of television." NY Times Book Rev

The torso in the town; a Fethering mystery. Berkley Prime Crime 2002 340p o.p.
ISBN 0-425-18502-8 LC 2002-18482

"A dinner party in a richly restored country house in a Sussex village that is 'riddled with class consciousness' is interrupted by a scream. A body, arms and legs neatly removed, has been discovered in the cellar. There to witness the discovery is an outsider, a middle-aged woman from the seaside village of Fethering. The woman, Jude brings news of the grisly find back to her pal Carole Seddon another middle-aged woman from Fethering, in hopes that a little mystery will pull her out of a depression brought on by a lapsed love affair. . . . The ladies from Fethering once again proceed totally outside the bumbling police investigation in a somehow utterly credible way, gaining access and insight where the police can't." Booklist

What bloody man is that?; a Charles Paris mystery. Scribner 1987 184p o.p.
LC 87-13000

In this novel Charles "Paris is engaged to play any number of small bits in a provincial theater company's production of the badluck play, 'Macbeth'. When a greatly disliked actor is found dead among the beer taps in a liquor storage room, Paris quickly becomes the chief suspect. A must read for its suspense, its theatrical atmosphere, its effortlessly witty dialogue, and its well-delineated characters." Booklist

Brin, David, 1950-

Brightness reef. Bantam Bks. 1995 514p o.p.
ISBN 0-553-89015-8 LC 95-17601

The first volume of a trilogy "set in the universe of Brin's Hugo-winning *The Uplift War* [1987]. It's a multivoice narrative concerning the six diverse cultures living on the banned planet Jijo—and what happens to their peaceful society when more humans arrive there via starship, searching for species to 'uplift' by bringing them to the next level of sentience." Publ Wkly

"Brin's rich world-building easily equals that displayed in classic series such as Herbert's Dune and Asimov's Foundation. Brin's resumption of Uplift is most welcome." Booklist

Followed by Infinity's shore

Earth. Bantam Bks. 1990 601p o.p.
LC 90-4

"In the mid-21st century, as the world is attempting to reconcile humanity's furious technological progress with its depletion of the planet's vanishing resources, the discovery of a pair of singularities (miniature black holes) deep in the Earth's core abruptly transforms an ongoing struggle for preservation into a desperate battle to prevent the Earth's imminent destruction. Combining the fast pacing of a techno-thriller with a unique array of characters, the author . . . delivers a thoughtful, persuasive message of hope and warning that embraces today's issues and tomorrow's possibilities." Libr J

Foundation's triumph. HarperPrism 1999 328p (Second Foundation trilogy) o.p.
ISBN 0-06-105241-8 LC 98-52683

"Near the end of his life's work, an aging Hari Seldon embarks on one final adventure that may reveal to him the ultimate secrets necessary to the unfolding of his grand plan for the future." Libr J

A "literate, intelligent coda to a grand vision of human evolution." Booklist

Brin, David, 1950-—*Continued*

Heaven's reach. Bantam Bks. 1998 447p o.p.
ISBN 0-553-10174-9 LC 98-4914

Final volume in the Uplift trilogy. "The narrative, which unfolds at frenzied speed, opens with the Earth under attack by an alliance of evil aliens, the essence of space itself shaking apart and the beleaguered *Streaker*, captained by Dr. Gillian Baskin, trying to outrun a Jophurian battleship that seeks to destroy it." Publ Wkly

"Brin's intellectual fertility is as prodigious as ever; indeed, readers coming to his work for the first time may feel a bit daunted. Brin doesn't fill all parts of his vast canvas with equal skill but manages enough of it at the top of his form to please all Uplift followers and many others as well." Booklist

Infinity's shore. Bantam Bks. 1996 524p o.p.
LC 96-32346

Second volume in the Uplift trilogy. "On the planet Jijo, the painfully developed cooperation among six sapient races (humans included) is rapidly crumbling under the impact of contact from space. The visitors include the dolphin crew of the ship *Streaker* and the Rothen, the race who may have 'uplifted' to intelligence most of the races of Jijo, except the humans, who because of their unique status are in greater peril than ever. The ensuing tale is well paced, immensely complex [and] highly literate." Publ Wkly

Followed by Heaven's reach

Kiln people. TOR Bks. 2002 459p $25.95
ISBN 0-7653-0355-8 LC 2001-54058

"A Tom Doherty Associates book"

"Thanks to the new technology of imprinting, people in a near-future America can copy their personalities into animated clay bodies (called 'dittos' or 'golems'), which last a single day. Albert Morris, private investigator, is his own sidekick as he attempts to uncover the murderer of a prominent imprinting research scientist, capture a criminal mastermind specializing in ditto copyright infringement and foil a conspiracy aimed at destroying the major ditto manufacturer and pinning the blame on several Alberts. Brin deftly explores the issues of identity, privacy and work in a world where everyone is supported with a living wage and has ready access to duplication technology." Publ Wkly

The postman. Bantam Bks. 1985 294p o.p.
LC 85-47647

This novel opens with the "familiar portrait of an America brought to the edge of extinction by nuclear war. An itinerant storyteller, Gordon Krantz, finds an old postman's uniform and bag and starts traveling across country, taking people's letters to loved ones and telling tales of a country on the road to recovery. Eventually he becomes a major force for that recovery, as the hope he gives the people rallies them." Booklist

"A well-crafted, realistic and often violent novel with diverse elements woven together in expert style." Best Sellers

Brink, André Philippus, 1935-

A chain of voices; [by] André Brink. Morrow 1982 525p o.p.
LC 82-80315

"The setting of this . . . polyphonic novel is the South African interior, 1825. The central voice is Galant, a black slave who might be part white and who, until adolescence, has been treated in some ways as a member of his master's family. When a series of extraordinarily cruel punishments proves to him that he will always be regarded as a slave, he leads a revolt in which his young master is murdered. Brink sees slavery as a sick product of corrupt moral righteousness and suppressed sexuality." Libr J

"This complex and powerful tale of a slave revolt in nineteenth-century South Africa lacks the hard-edged, polemic tone often found in novels that address racial issues." Booklist

Devil's Valley; {by} Andre Brink. Harcourt Brace & Co. 1999 401p o.p.
ISBN 0-15-100440-4 LC 98-40513

First published 1998 in the United Kingdom

"In South Africa, the mysterious death of a young acquaintance prompts a cynical crime reporter to investigate the boy's background and upbringing in Devil's Valley, a small, remote, and drought-ridden community closed to 'outsiders.' Ostensibly there to record a history of the people living within the confines, Flip Lochner finds himself drawn into the maelstrom of this odd colony, where spirits walk among the living, morality and values are twisted, and retribution is swift and uncompromising." Libr J

"It's difficult to build and maintain a convincing alternate world, but Brink succeeds with only a few signs of strain, and the book is vigorous, earthy entertainment that also sheds light on the darker reaches of South Africa's past." Publ Wkly

Imaginings of sand; {by} André Brink. Harcourt Brace & Co. 1996 352p o.p.
ISBN 0-15-100224-X LC 96-19316

"Kristien Muller prides herself on being a bad girl, well, headstrong. A rebellious expatriate Afrikaner, she has been living in London and trying to do her bit for the African National Congress. Now she returns to her small South African town after 11 years because her beloved grandmother (Ouma) is dying and wants outlaw Kristien to receive the family memory. It's a few weeks before the country's first democratic elections and Kristien's first-person narrative of the contemporary scene is woven together with Ouma's family saga, stretching back and back across generations." Booklist

This is "in many ways an ambitious book: in taking the South African elections as its backdrop, in its layering of history with mystery and in its use of the exclusive point of view of a woman who is herself aware that she may not strike the reader as likable. The structure of the narrative is complex and risky." N Y Times Book Rev

The other side of silence; [by] André Brink. Harcourt 2003 c2002 311p
ISBN 0-15-100770-5 LC 2002-32748

First published 2002 in the United Kingdom

This novel "takes as its point of departure a German program at the turn of the twentieth century whereby women were shipped out to Germany's colonies in South-West Africa (now Namibia) to be wives—or, failing that, sexual fodder—for the colonizers. Brink's protagonist, Hannah X., an abused orphan from Bremen, is eager for the imagined romance of the desert, but life in the colonies turns out to be even worse than what she has known before. . . .Brink's powerful and brutal story

Brink, André Philippus, 1935-—*Continued*

is an effective response to those who suspected that the end of apartheid would leave him without a subject, and a shrewd meditation on the dehumanizing power of hatred." New Yorker

The rights of desire; a novel; {by} André Brink. Harcourt 2001 311p o.p.

ISBN 0-15-100654-7 LC 00-46141

First published 2000 in the United Kingdom

"Ruben Olivier, a retired librarian, lives alone in an old family home in Cape Town, South Africa. . . . His only companions are his elderly housekeeper and the ghost of a 17th-century slave that haunts the property. Olivier, who is something of a prig, spends his days rereading the great books and listening to classical music. But his monastic lifestyle is threatened when he agrees to rent a room to 30-year-old Tessa, a troubled free spirit who drinks, smokes pot, and sleeps with a bewildering assortment of men, both black and white. Olivier is immediately attracted to her, but Tessa sends mixed signals, flirting with him outrageously one day, ignoring him the next." Libr J

"Although this isn't Brink's best effort, he remains a consummately professional storyteller, and the voice of his narrator, with its subtle wit and vulnerability, is a welcome one." Publ Wkly

Bristow, Gwen, 1903-1980

Calico Palace. Crowell 1970 589p o.p.

"San Francisco in the days of the Gold Rush (1849) is the setting for this lengthy, rather old-fashioned novel, which follows Kendra Morgan through two relatively unhappy marriages, the birth and death of a baby, and friendship with Marny, glamorous proprietress of Calico Palace, a gambling hall. In the eventual, traditional happy ending, both girls find true love." Libr J

Celia Garth. Crowell 1959 406p o.p.

This story "takes its background from South Carolina during the Revolutionary War. Its heroine is Celia Garth, a spirited orphan girl working as an apprentice dressmaker in Charleston, who witnesses the British siege of the city and returns during the occupation to become a spy for the rebels." Booklist

"Celia Garth's story is adventurous and romantic, patriotic and sentimental. Miss Bristow's historical novel presents abundant terror, but it is the terror endured by civilians more than the terror of bloody battle." Best Sellers

Deep summer
In Bristow, G. Gwen Bristow's Plantation trilogy p1-258

Gwen Bristow's Plantation trilogy; Deep summer, The handsome road, [and] This side of glory. Crowell 1962 812p o.p.

An omnibus volume of the three titles published originally 1937, 1938 and 1940, respectively

"The historical background material for each book was supplied by the author especially for this volume." Title page

In this trilogy "Judith Sheramy migrates to Louisiana in the 1800s and meets Philip Larne, the son of a wealthy South Carolina family. The two marry and struggle to keep their plantation through the Civil War. After the war, the lives of the wealthy Larnes and the poor Upjohns are followed to the period of the First World War." Jacob. To be continued

The handsome road
In Bristow, G. Gwen Bristow's Plantation trilogy p263-530

Jubilee Trail. Crowell 1950 564p o.p.

The Jubilee Trail was the traders' name for the great Spanish Trail, which in the 1840's led from Santa Fé to Los Angeles. This long novel describes the trek of a gently bred New York girl and her trader husband, along that trail. When she was left a widow and penniless, Garnet and the variety girl she had befriended managed to make their living. The story closes about the time of the California gold discovery

This side of glory
In Bristow, G. Gwen Bristow's Plantation trilogy p535-812

Brockmeier, Kevin

The truth about Celia. Pantheon Bks. 2003 216p $22

ISBN 0-375-42135-1 LC 2002-35513

This novel is "presented as if written by one Christopher Brooks, a science-fiction writer. In 1997, Christopher lives happily with his wife, Janet, and seven-year-old daughter, Celia, in a beautifully preserved 19th-century house in a peaceful small town. One morning, while Celia and her father are home alone, Celia vanishes from the backyard. There are no clues, no suspects. . . .The fragmented narration may deflect some readers, but others will cherish Brockmeier's seductive turns of phrase and sharp imagination." Publ Wkly

Bromell, Henry, 1947-

Little America. Knopf 2001 395p o.p.

ISBN 0-375-40684-0 LC 2001-89764

"In 1958, the C.I.A. agent Mack Hooper is posted to the desert kingdom of Kurash to save one small corner of the world from Communism. While Mack befriends its ruler, a twenty-two-year-old playboy enamored of fast cars, his ten-year-old son, Terry, plays doctor with the daughters of other spies in the Kurashian suburbs. Forty years later, Terry hunts through declassified documents for the truth about his father's role in the assassination of the king and the ultimate erasure of Kurash from the map. Bromell's critique of Cold War culture is more wistful than outraged, and his generosity makes his characters ring true." New Yorker

Bromfield, Louis, 1896-1956

Mrs. Parkington. Harper & Row 1943 330p o.p.

"From the vantage point of her 84 years, Mrs. Parkington looks back over her long life, beginning with that day in Leaping Rock, Nev., when newly orphaned by the mine explosion that killed both her parents, she married Augustus Parkington and set out with him on the buccaneering career that was to make him one of the richest men of his time. These glimpses of the past are interspersed among events of the present, as Mrs.

Bromfield, Louis, 1896-1956—*Continued*
Parkington guides and controls the complicated, often shady, affairs of the later generations of Parkingtons." Wis Libr Bull

The rains came; a novel of modern India. Harper 1937 597p o.p.
"A small state in India, where an enlightened native prince and his wife have labored for fifty years to establish modern standards and to abolish caste and religious antagonisms, is the scene also of the work of British officials, soldiers, American missionaries, and business men. Here Ransome, bitter, disillusioned expatriate, meets again his former mistress, now the wife of a fabulously wealthy nobleman; at the same time he experiences a slight awakening of chivalry when a missionary's daughter falls in love with him. A flood wipes out the ruler's work, cholera and plague follow, and in the desperate week before relief comes tragedy." Booklist

Brontë, Anne, 1820-1849

The tenant of Wildfell Hall. Modern Lib. 1997 510p o.p.
ISBN 0-679-60279-8 LC 97-14200
First published 1848
"This epistolary novel presents a portrait of debauchery that is remarkable in light of the author's sheltered life. It is the story of young Helen Graham's disastrous marriage to the dashing drunkard Arthur Huntingdon—said to be modeled on the author's wayward brother Branwell—and her flight from him to the seclusion of Wildfell Hall. Pursued by Gilbert Markham, who is in love with her, Graham refuses him and, by way of explanation, gives him her journal. There he reads of her wretched married life. Eventually, after Huntingdon's death, they marry." Merriam-Webster's Ency of Lit

Brontë, Charlotte, 1816-1855

Emma; by Charlotte Brontë and "Another Lady". Everest House 1980 201p o.p.
Fragments of a story left unfinished at Brontë's death form the opening two chapters of this novel completed by Constance Savery
"In the full-blown literary manner and circuitous storytelling characteristic of Charlotte Brontë, . . . an intriguing melodrama unrolls in this tale of wrongs finally righted. Most wronged is adolescent Martina, deprived of her natural mother by the machinations of her stepbrothers, led on by their sister, the cruel, enigmatic beauty Emma. The events that lead to familial reconciliation include Martina's sentence to ladies' boarding school, abduction to a French convent and graveyard visitations before some fancy detective work by an old friend unravels the ingenious but dastardly plot. The author of this Gothic romp is obviously steeped in the period and felicitous style of the brilliant English novelist, providing entertainment on the same grand scale." Publ Wkly

Jane Eyre; Charlotte Brontë with an introduction by Lucy Hughes-Hallet. Knopf 1991 xxxviii, 284p $20
ISBN 0-679-40582-8 LC 91-52968
"Everyman's library"
First published 1847
"In both heroine and hero the author introduced types new to English fiction. Jane Eyre is a shy, intense little orphan, never for a moment, neither in her unhappy school days nor her subsequent career as a governess, displaying those qualities of superficial beauty and charm that had marked the conventional heroine. Jane's lover, Edward Rochester, to whose ward she is governess, is a strange, violent man, bereft of conventional courtesy, a law unto himself. Rochester's moodiness derives from the fact that he is married to an insane wife, whose existence, long kept secret, is revealed on the very day of his projected marriage to Jane. Years afterward the lovers are reunited." Reader's Ency. 4th edition

The professor. Modern Lib. 1997 266p o.p.
ISBN 0-679-60273-9 LC 97-9957
First published 1857
"William Crimsworth, an orphan, after trying his hand at trade in the north of England, goes to seek his fortune in Brussels. At the girls' school where he teaches English he falls in love with Frances Henri, an Anglo-Swiss pupil-teacher and lace mender, whose Protestant honesty and modesty are contrasted with the manipulating duplicity of the Catholic headmistress, Zoraide Reuter. Crimsworth resists Mlle Reuter's overtures; she marries the headmaster of the neighbouring boys' school, M. Pelet, Crimsworth resigns his post, and, after finding a new and better one, is able to marry Frances." Oxford Companion to Engl Lit. 6th edition

Shirley. Modern Lib. 1997 656p o.p.
ISBN 0-679-60275-5 LC 97-9954
First published 1849
"Against the background of a changing world at the beginning of the nineteenth century, the story of a spirited heiress, Shirley Keeldar, is told. The author patterned her after her own sister, Emily. Robert Moore, millowner in Yorkshire, introduces labor-saving devices which cause workmen's riots. He persists, in spite of financial and physical hazards, and wins his point with a promise to give more jobs, and provide better housing. Caroline Helstone, his gentle cousin, is seeking a meaning to her life. Dissatisfied with doing nothing, she marries Robert, whom she adores, and finds direction in her decision to help him. Shirley also is a new type of woman. She marries Robert's brother Louis, a tutor, who has as much spirit as she." Haydn. Thesaurus of Book Dig

Villette. Modern Lib. 1997 575p o.p.
ISBN 0-679-60274-7 LC 97-9956
First published 1853
In Villette "Lucy Snowe makes her way by teaching, as she watches unhappily John Breton's infatuation for the flirt Ginevra Fanshawe, then falls in love herself with and transforms the professor, Monsieur Paul Emanuel." Haydn. Thesaurus of Book Dig
"The novel combines a masterly portrayal of Belgian daily life with a highly personal use of the elements of Gothic fiction." Oxford Companion to Engl Lit. 6th edition

Brontë, Emily, 1818-1848

Wuthering Heights; with an introduction by Katherine Frank. Knopf 1991 xxxiii, 385p $22
ISBN 0-679-40543-7 LC 91-52969

Brontë, Emily, 1818-1848—*Continued*

"Everyman's library"

First published 1847

Forced by a storm to spend the night at the home of the somber and unsociable Heathcliff, Mr. Lockwood has an encounter with the spirit of Catherine Linton. He gradually learns that Catherine's father, Mr. Earnshaw, had taken in Heathcliff as a young orphan. Heathcliff and Catherine began to fall in love, but after Mr. Earnshaw's death Catherine's brother treated Heathcliff in a degrading manner and Catherine married rich Edgar Linton. Heathcliff gradually worked his revenge against those who injured him

Brookner, Anita

Altered states. Random House 1996 229p o.p.
LC 96-17268

This novel's "protagonist is Alan Miller, a middle-aged widower who works as a solicitor, pays dutiful visits to his mother and her new husband, and pines away for an unrequited love. His obsession with Sarah, a distant cousin and a callous free spirit, progresses from admiration to stalking. After he accepts that she is out of reach, he settles into an unhappy marriage with her friend, Angela. But Sarah continues to drift in and out of his life, and Alan remains besotted with her, eventually putting his marriage at risk." Libr J

"The features are familiar: loneliness, misplaced affection, disillusionment, missed opportunity and the deadly power of propriety. Like an experienced holiday-maker, Anita Brookner revisits the same territory year after year, though each time approaching her favourite view from a slightly different angle. . . . Here, she gives form to the absence at the core of the lives she has created, shaping it and probing its effects with the delicate intrusiveness that has won her both acclaim and disdain since she began writing fiction in 1981." Times Lit Suppl

The Bay of Angels; a novel. Random House 2001 200p $23.95

ISBN 0-375-50582-2 LC 00-54299

"The daughter of a self-contained widow, Zoe is pleased when her mother agrees to marry elderly, wealthy and generous Simon Gould, who carries his new wife off to his villa in the south of France. When, after a few months, Simon dies suddenly, surprising events unfold. Simon, it seems, was about to run out of money and did not even own the sumptuous villa. Zoe, whose university degree has led to a series of freelance editing jobs in London—and, more important, the freedom that she craves—arrives in Nice to find that her mother has suffered a breakdown and is in a clinic undergoing a sleeping cure." Publ Wkly

"In language as voluptuous as her subjects are spare, Brookner offers bracing insights into the nature of sacrifice, the difference between men and women, and the adjustments that age and infirmity demand. There is quiet humor here and much affection for thoughtful people." Booklist

Brief lives. Random House 1991 c1990 260p o.p.
LC 90-38904

First published 1990 in the United Kingdom

This "novel covers the nearly 40 years of intertwining lives of two dissimilar, incompatible women. Flamboyant, selfish Julia was once a glamorous actress. Fay arranges her life around men—first her father, then her husband, then her lover—and eventually her friend, none of them her ideal; finally, she is alone." Libr J

"This short, subtle, beautifully organised and orchestrated novel positively gains from the deliberate restraint and detachment of the writing." London Rev Books

Dolly. Random House 1994 c1993 260p o.p.
LC 93-14537

First published 1993 in the United Kingdom with title: A family romance

"Jane, a successful young author, prefers a quiet life, unlike her Aunt Dolly, a flamboyant soul always on display and seeking admiration. Utterly dissimilar and not overly fond of each other, the two women are bound together by unexpected events and consequences dating from Jane's early childhood. As Jane narrates the story of their incongruous mutual dependencies, she speculates on the nature of human connections and the female experience." Libr J

"Certainly its first two-thirds are about as wonderful as anything Miss Brookner has ever written. Jane's apparently aimless ramblings, grounded with exacting detail and raised on a structure of steel, seem a faultless demonstration of authorial assurance." N Y Times Book Rev

Falling slowly; a novel. Random House 1999 227p o.p.

ISBN 0-375-50189-4 LC 98-12964

First published 1998 in the United Kingdom

Brookner "chronicles a turning point in the fortunes of two middle-aged sisters in London. Beatrice and Miriam Sharpe have spent their entire lives falling slowly through space: unattached, isolated from society, essentially passive. Miriam, the younger, sharp-tongued, divorced sister, who earns a comfortable living as a translator, is now dryly disillusioned and skeptical about the future. Beatrice, whose contract as a piano accompanist has not been renewed, is a fluttery, incurable romantic who has always expected to meet her Prince Charming. Both have lived cautiously, waiting for high points that have never arrived." Publ Wkly

"The ghastly power of Brookner's novels arises from their trenchant accuracy, and in this regard 'Falling Slowly' is a further testament to its author's gifts." N Y Times Book Rev

Family and friends. Pantheon Bks. 1985 187p o.p.
LC 85-6373

"We first see the widowed Sofka Dorn and her children—Frederick, Alfred, Mimi, and Betty—in London between the wars, after they have come from Eastern Europe, and we follow them from the children's adolescence through their middle age." N Y Times Book Rev

"Anita Brookner's prose is impeccably elegant and she is unsentimental with it. . . . There is a closeness of atmosphere, almost claustrophobic, in Family and Friends, as if we were alternating between a discreetly perfumed lady's boudoir and the smoking room of a superior gentleman's club. There is no mistaking the originality as well as the skill and consistency with which the novel so beautifully conforms to its genre and its intentions." N Y Rev Books

Brookner, Anita—*Continued*

Fraud. Random House 1992 262p o.p.
LC 92-20162

"Anna Durrant, immaculately turned out but dauntingly virginal and good, seems to have vanished. The doctor who cared for her and her recently deceased mother is perturbed enough to call the police, who question Mrs. Marsh, an elderly woman for whom Anna occasionally did favors. This precipitates a prolonged flashback and brings us, for a time, into the labyrinth of Mrs. Marsh's impressions and memories. In her eighties, stubborn, judgmental, and proud, Mrs. Marsh dislikes the perpetually cheerful Anna and wonders why she devoted her youth to her pretty but flaky mother, but Mrs. Marsh's real concern is combating the press of old age." Booklist

"Loneliness, deception, and the plight of midlife women are recurring themes in Brookner's novels. Yet 'Fraud' is not depressing. As Brookner explores these themes in her quiet elegant prose, she brings new insight to old dilemmas." Christ Sci Monit

Hotel du Lac. Pantheon Bks. 1985 c1984 184p o.p.
LC 84-20641

First published 1984 in the United Kingdom

"A sedate Swiss Hotel at end-of-season is the scene of Edith Hope's brief, melancholy exile (she's in disgrace for having jilted her fiancé on their wedding day). Edith observes her fellow guests with sympathy and amusement; writes long, unposted letters to her married lover; and works at her latest romantic novel, her life suspended and uneventful. When the worldly Mr. Neville plumbs her 'unused capacity' for mischief, she nearly acquiesces, at 39, to his quaintly treacherous proposal of marriage and respectability without the promise of love." Libr J

The tone of this novel is "oddly detached, very small-scale, faintly humorous. . . . It is by means of this very remoteness that Edith manages to hold our interest throughout this achingly uneventful holiday, with its empty chasms of time, its murmuring respectability, its dining room scattered sparsely with people who mean nothing to her. . . . There are some uncomfortable patches. . . . But generally, the writing is graceful and attractive." N Y Times Book Rev

Incidents in the Rue Laugier. Random House 1996 c1955 233p o.p.
LC 95-4720

First published 1995 in the United Kingdom

Maffy, the narrator of this novel, reconstructs events in the early life of her now deceased mother, Maud. As related by Maffy, Maud Gonthier is a "demure and serious young woman from Dijon who is introduced to desire by the fascinating, rich David Tyler. They meet one summer at her aunt's comfortable country home; the innocent Maud falls instantly and passionately in love. She follows Tyler to Paris, and when he abruptly disappears, Maud is left with his friend Edward to pick up the pieces of her life." Publisher's note

"As usual, Brookner reveals the passions percolating behind the facade of proper lives: the struggle of wills between parents and children and the paradoxes inherent in sexuality and marriage." Booklist

Making things better; a novel. Random House 2003 275p $23.95
ISBN 0-375-50888-0 LC 2002-69860

This novel "describes the daily routines and musings of Julius Herz, who at 73 has been forced into retirement when his shop is sold. He has been a passive player in his own life, not so much making decisions as accepting the anxieties and responsibilities thrust upon him by his inept family." Libr J

Brookner "never steps out from behind the curtain, never indulges in jazzy little riffs to show you how clever she is. All she does is tell her stories." N Y Times Book Rev

A private view. Random House 1995 242p o.p.
LC 94-26413

"At 65, George Bland has been looking forward to retirement and the commencement of his long-anticipated journey to the Far East with his good friend, Putnam. When Putnam suddenly dies, George begins to feel old and uncertain of the dull, restrained, responsible way he has lived his life. Though he never married, he has maintained a life-long friendship with Louise, his placid first girlfriend, who is now a widow and grandmother. His melancholy days of walks in London's parks and afternoons in museums are interrupted when young, brash Katy Gibbs moves into the flat across the hall. At first exasperated by Katy's rude and greedy nature, George becomes consumed by desire for her and her hedonistic lifestyle." Libr J

"Few writers can infuse a scene in which two people stand in a hallway without speaking with the suspense and tremendous intensity and delicacy of feeling Brookner achieves. Indeed, she is the poet of the silent skirmishes that rage behind the facade of dignified lives." Publ Wkly

The rules of engagement; a novel. Random House 2004 273p $23.95
ISBN 1-400-06165-2 LC 2003-58520

This novel is set in the world of "upper middle-class London. Elizabeth and Betsy are classmates who meet on their first day of school. Their relationship over time . . . is the focus of this book. Elizabeth, the protagonist, is worldly, unintellectual and unambitious. Her place in the world seems secure: Her family is well off, her father successful, her mother a beauty. Betsy, by contrast, is unsophisticated, intellectual, earnest and impecunious. Her place in the world is perilous: Her mother is dead, and her father dies soon after. She is raised by a dim and colorless aunt. Betsy timidly longs for inclusion into Elizabeth's family, but Elizabeth's cold and snobbish mother has other ideas." Washington Post Book World

"Brookner's spiritual and syntactic masters are Jane Austen and Henry James, and The Rules of Engagement contains, in places, passages worthy of these august forebears. Indeed, she pays specific homage to the shades whose style and concerns suffuse her prose." N Y Times Book Rev

Undue influence; a novel. Random House 2000 231p $24 o.p.
ISBN 0-375-50334-X LC 99-36282

"Having come through her father's long illness and her mother's recent death, [Londoner] Claire Pitt faces midlife longing for a significant attachment. She works in a used bookshop, sorting through the papers of the owner's father, which chronicled his largely uneventful life and observations. Into her musty basement one morning comes a handsome stranger, Martin Gibson, seeking out

Brookner, Anita—*Continued*
a novel by Fontane. On the pretext of delivering the book to his home, Claire becomes enmeshed in his life and his marriage to a sickly wife. The weird and wealthy Gibsons begin to occupy a new corner of Claire's life and provide a spark of previously unknown drama." Libr J

"The novel contains a fine brace of supporting characters whose behavior implicitly reflects on Claire's fall into limbo, and Brookner's narrative skill works like a scalpel exposing the complexity of each of their lives." Publ Wkly

Brooks, Geraldine

March; Geraldine Brooks. Viking 2004 280p $24.95

ISBN 0-670-03335-9 LC 2004-49496

This novel "imagines the Civil War experiences of Mr. March, the absent father in Louisa May Alcott's Little Women. An idealistic Concord cleric, March becomes a Union chaplain and later finds himself assigned to be a teacher on a cotton plantation that employs freed slaves, or 'contraband.' His narrative begins with cheerful letters home, but March gradually reveals to the reader what he does not to his family: the cruelty and racism of Northern and Southern soldiers, the violence and suffering he is powerless to prevent and his reunion with Grace, a beautiful, educated slave whom he met years earlier as a Connecticut peddler to the plantations. In between, we learn of March's earlier life: his whirlwind courtship of quick-tempered Marmee, his friendship with Emerson and Thoreau and the surprising cause of his family's genteel poverty. . . . [Brooks] relies heavily on primary sources for both the Concord and wartime scenes; her characters speak with a convincing 19th-century formality, yet the narrative is always accessible." Publ Wkly

Year of wonders; a novel of the plague. Viking 2001 308p o.p.

ISBN 0-670-91021-X LC 00-52757

"In 1665, the intense young pastor of a plague-stricken Derbyshire village persuades his parish to quarantine itself from the outside world. This selfless decision leads to the deaths of two-thirds of the inhabitants but saves the surrounding towns, as it did in the case of the historical village that inspired the tale. The novel glitters with careful research into such arcana as seventeenth-century lead-mining, sheep-farming, and of course, medicine, but its true strength is a deep imaginative engagement with how people are changed by catastrophe. . . . A rare few—including the narrator, a young widow who is a servant of the pastor—discover new strengths and abilities." New Yorker

Brooks, Janice Young, 1943-
See also Churchill, Jill, 1943-

Brooks, Terry, 1944-

Antrax. Del Rey Bks. 2001 375p (Voyage of the Jerle Shannara, bk2) o.p.

ISBN 0-345-39766-5

Sequel to Ilse witch

"Caught in a desperate race to discover a powerful form of ancient magic before it can fall into the hands of the Ilse Witch, Druid Walker Boh and his companions make their way to the city of Castledown. There, in the darkness below the city, Walker and the Ilse Witch meet in a confrontation that will change their world forever." Libr J

The black unicorn. Ballantine Bks. 1987 286p il (Magic Kingdom of Landover) o.p.

ISBN 0-345-33527-9 LC 87-1456

"A Del Rey book"

In this second book in the Magic Kingdom of Landover series "dreams of trouble, missing spell-books, and a black unicorn send Ben Holiday, Landover's newest king, his wizard, Questor, and the sylph, Willow, on three separate quests that converge in a battle for control of their magical kingdom." Libr J

Followed by Wizard at large

The druid of Shannara. Ballantine Bks. 1991 423p o.p.

ISBN 0-345-36298-5 LC 90-42424

"A Del Rey book"

In the second novel in the Heritage of Shannara tetralogy "Walker Boh, the 'Dark Uncle,' embarks on a perilous journey to recover the black Elfstone and restore the lost druid keep of Paranor." Libr J

"Broadening the landscape of his magic world, Brooks has produced a deep and thoughtful fantasy." Publ Wkly

Followed by The elfqueen of Shannara

The elfqueen of Shannara. Ballantine Bks. 1992 403p o.p.

LC 91-73257

"A Del Rey book"

Third volume of the Heritage of Shannara tetralogy. "While Par and Coll Ohmsford seek the lost Sword of Shannara and Walker Boh travels to the hidden city of Paranor to bring the Druids back to the Four Lands, young Wren Ohmsford journeys beyond the boundaries of the known world to fulfill the charge given to her by the shade of the Druid Allanon: to return the Elves to the lands of Men." Libr J

"Brooks's prose becomes more fluid and his world becomes more complex, ambiguous and credible with each volume." Publ Wkly

Followed by The talismans of Shannara

The Elfstones of Shannara; illustrated by Darrell K. Sweet. Ballantine Bks. 1982 469p il o.p.

LC 81-69187

"A Del Rey book"

Sequel to The sword of Shannara

"The Ellcrys Tree is dying and when she dies, hordes of demons will be released for a final epic battle. The Elves, despite the help of Allanon, the last Druid, are hopelessly outnumbered. It is up to Will Ohmsford and Amberle to carry an Ellcrys seed to the blood fire. A new Ellcrys will result and the demons will be banished." Voice Youth Advocates

This novel features "strong, believable women who aren't paper-doll characters, but substantial, important figures." SLJ

Followed by The wishsong of Shannara

Brooks, Terry, 1944-—*Continued*

First king of Shannara. Ballantine Bks. 1996 489p o.p.
LC 95-52321

"A Del Rey book"

"To defend his followers and escape subjugation from the evil Warlock Lord, Druid Bremen must possess the magical Black Elfstone. This . . . answers fans' questions about the early history of the Shannara family." Libr J

Ilse witch. Ballantine Pub. Group 2000 454p (Voyage of the Jerle Shannara, bk1) o.p.
ISBN 0-345-39654-5 LC 00-37863

"A Del Rey book"

"When evidence of an ancient magic surfaces in the Elven lands, a race begins between Walker Boh, the last Druid, and his implacable enemy, the young woman known as the Ilse Witch. Brooks . . . introduces a new and intriguing cast of characters along with a few familiar faces." Libr J

A Knight of the Word. Ballantine Pub. Group 1998 309p o.p.
ISBN 0-345-37963-2 LC 98-5471

"A Del Rey book"

"Haunted by his failure to prevent the death of innocent children, John Ross abandons his calling as a Knight of the Word and opens himself to corruption by the forces of the Void. His only hope for rescue lies with Nest Freemark, a young woman whose demon-blood once brought her to the edge of the Void but who now seeks to repay her debt to the Lady of the Word." Libr J

"Both a sprightly entertainment and a thoughtful allegory of the forces of Good and Evil at large in the modern world." Publ Wkly

Magic kingdom for sale—sold!. Ballantine Bks. 1986 324p (Magic Kingdom of Landover) o.p.
ISBN 0-345-31757-2 LC 85-26865

"A Del Rey book"

In this first novel in the author's Magic Kingdom of Landover series, dissatisfied lawyer "Ben Holliday buys a 'magic kingdom' for a million dollars, then finds that it is afflicted with an assortment of drawbacks, of which bankruptcy is the least important. More significant from Ben's point of view is the presence of a demon prince who challenges all the new human rulers and invariably defeats them." Booklist

"Despite a slow, pretentious beginning, Brooks displays an unexpected flair for light comedy in this not-so-standard fantasy quest." Libr J

Followed by The black unicorn

Morgawr. Del Rey Bks. 2002 401p (Voyage of the Jerle Shannara, bk3) o.p.
ISBN 0-345-43572-9 LC 2002-67386

In the conclusion of the Jerle Shannara trilogy the "fiendish creature known as the Morgawr commands a fleet of airships crewed by mindless creatures who were once men. Her goal: to find and destroy the Ilse Witch and any who try to lend her aid. As the survivors of the Morgawr's attack flee aboard the *Jerle Shannara,* they realize that they must inevitably confront their foe once and for all." Libr J

Running with the demon. Ballantine Bks. 1997 420p o.p.
LC 97-9381

"A Del Rey book"

"John Ross, a Knight of the Word, travels to Hopewell, Illinois, on the Fourth of July weekend to stop the horrendous future that he sees in his dreams. The demon of the Void arrives in town to set in motion the cataclysmic events that will make Ross's dreams a reality. Caught between them is 14-year-old orphan Nest Freemark, who has inherited magic from her mother and grandmother; the future of humanity depends on her action. In this realistic fantasy, Brooks skillfully explores good vs. evil." Libr J

Followed by A Knight of the Word

The scions of Shannara. Ballantine Bks. 1990 465p il o.p.
ISBN 0-345-35695-0 LC 89-37935

"A Del Rey book"

The first title in the Heritage of Shannara tetralogy finds the descendants of the heroes of the Shannara trilogy "summoned to the Hadeshorn in vivid dreams by the spirit of the Druid Allanon. The shade reveals the tasks they each must accept in order to save the Four Lands from total devastation. Par Ohmsford is ordered to find the missing Sword of Shannara; Wren must search for the Elves who mysteriously disappeared a long time ago, and Walker Boh must bring back the Druids." Voice Youth Advocates

Followed by The druid of Shannara

The sword of Shannara; illustrated by the Brothers Hildebrandt. Random House 1977 726p il o.p.
LC 77-151532

"Humans, trolls, dwarfs, elves, gnomes, sorcerers both good and evil, and battalions of knights and knaves populate this sweeping adult epic-fantasy. At the urging of a mysterious sorcerer, an adopted orphan named Shea reluctantly takes up the quest for the Sword of Shannara, a legendary elvin blade that alone can defeat the forces of evil engulfing the world." Booklist

"Reminiscent of Tolkien's fantasies though lacking the originality of his vision and the beauty of his language, this is still an engrossing saga of hardship and adventure with well-maintained action that will keep readers captive right up to a nicely-wrought finish." SLJ

Followed by The Elfstones of Shannara

The talismans of Shannara. Ballantine Bks. 1993 453p o.p.
LC 92-90377

"A Del Rey book"

The conclusion of the Heritage of Shannara tetralogy. "Having fulfilled the quests imposed upon them by the shade of the druid Allanon, the children of Shannara must now attempt to use their newfound powers and allies to defeat the Shadowen who are ravaging the Four Lands. . . . Brooks's appeal lies in his fidelity to tried-and-true quest fantasy and in his ability to create engaging protagonists." Libr J

The tangle box; a magic kingdom of Landover novel. Ballantine Bks. 1994 334p $22
ISBN 0-345-38699-X LC 93-47013

Brooks, Terry, 1944-—*Continued*

"A Del Rey book"

Sequel to Magic Kingdom for sale—sold!, entered in main catalog

"Sovereign Ben Holiday attempts to be merciful in allowing a couple of exiled sorcerers to return to Landover. Unfortunately, the exiles are stalking horses for the Gorse, a potent and evil sorcerer who seeks revenge upon the fairy folk. Ben ends up in the Tangle Box, his only hope for freedom the Lady Willow, who is unfortunately not available when she is needed." Booklist

The wishsong of Shannara; illustrated by Darrell K. Sweet. Ballantine Bks. 1985 499p il o.p.
LC 84-24185

"A Del Rey book"

In the concluding volume of the Shannara trilogy, "a third generation of Ohmsfords answers the druid Allanon's call to fight the forces of evil as Brin and her brother Jair carry their own version of elven magic—the wishsong—into the enemy's camp. Like its predecessors, . . . this fantasy quest features and entertaining variety of characters, impossible odds, and victory gained only through sacrifice." Libr J

Wizard at large. Ballantine Bks. 1988 291p (Magic Kingdom of Landover) o.p.
LC 88-47805

"A Del Rey book"

In this third Landover fantasy "a spell to restore the Court Scribe of Landover to human form backfires, and Landover's King embarks on a quest to his native world to rescue his friend and retrieve the medallion of Kingship from the clutches of a greedy wizard." Libr J

Followed by The Tangle Box

Brown, Carrie, 1959-

Confinement; Carrie Brown. Algonquin Books of Chapel Hill 2004 352p $24.95
ISBN 1-565-12393-X LC 2003-66441

"Arthur Henning, an Austrian Jew, had relocated to America with his nine-year-old son, Toby, after losing his wife and infant daughter when their building was bombed during World War II. Then Toby disappeared at the age of 18. Arthur has been sustained by his love, improper but never acted on, for Aggie Duvall, daughter of the banker for whom Arthur has been a driver for 17 years. It was Arthur, not Aggie's alcoholic mother or frequently absent father, who supported the girl emotionally when, pregnant at 17, she was sent away." Booklist

"The final revelation regarding Toby's relationship with Agatha is fairly predictable, and some of the time shifts get a bit jittery when Brown dramatizes Henning's climactic separation from Agatha. But Brown's deft shaping of their unconventional love makes the novel haunting and memorable." Publ Wkly

The hatbox baby; a novel. Algonquin Bks. 2000 333p $22.95
ISBN 1-56512-299-2 LC 00-44208

"Confirmed bachelor Dr. Leo Hoffman is a pioneer in neonatal intensive care who finances his research into and medical care of destitute babies by charging admission to his educational programs at fairs and amusement parks. During the summer of 1933, while working at his premature baby exhibit at the Chicago World's Fair, he saves the life of a special 'premie'—and finds love in the process. . . . This is a moving story about complex, interesting characters who love deeply." Libr J

The house on Belle Island and other stories. Algonquin Bks. 2002 248p $22.95
ISBN 1-56512-300-X LC 2001-55234

Contents: Friend to women; Miniature man; The correspondent; Wings; Father Judge Run; Postman; The house on Belle Isle

"Brown's prose is fluid and graceful and, despite the occasional use of romantic cliché, it eschews melodrama and unrealistic conclusions. These stories lack the economy usually associated with the form but, for this reason, they will probably appeal to readers who enjoyed Brown's novels." Publ Wkly

Lamb in love; a novel. Algonquin Bks. 1999 336p $21.95
ISBN 1-56512-203-8 LC 98-44580

Norris Lamb, "thought of as a confirmed bachelor at 55, is the postmaster of Hursley, a tiny village in rural England. Vida, at 41, has been the caretaker of severely retarded Manford Perry for 20 years, ever since his mother died giving birth to him. In July 1969, on the very day of the Apollo moon landing, Norris' perception of Vida, and ultimately himself, is suddenly, dramatically, and forever changed." Booklist

The author "reveals her characters not as others perceive them but as they are able to see one another, and as they come to understand themselves. Norris and Vida are full of depth and longing, passion and poetry, that continually startle and delight." N Y Times Book Rev

Brown, Dale, 1956-

Air Battle Force. Morrow 2003 xx, 426p $25.95
ISBN 0-06-009409-5 LC 2002-41092

In this thriller, the "Taliban have plans to take over oil-rich Turkmenistan, thus causing a global crisis. Maj. Gen Patrick McLanahan and the Air Battle Force are tasked to stop them." Libr J

"This absorbing techno-thriller follows the author's established pattern of fast action in the air and on the ground, its hard-driving protagonists equipped with an arsenal of futuristic hardware." Publ Wkly

Chains of command. Putnam 1993 479p o.p.
LC 93-7887

"It is the immediate future. Russia makes a low-level thermonuclear attack on Ukraine, trying to bring it back in line with the other former Soviet nations. When Turkey agrees to support the Ukrainian army, NATO becomes involved, and the U.S. Air Force Reserves are deployed. Brilliant but maligned maintenance officer Daren Mace joins forces with the beautiful and talented pilot Rebecca Furness in a last-ditch mission to destroy the blood-thirsty Russian leader before full-scale atomic war can erupt." Libr J

Flight of the Old Dog; a novel. Fine, D.I. 1987 347p o.p.
LC 86-46388

"It is not the Reagan Administration that has secretly been developing a Strategic Defense Initiative in this first book by retired USAF Captain Brown, but the Soviets, and as soon as the system comes on line, the Russians

Brown, Dale, 1956-—*Continued*
flagrantly attack American intelligence and military craft with their laser weapon . . . and the U.S. is left dangerously incapable of detecting a missile launch from the eastern U.S.S.R. Desperate, they decide to send a souped-up veteran B-52 bomber, the Old Dog, and its expert navigator Patrick McLanahan on a crucial mission into Siberia to neutralize the death ray." Publ Wkly

"Despite spinning his wheels in the opening portions of the book—labored attempts at developing character, a stumbling stab at establishing a love interest, a series of predictable Soviet low blows that bring the world to the precipice of nuclear war—Dale Brown finally . . . draws the reader into a tense, compelling adventure tale of the first order." Booklist

Hammerheads. Fine, D.I. 1990 478p o.p.
LC 89-46026

"Hammerheads are an elite force, part U.S. Coast Guard and part customs service, that use a powerful array of weapons, including a V-22C tilt-rotor Sea Lion (a combination helicopter and fixed-wing aircraft). The force is stationed on offshore platforms and led by General Brad Elliott and Major Mac McLanahan, and its purpose is to stop the operations of the South American drug cartels." Booklist

"This smooth blend of plot, action and gadgetry supports the debatable argument that drug smuggling can be checked by military methods. But forget ideologies—*Hammerheads* is a reader's delight from first page to last, a model of the genre." Publ Wkly

Night of the hawk. Fine, D.I. 1992 462p o.p.
LC 92-14138

"Lithuania, seeking to remove the last traces of Soviet rule, plans to get rid of a secret research facility where scientists have developed a Stealth-type bomber—with the involuntary aid of none other than David Luger, presumed killed in *Flight of the Old Dog*. Luger has instead been captured, brainwashed and given a new identity, but somehow he has retained his professional expertise. Informed of his survival, the U.S. government mounts a rescue." Publ Wkly

Shadows of steel. Putnam 1996 367p $24.95
ISBN 0-399-14139-1 LC 96-743

Patrick McLanahan "and his cronies are working to rescue a U.S. spy ship crew from some particularly thuggish Iranians and also keeping an Iranian aircraft carrier (acquired from the former-Soviet-armaments yard sale, so to speak) from catastrophically destabilizing the Persian Gulf region. They have available to them the resources of the CIA, a B-2 bomber . . . and some lengthy described and ingenious weaponry." Booklist

"Brown is a master of this school of fiction, bringing life to his characters with a few deft strokes. More than just a military thriller, this novel offers disturbing descriptions of possible political developments that are worthy of discussion." Publ Wkly

Storming heaven. Putnam 1994 399p o.p.
LC 94-12213

"Henri Cazaux is a terrorist with a grudge against the United States because MPs mistreated him in an army jail. In retribution, he decides to destroy the entire country by blowing up airports and, eventually, the Capitol. He is opposed by misunderstood retired Coast Guard admiral Ian Hardcastle." Libr J

"Over the top? Sure. But the author's view about the vulnerability of U.S. airports to aerial attack reads almost plausibly, and Cazaux is a fascinating monster." Booklist

The tin man. Bantam Bks. 1998 367p o.p.
LC 98-10254

In this suspense yarn, "international terrorism hits the streets of Sacramento, Calif., in the form of Gregory Townsend, who is apparently out to unite California's motorcycle gangs and corner the amphetamine market. His one mistake is wounding the brother of Brown's series hero, veteran Patrick McLanahan, during the robbery of a mall. The resulting mayhem is a tribute to Brown's storytelling abilities; it's an unlikely but successful mix of a revenge plot, a meditation on vigilante justice and a superhero-origin story." Publ Wkly

Warrior class. Putnam 2001 449p $25.95
ISBN 0-399-14714-4 LC 2001-19116

"Pavel Kazakov came out a winner in the sell-off of Soviet-era assets. Now his avarice turns to oil, specifically to the construction of a pipeline across the Balkans to the Adriatic Sea. Local potentates aren't keen on the scheme, but Kazakov's power, thanks to his Mt-179 stealth plane, which allows him to bomb them with impunity and anonymity, is unfairly persuasive. American superpilot Patrick McLanahan and his strike force are called upon to rescue a captured spy. And once McLanahan's 'Megafortress' B-1 bombers are aloft, the plot revolves around dogfight after dogfight." Booklist

Wings of fire. Putnam 2002 446p $25.95
ISBN 0-399-14860-4 LC 2002-23153

"Retired Air Force Gen. Patrick McClanahan returns, this time to do battle with a greedy and unscrupulous pretender to the Libyan throne. The self-proclaimed King Idris the Second, who led a coup ousting Qaddafi, has his heart set on invading Egypt, seizing its oilfields, and assassinating the Egyptian president. In the assassination attempt, his troops wound the Egyptian first lady, Susan Bailey Salaam, a former U.S. Air Force officer and a stunning beauty. When McClanahan's poorly planned assault on Libya goes awry and his wife is taken captive, he must join forces with Salaam and the rightful king of Libya to try to get her back." Libr J

"The politics and Middle East setting are spot on; the superweapons are eye-openers; and the villains deliciously evil" Publ Wkly

Brown, Dan, 1964-

The Da Vinci code; a novel. Doubleday 2003 454p $24.95
ISBN 0-385-50420-9 LC 2002-40918

"In a two-day span, American symbologist Robert Langdon finds himself accused of murdering the curator of the Louvre, on the run through the streets of Paris and London, and teamed up with French-cryptologist Sophie Neveu to uncover nothing less than the secret location of the Holy Grail. It appears that a conservative Catholic bishop might be on the verge of destroying the Grail, which includes an alternate history of Christ that could bring down the church. . . .The story is full of brain-teasing puzzles and fascinating insights into religious history and art." Booklist

Brown, Dee Alexander

Creek Mary's blood; a novel; [by] Dee Brown. Holt, Rinehart & Winston 1980 401p il o.p.
LC 79-9060

"Through the words and memories of Dane, grandson of Creek Mary (or Akusa Amayi), we follow the history of the men, children, and grandchildren in the life of that indomitable exemplar of the American Indian. The action—and there is plenty of it—takes place in the period after the Revolutionary War and continues through the nineteenth century. The customs, rituals, courting, fighting, and celebrating are all described in detail. One of the most painful sections of the book depicts the forced removal west of the Mississippi of Indian tribes. . . . The relationships among the various tribes—Creek, Cheyenne, Cherokee, and others—is of great interest. Many famous names are recalled, among them Tecumseh, Andrew Jackson, Teddy Roosevelt, and the great chiefs Crazy Horse and Sitting Bull." Shapiro. Fic for Youth. 3d edition

Killdeer Mountain; a novel; [by] Dee Brown. Holt, Rinehart & Winston 1983 279p o.p.
LC 82-15460

This "is the saga of a reporter for the Saint Louis Herald who sets out for the Dakota Territory in 1866. In his journey, he comes across the subject of Charles Riley, hero of the Civil War and Indian fighter. Reporter Sam Morrison finds conflicting stories as to the character of Major Rawley, thus planting the seeds of a quest for the truth as to the real story of Indian massacres, dishonor in battle, deserted love and planned rescue of an innocent Dakota Chief held captive in a desolate fort." Voice Youth Advocates

"The story of Major Rawley if it is indeed his story and not that of the mysterious stranger masquerading as Rawley—is told in a 'Rashomon'-like interweaving of different eyewitness accounts, and it is an intriguing and exciting tale." Libr J

The way to Bright Star; [by] Dee Brown. Forge 1998 352p $24.95
ISBN 0-312-86612-7 LC 98-14621

"A Tom Doherty Associates book"

This novel "opens in 1902, when narrator Ben Butterfield, a gimp-legged former circus horseback performer who is now the harried proprietor of a hardware store, attempts 'to set down the story of my wasted life' before he forgets the adventure that was its high point. Forty years earlier, in the spring of 1862 in northwest Arkansas, young Ben embarks on an unlikely journey. A Yankee officer assigns him, cavalry scout Johnny Hawkes and Egyptian cameleer Hadjee the duty of transporting two camels, the officer's own personal contraband, from Arkansas to his farm in Bright Star, Indiana." Publ Wkly

This "picaresque yarn whose main strength rests in its cast of colorful characters, whom readers quickly come to know as individuals and with whom they will want to spend time." Booklist

Brown, Elizabeth Inness- *See* Inness-Brown, Elizabeth, 1954-

Brown, Fredric, 1906-1972

The bloody moonlight
In Brown, F. Hunter and hunted

Compliments of a fiend
In Brown, F. Hunter and hunted

Dead ringer
In Brown, F. Hunter and hunted

The fabulous clipjoint
In Brown, F. Hunter and hunted

Hunter and hunted; the Ed and Am Hunter novels. Stewart Masters Pub. 2002 620p (Frederic Brown mystery library, pt. 1) $29.99
ISBN 0-9718185-0-9 LC 2002-8826

"The Ed an Am Hunter novels star a nephew (Ed) and uncle (Am) who begin as amateur sleuths but eventually become professional detectives. Of the four novels collected here-The Fabulous Clipjoint (1947), The Dead Ringer (1948), The Bloody Moonlight (1949), and Compliments of a Fiend (1950)—the best s the first, in which 18-year-old Ed helps his uncle solve the murder of Ed's father. The setting is a beautifully realized postwar Chicago. Like Hammett, Brown relishes specificity of place as he tracks Ed and Am's peregrinations across the city's North Side slum. . . . The streets are mean, but the characters are amiable, and the prose is almost jaunty." Booklist

Brown, Joe David, 1915-1976

Addie Pray; a novel. Simon & Schuster 1971 313p o.p.

"Set during the Depression this . . . picaresque novel follows the adventures of two con artists—the narrator Addie Pray, an eleven-year-old orphan, and Long Boy, her presumptive father. The pair travel the South selling gold-initialed Bibles to new widows, working a wallet-switching trick, and trading in nonexistent cotton, among other outrageous ploys, until they join Major Carter E. Lee in more sophisticated swindles culminating in a slick scheme to set Addie up as heiress to an enormous fortune." Booklist

"Brown has a special feeling for the Depression-era South. . . . [Addie's speech] is vulgar, pungent country talk, which adds greatly to the book's easygoing charm. Looking at Long Boy with his floozy, she observes that 'he got that silly, dazed grin like a tom cat being choked to death with cream.' Like that extravagant expression, the book is a long tall, oldtime tale. But as Addie might put it, in the right hands that kind of yarn has a lot of prance left." Time

Brown, John Gregory

Audubon's watch; a novel. Houghton Mifflin 2001 210p $24
ISBN 0-395-78607-X LC 2001-16914

This novel is narrated in part by the ornithologist John James Audubon. "A prologue introduces Audubon's foil, a doctor named Emile Gautreaux, and lays out the basic premise. Thirty years earlier, in the summer of 1821, the doctor's beautiful young wife, Myra, died under mysterious circumstances on a Louisiana plantation. Gautreaux

Brown, John Gregory—*Continued*
and Audubon, employed as a tutor by the plantation's owner, spent a night together keeping watch over the body—the first and last time they met. . . . Now, as Audubon is dying, he sends for Gautreaux. . . . As the novel progresses, Brown alternates between the two men while their recollections circle ever closer to the night of Myra's death." N Y Times Book Rev

"There are few moments of humor or cheer in this stream-of-consciousness study of two men whose genuine interests in science and nature were ruined by lust and its consequent remorse, but Brown . . . provides a delicate rendition of gloomy themes." Publ Wkly

Brown, Larry, 1951-2004

Fay; a novel. Algonquin Bks. 2000 487p $24.95
ISBN 1-56512-168-6 LC 99-88594

"When 17-year-old Fay walks out on her abusive, dirt-poor backwoods family, she is taken in by Mississippi trooper Sam Harris and his wife, Amy. First a surrogate for a dead daughter, Fay is soon Sam's lover and becomes pregnant after Amy dies (in a car accident involving alcohol), but then, more or less in self-defense, she shoots and kills Sam's ex-lover while Sam is on patrol. She flees, again on foot, this time ending up with Aaron, a volatile, violent, and bulked-up bouncer and part-owner of a Biloxi strip joint." Libr J

"The raw power of this novel, the clear, graphic accounts of both humble and perverted lives (in the bars and strip joints of Biloxi), is a triumph of realism and a humane imagination." Publ Wkly

Joe; a novel. Algonquin Bks. 1991 345p o.p.
ISBN 0-945575-61-0 LC 91-12026

A novel about "poor 'white trash' in rural Mississippi. Joe Ranson is a middle-aged redneck with a soul. He fights and spits, drinks beer by the gallon from a cooler embedded in his truck, and endures bad relationships with women. But within the society he inhabits, he is a moral man, more or less following the rituals and established 'codes' of fair play. Unfortunately, he is involved in a classic feud, the roots of which are never revealed, that threatens to destroy him. Also destined to cross paths with Joe is the nomadic Jones family. Gary Jones is a hardworking and painfully naive teenager. His father is pure evil, his mother nearly insane, and his siblings barely human. Joe offers Gary work, fueling hope that these two very different men will learn enough from each other to save themselves." Booklist

Brown is a "talented fiction writer in the whiskeyish, rascally Southern tradition of Faulkner and Erskine Caldwell. . . . The new novel is clear, simple and powerful, and it is great, rowdy fun to read." Time

The rabbit factory. Free Press 2003 339p $25
ISBN 0-7432-4523-7 LC 2002-45591

Set in or near Memphis, this novel focuses on "hooker Anjalee; older man Arthur along with his younger, sexually dissatisfied wife, Helen; 'gunslinger' Frankie and his just desserts; ex-prisoner Domino and his sordid attempts to make a go of it outside the big house, and other equally 'attractive' men and women working out their own destinies even when love, sex and money (or the lack of any or all of the three) get in their way. . . . You definitely can't go wrong with a novel that has dogs as fully developed characters in their own right." Booklist

Brown, Morna Doris MacTaggart, 1907-

For works written by this author under other names see Ferrars, E. X., 1907-

Brown, Rita Mae

Cat on the scent; by Rita Mae Brown & Sneaky Pie Brown; illustrations by Itoko Maeno. Bantam Bks. 1998 321p il o.p.
ISBN 0-553-09971-X LC 98-38104

"The small town of Crozet, VA, has its share of eccentric characters, social mainstays, money-driven individuals, powerful leaders, political intrigues, affairs of the heart, Civil War reenactment groups, and regular people. When all of the town's aforementioned parts clash, the result equals murder . . . twice. It takes most of the local folks to solve the first murder. The second one appears to be solved, but the truth becomes known only to readers and the three 'investigators' who solve both crimes—Mrs. Murphy, Pewter, and Tucker—the two cats and the dog owned by postmistress Mary Minor 'Harry' Haristeen. . . . A double treat for animal and mystery lovers." SLJ

Catch as cat can; {by} Rita Mae Brown & Sneaky Pie Brown; illustrations by Michael Gellatly. Bantam Bks. 2002 287p o.p.
ISBN 0-553-10744-5 LC 2001-35741

Crozet Virginia's "eccentric citizens are so caught up in the social whirl attending the annual Dogwood Festival that they ignore such unnatural events as the demise of a giant pileated woodpecker and the theft of the hubcaps on the widow Hogendobber's 1961 Ford Falcon. But when the rites of spring turn to murder, Mary Minor (Harry) Haristeen, the town postmaster and resident sleuth, is moved to investigate. Unlike Harry, who is only human and therefore oblivious of the urgently articulated advice of her house pets, readers are privy to their commentary, especially that of Mrs. Murphy, a bossy tiger cat who proves cleverer than the entire voting population of Crozet." N Y Times Book Rev

Dolley; a novel of Dolley Madison in love and war. Bantam Bks. 1994 382p o.p.
LC 93-44429

The author re-creates a "critical year in the life of the fourth president's wife, who loved politics and her husband and who had a great gift for friendship. In 1814, Napoleon's war with Britain spilled into its former colonies, and redcoats marching toward under-defended Washington constitute the backdrop of Brown's slice of Dolley Madison's life. Brown vivifies the capital hostess and covert political manipulator's doings by interspersing snippets from an imaginary diary with the main narrative. . . . Brown's Dolley Madison is full-blown and vibrant." Booklist

High hearts. Bantam Bks. 1986 464p o.p.
LC 85-48042

Set in Virginia, this "Civil War saga centers on the war-time experiences of Geneva Chatfield, who disguises herself as a boy and runs off to join her husband fighting on the Confederate side. In the process, Geneva discovers she can amount to something more than just a clinging vine, more than just a helpmeet for a man. Brown's purpose is to show how this terrible conflict had an effect on women and blacks, too—their participation in it,

Brown, Rita Mae—*Continued*
their sacrifices because of it, what they had at stake in the outcome." Booklist

"Although the chain of events is formulaic and the outcome less than surprising, Brown's style is energetic, her message humane, and her characters unconventional and lively." Publ Wkly

Loose lips. Bantam Bks. 1999 374p o.p.
ISBN 0-553-09972-8 LC 98-56079

"It is 1941 in the small Maryland town of Runnymede, and the two adult Hunsenmeir sisters, Julia Ellen and Louise, haven't gotten along since—well, since forever. . . . One day, their conflict actually erupts into an out-and-out brawl in the local drugstore. To pay for damages, the sisters decide to open a beauty salon. It doesn't take long for the Curl 'n' Twirl to become Gossip Central. For the next decade, we witness the sisters growing older and playing out the ups and downs in their relationship with each other and with the town they are so intimately involved in. . . . Brimming with Brown's comic sense of social posturing and missteps, her rich novel lets readers laugh with her at the personal foibles that seem to loom so large in small-town settings." Booklist

Murder at Monticello; or, Old sins; [by] Rita Mae Brown & Sneaky Pie Brown; illustrations by Wendy Wray. Bantam Bks. 1994 298p il o.p.
LC 94-16711

"Tiger cat Mrs. Murphy and corgi Tee Tucker . . . help Mary Minor 'Harry' Haristeen, postmistress of Crozet, Virginia, solve a nearly 200-year-old mystery. It begins with a skeleton discovered in a slave cabin during restorations at Monticello—and continues with the present-day murder of Kimball Haynes, head of archaeology there, who has discovered secrets of miscegenation recorded in a doctor's long-hidden journals. . . . An entertaining treat for animal-loving mystery/history fans." Booklist

Murder on the prowl; by Rita Mae Brown and Sneaky Pie Brown. Bantam Bks. 1998 320p il o.p.
ISBN 0-553-09970-1 LC 97-31153

"Two bogus obituaries that turn up in the local newspaper are just the sort of prank one expects of Crozet's eccentric residents; but when the non-deceased are then murdered—well, maybe that's to be expected too. Although it falls to Mary Minor (Harry) Haisteen, the postmistress, to unmask the culprit, the most impressive feats of detection are conducted by her cat, the estimable Mrs. Murphy. . . . The fond amusement with which Brown observes the foibles of Harry and her neighbors saves these upstanding citizens from becoming total idiots." NY Times Book Rev

Murder, she meowed; [by] Rita Mae Brown & Sneaky Pie Brown; illustrations by Wendy Wray. Bantam Bks. 1996 285p il o.p.
LC 96-20727

"A resourceful tiger cat named Mrs. Murphy . . . goes into a snit when her mistress, Mary Minor (Harry) Haristeen, the good-natured 'post office lady' of cozy Crozet, Va., leaves her behind to attend the steeplechase races at Montpelier. But when someone begins killing jockeys by sticking daggers into their hearts, the formidable Mrs. Murphy sends out the troops to (literally) dig up the dirt on this nasty human behavior. Harry is a sweet soul, but none of the bipeds has the brains of a cat." N Y Times Book Rev

Outfoxed. Ballantine Bks. 2000 409p o.p.
ISBN 0-345-42818-8 LC 99-44243

This novel is set in the "middle of Virginia fox-hunting country. When 70-year-old Jane Arnold, master of the prestigious Jefferson Hunt Club, sees the grim reaper crossing a field, she knows that it's time to choose a joint-master to secure the future of the club. The two rivals for the position are Crawford Howard, a crude Yankee outsider with money greatly needed by the club, and Fontaine Buruss, a popular local with good Southern manners and a taste for women and cocaine. On opening day, one of these candidates is murdered, and Jane realizes that the culprit is a club member." Libr J

"The antics of the anthropomorphic foxes, horses, hounds, cats, and dogs are as entertaining as those of the humans, especially because the animals are often the wiser ones. A quirky, adventurous, intriguing read." Booklist

Pay dirt; or, Adventures at Ash Lawn; [by] Rita Mae Brown and Sneaky Pie Brown; illustrations by Wendy Wray. Bantam Bks. 1995 251p il o.p.
LC 95-20021

Murder and mayhem come to the "sleepy little town of Crozet, Virginia, heralded by the arrival of a leatherclad biker who storms up to historic Ash Lawn (James Monroe's home) demanding to see the 'thieving slut' Malibu and upsetting the docents. Later, when the biker's body is found in Sugar Hollow, postmistress/detective Harry Haristeen, accompanied by the incorrigible cat Mrs. Murphy and Welsh corgi Tee Tucker, finds herself in the middle of the investigation." Libr J

"It's always a pleasure to visit this cozy world. True, there are never enough suspects around for any mystery resolution to come as a real surprise. But there's no resisting Harry's droll sense of humor about her eccentric neighbors." N Y Times Book Rev

Rest in pieces; [by] Rita Mae Brown & Sneaky Pie Brown; illustrations by Wendy Wray. Bantam Bks. 1992 292p il o.p.
LC 92-7257

This murder mystery "finds Mary Minor ('Harry') Haristeen, who is postmistress in the small southern town of Crozet, Virginia, and also runs a 120-acre farm, trying to discover the identity of a dismembered corpse, pieces of which are found on the property of her new neighbor Blair Bainbridge, a male model from New York." Booklist

"Ms. Brown's earthy prose breathes warmth into wintry Crozet and pinches color into the cheeks of its nosy, garrulous residents." N Y Times Book Rev

Riding shotgun. Bantam Bks. 1996 341p o.p.
LC 95-36103

"Virginia realtor Cig Blackwood is recently widowed, and with two children living at home, she struggles to make ends meet. Riding to the hounds is her passion, and one day, during a fox hunt, she is catapulted back in time to the year 1699, where she lives for a while with her own ancestors. In colonial times, she leads a whole new life and even falls in love. . . . Brown has

Brown, Rita Mae—*Continued*
done her homework well on the historical detail, and when it's time for Cig to come home again, Brown gives us a delightfully romantic ending." Booklist

Six of one. Harper & Row 1978 310p o.p.
LC 78-2057

The author "extols the vitality and variety of women by tracing the lives of two sisters, their families, and cronies. The women are rich and poor, heterosexual (mostly) and lesbian, but they are linked by emotional and physical experiences common to all women. . . . Structurally, the novel intersperses vivid scenes from the past with those from the present (1980 in the book). Despite flaws, the narrative is engrossing, as are the women." Libr J

Southern discomfort. Harper & Row 1982 249p o.p.
LC 81-47683

In this novel "the focus is on the rigid class and racial divisions of Montgomery, Ala., society during the early decades of this century. . . . Hortensia Banastre, ice goddess, model society matron, falls passionately in love with a young black boxer, and she bears and secretly raises his daughter. . . . Paris, Hortensia's beautiful and hateful son, figures it out—knowledge that figures in his shocking death." Publ Wkly

The author "seems to understand the way in which dark passions and unspeakable desires become magnified among a people segregated by unnatural laws concerning race, class and social position. She portrays well the suffering incurred by trying to defy such a system; she also captures the earthy quality of those who do what they must to get by." Best Sellers

Whisker of evil; [by] Rita Mae Brown & Sneaky Pie Brown; illustrations by Michael Gellatly. Bantam Books 2004 297p $24.95
ISBN 0-553-80161-9 LC 2003-56262

"Protagonist Mary Minor 'Harry' Harristeen, postmistress of tiny Crozet, Virginia, happens upon a dying man whose throat has been slashed. As if that weren't bad enough, he also had rabies. Snooping around the crime scene, Harry finds a ring belonging to a long-missing woman. Are the two connected? This is just one of the many puzzles that unfold in this suspenseful tale that also involves the disappearance of a famous studhorse. . . . Admirers of Mrs. Murphy will enjoy the expanding repertoire of animals she converses with: snakes, owls, mice, swallows, and foxes." Booklist

Wish you were here; {by} Rita Mae Brown & Sneaky Pie Brown; illustrations by Wendy Wray. Bantam Bks. 1990 242p il o.p.
LC 90-1071

"Mary Minor ('Harry') Haristeen, divorce in the works, runs the post office in Crozet, Virginia, with a pet cat and dog at her side. After two spectacularly gruesome murders rock the community, Harry attempts to gather helpful clues, while the pets (who converse with each other) do their best to protect her." Libr J

"Ms. Brown writes with wise, disarming wit about her country-bred characters and their not-always-neighborly ways." N Y Times Book Rev

Brown, Rosellen

Before and after. Farrar, Straus & Giroux 1992 354p o.p.
ISBN 0-374-10999-0 LC 92-81571

This novel begins "on the day that Carolyn Reiser, a New Hampshire pediatrician with two teenage kids, gets called to the emergency room. A girl has been bludgeoned to death. The chief suspect is Carolyn's son and he has disappeared." Newsweek

Brown is "tenacious in her examination of each major character. Deftly, artfully, she strips away the delicate shelter of conventional relationships." N Y Times Book Rev

Civil wars; a novel. Knopf 1984 419p o.p.
LC 83-48866

An "analysis of the falsehoods within the union of Teddy and Jessie Carll. Nearly two decades have passed since the exhilarating activism of the civil rights movement brought Teddy and Jessie together. The growing distance between them is barely realized and not at all defined when an automobile accident suddenly bequeaths the turbulent family with two more children, who have been raised in a racist, segregated environment. The novel alternates between Brown's third-person narration, which focuses on Jessie, and selections from the diary of one of the adopted orphans." Booklist

"This is a very fine novel. Its principal strength lies in the immense detail with which the characters are depicted. This is especially true of Jessie, from whose viewpoint the story is told." Best Sellers

Half a heart. Farrar, Straus & Giroux 2000 402p o.p.
ISBN 0-374-44013-1 LC 00-22926

"Miriam, a rich Houston housewife with three children, has a secret in her past: during a teaching stint at a black college in the Sixties, she had an affair with a black professor and gave birth to a daughter. When the baby's father challenged her for custody of the child, Miriam gave up without a fight and fled to Houston, soon marrying a rich doctor. For years she suffered feelings of guilt and loss yet felt smug that she wasn't as superficial or racist as her friends. As her own mother's health deteriorates, Miriam suddenly tracks down her daughter, Veronica, now 17 and entering Stanford. Veronica, for her part, intends to milk her new family for money for college." Libr J

"The situation is an intriguing one rendered all the more so by Brown's skillful and sympathetic handling of her two central characters." Time

Tender mercies. Knopf 1978 259p o.p.
LC 78-1315

"In a moment of high spirits, vacationing Dan Courser took the wheel of a powerboat, gunned the motor, and sucked his swimming wife [Laura] into its blades. Nine months later, Dan goes back home with his family—son Jon, daughter Hallie, and quadriplegic Laura, plucked abruptly from a rehabilitation institute—to come to terms with life. Now bright, lovely Laura must live in her head, her most intimate needs attended to by others. And Dan, weighed down with guilt, longs for pain to exceed hers but still needs some space of his own to keep himself and his family on an even keel." Libr J

"What impresses one most about Tender Mercies is its

Brown, Rosellen—*Continued*
dignity and restraint. While we learn a great deal about the physical details of paralysis, catheters and such, Brown makes no case for any horror of the body, nor does Laura's suffering prompt a garish loathing of the universe. . . . The language is spare and clean, with flashes of quiet poetry, perfectly suited to the plain but by no means simple New Englanders it portrays." Saturday Rev

Brown, Sandra, 1948-

The alibi. Warner Bks. 1999 490p o.p.
ISBN 0-446-51980-4 LC 99-31444
"When Charleston real estate developer Lute Pettijohn is murdered in the penthouse suite of the posh hotel he recently built, there is no shortage of likely suspects; Pettijohn is one of the most hated men in town. On the same night that the murder occurs, assistant district attorney Hammond Cross attends a county fair, where he meets a mysterious woman who refuses to tell him her name. . . . Later, when a witness places the woman, now identified as respected psychologist Dr. Alex Ladd, at the scene of the crime, she becomes the number one suspect. . . . A web of labyrinthine relationships becomes ever more intricate until the identity of the killer is revealed, a shock that would be implausible in a less carefully constructed tale." Publ Wkly

Charade. Warner Bks. 1994 405p o.p.
LC 93-38360
Following a successful heart transplant, soap opera star Cat Delaney "abandons stardom and Hollywood for San Antonio, Tex., where she hosts a local TV program featuring children up for adoption. Cat hardly has a chance to enjoy her change of heart and her new heartthrob, bad-boy crime novelist Alex Pierce, because a stalker is after her." Publ Wkly

Chill factor; Sandra Brown. Simon & Schuster 2005 389p $25.95
ISBN 0-7432-4554-7 LC 2005-44310
"Women have been mysteriously disappearing from the small mountain community of Cleary, NC, and a massive winter snowstorm has trapped Lilly Martin in a mountain cabin with the prime suspect, Ben Tierney. Lilly's ex-husband, local police chief Dutch Burton, is intent on rescuing her, but the cabin's remote location and the intensity of the storm significantly delay his efforts. Meanwhile, Lilly finds herself attracted to the charismatic Tierney. . . . Brown offers up her usual blend of steamy romance and suspense, as well as an entertaining subplot featuring the town's outwardly prudish high school English teacher." Libr J

The crush. Warner Bks. 2002 474p o.p.
ISBN 0-446-52704-1 LC 2002-25896
"Dr. Rennie Newton thought she was doing the right thing when she voted to acquit contract killer Ricky Lozada while serving on a jury. After all, the prosecution had not proved its case. But when Lozada is released, he begins calling her and leaving her flowers. When a rival doctor at Rennie's hospital is murdered, suspicion falls on Rennie, and the police suspect she has a connection to Lozada. Detective Wick Threadgill, who has deeply personal reasons to hate Lozada, begins to investigate Rennie. . . . This novel delivers a menacing villain and page-turning suspense." Booklist

Exclusive. Warner Bks. 1996 457p o.p.
LC 96-6252
TV journalist "Barrie Travis is looking for her ticket out of a second-rate Washington, D.C. TV station, but she has a reputation as a screw-up with little credibility. When First Lady Vanessa Merritt hints to her that [her] baby's death may not have been due to SIDs after all, Barrie has the big story she needs-but who will believe her? Before Barrie can learn more from the First Lady, President David Merritt sends his wife 'into seclusion,' where she's heavily drugged and kept under close guard." Publ Wkly
Brown provides an "exciting story line with enough twists and turns to keep you guessing. She is particularly successful here in making you feel like you're in the middle of the quagmire called public office." Booklist

Fat Tuesday. Warner Bks. 1997 454p o.p.
LC 97-7012
"Pinkie Duvall is evil, a prominent and powerful lawyer whose clients commit most of the crime in New Orleans. He met his wife when she was a child and had her educated to his requirements. He treats her as he treats his orchids but uses threats against her younger sister to keep her in line. Burke is the 'incorruptible cop' who sets out to avenge his buddy's death, clean out the bad cops, and get revenge against Pinkie." Libr J
"Brown's trademark mix of action and romance . . . is on display in this suspenseful, if rarely subtle, tale of revenge and corruption." Publ Wkly

French Silk. Warner Bks. 1992 403p o.p.
LC 91-50408
"Televangelist Jackson Wilde targets the catalog of Claire Laurent's mail-order lingerie business, French Silk, as part of his anti-pornography campaign. When Wilde's body is discovered in a New Orleans hotel room, Laurent becomes the number-one suspect in a murder investigation that also involves her mentally distracted mother; her partner, the beautiful model Yasmine; Wilde's wife and son, both working members of his ministry; and a local senator with a shady private life." Libr J
"Despite occasionally stilted and didactic dialogue, the novel is adroitly plotted and sleekly paced, and has just the right mix of menace and sex to keep pages turning." Publ Wkly

Hello, darkness. Simon & Schuster 2003 406p o.p.
ISBN 0-7432-4552-0 LC 2003-54447
"Paris Gibson is a late-night DJ who gives advice to the lovelorn. One night, she receives a call from a listener named Valentino, whom she's talked to many times before. This time, he's frighteningly sinister, threatening Paris and claiming that he's holding his latest girlfriend hostage and that he intends to kill her in three days. Paris takes him seriously and goes directly to the police. At the station, she's shocked to see a face from her past, handsome police psychologist Dean Malloy. Together with several detectives, Paris and Dean try to uncover Valentino's identity as well as the location of the girl he claims he's holding. . . . With an abundance of likely suspects, this sexy, engrossing thriller will keep readers guessing until the very end." Booklist

The switch. Warner Bks. 2000 469p $25.95
ISBN 0-446-52703-3 LC 00-42343

Brown, Sandra, 1948-—*Continued*

"On a whim, the same day she is artificially inseminated at a Dallas fertility clinic, Gillian Lloyd switches places with her identical twin sister, Melina, a professional celebrity escort assigned to chauffeur astronaut Col. Christopher Hart (or 'Chief,' as he is called by his NASA cohorts because his mother was a Native American). It's lust at first sight. Swept away by Chief, Gillian is caught up in a marathon frenzy of lovemaking in his hotel room. Slipping out in the wee hours of the night, she is found brutally butchered in her own bed the next morning. From an obscene blood-smeared scrawl on the bedroom wall, her sister realizes that the killing was related." Publ Wkly

White hot; Sandra Brown. Simon & Schuster 2004 419p $25.95

ISBN 0-7432-4553-9 LC 2004-52129

"Interior designer Sayre Lynch vowed never to return to her hometown of Destiny, LA, yet she finds herself on a plane headed there after learning about her little brother Danny's suicide. Wanting nothing to do with her ruthless family, she plans on attending the funeral only. But Sayre stays when the new deputy sheriff tells her Danny was murdered, perhaps by Chris, his own brother. Sayre also learns about past family crimes, gets involved with a labor dispute at the family-owned foundry, confronts her father for meddling in her affairs, and finds herself attracted to Beck Merchant, the family lawyer/lackey. . . . This should be a popular late-summer public library choice." Libr J

The witness. Warner Bks. 1995 422p o.p.

LC 94-42733

"This story pivots on the relationship between Kendall Deaton Burnwood, an idealistic public defender, and U.S. Marshal John McGrath, who is returning her to Prosper, S.C., as a material witness when their car crashes into a ravine in Georgia. With her three-month-old in tow, Kendall tries repeatedly to abandon John, who's hobbled by temporary amnesia and a leg injury. Kendall fears the town of Prosper for good reason: it's where she witnessed her husband and father-in-law, ringleaders of a white-supremacist vigilante group, ritualistically execute one of her clients. . . . The push-pull generated by John's memory loss and Kendall's terror sparks a sexual tension that is deftly and vividly consummated, and secrets keep popping out until the last page." Publ Wkly

Browne, Gerald A.

18mm blues. Warner Bks. 1993 372p o.p.

LC 92-54098

The title of this "thriller refers to the awesome size of rare blue Burmese pearls. . . . When Setsu and Michiko, the divers who located the uncommon treasure, are murdered by Bertin, the sleazy captain of their pearling boat, he's left with fantastic wealth *and* a witness to his crime. Switching locales to San Francisco, Browne homes in on Grady, a gem merchant, and his girlfriend, Julia, who are about to travel to Burma to purchase precious stones. As the tale unfolds, Thailand provides the setting for all manner of intrigue." Booklist

"Despite a dangerously cute love story . . . Browne's tale succeeds, thanks to a violent, satisfying ending and his mastery of fascinating gem lore." Publ Wkly

19 Purchase Street; a novel. Arbor House 1982 432p o.p.

LC 82-72051

This novel "deals with the big business of laundering dirty money. Purchase Street is the headquarters for a scam involving billions of dollars, carried piecemeal across the world. When Gainer's sister is killed while making a delivery for the group, he joins the organization to avenge her death. He becomes a carrier of money, as much as three million dollars at a time, to Europe, to be exchanged for 'clean' bills, that cannot be traced. Gainer becomes deeply entrenched in the workings of the organization, and makes his own plans to get even with the heads of it for causing his sister's death on one of her money-carrying trips." West Coast Rev Books

"Browne handles the material in this thriller of a tale expeditiously, particularly in a spectacular shoot-out in New York harbor, but some of the elaborate if creaky details that the author injects along the way are hardly for the squeamish or fastidious reader." Booklist

Hot Siberian. Arbor House 1989 424p o.p.

LC 88-7561

"Nikolai, a Russian, is assigned to the London bureau of the Soviet diamond export agency; his charge is to deal with the System, a private worldwide diamond company. Events reveal to Nikolai that the Soviet diamond agency is, in fact, supplying the System with the diamonds it supplies to the world market; and he must deal with contraband diamonds interrupting the System's control of the precious commodity issuing from the Soviet Union. Last but not least, Nikolai must deal with the lovely Vivian." Booklist

"Tautly written and absorbing, the thriller bears comparison with *Gorky Park*, which it closely resembles in mood and topical matter. And it's a noteworthy contribution to the subgenre of thrillers in which the heroes are Russians and some of the bad guys Westerners." Publ Wkly

West 47th. Warner Bks. 1996 390p o.p.

LC 96-60357

"When a gang of thieves makes off with $6 million in gems from the New Jersey home of an Iranian businessman, the insurance company calls in Mitch Laughton. A former Madison Avenue jeweler with a keen eye for precious stones, Mitch earns a nice living recovering stolen jewelry. . . . Mitch must locate the Iranian jewels ahead of Joe Riccio, an old mob boss, and Furio Visconti, a suave young hit man." N Y Times Book Rev

"Browne's plot combines thrills, romance, humor, and pathos." Booklist

Browne, Marshall, 1935-

Eye of the abyss. Thomas Dunne Bks. 2003 c2002 290p $23.95

ISBN 0-312-31156-7 LC 2003-47297

"Franz Schmidt, chief auditor for a family-owned bank in an unnamed south German city, loses his eye defending a Jew attacked by Nazi thugs in 1935. A quiet and meticulous man, he apparently bears no grudges, though his wife and best friend aren't so sure. Three years later, when his bank is chosen as a repository for large amounts of Nazi Party cash, the other shoe drops, and Schmidt becomes a man of action. First, he takes great risks trying to help a female bank employee whose moth-

Browne, Marshall, 1935-—*Continued*

er was Jewish. Then he dreams up a plan to punish Dietrich, the sleek and seductive party operative placed inside the bank." Publ Wkly

"Like the shifting reality of Schmidt's life, the changes in his character are as subtle as they are harrowing, a triumph of Browne's clean, exacting style." N Y Times Book Rev

Brownmiller, Susan

Waverly Place. Warner Bks. 1989 294p o.p.
LC 88-26072

"Brownmiller constructs a portrait of a man's brutality and a woman's destructive dependence. Criminal lawyer Barney Kantor is a psychopathic bully, conman, chiseler and cocaine addict; insecure, self-hating children's book editor Judith Winograd has a need to be dominated and abused; she's also a heroin addict. During the 17 years the couple live together, Kantor establishes a pattern of physical battery followed by grand gestures of contrition. When an adoption scam brings two babies into their lives, the children, especially Melinda, become innocent victims." Publ Wkly

"It would be clear with or without the author's introductory remarks that she has drawn upon the Joel Steinberg/Hedda Nussbaum case for inspiration. The parallels are unmistakable. But it is the colorful prose with which she describes the milieu of Greenwich Village, as well as the skill with which she maintains a balance between objectivity and a touching sense of humanity which make this story more than just investigative journalism disguised as fiction." West Coast Rev Books

Bruen, Ken

The guards. St. Martin's Minotaur 2003 291p $23.95
ISBN 0-312-30355-6 LC 2002-35855

"Ousted from Ireland's police force, the Garda Siochana (or Guards), Jack Taylor ekes out a living on the unmodernized margins of Galway. . . .When Ann Henderson walks into the pub that serves as Taylor's office, asking him to prove that her daughter Sarah was not a suicide but a murder victim, Taylor finds himself investigating a sex-and-murder tangle—and in love." Booklist

"Bruen's astringent prose and death's-head humor keep this quest for redemption from getting maudlin, just as his 'tapestry of talk' makes somber poetry of the barstool laments that serve as dialogue." N Y Times Book Rev

The killing of the tinkers; Ken Bruen. 1st U.S. ed. St. Martin's Minotaur 2004 244p $22.95
ISBN 0-312-30411-0 LC 2003-58559

"A year after the newly sober Jack Taylor left Galway to start a new life in London, the former member of the Gardai Sochna (the Irish police) returns home, a failed marriage behind him. The PI is sinking back into alcoholic oblivion when an Irish Gypsy, Sweeper, approaches Jack for help in solving the murders of a number of young men in his clan. . . . The quintessential outsider himself, Jack empathizes with the roaming Gypsies and feels comfortable in their company. Enlisting the aid of Keegan, a burly cop friend from London, Jack sets about investigating the killings, while at the same time he struggles to keep his own personal demons under control. Bruen's spare, lean style reads like prose poetry." Publ Wkly

Brulard, Henry *See* Stendhal, 1783-1842

Brunner, John, 1934-1995

Stand on Zanzibar. Grove Press 1968 505p o.p.
"Doubleday science fiction"

"Extrapolating from current politics, social and sexual mores, the communications revolution, the use of computers, brainwashing, drug use, psychology, philosophy, and sociology, Brunner has fashioned a mammoth work that is an intricate tapestry depicting a possible future. The dozens of characters interspersed in a complex fashion make the novel difficult to read but well worth the effort. Brunner's brand of cynicism and radical social commentary may not appeal to the taste of all readers, but in the time that has elapsed since the publication of the book, we have seen changes that bear startling similarities to several of Brunner's predictions." Shapiro. Fic for Youth. 3d edition

Bryan, Mike

The afterword. Pantheon Bks. 2003 195p $16
ISBN 0-375-42212-9 LC 2002-30710

In this "novel, Mike Bryan poses as an author writing a follow-up explanation of a wildly successful first novel. 'The Deity Next Door' supposedly described an ordinary man's discovery that he was 'a new and unexpected divinity' and the modest ways he put his powers to the test. . . . Supposedly hounded by readers for information about the book's genesis, the narrator of 'The Afterword' laces his thoughts on religion, contemporary society and the nature of fiction with various outtakes." N Y Times Book Rev

"Bryan brings a very human dimension to the spiritual crisis facing his protagonist by eschewing the hollow literary tricks of most postmodern fiction." Libr J

Buchan, John, 1875-1940

The thirty-nine steps. Doran, G.H. 1915 231p o.p.

"A bored, well-to-do Englishman, Richard Hannay, returns home to England after growing up in South Africa. Drifting between his club and the sights of London, he is drawn into the confidences of a secret agent in the thick of espionage. The agent is murdered in Hannay's apartment and Richard finds himself on the run from Scotland Yard and the cult of the 'Black Stone.'" Shapiro. Fic for Youth. 3d edition

Buchanan, Edna

Act of betrayal. Hyperion 1996 292p o.p.
ISBN 0-7868-6098-7 LC 95-38206

This "Britt Montero mystery involves the *Miami News* crime reporter in two cases. The first concerns a missing 12-year-old boy. In researching a story about the boy's disappearance, Britt uncovers a disturbing pattern in which a number of physically similar young boys have vanished. The other case begins spectacularly when a lo-

Buchanan, Edna—*Continued*
cal Hispanic television commentator is killed via car bomb." Booklist

The author "deftly captures the matter-of-fact quality of the police beat and its daily encounters with a world even stranger than fiction." N Y Times Book Rev

Cold case squad; a novel; Edna Buchanan. Simon & Schuster 2004 261p $22.95
ISBN 0-7432-5053-2 LC 2004-44992

This mystery focuses on "the Miami Police Department's Cold Case Squad, led by Sgt. Craig Burch. . . . Burch is backed by detectives Sam Stone and Pete Nazario and takes orders from Lt. K.C. Riley, who is grieving the death of ex-lover, Kendall McDonald. In fact, all of the squad members have problems both on and off the force, subplots that play out alongside the several murders that command most of the attention. Detective Stone is on the trail of a serial killer who specializes in old ladies, laying the bodies out in meticulously composed death scenes. Stone suspects the killer is an orthodox Jew, clued in by his feisty grandma, who used to work for a Jewish family. The chief case is 12 years old and involves Charles Terrell, who everyone thought was accidentally blown up while working on his car." Publ Wkly

Contents under pressure. Hyperion 1992 277p o.p.
ISBN 1-56282-932-7 LC 92-15949

"Blonde, green-eyed and game, Cuban American Britt Montero is, at 31, a respected crime reporter for a Miami daily. Nevertheless, she is stonewalled in her investigation of the death of former pro football player D. Wayne Hudson, a beloved figure in the city's black community who died in a car crash while being chased by officers on the midnight shift. . . . After Britt breaks her story about excessive police violence, the ensuing trial and verdict lead to a breathtaking explosion of arson and sniper fire, from which Britt barely escapes with her life." Publ Wkly

Garden of evil; a Britt Montero mystery. Avon Bks. 1999 319p o.p.
ISBN 0-380-97654-4 LC 99-36111

Miami crime reporter Britt Montero's "assignment is about a mysterious woman who kills a sheriff in north Florida and then weaves a southerly track downstate toward Miami, leaving a trail of corpses in her wake. Each is found with his pants down—his genitals mutilated, shot with Black Talon bullets, and graced with traces of lipstick. She becomes the 'Kiss-Me Killer.' Britt's coverage of the murders attracts the attention of the killer, who contacts Britt and draws her into a dangerous cat-and-mouse game that could cost Britt her life." Libr J

"Taut, terrifying, and suspenseful, Buchanan's hard-hitting novel takes this solid series to a new level." Booklist

The Ice Maiden. Morrow 2002 289p o.p.
ISBN 0-380-97332-4 LC 2002-24226

"This time out, Montero shows up at a jewelry store break-in. A would-be burglar, electrocuted by the much-victimized jeweler's trip wires, is stuck in the ceiling. The burglar's corpse is of interest to Miami PD's Cold Case Squad, as a possible suspect in a 14-year-old crime, in which a gang kidnapped two teens out on their first date, then tortured and left them for dead. One of the victims survived and, as Montero discovers, lives a reclusive life as an ice sculptor. Montero convinces the Ice Maiden to face her past and try to identify the long-ago killers. Prime Buchanan." Booklist

Margin of error. Doubleday 1997 290p o.p.
LC 96-49509

"Years of covering murders in Miami didn't prepare reporter Britt Montero for the lingering depression she felt after being forced to kill someone herself. Her editor decides the perfect antidote would be some 'light' duty—showing movie star Lance Westfell, in town for a film, what being an investigative reporter is all about. The 'light' duty merits hazard pay." Booklist

Buchanan's "reporter's eye doesn't miss much in Miami. She knows its poshest precincts, its poorest projects and the troubles lurking in both. She also knows how to reveal the vulnerable heart beating within Britt's tough exterior." Publ Wkly

Miami, it's murder. Hyperion 1994 244p o.p.
LC 93-4368

Miami police reporter Britt Montero "investigates a series of increasingly violent rapes and a selection of recent Miami murders, all involving old unsolved police cases. The rapist, who likes to powder his victims, writes to Britt and claims voodoo powers; and a retired, terminally ill cop pal of hers determines to bring to justice a powerful politician whom he is sure is guilty of the murder of a child many years before." Publ Wkly

"Buchanan knows crime inside and out: her dialogue is right, her plotting is clever, and her ambience captures every shade of sleaze in Miami's neon rainbow." Booklist

Pulse; a novel. Avon Bks. 1998 321p o.p.
ISBN 0-380-97331-6 LC 97-32292

"Wealthy Miami businessman Frank Douglas awakens from his heart transplant operation with an inexplicable taste for Tabasco, a phantom haunting his dreams, and an irresistible urge to contact his heart donor's family. Frank seeks out the widow and, immediately drawn to her, is instantly involved in the tangled mess of her life. Within days, Frank professes love for the widow, witnesses two murders, becomes convinced that the heart donor is not dead, and generally behaves so strangely that his wife prepares to have him committed. But led by an inner mystical voice, Frank eludes his wife and travels incognito across the county seeking the truth." Libr J

"This may not be the most surprising crime story in Buchanan's repertoire but, as a character study built around a mystery of psychological and physical clues, it deftly delivers on suspense and emotion." Publ Wkly

Suitable for framing. Hyperion 1995 243p o.p.
ISBN 0-7868-6047-2 LC 94-33133

Miami News crime reporter Britt Montero "confronts a mystery that cuts close to the bone: why she's suddenly losing her journalistic edge. Chance puts her on the spot to see a young woman killed and her toddler injured in the most horrible of a recent string of carjackings. Since then, however, the scoops have been gravitating toward young Trish Tierney, Britt's protégé and the *News's* newest reporter. Britt doggedly works her contacts in the Miami Police, especially Det. Bill Rakestraw, who is investigating the juvenile ring apparently respon-

Buchanan, Edna—*Continued*

sible for the car thefts." Publ Wkly

"Busy, busy plot but Buchanan's streamlined prose and genuine affection for Miami's weirdness make it a quick and entertaining read." Booklist

You only die twice; a Britt Montero mystery. Morrow 2001 292p $24

ISBN 0-380-97655-2 LC 00-49543

"When the body of a beautiful woman is found floating offshore, seaweed in her hair, veteran *Miami News* police-beat reporter Britt Montero gets the call. . . . Britt senses a good story in the making, and when the body remains unclaimed and foul play is established, she is sure of it. A fingerprint check identifies the well-cared-for mermaid as Kaithlin Jordan of the prominent department store family. One problem: she's been dead for 10 years, and her husband is scheduled to be executed for her murder." Publ Wkly

"A fascinating amalgam of red herrings, misdirection, and guilt by personality. . . . An intelligent, thoroughly entertaining crime novel." Booklist

Buchheim, Lothar-Günther, 1918-

The boat; translated from the German by Denver Lindley and Helen Lindley. Hyperion 1975 463p o.p.

Original German edition, 1973; first English translation published 1974 in the United Kingdom with title: U-boat

This novel focuses on the experiences of the crew of a German submarine patrolling the Atlantic during the fall and winter of 1941 in search of British convoys

"A memorable story of the power of the sea and of the horror of submarine warfare. . . . It is inevitable that his description of the oceans will be compared to Conrad's for example, but Buchheim's prose (with the superb English translation) stands on its own merit for sheer descriptive power. Toward the end there is a disingenuous and unnecessary espionage plot that is not fully developed and leads nowhere. . . . The excitement of the hunt, the chase and the ocean is more than enough to satisfy the most cynical armchair adventurer, and lifts this novel out of the trough of commonplace war stories." New Repub

Buck, Pearl S. (Pearl Sydenstricker), 1892-1973

Dragon seed. Day 1942 378p o.p.

Set in 20th century China, this novel shows the effects of the Japanese war on a family of sturdy, upright farmers, living not far from Nanking. Ling Tan, his wife, and their sons and daughters, and their families, at first cannot understand this type of war, and are unprepared to grasp its implications. But with the fall of Nanking, and the looting of the countryside, understanding and horror come. Ling Tan's sons take to guerilla warfare, and the family makes valiant attempts to continue some kind of decent life in the midst of chaos

East and West; stories. Day 1975 202p o.p.

Contents: Until tomorrow; Fool's sacrifice; The golden bowl; India, India; To whom a child is born; Dream child

East wind: west wind. Crowell 1930 277p o.p.

"A John Day book"

The theme of this novel is the conflict between Chinese traditions and Western ways. "The daughter of a noble family, trained for wifehood in the old customs and traditions and betrothed since childhood, is married to a Chinese of the new era who has received his medical training in America. It is only by adopting the Western habits which her husband esteems, that the little bride finds love and happiness. Her brother's love for an American girl is another phase of the conflict." Cleveland Public Libr

The good earth; introduced and edited by Peter Conn. Washington Square Press 1994 xxx, 379p il pa $14

ISBN 0-671-51012-6 LC 2002-522681

First published 1931 by Day

This novel set in pre-revolutionary China "describes the rise of Wang Lung, a Chinese peasant, from poverty to the position of a rich landowner, helped by his patient wife, O-lan. Their vigor, fortitude, persistence, and enduring love of the soil are emphasized throughout. Generally regarded as Pearl Buck's masterpiece, the book won universal acclaim for its sympathetically authentic picture of Chinese life." Reader's Ency. 4th edition

A house divided. Reynal 1935 353p o.p.

"A John Day book"

This concludes the trilogy which opened with The good earth and continued with Sons. China in revolution is its scene, the dilemma of the modern, educated young men and women its theme. Yuan, son of Wang the Tiger, grandson of Wang Lung spends some years in America as a student. He returns to find his country greatly changed and torn by the conflict between Eastern and Western forces, with the latter in ascendancy. Yuan marries a girl of his own race and class and resolves to forward the cause of the New China by teaching students modern methods of agriculture

Imperial woman; a novel. Day 1956 376p o.p.

A biographical novel about Tzu-hsi, last Empress of China, known as Old Buddha. Her life is pictured from the day she received the imperial summons to appear before the Emperor, to her death in 1908

"The accuracy or lack of accuracy will probably be of no particular concern to the readers of 'Imperial Woman.' . . . The details of the secluded life in the Forbidden City, the political jugglings of the court, and the increasing pressure from the Western powers as the Manchu Dynasty breaks up—these contribute to the novel's movement." N Y Times Book Rev

Pavilion of women. Day 1946 316p o.p.

On her fortieth birthday Madame Wu, a beautiful upper-class Chinese woman, voluntarily retires from married life. It is her plan to select a concubine for her husband and live a freer life as chief arbitrator of the house of Wu. The difficulties which ensue change the lives within this "pavilion of women"

"It is a searching, adult study of women written with high seriousness and sympathy, which should find a multitude of women readers. Mrs. Buck's grave unaccented prose is well suited to the delicate matters at hand." NY Times Book Rev

Sons. Day 1932 467p o.p.

This second volume of a trilogy, which began with The good earth, tells the story of Wang Lung's three sons who after the death of their father "are in great haste to divide the many fields he had spent his lifetime

Buck, Pearl S. (Pearl Sydenstricker), 1892-1973—*Continued*

accumulating. It is with the third son, fierce, haughty and hungry-eyed, and the use he makes of his patrimony that the story is mainly concerned. His rise and fall as a petty warlord, and his molding of his son to succeed him, only to have him revert to the land of his grandfather, make interesting reading though less gripping than the earlier novel." N Y Libr

Followed by A house divided

Buckley, Christopher Taylor, 1952-

Little green men. Random House 1999 300p $24.95

ISBN 0-679-45293-1 LC 98-36418

This novel's protagonist is John Banion, a Washington pundit, whose "Sunday-morning show [is] a D.C. must-see. . . . [He] is abducted by *things*, subjected to unpleasant procedures, and then abandoned on a golf course. . . . A second abduction convinces Banion that the alien threat is real. He has to become the 'Paul Revere of the Milky Way' and warn the world. The problem is that his world, the Washington world, doesn't want to know." Natl Rev

"Banion is endearing in his imperious, Princetonian way, and Buckley's satire is similarly poised—always sharp but never sour." New Yorker

No way to treat a First Lady; a novel. Random House 2002 288p o.p.

ISBN 0-375-50734-5 LC 2002-69926

"When philandering President Ken MacMann is found dead, his bossy wife, Beth, irreverently dubbed Lady Bethmac by the press, is charged with his murder. To represent her, Beth hires her law school sweetheart Boyce 'Shameless' Baylor, known for getting even the most deplorable defendents acquitted." Booklist

"This book is more plot driven than Buckley's earlier satires, making it more coherent and effective over the long haul. The political humor is first-rate as usual, as Buckley has plenty of fun with the slimy, silly mess that is Beltway politics." Publ Wkly

Buckley, Fiona

To shield the Queen; a mystery at Queen Elizabeth I's court, introducing Ursula Blanchard. Scribner 1997 278p o.p.

ISBN 0-684-83841-9 LC 97-15684

First published in the United Kingdom with title: The Robsart mystery

"In order to quell widespread rumors about their supposed murderous intentions, Elizabeth I and Sir Robert Dudley dispatch one of her ladies-in-waiting, young widowed mother Ursula Blanchard, to help tend Lord Dudley's sickly wife, Amy. Despite Ursula's friendly attentions, Amy dies violently. Ursula's subsequent search for the murderer of a trusted retainer uncovers evidence of Catholic scheming and tests her love for a dashing Frenchman. Buckley's tantalizing re-creation of Elizabethan life and manners is told with intelligence and gentle wit." Libr J

Buckley, William F. (William Frank), 1925-

Elvis in the morning. Harcourt 2001 328p il $25

ISBN 0-15-100643-1 LC 00-54484

In 1959 Orson Killere, whose mother works for the U.S. Army in Wiesbaden, "decides to 'liberate' two dozen Elvis records from the PX for German teens who can't afford them. His crime is reported in *Stars and Stripes*, and PFC Presley, stationed nearby, holds a private concert at Orson's home. Orson and Priscilla are soon regular visitors to Presley's off-base quarters. She ultimately moves to Memphis and, years later, becomes Mrs. Presley; Orson is expelled from the University of Michigan as a premature college radical, wanders the country, stumbles into the computer business, and throughout the 1960s and 1970s, plays a small but important role in the King's often troubled life." Booklist

"This is a low-key pleasure of a read, a nostalgic tale that eschews mush and a heartfelt tribute to the tragic figure who touched so many lives." Publ Wkly

Getting it right; a novel; by William F. Buckley Jr. Regnery Pub. 2002 311p $24.95

ISBN 0-89526-138-3 LC 2002-151632

"Woodroe (Woody) Raynor witnesses (and is shot in) the 1956 Hungarian Revolution while doing Mormon missionary work across the border in Austria. He returns to attend Princeton and becomes a Birch Society operative on graduation. At the founding meeting of the Young Americans for Freedom. . .Woody meets Leonora Goldstein, an acolyte in 'the Collective' surrounding Ayn Rand." Booklist

"Gussying up the epic struggle with a hearts-and-flowers romance between a Bircher and an Objectivist, Buckley has a lot of fun with the period. And if any reader doubts the truth of the story, there are footnotes aplenty." Libr J

Last call for Blackford Oakes; [by] William F. Buckley, Jr. Harcourt 2005 353p $25

ISBN 0-15-101085-4 LC 2004-25580

"Master spy Blackford Oakes hies to Russia to thwart yet another assassination plot against Soviet Communist Party chief Mikhail Gorbachev. . . . Back in the U.S.S.R., he's introduced to attractive, 40-year-old Moscow urologist Ursina Chadinov by his former partner Gus Windels, a CIA agent–cum–public affairs officer with the United States diplomatic legation. Immediately smitten by Ursina, Oakes asks her to marry him, but their romance takes a backseat once Oakes encounters Andrei Fyodorovich Martins, akahis old nemesis, spy and defector Kim Philby. The plot to assassinate Gorbachev soon resolves itself, shifting the suspense to the battle between the two master spies. The struggle quickly goes awry for Oakes, who must then make tough, life-altering decisions. As always, Buckley imparts erudite sidebars about American history, literature and his famous acquaintances as he spins a lively, entertaining tale." Publ Wkly

Mongoose, R.I.P; a Blackford Oakes novel; {by} William F. Buckley, Jr. Random House 1988 322p o.p.

LC 87-28344

This Blackford Oakes novel is a "retelling of the Kennedy assassination, which links Oswald to the Castro regime. Learning that the Soviets have secretly left behind a single missile after the U.S. challenge, Castro masterminds a scenario that will see Kennedy dead whether by bullet or ballistic missile." Libr J

"The best of the Blacky books, this is an entertainment

Buckley, William F. (William Frank), 1925-—
Continued
of the Graham Greene order that truly entertains, excites, and edifies. . . . The story builds with considerable suspense up to Blackford's horrendous dilemma on the day of JFK's assassination." Natl Rev

Nuremberg; the reckoning; {by} William F. Buckley, Jr. Harcourt 2002 366p o.p.
ISBN 0-15-100679-2 LC 2002-465
"Sebastian Reinhard, a German-born American, becomes an interpreter at the War Crimes Tribunal and an interrogator of one of the Nazi *Brigadeführers*. In this latter capacity, he learns disturbing truths about his national origin and about his father, an MIT-educated civil engineer who superintended the construction of an extermination camp. Buckley achieves a good working compromise between actual events and people (U.S. Chief Prosecutor Robert Jackson, defendants Hermann Göring, Joachim von Ribbentrop, Albert Speer, etc.) and the many fictional characters who weave in and out of his narrative." Libr J

The Redhunter; a novel based on the life and times of Senator Joe McCarthy; by William F. Buckley, Jr. Little, Brown 1999 421p $25
ISBN 0-316-11589-4 LC 98-31255
This is a novel about Senator Joseph McCarthy and the anticommunist movement. It is told from the viewpoint of Harry Bontecou, "who served in World War II, returned to an Ivy League college, . . . took a job as Joe McCarthy's administrative assistant in 1950, then reluctantly broke with him once it became all too clear that a deep-seated streak of irresponsibility was causing McCarthy to sink his own boats." Natl Rev
"The story is a powerful recreation of one of the most dramatic periods in contemporary political history. This new novel will attract younger readers for whom McCarthyism is but a Cold War bogeyman as well as those who have long enjoyed Buckley in whatever medium he is performing." Libr J

Spytime; the undoing of James Jesus Angleton: a novel; by William F. Buckley, Jr. Harcourt 2000 305p o.p.
ISBN 0-15-100513-3 LC 99-54977
This is a "fictionalized account of the life of James Jesus Angleton, the Yale graduate recruited by the U.S. government and sent to Italy as a spy during World II. After the war, Angleton was appointed chief of counterintelligence, responsible for—among other things—ferreting out spies in the U.S. government. Later, his relentless (some said obsessive) search for a double agent in the CIA almost destroyed his own life." Booklist
"Throughout the book, the intellectual appeal of espionage separates this from the usual cloak-and-dagger story." Libr J

Buffa, Dudley W., 1940-

The defense; {by} D.W. Buffa. Holt & Co. 1997 309p o.p.
ISBN 0-8050-5307-7 LC 97-12861
"A John Macrae book"
"Joseph Antonelli, the hero of this . . . legal thriller, is the most successful criminal defense attorney in Portland. When his mentor asks him to take a pro-bono case, Antonelli can't refuse, assuming the defense of Johnny Morel, who has been accused of raping his young stepdaughter. Though Antonelli thinks Morel is guilty, all he cares about is winning his case. When he gets Morel off, Antonelli sets in motion a chain of events that will change his life forever." Libr J
"In fine, flowing prose, 'The Defense' speaks bluntly of unspeakable crimes while presenting gripping courtroom briefs, stunning legal reversals and, yes, showy theatrics too. But in a genre loaded with hooey, its points of ethics land with the most devastating impact." N Y Times Book Rev

The judgment; [by] D. W. Buffa. Warner Bks. 2001 418p $24.95
ISBN 0-446-52737-8 LC 00-60013
A legal thriller set in Portland, Oregon featuring "attorney Joseph Antonelli. First, an old nemesis of Antonelli's, a judge who once made his life a living hell, is murdered. A suspect is quickly apprehended and makes a full confession. Several months later, another judge is murdered in the same fashion, and Antonelli agrees to represent the man accused of the crime. The police seem certain that it is nothing more than a copycat killing, but as Antonelli delves into the case, he begins to think that something more sinister is afoot. . . . [This novel] features well-drawn characters, clean writing, and a complex story line." Libr J

The prosecution; a legal thriller; {by} D.W. Buffa. Holt & Co. 1999 274p o.p.
ISBN 0-8050-6107-X LC 99-13417
"A John Macrae book"
Portland, Oregon defense attorney Joseph Antonelli is selected "to act as special prosecutor investigating the murder of Nancy Goodwin, wife of Chief Deputy D.A. Marshall Goodwin. A grungy sociopath named Travis Quentin admits to having slashed Nancy's throat, but claims he was hired by Goodwin and his new wife, the 'shapely and infinitely desirable' Assistant D.A. Kristin Maxfield. All Antonelli has to work with is the problematic Quentin's uncorroborated testimony." Publ Wkly
Buffa "provides readers with a thorough look at the legal system from an insider's viewpoint and relates Antonelli's struggles with dynamic writing and well-rounded characterization." Libr J

Buffett, Jimmy, 1946-

A salty piece of land; Jimmy Buffett. 1st ed. Little, Brown and Co 2004 462p $27.95
ISBN 0-316-90845-2 LC 2004-16508
"Waking from a ganja buzz on the beach in Tulum, [Cowboy Tully Mars] can't believe his eyes when a 142-foot schooner emerges out of the ocean mist. At its helm is Cleopatra Highbourne, the eccentric 102-year-old sea captain who will take him to a lighthouse on a salty piece of land that will change his life forever." Publisher's note
"Perhaps it is because Buffett has long been a writer of lyrics that his prose style now seems to flow in a fresh, fanciful, finely imagined fashion. . . . What makes the incredible so credible to the reader, what makes the old lighthouse shine again, is the spiritual savvy Buffett has gleaned from the beach of life as he's wandered in the raw poetry of time." N Y Times Book Rev

Bujold, Lois McMaster

Barrayar. Baen Books 1991 389p o.p.
ISBN 0-671-72083-X

"A Baen Books original"

"Cordelia Naismith and Aral Vorkosigan were once enemies in an interestellar war. Now a fragile peace has been established, and they're a married couple expecting their first child. Cordelia, a liberated woman, is ill at ease among the more conservative, less civilized people of Barrayar and, when her husband is named regent, she realizes that she, Aral, and their unborn baby are in great danger. Traditional space opera at its very best with a mild feminist tone and twist." Anatomy of Wonder 5

Cetaganda; a Vorkosigan adventure. Baen Pub. Enterprises 1996 302p o.p.
ISBN 0-671-87701-1 LC 95-33243

"When an unexplained death mars the funeral ceremonies for the Dowager Empress of the Cetagandan Empire, Barrayaran agent Miles Vorkosigan finds himself unwillingly drawn into a dangerous game of internal politics and affairs of the heart." Libr J

"Set in a vividly realized world where Machiavellian intrigues are played out behind a facade of aristocratic discretion, this novel . . . blends high adventure with wry commentary on the seemingly unbridgeable gulf between human ideals and political realities." Publ Wkly

Falling free; Lois McMaster Bujold. Baen Books 1988 307p o.p.
ISBN 0-671-65398-9 LC 96-117503

"Leo Graf, a welding engineer hired to train new workers on a space station, is astonished to discover that his new pupils are 'quaddies,' genetically engineeered living tools with extra arms where normal people have legs. Designed by the GalacTech corporation to be perfect zero-gravity employees, the quaddies have unfortunately failed to turn a profit for their owner/employers. Soon after Graf's arrival, the corporation decides to cut its losses and return the quaddies to Earth, where they will be presumably be dumped in nursing homes on a small pension. The quaddies, however, have other ideas, and convince Graf to join them in revolt. . . . This is an example of old-fashioned, Campbell-style hard SF at its best, but with a fascinating feminist twist." Anatomy of Wonder 5

The hallowed hunt; a novel. Eos 2005 470p $24.95
ISBN 0-06-057462-3 LC 2004-61936

Sequel to The paladin of souls

"Lord Ingrey kin Wolfcliff, sent by the kingdom's sealmaster to fetch orphaned Lady Ijada to trial, soon learns they both unwillingly bear animal spirits received in forbidden power rites stretching centuries back into the primeval Weald. With the aged Hallow King now dying, Ingrey and Ijada journey toward the king's hall at Easthome, falling into a love that appears doomed, while Ingrey's powerful fey cousin, Lord Wencel, spins a cunning web of bloodthirsty ambition that binds them to him in an unholy trinity. . . . Bujold's ability to sustain a breathless pace of action while preserving a heady sense of verisimilitude in a world of malignant wonders makes this big novel occasionally brilliant—and not a word too long." Publ Wkly

Mirror dance; a Vorkosigan adventure. Baen Pub. Enterprises 1994 392p o.p.
LC 93-39663

This science fiction adventure "features the deformed and undersized heir to the strongman of Barrayar, Miles Vorkosigan, who doubles as Admiral Naismith, leader of the Dendarii Mercenaries—and is secretly on the payroll of Barrayaran Imperial Intelligence. The tale begins with Miles' cloned sibling Mark masquerading as Miles in order to take a Dendarii ship to that free enterprise plague spot, Jackson's Whole, on an unauthorized mission to clean out the clone creches where he was raised. The mission goes awry, Miles comes to Mark's rescue, the rescue goes even more wrong. . . . The remaining pages complete as good a story as ever was offered as science fiction." Booklist

The paladin of souls. Eos 2003 456p $24.95
ISBN 0-380-97902-0 LC 2003-40884

Sequel to The curse of Chalion

"Three years free of the madness that kept her imprisoned in her family's castle, Ista is finally released from her last remaining duties by the death of her mother. She undertakes a pilgrimage, but doesn't get far before she is overtaken by trouble, sorrow, need, and a host of other adversities. Chalion is in trouble again, thanks to the plots, counterplots, machinations, and follies of men and of gods. . . . What really keeps one turning the pages is the fascinating cast of characters—not that the plot is anything to sneeze at." Booklist

Bulgakov, Mikhail Afanas´evich, 1891-1940

The master and Margarita; translated from the Russian by Michael Glenny. Knopf 1992 c1967 xxvii, 446p $19
ISBN 0-679-41046-5 LC 91-53220

"Everyman's library"

Written in the 1930s. Original Russian edition published 1966-67 in censored form. This translation, first published 1967 by Harper, is based on the unexpurgated version that was subsequently published 1973 in the Soviet Union

This novel "juxtaposes two planes of action—one set in Moscow in the 1930s and the other in Jerusalem at the time of Christ. The three central characters of the contemporary plot are the Devil, disguised as one Professor Woland; the 'Master,' a repressed novelist; and Margarita, who, though married to a bureaucrat, loves the Master. The Master has burned his manuscript and gone willingly into a psychiatric ward when critics attacked his work—a portrayal of the story of Jesus. Margarita sells her soul to the Devil in order to obtain the Master's release from the psychiatric ward. A parallel plot presents the action of the Master's destroyed novel, the condemnation of Yeshua (Jesus) in Jerusalem." Merriam-Webster's Ency of Lit

Bulwer-Lytton, Edward *See* Lytton, Edward Bulwer Lytton, Baron, 1803-1873

Bunn, T. Davis, 1952-

The great divide. Doubleday 2000 362p $19.95
ISBN 0-385-49615-X LC 99-86341

Bunn, T. Davis, 1952—*Continued*

"Devastated by a personal tragedy, Marcus Glenwood resigns from a prestigious law firm and returns to his childhood home of Rocky Mount, NC. There he confronts his most challenging case yet: Alma and Austin Hall come to him because their daughter, Gloria, has disappeared in China while investigating the labor practices of a factory owned by New Horizons, the world's largest maker of athletic shoes and equipment." Libr J

"The theme of underdog vs. the system is seductive and there are enough plot twists to keep even the most unforgiving of critics turning pages." Publ Wkly

Bunyan, John, 1628-1688

The pilgrim's progress; edited with an introduction and notes by W.R. Owens. Oxford University Press 2003 lvi, 333p il pa $8.95

ISBN 0-19-280361-1 LC 2003-283122

First published 1678

"The 'immortal allegory,' next to the Bible the most widely known book in religious literature. It was written in Bedford jail, where Bunyan was for twelve years a prisoner for his convictions. It describes the troubled journey of Christian and his companions through this life to a triumphal entrance into the Celestial city. Bunyan 'wrote with virgin purity utterly free from mannerisms and affectations; and without knowing himself for a writer of fine English, produced it.'" Pratt Alcove

Burdett, John

Bangkok 8. Knopf 2003 317p $24

ISBN 1-400-04044-2 LC 2002-40658

"The narrator, a Buddhist cop named Sonchai Jitplecheep, finds himself plunged into a dangerous investigation of the deaths of his partner Pichai Apiradee and U. S. Embassy Sgt. William Bradley. Sonchai is an unusual character on several levels, from the mysteries of his violent past to his conversations with the ghost of Pichai. His ambiguous feelings toward Kimberley Jones, an American FBI agent brought in to work the case, reflect his upbringing as the child of a Thai mother and an unknown American father. . . .The mix of detective work, Bangkok street life, the Thai sex trade and drug smuggling forms a powerful mélange of images and insight." Publ Wkly

Bangkok Tattoo. Knopf 2005 301p $24

ISBN 1-400-04045-0 LC 2005-5593

A mystery featuring Rayal Thai police detective Sonchai Jitpleecheep. "A devout Buddhist, Sonchai makes complex karmic calculations to justify his roles as law-bending cop and part-time papasan at his mother's gogo bar. When the bar's biggest moneymaker is suspected of killing her john, who turns out to be C.I.A., Sonchai initiates a coverup that eventually involves Muslim separatists in southern Thailand and American operatives eager to exploit post-9/11 paranoia for career advancement. The plot showcases Burdett's sly riffs on Third World stereotypes, Buddhism, and the gustatory pleasures of fried grasshoppers. It's a giddy, occasionally over-the-top performance, but mesmerizing: a comic tour of the underbelly of Bangkok in pursuit of both a murderer and the sublime." New Yorker

Burdick, Eugene

Fail-safe; by Eugene Burdick & Harvey Wheeler. McGraw-Hill 1962 286p o.p.

"With mounting tension this gripping thriller tells of a possible nuclear holocaust. An American attack squadron is accidentally and irretrievably launched to obliterate Moscow. The frantic U.S. president and the Russian premier begin a dramatic hotline race against time to halt the bombers' flight and prevent disaster. The crisis is seen through the eyes of several characters, and their differing perceptions provide an effective story-telling technique." Shapiro. Fic for Youth. 3d edition

(jt. auth) Lederer, W. J. The ugly American

Burford, Eleanor, 1906-1993

For works written by this author under other names see Carr, Philippa, 1906-1993; Holt, Victoria, 1906-1993; Plaidy, Jean, 1906-1993

Burgess, Anthony, 1917-1993

A clockwork orange. Norton 1963 c1962 184p o.p.

First published 1962 in the United Kingdom

"A compelling and often comic vision of the way violence comes to dominate the mind. The novel is set in a future London and is told in curious but readable Russified argot by a juvenile deliquent whose brainwashing by the authorities has destroyed not only his murderous aggression but also his deeper-seated sense of humanity as typified by his compulsive love for the music of Beethoven. It is an ironic novel in the tradition of Zamiatin's and Orwell's anti-Utopias." Sci Fic Ency

A dead man in Deptford. Carroll & Graf Pubs. 1995 272p o.p.

ISBN 0-7867-0192-7 LC 95-10410

In this posthumous novel, Burgess presents a fictional "re-creation of the life of . . . Elizabethan playwright and poet Christopher Marlowe." Booklist

This is "not just a very good novel; it may well be Burgess' masterpiece. His grasp of the age and its angsts is profound, and his portrait of Marlowe sympathetic, critical and brilliantly imagined all at once. The rich, deft language is a joy. Burgess uses Marlowe's own poetry and dramatic blank verse as subtext. He mirrors the poet's own risky life—espionage, homosexuality, London tavern lowlife, daring for power and inner freedom by means of necromancy and philosophy—with those of his fictional creations, notably Tamburlaine and Faustus." New Statesman Soc

Earthly powers. Simon & Schuster 1980 607p o.p.

LC 80-20978

The "narrator is an octogenarian writer whose novels, plays and stories, though they never aspired to art, have made him rich and world renowned. Kenneth Toomey's homosexuality imposed upon him early in life a triple exile: from his parents, who thought his proclivity willful; from England, which thought it a crime; and from the Roman Catholic Church, whose priests decreed it a sin. As the story begins, Toomey is asked to write an account of a miracle he once witnessed—a miracle performed by a priest who later became Pope and is now

Burgess, Anthony, 1917-1993—*Continued*
to be promoted to saint. Because Carlo Campanati was Toomey's relative by marriage and longtime friend, the request prompts Toomey to re-examine his life." Newsweek

This novel "is full of . . . parodic brilliancies as it is full of caricatured or modified people and events. But if it plays with the processes of fiction, with the transubstantiation of the actual into the preferred, Burgess does the actual itself with all his usual vividness. . . . [This] is a big, grippingly readable, extraordinarily rich and moving fiction." Times Lit Suppl

The pianoplayers. Arbor House 1986 208p o.p.
LC 86-20559

"In the first half of this fictional memoir Ellen Henshaw recalls her father, a piano player in silent movie houses. With the advent of the talkies the old man's only hope financially was to stage a 30-day nonstop piano marathon—a fatal mistake. In the second half Ellen describes her career as a teenage prostitute and then her opening a 'school of love' where wealthy gentlemen learn to play a woman's body like a musical instrument." Libr J

"First-rate satiric humor from a literary virtuoso." Booklist

Burgess, Trevor, 1920-1995

For works written by this author under other names see Hall, Adam, 1920-1995

Burke, James Lee, 1936-

Bitterroot. Simon & Schuster 2001 334p o.p.
ISBN 0-7432-0483-2 LC 00-66175

Defense attorney and former Texas Ranger Billy Bob Holland "travels to Montana's Bitterroot Valley to help an old friend, Doc Voss, who is having trouble with mining companies and a local right-wing militia group. Holland must also contend with a psychotic ex-convict rodeo clown who blames him for past tragedies." Libr J

"The region is infested with brutish bikers, psychotic ex-cons, fanatical militia types and best-selling novelists. Burke pours venomous contempt on the lot of them, and when he lights his literary match, the blaze is fierce and cleansing." N Y Times Book Rev

Black cherry blues. Little, Brown 1989 290p o.p.
LC 89-7977

"A former homicide cop is trying to run his fishing business, care for six-year-old orphan Alafair, and come to terms with the violent death of his wife, Annie. A chance encounter with an old friend haunted by a troubling secret sets off a chain of events that leaves Dave framed for murder. Desperate to prove his innocence and protect Alafair, Robicheaux is forced to conduct his own investigation." Libr J

"A stunning novel that takes detective fiction into new imaginative realms. . . . All the main characters in this darkly beautiful, lyric saga carry heavy emotional baggage, and Robicheaux's sleuthing is a simultaneous exorcism of demons of grief, loss, fear, rage, vengeance." Publ Wkly

Burning angel; a novel. Hyperion 1995 340p o.p.
LC 94-41921

In this "adventure, moody Louisiana deputy Dave Robicheaux confronts plaited evils: ages-old injustices based on race and class; the legacies suffered by modern-day mercenaries for their sins in Vietnam and central America; and the New Orleans mob. . . . Burke's lush, humid prose and the controlled, otherworldly aspects of this plot deftly capture the inhumanity of the bad guys and the more common frailties of ordinary folk." Publ Wkly

Cadillac jukebox. Hyperion 1996 297p o.p.
ISBN 0-7868-6175-4 LC 95-50045

This Dave Robicheaux mystery "starts with the escape from prison of a white-trash dirt farmer convicted of killing a black civil-rights activist. The ensuing reverberations affect everything from Louisiana gubernatorial politics to Robicheaux's marriage, but at the heart of the conflict is the detective's battle with his own personal demons: Will this case offer yet another opportunity to lose control, to jeopardize loved ones in an effort to take a stand against onrushing modernity?" Booklist

"For all the dirt it rolls around in, Mr. Burke's muscular prose is full of grace." N Y Times Book Rev

Cimarron rose. Hyperion 1997 288p o.p.
ISBN 0-7868-6258-0 LC 96-30745

"Texas Ranger-turned-lawyer Billy Bob Holland must defend his illegitimate son, Lucas Smothers, on a murder rap. Billy Bob knows that backwater Deaf Smith, Texas, will eat Lucas for lunch—especially the East Enders, the town's pocket of elite kids. He mounts his defense with sporadic help from sexy cop/possible federal agent Mary Beth Sweeney." Libr J

"Burke weaves in family history and regional legends and gives voice to a parade of local sadists and psychopaths, some of them in so-called law enforcement. But the story is a simple one about the cruelty of youth—how it's taught, how it's learned and what it does to both teacher and pupil." N Y Times Book Rev

Crusader's cross. Simon & Schuster 2005 325p $25.95
ISBN 0-7432-7719-8 LC 2005-44233

When Dave Robicheaux and "his brother, Jimmie, were teenagers, Jimmie fell hard for a young prostitute who was trying to get out of the business and who vanished soon after. Almost half a century later, a dying man whispers the woman's name to Dave, and soon Jimmie is out searching for her, with Dave unwillingly assisting in the pursuit. At the same time, Dave is tracking down a serial killer, trying to limit his involvement with a wealthy family who seems to have it out for him, and becoming romantically involved with a local nun. Never one to avoid trouble or confrontation, he manages to juggle all these complications in his own ham-handed, well-intentioned way. The story is a little crowded, but Burke's well-drawn characters and evocative writing more than compensate." Libr J

Dixie City jam. Hyperion 1994 367p o.p.
ISBN 0-7868-6019-7 LC 93-36228

In this Dave Robicheaux adventure the "foe is a neo-Nazi sadist who thinks Dave is the key to finding a German U-Boat that has been bouncing around the Gulf of

Burke, James Lee, 1936-—*Continued*
Mexico since World War II. Threats to Dave's wife and child draw Robicheaux into a violent confrontation." Booklist

"The preposterous plot implodes from . . . wretched excess, but in brief scene-by-scene doses, Mr. Burke's manic style has a life of its own. The sheer energy of his language has an uplifting effect on the characters, inspiring them to new heights of self-expression and new depths of brutality." N Y Times Book Rev

Heartwood. Doubleday 1998 341p o.p.
ISBN 0-385-48843-2 LC 98-40419

Country lawyer Billy Bob Holland is featured in this "narrative about the lawlessness that erupts in Deaf Smith, Tex., when Earl Deitrich, a rich, cruel man who thinks he can boss or buy everyone in town, tries to cheat a farmer out of his oil-rich land." N Y Times Book Rev

"Despite a circuitous, often confusing plot, the novel compels for its lush portrayal of exquisite countryside; its beautifully composed, mood-setting scenes that pace the action; and the leisurely introductions that give dimension to the many eccentric characters." Publ Wkly

Heaven's prisoners. Holt & Co. 1988 292p o.p.
LC 87-26878

"Ex-New Orleans cop Dave Robicheaux and his wife, Annie, are fishing in the Gulf one afternoon when a small plane crashes nearby. All of the plane's passengers—Nicaraguan refugees attempting to enter the U.S. illegally—are killed except one, a young girl whom Dave rescues. This chance encounter lands the Robicheaux family in the midst of an immigration squabble and then a vicious drug war." Booklist

"There is a pronounced streak of poetry in Mr. Burke's prose. He has the knack of combining action with reflection; he has pity for the human condition, and even his villains can have some sympathetic and redeeming qualities. Mr. Burke writes in an unhurried manner, but the book never loses tension because he is so wrapped up in his characters and their locale." N Y Times Book Rev

In the electric mist with Confederate dead. Hyperion 1993 344p o.p.
ISBN 1-56282-882-7 LC 92-26615

In this Dave Robicheaux mystery, Burke leads his "Cajun detective into a series of dreamlike encounters with a troop of Confederate soldiers under Gen. John Bell Hood. Soon after the severely mutilated body of a young woman is found in a ditch outside the southern Louisiana town of New Iberia, deputy sheriff Robicheaux busts Elrod Sykes, star of a Hollywood movie being filmed nearby, for drunk driving. Sykes says a skeleton wrapped in chains was unearthed during filming in a marsh where, in 1957, Robicheaux witnessed—but remained silent about—the killing of a chained black man by two white men. As the belatedly guilt-stricken detective tries to identify that victim, another young woman is brutally killed." Publ Wkly

"You can't write about Louisiana without at least nodding toward that supernatural realm hovering out there in the morning mist; somehow it seems right that Robicheaux, his eyes always on the past, would be the one to walk through the curtain." Am Libr

In the moon of red ponies; James Lee Burke. Simon & Schuster 2004 322p $24.95
ISBN 0-7432-4543-1 LC 2004-45430

"Moving to Montana fails to provide Billy Bob Holland with the peaceful, simple life of his dreams. The former Texas Ranger and federal prosecutor turned small-town lawyer is dismayed to learn that Wyatt Dixon, the psycho imprisoned for almost killing Billy Bob's wife, has been freed owing to a legal error. Soon enough, Wyatt arrives in Missoula, trying to make amends with the unbelieving Hollands for his past behavior. Meanwhile, a client of Billy Bob's seems to be getting railroaded by both the police and the government for crimes he didn't commit." Libr J

"While the shotgun spray of Burke's political complaints makes mincemeat of the plot, his passion is so real and raw that it redeems the ragged writing, giving voice to the new anxieties surfacing in genre fiction." NY Times Book Rev

Jolie Blon's Bounce; a novel. Simon & Schuster 2002 352p o.p.
ISBN 0-7432-0484-0

"The mysterious, seemingly indestructible Legion Guidry, once the overseer on a Louisiana plantation, where he raped numerous field hands, has resurfaced near New Iberia and may be linked to the murder of a teenager and a prostitute. Convinced that the drug-addicted blues singer under arrest for the first killing is innocent, Robicheaux goes after Guidry" Booklist

"No question about it, Legion is one of Burke's finest villains-a creature of immense force, fueled by pure malignancy, but not without the shred of humanity that makes a monster memorable." N Y Times Book Rev

Last car to Elysian Fields; a Dave Robicheaux novel. Simon & Schuster 2003 335p $25
ISBN 0-7432-4542-3 LC 2003-54386

"Dave Robicheaux, an Iberia Parish homicide detective with an 'abiding anger' for the corrupters of innocence and the despoilers of beauty, is roped into investigating [legendary R & B guitarist Junior] Crudup's fate by Jimmie Dolan, a priest whose moral crusades cause mobsters to put out a hit on him. Burke's heavies make great showpieces, but Max Coll, a stone killer who repents of his sins and causes all kinds of mayhem trying to do penance, knocks them all off the shelf. In the absence of plagues of locusts, a good hit man can really clean up a dirty town." N Y Times Book Rev

A morning for flamingos. Little, Brown 1990 294p o.p.
LC 89-77777

"Burke's Cajun detective, Dave Robicheaux, is once again battling personal demons—questions of fear and bravery, violence and compassion, pleasure and pain—and as he stalks an escaped killer and infiltrates the world of a Mafia drug lord, he finds reflections of his own torment wherever he looks. What it means to be Cajun is at the heart of Robicheaux's dilemma." Booklist

"Attentive to language and atmosphere, Burke delivers action on churning Gulf waters, in city streets, in deserted fields and within the souls of his memorable characters—and a fully satisfying resolution." Publ Wkly

The neon rain. Holt & Co. 1987 248p o.p.
LC 86-15222

"New Orleans homicide cop Dave Robicheaux has a passion for fishing. While pursuing his hobby on a back country bayou, Robicheaux finds a body. His discovery

Burke, James Lee, 1936-—*Continued*
pulls him into a network of small-time Mafiosi, Nicaraguan drug dealers, federal Treasury agents and retired two-star generals—all involved in a plot to ship arms to the Nicaraguan contras." Libr J

"With its fine local color and driving action, this novel is both chilling and first-rate entertainment." Publ Wkly

Purple cane road; a novel. Doubleday 2000 341p o.p.

ISBN 0-385-48844-0 LC 99-54080

New Iberia Parish Sheriff's investigator Dave Robicheaux "doesn't need much of a mental shove to bring to mind Vachel Carmouche, the state executioner who sent many a prisoner to glory (or damnation) until Letty Labiche chopped him up on the kitchen floor for having abused her and her twin sister, Passion, since childhood. Now Letty is about to die in Angola, and everyone from a 20-year-old prostitute named Little Face Dautrieve to Belmont Pugh, the governor, is begging Robicheaux to get her off. To add to his incentive, two corrupt cops who figure in the case might also have killed his mother." N Y Times Book Rev

"Burke is in top form, his words reading like poetry, his vivid descriptions effortlessly transporting the reader to Southern Louisiana." Libr J

A stained white radiance. Hyperion 1992 305p o.p.

LC 91-34213

"Sadistic villains and interior demons plague Cajun police detective Dave Robicheaux as the murder of a local cop draws him into the painful conflicts of the Sonnier family, with whom he grew up near the bayous." Publ Wkly

In this novel "the 'venal and meretricious' bear the unmistakable stench of the modern world: a drug-dealing mobster out to settle scores, a trio of swastika-sporting members of the Aryan Brotherhood, and, lurking on the respectable fringe, an impeccably coiffed former Klansman intent on snagging a senate seat. . . . Dave tackles them all, of course, and in the end establishes a tenuous calm into which he and his family are able to retreat. But the elegiac tone dominates." Booklist

Sunset limited; a novel. Doubleday 1998 309p o.p.

ISBN 0-385-48842-4 LC 97-23893

A Dave Robicheaux mystery set in New Iberia, Louisiana. "The Cajun detective finds good cause to be spooked when a clumsy thief called Cool Breeze runs afoul of New Orleans mobsters, when two bully boys shoot a rapist and dump his body in the swamp, and when the snooty Terrebonne family opens its plantation home to a company of filmmakers. . . . Whatever the misery at hand, Burke finds meaning for it in the old crimes of race hatred and class tyranny that obsess his brooding hero—and that the people in his books seem compelled to repeat." N Y Times Book Rev

White doves at morning. Simon & Schuster 2003 305p $25

ISBN 0-7432-4471-0 LC 2002-29436

In this historical novel set in New Iberia, Louisiana, "the author centers a constellation of characters around Willie Burke, a reluctant Confederate soldier who finds a skill for killing; Abigail Dowling, the abolitionist he loves; Flower, the slave girl he teaches to read; Ira Jamison, a southern aristocrat and Flower's father, and sundry friends, enemies, gunrunners, madams, and hired thugs." Booklist

"Although at times a bit forced, this moving morality play shows a different dimension of this gifted writer." Publ Wkly

Burke, Jan

Bloodlines; an Irene Kelly novel; Jan Burke. Simon & Schuster 2005 465p $25

ISBN 0-7432-2390-X LC 2004-52528

"In 1958, Conn O'Connor, a brash young reporter for the Las Piernas News-Express, is taken under the wing of veteran Jack Corrigan, who is nearly killed after claiming to have seen a blood-spattered car buried on a farm. In 1978, another brash youngster–Irene Kelly–in turn is taken under O'Connor's wing. By 1998, Irene is the veteran, mentoring two rookies. The sweep of events over such a long time span imparts a certain majesty. There are murders, to be sure, but little mystery, since it's clear early on who is responsible. The deaths serve more as a tragic link across the years and to the heartbroken families who grow old awaiting resolution. Several secondary characters from Burke's earlier novels appear in part three, furthering the sense of events coming full circle. In the end, it's the human relationships that stick in the mind and the heart." Publ Wkly

Bones; an Irene Kelly mystery. Simon & Schuster 1999 378p o.p.

ISBN 0-684-85551-8 LC 99-22207

"In order to escape the death penalty, a serial killer agrees to show authorities the grave of one of his victims in the Sierra Nevada mountains. Leaving a fretful detective husband behind, inveterate reporter Irene Kelly follows the taunting psychopathic killer, his guards, guides, two forensic anthropologists, a photographer, and one amazing canine into the wilderness. A traumatic reversal, however, turns the already risky journey into a lethal game of the hunter and the hunted." Libr J

Flight; a novel of suspense. Simon & Schuster 2001 396p o.p.

ISBN 0-684-85552-6 LC 00-52629

"In Las Piernas, Calif., newspaper reporter Irene Kelly, Burke's series heroine, takes backseat to her husband, prickly, tenacious homicide detective Frank Harriman. Ten years earlier, when brilliant police detective Philip Lefebvre disappeared in the middle of a triple homicide investigation, the cops believed he'd sold out to the suspected killer, drug lord Whitey Dane. When Lefebvre's 10-year-old corpse and sabotaged airplane are found in the San Bernadino Mountains, Frank reopens the case, suspecting that both Lefebvre and Dane were wrongly accused." Publ Wkly

"Burke handles her protagonist's intensifying isolation extremely well, keeping us in pleasurable suspense about his lonely investigation without giving too much away." N Y Times Book Rev

Hocus; an Irene Kelly mystery. Simon & Schuster 1997 348p o.p.

ISBN 0-684-80344-5 LC 96-34414

Burke, Jan—*Continued*

This "mystery places reporter Irene's husband in jeopardy. The homicide detective goes missing after busting a junkie, presumably held hostage by persons unknown." Libr J

"Switching between past and present, Burke writes a well-paced mystery with a heartrending climax, but her strength is the sympathy and depth with which she describes how the trauma of abduction haunts the victims." Publ Wkly

Liar; an Irene Kelly mystery. Simon & Schuster 1998 350p o.p.

ISBN 0-684-80345-3 LC 98-10197

"The murder of her long-lost aunt and the search for her missing cousin leads *Las Piernas News-Express* reporter Irene Kelly back to a decade-old murder that ties in with fresh ones." Libr J

"Kelly is a terrific heroine—feisty, tough, sensible, and smart—and Burke's suspenseful, action-filled plot, acerbic humor, and competent writing make this an entertaining entry in a popular series." Booklist

Remember me, Irene; an Irene Kelly mystery. Simon & Schuster 1996 303p o.p.

ISBN 0-684-80343-7 LC 95-52186

In this episode Southern California news reporter Irene Kelly is "married to her longtime lover, cop Frank Harriman. One day at a bus stop, Irene has a disturbing encounter with a homeless wino, only later discovering that the man, Lucas, was once her close friend, a gifted statistician who managed to get even the math-impaired Irene excited about numbers. Lucas has obviously fallen on hard times, so when Irene gets a cryptic message asking her to meet him, she's curious to learn more. But when she goes to the rendezvous, she discovers his dead body—and opens a Pandora's box of troubles. . . . Exciting action, clever dialogue, solid writing, and a smart, likable heroine produce a well-deserved thumbs-up." Booklist

Burke, Shannon

Safelight. Random House 2004 211p $23.95

ISBN 1-4000-6201-2 LC 2003-69549

"In the free-fire zone of early-1990s Harlem, emergency medical technician Frank Verbeckas drifts from one fresh horror to the next. Numbed by his father's suicide, Frank falls in with a rough-and-tumble ambulance crew that is as willing to deliver bruising blows to a rummy frequent flier as it is to provide topflight care to hopeless trauma cases. When he isn't boosting narcotics or encouraging insurance scams against the city, Frank snaps photos of the dead, the dying, and the down-and-out. His cowboy-surgeon brother, Norman, berates Frank for wasting his life. And he does seem headed for disaster-until he meets Emily Pascal, an HIV-positive competitive fencer. Against his better judgment, Frank eases into a romance. In punchy, cinematic chapters, Burke tenderly illustrates the transformative powers of love between people riding out tough emotional times." Booklist

Burley, W. J. (William John), 1914-

Wycliffe and the quiet virgin. Doubleday 1986 179p o.p.

LC 86-8856

"Published for the Crime Club"

"Scotland Yard Chief Superintendent Wycliffe is off for what seems an idyllic Christmas in Cornwall. Cornwall can be cold and bleak, however, and the house Wycliffe visits is even bleaker and beset by tensions. A young girl who plays the Virgin Mary in the local church play disappears on Christmas Eve. Then her mother is found murdered on Christmas morning. Burley's canny use of atmosphere—especially the way the sullen house overlooking the sea plays on one's nerves—is a strong point of this eerie tale." Booklist

Wycliffe and the redhead. St. Martin's Press 1998 189p o.p.

LC 98-33885

First published 1997 in the United Kingdom

Superintendent Wycliffe's present case "involves the shy and retiring Simon Meagor, an antiquarian bookseller in Falmouth from whom Wycliffe buys books. Some years ago, Simon's testimony convicted George Barker of murder. Now Barker is dead, and his redheaded daughter, Morwenna, has blackmailed Simon into giving her a job as his shop assistant. When Morwenna is found dead in her car in a flooded quarry, Simon is an obvious suspect." Publ Wkly

Burley, William John *See* Burley, W. J. (William John), 1914-

Burnard, Bonnie

A good house. Holt & Co. 2000 309p $25

ISBN 0-8050-6495-8 LC 99-87022

"Told from a variety of points of view, the book traces the upheavals and affirmations of the very ordinary Chambers family of Stonebrook, Ontario, from 1949 to 1997. The year after Sylvia's death, her husband, Bill, an injured WWII vet, remarries. His new wife, the unflappable Margaret, who used to work with him at the town hardware store, helps him raise his three children." Publ Wkly

"Though the usually subtle architecture of 'A Good House' suffers when Burnard occasionally inserts an overly symbolic contemporary event . . . it's easy to forgive these brief lapses in her otherwise strict policy of showing rather than telling what's on her characters' minds." N Y Times Book Rev

Burnett, W. R. (William Riley), 1899-1982

The asphalt jungle. Knopf 1949 271p o.p.

Story of the planning and execution of a million-dollar jewel robbery by underworld gangsters in a large Midwestern city. With the cooperation of the press, an honest and persistent police commissioner solves the case and also succeeds in curbing a disastrous local crime wave

Burnett, William Riley *See* Burnett, W. R. (William Riley), 1899-1982

Burnford, Sheila, 1918-1984

Bel Ria. Little, Brown 1978 c1977 215p o.p.
LC 77-21082

"An Atlantic Monthly Press book"

First published 1977 in the United Kingdom

"A British soldier who is fleeing before the advancing German troops first comes upon a small trick dog in a circus caravan. When its owners are killed he takes on the responsibility for it and a monkey that makes a habit of riding on its back. When he is evacuated from France, even when the ship is sunk and they must remain in the water for hours, the three stick together. Sinclair, however, is badly wounded and must be hospitalized, so he entrusts the animals to a sick berth attendant on the ship. The dog, who soon is named Ria, at first is lonely and afraid, while the monkey quickly adapts, though every effort is made to keep them apart. Back on shore briefly, Ria is left with someone who will return him to Sinclair. That night, however, the town is bombed and Ria winds up saving the life of a 76-year-old woman who has been entombed by the debris. She takes him under her wealthy wing and he changes her life." Publ Wkly

"A realistic portrayal of wartime life, and an unsentimental but delightful picture of a remarkable animal, self-reliant, independent, and loving." Libr J

The incredible journey; with illustrations by Carl Burger. Little, Brown 1961 145p il o.p.

"A half-blind English bull terrier, a sprightly yellow Labrador retriever, and a feisty Siamese cat have resided for eight months with a friend of their owners, who are away on a trip. Then their temporary caretaker leaves them behind in order to take a short vacation. The lonely trio decides to tackle the harsh 250-mile hike across the Canadian wilderness in search of home, despite the human and wild obstacles the group will encounter." Shapiro. Fic for Youth. 3d edition

Burns, Olive Ann

Cold Sassy tree. Ticknor & Fields 1984 391p $26; pa $13.95

ISBN 0-385-31258-X; 0-385-31258-X (pa)
LC 84-8570

"Young Will Tweedy lives in a small Georgia town called Cold Sassy in the early 1900s. He is hard working (when pushed) because he has chores to do at home and work to do at his Grandpa Blakeslee's store. That still leaves him time to plan practical jokes with his pals and to overhear family dramas. The biggest drama begins when Grandpa, only three weeks after the death of his wife whom he had dearly loved, marries Miss Love Simpson—young enough to be his daughter. Miss Love has to face not only the town gossip, but also rejection from Will's Mother and Grandpa's other daughter. The story has humor, excitement, and realistic family confrontations." Shapiro. Fic for Youth. 3d edition

Followed by Leaving Cold Sassy: the unfinished sequel (1992)

Leaving Cold Sassy; the unfinished sequel to Cold Sassy tree; with a reminiscence by Katrina Kenison. Ticknor & Fields 1992 290p il o.p.
LC 92-5561

"As she battled cancer, Burns (1924-1990) completed 14 chapters of a sequel to her 1984 bestseller *Cold Sassy Tree* leaving behind at her death part of a 15th chapter and notes on how she intended to develop the novel's characters and plot. This new visit to the fictional town of Cold Sassy, Ga., features the original novel's protagonist, Will Tweedy, now 25. . . . Encouraged by local matchmakers, Will nervously courts schoolteacher Sanna Klein." Publ Wkly

"These 15 chapters hint admirably at Ms. Burns's plans to turn from her first book's exterior small-town universe to the interior limbo of a marriage, from an adolescent's rites of passage to an adult's experience of disappointment and despair." N Y Times Book Rev

Burns, Tex, 1908-1988

For works written by this author under other names see L'Amour, Louis, 1908-1988

Busch, Frederick, 1941-

The children in the woods; new and selected stories. Ticknor & Fields 1994 338p o.p.
LC 93-5008

Contents: Bread; Bring your friends to the zoo; Is anyone left this time of year?; A three-legged race; The trouble with being food; How the Indians come home; Widow water; The lesson of the Hôtel Lotti; My father, cont.; What you might as well call love; The settlement of Mars; Critics; Stand, and be recognized; Ralph the duck; Dog song; One more wave of fear; The world began with Charlie Chan; Extra extra large; The wicked stepmother; Folk tales; Dream abuse; The page; Berceuse

"Busch's magical, moving stories cut to the bone, revealing concealed fears, pains and hopes as he surveys the wreckage of fractured families, embattled marriages, ruptured lives." Publ Wkly

Closing arguments. Ticknor & Fields 1991 288p o.p.
LC 90-28144

"Mark Brennan was a Marine pilot who became a prisoner of the Vietcong. Now a lawyer in upstate New York, he confronts a failing marriage, a troubled son, and a dangerously seductive client on trial for murdering her lover in a motel bed." Libr J

The author "delves unflinchingly into the dark, bleakly erotic, and terrifying realm of intimate violence, masterfully peeling back each layer of deception, brutality, and suicidal desire. . . . Busch has ventured boldly and surefootedly out into forbidding territory. A gripping, sorrowful, and potent work." Booklist

Don't tell anyone. Norton 2000 309p $25.95

ISBN 0-393-04973-6 LC 00-34871

Contains the novella A handbook for spies and the following short stories: Are we pleasing you tonight?; The baby in the box; Bob's your uncle; Debriefing; Domicile; Heads; Joy of cooking; Laying the ghost; Machias; Malvasia; The ninth, in E minor; Passengers; Still the same old story; The talking cure; Timberline; Vespers

A handbook for spies is "set during the Vietnam era. Willie Bernstein, the son of Holocaust survivors, is teaching in a small upstate New York college and experiencing anti-Semitism, hate-filled conservative ideology, a passionate love affair with a woman married to a deranged Vietnam vet, and the breakup of his parents' marriage." Publ Wkly

"Busch weds a dark, morally ambiguous world view to superbly composed prose." New Yorker

Busch, Frederick, 1941-—*Continued*

A handbook for spies

In Busch, F. Don't tell anyone

A memory of war. Norton 2003 352p $25.95

ISBN 0-393-04978-7 LC 2002-32668

"In the opening pages of Frederick Busch's. . .novel, a Manhattan psychologist named Alex Lescziak is confronted by a firts-time patient with a remarkable assertion: that he is Alex's half-brother. The patient, William Kessler, tells this story: during World War II, after Alex's late parents, Januscz and Sylvia, had escaped from Poland to England, and William's father, Otto Kessler, a German SS interpreter, was a prisoner of war there, Sylvia and Otto had an affair." N Y Times Book Rev

"While the novel's emotional landscape is bleak, Busch's portrait of a man trying to surmount his demons is masterful." Publ Wkly

The night inspector; a novel. Harmony Bks. 1999 278p il $23

ISBN 0-609-60235-7 LC 99-11890

The narrator of this novel "William Bartholomew, served as a Union sniper in the Civil War until an explosion maimed his face; now it's 1867, and Bartholomew works as an investor in New York City, hiding his scars behind a pasteboard mask. The Civil War may be over, but slavery isn't: slave children are stuck at a Florida school, and Jessie, a Creole prostitute romantically involved with Bartholomew, entangles him in a plot to bring them North to freedom. Bartholomew seeks help from Herman Melville, once a bestselling novelist, now a customs inspector . . . in Manhattan's shipyards." Publ Wkly

The novel "is a marvelously dark-hued story by a master craftsman, and watching mastery at work provides at least a part of the pleasure of reading it." N Y Times Book Rev

Bushnell, Candace

Lipstick jungle. Hyperion 2005 353p $24.95

ISBN 0-7868-6819-8 LC 2005-46379

"Victory Ford, Wendy Healy, and Nico O'Neilly are three movers and shakers in Manhattan who still find time to lunch at the hottest restaurants. . . . Victory is a world-famous fashion designer whose spring collection failed to impress at New York's all-important fashion week. As the president of Parador Pictures, Wendy is gearing up for the film she hopes will finally snag her the coveted Best Picture Oscar. Nico, editor in chief of Bonfire magazine, is working her way up the corporate ladder. The ladies' love lives are just as interesting as their careers. Victory is being courted by an eccentric billionaire; Wendy's handsome, lazy husband has just demanded a divorce; and married Nico finds herself drawn into a fling with a handsome, younger male model. Readers who want to immerse themselves in the trendy world of New York's high society will find themselves at home in this scintillating novel." Booklist

Butler, Gwendoline

See also Melville, Jennie

Coffin knows the answer. Thomas Dunne Bks. 2003 187p $22.95

ISBN 0-312-29033-0 LC 2002-41568

"Chief Commander of Police John Coffin. . .has been investigating a serial murderer in London, ultimately finding tie-ins to the 'stalker with a paedophile slant' who sent pictures to Coffin's wife. Fascinating British procedural intricacies from a talented hand." Libr J

A dark coffin. St. Martin's Press 1996 204p o.p.

ISBN 0-312-14577-2 LC 96-25900

"A Thomas Dunne book"

First published 1995 in the United Kingdom

"Commander John Coffin faces his most challenging case yet when a bizarre double suicide takes place in a local theater. The case becomes all the more intriguing when Coffin discovers that the victims, Joe and Josie Macintosh, were a same-sex couple whose deaths were not suicide but murder. . . . Gritty realism, characters of depth and complexity, innovative plots, and a look at the darker side of humanity characterize Butler's fine series." Booklist

Death lives next door; the first Inspector Coffin mystery. St. Martin's Press 1992 c1960 191p o.p.

LC 92-1581

"A Thomas Dunne book"

First published 1960 in the United Kingdom

"Keeping her detective in the wings, [Butler] begins by focusing her narrative on a gang of shabby, bitter academic types in Oxford, at the center of which dysfunctional clique is the famous and slightly mysterious Marion Manning, watched by a man who in time will claim to be her long lost husband. Everything in Marion's past is weird, and as Coffin is drawn out of London into this narrow little world, it is the investigation of this mysterious past that forms the heart of the book. Butler's regulars shouldn't pass up the chance for this peek at Coffin's past." Booklist

A double Coffin. St. Martin's Press 1998 232p o.p.

ISBN 0-312-18569-3 LC 98-3223

"A Thomas Dunne book"

First published 1996 in the United Kingdom

London policeman "John Coffin sees a possible connection between a former prime minister's nightmarish childhood memory and the murder of a young journalist." Libr J

Butler provides "an imaginative plot, gritty realism, tantalizing clues, stylish writing, and keen insights into the darker side of the human psyche." Booklist

Butler, Octavia E.

Adulthood rites. Warner Bks. 1988 277p (Xenogenesis) o.p.

LC 87-34620

In the second novel in the Xenogenesis trilogy "the alien Oankali have rescued the dying remnants of humanity after Earth's nuclear war. Now, though, the children of the two races, called constructs, are resented and feared by the original survivors. This is the story of one such construct, Akin, who possesses an adult mind and voice before he is two years old. Stolen by a barren human community, he grows up knowing both races." Publ Wkly

Followed by Imago

Bloodchild and other stories. 2nd ed. Seven Stories Press 2005 214p pa $14

ISBN 1-58322-698-2 LC 2005-18898

Butler, Octavia E.—*Continued*

First published 1995

Contents: Bloodchild; The evening and the morning and the night; Near of kin; Speech sounds; Crossover; Positive obsession; Furor scribendi; Amnesty; The Book of Martha

This volume comprises seven stories and two essays by the science fiction writer.

Dawn; {by} Octavia Butler. Warner Bks. 1987 264p (Xenogenesis) o.p.

LC 87-6195

In this first volume in the Xenogenesis trilogy "a band of nuclear holocaust survivors is in the hands of an alien race that offers to save them. The price is high though: the survivors must participate in the evolution of the aliens by bearing children that incorporate some of the aliens' characteristics. Butler is one of the few sf writers who can handle effectively a slow-moving plot that emphasizes characters' emotions. Her command of the language is superior, and her aliens are quite convincing creations." Booklist

Followed by Adulthood rites

Fledgling; a novel. Seven Stories 2005 317p $24.95

ISBN 1-58322-690-7 LC 2005-5664

"Awaking blind, in pain, confused, and alone, Shori Matthews manages to survive amnesia and what should be crippling injuries and starts looking for answers–who hurt her, who she is, and where she comes from. She quickly learns that she is not a young human girl but a genetically altered vampire. Her black skin allows her to survive sunlight and remain alert during the day, but she faces grave danger from those threatened by her strength and heritage. Accompanied by several human hosts who feed and love her, Shori tries to protect her new family and friends from an increasingly hostile threat." Libr J

"In the feisty Shori, Butler has created a new vampire paradigm–one that's more prone to sci-fi social commentary than gothic romance–and given a tired genre a much-needed shot in the arm." Publ Wkly

Imago. Warner Bks. 1989 c1985 264p (Xenogenesis) o.p.

LC 88-27975

First published 1985 in the United Kingdom

The concluding volume of the Xenogenesis trilogy "considers a post-holocaust humanity whose only chance for survival is to be absorbed by the alien Oankali. Totally uninterested in domination, this race thrives on a symbiosis that Earthlings find difficult to credit. That distrust hampers the narrator, an ooloi (neuter) named Jodahs, as it tries to find life partners in the same ratio as its five parents: a human couple, an Oankali couple and itself, the essential ooloi who joins all five and melds their genetic legacy. Butler's achievement here is less the abstract reassignment of sexual roles than a warmth and urgency that dramatizes and personalizes these conflicts and transformations." Publ Wkly

Kindred; Octavia E. Butler. 25th anniverary ed. Beacon Press 2003 287p (Black women writers series) pa $14

ISBN 0-8070-8369-0 LC 2003-62862

First published 1979 by Doubleday

"Dana, a well-educated contemporary African American woman, suddenly finds herself pulled into the past to save the life of a distant ancestor, an early-19th-century southern white boy named Rufus Weylin. Although she returns to the present moments later, she soon finds herself saving Rufus again and again. Although only a short time passes for her between each bout of time travel, years pass for Rufus, who gradually grows into adulthood and becomes a slave owner. This sometimes painful novel features superb character development." Anatomy of Wonder 5

Parable of the sower. Four Walls Eight Windows 1993 299p o.p.

ISBN 0-941423-99-9 LC 93-8703

"Written in diary form, *Parable* chronicles the sometimes grim adventures of Lauren Olamina, an adolescent girl living in a barricaded village in Southern California amid the rampant socioeconomic decay of the early twenty-first century. After her neighborhood is overrun by a cult of drug-demented pyromaniacs, Lauren takes to the road and bands together with other refugees of violent attacks." Booklist

The author "infuses this tale with an allegorical quality that is part meditation, part warning. Simple, direct, and deeply felt, this should reach both mainstream and sf audiences." Libr J

Followed by Parable of the talents (1998)

Parable of the talents; a novel. Seven Stories Press 1998 365p $24.95

ISBN 1-88836-381-9 LC 98-35863

"In this sequel to Parable of the Sower, Lauren Olamina "has founded a quiet community called Acorn, where she teaches people about Earthseed, her belief that God is simply another name for Change. Her community of believers is threatened, however, by the election of an ultra-conservative president opposed to any religion not his own. Among his followers are fanatical terrorists who will stop at nothing to destroy what Lauren has built, including forcibly separating parents from their children." Libr J

"The narrative is both impassioned and bitter. . . . Lauren, at once loving wife and mother, prophet and fanatic, victim and leader, gains stature as one of the most intense and well-developed protagonists in recent SF." Publ Wkly

Butler, Robert Olen

The deep green sea; a novel. Holt & Co. 1998 c1997 226p o.p.

ISBN 0-8050-3130-8 LC 97-28239

In this novel, "war veteran Ben Cole returns to Saigon to try to understand the source of his postwar emotional lethargy. When he meets Tien, the enchanting 26-year-old employee of a tourist company, both immediately . . . feel a compelling sexual attraction. The narrative is composed of their alternating voices, each describing their lovemaking in slow motion and with erotic explicitness. These sexual idylls are interspersed with flashbacks to Ben's war experiences and Tien's anguished memories of her mother's desertion when the conflict ended in 1975." Publ Wkly

This novel "has a tone that might best be called ruminative. Throughout the novel, Butler writes the kind of

Butler, Robert Olen—*Continued*
long, rhythmic, adjective-free sentences that are the sign of a writer working to cast a spell, and I was often willing to submit to it. His spare descriptions can be enormously evocative." N Y Times Book Rev

Had a good time; stories from American postcards. Grove Press 2004 267p il $23
ISBN 0-8021-1777-5 LC 2003-67771
Contents: Hotel Touraine; Mother in the trenches; The ironworkers' hayride; Carl and I; This is Earl Sandt; The one in white; No chord of music; Christmas 1910; Hiram the desperado; I got married to a milk can; The grotto; Up by heart; Uncle Andrew; Twins; Sunday
The author is an "ardent collector of early-twentieth-century American picture postcards, 15 of which, all neatly reproduced, inspired the 15 gloriously imaginative and utterly hypnotizing short stories gathered here in a book destined to enrapture a broad readership. Butler also frames his marvelously diverse tales with bizarre little items from newspapers published on August 7, 1910, a year, as his stories reveal, notable for the appearance of Halley's comet and its overall transitiveness." Booklist

They whisper; a novel. Holt & Co. 1994 333p o.p.
ISBN 0-8050-1985-5 LC 93-38261
"Middle-aged Vietnam vet Ira Holloway is obsessed with women, seeking a connection to life's deeper mysteries through his numerous sexual trysts. While this novel initially seems a mere sexual memoir, it soon becomes clear that Butler is concerned with hunger for God as much as flesh. Holloway recounts the breakdown of his marriage to the troubled Fiona, a woman whose fragile consciousness is held together by an increasingly fanatical devotion to Roman Catholicism. Throughout, Butler explores the contrast between Fiona's austere, guilt-based faith and Ira's search for spiritual meaning through the physical." Libr J
"While the descriptions of erotic love are integral to the plot, the highly charged sensuality, the details of the rising stages of lust and the relentless stream-of-consciousness monologue sometimes grow wearisome." Publ Wkly

Butler, Samuel, 1835-1902

The way of all flesh. Knopf 1992 374p $17
ISBN 0-679-41718-4 LC 92-52916
"Everyman's library"
First published posthumously 1903; first Everyman's library edition 1933
The theme of this semi-autobiographical novel "is the hypocrisy and smug complacency of English middle-class life, and particularly the relationship between parents and children, which is traced through several generations of the Pontifex family. . . . 'The Way of All Flesh' is generally regarded as a very original work: it exercised considerable influence on later English writers. 'It contains records of the things I saw happening rather than imaginary incidents,' said the author. Undoubtedly this novel has a strong vein of autobiography." Haydn. Thesaurus of Book Dig

Butters, Dorothy Gilman *See* Gilman, Dorothy, 1923-

Butterworth, W. E., 1929-
For works written by this author in collaboration with H. Richard Hornberger see Hooker, Richard;
For works written by this author under other names see Griffin, W. E. B.

Byatt, A. S. (Antonia Susan), 1936-

Angels and insects; two novellas. Turtle Bay Bks. 1993 c1991 339p o.p.
LC 92-56806
First published 1991 in the United Kingdom
"In 'Morpho Eugenia' penniless young entomologist William Adamson has just returned from a 10-year expedition in the Amazon. William is taken in by a titled clergyman with scientific pretensions, and soon marries his benefactor's beautiful daughter. Unable to undertake another Amazon adventure, he studies domestic ant colonies and discovers indecent parallels between the insects and his new family. 'The Conjugial Angel' involves a circle of spiritualists, chief among them Alfred Tennyson's sister Emily, in her youth engaged to Arthur Hallam, the man immortalized in Tennyson's *In Memoriam.* Emily has been branded faithless for having married years after Hallam's death, . . . but she is uncompromising in her pursuit of Hallam's ghost. . . . Complex and captivating, this fluid volume recasts itself on every page." Publ Wkly

Babel Tower. Random House 1996 625p o.p.
LC 95-53210
"At the dawning of the new feminist age, Frederica, a Cambridge-educated intellectual, finds herself in a stifling marriage to Nigel River, confined to his country estate and caring for her small son in the company of a severe housekeeper and hostile sisters-in-law. She finally bolts the oppressive household and her increasingly violent husband for London, where she takes refuge with understanding friends and in writing and teaching. Among her new acquaintances is Jude Mason, a troubled recluse, who is the author of 'Babel Tower,' the novel within this novel." Libr J
"In many ways, this is a book about language, and how it is used to conceal and reveal (there is a wonderfully satirical subplot about a commission examining English educational methods). But it also *employs* language, brilliantly, to create a large cast of characters whose struggles, anxieties and small triumphs are at once specific to a time and place, and universal." Publ Wkly

The biographer's tale. Knopf 2001 305p $24
ISBN 0-375-41114-3 LC 00-62012
This novel's protagonist is Phineas Nanson, a postgraduate student. He sets out to write the biography of Scholes Destry-Scholes, the biographer of the Victorian diplomat Elmer Bole, but finds it an increasingly complicated enterprise. He takes a job with a travel agency and meets Fulla, a Swedish bee taxonomist
"Theory and esoteric allusion dominate the action from start to finish. Byatt remains an author of daunting erudition and precious phrasing." Atl Mon

The conjugial angel
In Byatt, A. S. Angels and insects

Byatt, A. S. (Antonia Susan), 1936-—*Continued*

The djinn in the nightingale's eye

In Byatt, A. S. The djinn in the nightingale's eye: five fairy stories

The djinn in the nightingale's eye: five fairy stories. Random House 1997 274p o.p.

ISBN 0-679-42008-8 LC 96-46330

Contents: The glass coffin; Gode's story; The story of the eldest princess; Dragon's breath; The djinn in the nightingale's eye {novella}

The stories in this "collection adopt the conventions of folk or fairy tales: magic enchantments; the granting of three wishes; adventures that involve danger. . . . The title piece, a novella, is the most surprising and appealing. Middle-aged British narratologist Gillian Perholt acquires a beautiful bottle when she attends a convention in Turkey. The djinn she later releases not only grants her three wishes but also teaches her how to avoid the classic folk-tale irony by which the wisher lives to regret the fulfillment of his or her desires." Publ Wkly

Elementals; stories of fire and ice. Random House 1999 229p o.p.

ISBN 0-375-50250-5 LC 99-10627

Contents: Crocodile tears; A lamia in the Cérennes; Cold; Baglady; Jael; Christ in the house of Martha and Mary

Byatt's stories "have a delightful fairytale quality, reinforced by her extraordinary skill in creating leisurely, luxurious visual images." Atl Mon

Little black book of stories. Knopf 2004 2003 240p $21

ISBN 1-400-04177-5 LC 2003-65940

First published 2003 in the United Kingdom

Contents: The thing in the forest; Body art; A stone woman; Raw material; The pink ribbon

"Byatt has the sheer narrative skill to raise the hairs on the back of your neck and make your pulse race. In this fine and memorable collection, she attains a near perfect balance between low and high, body and mind, the Thing and its significance." N Y Times Book Rev

The Matisse stories. Random House 1995 c1993 134p il o.p.

LC 94-46131

First published 1993 in the United Kingdom

Contents: Medusa's ankles; Art work; The Chinese lobster

"A middle-aged academic wreaks havoc at her chic hair salon; a cleaning woman for an 'artistic' family picks up more around the house than her employers have bargained for; an anorexic art student with a grudge against Matisse accuses her adviser of molesting her. These three stories explore the sterility engendered by order and the ugliness born of despair, and in each of them one glimpses, like a flash of vermillion, a bright streak of rage." New Yorker

Morpho Eugenia

In Byatt, A. S. Angels and insects

(ed) The Oxford book of English short stories. See The Oxford book of English short stories

Possession; a romance. Modern Lib. 2000 605p o.p.

ISBN 0-679-64030-4 LC 99-56297

A reissue of the edition first published 1990 by Random House

The protagonist of this novel, Roland Mitchell, "is a postdoctoral research student. Working in the London Library of the Victorian poet Ash, he comes upon an interchange of letters between Ash and an unknown woman. . . . A series of clues lead him to believe the recipient of Ash's affections might be Christabel Lamotte, a Victorian poet of much interest . . . to feminist critics, and his quest for information about Lamotte leads him to the beautiful scholar Dr. Maud Bailey. Together Roland and Dr. Bailey unearth letters which establish the details of an intense and hitherto unsuspected relationship between these poets, and form one of their own." New Statesman Soc

"Intelligent, ingenious and humane, [this] bids fair to be looked back upon as one of the most memorable novels of the 1990s." Times Lit Suppl

A whistling woman. Knopf 2003 429p $26

ISBN 0-375-41534-3 LC 2002-72957

A "study of England in the Swinging Sixties. . . . Having abandoned university teaching, Frederica Potter finds herself the host of a cutting-edge TV show called Through the Looking-Glass that is bringing her some unwanted fame. She's a single mom struggling with young son Leo, who is having trouble learning how to read, and in addition can't commit to lover John, whose twin, Paul, heads up a rock band called Zag and the Syzgy Zy-goats. Events conspire to draw these characters to a Body-Mind conference at a northern university plagued by an Anti-University, even as a religious cult is getting started at a farm across the way." Libr J

"There is no other writer alive who is as interested as Byatt in creating characters who are thinking women and men while at the same time recognizing the limits of cognition in the face of unreason, or love." N Y Times Book Rev

Byatt, Antonia Susan *See* Byatt, A. S. (Antonia Susan), 1936-

Byrd, Max

Grant; a novel. Bantam Bks. 2000 362p $23.95

ISBN 0-553-09633-8 LC 99-56577

"As he covers Grant's potential candidacy and approaching death for the *Washington Post*, Nicholas Trist, a veteran of the Civil War who lost an arm at the battle of Cold Harbor (in which Grant was the commanding general), interacts with the major political and literary lights of the time. Washington in the 1880s resembles Washington of the 1990s: love affairs, leaks to the newspapers, jockeying for advantages, and even a best-selling anonymous novel purporting to give the inside scoop on Washington politicos. Historical fiction doesn't get any better than this." Booklist

Shooting the sun. Bantam Books 2004 306p $23.95

ISBN 0-553-80208-9 LC 2003-52403

This is the "tale of a scientific expedition to New Mexico in 1840. Joining the group as its official daguerreotype photographer is blond, talented, emancipated, and very well connected Selena Cott (she's part of scientist Charles Babbage's social circle in England); her job is to catch the total eclipse of the sun in a series of

Byrd, Max—*Continued*

images that will validate the mathematical genius of Babbage's Difference Engine-the first mechanical computer. Unbeknownst to her, the true purpose of the trip is to find Babbage's rich uncle, who had gone to America years before and wound up living with the Kiowas; if his death can be proven and recorded, his vast estate will finance the completion of Babbage's machine. Although well planned and equipped, the expedition runs into great difficulties." Libr J

"As the explorers work their way closer to Mexico and the day of the eclipse, Byrd ratchets up the dramatic tension with several ingenious surprises, including a truly Dantean fate for some of the least savory individuals west of the Mississippi." N Y Times Book Rev

C

Cabbage and bones; an anthology of Irish American women's fiction; edited and with an introduction by Caledonia Kearns; foreword by Maureen Howard. Holt & Co. 1997 xxii, 358p o.p.

ISBN 0-8050-5579-7 LC 97-13626

"An Owl book"

"The 24 contributions, . . . are filled with recurring themes of family, immigration, and religion. What makes these stories memorable are the depth and variety of emotions that each writer brings to her subject matter. A true celebration of Irish American women's fiction and an affirmation of this unique perspective in American literature." Libr J

Cadwalladr, Carole

The family tree; by Carole Cadwalladr. Dutton 2005 384p il $23.95

ISBN 0-525-94842-2 LC 2004-52756

"Set in late-20th-century Britain, the novel is narrated by Rebecca Monroe, a pop culture researcher who tells of her marriage to Alistair, a behavioral geneticist; her childhood leading up to her mother's suicide; and her grandmother's doomed biracial romance with Cecil, a Jamaican immigrant. In an effort to better understand herself, the child she can't decide whether or not to have, and the people she still can't believe make up her family, Rebecca considers both sides of the nature/nurture debate, with any romantic notions she might be on the brink of reaching debunked by her husband's passionless scientific postulations. Cadwalladr explicates her tale with a slew of definitions, scientific charts and graphs, detailed family anatomies, examples of deductive fallacies and footnotes expounding on such essential '70s pop culture references as Dallas and The Sale of the Century. Her mastery of time and place, wry humor and sporadic bouts of self-doubt will endear her to readers, while her fascination with the choices people make combined with a morbid curiosity about her own fate add depth and texture to this utterly winning tale of one lovable, dysfunctional family." Publ Wkly

Cain, James M. (James Mallahan), 1892-1977

Cain x 3; three novels; with a new introduction by Tom Wolfe. Knopf 1969 465p o.p.

Contents: The postman always rings twice (1934); Mildred Pierce (1934); Double indemnity (1943)

The first story concerns a young vagrant and a restaurant keeper's wife who plan to murder the latter's husband; the second is a study of a grass widow, her husband and a daughter who becomes a monster; the last deals with an insurance salesman who plots the perfect murder

Cain's "violent, sexually obsessed, and relentlessly paced melodramas epitomized the hard-boiled fiction that flourished in the U.S. in the 1930s and '40s." Merriam-Webster's Ency of Lit

Double indemnity
In Cain, J. M. Cain x 3 p363-465

Mildred Pierce
In Cain, J. M. Cain x 3 p103-362

The postman always rings twice
In Cain, J. M. Cain x 3 p1-101

Caldwell, Erskine, 1903-1987

Complete stories of Erskine Caldwell. Little, Brown 1953 664p o.p.

Contents: After-image; August afternoon; Automobile that wouldn't run; Autumn courtship; Back on the road; Balm of Gilead; Big Buck; Blue Boy; Candy-man Beechum; Carnival; Cold winter; Corduroy pants; Country full of Swedes; Courting of Susie Brown; Crownfire; Daughter; Day the presidential candidate came to Ciudad Tamaulipas; Day's wooing; Dorothy; The dream; Empty room; End of Christy Tucker; Evelyn and the rest of us; Evening in Nuevo Leon; First autumn; Fly in the coffin; Girl Ellen; Grass fire; Growing season; Hamrick's polar bear; Handy; Here and today; Honeymoon; Horse thief; Indian summer; It happened like this; Joe Craddock's old woman; John the Indian and George Hopkins; Kneel to the rising sun; Knife to cut the corn bread with; Lonely day; Mamma's little girl; Man and woman; Man who looked like himself; Martha Jean; Masses of men; Mating of Marjorie; Maud Island; Meddlesome Jack; Medicine man; Memorandum; Midsummer passion; Midwinter guest; Molly Cotton-Tail; Negro in the well; New cabin; Nine dollars' worth of mumble; Over the Green Mountains; People v Abe Lathan, colored; People's choice; Picking cotton; The picture; Priming the well; Rachel; Return to Lavinia; The rumor; Runaway; Saturday afternoon; Savannah River payday; The shooting; Sick horse; Slow death; Small day; Snacker; Squire Dinwiddy; Strawberry season; Summer accident; The Sunfield; Swell-looking girl; Ten thousand blueberry crates; Thunderstorm; Uncle Henry's love nest; Uncle Jeff; Very late spring; The visitor; Walnut hunt; Warm river; We are looking at you, Agnes; Where the girls were different; Wild flowers; The windfall; Woman in the house; Yellow girl

God's little acre. Viking 1933 303p o.p.

"A Georgia 'cracker,' Ty Ty Walden, has devoted 15 years to digging for gold on his farm. Always a 'religious man,' he has set aside one acre whose income

Caldwell, Erskine, 1903-1987—*Continued*
shall go to the church, but has had to shift 'God's little acre' constantly, so as not to interfere with the digging. Ty Ty's sincere but adaptable morality appears also in the shiftless lives of his children." Oxford Companion to Am Lit. 6th edition

Tobacco road. Scribner 1932 241p o.p.

"Jeeter Lester is an impoverished Georgia sharecropper who lives on Tobacco Road with his starving old mother, his sickly wife, Ada, and his two children, sixteen-year-old Dude and Ellie May, who has a harelip. A third child, Pearl, has been married at the age of twelve to Lov Bensey, a railroad worker. When Jeeter's widowed preacher sister, Bessie Rice, induces Dude to marry her by buying him a new automobile, Dude accidentally wrecks the car and kills his grandmother. Pearl runs away from Lov Bensey; Ellie May happily goes to live with him; and Jeeter and Ada, left alone one night, perish when their shack burns down." Reader's Ency. 4th edition

Caldwell, Ian

The rule of four; [by] Ian Caldwell & Dustin Thomason. Dial Press 2004 372p $24

ISBN 0-385-33711-6 LC 2003-70124

"A Princeton student has only twenty-four hours to complete his senior thesis—hardly the nail-biting stuff of thrillers, except that the thesis in question purports to solve the mystery of an erotic fifteenth-century allegory littered with ciphers and algorithms. . . . As the student races to meet his deadline, mayhem engulfs the campus: a chase through steam tunnels beneath the grassy quads, an inferno at the school's toniest eating club, and nude frolics in the snow (this last not fiction but a real Princeton tradition). The authors . . . keep up a frantic, somewhat exhausting pace, but the most riveting action sequences take place inside the mind, as the hero wrestles with the manuscript." New Yorker

Caldwell, Taylor, 1900-1985

Answer as a man. Putnam 1981 c1980 445p o.p.
LC 80-18187

"Set in a small Pennsylvania boomtown in the first decade of the 20th century, . . . this is the story of Jason Garrity, son of devoutly Roman Catholic, Irish immigrants who rises from delivery boy to wealthy resort hotel entrepreneur. In the course of his ascent, Jason confronts religious hypocrisy, political corruption, financial scandal, ethnic prejudice, martial discord, family upheavals." Publ Wkly

Captains and kings. Doubleday 1972 640p o.p.

This novel follows the growth of an Irish immigrant family from complete poverty to a position of wealth and political power. Joseph Armagh is ruled by the desire for money and overcome by ambition for his children. Along the way the family seems to have acquired a curse, so that the second generation of Armaghs reaps only misfortune and destruction

"Through all this saga one cannot help but find some parallels with the Kennedy saga, set back to the period 1850-1915. Portraits of some characters, rather bitterly slanted, are certainly more than coincidental." Publ Wkly

Ceremony of the innocent. Doubleday 1976 422p o.p.

Set in Pennsylvania and New York City at the turn-of-the-century this is an "allegory in which a naive servant girl (a cross between Candide and Cinderella) marries her Prince Charming. Always the innocent dupe of jealous and evil persons, she is eventually driven to suicide by her own avaricious children. Key to the allegory is a fatally ingenuous America drawn into the stock market crash of 1929 by her enemies." Booklist

Dear and glorious physician. Doubleday 1959 574p o.p.

This novel about Lucanus, or Luke, "physician and author of one of the Gospels, depicts him as an individual apart, plainly marked out for the service of God in spite of his almost lifelong protest against a deity who inflicted pain on men. Antioch, scene of his boyhood; Rome, where he visited his family in the intervals between his restless travels; Alexandria, where he was educated; and Judaea, where he learned the story of Jesus from his mother Mary and acknowledged him as the Christ, provide a background." Booklist

"Gripping and absorbing reading that illuminates a period and highlights the development of a man being prepared for God's purpose. The sweep and greatness of the story dwarf any defects in style." Wis Libr Bull

Great lion of God. Doubleday 1970 629p o.p.

Based upon the Biblical character, St. Paul, or Saul of Tarshish. "This very long novel covers Paul's life from the time of his birth and ends with his departure from Palestine for Rome, covering too the Biblical story of Jesus as it related to Paul, his first disbelief in the new Messiah and his conversion after the Crucifixion and Resurrection." Publ Wkly

"The book is backed by extensive research, supporting Miss Caldwell's obvious concern and seriousness about its religious and social implications." Libr J

I, Judas; [by] Taylor Caldwell and Jess Stearn. Atheneum Pubs. 1977 371p o.p.

"A first-person narrative which draws heavily on the four Gospel accounts and offers an explanation for Judas' betrayal of Jesus. It presents Judas as the betrayed: by authorities who promise acquittal, and by his own reasoning that the man who demonstrated power over death by raising Lazarus surely could not himself die. Wrong on both counts, his name became synonymous with treachery. By adhering closely to the biblical version in familiar parts of the story, the authors render their interpretation quite plausible and unthreatening to adherents of received word." Booklist

The authors "have dealt brilliantly with the issue of perspective and therein lies the value of their work." Best Sellers

Testimony of two men. Doubleday 1968 605p o.p.

"Jonathan Ferrier is the central character. He is dedicated to perfection—to perfect asepsis when few doctors yet acknowledged or even knew the need for it in 1901, and to perfect truth in human relations. Ironically, he himself has been tried for the murder of his wife and justly acquitted. The verdict was not acceptable to his community. Since they are incapable of the perfection he vocally demands, the people around him hate him and

Caldwell, Taylor, 1900-1985—*Continued*
are delighted by an apparent opportunity to condemn him." Libr J

"Caldwell combines incisive characterization with an absorbing description of nineteenth-century medical practices." Booklist

Calisher, Hortense

The collected stories of Hortense Calisher. Arbor House 1975 502p o.p.

Contents: In Greenwich there are many gravelled walks; Heartburn; The night club in the woods; Two colonials; The hollow boy; The rehabilitation of Ginevra Leake; The woman who was everybody; A Christmas carillon; Il ploe:r dã mõ koe:r, If you don't want to live I can't help you; A wreath for Miss Totten; Time, gentlemen; May-ry; The Coreopsis Kid; A box of ginger; The pool of Narcissus; The watchers; The gulf between; The sound of waiting; Old stock; The rabbi's daughter; The middle drawer; The summer rebellion; What a thing, to keep a wolf in a cage; Songs my mother taught me; So many rings to the show; One of the chosen; Point of departure; Letitia, Emeritus; The seacoast of Bohemia; Mrs. Fay dines on zebra; Saturday night; Little did I know; Night riders of Northville; In the absence of angels; The scream of Fifty-seventh Street

Sunday Jews. Harcourt 2002 694p $36

ISBN 0-15-100930-9 LC 2002-2517

At the source of this family saga is "the loving marriage of Zipporah Zangwill, a Jewish anthropologist, and her lapsed Catholic philosopher husband, Peter Duffy. Their large and elegant old New York apartment has been home to six children and the scene of ever-swelling Sunday family gatherings as these complicated individuals-some tall and blond, others short and Brillo-haired, some gay, some straight, some artistic, some theological, some professional-extend the family circle with friends, lovers, spouses, and children." Booklist

"Issues of identity, mortality and the passage of time are implicit in family sagas, and they are eloquently sounded out here by diverse characters, all of whom are in one way or another puzzling through the age-old conundrum 'Who is a Jew?' Zipporah is too intelligent, and 'Sunday Jews' too subtle, for an easy answer to emerge. Rather, like an animated group of Talmudic scholars, the characters in this lovely book delve ever deeper into the heart of its questions, valuing the multiplicity of opinions as much as any possible conclusion." N Y Times Book Rev

Callahan, John F.

Flying home and other stories; edited, with an introduction by John F. Callahan. Random House 1996 xxxviii, 173p o.p.

ISBN 0-679-45704-6 LC 96-27422

Includes the following stories: A party down at the Square; Boy on a train; Mister Toussan; Afternoon; That I had the wings; A coupla scalped Indians; Hymie's bull; I did not learn their names; A hard time keeping up; The black ball; King of the bingo game; In a strange country; Flying home

These "early stories (written between 1937 and 1954) are clearly apprentice work in which Ellison is struggling for control of voice, timing and structure. . . . His stories display, individually, the commitment to craft and, collectively, the acquired range that later enabled him to assemble, block by block, one of the great monuments of American literature." Publ Wkly

Calling the wind; twentieth century African-American short stories; edited and with an introduction by Clarence Major. HarperCollins Pubs. 1993 xxv, 622p o.p.

LC 92-52620

"An Edward Burlingame book"

"Fifty-nine African American authors, including Terry McMillan, Arna Bontemps, Richard Wright, Langston Hughes, James Baldwin, Toni Morrison, Alice Walker and Rosa Guy, have each contributed one short story to this collection." Book Rep

This "could become *the* anthology of black American short fiction for wide use in the high school and college classroom as well as by the general reading public." Booklist

Calvino, Italo

Baron in the trees; translated by Archibald Colquhoun. Harcourt 1977 c1959 217p pa $12

ISBN 0-15-610680-9 LC 76-039704

Original Italian edition, 1957; this translation first published 1959 by Random House

Calvino's "status as one of Italy's greatest writer's was confirmed by the acclaim which met the fantasy, The baron in the trees (1957), in which a nineteenth-century nobleman opts to pursue life without ever setting foot on the ground. The story examines the meeting-points of reality and imagination." Good Fiction Guide

If on a winter's night a traveler. Knopf 1993 c1981 254p $18

ISBN 0-679-42025-8 LC 92-54302

"Everyman's library"

Original Italian edition, 1979; this is a reissue of the edition published 1981 by Harcourt Brace Jovanovich

The novel "begins with a man discovering that the copy of a novel he has recently purchased is defective, a Polish novel having been bound within its pages. He returns to the bookshop the following day and meets a young woman who is on an identical mission. They both profess a preference for the Polish novel. Interposed between the chapters in which the two strangers attempt to authenticate their texts are 10 excerpts that parody genres of contemporary world fiction, such as the Latin-American novel and the political novel of eastern Europe." Merriam-Webster's Ency of Lit

Invisible cities; translated from the Italian by William Weaver. Harcourt Brace Jovanovich 1974 165p o.p.

"A Helen and Kurt Wolff book"

Original Italian edition, 1972

"Marco Polo, the traveler, describes to Kublai Khan (his patron) the various cities of the Khan's vast empire. The cities, which all have women's names, are metaphors for different kinds of people and the varied relationships they may form. . . . They progress from medieval to modern times, growing steadily in complexity

Calvino, Italo—*Continued*
and malignancy." Libr J

"Italo Calvino is recognized as one of the consummate stylists among writers today, a novelist whose superbly imaginative mind conjures up metaphorical fables of exquisite beauty to transcribe his personal visions of man and the universe." Choice

Mr. Palomar; translated from the Italian by William Weaver. Harcourt Brace Jovanovich 1985 c1983 130p o.p.

ISBN 0-15-162835-1 LC 85-5490

"A Helen and Kurt Wolff book"

Original Italian edition, 1983

"'A nervous man who lives in a frenzied and congested world, Mr. Palomar tends to reduce his relations with the outside world; and, to defend himself against the general neurasthenia, he tries to keep his sensations under control insofar as possible.' . . . Calvino [seeks to] lead the reader into three levels of experience—visual, cultural, speculative—in the life of Mr. Palomar. We watch Mr. Palomar on vacation, in the city, and silently thinking." Libr J

"There is an almost perfect sense of complementary relationships: Calvino is delicate and strong, his precision is lyric and mathematic; the equation between perceiver and perceived is made infinitely and effortlessly complex but remains exact. The care which Calvino has lavished on the formal arrangement of his book should not, however, lead us to think that it offers only a formal resolution of compositional intricacies, for Mr. Palomor is a work of cunning dialectics that goes beyond the delight in paradoxes for which Calvino is lazily praised." New Statesman (1913)

Under the jaguar sun; translated by William Weaver. Harcourt Brace Jovanovich 1988 86p o.p.

ISBN 0-15-192820-7 LC 88-835

"A Helen and Kurt Wolff book"

Contents: Under the jaguar sun; A king listens; The name, the nose

"Taste, hearing, and smell become the driving forces behind Calvino's characters in these three stories, which were to have been a part of the late Italian writer's projected series on the five senses. A couple vacationing in Mexico become inflamed by the local cuisine and by certain cannibalistic practices of the Aztecs; a mad monarch's paranoia is piqued by overheard rumblings; and a Parisian dandy goes off on the trail of a beautiful woman identified only by her alluring scent. With their mixture of the ordinary and the exotic, these stories are masterful miniatures." Booklist

Cambor, Kathleen

In sunlight, in a beautiful garden. Farrar, Straus & Giroux 2000 258p $23

ISBN 0-374-16537-8 LC 00-34772

"On Memorial Day, 1889, Pennsylvania's South Fork dam burst, and the resulting flood claimed over 2000 lives. The lake formed by the dam was the site of an exclusive summer club whose members included wealthy industrialists Henry Clay Frick, Andrew Mellon, and Andrew Carnegie. . . . The book centers on several characters, including Civil War veteran Frank Fallon, whose son Daniel becomes involved with Nora Talbot, one of the wealthy summer visitors to the lake. Meanwhile, Grace McIntyre, a woman with a mysterious past, becomes town librarian, befriending Frank's wife and eventually becoming enamored of Frank himself." Libr J

"The accomplishments of 'In Sunlight, in a Beautiful Garden' come close to matching its ambitions as it explores the blinding nature of class division, the difficulty of reaching out beyond one's own milieu and the caprice with which luck, love, and disaster play out within the divisive layers of society." N Y Times Book Rev

Cameron, Peter, 1959-

The city of your final destination. Farrar, Straus & Giroux 2002 312p $24

ISBN 0-374-28197-1 LC 2001-51127

In this "novel, Omar Razaghi, a graduate student in Kansas by way of Iran and Canada, travels to Uruguay to research a biography of Jules Gund, a critically ignored expatriate writer who published only a single novel before his death. In an attempt to obtain permission to proceed with his work, Omar finds himself entangled in, and even falling a bit in love with, the family Jules left behind: his homosexual brother, Adam; Jules's wife, Caroline; and his mistress Arden. . . . The characters discover themselves not through the books they have read (as Omar first believes) or the places they have been (as the title would suggest) but through Cameron's precisely rendered conversations." New Yorker

Camilleri, Andrea, 1925-

The snack thief; translated by Stephen Sartarelli. Viking 2003 $21.95p $21.95

ISBN 0-670-03223-9 LC 2003-41090

Original Italian edition, 1998

In this mystery, Sicilian Inspector Salvo Montaldo "suspects a link between the stabbing of a businessman in an apartment-house elevator and the shooting of a crewman on a fishing boat. Connecting the two are an enterprising Tunisian prostitute, now vanished, and her young son, who has been surviving by stealing lunches from schoolchildren. Montalbano fits the pieces together gradually, taking time, as always, for plenty of leisurely lunches but eventually exposing a wide-ranging plot fuelled by high-level corruption." Booklist

Camp, John, 1944-

See also Sandford, John, 1944-

Campbell, Bebe Moore

72 hour hold; a novel; by Bebe Moore Campbell. Knopf 2005 319p $24.95

ISBN 1-400-04074-4 LC 2004-57620

"Keri Whitmore hangs onto the hope that her daughter, Trina, who was about to enter Brown University, will overcome her bipolar disorder and become her lovely, promising child again. But part of Keri's struggle is realizing that mental illness can only be managed, never eradicated. The metaphor of Harriet Tubman and the Underground Railroad appears throughout, an apt image for Keri and Trina as they try to flee both physically and mentally from the slavery of mental illness. Flights of insanity and chaos are grounded in fresh descriptions of everyday life in Los Angeles, where Keri runs her own resale designer-clothing store, attends support group

Campbell, Bebe Moore—*Continued*

meetings, and deals with her actor boyfriend, alcoholic mother, and conservative ex-husband. There is a lot going on here, but Campbell deftly weaves the threads of Keri's life to form a rich and compelling tapestry that illustrates the tension between a woman's love for her child and her own need to have a fulfilling life." Libr J

Brothers and sisters. Putnam 1994 476p o.p.
LC 94-14196

"Set in the heart of a Los Angeles still troubled by the aftermath of the April riots, the novel draws a . . . portrait of the internal and external conflicts regarding race experienced by characters of varied backgrounds. The story centers on Esther Jackson, an African American with a promising career in banking who is torn between her need to succeed professionally and her loyalty to other people of color." Libr J

"What makes 'Brothers and Sisters' different from the traditional potboiler is Ms. Campbell's genuine attempt to address the complexities of race in the modern age." N Y Times Book Rev

Singing in the comeback choir. Putnam 1998 372p o.p.
ISBN 0-399-14298-3 LC 97-31649

"Professionally successful and newly pregnant, Maxine McCoy, an African American TV producer, tries to regain marital trust after her husband's brief infidelity. During a sweeps period that will determine her talk show's future, Maxine leaves L.A. and returns to North Philadelphia to attend to Malindy Walker, the grandmother who raised her. Once a moderately famous club singer, Lindy is depressed and rebellious after a recent mild stroke." Publ Wkly

"By the end of 'Singing in the Comeback Choir,' we have come to care deeply about Maxine and Lindy, which makes the novel's inventive resolution even more gratifying." N Y Times Book Rev

What you owe me. Putnam 2001 533p o.p.
ISBN 0-399-14784-5 LC 2001-19732

"The story of Hosanna Clark, a black maid in a Los Angeles hotel, and her surprising relationship with Gilda, a white Jewish émigrée from Poland. Just after World War II, the women join forces to promote a hand lotion that Gilda makes, with Gilda managing the financial end of their newborn partnership and Hosanna hustling the product. But just as they quit their jobs to make cosmetics for black women full time, Gilda disappears, as does all the cash in their joint bank account. Gilda starts her own cosmetics company, which brings her both fame and fortune, and Hosanna passes her jealousy, anger, and thirst for revenge on to her daughter, Matriece. Matriece goes to work for Gilda after Hosanna dies, with unfocused plans for revenge." Libr J

"Numerous subplots crowd the novel, covering issues from reparations and education to romance and betrayal. Campbell's detailed treatment of each accounts for the book's length, but all are credibly tied to the central tale." Publ Wkly

Your blues ain't like mine. Putnam 1992 332p o.p.
ISBN 0-399-13746-7 LC 91-45518

"In Ms. Campbell's story, a young black man, Armstrong Todd, visiting from Chicago in 1955, is murdered in Hopewell, Miss., by a white man. Reporters from New York are secretly summoned by an influential citizen of Hopewell, and as a consequence of the resulting news media attention there is, uncharacteristically, a trial. After the trial, the novel follows the lives of Armstrong's relatives in Mississippi—and in Chicago, where Armstrong's mother, Delotha Todd, starts a new and difficult life, raising another son. The novel also follows the lives of the murderer, Floyd Cox, and his family." N Y Times Book Rev

"Written in poetic prose, filled with masterfully drawn and sympathetic characters that a less able hand might have rendered in stereotypes, this first novel blends the irony of Flannery O'Connor's fiction and the poignance of Harper Lee's." Publ Wkly

Campbell, R. Wright, 1927-2000

In La-La Land we trust; [by] Robert Campbell. Mysterious Press 1986 528p o.p.
LC 86-47548

"A two-car collision at the rain-slicked corner of Hollywood and Vine results in one dead driver and one headless female corpse. When eyewitness Whistler, down-at-the-heels private eye, discovers a cover-up . . . he starts his own investigation. A blonde TV starlet and a mysterious millionaire are involved. Soon Whistler learns that the starlet, lured to New Orleans with promises of a movie role, is in danger, and he must stop the movie from turning into a 'snuff' film." Publ Wkly

"Although his dialogue can be bawdy, although the situations can be raw and gritty, Mr. Campbell does not play up the sex. All Mr. Campbell has to do, which he does, is have Whistler present a dispassionate account of the activity without any moralizing or indignation. Whistler is in many ways a very modern reincarnation of Hammett's Continental Op. . . . Mr. Campbell is one of the most stylish crime writers in the business." NY Times Book Rev

Pigeon pie; {by} Robert Campbell. Mysterious Press 1998 229p $22
ISBN 0-89296-665-3 LC 97-48921

Sleuthing Chicago sewer inspector Jimmy Flannery has "been around the block a few times by now, so he accepts the blessings of the party pols and agrees to run for alderman in the prestigious 11th Ward. But before the fatted calf is even cooked, someone sprays Jimmy's headquarters with bullets, killing his office manager, the transsexual cop Mabel Halstead. Mabel's passing is a sad occasion for fans of this series, but other familiar characters survive, talking a blue streak and reaffirming Jimmy's faith in the values that sustain his grand old neighborhood." N Y Times Book Rev

Campbell, Ramsey, 1946-

The Count of Eleven. TOR Bks. 1992 310p o.p.
LC 92-1097

"A Tom Doherty Associates book"

"Jack Orchard is not only a clumsy oaf with a genius for the ill-timed and inappropriate joke but also the victim of a stretch of very bad luck. He decides his ill fortune is caused by those who failed to pass on the chain letter he sent them—so he kills them with a blowtorch.

Campbell, Ramsey, 1946-—*Continued*

Comedy alternates with horror as Jack's personality becomes increasingly split between his own bumbling self and his efficiently murderous alter ego, the Count of Eleven. This novel will appeal to a broad group of readers beyond Campbell's horror-fan base." Libr J

The last voice they hear. Forge 1998 384p o.p.
ISBN 0-312-86611-9 LC 98-10256
"A Tom Doherty Associates book"
"The happy married life of young father and investigative reporter Geoff Davenport is shattered when his unbalanced, resentful, long-lost stepbrother, Ben, kidnaps Geoff's three-year-old son. . . . The plot unfolds without complication as a simple cat-and-mouse game in which Ben lures Geoff to an inevitable confrontation through clues keyed to shared childhood experiences." Publ Wkly

The long lost. TOR Bks. 1994 c1993 375p o.p.
LC 94-21751
"A Tom Doherty Associates book"
First published 1993 in the United Kingdom
"On vacation in Wales, David and Joelle Owain discover Gwen, an old woman asleep in a small cottage on a deserted island created by the tides. Amazingly, she claims to be a distant relative and returns with the Owains to Chester. After a backyard barbecue, where Gwen meets the family's friends and neighbors, misfortunes begin to dog the guests, causing David to wonder just who and what Gwen really is. . . . Disturbing and original, this neat mix of contemporary fiction with supernatural undertones is recommended for most collections." Libr J

Nazareth Hill. Forge 1997 383p o.p.
ISBN 0-312-86344-6 LC 96-6567
"A Tom Doherty Associates book"
"Nazareth Hill is an English apartment house with a varied history, rumored to have served in previous incarnations as a monastery, a mental hospital, an office complex, and, most iniquitously, a prison and torture chamber for the victims of witch hunts. Frightened by the house, where she lives with her father, teenager Amy Priestly uncovers its abominable past and soon finds herself and her father locked into a virtual reenactment of the hideous scenarios that occurred there years earlier." Libr J
"With consummate skill, Campbell gives this tale of the past's stranglehold upon the present the thick and suffocating texture of an inescapable nightmare." Publ Wkly

The one safe place. Forge 1996 c1995 383p o.p.
ISBN 0-312-86035-8 LC 96-2635
"A Tom Doherty Associates book"
First published 1995 in the United Kingdom
The protagonists of this suspense tale "are the Travises, American expatriates to England who run afoul of criminal lowlife Phil Fancy. After Phil is apprehended for forcing his way into the Travis home, events escalate tragically. Phil slips through legal loopholes with a light sentence. But Susanne Travis, a university instructor, is pilloried in the press for owning videos that violate Britain's tough censorship laws, and her husband falls prey to Phil's vengeful family. Equal horrors befall 12-year-old Marshall Travis, whom Phil's punk son, Darren, kidnaps and torments to win the regard of his relatives. Campbell is an expert at building terror subtly and indirectly." Publ Wkly

Pact of the fathers. Forge 2001 414p $26.95
ISBN 0-312-87869-9 LC 2001-40478
"A Tom Doherty Associates book"
"Acting student Daniella Logan is devoted to her father, and this adds to her burden of grief when he dies in a suspicious car crash at the novel's outset. The night of his funeral she inadvertently frightens a coven of knife-wielding men away from their inscrutable ritual at his graveside. Daniella's stubborn persistence investigating both events leads to the unsettling discovery that her dad may not have been the man she thought he was—and worse, that his surviving friends are inexplicably conspiring to silence her. . . . The novel's sinister B-movie imagery and sleekly paced frights put a dark gloss on what is ultimately a haunting reflection on the differences that painfully divide parents from children and the intransigence of the older and younger generations." Publ Wkly

Silent children. Forge 2000 352p $24.95
ISBN 0-312-87056-6 LC 00-24494
"A Tom Doherty Associates book"
"Years ago, a deranged man killed several children and then died himself; now a young boy and girl have disappeared, and their parents desperately try to find out what has happened to them and whether it's possible that the dead maniac isn't dead after all." Booklist
Campbell "has perfected a story style distinctive for its stifling atmosphere of dread and oblique approach to horror. Applying it here to the shocking theme of a serial child-killer, he has crafted a nail-biting psychological thriller." Publ Wkly

Campbell, Robert *See* Campbell, R. Wright, 1927-2000

Camus, Albert, 1913-1960

Exile and the kingdom; translated from the French by Justin O'Brien. Knopf 1958 213p o.p.
Original French edition, 1957
Contents: The adulterous woman; The renegade; The silent men; The guest; The artist at work; The growing stone
"Discipline of thought and style characterize [these] six short stories. . . The distinguishing marks of locales ranging from North Africa to Brazil are etched with telling detail, but it is the landscape of man's inner life which is most important here. The diverse protagonists—and it is intimated all men—are exiled from themselves, others, and the life of the spirit, but now and again a word or an action renews their courage to continue the pilgrimage." Booklist

The fall; translated from the French by Justin O'Brien. Knopf 1957 147p o.p.
Original French edition, 1956
"A former Parisian lawyer explains to a stranger in an Amsterdam bar his current profession of judge-penitent. His bitter honesty prevented him first from winning his own self-esteem through good deeds, then from exhausting his own self-condemnation through debauchery. Knowing that no man is ever innocent, he is still trying to forestall personal judgment by confession, by judging others, and by avoiding any situation demanding action." Reader's Ency. 4th edition

Camus, Albert, 1913-1960—*Continued*

The first man; translated from the French by David Hapgood. Knopf 1995 336p o.p.

ISBN 0-679-43937-4 LC 95-2668

Original French edition, 1994

"When Camus died in an automobile accident in 1960, a manuscript was found near him. It turned out to be the first chapters of his autobiographical novel. . . . The book covers the first 14 years of the life of Jacques Cormery, a.k.a. Albert Camus. First there is a 'search for the father,' the undercurrent of a boy's quest to fill a tragic vacuum created by his father's death when he is only a year old. The poverty and difficult circumstances in which he grows up in French Algeria make him feel like an outsider, even when he becomes an adult. Yet the memories of the child are filled with energy and physical intensity. The spontaneity of the narrative by an otherwise reserved writer makes this book a unique document for anyone interested in Camus." Libr J

The plague; translated from the French by Stuart Gilbert. Knopf 1948 278p o.p.

ISBN 0-394-44061-7

Original French edition, 1947

"Using an epidemic of bubonic plague in an Algerian city as a symbol for the absurdity of man's condition, Albert Camus has in this novel articulated his firm belief in mankind's heroism in struggling against the ultimate futility of life. The plague makes everyone in the city intensely aware both of mortality and of the fact that cooperation is the only logical consolation anyone will find in the face of certain death. Though each character, from doctor to priest, represents some aspect of mankind's attempts to deal with the absurd, none is a cardboard figure. The reader cares what happens to the men depicted here. One takes pleasure in the moments of deep human connection that leave us with the conviction that men are, on the whole, admirable." Shapiro. Fic for Youth. 3d edition

The stranger; translated from the French by Matthew Ward. Knopf 1988 123p $25

ISBN 0-394-53305-4 LC 83-48885

Original French edition, 1942; published in the United Kingdom with title: The outsider

"The new translation of Camus's classic is a cultural event. . . . With the domestications pruned away from the text, students will be as close to the original as another language will allow." Libr J

This novel "reveals the 'Absurd' as the condition of man, who feels himself a stranger in his world. Meursault refuses to 'play the game,' by telling the conventional social white lies demanded of him or by believing in human love or religious faith. The unemotional style of his narrative lays naked his motives—or his absence of motive—for his lack of grief over his mother's death, his affair with Marie, his killing an Arab in the hot Algerian sun. Having rejected by honest self-analysis all interpretations which could explain or justify his existence, he nevertheless discovers, while in prison awaiting execution, a passion for the simple fact of life itself." Reader's Ency. 4th edition

Canin, Ethan

Carry me across the water; a novel. Random House 2001 206p o.p.

ISBN 0-679-45679-1 LC 00-51812

"Living alone in a Boston apartment after his wife's death, 78-year-old millionaire beer magnate August Kleinman reviews the defining moments of his life: escape from Nazi Germany as a child, marriage to an Italian Catholic, and the reckless decision to start his own business. But mostly his thoughts turn to World War II and a tragic encounter he had with a young Japanese soldier." Libr J

This is a "short book, and it remains, despite its narrative sweep of time and geography, something of a chamber piece. But like the Bach cello suites that Kleinman plays on his stereo at night, it's a chamber piece that evokes intense and somber emotions." N Y Times Book Rev

For kings and planets; a novel. Random House 1998 335p o.p.

ISBN 0-679-41963-2

"When Missouri-bred Orno Tarcher comes to Columbia University and meets Marshall Emerson, the brilliant, unstable son of two charming New York professors, he tells himself, with anxious expectation, 'I am no longer among my own.' Marshall's wayward, debauched habits, in conjunction with his academic success, soon challenge Orno's long-held ideas about moral character and integrity. Their friendship's true test, however, comes when Orno falls in love with Marshall's sister, Simone, and discovers that the Emerson family's charisma masks a Jamesian history of manipulation and lies. In this bildungsroman, Canin writes about self-invention, loyalty, and the desire for experience with an uncomfortable, startling precision." New Yorker

The palace thief. Random House 1994 205p o.p.

LC 93-26888

Contents: Accountant; Batorsag and Szerelem; City of broken hearts; The palace thief

This "book presents us with four beautifully told long short stories. In each, a man muses over his past and realizes how little control he has had over pivotal moments in his life. . . . Canin proves himself adept at articulating moments of profound embarrassment followed by flashes of self-knowledge that are either invigorating or demoralizing. Moving and memorable." Booklist

Cannell, Dorothy

Bridesmaids revisited. Viking 2000 242p o.p.

ISBN 0-670-89205-X LC 00-38148

Interior decorator Ellie Haskell "hasn't thought about her late grandmother Sophia's three bridesmaids—Rosemary, Thora and Jane—in years. Then she receives a letter from Rosemary telling her that Sophia is trying to contact her from beyond the grave. With her saucy, uninvited helper, Mrs. Malloy, in tow, Ellie travels to the ancient Cambridgeshire village of Knells to investigate. . . . Cannell's smooth narration and her appealing, smart-mouthed characters charm you into suspending disbelief. The result is a thoroughly delightful puzzle." Publ Wkly

God save the Queen!. Bantam Bks. 1997 210p o.p.

LC 96-25041

"Gossingher Hall, in the middle of Lincolnshire, is the home of Sir Henry and his wife, Maud, who's been making her way up through the British class system.

Cannell, Dorothy—*Continued*

Gossinger Hall has been served faithfully by Hutchins the butler, who lives on the premises with his orphaned granddaughter, Flora. But when Sir Henry decides to leave Gossinger Hall to Hutchins, the butler winds up facedown in a twelfth-century privy. Flora, with the help of Sir Henry's heir, a young man named Vivian, are soon on the trail of the killer." Booklist

"Whether the action marches along in a stately country home or spins off in the bustling streets of London, there is no letup in the story's wit, charm and intrigue." Publ Wkly

How to murder your mother-in-law. Bantam Bks. 1994 261p o.p.

LC 93-31149

"After insisting that husband Ben's parents celebrate their anniversary with them at Merlin's Court, Ellie [Haskell] is dismayed when her in-laws reveal that their religious differences (she's Catholic, he's Jewish) prevented their legal marriage. . . . Then Ellie's father-in-law is caught skinny-dipping with a female friend, prompting mother-in-law Magdalene to leave him. Ellie seeks solace from friends in the village and discovers that everyone is suffering from a surfeit of mothers-in-law. A commiseration session among the afflicted daughters-in-law results in several vividly imagined murder scenarios—which, unfortunately, begin to happen." Booklist

The spring cleaning murders. Viking 1998 275p o.p.

ISBN 0-670-87571-6 LC 98-2827

"Ellie Haskell and husband Ben live in Chitterton Fells, where he runs a restaurant and she keeps house, tends their three-year-old twins, and occasionally investigates local murder. While attending a club meeting, Ellie discovers the fallen body of her new chairwoman, immediately suspects murder, and begins some insistent interrogating." Libr J

"Cannell's lively wit and acute insights into marriage, motherhood and murderous inclinations will delight fans as well as readers new to her high-spirited tales." Publ Wkly

The thin woman; an epicurean mystery. St. Martin's Press 1984 242p o.p.

LC 83-24565

"Overweight, overwrought interior designer Ellie Simons is reduced to hiring an escort for a family reunion at her Uncle Merlin's estate. Uncle Merlin dies shortly thereafter and leaves a strange will, specifying that Ellie lose 63 pounds, that her escort write a novel, and that they discover the estate's treasure. Their quest soon becomes an investigation into the murder of Uncle Merlin's mother 60 years before." Booklist

The trouble with Harriet. Viking 1999 274p $21.95

ISBN 0-670-88629-7 LC 99-17376

"Ellie Haskell and her husband, Ben, have left their three children with his parents and are about to depart Chitterton Falls, England, for a romantic vacation in France. But before they can get away, Ellie's gallivanting father, Morley, who abandoned her after her mother's death, returns with an urn containing the ashes of his most recent girlfriend, Harriet. . . . As Ellie hears the tale of her father's short tryst and his beloved's sudden death, she suspects that Harriet may have been involved in some shady business." Publ Wkly

"The fun is in the descriptions of Ellie's lovely home, the overwrought dialogue, and Ellie's distracted adoration of her perfect husband, the chef and cookbook writer." Booklist

The widows club. Bantam Bks. 1988 338p o.p.

LC 87-47913

"Ellie Simons has a great deal on her mind: her pending marriage to handsome Bentley Haskell; the opening of his restaurant in the charming English town of Chitterton Fells; the restoration of the castle Merlin's Court, where she and Ben live. Most compelling of all, Ellie must learn to feel comfortable with her newly thin body, celebrated in the first Cannell mystery, *The Thin Woman*. But from the bacchanalian wedding reception on, she runs into trouble. . . . Into her already chaotic life come Hyacinth and Primrose Tramwell, proprietors of Flowers Detection Agency, to enlist her help in an investigation. Chitterton Fells has been marked by a recent rash of murders, the victims all unfaithful husbands." Publ Wkly

Cannell, Stephen J.

Hollywood tough. St. Martin's Press 2003 346p $24.95

ISBN 0-312-29102-7 LC 2002-31878

"LAPD investigator Shane Scully agrees to return a favor to former snitch Nicky Marcella, a street hustler turned shady movie producer. He wants Shane to find Carol White, his former New Jersey high school classmate and an aspiring actress. What Shane finds is that she's abandoned her dreams for an abyss of drugs and prostitution, but her core of inherent decency touches him. When she's murdered he refuses to allow her to be dismissed as just another dead whore. . . . This is an entertaining mix of thrills, humor, and street justice." Booklist

Riding the snake; a novel. Morrow 1998 383p o.p.

ISBN 0-688-15805-6 LC 97-49674

"Drunken trust-fund jock Wheeler Cassidy is wasting his life and has lost his family's respect—especially when he's compared to his splendid brother, Prescott, a political power broker. When Prescott is murdered, Wheeler pairs up with beautiful Tanisha Williams, an African American detective in LAPD's Asian Crimes Task Force, to investigate. A second murder . . . sets them against formidable 'Willy' Wo Lap Ling, head of the notorious Hong Kong triad, and mainland éminence grise Chen Boda." Publ Wkly

Vertical coffin; Stephen J. Cannell. 1st ed. St. Martin's Press 2004 335p $24.95

ISBN 0-312-30425-0 LC 2003-58567

A thriller featuring LAPD cop, Shane Scully. "In this latest outing, he finds himself in the middle of a law enforcement territorial war when he begins to investigate the murder of one of his friends from the Los Angeles County Sheriff's Department. It seems as if both the sheriff and the feds arrived at the scene of the crime even though neither of their communications systems were compatible with the LAPD frequency. Shane is

Cannell, Stephen J.—*Continued*

teamed with a female sheriff, and together they find themselves without friends in any law enforcement agencies. . . . Cannell is, quite simply, one of the best police procedural writers today." Libr J

The Viking funeral. St. Martin's Press 2002 388p o.p.

ISBN 0-312-26960-9 LC 2001-48654

"It's been three years since LAPD cop Shane Scully's best friend and fellow cop Jody Dean blew his brains out—so what does it mean when Shane spots Jody driving in the next lane on the freeway? Shane's lover, Alexa Hamilton, herself a star in the LAPD, is skeptical of the sighting . . . until they find her boss dead in a faked suicide with a strange tattoo on his ankle. The tattoo is the symbol used by the Vikings, a group of brutal rogue cops in Jody's unit who were kicked off the force. A two-way radio at Sheperd's home leads Shane to Jody's hiding place, and it turns out he's involved in a lot more than just a rogue gang." Publ Wkly

"Scully is a likable protagonist who struggles with his personal life while staying a step ahead of a disturbed, dangerous adversary. A top-notch thriller with more than a little heart." Booklist

Cantor, Jay

Great Neck; a novel. Knopf 2002 703p $29.95

ISBN 0-375-41394-4 LC 2002-67123

This novel "starts in 1960 with a group of largely Jewish grade schoolers on Long Island learning the lessons of the Holocaust, then takes them through the radical decades of Freedom Summer, Weathermen, Black Power, bombs, and courts—as both defenders and defended. Meanwhile, the group is immortalized through comic-book characters drawn in their image by another member of the group (Billy Bad Ears, in the comic), a genius and best-selling cult favorite." Libr J

A novel "so rich in character and incident that you can't help wishing it a long shelf life and many devoted readers. Overflowing with brainpower—as though all the minds Cantor investigates were somehow networked and engaged in furious serial processing—it finds room for heart, too. It is, after all, anovel about friends." N Y Times Book Rev

Capote, Truman, 1924-1984

Answered prayers; the unfinished novel. Random House 1986 180p o.p.

ISBN 0-394-55645-3 LC 86-10110

"The first chapter, 'Unspoiled Monsters,' introduces the narrator, P. B. Jones, Capote's dark doppelgänger, who skids between high life and low life, working as a male prostitute to finance a promising first novel. The second, 'Kate McCloud,' introduces the odious Mr. Jones to an impossible love object, a mysterious society woman isolated by her sinister, rich husband. The third, 'La Côte Basque,' features Jones lunching *a deux* with a distressed Park Avenue matron who unloads her marital intimacies in a sodden aria of indiscretion. . . . Between the cloudbursts of malice there are flashes of prose in 'Answered Prayers' that bring the aching reminder of a more whole writer, prose that makes the heart sing and the narrative fly. Some of the character riffs are inspired." N Y Times Book Rev

Breakfast at Tiffany's

In Capote, T. Breakfast at Tiffany's: a short novel and three stories

Breakfast at Tiffany's: a short novel and three stories. Random House 1958 179p o.p.

ISBN 0-394-41770-4

Short stories included are: House of flowers; A diamond guitar; A Christmas memory

"'Breakfast at Tiffany's' tells the story of haunting and neurotic Holiday Golightly, Texan child-bride, girl-about-New York and friend of gangster czar, Sally Tomato, in a remarkable novelette that bears the Capote trademark of neat prose, multiple dimensions and unusual atmosphere." Ont Libr Rev

A Christmas memory. Random House 1966 c1956 45p o.p.

Appeared originally in Mademoiselle

An autobiographical story of a small boy's Christmas in Alabama and the joy of sharing it with his elderly cousin, Miss Sook Faulk

This book "is particularly a testimonial to the 60-year-old Miss Sook Faulk, who may not have been quite bright but who never stinted in her love of the boy she helped care for. Unpretentious, but touching." Best Sellers

also in Capote, T. Breakfast at Tiffany's: a short novel and three stories

The complete stories of Truman Capote; introduction by Reynolds Price. Random House 2004 300p $24.95

ISBN 0-679-64310-9 LC 2004-46876

Contents: The walls are cold; A mink of one's own; The shape of things; Jug of silver; Miriam; My side of the matter; Preacher's legend; A tree of night; The headless hawk; Shut a final door; Children on their birthdays; Master misery; The bargain; A diamond guitar; House of flowers; A Christmas memory; Among the paths to Eden; The Thanksgiving visitor; Mojave; One Christmas

"Now, for the first time, all of Capote's short stories are being published together, an event that signifies a renewed appreciation of his overall contribution to literature, for evidence is presented in this one volume that he should be ranked as a major American short story writer." Booklist

The grass harp. Random House 1951 181p o.p.

"After the death of his parents, Collin goes to live with his two aunts, Verna and Dolly. The former is wealthy and practical, the latter, whimsical and romantic. Dolly produces a cure for dropsy that she bottles and sells through the mail. Verna is ready to take over the operation and realize a large profit. To avoid this scheme, Collin, Dolly, and Catherine, a servant, go off to live in a treehouse, where they are joined by other eccentric characters. When Dolly dies, Collin is ready for his independence, having learned a valuable lesson about love and nonconformity." Shapiro. Fic for Youth. 3d edition

Other voices, other rooms. Random House 1968 231p o.p.

ISBN 0-394-43949-X

A novel describing the abnormal maturing of a loveless thirteen-year-old boy who goes to live with his father in a run-down Louisiana mansion peopled with ec-

Capote, Truman, 1924-1984—*Continued*
centric characters

"It is knowledge of the human heart which 'Other Voices, Other Rooms' gives us; and this is genuine achievement. It is not only a work of unusual beauty, but a work of unusual intelligence." N Y Her Trib Books

The Thanksgiving visitor. Random House 1968 c1967 63p o.p.
ISBN 0-394-44824-3

"If this volume seems thin . . . Capote has told his story with such precise economy that once inside the covers readers will no longer question the format. This is storytelling in the classic tradition." Times Lit Suppl

A tree of night, and other stories. Random House 1949 209p o.p.

Contents: Master Misery; Children on their birthdays; Shut a final door; Jug of silver; Miriam; The headless hawk; My side of the matter; A tree of night

Caputo, Philip

Acts of faith. Knopf 2005 669p $26.95
ISBN 0-375-41166-6 LC 2004-48982

"An evangelical Christian, a woman with a colonial past, and a crusading, multiracial Kenyan all have their reasons for joining Douglas Braithwaite as he flies supplies to the war-ravaged Sudan." Libr J

"Mr. Caputo writes with such authority that he's able to invest events that might seem improbable in another novelist's hands with an uncommon degree of verisimilitude, delineating not only the viewpoints of his Western visitors, but also those of the Sudanese rebels and their Islamic opponents with equally sure-handed drama and psychological ballast" N Y Times (Late N Y Ed)

Equation for evil; a novel. HarperCollins Pubs. 1996 488p o.p.
LC 95-46706

This novel opens "with a crime of fantastic brutality, the ambush and slaughter of a busload of Asian-American schoolchildren. With the gunman, Duane Boggs, dead by his own hand, a forensic psychologist named Leander Heartwood soon focuses his investigation on one of Boggs's acquaintances, Mace Weathers, a Mormon poster boy turned latter-day mystic. Aided by two detectives, Heartwood attempts to expose Mace's wickedness, even as he confronts his doubts about his own expertise." N Y Times Book Rev

The author "combines elements of a psychological thriller and police procedural in a novel that explores the issue of racial violence in considerable depth. The result is another riveting novel by one of America's master storytellers." Libr J

Horn of Africa. Holt & Co. 1980 487p o.p.
LC 79-27513

"Three men, two Americans and one Englishman, embark on a mission as mercenaries in Africa, involving gun-running and clandestine warfare. Their capacity for violence is related to events and drives in their own lives. Nordstrand, the most amoral of them, is a character that is indelibly drawn as are the horrible experiences lived through in desert treks. This author has been compared to Joseph Conrad and Graham Greene in his exploration of the deepest recesses of man's soul." Shapiro. Fic for Youth. 3d edition

The voyage. Knopf 1999 415p o.p.
ISBN 0-679-45039-4 LC 99-23568

In 1901, "a flinty New Englander suddenly orders his three sons, the oldest of whom is 16, to sail away from the Maine coast and stay away until September. 'Where are we supposed to go?' they ask. 'Don't much care,' he answers. So off they sail to face the series of adventures that make up most of the book, all the while trying to understand their seeming abandonment. Their story is reconstructed by one son's granddaughter, herself haunted by the mystery." Libr J

"Caputo, always a thoughtful, intelligent writer, has clearly researched his subject thoroughly and worked hard to integrate this haunted family's past and present." N Y Times Book Rev

Caras, Roger A.

(ed) Roger Caras' Treasury of great cat stories. See Roger Caras' Treasury of great cat stories

(ed) Roger Caras' Treasury of great dog stories. See Roger Caras' Treasury of great dog stories

Carcaterra, Lorenzo, 1954-

Apaches. Ballantine Bks. 1997 336p o.p.
ISBN 0-345-40101-8

This novel opens with the "brutal kidnapping of an innocent 12-year-old girl. But the kidnapper has made a deadly mistake. He has brought Boomer Frontieri back to life, back to the streets. And back into action. A New York City detective forced to retire after being wounded in a drug bust, Boomer thirsts to return to the life he loved—the life of a cop. When an old friend turns to him for help, Boomer has the excuse he needs." Publisher's note

Gangster. Ballantine Bks. 2001 376p o.p.
ISBN 0-345-40100-X LC 00-48594

Mafia boss "Angelo Vestieri lies dying in a hospital bed with two visitors by his side. One is Gabe, a man who as a child had been befriended and ultimately raised by Angelo. The other is Mary, initially introduced as a mysterious woman from Angelo's past who has come to witness his death. Through their recollections, we learn first of Angelo's rise from street urchin to boss, then of the development of his relationship with Gabe." Libr J

"What makes Carcaterra's portrait of Vestieri so effective is not only the 'adventures' Vestieri experiences in a career so cold and calculating, but also the author's psychological fathoming of the kind of character that turns to a life of organized crime." Booklist

Card, Orson Scott

Alvin Journeyman. TOR Bks. 1995 384p (Tales of Alvin Maker) o.p.
ISBN 0-312-85053-0 LC 95-22693

"A Tom Doherty Associates book"

Fourth title in the Tales of Alvin Maker series. "Driven from the Wobbish country by a girl's false accusation, [Alvin] returns to his birthplace in Hatrack River and promptly finds himself on trial for stealing the golden plough from Makepiece Smith and also facing lynching for helping fugitive slaves. Meanwhile, Alvin's younger brother, Calvin, is peddling his own Maker's skills with

Card, Orson Scott—*Continued*
more profit if many fewer scruples, both in America and in Europe. . . . From beginning to end, this novel is full of riches." Booklist
Followed by Heartfire

The call of earth. TOR Bks. 1993 304p il (Homecoming, v2) o.p.
LC 92-36971
"A Tom Doherty Associates book"
In this second volume of the Homecoming saga "the Oversoul must force a respected and brilliant general, nicknamed Moozh, to take over Basilica. He sets in motion forces that will destroy the city and thus disperse the Basilicans to spread the Oversoul's word throughout Harmony. . . . Although the plot unfolds at a more than leisurely pace, well-rounded characters keep it viable, and the dialogue is superb." Publ Wkly
Followed by The ships of earth

Children of the mind. TOR Bks. 1996 349p (Ender Wiggin) o.p.
ISBN 0-312-85395-5 LC 95-53262
"A Tom Doherty Associates book"
At the beginning of this fourth series title "Ender Wiggin has placed part of his consciousness and memory in two other bodies, one named after his brother Peter, the other after his sister Valentine. His own body is literally crumbling, and that is not the only problem. A human fleet is on the way to the planet of Lusitania to stop the deadly descolada virus by destroying the planet; meanwhile, the powers that be are also shutting down Ender's friend Jane, the sentient interstellar computer network who makes faster-than-light travel—and, therewith, discovery of the planet of origin of the descolada virus—possible." Booklist
Followed by Ender's shadow

The crystal city; Orson Scott Card. 1st ed. Tor 2003 384p (Tales of Alvin Maker) $25.95
ISBN 0-312-86483-3 LC 2003-55992
In this sixth of the Tales of Alvin Maker series, Alvin's precognitive wife, Peggy, sends Alvin to Nueva Barcelona (New Orleans) to rescue the slaves held there. At the same time a plague hits the city.

Earthborn. TOR Bks. 1995 378p (Homecoming, v5) o.p.
LC 95-5231
"A Tom Doherty Associates book"
The concluding volume of the Homecoming saga. "Of a group of humans from the distant planet Harmony searching for long-abandoned Earth, only one woman remains. Blessed and cursed with the immortality conferred upon her by the Cloak of the Starmaster, Shedemi watches from her orbiting starship as three Earth-born races struggle to overcome the prejudices that divide them. Card's protagonists confront their moral quandaries with a brutal and compassionate honesty." Libr J

Earthfall. TOR Bks. 1995 350p (Homecoming, v4) o.p.
LC 94-41993
"A Tom Doherty Associates book"
"The fourth volume of Homecoming, Card's grand saga of the human race's far-future return to Earth, takes the characters on a century-long starship voyage back to the old planet. They find it inhabited by two sapient races, one evolved from rats, the other from bats. The two are constantly hostile to each other but also symbiotically linked by their reproductive process. Meanwhile, the long-standing rivalry between the statesmanlike Nafai and the dictatorial Elemak nearly wrecks the voyage, then leads to open violence on Earth, with consequences for relations with the other two sapient Earth races." Booklist
"This action-packed, plot-rich installment features Card's typical virtues—well-drawn characters and a story driven by complex moral issues." Publ Wkly
Followed by Earthborn

Enchantment. Ballantine Pub. Group 1999 390p o.p.
ISBN 0-345-41687-2 LC 98-52444
"A Del Rey book"
"The fall of the Berlin Wall gives graduate student Ivan Smetski the opportunity to visit Russia, the land of his birth, and leads to the rediscovery of a magical woodland clearing he once stumbled upon as a child. His entry into that timeless place plunges him into an era of legends and fairy tales, entangling him in a web of sorcery and intrigue that crosses time and space and calls into question Ivan's ideas of love, honor, and bravery." Libr J
"The youthful protagonists, the elements of fantasy and romance, and Card's imaginative, humorous storytelling make this a winner for young adults." SLJ

Ender's game. TOR Bks. 1991 c1985 xxi, 226p $24.95; pa $6.99
ISBN 0-312-93208-1; 0-812-55070-6 (pa)
"A Tom Doherty Associates book"
A reissue of the title first published 1985
"Chosen as a six-year-old for his potential military genius, Ender Wiggin spends his childhood in outer space at the Battle School of the Belt. Severed from his family, isolated from his peers, and rigorously tested and trained, Ender pours all his talent into the war games that will one day repel the coming alien invasion." Libr J
"The key, of course, is Ender Wiggin himself. Mr. Card never makes the mistake of patronizing or sentimentalizing his hero. Alternately likable and insufferable, he is a convincing little Napoleon in short pants." N Y Times Book Rev

Ender's shadow. Doherty Assocs. 1999 379p (Ender Wiggin) $24.95
ISBN 0-312-86860-X LC 99-35824
In this fifth installment "Card has added a parallel novel that occupies the same time frame as *Ender's Game*, and chronicles many of the same events. Children are being tested, the best and the brightest being placed into a school where they will be trained for the eminent and final fight to the death between humanity and the insectlike 'Buggers.' *Shadow* shifts from Ender to Bean as the protagonist and presents the events from Bean's perspective, with his own unique viewpoints. Complex three-dimensional characters, a strong story line, and vivid writing all combine to make this an exceptional work." SLJ
Followed by Shadow of the Hegemon

Heartfire. TOR Bks. 1998 301p (Tales of Alvin Maker) o.p.
ISBN 0-312-85054-9 LC 98-3041

Card, Orson Scott—*Continued*

"A Tom Doherty Associates book"

This is the fifth title in the Tales of Alvin Maker series. "While Alvin Smith, blessed with the magical knack of Making, travels to the Puritan-controlled lands of New England in search of a way to realize his vision of a Crystal City, his wife, Peggy, seeks to use her own knack of seeing into the hearts of others to promote the abolition of slavery in the Crown Colonies of the South." Libr J

"Card's antebellum settings, dialogue and historical figures seem authentic and thoroughly researched, and, as always, he offers excellent differentiation of characters." Publ Wkly

Homebody; a novel. HarperCollins Pubs. 1998 291p o.p.

ISBN 0-06-017655-5 LC 97-37627

Widower Don Lark's efforts to restore the Bellamy "mansion to its former grandeur introduce him to a succession of women receptive to his emotional needs, including an amorous real estate agent, three dotty elderly neighbors who urge him to demolish the place and Sylvie Delaney, a squatter who has lived in the house secretly for a decade. All have been drawn to the mansion and its legacy of corrupted splendor through the shame of their private lives—and one turns out to be ghost. . . . The novel is a powerful tale of healing and redemption that skillfully balances supernatural horrors with spiritual uplift." Publ Wkly

Lost boys. HarperCollins Pubs. 1992 448p o.p.

LC 92-25506

"Step Fletcher, his wife DeAnne, and their children have just moved to Steuben, North Carolina, where there has been a rash of mysterious disappearances. Plagued by various problems, the religious Fletcher family slowly adjusts to the community. Eight-year-old son Stevie, however, spends all his spare time with his imaginary friends. Preoccupied with settling in their new home, Step and DeAnne fail to understand the connection between Stevie's friends and the young boys' disappearances. Almost too late, Stevie makes the ultimate sacrifice to convince his family that his imaginary friends are real." Libr J

"Most of this absorbing novel has the pull of family drama with an overlayer of rising suspense. . . . Though some readers may find the fantastic plot elements jarring, Card's easy and natural prose goes a long way toward authenticating the supernatural intrusion." Publ Wkly

Magic street. Del Rey/Ballantine Books 2005 397p $24.95

ISBN 0345416899 LC 2004065524

"The young boy known as Mack Street lives with his adopted parents in Los Angeles, aware of his strange origins (he was found in a grocery sack) and unique and sometimes terrifying gift–the ability to dream the dreams of others. As Mack grows up, he learns how to handle his gift, or so it seems until his talent leads him to the land of Fairy. Veteran award-winning sf author Card . . . turns to modern fantasy in his portrayal of a young African American man caught between two worlds and burdened with a responsibility to both of them. The author's always elegant prose and storytelling talent add a dimension of grace and morality to his work." Libr J

Maps in a mirror; the short fiction of Orson Scott Card. TOR Bks. 1990 675p $19.95

ISBN 0-312-85047-6 LC 90-38896

"A Tom Doherty Associates book"

This collection features "46 pieces by an exceptional writer. Card's talents are represented by fantasy, science fiction, horror, poetry, and the stories that launched his sagas of Alvin Maker and Ender Wiggins. A substantial amount of autobiographical discussion of each story's origin enhances the volume's high value." Booklist

The memory of earth. TOR Bks. 1992 xx, 294p (Homecoming, v1) o.p.

LC 91-36596

"A Tom Doherty Associates book"

The first novel of the Homecoming saga "introduces us to the city of Basilica on the far-future planet of Harmony. The Oversoul, the sentient computer that has kept the Harmonians from developing destructive cultural patterns or technology, is deteriorating, and it needs to be returned to Earth for restoration. To accomplish this, the computer must begin the technological and social development of Harmony in the direction of spaceflight. Its chosen method is 'visions,' which are sent to a trader and clan chief and his youngest son, an event that promptly puts the whole family in danger of life and fortune and drives them into exile." Booklist

"As a maker of visions and a creator of heroes whose prime directive is compassion, Card is not to be outdone." Libr J

Followed by The call of earth

Prentice Alvin. Doherty Assocs. 1989 342p (Tales of Alvin Maker) o.p.

LC 88-39927

"A TOR book"

In this third Tales of Alvin Maker title "a country schoolteacher and the child of a runaway slave find their destinies entwined with that of Alvin Miller, whose talent for 'making' has marked him for destruction by the evil force known as the Unmaker. Card's epic tale of a magical, alternate America demonstrates his skill in graceful storytelling." Libr J

Followed by Alvin Journeyman

Red prophet. Doherty Assocs. 1988 311p (Tales of Alvin Maker) o.p.

LC 87-50873

"A TOR book"

In this second volume of the Tales of Alvin Maker series "young Alvin Miller's magical talent for making things whole becomes the focus of a desperate race to prevent a bloodthirsty war between the Indians and the white settlers in North America." Libr J

"This novel superbly demonstrates Card's solid historical research, keen understanding of religious experience, and, most of all, his mastery of the art of storytelling." Booklist

Followed by Prentice Alvin

Seventh son. Doherty Assocs. 1987 241p (Tales of Alvin Maker) o.p.

LC 86-51490

"A TOR book"

A "fantasy set in early nineteenth century of an alternate-world America. Settlers beyond the Appalachians have brought with them powerful folk magic—charms,

Card, Orson Scott—*Continued*
hexes, petitions—to ease the hard work and danger of everyday life. Into this world is born Alvin Miller, a seventh son carrying powerful magic. Unfortunately, Somebody or Something is determined that Alvin won't grow up." Booklist

"This beguiling book recalls Robert Penn Warren in its robust but reflective blend of folktale, history, parable and personal testimony, pioneer narrative." Publ Wkly

Followed by Red prophet

Shadow of the giant. Tor 2005 384p $25.95
ISBN 0-312-85758-6 LC 2004-66083

"A Tom Doherty Associates book"

The eighth installment in the Ender Wiggins saga. "The imminent death of Bean, a superhuman 20-something Battle School graduate who suffers from uncontrolled growth due to a genetic disorder, leaves little time for Peter the Hegemon, Ender's older brother, to set up a single world government and for Bean and his wife and former classmate, Petra, to reclaim all their stolen children. When Card's focus strays from his characters into pure politics, the story loses power, but it's recharged as soon as he returns to the well-drawn interactions among Bean's Battle School classmates whose decisions will determine Earth's fate." Publ Wkly

Shadow of the Hegemon. TOR Bks. 2000 365p $25.95
ISBN 0-312-87651-3 LC 00-31678

"A Tom Doherty Associates book"

Sequel to Ender's shadow

This sixth installment "continues the exploits of Bean, Ender's strategist and friend, juxtaposing them with the deadly challenges faced by 14-year-old Petra Arkanian, another member of Ender's team. Now that the war against the buggers is over, the Battle School's graduates have returned home, and someone is kidnapping them." Booklist

"The complexity and serious treatment of the book's young protagonists will attract many sophisticated YA readers, while Card's impeccable prose, fast pacing and political intrigue will appeal to adult fans of spy novels, thrillers and science fiction." Publ Wkly

Shadow puppets. TOR Bks. 2002 348p $25.95
ISBN 0-7653-0017-6

Sequel to: Shadow of the Hegemon

The seventh installment in the Ender Wiggins saga. "In the aftermath of the war against the alien insectoid Formics, the people of Earth experienced a period of unity under the benevolent rulership of the Hegemon Peter Wiggin, brother of war hero Ender Wiggin. As the fragile political peace erodes and internal wars threaten to erupt, the child-warriors of the Battle School—now young adults skilled in the arts of leadership and politics—struggle to bring about a new kind of peace despite the efforts of traitors in their midst." Libr J

The ships of earth. TOR Bks. 1994 382p (Homecoming, v3) o.p.
LC 93-42549

"A Tom Doherty Associates book"

This third novel in the Homecoming series "is set on the distant planet Harmony, 40 million years after its settlement by control freaks who programmed a supercomputer to keep the peace forever by stunting technological development among their descendants. Now the supercomputer, known as the Oversoul, is breaking down; to carry on its mission, it has recruited a band of humans from the female-dominated city of Basilica to return to Earth for spare parts and perhaps new programming. To reach the long-forgotten space station, this band must travel through a desert wilderness guided only by the Oversoul." N Y Times Book Rev

"Throughout, Card weaves thoughts on such matters as religion, tradition and the needs of the community versus those of the individual, using Biblical allusions to drive home his points." Publ Wkly

Followed by Earthfall

Speaker for the Dead. TOR Bks. 1986 415p (Ender Wiggin) $24.95
ISBN 0-312-93738-5 LC 85-51765

"A Tom Doherty Associates book"

In this second title in the series Ender Wiggin becomes "Speaker for the Dead out of remorse over his role in the unnecessary destruction of the Buggers. In his new identity, Wiggin plays a vital role in preventing war when a second nonhuman intelligent race—even more incomprehensible than the Buggers—is discovered. This book lacks the sheer dramatic power of Ender's transformation from child into warlord as portrayed in its predecessor. However, it benefits from increased dramatic unity, a well-developed background and supporting cast on the colony planet Lusitania, and the author's customarily stylish writing." Booklist

Followed by Xenocide

Treasure box; a novel. HarperCollins Pubs. 1996 310p o.p.
LC 96-16248

"At age 11, Quentin Fears is devastated by his older sister Lizzy's death. Subsequently, he grows up to be a lonely man, obsessed with memories of Lizzy. He becomes extremely wealthy, yet everything he does centers around Lizzy. He even picks a wife who reminds him of her. Madeleine, the woman with whom he falls in love and marries in a matter of weeks, turns out to be an apparition invented by an evil witch." Libr J

"Although the story moves toward a powerful climax, its primary pleasures are more subtle: strong character development and complex motivations, a mystery to solve, the discovery of wheels within wheels." Publ Wkly

Xenocide. TOR Bks. 1991 394p (Ender Wiggin) o.p.
LC 90-27108

"A Tom Doherty Associates book"

Third title in the author's distant future series about Ender Wiggin. "As an armed fleet from Starways Congress hurtles through space towards the rebellious planet Lusitania, Ender Wiggin, his sister Valentine, and his family search for a miracle that will preserve the existence of three intelligent and vastly different species. As a storyteller, Card excels in portraying the quiet drama of wars fought not on battlefields but in the hearts and minds of his characters." Libr J

Followed by Children of the mind

Carey, Edward, 1970-

Alva & Irva; the twins who saved a city. Harcourt 2003 207p il map $24

ISBN 0-15-100782-9 LC 2002-13701

"Entralia, the fictitious metropolis at the heart of Edward Carey's. . . novel, exists not only in our imagination and in the pages of 'Alva & Irva' (which serves as Entralia's one and only guidebook) but in the form of tiny plasticine models of its streets and houses, seen in the appealingly smudgy photographs that punctuate the novel. A re-creation of Entralia also appears in the story of 'Alva & Irva,' since the twins of the book's title are the designer and sculptor, respectively, of their native city in miniature." N Y Times Book Rev

This novel is "mock epical in its consequential-ridiculous tone. . .and comedically symphonic in the precision and daffy chasteness of its diction. For all its ludicrousness, it is honorably pathetic, too—a genuine human comedy," Booklist

Carey, Jacqueline

The Crossley baby. Ballantine Bks. 2003 287p $23.95

ISBN 0-345-45990-3 LC 2003-545383

"Having a baby changes everything. But when your're congenitally competitive sisters, like Jean and Sunny Crossley, each vying for the right to raise their deceased sister's daughter, the more things change, the more they stay the same. A free-spirited single mom, Bridget dies during a routine operation, leaving custody of baby Jade in question. As a hotshot headhunter married more to her career than to her husband, Jean is childless by choice, but when Jade is orphaned, Jean surprises everyone by filing for adoption and surprises no one by simultaneously filing a malpractice suit. Meanwhile, Sunny, an overachieving soccer mom with two kids of her own, stays true to her nature, blithely assuming that Jade will live with her." Booklist

"If the book is a little too cluttered with interior monologues, Carey is nonetheless an engaging and often funny writer. . . . Her sharp descriptions of the sisters' various milieus give the novel its piquancy." Publ Wkly

Carey, Peter

Jack Maggs. Knopf 1998 c1997 306p $24

ISBN 0-679-44008-9 LC 97-36893

First published 1997 in the United Kingdom

"The central figure in this story, which contains many parallels to Dickens' life and work, is one Jack Maggs, . . . a convicted thief who has returned to London from Australia, where he has become a respected landowner, to seek out a young man he considers his son. Still a wanted felon in England, Maggs secures a position as a footman while he searches for his heir. Soon he has become embroiled in the affairs of his employer, Mr. Buckle, and in the life of a writer and would-be mesmerist, Tobias Oates." Booklist

"Call it Great Expectations through a Nabokovian prism (Maggs/Magwitch, Phipps/Pip and, of course, Oates as a likeness of Dickens); call it pomo and/or postcolonial faux-Victoriana, if you like. But whatever you call it, Jack Maggs is surely one of the most delightful packages of stories-within-stories around." Nation

My life as a fake. Knopf 2003 266p $24

ISBN 0-375-41498-3 LC 2003-52746

A novel told through the "eyes of Lady Sarah Wode-Douglass, editor of a struggling but prestigious London poetry journal, who one day in the early 1970s finds herself accompanying an old family friend, poet and novelist John Slater, out to Malaysia. There they encounter an eccentric Australian expatriate, Christopher Chubb, who concocted, Slater says, a huge literary hoax in Australia just after the war, creating an imaginary genius poet, Bob McCorkle, whose publication by a litle magazine led to the suicide of the magazine's editor. Now Chubb offers Lady Sarah a page of poetry that shows undoubted genius and claims it is from a book in his possession. Lady Sarah's every acquisitive instinct is inflamed, but to get her hands on the book she has to listen, as Chubb inflicts on her, Ancient Mariner-like, the amazing story of his own epic struggle with McCorkle." Publ Wkly

This work "is so confidently brilliant, so economical yet lively in its writing, so tightly fitted and continuously startling in its plot that something, we feel, must be wrong with it. It ends in a bit of a rush, and left several questions dangling in this reader's mind. Unfortunately, to spell out those questions would be to betray too much of an intricate fictional construct where little is as it first seems and fantastic developments unfold like scenes on a fragile paper fan." New Yorker

Oscar & Lucinda. Harper & Row 1988 433p o.p.

ISBN 0-06-015908-1 LC 87-46125

"Oscar is a shy, gawky, Oxford-educated Church of England minister with a tortured conscience; Lucinda is a willful, eccentric Australian who sinks her family inheritance into a glass factory; and the basis for the star-crossed love that develops between them is a shared passion for gambling. They meet on the boat to Sydney, Oscar becomes Lucinda's lodger after being defrocked for his 'vice' and, finally, leaving a trail of scandal behind them, they construct a glass church in the Outback, their wildest gamble yet." Publ Wkly

"Like the best fiction, Oscar and Lucinda does not require a choice between its alternative visions. It offers instead an enchanting contradiction, a mirror and a glass, a joyous reflection of how much and how little mere mortals are ever allowed to see." Time

True history of the Kelly gang. Knopf 2001 349p o.p.

ISBN 0-375-41084-8 LC 00-42853

This novel, purporting to be the confession of Australian outlaw Ned Kelly, is couched as an "apologia drawn from 13 parcels of dogeared papers Kelly has written while on the run, 'True History' is dedicated to the infant daughter he has yet to see." N Y Times Book Rev

"In this bracing narrative, Carey has given Kelly back his tongue with a style that rips like a falling tree. The Australian-born author is something of a genius in these acts of literary ventriloquism." Christ Sci Monit

Carlson, Ron, 1947-

At the Jim Bridger; stories. Picador 2002 194p $23

ISBN 0-312-28605-8 LC 2001-59065

Carlson, Ron, 1947-—*Continued*

Contents: Towel season; At the Jim Bridger; The clicker at tips; Disclaimer; The ordinary son; Evil Eye Allen; At Copper View; Single woman for long walks on the beach; The potato gun; Gary Garrison's wedding vows; At the El Sol

"With a precision and consistency rarely achieved in similar collections, this volume should earn Carlson continued, well-deserved recognition." Publ Wkly

Carr, Caleb, 1955-

The alienist. Random House 1994 496p o.p.
LC 93-32766

"A society-born police reporter and an enigmatic abnormal psychologist—the 'alienist' of the title—are recruited in 1896 by New York's reform police commissioner Teddy Roosevelt to track down a serial killer who is slaughtering boy prostitutes. The investigators are opposed at every step by crime bosses and city's hidden rulers (including J. Pierpont Morgan); they distrust the alienist's novel methods and would rather conceal evidence of the murders than court publicity." Libr J

"This story boasts a veracious historical feel and a tight plot that keeps open the murderer's identity to the end. An original that fits no established mystery niche." Booklist

Followed by The angel of darkness

The angel of darkness. Random House 1997 629p o.p.
LC 97-25063

Sequel to The alienist

In this mystery thriller set in turn-of-the century New York, pioneering child psychologist Dr. Laszlo Kreizler and his idiosyncratic cohorts "gather evidence against the monstrous Libby Hatch, a serial killer whose kidnapping of an infant gets Kreizler on her trail and smack up against society's sentiments about the sanctity of women. Carr also offers some courtroom dramatics as Libby is put on trial, defended by Clarence Darrow." Publ Wkly

Carr "is an adept miniaturist, and he succeeds in evoking the wonderful grotesqueries of old New York without straying into sub-Dickensian caricature." N Y Times Book Rev

Killing time; a novel. Random House 2000 274p o.p.
ISBN 0-679-46332-1 LC 00-59112

"The year is 2023, and narrator Dr. Gideon Wolfe, a noted criminal psychologist, has just been asked to solve the murder of a special-effects man. The victim left behind an encrypted computer disc that revealed the existence of conspiracies at the highest level. Someone out there has been manipulating information to mislead and even terrorize the public. Who are they, and why are they doing this?. . . . Carr's well-written prose deftly combines character development and a fast-paced plot." Libr J

Carr, Philippa, 1906-1993

For works written by this author under other names see Holt, Victoria, 1906-1993; Plaidy, Jean, 1906-1993

The black swan. Putnam 1990 350p o.p.
LC 89-28545

In this Daughters of England novel "Carr continues the story of Lucie, the devoted daughter of Benedict Lansdon, a member of Parliament and close friend of Prime Minister Gladstone—until they differed over the hotly contested issue of home rule for Ireland. Lucie's life is radically altered by the Irish question: it leads to her father's assassination and her marriage to a terrorist in disguise." Booklist

"The family's complex troubles are so deftly presented that readers willingly follow intimations of ghosts, disguises and violent events that bedevil the characters." Publ Wkly

Daughters of England. Putnam 1995 308p o.p.
LC 94-33987

This is a "coming-of-age novel set during the 20 years following Oliver Cromwell's rule. Sarah, raised in a strict Puritan family of moderate means is swept off her feet by Lord Rosslyn and innocently marries him, unaware that he is already married. Appalled by this sinful relationship, she immediately leaves him, and friends help her raise her daughter, Kate. However, illness strikes and Sarah dies at a young age. The novel continues as Kate relates the events in her life; she lives on her father's estate with her stepbrother and new friends as the turmoil in the country escalates. The complex plot moves quickly, and the characters are well developed and believable." SLJ

Voices in a haunted room. Putnam 1984 335p o.p.
LC 84-4220

In this installment in the author's multigenerational Daughters of England series "young Claudine de Tournville further tangles the family tree when she marries one of the twin sons of her stepfather. It is the other twin, however, mysterious and dashing Jonathan, to whom she is drawn and with whom she has an adulterous affair. How Claudine squares her guilt and contributes to the continuation of the comfortable family lifestyle is worked out mainly in an England that resonates with the imminence of Napoleon's sway and its consequences for the French relatives." Publ Wkly

Carroll, James

The city below. Houghton Mifflin 1994 422p o.p.
LC 93-40837

"In this sequel to *Mortal Friends* [1978] we again meet the Doyle brothers, who are no longer inseparable. Coming of age in the turbulent 1960s, Nick has turned to organized crime, while Terry has left the seminary for the promised Camelot of the Kennedys. Boston is a maelstrom of religion, politics, bigotry, and racism. Indeed, the city itself is the central character in this Cain-and-Abel saga. Terry returns home often as a Kennedy campaign worker and later as an aide to Senator Teddy, and with each return he clashes with the dark under-belly of Boston and with Nick." Libr J

"Mr. Carroll's story is a rich, seductive meld of characters real and fictive, of history and fancy, a tale that substantiates an Irish chestnut: every lie is a truth somewhere in time." N Y Times Book Rev

Carroll, James—*Continued*

Fault lines. Little, Brown 1980 248p o.p.
LC 80-36756

The title of this novel "alludes to the complexities of strained human relationships. David Dolan, once a notorious, draft-dodging radical, returns to the States after eight years in Canada and Sweden teaching contemporary American literature. Disappointment, remorse, guilt, and longing complicate his search for a new beginning as he confronts an old lawyer friend (who cannot help), his aging mother (who can), and his dead (in Vietnam) brother's widow, Eddie, a writer now married to, and estranged from, ultra-movie star Cheney McCoy. The three principals and their lines of fault and guilt converge on Hunter's Island, Maine, where Eddie has sent her son." Libr J

"Mr. Carroll has told his story from all the characters' points of view—which is to say that the narrator's voice jumps from one character's mind to another's even within a single conversation. And by doing so he's made his people too strong and complex to be reduced to mere agents of the action." Books of the Times

Memorial bridge. Houghton Mifflin 1991 495p o.p.
LC 90-28730

"An Irish Catholic seminarian who drops out just before final vows, Sean Dillon works in the famed Depression-era Chicago stockyards to finance his way through night law school. He nearly fails to get his law degree when he misses his final exam because he stayed late to pull the corpse of a murdered man from a blood drainage pipe in the slaughterhouse. In seeking justice for the murdered man, Sean finds both the love of his life, Cass Ryan, the victim's niece, and his life's work in the FBI. Finally, as a Pentagon general, he comes to agree with his conscientious objector son that America has created a slaughterhouse in Vietnam and that the war must be stopped." Libr J

"'Memorial Bridge' is meticulously researched, carefully judicious about still-controversial topics and, frequently, wonderfully written." N Y Times Book Rev

Prince of peace. Little, Brown 1984 531p o.p.
LC 84-14336

This novel "explores the complex world of faith, action, and personal conviction revealed when 50-year-old Benedictine lay brother Frank Durkin returns to 1982 New York to bury his best friend, renegade ex-priest Michael Maguire. Durkin's narration places Maguire firmly in the forefront—as athletic seminarian in Washington, D.C., as anti-war demonstrator and spokesman, as 'other man' to Durkin's ex-wife Carolyn (an ex-nun), and, finally, as symbol of moral integrity wronged when church authorities forbid his burial in consecrated ground." Libr J

"Carroll's narrative is gracefully rendered, his dialogue usually true, and, despite occasional lapses into left-wing propaganda, he ultimately reaffirms in many ways the hope and timeless resilience of the Catholic church." Booklist

Secret father. Houghton Mifflin 2003 344p $25
ISBN 0-618-15284-9 LC 2003-41725

This work "focuses on a single weekend in 1961, just before the Berlin Wall created an impenetrable barrier between East and West. On an idealistic lark, three American high school students travel to the Communistic side of Berlin for the May Day parade. Ensnared by the East Germans for alleged currency violations, they are clapped in jail. Meanwhile, their frantic parents mobilize, with two of them traveling to Berlin to pluck the kids loose. Surprisingly, this generic plot supports a beautifully textured exploration of relationships between husbands and wives, parents and sons, friends and lovers." Libr J

Carroll, Jonathan, 1949-

The wooden sea. TOR Bks. 2001 302p o.p.
ISBN 0-312-87823-0 LC 00-47938

"A Tom Doherty Associates book"

"Frannie McCabe, a mellowing middle-aged former bad boy who is now the police chief of a Hudson Valley town, opens the trunk of his car to discover the body of the pet pit bull he has just buried. But then things get weird . . . McCabe finds himself teamed up with his seventeen-year-old self in a time-travel fantasy-thriller, set almost entirely in his home town but involving aliens, cold fusion, and a sinister twenty-first-century Dutch entrepreneur. The result is a quirky piece of intelligent pop that is also surprisingly moving." New Yorker

Carson, Tom, 1956-

Gilligan's wake. Picador 2003 342p $25
ISBN 0-312-29123-X LC 2002-29256

Carson "uses characters from the Gilligan's Island TV series to explore 20th-century political, literary, and pop culture. Each character is allotted a chapter, starting with Gilligan, who thinks that he's hanging out with Lawrence Ferlinghetti in San Francisco when, in fact, he is in a mental institution in Minnesota. The skipper meets John Kennedy in the Pacific. Thurston Howell III helps Alger Hiss get a government job, and Howell's wife uses opium with Gatsby's love, Daisy Buchanan. Then there's Ginger, who explores Hollywood's low-budget film industry, as the Professor works with Oppenheimer on the bomb and Mary Anne moves from Kansas to Paris and has an affair with filmmaker Jean-Luc something or other." Libr J

"The pastiche is surprisingly smart and entertaining; it offers some genuinely inspired sketches for those who know their television—and their Cold War history." Publ Wkly

Carter, Angela, 1940-1992

Burning your boats; the collected short stories; with an introduction by Salman Rushdie. Holt & Co. 1996 462p o.p.
ISBN 0-8050-4462-0 LC 95-26312

"A John Macrae book"

Contents: The man who loved a double bass; A very, very great lady and her son at home; A Victorian fable; A souvenir of Japan; The executioner's beautiful daughter; The loves of Lady Purple; The smile of winter; Penetrating to the heart of the forest; Flesh and the mirror; Master; Reflections; Elegy for a freelance; The bloody chamber; The courtship of Mr. Lyon; The tiger's bride; Puss-in-boots; The Erl-King; The snow child; The lady of the house of love; The werewolf; The company of wolves; Wolf-Alice; Black Venus; The kiss; Our Lady of the Massacre; The cabinet of Edgar Allan Poe; Overture

Carter, Angela, 1940-1992—*Continued*

and incidental music for *A midsummer night's dream*; Peter and the wolf; The kitchen child; The Fall River axe murders; Lizzie's tiger; John Ford's *'Tis pity she's a whore*; Gun for the Devil; The merchant of shadows; The ghost ships; In Pantoland; Ashputtle; Alice in Prague; Impressions: The wrightsman Magdalene; The Scarlet House; The snow pavilion; The quilt maker

"Gathered from 30 years of Carter's writing life, this collection is arranged chronologically to reveal her evolution as a writer as well as her consistent preoccupation with the Gothic. . . . As her friend Salman Rushdie writes in his moving introduction, Carter is not an easy read, but there are many rewards for the persistent." Libr J

Nights at the circus. Viking 1985 294p o.p.
ISBN 0-670-80375-8 LC 84-40459

The protagonist of this novel is "a six-foot-two-inch woman aerialist with wings. The setting is turn of the century London, St. Petersburg, and Siberia. An American journalist, Jack Walser, has been sent to interview Sophia, known as Fevvers to her friends, and is so intrigued by her account of her childhood that he joins the circus as a clown." Libr J

"Carter describes a locale as exotic to the traditional reader as her women are to Walser and, by implication, all men; and she undercuts accepted Western history as she goes." New Republic

Wise children. Farrar, Straus & Giroux 1992 c1991 234p o.p.
ISBN 0-374-29133-0 LC 91-19920

First published 1991 in the United Kingdom

"On their 75th birthday, we meet Dora and Nora Chance, former dancers and illegitimate twin daughters of one of Britain's leading theatrical actors. They relate their colorful and amusing family history as the novel unfolds, describing their often strained relations with the legitimate branch of the family." Libr J

A "giddy souffle of a novel, mock memoir, mock confession, mock romance, a post-modernist parody of a familiar genre. . . . 'Wise Children' may not be Angela Carter's most provocative and arresting work of fiction, but it inhabits its own manic universe, and would probably translate, with the right talent, into a spirited, bawdy musical comedy-farce of the kind in which the Chance sisters themselves performed, long ago." N Y Times Book Rev

Carter, Stephen L.

The emperor of Ocean Park. Knopf 2002 657p $26.95
ISBN 0-375-41363-4 LC 2001-38227

This "tale of ambition, revenge and the power of familial obligations is set in the privileged environs of an Ivy League law school, Martha's Vineyard, and Washington, D.C. Oliver Garland is the demanding but emotionally distant patriarch of an elite, affluent African American family used to special privileges and close relationships with the powerful in government, business, and the criminal underworld. Oliver's death sparks renewed interest in his political career—as a vitriolic conservative, embittered by a failed bid for the U.S. Supreme Court—and concern in many quarters about 'arrangements' he has made in the event of his demise. Garland's son Talcott, a law professor, is very reluctantly drawn into the intrigue. . . . An elegantly nuanced novel, with finely drawn characters, a challenging plot, and perfect pacing." Booklist

Carter, Vincent O., 1924-1983

Such sweet thunder; foreword by Herbert R. Lottman. Steerforth Press 2003 537p $25.95
ISBN 1-58642-058-5 LC 2002-154280

"Written in 1963 and shelved, this hefty, astonishing novel by a black American expatriate who died in 1983 tells—in electric modernist vernacular prose—the story of a black child's life in Jim Crow America. In France during WWII, soldier Amerigo Jones thinks back on his youth in the 1920s and '30s in a black community resembling the author's native Kansas City." Publ Wkly

Carver, Caroline

Blood Junction. Mysterious Press 2002 323p o.p.
ISBN 0-89296-770-6 LC 2002-20099

This "thriller opens with the deadly massacre of an Aboriginal family, which took place almost 50 years ago in the town of Cooinda, earning it the nickname 'Blood Junction.' A half-century later, journalist India Kane is drawn to the town with the promise of information about her own past. What she gets instead is jail time, having been arrested for a double murder. India knows no one and must rely on strangers in her efforts to figure out the connections among the murders, the lost generation of Aborigines, and her own tangled history. Though the novel is set in present-day Australia, the author deftly evokes the claustrophobic feeling of a 19th-century Western frontier town." Libr J

Carver, Raymond

Cathedral; stories. Knopf 1983 227p o.p.
LC 83-47779

Contents: Feathers; Chef's house; Preservation; The compartment; A small, good thing; Vitamins; Careful; Where I'm calling from; The train; Fever; The bridle; Cathedral

A "Dickensian tension, the sense of holding back a wave of emotionalism, of heartbreak or rage or faith, galvanizes much of Cathedral—with character after character poised on the edge of some abyss, the verge of despair." N Y Rev Books

What we talk about when we talk about love; stories. Knopf 1981 159p o.p.
LC 80-21752

Contents: Why don't you dance; Viewfinder; Mr. Coffee and Mr. Fixit; Gazebo; I could see the smallest things; Sacks; The bath; Tell the women we're going; After the denim; So much water so close to home; The third thing that killed my father off; A serious talk; The calm; Popular mechanics; Everything stuck to him; What we talk about when we talk about love; One more thing

"In spare, deft, precise prose, whole lives are portrayed in a single second as Carver briefly exposes his doom-ridden characters to one startling flash of agonizing self-recognition. These disturbing images remain long in the memory even after their immediate impression has disappeared." Booklist

Carver, Raymond—*Continued*

Where I'm calling from; new and selected stories. Atlantic Monthly Press 1988 393p o.p.
LC 87-36778

Contents: Nobody said anything; Bicycles, muscles, cigarettes; The student's wife; They're not your husband; What do you do in San Francisco?; Fat; What's in Alaska?; Neighbors; Put yourself in my shoes; Collectors; Why, honey?; Are these actual miles?; Gazebo; One more thing; Little things; Why don't you dance?; A serious talk; What we talk about when we talk about love; Distance; The third thing that killed my father off; So much water so close to home; The calm; Vitamins; Careful; Where I'm calling from; Chef's house; Fever; Feathers; Cathedral; A small, good thing; Boxes; Whoever was using this bed; Intimacy; Menudo; Elephant; Blackbird pie; Errand

"Carver dwells on the commonplace: the outwardly small but personally consequential bad turn of fortune in ordinary lives. His people are the kind other people easily overlook. . . . But Carver, in his flat style, renders them resonant of common human experience: plain folks always having to face adversity." Booklist

Cary, Arthur Joyce Lunel *See* Cary, Joyce, 1888-1957

Cary, Joyce, 1888-1957

The horse's mouth; a novel. Harper & Row 1950 311p o.p.

The third volume in the trilogy that began with Herself surprised (1948) and To be a pilgrim (1949)

First published 1944 in the United Kingdom

Gulley Jimson is an "artist newly released from prison. At 67, he has finally gained some critical acclaim. His aspirations to paint and live comfortably off the fruits of his achievements are thwarted, however, by his own desire to change artistically and by his accidental killing of a former model, Sara Monday. Gulley is a charming and humorous hero, constanly spouting his ideas on art and London and vividly describing the people around him." Shapiro. Fic for Youth. 3d edition

"The book is crammed with characters and picaresque episodes, and its fire and gusto never once flag. It is a comic hymn to life, but it has nobility as well. Depicting low life, it blazes with an image of the highest life of all—that of the creative imagination." Burgess. 99 Novels

Casey, John, 1939-

Spartina. Knopf 1989 375p o.p.
LC 88-45765

"Dick Pierce is an angry man because he has seen property belonging to his family in his fishing village in Rhode Island bought up by affluent people for their summer homes. He works hard, not really making enough for his family, going out for crabs, lobsters, and swordfish. Pierce's relationship with his wife and his two sons is uneasy and his love for the boat he is building (Spartina—named for the tough grass that thrives on salt in marshy water) crowds out all other considerations. His discontent and need for money lead him to dangerous disregard for the law and into a passsionate affair with Elsie Buttrick, an unconventional and independent young woman. A stunning episode in the novel is Pierce's exposing his new boat to the force of a violent hurricane because there is no safe harbor for it." Shapiro. Fic for Youth. 3d edition

It is the author's "fearless romantic insistence on lyric, even mythic symbolism, coupled with the relentless salt-smack clarity of realistic detail, that makes 'Spartina' just possibly the best American novel about going fishing since 'The Old Man and the Sea,' maybe even 'Moby-Dick.'" N Y Times Book Rev

Cassirer, Nadine Gordimer *See* Gordimer, Nadine, 1923-

Cather, Willa, 1873-1947

Death comes for the archbishop. Knopf 1992 xxvii, 297p $15

ISBN 0-679-41319-7

"Everyman's library"

First published 1927

"Bishop Jean Latour and his vicar Father Joseph Vaillant together create pioneer missions and organize the new diocese of New Mexico. . . . The two combine to triumph over the apathy of the Hopi and Navajo Indians, the opposition of corrupt Spanish priests, and adverse climatic and topographic conditions. They are assisted by Kit Carson and by such devoted Indians as the guide Jacinto. When Vaillant goes as a missionary bishop to Colorado, they are finally separated, but Latour dies soon after his friend, universally revered and respected, to lie in state in the great Santa Fe cathedral that he himself created." Oxford Companion to Am Lit. 6th edition

also in Cather, W. Willa Cather, later novels

"A death in the desert"

In Cather, W. Early novels and stories

Early novels and stories. Library of Am. 1987 1336p $40

ISBN 0-940450-39-9 LC 86-10704

Omnibus edition of four novels: O pioneers! (1913); The song of the lark (1915); My Antonia (1918); One of ours (1922) and the story collection—The troll garden (1905)

Flavia and her artists

In Cather, W. Early novels and stories

The garden lodge

In Cather, W. Early novels and stories

A lost lady. Knopf 1923 173p o.p.

"The story of Marian Forrester is told by Niel Herbert, a Midwestern youth. Married to rugged old empire-builder Captain Forrester, Marian's graciousness sets her much above her commonplace neighbors. She becomes the lover of his friend, Frank Ellinger, however; and after the Captain's death due to a stroke, the lover of Ivy Peters, the man who acquires her home. Peters marries, and the impoverished Marian returns to the West, a 'lost lady' in the eyes of her youthful admirer, Niel. He later hears that Marian, married to a wealthy Englishman, won the respect and admiration of all in her new surroundings." Haydn. Thesaurus of Book Dig

also in Cather, W. Willa Cather, later novels

Cather, Willa, 1873-1947—*Continued*

Lucy Gayheart

In Cather, W. Willa Cather, later novels

The marriage of Phaedra

In Cather, W. Early novels and stories

My Antonia; with an introduction by Lucy Hughes-Hallett. Knopf 1996 xxxiii, 272p $20

ISBN 0-679-44727-X LC 96-223945

"Everyman's library"

First published 1918

"Told by Jim Burden, a New York lawyer recalling his boyhood in Nebraska, the story concerns Antonia Shimerda, who came with her family from Bohemia to settle on the prairies of Nebraska. The difficulties related to pioneering and the integration of immigrants into a new culture are clearly portrayed." Shapiro. Fic for Youth. 3d edition

also in Cather, W. Early novels and stories

O pioneers!.

First published 1913 by Houghton Mifflin

"The heroic battle for survival of simple pioneer folk in the Nebraska country of the 1880's. John Bergson, a Swedish farmer, struggles desperately with the soil but dies unsatisfied. His daughter Alexandra resolves to vindicate his faith, and her strong character carries her weak older brothers and her mother along to a new zest for life. Years of privation, are rewarded on the farm. But when Alexandra falls in love with Carl Linstrum, and her family objects because he is poor, he leaves to seek a different career. After Alexandra's younger brother Emil is killed by the jealous husband of the French girl Marie Shabata, however, Carl gives up his plans to go to the Klondike, returns to marry Alexandra and take up the life of the farm." Haydn. Thesaurus of Book Dig

also in Cather, W. Early novels and stories

One of ours

In Cather, W. Early novels and stories

Paul's case

In Cather, W. Early novels and stories

The professor's house

In Cather, W. Willa Cather, later novels

Sapphira and the slave girl. Knopf 1940 295p o.p.

This novel "centers on the family's matriarch, Sapphira Colbert, and her attempt to sell Nancy Till, a mixed-race slave girl. Sapphira's plot is foiled by her husband Henry and their widowed daughter Rachel Blake. A confident, strong-willed invalid, Sapphira has earned the respect of many of her slaves despite her subtle cruelty toward Nancy. Henry is a pious miller whose simple upbringing and passivity contrast with the aristocratic and manipulative nature of his wife. Henry's nephew Martin, a suave but lecherous ex-soldier, tries to seduce Nancy. Rachel, who helps Nancy flee to Canada, remains at odds with Sapphira over the issue of slavery until the death of Rachel's daughter reconciles the pair." Merriam-Webster's Ency of Lit

also in Cather, W. Willa Cather, later novels

The sculptor's funeral

In Cather, W. Early novels and stories

Shadows on the rock. Knopf 1931 280p o.p.

"A product of Cather's interest in Catholicism, this work is an episodic narrative of life in Quebec during the last days of Frontenac, centered upon the life of Cécile Auclair, a child recently emigrated from Old France." Benet's Reader's Ency of Am Lit

also in Cather, W. Willa Cather, later novels

The song of the lark. Houghton Mifflin 1915 580p o.p.

This novel "tells the story of Thea Kronborg, a Colorado girl, the daughter of a Swedish clergyman, who has a talent for music. She goes to Chicago to study, has an unhappy love affair with Fred Ottenburg, a wealthy young man who cannot obtain a divorce to marry her, and eventually becomes a soprano at the Metropolitan Opera House in New York City, famous for her Wagnerian roles." Reader's Ency. 3d edition

also in Cather, W. Early novels and stories p291-706

The troll garden

In Cather, W. Early novels and stories

In Cather, W. Willa Cather's collected short fiction, 1892-1912

A Wagner matinée

In Cather, W. Early novels and stories

Willa Cather, later novels. Library of Am. 1990 988p o.p.

ISBN 0-940450-52-6 LC 89-64130

Contents: The lost lady (1923); Death comes for the archbishop (1927); Shadows on the rock (1931); Sapphira and the slave girl (1940); The professor's house (1925); Lucy Gayheart (1935)

Willa Cather's collected short fiction, 1892-1912; edited by Virginia Faulkner; introduced by Mildred R. Bennett. [Rev. ed.] University of Neb. Press 1970 3v in 1 o.p.

First published 1965. This edition includes an attributed unsigned story: The elopement of Allen Poole

Contents: v 1 The Bohemian girl; v2 The troll garden [published separately, 1905]; v3 On the Divide

Short stories included are: v 1 The Bohemian girl; Behind the Singing Tower; The joy of Nelly Deane; The enchanted bluff; On the gulls' road; Eleanor's house; The willing muse; The profile; The namesake; v2 The troll garden; Flavia and her artists; The sculptor's funeral; The garden lodge; "A death in the desert"; The marriage of Phaedra; A Wagner matinee; Paul's case; v3 On the Divide; The treasure of Far Island; The Professor's commencement; El Dorado; A Kansas recessional; Jack-a-Boy; The conversion of Sum Loo; A singer's romance; The affair at Grover Station; The sentimentality of William Tavener; Eric Hermannson's soul; The westbound train; The way of the world; Nanette: an aside; The prodigies; A resurrection; The strategy of the Were-Wolf Dog; The Count of Crow's Nest; Tommy, the unsentimental; A night at Greenway Court; On the Divide; "The fear that walks by noonday"; The clemency of the court; A son of the Celestial; A tale of the white pyramid; Lou, the prophet; Peter

Caunitz, William J.

Chains of command. Dutton 1999 323p $23.95
ISBN 0-525-94514-8 LC 99-28778
"The book begins with the murder of a cop (with $5000 in his pocket) and his mistress (who has ties to the Cali drug cartel) in Washington Heights. Their deaths signal serious trouble for First Deputy Police Commissioner Suzanne Albrecht, who is in line to become the next commissioner and is worried that a scandal in the Heights will ruin her chances. So she enlists the aid of Matt Stuart, a lieutenant in the NYPD's intelligence division. When two street dealers are murdered, threatening to set off a territorial battle over the area's drug market, Albrecht and Stuart must act fast to avert a blood bath and save a political career." Libr J
"Christopher Newman deserves a hunk of credit for finishing the last book of his good friend William J. Caunitz, who died before he could complete the job himself. Whoever did what, this is one of the best police procedurals you're likely to read this season. The procedures are impeccable, the dialogue gleefully flouts all rules of grammar and the characters are poster children for their representative neighborhoods." N Y Times Book Rev

One Police Plaza. Crown 1984 369p o.p.
LC 83-14323
"This story details the tenacious search of a New York police detective for the murderer responsible for a heinous crime. Lt. Dan Malone is called in on the murder and is caught up in the apparent inconsistencies of the case. Despite threats, direct orders and attempts on his life, Malone refuses to back off. His tenacity pays off, . . . and he is able to solve the murder. The murder, though, includes elements of international terrorism and espionage as well as internal departmental vigilante activities." Best Sellers
The author "expertly depicts the stark reality of the police officer's life and work, and his hard-edged prose drives the story to a stunning conclusion." Booklist

Suspects. Crown 1986 374p o.p.
LC 86-13427
"The story begins with a double homicide in which one victim is a lionized police lieutenant and the other is the owner of a neighborhood candy store. But both victims have skeletons in their closets, as Lt. Tony Scanlon soon discovers as he investigates the crime. Lt. Scanlon is a solid character, a handicapped cop who must balance his loyalty to the job—that is, being a cop—with getting to the truth, something his superiors may not want him to discover." Publ Wkly
"The author's prose is not Joseph Wambaugh's, but his knowledge of life inside an urban police force is extraordinary, and his detailed word-pictures of ballistics tests, fingerprint techniques and department stag parties make this arcane blue world come alive." N Y Times Book Rev

Cavallo, Evelyn *See* Spark, Muriel

Cavell, Benjamin

Rumble, young man, rumble. Knopf 2003 191p $22
ISBN 0-375-41464-9 LC 2002-27525

Contents: Balls, balls, balls; All the nights of the world; Killing time; Evolution; The art of the possible; Blue yonder; The death of cool; Highway; The ropes
"Though Cavell occasionally comes on too strong, the collection is filled with dead-on, often hilarious dialogue and offers a thoughtful meditation on masculinity and class." Publ Wkly

Céline, Louis-Ferdinand, 1894-1961

Journey to the end of the night; translated from the French by John H. P. Marks. Little, Brown 1934 509p o.p.
Original French edition, 1932
"Ferdinand Bardamu, the cynical, disillusioned hero, wanders aimlessly through war-torn Europe, surrounded by destruction and putrefaction. Man, as Céline portrays him, attempts to flee from the solitude of his existence and the impossibility of helping his fellow humans but succeeds only in embracing evil and death. The novel caused a scandal when it was published because of the coarseness of its language and the unrelieved blackness of its pessimism. Yet the language is a highly original attempt to reproduce the proletarian *argot* that reflects the horror and intimacy of war, and the pessimism shows Céline's desire to arouse the reader and make him aware of his condition." Reader's Ency. 4th edition

A **Century** of great Western stories; edited by John Jakes. Forge 2000 525p $27.95; pa $18.95
ISBN 0-312-86986-X; 0-312-86985-1 (pa)
LC 99-462096

"A Tom Doherty Associates book"
This anthology of 30 short stories includes pieces by such writers as Owen Wister, Zane Grey, Max Brand, Bill Pronzini, Elmer Kelton and Marcia Muller
"Romance, murder, action, mystery and suspense are mixed with hefty doses of moral dilemma, guilt and redemption in these carefully plotted tales. . . . Many of the stories are appearing here for the first time since they were published in the pulps of the '30s, '40s and '50s, but their appeal is as fresh as ever." Publ Wkly

Cerf, Bennett, 1898-1971

(ed) Famous ghost stories. See Famous ghost stories

Cervantes Saavedra, Miguel de, 1547-1616

The colloquy of the dogs
In Cervantes Saavedra, M. d. Three exemplary novels p125-217

Don Quixote de la Mancha; [by] Miguel de Cervantes; translated, with a critical text based on the first editions of 1605 and 1615, and with variant readings, variorum notes, and an introduction by Samuel Putnam. Modern Library 1998 xl, 1239p $25.95
ISBN 0-679-60286-0 LC 97-47415
Original Spanish edition, published in two parts, 1605 and 1615
"Originally conceived as a comic satire against the chi-

Cervantes Saavedra, Miguel de, 1547-1616— *Continued*

valric romances then in literary vogue, the novel describes realistically what befalls an elderly knight who, his head bemused by reading romances, sets out on his old horse Rosinante, with his pragmatic squire Sancho Panza, to seek adventure. In the process, he also finds love in the person of the pleasant Dulcinea. Contemporaries evidently did not take the book as seriously as later generations have done, but by the end of the 17th century it was deemed highly significant, especially abroad. It came to be seen as a mock epic in prose, and the 'grave and serious air' of the author's irony was much admired. In the history of the modern novel the role of *Don Quixote* is recognized as seminal." Merriam-Webster's Ency of Lit

Man of glass
In Cervantes Saavedra, M. d. Three exemplary novels p75-121

Rinconete and Cortadillo
In Cervantes Saavedra, M. d. Three exemplary novels p9-71

Three exemplary novels; translated by Samuel Putnam; illustrated by Luis Quintanilla. Viking 1950 xxi, 232p il o.p.

Part of a collection first published 1613 in Spain

Rinconete and Cortadillo is a picaresque novella about thieves in early 17th century Seville. Man of glass is a philosophical tale set in 17th century Italy about a man intent on exposing the lie upon which human existence is based. The colloquy of the dogs describes life in 17th century Spain

Chabon, Michael

The amazing adventures of Kavalier and Clay; a novel. Random House 2000 639p $26.95
ISBN 0-679-45004-1 LC 00-29063

"Joe Kavalier, a Czech war refugee, and his American-born cousin Sammy Clay are [this] novel's protagonists. They create a comic-book crusader known as the Escapist. . . . A young artist with Harry Houdini's ability to pick locks while holding his breath, Kavalier has escaped Nazi-occupied Czechoslovakia by hiding in a coffin containing the mythic Golem of Prague." Time

"Themes are masterfully explored, leaving the book's sense of humor intact and characters so highly developed they could walk off the page." Newsweek

The final solution; a story of detection. Fourth Estate 2004 131p il $16.95
ISBN 0-06-076340-X LC 2004-53343

"In deep retirement in the English countryside, an 89-year old man, vaguely recollected by the locals as a once-famous detective, is more concerned with his beekeeping than his fellow man. Into his life wanders Linus Steinman, nine years old and mute, who has escaped from Nazi Germany with his sole companion: an African grey parrot." Publisher's note

"The writing here is taut and polished, and Chabon's characters and depictions of English country life are spot on." Publ Wkly

Wonder boys. Villard Bks. 1995 368p o.p.
ISBN 0-679-41588-2 LC 94-28921

"The book's hero is a fortyish novelist and writing teacher named Grady Tripp, who was once a literary phenomenon but is now stalled on a 2,600-page *magnum opus* called (of course) 'Wonder Boys.' . . . The reason for this sad state of affairs is Grady's lack of discipline and his endless need for thrills and chills in the various guises of drugs, booze, and love affairs." N Y Times Book Rev

"Bright promise gone awry is the theme of this exuberantly comic novel, whose convoluted plot sparkles with inventiveness and wit." Publ Wkly

Chadwick, Charles

It's all right now. HarperCollins 2005 688p $25.95
ISBN 0-06-074286-0

"The narrator, Tom Ripple, whose life we follow from the 1970s into the 21st century, is a lower-middle-class Englishman devoid of charm, intellectual curiosity and emotional warmth. Only gradually does the reader come to understand why Ripple's responses are stunted, why his preferred mode of communication is through excruciatingly bad puns and double entendres and why he subsists on a steady diet of television action films and paperback thrillers. When his wife leaves him, taking their two children, he is resigned to loneliness. As the years pass, Ripple cautiously engages in new relationships; he acquires the knack for tender paternal love and true friendship, and he develops an appreciation of music and books that brings him joy. Throughout, he continues to seek meaning in a postmodern world." Publ Wkly

"Ripple's voice is so convincing you don't just know him—you are him. Does it matter if he runs on a bit? . . . He alludes repeatedly to the poetry of Philip Larkin—whose dreary and solitary later life, in which he spent his evenings drinking and watching television, must have been partly a model for Ripple's. But [this novel], like its narrator, is radically original despite (and because of) its naivete. It doesn't rethink the novel: it thinks up the novel from scratch." Newsweek

Challans, Mary *See* Renault, Mary, 1905-1983

Chalmers, Robert

Who's who in hell. Grove Press 2002 360p $13
ISBN 0-8021-3924-8 (pa) LC 2002-21470

"Daniel, a former layabout, failed therapist and habitué of bars, writes rapier-witted obituaries for a large and unnamed London daily newspaper. His girlfriend, Laura, is an amateur sky diver who was born in America; the couple live together, eventually with their son, above the cafe she manages in London's Crouch End. . . . There are missteps, particularly in Chalmer's inept sketching of parenthood and in his largely impersonal relationship with novel's female characters, especially Laura, but these are probably to be expected—the book, to steal a title of Hornby's, is about a boy. And for that, it makes for fine and highly pleasurable reading." N Y Times Book Rev

Chandler, Raymond, 1888-1959

The big sleep. Knopf 1939 277p o.p.

"A tale of degeneracy in southern California, in which two Hollywood heiresses become mixed up in blackmail and murder; and Philip Marlowe is the private detective, who tells the story." Washington, D.C. Public Libr

also in Chandler, R. Stories and early novels p587-764

Farewell, my lovely

In Chandler, R. Stories and early novels p765-984

The high window. Knopf 1942 240p o.p.

"This early exploit of Philip Marlowe's is certainly high in the merit list. The Pasadena scene, the characterization, the tough-yet-literate style match the complex plot, involving counterfeiting and blackmail. Just how the photograph of the victim was obtained is glossed over, but all other details are clearly etched." Barzun. Cat of Crime. Rev and enl edition

also in Chandler, R. Stories and early novels p985-1177

The lady in the lake. Knopf 1943 216p o.p.

"A young wife has been missing for a month and Marlowe is hired by the husband whom she is about to leave for another man. The exposition of situation and character is done with remarkable pace and skill. . . . The scene shifts to Little Fawn Lake, where talk between a local woman, the caretaker of the missing wife's cabin, and Marlowe produces speculation about the absent girl, her lover, and also the missing wife of the caretaker; whereupon comes the dramatic discovery of the corpse in the lake. It is 'not' Marlowe's quarry. From then on this superb tale moves through a maze of puzzles and disclosures to its perfect conclusion. Marlowe makes a greater use of physical clues and ratiocination in this exploit than in any other. It is Chandler's masterpiece and true detection." Barzun. Cat of Crime. Rev and enl edition

In Chandler, R. Later novels and other writings

Later novels and other writings. Library of Am. 1995 1076p $35

ISBN 1-883011-08-6 LC 94-43705

Contents: The lady in the lake; The little sister; The long goodbye; Playback; Double indemnity; Selected essays and letters

The lady in the lake and The long goodbye are entered separately. In The little sister (1949), Marlowe takes on a case set in Hollywood involving a young starlet and her brother. In Playback (1958), "Marlowe is weakening (by his own standards), since he takes on an impossible girl who is running away from a quite imaginary threat and forces her to trust him. There is some silly back-and-forth with $5,000 of traveler's checks, a double fornication without much zest, and at last a transatlantic phone call summoning Marlowe to marry his true love." Barzun. Cat of Crime. Rev and enl ed

The little sister

In Chandler, R. Later novels and other writings

The long goodbye. Houghton Mifflin 1953 316p o.p.

Detective Philip Marlowe provides moral support for Terry Lennox who is running away to Mexico because he thinks he committed a murder

This novel is one of Chandler's "most meticulously plotted and by some stretches his most corrosive. What he gives us here is painful if exciting pleasure." N Y Her Trib Books

also in Chandler, R. Later novels and other writings

Playback

In Chandler, R. Later novels and other writings

Poodle Springs; [by] Raymond Chandler and Robert B. Parker. Putnam 1989 268p o.p.

LC 89-10414

When Chandler died he left "behind the opening chapters of this Philip Marlowe private investigator novel set in the 1950s, which Parker has completed. Here, Marlowe has a rich wife . . . and has moved from Los Angeles to the big-buck community of Poodle Springs, where he is hired by the area crime boss to track down a missing local who has run out on a gambling debt." Libr J

"Like Chandler's finest work, Poodle Springs has a haunted quality that comes from somewhere beyond the plot, a sense of things gone fundamentally wrong. . . . Chandler's great artistic flaw was his sentimentalizing of his detective. Parker isn't, even here, the writer Chandler was, but he's not a sentimentalist, and he darkens and deepens Marlowe." Atlantic

Raymond Chandler; collected stories; with an introduction by John Bayley. Knopf 2002 xxxvii, 1299p $27.50

ISBN 0-375-41500-9

"Everyman's library"

Contents: Blackmailers don't shoot; Smart-aleck kill; Finger man; Killer in the rain; Nevada gas; Spanish blood; Guns at Cyrano's; The man who liked dogs; Pick-up on Noon Street; Goldfish; The curtain; Try the girl; Mandarin's jade; Red wind; The king in yellow; Bay City blues; The lady in the lake; Pearls are a nuisance; Trouble is my business; I'll be waiting; The bronze door; No crime in the mountains; Professor Bingo's snuff; The pencil; English summer

"To read these 25 stories, 22 of which were originally published in the 1930s, consecutively is to watch Chandler's craft develop. . . . Only Chandler fanatics will want to read every word of this encyclopedic volume, but anyone with any interest in the history of hard-boiled fiction should sample its groundbreaking wares." Booklist

Stories and early novels. Library of Am. 1995 1199p $35

ISBN 1-883011-07-8 LC 94-45462

Contents: Pulp stories; The big sleep; Farewell, my lovely; The high window

The big sleep and The high window are entered separately. Pulp stories includes the following titles: Blackmailers don't shoot; Smart-aleck kill; Finger man; Nevada gas; Spanish blood; Guns at Cyrano's; Pick-up on Noon Street; Goldfish; Red wind; The king in yellow; Pearls are a nuisance; Trouble is my business; I'll be

Chandler, Raymond, 1888-1959—*Continued*

waiting

Farewell, my lovely (1940), a mystery featuring Philip Marlowe, is a "model of complexity kept under control, with a holocaust at the end. Its contents are the now familiar ones of political and personal corruption, double-crossing, and the woman killer." Barzun. Cat of Crime. Rev and enl edition

Chandra, Vikram

Red earth and pouring rain; a novel. Little, Brown 1995 542p o.p.

LC 94-48841

"Home from college abroad (in California), impulsive Abhay wounds a monkey outside his parents' Bombay home and finds that his victim is no ordinary beast. A reincarnation of the poet Sanjay, the failing monkey strikes a bargain with Yama, god of death: life in exchange for two hours of storytelling each day. Crowds gather at the Misra house to hear the epic of Sanjay and his warrior cousin Sikander, spun by the monkey at a typewriter. Abhay shares the monkey's burden by adding his own recollections of young, fast, aimless America." Libr J

"Clarity, order, logic and simplicity are Western demands. Forget them if you want to enjoy this riotous, sly and sophisticated saga, which . . . is an argument—sometimes quite a sharp challenge—deliberately aimed at Western canons, ethical as well as aesthetic." London Rev Books

Chaon, Dan

Among the missing. Ballantine Bks. 2001 258p o.p.

ISBN 0-345-44162-1 LC 00-66695

Contents: Safety Man; I demand to know where you're taking me; Big me; Prodigal; Passengers, remain calm; The Illustrated Encyclopedia of the Animal Kingdom; Among the missing; Prosthesis; Here's a little something to remember me by; Late for the wedding; Falling backwards; Burn with me

"People go missing both literally and figuratively in Chaon's beautiful and insightful stories, most of which are set in small, muffled Midwest towns. . . . Riveting and unpredictable, each pristine tale of absence looms like the proverbial tip of the iceberg as Chaon succeeds brilliantly in suggesting the immensity and mystery floating silently below the surface of everyday life." Booklist

You remind me of me; a novel; Dan Chaon. 1st ed. Ballantine Books 2004 356p $24.95

ISBN 0-345-44141-9 LC 2003-63776

This novel "begins with a self-possessed little boy named Jonah, who lives in Little Bow, South Dakota. His mother, who was forced, as an unwed teen, to give away her firstborn, is cruel, and her Doberman pinscher is vicious, eventually attacking Jonah and leaving him scarred for life both physically and psychologically. Now in his twenties, he's obsessed with finding his unknown half-brother. Meanwhile, Troy, a bartender in a small Nebraska town, is in crisis. Adopted as an infant by parents who soon divorce, he falls in with the town's druggies and marries one. She has disappeared, he has been arrested, and he is terrified that he'll lose custody of his son, the strangely watchful and solitary Loomis." Booklist

"Chaon has written an apparently claustrophobic novel that feels paradoxically large, generous and, ultimately, quite moving. This is thanks in no small part to his vivid, unadorned prose, which manages at once to be precise and dreamlike." Washington Post Book World

Chappell, Helen

A whole world of trouble; a novel. Simon & Schuster 2003 213p $23

ISBN 0-7432-1529-X LC 2003-42512

Carrie Hudson "comes home to Oysterback, Maryland, after her mother dies. Carrie, who scours estate sales and sells her treasures to antique dealers, doesn't get along with her sister Earlene on her bland husband, but the two are forced together to plan the burial of their mother, who died travellng to meet her latest boyfriend, and ex-con." Booklist

"Chappell sometimes lays on the folksy charm a little thick. . .but for the most part Carrie's sympathetic, wry voice gives some depth to what would otherwise be a predictable gallery of smalltown oddballs." Publ Wkly

Charles, Kate

A dead man out of mind. Mysterious Press 1995 c1994 339p o.p.

LC 95-15434

First published 1994 in the United Kingdom

In this mystery novel set in London, "painter Lucy Kingsley and solicitor David Middleton-Brown, her lover, become involved in a scandal surrounding two neighborhood Anglican churches. After an apparent burglar murders a priest, the vicar appoints a controversial female deacon as a replacement." Libr J

"Sensible Lucy and sensitive David make an odd but appealing couple. Ms. Charles's other slightly-off-the-beam characters range from the most imperious of deans to the fussiest of functionaries, and each one is a treat to find in your pew." N Y Times Book Rev

Chase-Riboud, Barbara, 1939-

The President's daughter. Crown 1994 467p o.p.

LC 93-42499

Sequel to Sally Hemings

"On her 21st birthday, Harriet, the daughter of Thomas Jefferson and Sally Hemings, his slave and mistress, is allowed to run north and pass into white society. Although Harriet's physical characteristics allow her outward passage to occur without difficulty, the psychological divisions she suffers endure for her lifetime. Obsessed by her desire for Jefferson to acknowledge his slave children, tormented by fears that her husband could be prosecuted for miscegenation and her children sold into slavery, Harriet struggles with the same questions that tear apart the Union and plunge the country into civil war." Libr J

The author "vividly captures the look and feel of Philadelphia from the 1820s to the 1870s. Just as in a romance novel, the beautiful and strong-willed Harriet succeeds in whatever arena she chooses. But her story goes beyond that of a feisty heroine in a heaving bodice; with intelligence and immediacy, 'The President's Daughter' illuminates the brutal politics of slavery." NY Times Book Rev

Chase-Riboud, Barbara, 1939-—*Continued*

Sally Hemings; a novel. Viking 1979 348p o.p.
LC 78-12682

"A Seaver book"

A novel about the relationship between Thomas Jefferson and his mistress Sally Hemings, a slave, whom he lived with for thirty-eight years

"If it indeed existed, the relationship must have been much as the author depicts it in this fine first novel: a mixture of love and hate, of tenderness and cruelty, and of freedom and bondage. The book is well researched, well written, insightful, and entertaining." Libr J

Followed by The President's daughter

Chatwin, Bruce

On the Black Hill. Viking 1983 c1982 248p o.p.
LC 82-10923

First published 1982 in the United Kingdom

"This is the story of Lewis and Benjamin Jones, reclusive and inseparable twins whose lives are untouched by events in the outside world from the turn of the century to the present day. Not rejecting modern life so much as innocent about it, the brothers preserve their parents' farm called The Vision in England, reluctantly capitulating to technology." Libr J

"Conventional plot structure and character development have little part here; we know Lewis, Benjamin, and their neighbors as we know some permanent figures of our own lives, not by dramatic revelation but by long association and accumulated sympathy." Harper's

Utz. Viking 1989 154p o.p.
LC 88-40310

This novel details the "existence of one Kaspar Utz, owner of a superb private collection of Meissen porcelain in Prague. The novel is narrated by a writer who goes to the Czech capital in 1967 to research the Holy Roman Emperor Rudolph II's passion for collecting objets d'art. His research—which he hopes will lead him to conclusions about the psychology of the compulsive collector—first leads him to the door of Kaspar Utz. What develops from this meeting affords the narrator a rich opportunity to observe and attempt to fathom human nature." Booklist

"The hero of Mr. Chatwin's provocative short novel is a successful survivor. He is part Jewish but has managed to survive Hitler. . . . [Utz is] required to bequeath the collection to the state, and what he does about that insult to his elegant eighteenth-century companions becomes his own peculiar final solution. Mr. Chatwin has created an intriguing proposition—that obedient passivity can amount to successful rebellion." Atlantic

Chayefsky, Paddy, 1923-1981

Altered states; a novel. Harper & Row 1978 184p o.p.
LC 77-11542

This novel tells the "story of an experiment in genetic regression. . . . Edward Jessup is a psychophysiologist with 'an extraordinary if monomaniacal mind'. His wife suspects that her coldly passionate husband may be a genius. . . . After numerous descents into the black water of an isolation tank he at last succeeds in regressing into a small, hairy, proto-human creature that eats gazelles in the university park and experiences 'the primal unity'. He smashes his way out of the laboratory and exults in the taste of warm blood." New Statesman (1913)

"What makes this shocking fantasy work is not only Chayefsky's dramatic skill . . . but also the authority of his prodigious research in chemistry, biology, and medicine. . . . The result is a marvelous and exciting work of the imagination." Saturday Rev

Chazin, Suzanne

Flashover. Putnam 2002 332p o.p.
ISBN 0-399-14850-7 LC 2001-48772

"Fire marshal Georgia Skeehan and her veteran sidekick, Randy Carter, are called to investigate a fire that took the life of a retired doctor with a history of denying pensions to firefighters disabled in the line of duty. To complicate matters, Georgia's best friend, NYPD detective Connie Ruiz, confirms that there is talk of a bomb threat to a fuel pipeline under the city and that whoever is behind it knew the retired doctor." Publ Wkly

"Fans of Patricia Cornwell will appreciate the gritty, realistic details Chazin provides concerning the techniques used to investigate suspicious fires. The appealing main character and the fast pace will keep readers turning the pages into the wee hours." Booklist

Cheever, John, 1912-1982

Bullet Park; a novel. Knopf 1969 245p o.p.

"The interplay between [suburbanites] Eliot Nailles, Paul Hammer, and Naille's son Tony forms the structure of a novel . . . embodying many contemporary issues and problems. Using the third person, Cheever depicts Nailles as an open-faced, conscientious man, driven to desperation when his son is ill. Hammer, in a first-person account, is revealed as criminally insane beneath his [middle-class] neighborly exterior. The third part portrays Hammer's attempt to murder Tony Nailles, an act narrowly averted by his father." Booklist

The author "mixes compassion and high comedy brilliantly, holding up to view an America that is fatally schizoid in many of its manifestations. The confrontation that finally comes between Hammer and Nailles is a horrifying dark allegory of our times." Publ Wkly

Falconer. Knopf 1977 211p o.p.

The novel's protagonist, Ezekiel Farragut, "is a well-read college professor, a drug addict convicted of murdering his brother, Falconer. Prison breaks Zeke Farragut of his addiction but embroils him in all the coarse, desperate gambits of prison life." Libr J

"John Cheever uses prison as an emblem for the world in this stunning novel about love, mysticism, and man's relationship with God. . . . The surface events include a prison riot, a massacre of prison cats by an enraged guard who had his steak stolen by one of them, a homosexual love affair, and a couple of breathtaking escapes, one by Farragut's lover, who dons a cassock to escape in a helicopter with a visiting bishop. Woven in and out are threads of Farragut's past life, his relationship to his wife and the other women in his life, the secret behind his hatred for his brother." Choice

Cheever, John, 1912-1982—*Continued*

Oh, what a paradise it seems. Knopf 1982 99p o.p.

LC 81-48109

"In a novella that focuses on an aging man's regret and anger at the erosion of time on the human body and the environment, John Cheever attempts a modern fable. Lemuel Sears, elegantly elderly, is rejuvenated via an impromptu, lively and offbeat love affair. His energy is galvanized to mount a legal attack on the despoilment by landfill of a once jewel-like pond near the home of his youth. A series of bizarre but somehow connected events, including a homosexual encounter, enhance Sears' appreciation of the mystery of life and the need for renewal in the waning of the 20th century." Publ Wkly

"Ever more boldly the celebrant of the grand poetry of life, Cheever, once a taut and mordant chronicler of urban and suburban disappointments, now speaks in the cranky, granular, impulsive, confessional style of our native wise men and exhorters since Emerson. The pitch of his final page is positively Transcendental." New Yorker

The stories of John Cheever. Knopf 1978 693p $45

ISBN 0-394-50087-3 LC 78-160

A "bringing together of 61 Cheever stories in a single binding. . . . Most of these pieces were initially published in 'The New Yorker.'" Choice

"Readers will delight in the delineation of Cheever's mythical landscapes. . . . Resonant with feeling and meaning, this is a collection to treasure." Publ Wkly

Thirteen uncollected stories; edited by Franklin H. Dennis; introduction by George W. Hunt. Academy Chicago 1994 227p $22

ISBN 0-89733-405-1 LC 93-49582

Contents: Fall River; Late gathering; Bock beer and Bermuda onions; The autobiography of a drummer; In passing; Bayonne; The princess; The teaser; His young wife; Saratoga; The man she loved; Family dinner; The opportunity

"These stories were nearly all published in the 1930s. . . . Several are Depression tales, set in dead mill towns or waterfront diners and informed by leftist politics. . . . Others are set among the Saratoga horse-racing set and appeared in such commercial magazines as *Collier's*. Surprisingly, women are at the center of many of the stories. . . . A fascinating example of one writer's beginning." Libr J

The Wapshot chronicle. Harper & Row 1957 307p o.p.

"Based in part on Cheever's adolescence in New England, the novel takes place in a small Massachusetts fishing village and relates the breakdown of both the Wapshot family and the town. Part One focuses on Leander, a gentle ferryboat operator harried by his tyrannical wife and his eccentric sister; he eventually swims out to sea and never returns. Part Two chronicles the disastrous lives of Leander's sons, Coverly and Moses. Told in a comic rather than a tragic vein, the novel uses experimental prose techniques to convey a nostalgic vision of a lost world." Merriam-Webster's Ency of Lit

Followed by The Wapshot scandal

The Wapshot scandal. Harper & Row 1964 309p o.p.

This sequel to The Wapshot chronicle "continues the tale of the decline of the fortunes of the Wapshot family and of the mythical New England town of St. Botolphs. The 'scandal' is the discovery that Aunt Honora has never paid her income taxes, and the principal disaster stems from the long-standing oversight. The novel also traces the misfortunes of two Wapshot nephews, Coverly, a public relations man at a missile site, and Moses, an alcoholic. Despite the somberness of the main line of events, the book is not depressing; it is lighted by the high gloss of Mr. Cheever's style, by glints of humor, and especially by the warm glow of human fortitude under stress." Libr J

Chekhonte, Antosha *See* Chekhov, Anton Pavlovich, 1860-1904

Chekhov, Anton Pavlovich, 1860-1904

Early short stories, 1883-1888; edited by Shelby Foote; translated by Constance Garnett. Modern Lib. 1999 642p o.p.

ISBN 0-679-60317-4 LC 98-20049

Following his introduction Foote presents seventy of Chekhov's early stories

Later short stories, 1888-1903; edited by Shelby Foote; translated by Constance Garnett. Modern Lib. 1999 628p o.p.

ISBN 0-679-60316-6 LC 98-20048

This volume contains forty-two short stories

Longer stories from the last decade; {by} Anton Chekhov; translated by Constance Garnett. Modern Lib. 1993 611p o.p.

ISBN 0-679-60063-9 LC 93-14536

Contents: The duel; The wife; Ward no. 6; An anonymous story; The black monk; A woman's kingdom; Three years; The murder; My life; Peasants; In the ravine

Cherryh, C. J., 1942-

Cloud's rider. Warner Bks. 1996 373p o.p.

LC 96-3147

In this sequel to Rider at the gate "colonists, stranded on a distant planet deadly to humans, struggle to survive in small, isolated communities. The native nighthorses provide a telepathic buffer between the humans and the wildlife—which projects violent images, driving humans insane. Here, young Danny Fisher and his nighthorse, Cloud, face a threat from an unseen predator." Libr J

The author "obviously knows where her strength lies. Her long, unhurried sentences keep digging deeper and deeper into the 'sense of whereness' that nighthorses and humans share." N Y Times Book Rev

The collected short fiction of C.J. Cherryh. DAW Bks. 2004 642p $23.95

ISBN 0-7564-0217-4

Contents: The only death in the city; The haunted tower; Ice; Nightgame; Highliner; The general; MasKs; Cassandra; Threads of time; Companions; A theif in Korianth; The last tower; The brothers; The dark king; Homecoming; The dreamstone; Sea Change; Willow; Of

Cherryh, C. J., 1942-—*Continued*
law and magic; The unshadowed land; Pots; The scapegoat; A gift of prophecy; Wings; A much briefer history of time; Gwydion and the dragon; Mech; The Sandman, the Tinman, and the BettyB

"Cherryh demonstrates a fine flair for compact storytelling that encompasses science, fantasy, and myth." Libr J

Destroyer. DAW 2005 480p $24.95
ISBN 0-7564-0253-0

In this title, set in the author's Foreigner universe, "Bren Cameron and his atevi allies finally return to their home world, where atevi natives and human colonists live in an uneasy truce. Their desperate, two-year mission has been a success; they've evacuated the humans stranded on distant Reunion Station and made tentative peace with the kyo, an enigmatic and heretofore hostile alien race. Bren soon discovers, however, that his troubles are far from over. . . . This volume, the first in a new trilogy, is hampered by the need to clarify what is now a considerable back story, but it features a healthy dose of the author's trademark well-developed characters, fine style and intense psychological realism." Publ Wkly

Finity's End. Warner Bks. 1997 471p o.p.
LC 96-37992

In this Merchanter universe novel, "The ship *Finity's End,* seriously shorthanded after the Union-Alliance War, returns to the Pell station to reclaim Fletcher Neihart, who grew up on the station after his mother was left there during the war. Young Fletcher, however, has a real gift for dealing with Pell's native inhabitants and no interest in being frog-marched aboard *Finity's End* or adjusting to the role of a new crew member." Booklist

"Despite an abundance of exciting action, this is character-driven drama that represents old-fashioned SF at its very best." Publ Wkly

Foreigner; a novel of first contact. DAW Bks. 1994 378p o.p.
LC 94-179662

"Set on an alien world where the descendants of humans marooned in a long-ago starship accident live segregated from the indigenous *atevi* on a remote island, this [novel] . . . addresses the complicated issue of how humans might have to compromise to survive on a planet where they are barely tolerated by the original, humanoid inhabitants." Publ Wkly

"Cherryh plays her strongest suit in this exploration of human/alien contact, producing an incisive study-in-contrast of what it means to be human in a world where trust is nonexistent." Libr J

Followed by Invader

Fortress of dragons. HarperCollins Pubs. 2000 422p o.p.
ISBN 0-06-105055-5 LC 00-25811

"The key element in this book is Cefwyn Marhanen's continuing efforts to be recognized as high king and thereby reclaim his wife Ninevrise's inheritance of Elwynor. Ninevrise hopes she is carrying Cefwyn's child, and another of his offspring is borne by Tarien Aswydd, whose desperately evil twin, Orien, tries to induce birth in time for evil wizard Hasufin Heltain to reincarnate in the newborn." Booklist

Hammerfall. Eos 2001 390p o.p.
ISBN 0-06-105260-4 LC 00-47621

"Brought before the powerful ruler known as the Ila, the madman known as Marak receives a command to seek out the silver tower of his mad dreams and return with the knowledge of what the tower holds. Marak discovers, however, that reaching his destination is only the beginning of a greater and more dangerous journey." Libr J

"Cherryh introduces the first wholly new world in her fiction in 30 years and makes it memorable with spare, clean, and elegant prose that lends a haunting quality to the story as it intriguingly conjures the desert setting and the close-to-the-bone way of life that it entails." Booklist

Inheritor. DAW Bks. 1996 410p o.p.
ISBN 0-88677-689-9 LC 96-140894

In this third volume set in the Foreigner universe "a spaceship returns after 200 years, and its human occupants threaten the balance of power between the human colony and the native, deadly atevi. Human translator Bren Cameron tries to avoid a human-atevi war while the atevi factions jockey for power. A good look at an alternative civilization where humans are not dominant, this nicely concludes a series but can stand on its own." Libr J

Followed by Precursor

Invader. DAW Bks. 1995 426p o.p.
LC 95-211942

Second title in the authors series set in the Foreigner universe. "After an absence of nearly 200 years, the starship *Phoenix* reappears in the skies above the human enclave of Mospheira, throwing both humans and the native atevi population into consternation and threatening the delicate balance between two distinctly alien civilizations. . . . Cherryh combines a flair for hard science with a keen insight into the complex rationales behind human—and nonhuman—actions." Libr J

Followed by Inheritor

Precursor. DAW Bks. 1999 438p $23.95
ISBN 0-88677-836-0

In this fourth title set in the Foreigner universe "Cherryh sends diplomat and translator Bren Cameron into space to conduct a tense three-sided negotiation among the Pilot's Guild on the recently returned human starship *Phoenix,* the *atevi*—the planet's indigenous sentient species, whom Bren now serves—and the Mospheirans, the human colonists whom the starship long ago abandoned in the *atevi's* world. . . . The novel features well-developed characters, Cherryh's trade-mark sophisticated political negotiations and strong prose." Publ Wkly

Rider at the gate. Warner Bks. 1995 437p o.p.
LC 95-7591

Set on "a distant world on which humans work closely with nighthorses—that is, psychic and sometimes psychotic equines. The plot is a whodunit revolving around the death of a nighthorse rider that affects many other people. Cherryh unfolds it by looking into the minds of a series of characters, some of whom are either illiterate or incoherent in their thoughts, or both." Booklist

"Cherryh never overwhelms the narrative with exposition, skillfully unfolding her society of humans and aliens so that the reader gradually understands past events and present situations." Publ Wkly

Followed by Cloud's rider

Cherryh, C. J., 1942-—*Continued*

Rimrunners. Warner Bks. 1989 327p o.p.
LC 88-27755

"Separated from her Freebooter (outlaw) ship, spacer Elizabeth ('Bet') Martin is stranded on Thule Station without papers and with a slim chance of getting hired. Unexpectedly, she secures a berth on the mysterious Union vessel *Loki*, which shows all evidence of being a 'spook' (intelligence-gathering) ship but turns out to be the bait in a dangerous plan to draw out and attack the Freebooters. . . . Cherryh has created a convincing shipboard setting, and her characters act and react realistically to the everyday minutiae and intrigue of life aboard the *Loki*." Booklist

Tripoint. Warner Bks. 1994 377p o.p.
LC 93-38247

A title in the author's saga set in the Merchanter universe. "Tom Bowe-Hawkins, young crew member of the family ship *Sprite*, was conceived in rape and is growing up with a chip on his shoulder. He is caught up in the revenge planned by his mother, Marie Kirgov Hawkins, against his father, Austin Bowe, captain of the *Corinthian*, a vessel suspected to be engaged in smuggling and piracy. When the two vessels find themselves docked at the same space station, Tom tries to keep his mother from getting the ship into trouble with station authorities. . . . Cherryh's satisfying novel delves deeply into the relations between families and crew members tied closely together in long and intimate voyages among the stars." Publ Wkly

Chesney, Marion

Snobbery with violence. St. Martin's Minotaur 2003 226p $22.95
ISBN 0-312-30451-X LC 2003-41351

"Capt. Harry Cathcart, youngest son of a baron, 'fixes' ackward situations for members of the British aristocracy. When he investigates the background of a potential suitor for an earl's daughter, Cathcart proves the suitor to be a cad. In the process, though, the daughter suffers the social consequences of scandal—ostracism. Her parents send her to a 'second chance' country-house party, where she's entangled in a murder mystery, which she and Cathcart solve together. This is a delightful costume melodrama, featuring wry humor and sleuthing protagonists with a pesky love/hate relationship." Libr J

Chesnutt, Charles Waddell, 1858-1932

Stories, novels, & essay; Stories, novels, & essays; [by] Charles W. Chesnutt. Library of Am. 2002 939p $35
ISBN 1-931082-06-5 LC 2001-38120

Contents: The conjure woman; The wife of his youth and other stories of the color line; The house behind the cedars; The marrow of tradition; Uncollected stories; Selected essays

The conjure woman (1899): Contents: The goophered grapevine; Po' Sandy; Mars Jeem's nightmare; The conjurer's revenge; Sis' Becky's pickaninny; The gray wolf's ha'nt; Hot-foot Hannibal

The wife of his youth and other stories of the color line (1899): Contents: The wife of his youth; Her Virginia mammy; The sheriff's children; A matter of principle; Cicely's dream; The passing of Grandison; Uncle Wellington's wives; The bouquet; The web of circumstance

Includes the following uncollected stories: Dave's neckliss; A deep sleeper; Lonesome Ben; The dumb witness; The march of progress; Baxter's Procrustes; The doll; White weeds; The kiss

The house behind the cedars (1900) is "concerned with a light-complexioned black woman who is undecided whether to enjoy comfort as a white man's mistress or the sincere love of a black man." Oxford Companion to Am Lit. 6th edition

The marrow of tradition (1901) explores the struggles of black and white half-sisters. Based on the 1898 massacre in Wilmington, North Carolina, the novel explores the emerging segregationist status quo

Chesterton, G. K. (Gilbert Keith), 1874-1936

Father Brown mystery stories; selected and edited with an introduction by Raymond T. Bond. Dodd, Mead 1962 246p o.p.

Contents: The blue cross; The queer feet; The flying stars; The invisible man; The sins of Prince Saradine; The absence of Mr. Glass; The dagger with wings; The oracle of the dog; The insoluble problem

The Father Brown omnibus; with a preface by Auberon Waugh. Dodd, Mead 1983 993p o.p.

First omnibus edition published 1933; this is a reissue of the 1951 edition analyzed in Short story index, with a new preface by Auberon Waugh

Contents: The wisdom of Father Brown: The absence of Mr. Glass; The paradise of thieves; The duel of Dr. Hirsch; The man in the passage; The mistake of the machine; The head of Caesar; The purple wig; The perishing of the Pendragons; The God of the Gongs; The salad of Colonel Cray; The strange crime of John Boulnois; The fairy tale of Father Brown

The incredulity of Father Brown: The resurrection of Father Brown; The arrow of heaven; The oracle of the dog; The miracle of Moon Crescent; The curse of the golden cross; The dagger with wings; The doom of the Darnaways; The ghost of Gideon Wise

The secret of Father Brown: The secret of Father Brown; The mirror of the magistrate; The man with two beards; The song of the flying fish; The actor and the alibi; The vanishing of Vaudrey; The worst crime in the world; The red moon of Meru; The chief mourner of Marne; The secret of Flambeau

The scandal of Father Brown: The scandal of Father Brown; The quick one; The blast of the book; The green man; The pursuit of Mr. Blue; The crime of the communist; The point of a pin; The insoluble problem; The vampire of the village

The incredulity of Father Brown
In Chesterton, G. K. The Father Brown omnibus p433-630

The innocence of Father Brown. Lane 1911 334p o.p.

Contents: The blue cross; The secret garden; The queer feet; The flying stars; The invisible man; The honour of Israel Gow; The wrong shape; The sins of Prince Saradine; The hammer of God; The eye of Apollo; The sign of the broken sword; The three tools of death

also in Chesterton, G. K. The Father Brown omnibus p1-226

Chesterton, G. K. (Gilbert Keith), 1874-1936— *Continued*

The scandal of Father Brown
In Chesterton, G. K. The Father Brown omnibus p815-974

The secret of Father Brown
In Chesterton, G. K. The Father Brown omnibus p631-811

The wisdom of Father Brown
In Chesterton, G. K. The Father Brown omnibus p227-431

Chesterton, Gilbert Keith *See* Chesterton, G. K. (Gilbert Keith), 1874-1936

Chevalier, Tracy, 1962-

Girl with a pearl earring. Dutton 2000 240p $21.95
ISBN 0-525-94527-X LC 99-32493

Chevalier examines the world of artist Johannes Vermeer and the city of Delft in the 17th century through the eyes of Griet, an illiterate 17-year-old. In this novel the fictional character of Griet, a servant in the Vermeer household, acts as the model for the artist's portrait Girl With a Pearl Earring

The author "has done very well in creating the feel of a society with sharp divisions of status and creed. . . . Griet is a memorable character—reserved, wary, observant, and, although she does not know it, afflicted with a serious and ultimately dangerous crush on her employer. The situation makes a fine story, which is exceptionally well told." Atl Mon

The lady and the unicorn. Dutton 2004 250p $23.95
ISBN 0-525-94767-1 LC 2003-57288

A "tale about a set of medieval tapestries known as the Lady and the Unicorn sequence. Nicolas des Innocents, a handsome, lascivious artist, is summoned to the home of Jean Le Viste, a nobleman who wants Nicolas to design a series of battle tapestries. Jean's wife, Genevieve, persuades Nicolas to talk her husband into a softer subject: the beguilement of a unicorn by a noblewoman. Nicolas shapes the tapestries with his own vision, dedicating five of the six to the senses and using the images of Genevieve and her daughter, Claude, with whom Nicolas is smitten, for the ladies. After finishing the paintings, Nicolas travels from Paris to Brussels, where Georges de la Chapelle will weave them. At first Nicolas is standoffish and scornful of Georges but gradually comes to respect him and take an interest in his blind daughter. But Nicolas' heart lies with the unattainable Claude." Booklist

"With great insight, invention and a remarkable eye for detail, Chevalier breathes life into artists and artisans, their subjects and surroundings and, most important, their magnificent creations." Washington Post Book World

Chiaventone, Frederick J., 1951-

Moon of bitter cold. Forge 2002 398p o.p.
ISBN 0-7653-0093-1 LC 2001-55585

"A Tom Doherty Associates book"

"Fought between 1866 and 1868, Red Cloud's War was precipitated by the construction of three military forts along the Bozeman Trail in the Wyoming Territory. Though abrasive and controversial, Red Cloud, a Lakota chief, manages to forge an unlikely alliance among the Sioux, Cheyenne, Arapaho, and Crow nations. Banding together under the leadership of Red Cloud, the tribes handed the U.S. Army a stunning defeat at Fort Phil Kearney. . . . The author's realistic representation of the major historical players results in a balanced account of a savage cultural clash." Booklist

Child, Lee

Echo burning. Putnam 2001 354p o.p.
ISBN 0-399-14726-8 LC 00-45910

Jack Reacher is "hitching a ride in Lubbock, Tex., when the Mexican wife of a sadistic landowner picks him up and gets his macho dander up with an ugly tale of physical abuse and mental torture. Although he refuses to play hit man for Carmen Greer, he agrees to hang around the family spread, keep the nasty in-laws at bay and see what happens when her husband gets out of prison for tax evasion. But things go wrong, and soon Reacher is looking for a criminal lawyer." N Y Times Book Rev

"Reacher is a one-man wrecking crew nourished only by the hunt. For anyone who thinks the hard-boiled genre is growing soft around the edges." Booklist

The enemy; a Jack Reacher novel. Delacorte Press 2004 393p $25
ISBN 0-385-33667-5 LC 2003-65282

This novel sends the military detective Jack "Reacher back to 1990. The Berlin Wall is being dismantled, and the United States Army's anti-Communist outlook is in disarray. . . . As the cold war winds down, Reacher finds himself embroiled in a Army scandal even as he wonders whether he has a future in uniform." N Y Times (Late N Y Ed)

"Known for his hold-your-breath action scenes, Child proves equally adept at portraying how a criminal investigation uses the smallest of building blocks . . . to construct a compelling circumstantial case." Booklist

One shot; a Jack Reacher novel. Delacorte Press 2005 376p $25
ISBN 0-385-33668-3 LC 2004-58246

"Accused of five murders in what looks like an open-and-shut case, the bad guy fires his last shot: he wants to speak to Jack Reacher." Libr J

"Mr. Child's idea of heroism has nihilism around the edges but a fierce, fighting spirit at its core. In marked contrast to the brooding figures who otherwise dominate contemporary detective stories, Reacher is not one for self-doubt. His is a two-fisted decency. But Mr. Child also gives him amazing powers of deduction, a serious conscience and the occasional touch of tenderness. It's a wildly improbable mixture, one that can't be beat." N Y Times (Late N Y Ed)

Persuader; a Jack Reacher novel. Delacorte Press 2003 342p $24.95
ISBN 0-385-33666-7 LC 2002-34965

Child, Lee—*Continued*

"Beginning with a stunning set-piece involving the apparent kidnapping of a college student, the novel offers the brooding Reacher, a former military policeman, the chance to settle a score with an old nemesis, renegade army intelligence officer Quinn, whom Reacher believed was dead until a chance encounter on a Boston street." Booklist

"What makes the novel really zing, though, is Reacher's narration—aunique mix of the brainy and the brutal, of strategic thinking and explosive action, moral rumination and ruthless force, marking him as one of the most memorable heroes in contemporary thrillerdom." Publ Wkly

Without fail. Putnam 2002 374p o.p.
ISBN 0-399-14861-2 LC 2001-48849

In this thriller Jack Reacher "is given the assignment of his career: to assassinate the newly elected vice president. Well, not exactly. More accurately, a nervous official high up in the Secret Service wants him to figure out . . . how the V.P. *might* be killed. When Reacher and a female confederate obligingly illustrate, the Secret Service contact reveals what Reacher has already surmised—that a serious assassination plot is under way and must be foiled." N Y Time Book Rev

This "novel is a stunner, packed with extraordinary detail regarding executive protection and overlaid with a genuine mystery that will baffle even the most astute armchair crime buffs." Booklist

Child, Lincoln, 1957-

(jt. auth) Preston, D. Brimstone
(jt. auth) Preston, D. The cabinet of curiosities
(jt. auth) Preston, D. Reliquary
(jt. auth) Preston, D. Riptide
(jt. auth) Preston, D. Still life with crows

Childress, Mark, 1957-

Crazy in Alabama. Putnam 1993 383p o.p.
LC 92-38334

"Peejoe, a successful screenwriter living in San Francisco, gets a call from his Aunt Lucille, who wants a part in the movie he's writing. Her request launches Peejoe into remembering the series of incredible events in both his and his aunt's lives in the summer of 1965, 'when everybody went crazy in Alabama.'" Booklist

"It is a measure of Mr. Childress's skill as a novelist—not to mention a triumphant example of style over content—that he soon had me eating out of his hand. I don't know how he did it but he managed to confront every cliché, every convention of the genre head on and pound it into submission, so that his novel seems not only fresh and original but also positively inspired." NY Times Book Rev

Tender; a novel. Harmony Bks. 1990 566p o.p.
LC 90-4298

This novel "features a poor Mississippi-born singer who in the 1950's rises to extraordinary fame, whose career is overseen by an eccentric Southern manager, whose greatest test of character occurs when he's drafted and who lives out his later years overweight and frequently in a drugged stupor." N Y Times Book Rev

"We see the world mostly from Leroy's point of view, and see it plain, we are on stage, watching and enticing the screaming girls, we are caught up in the hard work and technicalities of recording sessions, the heady bafflements of success. If we think of the book as trying to understand Leroy, we may find it engaging enough, but rather thin; if we see it as trying to situate him, to hold him up to the light, it seems a bold and rather austere experiment, a line of details refusing easy generalization." Times Lit Suppl

Chisholm, P. F., 1958-

See also Finney, Patricia, 1958-

Chkhartishvili, Grigory *See* Akunin, Boris, 1956-

Chong, Kevin

Baroque-a-nova. Putnam 2002 225p $23.95
ISBN 0-399-14825-6 LC 2001-19543

"Eighteen-year-old Saul's parents were a modestly successful folk duo, the St. Pierres, in the days of love-ins. Thirty years later, their greatest hit is enjoying a revival thanks to a techno band covering it, but the St. Pierres haven't faired as well. Long divorced, Saul's mostly absent father is living with two much younger women, having left Saul's stepmother. His entirely absent mother has just committed suicide. . . . What could easily have slipped into an archetypal teen-in-trouble novel is saved by a first-person narration that steadfastly refuses to be melodramatic and a protagonist who never loses the ability to make fun of himself." Booklist

Chopin, Kate, 1851-1904

Complete novels and stories; complete novels and stories. Library of Am. 2002 1071p $35
ISBN 1-931082-21-9 LC 2002-19450

Includes the novels At fault and The awakening; the story collections Bayou folk and A night in Acadie; and fifty-five uncollected stories

Bayou folk (1894): A no-account Creole; In and out of old Natchitoches; In Sabine; A very fine fiddle; Beyond the bayou; Old Aunt Peggy; The return of Alcibiade; A rude awakening; The Bênitous' slave; Désirée's baby; A turkey hunt; Madame Célestin's divorce; Love on the Bon-Dieu; Loka; Boulôt and Boulotte; For Marse Chouchoute; A visit to Avoyelles; A wizard from Gettysburg; Ma'ame Pélagie; La belle Zoraide; A gentleman of Bayou Têche; A lady of Bayou St. John

A night in Acadie (1897): A night in Acadie; Athénaise; After the winter; Polydore; Regret; A matter of prejudice; Caline; A Dresden lady in Dixie; Nég Créol; The lilies; Azélie; Mamouche; A sentimental soul; Dead men's shoes; At Chênière Caminada; Odalie misses mass; Cavanelle; Tante Cat'rinette; A respectable woman; Ripe figs; Ozème's holiday

The uncollected stories included are: Emancipation. A life fable; Wiser than a god; A point at issue!; Miss Witherwell's mistake; With the violin; Mrs. Mobry's reason; The going away of Liza; The maid of Saint Phillippe; A shameful affair; A harbinger; Doctor Chevalier's lie; An embarrassing position: comedy in one act; Croque-Mitaine; A little free-mulatto; Miss McEnders; An idle fellow; The story of an hour; Lilacs; The night came slowly; Juanita; The kiss; Her letters; Two summers and two souls; The unexpected; Two portraits; Fe-

Chopin, Kate, 1851-1904—*Continued*
dora; Vagabonds; Madame Martel's Christmas Eve; The recovery; A pair of silk stockings; Aunt Lympy's interference; The blind man; Ti Frère; A vocation and a voice; A mental suggestion; Suzette; The locket; A morning walk; An Egyptian cigarette; A family affair; Elizabeth Stock's one story; A horse story; The storm; The godmother; A little country girl; A reflection; Ti Démon; A December day in Dixie; Alexandre's wonderful experience; The gentleman from New Orleans; Charlie; The white eagle; The wood-choppers; Polly; The impossible Miss Meadows

At fault (1890) is a melodrama set in Louisiana centered on a love triangle between a young widow, a St. Louis businessman who purchases timber rights to her plantation, and his alcoholic wife. The awakening (1899) depicts a Southern woman's revolt against her husband and her quest for sexual and emotional fulfillment

Christensen, Kate

The Epicure's lament; a novel. Doubleday 2004 351p $23.95

ISBN 0-7679-1030-3 LC 2003-51503

"Composed as a series of journal entries by epicure and would-be hermit Hugo Whittier, this novel recounts the intrusions of a variety of family members and their friends into his solitary life at his home on the Hudson. The fortyish, misanthropic Hugo, who is presumably dying of the rare and painful Buerger's disease because he refuses to quit smoking, sets about causing trouble in the hopes of ridding himself of these interlopers, even as he insinuates himself into their lives." Libr J

"The real fun is watching Hugo squirm and rant like a crazed Frasier Crane as he desperately tries to avoid the company of his fellow characters, whom he despises almost as much as he hates himself." Time

Christensen, Lars Saabye, 1953-

The half brother; a novel; [translated by Kenneth Steven] 1st North American ed. Arcade Pub. 2004 682p $27

ISBN 1-559-70715-1 LC 2003-19905

Original Swedish edition, 2001; this translation first published 2003 in the United Kingdom

This novel "charts 50 years in the life of an unconventional Oslo family. . . . Narrator Barnum, an award-winning screenwriter, retraces his family's history, which begins with the rape of his mother, Vera, as a young girl at the end of World War II. From this crime, Barnum's half-brother, Fred, is conceived. Fred is angry, prone to mood swings and outbursts of verbal cruelty. But he is also street-smart, self-reliant and fiercely-if erratically-protective of Barnum, a small, sensitive boy who never grows to full height. The boys live with Vera and an extended family of spirited, loving women, including the Old One, Barnum's great grandmother (a former silent movie actress), and his beer-drinking grandmother, Boletta. Barnum's father is Arnold Nilsen, an itinerant con man, who woos and marries Vera. When Barnum is almost grown up, unpredictable Fred goes to sea and disappears, leaving Barnum angry and confused." Publ Wkly

"The Half Brother combines the meticulousness of a short story and the ambition of an epic and in doing so shows time passing in a new way. By favouring event over explication and imagination over analysis it allows readers to draw any appropriate conclusions. Kenneth Steven has helped by translating the novel superbly into precise, fluent English." Times Lit Suppl

Christie, Agatha, 1890-1976

The A.B.C. murders. Dodd, Mead 1936 248p o.p.

This novel is "about a serial killer who announces his apparently unmotivated killings in advance to Poirot; the only clue is a railway guide left at the scene of each crime. In the opinion of many critics, this is one of Dame Agatha's greatest detective novels." Ency of Mystery & Detection

And then there were none. Dodd, Mead 1940 c1939 218p o.p.

First published 1939 in the United Kingdom with title: Ten little niggers. Variant title: Ten little Indians

"A tour de force on the following trapeze: invitations go out to a group of people, all of whom have been responsible for the death of someone by negligence of intent. The island on which the party is gathered is owned by the would-be avenger of all those deaths. The events and the tension produced by the gradual polishing off of the undetected culprits are beautifully done. One improbability, well hidden, makes the whole thing plausible." Barzun. Cat of Crime. Rev and enl edition

At Bertram's Hotel. Dodd, Mead 1966 c1965 272p o.p.

"A solid, comfortable, respectable London hotel where Miss Jane Marple is spending a two weeks' vacation is suddenly of intense interest to the police. An elderly absent-minded clergyman has vanished from the hotel, and one or two other things seem very odd about the establishment. This London crime tale [is] complete with a clever Chief Inspector who cooperates with Miss Marple . . . [and is] brought to an end with a surprising stroke of horror." Publ Wkly

The body in the library. Dodd, Mead 1942 245p o.p.

"The body that turns up in the married colonel's library is that of a dancing hostess from a neighboring seaside hotel. The setting is St. Mary Mead, whence Miss Marple has drawn her knowledge of human evil and duplicity and applies it to the case at hand, predicting a second murder and averting a third." Barzun. Cat of Crime. Rev and enl edition

By the pricking of my thumbs. Dodd, Mead 1968 275p o.p.

The ingredients of this mystery plot "run all the way from the fancies of some old ladies in a home for the elderly, to dark hints at child murder, the machinations of a clever criminal gang, and the secret life of a supposedly peaceful English village. . . . [Solved by] the husband-and-wife team of Tuppence and Tommy [Beresford]." Publ Wkly

Curtain. Dodd, Mead 1975 238p o.p.

"In this her last book, which contrives Poirot's death *proprio motu*, the old grand master shows that her powers of invention and execution remained strong and fresh till the end. Her villain acts villainous in an entirely new

Christie, Agatha, 1890-1976—*Continued*
way and from an original yet convincing motive. As for Poirot's performance, it is charged with a new purposefulness, ending in a fine display of moral conscience. The story may have one or two moments of weak writing and even an unparsable sentence, but it is an astonishing piece of work nevertheless." Barzun. Cat of Crime. Rev and enl edition

Death on the Nile. Dodd, Mead 1938 c1937 326p o.p.

First published 1937 in the United Kingdom

Detective Hercule Poirot is aboard a Nile steamer in Egypt when the seemingly motiveless murder of a beautiful newly married young woman occurs. Complications quickly multiply as he investigates the case

Endless night. Dodd, Mead 1968 o.p.

First published 1967 in the United Kingdom

"A sharp break with all her previous work: none of her usual detectives. No résumé would be fair since the impact of the book depends upon a skillfully worked-out *volte-face* involving two characters. The creator of Roger Ackroyd has done it again, in a different way, but without any pretense at detection." Barzun. Cat of Crime. Rev and enl edition

Evil under the sun. Dodd, Mead 1941 260p o.p.

The body of beautiful Arlena Marshall is found in a cove and the untangling of the mystery presents Detective Poirot with one of the most baffling and surprising puzzles of his career

The harlequin tea set and other stories. Putnam 1997 281p o.p.

ISBN 0-399-14287-8 LC 96-51140

Contents: The edge; The actress; While the light lasts; The house of dreams; The lonely god; Manx gold; Within the wall; The mystery of the Spanish chest; The harlequin tea set

This collection contains "stories, most of which were published only in British newspapers and magazines during the 1920s. Hercule Poirot and Harley Quin make appearances, as do more 'normal' people dealing with murder." Libr J

Hercule Poirot's casebook. Dodd, Mead 1984 860p $18.95

ISBN 0-396-08417-6 LC 84-13488

All fifty short stories which involve the supersleuth's deductive skills are collected here in one volume for the first time

The Hollow. Putnam 1992 c1974 296p o.p.

ISBN 0-399-13727-0 LC 91-31855

"A Winterbrook edition"

First published 1946; copyright renewed 1974

"A triumph of Christie's art, not so much of characterization—for the detective story does not really permit true character study—but of *motive-building*. That is where A.C. is unrivaled. She knows how to make plausible the divergence between action and motive that maintains uncertainty until the physical clues, the times, and other objective facts mesh with motive to disclose the culprit. The great art is to multiply the ambiguities of feeling, action, and gesture without falling into obvious patterns about greed, revenge, and the like. Here the familiar figure of the able, virile, brilliant man whom women go for is admirably sketched and provided with three possible women murderers and their possibly jealous men. In addition, an elderly *femme folle* very well done—and Poirot." Barzun. Cat of Crime. Rev and enl edition

The mirror crack'd. Dodd, Mead 1962 246p o.p.

First published 1962 in the United Kingdom with title: The mirror crack'd from side to side

Miss Jane Marple, whose house in St. Mary Mead is close to the scene of the crime "gives Scotland Yard her gracious cooperation in solving a poisoning that takes place at a village reception where the hostess is a lovely film star." Publ Wkly

Miss Marple: the complete short stories. Putnam 1985 346p $16.95; pa $12.95

ISBN 0-396-08747-7; 0-425-09486-3 (pa) LC 85-10220

This volume contains "all 20 short stories that Christie centered on the elderly sleuth. . . . The bulk of the stories are gathered from *The Tuesday Club* murders, chronicling the meetings of a group formed by Miss Marple and a handful of her friends." Publ Wkly

Mr. Parker Pyne, detective. Dodd, Mead 1934 244p o.p.

First published in the United Kingdom with title: Parker Pyne investigates

Includes the following stories: Case of the city clerk; Case of the discontented husband; Case of the discontented soldier; Case of the middle-aged wife; Case of the rich woman; Gate of Baghdad; Have you got everything you want?; House at Shiraz; Oracle at Delphi; Pearl of price

Mrs. McGinty's dead. Dodd, Mead 1952 c1951 243p o.p.

First published 1951 in the United Kingdom with title: Blood will tell

"A Poirot story with Mrs. Oliver thrown in for humor, otherwise, an ingenious plot involving the discovery of one of the offspring of some scandals of 20 years earlier, so as to account for the murder of a charwoman who presumably found an incriminating photograph. Complex and well handled, as well as amusing." Barzun. Cat of Crime. Rev and enl edition

The murder at the vicarage; a detective story. Dodd, Mead 1930 319p o.p.

Colonel Protheroe, the heartily disliked squire of St Mary Mead, is the victim. The fact that his wife is desperately in love with another man seems to have supplied motive for murder on the part of two people at least. But shrewd Miss Marple points out several other possibilities

"The plot of this tale is intricate. . . . But it is well constructed and holds the reader's attention on the problem of who wanted Col. Protheroe out of the way. The byplay between the vicar and his flirtatious wife is also an amusing innovation." Barzun. Cat of Crime. Rev and enl edition

Murder in the Calais coach. Dodd, Mead 1934 302p o.p.

A man is murdered on a train going from Istanbul to Calais. The famous detective Hercule Poirot happens to be on board and unravels the mystery

"This is the tour de force in which Agatha makes con-

Christie, Agatha, 1890-1976—*Continued*
spiracy believable and enlivens it by a really satisfying description of the Taurus Express (part of the Orient system)." Barzun. Cat of Crime. Rev and enl edition

A murder is announced. Dodd, Mead 1950 248p o.p.
"A well-told story—her 50th—of blackmail and murder in an English village. Miss Marple does the detecting, and the author plays very fair with the reader in the laying down of a trail leading to the unmasking of a most satisfactory least likely person." Barzun. Cat of Crime. Rev and enl edition

The murder of Roger Ackroyd. Dodd, Mead 1926 306p o.p.
"Roger Ackroyd, a retired business man, is found dead in his study shortly after the suicide of the woman he was to have married. Suspicion and the police point to Ackroyd's adopted son as the murderer, but the outcome of the story is a complete surprise. As in others of Miss Christie's tales, the mystery is solved by . . . M. Poirot." Booklist

Murder with mirrors. Dodd, Mead 1952 182p o.p.
Published in the United Kingdom with title: They do it with mirrors
Inspector Curry of Scotland Yard and Jane Marple investigate a murder at Stonygates, a rehabilitation center for delinquent boys

The mysterious affair at Styles; a detective story. Lane 1920 296p o.p.
Mrs. Inglethorpe, step-mother of John and Lawrence Cavendish, holds their estate in trust for them, but since a recent marriage to a bounder much her junior, has treated her stepsons with less than her usual generosity. She dies suddenly of strychnine poisoning. A guest in the house sends for Hercule Poirot

The mystery of the blue train. Dodd, Mead 1928 306p o.p.
When Rufus Van Aldin bought the string of rubies containing the famous 'Heart of fire,' a flawless stone of great value, he made the mistake of his life. For he gave the necklace to his daughter, who was the only being whom he loved more than himself, and Ruth was murdered and the jewels stolen. The task of finding the murderer and the thief was given to Hercule Poirot

N or M!; the new mystery. Dodd, Mead 1941 289p o.p.
In the spring of 1940, Tommy Beresford, a middle aged man who once worked for British Intelligence, and his wife Tuppence, who worked with him on several cases, are bemoaning their lack of opportunity to contribute to the war effort. Then Tommy is assigned to track down two German agents who are organizing a Fifth Column which has already penetrated the defense and intelligence establishments. Tuppence quickly discovers Tommy's secret mission by her own means and joins in the hunt

The pale horse. Dodd, Mead 1962 c1961 242p o.p.
First published 1961 in the United Kingdom
A story of a Catholic priest who was murdered after hearing a dying woman's confession. "On his body was discovered a list of names, mysterious in that the people had nothing in common; yet when Mark Easterbrook came to inquire into the circumstances of the people named, he began to discover a connection between them, and an ominous pattern." Publisher's note
"This story relies on Mrs. Oliver without Poirot: detection is carried out by an oldish-young scholar called Mark Easterbrook, and what he investigates is superbly organized murder compounded with black magic. A classic treatment of the paralytic suspect-cum-wheelchair is thrown in for good measure." Barzun. Cat of Crime. Rev and enl edition

A pocket full of rye. Dodd, Mead 1953 211p o.p.
The elder Fortescue was killed by poison, but no one could explain the rye in his pocket or the practical joke of the blackbirds in the pie. Inspector Neele welcomed Miss Marple's appearance on the scene, but it was some time before the identity of the guilty person was discovered

Sad cypress. Putnam 1994 c1940 263p o.p.
ISBN 0-399-13924-9 LC 93-31257
"The Winterbrook edition"
A reissue of the title first published 1940. Copyright renewed 1968
"Mary Gerrard, a sweet, well-liked girl, lies dead of morphine poisoning. The evidence suggests murder, and points directly to the hands of Elinor Carlisle— or so it seems. The keen-minded detective Hercule Poirot is called in to explore the charges against her." Publisher's note

The secret of chimneys. Dodd, Mead 1925 310p o.p.
Years before World War I "the pretty little Parisian actress who had long been a member of a gang of international jewel thieves met an amorous Balkan monarch and exchanged her liberty for a few years of uneasy Queenship in a stormy capital. During the brief period before her husband's living subjects hurried him to a blood-stained grave she corresponded with her former associates using a code in which the whereabouts of certain jewels which have been hidden is described. Her letters are stolen; and the author cleverly sets a number of people to work at trying to recover them." Times Lit Suppl

Sleeping murder. Dodd, Mead 1976 242p o.p.
In this posthumously published novel spinster sleuth Miss Marple becomes involved "in an eighteen-year-old murder. Young Gwenda Reed buys a house on the coast only to find it seems oddly familiar; in time she realizes that she has lived in this house briefly when a child, and that what she has thought a nightmare was in fact her memory of seeing her stepmother strangled by a man with monkey's paws. Miss Marple warns her of possible danger unless she lets this 'sleeping murder' lie, but Gwenda and her husband are curious." Newsweek
This is not among Christie's "most skillful works, but it displays her personal sense of what she calls 'evil', of murder as an affront and a violation and an act of unique cruelty. She was not an imaginative or original enough writer to explore this, but when Marple tells us here that 'it was real evil that was in the air last night,' Christie makes us feel her curious primitive shiver." N Y Times Book Rev

Christie, Agatha, 1890-1976—*Continued*

Thirteen at dinner. Dodd, Mead 1933 305p o.p.

Published in the United Kingdom with title: Lord Edgeware dies

Hercule Poirot attends a dinner party as the guest of Lady Edgeware. In the course of conversation she speaks of the desirability of getting rid of her husband, who refuses to divorce her, so that she can marry the Duke of Merton. Within twenty-four hours Lord Edgeware is dead. Poirot investigates the murder

Three blind mice

In Christie, A. Three blind mice and other stories p1-91

Three blind mice and other stories. Dodd, Mead 1950 c1948 250p o.p.

Contents: Three blind mice; Strange jest; Tape-measure murder; The case of the perfect maid; The case of the caretaker; The third-floor flat; The adventure of Johnnie Waverly; Four and twenty blackbirds; The love detectives

A collection of eight stories and one novelette most of the puzzles solved either by Miss Marple or Hercule Poirot. The title story is a novelette, first published 1948, which was also published with the title: The mousetrap, and appeared as a play with that title. It involves a murder at a boarding-house where several people have taken shelter during a snowstorm. After a policeman arrives on skis, another murder takes place

Towards zero. Blakiston 1944 o.p.

"Agatha has always liked the combination of the big house on the cliff, the large party composed of relatives and in-laws at odds with one another, plus a couple of mysterious and possibly good-for-nothing male visitors. All these give sufficient reason for fastening the murder(s) upon almost any one of the group. The present brew is one of her best servings, enhanced by almost too many cleverly arranged clues, some of them laid by the murderer to bring off a double bluff. Poirot functions only to the extent of being wished for by Insp. Battle, who is solid and acceptable." Barzun. Cat of Crime. Rev and enl edition

The witness for the prosecution and other stories. Dodd, Mead 1948 272p o.p.

Contents: The witness for the prosecution; The red signal; The fourth man; S. O. S.; Where there's a will; The mystery of the blue jar; Sing a song of sixpence; The mystery of the Spanish shawl; Philomel cottage; Accident; The second gong

Churchill, Jill, 1943-

Fear of frying. Avon Bks. 1997 216p o.p.

ISBN 0-380-97324-3 LC 97-3188

In this Jane Jeffry mystery, "the amateur sleuth and single mom journeys to an isolated Wisconsin camp and conference center as part of a group to check it out for their school board and city council. All goes well until Jane and best friend Shelley find one of their own dead in the woods. The body disappears, however, and the 'dead' guy turns up alive and well." Libr J

"This is a pleasant, hard-to-solve mystery, with evocative autumnal atmosphere . . . lively writing, and often humorous dialogue." Booklist

A groom with a view; a Jane Jeffry mystery. Avon Twilight 1999 218p o.p.

ISBN 0-380-97570-X LC 99-16666

"Chicago sleuth Jane Jeffry tries her hand at planning a wealthy acquaintance's wedding—in a rather dingy hunting lodge that started life as a monastery. Murder forces Jane back into sleuthing mode, however, to the delight of series fans." Libr J

The merchant of menace; a Jane Jeffry mystery. Avon Twilight 1998 214p o.p.

ISBN 0-380-97569-6 LC 98-4493

"A muckraking journalist crashes series heroine Jane Jeffry's . . . holiday party looking for nasty gossip. The man's subsequent murder leads Jane and friend Shelley into a covey of likely suspects. A welcome addition to the series." Libr J

Chute, Carolyn

The Beans of Egypt, Maine. Ticknor & Fields 1985 215p o.p.

LC 84-8840

"The Beans are the unworthy poor with a vengeance, and the novel is a sequence of their dismal, cozy or audacious moments with one another and their angry or hapless encounters with outsiders. Between chapters about the Beans, Mrs. Chute narrates the life of the Beans' neighbor, Earlene Pomerleau. . . . Her story—in its entirety—consists of her progress from a childhood dominated by God-fearing Gram and Gram-fearing Daddy to a worse subjugation—through marriage—as a woman among the Beans." N Y Times Book Rev

The author "vividly evokes the substitutions rural poverty must make for everything from drinking glasses to romance, yet her imaginary Egypt can also echo with Old Testament allusions. The writing is uneven: sometimes striking and provocative, but mainly hovering uncomfortably between (perfectly caught) rural Maine speech patterns and a more literary spareness." Libr J

Other titles about the inhabitants of Egypt, Maine are: Letourneau's Used Auto Parts (1988) and Merry men (1994)

Ciresi, Rita

Sometimes I dream in Italian. Delacorte Press 2000 209p o.p.

ISBN 0-385-33493-1 LC 00-29451

"Each chapter covers a different period in the lives of two Italian American sisters, Angel and Lina. . . . We follow Angel and Lina through their youth and into adulthood. Lina's teenage pregnancy leads her into an unhappy yet prosperous marriage. Angel has an uninspired job writing Catholic greeting cards yet dreams of the house and kids that her sister has. As Angel begins a serious relationship with a man she met though the personal ads, she is forced to confront her dreams head on." Libr J

"Ciresi has a lovely ear for dialogue and the ability to nail the details in descriptions that are both funny and painfully accurate; the result is a book that manages to be simultaneously blunt and artful." N Y Times Book Rev

Cisneros, Sandra

Caramelo. Knopf 2002 443p o.p.
ISBN 0-679-43554-9 LC 2002-25488

"When Celaya (or 'Lala') Reyes takes a family vacation from Chicago to Mexico City, she begins a journey from girl to young adult and from the present to the past. Generous digressions trace roots and branches on the luxuriant family tree, telling the tales of ancestors, family members, and sometimes even walk-on players." Booklist

"Cisneros writes poetry as well as prose and her language-especially in the first section of the novel, mostly set in Mexico—is a lovely fusion of Spanish and English, idea and emotion, geography and spirit." N Y Times Book Rev

The house on Mango Street. Knopf 1994 134p $24
ISBN 0-679-43335-X LC 93-43564

"Originally published by Arte Público Press in 1984." Verso of title page

Composed of a series of interconnected vignettes, this "is the story of Esperanza Cordero, a young girl growing up in the Hispanic quarter of Chicago. For Esperanza, Mango Street is a desolate landscape of concrete and run-down tenements, where she discovers the hard realities of life—the fetters of class and gender, the specter of racial enmity, the mysteries of sexuality, and more." Publisher's note

This is "a composite of evocative snapshots that manages to passionately recreate the milieu of the poor quarters of Chicago." Commonweal

Woman Hollering Creek and other stories. Random House 1991 165p o.p.
ISBN 0-394-57654-3 LC 90-52930

"Unforgettable characters march through a satisfying collection of tales about Mexican-Americans who know the score and cling to the anchor of their culture." N Y Times Book Rev

Clancy, Tom, 1947-

The bear and the dragon. Putnam 2000 1028p $27.95
ISBN 0-399-14563-X LC 00-56499

Clancy "spins numerous plot strands—among them: a Sino-American spy seduces his way into Politburo secrets; enormous oil and gold reserves are discovered in Siberia; the new Papal Nuncio to Beijing is murdered; the Politburo orders a hit on a top Russian official—that lead to a Chinese invasion of Russia and a credible war scenario that occupies the novel's last quarter and that culiminates in a nuclear crescendo. . . . Add to that the excitement for Clancy fans of this being the first novel to feature not just Jack Ryan but also, in significant subordinate roles, Jack Clark and Ding Chavez of *Rainbow Six* and other tales." Publ Wkly

The Cardinal of the Kremlin. Putnam 1988 543p $27.95
ISBN 0-399-13345-3 LC 88-5818

In this novel Jack Ryan "is a CIA adviser to American arms negotiators. The talks are going well, but a chance sighting by a spy satellite reveals that the Russians are pursuing their own version of Star Wars just as they are demanding American concessions in that area at the bargaining table. Ryan and his colleagues hope for still more intelligence from a highly placed Russian mole, but the long-operating source is himself threatened with discovery." Publ Wkly

"Readers expecting the usual Clancy fare of highly-detailed battle scenes and lengthy descriptions of technology will be disappointed . . . but the details of the workings of the CIA and KGB will more than make up for his lack of discourse about hardware." West Coast Rev Books

Clear and present danger. Putnam 1989 656p o.p.
LC 89-10287

"A president decides that drug smuggling has become a 'clear and present danger' to national security. The response is a complex and covert military campaign against the 'Colombian Cartel.' Clancy presents the technology of special operations and the details of light infantry warfare with his usual facility. Superior even to his descriptions of tools and techniques, however, is Clancy's analysis of the legal and moral problems of operating in a twilight zone, where the rules are ambiguous and an open society makes secrecy impossible." Publ Wkly

Debt of honor. Putnam 1994 766p o.p.
ISBN 0-399-13954-0 LC 94-27313

"Jack Ryan, now the President's National Security Adviser, finds himself embroiled in the buildup to a new world war—one in which the stock market and national economic policy are as critical as advanced weaponry. A power-hungry Japanese financier, still blaming America for his parents' deaths in WW II, plans to use his immense wealth to purchase his revenge. . . . As always, Clancy instructs (sometimes didactically) as he entertains, teaching us about currency trading, Asian business etiquette and the daily life of an American politician." Publ Wkly

Executive orders. Putnam 1996 874p $27.95
ISBN 0-399-14218-5 LC 96-23388

Jack Ryan "must put together a government from the wreckage left at the end of *Debt of Honor*. While Jack, who assumed the U.S. presidency after the shocking deaths of the president and many congresspeople, attends to affairs of state, selecting a new Cabinet and arranging for special Congressional elections, enemies far and near continue to create nefarious plots against the United States. Political enemies prove themselves equally relentless, attacking the very legitimacy of Ryan's presidential role." Libr J

The author's "plotting here is masterful, as is his strumming of patriotic heartstrings." Publ Wkly

The hunt for Red October. Naval Inst. Press 1984 387p $27.95
ISBN 0-87021-285-0 LC 84-16569

"Based on a true incident—the attempted defection of a Soviet destroyer in 1975—the plot concerns the defection of the 'Red October', a Soviet submarine carrying 26 Seahawk missiles able to destroy 200 cities. Russia's fleet is ordered to find and destroy the sub; the U.S. Navy wants to find it and get it to an American port. An 18-day, 4,000-mile hunt across the Atlantic ensues." Booklist

Patriot games. Putnam 1987 540p $27.95
ISBN 0-399-13241-4 LC 87-6910

Clancy, Tom, 1947-—*Continued*

"On a visit with his wife and daughter in London, Ryan stumbles onto an attempt by a new Irish revolutionary group to kidnap the Prince and Princess of Wales and their eldest son. Using his Marine Corps training, Ryan saves the royals (which leads to several visits between the Ryans and the residents of Buckingham Palace), but Ryan becomes the target of the surviving terrorists." Publ Wkly

Rainbow Six. Putnam 1998 740p $27.95
ISBN 0-399-14390-4 LC 98-22301

"This thriller features ex-Navy Seal vigilante John Clark who now heads Rainbow Six, an international antiterrorist strike force. The novel also features Clark's longtime protégé 'Ding' Chavez. The story opens vigorously if arbitrarily, with an attempted airline hijacking foiled by Clark and Chavez, who happen to be on the plane. After that action sequence, the duo and others train at Rainbow Headquarters outside London, then leap into the fray against terrorists who have seized a bank in Bern, Switzerland." Publ Wkly

"Clancy obviously puts no credence in the advice that 'less is more,' but his mammoth book is meticulously researched and carefully plotted." N Y Times Book Rev

Red rabbit. Putnam 2002 618p
ISBN 0-399-14870-1 LC 2002-67958

This thriller relates the "story behind Mehmet Ali Agca's (real-life) failed attempt on the life of Pope John II in 1981. By going back 21 years, Clancy provides a fresh adventure for a young Jack Ryan . . . only a supporting player here. The book's main heroes are the husband-and-wife team of Ed Foley, CIA station chief in Moscow, and his agent-wife, Mary Pat, and Oleg Zaitev (code-named Rabbit), the mid-level employee in the KGB communications department who for conscience's sake decides to defect to America when he's asked to encrypt messages that reveal a plot, under the auspices of then-KGB chief Yuri Andropov, to kill the pope." Publ Wkly

Red Storm rising. Putnam 1986 652p o.p.
ISBN 0-399-13149-3 LC 86-9488

"A team of Moslem terrorists blows up a key Russian oil installation. Faced with a severe fuel shortage, the Soviets plan to seize the Persian Gulf, after establishing an elaborate smoke screen of hostilities against NATO. The cunning ruses used to justify the sudden Russian attack on Germany, the clever attempts to downplay Soviet firepower, and the subsequent land, sea, and air battles over Eastern Europe and the North Atlantic take up much of this book as the author weaves the various key offensives together." Booklist

The sum of all fears. Putnam 1991 798p o.p.
ISBN 0-399-13615-0 LC 91-11917

"In the late 1990s the world is cautiously emerging from the Cold War; even the Arab-Israeli conflict is being resolved, thanks to the cleverness of Clancy's hero Jack Ryan. But as confrontation yields to cooperation, what becomes of displaced terrorists? Palestinians without a cause and East Germans without a country seek to rekindle U.S.-U.S.S.R. animosity." Publ Wkly

The teeth of the tiger. G.P. Putnam's Sons 2003 431p $27.95
ISBN 0-399-15079-X LC 2003-47125

This book features Jack "Ryan's son, also known as Jack, as well as two of young Jack's cousins, fraternal twins Dominic and Brian Caruso, the former an FBI agent, the latter a Marine. All three are recruited to a privately funded vigilante organization, Hendley Associates, that aims to strike at America's enemies—particularly, terrorists—when the Feds can't or won't. . . . Their grapplings with the moral and logistical demands of their new jobs alternate with a villains' plot, as Islamic terrorists cut a deal with Colombian drug smugglers, sneak into the U.S. and move toward their killing-field objectives, four shopping malls in mid-America." Publ Wkly

Without remorse. Putnam 1993 639p $25.95
ISBN 0-399-13825-0 LC 93-13940

"John Kelly [introduced in The hunt for Red October] an ex-Navy SEAL in torment over the recent, accidental death of his wife and the murder of a friend (who was mixed up with a drug ring) takes on two free-lance jobs. First, he sets out to eliminate the man or men responsible for the murder by becoming judge and executioner (skip the jury) of any and all drug dealers who can lead him to the responsible party. Second, he agrees to return to Vietnam (this is 1970), where he has already earned three Purple Hearts. He leads a raid into the north where U.S. officers are being held for interrogation by the Soviets." Booklist

Clark, Carol Higgins

Decked; a Regan Reilly mystery. Warner Bks. 1992 230p o.p.
LC 91-50639

This mystery, finds "private detective Regan Reilly returning to Oxford for her tenth reunion. Discovery of a dead classmate's body on the estate of a former professor and his eccentric aunt, however, dampens any festivity. Regan accompanies the aunt on a week-long cruise to New York after someone poisons the original companion, but stays in touch with police. Danger lurks on the boat, of course, and Regan figures things out just in time." Libr J

Iced. Warner Bks. 1995 256p o.p.
LC 95-7592

"Thirtysomething private investigator Reilly is headed for the ski slopes of Aspen for the Christmas holidays, parents in tow. Mom and Dad are to be houseguests of television actress Kendra Wood while Regan visits with an old friend who's opening a new restaurant. But the Reillys walk into more than just a cheery holiday ski party—Kendra Wood's valuable art collection has been stolen, and her trusted housekeeper, Eben Bean, is missing. That's all Regan needs to know to send her off in pursuit of Eben and the sneaky thieves." Booklist

Snagged. Warner Bks. 1993 227p o.p.
LC 92-50568

In Miami for a friend's wedding L.A. based PI Regan Reilly "acquires a new friend in the bride's uncle, Richie Blossom, who has invented 'run-proof, snag-proof' pantyhose. If Richie can sell his patent to a manufacturer, he'll have the funds to buy the retirement home where he and his friends live. . . . Meanwhile Ruth Craddock of Calla-Lilly Hosiery, who has her hands on a pair of the prototype pantyhose, realizes that Richie's invention could put her out of business. When an aggressive driver nearly mows Richie down, Regan appoints herself his protector." Publ Wkly

Clark, Carol Higgins—*Continued*

Twanged. Warner Bks. 1998 259p $28
ISBN 0-446-51763-1 LC 97-32287

"It's summertime, and Regan Reilly is called back home from Los Angeles to the Hamptons on New York's Long Island to protect her friend Brigid O'Neill, an up-and-coming country singer with a knack for fiddling who'll be performing at the local Melting Pot Music Festival. Brigid has been given a legendary old fiddle by Ireland's champion fiddler, Malachy Sheerin, but legend has it that to take this fiddle out of Ireland will bring bad luck to the owner. Multimillionaire Chappy Tinka wants the instrument, which bears the initials C.T., and he's prepared to do anything to claim it for himself. An array of amusing but not necessarily deep supporting characters adds to this light but well-composed mystery." Libr J

(jt. auth) Clark, M. H. Deck the halls

Clark, Curt

For works written by this author under other names see Stark, Richard; Westlake, Donald E.

Clark, Martin

Plain heathen mischief; a novel; Martin Clark. Knopf 2004 397p $24.95
ISBN 1-400-04096-5 LC 2003-60475

This novel "begins when the Rev. Joel King is released from jail after a six-month sentence for the statutory rape of now-18-year-old gold digger Christy Darden. The question of whether Joel is actually guilty of the crime to which he confessed persists, but he keeps his lips sealed as he and parishioner Edmund Brooks drive from Roanoke, Va., to Missoula, Wyo., to be with Joel's recently single sister Sophie and his Alzheimer's-afflicted mother. It turns out the irascible Edmund is into insurance fraud, among other things, and, with Las Vegas attorney Sa'ad X. Sa'ad, is capable of unimaginable deceit and criminal activity. Facing divorce, jobless and desperate, Joel gets wrapped up in their latest scheme . . . . There is barely a false note in this comic novel of hope and redemption. Minor characters are rich and multilayered, and the dialogue is priceless." Publ Wkly

Clark, Mary Higgins

All around the town. Simon & Schuster 1992 301p o.p.
LC 92-7511

"When four-year-old Laurie Kenyon ventures out into the front yard to wave at a funeral procession against the strict rules imposed by her mother, nightmarish repercussions ensue. She is kidnapped by a child molester who is abetted by his wife. Even though Laurie is released a few years later and returned to her family, the horror is buried within her psyche. . . . A psychiatrist discovers that Laurie has four other personalities." Booklist

"Besides doling out the visceral thrills in well-calibrated increments [Clark] also knows how to translate more complex psychological terrors into simple, scary prose. There is cunning here, and much craft." N Y Times Book Rev

All through the night. Simon & Schuster 1998 170p o.p.
ISBN 0-684-85660-3 LC 98-36927

This "holiday tale of suspense and sentiment opens with a young unmarried woman leaving her newborn baby on the steps of a church on Manhattan's Upper West Side. At the same time, a young man steals the church's precious chalice. Both the child and the chalice then disappear, and it's up to Alvirah, Clark's lottery winner turned sleuth, and husband Willy to solve the mystery." Libr J

The Anastasia syndrome
In Clark, M. H. The Anastasia syndrome and other stories p9-157

The Anastasia syndrome and other stories. Simon & Schuster 1989 318p o.p.
LC 89-38841

Contents: The Anastasia syndrome; Terror stalks the class reunion; Lucky day; Double vision; The lost angel

In the title novella a "noted woman historian sets to work on a study of the British Civil War, juggling her research schedule with a love affair with a rising politician. But her writing is interrupted by strange mental sequences that seem to transport her back to Cromwell's time and involve her in plots against the monarchy. Moreover, these troubling events out of the past are mirrored in the present as a series of terrorist bombings seems to follow the historian's path around England." Booklist

Before I say goodbye. Simon & Schuster 2000 332p o.p.
ISBN 0-684-83598-3 LC 00-266596

"Nell MacDermott, a Manhattan political columnist with her eye on her grandfather's Congressional seat, has been hearing voices since she was 10 years old. But she doesn't tap into her gifts until her husband, Adam, dies in a boating accident and a sympathetic aunt takes her to a medium. Suddenly Nell is seeing black auras and having insights into her husband's shady character and dodgy business deals. There are limits to her powers, however, and she fails to spot the villain who is setting her up to die." N Y Times Book Rev

"The elements of Clark's plot masterfully converge to reveal the killer. A fast-paced, fun ride that leaves the reader guessing until the end." Booklist

The cradle will fall. Simon & Schuster 1980 314p o.p.
LC 80-121

"The story centers on what assistant prosecutor Katie De Maio may have seen when she was recovering in the hospital from a car accident. Katie believes, but isn't sure, that she saw a doctor load the body of a young woman into the trunk of a car. Katie has seen clearly, but she doesn't know it. The doctor, a fertility expert who murders his unsuccessful experimental subjects, has seen Katie and determines to get rid of her." Booklist

A cry in the night. Simon & Schuster 1982 317p o.p.
LC 82-10289

"After divorce from a callow actor, Jenny McPartland works hard at a Manhattan art gallery to support her two young daughters. At an exhibition of the works of Erich Krueger, the painter is thunderstruck when he meets Jenny. He is handsome, mature, kind, and he loves her children, so when he proposes, Jenny accepts. At first she is

Clark, Mary Higgins—*Continued*
impressed with Erich's magnificent mansion in rural Minnesota; but her new husband soon displays odd traits and jealous possessiveness. When Jenny's ex-husband shows up to scrounge, he quickly disappears; a too friendly stable boy nearly dies of poison; Jenny gives birth to Erich's child, which dies mysteriously—and all signs point to Jenny as either mad or criminal." Publ Wkly

In this neo-Gothic thriller "the clues are so subtle, so delicately woven into the fabric of the heroine's life, that even the reader begins to believe, with the heroine, that she herself is either criminal or insane." West Coast Rev Books

Daddy's little girl. Simon & Schuster 2002 291p o.p.
ISBN 0-7432-0604-5 LC 2002-21112
This novel's "heroine is Atlanta investigative journalist Ellie Cavanaugh, who was seven when her sister, Andrea, 15, was beaten to death by 20-year-old Rob Westerfield, scion of the wealthiest family in a small Westchester town. Now Westerfield is up for parole, so Ellie, now 30, returns home to speak out against him. When Westerfield is released, Ellie begins to write a book aimed at re-proving his guilt. . . . With its textured plot, well-sketched secondary characters, strong pacing and appealing heroine, this is Clark at her most winning." Publ Wkly

Deck the halls; [by] Mary Higgins Clark and Carol Higgins Clark. Simon & Schuster 2000 202p $18
ISBN 0-7432-1200-2 LC 00-49284
"Nora Reilly, the famous mystery writer, is laid up in a Manhattan hospital with a broken leg when her husband, a funeral director named Luke Reilly, and his driver, Rosita Gonzalez, are kidnapped by two ill-mannered young men. Fortunately, the Reillys' daughter, the private investigator Regan Reilly, has come in from Los Angeles for the Christmas holidays. . . . She teams up with Alvirah Meehan, a washerwoman-turned-lottery-winner who is also a renowned amateur detective." N Y Times Book Rev

"If the novel generates little suspense, it does go down like roasted chestnuts, and fans will greatly enjoy the pairing of two favorite detectives." Publ Wkly

I'll be seeing you. Simon & Schuster 1993 317p o.p.
LC 93-16584
The "heroine is Meghan Collins, a young reporter who's just landed a coveted spot on network news, but her satisfaction is tempered by sadness and worry as the investigation into her father's puzzling death flounders in uncertainty. . . . Then Meghan has a jolting experience while covering a news story at a Manhattan hospital. An unidentified young woman is rushed in, dying from a knife wound to the heart, and—there's no other way to put it—she's a dead ringer for Meghan." Booklist

"The story moves swiftly and plays cunningly on the universal fear of parental loss and abandonment. And by voicing our secret anxieties about designer genetics . . . Ms. Clark raises such horrid possibilities that, like Meghan, we have no patience for some silly killer lurking in the shadows." N Y Times Book Rev

Let me call you sweetheart; a novel. Simon & Schuster 1995 319p $24
ISBN 0-684-80396-8 LC 95-7331
This novel's protagonist Kerry McGrath "visits an eminent plastic surgeon and sees too many women come out of his office with the same beautiful face as his daughter, the victim in a 10-year-old domestic homicide. Kerry, a rising star in the prosecutor's office in Bergen County, N.J., opens a private investigation into the old case. This spooks some very dangerous people with some very good reasons for wanting to keep the past buried." N Y Times Book Rev

The lottery winner; Alvirah and Willy stories. Simon & Schuster 1994 265p o.p.
ISBN 0-671-86716-4 LC 94-241491
Contents: The body in the closet; Death on the Cape; Plumbing for Willy; A clean sweep; The lottery winner; Bye, Baby Bunting

"For readers who enjoy the nouveau riche approach to crime solving (á la Jonathan and Jennifer Hart or Nick and Nora Charles), these stories may prove . . . entertaining." Booklist

Loves music, loves to dance. Simon & Schuster 1991 319p o.p.
LC 91-10757
This novel focuses "on two friends, Erin and Darcy, who'd been college roommates and now, in their late twenties and each engrossed in her own profession, remain close. Thinking little of it, they become involved in a research project concerning people who utilize personal ads to meet people of potential romantic interest; but their efforts result in the murder of Erin." Booklist

"This Cinderella story turned sour reaffirms that Mary Higgins Clark deserves her reputation for creating splendid suspenseful fiction. Though the novel's characters are simple in more ways than one . . . the plot—surprisingly upbeat and thoroughly engaging—more than makes up for this flaw." N Y Times Book Rev

Moonlight becomes you; a novel. Simon & Schuster 1996 332p o.p.
LC 96-11529
In this suspense novel, "it goes unnoticed that someone is bumping off the residents of an exclusive retirement home in Newport, R.I.—until the killer jumps the gun and murders a woman who was only *thinking* of taking up residence. This faux pas alerts Maggie Holloway, the victim's former stepdaughter, that something is strongly amiss at the Latham Manor Residence. . . . Although the characters seem more peculiar than threatening, Ms. Clark has a sneaky way of injecting undertones of menace into a genteel place like Newport." N Y Times Book Rev

My gal Sunday. Simon & Schuster 1996 244p o.p.
ISBN 0-684-83229-1
Contents: A crime of passion; They all ran after the president's wife; Hail, Columbia!; Merry Christmas/Joyeux Noël

A husband-and-wife sleuthing team are the stars of this collection. The author's "protagonists are Henry Parker Britland IV, the 44-year-old former president of the U.S., and his recent bride, plucky congresswoman Sandra ('Sunday') O'Brien Britland. Debonair, wealthy Henry

Clark, Mary Higgins—*Continued*
and smart-as-a-whip Sunday enjoy their estates in New Jersey, Florida, the Bahamas and Provence, and other perks of Henry's patrician background, such as a private jet and an elegant yacht. But they keep getting embroiled in dicey situations. . . . Clark uses every occasion to celebrate her gorgeous newlyweds' delirious happiness and misses no opportunity to cater to those readers who favor a little romance with their mild suspense." Publ Wkly

Nighttime is my time. Simon & Schuster 2004 370p $25.95
ISBN 0-7432-0607-X LC 2004-273751
This book features "three females in peril, all targets of a serial killer who fancies himself a night-hunting predator. . . . The Owl kills his first victim, then it's off to attend his 20th high school reunion at Stonecroft Academy in Cornwall-on-Hudson, where he intends to do in the last several women who humiliated him when he was a geeky high school student. . . . The game here is figuring out which of the men who come to the reunion, all former nerds, is the Owl." Publ Wkly

No place like home; Mary Higgins Clark. Simon & Schuster 2005 368p $25.95
ISBN 0-7432-6489-4 LC 2005-42535
"At One Old Mill Lane, in Mendham, N.J., 10-year-old Liza Barton wakes to find her stepfather, Ted Cartwright, attacking her mother, Audrey. Liza grabs a gun in defense, but in the ensuing melee Audrey is killed and Ted is wounded. Dubbed 'Little Lizzie Borden,' Liza is taken away and almost convicted of murdering her mother and attempting to kill the lying, scheming Ted. Twenty-four years later, Liza, now known as Celia Foster Nolan, has just been presented with a surprise birthday present from her new husband, Alex: the house at One Old Mill Lane." Publ Wkly

On the street where you live. Simon & Schuster 2001 317p $26
ISBN 0-7432-0602-9 LC 2001-272623
"In the 1890s, three young women in the upscale seaside village of Spring Lake died at the hands of an unidentified killer. In the present day, two young women have disappeared from town—and their killer, whose first-person ruminations vein the third-person narrative, is preparing to strike again. His final target will be Emily Graham, an ambitious young attorney just moved to Spring Lake from upstate New York, where she'd been victimized by a stalker. . . . Clark's prose ambles as usual, but it takes readers where they want to go—deep into an old-fashioned tale of a damsel in delicious distress." Publ Wkly

Pretend you don't see her; a novel. Simon & Schuster 1997 318p $25
ISBN 0-684-81039-5
Lacey Farrell, "a 30-ish Manhattan real estate agent, witnesses the murder of a client, she is forced into hiding while the police slowly draw a net around the killer. But a puzzling last request from the victim means Lacey is still involved and still in danger, even as she assumes a new identity in another city. Somehow, in the midst of all this role-playing, while unraveling a growing number of knotted clues that seem to link her family to the crime, the frazzled Lacey also manages to meet Mr. Right." N Y Times Book Rev

Remember me. Simon & Schuster 1994 306p o.p.
ISBN 0-671-86708-3 LC 94-8762
"Just what is the mysterious presence that seems to haunt Menley Nichols and baby Hannah in their spectacular rented Cape Cod mansion? Menley is still trying to recover from the horror of her two-year-old son Bobby's death on the railroad crossing. Lawyer husband Adam is too busy dashing to and from New York, and defending a local hunk suspected of doing away with his wealthy bride, to be much help. And so the presence moves in on Menley, *Rebecca* style, with eerie middle-of-the-night sound effects and rocking cradles. As always with Clark, there are several plots going on at once, which are miraculously blended and resolved in the finale." Publ Wkly

The second time around; Mary Higgins Clark. Simon & Schuster 2003 302p $26
ISBN 0-7432-0606-1 LC 2003-271798
"Financial columnist Marcia 'Carley' DeCarlo finds herself squarely in the middle of a bizarre story about the mysterious disappearance of Nick Spencer, founder of the medical research firm Gen-stone, which had been on the brink of developing a cancer vaccine. When it's discovered that Spencer apparently stole thousands of investment dollars and either lied about or sabotaged the progress of the vaccine's development, Carley can't believe it. . . . Under the guise of doing an in-depth story on Nick Spencer, Carley conducts her own investigation, discovering dark forces behind Gen-stone's demise. The prolific and ever-popular Clark isn't the subtlest crime writer, but she knows how to spin an intriguing tale, and this time she's created a convincing heroine in Carley." Booklist

Silent night; a novel. Simon & Schuster 1995 154p o.p.
ISBN 0-684-81545-1 LC 95-36717
"The story is about seven-year-old Brian Dornan, whose leukemia-stricken dad is convalescing in a New York hospital. Brian, walking to the hospital with his mom, sees a woman pick up the wallet his mother has accidentally dropped. The wallet contains a St. Christopher medal that Brian is convinced will help make his dad okay again, so when the woman takes off, Brian follows. Unfortunately, the woman is Cally Hunter, sister of escaped convict Jimmy Siddons, who winds up taking Brian hostage." Booklist
"Clark blatantly, if cleverly, pulls all the sentimental strings here, but most readers will find this a heartwarming, affirmative tale of the power of faith." Publ Wkly

Stillwatch. Simon & Schuster 1984 302p o.p.
LC 84-14058
"Pat Traymore arrives in the nation's capital to produce a TV documentary on Sen. Abigail Jennings, rumored to be the President's choice to succeed the ailing, retired Vice-President. Disregarding dire warnings, Pat moves back into the house where, when she was a baby, her father had killed her mother and himself and tried to kill her too. The young woman begins to suspect something not quite admirable in Jenning's background as her research gets under way." Publ Wkly

Clark, Mary Higgins—*Continued*

A stranger is watching. Simon & Schuster 1978 c1977 314p o.p.

"When Steve Peterson's son and girl friend disappear, there is no apparent connection between this event and the murder of Steve's wife several years earlier. The latter crime had supposedly been solved, and, indeed, the convicted murderer is about to be executed. However, the kidnapping, the murder, and the execution are linked, as it turns out, and the common denominator is an expert mechanic and full-time psychopath named Arty." Best Sellers

Weep no more, my lady; a novel. Simon and Schuster 1987 315p o.p.

LC 87-4760

This novel "is a throwback to the romantic suspense of the thirties and forties. A beautiful leading actress, Leila LaSalle, dies in a fall from her high-rise terrace, leaving behind a wealthy fiancé who is arrested for her murder. Various 'friends' jockey for money and power and alibis, while her inconsolable little sister wanders around unaware that she is next on the killer's hit list." Wilson Libr Bull

"Although this novel is not quite as tightly plotted as other of Clark's best-sellers, . . . the author's legions of fans will find much to enjoy here—characters aplenty, multiple motives, and enough surprises to keep the action chugging along." Booklist

We'll meet again. Simon & Schuster 1999 320p o.p.

ISBN 0-684-83597-5 LC 99-20134

In this thriller Molly Carpenter Lasch "is convicted of murdering her faithless husband, the founder of a physician-run H.M.O. in Greenwich, Conn. When Molly gets out of prison five years later, still suffering from the 'dissociative amnesia' that blocked out the details of her husband's death, the real killer sets her up for another murder. Although Molly is more passive—and much dimmer—than she needs to be, . . . she suffers with becoming grace and dignity for the victim of the diabolical plot that Clark prepares so carefully and executes with such relish." N Y Times Book Rev

Where are the children? Simon & Schuster 1975 223p

This tale is "set against a background of Cape Cod in the dead of winter. Nancy Eldredge's past hides a terrible secret. She was once tried and almost convicted of the murder of her two young children from a first marriage. . . . She is now happily married again with another little boy and girl. When these children vanish from their front yard in a snowstorm, Nancy's past is raked up and the local police are certain she has killed again." Publ Wkly

While my pretty one sleeps; a novel. Simon & Schuster 1989 318p o.p.

LC 89-6078

"Fashion expert Neeve Kearney wonders why a controversial, unlikable writer, Ethel Lambston, suddenly disappears and is then murdered. Clark assembles a cast of suspects and skillfully juggles the possible motives and clues. As Neeve gathers evidence, a killer is hired to do her in. Meanwhile, Neeve's father, a former police commissioner, is haunted by a threat issued long ago against his daughter. He becomes convinced that the source of the present danger is the same organized crime figure accused of killing Neeve's mother 17 years earlier. Not the best of Clark's thrillers, but certain to be of interest to her widespread audience." Booklist

You belong to me. Simon & Schuster 1998 317p $25

ISBN 0-684-83595-9 LC 98-13064

This suspense novel features "Susan Chandler, a Manhattan clinical psychologist with a popular radio talk show. When Susan does a program on 'vanishing women,' it elicits fresh evidence in an unsolved murder case; but it also smokes out the predator, who hunts and kills the witnesses to protect his identity." N Y Times Book Rev

Clark, Nancy, 1952-

The Hills at home. Pantheon Bks. 2003 481p $25

ISBN 0-375-42203-X LC 2002-72314

"In the summer of 1989, septuagenarian Lily Hill's serenely solitary life in her ramshackle family home in Towne, MA, comes to a screeching halt. A torrent of Hill relatives with a richly diverse menu of dysfunctional quirks pours into her life, and they forget to leave." Libr J

"The plot is mild and ambling, and the darker emotions are kept strictly offstage, but plot and angst are not the point. The point is the revelation of a particular kind of life, and at that the book succeeds brillantly." N Y Times Book Rev

Clark, Walter Van Tilburg, 1909-1971

The Ox-bow incident. Random House 1940 309p o.p.

"Rustlers are systematically stealing cattle near Bridger's Gulch, Nevada, in the late 1880s. After a cattleman is killed, an illegal posse is formed to apprehend the criminals. In a remote valley they surprise three men, hold a makeshift trial, and hang the three. Soon afterward it is discovered that the wrong men have been punished. This is a western with psychological insight." Shapiro. Fic for Youth. 3d edition

Clarke, Arthur C., 1917-

2001: a space odyssey. New Am. Lib. 1968 221p o.p.

Astronauts of the spaceship Discovery, aided by their computer, HAL, blast off in search of proof that extraterrestrial beings had a part in the development of intelligent life forms on Earth millions of years ago.

"By standing the universe on its head, the author makes us see the ordinary universe in a different light. . . . [This novel becomes] a complex allegory about the history of the world." New Yorker

2010: odyssey two. Ballantine Bks. 1982 291p o.p.

LC 82-6850

"A Del Rey book"

"The Soviet Union and the United States send a joint mission, which includes Dr. Heywood Floyd, to find out what happened to David Bowman, HAL, and the 'Dis-

Clarke, Arthur C., 1917-—*Continued*
covery'. . . . Clarke has written a sequel to the movie, not the book, but it doesn't matter. This is another gripping adventure for which there is bound to be much demand." Libr J

2061: odyssey three. Ballantine Bks. 1987 279p o.p.
LC 87-47811

"A Del Rey book"

"Fifty years after the alien message forbidding humans to approach the moon Europa, an expedition to Halley's Comet is forced to violate the prohibition in the name of mercy." Libr J

"Clarke transforms his grasp of science into informed speculation while unleashing, with the understated skill of a master storyteller, several stunning narrative twists." Booklist

3001: the final odyssey. Ballantine Bks. 1997 263p o.p.
ISBN 0-345-31522-7 LC 96-49490

"*2001* astronaut Frank Poole, presumed dead and adrift in deep space near Jupiter, is recovered alive in the year 3001. Intent on saving humanity, he returns to Jupiter's satellite, Europa, to contact partner Dave Bowman, whose mind has become absorbed by a third monolith." Libr J

"3001 can stand alone from its predecessors in Clarke's Space Odyssey saga and is an intelligent romp, distinguished by Clarke's usual and inimitable wit and an unusual (perhaps unwelcome) strain of grumpiness about religion." Booklist

Beyond the fall of night; [by] Arthur C. Clarke and Gregory Benford. Putnam 1990 298p o.p.
LC 89-39736

"An Ace/Putnam book"

This volume contains the original text of Clarke's Against the fall of the night (a revised edition entitled The city and the stars was published 1956 and Benford's sequel which "takes place many years later: Earth is now under siege by the 'Mad Mind,' a being of pure mentality created by a much earlier galactic Empire. Cley, last of the seemingly primitive 'Urhumans,' initially refuses to help Alvin, Clarke's hero, in battle. But she begins to view her role differently with the aid of Seeker, a furry 'raccoon-creature' whose species avows 'a respect for evolution and one's place in it.'" Publ Wkly

Childhood's end. Ballantine Bks. 1953 214p o.p.

This novel is "paradigmatic of Clarke's more speculative, transcendental novels. Structured as a succession of apocalytic revelations, it depicts the sudden metamorphosis of humanity, under the protective midwifery of the alien Overlords, into the next evolutionary stage, a group mind that ultimately merges with the cosmic Overmind, destroying the Earth in the process. . . . The alien other that transcends humanity yet paradoxically represents humanity's destiny is a recurring theme in the author's speculative novels." New Ency of Sci Fic

The collected stories of Arthur C. Clarke. TOR Bks. 2001 c2000 966p $29.95
ISBN 0-312-87821-4

"A TOR book"

First published 2000 in the United Kingdom

"Although most of these stories date from between 1946 and 1970, seven earlier tales, rescued from what would now be called fanzines, extend coverage back to 1937, and a few snippets stretch it toward the present. At least two dozen stories bear titles that are household words among sf readers. . . . The stories demonstrate Clarke's dazzling and unique combination of command of the language, scientific and other kinds of erudition, and inimitable wit." Booklist

Earthlight. Ballantine Bks. 1955 186p o.p.

"Two hundred years after the moon had been meticulously explored and made habitable, man has learned the secret of extracting the previous heavy minerals buried 60 miles below its surface. These rich ore reserves trigger a war between Earth and the Federation of colonized planets. A reluctant young Central Intelligence agent is sent out from Earth, and through his eyes we see the moon's terrain and witness a spectacular space battle. This novel was first published 1955, but this well-known scientist and science fiction writer's vivid rendering of the moon's geography is as realistic as a telecast from a Lunar Rover. He imparts masses of scientific information painlessly and maintains suspense with a well-plotted war story." Publ Wkly

A fall of moondust. Harcourt, Brace & World 1961 248p o.p.

This futuristic "tale is about what happens when a sight-seeing vehicle, full of tourists, has an accident and is buried deeply under an enormous pile of fine volcanic dust in one of the Moon's craters, and how the expert technicians race against time in an effort to save the trapped people." Springfield Repub

"The fascination of this simple tale lies in its transferring a universal predicament to surroundings at once alien and possessed of verisimilitude. Mr. Clarke has thought out his Moon; he has thought it out with such thoroughness, consistency and care that we simply must believe him; and believing him, we are engrossed." Times Lit Suppl

The Garden of Rama; by Arthur C. Clarke and Gentry Lee. Bantam Bks. 1991 441p (Rama) o.p.
LC 91-2888

This is the third title in the Rama saga. "Trapped aboard the massive Raman spacecraft as it leaves Earth's solor system, three cosmonauts begin a 13-year voyage toward an unknown destination. Combining the best of space adventure (as the spacefarers encounter other life forms within the multi-habitat vessel) with human drama (as children are born and raised in an unearthly environment), this third novel in the Rama cycle asks as many questions as it answers." Libr J

Followed by Rama revealed

The hammer of God. Bantam Bks. 1993 226p o.p.
LC 93-22096

Expanded version of a short story that appeared 1992 in Time magazine

"As an asteroid named 'Kali' hurtles toward earth on a collision course that spells the end to life on the planet, a lone spaceship armed with a weapon to alter the asteroid's path attempts to carry out its perilous mission—unaware that others are simultaneously working for earth's destruction." Libr J

This is "vintage Arthur C. Clarke. While he takes

Clarke, Arthur C., 1917-*—Continued*
pains to persuade readers that the threat of destruction from outer space is real, he is optimistic about humanity's ability to meet any challenge if its keeps its collective head." N Y Times Book Rev

Rama II; by Arthur C. Clarke and Gentry Lee. Bantam Bks. 1989 420p o.p.
LC 89-15152

In this second installment in the Rama saga "another *Rama* appears in our galaxy with the same shape, the same unearthly vistas, and even more creatures running wild over its spacescapes. A childlike genius, a beautiful medical officer, and a deeply religious military man form the nucleus of the good guys, anxious to explore, befriend the creatures, and discover the true purpose of the spacecraft." Booklist

Followed by The Garden of Rama

Rama revealed; {by} Arthur C. Clarke and Gentry Lee. Bantam Bks. 1994 466p (Rama) o.p.
LC 93-31459

In this conclusion of the Rama saga "Cosmonaut Nicole Wakefield, the former governor of the human colony housed within the globe-shaped spaceship Rama III, is awaiting execution for opposing the fascistic powers that now run the colony. She is rescued from her cell by small robots sent by her husband Richard, whom she had thought dead. . . . Along with friends and family from the Earth sector, they begin traveling through the different alien environments housed in the vast Raman world." Publ Wkly

"Fans of skillfully crafted hard sf . . . will find plenty of Clarke and Lee's fascinating scientific speculations vividly given form in the marvels of Raman technology." Booklist

Rendezvous with Rama. Harcourt Brace Jovanovich 1973 303p (Rama) o.p.

A massive space capsule "is discovered approaching earth in the 22nd century. A team of scientists sent into space to make contact with and explore the monster at first believe it to be a dead artifact launched from an unknown galaxy a million years before. But as the machine approaches solar orbit it comes alive—with light, oxygen and biological life—and human reactions to it are mixed. A religious cult thinks Rama is a rescue ship come to save the faithful, while colonists on Mercury start making a bomb to keep the thing away." Publ Wkly

This work contains "flights of prose where the language fairly purrs. And here too one finds the questioning and probing of man and his place in the cosmos that marks good fiction and good science fiction." Libr J

Followed by Rama II

Clarke, Susanna, 1959-

Jonathan Strange & Mr. Norrell; illustrations by Portia Rosenberg. Bloomsbury; distributed by Holtzbrinck 2004 782p il $27.95
ISBN 1-582-34416-7 LC 2004-2402

"This fantasy novel is set in early-nineteenth-century England, where two men, Gilbert Norrell and his pupil Jonathan Strange, revive the once-thriving practice of the dark arts. After aiding the British against Napoleon, the magicians fall out over interpretations of wizardly philosophy. Meanwhile, a malevolent fairy accidentally set loose by Norrell enchants, among others, Strange's wife. Clarke's ability to construct a fully imagined world-much of it explained in long, witty footnotes-is impressive." New Yorker

Claudine, Sidonie Gabrielle *See* Colette, 1873-1954

Clavell, James

Gai-Jin; a novel of Japan. Delacorte Press 1993 1038p o.p.
ISBN 0-385-31016-1 LC 92-42129

The sixth volume in the author's Asian saga depicts the political and social intrigue that resulted when Japan slowly opened its doors to foreigners or gai-jin. This novel "opens in 1862 with a fictionalized version of the assassination of a British citizen, Charles Richardson, by samurai traveling with the rebellious lord of Satsuma on the great national highway known as the Tokaido. It ends with the British bombardment of Kagoshima in 1863, a seminal event on the road to the Meiji Restoration, which brought feudal Japan into the modern era." N Y Times Book Rev

Clavell "melds plot-driven storytelling and colorful characterization in vibrant collaboration with an exotic, dynamic setting." Publ Wkly

King Rat; a novel. Little, Brown 1962 406p o.p.

Third novel in the author's Asian saga

"A novel about corruption, fear and despair among the prisoners in a Singapore prison camp in World War II. 'King Rat,' so called because he breeds the prison rats and sells them for food, is an American corporal turned gambler and black marketeer. He has bribed his way into a position as real though unofficial ruler of the camp." Publ Wkly

This novel "is strong in narrative detail, penetrating in observation of human nature under stress, and thought-provoking in its analysis of right and wrong." Cincinnati Public Libr

Noble house; a novel of contemporary Hong Kong. Delacorte Press 1981 1206p o.p.
LC 80-26889

Fourth novel in the author's Asian saga

"Ian Dunross, head of Struan's, an old and respected China trade firm in Hong Kong, makes his appearance in the middle of a typhoon, and from there to the very end of this . . . saga the action never lets up. This action takes place during one week of 1963, with two plots going, and dozens of participants. . . . Along the way we are treated to the sights, sounds, smells, and history of Hong Kong. There is international finance and banking, the workings of multinational companies, smuggling of narcotics and gold, insight into how the Chinese regard sex, and their marvelously pragmatic view of how the world works." Libr J

Shogun; a novel of Japan. Atheneum Pubs. 1975 o.p.

First novel in the author's Asian saga

East and West meet in this "epic of feudal seventeenth-century Japan. When a gale casts John Blackthorne's ship ashore here, the English sea pilot and his crew must learn to sink or swim in an alien culture. Blackthorne's mentor is a feudal lord locked in a power

Clavell, James—*Continued*
struggle with another for control of all Japan. How Blackthorne makes himself useful and is rewarded with samurai status forms the bulk of this swashbuckler." Booklist

"Clavell creates a world: people, customs, settings, needs and desires all become so enveloping that you forget who and where you are. 'Shōgun' is history infused with fantasy. It strives for epic dimension and occasionally it approaches that elevated state. It's irresistible, maybe unforgettable." N Y Times Book Rev

Tai-Pan. Delacorte Press 1983 c1966 590p o.p.
LC 82-18339

Second novel in the author's Asian saga

A reissue of the title first published 1966 by Atheneum

"The time is 1841. England has just won the first Opium War with China and is determined to advance her interests there. Dirk Struan is tai-pan (supreme ruler) of the Noble House, the most powerful trading company in the orient. Struan realizes with a prophetic vision the value of Hong Kong and her port. He feels that England must use this area to branch out over the far East. Opposition to his plan comes from the apathy of politicians in England. Struan must also deal with Chinese pirates and with the multiple entity that is China and her people." Best Sellers

"The backgrounds—Hong Kong, the sailing ships, the trading preserve in Canton—surge with life, and the plot is neatly dovetailed with history. Superb storytelling; an utterly absorbing book." Publ Wkly

Whirlwind. Morrow 1986 1147p o.p.
LC 86-11293

Fifth novel in the author's Asian saga

"Andrew Gavallan, based in Scotland, runs a helicopter company operating in Iran during the Shah's reign. When Khomeini comes to power, Gavallan must get his pilots and their families, and his valuable helicopters, out of the riot-torn country. Complicating matters is his power struggle with his company's secret owner, the Noble House of Hong Kong. The pilots' escape efforts form the basic story [of the novel]." Libr J

"Clavell has done a fine job . . . of delineating the geography and politics of a country in turmoil. He seems less successful with the characters, however, as many of his Iranians are thinly disguised stereotypes. Still, the novel is rife with corporate and multinational intrigue, political drama, and romance." Booklist

Cleage, Pearl

Babylon sisters; a novel; Pearl Cleage. 1st ed. Ballantine Books/One World 2005 292p $23.95
ISBN 0-345-45609-2 LC 2004-51909

"For more than 17 years, Catherine Sanderson has not revealed the identity of her daughter's father and has kept the child's existence hidden from him. However, the universe, teenage curiosity, and two new work assignments conspire to put Catherine's past and present on a collision course. The plot is spun around a tale of women's empowerment, modern-day slavery, betrayal, and the survival of African American community institutions." Libr J

The author's "intelligent, lively narrative hits numerous notes–domestic drama, romance, thriller–right in tune." Publ Wkly

I wish I had a red dress. Morrow 2001 323p $24
ISBN 0-380-97733-8 LC 00-54620

"Joyce Mitchell is the social-worker founder of the Sewing Circus and Community Truth Center, dedicated to guiding young women from teenage pregnancies and violent relationships with the 'babydaddies' to free and independent adulthood. Joyce herself, five years a widow, longs for enough safety and assurance to wear a red dress, an ultimate symbol of freedom and abandon. When she meets former Detroit cop Nate Anderson, the new counselor at the high school, long-repressed feelings are awakened." Booklist

"With humor and sparkling dialog, Cleage balances the dark, abusive relationships of Joyce's clients with the delightfully healthy love between Joyce and Nate and the strength of women's friendships." Libr J

What looks like crazy on an ordinary day—; a novel. Avon Bks. 1997 244p o.p.
ISBN 0-380-97584-X LC 97-17708

This novel "focuses on an HIV-positive woman who seeks solace and refuge for the summer in her hometown with her widowed sister." Libr J

"Despite the early bad news, Cleage's funny, irreverent, and hopeful novel is stunningly real and evocative of the conditions behind the high unemployment, aimlessness, and drug culture that permeate the urban landscape and have invaded smaller towns as well." Booklist

Cleary, Jon, 1917-

The sundowners. Scribner 1952 290p o.p.

A story of one year in the life of a nomadic family in Australia. The chief characters are Paddy Carmody, a sheepdrover and his wife, Ida, and their fourteen year old son, Sean. The year saw ups and downs in their fortunes, hard times and good times, and the growth to maturity and understanding of the young boy

"The book is notable not so much for the action it develops as for the human qualities it depicts." N Y Her Trib Books

Clemens, Samuel Langhorne *See* Twain, Mark, 1835-1910

Clement, Hal, 1922-2003

Noise. TOR Bks. 2003 252p $23.95
ISBN 0-7653-0857-6 LC 2003-55987

"Linguist Mike Hoani arrives on the water planet Kainui to study the evolution of the language of its original Polynesian colonists. His travels on a planet with no fixed land except for floating artificial cities plunge him into a maritime adventure that tests his knowledge of both language and human nature." Libr J

"Clement skillfully weaves together challenging science, a unique familial society, and an encounter with a 'lost' city in a narrative that allows the reader to puzzle out Mike's questions along with him." Booklist

Clements, Marcelle

Midsummer. Harcourt 2003 291p $24
ISBN 0-15-100836-1 LC 2002-153525

Clements, Marcelle—*Continued*

"Taking place over eight summer weekends at a rented mansion in the Hudson River Valley, [this novel] is a portrait of a group of old friends—witty, middle-aged, neurotic, bourgeois-bohemian Manhattanites—who anticipate an idyll of leisure and gossip, only to find all their dissatisfaction and regret surfacing as they sift through past mistakes and missed opportunities." New Yorker

Cline, Rachel

What to keep; a novel; Rachel Cline. 1st ed. Random House 2004 290p $23.95

ISBN 1-400-06183-0 LC 2003-54810

"Divided into three sections, the story follows the life of Denny Roman, a daughter of brilliant but socially dysfunctional parents, and her relationship with Maureen, the family's de facto life secretary, who teaches Denny how to accept the good parts of herself and her parents and not obsess over the bad." Libr J

"This is a wryly funny novel that feels completely fresh. It has an odd but effective structure; depicts offbeat, memorable characters; and offers a perceptive, nuanced take on familial relationships." Booklist

Clute, John

Appleseed. TOR Bks. 2002 337p $25.95

ISBN 0-765-30378-7

"Nathaniel 'Stinky' Freer captains his ship, the Tile Dance, through space with the aid of a conjoined AI. . . . On a seemingly routine mercantile contract to the planet Trencher, he's nearly killed by the rampaging, cannibalistic, self-devouring alien, Opsophagos. On returning to his ship, Stinky discovers that he's somehow acquired two new AIs and that he has a stowaway: a topiary parthogenete, Mamselle Cunning Earth Link, who holds the key to the location of the planet where there are plaque-eating lenses. Opsophagos remains in hot pursuit as Stinky meets the mythic Johnny Appleseed, rediscovers his lady love and has a sexual encounter that just might save the universe." Publ Wkly

Clynes, Michael

For works written by this author under other names see Doherty, P. C.

Coben, Harlan, 1962-

Darkest fear. Delacorte Press 2000 285p o.p.

ISBN 0-385-33433-8 LC 99-89788

"Manhattan sports agent Myron Bolitar is shocked when his former college lover informs him he is the father of her 13-year-old son, who has anemia. But the girlfriend—now inimically divorced from her husband—only uses that fact to convince him to locate the boy's bone-marrow donor, who has disappeared." Libr J

"The Bolitar thrillers are always leavened with humor, no matter how grim the content, and this one is no exception. Even so, the darkness of the plot and the seriousness of the theme—the reponsibilities of parenthood—give this installment added impact." Booklist

Gone for good. Delacorte Press 2002 340p o.p.

ISBN 0-385-33558-X LC 2001-55292

"Will Klein was a nice Jewish boy from a nice Jersey suburb until his ex-girlfriend was found strangled next door and his brother became an international fugitive. Eleven years later, as his mother succumbs to cancer, Will gets the deathbed confession that his brother, Ken, is alive." Publ Wkly

"Through Klein, the psychological suspense turns on the question of guilt, surely but also on the transcendence of familial love and forgiveness. Watching Klein decide among dangerous alternatives, as the clockwork plot keeps picking up speed, is breathtaking." Booklist

The innocent. Dutton 2005 388p $26.95

ISBN 0-525-94874-0 LC 2005-1627

"A paralegal, devoted husband and soon-to-be father, Matt Hunter has a not-so-secret past: when he was 20, in an attempt to break up a fistfight, he killed a man and served four years in prison for it. He's been out five years, living in his New Jersey hometown, and life is pretty good. But when his beloved wife, Olivia, goes away on a business trip, he receives 15 seconds of digital video on his camera phone showing her in a hotel room with another man. Meanwhile, Loren Muse, Essex County homicide investigator, is working on an unusual case: an autopsy of a nun reveals breast implants, which hint at a previous, not so holy life. After the FBI is called in, evidence links Matt to the nun killing. . . . All the characters have extensive, interesting histories, which makes their actions believable under the extreme circumstances that engulf them." Publ Wkly

Just one look; by Harlan Coben. Dutton 2004 370p $25.95

ISBN 0-525-94791-4 LC 2004-2329

"While flipping through a set of newly developed photographs, Grace Lawson comes across an old picture of four people, one of whom resembles her husband, Jack. When she shows him the photo, he denies being the person or knowing anyone involved. Later that night, with the photo in his possession, Jack flees the house and promptly vanishes. When Grace uncovers proof that one of the strangers in the picture is now dead, her picture-perfect life starts to unravel. With each thriller, Coben just gets better and better." Libr J

No second chance. Dutton 2003 338p $24.95

ISBN 0-525-94729-9 LC 2002-192530

"Marc Seidman, a plastic surgeon near New York City, wakes up in a hospital to learn that he has been gravely wounded, his wife shot dead and his infant daughter, Tara, snatched. The ensuing narrative, which shuttles between third person and Marc's first person, covers more than a year in Marc's hunt for Tara." Publ Wkly

"The novel, spanning 18 months and jumping between the father and the kidnappers, sets off depth charges of meets, double-crosses, near-misses, and vengful acts. Coben holds it together with his hero's determination and smarts." Booklist

One false move. Delacorte Press 1998 322p o.p.

ISBN 0-385-32369-7 LC 97-51206

"Sports agent Myron Bolitar handles everything with panache: his relationships, his clients, and this search for two missing people. When a sports store mogul asks him to 'watch over' basketball star Brenda Slaughter, Myron winds up looking for her father, who disappeared a week ago, and her mother, who deserted the family some 20 years earlier. Myron not only discovers mob interest in

Coben, Harlan, 1962-—*Continued*

female basketball but also a connected suspicious death in a high-profile political family." Libr J

"After four paperback appearances, sports agent/sleuth Myron Bolitar makes his hardcover debut in a stylish mystery distinguished by memorably quirky characters and smart, tough narration." Publ Wkly

Cockey, Tim

Hearse case scenario. Hyperion 2002 338p o.p.
ISBN 0-7868-6711-6 LC 2001-24188

In this mystery "Hitchcock Sewell, Baltimore's wisecracking mortician/sleuth, sets out to exonerate his hapless childhood friend, Lucy, accused of murdering her low-life boyfriend, Shrimp Martin. Sure, Lucy shot him, but she wasn't the one who killed him." Publ Wkly

"Cockey effectively grounds Hitch's high jinks in the real world, placing his hero squarely in the comic-realistic tradition of Lawrence Block's Bernie Rhodenbarr and Janet Evanovich's Stephanie Plum." Booklist

Murder in the hearse degree. Hyperion 2003 324p $22.95
ISBN 0-7868-6712-4 LC 2002-27458

Wisecracking undertaker Hitchcock Sewell "finds out that his former squeeze, Libby Gellman, is back in town with her two children but sans husband and nanny. The nanny, surprisingly pregnant, is more than geographically distant: she's fallen from a very high bridge and drowned. Or was she pushed? The police support a knee-jerk suicide theory. The nanny's loyal mother doesn't. So Hitch sets off to see exactly what happened. . . . Brimming with humor—much of it dark—this book is perfect for the reader who has finished all the books by Janet Evanovich or Sue Grafton and doesn't know what to read next." Libr J

Cocteau, Jean, 1889-1963

The impostor; translated from the French by Dorothy Williams. Noonday Press 1957 132p o.p.

Original French edition, 1923; first English translation published 1925 by Appleton with title: Thomas the imposter

The setting of Cocteau's short novel "is the First World War; his imposter, a French youth, too young for the services, who in a borrowed uniform and under a borrowed name succeeds in obtaining a post in a curious nursing unit run by a Polish princess and her daughter. He plays the part he has adopted so well that in the end he succeeds in convincing even himself of his authenticity, and having finally been adopted as their mascot by a unit of Marines dies in the end a gallant death." Times Lit Suppl

Cody, Liza

Bucket nut. Doubleday 1993 c1992 236p o.p.
LC 92-30366

First published 1992 in the United Kingdom

The protagonist of this novel is "Eva Wylie, a fledgling professional wrestler working in London. Eva supports her new career with work as a security guard for a junkyard and as a courier for a shady Asian businessman. She lives with two protective dogs in a crumbling trailer amid the junk. She's a loner, very bitter, and not averse to working whatever side of the legal fence she finds herself on. Acting in her capacity as a courier, she becomes involved in a conflict between rival protection rackets. Her soul-deep bad attitude serves her well in the ensuing stroll through London's dark side. Eva's unremitting cynicism is certain to appeal to the hardest of the hard-boiled set." Booklist

Head case. Scribner 1986 197p o.p.
LC 85-25077

Working on a missing-person case, private detective Anna Lee "discovers her quarry, 16-year-old genius Thea Hahn, in a Dorset hospital, hysterical and apparently insane. Death has followed in Thea's wake—her tutor met with a fatal accident just before Thea's disappearance; another man is found shot to death in a hotel room—and Lee must sort through the vagaries of Thea's psyche, strange upbringing, and superficially tranquil past to discover whether the girl is victim or victimizer. A chilling, often funny, and finely plotted mystery." Booklist

Monkey wrench. Warner Bks. 1995 c1994 246p o.p.
LC 94-42737

First published 1994 in the United Kingdom

"Rough-and-tumble wrestler Eva Wylie . . . struts her attitudinal stuff around the tougher side of London. Having risen above her own humble beginnings and homelessness, Eva now divides her time between the gym and her night job, exhibiting an abrasive self-respect. Provoked by the murder of several of their number, a group of streetwalkers asks her for self-defense training, but she refuses until friend Crystal 'changes' her mind." Libr J

The author "delivers realistically raw scenes for the working girls and one slam-bang wrestling match for Eva. These loosely strung incidents don't make a story, but they do give Eva an opportunity to speak her piece, in a voice gruff with anger and pain." N Y Times Book Rev

Rift. Scribner 1988 240p o.p.
LC 88-17556

"Fay Jassahn, the narrator, is a young English freelance wardrobe assistant, who is completing a movie in Kenya in 1974. Deciding to visit Ethiopia, Fay agrees to deliver a letter across the border from a writer to his estranged lover, Natasha Beyer. Unwittingly, she involves herself in a game of dangerous intrigue. What begins as a romantic adventure—and a means of proving her independence—becomes a nightmare for Fay." Publ Wkly

Coe, Jonathan, 1961-

The closed circle. Knopf 2005 367p $25
ISBN 0-375-41415-0 LC 2004-57789

In this sequel to The Rotters' Club, " which was set in the 1970s, the circle of British teenagers is now teetering on the brink of middle age and struggling with infidelity and failed ambition. Benjamin Trotter is an accountant who has been working for decades on a novel that runs to thousands of pages and is to be accompanied by his own music; he is a victim of self-doubt and a paralyzing obsession with his first love. He becomes infatuated with young Malvina, who falls hard for Benjamin's

Coe, Jonathan, 1961-—*Continued*
brother, Paul, a rising political star. Coe interweaves the personal with the political as key developments over the past four years run continually in the background—the threatened closure of the Rover car factory, England's role in the war on terrorism." Booklist

"While Coe's political sensibility is readily apparent, this novel, with its incredibly well developed characters and its immensely engaging narrative, is no polemical tract. It's a compelling, dramatic and often funny depiction of the way we live now—both savage and heartfelt at the same time." Publ Wkly

The Rotters' Club. Knopf 2002 419p o.p.
ISBN 0-375-41383-9 LC 2001-42523

First published 2001 in the United Kingdom

"It is Birmingham, England, in the '70s and amidst IRA pub bombings, labor strikes, and immigration-related racism, Benjamin, Philip, and Doug are going about the business of adolescence. This means, among other things, changing their theoretical band's name from 'Gandalf's Pikestaff' to 'The Maws of Doom' and sneaking as much satire into the school paper as possible. . . . The narrative switches occasionally from third person to first (Benjamin), and includes diary excerpts, the boy's ridiculously pretentious attempts at music and theatre reviews, and other formatting diversions." SLJ

"The Rotter's Club, for all its occassional overegging and its selfconscious deployment of issues, is a superior entertainment. The pages seem to turn themselves, and Coe's oblique humor allows the romantic and satirical to combine without undercutting each other." New Statesman (1913)

Coe, Tucker

For works written by this author under other names see Stark, Richard; Westlake, Donald E.

Coel, Margaret, 1937-

The dream stalker. Berkley Prime Crime 1997 244p o.p.
ISBN 0-425-15967-1 LC 96-54797

"Arapaho lawyer Vicky Holden opposes the plan to construct a nuclear waste facility on the Wind River Reservation, but she receives death threats and the enmity of her people for her pains. Good friend John O'Malley, Jesuit priest at the local mission, believes that a murdered Indian he found has some connection to Vicky's troubles, so he investigates—against police advice. Financial problems at the mission, the personal crises of the new assistant, and O'Malley's own temptations of the flesh lend realistic touches to the author's usual commendable plotting and characterization." Libr J

The ghost walker. Berkley Prime Crime 1996 243p o.p.
ISBN 0-425-15468-8 LC 95-26164

In this mystery, "Father John O'Malley discovers a body dumped in a frozen ditch near his small church on the Arapaho reservation in Wyoming. His own truck disabled, Father John gets a ride from an edgy, evasive stranger. When police arrive at the snow-covered roadside, the body has vanished. The Arapahos say the ghost is walking around somewhere, causing trouble until the body is properly buried and the spirit can rest. Sure enough, Marcus Deppert, a troubled young Indian, disappears." Publ Wkly

"Coel's Catholic Irish Jesuit priest and his Arapaho friends and neighbors, each with individual worldviews and sensibilities, make for interesting contrasts in this excellent mystery that focuses on the strange place Native Americans occupy in their own land." Booklist

Coetzee, J. M., 1940-

Age of iron. Random House 1990 198p o.p.
LC 90-8310

This novel "takes the form of a letter-diary from Mrs. Curren, a former classics professor dying of cancer, to her daughter in America. She details a series of strange events that turn her protected middle-class life upside down. A homeless alcoholic appears at her door, eventually becoming her companion and confessor. Her liberal sentiments and her very humanity are tested as she experiences directly the horrors of apartheid. She comes to recognize South Africa as a country in which the rigidity of both sides has led to barbarism and to acknowledge her complicity in upholding the system." Libr J

"The word 'shame' throbs through the text like a recurrent pain. The principal character thinks she is dying of it. . . . One can, of course, read her death as a metaphor for the doom of liberalism in South Africa. . . . But Age of Iron is about dying as much as it is about apartheid, and that raises it above the level of a political novel or a *roman à thèse*, and gives resonance to the political message." N Y Rev Books

Disgrace. Viking 1999 220p o.p.
ISBN 0-670-88731-5

"At fifty-two, Professor David Lurie is divorced, filled with desire, but lacking in passion. An affair with one of his students leaves him jobless, shunned by his friends, and ridiculed by his ex-wife. He retreats to his daughter Lucy's isolated smallholding, where a brief visit becomes an extended stay as he tries to find meaning from this one remaining relationship. David's attempts to relate to Lucy and to a society with new racial complexities are disrupted by an afternoon of violence that shakes all his beliefs and threatens to destroy his daughter." Publisher's note

"A novel that not only works its spell but makes it impossible for us to lay it aside once we've finished reading it. . . . Coetzee's sentences are coiled springs, and the energy they release would take other writers pages to summon." New Yorker

Elizabeth Costello. Viking 2003 230p $21.95
ISBN 0-670-03130-5 LC 2003-60849

"Elizabeth Costello, a fictional aging Australian novelist who gained fame for a Ulysses-inspired novel in the 1960s, reveals the workings of her still-formidable mind in a series of formal addresses she either attends or delivers herself (an award acceptance speech, a lecture on a cruise ship, a graduation speech)." Publ Wkly

"There is no justice in the ability of youth to shame age, and yet it's a fundamental fact of the embodied life. Coetzee's unflinching exploration of this desolate and strangely beautiful terrain represents the cruelest and best use to which literature can be put." N Y Times Book Rev

Coetzee, J. M., 1940-—*Continued*

Foe. Viking 1987 c1986 157p o.p.
LC 86-40267

First published 1986 in the United Kingdom

"Cast adrift by a mutinous crew, Susan Barton washes ashore on an isle of classic fiction. For the next year, Robinson Cruso sculpts the land while Friday mutely watches Susan intrude upon their loneliness. Life is mere pattern for the two unquestioning castaways, but Susan is not of their story and she pushes Cruso for rationales that don't exist in a world of imagination. Finally rescued and returned to London, Susan leads Friday to Daniel Foe, the author who will write their tale. Foe, however, sees a different story and seeks 'to tell the truth in all its substance.'" Libr J

"In adding to Defoe's repertory company, Coetzee has introduced urgencies that are neither fresh nor illumined, only brilliantly disguised. Flashing back and forward, scattering allusions, adopting a series of poses and styles, the author is less reminiscent of a prior novelist than of contemporary street mimes who build hints until the audience shouts in recognition." Time

Life & times of Michael K. Viking 1984 c1983 184p o.p.
LC 83-47860

First published 1983 in the United Kingdom

"Born with a harelip and brought up in an uncaring orphanage, Michael K. struggles through a desperate life in South Africa. When his sick mother persuades him to bring her back to her homeland, he must endure not only the terrible journey, pulling her in a cart he has made, but also risk the dangers of military checkpoints since he does not have the necessary permits. His undying attachment is to the land, but he is not allowed to remain the gardener he wishes to be. The details of Michael's suffering in camps, hospitals, and labor gangs are harrowing and underscore a courage that never forsakes him." Shapiro. Fic for Youth. 3d edition

The master of Petersburg. Viking 1994 250p o.p.

"St. Petersburg is poised for revolution as Fyodor Dostoevsky returns from Germany to claim his deceased stepson's papers. Although the police rule Pavel's death a suicide, the famous writer is drawn into a group of shady characters, including the anarchist Nechaev, who is possibly Pavel's killer. Plagued by seizures and tormented by a torrid affair with his stepson's landlady, Dostoevsky struggles to ascertain once and for all a writer's responsibility to his family and society." Libr J

"The book's momentum is dependent finally on idea rather than incident, with the significance of events contingent on one's grasp of Dostoyevsky's complex frame of beliefs. All of which makes 'The Master of Petersburg' dense and difficult, a novel that frustrates at every turn. But despite that difficulty, the figure who emerges from these pages, the master himself, in his tortured unhappiness, his terror of the next epileptic seizure, his restless sexuality and his desperate gambling with God, will seize any imagination still susceptible to the complicated passions of the Slav soul." N Y Times Book Rev

Slow man. Viking 2005 265p $24.95
ISBN 0-670-03459-2 LC 2005-54693

"When photographer Paul Rayment loses his leg in a bicycle accident, his solitary life is irrevocably changed. Stubbornly refusing a prosthesis, Paul returns to his bachelor's apartment in Adelaide, uncomfortable with his new dependency on others. He is given to bouts of hopelessness as he looks back on his sixty years of life, but his spirits rise when he finds himself falling in love with Marijana, his practical, down-to-earth Croatian nurse who is struggling to raise her family in a foreign land. As Paul contemplates how to win her heart, he is visited by the mysterious writer Elizabeth Costello, who challenges Paul to taken an active role in his own life." Publisher's note

"What saves Slow Man from being a sterile, self-referential literary exercise is the vividness of the characters who animate it. Coetzee writes in a degree-zero style, purposely flat and unemphatic-he must be a translator's dream-yet in this book he has found a new access of warmth and humor, and displays a vivifying fondness for his characters. It is his triumph in Slow Man to bring a world into being with a minimum of literary effects." New Republic

Coffey, Brian, 1945-

For works written by this author under other names see Koontz, Dean R. (Dean Ray), 1945-

Coghlan, Peggie, 1920-

See also Stirling, Jessica

Cohen, Janet *See* Neel, Janet, 1940-

Cohen, Leah Hager

Heart, you bully, you punk. Viking 2003 214p $23.95
ISBN 0-670-03167-4 LC 2002-69191

"Cohen offers a bittersweet love story involving a 31-year-old math teacher at a Brooklyn private school, her star pupil, and the student's father. Ann James, the star student, breaks both heels when she slips (or jumps?) from the top of the bleachers. Her injuries render her immobile for a time; to help her keep up in math, Ann's teacher, Esker, volunteers to tutor her at home. After meeting Ann's father, Wally, Esker begins, despite herself, to fall in love with him. . . . Cohen demonstrates that there can be beauty even in sadness." Booklist

Cohen, Robert, 1957-

Inspired sleep; a novel. Scribner 2001 399p $25
ISBN 0-684-85079-6 LC 00-57337

"Bonnie Saks, divorced with two sons, a filmmaker ex-husband off in South America, an unfinished dissertation the point of which she has lost, an unsatisfactory job, and an unwanted pregnancy, finds her most debilitating problem to be an insurmountable case of insomnia. Her story is paralleled by that of Ian Ogelvie, a hapless sleep researcher." Booklist

"Smartly observed and stylishly written, Cohen's new novel is crammed with incidental pleasures. Yet underneath its clever examination of our current love affair with pharmaceuticals lie unsettling questions about the myths we choose to live by: it's not the interpretation of dreams but the meaning of our waking hours that is up for grabs here." New Yorker

Coldsmith, Don, 1926-

The long journey home. Forge 2001 400p $24.95

ISBN 0-312-87617-3 LC 00-48459

"A Tom Doherty Associates book"

"John Buffalo is a Lakota Sioux sent to a government school as a young boy in the 1890s. Proud of his Native American heritage, he vows to outdo the white man at his own game. Although he is a bright student, John's real success comes as an athlete—he plays football, baseball and track, and dreams of competing in the Olympics and later becoming a coach. Racism, however, derails his Olympic hopes and disrupts his budding romance with a U.S. senator's daughter. John later becomes a horse trainer and actor with a traveling Wild West show, performing around the world." Publ Wkly

Coldsmith portrays a "Native American athlete who bears an intentional resemblance to the great Jim Thorpe. . . . This well-researched piece of historical fiction interweaves a compelling life story with many of the pivotal events of the early twentieth century." Booklist

Raven Mocker; a novel. University of Okla. Press 2001 253p o.p.

ISBN 0-8061-3316-3 LC 00-61538

In this installment of his Spanish Bit Saga, Coldsmith "tells the tale of Granny Snakewater, née Corn Flower, an orphaned Cherokee girl who falls under the tutelage of her adoptive namesake and gradually replaces her as the conjure woman for the Real People. . . . The narrative flows well enough, although it is often slowed by intrusive folk tales and fairy stories. Still, this is a pleasant read." Publ Wkly

Tallgrass; a novel of the Great Plains. Bantam Bks. 1997 454p o.p.

LC 96-19672

Coldsmith's saga concerns "the opening of the Santa Fe Trail. Starting with the coming of the Spanish conquistadors in 1541, his work spans 300 years to a time when the fur trade has died, Eastern Native Americans have been relocated onto lands west of the Mississippi, and conflict is building between the Plains Indians and Eastern interlopers, both Indian and white. Coldsmith focuses on a tribe of Pawnee and the devastation that contact with whites brings. This powerful novel demonstrates the diversity of the Native American culture while treating the tribes and their history with dignity and understanding." Libr J

Colegate, Isabel

The shooting party. Viking 1981 c1980 195p o.p.

LC 80-54194

First published 1980 in the United Kingdom

"The time is October 1913, the place an estate in Oxfordshire where Sir Randolph Nettleby and his wife are hosting the biggest shoot of the season. Brought together are the privileged in pursuit of pleasure. For these guests shooting is a special ritual with the shooters, gamekeepers, beaters, and servants all playing specific roles, and the sport is marvelously and meticulously described. Woven through the story are the portrayals of the gentry, the allusions to romantic and adulterous affairs, the relationship between the classes, and the feeling of the vast changes soon to overtake the Edwardian period. The rising tension that accompanies the final hours of the shooting on this day explodes into unexpected tragedy." Shapiro. Fic for Youth. 3d edition

Winter journey. Counterpoint 2001 199p o.p.

ISBN 1-58243-122-1 LC 00-64449

First published 1995 in the United Kingdom

This "is the story of a brother and sister in late middle age who spend a few quiet days together at their childhood home between late December 1992 and early January 1993. . . . Alfred Ashby is 60, a well-known photographer who lives in the stone farmhouse in Somerset where he and his sister grew up. Edith, slightly older, is a former member of Parliament who runs a language school in London. . . . Neither is aware of the pain and disillusionment the other has suffered." N Y Times Book Rev

"Colegate employs a varied cast of background characters who, in addition to their fully dimensional portrayals, provide insight into Britain's still potent class system. In Colegate's assured hands, the natural landscape is rendered as clearly as her characters' interior landscapes, and she accomplishes this in a slim text remarkable for its lucidity, humor and precise observation." Publ Wkly

Coleman, Lonnie, 1920-1982

Beulah Land. Doubleday 1973 495p o.p.

This is the first volume of the Beulah Land trilogy

"This panoramic novel of pre-Civil War (1800-1861) life on a Georgia plantation follows the fortunes of the Kendrick family, owners of Beulah Land, through a multitude of births, marriages, and deaths, dished up with a heavy-handed dollop of sex. No subtle nuances here: the good guys and the bad guys are clearly differentiated—black and white—virtue is triumphant, and evil gets its just desserts in the end. One can fault the book only on characterization; Coleman gives us a splendid picture of the times, manners, and customs of the antebellum South." Libr J

Followed by Look away, Beulah Land

The legacy of Beulah Land. Doubleday 1980 430p o.p.

LC 79-7516

"The final volume of Coleman's Beulah Land trilogy finds life on the Kendrick/Davis plantation struggling back to normal during the last quarter of the nineteenth century. New dynastic troubles plague the land, however, as a poor farmer becomes a powerful threat to the family's inheritance. Although a bit of unsubtle soap opera, the novel benefits from a huge cast of characters, a long series of predicaments, and scenes of graphic violence—all of which produce a nonstop epic." Booklist

Look away, Beulah Land; a novel. Doubleday 1977 492p o.p.

LC 76-50759

Sequel to Beulah Land

"Two great Georgia plantations, Beulah Land and the neighboring Oaks, have already been drained of most of their menfolk when the victorious Yankees finally come—to plunder, rape, burn and kill. The Kendricks, the Davis's and their remaining freed slaves begin the painful task of reconstruction, though not before two of

Coleman, Lonnie, 1920-1982—*Continued*
them, accompanied by a Yankee deserter now settled at Beulah Land, take revenge on a murderous Union sergeant. The story that unfolds is intricate, encompassing several generations of whites, blacks and mulattoes whose passion-dominated lives, stirred to vigorous drama by the evil ambitions of a vengeful black, reflect the death of an old society and the birth of a new. This intricacy, however, is part of the charm and power of a tale that is history made back into life." Publ Wkly
Followed by The legacy of Beulah Land

Coleman, William Laurence *See* Coleman, Lonnie, 1920-1982

Colette, 1873-1954

Chance acquaintances
In Colette. Gigi. Julie de Carneilhan. Chance acquaintances p225-315

Chéri
In Colette. Six novels p411-534

Claudine and Annie
In Colette. The complete Claudine p516-632

Claudine at school
In Colette. The complete Claudine p1-206
In Colette. Six novels p1-234

Claudine in Paris
In Colette. The complete Claudine p209-364

Claudine married
In Colette. The complete Claudine p367-510

The collected stories of Colette; edited, and with an introduction, by Robert Phelps; translated by Matthew Ward, et al. Farrar, Straus & Giroux 1983 605p o.p.
LC 83-16449

Contents: The other table; The screen; Clouk alone; Clouk's fling; Chéri; The return; The pearls; Literature; My goddaughter; A hairdresser; A masseuse; My corsetmaker; The saleswoman; An interview; A letter; The Sémiramis Bar; "If I had a daughter . . ."; Rites; Newly shorn; Grape harvest; In the boudoir; The "master"; Morning glories; What must we look like; The cure; Sleepness nights; Gray days; The last fire; A fable: the tendrils of the vine; The halt; Arrival and rehearsal; A bad morning; The circus horse; The workroom; Matinee; The starveling; Love; The hard worker; After midnight; "Lola"; Moments of stress; Journey's end; "The strike, oh Lord, the strike"; Bastienne's child; The accompanist; The cashier; Nostalgia; Clever dogs; The child prodigy; The misfit; "La Fenice"; "Gitanette"; The victim; The tenor; The quick-change artist; Florie; Gribiche; The hidden woman; Dawn; One evening; The hand; A dead end; The fox; The judge; The omelette; The other wife; Monsieur Maurice; The burglar; The advice; The murderer; The portrait; The landscape; The half-crazy; Secrets; "Châ"; The bracelet; The find; Mirror games; Habit; Alix's refusal; The seamstress; The watchman; The hollow nut; The patriarch; The sick child; The rainy moon; Green sealing wax; In the flower of age; The rivals; The respite; The bitch; The tender shoot [novella]; Bygone spring; October; Armande; The rendezvous; The kepi [novella]; The photographer's wife; Bella-Vista; April

"Includes two novellas that rank as classics, not only in Colette's canon, but in all of 20th century French literature. The Tender Shoot is the story of a singularly nasty middle-aged roué's pursuit of a 15-year-old peasant girl. Upon this squalid tale, Colette lavished her most lyrical language and poetic fancies, heightening the sense of evil. . . . As Colette remarked of her writing, her 'great landscape was always the human face.' No work demonstrates this better than The Kepi, the portrait of a doomed 46-year-old French lieutenant." Time

The complete Claudine; Claudine at school, Claudine in Paris, Claudine married, Claudine and Annie; translated by Antonia White. Farrar, Straus & Giroux 1976 632p o.p.

Omnibus edition of four semi-autobiographical novels written by Colette in 1900-1903. The first three appeared under the pen name of her husband and the fourth novel was published under both their names. These translations have copyright dates 1956, 1958, 1960 and 1962 respectively. Variant title for English translation of third volume: Indulgent husband; of final volume: Innocent wife

In the first novel we meet Claudine as a precocious school girl peeping and spying on both her contemporaries and her boarding school teachers. The second novel depicts a girl approaching womanhood discovering the exciting world of Paris and meeting a varied assortment of escorts. Claudine married is not so much the story of the heroine's marriage as the story of Claudine's love affair with Rézi, another married woman. The final volume has Claudine as one of its principal characters, but it is largely the story of an innocent young wife, who during the absence of her domineering husband begins to see more of her sister-in-law and her sophisticated friends and her eyes open to the true ways of life and love

Gigi
In Colette. Gigi. Julie de Carneilhan. Chance acquaintances p9-74
In Colette. Six novels p649-97

Gigi. Julie de Carneilhan. Chance acquaintances. Farrar, Straus & Young 1952 315p o.p.

Gigi is the story of a young girl brought up to be a prosperous demimondaine who maneuvers a marriage proposal from a sophisticated man-about-town. Julie de Carneilhan tells of a much married aristocrat down on her luck who agrees with an ex-husband to blackmail his present wife and split the gain. The final novella concerns Madame Colette's involvement in the amorous schemes of visitors at a country lodge

Julie de Carneilhan
In Colette. Gigi. Julie de Carneilhan. Chance acquaintances p77-222

The kepi
In Colette. The collected stories of Colette p498-531

The last of Chéri
In Colette. Six novels p535-648

Mitsou
In Colette. Six novels p339-410

Colette, 1873-1954—*Continued*

Music-hall sidelights

In Colette. Six novels p237-337

Six novels. Modern Lib. 697p o.p.

Contents: Claudine at school; Music-hall sidelights; Mitsou; Chéri; The last of Chéri; Gigi

The tender shoot

In Colette. The collected stories of Colette p421-48

Collins, Larry, 1929-2005

The fifth horseman; a novel; [by] Larry Collins and Dominique Lapierre. Simon & Schuster 1980 478p o.p.

LC 80-14643

"Libyan leader Qaddafi gives a Carter-like President an ultimatum: the U.S. must force Israel to leave the West Bank and East Jerusalem, or a hydrogen bomb hidden in Manhattan will be detonated in less than two days." Libr J

This "novel is as expertly done as any [international thriller] you are likely to read. . . . Collins and Lapierre, a pair of high-powered journalists well known for deep research in their previous nonfiction works . . . have brought all their investigative skills to their first novel and the results are startingly effective." N Y Times Book Rev

Collins, Max Allan

Angel in black; a Nathan Heller novel. New Am. Lib. 2001 340p o.p.

ISBN 0-451-20263-5 LC 00-66844

"Nathan Heller, founder and president of Chicago's A-1 Detective Agency, is in Los Angeles in 1947 to forge a partnership with Fred Bradbury, an ex-Chicago cop running a small detective business. Nate is also on a honeymoon with his new bride, Peggy, who has visions of Hollywood stardom. Heller is schmoozing with a *Herald-Examiner* reporter when the scribe picks up a possible homicide alert on his police-band radio. That's how Heller finds himself on the scene of what will become L.A.s' most famous officially unsolved murder: the Black Dahlia case." Booklist

"Collins paints a web of interconnections in a tightly woven plot and posits a radical solution to a crime that still resonates in literature and movies." Publ Wkly

Chicago confidential; a Nathan Heller novel. New Am. Lib. 2002 292p o.p.

ISBN 0-451-20650-9 LC 2001-58702

"Nate Heller's A-1 Detective Agency is thriving in the fall of 1950, but there's trouble on the horizon. Heller generally stays on the right side of the law, but he was once friends with Al Capone's top lieutenant, Frank Nitti, which might make him an attractive witness for Estes Kefauver's Senate hearings on the Mafia. . . . Collins doesn't see the past through rose-colored glasses but rather down the sight lines of a nine-millimeter automatic. Excellent hard-boiled fare." Booklist

Flying blind; a novel of Amelia Earhart. Dutton 1998 343p $24.95

ISBN 0-525-94311-0 LC 98-4901

"In 1970, Chicago-based PI Heller is enjoying semi-retirement in Florida when he's approached by a wealthy Texan interested in making yet another attempt to solve the mystery of the disappearance of Amelia Earhart. This narrative reveals the truth about the disappearance of the world's most famous aviatrix as only Heller knows it, having been hired in 1935 by Earhart's husband, G.P. Putnam, to provide security for one of Earhart's triumphant appearances." Publ Wkly

Collins, Michael, 1964-

Lost souls; Michael Collins. 1st American ed. Viking 2004 260p $23.95

ISBN 0-670-03328-6 LC 2003-64535

"On Halloween night in a dead-end town in Indiana, local cop Lawrence discovers the body of a three-year-old girl, dressed as an angel, who appears to be the victim of a hit-and-run accident. Called into a private meeting with the mayor, Lawrence is told to steer the investigation away from a star athlete, who is set to quarterback a championship game. But as the investigation spirals out of control, the body count mounts, and Lawrence discovers an astounding level of hypocrisy at work among the town's most prominent citizens." Booklist

"Collins's style, which alternates between the clipped prose of a cop novel and some surreally introspective passages, gives the book the prose feel of a David Lynch film." Publ Wkly

The resurrectionists; a novel. Scribner 2002 304p $24

ISBN 0-7432-2904-5 LC 2002-67013

"The year is 1979, and narrator Frank Cassidy is stuck in a dead end job in New Jersey. Orphaned at the age of five when his parents were burnt to death in a fire, Frank is still huanted by his past and fights off fits of clinical depression. He's married to Honey and has two kids, 14-year-old Robert Lee and five-year-old Ernie. . . . When Frank discovers by chance that his adoptive father, Ward Cassidy, was shot and killed on his farm in Cooper, Mich., he packs up the family and returns to his hometown, in spite of his stepbrother Norman's advice not to come." Publ Wkly

"With memorable characters and a clever use of the time period, Collins depicts a desperate man stuck in an eternal rerun of the past." Booklist

Collins, Wilkie, 1824-1889

The moonstone. Knopf 1992 473p $19

ISBN 0-679-41722-2 LC 92-52918

"Everyman's library"

First published 1868

This novel "concerns the disappearance of the Moonstone, an enormous diamond that once adorned a Hindu idol and came into the possession of an English officer. The heroine, Miss Verinder, believes her lover, Franklin Blake, to be the thief; other suspects are Blake's rival and three mysterious Brahmins. The mystery is solved by Sergeant Cuff, possibly the first detective in English fiction." Reader's Ency. 4th edition

The woman in white. Knopf 1991 xxxvii, 569p $20

ISBN 0-679-40563-1 LC 91-52971

Collins, Wilkie, 1824-1889—*Continued*

"Everyman's library"

First published 1860; first Everyman's library edition 1910

"Practically the first English novel to deal with the detection of crime. The plot is based on the resemblance between the heroine and a mysterious woman in white, and involves an infamous attempt to obtain the heroine's money." Lenrow. Reader's Guide to Prose Fic

Colwin, Laurie

A big storm knocked it over; a novel. HarperCollins Pubs. 1993 259p o.p.

LC 92-56219

"For Jane Louise, even Teddy—her wonderful, new, rock-solid husband—and a baby on the way are not enough to stave off plenty of free-floating anxiety. Luckily, she shares her joy and her distress with best friends Edie and Mokie, who have decided to embark on parenthood at the same time. The extended family formed by these two couples must suffice emotionally for each of the four individuals, since not one of the four fits within his or her own family." Booklist

"The novel makes the idea of happy endings for decent people seem entirely plausible, almost inevitable—no small feat for a writer these days and no small pleasure for a reader." N Y Times Book Rev

Family happiness; a novel. Knopf 1982 271p o.p.

LC 82-23

"Polly Solo-Miller is the mainstay of an attractive, well-to-do New York Jewish family, a family so ensconced in society, so sure of itself and its eminently proper, aristocratic view of life that there is never a doubt in the minds of any of them but what the Solo-Miller way of doing things is the best. Polly loves her husband and two children, her parents, her siblings. She is, in fact, the perfect wife, mother, daughter. But underneath there is more than a hint of rebellion seething and when Polly falls headlong in love with a painter, Lincoln, and takes to spending long and very cozy afternoons in his studio, thoroughly enjoying the adulterous affair, her Solo-Miller conscience is sorely beset." Publ Wkly

"What is so striking about this wrenching novel is not the plot itself . . . but, rather, the absolutely convincing way that Colwin portrays Polly's slow awakening to selfhood." Booklist

Goodbye without leaving. Poseidon Press 1990 253p o.p.

LC 90-6797

This novel follows the "progress of Geraldine Coleshares' life, from mediocre graduate student to rock 'n' roll backup singer to wife and mother. She seems happily married to Johnny Miller, a lawyer but a music fanatic at heart. She worries (but not too much) about what she is doing with her life, and what it all means." Libr J

"The tone here is disarmingly light, the humor intimate, and the plot inventive. A cheerfully irreverent look at an identity crisis and its unexpected resolution." Booklist

Happy all the time; a novel. Knopf 1978 213p o.p.

LC 78-2425

Set in New York City, this love story involves four quite normal people, "two men, two women. The men are cousins and close friends, the women are very different from each other, but full of spunk and individuality. Guido and Holly come together first, Vincent and Misty meet later. The men, long-time associates, are terribly nervous about their women liking each other. The women, in turn, eye each other warily. What we, as readers are treated to, however, is one of the most engaging and funniest dual courtships in a long time. The dialogue is sparkling and crisp, the encounter situations perfectly believable and perfectly ridiculous, as these four people, who really are 'happy all the time,' go through the 'angst' of realizing it." Publ Wkly

Combs, Harry, 1913-2003

Brules; a novel. Lyford Bks. 1992 521p o.p.

LC 92-4235

"Cat Brules takes up his story in 1867 as a young hellraiser just off a cattle drive to Hays City, Kansas. He kills a man in a bordello and flees through Comanche country. Captured and tortured, he escapes, later loses his best friend to the Comanche. From there, the story is mainly about Brules's prowess as a killer of Indians, but in between the cold-blooded carnage he ably describes the almost mystical attraction of the glorious Western wilderness from Texas to Montana. He sees the demise of the buffalo herds, destruction of the Plains Indians' way of life, and the gradual introduction of civilization. A violent, brutal but well-written view of Western history." Libr J

Followed by The scout

The scout. Delacorte Press 1995 602p o.p.

LC 94-49068

"In the second installment of Combs' Western trilogy . . . Cat, now an elderly recluse, narrates his life's story to a young neighbor. Considering the Indian wars of the 1870s and 1880s, the author offers intriguing interpretations of historical characters and events, most notably Custer's annihilation at the Little Bighorn." Libr J

"Combs is a master of western narrative and dialogue, filling his story with rich descriptions of people, places and events; the Indian fights here swirl with dust and smoke, bullets and arrowheads, thudding warclubs and the crashing of rifle and pistol fire. This is a magnificent story of bravery, treachery, violence, beauty and love." Publ Wkly

Followed by The legend of the painted horse (1996)

Condé, Maryse, 1937-

I, Tituba, black witch of Salem; translated by Richard Philcox; foreword by Angela Y. Davis; afterword by Ann Armstrong Scarboro. University Press of Va. 1992 227p o.p.

ISBN 0-8139-1398-5 LC 92-8134

"A Caraf book"

Original French edition, 1986

This historical novel attempts to re-create the life story of the Barbadian slave who was arrested in 1692 "for witchcraft in Salem, Massachusetts. . . . As a child,

Condé, Maryse, 1937-—*Continued*

Tituba sees her mother executed. She is then raised by an old woman who teaches her the African art of healing and communicating with spirits. As a young woman, she is sold to a Puritan minister who leaves Barbados for America. Tituba uses her powers for good purposes, including the healing of her master's family. But her powers are misunderstood by the [Puritans]." Libr J

"Part historical novel, part literary fable, part exploration of the clash of irreconcilable cultures, [this] is most of all an affirmation of a courageous and resourceful woman's capacity for survival." N Y Times Book Rev

Condon, Richard

Prizzi's family. Putnam 1986 284p o.p.
LC 86-9338

Set chronologically prior to Prizzi's honor, the plot of this novel "revolves around Don Corrado Prizzi's granddaughter, Maerose, who aspires to become Donna Maerose of the brotherhood and who intends to use Charley to advance her ambitious plan in an unlikely liaison. Meanwhile, Charley has fallen in love with Mardell, who is not all she pretends to be and who herself is in love with another man." Booklist

An "entertaining depiction of high-level corruption. . . . Condon serves up this zesty mix with good humor, broadside slams at politicians and evangelism, and generous helpings of Sicilian food." Publ Wkly

Prizzi's glory. Dutton 1988 273p o.p.
LC 88-10194

This novel features "Don Corrado Prizzi, granddaughter Maerose, Charley and Angelo Partana, and financier Edward S. Price, aka Eduardo Prizzi. This time the plot turns on the Don's and Maerose's ambitions for respectability—and a more profitable, less labor-intensive criminal conglomerate. They franchise crime, producing 800-page procedural manuals for drug-dealing and flesh-peddling." Booklist

"The plot gives Mr. Condon ample elbow room for political and social satire that is always funny. Much of it is based on observations from the point of view of Charley Partanna or his cohorts, clear-thinking, pragmatic Sicilians whose values aren't learned from this season's television series. We like them for that, and Mr. Condon doesn't invest his characters with cute, endearing qualities; rather, the Prizzis' charms stem from their complete lack of hypocrisy." N Y Times Book Rev

Prizzi's honor. Coward, McCann & Geoghegan 1982 316p o.p.
LC 81-17366

"Charley Partanna, as enforcer for the Prizzi mob, is devoted to 'The Family,' virtual owners and operators of America. When Irene Walker appears in New York at a Prizzi relative's wedding, Charley falls instantly in love with her and follows her home to Los Angeles, where she operates as a tax consultant. This is a front; Irene is a free-lance killer for the Mafia and has also organized the theft of nearly a million dollars from the Prizzi operation in Las Vegas. Charley's dedication to 'doing the right thing' as a man of respect means killing Irene but he can't endure losing her. For her part, Irene is lethally determined to keep the money and Charley's love as well." Publ Wkly

"This is a book full of action and surprises. The stage is set quickly, and the action begins almost at once. Loaded with excitement, this novel is enthusiastically recommended." Libr J

Prizzi's money. Crown 1994 241p o.p.
LC 93-8983

"Julia Asbury sets out to swipe $800 million by raiding her husband's multinational companies. Supposedly, the money is to provide a ransom for the kidnapping that her husband (with the help of the Mob) organized. Julia, unaware of her husband's Mob connections, is in for a surprise when she is summoned by Don Corrado Prizzi for having stolen money that the Mob planned to steal. With enterprise and audacity, Julia convinces Mob bosses that rather than eliminate her, they should hire her." Booklist

"As is his wont, Condon uses these goings-on as a base from which to take pointed shots at the rich and powerful. . . . It's all great fun, even if the heavy-handed lampoonery goes over the top now and again." Publ Wkly

Conley, Robert J.

Mountain windsong; a novel of the Trail of Tears. University of Okla. Press 1992 218p o.p.
LC 92-54150

The author "chronicles the Trail of Tears—the forced removal of the tribe in the 1830s from its homelands in the southeastern U.S. to alien territory in Oklahoma. He gives this epic drama a human scale by focusing on the story of Oconeechee, daughter of a famous Cherokee chief, and Waguli (Whippoorwill), the young man she loves. Separated by the genocidal march—one-quarter of the participants died en route to Oklahoma—the pair spend much of the novel searching for each other. A young Native American named LeRoy . . . narrates their saga, related to him by his grandfather after he asks about the beautiful 'windsong' he has heard on a North Carolina reservation occupied by descendants of the Cherokees who escaped relocation." Publ Wkly

"Its historical accuracy and its political correctness aside, the novel is a timeless love story about young people buffeted by a changing world over which they have no control." Booklist

Connell, Evan S., 1924-

Deus lo volt!; chronicle of the Crusades. Counterpoint 2000 462p o.p.
ISBN 1-58243-065-9 LC 99-54831

A chronicle "of the crusades from the point of view of a French knight. Jean Joinville, a participant in the disastrous second crusade under Louis IX, begins his chronicle with the first crusade, in 1095, and ends with the taking of Acre in 1290 by the forces of Ashraf Khalil, which effectively ended the mad attempt to make Palestine a Christian protectorate." Publ Wkly

What enlivens Connell's historical fiction "is first, his boyish fascination with how much has been buried alongside the victims: lost books and alphabets, artworks, cities, enigmatic treasures of all kinds. Second, there is the glittering anger of his style." Yale Rev

Connell, Evan S., 1924-—*Continued*

Mr. Bridge; [by] Evan S. Connell, Jr. Knopf 1969 369p o.p.

This novel is made up "of fragments of experience from the life of a middle-aged suburban couple between the world wars. Brief episodes are juxaposed to reveal the stereotyped values and emotional and spiritual aridity of the prosperous, proper Bridges." Libr J

"Mr. Connell's art is one of restraint and perfect mimicry. His chapters are admirably short, his style is brevity itself. . . . Rarely has a satirist damned his subject with such good humor." N Y Times Book Rev

Mrs. Bridge; [by] Evan S. Connell, Jr. Viking 1959 254p o.p.

"India Bridge is a country club matron in Kansas City. Her husband, a successful lawyer, is seldom home so Mrs. Bridge copes—not too well—with her children, who are very different from one another. Ruth, the eldest, keeps aloft; Douglas, the youngest, is mostly off on his own projects and not interested in the fine rules of behavior that Mrs. Bridge finds essential. She seems able to communicate most easily with Carolyn, the middle child. We follow the family as the children grow. Mrs. Bridge, eager to be a proper upper-middle-class wife and mother, finds no happiness despite her affluence and good intentions." Shapiro. Fic for Youth. 3d edition

Connelly, Joe, 1963-

Crumbtown. Knopf 2003 259p $23
ISBN 0-375-41364-2 LC 2002-72930

"Set in a phantasmagoric dreamscape that is part New York City slum and part absurd parallel universe, Crumbtown is a place in which little is as it appears. The story centers on Don Reedy, in prison for a Robin Hood-style bank robbery, who is freed from jail to act as a consultant on a TV show based on his life. Once out, he quickly falls for Rita, a Russian émigré bartender, and teams up with half twins Tim and Tom, his former partners-in-crime, who sold him out to the police 15 years earlier. With them, he plots a new robbery set to take place during the filming of the bank robbery scene of the TV show. The result is a wildly inventive and darkly satiric take on a world constantly shifting and media image." Libr J

Connelly, Michael, 1956-

Angels flight; a novel. Little, Brown 1999 393p o.p.
ISBN 0-316-15219-6 LC 98-28507

LAPD detective Harry Bosch "and trusty partners Jerry Edgar and Kiz Rider are investigating the murder of Howard Elias, a high-profile black lawyer famous for suing L.A. police officers for racism and civil rights violations. The logical suspect? One of Elias's many LAPD defendants, of course, making for a touchy political situation in racially charged Los Angeles." Libr J

"Bosch is a wonderful old-fashioned hero who isn't afraid to walk through the flames—and suffer the pain for the rest of us." N Y Times Book Rev

The black ice. Little, Brown 1993 322p o.p.
LC 92-33500

Harry Bosch is a "smart, determined LAPD homicide detective who's driven by an inner sense of justice. This time out he arrives early on the scene of a fellow officer's suicide; then he's told it's not his case: back off. Fat chance. Harry senses the officer may have gone over to the bad guys and was killed when he tried to tiptoe back to the right side of the tracks. At every turn, Harry is confronted by dirty cops struggling to save their collective butts by lying and misdirecting the investigation. . . . A powerful novel." Booklist

Blood work. Little, Brown 1998 393p o.p.
ISBN 0-316-15399-0 LC 97-28240

"Terry McCaleb was an FBI profiler specializing in serial killers until his heart gave out. After waiting two years for a heart transplant, he's just happy to be alive—until Graciela, a beautiful woman with a disturbing story, draws him back into the game. Graciela's sister Glory was killed in a convenience story robbery, and she's come to seek McCaleb's help in solving the crime. . . . High suspense, masterful plotting, and smart prose make this a superior thriller." Libr J

Chasing the dime; a novel. Little, Brown 2002 371p o.p.
ISBN 0-316-15391-5 LC 2002-68311

"After a messy breakup, Henry Pierce is just settling into his new apartment and new life. However, any peace he might find ends as soon as he checks his phone messages for the first time. There are several, all left for a woman named Lilly. She apparently had the number before Henry, and the messages seem to indicate that she's in some sort of trouble. Becasue of an incident deep in his past, Henry decides to locate Lilly and attempt to help her. . . . Connelly takes what could have been a typical suspense thriller and turns it into something exceptional through nonstop action and suprising twists." Libr J

City of bones; a novel. Little, Brown 2002 393p o.p.
ISBN 0-316-15405-9 LC 2001-38399

This mystery opens with "the discovery of a human bone in the densely wooded hills around Laurel Canyon. Once the recovered skeleton is identified as that of a 12-year-old boy who had been repeatedly abused before his death, some 20 years earlier, Harry Bosch, the Los Angeles homicide detective . . . can go on the hunt for the killer. But before he does, Connelly works those initial scenes into a taut mini-drama in which even minor characters, like the elderly doctor whose dog dug up the first bone, play standout roles that burn with conviction." N Y Times Book Rev

The closers; a novel. Little, Brown 2005 403p $26.95
ISBN 0-316-73494-2 LC 2005-00076

"In Los Angeles in 1988, a sixteen-year-old girl disappeared from her home and was later found dead of a gunshot wound to the chest. The death appeared at first to be a suicide but some of the evidence contradicted that scenario, and detectives came to believe this was in fact a murder. Despite a by-the-book investigation, no one was ever charged. Now Detective Harry Bosch is back with the LAPD with the sole mission of closing unsolved cases, and this girl's death is the first he's given." Publisher's note

"Like James Ellroy and John Fante, both of whose work is referred to here, Mr. Connelly continues to make his doomy, secretive Los Angeles a living, breathing character in his stories." N Y Times (Late N Y Ed)

Connelly, Michael, 1956-—*Continued*

The concrete blonde. Little, Brown 1994 382p o.p.

LC 93-11802

LAPD detective Hieronymous "Harry" Bosch "is Exhibit A in a civil suit against the city filed by the family of a man Bosch killed: a man he and the police believe was the serial murderer of prostitutes and porn stars whom the media dubbed the Dollmaker. As Bosch's trial opens, however, a Dollmaker-style note directs the police to a woman's body buried in concrete, a 'concrete blonde' who turns out to have been murdered with all the Dollmaker's trademarks *after* Bosch killed the suspect." Booklist

"Mr. Connelly keeps a tight grip on his seesaw structure, boosting the suspense for the courtroom scenes and saving the gruesome details for the procedural work." NY Times Book Rev

A darkness more than night; a novel. Little, Brown 2001 418p o.p.

ISBN 0-316-15407-5 LC 00-31025

This mystery pits L.A.P.D. detective Harry Bosch and former FBI profiler Terry McCaleb against each other. "When approached by an old L.A.P.D. pal, McCaleb jumps at the chance to help on a baffling murder case, the ritualistic details of which suggest a serial killer. It doesn't take McCaleb long to focus in on a prime suspect: Bosch. . . . Readers familiar with Bosch's bend-but-don't-break morality won't be stumped for long, but Connelly's . . . novel is otherwise flawless, cleverly conceived, superbly plotted and morally complex." Publ Wkly

The Lincoln lawyer; a novel. Little, Brown 2005 404p $26.95

ISBN 0-316-73493-4 LC 2005-12863

"Mickey Haller defends low-life criminals who seem to offend habitually. With no actual office in which to hang his law degree, he works out of the backseat of his car. When a wealthy client lands in Mickey's lap, he thinks he has found a dream case. The evidence indicates a frame, and Mickey believes he might actually be defending his first truly innocent client. While he manipulates the system to his advantage, Mickey discovers that he is being maneuvered as well." Libr J

"The book is haunted by Mickey's worst nightmare: the thought of having to defend an innocent man. He starts out without the foggiest idea of what to do with someone like that. But by the end of the story an Honest Abe conscience has begun to kick in. That's when Mickey becomes a Connelly character through and through." N Y Times (Late N Y Ed)

Lost light; a novel. Little, Brown 2003 360p $25.95

ISBN 0-316-15460-1 LC 2002-36848

"The cop who failed to collar the person who strangled Angela Benton on her 24th birthday can't do much about it now; having taken a bullet in the spine, he's paralyzed from the neck down. But the man can talk, and he talks Harry Bosch into taking the cold case. . . . Despite some shockingly sunny developments in his personal life, Bosch wears his depression like armour, making him the perfect hero for our paranoid age." N Y Times Book Rev

The narrows; a novel. Little, Brown 2004 404p $25.95

ISBN 0-316-15530-6 LC 2003-25681

Private investigator Harry Bosch "confronts the most terrifying killer he's ever known—the monster known to millions as the Poet. FBI agent Rachel Walling finally gets the call she's dreaded for years. The Poet has returned. Years earlier she worked on the famous case tracking the serial killer who wove lines of poetry into his . . . crimes. Rachel has never forgotten the Poet-and apparently he has not forgotten her. Former LAPD detective Harry Bosch gets a call, too, from an old friend whose husband recently died. The death appeared natural, but this man's ties to the hunt for the Poet make Harry dig deep." Publisher's note

"Expertly juggling the narrative between Bosch's brooding, hardboiled voice and a broader third-person perspective that takes in the points of view of Walling and the Poet, Connelly builds tension exponentially through superb use of dramatic irony." Booklist

The poet. Little, Brown 1996 434p o.p.

ISBN 0-316-15398-2 LC 95-21896

"Crime reporter Jack McEvoy knows cops commit suicide, but he can't accept that his twin brother, Sean, the Denver police department's top homicide cop, would eat his gun—even if he was depressed and obsessed by a grisly unsolved murder. To understand what happened to his brother, Jack begins to investigate police suicides and discovers what appears to be the work of a peripatetic serial cop killer who somehow gets his tough victims to leave suicide notes drawn from the poems of Edgar Allan Poe." Booklist

"The villain's flamboyant character may be unbelievable, but his methods of killing and eluding detection are infernally ingenious, adding an intellectual charge to the visceral kick of the hunt." N Y Times Book Rev

Trunk music. Little, Brown 1997 383p o.p.

ISBN 0-316-15244-7 LC 96-18988

This Harry Bosch mystery "finds the LA detective back on the homicide squad trying to prove himself after his unwilling transfer to a desk job. He gets his chance when a wealthy Hollywood movie producer is found dead in the trunk of his Rolls Royce, taking Bosch to Las Vegas in search of clues. There he runs into an old flame, strip-show owner heavies, and the strangely interested Vegas police. Meanwhile, back in L.A., his team uncovers evidence of money laundering." Libr J

The author " has taken traditional motifs from crime, cop, private-eye, mystery, and noir novels and created a terrific read." Booklist

Void moon; a novel. Little, Brown 2000 391p $32

ISBN 0-316-15406-7 LC 99-37054

"Cassie Black, a crack burglar whose specialty is stealing from high rollers who break the bank in Las Vegas, ignores the astrological warning of a bad moon and inadvertently rips off a courier for the Chicago mob. 'Sometimes you can steal too much,' Cassie tells her panicked accomplice when they finish counting the mob's $2.5 million down payment for the Cleopatra Casino. 'We just did.' Connelly makes shrewd work of the manhunt, cranking up the suspense to keep Cassie a whisker ahead of her pursuer, a techno-savvy psycho named Jack

Connelly, Michael, 1956-—*Continued*
Karch, who is so adept at ruining a perfectly good hand that they call him the Jack of Spades." N Y Times Book Rev

Connelly, Neil O.

Buddy Cooper finds a way; [by] Neil Connelly. Simon & Schuster 2004 289p $24
ISBN 0-7432-4664-0 LC 2004-45282
"Semipro wrestler Buddy Cooper can't win. In his wrestling career, he is a stunning 0186. And in marriage, he is 01. Ex-wife Alix left him for Trevor (though she still comes by Buddy's apartment occasionally to have sex), and Buddy's resentment leads to angry fantasies of killing Trevor and winning back his family. Then the unthinkable happens: the head of the wrestling federation decides Buddy Cooper (aka the Unknown Kentucky Terror) will win a match. But fate intercedes as a crazed fan goes on a shooting spree, injuring Buddy and two fellow wrestlers and killing a referee. While recovering, Buddy fakes amnesia-a trick that just might get Alix back." Booklist
"Connelly clearly relishes his oddball plots and characters; the book is a comic romp with a darker side. Supernatural subplots . . . function surprisingly well as commentaries on everything from personal responsibility to the nature of the human condition." Booklist

Connolly, John

Bad men; a thriller; John Connolly. 1st Atria Books hardcover ed. Atria Books 2004 392p $25
ISBN 0-7434-8784-2 LC 2003-69639
"The small island of Sanctuary, off the coast of Maine, was once the scene of a bloody massacre. Now, three centuries later, evil has again come to the island, a modern-day evil with strange, eerie connections to the events of the late 1600s. Do two police officers have even a remote chance of stopping the carnage? This is one of those novels that refuses to be pigeonholed. It's a thriller; it's a mystery; it's a tale of the supernatural (sort of). At its center is Joe Dupree, the (literal) gentle giant of a cop, a man whose kindness and compassion would appear to make him a bad choice to defend the citizens of Sanctuary from the marauding evil that approaches." Booklist

Conrad, Joseph, 1857-1924

Almayer's folly
In Conrad, J. Tales of the East and West p1-128

The complete short fiction of Joseph Conrad; edited with an introduction by Samuel Hynes. Ecco Press 1991-1992 2v o.p.
LC 91-27115
Contents: v1 The idiots; The lagoon; An outpost of progress; Karain: a memory; The return; Youth: a narrative; Amy Foster; To-morrow; Gaspar Ruiz: a romantic tale
v2 An anarchist: a desperate tale; The informer: an ironic tale; The brute: an indignant tale; The black mate; Il conde: a pathetic tale; The secret sharer: an episode from the coast; Prince Roman; The partner; The Inn of the Two Witches: a find; Because of the dollars; The warrior's soul; The tale

The duel
In Conrad, J. Tales of land and sea p441-504

The end of the tether
In Conrad, J. Tales of land and sea p505-610

Great short works of Joseph Conrad. Harper & Row 1966 378p o.p.
"A Harper perennial classic"
Contents: The lagoon [short story]; The Nigger of the Narcissus (1914); Youth (1903); Heart of darkness (1899); Typhoon (1902); The secret sharer [short story]

Heart of darkness; with an introduction by Verlyn Klinkenborg. Knopf 1993 110p $15
ISBN 0-679-42801-1 LC 93-1855
"Everyman's library"
Originally published 1902 in the United Kingdom in the collection Youth, and two other stories
"Marlow tells his friends of an experience in the (then) Belgian Congo, where he once ran a river steamer for a trading company. Fascinated by reports about the powerful white trader Kurtz, Marlow went into the jungle in search of him, expecting to find in his character a clue to the evil around him. He found Kurtz living a depraved and abominable life, based on his exploitation of the natives. Without the pressures of society, and with the opportunity to wield absolute power, Kurtz succumbs to atavism." Reader's Ency. 4th edition
also in Conrad, J. Great short works of Joseph Conrad p175-256
also in Conrad, J. The portable Conrad p490-603
also in Conrad, J. Tales of land and sea p33-104

Lord Jim; a tale. Knopf 1992 xxxiii, 437p $19
ISBN 0-679-40544-5 LC 91-53223
"Everyman's library"
First published 1899; first Everyman's library edition 1935
"The title character is a man haunted by guilt over an act of cowardice. He becomes an agent at an isolated East Indian trading post. There his feelings of inadequacy and responsibility are played out to their logical and inevitable end." Merriam-Webster's Ency of Lit

The Nigger of the Narcissus; edited, with an introduction and notes, by Cedric Watts. Penguin Books 1989 151p map pa $12.95
ISBN 0-14-018094-X
First published 1897 with title: Children of the sea
"All life on board the *Narcissus* revolves around James Wait, a dying black sailor. Other members of the crew include the strong Captain Allistoun; Craik, an Irish religious fanatic; and Donkin, an arrogant, lazy Cockney. The superstitious sailors cater to Wait, even steal food for him, and rescue him when the ship capsizes during a fierce storm. However, he is also the cause of dissension aboard ship, leading to a near mutiny. The novel is notable not only for its vivid picture of life at sea but also as a study of evolving relationships among men amid the most extreme circumstances." Merriam-Webster's Ency of Lit
also in Conrad, J. Great short works of Joseph Conrad p21-140

Conrad, Joseph, 1857-1924—*Continued*

also in Conrad, J. The portable Conrad p292-453

also in Conrad, J. Tales of land and sea p106-210

Nostromo; a tale of the seaboard. Knopf 1992 532p $20

ISBN 0-679-40990-4 LC 91-53185

"Everyman's library"

First published 1904; first Everyman's library edition 1957

"Set in the South American republic of 'Costaguana,' it is an exciting, complicated story about capitalist exploitation and revolution on the national scene and about personal morality and corruption in individuals. Charles Gould's silver mine helps to maintain the country's stability and its reactionary government. Gould's idealistic preoccupation with the mine warps his character and makes him neglect his gentle wife, Dona Emilia. When the revolution comes, Gould puts a consignment of silver in the charge of Nostromo, the magnificent, 'incorruptible' *capataz de cargadores* ('foreman of the dock workers'). A chance happening makes Nostromo decide to bury the silver and pretend that it was lost at sea. He is eventually killed on the island where his riches are buried, when he is mistaken by his fiancée's father for a prowler. . . . Conrad's characterization is strong, his narration is complex and oblique. The story starts halfway through the events of the revolution and proceeds by way of flashbacks and glimpses into the future." Reader's Ency. 4th edition

The portable Conrad; edited, and with an introduction and notes, by Morton Dauwen Zabel. Viking 1947 760p o.p.

"Viking portable library"

Contains two novels: The Nigger of the 'Narcissus,' and Typhoon; three long stories; six shorter stories; and a selection from Conrad's prefaces, letters and autobiographical writings

Short stories included are: Prince Roman; Warrior's soul; Amy Foster; Outpost of progress; Il Conde; The lagoon; The secret sharer. The novelettes are: Youth; Heart of darkness

Secret agent

In Conrad, J. Tales of the East and West p353-544

Tales of land and sea; introduction by William McFee; illustrated by Richard M. Powers. Hanover House 1953 695p o.p.

Contents: Youth; Heart of darkness; The Nigger of the Narcissus; Il Conde; Gaspar Ruiz; The brute; Typhoon; The secret sharer; Freya of the Seven Isles; The duel; The end of the tether; The shadow-line

Tales of the East and West; edited and with an introduction by Morton Dauwen Zabel. Hanover House 1958 xxx, 544p o.p.

Contents: Almayer's folly [novelette]; Karain: a memory; The planter of Malata; An outpost of progress; Falk; Prince Roman; The warrior's soul; Amy Foster; The secret agent [novelette]

Typhoon

In Conrad, J. Great short works of Joseph Conrad p259-328

In Conrad, J. The portable Conrad p192-287

In Conrad, J. Tales of land and sea p287-347

Victory; an island tale; with an introduction by Tony Tanner. Knopf 1998 lxi, 385p $20

ISBN 0-375-40047-8 LC 98-27677

"Everyman's library"

First published 1915

The novel's "central character, Axel Heyst, a Swedish aristocrat, lives on an island in the Malay Archipelego. Influenced by the sceptical philosophy of his father, and trying to avoid forming any attachments, his way of life is challenged when he rescues Lena, who has been touring the islands as part of a Ladies' Orchestra, from the sexual harassment of the hotelkeeper, Schomberg. The novel explores their relationship and the difficulties precipitated by the arrival of the devilish 'Mr Jones' and his two companions." Oxford Companion to 20th-century Lit in Engl

Youth

In Conrad, J. The complete short fiction of Joseph Conrad p151-80

In Conrad, J. Great short works of Joseph Conrad p143-71

In Conrad, J. The portable Conrad

In Conrad, J. Tales of land and sea p7-32

Conroy, Frank, 1936-2005

Body & soul. Houghton Mifflin 1993 450p o.p.

LC 93-5163

Set in New York City in the 1950s, this novel is about "a fatherless street urchin, Claude Rawlings, [who] is blessed with remarkable talent and a nurturing mentor. Finding his true home in music, . . . Claude moves from the Blue Book for Beginners to performing his own prize-winning concerto with the London Symphony Orchestra, from snagging coins through street grates and languishing over condescending rich girls to professional acclaim and a mature capacity for love." Booklist

"It would be all too easy to be irreverent about 'Body and Soul,' with the simplicities of its structure, of its upstanding hero and of its affection for a bygone era. Yet the novel so fully embodies a certain romantic view of our country's past that one's irreverence can turn into something like nostalgia. Whatever its weaknesses, 'Body & Soul' comes across as a legitimate and moving piece of Americana." N Y Times Book Rev

Conroy, Pat

Beach music. Talese 1995 628p $32.50

ISBN 0-385-41304-1 LC 95-13563

This novel tells "the story of Jack McCall of Waterford, South Carolina, his five brothers, drunken father, . . . [his] mother, and Holocaust-surviving in-laws." Booklist

This "is an absolute attic of a book. It's overstuffed. Seemingly every memory, character, place, and event from not only Conroy's life, but from the lives of most of the people he's ever met are in it. And as in a proper

Conroy, Pat—*Continued*

attic, you wander through 'Beach Music' dazed and fascinated by the odd, clashing richness of the several lifestyles it contains." Christ Sci Monit

The lords of discipline. Houghton Mifflin 1980 499p

The story is set in the late sixties at the time of the Vietnam War. The narrator, "Will McLean, recounts his four years at 'Carolina Military Institute.' . . . We follow the fates of four roommates and their reactions to the Institute. Will has been given the responsibility of helping the Institute's first black cadet make it through the first year. In doing that Will runs into a mysterious secret society." Libr J

The novel "is engrossing and well written. Pat Conroy . . . writes dialogue that reeks of witty Hollywood repartee, but his descriptions and characterizations are both sensitive and entertaining. He carefully draws Will as the young man who disdains military formalities and defends plebes." Saturday Rev

The prince of tides. Houghton Mifflin 1986 567p $35

ISBN 0-395-35300-9 LC 86-10689

"Savannah Wingo, a successful feminist poet who has suffered from hallucinations and suicidal tendencies since childhood, has never been able to reconcile her life in New York with her early South Carolina tidewater heritage. Her suicide attempt brings her twin brother, Tom, to New York, where he spends the next few months, at the request of Savannah's psychiatrist . . . helping to reconstruct and analyze her early life." Libr J

Constantine, K. C.

Always a body to trade; a Mario Balzic mystery. Godine 1983 248p o.p.

ISBN 0-879234-58-X LC 82-48700

"Balzic finds his life about to be made miserable by the election of 34-year old mayor Kenny Strohn, an overbearing, idealistic, and obnoxious man who has no idea how government (or policing) works. . . . At this point, Balzic is distracted by a double burglary of two sumptuous and identical apartments owned by a local drug dealer, as well as the murder of a young woman. . . . He thinks the crimes are related. The new mayor, of course, wants instant results; Balzic hopes an informant will come forward. When none does, he is forced to seek the help of the Reverend Rufee, who presides over a kingdom of vice. The dialogue between Balzic and Rufee is wonderful, as is the dark humor that pervades the grisly story." Murphy. Ency of Murder and Mystery

Blood mud. Mysterious Press 1999 375p o.p.

ISBN 0-89296-647-5 LC 98-34909

Retired Rocksburg, Pennsylvania police chief Mario Balzic "is hired by an insurance lawyer to investigate a claimed loss of 40-plus handguns and 30,000 rounds of ammunition stolen from a firearms company. Bored with retirement, trying to ignore his wife's suggestions that he exercise more and they move to Florida, and the self-described 'old geezer' eagerly takes the job." Publ Wkly

"Constantine knows that Faulkner was right: the only subject truly worth writing about is the human heart in conflict with itself. The evocation of Mario's fears and inner conflicts, told through agonizingly wonderful dialogue between husband and wife, raises this latest Balzic novel to the level of the best contemporary literature." Booklist

Brushback. Mysterious Press 1998 278p $29

ISBN 0-89296-646-7 LC 97-10130

In this mystery set in Rocksburg, Pennyslvania "Ruggiero 'Rugs' Carlucci is investigating the brutal murder of Brushback Bobby Blasco, a local hero who once beaned the immortal Ted Williams, even though Williams was his Red Sox teammate. Blasco, who has a history of beating wives and girlfriends, has been bludgeoned to death with a Louisville Slugger autographed by the Splendid Splinter. But Rugs has many competing concerns: his mother's nightly anxiety attacks; his duties as acting police chief; byzantine city politics; undertrained, overworked cops; and summoning the courage to ask a beautiful woman for a date." Booklist

"This is another near-perfect game from Constantine. His working-class dialogue is always exacting and evocative, and his detective is a great guy with a good heart and a mouth that just never quits." Publ Wkly

Family values. Mysterious Press 1997 216p o.p.

LC 96-23330

Retired Rocksburg, Pa. police chief Mario Balzic is "working on special assignment for the state's Deputy Attorney General, who is bedeviled by a 17-year-old murder case that won't roll over and die. The plot isn't much: Balzic goes around interviewing people involved in the trial of Lester Walczinsky, who is doing serious prison time for killing a couple of no-good drug dealers, and digging up evidence of past perjury and police corruption. Plot doesn't really count for much in Mr. Constantine's books. Character does." N Y Times Book Rev

Grievance. Mysterious Press 2000 279p o.p.

ISBN 0-89296-648-3 LC 99-41380

This mystery, set in Rocksburg, Pa., begins with "the murder of J. D. Lyon, C.E.O. of the local steel outfit that pulled up stakes and relocated to Brazil, tossing this company town into an economic sinkhole. Ruggiero (Rugs) Carlucci, the young police sergeant who recently took over the peacekeeping chores . . . does his best to conduct a fair investigation. But he is driven to distraction by his mother's deteriorating mental state, and his work ethic is compromised by his compassion for the families whose lives were so casually destroyed by the murdered man. . . . The anguished voices of the broken people in this beat-up town would make a saint weep." N Y Times Book Rev

The man who liked slow tomatoes. Godine 1982 177p o.p.

LC 81-47321

This mystery features "Mario Balzic police chief of Rocksburg, Pennsylvania. . . . Wise and funny, Balzic swears profusely, loves his mother, weeps as he arrests a murderer, creatively manhandles a young punk, and vehemently refuses to endure the bureaucratic games of smalltown politics. His personality carries the book; the plot grows slowly and it is not until the last pages that we encounter in quick succession a corpse, a murderer and a pathetic suicide. Until then the suspense is provided by a missing husband, the crazy leitmotif of too-early-ripening tomatoes, and Balzic's mushrooming impatience with contract negotiations. Constantine is a genius with

Constantine, K. C.—*Continued*
conversation and reproduces various immigrant accents with uproarious accuracy. This is an intelligent, compassionate and moving book, as well as a top-notch entertainment." Publ Wkly

The man who liked to look at himself. Saturday Review Press 1973 156p o.p.
As police chief of Rocksburg, Pa. the novel's central character, Mario Balzic, is "confronted by parts of a body scattered through a hunting ground. As the case is out of his jurisdiction, he has to work with an unlovely specimen of a lieutenant in the state police, said lieutenant being a loud-mouth, a racist and, on top of all that, impulsive and not very smart. Balzic solves the case because he knows the people in his Pennsylvania town." NY Times Book Rev
"A top-grade blue-collar, small-town mystery. The dialogue is such that it might have been tape-recorded." Barzun. Cat of Crime. Rev and enl edition

Saving room for dessert. Mysterious Press 2002 294p o.p.
ISBN 0-89296-763-3 LC 2002-20096
This mystery "focuses on three Rocksburg cops who patrol the Flats, an area of the city known for domestic disputes that often become deadly. Officer William Rayford prays for a thunderstorm that will keep the feuding Bucyks and Hornyaks, not to mention the certifiable Scavellis, indoors. His prayers aren't answered, however, and Rayford and fellow cops Reseta and Canozza all find themselves drawn into a lunatic situation that ends tragically." Booklist
"Constantine is as eloquent as ever in speaking out on the inevitability of violence when people can't find the language to express themselves." N Y Times Book Rev

Cook, Elizabeth, 1952-

Achilles. Picador 2002 115p o.p.
ISBN 0-312-28884-0 LC 2001-52398
First published 2001 in the United Kingdom
"This forceful re-creation of the life of Achilles sacrifices nothing to modernity: gods mate violently with mortals, ghosts feast on sheep's blood, and Achilles rages and slays, unburdened by psychology. At the same time, this brief, intense novel is unmistakably modern in intent, turning a war epic into a meditation on the limits of human perfectibility." New Yorker

Cook, K. L.

Last call. University of Nebraska Press 2004 252p (Prairie schooner prize in fiction) $25
ISBN 0-8032-1540-1 LC 2004-3458
Contents: Easter weekend; Nature's way; Gone; Thrumming; Texas moon; Last call; Knock down, drag out; Costa Rica; Breaking glass; Marty; Pool boy; Penance
This short story cycle "chronicles the often fractious and brutal lives of the Tates of West Texas, who are indelibly scarred when the family matriarch clandestinely boards a bus one morning, never to return. . . . Although the stories are generally harsh and unforgiving, Cook transforms these attributes into a kind of grace." Libr J

Cook, Robin, 1940-

Acceptable risk. Putnam 1994 406p o.p.
LC 94-41273
In this medical thriller neuroscientist Edward Armstrong isolates a psychotropic drug with a dark history that is developed into an antidepressant with startling therapeutic capabilities. Ethical questions are raised when the drug's side effects are proven to be dangerous. How far will the medical and pharmaceutical establishments go to alter the parameters of acceptable risk?

Brain. Putnam 1981 283p o.p.
"Young women, repeating visits to the gynecology clinic [at Hobson University Medical Center in New York] because of abnormal Pap smears, develop seizures, blurred vision, and headaches, and smell strange odors. The women all vanish under mysterious circumstances except for Lisa Marino, who dies on the operating table. . . . Dr. Martin Philips, assistant chief of neuroradiology . . . [and] Denise Sanger, resident in radiology, discover—when they 'borrow' her body from the morgue—that someone stole Lisa's brain." Libr J

Chromosome 6. Putnam 1997 461p o.p.
ISBN 0-399-14207-X LC 96-53133
The body of underworld figure Carlo Franconi disappears before it can be autopsied. When the mutilated body of a "floater" surfaces, forensic pathologist Jack Stapleton and his colleague Dr. Laurie Montgomery identify the corpse as the missing Franconi. "Jack and Laurie's search for the truth leads them to the steamy jungles of equatorial Africa, where they discover a sinister cabal whose stock-in-trade involves surgical procedures a step beyond the latest in current technology and a Promethean leap beyond accepted medical ethics." Publisher's note

Coma; a novel. Little, Brown 1977 306p o.p.
LC 76-52951
"A female medical student uses her charms and femininity to obtain forbidden charts and computer read-outs on certain patients who have gone into coma on the operating table and never come out of it, remaining like vegetables due to extensive brain damage. Susan feels there is something wrong and sets out to find what it is. As a second-year med student, she knows practically nothing of medical terms or practices, so spends all of her class time in the library trying to learn the terminology before she can try to solve a mystery that has puzzled the finest surgeons in the hospital. She does manage to uncover a ring of doctors who are selling various organs for transplant from the coma victims as soon as they can declare them dead, and is almost a victim herself for her pains." West Coast Rev Books

Contagion. Putnam 1995 434p o.p.
ISBN 0-399-14106-5 LC 95-45375
"After he loses first his midwestern ophthalmology practice to a for-profit medical giant and then his family to a commuter airline tragedy, Dr. John Stapleton's life is transformed to ashes. Feeling less the golden boy than a jaded cynic, Stapleton retrains in forensic pathology and relocates to find an uneasy niche for himself in a city that suits his changed perspective: the cold, indifferent, concrete maze of New York. Stapleton thinks he is past pain and past caring, but as a series of virulent and extremely lethal illnesses . . . strikes the young, the old,

Cook, Robin, 1940-—*Continued*
and the innocent, his suspicions are aroused. When the apparent epicenters of these outbreaks are revealed to be hospitals and clinics controlled by the same for-profit giant that cannibalized his old ophthalmology practice, Stapleton fears he has stumbled upon a diabolic conspiracy of catastrophic proportions." Publisher's note

Godplayer. Putnam 1983 368p o.p.
LC 83-4507

"Someone is playing God on the surgery floor of Boston Memorial Hospital, causing unexplained patient deaths. Pathologist Robert Sieber, with the help of Dr. Cassandra Kingsley, is investigating these 'SSD's,' sudden surgical deaths. Meanwhile Cassi's husband, a top surgeon, is becoming estranged from her, and seems headed for a breakdown. When Cassi herself must be admitted for an eye operation, she isn't aware that she is the Godplayer's next target." Libr J

Marker; Robin Cook. Putnam 2005 533p $25.95
ISBN 0-399-15293-8 LC 2005-45812

This book "revisits medical examiners Jack Stapleton and Laurie Montgomery, whose romantic relationship has hit a major bump. Approaching her forty-third birthday, Laurie wants a family and has grown impatient with Jack's reluctance to commit. She walks out on Jack, but she can't avoid him at work. She soon finds herself absorbed in a puzzling case: 28-year-old Sean McGillan has landed on her table, and she can't determine what killed him. Sean had just undergone routine knee surgery, but she can't find any reason why he went into cardiac arrest in his hospital bed. When another young, seemingly healthy patient dies, she suspects foul play." Booklist

"True love runs a rocky course, and the plot thickens before the denouement crackles to an electric edge-of-the-seat finale." Publ Wkly

Mortal fear. Putnam 1988 364p o.p.
LC 87-29085

This suspense novel "centers around the startling death of an eminent biomolecular geneticist and the subsequent inexplicable and untimely deaths of a number of Dr. Jason Howard's patients. As Dr. Howard begins to investigate the deaths and even the possible discovery of the scientific breakthrough that the geneticist had made, we are immersed in an intricate journey that includes modern laboratories, seamy nightclubs, the wilds of the Northwest, and most particularly, Boston's erotic, sleezy backstreets." West Coast Rev Books

Mutation. Putnam 1989 367p o.p.
LC 88-31680

"Dr. Frank is an infertility expert, and when he learns that his wife can't conceive, he employs in vitro fertilization—but with genetic alterations in order to produce a superintelligent baby. Predictably, the experiment eventually backfires, and the horror begins. Cook marshals all the medical facts necessary to make this situation seem real, and he musters all the quick pacing necessary to keep the reader engrossed." Booklist

Outbreak. Putnam 1987 366p o.p.
LC 86-25390

"Dr. Marissa Blumenthal, pert, pretty, diminutive, is assigned by Atlanta's Centers for Disease Control to investigate a series of outbreaks of a mysterious, untreatable and highly contagious virus that is felling physicians and their patients in several hospitals around the country. Unless contained and checked, the deadly virus poses a threat to the entire populace. Unaccountably hampered by her superiors, Marissa persists in her sleuthing and, to her dismay, comes to suspect the viral contagion is the work of a sinister cabal of ultraconservative doctors trying to undermine the public's faith in prepaid health-maintenance facilities. Marissa finds her career endangered, her very life in peril. As in his previous medical whodunits, Mr. Cook is nimble at stitching together the ingredients of terror, suspense, intrigue and medical expertise." N Y Times Book Rev

Seizure. Putnam 2003 464p $24.95
ISBN 0-399-14876-0 LC 2003-43225

This "medical thriller centers around two men—Daniel Lowell, a brillant researcher and Ashely Butler, a powerful southern senator. Daniel and his girlfriend, Stephanie D'Agostino, are the cofounders of CURE, a medical research company, the existence of which relies heavily on biotechnology legislation that Butler is trying to block. . . . Cook is at his best when focusing on fascinating cutting-edge biotechnology procedures." Booklist

Terminal. Putnam 1993 445p o.p.
LC 92-30678

"The Forbes Cancer Center in Miami is experiencing unprecedented cure rates for patients stricken with medulloblastoma. Sean Murphy, a bright, brash, Harvard medical student, takes an elective at the center to learn as much as he can about the procedures and treatments. The icy atmosphere that greets him coupled with a warning to stay away from the unit in question fuels Sean's determination to discover why everything is veiled in such secrecy. To carry out his investigation, he enlists the help of his girlfriend, Janet Reardon, a nurse." SLJ

"Cook tells a beautifully woven story—keeping the various individuals and plots in meaningful operation—and winds up with a dramatic . . . denouement." Booklist

Toxin. Putnam 1998 356p o.p.
ISBN 0-399-14316-5 LC 97-52645

In this medical thriller a young boy dies as a result of E. coli poisoning. When his physician father attempts to find those responsible he runs into a conspiracy of silence enforced by violent thugs

Vector. Putnam 1999 404p o.p.
ISBN 0-399-14471-4 LC 98-49058

In this "novel, the People's Aryan Army (PAA) is planning a major terrorist attack against a big government building in New York, hoping that will spark nationwide revolution. PAA founder Curt recruits immigrant Russian technician Yuri to prepare bioweapons for the attack. Yuri sets up a basement lab to produce anthrax, and a package 'bomb' becomes the vector for the anthrax when Yuri tries it out on a Greek rug dealer. Desiring proof of the merchant's death. Yuri meets Jack Stapleton from the medical examiner's office, and Jack's sidekick, Laurie, gets involved. . . . *Vector* is Cook at his best, providing both thrills and an urgent message." Booklist

Cook, Robin, 1940-—*Continued*

Vital signs. Putnam 1991 396p o.p.
LC 90-46807

"Epidemiologist Marissa Blumenthal, seen before in *Outbreak* now has a successful pediatrics practice near Boston and an affluent health-care-entrepreneur husband. But her inability to become pregnant threatens both her marriage and her career. After unsuccessful visits to a local fertility clinic, she discovers a surprising and suspicious link between her medical records and those of an inordinate number of the clinic's clients. Traveling to Australia to learn more about a worldwide in vitro fertilization organization, Marissa and her friend Wendy are trailed, and tragedy occurs. Marissa, now accompanied by the physician whose work she had come to Australia to investigate, goes to Hong Kong and eventually China—fleeing murderous assailants every step of the way—before a billion-dollar international scam is revealed." Publ Wkly

Cook, Thomas H.

Breakheart Hill. Bantam Bks. 1995 264p o.p.
LC 94-26639

"The narrator is Ben Wade, the town doctor of Choctaw, Alabama: the story he tells is of 1962, his senior year in high school, and his unrequited love for Kelli Troy, the new girl in town, whose shattered body is found on Breakheart Hill at the end of that year. Ben's narration shuttles back and forth between an innocent past and a blighted present, where Ben and his former classmates struggle to free themselves of the sense of loss." Libr J

"Cook has crafted a novel of stunning power, with a climax that is so unexpected the reader may think he has cheated. But there is no cheating here, only excellent storytelling." Booklist

The Chatham School affair. Bantam Bks. 1996 292p o.p.
LC 96-4021

"The aged storyteller, a lawyer named Henry Griswald, was just a schoolboy when Elizabeth Channing arrived in his seacoast village in Massachusetts to teach art at his father's private school. But like more than one man in this staid community, young Henry was fascinated by Miss Channing, so unconventional and exotic by local standards, and by romanticizing her relationship with a married teacher, he contributed to her downfall. But did he also drive her to murder?" N Y Times Book Rev

"Cook is a marvelous stylist, gracing his prose with splendid observations about people and the lush, potentially lethal landscape surrounding them. Events accelerate with increasing force, but few readers will be prepared for the surprise that awaits at novel's end." Publ Wkly

Evidence of blood. Putnam 1991 319p o.p.
LC 91-476

"True-crime writer Jackson Kinley returns to his rural Georgia hometown to attend the funeral of longtime friend Ray Tindall, for years the county sheriff. When Tindall's daughter confides to Kinley that her father had recently grown withdrawn and had been doggedly investigating some case (certain files from which are now missing), Kinley decides to turn his own investigative talent toward the pursuit of Tindall's inquiry." Publ Wkly

"Highly satisfying story, strong in color and atmosphere, intelligent and exacting." N Y Times Book Rev

Instruments of night. Bantam Bks. 1998 293p o.p.
ISBN 0-553-10554-X LC 97-52760

"Paul Graves, the author of a popular series of thrillers, is hired to write about an unsolved murder that took place half a century ago in the small town of Riverwood. And the crime—a young girl was tortured and killed—bears a frightening resemblance to an incident from Paul's own past." Booklist

"Although it's easy to miss the very real clues that Cook drops so artfully into the story, there's no ignoring his savage imagery, or escaping the airless chambers of his disturbing imagination." N Y Times Book Rev

The interrogation. Bantam Bks. 2002 286p $23.95
ISBN 0-533-80095-7 LC 2002-280882

"It's 1952. Three cops take turns grilling one suspect in interrogation Room Number Three. They have 12 hours to solve the murder of a little girl, found strangled to death in a park, before the suspect must be released. . . . The ticking clock, in addition to the economy of scene, makes this an incredibly intense read, culminating in a true shocker of an ending." Booklist

Places in the dark. Bantam Bks. 2000 245p o.p.
ISBN 0-553-10563-9 LC 99-89644

A village on the coast of Maine "is torn apart by the arrival of a young woman, Dora March, who seems to bring death in her path. Dora awakens the interest and passions of two brothers. Central to the brothers' fascination with Dora is their half-knowledge of the childhood trauma that has maimed her spirit. One brother is murdered; Dora flees; the older brother embarks on a quest to find her and rid himself of obsession." Booklist

This novel "is swept along by Cook's artistry, his insights into broken people, his austere imagery of the barren landscapes that attract them." N Y Times Book Rev

Cookson, Catherine

The black velvet gown; a novel. Summit Bks. 1984 345p o.p.
LC 84-216472

"After her husband's death in a cholera epidemic, the widow Millican and her four children are homeless and nearly penniless, when the entire family is taken under the protection of an eccentric Northumberland bachelor. Eldest daughter Biddy is sent into service as a laundress at a neighboring estate, where she teaches the other servants to read and write, is promoted upstairs as a lady's maid, falls in love, and becomes the center of a family scandal. Cookson spices her story with blackmail, sexual passion, untimely death, and savage violence, but the novel's underlying message—it's not who you are but what you are that determines your destiny—emerges triumphant." Booklist

The desert crop. Simon & Schuster 1999 318p o.p.
ISBN 0-684-85683-2 LC 98-40561

Cookson, Catherine—*Continued*

First published 1997 in the United Kingdom

In 1880s Northern England "alcoholic widower Hector Stewart has subjected the family farm to near ruinous neglect. Though his children, Daniel and Pattie, object to his remarriage to Moira Conelly—she's *Irish,* they complain—their kind new stepmum turns out to be a blessing in disguise. Hector, the uncomplicated villian of the tale, treats Moira badly and denies Daniel the education he needs to become a doctor. Daniel makes the best of a bad situation, however, working hard and struggling to keep the farm from total deterioration, while emotionally supporting Moira and the increasing brood of half-brothers and sisters." Publ Wkly

"Told with insight, compassion, and humor, this coming-of-age story is sure to enrapture all the devoted fans Cookson attracted during her long and prolific career." Booklist

The glass virgin; a novel. Simon & Schuster [2004] c1969 356p $25

ISBN 0-7432-6126-7 LC 2005-295077

First published 1969 by Bobbs-Merrill

"Annabella Lagrange is a lovely 17-year-old lady-to-be . . . or not to be, whose aristocratic childhood comes to a crashing halt when her womanizing papa, who has just bankrupted his wife Rosina's glass factory, reveals that Annabella is actually the daughter of a local whorehouse madam. Manuel Mendoza, a predictably dark and handsome self-made workman, helps Annabella begin a new, humble life as a farmhouse maid with an invented past." Publ Wkly

"Readers will enjoy Cookson's lavish period detail and rich characterization, and how each twist in the plot becomes another step in the growth of a young girl into a woman." Booklist

A house divided. Simon & Schuster 1999 365p o.p.

ISBN 0-684-87121-1 LC 99-54730

This romance focuses on "Matthew Wallingham, scion of a wealthy military family who feels as though his life is over after being blinded in battle. He is brought back from the edge by Ducks, a nurse whom he believes to be a middle-aged, motherly woman but who is, in truth, the beautiful 24-year-old Liz Ducksworth, the daughter of a farmer. Released from the hospital, Matthew returns home with great plans to run the farm on the family estate, but during the war, his younger brother Rodney took control and wants to keep it. Matthew is rescued from utter despair by the news that an old comrade-in-arms, and nurse Ducksworth, have taken jobs at a nearby hospital. So he enrolls in a training program there and pursues Liz. But she has issues of her own that must be resolved. . . . Cookson fans will relish this posthumous romantic saga with its wonderful happily-ever-after ending." Booklist

The Maltese Angel; a novel. Simon & Schuster 1994 c1992 479p o.p.

LC 94-9729

First published 1992 in the United Kingdom

"Hayward Gibson, a nineteenth-century English farmer, finds his Maltese Angel on the stage in Newcastle, falls in love, and marries this dancer who brings beauty, happiness, and, eventually, generations of grief to his life. The woman he marries is not the cause of the sorrow. It is the woman he scorns, a neighboring country girl who had assumed her place would be beside Ward on his freehole farm. This girl, Daisie Mason, is avenged by her brothers, who torment Ward by damaging his farm property. Not content with that, Daisy catapults a stone at Ward's wife, killing her. Left to raise two young daughters, Ward lives only for the youngest, who so resembles her mother. Such preoccupation has chilling effects on the whole family." Booklist

The obsession. Simon & Schuster 1997 317p o.p.

ISBN 0-684-84241-6 LC 97-18688

First published 1995 in the United Kingdom

"Beatrice Steel's fanatic devotion to her family's north-country estate and to her unscrupulous father alienates her three sisters. The two oldest, Marion and Helen, escape by marrying. After the father's death reveals that his gambling and whoring have bankrupted the family, Beatrice's obsession only grows. Through deception, she convinces her youngest sister's fiancé to break his engagement so that Rosie will be forced to remain at home. Then Beatrice manipulates her own marriage to the local doctor, John Falconer, whose real love rests with Helen. Intriguing subplots, interesting and well-developed major and minor characters, and strong narrative movement demonstrate Cookson's mastery of the historical romance." Libr J

The upstart. Simon & Schuster 1998 348p o.p.

ISBN 0-684-84315-3 LC 97-28621

First published 1996 in the United Kingdom

"The son and grandson of cobblers, Samuel Fairbrother owns a series of boot factories. He buys a Newcastle mansion as a means of showing off his wealth and fortune. Totally out of his social depth, he relies on his butler Maitland to tell him how to dress, when to have a party, and whom to invite. . . . When Sam and his wife separate, he insists that his oldest child, Janet, trained as a librarian, stay with him. She and Maitland fall in love, but first one disaster and then another postpone their wedding. Cookson skillfully shows the class conflicts that result when a tradesman tries to climb beyond his station." Libr J

The year of the virgins; a novel. Simon & Schuster 1995 c1993 269p o.p.

LC 94-29796

First published 1993 in the United Kingdom

This novel, "set in England during the 1960s, focuses on a Catholic family about to celebrate the marriage of their youngest son. The wedding day, already a day of mourning for the groom's obsessively possessive mother, turns into a tragedy when the couple are involved in a car crash that leaves the groom crippled just as they embark on their honeymoon. From this bizarre opening, the story grows stranger as the mother is hospitalized in a mental institution, from which she escapes to wreak revenge on her troubled family." Booklist

"Cookson adeptly paints a stark, psychologically realistic portrait of the disintegration of the Coulson clan." Publ Wkly

Cooley, Martha

The archivist; a novel. Little, Brown 1998 328p o.p.

ISBN 0-316-15872-0 LC 97-38385

Cooley, Martha—*Continued*

Matthias Lane, a widower in his 60's, is an archivist and guardian to a collection of letters between T. S. Eliot and his friend Emily Hale. "This invaluable correspondence is off-limits until 2019, but Roberta, an attractive poet, is determined to gain access to it and draws Matthias into a tense tango of negotiations that unfreezes painful memories of his poet-wife's suicide." Booklist

The novel "treats serious questions in a humane and passionate manner, and leaves one thinking about these questions long after one has read the last page. Cooley is an accomplished stylist—there's scarcely a graceless or unintelligent sentence in the book—and a subtle chronicler of the inner life." N Y Times Book Rev

Coonts, Stephen, 1946-

America; a Jake Grafton novel. St. Martin's Press 2001 390p o.p.

ISBN 0-312-25341-9 LC 2001-34899

"*America*—the U.S. Navy's most advanced submarine—is pirated on her shakedown cruise by a mysterious crew of terrorists, just two months after the newly launched first satellite in an orbital antimissile system mysteriously disappeared. The missing sub then dispatches its Tomahawk missiles with magnetic pulse warheads to Washington and New York, devastating the government and Wall Street. Jake Grafton thinks these dire deeds are connected, and with various allies, he sets out to prove it and retrieve sub and satellite." Booklist

Cuba; a novel. St. Martin's Press 1999 390p $24.95

ISBN 0-312-20521-X LC 99-22070

In this speculative thriller "Rear Admiral Jake Grafton and staff operations officer Toad Tarkington are providing military cover for a shipment of American chemical and biological weapons—weapons that should have been destroyed long ago—out of Guantánamo Bay, where they have been in storage. When the shipment goes missing, it's Grafton's job to find it and get those weapons back. But that's the least of his worries, because Cuba is developing its own biological weapons." Publ Wkly

"Coonts has perfected the art of the high-tech adventure story. He juggles a multivoiced narrative with action taking place in a number of different locations but seldom loses sight of the direction of the story." Libr J

Final flight. Doubleday 1988 387p o.p.

LC 88-12001

Capt. Jake Grafton's "night-flying's over, thanks to failing eyesight. But the fate of the Middle East is hanging in the balance when his F-14 tears off into Mediterranean air-space. Coonts has cast the hero of his first novel, *The Flight of the Intruder,* as a wing commander aboard an aircraft carrier. He has also thrust him into the bulls-eye of an Arab plot to steal the ship's nuclear weapons. . . . The backdrop is Naples, and the well-detailed lives of Navy pilots. *Final Flight* has a long fuse, but its detonation is well worth the wait." Publ Wkly

Flight of the Intruder. Naval Inst. Press 1986 329p $26.95

ISBN 0-87021-200-1 LC 86-16440

"In the autumn of 1972, despite rumors of peace, United States Navy pilots flew A-6 Intruder attack planes in bombing raids over North Vietnam. Some of these pilots were angered by the relative insignificance of their targets—road intersections, sampan repair yards—which mocked the loss of life incurred carrying out the missions. So when the pilot Jake Grafton's best friend, a bombardier, is killed by a rifle bullet fired randomly from the ground, he decides 'to bomb something worth the trip' and plans a solo, unauthorized raid on Communist Party headquarters in downtown Hanoi." N Y Times Book Rev

Fortunes of war. St. Martin's Press 1998 376p o.p.

ISBN 0-312-18583-9 LC 97-52793

"Russia is in chaos, its economy in ruins; rich oil deposits in Siberia seem available to the most daring predator. When Japan mounts an invasion, the U.S. comes to Russia's defense. Air Force Colonel Bob Cassidy finds himself leading a squadron of irregular American troops—lent to Russia to fly the country's high-tech F-22s—against the attacking Japanese led by his old Air Force Academy buddy Jiro Kimura. Full of action and suspense, this is a strong addition to the genre." Publ Wkly

Hong Kong; a Jake Grafton novel. St. Martin's Press 2000 350p o.p.

ISBN 0-312-25339-7 LC 00-31766

"In Hong Kong to investigate the loyalty of American consul Virgil Cole, Grafton finds a tense city as protests against a failed bank take on anti-communist overtones. Constitutionally indisposed to the circumspect approach, Grafton bluntly confronts Cole with official suspicions that the consul is fomenting the unrest. Almost before the consul can concoct a lie, the aforesaid gangster nabs Grafton's wife, setting up the two agendas that drive Coonts' plot: Grafton's attempt to rescue his spouse, and Cole's sub rosa machinations with Chinese rebels. . . . This is an entertaining distraction within its genre's conventions." Booklist

The Intruders. Pocket Bks. 1994 344p o.p.

LC 94-213081

This Jake Grafton techno-thriller "takes the heroic Navy aviator back to 1973, immediately following the events of his debut in *Flight of the Intruder*. Disillusioned by the killing and dying 'for nothing' that he saw in Vietnam, Jake is at a crossroads. Should he try to find his way in civilian life, or stay in the service and make the demanding transition from hot shot jet jockey to professional Naval officer? He mulls over his decision while flying A-6 Intruders with a Marine squadron assigned to an aircraft carrier in the Pacific. As always with Coonts, the terrors and elations of flying take center stage." Publ Wkly

The minotaur. Doubleday 1989 436p o.p.

LC 89-11879

Jake Grafton's new assignment is "overseeing development of a navy stealth bomber. Jake's predecessor, he soon learns, was offed under mysterious circumstances, which the reader (if none of the navy brass) knows has to do with the dead man's top-secret computer-access code having been used by a Soviet mole code-named *Minotaur.*" Booklist

Coonts, Stephen, 1946-—*Continued*

The red horseman. Pocket Bks. 1993 344p o.p.
LC 93-1099

Jack Grafton "has been promoted to deputy director of the Defense Intelligence Agency—a desk job, in other words. But when Boris Yeltsin runs into trouble keeping 20,000 nuclear warheads out of terrorists' hands, only Grafton will do to save us all from death or a fate much worse. An ambitious reporter, Jack Yocke, and Grafton's earthy cohort, Toad Tarkington, also figure in the mix." Booklist

"The issues Coonts confronts—the frighteningly unprotected and undermaintained nuclear devices in the former Soviet Union; factionalism in the U.S. intelligence community; unrest in the Middle East—make this one of the most compelling post-*glasnost* thrillers to date." Publ Wkly

Under siege. Pockèt Bks. 1990 408p o.p.
LC 90-62714

This Jake Grafton novel is set "in contemporary Washington, D.C., where a Colombian drug lord has been brought for trial. His gunmen terrorize the capital with a series of spectacular mass murders while a hired assassin stalks top officials. . . . [Jake] is joined on the front lines by journalist Jack Yocke and undercover narc Harrison Ronald Ford." Publ Wkly

"Mr. Coonts has a tendency to see things in black and white. His heroes are too good to be true, and his villains are darker than a black hole. But in his prose he avoids the dreadful clichés of most of his colleagues. His dialogue is realistic, the story line mesmeric. That is the mark of a natural storyteller." N Y Times Book Rev

Cooper, J. California

The future has a past; stories. Doubleday 2000 265p $23.95
ISBN 0-385-49680-X LC 00-34602

Contents: A shooting star; A filet of soul; The eagle flies; The lost and the found

Stories about "African-American women struggling to make something of their smalltown lives. . . . Navigating poverty, unwanted pregnancy, single motherhood and inexperience, all Cooper's heroines triumph, to lesser and greater degrees, finding 'real love' despite being surrounded by 'no good men'." Publ Wkly

The wake of the wind. Doubleday 1998 373p o.p.
ISBN 0-385-48704-5 LC 98-21594

"Two good friends in Africa, Kola and Suwaibu, are taken from Africa and brought to America as slaves. The story of their great-great-great grandchildren, Mordecai (Mor) and Lifee, reunites these friends' families through marriage. Mor and Lifee's life together is chronicled through their marriage, freedom from slavery, the birth of their children and grandchildren, and their deaths." Booklist

Cooper, James Fenimore, 1789-1851

The Deerslayer; or, The first war-path, a tale; with an introduction by Donald E. Pease. Penguin Books 1987 xxvii, 548p il (Penguin classics) pa $12
ISBN 0-14-039061-8 LC 88-104322

This is the first title of the author's Leatherstocking saga featuring Natty Bumppo

First published 1841 in two volumes by Lea & Blanchard

Set in New York State this "is a record of Natty Bumppo's early days as a young hunter brought up among the Delaware Indians, engaged in warfare against the Hurons. He helps defend the family of Tom Hutter, a settler, from attack. Judith, who is really not Tom's daughter, but a girl of noble birth, loves Natty Bumppo and begs him not to return to the Iroquois, who have released him on parole from capture. Bumppo does return, but is rescued by the intervention of Judith, who thereafter disappears, and the Delaware Chief Chingachgook, who remains a lifelong friend." Haydn. Thesaurus of Book Dig

Followed by The last of the Mohicans

also in Cooper, J. F. The Leatherstocking tales p483-1030

The last of the Mohicans; introduction by Leslie A. Fiedler. Modern Library 2001 xxxii, 350p pa $9.95
ISBN 0-375-75764-3 LC 00-68105

First published 1826

This Leatherstocking tale "presents Chingachgook and his son Uncas as the last of the Iroquois aristocracy. Natty Bumppo, the scout Hawkeye, is in the prime of his career in the campaign of Fort William Henry on Lake George under attack by the French and Indians. The commander's daughters, Cora and Alice Munro, with the latter's fiancé Major Duncan Heyward, are captured by a traitorous Indian but rescued and conveyed to the fort by Hawkeye. Later Munro surrenders to Montcalm, and the girls are seized again by Indians. Uncas and Cora are killed, and the others return to civilization." Haydn. Thesaurus of Book Dig

also in Cooper, J. F. The Leatherstocking tales p467-878

The Leatherstocking tales. Library of Am. 1985 2v ea $40
ISBN 0-940450-20-8 (v1); 0-940450-21-6 (v2)
LC 84-25060

Contents: v1 The pioneers; or, The sources of the Susquehanna, a descriptive tale; The last of the Mohicans; a narrative of 1757; The prairie; a tale; v2 The Pathfinder; or, The inland sea; The Deerslayer; or, The first warpath

These novels "are linked together by the career of Natty Bumppo, or Hawkeye, Cooper's inimitable backwoodsman, a romantic embodiment of the virtues of both races, and of Chingachgook, his Indian counterpart, equally idealized. . . . There is little historical background; but the vivid descriptions of wood, lake, and prairie, and of the daily life of Indian and huntsman, gives the finest imaginable picture extant of natural scenes and human conditions that have long passed away." Baker. Guide to the Best Fic

The Pathfinder; or, The inland sea; edited with an introduction and notes by William P. Kelly. Oxford University Press 1992 xxxv, 484p pa $11.95
ISBN 0-19-283989-6

Cooper, James Fenimore, 1789-1851—*Continued*

First published 1840

The third in the Leatherstocking tales "finds Natty Bumppo at the age of forty. A small outpost on Lake Ontario is under attack. Mabel Dunham helps in the defense, and with the aid of Pathfinder, Chingachgook, and Jasper Western, a young sailor, the Iroquois are routed. Lieutenant Muir . . . arrests Jasper as a traitor, but when Muir is revealed as the guilty one, he is killed by Arrowhead, a Tuscarora Indian. Jasper wins the love of Mabel." Haydn. Thesaurus of Book Dig

Followed by The pioneers

also in Cooper, J. F. The Leatherstocking tales p1-482

The pilot; a tale of the sea; edited with an historical introduction and explanatory notes by Kay Seymour House. State University of New York Press 1986 xlvii, 479p il $59.50

ISBN 0-8739-5415-7 LC 84-8765

First published 1823

John "Paul Jones's adventures suggested the plot; which is, in brief, an attempt during the Revolutionary War to abduct some prominent Englishmen for exchange against American prisoners." Keller. Reader's Dig of Books

also in Cooper, J. F. Sea tales: The pilot, The red rover

The pioneers; edited with an introduction and notes by James D. Wallace. Oxford University Press 1999 465p map pa $10.95

ISBN 0-19-283667-6

First published 1822

In this fourth of the Leatherstocking tales Natty "first appears as an older man. The story takes place in the village of Templeton, founded by Judge Temple. The central conflict is between the laws of nature, upheld by Natty, and the laws of civilization. Symbolic of this opposition are two incidents, the first being the settler's hypocritical effort to punish Natty for killing a deer out of season for food, despite their own slaughter of pigeons purely for sport. The second is over the true ownership of the Judge's lands, which is resolved by the marriage of Elizabeth Temple and Edward Effingham, heir of the true owner. Natty, like Huck Finn, heads for the Far West to escape confining civilization." Reader's Ency. 4th edition

Followed by The prairie

also in Cooper, J. F. The Leatherstocking tales p1-465

The prairie; with an introduction by Blake Nevius. Penguin 1987 xxvi, 386p pa $13

ISBN 0-14-039026-X LC 87-2891

Sequel to The pioneers

First published 1827

This final installment in the Leatherstocking tales centers on the death of Natty Bumppo. "Cooper contrasts the noble, disinterested Natty with the squatter Ishmael Bush and his family. Lawless and self-seeking, the squatters portend ill for the future of democracy. Cooper's prairie descriptions . . . are derived from the *Journals* of Lewis and Clark." Reader's Ency. 4th edition

also in Cooper, J. F. The Leatherstocking tales p879-1317

The red rover

In Cooper, J. F. Sea tales: The pilot, The red rover

Sea tales: The pilot, The red rover. Library of America, Distributed to the trade in the U.S. and Canada by Viking Press 1991 902p $35

ISBN 0-940450-70-4 LC 90-52923

Contents: The pilot; The Red Rover

The pilot is entered separately. In The red rover (1827 in United Kingdom and France, 1828 in the United States), "Lt. Henry Ark, an officer in the British Navy about the middle of the 18th century, . . . takes the name Wilder and enlists as a common sailor on board the Dolphin in the hope of tracking down a mysterious pirate, the Red Rover." Reader's Ency. 2nd edition

The spy; a tale of the neutral ground. Wiley & Halsted 1821 2v o.p.

A story of the American Revolution. The hero, the spy, is a cool, shrewd, fearless man, who is employed by General Washington in service which involves great personal danger and little glory

Covers "the locality 'between the royal barracks in New York City and the American outposts on the Hudson' where a mixed population of loyalists and British sympathisers mistrusted one another. Not many historic figures or events are introduced . . . but the tale well illustrates the later Revolution period, and is full of allusions to such men as Burgoyne, Gates, Tarleton, Sumter, etc." Nield. Guide to the Best Hist Novels & Tales

Coover, Robert

Briar Rose. Grove Press 1996 86p o.p.

ISBN 0-8021-1591-8 LC 96-4917

This work of fiction is Coover's "retelling of the story of Sleeping Beauty. In this dark and unromantic world, a prince hacks his way through the briar hedge surrounding the castle, ever aware that the bodies of dead princes who went before him are swinging in the wind, and the princess dreams of the men who come and assault her as she lies helpless." Libr J

"Coover doesn't just spit in the eye of happily-ever-after; he gouges it out. But what makes Briar Rose more than a cynical tale for adult children is the startling complexity of its vision." Nation

Gerald's party; a novel. Linden Press 1986 316p

ISBN 0-671-60655-7 LC 85-15901

In this novel "Gerald and his (unnamed) wife are giving one of their famous parties. The guests are all 'creative' or pseudocreative types, in their 30s and 40s mostly. At the center of the night's events is a woman they all know, a celebrated sexy actress named Ros, who is found murdered on the living room floor as the book begins . . . More guests arrive, mayhem breaks out, more killings take place, toilets are stuffed up, the house is wrecked, sexual activity sprouts in every corner, chaos ensues, and the mystery is finally 'solved.'" New Repub

This novel is "relentless in its pursuit of outrage and its attempt to reduce the reader to a condition of helpless and exhausted voyeurism. It is also a work of considerable comic vitality, full of inspired mimicry and parody, gleeful in its unabashed sadism." N Y Rev Books

Ghost town; a novel. Holt & Co. 1998 147p o.p.

ISBN 0-8050-5884-2 LC 98-5713

Coover, Robert—*Continued*

This novel "retails the fever-dream misadventures of a nameless rider . . . as he moves back and forth through the gravity field of an archetypal Western frontier town, a place at times populated by . . . staple figures (the gruff barkeep, the saloon bawd, the grizzled drunk), at other times inexplicably stripped back to the tumbleweed streets and banging shutters suggested by the book's title." N Y Times Book Rev

"Genre isn't the only target of Coover's perversity: the goings on are often hilariously obscene, and perhaps truer to the old West than what we want to imagine. 'Ghost Town' is both warped and scintillating, a cross between 'No Exit' and 'The Canterbury Tales'." New Yorker

The origin of the Brunists. Grove Press 2000 441p pa $14

ISBN 0-8021-3743-1 LC 00-37670

First published 1966 by Putnam

Set in a small town in western Pennsylvania, this novel "fuses realism, satire, and fantasy in telling of a mystic cult founded by the survivor of an accident in a coal mine." Oxford Companion to Am Lit. 6th edition

Pinocchio in Venice. Linden Press/Simon & Schuster 1991 330p o.p.

ISBN 0-671-64471-8 LC 90-45706

"Pinocchio in Mr. Coover's novel has become an elderly professor of aesthetics and philosophy, . . . winner of two Nobel prizes and recipient of enough honors for an entire faculty. He returns to Venice, hoping that the scenes of his youth will inspire him to compose an adequate ending to the book he is writing, which is a tribute to the fairy with the blue hair, his mentor and lifelong inspiration. He encounters old friends in Venice, and even more old enemies; he blunders through nightmarish disasters; he is robbed, abused, and humiliated; and he gradually reverts to his original condition as a wooden puppet." Atlantic

"The ribaldry and the 'fun' are a lot more strenuous and obsessive than self-denial ever was. But then, that is Coover's specialism–the joke on the joker, that the world without soul, far from being easy, is absurdly hard." Times Lit Suppl

The Universal Baseball Association, Inc., J. Henry Waugh, Prop. Plume 1986 c1968 242p pa $15

ISBN 0-452-26030-2 LC 68-14517

First published 1968 by Random House

A novel "about a lonely accountant who fantasizes a rich, warm life in the imaginary baseball league he has invented and avidly follows." Oxford Companion to Am Lit. 6th edition

Corman, Avery

Kramer versus Kramer; a novel. Random House 1977 233p o.p.

LC 77-5654

"Joanna Kramer's answer to that locked-in feeling was to leave her husband and pre-school son for a life of her own. Ted Kramer tells of his minute-by-minute adjustments to the crises of single parenthood. Just when he has things under control, his wife brings suit to regain custody of the boy, with startling results. An intelligently wrought novel which depicts the role of single parenthood with convincing verisimilitude." Booklist

Prized possessions. Simon & Schuster 1991 320p o.p.

LC 90-22666

"Elizabeth Mason, her Manhattan family's 'prize possession,' is a dedicated student and talented singer who wins acceptance into Layton, a top liberal arts college near Albany, NY. With all her parents' hopes pinned on her, Liz goes off to Layton where, on the first weekend of her freshman year, she is asked to a party by senior Jimmy Andrews, star of the tennis team. They dance, they drink, they kiss. Then he gets her alone and he rapes her. . . . With Liz's story, Corman takes a tense, disturbing look at the nature of consent and raises critical questions about negative ways in which society still views female sexuality." Publ Wkly

Cornwell, Bernard

The archer's tale. HarperCollins Pubs. 2001 374p o.p.

ISBN 0-06-621084-4 LC 2001-24333

First published 2000 in the United Kingdom with title Harlequin

"Set in the early 1400s at the beginning of the Hundred Years War between England and France, this novel depicts one of the most bloody and violent periods in the history of conflict between these two nations. After the theft of the treasure of Hookton, a broken lance thought to have been the weapon St. George used to slay the dragon, young Thomas, the bastard son of the village priest and a skilled longbowman, joins the English army in hopes of recovering the relic. Instead, he finds himself caught up in the invasion of France." Libr J

"Authentically detailed and appropriately gruesome, the medieval battle scenes fairly crackle with tension; however, what sets Cornwell's work apart from most run-of-the-mill military adventures are his meticulously developed story lines and his razor-sharp characterizations." Booklist

Battle flag. HarperCollins Pubs. 1995 356p maps (Starbuck chronicles, v3) o.p.

LC 94-42288

This installment in the author's Civil War series is "set against the background of Lee and Stonewall Jackson's campaign against John Pope, the North's new commander, who was expected to end the war in the summer of 1862. Nate Starbuck, a renegade Bostonian who has become a Confederate officer, serves under Stonewall Jackson in that desperate summer. He distinguishes himself at the Battle of Cedar Mountain, but afterward his career is jeopardized through the suspicion and hostility of his brigade commander, the grandiose General Washington Faulconer." Publisher's note

Followed by The bloody ground

The bloody ground. HarperCollins Pubs. 1996 343p (Starbuck chronicles, v4) o.p.

ISBN 0-06-017500-1 LC 95-440503

The fourth volume in the saga "continues Nate Starbuck's story as he serves under General Robert E. Lee, culminating in the famous, bloody battle of Antietam." Publisher's note

Cornwell, Bernard—*Continued*

Copperhead. HarperCollins Pubs. 1994 375p (Starbuck chronicles, v2) o.p.

LC 93-29421

"Nathaniel Starbuck is a Northerner, the son of a Boston minister who becomes caught up in the South at the start of the Civil War and joins the Rebel cause, captivated more by the challenge and peril of war than the righteousness of either side. New-forged loyalties entice him to stay with the rebels even after his life and his family ties are put at risk when he must act as a spy to save his best friend from charges of espionage. Nate is a beguiling hero and Cornwell's balance of battle, romance, and historic scenes are neatly paced in this novel set against the 1862 battle for Richmond." Booklist

Followed by Battle flag

Enemy of God; a novel of Arthur. St. Martin's Press 1997 396p (Warlord chronicles, bk2) o.p.

ISBN 0-312-15523-9 LC 96-51740

In the second volume of the Warlord Chronicles trilogy, "having secured the throne of Dumnonia for the infant King Mordred, Arthur seeks to bring peace to the kingdom by uniting the various rival Celtic factions into the 'Brotherhood of Britain.' Derfel, one of Arthur's warriors and the book's narrator, sardonically notes that 'the Round Table, of course, was never a proper name, but rather a nickname.' But Arthur's good intentions are gradually undone: by Merlin's quest for the Thirteen Treasures of Britain; by Lancelot's and Guinevere's ambitions; by Mordred, now an unpleasant young man incapable of wise rule; and by the growing conflict between the old Druid religion and the new Christianity." Libr J

"This complex and superbly wrought narrative easily eclipses the more sanitized and tepid versions of Arthur's exploits." Booklist

Followed by Excalibur

Excalibur; a novel of Arthur. St. Martin's Press 1998 340p (Warlord chronicles, bk3) o.p.

ISBN 0-312-18575-8 LC 98-10247

In the concluding volumes of the Warlord Chronicles "Arthur temporarily halts the invading Saxons at the battle of Mynydd Baddon (during which Lancelot meets a coward's death and Guinevere is reconciled with her husband), [but] his dream of a unified Celtic kingdom is doomed. Thwarting him is the vicious Mordred who makes a pact with Nimue to bring back the old Druid gods and destroy the new Christian deity." Libr J

"The action is gripping and skillfully paced, cadenced by passages in which the characters reveal themselves in conversation and thought, convincingly evoking the spirit of the time. Ways of ancient ritual, battle and daily life are laid out in surprising detail." Publ Wkly

Gallows thief. HarperCollins Pubs. 2002 297p o.p.

ISBN 0-06-008273-9 LC 2001-58334

First published 2001 in the United Kingdom

"After successfully defending his country at Waterloo, Captain Rider Sandman returns to England to face bankruptcy and disgrace. . . . Looking for any type of honest work that will enable him to live and to pay off some of his father's creditors, he accepts an assignment to investigate the circumstances of the brutal rape and murder of the countess of Avebury. Though a hapless young portrait painter has already been convicted of the crime, Sandman begins to suspect well-connected members of the aristocracy have framed him." Booklist

Rebel. HarperCollins Pubs. 1993 308p (Starbuck chronicles) o.p.

LC 92-53344

This first volume of the Starbuck chronicles "follows the adventures of Nathaniel Starbuck, the rebellious and discredited son of a famous Boston abolitionist preacher. Nate flees the North after helping a *femme fatale* steal money she claimed was hers, winding up in Richmond as Fort Sumter falls and the Civil War begins. Unable to return home, distrusted by Southerners because of his parentage, Nate is taken under the wing of the mercurial and megalomaniacal Washington Faulconer, obsessed with building an independent army, answerable only to him, to fight for the Confederacy. Spanning the period from Sumter's capitulation in April 1861 to the First Battle of Bull Run in July, the book is well paced and filled with the historical details genre fans demand." Publ Wkly

Followed by Copperhead

Redcoat. Viking 1988 c1987 405p o.p.

LC 87-40018

First published 1987 in the United Kingdom

"The setting is Philadelphia and its environs at the time of the Revolution; the principal characters are Sam Gilpin, a Redcoat lured toward the Patriot cause by love, and Jonathan Becket, who is under his fiercely loyalist uncle's thumb until he makes a perilous break for freedom." Publ Wkly

"The grim and gory reality of war is skillfully played out against the gaiety of Loyalist society. Cornwell's fictional characters mingle well with the historical figures of the time." Libr J

Sharpe's battle; Richard Sharpe and the Battle of Fuentes de Oñoro, May 1811. HarperCollins Pubs. 1995 304p il o.p.

LC 95-10347

This adventure finds Sharpe "fighting the French and the hierarchy of Wellington's army. The encounter takes place in 1811, shortly after the destruction of Almeida (recounted in *Sharpe's Gold*. It is still Almeida that is under contention, for the French have mounted a massive campaign to supply the scant forces that still hold the fort. On another front, Sharpe is waging a private battle (which nearly gets him court-martialed) against the ferocious French Wolf Brigade. Vintage Cornwell." Booklist

Sharpe's company; Richard Sharpe and the Siege of Badajoz, January to April 1812. Viking 1982 280p o.p.

LC 81-69930

Sequel to Sharpe's gold

"The imaginary hero Captain Richard Sharpe is once again pitted against Napoleon's vast army as he attempts to seize the impenetrable Badajoz fortress in this third novel in the Sharpe series describing the Peninsular War. The battle itself is only one of Sharpe's problems, however, as he is savagely stalked by a figure from his early army days who proves more dangerous than the enemy. Further complications cause Sharpe still more anguish as he discovers that his gazette has not gone through, thus stripping him of his temporary captaincy and separating

Cornwell, Bernard—*Continued*
him from the very men he has trained and come to trust. Cornwell sustains his fine craftsmanship and adds a new realistic dimension to his portrayal of war as he depicts an army of men who fight for survival within their own ranks. Not even the smallest of details escapes the author's keen reconstruction of a series of events that made history more than a century ago." Booklist

Followed by Sharpe's sword

Sharpe's devil; Richard Sharpe and the Emperor, 1820-1821. HarperCollins Pubs. 1992 280p o.p.
LC 91-58360

Sequel to Sharpe's Waterloo

In this episode Richard Sharpe "finds himself in the Spanish colony of Chile during its fight for independence in 1820-21. Hired by the wife of a Spanish nobleman to locate her kidnapped husband, the captain-general of Chile, Sharpe and friend Patrick Harper sail halfway around the world on a mission complicated by political intrigue and corruption." Libr J

This is a "rousing read, full of invincible characters, deafening broadsides, roaring cannons, and smoking pistols as Cornwell writes of old-fashioned battles, blazing with glory." Booklist

Sharpe's eagle; Richard Sharpe and the Talavera campaign July 1809. Viking 1981 270p o.p.
LC 80-54081

First volume of a series set during the Napoleonic Wars

"As the Peninsular War against Napoleon is heating up in the summer of 1809, Lieutenant Richard Sharpe of the British 95th Rifles finds himself in Portugal separated from his battalion and in charge of a motley group of 30 men. When a battalion of greenhorn British troops arrives in Portugal, Sharpe and his detachment are put under the leadership of its colonel, a sadistic and incompetent bully. As they march along the Tagus to join their Spanish allies in a campaign against the French and Dutch at Talavera, Sharpe—who has risen from the ranks—finds himself catching more hell from snobbish British officers than from the enemy." Publ Wkly

This "is an engrossing and entertaining book. The action moves swiftly, and the characters are interesting, especially the hero." Libr J

Followed by Sharpe's gold

Sharpe's enemy; Richard Sharpe and the defense of Portugal, Christmas 1812. Viking 1984 351p o.p.
LC 83-47925

Sequel to Sharpe's sword

In this installment of Sharpe's adventures it is the "winter of 1812 and the Peninsular War is at its height. Sharpe, a major now, is given a dangerous mission: with a handful of men he is to rescue Lady Farthingale, wife of his poltroon of a superior . . . from the clutches of a villainous international band of deserters holed up in a village near the Spanish-Portuguese border." Publ Wkly

The author "writes in gruesome detail of the horrors faced by the dying soldiers and with glowing excitement of the satisfaction of victory. An appended historical note sets an even more realistic perspective on the events he has so smoothly chronicled." Booklist

Followed by Sharpe's honour

Sharpe's fortress; Richard Sharpe and the Siege of Gawilghur, December 1803. HarperCollins Pubs. 2000 294p o.p.
ISBN 0-06-019424-3 LC 00-59703

This installment in the Richard Sharpe saga finds "Sharpe, a junior officer in Her Majesty's army, stationed in India in 1803. Struggling to earn the respect of both his superiors and his troops, he . . . runs up against the unscrupulous Sergeant Obadiah Hakeswill. Uncovering an act of treason by Hakeswill, Sharpe must confront his sworn enemy in order to protect himself and recover a cache of stolen jewels. Set against the backdrop of the Maharatta War and the siege of the fortress of Gawilghur, this fast-paced historical adventure features plenty of electrifying military action." Booklist

Sharpe's gold; Richard Sharpe and the destruction of Almeida, August 1810. Viking 1982 c1981 250p o.p.
LC 81-51908

Sequel to Sharpe's eagle

In this second volume of the series "the time is 1810, and Lord Wellington's Peninsular army is tottering. Devoid of allies—the Spanish forces had been routed by the French—and badly in need of funds, Wellington's only hope for survival before his confrontation with Bonaparte is a cache of 16,000 gold coins hidden in the Portuguese hills. The gold must be stolen, and only one man is up to the task—Captain Richard Sharpe of the South Essex Regiment. The assignment, of course, is fraught with danger and adventure every step of the way." West Coast Rev Books

The author's "crisp, fast-paced style is engagingly suspenseful, and his rendering of characters wittily perspective." Booklist

Followed by Sharpe's company

Sharpe's havoc; Richard Sharpe and the campaign in northern Portugal, spring 1809. HarperCollins Pubs. 2003 306p $25.95
ISBN 0-06-053046-4 LC 2002-191284

"It is 1809, and Napoleon has plans to annex the Iberian Peninsula; British troops are sent to help the Portugese in their battle against the French. Sharpe and his small regiment of riflemen are separated from the main body of British troops, and once again find themselves in the thick of the action, which centers in and around the city of Oporto. Complicating matters is Kate Savage, the daughter of a British wine mechant in Oporto, whom Sharpe must find and escort to to safety. Meanwhile, a French spy marries Kate solely to get his hands on her fortune. The action shifts between battle scenes and the spy, whom Sharpe unmasks. Although the outcome is never in doubt, this nevertheless makes for a rousing story." Libr J

Sharpe's honour; Richard Sharpe and the Vitoria Campaign, February to June 1813. Viking 1985 320p o.p.
LC 84-40474

Sequel to Sharpe's enemy

"Fighting with Wellington's British forces in Spain, Major Sharpe is framed for murder and consequently court-martialed in an elaborate plot by a French master spy . . . to seal a treaty between Napoleon and King Ferdinand VIII. Sharpe is secretly spared from hanging

Cornwell, Bernard—*Continued*
only to be given the near-suicidal mission of uncovering the facts behind the conspiracy." Booklist

"The climactic battle of Vitoria is brilliantly presented, followed by an extraordinary scene of looting." Publ Wkly

Followed by Sharpe's regiment

Sharpe's prey: Richard Sharpe and the Expedition to Copenhagen, 1807. HarperCollins Pubs. 2002 262p o.p.

ISBN 0-06-000252-2 LC 2001-46501

"Richard Sharpe, though stuck in the lowly role of regimental quartermaster, finds himself in the thick of the 1807 British campaign to destroy the Danish navy anchored in Copenhagen before the French can seize the ships and pose another invasion threat. As ever, the story starts fast, here with the murder of an English army officer in London by Captain John Lavisser—a traitor working for the French and as vile a villain as any Sharpe has faced—and scarecely lets up until Sharpe's final confrontation with Lavisser during the British bombardment of Copenhagen." Publ Wkly

Sharpe's regiment; Richard Sharpe and the invasion of France, June to November 1813. Viking 1986 301p o.p.

LC 85-29541

Sequel to Sharpe's honour

"With the campaign against Napoleon about to enter France, Sharpe is informed that his South Essex regiment has been dissolved. Indignant, he returns to England and uncovers a scam of major proportions—the trainees lured into the prestigious South Essex are being sold off to less-popular regiments in the colonies. Sharpe and his Irish sergeant go undercover, posing as new recruits in hopes of determining the extent of the corruption." Booklist

"What really raises this story high above a mere action tale (including Cornwell's usual effectively gritty view of Army life) is the wonderful depiction of Regency London, from gaudy, bawdy Vauxhall Gardens to a reeking, dangerous slum to the perfumed, equally dangerous Royal Court. The book ends with a highly realistic battle that opens Sharpe's way into France." Publ Wkly

Followed by Sharpe's siege

Sharpe's sword; Richard Sharpe and the Salamanca Campaign, June and July 1812. Viking 1983 319p il o.p.

LC 82-40371

Sequel to Sharpe's company

In this fourth Captain Richard Sharpe novel, the nineteeth-century British infantryman "faces an inhumane adversary, Captain Leroux, who is Napoleon's most trusted and ruthless intelligence officer. While leading his company into numerous skirmishes in the battle of Salamanca, Sharpe must also search for Leroux, who has acquired, through torture and blackmail, the names of the British army's most valuable spies and is eliminating them. Cornwell not only delineates the political turmoil and battle scenes with incredible specificity, but he also draws in any number of other details that give this historical fiction its ghastly realism." Booklist

Followed by Sharpe's enemy

Sharpe's Trafalgar; Richard Sharpe and the Battle of Trafalgar, October 21, 1805. HarperCollins Pubs. 2001 293p o.p.

ISBN 0-06-019425-1 LC 00-53871

First published 2000 in the United Kingdom

"Sharpe finds himself on a homeward-bound ship to England after duty in India. He has some problems adjusting to sea life but learns quickly. When his ship is attacked by the French, Sharpe finds out that the French ship contains a treaty that could cause a new outbreak of hostilities between India and the British. The result is the 1805 Battle of Trafalgar. . . . Cornwell satisfyingly delivers action, adventure, and a great gallery of villains and heroes, plus the usual beautiful lady." Libr J

Sharpe's Waterloo; Richard Sharpe and the Waterloo campaign, 15 June to 18 June 1815. Viking 1990 378p o.p.

LC 89-40661

Sequel to Sharpe's revenge

"At Waterloo, Lieutenant-Colonel Sharpe serves as military adviser to the Dutch prince of Orange—a hapless military strategist who sends legions to their deaths before Sharpe takes matters into his own hands. . . . Along the way, Sharpe settles an old score with Lord John Rossendale, who previously cuckolded him and helped deprive him of his hard-earned fortune. Cornwell graphically depicts the grime and horror of the battlefield, including cavalry charges, cannon bombardments, and infantry attacks. A sublime work of historical fiction." Booklist

Followed by Sharpe's devil

Stonehenge, 2000 B.C.; a novel. HarperCollins Pubs. 2000 433p o.p.

ISBN 0-06-019700-5 LC 00-24288

A "novel that imagines the history behind Stonehenge. At the story's center are three brothers: Lengar, a warrior who takes the leadership of his tribe through patricide; Camaban, a crippled outcast who transforms himself into a sorcerer and seizes power from Lengar; and Saban, a craftsman who longs for the peaceful days of his father's reign. . . . Cornwell's depictions of the herculean efforts needed to move, shape and raise the stones of Stonehenge sound plausible, and his portrayal of the vitality and brutality of a society slowly creeping toward civilization is deft." N Y Times Book Rev

Vagabond. HarperCollins Pubs. 2002 405p $25.95

ISBN 0-06-621080-1 LC 2002-68884

"In this sequel to The Archer's Tale, gifted archer Thomas of Hookton continues his quest to avenge his father's murder and to find the Holy Grail, which King Edward III believes will help England defeat the French. Thomas finds himself embroiled in a series of events beginning with the Battle of Neville's Cross (October 1346) and ending with the English victory at La Roche—Derrien (spring 1347)." Libr J

"Cornwell is meticulous about historical facts and period detail, and his descriptions of butchery with arrow, mace and battleaxe are nothing if not convincing. As expected, the book culminates with battlefieldslaughter on an epic scale." Publ Wkly

Cornwell, Bernard—*Continued*

The winter king; a novel of Arthur. St. Martin's Press 1996 431p o.p.
LC 96-1421

First published 1995 in the United Kingdom

"Cornwell's Arthur is fierce, dedicated and complex, a man with many problems, most of his own making. His impulsive decisions sometimes have tragic ramifications, as when he lustfully takes Guinevere instead of the intented Ceinwyn, alienating his friends and allies and inspiring a bloody battle. The secondary characters are equally unexpected, and are ribboned with the magic and superstition of the times." Publ Wkly

Followed by Enemy of God

Cornwell, David John Moore *See* Le Carré, John, 1931-

Cornwell, Patricia Daniels

Blow fly; [by] Patricia Cornwell. Putnam 2003 465p $26.95
ISBN 0-399-15089-7 LC 2003-62314

"Booted out of her position as the chief medical examiner of Virginia, Scarpetta is reduced to living in a cottage in Delray Beach and hiring herself out as a consultant. But nothing lights her fire until she receives a message from Jean-Baptiste Chandonne, the monstrous killer she put on death row in an earlier novel, promising to fill her in on the atrocities currently being committed in Baton Rouge by his equally insane twin brother." N Y Times Book Rev

Postmortem. Scribner 1990 293p o.p.
LC 89-10177

This mystery about a serial killer features "Dr. Kay Scarpetta, Chief Medical Examiner for the Commonwealth of Virginia. . . . From the moment that the strangler makes his fourth killing (one of two that figure prominently in the plot), the tension is up. No less than the police, Dr. Scarpetta is baffled by the absence of the usual sick motivational pattern; but she can read the physical evidence, and she has the brains and the gizmos—computers, fingerprint-matching processor, DNA-testing equipment, F.B.I. profiling systems—to give the madman chase." N Y Times Book Rev

Cortázar, Julio, 1914-1984

Hopscotch; translated from the Spanish by Gregory Rabassa. Pantheon Bks. 1966 564p o.p.

Original Spanish edition published 1963 in Argentina

"Considered to be Cortázar's masterwork, it is an open-ended novel; after reading the first 56 chapters, the reader is asked to reread the chapters in a different order. . . . The novel's antihero is Horacio Oliveira, an Argentine existentialist who lives among cultured expatriates in Paris while searching for his telepathic mistress. Returning to Buenos Aires, Oliveira meets Traveler and Talita, who are the doubles of his mistress and himself. None of the characters understands or cares more than superficially about the others, and impulse motivates their choices and actions. Narrative progress in the story is insignificant and its end is inconclusive." Merriam-Webster's Ency of Lit

Coscarelli, Kate

Heir apparent. St. Martin's Press 1993 310p o.p.
LC 93-3681

"Lacey Haines, treasured daughter of California packaged food mogul Jack Gallagher, is stunned when her father's will leaves the control of Gallagher's Best, promised to her, to her beloved but lightweight younger brother Scott. When he winds up dead with her letter opener in his chest, all the evidence points first to Lacey, then to those closest to her." Publ Wkly

"Readers will enjoy this high-speed thriller in spite of some forced and obvious teases of evidence." Booklist

Costain, Thomas B., 1885-1965

The black rose. Doubleday, Doran 1945 403p o.p.

This novel set in the 13th century, is the story of a young English nobleman who fights his way to the heart of the Mongol empire and returns to find that he must choose between an English heiress and a girl of the East

"Its background of history is richly furnished with information and local color. . . . [It is] a story that, in spite of the attention given to the romance, derives its major interest from the remarkable tapestry of history against which it is enacted." Christ Sci Monit

The silver chalice; a novel. Doubleday 1952 533p o.p.

The silver chalice was a frame meant to hold the sacred cup from which Christ drank at the Last Supper. This novel, based on legends of the years following Christ's crucifixion, describes the life of Basil, the artisan, who fashioned the silver chalice. The scenes are laid in Antioch, Rome and Jerusalem

"Costain paints a tremendous canvas filled with warm color and life. . . . As those know who have read his many vigorous re-creations of the past, Costain has a magnificent talent for breathing life into history. . . . But over and above this the novel does something else. It will make real for thousands, perhaps for the first time, the whole world of the New Testament." Chicago Sunday Trib

Costello, Mark, 1936-

Big if. Norton 2002 315p $24.95
ISBN 0-393-05116-1 LC 2002-512

This novel focuses on the "world of Vi Asplund, a Secret Service agent assigned to protect the vice-president. As the daughter of an accident investigator, she saw things . . . that prepared her well for the tense uncertainties she faces on a daily basis. . . . Meanwhile, her brother, Jens, a computer genius who writes code for a war game, is starting to question the ethics of his creations, namely, the too-lifelike villains who are armed to the teeth." Booklist

"The novel ends not with a bang but a shiver—in a masterfully orchestrated scene that is vividly cinematic. But true to his materials and vision—and to life—Costello slyly defuses the emotional catharsis in a manner that would be anathema to the feel-good demands of a major Hollywood production." N Y Times Book Rev

Coughlin, William Jeremiah, 1929-1992

Death penalty; a novel; [by] William J. Coughlin. HarperCollins Pubs. 1992 353p o.p.
LC 92-52680

"Detroit trial lawyer Charley Sloan is defending a doctor accused of helping his patients die—for a fee. At the same time he is asked to handle the appeal in a five-million-dollar lawsuit involving Ford and a man injured in an accident. Sloan, whose reputation for alcohol consumption and legal shenanigans far outweights his current nondrinking, now-honorable self, is approached by a former Appellate judge who offers him a way to win the appeal." Libr J

"The first-person narrative form and wise-cracking humor give *Death Penalty* the flavor of a hard-boiled detective yarn, but the action all takes place on the battlefield of the courtroom. First rate in every respect." Booklist

The heart of justice; [by] William J. Coughlin. St. Martin's Press 1994 327p o.p.
LC 94-3783

"A Thomas Dunne book"

Judge Paul Murray has unwittingly "received his recently acquired position on the federal bench thanks to his new wife, beautiful socialite Hope Scott. Hope asked powerful corporate raider and old boyfriend Jordan Crandell to recommend Paul for the judgeship; Crandell obliged. Now Crandell is in a headline-grabbing legal fight with takeover king Lew Valentine to buy up the computer company Starwares. As fate and plotting would have it, the Starwares case ends up in federal court, with Paul presiding." Publ Wkly

"What's particularly appealing about Coughlin's treatment of a well-worn premise is his skillful development of the peripheral characters." Booklist

In the presence of enemies; [by] William J. Coughlin. St. Martin's Press 1993 309p o.p.
LC 92-29876

"A Thomas Dunne book"

In this courtroom suspense novel "Jake Martin, a probate attorney in a make-or-break race for partnership in a prestigious Detroit firm, starts as part of a team handling the estate of banking tycoon Augustus Daren. Daren's last will and testament favor his fourth wife, the sexy, 20-years-younger Elizabeth. The bank's president, Daren's millionaire children, and someone in Jake's firm don't want Elizabeth running things and contest the will based on an incompetency argument. Through twists of fate (maybe), Jake finds himself in a litigation situation for the first time. . . . Coughlin's forte is characterization, which carries the reader's interest." Booklist

Shadow of a doubt; [by] William J. Coughlin. St. Martin's Press 1991 390p o.p.
LC 90-27501

"A Thomas Dunne book"

"Attorney Charley Sloan has lost his lucrative Detroit practice, three wives and a considerable fortune—all to demon rum. Narrowly escaping disbarment, he has retreated to AA and the suburbs to pull his life together. Up pops Charley's high school girlfriend, Robin, who has gone from the backseat of his jalopy to the bed of multimillionaire septuagenarian Harrison Harwell. The mogul's daughter has just been arrested for his murder, and Robin offers Charley the chance to represent Angel Harwell—the media case of the decade—and reestablish his legal reputation. But the DA sees the case as a ticket to a congressional seat and drives full-tilt to discredit Charley." Publ Wkly

"A gripping mystery and reflective judicial drama that explores a number of relevant moral, ethical, and legal conundrums." Booklist

Coulter, Catherine

The heiress bride. Putnam 1993 303p o.p.
LC 92-15374

This "brings the cast from those previous novels to Scotland, where the sister of the Earl of Sherbrooke has just eloped with a Scottish laird. The new bride, Joan, is appalled to find herself the stepmother of two children and caretaker of a run-down castle, which she must share with a malevolent aunt and her spouse's fey sister-in-law (from her beloved's previous marriage). A murder mystery, feuding clans, and bridal-night terrors are also stirred into the plot, which features an appearance by a ghost called Pearlin' Jane. Coulter is more interested in detailed accountings of the newlywed's many sexual encounters than she is in the historical setting, but her story is moderately interesting and holds some surprises." Booklist

Impulse. New Am. Lib. 1990 390p o.p.
LC 89-77096

"Rafaella Holland, wealthy, shapely, Pulitzer Prize-winning reporter with a powerful karate kick, goes undercover at a Caribbean resort owned by the gangster who seduced and discarded her besotted mother many years before. Rafaella is his daughter. When her mother is hit by a car owned by the gangster's estranged wife, Rafaella decides to expose him for the snake he is." Publ Wkly

Coulter "proves why she has been dubbed the queen of romance. *Impulse* gives us dashing men, beautiful women, sex, intrigue, and international high stakes. It is a thoroughly enjoyable adventure." Booklist

The maze. Putnam 1997 373p o.p.
LC 97-12343

"San Franciscan Lacey Sherlock was just a teenager, dreaming of studying piano at Berkeley, when her older sister's life was brutally ended by the serial murderer that the media dubbed the String Killer. Now, seven years and one brief mental breakdown later, her career plans have changed. Having completed FBI training and learned to be addressed by her surname, she's assigned to agent Dillon Savich's Criminal Apprehension Unit, which, utilizing Dillon's specialized computer program for profiling, is responsible for pursuing serial killers. This places the obsessed Sherlock exactly where she wants to be when the String Killer strikes again, this time in Boston. It also puts her in position to become romantically involved with her attractive superior." Publ Wkly

Rosehaven. Putnam 1996 372p o.p.
LC 96-6494

This novel, set in medieval England, "pits willful young heiress Hastings of Trent against her new husband, doughty warrior Severin of Langthorne. The union has been decreed by Hastings's dying father, the Earl of

Coulter, Catherine—*Continued*
Oxborough, to save her—and the castle and estate—from the evil depredations of Richard de Luci. . . . Then, just as the relationship begins to grow, beautiful Lady Marjorie, Severin's long-lost first love, arrives at the castle, perhaps, Hastings fears, to try to win Severin back. Compounding her worries is her discovery that the earl had maintained a mysterious second household at Rosehaven, a keep on the English coast." Publ Wkly

The target. Putnam 1998 372p o.p.
ISBN 0-399-14395-5 LC 98-10563
"Federal Judge Ramsey Hunt is eluding the press in the mountains when he finds a frightened, injured little girl. When her mother locates them, she accuses Ramsey of kidnapping Emma. Soon, however, the three join forces to flee the bad guys, who attack again and again. FBI agents Sherlock and Savich, last seen in *The Maze* drop in occasionally, usually by telephone, to lend moral support." Libr J
"Coulter's plot doesn't always add up, and she can overdo her penchant for quirky characters . . . but her central figures—wary, quietly resilient Molly, musically gifted Emma and tough, decent Ramsey—make this an absorbing read." Publ Wkly

Coupland, Douglas

Eleanor Rigby; a novel. Bloomsbury 2005 249p $22.95
ISBN 1-582-34523-6 LC 2004-46437
"Liz Dunn is fat, lonely and has no friends. . . . The only exciting incident ever to brighten Liz's life was a class trip to Rome when she was 16, during which she attended a party where she drank so much she can't remember what happened. Nine months after she returned home, she gave birth to a son, an event hidden from her family because of her natural rotundness. Liz gave the child up for adoption and then launched into a life of perpetual loneliness (hence the title's nod to the lonely lady of Beatles fame). All this changes when her now 20-year-old son, Jeremy, shows up. He's a great kid, but his story is tragic-he bounced around foster homes until he could take care of himself, he has multiple sclerosis and his body is rapidly deteriorating. Coupland . . . avoids the pitfalls of weepy melodrama with sarcastic humor, inspired treatment of the weirdness of everyday life and dark mystical interludes." Publ Wkly

Microserfs. ReganBooks 1995 371p o.p.
LC 95-11472
This is the "tale of computer techies who escape the serfdom of Bill Gates's Microsoft to found their own multimedia company. The story is told through the online journal of Danielu'microsoft.com, an affable, insomniac, 26-year-old aspiring code writer. Together with his girlfriend Karla, a mousy shiatsu expert with a penchant for Star Trekky aphorisms, and a tight clique of maladjusted, nose-to-the-grindstone housemates, he relocates to a Lego-adorned office in Palo Alto. Calif., to develop a product called Object Oriented Programming (Oop!), a form of virtual Lego." Publ Wkly
"The characters are fascinating, and the relationships they develop, though unconventional in every way, are vivid and lovely." Booklist

Courter, Gay

The midwife; a novel. Houghton Mifflin 1981 559p o.p.
"Hannah Blau, licensed midwife, delivers her first child—the son of a czarist minister—in 1904. Two years later Hannah and her family flee the rising tide of anti-Semitism in Russia to start a new life in New York's Lower East Side. Soon Hannah is delivering children for the rich and for poor Jewish mothers in her area. At the same time she is supporting her ne'er-do-well husband, trying to keep her marriage afloat, and fighting the New York medical establishment, which is determined to wipe out midwifery because it threatens the male-dominated profession of obstetrics." Libr J
"In colorful vignettes of emerging life-styles among the immigrants, Courter gives freshness to traditional characteristics of the Jewish temperament, among them familial cohesiveness, endurance and a recognition of opportunity even in adversity." Publ Wkly
Followed by The midwife's advice

The midwife's advice. Dutton 1992 598p o.p.
LC 92-52869
This sequel to The midwife "covers 1913-22. The persistent questions of her patients at Bellevue Hospital drive Hannah to consult privately about sexual behavior. Each chapter/year deals with a different problem; medical or political details often slow this long book. Underlying the sexual and medical conditions are the political events of the day: World War I, the battle for birth control facts, and the Russian revolution. Hannah's love affair during her husband's prolonged absence in Mother Russia adds interest. While Hannah may be atypical in her professional successes . . . her efforts to work, be a wife and mother without much help will be familiar to many." Libr J

Coward, Noel

Bon voyage
In Coward, N. The collected stories of Noël Coward p562-630

The collected stories of Noël Coward. Dutton 1983 630p o.p.
LC 83-5704
Contents: The wooden Madonna; Traveler's joy; Aunt Tittie; What mad pursuit; Cheap excursion; The kindness of Mrs. Radcliffe; Nature study; A richer dust; Mr. and Mrs. Edgehill; Stop me if you've heard it; Ashes of roses; This time tomorrow; Star quality; Pretty Polly; Mrs. Capper's birthday; Me and the girls; Solali; Mrs. Ebony; Penny dreadful; Bon voyage [novelette]

Cox, Michael, 1948-

(comp) The Oxford book of English ghost stories. See The Oxford book of English ghost stories
(ed) The Oxford book of spy stories. See The Oxford book of spy stories
(ed) The Oxford book of twentieth-century ghost stories. See The Oxford book of twentieth-century ghost stories

Coyle, H. W. (Harold W.), 1952-

Bright star; a novel; by Harold Coyle. Simon & Schuster 1990 432p il o.p.

LC 90-30992

"When U.S. troops are sent to Egypt in a rapid-deployment exercise, the Soviet Union responds with a mini-buildup in Libya. Libyan terrorists turn international brinkmanship into regional conflict with attempts to assassinate the U.S. and Egyptian presidents. Egypt retaliates while Russians and Americans seek to avoid being drawn into another war. Coyle demonstrates mastery of tactical description—especially battalion-level narratives of armored warfare. Unusual in the genre, the women characters are convincing." Publ Wkly

Look away; a novel; by Harold Coyle. Simon & Schuster 1995 495p o.p.

ISBN 0-684-80392-5 LC 95-2077

"In December 1859, the state of New Jersey is perched undecidely between two political camps: one wanting to preserve the Union and the other made up of supporters of the Southern States. When his sons accidentally kill the woman they both love, wealthy entrepreneur Edward Bannon sees an opportunity to keep a foot in both camps. He sends his eldest son, James, to the Virginia Military Institute and the weaker son, Kevin, to the New Jersey Militia. When the Civil War begins, the brothers find themselves fighting on opposite sides. The story follows them from one battle to the next, culminating in the horror of Gettysburg." Libr J

Followed by Until the end

Until the end; a novel; by Harold Coyle. Simon & Schuster 1997 462p o.p.

LC 96-19347

In this sequel to Look away "Coyle plays out the saga of two estranged brothers, Kevin and James Bannon, against the last battles of the Civil War. The narrative alternates between Kevin, a captain in the 4th New Jersey, and James, a sergeant in the decimated 4th Virginia known as the Stonewall Brigade. Horror tales from the field hospital where Harriet Shields nurses wounded Union soldiers are juxtaposed with those of the decimated fields of the Virginia farm where Mary Beth McPhearson tries to keep her mother alive." Libr J

Coyle, Harold W. *See* Coyle, H. W. (Harold W.), 1952-

Cozarinsky, Edgardo

The bride from Odessa; translated from the Spanish by Nick Caistor. Farrar, Straus and Giroux 2004 161p $22

ISBN 0-374-11673-6

Original Spanish edition, 2001

Contents: The bride from Odessa; Literature; Real estate; Days of 1937; View of dawn over a lake; Budapest; Christmas '54; Obscure loves; Émigré hotel

"Any exploration of the past is necessarily incomplete and Cozarinsky has found the perfect form in these fragmentary stories. . . . His prose, as translated by Nick Caistor, is elegant, cool and precise. Occasionally the amassing of clauses might suggest the original Spanish, . . . but this is a book about moving between cultures, between continents and between generations; to be aware of the movement between languages is not necessarily a bad thing." Times Lit Suppl

Cozzens, James Gould, 1903-1978

By love possessed. Harcourt Brace & Co. 1957 570p o.p.

This novel concerns "49 hours in the life of Arthur Winner, . . . New England lawyer. The stability of Arthur's private and professional worlds is suddenly shaken both by repercussions of unhapppy and indiscreet episodes from his supposedly well-ordered past and by present events involving himself and those close to him." Booklist

"Cozzens is no peripheral observer of the human situation in which the Man of Reason finds himself; and all the vignettes of life in small-town Brocton involving the noble and the mean, the serious and the ridiculous, are viewed with sheer objectivity, boldly at one time, sensitively and delicately at another." Best Sellers

Crace, Jim

Being dead. Farrar, Straus & Giroux 2000 193p o.p.

ISBN 0-374-11013-1 LC 99-45082

First published 1999 in the United Kingdom

This novel's two central characters, Joseph and Celice, are biologists. "The story is told in two directions. As it opens, Joseph and Celice are recently dead, victims of a senseless murder. Subsequent chapters alternate between a counterclockwise retracing of the route they took to meet their bloody fate, and . . . descriptions of their physical decomposition." N Y Rev Books

"The style is agile, precise, and vigorous. Words hit their target directly and unerringly. Images are colorful, evocative, forceful." Commonweal

The devil's larder. Farrar, Straus & Giroux 2001 165p $20

ISBN 0-374-13859-1 LC 2001-23625

Crace has "written a set of teasing tales about how we are never so ignorantly alive as when we are eating ourselves to death. The 64 brief fictions that make up 'The Devil's Larder' are parables and parodies of knowingness. . . . Reading a collection of 64 apparently unconnected brief fictions, numbered and untitled and held together only by the odd title of the book, may not necessarily appear to be a tempting prospect. The form of the book is experimental in that it toys with the reader's willingness (or unwillingness) not to make too much sense of what is going on." N Y Times Book Rev

The gift of stones. Scribner 1989 c1988 169p o.p.

ISBN 0-684-19070-2 LC 88-31587

First published 1988 in the United Kingdom

"The protagonists of this novel are workers of flint in the Stone Age, chipping and hammering tools and arrowheads in a coastal village, exact time and place unspecified. They grow easy and complacent with the trading successes their skills bring them, and care little about the world without-though marauding bands of men on horseback sometimes come by. They are thus quite unprepared to discover, when ships appear from the great beyond and land on their coast, that bronze has been manufac-

Crace, Jim—*Continued*

tured, and that their livelihood is gone." Publ Wkly

"As the fabulist tale unwinds, Crace looks into the role of the artist in society-here, a storyteller-considering both the impact and limits of imagination in guiding us toward new horizons. A marvelous literary effort." Libr J

Quarantine. Farrar, Straus & Giroux 1998 c1997 242p o.p.

ISBN 0-374-23962-2 LC 97-61489

First published 1997 in the United Kingdom

"Five people come to the desert of Judea, for a quarantine, a fast of forty days. For four of them, the standard daytime fast will be enough. . . . They are Shim, part-Jew, part-Greek, sophisticate, religious dilettante, sceptic; Aphas, an old man with a new growth, looking for a simple miracle; Marti, the childless wife of a barren marriage, about to be cast off by her philoprogenitive husband; a nameless, perhaps Tourettic nomad, whose hopes remain unintelligible. And Jesus, a callow young man from Galilee with Messianic ambitions. He intends a total fast." Times Lit Suppl

Crace's "prose is startlingly specific about ancient life and Judea's harsh, terrible beauty. Unlike many authors of biblical fiction, he blends his research smoothly into his narrative and adds a leavening pinch of humor." Time

Crafts, Hannah

The bondswomans narrative; edited by Henry Louis Gates Jr. Warner Bks. 2002 lxxiv, 338p il $24.95

ISBN 0-446-53008-5 LC 2001-98325

This autobiographical novel "follows a female slave in her circumscribed existence on a North Carolina plantation and her flight to freedom in the North." Booklist

"Published from a manuscript bought at auction by Henry Louis Gates Jr., [this] is quite probably the first novel written by a black woman, as well as the only novel written by a female fugitive slave. It is also one of the few purely firsthand accounts of the slave experience available." N Y Times Book Rev

Craig, Alisa *See* MacLeod, Charlotte

Craig, Amanda, 1959-

Love in idleness; a novel. Talese 2003 340p $23.95

ISBN 0-385-50776-3 LC 2002-43570

"When eight adults and three children vacation together in a rented Italian villa, the children discover fairies, and the adults discover truths about themselves as they reunite with old lovers or find themselves changed and ready for new relationships." Libr J

"The novel reprises Shakespeare's mercurial farce about Athenian lovers and fairy royalty wandering around a forest at night, falling in and out of besottedness at the instigation of the mischievous Puck." N Y Times Book Rev

Craig, Patricia

(ed) The Oxford book of travel stories. See The Oxford book of travel stories

Craig, Philip R., 1933-

A deadly Vineyard holiday; a Martha's Vineyard mystery. Scribner 1997 282p o.p.

ISBN 0-684-19718-9 LC 97-4487

Retired Boston cop "J. W. Jackson and wife Zee become clandestine surrogate parents to the president's teenaged daughter. When someone kills the reporter who discovers her whereabouts, J.W. fears a conspiracy." Libr J

"Plenty of island lore and some simple seafood recipes spice the action." Publ Wkly

A fatal vineyard season; a Martha's Vineyard mystery. Scribner 1999 219p o.p.

ISBN 0-684-85544-5 LC 98-54710

"A Scribner crime novel"

"Instead of taking it easy now that the tourist season is over, year-round Martha's Vineyard resident and handyman J.W. Jackson, who's a retired cop, comes to the aid of a starlet in distress. . . . Carefully plotted, the novel has a companionable, relaxed atmosphere that's laced with J.W.'s insights on everything from coastal living and fishing to fatherhood and human relationships." Publ Wkly

A shoot on Martha's Vineyard; a Martha's Vineyard mystery. Scribner 1998 285p map $22

ISBN 0-684-83454-5 LC 97-51141

When "J.W. Jackson's long-time nemesis arrives in town and is murdered, J.W. can avoid suspicion only by finding the murderer. A handsome Hollywood movie scout, meanwhile, takes a shine to Jackson's new wife. A lively and entertaining addition to the series." Libr J

Vineyard enigma; a Martha's Vineyard mystery. Scribner 2002 242p $24

ISBN 0-7432-0523-5 LC 2001-57809

"The arrival on Martha's Vineyard of a strange man in search of two African soapstone eagles creates turmoil for series star J. W. Jackson. Murder, art-world intrigue, and jealousy of his wife's attraction to the man all complicate J. W.'s life." Libr J

A vineyard killing; a Martha's Vineyard mystery. Scribner 2003 229p $24

ISBN 0-7432-0524-3 LC 2002-42878

This installment "begins with a bang: an unknown assailant shoots someone outside the delicatessen where series private investigator J. W. Jackson is eating with his wife. Jackson is soon embroiled in a murder case involving grabby real estate developers and recalcitrant islanders. Off-season atmosphere and the usual high-caliber sleuthing." Libr J

(jt. auth) Tapply, W. G. First light

Crais, Robert, 1953-

Demolition angel; a novel. Doubleday 2000 386p o.p.

ISBN 0-385-49584-6 LC 00-29054

"Carol Starkey, an LAPD bomb-squad technician who nearly died in a blast three years earlier, is emotionally burned out. When a partner is killed by a bomb in what Starkey realizes is an assassination, she finds herself caught up in a deadly game with a serial bomber who targets individuals—including her." Libr J

Crais, Robert, 1953—*Continued*

"The book features one of the most complex heroines to grace a thriller since Clarice Starling locked eyes with Hannibal Lecter, a deliciously spooky villain in the person of a mad bomber known as Mr. Red, and an aggressively involving plot." Publ Wkly

The forgotten man; a novel. Doubleday 2005 352p $24.95

ISBN 0-385-50428-4 LC 2004-61857

"When an apparently homeless man is found shot in an alley, the first officer on the scene tells private investigator Elvis Cole that the dying man claimed to be Cole's father. Cole has never known the identity of his father. His mother was mentally unstable and would often go missing for extended periods. Cole was conceived during such a disappearance, and the only clue his mother gave him was the cryptic comment that his father was a 'human cannonball' in a circus. Long obsessed with finding his father, Cole backtracks through the years to learn the dead man's true identity. As he searches, Cole is unaware that he is the target of an associate of the dead man. . . . A deeply moving, heartfelt mystery." Booklist

Hostage; a novel. Doubleday 2001 373p o.p.

ISBN 0-385-49585-4 LC 2001-32577

"When three thieves botch a robbery, they take refuge in a nearby home and hold its owner and his two children hostage. Suburban police chief Jeff Talley, a burned-out former LAPD SWAT leader and hostage negotiator, is unwillingly drawn into the standoff." Libr J

"Thriller vets will have seen a lot of this before, but every virtuoso is allowed variations on a theme, and Crais, with his record and with the smart suspense offered here, has proven himself nothing less." Publ Wkly

Indigo slam; an Elvis Cole novel. Hyperion 1997 288p o.p.

ISBN 0-7868-6261-0 LC 97-966

In this mystery L.A. shamus Elvis Cole is "approached by three resourceful young children who would like their missing father located. That dad, Clark Hewitt, is soon revealed as a mystery man, a master printer and a possible junkie who fled the witness protection program he entered after informing on a counterfeiting operation run by Russian and Ukrainian mobsters. While Clark's kids clearly revere him, Elvis is suspicious. The feds want Clark back in their care and the Russians want revenge for his squealing." Publ Wkly

L.A. requiem. Doubleday 1999 382p o.p.

ISBN 0-385-49583-8 LC 98-52921

In this episode L.A. PI Elvis Cole, "drops his adolescent swagger in the heroic act of helping his friend and partner, Joe Pike, to stop the vengeful killer who is framing Pike for his own crimes. The writing doesn't fool around, either, and what starts as a routine search for a rich man's pampered daughter becomes a tense face-off with a killer and a serious examination of the limits of friendship." N Y Times Book Rev

The last detective; a novel. Doubleday 2003 302p $24.95

ISBN 0-385-50426-8 LC 2002-41507

This Elvis Cole thriller finds the "Los Angeles P. I. racing the clock to rescue his girlfriend's 10-year-old son, Ben, from a team of kidnappers who claim to be paying Cole back for atrocities they say he committed in Vietnam." N Y Times Book Rev

"Fast action, though guys, vivid Los Angeles details, and snappy dialog are Craig's trademarks, and this tale has them all." Libr J

Sunset express; a Elvis Cole novel. Hyperion 1996 274p o.p.

ISBN 0-7868-6096-0 LC 95-47250

Elvis Cole "is hired by high-profile attorney Jonathan Green to investigate the death of Susan Martin, wife of megamillionaire Teddy Green. The defense is basing its case on the Mark Fuhrman-like theory that evidence was planted at the scene by Detective Angela Rossi, a fallen star in the LAPD who could use a celebrity conviction as her ticket back to the fast track. . . . This hip, funny, and thought-provoking novel will delight Crais' growing legion of fans, and the fist-shaking, high-fiving conclusion offers at least the hope of ultimate justice when our system fails." Booklist

Crane, Stephen, 1871-1900

Active service

In Crane, S. The complete novels of Stephen Crane p429-592

The complete novels of Stephen Crane; edited with an introduction by Thomas A. Gullason. Doubleday 1967 821p o.p.

Includes: Maggie: a girl of the streets (1893); The red badge of courage (1895); George's mother (1896); The third violet (1897); Active service (1899); The O'Ruddy (1903)

The complete short stories & sketches of Stephen Crane; edited with an introduction by Thomas A. Gullason. Doubleday 1963 790p o.p.

Contains the following short stories: The king's favor; The camel; Dan Emmonds; Four men in a cave; Travels in New York; The broken-down van; The octopush; A ghoul's accountant; The black dog; Killing his bear; The Captain; A tent in agony; The cry of a huckleberry pudding; An explosion of seven babies; The mesmeric mountain; The holler tree; Why did the young clerk swear; The pace of youth; The reluctant voyagers; A desertion; An experiment in misery; An experiment in luxury; An ominous baby; A dark brown dog; Billie Atkins went to Omaha; Mr. Binks' day off; The men in the storm; Coney Island's failing days; In a Park Row restaurant; Stories told by an artist; When every one is panic stricken; When a man falls a crowd gathers; The duel that was not fought; A Christmas dinner won in battle; A lovely jag in a crowded car; A mystery of heroism; A gray sleeve; One dash—horses; A tale of mere chance; Three miraculous soldiers; A freight car incident; The little regiment; The veteran; The snake; Raft story; An Indiana campaign; In the Tenderloin; The voice of the mountain; Yen-Nock Bill and his sweetheart; Diamonds and diamonds; The auction; A poker game; A man and some others; The open boat; How the donkey lifted the hills; The victory of the moon; Flanagan and his short filibustering adventure; An old man goes wooing; A fishing village; The bride comes to Yellow Sky; Death and the child; The five white mice; The wise men; The monster; His new mittens; The blue hotel; The price of the harness; A self-made man; The clan of no-name; God rest ye, merry gentlemen; The lone charge of William B.

Crane, Stephen, 1871-1900—*Continued*
Perkins; The angel child; Lynx-hunting; The revenge of the 'Adolphus'; The sergeant's private madhouse; The battle of Forty Fort; The surrender of Forty Fort; "Ol' Bennett" and the Indians; The lover and the telltale; "Showin' off"; Virtue in war; Making an orator; Twelve o'clock; The second generation; An episode of war; Shame; The carriage-lamps; The Kicking Twelfth; The shrapnel of their friends; "And if he wills, we must die"; The upturned face; The knife; The stove; Moonlight on the snow; The trial, execution, and burial of Homer Phelps; An illusion in red and white; The fight; This majestic lie; The city urchin and the chaste villagers; Manacled; A little pilgrimage; At the pit door; The squire's madness; The man from Duluth; A man by the name of Mud

George's mother
In Crane, S. The complete novels of Stephen Crane p301-47
In Crane, S. The portable Stephen Crane p89-146
In Crane, S. Prose and poetry

Maggie: a girl of the streets (a story of New York); an authoritative text, backgrounds and sources, the author and the novel, reviews and criticism, edited by Thomas A. Gullason. Norton 1979 258p o.p.
ISBN 0-393-01222-0 LC 78-24596
"A Norton critical edition"
First published privately in 1893 under the pseudonym Johnston Smith
"Maggie Johnson is the daughter of a brutal father and a drunken mother. She goes to work in a collar factory, falls in love with Pete, a bartender who is a friend of her brother Jimmie, and is seduced by him. Her mother disowns her, she becomes a prostitute; and in despair she finally kills herself. Her final degeneration becomes almost an allegory." Reader's Ency. 4th edition
also in Crane, S. The complete novels of Stephen Crane p99-155
also in Crane, S. The portable Stephen Crane p3-74

Maggie: a girl of the streets [novelette]
In Crane, S. Prose and poetry

The monster
In Crane, S. Prose and poetry

The O'Ruddy
In Crane, S. The complete novels of Stephen Crane p593-790

The portable Stephen Crane; edited, with an introduction and notes, by Joseph Katz. Viking 1969 xxvi, 550p o.p.
"Viking portable library"
Short stories included are: A great mistake; An ominous baby; A dark-brown dog; The men in the storm; An experiment in misery; An experiment in luxury; An episode of war; The veteran; Flanagan and his short filibustering adventure; The open boat; The bride comes to Yellow Sky; The five white mice; The blue hotel; The monster; His new mittens; The knife

Prose and poetry. Library of Am. 1984 1379p $40; pa $15.95
ISBN 0-940450-17-8; 1-883011-39-6 (pa) LC 83-19908
Maggie: a girl of the streets and The red badge of courage are entered separately. George's mother (1896) focuses on a woman who sacrifices everything for her own son, whom she mistakenly believes to be destined for greatness. The third violet (1896-97) deals with an artist and his bohemian life. In The monster (1898) "Henry Johnson, a black servant in the home of Dr. Trescott, rescues the physician's son from a fire. He is terribly disfigured and loses his sanity, so that no home can be found for him in the town. Horrified by the 'monster,' the townspeople ostracize the doctor and his family because they harbor the man." Oxford Companion to Am Lit. 6th edition

The red badge of courage; an episode of the American Civil War; [by] Stephen Crane, with an introduction by Shelby Foote. Modern Library 1993 li, 246p $17.95
ISBN 0-679-60296-8
First published 1895
"A young Union soldier, Henry Fleming, tells of his feelings when he is under fire for the first time during the battle of Chancellorsville. He is overcome by fear and runs from the field. Later he returns to lead a charge that re-establishes his own reputation as well as that of his company. One of the great novels of the Civil War." Cincinnati Public Libr
also in Crane, S. The complete novels of Stephen Crane p197-299
also in Crane, S. The portable Stephen Crane p189-318
also in Crane, S. Prose and poetry
also in Crane, S. The red badge of courage and other stories

The red badge of courage and other stories; with biographical illustrations and pictures of the settings of the stories together with an introduction and captions by Max J. Herzberg. Dodd, Mead 1957 409p il o.p.
"Great illustrated classics"
Contents: The red badge of courage; The veteran; A mystery of heroism; An episode of war; Ouida's masterpiece; The gratitude of a nation

The third violet
In Crane, S. The complete novels of Stephen Crane p349-428
In Crane, S. Prose and poetry

Craven, Margaret

I heard the owl call my name. Doubleday 1973 166p $6.99 o.p.
ISBN 0-89966-854-2 (pa)
Not knowing that he has a fatal illness, a young Anglican priest is assigned to serve a parish of Kwakiutl Indians in the seacoast wilds of British Columbia. Among these vanishing Indians, Mark Brian learns enough of the meaning of life not to fear death
The author's "writing glows with delicate, fleeting im-

Craven, Margaret—*Continued*
ages and a sense of peace. Her characters' hearts are bared by a few words—or by the fact that nothing is said at all." Christ Sci Monit

Crayencour, Marguerite De *See* Yourcenar, Marguerite

Crews, Harry, 1935-

Body. Poseidon Press 1990 240p o.p.
ISBN 0-671-69576-2 LC 90-37459

"Female bodybuilding competition is the background for a tale of ambition, success, and failure. Shereel Dupont, a leading contender, has been trained to a fine-tuned perfection by Russell Morgan. At the Ms. Cosmos contest Shereel is confronted by her past as Dorothy Turnipseed {and by her} mother, father, sister, two brothers, and a former lover from the backwoods of Georgia." Libr J

"Crews lays his characters bare with incisive satire, derision, and ultimately some real compassion. By taking human behavior to bizarre extremes, he makes a powerful statement on the human condition. His is a unique and strong fictive voice" Choice

A feast of snakes. Atheneum 1976 177p o.p.
ISBN 0-689-107293 LC 76-8206

The novel is set in the backwoods hamlet of Mystic, Georgia, where the annual festival "begins with the crowning of the high-school Rattlesnake Queen, continues with a pit-bull championship fight, and ends with a Rattlesnake Roundup. The festival this year is a total nightmare: a black girl with a razor emasculates Sheriff Buddy Matlow, Big Joe Mackey kicks his losing dog to death, and Joe Lon Mackey–aged twenty-two, practically illiterate, miserably married, with two screaming babies, his years of glory as an all-around athlete . . . behind him–goes out of control with a twelve-gauge shotgun." New Yorker

Scar lover. Poseidon Press 1992 284p o.p.
ISBN 0-671-74489-5 LC 91-37810

"Protagonist Pete Butcher moves into a boardinghouse in Jacksonville, Florida, carrying a small suitcase and some heavy emotional baggage. Next door, in the personas of odd but beautiful Sarah Leemer, her father, Henry, and sick, embittered matriarch Gertrude, Pete finds both his future and his past, embroiled in guilt, magic, and scars, literal and figurative. Toss in a gymnastic octogenarian and a band of Rastafarians, and you have a scenario in which Pete's worst dreams come true even as he awakens to the possibilities of life." Booklist

"Crews darkly comic tale gives a disturbingly accurate portrayal of characters from the rural South, each fiercely shaped by sweat, grit, and cruel hardship" Libr J

Crichton, Michael, 1942-

Airframe. Knopf 1996 351p $26
ISBN 0-679-44648-6 LC 96-39154

"Casey Singleton works for Norton Aircraft in California. When an accident occurs on a Norton jet, it's her job to figure out what went wrong. . . . She is up against corporate intriguers, angry union members and Jennifer Malone, a young, cynical producer for Newsline, a TV newsmagazine." Time

"If Crichton uses the apparatus of the techno-thriller, it is always a means to an end—an unusual end for a writer of thrillers, since it is becoming increasingly apparent that he is, deep down, a moralist. . . . He now concentrates more and more on much debated issues of the day, which he picks up and turns into novels with a point of view and a moral." New Yorker

The Andromeda strain. Knopf 1969 295p o.p.
ISBN 0-394-41525-6

"In these days of interplanetary exploration, this tale of the world's first space-age biological emergency may seem uncomfortably believable. When a contaminated space capsule drops to earth in a small Nevada town and all the town's residents suddenly die, four American scientists gather at an underground laboratory of Project Wildfire to search frantically for an antidote to the threat of a world-wide epidemic." Shapiro. Fic for Youth. 3d edition

A case of need; by Michael Crichton, writing as Jeffrey Hudson. Dutton 1993 c1968 319p o.p.
ISBN 0-525-93802-8 LC 93-11277

First published 1968 under pseudonym Jeffrey Hudson by World

Boston pathologist John Berry "supports his colleague, Dr. Art Lee, who has been arrested for Karen Randall's death. The girl's socialite stepmother declares she has proof positive that Lee is guilty of the fatal operation, and her eminent surgeon father wants no mercy shown to him. The prosecutors and police are happy to oblige. Only Berry is willing to dig deeper into the seemingly open-and-shut case to save Lee. As his search for the truth takes him through hospital labs, mansions, and addicts' dens, from the depths of the sex and drug underworld to the heights of Boston society, John Berry meets with the shocking revelation that his own life, like the life of the colleague he is trying to save, is in deadly jeopardy." Publisher's note

Disclosure; a novel. Knopf 1994 397p $24
ISBN 0-679-41945-4 LC 93-34201

"Beautiful, bright, and talented Meredith Johnson arrives at Digital Communications Technology company to become the head of a division, a position that Tom Sanders thought was going to be his. Meredith, his former lover, invites him to her office after hours and attempts to seduce him. When he rejects her, she accuses him of sexual harassment. Tom hires Louise Fernandez to defend him and reverses the accusation to name Meredith as the aggressor." SLJ

"On one level Disclosure is a literary pebble tossed into a political pond, and the ripples just might dampen some of the strident howls and emotional spasms that currently dominate discussion of the issue. On another it is a refreshingly uncluttered and sinewy entertainment, free of pretension and eminently readable." Natl Rev

The great train robbery. Knopf 1975 266p o.p.

"Edward Pierce, a Victorian prince among rogues, meticulously plans the theft of £12,000 in gold bullion from the London-Paris train. The story is based on an actual heist that rocked Victorian England more than a century ago." Shapiro. Fic for Youth. 3d edition

"The caper is fraught with just enough misjudgment and happenstance to maintain constant tension. Crichton's reconstruction of London past, livened with heavy sprinklings of cockney dialect, is serendipitous." Booklist

Crichton, Michael, 1942-—*Continued*

Jurassic Park; a novel. Knopf 1990 399p $28.95
ISBN 0-394-58816-9 LC 90-52960
This novel "tells of a modern-day scientist bringing to life a horde of prehistoric animals." N Y Times Book Rev

"Crichton is a master at blending technology with fiction. . . . Suspense, excitement, and good adventure pervade this book." SLJ

Followed by The lost world (1995)

Prey; novel. HarperCollins Pubs. 2002 376p $26.95
ISBN 0-06-621412-2 LC 2002-32338
"Jack Forman has been laid off from his Silicon Valley job as a senior software programmer and has become a househusband, while his wife continues her career with a biotech firm involved in defense contracting. Jack is called in as a consultant to debug one of their products, and finds himself confronting a full-blown emergency, about which his wife and others in the organization have been suspiciously deceptive." SLJ

"Despite its absurd moments, 'Prey' is irresistibly suspenseful. You're entertained on one level and you learn something on another, even if the two levels do ultimately diverge." N Y Times Book Rev

Rising sun; a novel. Knopf 1992 355p $26
ISBN 0-394-58942-4 LC 91-53173
"On the forty-fifth floor of the Nakamoto Tower in downtown L.A.—the new American headquarters of the immense Japanese conglomerate—a grand opening celebration is in full swing. On the forty-sixth floor, in an empty conference room, the dead body of a beautiful young woman is discovered. The investigation . . . [involves a] conflict in which control of a vital American technology is the fiercely coveted prize." Publisher's note

"That Mr. Crichton effortlessly weaves a mesmerizing mystery comes as no surprise. . . . That he should now write so passionately and engagingly on matters of Japanese culture and the survival of a free and productive America—that is the surprise. . . . For that, indeed, is what he has done." N Y Times Book Rev

Sphere; a novel. Knopf 1987 385p o.p.
ISBN 0-394-56110-4 LC 86-46321
The author "sends a team of civilian experts to the floor of the Pacific to investigate an enormous spaceship that appears to have rested there for some 300 years. In it, they discover a huge sphere, made of a mysterious metal, which they cannot force open despite its having a door. Then, when one of the group inspects the ship on his own, it opens, he enters, and the real fun begins. . . . Crichton's prose, pedestrian but not clumsy, lets the story spin itself out, and few readers who grab its thread will let go until the web is broken in a 'Wizard of Oz'-style ending." Booklist

The terminal man. Knopf 1972 247p il o.p.
ISBN 0-394-44768-9
Harry Benson "is a brilliant computer expert, who is also an epileptic given to increasingly severe black-outs in which he attacks the nearest person at hand. A team of doctors, including surgeons and an attractive woman psychiatrist, will implant in Harry, literally, a miniature computer aimed at controlling his seizures. There is only one major problem. Harry is also slipping further and further into insanity, convinced that 'machines are taking over the world.'" Publ Wkly

"The book is filled with interesting details on what surely must be the latest in hospital procedure, neurosurgery, computers, and the like. . . . This is a very different piece of science-fiction because the suspense is centered around a hospital, and the battle is a psychological one between humans and machines." Best Sellers

Timeline. Knopf 1999 449p
LC 99-461985
In this novel, a billionaire planning a theme park uses time travel to send historians working on an excavation in the Dordogne back to the France of 1357, where they become involved in a war

"Crichton is a master of an odd hybrid: entertaining novels that educate. 'Timeline' is a page turner *and* a very lucid look at life in the late Middle Ages. He teaches you how to think like a knight during a joust by putting you in the saddle." Newsweek

Crichton, Robert

The Camerons; a novel. Knopf 1972 509p o.p.
"Turn-of-the-century Scotland is the setting for this novel of the now-familiar dilemma of modern man in an increasingly complex society. Ostensibly, it is the story of Maggie Drum's ambitions to escape from Pitmungo, an enslaving mining town; but Gillon Cameron, her husband, seems to wrestle the reader's attention from her. His strength alone carries the family through repeated conflict with the townspeople and the mine owners; his development and sensitivity to others increase as Maggie's remain static and cold. Finally, in one . . . dramatic scene when the Pitmungo miners storm his house, Gillon's humanity overwhelms all who observe; and the ambitions of Maggie and Gillon alike are fulfilled in an unexpected way." Choice

The secret of Santa Vittoria; a novel. Simon & Schuster 1966 447p o.p.
"Santa Vittoria, an Italian hill town devoted to the making of wine, is the setting for this story of a clash between the Italians and Germans at the close of World War II. Upon the death of Mussolini, the Fascists are thrown out of office and Bombolini, the town clown, elevates himself to the position of mayor. Having read Machiavelli 43 times, he feels able to handle any emergency. When the German occupation is imminent, he organizes the populace to hide their assets, one million bottles of wine. Captain Von Prum, whose mission is to confiscate the wine, cannot believe that these comic villagers can keep such an enormous secret. Their conspiracy in the face of torture and death make heroes of them, and a fool and madman of Von Prum." Libr J

"It takes a lot of courage—and no little craft—to blend the diverse and exotic ingredients that Robert Crichton has brought together in this heady brew of a novel, a mélange of allegory, symbolism, several kinds of comedy including comedies of error and opera bouffe, traces of Don Quixote and John Hershey's Major Joppolo, and a plot involving barely credible incidents of blind fate." NY Times Book Rev

Crider, Bill, 1941-

Death by accident; a Sheriff Dan Rhodes mystery. St. Martin's Press 1998 277p o.p.
ISBN 0-312-18080-2 LC 97-35452
"A Thomas Dunne book"
"The three dead men shared a taste for drinking in a roadhouse. They die nastily—burned up in a field, face down in a pond and behind the wheel of a car. Texas cop Dan Rhodes is soon caught in a triple murder investigation that involves womanizing by at least one of the dead threesome and some shoddy contract work on local houses by another." Publ Wkly
"Rhodes is an appealing character, a quiet man surrounded by supporting cast members who are . . . as vivid as any real-life next-door neighbors." Booklist

A ghost of a chance. Thomas Dunne Bks. 2000 263p o.p.
ISBN 0-312-20889-8 LC 00-27163
A Sheriff Dan Rhodes mystery set in Blacklin County, Texas. "Clearview is hardly a hotbed of crime, and the middle-aged sheriff's laid-back style seems a perfect fit. Neither the appearance of ghosts, first at the jail, then in a local cemetery; nor the body of a murdered man found in a grave newly dug for another body; nor the uproar over cemetery thefts raised by the Clearview Sons and Daughters of Texas, a historical preservation group, is enough to get Rhodes too worked up. . . . In some novels, two murders, a shootout, thefts and a drug factory would send the violence quotient over the top, but folksy Dan Rhodes handles it all with pleasing and entertaining aplomb." Publ Wkly

Murder is an art. St. Martin's Press 1998 246p o.p.
ISBN 0-312-19927-9 LC 98-41786
"A Thomas Dunne book"
"After a murderer strikes down a Texas community college department chair, police suspect the husband of a molested student. When the student, too, is killed, Dr. Sally Good begins sleuthing." Libr J

Murder takes a break; a Truman Smith novel. Walker & Co. 1997 184p o.p.
ISBN 0-8027-3308-5 LC 97-19939
In this mystery Truman Smith's "old friend Dino wants Tru to find college student Randall Kirbo, who came to Galveston for spring break nine months ago and hasn't been seen since. Tru interviews Randall's parents and friends and learns nothing, managing only to whet his appetite for the truth. As he investigates further, Tru crosses swords with the local cops and finds himself in the netherworld of alcohol, drugs, and date rape. Crider's down-home mysteries are always a delight." Publ Wkly

The prairie chicken kill; a Truman Smith mystery. Walker & Co. 1996 208p o.p.
ISBN 0-8027-3282-8 LC 96-4009
"A Walker mystery"
In this mystery Galveston PI Truman Smith "gets suckered into one of the craziest cases of all time. Lance Garrison, someone Tru went to high school with and didn't much like, wants Tru to investigate the death of a prairie chicken. Yep, that's right. A bird. But a rare, exotic bird. Lance thinks there's some government plot or maybe a loony-toons nut behind the prairie chicken's death. Tru agrees to investigate, partly for the $500-a-day fee and partly because he'll be in close proximity to Anne Lindemann, the still-beautiful high school sweetheart who ditched him for Lance years earlier. For pure fun and sheer entertainment, it doesn't get much better than Crider's Tru Smith stories." Booklist

Crime from the mind of a woman. See A moment on the edge

Crombie, Deborah

And justice there is none. Bantam Bks. 2002 318p o.p.
ISBN 0-553-10973-1 LC 2002-21459
In this "police procedural featuring Scotland Yard Superintendent Duncan Kincaid and Inspector Gemma James, the pair's relationship deepens. With the progression of Gemma's pregnancy . . . they consolidate households while working together to solve three murders. Dawn Arrowood, wife of prominent Notting Hill antiques dealer Karl, 25 years her senior, is newly pregnant and is having an affair when she is killed (her throat cut, her lung pierced) outside her home. It's no longer an isolated case when Kincaid finds similarities in the murder of antiques dealer Marianne Hoffman two months earlier, and police lose a prime suspect when Karl himself is found dead." Libr J
"For all the picturesque charms of its setting, . . . this is another hard-nosed piece of social criticism from Deborah Crombie, an American author with serious designs on the British cozy mystery." N Y Times Book Rev

Kissed a sad goodbye. Bantam Bks. 1999 322p $23.95
ISBN 0-553-10943-X LC 98-50186
"The murder of a beautiful businesswoman in London's Isle of Dogs neighborhood calls both local police and Scotland Yard into play. The Yard's Duncan Kincaid and Gemma James . . . create a psychological profile of the victim and thoroughly investigate the thriving family tea concern." Libr J

Mourn not your dead. Scribner 1996 281p o.p.
LC 95-26166
In this episode, Duncan Kincaid "has come down from Scotland Yard to the unspoiled hamlet of Holmbury St. Mary to investigate the murder of a top police official. At the risk of upsetting that fragile social equilibrium, Superintendent Kincaid and Sgt. Gemma James, who have a private dynamic of their own going on, cruise the town and discover that the victim was devoutly loathed as a bully and a brute. Ms. Crombie keeps this series on its toes with her smooth procedural techniques and engagingly eccentric characters." N Y Times Book Rev

Cronin, A. J. (Archibald Joseph), 1896-1981

The citadel. Little, Brown 1937 401p o.p.
"In 1921 Andrew Manson, newly graduated at the top of his medical-school class, accepts his first position as assistant to a dying physician in an impoverished Welsh mining town. Hard-working and conscientious at first, Andrew is promoted to a more socially desirable post in London, where he abandons his principles. A faulty operating-room procedure magnifies his increasing incompetence and jolts him back to a career of integrity." Shapiro. Fic for Youth. 3d edition

Cronin, A. J. (Archibald Joseph), 1896-1981— *Continued*

The keys of the kingdom. Little, Brown 1941 344p o.p.

ISBN 0-316-16189-6

"A child of Scottish fisher folk, Father Francis Chisholm, even as a young lad, yearned to enter the Catholic priesthood. After graduation from the seminary and a few years of parish work at home, he was sent to China as a missionary. With the years of toil he acquired saintliness and tolerance. Pestilence and famine, bandits and flood, and unappreciative superiors only served to strengthen his character and fortitude. Excellent character delineation." Libr J

A pocketful of rye. Little, Brown 1969 245p o.p.

Sequel to A song of sixpence

"Laurence Carroll, young British doctor with a background of completely selfish living, tired of medical work in poor districts, has with some fraud secured for himself a pleasant job in a clinic in Switzerland. To the clinic comes widowed Cathy with her ill son Daniel. Cathy had been Laurence's first love, abandoned with his usual disregard, and only gradually does he learn the story of her wretched marriage and that Daniel is his son." Libr J

A song of sixpence. Little, Brown 1964 344p o.p.

This novel depicts "the despair and joy of a Dickensonian childhood in Scotland at the turn of the century. . . . Its hero Laurence Carroll, is a Catholic and so an outcast in a Protestant Scottish community, but secure in his loving family circle, until his father dies of tuberculosis. After that, life is a struggle . . . but a struggle relieved by some rollicking good times, love for his mother and a pretty cousin, and help and sympathy from unexpected sources." Publ Wkly

"Much of the interest of this sympathy-evoking story of a Catholic boyhood lies in the many and varied adult characters who either helped or exploited Laurence. It is told with Cronin's expert professional skill." Libr J

Followed by A pocketful of rye

Cronin, Archibald Joseph *See* Cronin, A. J. (Archibald Joseph), 1896-1981

Cross, Amanda, 1926-2003

The collected stories of Amanda Cross. Ballantine Bks. 1997 184p o.p.

ISBN 0-345-40817-9 LC 96-42006

Contents: Tania's nowhere; Once upon a time; Arrie and Jasper; The disappearance of Great Aunt Flavia; Murder without a text; Who shot Mrs. Byron Boyd?; The proposition; The George Eliot play; The Baroness

"Kate Fansler, a university professor normally involved with things academic, also dabbles in solving mysteries. In these short stories, she deals with cases ranging from missing persons to murder. Cross presents a complex jumble of seemingly enigmatic clues that Kate proceeds to study and resolve into a simple answer based on logic and deduction. The author camouflages the clues, facts, and answers by placing them in total view during the entire story." SLJ

Death in a tenured position. Dutton 1981 156p o.p.

In this "mystery starring professor of literature, sleuth emeritus, and enemy of pomposity Kate Fansler, a millionaire offers Harvard a million if this bastion of male chauvinism will hire a woman English professor. Janet Mandelbaum, the chosen prof, not only shakes up the Harvard community, providing a litmus test for sexism and jealousy, she also invites murderous inclinations. Fansler investigates after Mandelbaum is slain." Booklist

"With its academic setting, literary flavor, and strong feminist point of view, this book won't appeal to everyone, but within its own framework it is a delight—witty and clever and perfectly true-to-life. The language is the best part." Libr J

Honest doubt. Ballantine Bks. 2000 259p $22

ISBN 0-345-44011-0 LC 00-41445

In this mystery Kate Fansler serves "as a consultant to private eye Estelle 'Woody' Woodhaven, who is investigating the murder of misogynistic Tennyson scholar Charles Hancock. Woody, a down-to-earth, overweight sleuth, is a likable foil to the elegant, erudite Kate. . . . Devotees of the series may be disappointed at Kate's relatively minor role, but they will be amply compensated by the delightful Woody." Libr J

An imperfect spy. Ballantine Bks. 1995 228p o.p.

LC 94-25357

Academic sleuth Kate Fansler "and husband Reed have each agreed to teach a course at New York's third-rate, racist, and chauvinistic Schuyler Law School, where they investigate the accidental death of the school's only woman professor and try to assist an imprisoned faculty wife who murdered her abusive husband. Highly sophisticated tone, carefully constructed prose, and nicely contrived plot make this a winner." Libr J

The James Joyce murder. Macmillan 1967 176p o.p.

"A Cock Robin mystery"

A village local found murdered practically on Professor Kate Fansler's own doorstep adds to her travail in "trying to unravel, with the help of a graduate student, the papers of a distinguished publisher who first introduced Joyce's writing to America." Publ Wkly

The author has "written a highly attractive specimen of the leisurely and witty academic mystery novel. . . . Not for action enthusiasts, but a happy souvenir of a once more popular school." N Y Times Book Rev

The players come again. Random House 1990 229p o.p.

LC 90-53122

"Kate Fansler, English professor and amateur detective, is asked by a major publisher to take on a bit of literary sleuthing for a biography of one Gabrielle Foxx, whose fame is rooted in the fact that she was married to an author of Joycean stature. As Kate debates whether to take on this project, she meets the surviving family members, three women who entice her through a maze of family secrets, dropping hints that Gabrielle's contributions to her husband's work involved far more than playing the roles of muse and housewife." Booklist

"This compelling novel is about motivation, rather than material motives, about the mystery of human character more than the details of a murder." Publ Wkly

Cross, Amanda, 1926-2003—*Continued*

The puzzled heart. Ballantine Bks. 1998 257p o.p.
ISBN 0-345-41883-2 LC 97-22686
This "Kate Fansler mystery starts with the kidnapping, just outside his Manhattan office, of attorney Reed Amhearst, the husband of English professor and amateur sleuth Kate. Told that her husband will be released after she publicly renounces feminism, Kate is frustrated by her unfamiliar powerlessness. She turns to Harriet Furst . . . now part-owner of a detective agency. The innocuous-looking but feisty Harriet and her businesslike partner, Toni, almost effortlessly rescue Reed. The remainder of this entertaining intellectual puzzle concerns the discovery of who kidnapped him and why." Publ Wkly

Sweet death, kind death. Dutton 1984 177p o.p.
LC 84-1469
"Patrice Umphelby, history professor at Clare College, maverick, and for many a general pain in the ass, has walked into the campus lake in a successful suicide. Her biographers . . . are suspicious, and they solicit the help of English professor cum sleuth, Kate Fansler." Best Sellers
"This likable whodunit is full to the brim with clever talk and literary allusions. Hard-boiled detective fans may find Fansler's book-learning a bit wearisome, but at least she drinks and smokes. On the other hand, for those who prefer their murder mysteries served with a side order of life according to the Bloomsbury Group . . . Amanda Cross remains the reigning champion." Booklist

A trap for fools. Dutton 1989 154p o.p.
LC 88-30204
"Kate Fansler, Cross' English professor detective, is asked by her superiors to determine whether a particularly unpopular university professor committed suicide or was murdered. The possible frame-up of a friend causes Kate to take the case. . . . Cross is a whiz at setting up a maze of evidence, dropping literary references, and portraying the ambience of academia." Booklist

Cross, Mary Ann Evans *See* Eliot, George, 1819-1880

Crowley, John, 1942-

Lord Byron's novel; the evening land. William Morrow 2005 465p $25.95
ISBN 0-06-055658-7 LC 2004-63575
"Documents discovered in a rotting old trunk in an English storage room prove that the manuscript of a novel by Byron once existed, and that it was saved from destruction, read, and annotated by Ada, Countess of Lovelace, a brilliant mathematician and Byron's abandoned daughter, during the final, agonizing months of her young life. While the mystery of what became of the manuscript itself is explored, we are permitted to read it—the whole of Byron's only novel—beginning to end." Publisher's note
"Crowley's real achievement in Lord Byron's Novel is not a convincing imitation of Byron—not even Byron, who was pudgy and pale and walked with a limp, could always pull that off. More persuasive by far is the suffocating world of encryption and code, coincidence and conspiracy, paranoia and parapsychology that Crowley summons from his 19th-century documents and 21st-century decoders." N Y Times Book Rev

The translator. Morrow 2002 295p o.p.
ISBN 0-380-97862-8 LC 2001-40324
In this novel, set during the Cuban missile Crisis of 1962, "Kit Malone, an aspiring writer at a small midwestern college, develops a relationship with exiled Russian poet Innokenti Falin. . . . Their friendship turns to romance as the international crisis builds. The world survives the Soviet-American crisis, but their relationship does not. Finally, on a trip to Russia years later, Kit can come to terms with their relationship." Booklist
"The fears 'The Translator' conjures seem eerily familiar, like a bad dream we've had before. At the same time, the novel gives us a world so suffused with beauty that its inhabitants manage to speak in fragments of poetry without sounding pompous or absurd." N Y Times Book Rev

Crumey, Andrew, 1961-

Mr. Mee. Picador 2001 344p o.p.
ISBN 0-312-26803-3
Mr. Mee is an English scholar who, late in life, has become fascinated with computers. On his screen is a picture of a naked woman reading a book, but Mr. Mee is excited mainly "by the title of the book she is reading, 'Ferrand and Minard,' which was written by a member of the faculty at the local university, one Dr. A.B. Petrie. . . . The book also goes back in time to meet Ferrand and Minard themselves. These are real-life figures who appear briefly in Book 10 of Rousseau's 'Confessions.'" N Y Times Book Rev
"Musing on Rousseau, the French encylopedists and the vagaries of chance and identity, Crumey . . . has written another novel of ideas in the grand tradition of Calvino, Borges and Kundera." Publ Wkly

Crumley, James, 1939-

Bordersnakes. Mysterious Press 1996 320p o.p.
LC 96-34405
"Milo Milodragovitch and Sonny Sughrue are former partners bent on revenge. . . . Milodragovitch, ex-lawman, p.i., and bartender in his mid-fifties, vows to locate the weaselly banker who absconded with his inheritance. Sughrue is a leathery cowboy looking for the men who tried to do him in. They crisscross Texas in Milo's new Cadillac, drinking hard, throwing money and punches, tricking bad guys, and coming upon a gruesome murder." Libr J
"The plot, such as it is, takes the pair from one violent encounter to the next, each with its separate cast of sublimely weird characters. . . . Mr. Crumley saves his fiercest prose for El Paso, where the villains of the piece have their day; but the sheer originality of his style tears up every pit stop on this hellishly funny adventure." NY Times Book Rev

The final country. Mysterious Press 2001 310p o.p.
ISBN 0-89296-666-1 LC 2001-30640
"Texas is no place for an old reprobate like Milo Milodragovitch to sober up and settle down. Except for laundering a little money through the bar he owns in the

Crumley, James, 1939-—*Continued*

Hill Country, James Crumley's saddle-sore private eye is keeping faithful to his woman and living a blameless life . . . when the payback murder of a drug dealer gives him an excuse to oil his gun, pack some drugs, jump in his black cherry El Dorado and hit the road again." N Y Times Book Rev

"Plot twists and details seem loose and easy, yet every thread is sewn tight as a hardball. This is a brilliant achievement, with Crumley returned to his full powers, seeming to say with each assured sentence, Yeah, I'm an old dog, but I still wag the baddest bone." Publ Wkly

The last good kiss; a novel. Random House 1978 259p o.p.

ISBN 0-394-41946-4 LC 77-90286

"C. W. Sughrue is hired to trace the missing and drunken writer Abraham Trahearne by the man's divorced first wife, Catherine. Catherine Trahearne is sexy, elegant, and ice-cold. She lives with Trahearne's ancient mother, Edna, across the creek from the house where Trahearne lives with Melinda, his second wife. The plot is episodic and keeps one bleary eye loosely focused on Trahearne's dysfunctional extended family." Murphy. Ency of Murder and Mystery

The wrong case; a novel. Random House 1975 272p o.p.

ISBN 0-394-49198-3 LC 74-29598

Milton "Milo" Milodragovitch is a private detective in Meriwether, Montana. This case involves the suicide of a homosexual heroin pusher

This is "an exceptionally good example of the genre. Properly deferring to hallowed conventions, Crumley writes about damaged people seen through a haze of jaded romanticism, but he asserts his own tone of voice . . . . Crumley is a vivid writer. He makes Milo much more vulnerable, more involved in this sordid case than Hammett or Chandler would have done." Newsweek

Crusie, Jennifer

Bet me; Jennifer Crusie. 1st ed. St. Martin's Press 2004 337p $22.95

ISBN 0-312-30346-7 LC 2003-58182

"Minerva Dobbs thought David Fisk might be the one she's been waiting for, until he dumps her three weeks before her sister Diana's wedding. Min soon realizes just how lucky she is to be rid of David when she overhears him at her favorite bar betting a handsome stranger, Calvin Morrisey, that Cal couldn't bed Min in a month. At first Min debates the idea of giving them both a piece of her mind, but then she remembers she still needs a date for the wedding. Why not use the all-too charming Cal just like he was going to use her, and then dump him? Of course, Min never expected that Cal might turn out to be the 'one.' . . . Finding exactly the right balance between cynicism and optimism, Crusie deftly blends snappy dialogue; quirky, irrepressible secondary characters; and two beautifully matched protagonists struggling against their romantic fate." Booklist

Crazy for you. St. Martin's Press 1999 325p o.p.

ISBN 0-312-19849-3 LC 98-37169

This novel, set in small-town Ohio, is "about a 35-year-old high school art teacher's chance at love. Quinn McKenzie leads a prosaic, dull existence until a stray mutt crosses her path and becomes the catalyst that changes her priorities. Suddenly, her safe relationship with reliable Bill Hilliard, the school sports coach, takes a downturn when Bill forbids her to keep the dog. Crusie delves into the amatory machinations of the town through the sparkling, gossipy dialogue that takes place at the local hair parlor where Quinn's best buddy, Darla, works." Publ Wkly

Faking it. St. Martin's Press 2002 340p $24.95

ISBN 0-312-28468-3

"Matilda Goodnight has put her days of forging art behind her, but when her niece accidentally sells one of the six paintings she did as the fictitious daughter of a reclusive painter, she fears her secret past will be discovered. Tilda determines to steal the painting from Clea Lewis, the conniving social climber who brought it. But when she sneaks into the house Clea shares with wealthy Mason Phipps, she runs right into Davy Dempsey, who is there to steal back the money Clea took from him. Sparks fly instantly between the two. . . . [This] is an entertaining, fast-paced romp with a pleasing love story at its heart." Booklist

Cullin, Mitch, 1968-

A slight trick of the mind; a novel. Nan A. Talese 2005 272p $23.95

ISBN 0-385-51328-3 LC 2004-46038

"It is 1947, and the long-retired Holmes, now 93, lives in a remote Sussex farmhouse, where his memories and intellect begin to go adrift. He lives with a housekeeper and her young son, Roger, whose patient, respectful demeanor stirs paternal affection in Holmes. Holmes has settled into the routine of tending his apiary, writing in journals, and grappling with the diminishing powers of his razor-sharp mind, when Roger comes upon a case hitherto unknown. It is that of a Mrs. Keller, the long-ago object of Holmes's deep-and never acknowledged-infatuation." Publisher's note

"Cullin is an unusually sophisticated theorist of human nature, and this book is first and foremost an analysis of Holmes—both as a fictional character and as an embodiment of the human drive to make fictions. . . . As the conclusion of this beautiful novel makes plain, lives aren't like cases or, for that matter, like narratives. They are never solved or resolved: they just one day come to an end." N Y Times Book Rev

Undersurface; a novel; art by Peter I. Chang. Permanent Press (Sag Harbor) 2002 166p il $24

ISBN 1-57962-077-9 LC 2001-36621

An "account of a Tucson teacher's descent into the lurid, furtive world of illicit gay sex, which lands him in the wrong place at the wrong time when a murder is committed. John Connor is the ordinary, sensitive narrator whose descent begins when he finds himself frequenting adult video stores after his sex life with his wife sours. . . . As a crime narrative based on a true story, the book is a chilling if somewhat dated tale of a misstep morphing into free fall; as a literary character study, Connor's attempt to come to terms with his situation is both haunting and compelling." Publ Wkly

Culver, Timothy J.

For works written by this author under other names see Stark, Richard; Westlake, Donald E.

Cumyn, Alan, 1960-

Losing it. St. Martin's Press 2003 365p $24.95
ISBN 0-312-30691-1 LC 2002-31882

"The Sterlings are ordinary members of the educated middle class living in Ottawa, but turmoil lurks beneath their surface calm. Bob Sterling, a professor of literature specializing in Edgar Allan Poe, is secretly obsessed with women's underthings; Julia, Bob's much younger wife and former student, is quietly losing her mind from the exhaustion of caring for Matthew, their two-year-old, and her mother, Lenore, who is tormented by Alzheimer's." Publ Wkly

"The nuanced persuasive characterization propels the story forward and provides depth and texture. . . . A bonus is that Cumyn spices up this essentially sad story with some horrifyingly funny scenes." Booklist

Cunningham, Michael, 1952-

Flesh and blood. Farrar, Straus & Giroux 1995 465p o.p.
ISBN 0-374-18113-6 LC 94-24628

This family chronicle begins "in 1935 in Greece, where a boy suffers poverty and neglect. Constantine Stassos eventually immigrates to the U.S., where he marries a lovely and industrious young woman, amasses a fortune, and turns his attractive home into a living hell. No one goes unscathed, from his suffocating wife, Mary, through his self-negating eldest daughter, his acerbic gay son, and his younger daughter, Zoe, a strangely feral child. As the years go by and abrupt social changes become the rack upon which families are wrenched and broken, each member of the Stassos clan struggles to achieve love and respect." Booklist

"Fairly brief episodes, often occuring years apart, recount key moments in the establishment, disintegration, and reconfiguration of the family. Thoroughly realized action, vivid character delineation, and the splendid control of language guarantee both the unity and powerful impact of this successful novel." Libr J

The hours. Farrar, Straus & Giroux 1998 229p $23
ISBN 0-374-17289-7 LC 98-34188

In alternating chapters, "three stories unfold: 'Mrs. Woolf,' about Virginia's own struggle to find an opening for *Mrs. Dalloway* in 1923; 'Mrs. Brown,' about one Laura Brown's efforts to escape, somehow, an airless marriage in California in 1949 while, coincidentally, reading *Mrs. Dalloway*; and 'Mrs. Dalloway,' which is set in 1990s Greenwich Village and concerns Clarissa Vaughan's preparations for a party for her gay—and dying—friend, Richard, who has nicknamed her Mrs. Dalloway." Publ Wkly

"After a brief prologue, the stories alternate in an intricate sequence, rather like a rhyme scheme. . . . The whole book does sound a little fussy in description, an exercise in echoes, but it doesn't read that way." N Y Times Book Rev

Specimen days. Farrar, Straus and Giroux 2005 308p $25
ISBN 0-374-29962-5 LC 2005-40518

"In 'In the Machine,' the first of three interrelated tales set in New York City, 13-year-old Lucas, who almost involuntarily spouts lines of Whitman's verse, confronts grief and the ambiguity of love as he tries to take his dead brother Simon's place. The setting, the Industrial 1920s, melds into the early 21st century in the second tale, 'The Children's Crusade,' in which African American police detective Cat investigates a band of Whitman-quoting children terrorizing the city. In the futuristic final story, 'Like Beauty,' an android with Whitman's poetry implanted in his circuits embarks on a journey with a young boy named Luke to meet his manufacturer." Libr J

"As much as Cunningham's novel is haunted by the ghost of Whitman's prophecies, it is profoundly informed by the events of September 11, 2001. . . . Cunningham's brilliantly imagined dystopian future represents the final betrayal of Walt Whitman's joyously democratic America." New Leader

Cussler, Clive

Atlantis found. Putnam 1999 534p $26.95
ISBN 0-399-14588-5 LC 99-39883

The threat in this Dirk Pitt suspense novel "comes from a family of genetically engineered superhumans that just may have Hitler as an ancestor. Basing a plan on relics discovered from an ancient civilization, the evilly insane Wolf family plans to split the Antarctic ice shelf, flooding the world. Then their superbreed can take over the world and bring about the creation of a Nazi 'Fourth Empire.' Dirk and sidekick Al Giordano are aided by a beautiful archaeologist and the NUMA staff in unraveling clues stretching back to 7000 B.C., in order to beat a doomsday countdown." Booklist

"This is a fascinating story with exotic locations, high-tech wizardry, heart-pounding suspense, the threat of a cataclysmic disaster, resourceful heroes, and an action-packed conclusion—all backed by meticulous research to make this a truly grand adventure." Libr J

Black wind; [by] Clive Cussler and Dirk Cussler. Putnam 2004 530p il $27.95
ISBN 0-399-15259-8 LC 2004-53536

"The story begins toward the end of World War II, and the Japanese have sent two submarines to the West Coast of the U.S. They are carrying a lethal new strain of biological virus, but neither vessel makes it to the designated target. Then, in 2007, a number of sea-lion deaths are reported along the western Alaska Peninsula, and birds and people in the area become sick and die, although no known environmental catastrophe or human-induced culprit is suspected. Called to the scene is Dirk Pitt, the head of the National Underwater Marine Agency, and his two sons, one a marine biologist, the other a marine engineer. Their task is to locate and recover the two subs from the ocean floor. There are the usual harrowing encounters, close calls, daring exploits, and—in the end—annihilation of the bad guys. Another win for NUMA." Booklist

Cyclops; a novel. Simon & Schuster 1986 475p il o.p.
LC 85-27704

"American scientists secretly send a manned space station to the moon; a Soviet plot to overthrow Fidel Castro erupts on the eve of a groundbreaking alliance between

Cussler, Clive—*Continued*
Cuba and America; and an American industrialist embarks on a treasure hunt in an antique blimp, only to disappear off the coast of Florida. The only constant in these seemingly unrelated events is Dirk Pitt, [who is involved] in every aspect of this complicated tale." Booklist

"The writing is brittle, but the reader is not likely to worry about that in a story whose plot resembles a box of exploding fireworks and poses some interesting questions regarding both Cuba and the militarization of space." Publ Wkly

Deep six; a novel. Simon & Schuster 1984 432p il o.p.

LC 84-5291

Salvage expert Dirk Pitt "is assigned by the U.S. Environmental Protection Agency to locate the source of a deadly nerve agent contaminating the ocean off Alaska. In the action-packed scenes that follow, Pitt uncovers an international plot to take over the U.S. Government through the use of mind control devices." Libr J

Dragon; a novel. Simon & Schuster 1990 542p il o.p.

LC 90-9650

In this "novel Cussler brings back Dirk Pitt, special projects director of the National Underwater and Marine Agency (NUMA), who has a 'razor hardness about him that even a stranger could sense,' a man who spends 'almost as much time on and under water as he does on land.' The plot involves a crashed B-29 bomber that was carrying a third atomic bomb to Japan in 1945—the nuclear cargo having been buried in the Pacific Ocean for 45 years—and a group of Japanese extremists who seek to blackmail the U.S. with nuclear weapons strategically planted in several large U.S. cities." Booklist

The author "offers a page-turning romp that achieves a level of fast-paced action and derring-do that Robert Ludlum and other practitioners of modern pulp fiction might well envy." Publ Wkly

Fire ice; a novel from the NUMA® files; {by} Clive Cussler, with Paul Kemprecos. Putnam 2002 434p o.p.

ISBN 0-399-14872-8 LC 2002-19050

Previous titles in the Kurt Austin series: Serpent (1999) and Blue Gold (2000), published in paperback

In this thriller Kurt Austin and "the men from NUMA (Native Underwater & Marine Agency) team up with former KGB spies to face down a Russian mobster with czarist aspirations and a zealot's hatred for the 'corruption and materialism' of the Western lifestyle. . . . Cussler is in top form here, working in a role for Old Ironsides and Czar Nicholas II's crown while throwing in enough derringdo and eco-lore to leave his fans breathless." Publ Wkly

Flood tide; a novel. Simon & Schuster 1997 511p o.p.

ISBN 0-684-80298-8 LC 97-26660

In this thriller, Dirk Pitt and "his sidekick, Al Giordino, are out to catch a Chinese shipping magnate who smuggles illegal Chinese immigrants into countries around the world to be worked as indentured slaves. On a lake near Seattle, Pitt stumbles across Qin Shang's heavily guarded compound. Pitt is the special projects director for the National Underwater & Marine Agency. . . . Searching the lake with a robotic observation device, Pitt finds heaps of mass-executed Chinese bodies. He then rescues a dozen still-living captives, including beautiful Immigration and Naturalization Service agent Julia Lee." Publ Wkly

Inca gold; a novel. Simon & Schuster 1994 537p o.p.

ISBN 0-671-68156-7 LC 94-6577

"A chance rescue of two divers trapped in a Peruvian sinkhole leads series hero Dirk Pitt . . . into a search for lost treasure that involves grave robbers, art thieves and ancient curses. Cussler's latest adventure novel features terrorists who aren't really terrorists and a respected archeologist who is not what he seems: it all boils down to a race between Pitt and some unscrupulous crooks for a cache of Inca gold hidden away from the Spanish and lost since the 16th century. . . . It's pure escapist adventure, with a wry touch of humor and a certain self-referential glee." Publ Wkly

Lost city; a novel from the NUMA files; [by] Clive Cussler with Paul Kemprecos. Putnam 2004 420p $26.95

ISBN 0-399-15177-X LC 2004-50556

"A body is discovered frozen in the Alps, scientists begin disappearing from a Greek lab, and death greets anyone intent on recovering a life-prolonging enzyme discovered deep in the ocean. . . . [These are some of the problems facing protagonist] Kurt Austin, leader of the National Underwater Marine Agency's (NUMA) Special Assignments Team." Libr J

"Kidnappings, hair's breadth escapes, fierce battles, strange science, beautiful women and plenty of action add up to vintage Cussler." Publ Wkly

Raise the Titanic!. Viking 1976 314p il o.p.

"It is the year 1988. United States scientists need a rare element, byzanium, the only existing supply of which was shipped in the Titanic's hold, to complete a missile defense system. The Russians try by various means to stop them from retrieving it. In order to get to the byzanium, the U.S. sets about bringing the Titanic, which lies under two and a half miles of water after its 1912 rendezvous with an iceberg, to the surface." Christ Sci Monit

"A great adventure thriller . . . [that] spins from one dizzying climax to another, holds its innermost secrets until the very end, and keeps you so audaciously entertained you won't want it to come to a close. . . . Simply super and very cleverly done, with just the right amount of tongue-in-cheek bravado." Publ Wkly

Sahara; a novel. Simon & Schuster 1992 541p o.p.

LC 92-5100

"In West Africa, a vicious plot launched by a military dictator and a French industrialist is killing thousands of people and threatening all the creatures in the world's seas with extinction. As Cussler's perennial hero Dirk Pitt hikes off across the Sahara to bring the world news of these evil doings, he discovers the secret behind Lincoln's assassination, hidden aboard a lost Confederate ironclad, and the disappearance of British aviatrix Kitty Mannock in 1931." Libr J

"Pepper the plot with human-rights abuse, cannibalism,

Cussler, Clive—*Continued*
state-of-the-art weaponry, espionage, and the evil General Zateb Kazim—and you've got more than enough action to keep the Cussler's thrill-craving fans satiated." Booklist

Shock wave; a novel. Simon & Schuster 1996 537p o.p.
ISBN 0-684-80297-X LC 95-30057
Protagonist Dirk Pitt "leads a National Underwater and Marine Agency expedition to discover why seals and dolphins have been disappearing on Seymour Island in the Antarctica. But the novel actually begins in 1859, when a British ship carrying convicts to Australia sinks. Eight survivors reach land, a deserted island. In the year 2000, naturalist Maeve Fletcher, one of the descendants of two of the survivors who'd married, is stranded on Seymour Island with passengers of a cruise ship and is rescued by Pitt." Booklist
"Readers will love this ripsnorting, old-fashioned sea adventure based on only slightly futuristic science. Cussler writes with tremendous confidence, creating bold characters to love or hate. They all act in situations of gripping intensity and palpable reality." Libr J

Treasure; a novel. Simon & Schuster 1988 539p o.p.
LC 88-1951
During a rescue mission in Greenland to recover a sabotaged airliner full of U.N. representatives, salvage expert Dirk Pitt runs across evidence of the location of a fabled Roman treasure, rescued from Alexandria in A.D. 391
"Cussler creates a world that is just believable enough for the reader to accept as true, a necessary prerequisite for audacious fiction such as this. Characters do and say what you'd expect in their situations. The scientific jargon, gadgets, and weaponry all seem authentic and fit smoothly into the plot. . . . Taken as a just-for-fun adventure, the book is solidly entertaining." West Coast Rev Books

Valhalla rising. Putnam 2001 531p o.p.
ISBN 0-399-14787-X LC 2001-19516
Dirk Pitt's "current nemesis is a timely one: Curtis Merlin Zale, an oil tycoon bent on taking over the U.S. by making it dependent on him for all its oil supplies. . . .He starts out by sinking an ocean liner with a revolutionary new propulsion system, and then he hijacks the research vessel sent to investigate the disaster. Fate keeps dropping Dirk Pitt in the middle of the action." Booklist
"Historical asides of submarine lore, Jules Verne minutiae and references to Viking runes in America add touches of real-life oddity to the mix, and nothing will prepare even longtime Cussler fans for the major surprise he drops at the end." Publ Wkly

White death; a novel from the NUMA files; [by] Clive Cussler with Paul Kemprecos. Putnam 2003 419p $26.95
ISBN 0-399-15041-2 LC 2003-46501
This thriller "chronicles the exploits of Kurt Austin, leader and hero of NUMA's Special Assignment Team. The plot involves Austin and his partner Zavala, who are investigating a feud between a radical environmentalist group and a Danish cruiser. Austin and Zavala must come to the rescue of men trapped on the ship. They find that a giant multinational corporation is seeking to kill anyone who attempts to stop its efforts to control the seas." Booklist

Cussler, Dirk
(jt. auth) Cussler, C. Black wind

Czaczkes, Shmuel Josef *See* Agnon, Shmuel Yosef, 1888-1970

D

Dahl, Roald

Ah, sweet mystery of life; stories; illustrated by John Lawrence. Knopf 1990 179p o.p.
LC 89-43292
First published 1989 in the United Kingdom
Contents: Ah, sweet mystery of life; Parson's pleasure; The ratcatcher; Rummins; Mr. Hoddy; Mr. Feasey; The champion of the world
"These seven stories date from the late 1940s when Dahl was living in England's Buckinghamshire countryside and just beginning his career. The remembered people and settings of this rural region come to life vividly, Dahl converting them into a series of tales that explore a surprisingly deep and engagingly humorous vision of humanity. . . . His characters are refreshingly ordinary and full of life." Booklist

Selected stories of Roald Dahl. Modern Lib. 1968 302p o.p.
These stories were selected by the author from two of his previous collections: Someone like you, published 1953 and, Kiss, kiss, published 1960
Contents: Lamb to the slaughter; Dip in the pool; The landlady; Taste; Parson's pleasure; Georgy Porgy; Royal jelly; Genesis and catastrophe; Mrs. Bixby and the Colonel's coat; Skin; The ratcatcher; Rummins; Mr. Hoddy; Mr. Feasy; The champion of the world
"These tales by a social satirist and moralist are a pungent blend of the macabre and the humorous." Chicago. Public Libr

Dailey, Janet

Calder pride. HarperCollins Pubs. 1999 358p o.p.
ISBN 0-06-017699-7 LC 97-23991
Chase Calder's "daughter, Cat, now a slender green-eyed brunette of 20, is his match in will if not in size. Thirsting for tough justice after her fiancé, Repp Taylor, is killed by a drunk driver, she helps ensure that culprit Rollie Anderson gets jail time, cold-shouldering his parents' plea for mercy and earning their vengeful hatred. Frankly lusting for a man to relieve her of the virginity Repp had insisted on honoring, she tumbles into bed with smoke-eyed treasury agent Logan Echohawk one torrid night in Fort Worth, Tex. . . . Cat becomes pregnant with a son she names Quint Benteen Calder and raises on her own in Calder country. Just before Quint's fifth birthday, Echohawk trades in his treasury job for the position of sheriff of Blue Moon." Publ Wkly

Dailey, Janet—*Continued*

Heiress; a novel. Little, Brown 1987 477p o.p.
LC 86-27538

"Abbie Lawson is 27 when her father, Dean, dies in an auto accident. Fully expecting to inherit millions from his petroleum-related business, Abbie is devastated to discover that not only was Dean in financial trouble, but that he left an enormous trust to his illegitimate daughter, Rachel Farr. Abbie and her mother are forced to sell the family estate, predictably purchased by Rachel, and so begins a bitter rivalry between the sisters, complicating their lives and those of their loved ones." Libr J

"Dailey doesn't hesitate to make full use of the clichés of the commercial fiction genre, but her wit, imagination and creation of a sardonic male romantic lead constitute solid entertainment." Publ Wkly

Daley, Robert

A faint cold fear; a novel. Little, Brown 1990 450p o.p.
LC 90-39021

"A dedicated New York cop, more interested in fighting crime than maintaining the political status quo, Ray Douglas finds himself unwanted in the Drug Enforcement Agency's Colombian field office. His path crosses that of Jane Fox, an ambitious journalist determined to prove that her abilities as a foreign correspondent are in no way limited by her gender. At first each sees the other only as a tool for their respective careers—he as her inside source, she as a means of reminding the NYPD of his existence—but their tentative friendship evolves into a more serious relationship." Libr J

"To say that Mr. Daley has written a wonderful cop novel may mean little. Considering how few writers do it well, however, what is most amazing is how easy Mr. Daley makes it look. This is popular entertainment of a high order." N Y Times Book Rev

Hands of a stranger. St. Martin's Press 1985 397p o.p.
LC 85-8193

"Joe Hearn, an ambitious inspector in the N.Y.P.D., finds himself falling in love with Judith Adler, the assistant district attorney for sex crimes. His neglected wife, Mary, comes close to having an affair but at the last second changes her mind. As she is about to leave an hourly-rate hotel room, Mary is raped. Her husband, ignoring his responsibilities and abusing the resources of the Police Department, obsessively investigates the assault." NY Times Book Rev

"Part soap opera, part compelling thriller, Daley's excellent novel paints a brutally vivid portrait of the turmoil within the criminal justice system and the humiliation of rape." Booklist

The innocents within; a novel. Villard Bks. 1999 438p o.p.
ISBN 0-375-50178-9 LC 99-14155

"An American pilot shot down over central France during WWII falls in love with the Jewish ward of a pastor who runs an underground resistance network in this novel based on the true story of pastor André Trocmé of LeChambon sur Lignon." Publ Wkly

"Daley's matter-of-fact narrative reflects the stark reality of an impoverished village in occupied France. The story makes clear the horror of having to conceal one's identity while never really knowing the identity or intentions of others." Booklist

Man with a gun. Simon & Schuster 1988 475p o.p.
LC 87-27695

"Foreign correspondent Phil Keefe has been selected right-hand man to New York Police Commissioner Timothy J. Egan. . . . Keefe is coached by a sergeant who has seen awful cruelties on the streets of New York. He is suspected by top brass who fear their power slipping into his hands. . . . He is in over his head, though, when police officials saddle him with a difficult hostage negotiation that results in the death of a distraught black trucker." Publ Wkly

"While Daley occasionally lets the plot wander as he explores the often dirty world of police politics, his characterizations are ruthlessly perceptive. Unlike many mysteries, all of the actors in this drama are painted in gritty, realistic shades of gray." Booklist

Nowhere to run. Warner Bks. 1996 460p o.p.
LC 96-3146

"When New York detective Jack Dilger's marriage to an interior designer deteriorates, he decides to bust one of her art-world pals who is dealing stolen paintings to South American drug lords. But it all goes bad: cops die, bad guys (including one of the infamous Zaragon brothers) die, and Jack is severely wounded. Forced to retire, he flees to France, the surviving Zaragon brother on his tail. There he meets Madeleine Leclerq, also a cop in deadly trouble." Booklist

"Daley's leads are likable and believable, his French local color is first-rate and his complicated plot turns, buoyed by tension and splashed with violence, work beautifully. The ending isn't happy, but it rings true." Publ Wkly

Wall of brass; a novel. Little, Brown 1994 409p o.p.
LC 94-14185

"When New York City Police Commissioner Harry Chapman is shot while jogging on Manhattan's Upper West Side, his former patrol-car partner, Bert Farber, now chief of detectives, is assigned to find the killer. Farber is also one of three top contenders to replace Chapman as commissioner, and his two chief rivals are doing their best to roadblock him in his search for the killer. Complicating the situation . . . [is] Farber's torrid romance with Chapman's wife, Mary Alice." Publ Wkly

"A tightly plotted, involving tale of law and disorder." Booklist

Dallas, Sandra

The diary of Mattie Spenser. St. Martin's Press 1997 229p o.p.
ISBN 0-312-15515-8 LC 96-53926

"Beginning in 1865, a week after her wedding in Fort Madison, Iowa, Mattie Spenser confides to her diary as she and her new husband travel by Conestoga wagon to the Colorado Territories. The building of a sod house; the births and deaths of children; the melting of narrow attitudes toward 'loose' women, Indians, and Negroes; and the growth of Mattie as a person are all visible in these pages, full of what seems like genuine details of prairie life." Booklist

Dallas, Sandra—*Continued*

The Persian Pickle Club. St. Martin's Press 1995 196p o.p.
ISBN 0-312-13586-6 LC 95-31032
"Hard times in Depression-era Harveyville, Kansas, are softened by the conviviality of a weekly quilting circle called the Persian Pickle Club. Queenie Bean, the 'talkingest' member of the group, narrates the novel. . . . When Queenie forms a fast friendship with the newest 'Pickle,' a flashy, big-city gal named Rita, the equilibrium of the group changes, for Rita is a novice newspaper reporter intent on making a name for herself. The story Rita most wants to crack involves the mysterious death of one of the club ladies' husbands." Libr J
This is a "simple but endearing story that depicts small-town eccentricities with affection and adds dazzle with some latebreaking surprises. Dallas hits all the right notes, combining an authentic look at the social fabric of Depression-era life with a homespun suspense story." Publ Wkly

D'Amato, Barbara

Good cop, bad cop. Forge 1998 301p o.p.
LC 97-35922
"A Tom Doherty Associates book"
In 1969 Chicago, "Nicholas Bertolucci was a rookie cop assigned to raid a Panther hideout. Three innocent victims died in the shootout, but the story was quickly hushed up. Years later, Nick has become Chicago's police superintendent, and his older brother, Aldo, a down-on-his-luck cop and a perpetual screwup, is filled with hate for his successful brother. When Aldo discovers a terrible secret from the past that could topple Nick and leave the CPD in tatters, the reader is left to watch in horror as the juggernaut rolls inexorably toward an explosive climax." Booklist

Hard evidence; a Cat Marsala mystery. Scribner 1999 255p o.p.
ISBN 0-684-83354-9 LC 98-31785
Cat Marsala "tosses her dog a bone bought from an expensive food store, but the bone turns out to be human. What a way to end a pleasant dinner and begin sleuthing." Libr J
"A vivid supporting cast, sprightly yet controlled wit and some fine cooking advice . . . combine to make for another delightful mystery from the ever-reliable author." Publ Wkly

Hard luck; a Cat Marsala mystery. Scribner 1992 242p o.p.
ISBN 0-684-19408-2 LC 91-37412
"Chicago freelance journalist Cat Marsala . . . watches the story of her career land—literally—in front of her when Jack Sligh, an Illinois lottery official, plummets to his death from a skyscraper. Cat recognizes the corpse because she'd made an appointment with Sligh in regard to an article she was writing on the proposed Central States Lottery. Convinced Sligh was pushed, Cat begins an indepth investigation of his co-workers at the Illinois state lottery." Publ Wkly
"D'Amato's descriptions of state lottery problems and procedures are factual and fascinating, and her characters—both series regulars and lottery folk—are lively and believable." Booklist

Hard road; a Cat Marsala mystery; [by] Barbara D'Amato; and an essay by Brian D'Amato, [The wooden gargoyles: evil in Oz] Scribner 2001 286p $24
ISBN 0-7432-0095-0 LC 2001-31393
"As freelance journalist Cat is squiring her young nephew, Jeremy, around a mythical Oz festival in Chicago's Grant Park . . . two people die before her eyes, one a stabbing victim. When bullets start to fly, Cat and Jeremy flee through a system of dark and dank tunnels." Publ Wkly
"Fans of L. Frank Baum's Oz books and all the history, controversy, and minutiae surrounding them will rejoice in D'Amato's merry weaving of all things Oz into this innovative mystery. Oz references are no mere gloss, however, but provide a satirical, sometimes spooky commentary on the action." Booklist

White male infant. Forge 2002 333p o.p.
ISBN 0-7653-0024-9 LC 2002-25029
"A Tom Doherty Associates book"
In this thriller about a baby-selling cartel D'Amato mixes "together a couple who are fighting against their suspicions that their greatly loved adopted son is not who they thought he was; a CNN reporter and her cameraman who see, firsthand, the deplorable conditions in European and Russian orphanages; and an FBI investigation into a highly profitable and corrupt international adoption agency. The separate strands of this complex but riveting story start coming together when the couple find evidence suggesting their son was not orphaned but kidnapped at the same time the CNN reporter discovers her cameraman brutally slain in their Russian hotel. Another D'Amato stunner." Booklist

Dams, Jeanne M.

Death in lacquer red; a Hilda Johansson mystery. Walker & Co. 1999 255p o.p.
ISBN 0-8027-3329-8 LC 98-45223
"With its fine churches and stately homes, its new industries and bustling downtown, South Bend, Ind., in 1900 looks like paradise to Hilda Johansson, a young Swedish maid who keeps house for the prominent Studebaker family. . . . When Hilda finds the battered body of a missionary lady, the sister of the grand political personage who lives next door, . . . [she] takes it upon herself to solve the crime before people look for a scapegoat among the city's immigrant population." N Y Times Book Rev

Dangerous visions; 33 original stories; illustrated by Leo and Diana Dillon. Doubleday 1967 xxix, 520p o.p.

"Doubleday science fiction"
Contents: Evensong, by L. Del Rey; Flies, by R. Silverberg; The day after the day the Martians came, by F. Pohl; Riders of the purple wage, by J. P. Farmer; The Malley system, by A. M. DeFord; A toy for Juliette, by R. Bloch; The prowler in the city at the edge of the world, by H. Ellison; The night that all time broke loose, by B. W. Aldiss; The man who went to the moon—twice, by H. Rodman; Faith of our fathers, by P. K. Dick; The jigsaw man, by L. Niven; Gonna roll the

Dangerous visions—*Continued*
bones, by F. Leiber; Lord Randy, my son, by J. L. Hensley; Eutopia, by P. Anderson; Incident in Moderan, by D. R. Bunch; The escaping, by D. R. Bunch; The dollhouse, by J. Cross; Sex and/or Mr. Morrison, by C. Emshwiller; Shall the dust praise thee, by D. Knight; If all men were brothers, would you let one marry your sister? by T. Sturgeon; What happened to Auguste Clarot? by L. Eisenberg; Ersatz, by H. Slesar; Go, go, go, said the bird, by S. Dorman; The happy breed, by J. T. Sladek; Encounter with a hick, by J. Brand; From the government printing office, by K. Neville; Land of the great horses, by R. A. Lafferty; The recognition, by J. G. Ballard; Judas, by J. Brunner; Test to destruction, by K. Laumer; Carcinoma Angels, by N. Spinrad; Auto-da-fé, by R. Zelazny; Aye, and Gomorrah . . ., by S. R. Delany

Daniel, Margaret Truman *See* Truman, Margaret, 1924-

Dann, Jack

Jubilee. TOR Bks. 2003 441p $27.95
ISBN 0-7653-0676-X LC 2002-73275
Contents: The diamond pit; Going under; Voices; Fairy tale; Marilyn; The black horn; Bad medicine; Tattoos; Camps; Da Vinci rising; Kaddish; The extra; A quiet revolution for death; Jumping the road; Blind shemmy; Tea; Jubilee
"The 17 stories in this collection illustrate the varied talents of one of the genre's most flexible and enduring writers." Libr J

Dannay, Frederic, 1905-1982
For works written by this author in collaboration with Manfred Lee see Queen, Ellery

Danticat, Edwidge, 1969-

The dew breaker. Knopf 2004 244p $22
ISBN 1-400-04114-7
This novel "focuses on the lives affected by a 'dew breaker,' or torturer of Haitian dissidents under Duvalier's regime. Each chapter reveals the titular man from another viewpoint, including that of his grown daughter, who, on a trip she takes with him to Florida, learns the secret of his violent past and those of the Haitian boarders renting basement rooms in his Brooklyn home. This structure allows Danticat to move easily back and forth in time and place, from 1967 Haiti to present-day Florida, tracking diverse threads within the larger narrative." Publ Wkly
"Beautifully written fiction about the real-life horror that is Haiti. Seamlessly blending the personal and political, it deals with what happens to a country and its people when mothers and fathers disappear for their political transgressions." USA Today

The farming of bones; a novel. Soho Press 1998 312p $23
ISBN 1-56947-126-6 LC 98-3655
"The book is based on a historical incident in 1937, when Dominican dictator Trujillo ordered the massacre of 15,000 to 20,000 Haitian emigrants living in his country. The Farming of Bones recounts the story through the eyes of Amabelle Désir, a young Haitian woman who is working in the Dominican Republic as the servant to a patrician family." Time
"It's a testament to Danticat's skill that Amabelle's musical, sorrowing voice never falters, even during her stark descriptions of the bloodbath." New Yorker

Krik? Krak!. Soho Press 1995 224p o.p.
ISBN 1-56947-025-1 LC 94-41999
The author "touches upon life both in Haiti and in New York's Haitian community, though we spend most of our time in Port-au-Prince and the country town of Ville Rose. The best of these stories humanize, particularize, give poignancy to the lives of people we may have come to think of as faceless emblems of misery, poverty and brutality." N Y Times Book Rev

Danvers, Dennis

The fourth world. Avon Eos 2000 336p $23
ISBN 0-380-97761-3 LC 99-52345
"When virtual reporter Santee St. John joins forces with the woman he loves in order to fight for a people's revolution in 21st-century Mexico, he uncovers a conspiracy that introduces a new element into the perennial battle between the First and Third Worlds. The author . . . crafts a mind-bending tale of paranoia, adventure, and unexpected love set in a near-future filled with web addicts deceived by powerful manipulators of the truth." Libr J

Darby, Catherine, 1935-
For works written by this author under other names see Black, Veronica, 1935-

Dargatz, Gail Anderson- *See* Anderson-Dargatz, Gail, 1963-

Dark, Alice Elliott

Think of England; a novel. Simon & Schuster 2002 271p $24
ISBN 0-684-86522-X LC 2002-17554
"While the MacLeod family anxiously awaits the Beatles performance on the *Ed Sullivan Show*, nine-year-old Jane is painfully aware of the escalating tensions between her parents. When a tragedy occurs later that night, Jane will relive every nuance of that evening, twisting the events like a set of rusty keys hoping to unlock the truth." Booklist
"Everything in this spare, eccentrically paced book is a pleasure to read, from the exposition of nine-year-old Jane MacLeod's home life in Pennsylvania to a family reunion, thirty-six years later. . . . It's almost impossible to write about the kind of subtle, inward sorrows and tensions that animate this story, and the author manages the challenge handsomely." New Yorker

Dark, Larry
(ed) The Literary ghost. See The Literary ghost

The **dark**; new ghost stories; edited by Ellen Datlow. 1st ed. TOR Bks. 2003 378p $25.95
ISBN 0-7653-0444-9 LC 2003-54336

The dark—*Continued*

Contents: The Trentino Kid, by Ford, J.; The ghost of the clock, by Lee, T.; One thing about the night, by Dowling, T.; The silence of the fallinf stars, by O'Driscoll, M.; The dead ghost, by Wilson, G.; Seven sisters, by Cady, J.; Subway, by Oates, J. C.; Doctor Hood, by Gallagher, S.; An amicable divorce, by Abraham, D.; Feeling remains, by Campbell, R.; The gallows necklace, by McCrumb, S.; Brownie, and me, by Grant, C. L.;Velocity, by Koja, Kathe; Limbo, by Shepard, L.; The hortlak, Link, K.; Dancing men; Hirshberg, G.

"Datlow has cast her net beyond the horror genre's usual names and pulled in contributors whose stories are the equal of their best work, as well as mystery, fantasy and SF writers whose tales seem to be the ghost story they've always wanted to tell." Publ Wkly

Dark matter; a century of speculative fiction from the African diaspora; edited by Sheree R. Thomas. Warner Bks. 2000 427p o.p.
ISBN 0-446-52583-9 LC 00-22288

This volume contains five essays and the following stories: Sister Lilith, by H. F. Jeffers; The comet, by W. E. B. DuBois; Chicago 1927, by J. Gomez; Black no more, by G. S. Schuyler; Separation anxiety, by E. Shockley; Tasting songs, by L. Ross; Can you wear my eyes, by Kalamu ya Salaam; Like daughter, by T. Due; Greedy choke puppy, by N. Hopkinson; Rhythm travel, by A. Baraka; Buddy Bolden, by Kalamu ya Salaam; Aye, and Gomorrah . . ., by S. R. Delany; Ganger (Ball Lightning), by N. Hopkinson; The becoming, by A. L. Hope; The goophered grapevine, by C. W. Chesnutt; The evening and the morning and the night, by O. E. Butler; Twice, at once, separated, by L. Addison; Gimmile's songs, by C. R. Saunders; At the huts of Ajala, by N. Shawl; The woman in the wall, by S. Barnes; Ark of bones, by H. Dumas; Butta's backyard barbecue, by T. Medina; Future Christmas, by I. Reed; At life's limits, by K. I. Salaam; The African origins of UFO's, by A. Joseph; The astral visitor delta blues, by R. Fleming; The space traders, by D. Bell; The pretended, by D. A. Smith; Hussy Strutt, by A. Patterson

"Ranging in variety from the lilting cadence of Nalo Hopkinson ('Greedy Choke Puppy') to the understated bleakness of Derek Bell ('The space traders'), this collection of 28 tales by African American sf and fantasy authors showcases a wealth of talent that spans over 100 years." Libr J

Darnton, John

The experiment. Dutton 1999 421p o.p.
ISBN 0-525-94517-2 LC 99-28860

"One way to achieve longer life might be to clone people who could provide body parts when yours wear out; clandestine research might reveal better but equally diabolical ways to extend life for those willing to pay large sums. When reporter Jude Harley discovers his apparent twin, a man raised in a mysterious island colony, he joins forces with a beautiful expert on twins, and the three uncover a genetic engineering plot of monstrous proportions, extending into the government and backward into their own childhoods as part of a secret project deep in an Arizona cavern." Libr J

"The central anxieties of 'The Experiment' strongly reflect the velocity of our technologies and the godlike desires of our nature." N Y Times Book Rev

Mind catcher. Dutton 2002 387p $25.95
ISBN 0-525-94662-4 LC 2002-25540

"When 13-year-old Tyler Jessup suffers profound brain injury, two neurosurgeons see conflicting opportunities. One wants to replace damaged brain cells with regenerated ones, the other wants to use a machine to separate the mind from its physical surroundings. Tyler's father, desperate to rescue his son, ultimately subjects himself to the latter experiment in order to find his son's psyche and bring it back." Libr J

"This is a dazzling, fast-paced novel that taps into issues about mind-body duality, cyberspace, artificial intelligence, and stem cell research. Well-drawn characters, tense emotions, and philosophical debates provide additional depth to this exciting scientific thriller." Booklist

Neanderthal. Random House 1996 368p o.p.
ISBN 0-679-44978-7 LC 96-11045

"Mat Morrison and Susan Arnot, archaeologists and ex-lovers, are summoned to investigate an odd find: an apparently new Neanderthal skull. They rush to Tadjikistan and foray into some of the least hospitable terrain in Asia. Not too unexpectedly, they find their quarry only to discover a long-lost mentor who is guarding unsettling moral, political, and archaeological secrets that threaten their lives and those of the reclusive Neanderthals. . . . When government agents intrude and threaten the scientific find, the two scientists must survive, rescue their old friend, deceive American and Russian intelligence gatherers, and balance a study of an astounding archaeological find with the interests of the tribes." Libr J

Dart, Iris Rainer

Show business kills; a novel. Little, Brown 1995 310p o.p.
ISBN 0-316-17334-7 LC 94-22947

This novel's protagonists "are four Hollywood players (two actresses, a writer, a producer) fast approaching obsolescence as they near fifty. As they grapple with the dog-eat-dog Hollywood world, falling faces, and encroaching flab, the four contemplate their pasts and try to come to terms with their presents. The shooting of their soap opera friend, Jan, by a thwarted actress from their college days grounds them once again in the things that matter in life." Libr J

"Dart's snappily paced tale is spiced with spot-on doses of black humor, while her insights into female friendships, as always, ring reassuringly true." Publ Wkly

The Stork Club; a novel. Little, Brown 1992 400p o.p.
LC 92-15612

"At age 50, Rick, a single movie producer and avowed Casanova combatting a midlife crisis, decides to adopt a baby. Ruthie and Shelley, a successful comedy-writing team, resolve to create a child even though he is gay and she is straight. Lainie and Mitch, owners of a chic California clothing boutique, contract with a surrogate mother to produce their child. These parents form the Stork Club led by Barbara, the child psychologist who guides the group as they struggle to make their atypical family cir-

Dart, Iris Rainer—*Continued*
cumstances work." Libr J

This novel is "hilarious, maudlin, warmhearted and surprisingly genuine in its emotions." Publ Wkly

Datlow, Ellen

(ed) The dark. See The dark

(ed) Snow white, blood red. See Snow white, blood red

Davidar, David

The house of blue mangoes. HarperCollins Pubs. 2002 421p o.p.

ISBN 0-06-621254-5

A multigenerational family saga set on the "Dorai estate in a tiny village in southern India. Tamil Christians, the Dorais are fortunate to have the contemplative patriarch Solomon at the helm in 1899, a time of violent unrest. Solomon has high hopes for his good-looking and athletic son, Aaron, but the heir apparent gets drawn into a radical terrorist group, so it's shy and studious Daniel, who makes a fortune in cosmetics, who takes his father's place. An avid student of the history and cultures of India, Davidar tracks the fortunes of the Dorai clan over the course of five turbulent decades as the independence movement coalesces, British rule ends, and India is drawn into two world wars." Booklist

Davidson, Diane Mott

The grilling season. Bantam Bks. 1997 322p o.p.

ISBN 0-553-10000-9 LC 97-20037

"Goldy Schulz, owner of Three Bears' Catering in Aspen Meadow, Colorado, has to deal yet again with her abusive ex-husband, this time arrested for the murder of his latest girlfriend. Their son, Arch, feels that Goldy should help prove his father's innocence. . . . Including all the requisite ingredients of a good puzzler, a riproaring finale, and the recipes from Goldy's catered affairs, this one is not to be missed." Booklist

Killer pancake. Bantam Bks. 1995 301p o.p.

LC 95-10852

"Careful planning for a cosmetics firm's lowfat luncheon fails to prepare Goldy [Schulz] for the sudden death of a gorgeous sales associate who was caught in the midst of an animal-rights demonstration." Libr J

The author "includes recipes as she brings events to a proper boil in this latest lively and satisfying outing for Goldy, who not only solves the mystery but also finds, much to her delight, that coffee can save your life." Publ Wkly

The last suppers. Bantam Bks. 1994 283p il o.p.

LC 94-18886

"Caterer Goldy Bear's wedding would have been perfect except for two minor problems—the priest is killed shortly before the wedding and her fiancé, homicide detective Tom Schultz, is kidnapped from the scene of the crime. Frustrated with waiting for updates from the police, Goldy attempts to find out who ruined her wedding." Booklist

"An appealing mixture of food and crime." Libr J

The main corpse. Bantam Bks. 1996 337p il o.p.

LC 96-23042

Caterer/sleuth Goldy Schulz's "wealthy friend Marla convinces Prospect Investment Partners, whose chief investment officer recently died in a car crash, to hire Goldy to cater a party. . . . As the party begins, Marla has a monumental argument with Prospect partner, Albert Lipscomb, about an assay report. Susequently, Albert disappears with Prospect's cash. Goldy decides to find out what happened, against the advice of her new husband, Tom Schulz, a Sheriff's Department Homicide investigator." Publ Wkly

Prime cut. Bantam Bks. 1998 305p o.p.

ISBN 0-553-10001-7 LC 98-33736

In this mystery "Aspen Meadows, Colo., caterer Goldy Schulz is ousted from her kitchen. Bilked, like many other residents, by local contractor Gerald Eliot, her workplace in a shambles, she agrees to help her old teacher, Chef André, as he caters a Christmas catalogue fashion shoot. On the way home from the acrimonious set, she stops by to visit her friend Cameron Burr, whose house has also been ravaged by Eliot. Searching for a coffee pot, she discovers Eliot's dead body." Publ Wkly

Davies, Linda, 1963-

Wilderness of mirrors. Doubleday 1996 355p o.p.

LC 95-35726

"Years back, British secret agent Eva Cunningham became a junky in a thwarted attempt to bust drug kingpin Robie Frazer, himself an underling to illegal arms mogul Ha Chin. Now Eva has a shot at revenge, and she calls on her old friend Cassie Stewart, a major force in the venture capital wing of a London bank, to help. . . . This fast-moving yarn parlays money, sex, and mayhem into an exciting read." Publ Wkly

Davies, Robertson, 1913-1995

The cunning man; a novel. Viking 1995 469p o.p.

LC 94-31874

This novel's "protagonist, Dr. Jonathan Hullah, is a holistic physician—a cunning diagnostician who is often able to get to the root of problems that have baffled others. A young reporter's query about the circumstances surrounding an Episcopalian priest's death at the high alter on Good Friday leads the doctor to reflect on his own life and career." Libr J

Robertson "entertains with an old-fashioned fictional mixture that he seems to have invented anew: keen social observations delivered with wit, intelligence and free-floating philosophical curiosity." Time

Fifth business. Viking 1970 308p o.p.

The first volume in the Deptford trilogy, followed by The manticore and World of wonders

"In the year 1908 in the Canadian Midwest, a woman is struck by a poorly aimed snowball. Her son is born prematurely as a result of her fright. Dunstan Ramsay describes his connection with four of his friends whose lives were affected by the incident: Boy Staunton who threw the snowball; Mrs. Amasa Dempster, who was hit by it; Paul, the son born prematurely; and Leola Cruikshank, a local beauty whom Staunton marries. The inter-

Davies, Robertson, 1913-1995—*Continued*
twining of their lives spans 60 years, three continents, and two wars." Shapiro. Fic For Youth. 3d edition

This novel "achieves a richness and depth that are exceptional in a modern novel and rare at any time. On its simplest and most obvious level it is a remarkably colorful tale of ambition, love and weird vengeance. At its deepest, it is a work of theological fiction that approaches Graham Greene at the top of his form." Book World

The lyre of Orpheus. Viking 1989 472p o.p.
LC 88-40311

Concluding volume of the Cornish trilogy

"This fable about the nature of artistic creation has two major plot lines. One thread concerns the production of an unfinished opera said to have been written by E.T.A. Hoffmann. The other concerns the discovery that the famous art collector Francis Cornish actually passed off one of his own paintings as a 16th-century masterpiece." Merriam-Webster's Ency of Lit

The manticore. Viking 1972 310p o.p.

The second volume in the Deptford trilogy

"The central figure is a highly successful Canadian lawyer, David Staunton, son of a Canadian millionaire, who is compelled to submit himself to the Jung Institute in Zurich for analysis when he feels insecure and no longer in command of his actions. Staunton himself relates the course of his Jungian analysis, revealing significant incidents and aspects of his past life and commenting from a different point of view on persons and actions." Booklist

This book "reflects in its style the buoyancy of the quick mind of its hero as well as his pomposity, his over confidence, and egotism. No doubt about it: Robertson Davies is a manipulator of words and he entrances the reader with a flowing flurry of dialogue and narrative. His book is well written, insightful, and a delightful psychological excursion." Best Sellers

Murther & walking spirits; a novel. Viking 1991 357p o.p.
LC 91-29844

"Connor Gilmartin ('Gil') is murdered in the novel's first sentence by a co-worker he discovers in bed with his (Gil's) wife. The indignity of being snuffed by 'the Sniffer,' a theater-cum-movie critic, is compounded when Gil is seemingly condemned to spend his after-life seated next to his nemesis at a film festival. But what Gil sees—unlike the rest of the audience—is a series of highly personal films starring an assortment of ancestors." Libr J

"The films convey more than sight and sound, making our hero eerily privy to his relatives' thoughts and feelings. Davies has great fun with this device, giving full rein to his sense of drama, love of gritty, historical detail, and delight in satire." Booklist

The rebel angels. Viking 1982 c1981 326p o.p.
LC 81-51907

First volume in the Cornish trilogy, followed by What's bred in the bone and The lyre of Orpheus

First published 1981 in Canada

"Set in a prominent Canadian university, the novel examines the dual themes of the distinction between knowledge and wisdom and the role of the university in contemporary society." Merriam-Webster's Ency of Lit

"The names of Rabelais and Paracelsus are not gratuitously invoked by the plot. There is a Rabelaisian quality . . . in Mr. Davies's own writing; while the hermetic and heterodox ideas associated with the name of Paracelsus are exploited in a fashion that is at once playful and serious." New Repub

What's bred in the bone. Viking 1985 436p o.p.
LC 85-40550

"An Elisabeth Sifton book"

Second volume in the Cornish trilogy

"Born in 1909 in the Canadian town of Blairlogie, Francis [Cornish] inherits a religious and cultural dichotomy: his mother is Canadian Catholic, his father English; both are also secret agents, and mostly absent. After college at Oxford and art school in Paris, Francis too becomes a spy, gathering intelligence in Hitler's Germany while apprenticed to a brilliant and devious art restorer. Three ill-fated loves leave Francis alone at the end, his life a puzzle to his descendants but not to his 'Daiman' and an Angel of Biography who unravel Francis's character and destiny." Libr J

"This novel nourishes the brain while it beguiles the senses. Even those who dislike its message must keep it in mind while they scramble for a rebuttal." Time

World of wonders. Viking 1976 c1975 358p o.p.

Final volume in the Deptford trilogy

"The world's premier illusionist, Magnus Eisengrim, tells his story to an audience of friends and filmmakers: his solitary childhood in a small, deeply Calvinistic village in rural Canada; his abduction by a carnival magician and his years of labor as a huckster; his initiation into the British theater by a grande dame and her husband, an egotistical star whom Magnus all but absorbs into himself; his work as a master repairman of gadgets, clocks, and mechanical toys; and finally his triumphant career on stage." Libr J

"If there is a single dominating theme, it is that we can never escape the consequences of our actions, and to ignore them is to be destroyed. . . . Among contemporary novelists, only Graham Greene has trod this ground and gleaned it so successfully. He and Davies stand alone, each in his own quarter of the field." New Repub

Davies, Valentine, 1905-1961

Miracle on 34th Street. Harcourt Brace & Co. 1947 120p o.p.

ISBN 0-15-160239-5

"Old Mr. Kringle believed he was Santa Claus, and he looked the part, but the home for the aged decided the delusion made him ineligible as a permanent resident so he went to stay with a friend who was a keeper of Central Park zoo. Quite by accident he became the official Santa Claus in Macy's department store where he inaugurated a new and profitable policy of good will between stores, but an irritated personnel manager tried to have him committed to a mental hospital. The case went to court and the judge was in a dilemma—what would happen to his political career if he declared Santa Claus a myth?" Booklist

"Nice blend of fantasy, fun and humor with the universal and wholesome appeal of the Christmas spirit." Libr J

Davies, William Robertson *See* Davies, Robertson, 1913-1995

Daviot, Gordon, 1896-1952

For works written by this author under other names see Tey, Josephine, 1896-1952

Davis, Amanda

Wonder when you'll miss me. William Morrow 2003 259p $24.95
ISBN 0-688-16781-0 LC 2002-24118

"After she is sexually assaulted under the school bleachers, 16-year-old Faith runs away from home, accompanied by the Fat Girl, a taunting, imaginary former self. At the circus, Faith finds a safe haven and a healing environment." Booklist

"Davis's writing is at its finest when the protagonist is struggling through the constant trials with her distant mother, her ineffectual teachers, and her one true friend's suicide. . . . The author succeeds in making this character unique, with flaws that teens will relate to. Readers will root for Faith, and the heartwarming conclusion will leave them satisfied." SLJ

Davis, Claire, 1949-

Winter range. Picador 2000 262p $23
ISBN 0-312-26140-3 LC 00-34701

"Winters are hard on the eastern edge of Montana, and a couple of bad ones in a row can force a rancher to sell his herd. But Chas Stubblefield refuses to unload his cattle, or even to slaughter them; he is letting them starve to death out on the range as a reproach to the merchants, the banks, and God, who he believes has turned against him. Local wisdom dictates that property is property: if Stubblefield wants to lose his reputation along with his farm, that's his business. But Ike Parsons, the sheriff, is an outsider, and he decides to intervene—a decision that has dire consequences for both his marriage and his community. This fine first novel—part thriller, part love story—explores the gradations between pity and mercy." New Yorker

Davis, Kathryn

Versailles. Houghton Mifflin 2002 206p $21
ISBN 0-618-22136-0 LC 2002-510048

This "idiosyncratic novel begins when Marie Antoinette, née Maria Antonia Josephina Johanna, Archduchess of Austria, aged fourteen, is riding in a blue-satin-lined carriage on her way to be married to the Dauphin of France. It ends with her death. Except for the brief, witty playlets studded throughout the narrative (in which various minor actors try to figure out what's going on), the Queen tells her own story, and the voice Davis has given her is by turns sage, mercurial, and ravishing. It is also edged with doom, each word bordered in black by the reader's own premonitions." New Yorker

Davis, Lindsey

The accusers; Lindsey Davis. Warner Books ed. Mysterious Press 2004 c2003 368p il map $25
ISBN 0-89296-811-7 LC 2003-65008

In this installment Marcus Didius Falco matches his "wits against two sleek lawyers intimately involved with the evident suicide of a Roman senator accused of corruption. Did he or didn't he? Of course, Falco uncovers the truth, though just barely; the ending is a surprise and surprisingly affecting. Meanwhile, the brothers of Falco's beloved Helen continue learning how hard the life of an informer can be and grow up just a little. Topnotch work in a topnotch series." Libr J

A body in the bath house. Mysterious Press 2002 c2001 354p o.p.
ISBN 0-89296-771-4 LC 2002-23071

First published 2001 in the United Kingdom

In this Marcus Didius Falco adventure "various circumstances—including a dead body under his father's new bathhouse, a sister in danger from a spurned love interest, and a request from the emperor for help in auditing a British building project—converge to send Falco, his family, and his frightened sister to the damp and uncivilized frontier. . . . Davis delivers her usual entertaining family dynamics and historically accurate details." Booklist

A dying light in Corduba. Mysterious Press 1998 428p maps o.p.
ISBN 0-89296-664-5 LC 97-25214

First published 1996 in the United Kingdom

In this mystery, "Marcus Didius Falco travels to the distant province of Baetica, pregnant girlfriend in tow, to investigate a possible olive oil cartel. The emphasis in this historical mystery is as much on historical as mystery, with solid detail and vivid insights that bring the ancient Roman alive. But the plotting, though leisurely, is nicely suspenseful and the ending worth the wait." Libr J

The iron hand of Mars; a Marcus Didius Falco mystery. Crown 1993 c1992 305p o.p.
LC 93-19265

First published 1992 in the United Kingdom

"In A.D. 71, the Emperor Vespasian sends his reluctant agent Marcus Didius Falco to Germany to bring a rebel chieftain into line and to find a missing legate whose battle-worn legion had surrendered him to a druidic sorceress." Publ Wkly

"Essential reading for historical mystery buffs and any lover of a good story." Libr J

Last act in Palmyra. Mysterious Press 1996 c1994 476p o.p.
ISBN 0-89296-625-4 LC 95-1612

First published 1994 in the United Kingdom

Court investigator Marcus Didius Falco "was denied a promised promotion into the upper class by the emperor Vespasian after his last escapade, a promotion required for him to marry his lover, the patrician Helena Justina. To get out of town with Helena, he takes on a job for one of the emperor's less trustworthy underlings, heading for Syria to do a little snooping. . . . While sightseeing, Falco and Helena discover, in a cistern, the body of a playwright who had been with an acting troupe out of Rome." Publ Wkly

"A delightful adventure that's charming, witty, intriguing, and clever." Booklist

One virgin too many. Mysterious Press 2000 356p $23.95
ISBN 0-89296-716-1 LC 00-31053

"Marcus Didius Falco, has just gotten a reward: Vespasian has appointed him Procurator of the Sacred Geese, a sinecure that allows him entrance into the world of Ro-

Davis, Lindsey—*Continued*

man cults. This knowledge comes in handy when a wellborn little girl, slated by her family to be a Vestal Virgin, disappears after telling Falco her family is trying to kill her. The girl's disappearance coincides with a brutal murder stumbled upon by Falco's brother-in-law." Booklist

"For sharply etched characters, wry humor, and a powerfully evoked Rome, this historical can't be beaten." Libr J

Poseidon's gold; a Marcus Didius Falco mystery. Crown 1994 336p o.p.
ISBN 0-517-59241-X LC 94-13060
First published 1993 in the United Kingdom

In this mystery Marcus Didius Falco "is challenged to locate both the art treasure hidden by his deceased brother as well as to clear his own name from a murder charge. His father, an auctioneer of (sometimes fine) art, and Helena, his fiancee, are able assistants. The first-person narrative immediately draws readers into the story. Falco's dry wit surfaces with puns and satirical asides, and the conversations are especially realistic—often with half sentences. Details of Roman art, architecture, military, etc. appear throughout." SLJ

Three hands in the fountain. Mysterious Press 1999 351p $30
ISBN 0-89296-691-2 LC 98-45058
First published 1997 in the United Kingdom

In this "mystery featuring Marcus Didius Falco, the Roman gumshoe teams with old friend Petronius Longus to discover who is assaulting and murdering young women during festival time and then tossing their chopped-up remains into the city's reservoirs." Libr J

"Davis weaves an intricate, irreverent plot filled with wittily imagined characters." Publ Wkly

Time to depart. Mysterious Press 1997 400p o.p.
LC 96-34381
First published 1995 in the United Kingdom

"When Balbinus Pius, a notorious underworld figure, is exiled from Rome by order of Emperor Vespasian, a power vacuum is created in the seamy underbelly of Roman society. While vice lords and hustlers scramble to claim a piece of Pius' territory, a virulent outbreak of crime sweeps the city, terrorizing honest citizens and infuriating the emperor. At the behest of Vespasian, Marcus Didius Falco, a renegade investigator with imperial ties, joins forces with staunch public officer Petronius Longus and launches an investigation. . . . An artfully crafted caper featuring plenty of suspense, comedy, and history." Booklist

Two for the lions. Mysterious Press 1999 390p o.p.
ISBN 0-89296-693-9 LC 99-19727
First published 1998 in the United Kingdom

In this adventure Falco "has a new gig: tax collector. Murder takes precedence, however, when Emperor Vespasian's executioner, a lion called Leonidas, is found dead. Falco follows the trail into the netherworld of gladiators and their handlers, called *lanista.* Meanwhile, Falco's patrician lover, Helena, must come to the aid of her black-sheep brother, who has run off to Tripoli, where the lanista buy their lions. Falco accompanies Helen to Africa, hoping to solve a family crisis and find a killer." Booklist

"The characterizations are terrific, the historical details are intriguing, and Falco is his rueful, wisecracking self." Libr J

Venus in copper; a Marcus Didius Falco novel. Crown 1992 c1991 277p o.p.
LC 91-37297
First published 1991 in the United Kingdom

A "mystery set in the Rome of Vespasian. Falco, the ancient equivalent of a private detective, ferrets out information for two nouveau-riche women about a 'professional bride' who wants to marry their husbands' business partner. When someone murders the partner, the fiancée hires Falco to find the murderer." Libr J

This novel "demonstrates Davis' solid historical knowledge as well as his quick wit." Booklist

Davis-Goff, Annabel

This cold country. Harcourt 2002 348p $31
ISBN 0-15-100847-7 LC 2001-3817

A "tale about a young English woman adjusting to new social, political and class demands when she moves to Ireland during World War II. A volunteer in England's Land Army, Daisy Creed works on a farm in Wales. Given the rare wartime occasion to meet an eligible bachelor, she quickly marries Patrick Nugent, a distant Anglo-Irish cousin of her employer. In a matter of days, Patrick is called on duty and Daisy joins Patrick's family in Ireland. Gothic touches abound; the Nugents are eccentrics, their home full of mysteries and reminders of better days." Publ Wkly

"A satisfying story told without sentimentality or melodrama but with a fine eye for detail." Booklist

Dawson, Carol, 1951-

The mother-in-law diaries; a novel. Algonquin Bks. 1999 284p $19.95
ISBN 1-56512-127-9 LC 98-27774

"When Lulu Penfield hears that her 19-year-old son, Treatie, has eloped, she takes the news badly. To her way of thinking, he has done the unspeakable: he's turned her into a mother-in-law, and she knows mothers-in-law. She's had four of them. Written in the form of a letter to Treatie, 'The Mother-in-Law Diaries' is Lulu's attempt to explain to her son what a crummy thing he's done to her. Thus she recounts her entire romantic history." N Y Times Book Rev

"When Lulu finally achieves insight about her sad marital record, it is to ruefully admit that she has been 'acting out the paradigm for an entire culture.' Meanwhile, the reader has bonded with an endearingly fallible heroine and traveled with her on a distinctive but also universal quest for happiness." Publ Wkly

Day, Cathy

The circus in winter; Cathy Day. 1st ed. Harcourt 2004 274p il $23
ISBN 0-15-101048-X LC 2003-25033

Contents: Wallace Porter; Jennie Dixianna; The last member of the Boela tribe; The circus house; Winnesaw; The Lone Star Cowboy; The Jungle Goolah Boy; The King and His Court; Boss man; The bullhook; Circus

Day, Cathy—*Continued*

people

In this "collection of interrelated short stories, [Day] succeeds in appropriating much of the garish pungency of the world of freaks, geeks and sideshow Houdinis without succumbing to its ready banalities. Although once or twice she treads close to cliche must the revelations of two-bit fortunetellers in fiction always turn out to be true? most of the time she steers clear of tired expectations. This is one circus act that doesn't rely on dependable gimmicks to keep the audience amused." N Y Times Book Rev

De Balzac, Honoré *See* Balzac, Honoré de, 1799-1850

De Beauvoir, Simone *See* Beauvoir, Simone de, 1908-1986

De Bernieres, Louis

Birds without wings; Louis de Bernieres. 1st American ed. Knopf 2004 553p $25.95

ISBN 1-400-04341-7 LC 2004-14529

"This novel tells of the inhabitants of a small coastal town in South West Anatolia in the dying days of the Ottoman empire: Iskander the Potter and fount of proverbial wisdom; Philothei, a Christian girl of legendary beauty who is courted almost from infancy by Ibrahim the Goatherd; . . . {and} Karatavuk and Mehmetcik, childhood friends who play in the hills above the town. . . . When jihad is declared against the Allies the young men of the town are sent to war. Karatavuk soon finds himself at Gallipoli where he experiences the . . . brutality of trench warfare, the loss of many comrades and of his own innocence." Publisher's note

"This epic about the tragedy of borders is likely to cross all borders, moving readers everywhere as it describes the harrowing cost of remaking faraway places in the image of our dreams." Christ Sci Monit

De Bernières, Louis, 1954-

Corelli's mandolin. Pantheon Bks. 1994 437p o.p.

LC 94-4783

"Set on the Greek island of Cephallonia, this . . . novel spans five decades beginning in the late 1930s just before the Axis forces occupy the island. . . . Corelli is an Italian army captain, a member of the first extraneous forces to occupy Cephallonia, and the lover of Pelagia Iannis. It is through Pelagia's voice that much of the story is revealed, but the chorus includes her father, various Greek villagers, Italian and Greek soldiers, and a goatherd." Libr J

The novel "has at times the rangy, expansive feeling of legend or saga, at other times the cozy intensities of chamber drama. The piece of Greek history it represents is composed of sufferings large and small, of national catastrophes and household agonies." N Y Times Book Rev

De Blasis, Celeste

The proud breed. Coward, McCann & Geoghegan 1978 571p o.p.

LC 77-20282

In this three-generational saga of old California, "beautiful Anglo-Spanish Tessa is rescued from a sadistic suitor by a handsome Yankee, Gavin—and theirs is to be a lifelong love affair only interrupted . . . when Gavin consorts with a whore because he can't bear the 'burden' of loving Tessa. They breed 'golden' palaminos on twin 'ranchos,' develop commercial enterprises in turbulent San Francisco (these are the bad old days of the Gold Rush, vigilante committees and anti-Chinese riots) and beget children, who keep the . . . story going by begetting other children." Publ Wkly

A season for Swans. Bantam Bks. 1989 676p o.p.

LC 88-37614

Concludes the Swan family trilogy

"Much of the action of this historical romance centers on the breeding and racing of thoroughbreds. . . . The novel opens dramatically with main character Gincie Culhane's murder of her brutal half-brother, Mark, followed by Gincie's and her family's flight to avoid prosecution. Then another tragedy shakes the family's foundation and threatens to destroy forever the family farm, Wild Swan, where many great thoroughbred racehorses were raised. A thoroughly engrossing, crisply told yarn spanning the final years of the nineteenth century, with a fine blend of historical realism and romantic imagination." Booklist

Swan's chance. Bantam Bks. 1985 547p o.p.

LC 85-5999

The second volume of the Swan family trilogy, follows Wild Swan (1984)

"Alexandria's world revolves around her beloved husband, her children and her horse farm in Maryland. Thoroughbred horse breeding and racing, carried on successfully after the death of her first husband, are important factors in Alex' life. The five children grow up, leave home to build their own lives and return to Wild Swan to share success, happiness and tragedy with their parents. Opposed to slavery, Alex and Rane run their farm and shipping business with free employees but nevertheless are touched by the political upheaval preceding the Civil War. The war brings hardships, tragedy and divided loyalties but the family is held together by a strong and caring Alex. Readers of family sagas, historic fiction and adult romance will find their preferences all in one very readable book." SLJ

De Crayencour, Marguerite *See* Yourcenar, Marguerite

De Hartog, Jan, 1914-2002

The captain. Atheneum Pubs. 1966 434p o.p.

"In 1942 Captain Martinus Harinxma, a Hollander escaped from the Nazis, is given command of a Dutch tugboat slated for convoy duty on the Iceland-Murmansk run. After the death of his liaison officer, complications pile up for the captain who becomes emotionally involved with the officer's widow. He also discovers that his ideas on war and heroism have changed drastically."

De Hartog, Jan, 1914-2002—*Continued*
Libr J

This sea story "is one of those rarities in contemporary fiction, a real spellbinder, a he-man story, full of action, in which the hero is brave and likeable. . . . The exposure and terror of that long and punishing convoy have never been so powerfully depicted. The art of this book lies in its unforced masculinity, for these men are real." Atlantic

The lamb's war. Harper & Row 1980 443p o.p.
LC 78-20201

The second volume in the author's trilogy about the Quakers

"This multifaceted novel . . . starts out in 1942 when the innocent 15-year-old Laura Martens arrives at a German concentration camp and demands to see her father. She does: the commandant rapes her in front of her gentle, Quaker father, who proceeds to attack the guards, who then beat him to death. She goes into shock, becomes amnesiac and lives for the next three years as the loving concubine of the SS doctor. This will always be her terrible, terrible guilt. A Quaker medic saves her from the camp, marries her out of sympathy and brings her to the U.S., where they become missionaries among a tribe of hostile Indians. There she begins to go mad until she learns to channel her rage and bitterness; she devotes the rest of her short life to saving the babies of the Third World." Publ Wkly

Followed by The peculiar people

The peaceable kingdom; an American saga. Atheneum Pubs. 1972 c1971 677p o.p.

This first volume in the author's trilogy about Quaker life "is set in England in 1652-53 and Pennsylvania in 1754-55. . . . In the first section, Margaret Fell, who falls in love with the Quaker preacher George Fox, must exorcise the passion of sexual desire in order to achieve grace. In her encounters she begins the work of reform in prisons, schools and mental institutions; in her progress she loses her property and possessions and is forced into prison. . . . In the second part of the novel, which takes place in colonial Pennsylvania, (there occur) Indian uprisings, massacres of Indians by whites, several murders of black slaves and ritual retribution by the blacks for the murders." N Y Times Book Rev

Followed by The lamb's war

The peculiar people; a novel. Pantheon Bks. 1992 321p o.p.
LC 92-11682

"A Cornelia & Michael Bessie book"

This novel is "set primarily in the American West of the 1830s, it concerns devout, individualistic members of the Religious Society of Friends . . . who struggle to put their ideals into practice as they confront divisive issues of human injustice. As they respond to the plights of slaves and American Indians—even as these issues divide their church—de Hartog's characters travel on private spiritual odysseys, grappling with doubts and profound personal weaknesses." Publ Wkly

Star of Peace; a novel of the sea. Harper & Row 1984 376p o.p.
LC 83-47552

"A Cornelia & Michael Bessie book"

"The hero of this novel, set in the summer of 1939, is Joris Kuiper, owner and captain of the small Dutch freighter 'Star of Peace.' Kuiper finds his recent rebirth through Christianity strongly challenged when his cargo—consisting of 250 Jews forced by the Nazis to emigrate from Germany—is refused admittance at the destination port in Uruguay or anywhere in North or South America. The novelist masterfully describes the tension aboard ship, focusing on key passengers and crew members as they each face the challenge in far different ways." Booklist

De Jonge, Peter *See* Jonge, Peter de

De Kretser, Michelle

The Hamilton case. Little, Brown and Co 2004 307p $24.95
ISBN 0-316-73548-5 LC 2003-60759

"Having come of age on the island nation of Ceylon, Sam Obeysekere is a lawyer whose life is guided by the British culture that dominates his homeland. . . . Sam's undoing arrives in the form of the Hamilton case, a scandalous murder that shakes the upper echelons of island society. Guided by grandiose visions of Sherlock Holmes, he becomes convinced he can solve the mysterious case-and that his good standing with the English will insulate him from the unrest the case has exposed." Publisher's note

"This is a miniature masterpiece of a mystery. . . . Obeysekere fancies himself a Holmesian observer in his own right and an instrument of English justice, but he can't see the treacherousness . . . of the territory he's treading. De Kretser's prose is stunning and subtle in depicting his downfall, evoking the glittering excesses of colonial life . . . and the tropical fecundity of Ceylon with equally irresistible power." Time

De la Mare, Walter, 1873-1956

Collected tales; chosen, and with an introduction, by Edward Wagenknecht. Knopf 1950 xxi, 467p o.p.

Contents: The riddle; The almond tree; In the forest; The talisman; Miss Duveen; The bowl; The tree; Ideal craftsman; Seaton's aunt; Lispet, Lispett and Vaine; Three friends; Willows; Missing; The connoisseur; The map; All Hallows; The wharf; The orgy; Cape Race; Physic; The trumpet; The creatures; The vats; Strangers and pilgrims

De la Roche, Mazo, 1879-1961

The building of Jalna. Little, Brown 1944 366p o.p.

"An Atlantic Monthly Press book"

"In this, the first volume, chronologically, in the Jalna series, the author goes back to the year 1850 and shows Adeline, the impulsive young wife with her blazing loyalty, and Captain Whiteoak, who sold his commission in order to migrate to the virgin country on the shore of Lake Ontario. Describes also the building of Jalna and the social life of the community." Ont Libr Rev

"In this, the first volume, chronologically, in the Jalna series, the author goes back to the year 1850 and shows Adeline, the impulsive young wife with her blazing loyalty, and Captain Whiteoak, who sold his commission in

De la Roche, Mazo, 1879-1961—*Continued*
order to migrate to the virgin country on the shore of Lake Ontario. Describes also the building of Jalna and the social life of the community." Ont Libr Rev

Centenary at Jalna. Little, Brown 1958 342p o.p.
"An Atlantic Monthly Press book"
Concluding volume in the author's Jalna series
"Traces the activities of the Whiteoak clan in the mid-fifties, a period climaxed by the one-hundredth anniversary celebration of Jalna, the oldest of the family residences. An alienated brother, a neurotic child, and a reluctant bride-to-be play stellar roles in an agreeably related though episodic tale of people to whom family ties and traditions are all-important." Booklist

Jalna. Little, Brown 1927 347p o.p.
"An Atlantic Monthly Press book"
Jalna is the family home of the Whiteoaks. Gathered under its roof are representatives of each generation from the time the grandparents drifted to Canada, via England from India and there built their homestead on a lavish scale. Renny, 37, is the present head of the household which includes Gran—a formidable old lady of 99—two uncles, an aunt, an elderly sister, and four half-brothers. An affectionate, warring group of strong personalities from the old lady down to Wakefield, the youngest, aged nine. Two of the boys marry and bring their wives home

De Lint, Charles, 1951-

Memory and dream. TOR Bks. 1994 400p o.p.
LC 94-21752
"A Tom Doherty Associates book"
"This is the story of a young Canadian artist whose paintings free (or unleash) ancient spirits into the modern world. The story moves from the spirit world into the everyday during a 20-year panorama of contemporary Ontario history." Booklist
The author's "multi-voiced, time-shifting narrative . . . beautifully evokes a sense of creative community, making it almost possible to believe that the rarified aesthetic atmosphere might well be capable of conjuring up a spirit or two." Publ Wkly

Someplace to be flying. TOR Bks. 1998 380p o.p.
ISBN 0-312-85849-3 LC 97-37443
"A Tom Doherty Associates book"
"A cab driver and a freelance photographer come together in the town of Newford to explore the existence of the mythical 'animal people' and discover the hidden world that lurks outside their normal perceptions. . . . DeLint's elegant prose and effective storytelling continue to transform the mundane into the magical at every turn." Libr J

Trader. TOR Bks. 1997 352p o.p.
ISBN 0-312-85847-7 LC 96-30646
"A Tom Doherty Associates book"
An urban fantasy set in the fictional "city of Newford. When quiet, responsible luthier Max Trader and egotistical loser Johnny Devlin wake up in each other's bodies, Max has a harder time dealing with it than Johnny, who had desperately wished for a change. Now homeless, Max receives help from a Native American fortune teller to get his life back." Libr J
"De Lint is a master at world building, at creating the apt image, and at making grippingly suspenseful a story in which the fate of the characters may have no cosmic significance but is vitally important to them and their closest friends." Booklist

De Loo, Tessa *See* Loo, Tessa de

De Moor, Margriet *See* Moor, Margriet de

De Saint-Aubin, Horace *See* Balzac, Honoré de, 1799-1850

De Saint-Exupéry, Antoine *See* Saint-Exupéry, Antoine de, 1900-1944

Dean, S. F. X.

It can't be my grave. Walker & Co. 1984 222p o.p.
LC 84-13192
First published 1983 in the United Kingdom
Professor Neil Kelly "is in London for the British publication of his surprise bestseller on the life of John Donne. There an old Oxford chum, now a famous thespian, and his actress wife tell Kelly of the possibility of running their own theater company devoted to lost plays by women writers and funded by tycoon Gordon Fairly. Sir Gordon, a man of power and charm, believes a 16th century female ancestor to have been the author of a newly found play attributed to Shakespeare or Marlowe, and wants to confirm her authorship. He offers Kelly a huge sum to play devil's advocate and prove his theories wrong, but before research can get under way, the rich man is murdered. . . . This mystery is worth reading for the sheer pleasure of its language." Publ Wkly

Deane, Seamus, 1940-

Reading in the dark. Knopf 1997 245p o.p.
ISBN 0-394-57440-0 LC 96-49635
First published 1996 in the United Kingdom
"A Catholic boy growing up hard by the border between Donegal and Derry is fascinated by the local ghost stories and neighborhood lore, and this fascination leads him to secrets at the heart of a family feud. His search for the truth runs through a labyrinth of Irish detours and delights: elaborate catechisms, mad poets, mute idiots, drunken hyperbole, deathbed revelations, and a clever reprisal involving an unwitting bishop." New Yorker

Deaver, Jeff

The bone collector; [by] Jeffery Deaver. Viking 1997 421p o.p.
LC 96-35457
"A brilliant forensics expert and ex-New York cop, Lincoln Rhyme wants to kill himself. Except he can't, not by himself. He is quadriplegic, able to move only his head, shoulders, and one finger. On the same day that Lincoln discusses his plight with a euthanasia doctor, some of his old police buddies show up at his door. A serial killer is on the loose, and Lincoln's help is needed. Reluctantly, he becomes involved. Helping him is Ame-

Deaver, Jeff—*Continued*
lia Sachs, a cop so pretty she could have been a model, who is new to crime-scene investigations. She becomes Lincoln's arms and legs. . . . Top-heavy with forensic details and police procedures, the work nonetheless offers suspenseful reading." Libr J

The Coffin Dancer. Simon & Schuster 1998 358p o.p.
ISBN 0-684-85285-3 LC 98-13537
Quadriplegic forensic specialist Lincoln Rhyme "is called in to track down a contract killer, known as the Coffin Dancer, who has been hired to eliminate three witnesses in the upcoming federal trial of Philip Hansen. The trial is set to begin just 48 hours from the novel's (literally) explosive beginning. Rhyme and his beautiful assistant, detective Amelia Sachs, have just that much time to ID the Dancer and keep him from murdering the remaining witnesses. . . . The pace, energized by Deaver's precise attention, never flags." Publ Wkly

The devil's teardrop; a novel of the last night of the century. Simon & Schuster 1999 296p o.p.
ISBN 0-684-85292-6 LC 99-26112
"When the FBI approaches former federal documents expert Parker Kincaid to assist with a ransom note asking for money to prevent massive killings in the Washington, DC, area, he hesitates. Kincaid has single-parented his children since his messy divorce from beautiful, unstable Joan. If she finds out he's taking dangerous risks by heading up the hunt for a genocidal killer, it could cost him custody. Assured that the FBI will keep him secret, Kincaid gets involved." Libr J

The empty chair. Simon & Schuster 2000 411p $25
ISBN 0-684-85563-1 LC 00-24220
Lincoln Rhyme "and his partner, Amelia Sachs, are in North Carolina to visit a hospital where a new experimental surgery technique might allow the paralyzed Lincoln partial use of his body. But something is going on in this town, and the authorities ask for his expertise. Two local girls have been kidnapped, and while the police know the culprit, they have no idea where the kidnapper has taken them. Lincoln is a fish out of water here, and it will take his complete forensic knowledge to find the two girls." Libr J
"Deaver is the master of the plot twist, and readers will only drive themselves crazy trying to outguess him. Better just to enjoy the ride. A magnificent thriller." Booklist

Garden of beasts; a novel of Berlin 1936; {by} Jeffery Deaver. Simon & Schuster 2004 404p $24.95
ISBN 0-7432-2201-6 LC 2004-45206
"Paul Schumann, a German American living in New York City in 1936, is a conscientious Mafia hit man known for agreeing to dispose of only the true dregs of society. When he is captured by the Feds, he is given an alternative to prison-travel to Berlin to assassinate Reinhardt Ernst, the man behind Nazi Germany's rearmament. Getting to know many of the locals while posing as a reporter covering the Olympics, Paul glimpses firsthand the horrors perpetrated by Hitler and his National Socialist Party. Finding himself the victim of a double-cross, Paul must choose between saving himself and completing his mission." Libr J
"Top Nazis, including Hitler, Himmler and Göring, make colorful cameos, but it's the smart, shaded-gray characterizations of the principals that anchor the exciting plot." Publ Wkly

A maiden's grave; [by] Jeffery Deaver. Viking 1995 422p o.p.
LC 95-21680
"Eight students and two teachers from a school for the deaf are kidnapped on a remote Kansas highway by three murderous escaped convicts. They are held hostage in an abandoned slaughterhouse for 18 hours while the FBI's top negotiator, Arthur Potter, attempts to secure their release. The situation is made more difficult because the leader of the convicts is as brilliant in his way as Potter is in his." Booklist
"Throughout, heartbreakingly real characters keep the wildly swerving plot from going off-track, even during the multiple-whammy twists that bring the novel . . . to its spectacular finish." Publ Wkly

The stone monkey; {by} Jeffery Deaver. Simon & Schuster 2002 425p o.p.
ISBN 0-7432-2199-0
This thriller's protagonist, "a quadriplegic forensics genius named Lincoln Rhyme who directs elaborate criminal investigations from his $3,000 customized bed, is the 'last hope' of government agencies clamoring for his aid in capturing the master criminal who sank a ship of illegal Chinese immigrants off the coast of Long Island. Rhyme's quarry, a sinister shapeshifter known as the Ghost, is 'probably the most dangerous human smuggler in the world,' and two desperate families will die if this fiend is not caught in the next 48 hours." N Y Times Book Rev

The vanished man; a Lincoln Rhyme novel; [by] Jeffrey Deaver. Simon & Schuster 2003 399p $25.95
ISBN 0-7432-2200-8 LC 2002-42826
In this thriller the "killer is a master magician who murders his victims in the style of classic magic acts. He is also able to change his appearance at will and plants evidence at the murder scenes to mislead the police. It is up to Rhyme and his paramour, cop Amelia Sachs, to sort out the few clues from manufactured ones." Libr J
"Among the crimes rendered with Deaver's customary grace and wit are sadistic variations on Houdini's Water Torture Cell, P. T. Selbit's neat trick of sawing a woman in half and one of Howard Thurston's animal acts, in which he brought a dead bird back to life." N Y Times Book Rev

Deaver, Jeffery *See* Deaver, Jeff

Deb, Siddhartha, 1970-

The point of return. Ecco Press 2003 304p $24.95
ISBN 0-06-050151-0 LC 2002-35300
This novel explores "what it was like to come of age in a provincial town during the nationalistic fervor in the time of Indira Gandhi's rule. Babu, the inquisitive son of a Bengali civil servant, grows up in a remote northeastern Indian state. His father, Dr. Dam, the director of the veterinary and dairy department of the state, was a prin-

Deb, Siddhartha, 1970-—*Continued*

cipled, devoted government official who grew up in the time of India's partition and fled with his family from East Pakistan, which became Bangladesh." Booklist

"To allow Dr. Dam to evolve through most of the book in a self-generated fog of benevolence and to shatter it in the last pages is a brillant stroke. . . . Storytelling of the kind Deb lavishes, for most of his book, on Dr. Dam is rare and precious and uplifting." N Y Times Book Rev

Dee, Ed

The con man's daughter; Ed Dee. Mysterious Press 2003 279p $23.95

ISBN 0-89296-794-3 LC 2003-50976

"Eddie Dunne's hands are swollen from fighting, his cell phone rings to the tune of 'When Irish Eyes Are Smiling,' and his spending money is in a metal box above his bathroom ceiling. Banished from the NYPD and retired from his job with the Russian mob, Eddie plays the ponies and baby-sits his six-year-old grandchild. Then, in the blink of an eye, his life is invaded when someone kidnaps his thirty-five-year-old daughter." Publisher's note

"Dee proves a sure hand when depicting the rough life of cops and criminals—and especially when creating Eddie Dunne, an amalgam of good and bad." Libr J

Dee, Jonathan

Palladio; a novel. Doubleday 2002 385p $24.95

ISBN 0-385-50179-X LC 2001-47174

"At the heart of this old-fashioned morality tale are two stories. Molly Howe, a pretty girl who knows how alluring silence can be, flees her bleak home town for Berkeley, circa 1989, and falls for an art-history student, John Wheelwright. Eight years later, John becomes the protégé of the imperious Malcolm Osbourne, who has founded a cutting-edge ad agency, Palladio—where, like characters in 'Cymbeline,' John and Molly are fated to meet again. Dee's skill in delineating loss and desire saves this extremely well-written book from its less successful attempts to skewer our material culture." New Yorker

Defoe, Daniel, 1661?-1731

A journal of the plague year. o.p.

First published 1722

An account "of the epidemic of bubonic plague in England during the summer and fall of 1665." Reader's Ency. 4th edition

Moll Flanders; with an introduction by John Mullan. Knopf 1991 xxxiii, 338p $19

ISBN 0-679-40548-8 LC 91-52994

"Everyman's library"

First published 1722. Variant title: The fortunes and misfortunes of the famous Moll Flanders

"This purports to be the autobiography of the daughter of a woman who had been transported to Virginia for theft soon after her child's birth. The child, abandoned in England, is brought up in the house of the compassionate mayor of Colchester. The story relates her seduction, her subsequent marriages and liaisons, and her visit to Virginia, where she finds her mother and discovers that she has unwittingly married her own brother. After leaving him and returning to England, she is presently reduced to destitution. She becomes an extremely successful pickpocket and thief, but is presently detected and transported to Virginia in company with one of her former husbands, a highwayman. With the funds that each has amassed they set up as planters, and Moll moreover finds that she has inherited a plantation from her mother. She and her husband spend their declining years in a atmosphere of prosperity and ostensible penitence." Oxford Companion to Engl Lit. 6th edition

Robinson Crusoe; with an introduction by John Mullan. Knopf 1992 xxxv, 261p $15

ISBN 0-679-40585-2 LC 91-52973

"Everyman's library"

First published 1719

"A minutely circumstantial account of the hero's shipwreck and escape to an uninhabited island, and the methodical industry whereby he makes himself a comfortable home. The story is founded on the actual experiences of Alexander Selkirk, who spent four years on the island of Juan Fernandez in the early 18th century." Lenrow. Reader's Guide to Prose Fic

Deighton, Len, 1929-

Berlin game. Knopf 1984 c1983 345p o.p.

LC 83-48104

The first volume of an espionage trilogy; other volumes are Mexico set and London match

British agent Bernard Samson must "help an undercover agent known as Brahms Four escape from East Berlin; unfortunately, a security leak high in the British organization threatens the continued success of the Brahms Four network." Libr J

This novel "is a decent entertainment that rattles swiftly along to its payoff. Two things especially recommend it—a devious contrivance of plot that has probably never been used before in an espionage novel; and the city of Berlin, mecca to spies and spy novelists. The second is the greater asset. Although the book is elaborately plotted, its best moments derive from the setting and from the force of this particular setting upon behavior and psychology." N Y Times Book Rev

also in Deighton, L. Game, set & match

Charity. HarperCollins Pubs. 1996 279p o.p.

LC 96-228083

In this final volume of the trilogy begun with Faith, and Hope, British agent Bernard Samson's "wife, Fiona, is back home after a dangerous flirtation with double-agentry that resulted in the tragic death of her sister, Tessa. Bernard, assigned to play second fiddle to head of station in Berlin, is frustrated at having to leave Fiona in London and his children in the care of Fiona's well-off parents. But Bernard has bigger problems: defending himself against the daily maneuverings for power, rationalizing the increasing emotional estrangement he feels from Fiona, intuiting subtle changes in his longtime mentor, and fending off his father-in-law's attempt to take custody of Bernard's kids. But most troubling of all is Bernard's feeling that something about Tessa's death [is suspicious]." Booklist

Deighton, Len, 1929-—*Continued*

City of gold. HarperCollins Pubs. 1992 375p o.p.

LC 92-52565

"City of Gold is Cairo, and the time is 1942. Rommel is on the move, and the city waits to see what will happen when he arrives. He has conquered Allied forces because somebody is feeding him information about their plans. A British captain is put in charge of an investigation to dig out the mole." N Y Times Book Rev

"Story lines concern not just the war but also black-market activities and the efforts of Jewish operatives to arm themselves for the anticipated battle for a homeland. Directing his varied characters and juggling his many subplots, Deighton demonstrates enviable legerdemain." Publ Wkly

Faith. HarperCollins Pubs. 1995 c1994 337p o.p.

LC 94-24663

First published 1994 in the United Kingdom

This novel "finds Samson leaving California to pick up VERDI, code name for a high-ranking East German Stasi officer who may be defecting to Britain's SIS. The operation goes disastrously wrong during a shoot-out in East Germany, but Samson manages to get back to London, where he encounters real danger and fighting: the take-no-prisoners politicking within the SIS, involving Samson, his duplicitous wife and a slew of internal enemies and possible friends. Deighton's penchant for explosive violence, telling detail and throwaway humor . . . are much in evidence here, and readers will enjoy some of the finest intramural politicking since C.P. Snow." Publ Wkly

Followed by Hope

Funeral in Berlin; a novel. Putnam 1965 c1964 312p o.p.

First published 1964 in the United Kingdom

A spy story in which a British agent is involved in smuggling a Russian scientist out of East Berlin with the connivance of a Russian security officer and a German contact man whose loyalties and motives are questionable

The author "writes well of the circles within circles at international crossroads where enemies can be closer than friends, and where horror and humor follow the agent." Libr J

Game, set & match. Knopf 1989 857p il o.p.

LC 88-45258

This omnibus edition first published 1986 in the United Kingdom. Each title is entered separately

Contents: Berlin game; Mexico set; London match

Hope. HarperCollins Pubs. 1996 295p o.p.

ISBN 0-06-017696-2 LC 95-44143

First published 1995 in the United Kingdom

In this second volume of the trilogy that began with Faith "it is the winter of 1987. Samson's brother-in-law, George Kosinski, has disappeared and Samson is stuck with his irascible boss, Dicky Cruyer, following leads across Poland's raw and inhospitable terrain. They trek from the Kosinski country estate, where Nazi tunnels and bunkers lurk for miles, to the black-market bazaars of Warsaw, where reality becomes dreamlike." Libr J

"Deighton gives readers unfamiliar with Samson's troubled life plenty of background information, so newcomers as well as old series hands should take equal pleasure in this subtly intense offering by perhaps the only author other than le Carré who deserves to be known as 'spymaster.'" Publ Wkly

Followed by Charity

The Ipcress file. Simon & Schuster 1963 c1962 287p o.p.

First published 1962 in the United Kingdom

"A British secret-service agent is assigned to help recover a kidnapped biochemist. The international intrigue, involving brainwashing, spies, and counter-spies of uncertain loyalties, takes the agent from London to the Far East, to an atomic test site in the Pacific, and behind the Iron Curtain." Shapiro. Fic for Youth. 3d edition

London match. Knopf 1985 i.e. 1986 407p o.p.

LC 85-40454

In this concluding volume of the Berlin-based trilogy "Agent Bernie Samson is faced with yet another problem. While one mole—Bernie's former wife—has been flushed from the London office, the Soviet defector's debriefing indicates there may be yet another double agent still operating. Bernie, of course, is a likely suspect, but this would be too obvious and, besides, there are numerous candidates for the office turncoat. Who could it be? Or could it be a cunning piece of subterfuge to further disrupt British intelligence gathering?" Booklist

"The strength of (this novel) is not in its plot but its characterization. . . . Mr. Deighton portrays each character of his large cast fully and sympathetically. However, the best character is the city of Berlin. It is a living presence, and in some of the descriptions one can almost hear the stones breathing." N Y Times Book Rev

also in Deighton, L. Game, set & match

Mexico set. Knopf 1985 373p o.p.

LC 84-48500

The second volume of the spy trilogy that began with Berlin game

"Fiona Samson—wife of our hero, British agent Bernard Samson—has defected to the KGB and become a diabolical alter ego to her husband, anticipating his moves and countermoves in ways only a spouse can do." Booklist

"Deighton displays prodigious talent here: while portraying sharply defined, sympathetic, and down-to-earth characters, he slowly but inexorably revs up the plot for a thoroughly exciting and satisfying conclusion." Libr J

also in Deighton, L. Game, set & match

Spy hook; a novel. Knopf 1988 291p o.p.

LC 88-11461

The first volume in a second spy trilogy featuring Bernard Samson

"Samson's story begins with a fruitless meeting in Washington with former colleague Jim Prettyman, who denies any knowledge of the slush fund Samson has been ordered to trace. Over half a million pounds is missing from money allocated to Bret Rensselear of the German desk by London Central before he was shot in Berlin. Later, in London, Samson learns at a briefing that Prettyman has been killed, another 'incident' pressuring Samson's superiors to widen his investigation in East and West Berlin and eventually in France. All the people he questions—even trusted friends—deepen Samson's fears that Central is using him to bait their own hook." Publ

Deighton, Len, 1929-—*Continued*

Wkly

"The entertainment lies in Deighton's eye for detail—landscape, fashion, cuisine, idiom—and in the sudden menace that erupts from the small talk and the brand names." Booklist

Spy line; a novel. Knopf 1989 291p o.p.

ISBN 0-394-55179-6 LC 89-45302

Second volume of the trilogy that started with Spy hook. The novel opens "with Samson in Berlin, a fugitive from England where the intelligence service accused him of spying for the Soviets. With the CIA and KGB also menacing him, Samson is suddenly cleared of the charge of treason and returned to London and to warm welcomes from colleagues, his lover Gloria and his children. The situation changes, however, when he's sent on a 'simple' mission to Vienna and a deep-cover meeting with Fiona." Publ Wkly

Spy sinker. Harper & Row 1990 374p o.p.

LC 89-46568

"A Cornelia & Michael Bessie book"

Final volume of the second spy trilogy featuring Bernard Samson

In this novel Bernard Samson, "steps backstage as his wife, Fiona, defects to East Germany after being groomed as a double agent. In place, Fiona is set to implement a plan facilitating the westward defection of East German professionals, leaving a gap in the economic structure which is expected to defeat the Communist regime." Publ Wkly

SS-GB: Nazi-occupied Britain 1941; a novel. Knopf 1979 343p o.p.

LC 78-14563

First published 1978 in the United Kingdom

"The King of England is a prisoner in the Tower, the Queen and Princesses have fled to Australia, Winston Churchill has been executed by a German firing squad, and the SS is in charge of Scotland Yard. Detective Superintendent Douglas Archer has started work on what seems to be a routine murder case until an SS official from Himmler's own staff comes to supervise the investigation. Archer finds himself involved in a resistance effort involving wealthy collaborators, high-level scientists, rivalry between the German military and the SS factions, and an attempt to remove King George from the Tower of London to the United States." Shapiro. Fic for Youth. 3d edition

XPD. Knopf 1981 339p o.p.

LC 80-7629

The plot involves "a face-to-face meeting between Winston Churchill and Adolf Hitler. Time: 1940. Place: a Belgian bunker. Topic: the surrender of Britain. . . . So sensitive is the clandestine rendezvous—one of the terms discussed is Nazi control of Ireland—that even two generations later, anyone who learns of it is marked for XPD—Expedient Demise. When the Führer's minutes of the affair threaten to surface, counter-intelligence launches a relentless search from Hollywood to Hamburg." Time

"Deighton's attention to detail and his appreciation of the delicacies of international politics give his book a plausibility too often lacking in spy novels." Best Sellers

Del Vecchio, John M., 1948-

The 13th valley; a novel. Bantam Bks. 1982 606p il o.p.

LC 81-70920

This Vietnam war novel "tells the story of a major combat assault by an infantry unit during August 1970. The narrative focuses on three men: Brooks, a black lieutenant who has just received divorce papers from his wife; Egan, a cynical platoon sergeant counting the days left in his tour of duty; and Chery, his new radio man, very scared, very eager, and very naive." Libr J

"The novel is almost documentary in style and conveys to an extraordinary degree the very 'feel' of ground combat in I Corps. . . . Two elements in this well-written novel are especially praiseworthy: the depiction of the explosive relations between white and black GIs, and the moral corruption by war of a decent, sensitive young man. . . . Despite the presence of too much historical exposition, this is one of the finest novels to come out of the Vietnam War." Publ Wkly

Carry me home. Bantam Bks. 1994 719p o.p.

LC 93-31585

In this novel "Del Vecchio focuses on veterans who returned home in the late '60s only to find themselves viewed largely as lepers. Back from his second tour in Vietnam, Marine Sgt. Tony Pisano, 20, bears a leg wound, is assigned to burial detail, marries student nurse Linda, tries out college and faces widespread hatred. Tony's story, central to the novel, melds with that of his doomed buddies, who are now rootless 'expatriates' in their own country. More grounded is the also returned Capt. Robert Wapinski, whose Pennsylvania farm becomes a haven for many vets fighting public castigation, post-traumatic stress disorder and the effects of Agent Orange." Publ Wkly

"Unabashedly polemical, often veering off into melodrama, the narrative is redeemed by its passionate affection for these soldiers who are attempting to build new lives." N Y Times Book Rev

For the sake of all living things. Bantam Bks. 1990 790p o.p.

LC 89-28066

In this novel "Samnang is an 11-year-old Cambodian peasant who is conscripted into the Khmer Rouge and rises, through brutal training and savage combat, to a position of leadership. His sister Vathana is also separated from their father, Chhuon, and grows up to marry a Frenchified heroin addict from Cambodia's upper class. As her country falls deeper and deeper into civil war, she goes to work in a hospital for refugees. There she meets and falls in love with an American Special Forces officer, John Sullivan, an adviser to the Cambodian military who has few illusions about that army's—or indeed his own nation's—ability to win." N Y Times Book Rev

"While interspersed reports filed by Special Forces Cpt. John Sullivan, Vathana's lover, put events in political perspective, this exhaustive, emotionally powerful novel ends on a note of desperate irony that sums up the Kafkaesque absurdity of Cambodia's torment." Publ Wkly

Delany, Samuel R.

Stars in my pocket like grains of sand. Bantam Bks. 1984 384p o.p.
LC 84-45180

This far future novel is the "dual story of Rat Korga, a slave and the last survivor of his devastated world, and Marq Dyeth, an industrial diplomat who introduces Korga to a future galaxy consisting of 6,000 human- and alien-inhabited planets." Booklist

"Reading this novel is like learning another language, only to realize how much it teaches you about your own, and how relative it makes your cultural assumptions." Publ Wkly

Time considered as a helix of semi-precious stones
In The Best of the Nebulas p329-57

Delbanco, Nicholas

What remains. Warner Bks. 2000 200p o.p.
ISBN 0-446-52416-6 LC 00-39895

The author presents a "portrait of a Jewish family with artistic and intellectual inclinations. The story encompasses several generations: Elsa, the proud and slightly eccentric matriarch; her sons Karl, who takes over the family business when his father dies, and Gustave, who is more interested in art; Karl's wife, Julia; and their little son, Jacob. Forced to leave their comfortable life in Hamburg when Hitler comes to power, they settle first in London. Not long after the war, Karl moves his family again, this time to America, and he sets up a branch of the family business." Booklist

"The mood is elegiac, meditative, yet delicate: a Chopin nocturne, perhaps, played out in words. The horror, the melodrama, is always held back. The memory and effects of the Holocaust are ever present but never dwelled on." N Y Times Book Rev

Delderfield, R. F. (Ronald Frederick), 1912-1972

Give us this day. Simon & Schuster 1973 767p o.p.

Sequel to Theirs was the kingdom

This third volume of the Swann family saga opens with Victoria's centennial celebration and closes with "the beginning of World War I. Against the background of Edwardian social and political history, Delderfield presents a third generation, the offspring of Adam and Henrietta, whose ventures, at times, become almost melodramatic. The characters are very real, especially Adam and his wife who are shown growing older and looking back over the years. In spite of some unneeded repetition of events, this is well written, good entertainment." Libr J

God is an Englishman. Simon & Schuster 1970 687p o.p.

The action, which takes place between 1857 and 1866, centers on the career of Adam Swann who returns from army service in the Crimea and in India to found a network of freight-hauling coaches bearing the name Swann-on-Wheels, and to marry Henrietta Rawlinson, daughter of a local mill owner. The vicissitudes of Swann's life mirror the ambition and enterprise that brought success to some amid the poverty of many during the period

Followed by Theirs was the kingdom

The green gauntlet. Simon & Schuster 1968 475p o.p.

This sequel to A horseman riding by follows the fortunes of the Craddock family from the Second World War through the postwar years, depicting three decades of modern English life

A horseman riding by. Simon & Schuster 1967 c1966 1150p o.p.

First published 1966 in the United Kingdom

Paul Craddock, a young soldier, returns from the Boer War, comes into a substantial inheritance and purchases a rundown Devonshire estate, consisting of seven tenancies. The story concerns the revitalization of the property by the new owner, the vicissitudes of the seven families that are his tenants, and the richly fulfilled life of the Squire, himself, and his family

Followed by The green gauntlet

Theirs was the kingdom. Simon & Schuster 1971 798p o.p.

This sequel to God is an Englishman "relates the careers of Swann, his indefatigable wife, and nine children. . . . Whereas Swann himself had been the dominant figure, the 'God' in 'God is an Englishman', the sequel turns to his satellites—to his enterprising children, who illustrate various facets of the Victorian scene, and to his business associates, who represent degrees of devotion and repulsion to the inevitability of change." Choice

Followed by Give us this day

To serve them all my days. Simon & Schuster 1972 638p o.p.

Concerns "the boys and masters of a West Country English public school in the years between World War I and II. . . . The central character is David Powlett-Jones, a shell-shocked youngster fresh from the Western Front, when we first meet him; a compassionate headmaster, whose personal life has known its full share of drama, sorrow and love, when we part company with him. In between, Mr. Delderfield has some eminently sane and sensible points to make about what education for life is really like. Academic rivalries, some bitter and vengeful; the loneliness of a small boy whose parents have no real feeling for him, and of a small girl whose mother and twin have died tragically; the development of an intense love affair between a mature man and woman are all elements in the storytelling." Publ Wkly

"Here is a schoolmaster's cavalcade of England between World Wars, told in the author's best stand-up style, and rife with episodes designed to pluck at the heartstrings." N Y Times Book Rev

Delderfield, Ronald Frederick *See* Delderfield, R. F. (Ronald Frederick), 1912-1972

DeLillo, Don

The body artist; a novel. Scribner 2001 124p o.p.
ISBN 0-7432-0395-X LC 00-58842

DeLillo, Don—*Continued*

"A young widow discovers that a dishevelled, vaguely autistic man has somehow taken up residence in her spare room—and that her dead husband's spirit may or may not be inhabiting her new boarder. This is a fertile premise—the novel plays with questions of identity, presence, ritual, memory, and sanity, and uses those questions to investigate the larger mystery of death—but the book's brevity forces DeLillo to treat his themes sketchily, and at times with an uncharacteristic sentimentality." New Yorker

Cosmopolis; a novel. Scribner 2003 209p $25
ISBN 0-7432-4424-9 LC 2002-30540

"Most of the action takes place inside a 'prousted' (cork-lined) stretch limo, as the reclusive financial wizard Eric Packer is chauffeured across Manhattan for a haircut. Thanks to a presidential visit, antiglobalization demonstrations, and a celebrity funeral, this journey takes up most of the day." Libr J

"DeLillo, master novelist and seer, tells the surreal, electrifying story of this dehumanized moneyman in English scrubbed so clean and assembled so exquisitely it seems like a new language." Booklist

Libra. Viking 1988 456p o.p.
LC 87-40649

DeLillo's "novel is his own personal vision—though anchored well enough in historical actuality—of what really was behind Lee Harvey Oswald's gun blasts from the book depository that day in Dallas. DeLillo follows Oswald through the marines and during his defection to the Soviet Union, as well as positing a scenario for how he came to be the vehicle for delivering the anti-Castro blow that resulted in Kennedy's death." Booklist

This novel "provokes the reader with its clever use of history, its dramatic pacing and its immaculate and detailed construction." Publ Wkly

The names. Knopf 1982 339p o.p.
ISBN 0-394-52814-X LC 82-48012

"Self-absorbed, rootless James Axton is a 'risk analyst' for insuring multinational corporations against political hazards. His ambiguous world—defined by an estranged family and the Iranian revolution—is bizarrely highlighted by the advent of an elusive ritual murder cult, 'The Names.' His compulsion to track down the meaning of the cult (it matches the initials of victims and place names) leads him as far off as India, and deep into 'memory, solitude, obsession, death.'" Libr J

"Nearly every page testifies to DeLillo's exceptional gifts as a writer." New Republic

Ratner's star. Knopf 1976 437p o.p.
ISSN 0-394-40083-6
LC 75-36808

This is a "grim, surreal novel, it's protagonist a 14-year-old mathematical genius and Nobel laureate, Billy Twillig, whose mission is to decode the message of a star and to invent a mathematical language to answer it." Oxford Companion to Am Lit. 6th edition

Underworld. Scribner 1997 827p o.p.
ISBN 0-684-84269-6 LC 97-13825

"On October 3, 1951, there occurred two 'shots heard round the world'—Bobby Thomson's last-minute homer, which sent the N.Y. Giants into the World Series, and a Soviet atomic bomb test. The fallout from these two events provides the nexus for this sagalike rumination on the last 50 years of American cultural history." Libr J

"The dialogue is a rockingly comic attack on our mental excreta: the distortions and sound bites of the television age. DeLillo was absent from his fiction before, an unbodied intelligence, but here is an undertow of personal pain he has never touched. This is his most demanding novel and yet his most transparent, giving the reader the privileged intimacy that comes from seeing a writer whole." N Y Times Book Rev

White noise. Viking 1985 326p o.p.
LC 84-40375

"An Elisabeth Sifton book"

"The chairperson of the department of Nazi studies at a midwestern college aches to escape the inevitable path of decline and death; a 'toxic event' that releases a dangerous cloud of pollution gives him the chance to break free in previously uncontemplated ways." Booklist

This "is a stunning performance from one of our finest and most intelligent novelists. DeLillo's reach is broad and deep, combining acute observation of the textures of American life and analytic rigor." New Repub

Delinsky, Barbara, 1945-

Coast road; a novel. Simon & Schuster 1998 365p o.p.
ISBN 0-684-84576-8 LC 98-24113

"Jack McGill's feelings for his artist ex-wife, Rachel, are put to the acid test when he receives news that she is lying comatose in a hospital after an automobile accident. Jack, a rising San Francisco architect and workaholic, still does not understand why Rachel left him and took their two daughters to live in Big Sur country, but he assumes the parental role for the teenage girls and moves into Rachel's house. Jack's second chance at being a real father is fraught with confrontations." Libr J

Flirting with Pete; a novel. Scribner 2003 355p $26
ISBN 0-7432-4642-X LC 2003-42721

"Therapist Casy Ellis knew she was a product of a one-night stand between her mother (now comatose) and her renowned psychologist father. But she never met him, and he never acknowledged her until after his death, when he left her his mortgage-free townhouse in Boston's upscale Beacon Hill. Casey has every intention of selling it and reaping a sizable nest egg, but circumstances cause her to linger. When she discovers writings about a young woman named Jenny Clyde among her father's belongings, she is determined to find out more about Jenny and to understand the father she never knew." Libr J

"Seamlessly and compassionately weaving Jenny's unsettling past with Casey's uncertain future. Delinsky delivers a scintillating study of each woman's search for answers and absolution." Booklist

For my daughters. HarperCollins Pubs. 1994 290p o.p.
LC 94-2233

"When Virginia St. Clair was a young married woman, she fell in love with the gardener of her vacation house in Maine. At the end of the summer, she chose duty to her husband over love and emotionally estranged herself from everyone who entered her life. Her three daughters,

Delinsky, Barbara, 1945-—*Continued*
born after that summer, suffered the most. Now, at 70, Virginia decides to correct her mistakes. She purchases her former vacation home in Maine and invites her daughters to join her there." Booklist
"Delinsky develops her characters well and creates a strong sense of place with beautiful, evocative descriptions of the landscapes." Libr J

Lake news. Simon & Schuster 1999 380p o.p.
ISBN 0-684-86432-0
"Falsely implicated in a scandal by an unscrupulous reporter, Lily Blake returns to Lake Henry, her small New England hometown. She is devastated by the loss of her job, privacy, and reputation and struggles to regain control of her life. Although distrustful of the media, she is drawn to John Kipling, the editor of the local *Lake News*. A wounded soul himself, Kip has also returned home to exorcise personal demons. Together they find justice for Lily and healing for themselves." Libr J
The author "plots this satisfying, gentle romance with the sure hand of an expert, scattering shady pasts and dark secrets among some of her characters, while giving others destructive family patterns and difficult family dynamics to contend with." Publ Wkly

The summer I dared; a novel; Barbara Delinsky. Simon & Schuster 2004 355p $24.95
ISBN 0-7432-4643-8 LC 2004-45339
The "tale of three people quite literally thrown together following a boating accident off the Maine coast that spares them while taking the lives of nine others. At 40 Julia is an obedient wife, dutiful daughter, and devoted mother, and has planned a visit to her aunt Zoe to reflect on her obligation to herself versus her ties to her family. Rescued by fellow passenger Noah Prine, Julia feels connected to him by virtue of their shared tragedy while also being drawn to Kim Colella, the other survivor, whose whereabouts at the time of the crash provide a shadowy subplot. As a gentle romance blossoms between Julia and Noah, each evaluates who they were before the accident and who they hope to become in its aftermath. Once again, Delinsky excels at combining a compelling mystery with an insightful portrayal of captivating people facing challenges both ordinary and dramatic." Booklist

A woman's place; a novel. HarperCollins Pubs. 1997 358p o.p.
LC 96-41299
"Clair Raphael has a less-than-admirable spouse, yet she is doing her best to be a superwoman, catering to her beloved children and husband and in her spare time building a $20 million business called WickerWise. Returning home from a visit to her dying mother, she finds her children at her in-laws and is presented with a court order to vacate the house and to stay away from the children. Dennis wants a divorce, the house, full custody of the children, a hefty alimony, and half of the business. Add a chauvinistic judge and a biased family court adviser to the mix, and the result is fast and furious reading to see what happens next." Libr J

DeMarinis, Rick, 1934-

Borrowed hearts; new and selected stories. Seven Stories Press 1999 322p $24
ISBN 1-88836-398-3 LC 98-55233
Contents: Under the wheat; Billy Ducks among the pharaohs; Life between meals; The smile of a turtle; Weeds; The handgun; Disneyland; Romance: a prose villanelle; Your story; Pagans; Your burden is lifted, love returns; Medicine man; Safe forever; Paraiso: an elegy; An airman's goodbye; Aliens; Horizontal snow; Wilderness; The Voice of America; Insulation; Borrowed hearts; A romantic interlude; Experience; Fault lines; Feet; Hormone X; Novias; On the lam; Sieze the day; The boys we were, the men we became; The singular we
"Dark humor, cosmic danger, and unglamorous romance snake through DeMarinis' compelling short stories." Booklist

Sky full of sand. Dennis McMillan 2003 250p $30
ISBN 0-939767-47-3
In this novel, set in El Paso, Uriah Walkinghorse is "suspended somewhere between a 'normal' existence and a descent into the bizarre and desperate world that surrounds him. Strained but strong ties still bind him to his odd assortment of adopted siblings—black and white and Korean—who include a school principal, an addict, a delivery driver and a corporate lawyer. At 42, he has lost his wife, abandoned his quest for a master's and manages derelict apartments of derelicts in exchange for rent. His one accomplishment was a bodybuilding title, Mr. West Side, and he still maintains a diet and exercise program. DeMarinis's exceptionally sharp wit slashes through the prose as Uri undertakes an odyssey through a world of kinky sex, drugs, high finance and the most vicious, most wasted dregs of humanity on either side of the border." Publ Wkly

Demetz, Hanna

The house on Prague Street; by Hana Demetz; translated from the German by the author. St. Martin's Press 1980 186p o.p.
LC 79-27312
Original German edition, 1970
This autobiographical novel tells the story of Helene Richter whose "adolescence in wartime Czechoslovakia coincides with the Holocaust, which intrudes more and more insistently into her life until its . . . violence destroys her romantic dreams. The house on Prague Street symbolizes her loss of innocence. At first the serene family homestead, it eventually shelters survivors of Auschwitz whose only familial ties are their shared memories of horror." SLJ

DeMille, Nelson

The charm school. Warner Bks. 1988 533p o.p.
LC 87-34637
"On an unorthodox vacation trip to Russia, Gregory Fisher, a young American tourist, stumbles onto a secret. . . . In a place called Mrs. Ivanova's Charm School, young Russians are being taught to imitate American citizens. And their instructors, none of whom have volunteered for the job, are Americans. . . . *The Charm School* offers much in the way of action and adventure, but the novel is more than an 'Us vs. Them' shoot 'em up. It is also a fascinating psychological study, one that forces the reader to ponder the true roles of good and evil, in connection with the individual mind as well as with international relations." West Coast Rev Books

DeMille, Nelson—*Continued*

The general's daughter. Warner Bks. 1992 454p o.p.
LC 91-51174

"Paul Brenner, a warrant officer in the army's criminal investigation unit, reluctantly teams with an old flame, Cynthia Sunhill, to investigate the murder of Captain Ann Campbell. Ann's body has been staked down with tent pegs on a rifle range; she's naked but she hasn't been brutalized. She's the daughter of a famous general, just back from the Gulf War, and she's also the Army's poster girl, a graduate with honors from West Point. And yet her chosen specialty, psychological operations, has raised some eyebrows, and Brenner and Sunhill soon discover other dark secrets about her." Booklist

"Characterization in general is fuzzy, though DeMille captures the often unquestioning regimen of life on a military base." Publ Wkly

The Gold Coast. Warner Bks. 1990 500p o.p.
LC 89-40465

"What happens to a priggish, WASPy, disillusioned Wall Street lawyer when a Mafia crime boss moves into the mansion next door in his posh Long Island neighborhood? He ends up representing the gangster on a murder rap and even perjures himself so the mafioso can be released on $5 million bail. . . . Attorney John Sutter has problems that would daunt even Fitzgerald's Jay Gatsby. His marriage is crumbling, despite kinky sex games with his self-centered wife, Susan, who's the mistress of his underworld client Frank Bellarosa. The IRS is after Sutter, and his law firm wants to dump him." Publ Wkly

"What makes 'The Gold Coast' glitter is Nelson DeMille's sharp evocation of the vulpine Bellarosa and of Sutter, a wonderfully sardonic, self-mocking man betrayed by a midlife crisis. In his way, Mr. DeMille . . . is as keen a social satirist as Edith Wharton." NY Times Book Rev

The lion's game; a novel. Warner Bks. 2000 677p $36
ISBN 0-446-52065-9

NYPD homicide detective John Corey, "now a special contract agent for the Federal Anti-Terrorist Task Force, is on the trail of a Libyan terrorist known as the Lion who vanished after arriving at New York's JFK Airport on a 747 filled with corpses. While the FBI and CIA think Asad Khalil has returned to Europe, Corey believes otherwise and teams up with Kate Mayfield, a leggy blonde FBI agent, to track Khalil down." Libr J

"DeMille artfully constructs a compulsively readable thriller around a troubling story line, slowly developing his villain from a faceless entity into a nation's all-too-human nemesis." Publ Wkly

Plum Island. Warner Bks. 1997 511p o.p.
LC 97-7221

"On Long Island's North Fork, . . . roguish NYPD bad-boy detective John Corey assists the local police chief at a crime scene that features a house deck garnished with a married couple dead of clean head shots. Investigators suppose that the pair, researchers at a heavily guarded lab on Plum Island, were involved in smuggling a viral antidote. But Corey, unpersuaded, soon discovers that local history and buried-treasure lore fascinated the victims." Booklist

"Key to the novel's sway is its boisterous plot, as DeMille expertly melds medical mystery, police procedural and nautical adventure, adding assorted love interests and capping matters with a ferocious storm at sea." Publ Wkly

Spencerville. Warner Bks. 1994 481p o.p.
LC 94-25759

"Keith Landry, his Cold War intelligence job a victim of the Soviet collapse, returns to the little Ohio town where he grew up and begins to tinker with thoughts of reviving the family farm. A former sweetheart, Annie, despondent after Keith went off to Vietnam, had married aggressive, good-looking Cliff Baxter on the rebound, but Keith and Annie had never ceased to correspond. Now that he's back, the old interest is rekindled in both, but Baxter, now police chief and a womanizing petty tyrant, is fiercely jealous—and the novel takes off as a deadly struggle between a man trained in the arts of deception and one with all the built-in advantages of police power in a remote spot." Publ Wkly

Up country. Warner Bks. 2002 706p o.p.
ISBN 0-446-51657-0 LC 2001-26414
Sequel to The general's daughter

Retired warrant officer Paul Brenner "is asked by his former boss in the U.S. Army's Criminal Investigation Division to go to Vietnam to find Tran Van Vinh, a North Vietnamese soldier who witnessed the murder of one American by another. . . . His first contact in Hanoi is Susan Weber, an expat who's a banker by day but who dreams of living more adventurously by night. Bright, well versed in local customs, and fluent in Vietamese, Susan convinces Paul to take her along as he attempts to find Vinh. Following a circuitous path as it becomes clear that there is much more at stake than a cold murder case. . . . DeMille's portrayal of the cocky soldier returning to enemy soil is moving and realistic." Booklist

Word of honor. Warner Bks. 1985 518p o.p.
LC 85-40005

A fictional version of the "My Lai massacre and the trial of Lieutenant William F. Calley. Calley's counterpart in this fictional account is Ben Tyson, a much-decorated Vietnam veteran and former Army lieutenant. One morning, on the way to work as an electronics executive in New York City, Tyson learns that a book has just been published about a military massacre at a French hospital in Hue, Vietnam. The book unhesitatingly accuses Tyson of staging the attack against nuns, children, and other civilians, and wounded soldiers on February 15, 1968. Based on evidence contained in the book and on testimony given by two of Tyson's former platoon members, the Army recalls Tyson to active duty in order to try him for murder." Booklist

"The flashbacks to Hue, the pre-trial investigation (involving an attractive female major), the court-martial proceedings, the emotions of the principal characters and the soul-sickness wrought by war (which is the story's effective subtext)—all are depicted with marvelous vividness." Publ Wkly

Denker, Henry

Mrs. Washington and Horowitz, too; a novel. Morrow 1993 333p o.p.

LC 92-32877

Sequel to Horowitz and Mrs. Washington (1979)

This is a "love story about a cantankerous 70ish widowed businessman and a sixtysomething widow. They become involved through the machinations of the marvelously manipulative black nurse, Mrs. Washington. She bullied Horowitz to recovery after his stroke and now works to help him recover his sense of purpose and self-worth. Harriet Washington involves Horowitz as a volunteer in the neonatal unit of Harlem Hospital, where he cares, sometimes too much, for the unloved, abandoned crack babies. In fact, he almost loses his job. But Mrs. Mendelson's help (engineered by the matchmaking Mrs. Washington) gets him reinstated. When the couple decides to marry, their children react with typical hostility. Mrs. Washington handles this, too. A very warm and true-to-life depiction of older persons." Libr J

This child is mine; a novel. Morrow 1995 330p o.p.

LC 94-32360

"Christie and Bill Salem, a couple whose son has died of SIDs (sudden infant death syndrome), find themselves unable to conceive and, so, adopt a baby born to a single mother named Lori Adams. Lori has refused her boyfriend's offers of marriage, deciding that it would ruin his acting career. Later, Lori and the child's birth father, Brett Manning (now a major soap opera star), decide to marry and he applies for custody of their child." Booklist

Dennis, Patrick, 1921-1976

Auntie Mame; an irreverent escapade. Vanguard Press 1955 280p o.p.

"A fond and somewhat baffled nephew reminisces about the aunt who guided his young footsteps in her unorthodox, inimitable fashion. Auntie Mame lived wholeheartedly in phases; whether she was being show girl, shopgirl, Southern belle, tweedy authoress, college widow, or society matron, she played each part to the hilt. Life with Auntie Mame was infinitely entertaining and unpredictable." Booklist

Followed by Around the world with Auntie Mame (1958)

DeRosso, H. A. (Henry Andrew), 1917-1960

Riders of the shadowlands; western stories; edited by Bill Pronzini. Five Star 1999 229p o.p.

ISBN 0-7862-1329-9 LC 98-42377

"Five Star standard print western series"

Contents: Killer; The ways of vengeance; Fear in the saddle; The return of the Arapaho Kid; Witch; Dark purpose; The happy death; Bad blood; Endless trail; Riders of the shadowlands

These 10 tales are "arranged chronologically and by theme: honor, hate and vengeance, the quest for self-respect or the simple triumph of right over wrong. Most are violent. Most have relatively conventional plots. Most are about men driven by internal demons. . . . And most provide stimulating, against-the-grain reading for western fans." Booklist

DeRosso, Henry Andrew *See* DeRosso, H. A. (Henry Andrew), 1917-1960

Desai, Anita, 1937-

Clear light of day. Harper & Row 1980 183p o.p.

LC 84-673511

"The novel begins with the triennial visit of the younger sister Tara and her diplomat husband to the old family home, a decaying suburban mansion on the banks of the Jumma outside Old Delhi. Here Bim the older sister, lives with the youngest brother, Baba. Baba is autistic, a childlike, speechless whisp of a man who spends his days playing 'I'm Dreaming of a White Christmas' and 'Donkey Seranade' on an ancient wind-up gramophone. The oldest brother, Raja, has moved away. The book divides itself equally between the present of Tara's visit and the sisters' memories of the past. . . . The visit is a strain—a series of under-the-surface estrangements and rapprochements, with sisterly love ebbing and flowing." Times Lit Suppl

This work "does what only the best novels can do: it totally submerges us. It takes us so deeply into another world that we almost fear we won't be able to climb out again." N Y Times Book Rev

Fire on the mountain. Harper & Row 1977 145p o.p.

LC 77-3788

"In this novel set in the hill country of India, Nanda Kaul's great-granddaughter is sent to spend the summer with her, thus breaking the solitude of the old and withdrawn woman, shattering the privacy she prizes most. But Raka, too, is clearly an outsider, a child living in and through her imagination, and one with a talent for disappearing. As Nanda Kaul finds herself attempting to draw out and communicate with the strange and unfathomable Raka, she discovers in the girl more of herself than she would have believed possible. Meanwhile, Nanda Kaul's lone friend, Ila Das, appears and hovers always on the brink of hysteria until that hysteria leads to a shocking rape and murder that is the book's climax." Publ Wkly

"This is a delicate wisp of a story that nevertheless possesses great tensile strength." Booklist

Destouches, Henri-Louis *See* Céline, Louis-Ferdinand, 1894-1961

Deutermann, Peter T., 1941-

Darkside. St. Martin's Press 2002 406p maps $24.95

ISBN 0-312-28120-X LC 2002-68393

An "account of some creepy goings-on at the U.S. Naval Academy in Annapolis. As the book opens, the school is buzzing with the news that a plebe has plummeted from a sixth-story window and died. Amid questions of suicide, a new twist emerges; the plebe was wearing a pair of panties belonging to Midshipman First Class Julie Markham, a perky senior at the academy and an acquaintance of the dead plebe, who then gets drawn into the investigation. Her father, a retired former fighter pilot and academy history professor, hires crack defense

Deutermann, Peter T., 1941-—*Continued*

lawyer Liz DeWinter, fearing that Markham will somehow be scapegoated by the Navy Criminal Investigation Service." Publ Wkly

Sweepers; a novel of suspense; by P.T. Deutermann. St. Martin's Press 1997 322p o.p.
ISBN 0-312-15669-3 LC 97-5772

"People who are important to Admiral Tag Sherman are dying under mysterious circumstances, leaving him large amounts of money. When a homicide detective starts asking embarrassing questions, Naval Commander Karen Lawrence is asked to investigate. Sherman suspects that he is being set up by an old enemy, a man he left behind in the swamps of Vietman, formally MIA but really one of the nastiest of the rogue CIA 'sweepers'—killers whose job is to get rid of other killers. . . . What the book lacks in clarity it makes up for in suspense, danger, and a disturbing vision of the CIA run amok." Libr J

DeVido, Brian

Every time I talk to Liston. Bloomsbury 2004 276p $22.95
ISBN 1-58234-458-2

"Aging and not as quick as he used to be, Amos 'Scrap Iron' Fletcher has finally arrived in Las Vegas, capital city of boxing. His years of slugging it out as a sparring partner for heavyweight contenders are about to pay off. But after his first big-league fight ends in defeat and when he's falsely accused of offering to sell secrets to his sparring partner's opponent he heads back home to Trenton to figure out his next move. It's there at his uncle's boxing gym that he's reunited with TNT, another boxer down on his luck. TNT is a reckless but kindhearted kid who just happens to throw some of the toughest punches Amos has ever seen. TNT's hunger for vindication rekindles Amos's passion for the sport, and he agrees to take the neglected young fighter under his wing." Publisher's note

The "writing shows quiet purpose in every move, carrying its insider knowledge with easy confidence. DeVido, at his best when showing how men tell stories about themselves with their bodies, pulls off the tricky feat of using boxing action to express character." N Y Times Book Rev

Dew, Robb Forman

The evidence against her; a novel. Little, Brown 2001 327p o.p.
ISBN 0-316-89019-7 LC 2001-29101

This novel is "set in the small town of Washburn, Ohio. The story begins with three children born on the same September day in 1888, and it ends with those same three, grown and with children of their own, in the summer of 1927. Lily Scofield, her cousin Warren Scofield and Robert Butler, son of the Methodist pastor, grow up as an inseparable group. . . . Even after Lily marries Robert in June 1913, she assumes that Warren will still somehow always be close by. . . . {But he meets} Agnes Claytor, who was a 14-year-old guest at Lily's wedding." N Y Times Book Rev

"A marvel of lyrical understatement, the narrative flows like a river—smooth, with surprising depths, some turbulence and the inexorability of time's passing." Publ Wkly

Dexter, Colin

The daughters of Cain. Crown 1995 c1994 295p o.p.

First published 1994 in the United Kingdom

In this Inspector Morse case "the crime is the murder of a retired Oxford don, and the stratagem is to make the homicide seem easy to solve. . . . Mr. Dexter is a superb technician who torments the reader with logistical details that contradict every previously established point in his puzzle. Red herrings are a specialty. But the canny author also strews the path with literary quotations to think on, polysyllabic words to look up and characters whose lives are so complicated they turn into richly distracting mini-dramas." N Y Times Book Rev

Death is now my neighbor; an Inspector Morse novel. Crown 1996 347p o.p.
ISBN 0-517-70786-1 LC 96-31781

This mystery "involves two senior Oxford dons and their ambitious wives in the death of a young woman with no obvious connections to any of them. Despite a medical scare that leaves him feeling 'unmanned' and has him behaving with uncharacteristic charity, Morse is brilliant at finding the links, filling in the blanks and coming up with the answers to this complicated case—if not to the ultimate questions that trouble his soul." N Y Times Book Rev

The jewel that was ours. Crown 1992 c1991 275p il o.p.
LC 91-45245

First published 1991 in the United Kingdom

This mystery finds British Inspector Morse "stymied by the theft of a rare artifact bound for the Ashmolean Museum and by the sudden deaths of both the American woman who owned it and the curator for whom it was intended. Challenged to keep track of several sneaky academics and frisky elderly tourists, the detective noses over British Rail timetables, handwritten notes and a smelly assortment of red herrings." N Y Times Book Rev

"The watertight solution is as tricky as it is dazzling." Booklist

Morse's greatest mystery and other stories. Crown 1995 c1993 242p o.p.

First published 1993 in the United Kingdom

Contents: As good as gold; Morse's greatest mystery; Evans tries an O-level; Dead as a dodo; At the Lulu-Bar Motel; Neighborhood watch; A case of mis-identity; The inside story; Monty's revolver; The carpet-bagger; Last call

The remorseful day. Crown 2000 363p o.p.
ISBN 0-609-60622-0 LC 99-59840

First published 1999 in the United Kingdom

"A two-year-old murder has baffled the police in Burford, a rural English village. Inspector Morse, who excels at this sort of puzzle, refuses to touch it, despite anonymous phone calls offering new evidence. Then his sidekick, Sergeant Lewis, discovers that the inspector knew the murdered woman." Libr J

"This finale to a grand series presents a moving elegy to one of mystery fiction's most celebrated and popular characters. . . . Dexter has fashioned another brilliantly intricate puzzle, one of his finest, with the valedictory

Dexter, Colin—*Continued*
tone of the narrative lending a particularly rich texture to the tale. Morse leaves us on the highest possible note, perfectly pitched." Publ Wkly

The secret of annexe 3. St. Martin's Press 1987 c1986 218p o.p.
LC 87-17590

First published 1986 in the United Kingdom

"Inspector Morse and Sergeant Lewis investigate a murder committed on New Year's Eve at a hotel in Oxford. Three couples are housed in the hotel annex, and one man, winner of the prize in the fancy-dress contest, is found dead in his room. The first problem facing Morse and Lewis is locating the other five guests, including the victim's wife, all of whom have fled, having registered under fake names and addresses. . . . Engrossed in the story that Dexter tells in his witty and stylish fashion, readers will savor the mystery of the masquerade and the detecting partners' ultimate triumph." Publ Wkly

The way through the woods. Crown 1993 c1992 296p o.p.
LC 92-40762

First published 1992 in the United Kingdom

"A student disappears, and Inspector Morse's only clue is a cryptic poem that the murderer might have sent." Libr J

"To say that the investigation is tricky is only to hint at the technical density of the plot, which, once all the tantalizing enigmas have been packed up, hinges on the most basic human frailties. Dazzling." N Y Times Book Rev

The wench is dead. St. Martin's Press 1990 c1989 200p il o.p.
LC 89-77807

First published 1989 in the United Kingdom

A mystery featuring Chief Inspector Morse of the Oxford police force. "In the hospital for an ulcer made worse by drink, and frustrated by the proximity of so many pretty young nurses, he finds distraction in an apparent case of gang rape and murder unsolved for over a hundred years." Booklist

"Mr. Dexter has fashioned a taxing brainteaser for Morse, whose superior wits and famously foul temper tug the reader into the detective's hospital bed to share his single-minded pursuit of the truth." N Y Times Book Rev

Dexter, Pete, 1943-

Brotherly love. Random House 1991 274p o.p.
LC 91-52666

"Peter Flood is the son of an Irish trade union leader with ties to the Mafia. In the space of a few days, eight-year-old Peter witnesses the death of his baby sister, his mother's mental collapse and removal to an institution, and his father Charley's bloody revenge on the man who set those events in motion, an act that leads to his own demise. Peter's uncle Phil, who betrayed Charley to the Mafia, inherits his brother's union position and his home; he raises Pete with his own son, Michael, encouraging the boys to think of themselves as brothers." Publ Wkly

"What deepens and darkens [Dexter's] writing, so that art is the precise word to describe it, is a powerful understanding that character rules, that we live with our weaknesses and die of our strengths." Time

Deadwood. Random House 1986 365p o.p.
LC 85-19635

"Deadwood (is) a vibrant, squalid late-nineteenth-century boomtown nestled in the forbidding Black Hills of the untamed Dakota Territory. When the legendary Wild Bill Hickok guides a wagon train full of prostitutes into the virtually lawless town, he becomes the target of Al Swearingen, a vengeful and cowardly pimp who hires an addlepated sot to kill him. Wild Bill's disquieted final days are spent in the company of a score of rough characters (including a riotously off-color Calamity Jane), each of whom is later bitterly haunted by the freakish circumstances of his murder." Booklist

This novel "is unpredictable, hyperbolic and, page after page, uproarious; a joshing book written in high spirits and a raw appreciation for the past." N Y Times Book Rev

The paperboy. Random House 1995 307p o.p.
LC 94-21523

"Set in the fetid swamps of northern Florida, the novel concerns the legal case of Hillary Van Wetter, who has been condemned to death for the murder of the county sheriff. Nineteen-year-old Jack James, son of the local newspaper publisher and delivery boy for the daily edition, narrates the story, which begins with Charlotte Bless, an interloping southern floozy just past her prime who takes an obsessive interest in Van Wetter's case. Jack's elder brother, Ward, a reporter in Miami, also detects a story in Van Wetter's predicament and returns to his native Moat County to investigate. He brings along the handsome, ambitious writer Yardley Acheman, whose stylistic flash is matched by his willingness to cut ethical corners. The group's inquiry drives this novel's action, taking them through the swamp, to death row, and on to Daytona Beach." Booklist

"Dexter's writing is rock-solid, he offers acute observations about the nature of reporting and his grip on the Southern male psyche is unquestionable." Publ Wkly

Paris Trout. Random House 1988 306p o.p.
LC 87-43314

"Paris Trout, the small-town Georgia store owner . . . sleeps with a sheet of lead under his mattress. He's afraid someone is going to hide under his bed and shoot him in the middle of the night—and for no good reason, as Trout sees it. He was only taking care of business, trying to collect on Henry Ray Boxer's debt. That little black girl, Rosie Sayers, who got shot and killed in the scuffle, shouldn't have got in his way, or the woman with Rosie, who still walks around with Trout's bullet in her chest. . . . Mr. Dexter has created a character whose racism is a blunt, unregenerate fact, as primitive and willful as an earthquake or a rainstorm—and just as sealed off from argument, examination or questions of mercy. What the town's polite society takes care to disguise in Sunday-go-to-meeting euphemisms, Paris sets in defiant, ugly relief; he makes it easy for them to believe they are innocent of racism." N Y Times Book Rev

Train; a novel. Doubleday 2003 280p $26
ISBN 0-385-50591-4 LC 2003-51946

Dexter, Pete, 1943-—*Continued*

Lionel "Train" Walk is a "young black caddy at an exclusive L.A. country club in 1953. Train is a self-taught golfer, too, and his natural ability catches the eye of an enigmatic cop, Miller Packard (or 'Mile-Away-Man,' as Train dubs him). As the stories of Train, Packard, and Norah Still, the survivor of a yacht hijacking (and eventually, Packard's wife), interject and ultimately implode, Dexter painstakingly reminds us that noir is all about disappointment, too." Booklist

Dezenhall, Eric

Money wanders. Thomas Dunne Bks. 2002 338p $24.95

ISBN 0-312-28275-3 LC 2001-54335

A "comic caper about a Jewish pollster put to work for an aging South Jersey/Philly Mafia don. Middle-aged Jonah Eastman, a D.C. spin doctor for hire whose business is in the doldrums, is summoned back to his Jersy home by his ailing grandfather Mickey, an old-school Jewish capo for the local Cosa Nostra kingpin, Mario Vanni. Mickey's cryptic deathbed missive to his nervous grandson directs Jonah to take on the don as a client." Publ Wkly

Di Lampedusa, Giuseppe Tomasi *See* Tomasi di Lampedusa, Giuseppe, 1896-1957

Diamant, Anita, 1951-

The red tent. Wyatt Bk. 1997 321p o.p.

LC 97-16825

This biblical tale "re-creates the life of Dinah, daughter of Leah and Jacob, from her birth and happy childhood in Mesopotamia through her years in Canaan and death in Egypt." Libr J

"Diamant's fiction debut links the passions of the early Israelites to the ongoing traditions of modern Jews, while the red tent of her title (where women retreat for menstruation, childbirth and illness) becomes a resonant symbol of womanly strength, love and wisdom. Despite a few unprofitable digressions, Diamant succeeds admirably in depicting the lives of women in the age that engendered our civilization and our most enduring values." Publ Wkly

Díaz, Junot, 1968-

Drown. Riverhead Bks. 1996 208p o.p.

LC 96-18362

Includes the following stories: Ysrael; Fiesta, 1980; Aurora; Aquantando; Drown; Boyfriend; Edison, New Jersey; How to date a browngirl, blackgirl, whitegirl, or halfie; No face; Negocios

"The 10 tales in this intense debut collection plunge us into the emotional lives of people redefining their American identity. Narrated by adolescent Dominican males living in the struggling communities of the Dominican Republic, New York and New Jersey, these stories chronicle their outwardly cool but inwardly anguished attempts to recreate themselves in the midst of eroding family structures and their own burgeoning sexuality." Publ Wkly

Dibdin, Michael

And then you die; an Aurelio Zen mystery. Pantheon Bks. 2002 183p o.p.

ISBN 0-375-42188-2 LC 2002-283086

"Zen has been given a new identity and use of a beachfront home in Versilia, a Tuscan coast resort town, while he awaits the beginning of a Mafia trial in America—a trial where he's supposed to be a surprise, and key, witness. . . . Zen's enforced idleness chafes, then evaporates as people too near him begin to die and the new strategies developed to conceal him seem to have (almost) fatal flaws." Publ Wkly

"You have to read between the lines—in scenes about a broken marriage, an empty home, a discredited occupation—to understand why Zen is really running for his life." N Y Times Book Rev

Blood rain; an Aurelio Zen mystery. Pantheon Bks. 2000 c1999 273p o.p.

ISBN 0-375-40915-7 LC 99-46938

First published 1999 in the United Kingdom

Posted to Sicily, Aurelio Zen's "nominal assignment, spying on the State Police's anti-Mafia operation for the rival Interior Ministry, is another example of corruption at work, and soon enough, he blunders into a lethal crossfire of power-hungry politicians, bureaucrats, and crime bosses. When his mother dies a suspicious death in Rome, and the woman he considers his daughter is killed in Sicily, Zen must ask himself a familiar question: Will finding the truth only make matters worse?" Booklist

Dibdin "uses the somber tones, circuitous locutions and dense plot structure appropriate to a region where every gesture—from a chess game to a political assassination—sends a subtle and dangerous message." N Y Times Book Rev

Così fan tutti; an Aurelio Zen mystery. Pantheon Bks. 1997 247p o.p.

ISBN 0-679-44272-3 LC 96-45387

First published 1996 in the United Kingdom

"Assigned to Naples, policeman Aurelio Zen takes time to assist a local wealthy widow: he refuses to let her daughters marry their supposedly Mafia-connected fiancés. Soon involved in a case of murder and mistaken for Mafia himself, Zen plays out Dibdin's . . . version of a darkly comic opera." Libr J

"Like the city that inspired it, this droll crime novel takes its frivolity very seriously." N Y Times Book Rev

Dead Lagoon; an Aurelio Zen mystery. Pantheon Bks. 1995 c1994 297p o.p.

ISBN 0-679-43349-X LC 94-27271

First published 1994 in the United Kingdom

"Rome's phlegmatic policeman, Aurelio Zen, takes a temporary transfer to his native Venice in order to earn some money on the side: a reclusive American millionaire has disappeared from his private island fortress. While in town, Zen observes troubling changes, both in Venice and in the people he knew as children." Libr J

The author's "earlier Aurelio Zen mysteries were so delicately complex they might have been spun by spiders. But here the author has transcended his own superb craftsmanship by working both story lines into a structure of pure steel—and by making it the foundation of a serious study of modern-day Venice." N Y Times Book Rev

Dibdin, Michael—*Continued*

A long finish; an Aurelio Zen mystery. Pantheon Bks. 1998 261p o.p.

ISBN 0-375-40429-5 LC 98-15764

When a leading Piedmontese "vintner is murdered and his son is charged with the gruesome deed, Zen is dispatched from Rome by a notable personage fearful that 'one of the great vintages of the century' will be compromised. . . . The all-embracing sense of place in Dibdin's mysteries extends here to the earthy sights and smells of dark woods (where the truffles grow) and lush vineyards (where the grapes ripen) and ancient farmhouses (where murder is done). Only when Zen learns to look past the beauty of these pastoral scenes can he identify the evil that lives in this village." N Y Times Book Rev

Medusa; an Aurelio Zen mystery; Michael Dibdin. 1st American ed. Pantheon Books 2003 259p $22

ISBN 0-375-42269-2 LC 2003-60893

"A long-dead body found in a mountain tunnel piques the interest of veteran Italian police officer Aurelio Zen (Blood Rain), who is especially intrigued by the inordinate attention paid to the case by the Defense Ministry and his own superior in the Interior Ministry. The corpse turns out to be that of Lt. Leonardo Ferraro, reportedly killed in a plane crash 30 years earlier. Its discovery brings to light a secret right-wing military group that prepared to overthrow the government in the 1970s. . . . Dibdin does a superb job of creating a complex background of Italian politics and society." Libr J

Thanksgiving. Pantheon Bks. 2001 182p o.p.

ISBN 0-375-42098-3 LC 00-58892

First published 2000 in the United Kingdom

This is a "portrait of a man stricken by grief after his wife is killed in an airplane crash. Anthony, a British journalist living in America, tracks down the first husband of his wife, Lucy, for reasons both unclear and sinister. . . . He meets the former husband, Darryl Bob, at the gas station he runs in the Nevada desert and learns that this crude braggart has an obsessive collection of snapshots, videotapes and audio recordings of Lucy's sexual encounters with various men. . . . Anthony leaves in a state of shock and soon learns that Darryl Bob has been killed and that the police have a photograph of him holding the murder weapon." N Y Times Book Rev

"This novel is a wonderful departure for Dibdin; nonetheless, this mystery writer keeps his psychodrama suspenseful and chilling." Booklist

Dick, Philip K.

The collected stories of Philip K. Dick. Underwood/Miller 1987 5v o.p.

Contents: Beyond lies the wub: Stability; Roog; The little movement; Beyond lies the wub; The gun; The skull; The defenders; Mr. Spaceship; Piper in the woods; The infinites; The Preserving Machine; Expendable; The variable man; The indefatigable frog; The crystal crypt; The short happy life of the brown oxford; The builder; Meddler; Paycheck; The great C; Out in the garden; The king of the elves; Colony; Prize ship; Nanny

Second Variety: The cookie lady; Beyond the door; Second Variety; Jon's world; The cosmic poachers; Progeny; Some kinds of life; Martians come in clouds; The commuter; The world she wanted; A surface raid; Project: Earth; The trouble with bubbles; Breakfast at twilight; A present for Pat; The hood maker; Of withered apples; Human is; Adjustment team; The impossible planet; Impostor; James P. Crow; Planet for transients; Small town; Souvenir; Survey team; Prominent author

The father-thing: Fair game; The hanging stranger; The eyes have it; The golden man; The turning wheel; The last of the masters; The father-thing; Strange Eden; Tony and the beetles; Null-o; To serve the master; Exhibit piece; The crawlers; Sales pitch; Shell game; Upon the dull earth; Foster, you're dead; Pay for the printer; War veteran; The chromium fence; Misadjustment; A world of talent; Psi-man heal my child!

The days of Perky Pat: Autofac; Service call; Captive market; The mold of yancy; The minority report; Recall mechanism; The unreconstructed M; Explorers we; War game; If there were no Benny Cemoli; Novelty act; Waterspider; What the dead men say; Orpheus with clay feet; The days of Perky Pat; Stand-by; What'll we do with Ragland Park?; Oh, to be a Blobel!

The little black box: The little black box; The war with the fnools; A game of unchance; Precious artifact; Retreat syndrome; A terran odyssey; Your appointment will be yesterday; Holy quarrel; We can remember it for you wholesale; Not by its cover; Return match; Faith of our fathers; The story to end all stories for Harlan Ellison's anthology *Dangerous visions*; The electric ant; Cadbury, the beaver who lacked; A little something for us tempunauts; The pre-persons; The eye of the sibyl; The day Mr. Computer fell out of its tree; The exit door leads in; Chains of air, web of aether; Strange memories of death; I hope I shall arrive soon; Rautavaara's case; The alien mind

Do androids dream of electric sheep? Ballantine Books 1996 244p pa $13.95

ISBN 0-345-40447-5 LC 96-96117

"A Del Rey book"

First published 1968

"In a future where technological sophistication has made the ersatz virtually indistinguishable from the real, the hero is a bounty hunter who must track down and eliminate androids passing for human. . . . A key novel in Dick's canon." Anatomy of Wonder 5

The man in the high castle. Vintage Books 1992 259p pa $12

ISBN 0-679-74067-8 LC 91-50895

First published 1962 by Putnam

"An alternate history in which Germany and Japan won World War II and partitioned the U.S., except for the Rocky Mountain States, which were left in a kind of political limbo. Faction-ridden Nazism oppressively rules the eastern U.S. In the west, the Japanese overlords are reconciling Oriental and American cultural values. . . . This is Dick's most important early book." Anatomy of Wonder 5

The minority report. Pantheon Bks. 2002 103p $12.95

ISBN 0-375-42187-4 LC 2002-72313

Originally published posthumously as a short story

"Police Commissioner John Anderton finds himself at the mercy of his own crime-prevention system when the prescient precogs he's hired to stop crime before it starts peg him as a soon-to-be murderer." Publ Wkly

Dick, R. A. *See* Leslie, Josephine Aimee Campbell, 1898-1979

The **Dick** Francis treasury of great racing stories; edited and introduced by Dick Francis and John Welcome. Norton 1990 c1989 221p o.p.
LC 89-72151

First published 1989 in the United Kingdom with title: Great racing stories

Contents: The dream, by R. Findlay; Silver Blaze, by A. C. Doyle; A glass of port with the proctor, by J. Welcome; Carrot for a chestnut, by D. Francis; The look of eagles, by J. T. Foote; Prime rogues, by M. Keane; The coop, by E. Wallace; The splendid outcast, by B. Markham; I'm a fool, by S. Anderson; Had a horse, by J. Galsworthy; The major, by C. Davy; What's it get you?, by J. P. Marquand; Harmony, by W. Fain; The bagman's pony, by E. de Somerville

Dickens, Charles, 1812-1870

Barnaby Rudge; a tale of the riots of 'eighty; with 76 illustrations by George Cattermole and Hablot K. Browne "Phiz" and an introduction by Kathleen Tillotson. Oxford Univ. Press 1961 634p il o.p.

ISBN 0-19-254513-2

First published 1841

"Gives a lurid account of the mad orgies and incendiarism of the 'No Popery' riots, introducing Lord George Gordon as an actor, the principal events being founded on fact. Intertwined with this is a private story containing a few characteristic traits." Baker. Guide to Hist Fic

"The plot is one of Dickens' weakest. The novel's chief interest lies in its depiction of the riots, shown to have been caused by a government heedless of the needs of its poor." Reader's Ency. 4th edition

Bleak House; with the original illustrations by Phiz; introduced by Barbara Hardy. Knopf 1991 xlix, 891p il $23

ISBN 0-679-40568-2 LC 91-52974

"Everyman's library"

First published 1853

"The heroine is Esther Summerson or rather Esther Hawdon, the illegitimate child of Lady Dedlock and Captain Hawdon. Esther, whom Lady Dedlock believes dead, is the ward of Mr. Jarndyce of the interminable case of Jarndyce and Jarndyce in Chancery Court, and lives with him at Bleak House. Lord Dedlock's lawyer, Mr. Tulkinghorn, gets wind of Lady Dedlock's secret past; and when Tulkinghorn is murdered, Lady Dedlock is suspected, disappears and is later found dead." Univ Handbk for Readers and Writers

"In this novel, Dickens attacks the delays and archaic absurdities of the courts, which he knew about first-hand." Reader's Ency. 4th edition

A Charles Dickens Christmas; A Christmas carol; The Chimes; The cricket on the hearth; with illustrations by Warren Chappell. Oxford Univ. Press 1976 308p il o.p.

Omnibus edition of the titles first published 1843, 1845 and 1846 respectively, the first and third of which are entered separately. The chimes is a fable about the fears and aspirations of the London poor. A porter and runner of errands, under the influence of the goblins of the church bells and/or a dish of tripe, has a nightmare or vision of awful misfortunes befalling his daughter, but conditions are ameliorated after he awakens

The chimes

In Dickens, C. A Charles Dickens Christmas p101-202

In Dickens, C. Christmas tales

A Christmas carol; with illustrations by Arthur Rackham. Knopf 1994 155p il $13.95

ISBN 0-679-43639-1 LC 95-163031

"Everyman's library children's classics"

Written in 1843

"This Christmas story of nineteenth century England has delighted young and old for generations. In it, a miser, Scrooge, through a series of dreams, finds the true Christmas spirit. . . . The story ends with the much-quoted cry of Tiny Tim, the crippled son of Bob Cratchit, whom Scrooge now aids: 'God bless us, every-one!'" Haydn. Thesaurus of Book Dig

also in Dickens, C. A Charles Dickens Christmas p3-98

also in Dickens, C. Christmas tales p11-77

also in Dickens, C. The complete ghost stories of Charles Dickens p89-151

Christmas stories; with 13 illustrations by E. G. Dalziel {et al.} and with an introduction by Margaret Lane. Oxford Univ. Press 1956 758p il o.p.

ISBN 0-19-254517-5

"New Oxford illustrated Dickens"

Contents: A Christmas tree; What Christmas is as we grow older; The poor relation's story; The child's story; The schoolboy's story; Nobody's story; The seven poor travellers; The holly-tree; The wreck of the Golden Mary; The perils of certain English prisoners; Going into society; The haunted house; A message from the sea; Tom Tiddler's ground; Somebody's luggage; Mrs. Lirriper's lodgings; Mrs. Lirriper's legacy; Doctor Marigold; Mugby Junction; No thoroughfare; The lazy tour of two idle apprentices

Christmas tales; with illustrations by contemporary artists and a foreword by May Lamberton Becker. Dodd, Mead 1947 c1941 414p il o.p.

"Great illustrated classics"

Contents: A Christmas carol; The chimes; The cricket on the hearth; The haunted man; A Christmas-tree; What Christmas is as we grow older; The poor relation's story; The seven poor travellers; The holly-tree; Doctor Marigold

The complete ghost stories of Charles Dickens; edited by Peter Haining. Watts 1983 c1982 341p il o.p.

LC 82-13481

First published 1982 in the United Kingdom

Contents: Captain Murderer and the Devil's bargain; The lawyer and the ghost; The queer chair; The ghosts of the mail; A madman's manuscript; The story of the goblins who stole a sexton; Baron Koëldwethout's apparition; A Christmas carol; The haunted man and the ghost's bargain; To be read at dusk; The ghost chamber;

Dickens, Charles, 1812-1870—*Continued*
The haunted house; Mr Testator's visitation; The trial for murder; The signalman; Four ghost stories; The portrait-painter's story; Well-authenticated rappings

The cricket on the hearth; a fairy tale of home. o.p.
First published in 1846
"In this short Christmas fairy tale of a happy English home, the cricket chirps when all is well, and is silent when sorrow enters. Mr. and Mrs. Perrybingle (John and Dot) give refuge to an old stranger, Edward Plummer. John sees the stranger, as a young man, without his disguise, put his arm around Dot. The cricket takes the form of a fairy and counsels him. John does not judge his young wife and is ready to forgive her. However, Edward bursts in with his bride, May Fielding, and explains everything." Haydn. Thesaurus of Book Dig
also in Dickens, C. A Charles Dickens Christmas p205-308
also in Dickens, C. Christmas tales p147-215

David Copperfield; with the original illustrations by "Phiz"; introduced by Michael Slater. Knopf 1991 xlii, 891p il $25
ISBN 0-679-40571-2 LC 91-52995
"Everyman's library"
First published 1850
This novel "incorporates material from the autobiography Dickens had recently begun but soon abandoned and is written in the first person, a new technique for him. Although Copperfield differs from his creator in many ways, Dickens uses many early personal experiences that had meant much to him—his own period of work in a factory while his father was jailed, his schooling and reading, his passion for Maria Beadnell (a woman much like Dora Spenlow), and (more cursorily) his emergence from parliamentary reporting into successful novel writing." Merriam-Webster's Ency of Lit

Dombey and Son; with forty illustrations by 'Phiz'; introduced by Lucy Hughes-Hallett. Knopf 1994 xlvii, 889p il $23
ISBN 0-679-43591-3 LC 94-4778
"Everyman's library"
First published 1848
"The proud, unfeeling Mr. Dombey has but one ambition: to have a son so that his firm might be called Dombey and Son. When his son Paul is born, he promises to fulfill this ambition, which overrides even grief at the death of Mrs. Dombey. Young Paul, a delicate, sensitive boy, is quite unequal to the great things expected of him; he is sent to Mr. Blimber's school and gives way under the strain of the discipline. . . . Mr. Dombey is embittered by Paul's death. Florence, his daughter, lives on with him, trying desperately to win his love, but she has succeeded only in incurring his hatred because she lives while her brother died. Dombey marries again, but his second wife, Edith Granger, runs off with Mr. Carker, his business manager. Florence marries the kind young Walter Gay. Dombey's firm fails, and alone and miserable, he finds himself longing for the sweet and kind daughter whom he treated so coldly. The two are reconciled, and Dombey tries to expiate his past through his grandchildren." Reader's Ency. 4th edition

Great expectations; illustrated by F.W. Pailthrope with an introduction by Michael Slater. Knopf 1992 xxxiv, 469p il $21
ISBN 0-679-40579-8 LC 91-53219
"Everyman's library"
First published 1861
"The first-person narrative relates the coming-of-age of Pip (Philip Pirrip). Reared in the marshes of Kent by his disagreeable sister and her sweet-natured husband, the blacksmith Joe Gargery, the young Pip one day helps a convict to escape. Later he is sent to live with Miss Havisham, a woman driven half-mad years earlier by her lover's departure on their wedding day. . . . When an anonymous benefactor makes it possible for Pip to go to London for an education, he credits Miss Havisham. . . . Pips benefactor turns out to have been Abel Magwitch, the convict he once aided, who dies awaiting trial after Pip is unable to help him a second time. Joe rescues Pip from despair and nurses him back to health." Merriam-Webster's Ency of Lit

Hard times. Knopf 1992 299p $19
ISBN 0-679-41323-5 LC 91-58704
"Everyman's library"
First published 1854. Variant title: Hard times for these times
The proprietor of an experimental private school in an English manufacturing town, "Thomas Gradgrind, a fanatic of the demonstrable fact, has raised his children Tom and Louisa in an atmosphere of grimmest practicality. Louisa marries the banker Josiah Bounderby partly to protect her brother who is in Bounderby's employ, and partly because her education has resulted in an emotional atrophy that makes her indifferent to her fate. Tom, shallow and unscrupulous, robs Bounderby's bank and contrives to frame Stephen Blackpool, an honest and long-suffering mill hand. Meanwhile, Louisa's dormant emotions began to awaken, stimulated by disgust for the vulgar Bounderby and the attentions of the charming, amoral James Harthouse. When she runs away to her father and when Tom's guilt is discovered, Gradgrind realizes how his principles have blighted his children's lives. . . . The novel is Dickens's harshest indictment of practices and philosophical justifications of mid-19th-century industrialism in England." Reader's Ency. 4th edition

The haunted man [variant title: The haunted man and the ghost's bargain]
In Dickens, C. Christmas tales

Little Dorrit. Knopf 1992 xxxvii, 836p il $22
ISBN 0-679-41725-7 LC 92-52919
"Everyman's library"
First published 1857
"Little Dorrit was born and brought up in the Marshalsea prison, Bermondsey, where her father was confined for debt; and when about fourteen years of age she used to do needlework to earn a subsistence for herself and her father. . . . Her father, coming into a property, was set free at length, and Little Dorrit married Arthur Clennam, the marriage service being celebrated in the Marshalsea, by the prison chaplain." Univ Handbk for Readers and Writers
"Satirizes the Civil Service under the style of the Circumlocution Office. Also pictures prison life. Little Dorrit's father being Father of the Marshalsea. The melodramatic element appears in the history of the House of

Dickens, Charles, 1812-1870—*Continued*
Clennam: with the usual complement of originals: Mr. F.'s Aunt, the Meagles, Pancks, Mr. Nanby, Mr. Casby, Flora Finching, Miss Wade, Tallycoram." Baker. Guide to the Best Fic

Martin Chuzzlewit; with forty illustrations by "Phiz"; introduced by William Boyd. Knopf 1994 xlvii, 851p il $20
ISBN 0-679-43884-X LC 95-136833
"Everyman's library"
"The story's protagonist, Martin Chuzzlewit, is an apprentice architect who is fired by Seth Pecksniff and is also disinherited by his own eccentric, wealthy grandfather. Martin and a servant, Mark Tapley, travel to the United States, where they are swindled by land speculators and have other unpleasant but sometimes comic experiences. Thoroughly disillusioned with the New World, the pair returns to England, where a chastened Martin is reconciled with his grandfather, who gives his approval to Martin's forthcoming marriage to his true love, Mary Graham." Merriam-Webster's Ency of Lit

The mystery of Edwin Drood; with 12 illustrations by Luke Fildes and 2 by Charles Collins, and an introduction by S. C. Roberts. Oxford Univ. Press 1956 278p il o.p.
ISBN 0-19-254516-7
"New Oxford illustrated Dickens"
First published 1870
"This novel Dickens left unfinished at his death. The striking opening scene shows John Jasper, precentor of Cloisterham cathedral, in an opium den. He is the uncle of Edwin Drood, and persecutes with his evil passion Rosa Bud, to whom Drood is betrothed by an arrangement made by the late respective fathers of the two orphans. Actually Edwin is cool to Rosa, and it is another orphan, Neville Landless, who is attracted to her. The sinister Jasper foments a quarrel between Edwin and Neville, not knowing that the engagement has already been broken off. The same night Edwin disappears, and there is circumstantial evidence pointing to Neville as his murderer. The latter is arrested, but as no body has been found, is released. There turns up in the neighborhood a white-haired stranger who calls himself Datchery and acts like a detective on the trail of Jasper. Here the story breaks off with no indication as to how it would have ended." Haydn. Thesaurus of Book Dig

Nicholas Nickleby; with an introduction by John Carey. Knopf 1993 lvii, 843p il $24
ISBN 0-679-42307-9 LC 93-1856
"Everyman's library"
First published 1839
After Nicholas Nickleby's father dies bankrupt, Nicholas, his sister and their mother go to London to seek aid from Nicholas' uncle, a moneylender. At the scheming miser's insistence, Nicholas "first serves as usher to Mr. Wackford Squeers, schoolmaster at Dotheboys Hall; the brutality of Squeers and his wife, especially toward a poor, half-witted boy named Smike, causes Nicholas to leave in disgust. Smike runs away from school to follow Nicholas, remaining his follower until he dies. Next Nicholas joins the theatrical company of Mr. Crummles, and finally he secures a good post in a counting house owned by the benevolent Cheeryble brothers, Ned and Charles, self-made merchants ready to help those struggling against ill fortune." Reader's Ency. 4th edition

The old curiosity shop; with seventy-five illustrations by Cattermole and 'Phiz'; introduced by Peter Washington. Knopf 1995 569p il $24
ISBN 0-679-44373-8 LC 95-75208
"Everyman's library"
First published 1841; first Everyman's library edition 1907
This is the "story of Little Nell Trent and the evil dwarf Quilp. When Little Nell's grandfather gambles away his curiosity shop to his creditor Quilp, the girl and the old man flee London. Nell's friend Kit Nubbles and a mysterious Single Gentleman (who turns out to be the wealthy brother of Nell's grandfather) attempt to find them but are thwarted by Quilp, who drowns while fleeing the law. Little Nell dies before Kit and the Single Gentleman arrive, and her brokenhearted grandfather dies days later." Merriam-Webster's Ency of Lit

Oliver Twist; with twenty-four illustrations by George Cruikshank; introduced by Michael Slater. Knopf 1992 xlvi, 427p il $20
ISBN 0-679-41724-9 LC 92-52899
"Everyman's library"
First published 1837-1838
"A boy from an English workhouse falls into the hands of rogues who train him to be a pickpocket. The story of his struggles to escape from an environment of crime is one of hardship, danger and the severe obstacles overcome." Natl Counc of Teachers of Engl

Our mutual friend; with an introduction by Andrew Sanders. Knopf 1994 xliii, 832p $22
ISBN 0-679-42028-2 LC 93-81033
"Everyman's library"
First published 1865
"John Harmon, 'our mutual friend,' will inherit a fortune if he marries Bella Wilfer. He assumes the names of Julius Handford and later John Rokesmith, and his supposed death helps him conceal his identity. John's father's foreman, Nicodemus Boffin, and his wife, Henrietta, help him with the ruse. He enters the employ of Boffin, who has adopted Bella. Bella has had her head turned by wealth, but reforms when her eyes are opened to its evils; she marries Harmon. Other characters are: Jesse Hexam; his son Charley, and daughter, Lizzie; Bradley Headstone, schoolmaster, who is jealous of Eugene Wrayburn's love for Lizzie Hexam; Fanny Cleaver (Jenny Wren), a doll's dressmaker; one-legged Silas Wegg, the villain in the main plot, as Headstone is in the secondary one. Here again Dickens protests against the poor laws through the character Betty Higder, who fears the workhouse." Haydn. Thesaurus of Book Dig

The posthumous papers of the Pickwick Club; with forty-three illustrations by Seymour and 'Phiz' and an introduction by Bernard Darwin. Oxford Univ. Press 1959 xxiii, 801p il o.p.
ISBN 0-19-254501-9
"New Oxford illustrated Dickens"
First published 1837
"Episodes of the doings and foibles of the Pickwick Club. . . . The book is made up of letters and manuscripts about the club's actions. Among the incidents are: the army parade; trip to Manor Farm; the saving of Rachel Wardle from the villain, Alfred Jingle; trip to Eatonsville; Mrs. Leo Hunter's party of authors, includ-

Dickens, Charles, 1812-1870—*Continued*

ing Count Smorltork and Charles FitzMarshall; ice skating. Pickwick's landlady, Mrs. Bardell, faints in his arms and compromises the unsophisticated gentleman. She sues him for breach of promise and an amusing court trial follows. Pickwick refuses to pay damages and is put in Fleet prison. Sam Weller, his faithful servant, accompanies him. Mrs. Bardell is also incarcerated for not paying the costs of the trial. When Pickwick is released he retires to a house outside London, with Weller, and the latter's new bride, Mary, as housekeeper. He dissolves the club and spends his time arranging its memoranda." Haydn. Thesaurus of Book Dig

Sketches by Boz. o.p.

The chapters are arranged under the following headings: Our parish; Scenes; Characters; Tales; Sketches of young gentlemen; Sketches of young couples; The Mudfog and other sketches

A tale of two cities; with an introduction by Simon Schama and sixteen illustrations by Phiz. Knopf 1993 xxviii, 413p il $20

ISBN 0-679-42073-8 LC 92-73542

"Everyman's library"

First published 1859

"Although Dickens borrowed from Thomas Carlyle's history, The French Revolution, for his sprawling tale of London and revolutionary Paris, the novel offers more drama than accuracy. The scenes of large-scale mob violence are especially vivid, if superficial in historical understanding. The complex plot involves Sydney Carton's sacrifice of his own life on behalf of his friends Charles Darnay and Lucie Manette. While political events drive the story, Dickens takes a decidedly antipolitical tone, lambasting both aristocratic tyranny and revolutionary excess." Merriam-Webster's Ency of Lit

Dickey, James

Deliverance. Houghton Mifflin 1970 278p o.p.

"The plot revolves around a canoe trip undertaken by four city men as a break in routine and to see a wilderness river before it is dammed. Early in the journey two of the men are attacked by brutal mountaineers and another member of the quartet is killed. Dickey probes the diverse personalities of each man, showing clearly that leadership devolves on the one most able to solve a problem rationally rather than the one most given to theorizing about how to cope with the issue of basic survival." Booklist

This "is a thriller—or, more strictly, a suspense story—that transcends its genre. . . . Dickey is to be praised for resisting the temptation of the poet to write 'poetical' prose. . . . He writes in a neat, terse, matter-of-fact prose, level in pitch and perfectly suited to carry the burden of the action." New Yorker

To the white sea. Houghton Mifflin 1993 275p o.p.

LC 93-1247

"A Marc Jaffe book"

WWII Air Force gunner Muldrow is shot down over Tokyo shortly before the "fire raid on that city. His position should be hopeless, but the man comes from a remote region of Alaska, where he grew up hunting, trapping, and studying game. His object is to find similarly cold country, and as he lurks and dodges his way north to Hokkaido, he uses every trick of camouflage and predation that he has learned from hare and wolverine." Atlantic

This novel "allows no easy assumption about nature or violence or war. What makes it so haunting, though, what keeps you reading, is the beauty of the prose." Newsweek

Dickinson, Charles, 1951-

A shortcut in time. Forge 2003 288p $24.95

ISBN 0-7653-0579-8 LC 2002-34688

"A Tom Doherty Associates book"

"Josh Winkler's settled life changes when he chooses a shortcut to town and ends up 15 minutes in the past. On the same path, he meets Constance, another bewildered time traveler from the year 1908. No one believes them, especialy Josh's doctor wife, who orders neurological tests. To validate their experiences, Josh researches Constance's disappearance in the local library's newspaper archives and discovers that Constance's boyfriend, a suspect in her disappearance, was hanged by an angry mob; Constance needs to find her way back to 1908 to prevent his death." Libr J

"Dickinson conjures a notably mundane environment, then makes it extraorinary" Booklist

Dickinson, Peter, 1927-

Skeleton-in-waiting. Pantheon Bks. 1989 154p o.p.

LC 89-42561

This sequel to King and Joker (1976) "focuses on the same fictional British royal family after the death of heroine Princess Louise's grandmother, Grand Duchess Marie Romanov. Dickinson juggles several subplots—a rumor of possible terrorist action; the odd behavior of Louise's sister-in-law—but concentrates mostly on the Grand Duchess's possibly scandalous letters and the strange woman hired to translate them from Russian." Libr J

This "is a most satisfying story, fast-paced and enthralling as a good detective thriller should be but also a study of extraordinary social and psychological perception." N Y Times Book Rev

Some deaths before dying. Mysterious Press 1999 251p $27

ISBN 0-89296-696-3 LC 98-37535

"Rachel Matson was a talented photographer and the devoted wife of Jocelyn, a World War II prisoner of war. Now a 90-year-old widow dying of an illness that has paralyzed her, Rachel is determined to hang on to her mental powers. When she discovers that Jocelyn's treasured antique pistol is missing, a long-buried secret comes back to torment her. With the help of her loyal nurse, Dilys, Rachel uses her photographs to come to terms with her past, piecing together a series of events that tore her family apart 39 years ago." Libr J

Dickinson's "radiant portrait of Rachel does honor to 'her long and steadfast campaign to keep hold of her mind,' just as he dignifies the other aged or inarticulate characters in his story by lending them the clarity of voice to express the thoughts they feared they'd lost forever." N Y Times Book Rev

Dickinson, Peter, 1927-—*Continued*

The yellow room conspiracy. Mysterious Press 1994 261p o.p.

LC 94-1980

"The yellow room was one of about 50 in Blatchards, an old mansion near Bury St. Edmonds. Owned by Lord Vereker, Blatchards was dominated by his five striking daughters whose politics and personal lives in the 1930s and '40s are at the heart of Dickinson's . . . tale. Flashbacks told in alternating chapters by Lucy Vereker, the third daughter, and her lover Paul Ackerley, now near the end of their lives, describe events that culminated in the 1956 fire that destroyed the house, an event that each one thought the other may have, in different ways, engineered. The fire covered up evidence about the death—accident, suicide or murder?—of Gerry Grantworth, the eldest daughter's husband." Publ Wkly

"Like the labyrinthine route one must take to the Yellow Room, the resolution of the mystery is lengthy and winding and delightfully disorienting." N Y Times Book Rev

Dickson, Gordon R., 1923-2001

The cloak and the staff
In The Hugo winners p209-43

The dragon and the djinn. Ace Bks. 1996 394p o.p.

LC 95-22447

This episode in the author's "series about Sir James of Malencontri, a twentieth-century scholar flung precipitously into a fantastic fourteenth-century England, has him accompanying his friend Sir Brian on a search for Sir Brian's father-in-law, missing in the Holy Land. What follows are encounters with classic, well-imagined *Arabian Nights*— like magic, a convoluted plot, and a great deal of exuberant action." Booklist

The dragon at war. Ace Bks. 1992 375p o.p.

LC 91-46350

In this installment of the author's Dragon series "the great mage Carolinus has been struck with a mysterious illness that leaves him despondent and unsure of his powers just as a sorcerous threat to England is developing, which pretty much leaves Jim, the dragon knight, to work his own lesser magic. As usual, Dickson provides a nice mixture of humor, action, and drama, not to mention interesting characters who reflect the medieval turn of mind regarding chivalry and brutality." Booklist

The dragon in Lyonesse. TOR Bks. 1998 381p (Dragon) o.p.

ISBN 0-312-86159-1 LC 98-23490

"A Tom Doherty Associates book"

"When the Dark Powers threaten to overwhelm the magical Kingdom of Lyonesse, Jim Eckert—the Dragon Knight—rides with his companions into a world of Old Magic to come to the aid of the legendary Knights of the Round Table." Libr J

"Dickson's is a distinctly original take on the Matter of Britain . . . distinguished by the humor arising out of the contrast between popular notions about the Middle Ages and its frequently grisly realities." Booklist

The dragon knight. Doherty Assocs. 1990 409p (Dragon) o.p.

LC 90-38897

"A TOR book"

A title in the author's Dragon series which began with The dragon and the George (1976). "Sir James Eckert, a 20th-century academician turned 14th-century baron in an alternate, magical Middle Ages, finds his idyllic existence disrupted by a call to arms to rescue his captive prince from the clutches of the French. Aided by his loyal companions and by the sudden emergence of his latent magical talents, Sir James brings his own modern sensibilities to bear in a confrontation with the forces of darkness." Libr J

"Dickson has further developed the intriguing medieval universe he posited in the first volume of the series . . . giving reality and texture to the actual life of the time while exploring the effects of magic. The scenes describing diplomatic relations among the dragons are particularly fine." Publ Wkly

The dragon on the border. Ace Bks. 1992 393p o.p.

LC 91-21270

In this title in the Dragon series "Dickson matches his contemporary-American-turned-medieval-knight-dragon against immortal and deadly sorcerers, the Hollow Men, and sets them against a background drawn from the Anglo-Scots border wars of great and bloody memory. The result is a mixture of humor and drama that recalls L. Sprague de Camp. Dickson is a good enough medievalist, humorist, and storyteller to sustain this combination." Booklist

The dragon, the Earl, and the troll. Ace Bks. 1994 442p o.p.

LC 94-7538

In this Dragon title Sir James must "contend with medieval court intrigues and the Dark Powers and other unworldly wildlife. He is helped by his wife, Angie; his master-in-magic Carolinus; the unforgettable English wolf Aargh; and his other friends. Although the yarn is unquestionably formulaic, that formula is a tried and tested winner allowing, in Dickson's capable hands, a wealth of wit and range of invention not found in the common ruck of thud-and-blunder romances." Booklist

Lost Dorsai
In The Hugo winners p137-206

Didion, Joan

A book of common prayer. Simon & Schuster 1977 272p o.p.

LC 76-50067

Charlotte Douglas, the novel's heroine, "is the quintessential American innocent. . . . Nothing alters her self-centered perception of events—not two disastrous marriages nor the fact that her daughter has turned overnight into a political outlaw. . . . Charlotte retires to Boca Grande, a shabby banana republic, to wait for things to turn out 'all right.' There she meets Grace Strasser-Mendana, the narrator of the novel, like Charlotte a 'norte-americana,' an anthropologist by training, and a local political power by marriage. Grace unwittingly involves Charlotte in a coup d'état. Charlotte in turn provides the subject matter for Grace's final inquiry into human be-

Didion, Joan—*Continued*
havior." Atlantic

Didion's "exposition of situations and details adroitly conceals their significance—until much later their meaning flares before our eyes. This is a remarkably good novel." Newsweek

The last thing he wanted. Knopf 1996 227p o.p.
ISBN 0-679-43331-7 LC 96-17084

"The year is 1984, and Elena McMahon is burned out. She has survived a bout with cancer, a divorce, and the death of her mother and has already reinvented herself several times over, but she is forced, once again, to adopt a false identity when her father, a quintessential fixer plugged into the deadly world of arms trading, takes ill. A journalist, Elena had been covering the presidential campaign, but she walks off the job, flies to Miami, and lands in the eye of a hurricane of deals, counterdeals, and political subterfuge, a storm of lies and power plays set in motion by the war in Nicaragua." Booklist

"There's an animating tension in Didion's fiction between her achingly sure control as storyteller and stylist and the numbing vagueness of the people she depicts. . . . Didion's novels are thus simultaneously lucid and surreal." New Yorker

Play it as it lays; a novel. Farrar, Straus & Giroux 1970 214p o.p.

"Using a phrenetic millieu of drugs, pills, sexual aberrancy, Didion elliptically etches the self-destructive life of Maria Wyeth. Didion with authorial legerdemain skillfully controls the suspense as Maria dangerously exists: she cannot relate and adjust. Her father has told her life was a crap game and to play it as it lays, not the hard way. But Maria plays it the hardest way, trying to anesthetize herself against pain (almost everyone, anything) and pleasure (Kate, her neurally damaged child), and trying to lose herself in the dead-end life around her." Choice

Diehl, William, 1924-

27. Villard Bks. 1989 559p o.p.
LC 89-40200

"Some of America's richest, most powerful men meet regularly at an exclusive resort on an island off Georgia. A Nazi 'sleeper agent,' code named 27, living in the U.S. since 1933, plans to kidnap these VIPs and hold them hostage in exchange for Roosevelt's guarantee that the U.S. will stay out of the war. Larger-than-life Francis Keegan, a wealthy American ex-bootlegger and friend of FDR, is agent 27's nemesis." Publ Wkly

The author "handles action scenes well, and the story keeps you turning the pages—but it's best while doing so to keep your capacity for willing disbelief in full working order." N Y Times Book Rev

Primal fear. Villard Bks. 1993 418p o.p.
LC 92-5728

This thriller "focuses on the maneuvers of Chicago defense attorney Martin Vail, a prosecutor's worst nightmare. . . . After discovering the mutilated body of Archbishop Richard Rushman in the rectory of his church, police find Aaron Stampler cowering in a confessional, blood-soaked and gripping the murder weapon. It seems like an iron-clad case—psycho slasher carves up 'the Saint of Lakeview Drive'—and a hostile judge appoints Vail as pro bono defense attorney, hoping to publicly humble him." Publ Wkly

"Taking the best elements of horror fiction, the psychological thriller, and the legal novel, best-selling author Diehl concocts an especially exciting chiller. . . . The ending may not hold up under a psychiatrist's professional scrutiny, but the general reader will find it an immensely successful finis!." Booklist

Reign in hell. Ballantine Bks. 1997 437p o.p.
ISBN 0-345-41144-7 LC 97-18214

"Illinois state attorney general Vail is called upon by President Lawrence Pennington to seek a trial case against one of the largest militia outfits in the country. The leader of this outfit, Gen. Joshua Engstrom, just happens to be an old adversary of the president, putting Vail in the middle of a dangerous situation. Vail must also relive the past when unwillingly faced with his nemesis from years ago, serial killer Aaron Stampler, who has now become blind Brother Transgression. The meshing of these storylines is intricate yet easily followed as the tension mounts." Libr J

Show of evil. Ballantine Bks. 1995 483p o.p.
LC 94-24112

"Defense attorney-turned-district attorney Martin Vail comes to regret having saved a murderer, Aaron Stampler, from the death penalty; Stampler wasn't suffering from multiple personality disorder but was merely a vicious killer who has many more scores to settle. When Stampler proves smart enough to convince an egotistical psychiatrist that he is now sane and can return to society, Vail has to out-think him to save not only his own life but the lives of everyone who contributed to the killer's ten years in a mental institution. The action is gripping, and the characters are well drawn." Libr J

Dierbeck, Lisa, 1963-

One pill makes you smaller. Farrar, Straus & Giroux 2003 312p $24
ISBN 0-374-22649-0 LC 2002-44675

This novel revolves around "11-year-old Alice Duncan, a Manhattan girl of declining privilege who has been left in the slipshod care of her 16-year-old half sister. Her young mother, Rain, has long since disappeared; her father, a 60-year-old failed artist, is in a mental institution. It's 1976. Alice and her sister, known as Aunt Esme, rattle around a tattered Upper East Side brownstone in a haze of nonsupervision, drugs, rock music and Esmes hippie boyfriends." N Y Times Book Rev

"This unsettling and disorienting—but also deliciously pop—account of deplorable actions and shattered innocence is a tour de force, a meshing of the myths of the counterculture with the fantastic universe of Lewis Carroll. It's a genuinely original, compulsively readable first novel, sure to stir up controversy." Publ Wkly

Dikty, Julian May *See* May, Julian, 1931-

Dinesen, Isak, 1885-1962

Last tales. Random House 1957 341p o.p.

Contents: The Cardinal's first tale; The cloak; Night walk; Of hidden thoughts and of heaven; Tales of two old gentlemen; The Cardinal's third tale; The blank page; Caryatids, an unfinished tale; Echoes; A country tale; Copenhagen season; Converse at night in Copenhagen

Seven Gothic tales; with an introduction by Dorothy Canfield. Modern Lib. 1994 c1934 422p o.p.

ISBN 0-679-60086-8 LC 91-50030

First published 1934 by H. Smith and analyzed in Short story index

Contents: The deluge at Norderney; The old chevalier; The monkey; The roads round Pisa; The supper at Elsinore; The dreamers; The poet

"Distinguished by a romantic style and an aura of mystery, these tales of nineteenth-century aristocratic life in northern Europe remain favorites of a wide audience. A major plot device in some stories is the revealing of illegitimacy (sometimes of legitimacy), while a strong element of the supernatural is to be found in others." Shapiro. Fic for Youth. 3d edition

Shadows on the grass. Random House 1961 c1960 149p il o.p.

Contents: Farah; Barua a Soldani; The great gesture; Echoes from the hills

"These finely drawn autobiographical stories not only re-create the Africans with whom Dinesen shared those years, but also convey, in every description and episode, the quality and texture of a past era in Kenya and in the author's life." Booklist

Winter's tales. Random House 1942 313p o.p.

Contents: The sailor-boy's tale; The young man with the carnation; The pearls; The invincible slaveowners; The heroine; The dreaming child; Alkmene; The fish; Peter and Rosa; Sorrow-acre; A consolatory tale

Dinosaurs; stories by Ray Bradbury, Arthur C. Clarke, Isaac Asimov and many others; edited by Martin H. Greenberg. Fine, D.I. 1996 288p o.p.

LC 95-46858

Contents: The fog horn, by R. Bradbury; Day of the hunters, by I. Asimov; Dino trend, by P. Cadigan; Time's arrow, by A. C. Clarke; Chameleon, by K. K. Rusch; Shadow of a change, by M. M. Sagara; Strata, by E. Bryant; Green brother, by H. Waldrop; Wildcat, by P. Anderson; Just like old times, by R. J. Sawyer; The last thunder horse west of the Mississippi, by S. N. Dyer; Hatching season, by H. Turtledove; A gun for dinosaur, by L. S. De Camp; Our Lady of the Sauropods, by R. Silverberg

These "are well-told tales calculated to rouse the interest of any dinosaur fan. Some are old enough that their scientific background is not up-to-date, but all score high in sheer readability." Booklist

Dixon, Stephen, 1936-

Frog. British Am. Pub. 1991 769p o.p.

ISBN 0-945167-43-1; 0-945167-41-5 (pa)

LC 91-12639

This fictional work presents stories about the life of a writer named Howard Tetch. He is "a New Yorker by birth and temperament, a teacher living in Baltimore who has come to academia late and almost by accident. . . . In the chapter 'Frog Remembers,' in which Howard seems to be elderly, divorced, and on his own, he tries to recall how he met Denise, his ex-wife, at a friend's house. Later in the text, however, in 'Frog Dances,' the story of the meeting is completely different, and in 'Frog Restarts,' in which it seems his wife has died, there is another version." Am Book Rev

"'Frog' is a narrative that leaps forward and lands sideways and flops over backward, croaking in dissonant pitches from chapter to chapter and contradicting itself whenever it pleases. . . . [The book], though billed as a novel, looks very much like a crazy quilt of short stories. Does that matter? Surprisingly, not very much. For no reader can fail to grasp that these often mutually exclusive scenarios for the family of a writer called Howard Tetch convey the jumpy landscape of that writer's mind." N Y Times Book Rev

Gould; a novel in two novels. Holt & Co. 1997 277p o.p.

ISBN 0-8050-4424-8 LC 96-19778

"Gould Bookbinder is obsessively driven by his desires–initially just for sex, then for children–regardless of consequences for the women in his life. . . . The first section, 'Abortions,' touches on five relationships over 40 years. Each includes an abortion or miscarriage. The second, 'Evangeline, explores what appears to be a version of one of those stories in greater depth." Libr J

"Given that his (anti) hero starts the narrative as a repellent, sex-driven creep, Stephen Dixon has effected a strange turnaround by the close of this remarkable book: we may not like Gould Bookbinder, but after being privy to the minutest contortions of his interior life, we may at least feel stirrings of forgiveness, if not outright sympathy." N Y Times Book Rev

Interstate; a novel. Holt & Co. 1995 374p o.p.

ISBN 0-8050-2654-1 LC 94-40174

In this novel, "eight narratives are alternative replays of a . . . moment that transpires in the book's opening pages: an act of random violence in which a man [Nathan Frey]and his two daughters are shot at by punks in a passing van, and one of the girls is killed." Libr J

"Italo Calvino and Alain Robbe-Grillet have also written novels that begin again and again, revising themselves, but the subjects of these novels are only themselves. Neither of them has brought off anything like the broken eloquence of Nathan's voice, which is as distinct and original and American as Mark Twain's, if otherwise very different. . . . Neither Italo Calvino nor Alain Robbe-Grillet ever brought off anything so cruelly audacious (although they tried) or so upsetting as 'Interstate' – or even attempted the muted beauty of the novel's last few pages, as Nathan performs the ordinary rituals of fatherhood, haunted by everything that has gone before." N Y Times Book Rev

Old friends; a novel. Melville House Pub 2004 220p $22.95

ISBN 0-9749609-2-6 LC 2004-16101

"Dixon follows the lives of two writers from the time they meet as young men until late middle age. Neither Irv nor Leonard has achieved any great fame, and though

Dixon, Stephen, 1936-—*Continued*

there's a good deal of writerly chatter, it's really background music to the story of the daily struggles of two aging men and their families. Their lives are tragic, but not dramatically so—Leonard slowly fades into Lyme disease-induced dementia while Irv is busy caring for his crippled wife. What makes this book so good is Dixon's ability to invent characters just average enough that readers can identify with the banality of their pain." Publ Wkly

The stories of Stephen Dixon. Holt & Co. 1994 642p o.p.
ISBN 0-8050-2653-3 LC 93-38509

Contents: The chess house; The new era; Making a break; Mac in love; Last May; Rose; The return; Parents; Man of letters; The Franklin stove; Em; 14 stories; Milk is very good for you; The signing; Love has its own action; Cut; The intruder; Streets; Movies; Layaways; The watch; Stop; Cy; The hole; Joke; The gold car; Darling; The frame; The bench; For a man your age; Goodbye to goodbye; Come on a coming; Time to go; Eating the placenta; The letter; Change; Moving on; The rescuer; Love and will; Grace calls; Dog days; In time; Said; The postcard; Windows; A sloppy story; The painter; Takes; Gifts; The student; All gone; The batterer; Magna as a child; Only the cat escapes; Frog's nanny; Frog dances; Frog made free; Frog takes a swim; Frog's mom; Man, woman and boy

"This volume contains some of Dixon's best short fiction, written over a 30-year period from 1963 to 1993. . . . Rich with the precise details of ordinary urban life, the stories are gently distorted by the introduction of fantastic and surreal elements." Libr J

Dobyns, Stephen, 1941-

Boy in the water; a novel. Metropolitan Bks. 1999 406p o.p.
ISBN 0-8050-6020-0 LC 98-56106

"When psychologist Jim Hawthorne takes the job of headmaster at a private school in remote New Hampshire, he is on the run from himself. Grieving and guilt-ridden after the deaths of his wife and daughter in a fire set by one of his patients, Hawthorne attempts to throw himself into his new job, but the task of setting the school on a new course leads to further tragedy. Simmering resentments among the faculty erupt into violence, and Hawthorne senses a deeper plot that may involve two other newcomers: a 15-year-old former stripper and a joke-telling cook. Dobyns tightens the screws on all these plot elements with great skill, using dramatic irony in place of traditional suspense." Booklist

The church of dead girls; a novel. Metropolitan Bks. 1997 388p o.p.
ISBN 0-8050-5103-1 LC 96-52525

A novel about "how the people in a small town change because of a series of murders. First, a promiscuous woman is murdered. Then three girls disappear in succession. The narrator reports how the symptoms of fear escalate into a raging disease consuming the community. Cloaking prejudice and fear with righteousness, certain citizens target individuals who are on the community's fringe. By the story's end, no one escapes suspicion." Libr J

"Methodically peeling back the veneer of civic pride and community harmony that holds the town together, Dobyns reveals the dark impulses and tangled relationships that lie underneath. He's not as interested in the pathology of the serial killer in their midst as he is in the pathology that exists within us all." Booklist

Saratoga backtalk. Norton 1994 221p o.p.
LC 93-48029

"Fearing that his wife wants him dead, a wealthy horse owner appeals to private eye Charlie Bradshaw for help. When a horse kicks the man to death shortly thereafter, Charlie and sidekick Victor Plotz uncover a host of bad feelings and nasty characters." Libr J

"With Charlie on jury duty, Victor draws the job of snooping about Logan's farm, and he quickly manages to offend everyone he encounters—except the reader, of course, who will fall totally under the hedonistic spell of the outrageously obscene, pleasure-craving, life-loving, 59-year-old Victor." Booklist

Saratoga bestiary. Viking 1988 256p o.p.
LC 88-14280

Detective Charlie Bradshaw is in "Saratoga Springs, where a stolen painting of Man o' War, a heist from an illegal gambling party, and a murdered grocery store owner have something in common. While unearthing the intricate connections—all of which lead to a very nasty villain who arranges pit bull dog fights and snuff videos—Charlie ponders the 'difficulties' of turning 50." Libr J

Saratoga haunting. Viking 1993 207p o.p.
LC 92-50750

"In the backwoods of upstate New York, laconic sleuth Bradshaw ruminates on his passing years, recalling his younger days when he was a brash career cop, married and miserable. The fluid narrative lures the reader into an ease that is rudely shattered by the eruption of two cases from the past." Publ Wkly

"Unlike most fictional detectives, who give the same flawless performance over and over again in a world outside time, Charlie is allowed by his creator to suffer changes and even to age. He is mortal, like us, and his struggles and successes matter." N Y Times Book Rev

Saratoga headhunter. Viking 1985 208p o.p.
LC 84-20955

"A headless corpse is found in Charlie Bradshaw's house. The corpse is that of a former jockey who was about to testify about crooked races before a grand jury. There are many people who wanted to prevent him from naming certain interests. It's said Bradshaw fingered the jock." N Y Times Book Rev

"None of this would be very interesting if it weren't for Bradshaw, who is such a miserable, guilt-ridden specimen that he eventually becomes paradoxically appealing. The Saratoga setting is another asset; buildings, locations and inhabitants are vividly described." Libr J

Saratoga snapper. Viking 1986 260p o.p.
LC 85-41075

Charlie Bradshaw's "mother owns the hotel where his friend Victor Plotz photographs a group at the bar. Later, a hit-run driver nearly kills Victor. While he's hospitalized, Charlie begins to unwind the tortured skein of events that are apparently unrelated: a young maid is found dead in the hotel; one of the people in the photo commits suicide; several local liquor stores are robbed.

Dobyns, Stephen, 1941-—*Continued*

Everything is unexpected in the ingeniously plotted adventure—most of all, the hair-trigger climax and Charlie's way of shielding the pitiful people innocently involved in a shocking crime." Publ Wkly

Saratoga strongbox; a Charlie Bradshaw mystery. Viking 1998 198p $21.95

ISBN 0-670-87692-5 LC 98-2886

This Bradshaw racetrack adventure "begins when his sometime partner, Vic Plotz, agrees to pick up a mysterious suitcase in Montreal for a wealthy Saratoga entrepreneur. Ex-cop Charlie is soon investigating an assortment of strange characters, looking for a murderer." Libr J

"Dobyns keeps a grip on his farcical plot and gives his rambunctious characters plenty of room to win, place and show off." N Y Times Book Rev

Doctorow, Cory

Down and out in the Magic Kindgom. TOR Bks. 2003 208p $22.95

ISBN 0-7653-0436-8 LC 2002-73277

"A Tom Doherty Associates book"

"Jules, a relative youngster at more than a century old, is a contented citizen of the Bitchun Society that has filled Earth and near-space since shortage and death were overcome. . . . What Jules wants to do is move to Disney World, join the ad-hoc crew that runs the park and fine-tune the Haunted Mansion ride to make it even more wonderful. When his prudently stored consciousness abruptly awakens in a cloned body, he learns that he was murdered; evidently he's in the way of somebody else's dreams. . . . Doctorow has served up a nicely understated dish: meringue laced with caffeine." Publ Wkly

Doctorow, E. L., 1931-

Billy Bathgate; a novel. Random House 1989 323p o.p.

LC 88-42820

"Having grown up poor but ambitious on the Bronx's Bathgate Avenue during the Depression, young Billy is now being educated in the ways of the world. . . . [He] is a gangster-in-training employed by [Dutch Schultz]. . . . Billy falls for 'the Dutchman's' latest lady—a beauty named Drew Preston who eventually reciprocates his youthful passion. Soon Billy is questioning the actions of the mob he was so eager to join as he seeks to protect Drew from its vengeance." Libr J

This is the "story of Billy's education, conducted on an extravagant scale. Doctorow brings a nice sense of moral ambiguity and creates characters who develop or deteriorate at an appropriate pace. His fecund run-on sentences are a pleasure to read. It all adds up to that rarity: a formal literary work that's also hugely entertaining." Newsweek

The book of Daniel; a novel. Random House 1971 303p o.p.

"The trial of Julius and Ethel Rosenberg in 1950-51 for espionage was a cause célèbre during the fifties. The justice of administering the death penalty to that pair is still argued, particularly by the sons of the Rosenbergs. In this novel, which is based on that case, Daniel Isaacson tells of the effect of that execution on his childhood, marriage, and career. The whole period of pre-World War II radicalism, the tyranny of the McCarthy era, the peace march on the Pentagon in 1967, the nature of left-wing politics in the United States are the elements that make this a provocative sociopolitical novel." Shapiro. Fic for Youth. 3d edition

City of God; a novel. Random House 2000 272p o.p.

ISBN 0-679-44783-0 LC 99-53215

"In fall 1999, a brass cross disappears from St. Timothy's Episcopal Church in Manhattan and reappears at an Upper West Side synagogue, forcing clergy deep into a religious mystery." Libr J

This is Doctorow's "most vital—and most difficult—work yet. . . . Without linear plot or unified voice, City of God is tessellated, a mosaic touching on love and loneliness, faith and physics. It glints and glimmers, reflecting off rather than building upon itself, and adding up to a sum greater than its multifarious parts." Nation

Lives of the poets; six stories and a novella. Random House 1984 145p o.p.

ISBN 0-394-52530-2 LC 84-42513

Contents: The writer in the family; The Water Works; Willi; The hunter; The foreign legation; The leather man; Lives of the poets

"The novella 'Lives of the Poets' ponders life and middle-aged love among East Coast literati. Here knowingness is all, with chat about 'Swiss-water-process decaffeinated coffee' overlaying narrator Jonathan's awareness that 'between the artist and simple dereliction there is a very thin line.'" Libr J

"The stories in this collection show Doctorow as an impeccable stylist, a man who writes with exceptional clarity and precision, who finds fresh, touching metaphors for the human condition. While the times and settings vary, all these tales picture the individual in a disintegrating society in which everyone lives in emotional isolation." Publ Wkly

Lives of the poets [novelette]

In Doctorow, E. L. Lives of the poets p81-145

Loon Lake. Random House 1980 c1979 258p o.p.

LC 79-5526

Set in the 1930's the narrative "covers several picaresque years in the life of a young roughneck from Paterson, the son of wretchedly poor mill hands, who runs away from home, joins a gang of hobos, becomes a carnival roustabout, and stumbles accidentally onto Loon Lake, the vast Adirondack estate of the steel tycoon F. W. Bennett. One of the old industrialist's toys is a gangster's moll who sneaks out of Loon Lake with Joe, and the two settle down for a while in a steel town owned by one of Bennett's many companies. She leaves him, and Joe goes back to Loon Lake [and] is taken in by the old man." Commentary

"Doctorow has written a myth about the inheritance of America. Many techniques enhance the epic feeling. The novel is set in 1936, yet ranges across the first half of the century, even as it shifts viewpoints from the young man's memories to the poet's verses." Books of the Times

The march. Random House 2005 363p $25.95

ISBN 0-375-50671-3 LC 2005-46452

Doctorow, E. L., 1931-—*Continued*

"The march in question is that of General William Tecumseh Sherman and his Union soldiers as they slash and burn their way through Georgia and the Carolinas, and the 'march to freedom' as liberated slaves fall in step with the liberating army. But it is also, given the poetic depth of Doctorow's vision, the great march of time and of humanity in all its cruelty and glory. As Doctorow dramatizes the fury, conviction, and chaos of the Civil War, he portrays historical figures, as he is wont to do, most electrifyingly Sherman himself. But he focuses most on brilliantly imagined characters who embody the epic conflicts of that cataclysmic era, including Pearl, the smart and courageous daughter of a slave and slave owner; an excessively clinical military surgeon; the valiant daughter of a Southern judge; a freed slave who becomes a war photographer; and Arly, a scheming Rebel soldier who provides shrewdly comic relief. Doctorow writes with blazing clarity about the 'brutal romance' of war and its gruesome realities, with lyrical splendor about nature, and with wry wisdom and nimble satire about human folly." Booklist

Ragtime. Modern Lib. 1994 320p o.p.

ISBN 0-679-60088-4 LC 93-43631

This is a reissue of the title first published 1975 by Random House

"The lives of an upper-middle-class family in New Rochelle; a black ragtime musician who loses his love, his child, and his life because of bigotry; and a poor immigrant Jewish family are interwoven in this early-twentieth-century story. There are cameo appearances by well-known figures of that period: Houdini, anarchist Emma Goldman, actress Evelyn Nesbit, Henry Ford, and J.P. Morgan, whose magnificent library plays an important part in the story. The book mingles fact and fiction in portraying the era of ragtime." Shapiro. Fic for Youth. 3d edition

Sweet land stories. Random House 2004 147p $22.95

ISBN 1-400-06204-7 LC 2003-58780

Contents: A house on the plains; Baby Wilson; Jolene: a life; Walter John Harmon; Child, dead, in the rose garden

"As one might expect of Doctorow, the title is ironic. In settings that range across the U.S., most of the alienated characters in the five stories here find life anything but sweet as they struggle to surmount the stigmas of poverty, lack of education and their instincts to gamble against the odds. . . . In this knowing treatment of the cynical abuse of power, Doctorow uses the spare, laconic style endemic to thrillers and builds suspense with sure strokes. Boring like a laser into the failures of the American dream, he captures the resilience of those who won't accept defeat." Publ Wkly

The waterworks. Random House 1994 253p o.p.

ISBN 0-394-58754-5 LC 93-44735

"Martin Pemberton, renegade son of rich, unscrupulous Augustus Pemberton and favorite freelance of the persevering editor of the New York *Telegram*, . . . narrates this tale. First, Martin claims to have seen his dead father on a horse-drawn omnibus, and then he disappears. The worried editor contacts Inspector Edmund Donne—the only honest cop in 1870s New York, where the Tweed Ring holds sway—and eventually they discover that the ailing Augustus is part of an experiment by the brilliant Dr. Sartorius to prolong the lives of several old men rich enough to foot the bill." Libr J

Welcome to Hard Times. Simon & Schuster 1960 180p o.p.

"A novel about a small town in the barren West at the close of the last century. . . . The tale revolves around a bad-man who destroys the town of Hard Times in one day, causally and cruelly; a mayor who is too weak to kill the bad-man but who is hopeful enough to rebuild the town; and a woman of easy virtue who waits, in terror and hatred, for the return of the bad-man." Springfield Repub

Docx, Edward

The calligrapher. Houghton Mifflin 2003 360p $24

ISBN 0-618-34397-0 LC 2003-51149

The novel's "protagonist, Jasper Jackson, is a Londoner whose current job is to transcribe the Songs and Sonnets of John Donne for a wealthy client. Like Donne, Jasper is also a relentless womanizer, a charming cad who lives for love affairs. When the woman of his dreams appears in his own garden, Jasper succumbs to real love for the first time and slowly begins to realize what it feels like to be the pursuer rather than the pursued." Publ Wkly

Dodd, Susan M., 1946-

Ethiopia

In Dodd, S. M. O careless love

O careless love; stories and a novella; {by} Susan Dodd. Morrow 1999 274p o.p.

ISBN 0-688-16999-6 LC 99-11468

This volume includes the novella Ethiopia and the following short stories: So far you can't imagine; The lost art of sleep; Lady Chatterley's root canal; I married a space alien; Lokey man; Adult education; Song and dance man; What I remember now; In France they turn to stone when they die

"The novella, 'Ethiopia,' is one of three stories where a black male protagonist and a white woman, both writers, take tentative steps toward love, and Dodd's turnabout plot, where each is almost destroyed by lack of self-worth, is spun with measured lucidity." Publ Wkly

Doenges, Judy, 1959-

God of gods

In Doenges, J. What she left me: stories and a novella p116-73

What she left me: stories and a novella. Middlebury College Press 1999 173p $22.95

ISBN 0-87451-937-3 LC 99-30945

"The Katharine Bakeless Nason literary publication prizes"

Contents: What she left me; MIB; Crooks; Solved; The money stays, the poeple go; Occidental; Disaster; The whole numbers of families; Incognito; God of Gods [novella]

"Marginal may be the best overall descriptor for these characters, who, whether working class or elite, and de-

Doenges, Judy, 1959—*Continued*
spite outward appearances, roil with inner turmoil. Certainly, the sad poignancy and the dark humor of their lives touch us deeply." Booklist

Doerr, Harriet

Consider this, señora. Harcourt Brace & Co. 1993 241p o.p.
ISBN 0-15-193103-8 LC 93-21471
This "novel focuses on expatriate Americans in Mexico searching for love, connection and meaning. Three women buy land on the hillside hard by a poverty-stricken village whose inhabitants view them with gentle bewilderment." Publ Wkly
"Doerr instills each of her memorable characters with great dignity and resilience, and bestows upon her entranced readers a deep sense of peace and wonder." Booklist

Stones for Ibarra. Viking 1984 214p o.p.
LC 83-47861
"When Sara and Richard Everton pack up their belongings and mortgage themselves to leave California for a small village in Mexico, their friends think they are crazy. Many of the Mexican natives in the village of Ibarra also consider the two gringos incredible. While Sara restores the house that had belonged to Richard's grandparents, Richard restores a copper mine that had been his family's, and thereby gives employment to many of the villagers. We learn that Richard has leukemia and has been given just a few years to live, but it is the lives of the villagers that are more full of tragedy, religious commitment, and reliance on talismans and prayers. There is a strength among these people and an acceptance of all that life brings which make them memorable. Learning from them, perhaps, Sara finally accepts the inevitability of her husband's death." Shapiro. Fic for Youth. 3d edition

The tiger in the grass; stories and other inventions. Viking 1995 210p o.p.
LC 95-32391
Contents: The flowering stick; Carnations; The extinguishing of Great-Aunt Alice; The seasons; Sun, pure air, and a view; The local train; Way stations; The watchman at the gate; Saint's Day; Please; Low tide at four; Like heaven; A sleeve of rain
"In this elegant collection of stories and 'inventions,' never before published in book form, Doerr opens the window on her own past: childhood in California, marriage, . . . child-rearing experiences and the bold decision to return to school after the death of her husband. These are revelatory tales full of tenderness, humor, and gratitude, but the jewels of the collection are Doerr's stories about life in Mexico, the place dearest to her heart." Booklist

Doherty, P. C.

The Anubis slayings; a story of intrigue and murder set in ancient Egypt. St. Martin's Minotaur 2001 c2000 308p o.p.
ISBN 0-312-27658-3
First published 2000 in the United Kingdom
An historical mystery set in ancient Egypt "where principal judge Amertoke must solve a series of gruesome murders. It is 1497 B.C.E. and the Pharaoh Queen Hatusu (Hatshepsut) is in the process of consolidating power and taking over as ruler after her husband's death. She has just defeated the Mitanni, and formal peace negotiations are in progress. Someone wearing a jackal mask that resembles the god Anubis is poisoning people." Booklist
"Although he's essentially working with the elements of a locked-room mystery, Doherty cloaks his technique in the morbid trappings of the Theban death industry." N Y Times Book Rev

The demon archer; {by} Paul Doherty. St. Martin's Press 2001 c1999 250p o.p.
ISBN 0-312-27287-1
First published 1999 in the United Kingdom
"It's 1303 and Edward I sends Corbett, Clerk of the Secret Seal, to Ashdown to investigate the death of Lord Henry Fitzalan, shot through the heart by an arrow. Lord Henry was Edward's proposd emissary to Phillip, the king of France, regarding the marriage of Edward's son Prince William, to Phillip's daughter, Isabella. . . . Of particular note are the inquiries conducted by Corbett that not only reveal the souls of the characters but create a vivid portrait of the evil Lord Henry." Publ Wkly

The devil's hunt. St. Martin's Press 1998 249p o.p.
ISBN 0-312-18084-5 LC 97-43668
First published 1996 in the United Kingdom
"Recently shed of his duty to King Edward as agent and courier, Sir Hugh Corbett finds he must reenter the king's service to route out another murderer. Someone in or near Oxford has murdered a series of beggars, leaving their grisly heads hanging in nearby trees. When treasonous proclamations appear on a church door and murder also strikes down the university's regent and others, Corbett begins to wield his astute powers of observation." Libr J
"Doherty's authentic historical detailing will appeal to discriminating fans of medieval mysteries." Booklist

The gates of hell; a mystery of Alexander the Great; [by] Paul Doherty. Carroll & Graf Pubs. 2003 292p il $24
ISBN 0-7867-1157-4
This mystery revolves "around the military exploits of Alexander the Great and the behind-the-scenes adventures of Telamon, his boyhood friend and personal physician. When Alexander's determination to invade and conquer Halicarnassus, a city inextricably linked to his infamous father, is threatened by an unsettling series of murders within his own inner circle, Telamon must use his considerable powers of detection in order to uncover a treasonous plot linked to the legendary Pythian manuscript. Booklist

The godless man; a mystery of Alexander the Great; [by] Paul Doherty. Carroll & Graf Pubs. 2002 303p $25
ISBN 0-7867-0995-2 LC 2002-67397
"After his mighty victory at the Granicus in 334 B.C., Alexander the Great sweeps deeper into Persia in this multilayered and entertaining mystery, but when his army captures the city of Ephesus, the march of conquest seems doomed to halt in the face of intrigue and multiple murders." Publ Wkly

Doherty, P. C.—*Continued*

The house of death; a mystery of Alexander the Great; {by} Paul C. Doherty. Carroll & Graf Pubs. 2001 276p o.p.

ISBN 0-7867-0853-0 LC 2001-28828

"Anxious to dominate the Persian empire in 334 B.C.E., Alexander the Great awaits a sign from the gods. He instead finds intrigue, secret agendas, spies, and murder. The appearance of boyhood friend Telamon gives him a trusted ear—he hopes." Libr J

"Fans of ancient historical mysteries will find themselves in superbly practiced hands." Publ Wkly

The masked man. St. Martin's Press 1991 174p o.p.

LC 91-20033

This novel "offers a plausible, fact-based solution to the identity of the Man in the Iron Mask. The Duke of Orleans frees imprisoned Englishman Ralph Croft so that the cunning forger can use his underworld contacts to determine the name of the disguised prisoner, now dead some 16 years. Forced to work with a dangerous archivist and a duplicitous soldier, Croft dodges assassins and tangles with secretive Knights Templar as he deciphers ambiguous clues." Libr J

"A tour de force of retrospective detection." Booklist

The slayers of Seth; a story of intrigue and murder set in ancient Egypt. St. Martin's Minotaur 2002 288p o.p.

ISBN 0-312-28264-8 LC 2002-24861

First published 2001 in the United Kingdom

"Lord Amertoke, chief judge of Pharaoh Queen Hatusu's court, has his hands full in his latest adventure. . . . A young scribe has been poisoned, and his lover, Lady Neshretta, is the prime suspect. Since she is from a noble family, the crime is a major topic of conservation in Thebes. While working hard to sort out the facts in this case, Queen Hatusu sends Lord Amertoke to the Temple of Seth to investigate another high-profile crime. . . . An outstanding historical mystery." Booklist

A tournament of murders; the Franklin's tale of mystery and murder as he goes on pilgrimage from London to Canterbury. St. Martin's Press 1997 249p o.p.

LC 97-16501

First published 1996 in the United Kingdom

A mystery based on the "ribaldly picturesque world of Chaucer's *Canterbury Tales*. It's 14th-Century England, and the Black Prince, black plague and bloody war with France are all raging. The narrator is the Franklin, who tells a tale of murder, treachery and honor. As Sir Gilbert Savage lies dying on the French field at Poitiers, he calls his young squire, Richard Greenele, to his side and tells him to flee back to England and there seek out a lawyer who will reveal his true parentage to him, as well as how his father was framed and betrayed by one of his five trusted knights. . . . This swiftly moving tale has it all." Publ Wkly

Doig, Ivan

Bucking the sun; a novel. Simon & Schuster 1996 412p o.p.

ISBN 0-684-81171-5 LC 96-3814

The author "begins this saga with adultery and death, then moves backward to examine the causes. Just as the building of the mammoth Fort Peck Dam transforms the Montana countryside, it radically alters the lives of its Depression-era inhabitants. In particular, members of the Duff clan abandon subsistence farming and move to the construction boomtowns. There a father, three brothers, and their wives confront the task of building the largest earthen dam in the world, brave the dangers of such labor, and battle among themselves. . . . This richly detailed narrative offers comedy, passion, and adventure." Libr J

Dancing at the Rascal Fair. Atheneum Pubs. 1987 405p o.p.

LC 87-18672

Chronologically the first in the author's Montana trilogy

"The settlement of Montana between 1890 and 1919 is recounted through the quiet but compelling life of Angus McCaskill, a young Scotsman who travels with his friend Rob Barclay to Montana's Two Medicine Country to homestead." Libr J

"If the thorny individualism of Rob and Angus results in lives that are never easy, they are rich in incident and growth, beautifully described in Doig's strong, savory prose. America's frontier history comes vividly to life in this absorbing saga filled with memorable characters." Publ Wkly

English Creek. Atheneum Pubs. 1984 339p o.p.

LC 84-45051

This volume in the Montana trilogy chronologically follows Dancing at the Rascal Fair

"In the summer of 1939, in the high country of western Montana, 14-year-old Jick McCaskill wants to understand who he is and why. He lives in a boy's dream of wilderness, mountains, sheep ranches, national forests, and an amazing variety of small-town characters. His father is a forest ranger, his mother a practical, hard-nosed local woman; his brother wants to forego college for a girl and a cowboy's life. The summer climaxes in a forest fire that leads Jick and his father to discuss and understand some painful hidden events of their personal histories." Libr J

This "is a sensitive coming-of-age story as well as a portrait of a society still looking to its frontier past, but about to be engulfed by the future. The result is both highly personal and deeply engaging." Best Sellers

Mountain time; a novel. Scribner 1999 316p o.p.

ISBN 0-684-83295-X LC 99-14324

This novel focuses on "sisters Lexa and Mariah McCaskell. Lexa's marriage to a forest ranger and her days as cook in Alaska are behind her; now sturdy, capable Lexa runs a catering service in Seattle. She lives with rugged environmental journalist Mitch Rozier, another escapee from rough life in northern Montana. At 50, Mitch is facing a double crisis: the newspaper where his column appears is about to fold, and his foxy, rapacious father, Lyle, a notorious land despoiler, is dying of leukemia and has summoned him back to Twin Sulphur Springs. Lexa goes back to Montana, too, bringing her sexy sister, Mariah, just returned to the States after a year-long photographing expedition around the world. Lyle's illness and death unleash complex memories and

Doig, Ivan—*Continued*

future shocks." Publ Wkly

"A worthy addition to Doig's impressive saga of the twentieth-century West." Booklist

Prairie nocturne; a novel. Scribner 2003 371p $26

ISBN 0-7432-0135-3 LC 2003-50385

"Susan Duff, ever the recalcitrant singer, is now approaching middle age and living alone after a love affair with the wealthy Wesley Williamson. When Williamson's chauffeur, former rodeo clown Montgomery Rathbun, comes to him with the idea of honing his vocal talents, Williamson brings him to Susan. But Monty is black, and when he and Susan begin late-night voice lessons in a secluded cabin, thinking no one the wiser, its revelation incites the local Ku Klux Klan. Monty flees to New York, where he establishes a brilliant career as a singer of spirituals. On a concert tour back out west, however, old feuds reignite." Libr J

"By multiplying, deepening and texturing the genealogy of the Two Medicine country in the course of six novels, Doig has staked his claim as one of Montana's essential literary witnesses. . . . And no other writer since A.B. Guthrie has been more determined to evoke the supersized grandeur of Big Sky country, especially in a time when it was emptier and more suited to mythologizing than it is today." Washington Post Book World

Ride with me, Mariah Montana. Atheneum Pubs. 1990 324p o.p.

ISBN 0-689-12019-2 LC 90-35834

Concluding volume of the author's Montana trilogy

"To explore the meaning of Montana's century of statehood, 65-year-old Jick McCaskill, his photographer daughter Mariah, and her newspaper columnist ex-husband Riley Wright tour the Treasure State in Jick's Winnebago. While Riley writes on-the-scene dispatches and Mariah takes photos of the places they visit, Jick, the narrator, recounts the state's—and his family's—good and bad times. A lengthy picaresque with innumerable well-crafted vignettes, this leisurely novel could easily serve as a tour guide of Montana's historic places. As the miles go by, Riley and Mariah again fall in and out of love, and Jick, a widower, unexpectedly finds a new mate." Libr J

Donaldson, Stephen R.

The Illearth war. Holt, Rinehart & Winston 1977 407p il o.p.

LC 77-8621

In this second volume, Lord Foul the Despiser continues his attack against the Land with the Illearth Stone. Covenant and the daughter of the High Lord, Elena, undertake a mission into a mountain region, where they hope they will find the ancient gnostic power that will combat the Stone

Lord Foul's bane. Holt, Rinehart & Winston 1977 369p il o.p.

LC 77-73868

Thomas Covenant, a man burdened with a stigma that has isolated him, is suddenly sent to a mysterious magic world known as the Land. The Land has an immortal enemy—Lord Foul the Despiser—who wishes to destroy it. In Thomas, who does not believe in the Land's life-restoring powers, Lord Foul thinks he has found the perfect tool for his purpose

The One Tree. Ballantine Bks. 1982 475p o.p.

LC 81-17596

"A Del Rey book"

This is the central volume of the second trilogy about the Land

"Covenant finds that his role as savior of the Land must be shared with another from our world, Dr. Linden Avery. . . . To stop Lord Foul's terrible concatenation of plagues, the Sunbane, they sail with giants on a granite ship in search of the One Tree. Covenant hopes to fashion from it a new Staff of the Law to restore the natural order Foul has overturned." Publ Wkly

Penance

In Donaldson, S. R. Reave the Just and other tales p149-203

The power that preserves. Holt, Rinehart & Winston 1977 379p il o.p.

LC 77-10814

In this final volume of the first trilogy Covenant makes his way to the stronghold of Lord Foul the Despiser. He is accompanied by his friend Saltheart Foamfollower, a Giant. But it is Covenant who must meet Foul in final combat, to ensure survival for the Land and to achieve salvation for himself

"Below the stirring adventure tale is a poignant and profoundly religious chronicle of a quest for self-esteem and peace." Booklist

Reave the Just and other tales; stories. Bantam Bks. 1999 370p o.p.

ISBN 0-553-11034-9 LC 98-24075

Included in this volume are the novellas The woman who loved pigs and Penance and the following short stories: Reave the Just; The djinn who watches over the accursed; The killing stroke; The kings of Tarshish shall bring gifts; What makes us human; By any other name

"The best pieces are the novellas 'The woman who loved pigs,' which vividly depicts the cunning of dueling magicians who alter the lives of ordinary folk, and 'Penance,' which sets the redemption of a vampire in a well-drawn medieval setting." Publ Wkly

The runes of the earth; Stephen R. Donaldson. G.P. Putnam's Sons 2004 xx, 532p (Last chronicles of Thomas Covenant) $26.95

ISBN 0-399-15232-6 LC 2004-50526

"It is 10 years since Thomas Covenant's death, and Linden Avery runs the small mental hospital in which Covenant's widow, Joan, is confined. Roger Covenant, newly turned 21, visits Avery and tries to get his mother released. Failing at that, he kidnaps Joan as well as Avery's adopted son, then commits several murders and flees to the Land, the other world of Covenant sagas. Roger is clearly doing Lord Foul's bidding, and Avery has no choice but to follow him. She discovers that in the Land three and a half millennia have passed. The Haruchai are now called the Masters and distrust Earthpower, and an old man, Anele, who is full of Earthpower, is key to finding the lost and essential Staff of Law. . . . Expect readers to swarm." Booklist

Donaldson, Stephen R.—*Continued*

This day all gods die: the gap into ruin. Bantam Bks. 1996 564p o.p.

LC 95-21037

"The struggle between Warden Dios, director of the United Mining Companies Police, and Horst Fasner, CEO of United Mining Companies itself, reaches a climax here. So does the tension between the human race and the alien Amnion, exacerbated by human development of a drug that prevents people from being mutated into the aliens. Meanwhile, much-victimized Morn Hyland and her motley crew are heading for Earth and arrive at the same time as an Amnion warship." Publ Wkly

White gold wielder. Ballantine Bks. 1983 485p il o.p.

LC 82-20640

"A Del Rey book"

This is the concluding volume of the second trilogy about the Land

"At the end of 'The One Tree,' Covenant failed to create a new Staff of Law to deliver the Land from the Sunbane, so he, Linden Avery, and their companions set out across the northern wastes to Revelstone, where Covenant extinguishes the Banefire. The paradox of white gold and venom has set him against his friends, however; when he faces Lord Foul at Mount Thunder, they believe that he will betray the Land, until that enigmatic created being, Vain, achieves his destiny." Libr J

The woman who loved pigs

In Donaldson, S. R. Reave the Just and other tales p205-55

The wounded Land. Ballantine Bks. 1980 497p il o.p.

LC 79-20644

"A Del Rey book"

This is the first volume of the second trilogy about the Land

"In the first of the second trilogy of his adventures, leper Thomas Covenant returns to the mysterious Land after nearly 4000 years have passed there (ten years in earth time). Dr. Linden Avery unexpectedly joins him and goes through the same denial and disbelief he had suffered before. Now the Land is suffering from unending plagues called the Sunbane, inflicted by the evil Lord Foul whom Covenant had defeated but not destroyed on his last visit. Although it is not necessary to have read the previous three to appreciate the breadth and scope of this grim fantasy, for those who have 'The Wounded Land' is absolutely compelling." SLJ

Donleavy, J. P. (James Patrick), 1926-

The ginger man. Complete and unexpurgated ed. Delacorte Press/Seymour Lawrence 1965 347p o.p.

Original French edition, 1955; first United States expurgated edition published 1958 by McDowell, Obolensky

"The central character, Sebastian Dangerfield, an American expatriate law student at Dublin's Trinity College, is the brawling outsider who lives in a world of fantasy to escape despair and loneliness. Donleavy uses the third person to describe what Dangerfield does, the first person to reveal his thoughts, enabling him to be both objective and subjective." Reader's Ency. 3d edition

The author's writing "is distinguished by humor, often inelegant, even coarse, but explosive and irresistible. Humor and poetry are his weapons. The whole novel is a wild and unpredictable outburst." Saturday Rev

The lady who liked clean rest rooms; the chronicle of one of the strangest stories ever to be rumored about around New York. St. Martin's Press 1997 126p il o.p.

ISBN 0-312-15563-8 LC 97-5852

"A Thomas Dunne book"

"Mrs. Jocelyn Guenevere Marchantiere Jones sweeps onto the scene as the doyenne of an estimable house and fortune in Scarsdale. . . . But Jocelyn's certainties are tested when her husband leaves her for a bit of 'fresh flesh.' Ever the lady, Jocelyn proposes modest terms for the divorce and holds her course through financial collapse. What follows is a freewheeling tour of our heroine's 'unexpurgated thoughts' as fortune bounces her down the peculiar social ladder that separates Scarsdale from Yonkers, Yonkers from the Bronx—and the New World nouveaux riches from the 'dignified homeless indigent.' Donleavy proves himself as much the master of certain New York social set and train corridor as he is of the psyche of a fresh-mouthed 43-year-old Daughter of the Confederacy." N Y Times Book Rev

Donleavy, James Patrick *See* Donleavy, J. P. (James Patrick), 1926-

Donoghue, Emma, 1969-

Slammerkin. Harcourt 2001 336p $30

ISBN 0-15-100672-5 LC 00-49867

First published 2000 in the United Kingdom

"Mary Saunders's mother scratches out a meager living as a seamstress in 1760s London, but Mary longs for a more luxurious life with fine ribbons and clothes. At 13, she sneers at her mother's suggestion that she take up the needle, then makes a fateful mistake that leads her into prostitution." Libr J

"In her storytelling, the author shrewdly alternates the point of view, a technique that, rather than feeling gratuitous and shticky as it so often does these days, works to put Mary in a delicious pickle, since the satisfaction of her deepest desires, and the revelation of her secret career, could crush those for whom she—and we—come to feel real affection." N Y Times Book Rev

Donohue, John J., 1956-

Sensei. Thomas Dunne Bks. 2003 258p $23.95

ISBN 0-312-28812-3 LC 2002-32507

"Someone who calls himself Ronin—masterless Samurai—is apparently killing off martial-arts masters across the U.S., and Connor Burke, a university professor and martial-arts student, is brought into the investigation by his brother, a New York detective assigned to the case. Connor recruits his own sensei, Yamshita, and this unusual pair uncover the facts with a combination of mental skill and good, old-fashioned (amateur) detective work." Booklist

Donovan, Anne

Buddha Da; Anne Donovan. 1st Carroll & Graf ed. Carroll & Graf Publishers 2004 330p pa $14
ISBN 0-7867-1336-4 (pa) LC 2004-45770
"Anne Marie's dad, a Glaswegian painter and decorator, has always been game for a laugh. So when he first takes up meditation at the Buddhist Center, no one takes him seriously. But as Jimmy becomes more involved in a search for the spiritual, his beliefs start to come into conflict with the needs of his wife, Liz. Cracks appear in their apparently happy family life, and the ensuing events change the lives of each family member." Publisher's note
"The transcribed brogue and gag-rich premise initially lend Buddha Da a slapstick feel. But as Jimmy's engagement with Buddhism deepens, the novel matures into an astute exploration of Donovan's enormously appealing characters." N Y Times Book Rev

Dorrestein, Renate

Without mercy; translated by Hester Velmans. Viking 2003 c2002 223p $23.95
ISBN 0-670-03188-7 LC 2002-44900
This translation first published 2002 in the United Kingdom
"First published in Holland, this work follows the grieving process of Franka and Phinus Vemeer as they attempt to deal with the senseless murder of their 15-year-old son. Dorrestein's novel . . . seems at first to be a straightforward exploration of parental grief but slowly transforms into a much darker story in which disturbing memories and relationship-destroying secrets are revealed in bits and pieces. The slow-building and well-crafted plot accurately illustrates the process by which guilt and denial become pathological." Libr J

Dorris, Michael

Cloud chamber; a novel. Scribner 1997 316p o.p.
ISBN 0-684-81567-2 LC 96-42544
Dorris's "first novel, 'A Yellow Raft in Blue Water,' traced the experiences of three generations of modern American Indian women. 'Cloud Chamber' stretches back farther still, to the 19th-century Irish immigrants whose descendants eventually fall in love with some of the black and Indian characters in that earlier book. . . . It tells the stories of five generations who live in Ireland, Kentucky and Seattle and on a Montana reservation." N Y Times Book Rev
"Though not unflawed—a few voices sound confusingly similar and a few characters are more types than people—this is a compellingly readable and emotionally satisfying novel, full of secrets and surprises." Booklist

The crown of Columbus; a novel; [by] Michael Dorris, Louise Erdrich. HarperCollins Pubs. 1991 382p o.p.
LC 90-55964
"Told in the very different voices of college professor lovers Vivian Twostar, Native American single mother, and Roger Williams, poet of an old New England family, the collaborative effort flows smoothly. Although estranged during Vivian's pregnancy, both are working on academic projects concerning the 500th anniversary of the discovery of North America by Columbus. The collision of their two lives is funny, vivid, and life-affirming." Libr J

Working men; stories. Holt & Co. 1993 286p o.p.
ISBN 0-8050-2296-1 LC 93-25558
Contents: The benchmark; Earnest money; Qiana; Name games; Groom service; Anything; The vase; Me and the girls; Jeopardy; The dark snake; Oui; Layaway; Shining agate; Decoration Day
"Dorris explores the inner terrain of dignified characters graced with exceptional patience and a profound, reflective reticence. In story after story, Dorris examines the power of unspoken emotions, the elusive but invaluable messages of silence, and the unforeseen leaps of faith that change lives and jump start love." Booklist

A yellow raft in blue water. Holt & Co. 1987 343p o.p.
ISBN 0-8050-0045-3 LC 86-26947
"The bitter rifts and inevitable bonds between generations are highlighted as a teenaged daughter, mother, and grand matriarch of an American Indian family tell their life stories. Humorous and poignant, with unique characters." SLJ

Dos Passos, John

The 42nd parallel. Harper 1930 426p o.p.
First volume of the author's U.S.A. trilogy
The characters "include Fainy McCreary ('Mac'), who eventually joins the Mexican Revolution; the ruthless J. Ward Moorehouse; Eleanor Stoddard, with whom he has an affair; and Charley Anderson, who later becomes a war hero and airplane manufacturer. These various interlocking strands are designed to show the U.S. on the eve of the First World War, rather than the development of particular individuals." Reader's Ency. 3d edition
Followed by 1919
also in Dos Passos, J. U.S.A.

1919. Harcourt Brace & Co. 1932 473p o.p.
In this second volume of the trilogy, the author continues his chronicle of life in America through the war years, giving glimpses of the lives and characters of five young Americans—a low caste sailor, the daughter of a Chicago minister, a young girl from Texas, a radical Jew, a young poet
"'1919' is literally what so many books are erroneously called, 'a slice of life.' With infinite skill that slicing is done by the author, and the raw surface which meets the reader's eye is the actual living, breathing record of a period in its most intense manifestation." Chicago Daily Trib
Followed by The big money (1936)
also in Dos Passos, J. U.S.A.

The big money
In Dos Passos, J. U.S.A.

Manhattan transfer. Harper 1925 404p o.p.
"Dos Passos creates a portrait of New York City in the first quarter of this century by telling the stories of many people. They include the daughter of an accountant, who loses hope for any future happiness when her first love

Dos Passos, John—*Continued*
commits suicide; a milkman who rises in status to become a union boss; and an immigrant sailor who starts as a bartender and becomes a wealthy bootlegger during Prohibition. There are happy and unhappy endings to these stories, but always the city plays an important role." Shapiro. Fic for Youth. 3d edition

also in Dos Passos, J. Novels, 1920-1925

Novels, 1920-1925; John Dos Passos. Library of America 2003 873p (The library of America, 142) $35

ISBN 1-931082-39-1 LC 2003-47529

Contents: One man's initiation, 1917; Three soldiers; Manhattan transfer

One man's initiation, 1917 (1920) focuses on a young American's experiences in France during a time of war. Three soldiers (1921) describes the lives of three men with three different backgrounds—an Indiana farmboy, an Italian-American store clerk, and a musician hoping to become a composer—and how they cope with life both on and off the battlefield. Manhattan transfer is entered separately.

One man's initiation: 1917
In Dos Passos, J. Novels, 1920-1925

Three soldiers
In Dos Passos, J. Novels, 1920-1925

U.S.A. Library of Am. 1996 1288p $40

ISBN 1-883011-14-0 LC 95-49282

An omnibus volume containing the trilogy titles: The 42nd parallel, first published 1930; 1919, first published 1932 and The big money, first published 1936

"U.S.A. tries to capture, through a diversity of fictional techniques, the variety and multiplicity of American life in the first decades of the 20th cent.; it presents various interlocking and parallel narratives, against a panoramic collage of real-life events, snatches of newsreel and popular song, advertisements, etc., with a commentary by the author as 'The Camera Eye.'" Oxford Companion to Engl Lit

Doss, James D.

The night visitor; a shaman mystery. Avon Twilight 1999 392p o.p.

ISBN 0-380-97721-4 LC 99-25049

Ute lawman Charlie Moon and Shaman Daisy Perika are featured in this "blend of modern murder and ancient beliefs, set on the Southern Ute Reservation in Colorado. Charlie investigates a murder associated with a paleontological dig, while Daisy senses a much older injustice. An excellent addition to the series." Libr J

The shaman's bones. Avon Bks. 1997 276p o.p.

ISBN 0-380-97424-X LC 96-52148

"Even though Ute police officer Charlie Moon's elderly aunt, a well-known visionary and shaman, warns him of impending violence on the Colorado reservation, he is ill prepared for what happens. Events begin with an Indian's bad check but escalate to child abandonment, a vicious attack on a female police trainee, murder, and the theft of another shaman's sacred objects. Doss uses setting and atmosphere to heighten the mystical aspects of his subject and astute characterization to enforce its credibility." Libr J

Dostoevskiĭ, Fedor Mikhaĭlovich *See*
Dostoyevsky, Fyodor, 1821-1881

Dostoyevsky, Fyodor, 1821-1881

The best short stories of Dostoevsky; translated with an introduction by David Magarshack. Modern Lib. 1992 xxvii, 348p o.p.

ISBN 0-679-60020-5 LC 92-50214

First Modern Library edition 1955

Contents: White nights; The honest thief; The Christmas tree and a wedding; The peasant Marey; Notes from the underground; A gentle creature; The dream of a ridiculous man

The brothers Karamazov; translated by Constance Garnett. Modern Library 1996 xxi, 880p $21

ISBN 0-679-60181-3

Written 1880

"The main plot involves Fyodor Pavlovich 'Karamazov' and his four sons: Dmitry, Ivan, Alyosha, and the bastard Smerdyakov. Fyodor Pavlovich, a depraved buffoon, is Dmitry's rival for the affections of the local siren, Grushenka, despite her checkered past and blemished reputation. Fyodor Pavlovich is a model of animation and irrationalism, who enjoys his depravity and is only encouraged by the shock and disapproval of others. After violent quarrels over Grushenka and over Dmitry's disputed inheritance, Fyodor Pavlovich is murdered. Dmitry is arrested and brought to trial for the crime. This basic line of action is complicated throughout the novel by a host of other factors masterfully linked to the main plot. . . . The literal, religious, social, and ethical levels of the novel are buttressed by the psychological probings for which Dostoyevsky is well known." Reader's Ency. 4th edition

Crime and punishment; translated from the Russian by Constance Garnett; with an introduction by Ernest J. Simmons. Modern Library 1994 xxiv, 629p $19.95

ISBN 0-679-60100-7

Written 1866

"The novel is a psychological analysis of the poor student Raskolnikov, whose theory that humanitarian ends justify evil means leads him to murder a St. Petersburg pawnbroker. The act produces nightmarish guilt in Raskolnikov. The narrative's feverish, compelling tone follows the twists and turns of Raskolnikov's emotions and elaborates his struggle with his conscience and his mounting sense of horror as he wanders the city's hot, crowded streets. In prison, Raskolnikov comes to the realization that happiness cannot be achieved by a reasoned plan of existence but must be earned by suffering." Merriam-Webster's Ency of Lit

The double
In Dostoyevsky, F. The short novels of Dostoevsky p475-615

The eternal husband
In Dostoyevsky, F. The short novels of Dostoevsky p343-473

The friend of the family
In Dostoyevsky, F. The short novels of Dostoevsky p617-811

Dostoyevsky, Fyodor, 1821-1881—*Continued*

The gambler; with Polina Suslova's diary; [by] Fyodor Dostoevsky; translated by Victor Terras; edited by Edward Wasiolek. University of Chicago Press 1972 xxxix, 366p o.p.

Written 1866

"The gambling mania of the tale's hero, Aleksey Ivanovich, is a reflection of the author's own weakness. The heroine of the story, Polina, is based on Polina Suslova, Dostoevski's lover in 1862-63." Reader's Ency. 4th edition

"The book contains, in addition to the main narrative, the diary kept by Polina Suslova detailing her affair with Dostoevskii, which he limns so graphically in the novel, a short story titled 'The stranger and her lover' also by Suslova, and a selection of letters exchanged between Dostoevskii and Suslova among others." Booklist

also in Dostoyevsky, F. The gambler, and other stories

also in Dostoyevsky, F. The short novels of Dostoevsky p1-126

The gambler, and other stories; by Fyodor Dostoevsky; from the Russian by Constance Garnett. Macmillan 1917 312p o.p.

First published 1914 in the United Kingdom

This volume contains two novelettes: The gambler and Poor people, written 1846, which has also appeared with the title: Poor folk. It also contains the story: The landlady

Poor people "tells of an impoverished, elderly clerk's hopeless struggle for respectability while concealing his love for an orphaned girl in a sentimentally expressed, paternal affection. An uncommon insight into the tragic futility of poor people in love is revealed, people victimized by cruel circumstances of contemporary society." Ency Britannica

The house of the dead; or, Prison life in Siberia. o.p.

First published in Russian in 1861-62; in English in 1881 under title: Buried alive. Variant titles: Prison life in Siberia, Memorials of a dead house and Memoirs from the house of the dead

"In this autobiography of a Russian landowner condemned to penal servitude in Siberia, Dostoevsky hardly troubles to disguise his own experiences. He traces the different effects of imprisonment on the moral nature, in the life-stories of a group of criminals. It is a terrible record of the anguish of the prisoner's lot." Baker. Guide to the Best Fic

The idiot; translated from the Russian by Richard Pevear and Larissa Volokhonsky; with an introduction by Richard Pevear. Everyman's Library 2002 xxxiii, 633p $23

ISBN 0-375-41392-8 LC 2001-33561

Written 1868

"Dostoevsky puts into a world of foolishness, vice, pretence, and sordid ambitions, a being who in childhood had suffered from mental disease, and who with an intellect of more than ordinary power retains the simplicity and clear insight of a child. . . . The deeply absorbing drama in which he is a protagonist turns on the salvation of a woman, Nastasya Filipovna who had been corrupted in young girlhood." Baker. Guide to the Best Fic

Notes from underground; translated from the Russian by Richard Pevear and Larissa Volkhonsky [sic]; with an introduction by Richard Pevear. Knopf 2004 xxxi, 126p $18

ISBN 1-4000-4191-0 LC 2003-59216

"Everyman's library"

Written 1864. Variant titles: Letters from the underworld and Memoirs from underground

"The work, which includes extremely misanthropic passages, contains the seeds of nearly all of the moral, religious, political, and social concerns that appear in Dostoyevsky's great novels. Written as a reaction against Nikolay Chernyshevsky's ideological novel What Is to Be Done? (1863), which offered a planned utopia based on 'natural' laws of self-interest, Notes from the Underground attacks the scientism and rationalism at the heart of Chernyshevsky's novel. The views and actions of Dostoyevsky's underground man demostrate that in asserting free will humans often act against self-interest." Merriam-Webster's Ency of Lit

also in Dostoyevsky, F. The best short stories of Dostoevsky p115-260

also in Dostoyevsky, F. The short novels of Dostoevsky p127-222

Poor people

In Dostoyevsky, F. The gambler, and other stories

The possessed; a novel in three parts; from the Russian by Constance Garnett. Macmillan Pub. Co. 1913 637p o.p.

Original Russian edition, 1892. Variant titles: Demons; The devils

"Loosely based on sensational press reports of a Moscow student's murder by fellow revolutionists, The possessed depicts the destructive chaos caused by outside agitators who move into a moribund provincial town. The enigmatic Stavrogin dominates the novel. His magnetic personality influences his tutor, the liberal intellectual poseur Stepan Verkhovensky, and the teacher's revolutionary son Pyotr, as well as other radicals. Stavrogin is portrayed as a man of strength without direction, capable of goodness and nobility. When Stavrogin loses his faith in God, however, he is seized by brutal desires he does not fully understand. In the end, Stavrogin hangs himself in what he believes is an act of generosity, and Stepan Verkhovensky is received into the church on his deathbed." Merriam-Webster's Ency of Lit

The short novels of Dostoevsky; with an introduction by Thomas Mann. Dial Press 1945 xx, 811p o.p.

Contents: The gambler; Notes from underground; Uncle's dream; The eternal husband; The double; The friend of the family

Uncle's dream

In Dostoyevsky, F. The short novels of Dostoevsky p223-342

Douglas, Carole Nelson

Cat in a midnight choir; a Midnight Louie mystery. Forge 2002 350p o.p.

ISBN 0-312-85797-7 LC 2001-58281

Douglas, Carole Nelson—*Continued*

"A Tom Doherty Associates book"

In this adventure Vegas cat sleuth "Louie's human roommate, Temple Barr, and her boyfriend, Max, are interested in a group of mysterious magicians called the Synth. Matters are complicated when a stripper is murdered, and police lieutenant C. R. Molina, a recurring character, identifies Max, also a magician, as a prime suspect. Alternating chapters—third-person human narration playing off against first-person Louie—move the action along briskly." Booklist

Cat in a neon nightmare; a Midnight Louie mystery. Forge 2003 365p $24.95

ISBN 0-7653-0680-8 LC 2002-45491

"A Tom Doherty Associates book"

In this episode sleuth and supercat Midnight Louie "and his human associates, Temple Barr and Max Kinsella, tangle with the Synth, a gang of outlaw magicians up to no good. Tracking down the elusive renegades takes Louie to a private magic club called Nightmare—imagine the bar in Star Wars but not quite as friendly." Booklist

Catnap; a Midnight Louie mystery. TOR Bks. 1992 241p o.p.

LC 91-33293

"A Tom Doherty Associates book"

"Midnight Louie, whose cat-memoirs bracket the discovery of a murdered book publisher at the American Booksellers Association, 'helps' public relations person Temple Barr discover the murderer's identity. Las Vegas provides a slightly surreal backdrop for Temple's 'smooth' friends and sly acquaintances, who alternately provide assistance or muck things up." Libr J

"Douglas's fine-turned sense of humor gives her tame plot enough of a spin to keep readers entertained." Publ Wkly

Douglas, Lloyd C. (Lloyd Cassel), 1877-1951

The Big Fisherman. Houghton Mifflin 1948 581p o.p.

"More than a fictional biography of the Apostle, Simon Peter, this . . . novel re-creates the Biblical background and personages of the time. Romance and adventure enter in the form of an Arabian prince who is searching for a beautiful Jewish-Arabian princess." Cincinnati Public Libr

"With the exception of the Arabian scenes, the story follows the biblical account of Peter, necessarily much condensed. The personalities of Peter and others of the disciples receive interesting and plausible interpretations; the modern idiom is used with somewhat startling effect, and frequent references are made to many persons actual and fictitious who appeared in 'The Robe'." Booklist

Magnificent obsession. Houghton Mifflin 1929 330p o.p.

The "magnificent obsession" that was the secret of the famous Dr. Hudson's success—a newly interpreted Christian teaching—was put into practice at Dr. Hudson's death by the young man who became his successor as a brain specialist, Bobby Merrick. Bobby, by continuing his 'personality-investments' in the way of secret philanthropies, as advocated by Dr. Hudson's formula, miraculously succeeds, and makes a famous surgical invention with which he is able to save the life of the woman he loves

Followed by Doctor Hudson's secret journal (1939)

The robe. Houghton Mifflin 1942 556p o.p.

"The story of Christ's robe and the influence it had on the wealthy young Roman soldier who won it at dice. Marcellus' personal affairs and conversion to Christianity are of chief interest, but with them is given a picture of the rise of Christianity in the first few years after Christ's crucifixion." Booklist

"Perhaps the narrative is a bit too diffuse and attempts to cover too much ground, but on the whole it is an interesting effort at explaining a time of crisis that has many points of similarity to our own. It is a skillful storytelling with high intent." Christ Century

Douglas, Michael *See* Crichton, Michael, 1942-

Douglass, Billie, 1945-

For works by this author see Delinsky, Barbara, 1945-

Dove, Rita

Through the ivory gate; a novel. Pantheon Bks. 1992 278p o.p.

LC 92-4456

"Virginia King, a talented young black woman, returns to her hometown of Akron, Ohio, as artist-in-residence at an elementary school. The story moves back and forth between the present, which finds her teaching puppetry to children, and her past, which includes memories of a constricting community and family life and the liberation offered by college and her stint with a communal puppet theater." Publ Wkly

"Whether she is evoking the look of a landscape or depicting the nuances of a family quarrel, Dove sees with the keen eye of an artist and writes with the finely honed diction of a poet. In Virginia King, she has created a distinctive, highly individualized heroine." Christ Sci Monit

Doyle, Sir Arthur Conan, 1859-1930

Adventures of Sherlock Holmes; by A. Conan Doyle. Harper 1892 307p il o.p.

Contains the following stories: Scandal in Bohemia; Redheaded League; Case of identity; Boscombe Valley mystery; Five orange pips; Man with the twisted lip; Adventure of the Blue Carbuncle; Adventure of the speckled band; Adventure of the engineer's thumb; Adventure of the noble bachelor; Adventure of the Beryl Coronet; Adventure of the copper beeches

also in Doyle, Sir A. C. The complete Sherlock Holmes

The best science fiction of Arthur Conan Doyle; edited by Charles G. Waugh and Martin H. Greenberg; with an introduction by George E. Slusser. Southern Ill. Univ. Press 1981 190p o.p.

LC 81-8884

"Alternatives"

Contents: The American's tale; The Los Amigos fiasco; The great Keinplatz experiment; The adventure of the devil's foot; The adventure of the creeping man; The ter-

Doyle, Sir Arthur Conan, 1859-1930—*Continued*
ror of Blue John Gap; Through the veil; The last galley; The great Brown-Pericord motor; The horror of the heights; Danger; The lift; The disintegration machine; When the world screamed

"The 14 pieces inevitably include a couple of Sherlock Holmes stories. They also include 2 of the not-so-readily-available Professor Challenger tales . . . and 10 other stories spread over more than 40 years of the author's career." Booklist

The case book of Sherlock Holmes
In Doyle, Sir A. C. The complete Sherlock Holmes

The complete Sherlock Holmes; with a preface by Christopher Morley. Doubleday 1960 c1930 1122p $27.95
ISBN 0-385-00689-6
First published 1930
Fifty-eight Sherlock Holmes stories which were originally published in nine separate volumes: A study in scarlet (1887); The sign of the four (1890); Adventures of Sherlock Holmes (1892); Memoirs of Sherlock Holmes (1894); The return of Sherlock Holmes (1905); The hound of the Baskervilles (1902); The valley of fear (1915); His last bow (1917); The case book of Sherlock Holmes (1927)

Conan Doyle's tales of medical humanism and values: Round the red lamp; being facts and fancies of medical life, with other medical short stories; edited with introduction, commentaries, and notes by Alvin E. Rodin and Jack D. Key. Krieger 1992 481p il $57.50
ISBN 0-89464-571-4 LC 90-24909
This volume includes the collection Round the red lamp which was first published in 1894
Round the red lamp includes the following stories: Behind the times; His first operation; A straggler of '15; The third generation; A false start; The curse of Eve; Sweethearts; A physiologist's wife; The case of Lady Sannox; A question of diplomacy; A medical document; Lot no. 249; The Los Amigos fiasco; The doctors of Hoyland; The surgeon talks
Other stories included in this volume are: Crabbe's practice; The great Keinplatz experiment; The ring of thoth

Famous tales of Sherlock Holmes. Dodd, Mead 1958 339p il o.p.
"Great illustrated classics"
Contents: A study in scarlet (1887); A scandal in Bohemia; The Red-headed League; The sign of the four (1890); The Boscombe Valley mystery

His last bow
In Doyle, Sir A. C. The complete Sherlock Holmes

The hound of the Baskervilles; introduction by Laurie R. King; notes by James Danly. Modern Library 2002 xx, 181p pa $7.95
ISBN 0-8129-6606-6 LC 2002-29505
First published 1902
This is the "case of the eerie howling on the moor and strange deaths at Baskerville. Sir Charles Baskerville is murdered, and Holmes and Watson move in to solve the crime." Haydn. Thesaurus of Book Dig
"By a miracle of judgment, the supernatural is handled with great effect and no letdown. The plot and subplots are thoroughly integrated and the false clues put in and removed with a master hand. The criminal is superb, Dr. Mortimer memorable, and the secondary figures each contribute to the total effect of brilliancy and grandeur combined. One wishes one could be reading it for the first time." Barzun. Cat of Crime. Rev and enl edition
also in Doyle, Sir A. C. The complete Sherlock Holmes

The lost world. Doran, G.H. 1912 309p il o.p.
"Two professors and two other Englishmen come across a region in the Amazon valley where the Jurassic period still persists, with its flora and fauna, pterodactyls, dinosaurs, iguanodons, and other beasts that we know only in fossil form, still flourishing. The scientific squabbles of Challenger and the other professor provide incidental comedy." Baker. Guide to the Best Fic

Memoirs of Sherlock Holmes
In Doyle, Sir A. C. The complete Sherlock Holmes

The return of Sherlock Holmes; a facsimile of the stories as they were first published in The Strand Magazine, London; with Sidney Paget's original illustrations and with a new introduction by Samuel Rosenberg. Schocken Bks. 1975 193p il o.p.
Originally published 1903-1904 in The Strand Magazine
Contents: The adventure of the empty house; The adventure of the Norwood builder; The adventure of the dancing men; The adventure of the solitary cyclist; The adventure of the Priory School; The adventure of Black Peter; The adventure of Charles Augustus Milverton; The adventure of the six Napoleons; The adventure of the three students; The adventure of the golden pinz-nez; The adventure of the missing three-quarter; The adventure of Abbey Grange; The adventure of the second stain
also in Doyle, Sir A. C. The complete Sherlock Holmes

Round the red lamp
In Doyle, Sir A. C. Conan Doyle's tales of medical humanism and values: Round the red lamp p15-302

The sign of four; with an introduction by Graham Greene. Doubleday 1977 134p o.p.
First published 1890 in the United Kingdom. Variant title: The sign of the four
Mary Morstan, the future wife of Dr. Watson, engages Holmes to trace her vanished father. Four years after his disappearance, Miss Morstan began receiving an annual gift of a large and lustrous pearl. Now her unknown benefactor has summoned her to a rendezvous outside the Lyceum Theater. As Holmes unravels the mystery, the Agra pearls are seen to be the center of a grim tale of murder and duplicity, which begins in India and ends in a chase through London's dockland
also in Doyle, Sir A. C. The complete Sherlock Holmes

Doyle, Sir Arthur Conan, 1859-1930—*Continued*
also in Doyle, Sir A. C. Famous tales of Sherlock Holmes p187-311

A study in scarlet; with an introduction by Hugh Greene. Doubleday 1977 145p o.p.

First published 1887

"A sensational story in two parts: the first deals with adventures in Utah and the wrong committed by two brutal Mormons on a girl and her lover; the second is the history of a mysterious double murder committed in London and, by the agency of Sherlock Holmes, shown to be the work of the wronged lover, who thus, after many years, attains his revenge." Baker. Guide to the Best Fic

also in Doyle, Sir A. C. The complete Sherlock Holmes

also in Doyle, Sir A. C. Famous tales of Sherlock Holmes p1-131

Tales of terror and mystery; introduction by Nina Conan Doyle Harwood; illustrated by Barbara Ninde Byfield. Doubleday 1977 224p il o.p.

"Although not as intricately plotted as the Sherlock Holmes stories, these 13 tales . . . display Doyle's attention to detail and uphold his reputation as a superb storyteller." SLJ

Uncollected stories; the unknown Conan Doyle; compiled and with an introduction by John Michael Gibson and Richard Lancelyn Green. Doubleday 1984 c1982 xxiii, 456p o.p.
LC 83-45159

First published 1982 in the United Kingdom

Contents: The mystery of Sasassa Valley; The American's tale; Bones. The April fool of Harvey's Sluice; Our Derby sweepstakes; That veteran; Gentlemanly Joe; The winning shot; An exciting Christmas Eve; Selecting a ghost. The ghosts of Goresthorpe Grange; The heiress of Glenmahowley; The cabman's story; The tragedians; The lonely Hampshire cottage; The fate of the Evangeline; Touch and go: a midshipman's story; Uncle Jeremy's household; The stone of Boxman's Drift; A pastoral horror; Our midnight visitor; The voice of science; The Colonel's choice; A sordid affair; A regimental scandal; The recollections of Captain Wilkie; The confession; The retirement of Signor Lambert; A true story of the tragedy of 'Flowery Land'; An impression of the Regency; The centurion; The death voyage; The Parish Magazine; The end of Devil Hawker; The last resource

This collection "runs the time gamut from 1879 to 1930 and includes ten tales never previously identified with Doyle. His work here is somewhat uneven but usually readable and covers a diverse range of styles and subjects. There are occasional Holmesian insights, but there's nary a sleuthing story in the lot." West Coast Rev Books

The valley of fear; a Sherlock Holmes novel; illustrated by Arthur I. Keller. Doran, G.H. 1915 320p il o.p.

First published 1914

"With the exception of 'The Hound of the Baskervilles,' our favorite among the long tales of Sherlock Holmes. Chapter 1 has in its ten pages some of the best wit and humor to be found anywhere, plus the solution of a cipher, and a stunning punch ending. Nor is there any serious letdown as Holmes, Watson, and Inspector MacDonald investigate the murder of John Douglas at Birlstone Manor in Sussex. The shadow of Moriarty appears early and comes into sharper focus at the end of the story after the long—and gripping—interlude dealing with Douglas' life among the 'scowrers' of the Pennsylvania coalfields." Barzun. Cat of Crime. Rev and enl edition

also in Doyle, Sir A. C. The complete Sherlock Holmes

The White Company; by A. Conan Doyle; pictures by N. C. Wyeth. Morrow 1988 366p il $24.99

ISBN 0-688-07817-6 LC 87-62625

First published 1891; this is a reissue of the edition published 1922 by Cosmopolitan Book Corporation

"The Hampshire hero joins an English Free Company, and, in the course of much wandering through France and the Pyrenees, meets with stirring adventures and performs many a deed of valour. The historical situation is that arising out of the Black Prince's decision to espouse the cause of Pedro the Cruel of Castile. Edward III, the Black Prince, Chandos, Sir William Felton, Bertrand du Guesclin, Don Pedro and others appear." Nield. Guide to the Best Hist Novels & Tales

Doyle, Conan *See* Doyle, Sir Arthur Conan, 1859-1930

Doyle, Roddy

Paddy Clarke, ha ha ha. Viking 1993 282p o.p.

"Set in the working-class environment of an Irish town in the late 1960s, the story is related by bright, sensitive 10-year-old Paddy Clarke, who, when we first meet him, is merely concerned with being as tough as his peers. Paddy and his best friend Kevin are part of a neighborhood gang that sets fires in vacant buildings, routinely teases and abuses younger kids and plays in forbidden places. In episodic fashion, Doyle conveys the activities, taboos and ceremonies, the daring glee and often distorted sense of the world of boys verging on adolescence." Publ Wkly

Doyle's "triumph in this novel is to replenish our sense of how children think and speak and explain the adult world to themselves." London Rev Books

A star called Henry. Viking 1999 343p o.p.

ISBN 0-670-88757-9 LC 99-25310

"The story is told in the voice of Henry Smart, born into harsh poverty in 1901 in Dublin. By age five, Henry was on his own, living in the streets of the city with his younger brother Victor in tow. . . . Fearless, more man than boy at 14, Henry was among the Irish rebels at the 1916 Easter Rising, pitching his own personal rage into the onset of Ireland's long and bloody battle for independence. Haunted by memories of a mother ravaged by poverty and repeated childbirths and by the fate of young Victor and his other siblings, Henry throws himself into the fight for the Republic." Booklist

"In Doyle's hands, the grand patriotic narrative is tempered with a sharp sense of humanity and human frailty." Times Lit Suppl

Doyle, Roddy—*Continued*

The woman who walked into doors. Viking 1996 226p o.p.
LC 95-41850

"Proud of her early-developed breasts, Paula O'Leary 'went with' lots of boys from her working-class Dublin neighborhood. With perfectly timed dance moves to 'My Eyes Adored You,' Charlo Spencer takes her. But he changes after their honeymoon. When Charlo first strikes her, she is stunned. His violent outbursts increase as slaps and bruises become yanked-out hair, broken fingers, and knocked-out teeth. While raising four children, she continues to be abused; she loses self-respect, denies how bleak things are, and drinks heavily." Booklist

Doyle "is a very, very good writer. 'The Woman Who Walked Into Doors' honors not the female experience in the abstract, but the experience of this one woman, Paula Spencer; it examines it with tenderness, but with fearless clearsightedness. And it's funny in places too. Paula Spencer is neither a victim nor a flawless Madonna; she inhabits the complexity of her mind and history; she acts to buy a better future for her children." N Y Times Book Rev

Dozois, Gardner R.

(ed) Year's best science fiction. See Year's best science fiction

Drabble, Margaret, 1939-

The gates of ivory. Viking 1992 463p o.p.
LC 91-39421

"Writer Stephen Cox, recently awarded the coveted Booker Prize, sets off for Cambodia after telling his friend, psychiatrist Liz Headleand, that there's nothing to keep him in London. No one hears from Stephen for months, and then Liz receives an odd package of his notebooks, newspaper clippings, manuscripts, and two finger bones. As she tentatively investigates Stephen's disappearance, the novel divides into a web of narratives." Booklist

"What seem mutually exclusive goals are realized: the characters are clear and compelling, objects of particular scrutiny; and the horrors of history are not trivialized by transposition to a tidily wrapped narrative. Drabble's achievement commands awe even as her subject matter rouses immeasurable stores of pity and terror." Publ Wkly

The middle ground. Knopf 1980 277p o.p.
LC 80-7630

"London life in the 1970's, with traditional British values surviving amidst foreign immigration, terrorism, and inflation, is the setting for [this] . . . novel. Kate Armstrong, daughter of a sewage worker, has become a popular journalist in the women's movement, but, at 40, begins to question her success. A recent failed love affair, an abortion, and exposure to a fiery young Arab radical, coinciding with a proposed documentary on women's choices, lead Kate to visit her old home town and to examine the paths taken by former schoolmates. Through these, and through the lives of Hugo and Evelyn, Kate's friends and co-narrators, Drabble explores . . . ways in which movements of recent decades have and have not changed the options open to men and women." Libr J

"Drabble, humane and wryly observant, has a certain grasp of life's silliness and dignity. She binds her readers to her with the same humorous intimacy that we find in the company of close friends." Harpers

A natural curiosity. Viking 1989 307p o.p.
LC 89-40166

In this "sequel to The Radiant Way, three middle-aged women, lifelong friends, continue their halting yet hopeful quest to find the lives they want amid the distractions and discontinuities of modern Britain. 'Life sets us unfair puzzles,' one of them says. 'Puzzles with pieces missing.' Supported by a rich cast of equally uncertain supporting characters, Drabble's women struggle gamely to find their missing pieces." Am Libr

Followed by The gates of ivory

The needle's eye; a novel. Knopf 1972 368p o.p.

"Rose Vassiliou, divorced from her mercurial husband Christopher and raising her children in near penury, is tossed between material needs and the desire to renounce her austere family's wealth and privilege. She comes under the protective, then loving eye of Simon Camish, a . . . barrister who sees Rose's heroic forbearance as a lesson against intrusions of unprinciple into his own tense, unhappy family life." Libr J

"It is hard not to hear these echoes [of Henry James and George Eliot] in the book's fine rendering of the close tangle of love and hate, truth and falsehood, integrity and corruption, in human emotion and human relationships, and its perception of how deeply these intangibles are affected by cruder realities like money—its presence or absence. . . . 'The needle's eye' is a novel that can enrich the reader's sense of his own humanity." Choice

The radiant way. Knopf 1987 407p o.p.
LC 87-45126

This first volume of a trilogy covers five years in the lives of three women who "met at Cambridge in the '50s. Liz Headleand is a Harley Street psychotherapist and mother of a large family; Alix Bowen teaches 'the poor, the dull and the subnormal' in government sponsored programs; Esther Breuer is an art scholar who has pared her life to minimal terms. Among them these women experience divorce, the death of a parent and of a lover, the loss of a job and a resulting sense of dislocation, an intimation of vulnerability as a ghastly murder affects their lives." Publ Wkly

Drabble "charts every hill and dale in the increasingly brighter landscape of middle-class women's roles (a progression that takes place, ironically, as Britain's economic power erodes). Drabble is a master of delicate phrasing set amid a big, robust narrative." Booklist

Followed by A natural curiosity

The realms of gold. Knopf 1975 354p o.p.

"Drabble juxtaposes the lives of distantly-related members of a family. Frances Wingate, middle-aging archaeologist, is a significant female protagonist who is granted intelligence, passion, ambition, foolishness, error, and goodness. The briefer portraits of her cousins Janet, small-town housewife trapped in despair, and David, solitary geologist, counterpoint Frances' struggles, underlining similarities as well as differences." Libr J

This "is an unusually stimulating novel of ideas—and something more. It is rare entertainment, shuttling bril-

Drabble, Margaret, 1939-—*Continued*
liantly between sandy African waters and tidy English villages. Perhaps as well as anyone now writing, Drabble can weave metaphysics into the homespun of daily life." Time

The witch of Exmoor. Harcourt Brace & Co. 1997 281p o.p.
ISBN 0-15-100363-7 LC 97-10952
First published 1996 in the United Kingdom
"The witch of Exmoor is Frieda Haxby Palmer, a writer 'social analyst, prophet, sage and sybil,' reluctant matriarch, and determined lone wolf. Bored with her three self-important and ambitious children and with all but one of her five grandchildren, and irritated by the viperish reviews of her last book, a historical novel about Queen Christina, she sold the family estate and bought a great, rotting mansion perched precariously above the sea. Here Frieda resides in eccentric solitude, working fitfully on her memoirs and enjoying her scheming family's increasing discomfort and concern over her sanity and her last will and testament." Booklist
"Can politics ever amount to more than the conspiracies we hatch against our parents and the spells we cast on our children? The humbling surprise of Drabble's novel is not that it refuses to resolve this question but that we gradually lose our lofty perspective and begin to have an emotional stake in the answer." New Yorker

Drake, Bonnie, 1945-
For works by this author see Delinsky, Barbara, 1945-

Drake, David, 1945-

Grimmer than hell. Baen Bks. 2003 373p $24
ISBN 0-7434-3590-7 LC 2002-34194
Contents: Rescue mission; When the devil drives; Team effort; The end; Smash and grab; Mission accomplished; Facing the enemy; Failure mode; The tradesmen; Coming up against it; With the sword he must be slain; Nation without walls; The predators; Underground
"Fourteen short stories and an introduction make up the latest, highly recommended collection from a leading light of military sf. . . . The intoduction puts everything in perspective with a minimum of apologetics, compressing Drake's psychological history since the Vietnam War into a short essay valuable to new and old fans alike." Booklist

Draper, Robert

Hadrian's walls. Knopf 1999 321p o.p.
ISBN 0-375-40369-8 LC 98-43203
"Shepherdsville, TX, is a prison town, dominated by the Hope Farm State Penitentiary and Sonny Hope—politician, con man, and director of the Texas Department of Criminal Retribution. Since childhood, Sonny has relied on others to do his dirty work for him and bail him out when things go wrong. His best friend, Hadrian Coleman, finds himself at age 15 serving a prison sentence for murder to protect Sonny. At 39, he is a long-term fugitive returned to Shepherdsville to receive a pardon arranged by Sonny. This is Hadrian's story—the murder, the escape, the pardon, the deal that follows—orchestrated by Sonny." Libr J
"Draper has found a modern Texas subject that is fresh and fertile: the exponential growth of the state's prison system and the rise of towns whose entire economies depend, with creepy exploitation, on incarceration." N Y Times Book Rev

Dreiser, Theodore, 1871-1945

An American tragedy. Boni & Liveright 1925 2v o.p.
"Clyde Griffiths, product of a poor and pious home, is driven by ambition to acquire money and social status. He is loved by Roberta, a factory coworker, but is dazzled by Sondra, who would be a passport to the country-club set. When Roberta, pregnant and no longer desirable, becomes an obstacle to Clyde's fulfilling his dream, he plans her death, for which he is caught and convicted." Shapiro. Fic for Youth. 3d edition

Jennie Gerhardt; a novel. Harper 1911 430p o.p.
"The fortunes of two families, German and Irish immigrants. Jennie, child of an unsuccessful German, falls a prey to the pleasure-loving son of the enterprising Irishman. Whether of deep-laid purpose or not, the book illustrates the rottenness of a complex social fabric resting on materialism." Baker. Guide to the Best Fic
also in Dreiser, T. Sister Carrie; Jennie Gerhardt; Twelve men

Sister Carrie; historical editors, John C. Berkey, Alice M. Winters; textual editor, James L.W. West III; general editor Neda M. Westlake; introduction by Alfred Kazin. Penguin Books 1994 499p pa $12.95
ISBN 0-14-018828-2
First published 1900
"A powerful account of a young working girl's rise to the 'tinsel and shine' of worldly success, and of the slow decline of her lover and protector Hurstwood." Oxford Companion to Engl Lit
also in Dreiser, T. Sister Carrie; Jennie Gerhardt; Twelve men

Sister Carrie; Jennie Gerhardt; Twelve men; . Library of America 1987 1168p il $40
ISBN 0-940450-41-0
Contents: Sister Carrie; Jennie Gerhardt; Twelve men
Sister Carrie and Jennie Gerhardt are entered separately. Twelve men (1919) presents brief biographical sketches of twelve men that have influenced the author's life

Drummond, Laurie Lynn, 1956-

Anything you say can and will be used against you; stories. HarperCollinsPublishers 2004 250p $23.95
ISBN 0-06-056162-9 LC 2003-51133
Contents: Something about a scar; Cleaning your gun; Taste, touch, sight, sound, smell; Finding a place; Under control; Katherine's elegy; Where I come from; Keeping the dead alive; Lemme tell you something; Absolutes
"Combining Southern grace and urban brutality, ex-cop Drummond debuts with 10 short stories grouped into five blistering fictional portraits of Baton Rouge policewomen. Each lady is tough even without her bul-

Drummond, Laurie Lynn, 1956-—*Continued*

letproof vest, and all are plagued by death and corruption as they undertake the bracing, dehumanizing enforcement of justice." Publ Wkly

Drury, Allen

Advise and consent; drawings by Arthur Shilstone. Doubleday 1959 616p il o.p.

"Robert A. Leffingwell, a liberal intellectual, is nominated by the President of the United States to be Secretary of State. The lives of four politicians are affected by the fight for his approval in the Senate. A suicide, a surprise witness at the hearings, a vote of censure, and some chicanery highlight the Washington political scene depicted in this novel." Shapiro. Fic for Youth. 3d edition

Dry, Richard, 1967-

Leaving; a novel. St. Martin's Press 2002 452p o.p.

ISBN 0-312-28331-8 LC 2001-41959

This novel "chronicles the efforts of an African-American family to overcome the inequities of racial injustice. The story begins in 1959, when matriarch Ruby Washington travels from her rural South Carolina home to Oakland in search of a better life. But by leaving, she unknowingly sets off a cycle of poverty and violence that will mar the lives of her children." Publ Wkly

"This brilliantly and beautifully written debut novel, with fully formed, realsitic characters, is dreadful in its stark glimpse at urban violence and disarray but beautiful in its portrait of family and love." Booklist

Du Maurier, Dame Daphne, 1907-1989

Daphne du Maurier's classics of the macabre; illustrated by Michael Foreman. Doubleday 1987 284p il $18.95

ISBN 0-385-24302-2 LC 87-9108

"Six of du Maurier's best stories admirably illustrated by a watercolorist, Michael Foreman, well able to catch their atmosphere. . . . Careful readers will notice that most of the creepy situations in these stories develop from marital stress and that sexual undertones sound everywhere. All readers ought to savor du Maurier's peerless narrative gift." Booklist

Don't look now. Doubleday 1971 303p o.p.

Published in the United Kingdom with title: Not after midnight and other stories

Contents: Don't look now; The breakthrough; Not after midnight; A border-line case; The Way of the Cross

The flight of the falcon. Doubleday 1965 311p o.p.

"An Italian tour guide in Rome recognizes a murder victim found on the steps of a Roman cathedral as his old nurse, whom he had last seen in Ruffano, a northern Italian town, when he was eleven. Afraid of being accused of the murder, but obsessed with finding out more about it, he deserts his tour and turns detective in Ruffano, now a university town." Publ Wkly

Frenchman's Creek. Doubleday, Doran 1942 310p o.p.

"The lovely Lady St. Columb fled by coach from the boredom of London society, and an unloved husband to their wild and unused Cornish coast estate. There she discovered an aristocratic French pirate who secreted his ship and crew in the hidden creek and as a game preyed gaily upon the dull Cornish gentry. [The book describes] the love between the two and the thrilling adventure they shared." Booklist

The house on the strand. Doubleday 1969 298p o.p.

"Richard Young, being in Cornwall as the guest of his biophysicist friend Magnus, takes 'trips' back into the 14th century under the influence of hallucinogens. Richard's absorption in the past, and the contrast with his own life with a difficult spouse and two stepsons, is tellingly portrayed." Barzun. Cat of Crime. Rev and enl edition

Hungry Hill. Doubleday, Doran 1943 402p o.p.

The story "follows a family of Irish mine owners through four generations. Copper John opened the mines on Hungry Hill and brought in Cornish miners, resented by the villagers. Money poured in, but each generation had its tragedy of weak characters and none had Copper John's strength of purpose." Booklist

Jamaica Inn. Doubleday, Doran 1936 332p o.p.

"A stirring tale of an old inn on the desolate moors of Cornwall, where Mary Yellan, left alone in the world at her mother's death, took refuge with her aunt. Her uncle, the landlord, directed smugglers who wrecked ships on the nearby coast, and the inn was a place of horror and mystery. Mary's hope of rescuing her aunt, and escaping, was soon complicated by her unwilling interest in the landlord's brother, who stole horses but drew the line at murder." Booklist

My cousin Rachel. Doubleday 1952 348p o.p.

The scene is Cornwall and Italy, the time probably the eighteenth century. The narrator is Philip Ashley, who had lived happily with his uncle on the family estate in Cornwall, until his uncle's ill health caused him to take a trip to Italy. There Ambrose met and married a distant cousin, Rachel, and not long after he died. Philip receives Rachel at Cornwall, falls under the influence of her charm, and seeks an unconventional way out when he thinks she may have poisoned his beloved uncle

Rebecca. Doubleday 1938 457p $29.95

ISBN 0-385-04380-5

"Rebecca, lovely and charming wife of English aristocrat Maxim de Winter, dies unexpectedly, and the mystery surrounding her death haunts all who remain at the Manderley country estate. Eight months after the sailing accident in which Rebecca lost her life Maxim remarries. Through his new wife's writing, the reader learns the truth about Rebecca's death and character." Shapiro. Fic for Youth. 3d edition

The scapegoat. Doubleday 1957 348p o.p.

"John, an Englishman, has just wound up a job of academic research in France. . . . In a station buffet in Le Mans he meets himself, a fantastic likeness, in the person of Jean, the Comte de Gué. . . . John, against his will, is compelled to become the Comte de Gué. In this role,

Du Maurier, Dame Daphne, 1907-1989—*Continued*
unaided by anything except the clues at which he snatches while everyone takes him for granted, he must cope with a pregnant and unhappy wife, a sick but domineering mother, a religiously obsessed young daughter, a sister and brother who loathe him, a valet-chauffeur devoted to him, and a mistress who gives without demanding." Saturday Rev

Dubus, Andre, 1936-1999

Dancing after hours; stories. Knopf 1996 233p o.p.
ISBN 0-679-43107-1 LC 95-32032
Contents: All the time in the world; At night; Blessings; The colonel's wife; Dancing after hours; Falling in love; The intruder; The last moon; A love song; The lover; Out of the snow; Sunday morning; The timing of sin; Woman on a plane
"Loneliness, fear, desire, grief—these are Dubus' themes, and he takes them on and never looks back. His gaze is absolutely fearless, and his observations are unerringly precise." Booklist

Ducornet, Rikki

Gazelle. Knopf 2003 189p $21
ISBN 0-375-41124-0 LC 2002-34000
"Recounts the sexual awakening of Elizabeth, a 13-year-old American girl in 1950's Cairo. While her father, an academic, plays war games with tiny toy soldiers and her mother moves out to satisfy her extramarital appetites, Elizabeth devours—and is awakened by—a provocatively illustrated edition of 'The Arabian Nights.'" N Y Times Book Rev
"Lushly detailed yet swiftly paced, this mythic coming-of-age novel archly traces the plexus of sensuality, intelligence, and imagination that defines the human soul." Booklist

Dudevant, Amantine Lucile Aurore Dupin *See* Sand, George, 1804-1876

Due, Tananarive, 1966-

The good house. Atria 2003 482p $25
ISBN 0-7434-4900-2
"After her 15-year-old son Corey's suicide, Angela Toussaint spent several months in a mental hospital. Now, divorced and focused on her work, she receives word of potential buyers of her grandmother's house in Sacajawea, Washington, in which Corey died. Realizing that she must put the tragedy to rest, Angela decides to go to the house to try to understand exactly what happened. Sacajawea is, however, a town beset by evil." Booklist
"Due handles the potentially unwieldy elements of her novel with confidence, cross-cutting smoothly from past to present, introducing revelatory facts that alter the interpretation of earlier scenes and interjecting powerfully orchestrated moments of supernatural horror that sustain the tale's momentum." Publ Wkly

My soul to keep. HarperCollins Pubs. 1997 346p o.p.
LC 97-4992
"Dawit's story spans 400 years and several countries. Yet, it is his current life, with wife Jessica and daughter Kira, that he wants to hold on to forever. His lives as a warrior, slave, jazz musician, teacher, husband, and father have all ended amid sorrow and extreme human conditions. He seeks to balance his mortality and immortality, yet with each mortal experience his perceptions of life are more human than wizardly." Booklist
"Smart psychological renderings, particularly of familial bonds, and a memorable set of African American protagonists highlight Due's . . . horror novel. Centering around the potent theme of immortality, this briskly told tale adds fresh blood—literally and figuratively—to a genre currently on life support." Publ Wkly

Dufresne, John, 1948-

Deep in the shade of paradise. Norton 2002 364p $25.95
ISBN 0-393-02020-7 LC 2001-44487
A novel set in the "Louisiana bayous and byways. Conceived the day his daddy Billy Wayne died in 1988, Boudou Fontana (short for Bergeron Boudeleaux deBastrop) has an eidetic memory and the knowledge that he's the last of the Fontana line. His mother, hillbilly songwriter Earlene deBastrop Fontana, is a cousin of Grisham Loudermilk, who is marrying Ariane Thevenot at Paradise, the family plantation in Shiver-de-Freeze (*chival de frise*), a small political subdivision outside Monroe, La." Publ Wkly
"The people in this small town are surprisingly endearing, despite their quirks. Numerous asides sprinkled throughout the novel make for a clever and memorable narrative style." Booklist

Duisberg, Kristin Waterfield

The good patient; a novel. St. Martin's Press 2003 328p $23.95
ISBN 0-312-30039-5 LC 2002-36877
"Darien Gilbertson is a 28-year-old Manhattan advertising executive known for her biting sarcasm, morbid humor and party-girl tendencies. But beneath the sleek facade, she hides the scars, bumps and bruises of her secret life—she enjoys violently hurting herself. Her husband, Robert, knows of her penchant for pain, but Darien can't seem to stop and refuses to get help. Then she goes too far and breaks her hand. . . . Robert forces her to see a psychiatrist, and despite herself, Darien begins to trust cool Dr. Rachel Lindholm." Publ Wkly
"From the facile duplicity of Darien's counseling sessions to the innocence of her interior dialogues, Duisberg's first-person narrative is electrifying in its unfeigned candor, harrowing in its unnerving vulnerability." Booklist

Dukes, Carol Muske- *See* Muske-Dukes, Carol, 1945-

Dukthas, Ann

For works written by this author under other names see Doherty, P. C.

Dumas, Alexandre, 1802-1870

The Count of Monte Cristo.
Original French edition, 1844
"Edmond Dantés, a young sailor unjustly accused of helping the exiled Napoleon in 1815, has been arrested and imprisoned in the Chateau d'If, near Marseille. After fifteen years, he finally escapes by taking the place of his dead companion, the Abbé Faria; enclosed in a sack, he is thrown into the sea. He cuts the sack with his knife, swims to safety, is taken to Italy on a fisherman's boat. From Genoa, he goes to the caverns of Monte Cristo and digs up the fabulous treasures of which the dying Faria had told. He then uses the money to punish his enemies and reward his friends." Haydn. Thesaurus of Book Dig

The iron mask. o.p.
Original French edition published 1850 as part of Le Vicomte de Bragelonne
The identity of the man in the iron mask—is an unsolved mystery. Dumas' "iron mask episode is found toward the end . . . of the third volume of 'Vicomte De Bragelonne'. . . . The present volume remains essentially the story of the . . . closing years of those four men who had performed such prodigies—attacking armies, assaulting castles, terrifying death itself—Athos, Porthos, Aramis, and their captain, D'Artagnan." Preface for the reader

The Queen's necklace. o.p.
Original French edition, 1848
Based on a scandal during the reign of Louis XVI, this tale of intrigue describes the efforts of Count Cagliostro, Countess Jeanne de la Motte, and Cardinal Rohan to discredit Queen Marie Antoinette. Their plot involves a coveted diamond necklace, an impersonator of the queen, and a web of suspicions of adultery and theft

Short stories. Black, W.J. 1927 10v in 1 o.p.
Contents: v1 Courtship of Josephine and Napoleon; Drowner; Blood union; Lady Hamilton and Admiral Nelson; Honor of Von Bulow; Gaetano and gorger; Provisional government; Cannibals; Confession of the district attorney; Vindication; Mme Dubarry; Storming the Bastile; Aurora; Branded; Tragedy of Nantes; Cripple and giant; Louis XIII; Death of Mirabeau; Anne of Austria; Black pearl
v2 Female defender; Great Copt; Scarlet sphynx; Real Bonaparte; Corneille; Wedding night; Bouquet; Tactics of love; Pipe and a man; Marat and Rousseau; Fate of a regicide; Scar of de Guise; Hollow voice; King and courtiers; Frankfort-on-Main; Bitter cup; Smuggler's in; Prodigal's favor; Sword of the Swiss; French breed
v3 Vive le roi; Mademoiselle; Uninvited visitors; Death of Richelieu; Vicomte's breakfast; Drum-head marriage; Sword and pistol; It rains; Melancholy tale; Isabella; Ransom of Isabella; Bridals; On to Rome; His oath; Legend; Some Prussian history; Count von Bismarck; Chalice; Avalanche; Little dog Jet
v4 King cobbler; Sweet smell; Citizen Bonaparte; Grecian slave-girl; Glove of Conde; Luisa San Felice; Chevalier San Felice; Martyr San Felice; Mad method; Historic fete; D'Orsay; Chimney-back; Modern Aspasia; Royal criminologist; Tenth muse; Ball of the victims—a sketch; Conquest of Circe; Inscription; Statistics; Birds of prey
v5 Caracciolo's capture; Wild boar hunt; Historic Banquo; Daughter of the Caesars; Three madames—a portrait; Vertigo; La Fontaine's first fable; Glimpse of Paris; Odoardo, the prisoner; Odoardo, the gentleman; Marseillaise; D'Artagnan, the Gascon; D'Artagnan meets the musketeers; Musketeers meet D'Artagnan; Voice of liberty; Dowry; Black tulip; Perennial Venus; Straw; Carnot and conspiracy
v6 Burgomaster; Sack of the Tuileries; Murat; Diana de Castro; Champion of beauty; Glory of love; D'Artagnan, detective; Narcotic dream; Instinct; Moliere; Moreau; View of the terror; Bismarck—his offer; Spanish surprise; Prison; Madam; Substitute; Man in the iron mask; Lame mendicant; Andre Chenier
v7 Career of a courtesan; Strange ending; People; Crossing the Alps; Battle of Langensalza; Diana de Meridor; Assassination; Fruit, a torch and a bouquet; Gourmand; Surprise; Cabaret; Picture; Bastard of Waldeck; Word of a king; Marie Touchet; Remember; Queen's perfumer; Madame de Sauve's chamber; Boxes; To Rusconise
v8 Saint Jean d'Acre; Men from Marseilles; Regent's letter; Regent's revenge; Marengo; Byron sees Kean; Son of a courtesan; Destiny; Call; Dock fight; Regal love; Balmasque; Chateau d'If; Story of no.27; Story of no.34; Cemetery of Chateau d'If; Madness; Paradise for hell; Battle of Charenton; Mercedes
v9 Death of the king's mistress; Theory of war; Two fugitives; Chastelard; Big spider; Count of Monte-Cristo; Slaughter; Italian lover; Dormice; First consul; Death of Hercules; Act of faith; Bernadotte; Pilgrimage; Conscience's dream; Mariettes dream; Vision of Athos; Le terrain de Dieu; Weird costume; Three against three
v10 Goddess of reason; Portrait; Thief; Jean Ouillier—a study; Eight long days; Gay prince; Remark; Augereau; Sacrifice of beauty; D'Artagnan-Marechal; Duel; Corsican mother; Corsican son; Corsican brother; Printing house—a sketch; Milan; Source of money: Hannibal; Brigand's faith; Mercy and Brigand; Reverses

The three musketeers; translated by Jacques Le Clercq. Modern Library 1999 xxi, 598p $24.95
ISBN 0-679-60332-8
Original French edition, 1844
"D'Artagnan arrives in Paris one day in 1625 and manages to be involved in three duels with three musketeers . . . Athos, Porthos and Aramis. They become d'Artagnan's best friends. The account of their adventures from 1625 on develops against the rich historical background of the reign of Louis XIII and the early part of that of Louis XIV, the main plot being furnished by the antagonism between Cardinal de Richelieu and Queen Anne d'Autriche." Haydn. Thesaurus of Book Dig

Twenty years after; edited with an introduction and notes by David Coward. Oxford University Press 1998 xxv, 845p il pa $15.95
ISBN 0-19-283843-1 LC 99-188043
Sequel to The three musketeers
Original French edition, 1845; first United States edition published 1846 by Taylor, Wilde and Company
"Anne of Austria's regency, the insurrection of the Fronde, and the execution of Charles I of England mark out the period (1648-9)." Baker. Guide to the Best Fic
Followed by The Vicomte de Bragelonne (1848-1850)

Dumas, Alexandre, 1824-1895

Camille. o.p.

Original French edition, 1848; first United States edition published 1857 by E.J. Hincken with title: The camelia-lady. Variant title: Lady with the camellias

Camille "is a beautiful courtesan who has become part of the fashionable world of Paris. Scorning the wealthy Count de Varville, who has offered to relieve her debts should she once more become his mistress, she escapes to the country with her penniless lover Armand Duval. Here Camille makes her great sacrifice. Giving Armand, whom she truly loves, the impression that she has tired of their life together, but actually at the request of his family, she returns to Paris and her life of frivolity. The tale concludes with the ultimate tragic reunion of Armand and the dying Camille." Reader's Ency. 4th edition

Dunant, Sarah

The birth of Venus; a novel. Random House 2004 394p $21.95

ISBN 1-400-06073-7 LC 2003-46932

"In this novel, the fictional narrator is Alessandra Cecchi, 14, the daughter of a wealthy cloth merchant in the Florence of Michelangelo and Botticelli. Alessandra yearns to live with a brush in her hand. For that matter, she would be happy just to get out of the house. But it's the 1490s, so her best hope is an agreeable arranged marriage." Time

"Part feverish thriller, part historical romance, the story of the outspoken heroine's sentimental education—a comprehensive curriculum including every conceivable transgression—sometimes comes off as a heady blend of Browning's My Last Duchess and Anaïs Nin. But Dunant's skill lies in combining these elements with a finely textured and pertinent depiction of a cultured citizenry in the grip of rampant fundamentalism." New Yorker

Duncan, Glen

Death of an ordinary man; y; Glen Duncan. Grove Press 2005 304p pa $13

ISBN 0-8021-7004-8 LC 2004-56727

"As this novel opens, Nathan finds himself falling into darkness and emerges to float above his own funeral. . . . Along with the reader, Nathan pieces together his life and death mosaiclike as he hovers around his family after the funeral, able to sense their feelings and falling into the memories thus invoked. We see his passion for his edgy, intense wife, who ultimately betrayed him with his best friend; we register his concern for his floundering son and budding, tough-as-nails older daughter. We learn that a younger daughter has died and are eventually rubbed raw by the details of her horrific death. Duncan layers on brilliant prose—sometimes a little heavily, as the narrative seems to slow halfway through. In the end, however, he has produced an arresting story, and he writes convincingly and affectingly of the consequences of a child's death, which is pretty rare indeed." Libr J

Dunlap, Susan

Cop out. Delacorte Press 1997 296p o.p.

LC 96-38245

"A Jill Smith mystery"

In this case, Berkeley California cop Jill "Smith tries to help p.i. Herman Ott, who also happens to be a murder suspect. The trail leads from a Telegraph Avenue jewelry vendor and a religious leader who surrounds himself with thugs to a tattoo artist, a patient defender, and ultimately a deadly pesticide." Libr J

"The seemingly unrelated clues do fit together, leading to a satisfying and surprising conclusion, but not before Jill faces the wrath of her superiors and more than a little danger." Booklist

Death and taxes. Delacorte Press 1992 247p o.p.

LC 91-33109

"A Jill Smith mystery"

Jill Smith, the "Berkeley detective is working homicide when 'one of the most hated employees of the nation's most-loathed bureaucracy' staggers off his bicycle and keels over dead, the victim of a poisoned hypodermic needle lodged in his bicycle seat. Since the I.R.S. field agent was not your run-of-the-mill public servant, but a rabid zealot . . . Jill could use a traffic cop to sort out all the suspects eager to dance on the dead man's grave." N Y Times Book Rev

"This poignant, suspenseful puzzler establishes Berkeley, Calif., homicide detective Jill Smith as one of the most interesting female series detectives." Publ Wkly

High fall; a Kiernan O'Shaughnessy mystery. Delacorte Press 1994 264p o.p.

LC 94-6047

"Nineteen-year-old movie stuntwoman Lark Sondervoil vows to be the first person in 10 years to attempt the 'Gaige move,' named for the late legendary stuntman Greg Gaige. Private eye Kiernan O'Shaughnessy, who once studied gymnastics with Gaige, arrives to watch the filming of Sondervoil's stunt. It goes wrong. Sondervoil misses her mark and plunges off a cliff to her death. Outraged to learn the fall was captured on film and will probably be used in an upcoming film, Kiernan decides to find out what went wrong." Booklist

The author "takes research seriously, which pays off in the uncanny authenticity of the various 'gags' staged to hair-raising effect by the stunt crew. With the same finicky attention to detail, she also covers all the technical minutiae necessary on an outdoor movie set where each day brings a fresh disaster." N Y Times Book Rev

Dunmore, Helen, 1952-

A spell of winter. Atlantic Monthly Press 2001 312p o.p.

ISBN 0-87113-782-8 LC 00-45334

First published 1995 in the United Kingdom

"In the years before World War I, Cathy, the narrator, and her brother grow up on their grandfather's impoverished English estate. Their mother abandoned them when they were small, and their father dies after being institutionalized. Except for the ministrations of the maid, Kate, and the interference of the repulsive governess, they are left on their own. It seems inevitable when their closeness takes an unnatural and destructive turn. . . . With a handful of characters and rich, ripe prose, Dunmore creates a compelling tale of obsession." Booklist

Dunmore, Helen, 1952-—*Continued*

With your crooked heart. Atlantic Monthly Press 1999 249p o.p.
ISBN 0-87113-773-9 LC 99-53739

"Louise, beautiful and sharp-edged at 31, washes out in an alcoholic fog of emotional paralysis by 40. Her wealthy ex-husband Paul provides for her daily needs even as he strip her of her one reason to live—daughter Anna who is, in fact, Paul's niece. Louise's forced encounter with Johnnie, Paul's beloved younger hoodlum brother, forever locks the three adults in a dark morass of self-destruction and leaves Anna forgotten." Libr J

"Dunmore is so skilled at drawing you into this story—it's about a doomed triangle involving two brothers and the woman they both love—that it's possible to be lulled into hoping for a happy ending." N Y Times Book Rev

Dunn, Katherine

Geek love. Knopf 1989 347p o.p.
ISBN 0-394-56902-4 LC 88-45776

"The narrator is a bald female albino hunchback dwarf, raised in her family's carnival show, Binewski's Fabulon. (By using drugs and other methods, her parents succeeded in producing children with physical 'attributes' perfect for performance in a freak show.) This picaresque tale follows the life of the narrator during her family's carnival existence, through times both strange and awful." Booklist

"This raw, shocking view of the human condition, a glimpse of the tormented people who live on the fringe, makes readers confront the dark, mad elements in every society. . . . A brilliant, suspenseful, heartbreaking tour de force." Publ Wkly

Dunn, Sarah

The big love. Little, Brown 2004 228p $21.95
ISBN 0-316-73815-8

"Alison Hopkins is devastated when her live-in boyfriend, Tom, walks out of their dinner party and back into the arms of his ex-girlfriend, Kate. Tom is only 33-year-old Alison's second lover, and she wonders if she wouldn't be better off if she had slept with more men. So when Henry, her handsome new boss at the free daily Philadelphia paper for which she writes a relationship column, seems interested in her, Alison seizes the opportunity. . . . Musing on everything from her evangelical Christian upbringing to men behaving badly . . . Alison's engaging voice carries this thoughtful, introspective, smart novel along and raises it far above the average novel about a young woman looking for love in the big city." Booklist

Dunne, Dominick

An inconvenient woman. Crown 1990 458p o.p.
LC 90-1602

This novel "concerns billionaire financier and presidential adviser Jules Mendelson; his high-society wife, Pauline, and fractious stepson, Kippie; a bunch of other gangsters and Hollywoodites who are either business associates, friends or antagonists; and Flo March, Jules' curvacious, decidedly nonblueblood mistress, who comes to know too much about everyone else's less-than-licit dealings for her own good." Booklist

"This is a smart novel because Dominick Dunne understands the distance between Los Angeles society and the spicy bazaars of Hollywood. And what makes Mr. Dunne not only first-rate, but also different from other writers who write about the very rich in late 20th-century America, is his knowledge that there's more to it than getting the labels and the street names right." N Y Times Book Rev

People like us; a novel. Crown 1988 403p o.p.
LC 88-353

In this novel about upper-crust New York life, "Loelia Manchester is leaving her husband for shoe designer Micki Mindaros; Hubie Altemous is dying of AIDS; Matilde Stewart is broke. Trying to break into this world are Elias and Ruby Renthal, the richest people in Cleveland, who soon become the toast of the Upper East Side by watching carefully and spending excessively. The story's two culminating events, Elias Renthal's Boesky-like fall and Gus Bailey's thirst for vengeance, shake the fabric of a world where custom and manners rule." Booklist

"Engaging us in his characters' concerns and then pulling multiple story strands into a tight knot, Dominick Dunne demonstrates with wit and accuracy the delicate, merciless distinction between 'people like that' and 'people like us'." N Y Times Book Rev

A season in purgatory. Crown 1993 377p o.p.
LC 92-42352

This novel "begins with the jury deliberating in the murder trial of Constant Bradley, a charming, handsome Congressman from an affluent Irish Catholic family in New England. He has been charged with a crime from his prep school days: the death of Winifred Utley, a pretty 15-year-old neighbor of the Bradleys who was clubbed to death with a baseball bat after a dance at the country club." N Y Times Book Rev

"The unforgettable Bradley family, their skeletons . . . and peccadillos offer an allure similar to a sidelong glance at tabloid headlines, though here told with wit and skill. Their machinations prove both fascinating and appalling—and always hypnotically readable." Publ Wkly

The two Mrs. Grenvilles; a novel. Crown 1985 374p o.p.
LC 85-445

"Basil Plant, a semisuccessful novelist tenuously clinging to the fringes of high society, narrates this haunting tale of two women destroyed by the virulence of their own twisted emotions. Alice Grenville, a respected woman of means, is initially appalled when her only son chooses to marry considerately beneath their fashionable set; still, rather than risk Junior's disaffection, Alice grudgingly accepts second-rate actress Ann Arden into her upper-crust family. The pathetic fates of the two Mrs. Grenvilles are sealed when Ann, in a jealous rage, murders her disenchanted husband. In order to avoid the sensationalism of a highly publicized scandal, Alice helps cover up the crime, forever binding herself to the woman she despises most. An affecting and disturbing tragedy replete with vivid portraits of spiritually crippled souls desperately struggling to inject some substance into their empty lives." Booklist

Dunne, John Gregory, 1932-2003

Nothing lost. Knopf 2004 335p $24.95
ISBN 1-4000-4143-0

Dunne, John Gregory, 1932-2003—*Continued*

This novel begins with the "torture-murder of a black man named Edgar Parlance, who has been skinned alive. It is also a detective story about its characters' pasts, {an} . . . inquiry into the lives of Edgar Parlance; his accused murderer, Duane Lajoie; and especially Duane's brilliant but tortured lawyer Teresa Kean. . . . Finally, it is a modern-day story about the media madness that routinely ensues with notorious trials, a story about celebrity and its consequences." N Y Times (Late N Y Ed)

The author "adeptly skewers the pretensions of the politicians, pundits, and celebrities who descend upon the trial, ready to use it to further their own agendas. This is a violent, sexually charged, and, at times, acidly funny tale of power and paranoia in contemporary America." Libr J

Playland; a novel. Random House 1994 494p o.p.

LC 94-4344

Hollywood screenwriter Jack Broderick featured in *The Red White and Blue,* "flies to Detroit to research story ideas. In a Michigan trailer park, he discovers a coupon-clipping bag lady named Melba Mae Toolate who claims to have been Blue Tyler, one of the biggest child movie stars of the 1940s. Melba tells Broderick her life story, focusing on her scandalous liaison with Jacob King, a flamboyant gangster and Las Vegas visionary." Libr J

"The most successful part of this novel is its bawdy, admiring portrait of that time and place, filled with jaundiced observations and half-familiar show-business anecdotes." N Y Times Book Rev

The red, white, and blue; a novel. Simon & Schuster 1987 475p o.p.

LC 86-26025

The author exhibits "a fascination with the invisible web that links certain disparate people and events. . . . 'The Red White and Blue' examines the most complicated web yet, a vast network extending halfway around the globe and across the past 20 years or so to encompass left-wing politics, big business, Hollywood and (yes, once again) a few figures in the Catholic Church. Its story line, if one may call it that, is a rambling rumination upon the career of a radical lawyer named Leah Kaye. Its real story is history's habit of ensnaring us in its meshes—even if we're apolitical, even if we're as uninvolved and wryly ironic as Jack Broderick, the narrator." N Y Times Book Rev

"An insightfully provocative slice of Americana." Booklist

True confessions. Dutton 1977 341p o.p.

"A Henry Robbins book"

This novel is "about brotherhood, the loss of innocence, and the frailty of the human condition. Corruption-ridden LA in the late 1940s provides the backdrop for this tale of two brothers, a cop and a priest, who are unable to detach themselves from their Irish Catholic milieu. The bizarre murder of a prostitute provides the focal point but not the main subject matter of this work, which is concerned with policeman Tom's investigation and his discovery of seemingly universal weakness among the multitude of characters." Libr J

Dunnett, Dorothy, 1923-2001

Caprice and Rondo. Knopf 1998 c1997 xxix, 539p (House of Niccolò) o.p.

ISBN 0-679-45477-2 LC 97-49458

First published 1997 in the United Kingdom

This seventh book in the House of Niccolo series "opens in 1474 as self-exiled Nicholas, holed up in Danzig with rowdy Polish cronies, licks his wounds from the family feud that destroyed his Scottish bank and alienated him further from his estranged wife (the obdurate, sharp-witted Gelis van Borselen). To protect Europe from the Turks, and to rebuild his financial empire, the globe-trotting Nicholas . . . mixes it up with Crimean Tartars, negotiates with the Shah of Persia and parries with Moscow traders before confronting Gelis in Ghent, where family skeletons tumble out of the closet. As usual, Dunnett brings her early modern financiers and aristocrats glitteringly to life." Publ Wkly

Checkmate. Putnam 1975 581p il o.p.

This concluding volume of the Francis Crawford saga "resolves Lymond's final mystery, the prophecy of astrologer John Dee: 'It is not one thing you seek, I fancy, but two. . . . The first you will have: the second you shall never have, nor would it be just that you should.' Lymond, an aggressive player in the political chess game of royalty, is also a key pawn in the quirky game of family bloodlines." Publ Wkly

"A thoroughly romantic action yarn which isn't an insult to the intelligence. Intricately plotted, atmospheric, and peopled with characters of magnetic complexity, this series combines literary quality with can't-put-down entertainment." Libr J

Gemini. Knopf 2000 xxxii, 672p il (House of Niccolò) $27.50

ISBN 0-679-45478-0 LC 00-25027

This "eighth and final installment of the 'House of Niccolò' series has as its backdrop the late 15th-century rift between King James III of Scotland and his brothers. Nicholas de Fleury has decided to return to Scotland to face two enemies: his family, the St. Pols, who still refuse to recognize him, and David Simpson, who stole the African gold in an earlier adventure. Nicholas immediately gets swept up in the fraternal strife of the royal family." Libr J

"It's remarkably easy for the neophyte to enter Dunnett's adventurous world, for the author does an outstanding job of keeping each personality distinct and each of the innumerable subplots coherent. . . . Dunnett's work sits triumphantly at the top of a crowded field: it is a sensational, emotionally resonant epic." Publ Wkly

Niccolò rising. Knopf 1986 470p (House of Niccolò) o.p.

LC 86-45306

In the first volume of the House of Niccolò series we meet Claus, later known as Niccolò, "an apprentice at the Bruges branch of the Charetty company, run by the widowed owner. Claus is an enigma, seemingly a buffoon getting into scrapes with Felix, the Charetty heir, but also capable of initiating a courier service in connection with the Charetty commercial and mercenary ventures. In an era of economic and political intrigue, Claus makes the most of all opportunities—romantic and business." Libr

Dunnett, Dorothy, 1923-2001—*Continued*

J

This novel "displays all the author's strengths: strong characterization, subtle wit (with a dash of slapstick), lively action, and labyrinthine plot." Wilson Libr Bull

Followed by The spring of the ram

Pawn in frankincense. Putnam 1969 486p o.p.

Previous titles in this series of interlocking novels about Scottish adventurer Francis Crawford are: The game of kings (1961); Queen's play (1964) and The disorderly knights (1966)

This installment of Crawford's adventures finds him in "the eastern Mediterranean region searching for his bastard son, who is being held hostage. Plots and counterplots, blood and gore lead to an excruciating climax in the form of a chess contest (a game this is not), in which Crawford and his old adversary Graham Mallett play with living pieces, themselves included. Penalty for capture is death, and Crawford's son, whom he can't recognize, is involved." Libr J

Followed by The ringed castle (1971)

Race of scorpions. Knopf 1990 534p (House of Niccolò) o.p.

LC 89-45292

Third volume in the Niccolò series. "At age 21, fifteenth-century Dutch adventurer Niccolò has lost his wife and her inheritance, but he has the rich resources of his personality and potential wealth in a trading business based in Venice to restore his fortunes in short order. Indeed, a dynastic power struggle over control of Cyprus draws him to that island, where both sides eagerly enlist his support and talents. Meanwhile, there are old wounds and debts to settle with the rulers of Anjou who have previously thwarted his ambitions." Booklist

"Through precisely rendered scenes, whether depicting a battle on the high seas, the operations of a dye works, a cleverly plotted ambush (using insects) or the gruesome tactics employed to destroy a proud city under siege, Dunnett furnishes fascinating images while spinning her admirable narrative web." Publ Wkly

Followed by Scales of gold

Scales of gold. Knopf 1992 519p (House of Niccolò) o.p.

LC 91-58554

First published 1991 in the United Kingdom

Fourth book in the House of Niccolò series. "In 1464, adventurer and merchant banker Nicholas van der Pole . . . returns to Venice to find his financial empire in jeopardy due to the Crusades and the onslaught of powerful, unscrupulous competitors. Closely guarding the specifics of his mission, Nicholas sets out for Africa and its gold trade." Publ Wkly

"Set within a rich tapestry of fifteenth-century Europe and Africa that is woven by a master of historical fiction, Nicholas' travels are constantly endangered by the greedy and vengeful figures he has tangled with in the past as well as by the natural hazards of the period." Booklist

Followed by The unicorn hunt

The spring of the ram. Knopf 1988 469p (House of Niccolò) o.p.

LC 87-37847

In the second volume of the House of Niccolò saga "Plucky 19-year-old Nicholas, fleeing his bitter foe Simon de Pol, journeys via Florence—where he gets funding from the Medicis—to the East. There he hopes to trade with the Emperor of Trebizond. . . . But the seductive Princess Violante, in diaphanous déshabillé, offers Nicholas protection—and much more." Publ Wkly

"Dunnett tells this story of love and money against a well-researched background of historical and cultural detail, taking her readers from Europe to Byzantium." Booklist

Followed by Race of scorpions

To lie with lions. Knopf 1996 xxiv, 626p (House of Niccolò) o.p.

ISBN 0-394-58629-8 LC 95-50422

First published 1995 in the United Kingdom

This sixth book in the House of Niccolo series focuses on 15th century adventurer Nicholas de Fleury's "marriage to quick-witted, self-sufficient Gelis van Borselen. It's a war of wills, egos and attrition that erupts in 1471 as de Fleury (aka Nicholas vander Poele) snatches his infant son, Jordan, from Gelis's arms and kidnaps the boy, a pawn in a bitter power struggle that will take the lives of friends and rivals. . . . With her usual dramatic flair, Dunnett mixes historical and fictive characters in a tale that sweeps from Venice to Antwerp, Edinburgh, Iceland, France and Cyprus." Publ Wkly

Followed by Caprice and Rondo

The unicorn hunt. Knopf 1994 656p (House of Niccolò) o.p.

LC 93-35692

First published 1993 in the United Kingdom

In the fifth volume of the saga fifteenth century banker/knight Nicholas vander Poele "sails to Scotland, where he confronts his archenemy, Simon de St. Pol, who may be the father of the child whom Nicholas's wife, Gelis van Borselen, is carrying. Months later, back in Flanders, vengeful Gelis, in order to punish Nicholas for fathering an illegitimate child by her sister, hides her newborn boy. Intrigue, betrayal and adventure follow as hardened Nicholas journeys from Florence, full of Medici machinations, to the Tyrol, where he uses a divining rod to find silver." Publ Wkly

"Dunnett's writing style is somewhat complex but rich in information. The reader can feel immersed in the environment she creates; the characters (there are many) have well-developed, unique identities." Libr J

Followed by To lie with lions

Dunning, John, 1942-

Booked to die; a mystery introducing Cliff Janeway. Scribner 1992 321p $24

ISBN 0-684-19383-3 LC 91-26889

Homicide detective and rare book collector Cliff "Janeway turns in his badge, opens a shop called Twice Told Books on Denver's Book Row and for a time becomes preoccupied with the enchanting lore of his trade. But Janeway discovers that not all book folk are gentlefolk. Two inoffensive book scouts are murdered after making a rare find, and the young clerk in Twice Told Books is dispatched with equal brutality. Thinking like a cop again, Janeway starts suspecting all his new friends on Book Row, including the woman with whom he has fallen in love. . . . This is a soundly plotted, evenly executed whodunit in the classic mode." N Y Times Book Rev

Dunning, John, 1942-—*Continued*

The bookman's wake; a mystery with Cliff Janeway. Scribner 1995 351p o.p.
ISBN 0-684-80003-9 LC 94-34328
"Unexpected danger and chilling intrigue attend a Denver bookstore owner's trip to Seattle for the purpose of escorting a purported book thief to jail. Ex-cop Cliff Janeway . . . agrees to act as bounty hunter because of his interest in rare books; he soon realizes, however, that his employer has a hidden agenda involving the years-ago murder of two brothers who were owners of a publishing company known for its limited editions." Libr J
The author "can't resist writing lengthy, luxurious passages about the craftsmanship of the great print men. Strictly speaking, these eloquent lectures on the art of the printer and the beauty of the book get in the way of the action; but that shouldn't bother anyone who loves books—and their covers." N Y Times Book Rev

The sign of the book; a Cliff Janeway novel; John Dunning. Scribner 2005 353p $25
ISBN 0-7432-5505-4 LC 2004-51190
"Rare books dealer Cliff Janeway agrees to help a friend of a friend, who's accused of murdering her husband. Coincidentally, the victim had an amazing book collection." Libr J
"It's great fun thumbing the pages with Janeway, who knows his business and takes a keen, almost sensual pleasure in a virgin edition." N Y Times Book Rev

Two o'clock, eastern wartime; a novel. Scribner 2001 478p $26
ISBN 0-7432-0195-7 LC 00-32218
"In 1942, writer/drifter Jack Dulaney breaks out of jail when he gets a mysterious message that his long-lost love, Holly, may be in trouble. He traces her to a small New Jersey shore town, changes his name, and finds work as a writer at the local radio station. Holly's father has vanished and is somehow linked to the disappearance of a famous radio actor six years ago. Dulaney quickly adapts to radio and discovers his true talent—writing scripts. But his life is ever in danger as he hunts for pieces to the puzzle." Libr J
"Dunning masterfully re-creates that brief moment when radio seemed to offer a means of changing the nature of artistic expression. Superb entertainment and fascinating media history." Booklist

Durham, David Anthony, 1969-

Gabriel's story. Doubleday 2001 291p o.p.
ISBN 0-385-49814-4 LC 00-25291
In this "novel, set in the eighteen-seventies, Gabriel, a fifteen-year-old black boy from Baltimore, resents his new life on the Kansas plains when his widowed mother marries a homesteader. But then he falls in with a charismatic cowpunch and horse thief, and as they travel west to New Mexico a series of violent episodes brings Gabriel to swift maturity. The moral gravity of Durham's narrative is offset by his attentiveness to the primacy of nature in the Western landscape." New Yorker

A walk through darkness. Doubleday 2002 292p o.p.
ISBN 0-385-49925-6 LC 2001-47673
Durham "tells the parallel tales of two men in antebellum America: William, a young fugitive slave, and Morrison, a white man hired to track him. William escapes from Maryland and makes his way toward Philadelphia in search of his pregnant wife, Dover. Morrison, an older Scottish immigrant, has lived a hard, violent life he's not proud of, whose dark secrets—such as his responsibility for the death of his brother—slowly emerge as the story unwinds." Publ Wkly

Durham, Marilyn

The man who loved Cat Dancing. Harcourt Brace Jovanovich 1972 246p o.p.
"The man who loved Cat Dancing is John Wesley [Jay] Grobart, an ex-army officer who married Cat, a Shoshone squaw, when she was only 14. . . . When we meet Grobart, he is about to rob a train: recently released from prison after serving a 10-year term for the killing of three Indians believed to have raped and killed his wife, he wants money to regain his son. . . . At the same time, we meet Catherine Crocker who is on her way to catch the same train to expedite flight from her husband. Instead of catching the train she is kidnapped by the robbers. . . . The story . . . takes place in the Wyoming Territory of the 1880s." New Repub

Durrell, Gerald M., 1925-1995

Marrying off mother and other stories; [by] Gerald Durrell. Arcade Pub. 1992 197p o.p.
LC 91-30895
Contents: Esmeralda; Fred; or, A touch of the warm South; Retirement; Marrying off mother; Ludwig; The jury; Miss Booth-Wycherly's clothes; A parrot for the parson
"These eight droll stories—linked only in that they may or may not have happened to Durrell—are told with the cleverness and wit of an accomplished after-dinner ranconteur who has put away most of a bottle of brandy." Publ Wkly

Durrell, Lawrence

The Alexandria quartet: Justine; Balthazar; Mountolive [and] Clea. Dutton 1962 884p o.p.
Omnibus edition of four titles entered separately

Balthazar; a novel. Dutton 1958 250p o.p.
The second volume of the Alexandria quartet
"Once again [Durrell] writes of Justine, Melissa, Clea, Nessim, Pursewarden, Scobie, Pombal—but from a fresh point of view. The new insights are provided by the psychiatrist, Balthazar, who convinces the narrator that the first volume of the story was almost wholly inaccurate. . . . So this second volume is a correction and an expansion of the first." N Y Times Book Rev
Followed by Mountolive

also in Durrell, L. The Alexandria quartet: Justine; Balthazar; Mountolive [and] Clea p205-390

Clea; a novel. Dutton 1960 287p o.p.
Final volume of the Alexandria quartet
"In this novel events are seen from the point of view of the Englishman Darley who, returning to Alexandria

Durrell, Lawrence—*Continued*
to see old friends and lovers, has a passionate affair with Clea, one of the women in the circle of friends. Again, the tone is philosophic, the language frequently overripe, and the characters, though individualistic, are symbolic. Heterosexual and homosexual affairs are prominent in each of the novels." Booklist

"'The Alexandria Quartet' is one of the major achievements of fiction in our time, distinguished not only by its power of language, by its evocation of a place, by its creation of character, by the drama of many of its incidents, but also by its boldly original design. 'Clea' perfects the work, as a spire crowns a cathedral, but the spire is not to be judged in isolation." Saturday Rev

also in Durrell, L. The Alexandria quartet: Justine; Balthazar; Mountolive [and] Clea p653-884

Justine. Dutton 1957 253p o.p.

First volume of the Alexandria quartet

"Set in Alexandria the story concerns the amorous adventures of a penniless young man, a prostitute who lives with him, the rich and beautiful Justine with whom he has an affair, and Justine's husband." Publ Wkly

Followed by Balthazar

also in Durrell, L. The Alexandria quartet: Justine; Balthazar; Mountolive [and] Clea p11-203

Mountolive; a novel. Dutton 1959 c1958 318p o.p.

Third volume of the Alexandria quartet

First published 1958 in the United Kingdom

The perspective is "that of David Mountolive, the British ambassador: and what appeared to be 'the intrigues of desire' are shown to be intrigues motivated by politics. We learn that the beautiful Jewess, Justine, and her Coptic (Christian) husband, Nessim, are passionately united by a common cause: he believes that the formation of a Jewish state will save other minorities in the Arab world from Muslim domination and he is the leader of a group which is smuggling arms to the Jews in Palestine. The discovery of this conspiracy by Nessim's loyal English friends, Pursewarden and the ambassador, and their reactions to it form the plot line of Mountolive." Atlantic

Followed by Clea

also in Durrell, L. The Alexandria quartet: Justine; Balthazar; Mountolive [and] Clea p391-652

Dwyer, Deanna *See* Koontz, Dean R. (Dean Ray), 1945-

Dwyer, K. R., 1945-

For works written by this author under other names see Koontz, Dean R. (Dean Ray), 1945-

Dybek, Stuart

I sailed with Magellan. Farrar, Straus and Giroux 2003 307p $24

ISBN 0-374-17407-5 LC 2003-49052

Contents: Song; Live from Dreamville; Undertow; Breasts; Blue boy; Orchids; Lunch at the Loypla Arms; We didn't; Qué quieres; A minor mood; Je reviens

The "episodes that intersect and surround young Perry Katzek's upbringing in the Polish-Mexican ghetto of Chicago's South Side are simultaneously daring and compassionate, intimate in detail and mythic in scale. Dybek has the rare ability to dart back and forth in time and slide around recklessly in space while carrying the reader effortlessly with him." Washington Post Book World

Dyja, Tom

Meet John Trow; a novel. Viking 2002 355p il $24.95

ISBN 0-670-03099-6 LC 2001-55905

Mired in a midlife crisis, Steven Armour "joins a ragtag group of Civil War re-enactors who on weekends play the roles of actual soldiers from the region in a historical theme park in Connecticut. Steven is transformed by his impersonation of Pvt. John Trow into a flinty, decisive backwoodsman to such an extent that he begins to suspect a supernatural connection between himself and his long-dead subject. . . . Dyja treats his somewhat silly premise with the right balance of suspense and good humor." N Y Times Book Rev

E

Eagle, Kathleen

The last true cowboy. Avon Bks. 1998 388p o.p.

ISBN 0-380-97522-X LC 97-44255

"Renowned horse trainer K.C. Houston arrives at the High Horse Ranch in Wyoming—just in time to attend his prospective boss's untimely funeral—and ends up helping to save both a ranch and a unique herd of wild mustangs. He also unexpectedly finds love, healing, and a home in the process. A burned-out social-worker heroine who finds a reason to care, an alienated, gentle hero with magic in his hands, and a cast of well-drawn, memorable characters . . . combine in a complex and emotionally captivating story of loss and reconciliation." Libr J

Eagles, Cynthia Harrod- *See* Harrod-Eagles, Cynthia

Earley, Tony, 1961-

Jim the boy; a novel. Little, Brown 2000 227p $23.95

ISBN 0-316-19964-8 LC 99-42901

This novel is set in "the Depression-era town of Aliceville, N.C. . . . The story opens on Jim's 10th birthday and ends a year later. In that time, Jim sees the ocean for the first time, plays ball in front of a stopped passenger train that might or might not have Ty Cobb on board, visits his dying grandfather and watches a traveling salesman court his widowed mother." Newsweek

"The genius of a novel like this is Earley's trust in the purity of his style and the plainness of his story. Perhaps all things done very well look simple." Christ Sci Monit

Early, Tom *See* Kelton, Elmer, 1926-

Earth song, sky spirit; short stories of the contemporary native American experience; edited with an introduction by Clifford E. Trafzer. Doubleday 1993 495p o.p.
LC 92-44296

Contents: From aboard the night train, by K. M. Blaeser; The moccasin game, by G. Vizenor; The prisoner of haiku, by G. D. Henry; The day the crows stopped talking, by Harvest Moon Eyes; The well, by N. S. Momaday; Lost in the land of Ishtaboli, by D. L. Birchfield; Faces, by J. L. Russell; Adventures of an Indian princess, by P. Riley; Lucy, Oklahoma, 1911, by C. Womack; Fear and recourse, by M. Kenny; Earl Yellow Calf, by J. Welch; Grandpa Kashpaw's ghost, by L. Erdrich; Sun offering, by A. Hansen; Lead horse, by D. Glancy; Bone girl, by J. Bruchac; Spirit woman, by P. G. Allen; The cave, by J. D. Forbes; Akun, Jiki Walu: Grandfather magician, by D. B. Wilson; Marlene's adventures, by A. Endrezze; The approximate size of my favorite tumor, by S. Alexie; Shadows and sleepwalkers, by C. Featherstone; For her with no regrets, by D. Niatum; Avian Messiah and Mistress Media, by A. Connors; Slaughterhouse, by G. Sarris; Joseph's rainbow, by I. Petersen; The dream, by P. Olson; Silver bass and alligator gar, by R. Salisbury; Danse d'amour, danse de mort, by L. Howe; Clara's gift, by M. Dorris; The return of the buffalo, by L. M. Silko

Easterman, Daniel

Brotherhood of the tomb. Doubleday 1990 c1989 295p o.p.
LC 89-49463

First published 1989 in the United Kingdom

"In 1968, in Jerusalem, a tomb is discovered that contains the bones of Jesus, his 'brother' James and their mother Mary. At the same time, at Trinity College in Dublin, young American student Patrick Canavan falls in love with Francesca Contarini, who wears a strange cross around her neck. Twenty-four years later, Francesca has apparently drowned, and Canavan, now ex-CIA has returned to Dublin to try to recapture his youthful peace of mind. But events from the past impinge on the present." Publ Wkly

"This is one of those down-to-the-wire books in which the hero accomplishes the impossible. Still, Mr. Easterman manages to carry it off. Perhaps the plotting will not withstand cold scrutiny. No matter. 'Brotherhood of the Tomb' is hard to put down." N Y Times Book Rev

The final judgement. HarperCollins Pubs. 1996 293p o.p.
ISBN 0-06-109206-1 LC 96-24831

"Although Aryeh Levin knew his adopted country of Sardinia was a haven for kidnappers, he never figured he would be a victim. When his son is kidnapped and an impossible ransom demand is made, Aryeh is grief-stricken. He asks his [Israeli] brother-in-law Yosef, a rabid right-winger and former member of a special armed forces unit, to help. But the boy is killed, and Yosef is left to extract revenge. Aided by a beautiful Arab Italian interpreter, Yosef soon tracks down the kidnappers but finds he's only uncovered the top layer of a complex plot that involves the execution of every existing survivor of Auschwitz. Building to a suspense-filled climax, the story takes readers on an emotionally disturbing, intellectually intriguing journey into the past." Booklist

Eco, Umberto

Baudolino; translated from the Italian by William Weaver. Harcourt 2002 522p $27
ISBN 0-15-100690-3 LC 2002-2345

Original Italian edition, 2000

An "adventure about a 12th-century Italian peasant gifted in learning languages, telling lies and putting himself in the middle of genuine historical situations." N Y Times Book Rev

"In this whimsical yet deadly earnest tale, Eco puts forth the question that perpetually beguiles him and with which he beguiles the rest of us: If a teller of tales tells us he's telling the truth, how can we know for sure what really happened?." New Yorker

Foucault's pendulum; translated from the Italian by William Weaver. Harcourt Brace Jovanovich 1989 641p $33
ISBN 0-15-132765-3 LC 89-32212

"A Helen and Kurt Wolff book"

Original Italian edition, 1988

A "student of philology in 1970s Milan, Casaubon is completing a thesis on the Templars, a monastic knighthood disbanded in the 1300s for questionable practices. At Pilades Bar, he meets up with Jacopo Belbo, an editor of obscure texts at Garamond Press. Together with Belbo's colleague Diotallevi, they scrutinize the fantastic theories of a prospective author, Colonel Ardenti, who claims that for seven centuries the Templars have been carrying out a complex scheme of revenge. When Ardenti disappears mysteriously, the three begin using their detailed knowledge of the occult sciences to construct a Plan for the Templars—only to discover too late that the Plan they have invented is in fact real." Libr J

This book "is not meant to be easy. . . . [But] great are the rewards for those who actually manage to read it. For while it is not a novel in the strict sense of the word, it is a truly formidable gathering of information delivered playfully by a master manipulating his own invention—in effect, a long, erudite joke." N Y Times Book Rev

The island of the day before; translated from the Italian by William Weaver. Harcourt Brace & Co. 1995 515p o.p.
ISBN 0-15-100151-0 LC 95-7594

Original Italian edition, 1994

In this novel, "set in 1643, Roberto della Griva is shipwrecked on a ship. His own ship has been rent apart by a storm, and, tied to a plank, he has drifted to the Daphne, anchored in the bay of a South Pacific island. The deserted Daphne has no boat, and Roberto can't swim, so he is effectively a prisoner. As he explores the Daphne, he recalls his life as a young man at the siege of Casale, his years spent in hot philosophical debate in Paris, and his devotion to an adored but unapproachable woman. But there is an intruder on board, which brings to mind Ferrante, the evil twin Roberto imagines he has. The intruder turns out to be a monk obsessed with issues of time and the meridians." Libr J

"Umberto Eco's narrative surface is sensually alluring, cool and glittery, but for all its lucidity and charm, there

Eco, Umberto—*Continued*
is always something else going on. . . . This novel is really a book about telling, reminding us that the only clarity we are capable of reaching is the story we tell to compel time and the universe to take on meaning." N Y Times Book Rev

The mysterious flame of Queen Loana; translated from the Italian by Geoffrey Brock. Harcourt, Inc. 2005 469p il $27
ISBN 0-15-101140-0 LC 2004-29105
Original Italian edition, 2004
"Giambattista Bodoni is an antiquarian book dealer, who has just lost all memory of his existence, except for his reading. . . . Bodoni discovers that he is a happily married, if philandering, husband, knowledge that quickly renders him eager to learn whether, before his recent neurological calamity, he was having an affair with his attractive assistant, Sibilla." N Y Times Book Rev
"Those who don't enjoy the occasional ramble through 'Bartlett's Quotations' may quickly lose patience with 'Queen Loana,' but bookworms will get an added kick out of puzzling out the dozens of literary allusions." Christ Sci Monit

The name of the rose; translated from the Italian by William Weaver. Harcourt Brace Jovanovich 1983 502p $35
ISBN 0-15-144647-4 LC 82-21286
"A Helen and Kurt Wolff book"
Original Italian edition, 1982
This mystery set in 14th century Italy "centers on William of Baskerville, a 50-year-old monk who is sent to investigate a death at a Benedictine monastery. During his search, several other monks are killed in a bizarre pattern that reflects the Book of Revelation. Highly rational, Baskerville meets his nemesis in Jorge of Burgos, a doctrinaire blind monk determined to destroy heresy at any cost." Merriam-Webster's Ency of Lit
This novel "is an antidetective-story detective story; as a semiotic murder mystery it is superbly entertaining; it is also an extraordinary work of novelistic art." Harpers

Eddings, David

Belgarath the sorcerer; by David Eddings and Leigh Eddings. Ballantine Bks. 1995 644p o.p.
"A Del Rey book"
The authors "return to the world of their multivolume sagas, *The Belgariad* and *The Malloreon*. This prequel to the earlier books, presented as Belgarath's memoirs, offers an absorbing story line and some memorable characters as, once again, the authors touch all the right fantasy bases, with warring gods, political intrigues, supernatural creatures and appealingly human magicians involved in a titanic war over the course of seven millennia." Publ Wkly

Guardians of the west. Ballantine Bks. 1987 454p (Malloreon, bk1) o.p.
LC 86-26588
"A Del Rey book"
"A follow-up to Eddings's popular five-book Belgariad series [published in paperback], this novel is the first in [the Malloreon series.] Garion's slaying of the evil god Torak in the last installment left the world peaceful enough for the current chapter to open with Polgara settling down in the bucolic Vale of Aldur with her husband Durnick, her ancient sorcerer father Belgarath and the orphan Errand. Garion himself, now on the Rivan Throne, tends to his responsibilities as Overlord of the West and concentrates on producing an heir. . . . Eddings once again delivers an appealing central story that is pleasing for the assured, leisurely pace of its narrative flow and the ease and charm with which it incorporates events of mundane life into a tale of gods, kings and adventure." Publ Wkly
Followed by King of the Murgos (1988); Demon lord of Karanda (1988); Sorceress of Darshiva (1989); The seeress of Kell (1991)

Polgara the sorceress; {by} David and Leigh Eddings. Ballantine Bks. 1997 643p o.p.
ISBN 0-345-41662-7 LC 97-14785
"A Del Rey book"
"Polgara, daughter of Belgarath and Poledra, narrates this epic final volume in the Eddingses' Belgariad and Malloreon fantasy cycles. Time-spanning EVENTS are crucial to the more than 33 centuries recapitulated here, as Polgara and her family are directed to shape history by keeping peace and spreading civilization, and as Polgara becomes the protector of generations of Rivan Kings in Exile, perpetuating the bloodlines that prophecies say will produce the Godslayer. . . . Never strikingly original, by now this fantasy world offers little new. Rather, it will attract readers for its familiarity, for its promise of one final hurrah among well-liked characters and places, spiced by the kind of humor and drama that have made bestsellers of previous entries in the series bestsellers." Publ Wkly

Eddings, Leigh
(jt. auth) Eddings, D. Belgarath the sorcerer
(jt. auth) Eddings, D. Polgara the sorceress

Eden, Dorothy, 1912-1982

The American heiress. Coward, McCann & Geoghegan 1980 251p o.p.
LC 80-15256
The author "tells the tried and true tale of an illegitimate girl who finds her way into the arms of an English lord. Hetty Jervis accompanies her stepsister, Clemency, across the Atlantic. Despite warnings that the voyage aboard the Luisitania could be dangerous, Clemency refuses to listen. She plans to marry Lord Hazzard, swapping her American millions for an aristocratic title. . . . When the Luisitania is torpedoed, Mrs. Jervis refuses to abandon ship until the girls take all the jewels. When an Irish rescue nurse asks Hetty what the gold monogrammed watch stands for, she repeats the name, Clemency Jervis. From that moment, Hetty decides to live the life of an American heiress." West Coast Rev Books
"All of this is melded together with consummate storytelling skill and fine period atmosphere. The surprise bittersweet ending is just right." Publ Wkly

The Salamanca drum. Coward, McCann & Geoghegan 1977 286p o.p.
LC 76-56143
Matilda Duncastle "is a strong-willed woman, whose whole life is dedicated to honoring and continuing the Duncastle code of military gallantry and sacrifice. Marry-

Eden, Dorothy, 1912-1982—*Continued*

ing not out of love but out of duty to save the family estate, she is willing to sacrifice her husband's devotion, her sons' lives, as one war after another bleeds Britain half to death, and her daughters' happiness and right to lives of their own—all for a dream of patriotic glory that is almost madness." Publ Wkly

This novel "combines rich characterizations, plenty of action, lush locales (London, Vienna, Ireland), war, love, madness, a mysterious disappearance, thwarted romance." Libr J

Edgerton, Clyde, 1944-

Killer diller; a novel. Algonquin Bks. 1990 247p o.p.

ISBN 0-945575-53-X LC 90-42778

"This sequel to *Walking across Egypt* focuses on Wesley Benfield, now 24 and a resident at a halfway house associated with a Baptist college, where he teaches masonry to a retarded teenager, starts a gospel-blues band, and wrestles with his feelings of faith and lust." Booklist

"Occasionally, Mr. Edgerton's sense of humor gets the best of him and he pushes a scene until the characters border on the cartoonish. And near the end the plot . . . seems a bit forced. But the bottom line is that there's an affecting story, authenticity of voice and moral complexity here." N Y Times Book Rev

Redeye; a western. Algonquin Bks. 1995 244p $17.95

ISBN 1-56512-060-4 LC 94-43341

This novel is "set in Colorado 100 years ago. The cliff dwellings of southwest Colorado attract a motley crew of explorers in 1892, each with a personal agenda. Abel Merriwether, a local rancher and amateur archaeologist, wants to explore and protect the site; Andrew Collier, an Englishman, wants to write about it; Billy Blankenship, a local businessman, wants to develop it for tourism; Bishop Thorpe, a Mormon saint, hopes to find proof that Jesus visited there 2000 years before; and Cobb Pittman, a drifter with a red-eyed dog, seeks revenge on Thorpe for the Mountain Meadows Massacre of 1875." Libr J

"A Hollywood pitchman might call 'Redeye' 'Eudora Welty meets Mark Twain.' An admirer of good fiction might say that Clyde Edgerton has combined structure, character and style to create a small gem of a novel." NY Times Book Rev

Walking across Egypt; a novel. Algonquin Bks. 1987 216p $17.95

ISBN 0-912697-51-2 LC 86-20645

"Mattie Rigsbee, at 78, is slowing down. She plans her funeral so as not to be a burden; she supports the local Baptist church and entertains herself with hymns at the parlor piano; she tries not to meddle in her children's lives, though she does wish they'd marry; she longs for grandchildren. Then comes Wesley. Reared in an orphanage until he graduated to the reformatory, Wesley touches her heart, revives a life gone to seed. Just as he needs a grandmother's love and stability, so Mattie needs his challenge, dependence, and love." Libr J

This novel is "warm, innocent, and has a charming central character." Booklist

Followed by Killer diller

Where trouble sleeps; a novel. Algonquin Bks. 1997 260p $18.95

ISBN 1-565-12061-2 LC 97-3151

This novel is "about a fugitive who underestimates the inhabitants of the small Southern town of Listre, N.C. Fleeing Alabama in a stolen Buick Eight, Jack Umstead stops in Listre where, in 1950, a new blinking traffic light signals modern progress. Cannily sizing up the townsfolk, he attempts to discover the places where their money might be hidden. . . . Whether through cunning, bashful or averted eyes, Edgerton reveals the innocent, the deluded and the hypocritical with an unerring sense of humor and truth." Publ Wkly

Edgeworth, Maria, 1767-1849

Castle Rackrent; edited by George Watson; with an introduction by Kathryn J. Kirkpatrick. Oxford University Press 2000 c1995 xliii, 127p (Oxford world's classics) pa $11.95

ISBN 0-19-283563-7 LC 94-48873

First published 1800 in the United Kingdom

"This work may be regarded as the first fully developed historical novel and the first true regional novel in English. Set, according to the title-page, 'Before the year 1782', the characters, the life of the country, and the speech, are unmistakably Irish. It is a brief, high-spirited work, narrated in his old age by the devoted Thady Quirk, steward to three generations of Rackrents." Oxford Companion to Engl Lit. 6th edition

Edghill, India

Queenmaker; a novel of King David's Queen. St. Martin's Press 2002 376p o.p.

ISBN 0-312-28918-9 LC 2001-48603

"When Saul, a simple farmer, is crowned the first king of Israel, his youngest daughter, Michal, thus becomes a princess. She meets and falls in love with a devastatingly handsome charmer, David." Booklist

"With its excellent writing, dynamic characters, and galloping pace, Edghill's work is highly recommended for all historical fiction collections." Libr J

Edmonds, Walter D., 1903-1998

Drums along the Mohawk. Little, Brown 1936 592p o.p.

A "regional novel about early settlers in the Mohawk river valley in New York state during the Revolutionary war. The little community is made up of . . . individuals to whom Indian raids, British invasions, and militia gatherings are evidences of a distraught world outside. Their own understanding of the difficulties is rather vague. Gil Martin and his wife, clearing their home in the forest, and their not-very-near neighbors, are the main characters." Booklist

Edric, Robert, 1956-

The book of the heathen. Thomas Dunne Bks. 2002 351p $24.95

ISBN 0-312-28888-3 LC 2002-75447

"At a declining British outpost in the Congo, a man stands accused of murdering a young native girl. The prisoner, Nicholas Frere, an intelligent and once-

Edric, Robert, 1956-—*Continued*

respected employee, denies none of the charges. His sole remaining friend, James Frasier (the narrator), is the only one who has not already judged and condemned Frere." Booklist

"There are no pretty characters or easy lessons here, but the book paints a memorable picture of this ravaged stretch of jungle and the misery of the people—both European and African—who inhabited it at the height of the European empires." Publ Wkly

Effinger, George Alec, 1947-2002

George Alec Effinger live! from planet Earth; featuring contributions by Neal Barrett Jr. ... {et al.}. Golden Gryphon Press 2005 360p $25.95
ISBN 1-930846-32-0 LC 2004016935

Contents: The aliens who knew, I mean, everything; All the last wars at once; Two sadnesses; Target: Berlin!; One; My old man; Everything but honor; Solo in the spotlight; At the bran foundry; Housebound; Glimmer, glimmer; From downtown at the buzzer; The wooing of Slowboat Sadie; The man outside; Afternoon under glass; Two bits; The day the invaders came; The wisdom of having money; Put your hands together; Seven nights in Slumberland

"Effinger was one of the acknowledged masters of satirical sf and a prolific short story writer whose prodigious stylistic gifts are showcased in this unusual collection selected by his fellow writers and editors. In tribute to Effinger's genius, 16 veteran authors, from Michael Bishop and Jack Dann to Mike Resnick and Neil Gaiman, introduce each selection with personal reflections on Effinger's character and legacy. . . . Constituting a special treat for Effinger's fans are the O. Niemand stories, here introduced by Gardner Dozois, in which Effinger mimics, without caricature, the styles of such literary legends as Steinbeck, Hemingway, and Twain, while in each tale exploring an sf theme." Booklist

Egan, Greg, 1961-

Schild's ladder. Eos 2002 342p $25.95
ISBN 0-06-105093-8 LC 2001-55583

First published 2001 in the United Kingdom

A novel "set some 20,000 years in the future. . . . At the start, an experiment in quantum physics goes badly astray, creating another universe with physical laws that differ from our own. Its border expanding at half the speed of light, this new universe swallows planetary systems whole. Fortunately, humanity is so highly developed that entire populations can be quickly evacuated with little if any loss of life. Soon the scientific community divides into two groups, those who would destroy the new universe, and those who would study it." Publ Wkly

"Egan writes rather forbidding novels, always grounded in real science and imbued with serious scientific speculations. This is his most uncompromising book to date." Booklist

Egan, Lesley, 1921-

For works written by this author under other names see Shannon, Dell, 1921-

Egleton, Clive, 1927-

Blood money. St. Martin's Press 1998 362p o.p.
LC 98-16335

First published 1997 in the United Kingdom

"Rogue SIS agent Peter Ashton becomes involved in a case that takes him from a multiple murder at a Yorkshire safe house to a dangerous confrontation in Moscow with his old nemesis, Russian agent Pavel Trilisser, and, finally, to northern Virginia and a head-to-head clash with a crazed perpetrator who's part of a plot to destroy the world economy." Booklist

This novel "would be a silly endeavor if Egleton weren't having so much fun tweaking the spy genre, never quite lapsing into burlesque despite his outlandish characters and brain-twisting narrative logic. It's all great fun from an accomplished yarn spinner." N Y Times Book Rev

A double deception. St. Martin's Press 1992 309p o.p.
LC 92-2753

"As the story opens, in September 1939, aristocratic Andrew Korwin has arranged for his younger sister and brother to leave their Warsaw home before the Nazis march in. The brother is killed, sister Christina gets away and we last see Andrew trying to escape from a burning hospital. In 1967 Christina's American daughter, Stefanie, appears in London in search of her uncle. She enlists the aid of Campbell Parker of the Foreign Office, and clues point to Polish émigré Arthur Kershaw, successful manufacturer of a new laser-equipped gun. Other players include a seedy PI, a German con man, a newly released war criminal and even Simon Wiesenthal." Publ Wkly

The honey trap. St. Martin's Press 2001 390p o.p.
ISBN 0-312-26924-2

First published 2000 in the United Kingdom

Peter Ashton of the British SIS "is detailed to investigate the grisly murder of a Queen's Messenger in Costa Rica. To uncover the hydra-headed monster lurking behind that torture killing, Ashton will have to explore links among terrorists as diverse as the IRA, the KGB, Turkish Cypriots and a former Cuban intelligence officer. . . . All in all, Egleton provides great entertainment, and if the novel's conclusion strains credulity, with Ashton always in the right place at the right time, it isn't enough to diminish the pleasure of the journey." Publ Wkly

Hostile intent. St. Martin's Press 1993 314p o.p.
LC 92-21219

"Peter Ashton, a British agent, investigates the death in 1991 of a colleague who was running a Soviet Army office, a woman, who has disappeared. The search for her leads from Europe to the United States, with Ashton having to avoid the members of a Russian hit team. They want the defector as much as the British and the Americans do. . . . The plotting is careful, the action constant but never heavy-breathing, the characters low-key and believable." N Y Times Book Rev

A killing in Moscow. St. Martin's Press 1994 346p o.p.
LC 93-44059

British agent Peter Ashton is "sent to the Moscow embassy to appraise the local security efforts, he gets caught up in the investigation of the murder of a British

Egleton, Clive, 1927-—*Continued*
subject. Puzzled by contradictions in the evidence, he enlists the help of a minor Russian functionary, a woman who is beaten and tortured for what she may know. Soon, the trail leads to Seattle and Serbia, where international commerce has been put to corrupt ends. Egleton is never fanciful but always imaginative, and his latest novel is densely plotted and peopled with full and convincing characters." Libr J

A lethal involvement. St. Martin's Press 1996 c1995 312p o.p.
ISBN 0-312-14313-3 LC 96-3506
First published 1995 in the United Kingdom
"Peter Ashton, now retired from the British Secret Intelligence Service (SIS), is asked to look into the suspicious disappearance of an army captain who was being considered for top-secret clearance. His investigation leads to the 1969 death of an Asian American woman in Hong Kong and another death in Germany." Libr J
"Chief among the novel's joys is Ashton's working through the cold, if often funny, SIS office politics. As usual, Egleton's plot complications can stun a horse, or a careless reader, but their intricacy is delicious and well worth the risk." Publ Wkly

Warning shot. St. Martin's Press 1997 410p o.p.
LC 97-7196
First published 1996 in the United Kingdom
British agent Peter Ashton is "asked to help stop a terrorist organization from carrying out an explosive attack on the United States. One bomb has already gone off in Berlin, in turn setting off an international game of hide-and-seek with Ashton and fellow agents, who are attempting to find the mastermind of a fundamentalist Islamic group determined to make its point to the world at all costs." Libr J
"Genre fans will relish the building suspense, fast pacing, and ingenious plot. This is an outstanding thriller from the old school." Booklist

Egolf, Tristan, 1971-2005

Skirt and the fiddle; a novel. Grove Press 2002 199p $23
ISBN 0-8021-1722-8 LC 2002-16442
"Narrator Charlie Evans, a violin virtuoso and orphan of Asian-Afro-American parentage, ends up in a skid-row boarding house in Philth Town, somewhere near New York City. Among the residents is Tinsel Greetz, an anarchist and troublemaker with whom Charlie reluctantly forms a friendship. . . . This energetic and entertaining work seems more like an expanded short story, but the author's vibrant writing and lunatic vision might be especially appealing to a younger . . . audience." Libr J

Eidson, Bill

One bad thing. Forge 2000 348p o.p.
ISBN 0-312-87646-7 LC 00-31696
"A Tom Doherty Associates book"
"After selling his business and house and buying a 38-foot sloop, The Wanderer, McKenna sets sail with his wife, Caroline, on a life-altering ocean voyage. When Caroline, unable to cope with their constant arguments, flies home from Tortolla in the Caribbean to Newburyport, Mass., young, blond, blue-eyed Tom Cain offers to be McKenna's mate. But Cain is not the experienced sailor or Harvard graduate he professes to be, and McKenna begins a journey home darker and more dangerous than the treacherous sea they endure en route." Publ Wkly

Elegant, Robert S.

Dynasty; a novel. McGraw-Hill 1977 625p o.p.
LC 76-58433
This novel "recounts the history of the Sekloongs, an influential Eurasian commercial family based in Hong Kong. The reader meets the Sekloong patriarch, Sir Jonathan (1853-1950), issue of an Irish father and Chinese mother, and observes his children and their children as they go about the business of birth, death, marriage, love affairs, politics, and, most of all, trade. . . . The Sekloong saga is told against the backdrop of larger events, specifically 20th-Century China in revolutionary turmoil." Libr J

Manchu. McGraw-Hill 1980 560p o.p.
LC 80-17452
This "novel of 17th Century China depicts the conquest of the great Ming Empire by the invading Tartars, or Manchus. The story, panoramic in scope, focuses on the life of Francis Arrowsmith, a European who comes to China at a young age in 1624 to serve the Christian cause as 'not a saint but a sinful soldier.' For the next 30 years Arrowsmith's military career places him at the center of tumultuous events." Libr J
The novel "has color and drama aplenty, and authentically captures the splendor, brutality and intrigue of the Ming dynasty in its decadence." Publ Wkly

Mandarin. Simon & Schuster 1983 527p o.p.
LC 83-18696
This "family saga cum historical epic has for background the tumultuous era of the Taiping Rebellion, which shook the Manchu empire to its foundations and led to the destruction by Western troops of Peking's Summer Palace. The principal characters are members of two wealthy merchant families, the Haleevies and the Lees, one Western and one Chinese, but partners in business and both Jewish by faith, and Yehenala, the decadent emperor's favorite concubine, who bears the heir to the throne and becomes de facto ruler of the empire." Publ Wkly

Eliot, Alice *See* Jewett, Sarah Orne, 1849-1909

Eliot, Alice C. *See* Jewett, Sarah Orne, 1849-1909

Eliot, George, 1819-1880

Adam Bede. Knopf 1992 xxxiii, 612p $20
ISBN 0-679-40991-2 LC 91-53187
"Everyman's library"
First published in 1859
"The title character, a carpenter, is in love with a woman who bears a child by another man. Although Bede tries to help her, he eventually loses her but finds happiness with Dinah Morris, a Methodist preacher. Adam Bede was Eliot's first long novel. Its masterly realism—evident, for example, in the recording of Derby-

Eliot, George, 1819-1880—*Continued*
shire dialect—brought to English fiction the same truthful observation of minute detail that John Ruskin was commending in the Pre-Raphaelites. But what was new in this work of English fiction was the combination of deep human sympathy and rigorous moral judgment." Merriam-Webster's Ency of Lit

Middlemarch; a study of provincial life; with an introduction by E.S. Shaffer. Knopf 1991 xxxix, 888p $22
ISBN 0-679-40567-4 LC 91-52976
"Everyman's library"
First published 1872
A novel "with a double plot interest. The heroine, Dorothea Brooke, longs to devote herself to some great cause and, for a time, expects to find it in her marriage to Rev. Mr. Casaubon, an aging scholar. Mr. Casaubon lives only eighteen months after their marriage, a sufficient period to disillusion her completely. He leaves her his estate, with the ill-intentioned proviso that she will forfeit if she marries his young cousin Will Ladislaw, whom she had seen frequently in Rome. Endeavoring to find happiness without Ladislaw, whom she has come to care for deeply, Dorothea throws herself into the struggle for medical reforms advocated by the young Dr. Lydgate. Finally, however, she decides to give up her property and marry Ladislaw. The second plot deals with the efforts and failure of Dr. Lydgate to live up to his early ideals." Reader's Ency. 4th edition

The mill on the Floss. Knopf 1992 xxxi, 597p $22
ISBN 0-679-41726-5 LC 92-52920
"Everyman's library"
First published 1860
"Deeply significant tragedy of the inner life, enacted amidst the quaint folk and old-fashioned surroundings of a country town (St. Ogg's is Gainsborough). The conflict of affection and antipathy between a brother and sister, and again in the family relations of their father, is a dominant motive; but the emotional tension rises to a climax in Maggie's unpremeditated yielding to an unworthy lover and betrayal of her finer nature. Brother and sister . . . are purified and reconciled only in death." Baker. Guide to the Best Fic

Romola. o.p.
First published in book form 1863
"Based on a special study of Florentine history in the epoch 1492-1509, the days of Lorenzo de' Medici, and the saintliness and all-conquering energy of Savonarola are finely portrayed. 'Romola' is a sternly tragic novel of temptation, crime and retribution." Baker. Guide to the Best Fic

Silas Marner; the weaver of Raveloe. Knopf 1993 xxx, 206p $18
ISBN 0-679-42030-4 LC 92-54293
"Everyman's library"
First published 1861
"Silas Marner is a handloom weaver, a good man, whose life has been wrecked by a false accusation of theft, which cannot be disproved. For years he lives a lonely life, with the sole companionship of his loom: and he is saved from his own despair by the chance finding of a little child. On this baby girl he lavishes the whole passion of his thwarted nature, and her filial affection makes him a kindly man again. After sixteen years the real thief is dicovered, and Silas's good name is restored. On this slight framework are hung the richest pictures of middle and low class life that George Eliot has painted." Keller. Reader's Dig of Books

Elkin, Stanley, 1930-1995

The Dick Gibson show. Random House 335p o.p.
ISBN 0-394-46215-7 LC 74-117660
"Look who's on the 'Dick Gibson Radio Show': Arnold the Memory Expert ('I've memorized the entire West Coast shoreline– except for cloud cover and fog banks'). Bernie Perk, the burning pharmacist. Henry Harper, the nine-year old orphan millionaire, terrified of being adopted. The woman whose life revolves around pierced lobes. An evil hypnotist. Swindlers. Con-men. And Dick Gibson himself." Publisher's note
This is Elkin's "best–a funny, melancholy, frightening, scabrous, absolutely American compendium that may turn out to be our classic about radio." N Y Times Book Rev

The MacGuffin. Linden Press 1991 283p o.p.
ISBN 0-671-67324-6 LC 90-13233
In this novel, Elkin "unleashes a Hitchcockian MacGuffin (the narrative spirit) which takes over the ebbing life of Bobbo Druff, 58, the fairly honest but bribable street commissioner of a mid-size American city. Kafkaesque unseen enemies and their supposed spies, perhaps including Bobbo's newly acquired mistress, Meg Glorioso, may be trying to nail him for an unspecified crime linked somehow to the hit-and-run death of the Lebanese Moslem Shiite girlfriend of his son Mikey, a 30-year-old ninny." Publ Wkly
"Here, MacGuffins of adultery, smuggling, and drug abuse merely provide a context for inspired, Joycean wordplay based on cliches, shoptalk, and technical jargon. Language itself is the real topic." Libr J

Mrs. Ted Bliss. Hyperion 1995 291p o.p.
ISBN 0-7868-6104-5 LC 95-5413
The protagonist of this novel is Dorothy Bliss. "After her husband's death, Dorothy stays on alone in The Towers, their Miami Beach retirement condo. Everyone continues to address her as Mrs. Ted Bliss, as if she had no identity of her own. But Dorothy adapts quickly to change, and soon she is on The Towers's A-list, hobnobbing with 'Tommy Overeasy', an elegant South American drug lord, and the building's chief engineer, a Yiddish-speaking Aztec." Libr J
"Elkin was always a better portrait artist than storyteller . . . . In this, the last of Elkin's books, Dorothy eventually figures out how to live a little for herself and to face what is coming. We leave her, in the end, staring down [a] hurricane." New Yorker

Stanley Elkin's The magic kingdom. Dutton 1985 317p o.p.
ISBN 0-525-24304-6 LC 84-21109
"When seven terminally ill English children [go] on a visit to Disney World . . . in the charge of five ostensibly healthy but odd adults, highly comic, and deeply tragic, things happen." Publ Wkly
"This is a book by an extraordinary artist in language.

Elkin, Stanley, 1930-1995—*Continued*

It is also extremely funny and its effect is often that of a strong emetic. That combination leaves the reader wondering which way to turn—not perhaps the worst position for a thoughtful reader to be left in. . . . Elkin is gentle yet tough with his forlorn children, funny yet kind with his distrait adults; as a whole, he has written a sensitive book. . . . His book challenges a resilient and imaginative reader." N Y Rev Books

Elkins, Aaron J.

Dead men's hearts; [by] Aaron Elkins. Mysterious Press 1994 227p o.p.

LC 93-43762

A mystery featuring anthropologist/sleuth Gideon Oliver. "After reluctantly agreeing to help film a documentary promoting Horizon House, a center for Egyptian studies located in the Nile Valley, Gideon and his wife, Julie, are looking forward to a relaxing few weeks. But soon after they reach Luxor, an ancient skeleton unearthed at a Horizon House dig in the 1920s is misplaced, and the illustrious head of the institute, Professor Clifford Haddon, is murdered. . . . A refreshingly funny, clever, entertaining mystery that will appeal to a broad range of readers." Booklist

A glancing light; [by] Aaron Elkins. Scribner 1991 243p o.p.

LC 90-25885

"When a stolen masterpiece surfaces in a shipment of inexpensive copies, [museum curator Chris Norgren] verifies its authenticity but questions the involvement of the seemingly innocent importer. During a business trip to Bologna, his suspicions are confirmed when he discovers the renowned art squad of the Italian carbinieri is conducting an investigation of a series of related thefts and forgeries. As the elaborate scam begins to unravel, Chris becomes the target of a desperately cunning colleague. An intelligent and superbly crafted caper." Booklist

Good blood; Aaron Elkins. 1st ed. Berkley Prime Crime 2004 293p $23.95

ISBN 0-425-19411-6 LC 2003-62799

In this mystery, forensic anthropologist Gideon Oliver and his park ranger wife, Julie, "are on holiday in Italy, helping a friend host a tour featuring canoeing and bicycle riding. Since neither activity is Gideon's idea of fun, he lounges around the picturesque town of Stresa and is pulled, consequently, into the investigation of recently uncovered bones, which turn out to be connected to a 40-year-old secret baby swap. In turn, the swap is tied to a recent kidnapping involving the wealthy, influential family to which Gideon's tour guide friend is related. . . . This is vintage Elkins: well-drawn supporting characters, lovely scenery, and a bit of interesting science." Libr J

Icy clutches; [by] Aaron Elkins. Mysterious Press 1990 294p o.p.

LC 89-49554

"Gideon Oliver, a 'skeleton detective' (he deduces how people got dead by examining their bones), thought Alaska would be a great spot for a getaway vacation. When human bones turn up at a 30-year-old avalanche site, however, play becomes work." Am Libr

"Mr. Elkins skates on thin ice with character and dialogue, but give him a mandibular fossa to analyze, or a glacial upheaval to describe, and he's right up there at 90 degrees north—on top of the world." N Y Times Book Rev

Skeleton dance; a novel; [by] Aaron Elkins. Morrow 2000 246p $23

ISBN 0-688-15928-1 LC 00-23278

"Celebrated Seattle 'skeleton detective' Gideon Oliver travels to the quaint French village of Les Eyzies to aid police in the identification of some human bones. At first, the bones were thought to be prehistoric fossils, common enough in a town famous for its Paleolithic caves and the world-class Institut de Préhistoire. But closer examination reveals the deceased to have been murdered sometime within the past five years, possibly by someone linked to the institute." Publ Wkly

"But for all the breezy humor, the satirical treatment of squabbling scientists respectfully illuminates their fascinating work, and in the end it is the scholarship that dazzles." N Y Times Book Rev

Twenty blue devils; [by] Aaron Elkins. Mysterious Press 1997 276p o.p.

LC 96-29085

This mystery finds forensic anthropologist Gideon Oliver "on Tahiti, picking over the exhumed remains of the manager of the Paradise Coffee plantation, a family-owned java empire plagued by misfortune. When Gideon declares this latest accident a homicide, the family can't go on blaming Pele, the hot-tempered Hawaiian fire deity, for its troubles." N Y Times Book Rev

"Zipping along at a smooth and rapid clip, the story combines masterfully etched characters and suggestions of lingering aromas of frangipani and coconut palms with the consummate panache of its hero." Publ Wkly

Ellis, Bret Easton, 1964-

Lunar Park. Alfred A. Knopf 2005 308p $24.95

ISBN 0-375-41291-3 LC 2005-40923

"At a fateful Halloween party [the protagonist] glimpses a disturbing (fictional) character driving a car identical to his late father's, his stepdaughter's doll violently 'malfunctions,' and their house undergoes bizarre transformations both within and without. Connecting these aberrations to graver events—a series of grotesque murders that no longer seem random and the epidemic disappearance of boys his son's age—Ellis struggles to defend his family against this escalating menace even as his wife, their therapists, and the police insist that his apprehensions are rooted instead in substance abuse and egomania." Publisher's note

"The whole book swirls, surreally, pushing the limits of tolerable confusion while sending up laughably familiar horror story shticks. For a while, it looks as if nothing will be resolved. It works precisely because it is a ghost story, replete with eviscerated livestock, freshly dug graves, and messages written in ash—and because everything, ultimately, is resolved." New Criterion

Ellis, David

Life sentence. Putnam 2003 390p $24.95

ISBN 0-399-14979-1 LC 2002-68137

Ellis, David—*Continued*

"Jon Soliday and Grant Tully share a dirty secret from their teenage years: after a night of drinking and drugs, Soliday climbed through the bedroom window of a beautiful young woman and then blacked out. Consequently, he doesn't remember anything after that—not even how she ended up dead. Via family connections, Soliday eludes prosecution, and 20 years later he is chief legal counsel to Senator Tully, who is running a fierce campaign for governor. . . . Elegant prose skillfully impels Soliday through a haze of deadly deceit, where no one is who he appears to be." Libr J

Ellison, Harlan

Adrift just off the Islets of Langerhans: latitude 38° 54′ N, longitude 77° 00′ 13″ W
In The Hugo winners p547-81

A boy and his dog
In The Best of the Nebulas p359-89

(ed) Dangerous visions. See Dangerous visions

The deathbird
In The Hugo winners p437-68

Ellison, Ralph

Invisible man; preface by Charles Johnson. Modern Lib. 1994 xxxiv, 572p $19.95; pa $12
ISBN 0-679-60139-2; 0-679-73276-4 (pa) LC 94-176953

A reissue of the title first published 1952 by Random House

"Acclaimed as a powerful representation of the lives of blacks during the Depression, this novel describes the experiences of one young black man during that period. Dismissed from a Negro college in the South for showing one of the founders how Negroes live there, he is used later as a symbol of repression by a Communist group in New York City. After a Harlem race riot, he is aware that he must contend with both whites and blacks, and that loss of social identity makes him invisible among his fellow beings." Shapiro. Fic for Youth. 3d edition

Ellroy, James

American tabloid; a novel. Knopf 1995 571p o.p.
ISBN 0-679-40391-4 LC 94-42898

This novel presents a "view of the American underworld from the late 1950s to the assassination of JFK. . . . The story hinges on the entanglements of three 40-something government mercenaries who play major, behind-the-scenes roles in such events as the Bay of Pigs and the assassination of the president." Publ Wkly

"The dizzying number of covert alliances and compromised loyalties that link the Mob, the C.I.A., Howard Hughes, J. Edgar Hoover, and the Kennedys comes across less like a cancer of epic proportions that like a kind of institutional dyspepsia. Ellroy's tabloidization of this chapter of American history makes it all the more queasy and real." New Yorker

Because the night
In Ellroy, J. L.A. noir p207-425

The black dahlia. Mysterious Press 1987 325p o.p.
LC 87-7952

"Using the basic facts concerning the 1940s' notorious and yet unsolved Black Dahlia case, Ellroy creates a kaleidoscope of human passion and dark obsession. A young woman's mutilated body is found in a Los Angeles vacant lot. The story is seen through the eyes of Bucky Bleichert, ex-prize fighter and something of a boy wonder on the police force." Libr J

"The author manages a gripping re-creation of LA street life in the 1940s, and his characters are powerfully written and terrifyingly real. The bare-bones plot, the slew of false conclusions, and the hazy evocation of the murder victim give the narrative a dreamlike atmosphere, ideal for a tale of immoral heroes and wasted lives." Booklist

Blood on the moon
In Ellroy, J. L.A. noir p1-206

The cold six thousand. Knopf 2001 672p $25.95
ISBN 0-679-40392-2

Sequel to American tabloid

A look "at the dark side of American life during the 1960s, focusing on a Las Vegas police officr, Wayne Tedrow Jr., and his inadvertent role in the cover-up of John F. Kennedy's assassination. The narrative spans a five-year period and traces Tedrow's dealings with the Mafia, the Ku Klux Klan, and various political and cultural icons of that time period." Libr J

"Ellroy's prose is easy to absorb sentence by sentence, thanks to his simple subject-verb-object constructions, but monstrous as it acquires cumulative force over hundreds of pages. . . . The novel is an exhausting, masochistic, often revelatory rereading of the allegedly idealistic sixties—an assassination, finally, of the decade rather than of its leaders." New Yorker

L.A. confidential. Mysterious Press 1990 496p $32
ISBN 0-89296-293-3 LC 89-40523

This novel focuses on three L.A. policemen: "Trashcan Jack Vincennes, a narcotics cop who makes a little cash on the side by setting up indiscreet celebrities for exposure in a Hollywood scandal sheet; Bad Bud White, whose favorite crime-stopping technique is to 'shoot everyone involved, then look for somebody a bit more intelligent to sort out the bodies'; and Ed Exley, a well-connected officer who believes in 'stern, absolute justice, whatever the price,' provided it doesn't impede his political ambitions." N Y Times Book Rev

The author "merges raw-edged period detail with sleazy celluloid lore, producing a dark and dazzling descent into the criminal underworld of the 1950s." Booklist

L.A. noir. Mysterious Press 1998 644p o.p.
LC 98-15470

Contents: In Blood on the moon (1984) Hopkins unearths a serial killer; Because the night (1984) concerns the disappearence of a hero cop and a multiple murder; Suicide hill (1986) explores corruption and betrayal when a kidnapping leads to an orgy of violence

Suicide hill
In Ellroy, J. L.A. noir p427-644

Ellroy, James—*Continued*

White jazz; a novel. Knopf 1992 349p o.p.
LC 92-52890

This novel unfolds in "the murky, decadent world of Los Angeles in the late 1950s, as seen through the cynical eyes of David Klein, age 42, the commanding officer of the LAPD's vice division. Klein makes up his own rules as he goes along, rules that involve money, mayhem, and murder as necessary. Klein isn't the only one to follow such rules, which apparently are the 'norm' for other members of the force as well. But Klein suffers the unthinkable when he becomes the scapegoat so that other officers can protect their own dirty laundry from the probing eyes of federal agents." Libr J

"Ellroy's clipped, telegraphic style, his use of real people and real events, and his creation of a world horrifyingly devoid of any conventional morality make *White Jazz* a harrowing, remarkable read." Booklist

Elward, James, 1928-1996

(jt. auth) Van Slyke, H. Public smiles, private tears

Emerson, Earl W.

Pyro. Ballantine Bks. 2004 307p $24.95
ISBN 0-345-46288-2

"Paul Wollf is a veteran Seattle firefighter whose firefighter father died in an arson blaze when Wollf was four. Fueled by his hatred for the killer, he achieves heroics that protect him from political infighting within the department. Work gets more complicated, however, when a new pattern of fires is detected, each one closer to Wollf's station; evidence points to the arsonist who caused his father's death." Libr J

This is a "fast-paced, smoke-filled, gripping story loaded with plot twists, snappy and graphic dialogue, and firefighting lore." Publ Wkly

Vertical burn; by Earl Emerson. Ballantine Bks. 2002 340p o.p.
ISBN 0-345-44589-9 LC 2001-35969

"One day, life is dandy for John Finney, . . . a veteran of Seattle's fire department. The next day he loses his friend and partner in a fire he suspects was set, and shortly after that he is being framed for arson and targeted for murder by conspirators who are planning to burn down the city's tallest building. . . . Emerson combines an intimate knowledge of fires and fire fighting with an intricate plot played out by characters you can love or hate." Booklist

Emmons, Cai

His mother's son. Harcourt 2003 366p $25
ISBN 0-15-100734-9 LC 2002-2990

"Dr. Jana Thomas has a secret that no one knows—not even her husband. Fifteen years before, she had a different life and a different name, which she abandoned when her younger brother murdered their parents and went on a killing spree at his school. Now Jana has a young son, and she begins to panic when she sees the warning signs that no one noticed in her brother." Libr J

"Those looking for domestic drama and hidden lives will enjoy Emmons' book and find the anxious and troubled character of Jana interesting." Booklist

Endō, Shūsaku, 1923-1996

Deep river; translated by Van C. Gessel. New Directions 1995 216p o.p.
ISBN 0-8112-1289-0 LC 94-38913

"A trip to India becomes a journey of discovery for a group of Japanese tourists playing out their 'individual dramas of the soul.' Isobe searches for his reincarnated wife, while Kiguchi relives the wartime horror that ultimately saved his life. Alienated by middle age, Mitsuko follows Otsu, a failed priest, to the holy city of Varanas." Libr J

This is a "beautifully wrought, lyrically suggestive story. . . . If Christianity holds up to us the lonely individual challenged by a God who entered history, Buddhism gives us people who are ready to surrender, finally, a measure of their human and spiritual particularity and who, with acceptance, join their fellow creatures as part of the great tide of humanity. Mr. Endo manages to merge both of these streams of faith, bringing them together in a flow that is, indeed, deep. His work is a soulful gift to a world he keeps rendering as unrelievedly parched." N Y Times Book Rev

The final martyrs; translated by Van C. Gessel. New Directions 1994 199p $21.95
ISBN 0-8112-1272-6 LC 94-746

Contents: The final martyrs; Shadows; A fifty-year-old man; Adieu; Heading home; Japanese in Warsaw; Life; A sixty-year-old man; The last supper; A woman called Shizu; The box

"This deftly translated collection, comprised of stories written as early as 1959 and as late as 1985, also includes semi-autobiographical tales in which Endo deals with the traumatic impact that his parent's divorce had on his boyhood. He also writes with grace, compassion and gentle humor about old age, love betrayed, Japanese tourists and the marks we leave on the lives of others." Publ Wkly

The girl I left behind; translated by Mark Williams. New Directions 1995 194p $21.95
ISBN 0-8112-1303-X LC 95-11038

Original Japanese edition, 1964

"Yoshioka Tsutomu, a typical Japanese salaryman, hears a disembodied voice in his head that says: 'It's not possible for someone to interact with a fellow human being without leaving some traces.' Specifically, the voice (which belongs to Jesus Christ) refers to a country girl named Morita Mitsu, whom Yoshioka seduced when he was a college student. Their affair was a shabby thing: Yoshioka exploited Mitsu's sympathy for his slight limp, caused by childhood polio, to get her into bed. . . . Inevitably, he meets her again, but under greatly altered circumstances, an encounter that leads Mitsu to a life of Christian charity. Flawed and awkward as it is, this early novel by a writer who has since come to be viewed as a master has moments of sparkling intelligence and clarity." Publ Wkly

The samurai; a novel; translated from the Japanese by Van C. Gessel. Harper & Row 1982 272p o.p.
ISBN 0-06-859852-1 LC 82-47851

Original Japanese edition, 1980

This historical novel is "set in the seventeenth century as a Franciscan missionary and a samurai travel to Span-

Endō, Shūsaku, 1923-1996—*Continued*

ish America and on to Rome as emissaries of the Eastern emperor to the Pope. Their journey begins under a veil of secrecy and subterfuge and ends in futility when the purpose of their lengthy voyage is negated by a twist of Japanese authority that commands a return to political isolation. This is an effective re-creation of both the Eastern and Western aspects of the tale and also a realistic portrayal of the cultural disjunction experienced by both of the main characters." Booklist

Scandal; a novel; translated from the Japanese by Van C. Gessel. Dodd, Mead 1988 261p o.p.
LC 87-27409

At age 65, "the harmony Suguro feels he has finally achieved between his life and work is shattered. . . . A drunken woman accosts him, accusing the venerated writer of frequenting the brothel district of Tokyo. In fact, she tells him a portrait of his degenerate self now hangs in a gallery there. And a journalist, Kobari, a dabbler in literature and Marxism who is intent on exposing the hypocrisy of this Catholic convert and celebrated artist, forces Suguro to pursue this allegation." N Y Times Book Rev

"This provocative, impassioned meditation manages to explore not only the nature of identity, but also the regions of sin, salvation, art and religion, all with the unerring grace that defines a novelist in the fullest command of his craft." Publ Wkly

Silence; translated by William Johnston. Taplinger 1979 c1976 294p o.p.
LC 78-27168

Original Japanese edition, 1966; this translation first published 1969 in Japan

"The story is based on events in early 17th-century Japan, when Japanese Christians and Christian missionaries were brutally persecuted. In the novel, Sebastian Rodrigues, a Portuguese seminarian, journeys to Japan to investigate why his former teacher, a missionary to Japan, has chosen apostasy over martyrdom. Pervading the novel is the belief that Christianity is incomparible with Japanese culture. In the end, seeing the selfishness of martyrdom, Rodrigues also chooses apostasy." Merriam-Webster's Ency of Lit

Engel, Howard, 1931-

The Cooperman variations; a Benny Cooperman mystery. Overlook Press 2002 279p $24.95
ISBN 1-58567-233-5 LC 2002-70410

"Canadian-Jewish P.I. Benny Cooperman . . . goes to work for Vanessa Moss, a former acquaintance who now heads the entertainment division of a television network. After a friend is murdered in her house, Vanessa fears for her own life." Libr J

"Readers new to Benny's world may find themselves a little confused from time to time, but this is only a minor inconvenience. Benny is a wonderful narrator, and once readers have spent a few minutes with him, they will feel like they've known him all their lives." Booklist

Engel, Mary Potter

Strangers and sojourners; stories from the lowcountry. Counterpoint 2004 222p $23
ISBN 1-582-43264-3 LC 2003-20892

Contents: Queen Esther Coosawaw; You got to learn how to read things right; All that we need; Let them big animals come back; Lowcountry cold; Why; A soldier's disease; Rat; Who calls each one by name; Philosophy of education; Unnatural acts; Redeeming the dead; Tongues of angels; What Addie wants; M to F; A better man; What we ought to be; Dis aliter visum; Those who shine like the stars; Epiphany; Strangers and sojourners

"Subtly interweaving the tale of each character, from a 114-year-old black woman to a cross-dressing outcast, Engel allows each to speak in his or her own distinctive voice, each of which she renders with pinpoint accuracy and astounding versatility. Their eccentricities notwithstanding, these are extraordinary characters, endowed by Engel with a sublime grace and humbling spirituality that is both penetrating and poignant." Booklist

Englander, Nathan

For the relief of unbearable urges. Knopf 1999 205p $22
ISBN 0-375-40492-9 LC 98-41727

Contents: The twenty-seventh man; The tumblers; Reunion; The wig; The gilgul of Park Avenue; Reb Kringle; The last one way; For the relief of unbearable urges; In this way we are wise

These nine stories focus on the "world of Orthodox Jews. In this world, ritual is reality, mystery lurks everywhere. Like Flannery O'Connor's God-haunted characters, Englander's people are constantly being waylaid by passions they neither control nor understand." Newsweek

Enquist, Per Olov, 1934-

The royal physicians visit; translated from the Swedish by Tiina Nunnally. Overlook Press 2001 312p $26.95
ISBN 1-58567-196-7 LC 2001-36475

Original Swedish edition, 1999

This historical novel about the royal court of Denmark in the 18th century focuses on "King Christian VII, who ascended to the Danish throne in 1766, at the age of 16, and who is now remembered in his country for the 'Struensee era' (1770-72), during which his German court physician, Johann Friedrich Struensee, served as the kingdom's de facto ruler." N Y Times Book Rev

"Enquist's spare, elliptical prose slowly gains dramatic momentum, especially when initially cool descriptions segue into sexual passion. The narrative reads like one of Brecht's political parables—an ironic vision of the collision between Enlightenment and madness." Publ Wkly

Ephron, Nora

Heartburn. Knopf 1983 179p o.p.
LC 82-48999

Cookbook author and TV personality Rachel Samstat "is truly in love with her second husband, Mark Feldman, a columnist prone to asking 'Do you think there's something to it?' when scouting daily life for column material. Rachel is seven months pregnant when she finds out Mark's in love with Thelma Rice." Publ Wkly

"Though 'Heartburn' bristles ferociously with wit, it's not entirely lacking in soul." N Y Times Book Rev

Epstein, Joseph, 1937-

Fabulous small Jews; stories. Houghton Mifflin 2003 339p $23
ISBN 0-395-94402-3 LC 2002-27621
Contents: Felix emeritus; Artie Glick in a family way; The third Mrs. Kessler; Moe; Love and The Guinness book of records; Family values; The executor; Saturday afternoon at the zoo with dad; Freddy Duchamp in action; Don Juan Zimmerman; Dubinsky on the loose; Coming in with their hands up; The master's ring; Howie's gift; A loss for words; My little Marjie; Postcards; Uncle Jack

"Like his emotionally candid, low-key protagonists, Epstein is intrinsically honest. Gratifying and genuine, this collection examines all sorts of respones to the encroachment of old age on human dignity." Publ Wkly

Epstein, Leslie

San Remo Drive; a novel from memory. Handsel Press 2003 238p il $26
ISBN 1-59051-066-6 LC 2002-35547
This novel "portrays one talented but troubled Hollywood family through the eyes of the elder son, Richard, who becomes a famous artist. His director father, Norman Jacobi, wittily mocks the HUAC during his televised hearing, his mother, Lotte, is beautiful and a bit of a loose cannon; and his strange little brother, Barton, is given to fits and visions, serving as a trickster figure, the fool who reveals the truth." Booklist

"There is something of 'The Winter's Tale' in the way Epstein pulls it all together, something of the miraculous second chance. Losing and finding, he shows us love between fathers and sons as the most powerful and enduring in life. . . . In doing so he has given us, along with F. Scott Fitzgerald's 'Last Tycoon,' Budd Schulberg's 'What Makes Sammy Run?' and his own 'Pandaemonium,' one of the four best Hollywood novels ever written." N Y Times Book Rev

Erdrich, Louise

The antelope wife; a novel. HarperFlamingo 1998 240p o.p.
LC 97-48894
This is the "tale of two mixed-blood Native American families: the Roys, who bear a set of twin girls in every generation, and the dogged Shawanos, ruled by the dual gods of coercion and love. Erdrich's shamanlike storytelling powers are in evidence from the start, when an Ojibwa baby vanishes during a cavalry raid; although she occasionally trips on the line between tragedy and farce, her smoky, resonant voice never falters." New Yorker

The Beet Queen; a novel. Holt & Co. 1986 338p o.p.
ISBN 0-8050-0058-5 LC 86-4788
Second installment in the author's North Dakota Quartet

This novel "concerns a brother and sister, Karl and Mary Adare, who are abandoned by their mother, who runs away with a barnstorming pilot. Flight is a recurring theme in this . . . tale of loneliness set against a stark North Dakota landscape. Karl spends his life as an itinerant salesman, running from his troubled family and his own sexual ambivalence; Mary, who grows up with her aunt and uncle, uses self-reliance as a way of hiding from the pain of human relationships; and Sita, Mary's cousin, retreats into insanity to avoid facing the realization that her idealized dreams of a glamorous life have evaporated. Only Celestine, Mary's friend and the mother of Karl's child, accepts reality on its own terms as she struggles to protect her daughter from the suffering that has engulfed those around her." Booklist

The bingo palace. HarperCollins Pubs. 1994 274p o.p.
LC 93-37684
Final volume in the author's North Dakota Quartet

"Immediately on returning to his North Dakota Chippewa reservation, Lipsha Morrissey—having failed in the outside world—falls head over heels in love with the beautiful Shawnee Ray. She is the fierce and ambitious mother of the illegitimate son of Lyman Lamartine, owner of the Bingo Palace and a powerful force on the reservation. Lyman is determined to marry Shawnee Ray, who is just as determined to elude him and go to college. When Lipsha goes to work for Lyman, he also enters into a battle for Shawnee Ray's affections, calling first on the magic of tribal elder Fleur Pillager, then on luck, and finally on traditional tribal religion." Libr J

"We're often uncomfortable when so much unadulterated feeling is spilled at our feet, but Erdrich is ready for our squeamishness, mixing romance and comedy with the skill of a master alchemist, diluting sentimentality while enhancing the emotional impact of the story." Booklist

Four souls. HarperCollins Publishers 2004 210p $23.95
ISBN 0-06-620975-7 LC 2003-65243
"Fleur Pillager takes her mother's name, Four Souls, for strength and walks away from her Ojibwe reservation to the cities of Minneapolis and Saint Paul. She is seeking restitution from and revenge on the lumber baron who has stripped her reservation." Publisher's note

"The shifting of voices and stories, ranging back and forth in time and place, may sound dauntingly complicated; luckily, it doesn't read that way. In fact, the progression of events feels natural and unforced, full of satisfying yet unexpected twists. The book begins with clean, spare prose, but finishes in gorgeous incantation and poetry." N Y Times Book Rev

The last report on the miracles at Little No Horse; a novel. HarperCollins Pubs. 2001 361p o.p.
ISBN 0-06-018727-1 LC 00-47198
This novel features characters who have appeared previously in Erdrich's work: Father Damien Modeste and Agnes DeWitt. "Now these two merge into one person. . . . From 1912 to 1996, Agnes, disguised as Damien and thus a sham as both man and priest, tries to bring Roman Catholicism to the Ojibwas of Little No Horse Reservation on a loney patch of North Dakota." Time

"Even the small incidents in this novel are moments of tremendous power, stripped of sentimentality or pretension. Erdrich has developed a style that can sound as serious as death or ring with the haunting simplicity of ancient legend." Christ Sci Monit

Love medicine; new and expanded version. Holt & Co. 1993 367p o.p.
ISBN 0-8050-2798-X LC 93-15166

Erdrich, Louise—*Continued*

Original version published 1984

"The story opens in 1981 when June Kashpaw, an attractive, leggy Chippewa prostitute who has idled away her days on the main streets of oil boomtowns in North Dakota, decides to return to the reservation on which she was raised. Before leaving Williston, N.D., however, June takes on one more client and, afterward, decides to walk back to her home. En route she dies in the freezing Dakota countryside. But her memory and the legacy she passes on to her family prompt various relatives and acquaintances to recall their relationships with her and to reminisce about their own lives." N Y Times Book Rev

The Master Butchers Singing Club. HarperCollins Pubs. 2002 289p $25.95

ISBN 0-06-620977-3 LC 2002-68501

"Erdrich tells the story of Fidelis Waldvogel, a WWI sniper and master butcher with a 'talent for stillness' and for singing. After marrying Eva, the pregnant fianceé of his best friend, who was killed in the war, he emigrates to America. Settling in Argus, N. Dak., he and Eva establish a butcher shop known for its Old World expertise and for housing Fidelis's beloved singing club." Publ Wkly

"Erdrich is demonstrably capable of pursuing a potent image or theme throughout a narrative. And although this novel's leitmotif of violent, gruesome death is a bit too obvious, its smaller symbols succeed better, perhaps because they're accompanied by less fanfare." N Y Times Book Rev

The painted drum. HarperCollins 2005 277p $25.95

ISBN 0-06-051510-4 LC 2005-40227

"Faye Travers, who narrates the first section, is a woman in her 50's who has come home to live with her mother in rural New Hampshire. Together they run the family's estates business, sorting through and selling the accumulations left behind by acquisitive lifetimes. . . . Faye, herself one-quarter Ojibwa, discovers a ceremonial drum among the possessions of an old New Hampshire family whose ancestor was an Indian trader. The drum begins to obsess her, as she increasingly questions her sense of self. The rest of the novel, told from various perspectives, follows the history of the drum in several episodes." N Y Times Book Rev

"There is searing pain and loss aplenty in this book, but one of Erdrich's strengths as a writer is the way in which she controls emotion. . . . Readers familiar with her works will recognize characters from the North Dakota native families who populate other of her works. But again, it doesn't really matter. Her themes transcend that terrain." Christ Sci Monit

Tales of burning love; a novel. HarperCollins Pubs. 1996 452p o.p.

LC 95-53315

This novel "opens with Jack Mauser drinking himself silly with a young pick-up, who subsequently freezes to death in her thin shoes in a North Dakota blizzard. Jack would certainly seem to be a loser, and someone any sane woman would stay away from, but this isn't a novel about him. It's a novel about his many wives, who come together at his funeral sometime later and get stuck in another blizzard, which gives them the opportunity to open up about their deepest secrets." Libr J

"Miracles and possibilities come together here to produce a kind of earthly magic that is more potent than magic realism. . . . Ms. Erdrich's saints are nearly as lively as her sinners, and that's a real achievement." N Y Times Book Rev

Tracks; a novel. Holt & Co. 1988 226p o.p.

ISBN 0-8050-0895-0 LC 88-9321

This third installment in the author's North Dakota Quartet depicts "the escalating conflict between two Chippewa families, a conflict begun when hapless Eli Kashpaw—who has passionately pursued the fiery, elemental Fleur Pillager—is made to betray her with young Sophie Morrissey through the magic of the vengeful Pauline." Libr J

"Ms. Erdrich is, as always, the generous kind of storyteller, passing along not only everything her characters know, but the story of the stories as well. Giving life and shape and sense to what's happened, she lets the designs spring clear." N Y Times Book Rev

(jt. auth) Dorris, M. The crown of Columbus

Erickson, Steve

Arc d'X. Poseidon Press 1993 298p o.p.

ISBN 0-671-74296-5 LC 92-30968

"The story opens on the life of a Thomas Jefferson crushed by a clash of ideals and desire. In 1789 Paris, his name on the lips of every revolutionary, he repeatedly rapes his slave Sally in a darkened hotel room. The X in the title refers to almost a year of days at the end of the millennium that—so a mathematician in the novel discovers—have accumulated because of inaccuracies in the Western calendar. In the year X, time and history collapse, and actors from various times reenact Jefferson's dilemma in all of its permutations." Booklist

"Erickson's idiosyncratic myths are troubling but palpably real. His complex plot and unorthodox chronology may puzzle many readers, but the persistent recurrence of Jefferson's phrase, 'the pursuit of happiness,' provides a unifying thread. Erickson skillfully shows that for those in such pursuit, the impulses of freedom and love are frequently in conflict and ever so occasionally harmonious." Libr J

The sea came in at midnight. Bard 1999 259p o.p.

ISBN 0-380-97766-4 LC 98-46851

"An Avon book"

In this novel, "a crackpot 'apocalyptologist' posits an alternative theory of recent history, marked by irrational and horrific events—assassination, terrorism, genocide, environmental disaster—which began in May of 1968. The cast includes a motherless teenage girl, a pair of snuff-film makers, a cartographer, and the daughter of a Japanese nuclear scientist, all haunted and seeking redemption. Against a background of chaos, Erickson has fashioned an ingenious Mobius strip of a book." New Yorker

Eskridge, Kelley

Solitaire. Eos 2002 353p $24.95

ISBN 0-06-008857-5 LC 2002-25381

"As one of the elite members of society on Ko Island, the world's first corporate country, Jackal Seguro is destined for political greatness until she discovers a secret

Eskridge, Kelley—*Continued*
that places her on the wrong side of the government. Arrested and sentenced to virtual solitary confinement, Jackal undergoes a social and psychological transformation that eventually leads her in a direction unforeseen by those who want to control her." Libr J

"Eskridge's evocation of Jackal's time in hightech solitary confinement is a stylistic and psychological tour de force. The horrors she confronts, the defenses she mounts, the things she learns are treated with a painful but bracing clarity." N Y Times Book Rev

Esquivel, Laura

Like water for chocolate; translated by Carol Christensen and Thomas Christensen. Doubleday 1992 245p $26

ISBN 0-385-42016-1 LC 91-47188

Original Spanish edition published 1989 in Mexico

Set in turn-of-the-century Mexico, this novel relates the story of Tita, "the youngest of three daughters. Practically raised in the kitchen, she is expected to spend her life waiting on Mama Elena and never to marry. Her habitual torment increases when her beloved Pedro becomes engaged to one of her sisters. Tita and he are thrown into tantalizing proximity and manage to communicate their affection through the dishes she prepares for him and his rapturous appreciation. Eventually, Tita's culinary wizardry unleashes uncontrollable forces, with surprising results." Booklist

"A poignant, funny story of love, life, and food which proves that all three are entwined and interdependent." Libr J

Swift as desire. Crown 2001 207p $22

ISBN 0-609-60870-3 LC 2001-28351

"Júbilo, a former telegraph operator, is suffering from Parkinson's disease; he has gone mostly blind and mute. His daughter, Lluvia, has the ingenious idea of installing telegraph equipment in Júbilo's bedroom. Now her father can tap out his thoughts in Morse code, which a computer program translates into written words. Flashbacks show us the glories and sorrows of Júbilo's life: his discovery of the power of words, his realization that people hardly ever say what they mean and his choice of telegraphy as a career." N Y Times Book Rev

Essex, Karen

Kleopatra. Warner Bks. 2001 385p o.p.

ISBN 0-446-52740-8 LC 00-44930

The author places "Kleopatra in the center of a deadly family controversy that pits her firmly against her brother. Forced into exile, she must raise an army in order to make her bid for the throne of Egypt. Unable to mount a successful assault on her own, she ultimately joins forces with the crafty Julius Caesar." Booklist

Essex's "rendering of the ancient world's culture and political machinations make this fast-paced treatment of Kleopatra's adventures particularly engaging. Exhaustive research is evident throughout." Publ Wkly

Pharaoh. Warner Bks. 2002 408p o.p.

ISBN 0-446-53025-5 LC 2002-16802

Sequel to Kleopatra

This second volume in the series, "which picks up as the 22-year-old queen of Egypt returns from exile in Rome, overflows with war, sex, political intrigue and the fruits of Essex's assiduous research on everything from ancient Egyptian religious ceremonies to traffic laws in Julius Caesar's Rome. . . . The careful balance Essex strikes between Kleopatra's intimate emotional life and her statecraft makes this a satisfyingly nuanced and approachable portrait." Publ Wkly

Esterházy, Péter, 1950-

Celestial harmonies; a novel; translated by Judith Sollosy. 1st ed. ECCO 2004 846p $29.95

ISBN 0-06-050104-9 LC 2003-53139

Original Hungarian edition, 2000

This Hungarian family saga is "divided into two books, the first containing fragmented glimpses of five centuries of the aristocratic Esterházy family, the second a somewhat more conventional narrative of the family's fortunes under Communism. Animating the book are a number of father figures—among them Esterházy's actual father—that owe much to the Central European literary tradition of the foolish, magical paterfamilias, and perhaps even more to Donald Barthelme's (dead) version. Ultimately, Esterházy's attempt to explode epic until it resembles the shards and mirrors of his own style doesn't quite live up to its ambition, though it yields many extraordinary moments." New Yorker

Esteves, Carmen C., 1952-

(ed) Green cane and juicy flotsam. See Green cane and juicy flotsam

Estleman, Loren D.

(ed) American West: twenty new stories from the Western Writers of America. See American West: twenty new stories from the Western Writers of America

Billy Gashade. Forge 1997 351p o.p.

ISBN 0-312-85997-X LC 96-27426

"A Tom Doherty Associates book"

"During the New York City draft riots of 1863, 16-year-old Billy Gashade lands on the wrong side of the Tammany Hall crowd and is forced to head West, where he winds up playing piano in a Kansas whorehouse. A visit from Quantrill's Raiders begins a series of adventures in which Billy encounters some of America's most infamous characters: Frank and Jesse James, Calamity Jane, Billy the Kid, Crazy Horse, and General Custer, among others." Booklist

"Mr. Estleman's novel succeeds not so much through the development of these historical figures as in Billy's comments on them. . . . 'Billy Gashade' is at once a lively coming-of-age story and an annotated pastiche of American history." N Y Times Book Rev

Black powder, white smoke. Forge 2002 318p $24.95

ISBN 0-7653-0189-X LC 2002-69266

"A Tom Doherty Associates book"

Honey Boutrille is a "freed slave who kills a white man to save a working girl in the New Orleans brothel he owns. 'Twice' Emerson is a career criminal on the run after a botched train robbery. Most of the time, Honey travels in Texas, while Twice hides out in the West. We know that they will eventually cross paths, but part of this story's charm is how it will happen." Libr J

Estleman, Loren D.—*Continued*

Bloody season. Bantam Bks. 1988 231p o.p.
LC 87-47573

A fictional retelling "of the gunfight at the O.K. Corral. Opening with the shootout itself, the narrative then recounts both the events leading up to the battle and its legacy, often doing so in a documentary fashion that focuses on the personal histories of the individuals involved." Libr J

"Estleman displays solid historical knowledge and his usual deft writing. The characters—especially Holliday, an alcoholic, tubercular woman-beater, and Wyatt Earp, a dandified womanizer interested mainly in money—spring indelibly to life. The feel, sights and smells of 1881 Tombstone are beautifully etched in this flawed but compulsively readable gem." Publ Wkly

City of widows. Forge 1994 254p o.p.
LC 94-4051

"A Tom Doherty Associates book"

"In an act of personal vengeance, Judge Harlan Blackthorne of Montana Territory sends deputy U.S. Marshal Page Murdock to San Sabado, New Mexico, to bring to justice murderers Ross and Frank Baronet. As a cover for his activities, Murdock . . . buys into a friend's saloon. His task is complicated by the fact that Ross is reputed to be dead in Mexico, and Frank is the sheriff of Socorro County, where Murdock's saloon is located." Libr J

The author "shows once again the difference between mere genre writing and artistry displayed in genre form." N Y Times Book Rev

Downriver. Houghton Mifflin 1988 210p o.p.
LC 87-16911

"An Amos Walker mystery"

Detroit private detective Amos "Walker's client, Richard DeVries, has just been paroled after serving 20 years on a riot-related arson and armed-robbery charge. He was framed and wants Walker to help him find the culprit. The search extends to an automobile manufacturer's headquarters 'downriver,' in the industrial area south of Detroit. Careful readers will have spotted the bad guy several chapters before the climax, but that only adds to the sense of inevitability, of the past taking its toll, that Estleman so effectively generates." Booklist

Edsel; a novel of Detroit. Mysterious Press 1995 291p o.p.
LC 94-36600

"Has-been Detroit journalist Connie Minor is handpicked by Henry Ford II to create the promotional campaign for his top-secret brainchild—the Edsel. . . . He's scarcely settled in when he gets caught between Walter Reuther and a Communist-hunting local politician who blackmails him into tapping his old underworld contacts for leads on a plot to kill Reuther. Bouncing from the mob to the union to the boardroom, Minor not only uncovers the murder plan but a stealthy scheme to sabotage the Edsel as well. . . . A swiftly entertaining story of Detroit in the 1950s with all the panache of a Raymond Chandler and a keen eye for historical detail." Libr J

Every brilliant eye. Houghton Mifflin 1985 252p o.p.
LC 85-10711

"An Amos Walker mystery"

Private eye Amos Walker is "hired by a Detroit newspaper to find a missing investigative reporter, Barry Stackpole, who has been summoned by the grand jury. Stackpole is also a Vietnam buddy of Walker's, so the case has its personal side. In following Stackpole's trail, Walker uncovers a murder-for-hire ring, unearths a skeleton in his friend's closet, and romances a svelte book editor who hopes to publish Stackpole's novel." Booklist

General murders. Houghton Mifflin 1988 232p o.p.
LC 88-1869

"An Amos Walker mystery"

Contents: Greektown; Robbers' roost; Fast burn; Dead soldier; Eight Mile and Dequindre; I'm in the book; Bodyguards shoot second; The prettiest dead girl in Detroit; Blond and blue; Bloody July

"Dating from 1982 to 1987, these [Amos Walker] samplings are good indicators of the pleasures in Estleman's longer works." Publ Wkly

The hours of the virgin. Mysterious Press 1999 296p $23
ISBN 0-89296-683-1 LC 98-48001

"Detroit private eye Amos Walker acts as bodyguard during a blackmail transaction involving a 15th-century illuminated manuscript. During the exchange, however, someone tries to kill him." Libr J

"Estleman doesn't write pretty travelogues; the pavements of his mean streets are always slippery with bodily fluids. But for all the noir trappings of his style, with its moody nightscapes of lonely streets and empty rooms, this is one genre author who follows the procedures without debasing the language or insulting the intelligence." N Y Times Book Rev

Jitterbug; a novel of Detroit. Forge 1998 303p o.p.
ISBN 0-312-86360-8 LC 98-21185

"A Tom Doherty Associates book"

In World War II Detroit "the heat is on Racket Squad leader Lieutenant Maximilian Zagreb and his three detectives . . . when someone starts killing people for hoarding ration coupons. Using some artful manipulation and some very unsubtle pressure, Zagreb leans on a couple of unlikely sources for help. Frankie 'The Conductor' Orr, a local mob boss, and Dwight Littlejohn, a black riveter in an airplane factory, are unwilling participants in Zagreb's efforts to smoke out the killer dubbed Kilroy by the newspapers." Publ Wkly

"This is historical crime drama at its highest level done by a consummate craftsman." Booklist

Journey of the dead. Forge 1998 251p o.p.
ISBN 0-312-85999-6 LC 97-34381

"A Tom Doherty Associates book"

A novel about "Billy the Kid's infamous killer, Sheriff Pat Garrett, a man lost at the end of his century and the Wild West he once knew. Two narrators tell this story. One is Garrett, the other an ancient Spanish alchemist, wise beyond his 100 years, still searching for the secret of turning lead into gold. Peace and contentment elude Garrett after his 1881 ambush of the Kid: even in death,

Estleman, Loren D.—*Continued*
Billy's fame is greater, Garrett's dreams constantly remind him that he killed a friend and the public seems not to care about his relentless self-justifications. . . . Estleman's Garrett is a convincingly tragic Western figure who never quite understands the praise and blame attached to him for an act he can never live down." Publ Wkly

Kill zone. Mysterious Press 1984 237p o.p.
This novel introduces "Detroit hit man Peter Macklin. Macklin is asked to do something unusually delicate, a departure from his ordinary line of work. When terrorists take over the world's largest passenger-carrying steamboat on Lake Erie and demand that the governor release 10 prisoners or the terrorists will kill the 800 hostages on ship, the Detroit mob, the FBI, and the Secret Service want Macklin to handle the negotiations." Booklist
This has "enough action and colorful characters for three ordinary thrillers. . . . Good guys, bad guys and 'ordinary' citizens are all distinctively portrayed, and the plot twists and turns are dazzling." Publ Wkly

King of the corner. Bantam Bks. 1992 294p o.p.
LC 92-742
Concluding volume in the author's Detroit trilogy
This novel is "set in the present day, during an uneasy experiment in minority rule. At the center is Doc Miller, whose pitching days ended with the drug-related death of a girl at a party he was throwing. After doing hard time at the Jackson county jail, he's struggling. Then he finds his way to Maynard Ance, a bail bondsman who makes a swell living bending the rules—putting his money on the poor 'scrouts' of the neighborhood and making it pay. Ance also has connections to a militant black outfit, the M&Ms, whose members dwell in that troubled world between heroism and terrorist fervor. And when the cops let it be known that they would like the inside dope, Doc isn't in a position to refuse." Booklist
"As a writer, Mr. Estleman plays in the majors. . . . Despite a shocking act of violence that brings his story to its bitter conclusion, the author plays a good clean game." N Y Times Book Rev

The master executioner. Forge 2001 270p $23.95
ISBN 0-312-86970-3 LC 2001-23181
"A Tom Doherty Associates book"
This novel set in the 19th century American West follows "Oscar Stone, a professional hangman, as he dispenses justice to axe murderers and army deserters. . . . Stone's calling causes his lovely young wife to flee in revulsion. But [he] is driven to exploit a gift that marries professionalism with mercy." Economist
"Estleman has created an unforgettable character in Stone. . . . A dark, compelling journey into a previously unexplored facet of the old West." Booklist

Motor City blue. Houghton Mifflin 1980 219p o.p.
LC 80-12716
"The hero is Amos Walker, a wry type who happens to be Detroit's best when it comes to finding murderers. In this case, however, events unfold as he investigates the whereabouts of a young woman, the ward of an aging gangster." Publ Wkly

Motown. Bantam Bks. 1991 292p o.p.
LC 91-6924
Second volume in the author's Detroit trilogy
"Choreographing the movements leading to the August 1966 Detroit riots, Estleman focuses on three main characters: Rick Amery, an ex-cop hired to spy on a Ralph Nader-like consumer advocate; inspector Lew Canada, trying to prevent a war between the Mafia and black gangs, and a likely race riot; and Quincy Springfield, numbers racketeer and 'blind pig' (after-hours club) operator." Publ Wkly
"Estleman seems more intent here on paying homage to the Motor City than on writing a mystery. Place is more important for Estleman than action, though this time several workable plots merge forcefully toward the novel's conclusion." Booklist

Never Street. Mysterious Press 1997 341p o.p.
ISBN 0-89296-633-5 LC 96-50130
Detroit private eye Amos Walker "finds himself in the middle of a film noir scenario when a distraught woman hires him to locate her husband, the creative partner in a video production company. Although this guy has led a blameless life, his obsession with cinematic crime leads his shrink to suspect him of enacting the bleak plot of his favorite film, 'Pitfall,' right down to the adultery, the intrigue and the murder. . . . For all the Chandleresque contortions that Mr. Estelman puts his story through, he never compromises form for cleverness. His language is strong enough to support the weight of its metaphors, his characters can't be pigeonholed and his hero doesn't faint under stress." N Y Times Book Rev

Poison blonde; an Amos Walker novel. Forge 2003 269p $24.95
ISBN 0-7653-0447-3 LC 2002-35242
"Latin singer Gilia Cristobal, the hottest commodity in show business, hires Detroit private eye Amos Walker to get to the botom of a scam involving the singer's designer gowns, but her real problem is blackmail. It turns out she's not really who she claims to be. . . . Walker is a classic hard-boiled private eye. He breathes air heavy with smoke and cordite, he delivers his dialogue through clenched teeth, and he operates by a murky moral code only he understands." Booklist

Port hazard; a Page Murdock novel; Loren D. Estleman. 1st ed. Forge 2004 301p $24.95
ISBN 0-7653-0190-3 LC 2003-49425
"Deputy U.S. Marshal Page Murdock usually roams the open trails and cow towns of the West in his dead-or-alive search for outlaws and miscreants. Federal judge Harlan Blackthorne has a different venue for Murdock's next assignment: California's Barbary Coast. A militant wing of the Sons of the Confederacy, located in San Francisco, is assassinating anyone who impedes its efforts to revive interest in secession from the union. . . . Estleman, at home in many genres, here mixes noir and the Old West, as Murdock literally walks off the trail and onto the mean streets. A wildly entertaining read with great period atmosphere and dialogue." Booklist

Retro; an Amos Walker novel; Loren D. Estleman. 1st ed. Forge 2004 286p $24.95
ISBN 0-7653-0448-1 LC 2003-71103

Estleman, Loren D.—*Continued*

"When time ran out on legendary Detroit madam Beryl Garnet, PI Amos Walker, a longtime acquaintance of Garnet, was asked to deliver her ashes to her son. The only problem was that the son, Delwayne, a Vietnam protestor implicated in a botched bomb plot, had been underground for 30 years. Walker finds Delwayne easily enough, but moments after meeting with him, he is murdered, and Walker becomes the prime suspect. Walker investigates to clear himself and learns the gun that killed Delwayne was the same gun used to kill his biological father in a celebrated but unsolved Motor City case 50 years earlier." Booklist

"Estleman makes his strongest stand for the pure, unvarnished glory of the classic American private eye in Retro, whose tongue-in-cheek title tells you what you need to know about Amos Walker." N Y Times Book Rev

Silent thunder. Houghton Mifflin 1989 202p o.p.
LC 88-32295

"An Amos Walker mystery"

Amos Walker "checks into this case when the murdered heir to an industrial fortune is discovered to have been hoarding enough illegal munitions in his whoopee room to wipe out Zambia. Walker's professional interest is in the victim's wife, who has been charged with the murder. . . . Mr. Estleman turns in a tight, well-oiled plot and some catchy characterizations of the leading local merchants in the illegal weapons trade." NY Times Book Rev

Sinister Heights. Mysterious Press 2002 262p o.p.
ISBN 0-89296-738-2 LC 2001-17797

In this case private eye Amos Walker "hires himself out to the widow of one of the old robber barons who built Detroit and left it in the hands of civic leaders who are busy tearing it down. Everyone but Walker can see that he's being set up for a double cross when this young temptress asks him to trace her late husband's illegitimate progeny so they can share the wealth. Walker knows that 'we're not talking about toothpick money'; but it takes a couple of killings, some savage beatings and the kidnapping of the industrialist's great-grandson before he gets the message." N Y Times Book Rev

A smile on the face of the tiger. Mysterious Press 2000 295p $24.95
ISBN 0-89296-706-4 LC 00-22284

Detroit gumshoe Amos Walker, "a serious drinker-thinker who lives by a tough-guy code that went out of fashion with the Edsel, is sick of hearing that he looks as if he just slouched out of a 1950's paperback novel. But when a publisher hires him to find Eugene Booth, a has-been pulp legend who skipped out on a lucrative contract to reissue his best book, Walker finds himself staring at a streaky mirror image of himself—if he lives so long. . . . Estleman pays handsome homage to Goodis and Woolrich and all the other 'paper tigers' to whom he dedicates this wonderful book." N Y Times Book Rev

Something borrowed, something black; a Peter Macklin novel. Forge 2002 236p $24.95
ISBN 0-312-87863-X LC 2001-54752

"A Tom Doherty Associates book"

Peter Macklin "has retired from the hit-man business and married Laurie, a young woman who knows nothing of his former career. They're on their honeymoon in Los Angeles when Macklin is forced back into his old calling by a Midwestern crime lord who's interested in expanding his territory. . . . Back in L.A., Laurie is being held hostage. At first she thinks the lanky cowboy named Abilene is just keeping her company while her husband is away 'on business,' but a fist in the face changes her take on things. . . . The story vibrates with letter-perfect details, and the plot, with changing locations and changing points of view, is deftly handled." Publ Wkly

Sudden country. Doubleday 1991 182p o.p.
LC 90-48441

This western set in 1890s Texas is "about a 13-year-old boy and a bunch of desperadoes on the trail of stolen gold." Booklist

Sugartown. Houghton Mifflin 1985 220p o.p.
LC 84-12910

"An Amos Walker mystery"

"Amos Walker's first client is a recent Polish immigrant who wants to find her adult grandson. His second client is a Russian writer who thinks his life is being threatened by the KGB. The cases dovetail when the two trails lead to a missing Polish silver cross. The writing includes a few melodramatic passages and unintentionally comic descriptions. . . . However, the story improves as it unfolds, the solution is satisfying, and the city, dirty Detroit, is always pulsing in the background." Libr J

Thunder City; a novel of Detroit. Forge 1999 252p o.p.
ISBN 0-312-86369-1 LC 99-40442

"A Tom Doherty Associates book"

"Harlan Crownover, the son of a wealthy coach maker, battles with his father to invest in Henry Ford's automobile plant. Rebuffed by the family, young Crownover turns to Big Jim Dolan, Detroit's ranking political heavyweight, and Sal Borneo, a young gangster who sees an opportunity to tie his criminal enterprises to Ford's burgeoning industrial revolution." Booklist

"Profiting from Estleman's . . . careful plotting, accurate backgrounds and crisp narrative, this is a gritty novel of high ideals and low morals, of men trying desperately to out-wit one another whatever the cost in the heady days of invention and industry in Detroit." Publ Wkly

Whiskey River. Bantam Bks. 1990 262p o.p.
LC 90-32895

First volume in the author's Detroit trilogy

This "chronicles the short business life of a young bootlegger named Jack Dance as he slashes his way among the gangs and gangsters that controlled Detroit's politics and economics as a direct result of the 18th Amendment. But this is not so much Jack Dance's story as it is that of his chronicler, a cynical, disillusioned newspaper columnist named Connie Minor, whose vocational rise and fall nearly parallel that of Dance. . . . At every opportunity, 'Whiskey River' strives for authenticity. And the immediacy of its atmosphere never waivers." N Y Times Book Rev

White desert. Forge 2000 236p o.p.
ISBN 0-312-86969-X LC 00-26764

Estleman, Loren D.—*Continued*

"A Tom Doherty Associates book"

This novel features "Page Murdock, a cynical 40-year-old deputy U.S. marshal working for tough-as-a-boiled-owl Judge Harlan Blackstone in the Montana territory in 1882. Lorenzo Bliss and Charlie Whitelaw, outlaws who have recently been plaguing Montana, are said to have fled north into Canada. . . . It's Canada's problem now, thinks Murdock, until he loses a billiard game to the wily judge and grudgingly crosses the border to assist the Mounties in tracking down the sadistic outlaws." Publ Wkly

"Wonderfully entertaining and filled with enough action and humor to satisfy the most demanding armchair buckaroos." Booklist

The witchfinder. Mysterious Press 1998 306p o.p.

ISBN 0-89296-663-7 LC 97-27461

Lawyer Stuart Lund summons PI Amos Walker "to a secret meeting at a Detroit airport hotel with Jay Bell Furlong, a world-famous architect who is supposedly dying in Los Angeles. Before he passes on, Furlong wants Walker to find the person who ended the architect's romance with a much younger woman eight years ago by sending him a photo of her in bed with another man. Furlong has just discovered that the photo was a fake." Publ Wkly

"Since this distinguished client is on his deathbed, Walker can't afford to waste any time; but then, Walker never does waste time—or words, or energy, or anything else. With his classical job skills and austere code of ethics, this no-nonsense shamus is one of the most efficient guys in his profession." N Y Times Book Rev

Estrin, Marc

Insect dreams; the half life of Gregor Samsa. BlueHen Bks. 2002 468p o.p.

ISBN 0-399-14836-1 LC 2001-35941

This novel follows Kafka's Gregor Samsa "from post-World War I Vienna through the Manhattan Project in Los Alamos, NM. In numerous behind-the-scenes actions, Gregor befriends historical figures like Charles Ives, President Franklin D. Roosevelt, and Robert Oppenheimer, as well as numerous other highly fascinating fictional characters." Libr J

Where the book "succeeds is in taking Kafka's character, and the knowledge and ideas we have about him, and using him for its own un-Kafkan purposes. The novel draws us in by offering us something we know, but keeps us there by giving us something new." Am Book Rev

Eugenides, Jeffrey

Middlesex. Farrar, Straus & Giroux 2002 529p $26

ISBN 0-374-19969-8 LC 2002-19921

A coming of age story about Cal, a hermaphrodite, born in 1960 Detroit as a baby girl and reborn in 1974 as a teenage boy

"Eugenides pitches a big tent, but one of the delights of 'Middlesex' is how soundly it's constructed, with motifs and characters weaving through the novel's various episodes, pulling it tight." N Y Times Book Rev

The virgin suicides. Farrar, Straus & Giroux 1993 249p o.p.

ISBN 0-374-28438-5 LC 92-33466

"The Lisbon girls, all five of whom committed suicide in the early 1970s, haunt the memories of boys next door in a wealthy Detroit suburb. A nameless narrator, one of the boys, 20 years later collects and weaves together the impressions that friends, neighbors, and parents had of the dead girls. Except for school and group outings to two ill-fated parties, the girls' lives played out confined to their dwelling, a cloistered existence protected by a mother vigilant for their virtue and by a meek father cowed by his feminized surroundings." Booklist

The author's "engrossing writing style keeps one reading despite a creepy feeling that one shouldn't be enjoying it so much. A black, glittering novel that won't be to everyone's taste but must be tried by readers looking for something different." Libr J

Eustace, Robert

(jt. auth) Sayers, D. L. The documents in the case

Evanovich, Janet

Eleven on top. St. Martin's Press 2005 310p $26.95

ISBN 0-312-30626-1 LC 2005-47846

Stephanie Plum "no longer wants to work for her cousin Vinnie, the bail bondsman in the Burg, a section of Trenton, New Jersey. Her first three tries at new gainful employment–the button factory, the local dry cleaner, and the infamous Cluck in a Bucket fast-food joint–engender firebombings, exploding cars, and even the death of a local everyone is way too happy to see go. Meanwhile, several local businessmen have disappeared, and a lowlife Stephanie has known since high school is leaving lurid and scary notes in her apartment. Although brimming with lines that will have readers howling with laughter, this installment also allows flashes of insight into the men in Stephanie's life, Morelli the cop and Ranger the bounty hunter, as well as into Stephanie herself and her (over)extended family." Booklist

Four to score. St. Martin's Press 1998 294p $24.95

ISBN 0-312-18586-3 LC 98-14627

New Jerseyan Stephanie Plum "works as a 'bounty hunter,' tracking down bail jumpers for her cousin Vinnie. Her latest assignment is to bring in Maxine Nowicki, who stole her boyfriend's car and then failed to show for her court date after she was arrested." Booklist

"Cracking the native idiom like a spicy new gum, the embattled heroine persists in her 'fugitive apprehension thing,' widening her search to the Tasty Pastry Bakery and Cluck in a Bucket, and lands in Atlantic City with a flamboyant posse that includes her 83-year-old grandmother and a seven-foot-tall transvestite named Sally Sweet. It doesn't make a lot of sense, but hey, it's a trip." N Y Times Book Rev

Hard eight. St. Martin's Press 2002 311p $25.95

ISBN 0-312-26585-9 LC 2002-21290

Evanovich, Janet—*Continued*

In this adventure Jersey bounty hunter Stephanie Plum drops "everthing to search for a missing child when Mabel Markowitz's granddaughter, Evelyn, skips town with her little girl, Annie, forfeiting Mabel's house as collateral on a child custody bond. . . . For all its zany elements, the plot turns logically on its own comically warped axis." N Y Times Book Rev

High five. St. Martin's Press 1999 292p $24.95
ISBN 0-312-20303-9 LC 99-21990

In this adventure "Stephanie Plum, New Jersey's Bombshell Bounty Hunter (as the local newspapers call her) has a full plate. Her cheapskate Uncle Fred has disappeared leaving behind some grisly photos of body parts in a garbage bag. She is being followed by a bookie who also wants to find Uncle Fred. In addition, the bounty-hunting business is in a slump; with her rent due, Stephanie is reduced to doing odd jobs for the sexy, mysterious Ranger." Libr J

"The combination of hilarious dialogue, oddball characters, and eye-popping action is hard to beat on its own, but the heroine, a righteous babe if ever there was one, is what sets the over-the-top series apart from all the competition in the comic mystery field." Booklist

Hot six. St. Martin's Press 2000 294p o.p.
ISBN 0-312-20540-6 LC 00-25208

"Stephanie Plum, Jersey Girl and bounty hunter extraordinaire, is on the hunt for Ranger, her mysterious and sexy co-worker, who has been implicated in a murder. At the same time, she is tracked by thugs Habib and Mitchell, who threaten bodily harm if she doesn't find Ranger for them." Libr J

One for the money. Scribner 1994 290p $25
ISBN 0-684-19639-5 LC 93-50733

"Stephanie Plum, a New Jersey native, is a laid-off discount lingerie buyer. Desperate for bucks, she decides to pursue a career as an 'apprehension agent,' tracking down scofflaws for her bail bondsman cousin, Vinnie. Her first mission: to bring in Joe Morelli, a cop accused of murder." Booklist

"A wonderful sense of humor, an eye for detail, and a self-deprecating narrative endow Stephanie Plum with the easy-to-swallow believability that accounts for her appeal as heroine. . . . A witty, well-written, and gutsy debut." Libr J

Seven up. St. Martin's Press 2001 309p $24.95
ISBN 0-312-26584-0 LC 2001-273613

Stephanie Plum's "employer, her bailbondsman cousin, Vinnie, gives her an easy job: pick up vicious senior citizen Eddie DeChooch, who is constantly sighted racing around Trenton in a borrowed white Cadillac, but whom no one can grab." Publ Wkly

Three to get deadly. Scribner 1997 300p $25
ISBN 0-684-82265-2 LC 96-42176

"Hunting for a local candy-store owner who jumped bail, Trenton's most famous bounty hunter, Stephanie Plum . . . is knocked out on the job. She awakens beside a dead man who happens to be in violation of a bond agreement with her cousin Vinnie, so homicide wants to give her the third degree." Libr J

"Stephanie Plum stands apart from the female series characters who are so popular in crime fiction. She's funnier, tougher, politically incorrect, and just loves her job to death." Booklist

To the nines; a Stephanie Plum novel. St. Martin's Press 2003 312p il $25.95
ISBN 0-312-26586-7

"Bounty hunter Stephanie Plum is at it again. Singh has jumped ship, abandoning his fianceé, stealing her dog, and owing his landlord back rent. Through their sleuthing, Stephanie and Ranger track him down in Vegas. Unfortunately, owing to a previous problem with the law, Ranger isn't allowed to go to Vegas. This leaves Stephanie with Lulu and Connie as her traveling companions." Libr J

Two for the dough. Scribner 1996 301p o.p.
ISBN 0-684-82592-9 LC 95-23888

In this novel bounty hunter Stephanie Plum tracks "a bond jumper through her blue-collar neighborhood known as the 'burg.' A local funeral home, a slimy undertaker and mutilated corpses figure large in the search for Kenny Mancuso, who, having shot an old high school friend in the knee, posted bail with Stephanie's boss, her cousin, and then disappeared. When the old friend is shot again, fatally, Stephanie reluctantly joins forces with her sexy enemy and love interest, Trenton homicide cop Joe Morelli. . . . Readers will likely stay a few steps ahead of the sleuths, but the sharp repartee and Stephanie's slightly cynical but still fond relationship with her family and the burg hold a treasury of urban-style charms." Publ Wkly

Evans, Nicholas

The horse whisperer. Delacorte Press 1995 404p $24.95
ISBN 0-385-31523-6 LC 95-17742

"The narrative begins with a frightful accident: teenage Grace Maclean, daughter of nice-guy lawyer Robert and tough, English-born magazine editor Annie, is out riding near their country home in upstate New York on a snowy day, and she and her beautiful horse Pilgrim are hit by a skidding tractor-trailer. Grace is crippled, Pilgrim desperately injured and mentally shattered. Annie takes things firmly in hand, finds a cowboy, Tom Booker, who is a wizard with horses and, with Grace and Pilgrim in tow, heads out to Montana in search of healing for the horse and ultimate recovery of Grace." Publ Wkly

"Evans can give equally clipped but clear descriptions of a prosthetic device or a Montana vista, and the lead characters emerge through carefully constructed, seemingly effortless scenes and dialog, not in histrionics." Libr J

The loop. Delacorte Press 1998 434p o.p.
ISBN 0-385-31700-X LC 98-12240

"Times are tense in the town of Hope, Mont., where sporadic wolf attacks have sparked a battle between ranchers . . . and Government officials whose 'wolf recovery' program has reintroduced these endangered predators into their old habitats. Arriving on the scene to take part in the fray is Helen Ross, a 29-year-old wolf biologist on the rebound from a failed relationship. . . . Helen soon becomes involved in a romantic triangle with Buck Calder, a . . . farmer and wolf hater, and his shy son, Luke, a loner with a speech impediment who's more comfortable with animals than people." N Y Times Book Rev

Evans "has a thing for strong and tender women char-

Evans, Nicholas—*Continued*

acters, a knack for clever dialogue, and a gift for wedding romance with suspense. And he's even handy with metaphors." Booklist

The smoke jumper. Delacorte Press 2001 432p o.p.

ISBN 0-385-33403-6 LC 2001-47089

"With fists over their hearts, best friends Connor Ford and Ed Tully shout out 'hearts of fire' before parachuting into devastating forest fires to extinguish them. Working side by side in life-threatening circumstances, this unlikely pair (Connor is a Montana cowboy and freelance photographer; Ed is a Chicago musician and would-be playwright) bond through their summer job. Ed's girlfriend, Julia, counsels troubled teens in the Montana wilderness and, though neither one acknowledged it, when Connor and Julia met sparks flew. All three of their lives change irreparably when Julia is trapped in a raging forest fire." Publ Wkly

Eve, Nomi, 1968-

The family orchard. Knopf 2000 316p $25

ISBN 0-375-41076-7 LC 00-40566

This is "a six-generation family memoir recast as fiction. . . . Set almost entirely in Israel, the book spans 160 years of tumultuous Israeli and family history, from the 1830's, when Palestine was part of the Turkish Empire, through the three major waves, or aliyahs, of Jewish immigration, the British mandate, modern statehood and warfare, up to the present. Historical figures and events flit past in the background of the characters' lives." N Y Times Book Rev

"This fascinating novel not only acknowledges that much of family history is imagined or embellished but glories in it." Booklist

Evelyn, John Michael *See* Underwood, Michael, 1916-

Everett, Percival L.

American desert; [by] Percival Everett. Hyperion 2004 291p $24.95

ISBN 0-7868-6917-8 LC 2003-056757

"While on his way to commit suicide, Ted Street, an untenured English professor and philandering husband, is beheaded in a car accident. Worse, he wakes up at his own funeral, his head clumsily stitched on his neck and his mouth sewn closed. From there, Ted embarks on a wide-ranging cruise through the American landscape, as he is kidnapped by a cult convinced that he is a devil; picked up by the military to be experimented on as a prototype of the perfect soldier; and sheltered by another cult, which worships him as a messiah." New Yorker

"Thoughtful, darkly comic and full of heart, the novel offers a wonderfully unusual story about retrospection and forgiveness." Publ Wkly

Exupéry, Antoine de Saint- *See* Saint-Exupéry, Antoine de, 1900-1944

F

Faber, Michel

The courage consort; three novellas. Harcourt 2004 232p $23.00

ISBN 0-15-101061-7 LC 2004-5912

"In 'The Courage Consort,' the soprano of a vocal quintet her husband directs progresses from suicidal anxiety to relative equanimity as the group rehearses a difficult new piece that sudden death prevents them from premiering. In 'The Hundred Ninety-Nine Steps,' a woman resolves her trauma over losing a leg and her lover because of a senseless accident; by means romantic and eerie, a handsome young doctor, his late father's dog, and a manuscript in a bottle are the catalysts of her transformation. In the entrancing 'The Fahrenheit Twins'—perhaps a coming-of-age parable—brother and sister Marko'cain and Tainto'lilith, born and reared in arctic isolation, quest far from home for a signal from the universe telling them what to do with their mother's corpse. Faber's literary artistry in all three pieces is consummate." Booklist

The courage consort [novelette]
In Faber, M. The courage consort

The crimson petal and the white. Harcourt 2002 838p $26

ISBN 0-15-100692-X LC 2002-24138

The protagonist of this novel, set in 1870s London, is a "young prostitute named Sugar. Intelligent and ambitious, Sugar yearns to escape from the livelihood forced on her at age 13. Enter William Rackham, a besotted philanderer and idle heir to a family perfume business, who installs Sugar as his secret mistress in a fashionable hideaway. When the incompetent William is forced into managing the family firm, he initially seeks advice from Sugar, who, fearful of losing his affection, schemes to gain closer proximity to the Rackham family. She succeeds by becoming governess to William's only child, young Sophie, who is cruelly ignored by her father and his insane and sickly wife, Agnes." Libr J

"The large themes that interwine the characters with one another—religion, health, sexuality, death, and, reluctantly, love—are juxtaposed against the most minute and intimate details of Victorian life. . . . This massive work is startling and absorbing." Booklist

The Fahrenheit twins
In Faber, M. The courage consort

The hundred and ninety-nine steps
In Faber, M. The courage consort

The **Faber** book of gay short fiction; edited by Edmund White. Faber & Faber 1991 586p o.p.

LC 91-173155

Stories included are: Trespasses, by P. Bailey; Just above my head, by J. Baldwin; Three wedding ceremonies, by N. Bartlett; Pages from Cold Point, by P. Bowles; The wild boys, by W. S. Burroughs; Good fortune, by S. Burt; In praise of Vespasian, by A. Chester; My Mark, by D. Cooper; BM, by J. M. Estep; Concerning the eccentricities of Cardinal Pirelli, by R. Firbank;

The Faber book of gay short fiction—*Continued*
Dr. Woolacott, by E. M. Forster; The list, by P. Gale; Denry Smith, by R. Gluck; Forced use, by A. Gurganus; Native, by W. H. Henderson; Sunday morning: Key West, by A. Holleran; The swimming-pool library, by A. Hollinghurst; The novice, by T. Ireland; Mr. Lancaster, by C. Isherwood; The pupil, by H. James; When you grow to adultery, by D. Leavitt; Southern skies, by D. Malouf; The changes of those terrible years, by A. Mars-Jones; Suddenly home, by A. Maupin; The secret of the gentiles, by D. Plante; Dawn, by J. Purdy; Another life, by L. Raphael; Pages from an abandoned journal, by G. Vidal; Darts, by T. Wakefield; When I was thirteen, by D. Welch; Skinned alive, by E. White; Two on a party, by T. Williams

Fain, Michael

For works written by this author in collaboration with Judith Barnard see Michael, Judith

Fairbairn, Ann, 1901 or 2-1972

Five smooth stones; a novel. Knopf 1966 756p o.p.

"Although born in poverty in New Orleans, David Champlin, a young black man, escapes this dreary background with the help of devoted grandparents, a Danish professor, and a scholarship to a Midwestern college. The book details his successful legal and diplomatic career and his love affair and marriage with Sara Kent, a white classmate. David becomes involved also in the Civil Rights movement. The book concludes on a triumphant but tragic note." Shapiro. Fic For Youth. 3d edition

Fairstein, Linda

The bone vault; a novel. Scribner 2003 386p $25

ISBN 0-7432-2354-3 LC 2002-26686

A thriller starring Alexandra Cooper, "a Manhattan assistant district attorney. This time out, she and her sidekick, cop Mike Chapman, are drawn into a particularly mysterious case: a Metropolitan Museum of Art intern is found dead in a sarcophagus, and though she's been dead for months, her body is perfectly preserved. When it is discovered that she died of arsenic poisoning, the plot thickens. This is fun reading." Libr J

Cold hit. Scribner 1999 413p o.p.

ISBN 0-684-84846-5 LC 99-24079

Assistant District Attorney Alexandra Cooper "teams up with detective Mike Chapman to track the killer of a woman found lashed to a ladder in the Hudson River. Their investigation takes them into the smarmy world of high-profile art galleries. . . . Smart, sexy, and indefatigable, bluestockingish Alex is relentlessly likeable; she holds her own with greedy art collectors and paranoid dealers and only needs rescuing when trapped by bullets pinging off a giant steel sculpture. But it is her empathy for victims of violence and unswerving determination to collar the scumbag that truly endear her to readers." Libr J

Entombed; [by] Linda A. Fairstein. Scribner 2005 400p $26

ISBN 0-7432-5488-0 LC 2004-52189

"Alexandra Cooper returns in another case featuring two seemingly unrelated crimes that the talented sex-crimes prosecutor is hell-bent on connecting. A serial rapist is terrorizing Manhattan's tony Upper East Side. Dubbed the Silk Stocking rapist, his usual M.O. is to terrorize the victim but not kill her. When one girl winds up dead, Alex and her trusted detective partners, Mercer Wallace and Mike Chapman, believe that perhaps a copycat perpetrator is out there who takes his crimes one step further. At the same time, Alex becomes obsessed with the stories of Edgar Allan Poe, especially after a young person's skeleton is found in an old home Poe once inhabited." Booklist

"It's a tribute to Fairstein's integrity and her clear, measured prose that the novel never tips into prurience. Her methodical presentation of authentic detail engages reader interest more than narrative flourish or cheap thrills." Publ Wkly

Final jeopardy. Knopf 1996 400p o.p.

LC 95-50619

Manhattanite Alexandra Cooper is "a middle-aged blonde heading the borough's prosecution of sex offenders. Cooper's typical day of counseling victims and working with the NYPD on sex crimes would probably keep readers fascinated, but her latest problem—the shooting murder of glamorous movie star Isabella Lascar at Cooper's getaway home on Martha's Vineyard—pitches the plot at high intensity right away. Though Cooper is warned by the DA not to play cop, she and homicide detective Mike Chapman, who's assigned to bodyguard her, work together unofficially to solve the crime, carrying on a sort of anti-romance all the while." Publ Wkly

Likely to die; a novel. Scribner 1997 393p o.p.

ISBN 0-684-81488-9 LC 97-10841

"A prominent woman neurosurgeon is sexually assaulted and stabbed in her own mid-Manhattan medical center office. Heroine Alexandra Cooper, who heads the Manhattan D.A.'s sex crimes unit, and her team of homicide detectives banter comically to cheer themselves as they winnow through witnesses, including transients who swarm the tunnels beneath the hospital and roam hospital corridors, snatching lab coats and trays of food. . . . [The] brittle police babble and mounting suspense make the pages crackle. Although there is little art to the language, it is crystal clear, and deft descriptions abound. " Libr J

Falconer, Colin, 1953-

Feathered serpent; a novel of the Mexican conquest. Crown 2002 374p $22.95

ISBN 0-609-61029-5 LC 2002-24711

"Born an Aztec princess and sold into slavery after her father's death, Malinali was at 15 given to conquistador Herman Cortes. A highly intelligent woman gifted in several languages, she made herself indispensable as an interpreter to the Spaniards. Her desire for revenge against Montezuma II, whom she held responsible for the murder of her father, and her belief that Cortes was actually the god Feathered Serpent, coupled with the Spaniards' overwhelming greed for gold, initiated a disastrous sequence of events that led to the fall of the Aztec empire." Libr J

"This enthralling reconstruction of the birth of modern Mexico is rooted in both genuine history and cultural myth." Booklist

Fallon, Martin, 1929- *See* Higgins, Jack, 1929-

Famous ghost stories; compiled and with an introductory note by Bennett A. Cerf. Modern Lib. 1944 361p o.p.

Contents: The haunted and the haunters, by E. Bulwer-Lytton; The damned thing, by A. Bierce; The monkey's paw, by W. Jacobs; The phantom 'rickshaw, by R. Kipling; The willows, by A. Blackwood; The rival ghosts, by B. Matthews; The man who went too far, by E. F. Benson; The mezzotint, by M. R. James; The open window, by "Saki"; The beckoning fair one, by O. Onions; On the Brighton Road, by R. Middleton; The considerate hosts, by T. McClusky; August heat, by W. F. Harvey; The return of Andrew Bentley, by A. W. Derleth; The supper at Elsinore, by I. Dinesen; The current crop of ghost stories, by B. A. Cerf

Fantasy & science fiction (Periodical)

The Best horror stories from the Magazine of fantasy and science fiction. See The Best horror stories from the Magazine of fantasy and science fiction

Farah, Nuruddin, 1945-

Links. Riverhead Books 2004 336p $24.95
ISBN 1-573-22265-8 LC 2003-65969

First published 2003 in South Africa

"Jeebleh, settled in the United States with an American wife and grown children, returns to Mogadishu with two purposes. One is to find the burial place of his mother; the other is to try to rescue the kidnapped niece of Bile, an old friend and onetime comrade in the early fight against the dictator Mohammed Siad Barre." N Y Times Book Rev

This novel is "both alien and familiar, a haunting exploration of the desire to help and the attendant costs of doing so." Christ Sci Monit

Farmer, Philip José

The classic Philip José Farmer, 1952-1964—1964-1973; edited and introduction by Martin H. Greenberg; foreword by Isaac Asimov. Crown 1984 2v o.p.

"Classics of modern science fiction"

Contents: 1952-1964: Sail on! Sail on; Mother; The God business; The Alley Man; My sister's brother; The king of beasts

1964-1973: The shadow of space; Riders of the purple wage [novelette]; Don't wash the carats; The jungle rot kid on the nod; The oogenesis of Bird City; The sliced-crosswise only-on-Tuesday world; Sketches among the ruins of my mind; After King Kong fell

The dark design. Berkley Pub. Group 1977 412p o.p.
LC 77-5138

The third volume of the Riverworld series

This volume "continues the adventures of explorer Sir Richard Burton, Mark Twain, and scores of others who are resurrected along the banks of the multimillion-mile-long River. . . . In dirigibles and riverboats, through heroism and treachery, a band of restless explorers attains the headwaters home of the mysterious Ethicals, who apparently are responsible for creating the Riverworld and resurrecting its confused populace." Booklist

"Some threads in the design are loose or overknotted, but the dash and grand scope of the project and this installment of it are compellingly fascinating." Publ Wkly

Followed by The magic labyrinth

Dayworld. Putnam 1985 320p o.p.
LC 84-17978

First volume in the Dayworld trilogy

"In the 35th century, people live only one day a week, spending the other six days in suspended animation. Jeff Caird, a policeman in Tuesday's World, is also a 'daybreaker,' illegally living seven different lives as seven different people—until the week he becomes both hunter and hunted in a mad chase across seven different cultures." Libr J

This novel "is cleverly crafted, fastmoving, and absorbing. Smooth transitions connect the days and Caird's various identities through which the author addresses many philosophical and political issues such as religious toleration, a classless society, marriage, monitoring of citizens by the government, and employer/employee relations." Best Sellers

Followed by Dayworld rebel (1987)

Dayworld breakup. Doherty Assocs. 1990 324p o.p.
LC 90-172386

"A TOR book"

The concluding volume of the Dayworld trilogy

"The infamous 'daybreaker' William Duncan continues to battle the powers-that-be in a future where humans live only one day in seven and a select few possess the knowledge that could overthrow a corrupt world government. This fast-paced conclusion to Farmer's 'Dayworld Trilogy' celebrates the power of the iconoclast and the triumph of idealism." Libr J

The fabulous riverboat; a science fiction novel. Putnam 1971 253p o.p.

This second novel in the Riverworld series "is set in an 'after-Earthlife' of resurrected people over the age of five from time immemorial. The main character is . . . Sam Langhorne Clemens, alias Mark Twain, who attempts to build a metal riverboat. His goal, not obtained in this novel, is to sail upriver to reach the Misty Tower and discover the secret of its guardians, the Ethicals." Libr J

Followed by The dark design

Gods of Riverworld. Putnam 1983 331p o.p.
LC 83-9552

The fifth volume of the Riverworld series

"The members of the intrepid band that achieved its quest for the end of the River in the previous books now find themselves in command of the Ethicals' polar control center. When they're not trying to track down an unknown enemy, they're building private worlds and resurrecting a few friends. . . . It's the two varieties of god-playing, culminating in a disastrous tea party in Alice Pleasance Liddell's Wonderland, that give the book its interest." Publ Wkly

Farmer, Philip José—*Continued*

The magic labyrinth. Berkley Pub. Group 1980 339p o.p.

LC 80-144

In this fourth volume in the Riverworld series "Farmer brings his large and bizarre cast of characters (including King John Lackland of England, Samuel Clemens, Sir Richard Burton, Hermann Göring, and Alice Liddell, who inspired 'Alice in Wonderland') to the end of their quest and reveals the secret of the Riverworld. For readers prepared to accept it on its own terms, this book will be rewarding, even exciting. Farmer's imagination does not flag from beginning to end." Booklist

Followed by Gods of Riverworld

Riders of the purple wage

In The Hugo winners p388-459

In Farmer, P. J. The classic Philip José Farmer, 1952-1964—1964-1973 p30-103

River of eternity. Phantasia Press 1983 205p o.p.

This is the original version of the novel written in 1952 that later formed the basis of the Riverworld series

"In 70,000 words this highly compressed rendering tells the essential story of the amazing Riverworld. It can't replace the later, grander work, but it is quite entertaining and a fascinating footnote to SF history." Publ Wkly

To your scattered bodies go; a science fiction novel. Putnam 1971 221p o.p.

The first volume of the Riverworld series

"The fabulous Riverworld, site of the resurrection of every human being who has died, is one of the great fictional creations. Sir Richard Burton, Victorian explorer and rogue, finds himself reborn and sets off on an epic journey to learn the truth of its existence." Shapiro. Fic For Youth. 3d edition

Followed by The fabulous riverboat

Farrell, James T. (James Thomas), 1904-1979

Judgment day

In Farrell, J. T. Studs Lonigan

Studs Lonigan; a trilogy; James T. Farrell. Library of America 2004 988p (The library of America, 148) $35

ISBN 1-931082-55-3 LC 2003-44207

First published as a trilogy 1935 by Vanguard Press

Contents: Young Lonigan; The young manhood of Studs Lonigan; Judgment day

A trilogy "about life among lower-middle-class Irish Roman Catholics in Chicago during the first third of the 20th century. . . . As a boy, William Lonigan (always referred to as 'Studs') makes a slight effort to rise above his squalid urban environment. However, the combination of his own personality, unwholesome neighborhood friends, a small-minded family, and his schooling and religious training all condemn him to the life of futility and dissipation that are his inheritance." Merriam-Webster's Ency of Lit

Young Lonigan

In Farrell, J. T. Studs Lonigan

The young manhood of Studs Lonigan

In Farrell, J. T. Studs Lonigan

Fast, Howard, 1914-2003

April morning; a novel. Crown 1961 184p pa $7.50 o.p.

ISBN 0-553-27322-1 LC 61-10306

"The spirit of the Revolutionary War, a country coming of age, and the life of a boy passing into manhood are captured in this historical novel. Fast focuses on one day in the life of Adam Cooper as his family and the community of Lexington rise to the events of April 19, 1775. Adam at first is caught up in the excitement, but by the end of the first skirmish the death of his father has brought home the horror and reality of war." Shapiro. Fic for Youth. 3d edition

The bridge builder's story; a novel. Sharpe, M.E. 1995 210p o.p.

LC 95-11018

"The plot centers on Scott Waring, a privileged New Yorker with a blue-blood heritage and a brilliant future. Waring's perfect life is shattered when his lovely young bride is killed during their honeymoon in Berlin, at the hands of Hitler's Gestapo. Carrying the burden of guilt over his wife's death, Waring himself bears witness to the Holocaust during the ensuing war years. The demons that distance Waring from others are ultimately exorcised through psychotherapy, and in an unexpected twist, he finds love again with a survivor of Dachau. Fast's acutely rendered, riveting tale is sure to satisfy readers." Booklist

Citizen Tom Paine. Duell, Sloan & Pearce 1943 341p o.p.

The author presents a "picture of Paine's mode of writing, idiosyncrasies, and character—generous, nobly unselfish, moody, often dirty, frequently drunken, a revolutionist by avocation." Libr J

Greenwich. Harcourt Brace & Co. 2000 290p $25

ISBN 0-15-100620-2 LC 99-46422

"Richard Castle, a successful Wall Street hustler, was once an assistant secretary of state who gave the orders for a massacre of nuns and priests in El Salvador. . . . Richard, meanwhile, married to beautiful and sweetly innocent trophy wife Sally, is trying to ascertain, through a local Jesuit monsignor and a nun who was in El Salvador, just how much is known about his role. These two are guests, along with a representative selection of Greenwich citizens, at a dinner party at the Castles' home, through which Fast portrays the social and political currents of the town." Publ Wkly

The immigrants. Houghton Mifflin 1977 389p o.p.

LC 77-9317

The first volume of the Lavette family saga. The main characters are Dan Lavette, son of French-Italian immigrants who builds a shipping and business empire with little but determination and luck; his overshadowed Jewish partner Mark Levy; his cold and beautiful society "wife Jean; May Ling, the Chinese woman he loves, but cannot marry without losing his empire. Around these people and their children, and against a background of the San Francisco earthquake, World War I and the Depression, Fast constructs a . . . story that ranges from fisherman's bar to tycoon's boardroom and pits the

Fast, Howard, 1914-2003—*Continued*

American Dream against the demands of conscience and love. It also underlines some of the bitter lessons of success." Publ Wkly

Followed by Second generation

The immigrant's daughter. Houghton Mifflin 1985 321p o.p.

LC 85-8251

The fifth volume of the Lavette family saga has "as its centerpiece, the campaign of Barbara Lavette for congresswoman from San Francisco's posh 48th district. Although Barbara—at 60 still in all ways breathtaking—loses, she is propositioned (and betrayed) by her Republican opponent, courted by her ex-husband, a newspaper publisher who sends her on assignment to El Salvador, and at book's end is up to her neck in ban-the-bomb plans." Publ Wkly

The legacy. Houghton Mifflin 1981 359p o.p.

LC 81-2906

The fourth volume of the Lavette family saga is set in the turbulent 1960s. Patriarch Dan is felled by a heart attack. "Daughter Barbara, whose psyche has been scarred by a prison sentence during the McCarthy era, is slowly coming to terms with her own volatile, independent nature, while her son and nephews are briefly involved in the civil rights struggle in the South, the Vietnam War, and the Six-Day War in the Middle East. The view of the Sixties is against Nixon, Johnson, big business, and war; and Fast lends . . . [a] wide-screen glamour to events most adult readers can still remember watching on the six o'clock news." Libr J

Followed by The immigrant's daughter

The outsider. Houghton Mifflin 1984 311p o.p.

"Young New Yorker David Hartman returns from the Second World War, marries Lucy Spendler, a U.S.O. volunteer, and accepts a position as rabbi in 'Leighton Ridge,' a small town in Fairfield County, Connecticut (Jewish population: 14) The narrative follows David's life—and world events—from memories of the Holocaust through blacklisting and the Rosenberg trial, civil rights marches in the South, Vietnam War. Through it all, David must respond to the needs of his growing congregation, his wife, son, and daughter, and his own spiritual questions." Libr J

Redemption; a novel. Harcourt Brace & Co. 1999 276p o.p.

ISBN 0-15-100455-2 LC 98-41373

This is "the story of Ike Goldman, a 78-year-old retired contract law professor at Columbia who becomes mixed up in a murder investigation after rescuing a mysterious woman from a suicide attempt. After preventing the much younger woman from jumping off the George Washington Bridge, and subsequently falling in love with her, Goldman is shocked when she is arrested for the murder of her beastly ex-husband." Booklist

"Fast's fast-paced story of love at any age and his indictment of a legal system that takes too many short cuts will be greeted warmly by his steadfast readers and is a wonderful introduction for those who are just discovering him." Libr J

Second generation. Houghton Mifflin 1978 441p o.p.

LC 78-5540

In the second volume of the Lavette family saga the author "traces the further activities of Dan Levette and his family, focusing upon his daughter Barbara, whose total involvement with the troubled times begins with aid to striking dockworkers, and then continues in prewar Nazi Germany and during journalistic encounters in the Eastern theaters." Booklist

Followed by The establishment (1979)

Faulkner, William, 1897-1962

Absalom, Absalom!; corrected text. Random House 1986 313p o.p.

ISBN 0-394-55634-8 LC 86-6488

First published 1936

"During the summer of 1910, prior to Quentin Compson's leaving the South for his first year at Harvard, old Rosa Coldfield insists upon a private conference with the youth to divulge her recollections of Thomas Sutpen. Driven by a great plan to become a Southern aristocrat, Sutpen builds a mansion, only to see his life ruined. The title of the book reveals the story's basic tragedy: Sutpen's disappointment in his children. One is a spinster and thus has no offspring to continue the family lineage; the other is a son who has disappeared. Sutpen himself falls victim to a murder for retribution. Faulkner depicts the South before and after the Civil War in this powerfully written novel." Shapiro. Fic for Youth. 3d edition

also in Faulkner, W. Novels, 1936-1940 p1-315

As I lay dying. Modern Lib. 2000 $16.95

ISBN 0-375-50452-4

This is a reissue of the title first published 1930 by H. Smith

"Experimental in both subject and narrative structure, this novel treats the events surrounding the illness, death and burial of Addie Bundren, wife of Anse and mother of Cash, Darl, Jewel, Dewey Dell, and Vardaman. It is divided into 59 short interior monologues, predominantly in the present tense, spoken both by the seven members of the family and by various other characters, including the Reverend Whitfield, Dr. Peabody, and the Bundrens' neighbours, Vernon and Cora Tull." Camb Guide to Lit in Engl

also in Faulkner, W. Novels, 1930-1935

Collected stories of William Faulkner. Random House 1950 900p o.p.

ISBN 0-394-41967-7

"Forty-two short stories, including all from These Thirteen (1931), all but two from Doctor Martino and other stories (1934) and seventeen published in magazines, 1932-1948. . . . Many of the stories deal with characters and incidents related to those in his novels set in the mythical Yoknapatawpha County, Mississippi." Libr J

A fable. Random House 1954 437p o.p.

ISBN 0-394-42400-X

"Set in France a few months before the end of World War I, 'A Fable' is both an allegory of the passion of Christ and a study of a world that has chosen submission

Faulkner, William, 1897-1962—*Continued*
to authority and the secular values of power and chauvinism instead of the individuality and the exercise of free will. The novel centers on the fate of a young corporal . . . [who] with the aid of twelve companions, incites a mutiny in the trenches which results in a temporary armistice. Betrayed by a member of his own regiment, the corporal is executed for cowardice along with two other military criminals, becoming a martyr to his principles and his belief in humanity." Benet's Reader's Ency of Am Lit

also in Faulkner, W. Novels, 1942-1954 p665-1072

Father Abraham; edited by James B. Meriwether; with wood engravings by John DePol. Random House 1984 c1983 70p o.p.
LC 83-43204

First published 1983 in a limited edition by the Red Ozier Press for the New York Public Library

This work was "written in 1926 as the beginning of the novel of which it became an important part, 'The Hamlet.' Several years later, Faulkner recast it in a different form as one of his best-known short stories, 'Spotted Horses.'" Publisher's note

The Faulkner reader; selections from the works of William Faulkner. Random House 1954 682p o.p.

Contains the following: The sound and the fury [complete] (1929); The bear, excerpt from Go down, Moses; Old man, excerpt from The wild palms; Spotted horses, excerpt from The hamlet; A rose for Emily; Barn burning; Dry September; That evening sun; Turnabout; Shingles for the Lord; A justice; Wash; An odor of verbena, excerpt from The Unvanquished; Percy Grimm, excerpt from Light in August; The courthouse, excerpt from Requiem for a nun

Flags in the dust; edited and with an introduction by Douglas Day. Random House 1973 370p o.p.

This is the uncut and complete version of Sartoris. "The introduction describes the bibliographic history of the narrative and makes clear that the present work is as complete a reproduction as possible of the extant composite typescript. Emphasis of 'Flags in the dust' is extended from the Sartoris family featured in the later novel to the full range of Faulkner's Yoknapatawpha social structure, resulting in a complete fictional documentation of the intense Faulknerian world which saturated all his writings." Booklist

Go down, Moses; introduction by Stanley Crouch. Modern Lib. 1995 xxii, 367p o.p.
ISBN 0-679-60174-0 LC 95-4715

A reissue of the Random House edition published 1942 with title: Go down Moses, and other stories which was analyzed in Short story index

"The voices of Faulkner's South—black and white, comic and tragic—ring through this sprawling tale of the McCaslin clan. The tone ranges from the farcical to the profound. As the title suggests, the stories are rife with biblical themes. Although the seven stories were originally published separately, *Go Down, Moses* is best read as a novel of interconnecting generations, races, and dreams." Merriam-Webster's Ency of Lit

also in Faulkner, W. Novels, 1942-1954 p1-281

The hamlet. 3rd ed. Random House 1964 366p o.p.
ISBN 0-394-42759-9

First published 1940

First volume in the trilogy about the "Snopes family who descended upon Yoknapatawpha County, Mississippi in the latter years of the nineteenth century. It "tells how Ab Snopes, ex-bushwhacker, horse trader and sharecropper won immunity in Frenchman's Bend because of his reputation as a barn burner and how his son Flem became a clerk in Will Varner's store. Before long other members of the family descend like swarming locusts on the village. . . . Led by Flem, who has set himself up in the world by marrying Eula Varner when she was pregnant with another man's child, they then move on to Jefferson, the county seat." Magill. Masterpieces of World Lit in Dig Form

Followed by The town

also in Faulkner, W. Novels, 1936-1940 p727-1075

also in Faulkner, W. Snopes p1-349

If I forget thee, Jerusalem

In Faulkner, W. Novels, 1936-1940 p493-726

Intruder in the dust. Random House 1948 247p o.p.
ISBN 0-394-43074-3

"When Lucas, an elderly Negro, is accused of murdering a white man, Charles, a 16-year-old white boy, works to save him from being lynched. Charles gets the help he needs in his sleuthing from an old aristocratic lady and a young black boy. The trio visits the church graveyard at night to dig up the corpse of the supposed victim. The book can be read as a mystery and, on a deeper level, as a social commentary on the South." Shapiro. Fic for Youth. 3d edition

also in Faulkner, W. Novels, 1942-1954 p283-470

Light in August. Random House 1967 c1959 480p o.p.
ISBN 0-394-43335-1

First published 1932 by Harrison Smith & Robert Haas, Inc.

The novel "reiterates the author's concern with a society that classifies men according to race, creed, and origin. Joe Christmas, the central character and victim, appears to be white but is really part black; he has an affair with Joanna Burden, a spinster whom the townsfold of Jefferson regard with suspicion because of her New England background. Joe eventually kills her and sets fire to her house; he is captured, castrated, and killed by the outraged townspeople, to whom his victim has become a symbol of the innocent white woman attacked and killed by a black man. Other important characters are Lena Grove, who comes to Jefferson far advanced in pregnancy, expecting to find the lover who has deserted her, and Gail Hightower, the minister who ignores his wife and loses his church because of his fanatic devotion to the past." Reader's Ency. 4th edition

also in Faulkner, W. Novels, 1930-1935

Faulkner, William, 1897-1962—*Continued*

The mansion. Random House 1959 436p o.p.

The mansion completes the trilogy of the Snopes family. Using his techniques of flashbacks and recombining earlier themes, Faulkner "covers a time span linking Jack Houston's murder with Flem's violent death at the hands of Mink Snopes thirty-eight years later. In this novel, however, much of Flem's trickery and greed for money and power fade into the background and Linda, Eula's daughter becomes the central figure." Magill. Masterpieces of World Lit in Dig Form

"Sometimes the reader grows tired of the tough repetitive monologues and the revelations of Southern decay, but in Faulkner there is a massiveness and even a majesty not easily found elsewhere in the American fiction of this century. . . . Turgid and difficult as he is, Faulkner is worth the trouble." Burgess. 99 Novels

also in Faulkner, W. Novels, 1957-1962 p327-721

also in Faulkner, W. Snopes p673-1065

Novels, 1930-1935. Library of Am. 1985 1034p $35

ISBN 0-940450-26-7 LC 84-23424

Contents: As I lay dying; Sanctuary; Light in August; Pylon

Novels, 1936-1940. Library of Am. 1990 1117p map $37.50

ISBN 0-940450-55-0 LC 89-62931

Contents: Absalom, Absalom!; The unvanquished; If I forget thee, Jerusalem (The wild palms); The hamlet

Absalom, Absalom!, The unvanquished, and The hamlet are entered seperately. If I forget thee, Jerusalem (published 1939 with title The wild palms) depicts, in alternating narratives, the "effects of a Mississippi flood on the lives of a hillbilly convict and a New Orleans doctor and his mistress." Oxford Companion to Am Lit. 6th edition

Novels, 1942-1954. Library of Am. 1994 1115p $35

ISBN 0-940450-85-2 LC 94-2942

Contents: Go down, Moses; Intruder in the dust; Requiem for a nun; A fable

Novels, 1957-1962. Library of Am. 1999 1008p $35

ISBN 1-88301-169-8 LC 99-18348

Contents: The town; The mansion; The reivers

Pylon. H. Smith and R. Haas, Inc. 1935 315p o.p.

The scene is a Southern city where a Mardi Gras celebration is in progress. The action covers four days in the lives of a strange set of people, all of them connected in some way with the airplane contests which are being held in celebration of the opening of a new airport. The main characters are: Shumann, an airplane pilot; Jiggs, his mechanic; Jackson, a parachute jumper; Laverne, Shumann's wife; and a nameless reporter who adopts the group for the time being

also in Faulkner, W. Novels, 1930-1935

The reivers; a reminiscence. Random House 1962 305p o.p.

"Told to his grandson as 'A Reminiscence,' Lucius Priest's monologue recalls his adventures in 1905 as an 11-year-old, when he, the gigantic but childish part-Indian Boon Hogganbeck, and a black family servant, Ned William McCaslin, become reivers (stealthy plunderers) of the automobile of his grandfather, the senior banker of Jefferson, Miss." Oxford Companion to Am Lit. 5th edition

also in Faulkner, W. Novels, 1957-1962 p722-971

Requiem for a nun. Random House 1951 286p o.p.

"Written in three prose sections, which provide the background, and three acts which present the drama in the courthouse and the jail, the novel centers on Temple Drake, one of the main characters of *Sanctuary*. In the interval of the eight years separating the events of the two books, Temple has married Gowan Stevens and borne two children; she is being blackmailed by Pete, brother of her lover in *Sanctuary*, and is planning to run away with him when Nancy Manningoe, her black servant, kills Temple's youngest child. Her attempts to gain a pardon from the governor for Nancy finally bring out Temple's own involvement in and responsibility for the crime." Reader's Ency. 4th edition

also in Faulkner, W. Novels, 1942-1954 p471-664

Sanctuary. J. Cape & H. Smith 1931 380p o.p.

"Horace Benbow, an ineffectual intellectual, becomes involved in the violent events centering on Temple Drake, a provocative, irresponsible young coed. Temple is raped by Popeye, who murders a man trying to protect her. Popeye is a figure of evil, but is also a victim of his environment. Carried off to a Memphis brothel by Popeye, Temple later protects him and testifies against Lee Goodwin, who is accused of the murder. Benbow defends Goodwin at the trial and unsuccessfully tries to give shelter to Goodwin's common-law wife. Temple's perjured testimony ends all hope for Goodwin, who is lynched by the townspeople." Reader's Ency. 4th edition

also in Faulkner, W. Novels, 1930-1935

Sartoris. Harcourt Brace & Co. 1929 380p o.p.

"A saga of the Sartoris family, the novel deals primarily with young Bayard Sartoris' urge for self-destruction. His beloved twin brother, John, having been killed in World War I, Bayard returns home haunted by the memories of his brother, and becomes involved in a number of accidents. Because of his reckless driving, his grandfather, old Bayard Sartoris, rides with him in an attempt to force him to drive carefully, but young Bayard runs the car off a cliff and his grandfather dies of a heart attack. Unable to face either himself or his family, Bayard goes to Ohio to become a test pilot and is killed. . . . Faulkner picks up the beginnings of the Sartoris family in 'The Unvanquished.'" Benet's Reader's Ency of Am Lit

A more complete version of this novel was published with title: Flags in the dust

Snopes; The hamlet, The town, The mansion; introduction by George Garrett. Modern Lib. 1994 1065p $27.95

ISBN 0-679-60092-2

Faulkner, William, 1897-1962—*Continued*

An omnibus volume of three novels entered separately

Soldiers' pay. Boni & Liveright 1926 319p o.p.

"Lieutenant Donald Mahon, an American in the British air force during World War I, is discharged from the hospital where he has been treated for a critical head wound, and makes his way home to Georgia. The wound leaves a horrible scar, and causes loss of memory and later blindness. On the train from New York he is aided by Joe Gilligan, an awkward, friendly, footloose ex-soldier, and Margaret Powers, an attractive young widow whose husband was killed in the war. Margaret, strangely attracted to the dying, subhuman Donald, decides to go home with him, as does Gilligan, who is in love with her. Their reception in the Georgia town reveals the character of the fickle people." Oxford Companion to Am Lit. 6th edition

The sound and the fury. New, corrected ed. Random House 1984 326p o.p.

ISBN 0-394-53241-4 LC 84-42626

First published 1929

"The story is told in four parts, through the stream of consciousness of three characters (the sons of the Compson family, Benjy, Quentin, and Jason), and finally in an objective account. The Compson family, formerly genteel Southern patricians, now lead a degenerate, perverted life on their shrunken plantation near Jefferson, Miss. The disintegration of the family, which clings to outworn aristocratic conventions, is counterpointed by the strength of the black servants, who include old Dilsey and her son Luster." Oxford Companion to Am Lit. 6th edition

also in Faulkner, W. The Faulkner reader p5-251

The town. Random House 1957 371p o.p.

ISBN 0-394-42452-2

This second volume in the Snopes trilogy "relates through three narrators of varying reliability the story of Flem Snopes' rise to prominence in the fictional Yoknapatawpha County. Flem's coldly calculated vengeance on his wife, Eula, and her lover culminates in Eula's suicide and Flem's rise to power in Jefferson, the county seat. Because Flem longs for respect as well as money, he turns against the clan of shiftless Snopes cousins who have followed him to town and forces them to leave Jefferson. In his hunger for social validation, he denies his own origins, and the book ends with a hint that the cousins' revenge will follow." Merriam-Webster's Ency of Lit

Followed by The mansion

also in Faulkner, W. Novels, 1957-1962 p1-326

also in Faulkner, W. Snopes p351-671

Uncollected stories of William Faulkner; edited by Joseph Blotner. Random House 1979 716p o.p.

ISBN 0-394-40044-5 LC 78-21803

Contents: Ambuscade; Retreat; Raid; Skirmish at Sartoris; The unvanquished; Vendée; Fool about a horse; Lizards in Jamshyd's courtyard; The hound; Spotted horses; Lion; The old people; A point of law; Gold is not always; Pantaloon in black; Go down, Moses; Delta autumn; The bear; Race at morning; Hog pawn; Nympholepsy; Frankie and Johnny; The priest; Once aboard the Lugger (I); Once aboard the Lugger (II); Miss Zilphia Gant; Thrift; Idyll in the desert; Two dollar wife; Afternoon of a cow; Mr. Acarius; Sepulture South; Gaslight; Adolescence; Al Jackson; Don Giovanni; Peter; Moonlight; The big shot; Dull tale; A return; A dangerous man; Evangeline; A portrait of Elmer; With caution and dispatch; Snow

The unvanquished; drawings by Edward Shenton. Random House 1938 293p il o.p.

Contents: Ambuscade; Retreat; Raid; Riposte in tertio; Vendée; Skirmish at Sartoris; An odor of verbena

This is "a collection of interlocking stories. . . . Set during the Civil War, these stories deal with the Sartoris family, whose modern history Faulkner recounted in Sartoris. Composed of seven stories, which first appeared separately in magazines, the book centers primarily on the adventures of Bayard Sartoris and his black companion, Ringo. Colonel John Sartoris and Miss Rosa, Bayard's grandmother, also figure prominently." Reader's Ency. 3d edition

also in Faulkner, W. Novels, 1936-1940 p317-492

Faulks, Sebastian

Birdsong. Random House 1996 c1993 402p o.p.

LC 95-23721

First published 1993 in the United Kingdom

"In 1910, England's Stephen Wraysford, a junior executive in a textile firm, is sent by his company to northern France. There he falls for Isabelle Azaire, a young and beautiful matron who abandons her abusive husband and sticks by Stephen long enough to conceive a child. Six years later, Stephen is back in France, as a British officer fighting in the trenches. Facing death, embittered by isolation, he steels himself against thoughts of love. But despite rampant disease, harrowing tunnel explosions and desperate attacks on highly fortified German positions, he manages to survive, and to meet with Isabelle again. . . . [The author] proves himself a grand storyteller here." Publ Wkly

Charlotte Gray; a novel. Random House 1999 399p o.p.

ISBN 0-375-50169-X LC 98-33658

First published 1998 in the United Kingdom

Charlotte Gray is a "young woman who, in 1942, leaves her home in Scotland to find work in London. Because of her fluency in French, she soon is recruited by G Section and sent to France to deliver a set of wireless crystals to the Resistance. Her personal mission is to find Peter Gregory, a missing RAF pilot with whom she had a brief but intense affair. Posing as Dominique Gulbert, Charlotte makes her way to the village of Lavaurette. Her official task accomplished, she decides to stay on, and her life becomes enmeshed with the lives of the villagers—in particular Julien Levade, a young architect who also works for the Resistance, and his father, a painter." Booklist

Faulks "has written one of those rare books that is adventurous enough to attract a popular audience while thoughtful enough to sustain the more serious reader." Libr J

Faulks, Sebastian—*Continued*

On Green Dolphin Street; a novel. Random House 2002 351p o.p.

ISBN 0-375-50225-4 LC 2001-41753

"It is 1960, and Mary and Charlie van der Linden are an English couple posted to Washington, where Charlie serves at the British Embassy. Mary is an exceptionally loyal wife—while Charlie, disillusioned by his own and the world's failures, is destroying himself through drink and pills, Mary uncomplainingly shores him up. Then she meets Frank Renzo, an American newspaper reporter, and enters into an affair." N Y Times Book Rev

"The outline of this archetypal love story may sound familiar, but everything about Faulks' telling of it is fresh. . . . It is a love story above all, but it is also a New York story, the sights, sounds, and smells of the city perfectly evoked to capture one of those moments when the forces of change collide with the proprieties of the past." Booklist

Faust, Frederick, 1892-1944

See also Brand, Max, 1892-1944

Feather, Jane

The widow's kiss. Bantam Bks. 2001 364p $19.95

ISBN 0-553-80181-3 LC 00-60823

"Lady Guinevere Mallory is placed in a precarious position when her fourth husband dies, and her wealth is brought to the attention of King Henry VIII and his avaricious Privy Seal, Lord Cromwell. They send Hugh of Beaucaire, who has a personal interest in the widow, believing that his son is entitled to some of her first husband's property, to investigate the deaths of all of her husbands. As Hugh looks into her past, he becomes intrigued with Lady Mallory herself, whose story seems full of contradictions." Booklist

"The story succeeds as romantic fiction, with fine characterizations, sound historical background and an effective evocation of the precarious times when a king's favor or disfavor meant life or death." Publ Wkly

Feist, Raymond E.

Mistress of the empire; by Raymond E. Feist & Janny Wurts. Doubleday 1992 613p o.p.

LC 91-24511

"A Foundation book"

Completes the trilogy about Lady Mara begun with Daughter of the empire (1987) and Servant of the empire (1990)

"Lady Mara of the Acoma, consummate player of the deadly game of intrigue that maintains the stability of the Tsurani Empire, pits her vision of a transformed society against an apparently unbeatable foe. . . . Feist and Wurts have created an exotic fantasy world that is rich in texture and alive with political machinations." Libr J

Rage of a demon king. Avon Bks. 1997 436p (Serpent war saga, v3) o.p.

LC 96-30715

In this third volume of the saga, "Erik von Darkmoor, no longer a young soldier (at least in spirit), and his scheming friend Rupert Avery are now at the very forefront of the physical battle against the Emerald Queen's invasion of Midkemia. Meanwhile, Pug, Miranda, and the sorcerer Macros are off on their own quest to foil the Demon King on his own home ground. . . . Feist remains honorably in the forefront of fantasists who continue to create well-told tales out of the genre's familiar elements." Booklist

Followed by Shards of a broken crown

Rise of a merchant prince. Morrow 1995 406p (Serpent war saga, v2) o.p.

LC 95-34380

The second book in the Serpent war saga focuses "on Rupert Avery's rise to power and influence in the mercantile class of the City of Krondor, the narrative follows 'Roo' as he forms a business alliance with a merchant, Helmut Grindle, whose daughter, Karli, he marries for a multitude of reasons, none of which is love. . . . Meanwhile, his friend and compatriot Erik von Darkmoor travels back down to the land of Novindus to battle the Pantathians." Publ Wkly

Followed by Rage of a demon king

Shadow of a dark queen; a novel. Morrow 1994 382p (Serpent war saga, v1) o.p.

LC 93-47455

In this first volume of the Serpent War saga "Erik von Darkmoor, bastard son of the local baron, flees to the city of Krondor after accidentally killing his legitimate and sadistic half-brother. Condemned to death, Eric and his childhood friend, Rupert (Roo) Avery, are provisionally spared to serve in a desperate mission against the reptilian Pantathians, who plan to conquer Midkemia and bring back their goddess, Alma-Lodaka, one of the ancient Dragon Lords. . . . A sensitive coming-of-age tale in which brutality and camaraderie are equally present." Publ Wkly

Followed by Rise of a merchant prince

Shards of a broken crown. Avon Eos 1998 417p (Serpent war saga, v4) o.p.

ISBN 0-380-97399-5 LC 97-44190

In this concluding volume of the saga, "Jimmy and Dash, the late Duke James' grandsons, take center stage. . . . They help persuade the late Emerald Queen's General Duko to change sides and enlist the thieves of Krondor in the resistance to the magically assisted Keshites. Their transformation from green if goodhearted youths to warriors much older than their years is the core of the book and a development Feist works out in some of his best writing ever." Booklist

Feldman, Ellen

See also Villars, Elizabeth, 1941-

Ferber, Edna, 1887-1968

Cimarron. Doubleday, Doran 1930 388p o.p.

"Yancey Cravat was a big, handsome man who quoted Shakespeare and the Bible and knew the law. He started a newspaper in Wichita, Kansas, in whose pages he protested the government's treatment of the Indians. Against the wishes of her family he married Sabra Venable, daughter of an aristocratic Southern family. Then, lured by the newly opened frontier, he took off with her to help settle Oklahoma, where he was instrumental in establishing law and order. Although he could have been governor of the state, his restlessness took him away for

Ferber, Edna, 1887-1968—*Continued*
weeks, months, and finally years, leaving Sabra with the responsibility for the newspaper. In the lives of these two strong-willed people, and of their son, Cim, Ferber has captured the drama, conflicts, and rewards of life in pioneer America." Shapiro. Fic for Youth. 3d edition

Giant. Doubleday 1952 447p o.p.
"The story unfolds as Leslie Lynnton, a patrician Virginian, marries Bick Benedict, a Texas cattle baron. The reader experiences Texas from Leslie's point of view, as she attempts to understand and to adapt to the customs and expansive way of life of Texans. Alongside her vivid descriptions of the crudeness of the newly rich oil men and cattle barons, Ferber observes their exploitation of the impoverished Mexicans who work for them." Merriam-Webster's Ency of Lit

Saratoga trunk. Doubleday 1941 352p o.p.
A "story of an adventuress making her way in the [18]80's. Clio, daughter of a New Orleans aristocrat and his French mistress, returned to scandalize New Orleans and levy a little blackmail from her father's family. A flamboyant Texas cowboy joined forces with her and they chose Saratoga in the racing season for their assault on society and big business, profiting by the rival railroad magnates' warfare." Booklist

Show boat; a novel. Doubleday, Page 1926 398p o.p.
"In this popular book appear three theatrical generations. First there is Captain Andy Hawks, who runs a showboat on the Mississippi and marries Parthy Ann, a prim New England schoolmarm. They have one daughter, Magnolia, who becomes an actress and runs off with the leading man, Gaylord Ravenal. Their daughter Kim is born on the showboat. The captain dies and Parthy Ann takes over; Ravenal takes Magnolia to Chicago, but ultimately leaves her, and she returns to the showboat. Kim meanwhile grows up to be a Broadway star." Benet's Reader's Ency of Am Lit

So Big. Doubleday, Page 1924 360p o.p.
Selina DeJong would look up from her work and say, 'How big is my man?' Then little Dirk DeJong would answer in the time-worn way, 'So-o-o big!' And he was so nicknamed. Though So Big gives the book its title his mother is the outstanding figure. Until Selina was nineteen she traveled with her gambler-father. At his sudden death she secured a teacher's post in the Dutch settlement of High Prairie, a community of hardworking farmers and their thrifty, slaving wives—narrow-minded people indifferent to natural beauty. Soon Selina married Pervus DeJong, a plodding, goodnatured boy. With her marriage the never-ending drudgery of a farmer's wife began. Through all the years of hardship she never lost her gay indomitable spirit. Unfortunately, she was unable to transmit these qualities to her son

Fergus, Jim

The wild girl: the notebooks of Ned Giles, 1932; a novel. Hyperion 2005 355p $23.95
ISBN 1-401-30054-5 LC 2004-54161
"After the death of his parents, 17-year-old Giles leaves behind his job at a Chicago country club to join the Great Apache Expedition, a journey organized by citizens of the U.S and Mexico to recover the kidnapped son of a Mexican rancher. Exploring Mexico's Sierra Madres is an opportunity too rich to resist for Giles, who lucks into a job as one of the expedition's photographers. But when he captures the chilling image of a wild Apache girl in a Mexican jail, the young man cannot, in good conscience, turn his back and walk away. . . . Fans of both Larry McMurtry and Louis L'Amour will relish this deftly rendered tale of survival, self-discovery, and the precarious boundaries between man and beast. " Booklist

Ferman, Edward L.

(ed) The Best from Fantasy & Science Fiction: a 40th anniversary anthology. See The Best from Fantasy & Science Fiction: a 40th anniversary anthology

(ed) The Best from Fantasy & Science Fiction: a 45th anniversary anthology. See The Best from Fantasy & Science Fiction: a 45th anniversary anthology

(ed) The Best from fantasy & science fiction: the fiftieth anniversary anthology. See The Best from fantasy & science fiction: the fiftieth anniversary anthology

(ed) The Best from Fantasy and Science Fiction: a special 25th anniversary anthology. See The Best from Fantasy and Science Fiction: a special 25th anniversary anthology

(ed) The Best horror stories from the Magazine of fantasy and science fiction. See The Best horror stories from the Magazine of fantasy and science fiction

Ferrars, E. X., 1907-

Blood flies upward. Doubleday 1977 c1976 186p o.p.
LC 76-18343
"Published for the Crime Club"
First published 1976 in the United Kingdom
"A young woman, posing as an abandoned wife, replaces her sister as housekeeper of an English country house after the sister disappears. Other members of the staff and the houseguests at first appear merely offbeat, and the puzzle seems to lead nowhere." Booklist

Thy brother death. Doubleday 1993 192p o.p.
LC 93-23187
"A Perfect crime book"
"Patrick and Henrietta Carey are visited by a well-mannered Scotswoman who is seeking the money owed her by her estranged husband, who she says is Patrick Carey. All three are bewildered, even after they realize that she had married Patrick's somewhat pathological brother David. The woman leaves before the Careys' planned party begins. Patrick is a university lecturer, and their guest list includes fellow faculty members, an American visitor, Patrick's spurned mentor, an insecure underling and other tweedy academics. That same evening the Scotswoman perishes in a fire at the mentor's home and, not long afterward, the bobbies appear to question Patrick." Publ Wkly

Ferrars, Elizabeth, 1907-

For works written by this author under other names see Ferrars, E. X., 1907-

Ferrigno, Robert

The Cheshire moon. Morrow 1993 285p o.p.
LC 92-22573

"When reporter Quinn's friend Andy is found dead after revealing to Quinn that he has observed a murder, the suspense in this novel begins. The victim is a TV producer, who was trying to blackmail a well-known talk-show host. Quinn, who works for a celebrity magazine, along with his friend Jen, a photographer, find themselves the hunted, as the murderer tries to eliminate all witnesses." Libr J

"The mean streets of southern California remain fertile ground for the stylish mystery novel, as demonstrated by Robert Ferrigno's 'Cheshire Moon.' The ingredients are familiar: a world-weary investigative reporter, his hard-as-nails, softer-than-silk love interest; the friend's murder that demands justice; puzzling connections to the Hollywood of the fabled, faded past. Mr. Ferrigno boils the pot tastefully and enjoyably." N Y Times Book Rev

Heartbreaker. Pantheon Bks. 1999 307p $24
ISBN 0-375-40124-5 LC 98-49029

"Val Duran, his undercover narco days behind him, is running from Junior, the only white-trash drug kingpin left in Miami. But what Val finds in Los Angeles proves every bit as lethal as Junior. First there's Kyle, a marine biologist whom Val falls hard for, and then there's her drunken stepbrother and his seriously bent girlfriend, who are plotting to murder Kyle's mother. Val lands in the middle of it all, with matters complicated by the arrival of Junior." Booklist

"The southern California atmospherics and razor-sharp dialogue are first-rate, and the villains are quirky and memorable." N Y Times Book Rev

The Horse Latitudes. Morrow 1990 294p o.p.
LC 89-38234

The plot of this novel "revolves around Danny DiMedici's search for his ex-wife Lauren, a celebrity psychologist who has disappeared after a scientist is murdered in her elegant beach house. . . . A former drug dealer, Danny is the prime suspect in the murder of Lauren's lover, Dr. Tohlson, who has found a way to use fetal tissue to preserve youth. To prove his innocence, Danny embarks on a journey through the culture of Southern California." Time

This novel "features superb writing, relentless action, and some memorably despicable characters." Booklist

Fesperman, Dan, 1955-

The warlord's son; a novel; by Dan Fesperman. Knopf 2004 319p $23
ISBN 0-375-41473-8 LC 2004-11841

"A burned-out war correspondent hoping for a last hurrah in Afghanistan, Skelly arrives on the Afghan border just as American bombs begin falling on the ruling Taliban. Seeking the scoop of a lifetime as witness to the capture of 'the biggest fish of them all,' he links up with an exiled warlord's quixotic expedition. Guiding Skelly's way is Najeeb, a tribal Pakistani with his own objective—U. S. visas for his girlfriend and himself, promised by Pakistani intelligence if he acts as an informant." Publisher's note

Fever, Buck *See* Anderson, Sherwood, 1876-1941

Fforde, Jasper

The Eyre affair; a novel. Viking 2002 374p o.p.
ISBN 0-670-03064-3 LC 2001-43775

First published 2001 in the United Kingdom

"It's 1985 in England, at least on the calendar; the Crimean War is in its hundred-and-thirty-first year; time travel is nothing new; Japanese tourists slip in and out of Victorian novels; and the literary branch of the special police, led gamely by the beguiling Thursday Next, are pursuing Acheron Hades, who has stolen the manuscript of 'Martin Chuzzlewit' and set his sights on kidnapping the character Jane Eyre, a theft that could have disastrous consequences for Bronte lovers who like their story straight. This rambunctious caper could be taken as a warning about what might happen if society considered literature really important—like, say, energy futures or accounting." New Yorker

Thursday Next in Lost in a good book; a novel. Viking 2003 399p il $24.95
ISBN 0-670-03190-9 LC 2002-71304

Companion volume to: The Eyre affair

First published 2002 in the United Kingdom with title: Lost in a good book

"Thursday Next, who literally jumps into books to do her detective work, must locate a surprise enemy in Poe's 'The Raven' to save her beloved." Libr J

"Time flies—and leaps and zigzags—while reading this wickedly funny and clever fantasy. Would-be wordsmiths and mystery fans will find the surreal genre-buster irresistible." Publ Wkly

Thursday Next in Something rotten; a novel. Viking 2004 383p $24.95
ISBN 0-670-03359-6 LC 2004-49497

Published in the United Kingdom with title: Something rotten

"Detective Thursday Next has had her fill of her responsibilities as the Bellman in Jurisfiction. . . . Packing up her son, Friday, Thursday returns to Swindon accompanied by none other than the dithering Danish prince Hamlet. Caring for both is more than a full-time job and Thursday decides it is definitely time to get her husband Landen back, if only to babysit. Luckily, those responsible for Landen's eradication, The Goliath Corporation-formerly an oppressive multinational conglomerate, now an oppressive multinational religion-have pledged to write the wrong." Publisher's note

The author's "penchant for plotting knows no bounds. . . . It's easy to be delighted by a writer who loves books so madly." N Y Times (Late N Y Ed)

Thursday Next in The well of lost plots; a novel. Viking 2004 c2003 375p il $24.95
ISBN 0-670-03289-1 LC 2003-62150

First published 2003 in the United Kingdom with title: The well of lost plots

Thursday Next "has beaten a strategic retreat into BookWorld, where as part of the Character Exchange Program, she hides out in an unpublished, by-the-

Fforde, Jasper—*Continued*

numbers police procedural. She's pregnant, her husband has been killed before he really existed, and her memories of him are being eaten away by a mindworm. She can't rest for long, however; she's still a trainee agent in the BookWorld police force, JurisFiction, and soon fiction itself is under a greater threat than ever before." Booklist

Field, Rachel, 1894-1942

All this, and heaven too. Macmillan 1938 596p o.p.

In fiction form the author tells the life story of her great-aunt by marriage, the French governess who in 1847 became involved in a famous murder trial, in which she was known as Mademoiselle D. Although she was acquitted, life became so difficult for her in France that Mademoiselle came to America, where she married an American minister and presided over a Gramercy Park salon, frequented by William Cullen Bryant, Harriet Beecher Stowe, Samuel Morse, and Fanny Kemble among others

Fielding, Helen

Bridget Jones: the edge of reason. Viking 2000 338p o.p.

ISBN 0-670-89296-3 LC 99-86499

Sequel to Bridget Jones's diary

First published 1999 in the United Kingdom

A novel in diary form. "The familiar cast is gathered. There are Bridget's friends Magda, Jude and Shaz, who compete in giving her disastrous advice from self-help books about dealing with Mark's apparently cavalier behavior and his involvement with a minx named Rebecca." Publ Wkly

"How can a reader not love this woman—not in spite of her faults but because of them? Bridget tries so hard. Her days are made up of glorious surges of hope followed by instant defeat or rash interpretations, or both." N Y Times Book Rev

Bridget Jones's diary; a novel. Viking 1998 271p $22.95

ISBN 0-670-88072-8 LC 98-18687

First published 1996 in the United Kingdom

This novel is the "purported diary, complete with daily entries of calories consumed, cigarettes smoked, 'alcohol units' imbibed and other unsuitable obsessions, of a year in the life of a bright London 30-something." Publ Wkly

"Brimming with a deliciously irreverent sense of humor and a keen sense of women's deepest insecurities, *Bridget Jones's Diary* is a must-read." Booklist

Fielding, Henry, 1707-1754

The history of Tom Jones, a foundling. Knopf 1991 xxxvi, 408, 427p $20

ISBN 0-679-40569-0 LC 91-52996

"Everyman's library"

First published 1749. Variant title: Tom Jones

"Squire Allworthy suspects that the infant whom he adopts and names Tom Jones is the illegitimate child of his servant Jenny Jones. When Tom is a young man, he falls in love with Sophia Western, his beautiful and virtuous neighbor. In the end his true identity is revealed and he wins Sophia's hand, but numerous obstacles have to be overcome, and in the course of the action the various sets of characters pursue each other from one part of the country to another, giving Fielding an opportunity to paint an incomparably vivid picture of England in the mid-18th century." Merriam-Webster's Ency of Lit

Joseph Andrews. o.p.

First published 1742

"Joseph Andrews, a prudent, brawny, pleasant young man, is intended to be the brother of Samuel Richardson's heroine Pamela. His widowed employer, Lady Booby, dismisses him from his position as footman for refusing her advances, and he flees London to rejoin his own true love, Fanny Goodwill. On hearing the news of his disgrace, Fanny rushes to meet him. Both are set upon by thieves but are providentially rescued by Parson Adams, and the three return to their parish, where Joseph and Fanny, after comic-opera reversals and discoveries, are married in triumph. The time of the novel is coincident with Pamela, *which* it parodies and transcends." Reader's Ency. 4th edition

Fielding, Joy

Don't cry now; a novel. Morrow 1995 356p o.p.

LC 94-42095

Protagonist "Bonnie Wheeler has a wonderful life wth handsome husband Rod and preschool daughter Amanda even though Rod's ex-wife, Joan, is a pest and Rod's children from his former marriage are less than warm to Bonnie. One of Joan's annoying phone calls leads Bonnie to an empty house where Joan is seated at the kitchen counter, dead. . . . Bonnie turns sleuth, questioning Joan's psychiatrist and anyone who befriended the dead woman." Libr J

"Just when things appear to be all worked out, new evidence points Bonnie in a different direction. With Fielding, nothing is as it appears, and like Bonnie, we can't help brooding on the vulnerability of what we all take for granted." Quill Quire

Missing pieces. Doubleday 1997 368p o.p.

LC 96-40901

"Practical Kate Sinclair, 47, a family therapist married for 24 years and the mother of two teenaged daughters, is losing control of her orderly, settled life. She fights with her rebellious elder daughter, Sara, who's 17. Her mother is diagnosed with Alzheimer's. Even her body is betraying her, as hot flashes startle her metabolism. Meanwhile, a chance encounter with an old high-school sweetheart inflames her in a totally different way. Worst of all, though, is the infatuation of her sexy half-sister, Jo Lynn, with a man on trial for the murder of 13 women." Publ Wkly

"As outlandish as the relationship between sister Jo Lynn and the serial killer seems, Fielding's talent makes it all quite credible." Booklist

See Jane run. Morrow 1991 364p o.p.

LC 90-22603

"Jane finds herself in downtown Boston, her dress covered with blood, nearly $10,000 in her coat pocket, and absolutely no idea of who she is. She seeks help at Boston City Hospital, where she discovers that she is the wife of handsome Michael Whittaker, a renowned sur-

Fielding, Joy—*Continued*
geon. The doctor seems to be the perfect husband, and as Jane learns the details of their ideal life together she is unable to understand her suspicions of him. However, as Jane's amnesia persists, it becomes clear that her model husband is threatening her sanity in order to conceal a sinister secret." Libr J

"Fielding handles her material with finesse; suspense is maintained at a high level, and the narrative is enriched by Jane's bracing sense of humor and a cast of sharply drawn, articulate characters." Publ Wkly

Tell me no secrets. Morrow 1993 352p o.p.
LC 92-43692

"Prosecutor Jess Koster is still distressed at the disappearance of her mother eight years before, but then her client disappears, and she starts receiving death threats in the mail." Libr J

"When Jess' ex rescues, or seems to rescue, her from the predictably sadistic stalker/rapist, her comment that 'it's just like in the movies' may seem like self-parody. Jess escapes this formula—and becomes not only real, but touching—when she visits her suburban sister and the brother-in-law she despises, when she talks with a woman juror in a rape trial about why the verdict was not guilty, and when we visit with her in her private fear." Booklist

Fifty years of the best from Ellery Queen's Mystery Magazine; edited by Eleanor Sullivan. Carroll & Graf Pubs. 1991 642p o.p.
LC 90-23928

Contents: The clue of the red wig, by J. D. Carr; Lost star, by C. D. King; The Bloomsbury wonder, by T. Burke; Dressing-up, by W. R. Burnett; Malice domestic, by P. MacDonald; I can find my way out, by N. Marsh; The fourth degree, by H. Pentecost; Midnight adventure, by M. Arlen; A study in white, by N. Blake; The phantom guest, by F. I. Anderson; As simple as ABC, by E. Queen; Money to burn, by M. Allingham; The gentlest of the brothers, by D. Alexander; One-way street, by A. Armstrong; Murder at the dog show, by M. G. Eberhart; Always trust a cop, by O. R. Cohen; The withered heart, by J. Potts; The girl who married a monster, by A. Boucher; Between eight and eight, by C. S. Forester; Knowing what I know now, by B. Perowne; Change of climate, by U. Curtiss; Life in our time, by R. Bloch; The special gift, by C. Fremlin; A neat and tidy job, by G. H. Coxe; Run—if you can, by C. Armstrong; Line of communication, by A. Garve; Danger at Deerfawn, by D. B. Hughes; The man who understood women, by A. H. Z. Carr; Revolver, by A. Davidson; The eternal chase, by A. Gilbert; Reasons unknown, by S. Ellin; Three ways to rob a bank, by H. R. Daniels; The perfect servant, by H. Nielsen; The marked man, by D. Ely; Flowers that bloom in the spring, by J. Symons; A nice place to stay, by N. Tyre; Paul Broderick's man, by T. Walsh; When nothing matters, by F. V. Mayberry; This is death, by D. E. Westlake; Woodrow Wilson's necktie, by P. Highsmith; The jackal and the tiger, by M. Gilbert; The fix, by R. Twohy; One moment of madness, by E. D. Hoch; Loopy, by R. Rendell; The plateau, by C. Howard; The butchers, by P. Lovesey; Burning bridges, by J. Powell; A good turn, by R. Barnard; Clap hands, there goes Charlie, by G. Baxt; Big Boy, Little Boy, by S. Brett

Finder, Joseph

Company man. St. Martin's Press 2005 520p $24.95
ISBN 0-312-31916-9

"Nick Conover, the youngish CEO of the Stratton Corporation, in Fenwick, Mich., has fired half of the high-end office furniture company's 10,000 employees at the bidding of new ownership in Boston. As a result, much of Fenwick hates Nick, including the person who has been breaking into his mansion and scribbling 'No Hiding Place' on the walls, and who then kills the Conover family dog—presumably Andrew Stadler, a fired employee and erstwhile mental patient. When Stadler accosts Nick one night, Nick, panicking, shoots him dead, and then, under the influence of his shady corporate security director, covers up the crime. The two cops assigned to the murder prove dogged, sending Nick into a generally beleaguered state that's slightly alleviated by his new romance with, of all people, the daughter of the murdered man, but exacerbated considerably by his discovery that his Boston masters intend to sell Stratton to Chinese government interests." Publ Wkly

This is "as much a novel about the chicanery of the business world as it is a mystery story. Takeovers and outsourcing are not news, but Mr. Finder weaves these prospects menacingly throughout the story, as Nick finds himself increasingly undermined by his colleagues." N Y Times (Late N Y Ed)

High crimes; a novel. Morrow 1998 341p o.p.
ISBN 0-688-14962-6 LC 97-37365

"Claire Heller Chapman seems to have it all: a successful career as a Harvard Law School professor and well-known defense lawyer; a loving, ruggedly handsome spouse and an adorable 6-year-old daughter. So imagine her shock when her husband, Tom, is hunted down by Federal agents and accused of being a ruthless member of a 'super-secret clandestine unit of the Pentagon' who slaughtered 87 innocent villagers during a mission in El Salvador in the 1980s. It turns out he's been on the run ever since, covering his tracks with an elaborately fabricated personal history that gradually unravels before Claire's eyes." N Y Times Book Rev

"As Claire defends 'Tom' in a secret trial where her civilian knowledge is of little value, she also probes to discover what truly happened in the Central American village. A lively, affecting story." Booklist

The Moscow Club. Viking 1991 548p o.p.
LC 90-50407

"The plot concerns a secret group called the Moscow Club, hardliners who want to overthrow Mikhail Gorbachev. Our hero is Charlie Stone, an analyst for the CIA. . . . The assignment is a personal one for Stone because this evil conspiracy is somehow linked to an episode years ago when his father was branded as a traitor by Senator Joseph McCarthy. Stone becomes the target of would-be assassins across the U.S. and Europe, is framed for a murder, but in the end . . . saves the world from global disaster." Booklist

"The story contains as many chases, murders, conspiracies and uncloseted ghosts as any thriller maven could want, as well as a credible love interest; in all, it's a superbly exciting read." Publ Wkly

Finder, Joseph—*Continued*

The zero hour; a novel. Morrow 1996 422p o.p. LC 95-25865

"A wealthy and bitter man, seeking revenge for the killing of his wife and child, hires Baumann, a brilliant but completely amoral terrorist who is justifiably known as 'The Prince of Darkness.' As Baumann prepares his plan to destroy not only people but also the very foundation of Western finance, FBI Special Agent Sarah Cahill assembles and directs a team of equally talented law enforcement agents to hunt him down." Libr J

"Henrik Baumann is a bad guy worthy of Nietzsche—able to snap spines with a twist, seduce his antagonist with a glance, and bring the world financial system to ruin with a laptop computer, some duct tape, and a screwdriver. We secretly root for him to bring down the avenging angel, Sarah Cahill, who is a fine F.B.I. agent and a terrific mom. In all, a thrilling chase through Europe, Wall Street, and cyberspace." New Yorker

Findley, Timothy

The piano man's daughter. Crown 1996 461p il o.p. LC 96-171372

First published 1995 in Canada

"Set in turn-of-the-century Canada, the story tells, in a series of evocative flashbacks, the engaging tale of Lily Kilworth, and her son, Charlie. Conceived when her mother, Ede, falls in love with a musician, Lily is born in a field of flowers and grows into an odd, lonely child whose world is exotically tip-tilted. As she matures, she becomes more and more alienated from real life, but this doesn't keep her from having a brief, mysterious affair while she's a student in wartime England. The result is her son, Charlie, who has perfect musical pitch and a high tolerance for his mother's eccentric ways. . . . Brilliantly told, powerfully affecting." Booklist

Finkelstein, Mark Harris *See* Harris, Mark, 1922-

Finney, Jack

From time to time; a novel. Simon & Schuster 1995 303p il o.p. LC 94-24497

In this sequel to Time and again, "time traveler Simon Morley leaves his voluntary exile in the 19th century to visit the 20th century of his origins and finds himself drawn into a desperate attempt to alter the events of history and prevent the onset of World War I." Libr J

"This mind-stretching escapist adventure is studded with period photos and news clippings that function as an integral part of the story." Publ Wkly

Time and again. Simon & Schuster 1970 399p o.p.

The author "re-creates the world of nineteenth-century New York City and at the same time critically appraises modernity. His hero, Simon Morley, agrees to live in the Dakota apartments and, assisted by hypnosis, to share a series of experiences in the year 1882. Eager to cooperate with the U.S. governmental agencies conducting the test Simon observes the manners and mores of the past and falls in love with Julia, a girl of the period. Simon's enthusiasm palls, however, when he is asked to alter historical events in the interest of the agency's evidently nefarious designs." Booklist

Followed by From time to time

Finney, Patricia, 1958-

Gloriana's torch. St. Martin's Press 2003 452p $24.95

ISBN 0-312-31285-7 LC 2003-58454

This "tale is set on the eve of the sailing of the Spanish Armada in 1588. David Becket, clerk of the ordnance and sometime spy for Elizabeth I, is ordered by the queen to discover the details of a top-secret Spanish plot dubbed the 'Miracle of Beauty.' In addition, Becket is commanded to rescue his fellow English spy and friend, Simon Ames, who has been condemned by the Spanish Inquisition as a heretic. . . . The various threads of this wide-ranging tale of intrigue do not come together neatly, but Finney's vivid prose and the high level of historical imagination on display make for a satisfying read." Publ Wkly

Fisher, Clay, 1912-1991

For works by this author under other names see Henry, Will, 1912-1991

Fisher, Vardis, 1895-1968

Mountain man; a novel of male and female in the early American West. Morrow 1965 372p o.p.

The author delves into the story "of Kate Bowden, whose family has been massacred by Indians, and into the life of the trapper Sam Minard who compassionately builds a cabin for Kate and then rides on to take and dearly love a Flathead bride. Sam . . . declares war against the Crow nation after the Crows murder his wife and unborn child." Publ Wkly

"Superb backgrounds, fascinating detail, and consistency of tone elevate this beyond the adventure story; as a picture of a mountain man, his love of nature and struggle to survive, it is a stirring piece of Americana." Libr J

Fitch, Janet

White oleander; a novel. Little, Brown 1999 390p $24.95

ISBN 0-316-28526-9 LC 98-50371

In this novel, "the title flower triggers a savage turn of events when the poet Ingrid Magnussen poisons her lover, consigning herself to jail life and her 12-year-old daughter to Los Angeles' foster-care system. Young Astrid gets off to a shaky start at the home of a born-again Christian who shoots her in a fit of righteous jealousy." Time

"This sensitive exploration of the mother daughter terrain . . . offers a convincing look at what Adrienne Rich has called 'this womanly splitting of self,' in a poignant, virtuosic, utterly captivating narrative." Publ Wkly

Fitzalan, Roger, 1920-1995

For works written by this author under other names see Hall, Adam, 1920-1995

Fitzgerald, F. Scott (Francis Scott), 1896-1940

Babylon revisited, and other stories. Scribner 1960 253p o.p.

Contents: The ice palace; May Day; The diamond as big as the Ritz; Winter dreams; Absolution; The rich boy; The freshest boy; Babylon revisited; Crazy Sunday; The long way out

The Basil and Josephine stories; edited with an introduction by Jackson R. Bryer and John Kuehl. Scribner 1973 xxix, 287p o.p.

Contents: Basil; That kind of party; The scandal detectives; A night at the fair; The freshest boy; He thinks he's wonderful; The captured shadow; The perfect life; Forging ahead; Basil and Cleopatra; Josephine; First blood; A nice quiet place; A woman with a past; A snobbish story; Emotional bankruptcy

The beautiful and damned. Scribner 449p o.p.

ISBN 0-684-15153-7

"Hudson River editions"

First published 1922; copyright renewed 1950

"Anthony Patch pursues and wins the beautiful and sought-after Gloria Gilbert. He decides that they can survive on his limited income until he comes into a large fortune he stands to inherit from his grandfather. Through the ensuing years, their lives deteriorate into mindless alcoholic ennui. Anthony's grandfather makes a surprise appearance at one of their wild parties and, in disgust, disinherits him. After his grandfather's death, Anthony institutes a lawsuit that takes years to settle. Although the Patches eventually win, by then Anthony's spirit is broken, he and Gloria have grown apart, and they care about nothing." Merriam-Webster's Ency of Lit

also in Fitzgerald, F. S. Novels and stories, 1920-1922 p435-795

The Fitzgerald reader; edited by Arthur Mizener. Scribner 1963 xxvii, 509p o.p.

Contents: The short stories are: Winter dreams; Absolution; "The sensible thing"; Basil and Cleopatra; Outside the cabinetmaker's; Babylon revisited; Crazy Sunday; Family in the wind; Afternoon of an author; "I didn't get over"; The long way out; Financing Finnegan; The lost decade

This representative selection of Scott Fitzgerald's work "includes the whole of his best novel, 'The Great Gatsby,' and considerable parts of his other two important novels, 'Tender Is the Night, and 'The Last Tycoon.' It also includes two novelettes ('May Day' and 'The Rich Boy'), the four or five best short stories from each period of his career, and his four most famous essays." Foreword

Flappers and philosophers

In Fitzgerald, F. S. Novels and stories, 1920-1922 p249-433

The great Gatsby; preface by Matthew J. Bruccoli. Scribner Classics 1996 170p $25

ISBN 0-684-83042-6 LC 96-16596

First published 1925

"The mysterious Jay Gatsby lives in a luxurious mansion on the Long Island shore. . . . Nick Carraway, the narrator, lives next door to Gatsby, and Nick's cousin Daisy and her crude but wealthy husband Tom Buchanan live directly across the harbor. Gatsby reveals to Nick that he and Daisy had a brief affair before the war and her marriage to Tom. . . . He persuades Nick to bring him and Daisy together again but ultimately he is unable to win her away from Tom. Daisy, driving Gatsby's car, runs over and kills Tom's mistress Myrtle, unaware of her identity. Myrtle's husband traces the car and shoots Gatsby, who has remained silent in order to protect Daisy. Gatsby's friends and business associates have all deserted him, and only Gatsby's father, and one former guest attend the funeral." Reader's Ency. 4th edition

"The power of the novel derives from its sharp and antagonistic portrayal of wealthy society in New York City and Long Island. . . . The 'Jazz Age,' Fitzgerald's constant subject, is exposed here in terms of its false glamor and cultural barrenness." Benet's Reader's Ency of Am Lit

also in Fitzgerald, F. S. The Fitzgerald reader p105-238

The last tycoon; an unfinished novel. Scribner 163p o.p.

ISBN 0-684-15311-4

"Hudson River editions"

First published 1941 with The Great Gatsby, and selected stories; copyright renewed 1969

In addition to providing a foreword to this unfinished novel "Edmund Wilson has assembled a tentative outline of the rest of the story as Fitzgerald intended to develop it, and has appended passages from the author's notes dealing with the characters and scenes." Publisher's note

"The work is an indictment of the Hollywood film industry, where Fitzgerald had had a disappointing career as a screenwriter. Monroe Stahr is a studio executive who has worked obsessively to produce high-quality films without regard to their financial prospects. He takes a personal interest in every aspect of the studio. At age 35 he is almost burned out, and the novel is the story of how he loses control of the studio and his life." Merriam-Webster's Ency of Lit

May Day

In Fitzgerald, F. S. The Fitzgerald reader p3-53

Novels and stories, 1920-1922. Library of Am. 2000 1082p $35

ISBN 1-88301-184-1 LC 00-24287

Contents: This side of paradise (1920); Flappers and philosophers (1920); The beautiful and the damned (1922); Tales of The jazz age (1922)

Flappers and philosophers includes the following stories: The offshore pirate; The ice palace; Head and shoulders; The cut-glass bowl; Bernice bobs her hair; Benediction; Dalyrimple goes wrong; The four fists

Tales of the jazz age includes the following stories: The jelly bean; The camel's back; May day; Porcelain and pink; The diamond as big as the ritz; The curious case of Benjamin Button; Tarquin of cheapside; "O russet witch!"; The lees of happiness; Mr. Icky; Jemina, the mountain girl

The rich boy

In Fitzgerald, F. S. The Fitzgerald reader p239-75

Fitzgerald, F. Scott (Francis Scott), 1896-1940— *Continued*

The short stories of F. Scott Fitzgerald; edited and with a preface by Matthew J. Bruccoli. Scribner Classics 1998 797p $37.50

ISBN 0-684-84250-5 LC 98-121806

Reissue of the 1989 edition analyzed in Short story index

Contents: Head and shoulders; Bernice bobs her hair; The ice palace; The offshore pirate; May Day; The jelly-bean; The curious case of Benjamin Button; The diamond as big as the Ritz; Winter dreams; Dice, brass-knuckles & guitar; Absolution; Rags Martin-Jones and the Pr-nce of W-les; 'The sensible thing'; Love in the night; The rich boy; Jacob's ladder; A short trip home; The bowl; The captured shadow; Basil and Cleopatra; The last of the belles; Majesty; At your age; The swimmers; Two wrongs; First blood; Emotional bankruptcy; The bridal party; One trip abroad; The hotel child; Babylon revisited; A new leaf; A freeze-out; Six of one—; What a handsome pair!; Crazy Sunday; More than just a house; Afternoon of an author; Financing Finnegan; The lost decade; 'Boil some water—lots of it'; Last kiss; Dearly beloved

Six tales of the jazz age, and other stories. Scribner 1960 192p o.p.

Contents: The jelly-bean; The camel's back; The curious case of Benjamin Button; Tarquin of Cheapside; "O'Russet witch"; The lees of happiness; The adjuster; Hot and cold blood; Gretchen's forty winks

The stories of F. Scott Fitzgerald; a selection of 28 stories; with an introduction by Malcolm Cowley. Scribner 1951 xxv, 473p o.p.

ISBN 0-684-15366-1

"The editor has attempted to make the best selection from all stages of Fitzgerald's career; the stories are arranged in chronological groups." Booklist

Tales of the jazz age

In Fitzgerald, F. S. Novels and stories, 1920-1922 p797-1054

This side of paradise. Scribner 282p o.p.

ISBN 0-684-15601-6

"Hudson River editions"

First published 1920; copyright renewed 1948

"Immature though it seems today, the work when it was published was considered a revelation of the new morality of the young in the early Jazz Age; and it made Fitzgerald famous. The novel's hero, Amory Blaine, is a handsome, spoiled young man who attends Princeton, becomes involved in literary activities, and has several ill-fated romances. A portrait of the Lost Generation, the novel addresses Fitzgerald's later theme of love distorted by social climbing and greed." Merriam-Webster's Ency of Lit

also in Fitzgerald, F. S. Novels and stories, 1920-1922 p1-248

Fitzgerald, Francis Scott *See* Fitzgerald, F. Scott (Francis Scott), 1896-1940

Fitzgerald, Penelope

The blue flower. Houghton Mifflin 1997 225p pa $13

ISBN 0-395-85997-2 (pa) LC 96-52911

First published 1996 in the United Kingdom

This "is a historical novel based on the life of the poet, aphorist, novelist, Friedrich von Hardenberg, a Saxon nobleman who wrote under the name of Novalis. . . . Novalis had a vision of a unique blue flower as the goal of a quest. . . . In the waking life of Fritz von Hardenberg the part of the flower was played by Sophie von Kuhn. She is 12 years old when he meets her and at once designates her his future bride and his incarnation of Wisdom. Reluctant parental permission is obtained for their betrothal, but Sophie (as well as not being noble) is tubercular. . . . Their relationship, and Fritz's dealings with his own family and Sophie's, are the main business of the novel." London Rev Books

This novel "ranges far beyond itself. It is an interrogation of life, love, purpose, experience and horizons, which has found its perfect vehicle in a few years from the pitifully short life of a German youth about to become a great poet." N Y Times Book Rev

The gate of angels. Doubleday 1992 167p o.p.

ISBN 0-385-42150-8 LC 91-4258

"A Nan A. Talese book"

First published 1990 in the United Kingdom

This novel is "set in 1912 Cambridge. A bicycle accident brings about the unlikely pairing of Fred Fairly, a junior fellow of physics at St. Angelicus College, and the enigmatic Daisy Saunders, unfairly dismissed from her place as a nursing probationer. By pursuing his love for Daisy, Fred jeopardizes his career, since St. Angelicus fellows must be celibate. The subsequent investigation into the bicycle accident reveals Daisy's questionable background, and she and Fred are devastated. But the . . . ending seems to hold out a second chance for their happiness." Libr J

"In the course of her charming parable, Mrs Fitzgerald sets about undermining the exciting certainties of the nuclear physicists, and more generally the closed-in male rationality that engendered them. . . . All this comes brightly wrapped in a tapestry of typically Fitzgerald eccentrics." Times Lit Suppl

The means of escape. Houghton Mifflin 2000 117p $18

ISBN 0-618-07994-7 LC 00-38914

Contents: The means of escape; The prescription; Desideratus; Beehernz; The axe; The red-haired girl; Not shown; At Hiruharama

"Strange, whimsical, sometimes gothic or bizarre, these tales demonstrate Fitzgerald's cool and civilized wit and the merciless eye she casts on worldly pretensions." Publ Wkly

Flagg, Fannie

Coming attractions; a wonderful novel. Morrow 1981 320p o.p.

This is a "novel in the form of a journal kept by Daisy Fay Harper from her 11th year (1952) to the day she is crowned Miss Mississippi at 17. Daisy has an alcoholic father, who is involved in money-making schemes such as self-taught taxidermy and a phony revival meeting,

Flagg, Fannie—*Continued*
with hilarious results; a classmate, Vernon Mooseburger, who is withdrawn and self-conscious because he is totally bald; and other friends with names like Pickle Watkins, Mustard Smoot, Peachy Wigham and Ula Sour. . . . This is a lively fictional memoir, full of 50s nostalgia." SLJ

Fried green tomatoes at the Whistle-Stop Cafe. Random House 1987 403p o.p.
ISBN 0-394-56152-X LC 87-12813
This novel is "set in a rural hamlet outside of Birmingham, Alabama. Bulletins from a gossipy town newsletter produced in the 1940s by Dot Weems are interspersed with the recollections of Mrs. Cleo (Vinnie) Throughgoode uttered (40 years later) in a nursing home to a depressed, menopausal visitor, Evelyn Couch (whose life is rejuvenated by these Sunday afternoon chats). Flagg also supplies basic narrative passages illuminating the news shared by Dot and Vinnie. The pace of the novel is as swift as the life of the small town is slow—at least it seems slow until Vinnie drops hints of a murder and of riotous pranks played upon the local minister. The story is carefully plotted, with the moods and people of pre- and post-World War II Alabama splendidly evoked." Booklist

Standing in the rainbow; a novel. Random House 2002 493p o.p.
ISBN 0-679-42615-9 LC 2002-21977
"We first met many members of this cast in *Welcome Back to the World, Baby Girl* (1998), one of whom is Dorothy Smith, the host of the daily radio show *Neighbor Dorothy*. The story begins in 1945. The war is over, the American economy is booming, and there is no better place in the world than Elmwood Springs, Missouri. At least that's what Bobby Smith thinks. He is the 10-year-old son of Neighbor Dorothy, and he's got the world wrapped around his little finger." Booklist
"Beneath the sentlmentality, there's a real celebration of life here, an affirmation that success and happiness are the results of simple kindness gratituder and courage." Sci Monit

Welcome to the world, baby girl!. Random House 1998 xxvi, 467p o.p.
ISBN 0-679-42614-0
"Set during the late '70s, the novel follows the career of Dena Nordstrom, a hard-charging TV anchorwoman. . . . Despite her aura of confidence, however, Dena is having a tough time. Plagued by a drinking problem and a bleeding ulcer, Dena finally consults a psychiatrist, who helps her face her traumatic feelings about her mysterious, emotionally distant mother and her nomadic childhood. Finally unlocking the secret of her racial heritage, Dena decides to chuck New York for the slower pace and friendly atmosphere of her hometown of Elmwood Springs, Missouri." Booklist
Flagg "has that gift that certain people from the theater have of never boring the audience. She keeps it simple, she keeps it bright, she keeps it moving right along." NY Times Book Rev

Flanagan, Richard, 1961-

Gould's book of fish; a novel in twelve fish. Grove Press 2002 404p il o.p.
ISBN 0-8021-1711-2 LC 2001-55747
The novel "tells the story of William Buelow Gould, a convict sent to a penal colony in Van Diemen's Land in the nineteenth century. Gould recounts his life story as he paints the island's native fish, a task given him by the fatuous prison doctor, convinced that such a taxonomic achievement will launch him into British society. As he completes each painting, Gould's story dips into his past, recalling his grim childhood and ill-fated life of crime." Booklist
"This remarkable novel is a meditation on colonialism—indeed, on history itself—couched in the story of an English guttersnipe." New Yorker

Flanagan, Thomas, 1923-

The end of the hunt. Dutton 1994 627p o.p.
LC 93-36478
"A William Abrahams book"
In this historical novel about Ireland, the author "covers the years following 1916's Easter Rebellion (an event more important to Irish consciousness than World War I), which will culminate in the creation of an Irish Free State and the waging of brutal civil war. Flanagan gives us history as moments, some dull and some dangerous, in the lives of scores of people, some invented and some actual." Libr J
The author manages "to sustain interest in the individual lives of his various characters while creating a sense of the monumental historical drama in which they are all players. . . . But it does more than re-create an era and satisfy the reader's appetite for a well-told tale. 'The End of the Hunt' is, in fact, a significant contribution to the historical interpretation of the period, an interpretation that possesses considerable relevance." N Y Times Book Rev

The tenants of time. Dutton 1988 824p o.p.
LC 87-13632
"A William Abrahams book"
"Set during three pivotal decades of Irish history, the narrative focuses on four men who participate in the short-lived Rising of 1867 and the irrevocable effects on their lives of the battle of Clonbrony Wood. . . . Except for Hugh, who is one of the narrators of this moving story, tragedy stalks each of the veterans of Clonbrony Wood." Publ Wkly
This "novel is enormously long and unfalteringly rich in its delineation of the sometimes thorny connection between the public associations and private needs and loyalties of people who live energetically, and even recklessly, through times of political turbulence." Commonweal

The year of the French; a novel. Holt, Rinehart & Winston 1979 516p o.p.
LC 78-23539
This historical novel is based on actual events. The year is 1798, when a band of "Irishmen rise up in County Mayo against their English rulers. The French, secure in the success of their own revolution, decide to come to the aid of the Irish, less for the sake of an ideal than to harass the English. Three shiploads of troops, under the brilliant General Humbert, set sail from France. Their arrival in Kilcummin Bay is the signal for the war of liberation to begin. . . . But by fall, disappointed in their hope for more troops from France and confronted by vastly superior forces under Lord Cornwallis, the Irish

Flanagan, Thomas, 1923-—*Continued*

are doomed." Publisher's note

The author "writes well, taking care to approximate . . . the spoken and written language of the time. The result is, I'm convinced, not only a serious book, free of the irony and satire that informs so many of the more literary historical fictions written today, but a distinguished one as well." Newsweek

Flaubert, Gustave, 1821-1880

Madame Bovary; patterns of provincial life; translated from the French by Francis Steegmuller; with an introduction by Victor Brombert. Alfred A. Knopf 1993 xxxviii, 330p $17

ISBN 0-679-42031-2 LC 92-54294

Original French edition, 1857

A novel about the "life and fate of the Norman bourgeoise Emma Bovary. Unhappy in her marriage to a good-hearted but stupid village doctor, Emma finds her pathetic dreams of romantic love unfulfilled. A sentimental, discontented, and hopelessly limited person, she commits adultery, piles up enormous debts, and finally takes her own life in desperation. The novel's subject, the life of a very ordinary woman, and its technique, the amassing of precise detail, make Madame Bovary one of the crowning works in the development of the novel." Reader's Ency. 4th edition

Sentimental education; or, The history of a young man. Magee c1904 2v o.p.

Original French edition, 1869

"The background of this novel is the decline and fall of the Monarchy of Louis Philippe and the Revolution of 1848. . . . The hero, Frederic Moreau, has many of the traits of young Flaubert. Madame Arnous, with whom he falls in love, is very like Madame Schlesinger whom Flaubert had admired at Trouville as early as 1836. The subject of the novel is really the futility of existence." Haydn. Thesaurus of Book Dig

Fleming, Ian, 1908-1964

Casino Royale. Macmillan 1954 c1953 176p o.p.

"Against the background of a French resort the book describes Bond's destruction of the French branch of SMERSH, the Soviet espionage ring. The climax of the story is a tense game of baccarat in which Bond ruins the leader of the ring, Le Chiffre. The girl in the case is a compliant Soviet agent named Vesper Lynd, and there is much closely described violence." Wakeman. World Authors, 1950-1970

Doctor No. Macmillan 1958 256p o.p.

The setting is the Caribbean, where James Bond is trying to trace the disappearance of two agents who had trespassed on the isolated island kingdom of the Eurasian Dr. No. The maniacal doctor, equipped with two pairs of steel pincers for hands, dreams of world conquest and is stockpiling a deadly arsenal for that time. Bond, with female companion in tow, survives a manhunt through the island's mangrove swamps to foil the doctor's plans

From Russia, with love. Macmillan 1957 253p o.p.

James Bond, the British secret agent here meets the Soviet murder organization SMERSH once more. His execution has been ordered but Bond's counter activities seem successful—until the last page

Goldfinger. Macmillan 1959 318p o.p.

"James Bond, British Secret Service Agent 007, must retrieve British gold from a Mr. Auric Goldfinger whose ruthless obsession is suggesting in his goal—personal possession of half the supply of mined gold in the world." Publ Wkly

"All this is, in some measure, a great joke, but Fleming's passion for plausibility, his own naval intelligence background, and a kind of sincere Manicheism, allied to journalistic efficiency in the management of his récit, make his work rather impressive." Burgess. 99 Novels

The man with the golden gun. New Am. Lib. 1965 183p o.p.

This adventure "begins with a brainwashed Bond ready to do the bidding of the K.G.B. in headquarters of the Secret Service, and thrashes through to a climax in Jamaica where the adversary is Scaramonga, the most ruthless death-dealing instrument forged in the 20th century." Libr J

On Her Majesty's Secret Service. New Am. Lib. 1963 299p o.p.

James Bond, British secret agent 007, forsakes his bachelorhood for Countess Teresa di Vicenzo, who involves him in another adventure with Ernst Stavro Blofeld, head of an international crime syndicate and architect of an atomic blackmail scheme. The story is set against an Alpine background

You only live twice. New Am. Lib. 1964 240p o.p.

"Bond, near-prostrate from his bride's death, is given a Japanese assignment to snap him out of his torpor. . . . [The story] involves Bond's making up as a Japanese and venturing into the den of a foreign 'death collector,' a madman who has set up a poisonous garden complete with noxious plants, volcanic geysers, snakes, and, in a lake, piranha fish. Very grisly and chilling. The ending is an epitome of horror." Publ Wkly

Fleming, Julia Spencer- *See* Spencer-Fleming, Julia

Fleming, Oliver *See* MacDonald, Philip, 1899-1981

Fleming, Thomas J., 1927-

Dreams of glory; [by] Thomas Fleming. Forge 2000 301p $24.95

ISBN 0-312-87743-9 LC 00-31810

"A Tom Doherty Associates book"

"Set during the frigid, bone-creaking winter of January 1780, when the Revolutionary War had seemingly quieted down, this . . . tale is based on an actual British plot to kidnap George Washington. . . . At the heart of the novel is the elusive British spy Twenty-Six, whose activities touch all the other characters. Meanwhile, Fleming

Fleming, Thomas J., 1927-—*Continued*
gives us an almost tactile sense of that cold winter and the desperate living conditions of the American troops in contrast to the near luxury of the British." Libr J

The officers' wives; [by] Thomas Fleming. Doubleday 1981 645p o.p.
LC 80-1063
In this "tale of military life, the overlapping destinies of . . . six characters unfold. Adam and Honor Thayer, Pete and Joanna Burke and George and Amy Rosser. . . . Adam Thayer, who quickly sours on his beautiful but dim wife, establishes himself as a brilliant strategist, serves valorously in the Special Forces in Southeast Asia, but is eventually undone by his peers for his vehement opposition to the Army's inept conduct of the Vietnam War. George and Amy Rosser, model military politicians, scheme their way up through the ranks to become Mr. and Mrs. General, not even daring to wonder if the struggle was worth it. Pete Burke . . . endures the nightmares of combat in Vietnam only to be broken by the failure of his marriage." N Y Times Book Rev

"Sometimes cumbersome, but often passionate or reflective, Fleming's fictional account of the alterations in our attitude toward military service recapitulates the entire course of recent American history." Atlantic

Time and tide; {by} Thomas Fleming. Simon & Schuster 1987 734p o.p.
LC 87-9896
"Having left the Battle of Savo Island under suspicious circumstances in 1942, the USS *Jefferson City* is a ship haunted by bad joss. Arthur McKay is sent to relieve the cruiser's captain, Win Kemble, also his Annapolis roommate and best friend. Accused of cowardice under fire, the men of the *JC* fight a constant battle to prove their valor to themselves and the rest of the Navy." Libr J

"Fleming performs a masterful job of blending the private, political, and military concerns faced by this huge, disparate crew, which ranges from movie stars to Annapolis graduates." Booklist

When this cruel war is over; [by] Thomas Fleming. Forge 2001 301p $24.95
ISBN 0-312-87204-6 LC 00-48444
"A Tom Doherty Associates book"
"In the last year of the Civil War, headstrong southern belle Janet Todd secretly works to rally support for the Sons of Liberty, a revolutionary conspiracy aiming to turn the northwest Union states into a second Confederacy. Her chief recruiting prospect is the dashing Major Paul Stapleton, a battle-scarred Union officer who is disillusioned by the grisly tactics of his army." Booklist

"Appearances by such historical figures as John Wilkes Booth and Mary Surratt and reprints of actual letters between President Lincoln and Colonel Gentry foster suspense." Publ Wkly

Fletcher, Lucille, 1912-2000

Sorry, wrong number
In Alfred Hitchcock presents: Stories not for the nervous

Flying Officer X *See* Bates, H. E. (Herbert Ernest), 1905-1974

Foe, Daniel *See* Defoe, Daniel, 1661?-1731

Foer, Jonathan Safran, 1977-

Everything is illuminated; a novel. Houghton Mifflin 2002 276p il $24
ISBN 0-618-17387-0 LC 2001-51610
"There are two plots here. The first is the story of Jonathan Safran Foer, who travels to the Ukraine hoping to find Augustine, the woman who helped save his grandmother from the Nazis. Jonathan; his Ukranian translator, Alexi (who narrates much of the novel in a hilarious broken English); Alexi's grandfather; and the family dog, Sammy Davis Junior Junior, all grow to love Augustine on their mad and hopeless search for her. The second story follows the history of one family in Trachimbrod, the shtetl for which Alexi and Jonathan are searching." Booklist

"Foer deftly handles the intricate story-within-a-story plot, and the layers of suspense build as the shtetl hurtles toward the devastation of the 20th century while Alex and Jonathan and Grandfather close in on the object of their search. An impressive, original debut." Publ Wkly

Extremely loud and incredibly close. Houghton Mifflin 2005 326p $24.95
ISBN 0-618-32970-6
"Oskar Schell is an inventor, Francophile, tambourine player, Shakespearean actor, jeweler, pacifist. He is nine years old. And he is on an urgent, secret search through the five boroughs of New York to find the lock that fits a mysterious key belonging to his father, who died in the attacks on the World Trade Center." Publisher's note

The author's "depiction of Oskar's reaction to phone messages left by his father as he awaited rescue in the burning World Trade Center, his description of Oskar's grandfather's love affair . . . and his experiences during the bombing of Dresden—these passages underscore Mr. Foer's ability to evoke, with enormous compassion and psychological acuity, his characters' emotional experiences, and to show how these private moments intersect with the great public events of history." N Y Times (Late N Y Ed)

Foley, Martha, 1897-1977

(ed) 200 years of great American short stories. See 200 years of great American short stories

(ed) Best of the Best American short stories, 1915-1950. See Best of the Best American short stories, 1915-1950

Follett, Ken, 1949-

Code to zero. Dutton 2000 356p o.p.
ISBN 0-525-94563-6 LC 00-42688
"Cold War tale about skullduggery in the early days of the space race. Set in 1958 shortly after the Soviets beat the Americans into orbit, the story tracks the frantic movements of Dr. Claude Lucas, who wakes up one morning in Washington, D.C.'s Union Station, dressed as a bum. A victim of amnesia, he has no recollection that he is a key player in the upcoming launch of Explorer 1, the army's latest attempt to get a rocket into space. While Lucas slowly unravels the clues to his identity, the CIA follows its own agenda." Publ Wkly

Follett, Ken, 1949-—*Continued*

A dangerous fortune. Delacorte Press 1993 533p o.p.

LC 93-21912

"In 1866, tragedy strikes at the exclusive Windfield School. A young student drowns in a mysterious accident involving a small circle of boys. Among them are scrappy Hugh Pilaster; his older cousin Edward, the weak, dissolute heir to the Pilaster banking fortune; and Micky Miranda, the darkly handsome son of a brutal South American landowner. The drowning and its aftermath initiate a spiraling circle of treachery that will span three decades and entwine many lives." Publisher's note

This novel contains "an authentic sense of history, a wonderfully complex and fascinating plot, mesmerizing characters, and a thoroughly entertaining story." Booklist

Eye of the needle; a novel. Arbor House 1978 313p o.p.

LC 77-90670

"It is 1944 and the Allies are preparing to invade France. Part of the preparations call for a vast deception that will draw the bulk of the German defending forces to the Calais area while the Allies go in at Normandy. Only one of the enemy smells out the fakery, a German spy called Die Nadel (for the stiletto which is his favorite murder weapon). Called variously Faber or Baker, the only spy Hitler trusts, he must get his information back to the homeland. The race by British Intelligence to thwart Die Nadel provides the story drive of the book." Best Sellers

"An absolutely terrific thriller, so pulse-pounding, so ingenious in its plotting, and so frighteningly realistic that you simply cannot stop reading, this World War II espionage tale is right up there with the best of them." Publ Wkly

The hammer of Eden; a novel. Crown 1998 404p o.p.

ISBN 0-609-60308-6 LC 98-26882

This thriller "concerns a secret California hippie commune whose existence is threatened when the state opts to build a power plant on the site. Priest, the commune's charismatic leader, vows to stay put no matter what. He figures the threat of a major earthquake is a perfect way to blackmail the state into abandoning the power-plant idea, and just in case he needs to deliver the goods, he thinks he knows how to produce a huge trembler that will bring the state to its knees. . . . Pitted against Priest is FBI agent Judy Maddox, who's hot to solve the case and convince her superiors she's ready for a major promotion. . . . Taut plotting, tense action, skillful writing, and myriad unexpected twists make this one utterly unputdownable." Booklist

Hornet flight. Dutton 2002 420p $26.95

ISBN 0-525-94689-6 LC 2002-37903

"Tale of amateur spies pursued by Nazi collaborators in occupied Denmark in 1941. Harald Olufsen is an 18-year-old physics student who stumbles into espionage when he accidentally discovers a secret German radar installation on the island where he lives. . . . Follett starts out fast and keeps up the pace, revealing how ordinary people who want to do the right thing are undone by their own enthusiasm and inexperience. He also paints a vivid and convincing picture of life in occupied Denmark, of easy collaboration with the Nazis and of the insidious, creeping persecution of the Jews. Publ Wkly

Jackdaws. Dutton 2001 451p o.p.

ISBN 0-525-94628-4 LC 2001-37087

This thriller is about a mission "to take out a German telephone exchange near Reims in the last few hours before D-Day. A full-frontal assault led by British SOE (Special Operations Executives) Felicity 'Flick' Clariet and her husband, a French Resistance leader, has failed, leaving the Allies with only a last-minute desperation plan: a team of six women, posing as a cleaning detail, will infiltrate the exchange and dismantle it. . . . The assembled team includes two lesbians, a German transvestite, and a gypsy. All of this may sound like cliched melodrama, but when Follett starts the clock and slips the narrative gearshift into synchromesh, one's literary misgivings are abandoned in the wake of the plot's forward thrust." Booklist

The key to Rebecca. Morrow 1980 381p o.p.

LC 80-16760

The story "opens in 1942, when Rommel successfully places a German spy in British-held Cairo. Alexander Wolff, a German of Egyptian nationality, infiltrates Egypt with great difficulty, only to attract the unwelcome attention of British Intelligence by knifing an Assyut corporal who threatens his cover. . . . [Wolff] eludes pursuer Major William Vandam [and] gains access to battle plans crucial to the defense of Tobruk and Mersa Matruh. . . . Using the call sign Sphinx, he transmits messages coded from a copy of DuMaurier's Rebecca while hidden on the houseboat of a locally famous . . . belly dancer." Libr J

The author "is no literary stylist, but his clean, purposeful prose is more than adequate to the demands of his tightly plotted, fast moving story. More to the point, he knows his people and his territory; his evocation of wartime Cairo is a marvel of concise atmospherics." Newsweek

Lie down with lions. Morrow 1986 333p o.p.

LC 85-25876

This novel is set in "Afghanistan, where the farmers and nomads are battling their Russian invaders. Jean-Pierre, a doctor fresh from residency, has volunteered two years to tend the wounded and offer general medical aid in the Valley of Five Lions; his real motive, however, is to spy on the rebels for the 'KGB'. Jane, his newly pregnant wife, serves as his nurse and his contact with the women of the villages. When local caravans bringing munitions are repeatedly attacked and the men killed, Ellis Thaler, a 'CIA' expert in explosives, arrives to consolidate the rebel's efforts, that he and Jane had been lovers complicates the situation. Separately they deduce Jean-Pierre's treachery. . . . This is fine adventure filled with passion, violence, and tension." Best Sellers

The man from St. Petersburg. Morrow 1982 323p o.p.

LC 81-22550

"Lydia, born a Russian noblewoman, now married happily into the English aristocracy, has carried with her for years the secret that daughter Charlotte was really sired by an anarchist-murderer lover, not by the man she believes to be her father. When that lover, whose freedom from prison and torture Lydia purchased by her 'safe' marriage, turns up in London, his mission to assassinate a visiting Russian prince, the past rises up to torment Lydia and all hell breaks loose. It doesn't take long for

Follett, Ken, 1949—*Continued*

nihilist Feliks to figure out that Charlotte is really his child and he sets out to make her acquaintance both to use her as an unwitting accomplice, and because he discovers he is capable of true, unselfish paternal love." Publ Wkly

This "novel beautifully reconstructs the era of pre-World War I London." Libr J

Night over water. Morrow 1991 400p o.p.
LC 91-17701

In this World War II-era thriller "the primary action takes place aboard a transatlantic flight of the Pan American Clipper bound for New York. The cast of characters who board the sumptuous seaplane in Southhampton includes an aristocratic Nazi sympathizer and his family, a renowned Jewish physicist, an American film star, an affable jewel thief, a bored housewife and her lover, and a Russian princess. The celebrated wayfarers are blissfully unaware that Eddie Deakin, the all-American aviation engineer, is being forced to sabotage the flight in order to necessitate a dangerous crash landing off the coast of Maine." Booklist

"Details of early aviation firmly establish the cast in their era and a tantalizing mosaic of subplots whisks the reader through a whirlwind of romance and intrigue." Publ Wkly

Paper money. Morrow 1987 c1977 216p o.p.
LC 87-7867

First published 1977 in the United Kingdom under the pseudonym Zachary Stone

"The novel's action takes place in a single day and involves gangsters, financiers, politicians, and journalists deliberately or unwillingly immersed in an oil scam, a monumental robbery, and a sex scandal." Booklist

"Though painted in broad brush-strokes, the characters seem compellingly real, as do their professional environments." Publ Wkly

Pillars of the earth. Morrow 1989 973p o.p.
LC 89-9405

This novel "chronicles the vicissitudes of a prior, his master builder, and their community as they struggle to build a cathedral and protect themselves during the tumultuous 12th century, when the empress Maud and Stephen are fighting for the crown of England after the death of Henry I." Libr J

"Follett has skillfully crafted an extraordinary epic buttressed by a succession of suspenseful subplots. A towering triumph of romance, rivalry, and spectacle from a major talent." Booklist

A place called freedom. Crown 1995 407p o.p.
ISBN 0-517-70176-6 LC 95-8404

In this novel, which begins in the coal-mining region of 18th-century Scotland, the author "evokes the grim, hard life of the miners, one of whom defies the brutal authority of the owner and is forced to flee. Mack ends up in London, but more defiance causes him to be deported to the American Colonies. Characters, whom he seems to find no matter where he goes, are Jay Jamisson, the weak-willed and bitter younger son of Sir George Jamisson, owner of the Scottish mines, and Lizzie, Jay's spunky, soft-hearted wife, who soon realizes what a horrid man she has married." Libr J

"If the dialogue sometimes seems lifted from a bodice-ripper, and if far-fetched coincidences keep flinging Lizzie and Mack together, these flaws are redeemed by Follett's vigorous narrative drive and keen eye for character." Publ Wkly

Triple; a novel. Arbor House 1979 377p o.p.
LC 78-73869

"The Egyptians are making nuclear weapons and the Israelis, in order to do the same, are obliged to steal 100 tons of uranium. A group of old acquaintances at Oxford in 1947 come together again in different roles: the Mossad agent who organizes the theft, the disgruntled Palestinian spying for Egypt, the Russian bureaucrat (actually a KGB colonel), and the American become a Mafia don. The hijacking plot is elaborate beyond description." Libr J

Folsom, Allan R.

The day after tomorrow; a novel; by Allan Folsom. Little, Brown 1994 596p o.p.
LC 93-30344

"A young American doctor haunted by his father's murder stumbles into a chilling international conspiracy and crosses paths with, among others, a weary L.A. cop investigating a series of surgically precise decapitations, a naive physical therapist and a hypercompetent German assassin." Publ Wkly

"In this ambitious and impressive first novel, Folsom covers vast amounts of territory at breakneck speed. . . . That Folsom manages to instill some genuine tension amidst all this is testimony to his skill." Libr J

Day of confession; a novel; [by] Allan Folsom. Little, Brown 1998 566p $35
ISBN 0-316-28755-5 LC 98-5470

"Four days after Cardinal Rosario Parma is assassinated in Rome, hotshot L.A. entertainment lawyer Harry Addison gets a frantic phone message from his estranged brother, Danny, a Vatican priest. Shortly thereafter, Harry hears that Danny has died in a bus explosion. When he flies to Rome to claim the body, he discovers that Danny is the prime suspect in Parma's murder-and that he's still alive. The novel then follows two parallel plots. Harry tries to find Danny and clear his name; meanwhile, the sinister Cardinal Umberto Palestrina, who thinks he's the reincarnation of Alexander the Great, plots to make China the site of a new Holy Roman Empire." Publ Wkly

Ford, Elbur, 1906-1993

For works written by this author under other names see Carr, Philippa, 1906-1993; Holt, Victoria, 1906-1993; Plaidy, Jean, 1906-1993

Ford, Ford Madox, 1873-1939

The good soldier; a tale of passion. Knopf 1991 (Everyman's library, 20) $24
ISBN 0-679-40665-4 LC 91-52977

First published 1915 in the United Kingdom

This novel "consists of the first-person narration of American John Dowell (an archetypally unreliable narrator), who relates the history of relationships that begin in 1904, when his wife Florence meet Edward and Leonora Ashburnham in a hotel in Nauheim. The two couples form a foursome, and meet regularly. In August 1913 the

Ford, Ford Madox, 1873-1939—*Continued*
Ashburnhams take their young ward Nancy Rufford to Nauheim with them, and Florence commits suicide. Later that year the Ashburnhams send Nancy to India (where she goes mad) and Edward also commits suicide. Dowell becomes Nancy's 'male sick nurse'; Leonora remarries. The substance of the novel lies in Dowell's growing understanding of the intrigues that lay behind the orderly Edwardian façade both couples had presented to the world." Oxford Companion to Engl Lit. 6th edition

The last post
In Ford, F. M. Parade's end

A man could stand up
In Ford, F. M. Parade's end

No more parades
In Ford, F. M. Parade's end

Parade's end. Knopf 1992 906p $22
ISBN 0-679-41728-1 LC 92-52922
"Everyman's library"
A reissue of the title first published 1950; A one volume edition of the author's tetralogy that includes: Some do not (1924); No more parades (1925); A man could stand up (1926); and The last post (1928)
This series of novels "describes the adventures in love and war of Christopher Tietjens, an old-fashioned gentleman of the English governing class. Ford draws a brilliant picture of the social changes brought about by the First World War. Before the war, Tietjens is nobly faithful to his impossible wife. But trench warfare seems to him a symbol of the disintegration of his whole society. He has a mental breakdown, goes to live with a woman he loves, and gives up his position, wealth, and historic family ties." Reader's Ency. 4th edition

Some do not
In Ford, F. M. Parade's end

Ford, Richard, 1944-

Independence Day. Knopf 1995 451p o.p.
LC 95-3126
This novel "picks up the story of Frank Bascombe where it left off in a previous novel, *The Sportswriter* (1986). The time is now the late 1980s, and Frank, divorced, is no longer sportswriting but selling real estate. Within the time span of preparing and participating in a Fourth of July weekend, Frank tells us in . . . detail about the Sisyphean boulders he has been forced to push uphill throughout his life: career, kids, ex-wife, current girlfriend, and the unpleasant people occupying his rental property. Frank's plan is to take his teenage son on the road over the Fourth to visit sports halls of fame, but, more significantly, to try to get the troubled youth somewhat straightened out." Booklist
One is "constantly struck by the rich, dense mixture of Ford's narrative. No one writes better—and with more inventive brio—about the bland wasteland of US suburbia; that shopping-malled, subdivisioned terrain that has rapidly become the true defining landscape of late 20th-century America." New Statesman (1913)

A multitude of sins; stories. Knopf 2002 286p o.p.
ISBN 0-375-41212-3 LC 2001-38402
Contents: Privacy; Quality time; Calling; Reunion; Puppy; Crèche; Under the radar; Dominion; Charity; Abyss
"Tracing the blueprint of human interaction in this latest collection . . . Ford signals the master text of lust standing behind the multitude of small sins he so tersely and poignantly chronicles. To err is human, and, in Ford's worldview, little is so human as the act of cheating on a wife or husband." Publ Wkly

Women with men; three long stories. Knopf 1997 255p o.p.
LC 97-5832
Contents: The womanizer; Jealous; Occidentals
In these "three powerful long stories, the author explores precarious and complicated relationships between men and women. Each tale revolves around the fractured emotions aroused by the dissolution of a marriage: feelings of failure and the dizzying sense of spinning unsteadily and off course through life, like a wheel without an axle. . . . All of Ford's magnetic characters seem permanently jet-lagged, woozy with displacement and disappointment, and their troubles escalate accordingly, with surreal and sickening inevitability." Booklist

Ford, Robert

The student conductor. Putnam 2003 289p $24.95
ISBN 0-399-15037-4 LC 2003-46514
"Eight years after dropping out of Juilliard, 30-year-old Cooper Barrow makes a bid to restart his career, going to work with Karlheinz Ziegler, a legendary conductor from prewar days who now teaches at a provincial music school. A strongly antagonistic relationship develops between them, exacerbated by Barrow's continuing anxiety, Ziegler's brusquely authoritarian manner and the young American's romantic interest in Petra Vogel, a young oboist in the student orchestra, a refugee from East Germany." Publ Wkly
"This is finally a novel about power—the power of a great conductor driving a well-trained orchestra, the power of the past to enslave us, the power of the future to free us, and the power of the individual to love and to forgive. There is hardly a wrong note, from the moment Ford lifts his baton to the final refrain." Booklist

Forester, C. S. (Cecil Scott), 1899-1966

Admiral Hornblower in the West Indies. Little, Brown 1958 329p o.p.
A collection of Horatio Hornblower's adventures set in the West Indies. "The first belongs chronologically with 'Lieutenant Hornblower.' The rest are set nearly 15 years later when, as rear admiral in command of His Majesty's fleet in the West Indies, he faces a new Bonapartist uprising, suppresses the slave trade, stamps out piracy, and maintains British diplomacy during the South American revolutions." Booklist
"Recounted with taste, with psychological insight, and with a sure sense of story. This is top grade adventure fiction." N Y Her Trib Books

The African Queen. Little, Brown 1935 275p o.p.
ISBN 0-89244-065-1

Forester, C. S. (Cecil Scott), 1899-1966—*Continued*

"At her brother's death Rose Sayer is left alone in an isolated African mission. She is determined to fight against the Germans, who have taken her brother's black converts into custody. She joins forces with a Cockney, Alnutt, and they take a long and dangerous trip downriver in Alnutt's dilapidated launch in order to reach the German boat they intend to blow up. The journey points up the differences between this ill-matched pair, and their bravery as well." Shapiro. Fic for Youth. 3d edition

Beat to quarters. Little, Brown 1937 324p o.p.

A sea story of the British navy in the early nineteenth century. Essentially it is a portrait of a man, captain of an English frigate. Hornblower, son of a country doctor, is a man uncertain of his own powers, of his technical skill and of the admiration of his men, yet when he is sent under sealed orders to the Pacific coast of Central America, he accomplishes his mission brilliantly, and fights two successful battles with the same Spanish warship

"There is plenty of action. But there is also an unusual character study." N Y Times Book Rev

Followed by Ship of the line

Commodore Hornblower. Little, Brown 1945 384p o.p.

"Hornblower returns to sea in command of a squadron on a delicate mission to the Baltic, reluctantly taking leave of his lovely wife Lady Barbara. In this expedition he combines brilliant naval strategy with diplomatic cunning to out-maneuver his old, unseen enemy Napoleon." Ont Libr Rev

"It is a spirited piece of work, and full of interesting detail where matters naval, military, and diplomatic in that year of decision are concerned." Times Lit Suppl

Followed by Lord Hornblower

Flying colours. Little, Brown 1939 294p o.p.

Third book in a series which began with Beat to quarters and Ship of the line. Captain Hornblower, his crippled first mate, Bush, and his servant, Brown, escape from their escort on the way to Paris to be tried for piracy. The story is of their recapture of an English vessel and return to England, where they are covered with honors

Followed by Commodore Hornblower

Hornblower and the Atropos. Little, Brown 1953 325p o.p.

This is a series of episodes in the early life of the Captain; a journey across England from Gloucester to London by canal; his part in the funeral of Nelson; and his battles on the coast of Turkey, where he recovers a huge treasure from a sunken English ship

Hornblower and the Hotspur. Little, Brown 1962 344p o.p.

ISBN 0-316-28899-3

"From the standpoint of sequence, this . . . title in the Hornblower saga follows 'Lieutenant Hornblower.'" Wis Libr Bull

"The story opens just before Horatio sails on a cruise in his first command. His rank is Commander; his ship something less than a frigate but something more than a sloop; his task to act as the eyes of the Channel Fleet which is to be in position to blockade Brest upon the imminent declaration of hostilities with France. In the course of action Hornblower is detained at sea for almost two years as, in his own inimitable and logically necessary style, he helps cripple the Napoleonic effort to invade England, the last block to conquest of Europe." Best Sellers

Hornblower during the crisis, and two stories: Hornblower's temptation and The last encounter. Little, Brown 1967 174p o.p.

ISBN 0-316-28915-9

"Posthumous novel fragment and two slender stories. The former concerns Hornblower's eventful voyage to London on another man's ship for reassignment on a spy mission to Spain. . . . In one story Mr. Hornblower is almost taken in by a seemingly harmless mission entrusted to him by a young Irishman before his shipboard execution. In the other tale a stranded traveler in distress, helped by Admiral Hornblower and wife, proves to be Napoleon Bonaparte." Booklist

"Because Forester died before completing this novel, the reader is left with a summary sketch and his own imagination for final details of the plot. For Forester devotees, this will not detract from the essential verve and dash of Hornblower's last chase." Christ Sci Monit

The last nine days of the Bismarck. Little, Brown 1959 138p o.p.

"Forester describes the pursuit and epic bombardment at sea in World War II when the German battleship 'Bismarck' broke into the Atlantic and sailed toward Brest with the whole British Home Fleet after her. Scenes on board the 'Bismarck' and the British ships have been given dialog to make the telling more vivid." Publ Wkly

Lieutenant Hornblower. Little, Brown 1952 306p o.p.

ISBN 0-316-28907-8

This novel details "Horatio's adventures as a Lieutenant until his promotion to Commander during the early years of the Napoleonic Wars." Best Sellers

The author "interprets the navy, certainly in its Napoleonic period, with the help of a character that represents the navy at its best and action that is grandly exciting without being melodramatic; helped, too, by a sense of order and a mastery of technique that puts his work on a high plane of artistry." Christ Sci Monit

Lord Hornblower. Little, Brown 1946 322p o.p.

ISBN 0-316-28908-6

In this "Hornblower novel Horatio continues his adventures and helps defeat Napoleon by aiding the heir to the Bourbon throne to enter France. Barbara goes to the Congress of Vienna to act as hostess for her brother while Horatio returns to France to visit old friends and renew an old love. When Napoleon escapes from Elba danger threatens Hornblower as he forms a guerrilla band in the south of France. But, saved by the defeat of the French at Waterloo, he returns to the arms of Barbara and new honors as Lord Hornblower." Booklist

Mr. Midshipman Hornblower. Little, Brown 1950 310p o.p.

ISBN 0-316-28909-4

Contents: Hornblower and the even chance; Hornblower and the cargo of rice; Hornblower and the penalty of failure; Hornblower and the man who felt queer; Hornblower and the man who saw God;

Forester, C. S. (Cecil Scott), 1899-1966—*Continued*

Hornblower, the frogs, and the lobsters; Hornblower and the Spanish galleys; Hornblower and the examination for lieutenant; Hornblower and Noah's Ark; Hornblower, the duchess, and the devil

Ship of the line. Little, Brown 1938 298p o.p.

In this sequel to Beat to quarters, Captain Hornblower is given command of the ship Sutherland and sent to join the forces blockading the Spanish coast in the war with Napoleon

Followed by Flying colours

To the Indies. Little, Brown 1940 298p o.p.

"The story of Narciso Rich who is lifted suddenly from his quiet life as a successful lawyer to join the swaggering, gold-hungry hidalgos who went with Columbus on his third voyage. He fights Indians at San Domingo, is kidnapped by renegades, shipwrecked off the coast of Cuba, and finally makes his way back to the settlement in time to return on the ship that carried Columbus in chains." Ont Libr Rev

Forester, Cecil Scott *See* Forester, C. S. (Cecil Scott), 1899-1966

Forrest, Katherine V., 1939-

Apparition alley; a Kate Delafield mystery. Berkley Prime Crime 1997 248p o.p.

LC 96-53688

"Wounded by 'friendly fire' during a burglary arrest gone awry, lesbian LAPD homicide detective Kate Delafield must undergo routine—but intrusive—psychological counseling before returning to duty. Meanwhile, officer Luke Taggart, a pariah among their colleagues, wants Kate to represent him at his disciplinary hearing. Luke believes that he has been set up by vindictive cops and that Kate's 'accident' could be part of the same conspiracy. Aptly described West Hollywood and L.A. settings, great counseling dialog, and subtle plot machinations underscore the author's talent." Libr J

Liberty Square; a Kate Delafield mystery. Berkley Prime Crime 1996 242p o.p.

ISBN 0-425-15467-X LC 95-46809

This mystery "featuring lesbian LAPD homicide detective Kate Delafield is also a moody meditation on the Vietnam War and the conflicted loyalties it engendered. For ex-marine Delafield begrudgingly attends a reunion with her military buddies from a quarter-century past, an event that not only stirs up troubled memories but also sets the scene for a grisly murder whose motives stem from the time when America's Southeast Asia involvement was bloodiest." Booklist

Sleeping bones. Berkley Prime Crime 1999 260p $21.95

ISBN 0-425-17029-2 LC 98-54294

This Kate Delafield "adventure takes her to the famous La Brea tar pits, where she breaks in new partner Joe on a bizarre case of murder. An excellent novel." Libr J

Forstchen, William R.

(jt. auth) Gingrich, N. Gettysburg

(jt. auth) Gingrich, N. Grant comes east

Forster, E. M. (Edward Morgan), 1879-1970

The collected tales of E. M. Forster. Knopf 1947 308p o.p.

The celestial omnibus: The story of a panic; The other side of the hedge; The celestial omnibus; Other kingdom; The curate's friend; The road from Colonus

The eternal moment: The machine stops; The point of it: Mr. Andrews; Co-ordination; The story of the siren; The eternal moment

Howards End. Knopf 1991 xxxiii, 359p $19

ISBN 0-679-40668-9 LC 91-52997

"Everyman's library"

First published 1910

This novel "deals with an English country house called Howards End and its influence on the lives of the materialistic Wilcoxes, the cultural and idealistic Schlegel sisters, and the poor bank clerk Leonard Bast. The Schlegels try to befriend Bast. Mr. Wilcox, whom Margaret Schlegel later marries, gives him financial advice which ruins him. Helen Schlegel becomes his mistress for a short time and bears his son; thereupon Charles Wilcox thrashes and accidentally kills him. The house passes from intuitive, half-mystical Mrs. Wilcox to her husband's second wife Margaret Schlegel, to Margaret's nephew, Leonard Bast's son. Illustrating Forster's motto 'Only connect,' the house brings together three important elements in English society: money and successful business in the Wilcoxes, culture in the Schlegels, and the lower classes in Leonard Bast." Reader's Ency. 4th edition

also in Forster, E. M. A room with a view and Howards End

Maurice. Norton 1971 256p o.p.

This novel was written between 1913 and 1914. It depicts the steps by which Maurice Hall, a shy, conventional young man, while a student at Cambridge, first discovers and then gradually comes to accept the fact that he is, by nature, sexually attracted to men, not women. "He enjoys a romantic friendship—idyllic, sentimental, chaste—with Clive, a fellow undergraduate at Cambridge. When Clive turns abruptly to women . . . the unhappy Maurice consults his family doctor and a hypnotist who fail to help him. On a visit to the now-married Clive's country estate he falls in love, physically this time, with a young gamekeeper to whom he commits his future on a brief acquaintance." Newsweek

"This posthumous novel with a homosexual theme would have been sensational had it been published when written in 1913. Appearing in the 1970's, it is not sensational, but it is an interesting novel—well written as all of E. M. Forster's works are. . . . It is filled with keen insight and sympathetic character analysis, valuable for an understanding of the author and his works." Choice

A passage to India; with an introduction by P.N. Furbank. Knopf 1991 xxxix, 293p $18

ISBN 0-679-40549-6

"Everyman's library"

First published 1924

"Politics and mysticism are potent forces in India just after World War I. Ronald Heaslop, magistrate of Chandrapore, has asked his mother, Mrs. Moore, to visit him along with his fiancee, Adela Quested. To add to their knowledge of the real India, Dr. Aziz, a young

Forster, E. M. (Edward Morgan), 1879-1970— *Continued*

Moslem doctor, offers to take them to the Marabar Caves outside the city. The visit is a shattering experience. Mrs. Moore is struck by the thought that all her ideas about life are no more than the hollow echo she hears in the cave. Adela, entering another cave alone, emerges in a panic and accuses Dr. Aziz of having attacked her in the gloom of the cave. The trial that results from her accusation divides the groups in the city so acutely that a reconciliation appears impossible." Shapiro. Fic for Youth. 3d edition

A depiction of the "clash between East and West, and of the prejudices and misunderstandings that foredoomed goodwill. Criticized at first for being anti-British and possibly inaccurate bias, it has been praised as a superb character study of the people of one race by a writer of another." Oxford Companion to Engl Lit

A room with a view. Putnam 1911 364p

First published 1908

The novel "is set mostly in Italy, a country which represents for the author the forces of true passion. The heroine, upper-class Lucy Honeychurch, is visiting Italy with a friend. When she regrets that her hotel room has no view, lower-class Mr. Emerson offers the friends his own room and that of his son. Lucy becomes caught between the world of the Emersons and that of Cecil Vyse, the shallow, conventional young man of her own class to whom she becomes engaged on her return to England. Finally, she overcomes her own prejudice and her family's opposition and marries George Emerson." Reader's Ency. 4th edition

also in Forster, E. M. A room with a view and Howards End

A room with a view and Howards End. Modern Lib. 1993 533p o.p.

ISBN 0-679-60069-8 LC 93-15340

A combined edition of two titles, both entered separately

Forster, Edward Morgan *See* Forster, E. M. (Edward Morgan), 1879-1970

Forsyth, Frederick, 1938-

Avenger. Thomas Dunne Bks. 2003 370p $24.95

ISBN 0-312-31951-7 LC 2003-53163

"World War II, Vietnam, Bosnia, and Cambodia take turns commanding center stage, held together by two protagonists: a middle-age lawyer and an aging business tycoon, who have both suffered devastating losses. The tycoon's loss, that of his grandson on a relief mission in Bosnia, becomes subsumed in the mission of attorney Calvin Dexter, grieving father and former 'Nam tunnel rat, whose mission in life is to bring justice to those who have gotten away with murder. . . . Forsyth's extraordinary care with detail, his solid voice, and his exquisite pacing make this a totally engrossing thriller." Booklist

The day of the jackal. Viking 1971 380p o.p.

"Dissident OAS officers hire a mercenary, known by the code name 'Jackal', to assassinate General Charles deGaulle. The officers hope to cash in on the political chaos that would follow. The methodical, ingenious preparations of 'Jackal' are paralleled by the attempts of the combined French law-enforcement agencies to uncover and stop the plot. The suspense is acute." Shapiro. Fic for Youth. 3d edition

The deceiver. Bantam Bks. 1991 480p o.p.

LC 91-13114

This novel presents four linked tales, "each dealing with a different episode in the career of Sam McCready, the head of a department of the British Secret Intelligence Service that is known as Deception, Disinformation and Psychological Operations." Times Lit Suppl

The devil's alternative. Viking 1980 432p o.p.

LC 79-25929

This novel's plot "involves a Russian crop failure, Ukrainian terrorists who assassinate the head of the KGB to embarrass the Soviet premier, a fanatic faction in the Soviet hierarchy that wants to topple the premier and attack the U.S., a plane hijacking, a ship hijacking (and a threat to kill everyone on board and dump tons of crude oil into the sea), the CIA, and a British spy in Moscow. Basically, the good guys want to keep the levelheaded Soviet premier in power to avoid World War III. It's a lot to wade through, but Forsyth is one of the best in the genre and worth the trip." Booklist

The dogs of war. Viking 1974 408p o.p.

A "novel about the carefully planned overthrow of the small African state of Zangaro. Behind the coup is a British multimillionaire, seeking control of the mining rites to the platinum within Zangaro's Crystal Mountain. He hires top mercenary Cat Shannon to do most of the planning and to carry out the attack. The bulk of the novel is devoted to each of the detailed transactions of the 100-day operation, from purchasing and smuggling arms to arranging a multitude of clandestine business deals." Libr J

The fist of God. Bantam Bks. 1994 544p o.p.

LC 93-47150

"Hero Mike Martin is a British Special Forces agent sent to Kuwait after the Iraqi invasion to assess the situation and build a resistance movement. When the British discover the existence of Saddam Hussein's double agent, Jericho, who had been feeding information to Israel, Martin is smuggled into Baghdad to contact Jericho and learn about Saddam's battle plans. What Martin finds out is that Saddam has a doomsday weapon he is planning to use against the Coalition Allies when they launch Operation Desert Storm." Publ Wkly

The author's "formula, consisting of well-researched backgrounds, technical detail and a dispassionate reportorial approach to fiction, almost always works well, and this book is no exception. There is general excitement without hysteria and plenty of credible action." N Y Times Book Rev

The fourth protocol. Viking 1984 389p o.p.

LC 83-40646

"The narrative reveals a Soviet plan to control England and destroy NATO by swaying the popular vote in England's election: the Russian's best undercover man will detonate a small nuclear device near an American base in Britain, thereby ensuring a wave of antinuclear sentiment." Libr J

Forsyth, Frederick, 1938-—*Continued*

This novel "succeeds magnificently on at least two . . . levels: as a scrupulously detailed study of spy 'tradecraft' and as a testament to the virtues of a well-constructed plot. We want to know what happens in this book not only because of the inherently dramatic situation, but also because we anticipate the sense of resolution that comes when the puzzle's last piece clicks securely into place." Booklist

The Odessa file. Viking 1972 337p o.p.

"Young German reporter Peter Miller comes upon the diary of a survivor of a World War II extermination camp at Riga. Its revelations lead him into the deadly pursuit of commandant Roschmann, known as the Butcher of Riga. Roschmann is engaged in an international scheme to destroy the Jewish state. The plan is promoted by the Odessa, a secret organization that protects the identities and fortunes of former SS members. Miller infiltrates the organization to find and expose Roschmann." Shapiro. Fic for Youth. 3d edition

"Forsyth skillfully blends fact and fiction into a suspenseful and detailed story which is often downright chilling in its credibility." Libr J

The veteran. St. Martin's Press 2001 367p o.p.
ISBN 0-312-28691-0

Contents: This collection contains the novella The whispering wind and the following short stories: The veteran; The art of the Matter; The miracle; The citizen

Whispering wind, set during the Indian wars in 1876, focuses on a frontier scout who survived the massacre at the Little Bighorn

These stories "showcase the author's ability to capture character and generate suspense in remarkably few words." Booklist

The whispering wind
In Forsyth, F. The veteran

Foster, Alan Dean, 1946-

Dinotopia lost. Turner Pub. (Atlanta) 1996 318p o.p.
LC 95-41352

"The plot revolves around a band of pirates whose ship miraculously survives the reefs around Dinotopia and who set out to turn what they find there to profit. Will Denison, the nineteenth-century discoverer of the symbiotic human-saurian society, is dragged into taking a leading part in defeating the pirates, most of whom are converted to the Dinotopian way of life. . . . Although the saurian characters are better limned than the human ones, Foster's addition to Dinotopiana will agreeably reward the fantastic place's many fans." Booklist

Kingdoms of light. Warner Bks. 2001 372p $24.95
ISBN 0-446-52667-3 LC 00-43501

"The fearsome sorcerer Khaxan Mundurucu has laid waste to the Gowdlands. While a host of goblins terrorize the land, leaching it of all color and destroying the will of the conquered populace, a dying wizard's final spell transforms his pets into a company of human heroes who possess the only chance of restoring hope and freedom to their world." Libr J

"Foster's brand of storytelling, lighthearted even at the darkest moments, doesn't leave much room for doubt about how it's all going to turn out. Fans of swift-moving plots and imaginative settings will overlook the thin characters and enjoy this pleasant fantasy tale." Publ Wkly

Mid-Flinx. Ballantine Bks. 1995 331p o.p.
LC 95-31803

"A Del Rey book"

Previous titles in the author's series featuring Philip Lynx published in paperback

The product of illegal genetic experiments, Philip Lynx—Flinx for short—is 20 in this adventure, "and his empathic abilities and poison-spitting pet snake, Pip, continue to land him in trouble. Touring the planet Samstead, Flinx crosses paths with a bullying aristocrat who insists on acquiring Pip for his menagerie. Using his own precocious wits as well as Pip's deadly fighting prowess, Flinx narrowly escapes to the safety of his orbiting spaceship and flees into uncharted space." Booklist

The mocking program. Warner Bks. 2002 279p o.p.
ISBN 0-446-52774-2 LC 2002-22851

"Angel Cardenas of the Namerican States Federales is a police inspector whose beat is the Strip, a megalopolis that encompasses Mexico and part of what used to be the United States. A routine investigation of what appears to be a mugging death soon leads to something unlike anything Cardenas has ever encountered." Libr J

"Like Anthony Burgess' *A Clockwork Orange,* this novel comes with a glossary to help readers translate the characters' slang (a combination of English and Spanish, mostly). Peppered with clever new technology and off-beat characters, the book successfully crosses genres and will appeal to both mystery and sf fans." Booklist

Phylogenesis. Ballantine Bks. 1999 327p o.p.
ISBN 0-345-41862-X LC 98-30777

"A Del Rey book"

"The insectoid race known as Thranx seeks to establish cordial relations with humankind through a careful process of gradual integration. An accidental meeting between a renegade Thranx poet and a human criminal, however, throws the best-laid plans into confusion." Libr J

A triumph of souls. Warner Bks. 2000 406p $24.95
ISBN 0-446-52218-X LC 99-41376

Concluding volume in the author's Journeys of the Catechist trilogy; previous titles Carnivores of light and darkness (1998) and Into the thinking kingdoms (1999)

"Bound by his promise to a dying stranger, the good-hearted herdsman and unlikely hero Etjole Ehomba continues his journey through strange and treacherous lands filled with odd creatures and marvelous sights." Libr J

"Set in a magical world with prehistoric overtones, the novel offers more wit and wandering than plot, but the inventive situations are engaging and the characters far more complex than they first appear. The ending is clever and will satisfy those who have made the fantastic trek through Foster's whimsical world." Publ Wkly

Fowler, Connie May, 1958-

Before women had wings. Putnam 1996 271p o.p.
ISBN 0-399-14129-4 LC 95-52431

Fowler, Connie May, 1958—*Continued*

"Avocet Jackson, called Bird, lives with her parents, Billy and Glory Marie, and her older sister, Phoebe, in a roach-infested Florida shack. When Billy, a frustrated country music singer who has squandered his talent in booze, commits suicide, a desperate Glory Marie takes the girls to the outskirts of Tampa, where they move into a dilapidated trailer. Terrorized by her mother's alcohol-fueled rages, Bird is further confused by the fire-and-brimstone strictures of the Bible, which she takes literally. . . . Fowler sweeps the narrative along with plangent, lyrical prose." Publ Wkly

Remembering Blue. Doubleday 2000 290p o.p.
ISBN 0-385-49842-X LC 99-22593

"After Mattie Blue's husband, a fisherman named Nick, disappears off Florida's Gulf Coast, the pregnant widow decides to tell the story of his life and of their love. . . . When Nick and Mattie meet, Nick has abandoned fishing and fled his native island, Lethe, in an attempt to avoid an untimely death. But predictably, he can't stay away; with Mattie, he returns to Lethe." N Y Times Book Rev

"There is true suspense in this seductively lyrical, mythlike drama. . . . [The author's] language is full of grace, and the beauty she conjures is a balm." Booklist

Fowler, Karen Joy

The Jane Austen book club; Karen Joy Fowler. Putnam 2004 288p $23.95
ISBN 0-399-15161-3 LC 2003-47244

This novel is "essentially a character study of six people who meet regularly over several months to discuss six of Austen's works. Jocelyn, in her 50s and never married, is the originator of the club, a control freak who handpicked all the members; Sylvia, her good friend, is in a funk because her husband of 32 years has just left her for another woman; Sylvia's daughter, Allegra, is an attractive 30-year-old lesbian who recently broke up with her lover; Prudie is a twentysomething high school French teacher; the much-married Bernadette, 67, is now single; and Grigg, in his 40s, would love to get married." Libr J

"In her portrait of a California reading group, Karen Joy Fowler turns a mirror on the gawking, voyeuristic presence that lurks in every story: the reader. What results is Fowler's shrewdest, funniest fiction yet, a novel about how we engage with a novel." N Y Times Book Rev

Sarah Canary. Holt & Co. 1991 290p o.p.
ISBN 0-8050-1753-4 LC 91-9746

"Chin Ah Kin is the reluctant hero of this search across Washington Territory for Sarah Canary. The year is 1873, one that holds promise for the emancipation of women, yet things couldn't be worse for Sarah. Chin first encounters her when she suddenly appears on the periphery of his camp. Because Sarah only speaks nonsense, Chin decides she is crazy and sets off with her to an asylum in Stellacoom. But because of her inability to communicate, Sarah soon becomes separated from Chin. Without her to justify his presence in the wilderness, Chin becomes the scapegoat for all the evil deeds around him." Libr J

"This novel is similar in scope to E. L. Doctorow's 'Ragtime,' and yet Ms. Fowler's book is as much a dreamscape as a panorama. Each of her 19 chapters has a contemporaneous and often cryptic epigraph from Emily Dickinson's poetry that, amazingly, seems to dictate the narrative that follows." N Y Times Book Rev

Sister Noon; a novel. Putnam 2001 321p $24.95
ISBN 0-399-14750-0 LC 00-46025

"A Marian Wood book"

"In Gilded Age-era San Francisco, fortyish spinster Lizzie Hayes is by any measure a good woman. She busies herself with worthy, conservative projects, especially her role as volunteer treasurer and fund-raiser for the Ladies' Relief and Protection Society Home. She does what is expected when it is expected. None in her circle suspects that a risk-taking spirit hides just beneath the surface. But when Lizzie crosses paths with the influential—and notorious—Mrs. Mary Ellen 'Mammy' Pleasant, opportunities for intrigue, passion, and subversion abound, and Lizzie plunges in with enthusiasm. This witty novel is a deft blend of historical fact, urban myth, social satire, and romance." Libr J

Fowles, John, 1926-2005

The collector. Little, Brown 1963 305p o.p.

"Frederick Clegg, a collector of butterflies, becomes obsessed with the idea of capturing a young, attractive art student, as he does insects. He finds the perfect, isolated spot for this adventure, and there ensues a tale of horror and suspense. It is told first by Frederick and then by Miranda, as she struggles valiantly, with intelligence and determination, for her freedom, to no avail." Shapiro. Fic for Youth. 3d edition

"Mr. Fowles is a powerful writer; this story has a nightmarish reality and immediacy. Both Miranda and Clegg are completely developed characters; the book is at once horrifying and fascinating." Best Sellers

Daniel Martin. Little, Brown 1977 629p o.p.

"Daniel Martin is a middle-aged Englishman, a successful playwright turned screenwriter, who is summoned from Hollywood to Oxford by the imminent death of a long-estranged friend, a Catholic philosopher named Anthony. In their student days, Dan and Anthony had been best friends and had married sisters. . . . [Dan's] marriage had collapsed in bitterness, and with it had gone Dan's friendship with Anthony and Jane. Now, in the unfailingly polite crucible of Anthony's death and a subsequent therapeutic trip up the Nile with his widow, Dan discovers the truth of something he had suspected ever since Jane crept up to his room that once so long ago at Oxford. He had married the wrong sister; Jane had knowingly married the wrong man." Newsweek

"In Fowles' hands [Martin's] pilgrimage becomes thoroughly absorbing, intellectually challenging—and not at all the snappy read his admirers have come to expect." Time

The French lieutenant's woman. Little, Brown 1969 467p o.p.

"The setting is Victorian England. The hero is Charles, respectable, well-to-do, thoughtful, progressive. He is engaged to Ernestina, a rich, attractive, but highly conventional girl, but he falls in love with the beautiful, tragic, mysterious Sarah who is known to Lyme Regis (where the action begins) as 'the French lieutenant's woman' because of some disreputable but romantic episode in her

Fowles, John, 1926-2005—*Continued*

past life. The situation, that of the amorous triangle, is familiar in fiction. What makes this book highly original is that it has three possible endings, all different. . . . We have here a highly readable and informative book, compelling, thrilling, erotic, but we are not permitted to relax as if we were reading Dickens or Thackeray. A very modern mind is manipulating us as well as the characters." Burgess. 99 Novels

A maggot. Little, Brown 1985 455p o.p.
LC 85-15937

This novel opens on "the final afternoon—the eve of May Day 1736—of a furtive four-day journey by five people on horseback to a small town in the English countryside, where they take lodging for the night. The party consists of a lord in disguise, his servant who cannot speak or hear, a professional actor hired to protect the disguise, a Welshman for a bodyguard and Rebecca the harlot, also hired but for purposes not yet revealed. . . . A few days after, Dick, the servant, is found hanged in a wood, the lord is missing, and the hirelings have also melted away, later to be tracked down by the agents of one Henry Ayscough, a barrister who investigates the case on behalf of the lord's estranged father. The rest of the book records the testimony of witnesses questioned by Ayscough." N Y Times Book Rev

The magus; a revised version; with a foreword by the author. Little, Brown 1978 c1977 656p o.p.
LC 77-17343

Originally published 1966; this version first published 1977 in the United Kingdom

"This novel follows the harrowing misadventures of Nicholas Urfe, a young British schoolmaster who takes a teaching post on a remote Greek island, Phraxos, where he is drawn into an emotional maelstrom of high intrigue." Newsweek

"With the narrative skill and literary sleight of hand . . . Fowles again provides hours of engrossing entertainment for an audience susceptible to a massive blend of sensuous realism, suspenseful romanticism, hypertheatrical mystification, psychic intervention, and a gallery of unusual or exotic characters in the vivid setting of the golden, craggy, threatening beauty of an isolated Greek island." Booklist

Fox, Paula

A servant's tale. North Point Press 1984 321p o.p.
LC 84-060679

"The narrator and heroine of this novel, Luisa de la Cueva, is the illegitimate daughter of a landowner's disinherited son and a servant girl on the fictional Caribbean island of San Pedro. Though her equivocal status bars her from fully entering into any social caste, she loves her homeland, and her father's sudden decision to uproot the family out of fear of an impending revolution is a wrenching blow. Settled in the barrio of Manhattan's Upper West Side, they find no happiness: Luisa's father cannot hold a job, her mother dies of cancer, and she herself is quickly locked into a pattern of defeatism that leads her to drop out of school, despite her lively intelligence, and hire out as a maidservant." Booklist

The author's "precision and grace in describing such things as Luisa's sudden longing to see her mother after the latter's death, the odd loneliness of a spring day and the eccentricities of Luisa's employers are breathtaking; the lives she creates are sharp-edged yet sympathetic." Publ Wkly

Frame, Ronald

The lantern bearers; a novel. Counterpoint 2001 224p $24
ISBN 1-58243-155-8 LC 2001-28897

"A Cornelia and Michael Bessie book"

First published 1999 in the United Kingdom

"Neil Pritchard, told that he will die of cancer within two years, presses forward with his book on the Scottish composer Euan Bone. He also tells in this book the story of his encounter with Bone shortly before the composer's death. Neil, 14 then and a superb boy soprano, was summering with his aunt in a southern Scottish coastal town when Bone enlisted him to help prepare a vocal score based on a Robert Louis Stevenson essay. All went beautifully, and Neil was falling in love with Bone; then his voice changed, ending the collaboration. . . . In a resentful funk, he told the lie that Bone had molested him, which led, Neil came to think, to Bone's demise." Booklist

"Subtly developed characters, a unique and enchanting setting, suspense, and lovely writing make this an exceptional work." Libr J

Francis, Clare

Night sky. Morrow 1984 c1983 631p o.p.
LC 83-17351

First published 1983 in the United Kingdom

"The story, which takes place between 1935 and 1945, concerns several characters whose disparate paths converge in Europe during the war. Julie Lescaux flees her home in England so her friends won't discover that she's pregnant out of wedlock. Julie has 'always thought of herself as an ordinary sort,' but after settling with an aunt and uncle in Brittany she becomes involved with the hazardous covert operation to evacuate Allied servicemen stranded in occupied Europe." N Y Times Book Rev

"The book is excellent and is completely absorbing, despite its length. Many scenes are like great landscapes and mirror the emotions of the characters during the war." Best Sellers

Wolf winter. Morrow 1988 c1987 558p o.p.
LC 87-24209

First published 1987 in the United Kingdom

"When Norwegian mountain climber Jan Johansen is killed in an incident on the Russian-Finnish border, his widow, Ragna, is drawn into a series of events with roots in World War II which set the stage for espionage in the Cold War of the 1960s. Ragna's attraction for two men, Jan's best friend and an Oslo journalist, brings them all together in a violent struggle for truth and survival in Lapland's frozen wastes." Libr J

"The skill with which the author counterpoints her several plot lines to create a mounting sense of tension is exemplary. . . . 'Wolf Winter' has a sure dramatic sense, minutely realized settings and—most important—the sort of casual style that easily delivers the large amounts of information that are essential to this sort of entertainment." N Y Times Book Rev

Francis, Dick

10 lb. penalty. Putnam 1997 273p $24.95
ISBN 0-399-14302-5 LC 97-28020

"As the action begins, Ben Juliard, a teen-age apprentice jockey, is tipped out of his job to find himself helping his father, George, win a seat in the House of Commons. Five years later, George Juliard is headed for national prominence when vicious rumors about an old crime are bruited about by his enemies and Ben, now an insurance investigator, returns to help solve it, risking his life in the process." N Y Times Book Rev

"As usual in a Francis novel, the sweetest parts are about family; here, especially the growing love and understanding between father and son. The villains aren't particularly scary, but this smooth, nimbly paced charmer isn't really about bad people anyway, but about how the rest of us cope and live, sometimes in their shadow." Publ Wkly

Banker. Putnam 1983 c1982 306p o.p.
LC 82-18122

First published 1982 in the United Kingdom

"The title figure is a young British investment banker who has no knowledge of racing until he becomes involved in the possibility of arranging a loan to buy a supposedly fabulous horse that will be put out to stud and sire a generation of winners. At the same time he is beginning to realize he is falling in love with the wife of an ailing colleague. Sandcastle is the horse, and very soon it becomes apparent that he is surrounded by violent death and some kind of medical manipulation." Publ Wkly

Bolt. Putnam 1987 318p o.p.
LC 86-25167

Jockey-sleuth Kit Fielding "must help his employer, Princess Casilia and her husband overcome pressure to convert their large industrial holdings to a munitions works. Murder and physical threats against his fiancée, the Princess's niece, force Kit to adopt a dangerous plan of action." Libr J

"As adept on a race-course as he is in an Eaton Square drawing room, Fielding is a match for any menace. . . . In mystery circles, Francis again demonstrates that he is both a win and a nice read." Time

Bonecrack. Harper & Row 1972 c1971 201p o.p.

"A Joan Kahn-Harper novel of suspense"

First published 1971 in the United Kingdom

"A gangster's spoiled son is redeemed through his burning desire to become a jockey." Booklist

"The ending is much too pat, not to say sentimental, but the man writes so agreeably and knowledgeably that 'Bonecrack' is a pleasant way to pass a few hours." NY Times Book Rev

Break in. Putnam 1986 317p o.p.
LC 85-25682

First published 1985 in the United Kingdom

"Kit Fielding, champion steeplechase jockey, comes to the rescue of his twin sister and her husband, horse trainer and estranged son of millionaire Maynard Allardeck. Someone is mounting a massive smear campaign against Allardeck, and his son is caught in the middle. Kit must find a way to make things right." Libr J

This novel "contains all the ingredients of the Francis formula: a well-written, fast-moving narrative; an attractive, likeable hero; and authentic racing scenes and background." Christ Sci Monit

Come to grief. Putnam 1995 308p o.p.
LC 95-32377

This mystery features "ex-jockey-turned-sleuth Sid Halley. . . . Smart, tough, cool, and controlled, Halley lost his left hand in an accident years earlier, but that doesn't stop him from investigating equine enigmas. When someone starts mutilating priceless racehorses by hacking off their feet, Halley can't wait to find the bloody bugger who's responsible. Outraged by the senseless attacks, Sid interviews owners, noses after leads, and slogs through muddy pastures looking for clues." Booklist

"A subplot about a little girl with leukemia offers some touching sentiment, and there are flashes of dry wit throughout as Francis . . . proves himself still at the top of his game." Publ Wkly

The danger. Putnam 1984 320p o.p.
LC 83-13973

First published 1983 in the United Kingdom

"This thriller follows a professional anti-kidnapping operative named Andrew Douglas as he works against an equally professional kidnapper known as Peter/Guiseppe. The key 'victim' is an Italian female jockey, whom Douglas works to free and then assists in rebuilding her shattered sense of security and confidence." Wilson Libr Bull

(ed) The Dick Francis treasury of great racing stories. See The Dick Francis treasury of great racing stories

Driving force. Putnam 1992 318p o.p.
LC 92-22793

"Freddie Croft is a 35-year-old former champion steeplechase jockey, knowledgeable about the British racing milieu and tolerant of its denizens, a bit of a loner, keen on honor and notably phlegmatic. His phlegm is sorely tested when two of his drivers—he owns 14 vans that transport racehorses from a Hampshire village—arrive with the body of a hitchhiker who died in the backseat during the ride." Publ Wkly

This novel is "rich in information—about Cockney rhyming slang, the Michelangelo computer virus, intercontinental smuggling and ticks (yes, ticks), among other subjects. Mr. Francis deals with the potential for boredom in exposition, or at least flatness, by putting the more obscure explanations in the mouths of completely charming, completely obsessed eccentrics." N Y Times Book Rev

Field of thirteen. Putnam 1998 287p $24.95
ISBN 0-399-14434-X LC 98-28720

Contents: Raid at Kingdom Hill; Dead on red; Song for Mona; Bright white star; Collision course; Nightmare; Carrot for a chestnut; The gift; Spring fever; Blind chance; Corkscrew; The day of the losers; Haig's death

"Many of the stories were written in the 1970s and originally appeared in British and American sporting magazines, but a few have never been published before, thus offering a rare and unexpected treat for Francis' legions of loyal fans." Booklist

Francis, Dick—*Continued*

Flying finish. Harper & Row 1967 c1966 249p o.p.

First published 1966 in the United Kingdom

"The young hero, heir to a title although he insists on working for a living, is both a private plane enthusiast and head groom in a busy operation that flies race horses and brood mares all over the world by cargo plane. There's more behind the operation than meets the eye and he is soon plunged into a terrifying race against time and sure death." Publ Wkly

"The combination of horse knowledge and aviation is excellent, the love story credible, and the hero—though, as usual, a depressed character—emerges triumphant and strong." Barzun. Cat of Crime. Rev and enl edition

For kicks. Harper & Row 1965 244p o.p.

"The owner of an Australian stud-farm is hired to find out how certain English steeplechase race horses have been doped. . . . He is determined to finish the job in spite of beastly living conditions (he has to masquerade as a stable boy), very real danger, and another kind of trouble from the very enticing promiscuous daughter of a lord." Publ Wkly

Forfeit. Harper & Row 1969 247p o.p.

"A Joan Kahn-Harper novel of suspense"

"James Tyrone, sports writer for the 'Sunday Blaze', always needs extra money for things that make life bearable for Elizabeth his almost totally paralyzed wife. He jumps at the chance to do a feature story for a racing magazine, but as he begins to gather rumors about favorites withdrawn just before starting time to upset odds and enrich bookmakers, he also begins to receive odd warnings, and sinister threats." Libr J

Francis possesses the "conventional merits of uproar and bloodshed, plus an attention to practical detail and a shrewd understanding of social maneuver that pull his stories out of that never-never land in which crime novels tend to wander." Atlantic

High stakes. Harper & Row 1976 c1975 201p o.p.

"A Joan Kahn-Harper novel of suspense"

First published 1975 in the United Kingdom

"A novice race horse owner, [Steven Scott, who is also] a rich inventor, fires his trainer [Jody] for a simple but effective swindle. The trainer steals a prize horse in revenge. The owner and his pals are lined up against the trainer and the hierarchy of the British racing elite, and outright war ensues." Libr J

Hot money. Putnam 1988 c1987 324p o.p.
LC 87-19193

First published 1987 in the United Kingdom

The narrator of this mystery novel is Ian Pembroke, a jockey. "The plot revolves around the protagonist's father, a multimillionaire whose many ex-wives and varied progeny [seem to be] after both his money and his life." Quill Quire

"Francis is sometimes faulted for wooden characterizations, but here he is believable and chilling as he takes on the pathology of a large, mutually destructive family. The whodunit puzzle at the book's core is unusually good, and its solution, like those the late Ross Macdonald used to devise, takes into account wounds dealt out and suffered decades before." Time

Knockdown. Harper & Row 1975 c1974 217p o.p.

First published 1974 in the United Kingdom

Shortly after Jonah Dereham, ex-jockey, "buys a horse for a client at the Ascot Sales, he loses the horse and is hit over the head. Then his stable is broken into and a thoroughbred valued at seventy thousand pounds is turned loose on a busy highway. Then his house is set on fire." New Yorker

Longshot. Harper & Row 1990 320p o.p.
LC 90-41145

John Kendall "is an expert on survival, having written several books on the subject before turning to fiction: when Longshot opens, he is awaiting the publication of his first novel, living very frugally, and (with many reservations) about to accept a commission for a biography . . . [of racehorse trainer] Tremayne Vickers." Times Lit Suppl

"Francis remains one of the most incandescent talents in the mystery game. His plot positively shimmers, and his sleuth easily hurdles that always difficult jump from credible character to believable amateur detective. Perhaps best of all, Francis extracts a wealth of weird and wonderful shadings from his suspects." Booklist

Nerve. Harper & Row 1964 273p o.p.

"Rob Finn, a young steeplechase jockey, had been near Art Mathews when Mathews shot himself at the Dunstable races. When asked why the man had killed himself, Finn replied, 'Mr Kellar might know.' Then other jockeys began having trouble and finally Finn was involved." Publisher's note

Proof. Harper & Row 1985 334p o.p.
LC 84-15940

"Wine merchant Tony Beach is engaged to supply a horse trainer's garden party. During the party a horse van careens into the marquee, bringing disaster. One of the casualties is a restaurant owner suspected of serving cheap liquor under false labels, and Beach, as an expert taster, is enlisted to track the bootleggers. Francis gives the same fascinating and authoritative detail about the liquor trade as he does about the racing world (which figures intermittently in this book as background)." Libr J

Rat race. Putnam 1971 214p o.p.

"A Joan Kahn-Harper novel of suspense"

"The hero's occupation in this tale is piloting an air taxi from one race meeting to another; horses are secondary to his rehabilitation as professional man and husband. As usual, the characters and incidents are well thought out, especially the bombing incident." Barzun. Cat of Crime. Rev and enl edition

Risk. Putnam 1978 c1977 240p o.p.
LC 77-11786

"A Joan Kahn book"

First published 1977 in the United Kingdom

"Absentee American owners of horses are being bled of much money by their unscrupulous English trainer, and Roland Britten, accountant and spare-time jockey, latches on to the business and has to be kept out of the way for a time. So he is shanghaied to Minorca, when a friendly schoolmistress helps to get him back to England, for a nicely calculated sexual price. Renewed trouble follows, not just once but twice." Barzun. Cat of Crime. Rev and enl edition

Francis, Dick—*Continued*

"The book is superbly constructed and the hero persecuted in a way that is mystifying, frightening and beautifully described." Times Lit Suppl

Shattered. Putnam 2000 289p $25.95

ISBN 0-399-14660-1 LC 00-55937

It was young glassblower Gerard Logan's "misfortune to have been entrusted with the videotape of a valuable medical secret by his best friend, a jockey who dies in a dreadful racing accident at Cheltenham. Not having the slightest clue as to the contents of the tape, which is stolen before he can blink, Logan enlists the aid of some brave and burly friends to trace the tape. . . . Francis' formula is made for excitement, not subtlety, so the eerie serenity of the glass blower's studio provides a nice breather from the choreographed displays of bruising action that keep the author on his toes." N Y Times Book Rev

Slayride. Harper & Row 1974 c1973 219p o.p.

First published 1973 in the United Kingdom

"Horse racing in Norway provides the locale for an absorbing first-person narrative related by British Jockey Club investigator David Cleveland. Called to Oslo to learn the facts concerning the theft of receipts from a day's racing, Cleveland enlists the help of Arnie Kristiansen, investigator for the Norwegian Jockey Club. Discoveries prove painful and results are tragic, but justice is served in solution of a murder." Booklist

Smokescreen. Harper & Row 1973 c1972 213p o.p.

"A Joan Kahn-Harper novel of suspense"

First published 1972 in the United Kingdom

"An English film star is persuaded by a dying friend to go to South Africa to see what is the matter with her eleven race horses—horses that could win races if they did not mysteriously collapse just before the finish." Newsweek

"Even given Francis's high standards [this novel is] an elegant construction, in which we see the parts and their potentialities, and are as much excited to discover how he put them together as what happens when he does. . . . A symphony tumultuous with thrills." Times Lit Suppl

Straight. Harper & Row 1989 323p o.p.

LC 89-36492

"When Derek Franklin, a steeplechase jockey nursing a shattered ankle from a bad spill, learns of the death of his older, long-estranged brother Greville, he's stunned to find himself named as both executor of the will and sole heir. But in rapid succession, Derek is mugged, his brother's gemology firm is robbed, and Derek himself is assaulted in another robbery attempt; understandably, he comes to suspect that Greville's death may not have been an accident." Publ Wkly

To the hilt. Putnam 1996 322p o.p.

ISBN 0-399-14185-5 LC 96-9805

Narrator "Alexander Kinloch, product of a privileged upbringing, has opted out of the family brewing business to take up painting in Scotland. But things change when his stepfather, Sir Ivan Westering, suffers a heart attack after learning that his trusted assistant has absconded with millions of dollars in profits. Against the wishes of his advisers, Sir Ivan asks Alexander to save the brewery." Booklist

"Like Alexander's paintings, which are sneered at in the art world because they actually sell, 'To the Hilt' delivers the pleasures people pay for: an exciting story told with great narrative drive and a hero who suffers 'fear and pain and humiliation' for the sake of his honor." NY Times Book Rev

Trial run. Harper & Row 1979 c1978 246p o.p.

LC 78-20204

"A Joan Kahn book"

First published 1978 in the United Kingdom

"Randall Drew, an expert steeplechase rider who is no longer able to ride because he wears glasses and cannot tolerate contact lenses, is persuaded to go to Moscow for the Olympics. He is asked to do this in order to insure the safety of a member of the Royal Family who is supposed to ride in the Olympics. There follows a suspenseful story of danger and pursuit. Francis's tautly written books appeal not only to mystery fans but also to those interested in horses and racing." Shapiro. Fic for Youth. 3d edition

Twice shy. Putnam 1982 307p o.p.

LC 81-15814

"Jonathan Derry, a physicist, is handed some cassettes, apparently Broadway musical scores, by a friend who then meets a violent death. The cassettes turn out to be a computer program for handicapped horses—guaranteed to make the user a rich man. When Jonathan tries to track down the tapes' rightful owner he becomes involved with a rough man and his violent son. The latter is brought to justice by Jonathan and then, after his release, he tries to avenge himself on Jonathan's brother. Computer buffs as well as mystery fans will enjoy this one." Shapiro. Fic for Youth. 3d edition

Whip hand. Harper & Row 1980 c1979 293p o.p.

"A Joan Kahn book"

First published 1979 in the United Kingdom

In this novel "Sid Halley, a famous ex-jockey crippled in an accident, is laboriously putting his life back together as a private investigator and making do with an artificial hand. Professionally he is successful. A top trainer's horses are failing in the home stretch; the jockey's repellent ex-wife gets caught in a fraudulent mail-order scheme; an aged peer is trapped as a front man in a crooked consortium. The jockey reluctantly agrees to investigate these mysteries, and they lead him into confronting his deepest fears." Libr J

"The book contains moments of breathless suspense, much information about the sport of kings, and perceptive insights into Halley's character that explain some of the reasons for the breakdown of his marriage." Shapiro. Fic for Youth. 3d edition

Wild horses. Putnam 1994 319p o.p.

LC 94-27262

"Filmmaker Thomas Lyon is making a movie—based on a best-selling book—of a real-life tragedy in the horse-racing world. Twenty-some years ago, the young, attractive wife of a horse trainer was found hanged. Although her death was ruled a suicide at the time, Thomas' old friend Valentine Clark, a famous racing writer, whispers a puzzling deathbed confession about the years-old mystery. Thomas feels compelled to investigate." Booklist

Francis, Dick—*Continued*

"Besides providing a many-faceted mystery and the author's trademark insights into the horse world, this novel offers an in-depth, fascinating behind-the-scenes view of filmmaking." Libr J

Frank, Jeffrey

Bad publicity; a novel. Simon & Schuster 2004 213p $22

ISBN 0-7432-4776-0 LC 2003-57342

"It's the eve of the 1988 presidential election, and everyone in Washington is angling for a role in the administration to come. Hank Morriday is a welfare expert in low-level orbit at a Democratic think tank, hoping that a Dukakis victory will bring him a White House job. Charlie Dingleman, on the other hand, has already had his time in the sun; he's a former three-term congressman bumped from office after a bad-and public-divorce. There's hope for Charlie, in the form of an adviser's role during Reagan's final few months in office, but first he's got to avoid any negative publicity-something he has an extraordinarily difficult time doing." Publ Wkly

"To describe this novel as darkly comic would be inadequate; it's funny, all right, but its vision isn't merely dark – it is so bleak as to be almost Hobbesian. Satirists traditionally take a dim view of humanity, and Frank is gleefully, unapologetically in that mordant tradition." N Y Times Book Rev

Frank, Pat, 1907-1964

Alas, Babylon; a novel. Lippincott 1959 253p o.p.

"Survival after a submarine nuclear attack is the focus of this story of a small group of people in Fort Repose, Florida. Rationing food, reestablishing law and order, and pondering whether there will be any future for the survivors are some of the concerns of organizer-leader Randy Bragg." Shapiro. Fic for Youth. 3d edition

"This is an extraordinarily real picture of human beings numbed by catastrophe but still driven by the unconquerable determination of living creatures to keep on being alive. The writing is simple and straightforward and practical." New Yorker

Franklin, Miles, 1879-1954

The end of my career; the sequel to My brilliant career; with a foreword by Verna Coleman. Harper & Row 1981 234p o.p.

First published 1946 in Australia with title: My career goes bung

Protagonist "Sybylla Melvyn, the Australian country girl who narrated My Brilliant Career, explains that while the earlier work was fiction, she will now tell the truth about how she came to write her book and the events that followed. The adventures of her fictional namesake have created a furor. Beyond her rural circle, whose members are indignant about their apparent depiction in My Brilliant Career, are others eager to fete the young author. They prompt a visit to Sydney, where Sybylla finds the supposedly cultured class just as flawed as those left behind." Libr J

"This book is at times a delicious satire on morals and manners. At other times it is a heart-rending tract for feminism. Always it is entertaining and filled with wisdom and universal truths." Christ Sci Monit

My brilliant career. Putnam 1980 232p o.p.

First published 1901 in Scotland

"The novel's heroine, Sybylla Melvyn, a girl of sixteen, rebels against the stagnant life on her parents' dairy farm at Possum Gully and against the inevitable fate of teaching or marriage that awaits her; both forms of 'slavery' are distasteful to her but she sees marriage as particularly degrading. Rescued temporarily by a period with her affluent grandmother at the congenial station homestead, Caddagat, she faces interwoven problems—her sexual ambivalence which is characterized by strong physical attraction to eligible young squatter, Harold Beecham, and an equally strong physical revulsion." Oxford Companion to Australian Lit

Followed by The end of my career

Franklin, Stella Maria Miles Lampe *See* Franklin, Miles, 1879-1954

Franklin, Tom

Hell at the breech; a novel. Morrow 2003 520p $23.95

ISBN 0-688-16741-1 LC 2002-40982

"When a storekeeper campaigning for the state legislature is assassinated, Mitcham Beat is swept by a wave of violence that includes lynchings and shootings, barn burnings, and robberies. A gang of hooded men known as the Hell-at-the-Breech gang is terrorizing the community, and the only man to stop them is an aging sheriff ready to retire with his whiskey bottle. It sounds like the wild, wild West, but Franklin. . . has taken a little-known event in Alabama history, the Mitcham Beat War, and transformed it into a Faulknerian tale of bloody revenge and vigilante justice." Libr J

Franzen, Jonathan

The corrections. Farrar, Straus & Giroux 2001 568p $25

ISBN 0-374-12998-3 LC 2001-33478

This work "follows the delamination of the Lambert family—Alfred, once a rigid disciplinarian, flounders against Parkinson's-induced dementia; Enid, his loyal and embittered wife, lusts for the perfect Midwestern Christmas; Denise, their daughter, launches the hippest restaurant in Philly; and Gary, their oldest son, grapples with depression, while Chip, his brother, attempts to shore his eroding self-confidence by joining forces with a self-mocking, Eastern-Bloc politician." Publ Wkly

The novel "has the absorbing treacheries of married life, the comic squalors of cruise-shop travel and the shenanigans of global capitalism. It also has language that builds in powerful, rolling strides. And it has characters, the separately unraveling Lamberts, who get very deeply under your skin." Time

Fraser, Antonia, 1932-

The cavalier case; a Jemima Shore mystery. St. Martin's Press 1991 c1990 228p o.p.

LC 90-41943

First published 1990 in the United Kingdom

This mystery "involves the ghost of a 17th-century poet, an upscale tennis club and modern London society. Ms. Fraser writes with zest and verve, and her primary interest is people." N Y Times Book Rev

Fraser, Antonia, 1932-—*Continued*

Cool repentance. Bantam Bks. 1982 222p o.p.
LC 82-8300

"Actress Christabel Cartwright, after a notorious affair with a young rock star, has returned to her husband and daughters, and even plans to appear in two plays at the local drama festival. Jemima Shore, arriving to televise the festival, discovers that, underneath her cool exterior, Christabel is terrified of someone. And the murders begin." Libr J

Jemima Shore at the sunny grave and other stories. Bantam Bks. 1993 174p o.p.
LC 92-21605

Contents: Jemima Shore at the sunny grave; The moon was to blame; The blude-red wine; House poison; Getting to know you; Cry-by-night; Dead leaves; Out for the Countess; The twist

This is a "collection of nine mystery stories, four of which feature 'stylishly presented' sleuth, Jemima Shore." Libr J

Oxford blood. Simon & Schuster 1985 224p o.p.
LC 85-15265

This "Jemima Shore mystery takes us into the exclusive reaches of Britain's titled aristocracy, as the glamorous TV investigator is drawn into the quest for an heir's true parentage. A nursemaid's deathbed confession of switched babies starts Jemima on her task, but it is a case—with its potentially unwelcome revelations—she would rather avoid. However, the scion in question, rakish Viscount Saffron, Oxford undergraduate and heir to the title of St. Ives, asks Jemima to investigate the matter." Publ Wkly

Political death; a Jemima Shore mystery. Norton 1996 c1994 208p o.p.
LC 95-37779

First published 1994 in the United Kingdom

A mystery revolving around "political doings in Britain. During a particularly nasty general election campaign, Lady Imogen decides to tell the world what she knows about the infamous 'Faber Mystery,' a political scandal as old as her wardrobe. She invites Jemima Shore, TV's consummately professional investigative journalist, to her dilapidated townhouse to reveal what happened to Franklyn Faber, who vanished without a trace in the middle of his 1964 trial for selling state secrets." Publ Wkly

"Fraser's trademark wry wit, dead-on plotting, and efficient writing style, plus her ever-spunky heroine, make this one a good choice for most collections." Booklist

A splash of red. Bantam Bks. 1981 213p o.p.
LC 81-9543

This novel starts "off when Jemima agrees to flat-and cat-sit for Chloe Fontaine, an author renowned for her fine but not financially profitable books and notorious for her many amours. Supposedly off to the Continent, Chloe never leaves the building; her mutilated body is found on the premises, whereupon Chloe's latest discarded lover is arrested. But Jemima shrewdly considers the possible guilt of apparently innocent people with links to the victim: the owner of the building where she lived; her noble editor; a woman friend betrayed by Chloe and others. With the help of the resident cat, Jemima traces clues that lead to evidence against the killer." Publ Wkly

Fraser, George MacDonald, 1925-

Flashman; from the Flashman papers, 1839-1842; edited and arranged by George MacDonald Fraser. World Pub. 1969 256p o.p.

"An NAL book"

The bounder of Thomas Hughes's Tom Brown's schooldays "left some memoirs, it appears, of which this is the first installment. After a true account of the circumstances of his expulsion from school we learn that he obtained a commission in the 11th Light Dragoons, under the Earl of Cardigan. . . . [Sent to fight in India and Afghanistan] he manages by undeviating cowardice and lack of principle to get himself acclaimed a hero." New Statesman (1913)

Followed by Royal Flash

Flashman & the angel of the Lord; from The Flashman papers, 1858-59; edited and arranged by George MacDonald Fraser. Norton 1995 c1994 394p o.p.
LC 94-47219

First published 1994 in the United Kingdom

In this installment, "Flashman is kidnapped in Cape Town, South Africa, and sails to Baltimore before being conscripted into abolitionist John Brown's doomed, bloody 1859 raid on a federal arsenal in Harper's Ferry, Va. U.S. government agents enlist Flashman as a spy to dissuade or forcibly prevent Brown from carrying out the raid, fearing that it might trigger civil war. . . . Combining wild imagination, sardonic commentary on American mores and meticulous historical research, Fraser tells a masterful historical tale and presents a magnificent portrait of John Brown as a fearless, autocratic, murderous iron-willed zealot." Publ Wkly

Flashman and the mountain of light; from the Flashman papers, 1945-46. Bantam Bks. 1991 365p maps o.p.
LC 90-45453

This installment in the Flashman papers is set in "the Punjab as the outnumbered British forces face a formidable Sikh army. Behind the scenes are a glamorous but corrupt maharani (who is bedded by Flashman), her son and various devious pretenders. Flashman, who speaks the lingo, is acting as secret agent on behalf of the British but somehow always gets involved in battles he seeks to avoid. The atmosphere is colorful in the extreme, the battle scenes are splendidly rendered and some decidedly odd British commanders are deftly sketched." Publ Wkly

Flashman and the tiger; and other extracts from The Flashman papers; edited and arranged by George MacDonald Fraser. Knopf 2000 347p o.p.
ISBN 0-375-41024-4 LC 00-20435

First published 1999 in the United Kingdom

In this installment "the aging antihero saves Emperor Francis Joseph of Austria from an assassination attempt, flees spear-throwing Zulu warriors in Africa and fights a duel in a salt mine. He consorts with various beautiful and mysterious women, exchanges quips with Oscar Wilde, . . . investigates a baccarat-cheating scandal at the behest of the Prince of Wales and crosses paths with Sherlock Holmes and Otto von Bismarck, among other luminaries of the Victorian age." N Y Times Book Rev

Fraser, George MacDonald, 1925-—*Continued*

Royal Flash; from the Flashman papers, 1842-3 and 1847-8; edited and arranged by George MacDonald Fraser. Norton 1970 257p o.p.

This second installment in the Flashman papers "finds 'Flashy' involved in a complicated intrigue engineered by Otto von Bismarck to topple the balance of power in Europe. Flashman is forced to pose as the double for Prince Carl Gustaf of Strackenz but before long Flashman finds himself a target for assassination. Forced to flee the bedroom for the countryside, Flashman stamps out the opposition and loses a fortune in jewels to Lola Montez before arriving back in England." Best Sellers

Other titles in the series are: Flash for freedom (1972); Flashman at the charge (1973); Flashman in the great game (1975); Flashman's lady (1978); Flashman and the redskins (1982); Flashman and the dragon (1986)

Frayn, Michael

Headlong; a novel. Metropolitan Bks. 1999 342p o.p.

ISBN 0-8050-6285-8 LC 99-20717

Martin Clay "seems to have all he might reasonably wish for: a new career as an art historian, a loving wife, an adorable baby daughter, and a summer cottage in the English countryside, where he is supposed to be completing his book on fifteenth-century Netherlandish art. Instead, he stumbles upon an unsigned Brueghel (at least, he's almost positive it's a Brueghel) stashed in a fireplace of his neighbor's crumbling estate. Overwhelmed by high-minded professional curiosity and base greed, Martin resolves to acquire it by whatever means necessary. What follows is part detective story, part art-history lesson, part cautionary tale, and entirely funny." New Yorker

A landing on the sun. Viking 1992 c1991 248p o.p.

LC 91-37594

First published 1991 in the United Kingdom

This "novel concerns a methodical British civil servant who is jolted out of his glum routine when he is ordered to investigate the death of [Summerchild], another civil servant who fell out of a window fifteen years earlier. Somebody upstairs has raised questions of espionage." Atlantic

"Michael Frayn is a deeply accomplished writer: his structure and timing are faultless, his control never wavers. The novel is beautifully written, and in places very moving." New Statesman Soc

Spies; a novel. Metropolitan Bks. 2002 261p o.p.

ISBN 0-8050-7058-3 LC 2001-39840

"Stephen Wheatley, now a grandfather living abroad, is drawn back to London to revisit his boyhood home, to deal with the complexities and eventual tragedy engendered by what seemed a harmless game of spy when he was just a schoolboy during WWII. His best friend at the time was Keith Hayward, the bright son of rather standoffish parents; Keith and Stephen embark on a childish adventure after Keith announces that his British mother is a German spy." Publ Wkly

"A compelling story about secrecy and betrayal. . . . What is truly remarkable about this novel, though, is the way Frayn perfectly captures the dynamics of childhood friendships." Booklist

Frazier, Charles, 1950-

Cold Mountain. Atlantic Monthly Press 1997 356p $19.95

ISBN 0-87113-679-1 LC 97-275

"After Inman, a Confederate soldier, is gravely wounded outside Petersburg, he decides to flee the war. With his fearsome LeMat's pistol for protection, he sets out for Cold Mountain, where he was raised and where he left Ada, the woman he loves, on uncertain terms four years earlier. In the meantime, Ada, a preacher's daughter transplanted to the country from Charleston, has begun to learn the hard reality of a farmer's life. This novel's landscape is finely drawn, full of dark beauty and presentiment, and so are its characters. They give voice to a classical, peculiarly American feeling of nostalgia—the pain of returning home" New Yorker

Freda, Joseph, 1951-

The patience of rivers; a novel. Norton 2003 351p $24.95

ISBN 0-393-05176-5 LC 2002-13330

"It is 1969, and Nick Lauria is spending his final summer before college hanging out with his best friend, Charlie Miles, while working at his family's campgrounds in Delaware Ford, a small New York town just up the road from the farm where Woodstock is to be held. Nick spends his spare time trying to bed Darlene Van Vooren, the youngest of the three gorgeous Van Vooren sisters. But beneath the surface of Nick's idyllic existence, his family is in trouble." Publ Wkly

"This is an appealing coming-of-age tale set to a classic rock soundtrack." Libr J

Fredriksson, Marianne

Hanna's daughters. Ballantine Bks. 1998 345p o.p.

ISBN 0-345-42664-9 LC 98-14086

"Set against the backdrop of the 1870s Swedish-Norwegian Union crisis and WWII, the plot . . . interweaves the stories of three generations of women. Born in 1871, grandmother Hanna Broman is a woman of 'sense and continuity,' but her life is blighted when she is raped and impregnated by a cousin at the age of 12. Marriage to miller John Broman restores her honor and produces three additional children: Johanna and . . . two more sons. As she matures, atheist-socialist Johanna is contemptuous of her mother, whose life has been so deprived that she must learn about mirrors, indoor plumbing and electricity. Johanna's daughter, Anna, is a writer living in the concrete suburbs, hungering to understand her antecedents." Publ Wkly

This tale should "appeal to American readers with its universal truths about women's lives and the constraints of society, family, and love." Libr J

Freed, Lynn

The curse of the appropriate man; Lynn Freed. Harcourt 2004 188p pa $13

ISBN 0-15-602994-4 (pa) LC 2004-5914

Contents: Under the house; Foreign student; The widow's daughter; Family of shadows; An error of desire; Liars, cheats, and cowards; The curse of the appropriate

Freed, Lynn—*Continued*
man; The mirror; Twilight; Selina comes to the city; William; Songbird; The first rule of happiness; Ma: a memoir; Luck

Freed is "expertly equipped to dissect the defiant longings and treacherous pleasures of the daughters and mothers, lovers and adventurers whom she imagines in her fiction." Washington Post Book World

Freedman, Benedict

Mrs. Mike; the story of Katherine Mary Flannigan; by Benedict and Nancy Freedman; drawings by Ruth D. McCrea. Coward-McCann 1947 312p o.p.

"At 16, Boston-reared Katherine Mary O'Fallon is sent north to Alberta, Canada, to find relief for the pleurisy from which she has been suffering. While residing with her Uncle John, she falls in love with Mike, a handsome Canadian Mounted Policeman. Life in the wilderness in the early 1900s is harsh, but the newly married couple finds joy and challenge in their adventures." Shapiro. Fic for Youth. 3d edition

Freedman, J. F.

House of smoke. Viking 1996 438p o.p.
LC 95-4772

This mystery features Kate Blanchard, a private investigator in Santa Barbara, California. Laura Sparks "hire's Kate to look into the death of her lover, Frank Bascomb. Frank had been the foreman of her family's ranch until he died in the county jail after being arrested for smuggling marijuana through the family's private dock. Laura's mother, Miranda, wants Kate and Laura to drop their investigation, so as not to disrupt a lucrative oil deal involving the family's land." Booklist

"Kate Blanchard is a smart, sexy, gutsy (though not especially tough) private eye whose fouled-up life does not smooth out any as her story progresses. . . . Within the conventions of detective fiction, she is reasonably three-dimensional." Time

Freedman, Nancy, 1920-

(jt. auth) Freedman, B. Mrs. Mike

Freeling, Nicolas

A dwarf kingdom. Mysterious Press 1996 213p o.p.
ISBN 0-89296-615-7 LC 96-11954

In this mystery Inspector Henri Castang "retires from the Brussels police force. Recoiling from the savage murders of two dear friends, Castang and his wife, Vera, retreat to a villa they have inherited in Biarritz. The living is easy, but Castang is too curmudgeonly to fall into a mental stupor. . . . Sure enough, someone kidnaps his infant granddaughter, and the real estate mogul who has been buzzing around his well-situated property grows increasingly menacing. For Castang, there is no escape, after all, from the 'dwarfish greed' or the gnomish values of his constant nemesis, the ruthless power elite of the abominable bourgeoisie." N Y Times Book Rev

Flanders sky. Mysterious Press 1992 207p o.p.
LC 91-50844

Henri Castang "has been kicked upstairs—or so he thinks. The assignment to the European Community Headquarters in Brussels seems to imply that he won't be needing his carefully honed street smarts. But as Henri ruminates . . . on his forthcoming ennui, his supervisor's wife is found murdered. And the boss is the prime suspect." Booklist

"Mr. Freeling takes the international *policier* to high ground here and does the genre proud." N Y Times Book Rev

One more river. Mysterious Press 1998 214p o.p.
ISBN 0-89296-616-5 LC 97-52323

"John Charles, a 70-year-old English expatriate living in the south of France, is jolted out of his complacency (as 'a writer of acknowledged distinction, with an individual prose style') when someone takes a shot at him in the garden of his secluded cottage—which his attackers later burn down. 'Pleased to find himself excited' by the violent turn his placid life has taken, Charles thinks he can escape danger by keeping on the move, in a trek that returns him to scenes (and secrets) of his youth in the Netherlands, Germany and England. . . . Despite the fatalism of the bleak ending, this is a wondrous, strange trip through a very fine mind." N Y Times Book Rev

Sand castles. Mysterious Press 1990 c1989 209p o.p.
ISBN 0-89296-372-7 LC 89-43144

First published 1989 in the United Kingdom

The author "restores to life his well-beloved Dutch detective, Commissaris Piet van der Valk, whom he killed off in 'Auprès de Ma Blonde' (1972). . . . In Groningen (a 'dusty corner of a tight, righteous little land'), van der Valk comes across a sordid child-pornography racket that confirms his belief in the moral hypocrisy beneath the 'stuffy sinless atmosphere' breathed by the Dutch." N Y Times Book Rev

"Like his idiosyncratic hero and heroine—he bashes the Dutch, she the French, for example—Freeling rewards with his oblique, subtly comic style." Publ Wkly

Freemantle, Brian

Bomb grade. St. Martin's Press 1997 407p o.p.
ISBN 0-312-14565-9 LC 96-48769

"A Thomas Dunne book"

First published 1996 in the United Kingdom with title: Charlie's chance

"The cold war is over, and Britain's spy agencies are being dismantled. Agent Charlie Muffin expects to be fired any day, so he's flabbergasted when the director-general gives him a plum assignment in Moscow: to help the Russian government curb the illegal smuggling of uranium from Russian nuclear silos. Charlie's delighted with the opportunity to revisit his beloved Moscow and possibly see Natalia, the Soviet agent he loved and then lost in a spy game gone wrong." Booklist

"Mr. Freemantle suggests that what makes Charlie's personal life so precarious is exactly what makes him so successful in his profession, since talk filled with deception and evasion is a basic tool of his trade. Watching this spy at work is like watching a stunted genius play Mozart perfectly, even as the rest of his life threatens to crumble around him." N Y Times Book Rev

Freemantle, Brian—*Continued*

The button man. St. Martin's Press 1993 390p o.p.
LC 93-17421

"A Thomas Dunne book"

This novel is "about a serial killer in Moscow who knocks off the niece of an important (but hateful) United States senator, clips her hair and cuts the buttons from her clothes. An honest, efficient Russian cop is on the case. Working with him is an American from the F.B.I." N Y Times Book Rev

"Every scene and conversation in this meticulously plotted tale is a fencing match or a chess game; every turn of events threatens to topple the dense edifice of politics, lust, subterfuge, and insanity. A real winner by thriller veteran Freemantle." Booklist

Charlie's apprentice. St. Martin's Press 1994 c1993 435p o.p.
LC 94-2347

"A Thomas Dunne book"

First published 1993 in the United Kingdom

"British intelligence officer Charlie Muffin, renowned for his unorthodox methods, has been grounded. Charlie's new female boss thinks his time is better spent teaching new operatives rather than working in the field. Although frustrated, Charlie does his best to instruct recent graduate John Gower in surviving as an agent—practical, life-saving tips of the trade that are not found in any of the training manuals. Charlie is suspicous when the inexperienced Gower is sent to Beijing on a tricky assignment; later, when Gower is arrested and imprisoned, Charlie is dispatched to China to extricate him." Libr J

"Charlie has a lesser role in this book than in his previous adventures, but when he has to go to China to bail out his apprentice, he demonstrates yet again that as a field operative nobody can touch him." N Y Times Book Rev

Comrade Charlie; a Charlie Muffin novel. St. Martin's Press 1992 c1989 443p o.p.
LC 92-26157

"A Thomas Dunne book"

First published 1989 in the United Kingdom

"Muffin has been relegated to a desk job by his superior, a twit who hates him and would love to see him demoted to dogcatcher. . . . Plugging away at his boring job, Charlie happens upon a Kremlin plot just as the Soviet Union is about to come apart. So his old adversaries at the K.G.B. decide to ruin him once and for all. They plan to use his former girlfriend, a Soviet spy, as bait for destruction. Charlie will be framed in what looks like a foolproof scheme." N Y Times Book Rev

"Freemantle is a wonderfully talented writer, a master at taut, fast-paced plots and deft characterizations, with a flair for making every nuance and detail of the dark world of espionage real and intriguing." Booklist

Dead men living. St. Martin's Press 2000 345p o.p.
ISBN 0-312-24379-0 LC 99-462044

"A Thomas Dunne book"

"British agent Charlie Muffin is surviving just fine in the new Russia, living with his lover, former KGB agent Natalia, and juggling his expense account to cover a snazzy Moscow apartment. Then three bodies turn up after a Siberian thaw, and the Cold War is jump-started. Two of the bodies—one American, one English—are wearing remarkably well-preserved World War II uniforms." Booklist

"Siberia's harsh climate and Moscow's volatile politics are in clear focus as slippery, upper-class Brits and powerful Americans toss monkey wrenches into Charlie's plans." Publ Wkly

Mind/reader. St. Martin's Press 1998 475p o.p.
ISBN 0-312-18654-1 LC 98-4484

"A Thomas Dunne book"

"Criminal profiler Claudine Carter has joined Europol, Europe's version of the FBI, after her husband's tragic suicide. Hoping to escape her grief, Claudine throws herself into a horrifying case involving a serial killer who is leaving bloody body parts at public sites across Europe. . . . Freemantle is at the top of his form, with a cunningly devious plot, riveting suspense, strong characters, and enough stunning twists to keep even seasoned readers from guessing the shocking conclusion." Booklist

French, Albert

Billy. Viking 1993 214p o.p.
LC 93-14676

"In 1937, in the small town of Banes, Miss., 10-year-old Billy Lee Turner lives with his mother in one of the miserable shanties of the black ghetto called the Patch. Headstrong Billy convinces another youngster to enter the white area of town, where they are attacked by teenaged cousins who are enraged to see black boys in 'their' pond. Seeking to escape, Billy impulsively stabs one of the girls; she dies, and the white community works itself into a paroxysm of rage and violence. Though Billy is too young to comprehend what he has done, he is sentenced to the electric chair." Publ Wkly

"The story, once in motion, gathers momentum like a landslide. . . . 'Billy' is tragedy in the classical mode, mythic in the sense that instead of the surprise, the twists of plot we might discover in a more typical contemporary novel, here we are confirmed in our worst dreads as destiny immutably and shockingly unfolds." NY Times Book Rev

French, Marilyn, 1929-

The bleeding heart; a novel. Summit Bks. 1980 337p o.p.
LC 79-26346

"This novel is the story of Dolores and Victor. They are adults, in the forties, successful in their careers, both parents, both Americans living in England for the year without their families. Dolores is a writer and professor of English, on sabbatical in Oxford to research a new book. Victor is a powerful executive with an American firm, assigned to the London office. When they meet in a compartment of the London-Oxford train, they instantly fall in love. They then discover that they agree on nothing." Publisher's note

The author "is a robust but controlled constructor of character and dialogue and exhibits deep understanding of both female and male consciousnesses." Booklist

French, Marilyn, 1929-—*Continued*

Her mother's daughter; a novel. Summit Bks. 1987 686p il o.p.

LC 87-7061

"Anastasia narrates her life experiences by blending them with those of her grandmother, mother, and daughter. Each woman has been determined not to make the sacrifices her mother made, instead seeking joy, freedom, and independence. And in doing so, each has become like her mother—emotionally drained, alienated from her children, and alone." Libr J

The author "continues to imbue what used to be dismissed as 'women's issues' with the significance they deserve. . . . Ms. French continues to write about the inner lives of women with insight and intimacy. What she's given us this time is a page-turner with a heart." N Y Times Book Rev

My summer with George. Knopf 1996 243p o.p.

ISBN 0-679-44774-1 LC 96-10574

"Hermione Beldame is a successful, self-made woman in her sixties who, ironically, is an author of romance novels. She becomes enamored of George, whom she meets at a party. For much of one summer, Hermione talks with many friends, trying to analyze and explain this relationship. French uses Hermione as the symbol of a generation of women who were raised on the myth of romantic love but were then disappointed." Libr J

"For much of society, a lovesick older woman is an off-putting sight. Once again, Marilyn French is challenging convention, pungently raising the possibility of a full romantic life rather than a surrender to the chaste compromise that the current culture encourages." N Y Times Book Rev

Our father; a novel. Little, Brown 1994 450p o.p.

ISBN 0-316-29390-3 LC 93-21190

"Four sisters, all with different mothers, congregate at the bedside of their dying father. First-born Elizabeth, an assistant secretary for the Treasury, is bitchy and alone; married Mary feels abandoned by everyone she ever loved; breathless, insecure Alex craves her sisters' approval; while the illegitimate and bitter youngest, Ronnie, knows she'll never really get it." Libr J

"This is a novel that is fueled by anger, revenge and the possibilities of recovery. It is overly long and often wildly melodramatic, but somehow these failings also give it an odd power." N Y Times Book Rev

The women's room. Summit Bks. 1977 471p o.p.

LC 77-24918

"Dealing with the interlocking lives of dozens of American women, who know each other at some point of time between the 1950s and the 70s, and concentrating in particular on the evolution of Mira from petted baby girl wife to independent womanhood, it speaks from the heart to women everywhere. . . . [The author's] dialogue, her characterizations, her knowledge of the changing relationships, sexual and otherwise, between men and women in a complex world of shifting values, are all extraordinary. Mira, the suburban housewife and mother, the unexpected divorcee groping her way out of a marriage that she never understood, going back to Harvard at 38 as a graduate student, meeting other women, some tougher, some weaker, coming to terms with herself against all odds, even if it means a bleak and lonely parting from a man she loves, is memorable." Publ Wkly

French, Nicci

Beneath the skin. Mysterious Press 2000 378p $24.95

ISBN 0-89296-726-9 LC 00-101483

Londoners "Zoe Haratounian (a pre-school teacher), Jennifer Hintlesham (a former model and mother of three) and Nadia Blake (a children's entertainer) are all petite, uniquely pretty women. They also are all involved in, or getting out of, bad relationships with men, and they are all the targets of a murderous stalker who haunts his victims through disturbingly personal letters." Publ Wkly

French "gives the killer terrifying presence through the perverse 'love' letters he sends to his victims. . . . But, in a stylistic twist that is rare for this genre, the focus of the suspense remains locked on his victims, smart, articulate women who reveal their escalating fears in intimate first-person narratives that are insightful and also sad, because the lessons learned come too late." N Y Times Book Rev

Land of the living. Warner Bks. 2003 341p $23.95

ISBN 0-446-53151-0 LC 2002-33149

In the "opening scenes, 25-year-old Abbie Devereaux finds herself blindfolded and shackled in some filthy hole, the victim of a kidnapping she can't recall. Through sheer luck Abbie escapes her prison, only to realize that no one in authority believes her story. . . . Although the thwarted killer who is still stalking Abbie is too real for us to share her terror of going mad, we're with her all the way in her gritty quest to forge a new identity and discover what went wrong with the old one." N Y Times Book Rev

French, Paul *See* Asimov, Isaac, 1920-1992

Freudenberger, Nell

Lucky girls; stories. HarperCollins Pubs. 2003 225p $22.95

ISBN 0-06-008879-6 LC 2003-44875

Contents: Lucky girls; The orphan; Outside the Eastern gate; The tutor; Letter from the last bastion

"A remarkably poised collection of stories about Americans abroad." N Y Times Book Rev

Frey, Stephen W.

The inner sanctum; [by] Stephen Frey. Dutton 1997 308p o.p.

ISBN 0-525-94206-8 LC 96-29869

"After her boss dies suddenly, IRS agent Jesse Hayes receives a mysterious, time-delayed E-mail message from him warning her of a powerful conspiracy involving senatorial candidate Elbridge Coleman. A wealthy businessman with ties to the military, Coleman is at the heart of some nasty business. Now Hayes is the only person with the information to derail him, but a dangerous killer is on her trail. Meanwhile, David Mitchell, who works for a Baltimore-based investment firm, hopes to insure that

Frey, Stephen W.—*Continued*
a company he has backed wins a huge government defense contract. He and Jesse meet, are attracted, and then seemingly wind up on opposite sides as the deadly conspiracy plays itself out." Libr J

The legacy; [by] Stephen Frey. Dutton 1998 296p o.p.
ISBN 0-525-94207-6 LC 98-12145
The author incorporates "JFK conspiracy lore in this yarn that spins around the second-shooter or 'grassy knoll' thesis. Since anything is possible in a novel, the proof lies in a literal smoking gun, filmed at the time but hidden for 35 years. This blockbuster evidence lands in the lap of Cole Egan, a Wall Street securities trader whose gambling habits have put him in hock to the Mob. Recognizing a magic bullet of his own when he sees it, Egan contemplates the multimillion-dollar value of the film, but his greed competes with filial curiosity about its source—his supposedly deceased father, whom he never knew." Booklist

The vulture fund. Dutton 1996 378p o.p.
LC 96-10617
"Hot-shot New York investment banker Mace McLain is recruited by his senior partner, Lewis Webster, to establish a $2 billion 'vulture fund' that will buy great chunks of Manhattan properties in what Webster insists will be an inevitable real estate bust. Mace's immediate boss in the venture will be Kathleen (Leeny) Hunt, smart, beautiful and predatory. Meanwhile, the country's vice president, a Democrat, is locked in a fierce struggle with the CIA director, who's the presumptive GOP presidential nominee." Publ Wkly
"Comparisons of Frey to Grisham and Clancy are apt—he's got the same ability to mesmerize his reader with fast-moving action, gripping intrigue, and larger-than-life characters." Booklist

Friedman, Bruce Jay, 1930-

A father's kisses; a novel. Fine, D.I. 1996 250p o.p.
LC 96-228084
"Needing to support his beloved daughter, recent widower and part-time tanning salon worker William Binny naively accepts smooth-talking Valentine Peabody's six-figure offer to assassinate some alleged ne'er-do-wells who have offended Peabody's billionaire boss." Libr J
"In short, Bruce Jay Friedman's book is an old-fashioned sort of comic novel: it is not cruel, it is not ill tempered and the humor comes from the combination of characters and events rather than from the sharp-wittedness of the author at the expense of everyone else. . . . One of the reasons the improbable scenario works is the complete success of William Binny as a character." N Y Times Book Rev

Friedman, Kinky, 1944-

Blast from the past. Simon & Schuster 1998 254p o.p.
ISBN 0-684-80379-8 LC 98-19620
This "is a prequel to Friedman's previous books, shifting back to the 1970's to show how the Kinkster got started as a detective. This time around, the cast includes a Vietnam casualty who returns from the grave, Abbie Hoffman (fleeing the Feds under the name of Barry Freed) and a band called the Shalom Retirement Village People. The 'mystery' is of the flimsiest and wouldn't mystify an idiot, being merely an excuse for Friedman to show off his inspired tomfoolery." N Y Times Book Rev

God bless John Wayne. Simon & Schuster 1995 253p o.p.
LC 95-16107
Kinky Friedman "is hired to find the birth mother of his friend Ratso (a.k.a. Larry Sloman). Among the obstacles in solving the case are the fact that Ratso doesn't tell him all he knows (including the death of a previous investigator) and that he brings yet another sleuth on to the case due to Friedman's lack of a P.I. license." SLJ
"It may not be everyone's cup of Jameson, but those with a taste for it will find Kinky's latest a delightfully potent draft." NY Times Book Rev

The love song of J. Edgar Hoover. Simon & Schuster 1996 238p o.p.
ISBN 0-684-80377-1 LC 96-3813
A mystery featuring amateur New York sleuth Kinky Friedman. "A case involving a leggy blond looking for her missing husband intertwines with that of Kinky's friend McGovern, who claims he's being hounded by the late Leaning Jesus (former cook for Al Capone and maybe the missing link to the Chicago gangster's hidden treasure). Kinky is soon led on a wild goose chase that gets him shot at by D.C. cops and a seat for a near-fatal limo ride in the Windy City." Booklist

Roadkill. Simon & Schuster 1997 252p o.p.
LC 97-10201
Kinky Friedman "is summoned by his old pal Willie Nelson . . . to join him in Texas on his 'floating city' of a tour bus, the Honeysuckle Rose, along with the singer's extended family, most of whom have names like Gator and Poodie. It seems that a bus accident has left 'Willie the Wandering Gypsy' guilt-stricken and skittish, but before Kinky has a chance to cheer him up, the salty-tongued sleuth is plunged into a mystery involving Indians, cops and former wives who may or may not be vengeful." N Y Times Book Rev
"Kinky's kvetching mope is an excellent counterpoint to Willie's Zen Texan. Let's hope we see them paired again." Booklist

Spanking Watson; a novel. Simon & Schuster 1999 218p o.p.
ISBN 0-684-85061-3 LC 99-22224
"A bunch of PI Kinky Friedman hangers-on are vying for the role of official sidekick, so the Kinkster suggests that they try to figure out who sent his upstairs neighbor a death threat. He doesn't realize until too late just how serious this death threat really is." Libr J
"Friedman refuses to let an excessively contrived plot handicap another entertaining, politically incorrect mystery." Booklist

Steppin' on a rainbow. Simon & Schuster 2001 208p o.p.
ISBN 0-684-86487-8 LC 2001-31159
This Kinky Friedman "mystery is about what happens when one of his band of merry crime solvers, the Village Irregulars, goes missing. Mike McGovern, blissfully childlike and peripatetic, vanishes while gathering recipes for a food book to be titled 'Eat, Drink and Be Kinky.'

Friedman, Kinky, 1944-—*Continued*

Through detective work that more resembles serendipity than deductive reasoning, Friedman's hero, who also happens to be known as Kinky Friedman, tracks Mike to Hawaii, where it seems he had disappeared into the surf." N Y Times Book Rev

Friedman, Philip, 1944-

Grand jury; a novel. Fine, D.I. 1996 595p o.p.
LC 96-5276

This novel "explores the secret workings of New York City's pretrial testing ground. An elderly Chinese couple is arrested for narcotics trafficking. One grand juror, herself part Chinese and oddly sympathetic to the pair, smells a rat. She inveigles another juror, a computer jock captivated by her beauty, into traveling with her to Asia, where love blooms. Back home, though, the local corruption squad has smelled the same rat, and the chase is on." Libr J

"The author's approach to the legal thriller owes more to Dickens than to Grisham . . . with social commentary and psychological exploration dominating plot concerns—and readers will finish this thoughtful, richly nuanced novel knowing more about the gloss and grit, the surface and soul, of 20th-century urban life than when they began." Publ Wkly

Inadmissable evidence; a novel. Fine, D.I. 1992 548p o.p.
LC 92-53075

"Manhattan prosecutor Estrada is beset by problems. His lover has moved to the West Coast and his career is idling on two-bit cases. Relief arrives when a sensational murder conviction is reversed, and Estrada is drawn into the retrial. He re-investigates the clues and witnesses surrounding the torrid relationship between Roberto Morales—real estate sharpie, popular Latino role model, defendant—and vivacious victim Mariah Dodge." Booklist

"If Friedman's insistence on day-to-day doings occasionally undercuts his novel's sense of drama and consequence, it also invests his story with authority, allowing a clear portrait of the give-and-take of the legal system and affording an even stronger sense of the ambiguities that arise from the pursuit of justice." Publ Wkly

Reasonable doubt; a novel. Fine, D.I. 1990 487p o.p.
LC 88-45381

The protagonist of this novel "is Michael Ryan, a widowed attorney whose only child, a son, has been murdered. Ryan's daughter-in-law, wealthy and sophisticated Jennifer Kneeland Ryan, is accused of the murder. Confoundingly, she asks Ryan to defend her; reluctantly, he says yes. In the course of the case, Ryan learns chilling and unsavory truths about both his dead son and his explosive daughter-in-law." N Y Times Book Rev

Fromm, Pete, 1958-

As cool as I am. Picador 2003 388p $24
ISBN 0-312-30775-6 LC 2003-49869

This "coming-of-age story follows Lucy Diamond of Great Falls, Mont., for two years, from 14 o 16. They're turbulent years, but more so for Lucy because her parents, themselves married as teenagers, are both self-centered, trying to recapture the youth they feel they missed. Chuck, her father, appears only for a few days every few months; he is a charmer, and Lucy has inherited his humor and smart mouth. Though he claims to be a logger, it becomes clear that there must be other reasons for his long disappearances. Lucy's mother, Lainee, frustrated by her absent husband, has a long string of boyfriends, all of whom, like her husband, eventually disappear. Lucy, meanwhile, drifts into an affair with her best friend, scrawny, funny Kenny, whose divorced mother is an alcoholic." Publ Wkly

"Fromm explores the sexual evolution of a cynical teenage girl who has the spunk and wit to survive two flaky parents and the urges of unbridled adolescence." Booklist

Fuentes, Carlos, 1928-

Apollo and the whores
In Fuentes, C. The orange tree p148-204

The campaign; translated by Alfred Mac Adam. Farrar, Straus & Giroux 1991 246p o.p.
LC 91-9723

Original Spanish edition, 1990

The focus of this novel is "on Argentina's complicated transition from colonial to free status. The protagonist is one Baltasar Bustos, a young man of certain privilege—the son of a wealthy ranchowner on the pampas—who performs an amazing act of defiance against the Spanish colonial regime. He sneaks into the house of the judge of the superior court of the viceroyalty of La Plata and substitute's the magistrate's newborn child with the child of a black prostitute. In the process, he not only causes the house to catch on fire, killing one of the babies, but also catches a glimpse of the judge's wife and falls in love with her. To assuage himself of guilt and to attempt to gain her love, Baltasar joins the independence army and follows the lady of his dreams all over South America." Booklist

"The novel takes on huge themes: revolution versus justice, the illusion of human perfectibility, the value of tradition against the appeal to reason. Though set in the past, it is not trapped in it. Mr Fuentes might equally be writing about modern revolutions." Economist

Constancia and other stories for virgins; translated by Thomas Christensen. Farrar, Straus & Giroux 1990 c1989 340p o.p.
LC 89-82138

Original Spanish edition, 1989

Contents: Constancia; La Desdichada; The prisoner of Las Lomas; Viva mi fama; Reasonable people

"Underneath the irony, the range of literary and historical reference, the brilliant, bawdy Fuentes finish and humanitarian social conscience, these stories are a set of variations on a macho theme of inner emptiness." Times Lit Suppl

The crystal frontier; a novel in nine stories; translated from the Spanish by Alfred Mac Adam. Farrar, Straus & Giroux 1997 266p o.p.
ISBN 0-374-13277-1 LC 97-11230

Original Spanish edition published 1995 in Mexico

Contents: A capital girl; Pain; Spoils; The line of oblivion; Malintzin of the maquilas; Las amigas; The crystal frontier; The bet; Rio Grande, Rio Bravo

"Leonardo Barroso is an unscrupulous Mexican oli-

Fuentes, Carlos, 1928-—*Continued*
garch whose fortress of a villa is only a short drive from the 'crystal frontier' of the title, and each one of the nine stories comprising this work explores the life of someone touched by him." Libr J

The death of Artemio Cruz; translated from the Spanish by Alfred MacAdam. Farrar, Straus & Giroux 1991 307p o.p.
LC 90-43280

Original Spanish edition published 1962 in Mexico; first English translation by Sam Hileman published 1964

"As the novel opens, Artemio Cruz, former revolutionary turned capitalist, lies on his deathbed. He drifts in and out of consciousness, and when he is conscious his mind wanders between past and present. The story reveals that Cruz became rich through treachery, bribery, corruption, and ruthlessness. As a young man he had been full of revolutionary ideals. Acts committed as a means of self-preservation soon developed into a way of life based on opportunism. A fully realized character, Cruz can also be seen as a symbol of Mexico's quest for wealth at the expense of moral values." Merriam-Webster's Ency of Lit

Diana, the goddess who hunts alone; translated from the Spanish by Alfred MacAdam. Farrar, Straus & Giroux 1995 217p o.p.
ISBN 0-374-13903-2 LC 95-10846

Original Spanish edition published 1994 in Mexico

"On New Year's Eve 1970, the narrator, an acclaimed Mexican novelist recently turned 40 (like Fuentes at the time), meets American actress Diana Soren, a character who draws from two mythic archetypes. One is the muse-like moon goddess alternately known as Cybele, Astarte or Diana; the second is the late Jean Seberg. . . . Despite his passion for Diana, the narrator learns that she is a 'goddess who hunts alone,' as their difficult affair undermines his confidence in his abilities as a Don Juan, his standing as a Mexican leftist and his prowess as an imaginative author." Publ Wkly

"The narrative is marked by digressions into Sixties revolutionary politics, the meaning of literary creation, and the Puritan origins of the United States. But these never distract from the central themes of the novel—the hunger with which Diana and Carlos consume each other, the tragic link between the eternity of desire and the finitude of love; the wish to create and the inexorable will to destroy." Libr J

The old gringo; translated by Margaret Sayers Peden. Farrar, Straus & Giroux 1985 199p o.p.
LC 85-16266

Original Spanish edition published in Mexico

"Fuentes fictionalizes the last days of the life of American journalist and author Ambrose Bierce, involving a mythic figure to the Mexican revolutionaries with whom Bierce fights and representing Bierce of the novel as an implanted, recurrent memory for the young American schoolteacher who witnesses his final passages through time." Choice

"We have in this novel a fastidious American governess stranded in Pancho Villa's revolution, where she attracts the erotic interest of an intellectual fellow countryman and a nature-boy Mexican general. On this inanely trite foundation Mr. Fuentes has erected a narrative of brilliant complexity and sophistication, describing brisk military action and philosophically contrasting national character, or social tradition, or styles of revolt, or regional strengths, weaknesses, and prejudices." Atlantic

The orange tree; translated from the Spanish by Alfred Mac Adam. Farrar, Straus & Giroux 1994 229p o.p.
ISBN 0-374-22683-0 LC 93-33608

Contents: The two shores; Sons of the Conquistador; The two Numantias; Apollo and the whores; The two Americas

In four of the five novelettes "here, Fuentes delves into the Hispanic world's past, with effective, even magical, results. The first, 'The Two Shores,' is a first-person narrative by a Spanish conquistador, who functioned as a translator between his troops and the Aztecs; his account of the conquest of Mexico is spoken from the grave, and offers sympathy to the defeated native inhabitants. . . . 'Sons of the Conquistador,' . . . is, as the title indicates, about the two sons of Cortés, both named Martin, one the son of his Spanish wife, the other the illegitimate son of his Indian mistress. . . . In 'The Two Numantias,' the Spain of Roman times is solidly conjured in brief space; and 'The Two Americas' both informs and entertains as it sees Columbus returning to Spain on a jet 500 years after he left. The remaining story, 'Apollo and the Whores,' . . . deals amusingly with an American grade-B movie actor visiting Acapulco and his phantasmagorical death there." Booklist

Sons of the Conquistador
In Fuentes, C. The orange tree p50-100

The two Americas
In Fuentes, C. The orange tree p205-29

The two Numantias
In Fuentes, C. The orange tree p101-47

The two shores
In Fuentes, C. The orange tree p3-49

The years with Laura Diaz; translated by Alfred MacAdam. Farrar, Straus & Giroux 2000 516p o.p.
ISBN 0-374-29341-4 LC 00-37648

"The novel begins in 1999 when photographer Santiago Lopez-Alfare arrives in Detroit to film a documentary about Mexican muralists in the U.S. There he comes across the image of an unnamed woman immortalized on the mural of the famous Diego Rivera. He soon realizes that 'those almost golden eyes, mestizo, between European and Mexican' belonged to his great-grandmother, Laura Diaz. Thereafter, the novel recounts the life of Diaz, from the settlement of her German grandparents in Mexico in the late 1800s . . . to her experience of the Mexican Revolution and its aftermath." Booklist

"Fuentes's emotional commitment to his subject shows in the lucidity of the book's underlying intellectual dialogues—the opposition of communism and fascism, the corrosion of individual identities by historical processes—which Fuentes is able to animate with a learned lyricism that should make this volume one of his most admired and memorable." Publ Wkly

Fujiwara, Murasaki *See* Murasaki Shikibu, b. 978?

Furst, Alan

Blood of victory; a novel. Random House 2002 237p o.p.
ISBN 0-375-50574-1 LC 2002-21312
This thriller "revolves around a plan to disrupt the flow of Romanian oil to the Third Reich. As usual, Furst adheres strictly to the rules of the genre: the protagonist, a Russian expatriate writer, is seduced into service both by the prospect of heroism and by a mysterious Frenchwoman, and embarks on a globetrotting, spy-versus-spy adventure. But his debts to convention work in his favor. Densely atmospheric and genuinely romatic, the novel is most reminiscent of the Hollywood films of the forties, when moral choices were rendered not in black-and-white but in smoky shades of gray." New Yorker

Dark voyage; a novel. Random House 2004 256p $24.95
ISBN 1-400-06018-4 LC 2004-46674
The protagonist of this novel is "E. M. DeHaan, the captain of the Dutch tramp freighter Noordenham, a ship without a home since the Nazis invaded Holland. It's 1941 when DeHaan accepts . . . his new assignment: disguised as a Spanish freighter, the Noordendam will be deployed on secret assignments for the British." Booklist
The author "lulls us into the atmosphere, allows us to imbibe his descriptions and then, in the last 50 pages, turns the screws. The denouement of Dark Voyage is both breathless and utterly relaxed, not so pellmell that Furst can't stop to be amused at the ironies of shifting alliances. If he ever breaks a sweat, it doesn't show." N Y Times Book Rev

Kingdom of shadows; a novel. Random House 2001 272p o.p.
ISBN 0-375-50337-4 LC 00-32344
"In Paris in 1938, Nicholas Morath, a Hungarian aristocrat, enjoys the benefits of his wealth and breeding—benefits that include the company of a beautiful young Argentine girlfriend and control of a successful advertising firm. But the rumblings of the Third Reich are drawing nearer, and when Morath's uncle and benefactor, Count Janos Polanyi enlists Nicholas to help fight Fascism back in Hungary the playboy becomes a political operative. . . . The novel's most attractive feature is its matter-of-fact suspense: Furst vigilantly restricts Nicholas's perspective, refusing to allow him anachronistic insight into the history being made around him, and this strategy helps reinvigorate one of the century's frequently told stories." New Yorker

Red gold. Random House 1999 258p o.p.
ISBN 0-679-45186-2 LC 98-24409
Sequel to The world at night (1996)
"It's 1941, and Jules Casson is back in Paris, on the run from the Gestapo and trying to stay alive without attracting attention. Drawn back into the resistance by an intelligence officer he knows from Dunkirk, Casson soon finds himself in the middle of an ill-advised plot to smuggle arms to the Communists. It all goes wrong, of course, as Casson and a Jewish girl he falls in love with struggle to tell the good guys from the bad." Booklist
"Furst proves himself a master at capturing the bleak and mean mood of wartime Paris." N Y Times Book Rev

Fyfield, Frances, 1948-

Blind date. Viking 1998 264p o.p.
ISBN 0-670-87889-8 LC 98-21218
First published 1992 in the United Kingdom
"Haunted by her sister's murder and humiliated by her failure, as a police officer on the case, to find the killer, [Elizabeth Kennedy] retreats to her womblike quarters in a London church belfry to recover from a near-fatal mugging that just about destroyed whatever strength and dignity she had left. Here she rages over her miserable condition . . . unaware of how close the killer is to her and to her family, and without a clue of the danger to three of her friends." N Y Times Book Rev
The plotting is "masterly, and Fyfield's critique of society—the real concern of the best crime thrillers—is seriously unsettling." Times Lit Suppl

Deep sleep. Pocket Bks. 1992 227p o.p.
LC 91-41030
"Lawyer Helen West, newly out of hospital, and DCI Geoffrey Bailey become interested in the 'accidental' chloroform poisoning death of a chemist's wife. Denizens of the chemist's London neighborhood include a policeman's estranged wife and insecure son as well as a docile-but-shrewd drug addict, so opportunities for psychological conflict abound. Tensions reach a snapping point with another murder, a bomb threat, and assault. Absorbing and crafted with care, this deserves every consideration." Libr J

Undercurrents. Viking 2001 278p $23.95
ISBN 0-670-89636-5 LC 00-43806
First published 2000 in the United Kingdom
American pharmacist Harry Evans "travels to the soaked seaside town of Warbling [England] to discover what happened to his lover from 20 years in the past. . . . Evans learns that his old girlfriend is serving time for the murder of her five-year-old son." Booklist
"Dark humor occasionally flashes through the narrative, but Fyfield's latest is primarily a grim, tense story about regret, loneliness and leaving well enough alone. In Warbling, she's created a memorable setting. It's a harsh, foreboding town populated by people—disappointed, judgmental, distrustful—who deserve such a place." Publ Wkly

G

Gabaldon, Diana

A breath of snow and ashes. Delacorte Press 2005 979p $28
ISBN 0-385-32416-2 LC 2005-51948
In this sixth title in the Outlander series, the author "unfolds the continuing story of the Frasers, heartbreakingly heroic highlander Jamie and his time-traveling wife Clare. Set during the three years leading up to the American Revolution, this . . . [novel] maps both violent loss and strong family ties. On the eve of war much is changing on Fraser's Ridge and Jamie and Claire encounter much harm. This vivid and haunting novel, therefore, brings an aching sadness, but it is balanced with sheer joy, revelation, and solace. The large scope of the novel allows Gabaldon to do what she does best, paint in exquisite detail the lives of her characters." Booklist

Gaddis, William, 1922-1998

Agapé agape; afterword by Joseph Tabbi. Viking 2002 113p o.p.
ISBN 0-670-03131-3 LC 2002-20676

"Gaddis has compressed 50 years of research on the social history of the player piano into a novel narrated by a dying elderly man who is as concerned with his own physical collapse as he is with his piano-based literary project. . . . As usual, Gaddis's avant-garde style requires patience and staying power from readers, who must parse long, elliptical sentences that wander from idea to idea while barely advancing the narrative. But his thoughts and ruminations remain fascinating and challenging." Publ Wkly

A frolic of his own; a novel. Poseidon Press 1994 586p o.p.
ISBN 0-671-66984-2 LC 93-26098

In this novel "Oscar Crease, middle-aged college instructor, savant, and playwright, is suing a Hollywood producer for pirating his play *Once at Antietam,* based on his grandfather's experiences in the Civil War, and turning it into a gory blockbuster called *The Blood in the Red White and Blue.* Oscar's suit, and a host of others—which involve a dog trapped in an outdoor sculpture, wrongful death during a river baptism, a church versus a soft drink company, and even Oscar himself after he is run over by his own car—engulf all who surround him." Publisher's note

"The medium is exceptionally dense. The mere effort of sorting out the voices, of tracking them, can be exhausting. . . . In any case, I hope the reader will persevere. 'A Frolic of His Own' is an exceptionally rich, even important novel." N Y Times Book Rev

J R. Knopf 1975 725p o.p.

"JR, ambitious sixth-grader in torn sneakers, bred on the challenge of 'free enterprise' and fired by heady mailorder promises of 'success' . . . parlays a deal for thousands of surplus Navy picnic forks . . . into a nationwide, hydraheaded 'family of companies.' The JR Corp and its Boss engulf brokers, lawyers, Congressmen, disaffected school teachers and disenfranchised Indians, drunks, divorcées, second-hand generals, and a fledgling composer." Publisher's note

The book is "frequently as turgid, monotonous, and confusing as the situation it describes. Yet Gaddis has . . . managed to reflect chaos in a fiction that is not itself artistically chaotic because it is imbued with the conserving and correcting power of his imagination." Saturday Rev

The recognitions; a novel. Harcourt Brace & Co. 1955 956p o.p.

"A novel about forgery. In it William Gaddis has attempted a full-scale portrait of our chaotic contemporary world, in all its hypocrisy and lack of love—a world in which the genuine is continually being discarded in favor of a successful facsimile. . . . Scores of characters move back and forth within the design, each one busy in pursuing his own desired deception." Publisher's note

"Rangy in settng, (New England, Greenwich Village, Paris, Spain, Italy, Central America), aswim in erudition, semi-Joycean in language, glacial in pace, irritatingly opaque in plot and character. The Recognitions is one of those eruptions of personal vision that will be argued about without being argued away." Time

Gaffney, Patricia

Circle of three; a novel. HarperCollins Pubs. 2000 421p $24
ISBN 0-06-019375-1 LC 00-33521

This tale "follows three generations of women through one tumultuous year. The book centers on recently widowed Carrie, who sees the grieving process as a chance to reinvent herself. But for Ruth, her 15-year-old daughter, it simply precipitates the onset of parent/child separation. Dana, Carrie's 70-year-old mother, isn't grieving; she's too busy trying to direct her daughter's life." Libr J

"Gaffney has each woman narrate in turn, providing added dimension to this poignant story of growing up and growing old." Booklist

Flight lessons; a novel. HarperCollins Pubs. 2002 388p o.p.
ISBN 0-06-018528-7 LC 2001-51934

"At 36, Anna Catalano is going home to the Eastern Shore of Maryland after finding her boyfriend in bed with her boss and best friend. For some reason she is more upset with her friend than with her boyfriend, maybe because history seems to be repeating itself. Anna walked in on her father and her aunt Rosa in the same position 20 years ago, and even though her mother was dead, Anna could never forgive Rosa, the guiding force in her life, although she did absolve her father. Now Anna is returning to help Rosa run the family restaurant, having flitted from job to job and man to man all this time. . . . The novel is filled with touching insights into family relationships." Booklist

Gage, Elizabeth

Pandora's box. Simon & Schuster 1990 717p o.p.
LC 90-9961

This novel "charts the careers of two alluring women born the same night in 1933. Secretive dark-haired Laura, given to mystical 'rainy day thoughts,' is left pregnant by a promiscuous art history prof at NYU. Nearly destroyed, she resurfaces as an acclaimed fashion designer and the greatest photographer since Steichen. Meanwhile, red-headed corporate climber Tess (aka Liz, Lisa, Bess), cold, bold and deliciously evil, plots her rise through the budding TV industry, then leaps to power in Washington." Publ Wkly

Gaiman, Neil, 1960-

American gods; a novel. Morrow 2001 465p $26
ISBN 0-380-97365-0 LC 2001-30407

"A noirish sci-fi road trip novel in which the melting pot of the United States extends not merely to mortals but to a motley assortment of disgruntled gods and deities. Early in 'American Gods' we are introduced to Shadow, a man who has been released from prison only to learn that his wife has died in a car crash. With nothing to return home to, Shadow accepts a job protecting Mr. Wednesday, an omniscient one-eyed grifter. . . . Soon the ex-convict finds himself in an alternate universe, where he is haunted by prophetic nightmares and visited by his dead wife." N Y Times Book Rev

Gaiman, Neil, 1960-—*Continued*

Anansi boys. William Morrow 2005 336p il $26.95

ISBN 0-06-051518-X LC 2005-47176

"Fat Charlie's life is about to be spiced up–his estranged father dies in a karaoke bar, and the handsome brother he never knew he had shows up on his doorstep with a gleam in his eye. Next thing he knows, Fat Charlie is being investigated by the police, his fiancée's falling in love with the wrong brother, and he finds out that his father was the god Anansi, Trickster and Spider, and that the beast gods of folklore are plotting their own revenge upon his family bloodline. A fun book with a little of everything–horror, mystery, magic, comedy, song, romance, ghosts, scary birds, ancient grudges, and trademark British wit." Libr J

Stardust. Avon Bks. 1999 238p o.p.

ISBN 0-380-97728-1 LC 98-8773

"Young Tristran Thorn has grown up in the isolated village of Wall, on the edge of the realm of Faerie. When Tristran and the lovely Victoria see a falling star during the special market fair, Victoria impulsively offers him his heart's desire if he will retrieve the star for her. Tristran crosses the border into Faerie and encounters witches, unicorns, and other strange creatures." Libr J

"Grounding his narrative in mythic tradition, Gaiman employs exquisitely rich language, natural wisdom, good humor and a dash of darkness to conjure up a fairy tale in the grand tradition." Publ Wkly

Gaines, Ernest J., 1933-

The autobiography of Miss Jane Pittman. Dial Press (NY) 1971 245p o.p.

LC 77-144380

"In the epic of Miss Jane Pittman, a 110-year-old ex-slave, the action begins at the time she is a small child watching both Union and Confederate troops come into the plantation on which she lives. It closes with the demonstrations of the sixties and the freedom walk she decides to make. This is a log of trials, heartaches, joys, love—but mostly of endurance." Shapiro. Fic for Youth. 3d edition

The gathering of old men. Knopf 1983 213p o.p.

ISBN 0-394-51468-8 LC 82-49000

"The story opens with the murder of Beau Boutan, a Cajun farmer, on the Louisiana plantation of Candy Marshall, a headstrong white owner. She claims to have done the shooting because she wished to protect one of her black workers, Mathu, who has been like a guardian to her following the death of her parents. In the plan to stand between Mapes, the local sheriff, and Mathu, Candy has set into motion an idea that has brought together a group of old black men with shotguns (unloaded), all claiming to have done the shooting. The threat of the South's way of punishing blacks by lynching hangs over the story like a pall. It meets opposition from Beau's young brother who has been friends with a black fellow-student and team-mate at his university." Shapiro. Fic for Youth. 3d edition

In my father's house. Knopf 1978 214p o.p.

LC 77-20357

"The sudden and unexpected appearance of his illegitimate son Etienne (or Robert X) throws Reverend Phillip Martin's life into disorder. His position as a religious figure in the community, a civil rights leader, and a stable family man is threatened, but the confrontation also brings to the fore many questions about father and son relationships and the conflict between the more conservative and militant factions in the black community." Shapiro. Fic for Youth. 2d edition

A lesson before dying. Knopf 1993 256p o.p.

ISBN 0-679-41477-0 LC 92-20335

"The story of two African American men struggling to attain manhood in a prejudiced society, the tale is set in Bayonne, La. . . in the late 1940s. It concerns Jefferson, a mentally slow, barely literate young man, who, though an innocent bystander to a shootout between a white store owner and two black robbers is convicted of murder, and the sophisticated, educated man who comes to his aid. When Jefferson's own attorney claims that executing him would be tantamount to killing a hog, his incensed godmother, Miss Emma, turns to teacher Grant Wiggins, pleading with him to gain access to the jailed youth and help him to face his death by electrocution with dignity." Publ Wkly

"YAs who seek thought-provoking reading will enjoy this glimpse of life in the rural South just before the civil rights movement." SLJ

Gaitskill, Mary, 1954-

Veronica. Pantheon 2005 227p $23

ISBN 0-375-42145-9 LC 2005-43143

Narrator Alison "discovers at an early age that her prettiness gives her power and leaves her vulnerable. She stumbles into modeling, barely survives a decadent interlude in Paris, then ends up in New York, worried that her modeling days are over. She takes a night-shift temp job and meets Veronica, who is older, unbeautiful, not hip, and joltingly cynical. Duncan, the love of Veronica's life, is a rampantly unfaithful bisexual who infects her with AIDS." Booklist

The author's "fierce, night-blooming new novel is about a close friendship between two women. But it should not be confused with anything cozy. Imagine a buddy story from the mind of William S. Burroughs, illustrated with images by Robert Mapplethorpe or David Cronenberg, and you get some idea of the tenderness to be found here. . . . Ms. Gaitskill writes so radiantly about violent self-loathing that the very incongruousness of her language has shocking power." N Y Times (N Y Late Ed)

Galbraith, Douglas

The rising sun. Atlantic Monthly Press 2001 535p o.p.

ISBN 0-87113-781-X LC 00-45336

A novel about pioneering "Scots of the 17th century seeking to establish a colony in modern-day Panama. Based on fact, the story is told from the viewpoint of the rather naive young Roderick Mackenzie, who signs on as a cargo supervisor of the *Rising Sun*, flagship of five vessels bound for the New World." Libr J

"Galbraith's greatest achievement is in finding a voice

Galbraith, Douglas—*Continued*
for his narrator, a tone and a vocabulary that sound plausibly like those of a 17th century clerk without resorting to the more onerous clichés and archaisms of historical fiction." N Y Times Book Rev

Galbraith, John Kenneth, 1908-

A tenured professor; a novel. Houghton Mifflin 1990 197p o.p.
LC 89-39559

"Can a tenured professor of economics at Harvard, creator of a stock forecasting model, put his vast yields toward liberal causes without upsetting the prevailing political-economic system? Montgomery Marvin develops the Index of Irrational Expectations (IRAT) after studying the euphoria which accompanies investment, and with his activist wife Marjie he puts IRAT earnings to such uses as labeling products based on their makers' number of women executives; establishing chairs in peace studies at the military academies; and setting up PRCs (Political Rectitude Committees)." Libr J

The author "juggles four victims in this irreverently satirical tale: Harvard, which is always a fine target for the deflationary knife jab; the mass hysteria that causes investors to assume that up is the only direction; official prattle about the American way; and the eccentricities of his own profession. He is in short, playing fairly as well as funnily." Atlantic

Galdós, Benito Pérez *See* Pérez Galdós, Benito, 1843-1920

Gallant, Mavis

The collected stories of Mavis Gallant. Random House 1996 887p o.p.
LC 96-6290

Published in Canada with title: The selected stories of Mavis Gallant

Contents: The Moslem wife; The four seasons; The Fenton child; The other Paris; Across the bridge; The latehomecomer; Señor Pinedo; By the sea; When we were nearly young; The ice wagon going down the street; The remission; The captive niece; Questions and answers; Ernst in civilian clothes; An unmarried man's summer; April fish; In transit; O lasting peace; An alien flower; The end of the world; New Year's eve; In the tunnel; Irina; Potter; Baum, Gabriel, 1935- ( ); Speck's idea; From the Fifteenth District; The Pegnitz Junction; Luc and his father; Overhead in a balloon; Kingdom come; Forain; A state of affairs; Mlle. Dias de Corta; Scarves, beads, sandals; The doctor; Voices lost in snow; In youth is pleasure; Between zero and one; Varieties of exile; 1933; The chosen husband; From cloud to cloud; Florida; A recollection; The colonel's child; Rue de Lille; Lena; A painful affair; A flying start; Grippes and poche; In plain sight

Gallico, Paul, 1897-1976

Mrs. 'Arris goes to Paris; drawings by Gioia Fiammenghi. Doubleday 1958 157p o.p.

"The unsinkable Mrs. 'Arris, a middle-aged London charwoman, who is fascinated with her wealthy employer's Dior gown, works and saves her money for her own Dior original. When she gets to Paris, she brings happiness to all she meets, and finally gets her dress." Jacob.

To be continued

Other titles in the series are: Mrs. 'Arris goes to New York (1960); Mrs. 'Arris goes to Parliament (1965); and Mrs. 'Arris goes to Moscow (1975)

The Poseidon adventure. Coward-McCann 1969 347p o.p.

"A large ocean liner converted to a cruise ship, the S.S. Poseidon, is caught by an underwater earthquake and capsizes. As the ship is slowly sinking, a group of survivors, with the help of an American mountaineer, inch their way upward through the bowels of the ship to safety. The interlocking stories of these passengers make for interesting reading." Shapiro. Fic for Youth. 2d edition

The snow goose. Knopf 1940 57p $19.95
ISBN 0-394-44593-7

"In 1930 Philip Rhayader, a hunchbacked painter, moves to an abandoned lighthouse, where he devotes himself not only to his painting but to maintaining a bird sanctury. Rejected by the world, he is a recluse until Fritha, a young girl, brings him a hurt Canadian snow goose to care for and heal. The bird becomes a bond in their deepening relationship. When Philip is killed in aiding the rescue at Dunkirk, Fritha continues to care for his birds until the lighthouse is destroyed." Shapiro. Fic for Youth. 3d edition

Galloway, Janice

Clara. Simon & Schuster 2003 425p $25
ISBN 0-684-84449-4 LC 2002-26800

First published 2002 in the United Kingdom

This work focuses on the life of "18th century composer and piano virtuoso, Clara Schumann. Schumann, better known as the wife of Robert Schmann, and the musical associate of such greats as Brahms and Mendelssohn, was a true artist in her own right. She was also the mostly submissive daughter of an egomaniacal and manipulative father and the long-suffering spouse to a mentally disturbed genius." Libr J

"The Schumanns' marriage was forged of perfectly dissonant material, and Galloway allows the collisions to speak for themselves." N Y Times Book Rev

Where you find it; stories. Simon & Schuster 2002 c1996 235p o.p.
ISBN 0-684-84450-8 LC 2001-49668

First published 1996 in the United Kingdom

Contents: Valentine; Where you find it; Sonata form; A night in; Test; After the rains; Waiting for Marilyn; Hope; Bisex; Peeping Tom; Baby-sitting; Someone had to; A proper respect; The bridge; Tourists from the south arrive in the independent state; The dreams of pleasing his mother; Last thing; Not flu; Proposal; Six horses

"The twenty stories in this unsettling, beautifully written collection take place in and around Glasgow, and the protagonists are mainly imperfectly loved girls and women. Galloway is particularly interested in moments of apprehension, times when a niggling intimation of something slightly out of kilter turns into really bad news. . . . In fact, Galloway's powers of observation are often so acute that the reader's impulse is to turn away." New Yorker

Galsworthy, John, 1867-1933

End of the chapter. Scribner 1934 897p o.p.
"The Forsyte chronicles"
Sequel to A modern comedy
Also known as the Cherrell saga (after family connections of the Forsytes) this book contains volumes 7-9 of the larger series, The Forsyte chronicles: Maid in waiting (1931), Flowering wilderness (1932), and Over the river (1933; published with title: One more river)
In Maid in waiting, Denny Cherrell undertakes the vindication of her brother whose army career has been ruined by an American archeological expedition leader's unjust accusations
In Flowering wilderness, Denny falls in love with Wifred Desert, a young poet back from the East. A meddlesome traveler spreads the rumor that Wilfred accepted Mohammedanism in order to escape death at the hands of Arab fanatics; English club and society people see this as an outrage to the British ruling class' code of honor. Ostracized and tortured by pride, the sensitive poet becomes in truth a coward and disappears, leaving his still loyal fiancée only her memories
In the final volume, Over the river, Denny's chief concern is her younger sister Clare's divorce from a sadistic husband. After learning of Wilfred's drowning in Siam, Denny decides to marry Dornford

Flowering wilderness
In Galsworthy, J. End of the chapter p331-592

The Forsyte saga; with a preface by Ada Galsworthy. Scribner 1922 xx, 921p o.p.
Contains volumes 1-3 of the Forsyte chronicles: The man of property (entered separately), In chancery (1920), and To let (1921). Two interludes are included: Indian summer of a Forsyte (1918) and Awakening (1920)
In chancery relates the further fortunes of the Forsyte family. Irene Forsyte's first effort toward emancipation from her husband Soames ended with the accidental death of the architect who loved her. Meeting Irene again, after a separation of fifteen years, awakens in Soames the old desire to possess her, and failing of her consent, files for divorce. This action forces his cousin Jolyon into the role of correspondent. Soames eventually marries Annette Lamotte, who presents him with a daughter, Fleur, instead of a longed-for male heir. Jolyon and Irene marry and have a son, Jon
The first interlude, Awakening, is about little Jon until he is eight years old. The second interlude, Indian summer of a Forsyte, goes back in time to the secret visit of Irene to old Jolyon at Robin Hill, the country place Soames had built for her before their separation. She captivates the older man by her gentleness, and he dies quietly one summer day
To let centers on the romance of Jon and Fleur who are brought together by chance and are ignorant of the enmity between Soames, and Irene and Jolyon. When Fleur proposes a hasty marriage to Jon, his father reluctantly discloses the reason for the feud. After Jolyon's death, Irene and Jon leave for America, and Fleur, disappointed, marries Michael Mont.
Followed by A modern comedy

The Galsworthy reader; edited by Anthony West. Scribner 1968 c1967 xxi, 702p o.p.
This omnibus volume includes: The man of property; Indian summer of a Forsyte (1918); excerpts from three other novels, four short stories and two plays
Short stories included are: The consummation; The meeting; A stoic; Virtue

In chancery
In Galsworthy, J. The Forsyte saga p363-639

The Indian summer of a Forsyte
In Galsworthy, J. The Forsyte saga p313-59
In Galsworthy, J. The Galsworthy reader p543-86

Maid in waiting
In Galsworthy, J. End of the chapter p1-330

The man of property. o.p.
First published 1906
"The 'man of property' . . . is Soames Forsyte. His wife Irene, whom he regards as just another piece of property, falls in love with Philip Bosinney, a young architect. Soames devotes all his money and power to punishing them, and Philip is killed in an accident." Reader's Ency. 4th edition
also in Galsworthy, J. The Forsyte saga p3-309
also in Galsworthy, J. The Galsworthy reader p15-294

A modern comedy. Scribner 1929 798p o.p.
"A Scribners/Macmillan Hudson River edition"
Sequel to The Forsyte saga
A reissue of the title first published 1929
This book contains volumes 4-6 of the Forsyte chronicles: The white monkey (1924); The silver spoon (1926); Swan song (1928)
The white monkey concerns Fleur and Michael Mont, and Fleur's father Soames. A son is born to the couple, thus strengthening the marriage which had been weakened by Fleur's affair with an artist and her unrequited love for her cousin Jon
The silver spoon, picks up the story line three years later in 1924 as Soames challenges a rival of Fleur's for calling his daughter a snob. A disagreeable libel suit evolves
As Swan song opens, Soames has mellowed. He guards with special tenderness the welfare of his daughter and son-in-law, but all his watchfullness and devotion are powerless to avert the tragedy of Fleur's deliberate revival of her love affair with Jon Forsyte when he returns to England with his American wife, Anne. The story ends as Soames saves Fleur from death, and in doing so, is killed himself. This sobers the girl and she returns to her husband.
Followed by End of the chapter

Over the river
In Galsworthy, J. End of the chapter p593-897

The silver spoon
In Galsworthy, J. A modern comedy

Swan song
In Galsworthy, J. A modern comedy

Galsworthy, John, 1867-1933—*Continued*

To let
In Galsworthy, J. The Forsyte saga p665-921

The white monkey
In Galsworthy, J. A modern comedy

Gann, Ernest Kellogg, 1910-1991

The high and the mighty. Sloane 1953 342p o.p.

"Story about 20 people on a Honolulu-San Francisco air liner and how they face the strong possibility that the plane will crash." Christ Sci Monit

Gao Xingjian, 1940-

Buying a fishing rod for my grandfather; stories; translated from the Chinese by Mabel Lee. HarperCollins Pubs. 2004 127p $17.95

ISBN 0-06-057555-7 LC 2003-51138

Original Chinese edition, 1989

Contents: The temple; In the park; Cramp; The accident ; Buying a fishing rod for my grandfather; In an instant

"Though few in number, the stories in this collection are richly diverse. One is a bittersweet reflection of a newlywed on his honeymoon; another a Pinteresque dialogue in a park; a third a traffic accident recounted in realtime with all its voyeuristic detail and authentic philosophical questioning, and still another, a strong memory-driven, first-person tale that follows the mental trail of a man who passes a fishing equipment shop and begins to remember his grandfather. For variety of content, stylistic experimentation, graceful language, and poignant insight, Xingjian is a writer who does it all beautifully." Booklist

Soul mountain; translated from the Chinese by Mabel Lee. HarperCollins Pubs. 2000 510p o.p.

ISBN 0-06-621082-8 LC 2001-269378

In this novel "a character called 'I' learns that he does not have lung cancer, as previously diagnosed, and embarks on a journey through China in search of spiritual tranquility." Time

"It is not easy to say what the novel is about—and yet the marvel is that somehow it is still both engaging and elegant." N Y Times Book Rev

García, Cristina, 1959-

The Aguero sisters. Knopf 1997 299p o.p.

ISBN 0-679-45090-4 LC 96-52204

"The story of the middle-aged Agüero sisters—independent Reina, an electrician living in Havana, and thoroughly urbanized Constancia, a successful cosmetics salesperson living in New York—is also the story of how personal tragedy and the legacy of Castro's revolution impact one family's history and collective memory. The narrative is filtered through many voices, both past and present, including the women's parents, famous naturalists, and Reina's daughter, a sometime prostitute who is sick to death of poverty-stricken Havana." Booklist

"Unmoored by the reverberating effects of the revolution, Garcia's characters search for stability and meaning in a world where fatalism is their only belief. They all endure 'the fidelity of certain, unshakable pain,' but sudden insights illuminate their different routes to salvation." Publ Wkly

Dreaming in Cuban; a novel. Knopf 1992 244p o.p.

LC 91-20755

Shifting back and forth between Cuba and Brooklyn, this novel "centers on three generations of a family torn apart by Fidel Castro's revolution. Celia del Pino is the matriarch whose passions alternate between a long-lost Spanish lover and service to El Lider. In Brooklyn, Celia's daughter Lourdes runs the Yankee Doodle Bakery. Haunted by the memory of being raped by a revolutionary soldier back home, she is obsessed by her hatred for Castro and communism and her mother's devotion to both. Lourdes's daughter, Pilar, scoffs at her mother's belief that she can 'fight Communism from behind her bakery counter' and plots a return to the island." Newsweek

"While taking very seriously those ideas that have truly riven so many families in recent years, leaving many obsessed with the politics of Cuba, Ms. Garcia also portrays the costliness of such an obsession and the fading of the light between mothers and daughters, between lovers, as communication fails." N Y Times Book Rev

Monkey hunting. Knopf 2003 251p $23

ISBN 0-375-41056-2 LC 2002-35916

This novel "chronicles the fortunes of Chen Pan, a Chinese who is enslaved in the Cuban sugar fields in 1857 and later becomes a prosperous businessman in Havana; the mulata slave Lucrecia, whose relationship with Chen Pan is poignantly rendered; and their descendants: Lorenzo, a doctor of herbal medicine in Havana; lesbian Chen Fang, a teacher imprisoned for counterrevolutionary activities in Mao's China; and Domingo Chen, an immigrant to New York City who serves in the U.S. Army in Vietnam." Libr J

"For all the ground Garcia covers, the most beautiful and moving parts of her novel are the chapters on Chen Pan's youthful sufferings. Here, horror and wonder alternate unblinkingly, as if they are random occurrences in a dark once-upon-a-time." N Y Times Book Rev

García Márquez, Gabriel, 1928-

The autumn of the patriarch; translated from the Spanish by Gregory Rabassa. Harper & Row 1976 269p o.p.

Original Spanish edition, 1975

"A highly sophisticated novel about an unnamed dictator (the patriarch), who, at the time of his death, is somewhere between 107 and 232 years of age. The patriarch embodies the archtypal evils of despotism, but even more significant is his extreme, and often pathetic, solitude, which becomes increasingly evident with his advancing age and which emerges as the principal theme. Despite its political and psychological overtones, the autumn of the patriarch can best be described as a lyrical novel, whose plot and character development are subordinate to formal design and symbolic imagery." Ency of World Lit in the 20th century

Big Mama's funeral
In García Márquez, G. Collected stories p97-200
In García Márquez, G. No one writes to the colonel, and other stories p65-170

García Márquez, Gabriel, 1928-—*Continued*

Chronicle of a death foretold; translated from the Spanish by Gregory Rabassa. Knopf 1983 c1982 120p $25

ISBN 0-394-53074-8 LC 82-48884

Original Spanish edition published 1981 in Colombia; this translation first published 1982 in the United Kingdom

Set in a provincial Colombian town, this novella "is a reconstruction of an actual episode in which the people of a whole neighborhood, if not in fact a whole town, stood by and did nothing while a couple of drunks planned, announced, and finally carried out a murder. The killers alleged motive was revenge for their sister's loss of honor and this claim, together with normal languor and stupidity, appears to have brought on collective paralysis and even collective complicity among their fellow citizens." Atlantic

This "investigation of an ancient murder takes on the quality of a hallucinatory exploration, a deep groping search into the gathering darkness of human intentions for a truth that continually slithers away." N Y Rev Books

also in García Márquez, G. Collected novellas p167-249

Collected novellas. HarperCollins Pubs. 1990 249p o.p.

LC 89-46106

English translations of the three novellas included in this volume were first published 1972, 1968 and 1982 respectively

Contents: Leaf storm; No one writes to the colonel; Chronicle of a death foretold

Collected stories. Harper & Row 1984 311p o.p.

LC 84-47826

This volume includes stories from the author's three previous collections: No one writes to the colonel, and other stories; Leaf storm, and other stories, and Innocent Eréndira, and other stories

The general and his labyrinth; translated from the Spanish by Edith Grossman. Knopf 1990 285p o.p.

ISBN 0-394-58258-6 LC 90-52957

Original Spanish edition, 1989

This novel attempts to portray the last days of Simon Bolivar. "Ousted from the presidency of Colombia while once adoring crowds jeer him as a tyrant, a dying 46-year-old Bolivar journeys to supposed exile. His route on the Magdalena River is a tropical Via Dolorosa, lined by war-ravaged towns, grieving widows, scheming generals and long-ago romances. What Bolivar encounters most, however, are delirious dreams and memories that expose his life's epic contradictions." Newsweek

"Seldom has there been a more fitting match between author and subject. Mr. Garcia Márquez wades into his flamboyant, often improbable and ultimately tragic material with enormous gusto, heaping detail upon sensuous detail, alternating grace with horror." N Y Times Book Rev

In evil hour; translated from the Spanish by Gregory Rabassa. Harper & Row 1979 183p o.p.

Original Spanish edition, 1968

This novel "is set in a squalid river town. . . . The village is weighed down by an immense inertia, the result of the natives' hatred of a corrupt dictatorship and of the seasonal rains that dampen their spirits. The mayor, a hired assassin of the new central government, dreams of wealth, not war. . . . Lampoons begin to haunt the town, in the form of slanderous posters that appear overnight on doors and walls. No one can trace the authors. . . . Prominent citizens become so upset by the ghostly terrorism that the mayor is forced to impose a curfew, which in turn triggers a resurgence of political opposition." Newsweek

"The reader is carried along effortlessly in the current of this gifted storyteller's prose. Both heroes and villains elicit sympathy because their basic human foibles, while true to local circumstances, can be recognized by people of any culture." Libr J

The incredible and sad tale of innocent Eréndira and her heartless grandmother

In García Márquez, G. Collected stories p262-311

In García Márquez, G. Innocent Eréndira, and other stories p1-59

Innocent Eréndira, and other stories. Harper & Row 1978 183p o.p.

Contents: The incredible and sad tale of innocent Eréndira and her heartless grandmother [novella]; The sea of lost time; Death constant beyond love; The third resignation; The other side of death; Eva is inside her cat; Dialogue with the mirror; Bitterness for three sleepwalkers; Eyes of a blue dog; The woman who came at six o'clock; Someone has been disarranging these roses; The night of the curlews

Leaf storm

In García Márquez, G. Collected novellas p1-106

In García Márquez, G. Leaf storm, and other stories p1-97

Leaf storm, and other stories; translated from the Spanish by Gregory Rabassa. Harper & Row 1972 146p o.p.

Short stories included are: The handsomest drowned man in the world; A very old man with enormous wings; Blacamán the Good, vendor of miracles; The last voyage of the ghost ship; Monologue of Isabel watching it rain in Macondo; Nabo

The title novella (originally published 1955) covers three generations of boom and decline in the mythical Colombian town Macondo. "The small river town changes with the leaf storm of people—strangers who come there as a result of civil war and the establishment of a banana company. Marquez begins with the end, the death of one mysterious wanderer, a doctor who . . . withdraws from the world. As the narrators, a man, his daughter, her young son, reveal the doctor's story, so too do the tellers' own melancholy lives emerge, symbolic yet specific, representing the everlasting variety of man's inhumanity to man." Publ Wkly

Love in the time of cholera; translated from the Spanish by Edith Grossman; with an introduction by Nicholas Shakespeare. Knopf 1997 xxxiii, 422p $22

ISBN 0-375-40069-9

García Márquez, Gabriel, 1928-—*Continued*

"Everyman's library"

Original Spanish edition published 1985 in Colombia, this is a reissue of the 1988 edition

"The story, which concerns the themes of love, aging, and death, takes place between the late 1870s and the early 1930s in a South American community troubled by wars and outbreaks of cholera. It is a tale of two lovers, artistic Florentino Ariza and wealthy Fermina Daza, who reunite after a lifetime apart. Their spirit of enduring love contrasts ironically with the surrounding corporeal decay." Merriam-Webster's Ency of Lit

No one writes to the colonel

In García Márquez, G. Collected novellas p107-66

In García Márquez, G. No one writes to the colonel, and other stories p3-62

No one writes to the colonel, and other stories; translated from the Spanish by J. S. Bernstein. Harper & Row 1968 170p o.p.

This volume contains the title novella (originally published 1961 in Colombia) and eight short stories (originally published together 1962 in Mexico; translated title: Big Mama's funeral)

Short stories included are: Tuesday siesta; One of these days; There are no thieves in this town; Balthazar's marvelous afternoon; Montiel's widow; One day after Saturday; Artificial roses; Big Mama's funeral

Of love and other demons; translated from the Spanish by Edith Grossman. Knopf 1995 147p o.p.

ISBN 0-679-43853-X LC 94-42904

Original Spanish edition, 1994

This novel is set in a Latin American port city during colonial times. The 12-year-old "offspring of a melancholy, ineffectual marquis and a mother yoked to 'insatiable vices,' Sierva Maria is raised by the family's West Indian slaves, who teach her the Yoruban language and magical practices. She is bitten by a rabid dog but shows no real symptoms; the local bishop, however, decides she is possessed by demons and orders her incarcerated in a convent where she will be exorcised by his gentle librarian, Father Delaura. But Delaura becomes possessed, too—by his love for this suffering child three decades his junior." Publ Wkly

"The novel is continuing proof that Garcia is the master of putting a lot of story into a small space. . . . A Latin American Abelard and Héloise? Not quite. Garcia tells a story of forbidden love, but he demonstrates once again the vigor of his own passion; the daring and irresistible coupling of history and imagination." Time

One hundred years of solitude; translated from the Spanish by Gregory Rabassa. Harper & Row 1970 422p o.p.

ISBN 0-06-011418-5

Original Spanish edition published 1967 in Argentina

This novel "relates the founding of Macondo by Jose Arcadio Buendia, the adventures of six generations of his descendants, and, ultimately, the town's destruction. It also presents a vast synthesis of social, economic, and political evils plaguing much of Latin America. Even more important from a literary point of view is its aesthetic representation of a world in microcosm, that is, a complete history, from Eden to Apocalypse, of a world in which miracles such as people riding on flying carpets and a dead man returning to life tend to erase the thin line between objective and subjective realities." Ency of World Lit in the 20th Century

Strange pilgrims; twelve stories; translated from the Spanish by Edith Grossman. Knopf 1993 188p o.p.

ISBN 0-679-42566-7 LC 93-12257

Contents: Bon voyage, Mr. President; The saint; Sleeping beauty and the airplane; I sell my dreams; "I only came to use the phone"; The ghosts of August; Maria dos Prazeres; Seventeen poisoned Englishmen; Tramontana; Miss Forbes's summer of happiness; Light is like water; The trail of your blood in the snow

"Exile and loss are the principal subjects of these 12 stories . . . which capture with lyrical precision the emotions of disorientation and fear, coupled with a sense of new possibility, experienced by Latin Americans in Europe." Publ Wkly

Garcia Morales, Adelaida

Bene

In Garcia Morales, A. and Deveny, T. G. The south and Bene

The south

In Garcia Morales, A. and Deveny, T. G. The south and Bene

The south and Bene; translated and with a preface by Thomas G. Deveny. University of Neb. Press 1999 117p o.p.

ISBN 0-8032-2178-9 LC 99-17852

"European women writers series"

Original Spanish edition, 1985

These two interwoven novellas are "narrated in the voice of Adriana, a young woman unraveling the painful secrets of her childhood. In a narrative set in a labyrinthine gothic landscape sometime after the Spanish Civil War, Adriana speaks almost exclusively to the ghost of her father, who committed suicide. . . . The second novella, . . . concerns the family's mysterious Gypsy maid, Bene, who may be a demon herself or the victim of diabolic machinations." Publ Wkly

García-Roza, Luiz Alfredo, 1936-

December heat; translated by Benjamin Moser. Holt & Co. 2003 273p $23

ISBN 0-8050-6890-2 LC 2002-38825

Original Portuguese edition published 1998 in Brazil

"This time the plot concerns Espinosa's friend, a retired policeman who appears to be the likely suspect when his hooker girlfriend is murdered. Confusing the issue, though, is a series of subsequent murders whose tenuous links to the first are fading as precious time passes." Booklist

"An exciting procedural, infused with exotic ambience, sympathetic detectives, and a little romance." Libr J

The silence of the rain; a mystery; {by} Luiz Alfredo Garcia-Roza; translated by Benjamin Moser. Holt & Co. 2002 261p o.p.

ISBN 0-8050-6889-9 LC 2001-51523

García-Roza, Luiz Alfredo, 1936-—*Continued*

Original Portuguese edition published 1996

In this mystery "Inspector Espinosa of the Rio de Janeiro police department, a jaded intellectual who'd rather visit a used bookstore than a crime scene, must catch the murderer of Richardo Carvalho, a corporate executive found shot to death in a parking garage, his briefcase and wallet missing. . . . The sultry Rio setting, whose exotic neighborhoods add definition to the action, and a most unorthodox detective should appeal to police procedural fans with a taste for the offbeat." Publ Wkly

Gardam, Jane

Faith Fox. Carroll & Graf 2003 416p $25

ISBN 0-786-71221-X

First published 1996 in the United Kingdom

In this novel set in the Britain of the early 1990s, Faith Fox's mother dies in childbirth. Her father won't take care of her and her grandmother "refuses to acknowledge the baby whose birth killed the daughter she loved. And so an extraordinary group of family, friends, and strangers converge to make sure that Faith Fox ends up raised well in the right hands." Publisher's note

Gardam's "characters, Dickensian in their number, variety, and abounding eccentricities, carry on so convincingly that she seems to be channeling, rather than creating, these people." Atl Mon

The flight of the maidens. Carroll & Graf Pubs. 2001 278p $25

ISBN 0-7867-0879-4 LC 00-343383

First published 2000 in the United Kingdom

"It is the summer of 1946 in Yorkshire England. . . . To the delight of the town, three local girls, best friends from secondary school, have won prestigious scholarships to universities in London and Cambridge. But before they depart, they must survive the summer. While Hetty struggles to escape from her battle-scarred father and possessive mother by reading books, Una haltingly asserts her emerging womanhood with a young man from the wrong side of the tracks and of a decidedly leftist political bent. Meanwhile, Liselotte, a Jewish refugee living with a Quaker family since her arrival in 1939 via the Kindertransport, is whisked off to California to meet her last surviving relative." Libr J

Gardam "has thrown out the usual too-sensitive-for-you boilerplate of the coming-of-age novel, for which we can be thankful. Luckily, the generational conflict that remains is usually all the better for her wry indirection." N Y Times Book Rev

The queen of the tambourine. St. Martin's Press 1995 226p o.p.

ISBN 0-312-13151-8 LC 95-15833

First published 1991 in the United Kingdom

This novel, constructed as a series of letters from Eliza Peabody to her neighbor, "examines what happens to a clever, imaginative, lively woman whose husband reaches the rank of senior civil servant and maroons her in a stodgy, semi-posh London suburb with no occupation but good works and no reliable company but the dog." Atl Mon

"With devilish wit, Ms. Gardam ushers Eliza into the ranks of heroines driven mad by splendid suburban isolation. . . . Yet Eliza's story takes on more and more sense as it emerges from her tragicomic vignettes." N Y Times Book Rev

Gardiner, John Rolfe

The Magellan House; stories; illustrations by Joan Gardiner. Counterpoint 2004 297p il $24

ISBN 1-582-43233-3 LC 2004-4932

Contents: The voyage out; Fugitive color; The doll house; The Ricus Adams; Morse operator; Leaving Port McHair; The head of Farnham Hall; The shape of the past; The Magellan House

"There is something tantalizingly sinister about Gardiner's short stories: a hint of intrigue and a soupcon of the illicit connect them all. This undercurrent of mystery and paranoia provides a thrilling tension that lurks just below the surface." Booklist

Gardner, Erle Stanley, 1889-1970

The case of the postponed murder. Morrow 1973 220p o.p.

This novel begins "with a girl trying to pass herself off as the younger of two daughters worried about the disappearance of her older sister. But Perry Mason, to whom she goes for help, is intrigued rather than taken in. The girl is accused of forgery, then a murder occurs in which she is a prime suspect." Best Sellers

The case of the sulky girl. Morrow 1933 303p o.p.

Defense attorney Perry Mason becomes embroiled in a murder case when he is contacted by a young woman worried about her father's will

Honest money, and other short novels. Carroll & Graf Pubs. 1991 204p o.p.

LC 91-12116

Contents: Honest money; The top comes off; Close call; Making the breaks; Devil's fire; Blackmail with lead

"First published in 1932 and 1933 by *Black Mask* magazine and starring the young crime-fighting lawyer Ken Corning and gutsy secretary Helen Vail, the six stories collected here provide the prototype for the late author's astoundingly successful Perry Mason crime novels." Publ Wkly

Gardner, John, 1933-1982

Grendel; illustrated by Emil Antonucci. Knopf 1971 174p il o.p.

ISBN 0-394-47143-1

"To the heroes of 'Beowulf,' the monster Grendel, devourer of men, represented chaos and death and pagan darkness. This is Grendel's side of the story. . . . Grendel perceives that what the primeval dragon has told him is true: he is the brute existent by which men learn to define themselves. 'Grendel' may be read for what it says about the human condition, for its implicit comments on men's art, wars, fears, and hopes." Publ Wkly

"The world, Mr. Gardner seems to be suggesting in his violent, inspiring, awesome, terrifying narrative, has to defeat its Grendels, yet somehow, he hints, both ecologically and in deeper ways, that world is a poorer place when men and their monsters cannot coexist." Christ Sci Monit

Mickelsson's ghost; a novel; illustrated with photographs by Joel Gardner. Knopf 1982 590p il o.p.

ISBN 0-394-50468-2 LC 81-48114

Gardner, John, 1933-1982—*Continued*

This novel "features a philosophy professor seeking to escape his students, the tax authorities, and a failed marriage by buying an old house in the country, only to encounter a series of paranormal events." Good Fiction Guide

Nickel mountain; a pastoral novel; with etchings by Thomas O'Donohue. Knopf 1973 312p il o.p.

The hero of this novel, "Henry Soames, is the fat owner of a truck-route diner deep in the forests of the Catskills. . . . A nice girl named Callie who helps in Henry's diner gets pregnant by a rich man's son, who then skips town. Soames marries her out of kindness. They go through the agony of childbirth. As the boy grows up, their domestic peace is variously threatened in small ways." Time

"Against considerable odds, Henry manages to survive with dignity and good conscience, and this is what the novel is really about—the survival of plain human goodness. Given a little thought, that is an exciting theme. Mr. Gardner has made an absorbing and provocative book out of it." Atlantic

October light; illustrated by Elaine Raphael and Don Bolognese. Knopf 1976 433p il o.p.

"One evening James Page, a 72-year-old Vermont farmer, chases his 80-year-old sister Sally upstairs with a piece of stovewood and locks her in her bedroom. James, part savage and part Green Mountain philosopher thinks the country has gone to hell—you can see it all on TV, which is why he shoots Sally's TV set to pieces right before her eyes. Sally is a liberal, believing in New York City and amnesty, and amuses herself in captivity with a 'trashy' novel about marijuana smugglers. . . . In them, Sally sees an allegory of Third World attacks on capitalism, even sees herself as the Third World and her brother as brutish capitalism. . . . At first James won't let Sally out [of her room], then she won't come out. . . . Family and friends gather to preach and cajole." Newsweek

"With splendid invention (including a marvelous novel within the novel), precise and emphatically drawn characters, superb writing, Gardner explores people and a place uniquely American." Libr J

The sunlight dialogues; illustrated by John Napper. Knopf 1972 673p il o.p.

"In 1966, Fred Clumly, age 64, was a stolid, law-and-order police chief in Batavia, a town in western New York. Law and order are disrupted by a bearded, babbling . . . madman, a magician of sorts who paints the word LOVE across one of the town streets. The Sunlight Man, Clumly calls him for lack of any other name, and locks him up. The lunatic stages a magical escape and then returns to free another prisoner, who murders a policeman as they leave. The hunt is on, and so is the pressure put on Clumly, who seems to do nothing right, though in fact the best fictional detectives—Inspectors Javert, Porfiry Petrovich and Maigret as well as Clumly—know that you catch your man after you have understood him." Newsweek

Gardner, John E., 1926-

Cold fall; [by] John Gardner. Putnam 1996 228p o.p.

ISBN 0-399-14149-9 LC 96-33671

This James Bond adventure "involves a British airliner that blows up while landing at Washington's Dulles Airport, killing almost 500 people. Bond's ex-lover is believed to be one of the victims. The evil doers belong to a group code-named COLD, the Children of the Last Days. Some are ex-Mob, some are dangerous crazies, and some are highly intelligent criminals who believe that the only way to fight crime is by putting criminals into the government." Booklist

License renewed; [by] John Gardner. Marek, R. 1981 285p o.p.

LC 81-1284

This continues the series of "novels about secret agent James Bond, Ian Fleming's literary creation of the 50s and 60s. . . . Bond now drives a Saab, eschewing the low-mileage Bentleys of his past years for one of those economical foreign models. His cigarettes are low tar, and he admits to cutting his alcohol consumption. But his license to kill has been renewed, for there is yet another mad genius loose in the world, one Anton Murik, nuclear physicist who happens to be Scottish laird as well. Anton has hatched an airtight scheme to make six nuclear power plants contract the China Syndrome unless the countries involved pay up." SLJ

The return of Moriarty; [by] John Gardner. Putnam 1974 366p o.p.

The novel is based on the concept that Professor James Moriarty, archrival of Sherlock Holmes, "had been saved from death at the Reichenbach Falls. Moriarty's notes of his criminal activities in the East End of London have recently been discovered and are now being published, together with footnotes. They outline the nefarious activities and the resounding capers of an English gang of the Nineties, its super-criminal leader, and the destruction of a rival gang of hoodlums." Libr J

"Holmes fans will enjoy Gardner's straight-faced humor—footnotes and all—as well as the colorful characters and their 19th century wickedness." Publ Wkly

Followed by The revenge of Moriarty

The revenge of Moriarty; [by] John Gardner. Putnam 1975 289p o.p.

Moriarty, "the arch enemy of Sherlock Holmes returns to London in 1896 with a hefty bankroll amassed in the U.S. He is burning for revenge—against the quartet of Continental supercriminals who betrayed him, and against Holmes and Scotland Yard's Inspector Crow. Simple murder is too good for his foes; he wants them utterly humiliated and ostracized from their professions. And Moriarty has all the time, money and staff he needs to devise complex schemes of retribution. . . . Superficially, the pace seems as leisurely as that of a Conan Doyle story, but a lot more is happening—including lots of bawdy sex—in a lovingly recreated Victorian London." Publ Wkly

Gardner, Lisa

Alone; Lisa Gardner. Bantam Books 2005 324p $24

ISBN 0-553-80253-4 LC 2004-57577

The protagonist of this thriller is "Massachusetts police sniper Bobby Dodge. He meets his match in Catherine Gagnon, who as a girl was snatched, raped and nearly murdered. Now she's the wife of erratic, rich Jimmy

Gardner, Lisa—*Continued*
Gagnon and mother of perpetually ill four-year-old Nathan. When Bobby kills Jimmy during a hostage situation at the Gagnons, he does it to save Catherine and Nathan. But was it a righteous shoot, or did Catherine engineer the killing? Judge James Gagnon and his wife, Maryanne, think Bobby murdered their son out of lust for Catherine. As other people start dying, very messily, and the DA and cops come down hard on Bobby, Gardner keeps the tension high and the pace fast." Publ Wkly

Garlock, Dorothy

The edge of town. Warner Bks. 2001 370p o.p.
ISBN 0-446-52769-6 LC 00-50346
"Since her mother's death, lovely Julie Jones has cared for her farmer father and five siblings. She dotes on her family, but she also dreams of the day a worthy love will come and whisk her away. When Evan Johnson, the son of the Joneses' despised neighbor, Walter, comes home to take over his father's farm, he proves a pleasant surprise. The handsome young WWI vet has a college education, and is nothing like his drunken, abusive father." Publ Wkly
"With settings and characters so authentic the reader believes they have a past and a future, Garlock's heartwarming romantic historicals are Americana at its best." Booklist

Garry, Jane
(ed) Trial and error. See Trial and error

Gash, Joe *See* Granger, Bill

Gash, Jonathan, 1933-

Moonspender. St. Martin's Press 1987 280p o.p.
LC 86-26199
"A Joan Kahn book"
In this caper "antiques dealer Lovejoy, perpetually penurious and even more impoverished than usual, finds himself simultaneously appearing on a TV game show, running a big wedding, receiving a job offer from his current lady friend, helping to redecorate a new restaurant and sniffing out antiquities in East Anglia. There are also a couple of antiques-related deaths, one definitely a murder. Lovejoy gets on with his chores, undeterred by a barrage of lawsuits and myriad romantic complications." Publ Wkly

The possessions of a lady. Viking 1996 324p o.p.
LC 96-17281
"Along with offending everyone he encounters at a fashion show, Lovejoy must deal with his failing antiques business and decide whether to help a friend find a missing teenage girl or join the mysterious Olga Maltravers Featherstone for what promises to be an evening of heady enchantment. . . . With his usual wit and style, Gash offers up another hilarious tale featuring one of the most appealing eccentrics in crime fiction." Booklist

Prey dancing; a Dr. Clare Burtonall mystery. Viking 1998 272p o.p.
ISBN 0-670-87764-6 LC 98-2830
"The unlikely team of cardiologist Clare Burtonall and her lover, male prostitute Bonn, risk murder when they attempt to carry out an AIDS patient's last request." Libr J
"Brilliantly written, mysterious, menacing, and filled with unforgettable characters." Booklist

A rag, a bone, and a hank of hair; the twenty-first Lovejoy novel. Viking 2000 344p o.p.
ISBN 0-670-88598-3 LC 99-52654
First published 1999 in the United Kingdom
"Pursued from East Anglia by the usual creditors and angry husbands, Lovejoy descends on London with a private commission to find out who is flooding the trade with bogus gemstones, a quest that takes him from trendy galleries on Chelsea's King's Road to the jumbled stalls of outdoor markets in Bermondsey, Camden Passage and Portobello Road." N Y Times Book Rev

The rich and the profane; a Lovejoy novel. Viking 1999 344p o.p.
ISBN 0-670-88346-8 LC 98-38951
First published 1998 in the United Kingdom
Lovejoy "takes on yet another persona when he impersonates a pop music impresario and produces a splashy variety show on the English Channel island of Guernsey—clever cover for an ingenious art fraud that draws the suckers like flies." N Y Times Book Rev
"With this dervish of comic activity and a romp that ends in a circuslike venue, Gash is in top form." Publ Wkly

The tartan sell. St. Martin's Press 1986 227p o.p.
LC 86-3754
"A Joan Kahn book"
"East Anglia antique dealer Lovejoy's passion for collecting takes him to the Highlands of Scotland, where he hides at a crossroads expecting the shipment of a fake antique bureau. Instead, he finds a deserted truck at the side of the road. When the driver is later found murdered, Lovejoy becomes the prime suspect, and to clear himself he switches identity and joins a traveling fair, hiding from the police and seeking out the culprits. Lovejoy's cynicism, his dashing way with women, and his superb knowledge of antiques all pull him through." Booklist

The Vatican rip. Ticknor & Fields 1982 c1981 221p o.p.
LC 81-14387
"A Joan Kahn book"
First published 1981 in the United Kingdom
"Antiques dealer Lovejoy is forced into a plan to steal a Chippendale table from the Vatican. After Italian lessons, he goes to Rome, where he takes up with an old lady con artist and works part-time in an antiques shop, while he perfects his heist plan and plots revenge on his boss. Lovejoy has a short temper, few scruples, and an obsession with antiques. His plans are original and fascinating, making a suspenseful caper novel." Libr J

Gaskell, Elizabeth Cleghorn, 1810-1865

Cranford; [by] Elizabeth Gaskell. Oxford University Press 1998 xxxii, 194p (Oxford world classics) pa $9.95
ISBN 0-19-283209-3 LC 98-204713

Gaskell, Elizabeth Cleghorn, 1810-1865—*Continued*

First published 1853

This novel "centres on the formidable Miss Deborah Jenkyns and her gentle sister Miss Matty, daughters of the former rector. Moments of drama are provided by the death of the genial Captain Brown, run over by a train when saving the life of a child; by the panic caused in the village by rumours of burglars; by the surprising marriage of the widowed Lady Glenmire with the vulgar Mr. Hoggins, the village surgeon; by the failure of a bank which ruins Miss Matty, and her rescue by the fortunate return from India of her long-lost brother Peter. But the greatest charm of 'Cranford,' which has kept it unfailingly popular, is its amused but loving portrayal of the old-fashioned customs and 'elegant economy' of a delicately observed group of middle-aged figures in a landscape." Oxford Companion to Engl Lit. 5th edition

Gaskin, Catherine, 1929-

The charmed circle. Scribner 1989 c1988 646p o.p.

LC 88-26401

First published 1988 in the United Kingdom

"The charmed circle of the Seymour family tantalizes outsiders, but those within it suffer tragedy. During WW II, Sir Michael Seymour, a renowned actor on the London stage, loses his wife, a concert pianist, when a fighter plane crashes into their home in southeast England. The RAF pilot bails out, saved, it seems, for a contrived, starry-eyed marriage with one of the Seymour daughters, Julia, a budding actress. When their idyll ends tragically, the young widow retires to her husband's crumbling Scottish castle to bear their son. Julia's sister, Alex, a talented journalist, learns that her husband has died in a Japanese prison camp, and takes up with a powerful newspaper mogul; only Connie, the third sister, has the common touch, choosing love with a stolid civil servant over a career of her own. After Julia marries an American movie star with a bad temper and a history of abuse, their glittering lives turn into a protracted nightmare." Publ Wkly

A falcon for a queen. Doubleday 1972 344p o.p.

"The atmosphere and countryside of the Scottish Highlands make a striking background for this turn-of-the-century gothic containing deft characterizations and a skillful blending of suspense, romance, and tragedy. Alone in China after her missionary father dies in a local uprising Kirsty Howard is drawn to her ancestral home Cluain where she is reluctantly accepted by her embittered grandfather, owner of a renowned whiskey distillery. Other main characters include the enigmatic housekeeper, her handsome illegitimate son to whom Kirsty is strongly attracted, and the neighboring Campbells, the family from whom her grandfather won his choice lands." Booklist

Gatewood, Robert, 1974-

The sound of the trees; a novel; [by] Robert Gatewood. Holt & Co. 2002 289p $25

ISBN 0-8050-6802-3 LC 2001-51703

This novel "begins on horse back in Depression-era New Mexico with Trude Mason, a taciturn 18-year-old, and his mother fleeing their impoverished family ranch in predawn desperation to escape the escalating brutality of the young man's father. Enroute to Colorado, Trude's steadfastness of purpose is tested by personal tragedy and sharpened by the treachery of man. His fate becomes entwined with that of a girl whom fortune has placed in the hands of scoundrels. . . . Gatewood has created a richly textured tableau threaded with mysticism and sustained by pitch-perfect dialogue laced with quiet dignity." SLJ

Gay, William

I hate to see that evening sun go down; collected stories. Free Press 2002 303p $24

ISBN 0-7432-4088-X LC 2002-73945

Contents: I hate to see that evening sun go down; A death in the woods; Bonedaddy, Quincy Nell, and the fifteen thousand BTU electric chair; The paperhanger; The man who knew Dylan; Those Deep Elm Brown's Ferry Blues; Crossroads Blues; Closure and roadkill on the life's highway; Sugarbaby; Standing by peaceful waters; Good 'til now; The lightpainter; My hand is just fine where it is

"Gay is richly gifted: a seemingly effortless storyteller, a writer of prose that's fiercely wrought, pungent in detail, yet poetic in the most welcome sense." N Y Times Book Rev

Gear, Kathleen O'Neal

People of the lakes; [by] Kathleen O'Neal Gear and W. Michael Gear. Forge 1994 608p il o.p.

LC 94-7145

"A Tom Doherty Associates book"

In this novel "an ancient Mask full of dark magic is found by Mica Bird, a young warrior. The spirit of his dead grandfather pleads with him not to use the Power of the Mask for his own gain—it will consume him. Mica Bird ignores the spirit and uses the Mask to manipulate, kill and seduce his own tribe and the tribes around him. But, Mica Bird is not the only one who wants the overwhelming Power of the Mask. Other clans want it for their own." Publisher's note

People of the lightning; [by] Kathleen O'Neal Gear and W. Michael Gear. Forge 1995 414p il o.p.

LC 95-34746

"A Tom Doherty Associates book"

This novel about a village of fisherfolk in ancient Florida focuses on the adventures of a youth with the ability to foretell the future

People of the masks; [by] Kathleen O'Neal Gear & W. Michael Gear. Forge 1998 416p o.p.

ISBN 0-312-85857-4 LC 98-8695

"A Tom Doherty Associates book"

"Great trouble begins for two tribes in what is now northeastern North America when Jumping Badger, a sadistic war leader, raids and destroys Paint Rock village and kidnaps the dwarf child Rumbler, whose power in the spirit world is legendary. Blue Raven, Jumping Badger's cousin, believes that the tribes need to work together to survive attacks from fiercer enemies. But as war-

Gear, Kathleen O'Neal—*Continued*
riors begin to die, Rumbler is accused of casting evil spells, and Blue Raven can no longer protect him." Libr J

People of the mist; [by] Kathleen O'Neal Gear and W. Michael Gear. Forge 1997 432p maps o.p.
ISBN 0-312-85854-X LC 97-14682
"A Tom Doherty Associates book"
"Red Knot has been betrothed to Copper Thunder in order to forge an alliance that will protect both their tribes. When she is murdered on the day of her wedding, it threatens to throw the tribal villages along the Chesapeake into a bloody war. Suspicion for the crime falls on Sun Conch, who had a relationship with the girl before she was promised away. Old Panther, a recluse, and possibly a powerful witch, is asked to look into the situation before it explodes." Booklist
"Simple prose brightened by atmospheric detail sweeps this fluid, suspenseful mix of anthropological research and character-driven mystery to a solid, satisfying resolution." Publ Wkly

People of the owl; a novel of prehistoric North America; [by] Kathleen O'Neal Gear and W. Michael Gear. Forge 2003 560p il maps $25.95
ISBN 0-312-87741-2 LC 2003-40019
"A Tom Doherty Associates book"
An "account of six prehistoric Native American clans living in the Lower Mississippi Valley. Salamander, the protagonist, is an unlikely leader of the Owl clan and struggles to maintain peace among the fractious clans. Even though many of his family, friends, and enemies believe him to be a naive young fool, a certain mystique surrounds him when his shamanistic visions empower him to keep violence at bay." Libr J
"Propelled by the Gears' spry storytelling, this sturdy epic skillfully navigates the ancient swamplands of Louisiana, with their lapping brown waters, hanging vines and brooding skies." Publ Wkly

People of the silence; [by] Kathleen O'Neal Gear and W. Michael Gear. Forge 1996 493p o.p.
LC 96-23402
"A Tom Doherty Associates book"
A "historical novel based upon the dissolution of the Anasazi empire. . . . Amid the confusion and chaos wrought by famine and warfare, two youngsters join forces in a hazardous quest for self-identity. While Cornsilk and Poor Singer seek to illuminate two pasts shrouded in secrecy, their mystical journey parallels the inevitable decline and collapse of the Anasazi culture. A grand, spell-binding adventure steeped in myth, legend, and spirituality." Booklist

The summoning God; [by] Kathleen O'Neal Gear, W. Michael Gear. Forge 2000 366p il o.p.
ISBN 0-312-86532-5 LC 00-28015
"A Tom Doherty Associates book"
Sequel to The visitant
The authors "tell the brutal story of one 13th-century tribe, the Katsinas' People, as they tumble down the path that leads to the sudden disappearance of the Anasazi. In parallel, the authors also tell the tale of a team of contemporary archeologists and anthropologists excavating the ancient site that bears witness to the Anasazi tragedy. . . . In the present, archeologist Dusty Stewart and anthropologist Maureen Cole each have their own intimate links to this past. As they excavate, those links and the fate of the puebloans become clearer. Their new novel is not for the squeamish, but the Gears offer unusual insight into Anasazi culture and history." Publ Wkly

Thin moon and cold mist. Forge 1995 380p o.p.
ISBN 0-312-85701-2 LC 95-15459
"A Tom Doherty Associates book"
"It is May 1864, and Robin Walkingstick Heatherton, a beautiful young woman of half-Cherokee descent, has again disguised herself as a 'Negro' soldier and infiltrated the Union Army in order to spy for her beloved Confederacy. Meanwhile, Union Army Major Thomas Corley, obsessed with Robin ever since her espionage work resulted in the death of his older brother, has offered $1000 in gold for information leading to her capture. . . . When her husband, a Confederate soldier, is shot by a firing squad commanded by Corley, Robin flees Virginia with their five-year-old son, Jeremy, for the West." Publ Wkly

(jt. auth) Gear, W. M. Dark inheritance
(jt. auth) Gear, W. M. People of the river
(jt. auth) Gear, W. M. People of the sea
(jt. auth) Gear, W. M. Raising Abel

Gear, W. Michael

Coyote summer. Forge 1997 427p o.p.
ISBN 0-312-86330-6 LC 97-5762
"A Tom Doherty Associates book"
Sequel to The morning river (1996)
"Richard Hamilton, the hero of this . . . western, rues the day when his father sent him west. Robbed and sold into indentured servitude on a keelboat, this young student of philosophy is forced to forsake his genteel Bostonian manners and breeding. In the harsh Upper Missouri country of the 1820s, it's kill or be killed. Dick learns that early, when he kills a Pawnee to save the life of an Indian woman, Heals Like the Willow. After a raiding party of Crows steals his company's horses, Dick is almost slaughtered himself when he accompanies brutal hunter Travis on a relentless pursuit of the thieves. Gear skillfully intercuts Dick's story with that of Willow." Publ Wkly

Dark inheritance; by W. Michael Gear and Kathleen O'Neal Gear. Warner Bks. 2001 519p $25.95
ISBN 0-446-52606-1 LC 00-32491
"A huge British pharmaceutical corporation has secretly invested hundreds of millions of pounds in experiments to raise the intelligence level of a species of chimpanzee in Equatorial Guinea. The company has also placed primates with specialists, such as American Jim Dutton, whose bonobo ape Umber is figuratively a sister to his 13-year-old daughter. . . . When Dutton's former wife, a widely known TV investigative reporter, looks into the company as it unexpectedly starts exerting its heavy-handed influence, it's inevitable that their paths will collide." Publ Wkly

People of the river; {by} W. Michael Gear and Kathleen O'Neal Gear. TOR Bks. 1992 400p o.p.
LC 92-2968
"A Tom Doherty Associates book"
A "tale of warring clans in a North American location around present-day Cahokia, Illinois. The time is A.D.

Gear, W. Michael—*Continued*
1300, and the Indian culture known as the Mississippians or Mound-Builders has a beautiful young priestess named Nightshade. This is her story, as well as the story of others like Flycatcher, Lichen, and a brave warrior—Nightshade's kidnapper and future partner—Badgertail. With a narrative that includes potent descriptions of art and artifacts (body ornaments, pottery, carvings, and weavings), this tale should appeal to readers seeking a novel containing authentic native American history, cultural rites, myths, and symbols." Booklist

People of the sea; [by] W. Michael and Kathleen O'Neal Gear. Forge 1993 425p il o.p.
LC 93-26556
"A Tom Doherty Associates book"
A "saga of prehistoric Native Americans in contemporary Arizona and California. Pregnant with twins by her lover, Iceplant, Kestrel flees westward from her abusive husband, Lambkill, who carves Iceplant to death with a hunting knife. Kestrel's only hope for survival is to travel to the seacoast and seek refuge with Iceplant's people." Libr J
The authors, "integrating a tremendous amount of natural and anthropological research into a satisfactory narrative, have again produced a vivid and fascinating portrait of early human life in America." Publ Wkly

Raising Abel; a novel; [by] W. Michael Gear & Kathleen O'Neal Gear. Warner Bks. 2002 572p o.p.
ISBN 0-446-52615-0
"Anthropologist Scott Ferris has secretly cloned embryos from glacier-frozen prehistoric cells and implanted the embryos in host mothers: now he has four-year-olds with superior traits that debunk the 'dumb Neanderthal' myth. He aims to derail creationists by revealing these living links to the human evolutionary chain, but is gruesomely murdered before he can do so. . . . The Gears lay credible anthropological and biochemical groundwork for this flight of fancy, and the nail-biting resolution is first-rate." Publ Wkly
(jt. auth) Gear, K. O. People of the lakes
(jt. auth) Gear, K. O. People of the lightning
(jt. auth) Gear, K. O. People of the masks
(jt. auth) Gear, K. O. People of the mist
(jt. auth) Gear, K. O. People of the owl
(jt. auth) Gear, K. O. People of the silence
(jt. auth) Gear, K. O. The summoning God

Geary, Joseph M.

Spiral. Pantheon Bks. 2003 355p $24.95
ISBN 0-375-42223-4 LC 2002-35679
"Biographer Nick Greer learns that a crucial missing source, Jacob Grossman, is alive and in Manhattan, but Grossman is killed shortly after Greer visits him and tapes his final interview. Grossman's untimely death hinders Greer in his efforts to track down a lost painting called the Incarnation that was the penultimate work of his subject, a controversial artist named Frank Spira who was romantically linked to Grossman." Publ Wkly
Lynch "has breathed life into a increasingly familiar mystery milieu—the art world—with assured detail and peopled it with a crowd of fascinating characters. He plants clues like a master and ratchets up the suspense so subtly we're lightheaded before we notice we haven't been breathing." Booklist

Gedge, Pauline, 1945-

House of illusions; a novel. Moyer Bell 1997 436p o.p.
ISBN 1-55921-200-4 LC 96-43474
Sequel to Lady of the reeds
First published 1996 in Canada
Sixteen years after her association with a failed plot to murder Ramses II, "Thu's desire for revenge against those who used and abandoned her burns stronger than ever. Living as a peasant along the banks of the Nile, Thu is considered a madwoman because of her frenzied attempts to find someone to carry her story back to the pharaoh. Eventually Kamen, an honorable junior army officer, takes pity on her and agrees to try to deliver her package. He does not suspect that his actions will resuscitate long-buried intrigues and deceits that will threaten Thu's life and also his own. . . . Gedge's gifts as a storyteller include full-blooded characterizations and vivid detail that brings ancient Egypt gloriously to life." Publ Wkly

Lady of the reeds. Soho Press 1995 c1994 513p o.p.
ISBN 1-56947-043-X LC 95-14837
First published 1994 in Canada with title: House of dreams
Set in the court of Egypt's Ramses III, this novel recounts the "wanton ambitions and unpredictable fortunes of its narrating heroine, Thu. Eschewing the humble life of a peasant girl, Thu persuades her brother to teach her all he learns at the temple school. When Pharaoh's famed seer, the royal physician Hui, anchors in Thu's village of Aswat, the girl steals to his barge. . . . Hui makes Thu his apprentice physician. Before long, Thu, though not yet 15, is called upon to treat the ailments of Pharaoh himself. Charmed by the aggressively capable and fiercely complicated young physician, the god-king honors her with a place in his harem. But as she luxuriates in Pharaoh's favor, Thu must contend with the treacherous vortex of court intrigue—and with her love for Pharoah's son, and her desire to be his queen." Publ Wkly
Followed by House of illusions

George, Elizabeth

Deception on his mind. Bantam Bks. 1997 616p o.p.
LC 97-7222
A mystery featuring New Scotland Yard Sergeant Barbara Havers. "Fearing for the safety of her Pakistani neighbors, in particular, sweet 10-year-old Hadiyyah, the chunky, self-deprecating Barbara impulsively follows the father and daughter to a seaside town where a racial conflict resulting from the death of a member of the Pakistani community is brewing. She's pleased when she's tagged by her former classmate, DCI Barlow, as community-police liaison—until she discovers that Hadiyyah's taciturn father, Taymullah, isn't in town just for vacation." Booklist
"This is an unusually elaborate and intricate mystery,

George, Elizabeth—*Continued*
but George keeps an unrelenting grip on her readers as the police constantly shift their focus among a dozen well-drawn suspects." Publ Wkly

For the sake of Elena. Bantam Bks. 1992 388p o.p.
LC 91-34865

"When student Elena Weaver jogs across a bridge spanning the River Cam and stumbles into a fatal ambush, a summons goes out to Scotland Yard's Thomas Lynley. . . . With his 'proletarian sidekick' Barbara Havers serving as a foil to the aristocratic dons lurking around the gothic spires of Cambridge U., Inspector Lynley interviews those who knew the victim, who emerges as casting a rather salacious spell on all men who met her." Booklist

"While elements of the plot are somewhat stretched, George's story never fails to engage." Publ Wkly

A great deliverance. Bantam Bks. 1988 305p o.p.
LC 87-47906

"Urbane inspector Thomas Lynley—a fascinating mix of public school bravado and appealing sensitivity—is sent to the wilds of Yorkshire, where an obese girl has been found sitting by the headless corpse of her father, covered in his blood and proclaiming her guilt. Pairing the suave Lynley with the plain, utterly charmless sergeant Barbara Havers, George creates a bizarre study in contrasts. . . . This first-rate whodunit has enough psychological interplay and character pyrotechnics to fuel several perfectly good mysteries." Booklist

In pursuit of the proper sinner. Bantam Bks. 1999 596p $25.95
ISBN 0-553-10235-4 LC 99-32503

In this mystery "Detective Inspector Thomas Lynley investigates the murder of two seemingly unconnected victims found together on a lonely British moor: a young man and the daughter of a former colleague. . . . Lynley, the local police, and Barbara Havers (on Lynley's team) pursue different suspects." Libr J

"George builds plausible motives for all of the suspects while simultaneously revealing the private lives of her admirable detectives with an engaging mix of subtlety and bravado." Publ Wkly

In the presence of the enemy. Bantam Bks. 1996 519p o.p.
LC 95-37670

"Ten-year-old Charlotte, daughter of Conservative MP Eve Bowen, is abducted after leaving a weekly music lesson not far from her London home. Dennis Luxford, editor for a tabloid-style, decidedly anti-Conservative newspaper, receives a message threatening Charlotte unless he acknowledges her paternity. Bowen, a rising star in the Home Office, chooses to avoid using the police, knowing that disclosure of her brief, long-ago fling with Luxford will ruin her politically. She agrees with Luxford to ask forensic scientist Simon St. James and his assistant Lady Helen (who is Lynley's lover) to investigate undercover. But soon a murder draws in Scotland Yard, allowing Lynley and Havers to lead a complicated investigation to its electrifying and astonishing conclusion." Publ Wkly

Missing Joseph. Bantam Bks. 1993 496p o.p.
LC 92-35630

This novel "examines relationships—mother-daughter, husband-wife, father-son, loved-lover—and the question of what is right versus what is moral. At the heart of the story are spirited Maggie Spence and her aloof, mysterious mother, Juliet, who's been accused of accidentally poisoning the village vicar. When Deborah St. James and her forensic scientist husband, Simon, visit the Spences' Lancashire village, they hear complaints from the locals that the murder investigation was mishandled, leaving critical questions unanswered and arousing suspicions of a cover-up. When St. James asks his old friend [Detective Inspector Thomas] Lynley to help investigate further, they find that the truth is infinitely complex. . . . This powerful and moving story won't be easily forgotten." Booklist

(ed) A moment on the edge. See A moment on the edge

Payment in blood. Bantam Bks. 1989 312p o.p.
LC 89-426

"On a country estate in Scotland, a troupe of actors has gathered to read through a new play. Alas, by dawn the playwright is found dead, impaled on a dirk, and by the time Scotland Yard arrives, the script has been burned and untold other clues have been disturbed. Inspector Thomas Lynley and his rebellious, class-conscious assistant, Sergeant Barbara Havers, have been assigned to the case. The presence of a woman Lynley loves adds complications to his police procedure, and further intrigue emerges within the marital and extramarital relations of the troupe's members. Red herrings abound in this intricate, finely drawn suspense story, which offers much more than the average locked-room mystery." Booklist

Playing for the Ashes. Bantam Bks. 1994 624p o.p.
LC 93-50153

"After cricket star Kenneth Fleming is found asphyxiated in a burned cottage on the estate of Miriam Whitelaw, his patron, [Detective Inspector Thomas] Lynley and Havers, with local Detective Inspector Isabelle Ardery, look into the victim's tangled domestic affairs." Publ Wkly

"There's more to think about in George's story than simply whodunit. Readers will be astounded by the ease with which she weaves complex relationships and provocative moral, emotional, and ethical questions into the compelling plot." Booklist

A suitable vengeance. Bantam Bks. 1991 371p o.p.
LC 91-10575

When Thomas Lynley, eighth earl of Asherton and a detective inspector of New Scotland Yard, brings his financée Deborah Cotton to Cornwall to meet his widowed mother they become embroiled in a series of local murders

A traitor to memory. Bantam Bks. 2001 422p o.p.
ISBN 0-553-80127-9 LC 2001-25488

"Violin virtuoso and former child prodigy Gideon Davies suddenly loses his ability to play. As he works with a psychiatrist to regain his gift, Gideon begins to dredge

George, Elizabeth—*Continued*

up memories from his childhood. Suddenly, people involved in an incident from his past, beginning with his mother, are being run over by a big black car. Detective Inspector Thomas Lynley and constables Barbara Havers and Winston Nkata are asked to investigate the hit-and-run murders and, like Gideon, must reconstruct the past in order to understand what is happening in the present." Libr J

Well-schooled in murder. Bantam Bks. 1990 356p o.p.

LC 90-117

Thomas Lynley "and Sergeant Havers focus their prodigious talents on uncovering the murderer of a young boy from an exclusive independent school near London. While author George necessarily centers the plot on solving the case, she adroitly plumbs the emotional and psychological depths of fully fleshed characters coping with various forms of personal stress in addition to the murder." Libr J

George, Margaret

Mary Queen of Scotland and the Isles; a novel. St. Martin's Press 1992 870p o.p.

LC 92-20975

This biographical novel is set "against the bloody turmoil of the 16th century's religious wars, in which decadence alternates with penitence, persecution and piety. From the luxury of her upbringing in a French palace to the harshness of her later years in Scotland's fortresses and England's royal prisons, Mary lives a tragic life. Her syphilitic drunkard husband plans her murder; her true love is thrown into a dungeon, shackled and left to rot; her brother and her trusted advisers betray her repeatedly; the Pope condemns her; and her last hope, her cousin, Queen Elizabeth, locks her away for almost 20 years until finally ordering her execution." NY Times Book Rev

"George enhances fact with both accurate and colorful embroidery, and the result is a huge but not cumbersome novel." Booklist

The memoirs of Cleopatra; a novel. St. Martin's Press 1997 964p o.p.

ISBN 0-312-15430-5 LC 96-51071

"Beginning with a memory at age three of witnessing her mother's death and ending with her own suicide, Cleopatra tells her story." Libr J

George "renders her myriad settings, whether in Athens, Syria, Actium or elsewhere, palpably real. The smell of the Alexandrian harbor, the taste of pomegranates, the visual grandeur of the pyramids and the clash of swords all come alive in her hands. Battles physical and political—Caesar's North African campaign, the Alexandrian War, the ill-fated struggle between Antony and Octavian for control of the world—are evoked with skill and passion, as are more domestic conflicts." Publ Wkly

Gerritsen, Tess

The apprentice; a novel. Ballantine Bks. 2002 344p $24.95

ISBN 0-345-44785-9 LC 2002-23185

Boston "detective Jane Rizzoli is called to a crime scene out of her jurisdiction. The victim is a wealthy doctor, found with his throat slashed, sitting on the floor of his living room in his pajamas, with a teacup in his lap. His wife is missing, but her nightgown is found folded neatly on a chair in the bedroom. There are unmistakable similarities to the work of serial killer Warren Hoyt, nicknamed 'the Surgeon,' but he is in prison, which leads Rizzoli to suspect a copcat killer." Libr J

Bloodstream. Pocket Bks. 1998 324p o.p.

ISBN 0-671-01675-X

In this novel, "widowed Dr. Claire Elliot takes her son Noah away from bad companions and potential trouble in Baltimore. She buys a practice in the summer resort of Tranquillity, ME, aiming for a new start. . . . Every 50 years or so when the rains are heavy and summers hot, the community's teenage boys, come autumn, boil over with uncontrollable rage. Desperately hoping all the violent occurrences have medical causes, Elliot comes up with a variety of theories, all of which involve placing a quarantine on Locust Lake, the town's main source of income. The real cause of the terror is even more ominous and frightening than Elliot ever imagines." Libr J

Body double; Tess Gerritsen. Ballantine Bks. 2004 339p $24.95

ISBN 0-375-43374-0 LC 2004-49807

"Medical examiner Dr. Maura Isles has just returned from a trip to France to encounter a grisly discovery. A woman has been found shot to death in front of her home, and the woman is a dead ringer for Maura. The woman, whose name is Anna Leoni, turns out to be Maura's twin; both were given up for adoption 40 years ago. The mystery deepens when Officer Rick Ballard shows up and tells Maura and Detective Jane Rizzoli that Anna was on the run from an abusive boyfriend and under police protection. But that still doesn't answer the question of what led Anna to Maura's door, and that question leads Maura to trace her sister's steps to an old house in Maine." Booklist

"An electric series of startling twists, the revelation of ghoulishly practical motives and a nail-biting finale make this Gerritsen's best to date." Publ Wkly

Gravity. Pocket Bks. 1999 342p o.p.

ISBN 0-671-04618-7

This "thriller is set aboard the International Space Station, where a team of six astronauts suddenly find themselves threatened by a virulent biohazard. . . . As astronaut Emma Watson, the station's onboard doctor, struggles to fight the outbreak, her colleagues are dying one by one." Publ Wkly

"Gerritsen creates believable characters and ably captures astronautical and scientific work in fashioning another fascinating story replete with cleverly intertwined subplots." Booklist

Harvest. Pocket Bks. 1996 344p o.p.

ISBN 0-671-55301-1 LC 96-1653

"Surgical resident Abby DiMatteo is on the fast track at Boston's fictional Bayside Hospital. But after she disobeys orders so she can give a heart transplant to a failing 17-year-old instead of to a failing middle-aged, rich woman, her career options look slim. Fighting back against hospital administrators, shyster lawyers and violent thugs, Abby . . . finds major discrepancies in the records of Bayside's organ-transplant procedures. Shocked, she finally learns the truth, experiences a major betrayal and, in the climax, must herself face the final harvest." Publ Wkly

Gerritsen, Tess—*Continued*

"Retired internist Gerritsen's first novel is a well-paced and smoothly written story that demonstrates she knows people as well as medicine." Booklist

Life support. Pocket Bks. 1997 326p o.p.
ISBN 0-671-55303-8 LC 97-15511

"Toby Harper, an overworked 38-year-old night-shift ER physician at a private Boston hospital, inadvertently allows a 76-year-old man with strange neurological symptoms to wander off and disappear into the night. She soon finds herself caught in a web of intrigue that centers around experimental anti-aging treatments administered by Dr. Carl Wallenberg, an imperious endocrinologist at Brant Hill, a retirement community catering to aging but upscale clientele . . . [The author] adeptly integrates medical details into a taut and troubling thriller." Publ Wkly

The sinner. Ballantine Bks. 2003 342p $24.95
ISBN 0-345-45891-5 LC 2003-59151

"When two Boston nuns are found brutally beaten—one fatally and one with a scintilla of life left in her—it's up to homicide detective Jane Rizzoli to find the perpetrator. Medical examiner Dr. Maura Isles, nicknamed the Queen of the Dead, has the unlucky fortune to discover that the murdered nun, a young woman about to make her final vows, hid untold secrets from the rest of the aging convent. . . . Woven within the horror of this gruesome story is the old allegory of good versus evil, but relating it through these two fascinating individuals, Gerritsen avoids cliches." Booklist

The surgeon. Ballantine Bks. 2001 359p o.p.
ISBN 0-345-44783-2 LC 2001-35901

Dr. Catherine Cordell "thought she had shot and killed her rapist and would-be murderer two years earlier in steamy Savannah, where he was a surgery intern at her hospital. Now, in Boston, as another hot summer begins, he appears to have miraculously returned and embarked once again on his grisly mission: he rapes women, then surgically removes their wombs. As two intrepid detectives—Thomas Moore and Jane Rizzoli—investigate, Cordell begins to doubt her own memories (or lack of) and discovers that not even her OR is safe." Publ Wkly

"A fascinating story with a gripping plot and believably human characters." Booklist

Ghosh, Amitav

The glass palace; a novel. Random House 2001 474p $25.95
ISBN 0-375-50148-7 LC 00-41477

This narrative "stretches from the British invasion of Burma, in 1885, through the country's independence, to the uneasy military rule of the present day. The novel is presided over by the Indian-born Rajkumar, a poor orphan, who falls for Dolly, a servant of the exiled queen. Ghosh renders the polite imprisonment of the Burmese royal family in India and the lush, dangerous atmosphere of teak camps in the Burmese forest with fine detail—a perfect balance for the broad stroke of romance and serendipity that drive the story forward." New Yorker

Gibbons, Kaye, 1960-

Charms for the easy life. Putnam 1992 254p o.p.
ISBN 0-399-13791-2 LC 92-40690

This novel "concerns three generations of strong Southern women: a grandmother who heals with herbs and native wisdom, a mother passionately in love with the wrong man, and the daughter who narrates this tale." Libr J

"A touching picture of female bonding and solidarity. Related with the simple, tart economy of a folktale, the narrative brims with wisdom and superstition, with Southern manners and insights into human nature." Publ Wkly

Divining women; Kaye Gibbons. G. P. Putnam's Sons 2004 205p $23.95
ISBN 0-399-15160-5 LC 2003-60661

In this "tale of marital strife and female resilience, Gibbons considers conflicts between blacks and whites and men and women within the context of the First World War and the Spanish influenza epidemic. Martha has sent her intelligent daughter, Mary, to North Carolina to help Martha's half-brother, Troop, and his expectant wife, Maureen, and Mary is amazed to find herself in a household as miserable as it is opulent. Troop is a cold-hearted, possibly insane despot; lovely and muddled Maureen is his prisoner; and Zollie and Mamie, their kind African American employees, are treated with appalling indifference. The hate, lies, and machinations at work in this psychotic hothouse rival that of the most gothic of southern melodramas, a tradition Gibbons shrewdly subverts as she divines the true nature of feminine power and points the way toward justice in this gorgeously moody and piquant fairy tale." Booklist

Ellen Foster; a novel. Algonquin Bks. 1987 146p $16.95; pa $11
ISBN 0-912697-52-0; 0-375-70305-5 (pa) LC 86-22136

A "novel narrated by an adolescent girl, Ellen, who relates the day-to-day experiences she endured as a child in a troubled family. Ellen's mother died young, her father was abusive, her other relatives were equally bad; it wasn't until she was taken into a foster home that she found the sort of peace and freedom to be innocent that most normal childhoods afford." Booklist

"What might have been grim, melodramatic material in the hands of a less talented author is instead filled with lively humor, . . . compassion and intimacy. This short novel focuses on Ellen's strengths rather than her victimization, presenting a memorable heroine who rescues herself." N Y Times Book Rev

On the occasion of my last afternoon. Putnam 1998 273p o.p.
ISBN 0-399-14299-1 LC 98-12947

"Now 70 and near death, Emma Garnet Tate begins her account by recalling her youth as a bookish, observant 12-year-old in 1842, living on a Virginia plantation in a highly dysfunctional family dominated by her foul-mouthed father, a veritable monster of parental tyranny and racial prejudice. Emma's long-suffering mother, of genteel background and gentle ways, is angelic and forgiving; her five siblings' lives are ruined by her father's cruelty; and all are discreetly cared for by Clarice, the clever, formidable black woman who is the only person Samuel Tate respects. . . . At 17, Emma marries one of the Boston Lowells, a surgeon, and spends the war years laboring beside him in a Raleigh hospital." Publ Wkly

"Gibbons is unsparing in her depiction of the gruesome

Gibbons, Kaye, 1960-—*Continued*
reality of the carnage, and unflinching in her effort to convey the madness of that time and the havoc it wreaked on people's souls." Booklist

Sights unseen. Putnam 1995 209p $19.95
ISBN 0-399-13986-9 LC 95-9781
"In flashback, Hattie describes the summer and fall of 1967, when she was 12 and living in Bend of the River, N.C., and when her beautiful, psychotically volatile mother, Maggie, was temporarily committed to the psychiatric ward at Duke University. A near-miracle occurs: for the first time in nearly two decades, Maggie becomes stabilized on medication. And, for the first time in her life, Hattie experiences a mother who relates to, touches and cares for her." Publ Wkly
"Gibbons has her quietly heroic narrator relate one wild and poignant incident after another, holding us rapt with wonder and empathy for Maggie and her loving, self-sacrificing family. This is a novel that deserves unwavering attention from start to finish." Booklist

A virtuous woman. Algonquin Bks. 1989 158p o.p.
LC 88-22026
"Jack Stokes and Ruby Pitt weave this strong, tightly knit love story in alternating chapters that begin when Jack, grieving over Ruby's death four months earlier, evokes the past. In flashbacks, the two richly cadenced Southern voices explore their vastly differing backgrounds, troubled histories and their unlikely but loving marriage." Publ Wkly
"A subtle, evocative, and romantic novel." Booklist

Gibson, William, 1948-

All tomorrow's parties. Putnam 1999 277p o.p.
ISBN 0-399-14579-6 LC 99-30997
"In this not quite sequel, characters from Gibson's last two books, 'Idoru' [1996] and 'Virtual Light,' converge upon the twenty-first-century shantytown occupying the Golden Gate Bridge to confront something momentous—though what, exactly, remains shimmeringly elusive. The pleasure is less in the plot, however, than in Gibson's coolly elegant prose, which creates a future that looks like Simon Rodia's Watts Towers: a science fiction constructed from glittering, broken artifacts of the present." New Yorker

Neuromancer; with a new introduction by the author; with an afterword by Jack Womack. 20th anniversary ed. Ace Books 2004 371p $25
ISBN 0-441-01203-5 LC 2004-48718
First published 1984
"In a highly urbanized future dominated by cybernetics and bioengineering, anti-hero Case is rescued from wretchedness and given back the ability to send his persona into the cyberspace of the world's computer networks, where he must carry out a hazardous mission for an enigmatic employer. An adventure story much enlivened by elaborate technical jargon and sleazy, streetwise characters—the pioneering 'cyberpunk' novel and arguably the most influential SF novel of the 1980s." Anatomy of Wonder 5

Pattern recognition. Putnam 2003 356p $25.95
ISBN 0-399-14986-4 LC 2002-67955
"Cayce Pollard is a brand consultant whose father disappeared on September 11th. She becomes fascinated by mysterious scraps of film footage—seemingly random scenes, luminously shot—that are disseminated on the Web and have spawned cults of viewers. Gibson wisely avoids addressing the import of 9/11 head on, but he somehow establishes a powerful correlative for it in Cayce's strange quest—through the Tokyo red-light district and the Moscow underworld—to find the anonymous filmmaker. In Gibson's eerie vision of our time, the future has come crashing upon us, fragmentary and undecipherable." New Yorker

Virtual light. Bantam Bks. 1993 325p o.p.
LC 93-7150
This novel focuses on "two young people in a near-future San Francisco, a bike messenger named Chevette and a security guard named Rydell, who may actually have a flesh-and-blood future of their own, together. Chevette, whose bike is moderately high-tech, gets her hands on a pair of super-high-tech sunglasses, which contain secrets that some powerful people are willing to kill for. Rydell, who discovers to his regret that he is working for the same people, eventually calls on a shadowy band of hackers for help." N Y Times Book Rev
"Rydell and Chevette are sympathetic without being as well-drawn as one would like. On the other hand, besides being a fun read, 'Virtual Light' performs the valuable service of bringing Gibson's social concepts into higher resolution." Christ Sci Monit

Gide, André, 1869-1951

The counterfeiters (Les faux-monnayeurs); translated from the French of André Gide by Dorothy Bussy. Knopf 1927 365p o.p.
Original French edition, 1925
"The novelist Edouard keeps a journal of events in order to write a novel about the nature of reality. The intrigues of a gang of counterfeiters symbolize the 'counterfeit' personalities with which people disguise themselves to conform hypocritically to convention or to deceive themselves. The adolescent boys Bernard Profitendieu and Olivier Molinier, having left home in order to be free to find and develop their true selves, encounter many varieties of hyprocrisy and self-deception in human relationships and barely escape falling into such poses themselves. Both begin by seeking a close emotional tie with Edouard. Each, however, comes to recognize that Edouard is inadequate as an ideal for emulation, particularly when the novelist cannot recognize the psychological reality of the schoolboy Boris' useless suicide, which is an indirect result of the counterfeiters' machinations." Reader's Ency. 4th edition

The immoralist; translated by Richard Howard. Modern Lib. 1984 c1970 171p o.p.
ISBN 0-394-60500-4 LC 83-42856
Original French edition, 1902. First United States edition, translated by Dorothy Bussy, published 1930 by Knopf; this translation first published 1970 by Knopf
"Michel takes his bride, Marceline, to North Africa, where he develops tuberculosis and becomes hyperconscious of physical sensations, particularly of his attraction to young Arab boys. Back on his French estate after being cured, he is encouraged by his friend Ménalque to rise above conventional good and evil and give free rein

Gide, André, 1869-1951—*Continued*

to all his passions. When Marceline falls ill with the tuberculosis she caught while nursing him, he takes her south. He neglects her demands on him more and more, however, in order to keep himself free, since his new doctrine demands that the weak be suppressed if necessary for the preservation of the strong. She dies, and he, guilt-ridden and debilitated by his excesses, tries to justify his conduct to a group of friends." Reader's Ency. 4th edition

Gifford, Barry, 1946-

Wild at heart; the story of Sailor and Lula. Grove Weidenfeld 1990 159p o.p.

ISBN 0-8021-1181-5 LC 89-36443

"Sailor Ripley, fresh from two years in a North Carolina prison farm, breaks parole and hits the road for dream-bright California. Along for the ride is his girlfriend, Lula Pace Fortune. On their tail is a private investigator, Johnnie Farragut, who's trying to win the affections of Lula's disapproving mother, Marietta. Sailor is thoughtful but spacey, a sweet boy who nonetheless suffers an amoral lack of judgment. Lula, barely out of her teens, is the one to reckon with dreamy, poetic, persevering, meditative, perspicacious, heartsore and practical to boot." N Y Times Book Rev

"There is a definite desperation in their frenzied flight that gives the story its edge, but there is also a marvelous tenderness and a wondrously life-affirming sexuality that make Sailor and Lula far more than just another randy couple used to evoke the steamy nihilism of Jim Thompson or David Goodis. . . . Wild hearts often grow cold, but Sailor and Lula make us remember what it is to burn." Booklist

Wyoming. Arcade Pub. 2000 129p $19.95

ISBN 1-55970-523-X LC 00-25046

A novel written almost entirely in "dialogue between a mother and her precocious nine-year-old son, Roy. The book takes place in the mid-1950s as Kitty and Roy drive across the American South and Midwest. Traveling from place to place–rarely leaving the car–they try to pass time in idle, soft-focus banter about their hopes and disappointments, occasionally musing about such big topics as fate, personal loss, divorce, death and the soul. The background unfolds: Kitty has left Roy's dishonest father, whose health is failing, while Roy craves reassurances that both parents still love him." Libr J

This is a "tender and understated story. . . . That Gifford forges these characters almost entirely out of dialogue makes their affecting humanity doubly impressive; by the novel's end, Roy and his mother are likely to live as vividly in the reader's mind as their unseen Wyoming lives in theirs." N Y Times Book Rev

Gilbert, Michael, 1912-

The black seraphim. Harper & Row 1984 216p o.p.

LC 83-48020

"Dr. James Pirie Scotland, an overworked London pathologist, takes a holiday in the quiet village of Melchester. What he finds, however, is a town embroiled in real estate scandals, with the local cathedral as the focal point of dissension. When the archdeacon dies suddenly, Dr. Scotland disagrees with the coroner's verdict of influenza and investigates a murder." Booklist

The author provides a "likable hero (complete with love interest) and an entertaining, if guessable, murder." Wilson Libr Bull

The killing of Katie Steelstock. Harper & Row 1980 293p o.p.

LC 79-3409

"A Joan Kahn book"

"Local girl makes good only to be murdered in her hometown. The town of Hannington, England, has one claim to fame; popular TV singer and personality Katie Steelstock. On a visit home, Katie attends a dance, slips out to meet someone, and is discovered later with her head smashed in. An investigation begins, with conflict quickly developing between local Detective Sergeant Ian McCourt and Scotland Yard Chief Superintendent Charlie Knott. Surprises and jolts abound with the story ending in an attempted murder and yet another mystery." Booklist

Gilbert, R. A.

(comp) The Oxford book of English ghost stories. See The Oxford book of English ghost stories

Gilchrist, Ellen, 1935-

The age of miracles; stories. Little, Brown 1995 260p o.p.

LC 94-37441

Contents: Among the mourners; The blue house; Death comes to a hero; The divorce; Going to join the poets; Joyce; Love at the Center; Love of my life; Madison at 69th, a fable; Paris; The Raintree Street Bar and Washerteria; A statue of Aphrodite; The stucco house; Too much rain; The uninsured; A wedding in Jackson

In several of the stories in this collection, the author recounts the adventures of her recurring heroine Rhoda Manning. "Elegant, independent, and successful, Rhoda is approaching 60 with unwavering nerve, delighted with the freedom age brings." Booklist

The cabal [novelette]

In Gilchrist, E. The cabal and other stories p1-132

The cabal and other stories. Little, Brown 2000 272p $35

ISBN 0-316-31491-9 LC 99-36893

Contents: The cabal [novella]; The sanguine blood of men; Hearts of Dixie; The survival of the fittest; Bare ruined choirs, where late the sweet birds sang; The big cleanup

The cabal "takes place in Jackson, Mississippi, upon Caroline Jones' arrival in town to begin a college teaching job. It just so happens that Caroline's arrival coincides with the mental breakdown of the psychiatrist who tends to the wellbeing of the town's artistic elite, a group called 'the Cabal,' all of whom are subsequently threatened with the public revelation of their deep, dark secrets." Booklist

Gilchrist, Ellen, 1935—*Continued*

The courts of love; a novella and stories. Little, Brown 1996 288p o.p.
LC 96-2901

Contents: Nora Jane and company; New Orleans; A man who looked like me; Paradise; Fort Smith; Desecration; Update; The dog who delivered papers to the stars; An ancient rain forest; Excitement, part I

"'Nora Jane and Company' reprises the eponymous character whom we last saw giving birth to twins, in *Light Can Be Both Wave and Particle* [1989]. Here, the twins are now 10; Nora Jane is 29 and happily married to Freddy Harwood. . . . In the course of the novella, Nora Jane, Freddy and the twins' godfather, journalist and film critic Neiman Gluuk, experience a terrorist assassination of one of their friends; enroll at Berkeley for graduate studies; survive an emergency in the California wilderness; and participate in a minor miracle that employs the long arm of coincidence. . . . Gilchrist's hand is sure, her vision keen and sometimes antic, and the world she has created in 12 previous books is expanded and enhanced by these luminous tales." Publ Wkly

Ellen Gilchrist: collected stories. Little, Brown 2000 563p $38
ISBN 0-316-29948-0

Contents: The famous poll at Jody's Bar; Revenge; There's a Garden of Eden; In the land of dreamy dreams; 1944; Summer, an elegy; Victory over Japan; Music; Jade Buddhas, red bridges, fruits of love; Miss Crystal's maid name Traceleen, she's talking, she's telling everything she knows; Traceleen, she's still talking; Drunk with love; The young man; Traceleen at dawn; Anna, part 1; Some blue hills at sundown; The Starlight Express; Light can be both wave and particle; Traceleen turns east; Mexico; A statue of Aphrodite; Among the mourners; The stucco house; The uninsured; Perhaps a miracle; Lunch at the best restaurant in the world; You must change your life; The brown cape; Fort Smith; A prologue; A tree to be desired; Witness to the crucifixion; A lady with pearls; The Southwest Experimental Fast Oxide Reactor

"Gilchrist is an important voice in contemporary Southern fiction, and this book belongs in every library." Libr J

Flights of angels; stories. Little, Brown 1998 327p $34 o.p.
ISBN 0-316-31486-2 LC 98-21420

Contents: A tree to be desired; While we waited for you to be born; The carnival of the stoned children; Mississippi; Miss Crystal confronts the past; A sordid tale; or, Traceleen continues talking; Phyladda; or, The mind/body problem; Battle; The triumph of reason; Have a *wonderful* nice walk; Witness to the crucifixion; Ocean Springs; Excitement at Drake Field; A lady with pearls; Excitement at Audubon Park; Free pull; Down at the dollhouse; The Southwest Experimental Fast Oxide Reactor

This collection "features some of Gilchrist's familiar, endearingly eccentric narrators. . . . There are also some new, young and engaging characters and, throughout the book, a convincing evocation of the changing South." Publ Wkly

Nora Jane and company
In Gilchrist, E. The courts of love

Giles, Janice Holt, 1909-1979

Hannah Fowler; with a foreword by Dianne Watkins. University Press of Ky. 1992 219p o.p.
ISBN 0-8131-1793-3 LC 92-14269

This is a reissue of the title first published 1956 by Houghton Mifflin

Hannah Moore and her father were on their way to Boonesborough in 1778 when Samuel got blood poisoning and died. A chance meeting with a frontiersman took Hannah on to Logan's Fort. There she married and went with her husband to make their own home. Capture by the Indians and an escape are part of the story

Gill, Bartholomew, 1943-2002

Death in Dublin; a novel of suspense. Morrow 2003 294p $24.95
ISBN 0-06-000849-0 LC 2002-32582

"Gill's final novel pits Police Chief Peter McGarr against a thief and murderer: a night watchman at Dublin's Trinity College has been killed and the irreplaceable Book of Kells stolen. McGarr suspects an infamous and most dangerous band of IRA zealots. Excellent work from a tried-and-true hand." Libr J

The death of a Joyce scholar; a Peter McGarr mystery. Morrow 1989 331p o.p.
LC 88-38560

"McGarr, chief superintendent of Dublin's murder squad, is faced with the brutal annihilation of a professor of English literature at Dublin's Trinity College, one Kevin Coyle. Not only was Coyle an expert on the work of James Joyce, he also had hired himself out on the day of his murder to narrate a guided tour of the Dublin neighborhoods that provide the setting for Joyce's *Ulysses.* Coyle had an odd wife—and her friends, to McGarr, seem even odder—and he was known to have aroused contention among the Trinity community for both personal and professional reasons. Investigating the suspects leaves McGarr up to his eyeballs in scholarly tomes and academic politics." Booklist

"An affectionate acquaintance with Joyce's Dubliners adds considerably to the pleasures of this profoundly clever literary mystery, the better to appreciate its careful Joycean parallels in plot and character." N Y Times Book Rev

The death of an Irish lover; a Peter McGarr mystery. Avon Bks. 2000 265p $23
ISBN 0-380-97797-4 LC 99-58663

"McGarr of the Dublin Police, who is the chief homicide cop in Ireland, is summoned to the village of Leixleap on the River Shannon to solve a double murder. Two local fisheries officers, known as the 'eel police' for their efforts to control the lucrative trade of eel poaching, are discovered dead at the local upscale inn. The older man and young woman apparently have been killed by a single bullet. The fact that the room was locked at the time of the murders is the least puzzling aspect of this case." Booklist

"The contradictions Gill manages to unearth in one small, placid patch of Irish ground are simply astonishing." N Y Times Book Rev

Gill, Bartholomew, 1943-2002—*Continued*

The death of an Irish sea wolf; a Peter McGarr mystery. Morrow 1996 296p o.p.

LC 96-15680

This novel is "part swashbuckling adventure . . . and part modern detective story about the disappearance of an old man with a dark past. Peter McGarr, head of the Serious Crimes Unit of the Garda Siochana, applies muscle to break through the sullen reserve of the islanders, an inbred lot who glare coldly at all outsiders. Mr. Gill gives a rough tongue to these crusty salts; but when he puts the town behind him and looks out to sea, there's poetry in his voice." N Y Times Book Rev

The death of an Irish tinker; a Peter McGarr mystery. Morrow 1997 295p o.p.

ISBN 0-688-14184-6 LC 97-12889

"Chief Superintendent Peter McGarr of the Dublin police has his hands full. Twelve years earlier, a man's body was found in a treetop, shackled and brutalized. Though no arrests were made, McGarr suspected Toddler Bacon, Dublin's most notorious drug dealer. Fast-forward to the present day, with Toddler still dealing and killing and still eluding the law. Biddy Nevins, an itinerant Irish 'traveler,' has become a famous photographer and is back in Dublin after years away. Unfortunately, she's spotted by Toddler, who recognizes her as the woman who witnessed the brutal 'treetop' murder he committed years earlier. Despite her distrust of the police, Biddy turns to McGarr for protection." Booklist

The death of love; a Peter McGarr mystery. Morrow 1992 320p o.p.

LC 91-27573

"Irish policeman Peter McGarr goes to the Irish resort of Parknasilla to determine whether the digitalis-induced death of a famous and beloved philanthropist, about to turn politician, was planned or accidental. With the aid of his much-younger wife and several undercover detectives, McGarr questions the man's doctor, his athletic ex-wife, his mistress/assistant, and several powerful politicians." Libr J

"Mr. Gill has constructed a devilishly intricate plot to tell this story; but typical of him, he manages to make the moral dilemma even more painful to resolve." N Y Times Book Rev

Death on a cold, wild river; a Peter McGarr mystery. Morrow 1993 251p o.p.

LC 93-7729

"In the opening scene Nellie Millar, 'the best fisher bar none in all of Ireland,' meets her picturesque death while casting for trophy salmon in the swollen floodwaters of the Owenea River. Peter McGarr, the chief of Dublin's murder squad and Nellie's former lover, carries his grief to the village in Donegal where she is being waked, only to discover that the drowning was no accident." N Y Times Book Rev

"Gill writes well, setting the tone for introspective passages with evocations of Ireland's wild coastal landscape on one page, while amusing us with witty pub banter on another. . . . Unpredictable, philosophical, funny, and ever so satisfying." Booklist

Gilman, Charlotte Perkins, 1860-1935

The Charlotte Perkins Gilman reader; "The yellow wallpaper" and other fiction; edited and introduced by Ann J. Lane. Pantheon Bks. 1980 208p o.p.

LC 80-7711

Contents: The yellow wallpaper; When I was a witch; If I were a man; The girl in the pink hat; The cottagette; The unnatural mother; Making a change; An honest woman; Turned; The widow's might; Mr. Peebles' heart; The crux; What Diantha did; Benigna Machiavelli; Unpunished; Moving the mountain; Herland; With her in Ourland

The editor "has selected representative pieces by the early-twentieth-century American feminist socialist, including her best known (and best) quasi-autobiographical story, 'The Yellow Wallpaper,' plus excerpts from four novels and three writings about utopias." Booklist

Charlotte Perkins Gilman's Utopian novels; edited and with an introduction by Minna Doskow. Fairleigh Dickinson Univ. Press 1999 389p o.p.

ISBN 0-8386-3761-2 LC 98-23510

Contents: Moving the mountain (1911); Herland; With her in Ourland

In Moving the mountain, an explorer, lost in Tibet for thirty years, returns to the United States in 1940 and finds a society totally transformed by women

Herland; with an introduction by Ann J. Lane. Pantheon Bks. 1979 xxiv, 147p o.p.

"Written in 1915, Herland was serialized in Gilman's monthly magazine, 'The Forerunner.'" Introduction

"On the eve of World War I, three American male explorers stumble onto an all-female society somewhere in the distant reaches of the earth. Unable to believe their eyes, they promptly set out to find the men of the society, convinced that, since 'this is a "civilized" country . . . there must be men.' . . . [The novel examines] what is masculine and what is feminine, what is culturally learned and what is biologically determined in our society." Publisher's note

also in Gilman, C. P. The Charlotte Perkins Gilman reader

also in Gilman, C. P. Charlotte Perkins Gilman's Utopian novels p150-269

Moving the mountain

In Gilman, C. P. The Charlotte Perkins Gilman reader

In Gilman, C. P. Charlotte Perkins Gilman's Utopian novels p37-149

With her in Ourland; sequel to Herland; edited by Mary Jo Deegan and Michael R. Hill; with an introduction by Mary Jo Deegan. Greenwood Press 1997 200p $100.95

ISBN 0-313-27614-5 LC 96-51135

"Contributions in women's studies"

Written in 1916, With her in Ourland was serialized in Gilman's magazine, The Forerunner

"He's a brash American adventurer; she's an independent, albeit sheltered, sociologist from Herland, a 2000-year-old, all-female society. Not surprisingly, when

Gilman, Charlotte Perkins, 1860-1935—*Continued*

Vandyck (Van) and Ellador marry, most everything becomes a point of negotiation, if not contention: sexual relations, family obligations and attitudes about race, class and the welfare state." Publ Wkly

also in Gilman, C. P. The Charlotte Perkins Gilman reader

also in Gilman, C. P. Charlotte Perkins Gilman's Utopian novels p270-387

Gilman, Dorothy, 1923-

The amazing Mrs. Pollifax. Doubleday 1970 234p o.p.

Mrs. Emily Pollifax, widow and grandmother, combats international espionage at the request of the C.I.A. in this spy adventure. The scene is Istanbul where Mrs. Pollifax must help a double agent escape. That she does, outwitting the enemy with her own special brand of logic

Caravan. Doubleday 1992 263p o.p.

LC 91-39459

"Born into a carnival family at the turn of the 20th century, 16-year-old Caressa Horvath finds her life taking a dramatic turn when she attempts to rob Jacob Bowman, a rich, eccentric anthropologist 20 years her senior. [Undaunted] by their unconventional introduction, he marries her, and they travel to Tripoli to explore the Sahara Desert. Nomadic Tuaregs attack their caravan but spare Caressa's life, launching her three-year adventure in the desert, where she befriends a young boy named Bakuli, gets sold into slavery, and eventually meets her great love, a wandering Scotsman named Jared MacKay." Libr J

"The story is as much a lesson on desert culture as a fine adventure saga and a love story with a delightful, fateful twist." Booklist

The elusive Mrs. Pollifax. Doubleday 1971 240p o.p.

Mrs. Pollifax "the genteel grandmother-heroine swings into action for the CIA by transporting in her hat some forged passports to the Bulgarian underground which turns out to be a group of five amateurs. In her travels Mrs. Pollifax meets some young Americans, one of whom is ostensibly imprisoned for espionage but actually held for ransom, and Mrs. Pollifax involves the underground and a paid informer in a daring rescue plan. Amusing spy adventure with more appeal for readers of light fiction than for espionage buffs." Booklist

Kaleidoscope; a Countess Karitska novel. Ballantine Bks. 2002 244p $21

ISBN 0-345-44820-0 LC 2002-277874

"Madame Karitska's trade as a fortune teller attracts a strange array of clients, including an artistic woman whose husband abandons her to join a religious cult and an Italian immigrant with a 'cursed' child. Karitska also helps her good friend, Detective-Lieutenant Pruden, solve the hit-and-run death of a young violinist and the murder of a local philanthropist. Her most troubling case, however, occurs when a subway incident leaves her with an attaché case full of diamonds. This [is a] well-written episodic adventure." Libr J

Mrs. Pollifax and the Golden Triangle. Doubleday 1988 184p o.p.

LC 87-13082

"Emily Reed-Pollifax and her husband, Curtis Reed, have planned a simple, relaxing vacation to Thailand. Their plans are slightly altered when Mr. Carstairs, Emily's boss at the CIA, receives a cryptic message from a mysterious operative in a small Thai village. He asks the pair of senior citizens to pick up a parcel of significant information while enjoying their trip. . . . Gilman is a pro at pacing her fiction, springing exciting surprises and timely coincidences to the very end." Booklist

Mrs. Pollifax and the Hong Kong Buddha. Doubleday 1985 181p o.p.

LC 85-4335

In this novel Mrs. Pollifax, the widow cum CIA operative is in "Hong Kong, and her assignment is to contact a young Chinese, whom she rescued in her previous mission. Intending to get a line on an apparently turncoat agent, she finds that a psychic and a cat-burglar-turned-Interpol-agent (and good friend) are on the same trail. What they turn up, besides murder, is a group of terrorists with a plan to take over and destroy Hong Kong." Booklist

Mrs. Pollifax and the whirling dervish. Doubleday 1990 196p o.p.

LC 89-25796

"Mrs. Pollifax's present assignment is to pose as the aunt of a C.I.A. agent while the two, in the guise of tourists, verify the bona fides of the informants, matching faces to photographs. To find the seven, Mrs. Pollifax and her escort are expected to spend a week traversing the desert and mountain areas that lie between Fez and the Algerian border. No sooner do they begin their mission than the first informant is murdered—and Mrs. Pollifax herself is in danger of becoming the killer's next victim." N Y Times Book Rev

"The countryside is depicted in great detail, and so are the native people. Gilman's eye for background matches her marvelous sense of adventure." Booklist

Mrs. Pollifax, innocent tourist. Fawcett Columbine 1997 203p o.p.

LC 96-47715

Mrs. Pollifax is on "a trip to the Middle East with her CIA friend Farrell to retrieve a manuscript written by a murdered dissident. The manuscript, thinly disguised as fiction, provides provocative details of Saddam Hussein's reign of terror. The pickup, arranged through an intermediary, proves much more difficult than Farrell or Mrs. Pollifax anticipated, what with smugglers disguised as businessmen, attacks by knife-wielding sheikhs, car chases, and rides on berserk camels. . . . Fun and entertaining, this one is sure to be a hit with the legion of Mrs. Pollifax fans." Booklist

Mrs. Pollifax on safari. Doubleday 1977 182p o.p.

Grandmotherly Emily Pollifax is "assigned by the CIA to join a safari in Zambia and take snapshots of others in the group. The intelligence agents hope one of the pictures will lead them to the identity of the international terrorist known only as Aristotle. The 'Unexpected Mrs. Pollifax' finds some unattractive people among the travelers but also a love interest, Cyrus Reed. When Emily

Gilman, Dorothy, 1923-—*Continued*
is kidnapped and nearly killed, Cyrus rescues her and both are sure they know who Aristotle is. This is a mistake, they discover, when they spot another of their companions aiming a gun at the president of Zambia." Publ Wkly

Mrs. Pollifax pursued. Fawcett Columbine 1995 198p o.p.
LC 94-27625
Mrs. Pollifax "discovers a young woman in her hall closet hiding from some men in a white van. Eager as always, she elicits the girl's story, eludes the villains, and enables the CIA to resolve the situation, which involves kidnapping, shady investments, attempted murder, and the grandson of Ubangiba's last king. Agents actually consult reference books for essential background information, and a few literary allusions build character or relate to earlier Pollifax appearances. This fast-moving tale sports a lively, energetic style." Libr J

A palm for Mrs. Pollifax. Doubleday 1973 226p o.p.
Emily Pollifax "registers as a guest at a posh resort-clinic in Switzerland where the C.I.A. thinks some stolen plutonium has been hidden. In the course of her investigation Mrs. Pollifax discovers the murdered body of her Interpol contact, meets a charming jewel thief who becomes her ally, befriends a frightened little boy who is the son of a leader in a Middle East nation, and escapes through a latrine chute from a mountain top castle where she and the boy are hiding from the killers who intend to use the plutonium to upset the balance of power in the Middle East." Booklist

Thale's Folly. Ballantine Pub. Group 1999 199p o.p.
ISBN 0-449-00364-7 LC 98-27657
"When New York City novelist Andrew Thale checks on some neglected family property in Massachusetts, he discovers four weird squatters—and subsequent mystery." Libr J
"At first, it seems Gilman is rounding up the usual literary suspects, but her genial and well-paced writing, vivid landscapes, and quirky characters are greater than the sum of the clichés." Booklist

The unexpected Mrs. Pollifax. Doubleday 1966 216p o.p.
"Published for the Crime Club"
A "tale of espionage with the chase in Mexico and through the mountains of Albania. Emily Pollifax, a widow of 63, was startled by her doctor's suggestion that the cure for her depression was a job. The only career that inspired Emily was spying, and despite her lack of qualifications, off she went to CIA headquarters in Langly, Virginia, to apply. How she became a routine courier, and why unexpected developments brought into play every scrap of skill and knowledge she had acquired in her former secure life, is an exciting discovery for the reader." Libr J

Gingrich, Newt

Gettysburg; a novel of the Civil War; {by} Newt Gingrich and William Forstchen; and Albert S. Hanser, contributing editor. St. Martin's Press 2003 463p il $24.95
ISBN 0-312-30935-X LC 2003-41381
"On July 1, 1863, the Army of Virginia, under the command of Gen. Robert E. Lee, and the Army of the Potomac, under Gen. George G. Meade, clashed in deadly combat near Gettysburg, PA. Of course, Union forces won, but Gingrich and Forstchen imagine a different outcome in which Confederate forces do a surprise march around Union lines to flank and cut off the Union troops from their supply and information routes. In the course of their narrative, the authors depict the gallantry and heroism of Lee, Longstreet, Chamberlain, Hancock, Hunt, and many other officers and enlisted men on both sides of the conflict." Libr J

Grant comes east; a novel of the Civil War; [by] Newt Gingrich, William R. Forstchen and Albert S. Hanser, contributing editor. 1st ed. Thomas Dunne Books\St. Martin's Press 2004 404p il map $24.95
ISBN 0-312-30937-6 LC 2004-43894
This alternate-history sequel to the author's Gettysburg "centers on the Union government's bringing General Grant eastward from his recent victory in Vicksburg; of course, the immediate ramification of Lee's win at Gettysburg . . . is the threatened safety of Washington, D.C.–and further down the line, the possibility of actual and official recognition of the Confederacy by the European powers. Gingrich and Forstchen's readjustments to history are notably original." Booklist

Gino, Carol, 1941-
(jt. auth) Puzo, M. The family

Gipson, Frederick Benjamin, 1903-1973

Old Yeller; [by] Fred Gipson; drawings by Carl Burger. Harper & Row 1956 158p il $23; pa $5.99
ISBN 0-06-011545-9; 0-06-440382-3 (pa)
LC 56-8780
A Newbery Medal honor book, 1957
"Travis at fourteen was the man of the family during the hard summer of 1860 when his father drove his herd of cattle from Texas to the Kansas market. It was the summer when an old yellow dog attached himself to the family and won Travis' reluctant friendship. Before the summer was over, Old Yeller proved more than a match for thieving raccoons, fighting bulls, grizzly bears, and mad wolves. This is a skillful tale of a boy's love for a dog as well as a description of a pioneer boyhood and it can't miss with any dog lover." Horn Book

Savage Sam; [by] Fred Gipson; decorations by Carl Burger. Harper & Row 1962 214p il o.p.
This is the story of Old Yeller's son. It is set in the East Texas of the 1870's, and deals with Savage Sam's pursuit of the Apaches who have seized Travis, Little Arliss, and Lisbeth
"Although the story is more contrived than its predecessor and overemphasizes the savagery of the Indians, there is good regional background of East Texas during the 1870's and readers will enjoy the fast-paced, sometimes humorous adventure." Booklist

Giroux, E. X.

A death for a dancer. St. Martin's Press 1985 198p o.p.
LC 85-10896

"Barrister Robert Forsythe and his vigilant secretary, Miss Sanderson, are pressed by another barrister into examining a case involving a body found inconveniently in a miniature Chinese Temple on one of England's most sumptuous estates. The victim is con artist Katherine St. Croix, whose demise throws the family of Sir Amyas Dancer into giddy paroxysms of speculation that can only be relieved, claims Dancer, by a private investigator. Enter Forsythe and Sanderson and exit normalcy as the Dancer family surrounds them with their bizarrely eccentric demeanor." Booklist

Death for a dietitian. St. Martin's Press 1988 182p o.p.
LC 87-28622

A mystery starring London barrister Robert Forsythe's secretary "Abigail 'Sandy' Sanderson. On leave from duty as her Robby's maternal secretary, Sandy joins members of a house party on an island where a game of solving a pretend murder mystery becomes real. . . . Then the chief suspect is also murdered, the group is marooned by a storm and the killer cuts the phone line. Red herrings abound in the story that nevertheless serves as a tense diversion with humorous moments leading to the brave and brainy spinster's triumph over the villain." Publ Wkly

A death for a dodo. St. Martin's Press 1993 230p o.p.
LC 92-42573

"A Thomas Dunne book"

"Murder in a swank English nursing home provides a neat puzzle for London barrister and criminologist Robert Forsythe, who nearly becomes a victim himself. . . . Convalescing from knee surgery in the Damien Day Health Home (known as DODO to the locals) near Hundarby, the temporarily crippled Forsythe is drawn into an oddly assorted group of well-known and powerful fellow patients. . . . Giroux's well-crafted page-turner has strong elements of suspense and careful characterization embedded in a classical setting." Publ Wkly

Girzone, Joseph F.

Joshua and the children. Macmillan 1989 224p o.p.
LC 89-2615

"Joshua, an unusual and attractive young man, comes to a village rent by partisan strife (e.g. Catholic vs. Protestant; guerrillas and political agitators) and immediately captures the hearts of the children, enchanting them with gentle stories and amusing sleight-of-hand until they carry his message to the adults." Publ Wkly

"A simple, moving, and inspirational parable presented in an uncomplicated fashion." Libr J

Joshua and the city. Doubleday 1995 242p o.p.
LC 94-41941

In this inspirational novel set in late 20th century New York "a mysterious stranger named Joshua appears, bringing with him a vision for healing the city's numerous social ills. As he walks the city streets, Joshua enters the lives of a number of people who are trapped in the downward spiral of their society, offering them love and strong hope for a brighter future. Joshua reaches out to both rich and poor as he tries to build God's kingdom on Earth." Libr J

Joshua in the Holy Land. Macmillan 1992 205p o.p.
LC 92-17264

As this novel "opens, the simple carpenter Joshua is wandering in the desert in the Middle East. Finding a lost lamb, he returns it to its owner, the prominent sheik Ibrahim Saud, then cures a little girl in the sheik's encampment of a deadly snakebite, thus gaining the Arab's eternal gratitude. Their ensuing friendship opens the possibility of success for Joshua's true mission, bringing peace to the Middle East. He unites like-minded Jews, Arabs and Christians as the Children of Peace, hoping to end strife by forming personal bonds between peoples." Publ Wkly

Joshua, the homecoming. Doubleday 1999 259p $19.95
ISBN 0-385-49509-9 LC 99-33129

In this inspirational novel set in 20th century America, the solitary carpenter Joshua returns to the small town of Auburn after a 20 year absence. Finding fear and spiritual insecurity among the new generation due to the coming Apocalypse, he calms the people with reminders of God's love

The shepherd. Macmillan 1990 246p o.p.
LC 90-2351

"On the eve of David Campbell's consecration as a Catholic bishop, he has an all-night vision that changes him from a strict observer of church law to a radical reformer." Libr J

"Girzone's story is a neat picture of where many American Catholics wish their church would head, but it may be far too unrealistically drawn to have an impact on real lives." Booklist

Glancy, Diane

Stone heart; a novel of Sacajawea. Overlook Press 2002 156p $21.95
ISBN 1-58567-365-X LC 2002-30820

"Sacajawea, the Shoshone native who accompanied Lewis and Clark on their famed expedition, narrates this fictional version of the magnificent, yet harrowing, journey. As told through the heart of a woman and through the spirit of a Native American, the Lewis and Clark expedition takes on entirely new contours." Booklist

Glass, Julia

Three Junes. Pantheon Bks. 2002 353p o.p.
ISBN 0-375-42144-0 LC 2001-55448

A "narrative of the McLeod family during three vital summers. . . . Paul McLeod, the reticent Scots widower introduced in the first section, is the father of Fenno, the central character of the middle section, who is a reserved, self-protective gay bookstore owner in Manhattan; both have dealings with the third section's searching young artist, Fern Olitsky, whose guilt in the wake of her husband's death leaves her longing for—and fearful of—beginning anew." Publ Wkly

Glass, Julia—*Continued*

"Free of gimmickry, 'Three Junes' brilliantly rescues, then refurbishes, the traditional plot-driven novel." N Y Times Book Rev

Glendinning, Victoria

Flight. St. Martin's Press 2003 260p $23.95
ISBN 0-312-31498-1 LC 2003-43125

The "protagonist is an aloof English structural engineer whose specialty is glass and whose innovations have made him a celebrity on the international design circuit. But his capacity to bear emotional loads has never been tested until he meets a French socialite whose ancestral chateau is to become the hotel for an airport he is designing. Glendinning has researched her architecture, and her glass, and she ingeniously explores the theme of responsibility in both work and love, managing to fashion her apparently airy material into a satisfying whole." New Yorker

Goddard, Robert

Beyond recall; a novel. Holt & Co. 1998 310p o.p.
ISBN 0-8050-5110-4 LC 97-28895

First published 1997 in the United Kingdom

When Chris Napier returns to Cornwall for "his niece's wedding, he is shocked to be confronted by childhood friend Nick Lanyon. Lanyon's father was hanged for the murder of Chris' great-uncle, an adventurer responsible for the Napier family fortune—money that would have gone to the Lanyons if there had been no murder. A mentally disturbed Nick promptly hangs himself after challenging Chris to find out the truth about the murder—that Lanyon's father was not the killer at all. Chris, feeling guilty about Nick's death, sets out to do just that." Booklist

"There's an elegant arc to Goddard's fluid style, which gracefully orchestrates the story over its broad time span and through the ambiguous testimony of its complex characters." N Y Times Book Rev

Into the blue. Poseidon Press 1990 415p o.p.
ISBN 0-671-70482-6 LC 90-42481

"When Heather Mallender, English schoolteacher, disappears while sightseeing in Greece with Harry Barnett, Barnett must discover whether she disappeared voluntarily or was a victim of malice. In Hitchcockian tradition, the hero finds himself trapped in a web of intrigue that threatens not only his reputation, but also his life. Barnett's quest leads him from Greece to England and back, followed everywhere he goes, encountering suspicion and resistance at every turn." Libr J

"During this quest, Harry's courage is tested as well as his judgment of people—all of whom turn out to be totally and depressingly human. An everyman's hero, against all mental and emotional odds, Harry finds Heather and renewed self-respect. A very satisfying novel in every way." Booklist

Godden, Rumer, 1907-1998

The battle of the Villa Fiorita. Viking 1963 312p o.p.

A "novel about the immediate effects of their parent's divorce on two English children who run off to Italy to persuade their mother to return home. She is enjoying a premarital honeymoon, days filled with sun, golden light, quiet and love, with an English film director. The two children crash into this peaceful pattern and the battle lines are drawn, children against adults." Publ Wkly

Godden's "characters live and linger in the mind, and the very feel of golden Italy counterpoints the sharp battle in which both sides so tragically lose." Libr J

Black Narcissus. Little, Brown 1939 294p o.p.

A "story of a small group of Anglican nuns newly settled in a convent, formerly a general's pleasure palace, on a high ledge facing Himalayan winds and snows. How the strange pagan environment and unusual experiences affect each of the Sisters, and how a year's effort to teach and heal the natives come to naught is related in a portrayal impressive for its beauty, poignancy and insight." Bookmark

An episode of sparrows. Viking 1955 247p o.p.

The sparrows of the title are the thin, wispy children of a bombed section of London. Tip Malone was almost thirteen; Lovejoy Mason was only eleven, but she was determined to have a garden. And to the surprise of people in the Square, and the joy of gentle Father Lambert, the children succeeded

"It is a deft, amusing, and touching story of a London neighborhood where wealth adjoins poverty. . . . It is a novel which rests lightly on the yearnings of childhood and the dreams of the unworldly. A false touch would tip it over, but Miss Godden stays this side of sentiment and of undue irony." Saturday Rev

The greengage summer; a novel. Viking 1958 218p o.p.

"The story tells of the summer adventures of a group of English children, in somewhat shadowed circumstances, at a second-rate hotel on the Marne, near the forest of Compiègne. . . . Their mother is taken seriously ill as they are enroute to the hotel Les Oeillets, at Vieux-Moutiers. Upon arrival, she is rushed to the hospital for a long stay. The disconcerted children are stranded at the hotel where neither the proprietress, Mademoiselle Zizi, nor her henchwoman, Mme. Corbet, want them. It is the somewhat mysterious Englishman, Eliot, apparently romantically involved with Mlle. Zizi, who takes them under his wing and casually superintends their stay." N Y Times Book Rev

"There is real evil in Miss Godden's novel as well as real good: sex and theft and even murder intrude upon her dewy world as baldly as on the daily papers. But even violence she handles with consummate delicacy. If she allows a moral to creep in, it is that we lose something valuable in gaining maturity." N Y Her Trib Books

In this house of Brede. Viking 1969 376p o.p.

The author writes "about a cloistered order of English Benedictine nuns (Roman Catholic), the way of life they follow in the 20th century, the very real problems, human and spiritual, with which they must grapple, and above all, the intense inner faith that infuses everything they do. . . . Her story centers on a successful career woman in her forties who renounces the world to enter Brede monastery, and what happens to her thereafter." Publ Wkly

"The reader gets an excellent insight into the daily life, rules, and rituals of a religious order." Libr J

Godden, Rumer, 1907-1998—*Continued*

Pippa passes. Morrow 1994 171p o.p.
LC 94-18336

"Pippa Fane, is the youngest member of the Midlands City Ballet. Chosen to go with the company on its Italian tour, she becomes fascinated with Venice, confused by romantic overtures from admirers of both sexes, and challenged by the demands of her dancing troupe." Libr J

"In less able hands, these highly romantic goings-on would seem contrived, but Godden's graceful storytelling keeps readers enthralled, with gorgeous Venice and the nitty-gritty of the dance troupe's routine providing a convincing backdrop for her winsome ingenue." Publ Wkly

Thursday's children. Viking 1984 249p o.p.
LC 83-40252

"Doone Penny, the sixth, the last and almost unwanted son of a London greengrocer and his starstruck wife, is literally born to dance. . . . At home, the center of attention is his only sister, the beautiful Crystal, for whom his mother, a one-time Gaiety girl, has dreams of theatrical grandeur. Following in Crystal's wake to dance classes, the eight-year-old endures the taunts of his macho brothers and the puzzlement of his tradesman father. Doone not only survives but absorbs Crystal's treacheries and other hardships to make his mark as an incandescent dancer." Publ Wkly

The author's "compassion and perceptions remain at perfect pitch. She obviously knows and cares about her children, their parents, the inbred world of ballet aspirants and principal dancers, in this behind-the-scenes fiction. If at times she seems to be speaking to children, perhaps she is addressing the child in each of us." Best Sellers

Godey, John, 1912-

The taking of Pelham one two three. Putnam 1973 316p o.p.

A suspense novel about a "New York subway train that is hijacked by four desperate men who threaten to murder sixteen passengers unless the mayor pays $1 million ransom. . . . Ryder, the brain behind the caper, is an amoral, asexual fatalist who killed for country in Vietnam and for profit as a mercenary in the Congo and Biafra. Longman, bitter at being sacked from his subway-motorman job, is willing to exploit his intimate knowledge of the transit system. Steever is a . . . hood who follows orders and Welcome is a surly Mafia reject who doesn't." Newsweek

"Brutally realistic and coarse in its details and language, but will be popular with suspense story readers." Booklist

Godwin, Gail, 1937-

Evensong. Ballantine Bks. 1999 405p o.p.
ISBN 0-345-37244-1 LC 98-15861

Sequel to Father Melancholy's daughter

Margaret Bonner (née Gower) "is now the pastor at All Saints High Balsam, a parish set in a conservative little resort community high in the Smokies in West North Carolina. She married the much older Adrian Bonner, who is struggling as headmaster of a local boys' school. . . . Into their lives, as they approach the millennium (the book is set a year from now, at Advent 1999) comes Tony, a strange old man with dyed hair who represents himself as a monk on the move; Grace Munger, a local woman with a grim past who has set up as an evangelical revivalist and seeks Margaret's participation in an end-time parade to bring salvation and healing to the mountains; and Chase Zorn, a bright but self-destructive orphaned youngster who is a student at Adrian's school." Publ Wkly

Godwin "has created a character who has enough flaws to satisfy contemporary skeptics but who also struggles convincingly with the old-fashioned task of being a good person. For all its leisurely pace, Evensong turns out, near the end, to have wasted few words." Time

Father Melancholy's daughter. Morrow 1991 404p o.p.
LC 90-13490

This "novel begins in the 1970s in a small Virginia town. Ruth, the Episcopal minister's young wife, leaves her husband and six-year-old daughter Margaret to pursue unfulfilled dreams that she had forsaken by marrying. Margaret and her idealistic father, a victim of recurring depression, find solace in each other as astounded church members look on. The child becomes the parent, assuming the burden of her father's unhappiness. Now, 16 years later and facing her own adulthood, she must come to terms with her conflicted past." Libr J

This novel "does have a number of real satisfactions, namely the characters that surround Margaret and her father. . . . Gail Godwin is almost Chaucerian in her delivery of these people." N Y Times Book Rev

Followed by Evensong

The finishing school. Viking 1985 322p o.p.
LC 84-40069

"Fourteen, yearning to grow up, and grieving for the world of Southern gentility she left behind when her widowed mother moved them up north to live with a determinedly middle-class aunt, Justin Stokes 'falls in love' that first summer in rural New York. Ursula DeVane, who shares the neighboring old mansion with her reclusive pianist brother, is 44, a sophisticated bohemian who dazzles . . . Justin with her worldliness and her attentions. A cabin in the woods becomes Justin's 'finishing school' as the . . . tale of Ursula's mysterious past unfolds. . . . [This story is] told from the point of view of a grown-up Justin, nearly 30 years later." Libr J

"'The Finishing School' is a strikingly accurate examination of the affinity between adolescence and middle age." N Y Times Book Rev

The good husband. Ballantine Bks. 1994 468p o.p.
LC 94-5651

Death "is the metaphorical 'good husband' whom brilliant professor Magda Danvers invokes as she lies dying, a process in which she participates with the same intellectual zest she has brought to her scholarship. While her body wastes away from cancer, she is devotedly tended by her own 'good husband,' Francis Lake, a former seminarian 12 years her junior. They are an unlikely pair: self-effacing Francis is content in his role as house husband and general factotum to flamboyant, iconoclastic Magda. In contrast, the union of Alice and Hugo Henry should constitute marital serenity. Hugo is a 50ish Southern novelist temporarily occupying a chair at Aurelia

Godwin, Gail, 1937-—*Continued*
College; Alice is the empathetic editor who shepherded to publication the work on which his celebrity rests. Yet an icy chill has descended between them after the loss, at birth, of their son. And Hugo's prickly abrasiveness has been exacerbated by writer's block." Publ Wkly

"Godwin's intensely drawn characters are vividly portrayed during the most intimate times of love, marriage, and death." Libr J

A mother and two daughters. Viking 1982 564p o.p.

LC 81-65286

"Suddenly widowed Nell Strickland and her two daughters, reunited in grief, are all on the verge of change as the story begins. Bohemian Cate is twice divorced, almost 40, out of a teaching job and threatened by losses, while younger Lydia, who just left her husband, is winning: a college degree, a new lover, and fame as a TV personality. Ambivalent about accommodation and possibility but 'hospitable . . . to whatever came next,' each has created herself anew by the end. The North Carolina setting is as precisely evoked as [are] the many unusual, amusing characters." Libr J

Mr. Bedford

In Godwin, G. Mr. Bedford and the muses p1-104

Mr. Bedford and the muses. Viking 1983 229p o.p.

LC 83-47870

Contents: Mr. Bedford; A father's pleasures; Amanuensis; St. John; The angry-year; A cultural exchange

"The longest story in this collection concerns itself with a group of young people living as boarders in London with an American couple of mysterious background. Each character is most interestingly described and the tensions and interrelationships among them keep the story moving. In other stories a writer is suddenly visited by a young girl who offers her services in the writer's home with a surprising development; a father's love for his son comes into conflict with his attraction to his son's friend; an author finds his life affected by the presence in his village of a woman with the same name as his. Godwin's writing is graceful and humorous." Shapiro. Fic for Youth. 3d edition

A Southern family. Morrow 1987 540p o.p.

LC 87-12381

This novel begins with a visit by Clare Campion, a successful novelist living in New York City, to her family, the Quicks, in Mountain City, North Carolina. During her visit, Clare's half brother Theo dies violently. The book then "focuses separately on each member of the Quick family, as well as some outside it. . . . Characters talk and think out their perceptions of Theo and themselves." N Y Times Book Rev

"Gail Godwin is something of a rarity today—a writer who not only maintains an elegant and suspenseful pace, but also has something worth saying and worth thinking about." Christ Sci Monit

Goethe, Johann Wolfgang von, 1749-1832

Novella

In Goethe, J. W. v. The sorrows of young Werther, and Novella p169-201

The sorrows of young Werther

In Goethe, J. W. v. The sorrows of young Werther, and Novella p1-167

The sorrows of young Werther, and Novella; translated by Elizabeth Mayer and Louise Brogan; poems translated by W. H. Auden; foreword by W. H. Auden. Modern Lib. 1993 c1971 xx, 201p o.p.

ISBN 0-679-60064-7 LC 93-5007

A translation of two of Goethe's works, originally published 1774 and 1828 respectively; this is a reissue of the 1971 edition published by Random House

"Werther is a sensitive artist, ill at ease in society and hopelessly in love with Charlotte, who is engaged to someone else. This novel, with the eventual suicide of the hero, caused a sensation throughout Europe." Oxford Companion to Engl Lit

Novella, is an example of a specific literary genre, the idyll. A tame tiger which escapes during a fire pursues a princess and is killed. The animal trainer and his family, lamenting its death, persuade the prince, who has been out hunting a lion, to let them tame that animal rather than kill it. According to W. H. Auden it is "a parable about the relation between wild nature and human craft"

Goff, Annabel Davis- *See* Davis-Goff, Annabel

Gogol´, Nikolaĭ Vasil´evich, 1809-1852

The collected tales of Nikolai Gogol; translated and annotated by Richard Pevear and Larissa Volokhonsky. Pantheon Bks. 1998 xxii, 435p o.p.

ISBN 0-679-43023-7 LC 97-37228

Contents: St. John's Eve; The night before Christmas; The terrible vengeance; Ivan Fyodorovich Shponka and his aunt; Old world landowners; Viy; The story of how Ivan Ivanovich quarreled with Ivan Nikiforovich; Nevsky Prospect; The diary of a madman; The nose; The carriage; The portrait; The overcoat

Dead souls; {by} Nikolai Gogol; translated and annotated by Richard Pevear and Larissa Volokhonsky. Pantheon Bks. 1996 xxiv, 402p o.p.

ISBN 0-679-43022-9 LC 95-24357

Original Russian edition, 1842

"Considered one of the world's finest satires, this picaresque work traces the adventures of the social-climbing Pavel Ivanovich Chichikov, a dismissed civil servant out to seek his fortune. It is admired not only for its enduring comic portraits but also for its sense of moral purpose." Merriam-Webster's Ency of Lit

The overcoat, and other tales of good and evil; [by] Nikolai V. Gogol; translated with an introduction by David Magarshack. Norton 1965 c1957 271p o.p.

This collection was first published 1957 in paperback by Doubleday with title: Tales of good and evil

Contents: The terrible vengeance; Ivan Fyodorovich Shponka and his aunt; The portrait; Nevsky Avenue; The nose; The overcoat

Goldberg, Myla

Bee season; a novel. Doubleday 2000 275p pa $13 o.p.

ISBN 0-385-49880-2 LC 99-47933

This novel concerns an eleven-year-old girl, Eliza Naumann, who wins the National Spelling Bee. "Eliza's supernatural gift for spelling thrills her father, Saul, a self-styled Jewish scholar who now believes he can train his daughter to literally talk to God. Unfortunately, that means shunting aside Eliza's older brother, Aaron, who joins a religious cult, and her scarily remote mother, Miriam, who begins breaking into houses in search of missing pieces of herself." Newsweek

"Some of the events that unfold . . . seem a little contrived. But Goldberg engenders considerable suspense around both Eliza's string of spelling successes and the fates of the other Naumanns." Time

Golden, Arthur

Memoirs of a geisha; a novel. Knopf 1997 434p il $26.95

ISBN 0-375-40011-7 LC 97-74747

"How nine-year-old Chiyo, sold with her sister into slavery by their father after their mother's death, becomes Sayuri, the beautiful geisha accomplished in the art of entertaining men, is the focus of this . . . novel. Narrating her life story from her elegant suite in the Waldorf Astoria, Sayuri tells of her traumatic arrival at the *Nitta okiya* (a geisha house), where she endures harsh treatment from Granny and Mother, the greedy owners, and from Hatsumomo, the sadistically cruel head geisha. But Sayuri's chance meeting with the Chairman, who shows her kindness, makes her determined to become a geisha. Under the tutelage of the renowned Mameha, she becomes a leading geisha of the 1930s and 1940s." Libr J

"Rarely has a world so closed and foreign been evoked with such natural assurance, from the aesthetics of the Kyoto geisha's 'art'—to the fetishized sexuality of Gion in the thirties and forties, at once delicate and crude, repressed and flagrant." New Yorker

Golding, William, 1911-1993

Clonk clonk

In Golding, W. The scorpion god: three short novels p63-114

Close quarters. Farrar, Straus & Giroux 1987 281p o.p.

LC 87-5351

This second volume of the trilogy begun with Rites of passage is a "tale of the tragic misadventures befalling an 18th century fighting ship now converted to transporting cargo and passengers on the treacherous voyage from England to Australia. The novel is cast as a journal written by Edmund FitzHenry Talbot, a well-meaning, somewhat uncertain, slightly pompous officer and gentleman enroute to Sydney and a career in His Majesty's service. As a result of a green sailor's blunder, the ship's masts shatter, and it founders. Golding's principal achievement is the vivid, detailed depiction of a disintegrating vessel in the tropical seas, its progressive decay, and the wretchedness and despair of its passengers." Publ Wkly

Followed by Fire down below

Darkness visible. Farrar, Straus & Giroux 1979 265p o.p.

LC 79-19206

"A child hideously maimed in the bombing of London during World War II grows up to inspire the messianic fantasies of the people with whom he comes in contact. In Golding's dark world the horrors of the physically deformed are mirrored in—but are no match for—the spiritual monsters who inhabit the novel's strange vision of contemporary life. A powerful contemplation of the evil at the root of human behavior." Booklist

Envoy extraordinary

In Golding, W. The scorpion god: three short novels p115-78

Fire down below. Farrar, Straus & Giroux 1989 313p o.p.

LC 88-18079

This is the concluding volume of the trilogy begun in Rites of Passage and continued in Close Quarters. "Narrated by young Edmund FitzHenry Talbot, the trilogy recounts his voyage from England to Australia on a former man-of-war during the Napoleonic era. The last of the three novels takes the badly damaged ship through several storms, an encounter with a gigantic iceberg (actually the continent of Antarctica, but the crew doesn't know it) and finally to the safe shelter of Sydney Harbor." N Y Times Book Rev

Golding is "translucent and economical. In his writing, allegorical motifs are revealed fleetingly in the everyday and in the ordinary. He is at once a complex and highly readable novelist." Economist

The inheritors. Harcourt 1962 c1955 233p o.p.

First published 1955 in the United Kingdom

A narrative "inhabiting the near-animal consciousness of Lok, a Neanderthal man, and describing in his clumsy terms and with great pathos the casual destruction of his species by *Homo sapiens*. The reader is shown his ancestors, already armed, arrogant, murderous, and corrupt—not superior to the Neanderthalers, only more clever and more evil." Wakeman. World Authors, 1950-1970

Lord of the Flies; a novel. Coward-McCann 1955 243p o.p.

First published 1954 in the United Kingdom

"Stranded on an island, a group of English schoolboys leave innocence behind in a struggle for survival. A political structure modeled after English government is set up and a hierarchy develops, but forces of anarchy and aggression surface. The boys' existence begins to degenerate into a savage one. They are rescued from their microcosmic society to return to an adult, stylized milieu filled with the same psychological tensions and moral voids. Adventure and allegory are brilliantly combined in this novel." Shapiro. Fic for Youth. 3d edition

The paper men. Farrar, Straus & Giroux 1984 191p o.p.

ISBN 0-374-22980-5 LC 84-27984

"The 'paper men' are famed English novelist Wilfred Barclay and American university professor Rick Tucker, and the two are engaged in a battle to the death over whether Tucker will write the aging author's biography. What begins as comedy . . . darkens as Tucker inadvertently destroys Barclay's marriage, provokes an alcoholic

Golding, William, 1911-1993—*Continued*

crackup, and finally pushes Barclay into taking a terrible revenge." Libr J

The author's "approach to this material is highly personal, projecting the portrait of a writer who struggles more within himself than with his craft and who is both victim and charlatan as he searches for a self that has become hidden in his art and altered by public adulation." Booklist

Rites of passage. Farrar, Straus & Giroux 1980 278p o.p.

LC 80-16809

In this first volume of a trilogy the author "is fascinated by what might have occurred on a long sea voyage to the Antipodes (Australia) in the Napoleonic era. The passengers are a motley lot out of Britain; the crew, officers and men, and a tough-minded captain who hates the clergy, find their scapegoat in a pitiable parson who has no idea of his own latent homosexuality. Told partly from the viewpoint of an aristocratic dilettante aboard and then in the words set down by the tormented victim in a journal meant for his sister but becoming almost a confession to God." Publ Wkly

"In a sense the novel seems highly artificial, not only in its careful, detailed recreation of the period, but also in the elaborate system of correspondences and parallels—some clear, some obscure—which underpins the narration. Yet at the same time it is an extremely lively, enjoyable piece of work. Readers who know only the early Golding will be surprised by its humor." Times Lit Suppl

Followed by Close quarters

The scorpion god

In Golding, W. The scorpion god: three short novels p9-62

The scorpion god: three short novels. Harcourt Brace Jovanovich 1972 c1971 178p o.p.

Contents: The scorpion god; Clonk clonk; Envoy extraordinary

In the title story "the Liar (a jester in the court of ancient Egypt) confounds the people of the land and reveals himself as the mysterious Scorpion God. In the second story . . . Charging Elephant (a tribal youth in Africa) passes into manhood through the services of She Who Names the Women and becomes the fierce Water Paw Wounded Leopard. In the third story . . . Panocles (an inventor in ancient Rome) impresses the Emperor by building a steamship and is rewarded with the post of Envoy Extraordinary and Plenipotentiary to China." New Yorker

"Entertaining if somewhat didactic, the three allegorical narratives are ironic, clever, and subtle in style and illustrate Golding's penchant for the unusual." Booklist

Goldman, William, 1931-

Marathon man. Delacorte Press 1974 309p o.p.

"'Babe' Levy, a graduate student, spends his free time running, and dreams of being a great marathon runner. The death of his brother in Babe's apartment starts a chain of mysterious and terrifying events. Pursued by government agents and ex-Nazis, Babe struggles to escape being assassinated. The torture scenes may make this suspenseful story an ordeal for some readers." Shapiro. Fic for Youth. 3d edition

Goldsborough, Robert

The bloodied ivy; a Nero Wolfe mystery. Bantam Bks. 1988 191p o.p.

LC 88-3513

"Rude, self-centered Nero Wolfe is persuaded by Archie Goodwin, the intelligent, good-natured narrator, to investigate the death of a well-known professor at Prescott University. Hale Markham attracted many students, but he also inspired jealousy among several coworkers. When Markham dies on campus, his friend asks Goodwin for help." Libr J

The missing chapter; a Nero Wolfe mystery. Bantam Bks. 1993 229p o.p.

LC 93-13714

A publisher hires Nero Wolfe and Archie Goodwin "to investigate the death, labeled a suicide, of Charles Childress, an ill-tempered author who had recently angered several people, including his agent, his editor and the possibly corrupt reviewer who had lambasted the latest Childress novel." Publ Wkly

"The publishing details ring true, and . . . Goldsborough does a masterly job with the Wolfe legacy." Booklist

Goldsmith, Olivia

Bad boy; a novel. Dutton 2001 324p $24.95

ISBN 0-525-94558-X LC 2001-524285

"Tracie Higgins is a young reporter for the *Seattle Times*. Though she has a musician-poet-lout boyfriend, every Sunday Tracie meets platonic chum Jonathan Delano for brunch. Jonathan is a techno-wizard for Micro/Con; he is responsible, dedicated, environmentally correct; good to his mother and stepmothers; and alas, an ugly duckling dweeb who hasn't had sex in a year. Tracie agrees to give him a 'make over': the clothes, the moves, the haircut, the lines—in short, attitude." Publ Wkly

"The book is kind of silly and sappy, but it works because Goldsmith infuses her story with much humor, general good cheer, a compulsively readable plot, and a hapless happy ending." Libr J

Pen pals. Dutton 2002 359p o.p.

ISBN 0-525-94644-6 LC 2001-47418

Protagonist Jennifer Spencer is "a rising star on Wall Street who is working at a prestigious firm and engaged to a brilliant lawyer. To help protect her trusted mentor-boss from exposure, Jennifer agrees to be the point person in an SEC investigation. After everything goes awry, Jennifer finds herself shackled in Jennings, a women's prison not at all like the country club, white-collar crime camp she envisioned. . . . The path from the despair of prison life to female conquest is glorious and satisfying without being man-hating; the cast of characters perfectly blends women from all walks of life, joined by their common goal." Booklist

Young wives; a novel. HarperCollins Pubs. 2000 512p $25

ISBN 0-06-017553-2 LC 99-48167

This novel features three protagonists: "sweet, innocent Angie, whose uptight but good-looking Boston lawyer husband is two-timing with her best friend; Jada, an African-American heroine who is at once a bank manag-

Goldsmith, Olivia—*Continued*

er, churchgoer and devoted mother . . . and whose husband is a ne'er-do-well lazybones; and houseproud Michelle Russo, whose dream-boat Italian mate is . . . a high-level drug dealer on the side. All three women are put through purgatory by their husbands, crooked lawyers and a bent legal system until . . . they fight back in all-for-one, one-for-all style." Publ Wkly

Goldstein, Lisa, 1953-

The alchemist's door. TOR Bks. 2002 286p o.p.
ISBN 0-7653-0150-4 LC 2001-59605
"A Tom Doherty Associates book"
"In the last years of the 16th century, Dr. John Dee, astrologer and alchemist to Elizabeth I, leaves England for the furthest reaches of Europe, in hopes of escaping a conjured demon intent on destroying his life and career. In Prague, Dee meets with the esteemed Rabbi Loew. Despite their differences in religion and social class, the two men embark on a mystical quest for the last righteous man, knowing that if they fail, the world will fall under the sway of darkness." Libr J
"Although Goldstein's story has a tendency to meander all over the map, diluting her strong message about the cost of power and pride, Dee and Loew's search for truth makes for a telling morality tale." Publ Wkly

González Echevarría, Roberto

(ed) The Oxford book of Latin American short stories. See The Oxford book of Latin American short stories

Gooden, Philip

The pale companion. Carroll & Graf Pubs. 2002 280p $24
ISBN 0-7867-1008-X LC 2002-67224
"Nick Revill is the sleuth-hero, an actor in Shakespeare's company, the Chamberlain's Men of the Globe Theatre. . . . It's the summer of 1601, and the Chamberlain's Men have been summoned to a great house in Salisbury to perform *A Midsummer Night's Dream* as part of the revels celebrating a noble marriage. But the great house is filled with strange happenings." Booklist
"Historical mystery fans are in for a treat." Publ Wkly

Goodman, Allegra

Paradise park; a novel. Dial Press (NY) 2001 360p o.p.
ISBN 0-385-33416-8 LC 00-49376
This novel's heroine-narrator Sharon Spiegelman "is on a lifelong tear through the world in search of God. . . . Abandoned in a fleabag hotel in Waikiki sometime in the mid-1970's by her folk-dancing partner, with little more than a macramé bikini to her name, she throws herself into a chaotic, all-consuming quest for human and divine love." N Y Times Book Rev
"Like Saul Bellow and Philip Roth before her, Goodman has achieved a breakthrough book by discovering and recording a thoroughly uninhibited narrative voice." Time

Goodrum, Charles A.

Dewey decimated. Crown 1977 190p o.p.
"A wealthy private library in Washington [receives] a series of anonymous letters [which] cast serious doubt on the value and authenticity of the library's most recherché books, and shortly afterwards the keeper of rare books is found impaled in the stacks. A . . . young public relations officer and a young scholar from Minnesota are joined by a distinguished retired librarian to investigate this murder as well as that of a secretive bookbinder." Libr J

GoodWeather, Hartley *See* King, Thomas, 1943-

Goonan, Kathleen Ann

Crescent city rhapsody. Avon Eos 2000 430p o.p.
ISBN 0-380-97711-7 LC 99-42227
"In 2012, a mysterious alien signal from space strikes Earth, sending the Information Age into a horrifying tailspin. An intermittent Silence descends on the planet, disrupting all electronic devices and sparking a virus that nine months later produces mutated children with a heightened receptivity to electromagnetic forces. In New Orleans . . . Marie Laveau, a mob chieftain and mulatto descendant of *voudoun* priestesses, is murdered by hit men, but then resurrected through the new science of nanotechnology. She launches a complex 20-year plan to save her city—and her world." Publ Wkly
"The rhythm of the story and the interaction of the characters brilliantly capture a time when everyone sees the future happening, each in a different way." Booklist

Light music. HarperCollins Pubs. 2002 406p $25.95
ISBN 0-380-97712-5 LC 2001-55602
Sequel to Crescent city rhapsody
In this concluding volume of the Nanotech Quartet "the microscopic machines of the 22nd century have gone beyond creating sentient cities and controlling all communications on Earth—they are themselves evolving. When mysterious lights point to an alien presence and disappearing people arouse stark fear, three human survivors, including Argentine refugee Angelina, set out to solve the mystery and measure the threat to humanity. A lot of picaresque adventures ensue. . . . This classic novel of ideas, with state-of-the-art technology as its subject, remains the work of a powerful imagination with a superior command of language." Publ Wkly

Gordimer, Nadine, 1923-

Burger's daughter. Viking 1979 361p o.p.
LC 78-20831
"A young Afrikaaner woman inherits a heavy burden from her father, a doctor and a leader of the South African Communist Party who is a martyr to the anti-apartheid cause—all the heavier because she shares his moral outrage but neither his confident analysis of a simple wrong and remedy nor his saintly selfessness. In the eyes of Rosa's father's friends (and foes), however, she is 'Burger's daughter'. . . . After her father dies in prison, when Rosa is in her mid-twenties, her secret ambivalence becomes unbearable, and she obtains a passport

Gordimer, Nadine, 1923-—*Continued*
and leaves South Africa, resolved to discover if there is any other way she can live." New Yorker

"What enables Gordimer's riveting poetic prose is her intellectual and political honesty—the scrupulous unsentimentality with which she affixes blame or despair, irrespective of color, status, or political orientation." Christ Sci Monit

The conservationist. Viking 1975 c1974 252p o.p.

First published 1974 in the United Kingdom

The author probes "the way of life that exists in South Africa today, and some aspects of the tensions that exist among English and Afrikaaners, Blacks, coloreds, Indian shopkeepers. . . . Mehring is rich, white, bored. His farm is a weekend pleasure place to which he once brought the mistress whose flirtations with left wing causes have now exiled her forever. His teenage son won't even come home for the holidays and wants out of all that South Africa stands for. Mehring is kind enough to his blacks, keeps them in their place, avoids his Boer neighbors with whom he has nothing in common. A loner, living for himself, deliberately isolated from any unpleasantness that might intrude, only gradually does he begin to perceive that there are forces at work in nature, in the closeness between the blacks and the land by which some day his way of life will be forever changed." Publ Wkly

A guest of honor. Viking 1970 504p o.p.

The hero of this novel, James "Bray is a 54-year-old former administrator for one of Her Majesty's former African colonies. . . . He was cashiered for showing too much sympathy for the local independence movement. After independence, Bray accepts an invitation to return as an educational consultant to Miss Gordimer's nameless, composite, new African nation. His professional commitment to the excruciating process of Third World nation building is complicated because the country's opposing political factions—one moderate, the other revolutionary—are led by two of his former protégés." Time

The house gun. Farrar, Straus & Giroux 1998 294p o.p.

ISBN 0-374-17307-9 LC 97-28787

In this novel, an upperclass South African "professional couple—insurance executive Harald and physician Claudia Lindgard—face the unthinkable when their 27-year-old-son, Duncan, in a fit of passion, picks up the 'house gun,' a staple item in many affluent households for protection against marauders, and shoots a man who has doubly betrayed him. . . . [The narrative depicts] the senior Lindgards' progression of emotions: disbelief that their son could commit such an act, followed by guilt about their shortcomings as parents and, finally, abandonment of their genteel ethics as they plead to Duncan's brilliant, suave black lawyer to just get their son off." Publ Wkly

"Gordimer is above all a writer of ideas, and she engages her audience in the discourse of morality and ethical conduct without deteriorating into the tedious language of a civics lesson." Women's Rev Books

July's people. Viking 1981 160p o.p.

LC 80-24877

"When revolution breaks out against the whites in South Africa, Bamford and Maureen Smales are forced to flee. Their black servant July, loyal to them for fifteen years, takes them away to his people in a bush village. His role changes slowly to one not only of savior but also overseer. The change in their manner of living from the good, clean, well-regulated life of 'the ruling class' to that of the customs of July's people raises havoc within both the white and black families and in the delicate tissue of understanding between the Smales and their servant. There is much to be learned from this powerful story written by an author who lives in South Africa and who writes with authority on a subject that has import for any society where race relations or colonial conditions are fragile and explosive." Shapiro. Fic for Youth. 3d edition

Jump and other stories. Farrar, Straus & Giroux 1991 256p o.p.

ISBN 0-374-18055-5 LC 91-2687

Contents: Jump; Once upon a time; The ultimate safari; A find; My father leaves home; Some are born to sweet delight; Comrades; Teraloyna; The moment before the gun went off; Home; A journey; Spoils; Safe houses; What were you dreaming?; Keeping fit; Amnesty

This "collection of tales features an insider's intensity about people caught in the savage particulars of southern Africa today; at the same time, the surprise of the stories and the slash of their endings make the words resonate with the revelations of an ever-widening universe." Booklist

Loot, and other stories. Farrar, Straus & Giroux 2003 240p $23

ISBN 0-374-19090-9 LC 2002-42601

Includes the novellas Karma and Mission statement and the following short stories: Loot; Visiting George; The generation gap; L,U,C,I,E.; Look-alikes; The diamond mine; Homage; An emissary

In Karma a deceased insurance executive's spirit makes successive returns to earth in various guises. Mission statement is about a middle-aged Englishwomanwho has a sexual relationship with a native while working for an international aid agency in an impoverished African country

"This compelling collection presents a bleak view of human existence in general and of Africa's colonial past in particular. Written with a sharp sense of irony, it should be a part of every fiction collection." Libr J

My son's story. Farrar, Straus & Giroux 1990 277p o.p.

ISBN 0-374-21751-3 LC 90-83232

"Sonny is a teacher of mixed race. He and his wife are . . . sympathetic to the plight of the 'real blacks,' yet ambitious that they may someday be accepted by the whites. Sonny's political education begins when he's fired for helping black children demonstrate in their township. Jailed for promoting boycotts and participating in illegal gatherings, Sonny meets and falls in love with a blond, blue-eyed woman who works for a human-rights organization. Sonny's adolescent son, Will, tells the story of his father's political and erotic development, the resentments and betrayals that ensue." Newsweek

This is a "thoughtful, poised, quietly poignant novel that not only recognizes the value and cost of political commitment, but also takes account of recent developments in South Africa and Eastern Europe in a way that Gordimer's previous work did not." Christ Sci Monit

Gordimer, Nadine, 1923-—*Continued*

None to accompany me. Farrar, Straus & Giroux 1994 324p o.p.

ISBN 0-374-22297-5 LC 94-7553

"In the final days of the old regime in South Africa, antiapartheid activists are released from prison or return home afters years of exile. Vera Stark, a white legal aid attorney representing the black community, recognizes many familiar faces from her youth, but she is shocked to see that they appear to have aged overnight. This unnerving experience causes her to reexamine her life. Known around her law firm as someone impervious to con games, Vera is ruthless in exposing her own lies and deceptions. She faces unpleasant truths about her marriages, her affairs, and the effect her actions may have had on her children. But rather than cling to the security of a flawed life, Vera finds that the rapidly changing political situation encourages radical personal change." Libr J

"A novel that raises more questions than it answers, 'None to Accompany Me' is an unflinching and perceptive exploration of people living on the brink of changes—political and personal—with little but their own sense of self-reliance to guide them." Christ Sci Monitor

The pickup. Farrar, Straus & Giroux 2001 270p $23

ISBN 0-374-23210-5 LC 2001-23041

To South African "Julie Summer, rebellious daughter of a rich white investment banker, the black mechanic she meets at a garage is initially merely an interesting person to add to her circle of bohemian friends. But as their relationship swiftly escalates, Julie comes to understand her lover's perilous tightrope attempts to find a country that will shelter him. Abdu, as he calls himself (it's not his real name), is an illegal immigrant from an abysmally poor Arab country. Now on the verge of deportation from South Africa, he's forced to return to his ancestral village. Julie insists on marrying him and going with him." Publ Wkly

"Gordimer writes so tenderly and so searchingly about Julie's gradual transcendence of her western self that she manages to hold sceptism at bay." Women's Review of Books

A sport of nature; a novel. Viking 1987 341p o.p.

LC 86-46150

This novel traces the adventures of its protagonist, Hillela Capran, a Jewish South African raised by her two aunts, one conventional, the other radical, through a series of love affairs and marriages which lead to her increasing involvement in African revolutionary causes. At the end of the book, she is the wife of the head of state of an African country and witnesses the end of apartheid in her native land

This is "fully a novel, grand-scale, rich and demanding, but it is also a thoughtfully documented history of postcolonial African nations." N Y Times Book Rev

Gordon, Mary, 1949-

The company of women. Knopf 1981 c1980 291p o.p.

LC 80-5284

In this novel "Felicitas is nurtured by a large circle of Catholic women. After attending only parochial schools, Felicitas goes to Columbia University, where she becomes sexually involved with a married professor, gives up her studies, and becomes pregnant. She returns to the company of women, gives birth to her baby, and later marries only to provide a father for her child." Merriam-Webster's Ency of Lit

"Given its scope, depth, and the perfection of its lyrical passages (which are the more impressive because of Gordon's natural inclination toward the austere), it is fair to call this a brilliant novel." Saturday Rev

Final payments. Random House 1978 297p o.p.

LC 77-90259

"Isabel Moore spends 11 years almost totally absorbed in caring for her invalid father, who suffered a paralyzing stroke after discovering his daughter in a compromising situation with one of his students. When she is thirty, her father dies; she is freed from responsibility for his welfare but not yet able to accept responsibility for her own life. Her involvement with two men adds complications as, guilt-ridden and filled with religious skepticism, Isabel searches for answers and begins to heal. Two childhood friends, Eleanor, an independent woman, and Liz, a tough married mother of two children, are instrumental in helping Isabel grow toward self-realization." Shapiro. Fic for Youth. 3d edition

Immaculate man

In Gordon, M. The rest of life: three novellas

Living at home

In Gordon, M. The rest of life: three novellas

Pearl; Mary Gordon. Pantheon Books 2005 354p $24.95

ISBN 0-375-42315-X LC 2004-48537

"The novel begins on Christmas night 1998 when Maria Meyers returns to her apartment on Manhattan's Upper West Side to discover a message that her twenty-year-old daughter, Pearl, who has been studying in Ireland, has chained herself to a flagpole at Trinity College, Dublin. Although she is not known to have any strong political opinions, Pearl has been starving herself for six weeks, and, we find out later, it is her intention to die for her complicity in the death of a young man whom she had insulted and who she thinks committed suicide as a result. Over her own protests, Pearl is taken by the authorities to a hospital, where her condition is considered grave. The challenge will be to convince her to continue to live. As Maria flies to her daughter's bedside, she meditates on her own life." Hudson Rev

"Gordon's job here was to show the intimacy in Pearl's grand stunt and the grandness in the intimate mother-daughter reunion that follows. In both of those tasks, she has most artfully succeeded." Washington Post Book World

The rest of life

In Gordon, M. The rest of life: three novellas

Gordon, Mary, 1949-—*Continued*

The rest of life: three novellas. Viking 1993 257p o.p.

LC 92-50753

"In 'Immaculate Lover,' a social worker falls in love with a Catholic priest and explains, with tremendous care and tenderness, the circumstances of their precarious relationship. 'Living at Home' is narrated by a doctor who works with autistic children. Her lover is a journalist who risks his life covering revolution and war. Here, Gordon probes the concept of home and the ways we define ourselves. The final novella, 'The Rest of Life,' records a 78-year-old woman's revelation upon returning to her native Italy for the first time since her exile at age 15. Paola was sent away after the boy with whom she'd made a half-hearted suicide pact went through with it on his own, leaving her alive and deeply ashamed." Booklist

"Gordon endows her heroines with a rich sexuality while engaging us in a probing debate about the complex relationship between our bodies, our pasts, and our sense of self." Libr J

Temporary shelter; short stories. Random House 1987 213p o.p.

LC 86-31627

Contents: Temporary shelter; The imagination of disaster; Delia; The only son of the doctor; The neighborhood; Watching the tango; Agnes; The magician's wife; Out of the fray; The thorn; Eileen; Now I am married; The murderer guest; The other woman; Billy; Safe; The dancing party; Violation; Mrs. Cassidy's last year; A writing lesson

"The 22 stories that make up this distinguished collection reaffirm Gordon's ability to create fully dimensional characters who speak in a variety of authentic voices. Though the narratives are poetically compressed, Gordon eschews minimalism and uses incident to sustain narrative energy." Publ Wkly

Gordon, Neil, 1958-

The company you keep. Viking 2003 406p $24.95

ISBN 0-670-03218-2 LC 2002-44905

"When limousine-leftist lawyer and single dad Jim Grant is unmasked as Jason Sinai, an ex-Weather Underground militant wanted for a deadly bank robbery, he abandons his daughter and goes on the lam. As he evades a manhunt and seeks out old comrades, the author introduces a sprawling cast of drug dealers, bomb-planting radicals turned leftist academics, Vietnam vets, FBI agents and Republicans who collectively ponder the legacy of the '60s." Publ Wkly

"If the book has a political stance, it might be called the radical center, training equal skepticism, even humorous contempt, on the excesses of both left and right." N Y Times Book Rev

Gores, Joe

Cons, scams & grifts. Mysterious Press 2001 324p $24.95

ISBN 0-89296-594-0 LC 2001-30637

"Daniel Kearny Associates—San Francisco private investigators and auto-repossession specialists—have been hired by Cal-Cit Bank to repossess cars being sold by a dealer who hasn't paid off his loans. The bank has also employed the firm to protect some very valuable property on a remote estate. Meantime, Kearney's investigators are working for a very different client—a local gypsy clan trying to clear one of its own of a murder charge." Booklist

"Although this episodic caper looks like a free-for-all, [Gores'] brazen schemes require high levels of intelligence and the underlying design of his ploys is quite breathtaking." N Y Times Book Rev

Contract null & void. Mysterious Press 1996 309p o.p.

LC 96-12769

"Repo men of Daniel Kearny Associates scour the streets of San Francisco for luxury cars and electric guitars. When a flamboyant union leader is murdered, their searches lead them into corrupt backwaters." Libr J

"Master of surreal comedic style, Mr. Gores keeps finding outlandish assignments for his repo men. But in the inspired ending, aptly called 'Walpurgisnacht,' the plot lines converge and all the insanity, believe it or not, makes perfect sense." N Y Times Book Rev

Gores, Joseph N. *See* Gores, Joe

Gorky, Maksim, 1868-1936

Selected short stories; [by] Maxim Gorky; with an introductory essay by Stefan Zweig. Ungar 1959 348p o.p.

Contents: Makar Chudra; Old Izergil; Chelkash; Afloat: an Easter story; Twenty-six men and a girl; Malva; Comrade; The ninth of January; Tales of Italy; The romancer; The Mordvinian girl; A man is born; The breakup; How a song was composed; The philanderer

Gorman, Ed

Breaking up is hard to do. Carroll & Graff Pubs. 2004 207p $24

ISBN 0-7867-1296-1

"In late October 1962, with Armageddon looming in the form of the Cuban missile crisis, life went on in Black River Falls, Iowa-except in the case of a young woman found murdered in gubernatorial candidate Ross Murdoch's under-construction bomb shelter. His political dreams dashed, Murdoch hopes to avoid the electric chair and hires young investigator-attorney Sam McCain to represent him. . . . Intelligent writing and great reading." Booklist

Save the last dance for me. Carroll & Graf Pubs. 2002 230p $24

ISBN 0-7867-0968-5

A mystery set in Black River Falls, Iowa in 1960. Sam McCain, "a part-time lawyer and part-time PI, gets hired by the town judge to investigate the murder of John Muldaur, a local fundamentalist preacher who used live rattlesnakes to test the 'purity' of his flock, after someone doses the preacher's bottle of Pepsi with strychnine. When he wasn't sleeping with the wife of one of his congregation, Muldaur was conducting a vigorous campaign to expose the conspiracy of Zionists and Roman Catholics to take over the world." Publ Wkly

A "dead-on perfect journey to the underside of the late

Gorman, Ed—*Continued*
'50s and early '60s, exposing the anti-intellectualism and anti-Semitism that lurked beneath the era's placid surface." Booklist

Gosling, Paula

The dead of winter. Mysterious Press 1996 c1995 328p o.p.
LC 95-39099

First published 1995 in the United Kingdom

"After the discovery of a body in an ice-fishing hole nearly scares a tipsy man sober, Sheriff Matt Gabriel knows what to do. Because the victim has mob connections, Matt fears unrest in the usually peaceful Blackwater Bay. One of Jess Gibbons's high school students, meanwhile, disappears." Libr J

"This complicated puzzler, pivoting from cozy sewing circles to talk of mafia hit men and cocaine dens, comes to its brilliantly staged conclusion at the annual ice festival where Gosling dramatizes the point that smooth and shiny surfaces can hide a lot of treachery." Publ Wkly

A few dying words. Mysterious Press 1994 344p o.p.
LC 94-18826

"A Blackwater Bay mystery novel"

"While bracing for the Blackwater Bay's annual Howl—a traditional Halloween celebration of carnival rides and pranks—Sheriff Matt Gabriel agrees to meet with clearly agitated retired pharmacist, Tom Finnegan. While driving to the sheriff's office, however, Finnegan is run off the road. Matt reaches the older man's side before he dies and hears him whisper 'not an accident.'" Publ Wkly

"Good writing, an inventive plot, and a nice balance of humor and horror make this an appealing mystery." Booklist

Goudge, Eileen

Garden of lies. Viking 1989 528p o.p.
LC 88-40395

"Sylvia seizes the opportunity offered by a hospital fire to switch infants, taking a newborn whose appearance resembles her husband. Her true child, fathered by Sylvia's lover, is left to make her own way in the world. Rachel, raised in luxury as Sylvia's daughter, becomes a doctor. When her career is jeopardized, she is defended by Sylvia'a real daughter, who has overcome poverty to become a lawyer. The two women of course compete for the same man, as Sylvia herself tries to decide whether to marry Nikos, her former lover." Libr J

"The characters intrigue, the situations hold attention, and the sex scenes simmer near the boiling point." Booklist

Followed by Thorns of truth

One last dance. Viking 1999 384p $24.95
ISBN 0-670-88575-4 LC 98-54891

"The Seagrave sisters are emotionally unfulfilled despite their accomplishments: Daphne, a novelist married to a doctor, cannot forget her childhood sweetheart, while homespun cafe entrepreneur Kitty yearns to adopt a child, and newly divorced real estate agent Alex is drowning in mounting debt. When their mother shoots their father without explanation or apology, the daughters investigate the rumors and suspicions they have ignored all their lives to confront the truth about their philandering parent." Publ Wkly

"Ideal for readers looking for a fairy tale: lovely, talented women, handsome men who love them, and little permanent trauma from a violent death and the awful secrets it unleashes." Libr J

Stranger in paradise. Viking 2001 321p o.p.
ISBN 0-670-89987-9 LC 2001-17747

This first volume of a projected trilogy set in Carson Springs, California focuses on "48-year-old Samantha 'Sam' Kiley and her daughters, Alice and Laura. As the story opens, Alice is about to marry Wes Carpenter, a Ted Turneresque entertainment mogul nearly 30 years her senior. Then Wes's son, Ian, takes a shine to Sam and the two become romantically involved, alarming Sam's daughters and setting the gossipy town abuzz. Laura, divorced because she couldn't bear children, and given to taking in strays, gets a new lease on life when she provides shelter for 16-year-old female runaway Finch." Publ Wkly

Such devoted sisters. Viking 1992 562p o.p.
LC 91-29103

"In 1954, Dolly Drake mails a letter addressed to Senator Joseph McCarthy that contains damning information about her famous film star sister Eve Dearfield. After leaving small-town America for Hollywood, Dolly has had enough of Eve stealing the spotlight. And she can't tolerate Eve stealing her man, either. Ruining the offending sister's career and her life seems the only thing to do. Years later, of course, she's regretting her actions, but Dolly's far away in Manhattan, with her own chocolate store and a lot of money. And it just so happens that Eve's two children, Annie and Laurel, have run away from home looking for Dolly, their long-lost aunt." Booklist

Thorns of truth. Viking 1998 398p o.p.
ISBN 0-670-87942-8 LC 97-53231

"Forty-six years after Sylvie Rosenthal abandoned Rose as a dark-haired newborn and stole blonde, blue-eyed baby Rachel to take her place, their lives are still intertwined, and Rachel still doesn't know the truth. Now Rose has problems of her own: her husband's death a year ago has left her with a law firm to manage; her stepdaughter is a drunk; and her eldest son, Drew, is planning to marry Rachel's mentally unstable daughter, Iris, against his mother's wishes. Rachel's life is starting to fray at the edges, too. Her job running a women's health clinic has caused a rift in her marriage to Brian, and, even medicated, Iris remains a constant worry." Publ Wkly

Trail of secrets. Viking 1996 443p o.p.
LC 95-39411

"In 1972, young Ellie's infant is stolen and privately offered to wealthy Kate and Will as an abandoned baby. Ellie's tragedy is heightened by her inability to conceive again, and her repeated attempts to adopt strain her marriage to Paul. Her daughter, Skyler, is now a lovely young woman, raised among love, money, and horses. She unexpectedly becomes pregnant by Tony, a policeman. Through a twist of events, she offers her baby to Ellie to adopt, not knowing that Ellie is her own mother and her unborn child's grandmother." Libr J

The author's "characters are sympathetic; her expres-

Goudge, Eileen—*Continued*

sions of the fierce emotions of motherhood are immediate; and her crafty decision to reveal likely plot turns to her readers but not to her characters will keep all who love a secret riveted." Publ Wkly

Goudge, Elizabeth, 1900-1984

Green Dolphin Street; a novel. Coward-McCann 1944 502p o.p.

Published in the United Kingdom with title: Green Dolphin country

This novel is set on one of the English Channel Islands and in frontier New Zealand. "The principal characters are two sisters and the boy who had been their neighbor and companion in Green Dolphin Street on the island. The sisters are Marianne, stern and intellectual, and Marguerite, radiant and beautiful. It is Marguerite whom William loves, but when he writes the letter from New Zealand asking her father for her hand he unaccountably confuses the names and it is Marianne, who comes to be his wife." Wis Libr Bull

The heart of the family. Coward-McCann 1953 337p o.p.

"Sebastian Weber, an Austrian refugee, once a famous pianist, is the mysterious character in this novel about the Eliot family. By sharing their daily lives, pervaded with a rare religious mysticism, he is purged of the hatred and despair caused by the loss of his family and years of incarceration in a concentration camp. The story is a simple one, yet the author's exquisite portrayal of children, grownups, animals, and the English countryside gives it the refreshing charm for which she is famous." Libr J

Gould, Judith

The best is yet to come. Dutton 2002 308p $24.95

ISBN 0-525-94659-4 LC 2002-23541

"After years of hard work, Carolina Mountcastle has finally made her flower shop the first choice of New York's most demanding hostesses. Factor in her storybook marriage to successful businessman Lyon, her 16-year-old son Richie and her great friends, and Carolina would appear to have it all. But when her husband suffers a fatal heart attack while traveling abroad for business and a mysterious woman and her daughter appear at the reading of his will, Carolina's world begins to unravel. . . . Gould's page-turning plot and deliciously evil villains distract artfully from some tone-deaf dialogue. . .and the flower descriptions are a delight." Publ Wkly

A moment in time. Dutton 2001 323p $24.95

ISBN 0-525-94607-1 LC 2001-25334

Valerie Rochelle has "found happiness, much to her society mother's bewilderment, working as a veterinarian in upstate New York. When Teddy, an old family friend, proposes, her mother is ecstatic, but Valerie is less than thrilled. Nonetheless, she accepts, but her reluctance is exacerbated when she pays a house call to the mysterious Stonelair estate to tend to an ailing horse. She and the estate's new owner, Wyn Conrad, connect on a level that she and Teddy never reach. . . . Gould's steamy tale about the lives of the rich and troubled is perfect for a read on the beach." Booklist

Time to say goodbye. Dutton 2000 291p $23.95

ISBN 0-525-94548-2 LC 99-89341

"Joanna and Josh are a perfect couple. They are blessed with great looks, a beautiful home on California's Central Coast, and a thriving orchid business. But their idyllic existence is about to be shattered when Joanna learns she has terminal cancer. Gould, however, takes an unexpected tack and has her strong and compassionate heroine come up with an altruistic plan to find a new love for her soon-to-be widowed husband. . . . But it isn't all bittersweet romance. Gould interweaves poignant interludes with lusty sex scenes and a subplot involving a hostile takeover attempt orchestrated by Josh's evil business rival, Joanna's avaricious and oversexed sister, and a treacherous maid." Booklist

Gowdy, Barbara

The romantic; a novel. Metropolitan Bks. 2003 305p $24

ISBN 0-8050-7190-3 LC 2002-29904

"At 10, a year after Louise's own mother left her and her father, the Richters, an older couple with an adopted son, move in next door. . . . Louise befriends Abel in order to get to Mrs. Richter, but her love soon transfers to the solitary, sensitive boy. The connection between the two flourishes, and Louise never stops thinking about Abel, even when he moves away. It is his return, when they meet at a high-school party, that marks the beginning of their adult relationship." Booklist

"Each of the characters, even minor ones, has a unique voice and a vivid, quirky personality. Louise's need to have Abel create the world for her resonates with unfulfilled passion." Publ Wkly

Grace, C. L.

For works written by this author under other names see Doherty, P. C.

Grady, James, 1949-

Six days of the condor. Norton 1974 192p o.p.

"When a branch of the CIA is mass murdered, Malcolm, the only survivor, becomes the object of an intense chase involving the Washington police, the CIA, the FBI, the NSC, and a host of other intelligence agencies. Trying to stay one jump ahead of his pursuers, Malcolm struggles to find out who within the agency has sold out his comrades." Libr J

Grafton, Sue

"A" is for alibi; a Kinsey Millhone mystery. Holt & Co. 1990 c1982 274p $27

ISBN 0-8050-1334-2

A reissue of the title first published 1982 by Holt, Rinehart & Winston

"California private eye, Kinsey Millhone, makes her debut in this story of a murder committed eight years before. Nikki Fife was convicted of killing her husband, but as soon as she's out of prison she hires Kinsey to find the true murderer." Libr J

"Kinsey Millhone is a cut above the usual woman private eye who flounces through fiction. Millhone is neither a sex bomb nor a detached cerebrum, but a believable, straightforward character." Booklist

Grafton, Sue—*Continued*

"B" is for burglar. Holt & Co. 1985 229p $27
ISBN 0-8050-1632-5 LC 84-22378

When Kinsey Millhone "is hired to locate Elaine Boldt, a well-to-do widow, she sets the wheels of a routine missing-persons investigation in motion. The bizarre, outlandish behavior of Elaine's sister and brother-in-law leads Kinsey to suspect a murder has been committed, but in order to solve the crime, a corpse must be uncovered." Booklist

"Grafton's plot is solid p.i. procedural, but it is her sense of style that will truly delight readers. Her characters, from a punk dope pusher to a brave and resourceful eighty-eight-year-old woman, are completely convincing, and Grafton's ear for natural dialogue is among the best in the business." Wilson Libr Bull

"C" is for corpse; a Kinsey Millhone mystery. Holt & Co. 1986 243p $27
ISBN 0-8050-2818-8 LC 85-24797

Kinsey Millhone "meets a young man, Buddy Callahan, at the gym where she works out and agrees to take his case. He wants her to investigate an auto accident in which he was badly injured because he claims that it was a murder attempt. When a second attempt results in his death, Kinsey, although she no longer has him as a client, pursues the matter and, in a hair-raising finale that takes place in a morgue, she unmasks the murderer." Shapiro. Fic for Youth. 3d edition

"D" is for deadbeat; a Kinsey Millhone mystery. Holt & Co. 1987 229p $27
ISBN 0-8050-0248-0 LC 86-25843

"Ex-con and drunken bum John Daggett hires Millhone to deliver a check for $25,000 to a teenage boy whose family was killed in a violent car crash in which Daggett was the offending drunk driver. Daggett's retainer check bounces, and in trying to recoup her losses, Kinsey is swept up in a tangled web of hate, violence, and families torn asunder." Booklist

"Social awareness and human weakness play a great part in the Millhone books, which always manage to finish with a heart-stopping climax." Libr J

"E" is for evidence; a Kinsey Millhone mystery. Holt & Co. 1988 227p $27
ISBN 0-8050-0459-9 LC 87-28100

"While private detective and former cop Kinsey Millhone is investigating a possible case of industrial arson involving a company owned by the family of a former schoolmate, someone tries to make it look as if she's on the take. A mysterious $5000 appears in her bank account. She sets out to clear herself, while two or possibly more cases of murder occur, including one by bombing." Publ Wkly

"The plot is just fine and does what a plot ought to in a good detective novel: it keeps us turning pages and serves as a vehicle for the really interesting stuff, an unveiling of the characters' foibles by the worldly-wise but uncorrupt private eye." NY Times Book Rev

"F" is for fugitive; a Kinsey Millhone mystery. Holt & Co. 1989 261p $27
ISBN 0-8050-0460-2 LC 88-27284

Kinsey Millhone "becomes involved in ugly doings in a California coastal town, where she attempts to prove a man's innocence on a 17-year-old murder rap. Floral Beach appears to be a cozy little place, but it's a hotbed of dirty secrets, most of them involving the long-dead Jean Timberlake, a confused yet apparently sexually quite precocious teenager. Kinsey's investigation opens closet doors, and some tawdry skeletons jump out." Booklist

"G" is for gumshoe; a Kinsey Millhone mystery. Holt & Co. 1990 261p
LC 89-24652

Private investigator Kinsey Millhone is hired to find and take "an elderly woman to a nursing home near her daughter. But the lady mysteriously disappears within hours of her arrival. Painfully aware of the fact that a contract has been arranged for her own murder, Kinsey unravels the events of the past." SLJ

"Millhone, whose background has made her believe that all families are dysfunctional, has unwittingly taken on another case of domestic violence. Grafton excels in this milieu. Never morally oblique, here she is slyly didactic about (among other things) attitudes toward the mentally ill." Newsweek

"H" is for homicide. Holt & Co. 1991 256p $27
ISBN 0-8050-1084-X LC 90-25016

Detective Kinsey Millhone is "hired by California Fidelity to investigate a string of fraudulent automobile insurance claims filed by someone named Bibianna Diaz. To track down the elusive Bibianna, Kinsey adopts an undercover identity as Hannah Moore, a wisecracking, reckless vamp. As Hannah, she befriends Bibianna, a sexy young woman on the run. Both are quickly swept up in an evening of kidnapping and gunplay that ends with the two of them in jail. Through her relationship with Bibianna, Kinsey also stumbles onto a much bigger network of crime." N Y Times Book Rev

"I" is for innocent. Holt & Co. 1992 286p $27
ISBN 0-8050-1085-8 LC 91-45165

Kinsey Millhone "lands the job of hunting up evidence for a wrongful-death suit against a high-living architect who couldn't be nailed in court for his wife's murder. It's a sobering case, weighted with the survivors' anger and suspicions and darkened by their sordid domestic affairs." N Y Times Book Rev

"J" is for judgment. Holt & Co. 1993 288p $27
ISBN 0-8050-1935-9 LC 92-35769

In this mystery, California P.I. Kinsey Millhone is "investigating a fraud case. Wendell Jaffe, a local businessman, set up a fraudulent Ponzi scheme and then disappeared, leaving his wife and business partner to deal with the creditors. His wife had Jaffe declared dead after five years and picked up a half-million-dollar life insurance settlement. Now Jaffe's supposedly been sighted in Mexico. If he's still alive, the insurance company wants its money back and hires Kinsey to find out what's what." Booklist

"Ms. Grafton writes a smart story and wraps it up with a wry twist; but she takes care to sweeten her tart characterizations with amused understanding and, in the case of Jaffe, even affection." N Y Times Book Rev

"K" is for killer. Holt & Co. 1994 284p $27
ISBN 0-8050-1936-7 LC 94-1242

"Grieving mother Janice Kepler asks Kinsey [Millhone] to investigate the nearly year-old death of her daughter Lorna. Janice believes Lorna was murdered,

Grafton, Sue—*Continued*

even though there were no signs of violence and the police concluded the young woman died of natural causes. Kinsey, always keen for a challenge, agrees to take the case and winds up working one of the oddest mysteries of her career." Booklist

"Despite an abrupt ending that has the reader frantically paging back for missed clues, the sturdily engineered plot drags Kinsey into the kind of joints that never seem to close: bars, nightclubs, diners, hospital emergency rooms. All this night crawling serves as an eye-opening experience for Kinsey, who is physically exhausted but mentally energized by her encounters with sad young prostitutes and other fascinating creatures of the night." N Y Times Book Rev

"L" is for lawless. Holt & Co. 1995 290p $27
ISBN 0-8050-1937-5 LC 95-12787

In this adventure "private investigator Kinsey Millhone is just doing a favor for a friend—checking the military status of a recently deceased neighbor—when she's sucked into a chase for the spoils of a 1941 bank heist. It's a lively outing with a couple of heart-pounding scenes, some interesting characters . . . and even a little detection. There are also hints of Kinsey's connecting with long-lost relatives, plus a romantic wedding of octogenarians." Libr J

"M" is for malice. Holt & Co. 1996 300p $27
ISBN 0-8050-3637-7 LC 96-30897

In this mystery set in Southern California, private eye Kinsey Millhone "looks for Guy Malek, the missing son and partial heir to a huge fortune. She finds him, but then he is murdered." SLJ

"This is a subtle and swiftly moving novel, pleasantly unpredictable, with an agreeable overlay of smoldering romance, as fellow PI and former lover Robert Dietz reenters Kinsey's life. Grafton's heroine—more introspective, yet still feisty and surefooted—leads this finely tuned and at times electrifying tale to a thoroughly satisfying conclusion." Publ Wkly

"N" is for noose. Holt & Co. 1998 289p $25
ISBN 0-8050-3650-4 LC 97-49320
"A Marian Wood book"

Kinsey Millhone "takes a case in tiny Nota Lake, Nevada, where deputy sheriff Tom Newquist has recently died of a heart attack. His grief-stricken widow, Selma, is convinced Tom died as a result of the terrible stress he was under during his last weeks, and she's determined to find out the source of that stress. . . . Apparently Tom was following up on a double homicide, and as Kinsey probes further into the bizarre details, she finds that he suspected the killer may have been one of his colleagues." Booklist

"Even when people are not nice to Kinsey, Grafton always deals fairly with them in this clean, well-constructed story about small-town insecurities." N Y Times Book Rev

"O" is for outlaw. Holt & Co. 1999 318p $26
ISBN 0-8050-5955-5 LC 99-14967
"A Marian Wood book"

"An unopened letter discovered in an abandoned storage locker is delivered, 15 years late, to P.I. Kinsey Millhone. It provides a possible alibi for Kinsey's first husband, Mickey, a cop who was accused of beating a man to death. The accusation ended Kinsey's marriage, and now guilt pangs lead her to reexamine her judgment of Mickey. When Mickey is shot with Kinsey's gun, Kinsey is only one step ahead of the police as she tries to solve the shooting and the crime attributed to Mickey." Libr J

"Everything that has always worked for this first class series works better here: the sturdy plotting, the animated characters, the breezy style and a heroine with foibles you can laugh at and faults you can forgive." N Y Times Book Rev

"P" is for peril. Putnam 2001 352p $26.95
ISBN 0-399-14719-5 LC 00-46024
"A Marian Wood book"

"Private investigator Kinsey Milhone is hired by Dr. Fiona Purcell to find her ex-husband, Dowan, a prominent physician who vanished with his passport and $30,000 in cash nine weeks earlier. Wondering what she can do that the Santa Rosa police haven't done already, Kinsey takes the case and quickly discovers that the nursing home Purcell administered is being investigated for Medicare fraud." Libr J

"Grafton gives us a truly complex heroine, marvelous depiction of Southern California architecture and interiors, and a writing style that can make a weed path interesting." Booklist

"Q" is for quarry. Putnam 2002 385p $26.95
ISBN 0-399-14915-5 LC 2002-68368
"A Marian Wood book"

"In the summer of 1969, the decomposed corpse of a young white female was discovered near a quarry off California's Highway 1. Her hands had been bound and her throat slashed. Despite months of investigation, 'Jane Doe' remained unidentified and the case unsolved. Now years later, Con Donlan and Stacey Oliphant, the police officers who had found her body, want Kinsey to help them to identify the girl and find her killer before they retire. At the same time, having learned that the body was found on a ranch owned by her estranged grandmother, Kinsey journeys into the past to retrace her own family history. Once again, an intriguing plot, fully drawn characters, and wry humor prove why Grafton's series is one of the best." Libr J

"R" is for ricochet; Sue Grafton. G.P. Putnam's Sons 2004 352p $26.95
ISBN 0-399-15228-8 LC 2004-44599

"Hired by dying millionaire Nord Lafferty to babysit his recently paroled daughter, Reba, Kinsey [Millhone] finds herself entangled in a complex money-laundering scheme when Reba decides to take revenge on the twotiming lover for whom she had gone to prison. Meanwhile, Kinsey's octogenarian landlord resigns himself to a loveless life after his interfering brothers sabotage a budding relationship with a lively widow. And the twice-divorced Kinsey has to decide whether to risk opening her heart to sexy cop Cheney Phillips. As demonstrated here, Grafton's series remains fresh and exciting, with complex plots and well-developed characters." Libr J

Graham, Caroline

Death in disguise. Morrow 1993 c1992 333p o.p.
LC 92-33300

First published 1992 in the United Kingdom

"Murder in a country manor inhabited by a cult of mystics tests the patience and skills of Detective Chief

Graham, Caroline—*Continued*
Inspector Tom Barnaby. . . . Graham's competent procedural works most effectively as a wickedly acid yet sympathetic portrayal of a group of society's misfits seeking comfort and a place in the world." Publ Wkly

Faithful unto death. St. Martin's Press 1998 311p o.p.
ISBN 0-312-18577-4 LC 98-17516
First published 1996 in the United Kingdom
Chief Inspector Barnaby "arrives in Fawcett Green looking for clues to the disappearance of a bell-ringer and the subsequent murder of her husband." Libr J
"What begins as a seemingly typical British small-town mystery ends as an eye-brow-raising shocker that will leave readers feeling a little dizzy." Booklist

The killings at Badger's Drift. Adler & Adler 1988 c1987 264p o.p.
LC 87-1284
First published 1987 in the United Kingdom
As Detective Chief Inspector Barnaby and Sergeant Troy "investigate the coniine (hemlock) poisoning death of 80-year-old spinster Emily Simpson, they encounter a bizarre mixture of eccentric village dwellers, starting with the little old cat-lady and gardener friend of the deceased. The murder, of course, causes a commotion in picturesque Badger's Drift, laden with quaint cottages and Georgian manor houses." Libr J

A place of safety; a Chief Inspector Barnaby mystery. St. Martin's Minotaur 1999 278p o.p.
ISBN 0-312-24419-3 LC 00-266710
"When an unpleasant (and disliked) man is found dead in the village of Ferne Basset, Barnaby is presented with a seemingly motiveless murder. His investigation is complicated by the fact that another resident of the village, a young woman, has disappeared." Booklist
"Graham is a master of pacing, and her dialogue is dark and worldly-wise enough to make this much fuller fare than most English-village cozies." Publ Wkly

Graham, James, 1929- *See* Higgins, Jack, 1929-

Graham, Tom *See* Lewis, Sinclair, 1885-1951

Graham, Winston

The angry tide; a novel of Cornwall, 1798-1799. Doubleday 1978 c1977 476p o.p.
LC 77-90809
Sequel to The four swans
First published 1977 in the United Kingdom
This is the "seventh novel in the Poldark saga. The darkly entwined destinies of the genteel Poldarks and the 'nouveaux riches' Warleggans, whose interests span the worlds of banking, mining and politics, continue to unfold. Ross Poldark, quick-tempered but agreeable hero of the piece, has now taken George Warleggan's seat in Parliament (for which he's roundly resented), in addition to being in love with George's wife—which is not to say he doesn't love his own wife, Demelza. Subsidiary characters include Demelza's two brothers, both love crossed, and Morwenna, married to an odious church minister who tries to get her put away as insane. There's a duel, a killing, a mine disaster and a near-drowning at sea." Publ Wkly
Followed by The stranger from the sea

Bella Poldark; a novel of Cornwall, 1818-1820. Macmillan 2002 530p $29.95
ISBN 0-333-98923-6
This is the twelfth and final novel of the Poldark series. "As the story opens, Valentine Warleggan's paternity still poisons the atmosphere, and his financial and marital trouble form a major narrative strand set firmly against the saga's familiar background of Cornwall. Meanwhile, Bella Poldark's desire for a musical career takes her to stages in London and France, where she is involved with rival suitors. Her widowed older sister, Clowance, must also choose between two men of vastly different backgrounds who propose marriage. A host of other characters and subplots, including a series of murders, keeps the action bubbling." Libr J

The black moon. Doubleday 1974 c1973 424p o.p.
First published 1973 in the United Kingdom
Set in Cornwall in the 1790's this "story of fates hanging in the balance: of England, its church, its social structure, and two of its families. Indeed, these fates form concentric circles about the old feud between George Warleggan and Ross Poldark and serve as metaphoric echoes of it." Libr J
Followed by The four swans

The four swans; a novel of Cornwall, 1795-1797. Doubleday 1977 c1976 479p o.p.
LC 76-18347
Sequel to The black moon
First published 1976 in the United Kingdom
As this sixth novel of the Poldark series opens it is a "bumptious era in British history; malcontents upset the country's equilibrium, Napoleon is thought to be mapping an invasion, upperclass cohesiveness falters before industrial expansion. In the middle of these events is Captain Ross Poldark. A respected man in civilian life or under arms, he parries the political ambitions of ruthless bankers and grapples with the emotional demands of four women who keep crisscrossing his career. Chief among them is wife Demelza, a smoldering vixen who never forgets one lost love. Further embellishing the serial-like chapters are revelations about the paternity of children and the discontents of a clergyman troubled by the pleasures of the flesh." Publ Wkly
Followed by The angry tide

The loving cup; a novel of Cornwall, 1813-1815. Doubleday 1985 c1984 440p o.p.
LC 85-4362
Sequel to The miller's dance
First published 1984 in the United Kingdom
In this tenth novel of the Poldark series, "Demelza and Ross Poldark oversees the escapades and marriages of their two oldest children and revel in the childish delights of their two youngest. The closing triumphs of Wellington's army, in which the Poldark cousins participate, are nicely integrated into the domestic drama." Booklist
"Set against a vivid Cornwall landscape, it is a tale high in readability, made even more enjoyable with a knowledge of the lineage explored in the earlier books." Publ Wkly
Followed by The twisted sword

Graham, Winston—*Continued*

The miller's dance; a novel of Cornwall, 1812-1813. Doubleday 1983 c1982 372p o.p.
LC 82-45596

Sequel to The stranger from the sea
First published 1982 in the United Kingdom
This "ninth novel of life on the Cornish coast in the late 18th century and the fluctuating fortunes of the Poldark family concentrates on the lives and complicated love affairs of the two oldest Poldark children, Jeremy and Clowance, rather than on their parents, Ross and Demelza. The Poldark story has emphasized events over character development, but *Miller's Dance* does so more than previous books. To the reader unfamiliar with the Poldark family, friends, and enemies, the large and varied cast of characters presented immediately and without introduction will be confusing." Libr J
Followed by The loving cup

Stephanie. Carroll & Graf Pubs. 1993 c1992 301p o.p.
LC 92-42462

First published 1992 in the United Kingdom
"Stephanie Locke is a 21-year-old student at Oxford who has an affair with 38-year-old Errol Colton, a married man. Shortly after she and Errol return from a trip to Goa, Stephanie is found dead in bed, an apparent suicide. At the inquest, Errol testifies that Stephanie became despondent when he decided to stop seeing her, but Stephanie's father knows that something happened during the couple's holiday that so distressed his daughter that she decided to end the affair although she was still very much in love. James Locke refuses to believe his daughter committed suicide, and his determination to investigate makes some people very nervous." Libr J
Graham "has written a dark, sophisticated, taut, and suspenseful story full of the strange ironies, sad coincidences, and small happinesses of life." Booklist

The stranger from the sea; a novel of Cornwall, 1810-1811. Doubleday 1982 c1981 445p o.p.

Sequel to The angry tide
First published 1981 in the United Kingdom
The action of this eighth novel in the Poldark series, begins in 1810 with the younger generation coming to maturity. Jeremy, Ross and Demelza Poldark's eldest, is engrossed in designing a steam engine that may expedite reopening a mine once owned by the Poldarks and now held by their longtime rival, George Warleggan. Jeremy and his sister Clowance have several romantic interests. Hers include Stephen Carrington, who is shipwrecked on the shores of Cornwall but whose origins are not altogether clear." Libr J
Followed by The miller's dance

The twisted sword; a Poldark novel. Carroll & Graf Pubs. 1991 c1990 510p o.p.
LC 91-4504

Sequel to The loving cup
First published 1990 in the United Kingdom
The eleventh and concluding novel in the author's Poldark saga, this adventure revolves "around Napoleon's defeat at Waterloo in 1815. When Ross Poldark undertakes a government assignment to assess the strength of Bonapartist sentiment in Bourbon, France, he and his beloved wife, Demelza, are swept into a giddy Parisian social whirl, belying the ominous threat of war. Meanwhile, young Jeremy Poldark, a lieutenant in the British army, and his bride enjoy a carefree honeymoon in Brussels. As fate and fortune conspire to reunite the Poldarks on the bloodiest of battlefields, life among their familiar band of friends and relatives in Cornwall continues to amuse and intrigue." Booklist

The walking stick. Doubleday 1967 278p o.p.

Handicapped Deborah "is persuaded by her lover and his criminal friends to help them rob the elegant London auction house for which she works." Publ Wkly
"What you begin with is a delicate and persuasive study of the sexual awakening of a highly intelligent girl, hitherto trapped into introversion by a withered leg. Almost a satisfactory novella in itself, this situation expands into a moving tragedy that represents one of those rare instances . . . in which formal suspense, technique and serious psychological novel reinforce each other." NY Times Book Rev

Granger, Bill

The el murders. Holt & Co. 1987 246p o.p.
LC 86-29399

This mystery features "Chicago homicide detective Terry Flynn and his lover, special investigator Karen Kovac. Flynn's case is the mugging-turned-murder of a gay man on an elevated-train platform. Kovac's case is a brutal rape that also takes place on an El platform. Flynn's key witness—the victim's lover—and Kovac's victim prove to be unacceptable witnesses, but neither Flynn nor Kovac retreats from the investigation." Booklist
"The two cases crisscross in this excellent police procedural filled with tough, streetwise characters and swift, rough action." Libr J

Grant, David, 1942-

For works written by this author under other names see Thomas, Craig, 1942-

Grant, John *See* Gash, Jonathan, 1933-

Grant, Linda

Vampire bytes; a crime novel with Catherine Sayler. Scribner 1998 285p o.p.
ISBN 0-684-82675-5 LC 97-38432

"Live Action Role Playing (LARP): Is it something teenagers do just for fun? Or is it satanism? That's the question when a young man is brutally murdered, his body drained of blood, and his girlfriend suddenly goes missing. . . . When private detective Catherine Sayler is called in to investigate, she encounters a group of young adults keeping dangerous and guilty secrets, as well as some grown-ups determined to prove that LARPing is a pastime inspired by the devil." Booklist
"Although many of the adults in this story find it easier to deal with satanic cultists then with self-dramatizing teen-agers . . . Grant doesn't share their aversion, and her open-minded attitude toward the adolescent imagination is refreshing." N Y Times Book Rev

Grant, Michael, 1940-

Officer down. Doubleday 1993 437p o.p.
LC 92-37205

"First a bomb explodes at New York City's police headquarters, killing an officer, then a policewoman is executed. While it is clear that the police are targets of a highly organized group, the motive behind the attacks is kept secret. FBI agent Chris Liberti, DEA undercover agent Donal Castillo, and deputy inspector Dan Morgan form a special task force to identify the people behind the violence. They know a terrorist group known as *Punyo Blanco* has been formed by the Colombian drug cartels to force the United States to stop pressuring Colombia into action against the drug lords. . . . The plot is timely, the characters realistic, the motive plausible, and the pace electrifying." Libr J

Grass, Günter, 1927-

The call of the toad; translated by Ralph Manheim. Harcourt Brace Jovanovich 1992 248p il o.p.
LC 92-20233

"A Helen and Kurt Wolff book"

The events recounted in this novel date from "November 2, 1989, only days before the Berlin Wall began to crumble. A chance encounter between a German art-historian, Alexander, and a Polish art-restorer, Alexandra, . . . [results in a plan to] found and develop a . . . Cemetery Association to enable exiles to opt for burial in their native Polish soil, uniting again those whom recent history has forced apart. . . . The plan snowballs out of control and into the hands of others more entrepreneurial and less naively idealistic than the quaint couple who had thought it all up." Times Lit Suppl

This book is a "skillful balancing act that juggles some very timely questions about the conflict between calls for ethnic self-determination and calls for international unity and cooperation." Christ Sci Monit

Cat and mouse; translated by Ralph Manheim. Harcourt, Brace & World 1963 189p o.p.

Original German edition, 1961

A novel about Mahlke, a teenager growing up in a Baltic port city during World War II who is set apart from his fellows by his huge Adam's apple. When a classmate attracts a cat to this 'mouse' he launches Mahlke on his career. Mahlke becomes an excellent swimmer and athlete, and later a hero to his nation. But the symbolic cat watching him is a society of petty men and Mahlke is eventually doomed

also in Grass, G. The Danzig trilogy

Crabwalk; translated from the German by Krishna Winston. Harcourt 2002 234p $25

ISBN 0-15-100764-0 LC 2002-13205

"The plot centers on the fate of the vessel Wilhelm Gustloff, which was built as a cruise ship in the Third Reich, was fitted out as a troop carrier in World War II and was turned into a refugee ship for German civilians fleeing the Russian Army. On Jan. 30, 1945, 12 years after the Nazis rose to power, it was torpedoed in the Baltic Sea by a Soviet submarine and, in what was apparently the biggest recorded disaster in maritime history, sank with the loss of some 9,000 souls." N Y Times Book Rev

"A writer who refuses to avert his eyes from unpleasant truths, Grassremains an eloquent explorer of his country's troubled 20th-century history." Publ Wkly

The Danzig trilogy; translated by Ralph Manheim. Harcourt Brace Jovanovich 1987 1030p o.p.

ISBN 0-15-123816-2 LC 87-8725

"A Helen and Kurt Wolff book"

Contents: The tin drum; Cat and mouse; Dog years

Dog years; translated by Ralph Manheim. Harcourt, Brace & World 1965 570p o.p.

"A Helen and Kurt Wolff book"

Original German edition, 1963

"A monumental parable on 'mass man,' materialism, and transcendence, written in the richly encrusted, playful, brutal, ironic, subtle, sensitive, surrealist, erudite, unique modern baroque. . . . [This novel tells] of Eduard Amsel, rumored to be half Jew, designer of fantastic scarecrows, endlessly ingenious and talented; of Walter Matern, athlete and compulsive tooth grinder, Amsel's blood brother, his defender, and helper until association with a Nazi S. A. group leads him to beat Amsel unmercifully; of Hitler's favorite dog Prinz of notable lineage and the howling dog days echoing down the centuries through World War II and aftermath. The cast is large; the canvas is chiefly Danzig and villages along the Vistula; and the scarecrow prevails as dominant symbol." Booklist

also in Grass, G. The Danzig trilogy

The flounder; translated by Ralph Manheim. Harcourt Brace Jovanovich 1978 547p o.p.
LC 78-53891

"A Helen and Kurt Wolff book"

Original German edition, 1977

"Grass's first-person narrator is the legendary fisherman who caught the magic fish and might have fared well had it not been for the foolishness of his wife Ilsebill. Grass uses the well-known fairy tale as a frame for his chronicler to relate his various lives' experiences (between the late Neolithic and [1970]) . . . to his pregnant wife Ilsebill in the course of nine months. While his story unfolds, the fish is on trial in a feminist courtroom after he has been caught again, this time by three women in West Berlin." Libr J

"It is perhaps best to take this fantasy . . . as a celebration of life in all its gross particularity, with Grass still telling the German people to beware of the abstractions that have too often made them flounder in a nordic mist." Times Lit Suppl

Local anaesthetic; translated by Ralph Manheim. Harcourt, Brace & World 1970 284p o.p.

"A Helen and Kurt Wolff book"

Original German edition, 1969

"At 17 the narrator, Eberhard Starusch, was the leader of a gang of juvenile delinquents in wartime Germany. Now, at the time of the novel, he is a 'quadragenarian schoolteacher' whose 17-year-old students are not at all impressed by the anecdotes of his youth and are preoccupied with their own projects, such as setting fire to a dog to protest the use of napalm in Vietnam. . . . Some or all of the action takes place while Starusch is sitting in a dentist's chair, undergoing [a] set of repairs to his teeth. The action moves forward simultaneously on three

Grass, Günter, 1927-—*Continued*

or more time-levels; the war period, the time after the war when Starusch was a cement-salesman and courting one Linde Krings, the daughter of an unreconstructed Nazi general, and the present." Christ Sci Monit

My century; translated by Michael Henry Heim. Harcourt Brace & Co. 1999 280p $31

ISBN 0-15-100496-X LC 99-38690

"A Helen and Kurt Wolff book"

Original German edition, 1999

In this fictional collage of 20th century Germany "each year has a story, and each story is told by a first-person narrator. Sometimes that narrator is Grass himself. Ironically, the stories highlight and celebrate the individual in this century of mass destruction, mass coercion, and mass consumerism; however, taken altogether, the narratives are like an album of snapshots from a dusty attic." Booklist

"The best thing [this book] offers non-Germans, even if inadvertently, is the opportunity to hear, or to overhear, how Germans speak to one another about their history when the rest of us are not supposed to be listening." Natl Rev

The tin drum. Knopf 1993 xxxvii, 551p o.p.

ISBN 0-679-42033-9 LC 92-54295

"Everyman's library"

Original German edition, 1959; this translation by Ralph Mannheim first published 1962 in the United Kingdom, 1963 in the United States by Pantheon Bks.

"Oskar Matzerath, born with an unusually sharp mind, describes the amoral conditions through which he has lived in twentieth-century Germany, both during and after the Hitler regime. This strange narrator stops growing when he is three years old and remains three feet tall until some time late, when he decides to grow a few inches more. After the war he escapes to West Germany, where he works in such capacities as an artist's model, a nightclub performer, and a black marketeer. Depicted as a freak (Oskar becomes a hunchback later in his life), this character symbolizes the deformed society of this century. It is through his tin drum, which he uses to stimulate recollections of his life, that Oskar describes his past while he is an inmate in a mental hospital." Shapiro. Fic for Youth. 3d edition

also in Grass, G. The Danzig trilogy

Too far afield; translated from the German by Krishna Winston. Harcourt 2000 658p $30

ISBN 0-15-100230-4 LC 00-29586

"A Helen and Kurt Wolff book"

Original German edition published 1995

The narrative's "focus is German reunification, in particular, the fate of the German Democratic Republic after the Wall came down in 1989. At the center of the novel are two characters, locked in a sort of political marriage: Theo Wuttke, a former East German cultural figure and long-winded raconteur, and Ludwig Hoffstaller, a professional spy who served for years as Wuttke's shadow. They are both about to turn 70 in this new Germany and are now both employees of the agency responsible for privatizing state-held companies." Booklist

Grau, Shirley Ann, 1929-

The condor passes. Knopf 1971 421p o.p.

This novel is set in New Orleans, where Thomas Henry Oliver "a 90-year-old multimillionaire is dying. His two middle-age daughters and the Cajun son-in-law the Old Man handpicked are at his side, and so is [Stanley] the Old Man's chauffeur. . . . In flashbacks we follow the . . . rags to riches rise of the Old Man, from an impoverished middle-western boyhood through adventurous years at sea and then on the make in New Orleans, building up out of brothels and bootlegging a great financial empire that eventually takes on the trappings of respectability. . . . Then we come to the story of the second generation, inevitably weakened and corrupted by sheer force and power of the Old Man's personality and need to dominate." Publ Wkly

The keepers of the house. Knopf 1964 309p o.p.

"This multigenerational novel deals with the twentieth-century heirs of a Southern dynasty, their relations to the past, and their involvement in the racial and political complexities of the present. The narrator is Abigail Mason Tolliver, granddaughter of William Howland, whose second wife had been a Freejack Negro. The townspeople have always assumed that she had been no more than William's mistress, but the truth of the legality of their marriage surfaces when Abigail's husband, John Tolliver, enters the race for governor. In addition to leading to Tolliver's defeat, the story of the marriage also incites a mob to burn down the old Howland house. Abigail saves the house but withdraws the economic support that the Howland family has always supplied the town, and lets it 'shrivel and shrink to its real size.'" Shapiro. Fic for Youth. 3d edition

Graver, Elizabeth

Awake. Holt & Co. 2004 288p $23

ISBN 0-8050-6540-7 LC 2003-55253

"Anna Simon has been living in the dark ever since she gave birth to Max, a child with a rare genetic disease for whom even an hour in sunlight could prove fatal. For years, Anna has homeschooled Max and structured her life around his schedule, despite the fact that her husband, Ian, favors mainstreaming and wants Max to attend school with his older brother. When Anna learns of a camp in upstate New York for children with light-sensitivity disorders, she sees room for a compromise between her own and Ian's approaches. . . . And so the summer that Max is nine, the family heads off to Camp Luna. At first, the place seems like the answer to their problems. But as Anna is drawn into life there and gets to know Hal, the camp's charismatic founder, freedom and safety soon prove to be complicated things." Publisher's note

"A beautifully constructed tribute to self-sacrificing parenting that segues into a clear-eyed anatomy of the inevitable destructive power of infidelity." Libr J

Graves, Robert, 1895-1985

Claudius, the god and his wife Messalina. H. Smith & R. Haas 1935 583p o.p.

"A vivid picture of profligate Rome during the years in which Claudius conquered Britain and instituted many reforms at home. A story complete in itself, though a continuation of 'I, Claudius.'" Booklist

Graves, Robert, 1895-1985—*Continued*

Complete short stories; edited by Lucia Graves. St. Martin's Press 1996 331p o.p.
ISBN 0-312-16055-0 LC 96-5343
Contents: Honey and flowers; My new-bug's exam; Thames-side reverie; The shout; Avocado pears; Old Papa Johnson; Interview with a dead man; Está en su casa; Bins K to T; School life in Majorca 1955; Bulletin of the College of St Modesto of Bobbio; Treacle tart; Week-end at Cwm Tatws; The full length; God grant your honour many years; 6 valiant bulls 6; Flesh-coloured net tights; Thy servant and God's; A man may not marry his . . .; An appointment for candlemas; The five godfathers; The white horse or 'The great southern ghost story'; Epics are out of fashion; Earth to earth; They say . . . they say; The abominable Mr Gunn; The Whitaker negroes; Trin-Trin-Trin; Cambridge upstairs; 'Ha, Ha!' Chort-led Nig-ger; Ditching in a fishless sea; Period piece; He went out to buy a rhine; Kill them! kill them!; Harold Vesey at the Gates of Hell; Life of the poet Gnaeus Robertulus Gravesa; Ever had a Guinea worm?; A bicycle in Majorca; Evidence of affluence; The French thing; A toast to Ava Gardner; The viscountess and the short-haired girl; She landed yesterday; The lost Chinese; You win, Houdini!; The tenement: a vision of Imperial Rome; The Myconian; Christmas truce; My best Christmas; No, Mac, it just wouldn't work; Miss Briton's lady-companion; My first amorous adventure
"Graves is a master storyteller, and the stories collected here are both masterly and charming. Especially noteworthy are the sweetly humorous tales about school days in Edwardian England and the breezy, gently witty stories about everyday life in Majorca, Graves's adopted home." Libr J

I, Claudius; from the autobiography of Tiberius Claudius, born B.C. 10, murdered and deified A.D. 54. H. Smith and R. Haas 1934 494p o.p.
"Claudius is lame and a stammerer who seems unlikely to carry on the family tradition of power in ancient Rome. Immersing himself in scholarly pursuits, Claudius observes and lives through the plots hatched by his grandmother, Livia, political conspiracies, murders, and corruption, and he survives a number of emperors. He becomes emperor at last and is a just and well-liked ruler, in contrast to those who preceded him." Shapiro. Fic for Youth. 3d edition
Followed by Claudius, the god and his wife Messalina

Gray, Alasdair

Poor things; episodes from the early life of Archibald McCandless M.D., Scottish public health officer; edited by Alasdair Gray. Harcourt Brace Jovanovich 1993 c1992 317p il o.p.
ISBN 0-15-173076-8 LC 92-40018
First published 1992 in the United Kingdom
"Scottish public health physician McCandless's manuscript describes his adventures in late-19th-century Glasgow with a Frankenstein-like doctor and scientist, Godwin Baxter, and Baxter's protegee, Bella, who, thanks to Baxter's surgical sorcery, has the body of a woman and the brain of a child." Newsweek
"Mr. Gray contrasts the political and moral bleakness of contemporary Britain with the civic energy that characterized the best of Victorian values, now lost. He underlines the harm done to Scotland. 'Poor Things' is a political book. It is also witty and delightfully written, if at times two-dimensional. Attention to Victorian Glasgow with its civic fountains, domestic interiors and medical schools gives the book texture. It is the characters, and strangely enough its phantasmagoria, that give it life." N Y Times Book Rev

Great racing stories. See The Dick Francis treasury of great racing stories

Great stories of the American West; stories by John Jakes [et al.]; edited by Martin H. Greenberg. Fine, D.I. 1994 290p il o.p.
LC 94-071113

Contents: The bandit, by L. D. Estleman; At Yuma crossing, by B. Garfield; The guns of William Longley, by D. Hamilton; The debt of Hardy Buckelew, by E. Kelton; Lost sister, by D. M. Johnson; The gift of Cochise, by L. L'Amour; The woman at Apache Wells, by J. Jakes; Law of the hunted ones, by E. Leonard; Snowblind, by E. Hunter; The corpse rides at dawn, by J. D. MacDonald; The time of the wolves, by M. Muller; Gamblin' man, by D. V. Swain; Vigilante, by H. A. DeRosso; Markers, by B. Pronzini; In the silence, by P. S. Curry; Wolf night, by B. Crider; Liberty, by A. Sarrantonio; Hacendado, by J. M. Reasoner; Death ground [novelette], by E. Gorman
"This excellent collection of 19 short stories is a suitable introduction to western fiction or a marvelous way to rekindle one's enthusiasm for the genre." Booklist

Greeley, Andrew M., 1928-

Ascent into hell. Warner Bks. 1983 371p o.p.
LC 82-61879
"A Bernard Geis Associates book"
Second volume of the author's Passover trilogy begun with Thy brother's wife
"Hugh Donlon fulfills his parents' wish that he become a Catholic priest. He then wrangles with his superiors, impregnates a nun and leaves the active priesthood to marry her, has numerous extramarital affairs, gets rich in commodities trading, becomes an ambassador, is jailed for shady finanical dealings, and finally must decide whether to return to the active ministry or marry the woman he has always loved." Libr J
"The narrative is packed with substance, strong characterizations and startling insights into Catholic politics, doctrine and attitudes." Publ Wkly
Followed by Lord of the dance

The bishop in the West Wing; a Blackie Ryan story. Forge 2002 255p il o.p.
ISBN 0-312-86873-1 LC 2001-58284
"A Tom Doherty Associates book"
"Bishop Blackie Ryan is summoned to Washington, D.C., by the newly elected Democratic president to investigate a possible poltergeist. Shortly after his inauguration, President Jack Patrick McGurn, a South Side Chicago Irishman dubbed Machine Gun McGurn by a national media eager to discredit him, is plagued by a series of inexplicable psychic phenomena. . . . An entertaining romp through the West Wing." Booklist

Greeley, Andrew M., 1928-—*Continued*

The cardinal virtues. Warner Bks. 1990 449p o.p.

LC 89-40463

"When Father Laurence ('Lar') McAuliffe, pastor of an affluent suburban Roman Catholic church, acquires an unconventional new assistant, reactionary elements within the congregation of St. Finian's show their displeasure. As Lar and young Father Jamie struggle to minister to the disparate needs of their flock, archdiocesan conservatives attempt to undermine their unorthodox methods. In addition to successfully challenging the ecclesiastical hierarchy, the dynamic spiritual duo also double as matchmakers, salvage disintegrating marriages, counsel spirited teens, and, most impressively, vanquish a regressive secret society flourishing within the clergy. Greeley appears more comfortable in this reversion to his pastoral roots than in his more sensationalistic fictional forays." Booklist

Irish cream; a Nuala Anne McGrail novel; Andrew M. Greeley. Forge 2005 319p $24.95

ISBN 0-7653-0335-3 LC 2004-56322

Psychic Nuala McGrail and her husband, Dermot Coyne "look into mysteries past and present: the first chronicled in the diaries of Father Richard Lonigan, a 19th-century parish priest in Donegal, Ireland, the second involving poor Damian 'Day' O'Sullivan, whom the couple hire to take care of their two Irish wolfhounds. Amid the troubled political and religious environment in Donegal, where mostly poor Catholic villagers are overseen by Protestant Lord Skeffington, Father Lonigan investigates two shootings while striving to prevent further violence. In present-day Chicago, Nuala and Dermot face opposition to hiring Day O'Sullivan from the lad's father, since Day is not only a profound disappointment to the O'Sullivan family but also a convicted felon." Publ Wkly

Irish lace; a Nuala Anne McGrail novel. Forge 1996 303p o.p.

LC 96-24519

"A Tom Doherty Associates book"

This novel "finds the winsome 20-year-old recently transplanted from Ireland to Chicago. Nuala is romantically involved with Dermot Coyne—just the backup she requires, given her penchant for attracting dicey situations. Nuala's 'gift,' experiencing visions from the past, allows the plot to careen back to Camp Douglas, a Union prison in Civil War-era Chicago. From thence the story proceeds, . . . to envelop a contemporary art theft, Irish terrorists, and corrupt city officials." Libr J

"Moving effortlessly between the (fictional) conspiracies of 1864 and 1995 Chicago, Greeley is at his top page-turning form, throwing in a few stinging words about racism and xenophobia and delivering a rousing defense of the Bill of Rights." Publ Wkly

Irish stew!; a Nuala Anne McGrail story. TOR Bks. 2002 303p o.p.

ISBN 0-312-87188-0 LC 2001-54805

"A Tom Doherty Associates book"

In this adventure, "set at an international music festival in Milan, the McGrails really have their hands full. Not only are there demands on Nuala professionally (in addition to sleuting, she is an international singing star), they must also solve the mystery surrounding one Seamus Costelloe, whose sinister personage is doomed according to Nuala's ESP. As usual with Greeley's fiction, there is a Chicago connection; in addition to everything else going on, Dermot tries to solve the 100-year-old mystery of who started the Haymarket riot. A light, entertaining read." Booklist

Lord of the dance. Warner Bks. 1984 401p o.p.

LC 83-40342

"A Bernard Geis Associates book"

Concluding volume of the author's Passover trilogy

"This is the story of the Farrell family, successful Irish Catholic contractors in contemporary Chicago. When 16-year-old Noele Farrell is assigned to write a term paper on family history, she becomes interested in the fate of her cousin Daniel, a U-2 pilot whose plane went down in China in the 1960s. Interviews with family members lead Noele to suspect the existence of skeletons in the family closet." Libr J

Second spring; a love story. Forge 2003 347p $24.95

ISBN 0-7653-0236-5 LC 2002-32549

"In this installation, Charles 'Chucky' O'Malley and his spirited family face the 1970s. Here we find Chucky approaching 50 and stuck in a vicious midlife and spiritual crisis. While O'Malley can count his blessings—an adoring wife, an amazing sex life, a prestigious career, and a large, happy family—he still feels unfulfilled. In addition, he is no longer able to take comfort in his faith. As a photographer of some importance, O'Malley travels the world snapping historical photos and searching for his own happiness." Booklist

September song. Forge 2001 317p o.p.

ISBN 0-312-87225-9 LC 2001-33552

"A Tom Doherty Associates book"

Fourth installment in the author's O'Malley Family saga; previous titles A midwinter's tale (1998); Younger than springtime; Christmas wedding (2000)

This installment "focuses on the spitfire Irish Chuck O'Malley and his gorgeous wife, Rosemarie. Set against the turbulent events of the 1960s following the Kennedy assassination, the novel opens with Chuck handing in his resignation as German ambassador to President Johnson. On a first-name basis with all the major political figures of the time, Chuck strongly opposes Lyndon's position on the Vietnam War. He returns to Chicago with his wife and five children, only to be notified by Bobby (Kennedy, that is) of the historic civil rights march in Selma, Ala. . . . Sprinkled with . . . silly endearments and some chaste love-making scenes, the novel proceeds along a predictable historic course, weaving a Forrest Gump-like path through the '60s." Publ Wkly

Thy brother's wife. Warner Bks. 1982 350p o.p.

LC 81-16239

"A Bernard Geis Associates book"

First volume of the author's Passover trilogy

The author "sets up two brothers, sons of Mike Cronin, an Irish-American power-broker who, from his Chicago mansion, destines one son, Sean, for the priesthood . . . and the other, Paul, for politics. . . . As both fulfill their father's wish—with interludes of doubt and sex along the way, despite Paul's arranged marriage to Nora, his quasi foster-sister—their personal lives are equally unfulfilling. Sean eschews his conservatism after a sojourn in Rome,

Greeley, Andrew M., 1928-—*Continued*

gives expression to his latent love for Nora before accepting a call to the Chicago archbishopric from Pope Paul. Senator-elect Cronin, with echoes of Kennedy Camelot days, rises to the threshold of the Presidency, famed as a sexual athlete, until his perhaps accidental death." Publ Wkly

This "novel makes strong statements about important matters—love, morality, power, belief and human frailty under the pressure of animal drives." N Y Times Book Rev

Followed by Ascent into hell

White smoke; a novel about the next papal conclave. Forge 1996 384p o.p.

LC 96-1412

"A Tom Doherty Associates book"

Bishop John Blackwood "Blackie" Ryan is "in Rome along with his boss, Sean, Cardinal Cronin of Chicago, as the College of Cardinals meets to choose the next pope. Covering the papal conclave is Dennis (Dinny) Molloy, a Pulitzer Prize-winning reporter for the *New York Times*, and his lovely ex-wife, Patricia McLaughlin, a correspondent for CNN. There is serious dissension in the ranks about whom should be the next spiritual leader of the world's one billion Roman Catholics. . . . While the clergy battle it out, sparks fly between Dinny and Patty as they rediscover each other. The situation heats up when Dinny unearths a new Vatican investment scandal and Cronin collapses." Libr J

Younger than springtime. Forge 1999 348p o.p.

ISBN 0-312-86572-4 LC 99-22198

"A Tom Doherty Associates book"

Sequel to A midwinter's tale (1998)

This novel about the O'Malley family of Chicago "chronicles the romantic and spiritual fortunes of returned soldier Chuck O'Malley, who comes home in 1949, having been stationed for two years in postwar Germany. . . . The central image, bookending the novel, is a snapshot Chuck takes of beautiful Rosemarie Clancy, the troubled alcoholic daughter of Chuck's father's best friend. The photo of Rosemarie, in *déshabillé,* gets Chuck into trouble at Notre Dame and concatenates his search for spiritual meaning within the strict prohibitions of the Church. Chuck and Rosemarie's lifelong mutual attraction permeates the novel, with Greeley shifting focus in the middle of the book to Chuck's father, John. The elder O'Malley tells of how he met Chuck's mother, and the part Rosemarie's father, Jim Clancy, played in the eventual union. John O'Malley's story is deftly set in the center of Chuck's saga." Publ Wkly

Green, George Dawes

The juror. Warner Bks. 1995 420p o.p.

LC 94-18831

"Annie Laird is a single mother, a part-time data entry clerk, an aspiring sculptor, and a juror selected for the murder trial of a mob boss. When a suave, handsome art broker buys some of her work and then invites her to dinner, she thinks her luck may be changing. Her supposed admirer, a Wall Street financier and Taoist nicknamed 'The Teacher,' is actually the brains behind the jailed mobster. The Teacher is incredibly charming; he's also a vicious killer. He promises Annie the continued safety of her son and the assurance of a lucrative artistic career in exchange for help in acquitting the mobster. . . . [This novel] is less a courtroom drama than a gripping psychological cat-and-mouse game." Libr J

Green, Gerald, 1922-

The last angry man; a novel. Scribner 1957 c1956 494p o.p.

The last angry man was a Jewish doctor in Brooklyn, who for forty years had lived in the slums, angry at all injustice, carrying on his profession as a general practitioner, believing in medical ethics and living up to his beliefs. A TV studio decided to do the story of his life for a new program, and in the process of setting up the program the story of the life and death of Dr. Samuel Abelman is told

Green, Hannah *See* Greenberg, Joanne, 1932-

Green, Norman, 1954-

The angel of Montague Street. HarperCollins Pubs. 2003 293p $24.95

ISBN 0-06-018819-7 LC 2002-32885

Silvano Iurata "should never be in Brooklyn in the first place. It's 1973, the city is broke and mean, and he's ben bumming around since he got out of Vietnam, avoiding his Mafia-employed family and keeping clear of his loco cousin, Domenic, who wants to settle and old family quarrel by killing him with his bare hands. But Iurata is on some private redemptive mission, and he figures that if he can find out what happened to his sweet, mildly retarded brother, last seen in Brooklyn Heights, he might be able to give up the dead and rejoin the living. . . . Green writes about mobster families with a knowledge that is unnerving in its intimacy." N Y Times Book Rev

Shooting Dr. Jack; a novel. HarperCollins Pubs. 2001 288p $25

ISBN 0-06-018822-7 LC 2001-16841

This novel is "set in a Brooklyn junkyard. Fat Tommy Roselli, a k a Tommy Bagadonuts, the shady boss of the operation; his partner, the hopeless alcoholic Stoney; and their young, street-smart apprentice, Tuco, are a bunch of losers trying to get by at the junkyard on Troutman Street. . . . When the novel opens, Tuco discovers two dead teenagers in the lot and then learns that the company's accountant has been found dead of gunshot wounds in a Bronx motel. The murders bring the police, whose investigation could put a crimp in the junkyard's off-the-book business." N Y Times Book Rev

"The sharply drawn characters and the clever nicknames will invite comparisons to Elmore Leonard, but there's little of Leonard's flash and cockiness here, only a gritty realism, an attention to detail, and a resolute avoidance of clichés." Publ Wkly

Green, Tim

The letter of the law. Warner Bks. 2000 341p o.p.

ISBN 0-446-52299-6 LC 00-22285

Texan Casey Jordan "helps clear Eric Lipton, a law professor at the University of Texas, of the charge of disemboweling and murdering Marcia Sales. An instant before the jury foreman reads the verdict, Lipton whis-

Green, Tim—*Continued*
pers his guilt to Jordan. After the trial, suspicion rests on Donald Sales, the victim's father. Distraught with grief, hating Lipton, and humiliated by Jordan's trial accusation of incest, Sales abducts Jordan to teach her some of the pain his daughter suffered." Libr J

Green cane and juicy flotsam; short stories by Caribbean women; Carmen C. Esteves and Lizabeth Paravisini-Gebert, editors. Rutgers Univ. Press 1991 xxix, 273p o.p.
ISBN 0-8135-1737-0 LC 91-4788

Stories included are: Widow's walk, by O. P. Adisa; Little Cog-burt, by P. S. Allfrey; Cotton candy, by D. Alonso; See me in me Benz an t'ing, by H. D. Campbell; They called her Aurora, by A. Cartagena Portalatin; Columba, by M. Cliff; A pottage of lentils, by M. T. Colimon-Hall; Three women in Manhattan, by M. Condé; Hair, by H. Contreras; Piano-bar, by L. Dévieux; Barred: Trinidad 1987, by R. Espinet; The poisoned story, by R. Ferré; Cocuyo flower, by M. Garcia Ramis; How to gather the shadows of the flowers, by A. Hernández; Opéra Station. Six in the evening. For months . . ., by J. Hyvrard; Girl, by J. Kincaid; No dust is allowed in this house, by O. Nolla; Parable II, by V. Pollard; Red flower, by P. Poujol-Oriol; The day they burned the books, by J. Rhys; Lola; or, The song of spring, by A. Roemer; Bright Thursdays, by O. Senior; Tétiyette and the Devil; ADJ, Inc., by A. L. Vega; Of nuns and punishments, by B. Vianen; Passport to paradise, by M. Warner-Vieyra; Of natural causes, by M. Yañez

"Throughout, [this anthology] the race and class issues unique to Caribbean women are explored but in diverse ways and on a small scale, so that one comes away from the book with a uniquely personal sense of a much larger political phenomenon." Booklist

Greenberg, Joanne, 1932-

I never promised you a rose garden; a novel; [by] Hannah Green. Holt & Co. 1964 300p o.p.
ISBN 0-8050-0872-1

Sixteen-year-old Deborah "is sick of rebelling against the lies she hears, the hatred she feels, and, at a summer camp, the antiSemitism she suffers. She is schizophrenic: she has invented for herself a mythical kingdom into which she retreats and only when her parents reluctantly commit her to an asylum does she begin with difficulty to face reality." Publ Wkly

"The hospital world and Deborah's fantasy world are strikingly portrayed, as is the girl's violent struggle between sickness and health, a struggle given added poignancy by youth, wit, and courage." Libr J

In this sign. Holt, Rinehart & Winston 1970 275p o.p.

"The life of deaf-mutes Abel and Janice Ryder is followed from their marriage to their old age. After they leave the cloistered world of the institution for those with their handicap, they are plunged, unprepared, into the terrifying world of the hearing. They are never fully assimilated into that society. When they have a daughter who can hear, they gain new perspectives, but poverty and personal tragedy—the death of a son—further separate them from others, even from other deaf people. Greenberg's insights into the lives of the deaf are sensitive and painful." Shapiro. Fic for Youth. 2d edition

No reck'ning made. Holt & Co. 1993 296p o.p.
ISBN 0-8050-2579-0 LC 93-10198

"Bitterness tinges this story of teacher Clara Coleman. Struggling to overcome a childhood of poverty in a rough Colorado mining town, Clara attends college, then returns to teach in a one-room schoolhouse, later becoming principal. As the decades pass, the valley changes and so, too, do the parents. Ignorant of past struggles and disdainful of old-fashioned methods, they threaten Clara's career with accusations that question her values." Libr J

"Greenberg creates a clear demographic picture to complement her map of the heart. Her unflinching eye and sense of irony prevent a facile or sentimental solution to Clara's and the community's problems. The lure of a good story, artfully told, is augmented here by the empathy and wisdom of the storyteller." Publ Wkly

Of such small differences. Holt & Co. 1988 262p o.p.
LC 88-4424

"Blind since birth and deaf since the age of nine, when his alcoholic father slammed him down in anger, John lives alone in a small, carefully ordered apartment, has a job, and writes poetry. But life is not easy: John's independence is rife with dependencies . . . and with potential everyday danger as he tries to make his way in a sighted-hearing world, whether it's fixing a simple meal at home, eating at a restaurant, crossing a street, or taking a wrong turn in the road. Then he meets and falls in love with Leda Milan, who, while trying to get started as an actress, drives one of the vans that transport the blind to work." Booklist

"Greenberg's accomplishment in this beautifully imagined and sensitive novel is to give us an awareness of how people with sensory handicaps apprehend and measure the world; she does so through the mind of an indelibly appealing character." Publ Wkly

Rites of passage. Holt & Co. 1972 197p o.p.

"The novella-length title story shows how an unloved boy becomes strongly attached to his paranoic, stern employer. . . . Most of the stories are introspective, slow, and intense; all . . . demonstrate Greenberg's penetrating understanding of human problems and conflicts." SLJ

Greenberg, Martin Harry

(ed) Dinosaurs. See Dinosaurs

(ed) Great stories of the American West. See Great stories of the American West

Greene, Graham, 1904-1991

3: This gun for hire, The confidential agent, The ministry of fear. Viking 1952 3v in 1 o.p.

A one-volume edition of three suspense stories. The titles were first published 1936, 1939 and 1943, respectively

Greene, Graham, 1904-1991—*Continued*

Brighton rock; an entertainment. Viking 1938 358p o.p.

"This novel presents the story of Pinkie Brown, a chilling, utterly evil 17-year-old gang leader who marries the plodding Rose in order to insure her silence about his crimes. Both Pinkie and Rose were reared as Roman Catholics, and that background continues to inform their thoughts, if not their actions. In the end Pinkie dies while attempting to kill Rose; later, a priest tells Rose that her love for Pinkie may have saved her, as the mercy of God may have saved Pinkie." Merriam-Webster's Ency of Lit

A burnt-out case. Viking 1961 c1960 248p o.p.

"The story opens as Querry, a European who has lost the ability to connect with emotion or spirituality, arrives at a leprosarium in the Belgian Congo. His spiritual aridity is likened to a medical burnt-out-case—a leper who is in remission but who has been eaten up by his disease. Querry is invigorated by his contact with the leprosarium and its inhabitants, and he begins to come to life. Parkinson, an opportunistic journalist, discovers that Querry is a distinguished architect with a lurid past and begins to write sensationalized newspaper articles about him. When Querry innocently consoles the wife of the manager of a local factory, he is shot dead by her husband." Merriam-Webster's Ency of Lit

The captain and the enemy. Viking 1988 188p o.p.

LC 87-40664

"The novel takes the form of a memoir of a young man named Victor, who recounts how the mysterious 'Captain,' posing as a friend of his father, removed him from school one day and set him up in residence with Liza, a kind but equally inscrutable woman. Victor is renamed Jim, the Captain—an apparent thief, a liar, and prone to jaunts to the Continent—returns only occasionally to give Liza money and 'instruct' Jim on survival in the world, and the boy grows up bewildered but, in time, aware that his position in life has been that of a kind of gift to Liza, who, as his real father's paramour, once underwent an abortion unwillingly." Booklist

The author "wastes not a word in distilling the fictional preoccupations of a lifetime, omitting descriptive padding and elaborate transitions. But stripped down, the narrative runs fast and true across that bleak and poignant emotional landscape that is uniquely, immortally his." Time

Collected stories; including May we borrow your husband? A sense of reality [and] Twenty-one stories. Viking 1973 c1972 561p o.p.

Contents: May we borrow your husband?; Beauty; Chagrin in three parts; The over-night bag; Mortmain; Cheap in August; A shocking accident; The invisible Japanese gentlemen; Awful when you think of it; Doctor Crombie; The root of all evil; Two gentle people; Under the garden; A visit to Morin; The blessing; Church militant; Dear Dr. Falkenheim; Dream of a strange land; A discovery in the woods; The destructors; Special duties; The blue film; The hint of an explanation; When Greek meets Greek; Men at work; Alas, poor Maling; The case for the defence; A little place off the Edgware Road; Across the bridge; A drive in the country; The innocent; The basement room; A chance for Mr. Lever; Brother; Jubilee; A day saved; I spy; Proof positive; The second death; The end of the party

The comedians. Viking 1966 309p o.p.

This "book concerns a back-slidden Catholic, a native of Monaco and owner of a rundown tourist hotel in Haiti; his affair with the German wife of a Latin American ambassador; and his involvement with a rascally British con man and an American Presidential candidate and his wife, in Haiti to propagate the cult of vegetarianism—most of them in varying degrees comedians on the stage of life, running a bluff, playing a role, substituting sham for sincerity." Libr J

The confidential agent

In Greene, G. 3: This gun for hire, The confidential agent, The ministry of fear

The end of the affair. Viking 1951 240p o.p.

"The novel is set in wartime London. The narrator Maurice Bendrix, a bitter, sardonic novelist, has a five-year affair with a married woman, Sarah Miles. When a V-1 bomb explodes in front of Bendrix's apartment and Sarah finds Bendrix pinned beneath the front door, she believes him dead. She promises a God in whom she does not believe that she will give Bendrix up if he is allowed to live. Just then, Bendrix walks into the room and Sarah begins her religious journey; she breaks off with Bendrix, railing against God even as she begins to take religious instruction. Gradually she comes to a profound religious faith." Merriam-Webster's Ency of Lit

The heart of the matter. Viking 1948 306p o.p.

"Set in West Africa, it is a suspense story ingeniously made to hinge on religious faith. . . . The hero is Scobie, an English Roman Catholic who has vowed to make his devout wife happy though he no longer loves her. He borrows money from a local criminal to send her out of harm's way to South Africa; then he falls in love with a young woman from a group of castaways whose ship has been torpedoed. The return of his wife, the development of an adulterous affair, and blackmail drive Scobie deeper into deception and lies. Forced to betray someone, he betrays his god and himself, and finally commits suicide." Reader's Ency. 4th edition

The honorary consul. Simon & Schuster 1973 315p o.p.

This "novel relates the story of the politically motivated kidnapping of a minor British functionary near Argentina's Paraguayan border. The novel's major characters exemplify the kinds of personal sacrifices one must make in order to live in good conscience in a world where there is too much tyranny and injustice. A minor machismo novelist endures privation; a priest joins the radical underground movement; a physician gives up a lucrative Buenos Aires practice." Libr J

The human factor. Knopf 1992 c1978 xxviii, 338p $18

ISBN 0-679-40992-0 LC 91-53189

"Everyman's library"

A reissue of the title first published 1978 by Simon & Schuster

"In the British Foreign Service 'the human factor' becomes a liability for employees and a conduit for suspense, intrigue, and tragedy. Maurice Castle, head of a

Greene, Graham, 1904-1991—*Continued*
division in which information seems to have been leaked, presents a very positive image that appears to assure his innocence, but Davis, directly responsible to him, is an object of speculation. For a secret agent, the normal relationships of love and family are fraught with danger. As is true of many of Greene's novels, there are questions in this book about the loyalty owed to a government whose activities are suspect." Shapiro. Fic For Youth. 3d edition

The last word and other stories. Reinhardt Bks. 1990 149p o.p.

LC 90-81665

Contents: The last word; The news in English; The moment of truth; The man who stole the Eiffel Tower; The lieutenant died last; A branch of the service; An old man's memory; The lottery ticket; The new house; Work not in progress; Murder for the wrong reason; An appointment with the General

"This modest volume gathers uncollected stories from the entire range of Greene's career. The earliest dates from 1923 (!) and the latest from 1989." Libr J

May we borrow your husband?
In Greene, G. Collected stories p1-161

The ministry of fear; an entertainment. Viking 1943 239p o.p.

"Probably the author's least remembered work, one showing the Buchan influence most clearly. A group of Fifth Column Englishmen attempt to corner and murder a neurotic fellow countryman who possesses a piece of military intelligence they want to pass on to Berlin." Smith. Cloak and Dagger Fic

also in Greene, G. 3: This gun for hire, The confidential agent, The ministry of fear

Monsignor Quixote. Simon & Schuster 1982 221p o.p.

LC 82-5937

"Father Quixote is a humble parish priest despised by his bishop. Through an accidental encounter with a stranded bishop, he is named Monsignor, much to his bishop's and his discomfort. He sets off on a journey with the communist ex-mayor of his town. The philosophy and thinking of the ex-mayor, Sancho, are diametrically opposed to that of the priest, and there is much provocative discussion between them as they follow paths similar to those taken by the priest's fictional forebear, Don Quixote. Some of their adventures bring the priest to some surprising places, such as an x-rated cinema and a church where religion is being commercialized and demeaned. There is much humor as well as theology to involve the reader in this delightful odyssey." Shapiro. Fic for Youth. 3d edition

Orient Express. Doubleday, Doran 1933 310p o.p.

First published 1932 in the United Kingdom with title: Stamboul train

This is the story of what happened to a number of people who board the Orient Express at Ostend to make the three-day journey across the continent to Constantinople

Our man in Havana; an entertainment. Viking 1958 247p o.p.

"Set in Cuba before the communist revolution, the book is a comical spy story about a British vacuum-cleaner salesman's misadventures in the British Secret Intelligence Service. Although many critics found fault with the book's overly farcical style, it was also admired for its skillful rendering of the Cuban locale." Merriam-Webster's Ency of Lit

The power and the glory; introduction by John Updike. Viking 1990 295p o.p.

LC 90-50052

First published 1940 with title: The labyrinthine ways

Set in Mexico, this novel "describes the desperate last wanderings of a whisky priest as outlaw in his own state, who, despite a sense of his own worthlessness (he drinks, and has fathered a bastard daughter), is determined to continue to function as priest until captured. . . . Like many of Greene's works, it combines a conspicuous Christian theme and symbolism with the elements of a thriller." Oxford Companion to Engl Lit

The quiet American. Modern Lib. 1992 c1955 247p o.p.

ISBN 0-679-60014-0 LC 92-50219

First published 1955 in the United Kingdom; first United States edition published 1956 by Viking

"The novel is set in Vietnam during the French war against the Vietminh, and revolves around the death of Alden Pyle (the Quiet American), a naive and high-minded idealist who has arrived in the country as a member of the Economic Aid Mission. . . . The narrator, Thomas Fowler, is a middle-aged English journalist, cynical and detached. . . . Estranged from his wife in England, Fowler lives with an Annamite girl, Phuong. The story alternates between the period immediately after Pyle's murder and the events leading up to it." Camb Guide to Lit in Engl

"Mr. Greene has always been a master of suspense, and the particular excellence of 'The Quiet American' lies in the way in which he builds up the situation finally to explode the moral problem which for him lies at the heart of the matter." Times Lit Suppl

A sense of reality
In Greene, G. Collected stories p164-323

The tenth man. Simon & Schuster 1985 157p o.p.

LC 84-29830

"The Tenth Man is a long forgotten film treatment that Greene wrote for MGM in 1947. A prosperous French lawyer is held hostage during World War II by the Gestapo. He and his fellow prisoners must draw lots to see who must die. He draws the marked paper and, panic-stricken, offers everything he has to save his life. A consumptive young man accepts and leaves his new found estate to his mother and sister. The war ends and this lawyer, in disguise, returns to his chateau. It is occupied by the young man's senile mother, who awaits the return of her son, and the sister, who hatefully awaits the return of the man who bought her brother 's life." West Coast Rev Books

"A fatal series of events follows, entwining narrative excitement with broader questions of identity, fate, and

Greene, Graham, 1904-1991—*Continued*
morality. As always with Greene, the basic plot is heightened by the novelist's compelling view of the human condition." Libr J

This gun for hire
In Greene, G. 3: This gun for hire, The confidential agent, The ministry of fear

Travels with my aunt; a novel. Viking 1969 244p o.p.
"Aunt Augusta, in her late 70's, embroils her bachelor nephew, an utterly respectable, dahlia-growing retired bank manager, in a series of wild escapades. The action moves from London, across the European continent to Istanbul, and ends in Paraguay. Most of the characters are from Aunt Augusta's somewhat murky past, although there are contemporary figures such as a C.I.A. agent and his hippie daughter, and Wordsworth from Sierra Leone, who lives with Aunt Augusta as her 'valet.'" Libr J

"The book unmistakably turns its back on the Orphic preoccupations with the hereafter that characterized Greene's Catholic novels, and wholeheartedly embraces a Bacchic emphasis on the here and now." N Y Times Book Rev

Twenty-one stories
In Greene, G. Collected stories p325-562

Greenfeld, Josh

Harry and Tonto; [by] Josh Greenfeld and Paul Mazursky. Saturday Review Press 1974 183p o.p.
"This amusing novel treats a serious subject: what it's like to be 70 years old in the 1970's. Harry, a retired schoolteacher, and his aging cat, Tonto, are forcibly removed from their West Side Manhattan apartment just before the building is demolished; thus uprooted, they wander from New York to California seeking a new home. This journey enables the authors to satirize various American life styles." Libr J

Greenleaf, Stephen

Blood type; the new John Marshall Tanner mystery. Morrow 1992 283p o.p.
LC 91-40057
San Francisco PI John Marshall Tanner "questions the supposed suicide of bar-buddy Tom, an ambulance driver whose beautiful, blues-singing wife has been dating a corporate raider of dubious integrity. Because he suspects murder, Tanner delves into Tom's background, tracks Tom's 'lost' schizophrenic brother, finds a motive, and uncovers a scheme involving San Francisco blood banks." Libr J

Greenleaf delivers "incisive social observations, compassionate characterizations and fine writing. . . . As befits an heir of Ross Macdonald, the author maintains his moral grip on what matters." N Y Times Book Rev

Ellipsis; a John Marshall Tanner novel. Scribner 2000 265p o.p.
ISBN 0-684-84955-0 LC 99-87721
"Chandelier Wells is a fabulously successful author who taps into readers' hearts in the manner of Oprah Winfrey. Not too many years ago, she was overweight and in an abusive relationship. That changed quickly, but on the way to success, she made enemies; among them, her greedy ex-husband, a rejected suitor, and jealous fellow authors. Someone is making threats, and they seem real enough to hire San Francisco private investigator Marsh Tanner to act as Wells' bodyguard as he determines the source of the threats." Booklist

"Greenleaf has fun picking apart the seamier aspects of the book trade: the embarrassing cases of plagiarism, the frenzied book-signing parties, the vicious author rivalries and those brittle business lunches with agents and publicists who are perpetually locked in a death grip with their cell phones. It's all Tanner can do to keep a straight face." N Y Times Book Rev

False conception; a John Marshall Tanner novel. Penzler Bks. 1994 273p o.p.
ISBN 1-883402-87-5 LC 94-17371
"Stuart and Millicent Colbert can't conceive a child, but they have the resources to hire a surrogate mother. San Francisco private eye, Marsh Tanner is employed to investigate the surrogate, Greta Hammond. The catch: Hammond must never know the identity of the Colberts nor that she's being investigated. . . . Tanner novels are never just mysteries; Greenleaf always weaves in a larger human dilemma, and here he does it more successfully than ever before." Booklist

Flesh wounds. Scribner 1996 318p o.p.
ISBN 0-684-81583-4 LC 95-24412
Private eye John Marshall Tanner "gives himself the masochistic pleasure of going to Seattle to do a job for an old flame. Although Tanner is still in love with this woman, he agrees to search for her fiancé's missing daughter, a stunning figure model who has run afoul of an exploitative photographer described as 'a carnivore.'. . . He discovers the city's richer, darker colors when he traces the photographer's previous victims to the sex clubs and prostitutes' turf where they ended up after appearing in a pernicious new line of pornography using advanced digital technology." N Y Times Book Rev

"The Tanner series continues to be among the most emotionally and intellectually challenging in the genre." Booklist

Past tense; a John Marshall Tanner novel. Scribner 1997 282p o.p.
ISBN 0-684-83249-6 LC 96-35476
San Francisco investigator Tanner, "rushes to the aid of his best friend, a veteran homicide cop named Charley Sleet, who shoots a man dead in open court and refuses to offer any explanation or defense. Tanner is one of the best listeners in the business, and he gets an earful when he goes around interviewing people who knew either Charley or his victim, a creep whose daughter was suing him for sexual abuse. The characters met on these rounds are prime specimens, and their talk is choice." N Y Times Book Rev

Southern cross; a John Marshall Tanner novel. Morrow 1993 320p o.p.
LC 93-17031
"John Marshall Tanner is closing the gap on 50 a little too rapidly—a fact made all the clearer by an upcoming college reunion. The reunion turns out to be the usual mix of memories, regrets, laughs, and love rekindled, but

Greenleaf, Stephen—*Continued*
more germane is the case Tanner picks up while worrying about how his life stacks up to those of his peers. Former roommate Seth Hartman, long a civil-rights champion, is now an attorney in Charleston. Recently he's been receiving threatening letters from the Alliance for Southern Pride. Troubling Hartman most is his estranged son's involvement with the Alliance. Tanner agrees to help." Booklist

Strawberry Sunday; a John Marshall Tanner novel. Scribner 1999 287p o.p.
ISBN 0-684-84954-2 LC 98-40955
"Tanner investigates the murder of a young woman who worked hard for labor reform among strawberry pickers in the Salinas Valley." Libr J
"The Tanner books often have been built around a specific social or political issue, and this one is no exception. Greenleaf takes a long, hard look at the miserable conditions in which many farmworkers live and toil, and builds a complex, absorbing plot around the topic." Publ Wkly

Greer, Andrew Sean

The path of minor planets. Picador 2001 273p $23
ISBN 0-312-27556-0 LC 2001-41818
"In 1965, several astronomers assemble on an island in the South China Sea to observe the comet Swift, but the event is marred by the accidental death of a young child. The tragedy seems to ignite a succession of relationship woes for two young scientists and their spouses. Like the galaxies they study, the progression of their lives and loves is updated as they reunite every six years to commemorate the anniversary of the comet's original appearance." Publ Wkly
"In this début novel, Greer pinpoints the 'tiny hidden madnesses in ordinary people' with unerring accuracy, and, in prose littered with sparks, makes palpable the longing for the celestial." New Yorker

Gregory, Philippa, 1954-

Earthly joys. St. Martin's Press 1998 440p o.p.
ISBN 0-312-19262-2 LC 98-8771
This story centers on "John Tradescant, gardener to several great lords and finally to the king himself during the darkest days of post-Elizabethan England. Tradescant is a loyal vassal of the old school. . . . The first great lord in Tradescant's life, Sir Robert Cecil, is a man of honor and intelligence, but none of his successors measure up. Under King James I and then his son, Charles I, the court sinks into corruption, decadence and greed, drawing Tradescant ever closer to its evil doings. His loyalty also leads him into a passionate and doomed affair with the most charming, favored and unscrupulous member of the court, the Duke of Buckingham. . . . This tale of forbidden love set against the turmoil of a country in chaos makes for both intelligent and satisfying reading." N Y Times Book Rev
Followed by Virgin earth

Virgin earth. St. Martin's Press 1999 576p o.p.
ISBN 0-312-20617-8 LC 99-48489
This sequel to Earthly joys "begins as John Tradescant the Younger, Charles I's gardener, sails to the New World in search of rarities for his gardens. Not only does he find exotic plants, but he also glimpses unimagined freedom. His father's death leads John to a marriage of convenience in England. Unwilling to fight for Charles I, he returns to Virginia, where he joins the Powhatan and finds a wife. But eventually John loses his place in the tribe because of his inability to kill settlers. Determined to maintain a commitment to his English family, he goes home to a country buffeted by civil war." Libr J

The wise woman. Pocket Bks. 1993 c1992 438p o.p.
LC 93-21824
First published 1992 in the United Kingdom
A novel of "passion and witchcraft in 16th-century England. Growing up as an ill-used apprentice to Morach, the much-feared wise woman of the moors, Alys finds respite by joining an order of Catholic nuns. When young Lord Hugo and his men burn the abbey to the ground during a drunken rampage, Alys is the only one to escape; she flees back to Morach. . . . Attracted to Hugo despite his murderous past, Alys begins to practice witchcraft in earnest to rid him of Catherine and become his wife." Publ Wkly

Grenville, Kate, 1950-

The idea of perfection. Viking 2002 401p $24.95
ISBN 0-670-03080-5 LC 2001-58133
First published 2000 in the United Kingdom
"Saving the picturesque Bent Bridge becomes both cause and catalyst for the most unlikely of love affairs when social outcasts Douglas Cheeseman and Harley Savage descend on a wayward village in the remote Australian outback." Booklist
"Grenville does her characters the honor of taking their pain seriously and is gracious enough to allow them their hard-earned pleasure. Her ability to move between these elements gives her novel a beautiful balance." N Y Times Book Rev

Grey, Zane, 1872-1939

The Arizona clan. o.p.
First published 1958 by Harper
Set in Arizona's Tonto Basin, this novel of feuding clans and illicit whiskey has the main character, Dodge Mercer, in search of the thieves who are making off with the sorghum supplies by night. Nan Lilley, lovely daughter of old Rock, the head of the Lilley Clan, provides romantic interest as Dodge risks his life to solve the mystery

Knights of the range. o.p.
Copyrighted 1936; first published 1939 by Harper
A girl, born and bred on the East coast finds herself heir to her father's great cattle empire and the problems caused by outlaw bands of cattle rustlers

Last of the Duanes; a western story. Five Star Western 1996 315p o.p.
ISBN 0-7862-0627-6 LC 95-47156

Grey, Zane, 1872-1939—*Continued*

Grey "wrote this novel in 1913, but it was rejected by his early publishers, who believed it contained too much gunplay and not enough sentimentality. Buck Duane is the son of an infamous gunfighter. Although Buck is warned by his family to avoid the outlaw trail, his quick temper, steady nerve and lightning-quick hand promptly get him into trouble. After killing a bully, Buck flees the law and heads off into the harsh badlands of southwest Texas, where outlaw gangs roam the Mexican border." Publ Wkly

Riders of the purple sage. Five Star 2005 368p $25.95

ISBN 1-59414-130-4 LC 2004-60017

First published 1912 by Harper

"Well handled melodramatic story of hairbreadth escapes from Mormon vengeance in southwestern Utah in 1871." Booklist

The trail driver. o.p.

First published 1936 by Harper

This is the story of a great cattle drive from Texas to Kansas in 1871

This book presents a "really solid and absorbing likeness . . . of the Southwest in a paramount phase and period of its turbulent evolution." N Y Times Book Rev

The vanishing American. o.p.

First published 1925 by Harper

"A young Nopah Indian, stolen from his tribe and educated in an eastern college where he distinguishes himself both in studies and in athletics, returns to help his people. His romance with the girl who comes from the East to share his struggles is set against a background which reflects the tragedy of the Indian people, despoiled by government agent and missionary." Carnegie Libr of Pittsburgh

West of the Pecos. o.p.

First published 1937 by Harper

"Romantic western which tells of Colonel Terrill, broken by the Civil War, and his tomboy daughter, their efforts to get a start in the new world of the west, the Colonel's brutal murder and Pecos Smith's ride to rescue the girl, left alone in a land of desperados." Wis Libr Bull

Woman of the frontier; a western story. Five Star 1998 320p $19.95

ISBN 0-7862-1156-3 LC 98-22717

"Five Star standard print western series"

"This tale, written in 1934, was rejected by magazines because of its vivid portrayal of the hardships of pioneer life, including the rape of Grey's heroine by a renegade Apache. A heavily edited version called *30,000 on the Hoof* was finally published in 1940, a year after the author's death. This version, completely restored by Grey's son, Loren, recounts the trials and tribulations of Arizona rancher Logan Huett, his heroic wife, Lucinda, their three sons, and a girl named Barbara, who is abandoned by wagon-train travelers and raised by the Huetts." Booklist

Griesemer, John

Signal & noise. Picador 2003 593p $26

ISBN 0-312-30082-4 LC 2003-42938

"Brilliant engineer Chester Ludlow is soon transformed into a mesmerizing showman when he becomes involved in the laying of the trans-Atlantic cable. Attempting to raise the cash needed to launch the initiative, Ludlow travels with a musical 'Phantasmagorium Show,' which bowls over willing investors with its complex scene-shifting and inspiring narration. Soon the money is pouring in, and Chester becomes a celebrity and begins a passionate affair with the beautiful piano player. Meanwhile, his wife, Lily, still grieving the death of their child some years before, embarks on an intense spiritual quest in an attempt to communicate with her dead daughter." Booklist

Griesemer "has created some fine set pieces of disaster: the failed launch of the Great Eastern, two spectacular fires, a train crash that wrecks Ludlow's invention of a great Civil War cannon and, best of all, a breathtaking storm at sea. At the other end of the scale, the detail that fleshes out the novel's world is equally convincing." N Y Times Book Rev

Griffin, Pauline

(jt. auth) Norton, A. Redline the stars

Griffin, W. E. B.

The aviators. Putnam 1988 409p (Brotherhood of war, bk8) o.p.

LC 88-12657

"Protaganist Johnny is a born soldier who distinguishes himself as a helicopter pilot in Vietnam and is promoted to aide-de-camp to the commanding officer of Fort Rucker. In his new post, he finds himself directly involved with the development of the Army's first Air Assault Division—a new force crucial to meet the challenge of guerrilla warfare in Vietnam. This is the story of Johnny's year of work and crisis, the making and breaking of rules, the development of friendships, and the awakening of love." Libr J

Blood and honor. Putnam 1996 553p o.p.

LC 96-19039

In this sequel to Honor bound "Marine pilot and OSS operative Cletus Frade is sent to Argentina, ostensibly as a military attaché to the U.S. ambassador. Actually, he is there to avenge his father's murder. An influential man in Argentine politics who was pro-Allies, Frade's father was killed by Nazi intelligence agents because they feared he might become president. Meanwhile, an SS intelligence officer arrives. Part of his mission is to help a German submarine infiltrate Argentine waters. The SS officer and Frade are soon playing cat and mouse, though they're hampered by Argentina's neutrality." Booklist

"There's no deep moral digging here as there is in, say, le Carré. But Griffin is a savvy old hand and here, working with an exotic setting and a complex plot, delivers the sort of sturdy entertainment his fans expect." Publ Wkly

Followed by Secret honor

By order of the President; W.E.B. Griffin. Putnam 2004 528p $26.95

ISBN 0-399-15207-5 LC 2004-53417

Griffin, W. E. B.—*Continued*

"This novel is about the effort to unravel and defeat a terrorist plot to crash a stolen 727 into the Liberty Bell in Philadelphia." N Y Times Book Rev

"Proving himself solidly in control of cutting-edge military material, Griffin bases his new series not on wars past but on today's murky exigencies of terrorism and international political intrigue. . . . In the end, there are a few bodies to account for, but it's the meticulous investigation that leaves readers standing on the tarmac waiting for Charley Castillo and his newly minted band of can-do compatriots to touch down and carry them away again on a new adventure." Publ Wkly

Close combat. Putnam 1993 383p (Corps, bk6) o.p.

LC 92-34677

Set in 1942 the sixth book in the series "revolves around a war bond tour featuring Marine heroes of the Guadacanal Campaign. Series fans will recognize the central characters, among them Marine general and presidential troubleshooter Fleming Pickering, his fighter pilot son Pick, and movie mogul Homer Dillon, a Marine for the duration. Griffin has Marine Corps lore and trivia down pat, and he uses the bond-tour story line to convey the public-relations aspects of modern war." Publ Wkly

Followed by Behind the lines (1995)

Counterattack. Putnam 1990 444p (Corps, bk3) o.p.

LC 89-10772

Books one and two Semper fi (1986) and Call to arms (1987) published in paperback

This volume in The Corps series "covers the period from Pearl Harbor to Guadalacanal. . . . Griffin explores the difficult adjustment of enlisted men suddenly given officers' commissions; the raising of a Marine parachute battalion; the impact of total war on peacetime routines." Publ Wkly

Followed by Battleground (1991)

Final justice. Putnam 2003 466p $26.95

ISBN 0-399-14926-0 LC 2002-68266

Philadelphia police "detective Sergeant Matthew Payne is working on three cases. In the first, a kitchen supervisor and a cop are murdered at a fast-food restaurant. The second is a case of rape and murder, and the third concerns a suspect who has fled the country, leaving behind a trunk containing the mummified body of his girfriend." Booklist

"What holds it all together is Griffin's infectious respect for and fascination with police work." Publ Wkly

Honor bound. Putnam 1994 c1993 474p o.p.

LC 93-36850

This "World War II novel pits U.S. Marine Captain Cletus Frade, late of Guadalcanal, against an ostensibly neutral ship in Buenos Aires in 1942. Naturally, the Nazis are angling for position in this vital South American port, and Clete's mission is to maintain Allied influence with the Argentine navy by destroying the German-controlled ship. Along the way, Clete encounters the father he's never met (now a top officer in the Argentine army), a sympathetic German Luftwaffe officer, and a beautiful Argentine 'virgin princess,' with whom he falls in love." Booklist

"Griffin's feel for the details of life in the military 50 years ago and the humanity of his characters on all sides of the covert war make this a superior war story in an interesting milieu." Libr J

Followed by Blood and honor

In danger's path. Putnam 1998 549p (Corps, bk8) o.p.

ISBN 0-399-14421-8 LC 98-18809

The hero of this novel is "Brigadier General Fleming Pickering, head of the OSS' Pacific operations during World War II. . . . Pickering is a can-do kind of guy, whose assignments include the rescue of some American ex-servicemen and their families who are fleeing the Japanese in the Gobi Desert, and the setting up of a weather station in the desert to aid in air attacks on the Japanese. As in Griffin's other novels, this one is packed with adventure." Booklist

The investigators. Putnam 1997 408p (Badge of honor) o.p.

ISBN 0-399-14308-4 LC 97-1842

Book seven of the series "continues the saga of the Philadelphia Police Department, focusing once again on the Special Operations unit. Detective Matt Payne is sent to Harrisburg to gather evidence against a narcotics unit that is suspected of stealing from the very people whom they have arrested. Payne is also working with the FBI in its attempt to locate several terrorists who, is 1968, blew up a scientific laboratory, killing 11 people. While walking in the footsteps of law-enforcement officers, Griffin gives a clear picture of what it is like to be a police officer, how police officers think, how politicians bring pressure to bear on their actions, and how the justice system works." Libr J

The last heroes. Putnam 1997 c1985 342p o.p.

ISBN 0-399-14289-4 LC 96-39458

First published 1985 in paperback

First volume of the author's Men at War trilogy about the OSS during World War II

It is June 1941 and "no operation may be more critical than the one being conducted by hotshot pilot Richard Canidy and his half-German wild-card friend Eric Fulmar: to secure the rare ore that will power a top-secret weapon coveted on both sides of the Atlantic—the atomic bomb." Publisher's note

Followed by The secret warriors

Line of fire. Putnam 1992 414p (Corps, bk5) o.p.

LC 91-29971

Book five in the Marine Corps saga "is centered mainly on the World War II battle for Guadalcanal, from August through September of 1942. But not only Guadalcanal: in keeping with the form of preceding volumes, *Line of Fire* is vast in geographical scope, with action occurring in such diverse and far-flung locations as Australia; the Japanese-held island of Buka in the Solomon Sea; Parris Island, South Carolina; and Washington, D.C. The cast is appropriately large and liberally stocked with brave heroes, beautiful heroines, and assorted tough guys, and their adventures are rendered in the wry, salty narrative voice ex-soldiers like Griffin so often employ when they turn to writing." Booklist

Griffin, W. E. B.—*Continued*

The murderers. Putnam 1994 396p (Badge of honor) o.p.

LC 94-34497

This sixth volume in the series, "set in 1975, centers around the murder of Philadelphia policeman Jerry Kellog, perhaps committed by a corrupt cop because Kellog's wife, who's left him for another cop, has revealed that her husband's narcotics unit is dirty. Meanwhile, bar owner Gerry Atchison hires a small-time hit man to kill his cheating wife and his thieving business partner. Finding solutions to the three murders unites Griffin's huge cast of characters, among them high-profile detective Matt Payne and take-charge Sgt. Jason Washington, both of Special Operations." Publ Wkly

"Griffin knows Philly, the Philadelphia PD, and cops, and he fills his novels with vast amounts of detail as proof of that knowledge." Booklist

The new breed. Putnam 1987 398p (Brotherhood of war, bk7) o.p.

LC 87-10570

Previous volumes in series published in paperback are: The lieutenants (1982); The captains (1983); The majors (1983); The colonels (1983); The Berets (1985); The generals (1986)

"The scene is the Congo in 1964, and . . . the enemy is a dual one: both the Congolese rebels, who are described in unrelievedly brutal terms, and the 'hand wringers' in the State Department and C.I.A. who prevent fighting Americans from mowing down blacks to rescue American and Belgian hostages." N Y Times Book Rev

Secret honor. Putnam 2000 497p o.p.

ISBN 0-399-14568-0 LC 99-35740

In this third novel in the Honor Bound series "a German general works toward the assassination of Adolf Hitler. In Buenos Aires, the general's son, codenamed Galahad, falls under suspicion by the SS after a Nazi operation suddenly goes bad. In the middle of it all is OSS agent Cletus Frade, who knows the identity of them both and what they will do next if they can survive that long. For not only are SS and Abwehr officers hot on their trails in both countries, but the OSS has branded Frade a rogue agent and is determined to shake the truth from him, at whatever cost." Publisher's note

The secret warriors. Putnam 1998 c1985 321p o.p.

ISBN 0-399-14381-5 LC 97-37485

First published 1985 in paperback

In this second volume of the Men at War trilogy the OSS drops agents into the Belgian Congo to locate and smuggle out uranium ore while avoiding German agents

Followed by The soldier spies

The soldier spies. Putnam 1999 c1986 352p $25.95

ISBN 0-399-14494-3 LC 98-33260

First published 1986 in paperback

"Secret agents Major Richard Caniday (who's really *not* a major) and Eric Fulmar, members of the fledging OSS, aim to smuggle out of Germany the scientist whose knowledge of metallurgy holds the key to the Third Reich's development of jet engines. . . . Cameos by such historical figures as William 'Wild Bill' Donovan, Joseph P. Kennedy Jr., David Niven and Peter Ustinov lend color." Publ Wkly

Special ops. Putnam 2001 665p (Brotherhood of war, bk8) $25.95

ISBN 0-399-14646-6 LC 00-62779

"In 1964, Cuba's Fidel Castro tried to export communism to Africa under the leadership of the legendary Che Guevera, and *Special Ops* details the efforts of the U.S. military and the CIA to stop him. With the world's attention focused on Vietnam and Europe, the deadly fighting in some of the world's most remote and primitive places went unnoticed. . . . This is an exciting, intriguing, and fast-paced novel about an often-ignored period in our recent history." Libr J

Under fire. Putnam 2002 576p o.p.

ISBN 0-399-14788-8 LC 2001-48245

In this novel "Captain Ken 'Killer' McCoy, a protege of ex-OSS officer Fleming Pickering, who knows a senator, who knows President Truman, has reported to General MacArthur that North Korea will be invaded. The report disappears, McCoy gets busted to the ranks . . . and the Communists start pouring across the thirty-eighth parallel. Truman, suspicious of MacArthur, gets wind of the report, and appoints Pickering and McCoy to the CIA. Boats, bullets, and carrier-launched avengers and corsairs make up the balance of this expansively told story." Booklist

Griffith, Bill *See* Granger, Bill

Grimes, Martha, 1931-

The Anodyne Necklace. Little, Brown 1983 250p o.p.

LC 83-880

"Sixteen-year-old Katie O'Brien, playing her violin in an underground London station to make some money, is mysteriously attacked. From that incident begins a mystery involving the theft of an emeral necklace, the murder of a young man whose fingers have been chopped off, and still another murder. The characters in this absorbing tale include not only the residents of Littlebourne, Katie's village, but some East End Londoners like the Cripps family, whose squalid home and bizarre behavior will not soon be forgotten by the reader. Satirical humor enlivens the careful and patient unraveling done by the special detective featured in Grimes' mysteries—the attractive Scotland Yard Superintendent Richard Jury." Shapiro. Fic for Youth. 3d edition

Belle ruin. Viking 2005 346p $25.95

ISBN 0-670-03461-4 LC 2005-42289

A mystery featuring "precocious 12-year-old Emma Graham. . . . Basking in the glow of newfound fame after narrowly escaping a murder attempt, Emma has her hands full reporting for the local newspaper, waitressing in her mom's seedy hotel restaurant and performing in her brother's low-budget production of 'Medea: The Musical.' She also creates havoc for the hotel's guests, hobnobs with the local sheriff and trades barbs with her archenemy, Ree-Jane Davidow. Nonetheless, Emma's never ending quest to discover the identity of a mysterious girl only she can see, as well as her passion for solving the 20-year-old mystery surrounding a baby kid-

Grimes, Martha, 1931—*Continued*
napped from the once famous Belle Rouen hotel are always her top priorities. Grimes' pungent prose and catchy dialog breathe life into her charming young narrator and the novels' idiosyncratic cast of characters." Publ wkly

Biting the moon; a mystery. Holt & Co. 1999 301p o.p.
ISBN 0-8050-5621-1 LC 98-42823
Grimes "sends two brave girls on a hair raising road trip from Santa Fe, N.M., to Salmon, Idaho, in pursuit of a child molester and animal abuser. . . . At 14, smart, shy Mary Dark Hope needs to come out of her shell, which she does on this coming-of-age odyssey with the big-eyed wonder of a true explorer. The young amnesiac who calls herself Andi Olivier and feels an affinity with the coyotes she frees from traps is more complicated. Too wise for her years, she's a sober realist with a romantic imagination that makes reality bearable." N Y Times Book Rev

The case has altered. Holt & Co. 1997 370p o.p.
ISBN 0-8050-5620-3 LC 97-20791
A mystery featuring Scotland Yard CID Inspector Richard Jury and aristocrat Melrose Plant. "Two murders have taken place in the bleak Lincolnshire fens: two weeks after glamorous actress Verna Dunn was found shot to death, plain kitchen-maid Dorcas Reese turned up, garroted and strangled. The local police have already identified the prime suspect, Jury's longtime friend, Jenny Kennington. Although the motive is murky, Jenny certainly had means and opportunity, and before long, she's arrested for both murders. Jury is understandably upset, and he and Plant determine to prove Jenny's innocence despite the steadily mounting evidence against her." Booklist
"Psychologically complex and muted in tone, with the characters' elliptical relationships reflecting the setting of England's dreamlike fen country, the novel also boasts Grimes's delicious wit." Publ Wkly

Cold Flat Junction. Viking 2001 390p o.p.
ISBN 0-670-89491-5 LC 00-43992
"Emma Graham, the 12-year-old narrator of this . . . coming-of-age mystery, related an earlier installment of this story in 'Hotel Paradise,' named for the once grand jewel of the decaying resort town where she lives. . . . [Emma's] obsession with Mary-Evelyn Devereau, a 12-year-old girl who drowned in Spirit Lake 40 years ago, has not gone unnoticed by her good friend the sheriff, who also suspects this observant child of poking into more recent deaths in the Devereau family." N Y Times Book Rev
"Listening to Emma grope for understanding in this most tangled town is fascinating, and watching as the seemingly unconnected bits come together is unnerving." Booklist

The Deer Leap. Little, Brown 1985 236p o.p.
LC 85-15916
This "novel is set in a Hampshire village and centralized in the quaint local pub of the title. Scotland Yard's Jury is summoned to Ashdown Dean after local mystery writer Polly Praed discovers a body in a telephone kiosk. The murder ties in with a series of pet poisonings and a controversy over blood sports. More murder follows before the unflappable Jury can sort things out in this satisfyingly cozy, old-fashioned tale that has the elegant/macabre feel of Edward Gorey's drawings." Booklist

The dirty duck. Little, Brown 1984 240p o.p.
LC 83-25629
"When a group of tourists on holiday in Shakespeare country are beset by brutal murder and kidnapping, with the murderer leaving Elizabethan couplets as a calling card, Superintendent Jury of Scotland Yard becomes drawn into work on the case." Libr J
The author is an "elegant writer who has a strong touch of poetry in her. Her prose flows limpidly, distinguished by its accurate dialogue, sophistication and quiet humor. She also has a sympathetic understanding of human foibles." N Y Times Book Rev

The five bells and bladebone. Little, Brown 1987 299p o.p.
LC 87-3148
"Visiting his friend Melrose Plant in Plant's ancestral village, Jury is at the local antique shop when Simon Lean's body is found in a flaptop desk. The dealer has just bought the piece from Lady Summerston, mistress of the lush estate of Watermeadows where Simon had lived with his wife Hannah, the lady's granddaughter. Questioning the women, Jury sees the strong resemblance between the widow and Sadie Diver, who was murdered in London's notorious Limehouse district. . . . The splendid mystery has a tragic core, but the gloom is offset by the author's quiet humor." Publ Wkly

Foul matter. Viking 2003 372p $25.95
ISBN 0-670-03259-X LC 2003-50153
"Best-selling author Paul Giverney will sign with publisher Mackenzie-Haack only if it drops literary author Ned Isaly and assigns Isaly's talented editor to Paul. Ambitious editor Clive Esterhaus wants Giverney for himself but isn't comfortable with the solution proposed by Bobby Mackenzie, owner of MackenzieHaack—hiring hit men." Libr J
"The serpentine plot is fun to follow, once Giverney realizes the extent of the mischief he has set in motion. But it's the nasty inside stuff—from the Dickensian names for authors and their publishing houses to the barbaric rituals of a power lunch—that incites rolling in the aisles." N Y Times Book Rev

Help the poor struggler. Little, Brown 1985 225p o.p.
LC 85-109
"An epidemic of child murders brings Jury and Chief Superintendent Macalvie, a local colleague, to reconsider the 20-year-old murder of a woman which had been witnessed by the victim's five-year-old daughter." Libr J
"This fine novel features a plot that startles, characters that convince, and an atmosphere that sparkles." Booklist

The Horse You Came In On. Knopf 1993 331p o.p.
LC 92-55069
"Scotland Yard superintendent Richard Jury joins his friend Melrose Plant in Baltimore, where they solve several seemingly unrelated mysteries and investigate the genealogy of a bunch of upstarts who claim to be descendants of Lord Baltimore." Libr J
"Notable for its themes of authorship and authenticity and for the cast of delightfully eccentric characters—who

Grimes, Martha, 1931-—*Continued*
gather each day at a blue-collar bar called The Horse You Came In On—this mystery, with its feathery plot and fey, lighthearted tone, moves in quite a different direction than earlier Jury tales. Not bad, just different." Publ Wkly

Hotel Paradise. Knopf 1996 347p o.p.
ISBN 0-679-44187-5 LC 95-49356
Twelve-year-old "Emma Graham, who works as a salad girl at the decaying resort hotel where her mother cooks, loves her mother's food almost as much as she loves investigating situations that stimulate her active imagination—like the mysterious death 40 years earlier of young Mary-Evelyn Devereau, who lived with three ugly aunts and drowned, silk-clad and sad, in nearby Spirit Lake. Emma pursues the Mary-Evelyn mystery with single-minded determination, and during the course of her investigation, finds answers to questions she didn't even know she wanted to ask." Booklist
"Emma's take on the colorful characters in her small-town world . . . makes this both a provocative study of lonely people and a delightful read." Publ Wkly

I am the only running footman. Little, Brown 1986 206p o.p.
LC 86-15305
"Scotland Yard's wise, kind Superintendent Richard Jury must determine if the case of Ivy Childess, strangled in London, is related to a similar crime in Devon. Ivy had left her sometime lover, David Marr, after a tiff in the Footman, so he heads the list of suspects. Jury's interrogation ends with Marr offering a strong alibi, backed by his prestigious family. Calling on the man's sister and other kin, the superintendent senses private fears behind a gracious facade. Jury is right, but his suspicions produce no evidence of collusion until a shocking truth sends him racing to save the killer's third intended victim. An artist at plotting, Grimes concludes this urbanely humorous, knife-edge thriller with a double twist." Publ Wkly

Jerusalem Inn. Little, Brown 1984 299p o.p.
LC 84-15495
Superintendent Richard Jury "taking a brief holiday a few days before Christmas, meets Helen Minton, a woman seeking answers about her past. Their acquaintanceship has no time to warm to love; Helen dies, of poisoning, it turns out. As Jury assists the local officials in the investigation, he chances upon a tangle of details that leads him to snowbound Spinney Abbey where occur a shot gun murder plus the apparent gradual poisoning of another woman." Best Sellers

The Lamorna wink; a Richard Jury mystery. Viking 1999 368p o.p.
ISBN 0-670-88870-2 LC 99-33525
This mystery "centers on Jury regular Melrose Plant/Lord Ardry, along with an intriguing, brilliant police friend of Jury's, Brian Macalvie, as they investigate the disappearance of one woman, the murder of another, and the horrific, four-year-old unsolved death of two children who lived in the Cornwall house Plant is renting. Ultimately, the events converge, and Jury appears to wrap things up." Libr J

The man with a load of mischief. Little, Brown 1981 263p il o.p.
LC 81-8251
"This book takes its intriguing title from the scene of one of several crimes perpetrated by a murderer with a macabre sense of humor and a penchant for depositing corpses in the vicinity or on the premises of English pubs. When a man is found strangled and deposited in a beer vat, likable but cunning Inspector Richard Jury spends his Christmas holidays in the 'picture postcard village' of Long Piddleton, determined to solve the growing number of crimes. Deft characterization and portrayal of English pub life add to the appeal of a cleverly contrived tale." Libr J

The Old Contemptibles. Little, Brown 1991 333p o.p.
LC 90-48647
Inspector "Jury is considering marriage to recently met widow Jane Holdsworth at the moment her teenaged son Alex finds her dead, apparently a suicide. Alex runs away, and Jury, required, as a suspect, to remain in London, sends old friend Melrose Plant up to the Lakes to learn what he can about the wealthy Holdsworth family, among whom Jane's death is the fourth suspicious one." Publ Wkly

The old fox deceiv'd. Little, Brown 1982 299p o.p.
LC 82-7719
"The central mystery that confronts Inspector Richard Jury of Scotland Yard is not whounit, but to whom was it 'dun.' Was the young woman found mutilated with an ice-pick-like instrument Dillys March, the ward of Colonel Titus Crael who left home 15 years previously and recently returned to reclaim her inheritance? Or was the victim Gemma Temple, Dillys' look-alike, who tried to pass herself off as Dillys to gain the inheritance? The tiny English fishing village of Rackmoor is divided and tormented by this mystery, which threatens to rock its social structure." Booklist

The Old Silent. Little, Brown 1989 425p o.p.
LC 89-31650
While vacationing in Yorkshire, at the inn of the title, Jury "observes a well-dressed, self-contained woman shoot her husband. With no question of who murdered whom, Jury is dogged by the whys. Officially off the case, he's irretrievably hooked when he learns that the victim's son, and the woman's stepson, is the musical prodigy presumed dead in a famous kidnapping case years before." Publ Wkly
"The calm moments in this moody mystery about parental ties and family schisms and relationships thicker than blood are as fine as anything Ms. Grimes has written." N Y Times Book Rev

Rainbow's end; a Richard Jury novel. Knopf 1995 383p o.p.
ISBN 0-679-44188-3 LC 94-48876
In this Richard Jury mystery, three women "die suddenly in public places: an aged textile restorer in Exeter Cathedral, a society matron in the Tate Gallery and an American tourist in the ruins of Old Sarum, near Salisbury. The deaths appear to be natural and unrelated, but the clever Brits come up with a connection: both Englishwomen had recently visited Santa Fe, N.M., where

Grimes, Martha, 1931-—*Continued*
the American had a silver shop. Once in the Southwest, Jury follows his wispy lead to eye-catching locations like a movie set in Santa Fe. . . . Meanwhile, back home, Jury's sidekick, Melrose Plant, pays nostalgic visits to people and places from previous novels, while mourning the passing of the grand old pubs." N Y Times Book Rev

The Stargazey; a Richard Jury mystery. Holt & Co. 1998 354p o.p.
ISBN 0-8050-5622-X LC 98-21214
"Jury is on the Fulham Road bus when he spots a beautiful blonde in a fur coat and feels compelled to follow her to the Fulham Palace grounds. Later she is found murdered on the palace grounds. But is it really she? Jury doubts it and follows a winding path to the truth." Libr J
Grimes "delivers a delightfully entertaining blend of irony, danger, and intrigue, liberally laced with wit and charm." Booklist

The train now departing
In Grimes, M. The train now departing: two novellas

The train now departing: two novellas. Viking 2000 185p o.p.
ISBN 0-670-89154-1 LC 99-53705
This volume "consists of a pair of atmospheric novellas. While both stories center on middle-aged, single women whose careful, well-ordered lives are gradually altered by meals they share with male acquaintances, these two novellas are quite distinct in their ambience and characterization. In 'The Train Now Departing,' Grimes eerily depicts a bright, analytical woman teetering into madness. 'When the Mousetrap Closes' is the story of Edith Parenger, a woman whose desperate loneliness is pitted against her keen powers of observation in an unflinching exploration of the power of illusion." Libr J

When the mousetrap closes
In Grimes, M. The train now departing: two novellas

The winds of change; a Richard Jury mystery. Viking 2004 407p $25.95
ISBN 0-670-03327-8 LC 2004-52636
This Richard Jury mystery involves "the murder of an anonymous five-year-old girl, shot in the back. . . . When he learns that the child was found near a house frequented by pedophiles, he's convinced there's a link. His suspicions grow stronger when the man supposedly behind the operation turns out to be the father of a child who mysteriously disappeared three years before from a country estate." Booklist

Grimsley, Jim

The ordinary; Jim Grimsley. 1st ed. TOR Bks. 2004 368p map $24.95
ISBN 0-7653-0528-3 LC 2003-71148
"Set in the same future world as Kirith Kirin (2000) . ., Grimsley's latest SF novel intimately explores the conflicts between magic and science, subconscious and conscious action, the past and the future. The planet of the tech-using Hormling of Senal is connected to the land of Irion, home of the magic-believing Erejhen, via the mysterious Twil Gate, a portal of unknown origins in the ocean. Although traders on both sides enjoy brisk commerce through the gate, Hormling leaders look more and more to Irion as a means to provide land and resources for their expanding civilization. Translator Jedda Martele, member of a Senal diplomatic mission to Irion, is caught in the middle when the delegation's true purpose is revealed. . . . Grimsley's finely textured societies have a clockwork intricacy that fascinates even as it dispels surprise." Publ Wkly

Grippando, James

The abduction; a novel. HarperCollins Pubs. 1998 386p o.p.
ISBN 0-06-018262-8 LC 97-28153
"It's the year 2000, and U.S. Attorney General Allison Leahy is the country's first female presidential candidate. When opponent Lincoln Howe's granddaughter, Kristen, is kidnapped, Leahy—whose own daughter was abducted eight years earlier—is torn between her political advisors, who tell her to stay far away from the investigation, and her memories of her own tragedy. . . . This is a gripping (and frightening) story about the Machiavellian world of American politics." Booklist

Found money. HarperCollins Pubs. 1999 336p o.p.
ISBN 0-06-018263-6 LC 98-24310
"Just before Frank Duffy dies, he tells his physician son, Ryan, that there is $2 million hidden in the attic, and that Frank got the money through blackmail—albeit off someone who 'deserved it.' The level-headed Ryan considers both claims unbelievable—until he finds the money. . . . Meanwhile, Amy Parkins, while struggling to support her daughter and her grandmother and to put herself through law school, receives $200,000 from an anonymous benefactor, apparently Frank Duffy, whom she'd never met. . . . As Ryan and Amy search for the money's source and meaning, they uncover a conspiracy involving high-ranking government officials, multi-billion-dollar corporations and a hidden crime committed on a hot summer night years ago. The final revelation is a real kicker." Publ Wkly

Hear no evil; James Grippando. 1st ed. HarperCollins Publishers 2004 310p $23.95
ISBN 0-06-056457-1 LC 2003-57138
This "Jack Swyteck mystery finds the Miami defense lawyer in unfamiliar territory. When a woman asks him to defend her against the charge of murdering her husband, Jack is initially reluctant: the victim is a U.S. naval officer; the crime took place at the naval base at Guantanamo Bay; and Jack has almost no experience with military courtroom procedures. But the woman has a very persuasive reason for Jack to take the case . . ., and soon Jack finds himself fighting for his client's life in an arena that is brand new to him." Booklist
"This character-driven, intricately plotted thriller will keep readers guessing up to the end." Publ Wkly

Grippando, James—*Continued*

The informant. HarperCollins Pubs. 1996 360p o.p.

LC 96-16310

"There's a serial killer out there, but the locations are disparate and the victims seemingly unconnected. FBI agent Victoria Santos has developed a psychological profile of the killer, whose attention to detail results in a dearth of clues. Then *Miami Tribune* reporter Mike Posten receives calls from someone who claims he's not the killer, but he thinks so much like him he can predict the killer's next move. The caller will talk for cash, which the FBI supplies. The finale takes place on a cruise ship and pits the killer against Santos and Posten." Booklist

"Although his prose is stilted, Mr. Grippando, . . . has a nice flair for the grotesque. More to his credit, he has done his homework on F.B.I. forensics, criminal profiling and the internal protocol for backstabbing." N Y Times Book Rev

A king's ransom. HarperCollins Pubs. 2001 426p o.p.

ISBN 0-06-019241-0 LC 2001-16786

"When lawyer Nick Rey's father is kidnapped during a business trip to Colombia it's up to Nick to save him. The chain of events designed to make the task as difficult as possible queues up behind him—Nick must battle his own law firm, the insurance company, the outrageously unhelpful FBI, and a group of merciless guerillas who refuse to budge from their ransom demands." Libr J

Grippando's "research into the kidnapping industry currently thriving in Latin America adds a harrowing dose of realism to a taut, well-constructed page-turner." Publ Wkly

Grisham, John

The brethren. Doubleday 2000 366p $30

ISBN 0-385-49746-6 LC 00-23841

This suspense novel revolves around two subplots. In the first three ex-judges, serving time in a federal prison in Florida, concoct a blackmail scheme that targets closeted gay men. The second storyline relates the CIA-backed presidential bid of a corrupt congressman

"Every personage in this novel lies, cheats, steals and/or kills, and while Grisham's fans may miss the stalwart lawyer-heroes and David vs. Goliath slant of his earlier work, all will be captivated by this clever thriller that presents as crisp a cast as he's yet devised, and as grippingly sardonic yet bitingly moral a scenario as he's ever imagined." Publ Wkly

The broker. Doubleday 2005 357p $27.95

ISBN 0-385-51045-4

"In his final hours in the Oval Office, the outgoing President grants a controversial last-minute pardon to Joel Backman, a notorious Washington power broker who has spent the last six years hidden away in a federal prison. What no one knows is that the President issues the pardon only after receiving enormous pressure from the CIA. It seems Backman, in his power broker heyday, may have obtained secrets that compromise the world's most sophisticated satellite surveillance system. Backman is quietly smuggled out of the country in a military cargo plane, given a new name, a new identity, and a new home in Italy. Eventually, after he has settled into his new life, the CIA will leak his whereabouts to the Israelis, the Russians, the Chinese, and the Saudis. Then the CIA will do what it does best: sit back and watch." Publisher's note

"If you will be satisfied with a workmanlike spy-cum-politics novel, with some first-rate cloak and dagger intrigue, an uplifting vignette of father-son redemption and a poignant pastiche of unrequited love, then 'The Broker' is the book for you." N Y Times Book Rev

The chamber. Doubleday 1994 486p o.p.

ISBN 0-385-42472-8 LC 94-11764

"The chamber in question is the gas chamber at the Mississippi State Penitentiary—and for 69-year-old Sam Crayhall, the road thence has been many years long. Sam was twice tried and twice acquitted for murder after a 1967 Ku Klux Klan scare bombing accidentally killed the twin sons of the intended target; 14 years later he was tried a third time, convicted and sentenced to death row. Now, in 1990, a young Chicago lawyer, employed by the firm that represented Sam but which he has just unceremoniously dumped, wants Sam as a client. Adam Hall, the 26-year-old rookie, is Sam Crayhall's grandson. . . . Though the countdown to an execution is a well-worn plot device, it has seldom been as effective, especially in the novel's last 100 pages." Publ Wkly

The client. Doubleday 1993 422p $29.95

ISBN 0-385-42471-X LC 92-39079

"While sneaking into the woods to smoke forbidden cigarettes, preteen brothers Mark and Ricky find a lawyer committing suicide in his car. Mark tries to save the man but is instead grabbed by him and told the location of the body of a murdered U.S. senator—a murder for which the lawyer's Mafia-connected client is accused. Witnessing the successful suicide sends Ricky into shock and Mark into a web of lies, half-truths, and finally into refusal to tell the confided secret to the police. Mark accidentally but fortuitously hires a lawyer, Reggie Love, who steers him through a maze of FBI agents, legal proceedings, judges, ambitious lawyers, and hit men. . . . This thriller is unique in its theme and in its suspense mixed with humor. A sure 'all-night' read." SLJ

The firm. Doubleday 1991 421p $30

ISBN 0-385-41634-2 LC 90-3945

"Fresh out of Harvard Law School, Mitchell McDeere is recruited by an elite Memphis law firm. . . . [His colleagues] put in 19-hour days for their front-office clients, while beavering behind the scenes on money-laundering operations for the Mafia. . . . Mitch, in fear for his life, agrees to work undercover for the F.B.I." N Y Times Book Rev

"The aphorism 'between a rock and a hard place' aptly describes the dilemma of a young attorney pressed by the FBI to reveal crime-related secrets of his firm, while also hounded by his employers to simply take his huge salary and zip his lip. No aphorism, though, can convey the suspense, wit, and polished writing of this laser-sharp candidate for the best recent updating of the David and Goliath story." Libr J

The last juror. Doubleday 2004 355p $27.95

ISBN 0-385-51043-8

"In 1970, one of Mississippi's more colorful weekly newspapers, The Ford County Times, went bankrupt. To the surprise and dismay of many, ownership was as-

Grisham, John—*Continued*
sumed by a 23-year-old college dropout, named Willie Traynor. The future of the paper looked grim until a young mother was brutally raped and murdered by a member of the notorious Padgitt family. Willie Traynor reported all the gruesome details, and his newspaper began to prosper. The murderer, Danny Padgitt, was tried before a packed courthouse in Clanton, Mississippi. The trial came to a startling and dramatic end when the defendant threatened revenge against the jurors if they convicted him. Nevertheless, they found him guilty, and he was sentenced to life in prison. . . . Nine years later Danny Padgitt managed to get himself paroled. He returned to Ford County, and the retribution began." Publisher's note

"The novel will satisfy those with an appetite for legal thrillers and those who believe Grisham possesses more talent than those breathless page-turners sometimes reveal. It ranks among his best-written and most atmospheric novels." USA Today

A painted house; a novel. Doubleday 2001 388p il $27.95
ISBN 0-385-50120-X LC 2001-266464

For "Lucas Chandler, the year 1952 is full of secrets—sweet, tragic, and mysterious. At 7, he still sleeps under the bed when he's scared and disappears behind his mother's skirts from time to time. But he's old enough to understand that prejudice, class rivalry (townies paint their houses; farmers don't), and violence are part of the fabric of his outwardly quiet farming community, and that he shouldn't be watching an unmarried teen give birth or pretty 17-year-old Tally bathing in the creek (even if she says it's okay). He also realizes that by confessing he's witnessed two vicious killings, he'll be threatening his family's livelihood and putting his loved ones in danger." Booklist

"Grisham is about as good a storyteller as we've got in the United States these days. . . . The plots and subplots twine. The pages turn. The characters take on their own lives." N Y Times Book Rev

The partner. Doubleday 1997 366p $30
ISBN 0-385-47295-1 LC 96-54702

"Money is essentially the principal character in [this novel]. It is a very large sum of it—$90 million, to be exact—that has motivated Gulf Coast lawyer Patrick Lanigan to concoct a scheme to disappear. . . . It is money that drove a crooked defense contractor to try to pry loose a huge sum from Washington, and got Patrick's greedy law firm involved in the first place. And it is varying sums of money that enable Patrick to bribe his way out of a collection of indictments against him a yard long—including one for first-degree murder—when he is eventually found in his Brazilian hide-away and brought back to the U.S. to face the music. . . . To call the plot of *The Partner* mechanical is at least partly a compliment: it is well-oiled, intricate and works smoothly." Publ Wkly

The pelican brief. Doubleday 1992 371p $30
ISBN 0-385-42198-2 LC 91-33235

"Set in the near future, the novel begins with an attention-getting double whammy, as two Supreme Court justices are assassinated within hours of each other. Brainy, self-possessed Tulane University law student Darby Shaw . . . proposes a theory about the murders in a brief that leaves chaos in its wake when it falls into the wrong hands." Publ Wkly

"Mr. Grisham has written a genuine page-turner. He has an ear for dialogue and is a skillful craftsman. Like a composer, he brings all his themes together at the crucial moment for a gripping, and logical, finale." NY Times Book Rev

The rainmaker. Doubleday 1995 434p $29.95
ISBN 0-385-42473-6 LC 95-2291

"When the modestly sized law firm that contracted for his future services unexpectedly merges with a tony Ivy League firm, . . . [attorney Rudy Baylor] finds himself without a job and bankrupt. . . . To make a living, Rudy finds himself chasing ambulances for a racketeering shyster, leading to his becoming enthralled with a beautiful young woman hospitalized by her husband's murderous attack. When Rudy agrees to represent the parents of a dying 22-year-old denied insurance coverage for bone-marrow transplant, he finds that he is up against the firm that broke contract with him." Publ Wkly

The runaway jury. Doubleday 1996 401p $30
ISBN 0-385-47294-3 LC 96-13872

"In a Mississippi Gulf Coast town, the widow of a lifelong smoker who died prematurely of lung cancer is suing Big Tobacco. Enter Rankin Fitch, a dark genius of jury fixing, who has won many such trials for the tobacco companies and who foresees no special problems here. Enter also a mysterious juror, Nicholas Easter, whom Fitch's army of jury investigators and manipulators can't quite seem to track—and his equally mysterious girlfriend Marlee. . . . The details of jury selection are fascinating." Publ Wkly

The street lawyer. Doubleday 1998 348p $27.95
ISBN 0-385-49099-2 LC 97-47484

"Michael Brock, a slick antitrust lawyer in a blue-chip Washington legal factory, experiences a profound shock when he and other lawyers are held hostage by a deranged man with a legitimate beef—and a gun. Reordering his values, Michael leaves his high-pressure job and sterile marriage to become an advocate for the homeless. In his zeal for his new mission . . . he also steals a file and tries to sue his old firm on behalf of the people they illegally evicted from a valuable piece of real estate." NY Times Book Rev

"The cat-and-mouse between Michael and the firm is vintage Grisham, intricately plotted, but the emphasis in this smoothly told, baldly manipulative tale is less on action and suspense, which are moderate, than on Michael's change of heart and moving exploration of the world of the homeless." Publ Wkly

The summons. Doubleday 2002 341p $27.95
ISBN 0-385-50382-2 LC 2001-58185

Ray Atlee, a 43-year-old law professor in Virginia is summoned to his family's home in Mississippi by his dying father, a respected judge. Following his father's death Ray discovers over $3 million in cash in the study

This Summons "is a swift, no-nonsense story written in a highly effective, uncluttered fashion. . . . Mr. Grisham seems genuinely interested in the questions of conscience that snare Ray, and he makes them matter." N Y Times Book Rev

The testament. Doubleday 1998 435p $30
ISBN 0-385-49380-0 LC 99-186246

Grisham, John—*Continued*

This novel "begins with the suicide of billionaire Troy Phelan, . . . who cuts his legitimate heirs out of his will and leaves his $11 billon to his illegitimate daughter, Rachel Lane, a missionary in Brazil. . . . [Nate Reilly's] firm dispatches him to the Brazilian back country to track down the heiress. . . . The physical journey turns into a spiritual quest for Nate midway through the novel." Newsweek

"Nate's search for redemption, which might have become hokey, is quite convincing. The big question—what will Rachel do upon learning she has inherited $11 billion—is nicely resolved." N Y Times Book Rev

A time to kill. Doubleday 1993 487p $30
ISBN 0-385-47081-9 LC 93-32545

A reissue of the title first published 1989 by Wynwood Press

In this novel, set in rural Mississippi, local criminal lawyer Jake Brigance defends a black man on trial for murdering the men who raped his daughter

Grøndahl, Jens Christian, 1959-

Lucca; translated from the Danish by Anne Born. Harcourt 2003 c2002 332p $26
ISBN 0-15-100594-X LC 2002-154301

Original Danish edition, 1998

"The title character is an actress who has renounced her career (for love) and then blinded herself in a drunken car crash after being dumped by her husband. Her doctor has become an emotional recluse since, or possibly before, being dumped by his wife. Over the course of many pages we get their back stories." N Y Times Book Rev

The author "proves himself to be master of the poetry of small moments that can lead to shattering discoveries." Libr J

Groom, Winston, 1944-

Such a pretty, pretty girl; a novel. Random House 1999 306p o.p.
ISBN 0-375-50161-4 LC 98-23263

"When Johnny Lightfoot, an Academy Award-winning screenwriter, runs into old flame Delia Jamison, now a successful Los Angeles TV anchorwoman, she tells him that she is being blackmailed by one of the many lovers she had dumped over the years. Still attracted to the seductive Delia despite his painful experience, Johnny offers to investigate. As he tracks down the men involved, Johnny learns more about Delia than he ever wanted to know." Libr J

Gross, Claudia

Scholarium; Claudia Gross. Toby Press 2004 400p $19.95
ISBN 1-592-64056-7

"The scene is set with a pervasive cloud of impending evil hovering over the Cologne Scholarium. Master Casall's murderer sends perplexing riddles to the frustrated and suspicious faculty. Casall's widow and select students disappear, the prior stirs potions in a shack, and Master Lombardi hides a guilty secret. In the midst of the debate surrounding the murder, brilliantly timed accusations of witchcraft and sorcery emerge, and rumors fly about pagan sex rites on crumbling altars. . . . Gross weaves a fascinating tapestry depicting the birth of the schism between church and state and showing how the search for truth becomes a life-and-death quest for a group of determined scholars." Booklist

Gross, Joel

The books of Rachel. Seaview Bks. 1979 440p o.p.
LC 79-4879

"The story follows a family of Jewish diamond merchants through six centuries, connecting its history by two threads: a fabulous diamond and the first-born female child in each generation. The child is always named Rachel, and the diamond becomes both symbol and talisman in each Rachel's personal drama, demanding and absorbing her heroisms, sacrifices, loves and even weaknesses." Best Sellers

"In tracing the fortunes of the family in all parts of the world, Gross exhibits thorough research into the social conditions of each country and period and considerable knowledge of the diamond industry. If the novel is floridly written, full of ponderous foreshadowings and mystical intuitions, it is also imaginative; the plot moves fast and the characters are vivid enough to keep readers involved." Publ Wkly

Prequel The lives of Rachel (1984)

Grossman, David

Be my knife; translated by Vered Almog and Maya Gurantz. Farrar, Straus & Giroux 2002 307p o.p.
ISBN 0-374-29977-3 LC 2001-33645

Original Hebrew edition, 1998

"When a thirty-three-year-old man named Yair catches a glimpse of Miriam at a class reunion, he senses a bond with her that goes beyond sexual attraction; because he is a practiced philanderer who is in search of something extraordinary, he implores her to enter a ruthlessly honest correspondence with him, on the understanding that they will never meet. . . . Most of the book is devoted to Yair's letters, and so we don't get to hear Miriam's responses until near the end. But it is Grossman's achievement that we understand from the start that Yair's vision of Miriam (and thus ours) is almost painfully incomplete." New Yorker

Someone to run with; translated by Vered Almog and Maya Gurantz. Farrar, Straus and Giroux 2004 343p $24
ISBN 0-374-26657-3 LC 2002-29778

Original Hebrew edition, 2000

In Jerusalem, teenage Assaf "a shy misfit, embarks upon a quixotic journey with a lost dog to find its mistress. Tamar, a caustic fifteen-year-old who can sing Mozart and Leonard Cohen on demand, runs away from home to find the criminals who have ensnared her older brother. A young street musician, in the grip of a heroin habit as formidable as his talent, stumbles through his routines with death close behind. The resulting picaresque is a cross between 'Run Lola Run' and 'Oliver Twist,' and as the reader waits for these solitary odysseys to intersect, the urgency becomes almost unbearable.

Grossman, David—*Continued*

Grossman evokes teenage nobility and self-hatred in all its pimply particularity, while slyly suggesting that the arduous quest for connections should never be outgrown." New Yorker

Gruber, Michael

Valley of bones. William Morrow 2005 436p $24.95

ISBN 0-06-057766-5

"When a Sudanese oil baron is thrown to his death from his hotel balcony, Miami detective Jimmy Paz finds a mysterious woman named Emmylou Dideroff vehemently praying at the scene of the crime; she quickly becomes the main suspect. The plot immediately thickens as Emmylou begins to write a lengthy confession about her disturbing childhood, how she reformed from a criminal to a woman of God, and what led her to the Miami hotel room that day. Is she crazy or does God really speak to her? Jimmy and criminal psychologist Lorna Wise investigate and are thrown into a whirlwind journey involving prostitution, white supremacists, the Sudanese civil war, and massive government cover-ups." Libr J

The author is "at least as eager to fathom the violent and the unknown as he is to exploit these things. Some books simply relish the darker sides of human nature. Mr. Gruber summons them with troubled inquisitiveness, with both brio and regret." N Y Times (Late N Y Ed)

Grumbach, Doris

The book of knowledge; a novel. Norton 1995 248p o.p.

LC 94-37901

This novel "follows the lives of four friends, each of whom departs from the sexual mores of the day in some way (homosexuality, incest, willful celibacy), from the summer of 1929—when, as prepubescent children, they first meet in an East Coast seaside town—through World War II and beyond." Libr J

"Grumbach's latest novel is grimly compelling in its portrayal of four lives filled with stifled desires, major depression, incest, self-sacrifice, and thwarted love. . . . Grumbach paints a glowing picture of warmth, security, and safety that is shattered by the Great Depression." Booklist

Chamber music. Dutton 1979 213p o.p.

LC 78-13033

"A Henry Robbins book"

"Caroline Newby Maclaren [is] the 90-year-old narrator of Chamber Music. Widow of an American composer who died in his 30's, Caroline has been requested (by a foundation established in her husband's memory) to leave a record of their life together. While they appeared happily married for 13 years, their 'secret lives' differed radically from their public image. Dominated by his mother, Robert was a homosexual who expended no feelings within his marriage. Caroline's only love affair was with Anna, Robert's nurse during his terminal illness." Libr J

"This is an elegant novel. Its style . . . combines clarity with a formal reserve that underplays a nudging eroticism." Newsweek

Guest, Judith

Killing time in St. Cloud; by Judith Guest & Rebecca Hill. Delacorte Press 1988 300p o.p.

LC 88-15068

"When charming psychopath Nick Uhler returns to his hometown of St. Cloud after a 12-year absence, he precipitates a series of deaths and initiates an irrevocable process in which old, unsavory secrets are revealed. Ruthlessly manipulating his former high school lover, Elizabeth, now married to surgeon Simon Carmody and in her ninth month of pregnancy, drug dealer Nick generates tragic tensions among three oldtime St. Cloud families." Publ Wkly

Ordinary people. Viking 1976 263p o.p.

"When his older brother drowns in a boating accident, seventeen-year-old Conrad Jarrett feels responsible and makes an unsuccessful attempt at suicide. After eight months in a mental institution, Conrad returns home to parents whose marriage is crumbling, friends who are wary of him, and a psychiatrist who works with him to help put the pieces together. The pain of adolescent anxiety and fragile family relationships are authentically depicted." Shapiro. Fic for Youth. 3d edition

The tarnished eye; Judith Guest. Scribner 2004 267p $24

ISBN 0-7432-5736-7 LC 2004-42999

"An entire family has been murdered in their summer cabin in northern Michigan, and the local sheriff faces a staggering uphill struggle in attempting to find an explanation. Guest carefully insinuates the reader into the lives of all the people involved in the case-not only the victims and the sheriff but also relevant townspeople and obvious and not-so-apparent suspects. At a fast but methodical pace, she follows the story of the crime's ramifications and draws a connection to a simultaneous series of coed murders in Ann Arbor. The gathering momentum is irresistible." Booklist

Guilfoile, Kevin, 1968-

Cast of shadows; by Kevin Guilfoile. Knopf 2005 319p $24.95; pa $13.95

ISBN 1-400-04308-5; 1-400-07826-1 (pa)

LC 2004-48983

"The time is the distant future, and human cloning has become legal. When the daughter of noted fertility doctor Davis Moore is brutally raped and murdered he uses a vial of DNA to clone the killer so that he can uncover the reasoning behind the gruesome crime. With both his marriage and his career in ruins, Davis faces the chilling prospect of eventually looking his daughter's killer in the eye. In logical yet compelling fashion, the novel takes on themes of good and evil, past lives, and scientific cloning in an intricately woven story." Libr J

Gulik, Robert Hans van, 1910-1967

The Chinese bell murders; three cases solved by Judge Dee; a Chinese detective story suggested by three original Chinese plots; with 15 plates drawn by the author in Chinese style. Harper 1959 c1958 262p il o.p.

First published 1958 in the United Kingdom

Judge Dee, a legendary magistrate and detective, who is based on a real 7th century Chinese person and was

Gulik, Robert Hans van, 1910-1967—*Continued*
the subject of Chinese detective tales during the 17th and 18th centuries, made his American debut in this murder-rape case. The judge solves three interwoven crimes in the provincial city of Pooyang. A postscript provides information on ancient Chinese detection and court procedure and on the Chinese sources of the story

The haunted monastery; a Chinese detective story; [by] Robert van Gulik; with eight illustrations drawn by the author in Chinese style. Scribner 1969 159p il o.p.

First published 1961 in Malaysia; first United States edition published 1963 in paperback

This mystery "finds Judge Dee and his family and retainers stranded because of a broken axle and a howling storm. He has to spend the night solving three murders and a problem of impersonation before he can proceed on his journey the following day." Ency of Mystery & Detection

The lacquer screen; a Chinese detective story; [by] Robert van Gulik; with ten illustrations drawn by the author in Chinese style. Scribner 1970 180p il o.p.

First published 1962 in Malaysia; first United States edition published 1963 in paperback

This tale is set in 7th century China. Magistrate detective Judge Dee and his lieutenant join the underworld in a district under the Judge's jurisdiction in order to solve three crimes. They share the life of the gangster-boss and his entourage while the underworld people unwittingly help them in their inquiries. The Judge eventually reveals the ugly secret hidden by the panels of a beautiful lacquer screen

The Red Pavilion; a Chinese detective story; [by] Robert van Gulik; with six illustrations drawn by the author in Chinese style. Scribner 1968 173p il o.p.

First published 1961 in Malaysia

Judge Dee, "solves more than one knotty criminal problem, all of them stemming out of the fact that he elects to stay in the infamous Red Pavilion on Paradise Island, not knowing it has been the scene of several mysterious deaths in the past. The Chinese atmosphere is suitably exotic and there is a lovely, mistreated courtesan for the judge to protect." Publ Wkly

The willow pattern; a Chinese detective story; by Robert van Gulik; with fifteen illustrations drawn by the author in Chinese style. Scribner 1965 183p il o.p.

"This adventure of the legendary Judge Dee, of Seventh Century China, is a strange, brooding tale of crime, cholera, and corruption. . . . The emperor and his court have fled the plague-ridden city and left the judge and his Colonels, Ma Joong and Chiao Tai, in charge of affairs. They quickly become involved in three murders: 'The Case of the Willow Pattern', 'The Case of the Steep Stairs', and 'The Case of the Murdered Bond-Maid.'" Libr J

Gunesekera, Romesh

Heaven's edge. Grove Press 2002 234p $24
ISBN 0-8021-1735-X LC 2002-35335

"Set on an environmentally devastated tropical island . . . (this) novel follows a Londoner named Marc, who comes to the island to find his father but instead gets caught up in a passionate affair with an ecological activist." Publ Wkly

"Lurking within the story of Marc's exile is, of course, an allegory about the human condition. 'Heaven's Edge' is a somewhat self-conscious reworking of the Edenic myth, but what gives the novel its power is an awareness of the irredeemability of that condition." N Y Times Book Rev

Gurganus, Allan

Blessed assurance: a moral tale
In Gurganus, A. White people p192-252

He's one, too
In Gurganus, A. The practical heart

A hog loves its life: something about my grandfather
In Gurganus, A. White people p139-80

The oldest living Confederate widow tells all. Knopf 1989 718p o.p.
ISBN 0-394-54537-0 LC 88-45870

"Ninety-nine year old Lucille Marsden, confined to a charity nursing home in North Carolina, is an American cousin of Joyce's Anna Livia Plurabelle. Lucy tells the story of her marriage to 'Captain' Will Marsden, ostensibly the Civil War's last survivor, whom she married when she was 15 and he was more than triple her age. She also tells about her husband's experiences in the war and after, the burning of her mother-in-law's plantation by Sherman's men, and the abduction from Africa of a former Marsden slave, midwife to Lucy's nine children as well as her best friend. But this novel is less about the War Between the States than about the war between the sexes." Libr J

"In a way, 'Oldest Living Confederate Widow Tells All' is as much about language and myth-making as it is about love and war. Whether one feels that it succeeds depends on how much leeway one is willing to give to this indomitable 'veteran of the veteran,' as Lucy describes herself." N Y Times Book Rev

The practical heart; four novellas. Knopf 2001 322p $25
ISBN 0-679-43763-0 LC 2001-32665

"In 'The Practical Heart,' the narrator recalls the proclivities of his great-aunt, daughter of a Scottish immigrant to Chicago. . . . 'Preservation News' is a fey portrait of a man who has just lost his battle with AIDS but who spent his last breath in the pursuit of the preservation of historic properties. . . . 'He's One, Too' offers an ironically sympathetic portrayal of a married man arrested for lewd acts with a younger man. And in the longest and most moving piece, 'Saint Monster,' a son remembers how the relationship between his ugly but kind father and his beautiful but faithless mother forced him into prematurely dealing with the rawer aspects of adulthood." Booklist

The practical heart [novelette]
In Gurganus, A. The practical heart

Preservation news
In Gurganus, A. The practical heart

Gurganus, Allan—*Continued*

Saint monster
In Gurganus, A. The practical heart

White people. Knopf 1991 c1990 252p o.p.
ISBN 0-394-58841-X LC 90-52943

Contents: Minor heroism: something about my father; Condolences to every one of us; Art history; Nativity, Caucasian; Breathing room: something about my brother; America competes; Adult art; It had wings; A hog loves its life: something about my grandfather {novella}; Reassurance; Blessed assurance: a moral tale {novella}

The novella A hog loves its life concerns a grandfather and his boyish grandson, the other novella Blessed assurance: a moral tale "is a funny, sad, confessional tale told by a man reflecting on his traumatic youth, when he collected funeral insurance premiums from poor blacks. Gurganus is a champion storyteller with particularly American roots, in the tradition of Mark Twain. This is a collection to be savored and reread." Publ Wkly

Gutcheon, Beth Richardson

Five fortunes; a novel; {by} Beth Gutcheon. Cliff St. Bks. 1998 398p o.p.
ISBN 0-06-017679-2 LC 97-48926

This is the "story of friendship and support among a group of five women who first meet on a week-long retreat at a health spa in Arizona. . . . During the following year, these strong, independent, and ambitious women face enormous challenges that bring them even closer: private detective Carter quits smoking and takes on drug dealers in L.A., the still vibrant Rae must face her husband's decline from Alzheimer's disease; Amy and her daughter, Jill, resolve old issues; and the recently widowed Laura declares her candidacy for the U.S. Senate." Booklist

More than you know; a novel; {by} Beth Gutcheon. Morrow 2000 269p o.p.
ISBN 0-688-17403-5 LC 99-45936

The novel opens "with an old woman named Hannah reminiscing about her youthful fling in the isolated, picturesque Maine coastal village of Dundee. . . . Hannah's romance is interwoven with a deadly love story, set 100 years earlier, that will in turn mysteriously haunt her. . . . The taut facility with which Gutcheon twines the two stories creates real suspense—both in the exact fates of the couples and the identity of the ghost, who grows viciously vengeful. While Gutcheon cannily evokes the ephemerality of passion, she also evinces, with stark and elemental resonance, the way love and hatred shape lives." N Y Times Book Rev

Saying grace; a novel; [by] Beth Gutcheon. HarperCollins Pubs. 1995 312p o.p.
LC 95-8677

"Rue Shaw is a wife, mother, and the dedicated headmistress of an elite California country day school. . . . When her daughter Georgia elects to drop out of Juilliard in favor of love and heavy metal, she sets off a chain of events that dramatically alters the lives of Rue, her husband, and her beloved school." Libr J

"As it follows Rue's trials, 'Saying Grace' provides a realistic portrait of both a good school and its gifted leader. Ms. Gutcheon knows private schools, and she knows her craft—and that's a winning combination." NY Times Book Rev

Guterson, David

East of the mountains. Harcourt Brace & Co. 1999 288p $25
ISBN 0-15-100229-0 LC 98-40512

This is the "story of one Ben Givens, a retired Seattle heart surgeon and widower who is dying of colon cancer. As the novel opens, Ben arises, depressed, after a sleepless night. . . . Ben is so depressed that he has decided to kill himself, and he wants to make it appear accidental; he will die while bird hunting in the dry eastern Washington canyons of his youth. With a surgeon's meticulousness, he sets out early with his dogs in his Scout and a cup of steaming lemon tea in hand." N Y Times Book Rev

"Guterson draws compelling characters and creates a haunting sense of place and of humankind's paradoxical relationship with the natural world." Libr J

Our Lady of the Forest. Knopf 2003 323p $25.95
ISBN 0-375-41211-5 LC 2002-43322

"When Ann Holmes starts having visions of the Virgin Mary, the bedraggled teen runaway becomes the last hope for the inhabitants of a dank, economically depressed logging town and the hordes of miracle-seekers who descend on it. In this panoramic, psychologically dense novel, she also becomes a symbol of the intimate intertwining of the sacred and the profane in American life." Publ Wkly

Snow falling on cedars. Harcourt Brace & Co. 1994 345p $20
ISBN 0-15-100443-9 LC 94-7535

"Japanese American Kabuo Miyomoto is arrested in 1954 for the murder of a fellow fisherman, Carl Heine. Miyomoto's trial, which provides a focal point to the novel, stirs memories of past relationships and events in the minds and hearts of the San Piedro Islanders. Through these memories, Guterson illuminates the grief of loss, the sting of prejudice triggered by World War II, and the imperatives of conscience. With mesmerizing clarity he conveys the voices of Kabuo's wife, Hatsue, and Ishmael Chambers, Hatsue's first love who, having suffered the loss of her love and the ravages of war, ages into a cynical journalist now covering Kabuo's trial." Libr J

Guthrie, A. B. (Alfred Bertram), 1901-1991

Arfive; [by] A. B. Guthrie, Jr. Houghton Mifflin 1971 c1970 278p o.p.

Another title in the author's loosely connected series of Western novels which began with The big sky

This novel is set in a small town in Montana at the beginning of the twentieth century. "Benton Collingsworth, the recently hired principal of the new town high school, arrives in Arfive by train and stagecoach with his wife and two children from Indiana. His eastern, disciplined determination mixed with Victorianism is met head-on by the loose attitude of the untamed West. This is not a 'western story' of all-conquering heroes and evil hombres quick on the draw. The characters are grey mixtures of virtue and vice from Benton's patient wife, May, to the hardbitten town prostitute, Eva Fox; from the realistic rancher, Mort Ewing, to the sadistic deputy sheriff Sarge

Guthrie, A. B. (Alfred Bertram), 1901-1991— *Continued*

Kraker. Benton is a non-hero in whom, taken together with the townsfolk, the reader can see the type that really built the West." Best Sellers

The big sky; [by] A. B. Guthrie, Jr. Sloane 1947 386p o.p.

"After a quarrel and fight with his father, 17-year old Boone Caudill leaves his home in Kentucky headed for St. Louis and the west, where he hopes to hunt buffalo and shoot Indians. The story follows his adventurous course, by foot and horseback, to the Mississippi, then by keel boat to the land of the big sky at the headwaters of the Missouri, where for 13 years he leads the typical life of a mountain man for his period and in that short times sees the Indian degraded, the game killed off and the life he loved destroyed." Wis Libr Bull

Fair land, fair land; [by] A. B. Guthrie, Jr. Houghton Mifflin 1982 262p o.p.

LC 82-3055

"Chronologically, this novel follows 'The Way West' and covers the years 1845 to 1870, relating the adventures of Dick Summers. At age 49, Summers . . . starts to explore some unspoiled areas of Montana. In the Bitter Root country, he marries a Blackfoot squaw and devotes his life to hunting and trapping. When gold fever hits the West, Dick goes to Wyoming and makes a living selling fresh meat to the miners. As he approaches 70, he finds game becoming scarce and the crowds of new settlers making life unpleasant; so he settles down with his wife's people and watches as tragic changes come to his world." Publ Wkly

The last valley; [by] A. B. Guthrie, Jr. Houghton Mifflin 1975 293p o.p.

"Covering the mid-20s to the mid-1940s, [this novel] is set in the same locale and has some of the same characters as the previous novel, 'Arfive'. It centers on an ex-military man, Ben Tate, who buys the mediocre local weekly and transforms it into a respected, profitable business. It is typical Guthrie fare in its graphic descriptions of the Western countryside, its rendering of the powers of nature exemplified in winds and floods, its gallery of small-town, sometimes eccentric characters, and its frank dramatizations of man's psychosexual needs. But 'The last valley' is more insistently political than the others in that the small town becomes the microcosm of our contemporary problems: freedom of the press, the influence of large corporations, appropriate and inappropriate modes of patriotism, the need for progress versus the demands of ecology." Choice

These thousand hills. Houghton Mifflin 1956 346p o.p.

Lat Evans, son of characters in The Way West, leaves his home in Oregon to help drive a herd of cattle to Montana. There he decides to stay and get a ranch of his own. His adventures, his love for the parlor house girl Callie, and his marriage to respectable Joyce, make a novel more conventional than the author's previous successes

The way West. Sloane 1949 340p o.p.

A story of an emigrant trek from Independence, Missouri, to Oregon in the 1840s. Dick Summers, one of the principal characters of the author's earlier novel, 'The Big Sky' reappears in this novel

"Where most writers of Western fiction concentrate on what their characters do, Mr. Guthrie concentrates on how they think and feel. It is this emphasis which gives his book depth and sense of reality." Christ Sci Monit

Guthrie, Alfred Bertram *See* Guthrie, A. B. (Alfred Bertram), 1901-1991

H

Ha Jin, 1956-

The bridegroom; stories. Pantheon Bks. 2000 225p o.p.

ISBN 0-375-42067-3 LC 00-28405

Contents: Saboteur; Alive; In the kindergarten; A tiger-fighter is hard to find; Broken; The bridegroom; An entrepreneur's story; Flame; A bad joke; An official reply; The woman from New York; After Cowboy Chicken came to town

"In this dazzling collection of stories, set in provincial China in the fairly recent past, most of the protagonists are emerging from the numbing predictability of totalitarianism, realizing that they must abandon the passivity that has insured their survival in the past." New Yorker

The crazed. Pantheon Bks. 2002 323p o.p.

ISBN 0-375-42181-5 LC 2002-22427

This novel is "set in 1989 China in the wake of the Tiananmen Square massacre. As Jian Wan sits by the bedside of his professor and future father-in-law, who has been felled by a stroke, he begins to discover peculiar yet arresting secrets about the professor's past. The seemingly delirious Yang is given to outbursts of shouting, singing, and talking to individuals who are not there. Scared but intrigued, Jian decides to delve deeper into the catalyst for Yang's mysterious behavior." Libr J

"Writing with a searing restraint born of long-brewing grief over the Chinese government's surreal savageness, Ha Jin depicts a warped society in which everyone is driven mad by viciousness and injustice. But Ha Jin's dramatic indictment does not preclude love, or the ancient power of story to memorialize, awaken compassion, and shore up hope." Booklist

In the pond; a novel. Zoland Bks. 1998 176p o.p.

ISBN 0-944072-92-5 LC 98-33493

"When Shao Bin, in post-Cultural Revolution China, is not among the chosen few for new housing, his wife berates him for not bribing the powers that be. Instead, Bin, a factory worker with a talent for cartooning, takes aim against the bosses' corruption and gets his cartoons published. Not surprisingly, the clownishly wicked bosses maintain an arsenal for zapping such gnats, and it seems that the war can have only the grimmest conclusion. But the author is as resourceful as his hero, and the simplicity of the narrative proves deceptive." New Yorker

Waiting. Pantheon Bks. 1999 308p $24

ISBN 0-375-40653-0 LC 99-21334

Ha Jin, 1956—*Continued*

This novel focuses on Ling Kong, a Chinese "military doctor who agrees, as his mother is dying, to an arranged marriage. His bride, Shuyu, turns out to be a country woman who looks far older than her 26 years and who has, to Lin's great embarrassment, lotus (bound) feet. While Shuyu remains at Lin's family home in Goose Village, nursing first his mother and then his ailing father, and bearing Lin a daughter, Lin lives far away in an army hospital compound, visiting only once a year. Caught in a loveless marriage, Lin is attacted to a nurse, Manna Wu, an attachment forbidden by communist strictures." Publ Wkly

This novel "provides a dual education: a crash course in Chinese society during and since the Cultural Revolution, and more leisurely but nonetheless compelling exploration of the less exotic terrain that is the human heart." N Y Times Book Rev

War trash; Ha Jin. Pantheon Books 2004 352p $25

ISBN 0-375-42276-5 LC 2004-43428

This is a "fictional memoir of a Chinese People's Volunteer, dispatched by his government to fight for the Communist cause in the Korean War. Yu Yuan describes his ordeal after capture, when P.O.W.s in the prison camp have to make a wrenching choice: return to the mainland as disgraced captives, or leave their families and begin new lives in Taiwan." New Yorker

"Written in the modest, uninflected prose of a soldier's letter home, Ha Jin's story, a mixture of authentic historical detail and realistic invention, is a powerful work of the imagination whose psychic territory is not the hunger and humiliation of the prison camp but the haunted past that was the old, lost China and the mysterious future that is in the process of becoming Mao Zedong's chimerical new China." Washington Post

Haasse, Hella S., 1918-

In a dark wood wandering; revised and edited by Anita Miller from an English translation from the Dutch by Lewis C. Kaplan. Academy Chicago 1989 574p o.p.

ISBN 0-89733-336-5 LC 89-17814

Original Dutch edition, 1949

This "book, whose action is set against the background of the Hundred Years War, deals with the internecine feuds among the French aristocracy and, in particular, with the life of the poet Charles d'Orléans, nephew of King Charles VI. When his father, the Duke of Orléans, is murdered by agents of Orléans's rival, Jean of Burgundy in 1407, the young, sensitive Charles promises his brokenhearted mother to avenge the deed. But Charles assumes his duties reluctantly; among these are his new conjugal responsibilities to an older cousin who soon dies in childbirth. He then allows himself to be married off to the daughter of Bernard d'Armagnac. . . . In this unlikely marriage Charles finds true love, but his happiness is short-lived. Captured in battle, he spends the bulk of his adult life as a prisoner in England, where he pens his famous poems of love and longing for his wife and homeland." N Y Times Book Rev

"This novel exemplifies historical fiction at its best; the author's meticulous research and polished style bring the medieval world into vibrant focus." Libr J

Haddam, Jane, 1951-

Bleeding hearts. Bantam Bks. 1994 311p il o.p.

LC 93-14466

This mystery "focuses on Valentine's Day as it's celebrated on Philadelphia's Cavanaugh Street, home to retired FBI agent Demarkian and a host of fellow Armenian immigrants. Everyone in the neighborhood is surprised when homely Hanna Krekorian turns up with a new man in her life, but Demarkian is especially shocked when he finds that Hanna's friend is none other than Paul Hazzard, who was once suspected of violently murdering his wife. Hazzard may have some kind of twisted motive for courting Hanna—but what?" Booklist

"Never quite cozy and never quite tough, this tale combines the best of both styles to stunning effect." Publ Wkly

Somebody else's music. St. Martin's Minotaur 2002 328p $24.95

ISBN 0-312-27186-7 LC 2001-58899

"A famous woman writer with a rock-star lover returns to the hometown where as a nerdy teenager she was traumatized by a nearby, still unsolved murder. The rock star asks FBI Behavioral Sciences Unit chief Gregor Demarkian. . . to solve this case—and more." Libr J

"Haddam movingly explores what that means for our lives—past, present and future—and how that happens and why." Publ Wkly

True believers. St. Martin's Press 2001 328p o.p.

ISBN 0-312-20929-0 LC 00-51794

"Retired FBI agent Gregor Demarkian . . . investigates an unusual apparent murder/suicide in a Philadelphia church, for which police blame the husband. A nun believes otherwise, however, and so the plot thickens." Libr J

"Haddam's large cast pulses with petty jealousies, vanities and fears as they confront the mysteries of life and religion. This is an engrossingly complex mystery that should win further acclaim for its prolific and talented author." Publ Wkly

Haddon, Mark

The curious incident of the dog in the night-time; a novel. Doubleday 2003 226p il $22.95

ISBN 0-385-50945-6 LC 2002-31355

Despite his overwhelming fear of interacting with people, Christopher, a mathematically-gifted, autistic fifteen-year-old boy, decides to investigate the murder of a neighbor's dog and uncovers secret information about his mother

"Unable to feel emotions himself, his story evokes emotions in readers—heartache and frustration for his well-meaning but clueless parents and deep empathy for the wonderfully honest, funny, and lovable protagonist. Readers will never view the behavior of an autistic person again without more compassion and understanding." SLJ

Hagen, George

The Laments; a novel. Random House 2004 370p $24.95

ISBN 1-400-06221-7 LC 2003-66882

Hagen, George—*Continued*

This novel "follows the lives of the Laments, a white South African family in the late 20th century. Howard is an engineer who marries the energetic and artistic Julia. In a twist of events, the Laments adopt Will, just delivered by a mother who has abducted their biological infant and is then tragically killed with the abducted child in an automobile accident. A few years later, Will's twin brothers, Marcus and Julius, are born as the Laments begin their nomadic flights from Rhodesia to the Persian Gulf, England, and, finally, the United States." Libr J

The author "has shaped an affectionate family portrait in which the characters come vividly to life, no matter how adrift they may be. The Lament parents are especially memorable, Julia for her sense of lost opportunity and Howard for his gradual way of losing heart. . . . Each of them sees new opportunity eternally on the horizon in ways that have the potential to make this a story of crushing disappointment. But Mr. Hagen somehow endows it with brightness and finds a universality here, too." N Y Times (Late N Y Ed)

Hager, Jean

The spirit caller. Mysterious Press 1997 257p o.p.

LC 96-42033

"Molly Bearpaw, major crimes investigator for the Cherokee nation, is drawn into the murder of her assistant's aunt, killed while trying to put a ghost to rest in the Tahlequah Native American Research Library." Libr J

"Hager offers readers a clever, well-written mystery that also provides an intimate and edifying look at Native Americans' beliefs, traditions, and lifestyle." Booklist

Haggard, H. Rider (Henry Rider), 1856-1925

King Solomon's mines; introduction by Alexandra Fuller; illustrations by Walter Paget; notes by James Danly. Modern Library 2002 xxv, 264p il pa $9.95

ISBN 0-8129-6629-5 LC 2002-29519

First published 1885

"Highly coloured romance of adventure in the wilds of Central Africa in quest of King Solomon's Ophir; full of sensational fights, bloodcurdling perils and extraordinary escapes." Baker. Guide to the Best Fic

She; edited with an introduction and notes by Daniel Karlin. Oxford University Press 1998 xxxviii, 332p pa $9.95

ISBN 0-19-283550-5

First published 1885

"'She,' or Ayesha, is an African sorceress whom death apparently cannot touch. The young English hero, Leo Vincey, sets out to avenge the murder of his ancestor, an ancient priest of Isis. The setting of this weird romance is an extinct volcano." Univ Handbk for Readers and Writers

Haggard, Henry Rider *See* Haggard, H. Rider (Henry Rider), 1856-1925

Haigh, Jennifer, 1968-

Baker towers; a novel. William Morrow 2005 334p $24.95

ISBN 0-06-050941-4 LC 2004-49073

This novel is "set in Bakerton, a mining town in post-World World II Pennsylvania. Haigh's focus is the Novak family, particularly the five children being raised by their Italian mother after their Polish father drops dead. All five make attempts to escape Bakerton at one point or another; some are successful, others are not. George, a veteran of WW II, neglects his Bakerton fiancee and marries a cold socialite. Dorothy goes to the nation's capital to work, but a nervous breakdown brings her home. Brilliant, cold Joyce thinks her future lies with the military, but she is sorely disappointed. Sandy is the golden son who escapes to dubious success. And Lucy is the youngest, who finds herself in college despite the nagging feeling that she never wanted to leave home in the first place. Haigh creates a real sense of a community and brings her mining town to life through a large cast of minor characters who pass in and out of the Novaks' lives." Booklist

Mrs. Kimble. Morrow 2003 394p $24.95

ISBN 0-06-050939-2 LC 2002-70304

The title "refers to three women, each of whom marries an opportunist named Ken Kimble. The first wife, Birdie, is Ken's student at a small Christian college. With her, he has two children. Then he seduces another student and deserts his family, leaving Birdie to bring up the children alone. The second Mrs. Kimble is a successful career woman, reassessing her priorities in the wake of her mastectomy. Ken capitalizes on Joan's neediness and sweeps her off her feet. He also ingratiates himself with her uncle, a real estate tycoon. When Joan and Uncle Floyd die, Ken inherits from both. The third Mrs. Kimble had been the first Mrs. Kimble's babysitter. . . . Original and compelling." Libr J

Hailey, Arthur

Airport. Doubleday 1968 440p o.p.

"In the space of a single night at the . . . Lincoln International Airport nearly every imaginable man, machine or function goes wrong. One of the worst snowstorms in history has been raging over the airport for three days. The longest and widest runway is blocked by a mired Boeing 707. A traffic controller is suicidally depressed. And a Rome-bound flight lifts off with a man carrying a bomb in his briefcase. How Airport Manager Mel Bakersfield and a score of other characters cope provides the [plot of this novel]." Time

"Here are many minor conflicts—of love, sex, business, and psychological problems—all building up to the tremendously exciting scenes of a shattered transoceanic plane trying to make its way back to the airport, and a runway that can't, but must, be cleared." Publ Wkly

Detective; a novel. Crown 1997 400p o.p.

LC 97-1204

The novel's "setting is the Miami Police Department, where Detective Sgt. Malcolm Ainslee, a former priest, hears the final confession of a killer he put on death row. Although Elroy Doil was tried for one horrible double murder, he's suspected of committing as many as seven others. His confession re-opens one of these cases, and

Hailey, Arthur—*Continued*

Ainslee is soon following leads into powerful political circles." N Y Times Book Rev

"It's a measure of Hailey's skill as a storyteller that he gives up the killer way before the end but still manages to maintain the suspense." Publ Wkly

Hotel. Doubleday 1965 376p o.p.

This novel reveals the inner workings of a large hotel during a hectic week. "Among the many events, the hotel changes ownership, royalty staying at the hotel are involved in hit-and-run deaths, there is an attempted rape, there is a racial incident, and a thief makes off with sizable loot. This is also the story of Peter McDermott. As an honest and intelligent assistant general manager of the St. Gregory Hotel, he thinks quickly and effectively in handling the many problems that beset this gracious old hotel in New Orleans. Yet his personal record is blemished by a single event which may keep him from rising higher in hotel echelons." Libr J

Strong medicine. Doubleday 1984 448p o.p.
LC 84-8019

This novel deals with "the controversial workings of the drug industry. Threaded into the brisk, clean lines of the story of Celia de Grey's rise to the top of a male-dominated, ultraconservative firm, Felding-Roth Pharmaceuticals, are numerous allusions to real-life events and issues, which make for a biting indictment of alarming medical and pharmaceutical practices. Celia seeks to change her firm's unethical and sometimes life-threatening eye-to-the-profit habits. Meanwhile, her husband, Dr. Andrew Jordan, fights his own battle for reform when he learns that his senior partner is a drug addict who, protected by his knowing colleagues, dangerously continues to practice medicine. While achieving their own ambitious goals, these two main characters also learn to compromise without losing their idealism. An inventive and remarkably insightful work." Booklist

Hailey, Elizabeth Forsythe, 1938-

A woman of independent means. Viking 1978 256p o.p.
LC 77-28414

This novel consists of letters tracing Bess Steed Garner's "life from childhood to old age, from the tranquility of Honey Grove, Texas, at the turn of the century to the turbulence of the late sixties. . . . Bess shares her triumphs and follies in love and marriage, in childbearing and child rearing, in travel, business, society." Publisher's note

The author "has succeeded in giving us a portrait of a woman, with all her frailties, strengths, failures and victories combining to prove that living a life is an accomplishment." Christ Sci Monit

Haldeman, Joe W., 1943-

The coming; {by} Joe Haldeman. Ace Bks. 2000 216p o.p.
ISBN 0-441-00769-4 LC 00-29306

"On 1 October 2054, astronomy professor Rory Bell receives a message, 'We're coming,' from an Earthbound object way out in space that will arrive on New Year's Day. Soon Rory, her composer husband, her chief faculty protege, the university president, a mob shakedown artist, a Gainesville cop, the mayor, the governor of Florida, and, finally, the president and her cabinet are all conniving away in response to the momentous announcement. . . . Haldeman's fast-paced, cannily constructed yarn is ultimately most like that granddaddy of first-contact flicks, The Day the Earth Stood Still. Maybe better." Booklist

Forever free; by Joe Haldeman. Ace Bks. 1999 277p o.p.
ISBN 0-441-00697-3 LC 99-33231

This novel "reintroduces readers to William Mandella [featured in Forever War] who has been living peacefully on the planet called Middle Finger, a refuge for humans who refuse to become part of the group mind known as Man. But after decades of this peace, Mandella and others are tired of living like zoo animals. They're ready for a challenge, and they'd like to see Earth again. So they steal a starship—and embark upon a voyage that will forever change their understanding of the universe . . . and themselves." Publisher's note

Forever peace; {by} Joe Haldeman. Ace Bks. 1997 326p o.p.
ISBN 0-441-00406-7 LC 96-52650

"It is 2043, and the U.S. and its allies are waging a seemingly endless war against a loose federation of Third World countries called Ngumi. Julian Class is a draftee, an infantryman, and part of a 'soldier-boy'—a mechanized, armor-plated, highly lethal unit run by a squad of men and women all of whom have been 'jacked' or linked together by surgical implantation. Add to the plot mix a plan to build a mammoth particle accelerator on Jupiter's moon, Io, and the rise of a fundamentalist, secretive religious sect, the Hammer of God, to the very highest military ranks." Booklist

The author "writes with uncommon intelligence and acuity about the terror of war and the horror of the human heritage in the middle of the next century." Publ Wkly

The forever war; [by] Joe Haldeman. St. Martin's Press 1975 c1974 236p o.p.

"Earth is battling the aliens from a planet in the constellation Taurus but in Haldeman's chronicle of the career of William Mandella from private to reluctant major, the war becomes an engrossing, poignant epic. Mandella was among the unlucky first recruits for a war that has been fought for 1,000 years." Booklist

"A naturalistic description of a war that lasts more than a thousand years, although the main characters age only a few years because of the relativistic effects of faster-than-light space travel. The situation of the soldiers fighting in this kind of war is complicated, however, by their alienation from their own societies by the time-dilation effect, and their growing disillusionment with the war." New Ency of Sci Fic

Hale, Edward Everett, 1822-1909

The man without a country. o.p.
First published 1863 in Atlantic Monthly

"This long short-story concerns Philip Nolan, a young officer of the United States Army who is tried for the Aaron Burr conspiracy. During the courtmartial he exclaims, 'Damn the United States! I wish I may never hear of the United States again!' The court thereupon

Hale, Edward Everett, 1822-1909—*Continued*
sentences him to live out his life on a naval vessel, and never hear news of the United States. The story recounts the mental torments of the countryless prisoner, who after fifty-seven years finally learns that his nation is thriving, and dies happy." Haydn. Thesaurus of Book Dig

Haley, Alex, 1921-1992

Mama Flora's family; a novel; {by} Alex Haley and David Stevens. Scribner 1998 393p o.p.
ISBN 0-684-83471-5 LC 98-5389
"A Lisa Drew book"
In this multigenerational family saga, the "lives of Mama Flora and her family provide a whirlwind survey of the 20th-century black experience. As a young woman in a small Tennessee town, Flora bears a son and sees his father killed at the hands of white racists. She realizes that education is the only way out of poverty. Soon, her daughter becomes a social worker while her son dabbles in communism and enlists to fight in World War II. As Flora lays dying, she can look back on her family and their accomplishments with pride." Libr J

Halkin, Hillel, 1939-

Tevye the dairyman and The railroad stories; [by] Sholom Aleichem; translated from the Yiddish and with an introduction by Hillel Halkin. Schocken Bks. 1987 xli, 309p o.p.
LC 86-24835
"Library of Yiddish classics"
"In the first eight stories of this collection, Tevye, the Russian Jew so familiar from *Fiddler on the Roof,* bemoans his fate. In these as well as the following 21 tales, the author displays his splendid storytelling skills." Booklist

Hall, Adam, 1920-1995

Quiller Balalaika. Carroll & Graf/Otto Penzler 2003 242p $24
ISBN 0-7867-1265-1
First published 1996 in the United Kingdom
"The detritus of the cold war in the former Soviet Union comprises self-serving bureaucracies, opportunistic ex-KGBers, and organized criminals who make their U.S. mafioso counterparts seem like mischievous delinquents. Into the mix drops pseudonymous Brit agent Quiller, with the intent of taking out a British national-Basil Seckes, aka Vasyl Sakkas-who is secretly heading up the burgeoning Russian criminal empire. To bring down Sakkas' empire, Quiller needs the help of one Marius Antonov, currently residing in a Gulag prison. Freeing Antonov entails Quiller making his way into the prison and then escaping with his target, no small feat because the prison is virtually escape proof. . . . The book is a typically atmospheric, exciting Quiller adventure." Booklist

The Quiller memorandum. Simon & Schuster 1965 224p o.p.
Published in the United Kingdom with title: The Berlin memorandum
"Quiller is a British 'Shadow executive', employed by 'the Bureau', a government agency assigned to carry out delicate tasks, and it is so secret it does not exist. As we follow Quiller's 'brain-think' sequences we learn that during the Second World War he was an infiltrator who arranged escapes from Nazi concentration camps. Quiller and others like him with specialised skills, do the jobs that M15 and M16 cannot do. Quiller is used only at the authorisation of the Prime Minister. In *The Quiller Memorandum* he exposes a large, well-organised neo-Nazi conspiracy in Berlin." McCormick and Fletcher. Spy Fic

Quiller Salamander. Penzler Bks. 1994 247p o.p.
ISBN 1-883402-40-9 LC 94-17372
British secret agent Quiller, "bored in London, takes on a rogue assignment—one the Bureau has not sanctioned but which is the private effort of one of the 'controls,' the enigmatic Flockhart. The mission: discover what Pol Pot is up to in his ongoing efforts to return the Khmer Rouge to power. Arriving in Phnom Penh, Quiller finds himself attracted to his first contact, a female French photographer who harbors an important secret, and suspicious of his field director. Following a narrow escape from a Khmer Rouge encampment, Quiller uncovers plans for yet another Cambodian bloodbath." Publ Wkly
"Mr. Hall, a master of intense prose and tense situations, has again come up with a story that wil not disappoint his admirers." N Y Times Book Rev

Quiller solitaire. Morrow 1992 286p o.p.
ISBN 0-688-10730-3 LC 91-31060
"When a fellow agent who has called upon him for protection is murdered before his eyes, an enraged and embarrassed Quiller pressures his superiors into giving him the dead man's assignment to investigate the murder of a British cultural attache in Berlin. The murder is apparently tied to former East German national Dieter Klaus, a madman who wants to gain attention for his terrorist splinter group." Publ Wkly

Hall, Brian, 1959-

I should be extremely happy in your company; a novel of Lewis and Clark. Viking 2003 419p $25.95
ISBN 0-670-03189-5 LC 2002-66376
"Narrated in multiple distinct voices, this retelling of the story of Meriwether Lewis and William Clark's legendary expedition is less a historical blow-by-blow than an engaging character study of the two men. Hall focuses on a few significant episodes in the journey—such as the hunting accident that wounds Lewis and causes him to sink into his famous depression—as seen through the eyes of Lewis, Sacagawea, Clark and Toussaint Charbonneau, Sacagawea's French fur trader husband. The result is a memorable portrait of the expedition leaders." Publ Wkly

Hall, James Norman, 1887-1951

(jt. auth) Nordhoff, C. Botany Bay
(jt. auth) Nordhoff, C. The Bounty trilogy
(jt. auth) Nordhoff, C. Men against the sea
(jt. auth) Nordhoff, C. Mutiny on the Bounty
(jt. auth) Nordhoff, C. Pitcairn's Island

Hall, James W., 1947-

Blackwater sound; a novel. St. Martin's Minotaur 2002 339p $24.95

ISBN 0-312-20384-5 LC 2001-48594

"When a passenger plane crash-lands near Thorn's boat in the Florida coastal waters, Thorn finds himself thrust into a rescue operation that leads him deeper and deeper into the lunatic world of the Braswell family." Publ Wkly

"Hall's quiet studies of loners—the old man in his fog of memory, the marlin in the freedom of the deep—are truly haunting." N Y Times Book Rev

Buzz cut; by James W. Hall. Delacorte Press 1996 374p o.p.

LC 95-50425

In this mystery, "Thorn and Sugar take security detail on a luxury Caribbean cruiseship only to find that a brilliant madman named Butler Jack has hijacked the ship for reasons clear only to himself. Butler creates general havoc on board, altering the ship's course, causing near collisions, and randomly killing crew and passengers in spectacularly bloody fashion. Thorn and Sugar slowly unravel the twisted tale of greed and madness that drives the mind of the hijacker, finally reaching a very surprising truth." Libr J

"Butler Jack's love of words comes to him naturally, from an author who uses language with great delicacy, even when his characters are sticking knives into one another." N Y Times Book Rev

Off the chart; a novel. St. Martin's Minotaur 2003 337p $24.95

ISBN 0-312-27178-6 LC 2002-191965

"Thorn's long-ago fling with a beautiful woman named Anne Joy comes back to haunt him years later when Anne's brother, Vic Joy, a modern-day pirate along the Gulf Coast, decides he needs to add Thorn's five-acre property to his ill-gotten business and real estate empire." Publ Wkly

"Yes, we like to imagine ourselves wearing Thorn's deck shoes, in a full-frontal assault on all those who endanger our world, but Hall, unlike most thriller writers, portrays the collateral damage wreaked when rugged individualists go into overdrive. This remains one of the best series in the genre." Booklist

Red sky at night; by James W. Hall. Delacorte Press 1997 326p o.p.

ISBN 0-385-31638-0 LC 96-45621

"Ensconced in his Key Largo beach house, Thorn seems to have carved a lasting separate peace with the modern world until a senseless crime drives the other side of his personality to the fore, the side that says, 'There's something broken, and I have to fix it.' What's broken this time, though, is Thorn himself, mysteriously paralyzed from the waist down after attempting to confront an apparent prowler. The story begins with the slaughter of several dolphins-killed for their endorphins, the key ingredient in a miracle, pain-killing drug-and extends to Thorn's distant past and his relationship with his best childhood friend, who has been nursing a grudge against Thorn for decades. . . . Popular fiction at its absolute best." Booklist

Rough draft; a novel. St. Martin's Press 2000 335p o.p.

ISBN 0-312-20383-7 LC 99-55532

In this suspense novel former Miami cop turned mystery writer Hannah Keller is trying to solve the murder of her parents when she finds a "copy of one of her books containing cryptic marginal notes that appear to be a message from the killer. Meanwhile, the FBI is tracking a psycho hit-man who dispatches his victims by crushing their hearts with his bare hands. The psycho is hunting the money launderer who may have killed Hannah's parents, and unbeknownst to her, she becomes the bait in the Bureau's elaborate sting operation. Hall weaves his contrapuntal plot strains beautifully, letting the reader know more than Hannah knows but never enough to be comfortable." Booklist

Hall, Radclyffe, 1886-1943

The well of loneliness; with a commentary by Havelock Ellis. Covici 1928 506p o.p.

This autobiographical novel traces "the life of the wealthy young woman Stephen Gordon from birth to her full realization that she is a 'congenital invert' (as she terms it), a lesbian by nature. . . . It is the first full, rich portrait of a lesbian in literature. At the time the publication was an act of outstanding bravery." British Women Writers

Hall, Steffie *See* Evanovich, Janet

Hallgrímur Helgason, 1959-

101 Reykjavik; a novel; translated by Brian FitzGibbon. Scribner 2003 339p $23

ISBN 0-7432-2514-7 LC 2002-29434

"Hlynur Björn is, by his own admission, a 33-year-old mommy's boy. He lives at home, spends his days watching porn and surfing the Web, and his nights at Reykjavik's nightclubs drinking and taking Ecstasy. He assigns every woman he encouonters a monetary value and refuses to commit to spending even a full night with his casual girlfriend, Hofy. When Hofy falls pregnant and his mother announces that her lesbian lover, Lolla, whom Hlynur slept with on New Year's Eve, is also pregnant, he must fight to protect his selfish and shallow way of life." Publ Wkly

"This novel uses caustic and irreverent humor to paint a vivid picture of Icelandic youth ideas and culture. . . . While the protagonist is confused, depressed, and futureless, the humor saves the book from being depressing." Libr J

Halpern, Daniel, 1945-

(ed) The Art of the story. See The Art of the story

Halter, Marek

The book of Abraham; translated by Lowell Bair. Holt & Co. 1986 722p o.p.

LC 85-17582

Original French edition, 1983

The author "begins his tome in 70 A.D. in Jerusalem, when a scribe named Abraham flees the conquering Roman army. The author follows the dynasty of scribes descended from Abraham through the centuries, until he links them to his own real-life ancestors, a line of print-

Halter, Marek—*Continued*
ers, one of whom worked with Gutenberg in Strasbourg. The book ends with death of Halter's grandfather, a printer, in the Warsaw ghetto, in 1943. The chronicle moves among dozens of cities in Asia and Europe, deftly encapsulating the historical events and social milieu of time and place, as each generation of this family hands down the so-called Book of Abraham, a record of births and deaths that also symbolizes the continuity of the collective Jewish memory." Publ Wkly

Sarah; a novel; Marek Halter. 1st American ed. Crown Publishers 2004 294p map $22
ISBN 1-400-05272-6 LC 2003-19648
Original French edition, 2003
"Sarah is the favorite daughter of a lord of Ur, a city-state of Sumeria. Raised in luxury and privilege, she defies her father on the day of her marriage and escapes into the lower city, where she meets Abraham of the nomadic mar.Tu people. Although soldiers take her home, she can't forget the young man who captured her heart and imagination. Owing to an injudicious use of infertility herbs in an effort to stave off marriage, Sarah renders herself sterile and is dedicated to the temple of Ishtar, where she serves as a revered Sacred Handmaid of the Blood for several years until she meets Abraham again. This time, she successfully escapes, and the two dedicate themselves to the one, true, invisible God and create a nation." Libr J
"Halter isn't afraid to present headstrong Sarah as bitter in her old age, and his complex portrait of the biblical matriarch gives this solid if predictable novel a dash of freshness." Publ Wkly

Hambly, Barbara

Days of the dead. Bantam Bks. 2003 314p il maps $23.95
ISBN 0-553-10954-5 LC 2002-38571
"An extreme case of culture shock awaits Benjamin January. . .when he leaves cosmopolitan New Orleans, a city that loves life, for bellicose Mexico, a country that lives for its dead. Traveling with his bride, Rose, by overland coach in 1835, this Paris-trained surgeon (and former slave) encounters bloodthirsty bandits, fierce soldiers from Santa Anna's army, rebellious Yankees from uncivilized Texas and a hacienda teeming with feuding relatives on the country estate of the Spanish grandee Don Prospero's only son." N Y Times Book Rev

Dead water; Barbara Hambly. Bantam Books 2004 297p $25
ISBN 0-553-10964-2 LC 2004-40766
This Benjamin January adventure "finds the amateur sleuth investigating a couple of mysteries. The bank that holds all his money has suddenly and suspiciously collapsed, and someone has apparently put a curse on a former student in the small school operated by January's wife, Rose. Just goes to show: New Orleans, circa 1836, is a wild and dangerous place. . . . Where many writers of historical mysteries get bogged down in exposition, or in cataloging details that most readers are not interested in, Hambly keeps things moving, always focused on her characters and her story, and not on showing off the quantity of research she's done." Booklist

A free man of color. Bantam Bks. 1997 311p o.p.
LC 96-44942
A romantic suspense novel set in 19th century New Orleans. "Benjamin January, a free Creole with dark brown skin, has returned to this society after living in Paris for more than a decade. He is trained as a surgeon, but in Louisiana, he makes his living playing the piano. Soon he is the main suspect in the death of a wealthy man's young mistress, found murdered at a ball. January spends the rest of the book gathering evidence in his defense." Libr J
"A few suspenseful moments not-withstanding, this isn't an action-packed or suspenseful whodunit. Rather, it's a richly detailed, telling portrait of an intricately structured racial hierarchy." Booklist

Graveyard dust. Bantam Bks. 1999 315p o.p.
ISBN 0-553-10259-1 LC 98-43456
A historical mystery set in 19th-century New Orleans featuring physician Benjamin January, a free man of color. "The year is 1834, and January seeks to free his sister, who has been jailed for a voodoo-related murder. As he follows the trail, aided by his friend Hannibal, his own life is threatened by a monstrous fellow with the fateful name of Killdevil. While the city struggles to keep cholera in check, January stays one step ahead of his would-be-assassin, interviewing the family and friends of the victim and the accused." Libr J
"Hambly's plot, which revolves around evils confined to no race or class, is complex and often hard to track, but its emotional authenticity, varied cast and rich historical trappings give the novel power and depth." Publ Wkly

Sold down the river. Bantam Bks. 2000 317p $23.95
ISBN 0-553-10257-5 LC 99-54845
A historical mystery "featuring Benjamin January, a freed slave whose Paris education earns him a living in New Orleans and whose refined sense of justice puts him in peril wherever he goes. . . . Ben bends his back to the pain and humiliation of being a slave again when he goes undercover at a sugar cane plantation 20 miles up the river, were a rebellion may be brewing." N Y Times Book Rev

Those who hunt the night. Ballantine Bks. 1988 296p o.p.
LC 88-47803
"A Del Rey book"
"Someone is killing the vampires of London and James Asher, an Oxford professor and former British foreign service agent, has been recruited by one of the oldest vampires in London to locate the murderer." Voice Youth Advocates
"The characters are well drawn (in the case of the vampire Don Simon Ysidro, positively compelling) and plausibly motivated, and the historical setting is both well researched and well depicted." Booklist
Followed by Traveling with the dead

Traveling with the dead. Ballantine Bks. 1995 343p o.p.
ISBN 0-345-38102-5 LC 95-30243

Hambly, Barbara—*Continued*

"A Del Rey book"

Sequel to Those who hunt the night

"Former British espionage agent James Asher is one of the few mortals aware of the existence of vampires. After he stumbles upon a meeting between an Austrian spy and the long-dead Earl of Ernchester, he embarks upon a dangerous journey across Europe to prevent a catastrophic alliance beteen human governments and the inhumane society of the undead." Libr J

"From beginning to end, the book succeeds as both a classic vampire tale and a specimen of the relatively new genre, the historical thriller." Booklist

Die upon a kiss. Bantam Bks. 2001 333p o.p.

ISBN 0-553-10924-3 LC 00-69666

In antebellum New Orleans "cultural war is declared between rival American and Creole opera houses when an Italian company attempts to open the season for the upstart Americans with an original and provocative version of 'Othello.' The composer is knifed in the alley, the lead soprano is poisoned, a prominent opera patron is murdered, and—oh, yes, the theater is torched. Benjamin January, a former slave and accomplished musician who plays in the orchestra, is well positioned for this backstage investigation." N Y Times Book Rev

Wet grave. Bantam Bks. 2002 288p o.p.

ISBN 0-553-10935-9 LC 2001-43401

Benjamin January, "the former slave and Creole surgeon looks into the murder of a drunken whore whom no one seems to care about. Despite his education and musical and medical accomplishments, January is only a short, catastrophic step up from bottom in the oddly stratified society of 1830s New Orleans." Publ Wkly

"As with any good historical mystery, we are at least as captivated by the characters, dialogue, and environment as we are with the mystery itself." Booklist

Hamill, Pete

Forever; a novel. Little, Brown 2002 613p $25.95

ISBN 0-316-34111-8 LC 2002-114241

"In 1740, an Irish Jew named Cormac O'Connor heads to New York in pursuit of the man who killed his father and gets tangled up in a rebellion against the English. Through a series of events involving an African slave with shamanistic powers, he is granted eternal life, provided that he never leaves Manhattan. There follows a tour of the city's history through Cormac's eyes: the political corruption and the poverty, but also the majestic growth of the metropolis through its culture, its buildings, and its people." New Yorker

Snow in August; a novel. Little, Brown 1997 327p o.p.

ISBN 0-316-34094-4 LC 96-36043

"In Brooklyn in 1947, Michael Devlin, an 11-year-old Irish kid who spends his days reading *Captain Marvel* and anticipating the arrival of Jackie Robinson, makes the acquaintance of a recently emigrated Orthodox rabbi. In exchange for lessons in English and baseball, Rabbi Hirsch teaches him Yiddish and tells him of Jewish life in old Prague and of the mysteries of the Kabbalah. Anti-Semitism soon rears its head in the form of a gang of young Irish toughs out to rule the neighborhood." Libr J

"Mr. Hamill is not a subtle writer, but his gift for sensual description and his tabloid muscularity . . . fit this page turner of a fable." N Y Times Book Rev

Hamilton, Clive *See* Lewis, C. S. (Clive Staples), 1898-1963

Hamilton, Jane, 1957-

Disobedience; a novel. Doubleday 2000 272p $24.95

ISBN 0-385-50117-X LC 00-29504

"Henry Shaw is a high school senior when he intercepts e-mail messages between his mother, Beth, a musician and specialist in ancient music, and violin maker Richard Pollico. As he secretly eavesdrops on the liaison between 'Liza38' and 'Rpol,' Henry's emotions, ranging from horror to fear of abandonment to rage to deep sadness, take on a new dimension when he himself falls in love with a girl he meets in summer camp. Meanwhile, his generally bemused and patient father, Kevin, a high school history teacher, seems unaware of Beth's infidelity, since he spends much of his time coaching Henry's rebellious sister, Elvira, 13, who is obsessed with her desire to join a Civil War reenactment disguised as a boy." Publ Wkly

"Hamilton has written a novel so disturbing that no one will enjoy reading it. But 'Disobedience' is so provocative that you must." Christ Sci Monit

A map of the world. Doubleday 1994 389p o.p.

ISBN 0-385-47310-9 LC 93-45723

"Alice Goodwin is caring for her best friend's children when two-year-old Lizzy Collins wanders to the pond on the Goodwin farm and drowns. The consequences of this tragedy reverberate through a small Wisconsin community, which never accepted Howard and Alice Goodwin. Theresa Collins, bereft at losing a child and a dear friend, draws on her Catholic religion and finds forgiveness. Alice, immobilized by guilt and grief and unable to function as a wife or mother to her own two daughters, is charged with abusing children in her part-time job as a school nurse." Libr J

This is "not an easy or light read; indeed, it takes on some of the toughest issues of modern life. But the writer's skill in describing a community and a way of life, as well as her insight into the hearts of her characters, render this story difficult to forget." Christ Sci Monit

The short history of a prince; a novel. Random House 1998 349p o.p.

ISBN 0-679-45755-0 LC 97-31627

This novel "alternates between two sections of narrative, set during two crucial years in [its protagonist's] life. The first introduces us to 15-year-old Walter in Illinois in 1972, coming to grips with his homosexuality, his lack of dancing skills and the fact that his confident, all-Amrican brother is dying of cancer. The second, which begins in September 1995, reveals 38-year-old Walter as a witty, warmhearted man full of regret for having spent his early adulthood pursuing 'The pleasures consigned to youth' in Manhattan's gay community—and full of determination to reorder his life by taking a job teaching high school English in a farm town near his family's summer home." N Y Times Book Rev

Hamilton, Jane, 1957-—*Continued*

"Hamilton has an amazing way with the varieties of human pain. Her characters live with ordinary and sometimes extraordinary torment, yet her writing remains bouyant and her sensibility full of light." Newsweek

Hamilton, Peter F.

Pandora's star; Peter F. Hamilton. 1st ed. Del Rey\Ballantine Books 2004 758p $26.95

ISBN 0-345-46162-2 LC 2003-68753

"By the 24th century, the vast human Commonwealth has spread from Earth via artificial wormholes. Various benign or seemingly indifferent alien races have been encountered during exploration of new planets, but an astronomer sparks curiosity by announcing that a pair of stars is enclosed by a mysterious energy barrier. Unfortunately, a space expedition discovers that the shield was created to imprison an insatiably greedy mass mind that sees any other race as a mortal threat. When the barrier somehow is lowered, the alien immediately attacks the largely unprepared Commonwealth, while humans begin wondering if yet another inhuman power has manipulated events that unleashed this threat. The author deftly juggles many characters in multiple plot lines." Publ Wkly

Hamilton-Paterson, James

Gerontius. Soho Press 1991 264p o.p.

ISBN 0-939149-48-6 LC 91-6441

This is a novel based on an episode in the life of Sir Edward Elgar. "In 1923 Sir Edward Elgar, in his mid-60s and acknowledged as England's finest living composer, takes a cruise to the Amazon port city of Manaos. Rootless and dissatisfied, he repudiates his life's work as insignificant. . . . Elgar wants only to escape from himself, but in Manaos he meets a woman from his past." Libr J

Loving monsters. Granta Bks. 2001 308p $24.95

ISBN 1-86207-425-9 LC 2001-536080

"A British biographer living in Tuscany takes on an unusual subject in [this novel] . . . set primarily in Egypt before WWII. Raymond Jerningham Jebb, known as JayJay to his friends, is the dying elderly man who talks James, the somewhat reluctant, semi-anonymous narrator, into writing his life story. . . . JayJay is raised in a middle-class, somewhat repressive British household, but when he goes to Egypt in 1936 to take a clerical job, he finds his true destiny among the shadowy figures of Suez and Cairo as a purveyor of pornography who occasionally smuggles drugs. . . . When the project stalls, James takes a brief hiatus to pursue another literary endeavor in the Far East, but when he returns JayJay surprises him by revealing the story of the love of his life, a British schoolboy whom he never approached or pursued." Publ Wkly

Hammett, Dashiell, 1894-1961

The big knockover; selected stories and short novels of Dashiell Hammett; edited and with an introduction by Lillian Hellman. Random House 1966 xxi, 355p o.p.

Contents: The gutting of Couffignal; Fly paper; The scorched face; This king business; The Gatewood caper; Dead yellow women; Corkscrew; Tulip [unfinished novel]; The big knockover; $106,000 blood money

Complete novels. Library of Am. 1999 967p $35

ISBN 1-88301-167-1 LC 98-53911

Contents: Red harvest (1929); The Dain curse (1929); The Maltese falcon (1930); The glass key (1931); The thin man (1934); the last three titles are entered separately

In Red harvest the nameless operative for the Continental Detective Agency in San Francisco known as the Continental Op fights political corruption in the town of Personville, referred to by its citizens as "Poisonville." In The Dain curse Continental Op solves a jewel burglary, multiple murders, and deals with drug addiction and a family curse

The Continental Op; selected and with an introduction by Steven Marcus. Random House 1974 xxix, 287p o.p.

Contents: The tenth clew; The golden horseshoe; The house in Turk Street; The girl with the silver eyes; The Whosis Kid; The main death; The farewell murder

Crime stories and other writings. Library of Am. 2001 934p $35

ISBN 1-931082-00-6 LC 00-54594

Includes the following short stories: Arson plus; Slippery fingers; Crooked souls; The tenth clew; Zigzags of treachery; The house in Turk Street; The girl with the silver eyes; Women, politics and murder; The Golden Horseshoe; Nightmare town; The Whosis Kid; The scorched face; Dead yellow women; The gutting of Couffignal; The assistant murderer; Creeping Siamese; The big knock-over; $106,000 blood money; The main death; This king business; Fly paper; The farewell murder; Woman in the dark; Two sharp knives

"The first great author in the hard-boiled detective genre, Hammett remains one of the most entertaining, as demonstrated by this largest single gathering ever of his short fiction. This collection's main distinction is that editor Steven Marcus uses the original story texts from their appearance in *Black Mask* magazine." Publ Wkly

The Dain curse

In Hammett, D. Complete novels

The glass key. Knopf 1931 282p o.p.

Appointed special investigator in the district attorney's office to track down the murderer of a Senator's son, Ned Beaumont becomes involved with political bosses, bootlegging gangsters and romance

"One of the two best novels by the man who is generally regarded as the creator and still the acknowledged master of the 'hard-boiled' school of detective fiction. Brutal in its subject matter but excellently written." Howard Haycraft

also in Hammett, D. Complete novels

The Maltese falcon. Knopf 1930 276p o.p.

This novel "called the best American detective novel by some critics, opens with Space accepting a case from Brigid O'Shaughnessy, a statuesque redhead masquerading as a Miss Wonderly. Almost immediately, his partner, Miles Archer is killed. Spade hated him and has been having an affair with his wife, but feels duty-bound to find his killer. He becomes involved with an odd assortment of characters, each searching for a statue of a black bird, about a foot high, said to be worth a fortune." Ency of Mystery & Detection

Hammett, Dashiell, 1894-1961—*Continued*
also in Hammett, D. Complete novels

Nightmare town; stories; edited by Kirby McCauley, Martin H. Greenberg, and Ed Gorman. Knopf 1999 396p o.p.
ISBN 0-375-40111-3 LC 99-37237
Contents: Nightmare town; House dick; Ruffian's wife; The man who killed Dan Odams; Night shots; Zigzags of treachery; The assistant murderer; His brother's keeper; Death of Pine Street; The second-story angel; Afraid of a gun; Tom, Dick, or Harry; One hour; Who killed Bob Teal?; A man called Spade; Too many have lived; They only hang you once; A man named Thin; The first thin man; Two sharp knives
These "short stories feature enigmatic plots of devilish intricacy, rife with fisticuffs and pistol shots, and populated by stiffs, laconic coppers, lowlifes and droll, world-weary detectives. Sam Spade shows up several times, as does the Continental Op." Publ Wkly

Red harvest
In Hammett, D. Complete novels

The thin man. Knopf 1934 259p o.p.
"Nick Charles, a San Francisco detective, is the narrator. He and his amusing wife, Nora (on a visit to New York), take time out from drinking and dancing to solve the problem of what happened to an inventor whose disppearance coincided with the murder of his mistress-secretary. There is the right amount of underworld, and in lieu of the usual tough stuff we are treated to an adolescent (son of the disappeared—and deceased), who battens on the more lurid aspects of toxicology and pathology." Barzun. Cat of Crime. Rev and enl edition
"One of the first works to bring humor, and of a distinctly native brand, to the detective story in this country." Howard Haycraft
also in Hammett, D. Complete novels

Tulip
In Hammett, D. The big knockover p238-74

Hammett, Samuel Dashiell *See* Hammett, Dashiell, 1894-1961

Hammond, Diane Coplin

Going to bend; a novel; [by] Diane Hammond. 1st ed. Doubleday 2004 293p $23.95
ISBN 0-385-50943-X LC 2003-51945
"Feisty Petie Coolbaugh and serene Rose Bundy, both 31, have been best friends for years while living in the small fishing town of Hubbard, OR. Despite the intermittent help of Petie's husband and Rose's boyfriend, they must work to support their families. They begin making soups for Souperior's Caf, run by Los Angeles transplants Nadine and her twin brother, Gordon. This collaboration ignites undiscovered talents in both Rose and Petie. Set in the late 1980s, this first novel reverberates with a small cast of memorable, working-class characters." Libr J

Hammond, Gerald, 1926-

Mad dogs & Scotsmen. St. Martin's Press 1996 185p o.p.
LC 96-25613
First published 1995 in the United Kingdom
This mystery finds "Scotsman Cunningham—dog breeder, kennel owner, and sometime sleuth—involved in a case of murder and industrial espionage. John has been boarding a black Lab named Jove for his friend Noel Cochrane. Then Noel shows up unannounced to take Jove with him to America, but in short order, Jove disappears, John's car is stolen, a woman's body is discovered, and Noel goes missing along with a briefcase full of documents that expose his company's falsification of the lab tests on a new rabies vaccine. As brisk and bracing as a walk in the Scottish Highlands." Booklist

Twice bitten. St. Martin's Press 1999 230p o.p.
ISBN 0-312-24256-5 LC 99-48487
"Dog breeder John Cunningham—and his family and staff at Three Oaks Kennels—face a crime that, if unsolved, could threaten their livelihood and their lives. When Dougal Webb, a young farm manager who was courting one of Cunningham's kennel maids, goes missing, he leaves behind evidence of some shady dealings. Since Webb had tried to blackmail Cunningham shortly before his disappearance, the breeder's entire household comes under suspicion. . . . Before the situation is set aright, the Cunninghams and the local police inspector must pick their way through a tangle of blackmail, chicanery, murder, fraud and old grievances that enmeshes the fates of characters high and low" Publ Wkly

Hammond, Gerald, 1945-

The hitch; Gerald Hammond. Severn House 2004 186p $27.95
ISBN 0-7278-6010-0
"Alice Dunwoodie has a flair for planning. Her friend Sarah is full of 'innocent' charm. Recently, the two used their skills to carry out a burglary in which Alice's father also became involved. While the girls escaped, Mr. Dunwoodie wasn't so lucky and ended up in prison. Following this disaster and Mr. Dunwoodie's release, all three have vowed to 'go straight.' But when Mr. Dunwoodie accidentally intercepts a fax from pop singer Mona Lisa to a Scottish castle, reserving the site for her lavish wedding, he immediately sees possibilities. If the trio can convince Mona Lisa that they represent the castle, and if they can keep the castle in the dark about the upcoming wedding, and if they convince Mona Lisa to send hefty deposits for the wedding expenses directly into an anonymous bank account, then take off with the money . . . well, they could all be a lot richer with very little effort. Entertaining fare, with appealing characters, an imaginative plot, and cracking good action." Booklist

Hamner, Earl, 1923-

The homecoming; a novel about Spencer's Mountain; [by] Earl Hamner, Jr. Random House 1970 115p o.p.
"Fifteen-year-old Clay-Boy of 'Spencer's Mountain' is again the protagonist in this short novel set in Virginia in the early 1930's. The story takes place one snowy Christmas Eve while the family of nine is anxiously

Hamner, Earl, 1923-—*Continued*

waiting for the father to come home from his out-of-town job. It tells of Clay-Boy's trip to the woods for a Christmas tree, of his encounter with a fabled albino deer, and of his adventures with neighbors as he searches for his father, who is delayed by the storm. This picture of everyday happenings in a small mountain community and of close family relationships amid the hardships of the Depression years is painted with simplicity and charm." Libr J

Spencer's Mountain; [by] Earl Hamner, Jr. Dial Press (NY) 1961 247p o.p.

An "account of a boy's growing up in a large and impoverished family in the Blue Ridge Mountains of Virginia. . . . His chief problems are love and the fact that his father feels that a college education is a waste of money." Publ Wkly

"A novel filled with joie de vivre, frank simplicity, a little sinning, and much human goodness." Libr J

Han, Suyin

The enchantress. Bantam Bks. 1985 345p o.p.

LC 84-45185

"Set in the eighteenth century, in Switzerland, China, and Thailand, the tale concerns the exploits of Colin and his twin sister, Bea, free spirits whose Celtic roots have endowed them with a special ability to commune with nature. As a child in Switzerland, Colin learns from his father how to make automatons, an early version of robots. After their parents' death, Colin and Bea travel to China, where craftspeople are needed to keep the automatons at the emperor's court in operating order. There, and subsequently in Thailand, they become embroiled in numerous affairs of the heart and state." Booklist

"This is an extremely well-told tale of life and love in the 18th Century. History comes alive, and there is a masterful blending of magic and science at a time when the division between the two were not so great." SLJ

Till morning comes; a novel. Bantam Bks. 1982 500p il o.p.

LC 81-19150

"This is a love story set in China during the period from World War II through the years of the Cultural Revolution. Stephanie Ryder, beautiful daughter of a rich Texan oilman, comes to China as a magazine correspondent and falls in love with Dr. Jen Yong, a physician from an upper class Chinese family who sympathizes with the Communist objectives. . . . Stephanie and Yong endure much censure, hardship and repression to sustain their relationship and marriage in the not very tolerant atmosphere of the Communist Revolution." Best Sellers

"Told with sensitivity, this is an engrossing story. Although her sympathies lie with the Communist uprising, Han does not spare that regime in depicting the purges." Libr J

Hand, Elizabeth, 1957-

Mortal love. Morrow 2004 364p $24.95

ISBN 0-06-105170-5 LC 2003-62398

"In Victorian London, psychiatrist Dr. Learmont collects paintings by artists on the edge of insanity. Painter Radborne Comstock (think the Pre-Raphaelites) walks that edge, haunted by the image of a beautiful 'green woman.' Meanwhile, in present-day London, writer Daniel Rowlands, researching a book on the legend of Tristan and Iseult, meets the mysterious and mesmerizing Larkin Meade, becoming more and more feverishly obsessed with her. Parallels emerge between Comstock and Rowlands. Each has been seduced by a dangerous muse; to follow her will bring more trouble than inspiration." Libr J

"What lies behind the complex, even violent process that we call artistic inspiration? That is the final mystery evoked in Elizabeth Hand's ambitious and richly imagined novel. By tracing the turbulence and reverberations of that process back to its source, Mortal Love offers its readers the satisfactions of a detective thriller. Here, however, the mystery goes deeper than murder. Nothing, Hand convinces us, is quite as mysterious as art." Washington Post Book World

Handke, Peter, 1942-

The left-handed woman; translated by Ralph Manheim. Farrar, Straus & Giroux 1978 87p o.p.

LC 78-5568

Original German edition, 1976

"Marianne, 30, decides that Bruno, her well-to-do executive husband, will some day leave her, so she throws him out on the spot. She takes long walks through nearby woods, through an unnamed West German city and through the halls and rooms of her rented house. A friend asks her to join what seems to be a women's consciousness-raising group, but Marianne does not. She works at a translation of a French book about a woman trying to achieve independence; if there is a message here for Marianne, she does not get it. Friends, relatives and casual acquaintances gather round her and then disperse as aimlessly as they came. At the end, the woman is virtually catatonic." Time

"There are echoes of Beckett, Sartre, and Kafka in this chilly little novel. . . . Handke at his best handles that moribund trinity of modern themes—alienation, failure of communication and absurdity—with quirky originality." Newsweek

My year in the no-man's-bay; translated by Krishna Winston. Farrar, Straus & Giroux 1998 468p o.p.

ISBN 0-374-21755-6 LC 97-48948

Original German edition, 1994

A "paean to the banlieue–the 'in-between spaces' of the Seine hills surrounding Paris. It is in this marginalized locale, inhabited by toads, muskrats, and the blue-collar regulars at the Bar des Voyageurs, that the narrator, an Austrian named Gregor Keuschnig, has installed himself to write. Keuschnig's exhaustively detailed meditation on the seemingly 'unwinnable struggle' to transform the visible into the readable is leavened by his exposes of nameless friends and his estranged wife." New Yorker

Repetition; translated by Ralph Manheim. Farrar, Straus & Giroux 1988 246p o.p.

ISBN 0-374-24934-2 LC 87-33065

Original German edition, 1986

"In 1960, Filip Kobal, an alienated, 20-year-old, nascent Austrian writer of Slovenian descent, embarks on a quest to the land of his forebears. Ostensibly a retracing of his much older brother's last steps 20 years before

Handke, Peter, 1942-—*Continued*
(he was a Slovenian patriot, lover and revivifier of the language and tradition, and a doomed member of the Resistance), the journey is in fact an odyssey of self-discovery for Filip the man and the writer." Publ Wkly

"The author invests this process of self-discovery with such originality and marvelous psychological detail that Filip's journey becomes at one with the writer's and the reader's as well." Booklist

Hannah, Kristin

Angel falls. Crown 2000 274p $23

ISBN 0-609-60592-5 LC 99-45488

"After Mikaela suffers a serious head injury in a fall from a horse, Liam, her physician husband, tries to do everything to awaken her from her coma. When he accidentally discovers some old photos and a beautiful diamond ring in her closet, he realizes that Mikaela's brief first marriage to Julian True meant a lot more to her than she ever admitted. Liam contacts Julian, now a very famous and attractive movie star, and asks him to come to his ex-wife's bedside and talk to her. Aided by Julian's voice, Mikaela rallies from unconsciousness and finds she must choose between the two men." Libr J

On Mystic lake. Crown 1999 323p $19.95

ISBN 0-609-60249-7 LC 98-26448

Annie Colwater "finds herself abandoned after 20 years by a faithless husband and a college-bound daughter. Having no identity of her own after spending her life nurturing them, she returns to her native Mystic, a logging town in Washington State. There she finds her old high school beau in crisis after his wife's suicide. His depression prevents him from caring for his small daughter, Izzy, who is also emotionally troubled. Annie is able to find meaning again through nurturing others." Libr J

"Never one to gush, [Hannah] is more than ever disciplined in her writing, and the result is a clean, deep thrust into the reader's heart." Publ Wkly

Hansen, Brooks, 1965-

The monsters of St. Helena. Farrar, Straus & Giroux 2002 306p $24

ISBN 0-374-27019-8 LC 2002-23433

This novel speculates on Napoleon's "second exile on the remote Atlantic island of St. Helena, where he spent his remaining years dictating his memoirs. Because his island residence is incomplete, the emperor-turned-prisoner stays with the Balcombe family, whose 14-year-old daughter Betsy befriends him. . . . As a contrast, the island's haunted history is revealed through its slaves, who all know the story of St. Helena's first exile, fallen nobleman Fernando Lopez, and his connection to the island." Libr J

"Hansen's characters, St. Helena aside, are obstinately alive, with their own plots, hopes and limits, especially with their own faith. The book's risky shape comes to seem almost as disciplined as a history—a matter of respect for the records Hansen has so precisely imagined." N Y Times Book Rev

Hansen, Erik Fosnes

Tales of protection; translated from the Norwegian by Nadia Christensen. Farrar, Straus & Giroux 2002 500p o.p.

ISBN 0-374-27240-9

Original Norwegian edition, 1998

"In present-day Norway, runaway Lea flees to her great-uncle Wilhelm's estate to escape a troubled past. . . . When Wilhelm dies, Lea finds herself entrusted to continue his vast business empire and lifework, which involves the connection between seemingly random events. From there, Hansen takes the reader on a journey to nineteenth-century Norway (where a lighthouse keeper's daughter battles illness) and to the escalating competition between two artists during the Italian Renaissance." Booklist

"Hansen favors the Russian doll approach to stories, in which one story is nested inside another. His 'serialism' is romantic in the deepest sense—allegories and narratives contain the deep structure of the world, while math and science are merely the mutable surface. The craft of 19th-century fiction and the complexity of 20th-century thought make this a gloriously rewarding novel." Publ Wkly

Hansen, Joseph

A country of old men; the last Dave Brandstetter mystery. Viking 1991 177p o.p.

LC 90-50550

"While investigating the murder of a drug-dealing musician and the kidnapping of a little boy who witnessed the killing, the gay detective stubbornly ignores the conspicuously poor state of his own health. But even as he drags his creaky bones on an exhausting and dangerous hunt for the killer, his fine, strong mind keeps turning to thoughts of mortality. . . . A cool stylist who never loses control over his emotional voice, Mr. Hansen trusts his lifelike characters to earn our compassion." NY Times Book Rev

Early graves; a Dave Brandstetter mystery. Mysterious Press 1987 184p o.p.

LC 87-15178

"Gay detective Dave Brandstetter tracks down a serial killer whose victims have all been young men dying of AIDS. Dave, in his 60s, has just returned to L.A. from a business trip, having been met at the airport by his young ex-lover, TV reporter Cecil, when he discovers the body of real-estate developer Drew Dodge on his porch steps. The man's death becomes linked to a string of stabbing murders, and it also becomes clear that he was killed first and then dropped at Dave's." Publ Wkly

Gravedigger; a Dave Brandstetter mystery. Holt, Rinehart & Winston 1982 183p o.p.

LC 81-6381

"A Rinehart suspense novel"

Insurance sleuth Dave Brandstetter "investigates the possible murder of a runaway teenage girl, who may have died by her own involvement with drugs, a strange cult, and the wrong kind of people. The missing girl's father, a corrupt lawyer engulfed by scandal, has run away, too, leaving Brandstetter with two cold trails and a lot of questions." Booklist

Hansen, Joseph—*Continued*

The little dog laughed; a Dave Brandstetter mystery. Holt & Co. 1986 184p o.p.
LC 86-12115

"A Rinehart suspense novel"

"Called in to investigate the death claims filed on the shooting demise of a globe-striding political journalist, insurance sleuth Brandstetter gets embroiled in international skulduggery. The writer was, of course, no suicide, and his death is linked to that of a young Latino sans green card who is from a Central American republic in turmoil." Booklist

Hansen, Ron

The assassination of Jesse James by the coward Robert Ford. Knopf 1983 304p o.p.
ISBN 0-394-51647-8 LC 83-47851

This "book begins with Jesse at the height of his notoriety. Waiting to hold up a train with his brother, Frank, and their gang, he meets Robert Ford, the 19-year-old brother of one of the gang members; Ford idolizes Jesse and [eventually murders him]." N Y Times Book Rev

"Hansen's Jesse is in no way romanticized; his interest derives from the complexity of his psychopathology. The Jesse that emerges here is prematurely decrepit; he'll murder when he doesn't need to, but he reads his Bible and talks about God's peace. Canny, intuitive, he seems to welcome the disciple who will betray him, even gives him the pistol for the job. . . . The novel works not despite our knowledge of what will happen, but because of it a sense of fatality hangs over every scene." Newsweek

Atticus; a novel. HarperCollins Pubs. 1996 247p o.p.
LC 95-38450

A novel "about Atticus Cody, a 67-year-old Colorado cattle man who goes to Mexico to retrieve the body of his younger son, an artist, alcoholic and, finally, a suicide. . . . A deeply grieving Atticus meets Scott's friends in the town of Resurrección and copes with the unknowns of a culture far removed from his ranch, where only recently 'carrots of ice were hanging from the roof's iron gutters.' As the Cody family history, which includes the death of Atticus's wife (mother of Scott, and his older, successful brother) in a car accident in which Scott was driving, is gradually revealed, Atticus comes to believe that Scott's death may have been at another's hand." Publ Wkly

"This is a didactic novel. It says that simplicity, purity and intelligence are good qualities to have. . . . It names great virtues and then looks at them glancingly, from all directions, finding them in unexpected forms. Mr. Hansen writes vigorously, and like an angel—so much so that 'Atticus' may end up giving didacticism a good name." N Y Times Book Rev

Hitler's niece; a novel. HarperFlamingo 1999 310p o.p.
ISBN 0-06-019419-7 LC 99-12656

"On September 18, 1931 Angelika (Geli) Raubal, the niece of Adolph Hitler, was found dead in her room in her uncle's flat, his pistol lying nearby. . . . Hansen's historically based novel offers one plausible scenario, that Hitler himself murdered her in a fit of anger over her attempts to escape his smothering jealousy. Using a variety of sources, including the memoirs and testimony of several of the principals involved, he attempts to dissect the nature of their relationship and show how such a conclusion is reasonable." Libr J

"Hansen's insightful, brilliantly interpretative, and frightening novel does more to illuminate the welter of evil that fueled Hitler than a dozen biographies." Booklist

Isn't it romantic?; an entertainment. HarperCollins Pubs. 2003 198p $17.95
ISBN 0-06-051766-2 LC 2002-69082

"Beautiful, self-possessed Parisian Natalie Clairvaux, a lover of all things American, decides to assuage her hurt feelings over her fiance's latest infidelity by taking a trip to the U.S. Appalled at Natalie's destination choice, the local travel agent grudgingly books her on a Greyhound See America tour. . . . When her fiance, Pierre, comes after her, they end up stranded by a flat tire in Seldom, Nebraska, and are lovingly embraced by the town's eccentric citizens." Booklist

"This is a preposterous plot, and at its best, 'Isnt It Romantic?' zips along like a Preston Sturges movie. Hansen slicks down his prose so the sentences are swift, and he punctuates them with a dry wit and some genuinely droll ripostes." N Y Times Book Rev

Mariette in ecstasy. Burlingame Bks. 1991 179p o.p.
ISBN 0-06-018214-8 LC 90-56362

This novel concerns "an early 19th-century monastery in upstate New York into which a beautiful young postulant comes in August 1906, only to be sent away in February 1907. The ostensible cause of neophyte Mariette's short-lived stay are her experiences of manifestations of the stigmata that begin four short months after her arrival and on the day of the death of her natural sister, who is 20 years her elder and also happens to be prioress of the monastery at the time." America

"The novel pulls its taut plot-thread smartly along from start to finish, weaving flash-forward patches of dialogue from the investigation of Mariette's 'case' into the unfolding action of her entry into the life of the convent. The finale is a stunner." N Y Times Book Rev

Hardesty, Sarah, 1950-

For works written by this author under other names see Roberts, Nora, 1950-

Hardie, Kerry

A winter marriage; a novel. Little, Brown 2003 394p $24.95
ISBN 0-316-07622-8 LC 2002-20781

"At a friend's wedding in England, widowed Hannie meets Ned Renvyle, a much older writer looking for a wife, and they agree to a pragmatic marriage—he gets a companion, she gets to share his money. Settling on Ned's farm in the Irish countryside, Hannie soon discovers that enduring the snooping of the snobbish community may be too high a price to pay for financial security, particularly when her disturbed teenage son, Joss, arrives." Publ Wkly

"This disquieting domestic drama effortlessly transforms itself into a taut psychological thriller featuring a harrowing back-story." Booklist

Harding, Paul

For works written by this author under other names see Doherty, P. C.

Hardwick, Mollie

The dreaming damozel. St. Martin's Press 1991 183p o.p.

LC 90-19457

This mystery features "Doran Fairweather, an English antiques dealer with a knack for discovering murder along with *objets d'art*. . . . Suffering from malaise after a miscarriage and the loss of her business partner to a more lucrative job, Doran hopes to spark new interest in her shop by branching into Pre-Raphaelite work; she is soon surprised to have a number of rare Rossetti drawings fall into her possession. Obsessed with Rossetti's dreaming figures and fascinated by a mysterious, eccentric man who entrusts her with one apparently rare artwork, Doran quickly links the art to murder." Publ Wkly

"The mystery plot seems a slender reed when stripped of its more piquant art-history references; but the story is gracefully written and full of interesting arcana about the antiques trade." N Y Times Book Rev

The Duchess of Duke Street; a novel. Holt, Rinehart & Winston 1977 c1976 303p o.p.

LC 76-29903

First published 1976 in the United Kingdom in two volumes with title The Duchess of Duke Street: Book 1: The way up; Book 2: The golden years

An "adaptation of a BBC television series. . . . The setting is 1900 London. Heroine Louisa Leyton sets out to be the best cook in England and ends up running a residential hotel and a catering service. The cast includes: Edward, Prince of Wales, whose interest in Luisa goes beyond her culinary skills; Augustus Trotter, who becomes Louisa's husband for propriety's sake and assists her as butler; and the Honorable Charles Tyrrel, who befriends Louisa in her post-Edward days. Although the episodic format is still evident in this novelization, it does not impair readability. There is enough adventure and humor here to entertain the reader willing to settle for a light-hearted if slightly unbelievable story." Libr J

Malice domestic. St. Martin's Press 1986 218p o.p.

LC 86-11376

This is the first novel featuring "Doran Fairweather, a humorously perceptive antiques dealer, and her love, the Reverend Chelmarsh, both of whom live in the isolated village of Abbotsbourne, Kent. A wealthy bachelor takes over the village's long-deserted great house. Events move from cozy to chilling when a series of deaths ensues, including a teen suicide. Graceful writing embellishes this stunning tale of evil." Booklist

Parson's pleasure. St. Martin's Press 1987 199p o.p.

LC 87-4437

This novel takes Doran Fairweather "to Warwickshire to track down the theft of priceless antiques from a rather eccentric elderly member of the aristocracy, Lady Timberlake. What starts off as a working holiday with her boyfriend, the prudish Rodney Chelmarsh, quickly turns serious when one of the leads Fairweather is investigating, a gypsy antiques dealer, is brutally murdered. Chelmarsh is the first to realize that Fairweather's own life may be in jeopardy. Hardwick has managed to breathe fresh life into this fairly conventional mystery. Everything is vaguely familiar, from the cast of dotty characters to the locale, but this only adds to the book's charm." Publ Wkly

Perish in July. St. Martin's Press 1990 205p o.p.

LC 89-77956

This Doran Fairweather mystery "finds the antiques dealer and her vicar husband involved in a parish fund-raising theatrical and the murder of its leading lady." Booklist

"Hardwick again writes about believable characters coping not only with murder and other disasters but with a true-to-life marriage." Publ Wkly

Hardy, Thomas, 1840-1928

Far from the madding crowd; with an etching by H. Macbeth-Raeburn and a map of Wessex. Knopf 1991 xxxiii, 243p $22

ISBN 0-679-40576-3 LC 91-52978

"Everyman's library"

First published 1874

"Bathsheba Everdene is loved by Gabriel Oak, a young farmer who becomes bailiff of the farm she inherits; by William Boldwood, who owns a neighboring farm; and by Sergeant Troy, a handsome inconsiderate young adventurer. She marries Troy, who mistreats her and squanders her money. When he leaves her and is presumed drowned at sea, Bathsheba becomes engaged to Boldwood. Troy, however, reappears, and is murdered by Boldwood, who goes mad as a result of his action and is sent to a mental institution. Bathsheba then marries Gabriel, the steadiest and most faithful of her three suitors." Reader's Ency. 4th edition

Jude the obscure. Knopf 1992 518p $20

ISBN 0-679-40993-9 LC 92-52925

"Everyman's library"

First published 1895

"Jude Fawley, a poor villager, wants to enter the divinity school at Christminster (Oxford University). Sidetracked by Arabella Donn, an earthy country girl who pretends to be pregnant by him, Jude marries her and is then deserted. He earns a living as a stonemason at Christminster; there he falls in love with his independent-minded cousin, Sue Bridehead. Out of a sense of obligation, Sue marries the schoolmaster Phillotson, who has helped her. Unable to bear living with Phillotson, she returns to live with Jude and eventually bears his children out of wedlock. Their poverty and the weight of society's disapproval begin to take a toll on Sue and Jude. . . . The novel's sexual frankness shocked the public, as did Hardy's criticisms of marriage, the university system, and the church." Merriam-Webster's Ency of Lit

The Mayor of Casterbridge; with an introduction by Craig Raine. Knopf 1993 362p map $18

ISBN 0-679-42035-5 LC 92-54297

"Everyman's library"

First published 1886. Variant title: The life and death of the Mayor of Casterbridge

"Michael Henchard, a hay-trusser, gets drunk at a fair and sells his wife and child for 5 guineas to a sailor, Newson. When sober again he takes a solemn vow not

Hardy, Thomas, 1840-1928—*Continued*

to touch alcohol for 20 years. By his energy and acumen he becomes rich, respected, and eventually the mayor of Casterbridge. After 18 years his wife returns, supposing Newson dead, and is reunited with her husband. She brings with her her daughter Elizabeth-Jane, and Henchard is led to believe that she is his child, whereas she is in fact Newson's. Through a combination of unhappy circumstances, and the impulsive obstinacy of Henchard, troubles accumulate." Oxford Companion to Engl Lit. 6th edition

The return of the native. Knopf 1992 xxxix, 497p map $22

ISBN 0-679-41730-3 LC 92-52901

"Everyman's library"

First published 1878

"The novel is set on Egdon Heath, a barren moor in the fictional Wessex in southwestern England. The native of the title is Clym Yeobright, who has returned to the area to become a schoolmaster after a successful but, in his opinion, a shallow career as a jeweler in Paris. He and his cousin Thomasin exemplify the traditional way of life, while Thomasin's husband, Damon Wildeve, and Clym's wife, Eustacia Vye, long for the excitement of city life. Disappointed that Clym is content to remain on the heath, Eustacia, willful and passionate, rekindles her affair with the reckless Damon. After a series of coincidences Eustacia comes to believe that she is responsible for the death of Clym's mother. Convinced that fate has doomed her to cause others pain, Eustacia flees and is drowned (by accident or intent). Damon drowns trying to save her." Merriam-Webster's Ency of Lit

Tess of the D'Urbervilles; with an introduction by Patricia Ingham. Knopf 1991 xlviii, 472p map $22

ISBN 0-679-40586-0 LC 91-52998

"Everyman's library"

First published in complete form 1891

"The tragic history of a woman betrayed. . . . Tess the author contends, is sinned against, but not a sinner; her tragedy is the work of tyrannical circumstances and of the evil deeds of others in the past and the present, and more particularly of two men's baseness, the seducer, and the well-meaning intellectual who married her. . . . The pastoral surroundings, the varying aspects of field, river, sky, serve to deepen the pathos of each stage in the heroine's calamities, or to add beauty and dignity to her tragic personality." Baker. Guide to the Best Fic

Under the greenwood tree. o.p.

First published 1872

"The first of the Wessex novels proper, the common groundwork of which is a very vivid delineation of the people of Dorset and the neighbouring counties, and of the natural life and scenery. . . . An idyll of village life, in which the members of a carrier's family and the village life choir, a gathering of rustic oddities, furnish a sort of comic chorus to the love-affairs of a rustic boy and girl." Baker. Guide to the Best Fic

Wessex tales. Wordsworth 1995 189p map pa $7.95

ISBN 0-19-283558-0

First published 1888

Contents: Three strangers; Tradition of eighteen hundred and four; Melancholy Hussar; Withered arm; Fellow-townsmen; Interlopers at the knap; Distracted preacher

Harfenist, Jean

A brief history of the flood; stories. Knopf 2002 212p $23

ISBN 0-375-41393-6 LC 2002-19068

Contents: Floating; Body count; Duck season; The gift; Salad girls; Voluntary breathers; Safety off, not a shot fired; Pixie dust; The road out of Acorn Lake; Fully bonded by the state of Minnesota; The history of the flood

"In 11 linked short stories set between 1959 and 1970, this jolting, highly colored narrative traces the life of Lillian Anderson from eight to 18. She and her sister and two brothers live in a perpetually flooded, rundown house in Acorn Lake, Minn. . . . The author's direct narrative style, though sometimes abrupt, gives Lillian's story a bright, three-dimensional quality." Publ Wkly

Harington, Donald

Ekaterina; a novel. Harcourt Brace Jovanovich 1993 373p o.p.

ISBN 0-15-128122-X LC 92-37830

This novel centers around an exiled Russian princess named Ekaterina Vladimirovna Dadeshkaliani "who arrives in the United States with a rudimentary knowledge of English, a passion for pubescent boys, and a deep-seated fear that her Russian psychiatrist tormentor, Bolshakov, is still on her trail. With the help of a ghost and an alcoholic art historian cum novelist, she discovers her own talent for fiction and makes enough money to take over a suite of rooms in an old mountain resort hotel (a la Nabokov). Eventually, however, both Bolshakov and her taste for 12-year-olds catch up with her and her world comes crashing down. Or does it?" Libr J

"It may be Harington's eccentric, second-person point of view that vaults his novel into completely postmodern territory, however; the 'I' who intrudes with long, literary asides . . . is actually an omniscient ghost who refers to Ekaterina throughout as 'you.' These conceits inside of conceits do add up to a marvelously entertaining novel, however, no doubt partly because Nabokov is the model: Harington has outdone himself." Booklist

With. Toby Press 2004 c2003 491p $19.95

ISBN 1-59264-050-8

In this novel, set in the Ozark town of Stay More, "a golden-haired seven-year-old girl is abducted and taken to a deserted house in the mountains by a retired cop. When he dies, she is left alone to fend for herself. Or almost alone: parts of the book dwell in the thoughts of a wise old dog who befriends her; others are narrated by the spirit of a young boy who had to leave Stay More when his parents moved to California, but who loved the place so much that part of him stuck around." New Yorker

"With is as whimsical as a paper-doll show while being deeply rooted in the earth; it gives the Garden of Eden myth a happy ending, and should find the wide readership that Harington so richly deserves." Washington Post Book World

Harlan, Thomas, 1929-

House of reeds; Thomas Harlan. 1st ed. TOR Bks 2004 414p map $25.95
ISBN 0-7653-0193-8 LC 2003-57060
"Gretchen Anderssen and her team are shunted from long-overdue leave to the investigation of a rumored First Sun artifact on the obscure planet Jagan. There they land in the middle of a 'flowery war' arranged by the priests to improve the emperor's youngest son, Tezozomoc's, reputation. And Gretchen can't get a permit for the main site on Jagan, because of university politics and the archaeologist already working at it. But then she gets a tip about one city's oldest building, the House of Reeds. She befriends an aging member of the other species present, though also nonnative, on Jagan. He is a former gardener, and with him she enters the House of Reeds. . . . The mystery of the long-gone forerunners of the empire Gretchen knows develops grippingly." Booklist

Harper, Karen

The Poyson garden. Delacorte Press 1999 310p o.p.
ISBN 0-385-33283-1 LC 98-36420
"Elizabeth Tudor, daughter of Henry VIII and Anne Boleyn, bides her time as her half-sister, Queen Mary I, burns heretics and sickens in the year 1558. Elizabeth's time may be short, however: a murderer, possibly backed by Mary, is poisoning anyone related to the Boleyn family. . . . Closely guarded at Hatfield by Thomas Pope and his wife, Beatrice, Elizabeth nonetheless determines to uncover the mysterious veiled woman behind the poisonings." Publ Wkly
"Elizabeth's active role may strain credulity a bit, but this one is great fun all the same." Booklist

The queene's Christmas; Karen Harper. 1st ed. Thomas Dunne Books 2003 287p map $24.95
ISBN 0-312-30175-8 LC 2003-46822
"It is the Christmas season of 1564, and Elizabeth wants her subjects to enjoy the holidays while she attempts to outwit her devious Catholic cousin, Mary Queen of Scots, who is plotting to steal the throne of England. Elizabeth has planned an elaborate holiday feast, but the preparations go awry when Master Hodge Thatcher, Dresser of the Queene's Privy Kitchen, is found hanging in his workroom adorned with the peacock feathers meant for decorating the roasted bird. Elizabeth must solve the crime before she becomes another victim. The wonderful historical detail mixed with intrigue and authentic Elizabethan recipes enliven this story." Booklist

The tidal poole; an Elizabeth I mystery. Delacorte Press 2000 290p o.p.
ISBN 0-385-33284-X LC 99-43315
"During her coronation procession into the city of London, Elizabeth I finds herself in the midst of crime and political intrigue. The murders of a lady of the court and another victim may be part of a plot to overthrow her government. This mystery full of scheming Tudors, Seymours, and Dudleys is a page-turner based on historical sources." Booklist

Harrar, George, 1949-

The spinning man. Putnam 2003 341p $24.95
ISBN 0-399-14983-X LC 2002-74532
This suspense novel "follows a philosophy professor under invesigation for the disappearance of a teenage cheerleader. Evan Birch gets pulled over by the police one evening on his way home from the supermarket with his 10-year-old twin sons. The police haul him in for interrogation, and he learns that a car much like his was spotted at the park where 16-year-old Joyce Bonner, a local high school student, was working the afternoon she disappeared. He's released after questioning, but damning circumstantial evidence continues to pile up." Publ Wkly
"A graceful and subtle writer, Harrar invites us to identify with the philosopher's struggles to maintain his mental equilibrium, even as the novel dangles the possibility that the mind might not always be in control of the body's behaviors." N Y Times Book Rev

Harries, Ann

Manly pursuits. Bloomsbury Pub.; distributed by St. Martin's Press 1999 339p $24.95
ISBN 1-58234-019-6
"Cape Town, 1899, Cecil Rhodes, arch-imperialist and tycoon, believes he has only months to live, and that he can be saved only by hearing the sound of British birdsong. . . . Professor Francis Wills, a reclusive Oxford don, arrives in Cape Town with two hundred songbirds . . . on the eve of the Anglo-Boer war. But the birds, confused by the change of season and hemisphere, refuse to sing. In Rhodes' gloomy, male-dominated estate, suffused with erotic undercurrents, Wills is drawn into intrigue - romantic, political and ornithological." Publisher's note
"This is a fascinating look at the turn of the last century, the infancy of industrialization, and the decline of imperialism, with hints of the decadence of the sexually repressed Victorian era." Booklist

Harrigan, Stephen, 1948-

The gates of the Alamo; a novel. Knopf 2000 581p $25
ISBN 0-679-44717-2 LC 99-33437
This novel is set during the struggle between Texans and Mexicans for the Alamo in 1836. Harrigan concentrates "on fictional characters caught up in a struggle not of their own making—an American naturalist, a female innkeeper and her son, [and] Mexican soldiers." Newsweek
"Harrigan has crafted a compulsively readable historical drama on a grand scale, peopled with highly believable frontier personalities—Mexican as well as American—and suffused with period authenticity." Publ Wkly

Harris, Deborah Turner

(jt. auth) Kurtz, K. The temple and the stone

Harris, E. Lynn

And this too shall pass; a novel. Doubleday 1996 347p o.p.
ISBN 0-385-48030-X LC 95-38844

Harris, E. Lynn—*Continued*

Among the African American characters featured in this novel are "Zurich Robinson, a gay pro-football quarterback; MamaCee, aka Miss Cora, his grandmother; Caliph Taylor, a Chicago cop who is devoted to his daughter; successful attorney Tamela Coleman; sports anchor Mia Miller; and gay sports reporter Sean Elliott. The major plot concerns Zurich's acceptance of his gayness and his developing relationship with Sean. Subplots involve Mia and Tamela, who both struggle with their careers, their relationships with men, and one another. . . . Ultimately both fun and moving, the book has something to impress nearly any reader." Booklist

If this world were mine; a novel. Doubleday 1997 318p o.p.

ISBN 0-385-48655-3 LC 97-18795

"Members of a monthly journal-writing group, four African American friends from college days who all live in the Chicago area, help each other through the dramas of their respective lives. They're all approaching 40 and looking for answers: Riley Woodson, a self-proclaimed Black Princess immured in a stultifying marriage; Yolanda Williams, a media consultant; gay psychiatrist Leland Thompson; and Dwight Scott, a computer engineer simmering with hatred for white people. . . . A supple raconteur, Harris explores the intimacies of friendship with a sensitive eye." Publ Wkly

Not a day goes by; a novel. Doubleday 2000 271p $19.95

ISBN 0-385-49824-1 LC 00-38368

"When John 'Basil' Henderson, ex-football player and sports agent on the rise, falls in love with haughty, ambitious Broadway star Yancey Harrington Braxton, it seems like a perfect match. But on the couple's wedding day, which opens the book, the extravagant nuptials are suddenly canceled. The narrative retraces the couple's rocky courtship. . . . Determined to mary, have children, and keep his homosexual proclivities a secret, Basil doesn't realize that Yancey has a few secrets of her own." Publ Wkly

Harris, Joanne

Chocolat; a novel. Viking 1999 242p o.p.

ISBN 0-670-88179-1 LC 98-21771

"When Vianne Rocher and her daughter arrive in the small French town of Lansquenet-sous-Tannes, they open a shop specializing in exquisite, voluptuous chocolates. This is the first breath of giddiness the town has ever felt. So isolated is the place, it still rigorously maintains Lenten abstinences, and the town priest takes umbrage at the effrontery of this *arriviste* scheduling a festival of chocolate for Easter Sunday. . . . Harris' writing conveys a multitude of images and captures the self-absorption of small town life in France." Booklist

Coastliners; a novel. Morrow 2002 350p o.p.

ISBN 0-06-019812-5 LC 2001-59045

A novel "set on the provincial French island of Le Devin. Madeleine Prasteau leaves her Paris apartment to return to the island village of Les Salants, where she discovers that her father, a widowed boat owner, is going downhill along with the village itself as the rival town of La Houssiniere grows and prospers. Despite her father's chilly greeting, Madeleine spruces up the family home, and when she meets an attractive, mysterious stranger named Flynn she gets involved in a project to save Les Salants." Publ Wkly

Harris "expertly weaves her themes of family, community, and loyalty and shows how these values can be affected by money. Most impressively, she vividly depicts how a bleak, patchy strip of land can be synonymous with home." Booklist

Five quarters of the orange. Morrow 2001 307p $25

ISBN 0-06-019813-3 LC 00-48952

"Framboise Dartigen, a stoic widow, is almost 65 and living a shadow life in the small French farmhouse she and her family abandoned after a mysterious tragedy that took place during the German occupation in World War II. . . . Having returned as an old woman, no longer recognizable to the families in the village that last saw her at 9, Framboise opens up a restaurant, using her mother's recipes. All might be well, until Framboise begins to decode what happened so many years ago by reading the tortured scribblings of her mother, hidden in an album she bequeathed to her." N Y Times Book Rev

"Harris has constructed a multilayered plot, punctuated with scrumptious descriptons of French delicacies and telling depictions of the war's jolting effects on one fragile family. This intense work brims with sensuality and sensitivity." Publ Wkly

Harris, Mark, 1922-

Bang the drum slowly; by Henry W. Wiggen; certain of his enthusiasms restrained by Mark Harris. Knopf 1956 243p o.p.

A baseball novel which centers on Bruce, a black catcher, who is slowly dying of Hodgkin's disease. The narrator tries to keep the matter a secret, but eventually it comes out. The rest of the book concerns the loyalty of Bruce's teammates to their doomed member

"Narrated by 'Author' in the raucous speech of the ball park, yet with an elegiac dignity." Booklist

Harris, Robert, 1957-

Archangel; a novel. Random House 1999 373p o.p.

ISBN 0-679-42888-7 LC 98-33655

This novel follows the "progress of Fluke Kelso, an academic who has dug up the diary of Stalin's last days. The failing dictator got a woman pregnant, the papers suggest, and she may have returned to Archangel, her home in the north." Time

"The sinewy plot never slackens, but what makes the book memorable are the vividly observed backgrounds. . . . No less authentic are the fragmented but undead relics of the old Soviet system." Natl Rev

Enigma. Random House 1995 320p o.p.

LC 95-11335

This thriller is set at "Bletchley Park, the remote, ultra-secret WW II British code-breaking center. In February 1943, having just cracked the key to the confoundingly complex Nazi code known as Shark, Thomas Jericho, an unworldly young academic, returns to his old digs at Cambridge to recuperate from nervous exhaustion and a broken heart. But Jericho has time to regain only a modicum of strength before he is pressed back into service to

Harris, Robert, 1957-—*Continued*
break the latest Nazi code—the putatively impregnable Enigma." Publ Wkly

"As one expects from a thriller-writer, Harris ensures the tension builds inexorably as the plot unfolds. Unlike some, however, he creates characters that linger in the mind, and he never bores his readers with gratuitous technical detail." New Sci

Fatherland. Random House 1992 338p o.p.
LC 91-51026

This thriller is "based on the premise that Hitler won the war and now rules a vast trans-European empire. On the eve of Hitler's 75th birthday, just when America's President Joseph P. Kennedy is expected in Berlin, the body of a once-important Nazi official washes up along the Rhine. Investigator Xavier March persists in checking out the case, despite orders to the contrary from the Gestapo itself, and soon he discovers a conspiracy whose roots date back to World War II." Libr J

"'Fatherland' is a bleak book. But what concerns the author is the indestructibility of the human spirit, as exemplified by Xavier March. If Hitler's Germany is hell, at least a few angels are floating around." N Y Times Book Rev

Pompeii. Random House 2003 278p $24.95
ISBN 0-679-42889-5 LC 2003-58446

A thriller about the "eruption of Mount Vesuvius in A. D. 79. It starts innocently enough; two days before the eruption, Marcus Attilius Primus, the engineer in charge of the massive Aqua Augusta Aqueduct, is summoned to the estate of Ampilatus. He is in the process of executing a slave for killing his fish. Attilius finds sulfur in the water and immediately realizes the problem is bigger than a few dead fish. With the approval of the famous admiral Pliny, Attilius sails to Pompeii and treks to the heart of the Aqua Augusta at the base of Mount Vesuvius. Attilius discovers the blockage that threatens to deprive a large chunk of the empire of water, but he is also troubled by the strange natural occurrences that may portend something far more serious than a blocked water supply." Booklist

"Lively writing, convincing but economical period details and plenty of intrigue keep the pace quick." Publ Wkly

Harris, Thomas, 1940-

Black Sunday. Dutton 2000 c1975 318p $26.95
ISBN 0-525-94555-5 LC 00-24649

A reissue of the title first published 1975 by Putnam

"In retaliation for American aid to Israel, an Arab terrorist group has determined to blow up the Super Bowl. Their prime weapon is Michael Lander, a former Navy pilot, whose own strange psyche, combined with his experiences as prisoner of war in Vietnam, has driven him to seek revenge against a world he believes has savaged him. As the pilot of the Aldrich television blimp that floats above professional football games and a brilliant technician, Lander is uniquely qualified to carry out the act of madness that obsesses him." Publisher's note

"All is neck and neck, quite excitingly to the very end. . . . The action is . . . very violent (violent sexy episodes, too) and the plot is packed with business. Not a bit believable, but successful entertainment." Libr J

Hannibal. Delacorte Press 1999 486p $27.95
ISBN 0-385-29929-X LC 99-29774

In this sequel to The silence of the lambs, "FBI agent Clarise Starling, is slated to take the fall for a botched arrest. Yet when a manipulative millionaire revives the FBI's interest in the still-at-large Lecter, Starling is reunited with her mentor, Jack Crawford, and sets to work on tracking the good doctor." Libr J

"Where Silence haunted and tantalized, Hannibal grosses out and gratifies. Yet there's still a basso ostinato of serious questions, and the answers are darker than in Silence." Nation

Red Dragon. Dutton 2000 c1981 348p $26.95
ISBN 0-525-94556-3 LC 00-22500

A reissue of the title first published 1981 by Putnam

This novel concerns "a psychopathic mass murderer with an intuitive FBI investigator on his trail. . . . [The ex-F.B.I. man] is Will Graham, whose acute perception gives him entree to murderers' minds. With two mass killers to his credit, he's lured from peaceful retirement and happy marriage to hunt the Red Dragon, slayer of two families within a month. A dedicated group of forensic experts and a dogged scandal sheet reporter also pursue the killer—born with a cleft palate, cruelly mistreated as a child, skewed by the sight of a powerful painting, and side-tracked by warm attention from a blind woman." Libr J

"This is a chilling, tautly written, and well-realized psychological thriller. . . . The suspense is sustained by deft characterizations, fascinating crime-lab details, a twisting plot, and understated prose." Saturday Rev

The silence of the lambs. St. Martin's Press 1988 338p $24.95
ISBN 0-312-02282-4 LC 88-18203

"Agent Clarice Starling of the FBI's behavioral science section is assigned to conduct a psychological profile of Hannibal Lecter, a psychiatrist imprisoned for serial murder. Uncooperative at first, Lecter then says he can help identify a serial killer who has eluded authorities for months. Lecter's aid proves invaluable, and Starling soon finds herself using one madman to catch another." Libr J

"Harris places his clues with precision, and his characterizations . . . are superbly developed and richly complex." Booklist

Followed by Hannibal

Harrison, Colin, 1960-

Afterburn. Farrar, Straus & Giroux 1999 438p $25
ISBN 0-374-10205-8 LC 99-13660

"Powerful businessman Charlie Ravich, a former Vietnam POW, thrives on the hectic world of global commerce. Columbia dropout Christina Welles has been in prison for four years when she is mysteriously released. Her boyfriend, Rick, is desperate to find her, believing that mobster Tony V. arranged her release and wants her killed." Libr J

"Harrison writes extremely well, and sections of 'Afterburn' are as elegant as you'll hope to find in any novel." N Y Times Book Rev

The Havana room. Farrar, Straus and Giroux 2004 385p $24
ISBN 0-374-29986-2 LC 2003-9238

Harrison, Colin, 1960-—*Continued*

"What goes on in the by-invitation-only Havana Room of a midtown steakhouse is certainly bizarre—but no odder than what happens in a Long Island potato field when a Chilean wine maker decides to expand his empire. Caught in the middle are two most unlikely heroes: Bill Wyeth, a real estate lawyer whose career and marriage are destroyed by a terrible accident involving a child, and Jay Rainey, a hulking, strangely sympathetic con artist. Linking these two is a touching and complicated woman, Allison Sparks, who manages the steakhouse but longs for more." Publ Wkly

"Most thrillers begin with a murder or a kidnapping or some other dread deed. 'The Havana Room' begins with a quote from Schopenhauer. The weighty epigraph signals an engagingly unconventional thriller, full of ruminations on the human condition. . . . Colin Harrison keeps the pages turning at a spanking clip." Economist

Harrison, Harry, 1925-

King and emperor. TOR Bks. 1996 384p (Hammer and the cross, bk3) o.p.

LC 95-53325

"A Tom Doherty Associates book"

In this concluding volume of the author's alternate history trilogy "protagonist Shef is now the unquestioned king of the North but faces the ultimate challenge of meeting the Holy Roman Empire. He succeeds in this and in love, too, and a saga's end, Europe enjoys a stable peace, Shef's technological and social innovations are spreading, and Shef has found a degree of personal happiness." Booklist

One king's way. TOR Bks. 1995 399p (Hammer and the cross, bk2) o.p.

LC 94-46358

"A Tom Doherty Associates book"

Sequel to The hammer and the cross (1993)

"Norse ruler, Shef Sigvarthsson, is finding that both Christians and less civilized Norsemen want him dead, that the Norse gods are not as well suited to an established religion as was expected, and that he will need all his statecraft and technical ingenuity to keep the proverbial alligators from biting him, never mind draining the swamp. One of his creations is a huge war fleet, which is to be used for defense but also creates the potential for empire building beyond the Channel." Booklist

"The story is richly laden with detailed accounts of period naval warfare and changes in technology and culture, but one of its most satisfying pleasures is the intertwining of pagan mythologies and Christian dreams." Publ Wkly

Followed by King and emperor

Return to Eden; illustrations by Bill Sanderson. Bantam Bks. 1988 348p il o.p.

LC 88-10436

The concluding volume of the Eden trilogy "sees contentions growing once more as rabble-rousers on both sides push for war. The pacifist Yilanè Daughters of Life are split while Kerrick's nemesis, the deposed Yilanè leader Vaintè, still seeks vengeance on him." Publ Wkly

"Harrison's conclusion to his alternate prehistory of Earth excels in its detailed depiction of an alien civilization that might have been. " Libr J

The Stainless Steel Rat joins the circus. TOR Bks. 1999 269p o.p.

ISBN 0-312-86934-7 LC 99-34005

"A Tom Doherty Associates book"

Following The Stainless Steel Rat goes to Hell (1996), the master criminal takes on a new assignment. "After taking a job infiltrating a suspicious circus on a four million credit a day retainer, DiGriz finds himself and his family bound up, literally at times, in a planet-wide swindle. Someone is robbing banks and other sources of wealth using The Rat's good name while he dutifully performs his magic act under the big top. Soon DiGriz is hunted by endless factions of the police, his son Bolivar is jailed, his wife Angelina kidnapped, his formerly benevolent employer is getting more sinister by the hour and worst of all, The Stainless Steel Rat is actually losing money!" Publ Wkly

The Stainless Steel Rat sings the blues. Bantam Bks. 1994 229p o.p.

LC 93-31809

"Caught in the act of robbing the new mint on the planet Paskonjak, master thief Jim DiGriz, a.k.a. the Stainless Steel Rat, is offered a deal by the Galactic League: discover a stolen artifact thought to be somewhere on the prison planet Liokukae within 30 days and go free—or die. In the same vein as previous adventures featuring Harrison's irrepressible antihero . . . this latest outing boasts fast-paced action, a hint of melodrama, and a sizable dose of satirical tweaks at modern culture." Libr J

Stainless steel visions; illustrated by Bryn Barnard. TOR Bks. 1993 254p il o.p.

LC 92-43879

"A Tom Doherty Associates book"

Contents: The streets of Ashkelon; Toy shop; Not me, not Amos Cabot!; The mothballed spaceship; Commando raid; The repairman; Brave newer world; The secret of Stonehenge; Rescue operation; Portrait of the artist; Survival planet; Roommates; The golden years of The Stainless Steel Rat

"Thirteen of Harrison's robust, fast-paced tales. One is a new tale of his best-known hero, Slippery Jim DiGriz, the Stainless Steel Rat. Another is 'Roommates,' the basis for the movie *Soylent Green*. The other 11 range widely over Harrison's 40-year career and many interests (not to mention more than a few prejudices). All reflect Harrison's acknowledged status as heir to the pulp tradition of keeping the story moving forward at all costs." Booklist

West of Eden; illustrated by Bill Sanderson. Bantam Bks. 1984 483p il o.p.

LC 84-6306

First volume of the author's Eden trilogy

"Alternate-history story in which the dinosaurs were not killed off and ultimately produced sentient, humanoid descendants devoted to biotechnology. Their civilized race is ultimately forced into contact and conflict with savage human beings, adding culture shock to crisis. Inventive, fast-paced narrative." Anatomy of Wonder 4

Followed by Winter in Eden

Harrison, Harry, 1925-—*Continued*

Winter in Eden; illustrations by Bill Sanderson. Bantam Bks. 1986 398p il o.p.

LC 86-14168

In the second volume of the Eden trilogy "the bitter struggle for dominance between the reptilian Yilanes and the human Tanus continues as Vainte, a cunning Yilane enraged by the destruction of her city, vows to annihilate not only her Tanu nemesis, Kerrick, but also the entire Tanu race." Booklist

Followed by Return to Eden

Harrison, Jamie, 1960-

Blue Deer thaw; a mystery. Hyperion 2000 271p $22.95

ISBN 0-7868-6422-2 LC 99-27230

A mystery featuring Blue Deer, Montana sheriff Jules Clement, "a chronically depressed cop with a Ph.D. in archaeology and a history of drug abuse. Jules is moonlighting at the Sacajawea Hotel, taking inventory of Halsey Meriwether's fabulous, if eccentric, collection of art. . . . Halsey is a very rich man who has written a very dumb will that practically begs his heirs to murder him." N Y Times Book Rev

"Clement continues to be one of the most interesting and believable mystery heroes working the American turf, and Harrison demonstrates once again that she's among the most talented writers to grace the genre in recent years." Publ Wkly

An unfortunate prairie occurrence. Hyperion 1998 369p o.p.

ISBN 0-7868-6260-2 LC 97-24087

This "novel about Sheriff Clement and the residents of Blue Deer, Montana, opens with a crazy autumn crime wave—everything from serial rape to a divorced couple battling for custody of a dog. Then campers find a human skeleton, and an elderly rancher perishes in a truck fire—an apparent suicide. While keeping the lid on the mayhem, Clement and his deputies try to identify the skeleton and determine if the suicide is really murder." Booklist

The author allows "us to linger in Blue Deer long enough to learn its history, drink in the scenery and laugh at the kinks and quirks of its idiosyncratic residents. No wonder the world-weary Jules came running back home the first chance he got—the place is heaven." N Y Times Book Rev

Harrison, Jim, 1937-

The beast God forgot to invent. Atlantic Monthly Press 2000 274p o.p.

ISBN 0-87113-821-2 LC 00-38620

"Three novellas from a master of the genre offer characters that have staying power: a wealthy 67-year-old man, describing events leading up to the drowning of a younger friend; a Native American tracking a double-dealing friend to recover a clan relic; his stolen bearskin; and a middle-aged writer of formulaic biographies who glibly narrates his tribulations." Booklist

The beast God forgot to invent [novelette]

In Harrison, J. The beast God forgot to invent

I forgot to go to Spain

In Harrison, J. The beast God forgot to invent

The road home. Atlantic Monthly Press 1998 446p $25

ISBN 0-87113-724-0 LC 98-8391

Sequel to Dalva (1988)

This novel "continues the multigenerational tale of Dalva's Northridge family, primarily Nebraska land baron John Northridge, his sons, his granddaughter Dalva, and Nelse, Dalva's son, who was taken from her at birth and is now trying to find her." Libr J

"This saga is as homespun as an old quilt. A woman and her grown son, whom she'd put up for adoption, are reunited. An old man makes his peace as he approaches death. Each family member stitches in a piece of the family history. They are such good company you forget they exist nowhere but in Harrison's imagination." Newsweek

Westward ho

In Harrison, J. The beast God forgot to invent

Harrison, Kathryn

The binding chair; or, A visit from the Foot Emancipation Society: a novel. Random House 2000 312p o.p.

ISBN 0-679-45000-9 LC 99-34559

"Hobbled at the age of five by traditional foot-binding, Mai is also crippled by 19th-century gender rules that demand female subservience. After an arranged marriage turns abusive, Mai flees to Shanghai and becomes a prostitute, the only vocation open to women without familial support. A subsequent second marriage to do-gooder Arthur Cohen, and her integration into his extended family, are the vehicles through which Harrison delves into . . . questions about race, class, assimilation, and gender." Libr J

"Harrison's vision is bold and unsparing, portraying a world in which a woman's survival comes at a terrible cost. . . . The novel continually surprises. Its narrative turns and its tonal shifts—from the rhythms of the epic to those of the erotic, with pauses for comedy along the way—are as deft as they are unexpected." N Y Times Book Rev

The seal wife; a novel. Random House 2002 224p o.p.

ISBN 0-375-50629-2 LC 2001-48979

"In 1915, 26-year-old Bigelow Greene is sent to establish a U.S. weather station in Anchorage. . . . Bigelow is a single-minded man; he first becomes obsessed with the idea of building a huge kite to measure air temperature high in the atmosphere and thus enable long-range forecasting. But he's soon smitten with a woman the locals call the Aleut. She's mysterious, enigmatic, virtually mute—sex between she and Bigelow is wordless—and when he discovers that she's left Anchorage, Bigelow almost goes mad with longing." Publ Wkly

"Painterly in its pearlescent evocation of the Alaskan landscape, steeped in myth and the magic of science, this is a delectably moody, erotic, and provocative cross-cultural love story." Booklist

Harrison, Payne

Storming Intrepid. Crown 1989 473p o.p.

ISBN 0-517-57133-1 LC 88-22905

Harrison, Payne—*Continued*

This thriller "tells the story of a U.S. space shuttle that carries the components for the Strategic Defense Initiative (SDI). Something goes wrong and the U.S. loses control of the craft to the Russians." Booklist

"After building a wonder of technical wizardry high above the earth, Harrison lets his heroes duke it out in a fierce showdown near ground level. This novel hums with vigor." Libr J

Harrison, Sue

Brother Wind; a novel. Morrow 1994 494p o.p.
LC 94-14271

This volume completes the trilogy about "the harsh and dramatic adventures of Kiin, Samiq and other Aleutian Islanders of 9000 years ago. When her husband is killed by Raven (of the Walrus People tribe), Kiin, an accomplished carver, is forced to abandon both her own tribe of the First Men and one of her twin sons and return with the killer to his village. In revenge, Samiq, chief hunter of the First Men and brother of the murdered man, seeks Raven's death. . . . Informed by Native American legends, myths and traditions and replete with convincing recreations of trading practices, seal hunting and vision fasts, this novel offers an emotionally compelling conclusion to a monumental saga." Publ Wkly

Call down the stars. Morrow 2001 446p o.p.
ISBN 0-380-97372-3 LC 2001-30541

The concluding volume of the author's Storyteller trilogy set in prehistoric Alaska. This installment "features two storytellers: Yikaas, a young, handsome, and fiery-tempered member of the River People tribe; and Qumalix, a beautiful, clever, and high-spirited member of the Sea Hunters tribe. These two quick-witted characters spend their evenings sparring verbally and weaving tales of their historic ancestors for their gathered tribespeople. . . . Well-written and meticulously researched, Harrison's powerful yarn details the hardships and simplicity faced by prehistoric people while also emphasizing their humanity." Booklist

Cry of the wind. Avon Bks. 1998 448p o.p.
ISBN 0-380-97371-5 LC 98-8837

The second volume of the Storyteller saga continues the story "of K'os, who seeks revenge for rape and enslavement by the Near River people, and Chakliux, the Cousin River Village's respected storyteller and K'os's adopted son." Libr J

"Harrison's research is clearly reflected in her meticulous attention to details as disparate as the careful sewing of a parka and the rituals of a caribou hunt. Her characters are based on ancient Native American mythologies and storytelling traditions." Publ Wkly

Mother earth, father sky. Doubleday 1990 313p o.p.
LC 89-25656

This is "the story of an Aleutian woman living around 7000 B.C. When her village is destroyed by a hostile tribe, Chagak flees to her grandfather in the Whale Hunter tribe. Along the way, she finds safety with old Shuganan, but her trails do not end there. She endures brutalization and childbirth. . . . Harrison's fine first novel is based on thorough research into the lifestyle and beliefs of ancient Aleutians; exquisite detail imparts great viability to her characters." Booklist

Followed by My sister the moon

My sister the moon. Doubleday 1992 449p o.p.
LC 91-29102

The second volume in the author's trilogy "picks up 16 years after 'Mother Earth Father Sky' leaves off. . . . The beautiful Kiin is promised to Amgigh, but has been in love with his brother Samiq for years. Violently abused by her father, marriage is a relief for Kiin. But her jealous younger brother brutally kidnaps and rapes her and tries to sell her as a slave into a marriage far from their homeland. The brutality and physical and sexual abuses are vividly portrayed, as well as the rigid roles of men and women." Baya Book Rev

Followed by Brother Wind

Song of the river. Avon Bks. 1997 484p map o.p.
ISBN 0-380-97370-7 LC 97-18455

The first book of the Storyteller saga tells the story "of poisonous revenge for the rape of a young woman, K'os, by men from a neighboring village. Most of it transpires several decades after that calamity, when K'os uses her sexual prowess and manipulative abilities to stir up a war with the offenders' village. . . . Complex and well imagined, the interlocking societies of Harrison's ancient Aleutians make a compelling backdrop for this tale of romance and revenge." Booklist

Followed by Cry of the wind

Harrod-Eagles, Cynthia

Blood lines; an Inspector Bill Slider mystery. Scribner 1996 281p o.p.
ISBN 0-684-80047-0 LC 96-8555

Inspector Slider investigates the "death of a prominent music critic who comes to a violent end in the men's room of a BBC recording studio. Each plot twist, including one devious turn that throws suspicion on a former member of Slider's murder squad, hangs on the testimony of the complicated characters, who are among the author's finest stock." N Y Times Book Rev

Death to go. Scribner 1994 c1993 281p o.p.
ISBN 0-684-19650-6 LC 93-10374

First published 1993 in the United Kingdom with title: Necrochip

"Detective Inspector Bill Slider is called on when a teenager finds a human finger among the fried potatoes she ordered at a London fish-and-chips shop. Body parts continue to surface as events expand to include a sinister business tycoon, a prostitutes' rooming house, three mysterious Asians, an odd mix of gay men and five murders." Publ Wkly

"Murder provides the foundation for this extraordinary novel, but, it's finally an examination of love, love lost, and ways in which people cope with both." Booklist

Death watch. Scribner 1993 c1992 280p o.p.
LC 92-30924

First published 1992 in the United Kingdom

"Grim reality and intimations of immortality confront London detectives Slider and Atherton when they respond to the arson murder of a womanizing salesman. The victim, a deceptive man of failing business, marriage, and personal aspirations, serves as a foil to Slider

Harrod-Eagles, Cynthia—*Continued*
(himself unhappily married) and ladies' man Atherton, who bounce theories off each other as they gather information and suspects." Libr J

"This is a fine example of the British procedural—a simmering rather than boiling narrative, plenty of quick wit, and a splash of romantic intrigue, all skillfully written and solidly plotted." Booklist

Grave music; an Inspector Bill Slider mystery. Scribner 1995 c1994 234p o.p.
ISBN 0-684-80046-2 LC 94-39222
First published 1994 in the United Kingdom with title: Dead end
"Just as the Royal London Philharmonic is about to start rehearsal, the famous conductor Sir Stefan Radek drops dead on the podium, shot by a mysterious stranger. Slider and his . . . partner Atherton get the case and quickly discover that there is no lack of suspects due to the widely held opinion that Sir Stefan was nasty, vindictive, and generally despicable—a view even shared by his family." Booklist
"Though readers may guess the murderer early on in this . . . [novel, Slider's] police cohorts, and his violinist love, Joanna, are among the most appealing cast in recent memory. Their relationships, the music world setting, and the clever dialog . . . recommend this to all collections." Libr J

Killing time; an Inspector Bill Slider mystery. Scribner 1998 313p o.p.
ISBN 0-684-83776-5 LC 97-26290
First published 1996 in the United Kingdom
In this mystery London's Inspector Bill Slider's "attention is divided between solving the murder of a male striptease dancer—a case that extends from seedy Soho cabarets to the posh country homes of cabinet ministers—and sorting out the needs and demands of his estranged wife and new lover. . . . Many readers may guess the killer early on, but that shouldn't interfere with their appreciation for the rumpled, empathetic Slider, whose ability to see the complexity in the people around him is both his strength and his weakness." Booklist

Orchestrated death; a mystery introducing Inspector Bill Slider. Scribner 1992 c1991 266p o.p.
ISBN 0-684-19388-4 LC 91-29042
First published 1991 in the United Kingdom
"Detective Inspector Bill Slider [is] taken advantage of at work and pummeled verbally at home by his incompatible spouse. His own dissatisfaction leads Slider to become immersed in solving the murder of a beautiful young violin player. With the help of best friend Sergeant Atherton and the sympathetic ear of new-found true love Joanna, Slider uncovers a far-flung conspiracy." Libr J
A novel "remarkable for its rich, romantic tone, assured technique and perfect literary pitch." N Y Times Book Rev

Shallow grave; a Bill Slider mystery. Scribner 1999 312p $22
ISBN 0-684-83777-3 LC 99-21351
First published 1998 in the United Kingdom
"It isn't Inspector Bill Slider's passion for architectural oddities that brings him to the Mimpriss Estate, but the body on the terrace of the Old Rectory. . . . The way the neighbors tell it, the victim was 'an unprincipled slut,' the unfaithful wife of a local builder, a 'jealous beast' with means and motive to throttle his spouse. But Slider, whose own convulsive extramartial affairs in this refreshingly grown-up series have made him sensitive to the complexities of modern relationships, believes in looking beneath surfaces." N Y Times Book Rev

Harry Patterson, Martin Fallon, Huge Marlowe, James Graham *See* Higgins, Jack, 1929-

Harstad, Donald

Code sixty-one; a novel. Doubleday 2002 370p o.p.
ISBN 0-385-50118-8 LC 2001-52736
When Deputy Sheriff Carl Houseman, of Nation County Iowa, answers an attempted entry call he "pays little attention to the woman's charge that a vampire was peering in at her. That changes when two bodies are found in the next 48 hours, one across the river in Wisconsin, the other in Iowa, in a small-town mansion. Both victims have deep neck wounds, forcing Houseman to investigative the unthinkable. Initially, the other cops treat both the usually sensible Houseman and a professional vampire hunter who joins the hunt as nuts, but even they become more and more spooked as local Goths make their tastes known. A terrific read—by turns, funny, eerie, and insightful." Booklist

Hart, Carolyn G.

Death in paradise; a Henrie O mystery; {by} Carolyn Hart. Avon Bks. 1998 275p o.p.
ISBN 0-380-97414-2 LC 97-29701
"Journalist Richard Collins died in a tragic accident in Hawaii six years ago. Now his widow, Henrietta O'Dwyer 'Henrie O' Collins has received an anonymous message implying that Richard was murdered. Henrie O, who has played amateur sleuth before, knows she won't rest until she learns the truth." Booklist
Hart is at her "best as she tightens the suspense and keeps the killer's identity out of focus until the cliffhanging finale." Publ Wkly

Letter from home; {by} Carolyn Hart. Berkley Prime Crime 2003 262p $22.95
ISBN 0-425-19179-6 LC 2003-51953
"A letter from her Oklahoma hometown spirits famous journalist Gretchen Gilman back to 1944, when someone murdered Faye Tatum. People believed Faye's husband, jealous of her flirtations, did it and then disappeared. Gilman believed otherwise and set out for proof." Libr J
"Set in a small-town America that lives only in memory, this artfully narrated whodunit observes the residents of an unnamed Oklahoma hamlet over the hot and dusty summer of 1944 as they ration their food, count their war dead and turn on their neighbors." N Y Times Book Rev

Mint julep murder. Bantam Bks. 1995 277p o.p.
ISBN 0-553-09463-7 LC 94-34244
"While ensconced on Broward's Rock Island, South Carolina, mystery bookstore owner and amateur sleuth Annie Darling serves as author liaison for the Dixie Book Festival on Hilton Head. Problems arise when a

Hart, Carolyn G.—*Continued*
self-serving, small-time publisher promises to write a scandalous roman à clef featuring Annie's five charges—all quite famous. After the would-be writer dies of poisoning, all evidence points to Annie." Libr J

"Hart combines genteel ambience, southern charm, a likable heroine, and some wonderfully nasty characters into a pleasantly entertaining mystery." Booklist

Murder walks the plank; a death on demand mystery; [by] Carolyn Hart. 1st ed. HarperCollins Publishers 2004 298p $23.95
ISBN 0-06-000474-6 LC 2003-51095

In this installment "mystery bookstore owner Annie Darling plans a mystery cruise as a benefit for the Island Literacy Council of Broward's Rock, South Carolina. Unfortunately, before the mystery is solved, one of the guests falls overboard. Or was she pushed? Annie believes she was pushed and becomes even more convinced when a suspicious death occurs soon after the cruise. Max and Acting Police Chief Cameron believe the two incidents are either accidents or suicides and are unconnected, leaving Annie, Emma Clyde (Broward's Rock's own mystery author), and mystery reader extraordinaire Henny Brawley no choice but to solve the crimes themselves." Booklist

This novel "can only reinforce Hart's high standing among the cozy mystery cognoscenti." Publ Wkly

Resort to murder; a Henrie O mystery; [by] Carolyn Hart. Morrow 2001 294p $24
ISBN 0-380-97773-7 LC 00-59446

"Recovering from pneumonia, Henrie O isn't sure she feels up to the task of dealing with the emotional maelstrom stewing around the Bermuda wedding of her son-in-law, Lloyd Drake, and beautiful Connor Bailey, a wealthy widow. . . . The hotel where the party has gathered witnessed tragedy the year before, when Roddy Worrell, the manager's husband, plunged to his death from a tower. According to rumor, Roddy had been infatuated with Connor, who spurned his advances. When a ghost is sighted at the tower, word spreads that Roddy has come back to haunt Connor. The subsequent death of a hotel employee who knew more than he should about the apparition puts Henrie O on the murder scent once again." Publ Wkly

Scandal in Fair Haven. Bantam Bks. 1994 275p o.p.
LC 93-40346

This Henrie O "adventure takes her to Fair Haven, Tennessee, where a local bookstore owner is accused of murdering his wealthy wife. . . . Hart offers a light and lively read with an appealing 'small-town America' ambience, a compelling plot, a potpourri of fascinating characters, and some revealing insights into what makes us humans tick." Booklist

Skulduggery. Five Star 2000 190p $22.95
ISBN 0-7862-2672-2 LC 00-30845

First published 1984 in the United Kingdom

"On a foggy San Francisco night, Jimmy Lee, a twentysomething Chinese man, comes to physical anthropologist Ellen Christie's Russian Hill apartment with the bones of Peking Man, which vanished in China in the chaos of World War II. Jimmy and Ellen quickly join forces, to protect the bones—and each other—from two, chillingly efficient hitmen. . . . The novel combines effective use of the San Francisco setting with solid characterizations and a 'McGuffin' as intriguing as Hammett's falcon." Booklist

Southern ghost. Bantam Bks. 1992 322p o.p.
LC 92-2543

"According to the news story published in the *Chastain* (South Carolina) *Courier* at the time, leading citizen Judge Augustus Tarrant suffered a fatal heart attack on May 9, 1970, after learning of the accidental shooting death of his 21-year-old son, Ross. What has prompted young Courtney Kimball to hire Max Darling to investigate this family tragedy 22 years later? . . . Hart's southern-gothic mystery offers a wealth of suspects . . . a generous scattering of literary allusions and peripheral ghost stories, and a chain of intriguing flashbacks that will leave most readers puzzled to the end." Booklist

White elephant dead; {by} Carolyn Hart. Avon Twilight 1999 277p $23
ISBN 0-380-97530-0 LC 99-20833

"After demanding that leading citizens of Broward's Rock donate priceless objects to the annual White Elephant sale, a wicked blackmailer turns up dead. The leading suspect is a top customer at Annie Darling's Death on Demand bookstore, so Annie must get involved." Libr J

This "Death on Demand mystery, delivers charming characters, . . . a tantalizing mystery, and plenty of appealing descriptions of coastal landscapes." Booklist

Yankee Doodle dead; a death on demand mystery; {by} Carolyn Hart. Avon Bks. 1998 273p o.p.
ISBN 0-380-97529-7 LC 98-13565

Sleuth Annie Darling, "owner of an island resort mystery bookstore, witnesses the murder of a much-hated man during a Fourth of July fundraiser for the local library." Libr J

Hart, Harry *See* Frank, Pat, 1907-1964

Hart, Josephine

Damage; a novel. Knopf 1991 195p o.p.
LC 90-53393

The narrator of this novel, "an English paterfamilias and Tory M.P., leads a passionless existence until he meets his son's fiancée, with whom he becomes erotically enthralled." Newsweek

"Erotic obsession is a risky subject for fiction. No matter how besotted the victims of this malady may be, their behavior is likely to strike mere witnesses, i.e., readers, as distasteful, hilarious or both. This first novel . . . sidesteps such unintended responses, thanks to old-fashioned British reserve. . . . The understatement works wonders." Time

The reconstructionist. Overlook Press 2001 218p $26.95
ISBN 1-58567-170-3 LC 2001-33963

"Jack Harrington, a well-to-do London psychiatrist, immerses himself in the familial problems of his patients' pasts, while admirably repressing his own childhood trauma. His sister, Kate, a seductive writer of 'fluffy things,'

Hart, Josephine—*Continued*
is less able to cope with that trauma, and readers learn early on that Jack's good-natured protectiveness toward his sister belies a far more disturbing sort of sibling bond. . . . Hart has packed this little gem of a novel with sparkling aphoristic insights befitting Jack's profession, and her sketches of fragile, childlike characters masquerading as capable adults are deftly drawn." Publ Wkly

Sin; a novel. Knopf 1992 163p o.p.
LC 92-53853

This novel "focuses on the sin of envy, embodied here in the person of narrator Ruth, corrosively jealous of her orphaned cousin Elizabeth, raised and cherished by Ruth's parents as their own daughter. Ruth hates the good, generous, kind Elizabeth and waits for the moment when she will be able to break her rival and take everything." Libr J

"Hart has constructed an arch and streamlined melodrama inlaid with some undeniably shrewd and provocative observations about human nature." Booklist

Harte, Bret, 1836-1902

The best short stories of Bret Harte; edited, and with an introduction, by Robert N. Linscott. Modern Lib. 1947 517p o.p.

Contents: The Luck of Roaring Camp; The outcasts of Poker Flat; Tennessee's partner; Brown of Calaveras; Iliad of Sandy Bar; Poet of Sierra Flat; How Santa Claus came to Simpson's Bar; Passage in the life of Mr. John Oakhurst; Heiress of Red Dog; Ingénue of the Sierras; Chu Chu; Devotion of Enriquez; Yellow dog; Salomy Jane's kiss; Uncle Jim and Uncle Billy; Dick Spindler's family Christmas; Esmeralda of Rocky Cañon; Boom in the "Calaveras Clarion"; Youngest Miss Piper; Colonel Starbottle for the plaintiff; Lanty Foster's mistake; Four guardians of LaGrange; Ward of Colonel Starbottle's; Convalescence of Jack Hamlin; Gentleman of La Porte

The Luck of Roaring Camp, and other tales; with pictures of the author and his environment and illustrations of the setting of the book together with an introduction by Louis B. Salomon. Dodd, Mead 1961 309p il o.p.

"Great illustrated classics"

Contents: The Luck of Roaring Camp; The outcasts of Poker Flat; Miggles; Tennessee's partner; The idyl of Red Gulch; Brown of Calaveras; High-water mark; A lonely ride; The man of no account; Mliss; The right eye of the Commander; Notes by flood and field; The mission Dolores; John Chinaman; From a back window; Boonder; How Santa Claus came to Simpson's Bar; Wan Lee, the pagan; Two Saints of the foothills; The fool of Five Forks; A ghost of the Sierras; My friend the tramp; The office-seeker

Hartog, Jan de *See* De Hartog, Jan, 1914-2002

Haruf, Kent, 1943-

Eventide. Knopf 2004 300p $24.95
ISBN 0-375-41158-5 LC 2003-60480

This novel takes up where the author's Plainsong left off, "in the windy high-plains country in and around the tiny town of Holt, Colorado. Distress is general: out on their ranch, two stolid elderly brothers discover loneliness after the wayward girl they took in leaves for college; various troubles—illness, death, basic inability to cope—afflict the adults in town; and some young children are set adrift from disintegrating homes, with dangerous consequences. Every action in Holt casts a long shadow, and the gist of Haruf's story is what happens when those shadows touch. (The results are equal parts grace and calamity.) It's rare that such slow, deliberate prose is this highly charged, but Haruf's writing draws power from his sense of character—its limitations and its possibilities—and how it propels action." New Yorker

Plainsong. Knopf 1999 301p $27.50
ISBN 0-375-40618-2 LC 99-15606

"Set in the plains of Colorado, east of Denver, the novel comprises several story lines that flow into one. Tom Guthrie, a high school history teacher, is having problems with his wife and with an unruly student at school—problems that affect his young sons, Ike and Bob, as well. Meanwhile, the pregnant Victoria Roubideaux has been abandoned by her family. With the assistance of another teacher, Maggie Jones, she finds refuge with the McPheron brothers—who seem to know more about cows than people." Libr J

"From simple strands of language and cuttings of talk, from the look of the high Colorado plains east of Denver almost to the place where Nebraska and Kansas meet, Haruf has made a novel so foursquare, so delicate and lovely, that it has the power to exalt the reader." N Y Times Book Rev

Harvey, Caroline *See* Trollope, Joanna

Harvey, Jack *See* Rankin, Ian, 1960-

Harvey, John, 1938-

Cold light. Holt & Co. 1994 370p o.p.
ISBN 0-8050-2046-2 LC 93-6263

This novel finds Charlie Resnick "and his fellow coppers in the industrial English city of Nottingham harried as usual, what with the customary run of Christmastime crimes. Matters take a decided turn for the worse, though, when a Social Services caseworker goes missing; messages from the kidnapper follow, indicating similarity to a previous case and suggesting that the perpetrator is very sick indeed." Booklist

"Nice men, murderers, child batterers, discarded lovers, grieving parents, weary probation officers, cynical cops—they all hurt, they all count and they all speak a kind of poetry in this writer's book." N Y Times Book Rev

Easy meat. Holt & Co. 1996 388p o.p.
LC 96-7307

"A Marian Wood book"

"Inspector Charlie Resnick, now in his mid-forties, investigates the apparent suicide of a 14-year-old delinquent boy. Resnick knows the boy's mother, the boy's older brother is a suspect in other crimes, and his teenaged sister is headed for trouble, too." Libr J

"As Resnick's eyes are opened, Mr. Harvey writes with painful urgency about the kind of sexual and psy-

Harvey, John, 1938-—*Continued*
chological abuse that no child can completely outgrow. If this is one of Mr. Harvey's darkest books, it is also one of his most enlightened." N Y Times Book Rev

Flesh and blood. Carroll & Graff Pubs. 2004 370p $25
ISBN 0-7867-1359-3
"After 30 years in the Nottinghamshire police, Frank Elder has retired to escape hassles and an unfaithful wife. Yet even fleeing to Land's End at the southwest tip of England can't prevent his being dogged by memories of the unsolved disappearance of a teenage girl. Soon Elder is drawn into helping the police investigate several violent crimes similar to those done by a man he helped catch 15 years ago. Past seems to merge with present, especially when Elder's own 16-year-old daughter is kidnapped." Libr J
"If anyone could make you feel sorry for a serial killer, it's John Harvey, who always writes with tender feeling about commonplace people killers among them damaged by criminal violence." N Y Times Book Rev

Last rites. Holt & Co. 1999 312p o.p.
ISBN 0-8050-4150-8 LC 98-33766
"A Marian Wood book"
First published 1998 in the United Kingdom
This final Charlie Resnick mystery "finds Resnick and colleagues attempting to end a local drug war and track down an escaped killer. As always, Resnick slouches his way to understanding, recognizing eventually that the catalyst for much of the mayhem is a love story, as perverted as it is wrenchingly tender. Meanwhile, strands of stories left incomplete in earlier novels come together, some offering more snapshots of wasted lives, others providing glimmers of hope. Harvey ends his story, yes, but he avoids wrapping it all into too neat a package. The great strength of the Resnick series has always been Harvey's grasp of the mess and muddle of human life and his ability to find poetry in the midst of that mess." Booklist

Still waters. Holt & Co. 1997 311p o.p.
ISBN 0-8050-4149-4 LC 97-12324
"A Marian Wood book"
"Charlie Resnick, the laconic British police investigator . . . is faced with the death of an abused woman, a friend of his lover, Hannah. At the same time, he tracks down the circumstances of an idiosyncratic art theft. This standard police procedural formula is given a bit of depth by passages detailing relationships, both business and personal, between the members of the Serious Crime Squad." Libr J

Wasted years. Holt & Co. 1993 339p o.p.
LC 93-247
Nottingham "Inspector Charlie Resnick's past comes back to mock him when a gang of armed robbers on a crime spree reminds him of a criminal who is up for parole. Ten years earlier Resnick put him away, under circumstances that cost the detective his marriage and made him a moody man. 'Boxing with shadows' is the police chief's opinion of Resnick's efforts to track his old enemy, resolve the old questions and maybe take back the lost years." N Y Times Book Rev
"By now Harvey's economy of prose is a given, as is his ability to pull together the many composite parts—the interlocking crimes, the boozing, infidelity and Resnick's very human bunch of underlings—that make a Charlie Resnick mystery such satisfying reading." Publ Wkly

Harvey, Kathryn, 1947-
See also Wood, Barbara, 1947-

Harwood, John

The ghost writer; John Harwood. Harcourt 2004 369p $25
ISBN 0-15-101074-9 LC 2003-24918
"Gerard Freeman grows up on the windswept southern coast of Australia in the late 20th century with a controlling mother strangely silent about the details of her childhood in England. His only solace is steadfast English pen friend, Alice, to whom he confides everything. What was Gerard's mother, Phyllis, hoping to escape when she left England? The protagonist slowly pieces together his mother's past with the aid of short stories written by his great-grandmother, Viola. These cunning tales, filled with supernatural occurrences and séances, are seamlessly embedded in the main narrative, offering Gerard—and readers—enticing clues into his troubled family's history. After Phyllis's death, her newly liberated son travels to England, hoping to learn more and to pursue elusive Alice. As he searches through the country house his mother inhabited long ago, Gerard finds past and present fusing in horrifying fashion." Publ Wkly

Hašek, Jaroslav, 1883-1923

The good soldier Svejk; and his fortunes in the World War; translated and introduced by Cecil Parrott; illustrated by Josef Lada. Knopf 1993 800p $22
ISBN 0-679-42036-3 LC 92-54304
"Everyman's library"
Original Czech edition published 1920-1923 in 4 volumes; this translation first published 1973 by Heinemann
"The novel reflected the pacifist, antimilitary sentiments of post-World War I Europe. The title character is classified as 'feeble-minded'; nevertheless, with the advent of World War I he is drafted into the service of Austria. Naive, instinctively honest, invariably incompetent, and guileless, Schweik is forever colliding with the clumsy, dehumanized military bureaucracy. Schweik's naiveté serves as a contrast to the self-importance and conniving natures of his superior officers and is the main vehicle for Hašek's mockery of authority." Merriam-Webster's Ency of Lit

Haskell, John, 1958-

American purgatorio; John Haskell. Farrar, Straus and Giroux 2005 239p $23
ISBN 0-374-10432-8 LC 2004-20087
"After stopping for gas on his way to his mother-in-law's house, the narrator, Jack, emerges from a convenience store to find that his car and his wife, Anne, are nowhere to be found. After making his way back home, Jack discovers a U.S. map marked with an apparent route; imagining that this will lead him to his wife, he buys another car and sets off." Publ Wkly
"The novel becomes more visual and distinct the far-

Haskell, John, 1958-—*Continued*
ther west Jack travels, and an undertow of regret begins to emerge, intimations of a marriage left unfulfilled. Gradually, Haskell creates a penetrating mood of loss. Turn the last page, and you'll realize that this strange, moving book has done just what a first novel should: it has left an impression." N Y Times Book Rev

I am not Jackson Pollock. Farrar, Straus & Giroux 2003 204p $20
ISBN 0-374-17399-0 LC 2002-33889
Contents: Dream of a clean slate; Elephant feelings; The judgment of Psycho; The faces of Joan of Arc; Capucine; Glenn Gould in six parts; Good world; Crimes at midnight; Narrow road
"Most of the nine stories are imaginative extrapolations of the lives of real people (or, in some cases, real animals), such as the eponymous painter and his wife, Lee Krasner; Psycho stars Janet Leigh and Anthony Perkins; Laika, the first dog in space; and Saartjie, the early 19th-century South African woman brought to London as the famous sideshow attraction the Hottentot Venus. . . . Haskell subtly explores questions of exploitation and agency through the eyes of his celebrity characters, winking all the while at his own attempts to get into their heads. His hypnotic writing creates its own genre, unsettling and quietly bizarre." Publ Wkly

Haslett, Adam

You are not a stranger here. Talese 2002 240p o.p.
ISBN 0-385-50167-6 LC 2001-54839
Contents: Notes to my biographer; The good doctor; The beginnings of grief; Devotion; War's end; Reunion; Divination; My father's business; The volunteer
"These are short stories that T. S. Eliot or Samuel Beckett might have come up with if they'd written conventional fiction about middle-class people. . . .{Haslett} writes stories of loss and illness, especially mental illness, and peoples them with the vanquished, the crazy and the soon to die—characters for whom there's no redemption." N Y Times Book Rev

Hassler, Jon

The dean's list. Ballantine Bks. 1997 396p o.p.
ISBN 0-345-41637-6 LC 97-10177
"In this sequel to Rookery Blues . . ., Hassler revisits Rookery State College in Minnesota some 30 years later. Leland Edwards, one of the faculty in the first book, is now dean of the college. In spite of growing older and more successful, however, he is still striving to understand his family and friends, tentatively exploring new relationship, and often simply trying to survive the follies of campus life in the 1990s." Libr J

Rookery blues. Ballantine Bks. 1995 484p o.p.
LC 95-2953
"Rookery is the name of a northern Minnesota state college where five faculty members get together to play the blues as well as endure them. The group—a beautiful singer, a tormented artist, a woebegone novelist, and two English teachers—includes a love triangle, and political strains arise as the members take different sides in a strike. Set in 1969, it feels like 1959—in large part because of its old-fashioned, four-square, apolitical humanism." New Yorker
Followed by The dean's list

The Staggerford flood. Viking 2002 199p $24.95
ISBN 0-670-03125-9 LC 2001-56808
"A natural disaster threatens the unique rural charm of Hassler's Minnesota village in the latest installment in his ongoing series. . . . Agatha McGee is the 80-year-old sixth-grade teacher who is beginning to dread the onset of old age, so much so that a local radio personality suggests that she hold her own memorial party in advance to try to get a lift from the tribute. What invigorates Agatha instead is the threat of a flood, which distracts her from her preoccupation with local gossip and causes her to offer shelter to several troubled residents, including a combative mother and daughter as well as several friends and acquaintances." Publ Wkly

Hatoum, Milton, 1952-

The brothers; translated from the Portuguese by John Gledson. Farrar, Straus & Giroux 2002 240p $23
ISBN 0-374-14118-5 LC 2002-17054
Original Portuguese edition, 2000
"Set in a Lebanese immigrant community in the Brazilian port town of Manaus, this is the story of identical twins, Yaqub and Omar, whose lives take radically different paths: one toward professional success in Brazil's metropolis São Paulo, the other to drunken dissipation in the lowly port of his birth. Set against the backdrop of a city whose very character is undergoing radical change, it is also the story of a family on the verge of conflagration from incestuous passion and riddled with secrets and guilt. . . . Hatoum suggests much while fully revealing little; he's content to unfold his lush narrative—replete with the dances, exotic sights, smells and fragrances of his luscious Brazil—one vivid bolt of cloth at a time." Publ Wkly

Hautman, Pete, 1952-

Doohickey; a novel. Simon & Schuster 2002 277p $24
ISBN 0-7432-0019-5 LC 2002-70671
"Nicholas Fashon and his pal Vince Love own a fashionable leather goods store in Tucson, Ariz. Nick's roguish granddad dies, leaving him a inheritance of useless inventions. Useless, that is, with one exception: a doohickey called the HandyMate, which performs numerous kitchen functions most efficiently. Yola Fuentes, a TV chef, is interested in the HandyMate and wants to use it on her TV show. Nick is grateful, especially since the building housing his store and the apartment upstairs containing all his worldly goods has just burned down." Publ Wkly
A "comic mystery that benefits greatly from deadpan humor; likable, eccentric characters; and a moral cleverly cloaked by the twisting plot." Booklist

Hawk, Alex, 1926-
For works written by this author under other names see Kelton, Elmer, 1926-

Hawke, Ethan, 1970-

Ash Wednesday; a novel. Knopf 2002 221p o.p.
ISBN 0-375-41326-X LC 2002-20811

"When he discovers that his girlfriend is pregnant and well into the process of leaving him, Jimmy Heartsock resolves to win her back whatever the cost—in his case going AWOL from the Army and giving up his carousing, coke-snorting ways. Christy, whose flight by bus from upstate New York to her Texas home sets off this interstate odyssey, is more leery about the shelf life of passion but is willing to find out how far the domestic kind of love will take them." N Y Times Book Rev

"Hawke's text at times reads raw, but the novel's conversational tone, dual first-person narration and, above all, direct exploration of the simple truths of life and love make this a worthwhile tale and an honest one." Publ Wkly

Hawkes, John, 1925-1998

The blood oranges. New Directions 1971 271p o.p.

"This novel focuses on an erotic quartet. Cyril and Fiona and Hugh and Catherine, two married couples who engage in mate swapping. . . . (Cyril) drifts into an affair with Catherine as easily as his wife does with Hugh. . . . But even in liberal Cyril we begin to detect traces of jealousy. Although trying to appear perfectly jolly and casual about his wife's lover, he is actually quite disturbed. . . . Just how involved is Fiona?" Saturday Rev

"This highly rhapsodic, sensual novel suggests both in title and substance the decline of vitality and enlightenment in the characters' lives as in each new day. Reminiscent of Lawrence in the concern with atmosphere and lushness of description, the book is powerfully evocative of a sometimes comic, sometimes hallucinatory sense of timelessness, obsession, and escape from reality." Choice

Second skin; preface by Jeffrey Eugenides. New Directions 2005 210p pa $14.95
ISBN 0-8112-1644-6 LC 2005-21516
First published 1964

"Skipper, the narrator . . ., interweaves past and present–what he refers to as his 'naked history'–to tell the story of a life marked by pitiful losses, as well as a more elusive, but overwhelming, joy. The past: the suicides of his father, wife, and daughter, the murder of his son-in-law, a brutal rape and mutiny at sea. The present: caring for his granddaughter, Pixie, on a 'northern' island where he works as an artificial inseminator of cows and attempts to reclaim some of the innocence of his earlier life." Publisher's note

"As with other contemporaries, such as Pynchon, Barth, and Nabokov, and predecessors such as Faulkner, Lautremont, and Blake, Hawkes has succeeded in creating a stylized, imagined world that doubles for the one in which we live and read his novels." Reader's Ency of Am Lit. 2d edition

Sweet William; a memoir of Old Horse. Simon & Schuster 1993 269p o.p.
LC 92-40125

In this novel, the author allows his narrator to "tell his own story in his own direct way. The twist is, this narrator is a horse. Called Sweet William in his prime, which didn't last long, and now called Old Horse, this equine character relates a life story full of grief, thwarted passion, fortitude, some humor, and a pinch of misanthropy and bitterness. Sweet William suffers through his adored mother's death, then loses his manhood to the knife when his lustiness inconveniences his owners. His feistiness persists even in his neutered state, leading to the demise of his brief but glorious racing career, and it's all downhill after that." Booklist

"Employing an uncharacteristically courtly tone that may surprise his longtime readers, Hawkes fills this account with rich color and winning detail; indeed, this is a virtuoso performance, with William's voice rendered in masterful prose." Publ Wkly

Hawkins, Anthony Hope *See* Hope, Anthony, 1863-1933

Hawthorne, Nathaniel, 1804-1864

The Blithedale romance. o.p.
First published 1852

"Blithedale, a Utopian community, is modeled on Brook Farm, the transcendentalist experiment at West Roxbury, Massachusetts, in which Hawthorne had participated ten years before he wrote the novel. Miles Coverdale, the narrator, is a coldly inquisitive observer; in revealing his knowledge of the other members of the community, he reveals himself." Reader's Ency. 4th edition

also in Hawthorne, N. Collected novels

Collected novels. Literary Classics of the United States, Distributed to the trade by the Viking Press 1983 1272p $39.50
ISBN 0-940450-08-9 LC 82-18031

Contents: Fanshawe; The scarlet letter; The House of the Seven Gables; The Blithedale romance; The marble faun

In Fanshawe (1828), two students at Harley College—one normal and outgoing, the other isolated and scholarly—both fall in love with a third student, Ellen Langdon. When Ellen is kidnapped, the isolated Fanshawe rescues her, only to turn down her marriage proposal afterward. The scarlet letter, The House of the Seven Gables, The Blithedale romance, and The marble faun are entered separately.

Complete short stories of Nathaniel Hawthorne. Hanover House 1959 615p o.p.

Contains the following stories: Gray champion; Wedding knell; Minister's black veil; Maypole of Merry Mount; Gentle boy; Mr. Higginbotham's catastrophe; Wakefield; Great carbuncle; Prophetic pictures; David Swan; Hollow of the three hills; Vision of the fountain; Fancy's show box; Dr Heidegger's experiment; Howe's masquerade; Edward Randolph's portrait; Lady Eleanore's mantle; Old Esther Dudley; Village uncle; Ambitious guest; The sister years; Seven vagabonds; White old maid; Peter Goldthwaite's treasure; Shaker bridal; Endicott and the Red Cross; Lily's quest; Edward Fane's rosebud; Threefold destiny; The birthmark; Select party; Young Goodman Brown; Rappaccini's daughter; Mrs. Bullfrog; Monsieur du Miroir; Hall of fantasy; Celestial railroad; Procession of life; Feathertop: a moralized legend; New Adam and Eve; Egotism; Christmas banquet; Browne's wooden image; Intelligence office; Roger Malvin's burial; P's correspondence; Earth's holo-

Hawthorne, Nathaniel, 1804-1864—*Continued*
caust; Passages from a relinquished work; Artist of the beautiful virtuoso's collection; Snow-image: a childish miracle; Great Stone Face; Ethan Brand; Sylph Etherege; Canterbury pilgrims; Man of Adamant; Devil in manuscript; John Inglefield's Thanksgiving; Wives of the dead; Little Daffydowndilly; My kinsman, Major Molineux; Antique ring; Graves and goblins; Dr. Bullivant; Old woman's tale; Alice Coane's appeal; Ghost of Doctor Harris; Young provincial; Haunted quack; New England village; My wife's novel; Bald Eagle

Doctor Grimshawe's secret; edited, with an introduction and notes, by Edward H. Davidson. Harvard Univ. Press 1954 305p il o.p.

Written 1883

"In a New England town in the early 19th century lives Dr. Grimshawe, an eccentric recluse, and two orphans, Ned and Elsie. The children are involved in a secret related to an estate in England, whence the doctor originally came. This estate has lacked a direct heir since the reign of Charles I, when the incumbent disappeared, leaving a bloody footprint on the threshold. After their guardian's death, the children are separated, but meet again years later, in England. Ned, now Edward Redclyffe, is injured while investigating the estate and is befriended by Colcord, his boyhood tutor. Lord Braithwaite, the estate's present owner, invites Edward to live at the Hall, where he meets Elsie, who warns him of a presentiment of danger. He finds the hiding place of an incredibly old man who 'haunts' the Hall, and recognizes him as the Sir Edward Redclyffe of the times of the bloody footprint. When the old man dies, Colcord produces a locket that proves Edward to be the heir." Oxford Companion to Am Lit. 6th edition

Fanshawe

In Hawthorne, N. Collected novels

The Hawthorne treasury; complete novels and selected tales of Nathaniel Hawthorne; edited by Norman Holmes Pearson. Modern Lib. 1999 1409p o.p.

ISBN 0-679-60322-0 LC 98-47424

This volume includes the complete text of the following novels: Fanshawe, The scarlet letter, The House of Seven Gables, The Blithedale romance, and The marble faun. Also included are stories from twice-told tales, Mosses from an old manse, and The snow-image and other twice-told tales

The House of the Seven Gables; introduction by Mary Oliver. Modern Library 2001 312p pa $8.75

ISBN 0-375-75687-6 LC 00-64585

First published 1851

"Follows the fortunes of a decayed New England family, consisting of four members—Hephzibah Pyncheon, her brother Clifford, their cousin Judge Pyncheon, and other cousin Phoebe, a country girl. At the time the story opens Hephzibah is living in great poverty at the old homestead, the House of the Seven Gables. With her is [her brother] Clifford, just released from prison, where he had served a term of thirty years for the supposed murder of a rich uncle. Judge Pyncheon, who was influential in obtaining the innocent Clifford's arrest, that he might hide his own wrongdoing, now seeks to confine him in an asylum on the charge of insanity. Hephzibah's pitiful efforts to shield this brother, to support him and herself by keeping a scentshop, to circumvent the machinations of the judge, are described through the greater portion of the novel. The sudden death of the malevolent cousin frees them and makes them possessors of his wealth." Keller. Reader's Dig of Books

also in Hawthorne, N. Collected novels

The marble faun; or, The romance of Monte Beni. Ohio State Univ. Press 1968 cxxxiii, 610p $83.95

ISBN 0-8142-0062-1

"Centenary edition of the works of Nathaniel Hawthorne"

First published 1860

"The novel's central metaphor is a statue of a faun by Praxiteles that Hawthorne had seen in Florence. In the faun's fusing of animal and human characteristics he finds an allegory of the fall of man from amoral innocence to the knowledge of good and evil. . . . The faun of the novel is Donatello, a passionate young Italian who makes the acquaintance of three American artists, Miriam, Kenyon, and Hilda, who are spending time in Rome. When Donatello kills a man who has been shadowing Miriam, he is wracked by guilt until he is arrested by the police and imprisoned. Both of the women are tainted by guilt." Merriam-Webster's Ency of Lit

also in Hawthorne, N. Collected novels

Mosses from an old manse

In Hawthorne, N. Tales and sketches, including Twice-told tales, Mosses from an old manse, and The snow-image; A wonder book for girls and boys; Tanglewood tales for girls and boys, being a second Wonder book

The portable Hawthorne; edited by Malcolm Cowley. rev. and expanded ed. Viking 1969 698p o.p.

"The Viking portable library"

First published 1948

This anthology contains the complete text of The scarlet letter with Hawthorne's introduction "The custom house." Thirteen of Hawthorne's stories are also included as are passages from his American notebook plus sections from his European journals and letters and excerpts from his novel The house of the seven gables

The scarlet letter; with an introduction by Alfred Kazin. Knopf 1992 xxvii, 273p $18

ISBN 0-679-41731-1 LC 92-52902

"Everyman's library"

"Set in 17th-century Salem, the novel is built around three scaffold scenes, which occur at the beginning, the middle, and the end. The story opens with the public condemnation of Hester Prynne, and the exhortation that she confess the name of the father of Pearl, her illegitimate child. Hester's husband, an old and scholarly physician, just arrived from England, assumes the name of Roger Chillingworth in order to seek out Hester's lover and revenge himself upon him. He attaches himself as physician to a respected and seemingly holy minister, Arthur Dimmesdale, suspecting that he is the father of

Hawthorne, Nathaniel, 1804-1864—*Continued*
the child. The Scarlet Letter traces the effect of the actual and symbolic sin on all the characters." Benet's Reader's Ency of Am Lit

also in Hawthorne, N. Collected novels

also in Hawthorne, N. The portable Hawthorne p337-546

The snow-image

In Hawthorne, N. Tales and sketches, including Twice-told tales, Mosses from an old manse, and The snow-image; A wonder book for girls and boys; Tanglewood tales for girls and boys, being a second Wonder book

Tales and sketches, including Twice-told tales, Mosses from an old manse, and The snow-image; A wonder book for girls and boys; Tanglewood tales for girls and boys, being a second Wonder book. Library of Am. 1982 1493p $39.50

ISBN 0-940450-03-8 LC 81-20760

The stories in this collection have appeared in the five books: Twice-told tales (1837); Mosses from an old manse (1846); The snow-image (1852); A wonder book for girls and boys (1851); Tanglewood tales for girls and boys, being a second wonder book (1853)

This volume contains all of Hawthorne's tales and sketches, which are arranged in order of their periodical publication

Twice-told tales; introduction by Rosemary Mahoney; notes by Gretchen Short. Modern Library 2001 xxiv, 404p pa $10.95

ISBN 0-375-75788-0 LC 2001-31480

First published 1837

Contents: The Gray Champion; Sunday at home; The wedding-knell; The minister's black veil; The May-pole of Merry Mount; The gentle boy; Mr. Higginbotham's catastrophe; Little Annie's ramble; Wakefield; A rill from the town-pump; The Great Carbuncle; The prophetic pictures; David Swan; Sights from steeple; The hollow of the three hills; The toll-gatherer's day; The vision of the fountain; Fancy's show box; Dr. Heidegger's experiment; Howe's masquerade; Edward Randolph's portrait; Lady Eleanore's mantle; Old Esther Dudley; The haunted mind; The village uncle; The ambitious guest; The sister years; Snow-flakes; The seven vagabonds; The white old maid; Peter Goldthwaite's treasure; Chippings with a chisel; The Shaker bridal; Night sketches; Endicott and the Red Cross; The lily's quest; Footprints on the seashore; Edward Fane's rosebud; The threefold destiny

also in Hawthorne, N. Tales and sketches, including Twice-told tales, Mosses from an old manse, and The snow-image; A wonder book for girls and boys; Tanglewood tales for girls and boys, being a second Wonder book

Hay, Elizabeth

Garbo laughs. Counterpoint 2003 294p $25

ISBN 1-582-43291-0 LC 2003-11989

A novel set in Ottawa. "Harriet, the Garbo-like star of the book, is a novelist who has developed the curious habit of writing but not mailing confiding letters to her hero, the then still-living film critic Pauline Kael, and discussing, at length, such burning cinematic questions as who is sexier, Cary Grant or Sean Connery, with her sweetly precocious and equality movie-mad son and daughter. As Harriet indulges her grand obsession with movies, she struggles with her less than passionate feelings for her real-life leading man and forges a warm but risky friendship with a new neighbor, the earthy Dinah." Booklist

"This rich, lovely novel makes us think about the ambivalences and contradictions of relationships and the patience of love." Quill & Quire

A student of weather. Counterpoint 2001 368p o.p.

ISBN 1-58243-123-X LC 00-64445

This novel "begins circa 1930 on the drought-ravished prairies of Saskatchewan, the home of two motherless sisters. The elder, Lucinda, is fair and diligent, Norma Joyce dark and willful, and both fall for a handsome, rambling botanist from fabled Ottawa, Maurice Dove. . . . As the sisters embark on a tragic rivalry that will determine the course of their lives, their story becomes a fairy tale in which solitude, work, art, and desire acquire mystical significance as Hay adroitly weaves their passions into luminous descriptions of extreme weather and the grand cycle of the seasons." Booklist

Haydon, Elizabeth

Destiny: child of the sky. TOR Bks. 2001 556p $27.95

ISBN 0-312-86750-6 LC 2001-27473

"A Tom Doherty Associates book"

Sequel to: Prophecy: child of earth

In this concluding volume of the first Rhapsody fantasy/romance trilogy "the harpist Rhapsody joins with the Firbolg king Achmed and his giant companion Grunthor to attempt to fight the powerful and elusive F'dor, a demon-born danger that threatens the fabric of existence." Libr J

"Though obviously inspired by music theory, Norse and Celtic folklore, and seemingly such authors as Tolkien, C.S. Lewis, Patricia A. McKillip, Anne McCaffrey and Palmer Brown (Cheerful), the author uses a fluid writing style to build a world uniquely and compellingly her own." Publ Wkly

Prophecy; child of earth. TOR Bks. 2000 480p $27.95

ISBN 0-312-86751-4 LC 00-26836

"A Tom Doherty Associates book"

Sequel to Rhapsody (1999)

"The skysinger Rhapsody and her two FirBolg companions seek to carve out a place for themselves in a new world even as their lives move inexorably toward the fulfillment of an ancient prophecy. As momentous events take shape around the three heroes, other forces work hard to undermine their hope and bring the powers of evil closer to victory. . . . Haydon's epic saga of the endless battle between light and darkness resounds with the richness of ancient myths reworked into new forms." Libr J

Haydon, Elizabeth—*Continued*

Requiem for the sun. TOR Bks. 2002 462p $27.95

ISBN 0-312-87884-2 LC 2002-28584

"A Tom Doherty Associates book"

First title in a second Rhapsody fantasy/romance trilogy

"Three years after she has helped bring peace and prosperity to the land of Navarne, Rhapsody, Lady Cymrian treasures her family and her people. When the death of the Dowager Empress at Sorbold leaves empty the line of succession, war threatens the fragile Cymrian Alliance—and an old and deadly foe of Rhapsody's rises up to threaten her and all she holds dear." Libr J

"Bears for neologisms may growl over words such as coronated and infrastructure, but even they will raise glasses to toast Haydon's generally high levels of achievement in characterization, world building through well-chosen detail, folkloric and musical expertise, and warmth of spirit." Booklist

Haymon, S. T.

A beautiful death. St. Martin's Press 1994 c1993 223p o.p.

LC 93-37005

First published 1993 in the United Kingdom

Inspector Ben Jurnet "plunges into his deepest fit of melancholia to date when his fiancée is blown to bits by a car bomb. . . . Racked with guilt for surviving the attack that was surely meant for him, the English copper stumbles through his grief, enduring the sympathy of his friends and the glee of his enemies, until he bolts for Ireland in pursuit of a neighborhood youth with terrorist clan connections in the old country. Ms. Haymon, an elegant and assured stylist whose esthetic juices are always stirred by a good, gloomy setting, finds the perfect lyric complement for Jurnet's dismal mood in the gray, misty drizzle of County Donegal in November." N Y Times Book Rev

Death of a hero. St. Martin's Press 1996 176p o.p.

LC 96-27968

"Posthumously published, Haymond's . . . final work details Detective Inspector Ben Jurnet's last case. Although still mourning the death of his fiancée, he investigates the murder of an idealistic protest leader in the local redlight district. A reliable police procedural." Libr J

Ritual murder. St. Martin's Press 1982 237p o.p.

LC 82-5781

"Arthur Cossey, an angelic choirboy, is murdered and sexually mutilated in imitation of the killing of Little St. Ulf during the 12th century in a small town, Angleby. St. Ulf was believed a victim of Jewish rituals; his death resulted in a vicious wave of anti-Semitism, and [Detective-Inspector] Jurnet fears the persecution of Jews will be repeated, a factor that intensifes his search for the murderer." Publ Wkly

"History serves as an eerie backdrop to present-day terror in this ably plotted tale." Booklist

Haynes, David

The full Matilda; a novel; David Haynes. 1st ed. Harlem Moon 2004 370p $14

ISBN 0-7679-1569-0 (pa) LC 2003-68773

"The Housewrights have a family legacy of service, their father, Jacob, having served as the venerable black retainer to a rich and powerful U.S. senator in Washington, D.C. But each successive generation scoffs at the service legacy, gravitating toward the catering business but anxious to drop the subservience of the serving class. Matilda Housewright, the strong-minded and willful daughter of Jacob, provides the focus for this intergenerational novel. After Jacob dies, Matilda's brother, Martin, embarks on a catering business and cuts out Matilda, leaving her on the sidelines. But her impervious nature and impeccable taste keep her at the center of the family as Martin's sons are sent to get the full-Matilda treatment. Alternating between the first-person accounts of Matilda and her brother and the third-person perspectives of Martin's sons, this vibrant family portrait tracks the rise of the Housewrights to a multimillion-dollar food distribution company." Booklist

Haynes, Melinda

Chalktown; a novel. Hyperion 2001 317p $23.95

ISBN 0-7868-6656-X LC 00-63217

"In the spring of 1961, 16-year-old Hezekiah ('Hez') Sheehand plans to walk to nearby Chalktown, a hamlet where folks are rumored to communicate only by writing on chalkboards. On his back he totes his mentally retarded five-year-old brother, Yellababy. Behind him, Hez leaves his mother, Susan-Blair, a slattern who hits her children; his father, Fairy, who lives in a bus in the yard; and his older sister, Arena, who has run off with a man who pays her to 'work on him with her hands.' As Hez nears Chalktown, Haynes slips back in time to 1955 to chart the silent community's history." Publ Wkly

Mother of pearl; a novel. Hyperion 1999 448p o.p.

ISBN 0-7868-6485-0 LC 98-47014

This "tells the story of twenty-eight-year-old Even Grade, a black man who grew up an orphan, and Valuable Korner, a fifteen-year-old white girl who is the daughter of the town whore and an unknown father. Both seeking the family, love, and commitment they never had." Publisher's note

Hays, Tommy

The pleasure was mine. St. Martin's Press 2005 255p $23.95

ISBN 0-312-33932-1 LC 2004-51311

This novel depicts the "transformation of a family in which an older man cares for his wife during her descent into Alzheimer's. The transformation begins when Prate Marshbanks, the remarkable, curmudgeonly protagonist, gets a visitor for the summer: his nine-year-old grandson, Jackson, whose mother died in a car accident several years before. But, despite Jackson's grieving presence, Marshbanks remains preoccupied with his own battle to ensure compassionate care for his wife, whom he has had to place in a nursing home. Hays's elegiac, penetrating description of Prate's marriage frames the landscape of this brilliant novel about love, loss, marriage and family. He offers a grim but hopeful treatment of a difficult subject, and his elegant writing and sharp, tender portraits of the Marshbanks make a potent combination." Publ Wkly

Hayter, Sparkle, 1958-

Bandit queen boogie. Three Rivers Press 2004 290p pa $13

ISBN 1-4000-4744-7 (pa) LC 2003-25853

"Two childhood friends travel across Europe the summer after their college graduation. The trip was meant for Chloe and her boyfriend, but after he dumps her, Blackie agrees to go instead. Unfortunately, brokenhearted Chloe is not much fun to be around—until the two decide to start robbing the sleazy married men who proposition them. Chloe soon perks up, getting addicted to the thrill and the possibility of being caught. Although the story centers on Chloe and Blackie, numerous characters and story lines come together when they steal a statue of the Hindu god Ganesh that contains a valuable treasure belonging to an Indian crime boss. . . . The characters are vividly rendered, and Hayter deftly weaves together the varying story lines and settings." Libr J

Hazzard, Shirley, 1931-

The great fire. Farrar, Straus & Giroux 2003 278p $24

ISBN 0-374-16644-7 LC 2003-49189

"The time is 1947-48, and the place is, primarily, East Asia. . . . Our hero, and indeed he fills the requirements to be called one, is Aldred Leith, who is English and part of the occupation forces in Japan; his particular military task is damage survey. He has an interesting past, including, most recently, a two-year walk across civil-war-torn China to write a book. In the present. . .he meets the teenage daughter and younger son of a local Australian commander. And, as Helen is growing headlong into womanhood, this novel of war's aftermath becomes a story of love—or more to the point, of the restoration of the capacity for love once global and personal trauma have been shed." Booklist

The transit of Venus. Viking 1980 337p o.p.

LC 79-21754

This novel centers on "the lives and loves of two Australian sisters who emigrate to England and America in the mid-20th Century. . . . [Focus is on the sister Caro]. Caro's transit is circular: seduction and abandonment, marriage, widowhood, reunion with her betrayer and—at last and fatally—with the astronomer who loved her secretly all along." Libr J

This "is an exceedingly ambitious novel; a stunning and at times bewildering galaxy of ideas. From a literary and intellectual standpoint it is a challenge. . . . Miss Hazzard's greatest achievement in this novel is the suspense she creates from unfinished relationships. Instead of spinning off in different directions through space, these characters collide once again, drawn together by an ineluctable magnetism." Christ Sci Monit

Head, Ann

Mr. & Mrs. Bo Jo Jones. Putnam 1967 253p o.p.

"A marriage of necessity between two pleasant high school youngsters led astray by their emotions barely holds up against unreadiness for love or marriage and differences in family background and families. After their premature baby's death, Bo Jo and young wife July find their separation, schooling, and return to opposite sides of town assumed and arranged for by their parents. They momentarily yield to seeming reasonableness but, gradually realizing the bonds that have grown between them during a year of marriage, pregnancy, and bereavement, decide to work out their destiny and education together." Booklist

"The relations between the youngsters and their parents are well handled and made painfully real." Publ Wkly

Healy, J. F. (Jeremiah F.), 1948-

Invasion of privacy; a John Francis Cuddy mystery; [by] Jeremiah Healy. Pocket Bks. 1996 340p o.p.

LC 96-1196

"Acting on behalf of successful bank employee Olga Evorova, Boston P.I. John Cuddy scopes out her secretive potential fiancé, a reclusive man of no apparent family or heritage. Cuddy's investigation stirs up trouble: representatives of the Milwaukee mob appear on the scene and apply pressure." Libr J

"The dialogue crackles, the plot is complex and clever, and Cuddy's relationship with his longtime lover faces a crisis in which machismo won't help." Booklist

Shallow graves; a John Cuddy mystery; [by] Jeremiah Healy. Pocket Bks. 1992 282p o.p.

LC 91-44059

"On the verge of a big-time modeling career in New York, Boston model Mau Tim Dani is strangled in her apartment. It looks like a burglary gone bad, but her modeling agency, which carried a 'key employee' insurance policy on her with Empire Insurance, wants to know for sure. Boston private eye John Cuddy used to investigate claims for Empire, which is why he's taken aback when the firm hires him to investigate the death." Booklist

"Healy gives his readers an array of distinctive characters while engaging them in a deftly plotted and satisfying story." Publ Wkly

Spiral; a John Francis Cuddy mystery; {by} Jeremiah Healy. Pocket Bks. 1999 359p o.p.

ISBN 0-671-00955-9 LC 99-25769

"Boston private investigator John Cuddy is reeling from the death of his love, Nancy Meagher, in an airline disaster. He can barely cope with the present, and the future seems bleak when his past comes calling. A fellow Vietnam vet enlists Cuddy's investigative skills on behalf of their old commander, Nicolas Helides, whose 13-year-old granddaughter was murdered during a party at the Helides' Florida estate." Booklist

Healy, Jeremiah F. *See* Healy, J. F. (Jeremiah F.), 1948-

Hearon, Shelby, 1931-

Ella in bloom. Knopf 2000 259p $23

ISBN 0-375-41038-4 LC 00-20311

"Ella is a single mother raising a precocious teenage daughter (a particularly annoying character) and eking out a precarious living by plantsitting and renting out part of her rundown duplex. To please her proper, disapproving Texas mother, who always favored Ella's more sucessful older sister, Ella writes long letters describing

Hearon, Shelby, 1931-—*Continued*
her 'gracious' life in Old Metairie, LA. But when Terrell, Ella's older sister, is killed in a plane crash on the way to meet her lover, Ella's illusions about her 'perfect' sister, as well as about her mother and her own life, are shattered, and she begins the process of blooming as her true self." Libr J

Footprints. Knopf 1996 191p o.p.
LC 95-42853

"Over 25 years, Nan Mayhall has made more than her share of compromises in return for a relatively stable marriage to Douglas, a successful academic. She finds the accompanying frustrations bearable until the shocking accidental death of Bethany, her adored daughter. Nan recoils from her husband's reaction to the tragedy: he becomes obsessed with the notion of part of Bethany living on through her transplanted heart. Douglas insists on establishing a relationship with the recipient, but he virtually ignores the grief experienced by his wife and their surviving child. Eventually, growing family divisions push Nan to seek a separate peace." Libr J

"Shelby Hearon takes a long, speculative look at the moment in the life of a family when a child departs. She has done a fine job of getting at this inevitable conflict between mother and child, between mother and father. She holds it to the light, turns and examines it with a caustic eye. We are the beneficiaries of a clear-eyed view that catches the humor and poignancy of the evolution of a woman's life." N Y Times Book Rev

Hedge, John *See* Buck, Pearl S. (Pearl Sydenstricker), 1892-1973

Heffernan, William, 1940-

The Dinosaur Club; a novel. Morrow 1997 303p o.p.
ISBN 0-688-14988-X LC 96-46637

"At age 49, Jack Fallon discovers that his life is plummeting out of control. In one fell swoop, his wife leaves him and corporate downsizing threatens his livelihood. Always the warrior, Jack organizes other fiftyish management employees to fight their ruthless corporate leaders, and the 'Dinosaur Club' is born. Working against formidable odds, the Dinosaurs engage in hilarious hijinks and serious espionage to foil their chief executives. What Jack does not count on is falling in love with Samantha Moore, legal counsel for the corporation. . . . Heffernan is masterly in examining the scruples of corporate downsizing with a discerning eye and blends levity in his cauldron of good and evil." Libr J

Red angel; a novel. Morrow 2000 273p $24
ISBN 0-688-16563-X LC 99-36638

"New York City special investigative detective Paul Devlin leaves behind an apparent gang war to help Adrianna, his Cuban American lover, with a family problem in Cuba. Only after arriving do they discover the death of Adrianna's aunt—widely known in Cuba as a heroine of the Revolution—and learn that members of a voodoo cult have stolen her body. With the assistance of a local policeman and Devlin's New York partner, Devlin and Adrianna struggle against the machinations of the Cuban secret police and other to uncover the truth. Deeply involving, expertly detailed, and strategically plotted." Libr J

Hegarty, Frances *See* Fyfield, Frances, 1948-

Heggen, Thomas, 1919-1949

Mister Roberts; with an introduction by David P. Smith. Naval Inst. Press 1992 xxii, 200p $34.95
ISBN 1-55750-723-6 LC 92-9422
"Classics of naval literature series"

A reissue of the title first published 1946 by Houghton Mifflin

"Douglas Roberts, First Lieutenant on the *Reluctant*, a U.S. Navy supply ship in the Pacific, is the leading inspiration for the undeclared war between the crew and the unreasonable skipper. The dull life on ship is eased by humorous antics and the resulting rage of the commander. When Roberts is transferred to a destroyer, the crew is saddened by his departure." Shapiro. Fic for Youth. 3d edition

"The leisurely narrative is told in a very few incidents, all centering about an admirable young lieutenant miserably defeated in his desire to get into fighting. A quiet, credible story of the corroding effects of apathy and boredom on men who, in battle, might have been heroes." New Yorker

Hegi, Ursula

The vision of Emma Blau. Simon & Schuster 2000 432p $25
ISBN 0-684-82997-5 LC 99-56392

This "novel follows three generations of family and its property. Stefan Blau, aged thirteen, ran away from a small German town in 1894, reached the United States, and would up as the proprietor of an elegant restaurant and the Wasserburg, . . . [an apartment house] on the shore of Lake Winnipesaukee, in New Hampshire. . . . His German-American family—one child by each of three wives—remained bicultural while splitting in various directions. Their affairs converge in a row over ownership of the now decaying Wasserburg." Atl Mon

"Hegi has created a milieu full of sexual energy—the book is often erotic—and has captured both the tension and love endemic to all tight-knit families. Compelling and absorbing, this old-fashioned saga is rife with passion, tragedy, and redemption." Libr J

Heidish, Marcy

A woman called Moses; a novel based on the life of Harriet Tubman. Houghton Mifflin 1976 308p o.p.

This is a fictionalized account of "the life of Harriet Tubman, born in slavery on Maryland's Eastern Shore, who escaped North and spent her life in conducting hundreds of blacks to freedom along the Undergound Railroad prior to the Civil War." Libr J

"This fictional life story, told in the first person, is filled with incandescent raw materials, namely the cruelties of slavery, and the itineraries of escape." N Y Times Book Rev

Heilbrun, Carolyn G., 1926-2003

For works written by this author under other names see Cross, Amanda, 1926-2003

Heinemann, Larry

Paco's story. Farrar, Straus & Giroux 1986 209p o.p.

LC 86-19527

"Lone survivor of a Viet Cong night attack that wipes out the 90-plus men of Alpha Company, Paco Sullivan returns to civilian life after much time spent in military hospitals. Narrated by a nameless dead soldier from Alpha Company, this . . . tale interweaves Paco's infantry days in Vietnam with his Valium- and Librium-soothed afterlife as a dishwasher in a smalltown cafe." Libr J

"Mr. Heinemann's carefully crafted, oblique narrative suggests that the right words are not going to be found in ever-more-graphic, frontal approaches to 'gruesome carnage.' Its horrors may be as forcefully conveyed by a haunting scene in a greasy spoon as by the tearing of human flesh." N Y Times Book Rev

Heinlein, Robert A. (Robert Anson), 1907-1988

Citizen of the galaxy. Scribner 1957 302p o.p.

"Although marketed as a juvenile novel, this work was serialized for adults in *Astounding.* The Horatio Alger hero is in an interstellar setting, except that his lad starts out closer to the edge than Horatio's bootblacks and newsboys: he is a slave on a far planet of a despotic empire. He escapes into space with a nomadic trading company and eventually gets back to Earth, where he assumes (by inheritance!) the headship of a giant financial corporation. This is a *bilungsroman,* except that the young hero never really grows up; but Heinlein's knack for creating sociologically plausible cultures is well displayed." Anatomy of Wonder 4

Friday. Holt, Rinehart & Winston 1982 368p il o.p.

LC 81-13221

"An artificially created superwoman, courier for a secret organization, has to fend for herself when the decline of the West reaches its climax; she ultimately finds a new raison d'être on the extraterrestrial frontier. Welcomed by Heinlein fans as action-adventure respite from his more introspective works." Anatomy of Wonder 4

Job: a comedy of justice. Ballantine Bks. 1984 376p o.p.

LC 84-3091

"A Del Rey book"

"Alexander Hergensheimer, a minister from an alternate-world America dominated by Bible Belt fundamentalism, is flipped from one alternate world to another in rapid succession, whereby his faith, his endurance, and his love for his Margrethe are supremely tested. There are occasional patches of discursive philosophical, religious, and ethical ramblings here, which will be familiar territory to most of Heinlein's readers. For the most part, however, this tightly written, provocative, and powerful book, with its large cast of intriguing characters and an irresistibly compelling love story, is eminently readable." Booklist

The moon is a harsh mistress. Putnam 1966 383p o.p.

"Colonists of the Moon declare independence from Earth, and contrive to win the ensuing battle with the aid of a sentient computer. Action-adventure with some exploration of new possibilities in social organization and fierce assertion of the motto 'There Ain't No Such Thing as a Free Lunch.'" Anatomy of Wonder 4

The puppet masters. Doubleday 1951 219p o.p.

ISBN 0-451-07339-8

"Heinlein's paranoia-laden tale of sluglike creatures, arrived in saucer-shaped craft to enslave humans by the particularly gruesome procedure of growing into each person's nervous system from a position on the upper back of the victim—making his or her profile humpbacked." Anatomy of Wonder. 3d edition

Stranger in a strange land. Putnam 1961 408p o.p.

"The hero is a human born of space travelers from earth and raised by Martians. He is brought to the totalitarian post-World War III world that is in many ways depicted as a satire of the U.S. in the 1960s, marked by repressiveness in sexual morality and religion. The plot, which tells how the heroic stranger creates a Utopian society in which people preserve their individuality but share a brotherhood of community, made Heinlein and his novel cult objects for young people dedicated to a counterculture." Oxford Companion to Am Lit. 5th edition

Heinrich, Will

The king's evil; a novel. Scribner 2003 195p $23

ISBN 0-7432-3504-5 LC 2003-42374

"Narrator Joseph Malderoyce knew passion only in his youth, when he vowed to be a painter, but that ambition was erased when an exhibition of Mondrians left him in hopeless awe. After working as a lawyer for many years, he resigns from his firm and moves to a remote rural village. . . . Joseph's quiet existence is abruptly altered when he discovers a strange teenager, Abel Rufous, asleep on his back porch. The boy has been beaten, and Joseph invites him in, sympathetically offering him a room and assistance." Publ Wkly

"Offbeat but undeniably well written—there are intriguing digressions on such topics as Piet Mondrian and the history of tuberculosis—this first novel about facing the darker forces of one's personality has psychological, philosophical and even biblical overtones." Libr J

Helgason, Hallgrímur *See* Hallgrímur Helgason, 1959-

Heller, Jane

Best enemies; Jane Heller. 1st ed. St. Martin's Press 2004 341p $24.95

ISBN 0-312-28849-2 LC 2003-61063

"Amy Sherman and Tara Messer, lifelong best friends, are now all grown up and living in New York City. There has always been some friction in their relationship because Amy feels overshadowed by the extravagantly beautiful and elegant Tara (a lifestyle guru). When Amy catches her fiance, Stuart, in a passionate embrace with Tara two weeks before the wedding, she cuts both of them out of her life. The two eventually marry each other, while Amy focuses on her demanding job as publicity director for a major publisher. Four years later, Amy and

Heller, Jane—*Continued*
Tara are thrown together when Amy is assigned to promote Tara's new book. The two women weave a web of deception, with Tara pretending her life is perfect (even though Stuart is a serial womanizer) while Amy invents a rich, handsome boyfriend, whom she then has to produce." Booklist

Heller, Joseph

Catch-22; a novel. Simon & Schuster 1999 415p $26
ISBN 0-684-86513-0 LC 00-265132
"A comic, satirical, surreal, and apocalyptic novel . . . which describes the ordeals and exploits of a group of American airmen based on a small Mediterranean island during the Italian campaign of the Second World War, and in particular the reactions of Captain Yossarian, the protagonist." Oxford Companion to Engl Lit. 6th edition
Followed by Closing time

Closing time; a novel. Simon & Schuster 1994 464p o.p.
ISBN 0-671-74604-9 LC 94-20604
"Just like the original *Catch-22*, this sequel opens with Yossarian in a hospital bed, flirting with the nurses. Now in his seventies, Yossarian is depressed by his perfect health: things can only get worse. He lives alone in a Manhattan apartment not far from most of his old war buddies, including Milo Minderbinder, a defense contractor straight out of *Dr. Strangelove*. Yossarian and company mourn the decline of New York City and American culture in general and look back longingly to the golden age of prewar Coney Island." Libr J
"Heller is richly paranoid about state paranoia, and his winning jokes are more vicious than anything even in Catch-22 itself. Besides which, although Closing Time is too often like an electricity grid in danger of fusing, there are many exchanges that display all the old verve." New Statesman Soc

Good as Gold. Simon & Schuster 1979 447p o.p.
LC 78-23894
"Dr. Bruce Gold, forty-eight-year-old professor (Jewish) of literature (English) and author of many seminal articles in small journals (unread), finds himself facing the prospect of becoming a high Washington official. The offer comes from Ralph Newsome (Protestant), a presidential aide. . . . [Gold accepts] and soon meets Andrea Conover, the tall, beautiful, gifted daughter (also Protestant) of a wealthy, retired career diplomat (anti-Semite), clearly the suitable mate for a man with a potential of becoming the country's (very first Jewish) Secretary of State." Publisher's note

Portrait of an artist, as an old man. Simon & Schuster 2000 233p $23
ISBN 0-7432-0200-7 LC 00-711802
"Eugene Pota, the hero, is an aging novelist whose imaginative powers have been in steady decline since his earlier, more successful works. The book is a record of Pota's attempts to cap off his career with another triumph, and consequently a collection of false starts: here a parody of 'The Metamorphosis,' there a Greek-myth burlesque set among lickerish gods. While these set pieces are almost uniformly unsatisfying (only a fantasia that anatomizes the melancholy of nineteenth-century authors really works), there is something bleakly bracing in Pota's obsession with his own literary desiccation." New Yorker

Something happened. Knopf 1974 569p o.p.
The protagonist of this novel "Bob Slocum, works for a large, nameless company that sells something. What, we never learn. Slocum has a wife without a name, a disgruntled 15-year-old daughter and adorable 9-year-old son, both also unnamed, and a retarded child, Derek, who has a name and nothing else. Slocum lives in terror at his office, where 'there are six people who are afraid of me, and one small secretary who is afraid of all of us. I have one other person working for me who is not afraid of anyone, not even me, and I would fire him quickly, but I'm afraid of him.' Slocum carries his anxieties home. . . . 'Only one member of the family is not afraid of any of the others, and that one is an idiot.' Between these dry equations Slocum circles and recircles the question of what went wrong with his life." Newsweek

Heller, Zoe

What was she thinking?; notes on a scandal. Holt & Co. 2003 258p $23
ISBN 0-8050-7333-7 LC 2002-38809
"Barbara Covett, a sixtyish history teacher, is the kind of unmarried-woman-with-cat whose female friends sooner or later decide she is 'too intense.' Thus when a beautiful new pottery teacher, Sheba Hart. . .chooses Barbara as a confidante, she is deeply, even rather sinisterly, gratified. Sheba's secret is explosive: married with two kids, she is having an affair with a fifteen-year-old student. . . .Equally adroit at satire and at psychological suspense, Heller charts the course of a predatory friendship and demonstrates the lengths to which some people go for human company." New Yorker

Helprin, Mark

Ellis Island
In Helprin, M. Ellis Island & other stories p128-96

Ellis Island & other stories. Delacorte Press 1981 196p o.p.
LC 80-18437
Contents: The Schreuderspitze; Letters from the Samantha; Martin Bayer; North light; A Vermont tale; White gardens; Palais de Justice; A room of frail dancers; La Volpaia; Ellis Island
This book "consists of a novella (the title story) and ten short stories whose variation in length, content, style, and theme attest to the remarkable versatility of the writer. . . . Written in the first person, 'Ellis Island' is a four-part story—the recollections of an enterprising Jewish immigrant who finds himself temporarily stranded on that famous stepping stone to the New World. His vulnerability to the arbitrary decisions of immigration functionaries, his efforts to keep from being deported, and his attempts to earn a living are adventures told with a whimsical humor by a raconteur with a zest for life." Best Sellers

Helprin, Mark—*Continued*

The Pacific and other stories. Penguin Press 2004 366p $25.95

ISBN 1-594-20036-X LC 2004-50505

Contents: Il colore ritrovato; Reconstruction; Monday; A billiant idea and his own; Vandevere's house; Prelude; Perfection; Sidney Balbion; Mar nueva; Rain; Passchendaele; Jacob Bayer and the telephone; Sail shining in white; Charlotte of the Utrechtseweg; Last tea with the armorers; The Pacific

This collection is "rich in big, life-shaping notions (love, honor, duty, regret) filtered through the language of longing and nostalgia in such a way that the world takes on a kind of fairy-tale luster." Washington Post

A soldier of the great war. Harcourt Brace Jovanovich 1991 792p $32

ISBN 0-15-183600-0 LC 90-45987

"In summer 1964, a distinguished-looking gentleman in his seventies dismounts on principle from a streetcar that was to carry him from Rome to a distant village, instead accompanying on foot a boy denied a fare. As they walk, he tells the boy the story of his life. A young aesthete from a privileged Roman family, Alessandro Giuliani found his charmed existence shattered by the coming of World War I. The war led to an onerous tour of duty, inadvertent desertion, near-execution, forced labor, service high in the Italian Alps that took advantage of his . . . skill at mountain climbing, capture by the enemy, and return home, dispossessed of most of his friends and family. Along the way, he gains, loses, and eventually rediscovers love." Libr J

"Helprin's big, rumbustious new novel is about four-fifths of a marvel. Helprin has simplified his language, though he still works up a good head of rhetorical steam, and he has moderated his enthusiasm for phantasmagoric set pieces. He has also picked themes—war and loss, youth and age—that suit a large, elaborate style. . . . For a very large chunk of the novel's center, Helprin writes with riotous energy and sustained brilliance." Time

Winter's tale. Harcourt Brace Jovanovich 1983 673p $35

ISBN 0-15-197203-6 LC 83-273

This novel "opens in the years just preceding World War I. Peter Lake, a burglar and mechanic with unparalleled skills, attempts to rob the mansion of the wealthy Isaac Penn—and falls in love with Beverly, Isaac's beautiful but sickly daughter. They marry. She dies. He departs on an involuntary journey through time. One hundred years later, he reappears, and with the help of younger Penns and various hangers-on leads the city of New York through the horrible waning hours of the 20th century, into the justice of the third millenium." Christ Sci Monit

The author "describes the impossible with microscopic precision, and he summons the moods and myriad landscapes of the city with breathtaking poetry. . . . Again and again Helprin celebrates selfless love, a devotion to beauty, the desire to explore, and an acceptance of responsibility. . . . Helprin's freewheeling use of fantasy at times eclipses his essential seriousness, diminishing the novel as a whole. Yet there is unquestionable genius in the book's marvelous individual pieces." Saturday Rev

Hemans, Donna

River woman. Washington Sq. Press 2002 232p $23

ISBN 0-7434-1039-4 LC 2002-282477

"Did Kelithe's son Timothy accidentally drown in the Rio Minho as the women washed their clothes, or did Kelithe stand by and watch Timothy die so that she could leave behind her life and join her mother in America? Though the women of Standfast, Jamaica, shun her and demand that she be put to justice, Kelithe remains mute and numb with grief. She can only wait for her mother, Sonya, to return from New York and stand by to defend her. . . .[This] novel is one of stark lyricism and shattering emotional honesty." Libr J

Hemingway, Ernest, 1899-1961

Across the river and into the trees. Scribner Classics 1998 272p $26

ISBN 0-684-84464-8 LC 98-159867

"This is the story of a peace-time army colonel, closely resembling the author, who comes to Venice on leave to go duck shooting, to see the young Italian countess he loves, and to make a significant pilgrimage to the place where he, Richard Cantwell (and Nick Adams, Frederic Henry, and the author himself), was wounded in World War I. . . . The novel is Hemingway's weakest. It points up sharply the importance of that war injury in the author's life and work, but in some of its postures and mannerisms it seems to read like a parody of his better fiction." Herzberg. Reader's Ency of Am Lit

A farewell to arms. Scribner Classics 1997 297p $27.50

ISBN 0-684-83788-9 LC 96-53356

A reissue of the title first published 1929

This novel "deals with a love-affair conducted against the background of the war in Italy. Its excellence lies in the delicacy with which it conveys a sense of the impermanence of the best human feelings; the unobstrusive force of its symbolism of mountain and plain; above all the vast scope of its vision of war—the retreat from Caporetto is one of the great war-sequences of literature." Penguin Companion to Am Lit

The garden of Eden. Scribner 1986 247p o.p.

LC 86-3701

A novel Hemingway "began in 1946 and worked on intermittently in the last 15 years of his life and left unfinished." N Y Times Book Rev

This novel is "based on Hemingway's honeymoon with Pauline in May 1927 at Le Grau-du-Roi, a . . . fishing village in the Camargue. David and Catherine Bourne at first lead an idyllic existence—tasting the pleasures of board, bottle, beach, and bed. . . . After the Bournes meet a beautiful . . . young woman, Marita, Catherine sleeps with her, urges Marita to sleep with David, and then become jealous of David's passion for the blank and passive girl. The love triangle brings out the deep-rooted tensions in the Bournes' marriage." Natl Rev

"Whatever its problems, this version of 'The Garden of Eden' deserves publication for what it says about writing and for the short story which Hemingway shows us David writing." Newsweek

Hemingway, Ernest, 1899-1961—*Continued*

The Hemingway reader; selected with a foreword and twelve brief prefaces by Charles Poore. Scribner 1953 xx, 652p o.p.

Partially analyzed in Short story index

This one volume selection includes two complete novels: The sun also rises and The torrents of spring; excerpts from A farewell to arms; Death in the afternoon; Green hills of Africa; To have and have not; For whom the bell tolls; Over the river and into the trees; The old man and the sea; and eleven short stories

The stories included are: In our time; A way you'll never be; Fifty grand; A clean well-lighted place; Light of the world; After the storm; The short happy life of Francis Macomber; Capital of the world; The snows of Kilimanjaro; Old man at the bridge; Fable of the good lion

In our time; stories. Scribner 156p pa $10

ISBN 0-684-82276-8

First published 1930

Several of these "stories" picture episodes in the life of a growing boy in the timber country of the Middle West

"Of 'stories' in the commonly accepted sense of the word there are few. . . . Most of the others are psychological episodes, incidents, sketches . . . call them what you will. They are soundly and movingly done." Lit Rev

Islands in the stream. Scribner 1970 466p o.p.

This posthumous novel is divided into three parts: Bimini, Cuba and At Sea. "'Bimini' is Thomas Hudson in the 1930s entertaining the three sons of his two wrecked marriages; they fish; their love leaves him open to his loneliness, and then the death of two of them leaves him nothing but lonely. 'Cuba' is Thomas Hudson clandestinely war efforting in about 1942; his other son (the eldest) has been killed as a pilot; Thomas Hudson drinks; he meets his first wife who is all he has ever wanted. 'At Sea' is Thomas Hudson commanding the pursuit of some German U-boat survivors; the Germans die, and it may be that the wounded Thomas Hudson is about to too." N Y Rev Books

Men without women. Scribner 1927 232p o.p.

Contents: The undefeated; In another country; Hills like white elephants; The killers; Che ti dice la patria; Fifty grand; A simple enquiry; Ten Indians; A canary for one; An Alpine idyll; A pursuit race; Today is Friday; Banal story; Now I lay me

The Nick Adams stories. Scribner 268p pa $12

ISBN 0-684-16940-1

First published 1972

Arranged chronologically, this collection of 24 tales contains all the semi-autobiographical Nick Adams stories

"The volume presents Nick as a child in the northern woods, as adolescent, as soldier, veteran, writer, husband and parent. The last Nick Adams story appeared in 1933, and what surprises here, in these . . . [stories] of varying length, quality and intent, is their freshness and immediacy." Publ Wkly

The old man and the sea; illustrations by C.F. Tunnicliffe and Raymond Sheppard. Scribner Classics 1996 93p il $20

ISBN 0-684-83049-3 LC 96-11419

A reissue of the title first published 1952

"The old fisherman Santiago had only one friend in the village, the boy Manolin. Everyone else thought he was unlucky because he had caught no fish in a long time. At noon on the 85th day of fishing, he hooked a large fish. He fought with the huge swordfish for three days and nights before he could harpoon it, but the battle came to nought when sharks destroyed the fish before Santiago could get back to the village." Shapiro. Fic for Youth. 3d edition

The short stories. Scribner Classics 1997 457p $30

ISBN 0-684-83786-2 LC 96-53349

Originally published 1938 in collection with the play The fifth column

Contents: The short happy life of Francis Macomber; The capital of the world; The snows of Kilimanjaro; Old man at the bridge; Up in Michigan; On the quai at Smyrna; Indian camp; The doctor and the doctor's wife; The end of something; The three-day blow; The battler; A very short story; Soldier's home; The revolutionist; Mr and Mrs Elliot; Cat in the rain; Out of season; Cross-country snow; My old man; Big two-hearted river; The undefeated; In another country; Hills like white elephants; The killers; Che ti dice la patria; Fifty grand; A simple enquiry; Ten Indians; A canary for one; An Alpine idyll; A pursuit race; Today is Friday; Banal story; Now I lay me; After the storm; A clean, well-lighted place; The light of the world; God rest you merry, gentlemen; The sea change; A way you'll never be; The mother of a queen; One reader writes; Homage to Switzerland; A day's wait; A natural history of the dead; Wine of Wyoming; The gambler, the nun, and the radio; Fathers and sons

The snows of Kilimanjaro and other stories. Scribner Classics 1995 143p $25

ISBN 0-684-86221-2 LC 95-4764

A reissue of the title first published 1961

Contents: The snows of Kilimanjaro; A clean, well-lighted place; A day's wait; The gambler, the nun, and the radio; Fathers and sons; In another country; The killers; A way you'll never be; Fifty grand; The short happy life of Francis Macomber

The sun also rises. Scribner Classics 1996 222p $25

ISBN 0-684-83051-5 LC 96-11420

A reissue of the title first published 1926

"Set in the 1920s, the novel deals with a group of aimless expatriates in France and Spain. They are members of the cynical and disillusioned post-World War I Lost Generation, many of whom suffer psychological and physical wounds as a result of the war. Two of the novel's main characters, Lady Brett Ashley and Jake Barnes, typify this generation. Lady Brett drifts through a series of affairs despite her love for Jake, who has been rendered impotent by a war wound. Friendship, stoicism, and natural grace under pressure are offered as the values that matter in an otherwise amoral and often senseless world." Merriam-Webster's Ency of Lit

also in Hemingway, E. The Hemingway reader p89-289

To have and have not. Scribner Classics 1999 174p $25

ISBN 0-684-85923-8 LC 00-266244

Hemingway, Ernest, 1899-1961—*Continued*

A reissue of the title first published 1937

This novel "deals with the effort of Harry Morgan, a native of Key West, to earn a living for himself and his family. He has operated a boat for rental to fishing parties, but, during the Depression of the 1930s, he is forced to turn to the smuggling of Chinese immigrants and illegal liquor. While assisting a gang of bank robbers to escape, he is shot and mortally wounded. He dies gasping, 'One man alone ain't got . . . no chance.'" Reader's Ency. 4th edition

The torrents of spring; a romantic novel in honor of the passing of a great race. Scribner 1926 143p o.p.

"A burlesque of 'Sherwood Anderson' and the 'Chicago school' of authors, this comic novel tells of Yogi Johnson and Scripps O'Neil, workers in a pump factory in Petosky, Mich.; of Scripp's amours with two waitresses in Brown's Beanery, and of Yogi's adventures with the Indians." Herzberg. Reader's Ency of Am Lit

also in Hemingway, E. The Hemingway reader p25-86

True at first light; edited with an introduction by Patrick Hemingway. Scribner 1999 319p $26

ISBN 0-684-84921-6 LC 98-55510

This is a "'fictional memoir' of the first phase of the 54-year-old Hemingway's final visit to East Africa in 1953-54. . . . His second son, Patrick, has extrapolated it from the untitled first draft of a manuscript." Natl Rev

"The tension of lion and leopard executions is superbly conveyed, as are the joking and teasing among the men and that peculiar, depersonalized alertness that comes with total concentration on the surrounding environment." Atl Mon

Hemon, Aleksandar, 1964-

Nowhere man; the Pronek fantasies. Doubleday 2002 242p $23.95

ISBN 0-385-49924-8 LC 2002-66208

This novel follows Joseph Pronek "from a peaceable childhood in Sarajevo through a strange respite in Kiev in 1991 to a series of often hilarious low-paid jobs in Chicago, including an improbable but edifying stint as a Greenpeace canvasser." NY Times Book Rev

"Pronek's constantly reconfiguring life makes the novel a wild, twisty read, and Hemon's inimitable voice and the wry urgency of his storytelling should cement his reputation as a talented young writer." Publ Wkly

Hendrie, Laura, 1954-

Remember me; a novel. Holt & Co. 1999 373p $24

ISBN 0-8050-6218-1 LC 99-13302

"Rose Devonic is not much liked in the little town of Quedero, NM, famed for its fine embroidery. . . . Rose's little brother and her uncle, regarded as a crazy dreamer/schemer, were killed along with her mother in an accident. Now Rose survives by embroidering for the tourist trade and living off-season for free in the Ten Tribes Motel, whose gruff but devoted proprietor, Birdie, taught her her stitches. But Birdie's sister Alice, who bought the motel for Birdie with the insurance money she got after her sister died in the same accident that felled Rose's family, wants to sell it. Birdie has a stroke, Alice is clearly developing Alzheimer's and Rose ends up caring for them both." Libr J

"Hendrie's beautifully crafted and gutsy novel is animated by an unusual and vivid cast and charged with sharp and knowing humor." Booklist

Henley, Patricia, 1947-

Hummingbird house; a novel. MacMurray & Beck 1999 326p $22

ISBN 1-87844-887-0 LC 98-31274

"For more than 20 years, over half her life, nurse-midwife Kate Banner and her oldest friend, Maggie Byrne, have been living and working in Central America. . . . In the early 1980s, after a devastating death and the end of a love affair, Kate decides to leave Nicaragua for Guatemala, the first step on the road home to Indiana. There, in the face of the increased violence, she finds comfort in the love she feels for eight-year-old Marta, whose brother is one of the many 'disappeared' children, and Father Dixie Ryan, a radicalized Catholic priest who came to Guatemala to help the people in their struggles to survive tragedy and make a better life for themselves." Booklist

"The prismatic trajectory of the tale may be deliberate, for the author's message is double-edged; that trying for a better world is necessary, demanding work, but no one can save herself through saving the world." Publ Wkly

In the river sweet. Pantheon Bks. 2002 291p o.p.

ISBN 0-375-42127-0 LC 2002-22018

"The heroine, Ruth Anne Bond, is a woman of 50, living in Indiana; Johnny, her husband of nearly 30 years, is the proprietor of an upscale restaurant. Everything seems picture perfect until devoutly Catholic Ruth Anne learns that their only daughter, Laurel, is a lesbian. While she adjusts to this revelation. . .her own secret past catches up with her: she is contacted by Tin, the illegitimate son she conceived with a blind Vietnamese boy when she was a teenager working in a convent in Saigon. . .(The author) balances long, stream-of-consciousness passages with short, potent sentences to wonderful effect, tilling the familiar ground of sexuality and spirituality with originality and grace." Publ Wkly

Hennissart, Martha

For works written by this author in collaboration with Mary J. Latsis see Lathen, Emma

Henry, April

Learning to fly. St. Martin's Minotaur 2002 308p $23.95

ISBN 0-312-29052-7 LC 2001-58549

"A gruesome freeway pileup (52 vehicles, 14 deaths) has unexpected benefits for a young woman whose hippie parents named her Free: a new identity plus a bag containing $750,000 in drug money. When a passenger in her car, killed in the carnage, is mistakenly identified as Free, suddenly our pregnant, unemployed heroine has a way out of her problems and the money to finance it. She becomes Lydia, and assembles a new life in what

Henry, April—*Continued*
she believes is the safe obscurity of another woman's persona. But then two dangerous men start to track her." Publ Wkly

Henry, O., 1862-1910

The best short stories of O. Henry; selected and with an introduction by Bennett A. Cerf, and Van H. Cartmell. Modern Lib. 1994 c1945 340p $22.95
ISBN 0-679-60122-8
First Modern Library edition published 1945
O. Henry "is best known for his observations on the diverse lives of everyday New Yorkers, 'the four million' neglected by other writers. He had a fine gift of humor and was adept at the ingenious depiction of ironic circumstances, in plots frequently dependent upon coincidence." Oxford Companion to Am Lit. 6th edition

Cabbages and kings
In Henry, O. The complete works of O. Henry p551-679

The complete works of O. Henry; foreword by Harry Hansen. Doubleday 1953 1692p $15.95
ISBN 0-385-00961-5
An omnibus volume of 13 short story collections: The four million (1906); Heart of the West (1907); The gentle grafter (1908); Roads of destiny (1909); Cabbages and kings (1904); Whirligigs (1910); Options (1909); Sixes and sevens (1911); Rolling stones (1912); The voice of the city (1908); The trimmed lamp (1907); Strictly business (1910); Waifs and strays (1917)

The four million
In Henry, O. The complete works of O. Henry p1-108

The gentle grafter
In Henry, O. The complete works of O. Henry p267-354

Heart of the West
In Henry, O. The complete works of O. Henry p109-266

Options
In Henry, O. The complete works of O. Henry p680-810

Roads of destiny
In Henry, O. The complete works of O. Henry p355-550

Rolling stones
In Henry, O. The complete works of O. Henry p941-1060

Sixes and sevens
In Henry, O. The complete works of O. Henry p811-940

Strictly business
In Henry, O. The complete works of O. Henry p1484-1631

The trimmed lamp
In Henry, O. The complete works of O. Henry p1365-1483

The voice of the city
In Henry, O. The complete works of O. Henry p1253-1364

Waifs and strays
In Henry, O. The complete works of O. Henry p1632-92

Whirligigs
In Henry, O. The complete works of O. Henry p1094-1252

Henry, Sue, 1940-

Cold company; an Alaska mystery. Morrow 2002 294p o.p.
ISBN 0-380-97882-2 LC 2001-44860
Jessie Arnold's "discovery of an old skeleton beneath her home sets her on the years-old trail of an infamous serial killer. When another woman disappears, Jessie's hunt becomes critical." Libr J
"One of the hallmarks of Henry's series is the beautiful and rugged Alaskan landscape, and she has never used it more effectively than she does here, as spring sets in motion new discoveries." Publ Wkly

Dead north; an Alaska mystery. Morrow 2001 280p o.p.
ISBN 0-380-97881-4 LC 00-48077
"While driving a friend's Winnebago to Alaska from Idaho, musher Jess Arnold . . . picks up a hitchhiking teenager trying to escape from the abusive stepfather who just murdered his mother. Friends, police, and the murderer all follow." Libr J
This "story offers a tough mystery, compelling characters, vivid scenery, endearing dogs, and a breakneck pace." Booklist

Death takes passage; an Alex Jensen mystery. Avon Bks. 1997 292p o.p.
ISBN 0-380-97469-X LC 97-4002
"Alaska state trooper Alex Jensen and girlfriend Jessie Arnold cruise down the Inside Passage as part of the 100th anniversary of the Klondike Gold Rush. When robbery and death strike the ship, Alex must investigate." Libr J
"Henry refreshingly blends classic mystery devices (a missing passenger, double identities, and locked rooms) with frontier and nautical history and the great beauty of Alaskan glaciers, mountains, night skies, and wildlife. In addition, Henry's enjoyable, well-paced novel displays little gratuitous violence and contains an intriguing mix of real and fictional characters." Booklist

Death trap; an Alaska mystery. Morrow 2003 273p $23.95
ISBN 0-380-97883-0 LC 2002-33734
"Sidelined from sled-dog racing this season because of a knee injury, musher Jessie Arnold agrees to help out a friend by working the Iditarod booth at the Alaska State Fair. The fun of the fair ends abruptly for Jessie when a man is found dead in a pond on the grounds, and her beloved lead dog, Tank mysteriously disappears from the booth. . . . Interesting developments in Jessie's personal life will please fans of this long-running series." Booklist

Henry, Sue, 1940-—*Continued*

Murder on the Iditarod Trail. Atlantic Monthly Press 1991 278p o.p.
LC 90-20925

"After three 'accidental' deaths early in the running of the torturous Iditarod Trail (from Anchorage to Nome) dog sled race, Alaskan police and race officials step up efforts to prevent further mayhem. State trooper Alex Jensen, single, brooding, handsome, and adept with physical evidence, falls upon the puzzling events with relish, comparing lists, visiting checkpoints, searching sled cargoes, etc. Consulting with race participant Jessie Arnold, he learns some of the inside facts, experiences delaying blizzards, and becomes emotionally attached." Libr J

"Henry provides suspense and excitement in this paean to a great sporting event and to the powerful Alaskan landscape." Publ Wkly

Murder on the Yukon Quest; an Alaska mystery. Avon Twilight 1999 291p o.p.
ISBN 0-380-97764-8 LC 99-21641

"Jessie Arnold has run the world-famous Iditarod dogsled race but is a rookie in the demanding Yukon Quest, which begins in Canada's Yukon Territory and extends over 1,000 dangerous miles to the finish line in Fairbanks. But Jessie has plenty of spirit and a fit, well-trained dog team. All of that hardly prepares her, however, for what happens when one of her fellow racers is kidnapped, and Jessie must deliver the ransom, rescue the victim, and capture the bad guys." Booklist

Henry, Will, 1912-1991

Mackenna's gold. Random House 1963 276p o.p.

A "Western melodrama with a touch of mystery and superstition. Set in Arizona in 1897, it tells of a tough young prospector who learns from a dying Apache of a valley filled with gold, and is then forced to lead a band of outlaws to the hidden treasure." Publ Wkly

"This Western, much better written and conceived than most, is an entertaining piece based on a first-rate Southwestern lost mine tale and a very good but little-read personal narrative." Libr J

Hensher, Philip

The Mulberry empire; or, The two virtuous journeys of the Amir Dost Mohammed Khan. Knopf 2002 486p o.p.
ISBN 0-375-41488-6

"In 1839, about 50,000 British troops entered Afghanistan to replace the amir with someone more palatable to the Empire. In this fictionalized account, we meet Burnes, a British explorer who ventures into the capital city of Kabul and befriends the soon-to-be-ousted Amir Dost Mohammed Khan." Libr J

"Hensher captures the mood of Western Victorian inquiry—mapping, botanizing, writing it all down—that seemed, in its bustle and energy, in its production of information, to underpin the whole imperial ideal. . . . The novel's plotting is smooth, its observations acute, and the minor and major characters are all beautifully drawn." N Y Times Book Rev

Herbert, Brian

Dune: House Atreides; [by] Brian Herbert and Kevin J. Anderson. Bantam Bks. 1999 604p o.p.
ISBN 0-553-11061-6 LC 99-17726

Set several decades before the first novel in the Dune series, this describes the origins, feuds and schemes that lay the foundation to the saga. "As Emperor Elrood's son plots a subtle regicide, young Leto Atreides leaves for a year's education on the mechanized world of Ix; a planetologist named Pardot Kynes seeks the secrets of Arrakis; and the eight-year-old slave Duncan Idaho is hunted by his cruel masters in a terrifying game from which he vows escape and vengeance." Publisher's note

"Though the plot here is intricate, even readers new to the saga will be able to follow it easily." Publ Wkly

Dune: House Corrino; [by] Brian Herbert and Kevin J. Anderson. Bantam Bks. 2001 496p o.p.
ISBN 0-553-11084-5 LC 2001-25777

"As Emperor Shaddam IV seeks to consolidate his power as Emperor of a Million Worlds through the monopoly of the spice trade, other forces array themselves in opposition to his increasingly tyrannical rule. . . . Though dependent on the previous books, this complex and compelling tale of dynastic intrigue and high drama adds a significant chapter to the classic Dune saga." Libr J

Dune: House Harkonnen; [by] Brian Herbert & Kevin J. Anderson. Bantam Bks. 2000 620p o.p.
ISBN 0-553-11072-1 LC 00-39804

In the second prequel "the young Duke Leto Atreides seeks to live up to his late father's expectations, [while] his rivals plot to bring about the downfall of House Atreides. Plots and counterplots involving the debauched Baron Vladimir Harkonnen, his Bene Gesserit enemies, and the treacherous schemers of the enigmatic Bene Tleilax escalate the tension among factions of a fragile galactic empire. Though power seems to reside in the hands of the emperor and his elite armies, the fate of many worlds hinges on the destiny of a single planet—the desert world known as Arrakis, or Dune." Libr J

Dune: The Butlerian jihad; [by] Brian Herbert and Kevin J. Anderson. TOR Bks. 2002 621p $27.95
ISBN 0-7653-0157-1 LC 2002-28581

"A Tom Doherty Associates book"

The authors "continue their prehistory of Frank Herbert's 'Dune' series with a new trilogy opener set in the distant past of Herbert's galactic saga. The authors reveal the origins of the Spacing Guild and the Bene Gesserit, as well as the root of the ancient feud between Houses Atreides and Harkonnen. This compelling saga of men and women struggling for their freedom is required reading for Dune fans." Libr J

Herbert, Frank, 1920-1986

Chapterhouse: Dune. Putnam 1985 464p o.p.
LC 84-17979

The sixth Dune novel "is set on the planet Chapterhouse, where the Bene Gesserits have installed their headquarters. They have fled from the slaughtering Honored Matres (a corrupt version of the Bene Gesserits), with plans to transform Chapterhouse into an-

Herbert, Frank, 1920-1986—*Continued*

other desert planet on which the valuable melange spice can be produced. The high point of the book is not the climactic raid on and capture of a group of Honored Matres, but rather a chapter in which a former Honored Matre undergoes the ritual spice agony to become a Bene Gesserit Reverend Mother." SLJ

Children of Dune. Berkley Pub. Corp. 1976 444p o.p.

This third volume in the saga of Dune "centers on the development of twins Leto and Ghanima and their decision to assume the mantle of political and religious leadership spurned by their father. Herbert expands on many of the questions raised in earlier books, especially prescience and the evolution of mankind." Booklist

Followed by God Emperor of Dune

Dune. Ace Bks. 1999 c1965 517p il $27.95

ISBN 0-441-00590-X

First published 1965 by Chilton

"Herbert combines several classic elements: a Machiavellian world of political intrigue worthy of fourteenth-century Italy, a huge cast of characters, and a detailed picture of a culture. Duke Leto Atreides and his family are coerced into exchanging their rich lands for a barren planet, Dune, which produces a unique drug. Duke's son, Paul, becomes the leader of a group that leads the Fremen of Dune against the enemy. This is a science fiction story with sociological and ecological import." Shapiro. Fic for Youth. 3d edition

Dune messiah. Putnam 1969 220p o.p.

In this second volume of the Dune series "the Bene Gesserit, a mystic sisterhood, plot to overthrow the god/emperor Paul Atreides, whom they created by special breeding but whom they cannot now control. Presented here via the narrative and quotes from journals and legends of the people of Dune, the imperial intrigue is engineered by such diverse characters as Bene Gesserit Mother Superior, a Tleilaxu face dancer, a 'ghola' recreation of Paul's dead friend, and the Princess Consort. Paul's eventual victory because of his future-vision makes fascinating reading." SLJ

Followed by Children of Dune

God Emperor of Dune. Putnam 1981 441p o.p.
LC 80-25149

In the fourth title of the Dune saga "Leto II, the God Emperor, combines melange, a spice drug, with religion in order to control his people. The scene is the planet now called Arrakis, since only a remnant of the desert, Dune, remains. It is 3,500 years after the events of 'Children of Dune,' which ended while Leto was young. After sacrificing his human body to melange in exchange for an estimated four-thousand year rule, Leto is still alive. Gradually the body of Shi-Hulud the Sandworm God is developing in him, while Leto the Emperor lives in the bosom of God, or so his followers believe. . . . His plan for the survival of humanity is the Golden Path, an enforced tranquility overriding man's desire for chaos, especially war." Best Sellers

Followed by Heretics of Dune

Heretics of Dune. Putnam 1984 480p o.p.
LC 83-16040

"The fifth installment of the 'Dune Cycle' follows the lives of the two children on different planets: On Gammu, a young Duncan Idaho trains relentlessly for the moment that will awaken the memories of his former lives; on Rakis, the fremen-child Sheeana discovers her ability to command the fearsome sandworms of the desert—and becomes an object of worship." Libr J

Followed by Chapterhouse: Dune

Herbert, Rosemary

(ed) The Oxford book of American detective stories. See The Oxford book of American detective stories

Herlihy, James Leo, 1927-1993

Midnight cowboy; [by] James L. Herlihy. Simon & Schuster 1965 253p o.p.

"The story of Joe Buck, a backward 27-year-old out of Albuquerque, who comes to New York to become a professional stud. In his fancy cowboy rig, Joe feels that he should be able to make his fortune. . . . He teams up with a handicapped pickpocket named Ratso Rizzo, who is just about as ineffectual a ponce as Joe is a hustler. . . . Living in an abandoned building with Ratso, he develops the strongest kinship with a human being since grandmother Sally Buck fell off a horse and died. He cares for Ratso when he is sick, steals for him, and tries to take him by bus to Florida, which he fancies as a land of greater opportunity. Eventually, Ratso breathes his last outside of Daytona—and once more Joe is left to face the world alone." N Y Times Book Rev

"An appalling story, told with great skill and important because Joe Buck is a characteristic product of the way we live and yet he cannot be adequately discussed outside of a novel." Saturday Rev

Hernández, Felisberto, 1902-1964

Around the time of Clemente Colling

In Hernández, F. and Allen, E. Lands of memory

Lands of memory; translated by Ester Allen. New Directions 2002 190p $24.95

ISBN 0-8112-1483-4 LC 2001-42589

Includes two novellas: Around the time of Clemente Colling and Lands of memory, and the following short stories: My first concert in Montevideo; Mistaken hands; The crocodile; The new house

The Lands of memory is an uncoventinal fictional autobiography and Around the time of Clemente Colling is a bildungsroman about a one-eyed blind piano teacher and his pupil

"Hernández revels in images that are simple and repetitive: arms, light and shadow, the houses of the wealthy and their odd contents. The stories acquire a luxurious sheen from the ease with which they navigate memories, taking pleasure in recounting them with no intention other than tracking the mind's twists and turns." Publ Wkly

Lands of memory [novelette]

In Hernández, F. and Allen, E. Lands of memory

Hersey, John, 1914-1993

A bell for Adano. Knopf 1944 269p o.p.

"The town bell of Adano is transformed into material for a cannon, and its loss symbolizes a moral loss to the very life of the people. When the town falls into the

Hersey, John, 1914-1993—*Continued*
hands of the Americans and the Fascist forces are in retreat, Major Joppolo, a Brooklyn-born Italian, becomes a favorite of the townspeople because of the concern he has for them. Not only does he help Tina find her missing sweetheart, but he finds a replacement for the bell, retrieving it from a U.S. ship named after an Italian-American hero of World War I. To the town's dismay, Major Joppolo is relieved of his command by an American general whose unreasonable orders he ignores." Shapiro. Fic for Youth. 3d edition

Key West tales. Knopf 1994 227p o.p.
ISBN 0-679-42992-1 LC 93-11094
Contents: God's hint; Get up, sweet slug-a-bed; Did you ever have such sport?; The two lives of Consuela Castanon; They're signaling!; A game of anagrams; Cuba libre!; Fantasy fest; Just like you and me; Page two; Amends; Piped over the side; To end the American dream; The wedding dress; A little paperwork
"In this final collection of stories, Hersey focuses on his theme of ordinary people facing momentous events in their lives: death by AIDS, the death of a friend from AIDS, loss of innocence and virginity, meeting the son one had given up for adoption two decades before, or retirement from military service. As interludes, Hersey presents brief, italicized vignettes of the famous or powerful people who have lived in or visited Key West." Libr J

A single pebble. Knopf 1956 181p o.p.
"An American engineer's trip by junk up the Yangtze to locate a dam site, as he relates it years later in retrospect, symbolizes the contrast between the Western idea of progress and tempo of living and the passive resignation of China's ancient culture and traditions. With mounting tension, the story brings into focus the subtle relationship between the young engineer and the owner of the junk, his wife, and the head tracker, Old Pebble, in a drama heightened by the physical grandeur of the Great River." Booklist

The wall. Knopf 1950 632p o.p.
"This novel is presented as a journal kept by a diarist during World War II. It tells of life in the Warsaw Ghetto, depicting Jewish interdependence in a struggle for survival. The writer's observations enrich our understanding of Jewish culture. Although the diarist dies of pneumonia in 1944, his escape from the enclosure within which the Germans confined the Jews is a testament to hope and courage." Shapiro. Fic for Youth. 3d edition

Hervey, Evelyn *See* Keating, H. R. F. (Henry Reymond Fitzwalter), 1926-

Hess, Joan

Busy bodies. Dutton 1995 246p o.p.
LC 94-46120
"A Claire Malloy mystery"
In this Claire Malloy mystery, "painter Zeno Gorgias, who has recently moved to the small Arkansas town's historic neighborhood, is staging performance pieces, starring a nearly naked young woman with a rubber snake, on his front lawn. Not only are Claire's hyperbolic teenage daughter and her friend involved, but Claire's policeman lover has his hands full with crowd control. Zeno's estranged wife arrives and threatens to have him institutionalized for incompetence; she is found murdered, her body recovered from charred ashes of Zeno's house after it—and half a million dollars' worth of his paintings—are burned." Publ Wkly

A conventional corpse; a Claire Malloy mystery. St. Martin's Press 2000 275p o.p.
ISBN 0-312-24662-5 LC 00-29686
"Arkansas bookseller/sleuth Claire Malloy organizes a mystery convention at Farber College that goes awry. Five major writers and attendant quirks create problems, as does the appearance/disappearance of a hated mystery editor and the suspicious death of an attendee." Libr J
"Offering a teasingly intricate puzzle along with some zinging satire of current publishing trends, Hess has produced another first-rate mystery." Publ Wkly

Death by the light of the moon. St. Martin's Press 1992 227p o.p.
LC 91-37884
"A Claire Malloy mystery"
"Bookstore owner/sleuth Claire Malloy . . . finds little but trouble when she and teenage daughter Caron attend the 80th birthday celebration of Miss Justicia, mother of Claire's late husband, at the family manor in the Louisiana bayous. Feuding relatives, mysterious hints about inheritances and terrible food begin a ghastly first night that will also include the drowning of the matriarch after she is seen careening drunkenly about the garden in her powered wheelchair." Publ Wkly
"Ms. Hess handles the complicated plot logistics with a deft touch, and although her overblown caricatures lack the affection she lavishes on the characters in her 'Maggody' series, she has a warm spot for teen-agers, whose insufferable ways elicit her funniest and kindest satirical swipes." N Y Times Book Rev

A diet to die for. St. Martin's Press 1989 199p o.p.
LC 89-34855
"A Claire Malloy mystery"
"Maribeth Galleston, heiress to the Farber fortune, is burdened with obesity, a bullying husband, and severe depression, but Claire Malloy's downstairs neighbor intends to help—by getting Maribeth to join the Ultima Diet Center. The diet, coupled with aerobics classes, seems to be succeeding . . . although Maribeth's behavior *is* becoming peculiar. When her car crashes through the glass door of Ultima, killing an employee, Detective Peter Rosen blames it on severe potassium deficiency caused by the diet, but Claire investigates and soon discovers that everyone involved seems to be having illicit affairs." Publisher's note

A holly, jolly murder. Dutton 1997 265p o.p.
ISBN 0-525-94240-8 LC 97-12895
"Small-town bookstore owner Claire Malloy lets curiosity get the best of her: she attends a Druid winter solstice festival. When the would-be celebrants discover their wealthy benefactor murdered, the Arch Druid (a feisty old lady) asks Claire's help." Libr J

Madness in Maggody. St. Martin's Press 1991 231p o.p.
LC 90-49306
"Chief of police Arly Hanks, lately of New York City, takes an offhand attitude toward crime or the lack of it in Maggody, Arkansas, until the tamales hit the fan dur-

Hess, Joan—*Continued*

ing the grand opening of a supermarket that none of the other merchants in town wants to see succeed. Now Arly's got one death, and reams of rumors to unravel. Although the situation is loaded with humor and small-town high jinks, the solution to the murder shocks Arly so much she promises herself that in the future she will take her job more seriously." Booklist

Maggody and the moonbeams; an Arly Hanks mystery. Simon & Schuster 2001 254p o.p.

ISBN 0-7432-0229-5 LC 2001-20208

Police chief Arly Hanks, "to her extreme horror, gets railroaded by Mrs. Jim Bob Buchanon into acting as chaperone for a church youth group at Camp Pearly Gates in nearby Dunkicker. Unbeknownst to all, the camp is also the home of a weird commune, the Daughters of the Moon, which is made up of a group of women (known locally as 'Beamers') who sport shaved heads, magenta lipstick, and white robes. The typical Maggody madness and mayhem begins when one of the campers stumbles over the body of a Beamer whose head has been pulverized." Booklist

Mischief in Maggody; an Ozarks murder mystery. St. Martin's Press 1988 202p o.p.

LC 88-1867

"Maggody, a little Ozark town where nothing ever happens, has problems. Its first female police chief, Arly Hanks, . . . comes back from vacation to find the community in an uproar . . . local prostitute and moonshiner Robin Buchanon has disappeared, leaving behind five hungry children. . . . Arly manages to foist them onto Mrs. Jim Bob while she goes hunting for the mother, whom she finds with her head blown off in the middle of a marijuana patch. . . . Another death and the public humiliation of two of the town's most righteous citizens take place before peace comes to Maggody once again. Hess writes an engaging tale, although the raunchy characters impart a certain vulgarity to the text." Publ Wkly

Misery loves Maggody; an Arly Hanks mystery. Simon & Schuster 1999 285p $22

ISBN 0-684-84562-8 LC 98-28728

Maggody, Arkansas police chief Arly Hanks "investigates after out-of-town police arrest the mayor of Maggody in connection with the death of a riverboat showgirl." Libr J

Murder@maggody.com. Simon & Schuster 2000 253p o.p.

ISBN 0-684-84563-6 LC 99-46821

"It's a new headache for Arly Hanks, chief of police . . . when funding is provided for a community computer lab, and everyone in the sleepy backwoods Arkansas town of Maggody is standing on line to get on-line. Everyone is already in a stew provoked by the newest resident, the fetching Gwynnie, who, in the opinion of Maggody's women, caught the eye of too many of their men. When Gwynnie turns up murdered, a trace of her e-mails suggests someone in town could have done her in." Publisher's note

"Maggody's eccentric inhabitants and Hess's comic touch infuse this cozy with a refreshing dose of spunk, resulting in another triumph for both small-town America and Hess." Publ Wkly

Out on a limb; a Claire Malloy mystery. St. Martin's Minotaur 2002 306p o.p.

ISBN 0-312-26680-4 LC 2002-69939

"When a local developer tries to level a bunch of trees, a protester chains herself to one of them—while the developer's daughter apparently abandons her baby on bookseller-sleuth Claire Molloy's doorstep. By the time Claire tracks her down, the woman has been charged with murdering her father." Libr J

"The author deftly juggles the various plot strands, letting the local news reporter fill in the action in which Claire is uninvolved. The surprising denouement comes off with éclat." Publ Wkly

Hesse, Hermann, 1877-1962

Demian. Boni & Liveright 1923 215p o.p.

Original German edition, 1919

A novel "featuring young Emil Sinclair. Largely through the crude aggression of a school bully, Sinclair becomes troubled by the realization that life consists of conflicting, opposite forces. His confusion is both cleared and compounded by the appearance of a mysterious older boy named Max Demian. Both Demian and his mother become central influences in Sinclair's life, although their encounters are sporadic. In a letter, Demian tells Sinclair of the devil-god Abraxas, who is the embodiment of a fusion of all good and evil, of destruction and creation. When he is wounded in the war, Sinclair has a vision of Demian, in which his death is implied. From that time on, Sinclair feels himself to be the possessor of the wisdom and understanding he had attributed to Demian. The novel is one of Hesse's most poignant statements of the terrors and torments of adolescence." Reader's Ency. 4th edition

The fairy tales of Hermann Hesse; translated and with an introduction by Jack Zipes; woodcut illustrations by David Frampton. Bantam Bks. 1995 xxxi, 266p il o.p.

LC 94-49166

"Quirky and evocative, Hesse's fairy tales stand alone, but also amplify the ideas and utopian longings of such counterculture avatars as *Siddhartha* and *Steppenwolf*." Publ Wkly

Gertrude; translated by Hilda Rosner. Rev. translation. Boni & Liveright 1969 237p o.p.

Original German edition, 1910; this translation first published in the United Kingdom

"The story has three major characters: Herr Kuhn, Herr Muoth, and Fräulein Gertrude Imthor, later Frau Muoth. Narrated by the aging Kuhn, the novel recounts his travails as a youth, his success as a composer, his frustrated love for Gertrude Imthor, and his strange friendship with Heinrich Muoth. . . . As a young man Kuhn had his leg crippled in an accident. The physical disability which prevents him from achieving happiness in life, especially with women, measurably accounts as well for his creativity." Saturday Rev

The glass bead game (Magister Ludi); translated from the German by Richard and Clara Winston; with a foreword by Theodore Ziolkowski. Holt, Rinehart & Winston 1969 558p o.p.

Original German edition, 1943; first published 1949 in the United States with title: Magister Ludi

This "novel follows the intellectual and spiritual odys-

Hesse, Hermann, 1877-1962—*Continued*

sey of Josef Knecht, who lives in a utopian society in the 23rd century. The culture is dominated by a glass-bead game, practiced in its highest form (in which beads are not even used) by an intellectual elite. The game represents a balanced fusion of the active and contemplative disciplines; it is a combination of music and mathematics (art and science) but includes elements from virtually every cultural endeavor. Knecht becomes master of the game (Lat, *Magister Ludi*) but has doubts about the virtues of pure intellect. He renounces his order and departs to the outer world, where he eventually dies, the tragic result of a life dedicated entirely to the world of the spirit." Reader's Ency. 4th edition

Narcissus and Goldmund; translated by Ursule Molinaro. Farrar, Straus & Giroux 1968 315p o.p.

Original German edition, 1930; English translation published 1932 with title: Death and the lover; also 1959 in the United Kingdom, with title: Goldmund

"The setting is Germany in the late Middle Ages—dark forests, wandering scholars, sheltered monasteries, flourishing imperial cities, the plague. The problem is the conflict of the intellectual and the sensual, the scholar and the artist. The device is the biographical novel, half picaresque, half philosophical." Choice

"Hesse's prose, ranging from lyricism to allegory, and from unabashed sentimentality to an intellectuality of a high order, is not easily rendered into another language. . . . The present version . . . is close to perfection." Saturday Rev

Siddhartha; translated by Hilda Rosner. New Directions 1951 153p $16.95; pa $6.95

ISBN 0-8112-0292-5; 0-8112-0068-X (pa)

Original German edition, 1923

"The young Indian Siddhartha endures many experiences in his search for the ultimate answer to the question, what is humankind's role on earth? He is also looking for the solution to loneliness and discontent, and he seeks that solution in the way of a wanderer, the company of a courtesan, and the high position of a successful businessman. His final relationship is with a humble but wise ferryman. This is an allegory that examines love, wealth, and freedom while the protagonist struggles toward self-knowledge." Shapiro. Fic for Youth. 3d edition

Steppenwolf; translated from the German by Basil Creighton. Holt & Co. 1929 309p o.p.

Original German edition, 1927

"The hero, Harry Haller . . . is torn between his own frustrated artistic idealism and the inhuman nature of modern reality, which, in his eyes, is characterized entirely by philistinism and technology. It is his inability to be a part of the world and the resulting loneliness and desolation of his existence that cause him to think of himself as a 'Steppenwolf' (wolf of the Steppes). The novel, which is rich in surrealistic imagery throughout, ends in what is called the magic theater, a kind of allegorical sideshow. Here, Haller learns that in order to relate successfully to humanity and reality without sacrificing his ideals, he must overcome his own social and sexual inhibitions." Reader's Ency. 4th edition

Stories of five decades; edited and with an introduction by Theodore Ziolkowski; translated by Ralph Manheim. With two stories translated by Denver Lindley. Farrar, Straus & Giroux 1973 c1972 xx, 328p o.p.

Contents: The island dream; Incipit vita nova; To Frau Gertrud; November night; The marble works; The Latin scholar; The wolf; Walter Kompff; The field devil; Chagrin d'amour; A man by the name of Ziegler; The homecoming; The city; Robert Aghion; The cyclone; From the childhood of Saint Francis of Assisi; Inside and outside; Tragic; Dream journeys; Harry, the Steppenwolf; An evening with Dr. Faust; Edmund; The interrupted class

Hewson, David

Lucifer's shadow. Delacorte Press 2004 369p $21.95

ISBN 0-385-33794-9

"In 1733, a wealthy patron of the arts supplies a lovely and talented Jewish woman with a Guarneri violin and the venue for her debut as a concert soloist in a world hostile to both women and Jews. In modern Venice, a young scholar is manipulated into selling a stolen antique violin and pretending authorship of a brilliant concerto recently unearthed in his employer's basement. Both stories follow naive young men who fall in love with gifted and troubled women musicians, then become involved in tracking killers who leave behind only traces of their female victims. The pungent canals of beautiful Venice carry readers on a metaphorical journey, tracing the spread of evil through ghetto, church, concert hall, and even the mansions of the elite." Booklist

A season for the dead; David Hewson. Delacorte Press 2004 386p $21.95

ISBN 0-385-33722-1 LC 2003-62522

This mystery "introduces Nic Costa, a 27-year-old Rome Questura detective, Caravaggio aficionado, and son of a prominent Italian Communist. Initially on pickpocket detail around Saint Peter's, Costa and his partner become involved in an incident on Vatican turf that reveals the complex relationship between the sovereign Vatican state and surrounding Rome. By responding to a situation at the Vatican Library, the pair begins the hunt for a serial killer who uses his victims to create tableaux of famous martyr portraits." Libr J

"Outsized, eccentric characters, a complex story and an abundance of historical detail make this engrossing book more than just another cookie-cutter, religious-nut serial killer thriller." Publ Wkly

Heyer, Georgette, 1902-1974

Cousin Kate. Dutton 1968 317p o.p.

In this Regency novel "Cousin Kate, a poor relation [is] brought into the aristocratic English Broome household with a very nasty fate indeed planned for her. . . . Kate, aided by a dashing cavalier and the earthy family of her old nurse, wins out. The Gothic gloom and doom is nicely leavened with wit, romance and wonderful period slang." Publ Wkly

The grand Sophy. Putnam 1950 307p o.p.

"On the Continent, where she had grown up and knew everyone in military, court, and diplomatic circles, Sophy was famous for her delightfully unexpected behavior, and

Heyer, Georgette, 1902-1974—*Continued*
for her irrepressible habit of managing less energetic people for their own good. When she returned to England, Regency London was also amused and startled by her antics, and her Rivenhall cousins, who offered her hospitality, were subjected to a reorganization of their lives. Sophy had learned the value of surprise attack from the Duke of Wellington, and applied it with shock tactics of her own to untangling the eldest Rivenhall cousins from unsuitable engagements, incidentally winning a husband for herself." Booklist

Lady of quality. Dutton 1972 254p o.p.
"The Lady of Quality is a Miss Annis Whychwood: wealthy, independent—and twenty-nine! She is finally mastered by her love for the pseudo-villain who of course reforms in order to win her after she has won his admiration by 'sparring' with him in what he calls a hornet-like manner of conversation." Best Sellers

Penhallow. Doubleday, Doran 1943 309p o.p.
A "story about a family of terrorizing and oversexed males, embroiled with one or two victimized females, halfwits, illegitimate boot boys, and others. Very British, rural, and somewhat artificially 'tense.' . . . Here technique is equal to all improbabilities." Barzun. Cat of Crime. Rev and enl edition

Hiaasen, Carl, 1953-

Basket case. Knopf 2002 317p o.p.
ISBN 0-375-41107-0 LC 2001-38317
"In laying out the tale of Jack Tagger, a maladjusted, middle-aged Florida obituary writer who stumbles across a hot news story in the supposed scuba-diving death of Jimmy Stoma, former lead singer for a band called Jimmy and the Slut Puppies, Hiaasen skewers both corporate media operations and the world of pop stardom." N Y Times Book Rev

Lucky you; a novel. Knopf 1997 353p o.p.
ISBN 0-679-45444-6 LC 97-36885
"Sharing $28 million worth of lottery money with the holder of one other winning ticket wouldn't seem to be much of a burden to bear, but it is for Bodean Gazzer and his pal Chub, who crave all the cash to launch their own personal hate group, the White Clarion Aryans. The other winner, a black woman named JoLayne Lucks, plans to use her money to save a patch of Florida swamp, but that's before the Aryans assault her and steal the ticket. With the help of maverick journalist Tom Krome, JoLayne attempts to steal it back." Booklist
"Hiaasen writes witty dialogue that crackles, and his characters are eccentrically colorful." N Y Times Book Rev

Native tongue. Knopf 1991 325p o.p.
LC 91-52713
This novel is set in the Florida keys. "There, just a few hundred miles south of Disney World, Francis X. Kingsbury, a k a Frankie King, a one time racketeer now enrolled in the Federal witness relocation program, has assembled a giant parcel of Florida real estate. . . . Kingsbury turns some of the property into an amusement park, the Amazing Kingdom of Thrills, and sets about developing the rest into a turf of condominiums, villas and golf links. Trouble is, the ecologically minded grow enraged. . . . [They] set out to destroy Kingsbury and his developments." N Y Times Book Rev
"Hiaasen writes to a formula with brilliant success. His books are addictive. . . . One may miss the sour bite of bleaker comedy, found in the best crime stories of a more realistic kind, but for entertainment few can match him." London Rev Books

Sick puppy; a novel. Knopf 2000 341p o.p.
ISBN 0-679-45445-4 LC 99-33435
"Twilly Spree, an independently wealthy, psychologically unstable pseudo-ecologist, spends his time on a one-man crusade to preserve Florida's wildlife and natural beauty. When Twilly sees Palmer Stoat toss a Burger King wrapper from a car window, he vows to teach the litterbug a lesson. Twilly hits paydirt when he realizes that Palmer is a legislative lobbyist working for a land developer intent on building a mall, golf course, and condos on one of Florida's few undeveloped offshore islands. In a wild plot to get Palmer's attention, Twilly kidnaps Palmer's Labrador retriever but ends up with his wife as well." Libr J
"While there may be nothing laughable about unchecked environmental exploitation, Hiaasen has refined his knack for using this gloomy but persistent state of affairs as a prime mover for scams of all sorts. In *Sick Puppy,* he shows himself to be a comic writer at the peak of his powers." Publ Wkly

Skin tight. Putnam 1989 319p o.p.
LC 89-31580
"When Mick Stranahan, a retired investigator, is the attempted victim of murder, he becomes a little curious to find out who wants him dead. He trails the killer to a quack plastic surgeon who was a suspect in a murder case Stranahan investigated four years before. Someone is about to blab that the surgeon had a more than passing interest in the old case and Stranahan gets back in the harness to investigate." West Coast Rev Books

Skinny dip; a novel. Alfred A. Knopf 2004 355p $24.95
ISBN 0-375-41108-9 LC 2004-44106
"Joey Perrone and her husband, Chaz, are taking a cruise to celebrate their wedding anniversary. One night, as the rain pours down, Chaz throws Joey overboard. He then proceeds to convince the authorities that he has no idea what happened to her. Unfortunately for him, Joey is rescued and begins to plot her ultimate revenge against her soon-to-be-patsy of a husband. The squirm-inducing mayhem that follows in this sometimes sidesplitting novel almost makes you feel sorry for Chaz. It has rarely been this much fun to read about the act of revenge. All of the trademark characters and Florida locales are used to maximum effect." Libr J

Stormy weather; a novel. Knopf 1995 335p o.p.
ISBN 0-679-41982-9 LC 95-78487
A Florida hurricane "puts on a collision course a demented cast of tourists, scam artists and eccentrics: New York ad exec Max Lamb, who decides to spice up his Orlando honeymoon by taking his bride and his camcorder into the teeth of the storm; Skink, the swamp-dwelling former Florida governor . . . who kidnaps Max in an effort to teach him to respect the land; Edie March, a seductive drifter who hatches a half-baked personal-injury scam with the help of Snapper, a sadistic ex-con; and Augustine, the altruistic son of a jailed drug smuggler, who juggles skulls to relax." Publ Wkly

Hiaasen, Carl, 1953-—*Continued*

"The crimes plotted are minor aspects of a fiction that explores the intersection of the grotesque and the human." Libr J

Strip tease; a novel. Knopf 1993 353p o.p.
LC 93-12358

"At the Eager Beaver, a topless bar in Fort Lauderdale, former FBI clerk Erin Grant dances nightly to pay for legal fees in her custody fight for her young daughter. There David Dilbeck, a poorly disguised, somewhat kinky and imbecilic U.S. Congressman owned by the state's sugar interests, is recognized by a sharp-eyed regular who, infatuated with Erin, initiates a blackmail plan meant to influence her court case. The resulting mayhem, occuring in an election year, involves machinations up to the highest state level." Publ Wkly

In among Hiaasen's "freaks and obsessives, his corrupters and corrupted, his brain-dead and his frenetically active, the author has dropped a real honest-to-God human being, an appealing young woman named Erin Grant. Her presence, her history and goals, make the cartoon nastiness around her less cartoony and more nasty than in previous Hiaasen novels." N Y Times Book Rev

Hickam, Homer H.

The keeper's son; a novel; [by] Homer Hickam. 1st ed. Thomas Dunne Books 2003 353p $24.95
ISBN 0-312-30189-8 LC 2003-54964

"This is the first novel of a planned series about rough and tumble Coast Guard Lt. Josh Thurlow and his unusual patrol boat crew during WWII. Josh, 31, is a career officer assigned to Killakeet Island, along North Carolina's treacherous Outer Banks. Both he and his father-the keeper of the Killakeet Lighthouse-are haunted by the loss at sea and presumed death of Josh's two-year-old baby brother 17 years earlier. Shaken from his brooding by the appearance of German U-boats, Josh must try to protect the merchant ships torpedoed every night offshore. . . . Well-crafted characters, gripping naval warfare and colorful island life come together in this dynamic and exciting tale." Publ Wkly

Hickman, Tracy

(jt. auth) Weis, M. Guardians of the lost
(jt. auth) Weis, M. Well of darkness

Higgins, George V., 1939-1999

The agent; a novel. Harcourt Brace & Co. 1998 341p o.p.
ISBN 0-15-100357-2 LC 98-14624

In this novel, Alex Drouhin is a sports agent who "protects his clients from everyone who would prey on them, from reporters to folks who would steal their underwear and sell it to sports memorabilia collectors. When Drouhlin is murdered, his partners, servants and clients are all suspects." Libr J

"A riveting look at the world of big-time sports provides veteran storyteller Higgins . . . another opportunity to show off his skills at writing the most addictive dialogue since John O'Hara." Publ Wkly

At end of day; a novel. Harcourt Brace & Co. 2000 383p $30
ISBN 0-15-100358-0 LC 99-46414

This novel explores the "underworld of south Boston. Much of the story drills into the domain of two gangsters, Nick Cistaro and Arthur McKeath, and their unusual relationship with the city's top FBI men, tough veteran Jack Farrier and bumbling sycophant Darren Stoat. Both sides meet regularly for a civilized dinner, slipping each other just enough information so they can succeed at their respective pursuits." Publ Wkly

"The last novel of the late George V. Higgins shows no hint of failing skill or mellowing temper. The dialogue is as raffisly elegant as ever, the action as disconcerting to the lawfully minded, and the author's underlying attitude what it has regularly been—a plague on all your houses. . . . Questions of law and justice, as discussed by the characters, become almost equally unnerving. Higgins was a brilliantly clever, savagely bitter observer of society." Atl Mon

Bomber's law; a novel. Holt & Co. 1993 296p o.p.
ISBN 0-8050-2329-1 LC 93-26006

"A John Macrae book"

"A young detective, Harry Dell'Appa, discovers that his fellow detective and nemesis, Bob Brennan, has become curiously lax in his efforts to nail Short Joey Mossi, an aging Mafia hit man. Dell'Appa, who has been assigned to take over the Mossi case, begins to suspect that Brennan has gotten to know his subject a little too well—or rather, that he sympathizes too fully with Mossi. As the cops sit together in a cold car, waiting for Mossi to appear, Brennan talks on and on, digressing into stories about other criminals and about his own life. Dell'Appa listens fitfully." Commonweal

"A whiz of a stylist with a black belt in dialogue, Higgins lets his characters' conversation carry the story. This is our language as it is spoken, full of false stops and loony poetry." Newsweek

A change of gravity. Holt & Co. 1997 456p o.p.
ISBN 0-8050-4815-4 LC 97-6892

"A John Macrae book"

This novel "begins as two old-style, bent but not crooked Massachusetts pols discover that the Feds are about to indict one of them. The charges against former state representative Dan Hilliard are ultimately bogus yet grounded in fact, leaving Hilliard and his loyal campaign manager, Ambrose Merrion, in a major pickle." Booklist

"The story unfolds in a nonlinear way; it does so almost entirely through superb dialogue that reveals character in a far more complex and interesting way than does an omniscient author. . . . Characters often speak continuously for several pages, but convey such nuances about the mores and social strata of their time that we welcome their loquaciousness." N Y Times Book Rev

Defending Billy Ryan; a Jerry Kennedy novel. Holt & Co. 1992 245p o.p.
LC 92-7800

"A John Macrae book"

This is Higgins's "third tale about Jerry Kennedy, a frazzled Boston criminal lawyer paid, in this case, a hundred thousand bucks to defend Billy Ryan, a corrupt public official. Billy Ryan, the commissioner of the Department of Public Works, has finally been indicted after many years of sleazy dealings and conflicts of interest. He does not like his lawyer, which is fine with Jerry Kennedy because the feeling is quite mutual. The story is vintage George Higgins." N Y Times Book Rev

Higgins, George V., 1939-1999—*Continued*

The friends of Eddie Coyle. Knopf 1972 c1971 183p o.p.

The action of the story "involves a series of bank robberies. Eddie Coyle is a small-time [Boston] crook who is trying to crash the big time by providing the armament for the robbers. His 'friends' use him, are used by him, and ultimately there is double-crossing all the way along the line." Publ Wkly

"Written entirely in riveting dialogue, this novel is a compelling study of motive." Oxford Companion to Am Lit. 6th edition

The Mandeville talent. Holt & Co. 1991 278p o.p.

LC 91-9232

"A John Macrae book"

This book is about "a 23-year-old unsolved murder in Goshen, Mass. When the granddaughter of murder victim James Mandeville is offered a teaching post at Mount Holyoke, her husband, Joe, a young lawyer in a big Manhattan firm, grabs the chance to resign from the corporate rat race, solve the old murder case and set up private practice in the Berkshires. The local law can't help (for diverse reasons) and sends him to retired Defense Department investigator Baldad ('Baldo') Ianucci, who is bored and looking for something to do." Publ Wkly

"The drama in this book comes simply from watching the protagonists' minds work. Higgins makes us believe that the paper trail of contemporary life actually leads not to obfuscation but to clarity." Booklist

The patriot game. Knopf 1982 237p o.p.

LC 81-18655

The novel is set in "Boston's underside with its smalltime political hacks, Irish-Catholic ghetto and real lace country clubs. The hero of this piece is a tough-talking Justice Department agent, Pete Riordan. . . . On the path of an IRA gunrunner, Riordan wants to know why so many proper Bostonians are eager to get a convicted murderer out of prison." Publ Wkly

Swan boats at four; a novel. Holt & Co. 1995 228p o.p.

LC 94-40985

"A John Macrae book"

"David Carroll is a Boston banker whose institution is under federal investigation at the time his wife, Frances, forces him to take a vacation aboard the Atlantic cruise ship *America*. On the voyage, Carroll renews an old affair, and he and Frances meet Burton Rutledge, ostensibly a lawyer from a small Massachusetts town. Most of the story unfolds via flashbacks embedded in the mealtime conversations among these three characters, a narrative device that is extremely effective and gives Higgins room to create layers of irony and past-present interactions." Libr J

Higgins, Jack, 1929-

Bad company. Putnam 2003 287p $25.95

ISBN 0-399-14970-8 LC 2003-41365

"As the war is drawing to a close in 1945, Hitler gives his diary to an aide for safekeeping. The diary contains an account of a meeting between representatives of Hitler and President Roosevelt at which they discussed ways to negotiate a peace treaty and then to attack Russia. The aide, Max von Berger, is now (in 2003) a billionaire industrialist and a silent partner with an international crime family. Seeking revenge for a killing, Berger vows to reveal the diary's secret that would destroy the current U.S. president. It's up to an American and a British agent to get the diary before it falls into the hands of the president's enemies." Booklist

Cold Harbour. Simon & Schuster 1990 318p o.p.

LC 89-26198

A "tale of deception set in World War II Europe. Cold Harbour, a tiny village on the English Channel in Cornwall, is being used by the Special Operations Executive . . . as a base for running secret agents into and out of occupied France. To safeguard that operation, Englishmen masquerading as Germans patrol the Channel in a captured German vessel and fly planes bearing Luftwaffe insignia. But these deceptions are just the beginning. At a French chateau occupied by the German High Command, the resident family—now reduced to an elderly countess and her young niece, AnneMarie—pretend to be collaborators." N Y Times Book Rev

Confessional. Stein & Day 1985 278p o.p.

LC 884-40777

"The hero of this spy-thriller is three people—a KGB agent, an ordained Catholic priest and an IRA terrorist, which means that he goes through a lot of cloak-and-dagger changes as he slips from role to role. In 1958 the Russians set up a mock Irish village in the Ukraine to train future KGB agents so that they could more easily blend into the Irish landscape and go about their nefarious activities of destabilizing English-Irish relations by working through the IRA. Mikhail Kelly was a first-rate candidate because his Irish father had been hung by the British as an IRA activist and he had been raised by his Russian mother in Ireland." Best Sellers

This novel is "tense. It is riveting. It is what a thriller should be. If Mr. Higgins's prose is dull and his understanding of humanity shallow, it may only be because good prose and a deeper understanding would inhibit the race to the plot's final twist." N Y Times Book Rev

Day of judgment. Holt, Rinehart & Winston 1979 263p o.p.

LC 78-15043

"The time of the story is Spring 1963, just prior to President Kennedy's planned visit to Berlin. To discredit his good-will tour, members of the East German Intelligence have kidnapped a [Jesuit] Catholic priest known to be a foe of Communism and a member of an organization that has been smuggling refugees from the East into the West. They imprison him in a castle just fifty miles inside the East German border, to try to break his will and make him reveal certain facts that could prove an embarrassment to the Free World, through brainwashing. But they reckon without dedicated people, including members of the Catholic Church and the members of a non-Catholic monastery in the town where they are holding the priest. The rescuers also have the help of a Jesuit father, a woman doctor and a British Intelligence Officer." West Coast Rev Books

The author "has used an episode in history to write a finely crafted thriller with excellent characterization." Booklist

Higgins, Jack, 1929-—*Continued*

Day of reckoning. Putnam 2000 295p $25.95
ISBN 0-399-14585-0 LC 99-34847

The journalist wife of Sean Dillon's "old comrade Blake Johnson is killed in Brooklyn on orders of her latest object of investigation, Jack Fox, heir apparent to the powerful Solazzo crime family. The law can't touch Fox, but Blake and Dillon can and will. Aided by Dillon's black-ops boss Brigadier Charles Ferguson, and his crew, plus a father/son team of British gangsters, Blake and Dillon strike again and again at Fox's wallet: shutting down his London gambling den; sinking a boat laden with his gold; destroying a cache of his weapons in Ireland; foiling his plans for a major robbery in London. . . . The action is sleek and intensely absorbing." Publ Wkly

Drink with the Devil. Putnam 1996 311p o.p.
LC 96-3821

This Sean Dillon adventure "finds the former terrorist involved with a group of Irish Protestant paramilitaries in 1985 as they hijack a truck carrying £100 million in gold bullion. Ten years later, Sean is working for British Intelligence when he is ordered to go after the gold again. Now he is to prevent the bullion from disrupting the peace between the Catholics and Protestants. Dillon, boss Brigadier Ferguson, and partner Hannah Bernstein must also deal with the Mafia. They ask 85-year-old Liam Devlin for help, and the IRA legend of past Higgins books is only too pleased to participate. The excitement never lags as each side double-crosses the others." Libr J

The eagle has flown; a novel. Simon & Schuster 1991 335p o.p.
LC 91-4368

In this sequel to The eagle has landed, "Devlin is asked by the Germans to parachute into England and free Steiner from St. Mary's Priory, where he has been taken after being held captive in the Tower of London. This [adventure also] involves a plot to thwart the assassination of Hitler in order to prevent the nation's takeover by Himmler and the SS." Booklist

"Mr. Higgins is an expert storyteller, and he goes about 'The Eagle Has Flown' with typical gusto. Everything is carefully arranged, little pieces fitting into other little pieces to form an action-packed mosaic." NY Times Book Rev

The eagle has landed. Simon & Schuster 1991 399p o.p.
LC 90-44042

A revised edition containing the full text of the title first published 1975 by Holt, Rinehart & Winston

"After intense training a small force of German paratroopers lands on the Norfolk coast in November 1943, with the aim of capturing Churchill, who is spending the weekend at a neighbouring country house." Times Lit Suppl

"There are elements of heroism, duplicity, and heavy irony, plus considerable bloodshed, in this action-oriented yarn." Christ Sci Monit

Followed by The eagle has flown

Edge of danger. Putnam 2001 273p $25.95
ISBN 0-399-14701-2 LC 00-40268

"Pitting returning antihero Sean Dillon, once of the IRA, now with British intelligence, against an aristocratic English-Arab family bent on vengeance that threatens world order, the story whips along. From London to the Middle East, from Ireland to the White House, it swirls with intrigue and snaps with violence." Publ Wkly

Eye of the storm. Putnam 1992 320p o.p.
LC 91-46736

"Early in 1991, while the Gulf war is in full bloom, operatives of Saddam Hussein hire legendary terrorist Sean Dillon to take the war to the enemy. A master of disguise and subterfuge, Dillon began his career with the IRA, earning the enmity of Liam Devlin—the unforgettable antihero of *The Eagle Has Landed*, who makes a featured appearance here—and of Martin Brosnan, an American Special Forces hero and IRA member turned college professor. After Dillon's attempt to assassinate former Prime Minster Margaret Thatcher during a visit to France fails, he decides to go after her successor John Major. . . . Although readers can be sure that Dillon's scheme will be foiled, fun remains in the how and why." Publ Wkly

Followed by Thunder point (1993)

Flight of eagles. Putnam 1998 328p o.p.
ISBN 0-399-14376-9 LC 97-37582

The author traces the exploits of twins Max and Harry Kelso "from 1917, when their wealthy American father marries a German baroness, through 1944. . . . Upon her husband's death in 1930, the baroness returns to Germany with Max in tow, leaving Harry in the care of his American grandfather. By the early 1940s Max is Germany's premier flying ace–he eventually downs more than 300 Allied planes–and is famed as the Black Baron. Harry, meanwhile, has enlisted with the RAF and distinguished himself equally in the Battle of Britain and beyond. The narrative cuts briskly from one twin's adventures to the other's as the dashing, daring young men intersect with historical greats including Hitler, Himmler, Goring, FDR and Eisenhower." Publ Wkly

Luciano's luck. Stein & Day 1981 238p o.p.
LC 881-40330

"It is 1943 and the Allied invasion of Sicily is imminent. General Eisenhower plans to enlist Sicilian Mafia support for the invasion by sending two emissaries into Sicily to sway Luca, the Sicilian 'capo di tutti capi.' Logically, perhaps, one emissary is the chief U.S. capo, Lucky Luciano (who is in prison); the second is Luca's alienated granddaughter. The commando expedition to effect a meeting between these three in German-occupied Sicily forms the basis for a fast-paced, action-crammed plot, suspenseful to the last page. The fictionalized Luciano is sympathetically portrayed, and although the romanticizing of the Mafia figures jars a little, the historical premises are acceptably plausible." Libr J

Midnight runner. Putnam 2002 289p o.p.
ISBN 0-399-14833-7 LC 2001-48124

This suspense novel finds "former IRA enforcer Sean Dillon and his present boss, Gen. Charles Ferguson, . . . responding to various revenge gambits by the beautiful and fabulously wealthy half-bedu, half-English Lady Kate Rashid, countess of Loch Dhu and head of the Rashid Bedu tribe of Hazar, whose three brothers were killed by Dillon and his comrades . . . after, among other acts of infamy, a Rashid assassination attempt on U.S. President Jack Cazalet." Publ Wkly

Higgins, Jack, 1929-—*Continued*

Night of the fox. Simon & Schuster 1986 316p o.p.

LC 86-29662

"Taking the form of a continuous flashback, 'Night of the Fox' begins with the aftermath of a U-boat attack off the coast of German-occupied Jersey, which results in the wounded body of an American soldier being washed ashore. For the Allies, Hugh Kelso is a dangerous liability; if the Germans learn what he knows about the proposed Normandy invasion, disaster would be inevitable. British agents Harry Martinique and Sarah Drayton secretly enter Jersey, posing as an SS officer and his mistress. Another form of deception is also taking place, as a gifted Jewish actor arrives on the island, impersonating Field Marshall Rommel and covering for the real 'Desert Fox,' who is in France on secret talks. The three imposters join forces in a daring and dangerous mission." Booklist

"Higgins combines powerful narrative with documentary detail in an exceptional tale that relies upon the interweaving histories of the various characters." Libr J

The president's daughter. Putnam 1997 278p o.p.

ISBN 0-399-14239-8 LC 96-48654

In this suspense novel, Sean Dillon, "now with British Intelligence, finds himself working on behalf of the U.S. president. . . . Dillon, Brigadier Charles Ferguson and Chief Inspector Hannah Bernstein are on the track of a Jewish extremist who calls himself Judas Maccabeus and is pressing President Jake Cazalet to sign off on a thorough bombing attack on Iraq, Iran and Syria. If Cazalet doesn't authorize the strikes, Judas will kill Contesse Marie de Brissac, Cazalet's illegitimate daughter, who was conceived in 1969 in Vietnam when Cazalet, then a Special Forces lieutenant, bedded Marie's mother." Publ Wkly

"Higgins offers the usual cast of characters—beautiful women and tough guys—and exotic locales, including London, Corfu, Sicily, Ireland, France, and the eastern Mediterranean. . . . [This] is another 'race against the clock' thriller, and Higgins' fans won't be disappointed." Booklist

Storm warning; a novel. Holt, Rinehart & Winston 1976 311p il o.p.

"Late in the Second World War, a German sailing ship disguised as a Swedish vessel sets out from Belém, Brazil, for Kiel, Germany—5,000 miles across the Atlantic—taking home a crew and group of passengers wishing to return to their collapsing fatherland. The trip is arduous, ending when the ship strikes a reef in the Outer Hebrides Islands off the coast of Scotland." Booklist

"What does work, exceedingly well, are the action at sea scenes, building up to the climax. . . . Basically what we have are decent people on both sides of the war, some of whom survive, some of whom do not, who come together in a desperate attempt to save the lives of the Germans aboard the ship who have fought so bravely to make it home." Publ Wkly

Touch the devil. Stein & Day 1982 251p o.p.

LC 82-40080

"Charles Ferguson of British intelligence persuades Devlin [featured in the Eagle novels] to join forces with Martin Brosnan, former comrade in the fight for Irish independence, to find and stop (by killing if necessary) another onetime rebel, Frank Barry, now in the pay of the Soviets. Barry, a cold assassin and thief of NATO secret weapons, is a match in cunning for Devlin and Brosnan, and he learns about the plot against him from a mole in Ferguson's office. He knows that Devlin and Brosnan's lover, Anne-Marie Audin, get help from the British to spirit Brosnan from a French prison, as grim as Devil's Island, where his revolutionary activities have landed him. Anne-Marie takes the two men to her secluded farm house in southern France, where Barry and his hirelings lurk in ambush." Publ Wkly

The Valhalla exchange; [by] Harry Patterson. Stein & Day 1976 224p o.p.

The novel "tells the story of Martin Bormann's escape from Berlin and his 'insurance' plan involving U.S. war hero Hamilton Canning, one of five important prisoners of war tucked away in a small Austrian town during the last days of the Third Reich. General Canning tells the story to a correspondent in South America years later as he searches for Bormann or proof of his death." Booklist

The White House connection. Putnam 1999 323p $25.95

ISBN 0-399-14489-7 LC 98-42577

"Sean Dillon, a former IRA gunman, now works for the British prime minister; Blake Johnson heads a secret office for the U.S. president. Both have their various talents severely tested while trying to stop a vengeful 66-year-old woman who is assassinating members of the Sons of Erin, including a senator, thereby threatening both governments." Libr J

"When it comes to thrillers, Jack Higgins wrote the book. In fact, he wrote lots of them, and this is one of the best." Booklist

Highet, Helen MacInnes *See* MacInnes, Helen, 1907-1985

Highsmith, Patricia, 1921-1995

The boy who followed Ripley. Lippincott & Crowell 1980 291p o.p.

LC 79-29678

In this novel "two people meet casually, but their fates become inextricably, and dangerously, joined. Tom Ripley is an American expatriate living on the outskirts of Paris; he meets a 16-year-old American runaway, who turns out to be the son of a recently deceased food products tycoon. The boy is haunted by guilt over his father's death and pursued through Europe by kidnappers. Engrossing and shiver packed." Booklist

Ripley under ground

In Highsmith, P. The talented Mr. Ripley; Ripley under ground; Ripley's game

Ripley's game. Knopf 1974 267p o.p.

"Tom [Ripley], an American married to a lovely French woman and living in luxury in country France, is a diabolically clever killer and con artist. What he begins here starts as a fairly vicious practical joke to worry an Englishman who has snubbed Tom. Before the last ploy has been played out, several murders have taken place, the Mafia has embarked on ruthless revenge against Tom and the Englishman, the latter's happy marriage has been

Highsmith, Patricia, 1921-1995—*Continued*
hopelessly damaged and Tom has survived as only someone as totally amoral as he can succeed in doing." Publ Wkly

"Highsmith uses a matter-of-fact, almost reportorial, tone to effect her measured, driving pace and to construct her tightly woven web. The second half of this literate and imaginative thriller is especially brilliant—all the way to the dazzling last page." Libr J

also in Highsmith, P. The talented Mr. Ripley; Ripley under ground; Ripley's game

The selected stories of Patricia Highsmith; with a foreword by Graham Greene. Norton 2001 724p $27.95

ISBN 0-393-02031-2 LC 2001-30878

Contents: Chorus girl's absolutely final performance; Djemal's revenge; There I was, stuck with Bubsy; Ming's biggest prey; In the dead of truffle season; The bravest rat in Venice; Engine horse; The day of reckoning; Notes from a respectable cockroach; Eddie and the monkey robberies; Hamsters vs. Websters; Harry: a ferret; Goat ride; The hand; Oona, the jolly cave woman; The coquette; The female novelist; The dancer; The invalid; or, The bedridden; The artist; The middle-class housewife; The fully licensed whore; or, The wife; The breeder; The mobile bed-object; The perfect little lady; The silent mother-in-law; The prude; The victim; The evangelist; The perfectionist; The man who wrote books in his head; The network; The pond; Something you have to live with; Slowly, slowly in the wind; Those awful dawns; Woodrow Wilson's necktie; One for the islands; A curious suicide; The baby spoon; Broken glass; Please don't shoot the trees; Something the cat dragged in; Not one of us; The terrors of basket-weaving; Under a dark angel's eye; I despise your life; The dream of the Emma C; Old folks at home; When in Rome; Blow it; The kite; The black house; Mermaids on the golf course; The button; Where the action is; Chris's last party; A clock ticks at Christmas; A shot from nowhere; The stuff of madness; Not in this life, maybe the next; I am not as efficient as other people; The cruelest month; The romantic

The talented Mr. Ripley

In Highsmith, P. The talented Mr. Ripley; Ripley under ground; Ripley's game

The talented Mr. Ripley; Ripley under ground; Ripley's game. Knopf 1999 877p $26

ISBN 0-375-40792-8 LC 99-38147

"Everyman's library"

In the talented Mr. Ripley "Tom Ripley is hired by the wealthy Herbert Greenleaf to help him find his son, Dickie. Ripley travels to Europe and catches up to Dickie in Italy, meanwhile corresponding with Greenleaf through the mail. Later, after he has assumed Dickie's identity himself, he keeps up the imposture by writing to Dickie's friends and avoiding personal contact. He continues, however, to be 'Tom Ripley' when the occasion demands. Highsmith takes us into the mind of a repellent character but, through the sheer force of her communication of his personality, compels a sympathetic fascination on the part of the reader." Murphy. Ency of Murder and Mystery

In Ripley under ground Tom impersonates a dead artist and is drawn into murder when his deception is about to be discovered

Hijuelos, Oscar

Empress of the splendid season; a novel. HarperFlamingo 1999 342p o.p.

ISBN 0-06-017570-2 LC 98-34798

Once called the "'Professor of Cuba' by her father, Lydia is a long way from Havana in this novel, set in New York City from the 1950s to the mid-1980s. Disowned by her family, Lydia moves to New York and finds work as a seamstress. She marries and has two children, but her hopes of becoming a housewife come to an end when her husband suffers the first of many heart attacks. Lydia goes to work cleaning homes for wealthy New Yorkers." Libr J

The author "tells his story without condescension or false sentimentality, in the tone of a neighborhood gossip. The literary device of the cleaning lady also provides a new and unexpected angle of vision on Manhattan's old money. . . . Hijuelos reaffirms his place in the front rank of American novelists and forces the Hispanic immigrant experience closer to the center of our cultural consciousness." Natl Rev

The fourteen sisters of Emilio Montez O'Brien; a novel. Farrar, Straus & Giroux 1993 484p o.p.

ISBN 0-374-15815-0 LC 92-41935

This novel "tells the story of the family of Nelson O'Brien, an Irish immigrant to the U.S. who travels to Cuba as a photographer during the Spanish-American War. There he falls passionately in love and marries the young and beautiful Mariela Montez. After the couple returns to the farm O'Brien owns in a small Pennsylvania town, he works as the local photographer and operates the community's movie theater, while she keeps busy bearing and rearing their 14 daughters and, finally, one son, Emilio Montez O'Brien." Time

"The sprawling narrative is sustained by the author's leniency in enforcing whatever conventions he adopts. Its pace speeds up and slows down, depending as much, it seems, on Mr. Hijuelos's mood as his material. . . . The changing degree of connectedness discernible among the characters and plot lines mirrors nothing so much as family life the way it is actually lived, by both great broods and small." N Y Times Book Rev

The Mambo Kings play songs of love; a novel. Farrar, Straus & Giroux 1989 407p o.p.

LC 89-1248

"The Mambo Kings are two brothers, Cesar and Nestor Castillo, Cuban-born musicians who emigrate to New York City in 1949. They form a band and enjoy modest success, playing dance halls, nightclubs and *quince* parties in New York's Latin neighborhoods. Their popularity peaks in 1956 with a guest appearance on the *I Love Lucy* show, playing Ricky Ricardo's Cuban cousins and performing their only hit song in a bittersweet event that both frames the novel and serves as its emblematic heart." Publ Wkly

"The novel alternates crisp narrative with opulent musings—the language of everyday and the language of longing. When Mr. Hijuelos falters, as from time to time he does, it's through an excess of self-consciousness: he

Hijuelos, Oscar—*Continued*
strives too hard for all-encompassing description or grows distant and dutiful in an effort to get period details just right." N Y Times Book Rev

A simple Habana melody: from when the world was good; a novel. HarperCollins Pubs. 2002 342p o.p.

ISBN 0-06-017569-9 LC 2002-512611

"The story begins in 1947, when the 58-year-old Israel Levis returns to his native Habana after spending most of the 1930s in Paris and then enduring two years in Buchenwald (Levis, a Catholic, was assumed by the Nazis to be a Jew because of his name). Hijuelos jumps. . .between past and present, lingering on Levis' early years in Cuba, when he emerged as a musician and composer." Booklist

"While there is a faintly contrived air about Levis's experience of the Holocaust. Hijuelos triumphs in capturing the sights and sounds of Habana at the edge of modernity." Publ Wkly

Hill, John *See* Koontz, Dean R. (Dean Ray), 1945-

Hill, Rebecca

(jt. auth) Guest, J. Killing time in St. Cloud

Hill, Reginald, 1936-

Arms and the women; an elliad. Delacorte Press 1999 408p $23.95

ISBN 0-385-33279-3 LC 99-35873

"Andy Dalziel and Peter Pascoe, the ranking Yorkshire police officers in this series, marshal the troops when Pascoe's wife, Ellie and their little girl narrowly escape being abducted in broad daylight from their home. Suspicion naturally falls on any number of criminals with deep grudges against Pascoe; but once these obvious bad guys are eliminated, it begins to look as if Ellie has acquired an enemy of her own, perhaps within the circle of strong-minded political activists in her women's rights group." N Y Times Book Rev

Blood sympathy. St. Martin's Press 1994 c1993 220p o.p.

LC 94-26216

"A Thomas Dunne book"

First published 1993 in the United Kingdom

This mystery "features unlikely hero Joe Sixsmith, a balding, middle-aged, recently laid-off lathe operator from Luton, Bedfordshire, and Joe's partner, Whitey, a curmudgeonly feline that loves beer, pork rinds, and an occasional taste of champagne. Joe decides that if he can't make a living operating lathes, maybe his real calling is private investigation. Before he can have business cards printed, Joe is juggling a mysterious multiple murder, a cache of illicit drugs, his meddling, matchmaking Aunt Mirabelle, and two thugs whose sole aim in life seems to be inflicting pain on Joe." Booklist

Bones and silence. Delacorte Press 1990 332p o.p.

LC 89-48836

"Set in a cathedral city which will host a contemporary enactment of medieval mystery plays, Hill's narrative features the police duo Andrew Dalziel and Peter Pascoe looking into a series of related murders and disappearances tied to a builder who is coincidentally constructing garages for the police station. Meanwhile, the galvanizing director of the mystery plays, Eileen Chung, has cast Dalziel as God and the builder in question as Lucifer." Publ Wkly

"A complex, challenging and diverting novel, from one of the most cogent of detective writers." Times Lit Suppl

Child's play. Macmillan 1987 296p o.p.

LC 86-8712

"A Dalziel-Pascoe murder mystery"

This novel "has two plots. One concerns the will of a dotty, wealthy old woman who leaves her money to a son missing in action since 1944 and presumed dead. Hungry, greedy, angry relatives gather to see what can be done about breaking the will. . . . The other side of the story has to do with a tough cop who lives a secret life as a homosexual. Mr. Hill handles this aspect with grace; there also is a good deal of humor in the way Dalziel goes into action when, on orders from above, he has to track down the homosexual. He takes care of things in his own inimitable manner. Mr. Hill, as always, has a fine time jousting against hypocrisy and the hollow men of the bureaucracy." N Y Times Book Rev

A clubbable woman. Countryman Press 1984 c1970 256p o.p.

LC 84-17604

"A Foul Play Press book"

First published 1970 in the United Kingdom

This police procedural features "police superintendent Andrew Dalziel and the refined, bookish detective sergeant Peter Pascoe. . . . The wife of a onetime rugby star has her head bashed in as she sits watching television. The murder investigation reveals the adulterous and hateful relationships that form the backbone of what seems a peaceful suburban development." Booklist

Deadheads; a murder mystery. Macmillan 1984 c1983 275p o.p.

LC 83-26735

First published 1983 in the United Kingdom

This novel "finds inspectors Dalziel and Pascoe investigating Patrick Aldermann, a young accountant and obsessive rose gardener, whose good fortune in life comes from a series of highly convenient accidental deaths." Libr J

Dialogues of the dead; or, Paronomania!; a word game for two players. Delacorte Press 2002 424p o.p.

ISBN 0-385-33600-4 LC 2001-42392

First published 2001 in the United Kingdom

In this mystery a madman comes to the attention of the authorities "when his anonymous entries in the Mid-Yorkshire Short Story Competition—little tales of murder steeped in gore and classical references—turn out to be records of fact. . . . As West Yorkshire's brightest intellectuals fall to the killer like so much dried cordwood, it is left to Pascoe's patient deconstruction of clues and Dalziel's infallible intuition to cut through the thickets of this madman's mind." N Y Times Book Rev

Hill, Reginald, 1936-—*Continued*

Dream of darkness; {by} Patrick Ruell. Countryman Press 1991 204p o.p.
LC 90-38677

"A Foul Play Press book"

"In London 18-year-old Sairey Ellis suffers from a recurring, debilitating nightmare that shows the young Sairey viewing the open coffin of her mother in Uganda years ago. That did not happen, say her retired British security officer father, Nigel, and his sister, who raised Sairey after her mother's death. Sairey's analysis-prompted returning memory of the brief time with her mother in Uganda holds the key to her nightmare and seems to threaten family and friend—as does Nigel, who is writing his African memoirs." Libr J

"The story of Sairey's haunted nights and days alternates with selections from her father's memoirs, which detail his diplomatic career in Uganda during the Amin years. Ruell effectively uses these parallel narratives to slowly unravel the mystery of Sairey's mother's death. A gem of a book with a startling finale." Booklist

Good morning, midnight; Reginald Hill. 1st ed. HarperCollins 2004 433p $24.95
ISBN 0-06-052807-9 LC 2003-67603

Detectives Andy Dalziel and Peter Pascoe investigate "a locked-room suicide. . . . The case seems as closed as the room in which the local businessman's body was found until Hill and Pascoe discover that this suicide was committed 10 years to the day after the victim's father committed suicide in the same way and that the new suicide has left a very damning cassette tape. A cut-and-dried case morphs into a cold-case scenario in this wickedly clever, classic Brit-mystery puzzle, loaded with Yorkshire atmosphere and mordant wit." Booklist

Killing the lawyers. St. Martin's Press 1997 287p o.p.
ISBN 0-312-16877-2 LC 97-16249

"A Thomas Dunne book"

Joe Sixsmith is a "black PI in the not especially famous English town of Luton. He solves crimes less by detection than by his own brand of scrupulous honesty, which creates a kind of white light in which the bad guys invariably stand out. After Joe's insurance company undervalues his wrecked and beloved old car, he seeks the counsel of a rude and fancy lawyer. The visit ends in shouting—and becomes a case when the lawyer is murdered. Another lawyer in the dead man's firm is killed, and Joe, after being cleared as a suspect, is hired to investigate by a remaining partner in the firm." Publ Wkly

On Beulah Height. Delacorte Press 1998 374p o.p.
ISBN 0-385-33278-5 LC 97-40673

"When a 7-year-old girl goes missing from the Yorkshire hamlet of Danbydale, everyone shivers with dread, recalling the unsolved 15-year-old disappearances of three other little girls from the neighboring valley of Dendale. Since most of Dendale's residents had relocated to Danbydale when their homes were demolished to make way for a reservoir, Detectives Andy Dalziel and Peter Pascoe are forced to root up the still-raw memories and imperfectly buried secrets of this traumatized community." N Y Times Book Rev

"Cascading imagery and sinuous plotlines flow into a flawless blend of mystery, ghost story and psychological thriller." Publ Wkly

Pictures of perfection; a Dalziel/Pascoe mystery in five volumes. Delacorte Press 1994 307p o.p.
LC 93-47449

"The intrepid trio of Sergeant Wield and detectives Dalziel and Pascoe are called to the tiny hamlet of Enscombe to investigate the mysterious disappearance of a rookie constable. When they arrive, however, they find there are more problems than just a missing copper; skulduggery, thievery, forgery, lust, lechery, libel, and passion all lie in wait for the three unwitting chaps. This is an intelligent, stylish, scintillating, witty mystery that transcends its cozy trappings." Booklist

Recalled to life. Delacorte Press 1992 359p o.p.
LC 92-1380

A mystery set in England and the U.S. "As Inspector Dalziel and partner Pascoe work unofficially to refute new evidence concerning a 1963 case, they threaten to unearth various nasty political secrets." Libr J

"Though Hill relies too much on coincidence, the complex plot here sustains interest. The novel's chief rewards, however, are those of character: Dalziel is a brilliant, bearish delight and the supporting players, including a brash black woman CIA agent, provide a constant parade of pleasures." Publ Wkly

Singing the sadness; a private eye Joe Sixsmith mystery. Thomas Dunne Bks. 1999 251p o.p.
ISBN 0-312-24238-7 LC 99-16864

Black private eye Joe Sixsmith "a member of the local choir, is traveling with his fellow singers to the Llanffugiol Choral Festival when the bus passes a burning cottage; without thinking, Joe rushes into the inferno and rescues a woman from the flames. He is pronouced a hero, but there's a mystery brewing: the cottage was supposed to be empty, so who is the woman Joe rescued?" Booklist

The Stranger House. HarperCollins 2005 480p $24.95
ISBN 0-06-082081-0 LC 2005-40274

"Twentysomething Aussie math whiz Samantha Flood has fiery red hair and a fierce determination to learn the truth about her paternal grandmother, an orphan shipped from her native England to Australia under suspicious circumstances. Sober Spaniard Miguel Madero, who experiences ghostly visions and painful sensations in his feet and hands, has abandoned pursuit of the priesthood to engage in research about English Catholics during the Reformation. The paths of Samantha and Miguel (known to all as 'Mig') cross in the tiny English village of Illthwaite, home to the Stranger House, an inn that has hosted weary travelers for more than 500 years. Samantha and Mig, an unlikely duo, are drawn to one another as each discovers secrets simmering beneath the surface of Illthwaite's deceptively serene facade." Booklist

The wood beyond. Delacorte Press 1996 358p o.p.
LC 95-32319

"Chief Inspector Andy Dalziel and Peter Pascoe investigate the discovery of some old bones near a large pharmaceutical research laboratory in Yorkshire. As the case

Hill, Reginald, 1936-—*Continued*

progresses, Pascoe unearths surprising facts about his own grandfather, a World War I soldier." Libr J

"The theme of personal honor in a dishonorable world gives passion to the characters and urgency to their individual causes and obsessions." N Y Times Book Rev

Hill, Ruth Beebe

Hanta yo. Doubleday 1979 834p o.p.
LC 77-74792

"The story is a fictional elaboration upon the chronological record kept on a tanned hide by a member of the Mahto band of the Teton Sioux. Hill follows the tribe from 1794 to 1835 in the seasonal moves across the plains. She unfolds . . . the tale of two families, and in particular, the . . . friendship between Ahbleza and Tonweya, the son of a warrior-leader and the son of a hunter." New Repub

"The practice of using the multi-generational family story to reflect changing times and/or historical events is almost a genre unto itself. This is such a novel. . . . The historical accuracy, linguistic acrobatics, and ethnological acuity do not limit the book's appeal. A superb style transcends the few minor flaws, and despite the scholarly impression given by the introduction, chronology notes, and glossaries, this book is first and foremost a well-written story." Libr J

Hill, Susan, 1942-

Mrs. de Winter; a novel. Morrow 1993 349p o.p.
LC 93-5347

"What happened to Maxim de Winter and his second wife after Manderley burned? This suspenseful 'completion' of Daphne du Maurier's *Rebecca* begins with the couple's return to England, following a ten-year, self-imposed exile, for the funeral of Maxim's sister Beatrice. In a voice true to the original story, Hill's Mrs. de Winter chronicles Rebecca's continuing shadow on their life; a mysterious wreath bearing a card with the initial 'R' is discovered near Beatrice's grave, and unwelcome visitors include Jack Favell, who has visions of blackmail, and Mrs. Danvers, who seeks revenge." Libr J

Hill, Tobias, 1970-

The love of stones. Picador 2002 396p o.p.
ISBN 0-312-28773-9 LC 2001-50038

"Obsessed with finding a legendary stone set called 'The Three Brethren,' [jewel dealer Katharine] Sterne starts her search in Turkey, where she must first locate a rich, eccentric British woman who teases her with a lead about the whereabouts of the gems. As Sterne's quest continues, Hill introduces a parallel historical subplot dealing with the provenance of the stones." Publ Wkly

"Stories of jewels are often detective fictions. They involve a certain amount of theft, betrayal, royalty, beautiful women and hard travelling. Hill's novel contains all these things. The story takes us from Turkey to London via Baghdad, then heads east, from Tokyo to the remote coast of Japan. The quest also travels through time. Queen Victoria has a delightful cameo role." New Statesman (1913)

Hillerman, Tony

(ed) The Best American mystery stories of the century. See The Best American mystery stories of the century

The blessing way. Harper & Row 1970 201p o.p.

"A Joan Kahn-Harper novel of suspense"

"When Bergen McKee, a disillusioned anthropologist, goes to the reservation to continue his research on Navajo witchcraft, he finds himself involved in murder, intrigue, adventure, and, worst of all, what appears to be genuine witchcraft. . . . Investigating the crime is Lt. Joe Leaphorn of the Navajo Law and Order Division." Libr J

"Here's suspense enough for anyone, but what makes the first mystery by Tony Hillerman outstanding is the wealth of detail about the Navajo Indian—customs, rites, way of life—with which he has crammed his pages." Saturday Rev

also in Hillerman, T. The Joe Leaphorn mysteries

Coyote waits. Harper & Row 1990 292p o.p.
LC 89-46098

Lieutenant Joe Leaphorn of the Navaho Tribal Police is investigating the murder of "his fellow policeman Delbert Nez. Meanwhile, [Jim] Chee, the erstwhile medicine man and Tribal Police officer, is also on the trail of Nez's murderer and believes he has already arrested the culprit in the person of a fellow Navajo, the old shaman Ashie Pinto." N Y Times Book Rev

"The story line has more twists, turns, and bumps than one of the many back-country roads on the Navajo reservation. . . . Hillerman's characters are not just there to provide dialogue for a story that dances along to a clever ending. Leaphorn and Chee each have a past they remember, a present they puzzle over, and a future they anticipate with mixed feelings." Christ Sci Monit

Dance hall of the dead. Harper & Row 1973 166p o.p.

"A Joan Kahn-Harper novel of suspense"

Navajo police lieutenant Joe Leaphorn faces a "mystery and possible murder in the disappearance of a Zuni youth and his Navajo best friend shortly before an important annual Zuni religious ceremony." Booklist

"While Leaphorn discovers the real truth, the white men concoct another 'truth' that satisfies their preconceptions. The lack of trust in and respect for the independence of the Native Americans by the white authority is forcefully brought home." Murphy. Ency of Murder and Mystery

also in Hillerman, T. The Joe Leaphorn mysteries

The dark wind. Harper & Row 1982 214p o.p.
LC 81-47793

"Jim Chee of the Navajo Tribal Police is drawn into the mystique of the Hopi tribal ways, which are very different from his own, as he follows a trail that leads him to a father seeking revenge for his son's death, a corrupt lawman and a fortune in cocaine." Publ Wkly

"Fascinating background and atmosphere makes something special out of an otherwise ordinary story." Libr J

also in Hillerman, T. The Jim Chee mysteries

Hillerman, Tony—*Continued*

The fallen man. HarperCollins Pubs. 1996 294p o.p.

LC 96-29469

"A skeleton is found on a high ledge of Ship Rock mountain, a place sacred to the Navahos. Tribal Police Lieutenant Chee and the now retired Leaphorn suspect correctly that it belongs to a wealthy rancher missing for 11 years, and Chee tries to discover if it is murder or an accidental death. Meanwhile, Leaphorn is hired by a lawyer to look into the investigation for the rancher's Eastern family, who want to own his land legally so they can accept a lucrative bid for the mining rights." SLJ

"In dealing with the pragmatic older cop and his dreamy young protege. Mr. Hillerman has always kept the frictions carefully contained. Here he gives his heroes more room to rub each other the wrong way. The personal tensions add another facet to the story, which continues the author's fascination with the savagery that men do to themselves and to the land they claim to hold sacred." N Y Times Book Rev

The first eagle; a novel. HarperCollins Pubs. 1998 278p o.p.

ISBN 0-06-017581-8 LC 98-6955

"Joe Leaphorn didn't believe in coincidences when he was a police officer, and he doesn't believe in them now that he's retired and working as a private investigator. So he's suspicious when his inquiry into the disappearance of a 'flea catcher,' a young woman working for the Arizona Health Department, leads him to the vicinity of the murder of a member of the Navajo Tribal Police. Acting Tribal Police Lieutenant Jim Chee isn't convinced there's a connection, but he knows there's something amiss about the story told by the accused cop killer, Robert Jano." Booklist

"Surrendering to Hillerman's strong narrative voice and supple storytelling techniques, we come to see that ancient cultures and modern sciences are simply different mythologies for the same reality." N Y Times Book Rev

The ghostway. Harper & Row 1985 c1984 213p o.p.

LC 84-48165

"A Harper novel of suspense"

Originally published 1984 in a limited edition by Dennis McMillan Publications

"The story concerns Navaho tribal detective Jim Chee's pursuit of the men who killed three Navaho of the Turkey clan. Chee solves the murders through his knowledge of the Indian way of life, which is gradually being eroded by white culture. As Navaho rituals help to solve Chee's murders, they also reinforce his doubts about the Indian in him. In an entertaining and fact-filled narrative, Hillerman offers a good look at the plight of contemporary Indians in the West. It is an engrossing and intelligent book for mystery fans and armchair anthropologists alike." Booklist

also in Hillerman, T. The Jim Chee mysteries

Hunting badger. HarperCollins Pubs. 1999 275p o.p.

ISBN 0-06-019289-5 LC 99-47906

This "mystery opens with the robbery of the Ute casino. The head of security is killed; a Navajo police officer working off-duty as a rent-a-cop is wounded; and the perpetrators flee into canyon country. Back from vacation, Jim Chee is reluctantly drawn into the hunt for the three men. . . . Retired Lt. Joe Leaphorn gets involved when a rancher gives him the names of the perpetrators." Libr J

This offers "several new insights into the mysteries of Navajo culture and a story with enough twists and surprises to make readers glad they checked in." Publ Wkly

The Jim Chee mysteries. HarperCollins Pubs. 1990 566p $26.95

ISBN 0-06-016478-6

Contents: People of darkness; The dark wind; The ghostway

The Joe Leaphorn mysteries; three classic Hillerman mysteries featuring Lt. Joe Leaphorn. Harper & Row 1989 499p o.p.

LC 89-45079

Contents: The blessing way; Dance hall of the dead; Listening woman

Listening woman. Harper & Row 1978 200p o.p.

LC 77-11788

"A Joan Kahn-Harper novel of suspense"

In this novel detective "Joe Leaphorn of the Navajo Tribal Police . . . [is] tracking down the murderer of a harmless old man and searching for a missing helicopter used for the getaway in a Brinks-style robbery pulled off by a militant Indian-rights group called the Buffalo Society. The desecration of some ritual sand paintings and the rumor of a sacred cave lead Leaphorn into a violent confrontation with the fanatical Buffalo Society. The terrorists are plotting to avenge the victims of a long-forgotten atrocity by recreating it—with white children as the pawns—in a vicious kidnapping/mass-murder scheme." N Y Times Book Rev

also in Hillerman, T. The Joe Leaphorn mysteries

(ed) The Mysterious West. See The Mysterious West

(ed) The Oxford book of American detective stories. See The Oxford book of American detective stories

People of Darkness. Harper & Row 1980 202p o.p.

LC 80-7605

"A Joan Kahn book"

"Navajo Tribal Police Detective Jim Chee, constantly confronted by the split between the ways of the Indian and those of the white man, is led into an investigation that challenges and torments him. A wealthy woman asks Chee to find a stolen box of keepsakes, which contains the key to a mysterious Navajo cult called 'The People of Darkness,' a buried Indian, peyote abuse, and danger. Hillerman has written an absorbing mystery and a fascinating cultural study." Booklist

also in Hillerman, T. The Jim Chee mysteries

Sacred clowns. HarperCollins Pubs. 1993 305p o.p.

LC 91-50470

"Lt. Joe Leaphorn and Officer Jim Chee of the Navajo police resolve personal issues as they investigate the murders of a tribal dancer and a white schoolteacher."

Hillerman, Tony—*Continued*
Publ Wkly

"The author skillfully employs the elements of detection and routine police work while providing readers with an intriguing glimpse of Navajo culture. The relationships between the officers and between the other well-defined characters give depth to the story, which is spiced with both men's romantic interests." SLJ

The sinister pig. HarperCollins Pubs. 2003 228p $25.95

ISBN 0-06-019443-X LC 2003-42316

"A barren desert landscape is quickly filled with Navajo tribal police, customs patrol officers, and the FBI when a dumped, unidentified body is discovered on the Navajo Reservation. The gathering of experts gives Hillerman the chance to bring back both Lieutenant Joe Leaphorn, whom he retired but can't bear to live without, and Officer Bernie Manuelito, now reassigned to the customs patrol and still ambivalent about her on-again, off-again romance with Sergeant Jim Chee." Booklist

"With his usual up-front approach to issues concerning Native Americans such as endlessly overlapping jurisdictions, Hillerman delivers a masterful tale that both entertains and educates." Publ Wkly

Skinwalkers. Harper & Row 1987 216p o.p.

In this mystery "Leaphorn has three unsolved murders to contend with, and then an attempt is made on Chee's life. Much to Leaphorn's dismay bone head figures are the sole clues found, indicating the work of a skinwalker or witch. Hillerman's Leaphorn and Chee novels convey the Navaho culture with all its intricacies set forth in a meaningful way." Libr J

Talking God. Harper & Row 1989 239p o.p.

LC 88-45914

This "complex tale hinges on the mysterious murder of a man in shiny old shoes who was apparently killed on his way to an ancient tribal ceremony. Leaphorn and Chee's investigation reveals a conflict over ceremonial masks, which in turn takes them from their familiar New Mexico haunts to Washington, D.C., where they must foil an assassination attempt. As in his previous works, Hillerman combines P. D. James' taut, precise narrative style with a consistently sensitive portrayal of the native American experience. The rural landscapes shimmer with realism, while the plot is crafted with skill and passion, like the masks that figure so strongly in the action." Booklist

A thief of time; a novel. Harper & Row 1988 209p o.p.

LC 87-46147

In this novel "Lieut. Joe Leaphorn and Officer Jim Chee of the Navajo Tribal Police . . . combine forces . . . in the search for a missing archeologist, Prof. Eleanor Friedman-Bernal. A specialist in Anasazi pots, she's on the verge of a major breakthrough—the identification of a specific artist, dead a thousand years—when, beneath a full desert moon, she seems simply to vanish." N Y Times Book Rev

"It is the complex relationship between Leaphorn and Chee and the rich view of Navaho culture that give the book its depth and resonance." Booklist

The wailing wind. HarperCollins Pubs. 2002 232p o.p.

ISBN 0-06-019444-8 LC 2001-51734

"Sergeant Jim Chee lures his old boss, Lieutenant Joe Leaphorn, out of retirement with news of a murder that reaches back to an unsolved mystery that has long haunted both Chee and Leaphorn." Booklist

"Hillerman is never better than when he is circling a puzzle from various angles, playing with the perceptions of his detectives as well as the reader's." N Y Times Book Rev

Hillhouse, Raelynn

Rift zone; Raelynn Hillhouse. 1st ed. Forge 2004 349p $24.95

ISBN 0-7653-1013-9 LC 2003-71102

"It's April 1989: discontented East Germans have plotted to assassinate Soviet leader Mikhail Gorbachev and restore the old order before it's too late. Meanwhile, Faith Whitney, a smuggler of antiquities, reluctantly agrees to deliver a package to Moscow when the Ministry for State Security (Stasi) hints that they will reveal the whereabouts of her father, long thought dead. However, she soon learns that she is carrying high explosives that can be traced to the Americans. Aided by a lesbian KGB colonel and a former boyfriend, a Navy SEAL trained in defusing explosives, Faith must use all her wiles to save her own life and to prevent a cataclysm. . . . An original voice of unusual authority, a resourceful female protagonist, sexual undertones, explosive tension, and tradecraft galore add up to a spellbinding tale." Libr J

Hilton, James, 1900-1954

Good-bye Mr. Chips; illustrated by H.M. Brock. Little, Brown 1962 c1934 132p il $22

ISBN 0-316-36420-7

"An Atlantic Monthly Press book"

First published 1934

"In 1870 Mr. Chipping begins a career teaching the classics at Brookfield Boys' Boarding School in England. After teaching three generations of Brookfield boys, Mr. Chips, as he is fondly called, retires to the boarding house directly across the street from the school. He continues to keep a close watch over the new group of boys and host afternoon teas as a way of sharing his reminiscences. This is a warm testimonial to a caring teacher." Shapiro. Fic for Youth. 3d edition

Lost horizon; a novel. Morrow 1995 c1933 262p o.p.

ISBN 0-688-14656-2 LC 96-160022

A reissue of the title first published 1933

"Hugh Conway is a British consul at Baskul when trouble erupts in 1931 and all civilians are evacuated. He and three others board a plane lent by a Maharajah. After they are airborne for several hours, they realize that they are headed in the wrong direction. When the pilot finally lands, the passengers find themselves in Shangri-La, a utopian lamasery whose inhabitants know the secret of attaining long life. Believing that war is going to destroy all civilization, the High Lama summons the newcomers to form the nucleus of a new civilization." Shapiro. Fic for youth. 3d edition

Random harvest. Little, Brown 1941 326p o.p.

"An Atlantic Monthly Press book"

"Charles Rainier, wealthy business man and M.P., for nearly twenty years unable to recall that period of his

Hilton, James, 1900-1954—*Continued*

life between his World War injury and 1919 suddenly has his memory restored. The dramatic suspense is great as Rainier faces his two pasts, passionately resolved to find the Paula of his lost years, at whatever cost to his present marriage and position. . . . Part of the story is related in the first person by Rainier's secretary and confidante who is interested in psychology." Libr J

Himes, Chester, 1909-1984

The collected stories of Chester Himes; foreword by Calvin Hernton. Thunder's Mouth Press 1991 429p o.p.

LC 90-25682

Contents: Headwaiter; Lunching at the Ritzmore; All God's chillun got pride; A nigger; Let me at the enemy-an' George Brown; With malice toward none; A penny for your thoughts; Two soldiers; So softly smiling; Heaven has changed; Looking down the street; The song says 'Keep on smiling'; Her whole existence; He seen it in the stars; Make with the shape; Dirty deceivers; A modern marriage; Black laughter; A night of new roses; The night's for cryin'; Face in the moonlight; Strictly business; Prison mass; Money don't spend in the stir; I don't want to die; The meanest cop in the world; On dreams and reality; The way of flesh; The visiting hour; The things you do; There ain't no justice; Every opportunity; I'm not trying to hurt you; Pork chop paradise; Friends; To what red hell; His last day; In the rain; The ghost of Rufus Jones; Whose little baby are you?; Mama's missionary money; My but the rats are terrible; The snake; In the night; All he needs is feet; Christmas gift; The revelation; Daydream; Da-da-dee; Marihuana and a pistol; One more way to die; Naturally, the Negro; Winter coming on; Spanish gin; The something in a colored man; Tang; One night in New Jersey; A modern fable; Prediction; Life everlasting

Cotton comes to Harlem. Vintage Books 1988 c1965 159p pa $11.95

ISBN 0-394-75999-0 LC 88-40045

First published 1965 by Putnam

In this mystery featuring "Coffin" Ed Johnson and "Grave Digger" Jones " which, revolves around a cotton bale filled with $87,000, [the author] parodies Marcus Garvey's back to Africa movement. Himes treats the black community with humor and respect, but does not hesitate to show blacks victimizing each other." Murphy. Ency of Murder and mystery

Yesterday will make you cry. Norton 1998 363p o.p.

ISBN 0-393-04577-3 LC 97-40364

Written in 1937; first published in different form 1953 with title: Cast the first stone

"This edition restores the work to its original form and chronicles the directionless life of Jimmy Monroe, a smart loser born poor white and rural, who bounces self-destructively through life until sentenced to 20 years in prison for robbery." Publ Wkly

"Is Himes's unexpurgated work anything more than a literary footnote? Some phrases still come off as pulp hardball, but the novel's emotional core continues to smolder. Rage tempered with compassion is the backbone of this story—and what makes it eminently worth reading." N Y Times Book Rev

Hiraoka, Kimitake *See* Mishima, Yukio, 1925-1970

Hirshberg, Glen, 1966-

The Snowman's children. Carroll & Graf Pubs. 2002 324p $24

ISBN 0-7867-1082-9

"Troubled 29-year-old Mattie Rhodes returns to Detroit in search of hs childhood friend Theresa, a brilliant, strange, and mysterious girl who, even now, haunts him. For a few magical months in 1977, Mattie, Theresa, and their friend, Spencer, the lone black boy bused to their school as part of Detroits' desegregation mandate, form a special bond, united by their outsider status. At the same time, a serial killer called the Snowman has been preying on children, snatching them in broad daylight. . . . As Mattie and Spencer begin to sense that Theresa is in danger of slipping away from them and descending into mental illness, they concoct a desperate plan to save her and instead condemn their families to the nightmare of media publicity." Booklist

Hitchcock, Alfred, 1899-1980

(ed) Alfred Hitchcock presents: Stories not for the nervous. See Alfred Hitchcock presents: Stories not for the nervous

Hoag, Tami

Dark horse. Bantam Bks. 2002 435p o.p.

ISBN 0-553-80192-9 LC 2002-74583

"Elena Estes is a former cop whose bravado on the force resulted in a colleague's death; it also cost her her job and her self-esteem. . . .She's been keeping a low profile at a friend's Florida ranch, but her world is disrupted when 12-year-old Molly Seabright, wise beyond her years, attempts to hire Elena to find her older sister, Erin, who has been missing for two days." Publ Wkly

"A tangled web of deceit and double-dealing makes for a fascinating look into the wealthy world of horses juxtaposed with the realistic introspection of one very troubled ex-cop." Booklist

Dust to dust. Bantam Bks. 2000 354p o.p.

ISBN 0-553-10634-1 LC 00-39786

"Minneapolis detective Sam Kovac and his young female partner, Nikki Liska, find themselves hot on the trail of some bad cops. It all starts when they are called to the scene of a homicide, where they find the nude, hanging body of a young Internal Affairs officer, the son of a department hero. Department brass want to declare the case a suicide and close it quickly. But after nosing around a bit, Kovac and Liska begin to suspect something much more sinister. . . . A classic whodunit with many twists and turns and a surprise ending." Booklist

Guilty as sin. Bantam Bks. 1996 470p o.p.

LC 95-38214

Sequel to Night sins

This suspense novel opens "with an accused kidnapper and child molester sitting in jail awaiting trial. But is the suspect—a respected and beloved college professor—really the author of a devilishly sick scheme to terrorize the families of idyllic Deer Lake, Minn.? Ellen North is the tough county prosecutor, armed with evidence and

Hoag, Tami—*Continued*
anger; Tony Costello is the flashy big-town lawyer intent on winning fame and fortune with a headline case; and Jay Butler Brooks is the reporter, a self-centered firebrand who appears to derive pleasure from the suffering of others. . . . As the criminal's clever plot unravels and North and her team come closer to the truth, the tangled relationships that lie just beneath the surface of Deer Lake are tantalizingly revealed." N Y Times Book Rev

Kill the messenger; Tami Hoag. Bantam Bks. 2004 419p $26
ISBN 0-553-80195-3 LC 2004-47612
Nineteen-year-old L. A. Bike messenger Jace Damon "picks up a package from a shady lawyer, but when he gets to the delivery address, he finds an empty lot; suddenly, someone attacks him and tries to grab the package. The bike messenger takes off, but the attacker pursues him, nearly runs him over with a car, and takes a couple of shots at him. Injured and frightened, Jace returns to Lowell's office only to find the place swarming with cops and the attorney murdered. The plot thickens as Jace attempts to elude both homicide detective Ken Parker, who wants some answers, and a menacing, shadowy figure, who is trying to get that package." Booklist
"A link to Hollywood provides a burst of fresh energy in the later chapters of this character-driven, solidly constructed thriller." Publ Wkly

Night sins. Bantam Bks. 1995 483p o.p.
LC 94-23910
The "community of Deer Lake, Minn., takes a turn toward Stephen King territory when the local lady doctor's son is snatched by a fiend who leaves enigmatic notes. Attempting to crack the case, feisty feminist Megan O'Malley—who hopes to become the first female field agent for the male-dominated Minnesota Bureau of Criminal Apprehension—finds herself paired with Mitch Holt, the town's love-scarred sheriff (and recovering alcoholic) who is facing assorted personal demons." Publ Wkly

Hoban, Russell

Angelica's Grotto; a novel. Carroll & Graf Pubs. 2001 271p $25
ISBN 0-7867-0878-6 LC 2001-35121
First published 1999 in the United Kingdom
To Harold Klein, 72-year-old art historian, "sexuality is an unavoidable element of art. But from these rarified artistic heights, Klein descends to a more prurient level when he clicks onto a Net sex site called Angelica's Grotto. Klein is already going through a crisis, having suffered a puzzling psychological breakdown similar to Tourette's syndrome. . . . In her cyber-grotto, Angelica (real name, Melissa) is eliciting responses from male viewers for a thesis on sexuality she is writing, and chooses Klein as a chat partner. Eventually, they meet in person (after the near-rape of Klein by one of Melissa's associates) and act out their fantasies in a sadomasochistic, May/December affair." Publ Wkly
"Harold's esoteric musings on art, sex, philosopy, sailing, and everything in between will not appeal to everyone, but those willing to follow his meandering thoughts will be rewarded by an intelligently bizarre novel." Booklist

Her name was Lola; by Russell Hoban. 1st U.S. ed. Arcade Pub. 2003 207p $24
ISBN 1-559-70726-7 LC 2003-20375
"Max, a writer struggling with his next novel and meanwhile paying the bills with his children's books starring hedgehog Charlotte Prickles, is torn between two lovers. First, he met Lola, an aristocrat from a British family, and proclaimed her his destiny woman. A few days later, as he and Lola are exploring the National Gallery, he meets Lula Mae, a Texan transplant working in London for a technology company. Suffering from writer's block and the guilt of romancing two women at once, Max argues with himself about the best course of action. Inevitably, he is found out. Lola cannot believe he has been two-timing her and leaves in a hurry. Soon after, Lula Mae, who is pregnant with Max's child, takes off for the States, saying she doesn't need him." Libr J
"Hoban apparently wants to see how much outrageous artifice and wilful exposure of literary technique he can get away with while still working his magic on the reader. The answer is plenty. Far from being an arid exercise, the novel has great charm and grace." New Statesman

Riddley Walker; afterword, notes, and glossary by Russell Hoban. Expanded ed. Indiana Univ. Press 1998 235p il o.p.
ISBN 0-253-33448-9 LC 98-14996
A reissue of the title first published 1980 by Summit Bks.
"About 2,000 years before this novel begins, civilization was shattered by a great barm [bomb]—a flash of light followed by centuries of darkness and ignorance. Riddley [the narrator and interpreter] having reached manhood at 12 and having witnessed the crushing of his father during the unearthing of an ancient machine, sets off on foot across the ruined landscape of Inland [England]. Riddley's quest involves the reader in learning a new language based on English . . . a written language in which spelling is a rusty approximation of sounds handed down orally during the dark centuries." Newsweek
"No review can do more than suggest the range and effect of this extraordinary book. It is 'sui generis,' its inspirations both particular and diverse, its references legion, its craft remarkable—contributing to a whole that is vivid, compelling and certainly unforgettable." Encounter

Turtle diary. Random House 1976 c1975 211p o.p.
First published 1975 in the United Kingdom
"Two middle-aged, unattractive, reclusive, and slightly daft idealists, William G. and Neaera H., record in their diaries a shared obsession: to capture from the aquarium of the London Zoo all the mature sea-turtles and set them free in the ocean. Encouraged by George Fairbairn, the head keeper of the zoo, the two conspirators succeed with astonishing ease, then set their dark plans to free the remaining immature turtles at an appropriate time. Otherwise, nothing much else happens to William G.; his brief fling with Harriet lapses into bored neglect. Similarly, Neaera H. continues her drab life, writing uninspired children's books, tending her water-beetle, and mothering her new sleeping partner." Choice
"Turtle Diary is very intelligent and very funny. I know perfectly well that some people will find it whimsical and irritating; and the journal technique makes it all

Hoban, Russell—*Continued*
too easy to include a lot of 'writer's diary' observation of people in buses and shops—there is an air of no material being wasted. But no one else could have written this bizarre book, and it is . . . most distinguished and memorable." New Statesman (1913)

Hobb, Robin

The mad ship. Bantam Bks. 1999 647p o.p.
ISBN 0-553-10333-4 LC 98-51188
In the second volume of the Liveship trilogy "Althea Vestrit is now a seasoned sailor, and with the aid of her family, her lover Brashen Tell, and the curious woodcarver Amber, she restores the abandoned, blind liveship Paragon, the 'mad ship' of the title. Aboard him (Paragon is male), they set out on a bold quest to find and recover the Vestrit family's liveship Vivacia." Booklist

Ship of magic. Bantam Bks. 1998 685p o.p.
LC 97-32216
First book in the author's Liveship traders trilogy
"The untimely death of Old Trader Ephron Vestrit deprives his daughter Althea of her inheritance and places her ambitious brother-in-law Kyle in command of the live ship *Viveca* and the family fortunes. . . . [This novels is] set in a world of sentient ships, merchant traders, ruthless pirates, dangerous treasures, seagoing dragons, and a mysterious elder race. Hobb excels in depicting complex characters; even her villains command respect, if not sympathy, for their actions." Libr J
Followed by The mad ship

Hobson, Laura Keane Zametkin, 1900-1986

Consenting adult; [by] Laura Z. Hobson. Doubleday 1975 256p o.p.
"What happens when a truly liberated, middle-aged, professional woman receives a letter from her son that says, 'I am a homosexual'? Since she is also liberated from religion, to whom can she turn for strength and advice? Her husband Ken, is recovering from a stroke, so she feels that she has to hide it from him as long as possible. Basically, this story is the thirteen-year history of her efforts to cope with this singular event in her family." Best Sellers
"Never patronizing, Hobson exhibits crystal perception in fashioning a cogent statement about homosexuality as viewed from a parental standpoint." Booklist

Gentleman's agreement; a novel; by Laura Z. Hobson. Simon & Schuster 1947 275p o.p.
"Phil Green, a member of the editorial staff of 'Smith's Weekly,' is assigned to write a series of ariticles about anti-Semitism in America. He decides to pose as a Jew for six months, and he has some extraordinary experiences." Benet's Reader's Ency of Am Lit

Hodgins, Eric, 1899-1971

Mr. Blandings builds his dream house; illustrated by William Steig. Simon & Schuster 1946 237p il o.p.
"Expanded from a 'Fortune' short story, this book is an amusing tale of a New York advertiser who found his apartment much too small and bought 50 acres and a farmhouse in the country. Mr. Blandings' trials and tribulations from the time when the architect, after spending a great deal of time and money, decided that the farmhouse should be torn down instead of remodelled until the new home was finished at a cost of $45,000 more than they expected make hilarious reading." Ont Libr Rev

Høeg, Peter, 1957-

Borderliners; translated by Barbara Haveland. Farrar, Straus & Giroux 1994 277p o.p.
ISBN 0-374-11554-0 LC 94-18892
Original Danish edition, 1993
"Hoeg portrays the closed world of Biehl's, a Danish private school where a bizarre social experiment is underway. The narrator, Peter, is now a student at Biehl's after spending all of his life in children's homes and reform schools. He is a borderline case, along with Katarina, whose parents both died in the past year, and August, severely disturbed after killing his abusive parents. Although allowed no social interaction, the children conspire to conduct their own experiment to discover what plan is being carried out at Biehl's." Libr J
"The author avoids simple storytelling, preferring instead to explore the nature of time. 'What is time?' are the book's opening words, and later Mr. Hoeg actually provides brief historical passages on the development of theories of time. In a related device, the novel employs a dreamy, associative narrative, moving back and forth through the years, including flash-forwards to the adult Peter's family life. . . . 'Borderliners' is written from the heart, and its portrait of the embittered survivor Peter is moving." N Y Times Book Rev

The history of Danish dreams; translated by Barbara Haveland. Farrar, Straus & Giroux 1995 356p o.p.
ISBN 0-374-17138-6 LC 95-18355
Original Danish edition, 1988
A satiric family saga set in Denmark. "Introduced in the first section are four characters born around the turn of the century: Carl Laurids, whose ambitions lead him beyond his estate, where, in the 16th century, the resident count had banned the keeping of time; Amalie Teader, a girl whose delusion that she has been 'chosen' springs from a wealthy and powerful grandmother, who writes a newspaper that predicts the future; Anna Bak, a pastor's innocent child who is deemed worthy of bearing 'the new Messiah'; and Adonis Jensen, the son of roving thieves, who refuses to learn how to steal because of 'his compassion for mankind.' In Part II, which ends at 1939, these four become couples: Carl and Amalie have a golden child, Carsten, for a son, while Anna and Adonis produce rebellious Maria; in the final section, Carsten and Maria marry and have children of their own." Publ Wkly
"If *Dreams* is regarded not as a novel, but as a marvelous trunkful of loosely related funny bits, . . . it is a great success." Time

Smilla's sense of snow; translated by Tiina Nunnally. Farrar Straus Giroux 1993 453p o.p.
ISBN 0-374-26644-1 LC 93-17742
Original Danish edition, 1992; published in the United Kingdom with title: Miss Smilla's feeling for snow
This novel "is set in Copenhagen and features Smilla Qaavigaaq, a 37-year-old, part-Eskimo, part-Danish heroine who is investigating the death of Isaiah, her young

Høeg, Peter, 1957-—*Continued*

neighbor. Although police officially rule Isaiah's death an accident, Smilla is convinced that he has been pushed off the roof of her apartment building. Discouraged by Danish officials, the tough, persistent, and resourceful Smilla follows Isaiah's trail to a ship that is docked off the coast of Greenland with a crew that is involved in drug trafficking and mysterious scientific experiments." Libr J

"Selfishness, menace and systematic corruption form the fabric of this mysterious novel. Relationships are all based on suspicion, and love has to be 'like a military operation.'. . . Peter Høeg has a remarkable feeling for sinister surprises." Times Lit Suppl

Tales of the night; translated by Barbara Haveland. Farrar, Straus & Giroux 1998 278p $23

ISBN 0-374-27254-9 LC 97-26664

Original Danish edition, 1990

Contents: Journey into a dark heart; Hommage à Bournonville; The verdict on the Right Honorable Ignatio Landstad Rasker, Lord Chief Justice; An experiment on the constancy of love; Portrait of the avant-garde; Pity for the children of Varden Town; Story of a marriage; Reflection of a young man in balance

These "stories take us to eight separate corners of the world on the night of March 19, 1929. . . . The deep despair and foreboding of well-intentioned Europeans victimized by the very culture that was supposed to educate them is often painfully credible. Potent but problematic, this collection lays bare the difficulties of love, even if it must make do without the dazzling lucidity of Hoeg's more recent works." Publ Wkly

The woman and the ape; translated by Barbara Haveland. Farrar, Straus & Giroux 1997 261p o.p.

ISBN 0-374-29203-5 LC 96-27289

"Madelene Burden is a 30-year-old Danish woman, a closet tippler trapped in a loveless marriage with Adam, a famous British zoologist. One day, Adam's horrid sister, Andrea, turns up with a wounded ape named Erasmus, who has escaped from some smugglers. The ape, we are initially led to believe, may be a member of a previously unknown species; receiving credit for this amazing discovery would win Adam the most important zoological post in Europe, perhaps the world. So the ape is spirited off to the conservatory behind Adam and Madelene's London mansion. But then strange things start happening. . . . Bored by her status as a trophy wife, she decides to discover precisely what's going on in that conservatory. Along the way, she develops a genuine affection for her 'irreplaceable playmate,' ultimately helping it to escape. But Erasmus is no ordinary ape. Erasmus is an ape that can talk." N Y Times Book Rev

This novel is "too fresh in its writing and its perceptions to fall into the sentimentality one might expect. An air of freedom surrounds Madelene's eventual abduction by the ape, and though their sexual involvement may seem over the top to some readers, you can't help but be carried along by Hoeg's convictions." Libr J

Hoffman, Alice, 1952-

At risk. Putnam 1988 219p o.p.

LC 87-33240

"The Farrells are your typical New England upper middle class family. Ivan, the father, is an astronomer, and Polly, the mother, is a free lance photographer. Amanda is a typical 11-year old girl with a passion for gymnastics, and Charles is an 8-year old budding biologist, interested in specimens of frogs and insects and books on dinosaurs. Their comfortable lifestyle is shattered when Amanda is diagnosed as having AIDS. The family goes through stages of disbelief, denial, anger, despair, and finally numbing acceptance as Amanda withers away and is hospitalized at the end presumably with death close at hand." West Coast Rev Books

"Such is Ms. Hoffman's tenderness and perceptiveness that we come to care about her creations despite their imperfections the way we would care about those we love despite theirs." N Y Times Book Rev

Blackbird house. Doubleday 2004 225p $21.95

ISBN 0-385-50761-5 LC 2004-07958

Contents: The edge of the world; The witch of Truro; The token; Insulting the angels; Black is the color of my true love's hair; Lionheart; The conjurer's handbook; The wedding of snow and ice; India; The pear tree; The summer kitchen; Wish you were here

"The relationship of the characters to their surroundings is seen as a kind of magical bond, expressed in language that is both eerie and beautiful. The house of the title is one in which, from story to story, we glimpse various families over the course of two centuries. . . . Hoffman lets Blackbird House stand as an emblem for the transforming power of any long-established home, while reveling in the haunting quality of her own distinctive literary style." N Y Times Book Rev

Blue diary. Putnam 2001 303p o.p.

ISBN 0-399-14802-7 LC 2001-19517

Ethan Ford is "suddenly arrested on suspicion of the rape and murder of teenager Rachel Morris 15 years earlier in Maryland. Ethan confesses to the crime, but says that he is now 'a different man,' who has redeemed himself through exemplary behavior. What this revelation means to his beautiful wife of 13 years, Jorie [and] his 12-year-old son, Collie . . . allows the novel to investigate the themes of devotion, betrayal, guilt and forgiveness in trenchantly effective ways." Publ Wkly

Here on Earth. Putnam 1997 293p o.p.

ISBN 0-399-14313-0 LC 97-5382

"Set in Jenkintown, a seemingly isolated village within easy driving distance of Boston, [this novel] tells the story of the obsessive love between March Murray, a successful jeweler who lives in California with her professor husband and their 15-year-old daughter, and March's onetime teen-age heartthrob, the malevolent Hollis." N Y Times Book Rev

The novel "is a surprisingly successful recasting of Wuthering Heights. Like that book, it is charged with passion, but unlike their prototypes, the modern-day lovers indulge their lust to their demise. . . . [Hoffman] not only covers the much-furrowed ground of renewing old romances with startling energy, she evokes the tricky relationship between mother and teenage daughter with bitter-sweet insight." Times Lit Suppl

The ice queen; a novel. Little, Brown 2005 224p $23.95

ISBN 0-316-05859-9 LC 2004-26610

"Ever since she was eight years old, Hoffman's narrator, a devoted reference librarian, has believed that her temper tantrum caused her mother's death. Her guilt turned her solitary, stoic, and somewhat misanthropic,

Hoffman, Alice, 1952—*Continued*
and she envisions herself as an ice queen. Even after she is struck by lightning. As her damaged narrator reluctantly joins a lightning-strike-survivor support group, Hoffman dramatizes the bizarre effects experienced by real-life lightning strike survivors, and orchestrates a highly erotic and risky romance between the ice queen and a fellow survivor known as Lazarus, whose breath ignites paper. As Hoffman's spellbinding and wonderfully insightful tale unfurls, she pays charming tribute to librarians, revels in metaphors of hot and cold, and poetically explores the meaning of trust, the chemistry of healing, and the reach of love." Booklist

Illumination night. Putnam 1987 224p o.p.
LC 86-30472

"A young couple's marriage has survived struggles and poverty in a countercultural transplant to the off-season isolation of Martha's Vineyard only to face a more unlikely and dangerous threat. A teen-age girl, who has moved next door to care for her sick grandmother, develops an erotic fixation on the husband. Hoffman probes the mythic connotations of the situation as she supplies convincing portraits of the man and woman and of the young girl who is determined to come between them. . . . All of this is delineated with both depth and clarity in a novel that encapsulates and transforms the characters' experiences into broader symbols of yearning and passion." Booklist

Local girls. Putnam 1999 197p $22.95
ISBN 0-399-14507-9 LC 98-50632

Contents: Dear diary; Rose Red; Flight; Gretel; Tell the truth; How to talk to the dead; Fate; Bake at 350°; True confession; The rest of your life; The boy who wrestled with angels; Examining the evidence; Devotion; Still among the living; Local girls

A collection of "interlinked stories about a Jewish Long Island family locked in a downward spiral after the parents' divorce. Most of the stories are told from the viewpoint of Gretel Samuelson as she moves from high-school years to young adulthood. . . . Hoffman doesn't sentimentalize her characters' lives: the tragedies they suffer are ordinary, after all. She has a light touch and a poet's knack for making diffuse elements fall into place with seeming effortlessness." Publ Wkly

Practical magic. Putnam 1995 244p o.p.
LC 94-47013

This novel is set in Massachusetts. "A family of women notorious for their witchcraft is at the book's center: the Owens sisters and the nieces they're raising, Sally and Gillian. The aunts are famous for dispensing potions to the lovelorn, but the old women are pariahs, too; so when Sally and Gillian grow up, they escape to what they hope will be normality, Sally becomes a perfect homemaker and Gillian a wild thing, but their inheritance can't be dismissed." Newsweek

"The tale of the Owenses' struggle is charmingly told, and a good deal of fun. Dark comedy and a light touch carry the story along to a truly Gothic climax." N Y Times Book Rev

The probable future. Doubleday 2003 322p $24.95
ISBN 0-385-50760-7 LC 2003-40960

"In a New England family in which generations of women have magical powers, young Stella foresees a murder, a crime that her father is then accused of committing." SLJ

"Filled with vivid (if sometimes sketchy) characters and cinematic descriptions of New England landscapes, this book will be a hit wherever Hoffman is in demand." Libr J

The river king. Putnam 2000 324p o.p.
ISBN 0-399-14599-0 LC 00-23870

A novel set in the "small Massachusetts town of Haddan, where the locals resent the snotty denizens of a posh prep school. But not all of Haddan's students are privileged and arrogant. Poor, beautiful, and smart, Carlin is attending Haddan on a swimming scholarship and finds most of her peers callow at best. Gus is also smart, self-possessed, and defiant, and he cannot believe his good luck in befriending a girl as amazing as Carlin. But the boys in his dorm despise and torment him, and no one comprehends the severity of his situation. When his body is pulled from the river, Haddan's legacy of suicide is reexamined, but neither Carlin nor Abe, a maverick policeman, believe that Gus killed himself." Booklist

"It can be hard to find an example of good old-fashioned storytelling these days, but storytelling, refreshingly, is Alice Hoffman's strength." N Y Times Book Rev

Second nature. Putnam 1994 254p o.p.
LC 93-11595

"Robin Moore rescues a wild, unspeaking young man—called the Wolf Man because he was found, injured, in a wolf trap—from impending transfer to a mental hospital. In the process of teaching Stephen how to live in 'civilized' suburban society, she falls in love with him. Meanwhile, neighborhood animals are found with their throats slit, and a teenage girl is murdered; the Wolf Man is naturally a suspect." Libr J

"In the end, Ms. Hoffman suggests that it is love in all its wondrous forms, from a parent's love for a child to the most consuming sexual passion that truly delineates mankind. Her abiding vision of this ineluctable and uniquely human power informs 'Second Nature' with grace and beauty, making it at once her richest and wisest, as well as her boldest, novel to date." N Y Times Book Rev

Seventh heaven. Putnam 1990 256p o.p.
LC 89-28737

"The setting is a Long Island, N.Y., housing development from 1959 to 1960, a place of conforming, happy families where husbands mow the lawns of the tract houses and wives meet for coffee, where 'safety hung over the neighborhood like a net.' The arrival of Nora Silk, a brassy divorcée with two young children, is the catalyst for disturbing changes and events, some of them violent. Plucky, impetuous, innocently seductive and a messy housekeeper, Nora is anathema to the subdivision wives, who ostracize her and whose children torment her eight-year-old clairvoyant son, Billy. But as Nora's presence disturbs the community, it is slowly revealed that behind the identical facades of the houses are secret lives of turmoil, restlessness and longing." Publ Wkly

This is "one of those rare novels so abundant with life it seems to overflow its own pages, these aren't the sort

Hoffman, Alice, 1952-—*Continued*
of fictional characters who are all used up by the end of the book; on the contrary, they seem ready to leap straight into another volume." Newsweek

Turtle Moon. Putnam 1992 255p o.p.
LC 91-37222

"Julian Cash, policeman, and Lucy Rosen, obit writer, both with hardened shells covering events that shattered their younger selves, are thrown together when they try to solve a murder that endangers Lucy's son and the murdered woman's child. In the ensuing days they gradually draw solace from each other and revisit their pasts in search of the solution to the murder; Lucy to Great Neck, New York where she lived after her parents died when she was 16; Julian to the foster mother who raised him and the gumbo-limbo tree where an imprisoned angel waits, the cousin Julian killed in a car accident 20 years earlier." Libr J

"Hoffman handles romance, suspense, and the healing properties of love and understanding with aplomb and a dash of magic." Booklist

Hoffman, Eva

The secret; a novel. PublicAffairs 2002 265p $25
ISBN 1-58648-150-9 LC 2002-73433

"The time is 2022, the place is Chicago, and Iris Surrey has an unusually close relationship with her chilly mother, Elizabeth. At 17, Iris is wearying of the odd stares she triggers in others, especially when her look-alike mother is with her. Iris wants to learn the identity of her father, which, alas, is not possible; the reader will figure out before Iris does that she is the product of genetic engineering. When Iris uncovers the truth, she goes on an emotional rampage, intent on tracking down any blood relatives in the hope that they will make her feel more authentic." Libr J

This work "is compelling throughout for Hoffman's prose, for her insights on identity, for her reflections on history." N Y Times Book Rev

Hoffman, Jilliane

Retribution; Jilliane Hoffman. G.P. Putnam's Sons 2004 420p $24.95
ISBN 0-399-15127-3 LC 2003-46502

"In the late 1980s, law student Chloe Larson was brutally raped and left for dead in her New York apartment. Fast-forward 12 years; Chloe, now known as C.J. Townsend, is one of the top prosecutors in Miami. It is in this capacity that she finds herself face to face with the man who terrorized her." Libr J

"The twists and turns are a suspense lover's dream the climax is chillingly good. An absolutely remarkable first outing." Rendezvous Magazine

Hoffman, William, 1925-

Wild thorn. HarperCollins Pubs. 2002 293p $24.95
ISBN 0-06-019798-6 LC 2001-58336

"Charley LeBlanc, the black sheep of a prominent family first introduced in Hoffman's Tidewater Blood, returns from Montana to his native Shawnee County in West Virginia for what he thinks will be a short visit. He is accompanied by his tough, sexy girlfriend, Blackie, whose hillbilly argot belies her extensive reading. When he calls on his old friend, the aging Aunt Jessie Arbuckle, he finds her isolated home crawling with police. She has been found dead under mysterious circumstances." Publ Wkly

"This entertaining murder mystery is replete with corrupt lawmen, betraying kin, dignified country folk, and the genteel residents of Wild Thorn manor. Further intrigue results over the true identity of two women: Esmerelda, who lives wild in the forest, and Jennie Bruce, the seductive mistress of Wild Thorn." Libr J

Hofmann, Gert

Lichtenberg and the little flower girl; translated and with an afterword by Michael Hofmann. New Directions 2004 245p $19.95
ISBN 0-8112-1568-7 LC 2003-28140
Original German edition, 1994

"Georg Christoph Lichtenberg, an eighteenth-century Göttingen mathematician, physicist, and astronomer, is remembered for the satiric aphorisms he wrote in his spare time, which have been celebrated by luminaries from Nietzsche to Einstein. He was also a dwarf and a hunchback, attributes crucial to this lively fictionalization of his life by the late German novelist, which charts Lichtenberg's love affair with the progress of civilization and, in parallel, his failure to find a wife. Hofmann gives the scientist a delirious, childish glee at the universe's workings, and a sweetness of character that, true to Lichtenberg's biography, eventually wins him the love of a thirteen-year-old beauty. The author shares with his hero a gift for the epigram, which makes the book seem at first a rather weightless affair. But a mass of loneliness and longing just beneath the comedy keeps it from floating away." New Yorker

Luck; translated from the German by Michael Hofmann. New Directions 2002 266p $23.95
ISBN 0-8112-1502-4 LC 2002-3556
Original German edition, 1992

This novel "chronicles the bitter end of a marriage, capturing. . .the relationship's final day as experienced by father, mother, son and daughter. The son serves as the novel's nameless narrator, and in many ways the story itself, as well as the act of its telling, marks the end of his adolescence." N Y Times Book Rev

"Stripped, spare prose creates the impression that the boy is merely a detached witness to his parents' separation, but subtle clues belie his neutrality. . . .While Hofmann's desolate emotional landsapes and darkly comic observations are not for those seeking a literary lark, readers will appreciate his deft handling of the minimalist plot and his authentic rendering of a precociously perceptive boy baffled by his elders." Publ Wkly

Holden, Craig

The jazz bird. Simon & Schuster 2002 314p $25
ISBN 0-7432-1296-7 LC 2001-32259

"Charlie Taft is a prosecutor in late 1920s Cincinnati. . . . When bootlegger George Remus turns himself in, in October 1927, for shooting his society wife, Imogene, Charlie thinks he's been handed a career maker. But all

Holden, Craig—*Continued*

is not as simple as it seems." Publ Wkly

This novel "is based on an actual murder that place in Cincinnati in 1927. In addition to its exploration of the Remus murder case, the book offers a portrait of a now-lost Cincinnati, with its jazz clubs, its great Roebling suspension bridge and its neighborhoods with names like Over the Rhine and Eden Park." N Y Times Book Rev

Holland, Cecelia, 1943-

The angel and the sword. Forge 2000 304p $23.95

ISBN 0-312-86890-1 LC 00-30668

"A Tom Doherty Associates book"

Set in "ninth-century Paris, the novel centers on King Charles the Bald's fight to save the city when the continued demands of the Vikings can no longer be met. To his aid comes the young, intensely spiritual Lord Roderick. Roderick is in fact the Princess Ragny, who fled her native Spain and incestuous father by disguising herself as a man. As Roderick, Ragny struggles with her sin of deception, her personal identity, womanhood, and the privileges and restrictions of manhood. She also manages to become a hero in battle. . . . A wonderful story of faith, love, hope, and justice." Libr J

The Bear Flag. Houghton Mifflin 1990 422p o.p.

LC 89-71670

"A Peter Davison book"

This novel is set in California during the 1840s. The protagonist, Catharine Reilly, "loses everything—including her husband—on the brutal trek to California. She reaches Sutter's Fort and falls in love with Count Sohrakoff, a Russian agent for the Mexican dons who rule California. The settlers' uprising in 1846 places Cat and the Count on opposing sides." Libr J

"Holland's splendidly researched historical novel makes the confusion and brutality of the American takeover of California during the Mexican War believable and steadily interesting. Most of her characters are—or were—real people. She is particularly adroit in recreating the subsurface tension between Frémont . . . and his scout, the experienced Kit Carson." Atlantic

The firedrake. Atheneum Pubs. 1966 c1965 243p o.p.

A "picaresque tale set in 11th century Germany, Flanders, Normandy and England. The Irish hero, named Laeghaire, the Gaelic spelling of Lear, is a brave, hard-fighting mercenary in the forces of William of Normandy. He is impetuous, brawling, very proud, with a plain and cutting tongue. Laeghaire kills men in battle with no hesitation, but he is haunted with nightmares about an ugly future. He is a restless adventurer, he is briefly a man in love, he is a violent man of action. This vital central character is placed against a colorful medieval background of castles and wild countryside and in the middle of one fight after another." Publ Wkly

Jerusalem. Forge 1996 318p o.p.

LC 95-38814

"A Tom Doherty Associates book"

This historical novel "takes place in the Holy Land, during the 12th century, in the years before Crusader Jerusalem fell to the Muslims—a time when the Christian leaders fought among themselves whenever Saladin gave them respite. . . . [Holland centers] her story on the Knights Templar, ferocious warriors who took vows of chastity and attempted to live like monks." N Y Times Book Rev

"The narrative structure may be simple, but Holland's masterful layering of subplots, historical detail and multiple perspectives makes for a great read." Publ Wkly

Lily Nevada. Forge 1999 224p $22.95

ISBN 0-312-86670-4 LC 99-36339

"A Tom Doherty Associates book"

"Detective Brand is dismayed to learn that the man he's after may be a member of Lily Nevada's roving theater troupe. Brand has already killed young Lily's biological and adoptive fathers, both outlaws, in *Railroad Schemes* . . . and he is not eager to go after her new-found friends and coworkers. Meanwhile, Lily, along with members of her troupe, is headed for San Francisco to stage *Hamlet* in a posh new theater." Booklist

"Holland has created a truly independent, compassionate and headstrong frontier woman in Lily. . . . Gutsy and gritty, but touchingly vulnerable, she's an exemplary historical heroine." Publ Wkly

An ordinary woman; a dramatized biography of Nancy Kelsey. Forge 1999 223p o.p.

ISBN 0-312-86528-7 LC 98-48929

"A Tom Doherty Associates book"

A "fictionalized biography of Nancy Kelsey, the first American woman to reach California. Traveling by horse and on foot, 17-year-old Nancy leaves Missouri with a baby on her hip in search of California's holy grail. Part of the 1841 Bidwell-Bartleson party, Nancy and her husband, Ben, decide against the meandering Santa Fe Trail in order to take a more—direct and uncharted—course directly across the continent: traversing the Great Plains, the Rockies, the desert and the Sierra Nevadas. . . . The thorough research lends authority to a vivid and engaging narrative that suffers only a little from Holland's evident fervent admiration for her heroine." Publ Wkly

Pacific Street. Houghton Mifflin 1992 260p o.p.

LC 91-27314

"A Peter Davison book"

This novel creates a "montage of San Francisco in its wild beginnings. The aptly named Frances Hardheart, an escaped slave with a quick wit, a sharp tongue and a knack for using people, has found the Shining Light, a haven for non-whites. With her protégée, the beautiful and white Daisy Duncan, she sets up a stage show and bar, enlisting the aid of such likable characters as good-natured, white Gil Marcus and taciturn, Indian Mitya. Frances, aka Mammy, soon extends her influence to the city's rising political and social elite." Publ Wkly

"The plot's credibility runs a little thin at times, but Holland captures the lawlessness of early San Francisco with style and imagination and tells a story both engaging and romantic." Libr J

Pillar of the Sky; a novel. Knopf 1985 534p o.p.

LC 84-48659

The novel is set in prehistoric England, the "central character is Moloquin, who has lived as a wild child since his mother, Ael, was banished from her village by her brother Ladon, the ruler of the People. When Moloquin is adopted by Karella, the clan's storyteller, he joins the tribe, eventually overthrowing Ladon and be-

Holland, Cecelia, 1943-—*Continued*
coming the People's new chief. Discovering the dark secret of his father's true identity, the demon-possessed Moloquin buries his shame by overseeing the construction of Stonehenge in the Pillar of the Sky, an ancient burial ground." N Y Times Book Rev

"Part Christ figure and part avenger, [Moloquin] is companionable with women, but also amazingly brutal. The tale is full of subtleties and contradictions and depicts a long struggle between the forces of change and those favoring stability. . . . This is more a story of power and customs than of Stonehenge and the early Britons." Libr J

Railroad schemes. Forge 1997 271p o.p.
ISBN 0-312-86405-1 LC 97-19555

"A Tom Doherty Associates book"

"Set in 1850s California as the transcontinental railroad is gobbling up land near Los Angeles, the . . . narrative pits a charismatic bank robber, King Callahan, against his one-armed nemesis, a Southern Pacific Railroad detective called Brand. King's robbery of a stagecoach, during which he humiliates Brand, locks them in enmity; 15-year-old orphan Lily Viner is the innocent catalyst who influences their fates. . . . King vows to take care of Lily and to marry the indomitable Mexican widow Serafa, and he's even willing to give up a life of crime to protect them both." Publ Wkly

"Holland's renditions of the desolately beautiful landscapes of the region, with its dusty frontier towns and vast stretches of dry wilderness, bring a sharply haunting physicality to her story." N Y Times Book Rev

Followed by Lily Nevada

Valley of the Kings; a novel of Tutankhamun. Forge 1997 231p o.p.
LC 97-5499

"A Tom Doherty Associates book"

First published 1977 by Dutton under the pseudonym Elizabeth Eliot Carter

The first half of the "novel is narrated by a fictionalized Howard Carter, the Englishman who discovered Tut's tomb in 1922. Holland does an excellent job of rendering Carter's strained relationship with his upper-crust patron, Lord Carnarvon, while surrounded by obtuse British bureaucrats, archeologists more interested in treasure than history and a culture that Carter loves despite its otherness. . . . The second half of the book flashes back to the ancient Egypt of Tut and concerns three common Egyptians—a mason, a beggar and a maid—who are variously damaged and nurtured by the royals, who have their own problems." Publ Wkly

Holland, Isabelle

A death at St. Anselm's. Doubleday 1984 229p o.p.
LC 83-11668

"An Episcopal church is rocked by the brutal murder of the parish's business manager, Dick Grism. Grism's helplessness as a paraplegic underscores the savagery of the crime, leading New York City police to search for suspects among the drug addicts and mentally unbalanced who frequent St. Anselm's—including the disturbed, anorexic daughter of the female pastor." Booklist

"Holland remains one of the best of modern romantic suspense writers. Her characters (except for her maniacal murderer) are believable, and her settings (in this case, a modern urban church) are uncommon without being wildly exotic." Wilson Libr Bull

Holman, Sheri

The dress lodger. Atlantic Monthly Press 1999 291p o.p.
LC 99-18153

"Dr. Henry Chiver relocates from London to the town of Sunderland, England, in 1830. Haunted by past dealings with 'resurrectionists,' grave robbers who furnish bodies for autopsies, Henry is torn by a desire to refocus his attention on the living and the need for fresh specimens for his students. . . . Gustine works as a potter's assistant by day and walks the streets at night, wearing a fancy gown rented to her by her landlord. . . . Gustine's only desire is for her baby, born with an extremely rare anatomical defect, to live to adulthood. She is able to see how her desire and those of Henry Chiver are intertwined—until an outbreak of cholera puts the entire town at risk." Booklist

"While the topic may seem morbid and the setting alien, Holman offers both a well-told story with affecting characterizations and insight into the human response to the unknown." Libr J

The mammoth cheese; a novel. Atlantic Monthly Press 2003 442p $24
ISBN 0-87113-900-6 LC 2003-41796

This novel "begins with the media circus surrounding the birth of 11 infants to Manda Frank, a hapless young dog breeder living in the rural Virginia town of Three Chimneys. It's a situation ripe for satire or social commentary, but Holman isn't interested in anything so obvious. Her focus quickly widens to encompass a handful of Frank's neighbors and their ordinary, deeply eccentric lives." N Y Times Book Rev

Holt, Victoria, 1906-1993

For works written by this author under other names see Carr, Philippa, 1906-1993; Plaidy, Jean, 1906-1993

The black opal. Doubleday 1993 275p o.p.
LC 92-33830

In this "romantic mystery, Dr. Marline and his ailing wife adopt young Carmel March after she is found wandering among the azaleas on their estate, Commonwood House. Soon she is on her way to a new life in Australia. When Carmel finally returns as a young woman, she realizes that she was hustled away to shield her from a mysterious murder at Commonwood House, and she is convinced that the wrong man has been convicted for the crime." Libr J

Bride of Pendorric. Doubleday 1963 288p o.p.

Favel Farrington is a young bride, married to handsome Roc Pendorric. She is fearful that he has chosen her for her money and that she will become another of the legendary brides of Pendorric Castle to die young and tragically

The India fan. Doubleday 1988 404p o.p.
LC 87-36497

"As a motherless girl whose father is totally engrossed in classical history, Drusilla is grudgingly taken in by the Framlings as a companion to Lavinia, a high-spirited

Holt, Victoria, 1906-1993—*Continued*

young woman with a taste for sexual escapades. Plain, commonsensical Drusilla is sent, along with Lavinia, to boarding school in England, finishing school in France, and finally India, where Lavinia lives as imprudently as ever as the wife of a young man who once intended to marry Drusilla, until he inherited a title and estate." Booklist

The Judas kiss. Doubleday 1981 400p o.p.
LC 81-43138

"Pippa Ewing discovers that her beloved older sister Francine has been murdered as she lay in bed with her husband Baron Rudolph. As evidence accumulates to show that Francine had not married him after all, Pippa is launched on a quest to solve her sister's murder and vindicate her name, a journey that takes her to the duchy of Bruxenstein; a job as a governess; and another encounter with Nordic, handsome Conrad, who had caused Pippa to 'fall down the slippery slope' one romantic evening. Mysteries pile up as two similar midnight fires take the lives of a pious and cruel grandfather and a young countess. . . . Plenty of romance, an agreeable amount of sex, lots of danger and suspense in Gothic and exotic settings ensure that this will please Holt fans." Publ Wkly

Kirkland Revels. Doubleday 1962 312p o.p.

"Kirkland Revels, a magnificent manor house, standing grand and aloof on the Yorkshire moors, hides many secrets from Catherine Rockwell, its newest resident. The strange suicide of her young husband prompts Catherine to try to prove his death murder despite certain danger." Cincinnati Public Libr

Mistress of Mellyn. Doubleday 1960 334p o.p.

In this romantic novel set in late 19th century England, the heroine is an attractive, young English governess. "She takes charge of the motherless child of a handsome, arrogant gentleman who lives in a large creepy mansion in Cornwall. The plot is lively and complicated. Eventually, our bright heroine discovers that her little pupil's mother was murdered and she narrowly escapes being murdered herself." Publ Wkly

My enemy the Queen. Doubleday 1978 348p o.p.
LC 77-11366

This novel of the Elizabethan era is narrated by Lettice Knollys, cousin of the queen and wife of the Earl of Essex. "Aware that Robert Dudley is the favorite of Elizabeth I and of dark rumors about the death of his wife, Lettice becomes one of Dudley's closet strumpets anyhow. When her husband dies, the Countess dares the axe by marrying Robert, but then betrays him by carrying on with a young man who becomes her third husband when Dudley dies. All the events of a momentous age are colored by Lettice's vanity, even the beheading of her own son, the second Essex, who supplants his stepfather in the affections of the queen." Publ Wkly

Secret for a nightingale. Doubleday 1986 371p o.p.
LC 86-2206

"In this Victorian romance, Susanna Pleydell loses her husband to drugs and her dearly loved child to her husband's neglect. She develops an obsessive hatred for Damien Adair, the physician she holds responsible for both tragedies. She tries to forget by taking up a nursing career, eventually going to the Crimea. There, working beside Dr. Adair, she finds herself attracted to him despite her hatred. . . . This is one of the better Holt novels, with a well-drawn historical background." Libr J

Holthe, Tess Uriza

When the elephants dance; a novel. Crown 2002 368p il o.p.
ISBN 0-609-60952-1

A novel set "in the final days of the battle for the Philippines. During MacArthur's assault on Manila, a group of neighbors seek shelter in the cellar of an abandoned house. Cramped, starving and terrified, they begin to tell each other stories in order 'to stay alive when you have died inside'. . . . Full of weird, fantastic twists and folkloric wisdom, the stories become both a touchstone to and a respite from the horrific events unfolding outside." N Y Times Book Rev

Hood, Ann, 1956-

An ornithologist's guide to life; Ann Hood. 1st ed. W.W. Norton 2004 237p $23.95
ISBN 0-393-05900-6 LC 2004-6112

Contents: Total cave darkness; The rightness of things; The language of sorrow; After Zane; Joelle's mother; Escapes; Lost parts; Dropping bombs; Inside Gorbachev's head; New people; An ornothologist's guide to life

"Hood is a seductive storyteller, given her emotionally reckless and nonconformist characters, sensuous detail, precise dialogue, and keen rendition of the inner monologue that so often contradicts what we say and do. She also engineers just the sort of painful and inexplicable familial and romantic predicaments friends spend hours attempting to decipher." Booklist

Places to stay the night. Doubleday 1993 275p o.p.
LC 92-10526

"Small-town life in Holly, Massachusetts, serves as the backdrop for two family crisis. The lives of former high school classmates Tom and Libby Harper and Renata Handy intersect when beautiful but unhappy Libby decides to leave Tom and their children and Renata the outsider returns. While Libby seeks fulfillment, Renata only wants to give her fatally ill daughter a moment of normalcy. Despite their own confusion and anger, Tom and his teenage children provide a temporary refuge for Renata." Libr J

"Hood, an accomplished scene setter and dialogist, works out the consequences of the characters' confusion of dream with fantasy and their groping return to truth with a wonderful frankness that illuminates the lessons of paradox and our belief in romance. An exceptionally fluent tale about the unending process of growing up." Booklist

Ruby. Picador 1998 225p o.p.
LC 98-23451

"In the year since her husband David was hit by a car and killed while jogging at their Rhode Island summer place, Olivia hasn't come to terms with his senseless death. . . . She's about to sell the summer house when Ruby, a pregnant, 15-year-old runaway, arrives on her doorstep. The teen's a hard case: sullen, deceptive, ma-

Hood, Ann, 1956-—*Continued*

nipulative. . . . But she's carrying what Olivia wants, the baby she and David never got around to making." Libr J

"While lies, betrayals and manipulations give the plot its undeniable page-turning pull, Hood's caustic wit, brightly detailed prose and thoughtful delineations of two women struggling with private, powerful regrets supply 'Ruby' with rich and surprising emotional depths." N Y Times Book Rev

Hooker, Richard

MASH. Morrow 1968 219p o.p.

"Captains Hawkeye Pierce, Duke Forrest, and 'Trapper' John McIntyre, all M.D.'s, are stationed in Korea with the 4077th MASH (Mobile Army Surgical Hospital). The reader is soon involved in many operations and medical jargon. It is, however, the off-duty activities of these three that engages one's attention and laughter. Full of martinis, or bored, or tired, or all three, the men soon start raising hell. . . . Hilarious, occasionally very serious, full of warm, appealing eccentric characters, one could enjoy a very pleasant evening with this sMASHing novel." Libr J

Hooper, Chloe, 1973-

A child's book of true crime. Scribner 2002 238p $23

ISBN 0-7432-2512-0

"Kate Byrne, a primary-school teacher in Tasmania, is having an affair with the father of one of her students. But even as she obligingly plays the part of the slutty young mistress, she waits, like a child, to be punished; her lover's wife has just written a highly colored account of a local sex crime, and Kate is convinced that the older woman means to harm her. Hooper's first novel is at once suspenseful and self-conscious; crammed with fragments of animal fables, erotic fantasies, deaths remembered and foretold, it becomes a witty and unsettling meditation on innocence and experience." New Yorker

Hooper, Kay

Finding Laura. Bantam Bks. 1997 322p il o.p.
LC 97-10116

At the Kilbourne estate auction in Atlanta "striking redhead Laura Sutherland is delighted to acquire a beautiful 200-year-old mirror for her collection. But she's no longer convinced her purchase is a bargain when magnetic Peter Kilbourne turns up dead only hours after attempting to buy back the mirror, and the police immediately consider her a suspect. . . . Hooper keeps the intrigue pleasurably complicated, with gothic touches of suspense and a statisfying resolution." Publ Wkly

Haunting Rachel. Bantam Bks. 1998 346p o.p.

ISBN 0-553-09950-7 LC 98-607160

"Rachel Grant's fiancé, Thomas, was lost in the jungles of South America ten years ago, just before their wedding, and she has never found another man to replace him. After her parents die in a plane crash, Rachel begins to catch glimpses of a man who looks very much like Thomas, always right before suspicious accidents threaten her life. As the threats become more deadly and Rachel comes to know the mysterious stranger who resembles her dead lover, messages that seem to come from beyond the grave warn her away." Libr J

"The book keeps you on your toes with plenty of suspects and motives to choose from as well as a ghostly intervention or two." Booklist

Hope, Anthony, 1863-1933

The prisoner of Zenda; being the history of three months in the life of an English gentleman. Holt & Co. 1894 226p o.p.

"Rudolf Rassendyll, an Englishman, makes a three month's visit to the kingdom of Ruritania. He arrives on the eve of the coronation of King Rudolf. The king has an enemy in his brother, Duke Michael, who aspires to the throne himself. During the festivities at Zenda Castle, the Duke drugs King Rudolf so that he is unable to attend his own coronation. Later, Rassendyll, . . . succeeds in impersonating the King and is crowned in his stead. In the meantime, Princess Flavia, the king's betrothed, falls in love with Rassendyll, who in turn loves her. After many dramatic and dangerous escapades, duels, and intrigues King Rudolf is rescued from Zenda Castle where he is held prisoner by Duke Michael. Rassendyll and Princess Flavia renounce each other when the King is restored, and Rassendyll returns to England." Haydn. Thesaurus of Book Dig

Horgan, Paul, 1903-1995

A distant trumpet. Farrar, Straus & Cudahy 1960 629p o.p.

A novel of the Southwest in the 1870's. The chief scene of action is at a U.S. Army outpost in Arizona during the Apache Indian Wars. Chief protagonists in the story are Lieutenant Matthew Hazard and his wife, Laura; Major General Alexander Upton Quait, Laura's resourceful eccentric uncle; Colonel and Mrs. Prescott and other officers and their wives; and, White Horn, an Apache scout

"The author evokes the arid landscape of the Southwest with his usual great skill and feeling; in the characterization of a general officer Mr Horgan appears to have accomplished a real tour de force!" Libr J

Hornberger, H. Richard, 1924-1997

For works written by this author in collaboration with W. E. Butterworth see Hooker, Richard

Hornby, Nick

About a boy. Riverhead Bks. 1998 307p o.p.

ISBN 1-57322-087-6 LC 97-46499

The protagonist of this satire set in London is 36-year-old underachieving bachelor Will Lightman. "Targeting single mothers, he joins a single parents' group under false pretenses and is soon drawn into the lives of depressed Fiona and her bright 12-year-old son, Marcus. Suddenly, his life is messy and complicated. . . . [Hornby] has an uncanny ability for homing in on wholly contemporary, often serious topics and serving them up in truly hilarious fashion." Booklist

High fidelity. Riverhead Bks. 1995 323p o.p.

ISBN 1-57322-016-7 LC 95-8469

Hornby, Nick—*Continued*

"Owner of a small London record shop and musical snob of a high degree, [thirty-five-year-old protagonist Rob Fleming] . . . finds his life thrown into turmoil when live-in girlfriend Laura suddenly leaves. He embarks on a journey through the past, tracking down old lovers while finding solace with Marie, an American folk/country singer living in London, even as he yearns for Laura's return." Libr J

"Happily, Hornby does not rely on pop-cultural allusion to limn his characters' inner lives, but uses it instead to create a rich, wry backdrop for them." Time

How to be good. Riverhead Bks. 2001 305p o.p.

ISBN 1-57322-193-7 LC 2001-19395

"'I'm not a bad person. I'm a doctor,' says Katie Carr, liberal 1990s North London mother of two. This is her hollow mantra, the only comfort that she can feign while her 20-year marriage to surly David falls to pieces. Just when she is about to be kicked out of the house after confessing to an affair, David returns from a visit with an ecstasy-dropping club kid-turned-faith healer named DJ GoodNews a changed—a *good*—man." Libr J

This novel "hits the funny bone but bruises the conscience. . . . Hornby draws the curtain aside and drags our ethics onto center stage where we can watch them squirm." Christ Sci Mount

A long way down. Riverhead Books 2005 333p $24.95

ISBN 1-57322-302-6 LC 2004-58837

"Hornby follows four depressed people from their aborted suicide attempts on New Years Eve through the surprising developments that occur over the following three months. Middle-aged Maureen has been caring for her profoundly disabled son for decades; Martin is a celebrity-turned-has-been after sleeping with a 15-year-old girl; teenage Jess, trash-talker extraordinaire, is still haunted by the mysterious disappearance of her older sister years before; and JJ is upset by the collapse of his band and his breakup with his longtime girlfriend." Booklist

"Whatever limited consolations the book's survivors find in each other, Hornby resists melodramatic resolutions or glorious moments of redemption, and he doesn't smuggle away or refute all the reasons his characters took with them to the rooftop where they met, the ones that urged them toward the edge rather than down to the ground the slow way, back into the world." N Y Times Book Rev

Hornsby, Wendy

A hardlight; a Maggie MacGowen mystery. Dutton 1997 261p o.p.

LC 97-8750

Amateur sleuth and freelance filmmaker Maggie MacGowen "is making a documentary on teenage criminals when a Vietnamese friend is robbed. Puzzlingly, the thief, also Vietnamese, is an acquaintance of the victim. Maggie becomes inextricably involved in the crime when she decides to sell the house she and her ex-husband, Scott, bought years ago. The sale of the house leads to the deaths of Scott and his longtime client, a Vietnamese. . . . With the help of LAPD detective and boyfriend Mike Flint, Maggie unravels the complex story behind the case—a story that goes back to the last tragic days of the Vietnam War. Smart, tough, and idealistic, Maggie MacGowen is an appealingly unorthodox heroine in a fine series." Booklist

Hospital, Janette Turner, 1942-

Due preparations for the plague. Norton 2003 401p $24.95

ISBN 0-393-05764-X LC 2002-156598

"Lowell is a single father whose mother died when terrorists hijacked an Air France plane she was on in 1987. That event continues to haunt him and the other children of the victims, one of whom, Samantha, is convinced that the whole story of the hijacking has never been told and wants Lowell's help in unearthing it. When Lowell's father, a CIA agent, dies suspiciously and leaves his son incriminating evidence about the U.S.' role in Air France 64, Lowell reluctantly joins forces with Sam." Booklist

"Using the form of a politico-literary thriller, Janette Turner Hospital has attempted a meta-physical novel of evil. . . . 'Due preparations for the Plague'—the title and the frequent quotes from Camus indicate the author's larger intentions—is a descent through Dantean circles of governmental conspiracy and betrayal." N Y Times Book Rev

North of nowhere, south of loss; Janette Turner Hospital. 1st American ed. Norton 2004 c2003 286p $24.95

ISBN 0-393-05991-X LC 2004-54723

Contents: The ocean of Brisbane; North of nowhere; For Mr. Voss or occupant; Unperformed experiments have no results; Our own little Kakadu; Cape Tribulation; Flight; Frames and wonders; Nativity; Credit repair; South of loss; Night train; Litany for the homeland; The end-of-the-line end-of-the-road disco

"Hospital's strength lies in capturing her character's interior lives with a poet's grace and precision. . . . The collection is thematically linked: each story explores the geographies and memories that define and bind us even as they change shape over time. How we embroider past events or alter and manipulate memories from actual occurrences are key elements in many of the tales." Booklist

Oyster. Norton 1998 c1996 400p o.p.

ISBN 0-393-04618-4 LC 97-34071

First published 1996 in the United Kingdom

"In a part of the Australian Outback so remote it is literally off the charts, a tiny opal-mining and ranching community faces the end of its world. A place of closed minds and closely held secrets, Outer Maroo has become dangerous since the arrival and departure of the fascinating, sinister spiritual leader calling himself Oyster. Since Oyster's coming, certain areas of conversation are taboo, minds are unhinged, and reality seems hard to define. Outsiders are met with distrust, dislike, and worse, while a seemingly endless drought heightens tension unbearably. When two particularly stubborn strangers demand information about their lost children, disciples of Oyster, they initiate Armageddon for Outer Maroo" Libr J

"With language that slips between the surreal and the all-too-real, the sign of the beast and the meteorological formation of a rain cloud [Hospital] delivers a world that is at once our own and a place from another time, from the old West, the Bible." N Y Times Book Rev

Hosseini, Khaled

The kite runner. Riverhead Bks. 2003 324p $24.95

ISBN 1-57322-245-3 LC 2003-43106

"Amir, the son of a well-to-do Kabul merchant, is the first-person narrator, who marries, moves to California and becomes a successful novelist. But he remains haunted by a childhood incident in which he betrayed the trust of his best friend, a Hazara boy named Hassan, who receives a brutal beating from some local bullies. After establishing himself in America, Amir learns that the Taliban have murdered Hassan and his wife, raising questions about the fate of his son, Sohrab. Spurred on by childhood guilt, Amir makes the difficult journey to Kabul, only to learn the boy has been enslaved by a former childhood bully who has become a prominent Taliban official." Publ Wkly

"Khaled Hosseini gives us a vivid and engaging story that reminds us how long his people have been struggling to triumph over the forces of violence." N Y Times Book Rev

Houellebecq, Michel

Platform; a novel; translated from the French by Frank Wynne. Knopf 2003 259p $25

ISBN 0-375-41462-2 LC 2002-40634

Original French edition, 2001

"Michel, a 40-year-old bachelor, is a civil servant working in the ministry of Culture. He falls for Valerie, a woman he first meets on a group tour vacation to Thailand. The point of his trip—which he pays for with money that he inherits when his father is murdered by the Muslim brother of his father's cleaning lady/lover—is to see if Thai prostitutes are as pretty, expert and reasonable as he imagines. . . . Valerie works for Aurore, a multinational hotel and resort chain. She and Michel persuade her boss, Jean-Yves Frochot, to invest in sex tourism resorts, but the plan goes terribly awry because of a terrorist attack by puritanical Islamic fanatics on a resort in Thailand." Publ Wkly

"Houellebecq can be a terrific writer, funny and prophetic, more feverishly alive to the world around him than are many authors more tasteful, less offensive, less willing to take risks." N Y Times Book Rev

Hough, Robert

The stowaway. Arcade Pub. 2004 232p $24

ISBN 0-679-31146-7 LC 2004-9347

Based on an actual incident, this novel "relates how two stowaways are discovered on a container ship bound for North America. The stowaways, who speak only Romanian, are set adrift and soon drown. Several crew members agonize over this, with Rodolfo, the bosun, particularly afflicted, since he notified the captain of the stowaways' existence, assuming that they would be integrated into the work of the ship. Later, when two more stowaways are discovered, Rodolfo and the rest of the crew must decide whether to obey orders or to follow their conscience." Libr J

"This is a moving, haunting novel, full of deeply sympathetic portraits of common people being uncommonly brave." Publ Wkly

House, Silas, 1971-

A parchment of leaves; a novel. Algonquin Bks. 2002 278p $23.95

ISBN 1-565-12367-0 LC 2002-66570

"In 1917 rural Kentucky, a young Cherokee woman named Vine, rumored to cast spells on unsuspecting men, falls in love with local Irishman Saul Sullivan, whom she eventually marries. . . (This novel) tells the story of Vine and Saul's tender relationship and the prejudice they face and eventually overcome." Libr J

"This is a moving love story set against a stunningly beautiful background, and House seems to capture it all—the deep emotion, the love of land, the customs of mountain people—in quietly eloquent prose." Booklist

House, Tom

The beginning of calamities; a novel. Bridge Works 2005 288p $24.95

ISBN 1-88259-369-3 LC 2002-152049

This novel is "set in the mid-1970s in a blue-collar Long Island town. Shy, awkward, 11-year-old Danny recreates the Passion of Christ as a school play to be performed for his fellow parochial school students during Holy Week. Impressed by his initiative, Danny's young teacher, Liz Kaigh, gets caught up in producing and directing the piece, whose troupe of players is eventually composed of the class misfits. The author effectively depicts Danny's constant personal angst and spiritual longings within the context of religious suffering but also manages to add a note of dark humor." Libr J

Houston, Pam

Cowboys are my weakness; stories. Norton 1992 171p o.p.

LC 91-12920

Contents: How to talk to a hunter; Selway; Highwater; For Bo; What Shock heard; Dall; Cowboys are my weakness; Jackson is only one of my dogs; A blizzard under blue sky; Sometimes you talk about Idaho; Symphony; In my next life

"Short stories, mostly first-person, told with verve and perfect pitch by women entangled with wild men in a cruel world." N Y Times Book Rev

Waltzing the cat. Norton 1998 288p o.p.

ISBN 0-393-02749-X LC 98-10562

Contents: The best girlfriend you never had; Cataract; Waltzing the cat; Three lessons in Amazonian biology; The moon is a woman's first husband; Moving from one body of water to another; Like goodness under your feet; Then you get up and have breakfast; The kind of people you trust with your life; The whole weight of me

This collection "is far from perfect, but Houston's vigorous voice and lively take on what it's like to be a woman both physically bold and hopelessly romantic are to be cherished nonetheless." N Y Times Book Rev

Howard, Maureen, 1930-

Big as life; three tales for spring. Viking 2001 225p il $23.95

ISBN 0-670-89978-X LC 2001-17904

Howard, Maureen, 1930-—*Continued*

"In 'Children with Matches,' a history professor unexpectedly inherits her family's dilapidated estate, while her lover, a famous economist, fears for his life in war-warped Africa. A young Irish woman's beauty brings her nothing but grief until she finds her calling as an army nurse in World War II, in 'The Magdalene.' And Audubon and his longsuffering wife are the subjects of the title story." Booklist

"Although Howard's style can be too ellipitical for its own good (a fault that sometimes extends to her dialogue and that produces the odd longueur), it just as often succeeds in gorgeously evoking the movement of lives and minds and emotions. . . . This is a quiet and contemplative book of subtlety and grace, passion and commitment." Atl Mon

Big as life [novelette]
In Howard, M. Big as life

Children with matches
In Howard, M. Big as life

The Magdalene
In Howard, M. Big as life

Natural history; a novel. Norton 1992 393p il o.p.
LC 92-7041

This novel "relates the tortured history of the Brays, an Irish-American family living in Bridgeport, Connecticut, at the close of World War II. As adults, James and Catherine leave home but cannot come to terms with their lives, for they are trapped in the shadow of their bigger-than-life father. . . . [One section of the book] juxtaposes the storyline with facts and myths about Bridgeport notables, among them P.T. Barnum, Robert Mitchum, and Walt Kelly of Pogo fame." Libr J

This is a "novel always in the midst of breaking free of itself, its pages filled with brilliant variations on the screenplay, the encyclopedia, the diary, and, of course, the history book." New Repub

Howatch, Susan

Absolute truths; a novel. Knopf 1995 559p o.p.
LC 94-27510

Sixth in the Church of England series, this novel "is set during the mid-1960s, the period during which the Church of England . . . was rocked by widespread challenges to tradition. Again representing tradition is narrator Charles Ashworth, The Anglican Bishop of Starbridge. . . . Ashworth's archenemy—and doppelgänger—is Neville Aysgarth, the Dean of the Cathedral who is, according to Ashworth, unorthodoxly open to using the trappings of a capitalistic marketplace to benefit the financially deteriorating church building. To make matters worse, Aysgarth is an alleged dipsomaniac and womanizer, who once made a pass at Ashworth's beloved wife, Lyle. When Lyle dies suddenly, the bereaved widower strays dangerously from the fold." Publ Wkly

Cashelmara. Simon & Schuster 1974 702p o.p.

Divided into six sections, each narrated by a different character, this novel charts "the lives of three generations of the Anglo-Irish de Salis family between 1859 and 1891. They move between London homes, a Warwickshire estate, New York and Boston—where two Lords de Salis find their wives—but end always at the great white house on their Irish estate, Cashelmara. In the background are the simmering troubles between starving Irish tenants and callous English landlords." Christ Sci Monit

"With a copiousness of detail studded with adventure, rape, depravity, intrigue, and murder, the story plays out with clarity and brilliance." Best Sellers

Glamorous powers. Knopf 1988 403p o.p.
LC 88-45347

This "novel, the second in the Church of England series that began with 'Glittering Images,' weaves an intriguing and wholly involving story out of the otherwise sober subject of Christian mysticism in the 20th-century Church of England. Howatch's chief characters are a clerical odd couple, rivals since their Cambridge days: Jonathan Darrow, a 60-year-old Anglo-Catholic monk with 'glamorous' psychic powers, and his Abbot-General, Francis Ingram, a practical, eloquent, urbane man with sophisticated insight into modern psychology. . . . The wisdom of 'Glamorous Powers' lies in the deft way it aligns psychological and spiritual truths to bring about healing in the broadest sense." N Y Times Book Rev

Followed by Ultimate prizes

Glittering images. Knopf 1987 399p o.p.
LC 87-45130

This, the first in the Church of England series, "takes place in pre-World War II England, just after Edward VIII abdicated to marry the divorced Wallis Simpson. The event is emblematic, for this novel is about marriage and divorce and proper behavior within a religious context. . . . The narrator is a young intellectual cleric, Charles Ashworth, who is sent by the Archbishop of Canterbury to spy on Alex Jardine, the charismatic, liberal Bishop of Starbridge. Ashworth uncovers evidence in Jardine's household—which includes a depressive wife and her pretty female companion—of sexual scandal and a highly irregular interpretation of Anglican dogma. The revelation of the mystery of Starbridge sends Ashworth into a personal crisis of faith." N Y Times Book Rev

"An ambitious and lifelike work of uncommon depth." Booklist

Followed by Glamorous powers

The heartbreaker. Knopf 2004 c2003 483p $25
ISBN 1-4000-4147-3 LC 2003-62493

This title "in Howatch's series of novels investigating the juncture of the sacred and the profane in contemporary British life is set a little more than a decade ago in London's financial center, known as the City. Carta Graham, a former lawyer, had come somewhat unglued upon the death of her husband, and the good people at St. Benet's Church helped her through this life crisis. In turn, she now works for the church as its chief fundraiser. An old friend announces his intention to donate a large sum of money and the fact that he is besotted by a person he's been seeing outside his marriage. When he dies soon after these proclamations, Carta discovers that the person he had been head over heels in love with is a male prostitute, Gavin by name." Booklist

"Plot improbabilities and long sections of spiritual musing are redeemed by Howatch's strongly drawn characters: if Carta can come across as brittle and prudish, Gavin's self-absorbed cant is continually entertaining." Publ Wkly

Howatch, Susan—*Continued*

The high flyer; a novel. Knopf 2000 500p o.p.
ISBN 0-375-41057-0 LC 99-58953
First published 1999 in the United Kingdom
In this novel "success-driven London lawyer Carter Graham is suddenly confronted with phenomena that test the coping abilities of her liberated, modern mind. The quintessential 'high flyer,' Carter has broken through the glass ceiling and become a partner in the prestigious law firm of Curtis, Towers. Recently married to Kim Betz, a handsome banker almost 15 years her senior, Carter lives in the 'right' apartment complex, drives a Porsche and is thinking of having a baby. However, Kim's hidden past (involvement with Nazis, the occult, group sex and an unsavory psychic healer named Mrs. Mayfield) threatens Carter's carefully orchestrated life plan." Publ Wkly
"A suspense novel mixed with Gothic overtones and spiritual dimensions, this story works on almost every level." Libr J

Mystical paths; a novel. Knopf 1992 433p o.p.
LC 91-58557
This novel is fifth in the Church of England series. "At 25, Nicholas Darrow, scion of eminent churchman Jonathan Darrow [featured in Glamorous powers] has inherited his father's psychic gifts, but overconfidence in his abilities and a dangerously frayed relationship with his father lead him close to the edge of an emotional abyss. Asked by the widow of his friend Christian Aysgarth to investigate her husband's death—Christian was drowned when swept overboard while sailing, but she fears that he committed suicide—Nick embarks on a quest that uncovers dark secrets in the linked lives of his friends and family." Publ Wkly
"Although this is all rather formulaic, Howatch has discovered that the Christian story is essentially a romance, and she has exploited this with considerable intelligence." Booklist
Followed by Absolute truths

Penmarric. Simon & Schuster 1971 735p o.p.
Set against the landscape of Cornwall, this novel relates the "life and amours of brutally selfish Mark Castallack through the end of the Victorian era and . . . the lives and amours of his children, legitimate and illegitimate and their progeny." America
"Throughout the story, the author keeps the reader aware of the great historical precedent and parallel for her fiction; the love of Henry II and Eleanor of Aquitaine; preceding each chapter are two pertinent quotations about that royal couple and the king's progeny. It is a neat and useful device, adding piquancy and historical flavor to an interesting tale." Best Sellers

Scandalous risks. Knopf 1990 385p o.p.
LC 90-53076
This novel, fourth in the Church of England series, is "narrated by Venetia Flaxton, a young woman of intellect and means but no direction, and centers around her strange affair in 1963 with 61-year-old Neville Aysgarth, dean of Starbridge Cathedral. Related mainly through their letters and conversations, the progress—and explosive dissolution—of their relationship is set in the context of a real-life theological controversy in England crystallized by the publication of *Honest to God*, a best-selling, situational-ethics view of God's relevance to modern man." Publ Wkly
"With sculptor's hands fashioning rich, lustrous three-dimensional characters, Howatch brilliantly shows how and why the situation between Venetia and her 'Mr. Dean' arose, flourished, then died away." Booklist
Followed by Mystical paths

Sins of the fathers. Simon & Schuster 1980 608p o.p.
"A sequel to 'The Rich Are Different,' (1977) this . . . family saga traces the fortunes of the Van Zales of New York City from the late 1940's through the 1960's. Cornelius, head of the clan and president of the Van Zale Bank, has not shed his killer instinct, and habitually uses raw power to mask his personal inadequacies. His cut-throat tactics have far-reaching adverse effects on friends and family, particularly on his vulnerable daughter Vicki. . . . The novel is narrated by six characters in sequence." Libr J
The author, "witty storyteller that she is, picks her way through a mind-boggling tangle of marriages and motives with the greatest of ease, never losing or confusing the reader." Publ Wkly

Ultimate prizes. Knopf 1989 387p o.p.
LC 89-45303
This, third novel in the Church of England series, "is narrated by Neville Aysgarth, an ambitious archdeacon in the fictional English diocese of Starbridge. A brilliant administrator with a firm, practical faith in God and the Church of England, Neville has steadily moved up in life by 'chasing the prizes,' overcoming his humble birth and troubled youth to win for himself a perfect wife, a flock of delightful children and a powerful position, all before age 40. During his climb to success he has kept his mind as tidy as his diocese by relentlessly 'ringing down the curtain'—a mental curtain, that is—on disturbing memories and desires. But alas for Neville, his curtain is shortly to be twitched off its rod, first by an infatuation with a young society girl, then by a death in his family." N Y Times Book Rev
Followed by Scandalous risks

The wheel of fortune. Simon & Schuster 1984 973p o.p.
LC 84-5357
This "saga, based loosely upon the tragedies that beset Edward of Woodstock (the Black Prince) and his descendants, is 'a recreation in a modern dimension.' A cycle of tragedy plagues the descendants of a lecherous Robert Godwin, who allows the glittering family manor, Oxmoon, to disintegrate into rat fodder until his heirs take decisive action. The treasured Welsh estate is restored to its former grandeur, but a legacy of enormous guilt and a pattern of adultery and murder haunt further inheritors of Oxmoon." Booklist
This "absorbing novel convincingly demonstrates that a family saga can be more than the mere 'show and tell' of one generation following another. By using six different narrators to recount five generations of a 20th-century Welsh family, the author deftly supplies multiple viewpoints of events." Libr J

The wonder-worker. Knopf 1997 529p o.p.
ISBN 0-375-40102-4 LC 97-36886
"The narrative examines the self-delusions to which priests are susceptible as they deal with their own humanity. Nicholas Darrow, 45, first met in *Mystical Paths* is a gifted healer whose pre-conversion past is filled with

Howatch, Susan—*Continued*
hobgoblins and parlor tricks. He is sexually alluring but seems capable of keeping his responsibilities wisely in balance. Everyone is just waiting for him to show himself as fallible. And it happens, with disastrous consequences for the people within his orbit: Lewis, an older priest; a homely cook named Alice; a younger priest, Stacy; and Darrow's wife, Rosalind." Publ Wkly

"The setting is St. Benet's, a London parish church, and while every character displays a level of eccentricity verging on the gothic, Howatch's good-humored tone keeps the whole—just—from collapsing." New Yorker

Howells, William Dean, 1837-1920

A foregone conclusion
In Howells, W. D. Novels, 1875-1886

Indian summer
In Howells, W. D. Novels, 1875-1886

A modern instance
In Howells, W. D. Novels, 1875-1886

Novels, 1875-1886; . Literary Classics of the U.S. 1983 1217p $40
ISBN 0-940450-04-6 LC 82-112

Contents: A foregone conclusion; A modern instance; Indian summer; The rise of Silas Lapham

A foregone conclusion (1875) describes the love triangle between American expatriate Florida Vervain, American painter Henry Ferris, and lapsed priest Don Ippolito. In A modern instance (1882), Bartley Hubbard, an unscrupulous and philandering journalist is divorced by his wife and subsequently murdered by one of the individuals scandalized in his newspaper. In Indian summer (1886), Theodore Coville, a middle-aged American vacationing in Florence meets an old acquaintance and one of her young friends, eventually sparking relationships with each of them. The rise of Silas Lapham is entered separately.

The rise of Silas Lapham; with an introduction by Kermit Vanderbilt. Penguin Books 1986 xxxi, 368p pa $12
ISBN 0-14-039030-8

First published 1885

"Silas is a crude, uneducated man who makes his fortune by methods not above criticism, but manly and capable of better things when his conscience is awakened—a compendium of human virtues and vices, drawn with insight, tenderness and humor. The efforts of the prosperous Laphams to get into Boston society, with their mistakes and disillusionments, the sentimental tragicomedy of the two daughters, in love with the same young man; and Lapham's business troubles, are more or less neatly woven in to make the plot." Baker. Guide to the Best Fic

also in Howells, W. D. Novels, 1875-1886

Hrabal, Bohumil, 1914-1997

I served the King of England; [translated by Paul Wilson] Harcourt Brace Jovanovich 1989 243p o.p.
ISBN 0-15-145745-X LC 88-16482

This novel "is a picaresque allegory of 20th-century Czechoslovak history as lived and narrated by a short hotel waiter by the name of Ditie, meaning child. Rising from one hotel to another, each a stage of his country's history, he marries a Nazi during the war, and in the postwar years at last realizes his dream of becoming a millionaire, only to see his wealth vanish under Communism." N Y Times Book Rev

This novel "is a flood of meandering garrulous narration, with dreamlike, filmlike sequences, hyperbolic, grotesque and farcical analogues of familiar historical fact. No sober account, this, of how it might actually have been, yet still it projects through its debunking prism the shallowness, absurdity and cruelty of how it indeed was." Times Lit Suppl

Too loud a solitude; translated from the Czech by Michael Henry Heim. Harcourt Brace Jovanovich 1990 98p o.p.
ISBN 0-15-190491-X LC 90-4313

"In this novella, written in 1976, . . . [the narrator] Hanta meditates on the 35 years he has spent at a hydraulic press in a dark cellar, compacting waste paper and books proscribed by various regimes. Though he no longer weeps or protests when rare treasures appear in his press, the books that he must destroy become his whole life, his only companions. When he is to be replaced by young workers with a more productive machine, Hanta dreams of a gigantic press that destroys not only himself but the entire city, with its traditions and culture." Libr J

"This is indeed Franz Kafka's Prague. . . . The book is funny, in its desperate, knockabout way. Along with Hant'a's incessant reading goes excessive swilling of beer, and the tone throughout is at once strident and woozy, so that the reader has the impression of being trapped in that basement room as the press grinds and the drunken operator rummages through the tatters of a ruined culture." N Y Rev Books

Huddle, David, 1942-

La Tour dreams of the wolf girl. Houghton Mifflin 2002 196p $24
ISBN 0-618-08173-9 LC 2001-16915

"Shifting between two narratives—one concerning an unhappy wife in present-day Vermont, the other involving the 17th-century French painter Georges de La Tour and a 15-year-old model—the novel's premise sounds like a prescription for historical, escapist entertainment. But anyone looking for easy distraction or predictable romance will be disappointed; Huddle's book offers more complex pleasures. A study of the relation between art and life, the novel has an honesty and psychological depth that are at times painfully real and quietly moving." N Y Times Book Rev

Hudson, Jeffery *See* Crichton, Michael, 1942-

Hudson, W. H. (William Henry), 1841-1922

Green mansions; a romance of the tropical forest. Putnam 1904 315p o.p.

"The hero, Mr. Abel, tells the tragic story of his love for the bird girl, Rima, an ethereal maiden whose jungle upbringing has brought her close to the powers and beau-

Hudson, W. H. (William Henry), 1841-1922— *Continued*

ty of nature. Abel has just succeeded in awakening the human emotion of love in the half-wild girl when she is killed by a band of savages." Reader's Ency. 3d edition

Hudson, William Henry *See* Hudson, W. H. (William Henry), 1841-1922

Huebner, Andrew

We Pierce; a novel. Simon & Schuster 2003 278p $24

ISBN 0-7432-1277-0 LC 2003-41618

This autobiographical novel "relates the story of two brothers: one whose sense of duty propels him into the Gulf War as a tank commander, the other whose equally strong sense of his duty to protest war leads him eventually to New York to ultimately fight a war of his own." Booklist

"The emotional impact builds even when the events being described are somewhat predictable, and the characters are richly individualized." Publ Wkly

Hueffer, Ford Madox *See* Ford, Ford Madox, 1873-1939

Hughes, Langston, 1902-1967

Laughing to keep from crying. Holt & Co. 1952 206p o.p.

Contents: Who's passing for who?; Something in common; African morning; Pushcart man; Why, you reckon; Saratoga rain; Spanish blood; Heaven to hell; Sailor ashore; Slice him down; Tain't so; One Friday morning; Professor; Name in the papers; Powder-white faces; Rouge high; On the way home; Mysterious Madame Shanghai; Never room with a couple; Little old spy; Tragedy at the Baths; Trouble with the angels; On the road; Big meeting

Not without laughter. Knopf 1930 324p o.p.

This novel portrays the lives of a poor black family in a small Kansas town

"A sympathetic portrayal, unmarred by bitterness or sentimentality, of a people to whom life, no matter how hard, was not without laughter." Booklist

Short stories of Langston Hughes; edited by Akiba Sullivan Harper; with an introduction by Arnold Rampersad. Hill & Wang 1996 299p o.p.

ISBN 0-8090-8658-1 LC 95-19554

"Dating from 1919 to 1963, these pieces vary in theme, covering life at sea, the trials and tribulations of a young pianist and her elderly white patron, a visiting writer's experience in Cuba, a young girl's winning an art scholarship but losing it when it's learned she is black, and an ambitious black preacher trying to gain fame by being nailed to a cross. If you crave good reading don't pass up this gem." Libr J

Simple speaks his mind. Simon & Schuster 1950 231p o.p.

The central figure, is a Harlem black who expresses his views on many subjects, but always from the point of view of his own race. He dislikes whites, and makes no bones of it. Some of his favorite topics are women, landladies especially, parties, and beer

"Simple is completely frank in his opinions about white people; he dislikes them intensely. The race problem is never absent, but the flow of the book is lighthearted and easy." N Y Times Book Rev

Simple stakes a claim. Rinehart 1957 191p o.p.

In this book Simple, of Harlem, speaks his mind on a variety of subjects, ranging from housing conditions, to sex magazines

Simple takes a wife. Simon & Schuster 1953 240p o.p.

"Before Mr. Jesse B. Semple, the untutored philosopher of the Harlem rooming-house set, can divorce his wife and espouse the morally impeccable Joyce, he has to run the gauntlet of many problems. He discourses on them in Harlem bars over beers he has cadged from his sympathetic and more literate listener. Under the folklike humor of 'Simple's' monologs runs a bitter undercurrent of racial consciousness." Booklist

Simple's Uncle Sam. Hill & Wang 1965 180p o.p.

Contents: Census; Swinging high; Contest; Empty houses; The blues; God's other side; Color problems; The moon; Domesticated; Bomb shelters; Gospel singers; Nothing but a dog; Roots and trees; For President; Atomic dream; Lost wife; Self-protection; Haircuts and Paris; Adventure; Minnie's hype; Yachts; Ladyhood; Coffee break; Lynn Clarisse; Interview; Simply Simple; Golden Gate; Junkies; Dog days; Pose-outs; Soul food; Flay or pray; Not colored; Cracker prayer; Rude awakening; Miss Boss; Dr. Sidesaddle; Wigs for freedom; Concernment; Statutes and statues; American dilemma; Promulgations; How old is old; Weight in god; Sympathy; Uncle Sam

Hughes, Richard Arthur Warren, 1900-1976

A high wind in Jamaica; [by] Richard Hughes; introduction by Francine Prose. New York Review Books 1999 c1929 279p pa $12.95 o.p.

ISBN 0-940322-15-3 LC 99-14565

First published 1929 by Harper with title: The innocent voyage

"A family of children living in Jamaica in the 19th century are sent to England after a hurricane has partly destroyed their home. Amiable pirates capture them by mistake, and the children bring about the pirates' ruin; one girl becomes a murderess. The irrational, amoral world of children is powerfully conveyed." Reader's Ency. 4th edition

Hugo, Victor, 1802-1885

The hunchback of Notre Dame; revised translation and notes by Catherine Liu; introduction by Elizabeth McCracken. Modern Library 2002 xxviii, 483p pa $11.95

ISBN 0-679-64257-9 LC 2002-18917

Original French edition, 1930. Variant title: Notre Dame de Paris

The hidden force of fate is symbolized by the superhuman grandeur and multitudinous imageries of the cathedral. "The first part . . . is a panorama of medieval

Hugo, Victor, 1802-1885—*Continued*
life—religious, civic, popular, and criminal—drawn with immense learning and an amazing command of spectacular effect. These elements are then set in motion in a fantastic and grandiose drama, of which the personages are romantic sublimations of human virtues and passions—Quasimodo the hunchback, faithful unto death; Esmeralda, incarnation of innocence and steadfastness; Claude Frolla, Faust-like type of the antagonism between religion and appetite. Splendors and absurdities, the sublime and the grotesque are inextricably mingled in this strange romance. The date is fixed at the year 1482." Baker. Guide to the Best Fic

Les misérables; translated from the French by Charles E. Wilbour; with an introduction by Peter Washington. Knopf 1997 xxxvii, 1432p $27
ISBN 0-375-40317-5 LC 98-156450
"Everyman's library"
Original French edition, 1862
"A panorama of French life in the first half of the [nineteenth] century, aiming to exhibit the fabric of civilization in all its details, and to reveal the cruelty of its pressure on the poor, the outcast, and the criminal. Jean Valjean, a man intrinsically noble, thru the tyranny of society becomes a criminal. His conscience is reawakened by the ministrations of the saintly Bishop Myriel . . . and Valjean, reformed and prosperous, follows in the good bishop's footsteps as an apostle of benevolence, only to be doomed again by the law to slavery and shame. The 'demimondaine' Fantine, another victim of society; her daughter Cosette one of those whom suffering makes sublime; Marius, an ideal of youth and love; Myriel, the incarnation of Christian charity, are the leading characters of this huge morality, which is thronged with representatives of the good in man and the cruelty of society. Magnificent description . . . scenes invested with terror, awe, repulsion, alternate with tedious rhapsodies. Realism mingles with the incredible." Baker. Guide to the Best Fic

The **Hugo** winners; edited by Isaac Asimov. Doubleday 1962-1986 5v

v1 Novelettes are: The darfsteller, by W. M. MIller; Exploration team, by M. Leinster; The big front yard, by C. D. Simak; Flowers for Algernon, by D. Keyes ; The longest voyage, by P. Anderson. Short stories are: Allamagoosa, by E. F. Russell; The star, by A. C. Clarke; Or all seas with oysters, by A. Davidson; The hellbound train, by R. Bloch

v2 Novelettes are: The last castle, by J. Vance; Weyrsearch, by A. McCaffrey; Riders of the purple wage, by P. J. Farmer; Gonna roll the bones, by F. Leiber; Nightwings, by R. Silverberg; The sharing of flesh, by P. Anderson. Short stories are: The dragon masters, by J. Vance; No truce with kings, by P. Anderson; Soldier, ask not, by G. R. Dickson; "Repent, Harlequin!", said the Ticktock-man, by H. Ellison; Neutron star, by L. Niven; I have no mouth, and I must scream, by H. Ellison; The beast that shouted love at the heart of the world, by H. Ellison; Time considered as a helix of semi-precious stones, by S. R. Delany

v3 Novelettes are: Ship of shadows, by F. Leiber; III met in Lankhmar, by F. Leiber; The Queen of Air and Darkness, P. Anderson; The word for world is forest, by U. K. LeGuin; Goat song, by P. Anderson. Short stories are: Slow sculpture, by T. Sturgeon; Inconstant moon, by L. Niven; The meeting, by F. Pohl; Eurema's dam, by R. Lafferty; The girl who was plugged in, by J. Tiptree; The deathbird, by H. Ellison; The ones who walk away from Omelas, by U. K. LeGuin; A song for Lya, by G. R. R. Martin; Adrift just off the islets of Langerhans: lattitude 38° 54' N, longitude 77° 00' 13' W, by H. Ellison; The hole man, by L. Niven

v4 Novelettes are: Home is the hangman, by R. Zelazny; By any other name, by S. Robinson; Houston, Houston, do you read? by J. Triptree; The Bicentennial Man, by I. Asimov; Stardance, by S. Robinson; The persistence of vision, by J. Varley; Hunter's moon, by P. Anderson. Short stories are: The borderland of Sol, by L. Niven; Catch that Zeppelin, by F. Leiber; Tricentennial, by J. Haldeman; Eyes of amber, by J. D. Vinge; Jefftyis five, by H. Ellison; Cassandra, by C. J. Cherryh

v5 Novelettes are: Enemy mine, by B. B. Longyear; Sandkings, by G. R. R. Martin; Lost Dorsai, by G. R. Dickson; The cloak and the staff, by G. R. Dickson; The Saturn game, by P. Anderson. Short stories are: The way of cross and dragon, by G. R. R. Martin; Grotto of the dancing deer, by C. D. Simak; Unicorn variations, by R. Zelazny; The pusher, by J. Varley

The stories and novelettes included in these volumes won the Hugo Awards from 1939-1982

Hulme, Juliet *See* Perry, Anne, 1938-

Hulme, Kathryn, 1900-1981

The nun's story. Little, Brown 1956 339p o.p.
"Convent life, with its rigors and its compensations, has seldom been as fairly depicted as in this biographical account. An unhappy love affair was one of the reasons why 'Gabrielle Van der Mal' [fictitious name] entered a convent in Belgium, but her love of God and desire to serve her fellow men were also important influences. For 17 years she tried diligently to discipline her analytical and independent mind through prayer and hard work as a nurse, first in a hospital for the insane, then in a Congo mission, and finally in a TB sanatorium in occupied Holland. Ultimately, she faced the bitter truth that the religious life, with its inflexible authority, was not for her, and she was released from her vows." Libr J

Hulme, Keri

The bone people; a novel. Louisiana State Univ. Press 1985 c1983 450p o.p.
LC 85-12937
First published 1984 in New Zealand
"Hulme's novel tells the story of three people in rural New Zealand, Kerewin, a part-Maori woman; Joe, a Maori man; and Simon, Pakeba (European) child whom Joe finds washed up on the shore during a storm. Joe alternately loves the child passionately and thrashes him brutally. Although they are 'different and difficult people,' isolated from those around them, they are drawn into an intense relationship." Choice

"This novel is unforgettably rich and pungent. . . . Set on the harsh South Island beaches of New Zealand, bound in Maori myth and entwined with Christian symbols, Miss Hulme's provocative novel summons power with words, as in a conjurer's spell." N Y Times Book Rev

Humphreys, Helen, 1961-

Afterimage; a novel. Metropolitan Bks. 2001 240p $23

ISBN 0-8050-6666-7 LC 00-46907

First published 2000 in Canada

"It's 1865, in England, and both Isabelle Dashell and her husband, Eldon, are making pictures. She's intent on mastering a new medium, photography, and he's seeking renown as a cartographer. When Annie Phelan, a sober beauty orphaned by the Irish famine, answers their ad for a housemaid, she becomes Isabelle's muse and Eldon's confidante, and finds herself pressed into the service of art. Inspired by the work of Julia Margaret Cameron, this urgent, well-made novel charts the boundaries where light becomes shadow, and the known can suddenly appear awful and astonishing." New Yorker

The lost garden. Norton 2002 183p $23.95

ISBN 0-393-05183-8 LC 2002-26308

In this novel, set in the English countryside of 1941, "Gwen Davis, a desperately lonely botanist employed by the Royal Horticultural Society to investigate canker in parsnips, has signed up to direct young women agricultural volunteers on an estate requisitioned for the war effort. Humphreys is a metaphysical novelist; for her, intricate emotional content finds specific analogues in the made world—an astonishing photograph or, as here, an overgrown garden that, once cleared, reveals its consoling secrets." New Yorker

Humphreys, Josephine

The fireman's fair. Viking 1991 263p o.p.

ISBN 0-670-83907-8 LC 90-50575

"Rob Wyatt, unmarried at 32, has quit his job as a lawyer, moved out of a luxury apartment to poor housing, sold his Alfa for a cheap used car, and is looking for a new kind of life. Hurricane Hugo almost devastates the southern town in which he lives and also seems to have swept an uprooting storm through his personal life. His unceasing love for Louise, now married to wealthy Frank Camden, becomes not so firm when Billy Poe, 18 years old and naively innocent (or precociously wise) comes into Rob's life. She is a healer in her innocent wisdom and the novel has an ending especially welcome as a change from many violent and depressing contemporary novels." Shapiro. Fic for Youth. 3d edition

Nowhere else on earth. Viking 2000 341p o.p.

ISBN 0-670-89176-2 LC 00-36666

"In 1864, Rhoda Strong is a teenager of mixed ancestry in Scuffletown, an Indian settlement on the Lumbee River, in North Carolina. As the town's inhabitants find themselves caught between marauding Union soldiers and Confederates attempting to conscript their children for labor, Rhoda falls in love with a local outlaw who is fighting to protect the community. Humphreys has always been a master of telling a larger story through a deceptively intimate narrative, and Rhoda's tale, with its clear, distinct voice, is no exception." New Yorker

Hunt, Walter H.

The dark path. TOR Bks. 2003 413p $27.95

ISBN 0-7653-0606-9 LC 2002-38757

"A Tom Doherty Associates book"

Sequel to: The dark wing (2001)

"The war between the human and zor races has ended, and both have learned to coexist on the borders of the Solar Empire. When some Exploration Service vessels disappear, Ch'k'te, a young zor 'Sensitive,' senses a dark presence at the root of the trouble. Ordered to deal with the escalating series of events, Commodore Jacqueline Lapierre must draw upon her own skills, along with zor mysticism, to confront an enemy that threatens the existence of both races." Libr J

Hunter, Evan, 1926-2005

For works written by this author under other names see McBain, Ed, 1926-2005

The blackboard jungle. Simon & Schuster 1954 309p o.p.

A story "of an idealistic young man, facing the bitter realities of being a teacher in the frighteningly brutal world of a big city vocational high school. A near-rape, student sluggings, a knifing—all these plus a strong indictment of the inadequacies of routine teachers college preparation in helping teachers to learn how to discipline near-morons and prospective or actual delinquents." Libr J

"The author has not used his shocking material merely to appall. With a superb ear for conversation, with competence as a storyteller, and with a tolerant and tough-minded sympathy for his subject, he has built an extremely good novel." N Y Her Trib Books

Candyland; a novel in two parts; [by] Evan Hunter and Ed McBain. Simon & Schuster 2001 301p $25

ISBN 0-7432-1316-5 LC 00-49684

This novel "is written in two parts. The first half, attributed to Hunter, probes the psyche of Benjamin Thorpe, a sexually obsessed Los Angeles architect on the prowl in New York. The second half, attributed to McBain, is a police procedural in which a detective, Emma Boyle, investigates the murder of a prostitute and identifies the architect as a prime suspect. The novel is a gimmick, and it is a surprise that it works at all. That it works so superbly is a tribute to the skills of this great storyteller." N Y Times Book Rev

The Chisholms; a novel of the journey West. Harper & Row 1976 208p o.p.

This novel about the early nineteenth-century pioneer experience "tracks Hadley Chisholm and family, leaving their unproductive Virginia homeland to find a better life in California; the journey [which is followed up to their departure from Fort Laramie in Wyoming] is arduous, to say the least, for every member of the household." Booklist

"An affectingly spare, closely seen recreation of the pioneer spirit and what the search for new opportunity signified." Publ Wkly

Lizzie. Arbor House 1984 430p o.p.

LC 83-15642

"By legend, Lizzie Borden, a New England spinster, axed her father and stepmother to death one summer day in 1892. Writing fictionally about Lizzie and those horrible crimes, popular novelist Hunter uses actual inquest and trial material, but counterpoints the attempted resolu-

Hunter, Evan, 1926-2005—*Continued*
tion of the murders in that small Massachusetts town with invented events during a European trip that Lizzie took a couple of years previous. It is this trip wherein lie the seeds for the slaying of Mr. and Mrs. Borden, for Lizzie's latent lesbianism surfaces in Europe and leads her to desperate acts when she returns home." Booklist

"The portrait of Lizzie that emerges is fascinating, ultimately sympathetic: a murderess yes, but the victim of the repression and sexual exploitation of her time." Libr J

The moment she was gone; a novel. Simon & Schuster 2002 208p $25
ISBN 0-7432-0269-4 LC 2002-70532

"Andrew Gulliver is the first-person narrator, a New York teacher who learns that his flighty, erratic sister, Annie, has disappeared, leaving her family with no clue as to her destination or whereabouts." Publ Wkly

Hunter "is a masterfully adept storyteller and a very shrewd observer of human behavior. . . . Powerful reading." Booklist

"Carella and Meyer must team up on a murder investigation with Fat Ollie Weeks of the 88th because the lion habitat at the Isola Zoo straddles the boundary between the two precincts and one of the lions dragged part of a victim's body onto the 88th's turf. The body in the lion's den leads the detectives to several things: to a burglary, or at least the burglar; to some strange doings by the Secret Service; to some pretty big local drug dealers; and, finally, to some big-time dealers who don't mind leaving bodies strewn about." Libr J

Privileged conversation. Warner Bks. 1996 326p o.p.
LC 95-11148

"Psychiatrist David Chapman intervenes as Kate Duggan is mugged in Central Park on a beautiful summer day. While his wife vacations with their daughters, Chapman finds himself drawn into a passionate affair with Duggan. The novel, told from Chapman's point of view, moves back and forth from his sessions with patients to his deepening involvement with Duggan. Chapman sneaks back into New York City during his annual August vacation to spend time with Duggan, just as she begins getting letters and veiled threats from a stalker." Booklist

"Mr. Hunter is smart enough to poke fun at the book's echoes of 'Fatal Attraction.' Even better, he has a good feel for Dr. Chapman's midlife crisis and for the petty annoyances of New York social life." N Y Times Book Rev

Hunter, Stephen, 1946-

Black light. Doubleday 1996 463p o.p.
LC 95-43079

This suspense "novel pairs Russ, the son of State Trooper Bud Pewtie from *Dirty White Boys* and sharpshooter Bob Lee Swagger (*Point of Impact*, 1993) as they dig into a decades-old cover-up that has the entire Arkansas power structure in a lather trying to keep buried. In a parallel story, Bob Lee's father, Earl, is trying to solve a mysterious abduction and murder that crosses the strictly divided racial lines of the time and place while trying to bring down an escaped convict he swore to reform in a battlefield oath." Libr J

"Mr. Hunter, who is a powerful and disturbing writer, tells this unholy story in a heroic style that gives mythic sweep to the generational waves of violence that seem to have had no beginning and threaten to have no end." N Y Times Book Rev

Dirty white boys; a novel. Random House 1994 436p o.p.
LC 94-15359

"After killing a black inmate, the brutal Lamar Pye breaks out of the Oklahoma State Penitentiary along with his retarded cousin, Odell, and a hapless artist-turned-felon named Richard. They embark on a desperate run across Oklahoma and Texas, pursued by state troopers. The escapees hide out with a convict groupie who has lived alone since murdering her parents as an adolescent. In a parody of domesticity, Lamar embraces these losers as the family he never knew." Libr J

"The blood-soaked packaging of Mr. Hunter's big, mythic theme is thrilling, in the manner of the ancient storytellers, with battles fierce enough for a war and characters crazy enough to fight them to the death. There is no place to run for cover from this author's prose—no glades of pretty writing to cool his vision of a land of lost children, forgotten values and total desolation." NY Times Book Rev

Havana; an Earl Swagger novel. Simon & Schuster 2003 403p $24.95
ISBN 0-7432-3808-7 LC 2003-54461

"Fifty years ago the mob was enjoying huge profits from its extensive Cuban enterprises. The only cause for concern is a young lawyer named Fidel Castro. Under the auspices of the CIA, an assassination plot is advanced and an unsuspecting Earl Swagger, a Medal of Honor winner and legendary tough guy, is brought in as the shooter. The Communists are also interested in Fidel, and Speshnev, a KGB operator, is brought in to protect their investment. Earl and Speshnev soon discover their efforts are better directed at neutralizing the mob, the corrupt government, and their respective spy agencies." Libr J

"Havana's story line bobs and weaves like a prizefighter, taking the reader in many directions, from barely exciting scenes to intense ones." USA Today

Hot Springs; a novel. Simon & Schuster 2000 478p $25
ISBN 0-684-86360-X LC 99-88530

Earl Swagger is "a no-nonsense marine who was awarded the Medal of Honor for heroism on Iwo Jima. After the war, Earl works as a foreman in a sawmill. But when he is offered a job training a group of young lawmen whose mandate is to rid Hot Springs, Ark., of its mob-run gambling houses, he eagerly accepts. . . . As Earl's deputies attempt to clean up Hot Springs, Earl's fearlessness makes his boss think he has a death wish. When he hires an investigator to look into Earl's background, the pious myths that surround Earl's father, a respected Arkansas sheriff, are shattered." N Y Times Book Rev

"Once upon a time, *hard-boiled* implied more than a style; Hunter shows us what the real thing was all about." Booklist

Pale horse coming; a novel. Simon & Schuster 2001 491p o.p.
ISBN 0-684-86361-8 LC 2001-47386

Hunter, Stephen, 1946-—*Continued*

In this sequel to Hot Springs, "Hunter continues the story of Arkansas state cop Earl Swagger. It's 1951, and Swagger is once again called on to clean up an evil empire. Deep in the swamps of Thebes, Mississippi, a prison for black criminals run by a gang of redneck thugs harbors a sinister conspiracy. After rescuing his friend Sam Vincent from Thebes and narrowly escaping from the prison himself, Earl gathers a team of legendary gunfighters . . . and sets out to liberate Thebes the only way he knows how—violently. . . . The character of Earl Swagger, equal parts gristle and determination, remains compelling, both as archetype and as complex human being." Booklist

Time to hunt; a novel. Doubleday 1998 467p o.p.

ISBN 0-385-48043-1 LC 97-46985

This novel featuring Bob Lee Swagger "begins in the early 1970s in Washington, when Marine Corporal Donny Fenn gets himself sent back to Vietnam for refusing to betray a fellow platoon member suspected of collaborating with student dissidents. Once in Southeast Asia, Fenn finds himself working as a spotter for the inimitable Swagger, and the two manage to save a pinned-down battalion before Fenn is killed by a Russian adversary who has been sent to Vietnam to hunt down the dynamic duo. After Fenn's death, Swagger leaves the Marine Corps to marry Fenn's widow, Julie, and start a family, but his Russian rival remains intent on finishing the job." Publ Wkly

"Swagger is a near-mythic character without peer in mystery fiction. He was born to soldier but longs to stop. As we revel in his adventures and triumphs, we also experience his pain." Booklist

Hurston, Zora Neale, 1891-1960

The bone of contention
In Hurston, Z. N. Novels and stories p968-78

Book of Harlem
In Hurston, Z. N. Novels and stories p979-84

The complete stories; introduction by Henry Louis Gates, Jr. and Sieglinde Lemke. HarperCollins Pubs. 1995 xxiii, 305p o.p.

LC 91-50438

This collection of Hurston's short fiction contains nineteen stories originally published between 1921 and 1951, arranged in the order in which they were published, and seven previously unpublished stories

Drenched in light
In Hurston, Z. N. Novels and stories p940-48

The fire and the cloud
In Hurston, Z. N. Novels and stories p997-1000

The gilded six-bits
In Hurston, Z. N. Novels and stories p985-96

John Redding goes to sea
In Hurston, Z. N. Novels and stories p925-39

Jonah's gourd vine
In Hurston, Z. N. Novels and stories p1-171

Moses, man of the mountain
In Hurston, Z. N. Novels and stories p335-595

Novels and stories. Library of Am. 1995 1041p $35

ISBN 0-940450-83-6 LC 94-25757

Companion volume to Folklore, memoirs, and other writings

This collection contains Hurston's four novels: Jonah's gourd vine, Their eyes were watching God, Moses, man of the mountain, and Seraph on the Suwanee. Also included are nine short stories

"Libraries without a complete set of Hurston's fiction will find this volume a necessary and easy purchase to fill that unfortunate gap." Booklist

Seraph on the Suwanee
In Hurston, Z. N. Novels and stories p597-920

Spunk
In Hurston, Z. N. Novels and stories p949-54

Story in Harlem slang
In Hurston, Z. N. Novels and stories p1001-10

Sweat
In Hurston, Z. N. Novels and stories p955-65

Their eyes were watching God
In Hurston, Z. N. Novels and stories p173-333

Hustvedt, Siri

What I loved; a novel. Holt & Co. 2003 370p $25

ISBN 0-8050-7170-9 LC 2002-27358

The author "co-opts New York's competitive and faddish art world for its symbol-laden milieu. Leo Hertzberg, a thoughtful art historian, narrates a measured and mesmerizing tale of passion and tragedy that spans 20 years and involves his wife, Erica, a literary scholar, his close friendship with highly provocative painter Bill Wechsler; and his hidden infatuation with Bill's sexy muse and second wife, Violet, an expert in psychotic disorders associated with women's body images." Booklist

"The imprint of Henry James turns out to have reference not to the novel's prose style, which is cleanly colloquial, but to a tragic vision in which surface decorum hides subterranean upheaval. 'What I Loved' is a rare thing, a page turner written at full intellectual stretch, serious but witty, large-minded and morally engaged." N Y Times Book Rev

Huxley, Aldous, 1894-1963

Brave new world; a novel. Doubleday, Doran & Co. 1932 311p o.p.

"The ironic title, which Huxley has taken from Shakespeare's *The Tempest*, describes a world in which science has taken control over morality and humaneness. In this utopia humans emerge from test tubes, families are obsolete, and even pleasure is regulated. When a so-called

Huxley, Aldous, 1894-1963—*Continued*
savage who believes in spirituality is found and is imported to the community, he cannot accommodate himself to this world and ends his life." Shapiro. Fic for Youth. 3d edition

Collected short stories. Harper & Row 1957 397p o.p.
Contents: Happily ever after; Eupompus gave splendour to art by numbers; Cynthia; The bookshop; The death of Lully; Sir Hercules; The Gioconda smile; The Tillotson banquet; Green tunnels; Nuns at luncheon; Little Mexican; Hubert and Mimmie; Fard; The portrait; Young Archimedes; Half holiday; The monocle; Fairy godmother; Chawdron; The rest cure; The Claxtons

Point counter point. Doubleday, Doran & Co. 1928 432p o.p.
The book "presents a satiric picture of London intellectuals and members of English upper-class society during the 1920's. Frequent allusions to literature, painting, music, and contemporary British politics occur throughout the book, and much scientific information is embodied in its background. The story is long and involved, with many characters; it concerns a series of broken marriages and love affairs, and a political assassination. The construction is elaborate, supposedly based on Bach's 'Suite No. 2 in B Minor.' It is also a novel within a novel. Philip Quarles a leading character . . . is himself planning a novel, which echoes or 'counterpoints' the events going on around him." Reader's Ency. 4th edition

Huyler, Frank, 1964-

The laws of invisible things. H. Holt 2004 320p $25
ISBN 0-8050-7330-2 LC 2003-51116
This novel "focuses on Michael Grant, a newly divorced doctor who has just moved to North Carolina and joined the practice of widower Ronald Gass, a much older physician. Grant's lonely personal life is soon in turmoil as it intersects with the black Williams family. Soon after his arrival, Grant treats the granddaughter of Rev. Thomas Williams; the little girl dies, probably due to an oversight by Grant. As a favor to the minister, Grant agrees to see his son Jonas, the girl's father, who has bizarre symptoms that Grant thinks may indicate a previously unknown disease; Gass is skeptical, almost scornful of this idea. Within days, Gass dies of natural causes, Jonas is dead from the disease, and Grant himself is hospitalized with the same symptoms." Libr J
"Although the story elements are melodramatic, the intimate tone of Huyler's elegiac voice invites us to rise above our disgust and think again about the things we think we know." N Y Times Book Rev

Hynes, James

Kings of infinite space; James Hynes. St. Martin's Press 2004 341p $24.95
ISBN 0-312-45645-X LC 2003-58563
"According to Paul Trilby, there's something weird going on at the Texas Department of General Services, where he slaves away as the lowliest-of-lowly corporate workers, the office temp. . . . Divorced, destitute, and driving a rattletrap clunker amidst a sea of sleek SUVs, Paul's down-and-out existence is a far cry from his former glory days as an up-and-coming university professor. Confronted by his smarmy coworkers (who are not above selling their souls for a better gig), Paul is introduced to a mysterious world of former employees, equally downtrodden middlemen downsized in state budget cuts. The only difference is—they're dead." Booklist
This "is social satire that slides smoothly and surreally into horror, and if it loses a little of its emotional heft in the process, you don't really miss it. The glee with which Hynes choreographs an in-office zombie-vs.-stapler fight scene is compensation enough." Time

The lecturer's tale. Picador 2001 388p $25
ISBN 0-312-20332-2 LC 00-47836
"The protagonist is Nelson Humboldt, a once bright star in the English department at Midwest University but now reduced to teaching composition classes. Never one to publish much, Nelson's academic career is on the verge of perishing. That is until he realizes he has accidentally (in the literal sense) acquired a magic power over people that allows him to bend them to his will." Booklist
"The culture wars of the ivory tower may be well-charted waters, but Hynes wades in with Swiftian glee." Am Book Rev

I

Iagnemma, Karl

On the nature of human romantic interaction. Dial Press (NY) 2003 212cmp il $22.95
ISBN 0-385-33593-8 LC 2003-40953
Contents: On the nature of human romantic interaction; The phrenologist's dream; Zilkowski's theorem; The confessional approach; The Indian agent; Kingdom, order, species; The ore miner's wife; Children of hunger
"The meticulousness of science and mathematics is applied to the mysteries of love in Iagnemma's debut collection, which features eight complex, multilayered stories in which protagonists try to balance the demands of the heart against their need for rational, orderly thinking." Publ Wkly

Ibáñez, Vicente Blasco *See* Blasco Ibáñez, Vicente, 1867-1928

Ignatius, David, 1950-

A firing offense. Random House 1997 333p o.p.
LC 96-29518
In this "espionage thriller, an up-and-coming journalist finds he has made a Faustian bargain when he takes information from the CIA. *New York Mirror* foreign correspondent Eric Truell's exposé of French governmental corruption leads him to probe the dynamics of power behind a pending French-Chinese communications contract—a deal that could mean the loss of billions for American businesses. Truell's CIA sources use their information to lure the ambitious but naive reporter into playing their own dangerous game in the murky new world order, where real power resides not with governments but with private enterprise." Libr J
"Thanks to great writing and an all-too-human protago-

Ignatius, David, 1950-—*Continued*
nist, the preaching is kept to a minimum, but the sermon—about good journalism and bad, truth and lies—is there in bold letters." Publ Wkly

The Sun King; a novel. Random House 1999 305p o.p.
ISBN 0-679-44861-6 LC 99-13490
"Publishing mogul Sandy Galvin, a.k.a. the Sun King, arrives in Washington, DC, one day with plans to revive a dying newspaper. He hires David Cantor, a cynical lifestyle writer with a profound appreciation for fluff journalism, and Candace Ridgway, a former flame and scrupulous foreign affairs writer also known as The Mistress of Fact. Shortly, both men are deeply involved with the Mistress, and the threesome spend the rest of the book sparring about love and journalistic ethics." SLJ
"A thoroughly involving narrative with a sharp, satiric edge, Ignatius's contemporary take on the tragic confluence of love, power and ambition is a sophisticated look at the media mystique and the movers and shakers in our nation's capitol. His stylish, fluent prose, anchored with fine atmospheric detail, gives the story texture and momentum." Publ Wkly

Iguana dreams; new Latino fiction; edited by Delia Poey and Virgil Suarez; with a preface by Oscar Hijuelos. HarperCollins Pubs. 1992 376p il o.p.
LC 92-52628

This "anthology brings together 29 short stories that reflect different aspects of Latino life from the despair of the barrio to the unease of working within the Anglo status quo, yet also embody humanity's archetypal dramas. . . . While each magnetic narrative is unique, they all radiate an aura of deliberateness, astuteness, and power." Booklist

Iles, Greg

Black cross. Dutton 1995 516p o.p.
LC 94-34642
This novel "tells the story of a physician from Georgia and a German Jew who manage to forestall Hitler's use of poison nerve gas during World War II by destroying a secret laboratory hidden in a Nazi death camp. The rash plan for infiltrating the camp and destroying the laboratory has been developed by the Allies and led by Winston Churchill and will require nerves of steel, physical and emotional stamina, unparalleled bravery, and incredible luck. If it works, millions of lives will be saved. But there is a horrible price to pay for the larger victory—hundreds of Jewish prisoners interred in the camp may also die. From the very first page, Iles takes his readers on an emotional roller-coaster ride, juxtaposing tension-filled action scenes, horrifying depictions of savage cruelty, and heart-stopping descriptions of sacrifice and bravery." Booklist

The footprints of God. Scribner 2003 459p $25.95
ISBN 0-7432-3469-3 LC 2003-45733
As the novel opens Dr. David Tenant is "contemplating his life after friend and mentor Andrew Fielding is found dead in his lab. A stroke is the suspected cause, but David knows better because both men were part of an ultra-top-secret project known as Project Trinity, a quantum leap in the future of supercomputing and artificial intelligence. Both men had warned their managers about the experiment's dangers, and now David believes that he is next on the hit list." Libr J
"Readers interested in the exploration of religious themes without the usual New Age blather or window-dressed dogma will snap up this novel of cutting-edge science." Publ Wkly

Mortal fear. Dutton 1997 564p o.p.
LC 97-194514
"When futures trader Harper Cole, who moonlights as the systems operator of an erotic online services called EROS, contacts the New Orleans police with information about the murder of celebrated author—and EROS subscriber—Karin Wheat, he immediately becomes the prime suspect in six other murders of EROS subscribers across the country." Publ Wkly
"Despite the artifice of the characters operating it, the technology involved in their ingenious computer chase—which gives new meaning to the term 'network'—is fascinating." N Y Times Book Rev

Ingram, Willis J. *See* Harris, Mark, 1922-

Inman, Robert, 1943-

Captain Saturday; a novel. Little, Brown 2002 455p $24.95
ISBN 0-316-41502-2 LC 2001-23529
"Will Baggett has settled into a comfortable existence: he's a fixture of the Raleigh community as its most popular TV weatherman; his beatiful wife, Clarice, is a successful real estate broker; and his son, Palmer, is a medical student at UNC-Chapel Hill. Yet Will's seemingly perfect facade is destroyed when his news station is bought out and he is abruptly fired. This upset to his routine has a ripple effect; Clarice announces she wants a divorce, his relationship with Palmer is proven to be not as solid as he once believed, and Will finds himself accidentally embroiled in legal problems." Booklist
"Peopled with vivid, endearlingly quixotic characters and filled with dead-on insights into a shallow New South that defines itself by club memberships and designer labels, this richly textured epic is paean to the vagaries of the human heart." Publ Wkly

Innes, Hammond, 1913-1998

The wreck of the Mary Deare. Knopf 1956 296p o.p.
"When narrator John Sands first sights the freighter 'Mary Deare' from the deck of his salvage boat, she appears to be a ghostly derelict drifting toward the Channel reefs. Boarding her, however, he encounters her specter-ridden captain, Gideon Patch, and becomes dangerously involved in the suspect seaman's desperate attempt to expose the conspiracy behind her last voyage." Booklist

Inness-Brown, Elizabeth, 1954-

Burning Marguerite. Knopf 2002 237p $23
ISBN 0-375-41196-8 LC 2001-29860

Inness-Brown, Elizabeth, 1954-—*Continued*

"When James Jack finds his 94-year-old Tante Marguerite frozen in the snow outside their house on a remote New England island, he sets out to give her the very private funeral she desired. . . . The narrative jumps from James Jack's point of view to Marguerite's, as gradually we learn the tragedy of her young life, which led to a period of exile in New Orleans and finally to her return to the isolated island, where she raised James Jack after the sudden death of his parents. This is a remarkably quiet novel, one that draws its power and beauty as much from silence as from human interaction." Booklist

Irving, Clifford

Final argument; a novel. Simon & Schuster 1993 333p o.p.

LC 92-42693

"Ted Jaffe is a successful lawyer with a nice family, a six-figure income, and an expensive house. Then a series of events changes his life forever. Twelve years earlier, just after Jaffe had ended a torrid affair with rich, sexy Connie Zide, he had successfully convicted a young black man of killing Connie's husband. Now, one of the men who testified at the trial says he was bribed. Jaffe's interest is piqued, but the truth is elusive. Witnesses are reluctant to talk, and when they do, they end up dead. The case quickly becomes an obsession while Jaffe's personal life disintegrates." Booklist

"A fast-moving legal thriller noteworthy for its virtuoso interweaving of story lines, numerous plot twists and superior characterizations. . . . Culminating in an edge-of-the-seat courtroom showdown with plenty of surprises, this superior thriller is a top example of the genre." Publ Wkly

Irving, John, 1942-

3 by Irving. Random House 1980 718p o.p.

LC 79-5536

Contents: Setting free the bears (1969); The water-method man (1972); The 158-pound marriage (1974)

The first of these novels "involves a madcap scheme to liberate zoo animals, the second chronicles the misadventures of a bungling graduate student, and the third features a ménage-à-quatre in academe. . . . Irving's early fictions are noteworthy not only as forerunners to the remarkable *Garp* but also on their own merits. Possessing much of the same narrative inventiveness, zany wit, and sheer verve that so distinguish Irving's best-seller, they also maintain a *Garp*-like balance between the humorous and the macabre." Choice

The 158-pound marriage
In Irving, J. 3 by Irving p561-718

The cider house rules. Morrow 1985 560p o.p.

LC 84-27195

"Homer Wells wants to be neither an orphan nor an abortionist. But he has little choice in either matter; failing to be adopted, he is fated to always return to Maine's Saint Cloud's Orphanage and his surrogate father, Dr. Larch, head administrator and resident abortionist. Although still in his teens, Homer learns 'perfect obstetrical procedure' while assisting Larch, but his unwillingness to perform abortions eventually leads him away from Saint Cloud's and into a head-on collision with life and its mysterious rules." Libr J

"The book is, to be sure, a novel . . . not a tract; it follows several human lives from youth to maturity, gripping our attention as chronicle rather than argument. But it is also a book about abortion, and the knowledge and sympathy directing Mr. Irving's exploration of the issue are exceptional." N Y Times Book Rev

The fourth hand; a novel. Random House 2001 316p o.p.

ISBN 0-375-50627-6 LC 2001-18155

This novel's hero, "Patrick Wallingford, is a television reporter whose left hand is eaten by a lion while he is covering a story about the circus in India. Patrick eventually receives a transplanted hand from a man named Otto Clausen, who accidentally shot himself. . . . Otto's widow, Doris, who has chosen Patrick to be the hand recipient, not only declares that she has visiting rights with her late husband's hand, but also sexually assaults Patrick in order to become pregnant with his child." N Y Times

"Irving's set pieces are on that high level of American gothic comedy he has made uniquely his own." Publ Wkly

The Hotel New Hampshire. Dutton 1981 401p o.p.

LC 81-2610

"A Henry Robbins book"

This is "a family chronicle—a tale of generations of parents coping with children and siblings coping with each other. The chief parents are Win and Mary Berry of Dairy, New Hampshire, a couple brought together after high school at a seaside resort where, on summer jobs, they catch a glimpse of a joyous vocation (innkeeping). The Berry union produces five spirited and amusing children. . . . The story covers a quarter-century, beginning round about 1940, and the principal action takes place in three hotels, each called . . . The Hotel New Hampshire. (The hotels are situated in New Hampshire, Austria, and Maine.)" Atlantic

The author "keeps us moving, sacrificing rhetoric to pace, as in the most primitive narrative forms, the fable and the fairy tale. In fiction like this, meaning lies near the surface of the story and in the voice of the storyteller." New Repub

A prayer for Owen Meany; a novel. Morrow 1989 543p o.p.

LC 88-13839

This novel is set in New Hampshire in the 1950s and 1960s. Owen Meany is a short boy with a squeaky voice, who foresees his own death and sees himself as an instrument of God. He hits a baseball that kills the mother of John Wheelwright, the novel's narrator. Because of Owen, John becomes a Christian

"Despite its theological proppings, A Prayer for Owen Meany is a fable of political predestination. As usual, Irving delivers a boisterous cast, a spirited story line and a quality of prose that is frequently underestimated even by his admirers. On the other hand, the novel invites trespass by symbol hunters. . . . To get lost in critical rummage would be to miss the point. Irving's litany of error and folly may strike some as too righteous; but it is effective." Time

Setting free the bears
In Irving, J. 3 by Irving p1-284

Irving, John, 1942-—*Continued*

A son of the circus. Random House 1994 633p o.p.

LC 93-44750

"At center stage is Farrokh Daruwalla, an alienated, middle-aged, Bombay-born doctor who returns to his birthplace to study circus dwarfs. Farrokh becomes entangled in a case involving a serial murderer who carves the image of a winking elephant on his victims' torsos. This storyline bounces around like the proverbial three-ring circus and features a cast of eunuchs, hippies, movie stars, transsexuals, and clergymen." Libr J

Irving "is at the peak of his powers in this new novel. He plunges the reader into one sensual or grotesque scene after another with cheerful vigour and a madcap tenderness for life. . . . The author knows what he is doing from first to last, and handles the dozens of strands of his plot with exuberant ease." Economist

Until I find you; a novel. Random House 2005 824p $27.95

ISBN 1-400-06383-3

This novel "recounts the life of an actor as he tries to find the father who abandoned him and to come to terms with the traumas of his youth: a mother who was an itinerant tattoo artist and occasional prostitute, schooling at an all-girls academy where he was tormented by older classmates, sexual molestation at the hands of a woman who had been a kind of nanny." New Yorker

"The fatal difference between Irving and his master is that in a Dickens novel the smallest components are thematically and even poetically tied to the central idea, rather than unnecessary and irrelevant. Still, Irving is a skillful, powerful writer, and his novels are nearly always worth the considerable time they demand. His latest, Until I Find You, is in many ways characteristic: generous, sprawling, vivid, and, as with all his work, quintessentially masculine." New Leader

The water-method man

In Irving, J. 3 by Irving p285-560

A widow for one year; a novel. Random House 1998 537p o.p.

ISBN 0-375-50137-1 LC 97-49166

The first half of this novel "tells the story of Eddie O'Hare, a prep school student with literary aspirations who lands a job as a personal assistant to noted children's author Ted Cole in the summer of 1958. O'Hare spends most of the time in bed with Cole's wife, Marion. The second half of the book describes O'Hare's acquaintance, decades later, with Ruth Cole, Ted's daughter, who is also a successful writer. While researching her latest novel, Ruth witnesses the murder of an Amsterdam window prostitute." Libr J

"It is clearly not the outline of the plot that makes the book obstinately memorable. Rather, it is Irving's special gift for farcical incident . . . his piercing sense of the wonderful and terrible vulnerability of children, his poetic evocation of the ravages of time." Publ Wkly

The world according to Garp. Dutton 1978 437p o.p.

LC 77-15564

"A Henry Robbins book"

"Jenny Fields is the black sheep daughter of an aristocratic New England family; she becomes, almost by accident, a feminist leader ahead of her time. Her son, T. S. Garp (named for a father he never saw), has high ambitions for his artistic career, but he has an even higher, obsessive devotion to his wife and children. Surrounding Garp and Jenny are a wide assortment of people: schoolteachers and whores, wrestlers and radicals, editors and assassins, transsexuals and rapists, and husbands and wives." Publisher's note

This "is a long family novel, spanning four generations and two continents, crammed with incidents, characters, feelings and craft. The components of black comedy and melodrama, pathos and tragedy, mesh effortlessly in a tale that can also be read as a commentary on art and the imagination." Time

Irving, Washington, 1783-1859

The complete tales of Washington Irving. Doubleday 1975 xxxvii, 798p o.p.

Contents: Rip Van Winkle; The spectre bridegroom; The legend of Sleepy Hollow; The stout gentleman; The student of Salamanca; Annette Delarbe; Dolph Heylinger; The hunting-dinner; The adventure of my uncle; The adventure of my aunt; The bold dragoon; Adventure of the German student; Adventure of the mysterious picture; Adventure of the mysterious stranger; The story of the young Italian; Literary life; A literary dinner; The club of queer fellows; The poor-devil author; Notoriety; A practical philosopher; Buckthorne; Grave reflections of a disappointed man; The booby squire; The strolling manager; The inn at Terracina; Adventure of the little antiquary; The belated travellers; Adventure of the Popkins family; The painter's adventure; The story of the bandit chieftain; The story of the young robber; The adventure of the Englishman; Hell gate; Kidd the pirate; The devil and Tom Walker; Wolfert Webber; Adventure of the black fisherman; The adventure of the mason; Legend of the Arabian astrologer; Legend of Prince Ahmed al Kamel; Legend of the Moor's legacy; Legend of the three beautiful princesses; Legend of the rose of the Alhambra; The governor and the notary; Governor Manco and the soldier; Legend of the two discreet statues; Spanish romances; The legend of the enchanted soldier; Wolfert's roost; The Creole village; Mountjoy; The widow's ordeal; The grand prior of Minorca; A contented man; Guests from Gibbet Island; The early experiences of Ralph Ringwood; The Count Van Horn; Don Juan: a spectral research; Legend of the engulphed convent; The phantom island

Isaacs, Susan, 1943-

After all these years. HarperCollins Pubs. 1993 343p o.p.

LC 92-56200

"Rose Meyers was just an ordinary Jew from Queens who married her sweetheart, became a teacher, moved to the suburbs, and had two kids. Then her husband's business made him a millionaire. Suddenly, Rose and Richie have a Long Island mansion, a fleet of BMWs, and invitations to all the soirees. Rose is in for a shock, though, when Richie announces he's leaving her for a younger woman. The divorce papers aren't even signed when Rose, stricken with insomnia, goes downstairs one night for a glass of milk and trips over Richie's corpse. The cops immediately peg Rose as the prime suspect, but she

Isaacs, Susan, 1943-—*Continued*
knows she didn't kill her husband, and she's determined to find out who did." Booklist

Isaacs "has a field day lampooning upper-class mores . . . but also weaves into this thoroughly diverting caper unexpected moments of genuine tenderness and sly social commentary." Publ Wkly

Almost paradise. Harper & Row 1984 483p o.p.
LC 83-48357

"Nicholas is the scion of a wealthy family, although Jane's bloodline is anything but aristocratic. They marry after Jane convinces Nick that his true talent lies with acting rather than law. In no time Nick is the rage of Broadway and Hollywood. The marriage remains idyllic until Jane develops a fear of crowds so great she is unable to walk to her own mailbox. But she continues to make their Connecticut farmhouse the ideal place for her husband to entertain his many guests. The arrangement works for twenty years, as Nick resists the attempts of countless women to seduce him. Nick finally succumbs to a timid film student and Jane takes up with her shrink." West Coast Rev Books

Close relations. Lippincott 1980 270p o.p.
LC 80-7858

"David Hoffman would appear to be everything a girl could want—and he appears in Marcia Green's life when the politician she writes speeches for is lagging in the gubernatorial primary and her lover Jerry Morrissey is stubbornly resisting the longterm commitment she longs for. But here's one big strike against David: Marcia's family approves of him. Flashbacks to her childhood, her first marriage, her unhappy promiscuity show the reasons for her rebellion. Ultimately, she and David decide they need each other enough to be happy despite the past." Libr J

"Besides being simultaneously romantic, feminist, and political, the novel is also a satire: of Jewish mothers and success-orientation, late-marrying Irishmen, American political campaigns, WASP mores, and human relations." Best Sellers

Compromising positions. Times Bks. 1978 248p o.p.
LC 77-13896

"Judith Singer is a nice, average Jewish housewife—on the surface—but beneath that placid exterior lurks a secret longing for high adventure. . . . When a local dentist-Lothario is murdered in his office and a neighbor who was his last patient is a suspect, Judith cannot resist getting into the act. Meddling, gossiping, she turns detective, and when she learns that the elegant late Dr. Fleckstein was not only bedding virtually every woman in town but getting them to pose for exceedingly porno photos, there's no stopping her. Enter detective Nelson Sharpe, much more attractive than Judith's stodgy husband. The two make a wild pair of sleuths as Sharpe tracks down the murderer and an accomplice and exposes smug suburban hypocrisy." Publ Wkly

Lily White; a novel. HarperCollins Pubs. 1996 459p o.p.
LC 96-17399

"Told in chapters alternating between her personal life and her work, this is the story of Lily White, a funny, ambitious, criminal-defense attorney. Lily becomes overinvolved in the case of her current client, Norman Torkelson, a con man who woos and then bilks desperate, lonely women. Something went terribly wrong in his last con, and the mark ended up dead. . . . As Lily pulls out all the stops in trying to determine what really happened, she also reveals her painful personal life—her increasing distance from her blue-blooded, ne'er-do-well husband, his startling revelation that he is in love with her sister, and her subsequent efforts to build a makeshift family with her best friend and mentor, an elegant gay black man." Booklist

"Susan Isaac's real subject here isn't murder or legal thrills, of course, but the drama and suspense of middle-class women's lives. In her rendition, it's white-knuckle stuff." N Y Times Book Rev

Magic hour. HarperCollins Pubs. 1991 412p o.p.
LC 90-55570

Isaacs' setting, "the various sections of Long Island's Hamptons (N.Y.), allows her to depict the tension between the hardworking locals, many of whom live on the edge of poverty, and the snooty summer people, phony Manhattan culture hounds and social climbers. Movie producer Sy Spencer is clearly among the latter, and when he is shot by the side of his glitzy Southampton swimming pool, homicide detective Steve Brady is not surprised to discover plentiful evidence of widespread resentment and hatred of Spencer." Publ Wkly

"Best of all . . . is the subplot, an old-fashioned love story (think 1940s movie) in which Brady falls hard for his leading suspect, the dead producer's first wife. There's no good reason why we should buy into this romance—it rests on a totally improbable premise—but Isaacs sets the hook and reels us in anyway." Booklist

Red, white and blue; a novel. HarperCollins Pubs. 1998 402p o.p.
ISBN 0-06-017608-3 LC 98-34568

"Investigation of a radical Wyoming militia group brings together two unlikely people—Charlie Blair, an FBI agent and Wyoming native, and Lauren Miller, a New York reporter. Before focusing on the investigation and the developing relationship between Charlie and Lauren, Isaacs tells the story of their Jewish immigrant ancestors, showing how two such different individuals can be descended from the same roots." Libr J

"It is no easy task to hold a reader's attention when a novel's outcome is obvious from the very first page. But Susan Isaacs has such a knack for entertaining her reader with the details of American pop culture . . . that it's easy to be distracted from the predictability of her plot." N Y Times Book Rev

Shining through. Harper & Row 1988 402p o.p.
LC 87-45630

"Linda Voss is a 31-year-old secretary to the dreamiest looking man on Wall Street, international lawyer John Berringer, with whom she is secretly and hopelessly in love: she is a poor girl from Queens, and he boasts an Ivy League background along with his perfect profile. When circumstances lead to their unlikely marriage, however, sexual fireworks keep them together. As World War II engulfs Europe, the Berringers move to Washington, where both become involved in undercover work for the COI, soon to become the OSS. Heartbreak, plus a feeling of kinship for the victims of Nazism, leads Linda, whose childhood was spent in a German-speaking house-

Isaacs, Susan, 1943-—*Continued*
hold, to volunteer for a dangerous mission in Berlin." Publ Wkly

"Whether completely believable or not, Isaacs' tale of bravery and romance makes exciting, entertaining reading." Booklist

Isegawa, Moses, 1963-

Snakepit. Knopf 2004 259p $24

ISBN 0-375-41454-1 LC 2003-60479

This novel is "set in Uganda in the 1970s. . . . Bat Kaanga is a Ugandan just returned to his homeland after two years in Britain. While he completed a postgraduate degree at Cambridge, he watched from afar as 'flag independence [gave] way to economic independence' in Uganda, his chances to make a fortune there increasing with each 'reform' imposed by Idi Amin. Now, when Bat lands a job as Bureaucrat Two in the Ministry of Power and Communications, he feels himself entering the top echelons of government." Publisher's note

"This is a headlong and blurry novel filled with violence and sex, deceit and revenge-a messy, captivating portrait of a desperate time and place." Publ Wkly

Isherwood, Christopher, 1904-1986

The Berlin stories; The last of Mr. Norris; Goodbye to Berlin; with a preface by the author. New Directions 1954 2v in 1 o.p.

The two titles included in this combined edition were originally published separately; the first in 1935 in the United Kingdom with title: Mr. Norris changes trains and the latter in 1939 by Random House, which is analyzed in Short story index

The last of Mr. Norris, set in Berlin during Hitler's rise to power, "is the story of the narrator's innocent friendship with odd, corrupt Mr. Norris. While pretending to be a sincere Communist, Mr. Norris is actually selling information to fascists and foreigners. Mr. Norris's masochistic sexual aberrations add to the impression that he is a symbol of the whole corrupt, disintegrating society." Reader's Ency. 4th edition

Goodbye to Berlin contains six short stories or sketches of life in Berlin in the last years before Hitler came to power. Though written in first person by one calling himself Christopher Isherwood, according to the author's statement, the material is not to be regarded as autobiographical. The sketches are entitled: A Berlin diary (Autumn 1930); Sally Bowles; On Ruegan Island (Summer 1931); The Nowaks; The Landauers; A Berlin diary (Winter 1932-3)

Goodbye to Berlin
In Isherwood, C. The Berlin stories

The last of Mr. Norris
In Isherwood, C. The Berlin stories

Ishiguro, Kazuo, 1954-

An artist of the floating world. Putnam 1986 206p o.p.

LC 85-25759

"Like figures on a Japanese screen, the painter Masuji Ono and his daughters Setsuko and Noriko are fixed in the formal attitudes that even their private conversations reflect. In the postwar 1940s, the father is a relic of traditional Japan, of teahouses, geishas and patterned gardens not yet destroyed by industry and Westernized thinking. He is unable to communicate with his daughters, unsure of the propriety of his wartime nationalism yet unwilling to exchange it for what seem to him doubtful modern values." Publ Wkly

"The tensions stay tight. And this is what makes Mr. Ishiguro not only a good writer but also a wonderful novelist." N Y Times Book Rev

Never let me go; Kauzo Ishiguro. Knopf 2005 288p $24

ISBN 1-400-04339-5 LC 2004-48966

"Kathy, Ruth and Tommy were pupils at Hailsham-an idyllic establishment situated deep in the English countryside. The children there were tenderly sheltered from the outside world, brought up to believe they were special, and that their personal welfare was crucial. But for what reason were they really there? It is only years later that Kathy, now aged 31, finally allows herself to yield to the pull of memory. What unfolds is the . . . story of how Kathy, Ruth and Tommy slowly come to face the truth about their seemingly happy childhoods—and about their futures." Publisher's note

"Ishiguro serves up the saddest, most persuasive science fiction you'll read. Set in 'England, late 1990s,' the novel posits a technological breakthrough whose effect is to condemn the children of Hailsham to a fate that was, until this novel, unthinkable. Ishiguro's imagining of the children's misshapen little world is profoundly thoughtful, and their hesitant progression into knowledge of their plight is an extreme and heartbreaking version of the exodus of all children from the innocence in which the benevolent but fraudulent adult world conspires to place them." Atlantic Monthly

The remains of the day. Knopf 1989 245p o.p.

LC 89-80445

"Mr. Stevens is a butler of high quality now employed by the American owner of Darlington Hall. His position as butler was quite different when Lord Darlington was his employer. Then there was a large staff, including Miss Kenton, whose friendly overtures to Stevens were met only by his inability to unbend or find some humor as an outlet offsetting his customary snobbish personality. As Stevens reflects on the past the reader gains insight into Lord Darlington's political connections after World War I with important government officials including Ribbentrop, representive of Germany's movement toward a dictatorship. Questions regarding an employee's unquestioning loyalty toward his employer and awareness of the political situation in the period just before Hitler's rise to power make this a thought-provoking novel." Shapiro. Fic for Youth. 3d edition

The unconsoled. Knopf 1995 544p o.p.

LC 95-15829

In this novel, "prominent concert pianist Ryder is at odds with his surroundings. Ryder arrives in an unidentified European city at a bit of a loss. Everyone he meets seems to assume that he knows more than he knows, that he is well acquainted with the city and its obscure cultural crisis. A young woman he kindly consents to advise seems to have been an old lover and her son quite possibly his own; he vaguely recalls past conversations. The world he has entered is a surreal, Alice-in-Wonderland

Ishiguro, Kazuo, 1954-—*Continued*
place where a door in a cafe can lead back to a hotel miles away. The result is at once dreamy, disorienting, and absolutely compelling; Ishiguro's paragraphs, though Proust-like, are completely lucid and quite addictive to read." Libr J

When we were orphans. Knopf 2000 335p $25
ISBN 0-375-41054-6 LC 00-26120
"Christopher Banks is an Englishman born in early 20th-century Shanghai whose parents disappear mysteriously when he is nine. He is escorted to England, grows up to be a famed detective, and returns to Shanghai, convinced that his parents are still alive and that he must find them." Libr J
"For all its ellipses and evasions, When We Were Orphans, will linger in the mind as an often fascinating, imaginative work of surpassing intelligence and taste." Times Lit Suppl

Itani, Frances, 1942-

Deafening. Atlantic Monthly Press 2003 378p $24
ISBN 0-87113-902-2 LC 2003-45108
"Grania O'Neill has been deaf since an early childhod fever. . . . Leaving her intimate Canadian hometown for the Ontario School for the Deaf, she learns sign language and finds Jim, who expresses his love for her by describing beautiful sounds. Unfortunately for their marriage, Jim is off to the trenches of World War I, where the sounds (and sights) are horrifying indeed." Booklist
"This novel is not only a beautifully crafted love story but also an exploration of the possibilities of language and the eloquence of silence." Libr J

Iyer, Pico

Abandon; a romance. Knopf 2003 353p $24
ISBN 0-375-41505-X LC 2002-70059
"John Macmillan is a student at a Santa Barbara, Calif., university trying to finish his thesis on the lesser works of Sufi master Rumi. John begins searching the globe for a secret Islamic manuscript, reputedly smuggled out of Iran after the Shah's downfall, that may contain lost poems by Rumi. He travels through Syria, Iran, Spain and India; though the search is mostly fruitless, along the way he finds himself drawn into a romance with the flighty, fragile, slightly New Agey Camilla Jensen." Publ Wkly
"Lyer's writing is often poetic, and in presenting the Persian diaspora in Southern California, he has an intriguing way of peeling back familiar landscapes to reveal hidden sights." Booklist

J

Jaber, Diana Abu- *See* Abu-Jaber, Diana

Jackson, Charles, 1903-1968

The lost weekend. Rinehart 1944 244p o.p.
Psychological study of a drunkard. The actual time covered is five days, but in those five days the story of a man's life is told. Don Biram, a sensitive, charming and well-read man, left alone for a few days by his brother, struggles with his overwhelming desire for alcohol, succumbs to it, and in the resulting prolonged agony, goes over much of his life up to and including the long weekend
"It's written with complete lack of literary pretensions; yet Jackson's sheer ability to lick the problems of flashback, stream of consciousness, mind wandering, twisted recollection and alcoholic delirium is spectacular. . . . Its frankness is sometimes shocking but never aimed to shock. The aim, and it is unerring, is always for accuracy and the complete truth" Book Week

Jackson, Jon A.

No man's dog; a Detective Sergeant Mulheisen mystery. Atlantic Monthly Press 2004 355p $24
ISBN 0-87113-920-0 LC 2003-69500
Detective Sergeant Fang Mulheisen retired from the force "to nurse his mother after she was injured in an apparent terrorist bombing of a suburban Detroit courthouse. That bombing has the curious effect of making partners of former antagonists Service and Mulheisen. Joining forces for different reasons to track down the bombers, these strange bedfellows-two of the most appealing, well-grounded characters in the genre-traipse about in the woods near Traverse City, sparring with a local militia roughneck. Jackson tackles the whole Patriot Act mess from an engaging everyman point of view." Booklist

Jackson, Mick

Five boys. Morrow 2002 279p $24.95
ISBN 0-06-001394-X
First published 2001 in the United Kingdom
In this novel "a close-knit gang of five boys forms a prism that refracts the idiosyncrasies of WWII English life in a small village in Devon. Ostensibly, the story is about Bobby, a newcomer evacuated from London and the Blitz, who is terrorized and then befriended by the gang. But the real protagonist is the town itself and its unusual denizens. . . . The narrative is episodic, more an integrated collection of seriocomic short stories than a novel with dramatic unity, but these vignettes are a testament to Jackson's writerly skill and imagination. Highly evocative of both time and place, the novel is about the bizarre ways the war affected those left at home and how it changed virtually everything about English life, particularly for the generation too young to serve." Publ Wkly

Jackson, Sheneska

Caught up in the rapture. Simon & Schuster 1996 270p o.p.
ISBN 0-684-81487-0 LC 95-47337
In this novel, "two young African Americans hoping for pop-music stardom become lovers—and pawns in a record-company power struggle. . . . Jazmine Deems, a 26-year-old UCLA student anxious to escape her father's strict household, envies the freedom enjoyed by her best friend, Dakota, who introduces her to popular music, current fashion and sexy guys. Life hasn't been as smooth for Xavier Honor, aka X-Man, whose 'family' consists of two street buddies and who hopes to rap his way out of the 'hood. X-Man and Jazmine meet at a party thrown

Jackson, Sheneska—*Continued*
by Black Tie Records." Publ Wkly

"This first novel is vivid, realistic, and strong, with perfectly fleshed-out characters. Readers will be bound by each word as they watch Jazmine struggle with life and the pursuit of happiness." Libr J

Jackson, Shirley, 1919-1965

Come along with me; part of a novel, sixteen stories, and three lectures; edited by Stanley Edgar Hyman. Viking 1968 243p o.p.

Contents: Short stories included are: Janice; Tootie in peonage; A cauliflower in her hair; I know who I love; The beautiful stranger; The summer people; Island; A visit; The rock; A day in the jungle; Pajama party; Louisa, please come home; The little house; The bus; The night we all had grippe; The lottery

The haunting of Hill House. Viking 1959 246p o.p.

"Dr. John Montague, an anthropologist, is interested in the analysis of supernatural manifestations. He rents Hill House, which is reported to be haunted, and plans to spend the summer there with research assistants. Eleanor Vance, one of the researchers, is at first repelled by the house but soon adjusts. Other people come and signs of psychic activity are rampant, many of them centered on Eleanor. When Dr. Montague insists that she leave to insure her safety, the house does not release her." Shapiro. Fic for Youth. 3d edition

Just an ordinary day. Bantam Bks. 1997 388p o.p.

LC 96-23871

This collection includes unpublished and uncollected stories

Contents: The smoking room; I don't kiss strangers; Summer afternoon; Indians live in tents; The very hot sun in Bermuda; Nightmare; Dinner for a gentleman; Party of boys; Jack the Ripper; The honeymoon of Mrs. Smith (versions I and II); The sister; Arch-criminal; Mrs. Anderson; Come to the fair; Portrait; Gnarly the King of the Jungle; The good wife; Devil of a tale; The mouse; My grandmother and the world of cats; Maybe it was the car; Lovers meeting; My recollections of S. B. Fairchild; Deck the halls; Lord of the castle; What a thought; When Barry was seven; Before Autumn; The story we used to tell; My uncle in the garden; On the house; Little old lady in great need; When things get dark; Whistler's grandmother; Family magician; The wishing dime; About two nice people; Mrs. Melville makes a purchase; Journey with a lady; The most womderful thing; The friends; Alone in a den of cubs; The order of Charlotte's going; One ordinary day, with peanuts; The missing girl; The omen; The very strange house next door; A great voice stilled; All she said was yes; Home; I.O.U.; The possibility of evil; Fame

The lottery and other stories; introduction by Patrick McGrath. 2000 Modern Library ed. Modern Lib. 2000 292p o.p.

ISBN 0-679-64039-8 LC 00-36064

A reissue of The lottery; or, The adventures of James Harris, published 1949 by Farrar, Straus

Contents: The intoxicated; The daemon lover; Like mother used to make; Trial by combat; The villager; My life with R. H. Macy; The witch; The renegade; After you, my dear Alphonse; Charles; Afternoon in linen; Flower garden; Dorothy and my grandmother and the sailors; Colloquy; Elizabeth; A fine old firm; The dummy; Seven types of ambiguity; Come dance with me in Ireland; Of course; Pillar of salt; Men with their big shoes; The tooth; Got a letter from Jimmy; The lottery

We have always lived in a castle. Viking 1962 214p o.p.

"Since the time that Constance Blackwood was tried and acquitted of the murder of four members of her family, she has lived with her sister Mary Catherine and her Uncle Julian in the family mansion. Mary Catherine takes care of family chores and Uncle Julian is busy with the writing of a detailed account of the six-year-old murders. Cousin Charles's arrival on the scene disrupts the quiet peace of the family, and Mary Catherine's efforts to get rid of him unloose a chain of events that bring everything down in ruins." Shapiro. Fic for Youth. 3d edition

Jaffe, Rona

Class reunion; a novel. Delacorte Press 1979 338p o.p.

LC 78-25838

"In the Fifties, when rules were rules, college campuses were husband-hunting grounds, and 'going all the way' could ruin a girl's reputation, four Radcliffe students pursue the dream of Mr. Right, Marriage, and Living Happily Ever After. Jaffe builds this book around their 20th reunion, using alternate chapters to flash back through the tales of beautiful Annabel, witty Chris, golden girl Daphne, and insecure Emily. [The author focuses on these women's lives] from college romances to crises which rock them—loveless marriage, divorce, adultery both homosexual and heterosexual, murder, nervous breakdown, birth of a mongoloid child." Libr J

The room-mating season. Dutton 2003 326p $24.95

ISBN 0-525-94713-2 LC 2002-73855

"The year is 1963, and college friends Leigh and Cady are determined to begin their adult lives amid the cosmopolitan social whirl of New York City. An ad for roommates brings two more young women into the circle: Vanessa, a sophisticated airline stewardess, and awkward, needy misfit Susan. . . . Jaffe traces the lives of her characters over the next four decades with wit and poignancy." Booklist

Jakeman, Jane

In the Kingdom of mists. Berley Prime Crime 2004 c2002 355p $23.95

ISBN 0-425-19512-0 LC 2003-62800

A novel about Claude Monet, "murder, and London in the year 1900. Oliver Cranston is trying to get out from under the thumb of his overbearing father by working for the Foreign Office. Oliver's job brings him to the Savoy, where the French painter Monet tries to capture the light and mist he sees on the Thames every morning and where an entire floor is devoted to the care of officer victims of the Boer War. It is Oliver's unlucky fate to see a woman's body wash up from the Thames, brutally and surgically murdered; he is luckier to make the ac-

Jakeman, Jane—*Continued*
quaintance of the painter's son, Michel." Booklist

"The novel tells a dramatic story about crime and perception, art and reality through the eyes of the famous painter, the policeman and a young diplomat. Multilayered and voiced, this is a fascinating attempt to add an extra dimension to this historical crime novel." Guardian

Jakes, John, 1932-

American dreams. Dutton 1998 495p o.p.
ISBN 0-525-94437-0 LC 97-49163

In the second volume of the "Crown family chronicles, Jakes portrays American during the turbulent period from 1906 to 1917. Once again, the story centers on the family of German-American patriarch and Chicago beer baron Joe Crown, whose headstrong daughter Fritzi defies her father to pursue a dreadfully unsuccessful New York stage career. In desperation, she surrenders to the lure of performing in moving pictures, which takes her to 'empty, rural, and uncivilized' Hollywood, where she falls in love and achieves a measure of fame as a comic actress. Meanwhile, her brother Carl gets tossed out of Princeton, goes to work for eccentric car manufacturer Henry Ford, becomes a race-car driver with Barney Oldfield, 'Speed King of the World', and flies as an ace pilot during WWI. Their cousin Paul is a professional news cameraman driven to record the horrors of war." Publ Wkly

The best western stories of John Jakes; edited by Bill Pronzini and Martin H. Greenberg. Ohio Univ. Press 1991 275p o.p.
LC 90-49427

Contents: Shootout at White Pass; The woman at Apache Wells; Hell on the high iron; A duel of magicians; Death rides here!; The winning of Poker Alice; To the last bullet; Little Phil and the daughter of joy; The tinhorn fills his hand; The naked gun; Dutchman

"This collection combines new material with several of Jakes's better efforts published earlier in the pulp magazines of the 1950s." Libr J

California gold; a novel. Random House 1989 658p o.p.
LC 89-3779

"Driven by his father's failed California dream, young Mack sets out from an Appalachian coal mine and lands eventually on Nob Hill, becoming a maverick real estate and business tycoon who sets out to challenge the San Francisco establishment. As he's faced with mounting adversity, his affairs begin to crumble, and so, in 1906, does a large chunk of the city. 'California Gold' is the story of one man, one state and three women." N Y Times Book Rev

"The novel potently conveys the raw, irrepressible vitality of California, but the historical backdrop (especially the 1906 earthquake) outshines the conventional rags-to-riches plot. Jake's impressive research . . . enriches the story considerably." Publ Wkly

(ed) A Century of great Western stories. See A Century of great Western stories

Charleston; a novel. Dutton 2002 506p o.p.
ISBN 0-525-94650-0 LC 2002-21251

This novel "details the shifting fortunes of several generations of a powerful southern dynasty, the Bell family, set against the dramatic and fiery backdrop of the American Revolution and the Civil War. Told in three parts, the story follows the lives, loves, and changing fortunes of the Bells and the Charleston aristocracy to which they belonged. Never one to gloss over details, the author manages to show the bleak horrors of slavery, war, and greed while also confirming the essential goodness of American ideals. Jakes is in tiptop shape here." Booklist

Heaven and hell. Harcourt Brace Jovanovich 1987 700p o.p.
LC 87-17652

The concluding volume of the North and South trilogy "centers on Charles, Orry Main's cousin, a Southerner totally devastated by the Civil War. Displaced and just having lost his beloved Augusta, Charles heads West with his infant son hoping to make a new life. With Charles as the focal point, the narrative continually shifts to all the other family members, including . . . a madman bent on destroying both families." Libr J

"Mr. Jakes sets this fictional action against a meticulously detailed historical backdrop. Although his characters are not as vivid as his storytelling, his portrait of a divided, demoralized nation, inflamed with hatred, still emerges as an enjoyable work of popular historical fiction." N Y Times Book Rev

Homeland. Doubleday 1993 785p o.p.
LC 92-43894

"In 1892, a Berlin street urchin named Pauli Kroner, 14 years old, scrapes up steerage fare for America with the help of his dying Aunt Lotte. Pauli is robbed of his papers and what little money he has just before his arrival. But he still manages to pass customs and make his way to Chicago, where his uncle is one of the city's leading brewers. . . . Paul yearns to be a painter, but lacks the skill. George Eastman's recent invention, the Kodak camera, offers him a chance to overcome that problem. When Paul has a chance to assist in the birth of cinematography, his life's course is set." N Y Times Book Rev

"Chockfull of fascinating period detail, Jakes' captivating story brings to life the sounds, smells, and tastes of turn-of-the-century America." Publ Wkly

Followed by American dreams

Love and war. Harcourt Brace Jovanovich 1984 1019p o.p.
LC 84-12895

This sequel to North and South "carries forward the entwined sagas of the Hazards of Pennsylvania, industrialists, and the Mains of South Carolina, plantation owners. . . . The story moves from action on the battlefield to the corridors of Washington to the shipyards of Liverpool. It encompasses deeds heroic and dastardly; passions licit and illicit; spying, assassination plotting and cynical profiteering; and the trying out of new military interventions." Publ Wkly

Followed by Heaven and hell

North and South. Harcourt Brace Jovanovich 1982 740p o.p.
LC 81-47898

In this first novel of a trilogy the author "introduces two families: The Main family of South Carolina, and the Hazard family of Pennsylvania. The families are ba-

Jakes, John, 1932-—*Continued*
sically different. The Mains from the South grow rice and represent the old ways while the Hazards of the North produce iron and are examples of the Industrial Revolution. Their paths converge however, when Orry Main meets George Hazard as the two are entering West Point in 1842. Their friendship is immediate and strong. Orry's family owns slaves, and George, while loving his friend, cannot understand it. As the years pass each grows more entrenched in his beliefs. . . . George's sister Virgilia, an avowed abolitionist, seeks to pry the friendship apart and nearly succeeds. George and Orry's struggles are representative of that which plague the nation." West Coast Rev Books

Followed by Love and war

On secret service; a novel. Dutton 2000 448p o.p.

ISBN 0-525-94544-X LC 99-47951

"In 1861, Washington was located on the frontier between the Union and Confederacy; despite being the Union capital, it was a hotbed of Confederate sympathizers, some of whom were actual spies and even involved in the conspiracy to assassinate President Lincoln. . . . Jakes follows, throughout the four-year war period, a handful of individuals with intertwined allegiances as they worked both aboveboard and below for their various causes." Booklist

"Numerous historical figures are represented accurately and plausibly, and lesser-known events like the horrific Draft Riots in New York are vividly portrayed." Libr J

Savannah; or, A gift for Mr. Lincoln; John Jakes. Dutton 2004 288p il $23.95

ISBN 0-525-94803-1 LC 2004-49417

This "historical novel recounts the taking of Savannah by Gen. William Tecumseh Sherman's Union Army during Christmas 1864. Fundamentally, it is the story of Sara Lester and her precocious 12-year-old daughter, Hattie, who has an aversion to General Sherman until she finds herself in need of his help. The novel includes a rich cast of characters who, as Union forces move north, are ultimately left to their own devices. The narrative offers adventure, romance, humor, and crime along with the trials of an American city living under what is, to its citizens, occupation by a foreign army." Libr J

James, Henry, 1843-1916

The ambassadors; edited with an introduction by Harry Levin. Penguin Books 1986 517p pa $7

ISBN 0-14-043233-7 LC 87-29773

First published 1903 by Harper

"The central character and first 'ambassador,' Lambert Strether, is sent to Paris by Mrs. Newsome, a wealthy widow whom he plans to marry, in order to persuade her son Chad to come home. Chad is deeply involved with a charming French woman, Madame de Vionnet, and the novel deals chiefly with Strether's gradual conversion to the idea that life may hold more real meaning for Chad in Paris than in Woollett, Massachusetts. Strether comes to this conclusion in spite of his discovery that Chad and Mme de Vionnet are, in fact, more than just good friends. After the arrival of a second ambassador, Chad's sister Sarah, Strether decides to return to Woollett, urging Chad to remain in Paris. The essence of the novel is in Strether's remark, 'Live all you can; it's a mistake not to.'" Reader's Ency. 4th edition

The American; edited with an introduction and notes by Adrian Poole. Oxford University Press 1999 xxxiv, 400p pa $10.95

ISBN 0-19-283322-7 LC 98-42570

First published 1877 by J. R. Osgood and Company

"A self-made American goes to Europe to enjoy his 'pile,' and becomes engaged to a French widow of noble family. The match is a good one for both parties, but at length the powers that rule this exclusive social world deliver their verdict: the engagement must be annulled. The American's pluck and good nature are happily contrasted with the colossal pride and essential meanness of the old noblesse." Baker. Guide to the Best Fic

"With much humour and delicacy of perception, the author depicts the reaction of different American types to the European environment." Oxford Companion to Engl Lit

The Aspern papers
- *In* James, H. Complete stories, 1884-1891
- *In* James, H. The complete tales of Henry James
- *In* James, H. The Henry James reader p165-254
- *In* James, H. Short novels of Henry James p257-354

The author of "Beltraffio"
- *In* James, H. Complete stories, 1874-1884
- *In* James, H. The complete tales of Henry James
- *In* James, H. The Henry James reader

The beast in the jungle
- *In* James, H. Complete stories, 1898-1910
- *In* James, H. The complete tales of Henry James
- *In* James, H. The Henry James reader p357-400

The Bostonians. Knopf 1992 394p o.p.

ISBN 0-679-41750-8 LC 92-52889

"Everyman's library"

First published 1886 by Macmillan

In this satirical novel, "Basil Ransom, a Mississippi lawyer, comes to Boston to seek his fortune, and becomes acquainted with his cousins, the flirtatious widow, Mrs. Luna, and her neurotic sister, Olive Chancellor. He is taken by Olive, a radical feminist, to a suffragette meeting. . . . They hear an address by beautiful young Verena Tarrant, whose gift of persuasion interests Olive as an instrument for her own use. Olive removes the girl to her own luxurious home, converts her to the feminist cause, and even urges her to vow that she will never marry. Fleeing the attentions of Mrs. Luna, Ransom attempts to win Verena to his belief that her proper sphere is a home and a drawing room, not a career as lecturer for a preposterous political movement." Oxford Companion to Am Lit. 6th edition

This was "one of the first American novels to deal more or less explicitly with lesbianism." Reader's Ency. 4th edition

Complete stories, 1864-1874. Library of Am. 1999 972p $40

ISBN 1-883011-70-1 LC 98-53919

James, Henry, 1843-1916—*Continued*

Contents: A tragedy of error; The story of a year; A landscape painter; A day of days; My friend Bingham; Poor Richard; The story of a masterpiece; The romance of certain old clothes; A most extraordinary case; A problem; De Grey: a romance; Osborne's revenge; A light man; Gabrielle de Bergerac; Travelling companions; A passionate pilgrim; At Isella; Master Eustace; Guest's confession; The madonna of the future; The sweetheart of M. Briseux; The last Valerii; Madame de Mauves [novelette]; Adina

Complete stories, 1874-1884. Library of Am. 1999 941p $35

ISBN 1-883011-63-9 LC 98-19252

Contents: Professor Fargo; Eugene Pickering; Benvolio Crawford's consistency; The ghostly rental; Four meetings; Rose-Agathe; Daisy Miller: a study [novelette]; Longstaff's marriage; An international episode [novelette]; The pension beaurepas; The diary of a man of fifty; A bundle of letters; The point of view; The siege of London [novelette]; The impressions of a cousin; Lady Barberina [novelette]; Pandora; The author of "Beltraffio" [novelette]

Complete stories, 1884-1891. Library of Am. 1999 904p $35

ISBN 1-883011-64-7 LC 98-19250

Contents: Georgina's reasons; A New England winter; The path of duty; Mrs. Temperly; Louisa Pallant; The Aspern papers [novelette]; The liar; The modern warning; A London life; The lesson of the master; The Patagonia; The solution; The pupil [novelette]; Brooksmith; The marriages; The chaperon; Sir Edmund Orme

Complete stories, 1892-1898. Library of Am. 1996 948p o.p.

ISBN 1-883011-09-4 LC 95-23463

Contents: Nona Vincent; The real thing; The private life; Lord Beaupré; The visits; Sir Dominick Ferrand; Greville Fane; Collaboration; Owen Wingrave; The wheel of time; The middle years; The death of the lion; The Coxon Fund; The altar of the dead; The next time; Glasses; The figure in the carpet; The way it came; The turn of the screw [novelette]; Covering end; In the cage [novelette]

Complete stories, 1898-1910. Library of Am. 1996 946p $35

ISBN 1-883011-10-8 LC 95-23462

Contents: John Delavoy; The given case; "Europe"; The great condition; The real right thing; Paste; The great good place; Maud-Evelyn; Miss Gunton of Poughkeepsie; The tree of knowledge; The abasement of the Northmores; The third person; The special type; The tone of time; Broken wings; The two faces; Mrs. Medwin; The Beldonald Holbein; The story in it; Flickerbridge; The birthplace; The beast in the jungle [novelette]; The papers; Fordham Castle; Julia Bride; The jolly corner; "The Velvet Glove"; Mora Montravers; Crapy Cornelia; The bench of desolation; A round of visits

The complete tales of Henry James; edited with an introduction by Leon Edel. Lippincott 1962-1965 12v o.p.

Contents: v1: 1864-1868: A tragedy of errors; The story of a year; A landscape painter; A day of days; My friend Bingham; Poor Richard; The story of a masterpiece; The romance of certain old clothes; A most extraordinary case; A problem; De Grey: a romance

v2: 1868-1872: Osborne's revenge; A light man; Gabrielle de Bergerac; Travelling companions; A passionate pilgrim; At Isella; Master Eustace; Guest's confession

v3: 1873-1875: The Madonna of the future; The sweetheart of M. Briseux; The last of the Valerii; Madame de Mauves [novelette]; Adina; Professor Fargo; Eugene Pickering; Benvolio

v4: 1876-1882: Crawford's consistency; The ghostly rental; Four meetings; Rose-Agathe; Daisy Miller: a study [novelette]; Longstaff's marriage; An international episode [novelette]; The pension Beaurepas; The diary of a man of fifty; A bundle of letters; The point of view

v5: 1883-1884: The siege of London [novelette]; The impressions of a cousin; Lady Barberina [novelette]; The author of "Beltraffio" [novelette]; Pandora

v6: 1884-1888: Georgina's reasons; A New England winter; The path of duty; Mrs. Temperly; Louisa Panant; The Aspern papers [novelette]; The liar

v7: 1888-1891: The modern warning; A London life; The lesson of the master; The Patagonia; The solution; The pupil [novelette]

v8: 1891-1892: Brooksmith; The marriages; The chaperon; Sir Edmund Orme; Nona Vincent; The private life; The real thing; Lord Beaupré; The visits; Sir Dominick Ferrand; Collaboration; Greville Fane; The wheel of time

v9: 1892-1898: Owen Wingrave; The middle years; The death of the lion; The Coxon Fund; The next time; The altar of the dead; The figure in the carpet; Glasses; The way it came (The friends of the friends); John Delavoy

v10: 1898-1899: The turn of the screw [novelette]; In the cage [novelette]; Covering end; The given case; The great condition; "Europe"; Paste; The real right thing

v11: 1900-1903: The great good place; Maud-Evelyn; Miss Gunton of Poughkeepsie; The tree of knowledge; The abasement of the Northmores; The third person; The special type; The tone of time; Broken wings; The two faces; Mrs. Medwin; The Beldonald Holbein; The story in it; Flickerbridge; The beast in the jungle [novelette]; The birthplace

v12: 1903-1910: The papers; Fordham Castle; Julia Bride; The jolly corner; The Velvet Glove; Mora Montravers; Crapy Cornelia; The bench of desolation; A round of visits

Daisy Miller; introduction by Elizabeth Hardwick; notes by James Danly. Modern Library 2002 xxiv, 80p pa $14.50

ISBN 0-375-75966-2 LC 2001-44626

First published 1878

"The book's title character is a young American woman traveling in Europe with her mother. There she is courted by Frederick Forsyth Winterbourne, an American living abroad. In her innocence, Daisy is compromised by her friendship with an Italian man. Her behavior shocks Winterbourne and the other Americans living in Italy, and they shun her. Only after she dies does Winterbourne recognize that her actions reflected her spontaneous, genuine, and unaffected nature and that his suspicions of her were unwarranted." Merriam-Webster's Ency of Lit

also in James, H. Complete stories, 1874-1884

James, Henry, 1843-1916—*Continued*

also in James, H. The complete tales of Henry James

also in James, H. The Henry James reader p403-61

also in James, H. Short novels of Henry James p1-58

The Europeans; a sketch; edited with an introduction and notes by Ian Campbell Ross. Oxford University Press 2000 pa $14.50

ISBN 0-19-283500-9 LC 00-703219

First published 1878

"Two expatriates, the Baroness Muenster and her brother Felix Young, come to Boston to visit some relatives they have never seen. The baroness futilely tries to make a wealthy marriage, and Felix seeks to paint portraits of the Bostonians he meets. A contrast is drawn between the sophistication of the pair and the strict New Englanders. Felix marries one of his kinswomen, who is eager to escape from her bleak environment." Benet's Reader's Ency of Am Lit

The golden bowl. Knopf 1992 596p $22

ISBN 0-679-41733-8 LC 92-52927

"Everyman's library"

First published 1904 by Scribner

Maggie Verver, daughter of an American millionaire living in London, marries an indigent "Italian prince who has had a love affair with Maggie's closest friend, Charlotte Stant. Charlotte visits the pair and continues her intimacy. Then she marries Maggie's father. Everybody tries to keep secret from the others that he or she knows all that has happened or is happening. The complications are solved when Maggie's father goes back to America with Charlotte. James depicts with all the subtlety of his late style the cultural and moral involvements that follow on international marriage and irregular sex relationships." Benet's Reader's Ency of Am Lit

The Henry James reader; selected with a foreword and headnotes by Leon Edel. Scribner 1965 626p o.p.

Analyzed in Short story index

Contains the short novels: Washington Square (1881); The Aspern papers (1888); The turn of the screw (1898); The beast in the jungle (1903); Daisy Miller (1878); The author of Beltraffio (1884); also the following short stories: Pandora; Owen Wingrave; The real thing; The two faces

In the cage

In James, H. Complete stories, 1892-1898

In James, H. The complete tales of Henry James

In James, H. What Maisie knew, In the cage, The pupil

An international episode

In James, H. Complete stories, 1874-1884

In James, H. The complete tales of Henry James

Lady Barberina

In James, H. Complete stories, 1874-1884

In James, H. The complete tales of Henry James

Madame de Mauves

In James, H. Complete stories, 1864-1874

In James, H. The complete tales of Henry James

The portrait of a lady. Knopf 1991 xxv, 626p $18.95

ISBN 0-679-40562-3 LC 91-52999

"Everyman's library"

First published 1881 by Houghton

"This is one of the best James's early works, in which he presents various types of American character transplanted into a European environment. The story centres in Isabel Archer, the 'Lady,' an attractive American girl. Around her we have the placid old American banker, Mr. Touchett; his hard repellent wife; his ugly, invalid, witty, charming son Ralph, whom England has thoroughly assimilated; and the outspoken, brilliant, indomitably American journalist Henrietta Stackpole. Isabel refuses the offer of marriage of a typical English peer, the excellent Lord Warburton, and of a bulldog-like New Englander, Casper Goodwood, to fall a victim, under the influence of the slightly sinister Madame Merle (another cosmopolitan American), to a worthless and spiteful dilettante, Gilbert Osmond, who marries her for her fortune and ruins her life; but to whom she remains loyal in spite of her realization of his vileness." Oxford Companion to Engl Lit. 6th edition

The pupil

In James, H. Complete stories, 1884-1891

In James, H. The complete tales of Henry James

In James, H. Short novels of Henry James p355-405

In James, H. What Maisie knew, In the cage, The pupil

Roderick Hudson; edited with an introduction by Geoffrey Moore and notes by Patricia Crick. Penguin Books 1986 397p pa $12

ISBN 0-14-043264-7

First published serially 1875 in The Atlantic Monthly; in book form 1876 by J. R. Osgood and Company

"The titular hero is a talented young American sculptor who goes to study in Rome at the insistance of a wealthy benefactor and becomes gradually disillusioned about his art and utterly demoralized by his experience. He neglects his New England fiancée; becomes involved in a love affair with Christina Light and finally leaps over a cliff." Univ Handbk for Readers and Writers

Short novels of Henry James; with eight full-page illustrations; introduction by E. Hudson Long. Harcourt Brace Jovanovich 1961 530p il o.p.

"Great illustrated classics"

Contents: Daisy Miller (1878); Washington Square (1881); The Aspern papers (1888); The pupil (1892); The turn of the screw (1898)

The first, second and the last titles are entered separately. The pupil is entered in a combined edition with: What Maisie knew, In the cage and The pupil. "In 'The Aspern Papers,' an unnamed American editor rents a room in Venice in the home of Juliana Bordereau, the elderly mistress of Jeffrey Aspern, a deceased Romantic poet, in order to procure from her the poet's papers." Merriam-Webster's Ency of Lit

James, Henry, 1843-1916—*Continued*

The short stories of Henry James; selected and edited with an introduction by Clifton Fadiman. Dodd, Mead 1945 xx, 644p o.p.

Contents: Four meetings; A bundle of letters; Louisa Pallant; The liar; The real thing; The pupil [novelette]: Booksmith; The middle years; The altar of the dead; "Europe"; The great good place; The tree of knowledge; The tone of time; Mrs. Medwin; The birthplace; The beast in the jungle [novelette]; The jolly corner

The siege of London

In James, H. Complete stories, 1874-1884

In James, H. The complete tales of Henry James

The spoils of Poynton; edited with an introduction by David Lodge and notes by Patricia Crick. Penguin Books 1987 247p pa $13

ISBN 0-14-043288-4

First published 1896 by Houghton

"Owen Gareth, heir to the great house at Poynton, spurns his mother's favorite, Fleda Vetch, to marry Mona Brigstock. Old Mrs. Gareth thereupon removes her art treasures from Poynton. Owen was in fact in love with Fleda, and offers her any object she may desire at Poynton, but suddenly the house is ruined by an accidental fire, which ruins the spoils that have warped so many lives." Haydn. Thesaurus of Book Dig

The turn of the screw; edited by Allan Lloyd Smith. J.M. Dent 1993 xxxii, 139p pa $8.95

ISBN 0-460-87299-0 LC 94-125860

First published 1898

This novella "is told from the viewpoint of the leading character, a governess in love with her employer, who goes to an isolated English estate to take charge of Miles and Flora, two attractive and precocious children. She gradually realizes that her young charges are under the evil influence of two ghosts, Peter Quint, the ex-steward, and Miss Jessel, their former governess. At the climax of the story, she enters into open conflict with the children, as a result of which Flora is alienated and Miles dies of fright." Reader's Ency. 4th edition

also in James, H. Complete stories, 1892-1898

also in James, H. The complete tales of Henry James

also in James, H. The Henry James reader p255-356

also in James, H. Short novels of Henry James p407-530

Washington Square. Modern Lib. 1997 248p o.p.

ISBN 0-679-60276-3 LC 97-25219

First published 1881 by Harper

"The novel concerns Catherine Sloper, the shy and stolid daughter of wealthy, urbane, sardonic Dr. Austin Sloper. When young Morris Townsend, who is courting Catherine for her money, learns that her father will disinherit her if she marries him, he leaves her. Renewing his courtship after Dr. Sloper dies and leaves Catherine a small fortune, Morris is rejected sadly but firmly by Catherine, who lives on at Washington Square and is by then a spinster. Thus Catherine, plain and unintelligent, nevertheless withstands the world's assaults." Benet's Reader's Ency of Am Lit

also in James, H. The Henry James reader p1-163

also in James, H. Short novels of Henry James p59-256

What Maisie knew

In James, H. What Maisie knew, In the cage, The pupil

What Maisie knew, In the cage, The pupil. Kelley 1936 xxi, 576p $45

ISBN 0-678-02811-7

"The Novels and tales of Henry James. New York edition v11"

A combined edition of one novel and two novelettes first published 1897, 1898 and 1891 respectively

What Maisie knew, concerns a twelve-year-old girl whose parents have divorced and remarried. Living alternately with each parent she learns that her stepmother and stepfather are having an adulterous affair, just as she had learned of her parents' earlier infidelities. She decides to go to live with her old governess rather than with either parent. In the cage concerns a young woman who works as a telegram dispatcher in a London grocery store. She experiences vicarious enjoyment by imagining details in the lives of her well-to-do customers and even puts off marriage to her working-class fiance while she tries to aid in the affairs of an aristocratic lady and her lover. But when she learns the unsavory truth about the couple from an outside source she decides to proceed with her marriage at once. The pupil deals with an American student who becomes a tutor for the sickly son of a shabby American family traveling about in Europe, develops a strong attachment to the boy, and tries to help him leave his despicable family—with tragic results

The wings of the dove. Modern Lib. 1993 711p o.p.

ISBN 0-679-60067-1 LC 93-15338

First published 1902 by Scribner

"The story is set in London and Venice. Kate Croy is a Londoner who encourages her secret fiancé, Merton Densher, to woo and marry Milly Theale, a wealthy young American who is dying of a mysterious malady. This, Kate reasons, although Milly will die soon, she will at least be happily in love, Merton will inherit her fortune, and Kate and Merton can marry and be rich. Shortly after Milly learns of Merton's and Kate's motives, she dies, leaving Merton a legacy that he is too guilt-ridden to accept. Kate is unwilling to forgo the inheritance, and she and Merton part forever, their relationship destroyed by Milly's unwittingly prescient gift." Merriam-Webster's Ency of Lit

James, P. D.

The black tower. Scribner 1975 271p o.p.

"Adam Dalgliesh, convalescing after a severe illness, arrives at Toynton Grange (Dorset coast), the rest home for the young disabled, just too late to find out why his old friend Father Baddeley had sent for him. The monk-robed Wilfred Anstey and his staff are an odd lot, as are

James, P. D.—*Continued*
the few patients, all in wheelchairs. There's already been a suspicious suicide, and Dalgliesh is not satisfied that the old priest's death was caused by myocarditis alone. Handicapped by poor health, he finally manages to unearth the secret of the grange." Barzun. Cat of Crime. Rev and enl edition

A certain justice. Knopf 1997 364p $25
ISBN 0-375-40109-1 LC 97-36889
"Called in to investigate the murder of barrister Venetia Aldridge in Temple Court, Scotland Yard Commander/poet Adam Dalgliesh and his team find that the death is merely the centerpiece around which swirl other crimes and the dirty little secrets of Aldridge's fellow barristers." Libr J
"In obedience to the classic crime-writing genre, James finally offers up the guilty party, resolving a complicated plot with impeccable logic. But there the symmetry ends, for the moral and emotional questions she asks do not admit of such neatness." N Y Times Book Rev

Death in holy orders. Knopf 2001 415p o.p.
ISBN 0-375-41255-7 LC 2001-88108
In this mystery "almost everything happens behind the closed doors of St. Anselm's, a small Anglican theological college set on a windy cliff abutting the sea. Commander Adam Dalgliesh, as always both wistful and stern, returns to St. Anselm's, where he spent a few blissful boyhood summers, to investigate the death of a student, but the case quickly expands as bodies begin to fall like so many dominoes. It's a pleasure to read James at the top of her form, as she often is here." New Yorker

Death of an expert witness. Scribner 1977 322p o.p.
LC 77-21530
The setting of this novel is "a forensic-science laboratory in a small East Anglia village. One of the senior biologists is found murdered in his triple-locked and delicately alarm-wired office, and Commander Adam Dalgliesh of Scotland Yard . . . is assigned to the case." New Yorker
"Basically James is a novelist who happens to put her character into mystery stories. She is just as much interested in people and their relationships as she is in the conventions of the genre. And being the perceptive and sensitive writer she is, she constructs books that can be read on several levels." N Y Times Book Rev

Devices and desires. Knopf 1990 c1989 433p o.p.
LC 89-45305
First published 1989 in the United Kingdom
"Commander Adam Dalgliesh, travels to the coastal Norfolk community of Larksoken to settle up the estate of his recently deceased aunt. Inevitably, Dalgliesh becomes embroiled in the affairs of the locals, many of them connected with the Larksoken nuclear power plant, which has brought a new economy to the area but has also stirred the juices of antinuclear protestors. Meanwhile, a mad killer called the Whistler is aprowl, savaging women with a bizarre modus operandi." Booklist
"As always with P. D. James, the whodunit element is the lagniappe, so interesting are her characters, so absorbing her depiction of time and place, so rich the texture of the tale she tells." N Y Times Book Rev

Innocent blood. Scribner 1980 311p o.p.
LC 79-28699
"What starts things moving in the tale is a young (adopted) woman's determination to find her real parents. This headstrong wish is gratified, creating social difficulties, deep changes in personal relations, the plotting of a murder, the experience of jail, and miscellaneous sexual activity. The diverse characters are admirably drawn and the author's fingerwork in tying and untying threads is as deft as her touches of sordid life and as nimble as her prose." Barzun. Cat of Crime. Rev and enl edition

Original sin. Knopf 1995 c1994 416p o.p.
LC 94-26094
First published 1994 in the United Kingdom
A mystery featuring Commander Adam Dalgliesh of Scotland Yard. "Innocent House, a nineteenth-century pile on the Thames that accommodates the Peverell Press, presides over this novel of revenge. After Gerard Etienne, the new chairman of the press, announces his plan to sell the house, he ends up dead, with the head of a toy snake stuffed in his mouth. In this elaborate novel, the author . . . does what she does best: shows that guilt and blame have no single address." New Yorker

The skull beneath the skin. Scribner 1982 328p o.p.
LC 82-5981
"Fading actress Clarissa Lisle has been receiving frightening notes and is terrified of failing in her comeback performance, a revival of 'The Duchess of Malfi', held on a small private island off Dorset. Her husband hires detective Cordelia Gray to stop the notes. Once on the island, Cordelia discovers that nearly everyone there has a good reason to hate Clarissa, who is soon found gruesomely battered to death. The isolated group of suspects, hidden clues, and macabre atmosphere of an island castle complete with skulls and underground passageways make a pleasant traditional mystery. But James is never superficial, and her in-depth characterizations and excellent writing reveal complex relationships, motives, and human frailties." Libr J

A taste for death. Knopf 1986 459p o.p.
LC 86-45273
Sir Paul Berowne, a minister of the Crown, is found with his throat cut in the vestry of St. Matthew's church in London. A tramp has also been killed. Dalgliesh and his assistant Kate Miskin seek the solution to the mystery in the victims' past. All the family members and witnesses have something to conceal
This "book is about murder and the way murder changes everything. . . . It is also about the human condition in London today, enlarged by a sense of the British past that stretches back like a rich and barely dwindling perspective." N Y Times Book Rev

An unsuitable job for a woman. Scribner 1973 c1972 216p o.p.
First published 1972 in the United Kingdom
"In this book James's usual investigator, Chief Superintendent Dalgliesh, plays only a minor part. It is Cordelia Gray, the young, intelligent, and clear-thinking owner of an unsuccessful detective agency, who solves the case. She is hired by Sir Ronald Callender to investigate the death by suicide of his son, Mark. Miss Gray's

James, P. D.—*Continued*

meticulous research leads her to suspect that Mark was murdered and makes her a prime target for murder. There are suspenseful moments, close calls, and a very surprising encounter, at last, between Cordelia and Supt. Dalgliesh." Shapiro. Fic for Youth. 3d edition

Jance, Judith A., 1944-

Birds of prey; a novel of suspense; [by] J.A. Lance. Morrow 2001 390p o.p.

ISBN 0-380-97407-X LC 00-59445

"Retired Seattle cop J. P. Beaumont accompanies his newlywed, eightysomething grandmother and her crusty hubby, Lars Jenssen, on an Alaskan cruise to act as a chaperone of sorts. The jaded protagonist is inadvertently forced to masquerade as an FBI agent when Dr. Harrison Featherman's shrill blonde wife Margaret is tossed overboard, and the crime is captured on ship security cameras." Libr J

Breach of duty; a J.P. Beaumont mystery; [by] J.A. Jance. Avon Bks. 1999 343p o.p.

ISBN 0-380-97406-1 LC 98-42112

In this J.P. Beaumont "mystery, the sensitive Seattle police detective, a recovering alcoholic, juggles several mysteries, including the arson-induced death of an older woman and a series of crimes related to the stolen bones of a Native American shaman. Meanwhile, partner Sue Danielson is hounded by her ex-husband, and all three 'cases' move to violent conclusions almost simultaneously." Libr J

Dead to rights; a Joanna Brady mystery; [by] J. A. Jance. Avon Bks. 1996 373p o.p.

LC 96-24634

"When veterinarian Amos Buckwalter is murdered, all fingers point to Hal Morgan, the angry husband of a woman the drunken vet killed in a car accident the previous year. When she alone thinks he's innocent, Brady, herself a bereaved widow, is unsure if her personal feelings are getting in the way of her professional judgment. More deaths follow as the emotionally fragile Brady attempts to juggle her own family problems . . . with the trials of her job and a potential new love interest." Booklist

"Jance skillfully ties the mystery to the southeastern Arizona landscape, its historic mining towns and their modern problems." Publ Wkly

Devil's claw; a Joanna Brady mystery; [by] J.A. Jance. Morrow 2000 374p o.p.

ISBN 0-380-97501-7 LC 00-25805

Set "in Cochise County, Arizona. This time County Sheriff Joanna Brady is working two cases in the weeks before her wedding to Butch Dixon. The first involves the death of her octogenarian handyman, friend, and neighbor, Clayton Rhodes. . . . The other case involves the murder of a woman freshly released from prison after serving eight years for murdering her husband." Booklist

"The Arizona desert, as usual in Jance's mysteries, plays an unforgettable part in this atmospheric tale." Publ Wkly

Kiss of the bees; [by] J. A. Jance. Avon Bks. 2000 389p o.p.

ISBN 0-380-97747-8 LC 99-35465

"In Tucson, twenty years ago, a psychopath named Andrew Carlisle brought blood and terror into the home of Diana Ladd Walker and her family [Hour of the hunter]. When Carlisle died in prison, Diana and her husband, ex-county sheriff Brandon Walker, believed their long nightmare was finally over. They were wrong. Their beloved adopted daughter Lani has vanished—a beautiful Native American teenager destined, according to Tohono O'othham legend, to become a woman of great spiritual power. A serial killer is dead, but his malevolence lives on in another—and now the fiend holds Lani's innocent life in his eager hands." Publisher's note

Lying in wait; a J.P. Beaumont mystery; by J.A. Jance. Morrow 1994 303p o.p.

LC 94-15565

Police detective J.P. Beaumont "tackles a case with its origins in the Nazi death camps of World War II. When not one but two grisly torture-murder victims are discovered in the Seattle area, Beau and his new partner, Sue Danielson, are called in to investigate. Much to Beau's surprise, he finds that one of the victims was married to a former high school classmate, Else Didricksen." Booklist

"Beau and Sue probe Else's high school romance, the missing accident victim and the Nazi connection before they come up with the killer in this red hot, fast-paced story." Publ Wkly

Skeleton canyon; a Joanna Brady mystery; [by] J. A. Jance. Avon Bks. 1997 373p o.p.

LC 97-3217

"When high-school valedictorian Bree O'Brien is found dead in the southeastern Arizona mountains, suspicion falls on her boyfriend, Ignacio Ybarra, who refuses to explain his fresh cuts and bruises. But the case isn't that simple, as Coshise County Sheriff Joanna Brady learns. . . . Jance's regional knowledge runs deep, whether she writes about troubled Anglo-Hispanic relations along the border or the surprising power of Arizona thunderstorms." Publ Wkly

Jen, Gish

The love wife. Knopf 2004 379p $24.95

ISBN 1-400-04213-5 LC 2004-40917

"A meddlesome Chinese-American mother bequeaths a Chinese nanny to her ambivalent son and his big blonde wife in this darkly comic fairy tale about cultural assimilation, biological destiny and domestic warfare." Publ Wkly

"In a story told from multiple points of view, Jen turns stereotypes upside down by giving each character an issue, label or characteristic you might not expect." USA Today

Mona in the promised land. Knopf 1996 303p o.p.

LC 95-44447

This continues the story of the Chang family which began in Typical American. "This time, the focus is on Ralph and Helen's brash teenager, Mona. The success of their pancake restaurant has enabled the Changs to move to 'the promised land': Scarshill, New York, circa 1968. Drawn by the good schools and the majestic landscaping, the Changs are unprepared to deal with their daughter's attempts to assimilate into the community, namely, her

Jen, Gish—*Continued*

decision to convert to Judaism. As Mona takes instruction from an unconventional rabbi, participates in rap sessions with her fellow temple-goers, and has her first sexual encounter with a smart, politically active college dropout, the Changs are at first bemused and then thunderstruck by their daughter's un-Chinese-like behavior." Booklist

This work "has a wide-ranging exuberance that's unusual in what is still—to its credit—a realistic novel. Ms. Jen doesn't sacrifice her characters to satire. And her story can take the broad view even while it focuses on smaller, more personal matters because she works in so many voices and because she includes so many perfectly timed set pieces." N Y Times Book Rev

Typical American. Houghton Mifflin 1991 296p o.p.

LC 90-48423

"Yefing Chang becomes Ralph Chang in America and begins a hard struggle to achieve the American dream—a career, a family and a home of his own. In poverty, he succeeds finally to win a doctoral degree, a college position, a happy marriage to Helen, two delightful daughters and a close reunion with his older sister, Theresa. The dream becomes a nightmare when he meets Grover Ding whose corrupt influence over Ralph and Helen begins to unravel all that the Changs have managed to achieve. This is an honest novel that does not promise happy endings and recognizes the human weaknesses that can destroy a family's stability." Shapiro. Fic for Youth. 3d edition

Followed by Mona in the promised land (1996)

Who's Irish?; stories. Knopf 1999 207p $22

ISBN 0-375-40621-2 LC 98-42801

Contents: Who's Irish?; Birthmates; The water faucet vision; Duncan in China; Just wait; Chin; In the American society; House. House. Home

"Jen's characters, Chinese immigrants and their American-born children, find themselves commuting between two cultures, between familial expectations and their own yearnings for self-definition, between remembered traditions and shiny, new dreams." N Y Times Book Rev

Jenkins, Will F., 1896-1975

Exploration team

In The Hugo winners p95-142

Jennings, Gary

Aztec. Atheneum Pubs. 1980 754p o.p.

LC 80-55608

"Mixtli (Dark Cloud), the book's hero, is a Mexicatl who is born on the outskirts of the capital city of Tenochtitlan a half-century before the arrival of Cortés. He becomes, in turn, a student, a scribe, a soldier, a merchant, a cultural anthropologist, an adviser to noble rulers, and finally an involuntary chronicler of his people's past for the victorious Spaniards. The book is presented as the verbatim transcript of the reminiscences of this 'elderly male Indian,' recorded at the command of Emperor Charles I, who is eager to learn more about his recently acquired colony of New Spain." N Y Times Book Rev

Aztec blood. Forge 2001 525p o.p.

ISBN 0-312-86251-2 LC 2001-40130

"A Tom Doherty Associates book"

An adventure tale set in "17th-century Mexico as seen through the eyes of a teenage boy. . . . Cristo is a *lepero*, a scorned *mestizo* beggar who lives by his wits, conniving and scheming merely to stay alive. He is taught to read, write, and converse in foreign tongues by Fray Antonio, a Catholic friar. When the friar is murdered, Cristo must flee for his life, although he doesn't know why. On the way to discovering the truth about himself, he encounters many colorful characters and adventures." Libr J

"Injustice has seldom been so keenly sketched nor valor so compellingly portrayed as in this swashbuckling adventure." Publ Wkly

Raptor. Doubleday 1992 980p o.p.

LC 92-9433

In this "historical novel about the Gothic conquest of the Roman Empire, Thorn, the hermaphrodite hero/heroine, is seduced first by a monk and then by a nun. Evicted from a monastery and a convent, Thorn is then schooled in the ways of the world by the grumpy, blasphemous woodsman Wyrd. Rugged yet sensitive, usually dressed as a man, Thorn is raptorial (i.e., predatory) in his thirst for lovers, male and female, and for adventure. He serves as field marshal, sidekick and spy for bloody Theodoric (A.D. 454-526), king of the Ostrogoths, depicted here as a benevolent despot." Publ Wkly

"Like Michener, Jennings fills his boldly sketched historical canvas with lively action and dense, well-researched detail; in the works of both, a strong plot and interesting characters often camouflage an absence of style. But readers will enjoy this trip to an exotic world." Booklist

Jensen, Mrs. Oliver *See* Stafford, Jean, 1915-1979

Jewett, Sarah Orne, 1849-1909

The best stories of Sarah Orne Jewett; selected and arranged with a preface by Willa Cather. Houghton Mifflin 1925 2v o.p.

"The Mayflower edition"

Contents: v1 Return; Mrs. Todd; Schoolhouse; At the schoolhouse window; Captain Littlepage; Waiting place; Outer island; Green island; William; Where penny-royal grew; Old singers; Strange sail; Poor Joanna; Hermitage; On Shellheap island; Great expedition; Country road; Bowden reunion; Feast's end; Along shore; Dunnett shepherdess; Queen's twin; William's wedding; Backward view

v2 A white heron; The flight of Betsy Lane; The Dulham ladies; Going to Shrewsbury; The only rose; Miss Tempy's watchers; Martha's lady; The guests of Mrs. Timms; The town poor; The Hilton's holiday; Aunt Cynthy Dallett

The country of the pointed firs. Houghton Mifflin 1896 213p o.p.

"Highly regarded for its sympathetic yet unsentimental portrayal of the town of Dunnet Landing and its residents, this episodic book is narrated by a nameless summer visitor who relates the life stories of various inhabi-

Jewett, Sarah Orne, 1849-1909—*Continued*

tants, capturing the idiomatic language, customs, mannerisms, and humor peculiar to Down-Easters." Merriam-Webster's Ency of Lit

also in Jewett, S. O. The best stories of Sarah Orne Jewett

also in Jewett, S. O. The country of the pointed firs and other stories p1-139

The country of the pointed firs and other stories. Modern Lib. 1995 247p o.p.

ISBN 0-679-60173-2 LC 95-2831

In addition to the title story, this volume also includes the following: The queen's twin; A Dunnet shepherdess; The foreigner; William's wedding

Jhabvala, Ruth Prawer

East into Upper East; plain tales from New York and New Delhi. Counterpoint 1998 314p o.p.

ISBN 1-88717-850-3 LC 98-34881

Contents: Expiation; Farid and Farida; Independence; Development and progress; A New Delhi romance; Husband and son; The temptress; A summer by the sea; Great expectations; Parasites; Fidelity; Bobby; Broken promises; Two muses

"Jhabvala is a connoisseur of divided souls, conceiving characters whose inner longings are at odds with their outer protective coloration—Indians who covet and achieve more tidy, 'modernized' existences, then feel as if someone had stolen their life force; Westerners who eagerly hand themselves over to India's chaotic bliss, then find it too rigorous to endure." N Y Times Book Rev

Heat and dust. Harper & Row 1976 c1975 181p o.p.

"A Joan Kahn book"

First published 1975 in the United Kingdom

"The juxtaposition of past and present India is explored in this novel. The 1923 storyline tells of Olivia, who, though married to a British officer stationed in India, falls madly in love with an Indian prince. It is also about Olivia's husband's granddaughter by a second marriage, who has come to India to discover the details of Olivia's life but finds that, although India and women have become modernized, she must face many of the same choices as Olivia. The intrusion of British culture on India's own traditions and values is a second theme in the novel." Shapiro. Fic for Youth. 3d edition

My nine lives. Shoemaker & Hoard 2004 277p $25

ISBN 1-59376-028-0

In this autobiographical novel the author turns the lens "upon herself in a series of self-described invented memories. Each of the nine chapters presents a possible past for its first-person narrator. The familial relationships depicted vary as much as the locales, spanning relations between parents, siblings, lovers, or husbands in settings as far-reaching as England, India, and the United States." Libr J

"Jhabvala name-drops Chekhov, and this is no pretension given the grace of her spiraling plots, the depth of her psychology, the elegance of her humor, the subtly of her eroticism, and her masterfully concise descriptions of imperiled households, eccentric personalities, sexual enthrallment, unexpected alliances, and transcendent love." Booklist

Out of India; selected stories. Morrow 1986 288p o.p.

LC 85-25961

Contents: My first marriage; The widow; The interview; A spiritual call; Passion; The man with the dog; An experience of India; The housewife; Rose petals; Two more under the Indian sun; Bombay; On bail; In the mountains; How I became a holy mother; Desecration

"Out of a web of subtle but not precious ironies, couched in a limpid style, arises a sense of the author's obvious love-hate attitude toward this land that is so difficult to live in, for foreigner and native alike. Jhabvala sensitively explores the tense juncture between Western and Indian cultures; plots and characters glow with realism and energy." Booklist

Shards of memory. Doubleday 1995 221p o.p.

LC 94-45311

This novel chronicles "four generations of a family who, in varying degrees, follow a charismatic leader known as the Master. Told in the form of remembrances of people who were involved with the Master, as collected by Henry, his possible successor, the story becomes intensely personal because of the way it weaves its multiple memories. . . . Every member of the family is touched by the Master in a unique way. Elsa, the tempestuous woman who becomes his devoted follower, is the mother of Baby, who is able to experience the guru as more than master. Baby's lackluster daughter, Renata, comes to the Master's teachings late, but she is never sure whether he has given her a more profound gift than enlightenment—her son, Henry." Booklist

"Jhabvala's understanding of character is shrewd, and her language is controlled and lucid. . . . [Her] technical fluency and poise are admirable; combined with Jhabvala's sensitivity, and her understanding of characters, they make the novel feel startlingly realistic, so that the vagueness of the central themes, and the sometimes slow development of plot seem almost irrelevant." Times Lit Suppl

Jiles, Paulette, 1943-

Enemy women. Morrow 2002 321p o.p.

ISBN 0-06-621444-0 LC 2001-40200

"For Adair Randolph Colley, at 18 the eldest daughter of a widowed Missouri Ozarks schoolmaster and justice of the peace, the Civil War becomes personal when her father, who has remained neutral in the conflict, is arrested by the Union militia, their home is nearly burned and their possessions stolen. At the start of this . . . novel, Adair and her two younger sisters try to follow their father's captors, but Adair is falsely denounced as a Confederate spy. At the prison in St. Louis, upright commandant Maj. William Neumann is . . . touched by Adair's beauty and spirit and asks her to give him some information so she can be released. Instead, she writes the story of her life, augmented by folk tales and fables, and he finds himself falling in love. When he gets his reassignment orders, he proposes marriage and asks her to escape, promising to find her after the war. Thus begins a long and terrible journey for each of them." Publ Wkly

Jin, Ha *See* Ha Jin, 1956-

Joe, Yolanda

My fine lady; Yolanda Joe. Dutton 2004 221p $23.95
ISBN 0-525-94808-2 LC 2003-17788
"Imani Holland has a voice like 'velvet on fire,' and she raps the lyrics her boyfriend, Taz, writes; together they're gonna make it big. At an unofficial competition at the local college campus, Imani catches the attention of Orenthal Hopson, a gifted young musician and academic. Hopson's been butting heads with department chair Perkins over his theory of music's transformative powers, and Imani's raw talent makes her the perfect test—Perkins will give Hopson three months to make Imani into a jazz diva." Publ Wkly
"A fantastic update of Pygmalion and hip Americanization of My Fair Lady . . ., Joe's compelling tale about one woman's coming into her own and the dichotomy between educated African Americans and those living in poverty may well become a popular classic in its own right." Booklist

Johansen, Iris

And then you die—. Bantam Bks. 1998 344p o.p.
LC 97-40073
"When photojournalist Bess Grady is sent on assignment to a small town in Mexico, she unwittingly finds herself in the midst of a horrific nightmare. Every citizen of the town has died of anthrax poisoning as a result of a terrorist germ-warfare attack. Because she survived, Bess is sought by both the terrorists and a hard-hearted CIA man. The plot is filled with clever detours that twist and turn and cast suspicion on all of the main players until Bess doesn't know who to trust." Booklist

Blind alley; Iris Johansen. Bantam Books 2004 344p $25
ISBN 0-553-80341-7 LC 2004-54410
In this thriller featuring "Atlanta detective Joe Quinn and the love of his life, forensic sculptor Eve Duncan, Joe gives Eve a skull to reconstruct. Eerily enough, the face resembles 17-year-old Jane MacGuire, who has been offered sanctuary by Eve and Joe after surviving a rough-and-tumble life on the streets. . . . Several look-alikes have already been killed in Europe, and Scotland Yard sends in hunky Mark Trevor to help. Eve mistrusts him, but Jane, who has had recurring nightmares related to the killings, believes that he's there to help her. Eve and Joe want to protect Jane, but the intrepid teenager knows that unless she confronts the killer, she will live the rest of her life in fear. Johansen has become adept at mixing supernatural elements with intriguing suspense." Booklist

The face of deception. Bantam Bks. 1998 354p o.p.
ISBN 0-553-10623-6 LC 98-24713
Forensic sculptor Eve Duncan "is swept into a maelstrom of murder, deception, and political intrigue when she is coerced into rebuilding the face of an adult whose remains consist of a burned skull. Obsessed with establishing the identities of the skeletal remains of murdered children ever since her daughter was killed and the body was never found. Eve resists the request of billionaire John Logan to work on this mysterious case until her lab is destroyed and her mother threatened." Booklist
"With the help of well-timed, steady disclosures and surprising revelations, the book's twists and turns manage to hold the reader hostage until the denouement." Publ Wkly

Final target. Bantam Bks. 2001 340p $24.95
ISBN 0-553-80094-9 LC 00-65124
At the center of this thriller "is the Wind Dancer, a priceless gold statue of the winged horse Pegasus. The statue has been in the Andreas family since the fall of Troy and now, centuries later, U.S. President Jonathan Andreas is in Paris to lend the family heirloom to a museum. On the night of the ceremony, his daughter, seven-year-old Cassie, is awakened at the family's farmhouse in the south of France by masked men who murder her nanny and her nurse, intent on kidnapping Cassie and ransoming her in exchange for the Wind Dancer. Cassie is saved in the nick of time by the arrival of Michael Travis, international underworld information dealer, but eight months later, the child is being treated in the Virginia home of psychiatrist Dr. Jessica Riley and Jessica's psychically extrasensitive sister, Melissa, for severe catatonic trauma. . . . Michael Travis then reappears and lures Cassie and the Riley sisters into a web of intrigue." Publ Wkly

The killing game. Bantam Bks. 1999 355p o.p.
ISBN 0-553-10624-4 LC 99-20999
Following the abduction and murder of her daughter in The face of deception, forensic sculptor Eve Duncan "has abandoned the day-to-day world for life on a Tahitian island. Eve's tropical exile is interrupted, however, when Joe [Quinn] shows up to tell her that a pile of bodies has been discovered in the Georgia woods, including that of a young girl he believes may be Eve's daughter. Determined to reconstruct the skull and hoping to lay her daughter to rest, Eve returns to the U.S. Her arrival draws the attention of Dom, the psychotic serial killer responsible for the Georgia murders. Random attacks on social outcasts don't produce the rush they once did for Dom, and now he needs to up the ante, by stalking and murdering more prominent people and interacting with his victims before he attacks. Eve, whose story he has long followed in newspaper accounts, becomes his next target." Publ Wkly
"Johansen's novel of psychological suspense features a hair-raising plot, a fiendish killer, a brave heroine, and dozens of heartstopping plot twists." Booklist

Long after midnight. Bantam Bks. 1997 371p o.p.
LC 96-24957
"Genetic research and industrial espionage are at the center of this story about Kate Denby, a research scientist working on a new way for medicine to be delivered to the human cell. Another researcher, who owns his own company, wants Kate to work for him. He needs what she's working on because it dovetails with the project he's working on: a powerful new drug that will strengthen the immune system beyond anything currently available. But there's somebody out there who doesn't want Kate to succeed." Booklist
"Johansen knows how to take the formula and run with

Johansen, Iris—*Continued*
it, and readers will be won over by her flesh-and-blood characters, crackling dialogue and lean, suspenseful plotting." Publ Wkly

The ugly duckling. Bantam Bks. 1996 378p o.p.
LC 95-36175
"Nell Carter is plain and plump—and, for some mysterious reason, the target of a drug cartel hit that maims her but wipes out her husband and young daughter. Her world destroyed, Nell wills herself to die, until a stranger gives her a purpose to live: revenge. The mysterious Nicholas Tanek, once master of his own criminal network, will do anything and use anyone to destroy the drug cartel that, he tells Nell, murdered a 'very close' friend. . . . Given a new face and identity, Nell throws herself into guerrilla and martial arts training with Nicholas." Publ Wkly
"A forceful, enigmatic hero with a dangerous past and a mission of his own; a focused, determined, and refreshingly creative heroine who develops quite nicely; and a few interesting secondary characters join forces in a well-executed story that deftly provides chilling suspense without sacrificing a warm romance." Libr J

Johnson, Adam

Parasites like us; a novel. Viking 2003 341p $24.95
ISBN 0-670-03240-9 LC 2002-41181
"Anthropology professor Hank Hannah studies the Clovis people, a prehistoric tribe of hunter-gatherers. His theory is that their hunting habits helped kill off 35 species of large mammals. The discovery of a Clovis arrowhead helps substantiate his claim, but disaster strikes when Hannah and two graduate students, publicity hound Brent Eggers and formidable Trudy Labelle, try to dig up the remains of a Clovis male. The police appear and Hannah is arrested for assaulting the officer who defiles the grave site. His stint at a luxury low-security prison, Club Fed, is interrupted by the outbreak of a deadly epidemic, transmitted from pigs to humans and triggered when Eggers and Labelle use the Clovis arrowhead to kill a pig." Publ Wkly
"Johnson relates all of this with great ingenuity and bravado—as well as a good deal of unfocused energy. . . . The most daring element in this heterogeneous mix, however, may well be the vein of earnest solemnity that Johnson adds to it. Unlike most satirists, he's not afraid to let the mask of irony fall occasionally." N Y Times Book Rev

Johnson, Charles Richard, 1948-

Dr. King's refrigerator and other bedtime stories; [by] Charles Johnson. Scribner 2005 123p $20
ISBN 0-7432-6453-3 LC 2004-56642
Contents: Sweet dreams; Cultural relativity; Dr. King's refrigerator; The gift of the Osuo; Executive decision; Better than counting sheep; The queen and the philosopher; Kwoon
"Johnson is once again at the ready with his quirky, professorial writing style and his melange of Buddhism, Western philosophy and African magic realism." N Y Times Book Rev

Dreamer; a novel; [by] Charles Johnson. Scribner 1998 236p o.p.
ISBN 0-684-81224-X LC 98-10201
"Chaym Smith doesn't have much going for him, except for his uncanny resemblance to Civil Rights leader Martin Luther King Jr. After a tour of duty in Korea, where he was severely wounded, Smith drifted around the East for several years. . . . Now, in the late 1960s, this modern-day Cain hopes to redeem himself by acting as a decoy for Dr. King at his increasingly dangerous public appearances. He quickly accepted into King's inner circle, where he learns to dress and speak like his hero. But as their partnership grows, King seems to take on some of Smith's characteristics. There are sinister hints that this mysterious doppelganger may be working for the FBI." Libr J
"It's a joy to read fiction in which there is a cultivated vision at work. Among the accomplishments of 'Dreamer' is an overarching argument that the Truth is an amalgamation, a messy mosaic full of contradictions . . . and that the best way to get at it is to include a lot." N Y Times Book Rev

Middle passage; [by] Charles Johnson. Atheneum Pubs. 1990 209p o.p.
LC 90-32713
The protagonist of this novel, set in 1830, "is Rutherford Calhoun, a newly freed slave leading a dissolute life in New Orleans. Rutherford finds himself forced into marriage with Isadora Bailey, a proper yet severe Boston schoolteacher, and, to quickly escape both wedlock and his Louisiana debts, he stows away on the first available ship. To his shock and horror, Rutherford learns that the vessel, the Republic, is a slave ship bound for Africa. Its captain is the American soldier of fortune, Ebenezer Falcon, a buccaneer and empire-builder. . . . The Republic's mission is to transport the last survivors of a nearly legendary tribe, the Allmuseri, from their devastated homeland to the New World." Publisher's note
"Johnson's exciting sea narrative provides an unusual historical look at the horrifying Middle Passage experience. . . . Like Moby-Dick's Ahab, the captain of the Republic is on his own special quest (in this case, the capture of the African trickster god). . . . Above all, the book is valuable in offering a rare perspective of the shocking experience of the slave trade and the consequences of that event for American blacks." Choice

Johnson, Diane, 1934-

Le divorce. Dutton 1997 309p o.p.
LC 96-9644
"A William Abrahams book"
"Film-school dropout Isabel Walker arrives in Paris intending to baby-sit for her sister Roxeanne and figure out her next move. Unfortunately, Roxeanne's French husband, Charles-Henri Persand, has abandoned her for another woman, and the pregnant Roxeanne seems suicidal. As the divorce proceedings heat up, the rights to an extremely valuable painting that Roxeanne has had since childhood are suddenly in dispute. Meanwhile, Isabel has become the mistress of a famous 70-year-old Persand relative, much to the Persands' distress, and as Isabel and Roxy's family descend on Paris, the American and French families face off." Booklist
"The author pokes fun at the Americans for moraliz-

Johnson, Diane, 1934-—*Continued*

ing, and at the French for being amoral; and she manages to be even-handed because she displays admiration for French elegance of behavior, and affection for American earnest good will." N Y Rev Books

L'affaire. Dutton 2003 340p $24.95
ISBN 0-525-94740-X LC 2003-13725

"Amy Hawkins, a beautiful, naive, suddenly very rich Californian dot-com entrepreneur, comes to a posh ski resort in the French Alps as part of her plan for cultural self-improvement. When she generously pays for transporting the dying Adrian Venn, a publisher crushed in a landslide, back to his native England, her humanitarian gesture backfires with exquisite irony. Venn's two grown English children, his illegitimate French daughter, his new much younger American wife and their toddler son become embroiled in a classic scenario of quarreling heirs, each seething with expectations at the expense of the others." Publ Wkly

"Much of the wit comes from Johnson's shrewd view of her characters' cultural assumptions, which are both simplistic and devilishly on target." N Y Times Book Rev

Le mariage; a novel. Dutton 2000 322p $23.95
ISBN 0-525-94518-0 LC 99-89849

This companion to Le divorce is "set again in Paris with a few overlapping characters, the plot revolves around two couples—Tim Nolinger, a Belgian American journalist engaged to the very French Anne-Sophie, a dealer in equine collectibles; and the very beautiful American Clara, a former actress married to the reclusive film director Serge Clay. Thrown into the entertaining mix is a stolen illuminated manuscript, a murdered flea market dealer, Y2K cults, an adulterous liaison, and of course Johnson's perceptive and witty insights on love, marriage, and Anglo-French relations." Libr J

Johnson, Stephanie, 1961-

The sailmaker's daughter. St. Martin's Press 2003 255p il map $23.95
ISBN 0-312-30693-8 LC 2003-40639

First published 1996 in the United Kingdom with title: The heart's wild surf

"The book follows 12-year-old Olive McNab during the month she is sent to her aunt and uncle's plantation while her mother is dying of influenza. Olive is haunted by ghosts of the family dead, appalled by her uncle's coarse brutality, fascinated by two free-spirited British lady travelers who are passing through, and, most of all, anguished by her mother's approaching death. In Johnson's poetic hands Olive and her eccentric family come to life." Libr J

Johnson, Wayne

The devil you know; a novel; Wayne Johnson. 1st ed. Shaye Areheart Books 2004 381p $23
ISBN 0-609-60964-5 LC 2003-11616

"Set in Minnesota in the 1970s, this . . . is at once a coming-of-age tale and a survival story. Fifteen-year-old David Geist is the product of a troubled family. His father, Max, physically abused him before abandoning the family. A budding track star, David is now being bullied by a lunkish football player at school. When his estranged father returns, he proposes that David and his younger sister, Janie, take a trip to the north woods with him as a way of healing old wounds. Once there, the family runs afoul of a group of smalltime criminals. After David wards off a brutal attack on their campsite, he has to find a way to get his injured father and sister to safety while being pursued by the remaining thugs." Libr J

"Johnson surrounds a mythic, Deliverance-like confrontation with evil . . . with a subtly realsitic coming-of-age story about a teenager's conflict with his abusive father. Rising above cliché at every seemily predictable turn, the novel works on both levels: a literary thriller with an abundance of heart." Booklist

Johnston, Terry C., 1947-2001

Cry of the hawk; a novel. Bantam Bks. 1992 391p o.p.
LC 92-46

"To get out of the Union prison at Rock Island, Illinois, Confederate Jonah Hook volunteers to go West and fight Indians as a 'galvanized Yankee.' When the Civil War and his service for the hated North end, he returns home to find his family has been abducted by a roaming band of Mormon Danites. Jonah's turbulent search for them over the Western plains develops into a stunning narrative of violent life on the frontier." Libr J

Followed by Winter rain

Dance on the wind. Bantam Bks. 1995 517p o.p.
LC 95-7558

"Johnston here reprises Titus Bass, the central character in several of his earlier novels. In this story of Bass's coming of age, the itchy-footed adolescent runs away from the sameness of his father's Kentucky farm in 1810. Teaming with flatboaters floating supplies down the Ohio and Mississippi rivers to New Orleans, he experiences the dangers and earthly pleasures of that breed of adventurer. But he finds river life unsatisfying and soon settles down at a blacksmith's forge in St. Louis—until a mountain man resurrects his restless desire to move West." Libr J

The author "is a deservedly popular western author whose appeal lies not so much in the adventures he dramatizes as in the depth of his characters. They love, grieve, laugh, and feel guilt, anger, and jealousy. They're real people, not just providers of vicarious thrills." Booklist

Death rattle; a novel. Bantam Bks. 1999 429p $24.95
ISBN 0-553-09084-4 LC 99-15684

"The frontier that Titus Bass has known is shrinking. The beaver-skin trade is virtually over. . . . Not ready to give in to civilization, Bass embarks, with some of his fellow trappers, on an adventure to Southern California, where they plan to steal horses that can then be sold to settlers. The ex-trappers get the horses but find themselves the objects of a relentless pursuit by Mexican soldiers. Indians attack them as well, and, finally, they find themselves in the middle of the legendary Taos rebellion." Bookist

Johnston, Terry C., 1947-2001—*Continued*

Dream catcher. Bantam Bks. 1994 446p o.p.
LC 94-11547

"In this final entry in the Jonah Hook trilogy, the battle-weary Civil War veteran finally rescues his kidnapped wife, Gritta, after a decade-long search. After returning from the war, Hook discovers that his wife and family are prisoners of renegade Mormon zealot Jubilee Usher, who adds Gritta to his harem despite her continued physical and emotional resistance, which only fuels his sadism. All the while Gritta is held captive, Jonah, son Jeremiah, and Indian companion Two Sleep search ceaselessly for her. On the trail, they endure the vagaries of nature, outlaws, and hostile Indians. . . . Though there are too many peripheral characters and adventures her, the novel's reach never quite exceeds its grasp." Booklist

Lay the mountains low; the flight of the Nez Perce from Idaho and the Battle of the Big Hole, August 9-10, 1877. St. Martin's Press 2000 xxii, 495p il o.p.
ISBN 0-312-26189-6 LC 00-24201

"In this tale of five Nez Perce tribal leaders who choose to resist the encroaching white settlers and who refuse to make treaties with the U.S. government, Johnston provides gripping, authentic details of historically accurate events; readers see the Nez Perce wars through the eyes of those involved and read actual letters and newspaper clippings of the day. Besides the historical details, the novel presents a compelling, action-packed story." Libr J

Turn the stars upside down; the last days and tragic death of Crazy Horse. St. Martin's Press 2001 329p o.p.
ISBN 0-312-27757-1 LC 2001-19264

This installment in the author's "Plainsmen series recounts Crazy Horse's surrender to the U.S. Army at Camp Robinson, Neb. Here the {author} . . . attempts to set straight the diverse and highly questionable account of the shameful events leading up to Crazy Horse's mortal stabbing while he was resisting incarceration in an Army guardhouse on September 5, 1877. The perfidy begins scarcely a day after Crazy Horse's surrender, when the U.S. decides not to honor its promise to give him agency to the north. It is further compounded when the Army reneges on its pledge to allow him to take a hunting party to gather meat to see his people through the winter. When Crazy Horse is offered the opportunity to scout for the Army to quell a new Nez Percé uprising, he responds eagerly, but a malevolent interpreter bearing an old grudge misquotes him." Publ Wkly

Wind walker. Bantam Bks. 2001 461p map $24.95
ISBN 0-553-09090-9 LC 00-48570

This final installment in the Titus Bass series "covers six years (1847-1853) and sees the scarred, aging, one-eyed mountain man struggling to find peace and sanctuary in a changing world. The fur trade is finished, free mountain men are few and white immigrants are flooding the pristine and untamed wilderness. Bass knows his independent way of life is over, so he takes his Indian family north, hoping to settle with his wife's Crow relatives. Bass's final journey, however, will not be easy. . . . Titus Bass is a believable, enduring character, a solitary man who lives by his wits, believes in mountain justice and is willing to use rifle or tomahawk to settle a score when he knows right is on his side." Publ Wkly

Winter rain. Bantam Bks. 1993 419p o.p.
LC 93-15242

In this sequel to Cry of the hawk, Jonah Hook returns "home to Missouri after a stint in a Yankee prison camp and service in the Indian wars out West, [Jonah Hook] the former Confederate finds that his wife Gritta, their daughter Hattie and two sons have been kidnapped by raiders. He begins a seven-year quest, reminiscent of John Ford's epic film *The Searchers*, to find his family. . . . Told in a flashback from 1908, when the aged Jonah recounts his ordeal to a newspaper reporter, the narrative follows him as he recovers Hattie and one of the boys. . . . Johnston has a good sense of place and a fine knowledge of history." Publ Wkly

Followed by Dream catcher

Johnston, Wayne

The colony of unrequited dreams. Anchor Bks. (NY) 1999 562p o.p.
ISBN 0-385-49542-0 LC 99-19144

This is the "fictional biography of Joe Smallwood, one of Newfoundland's most controversial political figures, and focuses on his early years and arduous rise to power: union organizer, newspaperman, socialist turned liberal, and Newfoundland's first premier after confederation with Canada in 1949. . . . [In] counterpoint are the views of Smallwood's lifelong friend, Sheilagh Fielding, as set forth in her acerbic newspaper columns, personal journals, and irreverently entertaining *Condensed History of Newfoundland*." Booklist

"The very human story of Smallwood and Fielding and its historical counterpoint may both appear inauspicious, even contrived, at first, but as the book proceeds they and their pairing gather momentum to achieve a mesmerizing inevitability." N Y Times Book Rev

Human amusements. Anchor Bks. 2004 326p pa $13.95
ISBN 1-4000-3197-4 (pa)

"Substitute teachers Audrey and Peter Prendergast are struggling to get by in Toronto in the 1950s when Audrey's idea for a TV show for preschoolers becomes a runaway success. She goes on to write a series starring their son, Henry, as Philo Farnsworth, the teenage inventor of the television set. It becomes a huge cult favorite, inspiring fanatical followers dubbed Philosophers who re-enact the episodes. Peter, struggling to complete a novel he has been working on for 15 years, offers caustic running commentary on popular culture, with especially vitriolic remarks reserved for the role of television, and amuses himself by staging mock fights with Henry for the tabloids. As the eccentric Prendergasts seem about to collapse under the weight of their enormous success, they each take drastic action to preserve their family. Johnston brings both high jinks and humanity to his highly original portrait of a more innocent era." Booklist

The navigator of New York; a novel. Doubleday 2002 483p $27.95
ISBN 0-385-50767-4 LC 2002-71418

Johnston, Wayne—*Continued*

"Devlin Stead is the orphaned protagonist raised by his aunt and uncle in Newfoundland after his physician father dies in a polar expediation under the aegis of Robert Edwin Peary and Dr. Frederick Cook. The boy's sheltered existence is shattered when he receives a series of letters from Cook that reveal the explorer—who had committed an indiscretion with Devlin's mother—to be the boy's real father. Cook invites Devlin to New York, where he takes him under his wing and makes him an assistant." Publ Wkly

"Polar exploration—with its incredible hardships, its months of freezing isolation, darkness and despair—makes an irresistable metaphor for a lonely and uncertain childhood. The story itself is told through Devlin's deliberately understated narration and Cook's long expository letters and monologues, which can be tedious at times but which echo the straightforward humble-heroic tone of a Victorian explorer." N Y Times Book Rev

Jones, Diana Wynne

A sudden wild magic. Morrow 1992 412p o.p.

LC 92-10860

"Computer expert Mark Lister, incidentally the only male member of the Inner Ring of witches in Great Britain, unexpectedly comes across evidence that Earth is being manipulated by a distant planet called Arth. This pirate world, an all-male society sworn to celibacy, is sending wars, plagues, and environmental disasters (notably global warming) to Earth and then observing and appropriating Earth's leaders' solutions. In defense, the witches' council decides to transport some attractive female recruits to Arth to sabotage the inhabitants' oaths and restore the balance of power." Booklist

"Jones's sly sense of humor and her accurate, affectionate depiction of relations between women and men give an extra kick to this effervescent tale." Publ Wkly

Jones, Douglas C., 1924-1998

Arrest Sitting Bull. Scribner 1977 249p o.p.

LC 77-7645

In this second volume of a western historical trilogy, the author tells it "as it really *did* happen when the order went out: 'Arrest Sitting Bull.' We begin with the Ghost Dance, when that confusion of Indian mythology and missionary-brought Christianity has fired the Plain Indians to a belief in the coming of an Indian Messiah. Sitting Bull, already the conqueror of Custer, the veteran of Buffalo Bill's Wild West Show, is back on the reservation, but at the center of a growing revolt against the white man. . . . Jones makes us understand the torment of a minority of decent white men and women who really cared about the Indians and of the Indians, trapped between a fight to the death (the novel closes with Wounded Knee three days off), and a willingness to try to assimilate themselves to the white man's ways." Publ Wkly

Followed by A creek called Wounded Knee

The court-martial of George Armstrong Custer. Scribner 1976 291p o.p.

In this novel, the first of a trilogy, history is reshuffled. "Custer survives the Little Big Horn, leaving behind 260 dead comrades. Professionally scandalized, the army under William Sherman charges Custer with insubordination although the man is a folk hero often puffed up in the papers. Marshalling evidence for the government falls to Judge Advocate General Asa Gardiner. A determined idealist, he senses that superiors deem Custer a menace, a 'Golden Cavalier' with dubious ambitions. The defense ostensibly rests on a breakdown in communication and bad field intelligence; actually the implications cut deeper: Custer knows enough to have his Civil War cronies (Schofield, Miles, Sheridan) put in the stockade." Publ Wkly

"Slowly building the cases for the prosecution and defense, Jones does well by mixing the drama of courtroom proceedings with the color of a controversial incident." Booklist

Followed by Arrest Sitting Bull

A creek called Wounded Knee. Scribner 1978 236p o.p.

LC 78-16660

In the concluding volume of the trilogy, the author "tells the story of the Wounded Knee tragedy through the eyes of the principals: the Indians, the Federal troops, and the Press. Each chapter of the novel begins with a verbatim lead from an 1890 newspaper that if not finding the war inevitable at least found it irresistable. The Press did much to make the day." Best Sellers

"We all know what will happen here, and Jones vividly dramatizes it, but, perhaps more important, he dramatizes how it had to happen. For him people create history, and their actions, beliefs, foibles, aspirations, and apprehensions combine to make his 'Wounded Knee' not a historical pageant but a very human tragedy." Libr J

Elkhorn Tavern. Holt, Rinehart & Winston 1980 311p o.p.

LC 79-27818

The author "conveys the turmoil faced by a family caught in the Civil War. Ora Hasford and her two teenage children struggle to preserve the family farm, first against scavenging jayhawkers and later from the artillery launched during the Battle of Pea Ridge, which was waged in their fields and in the nearby town. Not only has Jones used actual wartime events and military figures, but also the Hasford family is itself based on the author's ancestors." Booklist

The search for Temperance Moon. Holt & Co. 1991 324p o.p.

LC 90-25134

"A Donald Hutter book"

"Oscar Schiller, cashiered U.S. deputy marshal, is summoned to Fort Smith, Arkansas' most famous bordello where the madam, Jewel Moon, asks him to solve the murder of her outlaw mother Temperance. The murder has been committed across the river in the Indian Nations, where only tribal police forces and federal courts have jurisdiction. Oscar develops a psychological portrait of Temperance from interviews and enlists the aid of several police comrades in his investigation." Libr J

"Taking obvious delight in his colorful and complex characters, Jones offers a particularly unsentimental view of the post-Civil War West." Booklist

Season of yellow leaf. Holt, Rinehart & Winston 1983 323p il o.p.

LC 83-117

"In the Texas area during the first half of the 1800s the Parry family, Welsh settlers, are eking out a living and facing the usual dangers of frontier life. Their ten-

Jones, Douglas C., 1924-1998—*Continued*

year-old daughter and her younger brother are captured in a raid by Comanche Indians led by Sanchess, son of Iron Shirt. Morfydd is taken into the tribe, since the Indians looked upon all females as potential bearers of warrior sons. She gradually becomes part of the Indian culture and is renamed Chosen. The novel portrays the precarious life of the Indians who had to worry about battles not only with the white man but also with other Indian tribes. Iron Shirt, a respected peace chief of the tribe, foresees the 'season of yellow leaf,' the eventual disappearance of the Indian as the white man moves farther into the West usurping the land and killing buffalo for hides rather than for food." Shapiro. Fic for Youth. 3d edition

Followed by Gone the dreams and dancing (1984)

This savage race. Holt & Co. 1993 401p il o.p.
LC 92-36881

"In 1808, Boone Fawley takes his family out of the relatively civilized city of St. Louis and enters the territory that will soon be called the Louisiana Purchase. They make a hard living near the Mississippi, mostly at the mercy of the Osage and Cherokee or the equally dangerous fur traders. Boone's son Questor exemplifies the agricultural virtues, but son John becomes a hardened wilderness man. When the earthquake of 1811 wipes out the family, they move to Arkansas, where they find that the rudimentary civilization there is even more treacherous than the wilderness." Libr J

"To watch the Fawleys take, pick up stakes, move and then take again, is to watch the American spirit as it is born, for both better and worse." N Y Times Book Rev

Jones, Edward P.

The known world. Amistad 2003 388p $24.95
ISBN 0-06-055754-0 LC 2003-40389

"Henry Townsend, born a slave, is purchased and freed by his father, yet he remains attached to his former owner, even taking lessons in slave owning when he eventually buys his own slaves. Townsend is part of a small enclave of free blacks who own slaves, thus offering another angle on the complexities of slavery and social relations in a Virginia town just before the Civil War." Booklist

"There are few certified villains in the novel, white or black, because slavery poisons moral judgements at the root. . . . The freshness of this story lies in its very incongruity and strangeness." N Y Times Book Rev

Jones, James, 1921-1977

From here to eternity. Scribner 1951 861p o.p.

A story of Army life in Hawaii in the last months before Pearl Harbor. The chief characters are two soldiers—Pfc Robert Prewitt and First Sergeant Milton Warden—and the women they loved

"Mr. Jones has grappled with a variety of materials and handles some of them less successfully than others. There is a good deal of weak stuff in the two love affairs and the characterizations of the women, and the sorties into the field of general ideas are unimpressive. The book as a whole, however, is a spectacular achievement; it has tremendous vitality and driving power and graphic authenticity." Atlantic

The thin red line. Scribner 1962 495p o.p.

"The Thin Red Line is a kind of companion piece [to From here to eternity] which describes the Guadalcanal campaign. . . . Company C-for-Charlie is the 'hero' of this novel which has no hero—except the collective behavior of a wide and varied cross-section of American military men. . . . From the abstract strategy of the Guadalcanal campaign and the Big Brass who have come to watch the show, down to the fighting men who carry out the battle plans without knowing or caring about them, [it] is a many-leveled chronicle of the whole amphibious military operation." N Y Times Book Rev

"This novel will surely offend some readers, lavishly bespattered as it is with Anglo-Saxon words and physiological detail. Nevertheless, it bears the Jones stamp of authenticity and is a major combat novel of World War II." Ont Libr Rev

Followed by Whistle

Whistle. Delacorte Press 1978 457p o.p.
LC 77-11980

This is the final installment of Jones' war trilogy, which also includes From here to eternity and The thin red line. This book begins in 1943, when "four soldiers from an infantry company in the Pacific are sent by boat and train to an army hospital in Tennessee. . . . These men, who have known no security except what the company provided, are quickly unhinged by faithless wives and intolerable families, by their rage and despair at the human condition. . . . To stave off disintegration, these out-of-work warriors resort to . . . drink and brawls, politics and sex. . . . The outline for the conclusion of the book . . . has been pieced together [following his death] from Jones's notes and conversations by his friend and fellow writer Willie Morris." Newsweek

Jones, Stephen, 1953-

(ed) The Best horror from Fantasy tales. See The Best horror from Fantasy tales

Jong, Erica

Fear of flying; a novel. Holt, Rinehart & Winston 1973 340p o.p.

Isadora Wing, the heroine "is twice-married, Barnard-educated, under thirty, and . . . fiercely restless. . . . In Vienna with her psychiatrist husband, she meets an English Laingian who . . . exhorts her to cast off marital ties and live by his self-proclaimed existentialist nonrules. . . . After two weeks of roaring about the Continent in a Triumph, coupling with each other and with strangers met in roadside camps, they split: it's time for the English existentialist to rejoin his wife and kids. Spirits intact, Isadora hunts up her husband's holiday digs; finding him away when she calls, she awaits his return (on the closing page) in his tub." Atlantic

"At times, Jong gets caught in clichés about women, men, sex, and Jewish mothers, all [of] which she could do without. However, when she takes herself more seriously, the language is penetrating, paying tribute to her worth as a poet." Libr J

Followed by How to save your own life (1977) and Parachutes and kisses (1984 paper only)

Sappho's leap; a novel. Norton 2003 316p $24.95
ISBN 0-393-05761-5 LC 2002-155113

Jong, Erica—*Continued*

A "interpretation of the life of the first known woman poet, Sappho, who lived on the island of Lesbos 2,600 years ago and wrote and performed poems of indelible candor and eroticism. Jong envisions Sappho as an ardent and adventurous soul who, while still in her teens, meet the love of her life (the rebel poet Alcaeus), reveals her poetic talents, and is forced into exile and marriage to a wealthy old drunk." Booklist

Jong's "effort to bring to life an ancient writer engrossed in politics, family and the creation of poetry is a relief from the relentlessly everyday sincerity of much current 'women-oriented' writing." N Y Times Book Rev

Jonge, Peter de

(jt. auth) Patterson, J. The beach house

Jönsson, Reidar, 1944-

My life as a dog; translated by Eivor Martinus. Farrar, Straus & Giroux 1990 219p o.p.

LC 89-46390

Original Swedish edition, 1983; this translation first published 1989 in the United Kingdom

"This novel focuses on "the thirteenth and fourteenth years of a Swedish boy named Ingemar Johansson. Ingemar's mother is dying of tuberculosis, and his absentee father is away at sea. Somehow Ingemar repeatedly falls into exploits, scrapes, and disasters that, he thinks, make his mother's condition worse. Ingemar is . . . sent away to live with his uncle. . . . [His dog Sickan] is put to sleep because no one can spare the time and attention to care for it." Horn Book

"The novel's anecdotal style accommodates a boy's confabulation. Occasionally wayward and a bit too long in their descriptions, his comedic exploits cast Ingemar as schlemiel, underdog and, yes, dog. . . . It is Sickan's fate that finally helps Ingemar come to terms with his dead mother." N Y Times Book Rev

Jordan, Anne Devereaux, 1943-

(ed) The Best horror stories from the Magazine of fantasy and science fiction. See The Best horror stories from the Magazine of fantasy and science fiction

Jordan, Laura, 1948-

For works written by this author under other names see Brown, Sandra, 1948-

Joyce, Graham

The limits of enchantment. Atria 2005 263p $22

ISBN 0-575-07231-8

"Although it's 1966, Mammy Cullen, a beloved midwife in rural Hallaton, still dispenses a kind of herbal medicine that women have practiced since time immemorial. But times are changing and prejudices are building. When one of her remedies appears to kill a patient, the locals turn on Mammy. Her practice falls to Fern, her adopted daughter and apprentice, who soon finds herself confronting contemporary reality in several forms: Arthur, an amorous biker with marriage on his mind; an intrusive commune of feckless hippies who settle next door; and a devious landlord who schemes to evict her from her cottage." Publ Wkly

"Generally the prose is economical, hurrying along a plot which engages as a whole, despite the weight of Fern's introspection." Times Lit Suppl

Joyce, James, 1882-1941

Dubliners. Knopf 1991 lxvii, 7-287p $18

ISBN 0-679-40574-7 LC 91-53001

First published 1914 in the United Kingdom; first United States edition published 1916 by Huebsch

Contents: The sisters; An encounter; Araby; Eveline; After the race; Two gallants; The boarding house; A little cloud; Counterparts; Clay; A painful case; Ivy day in the committee room; A mother; Grace; The dead

"This collection of 15 stories provides an introduction to the style and motifs found in Joyce's writing. The stories stand alone as individual scenes of Dublin society and are intertwined by the use of autobiography and symbolism." Shapiro. Fic for Youth. 3d edition

Finnegans wake. Viking 1939 628p o.p.

This novel is "written in a unique and extremely difficult style, making use of puns and portmanteau words, (using at least 40 languages besides English) and a very wide range of allusion. The central theme of the work is a cyclical pattern of history, of fall and resurrection inspired by Vico's Scienza nuova. This is presented in the story of Humphrey Chimpden Earwicker, a Dublin tavern-keeper, and the book is apparently a dream-sequence representing the stream of his unconscious mind through the course of one night. Other characters are his wife Anna Livia Plurabelle, their sons Shem and Shaun, and their daughter Isabel." Oxford Companion to Engl Lit. 6th edition

A portrait of the artist as a young man; with an introduction by Richard Brown. Knopf 1991 xli, 318p $18

ISBN 0-679-40575-5 LC 91-52979

"Everyman's library"

First appeared serially, 1914-1915 in the United Kingdom; first United States edition published 1916 by Huebsch

This autobiographical novel "portrays the childhood, school days, adolescence, and early manhood of Stephen Dedalus, later one of the leading characters in Ulysses. Stephen's growing self-awareness as an artist forces him to reject the whole narrow world in which he has been brought up, including family ties, nationalism, and the Catholic religion. The novel ends when, having decided to become a writer, he is about to leave Dublin for Paris. Rather than following a clear narrative progression, the book revolves around experiences that are crucial to Stephen's development as an artist; at the end of each chapter Stephen makes some assertion of identity. Through his use of the stream-of-consciousness technique, Joyce reveals the actual materials of his hero's world, the components of his thought processes." Reader's Ency. 4th edition

Ulysses; with an introduction by Craig Raine. Knopf 1997 xlv, 1076p $25

ISBN 0-679-45513-2

Joyce, James, 1882-1941—*Continued*

"Everyman's library"

First published 1922

"The novel is constructed as a modern parallel to Homer's Odyssey. All of the action of the novel takes place in Dublin on a single day (June 16, 1904). The three central characters—Stephen Dedalus (the hero of Joyce's earlier Portrait of the Artist as a Young Man), Leopold Bloom, a Jewish advertising canvasser, and his wife Molly Bloom—are intended to be modern counterparts of Telemachus, Ulysses, and Penelope, and the events of the novel parallel the major events in Odysseus' journey home. The main stream of *Ulysses* lies in its depth of character portrayal and its breadth of humor." Merriam-Webster's Ency of Lit

Judd, Alan

Legacy. Knopf 2002 245p $24

ISBN 0-375-41484-3 LC 2002-16262

First published 2001 in the United Kingdom

This "spy thriller, set in the 1970s, begins when fledgling British agent Charles Thoroughgood receives an assignment: he is to persuade his former Oxford classmate, Viktor Koslov, now a liaison at the Soviet Embassy and apparently an undercover operative, to defect. But before he can do it, Koslov stuns him with the revelation that Thoroughgood's late father, an engineer who also had a military career, was working as a KGB agent." Publ Wkly

"Comparisons with John le Carre are inevitable, but Judd's style is more straightforward and his worldview far more benign. While fans of explosive action may find it slow going, this elegant and understated literary thriller is a worthy addition to the growing genre of historical espionage fiction." Libr J

Just, Ward S.

An unfinished season. Houghton Mifflin 2004 256p $24

ISBN 0-618-03669-5 LC 2004-42722

"Set in 1950's Chicago during a single summer, this novel recounts the story of the owner of a printing company, the narrator's father, who is on the management side of a vicious union dispute and begins to carry a gun. Wilson Raven, his son, takes a summer job at a scandal rag, where no amount of ink on his sleeves lives down the day he arrives at work wearing his bowed dancing shoes from debutante balls on the ritzy North Shore." Economist

"Even if the setting of Just's . . . novel is the Midwest instead of Washington, Saigon or Paris, the territory is familiar: it's the world of memory tinged with regret. It's the early 1950s, the dawn of the cold war and the Red scare. . . This is vintage Just: elegant writing that captures the wounded spirit of the times." Newsweek

The weather in Berlin; [by] Ward Just. Houghton Mifflin 2002 305p $24

ISBN 0-618-03668-7 LC 2001-51885

This novel "follows a burned-out American movie director on a three-month stay at an artists-and-intellectuals institute in the capital of the new Germany. At 64, Dix Greenwood is remembered for a film made decades ago, an art-house favorite set in a German lake village just after World War I. . . . Ailing physically, tantalized by a fading memory of artistic inspiration, resenting his actress wife for her still-active career, Greenwood repairs to the city Willy Brandt once called Germany's Schicksalstadt, city of destiny. Berlin is experiencing a rebirth; perhaps Dix will too." N Y Times Book Rev

K

Kadare, Ismail

Spring flowers, spring frost; a novel; translated from the French of Jusuf Vrioni by David Belos. Arcade Pub. 2002 182p $23.95

ISBN 1-55970-635-X LC 2002-20877

Original Albanian edition 2000

"Mark Gurabardhi, an artist in his late twenties, experiences the unfamiliarity of life after Communism in the provincial Albanian town where he was posted by the former regime. It feels almost like a loss not to be spied on, and he and his girlfriend thrill to words like 'heist,' so modern and Western do they seem. The couple discover, however, that dictatorship is replaced not so much by modernity as by old, crippling superstitions and family feuds. Throughout the book, images of icebergs, the Titanic, and enchanted snakes recur. . . . The result is like a dream-seemingly full of stirring meanings whose interpretations remain tantalizingly out of reach." New Yorker

The Successor; a novel; translated from the French of Tedi Papavrami by David Bellos. Arcade Publishing 2005 207p $24

ISBN 1-55970-773-9 LC 2005-10311

Original Albanian edition, 2003

This novel "depicts an Albania governed by the whim and vanity of the aging Guide when the Successor, second in command, is found dead in his bedroom. The international intelligence community and the citizens of Albania contemplate the questions of how the Successor fell from grace and whether he died through murder or suicide. From day to day, the official word varies as the Guide decides whether the Successor is an enemy of the state or a martyr for the party. Drawing on real events–Mehmet Shehu was poised to succeed Albanian dictator Enver Hoxha in 1981 when he mysteriously died–Kadare successfully builds suspense by portraying multiple suspects with the motivation to commit murder; all believe they are guilty of the crime in some small or large way. The story unfolds through the intimate conversations of brothers and sisters and husbands and wives, all potential victims of the Guide's unpredictable behavior, before concluding with the Successor speaking from the dead about his life and death." Libr J

"It is possible to read 'The Successor' as something of a coded commentary on Kadare's own life. Just as we long to know the cause of the Successor's death, so do we long to resolve Kadare's true place in Hoxha's Albania. . . . This novel finds its truth in the imagined words of a dead man, setting the individual over the many. It valorizes the imagination by arguing that the truth of a man is not always found in what he does or says but in his numinous interior, the place all great literature celebrates." N Y Times Book Rev

Kadare, Ismail—*Continued*

The three-arched bridge; translated from the Albanian by John Hodgson. Arcade Pub. 1997 184p o.p.

ISBN 1-55970-368-7 LC 96-41236

Originally written 1976-1978; published in French translation 1993

In this "matter-of-fact parable, a fourteenth-century Albanian monk attempts to 'record the lie we saw and the truth we did not see' about the building of a stone bridge that is a threatening wonder to the local people. The lie is the myths and legends exploited by the foreign builders to destroy their competitors; the truth is the mercenary nature of their crime. Kadare manages to appeal to a sense of outrage and hunger for evidence even as he suggests the outlines of today's Balkans." New Yorker

Kafka, Franz, 1883-1924

Amerika; the man who disappeared; translated and with an introduction by Michael Hofmann. New Directions 2002 216p $23.95

ISBN 0-8118-1513-X

Original German edition, 1927; this translation first published 1996 in the United Kingdom

The narrative of this unfinished novel "concerns the efforts of young Karl Rossmann, newly arrived in America, to find his place in an enigmatic and hostile society."

"Kafka left six completed chapters and a number of additional scenes, two of which appear in English for the first time in this new translation. . . . Anything by Kafka is worth reading again, especially in the hands of such a gifted translator as Hofmann." N Y Times Book Rev

The castle. Knopf 1992 xxxviii, 378p $17

ISBN 0-679-41735-4 LC 92-52904

"Everyman's library"

Original German edition, 1926; this translation first published 1930

In this unfinished novel, the hero, "known only as K., is constantly frustrated in his efforts to gain entrance into a mysterious castle to which he believes he has been summoned to work as a land surveyor. The castle is administered by an extraordinarily complicated and incompetent bureaucratic hierarchy that refuses to either recognize or reject K.'s claim. He is put to work instead as a school janitor and is denied his right to practice his craft. According to Brod, Kafka intended K., an ailing man throughout the novel, to die of exhaustion at the end of the novel." Reader's Ency. 4th edition

Collected stories; edited and introduced by Gabriel Josipvici. Knopf 1993 lv, 503p $21

ISBN 0-679-42303-6 LC 93-1858

"Everyman's library"

Contents: Children on a country road; Unmasking a confidence trickster; The sudden walk; Resolutions; Excursion into the mountains; Bachelor's ill luck; The tradesman; Absent-minded window-gazing; The way home; Passers-by; On the tram; Clothes; Rejection; Reflections for gentlemen-jockeys; The street window; The wish to be a red Indian; The trees; Unhappiness; The judgment; The stoker; The metamorphosis; In the penal colony; The new advocate; A country doctor; Up in the gallery; An old manuscript; Before the law; Jackals and Arabs; A visit to a mine; The next village; An imperial message; The cares of a family man; Eleven sons; A fratricide; A dream; A report to an Academy; The bucket rider; First sorrow; A little woman; A hunger artist; Josephine the singer; Description of a struggle; Wedding preparations in the country; The student; The angel; The village schoolmaster {the giant mole}; Blumfeld, an elderly bachelor; The Hunter Gracchus; The proclamation; The bridge; The Great Wall of China; The knock at the manor gate; An ancient sword; New lamps; My neighbor; A crossbreed {a sport}; A splendid beast; The watchman; A common confusion; The truth about Sancho Panza; The silence of the sirens; Prometheus; The city coat of arms; Poseidon; Fellowship; At night; The problem of our laws; The conscription of troops; The test; The vulture; The helmsman; The top; Hands; A little fable; Isabella; Home-coming; A Chinese puzzle; The departure; Advocates; Investigations of a dog; The married couple; Give it up!; On parables; The burrow

The complete stories; edited by Nahum N. Glatzer; with a new foreword by John Updike. Centennial ed. Schocken Bks. 1983 xxi, 486p il o.p.

LC 83-3233

First published 1971

"All of Kafka's writing, with the exception of his three novels, is collected here and includes a number of fairly long stories followed by a group of shorter pieces varying in length from several pages to a single paragraph." Booklist

Metamorphosis. Vanguard Press 1945 98p il o.p.

Written in 1915 this is "often regarded as Kafka's most perfectly finished work. 'The Metamorphosis' begins as its hero, Gregor Samsa, awakens one morning to find himself changed into a huge insect; the story proceeds to develop the effects of this change upon Samsa's business and family life and ends with his death. It has been read as everything from a religious allegory to a psychoanalytic case history; it is notable for its clarity of depiction and attention to significant detail, which give its completely fantastic occurrences an aura of indisputable truth, so that no allegorical interpretation is necessary to demonstrate its greatness." Reader's Ency. 4th edition

also in Kafka, F. Collected stories p73-128

also in Kafka, F. The complete stories

also in Kafka, F. The metamorphosis and other stories p117-92

also in Kafka, F. The penal colony: stories and short pieces

also in Kafka, F. Selected short stories of Franz Kafka

The metamorphosis and other stories; translated by Joachim Neugroschel. Scribner 1993 xxiii, 227p o.p.

ISBN 0-684-19426-0 LC 92-43912

This is a collection of thirty stories, some of which are quite short. The stories are arranged in order of their original publication dates

The penal colony: stories and short pieces; translated by Willa and Edwin Muir. Schocken Bks. 1948 320p il o.p.

Stories included are: The judgment; The metamorphosis; A country doctor; In the penal colony; A hunger artist

Kafka, Franz, 1883-1924—*Continued*

Selected short stories of Franz Kafka; translated by Willa and Edwin Muir; introduction by Philip Rahv. Modern Lib. 1993 xxv, 346p o.p.
ISBN 0-679-60061-2 LC 93-14747
First Modern Library edition published 1952
Contents: The judgment; The metamorphosis; In the penal colony; The Great Wall of China; The country doctor; Common confusion; New advocate; Old manuscripts; A fratricide; Report to an Academy; Hunter Gracchus; A hunger artist; Investigations of a dog; The burrow; Josephine the singer

The trial; translated from the German by Willa and Edwin Muir; revised, with additional notes, by E. M. Butler. Knopf 1992 299p $19
ISBN 0-679-40994-7
"Everyman's library"
Original edition 1924; first Everyman's Library edition, 1922
"Joseph K., a respected bank assessor, is arrested and spends his remaining years fighting charges about which he has no knowledge. The helplessness of an insignificant individual within a mysterious bureaucracy where answers are never accessible is described in this provocative and disturbing book." Shapiro. Fic for Youth. 3d edition

Kafka, Kimberly

Miranda's vines. Dutton 2004 258p $23.95
ISBN 0-525-94763-9
"Since college, Miranda and Bridie's relationship has been that of sisters, surpassing any friendship by the depth of their commitment. It was Bridie Miranda relied upon when her husband died before their son could be born, and it was Bridie Miranda called again when her father died, bequeathing her the struggling Oregon vineyard to which he'd devoted his life. Now it's Miranda's turn. When Bridie, a champion Idatarod sledder, is critically injured, legs paralyzed and dangerously depressed, Miranda brings Bridie back to the vineyard she is reluctantly calling home again. In this lustrous tale of loyalty and devotion, Kafka limns the depths of intimacy and explores the nature of relationships, from mother to son, father to daughter, neighbor to stranger, and friend to friend." Booklist

Kalfus, Ken

The commissariat of enlightenment; a novel. Ecco Press 2003 295p $24.95
ISBN 0-06-050136-7 LC 2002-69308
"For Comrad Astapov of the Agitprop Section of the Commissariat of Enlightenment, the filmmaker protagonist of this début novel, 'life's struggle was not to control events, but the way in which they were remembered.' His story begins in 1910, at the press-besieged deathbed of Tolstoy, where his talent for manipulating film to satisfy events earns the notice of Stalin. Astapov's distortions are the perfect metaphor for Kalfus's own special effects: Stalin, of course, wasn't there when Tolstoy died. Preoccupied with truth, media, history, and politics, this novel shows its mechanisms proudly." New Yorker

Kallos, Stephanie

Broken for you; Stephanie Kallos. 1st ed. Grove Press 2004 371p $24
ISBN 0-8021-1779-1 LC 2004-40631
"Margaret Hughes lives alone in a Seattle mansion, divorced from her husband after the death of their son. She talks to her father's priceless antique porcelain collection and spends her days dusting. Wanda Schultz, abandoned as a child by her parents, cannot accept the rejection of her lover, Peter, whose solitary postcard brings her across the country in search of him. When cancer sends Margaret a wakeup call, she opens her home and her heart: first to Wanda and then to a flood of other new 'family' members as she learns to interact with people and eventually to atone for a past crime she only gradually understands." Booklist
"The novel itself is a mosaic of eccentric characters and their interlocking storylines, which sometimes border on the fantastic. . . . So lovely is the world Kallos has created that it seems more reparative to curl up on the couch with this book and suspend belief than to deconstruct the plot." Washington Post Book World

Kaminsky, Stuart M.

The big silence; an Abe Lieberman mystery. Forge 2000 268p $23.95
ISBN 0-312-86926-6 LC 00-31811
"A Tom Doherty Associates book"
Chicago cop Lieberman and "his morose partner, Bill Hanrahan, find themselves backed into a corner by a blackmailer who kills a mob informant's ex-wife, kidnaps his 17-year-old son and threatens to do away with the boy unless the informer pledges ultimate silence—by committing suicide. And that's only the first labor of the day for this herculean cop. Heaping one calamity on top of another, Kaminsky piles up a whole stack of woe to try his hero's soul." N Y Times Book Rev

Blood and rubles; a Porfiry Petrovich Rostnikov novel. Fawcett Columbine 1996 257p o.p.
ISBN 0-449-90949-2 LC 95-23885
"Rubles are scarce in Moscow, but Chief Inspector Porfiry Rostnikov and his subordinates are up to their shoe tops in blood: a shootout apparently involving a Mafia scheme to sell fissionable material to the highest bidder; three nearly feral small boys who kill passerbys for whatever they carry; and the kidnapping of a wealthy businessman that turns into multiple murders. . . . It's hard not to feel compassion for the cops and the Moscovites in general, and Kaminsky is deft at creating this feeling with small, telling details of ordinary life." Booklist

A cold red sunrise; an Inspector Porfiry Rostnikov mystery. Scribner 1988 210p o.p.
LC 88-15359
"Inspector Porfiry Rostnikov of the Moscow police . . . is assigned to Tumsk in deepest Siberia. . . . Two people have died mysteriously—the young and beautiful daughter of a famed dissident father who is scheduled, in the new climate of 'glasnost,' to depart for the West, and the police Commisar from Moscow who was sent to Tumsk to investigate her death. With him on this mission is his trusted associate, Emil Karpo." West Coast Rev Books

Kaminsky, Stuart M.—*Continued*

"The author has fine-tuned Porfiry and Karpo into a delightful sleuthing team and a fascinating study in odd contrasts." Booklist

Dancing in the dark. Mysterious Press 1996 228p o.p.

LC 95-13095

"In 1943, Arthur Forbes is a respected California businessman, but not too many years earlier he lived in Detroit and was known as Fingers Intaglia because he liked to remove the fingers of his victims. Luna, his mistress, wants to learn to dance, and she wants Fred Astaire to teach her. . . . To get Luna and her lover off his back, Astaire hires Toby Peters, private eye to the stars. When Luna drops dead at Toby's feet, Fingers is ready to resume his former profession but doesn't want a scandal. A deal is cut: If Toby can find the killer, he can live." Booklist

The author "effortlessly choreographs Hollywood history, colorful cast and dirty doings." Publ Wkly

Death of a Russian priest. Fawcett Columbine 1992 223p o.p.

LC 91-58638

In this Inspector Porfiry Rostnikov mystery "two crimes need solving: the disappearance of a Syrian diplomat's daughter and the ax murder of a prominently outspoken priest. The missing girl becomes the preoccupation of Rostnikov's emotionally messed-up young assistant Sasha, while Rostnikov himself, working with the vampiric Karpo, uncovers the priest's secret life, hindered by silent friends who seem to be dying for their loyalty." Booklist

The dog who bit a policeman. Mysterious Press 1998 275p o.p.

ISBN 0-89296-667-X LC 98-13385

This Inspector Rostnikov novel "interweaves three crimes, all set amidst corrupt, Mafia-ridden contemporary Moscow: the disappearance of a politician, the serial murder of members of two rival gangs, and an illegal, big-money dogfight ring." Libr J

"Kaminsky takes care not to rob the beleaguered cops of their human core—a courtesy he also extends to Moscow, which comes across as a character in its own right: rough and dangerous and somehow tragic." N Y Times Book Rev

A fatal glass of beer. Mysterious Press 1997 246p o.p.

LC 96-49494

Hollywood private investigator Toby Peters "and W.C. Fields cross the country (chauffeured by a Swiss midget) in search of Lester O. Hipnoodle, the villian who has somehow gained access to Field's numerous hidden bank accounts." Libr J

The author "balances one-liners from Fields with headlines about the war effort in this amiable adventure that delivers a nicely twisted plot with fully dimensioned characters, including the usually caricatured misanthropic comedian." Publ Wkly

Hard currency. Fawcett Columbine 1995 247p o.p.

LC 94-28273

This Inspector Porfiry Rostnikov mystery takes the "Moscow detective to Havana, where he investigates the murder of a Cuban woman who was apparently killed by a minor intelligence officer in the Russian embassy. . . . Meanwhile, back in Moscow, Rostnikov's associate Emil Karpo is tracking down a vicious serial killer whose single-minded precision chillingly matches Karpo's own thought processes. Kaminsky, one of the genre's finest storytellers, is at the peak of his powers here." Booklist

Lieberman's choice; [by] Stuart Kaminsky. St. Martin's Press 1993 216p o.p.

LC 92-40797

"A Thomas Dunne book"

Abe Lieberman is "an aging Jewish Chicago cop who's comfortable and at ease on the street but troubled by his domestic life. He can handle the perpetrators but is puzzled by the paths that end in violence. The case here involves a cop who kills his wife and her lover and then barricades himself atop an apartment building. Political expediency clashes repeatedly with prudence as Abe struggles with the situation." Booklist

"Abe's conversation—whether with his old Jewish buddies, some small-time cons or his family—is pure pleasure, with never a false, extraneous note." Publ Wkly

Lieberman's day; [by] Stuart Kaminsky. Holt & Co. 1994 260p o.p.

ISBN 0-8050-2575-8 LC 93-22910

Chicago homicide detective Abe Lieberman's "nephew, David, and David's pregnant wife are shot in a late night mugging. David dies; his wife and unborn child survive, barely. Lieberman gets the case and in the following 24 hours deals with the grief of his brother and sister-in-law, the aftereffects of the collapse of his daughter's marriage, the desperate deal he cuts with a violent drug-dealer called El Perro to catch the killers and the busting of two con artists." Publ Wkly

The author is "extraordinarily attuned to the domestic minutiae of his detectives' lives." N Y Times Book Rev

Lieberman's folly; [by] Stuart Kaminsky. St. Martin's Press 1991 216p o.p.

LC 90-49309

"A Thomas Dunne book"

This mystery "features the partnership of Chicago cops Abe 'Rabbi' Lieberman and Bill 'Father Murphy' Hanrahan. When prostitute Estralda Valdez, a past informer, asks the pair for protection, tippler Hanrahan agrees to watch her apartment from a Chinese restaurant across the street. After Valdez is murdered during Hanrahan's watch, he and Lieberman investigate her death, despite the objections of their captain, who is unhappy about negative publicity." Publ Wkly

Lieberman's thief; [by] Stuart Kaminsky. Holt & Co. 1995 238p o.p.

ISBN 0-8050-2576-6 LC 94-27304

"George Patniks is a professional burglar and a good one. Unfortunately, the day he has chosen to burgle the Rozier home turns out to be the same day Mr. Rozier has chosen to kill Mrs. Rozier. . . . Chicago homicide detective Abe Lieberman and his partner Bill Hanrahan immediately suspect Rozier, but they have nothing on which to build a case. Kaminsky captures the sights and sounds of his Chicago setting most convincingly." Booklist

Kaminsky, Stuart M.—*Continued*

The man who walked like a bear; an Inspector Porfiry Rostnikov novel. Scribner 1990 261p o.p. LC 89-29082

"Beset by the usual demons (including the plumbing in his apartment), visited by a few new ones, and still a thorn in the side of the Soviet bureaucracy, Rostnikov must deal with a host of problems: . . . a plot to kill a Politburo member, shady deals in a Moscow shoe factory, and several demented nationalists who mastermind a scheme to destroy Lenin's tomb. Then there's the inspector's sick wife to visit in the hospital and the matter of getting his son out of the military." Booklist

"Kaminsky masterfully balances stories of family life, humorous anecdotes and riveting suspense involving his distinctive characters." Publ Wkly

Murder on the Trans-Siberian Express. Mysterious Press 2001 277p o.p.

ISBN 0-89296-747-1 LC 2001-26218

"The action reaches back to Siberia in 1894, when one man in a band of starving, disease-ridden convicts, sentenced to work on constructing the great rail line from Moscow to Vladivostok, buries his treasure—a leather pouch containing a tiny gold box with a letter inside. More than a century later, Inspector Porfiry of the Moscow Police is sent on the 6,000-mile rail line to find this box. Porfiry leaves behind two other investigations: the kidnapping of a skinhead rock star and a series of murders in the Moscow Metro. How Kaminsky weaves these tangled plot lines into a taut suspense fabric, while providing fascinating, sad-funny commentary on his characters and the tensions inherent in the new Russian social order, is a matter of wonder." Booklist

Not quite kosher; an Abe Lieberman mystery. Forge 2002 254p $23.95

ISBN 0-312-87453-7

This installment "finds Lieberman trying to cope with a jewelry heist gone bad, a potential gang war, two corpses washed up from Lake Michigan and his grandson's bar mitzvah." N Y Times Book Rev

"Although Kaminsky can plot with the best of them, his characters are the real delights of the book." Publ Wkly

Retribution; a Lew Fonesca novel. Forge 2001 272p o.p.

ISBN 0-312-87452-9 LC 2001-40483

"A Tom Doherty Associates book"

Lew Fonesca "rescued a teenage prostitute named Adele in 'Vengeance' and left her in the care of a rich and vulgar (but really sweet and lonely) widow who promised to put the girl through high school. Adele is in trouble again . . . and Lew has been charged with finding out why she skipped town with a cache of manuscripts, the unpublished life's work of the reclusive, Salingeresque author who was tutoring her." N Y Times Book Rev

The Rockford files: Devil on my doorstep. Forge 1998 304p o.p.

ISBN 0-312-86444-2 LC 97-29851

"A Tom Doherty Associates book"

Jim Rockford's "trashy beachfront trailer home becomes a safe haven for Melisa Conforti, the teenage daughter of Jim's former lover Rene. Melisa shows Jim a letter, signed by Rene, that indicates Melisa is his daughter. . . . Then Rene is killed, the feds seize Melisa, and a poetry-loving hit man named Wright enters the picture. . . . [Kaminsky] is a stellar talent and shows great skill in creating a carefully updated version of the much loved TV PI." Publ Wkly

The Rockford files: the green bottle. Forge 1996 318p o.p.

ISBN 0-312-86229-6 LC 96-17316

"A Tom Doherty Associates book"

"Jim Rockford is still a struggling private eye living in a house trailer near the beach in Malibu. His knees are aching and his bank account depleted when he strikes a deal to find an orthopedic surgeon's niece. If Rockford finds aspiring actress Barbie, he gets a discount on knee surgery. Then the man Barbie was staying with is killed with Jim's gun. All the characters we've grown to know from the Rockford television show are present." Booklist

Rostnikov's vacation; an Inspector Porfiry Rostnikov novel. Scribner 1991 244p o.p. LC 91-13874

"While on forced vacation in Yalta, Rostnikov chances upon the murder of an acquaintance from military intelligence. He also befriends an American policeman, who points out the man tailing Rostnikov. Back in Moscow, meanwhile, Rostnikov's subordinates track a beautiful young woman and two accomplices connected with the murder of a German businessman. Kaminsky solidly and ably controls all these complications, but not without offering certain political vagaries, a cold-blooded atmosphere, and a certain dry humor." Libr J

To catch a spy; a Toby Peters mystery. Carroll & Graf Pubs. 2002 230p $24

ISBN 0-7867-1023-3 LC 2002-67254

"An Otto Penzler book"

In this installment the author supposes Cary Grant "to have been a British intelligence agent, his job to detect the activities of Nazi sympathizers in Hollywood. Married to Woolworth heiress Barbara Hutton at the time, he finds more pro-Nazis among his wife's rich friends than among the acting community. Grant hires Toby, who packs a .38 with which he's unable to hit the broad side of a sound stage, to deliver a satchel of money in the dark of night to a man who'll give him an envelope in return." Publ Wkly

Tomorrow is another day. Mysterious Press 1995 201p o.p. LC 94-18987

"Set during World War II, when Hollywood was at its most glamorous, the plot involves the mysterious stabbing death of an extra on the set of Selznick International's *Gone with the Wind.* Five years after the murder, the debonair Clark Gable approaches Toby [Peters] to ask for help—seems Gable's been receiving bizarre death threats in the form of poems. . . . Nostalgic readers with a yen for the good old days—when men were men and movies were *movies*—will find Kaminsky's story entertaining, clever, eminently readable, and chock-full of snippets from Hollywood's Golden Age." Booklist

Vengeance; a Lew Fonesca mystery. Forge 1999 328p o.p.

ISBN 0-312-86927-4 LC 99-38393

Kaminsky, Stuart M.—*Continued*

"A Tom Doherty Associates book"

"Fonesca is a middle-aged, widowed process server, a transplanted Chicagoan who has made a new home in Sarasota, Fla. . . . Occasionally he uses the investigative skills he developed while employed by the state attorney's office in Chicago to do a little ad hoc sleuthing. In [this novel] his skills and fortitude get stretched to the limit as he tries to locate two missing persons: a teenage girl whose sexually abusive and violent father has lured her away from her poverty-stricken mother, and a woman who has run away from her wealthy husband." Publ Wkly

Kanon, Joseph

The good German; a novel. Holt & Co. 2001 482p o.p.

ISBN 0-8050-6422-2 LC 2001-16968

"Jake Geismar, a U.S. reporter assigned to cover the Potsdam Conference for *Collier's* magazine, stumbles upon a story that is intertwined with his own life. Though he has returned to Berlin primarily to reunite with his prewar lover, Geismar confronts a Germany he no longer recognizes. Further, he is compelled to solve the murder of an American soldier found with a money belt stuffed with black market cash." Libr J

"Kanon hits every note just right, from the wide-angle descriptions of Berlin's pockmarked moonscape to the tellingly detailed portraits of the city's shellshocked survivors. Superb popular fiction, combining propulsive narrative drive with a subtle grasp of character and a fine sense of moral ambiguity." Booklist

Los Alamos; a novel. Broadway Bks. 1997 403p o.p.

LC 96-44055

This book's plot involves the murder of a security officer of the Manhattan Project, which developed the atomic bomb. "Michael Connolly, a civilian intelligence expert called to New Mexico to investigate the murder, soon finds himself entangled in the insular, secretive world of Los Alamos: first he falls in love with one of the scientist's wives, and then he comes under the . . . spell of Oppenheimer himself." Booklist

"'Los Alamos,' besides being a terrific mystery, wonderfully evokes the Southwest in the '40s, reminding us in a dozen subtle ways that life goes on even while history is being made." Newsweek

Kantner, Seth, 1965-

Ordinary wolves; Seth Kantner. 1st ed. Milkweed Editions 2004 324p $22

ISBN 1-571-31044-4 LC 2003-24025

"Growing up in the unforgiving wilderness with his back-to-the-land artist father and siblings, Cutuk learns all the traditional skills necessary for living off the tundra and develops an abiding love for wolves. But Cutuk is white, and although he reveres traditional native Alaskan ways and wants to be a great hunter, he remains an outsider. Then when the 1970s bring radical change even to this distant realm and his indigenous neighbors trade in their dogsleds for snowmobiles, he becomes even more of an anachronism. So he tries his luck in Anchorage, discovers an alien form of wilderness, and hastily acquires a whole new set of survival skills. At every turn, Kantner fearlessly orchestrates dramatic communions between humans and the wild, hilarious incidents of culture shock." Booklist

Kantor, MacKinlay, 1904-1977

Andersonville. World Pub. 1955 767p il o.p.

"After twenty-five years of research Kantor wrote this novel, which realistically portrays the atrocities of Andersonville Prison, home of many Yankee soldiers during the Civil War. Ira Claffey, Georgia planter and owner of the property on which Andersonville is built, serves as a humane central character whose sorrows and frustrations serve to point up the brutality of war. The primitive, indeed horrible, existence of the prisoners is described in detail." Shapiro. Fic for Youth. 3d edition

Kanwar, Asha

(ed) The Unforgetting heart: an anthology of short stories by African American women (1859-1993). See The Unforgetting heart: an anthology of short stories by African American women (1859-1993)

Kao, Hsing-chien *See* Gao Xingjian, 1940-

Kaplow, Robert

Me and Orson Welles; a novel. MacAdam/Cage Pub. 2003 269p $18.50

ISBN 1-931561-49-4 LC 2003-14982

"A comic coming-of-age novel set against the background of the twenty-two-year-old Orson Welles's debut production at the Mercury Theatre on Broadway. Richard Samuels is the stage struck seventeen-year-old from New Jersey who wanders onto the set one day and gets a small role in Welles's Julius Caesar. His life will never be the same." Publisher's note

"A delightful escape into a prewar coming-of-age, and coming-of-stage, story-perfect for a quick and totally entertaining read." Booklist

Karbo, Karen

Motherhood made a man out of me. Bloomsbury Pub. 2000 212p $23.95

ISBN 1-58234-083-8

This novel "contains two plots that are intertwined and equally weighted. There's the story of Brooke, the new mother of baby Stella, and her husband, Lyle—a mildly annoying, mildly dim would-be artist who can't understand why the fact that he looked after Stella for one evening a few weeks ago doesn't prove he's a good father. Then there's the story of Brooke's best friend, Mary Rose, a pregnant gardener who's engaged to marry Brooke's cousin Ward—a mildly annoying, mildly dim director of 'high-profile commercials' who forgot to tell Mary Rose that he's still married." N Y Times Book Rev

"Karbo writes about the intricacies of human nature and relationships with insight and humor, and her characters are realistic yet wonderfully over-the-top. The result is a fast-paced and delightful novel." Publ Wkly

Karnezis, Panos, 1967-

The maze. Farrar, Straus and Giroux 2004 376p $24

ISBN 0-374-20480-2 LC 2003-60261

"This novel is set in the 1920s, while Turkey was fighting for independence from Greece. The characters are either soldiers in the retreating Greek army, or Greek residents of a sleepy, doomed town where Christians used to live well. . . . The brigadier is addicted to morphine, his chief of staff is a secret communist and the padre, Father Simeon, is a hopeless kleptomaniac. In the town, the mayor and the schoolmaster compete for the attentions of the local courtesan, a Frenchwoman who is nurturing her own guilty secrets." Economist

"As with many an imperial expedition, the soldiers seem to be lost without honor; they massacre civilians on their fool's errand undertaken for worthless ends. Karnezis dramatizes their plight with remorseless clarity and dry humor." N Y Times Book Rev

Karon, Jan, 1937-

A common life; the wedding story. Viking 2001 186p il $24.95

ISBN 0-670-89437-0 LC 00-31984

This novel in the author's Mitford series focuses "on a key event in the life of Father Tim Kavanaugh—his marriage. The book begins with Father Tim's proposal to next-door-neighbor Cynthia and ends with their honeymoon at the bishop's summer cottage in Maine. In between, Mitford's various residents prepare for the big day, each in his or her own way." Booklist

In this mountain. Viking 2002 382p $24.95

ISBN 0-670-03104-6 LC 2002-16877

In this Mitford novel "three years have passed since Father Tim Kavanagh and his wife, Cynthia, returned to Mitford from Whitecap Island, and depression and discontent are gnawing away at the good cleric as he faces the big '7-0.' As Cynthia's career reaches new heights, Father Tim makes some personal decisions that lead to tragedy. . . . Homespun dialogue, fresh and lively descriptions, laugh-out-loud moments and poignant scenes mark the heartfelt book, which is a happy reunion form Mitford devotees." Publ Wkly

A new song. Viking 1999 400p $24.95

ISBN 0-670-87810-3 LC 98-55141

In this episode in the Mitford series "Father Tim Kavanagh heads for the islands to serve as an interim priest. Although most of the book takes place in his new parish, fans of Mitford's eccentric citizens are not left bereft. Frequent bulletins keep Father Tim up-to-date as well as worried about his former flock. While juggling news of mysterious thefts, the arrest of his adopted son, Dooley, and fights over historic properties, he also must deal with congregational squabbles, being a foster parent to an active three-year-old, surviving a terrible storm, and bringing a lonely man out of decades of solitude." Libr J

Out to Canaan. Viking 1997 342p $23.95

ISBN 0-670-87485-X LC 97-5867

"Racing from one good deed to another, Father Timothy takes in stray sick folk, finds an abandoned child, and helps his favorite baker write a winning jingle. A mayoral race pitting the long-time mayor Esther Cunningham against the possibly corrupt Mack Stroupe makes for some colorful sparring. Father Timothy applies his own unique, time-honored method of intuition, prayer, or dietary indulgence to a multitude of problems big and small. His late-in-life marriage to Cynthia continues to be a blessing readers will feel privileged to share." Libr J

Kasischke, Laura, 1961-

The life before her eyes. Harcourt 2002 273p $24

ISBN 0-15-100888-4 LC 2001-24311

"Diana and her best friend are confronted by a schoolmate killer, but only Diana is spared. Fast-forward 20 years: Diana, now middle-aged and still beautiful, is a housewife and artist living in the same idyllic university town with a handsome professor-husband and a young daughter. She has seemingly repressed her memory of the event as well as her survivor's guilt, but her perfect world and her grip on reality are both starting to crack." Libr J

This novel "evokes terror and redemption, shadows and light. Kasischke treads a delicate line with the precision and confidence of a tightrope walker." N Y Times Book Rev

Katkov, Norman

Blood & orchids. St. Martin's Press 1983 503p o.p.

LC 83-2889

"Set in Hawaii in the early '30s, [this] crime novel is based on an actual case. The story begins when a quartet of beach boys play Good Samaritan and end up accused of beating and raping the U.S. naval officer's wife they rescued, Hester Murdock. The trial brings to a boil the simmering racial tensions in the islands, and when it ends in a hung jury, vigilante justice takes over. Three of the boys are kidnapped and flogged by sailors, while the other is shot to death. A flamboyant trial lawyer named Bergman is imported from the States to defend the accused: Hester's husband, Gerald; Doris Ashby, her mother; and a hapless gob who was in the wrong place at the wrong time. As Honolulu detective Curt Maddox digs deeper into the matter, the situation is revealed to be even more sordid and scandalous than originally supposed. Studded with vivid characterizations, the story rolls inexorably to an awesome, tragic conclusion." Publ Wkly

Katzenbach, John

The analyst. Ballantine Bks. 2002 424p o.p.

ISBN 0-345-42626-6 LC 2001-43841

"On his 53rd birthday, a stodgy Manhattan psychoanalyst named Frederick Starks is given a life-or-death challenge by a cunning psychopath calling himself Rumplestiltskin. Starks has 15 days to identify his tormentor and the source of his grievance, or else commit suicide—unless he is willing to have some blameless relative die in his stead." N Y Times Book Rev

The author has "potently chronicled a long journey of revenge and redemption. Some of his psychological plot points . . . are a stretch, but the novel's fine sense of pacing, sudden switchbacks and chilling characterizations far overshadow its minor faults." Publ Wkly

Katzenbach, John—*Continued*

Hart's war; a novel. Ballantine Pub. Group 1999 490p o.p.
ISBN 0-345-42624-X LC 98-29890
"In 1942, Tommy Hart's B-25 is shot down over German territory. Prison life in Stalag Luft Thirteen is disrupted by the arrival of a young Tuskegee airman named Lincoln Scott. Capt. Vincent Bedford, a popular officer, is found murdered, and Scott is accused of the crime. Hart, formerly a Harvard law student, is assigned the nearly impossible task of defending a man who is presumed guilty because of his race and the preponderance of evidence pointing to him." Libr J
"Katzenbach's setting is flawlessly grim, and his characters chillingly reveal the divisive bigotry of soldiers ostensibly fighting for the same values, as well as some unexpected sources of redemption." Publ Wkly

Just cause. Putnam 1992 431p o.p.
LC 91-15135
"Matthew Cowart is at the top of his profession—a member of the editorial page staff of a major Miami newspaper. Cowart thinks his days as a crime reporter are behind him until he receives a letter from death row inmate Robert Ferguson, who not only proclaims his innocence, but also to have learned the identity of the real murderer. Cowart, his personal life a mess, takes the bait, hits the crime beat again, and writes a series of articles that lead to Ferguson's release and win the journalist a Pulitzer Prize. But Cowart has opened a Pandora's box of events which leads him to a showdown with the killer." Libr J
"Despite some extraneous subplots, the story generally proceeds at a breakneck pace, enhanced by ear-perfect dialogue and complex characterization." Publ Wkly

The madman's tale. Ballantine Bks. 2004 438p $24.95
ISBN 0-345-46481-8
"When Francis Petrel, a former inmate of the Western State Hospital, returns for a commemoration, he begins to remember events surrounding the brutal rape and murder of a young nurse 20 years before. At the same time, prosecutor Lucy Jones has arrived to determine whether the nurse's death could be related to several recent killings. Despite the lack of help from hospital authorities, Lucy puts together a team made up of Francis, another inmate, and two orderlies. As his long-suppressed recollections become clearer, Francis goes off his medications and begins hearing voices and maybe having hallucinations. Poised between sanity and madness, he is able to empathize with others, much like a profiler, and begins to understand the killer, placing Lucy and her team in great danger." Libr J
The author "delivers an uplifting story of justice, friendship, mystery and, above all, the courage of certain men and women who rise up, no matter the circumstances, to defeat evil, no matter the consequences." Publ Wkly

State of mind. Ballantine Bks. 1997 409p o.p.
ISBN 0-345-38631-0 LC 97-1415
"The U.S. has become more horrible than anyone could imagine; crime is rampant, and all citizens carry semiautomatic or even automatic weapons. When a teenage girl is found dead in a supposedly crime-free area controlled by the government, called the Fifty-first State, the murder appears to be one of a series that began a number of years prior. The Fifty-first authorities turn to criminal-mind expert Jeffrey Clayton, who has little choice but to help out, even though it means he will meet with personal demons he didn't want to resurrect." Booklist
"Katzenbach is a master at creating believable people caught up in horrific situations." Libr J

Kaufman, Bel

Up the down staircase. Prentice-Hall 1964 340p il o.p.
"Fresh from graduate study in English and crammed with pedagogy courses, young Sylvia Barrett begins her first year as a teacher in Calvin Coolidge High School. The experiences of this first year teacher, determined to remain true to her ideals despite the administrative confusion and organizational chaos of a New York City high school, form the core of Up the Down Staircase. . . . It tells its story through a series of letters, administrative memoranda, student compositions, suggestion box contributions, and intraschool communications." Best Sellers

Kaufman, Sue

Diary of a mad housewife. Random House 1967 311p o.p.
"Bettina Balser, in her mid-thirties, with a husband, two daughters ages nine and seven, and a bright apartment on Central Park West, (New York City), has arrived at a point in her life where she has completely lost her way, her purpose, her identity. She is literally terrified of so many things . . . that she is also afraid she is losing her mind. She decides to write out the things that so alarm her, as a form of therapy." Best Sellers

Kavanagh, Paul *See* Block, Lawrence, 1938-

Kawabata, Yasunari, 1899-1972

Snow country
In Kawabata, Y. Snow country, and Thousand cranes p1-175

Snow country, and Thousand cranes; the Nobel Prize edition of two novels; translated from the Japanese by Edward G. Seidensticker. Knopf 1969 2v in 1 o.p.
First United States editions published 1957 and 1959, respectively
Snow country "describes the three visits of Shimamura, a rich Tokyo dilettante, to a hotspring in the west of Japan, the snowiest region in the world. Here a young geisha, Komako, becomes his mistress and falls in love with him. . . . Komako's sparkling freshness stirs him, and he is touched by the 'irresistible sadness' she makes him feel, a sense of beauty going to waste and of immanent decay. But he cannot return her love; and their strange relationship, to which she gives so much, is doomed from the start." Atlantic

Kawabata, Yasunari, 1899-1972—*Continued*

The sound of the mountain; translated from the Japanese by Edward M. Seidensticker. Knopf 1970 276p o.p.

"This translation of the 1954 novel . . . is set in post-occupation Tokyo and Kamakura. An elderly businessman, nearing retirement, attempts to come to grips with the practical problems of the failing marriages of both his children and the psychological problems resulting from deaths of close friends and abortions completed or desired by his daughter-in-law and his son's mistress. Behind all is the nagging suspicion that his affection for his daughter-in-law is greater than that he has for his own daughter because the daughter-in-law resembles his early lost love, his wife's sister." Libr J

"The language is delicate, allusive, intensely Japanese; and, since plot and character development count for little, the style is all-important. We are fortunate that it should have been a writer with Mr. Seidensticker's gifts who ventured to convey [Kawabata's] rarefied novels into English." N Y Times Book Rev

Thousand cranes; translated by Edward G. Seidensticker. Knopf 1959 c1958 147p o.p.

Original Japanese edition, 1949

"This melancholy tale uses the classical tea ceremony as a background for the story of a young man's relationships to two women, his father's former mistress and her daughter. Although it has been praised for the beauty of its spare and elegant style, the novel has also been criticized for its coldness and its suggestion of nihilism." Merriam-Webster's Ency of Lit

also in Kawabata, Y. Snow country, and Thousand cranes p3-147

Kay, Guy Gavriel

The last light of the sun. ROC 2004 504p $24.95

ISBN 0-451-45965-2

A novel set during the "times when Vikings roamed the Anglo-Saxon and Welsh shores. . . . At the centre of the story is a young, self-exiled Viking who joins a Viking mercenary band. Set against the band are rival Welsh clans and their relations with Anglo-Saxon royalty. A fantastic element {in the novel concerns} . . . a faerie queen who claims the soul of a fallen prince." Publisher's note

"Kay's novel is an ambitious entertainment that transcends the historical record, offering cogent observations on fathers and sons, on the power of grief, on faith, courage, loyalty and the inevitability of change." Quill Quire

Kay, Terry

The runaway. Morrow 1997 406p o.p.

LC 97-16737

"Naively defying the mores of their small Georgia hometown, 12-year-olds Tom Winter, white, and Son Jesus Martin, black, have been friends their whole lives. But their twelfth summer brings change. Their accidental discovery of a human bone buried in a sawdust pile at an abandoned mill they pass while running away from home and the vicious rape of Son Jesus' sister by the family's white landlord set in motion events that forever change the boys' relationship and the way they see the world." Booklist

"The dialog is authentic and the storytelling has a homespun Southern texture." Libr J

Shadow song. Pocket Bks. 1994 388p o.p.

LC 94-15369

"Naive and gentlemanly Madison Lee ('Bobo') Murphy is 17 when, in 1955, he leaves rural Georgia to work at a resort in the Catskills, where he experiences instant culture shock among the inn's Jewish clientele. He comes under the influence of Avrum Feldman, an elderly eccentric who has devoted his life to the memory of Amelita Galli-Curci, the legendary soprano. . . . Avrum encourages Bobo when he falls chastely in love with Amy Lourie, a rich Jewish girl from New York visiting the resort with her protective parents. . . . Now, 38 years later, Bobo has returned to the Catskills to bury Avrum—and discovers that Amy is there too." Publ Wkly

"An absolutely enchanted and lyrical testimonial to the indomitable spirit of friendship and the tenacity of true love." Booklist

Kaye, M. M. (Mary Margaret), 1908-2004

Death in Berlin. St. Martin's Press 1985 254p o.p.

LC 85-1733

First published 1955 with title: Death walked in Berlin

This murder mystery is "set mainly in West Berlin in 1953, before cold war preoccupations had overshadowed concern about the Nazi evil. Young Miranda Brand, its English heroine, is appealing in the innocent way fictional characters nowadays rarely are. An orphan, she is wraith-thin, lovely-looking, intelligent and compassionate. Simon Lang, the mysterious hero, can't resist her. The plot revolves around a fortune in Dutch diamonds that was stolen by the Nazis and then disappeared—along with Herr Ridder, the functionary entrusted with them, and his wife. . . . This well-paced mystery has a nicely sustained atmosphere of menace." N Y Times Book Rev

Death in Kashmir. St. Martin's Press 1984 332p o.p.

LC 84-11748

Revised version of the novel first published 1953 in the United Kingdom with title: Death walked in Kashmir

Set in Kashmir, the book "involves the efforts of an intrepid heroine to uncover the circumstances surrounding a bizarre series of murders. Young Sarah Parrish becomes unwittingly entangled in a treacherous plot that threatens the safety of the entire free world, and during the course of her investigations she stumbles onto important evidence, places her own life in grave jeopardy, and finds true love." Booklist

"The setting—Kashmir's mountains, lakes, houseboats and hotels—comes exotically, enticingly alive. And the narrative unfolds superbly." N Y Times Book Rev

The far pavilions. St. Martin's Press 1978 957p o.p.

LC 78-3975

This historical novel of India between the Mutiny of 1857 and the second Afghan war focuses on "the early life, loves, and military career of Ashton Pelham-Martyn, an impetuous Englishman born in mid-Victorian India,

Kaye, M. M. (Mary Margaret), 1908-2004— *Continued*

reared by a Hindu serving-woman, and educated in the stuffiest of British schools. Considered an odd duck by his fellow Englishmen for his liberal view on race, and held at arm's length by his Indian friends, Pelham-Martyn resolves undivided loyalties by serving as a secret agent for the British Guides. . . . A romantic subplot concerns his quest for an Indian princess he has loved all his life, and lost to a Rajah." Libr J

"It's a leisurely, panoramic, enjoyable tale, convincing and varied in characterization, rich in adventure, heroism, cruelty and love, rich in India." Publ Wkly

Shadow of the moon. St. Martin's Press 1979 614p o.p.

LC 79-5033

First published 1957 in the United Kingdom; an abridged version of this novel was published 1957, in the United States by Messner

The historical background of this novel "deals with the events leading up to and encompassing the Indian Mutiny of 1857, a rather haphazard rebellion by the Indian soldiers (Sepoys) against cruel and scornful British officers. . . . The novel tells the story of lovely Winter de Ballesteros, her premature engagement and marriage to the British Commissioner of Lunjore, her love for Captain Alex Randall, and her life and adventures in India. The book culminates in the bloody rebellion against the English which forces Alex and Winter, with two others, to flee into the shelter of the jungle." Best Sellers

The author exhibits "an intimate knowledge of Indian history, a deep feel for the land, unflagging vitality and an unfailing instinct for suspense. These qualities make her story delightfully readable." Publ Wkly

Trade wind. St. Martin's Press 1981 553p il o.p.

LC 80-28302

Rewritten and expanded version of a novel first published 1963 in the United Kingdom and 1964 in the United States

"Twenty-one year old Hero Athena Hollis sets out from Boston for Zanzibar to fulfill her mission in life—to stop slave trading. On the journey she is washed overboard and rescued by Rory Frost, a piratical slave trader. Stubborn, spoiled Hero clashes with equally stubborn, overconfident, wicked Rory. Disagreements come in rapid succession about her naive assumptions, his overbearing manner, her proposed marriage, his occupation, etc. Palace intrigue, revolution, a pirate raid on the island, and a murder lead up to Rory's kidnapping of Hero." Libr J

Kaye, Mary Margaret *See* Kaye, M. M. (Mary Margaret), 1908-2004

Kazan, Elia

America, America; with an introduction by S. N. Behrman. Stein & Day 1962 190p o.p.

Copyright 1961 as an unpublished dramatic work with title: Hamal

"A young Greek boy, Stavros, pursues his intense desire to leave the tyranny of his land and seek a new life in America. As a means of attaining his goal, he accepts his family's offer to go to Constantinople with wealth and prized possessions where he is to establish himself in his uncle's rug business. After losing his family fortune enroute, he sinks to degradation in an effort to secure money for passage to America. After suffering incredible hardships his dream of America is realized." Wis Libr Bull

"Elia Kazan's book is a scenario, with the spareness, emphasis on the concrete, the appeal to eye and ear of the film story. It has a rugged simplicity, vividly sketched characters, and a strong story line." Libr J

Followed by The Anatolian (1982)

Kazantzakis, Nikos, 1883-1957

The last temptation of Christ; translated from the Greek by P. A. Bien. Simon & Schuster 1960 506p o.p.

"This novel is a retelling of the life story of Jesus of Nazareth as Kazantzakis imagined it might actually have happened, the human events from which the worshipful Gospel account was derived and their meaning to the people who experienced them." Atlantic

"The Christ created here by Kazantzakis is definitely not the Christ of the Gospels. . . . Far from it. Kazantzakis has composed a fictional biography of Jesus that is written with passion, a colorful, lyric testimony of his, Kazantzakis' own anguished search for God." Best Sellers

Zorba the Greek; translated by Carl Wildman. Simon & Schuster 1952 311p o.p.

"The spirit of Zorba, full of energy and peasant philosophy, is contrasted with that of the narrator, a learned but staid Englishman who comes to Crete for adventure. The relationship between the two men deepens despite Zorba's mismanagement of the narrator's mining business, and despite Zorba's attempts to change his friend's behavior to a more zestful one. Kazantzakis creates in Zorba a character that represents the vitality sapped by the inhibitions civilization has created." Shapiro. Fic for Youth. 3d edition

Kearns, Caledonia

(ed) Cabbage and bones. See Cabbage and bones

Keating, H. R. F. (Henry Reymond Fitzwalter), 1926-

The bad detective. St. Martin's Minotaur 1999 279p o.p.

ISBN 0-312-24371-5 LC 99-33531

First published 1996 in the United Kingdom

"British copper Jack Stallworthy isn't a bad detective, exactly, but occasionally the opportunity has arisen for him to suppress evidence and, in the process, stash away a few pounds in his secret retirement fund. Jack's wife has decided on Ko Samui, a remote island paradise, as the perfect retirement spot, but Jack knows that his pension—even with the secret stash—won't be enough. So when a local entrepreneur asks Jack to steal a file from police headquarters in exchange for the deed to a hotel in Ko Samui, Jack can hardly believe his 'good luck.'" Booklist

"Keating's low-key sense of humor and his dexterity at

Keating, H. R. F. (Henry Reymond Fitzwalter), 1926-—*Continued*

making a crooked protagonist sympathetic are firmly in place, as is the story's satirical edge, which explores the disparity between the financial rewards received by criminals and police and the symbiotic relationship between cops and robbers." Publ Wkly

Bribery, corruption also. St. Martin's Press 1999 282p $23.95

ISBN 0-312-20502-3 LC 99-15494

"A Thomas Dunne book"

"Inspector Ghote, of the Bombay police, accompanies his wife to Calcutta in order to take possession of an inherited house. The hassles they encounter reveal corruption, conspiracy, and more." Libr J

Cheating death. Mysterious Press 1994 172p o.p.

LC 94-9502

This "Inspector Ghote novel finds the lovable Indian detective embroiled in an academic cheating scandal, under pressure from his superiors and vexed by pressing domestic business. When a final exam paper is circulated throughout Bombay's Oceanic College prior to the test, Ghote is sent to investigate, only to find his prime suspect in a coma, having tried to commit suicide (Or was it a murder attempt?)." Publ Wkly

Doing wrong; an Inspector Ghote novel. Penzler Bks. 1994 218p o.p.

LC 94-9287

"From Bombay, the exquisitely courteous, ever persistent police detective, Inspector Ghote, travels to the holy city of Banaras to find the murderer of the much loved Mrs. Popatkar, 'veteran freedom fighter, former Minister, upholder of a hundred good causes'. . . . In spite of a leisurely pace befitting a country where foot-sore pilgrims, sacred cattle and auto rickshaws clog the roads, this is an absorbing tale and an illuminating tour of Banaras." Publ Wkly

The good detective; a mystery. Scribner 1995 199p o.p.

LC 95-9078

"Detective Ned French is smooth talking, ambitious, talented, and sure to move up quickly in the Norchester police. . . . Trouble is, Ned's so obsessed with keeping Norchester free of crime that he completely loses his good judgment. First, there's an illicit and ill-advised affair with attractive barrister Deborah Brooke, and then he foolishly covers up a damning incident from his past. Finally Ned makes his biggest mistake—a unilateral and extremely unwise decision about how to deal with a gang of 'London thugs' who are threatening Norchester. Deeply affecting and superbly written, this is an outstanding police procedural and a moving human drama." Booklist

Inspector Ghote trusts the heart. Doubleday 1973 c1972 201p o.p.

"Published for the Crime Club"

First published 1972 in the United Kingdom

In this mystery "Inspector Ghote is the go-between in a kidnapping case. The child of a rich man is snatched. A mixup follows, and it is a poor man's son who is taken. The kidnappers still hold the rich man up for ransom, posing him with a terrible dilemma." N Y Times Book Rev

The author "writes with wonderful ease and energy—his understanding of the individuality of human beings is profound." New Yorker

The soft detective. St. Martin's Press 1998 268p o.p.

ISBN 0-312-19335-1 LC 98-8817

First published 1997 in the United Kingdom

"When Detective Chief Inspector Phil Benholme begins investigating the murder of a Nobel Prize-winning physiologist, he can scarcely believe what he discovers: his own teenage son may be involved. Keating's latest is a gripping examination of one of a police officer's worst nightmares—a portrait of a man faced with the choice between defending his son and helping to prove he's a killer." Booklist

Keating, Henry Reymond Fitzwalter *See* Keating, H. R. F. (Henry Reymond Fitzwalter), 1926-

Keillor, Garrison

Happy to be here. Atheneum Pubs. 1982 210p o.p.

LC 81-66033

Contents: Jack Schmidt, Arts Administrator; Don: the true story of a young person; My North Dakota railroad days; WLT (The Edgar era); The Slim Graves Show; Friendly neighbor; Attitude; Around the Horne; The new baseball; How are the legs, Sam?; U.S. still on top, says rest of world; Congress in crisis: the proximity bill; Re the tower project; How it was in America a week ago Tuesday; Shy rights: why not pretty soon; Mission to Mandalla; Nana hami ba reba; Plainfolks; The people's shopper; Your wedding and you; The lowliest bush a purple sage would be; Local family keeps son happy; Oya life these days; Your transit commission; Be careful; Ten stories for Mr. Richard Brautigan, and other stories; The drunkard's Sunday; Happy to be here; Drowning 1954

Lake Wobegon days. Viking 1985 337p o.p.

LC 85-40029

This book is the author's "history and season-by-season chronicle of his imaginary hometown, [Lake Wobegon]. . . . It's a town 'where nobody locks the doors or knows where the keys are,' where wearing black tennis shoes marks a boy for life and where it's thought that newfangled contraptions like dishwashers lead to degeneracy." Newsweek

"Much of this is satirical, but Keillor's subtle humor is gentle, rather than biting or mocking, as he exposes the foibles and faults of Lake Wobegonians with affection and sympathy." Publ Wkly

Lake Wobegon summer 1956. Viking 2001 291p o.p.

ISBN 0-670-03003-1 LC 2001-26312

"It is summer, and as the denizens of Lake Wobegon sit on their front porches, listening to the radio and to the swish of sprinklers on their lawns, 14-year-old Gary struggles to find his own place within the community. . . . Gary has, by his own admission, been a good boy, but he is now exploring what it means to be bad-as 'bad'

Keillor, Garrison—*Continued*

is defined in 1950s Lake Wobegon. Keillor's wry vignettes of Gary's summer of change and turmoil are laced with his trademark self-deprecating humor." Libr J

Leaving home. Viking 1987 xxiii, 244p o.p.
LC 87-40219

Contents: A trip to Grand Rapids; A ten-dollar bill; Easter; Corinne; A glass of Wendy; The speeding ticket; Seeds; Chicken; How the crab apple grew; Truckstop; Dale; High rise; Collection; Life is good; Lyle's roof; Pontoon boat; State Fair; David and Agnes, a romance; The killer; Eloise; The royal family; Homecoming; Brethren; Thanksgiving; Darlene makes a move; Christmas dinner; Exiles; New Year's; Where did it go wrong?; Post office; Out in the cold; Hawaii; Hansel; Du, du liegst mir im herzen; Aprille; Goodbye to the lake

"These radio monologues [from A Prairie Home Companion] read easily, and listeners to the weekly radio show will find the flow of Keillor's distinctive flat rendition ringing in their ears." Wilson Libr Bull

Love me. Viking 2003 272p $24.95
ISBN 0-670-03246-8 LC 2003-52540

This novel is "about fame, seduction and downfall as experienced by a Midwestern writer named Larry Wyler, whose common sense is hijacked by best-sellerdom. When his first novel, a prairie potboiler called 'Spacious Skies,' improbably takes off, so does Wyler. He abandons ho-hum St. Paul and his wife, Iris, for the diamond glitter of Manhattan, where he gets an apartment on Central Park, an office at The New Yorker and a killer case of creative constipation." N Y Times Book Rev

The author "blends humor and compassion with just a touch of cynicism, cooking up a funny, insightful, and touching story of ambition, sacrifice, and love." Booklist

WLT; a radio romance. Viking 1991 401p o.p.
LC 91-50160

This novel "chronicles the story of the birth (in 1926), ripening and decline of a Minneapolis radio station, the brainchild of the brothers Ray and Roy Soderbjerg. Its characters are WLT's principal staffers, both those on the mike and those behind it." N Y Times Book Rev

"Garrison Keillor's mythical America, unlike the faded and inoffensive Midwest of Sandburg, is dreamed with an unblinking eye. His characters are idiosyncratic. They are culled from who knows where—from our collective past, certainly, but also from the demotic oral tradition of a rich and very real community that is gone and now exists only in recollection." Nation

Kellerman, Faye

Day of atonement; a Peter Decker/Rina Lazarus mystery. Morrow 1991 359p o.p.
LC 90-22682

"When Los Angeles detective Peter Decker and new wife Rina Lazarus visit her Jewish kinfolks in Brooklyn, startling events disturb their honeymoon. Quite unexpectedly and with great antipathy, Decker—an adoptee—recognizes his natural mother at a holiday gathering. Before he can confront her, though, her troubled 14-year-old grandson goes missing and Decker, fortuitously on hand, begins the search. . . . Hard-hitting details, vignettes of Jewish life, and uncomfortably close glimpses of a cold-hearted psycho make this an entrancing page turner." Libr J

The forgotten. Morrow 2001 374p o.p.
ISBN 0-688-15614-2

In this mystery Kellerman "balances Rina Lazarus's consuming Orthodox Judaism with the broader societal issues faced by her husband, L.A. homicide detective Peter Decker. Here they intertwine when the vicious defacement of their synagogue reverberates in a widening circle of murders. Ernesto Golding, a troubled, spoiled youth and acquaintance of Rina's son, Jacob, confesses to the crime, but several months later Ernesto and his therapists, Mervin and Dee Baldwin, are murdered." Publ Wkly

"The depiction of how teens and parents push and pull at one another's emotions is dead on." Booklist

Grievous sin; a Peter Decker/Rina Lazarus mystery. Morrow 1993 368p o.p.
LC 93-12344

"Complications in the delivery room lead to major surgery for Rina Decker, who, when last seen in *False Prophet*, [1992] was pregnant with her and husband Peter Decker's first child. She is barely out of danger when an infant vanishes from the hospital's understaffed nursery, and proud father Peter, an LAPD detective sergeant, declares . . . 'I *owe* it to that little baby girl to find her.'" Publ Wkly

"While the plot comes dangerously close to being overly saccharine and annoyingly artificial, Kellerman does know how to hook her readers. First, she tantalizes them with ambiguous clues and ominous glimpses of an unbalanced villain's psyche, then she teases them with a blend of pulse-quickening suspense and heartwarming family tableaux. Only then does she deliver the shocking climax." Booklist

Jupiter's bones; a novel. Morrow 1999 375p o.p.
ISBN 0-688-15612-6 LC 99-33356

"When Emil Euler Ganz, a brilliant former astrophysicist turned cult leader, is found dead with an empty fifth of vodka under his bed, it looks like suicide. But LAPD lieutenant Peter Decker is suspicious and begins to ask questions about the man who disappeared 25 years ago only to turn up ten years later as Father Jupiter, the charismatic leader of the Order of the Rings of God." Libr J

"Kellerman has pulled together elements of suspense, violence, humor, pathos, and love and wrapped them into a potent plot certain to captivate genre fans." Booklist

Justice. Morrow 1995 388p o.p.
LC 95-14268

"A Peter Decker/Rina Lazarus novel"

In this mystery "a high school prom queen is strangled to death after a wild night of drugs, drink and boisterous group sex. Peter Decker, a Los Angeles homicide detective, who lies awake nights worrying about his own children, coaxes a confession from the dead girl's date. 'He's cold, he's calculating, he's eerie,' Decker says of this preternaturally self-contained youth, the nephew of a Mafia crime boss. . . . Rina Lazarus, Decker's wife and helpmate in this series, is uncharacteristically subdued here, which gives this sympathetic cop a rare chance to work independently on a case that raises touchy issues like ethnic stereotyping and religious prejudice." N Y Times Book Rev

Kellerman, Faye—*Continued*

Milk and honey; a novel. Morrow 1990 384p o.p.
LC 89-39592

"On a summer night in a housing development near Los Angeles, police sergeant Peter Decker finds a winsome two-year-old girl playing on a swing set—and wearing blood-soaked pajamas. Unclaimed, 'Sally' is placed in a foster home while Decker and partner Marge Dunn try to learn her identity. Bee stings on her arms lead them days later to the scene of a bloody multiple murder at a honey farm. While piecing together a bizarre puzzle of betrayal and revenge . . . Peter is also investigating rape and assualt charges brought against an old army buddy from Vietnam. The pressures of the murder case and doubts about his friend's innocence compound Peter's anxiety as he waits for young Orthodox Jewish widow Rina Lazarus to decide if she will marry him." Publ Wkly

Moon music; a novel. Morrow 1998 424p o.p.
LC 98-6735

Las Vegas homicide cop Romulus Poe finds himself "in charge of investigating the gruesome death of a showgirl turned hooker. The case reminds Poe of a brutal, unsolved murder 25 years in his own past and brings up his unresolved feelings for his partner's troubled wife. When a second, similarly mutilated body is found, Poe and his team must uncover the truth, even if it involves confronting a powerful, corrupt casino owner. Kellerman's characters have complex interrelationships that often seem more important than the murder investigation itself." Libr J

Prayers for the dead. Morrow 1996 406p o.p.
LC 96-7494

"A Peter Decker/Rina Lazarus novel"

This "mystery begins with the brutal murder and mutilation of renowned heart surgeon, researcher and fundamentalist Christian Azor Sparks. LAPD Lieutenant Decker gets the call. He also gets an abundance of suspects. . . . Religion and morality are integral to Kellerman's mysteries—built on the bedrock of the Deckers' orthodox Judaism. Here she deftly casts her net around the commanding victim, whose shadow lay equally over family and colleagues, and his son, the theologian Father Abram, whose past connection with Rina may force Decker off the case." Publ Wkly

The quality of mercy; a novel. Morrow 1989 607p o.p.
LC 88-29275

"Rebecca Lopez and William Shakespeare first encounter each other in a London graveyard where she is burying her betrothed and he his mentor and best friend. Their paths cross again as they seek to avenge these untimely deaths, she joining in her family's mission to rescue fellow Jews from the Spanish Inquisition, he searching for the murderer among London's criminals. Shakespeare offers excitement and intellectual stimulation to the brilliant, adventurous Rebecca, stifled by the restricted life of an Elizabethan woman, but political and religious events overtake them and doom the relationship." Libr J

"Deft characterization and dazzling prose evoke the ambiance of the period. More than just a mystery, the novel is a spectacular epic—romantic, bawdy, witty and abounding with adventure." Publ Wkly

Sanctuary; a Peter Decker/Rina Lazarus mystery. Morrow 1994 396p o.p.
LC 94-11350

"L.A.P.D. sergeant Pete Decker and his Orthodox Jewish wife, Rina Lazarus, the parents of a baby daughter, are caught up in a case involving Rina's old school chum, Honey Klein, who comes to stay with the Deckers after leaving her diamond-merchant husband. When Honey and her children mysteriously disappear, Rina is first puzzled and then alarmed, especially considering that Pete is working on a double homicide involving another Jewish diamond merchant and his family. To solve the case, the Deckers travel to Israel and find themselves risking their lives to track down the disturbing truth." Booklist

Serpent's tooth; a Peter Decker/Rina Lazarus novel. Morrow 1997 400p o.p.
ISBN 0-688-14368-7 LC 97-10685

"LAPD detective Pete Decker's latest case is a shocker. Estelle's, the watering hole favored by L.A.'s rich and famous, is the scene of a mass shooting that leaves a dozen dead and scores wounded. There is no need to look for the murderer, who shot himself following his killing spree, but Pete does have to figure out the killer's motive, wrap up loose ends, and make the LAPD come out looking good." Booklist

"The scope of the investigation is broad and the moralizing is kept to a minimum, giving Decker a rare chance to do some solid police work." N Y Times Book Rev

Stone kiss; a Peter Decker/Rina Lazarus novel. Warner Bks. 2002 390p $25.95
ISBN 0-446-53038-7 LC 2002-16886

In this mystery LAPD detective Decker and his wife Rina "come to New York to investigate the homicide of a distant relative in Decker's family. Natural grief and shame aside, there is something profoundly unpleasant about the rigidly closed-minded family of Hasidic Jews that rebuffs Decker's efforts to find out who murdered a rabbi's bookish son in a seedy Manhattan hotel room—and what become of the 15-year-old niece who was in his care." N Y Times Book Rev

"Whether Kellerman is depicting the ultra-Orthodox Jewish community or a pornographer's studio she is utterly convincing. Amid the wreckage of lives taken or thrown away, Kellerman's heroes find glimmers of hope and enough moral ambiguity to make even her most evil villain look less than totally black." Publ Wkly

Street dreams. Warner Bks. 2003 420p $25.95
ISBN 0-446-53131-6 LC 2003-45079

"Cindy, a rookie cop and Peter's 28-year-old daughter by his first marriage, takes center stage here. Both her rocky history with the department and with her dad come to the fore as she digs into the case of a developmentally disabled teenager who abandoned her baby, insists she was raped, and may have witnessed a murder. Following the strangely coincidental hit-and-run of another disabled teen from the same area, the case blossoms into a mystery that requires help from Peter." Booklist

Kellerman, Jonathan

Bad love. Bantam Bks. 1994 386p o.p.
LC 93-26678

Child "psychologist Alex Delaware receives a terrifying audiotape full of bloodcurding screams and a disjointed voice chanting, 'Bad love, bad love.' Alex can't connect the tape with anything, but when he begins to get threatening phone calls, and someone brutally harpoons one of his beloved koi fish, he realizes he could be in danger. With the help of his friend, Detective Milo Sturgis, Delaware begins to unravel the complex, multilayered plot that seems to be linked to a conference he chaired 20 years ago. Delaware finally discovers he's being pursued by a tormented, relentless, deranged killer." Booklist

The author "spins a tight, complicated plot and is careful to balance his grisly murder scenes with substantive shoptalk about childhood trauma and the devastating effects of authoritarian discipline." N Y Times Book Rev

Billy Straight; a novel. Random House 1999 467p o.p.
ISBN 0-679-45959-6 LC 98-19583

Hollywood homicide detective Petra Connor "frantically scours the city in search of a runaway 12-year-old boy who witnessed the vicious stabbing of a woman in Griffith Park. This case quickly draws the media carrion crows when it comes out that the victim was recently divorced from the popular star of a television series. Like Connor, the investigation is competent but strictly by the book—and not the reason you're turning the pages so fast. That distinction goes to the winsome title character and frequent narrator, a self-taught street kid with an artless affection for books." N Y Times Book Rev

The clinic. Bantam Bks. 1997 370p o.p.
LC 96-24626

Alex Delaware conducts "an investigation into the savage stabbing murder of Hope Devane, a psychology professor and celebrity author. The LAPD, unable to solve the case after three months, reassigns it to Lieutenant Milo Sturgis. Milo calls on his friend Alex, a compassionate, astute psychologist, for insight into the victim, who had a seemingly routine academic career and marriage until writing a pop-psych relationship book." Publ Wkly

The author "has crafted another masterly, darkly psychological tale, drawing upon timely issues ranging from abortion to organ harvesting." Libr J

Devil's waltz. Bantam Bks. 1993 416p o.p.
LC 92-18089

"Alex Delaware, the child psychologist and amateur sleuth . . . returns to the beleaguered Los Angeles pediatrics hospital where he was trained. Called in to consult on the baffling case of a 2-year-old girl with phantom ailments, Alex performs his clinical chores with his customary tenderness, while bearing the details of the child's extraordinary medical history. Despite Mr. Kellerman's overelaborate approach, he maintains the harrowing suspense of a medical mystery too horrid to be anything but real." N Y Times Book Rev

Dr. Death; a novel. Random House 2000 352p o.p.
ISBN 0-679-45961-8 LC 00-29065

In this mystery Dr. Alex Delaware works "with old LAPD buddy Detective Milo Sturgis on a particularly gruesome murder. Dr. Eldon Mate, a Kervokian-like 'Dr. Death,' is found vivisected in the back of an Econoline van, hooked up to his 'humanitron' suicide machine. A crass farewell note is stapled to his chest. It's obviously the work of an extremely intelligent and bold killer, and suspects abound." Libr J

"A heady blend of criminal profiling and police procedural." Booklist

Monster; a novel. Random House 1999 396p o.p.
ISBN 0-679-45960-X LC 99-20098

"A handsome young actor is found murdered and mutilated, a female psychologist meets a similar fate, and twin brothers are gruesomely dispatched—all in separate events, on the same evening. The murders, though different, seem to be the work of the same killer. As Dr. Alex Delaware, psychologist and consultant to the LAPD, and detective Milo Sturgis unravel the mystery of the killer's identity, it becomes clear that Ardis Peake (a.k.a. 'Monster'), incarcerated in a psychiatric hospital for the criminally insane for the past 16 years, is somehow involved." Libr J

The murder book. Ballantine Bks. 2002 408p o.p.
ISBN 0-345-45253-4 LC 2002-74733

In this "caper starring Delaware and his mentor in police work, homicide detective Milo Sturgis, Delaware receives a package in the mail. It contains an official police case file, known as a 'murder book,' filled with stark crime scene photos and terse reports of some 40 cases. What Delaware finds most shocking, however, is the horrified reaction his hard-bitten detective pal Milo has upon seeing one particular scene. Kellerman departs from his standard focus on Delaware to a telling of Sturgis' story, going back to his struggles as a young black, gay cop and showing how his first victim, the girl depicted in the murder book, still haunts him." Booklist

Over the edge. Atheneum Pubs. 1987 373p o.p.
LC 86-47936

This novel featuring "child psychologist Alex Delaware begins with a desperate, garbled phone call from former patient Jamey Cadmus, genius of record and heir to a construction fortune. The next day, Jamey is accused of the Lavender Slashings, a series of grisly homosexual murders that have rocked Los Angeles. The teenager's lawyer asks Alex to examine Jamey's recent history with the hope that a plea of diminished capacity will protect Jamey from a prison sentence. Though soon fired, Alex continues his investigation." Publ Wkly

Private eyes. Bantam Bks. 1992 475p o.p.
LC 91-17314

"Harvard-bound, 18-year-old heiress Melissa Dickinson, whom child psychologist Alex Delaware had successfully treated for anxiety 10 years earlier, calls him with concerns about leaving her wealthy mother, an agoraphobe. Years before Melissa's birth, Gina Dickinson Ramp had been disfigured by acid thrown for never-revealed reasons by a former lover, now out of prison and back in town. Widowed for many years, recently remarried and making progress in her own intensive therapy with a noted husband-and-wife team of behaviorial psychologists, Gina is still fragile. When she disappears,

Kellerman, Jonathan—*Continued*

Melissa enlists Delaware's help and that of his friend, Milo Sturgis, on leave from the LAPD. . . . Kellerman deftly handles the strings of his plot." Publ Wkly

Self-defense. Bantam Bks. 1995 390p o.p.
LC 94-26175

Psychologist Alex Delaware "is treating 25-year-old Lucy Lowell for a recurring nightmare that she has been having ever since serving on the hanging jury that convicted a serial killer. . . . When Lucy's terrifying dream is complicated by incidents of sleepwalking, bed-wetting, narcolepsy and a possible suicide attempt, Alex suspects a repressed childhood memory. After putting his patient through hypnotic regression, he is convinced that she witnessed a murder and he sets out to prove it. . . . An exciting story that is loaded with tension and packed with titillating insights into abnormal psychology." N Y Times Book Rev

Silent partner. Bantam Bks. 1989 404p o.p.
LC 89-6490

"At a glitzy party, child psychologist Alex Delaware meets a woman from his past who seems troubled. When she is found dead later that night, Delaware decides to investigate. Combining a judicious use of psychological detail with suspenseful sleuthing, Kellerman's . . . novel is certain to increase the author's already substantial audience." Booklist

Survival of the fittest; a novel. Bantam Bks. 1998 401p o.p.
LC 97-3182

In this mystery, psychologist Alex Delaware, "helps his friend, detective Milo Sturgis, solve a cold case: a deaf and mildly retarded Israeli girl, the daughter of a diplomat, is strangled in a park, and letters 'D-V-L-L' are found on a scrap of paper in her pocket. Authorities have failed to come up with a suspect or any leads, so the victim's father brings in a detective of his own, the great Daniel Sharavi." Libr J

"Kellerman has things down to a science now, knowing instinctively what his fans want: suspense, adventure, romance, and a leading man to die for." Booklist

Therapy. Ballantine Bks. 2004 387p $26.95
ISBN 0-345-45259-3

"To help solve a young couple's murder, Alex Delaware needs to dig secrets out of a testy celebrity psychologist." Libr J

The author "manages to take the story of a lovers' lane double murder near Mulholland Drive to the point where it involves human rights atrocities in Rwanda. Along the way Mr. Kellerman packs in the descriptive detail that is one of his hallmarks and one of the incidental attractions in his fiction." N Y Times (Late N Y Ed)

Time bomb; a novel. Bantam Bks. 1990 468p o.p.
LC 90-349

This novel featuring "child psychologist and private detective Alex Delaware begins when Delaware is called upon to deal with the potential trauma to elementary-school children of a sniper killed in their midst during lunch recess. He quickly learns that the sniper's target may not have been the children at all, but either a right-wing politician holding a news conference at the school or his liberal counterpart, a publicity-hungry, former 1960's radical who had appeared unexpectedly for an impromptu debate and whose bodyguard shot the sniper to death." N Y Times Book Rev

The web. Bantam Bks. 1996 342p o.p.
LC 95-32161

Child psychologist Alex Delaware "and his paramour Robin land on Aruk, a tiny Micronesian island, and unwittingly begin the vacation from hell. Alex has been invited by Dr. Moreland, the island's richest and most influential resident, to collaborate on a writing project. The eccentric Moreland, who keeps a zoo of large, creepy insects, seems literally to vanish after sunset, leaving Alex written clues based on the works of great thinkers." Libr J

"An intriguing, keep-'em-guessing plot, Kellerman's usual mix of psychologically fascinating characters, a megadose of suspense, and that always reliable heart-throb, Dr. Alex Delaware, make this one a must-have for all mystery collections." Booklist

When the bough breaks. Atheneum Pubs. 1985 293p o.p.
LC 81-16805

Psychologist Alex Delaware "turns detective when he is called upon to interview a young girl who is the only living witness to a brutal dual murder. Whatever the girl may have seen, the actual crime veils an even more horrible contemporary phenomenon: a ring of child molesters at a school in Southern California. The psychologist is soon out of his professional depth in pursuing clues and leads, but he plods onward to solve the case, nearly at the expense of the girl's and his own life. Kellerman's story is long on sensational descriptions and short on believable disclosures—too many of the good turns of fortune seem coincidentally opportune—but as a suspenseful drama, the novel does rack up its points." Booklist

Kellogg, Marjorie

Tell me that you love me, Junie Moon. Farrar, Straus & Giroux 1968 216p o.p.

"Junie Moon, in a rehabilitation center after a crazy boyfriend threw acid in her face, meets Warren, a paraplegic who has been shot in the spine on a hunting trip, and Arthur, who is slowly dying of a degenerative nerve disease. Amid the protests of the hospital staff the three decide to leave the center to set up a household. The reaction of their new neighbors is anything but encouraging, but one of them, an Italian fish merchant, befriends them and sends them on a vacation in his truck. It is a wonderful interlude until Arthur, recognizing that he is in the last stages of his illness, asks to be taken home to die." Shapiro. Fic for Youth. 3d edition

Kelly, Thomas, 1961-

Empire rising; Thomas Kelly. Farrar, Straus and Giroux 2005 390p $25
ISBN 0-374-14781-7 LC 2004-8580

"It is 1930, and ground has just been broken for the building dubbed 'the Eighth Wonder of the World.' One of the thousands of men working high above the city is Michael Briody, an Irish immigrant torn between his desire to make a new life in America and his pledge to gather money and arms for the Irish republican cause. When he meets Grace Masterson, an alluring artist who

Kelly, Thomas, 1961—*Continued*
is depicting the great skyscraper's rise from her houseboat on the East River, Briody's life turns exhilarating and dangerous, for Grace is also a paramour of Johnny Farrell, Mayor Jimmy Walker's liaison with Tammany Hall and the New York underworld." Publisher's note

"The canvas is epic in scale, peopled with numerous arresting characters, recognizable in both senses: 'real' persons like Jimmy Walker, Babe Ruth, Primo Camera, the famously 'missing' Judge Crater and the many engaging but no less real inventions of his own. [Kelly's] special gift as a novelist is his ability to maintain a galloping tilt of narrative suspense, despite countless shifts in plot development, without overwhelming or confusing the reader. Unusual in an epic, to say the least, this novel is a page-turner; there is no plot-padding or authorial longueurs slackening the pace." America

Kelman, James

How late it was, how late. Norton 1995 373p o.p.

ISBN 0-393-03817-3

"Sammy, the novel's central figure, is an ex-convict who wakes on a Glasgow street after a two-day binge. . . . He gets himself into a fight with some soldiers. They beat him up, and then he is arrested and beaten some more by the police. The beatings cause him to lose his sight. He's released, blind, into the Glasgow streets, and must try to find his way home." N Y Times Book Rev

The novel "is a tour de force, both in its convincingly claustrophobic rendering of what it's like to be newly sightless and in its rhythmic prose." Newsweek

Kelman, Judith

Summer of storms. Putnam 2001 288p $24.95

ISBN 0-399-14674-1 LC 00-45728

This thriller "chronicles the rekindling of a long-dormant murder investigation and the return of a ruthless killer. Thirty years after her young sister's death, Anna Jameson is haunted by memories of what was dubbed the Sleeping Beauty Murder. On a stormy summer night, five-year-old Julie Jameson was killed in her bedroom while her family slept. . . . Fast-forward to Anna, now 33 and an aspiring photographer, who returns to New York to work as a photojournalist for a high-powered media conglomerate and to confront family demons." Publ Wkly

Kelton, Elmer, 1926-

Badger boy. Forge 2001 286p o.p.

ISBN 0-312-87319-0 LC 00-48457

"A Tom Doherty Associates book"

Sequel to The buckskin line

As the Texas Rangers disband, Badger Boy, a white boy whose parents were murdered by Comanches and who was himself captured and raised by a Comanche warrior, falls prisoner to David "Rusty" Shannon

Slaughter. Doubleday 1992 369p o.p.

LC 92-10317

"Set on the Great Plains shortly after the end of the Civil War, the story focuses on the intertwining lives of a half dozen characters. Among them are Jeff Layne, a bitter, middle-aged Confederate veteran; Crow Feather, a proud Comanche warrior; Sully, a recently freed slave; and Arletta Browder, a displaced easterner who takes over her dead father's buffalo-hunting business. It is buffalo that throw them all together, the whites hoping to slaughter the great beasts for profit, the Indians hoping to preserve a way of life that requires the buffalo's survival." Booklist

"Well written and fast-paced, this powerful, moving novel proceeds inexorably toward the extinction of the great herds and of the indigenous peoples' way of life" Publ Wkly

Followed by The far canyon (1994)

Texas vendetta; Elmer Kelton. 1st Hardcover ed. Forge 2004 301p $24.95

ISBN 0-7653-0572-0 LC 2003-17352

Texas Ranger "privates Andy Pickard, the onetime Comanche captive called Badger Boy, and the war-anguished Farley Brackett, are assigned to deliver a prisoner to the sheriff of a county some distance from the ranger camp on the San Saba River. The prisoner, Jayce Landon, has recently killed a man named Ned Hopper and is to stand trial for murder. The rangers quickly learn that the Landon and Hopper families are involved in a blood feud and that Jayce Landon is the target of both clans." Publisher's note

"Within the exciting context of a western adventure, [Kelton] explores paternal relationships-good and bad-and the crippling consequences of hanging on too tightly to a painful past." Booklist

The way of the coyote. Forge 2001 283p o.p.

ISBN 0-312-87318-2 LC 2001-40482

"A Tom Doherty Associates book"

"Rusty Shannon, who was kidnapped by the Comanche as a child, rescues 10-year-old Andy Pinkard from the same fate. Andy's memories are all Comanche, and he struggles to adjust to the white life. Meanwhile, the young son of a woman Rusty once loved is kidnapped by the Comanche, and two rivals from Rusty's Texas Ranger days arrive as representatives from the corrupt state government and twist the law to confiscate Rusty's ranch." Booklist

"Kelton covers a wide swath of history with aplomb, illuminating a little-known period in Western history. California is still Mexican, Indians are a real threat and outlaws rule the land in this rough-riding adventure tale." Publ Wkly

Kemelman, Harry

The day the rabbi resigned. Fawcett Columbine 1992 273p o.p.

LC 91-72891

"Twenty-five years after coming to the Boston suburb of Barnard's Crossing, Rabbi David Small is considering retirement. But before he can get so much as one foot out of the pulpit, a local college professor dies in a car accident and the weary clergyman finds himself once again drawn from his own everyday concerns into more serious matters." Publ Wkly

"Mr. Kemelman's fans will be mollified by his clever resolution of Rabbi Small's career crisis, which is woven into a deft murder mystery involving several characters of different faiths." N Y Times Book Rev

Kemelman, Harry—*Continued*

Friday the rabbi slept late. Crown 1964 224p o.p.

"Rabbi Small, an unstylish young scholar, is up for contract renewal in a fashionable New England community, when a young girl's murdered body is found on the Temple grounds. Her purse is in his car. Because of his character, he is not a leading suspect and works with the Catholic police chief to find the killer." Book Week

"Here are conflict and suspense, understanding and conversation, and a remarkable Biblical explanation of the differences between priests, ministers and rabbis." Libr J

Monday the rabbi took off. Putnam 1972 316p o.p.

"The rabbi and his family set out for Israel. The action alternates between Massachusetts, where Rabbi Small may or may not be losing his congregation to the rabbi substituting for him, and Jerusalem, where he soon becomes embroiled in troubles involving a TV commentator, the commentator's son, and plotting Arab militants." Saturday Rev

"This is not so much a novel of mystery and detection as it is a beautifully conceived and executed novel of conditions in Israel and a rabbi's dilemma." Best Sellers

One fine day the rabbi bought a cross. Morrow 1987 234p o.p.

LC 86-23571

"Central to the plot is a Palestine Liberation Organization arms cache that Druse fighters would dearly love to steal. An American professor unwittingly delivers a letter with a map of the cache to a Druse agent in Jerusalem. The American is promptly murdered. Rabbi Small is in Jerusalem and solves the case." N Y Times Book Rev

Saturday the rabbi went hungry. Crown 1966 249p o.p.

"The absent-minded knowledgeable young Rabbi, leader of a Conservative congregation, collaborates with his friend the Irish Catholic police chief in solving a mystery, this time deciding whether a death is murder or suicide and, if it is murder, who did it. The story is a good mixture of Jewish folk wisdom with modern community problems and with a murder mystery all nicely seasoned with humor." Publ Wkly

Sunday the rabbi stayed home. Putnam 1969 253p o.p.

"After six years at the Temple in Barnard's Crossing, Rabbi David Small is a little weary of the politics, dissention and factionalism of his congregation, and slightly disconcerted by the idea of a 'swinging Passover Service.' The weekend visit to Massachusetts College doesn't provide the release he expects, but neither does it prepare him for dealing with the rash of modern urban problems that confront him on Sunday when the body of Moose Carter is found in the empty house on the beach after a college student cookout." Libr J

Thursday the rabbi walked out. Morrow 1978 250p o.p.

LC 78-8466

"Kemelman's famous town, Barnard's Crossing, is in a turmoil after the murder of mean, anti-Semitic Ellsworth Jordan. Again Police Chief Lanigan asks Rabbi Small for help with the case, complicated by too many suspects. Those with motive and opportunity include members of Small's flock. Maltzman, president of the Temple, is one. So are the head of the local bank and his secretary as well as the dead man's illegitimate son by a Jewish mother." Publ Wkly

Wednesday the rabbi got wet. Morrow 1976 312p o.p.

In this story Rabbi Small "champions a young hippie, Akiva, suspected of causing a death. He has filled two prescriptions at his father's pharmacy. On the wet Wednesday, a wheeler-dealer member of Small's congregation, Safferstein, picks up the pills—a vial for his ailing wife and one for crotchety old Kestler. Kestler dies. His prescription is not what the doctor ordered. Dissension within the Temple's membership, with Small at odds with powerful men among them, adds to the excitement as the Rabbi applies Talmudic 'pilpul' (logical reasoning) to solve the problem of the switched dosage and exonerate the boy." Publ Wkly

Kempadoo, Oonya

Tide running. Farrar, Straus & Giroux 2003 215p $22

ISBN 0-374-27757-5 LC 2002-37914

This is the "story of a ménage à trois involving a beautiful Tobagan man and some recent arrivals—a wealthy mixed-race couple, recklessly 'flirting with newness' in a place that still bears the historical scars of the slave trade. With a finely tuned ear for the cadences of the Caribbean, Kempadoo, . . . examines the strange symbiosis between the newcomers, seduced by local color, and the impoverished islanders, hungry for consumer goods. As the trio's relationship presses to its disastrous conclusion, she succeeds in turning an unsettling tale into an exploration of the global politics of desire." New Yorker

Kemprecos, Paul

(jt. auth) Cussler, C. Fire ice
(jt. auth) Cussler, C. White death

Keneally, Thomas, 1935-

Confederates. Harper & Row 1980 c1979 427p o.p.

LC 80-7606

First published 1979 in the United Kingdom

"Several impressionistic stories, blends of fact and fiction, are woven into [this novel] of American Civil War as seen from the Southern side. The focus is not so much on the strategy of generals or the schemes of politicians as on the lot of the white farm boys who made up the core of the Confederate armies. There is Usaph, a Shenandoah Volunteer, tortured by the thought that the beautiful wife he left behind may be unfaithful (as she is); an intrepid widow who is both a hospital matron and, from deep moral conviction, a Union spy; an English journalist who loves the widow and is himself a Union spy; and the moody and brilliant Stonewall Jackson, victor of many battles against the odds." Publ Wkly

This book "transcends historical issues of right and wrong; it is a gripping, deeply satisfying work of art." Newsweek

Keneally, Thomas, 1935-—*Continued*

A family madness. Simon & Schuster 1986 336p o.p.

LC 85-26121

"Approximately half of the chapters of 'A Family Madness' are set in the present and concern a young working-class Australian, Terry Delaney, who becomes involved with a family of Byelorussian origin, the Kabbels (originally Kabbelski), who immigrated to Sydney in the late 1940's. The other half deals with the terrible modern history of that family, a history reaching back to the early days of World War II." N Y Times Book Rev

"Keneally brilliantly combines three diverse narrative techniques, and while the book is not light or easy reading, it is enormously rewarding." Publ Wkly

Flying hero class. Warner Bks. 1991 289p o.p.
ISBN 0-446-51582-5 LC 90-50524

"A troupe of Australian aboriginal dancers is flying from New York to Frankfurt on the last leg of a world tour when their jetliner is hijacked by Palestinian terrorists, and Frank McCloud their manager is identified as an enemy of the people and sentenced to death. In . . . [an] account of the next 48 hours Keneally relates blow-by-blow the hijackers' plot to intimidate, demoralize, and manipulate the minds of a plane load of people." Libr J

This is "despite some problems, a good book. Unlike many suspense novels, it never deadens our sensibilities with predictable characters, simpleminded politics or slick prose. Mr. Keneally's people are always fascinating, and so are the ideas his plot generates, making the hijacking a metaphor for the complex relationship between the West and third world peoples deprived of land and dignity." N Y Times Book Rev

Office of innocence. Doubleday 2003 319p $25
ISBN 0-385-50763-1 LC 2002-73653

A novel "about one young priest's crisis of faith in Sydney during World War II. Father Frank Darragh already feels conflicted about being out of the fighting when his regular duties as a soft-hearted confessor at St. Margaret's begin to put him in touch with war widows and American GIs. He is especially intrigued by Kate Heggarty, who seeks spiritual guidance when she's tempted to cheat on her P.O.W. husband. The monsignor objects to Father Frank's becoming so involved in her case, which explodes in the young priest's face when Kate turns up strangled." Libr J

Keneally moves his "protagonist, as confessor, from the banal to the transcendent: from insipid negotiations with schoolchildren to a primal reckoning in a war-ravaged landscape; from an innocence barely aware of its own spiritual vanity to a disillusioned acceptance of the ubiquity of sin and the stubborn mystery of fate." N Y Times Book Rev

River town. Talese 1995 324p o.p.

LC 94-48664

This is the "turn-of-the-century story of Tim Shea, an Irish storekeeper struggling with his own and society's demons to make a life for his family in New South Wales. Deaths frame the novel: Tim is haunted by the image of a nameless young woman, dead from an abortion, whose severed head is trotted around in a jar by the local constable in an effort to identify her; and after attending to a farmer killed in a gory buggy accident, Tim feels obliged to support the farmer's elder child, Lucy. First regarded as a hero for his quick action after the cart accident, then excoriated publicly for his anti-Boer War sentiments, Tim fears losing his business. A final quarantine after exposure to the black plague ends Tim's tribulations." Libr J

"There are times when Keneally's lapsed-Catholic sensibility and his not-at-all-lapsed Irish sensibility turn mawkish. . . . Nevertheless, Keneally's lapses are redeemed and overshadowed by his meticulous attention to psychological details which have nothing to do with his political agendas and which in fact subvert them." London Rev Books

Schindler's list. Simon & Schuster 1982 400p $25; pa $14
ISBN 0-671-51688-4; 0-671-88031-4 (pa)

LC 82-10489

"An actual occurrence during the Nazi regime in Germany forms the basis for this story. Oskar Schindler, a Catholic German industrialist, chose to act differently from those Germans who closed their eyes to what was happening to the Jews. By spending enormous sums on bribes to the SS and on food and drugs for the Jewish prisoners whom he housed in his own camp-factory in Cracow, he succeeded in sheltering thousands of Jews, finally transferring them to a safe place in Czechoslovakia. Fifty Schindler survivors from seven nations helped the author with information." Shapiro. Fic for Youth. 3d edition

To Asmara. Warner Bks. 1989 290p o.p.

LC 89-40035

"An Australian journalist named Darcy disappears in the remote Ethiopian province of Eritrea, where rebels are fighting a savage war of independence against the ruling Marxist regime. His legacy: a number of cassette tapes and notebooks, in which he has recorded the details of his mysteriously aborted journey. From these sources we learn that Darcy had gone to Eritrea to investigate reports of rebel attacks on UN food shipments to that famine-oppressed region. In his company were an American aide seeking the rescue of his imprisoned Somali lover, an aging English feminist bent on putting an end to the ritualized mutilation of females, and a young French girl searching for her missing photojournalist father. After touring rebel-controlled territory and surviving many close scrapes with Ethiopian forces, Darcy learns that many of his basic assumptions about the famine are in error. Spurred on by this knowledge, he commits himself to a course of action that may or may not have claimed his life." Booklist

This novel "is a rare entity in contemporary fiction, a work of advocacy and engagement that unhesitatingly takes sides in one of the world's longest-running and least understood wars." N Y Times Book Rev

The tyrant's novel; Thomas Keneally. 1st ed in the U.S.A. Nan A. Talese 2004 235p $25
ISBN 0-385-51146-9 LC 2003-59670

The protagonist of this "novel is a successful author in a country that bears more than a passing resemblance to Iraq. One day, he is ordered to write a novel to be published under the name of the country's dictator—and given only a month for the task. As luck would have it, he has recently completed a novel that, with slight modification, will fit the bill. However, he has buried the novel

Keneally, Thomas, 1935-—*Continued*

with his late wife. Can he bear to disinter the manuscript in order to save himself? Though concerned with current events, Keneally takes care to give his tale wider resonance. The Middle Eastern characters go by English names, a technique that makes them less foreign to the reader and draws parallels between the subtle self-censorship of Western commercialism and the blunter kind practiced by the arts community in a dictatorship." New Yorker

Woman of the inner sea. Doubleday 1993 c1992 277p o.p.

LC 92-28554

First published 1992 in the United Kingdom

"In the Australian state of New South Wales, Kate Gaffney-Kozinski, in her early thirties, has a marriage that's unworkable, despite all outward appearances of its success. Not ordinarily the kind of person who would do so, Kate nonetheless is pushed to the limit and flees—to the outback, where she hides her identity yet, tested again, comes into her own as a person." Booklist

This novel "succeeds on many fronts. It is a picaresque and often hilarious adventure story, recounting one woman's unforgettable if improbable travels. It is a series of love stories, as Kate meets the man who is appropriate for her at each stage of her life, and it is a mystery story as well. But the novel is also very much an exploration of ethics." N Y Times Book Rev

Kennedy, Douglas, 1955-

The big picture. Hyperion 1997 374p o.p.

LC 96-44446

"Ben and Beth Bradford, who once dreamed of being hippie artists, bought into the American dream instead. Ben is a successful lawyer pulling down a six-figure salary, and Beth is a bored surburban housewife with everything Ben's money can buy. But the Bradford's are miserable, imprisoned in a loveless marriage, and tied to a lifestyle they hate. To relieve her tedium, Beth takes a lover, an aging hippie who, unlike Ben, hasn't given in to the almighty dollar. Naturally, Ben finds out about Beth's affair. The worst happens, and in a moment, the Bradfords' lives change forever." Booklist

"The book is more than just a compelling read: it also has poignant and moving things to say about lost opportunities and wasted lives in America, the cynical quality of sudden fame, the awfulness of willed seperation from deeply loved children." Publ Wkly

Kennedy, William, 1928-

Ironweed. Viking 1983 227p o.p.

LC 82-40370

With this "tale of skid-row life in the Depression, Kennedy adds another chapter to his 'Albany cycle'—a group of novels set in the Albany, New York, underworld from the 1920s onward. Following 'Legs' and 'Billy Phelan's Greatest Game,' 'Ironweed' tells the story of Francis Phelan, a 58-year-old bum with muscatel on his breath and hallucinations on his mind. Chief among the latter is a vision of his infant son, who died after falling out of Francis' arms. It is the desire to reconcile himself to the memory of his dead son that brings Francis home to Albany, ultimately opening the door to a possible reconciliation with his family." Booklist

Quinn's book. Viking 1988 289p il o.p.

LC 86-45858

This novel is set in Albany, New York from 1849 to 1864. The narrator, "Daniel Quinn, America's foremost Civil War reporter, recalls his adolescent years . . . and his 15-year pursuit of the mysterious Maud Fallon, a theater star world-renowned for her nude interpretations of Byron and Keats." Libr J

"In the past, Kennedy has excelled at revealing the dignity hidden within mean, pinched lives. This time he gives his characters plenty of elbowroom and lets them move toward folly or heroism. But the end result is the same: a novel that is both engrossing and eerily profound." Time

Roscoe. Viking 2002 291p $24.95

ISBN 0-670-03029-5 LC 2001-33237

"Roscoe Owen Conway, fifty-five, fat, and in failing health, is the brains who protects and preserves Albany's Democratic Party, and, as Kennedy's seventh 'Albany Cycle' novel opens, Roscoe has plenty of protecting and preserving to do. It's V-J Day, 1945, and though the war in the Pacific is over, the war at home has just begun: the Democratic machine is facing a stiff challenge from the state's Republican governor. . . . When Elisha Fitzgibbon, the city's major Democratic funder and one of Roscoe's oldest friends, commits suicide, it looks as if the city's entire political tapestry might unravel." New Yorker

"As in all of Kennedy's Albany novels, the town is rendered with a hallucinatory, three-dimensional density. . . . This is an engrossing, comic vision of the dark side of politics." Publ Wkly

Very old bones. Viking 1992 292p o.p.

LC 91-40723

The protagonist and narrator in this installment of The Albany cycle is "Orson Purcell, the bastard son of artist Peter Phelan. . . . Building his tale around a family gathering in 1958, Purcell relates his own life story as well as episodes in the history of each family member, both living and dead, who struggle to overcome their collective and individual pasts." Libr J

"Orson is wounded, pompous, a bit pedantic in his initial attempt at family history. What transpires in [the book] is the growth and increasing authenticity of his voice. . . . Beneath the mete and just end of this closely worked novel lie bitter bones of estrangement, of love hidden or misplaced, lives wasted by jealousy and fear." N Y Times Book Rev

Kent, Alexander

See also Reeman, Douglas

Kerley, Jack

The hundredth man. Dutton 2004 307p $23.95

ISBN 0-525-94821-X LC 2004-696

"A serial killer who leaves behind headless corpses is on the loose in Mobile, AL. Detectives Carson Ryder and Harry Nautilus are first assigned to the case but are later removed when their clues to the murderer lead them too close to the law enforcement community. Carson's older brother, a twisted serial killer who is serving a life sentence, understands enough to give them a disturbing insight into the killer's identity." Libr J

"Kerley jacks up the tension effectively with nicely

Kerley, Jack—*Continued*
placed jumps between Carson's narration and the tortured thoughts of the killer, building to an all-stops-out climax involving a raging river and a supremely horrific home movie." Booklist

Kerouac, Jack, 1922-1969

The Dharma bums. Viking 1958 244p o.p.

"This novel deals with Zen Buddhism. It's about two young men who are seeking to find themselves through meditation, voluntary poverty, separation from society, and intimate contact with nature, especially the Western mountains. . . . Sometimes Kerouac seems a little foolish, often he is extreme, but he is genuine, he is alive, and he is native." Libr J

On the road. Viking 1957 310p o.p.

"Sal Paradise (a self-portrait of Kerouac), a struggling author in his mid-twenties, tells of his meeting Dean Moriarty (based on Neal Cassady), a fast-living teenager just out of a New Mexico reform school, whose soul is 'wrapped up in a fast car, a coast to reach, and a woman at the end of the road.' During the next five years they travel coast to coast, either with each other or to each other. Five trips are described." Oxford Companion to Am Lit. 6th edition

Kerouac, Jean *See* Kerouac, Jack, 1922-1969

Kerouac, Jeanlouis *See* Kerouac, Jack, 1922-1969

Kerr, Katharine

Snare; a novel of the far future. TOR Bks. 2003 591p $27.95

ISBN 0-312-89045-1 LC 2002-40947

"A Tom Doherty Associates book"

"Three very different groups of human settlers go, not all willingly, to the planet Snare: a band of Islamic fundamentalists, a group of horse tribes and the pragmatic Cantons people. All descend on Snare's indigenous repitilian species the ChaMeech, and eight centuries of territorial and social turmoil follow." Publ Wkly

"Compelling male and female characters and a thoughtful premise make this epic adventure a strong addition to most sf collections." Libr J

Kerr, Philip

Dark matter; the private life of Sir Isaac Newton. Crown 2002 345p o.p.

ISBN 0-609-60981-5 LC 2002-24155

"One of the seventeenth century's greatest minds, Isaac Newton, is appointed warden of the Royal Mint during England's Great Recoinage. Aided by educated yet slow-witted sidekick and narrator Christopher Ellis, Newton employs the scientific method and logical deduction to thwart a high-reaching conspiracy to murder thousands of Catholics, pass counterfeit guineas, and reignite the war with France." Booklist

"Plot devices such as secret coded documents, the pseudoscience of alchemy, and a string of strange murders make for an exciting read. Using as backdrop the Tower of London, the Royal Mint, Bedlam madhouse, and Newgate Prison. . . [The author] weaves a rich tapestry of interesting characters and period details." Libr J

Kesey, Ken

One flew over the cuckoo's nest; a novel. Viking 1962 311p $24.95; pa $6.99

ISBN 0-670-03058-9; 0-14-004312-8 (pa)

"Life in a mental institution is predictable and suffocating under the iron rule of Nurse Ratched, who tolerates no disruption of routine on her all-male ward. Half-Indian Chief Bromden, almost invisible on the ward because he is thought to be deaf and dumb, describes the arrival of rowdy Randle Patrick McMurphy. McMurphy takes on the nurse as an adversary in his attempt to organize his fellow inmates and breathe some self-esteem and joy into their lives. The battle is vicious on the part of the nurse, who is relentless in her efforts to break McMurphy, but a spark of human will brings an element of hope to counter the despotic institutional power." Shapiro. Fic for Youth. 3d edition

Sailor song. Viking 1992 535p o.p.

LC 92-5406

"The story, set some 30 years hence, involves Ike Sallas, a once-famous ecoterrorist now living in an Alaskan fishing village. Ike's carefully cultivated disengagement is threatened first by the arrival of a Hollywood film company, there to make a movie based on a children's book, and then by his thawing relations with Alice Carmody, a fisherman's wife whose marriage is on the rocks. When Ike discovers that the film company has a sinister motive, he tries to rally the town, yet defeat seems imminent until an environmental apocalypse throws a monkey wrench into everyone's plans." Libr J

The author "includes a great deal of purposeful foolery, flooding the narrative with farcical incongruities, crude asides, wacky in-jokes, and countless allusions to literary classics and popular culture. . . . In sum, Sailor Song is vintage Ken Kesey: not for the faint-hearted, perhaps, but certainly instructive, and never boring." New Leader

Sometimes a great notion. Viking 1964 628p o.p.

"This novel focuses on the person of Hank Stamper, raw and aggressive scion of an Oregon lumber empire. The struggle is . . . with a society unwilling to accommodate a strong individualist, but the issues are deepened and complicated by the fact that Hank's principal antagonist turns out to be his cerebral, introspective half-brother, Lee, and by Kesey's development of Lee as an equally appealing character, Kesey manipulates the clash of fraternal egos to a powerful climax, before reconciling the brothers to a tragic understanding of their own vulnerability to an indifferent fate and to a group of townspeople who have been made intolerably uncomfortable by the sight of the Stampers' strength." Ency of World Lit in the 20th Century

Keyes, Daniel, 1927-

Flowers for Algernon. Harcourt Brace Jovanovich 1966 274p o.p.

"Charlie Gordon, aged thirty-two, is mentally retarded and enrolls in a class to 'become smart.' He keeps a journal of his progress after an experimental operation that increases his I.Q. Although Charlie becomes brilliant, he is unhappy because he cannot shed his former

Keyes, Daniel, 1927-—*Continued*
personality and is tormented by his memories. In the end he begins to lose the mental powers he has gained." Shapiro. Fic for Youth. 3d edition

Flowers for Algernon [novelette]
In The Hugo winners p245-73

Keyes, Marian

Last Chance Saloon. Morrow 2001 c1999 370p $25
ISBN 0-688-18072-8 LC 00-67891
First published 1999 in the United Kingdom
This novel's "protagonists are two London women who grew up together in the small, repressive Irish town of Knockavoy. Tara, a computer analyst, lives with Thomas, a bitter and miserly high school geography teacher. . . . Katherine Casey, an accountant for an advertising agency, wears boring suits, has a hyperorganized underwear drawer and brushes off all advances, including those of attractive advertising account executive Joe Roth. As they turn 31, each woman is full of suggestions for improving the other's life and full of excuses for doing nothing about her own. That begins to change when Fintan O'Grady, their gay pal and fellow Knockavoy refugee, falls ill with a mysterious disease." Publ Wkly

The other side of the story; Marian Keyes. 1st ed. W. Morrow 2004 516p $24.95
ISBN 0-06-052051-5 LC 2003-64939
This novel "follows the lives of three dynamic women-jilted Gemma Hogan; literary agent Jojo Harvey; and bestselling English author Lily Wright, who 'stole' Gemma's boyfriend Anton. Gemma, hurt and betrayed by her best friend's actions, must put her emotions on hold to care for her mam after her dad takes off with a younger woman." Publ Wkly
"Packing every page with her trademark one-liners, the insightful Keyes has the ability to examine life, love, and work issues with great wit and aplomb." Booklist

Khadra, Yasmina *See* Moulessehoul, Mohammed, 1955-

The swallows of Kabul; translated from the French by John Cullen. Nan A. Talese\Doubleday 2004 195p $18.95
ISBN 0-385-51001-2 LC 2003-50769
"Before the destruction wrought by the Soviet war and Taliban rule, Mohsen was an affluent merchant; now he wanders the streets while his beautiful wife is confined to home and burka. Atiq, a volatile ex-mujahideen, guards the prisoners awaiting public execution. One day, Mohsen stops to observe the public stoning of a prostitute, one of Atiq's charges. Caught up in the frenzy, he joins in, initiating a series of tragic events." New Yorker
The author is "intimately familiar with the consequences that war and religious extremism have on people's daily lives, and in this book he gives the reader a tactile sense of what life under the Taliban might have been like." N Y Times (Late N Y Ed)

Kidd, Sue Monk

The mermaid chair. Viking 2005 352p $24.95
ISBN 0-670-03394-4
"Forty-three-year old Jessie Sullivan is pulled out of her staid life in Atlanta with her husband and daughter, back to her childhood home on Egret Island after her mother, Nelle, cuts off one of her own fingers. Jessie has been uneasy with the island since her beloved father died when she was nine in a boating accident, a tragedy Jessie has always felt partially responsible for. At the behest of her mother's best friend, Jessie journeys back to the island to try to reconnect with the mother she's never been close to. Jessie wants to know what drove her obviously disturbed mother to sever her finger, and she thinks Father Dominic, one of the Benedictine monks who resides in a nearby monastery, might know more about her mother's state of mind. But it is another monk who claims Jessie's attention—handsome Brother Thomas, who ignites in Jessie a passion so intense it overwhelms her, leading her to question her marriage and rediscover her artistic drive." Booklist
This is an "emotionally rich novel, full of sultry, magical descriptions of life in the South." Publ Wkly

The secret life of bees. Viking 2002 301p $24.95
ISBN 0-670-89460-5 LC 2001-26310
This is the "tale of a 14-year-old white girl named Lily Owen who is raised by the elderly African American Rosaleen after the accidental death of Lily's mother. Following a racial brawl in 1960s Tiburon, S.C, Lily and Rosaleen find shelter in a distant town with three black bee-keeping sisters." Libr J
"Lily is a wonderfully petulant and self-absorbed adolescent, and Kidd deftly portrays her sense of injustice as it expands to accommodate broader social evils." N Y Times Book Rev

Kienzle, William X., 1928-2002

Assault with intent. Andrews & McMeel 1982 273p o.p.
LC 82-1628
"The action takes place in a seminary in Detroit and it involves an apparent plot to kill some or all of the priests in seminaries. It is a perfect setting for one of the instructors at the seminary, Father Koesler, a priest-detective. . . . The attempts at murdering the priests are continuously foiled either by circumstances or the ineptitude of the assailant. We are led from one seminary to the other as the would-be murderers change their targets. The plot attracts such media attention that a TV movie is filmed at the major seminary to document the plot against the priests. In the process of the investigation attention is focused on a group of ultraconservative Catholics and their leader, Roman Kirkus." Best Sellers

Body count. Andrews & McMeel 1992 266p o.p.
LC 92-3266
This mystery involves Father Koesler, "Detroit detective-priest in conflicts between old and new Catholic theology. Hitman Guido Vespa loudly confesses to Koesler that he has bumped off Father Keating, the spiritual leader of a nearby parish, and buried the body in the grave of the long-dead, much beloved Monsignor Kern. Overhearing the confession, exuberant new resident priest Nick Dunn is delighted: one of the reasons he came to St. Joseph's was to be near its sleuthing pastor. Nick's enthusiasm increases when the police ask Koesler for help with Keating's disappearance." Publ Wkly

Kienzle, William X., 1928-2002—*Continued*

Chameleon. Andrews & McMeel 1991 289p o.p.
LC 91-6433

"When a prominent nun, a diocesan bureaucrat, and a retired archbishop are targeted for murder, [Father Robert] Koesler dubiously agrees to shepherd Lieutenant Alonzo 'Zoo' Tully of the Detroit police department through the arcane intricacies of the Roman Catholic church. Father Bob and Zoo must work in concert in order to unravel a deadly game of revenge mired in the complexities of canon law. An intriguing blend of glory and gore from the master of the theological mystery." Booklist

Death wears a red hat. Andrews & McMeel 1980 304p o.p.
LC 79-28353

"Detroit is the setting of a series of baffling murders. Some puzzling motive brings the murderer to decapitate his victims and deposit the heads on church statues. Each head has the same horror stricken countenance, as if the victim was frightened to death. The police and press are baffled by the case, but Father Robert Koesler . . . suspects that there is some logic in it all. This is a swiftly paced narrative, expertly plotted to juxtapose the progress of the investigations of the police, the press and Father Koesler. Koesler's knowledge of church history, mythology, and his fellow clergymen gives him insight while the police and newsmen remain confused." Best Sellers

The gathering. Andrews McMeel Pub. 2002 280p $22.95
ISBN 0-7407-2229-8 LC 2001-55969

Father Koesler "reaches back in time and memory to clarify the ambiguous details surrounding the death of an old friend and fellow priest. Father Stan Benson is declared accidentally dead by carbon monoxide poisoning. Nursing his own doubts, Koesler convenes a reunion with the five remaining members of a close-knit group of friends who all initially chose religious vocations as a way of life. . . . Koesler's natural flair for detection is surpassed only by his deep and abiding compassion for the human condition." Booklist

The greatest evil. Andrews McMeel Pub. 1998 278p o.p.
LC 97-37738

"Father Robert Koesler is excited at the prospect of having Father Zachary Tully join his parish. Unfortunately, Bishop Vincent Delvecchio has misgivings about Tully's appointment. As Koesler and Tully discuss the matter, Koesler discovers a long-hidden mystery, which takes a back seat to numerous discussions that give fascinating insight into the working of the Catholic Church before Vatican II." Libr J

The man who loved God. Andrews & McMeel 1997 274p o.p.
LC 96-34604

"Father Bob Koesler, the popular amateur sleuth and Detroit priest, takes a vacation literally and figuratively away from the action. Taking his place is Father Zachary Tully, who comes to Detroit (from Dallas) to present an award to banker and philanthropist Thomas A. Adams. Father Tully is also eager to meet the half-brother he never knew he had, Detroit police lieutenant Alonzo 'Zoo' Tully. When one of Adam's vice-presidents is murdered just after being named to head a new inner-city bank branch, Father Tully and his brother find themselves working together." Publ Wkly

No greater love. Andrews McMeel Pub. 1999 292p o.p.
LC 98-44577

"Lured out of retirement by his old friend Bishop Patrick McNiff, Father Koesler, the former pastor of an urban parish in the heart of downtown Detroit, moves into St. Joseph's seminary on the pretext of counseling students and teaching a class or two. His actual assignment is to attempt to bridge the ever-widening gulf between conservative and liberal faculty members and students. An experienced veteran with a decidedly open mind, Koesler seems to be the ideal candidate for a difficult job until he gets sidetracked by a chilling chain of events that culminates in tragedy." Booklist

The rosary murders. Andrews & McMeel 1979 257p o.p.
LC 78-31833

"From Ash Wednesday, when the murderer first struck Detroit's Catholic community, the police seemed helpless to solve the string of senseless murders. The weeks that followed became a nightmare for the crack homicide team of investigators headed by Lieutenant Walter Koznicki, until Father Koesler broke the madman's code." Publisher's note

Kijewski, Karen

Alley Kat blues. Doubleday 1995 342p o.p.
LC 94-35200

In this mystery, Kat Colorado, "investigator and girlfriend of Las Vegas cop Hank Parker, becomes embroiled in a family controversy and murder investigation when she discovers a young girl's mangled body, an apparent hit-and-run victim. The girl's mother begs Kat to look into her daughter's death but her religious husband refuses to cooperate. To add to Kat's problem, Hank is involved with a murder investigation of his own." SLJ

The author "has written a solid narrative in a snappy style that fits Kat's clear-eyed intelligence and unpretentious methods of dealing with difficult people." N Y Times Book Rev

Copy Kat. Doubleday 1992 261p o.p.
LC 92-14482

"A Perfect crime book"

"Hard-boiled female private eye Kat Colorado . . . takes on a new identity as Kate, the dyed-blonde bartender, to try to discover who murdered Diedre Durkin, the local bartender's wife. As she investigates motives, suspects, and alibis, Kat encounters blackmail and infidelity, a deep-seated and dangerous sibling rivalry, twisted family jealousies, and a web of bitter deceit and hatred." Booklist

Honky tonk Kat. Putnam 1996 323p o.p.
LC 95-49335

"Country-western singing star Dakota Jones, a friend of Kat's since childhood, is worried. Like most stars, she has enemies, but someone has been sending her unusually unnerving letters and really nasty gifts. Dakota, afraid that her one out-of-control fan might do something stupid, asks Kat to join her entourage and find out who's up to what." Booklist

Kijewski, Karen—*Continued*

The author "captures the sweaty thrills of road life while taking a clear-eyed view of the boozy dives and greasy food and the scary adoration of desperate fans." N Y Times Book Rev

Kat scratch fever. Putnam 1997 323p o.p.
LC 96-51141

In this mystery Sacramento PI Kat Colorado "exposes embezzlement and extortion at Hope for Kids, a charity that aids crippled and disfigured children." Publ Wkly

"Taking the direct approach here, Kat marches up to the charity's most generous givers and demands to know if they were being blackmailed. When that doesn't work, she tries bullying, wheedling, groveling and breaking and entering. And when all her muscle and charm run out, she uses her brain." N Y Times Book Rev

Kat's cradle. Doubleday 1992 244p o.p.
LC 91-32218

"A Perfect crime book"

"Narrator Kat Colorado, a socially conscious Sacramento private investigator with a Las Vegas policeman lover, accepts the challenge of finding the birth parents of an 'orphan' whose autocratic-but-rich grandmother has just died. Paige Morrell and scruffy boyfriend Paul may be more interested in proving her right to inherit; however, Kat thinks she has a right to know about her folks." Libr J

"Outstanding among today's female detectives, PI Kat Colorado exhibits conscience and compassion, muscle and wisecracking savvy in an appealing and believable combination." Publ Wkly

Stray Kat waltz. Putnam 1998 311p o.p.
ISBN 0-399-14368-8 LC 97-46986

Sacramento P.I. Kat Colorado is recovering from the murder of her fiancé Hank Parker. "Although the heartache that makes Kat weep into her pillow sensitizes her to the plight of a battered wife who comes to her for help, it also blunts the P.I.'s normally sharp instincts for deceit and danger. Sara Bernard might well be the stalking victim she claims to be. Her husband might also be the model-cop-gone-nuts she says he is. But both their stories seem fishy, and Kat's judgment is too clouded by emotional cobwebs for her to think clearly. She perks up, though, for some undercover scenes at a fancy rehab clinic, where the pretentiousness is enough to restore her mental equilibrium, not to mention her sense of humor." N Y Times Book Rev

Wild Kat. Doubleday 1994 343p o.p.
LC 93-25740

Sacramento private eye Kat Colorado is drawn into a "case of corporate criminality when she is hired to protect Amanda Hudson, an accountant who has blown the whistle on a medical supplies company for manufacturing artificial hearts with defective valves." N Y Times Book Rev

The author's in "fine form here, combining her easy, breezy style and deadpan humor with a sinister, suspenseful plot that's thought-provoking, fast-paced, and entertaining." Booklist

Kim, Suki, 1970-

The interpreter. Farrar, Straus & Giroux 2003 294p $24
ISBN 0-374-17713-9 LC 2002-72120

This novel introduces Korean American "Suzy Park, a 29-year-old interpreter whose work involves her in a bevy of agencies throughout the five boroughs, from the Immigration and Naturalization Service to the criminal courts. Park is blasé about her occupation until a routine translating job reveals that her greengrocer parents were not murdered by random violence, as the police had indicated, but instead had been shot by political enemies. These data provide fodder for Park, and the novel tracks her investigation into what really happened." Libr J

"This is an intriguing, tortured portrait of a second-generation Korean-American by a promising young writer." Publ Wkly

Kimmel, Haven

Something rising (light and swift). Free Press 2004 273p $24
ISBN 0-7432-4775-2 LC 2003-49114

This tale is set in a "small town in Indiana. Cassie Claiborne, the most grounded person in her family, longs for her feckless father to return home but in the meantime, she grows into a young woman and shoulders the burden herself. On one of his increasingly rare visits, her father takes her to a pool hall, and she watches him play. When she takes her turn with the cue, it becomes clear that Cassie has an innate talent for the game. She starts playing for money and routinely beats arrogant men who think they can easily best a young girl. Her skill ultimately leads her to a match with her father, but even pool playing can't make up for his abandonment of her, or the fact that Cassie's destiny might lie beyond Roseville." Booklist

"Kimmel's idea of a plot is not very linear. It's more like a net that hauls in great scenes. But while things may look superficially languid, this is one author who will not waste your time." Newsweek

Kincaid, Jamaica

Annie John. Farrar, Straus & Giroux 1985 148p pa $11 o.p.
ISBN 0-374-52510-2

"Episodes from the young life of Annie John, aged 10 to 17, as she grows up on the Caribbean island of Antigua. This is a magical coming-of-age tale, ripe with the special ambience of its tropical setting and sustained by Annie's far from naive awareness of the world around her. Death, illness, and poverty intrude on the narrator's perceptive sensibility from time to time, but even these experiences instruct her and expand her understanding of life and its shifting reality. . . . A poetic and intensely moving work." Booklist

Autobiography of my mother. Farrar, Straus & Giroux 1995 228p o.p.
ISBN 0-374-10731-9 LC 94-24580

The narrator of this novel is Xuela Claudette Richardson. "Raised without love and self-defined by her mother's death at the moment of her birth, Xuela regards life in her Dominican villages with disturbing disinterest and keen penetration. . . . Haunted by her mother's absence, Xuela ensures her own barrenness, endures a loveless affair with and marriage to the English doctor Philip, who loves her, and rejoices with stevedore Roland, whom she loves—or claims to." Libr J

Kincaid, Jamaica—*Continued*

In Kincaid's "poised and crystalline prose, precise and serene as a knife drawn through water, she now gives us this starkly memorable 'self-portrait' of a calm, thoughtful, utterly alienated woman who has learned to lead a life devoid of love, but not devoid of dignity." Christ Sci Monit

Lucy. Farrar, Straus & Giroux 1990 163p o.p.
LC 90-83987

The narrator, Lucy Potter, a nineteen year old from Antigua, tells of her experiences as an *au pair* for a wealthy family in a large North American city

"The great motifs of Western literature, like goodness and evil, innocence and experience, resonate in Kincaid's novel in a completely updated and unselfconscious way. In other hands, this story of a West Indian *au pair* would just be sociology. In Kincaid's recasting, it is both art and argument." Christ Sci Monit

Mr. Potter. Farrar, Straus & Giroux 2002 195p $20
ISBN 0-374-21494-8

"Mr. Potter is a man without qualities, an illiterate taxi driver on Kincaid's native island of Antigua, whose life, though full of loss and suffering, is essentially uneventful. His illegitimate daughter, Elaine Cynthia, returns to the island after his death to write his story—in fact, to narrate this novel." N Y Times Book Rev

"Kincaid has exquisite control over her narrator's deep-seated rage, which drives the story but never overpowers it and is tempered by a clear-eyed sympathy. Her prose here is more incantatory and hypnotic than ever." Publ Wkly

Kincaid, Nanci

Verbena; a novel. Algonquin Bks. 2002 338p $24.95
ISBN 1-56512-348-4 LC 2001-56531

"A Shannon Ravenel book"

Sixth-grade teacher Verbena Eckerd "was happily married to Bob, or so she thought, until he died in a car accident with another woman at his side. She thinks she has raised her five children well, until her two oldest daughters run off with no-account men, her third moves away with Bena's arch rival, and her eldest son chooses the one woman in the world whose very name causes Bena anguish. She can't believe that good-natured mailman Lucky McKale really loves her, since he is married to Sue Cox, the most beautiful and richest woman in Baxter County, Ala. But after Sue Cox herself agrees to a divorce and blesses their union, Bena finally feels she can accept Lucky's proposal. A new kind of domestic unit is formed, with exes and stepchildren integrated into one colorful family. Then disaster strikes—Lucky disappears. Kincaid is both warmhearted and clear-eyed about the compromises people make to find happiness." Publ Wkly

Kinder, Chuck

Honeymooners; a cautionary tale. Farrar, Straus & Giroux 2001 357p $24
ISBN 0-374-17258-7 LC 00-63616

"Chronicle of two writers who share a 'stupendous dream' of fame and freedom in the Bay Area in the 1970s, the heyday of drugs, booze and indiscriminate sex. Aspiring writer Ralph Crawford (based loosely on Raymond Carver); Jim Stark, his sidekick in friendship, ambition and general fecklessness; and the two writers' mistresses and wives never quite recover from their adolescent pranks, cheerful amorality and determined debauchery, despite Crawford's rise to fame." Publ Wkly

"Both wives emerge as major characters, reflecting the humor and anguish of living with men who, despite their successes, seem headed for rock bottom. Kinder's speedy, wry prose transports the reader to a time when drug use and personal freedom were unquestioned." Libr J

King, Dave, 1955-

The ha-ha; a novel. Little, Brown and Co 2005 340p $23.95
ISBN 0-316-15610-8 LC 2004-7398

"First-person narrator Howard Kapostash is unable to read or to speak coherently, the result of injuries suffered in Vietnam. Now middle-aged and living a low-key life in a large house he inherited from his parents, Howard is still friends with his former high school sweetheart, Sylvia. Before entering a drug rehab program, she entrusts Howard with her nine-year-old son, Ryan, completely upending Howard's lonely, disorganized existence. Also sharing his house are a Texas-raised Vietnamese woman, who runs a catering business, and two freewheeling young house painters. This unlikely family—heretofore all but strangers to one another—becomes a thriving parental unit centered on young Ryan. Everything begins to deteriorate, however, as the mother signals her return, and Howard fights in the only way he knows how to retain ties with Ryan." Libr J

"With Howard as a guide, a potentially corny situation develops into a complex exploration of loss and loneliness that packs a potently bittersweet punch." Washington Post Book World

King, Laurie R.

The beekeeper's apprentice; or, On the segregation of the queen; [by] Laurie King. St. Martin's Press 1994 347p $23.95
ISBN 0-312-10423-5 LC 93-43522

"A Thomas Dunne book"

"In the early years of WWI, 15-year-old American Mary Russell encounters Holmes, retired in Sussex Downs where Conan Doyle left him raising bees. Mary, an orphan rebelling against her guardian aunt's strictures, impresses the sleuth with her intelligence and acumen. Holmes initiates her into the mysteries of detection, allowing her to participate in a few cases when she comes home from her studies at Oxford. The collaboration is ignited by the kidnapping in Wales of Jessica Simpson, daughter of an American senator." Publ Wkly

"A wonderfully original and entertaining story that is funny, heartwarming, and full of intrigue. . . . Holmes fans, history buffs, lovers of humor and adventure, and mystery devotees will all find King's book absorbing from beginning to end." Booklist

A darker place. Bantam Bks. 1999 384p o.p.
ISBN 0-553-10711-9 LC 98-29835

King, Laurie R.—*Continued*

For 18 years, Professor Anne Waverly "has divided her time between teaching theology and working as an undercover operative for the FBI. This novel takes Anne inside a religious community called Change for what she vows will be her last investigative assignment. At its Arizona outpost she confronts not only the distorted goals and values of the community but the phantoms that lurk in her own past." Libr J

"King's solid research into alternative religious sects makes the desert commune feel like a real place, while her taut pacing insures that an air of menace hangs over the strange rituals that go on there. But the strongest appeal of the story lies in its superb characters, especially the children who become Anne's charges." N Y Times Book Rev

The game; a Mary Russell novel; Laurie R. King. Bantam Books 2004 368p map $23.95
ISBN 0-553-80194-5 LC 2003-55684

"Mycroft Holmes sends his brother, Sherlock, and Sherlock's wife, Mary Russell, to India to investigate the disappearance of master spy Kimball O'Hara, the legendary 'Kim' made famous by Rudyard Kipling." Libr J

"Whatever this grueling land journey lacks in urgency, it repays in scenes of vibrant local color, described by Russell in the droll tongue of a woman with the wit to realize that, while she may be dirty and tired and in constant danger, she is having the time of her life." N Y Times Book Rev

Justice Hall; a Mary Russell novel. Bantam Bks. 2002 331p o.p.
ISBN 0-553-11113-2 LC 2001-37945

"Mary Russell is Sherlock Holmes' partner and wife. In the England of the 1920s, the pair find themselves shocked by the appearance of Ali and Mahmoud Hazr, their mysterious Arab associates from *O Jerusalem.* Ali is Alistair, and Mahmoud is Maurice (called Marsh). Who would have divined that this pair of cousins is actually British, and Marsh is about to be named duke to his family's ancestral manse, the Hall of the title? King breaks most of the rules of mystery narrative with voluptuous abandon, and we don't care." Booklist

Keeping watch. Bantam Bks. 2003 383p $23.95
ISBN 0-553-80191-0 LC 2002-34266

"At its simplest, this is the story of a man who helps rescue women and/or children from dangerously abusive men. King's lengthy, brillantly executed backstory of Allen Carmichael's experiences in Vietnam, his disastrously unhappy return home and his eventual discovery of his 'calling' showcase some of her finest writing. Now in his early 50s, Allen is ready to retire from his dangerous vocation, to settle on his remote island and perhaps serve as a consultant to those who continue the struggle. But his last rescue, that of a 12-year-old boy trapped in a horrible situation, continues to haunt him." Publ Wkly

A letter of Mary; a Mary Russell novel. St. Martin's Press 1996 276p o.p.
LC 96-22424

"A Thomas Dunne book"

In this mystery "featuring Mary Russell, Oxford scholar, detective, and wife of Sherlock Holmes, Russell and Holmes are visited by Palestinian archaeologist Dorothy Ruskin, who leaves the pair an ancient parchment that is purportedly a letter from Mary Magdalene in which Mary calls herself an apostle of Jesus. Soon after, Ruskin is killed by a hit-and-run driver, and the Holmes' house is ransacked, presumably by people who want the document." Booklist

"For all the disparity of their investigative techniques, the ultra-perceptive Holmes and the super-scholarly Russell make an engaging pair of sleuths. Their quick minds and quirky personalities insure a lively adventure in the very best of intellectual company." N Y Times Book Rev

Locked rooms; a Mary Russell novel. Bantam Books 2005 402p $24
ISBN 0-553-80197-X

"Tormented by recurring nightmares, Mary Russell . . . returns to San Francisco after a ten-year absence. She swears to husband Sherlock Holmes that she wasn't in the city during the 1906 fire, but events soon prove her wrong. What memories is she hiding from herself? Holmes suspects they are connected somehow to the terrible car crash that claimed the lives of Russell's father, mother, and younger brother in 1915. With his normally capable wife distracted by her emotions, it is up to Holmes to recruit new Irregulars and uncover the truth behind the 'locked rooms' that Russell dreams about." Libr J

"In alternating sections, told in first person for Mary and third for Holmes, the unraveling of long-buried and terrifying memories also unwinds a skein of wonderful historical texture: the place of Chinese immigrants and the use of feng shui; the nightlife of a city during the age of jazz, Prohibition, and flappers; and the presence of Dash Hammett, who plays a fascinating role as a very different sort of Irregular." Booklist

The moor; a Mary Russell novel. St. Martin's Press 1998 307p il o.p.
ISBN 0-312-16934-5 LC 97-31886

"A Thomas Dunne book"

Mary Russell "drops everything to join husband Sherlock Holmes in Devonshire, where the pair investigate an ancient family curse near the scene of *The Hound of the Baskervilles*—published some 20 years earlier. The forbidding moor nearby provides them both danger and inspiration." Libr J

"Sherlockians have their choice of being amused or affronted by these artful embellishments on the Holmes canon, and few will appreciate the curiously wan characterization of the great detective. But there's no resisting the appeal of King's thrillingly moody scenes of Dartmoor and her lovely evocation of its legends." N Y Times Book Rev

O Jerusalem. Bantam Bks. 1999 367p o.p.
ISBN 0-553-11093-4 LC 98-56124

In 1918, Sherlock Holmes and Mary Russell, "the 19-year-old Oxford student whom he takes under his wing as an apprentice and partner, are sent on a mission to Palestine by Mycroft, Sherlock's powerful older brother. When Russell and Holmes are deposited, under cover of darkness, on the shores of Palestine, the British, under General Allenby, have just wrested control of the area from the Turks. . . . Eventually they encounter Joshua, a British agent, and Allenby himself." Publ Wkly

"With the feminist heroine chronicling events and the cerebral detective stirring the pot, readers can't lose." Booklist

King, Roger, 1947-

A girl from Zanzibar. Books & Co./Helen Marx Bks. 2002 307p $14.95

ISBN 1-885586-60-4 (pa) LC 2002-105487

A picaresque novel about a young East African woman's adventures and loves across a dozen years and three continents.

"Marcella is the author's mouthpiece, his stage manager, theorizing, summing up the action, signaling transitions, and at times these extra roles blur her outline. But the minor characters are just themselves, seen whole with tragic clarity." N Y Times Book Rev

King, Ross, 1962-

Domino. Walker & Co. 2002 435p $26

ISBN 0-8027-3378-6 LC 2002-29620

"When a talented young artist, Sir George Cautley, goes to London from Shropshire in 1780 to make something of himself, he meets a glamorous, mystifying woman named Lady Petronella Beauclair. As he paints her portrait, she tells him the labyrinthine story of an old man named Tristano, one of Europe's most renowned castrati from decades ago, who is a dormant social presence in London. As Cautley begins studies with Sir Endymion Starker, a famous artist he meets while gambling, he also makes the acquaintance of Starker's mistress, Eleanora, who has her own sad tale to tell." Publ Wkly

"Replete with mystery and suspense and immersed in vivid historical details, this work is also a sharp, philosophical musing on the disguises of the world and the search for the truth that lies beneath." Libr J

King, Stephen, 1947-

Apt pupil
In King, S. Different seasons p103-296

The Bachman books: four early novels by Stephen King. New Am. Lib. 1985 692p o.p.

LC 85-11411

An omnibus edition of four novels first published in paperback under the author's pseudonym Richard Bachman

Contents: Rage (1977); The long walk (1979); Roadwork (1981); The running man (1982)

"In *Rage*, a high-school student goes berserk in the classroom, killing the teacher and holding the class hostage. Set in a militaristic ultra-conservative America, *The Long Walk* pits 100 teenagers against each other in a grueling 450-mile marathon walk in which the penalty is death. *Roadwork* is a novel of societal conflict, man vs. progress. The first three thrillers, while entertaining and gripping, occasionally suffer from unfocused and uneven writing. Unresolved questions cause the books to be somewhat unsatisfying. However the fourth novel, *The Running Man* . . . is an action-packed futuristic romp. Protagonist Ben Richards bets his life on a TV show in order to win the money to save the life of his deathly ill daughter. The story combines social commentary, adventure and science fiction, set against the backdrop of a decaying society." SLJ

Bag of bones. Scribner 1998 529p o.p.

ISBN 0-684-85350-7 LC 98-23801

Suspense writer Mike Noonan is "mourning the untimely death of his wife. Plagued by vivid nightmares, writer's block, and ghostly visitations, Noonan nonetheless becomes willingly involved in a bitter custody dispute between a beautiful young woman and a wealthy computer magnate. All is not as it seems, however, and Noonan soon finds himself and his charges pawns of forces seeking revenge for an unspeakable, century-old crime." Libr J

"The big surprise here is the emotional wallop the story packs, particularly in the scenes where Noonan grieves for his dead wife. These are among the most disconsolate moments King has ever created." Newsweek

Black house; a novel; [by] Stephen King [and] Peter Straub. Random House 2001 624p o.p.

ISBN 0-375-50439-7 LC 2001-31657

Sequel to The talisman (1984)

"In French Landing, Wis., a serial killer called the Fisherman is doing unspeakable things to local children. But a retired Los Angeles homicide detective named Jack Sawyer, who has done a mighty job of repressing his boyhood trials in an alternate world called the Territories, knows that there's more to these crimes than mere banal human cruelty. . . . What elevates 'Black House' beyond ordinary horror novels is the richness of its cast, from a bunch of philosophy-reading bikers to a sleazy journalist to a grieving mother on the brink of madness." N Y Times Book Rev

The body
In King, S. Different seasons p299-451

The breathing method
In King, S. Different seasons p453-518

Carrie. Doubleday 1974 199p $32.50

ISBN 0-385-08695-4

"Carrie is 16, lonely, the butt of all her Maine classmates' tricks and jokes, an object of scorn even to her own mother, who is fanatically religious and believes anything remotely sexual is from the devil. Then one girl becomes ashamed of the cruelty being vented on Carrie and plans an act of kindness that will give her the first happiness in her young life. The only trouble is the act backfires horribly and Carrie is worse off than ever before. It is at this point, at the senior prom, that Carrie begins to put into effect her awesome telekinetic powers, powers with which she has only toyed before." Publ Wkly

"A terrifying treat for both horror and parapsychology fans." SLJ

Christine. Viking 1983 526p $35

ISBN 0-670-22026-4 LC 82-20105

"Arnie Cunningham—a teenager who has never fit in—buys a dilapidated 1958 Plymouth Fury from an equally broken-down Army veteran, Roland LeBay. But Christine—and the soon-dead LeBay—have mysterious regenerative powers; Christine's odometer runs backwards and the car repairs itself. Arnie becomes obsessed by the car and possessed by its previous owner, losing his girlfriend and his best friend as they work together to save him from Christine's clutches." Publ Wkly

"As always, there is the sense of descriptive detail that is the author's trademark. Yet the strength of King's prose is best seen here in the remarkable accuracy of language and attitude that captures the spirit of the teenage characters." Libr J

King, Stephen, 1947-*—Continued*

Cujo. Viking 1981 319p o.p.
ISBN 0-670-45193-2 LC 81-50265

"A Saint Bernard gone berserk, Cujo is the 200-pound family pet who is bitten by a rabid bat one very hot summer in Castle Rock, Maine. Victims of his violence are two families—that of his owner, backwoods auto mechanic Joe Cambers, and of Vic Trenton, an ad man struggling to keep an important account while 'dealing with his wife's infidelity and his four year old's fears.' Counterpoint to the ad campaign's folksy slogan and the writer's lush reveries are . . . vigils in stalled Pintos where one awaits deadly assault." SLJ

"Carefully plotted, the novel throbs with the malignant evil that permeates all of King's fiction." Saturday Rev

The dark half. Viking 1989 431p o.p.
LC 88-40628

The protagonist of this novel "is literary novelist Thad Beaumont, whose greatest success has come with three gory thrillers written under the pseudonym George Stark. . . . When a blackmailer threatens to reveal Stark's identity . . . Beaumont and his literary agent decide to foil the plan and capitalize on Stark's 'demise.' But Stark, who of course was never alive, will not stay dead either. Beaumont's alter ego . . . seeks revenge against all those involved in killing him off." Publ Wkly

The author is "a very good storyteller. 'The Dark Half' mostly succeeds, as both parable and chiller, in spite of occasional clichés of thought and expression and bits of sophomoric humor." N Y Times Book Rev

The dead zone. Viking 1979 426p o.p.
ISBN 0-670-26077-0 LC 79-12785

"Following a car accident, New England high school English teacher Johnny Smith is unconscious for five years only to wake a bewildered psychic in post-Watergate America. He quickly runs afoul of a national scandal sheet that wants to exploit his power to see the future. He also catches a sex murderer and eventually takes an interest in presidential politics. In the end he turns assassin to save the country from a Hitler-like congressman with White House aspirations." Libr J

Desperation. Viking 1996 690p o.p.
LC 96-17259

This horror tale shares character's with The regulators, entered below. An "alien force is loose in Desperation, Nevada, and, having occupied the bodies of a succession of citizens . . . has gruesomely slaughtered everyone else in town. Now in the body of a patrolling cop, it is picking up people motoring by on U.S. 50. Foremost among those are burned-out novelist Johnny Marinville and 11-year-old David Carver, who barely a year ago underwent a serious religious conversion and occasionally hears the voice of God. It is God—the God of the Christian Bible, both Testaments—who eventually saves Johnny, David, and the rest of those who survive Desperation, but saves them only by means of their own free will and their own heroic and gory exertions. If King wants to show how to inject religion honestly and effectively into the normally crass horror genre, he succeeds beautifully." Booklist

Different seasons. Viking 1982 527p $37.95; pa $7.99
ISBN 0-670-27266-3; 0-451-16753-8 (pa)
LC 82-70145

This "is a collection of four novellas. . . . The first tale is about how one self-contained individual coped with life in a Maine jail. The second is not so much about Nazism today as it is about how victim and victimizer can develop a symbiotic relationship. In the third a search by 12-year-olds for a body in the woods has implications for their innocence. The last is a good old-fashioned horror story." Libr J

Dolores Claiborne. Viking 1993 305p o.p.
LC 92-15467

This novel unfolds in the form of a monologue "by the title character, who is suspected of murdering her loutish, insensitive husband and the difficult, rich, and senile woman for whom she has kept house for many years. As Dolores tells her story to the local authorities, the details of a life of drudgery and marital unhappiness emerge, along with the ironic truth behind the deaths." Libr J

"What drives Dolores Claiborne is a powerful characterization of the title figure, a cranky old Maine islander who takes no guff from life or death. . . . King's mimicry is startlingly good." Time

Dreamcatcher; a novel. Scribner 2001 620p $28
ISBN 0-7432-1138-3 LC 00-67990

"One November afternoon in the Maine woods, four men, friends since childhood are on their annual hunting trip that has become as much a time for catching up on one another's lives as it is a time for drinking beer and pursuing game. But this congenial respite ends quickly for Pete, Beaver, Henry, and Jonesy when a dazed and disheveled stranger wanders into their campsite. The hours and days that follow are filled with spaceships, evil gray aliens, a toxic parasite called byrus, and a military search-and-destroy mission. . . . [King] serves up a powerful work that examines the interconnections between memory and imagination and studies the influence of friendship on the human condition." Libr J

Everything's eventual: 14 dark tales. Scribner 2002 459p $28
ISBN 0-7432-3515-0 LC 2002-17738

"Fourteen stories, most of them gems, featuring an array of literary approaches, plus an opinionated intro from King about the '(Almost) Lost Art' of the short story." Publ Wkly

Firestarter. Viking 1980 428p o.p.
ISBN 0-670-31541-9 LC 80-14793

"Two college students sign up as paid guinea pigs for a secret and unknowingly dangerous government experiment in telekinesis. . . . When the subjects marry and have a baby, however, their child develops not only telekinesis but pyrokinesis as well; in short, the tot can not only push things with her mind, but set them ablaze as well. The government's plan to use the girl as a human weapon set [the author's] plot into action, and an extended chase ensues with expected havoc wreaked in vivid detail." Booklist

"This is your advanced post-Watergate cynical American thriller with some eerie parapsychological twists, and it's been done so distinctively well that we'd better talk about genius rather than genre." Quill Quire

Four past midnight. Viking 1990 763p o.p.
LC 90-50046

This volume contains four novellas: The Langoliers; Secret window, secret garden; The library policeman; The sun dog

King, Stephen, 1947-—*Continued*

This book "is hard to put down, truly chilling, and sure to be enjoyed by YA horror afficionados everywhere." SLJ

From a Buick 8; a novel. Scribner 2002 356p $28

ISBN 0-7432-1137-5 LC 2001-55118

"In 1979, an odd man drives what at first glance looks like a 1954 mint-quality Buick Roadmaster up to a service station in rural Pennsylvania, then vanishes, leaving behind the car. The state police of Troop D deposit the vehicle in a shed near their barracks, where, up to the present, it remains a secret from all but cop colleagues—for the car isn't exactly a car; it may be alive, and it certainly serves as a doorway between our world and. . . what? Another dimension? Another galaxy?" Publ Wkly

This is a "horror novel, but it's one that gnaws away at the very premises of the horror novel. It knows what you want and expect from it, but it deftly gives you something else instead, something equally worth having and all the more pleasing for being a surprise." N Y Times Book Rev

Gerald's game. Viking 1992 332p o.p.

LC 91-47628

"Jessie and Gerald Burlingame have been married for 20 years. Kinky sex is Gerald's game; lately he has taken to handcuffing his wife to the bedposts. During one such session, via a series of bizarre circumstances, Jessie accidentally kills her husband, and for the next 28 hours she is trapped." Publ Wkly

Even after escaping, Jessie "still has to deal with the corpse-like figure she thinks invaded the cabin just as she freed herself and that pursued her to her car and has haunted her during her convalescence. Was—is—it real? Somewhat like King's earlier naturalistic shocker, *Misery*, this book is grim and nasty. Unlike *Misery*, it's not semiconsciously misogynistic. Quite the reverse: it seems to say that virtually no man and no men's institution can treat a woman decently. A very disturbing stylistic tour de force, this may be King's darkest book." Booklist

The girl who loved Tom Gordon; a novel. Scribner 1999 224p $16.95

ISBN 0-684-86762-1 LC 99-13109

"Nine-year-old Trisha McFarland is hopelessly lost in the woods. Out for a morning hike with her bickering mother and brother, she runs off to relieve herself and discovers she can't find her way back to the path. . . . Trisha wanders for a week in the mosquito-infested forest with nothing but her wits, her Walkman and the pitching prowess of her hero, the dreamy Red Sox reliever Tom Gordon, to guide her. As Trisha fights to stay alive, King demonstrates his empathy for the inner lives of children and an outdoorsman's knowledge of the edible wild flora of Maine." N Y Times Book Rev

Hearts in Atlantis. Scribner 1999 523p $28

ISBN 0-684-85351-5 LC 99-23889

Five interconnected fictions follow three friends from their sixth-grade year, 1960, to 1999. The war in Vietnam serves as a unifying theme

"The characters are compelling and well drawn, the action is ingeniously interwoven from story to story, and the feel of the 60s, and the baggage carried into later decades, is vivid, harsh, and absolutely true." SLJ

Insomnia. Viking 1994 787p o.p.

LC 94-784

"On one of the long, exhausting walks old Ralph Roberts starts taking as a brain tumor slowly kills his wife, he witnesses a friendly young neighbor, Ed Deepneau, behaving totally out of character—indeed, like someone possessed. About a year later and after his wife's death, Ralph begins waking early and then earlier and earlier. He also starts seeing things—intense colors streaming off people and animals. Meanwhile, Ed has turned into an antiabortion fanatic and wife-beater. Ralph intervenes to help Helen Deepneau escape from Ed, for which Ed threatens him. Or is it Ed? Ralph senses that someone or something else is in control of the troubled man. Ralph's right, of course. Ed has been involuntarily recruited on one side, and, it develops, Ralph and his also-widowed neighbor, Lois Chasse, on the other, of a supercosmic struggle the import of which King reveals with deliciously tantalizing gradualness." Booklist

It. Viking 1986 1138p o.p.

LC 85-41062

"Six adults, living separately in a blessed fog of forgetfulness, are summoned back to their hometown to complete the destruction of a horrific, shape-changing entity who breakfasts on the city's children. This same group first encountered the menace more than a quarter century before, as schoolchildren in the 1950s. Their quest breeds some riveting chase scenes as adults and children alike flee from an assortment of menacing humans and slavering monsters—most of which are manifestations of an evil so vile its true nature can never be known. King's considerable talent for grounding this supernatural stuff in the minutiae of everyday life is evident." Booklist

The Langoliers

In King, S. Four past midnight p1-246

The library policeman

In King, S. Four past midnight p401-604

The long walk

In King, S. The Bachman books: four early novels by Stephen King

Misery. Viking 1987 310p o.p.

LC 86-40504

"Paul Sheldon is a serious novelist plagued by the commercial success of his 'Misery Chastain' romance series. He fictionally kills off his irritating heroine and finally writes his great American novel, celebrating with a drunken drive through a rural Colorado blizzard; but he learns what real misery means when he wrecks his car and awakens as the crippled prisoner/patient of a psychotic ex-nurse named Annie Wilkes—Misery's biggest, and angriest, fan. In a graphically gruesome story, Paul must bring Misery back to life just for Annie; but will this new novel buy his freedom, or is he only prolonging his physical and mental torture?" Libr J

"Even if 'Misery' is less terrifying than his usual work—no demons, no witchcraft, no nether-world horrors—it creates strengths out of its realities. Its excitements are more subtle. And, as such, it is an intriguing work." N Y Times Book Rev

Needful things. Viking 1991 690p o.p.

ISBN 0-670-83953-1 LC 91-50148

King, Stephen, 1947—*Continued*

A mysterious entrepreneur named Leland Gaunt arrives in Castle Rock, Maine, and sets up an old curiosity shop. Calling his shop "Needful Things", Gaunt "sells objects that revive his customers' deepest and most selfish desires—things they must have at any cost. As part of the bargain, he requires that his purchasers carry out various 'pranks' on each other. One thing leads to another and an eventual bloodbath." Times Lit Suppl

"As the dreams of each strikingly memorable character, major and minor, inexorably turn to nightmare, individuals and soon the community are overwhelmed, while the precise nature of Gaunt's evil thrillingly stays just out of focus. King, like Leland Gaunt, knows just what his customers want." Publ Wkly

Night shift. Doubleday 1978 xxii, 336p $35
ISBN 0-385-12991-2 LC 77-75146

The stories "all begin in our normal world, where everything is safe and warm. But in almost every instance, something slips, and we find ourselves in the nightmare world of the not-quite real. . . . Such stories require a willing suspension of disbelief, of course, but they also require an author who is an expert manipulator. . . . King is an expert." Best Sellers

Nightmares & dreamscapes. Viking 1993 816p o.p.
LC 92-46881

Includes the following stories: Dolan's Cadillac; The end of the whole mess; Suffer the little children; The Night Flier; Popsy; It grows on you; Chattery teeth; Dedication; The moving finger; Sneakers; You know they got a hell of a band; Home delivery; Rainy season; My pretty pony; The ten o'clock people; Crouch End; The house on Maple Street; The fifth quarter; The doctor's case; Umney's last case

"There's certainly nothing skimpy about this collection of large, leisurely short stories. . . . Fans of Mr. King's work will find here his usual menu: wild conspiracies; repellent, zestful monsters; scenes speckled and splashed with gore." N Y Times Book Rev

Pet sematary. Doubleday 1983 373p o.p.
ISBN 0-385-18244-9 LC 82-45360

"For Dr. Louis Creed and his family, their new house is perfection, with a fairyland forest within walking distance. But the woods contain a bizarre pet cemetery tended by local children, and eventually the Creeds discover its secret—an ancient burial ground with the power to raise the dead." Libr J

"King's characters are so solid and next-door neighborly that we are drawn quite naturally and trustingly into their lives. And then, a single note at a time, the eerie music begins and we are entranced." Best Sellers

Rage
In King, S. The Bachman books: four early novels by Stephen King

The regulators; [by] Richard Bachman. Dutton 1996 466p o.p.
LC 96-8931

This novel is "set in an idyllic Ohio suburb where a group of residents are treated to a day-long horror show courtesy of an autistic child who is serving as host to an alien intelligence." Libr J

"The premise owes a big unacknowledged debt to the classic *Twilight Zone* episode 'It's a Good Life'; echoes of earlier Kings resound often as well. . . . But King makes hay in this story in which anything can happen, and does, including the warping of space-time and the savage deaths of much of his large cast. The narrative itself warps fantastically, from prose set in classic typeface to handwritten journals to drawings to typewritten playscript and so on." Publ Wkly

Rita Hayworth and Shawshank redemption
In King, S. Different seasons p1-101

Roadwork
In King, S. The Bachman books: four early novels by Stephen King

Rose Madder. Viking 1995 420p o.p.
ISBN 0-670-85869-2 LC 95-14376

"In the book's first scene, having beaten his cowed, pregnant wife badly enough to induce a miscarriage, Norman blithely makes himself a sandwich while waiting for the ambulance to arrive. And when Rose suddenly flees, after 14 years of abuse, Norman calmly begins trolling for her, leaving in his wake a string of mutilated corpses. Rose doesn't leave Norman because she's afraid he'll kill her—she's driven to escape by the fear that he won't, that his cruel torments will simply go on and on. Her despair, her gradual creation of a new life in a Midwestern city, her hesitant romance with a wry, gentle pawnbroker, are all convincingly rendered." N Y Times Book Rev

The running man
In King, S. The Bachman books: four early novels by Stephen King

Salem's Lot. Doubleday 1975 439p $35
ISBN 0-385-00751-5

"The small Maine town of Jerusalem's Lot, or Salem's Lot as the natives call it, has become what appears to be a ghost town. Its streets, however, are deserted only in the daylight hours, for the villagers have turned into vampires." Booklist

"It is to Stephen King's credit as a stylist that he has charmed us into such familiar territory. Sparing the endless atmospheric creaks and cobwebs and cupolas of this New England landscape, he thrusts us into the private terror of his characters." Best Sellers

Secret window, secret garden
In King, S. Four past midnight p247-399

The shining. Doubleday 1977 447p $35
ISBN 0-385-12167-9 LC 76-24212

"The Overlook Hotel, high in the mountains of Colorado, has in the past played host to a colorful selection of visitors, from gangsters to presidents. But a few even more extraordinary guests are in residence when Jack Torrance comes to the Overlook with his wife, Wendy, and son, Danny, to be winter caretaker. Danny is precognitive and telepathic, a condition that allows him to outmaneuver the hotel's spirits of the dead that attempt to lay claim to the entire Torrance family." Booklist

"In a fast-paced and gory denouement, the terror comes to a violent end. King is a masterful technician of suspense whose readers as well as characters are the victims of his relentless heightening of horror." Libr J

King, Stephen, 1947-—*Continued*

Skeleton crew. Putnam 1985 512p o.p.
LC 84-15947

This "collection of King's shorter work is a hefty sampler from all stages of his career, and demonstrates the range of his abilities. . . . There are several stories here that must rank among King's best." Publ Wkly

The stand. Doubleday 1978 823p o.p.
LC 77-16928

"A flu-like plague escapes from an experimental lab. Within days it devastates the country, leaving only a few thousand immune people. Besides their immunity, the survivors have in common a terrible dream pitting a faceless man of evil against a woman of goodness. The survivors make their choices and head west, gathering for the confrontation between the satanic Randall Flagg and the God-anointed Mother Abigail." Libr J

"Stephen King takes liberties permitted in science fiction and thrillers (the good guys share clairvoyant powers, and the plot often turns on lucky coincidences), but he grounds his apocalyptic fantasy in a detailed vision of the blighted American vista, and he avoids the formulas of less talented popular novelists." New Yorker

The sun dog
In King, S. Four past midnight p605-763

Thinner; [by] Richard Bachman. New Am. Lib. 1984 309p o.p.
LC 84-11462

"While driving, Billy Halleck is distracted by his wife and accidentally strikes and kills an old gypsy woman. After he's acquitted through the aid of two influential friends, all three are cursed by the gypsy leader. Halleck begins to lose weight rapidly, and must race with death to try to have the curse removed." Libr J

"Bachman blends extraordinary events so cleanly and credibly into the fabric of his characters' lives that we are compelled to read on to the story's chilling conclusion. A superbly crafted drama." Booklist

King, Tabitha, 1949-

Survivor. Dutton 1997 433p o.p.
LC 96-26347

"A William Abrahams book"

Maine college student Kissy Mellors "is the driver who stopped in time to avoid killing two young women—but the drunk who passed her did not. One woman dies, and the other goes into a coma that lasts for years. Kissy's life is changed forever by this event and by the relationships she forms because of it—with the comatose victim and her family, with the dead girl's boyfriend (a hockey player Kissy later marries), with the investigating officer, even with the drunk driver." Libr J

"King's brutally frank 'warts and all' writing style and bizarre dissection of ordinary events lend a chilling, vaguely eerie element to this suspenseful, enjoyable novel." Booklist

King, Thomas, 1943-

Truth & Bright Water. Atlantic Monthly Press 2000 266p o.p.
ISBN 0-87113-818-2 LC 00-38618

"Truth is a railroad town in the United States, and Bright Water, an Indian reserve right across the river in Canada. Tecumseh is a 15-year-old who regularly crosses between the two with his dog, Soldier, and his cousin and almost constant companion, Lum. The novel is written in the first person, and the action takes place during a few short weeks in the summer." Libr J

"This book exhibits the author's keen powers of observation and captures the essence of reservation life with dark humor and cutting satire. But the wry humor mediates and belies desperation, with 15-year-old Tecumseh fixated on getting his mother to reconcile with his dreamy but shiftless father." Publ Wkly

Kingsolver, Barbara

Animal dreams; a novel. HarperCollins Pubs. 1990 342p o.p.
LC 89-46571

This novel is set in Grace, Arizona. The narrator is Cosima (Codi) Noline, who returns home after abandoning a career in medicine. Codi looks after her aging father, the local doctor, and teaches high school biology. Her sister Halimeda (Hallie) is an agronomist helping the Sandinistas in Nicaragua. In Grace, Codi becomes involved with a former boyfriend, Loyd Peregrina, a Native American. She struggles to come to terms with her past and works to save the town from an impending ecological disaster

"Like all good novels, Animal Dreams is a web of interlacing news. It is dense and vivid, and makes ever tighter circles around the question of what it means to be alive." Nation

The bean trees; a novel. 10th anniversary ed. HarperFlamingo 1997 261p $19.95
ISBN 0-06-017579-6 LC 97-2691

A reissue of the title first published 1988

In this novel, "Taylor Greer, a poor, young woman, flees her Kentucky home and heads west. . . . While passing through Oklahoma, she becomes responsible for a two-year-old Cherokee girl. The two continue on the road. When they roll off the highway in Tucson, Taylor and the child, whom she has named Turtle, . . . meet Mattie, a widow who runs Jesus Is Lord Used Tires and is active in the sanctuary movement on the side." Ms

This book "gives readers something that's increasingly hard to find today—a character to believe in and laugh with and admire." Christ Sci Monit

Followed by Pigs in heaven (1993)

Pigs in heaven; a novel. HarperCollins Pubs. 1993 343p o.p.
LC 92-54739

In this sequel to The bean trees, Taylor Greer and her adopted Cherokee Indian daughter Turtle "are on a trip to the Hoover Dam, where Turtle is the only person to see a man fall over the side. . . . The rescue makes Turtle a heroine. But becoming a heroine, which culminates in an appearance on 'Oprah,' engenders a new disaster. Annawake Fourkiller, an Indian-rights lawyer, sees the white mother with her Cherokee daughter on TV and decides the child must be returned to the Cherokee Nation. . . . But Taylor isn't about to let go of the little girl. . . . They pack up and run." Newsweek

"Possessed of an extravagantly gifted narrative voice, [Kingsolver] blends a fierce and abiding moral vision with benevolent, concise humor." N Y Times Book Rev

Kingsolver, Barbara—*Continued*

The poisonwood Bible; a novel. HarperFlamingo 1998 546p $26; pa $15

ISBN 0-06-017540-0; 0-06-093053-5 (pa) LC 98-19901

"In 1959, evangelical preacher Nathan Price moves his wife and four daughters from Georgia to a village in the Belgian Congo, later Zaire. Their dysfunction and cultural arrogance proves disastrous as the family is nearly destroyed by war, Nathan's tyranny, and Africa itself. Told in the voices of the mother and daughters, the novel spans 30 years as the women seek to understand each other and the continent that tore them apart." Libr J

"Buttressing her suspenseful chronicle with authentic background detail, Kingsolver's narrative is at once a compelling family saga and an astute look at Western imperialism in Africa." Publ Wkly

Prodigal summer; a novel. HarperCollins Pubs. 2000 444p $26

ISBN 0-06-019965-2 LC 00-61361

"A corner of southern Appalachia serves as the setting for the stories of three intertwined lives. . . . In the chapters called 'Predator,' forest ranger Deanna Wolfe is a 40-plus wildlife biologist and staunch defender of coyotes, which have recently extended their range into Appalachia. . . . Meanwhile, in the chapters called 'Moth Love,' newly married entomologist Lusa Maluf Landowski is left a widow on her husband's farm with five envious sisters-in-law, crushing debts—and a desperate and brilliant idea. Crusty old farmer Garnett Walker ('Old Chestnuts') learns to respect his archenemy, who crusades for organic farming and opposes Garnett's use of pesticides." Publ Wkly

The novel is full of "tenderness, humor, and earthy spirituality. . . . As usual, Kingsolver's dialogue is absolutely natural, often funny, and sometimes heartbreaking." Chris Sci Monit

Kipling, Rudyard, 1865-1936

The best short stories of Rudyard Kipling; edited by Randall Jarrell. Hanover House 1961 o.p.

Contents: Lispeth; At the pit's mouth; A wayside comedy; The story of Muhammad Din; A bank fraud; At the end of the passage; Without benefit of clergy; Jews in Sushan; The return of Imray; The phantom 'rickshaw; Moti Guj—mutineer; The drums of the fore and aft; On Greenhow Hill; The man who would be king; Baa baa black sheep; In the rukh; A matter of fact; The disturber of traffic; "The finest story in the world"; "Brugglesmith"; The Children of the Zodiac; The Maltese Cat; The miracle of Purun Bhagat; The undertakers; Kaa's hunting; The King's ankus; Red Dog; A Centurion of the Thirtieth; On the Great Wall; The Winged Hats; Marklake witches; "Wireless"; A Sahib's war; As easy as A.B.C.; "They"; An habitation enforced; The village that voted the earth was flat; Regulus; The propagation of knowledge; "My son's wife"; Friendly Brook; Mary Postgate; "In the interests of the brethren"; A madonna of the trenches; Dayspring mishandled; The Janeites; The Wish House; The manner of men; Unprofessionl; The Eye of Allah

Collected stories; selected and introduced by Robert Gottlieb. Knopf 1994 xxxvii, 911p $25

ISBN 0-679-43592-1 LC 94-5854

"Everyman's library"

"There is an enormous range of subject matter, genre, styles, and tones in Kipling's prose work. . . . [He] is undoubtedly one of the great short-story writers in English and the subtlety of his early narrative technique has led some to claim him as a proto-Modernist." Oxford Companion to 20th Cent Lit in Engl

Kirn, Walter

Mission to America. Doubleday 2005 271p $23.95

ISBN 0-385-50764-X LC 2005-45477

"Founded in the 19th century, the Aboriginal Fulfilled Apostles are a doctrinal smorgasbord of health food enthusiasm, Swedenborgism, matriarchy and semicommunal living. Isolated in Bluff, Mont., the group is dying out, so its only prosperous member, Ennis Lauer, finances some missionary work to Terrestria–aka the on-the-grid U.S. Narrator Mason Plato LaVerle is plucked from his ongoing courtship of young Sarah to trawl for converts with the (as it turns out) tragically temptable Elder Stark. As he and Elder drive through Wyoming, Elder is introduced to crank by a decrepit dealer, and Mason is introduced to sex by a 15-year-old Wiccan. In the Aspen-like Snowshoe, Colo., the two fall into the circle around Errol Effingham Sr., a billionaire constructed mainly of bogus takes on Ayn Rand and a bad stomach, while Mason falls for the lovely Becky, whose former incarnation can still be viewed with a tripleX mouse click. Mason's flat voice, which levels everything to a certain calm, makes overconsumption and dissipation seem funny again." Publ Wkly

Kirshenbaum, Binnie

An almost perfect moment. Ecco 2004 321p $23.95

ISBN 0-06-052086-8 LC 2003-54961

The protagonist of this novel is Valentine Kessler. "A nice Jewish girl growing up in late-1970s Brooklyn, she becomes infatuated with her Polish American math teacher and with the Virgin Mary, for she mysteriously resembles the vision of Mary seen by Bernadette of Lourdes. Valentine's father left when she was a baby, and ever since her mother, Miriam, indulges her beautiful, newly withdrawn daughter while eating herself into obesity and playing mah-jongg every afternoon with her buddies. The so-called Girls are like a Greek chorus, commenting on life around them and wondering at Valentine's inspired silence. . . . Bursting with hyperbole, this is a hilarious and uncanny snapshot of a bygone era." Libr J

Kirst, Hans Hellmut, 1914-1989

Forward, Gunner Asch!; translated from the German by Robert Kee. Little, Brown 1956 368p o.p.

Sequel to The revolt of Gunner Asch

Original German edition, 1954; published in the United Kingdom as part two of the trilogy: Zero eight fifteen, with title: Gunner Asch goes to war

"The action of the book alternates between a sector of the Russian front in late winter of 1941-2, and a base depot somewhere in Germany. Gunner Asch and his com-

Kirst, Hans Hellmut, 1914-1989—*Continued*

panions, whom we met in the first volume training at home, have now gone to war. . . . The characters move like Breughel peasants against a bleak winter landscape; unshaven, filthy, swaddled in greatcoats and sacking, their minds set only on self-preservation, food, and, where possible, women." New Statesman (1913)

Followed by The return of Gunner Asch

The return of Gunner Asch; translated from the German by Robert Kee. Little, Brown 1957 310p o.p.

Sequel to Forward, Gunner Asch!

Original German edition, 1955; published in the United Kingdom as third part of the trilogy: Zero eight fifteen

The third volume in the author's series about the adventures of a German army sergeant in World War II describes "the disintegration of the front-line units of the German Army as the Allies advanced in the closing days of combat in Europe in 1945. Asch becomes involved in an effort to track down two officers who left their men to needless slaughter to catch up with a black-market cache." Booklist

Followed by What became of Gunner Asch (1964)

The revolt of Gunner Asch; translated from the German by Robert Kee. Little, Brown 1955 311p o.p.

First in a series of four novels about Gunner Asch; Original German edition, 1954; published in the United Kingdom as part of the trilogy Zero eight fifteen, with title: The strange mutiny of Gunner Asch

This is "a German novel poking fun at the more idiotic aspects of Army discipline. Set in a garrison town just before the last war, it tells of a one-man battle fought by Gunner Asch, a nice young man with a capacity for indignation, against the bullying N.C.O.'s of his company." Manchester Guardian

"A tale in which elements of drama and suspense are skillfully fused with high comedy—a tale which the author brings to a startling and altogether delightful conclusion. . . . Kirst has succeeded in distilling robust fun out of brutal realities without ever suggesting that the realities were other than brutal." Atlantic

Followed by Forward, Gunner Asch!

Kitchen, Judith

The house on Eccles Road. Graywolf Press 2002 221p $22

ISBN 1-55597-368-X

"Eight years, after the death of their only child, Molly O'Rourke and Leo Bluhm are still tiptoeing around each other. While Leo is able to lose himself in academia, Molly has found it impossible to resume work as a singer. Both continue to mourn, albeit separately and wordlessly. . . . By focusing on a single day (much like *Ulysses,* which it hints at), the novel captures both the nuances of routine and the serendipity of chance." Libr J

Klein, Joe, 1946-

Primary colors; a novel of politics; [by] Anonymous. Random House 1996 366p o.p.

LC 95-39823

This is a "romance à clef about the 1992 Democratic Presidential primary campaign, featuring an ambitious . . . Southern governor named Jack Stanton seen through the eyes of [Henry Burton], a disillusioned aide." London Rev Books

"This is, in short, a quite outstanding novel of political process and motive that reads like a slightly hipper version of Gore Vidal." New Statesman (1913)

The running mate; a novel. Dial Press (NY) 2000 403p $26.95

ISBN 0-385-33386-2 LC 00-27933

This novel's protagonist, Charlie Martin, appeared in the author's Primary Colors (1996) "as a presidential candidate—a U.S. Senator from the Midwest. . . . Charlie returns to his home state . . . to run for a third Senate term. But he succumbs to unexpected distractions—including a romance with a glamorous Manhattan designer and the appearance of a previously unknown . . . illegitimate son. The most unexpected distraction of all: a tough re-election opponent named Lee Butler." Time

"Klein retains his affinity for a kind of novel written too seldom nowadays: the comic novel of strategy and machinations." Times Lit Suppl

Klein, Rachel, 1953-

The moth diaries; a novel. Counterpoint 2002 249p $24

ISBN 1-58243-205-8 LC 2001-7226

"The unnamed narrator of Klein's first novel is a studious, thoughtful 16-year-old at an elite boarding school in the late '60s. Her closest friend is her sweet, friendly roommate, Lucy, who navigates the school's social system with ease. The arrival of quiet, mysterious Ernessa upsets the balance between the friends when Ernessa befriends and seemingly takes Lucy away from the narrator. . . . Thanks to reading LeFanu's vampire story 'Carmilla' and other tales, and to Ernessa's odd behavior and Lucy's mysterious wasting illness, the narrator begins to suspect that Ernessa is a vampire. . . . The diary format of Klein's story gives it immediacy, and a menacing atmosphere permeates it." Booklist

Klíma, Ivan

No saints or angels; translated by Gerald Turner. Grove Press 2001 267p $24

ISBN 0-8021-1695-7 LC 2001-33994

Original Czech edition, 1999

"Kristýna, a divorced mother in her 40s, works as a dentist in Prague. Burdened with responsibilities, she is the sole caregiver for her aging, widowed mother; her terminally ill ex-husband; and her 15-year-old daughter, Jana, who may or may not be using hard drugs. Lonely and starved for affection, Kristýna begins dating Jan, a former student of her ex-husband and her junior by 15 years. While she tries to use the romance and morning glasses of wine to erase mounting concerns, Kristýna is unable to overcome her own unsentimental perceptions." Publ Wkly

Klíma, Ivan—*Continued*

"In Klima's world bureaucracy is a metaphor for the human condition: our dearest allies now are those who gassed our grandmothers, the young of the past had more purpose under interrogation than those of today have on the Internet, and we long for a God grown wholly inadequate to his creatures in the 21st century. Against this cosmic mismatch, frail, flawed human beings play out their volatile longings and their inglorious heroisms." N Y Times Book Rev

Kluge, Alexander, 1932-

The devil's blind spot; tales from the new century; translated by Martin Chalmers & Michael Hulse. New Directions 2004 322p $23.95

ISBN 0-8112-1595-4 LC 2004-19286

Contains 173 of the 500 stories in the original German edition, 2003

The stories "range from a dozen pages to just half a page in length: these tales, like novels in pill form, are arranged in five chapters. The first group illustrates the little-known virtues of the Devil; the second explores love (from Kant to the opera); the third (entitled 'Sarajevo Is Everywhere') addresses power; the fourth considers the cosmos; and the fifth ranges all our 'knowledge' against our feelings." Publisher's note

"Kluge provides us with . . . stories that are in effect metaphysical or occult signs that flash and disappear and then flash again. In this respect, his book, like a silent movie, appeals to our need to make patterns and highlights how words themselves can blind us. A beautiful and chilling collection that is simply unforgettable, it insists we must adapt to our 'new century' of continually shifting alliances and uncertainties." Review of Contemporary Fiction

Knebel, Fletcher, 1911-1993

Seven days in May; by Fletcher Knebel and Charles W. Bailey II. Harper & Row 1962 341p o.p.

"The story set against a . . . political Washington background, is about a military plot to take over the government. Its hero is a President of the U.S. in the 1970's, who with six men he trusts, sets out to prove the plot exists and to foil it." Publ Wkly

Knight, Damon Francis, 1922-2002

The best of Damon Knight; with an introduction by Barry N. Malzberg. Taplinger 1978 c1976 307p o.p.

First published 1976 in paperback by Pocket Books

Contents: Not with a bang; To serve man; Cabin boy; The analogues; Babel II; Special delivery; Thing of beauty; Anachron; Extempore; Backward, O time; The last word; Man in the jar; The enemy; Eripmav; A likely story; Time enough; Mary; The handler; The big pat boom; Semper fi; Masks; Down there

"A writer of estimable talent, as these twenty-two stories from 1948-73 prove. Knight's motifs are common—time travel, after-the-holocaust, cyborgs, alien visitors to earth—but the wit, penetrating social satire, and quick narrative twists are distinctly his own." Booklist

Knight, Michael, 1969-

Goodnight, nobody. Atlantic Monthly Press 2002 160p $23

ISBN 0-87113-867-0 LC 2002-27944

Contents: Birdland; Feeling lucky; Killing Stonewall Jackson; The end of everything; The mesmerist; Keeper of secrets, teller of lies; Mitchell's girls; Ellen's book; Blackout

"Stylistically, Knight slaloms through old-fashioned noir and snarky postmodernism, and from Barthelmean set pieces to a riff on Stonewall Jackson that evokes one of Barry Hannah's Civil War fever dreams." N Y Times Book Rev

Knode, Helen

The ticket out. Harcourt 2003 340p $24

ISBN 0-15-100184-7 LC 2002-7804

The morning after a party, film critic Ann Whitehead "discovers aspiring moviemaker Greta Stenholm in the bathtub, dead from knife wounds. Even though the knife used to kill Greta belongs to her, Ann's primary concern is using the story as her ticket out of the movie-reviewing business and into feature writing. Even as she patiently answers taciturn Detective Doug Lockwood's questions about the murder scene, she's busily hiding evidence. . . . Her increasingly intimate relationship with the complicated Lockwood is the high point in this very entertaining novel." Booklist

Knopf, Marcy, 1969-

(ed) The Sleeper wakes. See The Sleeper wakes

Knowles, John, 1926-2001

Indian summer. Random House 1966 242p o.p.

A "study of a lifelong friendship that has an unrecognized source of tragedy. Cleet Kinsolving's idealization of the friendship is destroyed when he realizes that Neil Reardon is disguising envy by using his wealth to turn Cleet into a hanger-on. Cleet breaks off the association and starts his life over with the knowledge that his revenge, an attack on Neil's wife, is animalistic and reveals his own weaknesses." Booklist

"The theme of individualism is explored with great energy and charm; and the commentaries on the rich, the poor, success, failure, and politics are dipped in truth and rolled in humor." Libr J

Peace breaks out. Holt, Rinehart & Winston 1981 193p o.p.

LC 80-19678

Set in the Devon School in New Hampshire, scene of A separate peace, this novel takes place during the 1945-46 term. "Pete Hallam—Class of '37—returning . . . as a teacher, hopes to recover there from wartime traumas. But the boys in the class of '46 are an edgy bunch, frustrated and guilty because they won't be graduating from the prep school to the armed forces like the classes before them. There's a simmering air of violence among them during the long winter as Pete in his low-keyed way tries to help them across the threshold to adulthood." Publ Wkly

A separate peace; a novel. Macmillan 1960 c1959 186p o.p.

ISBN 0-02-564850-0

Knowles, John, 1926-2001—*Continued*

First published 1959 in the United Kingdom

"Gene Forrester looks back on his school days, spent in a New England town just before World War II. He both admires and envies his close friend and roommate, Finny, who is a natural athlete, in contrast to Gene's special competence as a scholar. When Finny suffers a crippling accident, Gene must face his own involvement in it." Shapiro. Fic for Youth. 3d edition

Knox, Elizabeth, 1959-

Billie's kiss. Ballantine Bks. 2002 343p $24

ISBN 0-345-45052-3

A "romantic mystery set in 1903. Billie Paxton, an uneducated but perspicacious young woman, thinks the worst is over after a rough voyage on the *Gustav Edda,* a Swedish steamer that has taken her to the outer Scottish island of Kissack and Skilling, along with her pregnant sister, Edith, and her brother-in-law, Henry Maslen, a tutor who has accepted a position with the local squire, Lord Hallowhulme, at Kiss Castle. But just as the *Gustav Edda* is docking in port, an explosion shatters the hull, leaving Edith dead and Henry injured. An excellent swimmer, Billie immediately jumps off the stricken ship and scrambles to shore." Publ Wkly

Knox's "characters are unique and yet somehow familiar, in the sense that they are reminiscent of famous characters in Victorian literature." Booklist

Daylight. Ballantine Bks. 2003 356p map $23.95

ISBN 0-345-45795-1 LC 2003-544868

"Saint or vampire? The identity of the Blessed Martine Raimondi, a French nun murdered by the Nazis in 1944 for her part in the daring cave escape of rebel partisans, is only one question answered in this illuminating tour-de-force set in the south of France. . . . Brian 'Bad' Phelan, a New South Wales bomb tech and expert 'caver' on paid injury leave, helps retrieve Martine's blistered corpse outside a cave near the Italian border and discovers she bears a shocking resemblance to a woman he'd encountered years before in another flooded cave. He's further struck by Martine's resemblance to Eve Moskelute, the subject of a painting by Jean Ares, her Picasso-esque deceased husband. The author constructs an impressive mystery that dissects the meaning of miracles while putting a fresh spin on the vampire archetype." Publ Wkly

Koen, Karleen

Through a glass darkly. Random House 1986 743p o.p.

LC 86-422

Set in early eighteenth century England and France, this novel "tells the story of Barbara Alderley, who is fifteen when the story begins, and about to be bartered in marriage to the middle-aged but gorgeous Roger Montgeoffry. The barterer is her own mother, [Diana]. . . . Barbara is in love with Roger, Roger is in love with Bentwoodes, the family seat that is to be her dowry, and Diana is in love with money and power." N Y Times Book Rev

"Expertly paced, the novel blends quaint historical romance with a sharp-edged, contemporary psychodramatic style. Its characters are memorable and full-bodied, maturing through a series of rapidly escalating tragedies that bring the sweetly naive heroine into full womanhood and force her to make a decision that will forever change her life. A sophisticated, atmospheric work." Booklist

Koeppen, Wolfgang, 1906-

The hothouse; translated by Michael Hofmann. Norton 2001 221p $23.95

ISBN 0-393-04902-7 LC 00-69573

Original German edition, 1953

This novel "tells the story of the final days of a widower who is a member of the German parliament. As his sadness over his loss expands to encompass not only the death of his much younger wife but also the destruction and division of Germany and the present political corruption of which he finds himself a part, he moves deeper into depression." Booklist

"Gloom pervades these pages, lighted from within by the fireworks of Koeppen's dazzling prose, rich with allusions to classical and German literature and masterfully translated by Hofmann. Almost eerily contemporary in its concerns, and remarkable as a sidelong, searing appraisal of the legacy of the Nazi years, it is a recovered masterpiece." Publ Wkly

A sad affair; translated with an introduction by Michael Hofmann. Norton 2003 176p il $23.95

ISBN 0-393-05718-6 LC 2003-2212

Original German edition, 1934

This novel "follows the uncertain steps of young Friedrich, a university student who falls in love with an actress named Sibylle. Beautiful and unconventional in a Sally Bowles kind of way, Sybille has the usual ingénue's coterie of lovestruck suitors orbiting around her, and Friedrich is quickly drawn into what looks like a hopeless obsession. In this flowing translation by Michael Hofmann, Koeppen's narration is ellipitical and dreamlike." N Y Times Book Rev

Koestler, Arthur, 1905-1983

Darkness at noon; translated by Daphne Hardy. Macmillan 1987 267p o.p.

ISBN 0-02-565210-9 LC 86-31273

First published 1940 in the United Kingdom; this is a reissue of the 1941 edition

This novel "deals with the arrest, imprisonment, trial, and execution of N. S. Rubashov in an unnamed dictatorship over which 'No. 1' presides. Koestler describes Rubashov as 'a synthesis of the lives of a number of men who were victims of the so-called Moscow trials,' and the novel did much to draw attention to the nature of Stalin's regime." Oxford Companion to Engl Lit. 6th edition

Koontz, Dean R. (Dean Ray), 1945-

The bad place. Putnam 1990 382p o.p.

LC 89-10861

"Married detectives Julie and Bobby Dakota agree to help frightened amnesiac Frank Pollard figure out what he does when he's asleep. . . . In due course, Frank and the Dakotas join forces against murderer Candy Pollard and his weird sisters, who want to kill Frank—evidently

Koontz, Dean R. (Dean Ray), 1945-—*Continued*
the sole human in the monstrous family. Candy extends psychic feelers toward potential victims, emanations that are sensed by Julie's younger brother Thomas. A Down's syndrome child, Thomas is telepathically gifted and able to warn Bobby of the demons who threaten Julie." Publ Wkly

By the light of the moon; [by] Dean Koontz. Bantam Bks. 2002 431p $26.95
ISBN 0-553-80143-0 LC 2002-29902
The author "introduces readers to a twentysomething trio consisting of artist Dylan O'Conner, his autistic younger brother, Shep; and a stand-up comedienne named Jilly Jackson. One momentous evening, these threeunexpectedly find themselves coping with the bizarre effects of mysterious injections forced upon them by mad scientist Lincoln Proctor in an Arizona motel. With a generous helping of dark humor, Koontz quickly charges his characters with the task of harnessing their paranormal abilities as weapons against real-world violence and evil in a setting littered with present-day totems ranging from fast-food restaurants to sensation-mongering radio personalities." Libr J

Cold fire. Putnam 1991 382p o.p.
LC 90-46806
Teacher Jim Ironheart "is sent by forces unknown to save chosen people in life-threatening situations. By chance, [Holly Thorne], a young but jaded reporter stumbles onto his missions, and joins him to investigate who is controlling him and why. Shared nightmares begin to point to an extraterrestrial influence, and the pair are forced to confront Ironheart's forgotten past for answers." Libr J
"Koontz is perhaps the least given to verbal pyrotechnics of the current horror masters. His work displays a subdued prose style; cultural sidebars are kept to a minimum; and blood spills are few and far between. But he also knows how to generate genuine terror without gore." Booklist

Dark rivers of the heart; a novel; [by] Dean Koontz. Knopf 1994 487p o.p.
LC 94-12090
"Spencer Grant is on the run from a nameless, violent government agency. His goal is to keep away from his pursuers long enough to find the woman he met the night before, who appears to be their real target. Spencer has no idea why they want to kill Valerie Keene, but his brief acquaintance with her has convinced him that the killers have no good reason for wanting her dead. With his . . . dog, Rocky, Spencer leads the killers on a frustrating chase." Libr J
"Koontz has succeeded where many genre writers have failed: he has switched gears, put the zombies and creepy crawlers aside, and written a believable high-tech thriller." N Y Times Book Rev

Dragon tears; [by] Dean Koontz. Putnam 1993 377p o.p.
LC 92-28854
"In southern California, police detective Harry Lyon and his partner, Connie Guliver, find themselves hounded by a golem who appears in the shape of a towering vagrant. Called Ticktock because he grants his victims only hours to live, the vagrant has tremendous physical power, a taste for gruesomely described violence and the ability to stop time and rearrange reality. Koontz romps playfully and skillfully through this grown-up enchantment." Publ Wkly

The face; [by] Dean Koontz. Bantam Bks. 2003 608p $26.95
ISBN 0-553-80248-8 LC 2003-40354
"The eponymous Face is the world's biggest movie star; he doesn't appear in the novel, but his smart, geeky 10-year-old-son, Fric, takes center stage, as does Ethan Truman, cop-turned-security chief of the Face's elaborate estate and Fric's main human protector when one Corky Laputa, who's dedicated his life to anarchy, decides to sow further disorderby kidnapping this progeny of the world's idol. . . . Koontz's characters are memorable and his unique mix of suspense and humor absorbing." Publ Wkly

False memory; [by] Dean Koontz. Bantam Bks. 2000 627p o.p.
ISBN 0-553-10666-X LC 99-54782
"The heroes are Southern Californians Dusty and Martie Rhodes, he a housepainting contractor, she a computer game designer. . . . As Martie shepherds her terrified, agoraphobic friend, Susan, on a visit to Susan's shrink (Ahriman), Dusty deals with his drug-addled stepbrother/employee, Skeet, about to jump to his death from the roof of Dusty's latest project. Skeet leaps, taking Dusty with him, but both survive; as Dusty checks Skeet into rehab, Martie suffers her first of several horrific phobic episodes, in which she imagines mutilating Dusty with household items. Seeking help, she and Dusty turn to Ahriman, who, it's eventually revealed first to the reader, then to the couple, is responsible for all the trouble. . . . An expertly crafted, ornate suspenser." Publ Wkly

Fear nothing; by Dean Koontz. Bantam Bks. 1998 391p o.p.
LC 97-41129
"Tale of one night in the California coastal town of Moonlight Bay as experienced by Chris Snow. Saddled with a genetic defect that makes direct sunlight toxic to him, Snow is a nocturnal creature whose father has just died. When he discovers that his father's corpse has been stolen, he begins pursuit. Koontz expertly illuminates Snow's nocturnal world and friends, and incrementally, cleverly, the crises erupting in Moonlight Bay take shape. The plot is wonderfully unpredictable, and though the surfer slang wears thin after a while, the narrative remains taut." Libr J
Followed by Seize the night

From the corner of his eye; [by] Dean Koontz. Bantam Bks. 2001 622p o.p.
ISBN 0-553-80134-1 LC 00-48619
This novel "chronicles the lives of three unique individuals. Bartholomew Lampion, born under miraculous yet tragic circumstances, has the most unusual and mesmerizing eyes ever seen. As he grows, he begins to exhibit abilities that defy physics. Angel, born in another city at the same time as Bartholomew, is also a miracle child; as she grows, she demonstrates the ability to see the world as it really exists. At the time of their births, ruthless and cunning Junior dreams that someone named Bartholomew will lead to his downfall. While attempting

Koontz, Dean R. (Dean Ray), 1945-—*Continued*
to find the nemesis he knows only by name, Junior is relentlessly pursued by a police detective." Libr J

"The large cast of characters, particularly the fully developed main players, is richly imagined. The plot is suspenseful and complex. Informing the novel throughout is a fascinating theory that involves quantum mechanics, faith, and human relationships." Voice Youth Advocates

Hideaway. Putnam 1992 384p o.p.
LC 91-29786

"When Californians Hatch and Lindsey Harrison are run off a mountain road, Hatch drowns. A helicopter lifts him to an Orange County state-of-the-art hospital, however, and after being dead for 80 minutes Hatch is resuscitated. Weeks later, impelled by newfound joy in life, Hatch and Lindsey adopt bright, crippled 10-year-old Regina. The only clouds in their delight are visions that Hatch seems to share with a deranged killer." Publ Wkly

Intensity; a novel; by Dean Koontz. Knopf 1995 307p o.p.
ISBN 0-679-42525-X LC 95-33591

Chyna Shepherd, 26, child of a woman who "exposed the girl to plenty of mayhem until she fled Mom at age 16, goes for a pleasant Napa Valley weekend visiting the vintner parents of her best college friend, only to become the covert witness to the family's murder at the hands of thrill-addicted serial (and mass) murderer Edgler Foreman Vess. Hardened by her childhood . . . Chyna determines to keep on the killer's trail until she can bring him to justice or exact it herself." Booklist

"The velocity of the plot is the book's true pleasure; the story does not move so much as rocket up the portentously gloomy highway with the reader in violent pursuit." N Y Times Book Rev

Lightning. Putnam 1988 351p o.p.
LC 87-21649

"On the night of Laura Shane's birth, a stranger appears from the lightning to prevent her delivery's being botched by an alcoholic physician. Throughout Laura's childhood the stranger reappears at times of danger. He protects rather than threatens, yet menace seems to follow him. Thirty years later another storm flashes and the stranger collapses, shot, at Laura's door. Now Laura protects her erst-while guardian from mysterious hunters. He reveals that he and the hunters are time travelers. Laura, quick-witted and brave, leads the way to a bloody showdown." Libr J

The author "quickly grabs the reader's attention. But then he kicks in with his usual stop-start suspense rhythm, giving rise to a certain impatience with the heroine's roller-coaster perils. Nonetheless, there are enough imaginative twists here, along with likable characters . . . to win him new fans and please old ones." N Y Times Book Rev

Midnight. Putnam 1989 383p o.p.
LC 88-22830

"A set of mysterious disappearances and suspicious deaths in the northern California town of Moonlight Cove brings together an undercover F.B.I. agent named Sam Booker and Tessa Lockland, a documentary film producer who suspects that the local police report of her sister's suicide has been falsified. They discover that someone has been turning the town's citizens into humanoids." N Y Times Book Rev

Night chills. Atheneum Pubs. 1976 334p o.p.

"It all begins with a plausible network of self-serving types—a scientist peddling a chemical formula, a businessman mindful of profits, a Pentagon superpatriot. All three see a chance for millions by injecting potable water with a drug that causes people to heed subliminal suggestions transmitted personally or through the media. Taking over an Arab emirate saturated with petro-resources is a possibility, but first comes the trial run and this involves the New England township of Black River in a grizzly shakedown exercise. Villagers act like zombies, ignoring the murder of a child, the son of a tourist, just as long as code phrases prompt Pavlovian responses. Yet the boy's father Paul Annendale undercuts mass manipulation by exploiting a trauma buried with scientist Paul Salsbury's perverse psyche." Publ Wkly

One door away from heaven; [by] Dean Koontz. Bantam Bks. 2001 606p o.p.
ISBN 0-553-80137-6 LC 2001-49952

The "story coalesces from two converging subplots steeped in the weirdness of fringe ufology: in one, loser Michelina Bellsong struggles to save crippled nine-year-old Leilani Klonk from an evil stepdad planning to pass off her imminent disposal as a benevolent alien abduction; in the other, a strange boy who goes by the alias Curtis Hammond is the quarry of two cross-country manhunts, one led by the FBI and the other by mass murderers who, like the messianic Curtis, may not be what they seem. En route to a pyrotechnic finale in rural Idaho, Koontz shoots bull'seyes at target issues that shape his theme, including assisted suicide, substance abuse, the irresponsibility of the counterculture and the goofiness of true-believer ET enthusiasts." Publ Wkly

Seize the night; by Dean Koontz. Bantam Bks. 1999 401p o.p.
ISBN 0-553-10665-1 LC 98-31410

In this second novel featuring Christopher Snow, "the horrifying tale of Chris's hometown, Moonlight Bay, continues to unfold. Chris and his tight band of friends take up the search for four missing children in this town, where experiments with a genetically engineered retrovirus have begun to turn several local residents into creatures that are less than human. Koontz successfully blends his special brand of suspense from generous measures of mystery, horror, sf, and the techno-thriller genre. But his greatest triumph in this series is the creation of Christopher Snow, a thought-provoking narrator with a facility for surfer-lingo and dark humor who, despite his extreme situation, is an undeniably believable character." Libr J

Sole survivor; a novel. Knopf 1997 321p o.p.
ISBN 0-679-42526-8 LC 96-80209

"Joe Carpenter, a former California crime reporter, loses his wife and daughters in a mysterious plane crash. Soon, a series of strange visits, violent chases, and quasispiritual encounters points to an amazing idea: that a scientist aboard the doomed aircraft had discovered irrevocable proof of life after death and that a secret government organization will stop at nothing to keep this knowledge from the public." Libr J

"Mr. Koontz is a master of his trade. Sure, he sometimes gets bogged down in unnecessary, flowery descriptions, and his paranoid perspective is often unbelievable and downright annoying. But he does know how to tell an exciting story." N Y Times Book Rev

Koontz, Dean R. (Dean Ray), 1945—*Continued*

Strangers. Putnam 1986 526p o.p.
LC 85-25677

"Eight characters—all strangers to each other—form the core of the novel. Each is plagued by suspiciously similar fears and anxieties. Ernie Block, who runs a Nevada motel, fears the dark. Ginger Weiss, a Boston cardiology resident, suffers from panic attacks. Southern California horror novelist Dom Corvaisis is vexed with somnambulism. These and other seemingly disparate characters share only one link aside from their bewildering array of related symptoms—all had spent three days during the previous July at Block's motel, not far from a secret military depository." Booklist

The taking; [by] Dean Koontz. Bantam Bks. 2004 388p $27
ISBN 0-553-80250-X

"In a small California town, Molly and Neil Sloan wake in the night to find the world experiencing the communication breakdown and extreme weather phenomena that will presage an extraterrestrial annexation of Earth. Along with the assistance of some intelligent and intuitive dogs . . ., Molly and Neil try to save as many children as they can from being 'taken' or killed outright. In The Taking, Koontz continues his ongoing exploration of the capacity of human nature for hope, goodness, and innocence in the face of evil." Libr J

Velocity; [by] Dean Koontz. Bantam Books 2005 400p $27
ISBN 0-55380-415-4

"Billy Wiles, a 30-something bartender and former writer, is content with his solitary Napa County existence listening to 'beer-based psychoanalysis' from tavern regulars; visiting his hospitalized, comatose fiancée, Barbara; and carving wood sculptures. But the simple life gets mighty complicated when he finds a note with a deadly, time-sensitive ultimatum: he must choose between the death of a young schoolteacher or an elderly humanitarian in six hours. Reluctant local sheriff Lanny Olsen dismisses it as a joke until a comely teacher is found strangled and another threatening note appears—offering even less time for Billy to decide the fate of two more people. Who would have guessed that one of those people would be Olsen? After his friend's murder, Billy finds that the cunning killer has gained access to every aspect of his life as the ultimatums grow increasingly more personal. . . . Graphic, fast-paced action, well-developed characters and relentless, nail-biting scenes show Koontz at the top of his game." Publ Wkly

Watchers. Putnam 1987 352p o.p.
LC 86-22687

"When the Russians sabotage a genetic research project in California, two mutated creatures escape from the lab. One is a golden retriever with high enough intelligence to think and communicate with humans; the other is the Outsider, a vicious monster created from a baboon and bred to kill. Both the man who befriends and adopts the dog and his new bride find themselves stalked by government agents anxious to find the dog, a particularly repulsive Mafia hit man intent on stealing him, and the Outsider, with whom the dog is linked telepathically." Libr J

Korda, Michael, 1933-

Curtain; a novel. Summit Bks. 1991 378p o.p.
LC 90-23198

"Robert Vance is a superb Shakespearean actor. He falls in love with an actress, Felicia Lisle, whose fastidious beauty conceals fierce passion. Unable to escape their marriages, they become Britain's favorite adulterous celebrity couple, playing the role of lovers both on stage and in private. Korda opens this page-turner with a prologue set 40 years in the future and hinting at dark, long-hidden secrets. He then flashes back to the 1940s when Vance and Felicia are stranded in Hollywood, broke after a disastrous attempt at taking *Romeo and Juliet* on the road in the U.S. Felicia, drinking and pill-popping, is on the verge of a breakdown, and Robby is anxious to return to London and serve in the RAF. . . . Having set his novel on stage, Korda can pull out all the stops—nothing is too theatrical. And it's a hit." Booklist

The fortune. Summit Bks. 1989 481p o.p.
LC 88-37980

"The wealthy, snobbish Bannerman family is a fictional hybrid of the Rockefellers and the Binghams. It's bad enough that Arthur Bannerman has the poor taste to die in the bed of an attractive young woman. But when she declares herself his widow and delivers a will giving her control of the family fortune, his son Robert and the redoubtable matriarch Eleanor haul out the heavy artillery. Korda has a wonderful ear for bitchy, brittle society chatter, and he takes satirical swipes in every direction." Publ Wkly

The immortals; a novel. Poseidon Press 1992 559p o.p.
ISBN 0-671-74526-3 LC 92-22265

A "novel about the love affair between John F. Kennedy and Marilyn Monroe. The theme it rests on is this: as JFK's star ascended, MM's descended, and as their stars crossed, heat was definitely generated. Korda understands politics as well as fatal attraction, so his fiction is several notches above your basic steamy romance." Booklist

Worldly goods. Random House 1982 353p o.p.
LC 81-40213

A saga about a "Hungarian family torn apart by various fortunes, a terrible betrayal back in Nazi days (there are flashbacks to Hitler, Himmler, and the Holocaust), and insatiable lust for money, power, and vengeance now. Paul Foster (née Grunwald) survived Auschwitz and has at last amassed the worldly wherewithal to avenge his father, all unbeknownst to his betraying uncle and cousin. Foster is a cold fish (though there's a heroine to adhere to him), but he only wants to take enough fortune away from his uncle to make him cry 'uncle.'" Saturday Rev

"At once a Holocaust novel from a new point of view, and a look at love, hate, power, and sex in the stratosphere of the modern corporation, this book is tightly constructed." Libr J

Korelitz, Jean Hanff, 1961-

The Sabbathday River. Farrar, Straus & Giroux 1999 499p o.p.
ISBN 0-374-25323-4 LC 98-6636

Korelitz, Jean Hanff, 1961-—*Continued*

"Naomi Roth, a New York transplant living in a small New Hampshire town, finds herself drawn to the plight of Heather, a young social outcast who is accused of murdering her baby. Though a local in the area for nine years, Naomi still feels like an outsider herself and is compelled to offer support to Heather when the townspeople rush to judgment over the case and subsequent trial." Libr J

"Korelitz securely navigates the scientific shoals surrounding the crime. Her rich, often lyrical language occasionally becomes fussy but in general serves her well in conveying local color and atmosphere and in describing the moments of passion and betrayal in this compelling study of modern women with old-fashioned desires." Publ Wkly

Kornbluth, C. M. (Cyril M.), 1923-1958

(jt. auth) Pohl, F. The space merchants

Kornbluth, Cyril M. *See* Kornbluth, C. M. (Cyril M.), 1923-1958

Koryta, Michael

Tonight I said goodbye; Michael Koryta. 1st ed. Thomas Dunne Books\St. Martin's Minotaur 2004 290p $21.95

ISBN 0-312-33245-9 LC 2004-46781

"The Cleveland police would charge private investigator Wayne Weston with murdering his wife and daughter except that their bodies can't be found and he's dead, apparently a suicide. Weston's father isn't buying it, however, and he hires private investigators Lincoln Perry and Joe Pritchard to clear his son's name and find his family. Perry is a former cop whose cheating ex-fiancée set him off on a bender that cost him his job. Pritchard, his old partner, is ready to retire and become what all retired cops become, a P.I. The hardboiled cliché works beautifully here as these two men find themselves chasing Russian Mafiya, a real estate mogul, and an ex-Marine while dodging bullets, cops, and the FBI. The Cleveland setting is a nice change from the usual East Coast/West Coast locales." Libr J

Kosinski, Jerzy N., 1933-1991

Being there; [by] Jerzy Kosinski. Harcourt Brace Jovanovich 1971 c1970 142p o.p.

"An illiterate gardener, Chance, knows the world only through his gardening and by watching television, to which he is addicted. Without education or any identifiable background, he is evicted into the outside world when his employer dies. He makes horticultural analogies to current events, which give him a reputation for wisdom that he really does not have, and which catapult him into national prominence. Chance's simple statements are interpreted by his listeners to be profound observations, and we see him being considered for positions of great importance. This is a satire on human behavior in the worlds of power, government, and the media." Shapiro. Fic for Youth. 3d edition

The devil tree; [by] Jerzy Kosinski. Harcourt Brace Jovanovich 1973 208p o.p.

This novel "confronts the disintegration of the American dream as seen through the eyes of Jonathan James Whalen, the man-who-has-everything. For Whalen and many of the people who surround him, the American dream has become the American nightmare. Their efforts to escape their roots become a frenetic search to find their roots, until, like the devil tree, they get turned upside down and confirm the fact of their own extinction. Jonathan Whalen is as empty as the life he leads, although on the surface he is a man who can be and do anything he wants." Publ Wkly

The painted bird; [by] Jerzy Kosinski. 2nd Modern Library ed. Modern Lib. 1983 c1965 234p o.p.

LC 82-42869

First published 1965 by Houghton Mifflin

"In Eastern Europe during World War II a ten-year-old boy is separated from his parents and struggles to survive in primitive villages where he is viewed as an unwanted outsider. Dark-haired and dark-eyed, he is unlike the Polish villagers among whom he tries to find refuge. He is the gypsy, the 'painted bird,' and savage abuse is heaped upon him time after time. He has, nevertheless, the will to transcend the sadism and superstition of these ignorant people." Shapiro. Fic for Youth. 3d edition

Passion play; [by] Jerzy Kosinski. St. Martin's Press 1979 271p o.p.

LC 79-5035

"Fabian, the protagonist, is a peripatetic polo-player who travels in an hermetic recreational vehicle, his Van-Home. He is past his prime, obsessed with aging and poverty, stricken from the ranks of 'good team players,' seeking financial support through odd jobs and friendships on the playing fields of the idle rich and by one-on-one polo jousts. This latter-day Knight of the Sad Countenance is also obsessed with sexual dominance, proving his mastery with a string of underage Dulcineas." West Coast Rev Books

The author's "descriptions of equestrian combat belong on the same shelf with Hemingway and Tolstoy. His accounts of a South American republic where the main sources of power are the ox and the jet are masterpieces of irony and pure narrative. He tirelessly examines what he terms 'the regency of pain.' Like Dostoyevsky's, Kosinski's characters explore their own souls, always reaching for limits." Time

Kostova, Elizabeth

The historian; a novel; Elizabeth Kostova. 1st ed. Little, Brown and Co 2005 642p $25.95

ISBN 0-316-01177-0 LC 2004-22563

"In the early 20th century, Paul, a young graduate student, learns from his advisor, Professor Rossi, that Prince Dracula is still alive as one of the undead. When the professor disappears one terrifying night, Paul goes in search of his mentor, whom he knows to be in Dracula's clutches. His search takes him to secret archives and libraries of ancient monasteries throughout Eastern Europe; he is joined by his daughter, his wife, and friends, all historians and scholars themselves." Libr J

"Kostova's vampire is no campy Lugosi knockoff but

Kostova, Elizabeth—*Continued*

a blend of the cunning, powerful count who debuts in Bram Stoker's 1897 classic novel and the actual Dracula, Vlad the Impaler, a 15th-century Romanian prince who was both a nationalist hero and a sadistic torturer. Blending history and myth, Kostova has fashioned a version so fresh that when a stake is finally driven through a heart, it inspires the tragic shock of something happening for the very first time." Newsweek

Kotzwinkle, William, 1938-

The bear went over the mountain. Doubleday 1996 306p o.p.
ISBN 0-385-48428-3 LC 96-2296

"Kotzwinkle has imagined a disconsolate Maine professor, Arthur Bramhall, who sets out to write a bestseller, only to have a bear steal it, thinking it's something to eat. This is no ordinary bear, however; he has aspirations to becoming a person. . . . What better way to establish an identity than by becoming a celebrity novelist? Soon, the bear has found a pseudonym, Hal Jam, an agent and a publisher. With his distinctively masculine presence, and a monosyllabic way of talking that reminds many of Hemingway, he's on his way to stardom with a novel that everyone agrees has its roots deep in the natural world." Publ Wkly

"This genuine parable for our time is as full of truth as it is of humor." Nation

E.T.; the extra-terrestrial; a novel. Putnam 1982 246p o.p.
LC 82-9078

"A ten million year old alien botanist is accidentally marooned on Earth. He is befriended by three children and in particular by Elliott, whose bedroom closet becomes his hideout. With their help he learns something of our planet's bewildering ways, puts together a beacon to call for rescue and thrives on a diet of M&Ms, Oreos and, even more important, the children's love. Of course, the government suspects his presence and is hunting him, but after he is captured Elliott helps him escape in time to rendezvous with his ship." Publ Wkly

"Kotzwinkle's many gifts, particularly for realistic detail and black humor, make this a book capable of standing on its own merits apart from the motion picture." Booklist

Kozak, Harley Jane

Dating dead men; Harley Jane Kozak. 1st ed. Doubleday 2004 326p $22.95
ISBN 0-385-51018-7 LC 2003-46236

"Los Angeles greeting-card artist Wollie Shelley is dating forty men in sixty days as research for a radio talk-show host's upcoming book, How to Avoid Getting Dumped All the Time. Wollie is meeting plenty of eligible bachelors but not falling in love, not until she stumbles over a dead body en route to Rio Pescado a state-run mental hospital and is momentarily taken hostage by a charismatic 'doctor' who is on the run from the Mob. Wollie fears that her beloved brother, a paranoid schizophrenic living at Rio Pescado, is involved in the murder, so rather than go to the authorities, she decides to solve the crime on her own." Publisher's note

"Kozak has written a finely calibrated story about a cheerfully seedy section of Los Angeles with characters of all ages all very human and real. While not stupid, her heroine is no superhero either. And the eccentricity of characters and plot always stops short of being annoying or unrealistic." Washington Post

Krantz, Judith

Mistral's daughter. Crown 1983 c1982 531p o.p.
LC 82-17966

"Three generations of Lunel women are intimately involved with Julien Mistral, France's greatest artist. Maggy is his model, the inspiration for a series of remarkable nude paintings in 1925, and he is her first lover. Years later Teddy, star of her mother Maggy's New York modeling agency, meets Mistral on assignment and lightening strikes; she becomes his mistress and the mother of Fauve. And Mistral's daughter Fauve, though an 'enfante adulterine,' has some of his talent and brightens his life before their estrangement." Libr J

The author "possesses an undeniable talent for plot-weaving and descriptive detail." Best Sellers

Krauss, Nicole

The history of love. Norton 2005 252p $23.95
ISBN 0-393-06034-9 LC 2005-00936

"A boy in Poland falls in love and writes a book when World War II arrives, and both the love and the book are lost. Leo Gursky, now in his eighties and living in New York City, struggles to be noticed each day so that people will know he has not yet died. Meanwhile, 14-year-old Alma Singer wants her brother to be normal and her mother to be happy again after the death of Alma's father. In a quest for the story behind her name, Alma and Leo find each other, and Leo learns that the book he wrote so long ago has not been lost." Libr J

"Beyond the vigorous whiplash that keeps Ms. Krauss's [book] moving (and keeps its reader off-balance until a stunning finale), this novel is tightly packed with ingenious asides. They range from parodying various publications' characteristic obituaries of a very famous writer, a man who was best known for a single, ecstatic five-page paragraph (Ms. Krauss perfectly mimics the syntax of both The Times and The New Republic) to skewering the kind of editor whom all writers dread." N Y Times (Late N Y Ed)

Man walks into a room. Talese 2002 248p o.p.
ISBN 0-385-50399-7 LC 2001-53699

"When a tumor in his brain is discovered and removed, Samson Greene, an English professor in his thirties, finds himself afflicted by a peculiar kind of amnesia: he cannot remember anything that happened after he was twelve. Even as he struggles to connect with his wife, Anna, he thinks that he might prefer the blankness of his new life. Samson's loss takes place against a backdrop of secret experiments on human memory and the social implications of atomic testing, but it is his shadow-filled scrutiny of intimacy—as he wonders why he might have married this beautiful stranger, and whether he can love her—that is the book's real strength." New Yorker

Krentz, Jayne Ann, 1948-

For works written by this author under other names see Quick, Amanda, 1948-

Krentz, Jayne Ann, 1948-—*Continued*

Lost and found. Putnam 2001 341p o.p.
ISBN 0-399-14669-5 LC 00-44563

"Cady Briggs, a Santa Barbara-based art consultant specializing in decorative arts and antiques, has been doing some work for Mack Easton, who runs a company called Lost and Found that tracks the movement of art and antiquities. When her eccentric aunt Vesta, an excellent swimmer, drowns, Cady has a hunch that something isn't right, especially since Vesta left controlling shares of Chatelaine, her tony art gallery, to her instead of to cousin Sylvia, Chatelaine's much more business-oriented CEO. . . . Cady enlists Mack to help uncover the truth." Booklist

"This is romantic suspense at its most enjoyable, enhanced by Krentz's . . . trademark humor and quirky characters." Libr J

Smoke in mirrors. Putnam 2002 320p $23.95
ISBN 0-399-14792-6 LC 2001-19361

"The news of Meredith Spooner's death comes as no surprise to her half-sister, Leonora Hutton; after all, Meredith was a con artist who was adept at making enemies. But when Thomas Walker, a victim of Meredith's most recent scam, confronts Leonora, demanding that she help him find the $1.5 million that Meredith filched from the Bethany Walker memorial fund and intimating that Meredith may have been murdered, Leonora drops her reference desk position in California to do some amateur sleuthing in Wing Cove, Wash." Publ Wkly

"The politics of academe, eerie antique mirrors, secret passages, and psychic contact contribute a haunting quality to Krentz's enticing blend of suspense and top-notch romance." Booklist

Kress, Nancy, 1948-

Beggars & choosers. TOR Bks. 1994 315p o.p.
ISBN 0-312-85749-7 LC 94-21753

"A Tom Doherty Associates book"

Sequel to Beggars in Spain

"As a byproduct of their genetic mental enhancements, the Sleepless neither sleep nor age. For those reasons, they are reviled by the unmodified majority of humans. Yet in a world of overpopulation, chronic joblessness, environmental depletion, and uncontrolled plagues of nanotechnological origin, the Sleepless may hold the key to humanity's salvation—if only they can be persuaded to come out of their self-imposed hiding." Libr J

"Kress's work remains strongly character driven, an approach that in her hands raises social-speculation sf to about as high a level as one can reasonably expect." Booklist

Followed by Beggars ride

Beggars in Spain. Morrow 1993 438p o.p.
LC 92-25070

"An AvoNova book"

Based on a novella of the same title

In this novel, "genetic enhancements have placed Leisha Camden and a few other individuals in a category of their own. Smarter and healthier than normal humans, born without the need to sleep, the 'Sleepless'—as they are called—grow up in a world that turns increasingly hostile toward the super-achievers in their midst." Libr J

"This book is an intellectual roller-coaster ride, supplying no simple conclusions about right and wrong, and racing along with its brisk prose, stimulating ideas, and a variety of challenging characters." SLJ

Followed by Beggars & choosers

Beggars ride. TOR Bks. 1996 304p o.p.
ISBN 0-312-85817-5 LC 96-19956

"A Tom Doherty Associates book"

In this concluding volume of the Beggars trilogy, "the near-utopia that the genetically altered Sleepless finally realized is . . . well on the way to crumbling under the onslaught of warfare waged with tailored viruses. Society is devolving into a host of subgroups, some of which are virtually abandoning technology and surviving or failing as much through luck as through resistance to the viruses. Gradually, communication among tribes is restored, lost knowledge regained, disused knowledge again put to use, and the survival of the race assured." Booklist

"The scale of Kress's vision is large as she lays out a drama that-convincingly if unsurprisingly-argues that moral quandaries can't be addressed by technology." Publ Wkly

Probability moon. TOR Bks. 2000 334p $23.95
ISBN 0-312-87406-5 LC 00-27117

"A Tom Doherty Associates book"

"In this novel set in the distant future, humans explore the universe through tunnels that propel them to the far reaches of space. The most recent expedition takes an anthropological team to World, a planet with a peaceful sentient civilization. Anthropological answers are not all that humans seek on World. A covert military operation accompanies the team to study a strange moon that might have military significance." Voice Youth Advocates

"The climax of the book is a four-way conflict among the scientists, the two alien races, and the scientists' military superiors, each charging from a different corner, so to speak. Kress' characterizations are as sound as ever, but many will be agreeably surprised at her proficiency with military hardware and action scenes. Very impressive." Booklist

Probability sun. TOR Bks. 2001 348p $24.95
ISBN 0-312-87407-3 LC 2001-27119

"A Tom Doherty Associates book"

This sequel to Probability moon "continues humanity's war against the alien Fallers, a war humanity is losing. It again shows scientists and the military at odds if not in outright conflict while portraying the strengths and limitations of both with admirable even-handedness. A shipload of scientists has come to study the alien artifact discovered on the planet World, and the ship's military crew is holding the only Faller POW as a secret captive." Booklist

Krist, Gary

Chaos theory; a novel. Random House 2000 347p o.p.
ISBN 0-375-50080-4 LC 99-13411

"On a whim, two middle-class high-school boys, one African American, the other white, venture into one of Washington, D.C.'s less savory neighborhoods to buy drugs. . . . A wacko with a gun greets them in an alley, and they break his arm in the course of escaping. Imagine their surprise when police question them regarding a dead undercover cop found in the same alley. A caring

Krist, Gary—*Continued*

teacher enlists the aid of an FBI agent, who steps in to uncover a scam involving corruption at the highest level of city government." Booklist

"Spinning a plausible situation into an extraordinary story while training a marksman's eye on character, Krist has conceived a sleek and thoughtful thriller." Publ Wkly

Krüger, Michael, 1943-

The cello player; translated from the German by Andrew Shields. Harcourt 2004 200p $23

ISBN 0-15-100591-5 LC 2003-13369

The narrator of this novel is a "middle-aged German composer who writes serious avant-garde music, but makes a living writing theme music for television. When Judit, an ambitious young cello player from Budapest (whose mother was once the composer's lover and who may or may not be his daughter), shows up on his doorstep, he agrees to take her in while she studies at the conservatory in Munich." Publisher's notes

"Packed into this small, powerful novel is a dazzling array of well-chiseled, colorful characters, extracted from the grand tableau of history and from the author's imagination." New York Times Book Rev

Kundera, Milan

The book of laughter and forgetting; translated from the Czech by Michael Henry Heim. Knopf 1980 228p o.p.

LC 80-7657

First published 1979 in France

"The novel is written in seven parts with an interwoven structure that the author likened to polyphonic music. The repetition of incidents, characters, and themes provides *The Book of Laughter and Forgetting* with its formal shape. Memories, which the characters want to keep or to forget, are a recurring subject, as is laughter, which is as often ironic as joyous." Merriam-Webster's Ency of Lit

Identity; a novel; translated from the French by Linda Asher. HarperFlamingo 1998 168p o.p.

ISBN 0-06-017564-8 LC 97-31907

"Recently divorced ad executive Chantal, on a vacation with her younger boyfriend, Jean-Marc, believes that she is too old to be considered attractive by other men. For Chantal, identity is defined by the perceptions of strangers. . . . When she returns from her vacation, she begins to receive letters from an anonymous admirer. She suspects each new man she encounters to be the mysterious scribe and fantasizes how each might perceive her. Gradually, these letters, along with a few dreams, affect how Chantal views herself and her relationship with Jean-Marc, until her feelings and identity become unrecognizable both to her lover and to herself." Publ Wkly

Ignorance; a novel; translated from the French by Linda Asher. HarperCollins Pubs. 2002 195p o.p.

ISBN 0-06-000209-3

"After nearly 20 years in Paris and after the fall of Czech communism, Irena considers moving back to her country and returns for a visit. In the airport, she meets Josef, also an immigrant, with whom she shared a single evening years ago in Prague. Irena remembers their initial meeting with detailed intensity and has always regretted its abrupt, chaste conclusion. Josef doesn't even recognize Irena, but he lies and a passionate climax follows." Booklist

"Kundera knows how to keep us turning the pages. He cuts his scenes skillfully, withholding essential information. . . . His characters may not linger on in the mind. But he is able in Ignorance to turn his house of ideas into a believable and moving edifice." New Leader

Immortality; translated from the Czech by Peter Kussi. Grove Weidenfeld 1991 345p o.p.

LC 90-28628

"Kundera, himself a prominent character in the circular narrative, here contrasts the troubled, comic relationships among Goethe; his wife, Christiane; and Goethe's much younger friend Bettina von Arnim to the modern-day triangle of three imaginary Parisians: Paul; his wife, Agnes; and Agnes's sister Laura." Publ Wkly

"Immortality swings easily, almost imperceptibly, from narrative to rumination and back again, collapsing the distinction between action and concepts. . . . Out of a story about contemporary neuroses, Kundera has fabricated a context in which everything, literally, can be claimed to matter. What is more, the author indulges this obsessiveness without ever droning or turning out a dull page. In its inventiveness and its dazzling display of what written words can convey, Immortality gives fiction back its good name." Time

The joke. definitive version, fully revised by the author. HarperCollins Pubs. 1992 317p o.p.

LC 91-58349

Original Czech edition, 1967; first English translation published 1969 by Coward, McCann

In this novel "a young communist intellectual, Ludvik, is imprisoned, then stigmatized for life for having written an irreverent postcard to a girlfriend ('Optimism is the opium of the people! . . . Long live Trotsky!'). Years later he seeks revenge in another 'joke'; he will cold-bloodedly seduce the wife, Helena, of the party leader who denounced him." Newsweek

"Kundera's brilliance resides in his ability to strip away the lies and disguises which Ludvik and the others need to survive, and which their society has institutionalized and sanctified." New Repub

Laughable loves; translated from the Czech by Suzanne Rappaport. Knopf 1974 242p o.p.

Original Czech edition, 1970

Contents: The hitchhiking game; Let the old dead make room for the young dead; Nobody will laugh; The golden apple of eternal desire; Symposium; Dr. Havel after ten years; Edward and God

"The stories in [this volume] are buoyantly energetic and virtuosic. . . . The politics here is sexual: male dominance and impotence, role-playing and fantasizing detonate with startling effect." Newsweek

Slowness; translated from the French by Linda Asher. HarperCollins Pubs. 1996 156p o.p.

LC 96-6253

"The narrator (the writer himself, 'Milanku) and his wife decide to vacation at a château, and en route he immediately begins meditating on slowness versus speed when they find themselves impeding the progress of the

Kundera, Milan—*Continued*

driver behind them. Before the end, Kundera has converted his philosophical ruminations into a . . . fictional piece in which the action takes place at the château. The writer sets up parallel stories of seduction; one set in the eighteenth century, the other contemporary." Booklist

"Mr. Kundera comes closer to polemic here than in his other fiction, but he is fiercely defending the 'spirit of complexity' that the novel embodies. . . . So it seems almost churlish to point out shortcomings in a writer of his spirit of play, breadth of reach and perspicacity—all admirably at work once again in 'Slowness.'" N Y Times Book Rev

The unbearable lightness of being; translated from the Czech by Michael Henry Heim. Harper & Row 1984 314p o.p.

LC 83-48363

"Set against the background of Czechoslovakia in the 1960s, the novel concerns a young Czech physician who substitutes a series of erotic adventures over which he thinks he can maintain control for becoming involved in his country's politics, where he feels he can have no power or freedom. Inevitably, he is drawn into Czechoslovakia's political unrest. In a parallel vein, he is forced to choose among the women with whom he is involved." Merriam-Webster's Ency of Lit

Kunetka, James W., 1944-

(jt. auth) Strieber, W. Warday

Kuniczak, W. S., 1930-

The thousand hour day. HarperCollins Pubs. 1967 c1966 628p o.p.

First volume of a trilogy that includes The march (1979) and Valedictory (1983)

"The time of this novel is 1939; the setting, Poland. Mr. Kuniczak covers the first 1000 hours of World War II when the small, ill-equipped Polish army made a magnificent holding action before the final surrender to the attacking Germans. Against the speeding background of the war evolves the story of General January Prus, a gentle man of strong character, and his influence on his government and on the men and women around him." Libr J

The story "usually sustains its interest. The few flat scenes are more than overbalanced by compelling episodes. . . . There are the vivid battle scenes. . . . We also see a good deal of the countryside, with its peasants and hunters and wandering armies." Saturday Rev

Kunkel, Benjamin

Indecision; a novel. Random House 2005 241p $21.95

ISBN 1-4000-6345-0 LC 2004-62894

"Twentysomething Manhattanite Dwight Wilmerding suffers from a fictional condition called abulia–the inability to make up his mind. Paralyzed by indecisiveness about his tech-support job, his complicated love life (there's Dutch bombshell Natasha who lives in Ecuador and coy Vaneetha in New York), and a distressing attraction to his psychiatrist sister, Dwight signs up for the trial drug Abulinix, which claims to tackle tentativeness with a little blue-and-white pill. Dwight travels to South America, only to discover that even the most potent pharmaceuticals are virtually powerless against the forces of fate." Booklist

"Ever the clever chef, Kunkel reduces the sprawling, indigestible postmodern novel to an amiable pop confection that goes down like a milkshake. The result is a stylistic triumph of sorts. The half-serious pastiche is the ideal vehicle for bright apercus, capers, riffs, and dreamy ruminations." New Leader

Kunzru, Hari

The impressionist. Dutton 2002 383p o.p.

ISBN 0-525-94642-X LC 2001-47137

"Until 1918, his 15th year, spoiled Pran Nath believes that he is the son of a wealthy Kashmiri merchant and a disturbed woman, Amrita, who died giving birth to him. When the housekeeper reveals that he is actually an Englishman's child, and thus a despised half-breed, he's thrown out on the street. After an involuntary stay in a brothel, a stint as a servant in the depraved household of the Nawab of Fatehpur, and a sojourn at a Bombay missionary's home, he moves on to England, where he pretends to be an orphaned heir, Jonathan Bridgeman." Publ Wkly

This novel "includes a multitude of richly imagined characters. A bold, unfashionably omniscient voice narrates the story as it tackles such subjects as race, class, colonialism, and the roots of personal identity" New Leader

Transmission. Dutton 2004 276p $24.95

ISBN 0-525-94760-4 LC 2004-3295

"This novel introduces a daydreaming Indian computer geek whose luxurious fantasies about life in America are shaken when he accepts a California job offer. Lonely and naive, Arjun Mehta bides his time as a lowly assistant virus tester, pining away for his free-spirited colleague Christine. Despite building digital creatures in a feeble attempt to enhance his job security, Arjun gets laid-off like so many of his Silicon Valley peers. In an act of desperation to keep his job, he releases a mischievous but destructive virus around the globe that has major unintended consequences." Publisher's note

"Transmission is a tragicomedy, a subtle exploration of the relations between feeling, fiction and technology. . . . Martin Amis is a clear influence on Kunzru. His characters have the same foam-rubber resilience, his women are devastatingly sexy, his baddies grotesquely bad. This, together with a romping plot, makes Transmission enormous fun. It is also a thoughtful, and thought-provoking novel, which engages with important questions about twenty-first-century life." Times Lit Suppl

Kurtz, Katherine

The harrowing of Gwynedd. Ballantine Bks. 1989 384p (Heirs of Saint Camber, v1) o.p.

LC 88-7414

"A Del Rey book"

This is the first volume of The heirs of Saint Camber trilogy; other titles are: King Javan's year (1992) and The bastard prince (1994). An earlier Deryni tale: The quest for Saint Camber, is entered below

This is a "tale of the events immediately after Saint Camber's death. The persecution of the Deryni is widespread and brutal, their own leadership is beginning to

Kurtz, Katherine—*Continued*
descend from the high culture of Camber's time to the petty politics of a later era, and Camber's daughter must face death to continue her father's work. Kurtz also manages to be sufficiently graphic about the violence without being gratuitous, and in short has added another well-told tale to the Deryni canon." Booklist

King Kelson's bride. Ace Bks. 2000 387p il (Histories of King Kelson, v4) o.p.
ISBN 0-441-00732-5 LC 99-48047
A fantasy "set in a land analogous to medieval Wales and featuring the Deryni, a human minority with magical powers. It also resolves the longstanding question of when King Kelson Haldane of Gwynedd is going to get married. He has missed two opportunities, one due to a lady's death and the other to family treachery." Publ Wkly

The quest for Saint Camber. Ballantine Bks. 1986 xxvi, 435p (Histories of King Kelson, v3) o.p.
LC 86-8249
"A Del Rey book"
Earlier titles in the King Kelson series are The bishop's heir (1984) and The King's justice (1985)
"The reported death of King Kelson on a quest for the tomb of the Deryni Saint Camber throws the Kingdom of Gwynedd into turmoil. As Kelson's friends set out to search for the truth, a power struggle at court brings deceit and murder in its wake. [This installment in the author's] Deryni series . . . skillfully combines magic with the medieval in a novel that will appeal to fantasy readers and medievalists alike." Libr J

St. Patrick's gargoyle. Ace Bks. 2001 233p $21.95
ISBN 0-441-00725-2 LC 00-36275
"When Dublin's St. Patrick's Cathedral becomes the target of an act of vandalism, the gargoyle guardian of the building enlists the aid of an aging Knight of Malta to assist him in his pursuit of the vandals. Combining an interest in Irish history with snatches of Templar lore, the author. . . creates a story of angelic powers and demonic forces locked in an eternal struggle." Libr J

The temple and the stone; [by] Katherine Kurtz and Deborah Turner Harris. Warner Bks. 1998 456p o.p.
ISBN 0-446-52260-0 LC 98-14344
"Following a vision that foretells the formation of a new Temple of Solomon in Scotland, Brother Arnault de Saint Clair, a member of a secret magical order within the Order of the Knights Templar, becomes involved in the struggle for Scottish independence. The authors . . . vividly recreate one of Scottish history's most compelling periods, as Robert the Bruce and William Wallace share the limelight with fictional, but no less credible, characters." Libr J

Two crowns for America. Bantam Bks. 1996 375p o.p.
LC 95-32372
This novel presents an "alternate American Revolution driven by the occult machinations of an age-old Master as well as destiny and Masonic solidarity. . . . The Wallace family—Jacobite Andrew; his son Simon; Simon's wife, Arabella; and Arabella's brother, Justin Carmichael—provide viewpoints for most of the important action." Publ Wkly
"Vivid portrayals of Washington and Charles Edward Stuart ('Bonnie Prince Charlie') are at the core of the book, which is otherwise well up to Kurtz's historically well-informed standards." Booklist

Kurzweil, Allen

The grand complication. Hyperion 2001 359p o.p.
ISBN 0-7868-6603-9 LC 2001-16811
"Henry James Jesson III, the kind of wealthy eccentric who seems to exist only to send other men on wild-goose chases, hires Alexander Short, a down-on-his-luck librarian, to help solve the mystery of an eighteenth-century cabinet of wonders that is missing one of its objects. Eager to escape his problems with his wife, a French artist and pop-up-book designer, Short discovers that the missing item is a fantastically precise timepiece that allegedly belonged to Marie Antoinette, and he is soon consumed by the quest for the watch. Kurzweil's intricately constructed novel has no shortage of esoterica, and the author's fondness for sexual comedy supplies a welcome counterweight." New Yorker

KuznetSsSov, Anatoliĭ Vasil´evich *See* Anatoli, A., 1929-1979

L

La Farge, Oliver, 1901-1963

Laughing Boy. Houghton Mifflin 1929 302p o.p.
"This novel takes place in the early years of the twentieth century in Navajo country in the American Southwest. It is the story of the ill-fated love of Laughing Boy, worker in silver and maker of songs, and Slim Girl, whose education in American schools has embittered her. The reader is immersed in their tender romance but also learns a great deal about the culture and philosophical outlook of the Native American." Shapiro. Fic for Youth. 3d edition

La Plante, Lynda

Cold blood. Random House 1997 402p o.p.
LC 98-107026
First published 1996 in the United Kingdom
"One night during the Mardi Gras in New Orleans, 18-year-old Anna Louise Caley vanishes. Eleven months later, when all other efforts have failed, the girl's mother (aging film star Elizabeth Caley) hires an ex-cop and recovering alcoholic named Lorrain Page and offers her a $1 million bonus if she finds Anna Louise, dead or alive. The investigation leads Lorraine and her team into a world of drugs, booze, adultery, suicide, voodoo, and murder." Libr J
"The mystery of what happened to Anna Louise is interesting, but the real suspense concerns whether Page—who finds herself drinking again and in bed with the missing girl's father—will fall apart." Publ Wkly

Labiner, Norah, 1967-

Miniatures. Coffee House Press 2002 381p $23
ISBN 1-566-89136-1 LC 2002-71283
"Fern Jacobi, the restless 29-year-old narrator of this eccentric novel . . . recounts an unhappy two months spent as a housekeeper in the home of two expatriate writers from America named Owen and Brigid Lieb. Owen is nearly three decades older than Brigid. The house where the Liebs live in Ireland carries the memory of Owen's first wife, Franny, a novelist who died of either suicide or murder when she was electrocuted in a bathtub." (NY Times Book NY Times Book

"This is a haunting novel, written in the first person and switching from past to present, from Fern's life to the other characters' lives. It slowly and achingly reveals secrets, evokes literary figures from the Bronte sisters to Marcel Proust, and explores biography as a literary form." Booklist

LaBute, Neil

Seconds of pleasure; stories. Grove Press 2004 221p $22
ISBN 0-8021-1785-6 LC 2004-49137
Contents: Perfect; Maraschino; Timeshare; Booboo; Opportunity; Spring break; Wait; Layover; A second of pleasure; Look at her; Ravishing; Open all night; Full service; Loose change; Switzerland; Los Feliz; Some do it naturally; Grand slam; Whitecap; Soft target

"All in all, expect the unexpected as some simple truths are revealed during these seconds of pleasure. Terse and potent with sharp, realistic dialog, these stories reflect LaBute's harsh and often unnerving view of human nature." Libr J

Lackey, Mercedes

The fairy godmother. Harlequin 2004 432p $24.95
ISBN 0-373-80202-1
This fantasy is "set in a world where The Tradition tries its magical—and surreptitious-best to force the characters into their 'legendary' roles. But things sometimes go awry, and when Elena is denied her predestined Cinderella role because her kingdom's prince is too young, she is chosen as an apprentice by the local Fairy Godmother and ends up creating a legend of her own. A spirited, resourceful, though somewhat impulsive heroine, a prince who needs to learn a lesson in manners, humility, and compassion, and a host of magical creatures—including some delightful house elves and besotted unicorns—result in a lively, humorous fantasy romance." Libr J

Firebird. TOR Bks. 1996 352p o.p.
LC 96-23841
"A Tom Doherty Associates book"

In this coming-of-age fantasy, "the author transports readers to a medieval Russian world based on the folktale of 'The Firebird.' Ilya Ivanovitch is beaten and teased by his ruffian brothers and ignored by his father, a *boyar* or Russian prince, whose singular concern is his stolen cherries. While trying to catch the thief, Ilya Ivanovitch is unknowingly cursed just by glimpsing at the Firebird, which is half maiden and half bird. During his brother's prewedding boar hunt, the young man gets lost, but becomes much wiser as the enchanting adventures unfold." SLJ

Joust. DAW Bks. 2003 373p il $24.95
ISBN 0-7564-0122-4 LC 2003-544990
Vetch, an Altan serf, must learn the secret of the Tian jousters and their dragons in order to save his people

"This uplifting tale, which contains a valuable lesson or two on the virtues of hard work, is a must-read for dragon lovers in particular and for fantasy fans in general." Publ Wkly

The serpent's shadow. DAW Bks. 2001 343p $24.95
ISBN 0-88677-915-4 LC 2002-265143
"To an alternative Victorian London Dr. Maya Witherspoon, [daughter] of a Brahmin lady and an English physician, comes to practice. Besides standard Western medicine, Maya knows the magic of India, where she grew up. Maya's aunt Shivani has also come to England, but as a devotee of Kali, she hates her sister's marriage and is determined to wreak havoc on the English. Maya must seek the aid of British magical masters before the powers of Kali devastate London." Booklist

Winds of fate. DAW Bks. 1991 385p il (Mage winds, bk1) o.p.

This first volume of a trilogy is set in the "imperiled land of Valdemar, encountered earlier in Lackey's Heralds of Valdemar series. The heir to the throne, Herald Elspeth, sets out with Gwena, her Companion (a Guardian Spirit embodied as a horse), to find an Adept who can teach her people both to use and to deflect the power of magic. . . . Lackey's delightful world of magic is inhabited by strong and believable men, women and creatures." Publ Wkly

Followed by Winds of change (1992)

Winds of fury. DAW Bks. 1993 387p il (Mage winds, bk3) o.p.
LC 93-219013
"In this concluding book of the Mage Winds trilogy . . . Elspeth returns home via the Forest of Sorrows where the manifest spirit of Vanyel and his lover, the bard Stefan, pull her from her intended destination to explain the now diminished shields against magic and the interlocking mind-web he once placed on Valdemar and how Elspeth must prepare to fight the evil and voracious Ancar of Hardorn." Voice Youth Advocates

(jt. auth) Norton, A. The elvenbane
(jt. auth) Norton, A. Elvenblood

Lagerkvist, Pär, 1891-1974

Barabbas; translated by Alan Blair; with a preface by Lucien Maury and a letter by André Gide. Random House 1951 180p o.p.

Original Swedish edition, 1950

This "is a psychological study of the spiritual journey of Barabbas, the criminal in the New Testament who was offered to the mob in place of Jesus but was spared from execution. The widely translated work was noted for its economical writing style, and it brought Lagerkvist international fame." Merriam-Webster's Ency of Lit

Lahiri, Jhumpa

Interpreter of maladies; stories. Houghton Mifflin 1999 198p $23

ISBN 0-618-10136-5 LC 98-50895

First published in paperback

Contents: A temporary matter; When Mr. Pirzada came to dine; Interpreter of maladies; A real durwan; Sexy; Mrs. Sen's; This blessed house; The treatment of Bibi Haldar; The third and final continent

"The rituals of traditional Indian domesticity—curry-making, hair-vermilioning—both buttress the characters of Lahiri's elegant first collection and mark the measure of these fragile people's dissolution. . . . Lahiri's touch in these nine tales is delicate, but her observations remain damningly accurate, and her bittersweet stories are unhampered by nostalgia." Publ Wkly

The namesake. Houghton Mifflin 2003 291p $24

ISBN 0-395-92721-8 LC 2003-41718

"A novel about assimilation and generational differences. Gogol is so named because his father believes that sitting up in a sleeping car reading Nikolai Gogol's 'The Overcoat' saved him when the train he was on derailed and most passengers perished. After his arranged marriage, the man and his wife leave India for America, where he eventually becomes a professor. They adopt American ways, yet all of their friends are Bengalis. But for young Gogol and his sister, Boston is home, and trips to Calcutta to visit relatives are voyages to a foreign land." SLJ

"Its incorrigible mildness and its ungilded lilies aside, Lahiri's novel is unfailingly lovely in its treatment of Gogol's relationship with his father. This is the classic American parent-child bond." N Y Times Book Rev

Laker, Rosalind, 1925-

Banners of silk. Doubleday 1981 469p o.p.

LC 80-1453

"A historical romance portraying the rags-to-riches climb of two likable and hard-working couturiers in the nineteenth-century Parisian fashion world. Fate brings Charles Worth and Louise Vernet together when they are young and poor. Although they separate and lose touch, they again meet as colleagues after both have gained reputations as innovative dress designers." Booklist

The golden tulip. Doubleday 1991 585p o.p.

LC 90-27591

This novel "follows the exploits of Francesca Visser and her family during late seventeenth-century Holland, as they move in the circles of Rembrandt, Vermeer, and William of Orange. Francesca's dream to become a master artist threatens to be thwarted by the devious Ludolf van Deventer, who manipulates her heavily indebted father into signing a marriage contract for her. Only her own determination and the constant support of Pieter van Doorne—the tulip grower who loves her selflessly—and her sisters guide Francesca toward her goal." Booklist

"The suspense rarely slackens, for Francesca's spirited younger sisters, Aletta and Sybylla, enter into highly entertaining and surprising romances of their own. Laker's . . . tightly woven novel, swift-moving and filled with lusty characters, is weakened only by a convoluted, lengthy cloak-and-dagger finale." Publ Wkly

To dance with kings. Doubleday 1988 564p o.p.

LC 88-3698

"Set during the reigns of Louis XIV and Louis XVI, the sweeping saga takes place mainly in the Chateau of Versailles and the surrounding town from which the magnificent edifice took its name. . . . Spanning four generations, the protagonists are the women of one family, named, in turn, Marguerite, Jasmin, Violette and Rose, all of whose destinies are entwined with those of their monarchs as well as the dashing men who bring them love and heartache." Publ Wkly

Lamb, Wally

I know this much is true. HarperCollins Pubs. 1998 901p $27.50

ISBN 0-06-039162-6 LC 98-167337

"Lamb's narrator, Dominick Birdsey, has lost his mother, his wife, his infant daughter, his career. His identical twin brother, the gentle Thomas has lost his mind. A paranoid schizophrenic . . . Thomas goes into the public library one morning during the early rumblings of Desert Storm and cuts off his hand in a biblically inspired protest against the impending war. What follows is the 40-year-old Dominick's meltdown. In his struggle to do right by Thomas, the brother he loves, resents and envies in equal measure, he is forced to face not just his own demons but the entire cavalcade of nightmares that have bedeviled the Birdsey clan." N Y Times Book Rev

"The novel explores the subjects of mental illness, dysfunctional families and domestic abuse, but it also rings with humor and tenderness." Publ Wkly

Lambdin, Dewey

King's captain; an Alan Lewrie naval adventure. St. Martin's Press 2000 358p o.p.

ISBN 0-312-26885-8 LC 00-31764

Fresh from a stunning victory against the formidable Spanish Armada in the Battle of St. Vincent's Cape, Lewrie is promoted and rewarded with the command of an enviable new warship. Shortly after being installed as the captain of the H.M.S. Prote*us, he m*ust contend with a treasonable mass mutiny, a bitter enemy bent on revenge, and several rather complicated romantic entanglements. A rip-roaring sea yarn brimming with riveting action and lusty diversions." Booklist

Lambrecht, Patricia *See* Tracy, P. J.

Lambrecht, Traci *See* Tracy, P. J.

Lamott, Anne

Blue shoe. Riverhead Bks. 2002 291p o.p.

ISBN 1-57322-226-7 LC 2002-22824

This novel "tracks the efforts of Mattie Ryder to cope with her divorce, find a new man, deal with her mother's aging and restore the emotional equilibrium of her two young children." Publ Wkly

"The acceptence of one's imperfections is a pillar of wisdom in Lamott's New Age Christianity. Mattie is an embodiment of that philosophy, but she's better written than that makes her sound. She and her family are hilariously specific." NY Times Book Rev

L'Amour, Louis, 1908-1988

Bendigo Shafter. Dutton 1979 324p o.p.
LC 78-15280

"This book's hero is 18-year-old Bendigo Shafter. He is part of a small band of migrants that breaks off its westward trek and builds a small community. The group increases with the coming of other members. It has to fight off the dangers of the frontier both within and outside its confines. Among the main influences on Ben's life are the Widow Macken, who inspires him to read Locke, Rousseau, and Blackstone; Uruwishi, an old Indian brave; and Ethan Sackett, woodsman nonpareil. There are heroes and villains, both white and red, and shooting from the hip in old Western style as Ben demonstrates all the traditional values of courage, honesty, loyalty, and stamina." Shapiro. Fic for Youth. 3d edition

Beyond the Great Snow Mountains. Bantam Bks. 1999 282p o.p.
ISBN 0-553-10963-4 LC 99-11757

The stories in this collection were written in the 1940s and 1950s

Contents: By the waters of San Tadeo; Meeting at Falmouth; Roundup in Texas; Sideshow champion; Crash landing; Under the hanging wall; Coast patrol; The gravel pit; The money punch; Beyond the Great Snow Mountains

The Californios. Saturday Review Press 1974 188p o.p.

"Eileen Mulkerin is about to lose her ranch because of debts but an ancient Indian, survivor of the Old Ones, leads her to a hidden cache of gold while her son fights off the killers sent to do them in." Booklist

"An expert blend of the fascinating settling of California in the 1840's; strong, self-reliant characters . . . and a plot of evil doings but triumphant good. The theme of mysticism and the legends of The Old Ones is what lifts this book above the typical western. Intriguing even for those who aren't westerns fans." Libr J

The Cherokee Trail. Bantam Bks. 1982 179p o.p.
LC 82-90288

"The leading character [of this novel] is a woman, Southern born and bred, who is left a widow with a small girl in Colorado of the 1860's. She is a tough lady who believes anything a man can do, she can do, and does. As the only woman operator of a station on the Cherokee Trail, Mary Breydon battles enemies with her guns, brains, and supportive friends, male and female. . . . As always, L'Amour respects the history and nature of the West: His characters and language are representative; his details of life on a station are accurate." Libr J

The daybreakers
In L'Amour, L. The Sacketts: beginnings of a dynasty

End of the drive. Bantam Bks. 1997 257p o.p.
LC 96-36872

Contents: Caprock rancher; Elisha comes to Red Horse; Desperate men; The courting of Griselda; End of the drive; The lonesome gods; Rustler roundup; The skull and the arrow

The haunted mesa. Bantam Bks. 1987 357p o.p.
LC 86-47576

This novel is a "combination of western and occult adventure, with the former given a decided edge. Mike Raglan, the hero, is an investigator of occult phenomena, but he is also a tough loner who knows how to use a six-gun. When he travels to a remote Southwest mesa to investigate the mystery of the Anasazi—a race of vanished cliff-dwellers—he manages to cross over to the Other Side, a fourth dimension that turns out to be very much another western frontier, replete with hidden gold, treacherous landscapes and plenty of Indians to shoot down." N Y Times Book Rev

"Although L'Amour's didactic approach and his needless repetition of details get in the way, this curious hybrid should satisfy fans of both genres." Booklist

Jubal Sackett. Bantam Bks. 1985 375p o.p.
LC 84-91724

This installment of the Sackett saga "features Jubal Sackett, a wily, homespun seventeenth-century hero who sets off to traverse the vast, unexplored North American hinterland. As he ranges through and beyond the mountains, Jubal befriends Keokotah, a fiercely proud Kickapoo brave, and together they help shield an astonishingly beautiful Natchez princess from a vengeful renegade Indian and an unscrupulous Spanish soldier." Booklist

"An absorbing story filled with adventure, romance, a hint of the occult, and information about Indian tribes and life in the mountains in the 17th century." Libr J

Lando
In L'Amour, L. The Sacketts: beginnings of a dynasty

Last of the breed. Bantam Bks. 1986 358p o.p.
LC 86-3622

The setting "is modern-day Siberia; the main character [is] Maj. Joe Makatozi, a part Sioux, part Cheyenne Air Force pilot who has been forced down over the Soviet Union and imprisoned in a desolate region roughly equidistant from Moscow and the western tip of Alaska. . . . The athletically inclined 'Joe Mack' slips out of his cell, pole-vaults over the wall and begins heading east with the Russians, and most particularly a hulking Yakut named Alekhin, in hot pursuit." Newsweek

"Joe Mack is a classic American hero, thrown back into the wilderness and forced to rely on his wits and his ancestral skills to survive the deadly cold and elude his Soviet pursuers, including his nemesis, a Siberian tracker. L'Amour brings the same colorful realism to this sweeping adventure that has made his Westerns so beloved." Publ Wkly

The lonesome gods. Bantam Bks. 1983 450p o.p.
LC 82-45945

"In the early 1840s six-year-old Johannes Verne survives abandonment in the desert to spend his growing years dreaming of vengeance for the murder of his father and defending himself against enemies, including his grandfather, who are determined to kill him. The pace is almost leisurely, and the book is filled with splendid descriptions of the desert country, historical facts, and nature lore. An absorbing story of the early years of California with plenty of action, gun play, heroes, and villains." Libr J

L'Amour, Louis, 1908-1988—*Continued*

May there be a road. Bantam Bks. 2001 276p o.p.
ISBN 0-553-80213-5 LC 2001-18127
Contents: Friend of a hero; May there be a road; Fighter's fiasco; The Cactus Kid; Making it the hard way; The hand of Kuan-yin; Red Butte showdown; The ghost fighter; Wings over Brazil; The vanished blonde
In this collection of 10 previously uncollected stories with settings ranging from the coasts of Brazil to the border of Tibet to the very heartland of America . . . [the author] takes us into those sudden moments when lives and futures are altered forever, when men and women face a deadly enemy, meet a kindred spirit, or confront their own mortality." Publisher's note

Monument Rock. Bantam Bks. 1998 264p o.p.
ISBN 0-553-10833-6 LC 97-43622
Contents: A man named Utah; Battle at Burnt Camp; Ironwood Station; Here ends the trail; Last day in town; Strawhouse trail; The man from the Dead Hills; Monument Rock
"The seven short stories and one short novel collected here are newly discovered among his papers and have never been published before. Often, works left behind by authors are deficient in some manner, but that's not the case here. . . . This is top-drawer L'Amour complete with taciturn heroes, strong women, amoral villains, and loyal friends." Booklist

Monument Rock [novelette]
In L'Amour, L. Monument Rock p141-249

Off the Mangrove Coast. Bantam Bks. 2000 277p o.p.
ISBN 0-553-80160-0 LC 99-86061
Contents: Fighters should be hungry; It's your move; Off the Mangrove Coast; The cross and the candle; The diamond of Jeru; Secret of Silver Springs; The unexpected corpse; The rounds don't matter; Time of terror
"This batch of stories is something of a mixed bag, ranging from as far back as the 1920s up through the last days of World War II. There are a couple of boxing yarns, a pair of thrillers . . . and some fascinating pieces that came from L'Amour's worldwide travels." Booklist

The outlaws of Mesquite; frontier stories. Bantam Bks. 1990 199p il o.p.
LC 89-18254
Contents: The outlaws of Mesquite; Love and the Cactus Kid; The Ghost Maker; The drift; No rest for the wicked; That Packsaddle affair; Showdown on the Tumbling T; The sixth shotgun

Rustler roundup
In L'Amour, L. End of the drive p93-239

Sackett
In L'Amour, L. The Sacketts: beginnings of a dynasty

The Sacketts: beginnings of a dynasty. Saturday Review Press 1976 3v in 1 o.p.
Contains The daybreakers, Sackett, and Lando, originally published by Bantam Books in 1960, 1961 and 1962 respectively. The three novels included in this omnibus edition all concern members of the Sackett family during the great frontier heyday of the 1850s and 1860s
"The first tale takes Tyrel and Orrin from the Tennessee hills to Santa Fe. The second adventure is told by William Tell Sackett, the third by Lando. All are well-drawn portraits of a unique period, unmistakably L'Amour, unmistakably among his best." Booklist
Other titles about the Sacketts are: Mojave crossing (1964); Sackett brand (1965); Mustang man (1966); The lonely man (1966); The sky-liners (1967); Galloway (1970); Treasure Mountain (1972); Ride the dark trail (1972); Sackett's land; To the far blue mountains; The warrior's path (1980); Lonely on the mountain (1980); Ride the river (1983); and Jubal Sackett

To the far blue mountains. Saturday Review Press 1976 287p o.p.
In this Sackett novel Barnabas returns from America with a cargo of goods. He "is in Lincolnshire on business when he learns that there is a queen's warrant out for him because he is suspected of stealing the crown jewels. He is thrown in prison but manages to escape and make his way to Bristol and a ship back to Raleigh's Land. In Virginia, he recruits a band of brave settlers and strong women and they take boats up the James River in the direction of the blue mountains until they find rich land to farm. There Barnabas's children are born and the community flourishes even though there is ever-present danger from hostile Indians. This tale is much more leisurely and nonviolent than the usual L'Amour story, but it has its share of suspense and gives us a different kind of look at colonial America." Publ Wkly

The trail to Seven Pines; a Hopalong Cassidy novel. Bantam Bks. 1992 244p o.p.
LC 91-43760
First published 1951 with title: Hopalong Cassidy and the trail to Seven Pines, by the author writing as Tex Burns
"Hopalong was headed northeast toward open country when he crossed the path of six suspicious-looking men wearing silver-plated Colts. By the time he heard the gunshots, he was too far up the trail to do anything—riding back in time to find a robbed stagecoach and two bodies lying sprawled and bloody in the dust. The shipment of gold was the fourth to be hijacked in only three months, and appeared to be connected to the range war exploding around the Rocking R Ranch in the nearby town of Seven Pines. Hiring on at the Rocking R, Hopalong organizes a rough and ragtag outfit to save the ranch, only to find himself accused of murder and the target of a ruthless gunman." Publisher's note

The walking drum. Bantam Bks. 1984 423p o.p.
LC 83-25703
"In 12th century Brittany, young Mathurin Kerbouchard, escaping from the evil baron who has slain Mathurin's mother and plundered their estate, is forced into galley slavery. He gains control of the boat and lands in Moorish Spain, where he quickly makes powerful friends and enemies. Mathurin's quest is to rescue his corsair father, prisoner in the Persian stronghold of the Assassins. On the way the youth becomes a famed scholar . . . warrior, merchant, doctor and lover." Publ Wkly

Lampedusa, Giuseppe Tomasi di *See* Tomasi di Lampedusa, Giuseppe, 1896-1957

Lanchester, John

Fragrant Harbor. Putnam 2002 342p o.p.
ISBN 0-399-14866-3 LC 2001-57876
"A Marian Wood book"
"In 1935, young Englishman Tom Stewart sails to Hong Kong in search of adventure. During the six-week voyage, he is taught Cantonese by a young Chinese missionary nun, Sister Maria. Upon his arrival in Hong Kong, his proficiency in the language leads to a career as a hotel manager. When the Japanese invade, Sister Maria urges him to flee with her, but he's given his word that he'll work as an undercover agent for the British. After the war, which Tom spends mostly in the notorious Stanley prison, his life and Sister Maria's continue to entwine." Publ Wkly

This "is not an enormous novel, but it feels like one—it is bursting with ideas. Lanchester takes on almost every major theme and succeeds with most of them: race, class, love, war, the fall of rulers and the rise of the ruled." N Y Times Book Rev

Landers, Scott, 1952-

Coswell's guide to Tambralinga; a novel; Scott Landers. Farrar, Straus and Giroux 2004 338p $24
ISBN 0-374-13021-3 LC 2003-21116
A novel set on a fictional Southeast Asian island. "At the center is Conrad, a meek computer systems analyst on a desperate second honeymoon with Lucy, who's furious at him for losing her all-important guidebook. Fearing 'that he was missing it, that better half of existence, the throbbing center of what it meant to be alive,' Conrad heads to a brothel on another island, while Lucy finds the guidebook and embarks on her own adventure." Publ Wkly

"In this offbeat first novel, Landers puts a wry spin on the theme of self-discovery, suggesting that jealousy, hardship, and disillusionment are good for the soul." Booklist

Lange, John *See* Crichton, Michael, 1942-

Langton, Jane

The Dante game; illustrations by the author; blackboard sketches by Giovanni Zibo. Viking 1991 325p il o.p.
LC 90-50427
This "Homer Kelly mystery unfolds in Italy, where he joins the faculty of the newly formed American School of Florentine Studies. As students and professors read their way through Dante's *Divine Comedy*, they and the author draw parallels to modern-day Florence, where a bank official (and secret heroin smuggler) plots to assassinate the anti-drug-crusading Pope, using a Beatrice-like student as hostage. After three murders at the school, Homer and a friend investigate." Libr J

"A little pixilated, perhaps, by the richness of her setting, Ms. Langton stuffs too many criminal plots into her busy story, which features the Pope himself in its teeming cast. But her descriptions of the city's visual delights are as voluptuously detailed as any armchair traveler might desire." N Y Times Book Rev

Dead as a dodo; a Homer Kelly mystery. Viking 1996 339p il o.p.
ISBN 0-670-86221-5 LC 96-6724
In this adventure "Homer takes a leave from Harvard to lecture at the Oxford University Museum. Exposed to the natural history scholarship at this seat of learning, he discovers Charles Darwin and is 'flabbergasted' by 'The Origin of Species.' . . . Homer is floored by a number of other things, including the theft of a 17th-century painting of a dodo, the discovery of some long-lost crustacean specimens collected by Darwin and two suspicious deaths. Adopting the style of a famous Oxonian, Charles Dodgson, Ms. Langton makes a Mad Tea Party of Homer's investigation of these curious events, which strike him as a Jabberwockian version of natural selection." N Y Times Book Rev

The deserter; murder at Gettysburg. St. Martin's Minotaur 2003 322p il $23.95
ISBN 0-312-30186-3 LC 2002-191961
"Homer Kelly's wife, Mary, wants to clear the name of her Civil War ancestor, purported to have been a deserter. As the narrative alternates between past and present, the Kellys find evidence of false identity and murder." Libr J

"The suspense builds as the author adroitly shifts between past and present. Period photos, an 1860 playbill for the Hasty Pudding show, quotations from Walt Whitman and loads of Harvard lore add historical weight." Publ Wkly

Divine inspiration; a Homer Kelly mystery. Viking 1993 406p il o.p.
LC 93-1693
Homer Kelly "investigates a puzzling set of events involving the First Church of the Commonwealth in Boston. A fire has destroyed the church's organ and left its sexton dead. Now that the glorious new organ is being installed, strange things are happening: an apparently abandoned baby crawls into the church, inexplicable accidents keep delaying the organ's installation, a former musical genius reappears in a homeless shelter, and the church is literally coming apart at the seams. Langton has a knack for weaving dozens of seemingly unrelated plot threads together to form a satisfying and entertaining mystery." Booklist

Emily Dickinson is dead; a novel of suspense; illustrations by the author. St. Martin's Press 1984 247p il o.p.
LC 83-24451
"A Joan Kahn book"
"In a mystery that pokes fun at the behavior of professors in the academic world, a famous poet is chosen as a theme for a literary conference. Stemming from a photograph that an undistinguished professor from a small midwestern college claims is an authentic photo of Emily Dickinson, the faculty of an elite university begin to fight among themselves—sometimes even physically—about who will star at the conference. Entangled in that is Winifred Gaw, an overweight graduate student, and the professor whom she worships, as well as beautiful Allison Groves who becomes the object of Winifred's jealousy and hatred. Emily Dickinson, quietly dead for so many years, becomes a motivation for arson, forgery, and murder." Shapiro. Fic for Youth. 3d edition

The Escher twist; a Homer Kelly mystery. Viking 2002 240p il o.p.
ISBN 0-670-03067-8 LC 2001-26806

Langton, Jane—*Continued*

This "Homer Kelly book follows crystallographer Leonard Sheldrake as he pursues the enigmatic Frieda, who disappears after they meet at an Escher exhibition at a Cambridge, Mass., art gallery. The mystery here is less about the murders that crop up occasionally in this whimsical narrative than about identity." Publ Wkly

The face on the wall. Viking 1998 291p il o.p.
ISBN 0-670-87674-7 LC 98-2832

"Amateur sleuth Homer Kelly goes to the aid of his wife's niece, a book illustrator whose dream house has become the scene of murder." Libr J

"Overlaying her mythic design with a trim narrative of modern-day wickedness, [Langton] steps back to let us marvel at the patterns of evil that she traces from Mother Goose to the murderer next door." N Y Times Book Rev

God in Concord; illustrations by the author. Viking 1992 338p il o.p.
LC 91-42940

As Homer Kelley, the "transcendentalist detective and his tiny band of partisans stand by fuming, a rapacious Boston developer swoops down on Concord to poison 'the sacred water' of Walden Pond with commercial real estate complexes. Transfixed by the dragon's enticements of new sewage plants and an enriched tax base, the simpleton townsfolk don't even notice when the elderly residents of a choicely situated trailer camp begin to die mysterious deaths." N Y Times Book Rev

Murder at Monticello; a Homer Kelly mystery; illustrations by the author. Viking 2001 256p il $22.95
ISBN 0-670-89462-1 LC 00-43369

"It's the bicentennial of Jefferson's election to the presidency, and Homer and his wife, Mary, are invited to a Fourth of July celebration at Monticello, Jefferson's Virginia home, where, incidentally, a serial killer has been murdering young women. Like the previous Kelly novels, this one features a smart mystery, delightful characters, and vastly entertaining dialogue." Booklist

Murder at the Gardner; a novel of suspense; illustrations by the author. St. Martin's Press 1988 353p il o.p.
LC 87-27452

"A Joan Kahn book"

"Within the palatial walls of Boston's Gardner Museum, paintings by Botticelli and Titian shed artistic light on a hodgepodge of lesser collectibles, all forever fixed in place as decreed by the inflexible terms of Isabella Stewart Gardner's will, which demands that the whole collection be auctioned off should any changes or unwelcome disturbances occur. The museum's very boyish director, Titus Moon, turns a blind eye to such pranks as tadpoles in the courtyard fountain and ghostly music in the galleries, but even he is appalled when a particularly awful benefactor meets an untimely end." Publ Wkly

Natural enemy; illustrations by the author. Ticknor & Fields 1982 282p il o.p.
LC 81-16618

"A Joan Kahn book"

"Young John Hand, amateur spider expert, has a summer job as live-in-handyman for Barbara and Virginia Heron, whose father has just died. But their pushy neighbor Buddy Whipple moves in too and begins to manipulate everything—including Virginia—in a sinister way. John, whose schoolboy crush on Virginia has not abated, calls on his uncle Homer Kelly to help." Libr J

The shortest day; murder at the Revels. Viking 1995 262p il o.p.
LC 95-14266

This novel, featuring the amateur detective Homer Kelly, is set in Cambridge, Massachusetts during the Revels, a "Christmas festival featuring ancient rituals and Morris dancing. . . . Director Sarah Bailey is determined that the celebration will be the best yet, but she's finding it hard to concentrate on the Revels because she's just found out she's pregnant. . . . But what's really upsetting is that Sarah's star Revels performers are dying at an alarming rate—and she's terrified there may be a murderer loose among the cast." Booklist

"Langton's witty line drawings enrich the proceedings as journalists, do-gooders and a fine crew of sharply drawn academics (ambitious, competitive, jealous and psychotic) come in for some delicate ribbing. Neither the occasional moralizing nor the crude deus ex machina can slow the merry spin of this colorful and absorbing tale." Publ Wkly

The thief of Venice. Viking 1999 247p il o.p.
ISBN 0-670-88210-0 LC 98-54894

"A Homer Kelly mystery"

Homer Kelly, "a policeman-turned-scholar, and his professor wife, Mary, have ventured to Venice to attend a scholarly conference on rare books. Homer is intoxicated by the riches afforded in the Biblioteca Marciana, while Mary prowls the streets of the Italian city, camera in hand. An expatriate English doctor, Richard Henchard, seeking an apartment for his demanding mistress, stumbles upon a cache of golden artifacts. He kills twice to protect his secret, and his path soon intersects Mary's. . . . With a master hand, Langton develops the various subplots into a sophisticated, elegantly constructed thriller." Publ Wkly

Lankford, Terrill

Earthquake weather. Ballantine Bks. 2004 293p $24.95
ISBN 0-345-46777-9 LC 2004-41068

This novel starts with the "L.A. earthquake of 1994. Suffering from post-quake shell shock, Mark Hayes, D-Boy (or script reader) for schlocky producer Dexter Morton, finds his career in tatters, just like his quake-damaged apartment in the Valley. Then he finds a body floating in Dexter's pool and becomes a murder suspect. Along with a motley crew of similarly dysfunctional cronies, including a washed-up writer who spouts cliches about 'killing creativity for a paycheck,' Mark slouches toward Armageddon or a jail cell, whichever comes first. Lankford nails the updated noir mood, and he fills the tale with juicy insider stuff about the 'industry'." Booklist

Lansdale, Joe R., 1951-

The bottoms. Mysterious Press 2000 328p $30
ISBN 0-89296-704-8 LC 00-32886

Lansdale, Joe R., 1951-—*Continued*

A tale of "race violence and serial murder in a small East Texas town during the Depression. The aged narrator, Harry Collins, is lying in a rest home and letting his mind drift back to the events that changed his life in 1933 . . . when he and his little sister find the mangled body of a black prostitute in the deep bottom lands along the Sabine River. Harry's father, the town barber and constable, does his best; but when the killer claims a white victim, he can't stop his Klan neighbors from lynching an old black man for the crimes." N Y Times Book Rev

"An emotionally charged tale very reminiscent of *To Kill a Mockingbird.* Effectively combining mystery and family history, it offers a vivid, multifaceted glimpse back to a simpler, but not necessarily better, time." Booklist

A fine dark line. Mysterious Press 2003 307p $24.95

ISBN 0-89296-729-3 LC 2002-71387

A regional mystery "which harks back to 1958. Thirteen-year-old Stanley Mitchel, Jr., has enough on his hands just growing up in Dewmont, Tex., when he literally stumbles on a buried cache of love letters. Stanley pursues the identity of the two lovers with help from the projectionist at his family's drive-in, an aged black man who quotes Sherlock Holmes and doesn't mince words about the world's injustices. As the truth of a gruesome 20-year-old double murder comes to light in the sleepy town, so do the facts of life, death, men, women and race for young Stanley." Publ Wkly

"Stanley doesn't unravel everything, but race and power, and what people do to each other in the name of desire and religion, coalesce to a mighty climax." Booklist

Sunset and sawdust; Joe R. Lansdale. 1st ed. Alfred A. Knopf 2004 321p $22

ISBN 0-375-41453-3 LC 2003-60478

This novel is set in Depression-era East Texas. "After shooting her spouse during conjugal rape, spunky redhead Sunset Jones winds up with his job as constable of the roughhewn lumber town of Camp Rapture, thanks to the influence of a mother-in-law whose own marital woes are brought to an abrupt and gory end when her man lies down on the job at the sawmill. Already unpopular for thwarting a lynching, Sunset and her deputies—a devilishly handsome vagabond and his mulish rival—get in over their heads in a stew of greed and brutality when the oil-covered corpses of a mother and her newborn are plowed up in a black farmer's field." Libr J

"The mystery is only mildly engrossing here; the great pleasure of Lansdale's work lies in his pitch-perfect vernacular prose. . . . The book opens with a cyclone, ends with a plague of grasshoppers and in between there's insanity, extreme violence, sex, grotesques aplenty and an excellent dog. What's not to like?" Publ Wkly

Lapcharoensap, Rattawut

Sightseeing; stories; Rattawut Lapcharoensap. Grove Press 2005 250p $22

ISBN 0-8021-1788-0 LC 2004-54131

Contents: Farangs: At the Café Lovely; Draft day; Sightseeing; Priscilla the Cambodian; Don't let me die in this place; Cockfighter

"The Thailand of Westerners' dreams shares space with a Thailand plagued by social and economic inequality in this auspicious debut collection. . . . Young or old, male or female, all of Lapcharoensap's spirited narrators are engaging and credible. Anger, humor and longing are neatly balanced in these richly nuanced, sharply revelatory tales." Publ Wkly

Lapierre, Dominique

(jt. auth) Collins, L. The fifth horseman

Lardner, Ring, 1885-1933

The best short stories of Ring Lardner. Scribner 1976 c1957 346p o.p.

ISBN 0-684-14743-2

"Hudson River editions"

A reprint of the 1957 edition

"A selection of twenty-five stories by one of the most original figures in American literature, the colorful personality who was noted as a sports writer, humorist and columnist, as well as short-story writer." N Y Her Trib Books

Ring around the bases; the complete baseball stories of Ring Lardner; edited and with an introduction by Matthew J. Bruccoli; foreword by Ring Lardner, Jr. Scribner 1992 609p il $35

ISBN 0-684-19374-4 LC 91-38363

"This volume collects all [of Lardner's baseball] tales, including the famous Jack Keefe epistolary stories that made up the well-known volume *You Know Me Al* (1914), plus some prime journalistic pieces. . . They all display the writer's excellence in capturing the idiom and nuances of baseball talk." Libr J

You know me, Al

In Lardner, R. Ring around the bases

Larminie, Margaret Beda *See* Yorke, Margaret

Larsen, Deborah

The white; a novel. Knopf 2002 219p $22

ISBN 0-375-41359-6 LC 2001-53977

A reinterpretation of the "life of Mary Jemison, a white woman who was captured in 1758 by a Shawnee raiding party at her home in Gettysburg, Pa., while the rest of her family was murdered and scalped. . . . Mary is eventually adopted by another tribe, the Seneca. Learning their language and culture, marrying and bearing six children, Mary ultimately finds herself at home with them and no longer feels the compulsion to escape or return to white society at all." Publ Wkly

This novel "has escaped many of the dangers that ensnare fiction with this sort of subject. It is neither epic nor sentimental, nor does it bang any political or anthropological drum. Beneath the smooth beauty of its descriptive language, there is some terrific concision and lightness." N Y Times Book Rev

Larsen, Jeanne

Silk road; a novel of 8th century China. Holt & Co. 1989 434p il o.p.

LC 88-27286

The author has "several ideas going in this novel set in eighth-century China and seen through the eyes of a young girl transformed into a beautiful woman and even-

Larsen, Jeanne—*Continued*

tually a wandering warrior. First, there's a romantic tale of how a heroine, snatched as a child from her parents, is sold into slavery and trained as a concubine. Second, there's a story of mystical revenge, with the girl seeking justice for the mother she barely knew. Superimposed on these stories are the details of Chinese history and culture." Booklist

This novel "maintains a wonderfully mellow tone, perhaps so even a tone as to subvert intensity. But it accommodates much merriment, and moments of sadness and joy, as this feminist fable of mother- and sister-bonding draws together." N Y Times Book Rev

Larson, Charles R.

(ed) Under African skies. See Under African skies

Lasdun, James

The horned man. Norton 2002 193p $24.95

ISBN 0-393-00336-1 LC 2002-539

"Brit Lawrence Miller, a professor of gender studies at Arthur Clay College, becomes convinced that a stranger is camping out nightly in his office. Though preoccupied by his wife's recent decampment and his membership on the college's sexual harassment committee, Lawrence fixates on the illustrious Professor Trumilcik, an Eastern European womanizer and ex-board member, who went mad on campus one afternoon and never returned." Publ Wkly

"This arch, assured satire is a psychological thriller, too, and it races cleanly and hungrily to unexpected (and expected) revelations; the academic and sexual politics that ground it are familiar, but this almost doesn't matter, since Lasdun is interested in the inevitability of error when we mistake trendiness for truth." New Yorker

Laskas, Gretchen Moran

The midwife's tale. Dial Press (NY) 2003 243p $23.95

ISBN 0-385-33551-2 LC 2002-41010

"Set in pre-World War I West Virginia, this novel flows along like the tributaries that feed the book's Appalachian foothills, as narrator Elizabeth Whitely traces the arc of four generations of midwives in her family, she being the last of the line. Poverty, lack of clean water, unemployment, an influenza epidemic, and severe weather also figure in this often melancholy tale. Laskas has injected many period details into her first book and a lot of verve into her characters to make them come alive." Libr J

Laskowski, Tim, 1957-

Every good boy does fine; a novel. Southern Methodist Univ. Press 2003 176p $23.95

ISBN 0-87074-477-1 LC 2003-40726

"Robert was a recent college graduate with a promising future as a pianist when he fell in a mountain-climbing accident. After weeks in a coma and years in a nursing home, he is placed in a rehabilitation program. At the novel's beginning, he is accepted into an accelerated program that might prepare him for relatively independent living—if he can adapt." Libr J

"Laskowski keeps the focus on Robert's daily struggles in the early going, but as the book progresses he begins to pose wrenching questions about the nature of illness and sanity. The book closes with an elegiac recovery fantasy that serves as a poignant reminder of the strength of the human spirit in the face of devastating disability." Publ Wkly

Latham, Aaron

Code of the West. Simon & Schuster 2001 494p $26

ISBN 0-7432-0117-5 LC 00-51618

"Set in Texas during the 1860's, Aaron Latham's . . . novel transplants the Arthurian legend into the Wild West, where his hero—a cowboy named Jimmy Goodnight—employs a Colt revolver rather than Excalibur. Stolen as a child by Commanches who killed his family, Goodnight is an outsider who returns to white society when he coaxes an ax from a stone. He then collects a band of ruffians and establishes his own dusty Camelot in an immense canyon, successfully woos his Guinevere and befriends Jack Loving, a handsome, sharpshooting drifter who becomes his Lancelot." N Y Times Book Rev

"Latham is booth a lyrical and an economical writer, and his ability to bring Jimmy Goodnight fully to life even in the stolen chain mail of a much larger figure transforms this compulsively readable novel from a farce into a good western." Booklist

Lathen, Emma

Brewing up a storm; a John Thatcher mystery. St. Martin's Press 1996 248p o.p.

LC 96-22116

"A Thomas Dunne book"

In this novel "a protest organization sues a local brewery, claiming that the firm's new nonalcoholic beer contributed to the alcohol-related death of a teenager. When someone murders the protest leader, the brewery calls on series sleuth John Thatcher, a Wall Street banker." Libr J

Double, double, oil and trouble. Simon & Schuster 1978 255p o.p.

LC 78-5151

"A negotiation vital to construction in the North Sea oil fields is interrupted when an executive is kidnapped. A large ransom is paid and the British government awards the contract to the victim's firm, unfairly in the view of the competition. Matters become complicated when the victim is killed in a car bombing in Houston, and personal rather than business considerations become paramount." Libr J

"The scene shifts from London to Istanbul and Houston to Switzerland, in a story that wouldn't work in the hands of a less skilled writer. Lathen knows how to keep her novels from becoming bogged down by excess verbiage and unnecessary violence." Booklist

East is east. Simon & Schuster 1991 268p o.p.

LC 91-32789

This John Putnam Thatcher adventure "takes the senior banking executive from the Sloan Guaranty Trust building in Manhattan on evenly paced travels to Japan, Alas-

Lathen, Emma—*Continued*
ka and England. Lackawanna Electric Industries, rebounding from bankruptcy under the forceful leadership of Carl Kruger, is about to pull off a distribution coup with Yonezawa Trading, one of Japan's largest corporations. Thatcher is present at the Tokyo signing, which is delayed by the discovery of a murdered accountant in Japan's Ministry of International Trade and Investment and a note suggesting a $1-million bribe." Publ Wkly

Ms. Lathen "has a wonderful knack for turning the driest, most complicated corporate maneuvers into high drama, and occasionally burlesque." N Y Times Book Rev

Going for the gold. Simon & Schuster 1981 251p o.p.

"Unprecedented banking demands in Lake Placid during the Winter Olympics have caused the Sloan to open a branch. But the man in charge is not what he seems and his doings are followed by two murders and a blizzard. Thatcher and Co. have 48 hours to straighten out the mess. As usual, the background—here athletic—is worked into the plot without seeming forced or padded." Barzun. Cat of Crime. Rev and enl edition

Right on the money; a John Putnam Thatcher mystery. Simon & Schuster 1993 256p o.p.
LC 92-35673

A "Wall Street mystery featuring banker John Thatcher of Sloan Guaranty Trust. When a Princeton manufacturing firm represented by a sister bank targets a Sloan family-owned business client for takeover, Thatcher monitors the ensuing negotiations. Friction erupts into fracas, however, when rumors fly, financial records burn, and possible industrial sabotage culminates in murder." Libr J

A shark out of water; a John Thatcher mystery. St. Martin's Press 1997 293p o.p.
ISBN 0-312-17018-1 LC 97-23036
"A Thomas Dunne book"

"Wall Street's Sloan Guaranty Trust sends banker John Thatcher to Poland to research possible investment in a scheme to modernize the Kiel Canal, the link between the North and Baltic seas. While there, of course, he becomes involved in hidden problems, personal agendas, and murder." Libr J

"Without ruffling his fabled composure, Thatcher manages to clarify the intricacies of international finance for the Polish police officer investigating the crime, and for the rapt reader too." N Y Times Book Rev

Something in the air. Simon & Schuster 1988 270p o.p.
LC 88-4491

This mystery featuring "John Thatcher of New York's Sloan Guaranty Trust is set mainly in Boston, headquarters of the commuter airline Sparrow Flyways. A product of airline deregulation, Sparrow is a nonunion operation surviving on horizontal management and project development teams. Mitchell Scovil, CEO and guiding figure of the founders, dreams of expansion, but a group of lower-level employees (and shareholders) is worried about their investment. When their arrogant spokesperson is murdered, the Sloan, holding 20% of unsalable Sparrow stock in a trust, becomes involved." Publ Wkly

A stitch in time. Macmillan 1968 185p o.p.
"A Cock Robin mystery"

John Putnam Thatcher, bank vice-president "has problems in settling the estate of the late Pemberton Freebody because Atlantic Mutual Insurance says Freebody was a suicide, and therefore refuses to pay the $100,000 policy on his life to Hanover University. The university takes the case to court, and the trial of the century begins when the company calls Dr. Wendell Martin of Southport Memorial Hospital to the stand." Libr J

Latour, José

The Havana World Series; José Latour. 1st ed. Grove Press 2003 320p $23
ISBN 0-8021-1754-6 LC 2003-60716

The author "tells the story of a gang of Cuban crooks, funded by New York Mob boss Joe Bonanno, who sets out to rob Meyer Lansky's Capri casino on the last day of the 1958 World Series (when the coffers are overflowing). The portraits of Lansky, Bonnano, and the other gangsters are full-bodied, but it's the fictional blue-collar crooks, led by mastermind Ox Contreras, who give the novel its appeal and afford the best view of Cuban life. Although the documentary style occasionally seems flat, it contrasts nicely with the richness of detail and quirkiness of character." Booklist

Latsis, Mary J., 1927-1997

For works written by this author in collaboration with Martha Hennissart see Lathen, Emma

LaValle, Victor D., 1972-

The ecstatic; or, Homunculus; [by] Victor Lavalle. Crown 2002 272p $22.95
ISBN 0-609-61014-7 LC 2002-6766

The protagonist of this novel is "Anthony James, a 318-pound, 23-year-old, Cornell-educated schizophrenic. In order to keep a semblance of order in his unstable mind, he narrates his family's slow road to destruction. Stops along the way include a small-town beauty pageant in Virginia, a weight-loss clinic, and a McDonald's beseiged by protesting college students. Throughout, Anthony remains sarcastic, intelligent, and conscious of his condition, though control of it increasingly eludes him. His experience is brought to life by Lavelle's acute sensory details and hyperbolic wordplay." Libr J

Lawhead, Stephen R. *See* Lawhead, Steve, 1950-

Lawhead, Steve, 1950-

Avalon; the return of King Arthur; by Stephen R. Lawhead. Avon Eos 1999 442p $25
ISBN 0-380-97702-8 LC 99-25048

"In a near-future Britain, the death of King Edward IX throws the succession into disarray until a young man named James Arthur Stewart discovers his identity as the reborn King Arthur and claims his rightful throne." Libr J

"In revisiting nearly every romantic Arthurian cliché and playing off snappy contemporary derring-do against the powerful shining glimpses of the historical Arthur he created, Lawhead pulls off a genuinely moving parable of good and evil." Publ Wkly

Lawless, Anthony *See* MacDonald, Philip, 1899-1981

Lawrence, D. H. (David Herbert), 1885-1930

Collected stories; with an introduction by Craig Raine. Knopf 1994 xxxv, 1397p o.p.
LC 94-2493

"Everyman's library"

Contents: A modern lover; The old Adam; Her turn; Strike-pay; The witch à la mode; New Eve and old Adam; A prelude; Love among the haystacks; A chapel and a hay hut among the mountains; Once; A fly in the ointment; Lessford's rabbits; A lesson on a tortoise; The Prussian officer; The thorn in the flesh; Daughters of the vicar; A fragment of stained glass; The shades of spring; Second best; The shadow in the rose garden; Goose fair; The white stocking; A sick collier; The christening; Odour of chrysanthemums; England, my England; Tickets, please; The blind man; Monkey nuts; Wintry peacock; You touched me; Samson and Delilah; The thimble; The mortal coil; The primrose path; The horse dealer's daughter; Delilah and Mr. Bircumshaw; Fanny and Annie; The ladybird; The fox; The captain's doll; St. Mawr; The princess; Two blue birds; Sun; The woman who rode away; Smile; The border line; Jimmy and the desperate woman; The last laugh; In love; Glad ghosts; None of that; The man who loved islands; The lovely lady; Rawdon's roof; The rocking-horse winner; Mother and daughter; The blue moccasins; Things; The virgin and the gipsy; The man who died

Lady Chatterley's lover; the historic unexpurgated Grove Press edition; with Archibald MacLeish's letter to Barney Rosset, an introduction by Mark Schorer, and Judge Bryan's decision in the obscenity case. Modern Lib. 1993 liii, 491p o.p.
ISBN 0-679-60065-5 LC 93-15337

First published 1928 in a limited edition in Florence

A novel "presenting the author's mystical theories of sex in the story of Constance, or Connie, the wife of an English aristocrat, who runs away with her gamekeeper. Her husband, Sir Clifford, has been rendered impotent by a war wound and is also an emotional cripple. The gamekeeper, Mellors, is a forthright individualistic man, uncontaminated by industrial society." Reader's Ency. 4th edition

The plumed serpent (Quetzalcoatl). Knopf 1926 445p o.p.

This novel is "a powerful, vivid evocation of Mexico and its ancient Aztec religion. Kate Leslie, an Irish visitor to Mexico, goes to a bullfight and is horrified by the vulgar cruelty of modern Mexico. But then she meets Don Ramón, a scholar and political leader, and General Cipriano, a military leader, and becomes involved in their resurrection of the ancient Mexican religion. For Lawrence, this religion is characterized by 'blood consciousness,' emotional and symbolic depth, and sex awareness. It is marked by dominance of the male over the female and the political leader over the masses, Lawrence's distorted interpretation of the Nietzschean superman. Don Ramón, the sexual, political, and religious hero of the book, is regarded as the reincarnated Quetzalcoatl, the Plumed Serpent that the Aztecs used to worship. He rises to lead the people, drawing them away from 'outworn' Christianity toward the Aztec religion. Eventually the cult spreads over the whole of Mexico and Kate, too, comes under its spell." Reader's Ency. 4th edition

The rainbow; with an introduction by Barbara Hardy. Knopf 1993 xxxv, 460p $20
ISBN 0-679-42305-2 LC 93-1860

"Everyman's library"

First published 1915

"The story line traces three generations of the Brangwen family in the Midlands of England from 1840 to 1905. The marriage of farmer Tom Brangwen and foreigner Lydia Lensky eventually breaks down. Likewise, the marriage of Lydia's daughter Anna to Tom's nephew Will gradually fails. The novel is largely devoted to Will and Anna's oldest child, the schoolteacher Ursula, who stops short of marriage when she is unsatisfied by her love affair with the conventional soldier Anton Skrebensky. The appearance of a rainbow at the end of the novel is a sign of hope for Ursula, whose story is continued in Lawrence's *Women in Love*." Merriam-Webster's Ency of Lit

Followed by Women in love

Sons and lovers. Knopf 1991 xxvii, 403p $17
ISBN 0-679-40572-0 LC 91-53002

"Everyman's library"

First published 1913

"Paul Morel, adored youngest son of a middle-class mother who feels that her coal-miner husband was unworthy of her, has difficulty in breaking away from her. Mrs. Morel has given her son all her warmth and love for so long a time that Paul finds it impossible to establish a relationship with another women. Miriam is supportive and understanding of his artistic nature but appeals mainly to his higher nature; Clara Dawes becomes his mistress but she is married and will not divorce her husband. After the death of his mother, Paul arranges a reconciliation between Clara and her husband and, after months of grieving for his mother, at last finds the strength to strike out on his own." Shapiro. Fic For Youth. 3d edition

The white peacock. o.p.

First published 1911

"A story of rural England, its characters being farmers and sons of farmers, and its scenes all enacted in the midst of crops and harvests, woods and country lanes. Everywhere we come in close contact with the life of the open, free out-of-doors; everywhere we get the scent of the soil. The tragedy of a rabbit mangled by the steel teeth of a trap, a nest of field-mice dug up and crushed remorselessly, one by one; the sordid wretchedness of a hovel swarming with dirty, quarreling, half-clad children, mismanaged by a slatternly, overworked drudge of a woman who occasionally relieves her feelings by hitting them over the head with a battered saucepan—such scenes as these are done with relentless skill that makes them actually hurt as you read them." Bookman's Manual

Women in love. Knopf 1992 475p o.p.
ISBN 0-679-40995-5 LC 91-53191

"Everyman's library"

Sequel to The rainbow

First published 1920

This novel "examines the ill effects of industrialization

Lawrence, D. H. (David Herbert), 1885-1930—*Continued*

on the human psyche, resolving that individual and collective rebirth is possible only through human intensity and passion. *Women in Love* contrasts the love affair of Rupert Birkin and Ursula Brangwen with that of Gudrun, Ursula's artistic sister, and Gerald Crich, a domineering industrialist. Birkin, an introspective misanthrope, struggles to reconcile his metaphysical drive for self-fulfillment with Ursula's practical view of sentimental passion. Their love affair and eventual marriage are set as a positive antithesis to the destructive relationship of Gudrun and Crich." Merriam-Webster's Ency of Lit

Lawrence, David

The dead sit round in a ring; David Lawrence. 1st U.S. ed. Thomas Dunne Books 2004 435p $24.95

ISBN 0-312-32710-2 LC 2004-41878

"Three of the four bodies sitting in a ring in a London flat are identified as elderly siblings in a suicide pact. The fourth turns out to be Jimmy Stone, a gofer for the notorious Tanner family, runner of drugs, guns, and girls. So begins Det. Sgt. Sheila Mooney's bedevilment. Dogged in her investigation of the murder, she disrupts a neighboring undercover operation and turns over another stone: the sexual exploitation of women lured from Eastern Europe by promises of visas and jobs. Nearing the breaking point at work, Sheila also has to wrestle with personal issues." Libr J

This mystery offers a "perspective on London that is darker and grittier than in conventional treatments. But the writing is the thing. Whether he's describing a bizarre death scene . . . or observing a group of streetwalkers plying their night trade . . . Lawrence, a published poet, writes with a delicacy and restraint rare in the genre." N Y Times Book Rev

Lawrence, David Herbert *See* Lawrence, D. H. (David Herbert), 1885-1930

Lawrence, Margaret K.

The burning bride; [by] Margaret Lawrence. Avon Bks. 1998 387p o.p.

ISBN 0-380-97620-X LC 98-4491

This novel finds eighteenth-century midwife Hannah Trevor hesitating on the brink of marriage. Her tormented lover, town militia commander Daniel Josselyn, father of her daughter, Jennet, and of the child Hannah now carries, is finally free to wed. But will Daniel insist that she give up her fierce independence and assume the duties of a gentleman's lady? Before she has a chance to find out, a man is murdered and violence erupts in the small Maine community, testing both Hannah and Daniel's loyalties and opening a Pandora's box of dark secrets." Booklist

Hearts and bones; [by] Margaret Lawrence. Avon Bks. 1996 307p il o.p.

LC 96-2394

"The year is 1786; the place a rural community in Maine. Hannah Trevor, a midwife, healer, and Enlightenment thinker, finds Nan Emory apparently raped and murdered in her bed. A damaging letter in which Nan accuses her attackers is left behind. All evidence seems to point to Hannah's former lover, Daniel Josselyn. Daniel's invalid wife, Charlotte, turns to Hannah, who is convinced that Daniel was framed by an enemy, explores the evidence, and discovers the real murderer." Libr J

"Through a combination of diary entries, trial records, autopsy reports, and engrossing narrative, Lawrence reveals the story of a witness and a participant in a brutal war crime and their decade-long silence." Booklist

Lawson, Mary, 1910-1941

Crow Lake. Dial Press (NY) 2002 291p o.p.

ISBN 0-385-33611-X LC 2001-53779

In this novel "four children living in northern Ontario struggle to stay together after their parents die in an auto accident. . . . Kate Morrison narrates the tale in flashback mode, starting with the fatal car accident that leaves seven-year-old Kate; her toddler sister, Bo; 19-year-old Luke; and 17-year-old Matt to fend for themselves." Publ Wkly

"Lawson achieves a breathless anticipatory quality in her surprisingly adept first novel, in which a child tells the story, but tells it very well indeed." Booklist

Lawton, John, 1949-

Old flames. Atlantic Monthly Press 2003 416p $24

ISBN 0-87113-864-6 LC 2002-28025

"April 1956, Nikita Krushchev is in London on a diplomatic errand. Chief Inspector Frederick Troy of Scotland Yard is assigned as a bodyguard to the Russsian leader. But he has a secret mission, too: Troy, fluent in Russian, is to spy on Khrushchev (who doesn't know the British cop speaks his language) by evesdropping on private conversations and reporting back to his superiors. It's a tough assignment, with a handful of tricky moral qualms, and it gets a heck of a lot tougher when a Royal Navy diver turns up dead." Booklist

"Lawton has created an effective genre-bending novel that is at once a cerebral thriller and an uproarious, deliciously English spoof." Publ Wkly

Le, Thi Diem Thuy, 1972-

The gangster we are all looking for. Knopf 2003 160p $18

ISBN 0-375-40018-4 LC 2002-33999

"The nameless first-person narrator is born in Vietnam, carried across the ocean by her father and 'washed to shore' in Linda Vista, a section of San Diego. Her 'Ba' finds work as a house painter, a welder and finally a gardener. It is two years before her mother joins them and her parents' tempestuous marriage moves to center stage, but the father is always a haunted, brooding presence in this drama of the narrator's coming-of-age." N Y Times Book Rev

"The story opens slowly but gathers strength, and though it remains somewhat muted, Le's lyrical writing and skill with the telling vigette will reward patient readers." Libr J

Le Carré, John, 1931-

Absolute friends. Little, Brown 2004 455p $26.95

ISBN 0-316-00023-X LC 2003-61196

Le Carré, John, 1931-—*Continued*

"The central characters in this novel are Ted Mundy, an old-school Englishman, the misfit son of a disgraced British Army major and once a spy but now a tour guide at one of Mad King Ludwig's Bavarian castles; and Sasha, a 1960's German radical. . . . Sasha, whose father was a Lutheran minister with Nazi ties, is a double and possibly a triple agent. . . . Their lives as friends, secret agents and idealists have been intertwined for more than 40 years." N Y Times (Late N Y Ed)

"If le Carre's symbols are a little obvious and his rhetoric a little heated, his technical skill is pure joy." New Leader

The constant gardener; a novel. Scribner 2001 492p o.p.

ISBN 0-7432-1505-2 LC 00-53340

"Tessa Quayle, a beautiful young lawyer, is posted to Nairobi as the wife of British diplomat Justin Quayle. In the course of the voluntary work in which she becomes involved, she uncovers a trail of intentional malfeasance by the vast pharmaceutical multinational KVH, which is fast-tracking a new TB drug using Africans as guinea pigs. She first calls on the British government to intervene and then decides to take her evidence to Richard Leakey. Le Carre's latest novel opens with Tessa's being murdered on her way to Leakey. Tessa was accompanied by her friend Arnold Bluhm, whom the official investigation finds guilty of her murder. But Tessa's husband begins his own probe, following her trail of contacts around the world." Libr J

"Globalization in its uglier aspects . . . has replaced the Cold War as the moral backdrop in Le Carre's work. His Cold War novels did not spare the conscience even of citizens on the 'right' side, confronting them with crimes committed in their names, and the globalization novels do not spare the stockholder." Atl Mon

The honourable schoolboy. Knopf 1977 533p o.p.

LC 77-75001

Jerry Westerby is the honorable schoolboy of the title. He works with George Smiley of the British Secret Service, described by the author as The Circus, to discover why the Russian Secret Service is paying $25,000 a month into the bank account of the prosperous Hong Kong business man, Drake Ko. The action takes place in London and Southeast Asia. The story opens in the Hong Kong press club

This "is superbly well-organized, combining a grandiose sweep with an intricate pattern. It has hard-edged reality instead of fuzzy near-fantasy, a host of sharply etched characters instead of a few eccentric caricatures, and a style which, subtle and flexible . . . . never obtrudes, yet never goes unnoticed." Times Lit Suppl

also in Le Carré, J. The quest for Karla p253-678

The little drummer girl. Knopf 1983 429p o.p.

LC 82-48733

"A series of bomb-attacks upon Israeli officials throughout Europe is investigated by Kurtz and his assistant Litvak . . . who plan not merely to track down the terrorists but to infiltrate the core of the illicit Palestinian organisation and explode it from within. Charlie, a footloose actress with radical affinities, is taken up by a . . . stranger who gradually introduces her into a network of political altruism. She is schooled to succumb to the charms of a Palestinian guerrilla yet at a deeper level to be still working for the Israelis." New Statesman (1913)

"Mr. le Carré's novel is certainly the most mature, inventive and powerful book about terrorists-come-to-life this reader has experienced. It transcends the genre." NY Times Book Rev

The looking glass war. Coward-McCann 1965 320p o.p.

This spy story "concerns a former military espionage department in London (small, left over from the . . . days of World War II) and its struggle to train one of its former agents for a mission into East Germany." NY Times Book Rev

"A bitter, cruel, dispassionate—yet passionate—study of an unimportant piece of espionage and the unimportant little men who are involved in it." Book Week

The night manager; a novel. Knopf 1993 429p o.p.

LC 92-55070

"Jonathan Pine, hotel night manager and volunteer spy, [sets] out to avenge the death of Sophie, a high-class Egyptian prostitute whom he loved and betrayed. . . . With the help of a maverick branch of British Intelligence determined to wrest operational control from the latter-day cold warriors, Pine sets out to trap Dicky Roper, the man responsible for Sophie's death, a world-class arms dealer about to embark on a massive drugs-for-guns deal." Booklist

Le Carré "brings to the world of the drug wars the same skilled characterization, perceptive detail, and dramatic storytelling that made him the undisputed master of the Cold War spy novel. This novel is precisely what we have come to expect from him: a work of high literary merit that's also great entertainment." Libr J

Our game; a novel. Knopf 1995 301p o.p.

LC 95-2666

The "narrator is Tim Cranmer, former secret agent turned winemaker in rural Somerset. Tim's great espionage success was the recuiting of brilliant gadfly Larry Pettifer, who ended up not only stealing Tim's beautiful mistress, the enigmatic Emma, but also disappearing, apparently with a fortune lifted from Russian banks to aid the rebels through shady arms deals. Now the police are looking for Larry, the 'Office' is convinced Cranmer must be in on his schemes, and, using all his old spycraft, he sets out to find Larry and Emma." Publ Wkly

"This is classic le Carré, spun out beautifully: the ex-spy treated shabbily by his two-bit successors, then besting them by virtue of his superior spycraft. Delicious. But as the plot grows more complex, both politically and psychologically, it becomes clear that even after 14 novels, le Carré has no intention of repeating himself." Newsweek

A perfect spy. Knopf 1986 475p o.p.

LC 85-45587

"The protagonist of the story, Magnus Pym, aged 53, is . . . a senior partner in 'the firm' of British intelligence, working out of the British Embassy in Vienna. He is a man respected and admired for his intelligence and common sense. He is also a man of mystery . . . [His disappearance] sets the plot in motion. Friends, colleagues, and family haven't a clue to his whereabouts.

Le Carré, John, 1931-—*Continued*
His superiors fear that 'the perfect spy' has defected and that British agents in Czechoslovakia, a group supervised by Pym, may be targeted. Jack Brotherhood, Pym's agency superior, begins an investigation." West Coast Rev Books

"Not a spy novel in the usual sense . . . but a skillfully manipulated, complex, and probingly written study spiced with lively anecdotes. To be savored." Libr J

The quest for Karla. Knopf 1982 952p o.p.
LC 82-47961

Contents: Tinker, tailor, soldier, spy; The honourable schoolboy; Smiley's people

The Russia house. Knopf 1989 353p o.p.
LC 88-46159

"A mysterious manuscript purporting to prove the Soviet defense system is unworkable is smuggled out of Moscow. It was intended for a flaky English publisher, a womanizing saxophone-playing boozer, but the smuggler has turned it over to British intelligence. In order to prove its authenticity, they recruit the publisher as an amateur spy and send him to Moscow to reestablish contact with the author. But the 'truth' Barley Blair finds there is love and a purpose for his shambles of a life." Libr J

"With scarcely an intimation of sex, no violence and not a side arm visible, Le Carre has again managed to construct a plot of commanding suspense. . . . The Russia House is both afire and thought provoking, a thriller that demands a second reading as a treatise on our time." Time

The secret pilgrim. Knopf 1990 335p o.p.
LC 90-52944

This novel "takes the form of a reverie-memoir, a series of reflections on a long life in the espionage business recalled by a surnameless man called Ned. . . . Now on the verge of retirement, Ned is running Sarratt, the training school for new recruits to British intelligence. He invites the legendary George Smiley to address the impending graduates and, after dinner, the night is whiled away as the next generation of spies picks the brains of a past master. As Smiley responds to their questions, allusions and remarks that he makes trigger Ned's recollections about his own past." N Y Times Book Rev

"There's always been a didatic quality to le Carré's work that has been part of his novels' charm, but in no other book has he said so much about the ravages that the spying profession works upon the agent." Newsweek

Single & Single; a novel. Scribner 1999 345p $26

ISBN 0-684-85926-2 LC 98-47174

This book's title "is the name of a London family firm whose members seem to be investment bankers, but of a very peculiar and contemporary sort. In fact, they work with the kind of people—Russian gangsters, Swiss lawyers, creators of dummy corporations around the world—that specialize in making big money out of drugs and arms, and laundering the proceeds. The firm is run by Tiger Single, a modern buccaneer who wants his son, Oliver, to move up in the business." Publ Wkly

Le Carré "provides a fascinating journey through the new landscape of corruption. . . . The power of [this novel] stems from the author's portrait of a world in which individuals are no match for the organized mania of greed." Time

A small town in Germany. Coward-McCann 1968 383p o.p.

"Alan Turner arrives from London to investigate a breach in security [of the British Embassy at Bonn]. A temporary employee, Leo Harting, has apparently absconded with the crucial Green File and a mass of other secret papers. Turner's job: find them. The permanent staff, an encyclopedia of the English class system, dislikes Turner, the angriest of young men, and tries to keep him at arm's length. Turner stops at nothing." Newsweek

"The plot is ingeniously constructed with ever-mounting suspense and it is related with the deftness of a writer who possesses an enviable command of description and narration." Best Sellers

Smiley's people. Knopf 1980 c1979 374p o.p.
LC 79-2299

First published 1979 in the United Kingdom

"George Smiley, who retired as master of the British secret service known as the Circus when the Cold War was supplanted by détente, is . . . recalled to duty when one of his former 'people,' a brilliant anti-Soviet Estonian emigré called the General, is murdered on Hampstead Heath. The General, as Smiley patiently works it out, had been trying to reach him with what was understood to be documentary evidence that could destroy the infamous Russian spymaster Karla." New Yorker

This novel "is a complete winner, exciting, well-paced, and convincing. . . . There is a lot of the Le Carré gloom, but now it seems almost elegiac and touching. Absolutely not to be missed." Libr J

also in Le Carré, J. The quest for Karla p679-952

The spy who came in from the cold. Coward-McCann 1964 c1963 256p o.p.

First published 1963 in the United kingdom

"The story of Alec Leamas, 50-year-old professional [secret agent] who has grown stale in espionage, who longs to 'come in from the cold'—and how he undertakes one last assignment before that hoped-for retirement. Over the years Leamas has grown unsure where his workday carapace ends and his real self begins. . . . Recalled from Berlin after the death of his last East German contact at the Wall, Leamas lets himself be seduced into a pretended defection—thereby providing the East Germans with data from which they can deduce that the head of their own spy apparatus is a double agent." N Y Times Book Rev

The tailor of Panama. Knopf 1996 331p o.p.

ISBN 0-679-45446-2 LC 96-34802

This is an "account of a British tailor in Panama whose manufactured universe collides tragically with reality. . . . Harry Pendel is pressured into becoming a spy by an amoral British agent. Desperate to avoid exposure as an ex-con, Harry fabricates a network of sources and plies the giddy Brits with tales of a coming Panamanian revolution." Booklist

Le Carré "reveals in the contortions of British diplomats, aghast at the *arriviste* spy masters whom they pretend to accept, all the while struggling to extricate them-

Le Carré, John, 1931-—*Continued*

selves from absurd but inevitable catastrophe. Readers who wonder whether Graham Greene was not here 40 years ago are right, and Mr le Carré acknowledges his debt to 'Our Man in Havana'. This tale, told with wit and ingenuity, is a splendid homage from one master of political thrillers to another." Economist

Tinker, tailor, soldier, spy. Knopf 1974 355p o.p.

The novel's protagonist, British agent George Smiley, "is asked to come out of retirement and root out as unobtrusively as possible the 'mole,' or Russian agent, that has burrowed his way to the center of England's secret intelligence organization, the Circus. Smiley is feeling glum. His wife has left him and his retirement was forced upon him the year before when power was reshuffled at the Circus. It is clear, too, that the mole must be one of Smiley's old colleagues." Newsweek

Smiley "instinctively realises from the outset who the traitor is but refuses to confront the embarrassing truth. A perceptive reader will sense the secret too, but one goes on reading entranced not so much by the ramifications of the plot, beautifully engineered though it is, as by concern for the characters, a rare thing in thrillers." New Statesman (1913)

also in Le Carré, J. The quest for Karla p1-252

Le Guin, Ursula K., 1929-

The beginning place. Harper & Row 1980 183p o.p.

LC 79-2653

"For Hugh, on the run from the demands of his domineering mother and from the dullness of his job as a checkout boy at a local market . . . and for Irene, fearful of sexual harrassment at the hands of her stepfather and other men, [a fantastical] world becomes a refuge. Then an unknown evil begins to pervade their paradise and they are chosen to face the 'fear.' Irene, jealous of newcomer Hugh's acceptance into the world she has been visiting for so long, reluctantly acts as guide for Hugh who, as sword-wielder, is to be the savior. Having finally slain a monster, Irene and Hugh seek to escape Eden turned nightmare." SLJ

"The style is fluent, concise and elegant, and the story that is told is easily understood by anyone who has ever found himself at a loss to deal with the realities of modern life." Best Sellers

Betrayals

In Le Guin, U. K. Four ways to forgiveness p1-34

The birthday of the world and other stories. HarperCollins Pubs. 2002 362p $24.95

ISBN 0-06-621253-7 LC 2001-39508

Contents: Coming of age in Karhide; The matter of Seggri; Unchosen love; Mountain ways; Solitude; Old music and the slave women; The birthday of the world; Paradises lost

"Le Guin appears to have the most fun with her investigations of sex and gender . . . but the costs of revolution, religious bliss, and technology are also provicatively explored, and one returns to the current headlines with a fresh awareness of the exotic providional nature of human arrangements." New Yorker

Changing planes; illustrated by Eric Beddows. Harcourt 2003 246p il $22

ISBN 0-15-100971-6 LC 2002-14919

Contents: Sita Dulip's method; Porridge on Islac; The silence of the Asonu; Feeling at home with the Hennebet; The ire of the Veksi; Seasons of the Ansarac; Social dreaming of the Frin; The royals of Hegn; Woeful tales from Mahigul; Great Joy; Wake Island; The Nna Mmoy language; The Building; The fliers of Gy; The Island of the Immortals; Confusions of Uñi

This is "philosophical fiction in the manner of Jonathan Swift and Jorge Luis Borges. . . . The narrator explains that a friend of hers, suffering from the 'tense misery, indigestion and boredom' of airport waiting rooms, discovered that with a slight twist of her mind she could transport herself to other 'planes' of existence. The 15 tales that follow are reports, ranging from the satirical to the gnomic, abut the strangely familiar societies one encounters during 'interplanary travel.'" N Y Times Book Rev

City of illusions. Harper & Row 1978 c1967 199p o.p.

First published 1967 in paperback by Ace Books

This novel "chronicles the search for identity by a man without a past, named Falk, as he wanders through a world where scientists and shamans live in separate societies. In the city of Shing, a city of illusion and trickery, Falk regains his memory and becomes a threat to the ruling Shing. Standard adventure fare raised from the ordinary by Le Guin's richly drawn background of Earth taken over by aliens." Booklist

The dispossessed; an ambiguous Utopia. Harper & Row 1974 341p il o.p.

"Shevek, a brilliant physicist, is caught between the prejudices and hatreds of two worlds. His quest to bridge the gap between Ararres, an anarchist, egalitarian society, and Varas, a structured, capitalistic world, unleashes a storm of intrigue and drama. The two distinct cultures provide insights into the role of women in society, the issue of free will versus obligation to the state, human rights, and ecomonic systems." Shapiro. Fic for Youth. 3d edition

A fisherman of the inland sea; science fiction stories. HarperPrism 1994 191p il o.p.

LC 94-5397

Contents: The first contact with the Gorgonids; Newton's sleep; The ascent of the north face; The rock that changed things; The kerastion; The Shobie's story; Dancing to Ganam; Another story; or, A fisherman of the inland sea

"Le Guin demonstrates her storytelling virtuosity in each of these diverse tales." Voice Youth Advocates

Forgiveness day

In Le Guin, U. K. Four ways to forgiveness p35-92

Four ways to forgiveness. HarperPrism 1995 228p o.p.

LC 95-11459

Contents: Betrayals; Forgiveness day; A man of the people; A woman's liberation

"Four interrelated novellas deal with the Hainish culture on the twin planets of Werel and Yeowe and examine the relationship between love, freedom and forgiveness." Publ Wkly

Le Guin, Ursula K., 1929-—*Continued*

The lathe of heaven. Scribner 1971 184p o.p.

"A psychiatrist sets out to use a patient whose dreams can alter reality to create utopia, but in usurping this power he is gradually delivered into madness." Anatomy of Wonder 4

"The author has done some profound research in psychology, cerebro-physiology and biochemistry. . . . In addition, her perceptions of such matters as geopolitics, race, socialized medicine and the patient/shrink relationship are razor-sharp and more than a little cutting." Natl Rev

The left hand of darkness; with a new afterword and appendixes by the author. 25th Anniversary ed. Walker & Co. 1994 345p o.p.

ISBN 0-8027-1302-5 LC 94-27147

A reissue of the title first published 1969 by Walker & Company

"This is a tale of political intrigue and danger on the world of Gethen, the Winter planet. Genly Ai, high official of the Eukeman—the commonwealth of worlds—is on Gethen to convince the royalty to join the Federation. He soon becomes a pawn in Gethen's power struggles, set against the elaborate mores of the Gethenians, a unisex hermaphroditic people whose intricate sexual physiology plays a key role in the conflict. Allied with Estraven, fallen lord, Genly is forced to cross the savage and impassable Gobrin Ice." Shapiro. Fic for Youth. 3d edition

Malafrena. Putnam 1979 369p o.p.

LC 79-11042

"Sorde is the heir of a well-to-do landowner in Malafrena. He goes off to college and finds that he does have something to live for—his concept of freedom. His fight for that freedom leads him to publish revolutionary tracts, spend two years in prison, and then lead a short-lived insurrection." Best Sellers

Set in "the 19th Century in an imaginary European country. . . . Le Guin portrays Sorde's coming of age—and how he and those who love him discover their life's work and personal strengths—with a Tolstoyesque flavor and grandeur. A book about freedom and commitment that should win a grateful, enthusiastic audience." Libr J

A man of the people
In Le Guin, U. K. Four ways to forgiveness p93-144

(ed) The Norton book of science fiction. See The Norton book of science fiction

Orsinian tales. Harper & Row 1976 179p o.p.

Contents: The fountains; The barrow; Ile Forest; Conversations at night; The road east; Brothers and sisters; A week in the country; An die Musik; The house; The lady of Moge; Imaginary countries

This is a cycle of interrelated short stories. "Set in a vaguely Middle-European country, Le Guin's tales deal with love, freedom, and tyranny in a society which over a series of historical periods appears to be perpetually in the last stages preceding cataclysm." Booklist

The other wind. Harcourt 2001 246p o.p.

ISBN 0-15-100684-9 LC 2001-24632

"Alder, the man who unwittingly initiates the transformation of Earthsea, is a humble sorcerer who specializes in fixing broken pots and repairing fence lines, but when his beloved wife, Lily, dies, he is inconsolable. He begins to dream of the land of the dead and sees both Lily and other shades reaching out to him across the low stone wall that separates them from the land of the living. Soon, more general signs and portents begin to disturb Earthsea." Publ Wkly

"The Earthsea saga, begun in 1968 as a young adults' series, has evolved into one of Le Guin's, and modern science fiction's, signature achievements." N Y Times Book Rev

Searoad; chronicles of Klatsand. HarperCollins Pubs. 1991 193p o.p.

LC 91-55160

Includes the following stories: Bill Weisler; Crosswords; Foam women, rain women; Geezers; Hand, cup, shell; Hernes; In and out; Quoits; The Ship Ahoy; Sleepwalkers; Texts; True love

"In these stories, connected loosely but powerfully by their rugged Pacific Northwest setting, LeGuin portrays residents of a small Oregon shore town with sympathy and no sentiment. Many of the tales center around women drawn together in threes—mother, daughter, grandmother—by illness or death. Passionate, independent and questioning, these characters generally choose, sooner or later, personal freedom over convention, but not without pain." Publ Wkly

The telling. Harcourt 2000 264p o.p.

ISBN 0-15-100567-2 LC 00-29574

A title in the authors Hainish cycle. "As a member of the Ekumen's embassy on the planet Aka, Sutty undertakes a delicate mission that leads her to a mountain village reported to contain the last remnants of a dying culture. Following a trail of subtle clues concealed in stories and folk sayings, Sutty discovers the suppressed history of a planet willing to abandon its old ways in the name of progress. . . . This parable of the modern world's headlong rush toward monocultural sterility exemplifies the author's elegant simplicity and keen insight." Libr J

A woman's liberation
In Le Guin, U. K. Four ways to forgiveness p145-208

The word for world is forest
In The Hugo winners p225-327

Lear, Peter *See* Lovesey, Peter

Leavitt, David, 1961-

The body of Jonah Boyd. Bloomsbury 2004 215p $23.95

ISBN 1-582-34188-5 LC 2003-20904

"Thirty years later, Judith 'Denny' Denham recalls the fateful Thanksgiving of 1969, which she spent with the family of her employer, Dr. Ernest Wright of Wellspring University's psych department. Momentous at the time because Nancy Wright's best friend from back East was visiting with her new husband, novelist Jonah Boyd, the day became more momentous because during it Boyd lost his magnum-opus third novel. A few years later, he fell off the wagon and drove into a bridge." Booklist

Leavitt, David, 1961-—*Continued*

"The book, with its acerbic tone and tight plot, is an unlikely vehicle for a paean to domesticity, yet it's this odd fit that makes 'The Body of Jonah Boyd' such a pleasure. And Leavitt is once again having a surprisingly good time messing about with the idea of authorship." N Y Times Book Rev

The lost language of cranes. Knopf 1986 319p o.p.

LC 86-45277

"The story focuses on Philip Benjamin, a 25-year-old New Yorker, . . . gay, who is involved in his first 'serious' romance. This situation is complicated by the struggle of Philip's father to deal more openly with his own long-standing, but thus far closeted, homosexual inclinations. With Philip's coming out, father is thrown into even greater turmoil, mother begins to realize the complete truth, and all are forced to reexamine the ties that bind them." Libr J

"Mr Leavitt's sense of pacing, his graceful sentences and his storytelling ability dovetail nicely. On the other hand, the book feels young—experientially thin, intellectually timid, contrived, erratic and, understandably, not yet wise. . . . 'The Lost Language of Cranes' lingers in the mind, greater than the sum of its problematic parts." N Y Times Book Rev

The marble quilt; stories. Houghton Mifflin 2001 241p $25

ISBN 0-395-90244-4 LC 2001-24522

Contents: Crossing St. Gotthard; The infection scene; Route 80; We meet at last; Black box; Speonk; The scruff of the neck; The list; Heaped earth; The marble quilt

"A masterly collection of stories that transport us from Italy at the turn of the 19th century, where we follow a small family on their first trip to Europe, to England and a fictional account of Lord Alfred Douglas's life (he was one of Oscar Wilde's lovers) to the United States and the tragedy of a plane crash off the Atlantic Coast. . . . As always, Leavitt creates some of the most finely polished characters in fiction today; even minor characters feel real." Libr J

Martin Bauman; or, A sure thing. Houghton Mifflin 2000 387p $26

ISBN 0-395-90243-6 LC 00-27589

"Martin Bauman, the gay writer protagonist of Leavitt's self-referential novel, has not even come out to himself let alone his parents or friends when he enters college in 1980. Happiest in the company of lesbians and seemingly immune to lust or love, he assiduously cultivates his literary ambitions under the brutal tutelage of professor Stanley Flint, who warns him that his need for approval and preference for 'a sure thing' could turn him into a mere hack. Flint continues to be his nemesis even after Martin achieves instant fame by disclosing his homosexuality in the first 'gay' short story ever published in *the* New York literary magazine, and Martin, analyzing himself two decades later, acknowledges Flint's prescience as he relates, in detail both mesmerizing and maddening, the story of his early success and rapid comeuppance." Booklist

(ed) Penguin book of gay short fiction. See Penguin book of gay short fiction

While England sleeps. Viking 1993 304p o.p.

LC 92-45878

This novel is narrated by "English public school boy Brian Botsford. During a promiscous post-university period in the 1930s, Brian dallies with both leftist political interests and the affections of a working-class Underground ticket taker, Edward Phelan, in a highly charged sexual affair. He also convinces himself that he is in love with a young woman of his own class, Philippa Archibald, with whom he has a sexual liaison. Having discovered Brian's affair with Philippa, Edward flees to Spain to join the International Brigade. Risking prison, he later deserts, and Brian rushes to Spain to help." Libr J

"A narrative that for the most part rings true, though in a curiously mannered way. The reader ends up with a feeling of respect for the assiduous research that has been undertaken, rather than with any sense of deep involvement with the characters." N Y Times Book Rev

Lebrecht, Norman, 1948-

The song of names; Norman Lebrecht. Anchor Bks. 2004 c2002 311p pa $14

ISBN 1-4000-3489-2 (pa) LC 2003-67451

In this novel, "two men who became friends as children in London during WWII are reunited after 40 years. In 1939, nine-year-old Martin Simmonds meets Dovidl Rapoport, a violin prodigy the same age. Martin's father is a music impresario, and when Dovidl is sent by his Polish parents to study in England, he offers the boy lodging in his own home. Dovidl and Martin quickly become best friends. Dovidl's parents perish in the Holocaust; then, in 1951, Dovidl-his name changed to the more palatable Eli-is about to embark on a career as a concert virtuoso when he disappears on the day of his debut. Martin becomes obsessed with his friend's disappearance, and after decades of searching finally finds him in a dreary town in the north of England." Publ Wkly

"Lebrecht's story delves into the horrors of the Holocaust and the Blitz, as well as the quiet communities of Hasidic Judaism that developed in Britain after the flight of so many refugees. What emerges is a vivid and outstanding story that sings about artistry, genius, music, love, envy, friendship, and revenge." Booklist

Lederer, William J., 1912-

The ugly American; [by] William J. Lederer and Eugene Burdick. Norton 1958 285p o.p.

Contents: Lucky, Lucky Lou #1; Lucky, Lucky Lou #2; Nine friends; Everybody loves Joe Bing; Confidential and personal; Employment opportunities abroad; The girl who got recruited; The ambassador and the working press; Everyone has ears; The ragtime kid; The iron of war; The lessons of war; What would you do if you were President; How to buy an American junior grade; The six-foot swami from Savannah; Captain Boning, USN; The ugly American; The ugly American and the ugly Sarkhanese; The bent backs of Chang 'Dong; Senator, Sir; The sum of tiny things

Lee, C. Y., 1917-

The flower drum song. Farrar, Straus & Cudahy 1957 244p o.p.

A story of family life in San Francisco's Chinatown. The principal characters are the elderly Mr. Wang and his oldest son, Wang Ta, torn between Chinese tradition and western custom

"A first novel that is always fascinating, and by turns amusing and pathetic—a novel written with grace and decorum in the even, unimpassioned narrative style that is characteristic of classical Chinese fiction." Chicago Sunday Trib

Lee, Chang-Rae

Aloft. Riverhead Books 2004 343p $24.95

ISBN 1-573-22263-1 LC 2003-58630

"Set on affluent Long Island, [this novel] follows the life of a suburban, upper-middle-class man during a time of family crisis. Jerry Battle's favorite diversion is to fly his small plane over the neighboring towns and villages. When his daughter and her fiance arrive from Oregon to announce their marriage plans, he looks back on his life and faces his disengagement with it . . . and the people he loves." Publisher's note

The author "creates a pointillist portrait of three generations of a family as it has motored its way from blue collar immigrant hopes to bourgeois respectability to new money indulgence, and in doing so he gently nudges Jerry and his relatives into holding up a mirror to the American Dream in all its glittering and treacherous promise." N Y Times (Late N Y Ed)

A gesture life. Riverhead Bks. 1999 356p o.p.

ISBN 1-573-22146-5 LC 99-28382

"Doc Hata lives an exemplary American small-town life, but . . . his decorum conceals an immigrant's tragic past. Born to poor ethnic Koreans but raised by wealthy Japanese, Hata falls in love with a comfort woman during the war. Haunted by her dire fate, he adopts a Korean girl, but, unable to express his love, he nearly loses her, too." Booklist

"This is a wise, humane, fully rounded story, deeply but unsentimentally moving, and permeated with insights about the nature of human relationships." Publ Wkly

Lee, Don, 1959-

Country of origin. W.W. Norton & Co 2004 315p $24.95

ISBN 0-393-05812-3 LC 2004-4722

"Set in Tokyo in 1980, the book centers on the disappearance of Lisa Countryman, a half-Japanese, half-black Berkeley graduate student who goes to Japan to research the 'sad, brutal reign of conformity' for her dissertation and, perhaps more importantly, embark on an identity quest. . . . When she vanishes, it is first brought to the attention of Tom Hurley, a vain and careless junior diplomat at the U.S. Embassy who tells people he's Hawaiian, though he's really half-Korean and half-white. The case is turned over to Kenzo Ota, a glum, divorced police inspector, who spent three hard years of his adolescence in Missouri." Publ Wkly

"Issues of race, class, and national identity drive this clear-eyed story of closure, redemption, and carving out a place in the world." Booklist

Lee, Gentry

(jt. auth) Clarke, A. C. The Garden of Rama
(jt. auth) Clarke, A. C. Rama II
(jt. auth) Clarke, A. C. Rama revealed

Lee, Gus

China boy; a novel. Dutton 1991 322p o.p.

LC 90-21687

"The rough-and-tumble tale of Kai Ting, the only son of an aristocratic Shanghai couple whose escape from the Communists landed them in San Francisco's tough, predominantly black, Panhandle district. When Kai Ting's mother dies, his father marries a white woman who tries to eradicate her stepchildren's Chinese heritage. She sends the skinny, sheltered, and bewildered boy out into the neighborhood, where he becomes everyone's favorite punching bag." Am Libr

"Based on events in his own childhood, Mr. Lee's depiction of Kai's efforts to reconcile his Chinese heritage with the several equally bewildering worlds of American culture he is simultaneously exposed to . . . is vivid and moving." N Y Times Book Rev

Followed by Honor & duty (1994)

Honor & duty. Knopf 1994 425p o.p.

LC 92-42711

This novel "continues the saga of Kai Ting's struggle to become an American without abandoning Chinese cultural values. Now, Kai faces the challenge of West Point. Having survived his brutal stepmother and life on San Francisco's mean streets, first-year hazing seems insignificant, but other problems arise. Kai is required to pass engineering courses with no math ability; he is an Asian in the military at a time when America's involvement in Vietnam is deepening; and he is a man of honor faced with a cheating scandal." Libr J

"Although his plot becomes maudlin at times, Lee fashions a generally convincing first-person narrative in Kai's voice, skillfully drawing the reader into each of his young narrator's painful dilemmas." Publ Wkly

Lee, Harper, 1926-

To kill a mockingbird. 40th anniversary ed. HarperCollins Pubs. 1999 323p $19.95

ISBN 0-06-019499-5

A reissue of the title first published 1960 by Lippincott

"Scout, as Jean Louise is called, is a precocious child. She relates her impressions of the time when her lawyer father, Atticus Finch, is defending a black man accused of raping a white woman in a small Alabama town during the 1930's. Atticus's courageous act brings the violence and injustice that exists in their world sharply into focus as it intrudes into the lighthearted life that Scout and her brother Jem have enjoyed until that time." Shapiro. Fic for Youth. 3d edition

Lee, Lilian *See* Li, Pi-hua

Lee, Manfred, 1905-1971

For works written by this author in collaboration with Frederic Dannay see Queen, Ellery

Lee, Mark, 1950-

The canal house. Algonquin Bks. 2003 353p $23.95

ISBN 1-56512-379-4 LC 2003-40401

This is the "story of the life and death of war correspondent Daniel McFarland, who after a brush with death in Uganda develops a new sense of mission and responsibility toward those whose wracked lives he is covering. He is drawn into an affair with Julia Cadel, an English doctor who idealistically ministers to the suffering in war zones, and the book's title refers to a brief idyll they share in London before setting out again on dangerous missions. Their new one is in East Timor." Publ Wkly

"Lee is a foreign correspondent who creates a powerful aura of realism that will forever alter your perception of the news." Booklist

Lee, Tanith

White as snow. TOR Bks. 2000 319p o.p.

ISBN 0-312-86993-2 LC 00-41160

"A Tom Doherty Associates book"

In this reworking of Snow White "evil queen, Arpazia, first appears as an innocent princess of 14, who is terrified when Draco, a rising new leader, conquers her father's castle and rapes her. Soon after he has her sister, Lilca, hanged because Lilca betrayed the castle. Draco forces Arpazia to travel with him and his barbaric army. She later bears him a girl, Candacis, whom she immediately shuns as an incarnation of evil, mumbling death spells as the infant tries to suckle her." Publ Wkly

"Incorporating many traditional fairy-tale elements, Lee's Gothic story is set in a medieval world filled with castles, wars, dwarves, pagan lore, and Christian ritual." Libr J

Leebron, Fred G.

In the middle of all this. Harcourt 2002 251p $30

ISBN 0-15-100834-5 LC 2001-5955

"Martin Kreutzel teaches college in a small Pennsylvania town, where his house is leaking, his children seem to be normal, and his colleagues are facing such vicissitudes as a spouse's substance abuse and a student's suicide. His main concern at the moment is his London-based sister, Elizabeth, a vigorus woman who is dying of cancer. When Elizabeth's husband disappears for a few days, Martin rushes to London to be with her. After Martin returns home, Elizabeth herself disappears, presumably to make her own peace with her foreshortened future." Libr J

"Leebron's exceptional skills as a storyteller and observer of humanity produce a novel both tremendously enjoyable and grandly poignant, a novel almost anthropological in its keen examination of man's fate." Publ Wkly

Lefcourt, Peter

Eleven Karens; a novel. Simon & Schuster 2003 223p $24

ISBN 0-684-87034-7 LC 2002-21792

Lefcourt's "novel is essentially a series of short stories that reflect a statistical quirk—11 of his protagonist's loves have been named Karen. These femmes fatales range from the girlish—a kissing partner whom Lefcourt's hero pretends to marry in the fifth grade—to the matronly, as in the married fellow tourist who lures the narrator into an afternoon of stockings and heels in a Paris hotel." N Y Times Book Rev

"A blithe bacchanal, a lurid love song, one part travelogue, one part spoof, Lefcourt's narcissistic novel would work equally well on the big screen." Booklist

Legal briefs; stories by today's best legal thriller writers; edited by William Bernhardt. Doubleday 1998 292p o.p.

LC 97-53089

Contents: The divorce, by G. Stockley; Poetic justice, by S. Martini; Stairwell justice, by J. Brandon; The client, by R. N. Patterson; What we're here for, by W. Bernhardt; Cook County redemption, by M. A. Kahn; The jailhouse lawyer, by P. M. Margolin; Voir dire, by J. Healy; The birthday, by J. Grisham; Roads, by P. Friedman; Carrying concealed, by L. Scottoline

"This enjoyable collection lets readers laugh both at and with the legal profession." Booklist

Legal fictions; short stories about lawyers and the law; edited by Jay Wishingrad. Overlook Press 1992 402p o.p.

LC 91-46664

Contents: The tender offer, by L. Auchincloss; About Boston, by W. Just; The balloon of William Fuerst, by L. B. Komie; The contract, by H. Jacobs; Still life, by M. Thurm; After you've gone, by A. Adams; Weight, by M. Atwood; Puttermesser: her work history, her ancestry, her afterlife, by C. Ozick; Centaurs, by J. S. Marcus; Discipline, by L. Brown; Witness, by M. S. Bell; Earthly justice, by E. S. Goldman; The most outrageous consequences, by J. R. Parker; The colonel's foundation, by L. Auchincloss; Justice is blind, by T. Wolfe; Triumph of justice, by I. Shaw; The paradise of bachelors, by H. Melville; The web of circumstance, by C. W. Chesnutt; Bartleby, the scrivener, by H. Melville; Congress in crisis: the proximity bill, by G. Keillor; Szyrk v. Village of Tatamount et al., in the United States District Court, Southern District of Virginia, No. 105-87, by W. Gaddis; Coyote v. Acme, by I. Frazier; Before the law, by F. Kafka; The litigants, by I. B. Singer; Crimes of conscience, by N. Gordimer; A few selected sentences, by B. S. Johnson; Heart of a judge, by R. S. Easmon; Joy and the law, by G. Di Lampedusa; The condemned man's last night, by B. Peret; Legal aid, by F. O'Connor; General bellomo, by P. West; The Clairvoyant, by K. Čapek; The case for the defence, by G. Greene; Rumpole for the prosecution, by J. Mortimer; The judge's wife, by I. Allende

LeGuin, Ursula *See* Le Guin, Ursula K., 1929-

Lehane, Dennis

Gone, baby, gone; a novel. Morrow 1998 374p o.p.

ISBN 0-688-15332-1 LC 98-14042

Lehane, Dennis—*Continued*

"Four-year-old Amanda McCready has disappeared without a trace, and after several days, the police have no leads. Boston PIs Patrick Kenzie and Angela Gennaro reluctantly take the case, knowing that the odds are that Amanda is already dead. Their investigation is complicated by Amanda's mother, Helene, who seems more interested in drinking at the local bar than in finding her daughter. After a second child disappears, Kenzie and Gennaro are drawn into a dark nexus of pedophiles, drug dealers, and a shady police unit with a hidden agenda." Libr J

"The wrenching portrait of a bent cop whose instincts are admirable but whose actions are appalling only adds to the emotional impact of this grim, utterly unsentimental blue-collar tragedy." Booklist

Mystic river. Morrow 2001 401p il $25
ISBN 0-688-16316-5 LC 2001-273012

"Lehane identifies that turning point in the life and spiritual death of a working-class Boston neighborhood as the day in 1975 when 11-year-old Dave Boyle climbed into a car with two strange men—and his best friends, Sean Devine and Jimmy Marcus, did not. A quarter-century later, when the murder of Jimmy's 19-year-old daughter forces the three of them into a heart-scorching reunion, they still carry the scars of that childhood trauma. 'Maybe they *had* gotten in that car. All three of them,' Sean thinks. 'And what they now thought of as their life was just a dream state.' Lehane spares nothing in his wrenching descriptions of how a crime in the neighborhood kills the neighborhood, taking it down house by house, family by family." N Y Times Book Rev

Prayers for rain; a novel. Morrow 1999 337p $25
ISBN 0-688-15333-X LC 99-22048

"In what he thinks is an open-and-shut case, Boston private investigator Patrick Kenzie and his sidekick Bubba Rowgoski convince Cody Falk, a stalker with a nasty record of rape and sexual assault, to cease his harassment of Patrick's client, Karen Nichols. But six months later, a naked Karen leaps to her death off the observation deck of the Custom House tower. . . . Aided by Bubba and ex-partner/ex-lover Angie Gennaro, Patrick decides to investigate Karen's death. . . . Lehane's love of Boston, its neighborhoods, and its people shines through his hard-edged prose." Libr J

Sacred. Morrow 1997 288p o.p.
ISBN 0-688-14381-4 LC 96-53115

"When detectives Patrick Kenzie and Angela Gennaro are kidnapped by dying billionaire Trevor Stone and forced to find his lost daughter, they become entwined in a vicious whodunit in which 'up is down and north is south.' The case takes them to Grief Release Inc., a Boston-area church/cult whose members purge their sins, secrets, and financial records; then, accompanied by Stone's henchmen, to Tampa, Florida, where a top-of-the-line sports car and all the money they can spend are put at their disposal. . . . When the detectives finally find their prize, the perfecto, leggy Desiree Stone, she turns out to be much more than they bargained for." Libr J

Shutter Island. Morrow 2003 325p $25.95
ISBN 0-688-16317-3 LC 2003-48744

"From the 1993 perspective of the prologue, Shutter Island is one of those unpopulated islands in Boston's outer harbor that always look so mysterious from a distance and so scruffy up close. But in 1954, when the United States marshall Teddy Daniels and his partner, Chuck Aule, alight on its rocky shores to hunt for an escaped murderess, this bleak spot is home to Ashecliffe Hospital, a maximum-security institution for the criminally insane. . . . The atmosphere is properly dark and moody, and so long as Teddy and Chuck stick to the manhunt and their investigation of Ashecliffe's creepy medical staff, they play their roles with muscle and grace." N Y Times Book Rev

Lehrer, Jim

The last debate. Random House 1995 318p o.p.
LC 95-211383

"Four journalists are scheduled to moderate a debate between two presidential candidates. The Republican is a born-again racist, while the Democrat is not too swift but a decent fellow. The journalists decide to torpedo the Republican by bringing up his background of abuse and violence. The television presentation goes off the wall with the Republican going berserk. . . . When he loses the election, the journalists are rocketed to fame and notoriety." Libr J

"Mr. Lehrer is at his best when presenting his fictional version of the Washington journalism scene, which is close enough to reality to be truly funny." N Y Times Book Rev

Purple dots; a novel. Random House 1998 262p $23.95
ISBN 0-679-45237-0 LC 98-12962

This novel, set in Washington, D.C., is a "tale of a stalled presidential nomination. One senator objects to promoting Joshua Bennett from DCI to director of the Central Intelligence Agency, and someone within the agency is passing information to the senator's aide. When Bennett can't figure out what's going on, a group of ex-spooks who support him take on the assignment." Booklist

"The bad guys in this comedy of errors are uniformly inept and arrogant. The good guys behave like overgrown kids. Lehrer . . . has produced a very funny novel of Washington politics, broad and subtle by turns, and sly throughout." Libr J

The special prisoner; a novel. Random House 2000 227p o.p.
ISBN 0-375-50371-4 LC 00-701284

"A chance airport encounter sends retired Methodist bishop John Quincy Watson to San Diego, following a man whose too-familiar eyes drag Watson 50 years into the past, to a Japanese prisoner of war camp, where the then youthful, red-haired B29 pilot became a 'special prisoner' when captured after parachuting from his dying plane. His pursuit of the interrogator he knew as Tashimoto, the Hyena, alternates with the minister's memories of the horrors of Camp Sengei 4." Booklist

Leiber, Fritz, 1910-1992

Gonna roll the bones
In The Best of the Nebulas p211-27
In The Hugo winners p460-83

Leiber, Fritz, 1910-1992—*Continued*

Ill met in Lankhmar
In The Hugo winners p55-115

Ship of shadows
In The Hugo winners p5-50

The Wanderer. Walker & Co. 1970 c1964 318p o.p.

First published 1964 in paperback by Ballantine Books

A "novel telling of the havoc caused by the arrival of a strange planet in the Solar System. Its mosaic narrative technique, through which events are observed through a multiplicity of viewpoints, foreshadowed the profusion of such novels and films in the 1970s." Ency of Sci Fic

Leinster, Murray *See* Jenkins, Will F., 1896-1975

Leithauser, Brad, 1953-

A few corrections; a novel. Knopf 2001 273p $24

ISBN 0-375-41149-6 LC 00-62010

"At first, this exploration of a small-town Midwestern Lothario's life is like something out of Dreiser: Wesley Sultan—Rotarian, Episcopalian, and aspiring business-man—seems emphatically ordinary. The relevant characters, however, are Wesley's second wife, the brilliant, self-deprecating Sally, in France, who speaks in the style of the novels that fuel her mental life; and his brother Conrad, in Miami, riddled with disease and quite definitely raging against the dying of the light. The novel is formally constructed, each chapter offering a correction to the obituary of Wesley that appears on the first page, and this sobriety of design contrasts with the inventiveness of Leithauser's portraits." New Yorker

Lelchuk, Alan

Ziff; a life? : a novel. Carroll & Graf Pubs. 2003 408p $25

ISBN 0-7867-1115-9 LC 2002-191184

"Dimming literary light Danny Levitan takes a last shot at glory by penning a biography of his onetime mentor and sometime friend, Arthur Ziff, a great American writer whom many Jews consider a traitor, and whose sex-charged novels have been overlooked by the Pulitzer and Nobel committees. What gives this story frisson is author Lelchuk's similar relationship with Philip Roth." Booklist

Lem, Stanisław

Eden; translated by Marc E. Heine. Harcourt Brace Jovanovich 1989 262p o.p.

LC 89-1963

"A Helen and Kurt Wolff book"

This novel "details the adventures of the crew of a crash-landed spaceship on an alien planet. The crew, composed of Captain, Engineer, Physicist, Cyberneticist, Doctor and Chemist, and remaining mostly nameless . . . sets about repairing the ship and exploring the beautiful, unmapped planet. They encounter increasingly exotic creatures and phenomena which they assume they understand, but all-too-human errors lead them to misinterpret nearly everything. Finally, when a communication of sorts is initiated with one of the planet's natives, the crew learns the full extent of their illusions." Publ Wkly

"No one writes sf more intellectually challenging or of greater literary distinction than Lem." Booklist

Fiasco; translated from the Polish by Michael Kandel. Harcourt Brace Jovanovich 1987 322p o.p.

LC 86-31816

"A Helen and Kurt Wolff book"

Original Polish edition, 1986

The author "imagines a time when Earth has found evidence of life on the planet Quinta and has sent a spaceship, the Hermes, to open communications with its inhabitants. For reasons impossible to know, Quinta is a silent planet; the goal of the expedition is to make it speak. The Hermes is manned with specialists in logic, game theory and 'exobiology,' as well as a Dominican monk called Arago (after the 19th-century French physicist) and a master computer whimsically named DEUS." N Y Times Book Rev

"The crew's dense, challenging discussions—of physics, philosophy, military tactics, morality, cybernetics, psychology, game theory, etc.—are punctuated by bursts of action whose initial release only serves to increase the tension, as new data disproves old theses and one fiasco follows another. Brilliant and demanding, this is one of Lem's best novels, putting the reader through an intellectual and emotional wringer." Publ Wkly

His Master's Voice; translated from the Polish by Michael Kandel. Harcourt Brace Jovanovich 1983 c1968 199p o.p.

LC 82-15765

"A Helen and Kurt Wolff book"

Original Polish edition, 1968

"A stream of 'signals' from outer space is the subject of various attempted decodings and an excuse for all kinds of wild hypotheses about who might have sent the message and why, in which are reflected various human hopes and fears. Good satire." Anatomy of Wonder 4

Memoirs of a space traveler; further reminiscences of Ijon Tichy; drawings by the author; translated by Joel Stern and Maria Swiecicka-Zirmionek. Harcourt Brace Jovanovich 1982 153p il o.p.

LC 81-47310

"A Helen and Kurt Wolff book"

Contents: The eighteenth voyage; The twenty-fourth voyage; Further reminiscences of Ijon Tichy; Doctor Diagoras; Let us save the universe

"These stories of Ijon Tichy appeared in the original 1971 Polish edition of 'The Star Diaries' but were omitted from the English language editions of 1976. Some of these space age tall tales are funny, some are serious, but all are pointed. The targets range from SF itself to politics and commercialism." Publ Wkly

Solaris; translated from the French by Joanna Kilmartin and Steve Cox; afterword by Darko Suvin. Walker & Co. 1970 216p o.p.

ISSN 0-8027-5526-7

LC 75-123267

Original Polish edition, 1962

"This novel combines profound philosophic speculation with the structure of action-adventure SF, embodied in a clear, vivid writing style that somehow survived two

Lem, Stanisław—*Continued*
translations. A planet under study by Earth scientists is swathed in a world-girdling ocean, which the scientists conclude is sentient. For unknown reasons, the ocean 'reads' the deepest memories of the four men and sends each a double of a woman in his past. The mysterious world-ocean, constantly flinging up strange shapes that defy the savants' efforts at classification, may be the first, infantile phase of an emerging 'imperfect God.' A major work by any measure." Anatomy of Wonder 5

Lemann, Nancy

Malaise; a novel. Scribner 2002 253p $23
ISBN 0-7432-1548-6 LC 2002-17584

"Fleming Ford is the sometimes outrageous narrator, former belle from Alabama who finds herself pregnant and stranded in Southern California as her husband, the endearingly oafish Mac MacMoreland, works on a project to discover underground water that can be piped to Mexico for an enormous profit. Fleming has little interest in her husband's efforts and she seems mildly terrorized by the prospect of caring for her two toddler daughters, so she turns her attention to Mr. Lieberman, the reserved widower who once signed her paychecks when she worked for his New York newspaper." Publ Wkly

Lemann's "novel is full of her customary antic charm, but here she has come up with something more: a beautifully nuanced anti-'Lolita,' in which the object of desire, wandering around L.A. in a brocade dressing gown and alligator slippers, is the now vanished twentieth century." New Yorker

L'Engle, Madeleine, 1918-

Certain women. Farrar, Straus & Giroux 1992 351p o.p.
ISBN 0-374-12025-0 LC 91-34048

In this novel, "terminally ill David Wheaton, a prominent and much-married American actor, obsessively recalls an unfinished play about King David, a role he coveted. L'Engle explores Christian faith, love, and the nature of God by framing the delayed-maturation story of Emma, Wheaton's daughter, within three subplots: the Wheaton family saga, the story of King David, and the history of the play's development. The characterizations of both Davids are compelling, but the primary interest here is the community of women which surrounds each man. L'Engle describes complex truths very simply. . . . Because she also details the emotional cost of discovering and accepting such concepts, many readers will find these observations memorable but never simplistic." Libr J

A live coal in the sea. Farrar, Straus & Giroux 1996 323p o.p.
LC 96-4909

This "is a family drama centered around astronomy professor Camilla Dickinson. In . . . present and flashback story lines, we learn all about the skeletons in the family closet. When 18-year-old granddaughter Raffi asks Camilla why her father—Camilla's son Taxi, a soap opera star—claims she's not really her grandmother, the complicated true story starts to spill out. Camilla's young, pretty mother, Rose, cheated on her husband. Camilla's husband, Macarios Wanthakos, an Episcopal priest and son of a bishop, had his own dark family stories." Libr J

"The story is not always pretty; it involves desertion, infidelity, miscarriages, untimely death, a four-year-old torn from his parents, and an eight-year-old seeing his father sodomized. But neither is it explicit. In fact, in L'Engle's hands it is infused with the warmth of love and mercy. A complex, modern saga that is most of all genteel." Booklist

The love letters. Farrar, Straus & Giroux 1966 365p o.p.

A "counterpoint tale of two young women, three centuries apart in time, tormented by their experience of love, each needing to understand love in its deepest sense for her salvation. One is Mariana, long-ago Portuguese nun, won from her vow and soon deserted by a French soldier. The other is Charlotte Napier whose disintegrating marriage, built on an emotionally insecure childhood, has sent her in flight to Beja, Portugal. Learning about Mariana, lingering over her published letters, and pondering her fate, Charlotte comes to understand what love demands of her." Booklist

The other side of the sun. Farrar, Straus & Giroux 1971 344p o.p.

"Set in the post-bellum era, [this Gothic novel] chronicles the experiences of a 19-year-old English girl, Stella, who shortly after her marriage is sent alone to the South while her husband embarks on a secret . . . mission to Africa. . . . Through a brace of aging, eccentric relatives and some violent encounters with the blacks who inhabit the nearby scrub, she comes to know something of the Renier family. Her curiosity grows until it plunges her into a cauldron of racial strife. . . . [Woven into the plot are] richly drawn characters, the scars and guilt of the Civil War, and scattered bits of brilliant insight into the human condition." Libr J

A severed wasp. Farrar, Straus & Giroux 1982 388p o.p.
LC 82-15694

In this sequel to The small rain, "international pianist Katherine Vigneras settles into her comfortable brownstone on Greenwich Village's 10th Street . . . [expecting] a music-dominated retirement, peaceful and restorative. Instead, she becomes involved, through friendship with one of her tenents, a Jewish doctor stationed at nearby St. Vincent's Hospital, with the Episcopal community of the great Cathedral of St. John the Divine. . . . At the cathedral she finds connections with her own tortuous past through her music, her friendship with a retired bishop and with the young family of the cathedral's present dean." Publ Wkly

The small rain. Vanguard 1945 371p o.p.

The story of Katherine Forrester from the age of ten to twenty. The daughter of musicians, Katherine is to become a pianist but before she can begin her career she must pass thru the heartaches and joys and disappointments of adolescence, school days and early love affairs

Followed by A severed wasp

Lent, Jeffrey

Lost nation. Atlantic Monthly Press 2002 370p $25
ISBN 0-87113-843-3 LC 2001-56495

Lent, Jeffrey—*Continued*

"In 1838, a man called Blood opens a tavern and one-girl brothel in an ungoverned area on the New Hampshire—Canada border. His prostitute, Sally, is a teenager he won in a game of cards. While the territory is already home to a number of society's escapees, Blood's presence introduces a new volatility. Blood and Sally's relationship grows in unpredictable ways, the law threatens to descend, and Blood's secret past returns in a surprising manner. . . . The author has tremendous literary gifts: a fine ear for speech, a keen eye for period detail, the ability to craft a well-turned phrase and create rich interior lives for his characters." Booklist

Leon, Donna

Doctored evidence; Donna Leon. Atlantic Monthly Press 2004 245p $22

ISBN 0-87113-918-9 LC 2003-63941

"The crime at first seems an open-and-shut case: a Romanian housekeeper, accused of brutally murdering her miserly, elderly Venetian employer, is killed while fleeing the police. But when a neighbor steps forward to clear the housekeeper's name, Commissario Guido Brunetti seeks to find the real killer, especially when he learns that the original officer on the case is his enemy, the malevolent Lieutenant Scarpa." Libr J

"The detective's humane police work is disarming, and his ambles through the city are a delight; but it is this peculiar insistence on turning every case into a morality tale that gives Leon's fiction its subtlety and substance and makes us follow Brunetti wherever we must even into the sea." N Y Times Book Rev

Uniform justice. Atlantic Monthly Press 2003 259p $24

ISBN 0-87113-903-0 LC 2003-44326

In this Guido Brunetti mystery "the Venetian police detective and family man is summoned to the exclusive San Martino Military Academy, where Cadet Ernesto Moro has been found dead, hanging in the lavatory." Publ Wkly

"As a thinking man, Brunetti reads Cicero for moral direction, looks to his wife for doses of cynical realism and humbly consults his secretary, the terrifyingly efficient Signorina Elettra, on practical matters. But it is as a man of sensibility that this endearing detective most engages us." N Y Times Book Rev

Leonard, Elmore, 1925-

Bandits. Arbor House 1987 345p o.p.

LC 86-14104

"Ex-con Jack Delaney, a former hotel burglar turned mortician's assistant, finds his 'window of opportunity' in the form of a Calvin Klein-clad ex-nun, Lucy Nichols, who enlists his help in a plot to steal five million dollars from Colonel Dagoberto Godoy, a Nicaraguan contra visiting New Orleans to raise money. Jack, Lucy, and two other ex-cons form a motley crew of bandits, each with a different set of motives and illusions." Booklist

"At its heart, the novel is about taking sides, the politically charged background of Contra aid used as one more tool to pull the reader in and out of the moral quicksand. Leonard is no Graham Greene, but the ethical issues called into play here give the novel depth and immediacy. This, then, is not just another gritty adventure novel; it's a top-notch thriller with a real moral resonance." Publ Wkly

Be cool. Delacorte Press 1999 292p o.p.

ISBN 0-385-33391-9 LC 98-36601

Sequel to Get Shorty

"Ex-loan-shark-turned-movie-producer Chili Palmer needs a new hit. *Get Lost*, the sequel to his successful first film *Get Leo*, tanked at the box office. . . . Despite being pursued by several assassins (he promises one a screen test), the always unflappable Chili uses his own life to develop his movie, manipulating the people he meets and staging events to see how they would fit in a screenplay." Libr J

"Aside from the wit, the fun and the colorful figures that populate Elmore Leonard's novels, the real magic of his work is in the language. . . . This is Elmore Leonard at his best, the sweeping synaptic prose effortlessly echoing the argot of the gutter." N Y Times Book Rev

Cat chaser. Arbor House 1982 283p o.p.

LC 81-71687

"Ex-Marine George Moran intends to lead a quiet life at his Florida motel, but then he falls in love with the American wife of exiled Dominican General Andres de Boya. After a visit to the Dominican Republic, he's pestered by con men and private eyes, getting caught in the crossfire between them and de Boya, and it's hard to tell which is more dangerous." Libr J

This "is a tidy little thriller with sufficient twists and turns (not to mention sex and violence) to keep you intrigued and entertained. The characters are well drawn, the plotting is complicated but clear, and the suspense is strong without being too painful." Best Sellers

The complete Western stories of Elmore Leonard. 1st ed. William Morrow 2004 528p $27.95

ISBN 0-06-072425-0 LC 2004-55969

Contents: Trail of the Apache; Apache medicine; You never see Apaches . . .; Red hell hits Canyon Diablo; The colonel's lady; Law of the hunted ones; Calvary boots; Under the friar's ledge; The rustlers; Three-ten to Yuma; The big hunt; Long night; The boy who smiled; The hard way; The last shot; Blood money; Trouble at Rindo's station; Saint with a six-gun; The captives; No man's guns; The rancher's lady; Jugged; Moment of vengeance; Man with the iron arm; The longest day of his life; The nagual; The kid; Only good ones; The Tonto woman; "Hurrah for Captain Early!"

Cuba libre. Delacorte Press 1998 343p o.p.

ISBN 0-385-32383-2 LC 97-24541

This novel is set at "the onset of the Spanish-America War. Ben Tyler, a cowboy cum bank robber, is recruited by an old partner to assist in a scheme to run guns to insurgent Cubans, under cover of horse trading. When they arrive, they find the U.S.S. Maine's wreckage in the harbor at Havana, and Tyler and his partner must cope with a rapidly developing chain of events." Libr J

"What makes Leonard's invocation of Cuban history more than ornamental is the way the double cross of his own narrative matches the double cross of the historical narrative." New Yorker

Leonard, Elmore, 1925–—*Continued*

Elmore Leonard's Dutch treat: 3 novels; introduction by George F. Will. Arbor House 1985 568p o.p.
LC 85-11246

An omnibus edition of three of the author's mid-1970s novels

Contents: Mr. Majestyk (1974); Swag (1976); The hunted (1977)

In "*Mr. Majestyk*, a California melon grower, is set upon by professional killers but manages to turn his predators into prey. In *Swag*, originally called *Ryan's Rules*, two small-time Detroit thieves prosper until they go for bigger loot. Riveting though these two tales are, they will strike readers as mere curtain raisers for *The Hunted*. Set in Israel, it focuses on the perilous state of Al Rosen, an American who receives large sums of money regularly from his lawyer in Detroit. When news of Rosen's whereabouts gets back to his home city, a gang of paid hoods jets to Tel Aviv and goes gunning for him. Sgt. Davis of the U.S. Marines, perceiving their lethal intentions, drives Rosen to a desolate spot in hopes of getting the drop on the pursuers. The climax to this story is a stunning, unforgettable surprise." Publ Wkly

Freaky Deaky. Arbor House 1988 341p o.p.
LC 87-19466

"Soon after Chris Mankowski—lately transferred from the bomb squad to sex crimes—visits rich, mindless alcoholic Woody Ricks on a rape complaint, someone blows up Woody's limousine—along with Woody's brother Mark. Ghosts from their student activist past have returned to haunt them. One ex-Panther even now takes care of Woody, and two ex-demonstrators hope to extort cash." Libr J

Leonard "excels here with his trademark menace and his deadpan, throwaway humor. His superlative ear for the vernacular makes all the characters spring to life; Woody, 'always in low with his dims on,' is a brilliant creation." Publ Wkly

Get Shorty. Delacorte Press 1990 292p o.p.
LC 89-25816

When Chili Palmer, a Miami extortionist, "agrees to help a fellow mobster track down a movie producer trying to evade his Las Vagas debts, a new world of opportunities opens up before him." Quill Quire

"Leonard's strongest books make you stand up and sit down a lot during their tight moments, but 'Get Shorty,' despite its occasional white-knuckle passages, belongs to that vast vinegary canon known as the Hollywood novel. . . . Best of all is the portrait Leonard gives us of a seven-million-dollar-a-picture star named Michael Weir." New Yorker

Followed by Be cool

Glitz. Arbor House 1985 228p o.p.
LC 84-16794

This novel is "set in the high-roller world of casino gambling, alternating between Puerto Rico and Atlantic City. Miami cop Vincent Mora is on medical leave in San Juan when two seemingly unrelated events conspire to end his vacation: a paroled rapist who Mora arrested turns up bent on revenge, and a Puerto Rican girl employed by an Atlantic City casino owner turns up dead." Booklist

"There is a steady flow of intrigue and action set just outside the law in a world both dirty and glamorous. Several characters develop into complex personalities, but Mora is never quite clear." Libr J

The hot kid. William Morrow 2005 312p $25.95
ISBN 00-6072422-6

"The Hot Kid is part-Cuban, part-Indian Carlos Webster, who inadvertently gets his start in law enforcement at age 15 when he shoots a cattle thief. The investigating U.S. marshal thinks Carlos has potential and tells the kid to give him a call in five or six years. Carlos does and becomes Carl, though the next guy he shoots is a bank robber who once called him a 'greaser.' Carl Webster thrills the public with his soon-to-be signature line, 'If I have to pull my weapon I'll shoot to kill.' He's so cool he doesn't even know he's saying it—or does he? This Dust Bowl-era Okie ambler captures the era of Pretty Boy Floyd, Bonnie and Clyde, and John Dillinger with a slow-simmering feud between Webster and Jack Belmont, a pea-brained oil scion who wants to be a most-wanted outlaw. Trailing them both is Tony Antonelli, a journalist with a knack for turning gunfights into heroic battles." Booklist

"Where so much of Leonard's recent fiction has a sharp, almost hyperrealistic quality, 'The Hot Kid' is noirish and even a little pulpy at times, in the fashion of 30's movies and detective magazines. . . . Tony Antonelli isn't a portrait of the artist as young man, exactly, but rather a fond wink at the tradition of potboilers and genre writing that gave rise to Leonard himself and from which, for all his success, he has never cut himself off." N Y Times Book Rev

The hunted

In Leonard, E. Elmore Leonard's Dutch treat: 3 novels

Killshot. Arbor House 1989 287p o.p.
LC 88-31532

"When a professional hit man gets in on a shakedown planned by a psychotic killer, the luck that's kept him alive for 50 years starts running out. Trying to make the score, they run into not the realtor they'd targeted, but Carmen Colson and her ironworker husband, Wayne, who rough them up and run them off. The thugs decide to kill the couple, but that's not easily done. Electing protection by the Federal Witness Security Program, the Colsons have no picnic, either. The cops treat them like dirt, the home they're given by the program is a dump, and the deputy marshal guarding them puts the make on Carmen." Booklist

"Mr. Leonard has either done his homework or he's been there—up on the high beams in Detroit, on the Mississippi towing barges from Baton Rouge to Hickman, Ky., looking into the flat stare of an irritated cop, and somehow, improbably, inside the head of a woman who has had it with being treated like 'the wife.' 'Killshot' is pure, distilled, vintage Leonard." N Y Times Book Rev

LaBrava. Arbor House 1983 283p o.p.
LC 83-72676

"The time is now; the scene, Miami's South Beach area. Joe LaBrava is a former Secret Service agent turned freelance photographer. A friend of his has been taking care of Jean Shaw, a middle-aged beauty who was once a movie actress. LaBrava fell in love with Jean's image when he was 12. She played the spider-woman

Leonard, Elmore, 1925-—*Continued*

role: she enticed second leads to their deaths and never married the hero. Now in real life the predator may be cast as the victim: a psychotic extortionist and his creepy Cuban sidekick are looking for her. Jean receives a crudely typed note demanding that she pay $600,000 for the privilege of remaining alive." Newsweek

"What makes the author's work memorable is his uncompromisingly direct prose, his affectionately crafted yet very real characters, and, of course, the fact that Leonard knows that providing entertainment is the novelist's first commandment. Nobody brings the illogic of crime and criminals to life better." Christ Sci Monit

Maximum Bob. Delacorte Press 1991 295p o.p.
LC 91-6539

"Maximum Bob is a Florida judge famous for his tough sentencing and, among women who have to work with him, as a fairly crude lecher. Parole officer Kathy Diaz Baker is the book's protagonist, though. For a slight violation, her parolee Dale Crowe Junior gets one of Bob's stiff sentences, by which he's not too pleased. Moreover, Dale's uncle Elvin, just out after doing 10 years from Bob on a murder conviction, conceivably could be nursing a grudge. What's more, Elvin hooks up with rich Dr. Tommy Vasco, who's under house arrest for illegal drugs—a sentence given him by guess who. When a live and lively alligator shows up in the judge's backyard, swallowing his wife's dog and scaring its owner clean out of town, and then when shots are fired through hizzoner's windows, Kathy gets suspicious and suspiciouser. Leonard's trademark toughness, grit, and sleaze are on every page." Booklist

Mr. Majestyk
In Leonard, E. Elmore Leonard's Dutch treat: 3 novels

Mr. Paradise. Morrow 2004 291p $25.95
ISBN 0-06-008395-6 LC 2003-64867

"Roommates Kelly and Chloe are enjoying their lives and their downtown Detroit loft just fine. Kelly is a Victoria Secret catalog model. Chloe is an escort, until she decides to ditch her varied clientele in favor of a steady gig as girlfriend to eighty-four-year-old retired lawyer Tony Paradiso, a.k.a. Mr. Paradise. Evenings at Mr. Paradise's house, there's always an old Michigan football game on TV. And when Chloe's around, there's a cheerleader, too, complete with pleated skirt and blue-and-gold pompoms. One night Chloe convinces Kelly to join in the fun, along with Montez Taylor, Tony's smooth-talking right-hand man. But things go awry." Publisher's note

"Leonard addresses those who think they hear the same music he does, but who are open to questioning the familiar, to listening carefully and seeing when something has a different emphasis. . . . 'Mr. Paradise' is about deception. People deceive through false identity (appropriating, dissembling), just as they, themselves, have been deceived whether by the implied promise of collapsed dot-coms or by positive, false assumptions about family." N Y Times Book Rev

Out of sight. Delacorte Press 1996 296p o.p.
LC 96-8030

"U.S. Marshall Karen Sisco, 29, wearing a $3500 Chanel suit, meets escaping con, bank robber Jack Foley, 47, and can't get him out of her mind. The attraction is mutual, and as their paths diverge and converge, the Leonard-ian plot predictably gets more convoluted and the characters more bizarre. Foley and Co.'s hit on the house of an ex-junk bond trader who reportedly has a million stashed away there brings the star-crossed lovers together once more." Libr J

"A few stitches in the plot don't quite mesh, like the big part played by Foley's ex-wife, a magician's assistant. But even the finest silk suit can develop an errant thread, and this one, as sexy and well-tapered as Leonard's two new principals, will fit the author's fans just right." Publ Wkly

Pagan babies. Delacorte Press 2000 263p o.p.
ISBN 0-385-33392-7 LC 00-29506

"Father Terry Dunn, an American priest working in Rwanda, is forced to return to the United States after exacting penance from a group of local Hutu murderers. Upon returning to Detroit, ostensibly to raise money for African orphans, he becomes involved with Debbie, a recently released ex-convict hoping to strike it rich as a stand-up comedian. A plan for both Terry and Debbie to attain the riches they desire soon gives way to a mix of deceit and false loyalties." Libr J

This "is one of Mr. Leonard's funniest books, with a typically colourful cast of oddballs. The dialogue, too, is snappy. . . . Mr. Leonard steers the reader effortlessly through a maze of plots and counterplots, then brings the whole thing in with a bravura flourish and stops on a dime." Economist

Pronto. Delacorte Press 1993 265p o.p.
LC 93-2999

This novel "tracks the misadventures of Harry Arno, a small-time operator who runs a sports book for the Miami syndicate. Federal investigators try to pressure him to rat on his boss, Jimmy Cap, by planting a rumor that he is skimming. As, of course, he is. Squeezed by both sides, Harry takes his nest egg and flees to Rapallo, a harbor town on the Italian Riviera." N Y Times Book Rev

"Leonard's spare language and propulsive plotting still leave room for expositions of Sicilian slang, gamblers' lingo and Ezra Pound's private life. His colorful characters work together splendidly." Publ Wkly

Riding the rap. Delacorte Press 1995 294p o.p.
LC 94-38211

Two characters from Leonard's novel, Pronto, appear in this story set in Florida's Palm Beach. They are Harry Arno, a mob-connected bookie, and US Marshal Raylan Givens. As the book opens, Harry is "drinking too much Absolut vodka and making the mistake of hiring Puerto Rican tough guy Bobby Deo to collect 16.5K from a deadbeat who hasn't paid his sports bets. When the deadbeat and his cronie, a Bahamanian con man named Louis Lewis, join forces with Bobby Deo to abduct Harry, . . . Raylan gives chase with the help of a slightly bent fortune teller." Booklist

"Leonard's brilliance consists in having matched his style to his subject perfectly. These are not characters who would bloom into life in the hands of a more sophisticated writer. They are complete, because they are shallow." Commonweal

Leonard, Elmore, 1925-—*Continued*

Rum punch. Delacorte Press 1992 297p o.p.
LC 91-38738

"A combination of coincidence and choice connects the fates of Jackie Burke, a 44-year-old, thrice-married stewardess, bail bondsman Max Cherry, overweight and in his 50s, and brash young gun dealer Ordell Robbie, in Miami. When Jackie is caught bringing cash into the U.S. from the Bahamas for Ordell, she agrees to cooperate with federal and state agents to catch him in a sting operation. Max, who has posted Jackie's bond and is drawn to her, becomes her sounding board as she contemplates a sting of her own." Publ Wkly

"Mr. Leonard never tells you; he shows you. The story is all action, a scam within a scam. . . . His style is the absence of style, stripped of fancy baggage . . . the absence, as far as it's possible, of an authorial ego." NY Times Book Rev

Split images. Arbor House 1982 282p o.p.
LC 81-67524

"When millionaire Robbie Daniels hires a trigger-happy cop as bodyguard, reporter Angela Nolan, who's been doing a story on Daniels, becomes worried. Daniels has killed people—supposedly by accident and in self-defense— and seems to be getting a taste for it. She and policeman Bryan Hurd find themselves in a deadly race to thwart Daniels' plans, which include video taping his killings. This is a fast-paced suspense novel with interesting characters and a warm-hearted romance between Hurd and Nolan." Libr J

Stick. Arbor House 1983 304p o.p.
LC 82-72073

"After seven years in a Michigan prison for armed robbery, Ernest Stickley, Jr. heads for Florida and gets together with a friend who served a three-four year sentence at the same prison for possession with intent to deliver. Stick is soon in the center of Miami's underworld of big money and illegal drugs. He barely escapes from the scene of a slaying, which is more of a human sacrifice than a murder. Soon a couple of drug-pushing czars and their goons are on his trail. But Stick is not exactly hiding, and his trail leads across yachts, through mansions, and to a country club gala." Best Sellers

"Despite his violence, Stick is likeable, and the scam he pulls on the drug dealers has the reader firmly on his side. Escapist but not shallow." Libr J

Swag

In Leonard, E. Elmore Leonard's Dutch treat: 3 novels

Tishomingo blues; a novel. Morrow 2002 308p o.p.

ISBN 0-06-000872-5 LC 2001-44405

Dennis Lenahan, an itinerant high diver setting up for a Mississippi casino show, watches a Dixie drug-ring murder from his eighty-foot diving platform. Various factions-a smooth-talking Detroit con man, a mob-backed explosives expert, redneck crank dealers, local police on either side of the law-try to badger or buy his silence or cooperation, but Lenahan stays cool and uncommitted, until a 'Shane'-like showdown at a local Civil War reenactment. Lenahan's composure and his easy acrobatics feel like a stand-in for the author's; both seem to play it by ear even after the guns start firing. And the hurtling plot twists keep coming, right up to the perfect rip of a finish."New Yorker

The Tonto woman and other western stories. Delacorte Press 1998 345p o.p.

ISBN 0-385-32386-7 LC 98-21566

"A Delta book"

The stories in this collection were originally published in various magazines

Contents: Trouble at Rindo's Station; The nagual; Saint with a six-gun; Moment of vengeance; "Hurrah for Capt. Early"; The boy who smiled; Three-ten to Yuma; Blood money; The hard way; Jugged; No man's guns; Apache medicine; The big hunt; The kid; The colonel's lady; You never see Apaches . . .; Only good ones; The captives; The Tonto woman

Touch. Arbor House 1987 245p o.p.
LC 87-12624

"Charlie Lawson once served as Brother Juvenal in a Catholic order; now he cares for alcoholics in a Detroit hospice. Charlie/Juvenal cures those he touches through miracles manifested by the Stigmata, the wounds of Christ that appear on Charlie's body. The phenomenon lures a flashy promoter, Bill Hill, aiming to get rich by exploiting the reclusive, gentle man who is also the intended prey of rabid right-winger August Murray." Publ Wkly

"The hard-as-nails-and-twice-as-real dialogue and sharp characterizations make this weird nonviolent thriller . . . as absorbing as Leonard's usual, more menacing fare." Booklist

When the women come out to dance, and other stories. Morrow 2003 228p $24.95

ISBN 0-06-008397-2 LC 2002-26426

Contents: Sparks; Hanging out at the Buena Vista; Chickasaw Charlie Hoke; When the woman come out to dance; Fire in the hole; Karen makes out; Hurrah for Capt. Early; The Tonto woman; Tenkiller

"Reading the clipped, unfailingly accurate dialogue that comes out of the mouths of Leonard's characters can make you feel as if you're in the presence of a writer who is both ventriloquist and psychic. It's not just that Leonard captures the cadences and elisions of each character's speech, it's that he has an uncanny sense of knowing what each will say next." N Y Times Book Rev

Leroy, Margaret

Postcards from Berlin; a novel. Little, Brown 2003 391p $22.95

ISBN 0-316-73813-1 LC 2003-40069

"On the surface, Catriona (Cat) Lydgate enjoys a contented, middle-class life with a devoted husband, two lovely daughters, an elegant home, and a room to call her own: an attic where she dabbles at art. Things begin to unwind when Daisy, her younger daughter, comes down with the flu, which develops into a mysterious, malingering illness that causes her to stop eating and leaves her lethargic and achy. As specialist after specialist can find no physical explanation for the illness, they begin to suspect psychological causes." Libr J

"The resolution of Leroy's novel has a fairy-tale aspect, but fairy tales can nevertheless be very absorbing. Despite the occasional straining of her plot, Leroy succeeded in making me care about these characters; even at my most incredulous." N Y Times Book Rev

Lescroart, John T.

The 13th juror; a novel. Fine, D.I. 1994 484p o.p.

LC 93-74487

"Jennifer's fairytale life as the wife of Dr. Larry Witt seems perfect. When Larry and their seven-year-old son are murdered while Jennifer is out jogging, the newspapers have a field day weeping with the photogenic young widow. After she is arrested for the crime, a full-fledged tabloid feeding frenzy erupts. Into this fray steps Dismas Hardy, a fortysomething former district attorney's office hotshot and an ex-bartender who is 43 days into his new job with a prestigious law firm." Libr J

"The story gets off to a slow start, and sometimes Lescroart belabors the obvious. . . . Despite these flaws, however, an intricate story and satisfying courtroom scenes carry the day." Publ Wkly

A certain justice; a novel; [by] John Lescroart. Fine, D.I. 1995 435p o.p.

LC 94-61908

This novel "takes place over a few stress-filled summer days in San Francisco. When a drug-related murder results in strained race relations in the city, events escalate until a drunken mob lynches a young black attorney. A young white man, Kevin Shea, tries with all his body and soul to stop the crime from happening, but his efforts are wasted, and an irresponsible photographer snaps a shot of Kevin that gets misinterpreted by everyone. The city goes nuts—riots, fires, and a $200,000 reward is posted for Kevin's apprehension. But Kevin, now on the run with his spunky girlfriend, insists on making his role in the event clear and his innocence known. He calls an old friend, attorney Wes Farrell, to help." Booklist

"By showing the political maneuvering that can accompany an outbreak of violence, Lescroart offers an unusually thoughtful, exciting thriller that evinces insight into incidents and attitudes that seem all too real." Publ Wkly

The first law; a novel; by John Lescroart. Dutton 2003 403p $25.95

ISBN 0-525-94705-1 LC 2002-37902

"The popular lawyer-cop team of Dismas 'Diz' Hardy (lawyer) and Abe Glitzky (cop) returns for another episode of legal maneuvering on the streets of San Francisco. The bullet wound sustained by Abe in Lescroart's last adventure. . . confines him to a desk job, so he's no help to Diz when he goes up against the Patrol Special, a private-enterprise neighborhood security system supervised by the SFPD. It seems that Diz's good friend, John Holliday, a bar owner in one of the patrolled areas, is fingered as a murder suspect; however, John contends the corrupt beat 'cops' framed him. . . . Lescroart's expert crafting turns this legal thriller into quite a wild ride." Booklist

Guilt; [by] John Lescroart. Delacorte Press 1997 462p o.p.

ISBN 0-385-31655-0 LC 96-43756

"Mark Dooher, head of a high-powered San Francisco law firm, pushing 50 and tired of his alcoholic wife, is smitten with beautiful law student Christina Carrera. He begins a subtle campaign to woo her, revealing himself to readers . . . as manipulative, but believably so. When Dooher's wife is murdered in an apparent burglary, SFPD detective Abe Glitsky finds enough odd clues to press for a murder charge against Dooher. With Dooher's best friend, Wes Farrell, leading the defense (with Christina as second chair), the cold-blooded attorney takes on the police, the court and various hostile witnesses." Publ Wkly

"Lescroart effectively dramatizes the many moral dilemmas that emerge in this case, not the least of which is posed by the role of the Catholic Church." Booklist

Hard evidence. Fine, D.I. 1993 478p o.p.

LC 92-54457

"Dismas Hardy, the grief-stricken former district attorney turned bartender who first appeared in *The Vig* (1991) and *Dead Irish* (1990), returns with a new wife, a child, and his old job with the prosecutor's office. Pushing 40, Dis thought he'd paid his dues during his previous stint as a D.A., but now he's back at the low end of the totem pole, prosecuting small-time drug dealers, hookers, and other losers. He needs a case, a real case, to relaunch his career. It comes in the form of a hand in a dead shark's stomach. The hand is soon connected (figuratively, of course) to a recently murdered silicon-chip king." Booklist

"Lescroart blends an intricate plot, a great locale, wonderfully colorful characters, and taut courtroom drama to create a book that will leave readers eager for more." Libr J

The hearing; [by] John Lescroart. Dutton 2001 451p $25.95

ISBN 0-525-94575-X LC 00-34119

In this legal thriller "attorney Dismas Hardy not only defends confessed murderer Cole Burgess but is forced to confront the fallibility of his friend, Abe Glitsky, chief of the San Francis Police Department's homicide division. Burgess, a heroin addict, is found near the lifeless body of a prominent female attorney, unable to remember the events that brought him there. Lescroart tantalizes readers with a tightly constructed plot in which Hardy and Glitsky track crime and political corruption to an unexpected source." Libr J

The mercy rule; a novel; by John Lescroart. Delacorte Press 1998 466p o.p.

ISBN 0-385-31658-5 LC 98-16726

In this "legal thriller, attorney Dismas Hardy agrees to defend his friend Graham Russo, accused of murdering his own father. Sal Russo, suffering from Alzheimer's disease and an inoperable brain tumor, is losing his capacity to take care of himself and is beginning to experience severe pain, making no secret of his plan to inject himself with morphine and eventually use the drug to end his suffering. When Sal is found dead of an overdose, his apartment in disarray, and $50,000 missing, the police suspect that his death was not a suicide." Libr J

"Lescroart has the technical clues of the plot perfectly arranged, locking in the attention of mystery mavens until the connections are revealed, but it's his credible characters who cement this entertaining front-rank whodunit." Booklist

Nothing but the truth; [by] John Lescroart. Delacorte Press 1999 435p o.p.

ISBN 0-385-33353-6 LC 99-32584

Lescroart, John T.—*Continued*

"San Francisco lawyer Dismas Hardy has 72 hours to solve a murder that happened three weeks ago. Time is crucial because his wife, Frannie, has been jailed for contempt after refusing to reveal a secret (confided to her by her friend Ron Beaumont) to the grand jury investigating the murder of Beaumont's wife, Bree." Publ Wkly

"Lescroart orchestrates a cadre of multidimensional characters through a plot full of political subterfuge and action without losing track of the subtlety of modern personal relationships." Libr J

The oath; [by] John Lescroart. Dutton 2002 408p o.p.

ISBN 0-525-94576-8 LC 2001-47055

San Franciso attorney Dismas Hardy "finds himself representing Dr. Eric Kensing, who stands accused of murdering his boss, Tim Markham, the CEO of the Parnassus Medical Group, a struggling HMO providing health services to all the city's employees. An autopsy shows that Markham, hospitalized in critical condition following a hit-and-run, died not of his injuries but of a potassium overdose. . . . The author wisely steers clear of taking cheap shots at the HMO industry, yet manages to direct a sharp beam into some of its darker crevices." Publ Wkly

The second chair; [by] John Lescroart. Dutton 2004 390p $25.95

ISBN 0-525-94775-2 LC 2003-19782

An installment in the "San Francisco legal/detective series featuring lawyer Dismas Hardy and police detective Abe Glitzky. Amy Wu, a young attorney in the law firm now headed by Dismas, has a high-profile client in Andrew Bartlett, a high school student accused of shooting his girlfriend and drama coach. The evidence against Andrew is extremely damning, and Amy arranges a plea-bargain whereby Andrew would agree to admit guilt in exchange for the case remaining in the juvenile justice system. She's forced to antagonize the court and the district attorney, however, by reneging on the deal when Andrew continues to claim his innocence. Dismas appoints himself to the case as 'second chair' to salvage the reputation of his firm, just as it seems that Andrew might not be guilty after all." Libr J

Leslie, Josephine Aimee Campbell, 1898-1979

The ghost and Mrs. Muir. Ziff-Davis 1945 174p o.p.

"When Lucy Muir, a pretty young widow, bent on living her own life at long last, flees from her domineering inlaws, she falls in love with Gull Cottage in an English coast town and rents the place, thus inheriting a ghost who has made things so disagreeable for previous tenants that none of them would stay in the haunted house. Though no one she has ever met has been on intimate terms with a ghost, Lucy soon finds herself hobnobbing with the gruff old sea captain and comes to depend on the old fellow in all the crises, emotional and financial, in her life." Bookmark

Lessing, Doris May, 1919-

African stories; [by] Doris Lessing. Simon & Schuster 1965 636p o.p.

A collection of "tales which taken together reflect myriad aspects of African existence. Vivid personality delineation, narrative integrity, and artistry dominate each story whatever its subject or theme." Booklist

Ben, in the world; the sequel to The fifth child; [by] Doris Lessing. HarperCollins Pubs. 2000 178p o.p.

ISBN 0-06-019628-9 LC 99-89804

Ben Lovatt's "abnormal appearance and strength distinguishes him from other people. Rejected by his older siblings, he is now homeless in London. He has been fed and sheltered by the sickly Mrs. Biggs, but when she enters the hospital, Ben ends up staying with a prostitute named Rita. Rita's boyfriend enlists Ben's unknowing assistance to transport drugs to Paris, where he meets Alex and is taken to Brazil to make a movie. There, Ben meets a scientist who wants to run genetic tests on him. Ben is treated inhumanely but is excited when he hears that he may meet more people like himself." Libr J

"Lessing's unsentimental yet excruciating moral fable forces us to accept the Lovatts' dilemma as our own." New Yorker

Children of violence; [by] Doris Lessing. v1-5 o.p.

v1-4 published by Simon & Schuster; v5 published 1969 by Knopf with title: The four-gated city

Contents: v1 Martha Quest (1964; United Kingdom edition 1952); v2 A proper marriage (1964; United Kingdom edition 1954); v3 A ripple from the storm (1966; United Kingdom edition 1958); v4 Landlocked (1966; United Kingdom edition 1965); v5 The four-gated city (1969)

This "is an account of the life of Martha Quest and of her search for self-definition, which for her is to be achieved through total commitment to a person or a cause. We follow her from her beginnings as a wayward but intelligent child on a Rhodesian farm, through two unsuccessful marriages and active involvement in the Communist party in Salisbury during World War II. After the war Martha goes to London and becomes an increasingly disenchanted observer of London life and behavior in the 1950s; the last volume of the sequence anticipates an apocalyptic, science-fiction future, as Martha dies in a devastated, radioactive world at the end of the twentieth century." Wakeman. World Authors, 1950-1970

The fifth child; {by} Doris Lessing. Knopf 1988 133p o.p.

LC 88-2680

"Mildly eccentric English couple Harriet and David Lovatt are the contented parents of four healthy children. Suddenly, their peace is forever shattered by their fifth child, Ben, a fiercely malevolent goblin-child with a penchant for violence. . . . Only Harriet tries to civilize the boy, and he gradually learns to function on a primitive level and even collects a band of similar outcasts about him. Unwanted, they leave their homes to wander England." Libr J

"Acting as a social moralist, Lessing exposes the division between the warm and comfortable domestic scene and the harsh reality of the outside world, piercing the

Lessing, Doris May, 1919-—*Continued*
boundary between the two as human desires clash with a more brutal vision of existence. A psychologically probing and emotionally powerful performance." Booklist
Followed by Ben, in the world

The four-gated city
In Lessing, D. M. Children of violence

The golden notebook; [by] Doris Lessing. Simon & Schuster 1962 567p o.p.
"Regarded as one of the key texts of the Women's movement of the 1960s, it opens in London in 1957 with a section ironically entitled 'Free Women', a realistic account of a conversation between two old friends, writer Anna Wulf, mother of Janet, and Molly, divorced from Richard, and mother of disturbed son Tommy, who will later attempt suicide. The novel then fragments into the four sections of Anna's 'Notebooks.' . . . This pattern of five non chronological overlapping sections is repeated four times, as it tracks both the past and the present, and although one of Lessing's concerns is to expose the dangers of fragmentation, she also builds up through pastiche and parody, and through many refractions and mergings, a remarkably coherent and detailed account of her protagonists and the world they inhabit." Oxford Companion to Engl Lit. 6th edition

The good terrorist; [by] Doris Lessing. Knopf 1985 375p o.p.
LC 85-40214
"Alice Mellings is the 'good' terrorist, a sort of house mother for a group of London radicals who take over an abandoned and badly vandalized house as communal home and headquarters. Picketing with trade unionists and spray-painting bridges with slogans protesting vivisection, chemicals in food, Trident, and sexism, these smalltime revolutionaries get involved in something big, and very dangerous, as the story progresses. Alice, whose contempt for her mother's middle-class values informs her rebellion, winds up just like her mother, decorating the squatters' squalid home and cooking for her comrades. [This is] a novel about home, family, and revolt." Libr J
"Unsparingly, fiercely, often satirically, Lessing is writing a narrative about death: the death of the heart when ideology tyrannizes over just, kindly human relations, abstractions over common sense." Ms

The grass is singing; [by] Doris Lessing. Crowell 1950 245p o.p.
The novel begins with the newspaper notice of the death of Mary Turner, wife of an unsuccessful South African farmer. There seems to be some reluctance among the other whites about discussing the case. The author then turns back to the story of Mary Turner's life, showing her gradual disintegration as a person, and ending with her murder by a Kaffir houseboy
This novel "besides being very well-written is an extremely mature psychological study. It is full of those terrifying touches of truth, seldom mentioned but instantly recognized. By any standards, this book shows remarkable powers and imagination." New Statesman (1913)

Landlocked
In Lessing, D. M. Children of violence

Love, again; a novel; [by] Doris Lessing. HarperCollins Pubs. 1996 352p o.p.
LC 95-53317
"Sarah Durham was widowed young; now in her mid-60s, she is manager of and playwright for a London fringe theater group. A production of a play based on the journals and music of a 19th-century quadroon from Martinique, Julie Vairon, inflames Sarah's dormant sexual impulses. And she is not the only one: all of the actors, the director and a rich patron, Stephen Ellington-Smith, are also sublimely seduced by Julie's words, music and the few portraits of her that survive. . . . Although the book is long and rambling, asking much of a reader's patience and willingness to spend so much time inside Sarah's head, Lessing, wields a formidable analytic intelligence that makes this work provocative and often astonishingly beautiful." Publ Wkly

Mara and Dann; an adventure; [by] Doris Lessing. HarperFlamingo 1999 407p o.p.
ISBN 0-06-018294-6 LC 98-30782
"In this futuristic novel, in Ifrik, a land savaged by war and environmental disaster, seven-year-old Mara and her little brother Dann are snatched from their home and severed from their pasts. The children grow up literally on the run, made to fight for their enemies one moment and left to starve the next. But their love for each other remains as fierce as their surroundings are terrifying, and it transfigures their brutal trials. On the surface a grand adventure, this novel at its heart makes a fascinating argument for the force of affection and the power of the questioning mind." New Yorker

Martha Quest
In Lessing, D. M. Children of violence

The memoirs of a survivor; [by] Doris Lessing. Knopf 1975 c1974 213p o.p.
First published 1974 in the United Kingdom
This "novel is a projection into the near future when technological structures have broken down and society is forging new patterns among the chaos. [The] speaker, never named, lives through progressive disorientation in an English city, (also never named) where bands of children terrorize those people who haven't left yet. As her everyday life becomes more and more survival-bound, she fashions an imaginary world beyond her living room wall. When [Emily], a young girl, comes into her care, she is forced to see her emerging strength and womanhood as the hope of an uncertain future." Libr J
This is "an extraordinary and compelling meditation about the enduring need for loyalty, love and responsibility in an unprecedented time that places unbearable demands upon people." Time

The other woman
In Lessing, D. M. Stories p157-211

A proper marriage
In Lessing, D. M. Children of violence

The real thing; stories and sketches; [by] Doris Lessing. HarperCollins Pubs. 1992 214p o.p.
LC 91-59932
Published in the United Kingdom with title: London observed
Contents: Debbie and Julie; Sparrows; The mother of the child in question; Pleasures of the park; Womb ward;

Lessing, Doris May, 1919—*Continued*
Principles; D.H.S.S.; Casualty; In defence of the underground; The new café; Romance 1988; What price the truth?; Among the roses; Storms; Her; The pit; Two old women and a young one; The real thing

In this "sharply observed collection of short works, Lessing offers a rich portrait of life and love in contemporary London." N Y Times Book Rev

A ripple from the storm
In Lessing, D. M. Children of violence

Shikasta; re: colonised planet 5; personal, psychological, historical documents relating to visit by Johor (George Sherban) emissary (grade 9) 87th of the period of the last days; [by] Doris Lessing. Knopf 1979 364p (Canopus in Argos: archives) o.p.

LC 79-11295

"First of the Canopus in Argos: Archives five-volume series. Shikasta is Earth, whose history—extending over millions of years—is here put into the cosmic perspective, observed by Canopeans who seem to be in charge of galactic history although responsible to some higher, impersonal authority. The sequels follow the exploits of various human cultures whose affairs are subtly influenced by the Canopeans; all share the remotely detached perspective that transforms the way in which individual endeavors are seen. Thoughtful and painstaking." Anatomy of Wonder 4

Followed by The marriages between zones three, four, and five (1980); The Sirian experiments (1981); The making of the representative for Planet 8 (1982); Documents relating to the sentimental agents in the Volyen Empire (1983)

Stories; [by] Doris Lessing. Knopf 1978 625p o.p.

LC 77-20709

Contents: The habit of loving; The woman; Through the tunnel; Pleasure; The witness; The day Stalin died; Wine; He; The eye of God in Paradise; The other woman; One off the short list; A woman on a roof; How I finally lost my heart; A man and two women; A room; England versus England; Two potters; Between men; Our friend Judith; Each other; Homage for Isaac Babel; Outside the ministry; Dialogue; Notes for a case history; To room nineteen; An old woman and her cat; Side benefits of an honourable profession; A year in Regent's Park; Report on the threatened city; Mrs. Fortescue; An unposted love letter; Lions, leaves, roses; Not a very nice story; The other garden; The temptation of Jack Orkney

"All of Lessing's non-African stories are brought together from three of her previous collections: 'The habit of Loving,' 'A Man and Two Women,' and 'The Temptation of Jack Orkney and other Stories'. In addition, 'The Other Woman,' a short novel, previously published only in Great Britain, is also included." Booklist

The sweetest dream; [by] Doris Lessing. HarperCollins Pubs. 2002 478p o.p.

ISBN 0-06-621334-7 LC 2002-279950

The epicenter of this novel "is a grand old house in London, the holdfast of the seemingly impervious widow Julia. It's the early 1960s and when her selfish and feckless communist son, Johnny, callously abandons his wife, Frances, and their two young sons, Julia persuades her resilient daughter-inlaw to move in with her. Soon Frances, a self-possessed yet endlessly empathic and accommodating earth mother, is presiding over a contentious commune of moody teenage 'waifs and strays.'" Booklist

"Lessing's understanding of relationships-both personal and political-has always been keen; now . . . it is unparalleled. This novel is warm and heartfelt, old-fashioned and ambitious in its historical sweep." New Statesman

Lester, Julius

Do Lord remember me; a novel. Holt & Co. 1985 c1984 210p o.p.

LC 84-3845

"The final day of Rev. Joshua Smith's earthly existence is a reminiscence: of his turn-of-the-century boyhood in a hardscrabble county in Mississippi as the son of sharecroppers; of his gift as the 'singing preacher' for churches all over the segregated South; of his disappointment at never leading a big church in Detroit or Chicago; of his love for his fair-skinned wife and the trouble her appearance caused them." Publ Wkly

"Smith's memories link with those of older people in his past, whose stories take him back to slavery times. What emerges is a picture of black experience covering more than 150 years, with memory and storytelling providing continuity between present and past. A rich and moving reading experience." Booklist

Lethem, Jonathan

The fortress of solitude; a novel. Doubleday 2003 511p $26

ISBN 0-385-50069-6 LC 2003-43535

"Dylan Ebdus is a white kid on a black-and-brown street. As he struggles through public school in 1970s Brooklyn, he is 'yoked'-put in a headlock-and frisked for change on a daily basis. Testing into a good Manhattan school, he steps into a long-lasting role: vulnerable among street kids, he's street-smart compared to his new, privileged pals, and loathes himself as a poseur with both crowds. When he finds a ring that grants the power of flight, he's afraid to use it, but his black friend, Mingus, is not." Booklist

"The plot manages to encompass pop music from punk rock to rap, avant-garde art, graffiti, drug use, gentrification, the New York prison system-and to sing a vibrant, sometimes heartbreaking ballad of Brooklyn throughout. Lethem seems to have devoured the '70s, '80s, and '90sinhaled them whole-and he reproduces them faithfully on the page, in prose as supple as silk and as bright, explosive and illuminating as fireworks." Publ Wkly

Men and cartoons; stories. Doubleday 2004 160p $19.95

ISBN 0-385-51216-3 LC 2004-50039

Contents: The vision; Access fantasy; The spray; Vivian Relf; Planet Big Zero; The glasses; The dystopianist, thinking of his rival, is interrupted by a knock on the door; Super goat man; The national anthem

"Funny, strange, and sometimes impenetrable, Lethem's new collection of stories . . . deals in themes of loneliness, missed connections, and betrayal, set against futuristic and near apocalyptic backdrops. Despite

Lethem, Jonathan—*Continued*
this, the stories never feel heavy or particularly dark the writing is playful, and the narrators are keenly aware of the absurd." Libr J

Motherless Brooklyn. Doubleday 1999 311p o.p.
ISBN 0-385-49183-2 LC 99-18194
"The short and shady life of Frank Minna ends in murder, shocking the four young men employed by his dysfunctional Brooklyn detective agency/limo service. The 'Minna Men' have centered their lives around Frank. . . . Tourette's-afflicted Lionel has found security as a Minna Man and is shattered by Frank's death. Lionel determines to become a genuine sleuth and find the killer. The ensuing plot twists are marked by clever wordplay, fast-paced dialog, and nonstop irony." Libr J

Letts, Billie, 1938-

Shoot the moon; Billie Letts. Warner Books 2004 333p $24
ISBN 0-446-52900-1 LC 2004-3447
"No one in sleepy DeClare, Oklahoma, has forgotten the 1972 murder of pretty Cherokee Gaylene Harjo and the abduction of her infant son, Nicky Jack. Hard-nosed deputy sheriff Oliver 'O Boy' Daniels pinned the blame on local preacher Joe Dawson, but few in town believed the kindly Joe was capable of such an act. Powerful emotions resurface 30 years later, when Nicky Jack, adopted and raised by a rich couple in Beverly Hills, mysteriously reappears, determined to learn about his mother and the circumstances surrounding her death. . . . Letts peppers her prose with a cast of quirky characters." Booklist

Leung, Brian, 1967-

World famous love acts; stories; by Brian Leung. 1st ed. Sarabande Books 2004 202p pa $14.95
ISBN 1-88933-016-7 (pa) LC 2003-11923
Contents: Six ways to jump off a bridge; Executing Dexter; Leases; White hand; Dog sleep; Fire walk; Who knew her best; Desdimona's ruins; Drawings by Andrew Warhol; After; World famous love acts
"As diverse as they are similar, Leung's characters and their conditions run the gamut from elderly widower to precocious youngsters, porn star to AIDS victim, serial killer to estranged sisters, and all are lucidly portrayed in prose that is achingly lyrical and elegantly refined." Booklist

Levenkron, Steven, 1941-

The best little girl in the world. Contemporary Bks. 1978 196p o.p.
LC 78-9063
"Francesca is 15, an excellent student, a docile girl at home in her affluent parents' Manhattan apartment. But Francesca sets about killing her 'fat' self to become imaginary Kessa—slim and firm. Within weeks she starves herself, so that she drops from 98 to an alarming 84 pounds and is hospitalized, another young victim of anorexia nervosa. The reader is drawn into the arena where dedicated professionals battle to save Francesca's life and the lives of others like her. This book, fiction in name only, proves what an impassioned and skillful author can do to make a novel more powerful than dry facts." Publ Wkly

Levenson, J. C. (Jacob Claver), 1922-

(ed) Crane, S. Prose and poetry

Levenson, Jacob Claver *See* Levenson, J. C. (Jacob Claver), 1922-

Leventhal, Alice Walker *See* Walker, Alice, 1944-

Levi, Primo, 1919-1987

If not now, when?; translated from the Italian by William Weaver; introduction by Irving Howe. Summit Bks. 1985 c1982 349p o.p.
LC 85-2526
Original Italian edition, 1982
"The author, himself a victim of Nazi atrocities, has based his novel on true events. A band of Jewish partisans makes its way from Russia to Italy waging their personal war against the Nazis. They blow up trains, rescue concentration camp inmates, and face incredible dangers in their efforts to strike back against a ruthless, seemingly invincible enemy. The story is a testament to human endurance and courage." Shapiro. Fic for Youth. 3d edition

The monkey's wrench; translated from the Italian by William Weaver. Summit Bks. 1986 171p o.p.
LC 86-5803
Original Italian edition, 1978
"In this tale of two lonely and quite different men, a steel rigger entertains a chemist with memories of his world travels." Booklist
"Among other things, The Monkey's Wrench is a model of the interplay between storytellers and listeners. For their part, readers can envy Levi's sixth sense about building bridges between what can be seen and what must be imagined." Time

The sixth day, and other tales; translated by Raymond Rosenthal. Summit Bks. 1990 222p o.p.
LC 90-9734
Contents: The mnemogogues; Angelic butterfly; Order on the cheap; Man's friend; Some applications of the Mimer; Versamina; The sleeping beauty in the fridge: a winter's tale; The measure of beauty; Full employment; The sixth day; Retirement fund; Westward; Seen from afar; The hard-sellers; Small red lights; For a good purpose; Psychophant; Recuenco: the nurse; Recuenco: the rafter; His own blacksmith: to Italo Calvino; The servant; Mutiny: to Mario Rigoni Stern; Excellent is the water
"These bizarre stories from master storyteller Levi are full of shadowed meanings, conveying truths about our technological society and how our scientific appetites have outstripped our moral capacities." Libr J

Levin, Ira

The boys from Brazil; a novel. Random House 1976 312p o.p.

"Ninety-four potential Hitlers are created through the technique of cloning by Dr. Mengele, infamous doctor of Auschwitz. Striving to re-create the early environment of the original Hitler, Mengele plots the murder of the fathers of these ninety-four children. Yakov Liebermann, a pursuer of Nazis, tries to stop the murders at the cost of great, almost mortal, danger to himself." Shapiro. Fic for Youth. 3d edition

A kiss before dying. Simon & Schuster 1953 244p o.p.

"An Inner sanctum mystery"

"The plot has to do with a remarkably ingenious, subtle, and relentless murderer, who does away with a pregnant college girl, goes on from there to kill her sister and a more or less innocent bystander, and is cheated of the fortune that has driven him to these desperate measures only by a couple of tiny oversights that might easily have escaped Sherlock Holmes. The book is a succession of solid and quite legitimate surprises, the suspense is admirably sustained, the detail is thorough and convincing, and the writing is considerably above the level usually associated with fictional crime and passion." New Yorker

Rosemary's baby; a novel. Random House 1967 245p o.p.

"Guy and Rosemary Woodhouse dismiss the warnings of friends and move into a luxurious Manhattan apartment building where, supposedly, rites of witchcraft and suicides have occurred. Rosemary's instincts warn her to beware of their neighbors, the Castevets, but her husband is not convinced and they become a dominant influence on Guy when Rosemary becomes pregnant. She is alone in her fear and becomes a helpless victim." Shapiro. Fic for Youth. 3d edition

Son of Rosemary (1998)

The Stepford wives. Random House 1972 145p o.p.

"Attractive, talented Joanna moves with her husband and kids to a suburb, where she comes to suspect that the village housewives have all been murdered and replaced by robots, the suspected villain being a chauvinistic Men's Association . . . and so Joanna begins to fear for her life." Libr J

"There is a broad current of humor beneath the horrific surface of this little ambush of Women's Lib, life and the pursuit of happiness." N Y Times Book Rev

Levin, Meyer, 1905-1981

Compulsion. Simon & Schuster 1956 495p o.p.

Using fictionalized names and probing deeply into the psychological aspects of the crime, this is a retelling of the Loeb-Leopold murder case

"The writing shows the hand of a master. Despite the fact that the reader who is familiar with the history of the case knows the outcome, Mr. Levin manages to fill this book with sustained suspense." N Y Times Book Rev

Levine, Paul

Flesh and bones; a Jake Lassiter novel. Morrow 1997 303p o.p.

LC 96-35364

"Pro football player turned lawyer Jake Lassiter is savoring a drink at a South Beach bar when a beautiful young woman shoots the man on the next bar stool and faints in Lassiter's arms. It's one way to get clients, he figures. The woman, Chrissy Bernhardt, is charged with the first degree murder of her father, whom Chrissy believes abused her as a child. Lassiter takes the case. . . . Lassiter is smart, tough, funny, and very human." Booklist

Lewin, Michael Z.

And baby will fall. Morrow 1988 261p o.p.

LC 88-1089

A mystery introducing social worker/detective Adele Buffington. "Working late one evening, Buffington is pushed around by an intruder who only wants information from the social agency files. When a former colleague is apparently murdered soon thereafter, Detective Sergeant Homer Proffitt of the Indianapolis P. D. investigates. He and Buffington unearth a seamy ring of baby brokers who deal in illegal adoptions. . . . Wonderful entertainment from an underappreciated master." Booklist

Lewis, C. S. (Clive Staples), 1898-1963

The dark tower and other stories; edited by Walter Hooper. Harcourt Brace Jovanovich 1977 158p o.p.

Contents: The dark tower; The man born blind; The shoddy lands; Ministering angels; Forms of things unknown; After ten years

Out of the silent planet. Scribner Classics 1996 158p $22

ISBN 0-684-83364-6 LC 96-30110

A reissue of the title first published 1938 in the United Kingdom; first United States edition published 1943 by Macmillan

"The trilogy can be read on two levels: first for its exciting plot and second as a theological allegory, although Lewis denied this interpretation. The stories are about temptation. They concern the classic battle between good, as represented by Ransom, the philologist, and evil, as represented by Weston, the physicist. The battle is played out on the planets of Malacondra (Mars), Perelandra (Venus), and Earth." Shapiro. Fic for Youth. 3d edition

Followed by Perelandra (1943) and That hideous strength (1945)

Perelandra; a novel. Scribner Classics 1996 190p $22

ISBN 0-684-83365-4 LC 96-20724

A reissue of the title first published 1944 by Macmillan

In the second volume of the fantasy trilogy Dr. Ransom "is ordered to Perelandra (Venus) by the supreme being and finds there a paradise threatened by the villainous scientist Weston, who becomes the devil incarnate." Booklist

Followed by That hideous strength

Lewis, C. S. (Clive Staples), 1898-1963—*Continued*

That hideous strength; a modern fairy-tale for grown-ups. Scribner Classics 1996 380p $23
ISBN 0-684-83367-0 LC 96-20722
A reissue of the title first published 1946 by Macmillan
In the final volume of the fantasy trilogy Ransom and Weston again represent the struggle between good and evil, this time in a college community on Earth. Mark Studdock learns the error of his attempts to play faculty politics, and his wife discovers the footlessness of modern theories of love and life

Till we have faces; a myth retold. Harcourt Brace & Co. 1957 c1956 313p il o.p.
First published 1956 in the United Kingdom
"Introducing his own version of the myth of Psyche and Cupid the author weaves it into a fantasy in which he gives expression to some of his persisting ideas on the forces at work in the soul of man. Orual, queen of a fictional kingdom of the Near East in ancient times, tells the story." Booklist
"The religious allegory is plain to read. In Mr. Lewis's sensitive hands the ancient myth retains its fascination, while being endowed with new meanings, new depths, new terrors." Saturday Rev

Lewis, Clive Staples *See* Lewis, C. S. (Clive Staples), 1898-1963

Lewis, Hilda Winifred, 1896-1974

I am Mary Tudor; [by] Hilda Lewis. McKay, D. 1972 c1971 422p o.p.
First published 1971 in the United Kingdom
The author "traces the life of Mary Tudor, daughter of King Henry VIII and his queen, Catherine of Aragon, from her birth in 1516 to her accession. Mary was at first favored and treated royally but, by the age of nine, she began to suffer the disfavor of her father. Henry's great desire for a male heir, plus his later passion for Anne Boleyn, made him take the matters of marriage and religion into his own hands. Through Mary's eyes, readers watch Henry declare himself head of the Church of England; declare Mary a bastard; and marry, one after the other, five unlucky women. With her half-sister, Elizabeth, and half-brother, Edward, Mary waited upon the father she both loved and hated until she finally ascended the throne." Libr J

Lewis, Jim, 1963-

The king is dead. Knopf 2003 259p $24
ISBN 0-375-41417-7 LC 2002-43288
Walter Selbly "was born in 1925 and became a World War II hero, lawyer, and indispensable aide to the governor of Tennessee. His life seemed complete when he marrried beautiful Nicole Lattimore, whom he adored, and they had a son, Frank, and a daughter, Gail. Then, on a single day, Walter's professional and personal lives were destroyed, and his young children were left without parents. Thirty-five years later Frank Cartwright (with his adoptive parents' name), an attractive, womanizing actor whose career is languishing, is provoked by a film proposal from a fabled dowager to find his roots. . . . Even if the parts of this novel outshine the whole, Lewis' language often soars." Booklist

Lewis, M. G. (Matthew Gregory), 1775-1818

The monk; by Matthew Lewis, with an introduction by Stephen King. Oxford Univ. Press 2002 442p (Oxford world's classics) $20
ISBN 0-19-515136-4 LC 2002-25111
First published 1796 in the United Kingdom
"Ambrosio, the worthy superior of the Capuchins of Madrid, falls to the temptations of Matilda, a fiend-inspired wanton who, disguised as a boy, has entered his monastery as a novice. Now utterly depraved, Ambrosio falls in love with one of his penitents, pursues the girl with the help of magic and murder, and finally kills her in and effort to escape detection. But he is discovered, tortured by the Inquisition, and sentenced to death, finally compounding with the devil for escape from burning, only to be hurled by him to destruction and damnation. Although extravagant in its mixture of the supernatural, the terrible, and the indecent, the book contains scenes of great effect. It enjoyed a considerable contemporary vogue." Oxford Companion to Engl Lit. 6th edition

Lewis, Sinclair, 1885-1951

Arrowsmith. Harcourt Brace & Co. 1925 448p o.p.
ISBN 0-15-108216-2
"Although he is most interested in bacteriology and research, Martin Arrowsmith turns from that area to general medicine and then to public health. He is unable, however, to deal with the political aspects of the public health field and returns to laboratory work and research. Martin develops an antitoxin that he believes will be effective against bubonic plague, but when he gets the chance to test the serum during an epidemic in the West Indies, he invalidates the results by not adhering to a control situation. Returning to the States, he feels that he is a failure and refuses the offer of a prestigious position in order to join an old friend at a rural laboratory in a search for a cure for pneumonia." Shapiro. Fic for Youth. 3d edition
also in Lewis, S. Arrowsmith; Elmer Gantry; Dodsworth

Arrowsmith; Elmer Gantry; Dodsworth; .; Sinclair Lewis. Library of America, Distributed to the trade in the U.S. by Penguin Putnam 2002 1346p $40
ISBN 1-931082-08-1 LC 2002-19451
Contents: Arrowsmith; Elmer Gantry; Dodsworth

Babbitt; with an introduction and notes by James M. Hutchisson. Penguin Books 1996 xxxii, 365p il pa $9.95
ISBN 0-14-018902-5 LC 95-36188
First published 1922 by Harcourt, Brace
Satire on American middle-class life in a good-sized city. George F. Babbitt is a successful real estate man, a regular fellow, booster, Rotarian, Elk, Republican, who uses all the current catchwords, molds his opinions on those of the Zenith Advocate-Times and believes in "a sound business administration in Washington"

Lewis, Sinclair, 1885-1951—*Continued*

"The novel's scathing indictment of middle-class American values made Babbittry a synonym for adherence to a conformist, materialistic, anti-intellectual way of life." Merriam-Webster's Ency of Lit

also in Lewis, S. Main Street & Babbitt

Cass Timberlane; a novel of husbands and wives. Random House 1945 390p o.p.

Cass Timberlane at forty-one was sober, thoughtful, and respected by the Minnesota town in which he was a judge. This story of Cass's second marriage to a girl in her early twenties is punctuated by stories of the married lives of many of his friends

Dodsworth; a novel. Harcourt Brace & Co. 1929 377p o.p.

"The book's protagonist, Sam Dodsworth, is an American automobile manufacturer who sells his company and takes an extended European vacation with his wife, Fran. *Dodsworth* recounts their reactions to Europeans and European values, their various relationships with others, their estrangement, and their brief reconciliation." Merriam-Webster's Ency of Lit

also in Lewis, S. Arrowsmith; Elmer Gantry; Dodsworth

Elmer Gantry. Harcourt Brace 1927 432p o.p.

This novel "deals with a brazen ex-football player who enters the ministry and, through his half-plagiarized sermons, his physical attractiveness, and his unerring instinct for promotion, becomes a successful evangelist and later the leader of a large Middle Western church. Carefully researched, the novel was realistic enough to shock both the faithful and unfaithful." Reader's Ency. 3d edition

also in Lewis, S. Arrowsmith; Elmer Gantry; Dodsworth

It can't happen here; a novel. Doubleday, Doran 1935 458p o.p.

"Doremus Jessup, editor of a small New England newspaper, follows the rise to the presidency of the United States of a fascist demagogue, Berzelius Windrip. Doremus and his friends publish an underground newspaper that tells the truth about what is happening. Doremus is imprisoned, escapes to Canada, and joins the underground movement, which is headed by the man who had opposed Windrip in the election. The novel inveighs against some aspects of capitalism as well as fascism, and communists come in for their share of criticism also." Shapiro. Fic for Youth. 3d edition

Main Street & Babbitt. Library of Am. 1992 898p $40

ISBN 0-940450-61-5 LC 91-58224

Contents: Main Street; Babbitt

Main Street [novelette]

In Lewis, S. Main Street & Babbitt

Main Street, the story of Carol Kennicott. Harcourt, Brace and Howe 1920 451p o.p.

"Carol Milford, a girl of quick intelligence but no particular talent, after graduation from college meets and marries Will Kennicott, a sober, kindly, unimaginative physician of Gopher Prairie, Minn., who tells her that the town needs her abilities. She finds the village to be a smug, intolerant, unimaginatively standardized place, where the people will not accept her efforts to create more sightly homes, organize a dramatic association, and otherwise improve the village life." Oxford Companion to Am Lit. 6th edition

Lewis, William Henry, 1967-

I got somebody in Staunton; stories; William Henry Lewis. 1st ed. Amistad 2005 202p $22.95

ISBN 0-06-053665-9 LC 2004-55128

Contents: Shades; Kudzu; In the swamp; I got somebody in Staunton; Urban renewal; For the brothers who ain't there; Why we jump; Crusade; Potcake; Rossonian days

"Lewis is not a trendy hip-hop stylist or a viciously satirical postmodernist with a knack for making fun of America's racial obsession. He is a quieter sort of writer who reminds us that beneath the hype are ordinary people struggling with racist employers, lost fathers, lack of education and fears of stepping out of line and threatening the status quo. Some of those people live in Washington power circles and upscale Manhattan; some of them live in Staunton, Va." Washington Post Book World

Li, Pi-hua

Farewell to my concubine; {by} Lilian Lee; translated by Andrea Lingenfelter. Morrow 1993 255p o.p.

LC 93-16777

The author "sets an intricate love triangle against the backdrop of China during the warlord period, the Japanese occupation, the Communist victory, and the Cultural Revolution. Singers Duan Xialou and Cheng Dieyi grow up together and come to play leading roles at the Peking Opera; their bravura performance is *Farewell to My Concubine*, in which the devoted mistress of a general kills herself rather than face her man's defeat. Cheng incarnates female roles so totally that he falls passionately in love with Duan, who feels only brotherly affection for his stage partner and marries a beautiful courtesan. The obsessive Cheng tries repeatedly to undermine the marriage. Unlike most Chinese fiction, this novel seamlessly integrates the personal and the social; its riveting drama of a *menage á trois* also reveals the burden of recent Chinese history." Libr J

Lieberman, Herbert H., 1933-

The girl with Botticelli eyes; by Herbert Lieberman. St. Martin's Press 1996 308p o.p.

LC 96-5193

"A Thomas Dunne book"

"To commemorate the 550th birthday of Botticelli, Mark Manship, curator of Renaissance painting at the Metropolitan Museum of Art, is assembling a major retrospective that could catapult him into the position of museum director. In Europe to track down three drawings for the show, Manship meets the eponymous Isobel Cattaneo, a direct descendant of Botticelli's famed model and mistress, Simonetta. Meanwhile, in a parallel plot line, a neo-fascist Italian count, Ladovico Borghini, determined to preserve his country's heritage, is planning

Lieberman, Herbert H., 1933-—*Continued*

to prevent the transfer of the drawings, which he has stolen, to the States." Publ Wkly

"Borghini is a brilliant and wily opponent, and it takes every ounce of Manship's intellect and courage to play—and win—the high-stakes game into which he is thrown. Lieberman provides a literate plot, graceful prose, lovely settings and tantalizing glimpses into the competitive politics of the art world." Booklist

Lightman, Alan P., 1948-

The diagnosis; [by] Alan Lightman. Pantheon Bks. 2000 369p o.p.

ISBN 0-679-43615-4 LC 00-24543

"Bill Chalmers is an executive at an 'information company' in Boston who on his way to work one day forgets completely who he is, what he does or where he is supposed to be going. After a number of nightmarish experiences, in which he rapidly becomes a homeless bum, he awakens in a hospital, more or less his old self—except that his body is beginning to turn numb." Publ Wkly

"A work of vivid sensuousness, sparkling intelligence, and poignant beauty, Lightman's gripping tale contrasts the needs of the body and spirit with the acquisitiveness of the mind and ponders the potential lethality of ideologies, be they cultural or technological." Booklist

Einstein's dreams; {by} Alan Lightman. Pantheon Bks. 1993 179p il o.p.

LC 92-50465

"In 1905, while working as an examiner at the Swiss Patent Office in Bern, Einstein published three important papers in Annals of Physics. Here Lightman re-creates the dreams that allegedly culminated in the famous essay on the relativity of time." Libr J

"Lightman starts out with commonplaces, neurological conditions or abstractions of our personal experience of time. Then, with one or two exceptions, he embodies the concept in brilliant, folkloric tales with extraordinary assurance." New Statesman Soc

Reunion; [by] Alan Lightman. Pantheon Bks. 2003 231p $23

ISBN 0-375-42167-X LC 2002-34575

"Charles, a 'small-college professor' in his early 50's, more or less amicably settled into domestic banality in a leafy suburb, decides to attend his 30th college reunion. Once back at his unnamed alma mater . . . he is struck with eidetic force by recollections of his first passionate love affair, with an aspiring ballerina, Juliana. A narrative of this love affair and reflections upon it form the bulk of the novel." N Y Times Book Rev

"Lightman infuses even the simplest scenes with quiet menace as he explores the cataclysmic power of both erotic love and shocking betrayal." Booklist

Ligon, Samuel

Safe in heaven dead. HarperCollins Pubs. 2003 245p $23.95

ISBN 0-06-009910-0

"After stealing nearly half a million dollars of money skimmed by his bosses at the County Executive's office and deserting his wife, son and daughter, Elgin is mowed down by a bus 'while pursuing a woman he could not live without'—a woman who is a graduate student by day and and a high-priced call girl by night. How Elgin winds up in this predicament is the complex morality tale that Ligon tells in flashbacks that alternate between a third-person account shadowing Elgin's cross-country flight in search of salvaton and a first-person narration by Carla, the cynical young woman who has captured his heart." N Y Times Book Rev

Lin Yutang, 1895-1976

Moment in Peking; a novel of contemporary Chinese life. Day 1939 815p o.p.

A story of family life among the upper middle class of China, covering forty years from the time of the Boxer Rebellion to the Japanese invasion

"There are many scenes and passages of great beauty in the book, excerpts from the classics, poetry and philosophy. There are also incidents of humor, delicate and subtle. Equally skillful is the author in depicting scenes of dramatic intensity, stark tragedy of war and acts of heroism" Springfield Repub

Lindgren, Torgny, 1938-

Hash; a novel; translated from the Swedish by Tom Geddes. 1st ed. Overlook Press 2004 236p $23.95

ISBN 1-585-67408-7 LC 2003-63976

Original Swedish edition, 2002

"In December 1947, for the newspaper to which he corresponds from northern Sweden, a middle-aged man is writing about two newcomers to the village of Avaback: a schoolteacher, just released as cured from the tuberculosis sanitarium in which he spent his youth, and a middle-aged clothing peddler, who the writer believes is missing Nazi leader Martin Bormann. Then a messenger arrives with a termination letter from the newspaper editor, who has researched the places the writer reports on, only to be told that they don't exist. The writer stops writing, for 53 years, resuming at age 107, only after he has outlived old age and is regaining lost powers and attributes." Booklist

"Lindgren delivers a story that's a clever sendup of the conceits of storytellers and a bittersweet meditation on life and the pleasures that bind us to it." N Y Times Book Rev

Lindsay, Jeffry P.

Darkly dreaming Dexter. Doubleday 2004 288p $22.95

ISBN 0-385-51123-X LC 2004-45460

Dexter Morgan is a "Miami police-department blood-spatter analyst with a weakness for bowling shirts and batidos, who, when the moon is full, carves up villains in a careful ritual, keeping a single drop of blood on a slide as a souvenir. (He's collected thirty-six so far.) When other victims start popping up, dispatched with the same creativity as Dexter's, he pursues the copycat murderer with acute professional self-interest. Like other charismatic killers—Hannibal Lecter, say, or Tom Ripley—Dexter has a set of motives that are tough to untangle. But his quest proves weirdly convincing as he ponders whether to turn his doppelgänger over to the cops or take care of the problem himself." New Yorker

Lindsey, David L.

An absence of light. Doubleday 1994 519p o.p.
LC 93-35730

"When a member of Houston's Police Intelligence Division turns up an apparent suicide, a chilling chain of events is triggered, unveiling the compromise of highly sensitive data, a sophisticated drug smuggling scam, and the relocation of vast sums of money. To avoid publicity and scandal, Capt. Marcus Garver hires an old friend in the 'intelligence-for-profit business' to assist him and a tight crew from the force in the pursuit of the wily kingpin of the enterprise." Libr J

"Along with deft plotting and abundant surprises, . . . Lindsey offers suspense shrewdly balanced by a number of thoughtful meditations on the nature of betrayal and deceit." Publ Wkly

The color of night; [by] David Lindsey. Warner Bks. 1999 480p $32
ISBN 0-446-52361-5 LC 98-30770

"Harry Strand, a retired U.S. intelligence officer, thinks he's finally put his life back together after the tragic death of his wife. He has become a successful art dealer, and he's fallen in love with Mara Song, a beautiful collector. But everything changes abruptly when Harry discovers a tape in Mara's VCR that clearly shows his wife being murdered. Finding out who is responsible for her death proves to be far more complicated than this former spy can imagine. This is a fast-paced and exciting thriller." Booklist

The rules of silence; [by] David Lindsey. Warner Bks. 2003 405p $24.95
ISBN 0-446-53163-4 LC 2002-33059

"Multimillionaire Titus Cain is approached with a strange proposition: if he doesn't give a certain man $64 million, this same man will kill off some (or perhaps all) of Cain's friends and loved ones. The money has to be given to the extortionist in such a way that no one suspects anything is going on . . . and if Cain even tries to seek help, the killings will start instantly. . . . Lindsey's novels sometimes suffer from lethargy, as though he's just sort of wandering through his story, but this one moves swiftly to its rousing finale." Booklist

Lindskold, Jane M.

(jt. auth) Zelazny, R. Donnerjack
(jt. auth) Zelazny, R. Lord Demon

Linington, Elizabeth, 1921-

For works written by this author under other names see Shannon, Dell, 1921-

Linscott, Gillian

Blood on the wood; a Nell Bray mystery; Gillian Linscott. 1st St. Martin's Minotaur ed. St. Martin's Minotaur 2004 311p $24.95
ISBN 0-312-33148-7 LC 2003-69721

"After Edwardian British suffragette Bray discovers that a valuable painting bequeathed to the suffragettes is fake, she breaks into the owner's house to substitute the fake for the real. When she does, she chances upon murder." Libr J

"Readers will soak up fascinating detail about the Fabians, the Scipians, and the Arts and Crafts Movement while following the action in this delightful romp through England at the turn of the century." Booklist

Lipman, Elinor

The dearly departed; a novel. Random House 2001 269p $23.95
ISBN 0-679-46312-7 LC 00-67368

The author sets her "novel in King George, N.H., a small town where the sudden accidental deaths of a secretly engaged couple summon their two grown-up children to sort out the conundrum of their relation to each other. Both the dead woman's stoical daughter, Sunny Batten, and the man's cranky son, Fletcher Finn, possess an identical corona of satiny gray hair; both are 31; and neither has ever met the other, although their parents have been on-and-off lovers for years." Publ Wkly

The novel "entertains the reader with quirky details and amusing dialogue, but most nourishing is its picture of small-town life, in which everyone knows everyone else's business but they love one another just the same." Atl Mon

The Inn at Lake Devine. Random House 1998 253p o.p.
ISBN 0-679-45693-7 LC 97-1307

"Casting her eye on the social mores of the 1960s and '70s, [Lipman] focuses most notably on the not-so-dainty dance that pulled Jews and WASPs into an assimilationist détente. Natalie Marx of Newton, Mass., is 13 in 1962 when she learns that the Inn at Lake Devine in Gilbert, Vt., strongly suggests to Jewish would-be guests that they would be more comfortable elsewhere. Her crank calls and letters to owner Ingrid Berry have no impact; only when she wangles an invitation from summer-camp friend Robin Fife does Natalie succeed in insinuating herself into this gentile enclave. When she and Robin meet again years later, Natalie finds herself re-entangled in the fate of the Inn." Publ Wkly

"Skillfully interweaving the bittersweet narrative with threads of both tragedy and comedy, Lipman displays a healthy amount of empathy and affection for her flawed and slightly eccentric cast of characters." Booklist

The ladies' man; a novel. Random House 1999 260p o.p.
ISBN 0-679-45694-5 LC 98-56450

"The basic premise of the book is that Nash Harvey, né Harvey Nash, has a crisis of conscience over an engagement he walked out on 30 years ago. He returns to Boston to see Adele Dobbin, his spurned fiancée. Nash's visit teaches Adele and her two unmarried sisters a new lesson 'about dignity being less important than love.' Nash is a shallow smooth talker, seemingly addicted to lust and unfamiliar with love." Libr J

"'The Ladies' Man' never suggests that all men are like Nash Harvey. . . . This book isn't even angry with its villain; it just shakes its head in amused amazement and, a little wiser, walks away." N Y Times Book Rev

The pursuit of Alice Thrift; a novel. Random House 2003 269p $23.95
ISBN 0-679-46313-5 LC 2002-31864

Lipman, Elinor—*Continued*

"The eponymous Alice is a sleep-deprived surgical intern at a Boston hospital. A graduate of MIT and Harvard and a congenital workaholic, she's also devoid of social skills, a sense of humor or elementary tact. Though miserably unequipped with self-esteem, Alice is an intelligent, well-brought-up offspring of upper-middle-class parents. Why, then, does she fall prey to the romantic blandishments of Ray Russo, a vulgar loudmouth and con artist who—it turns out—lies every time he opens his mouth? That Lipman can make this story plausible, and tell it with humor, pschological insight and rising suspense, is a triumph." Publ Wkly

Lipsyte, Sam

Home land; a novel; Sam Lipsyte. 1st Picador ed. Picador 2005 c2004 229p pa $13

ISBN 0-312-42418-3 LC 2004-57318

First published 2004 in the United Kingdom

"The hero of this comic novel, Lewis Miner, a.k.a. Teabag, was a highschool stoner, and now makes it his mission to write extremely candid letters to the alumni newsletter. His life, as he writes, 'did not pan out.' He works as a dishwasher in his father's cheesy catering business and spends his free time moping with his friend Gary, who sued his parents for molestation and then sued the shrink who conjured up these false memories. Teabag's letters detail his sexual fantasies (most of which involve the leg warmers of the school's jazz-dancing squad), his stalled ambition, and the misshapen pearls of wisdom he's garnered from his bottomed-out life. The story ends in an improbable shootout, but Lipsyte transfigures Teabag's self-loathing into a sensibility that is both hilarious and noble." New Yorker

Liss, David

A spectacle of corruption. Random House 2004 381p $24.95

ISBN 0-375-50855-4 LC 2003-54806

"Moments after his conviction for a murder he did not commit, at a trial presided over by a judge determined to find him guilty, Benjamin Weaver is accosted by a stranger who cunningly slips a lockpick and a file into his hands. In an instant he understands two things: Someone had gone to a great deal of trouble to see him condemned to hang and another equally mysterious agent is determined to see him free. . . . After a daring escape from eighteenth-century London's most notorious prison, Weaver must face another challenge: how to prove himself innocent of a crime when the corrupt courts have already shown they want only to see him hang." Publisher's note

Weaver "turns out to be the hard-outside, soft-inside private investigator of the noir thrillers inserted into 1720s London: Philip Marlowe done up in a wig and buckles." Washington Post Book World

The **Literary** ghost; great contemporary ghost stories; edited and with an introduction by Larry Dark. Atlantic Monthly Press 1991 369p o.p.

LC 91-15052

The ghost story "is alive and more than well, as proved by this anthology of 28 examples. . . . From the U.S., Britain, Canada, South Africa, and India, the authors showcased here who have taken their fiction in the direction of the supernatural are, specifically, such modern luminaries as Joyce Carol Oates, Nadine Gordimer, Graham Greene, and Isaac Singer. . . . The variety of approaches . . . represented here promises wide appeal." Booklist

Littell, Robert, 1935-

The company; a novel of the CIA. Overlook Press 2002 894p $27.95

ISBN 1-58567-197-5 LC 2001-51383

"Mixing real events and real people with the story of four fictional spies, Littell presents the history of the CIA, from post-war Berlin to the present. As we follow the intersecting careers of three Company agents and one KGB operative, we see the major events and personalities of the cold war from the inside." Booklist

"There is plenty here to amuse anyone with even a network news interest in current events—and a gold mine for true conspiracy theorists." N Y Times Book Rev

Walking back the cat. Overlook Press 1997 220p o.p.

ISBN 0-87951-764-6 LC 96-49507

In this thriller, "'Parsifal,' a Soviet mole, discovers that he no longer carries out his 'wet work' (contract killing) for the KGB but for an unknown party who is using a New Mexico casino run by 'all that's left on earth of the Suma Apaches, the smallest Indian tribe in America, living on the smallest Indian reservation in America' to launder money. Parsifal joins forces with his final intended victim, a Gulf War dropout named Finn. Together they 'walk back the cat,' retracing the chain of command between Parsifal and the hidden executive who ordered Finn's execution." Libr J

"Sinister deeds and playful characterizations ricochet the reader through a complex plot, replacing the genre's usual hightech gizmos with the strengths and skills of lone-wolf heroes." Publ Wkly

Litwos *See* Sienkiewicz, Henryk, 1846-1916

Lively, Penelope, 1933-

City of the mind; a novel. HarperCollins Pubs. 1991 231p o.p.

LC 90-56365

"Architect Matthew Halland is tuned into the physical world. London's night sky asks him unanswerable questions about time and space. The dilapidated old buildings and blackened brick walls resound with human experience. Everything Matthew knows of London pulls him out of its present and into its past, leaving him spellbound by the realization that some things will never change for its inhabitants. . . . Like countless Londoners before him, he is tested by the pressures of city life, and his knowledge of the past sustains him until a chance meeting with Sarah Bridges focuses his sights on the future." Libr J

"This book is largely a meditation on time and the individual experience. . . . The 'allusions' in the novel are

Lively, Penelope, 1933-—*Continued*
to figures, major or minor, from London's past, recent or remote. . . . Penelope Lively evokes these personalities and their stories with great power and charm." London Rev Books

Cleopatra's sister. HarperCollins Pubs. 1993 281p o.p.
LC 92-54424

In alternating chapters, the author "depicts the lives of paleontologist Howard Beamish and crusading journalist Lucy Faulkner, both successful in their careers but unfulfilled because they have not established enduring relationships. They meet when the plane they are taking to Cairo makes a forced landing in Callimbia, a fictional country in the throes of a bloody revolution led by a lunatic dictator. Lively's . . . construction of Callimbia's history ranges from its establishment by Cleopatra's sister Berenice through the rise of the 'moral renegade' who orders the plane's British passengers taken hostage. Through the eyes of Howard and Lucy, and in counterpoint to their growing love for each other, Lively depicts the passengers' responses to their plight." Publ Wkly

Heat wave; a novel. HarperCollins Pubs. 1996 214p o.p.
LC 96-19893

The novel's heroine, Pauline "is a freelance copyeditor. She is spending the summer in her [English] country cottage, working on the typescript of an epic novel about knights and maidens. Her daughter, Teresa, is staying next door with her husband, Maurice, and their infant son. From her cool, 'slightly opportunistic life of the unattached,' Pauline gradually becomes aware of the emotional shifts in her daughter's marriage." Times Lit Suppl

"Outwardly, the mother herself seems cool, but she is still seething over her own husband's infidelities, many years earlier. Wisdom tends to substitute for drama here, yet you don't want to part company with these characters, who, time and again, elicit a sensation of intense familiarity." New Yorker

Moon tiger. Grove Press 1988 c1987 208p o.p.
LC 87-23798

First published 1987 in the United Kingdom

"The heroine is Claudia Hampton, an unconventional historian and former war correspondent who lies in a hospital bed dying of cancer. Forced inward, Claudia moves randomly across time and place to reconstruct the strata of her life." Libr J

"Moon Tiger is an extremely accomplished novel which tells an interesting story with an impressive variety of fictional techniques." Quill Quire

Pack of cards and other stories. Grove Press 1989 c1986 323p o.p.
LC 89-1851

First published 1986 in the United Kingdom with title: Pack of cards: stories, 1978-1986

Contents: Nothing missing but the samovar; The voice of God in Adelaide Terrace; Interpreting the past; Servants talk about people: gentlefolk discuss things; Help; Miss Carlton and the pop concert; Revenant as typewriter; Next term, we'll mash you; At the Pitt-Rivers; Nice people; A world of her own; Presents of fish and game; A clean death; Party; Corruption; Venice, now and then; Grow old along with me, the best is yet to be; The darkness out there; The pill-box; Customers; Yellow trains; The ghost of a flea; The art of biography; What the eye doesn't see; The emasculation of Ted Roper; A long night at Abu Simbel; Bus-stop; Clara's day; The French exchange; The dream merchant; Pack of cards; The Crimean hotel; A dream of fair women; Black dog

"These witty, profoundly civilized stories display Lively's compassion, intelligence, and versatility." Libr J

Passing on. Grove Weidenfeld 1990 c1989 210p o.p.
LC 89-7459

First published 1989 in the United Kingdom

This novel describes the reactions of Helen and Edward Glover to the death of their mother Dorothy. "Long years in Greystones, the family nest in a pleasant Cotswold village, have all but atrophied their desire to make lives of their own, free of their widowed mother's commanding presence; both have remained unmarried. . . . Opening the novel with Dorothy's funeral, Lively traces the events of the months that follow and poses the question whether real change is possible in the lives of such repressed and gentle characters." Times Lit Suppl

"Penelope Lively is blessed with the gift of being able to render matters of great import with a breath, a barely audible sigh, a touch. The result is wonderful writing, and a marvelous book." N Y Times Book Rev

The photograph. Viking 2003 231p $24.95
ISBN 0-670-03205-0 LC 2002-32420

Widower "Glyn Peters, a famous British archeologist, discovers a compromising photograph of his wife, Katherine Targett, sealed in an envelope in a closet at home. Peters specializes in excavating the long defunct gardens, buried fields and covered-over roads of the British landscape. Reverting to professional habits, he treats Kath's infidelity as a sort of archeological dig. The photo depicts Kath and Nick Hammond, the husband of Kath's sister, Elaine, surreptitiously holding hands on some outing, with Elaine and Mary Parkard, Kath's best friend, in the background. Glyn decides to interview this cloud of witnesses, beginning with Elaine." Publ Wkly

"Lively's characters are shallow, their efforts at introspection often hilarious, but they are all obliged to confront their complicity in the premature death of a woman they each claim to have loved." N Y Times Book Rev

The road to Lichfield. Grove Weidenfeld 1991 215p o.p.
LC 90-47673

First published 1977 in the United Kingdom

This novel "centers around British housewife Anne, whose father is dying in a nursing home. Anne goes to see him, in Lichfield, and in the process of cleaning out his house discovers that her father was someone she hadn't known well at all. 'I knew my father in one dimension only,' she realizes. Her relationships with her husband, brother, and lover might be similarly described. Lively's prose is clean and readable." Libr J

Spiderweb; a novel. HarperFlamingo 1999 218p o.p.
ISBN 0-06-019233-X LC 98-45696

First published 1998 in the United Kingdom

Anthropologist Stella Brentwood "is about to retire, so she buys a cottage in Somerset, England, and sets about

Lively, Penelope, 1933—*Continued*
learning to live the country life. Of course, Stella is *still* an anthropologist, observing the strange customs of her neighbors. . . . In the process, Stella gets reacquainted with the husband of her oldest friend, now dead, whose life was decidedly more domestic. . . . Stella also has occasion to encounter her neighbors, a family that seems far more uncivilized and violent than any Stella may have encountered during her work. Stella's new life is . . . shattered by a terrible incident involving this family." Libr J

"Though the leisurely pace and purposefully digressive narrative are somewhat slow to build suspense, Lively's perceptive vision about the insularity of modern life rings true." Publ Wkly

Livesey, Margot

Banishing Verona; a novel. Henry Holt 2004 321p $24

ISBN 0-8050-7462-7 LC 2004-52383

The author relates the "love story of Zeke, a 29-year-old painter and carpenter . . ., and 37-year-old Verona, a pregnant radio host. In the 17 hours they spend together, they fall in love-only to be separated and put through impossible and unbearably stressful situations." Libr J

"Both Zeke and Verona have just enough quirks to be endearing without being implausible; the supporting characters are similarly well realized. As Livesey . . . probes the depths of longing, betrayal and forgiveness, her gift for creating sublimely unexpected sentences is abundantly on display." Publ Wkly

Criminals; a novel. Knopf 1996 271p o.p.

LC 95-31512

"On his way to see his sister in rural Scotland, Ewan, a dour, middle-aged investment banker, finds an abandoned baby in the washroom of a roadside bus stop. As he emerges with the baby, the bus carrying his belongings roars into motion, forcing him back on board with the intention of turning the baby over to the proper authorities when he arrives at his sister's. Mollie, his sister, recently separated from her long-time lover, is on emotionally shaky ground and views the arrival of a baby on her doorstep as providential. Conspiring to keep the baby, Mollie plunges herself and Ewan into morally murky waters." Libr J

The reader becomes "enmeshed in the complex windings of Ms. Livesey's plot, a web of criminal circumstance and moral consequence that conveys the awful randomness of life even as it offers the abiding pleasures of artfully constructed fiction." N Y Times Book Rev

Eva moves the furniture. Holt & Co. 2001 232p o.p.

ISBN 0-8050-6801-5 LC 00-143895

"Eva McEwen grows up engulfed by a vast and hopeful loneliness. She lives in a small Scottish town with her father and an overprotective aunt, her mother having died of the flu at her birth, in 1920. After Eva turns six, her solitary play is interrupted at unpredictable moments by a girl and a woman who, more than once, come to her aid. Only when she starts school does she realize that these two are invisible to everyone else-and, moreover, jealous of new acquaintances. At eighteen, Eva is desperate to escape the emotional tyrannies of her upbringing, but she eventually comes to feel the fullness of her love for both the real and the imaginary companions of her childhood. Livesey has written a ghost story, of sorts, minus the theremin musiclike 'Our Town,' with its speakers from the grave-and, if it moves you, the end will send you back to the beginning again." New Yorker

The missing world; a novel. Knopf 2000 325p o.p.

ISBN 0-375-40581-X LC 99-35785

"Hazel loses three years of her past when a traffic accident wipes out her memory. She doesn't remember that she and Jonathan quarreled, and she moved out of their apartment. All she knows is that he has dropped everything to care for her. But she becomes a virtual prisoner when Jonathan decides he can't let her out of his sight for fear someone will 'remind' Hazel of what really happened." Booklist

"Adroitly paced, meticulously plotted and increasingly suspenseful, the novel transcends its genre as psychological thriller." Publ Wkly

Llewellyn, Richard, 1906-1983

Green, green, my valley now. Doubleday 1975 236p o.p.

In this concluding novel about the Morgan family, "Huw with his wife Sus, returns to Wales from his self-imposed exile in Patagonia. He's rich now, and prepares to retire in comfort after spending a great deal of time and money in renovating an ancient house in a small village. Then his wife dies suddenly, and he finds himself innocently mixed up with some fanatical IRA members who have represented themselves as his relatives, and who hope to use his land as a front and a base for their illegal activities. . . . The plotters are discovered and arrested, and the book ends with Huw's remarriage." Libr J

"Llewellyn's belief in the value of life is strong enough to carry his hero through the vicissitudes of great wealth, on the wings of prose that is nearly poetic." NY Times Book Rev

How green was my valley. Macmillan 1940 495p o.p.

In this "novel of the Welsh mining country the story is told by Huw Morgan, youngest son of a miner's family. In his boyhood, in the '80's, the valley was green and beautiful, the people were prosperous and law abiding; gradually the countryside was changed to a place of desolation as slag-heaps of mine refuse covered the mountain slopes; hard times, with strikes and layoffs, brought suffering, and a wholesome way of life was destroyed." Booklist

"A remarkably beautiful novel of Wales. And although it follows stirringly in the romantic traditions, there is the resonance of a profound and noble realism in its evocation, its intensity and reach of truth." N Y Times Book Rev

None but the lonely heart. Macmillan 1969 518p o.p.

"First published in 1943, this novel of London low-life has been revised and finished—author Llewellyn was called into the armed services before the work was completed." Best Sellers

This is an intimate character study of a young Cockney, Ernie Mott, living in the London slums. Ernie's fa-

Llewellyn, Richard, 1906-1983—*Continued*
ther, who had been an artist, was killed at Verdun; his mother ran a second hand shop. Ernie himself worked with a firm of commercial artists, and it was when he lost his job and was faced with the bitterness of telling Ma, that he met Henry Twite, an elderly eccentric Robin Hood, and began his career of crime

The "additional chapters make it a stronger book. For the first time the career and character of Ernie Verdun Mott are rounded out and the Cockney adolescent becomes a man." Libr J

Llosa, Mario Vargas *See* Vargas Llosa, Mario, 1936-

Lloyd, Levanah, 1935-

For works written by this author under other names see Black, Veronica, 1935-

Llywelyn, Morgan

1916. Forge 1998 447p o.p.
ISBN 0-312-86101-X LC 97-29838
"A Tom Doherty Associates book"

"A novel set in Ireland at the time of the Easter Rebellion. Llywelyn tells the tale of 15-year-old Ned Halloran, a young *Titanic* survivor who lost both of his parents in that disaster. Upon his return to his native Ireland, he becomes embroiled in its rapidly changing political scene. The headmaster of his school is a renowned scholar and also a rebel and patriot for the Irish cause. Ned acts as a courier for the rebels, becoming more and more supportive of their struggle." SLJ

"Battle scenes are both accurate and compelling. The betrayals, slaughters and passions of the day are all splendidly depicted as Llywelyn delivers a blow-by-blow account of the rebellion and its immediate aftermath. The novel's abundant footnotes should satisfy history buffs; its easy, gripping style will enthrall casual readers." Publ Wkly

1921. Forge 2001 445p $25.95
ISBN 0-312-86754-9 LC 00-49021
"A Tom Doherty Associates book"
Sequel to 1916

"Incessantly haunted by the rather passive role he played in the doomed Easter Rebellion, Henry Mooney, a journalist struggling for objectivity in the midst of controversy and mayhem, reevaluates his own convictions and commitment to the cause of a free Ireland. When Henry falls in love with an Anglo-Irish woman, simmering tensions wrought by centuries of domination and repression are reflected in a microcosm of passion and agony. The lucid narrative and the compelling subject matter will enthrall both Irish history buffs and fans of sweeping historical fiction." Booklist

1949; a novel of the Irish Free State. Forge 2003 414p $25.95
ISBN 0-312-86753-0 LC 2002-32525
"A Tom Doherty Associates Book"
Sequel to: 1921

"The story focuses on the indomitable Ursula Halloran . . . a young woman who first works for the Irish radio service and later the League of Nations. The unwed Ursula discovers how oppressive the new Catholic state can be when she becomes pregnant and must flee the country. Eventually, Ursula must choose between the two men in her life, one an Irish civil servant, the other an English pilot." Publ Wkly

"Llywelyn's great strength is her ability to communicate sweeping historical events through the eyes of both passive bystanders and active participants." Booklist

1972; a novel of Ireland's unfinished revolution. Forge 2005 365p $24.95
ISBN 0-312-87857-5 LC 2004-51246
Sequel to 1949

The author "tells the story of Ireland from 1950-1972 as seen through the eyes of young Barry Halloran, son and grandson of Irish revolutionaries. Northern Ireland has become a running sore, poisoning life on both sides of the Irish border. Following family tradition, at eighteen Barry joins the Irish Republican Army to help complete what he sees as 'the unfinished revolution.'" Publisher's note

Druids. Morrow 1991 456p o.p.
LC 90-44292

"Caesar's Gallic Wars are recounted from the viewpoint of the losers in this . . . evocation of the culture of the European Celts. Ainvar of the Carnutes, a young orphan druid-in-training, receives instruction for the 'manmaking' rituals with prince Vercingetorix of the Arverni, forging a bond that will later unite them in an effort to free Celtic Gaul from Roman domination." Publ Wkly

"Llywelyn's skill at making ancient history come alive for a modern audience without sacrificing authenticity of fact or detail is nothing short of brilliant. A richly atmospheric tale filled with subtle flashes of humor, perceptive characterizations, and heart-stopping suspense." Booklist

The elementals. TOR Bks. 1993 303p o.p.
LC 93-12760

"Remnants of humanity escape the great flood and make their way to safety in prehistoric Ireland. A singer and his companions survive the volcanic eruption that destroys the palace of Minos in Crete. A farmer's wife in 19th-century New Hampshire discovers the secrets of a sacred stone, and in the 21st century, George Burning Feather seeks the wisdom of the past to combat the ultimate natural disaster—the death of the air. . . . Though the connections among the four stories comprising this volume emerge only in the final story, each tale bears its own compelling message." Libr J

The horse goddess. Houghton Mifflin 1982 417p o.p.
LC 82-6234

"The Celts of 700 B.C. were a variety of tribes spread over Central Europe. Epona, a teenage Celt has just been initiated into womanhood when four strange horsemen visit her community. She is drawn to the leader, Kazhak, and leaves with the Scythians to escape the lecherous Druid priest. Epona's affinity for animals is held in awe by her new tribe, as is her boldness in a world where women are seen in veils only and never heard. Epona is eventually forced to flee the Russian steppes and returns to her old home, where her acquired wisdom helps her become the new Druid priestess." Libr J

"The author emphasizes the independent status of Celtic women, a proto-feminist characteristic that should heighten the appeal of the book." Publ Wkly

Llywelyn, Morgan—*Continued*

The last prince of Ireland. Morrow 1992 368p o.p.
LC 91-42516

Published in the United Kingdom with title: O'Sullivan's march

This "novel takes place in 17th-century Ireland as Queen Elizabeth I of England seeks to obliterate 2000 years of Celtic tradition and religion. It begins on December 30, 1602, soon after the Battle of Kinsale sounded the death knell for Irish independence. Fugitive nobleman Donal Cam O'Sullivan, the 'prince' of the title, denounces the queen and seeks to march 1000 followers to safety across wintry, dangerous terrain. Death, desertion, and near-constant fighting with the enemy, both English and Irish, reduce his band to a starving and exhausted group of 35 survivors." Libr J

"This tale of courage, love, cruelty and treachery, one of the great legends of Ireland, receives vivid, evocative treatment here." Publ Wkly

Pride of lions. Forge 1996 351p il o.p.
LC 95-42566

"A Tom Doherty Associates book"

"The perils of royal succession and a choice between love and glory form the dominant themes of Llywelyn's . . . sequel to *Lion of Ireland* (1979). That novel described the rise of High King Brian Boru, who became known as the 'Charlemagne of Ireland' after he managed to briefly unite the tribes of the Emerald Isle at the end of the 10th century. Here it's Brian's 15-year-old son, Donough, who aspires to the throne, made ambitious by a brief initial success in battle against the Vikings at Contarf, where Brian has met his death. But Donough's brother Teigue also claims the crown. . . . Llywelyn tells a strong story distinguished by its psychological depth and by his knowledge of ancient Irish history." Publ Wkly

Red Branch. Morrow 1989 558p o.p.
LC 88-13508

In this novel the author has created a legendary world "based on disparate tales of Ireland's mythical warrior-hero Cuchulain. . . . The story begins with a boy, Setanta, born in mysterious circumstances to Dectera, the King's half sister. Either Dectera's husband, the King, or a god is Setanta's father. But the truth is concealed from him, and in a land where status and privilege derive from birthright, his uncertain paternity is a painful mark of difference. Though still a youth, Setanta's ferocity while in combat with a monstrous wolfhound owned by a blacksmith, Cullen, earns him the name Cuchulain, or hound of Cullen. Soon after, he enters a warrior clan, the 'Red Branch' of the book's title." NY Times Book Rev

"Llywelyn works a massive canvas, peopling it with larger-than-life characters, yet shaping them with intimate insights." Publ Wkly

Silverhand; [by] Morgan Llywelyn, Michael Scott. Baen Pub. Enterprises 1995 416p o.p.
ISBN 0-671-87652-X LC 94-44443

"Young Caeled lives in a Celtic-like future of alternate world that is spotted with areas of 'gray nothingness' marking pockets of the Void in which nothing can exist. Returning to his village, he finds every organic thing has dissolved into a reeking, gelatinous sludge. He heads south and ends up in a community of scholars in which he learns his destiny is to be the Spoken One, the instrument for defeating the evil Duet-royal twins, brother and sister, who through their sexual passion can use the Void to kill." Booklist

"This rich tale shows how good fantasy can be when its authors neither denigrate their audience's intelligence nor obscure their ideas with overwrought language and overblown symbologies." Publ Wkly

Followed by Silverlight

Silverlight; [by] Morgan Llywelyn, Michael Scott. Baen Pub. Enterprises 1996 406p o.p.
ISBN 0-671-87728-3 LC 96-7635

Sequel to Silverhand

Caeled "possesses two magical artifacts that allow him to affect events but cause him to age with every use. Joined by three companions who hate the despotic twins who rule the world, Caeled seeks the remaining two Arcana artifacts that he will use to restore order to the world. A morality tale about how much power one can have and whether to use it that belongs in most fantasy collections." Libr J

Lockridge, Ross, 1914-1948

Raintree County. Houghton Mifflin 1948 1066p il o.p.

An epic novel describing a day, the Fourth of July of 1892, in the life of school teacher Johnny Shawnessy in which he participates in the holiday ceremonies of his small Indiana town and meets two old boyhood friends. These events set off a series of flashbacks in his mind and he relives his schooldays, his Civil war experiences, his brief political life, his two marriages, and a love affair that ends badly

"The book is full-blooded, it has gusto, ribaldry, vision, beauty, and narrative skill. It is also repetitious, overly 'organized,' reminiscent of a variety of predecessors, 'literary' in the wrong sense, and too dependent upon source material. But the breath of life sweeps through its voluminous pages." Saturday Rev

Lodge, David, 1935-

Nice work. Viking 1989 277p o.p.
ISBN 0-670-82806-8 LC 88-40480

A satirical look at "Thatcher's England. Two representatives from different worlds–the groves of academe and the dark satanic mills–meet and fall in (a semblance of) love as they aim to satisfy their physical passions and also open their emotions to new experiences. The academic is a young female professor of literature, and her industrial counterpart is a middle-aged factory manager. Their initial meeting does set off sparks but only to fan the flames of mutual antagonism before an attraction of sorts takes place." Booklist

"Lodge spoofs in a nonjudgmental way both the pretensions of academia and the materialism of the upper-middle business class. While lacking in stylistic elegance, this is a well-told tale full of gentle humor." Libr J

Paradise news; a novel. Viking 1992 293p o.p.
ISBN 0-670-84228-1 LC 91-32128

First published 1991 in the United Kingdom

"Bernard Walsh is planning a quiet visit to his sick aunt in Hawaii. A cynical ex-priest in search of a well-

Lodge, David, 1935-—*Continued*
needed vacation, he is unprepared for this zany package tour from Hell populated with all the 'types': dueling newlyweds, boring salesmen, video happy seniors, romance starved spinsters, and a sexy native girl on a collision course with fate (or at least Walsh's father)." Libr J

"Mr. Lodge is a serious author who bravely uses coincidence and contrivance to tie up loose ends. And just under the surface of the spirited and often comic adventures of his travelers he runs an undercurrent of understanding about their longings for the perfection of paradise. This comes to us in graceful and disciplined prose that offers vivid glimpses of what lies beyond the tourist hotels of Waikiki–the natural and imperfect world." N Y Times Book Rev

Therapy; a novel. Viking 1995 320p o.p.
ISBN 0-670-86358-0 LC 95-16337

"Laurence 'Tubby' Passmore is a successful British TV sitcom writer. He has plenty of money, homes in London and Rummidge, a fast car, and all the therapists his calendar will hold. Yet Tubby is chronically unhappy. In fact, he is so wrapped up in dismal self-contemplation that he does not notice when his daughter's pregnancy is announced or his wife of 30 years demands a divorce. He discovers and obsesses about Kierkegaard, seeing many similarities between his own life and that of the philosopher. When his world begins to crumble around him, Tubby sets off on a pilgrimage to find Maureen Kavanaugh, his first girlfriend." Libr J

"The novel is almost Victorian in its earnest goodness, which shines through its humor straight to the enormously moving and exultant ending." New Yorker

Thinks—; a novel. Viking 2001 341p o.p.
ISBN 0-670-89984-4 LC 2001-17555

"At a grim and insular provincial university, Ralph, a married scientist who runs an artifical-intelligence program, is drawn to the newly arrived Helen, a novelist and a recent widow. In Lodgian fashion, adultery quickly becomes their chief preoccupation, as the narrative unfolds in shifting points of view (Ralph dictating into a tape recorder, Helen adding to a diary), with occasional third-person authorial assistance." New Yorker

"This is the first Lodge novel set in the world of science, and it paints an utterly persuasive portrait of it. The story is a cracking tale, but read it, too, for the ideas. It's obvious that Lodge has become fascinated by the science of thought. Reading this is, so will you." New Sci

Lofts, Norah, 1904-1983

Gad's Hall. Doubleday 1978 c1977 282p o.p.
LC 77-92220

First published 1977 in the United Kingdom

"Dismissing Mrs. Spender's claims that Gad's Hall is haunted, her son Bob and daughter-in-law Jill buy the grand English country estate. . . . With this setup, Lofts deserts her modern family to describe the lives of the Thorleys who founded Gad's Hall in the 1800s. The widowed Mrs. Thorley of that era exerts firm control over the affairs of her children and stepchildren. When unwed Lavinia becomes pregnant, Mrs. Thorley hides the girl until the baby is born. The tragedy that results creates the ghosts that haunt the manor, to affect the Spenders, more than 100 years later." Publ Wkly

Followed by The haunting of Gad's Hall

The haunting of Gad's Hall. Doubleday 1979 c1978 281p o.p.
LC 78-62603

First published 1978 in the United Kingdom with title: Haunted house

The author "continues to relate the problematic history of the Thorleys as each of the daughters marries well but meets various troubles to do with love and money. Their final years are . . . summed up so that the plot may return to the present-day inhabitants whose discovery of the source of the evil that haunts a locked attic room finally results in its exorcism and the restoration of earlier harmony." Booklist

"The chief attraction here is Lofts' spotlight on the effects of manners and mores on females in 19th-century England." Publ Wkly

The lost queen. Doubleday 1969 302p o.p.

A novel about "the life of Princess Caroline Matilda, sister of George III, who left England at age fifteen to become the bride of King Christian of Denmark. Unhappy in her marriage to the mentally unbalanced King Christian, Caroline was led into an affair with the politically liberal court physician. Her lover was executed but Caroline was accused of treason and exiled to an unhappy life in Hanover." Booklist

"The book is rich in the atmosphere of the 18th century. Both extremes of the economic scale are revealed and the great social cruelties and injustices of the time come to light in the author's skillful weaving of the plot. The characters are vividly drawn and Mrs. Lofts is extremely sympathetic to her heroine." Best Sellers

Logue, Mary, 1952-

Bone harvest. Ballantine Bks. 2004 239p $23.95
ISBN 0-345-46222-X

This mystery featuring deputy sheriff Claire Watkins is set in the "small Wisconsin town of Fort St. Antoine. Someone has stolen deadly pesticides and is using them in a series of escalating crimes: first, a bed of flowers is wiped out, then a flock of chickens, and finally the lemonade at a Fourth of July celebration is contaminated. Claire soon links the poisonings to the 50-year-old unsolved slaughter of seven members of a local farm family, the Schulers. Each of the Schulers had a finger removed; now the dried bones of those fingers are showing up at the scenes of the recent crimes, and Claire is convinced that the 50-year anniversary of the killings will end in disaster if she can't find the person responsible. Her daughter, 11-year-old Meg, is sent safely out of town, but boyfriend Rich is still in the picture and bent on asking Claire to marry him. All these continuing characters are winning, and even the killer, once exposed, is sympathetic." Publ Wkly

Loh, Vyvyane

Breaking the tongue; a novel; Vyvyane Loh. 1st ed. W.W. Norton 2004 407p map $24.95
ISBN 0-393-05792-5 LC 2003-15870

Loh, Vyvyane—*Continued*

"On the eve of World War II, Claude Lim, a Chinese youth, uncertain of himself and his nationality, is being raised in a family that strongly identifies with the British colonists in Singapore. The family neither speaks nor understands Chinese and is proud of that fact. Their placid lives are disturbed by the hodgepodge of Asians, Eurasians, and British expatriates shifting in their roles and political sensibilities as the threat of invasion approaches. Prickly, pretentious Claude slowly metamorphoses into a young man with a budding Chinese identity and a wisdom wrought from the tortures and tragedies of war." Booklist

The author "explores such concepts as loyalty to one's family and country, the place of language in culture, and the roles of race, racism and ethnicity in how we perceive ourselves and others. In doing so, she has skillfully touched on questions at the very heart of politics, culture and global relations today." Washington Post Book World

London, Jack, 1876-1916

The call of the wild; pictures by Wendell Minor. Atheneum Books for Young Readers 1999 112p il $24

ISBN 0-689-81836-X LC 97-45019

First published 1903 by Macmillan

"Buck, half-St. Bernard, half-Scottish sheepdog, is stolen from his comfortable home in California and pressed into service as a sledge dog in the Klondike. At first he is abused by both man and dog, but he learns to fight ruthlessly. He becomes lead dog on a sledge team, after bettering Spitz, the vicious old leader, in a brutal fight to the death. In John Thornton, he finally finds a master whom he can respect and love. When Thornton is killed by Indians, Buck breaks away to the wilds and becomes the leader of a wolf pack, returning each year to the site of Thornton's death." Reader's Ency. 4th edition

also in London, J. Novels & stories

The complete short stories of Jack London; edited by Earle Labor, Robert C. Leitz, III, and I. Milo Shepard. Stanford Univ. Press 1993 3v $195

ISBN 0-8047-2058-4 LC 92-44856

"The London scholar and enthusiast will find this collection of Jack London's short fiction invaluable for the 5 previously unpublished stories it contains and for the 28 others it collects for the first time since their original publication in magazines." Choice

Martin Eden. Macmillan 1909 411p o.p.

A semi-autobiographical novel. "Eden has had a knock-about life as a sailor, and falling in love with a girl used to middle-class refinement and luxuries, tries to write. He is rejected by editors, and the girl jilts him. The abysmal contrast between the genius of this man, his vital ideals and the big realities of life, and on the other hand, the narrow, unintelligent mediocrity of the 'cultured classes' is brought out with characteristic force." Baker. Guide to Hist Fic

Novels & stories; Jack London. Literary Classics of the United States, Distributed to the trade by Viking Press 1982 1020p $30

ISBN 0-940450-05-4 LC 82-249

Contents: The call of the wild; White fang; The sea-wolf; Short stories

The Sea-Wolf; with illustrations by W.J. Aylward. Macmillan 1904 366p o.p.

"Wolf Larsen, ruthless captain of the tramp steamer 'Ghost,' receives an unexpected passenger on the high seas, Humphrey Van Weyden, a wealthy ne'er-do-well. In spite of his selfish brutality, Larsen becomes an instrument for good. The treatment he gives to the dilettante Van Weyden teaches the latter to stand on his own legs. He and the poet Maude Brewster, whom the 'Sea-Wolf' loves also, escape to an island as the 'Ghost' sinks and Larsen, mortally sick, is deserted. The lovers later return to civilization." Haydn. Thesaurus of Book Dig

also in London, J. Novels & stories

Short stories of Jack London; authorized one-volume edition; edited by Earle Labor, Robert C. Leitz III, I. Milo Shepard. Macmillan 1990 xli, 738p o.p.

LC 90-6175

Contents: Story of a typhoon off the coast of Japan; The white silence; To the man on trail; In a far country; An odyssey of the north; Semper idem; The law of life; A relic of the pliocene; Nam-Bok the unveracious; The one thousand dozen; To build a fire (1902); Moon-face; Bâtard; The story of Jees Uck; The league of the old men; Love of life; The sun-dog trail; All gold canyon; A day's lodging; The apostate; The wit of Porportuk; The unparalleled invasion; To build a fire (1908); The house of pride; The house of Mapuhi; The Chinago; Lost face; Koolau the leper; Chun Ah Chun; The heathen; Mauki; The strength of the strong; South of the Slot; Samuel; A piece of steak; The madness of John Harned; The night-born; War; Told in the drooling ward; The Mexican; The pearls of Parlay; Wonder of woman; The red one; On the Makaloa mat; The tears of Ah Kim; Shin bones; When Alice told her soul; Like Argus of the ancient times; The princess; The water baby

South Sea tales. Macmillan 1911 327p o.p.

Contents: The house of Mapuki; The whale tooth; Mauki; "Yah! Yah! Yah"; The heathen; The terrible Solomons; The inevitable white man; The seed of McCoy

The star rover. Macmillan 1915 329p o.p.

In this science fiction novel about transmigration of the soul, Darrell Standing is condemned to solitary confinement in a corrupt prison. He discovers how to free his soul from his body and escapes through time and space to relive the experiences of his past lives, which include being a caveman, a Danish soldier in the Roman legions, a French swordsman, and an American pioneer boy

Stories of Hawaii; edited by A. Grove Day. Appleton-Century 1965 282p o.p.

Contents: The house of pride; Koolau the leper; Good-by, Jack; Aloha oe; Chun Ah Chun; The sheriff of Kona; On the makaloa mat; The bones of Kahekili; When Alice told her soul; Shin bones; The water baby; The tears of Ah Kim; The Kanarka surf; A royal sport: Surfing at Waikiki; From "My Hawaiian aloha"

"These are stories written when London was living in Hawaii. . . . With a wide range of themes he covers many superstitions, beliefs, problems, and pleasures of those glamorous and fascinating islands and captures the flavor of the life there at the turn of the century." Libr J

London, Jack, 1876-1916—*Continued*

White Fang; pictures by Ed Young. Atheneum Books for Young Readers 2000 260p il $25
ISBN 0-689-82431-9 LC 98-19241
First published 1906
White Fang "is about a dog, a cross-breed, sold to Beauty Smith. This owner tortures the dog to increase his ferocity and value as a fighter. A new owner Weedom Scott, brings the dog to California, and, by kind treatment, domesticates him. White Fang later sacrifices his life to save Scott." Haydn. Thesaurus of Book Dig

also in London, J. Novels & stories

also in London, J. White Fang, and other stories p1-230

White Fang, and other stories; with photographs of the author and his environment as well as illustrations from early editions, together with an introduction by A.K. Adams. Dodd, Mead 1963 308p il o.p.
"Great illustrated classics"
Short stories included are: The one thousand dozen; All Gold Canyon; The son of the wolf; In a far country
The title novel (entered separately) and short stories are about dogs in Canada's Yukon Territory

Long, Jeff

The reckoning; Jeff Long. 1st Atria Books hardcover ed. Atria Books 2004 278p $25
ISBN 0-7434-6300-5 LC 2004-43657
A "journey into the dark past-and present-of Cambodia's former killing fields. Molly Drake, a would-be photojournalist, accompanies a U.S. Army-led search for the bones of a pilot shot down during the war. She meets Duncan O'Brian, an archeologist at a local dig, and John Kleat, who has come back to the country repeatedly, seeking his brother's remains. When bones unexpectedly turn up, Molly photographs them, breaking her agreement with the army not to take pictures of bodies. The captain in charge dismisses her along with O'Brian and Kleat, and the trio make their way to an ancient, fog-enshrouded Angkor-like city where they have evidence an army patrol went missing years ago. . . . Long's considerable knowledge of Cambodian folklore and history is put to good use as he superbly depicts the war-scarred country, its people and its beautiful, hazardous landscape." Publ Wkly

Longyear, Barry B.

Enemy mine

In The Hugo winners p5-67

Loo, Tessa de

A bed in heaven; translated from the Dutch by Ina Rilke. Soho Press 2003 120p $21
ISBN 1-56947-316-1 LC 2002-30295
Original Dutch edition, 2000
"When the novel opens, narrator Kata Roszavolgyi, in her 40s, has just buried her father and is now 'lying in bed with his son.' Kata recalls growing up in Holland in the 1950s with a Dutch mother and Hungarian Jewish father, the latter a renowned composer. As a teenager she falls in love with another student named Stefan; as they grow closer, Kata learns that Stefan's mother, Ida Flinck, hid Kata's father from the Nazis during WWII. From there, the revelations pile up. . . . As the novel moves toward a climactic encounter between Kata's father and Stefan, de Loo explores the legacy of the war—loss, guilt, families set adrift—for the generation of Europeans born in its wake." Publ Wkly

Looking for a rain god: an anthology of contemporary African short stories; edited by Nadežda Obradovic. Simon & Schuster 1990 284p o.p.
LC 89-48685

Contents: The madman, by C. Achebe; Maruma, by I. N. C. Aniebo; In the cutting of a drink, by A. A. Aidoo; Heart of a judge, by R. S. Easmon; Emente, by O. O. Enekwe; Noorjehan, by A. Essop; Blankets, by A. La Guma; Looking for a rain god, by B. Head; A man can try, by E. D. Jones; The winner, by B. Kimenye; Black skin what mask, by D. Marechera; The criminals, by S. Mpofu; Some kinds of wounds, by C. Mungoshi; A different time, by C. Nkosi; The doum tree of Wad Hamid, by T. Salih; Thoughts in a train, by M. Tshabangu; The soldier without an ear, by P. Zaleza; The spider's web, by L. Kibera; Call me not a man, by M. Matshoba; The spearmen of Malama, by K. Mubitana; A present for my wife, M. Mzamane; The rain came, by G. Ogot; The will of Allah, by D. Owoyele; The nightmare, by W. Saidi; The return, by Ngugi wa Thiong'o; The point of no return, by M. M. Tlali

Lopez, Barry Holstun, 1945-

Resistance; Barry Lopez. 1st ed. Alfred A. Knopf 2004 163p il $18
ISBN 1-400-04220-8 LC 2003-65986
This novel is comprised of "nine fictional testimonials that chronicle a group of activists who have been called before the 'Office of Inland Security' for the crime of 'terrorizing the imaginations of our fellow citizens.' These narrators—who come from various backgrounds (e.g., veteran, linguist, artisan) and parts of the world—focus on the transformative moment in their lives that led them to discover the injustices of the world." Libr J
"If it's true the author's erudite, well-meaning characters all sound very much alike, it's also true that one of his goals is to underscore the responsibility of artists to speak as one when speaking truth to power. To his credit, Lopez never sacrifices craft to politics." N Y Times Book Rev

Lord, Bette Bao

The middle heart; a novel. Knopf 1996 370p $25
ISBN 0-394-53432-8 LC 95-36165
The story begins in early 1930s China, "when three young people forge an unlikely alliance that survives five decades of loss and love. There's Steele Hope, the second son of the head of the once noble and powerful Li family; Mountain Pine, his 'bookmate' and retainer; and a destitute girl posing as a boy named Firecrackers. The novel's early sections sparkle with hope and joy as the three devoted friends romp and grow, but personal tragedy and war soon intrude." Booklist

Lord, Bette Bao—*Continued*

Spring Moon; a novel of China. Harper & Row 1981 464p o.p.

LC 78-20210

This novel "follows the history of a Mandarin Chinese family from 1892 until 1927, with an epilogue that updates the story to 1972. Through the eyes of Spring Moon, a lively and intelligent daughter of the house of Chang, we see the beauty of the inner courtyard society and observe its respect for family, order and harmony, scholarship and poetry. But we see, too, how Chinese society's rigid etiquette hobbles the lives of its women as surely as their bound feet. Unlike most women of her class and time, Spring Moon learns to read and write. The two men she loves, her eldest uncle and her husband, have both studied in America and have modern ideas. But her husband is killed in the Boxer Rebellion, and Spring Moon herself is forced into hiding for her role in the assassination of a Manchu official. She gives birth to a son she can't acknowledge and sees her daughter become a Communist revolutionary." Saturday Rev

Lordan, Beth

But come ye back; a novel in stories. Morrow 2004 278p $23.95

ISBN 0-06-053036-7 LC 2003-56217

This is the "story of Mary Curtin, an Irish nanny, and Lyle Sullivan, an American accountant, who fall in love, marry, and raise their two sons. When Lyle retires, Mary persuades him to relocate to her native Galway. She wants to live among her remaining family again and assures Lyle that he will love Ireland. Predictably, as in their earlier life together, there are joys and complications that stretch the ties that bind them, yet their marriage endures. Lyle reluctantly adapts to the idiosyncrasies of their small Irish community, and each spouse rediscovers the other in their new surroundings." Libr J

"Lordan's muted prose and fluting Irishisms ('Right, so,' 'Grand') are pleasant if rather selfconscious, and her characters are human, breathing people, forthrightly crafted. The novel-in-stories structure produces some inconsistencies and redundancies, but this is a quietly engaging effort." Publ Wkly

Lovecraft, H. P. (Howard Phillips), 1890-1937

At the mountains of madness, and other novels; selected by August Derleth; with texts edited by S.T. Joshi and introduction by James Turner. Arkham House Pubs. 1985 c1964 458p o.p.

ISBN 0-87054-038-6 LC 85-1254

A reissue of the title first published 1964 and analyzed in Short story index

Contents: At the mountains of madness; The case of Charles Dexter Ward; The shunned house; The dreams in the witchhouse; The statement of Randolph Carter; The dream-quest of unknown Kadath; The silver key; Through the gates of the silver key

The Dunwich horror, and others; selected by August Derleth, with texts edited by S.T. Joshi and an introduction by Robert Block. Arkham House Pubs. 1985 c1963 433p o.p.

ISBN 0-87054-037-8

A reissue of the title first published 1963 and analyzed in Short story index

Contents: In the vault; Pickman's model; The rats in the walls; The outsider; The colour out of space; The music of Erich Zann; The haunter of the dark; The picture in the house; The call of Cthulhu; The Dunwich horror; Cool air; The whisper in darkness; The terrible old man; The thing on the doorstep; The shadow over Innsmouth; The shadow out of time

H.P. Lovecraft; tales; edited by Peter Straub. Library of America 2005 838p $35

ISBN 1-93108-272-3 LC 2004-48979

Contents: The statement of Randolph Carter; The outsider; The music of Erich Zann; Herbert West—animator; The lurking fear; The rats in the walls; The shunned house; The horror at Red Hook; He; Cool air; The call of Cthulhu; Pickman's model; The case of Charles Dexter Ward; The colour out of space; The Dunwich horror; The whisperer in darkness; At the mountains of madness; The shadow over Innsmouth; The dreams in the witch house; The thing on the doorstep; The shadow out of time; The haunter of the dark

"If you spend enough time in Lovecraft's lonely landscapes, fear really does develop: not the fear that you will come across unearthly creatures, but the fear that you will come across little else. And what first seems horridly overdone accumulates a creepy minimalism. Taken as a whole, Lovecraft's work exhibits a hopeless isolation not unlike that of Samuel Beckett: lonely man after lonely man, wandering aimlessly through a shadowy city or holing up in rural emptiness, pursuing unspeakable secrets or being pursued by secret unspeakables, all to little avail and to no comfort. There is something funny about this—in small doses. But by the end of this collection, one does not hear giggling so much as the echoes of those giggles as they vanish into the ether lonely, desperate and, yes, very, very scary." N Y Times Book Rev

The horror in the museum, and other revisions; with texts edited by S. T. Joshi, and an introduction by August Derleth. Arkham House Pubs. 1989 450p o.p.

LC 88-7921

Contents: The green meadow; The crawling chaos; The last test; The electric executioner; The curse of Yig; The mound [novelette]; Medusa's coil; The man of stone; The horror in the museum; Winged death; Out of the aeons; The horror in the burying-ground; The diary of Alonzo Typer; The horror at Martin's Beach; Ashes; The ghost-eater; The loved dead; Deaf, dumb, and blind; Two black bottles; The trap; The tree on the hill; The disinterment; 'Till a' the seas'; The night ocean

"The volume is divided into 'Primary Revisions,' those stories that are all Lovecraft but for an idea, and 'Secondary Revisions,' clients' manuscripts heavily edited and revised." Publ Wkly

The mound
In Lovecraft, H. P. The horror in the museum, and other revisions p96-163

Tales of H.P. Lovecraft; major works selected and introduced by Joyce Carol Oates. Ecco Press 1997 328p o.p.

ISBN 0-88001-541-1 LC 96-47196

Lovecraft, H. P. (Howard Phillips), 1890-1937—
Continued

Contents: The outsider; The music of Erich Zann; The rats in the walls; The shunned house; The call of Cthulhu; The colour out of space; The Dunwich horror; At the mountains of madness; The shadow over Innsmouth; The shadow out of time

Lovecraft, Howard Phillips *See* Lovecraft, H. P. (Howard Phillips), 1890-1937

Lovesey, Peter

Bertie & the crime of passion. Mysterious Press 1995 244p o.p.
LC 94-28274

First published 1993 in the United Kingdom

Prince Albert sets out to "help his old friend, Jules d'Agincourt, whose daughter's fiance has been shot at the trés chic Moulin Rouge. Enlisting the aid of such notable celebrities as actress Sarah Bernhardt and curmudgeonly painter Henri Toulouse-Lautrec, Bertie surpasses even the considerable skills of the Paris Sûreté." Booklist

Bertie and the seven bodies. Mysterious Press 1990 196p o.p.
LC 89-12405

In this mystery "Albert Edward, the Prince of Wales—Bertie to the ladies—sallies forth on an elaborate hunt in Buckinghamshire and bags a murderer along with the other game." N Y Times Book Rev

"Narrated by Bertie himself, the voice here is perfectly accurate; Lovesey gives his main character just the right tone of sophistication, charm, anti-intellectualism, and savoir faire—mixed in with ennui. A wonderfully put together puzzle." Booklist

Bertie and the Tinman. Mysterious Press 1987 212p o.p.
LC 87-40426

Prince Albert is shocked to learn of the apparent suicide of his friend Fred Archer, known as the Tinman and as England's greatest jockey. When the inquest presents discrepancies known only to Bertie, he begins sleuthing in London's underworld

"Mr. Lovesey is a specialist in the Victorian crime novel, and in 'Tinman' he has done his usual impeccable research. . . . The racetrack scenes and backgrounds crackle with authenticity. There is a great deal of humor in the book, even a strong dash of P.G. Wodehouse." N Y Times Book Rev

Bloodhounds. Warner Bks. 1996 359p o.p.
LC 96-22244

In this takeoff on the traditional "locked room" mystery "Lovesey's wise but beleaguered hero Peter Diamond confronts a homicide case as perplexing as any he's faced. The perpetrator appears to be both brilliant and devious, composing a series of riddles designed to offer clues to upcoming crimes while effectively throwing the police off the scent, then stealing a priceless postage stamp while the coppers' collective backs are turned." Booklist

Lovesey "skillfully pays homage to the old style whodunit in this thoroughly modern mystery." Publ Wkly

The detective wore silk drawers. Dodd, Mead 1971 188p o.p.

"A Red badge novel of suspense"

"Three London detectives of the 1880s, all boxing fans, uncover a clandestine center of the sport while investigating several headless corpses." Booklist

"Although the mystery is nothing special, it suffices, and the kicks come from the 19th century atmosphere of Victorian sex and mild sadism." Publ Wkly

Diamond dust. Soho Press 2002 343p $24
ISBN 1-56947-291-2 LC 2002-17567

This "mystery, starring Peter Diamond, head of the murder squad in Bath, England, has the avuncular copper off the murder beat and assigned to an investigation of Bath's Mafia family. News of a murder in the city's Victorian formal gardens sends Diamond's spirits soaring, confident he will be returned to his home turf. As he draws back the plastic sheet over the woman's body, however, he discovers that the victim is his own wife." Booklist

"In a bold display of virtuosity, Lovesey takes his hero to emotional places he's never been before while constructing a plot of infernal ingenuity." N Y Times Book Rev

Diamond solitaire. Mysterious Press 1993 c1992 343p o.p.
ISBN 0-89296-535-5 LC 92-50660

First published 1992 in the United Kingdom

"Peter Diamond is plagued by bad karma. Formerly detective superintendent of police in Bath, he's sunk to being a security guard at Harrod's—until a small Asian child is found in the area of the store Peter patrols. Out of a job once again (security breaches are no laughing matter at terrorist-obsessed Harrod's), Diamond becomes intrigued by the Asian child, who is autistic and who remains unclaimed despite massive publicity. What starts out as a kindly effort to restore the child to her parents turns into an international adventure as Diamond travels from London to New York to Japan and confronts millionaire sumo wrestlers, unethical drug researchers, and corrupt businessmen." Booklist

The house sitter. Soho Press 2003 346p $25
ISBN 1-56947-326-9 LC 2002-42626

"Initially brought in as an auxilliary police consultant, Bath's Inspector Peter Diamond soon proves himself indispensable to a missing person case turned murder investigation. A woman from Bath discovered dead on a Sussex beach turns out to have been strangled—apparently right there in the midst of a crowd. The main witnesses, a family of three, seem to be hiding something. The victim was a psychological offender profiler, apparently working on the case of a serial murderer." Libr J

"The identity of the killer, when finally revealed, is genuinely startling, and not because of authorial obfuscation. The writing is as smooth as polished steel." Publ Wkly

The last detective. Doubleday 1991 331p o.p.
LC 91-11859

"A Perfect crime book"

"Irascible, corpulent, cynical Chief Superintendent Peter Diamond of the Avon and Somerset murder squad attributes Britain's decline as a world power to the abolition of capital punishment in 1964. Spurning computer

Lovesey, Peter—*Continued*
gadgetry, he sticks to common sense, index cards and gumshoeing: 'Knocking on doors. That's how we get results.' The almost clueless case of the naked woman's body found floating in Chew Valley Lake poses a supreme challenge for the detective, who is anxious to clear his name of recent charges of brutality." Publ Wkly

"An intricate, many-tiered examination of police work, especially modern forensic technology, complete with computers and genetic fingerprinting. Everything meshes perfectly in this airtight tale." Booklist

On the edge. Mysterious Press 1989 204p o.p.
LC 88-13549

"Set in Britain immediately after World War II, this is a novel that balances wit and wickedness, ambitions and just desserts. Rosie married badly—to a penniless philanderer. Antonia married well—to a wealthy man—but her lover is going to the U.S. and she wants to join him there. Rosie and Antonia meet by chance, talk, and a plan is gradually hatched. With a helpful shove from Antonia, Rosie's hubby comes to a bad end beneath a tube train. The second half of the deal becomes more convoluted, as Antonia's past (she having murdered her husband's first wife) and several secret agendas throw a wrench in the works." Booklist

"Told mostly in racy, ear-perfect dialogue that magnifies the impact of events, the story dodges from one unguessable outcome to the next." Publ Wkly

Rough cider. Mysterious Press 1986 216p o.p.
LC 86-18212

"A tightly knit tale that has its roots in the hanging for murder in England of an American G.I. Twenty years later his daughter, who lives in the U.S., attempts to exonerate his name by enlisting the aid of an English professor whose childhood was marked by the crime. Readers incidentally learn about cider making and discover some grisly evidence of murder and guilt in the course of the demonstration." Barzun. Cat of Crime. Rev and enl edition

Upon a dark night. Mysterious Press 1998 374p o.p.
LC 97-48922

First published 1997 in the United Kingdom

Peter Diamond, "head of the murder squad in Bath, England, annoys his peers by poking around in two seemingly clear-cut suicides—an unknown woman who leaped to her death and a farmer who blew his head off with a shotgun. His poking soon uncovers murder, and eventually the two deaths become linked to the disappearance of an amnesia victim." Booklist

A "triumph of plotting from this master of the classic puzzle form." N Y Times Book Rev

The vault. Soho Press 2000 331p $23
ISBN 1-56947-208-4 LC 00-41010

First published 1999 in the United Kingdom

This mystery "relies on Peter Diamond, a British copper of eclectic cultural tastes, to unravel the complexities of a story that begins when a human hand is disinterred from a burial vault beneath the now-vanished house in Bath where Mary Shelley finished the classic horror story she famously started on a dark and stormy night at Lake Geneva." N Y Times Book Rev

"A wealth of good things fills this novel: Lovesey's deft plotting, his hilarious send-ups of the Brits through the perspective of the American professor, and his intriguing allusions to the architecture and literary history of Bath." Booklist

Waxwork. Pantheon Bks. 1978 239p o.p.
LC 77-90420

"There is certainly enough here to warrant the praise given this tale by more than one highly regarded colleague in crime. Set in the London and Kew of 1888, a case of KCN poisoning following upon blackmail taxes the abilities of the police, but in the end Sgt. Cribb really does distinguish himself. The title alludes to Tussaud's Waxwork Exhibition." Barzun. Cat of Crime. Rev and enl edition

Lovric, Michelle

The floating book; a novel; Michelle Lovric. 1st ed. Regan Bks. 2004 480p $25.95
ISBN 0-06-057856-4 LC 2003-58400

A novel set in Venice in 1486. "Sosia Simeon, married to a Jewish doctor who is repulsed by her, finds comfort in the arms of many other men. German-born Wendelin von Speyer comes to Venice to capitalize on the invention of the printing press. Sosia bewitches handsome young Bruno, Wendelin's editor, but it is the cold, disinterested Felice, his scribe, who captivates her. Wendelin falls in love with Lussieta, the beautiful daughter of a bookseller, and marries her. All of them are drawn in by the amorous poems of the Latin poet Catullus, which Wendelin intends to print. . . . Meticulous historical detail and a splendid, complex story make this portrait of Venice and its denizens memorable and moving." Booklist

Lowell, Elizabeth

Die in plain sight. Morrow 2003 385p $24.95
ISBN 0-06-050412-9 LC 2003-40606

"Art buyer and struggling southern California artist Lacey Quinn shows a few of her grandfather's paintings to renowned artist Susa Donovan, in the area for a charity event. The paintings are mostly landscapes, but also include a few samples from his dark later work, including detailed depictions of murder and death by fire and drowning. Believing that the landcapes are really the work of famous California plein air painter Lewis Marten, Susa asks Lacey to have them professionally appraised. Lacey resists Susa's pleas, fearing that her grandfather may have been guilty of forgery, but she discovers something far more complicated and horrifying. The murders her grandfather depicted actually took place." Publ Wkly

Lowry, Malcolm, 1909-1957

Under the volcano. Reynal & Hitchcock 1947 375p o.p.

This novel "presents in detail the events of [a] single day in a single place—the Day of the Dead in a town in Mexico, with Popocatepetl and Ixtaccihuatl looking down. It is the last day on earth of the British Consul, Geoffrey Firmin, and he is dying of alcoholism. Like any tragic hero, he is fully aware of the choice he has made: he clings to his sloth, he needs salvation through love but will not utter the word which will bring it, he lets his morbid lust for drink drag him from bar to bar. In other

Lowry, Malcolm, 1909-1957—*Continued*
words, he has made a deliberate choice of damnation. . . . We don't despise or even dislike Firmin, despite his weaknesses and his self-destructive urge. As with all tragic heroes (and this novel is a genuine tragedy) he sums up the flaws which are latent or actual in all of us." Burgess. 99 Novels

Ludlum, Robert, 1927-2001

The apocalypse watch. Bantam Bks. 1995 645p o.p.

LC 95-1860

"Brilliant deep-cover American agent Harry Latham is captured and implanted with a mind-control microchip after he penetrates the secret Austrian headquarters of a contemporary movement to restore the Nazis to world domination. Programmed with false information incriminating legions of high-level officials around the free world, Harry is allowed to escape. Debriefed by the CIA in London, he contacts his brother Drew, also a secret agent for American Consular Operation in Paris. After revealing the name of one Nazi, Harry is assassinated by the sinister Brotherhood of the Watch, prompting Drew—aided by Karin de Vries, the beautiful and mysterious widow of Harry's former partner—to assume his identity." Publ Wkly

"A powerful, exploding novel that, frightening as it sounds, may not be so far reaching, for it touches on the issues of hate, ethnic cleansing, and racism that we read about every day." Booklist

The Aquitaine progression. Random House 1984 647p o.p.

LC 83-19078

This novel "features five present or former generals from five different countries who mean to take over the world. They have decided to put an end to the quagmire of Western politics and set up a super-fascist state with themselves in control. The hub of this enterprise is Gen. George Marcus Delavane, a fanatic who makes Genghis Khan look like a Peace Corps volunteer. Joel Converse, an international lawyer, has reason to know and hate Delavane. It was Delavane who insisted on an Air Force mission in Vietnam that resulted in Converse's capture and subsequent agonies at the hands of the enemy. While in Geneva working on a case for his New York law firm, Converse is contacted by one A. Preston Halliday, who gives him information he finds hard to believe. But there follows a series of entanglements and murders that clearly prove Halliday's assertions." N Y Times Book Rev

The Bourne identity. Marek, R. 1980 523p o.p.

LC 79-23638

"Jason Bourne is shot and left for dead. He survives, but without a memory. Slowly, painstakingly, he retraces his past, only to find himself hunted by assassins of several governments, including his own. He fights against seemingly insurmountable odds—especially his very limited knowledge of his past—to discover his identity and stop his enemies before it is too late." Libr J

Followed by The Bourne supremacy

The Bourne supremacy. Random House 1986 597p o.p.

LC 85-18318

"In this sequel to The Bourne Identity David Webb, still suffering flashbacks to his Jason Bourne persona, is forced to undertake a final, possibly fatal mission after his wife is kidnapped. He must find and capture an assassin who is posing as Bourne in Hong Kong. By so doing he'll foil a plot that could plunge the Far East and then the world into war." Libr J

"Every chapter ends with a cliff-hanger; the story brims with assassination, torture, hand-to-hand combat, sudden surprise and intrigue within intrigue. It's a surefire bestseller." Publ Wkly

Followed by The Bourne ultimatum

The Bourne ultimatum. Random House 1990 611p o.p.

LC 89-43201

"When the international terrorist known as Carlos the Jackal penetrates his civilian identity, Webb must again assume the Bourne persona to protect his wife and small children. In their renewed struggle, the two master assassins uncover the revived existence of Medusa, the sinister alliance that originally led to the establishment of the Bourne identity." Publ Wkly

The Gemini contenders. Dial Press (NY) 1976 402p o.p.

"The twin sons of a former Italian government official search for a mysterious document he was forced to leave behind when fleeing his fascist-dominated homeland in 1939." Smith. Cloak and Dagger Fic

Ludlum is "at the top of his form here as he tells a suspenseful story that gives fresh slants to old themes." Publ Wkly

The Holcroft covenant. Marek, R. 1978 542p o.p.

LC 77-95295

"Thirty years after Hitler, Noel Holcroft sees an astounding document, drawn up by three supposedly contrite Nazis (all now dead), one of them his own father. If he signs it and collects signatures from the sons of the other two men, the Holocaust victims' heirs should become the beneficiaries of a gigantic fund. The fund's 'real' purpose is to establish the Fourth Reich, not atone for the Third, but Holcroft doesn't realize this as he flings around the world in search of those signatures, precipitating . . . ruthless clashes between secret Nazi and anti-Nazi organizations." Publ Wkly

The Janson directive. St. Martin's Press 2002 547p $27.95

ISBN 0-312-25348-6 LC 2002-5136

"The hero is Paul Janson, a private security consultant who retired a few years ago after a notorious career as the U.S. government's go-to guy for nasty jobs no one else was willing to take. Against his better judgment, Janson accepts an assignment to rescue Peter Novak, a Nobel Peace Prize-winning philanthropist and international troubleshooter held captive by Islamic extremists on an island in the Indian Ocean. . . . Extremely engaging and agonizingly suspenseful, Ludlum's plot bolts from scene to scene and locale to locale—Hungary, Amsterdam, London, New York City—never settling for one bombshell when it can drop four or five." Publ Wkly

Ludlum, Robert, 1927-2001—*Continued*

The Matarese Circle. Marek, R. 1979 601p o.p.
LC 78-31673

This novel of international intrigue "features the world's top secret agents: Scofield, American, and Taleniekov, Russian. They have sworn to kill each other—Scofield was responsible for the death of Taleniekov's brother, Taleniekov for that of Scofield's wife—yet they have much in common besides their brilliance: both are semiretired, held in suspicion by their respective governments and encumbered (occasionally) by the humane streak in their characters. And now they are drawn into cooperation, as the only men capable of destroying an international circle of killers, The Matarese, originally Corsican, which is dedicated to reducing the world to chaos via assassination and terror." Publ Wkly

The Matlock paper. Dial Press (NY) 1973 312p o.p.

"James Matlock, instructor in Elizabethan literature at Carlyle University in Connecticut, formerly an Army officer in Vietnam, is drawn into the most personally dangerous and violent struggle of his life when he is requested to cooperate with a government narcotic agent in exploring Carlyle's connection with the expanding drug traffic in New England." Publ Wkly

The Parsifal mosaic. Random House 1982 630p o.p.
LC 84-8925

The novel "centers around the background figure of superstar Secretary of State Anthony Matthias, whose unhinged brilliance nearly leads to nuclear disaster. In the foreground is accomplished and durable U.S. deep-cover agent Michael Havelock (nee Mikhail Havliček), protégé and surrogate son of fellow Czech Matthias. Forced to order the execution of the woman he loves, believing her to be an agent of the Soviet terrorist group VKR, Havelock leaves espionage service. But when he spots her alive in Rome he's back in, on a convoluted trial of international intrigue that leads to the highest levels of government." Libr J

"The tale has all the hallmarks of vintage Ludlum: non-stop action, precisely timed curtain-raisers, the darksome deeds of agent and double agent, a deadly secret ultimately revealed and an underlying theme of the whole world jeopardized by a few fanatics." Publ Wkly

The Prometheus deception. St. Martin's Press 2000 509p o.p.
ISBN 0-312-25346-X LC 00-62585

"Nick Bryson works for an ultrasecret intelligence organization; after making a mistake during a mission, he's put out to pasture. Later, he's brought back into the game by a different intelligence group, and he learns that everything he believed about his former bosses was a lie-until, that is, he discovers that everything the second organization has told him is also a lie. Bryson winds up trying singlehandedly to save the world from a shadowy terrorist group, while simultaneously trying to figure out which of the various 'good guys' he should believe. . . . The pace is fast, the action plentiful, and the story confusing enough to keep us turning the pages." Booklist

The Rhinemann exchange. Dial Press (NY) 1974 460p o.p.

"A World War II espionage novel detailing an attempted treasonous exchange between the Germans and the Americans—the technological secret of a gyroscopic guidance system in return for industrial diamonds. This is to be brought off by a disenfranchised German Jew in Buenos Aires, tracked by an American agent not quite in the know and thus in jeopardy." Booklist

The Scarlatti inheritance; a novel. World Pub. 1970 358p o.p.

"An American agent becomes concerned about the decline in his family's fortune and looking into the matter finds that his relative, Ulster Scarlatti, is using the money to bankroll Hitler's World War II effort." Smith. Cloak and Dagger Fic

The scorpio illusion. Bantam Bks. 1993 534p o.p.
LC 93-9272

In this thriller, "the beautiful, anarchistic Basque terrorist Amaya Bajaratt . . . modestly sets out to eliminate the leaders of the United States, Britain, France and Israel. The only person able to stop her and thus save civilization as we know it is Tyrell Nathaniel Hawthorne 3d, a disillusioned former United States Naval Intelligence officer, now going to seed in the Caribbean. The two adversaries circle warily, each desperate to eliminate the other, neither able to strike the fatal blow." N Y Times Book Rev

The Sigma protocol. St. Martin's Press 2001 535p o.p.
ISBN 0-312-27688-5 LC 2001-48240

"Anna Navarro, a U.S. homicide specialist for the enigmatic Internal Compliance Unit is sent to look into a spate of mysterious deaths around the world. All the victims are very old wealthy men, and all are connected to the secretive corporation Sigma A.G., founded in Switzerland during WWII. When her only living lead is murdered moments before Anna lands in Switzerland, she crosses paths with Ben Hartman, a New York financier who is dodging the killer who murdered his twin brother, Peter, when Peter discovered that their father, Max, was part of Sigma." Publ Wkly

"Ludlum keeps things moving with plenty of gunplay and running about. Uncharacteristically, he also lets things slow down from time to time, long enough for us to get to know the players in this complicated story." Booklist

Lupica, Mike

Wild pitch. Putnam 2002 352p o.p.
ISBN 0-399-14927-9 LC 2002-21952

An "account of the comeback of Showtime Charlie Stoddard, a pitching phenom for the New York Mets forced into early retirement by a ruined arm. Five years after his final sorry major league appearance, Charlie encounters a mysterious therapist named Chang, whose treatments make his tortured arm feel so good he dreams of pitching again. . . . How Charlie ends up pitchings for the Red Sox as they try to hold off the Yankees in a tight pennant race and just possibly shake off the collective curses of the Bambino, Bill Buckner and Bucky Dent, is fast and funny and occasionally brings a tear to the eye." Publ Wkly

Lurie, Alison

Foreign affairs. Random House 1984 291p o.p. LC 84-42657

This novel follows "the actions and reactions of two English professors, both Americans, both from the same university, who are on leave in London to do research: Virginia Miner, 54, unmarried, happy to be back in the city she adores, and Fred Turner, 28, separated from his wife and depressed over being more or less in exile. Both Vinnie and Fred indulge in, while there, affairs with unlikely persons, with the result that they learn more about themselves from the experiences." Booklist

"Lurie portrays these entanglements with her customary astute wit and deft characterization, but also with unexpected warmth and generosity. A wry, wonderful book." Libr J

The last resort; a novel. Holt & Co. 1998 321p o.p.

ISBN 0-8050-5866-4 LC 97-42985

In this novel a "forbearing New England wife puts up with an overbearing nature-writer husband; he's twenty-four years her senior, famous, and secretly thinks he's dying. During a sojourn in the Florida Keys, opportunities for mixing and rematching abound: she is coveted by a celebrated poet and by a lush lesbian, while he is worshipped by a would-be savior of manatees. Lurie sets this gavotte in a Key West whose pastels take on a tasty acidity, and the novel goes down like Key-lime pie." New Yorker

The nowhere city. Coward-McCann 1966 c1965 276p o.p.

First published 1965 in the United Kingdom

"Paul Cattleman, a young Harvard historian, goes West to spend a year writing the history of the Nutting Electronics Corporation; he is unwillingly followed by his wife Katherine. . . . He takes to transplantation . . . [but] his wife doesn't until she falls in with an ex-Mittel-Europa analyst." New Statesman (1913)

The author describes the Los Angeles "scene with such a cool and penetrating eye, such total disbelief in its existence, that she is able to portray it with a pristine freshness. . . . Transformed by her wicked wit, the most exhausted clichés come alive, galvanized into original revelation." Newsweek

Only children. Random House 1979 259p o.p. LC 78-21994

"The novel spans the Fourth of July weekend [of 1935]. Bill and Honey Hubbard and their eight-year-old daughter Mary Ann, and Dan and Celia Zimmern and their daughter Lolly (and Dan's sullen adolescent son from a previous marriage) abandon New York City and its suburb, Larchmont, for the Catskill farm owned by Anna King, headmistress of the progressive school the two girls attend. This innocent outing doesn't turn out to be a relaxing weekend. . . . Instead the grownups start romping in an unseemly way and end up fighting while the two little girls look on, bewildered." New Repub

"Lurie has a sharp, ironic eye for the man-woman game and a dramatic deftness for setting the scene. Her rendering of the children is particularly effective." Libr J

(ed) The Oxford book of modern fairy tales. See The Oxford book of modern fairy tales

The war between the Tates. Random House 1974 372p o.p.

The setting of the novel is the community of Corinth, New York during late 1969 and early 1970. "Brian Tate, a university professor, complete with neuroses, approaching 50, and not nearly so successful as he had hoped to be, becomes entangled with Wendy Gahaghan, a graduate student, who, unlike Erica Tate, gives of herself so freely that Brian consents to attempt to alleviate her infatuation. Wendy slowly moves into what little there is of the Tate's family life so that she can tell Erica everything. The personality and sexual problems of these characters, compounded by the rebelliousness of the obnoxious and beautifully drawn Tate children, are intriguingly set off against recurring metaphors which are tied to the Vietnamese war." Choice

"An outline of the plot does scant justice to the substance and wit of Lurie's novel. What makes the lines sing is her skill in catching the idiosyncracies of the mind and the tongue, the twists and turns of sophisticated sensibilities trapped in absurd situations." America

Women and ghosts. Talese 1994 179p o.p. LC 93-46332

Contents: Ilse's house; The pool people; The highboy; Counting sheep; In the shadow; Waiting for baby; Fat people; Another Halloween; The double poet

"In each tale Lurie pits a female protagonist against an apparition of varied, often comical, spectral persuasions. . . . These entertaining and enchanting tales deliver far more than one might bargain for, with afterimages that reverberate long after the initial delight with Lurie's dexterous prose has worn off." Booklist

Lustbader, Eric Van, 1946-

Black Blade; [by] Eric Lustbader. Fawcett Columbine 1993 518p o.p. LC 91-72890

New York homicide cop "Wolf Matheson is assigned to investigate a chain of murders perpetrated by the furtive Black Blade Society. That's a nationalistic, militaristic, but intellectual cabal that, for centries, has been nurturing the 'Oracle,' an enhanced mental state in which practitioners are able to predict the future and attain long lifespans. Alas, the Black Blade is bent on world domination and has been maneuvering events in both the U.S. and Japan toward world war. Wolf, with his sexy-but-clairvoyant Japanese girl friend, Chika, at his side, is equal to the task of saving the world, but he wouldn't be if it weren't for his Shoshone childhood, where shamans knew the same kind of stuff the Black Blade know." Booklist

Dark homecoming; [by] Eric Lustbader. Pocket Bks. 1997 353p o.p.

ISBN 0-671-00329-1 LC 96-48909

"Seeking refuge from his former life as a cop, Lew Croaker finds his reverie on his fishing boat in Miami cut short when his estranged sister, Matty, reappears. Matty begs him to find a kidney donor for her daughter, Rachel, whose self-abusive lifestyle has left her near death. Suddenly, Croaker is catapulted into the nefarious world of the feral Bonita twins, who murder people to harvest their organs. In a race against time to save Rachel, he agrees to murder a Latin American drug lord in exchange for a kidney; and then his friends become his

Lustbader, Eric Van, 1946-—*Continued*
enemies." Libr J

"An accomplished crime novel from a writer whose work has grown in depth without sacrificing thrills." Booklist

Floating city; a Nicholas Linnear novel; by Eric Lustbader. Pocket Bks. 1994 404p o.p.
LC 93-49360

"Nicholas Linnear and his private-eye buddy, Lew Croaker, dash around the globe attempting to thwart the murder of the Yakuza boss of bosses and stop the development of a terrible new weapon and a supercartel bent on world domination." Booklist

Jian. Villard Bks. 1985 448p o.p.
LC 85-40184

This "tale pits American superspy Jake Maroc and his cohorts in the Quarry (U.S. intelligence) against the formidable Japanese KGB agent Nichiren and a web of Oriental double-dealings and counter-allegiances, all of which are metaphorically played out as 'wei qi,' the ancient Chinese game of military strategy. Brutal killings, deadly females, and an acceptably diverting amount of steamy erotica are the hallmarks of Lustbader's story, which, considering its imposing use of italicized Japanese terms, may put off all but his most rabid fans." Booklist

Mistress of the pearl; Eric Van Lustbader. 1st ed. TOR Bks. 2004 588p map $27.95
ISBN 0-312-87237-2 LC 2003-60698

"As Riane, the prophesied Dar-Sala-at destined to deliver the people of Kundala from their V'ornn conquerors, continues her search for the legendary Pearl believed to hold the key to deliverance for her people, other forces for change are at work within the world. A Resistance movement unites Kundalans with sympathetic V'ornns even as a group of V'ornn scientists conduct ruthless experiments to master a rare radioactive substance." Libr J

This novel "builds powerfully upon its predecessors, thanks to characters of uncommon depth and complexity, lots of perplexing dilemmas for them to wrestle with, and plenty of exciting swordplay and gore." Booklist

Second skin; a Nicholas Linnear novel. Pocket Bks. 1995 454p o.p.
LC 95-14365

In this adventure Nicholas Linnear "heads a computer firm on the verge of a mega-breakthrough that here is threatened by: a crazed Nietzsche-spouting American gangster who is Nicholas's doppelganger; the gangster's equally crazed, California-based brother, who's trying to take over the Eastern U.S Mafia family run by a middle-aged suburban matron; an unholy mix of Japanese tycoons, pols and Yakuza; and a creepy, untrustworthy aide to Nicholas's ailing mentor." Publ Wkly

Shan. Random House 1987 c1986 503p o.p.
LC 86-10027

This novel "follows the spectacular career of a former U.S. intelligence agent, the half-Chinese Jake Maroc. Jake's Chinese father (the subject of Lustbader's 'Jian') was the guiding light behind the Cultural Revolution. Following in his father's footsteps, Jake becomes the 'zhuan,' the instrument through which the Jian's vision is to come to fruition, with China asserting itself as a world economic power. The gateway to this power is Hong Kong. Within a world of cutthroat diplomacy and espionage, Jake rises to the summit, helped by Bliss, the beautiful and dangerous woman he loves." Booklist

White Ninja; [by] Eric V. Lustbader. Fawcett Columbine 1990 518p o.p.
LC 89-92008

This installment centers on the adventures of the ninja Nicholas Linnear. As this novel opens, Linnear is having marital problems, and his best friend, chairman of a large corporation, is fighting off a computer virus and pressure from a Japanese business coalition

"A distinctly good time for the unabashed thriller-reader, particularly those with a taste for the mystical, exotic and sexually kinky." Publ Wkly

Lutz, John, 1939-

Burn. Holt & Co. 1995 278p o.p.
ISBN 0-8050-3480-3 LC 94-32187

Florida private eye "Fred Carver's new client, an attractive, widowed housing developer with the 'guileless blue eyes' of a serial killer, claims he is being persecuted by a woman who has accused him of stalking her. Keeping an open mind, Carver sets out to determine whether the frantic businessman is your 'typical compulsive male sexual psychopath' or a much-maligned guy." N Y Times Book Rev

This mystery, "in which the motive isn't greed or passion but rather grief and loss, is one of the best in a fine series." Booklist

Dancing with the dead. St. Martin's Press 1992 208p o.p.
LC 92-2997

"A Thomas Dunne book"

"St. Louis realtor Mary Arlington, whose mother is alcoholic and whose lover is physically abusive, lives for her mambo, cha-cha and tango lessons with Mel Holt at the Romance Studio. After kicking her lover out of her life and checking her mother into a detox center, Mary agrees to dance with Mel in the Ohio Star Ball, a major competition. Meanwhile in Seattle and New Orleans, women dancers resembling Mary are murdered. Rene Verlane, the husband of the New Orleans victim, insists the crime is related to his wife's dancing. Mary follows the case on TV and one night calls Verlane to offer her help in finding the killer." Publ Wkly

Death by jury. St. Martin's Press 1995 291p o.p.
LC 95-11363

"A Thomas Dunne book"

St. Louis detective Alo Nudger "is hired by Lawrence Fleck, an odious and permanently small-time attorney, to investigate his client, banker Roger Dupont, who is about to stand trial for the murder of his wife. The twist is that Fleck wants Nudger to find incriminating evidence because he wants his client to accept a plea bargain. Lutz is a master storyteller, and this plot is an intricate masterpiece." Booklist

Final seconds; by John Lutz and David August. Kensington Bks. 1998 316p o.p.
ISBN 1-57566-259-0 LC 97-75929

"Will Harper, a member of the NYPD bomb squad, lost part of a hand in an explosion at a city high school. While Harper is in Florida visiting his former partner,

Lutz, John, 1939-—*Continued*
Jimmy Fahey, who works for a Tom Clancy-like writer, a letter bomb arrives at the author's compound. The explosion kills Fahey and two colleagues. Loyalty to his dead partner prompts Harper to investigate." Booklist

"The most welcome realism in the book comes from the authors' resistance to the far-fetched elements that creep into many thrillers. Their seamless collaboration is notable for the efficiency of the plotting and for the unusual credibility of the story, its characters and the methodical way they do their work." Publ Wkly

Hot. Holt & Co. 1992 273p o.p.
LC 91-3153

"Fred Carver, an Orlando private eye who normally thrives in soaring temperatures, takes on a dull surveillance job for a retired cop named Henry Tiller who lives on Key Montaigne . . . where he keeps an eye peeled on the neighbors. The old man's suspicion that 'one of them neighbors ain't right' takes on ominous weight when Tiller is struck by a hit-and-run driver, leaving Carver to sweat out the watch for whatever mischief the guy next door is up to." N Y Times Book Rev

"Lutz creates terrific characters in this concise, crisply told escapade. . . . Carver remains one of the genre's most credible protagonists." Publ Wkly

Lightning. Holt & Co. 1996 296p o.p.
ISBN 0-8050-4379-9 LC 95-43273

"This time out, crime strikes very close to private detective Fred Carver's home. His significant other, journalist Beth Jackson, is pregnant with their child. Carver is delighted when she changes her mind about having an abortion—until she goes to the clinic to cancel her appointment. As she enters, a bomb explodes, killing two clinic workers. Beth loses the baby. Local police and the FBI very quickly arrest a likely suspect, but driven by loss and anger, Carver begins to investigate other possibilities." Booklist

"Behind the intransigent and hackneyed rhetoric of both sides, Carver finds venality aplenty as he and Beth attempt to come to terms with their loss. Veteran novelist Lutz ties some nifty twists into his plot, which moves quickly towards a final deadly confrontation." Publ Wkly

Oops!; a Nudger mystery. St. Martin's Press 1998 278p o.p.
ISBN 0-312-18152-3 LC 97-36529

"A Thomas Dunne book"

"St. Louis private investigator Alo Nudger doesn't usually accept referrals from other PI's, but this time Lacey Tumulty does the referring. Her friendship and his dwindling bank account induce Nudger to attempt to find out if Betty Almer's death was an accident, as the police believe, or something else, as her father contends." Booklist

"Nudger's novice partner Lacey . . . provides sometimes humorous complications." Libr J

Lychack, William

The wasp eater; William Lychack. Houghton Mifflin 2004 164p $21
ISBN 0-618-30244-1 LC 2004-42728

In this "novel, 10-year-old Daniel tries to reunite his parents after his father, Bob . . . is kicked out of the house for having an affair with a waitress. On one of Bob's fleeting visits home, Daniel is given a pawnshop receipt for his mother's engagement ring. Thinking the ring might be the key to reconciliation, Daniel takes a bus from New England to New York to buy it back, but he runs into trouble and his father has to come and get him. Rather than return home, father and son set off on a road trip." Publ Wkly

"Just when the dysfunctional family drama seems entirely wrung out, along comes a book so freshly original that it seems to have invented the genre. What's so remarkable here is the understatedness, the quietly intense writing carefully containing more emotion than many louder novels have to show. Original, too, is the impulse to heal rather than break away-however mixed the outcome." Libr J

Lynn, Allison

Now you see it; a novel; Allison Lynn. Touchstone 2004 281p pa $13
ISBN 0-7432-5026-5 LC 2003-70450

In this "novel, a Manhattan couple decides to infuse their lives with meaning by having a child. David hangs out in the middle of the masthead at a middlebrow magazine while Jessica teaches school, but after several failed fertility treatments, they focus on clearing hurdles in the adoption process. And then one day, Jessica vanishes, her keys left on the counter, a bedroom window ajar. . . So without evidence of a crime, the detached David and Jessica's increasingly desperate mother must come to grips with the jarring disappearance in their own way and time. David does so by revisiting the story of a U.S. businessman gone missing in Peru—the one real scoop of his career, which he landed on his honeymoon. Although Jessica is more plot device than compelling character, Lynn deftly employs David's journey to explore how someone might rediscover his internal compass when he no longer has any reason to lie to himself." Booklist

Lytton, Edward Bulwer Lytton, Baron, 1803-1873

The last days of Pompeii. Harper 1834 2v o.p.

The setting is Pompeii just before and during the famous eruption of Vesuvius, A.D. 79. "The simple story relates principally to two young people of Grecian origin, Glaucus and Ione, who are deeply attached to each other. The former is a handsome young Athenian, impetuous, high-minded, and brilliant, while Ione is a pure and lofty-minded woman. Arbaces, her guardian, the villain of the story, under a cloak of sanctity and religion, indulges in low and criminal designs. His character is strongly drawn; and his passion for Ione, and the struggle between him and Glaucus, form the chief part of the plot. . . . The book, full of learning and spirit, is not only a charming novel, but contains many minute and interesting descriptions of ancient customs; among which, those relating to the gladiatorial combat, the banquet, the bath, are most noteworthy." Keller. Reader's Dig of Books

M

Maalouf, Amin

Balthasar's odyssey; a novel; translated from the French by Barbara Bray. Arcade Pub. 2002 391p $25.95

ISBN 1-55970-666-X LC 2002-74630

Original French editon, 2000

The author "sets this historical novel mostly in the Mediterranean of the mid-1600s. Balthasar Embriaco, an exiled Italian merchant, becomes fixated on retrieving a mysterious religious text called The Hundreth Name that he mistakenly sold to a traveler who stopped in his shop in the Levant. He thus sets out on a long journey, accompanied by his two nearly grown nephews, his manservant, and a woman seeking her estranged husband." Libr J

"Maalouf has considerable success using cultural details to create an authentic atmosphere, and the novel effectively captures the flavor and spirit of 17th-century Europe." Publ Wkly

Maas, Peter, 1929-2001

China white. Simon & Schuster 1994 270p o.p.

LC 94-20327

"An influential Chinese business tycoon plots to transfer the assets of the Hong Kong crime syndicate to the United States in a single huge shipment of high-grade heroin. With the guidance of a law firm populated by former CIA operatives, he sets about relocating his businesses in New York's Chinatown. His counsel, Tom MacLean, is a new recruit from the U.S. attorney's office, hired by the firm specifically for his father's CIA connections. From the outset, young MacLean is caught in the crossfire between Chinese and Mafia warlords, the New York crime syndicate, and the Chinatown gangs." Libr J

"In presenting a picture of these gangs working together, Mr. Maas pulls no punches; like many political thrillers, 'China White' not only refuses to bow to political correctness, it slaps it in the face." N Y Times Book Rev

Father and son; a novel. Simon & Schuster 1989 316p o.p.

LC 88-13865

"Widower Michael McGuire is a New York ad exec with dwindling emotional ties to his Irish heritage, but his young son Jamie (with some indoctrination from his grandfather) becomes an outspoken supporter of the IRA at an early age. At 19, he attends Harvard but moonlights as a coffeehouse balladeer whose songs about 'the Troubles' capture the attention of a gunrunning network that decides to use him as a pawn. In alternate chapters, the author probes Michael and Jamie's relationship and strips away the layers of an IRA network that, in his portrayal, extends through every level of American government." Publ Wkly

This "novel is a thriller that brings the reader face to face with political violence, showing how the tortured intricacies of the Irish struggle can create the awful tragedies that mar its history." N Y Times Book Rev

MacDonald, Ann-Marie

The way the crow flies; a novel. HarperCollins Publishers 2003 722p $26.95

ISBN 0-06-057895-5 LC 2003-61076

This novel is "set during the early sixties on a suburblike Canadian air force base. . . . Madeleine is an exuberant eight-year-old still attached to her stuffed Bugs Bunny. When her creepy new teacher begins keeping her and other girls after school for 'exercises,' which gradually morph into full-blown sexual abuse, she feels she cannot talk about it because it is so alien to the sunny, wholesome world of her family. Meanwhile, her straight-arrow father, Jack, has been recruited by his revered former flying instructor, who now works for intelligence, to babysit an ex-Nazi scientist; Jack is soon faced with a moral dilemma tinged with the cynical overtones of realpolitik." Booklist

This is "a brilliant portrayal of child abuse and its consequences, but it is much more than that. It is a fiercely intelligent look at childhood, marriage, families, the 1960s, the Cold War and the fear and isolation that are part of the human condition." Washington Post Book World

Macdonald, Filip *See* MacDonald, Philip, 1899-1981

MacDonald, John D. (John Dann), 1916-1986

Cinnamon skin; the twentieth adventure of Travis McGee. Harper & Row 1982 275p o.p.

LC 81-48159

"Travis McGee and his friend Meyer search for Meyer's niece's new husband, who has killed his wife and faked his own death in an explosion. The search is plodding and long, but MacDonald makes it interesting through the diverse and lively characters involved. The showdown, on Mexico's Yucatán Peninsula, is a bit slow but colorful and original." Libr J

A deadly shade of gold. Lippincott 1974 c1965 336p o.p.

"The Travis McGee series"

First published 1965 in paperback by Fawcett Books

An old friend of Travis McGee's is found dead, and an Aztec idol worth more than its weight in gold disappears. McGee's search for the perpetrator (or perpetrators) leads him to Florida, New York, California and Mexico

The deep blue good-by. Lippincott 1975 c1964 200p o.p.

"The Travis McGee series"

First published 1964 in paperback by Fawcett Books

"Travis McGee, as usual helping out a damsel in distress, encounters a psycho ladykiller who makes most of the women he fancies soon wish they were dead. Plenty of action on the 'Busted Flush,' McGee's houseboat and on the deep seas off the Florida coast, but the deep blue of the title is that of a stolen sapphire. McGee's probings go back to the fly-boys of World War II, including some who came home from the China run with more gold than good conduct medals." Booklist

MacDonald, John D. (John Dann), 1916-1986—
Continued

The dreadful lemon sky. Lippincott 1975 c1974 228p o.p.

"The Travis McGee series"

"After successfully smuggling a huge quantity of Jamaican marijuana into Florida in a plane and boat operation, a team of felons fall victim to greed and treachery among themselves. A member of the team, a girl who had once been Travis's lover, entrusts him with her share of the loot for safekeeping (not specifying its origin, of course). Then she's murdered. As Travis investigates this death, with the aid of his philosophical friend Meyer, he finds himself investigating a whole series of related deaths, none of them accidental." Publ Wkly

Dress her in indigo. Lippincott 1971 c1969 255p o.p.

"The Travis McGee series"

First published 1969 in a paperback edition

"Travis McGee and friend Meyer [go] to the Mexican village of Oaxaca, among the gay, the depraved, [the drug addicted] and the violent, to find out about the kind of life Bix Bowie led there before her tragic death." Libr J

The empty copper sea. Lippincott 1978 239p o.p.

LC 78-17868

This episode finds McGee "in his familiar Florida Gulf Coast territory. A friend and former alcoholic has been boat skipper for an enterprising young land developer. Unfortunately, his boss disappears in the murky sea, and is presumed drowned after the friend passes out on the bridge while apparently drunk. He loses his license, reputation and his livelihood and comes to McGee for help." Best Sellers

Free fall in crimson. Harper & Row 1981 246p o.p.

LC 80-7871

"The Travis McGee series"

"A jig-saw trail takes Trav to a small Iowa town where Peter Kesner is making 'Free Fall' a movie about balloon racing he hopes will salvage his career after several flops. Financing the current flick is Josie Laurant, Kesner's lover. She has inherited a fortune from her former husband and daughter, both victims of unsolved murders McGee is investigating. Adding to the bank roll are porn flicks made by Desmin Grizzel, a real-life biker Kesner had featured in a film about motorcycle gangs. Grizzel has seduced local minors and forced them to take part in the scabrous movies, outraging the citizens. A mob attacks the film crew and a pitched battle leaves scores dead and injured." Publ Wkly

The green ripper. Lippincott 1979 221p o.p.

LC 79-12063

"Gretel, Trav's fiancée, mentions the suspicious, secret visit of a leader in the Church of Apocrypha to a posh local resort. Soon after, Gretel dies, supposedly of a mysterious virus. But Trav's grief is increased by instincts that tell him his love was murdered. He leaves Florida on the trail of the cult members." Publ Wkly

"MacDonald is unsurpassed at showing the American brand of loneliness. He catches foibles in a phrase and gives us many-sided, wounded but courageous, characters." Booklist

The lonely silver rain. Knopf 1985 c1984 232p o.p.

LC 84-23373

"The Travis McGee series"

"Travis McGee is growing older, and here he has good reason to feel his age. Besides combating a drug-smuggling potentate out to kill him, he finds himself the father of a young woman, all of which make the sleuth-philosopher reflect even more somberly on his life, his friends, his lonely job. One of the last MacDonald stories, it is also one of the best." Barzun. Cat of Crime. Rev and enl edition

The long lavender look. Lippincott 1972 c1970 264p o.p.

"The Travis McGee series"

First published in paperback 1970 by Fawcett Books

When McGee avoids running his Rolls Royce into a young girl, he finds himself embroiled in intrigue

Nightmare in pink. Lippincott 1976 c1964 191p o.p.

"The Travis McGee series"

First published 1964 in paperback by Fawcett Books

"Travis McGee, whose moral and social creed in the tradition of Chandler's Marlowe is given on p. 21, leaves his beach bum's paradise in Florida to solve in New York City the murder of the man who was to marry Travis' war buddy's sister. The suspense is expertly done as usual, the sex is explicit but poeticized, the evil of riches and cities is virtually out of the Bible, and the hanky-panky of the sanatorium, though outré, is scientifically sound." Barzun. Cat of Crime. Rev and enl edition

One fearful yellow eye. Lippincott 1978 c1966 286p o.p.

LC 77-24165

"The Travis McGee series"

First published 1966 in paperback by Fawcett Books

Travis McGee "answers an SOS from Glory Geis. She tells him that her late husband had secretly disposed of a fortune in cash before his death, money Geis's other heirs accuse the widow of stealing. Smelling blackmail, McGee digs into the dead man's past and finds evidence of a venomous plot. A gang of Nazi criminals, passing for respectable citizens, had extorted Geis's money by threatening the lives of his wife and children." Publ Wkly

One more Sunday. Knopf 1984 311p o.p.

LC 83-48858

"John Tinker Meadows and his sister Mary Margaret head the Eternal Church of the Believer, a fundamentalist sect headquartered in the South. From a small country church, ECB has grown into a huge conglomerate, exuding power and wealth, masking a variety of sins—lust, greed, corruption, and murder." Libr J

The author "is far too wise to fall into any simplistic traps, nor does he dismiss all of the religious work as worthless. His descriptions of the church's organization and its power over ordinary mortals are brilliantly done, and the questions of conscience come vividly to life." NY Times Book Rev

A purple place for dying. Lippincott 1976 c1964 204p o.p.

"The Travis McGee series"

First published 1964 in paperback by Fawcett Books

"Travis McGee is pondering whether to take on the

MacDonald, John D. (John Dann), 1916-1986— *Continued*

beautiful Mona Yeoman as a client when someone decides for him by shooting her in the back and hiding the body. Mona's husband soon dies of poison, and the killers might have been in the clear if they had not tried to add McGee (and one of those lovely women he always attracts) to their list. The usual literate and fast-paced stuff expected from MacDonald." Booklist

The scarlet ruse. Lippincott 1980 c1973 262p o.p.

LC 79-24843

"The Travis McGee series"

First published 1973 in paperback by Fawcett Books

Private detective Travis McGee, "who lives on a houseboat, is told that the owner is planning on cleaning up the waterfront so he's going to lose his mooring place. McGee is bothered by this but to take his mind off this impending disaster, he takes on a case wherein a dealer of rare stamps is being made the victim of a stamp collector who is substituting 'junk' stamps—worthless stamps for valuable one-of-a-kind stamps. MacDonald keeps the pot boiling as McGee conducts his investigation and, as tradition would have it, runs into all kinds of unforeseen difficulties in settling this case, up to and including murder." West Coast Rev Books

The turquoise lament. Lippincott 1973 287p o.p.

"The Travis McGee series"

McGee goes to the rescue of the daughter of a man who saved his life

"One of the best McGee adventures." Publ Wkly

Macdonald, Malcolm *See* Ross-Macdonald, Malcolm

Macdonald, Malcolm Ross- *See* Ross-Macdonald, Malcolm

MacDonald, Philip, 1899-1981

The list of Adrian Messenger. Doubleday 1959 224p o.p.

"Published for the Crime Club"

"A piece of paper listing ten men, six of them died 'accidentally,' sends Anthony Gethryn on a desperate man hunt for a diabolical killer." Publ Wkly

"If some readers find Mr. MacDonald's style a bit stiff and old-fashioned, they will also find that he provides such other old-fashioned elements as honest clues, characters who stick in the mind from page to page, an original idea, and, in Anthony Gethryn, a detective who inspires utter confidence." New Yorker

Macdonald, Ross, 1915-1983

Archer in Hollywood; with a foreword by the author. Knopf 1967 528p o.p.

A combination of three titles published separately 1949, 1951, and 1956 respectively, starring Lew Archer, private detective

Archer in jeopardy; with a foreword by the author. Knopf 1979 757p o.p.

LC 79-63807

An omnibus volume of three titles published separately 1958, 1962 and 1968 respectively

Contents: The doomsters; The zebra-striped hearse; The instant enemy

Three mysteries featuring Lew Archer. In The doomsters the activities of an unscrupulous doctor occupy the sleuth; in The zebra-striped hearse the detective becomes involved in an ice pick murder, and in The instant enemy it is the high school runaway that is the focus of Archer's attention

"Three classic Lew Archer mysteries. . . . This stunning trilogy is a must for all mystery enthusiasts." Booklist

The barbarous coast

In Macdonald, R. Archer in Hollywood p171-346

The doomsters

In Macdonald, R. Archer in jeopardy

The drowning pool. Knopf 1950 244p o.p.

"Admirers of the later Ross Macdonald will detect in this early book the capacities subsequently so well exploited. Lew Archer started as he continued: tough and straight; clever and informed, but not omniscient; full of love and hostility toward Southern California. This story, of a woman who has made a bad marriage to a mother-dominated husband of ambivalent sexual character, has a bit too much violence, but the character-drawing shows a sure hand, and the tangle is so capably manipulated that it does not annoy." Barzun. Cat of Crime. Rev and enl edition

The far side of the dollar. Vintage Books 1996 247p pa $12

ISBN 0-679-76865-3 LC 97-120671

First published 1965 by Knopf

This mystery "begins with Lew Archer's visit to a school for troubled boys, in search of a lead on Tommy Hillman, who has just escaped. . . . It turns out that Hillman had borrowed and wrecked a neighbor's car, and was put in the school by his father to teach him a lesson. Next, Archer learns that a ransom of $25,000 has been demanded for the return of Tommy Hillman. The Hillmans are a typically horrifying wealthy couple whose life has become unmoored through too much lying. The investigation of their past at one point brings up a connection to Archer's, showing that he has more in common with these people than he at first supposed." Murphy. Ency of Murder and Mystery

The Galton case. Vintage Books 1996 242p pa $12

ISBN 0-679-76864-5 LC 97-118474

First published 1959 by Knopf

"Archer is hired by Lawyer Gordon Sable on a hopeless case: to search for the elderly Mrs. Galton's son and heir, Anthony Galton. What he quickly turns up is a decapitated corpse buried on the spot where Anthony had lived twenty years before, and a young man working in a gas station who looks exactly like Anthony and may be his son. . . . The Galton trail leads to a bleak provincial town in Canada, and Macdonald's wry and funny

Macdonald, Ross, 1915-1983—*Continued*
glance at the beatnik poetry scene in San Francisco enriches the early part of the novel, putting on display the strength and flexibility of Macdonald's mature style. With The Galton case, Macdonald had 'arrived' precisely by finding a mythical form for his own beginnings." Murphy. Ency of Murder and Mystery

The goodbye look. Knopf 1969 243p o.p.
Private detective Lew Archer is brought "into the affairs of the Chalmers family because their lawyer thinks they are worried about a theft from their safe. But the Chalmers have other problems, and Lew becomes involved with murders old and new." Libr J

The instant enemy
In Macdonald, R. Archer in jeopardy

The moving target
In Macdonald, R. Archer in Hollywood p3-169

Ross Macdonald's Lew Archer, private investigator. Mysterious Press 1977 245p o.p.
LC 77-81870
Contents: Find the woman; Gone girl; The bearded lady; The suicide; Guilt-edged blonde; The sinister habit; Wild goose chase; Midnight blue; Sleeping dog

Sleeping beauty. Knopf 1973 271p o.p.
The scene "is California and the concern is with what power and money can do to wreck a family. Lew [Archer] befriends a lost lady who is running away from fears and responsibilities and from her young husband. Before very long word comes that the girl has been kidnapped and a ransom is demanded of her oil rich family. Bit by bit, as Archer probes deeper into the family relationships, he begins to see that nothing is what it seems and the key to the present lies deep in the past." Publ Wkly

The underground man. Knopf 1971 272p o.p.
"With his customary skill and economy of means, the author gets us, through Archer, into a tangle of passions about runaway spouses, disaffected and drug-taking children, amateur blackmail, and, of course, murder." Barzun. Cat of Crime. Rev and enl edition

The way some people die
In Macdonald, R. Archer in Hollywood p347-528

The zebra-striped hearse
In Macdonald, R. Archer in jeopardy

MacInnes, Helen, 1907-1985

Above suspicion. Harcourt Brace & Co. 1954 333p o.p.
ISBN 0-15-102707-2
A reprint of the title first published 1941 by Little, Brown
"An Oxford don and his pretty wife are chosen to perform a secret mission to Germany in late 1939. While using their vacation as a cover, they are to locate the whereabouts of an anti-Nazi agent. The plan seems foolproof—until someone betrays it and them." Smith. Cloak and Dagger Fic

Prelude to terror. Harcourt Brace Jovanovich 1978 368p o.p.
"Colin Grant, art consultant, is asked by a wealthy art collector to purchase a specific seventeenth-century painting at an art auction in Vienna. The owner of the painting needs money to escape from Hungary, and the transaction must be kept secret. When Colin arrives in Vienna, he finds that the auction conceals a conspiracy for laundering money that is used to buy weapons for terrorist groups. In spite of great personal danger Colin searches for the key piece of information that will stop this source of financing." Shapiro. Fic for Youth. 2d edition

Ride a pale horse. Harcourt Brace Jovanovich 1984 355p o.p.
LC 84-9037
"Karen Cornell, journalist for an American world affairs magazine, is about to leave a peace convention in Prague disgruntled by her treatment and the lack of material when she is approached by a Czech intelligence officer who is about to defect. The papers he gives her to relay to a CIA expert on 'disinformation' start her on a harrowing course from Prague to Vienna, Rome, and Washington." Libr J
"The device of dual protagonists moves the plot along smartly, and the demonstration of the insidious uses of disinformation could hardly be more timely." Booklist

The Venetian affair. Harcourt, Brace & World 1963 405p o.p.
This "suspense novel is set in Paris and Venice in 1961. An American newspaperman on vacation picks up the wrong raincoat on arrival at Orly airport, and finds himself involved in a communist plot to assassinate De Gaulle and implicate the United States. American agents enlist his help to thwart the plotters and to unmask the mysterious and ruthless spymaster." Publ Wkly

Mackin, Edward, 1929-
For works written by this author under other names see McInerny, Ralph M., 1929-

Mackintosh, Elizabeth *See* Tey, Josephine, 1896-1952

MacLean, Alistair, 1922-1987

Breakheart Pass. Doubleday 1974 178p o.p.
The setting for his novel "is the era just after the Civil War. An Army relief train is proceeding to a fort in Indian territory, which is reportedly suffering from an epidemic of cholera. The chief characters are the Governor of Nevada, a U.S. Marshall, a major who was a renowned Civil War hero, the Governor's niece, and John Deakin, a prisoner of the marshall's wanted for atrocious crimes, including murder. As the train proceeds various mysterious accidents happen [and] . . . Deakin is revealed as a Secret Service agent." Best Sellers

Floodgate. Doubleday 1984 c1983 369p o.p.
LC 83-45013
First published 1983 in the United Kingdom
"The novel is set in and around Amsterdam, where a band of canny, sophisticated terrorists are threatening to flood the Netherlands by blowing up dikes and exploding offshore nuclear devices. The terrorists demand that Hol-

MacLean, Alistair, 1922-1987—*Continued*
land must negotiate with Great Britain for the withdrawal of all British troops from Northern Ireland. Peter van Effen, senior detective and explosives expert, eventually saves the nation, a task he carries out with cool, dispassionate efficiency." Booklist

"Readers accustomed to thrillers of a more lurid hue may well appreciate MacLean's stylistic restraint, neat plotting and attention to characterization." Publ Wkly

Force 10 from Navarone. Doubleday 1968 274p o.p.

The three heroes of The guns of Navarone, Mallory, Miller and Stavros are assigned a new mission during World War II. "They are dropped into Yugoslavia to join the Partisans, prevent a German attack, blow up a dam, and provide a diversion to draw German troops out of Italy." Publ Wkly

The guns of Navarone. Doubleday 1957 320p o.p.

"World War II is being fought, and the Germans control the island that guards the approaches to the eastern Mediterranean with big guns. After all other attempts have failed, a five-man British army team is chosen to silence the guns of Navarone. They land on the island, elude the Nazis, and scale a seemingly unclimbable cliff." Shapiro. Fic for Youth. 3d edition

Followed by Force 10 from Navarone

Ice Station Zebra. Doubleday 1963 276p o.p.

A novel of suspense and intrigue that begins on "a bitter-cold morning in Holy Loch, Scotland, when a British doctor with top-level endorsements from the American and British military forces seeks admission to an American nuclear submarine. The submarine is slated for a perilous trip to rescue the starving, freezing British crew of a meteorological station situated on an ice floe in the Arctic." Publ Wkly

Night without end. Doubleday 1960 287p o.p.

"An airliner crash lands on the Greenland icecap near a small I.G.Y. observation station. It soon becomes clear that the landing was planned and certain of the passengers and crew murdered for reasons unknown, while at least eight of the 10 survivors were drugged into insensibility—the other two of course, being the killers. But which two? . . . A sometimes barely credible, but always absorbing, thriller that combines elements of the espionage story and murder mystery with those of the 'castaway' adventure tale." Libr J

When eight bells toll. Doubleday 1966 288p o.p.

"Sure and deadly with guns and knives, an expert at underwater work, Philip Calvert, British secret service agent, polishes his skills to a high gloss in this tense adventure story set in the western Scottish Highlands. Calvert and his friends oppose a gang of killers who operate at sea and in harbors. What the killers are doing, why they are busy in this cold, rainy, windy part of Scotland, and whether Calvert will survive his fight against them are questions that provide suspense." Publ Wkly

Where eagles dare. Doubleday 1967 312p o.p.

"Secrecy and stealth are essential to the mission of an assorted crew from MI 6 who must rescue an American general, the coordinator of Overlord, from Schloss Adler, a castle built by a mad Bavarian prince, which is the combined HQ of the German Secret Service and the Gestapo of South Germany in the bitter winter of 1943-44. And if that isn't enough, there is Major Smith's second assignment to bring out the pyrotechnic display of excitement and suspense." Libr J

MacLeod, Alistair

Island; the complete stories. Norton 2001 434p $25.95

ISBN 0-393-05035-1 LC 00-51524

Contents: The boat; The vastness of the dark; The golden gift of grey; The return; In the fall; The lost salt gift of blood; The road to Rankin's Point; The closing down of summer; To every thing there is a season; Second spring; Winter dog; The tuning of perfection; As birds bring forth the sun; Vision; Island; Clearances

"The author, an expatriate from Cape Breton, Nova Scotia, writes about his homeland and its dying traditions, in tales that marry the elemental themes of Gaelic song (loneliness, sorrow, work, death) with a simple but deceptively modern narrative style. In the course of the sixteen stories (presented in order of publication, from 1968 to 1999), MacLeod's spare style grows more artful, but the ache of loss is constant as he captures the direct eloquence of the islanders-the coal miners, lobstermen, farmers, and lighthouse keepers who know they are the last of their kind." New Yorker

MacLeod, Charlotte

The corpse in Oozak's Pond. Mysterious Press 1987 213p o.p.

LC 86-62775

"History eerily repeats itself in this . . . mystery set on the rustic campus of an agricultural college in Balaclava Junction, Mass. When a corpse is found floating in Oozak's Pond dressed in turn-of-the-century costume, outfitted with a false beard, stabbed through the neck with an ice pick and weighted down with rocks, it is almost an exact reenactment of the 1905 demise of Augustus Buggins, grandson of the college's founder Balaclava Buggins, to whom the unidentified corpse bears a startling resemblance. When the bodies of the aging but still sprightly couple Trevelyan and Beatrice Buggins are discovered the same day, it is clear to Peter Shandy, professor of agronomy at the college, that a conspiracy is afoot." Publ Wkly

Exit the milkman. Mysterious Press 1996 311p o.p.

LC 96-18337

In this mystery Balacava Agricultural College's "Peter Shandy is the last person to see fellow professor Jim Feldster—a man who welcomes any excuse to get away from his wife—before he disappears. When Feldster's wife accuses the Shandys of hiding her husband, they begin sleuthing. Another series charmer." Libr J

The Gladstone bag. Mysterious Press 1990 218p o.p.

LC 89-43143

"Six feisty and contentious characters with inventive names surround aging-but-active Emma Kelling during her stay at a friend's Maine retreat. Strange events, attempted theft, and a sodden body propel her to consult niece and nephew-in-law/detectives Sarah and Max

MacLeod, Charlotte—*Continued*

Bittersohn . . ., as well as cousin-in-law Theonie. Tongue-in-cheek eccentricities, the usual casual but astute deductions, and a certain luxuriousness of language make this a most welcome addition to the MacLeod canon." Libr J

Rest you merry. Doubleday 1978 182p o.p.
LC 77-27713

"Published for the Crime Club"

"Christmas time at Balaclava Agricultural College is the background for this academic mystery tale. Professor Peter Shandy capitulates to the badgering of a resident busy-body Jemima Ames and shows his Christmas spirit—by decorating his house with plastic reindeer, flashing lights, and leering Santas. . . . He then flees, but driven back by his conscience, he returns to find the body of Jemima in his living room. Helen Marsh, the new librarian, joins the professor in the investigation of the murder." Publisher's note

The resurrection man; a Sarah Kelling and Max Bittersohn mystery. Mysterious Press 1992 250p o.p.
LC 91-58024

"Initial suspicions about Bartolo Arbalest, the 'resurrection man' who has suddenly appeared in Boston, concern his business of art and furniture restoration, his secretive nature, and his insistence on his helpers all living with him in seclusion. He does fine work, commands high fees, employs a bodyguard, and cooks sumptuous dinners for his chosen acolytes, a rum bunch of dubious ne'er-do-wells and Beantown society types down on their luck. To Max and Sarah, the whole enterprise fairly screams of illegality. Then events grow more labyrinthine, as works recently restored start to vanish, and owners meet bad ends." Booklist

"MacLeod's sure touch with the cheerily eccentric and her keen eye for the often strange social habits of apparently staid society make this another delight." Publ Wkly

The Silver Ghost; a Sarah Kelling mystery. Mysterious Press 1988 213p o.p.
LC 87-35027

Sarah and her husband Max are hired by cousin Bill "to find out who stole his vintage 1927 Phantom Rolls Royce. Since Bill suspects that someone close to him may be responsible, he invites Max and Sarah to do their sleuthing at his annual Renaissance Revel. All the possible culprits are gathered. . . . But before the two can form any theories, another of Bill's classic Rolls Royces, the Silver Ghost, disappears. The gateman who was guarding it is found murdered. And Sarah's Aunt Boadicea, last seen heading out to the garage, is nowhere to be found." West Coast Rev Books

Vane pursuit; a Peter Shandy mystery. Mysterious Press 1989 185p o.p.
LC 88-25595

"Detective Peter Shandy, and his redoubtable wife, Helen the librarian, are swept up in the diabolical theft of antique weather vanes by crooks who use arson as their *mode d'accomplis*. . . . Endless puns punctuate MacLeod's delightfully absurd tale, which, beneath all the frivolity, is masterfully executed." Booklist

The withdrawing room. Doubleday 1980 186p o.p.

"Published for the Crime Club"

"Widowed Sarah Kelling takes boarders into her stately home on Boston's Beacon Hill to pay the heavy mortgage, a move that means trouble. Mr. Quiffen, who settles into the former 'withdrawing room,' is killed and so is Mr. Hartler, who rents the vacated premises. Sarah appeals to her brainy, attractive friend Max Bittersohn for help but begins to investigate her guests personally, afraid that one may be the murderer." Publ Wkly

The wrong rite; [by] Charlotte MacLeod writing as Alisa Craig. Morrow 1992 284p o.p.
LC 91-30374

When Canadian Mounted Police inspector Madoc Rhys and his wife Janet visit the Rhys ancestral home in Wales for a family reunion "dark deeds . . . commence: Janet spots a ghost; Madoc finds the local crows feasting on a slaughtered sheep and spots a badly bruised shepherd resting nearby. Then table conversation leads to fertility dances and leaping through fires. Later, a distant cousin makes the fatal fiery jump." Booklist

"If the investigation lacks thrills, the portrayal of old Welsh customs and engaging family eccentrics is delightful." Publ Wkly

MacNeil, Duncan *See* McCutchan, Philip, 1920-

MacNeil, Robert, 1931-

Breaking news; a novel. Doubleday 1998 371p $24.95
ISBN 0-385-42020-X LC 98-19562

"Network anchor, Grant Munro, opens the book with a speech to the Radio and Television News Directors dinner comparing the media's Monica Lewinsky feeding frenzy to the behavior of the Bible's Gadarene swine. . . . Munro is under pressure: he is close to 60; ratings are dropping; and he is surrounded by kids (reporters, producers, etc.) who think sensation and sentimentality have much more appeal than what's happening in Washington or Kosovo." Booklist

"By the novel's end, MacNeil has delivered some extremely disheartening news about the state of our national news media wrapped neatly in a shiny literary package: Jim Lehrer's loss is fiction's gain." N Y Times Book Rev

Burden of desire. Doubleday 1992 466p o.p.
LC 91-28919

"The story begins with a bang—literally, as a munitions ship blows up in Halifax, Nova Scotia, in 1917 in what will be the biggest, most destructive man-made explosion until the atomic bomb. Picking up the pieces in the well-evoked ruined city are young parson Peter Wentworth, an ambitious man in an unhappy marriage, and Stewart MacPherson, a psychiatrist just beginning to treat shell-shocked returning soldiers. The two read a diary accidentally lost in the wreckage, belonging to Julia Robertson, a young, unconventional woman whose beauty and self-acknowledged sensuality ensnares each of them in turn." Publ Wkly

This novel "is at once a wonderful romance involving one of the more appealing triangles in recent fiction and a thoughtful dissection of the glacial pace of social change." N Y Times Book Rev

MacNeil, Robert, 1931-—*Continued*

The voyage. Talese 1995 288p o.p.
LC 95-22795

"David Lyon is a senior Canadian diplomat, consul general in New York. . . . A colleague's phone call alerts him to the fact that one Francesca D'Anielli is missing, presumed drowned, off the coast of Finland. The sole clue to the mystery is a letter left on her abandoned yacht, addressed to David. . . . [Francesca] was for many years David's . . . [mistress]. Mr. MacNeil alternates his narrative between them, with David's sections telling their history and Francesca's focusing on her life after their breakup." N Y Times Book Rev

"This is an original, bittersweet romantic drama." Publ Wkly

Maguire, Gregory

Son of a witch; a novel. ReganBooks 2005 337p il $26.95
ISBN 0-06-054893-2 LC 2005-46232

"This sequel to the adult fairy tale Wicked (1995) . . . begins ten years after the destruction of Elphaba, a.k.a. the Wicked Witch of the West. In Maguire's dark version of the Land of Oz, there's not much to ring the bells for in the Emerald City, despite the tyrannical Wizard's departure. Corruption is rife, political factions compete for power, and radicals proclaim 'Elphaba lives!' Elsewhere, a horribly injured young man called Liir wakes in the religious House of Saint Glinda to many puzzles. . . . Above all, was Elphaba his mother? These and other questions drive a tale that adroitly mixes drama, humor, and political satire into a well-knit examination of good and evil-and leaves several doors open for future journeys over the rainbow into this cleverly constructed dystopia." Libr J

Mahfouz, Naguib *See* Maḥfūẓ, Najīb, 1911-

Maḥfūẓ, Najīb, 1911-

Children of the alley; by Naguib Mahfouz; translated by Peter Theroux. Doubleday 1996 448p o.p.
LC 95-15510

Original Arabic version serialized 1959 in Cairo newspaper; previous English translation with title: Children of Gebelaawi, published 1981 in paperback by Three Continents Press

"Gabalawi's mansion sits at the desert's edge, surrounded by high-walled gardens. His sons, however, quarrel over his estate, and the omnipotent gangster banishes them from his earthly paradise. Their descendants settle outside the wall, desperately poor but always praying to Gabalawi for salvation. As each succeeding generation spawns its messiah, the people rise up against the ruling gangsters, seizing their portion of the estate, but greed and ignorance prove their ultimate undoing, poverty and suffering their inescapable fate." Libr J

Theroux "skillfully conveys Mahfouz's fierce egalitarian message while capturing his gift for masterly storytelling. Mahfouz combines the universal appeal of archetypal dramatic conflicts—brother murders brother; wife betrays husband into the hands of his enemies; father expels defiant son—with the originality of his own inventive narrative structures." Publ Wkly

Midaq Alley; [by] Naguib Mahfouz; translated by Trevor Le Gassick. Anchor Bks. (NY) 1992 286p o.p.
LC 91-27459

"Written in the 1940s, this novel . . . deals with the plight of impoverished classes in an old quarter of Cairo. The lives and situations depicted create an atmosphere of sadness and tragic realism. Indeed, few of the characters are happy or successful. Protagonist Hamida, an orphan raised by a foster mother, is drawn into prostitution. Kirsha, the owner of a café in the alley, is a drug addict and a lustful homosexual. Zaita makes a living by disfiguring people so that they can become successful beggars. Transcending time and place, the social issues treated here are relevant to many Arab countries today." Libr J

Palace of desire; translated by William M. Hutchins and Olive E. Kenny. Doubleday 1991 422p o.p.
LC 90-3753

Original Arabic edition, 1957

"Al-Sayyid Ahmad is mellowing as he leaves middle age. As this second novel of 'The Cairo Trilogy' opens, he is ending his self-imposed abstention from liquor and women, begun five years earlier upon the death of his son, Fahmy. . . . Meanwhile, his children are struggling with life beyond their father's domination. Yasin is twice divorced and incapable of resisting any woman. The two married daughters are split by an open feud. And Kamal, the intellectual center of this novel, enters college [and grapples with] . . . religion, science, and romance." Libr J

"Mr. Mahfouz excels at fusing deep emotion and soap opera. Fortunately, the translators . . . are equal to the task of animating rather than embalming Mr. Mahfouz's elegant and often explosive text." N Y Times Book Rev

Followed by Sugar Street

Palace walk; [by] Naguib Mahfouz; translated from the Arabic by William M. Hutchins with Olive E. Kenny. Doubleday 1990 c1989 498p o.p.
LC 89-23348

Originally published in Arabic

This is the first volume in the author's trilogy "dealing with three generations of a Cairo family in the first half of the twentieth century. The emotional and physical struggles of these middle-class people are depicted with a great deal of sympathy and honesty, from the torments of adolescent love through the banked passions of an established marriage. The novel begins with a series of domestic scenes featuring the five children of a merchant and his wife; later, the setting shifts to Cairo nightclubs, coffee shops, and stores as Mahfouz re-creates the everyday existence of his characters in almost Dickensian detail." Booklist

Followed by Palace of desire

Sugar Street; [by] Naguib Mahfouz; translated by William Maynard Hutchins and Angele Botros Samaan. Doubleday 1992 308p o.p.
LC 91-12938

Original Arabic edition, 1957

This is the concluding volume of the author's Cairo trilogy. "The novel opens in 1935 as Egypt smolders under British occupation, and it extends through the war. Kamal, son of the gaunt, wasted patriarch, is a grade-

Maḥfūẓ, Najīb, 1911—*Continued*
school teacher and philosopher who veers between lusty debauches and reading Spinoza. One of his nephews, Abd Al-Muni'm, becomes a Muslim fundamentalist; another nephew, Ahmad, takes Marx as his prophet. These two diametrically opposed brothers will share the same fate—a jail cell. The inadvertent cause of their undoing may be another scion of the patriarch, young Ridwan, a closet homosexual whose liaison with a prominent politician apparently backfires." Publ Wkly

"The ordinary nature of Mr. Mahfouz's world, with its willingness to confront the complexities of human intentions, makes it an extraordinary exception in a marketplace of manufactured ideas and is, for that, all the more admirable." N Y Times Book Rev

Mailer, Norman, 1923-

Ancient evenings. Little, Brown 1983 709p o.p.
LC 82-22839

"Set in the span between the reigns of Ramses II and Ramses IX, Mailer's . . . novel is narrated by the remnant spirits of Menenhetet I and his great-grandson as they join mutuality to survive the land of the Dead and to ascend to Ra. The story is largely the account of Menenhetet's first life (he has had four) as he rises from peasant stock to become first charioteer to Ramses II, then general, then overseer of the harem." Libr J

"This novel is perhaps the best reconstruction of the far past since Flaubert's 'Salammbo,' but Mailer's eye is on the modern age, especially the psychic problems of America. These problems may find a solution through an understanding of the repressed areas of human sexuality, with the reality of magic. Our own rationality has failed. Here, he seems to say, is a complex civilization of high achievement based on the irrational, on the radial power of magic whose centre is both decay and resurrection. This is a different book, on whose writing and research Mailer spent over ten years, but it is not only about magic, it is magical in itself." Burgess. 99 Novels

The executioner's song. Modern Lib. 1993 1002p o.p.
ISBN 0-679-42471-7 LC 92-51066

A reissue of the title first published 1979 by Little, Brown

A "documentary narrative of 'the activities of Gary Gilmore and the men and women associated with him' between his release from prison in April 1976 and his execution for murder in early 1977. . . . The first half of the book, called 'Western Voices,' is the story of Gilmore's . . . attempt to fit in between the time he is released from prison and the time he is arrested, tried, and found guilty of two murders on two successive nights. But the second half, 'Eastern Voices,' is really the story of the marketing of Gilmore as he awaits—and demands—death in the Utah state prison." New Repub

"In this study of a condemned murderer Mailer not only vividly portrays the character in a real-life drama but also invokes the whole history of westward migration of the Mormons of Utah." Reader's Ency. 3d edition

The Gospel according to the Son. Random House 1997 242p o.p.
LC 96-48018

This is a "novel that purports to be a first-person memoir written by Jesus." Time

Mailer's "gospel is written in a direct, rather relaxed English that yet has an eerie, neo-Biblical dignity." New Yorker

Harlot's ghost. Random House 1991 1310p o.p.
LC 90-53152

"Harry Hubbard is a bright young man whose father and whose mentor, Hugh Montague (also known as Harlot), are both senior CIA figures and induct him into the Agency. Most of the book . . . is one long flashback, Harry's autobiographical account of his early career—partly in his own words, partly in an exchange of letters with Harlot's beautiful, brilliant wife, Kittredge, whom Harry admires from afar and will one day steal." Publ Wkly

"An immensely long but never laborious book, one where Mailer works compelling variations on his quintessential themes." Libr J

The naked and the dead. Holt & Co. 1948 721p o.p.

"In 1944 an American platoon takes part in the invasion and occupation of a Japanese-held island. The action is divided into three parts: the landing on the island, the counter-attack by night, and a daring patrol by the platoon behind enemy lines. The style is simple realism and therefore the language is rough, in keeping with the army setting." Shapiro. Fic for Youth. 3d edition

"The book is encyclopedic yet particular, both realistic and symbolic. It is one of the best novels by an American about World War II." Benet's Reader's Ency of Am Lit

Tough guys don't dance. Random House 1984 229p o.p.
LC 84-42514

"Tim Madden is a writer who lives in Provincetown, where the action takes place one dreary November. . . . After a night of monumental drinking, Madden awakens with a mysterious tatoo on his arm, blood all over the passenger seat of his Porsche, and no memory of his actions. Later he discovers one, then another decapitated head buried with his stash of marijuana. Madden is obviously the prime suspect in the murders, and his task is to find which of the many unsavory characters of his acquaintance is responsible." Publ Wkly

"This genre is not exactly Mailer's forte, but the nononsense prose and the hard-as-nails style . . . may attract readers." Booklist

Maillard, Keith, 1942-

The clarinet polka. Thomas Dunne Bks. 2003 406p $24.95
ISBN 0-312-30889-2 LC 2002-32511

"Jimmy Koprowski returns from his stint in the Air Force in 1969 consigned to his boyhood attic bedroom and a minimun-wage job at a TV repair shop. He drifts into an alcohol-fueled, sexually charged affair with a doctor's wife and engages in ongoing arguments about his 'life plan' with his hard-working dad. . . . Then his ethonmusicologist sister decides to start an all-girl polka

Maillard, Keith, 1942-—*Continued*

band, and that's when he meets singer Janice Dluwiecki." Booklist

"Jimmy is a wry, down-to-earth, irresistable narrator, and Maillard draws all the characters in the working-class community with compassion and obvious affection. This moving, well-drawn story of sin and redemption in a fading industry town may remind readers of Richard Russo." Publ Wkly

Maine, David

The preservationist. St. Martin's Press 2004 230p $24.95

ISBN 0-312-32847-8 LC 2003-70881

"Noah's family (or Noe as he's called here) his wife, sons, and daughters-inlaw tell what it's like to live with a man touched by God, while struggling against events that cannot be controlled or explained. When Noe orders his sons to build an ark, he can't tell them where the wood will come from. When he sends his daughters-inlaw out to gather animals, he can offer no directions, money, or protection. And once the rain starts, they all realize that the true test of their faith is just beginning." Publisher's note

This is an "elegant, inventive book and in no way a cynical one, despite the author's keen appreciation of the incongruous. . . . The book resounds with the gravity of Noe's mission even as it invents the quotidian details of his story." N Y Times Book Rev

Mainwaring, Marion

(jt. auth) Wharton, E. The buccaneers

Major, Clarence

(ed) Calling the wind. See Calling the wind

Makine, Andreï, 1957-

Dreams of my Russian summers. Arcade Pub. 1997 241p o.p.

ISBN 1-55970-383-0 LC 97-2720

Original French edition, 1995

This is the story "of Charlotte Lemonnier, born in France at the turn of the century, who as a child moved to Russia, where her father practiced medicine. Traveling back and forth over the years, she found herself in France on the eve of World War I, only to return to Russia with a Red Cross mission during the Revolution. There she remained to see the horrors of civil war and famine, and later witnessed the Stalinist purges, the war with Germany, the dehumanizing industrialization of the country and ultimately the fall of Communism's idols. By the time her grandson, the novel's narrator, begins visiting her for his summer holidays, she has been long settled in the sleepy Siberian town where her Russian husband lies buried." N Y Times Book Rev

"At first, the narrator's lyrical and poetic memoir is so Proustian that it seems almost a pastiche, but insidiously it brings home the surreal and heartbreaking wonder of this woman's life." New Yorker

Music of a life; translated from the French by Geoffrey Strachan. Arcade Pub. 2002 109p $21.95

ISBN 1-55970-637-6 LC 2002-25854

Original French edition, 2001. Published in the United Kingdom with title: A life's music

"It is 1941, and Alexei, a budding concert pianist, is returning to his Moscow apartment two days before his first public recital when a neighbor warns his off: his parents are being arrested. Knowing that he will be sent to the Gulag, too, Alexei flees to the home of relatives in the countryside. Then the Germans invade, decimating his family's village but providing a plethora of bodies from which he can pillage an identity. . . . Stalin's atrocities are made visceral in this wisp of a book." New Yorker

Malamud, Bernard, 1914-1986

The assistant; a novel. Farrar, Straus & Giroux 1957 246p o.p.

This novel is "set in the prison of a failing grocery store, where Morris Bober, its elderly, long-suffering Jewish owner, teaches his assistant, Frankie Alpine, what it means to be a Jew, and what it means to be a man. After decades in which Jewish protagonists struggled to assimilate to the non-Jewish world around them, *The Assistant* is a tale about reverse assimilation, one in which Frankie takes over the store on Morris's death and undergoes a painful conversion to Judaism." Benet's Reader's Ency of Am Lit

also in Malamud, B. A Malamud reader p75-305

The complete stories; introduction by Robert Giroux. Farrar, Straus & Giroux 1997 634p o.p.

ISBN 0-374-12639-9 LC 97-12394

"Whether, stark, comic or fanciful, Malamud's stories give us immigrant Jews and their descendants pondering moral questions and experiencing moments of magical intervention while enduring life's ridiculous situations. Yet the stories transcend their ethnic settings and achieve a universal resonance." Publ Wkly

Dubin's lives. Farrar, Straus & Giroux 1979 361p o.p.

LC 78-23897

"William B. Dubin is one of America's foremost writers. His biographies of Lincoln, Mark Twain, and Thoreau have won universal praise and a presidential medal; now, after several years of research, he is about to begin a life of D. H. Lawrence. Dubin lives with his wife of more than 25 years in a small town in upstate New York near the Vermont border. . . . The main action of the novel is Dubin's on-again, off-again love affair with Fanny Bick, a 22-year-old college dropout whom his wife first hires as a part-time cleaning lady." Saturday Rev

"Seldom have the travails of advancing age—of late middle-age constantly haunted by thoughts of lost youth and coming old age—been captured so tellingly, so movingly. In Dubin's lives the reader is likely to recognize, alas, all too much of his/her own." Choice

The fixer. Farrar, Straus & Giroux 1966 355p o.p.

"Yakov Bok, a handyman, is arrested and charged with the killing of a Christian boy. Innocent of the crime, he is only guilty of being a Jew in Czarist Russia. In jail he is mentally and physically tortured as a scapegoat for a crime he insists he did not commit. Although his suffering and degradation are unrelenting, Bok emerges a hero

Malamud, Bernard, 1914-1986—*Continued*
as he maintains his innocence. Malamud has fashioned a powerful story of injustice and endurance based on a true incident." Shapiro. Fic for Youth. 3d edition

A Malamud reader. Farrar, Straus & Giroux 1967 528p o.p.

Short stories included: The mourners; Idiots first; The first seven years; Take pity; The maid's shoes; Black is my favorite color; The Jewbird; The magic barrel; The German refugee; The last Mohican

The natural. Harcourt Brace & Co. 1952 237p o.p.

"The fanaticism and seriousness of baseball to both players and fans are vividly pictured in this novel about a man whose sole ambition was to be 'the greatest ever.' Roy Hobbs, who has made his own bat, Wonderboy, starts off at nineteen years of age to a possible spot on a big team. That promising beginning is blasted when he has an encounter with an erratic, seductive woman. When we next meet Roy fifteen years later, he is trying again to realize his dream as the best baseball player. His wrong-headed decisions and the exciting descriptions of the games played by his team, The Knights, make this a tense story up to the last out." Shapiro. Fic for Youth. 3d edition

The tenants. Farrar, Straus & Giroux 1971 230p o.p.

A novel "about Harry Lesser, a Jewish writer whose third novel is not completed after nearly ten years of incessant work. Lesser lives alone, the last occupant of an apartment building located in a dying neighborhood. The clash between Lesser and Willie Spearmint, an aspiring but as yet unpublished black writer who takes over one of the empty apartments, serves as the focus of the novel." Libr J

"A magnificent story is told with grieving insight into some of life's more damaging conflicts and betrayals." Saturday Rev

Mallinson, Allan

A close run thing; a novel of Wellington's army of 1815. Bantam Bks. 1999 306p o.p.

ISBN 0-553-11114-0 LC 98-52512

First volume is a projected "series featuring Cornet Matthew Hervey, a young cavalry officer in Wellington's army of 1815." Publisher's note

"Hervey's story begins in 1814, with Napoleon's defeat. Hervey narrowly escapes a court martial for impetuous, albeit brave, action in the Peninsular Campaign against the French, and is invited to purchase his lieutenancy. He returns to Britain, rekindles his affections for his childhood sweetheart, and is posted to Ireland: there he explores the country's religious strife, rides horses and reads Pride and Prejudice. But when Bonaparte escapes from Elba and raises a new army for a rematch with Wellington, Hervey's dragoons must return to war." Publ Wkly

"An exciting historical adventure steeped in authentic military detail." Booklist

Mallon, Thomas, 1951-

Bandbox. Pantheon Books 2004 305p $24.95

ISBN 0-375-42116-5 LC 2003-54861

"Bandbox is a hugely successful magazine, a glamorous monthly cocktail of 1920s obsessions from the stock market to radio to gangland murder. Edited by the bombastic Jehoshaphat 'Joe' Harris, the magazine has a masthead that includes, among many others, a grisly, alliterative crime writer; a shy but murderously determined copyboy; and a burned-out vaudeville correspondent. . . . As the novel opens, the defection of Harris's most ambitious protege has plunged Bandbox into a death struggle with a new competitor on the newsstand." Publisher's note

"Mallon, in his other books, has gravitated toward previous eras out of an affinity for something like reticence. 'Bandbox,' then, is a real departure: antic, stylized, and up-tempo. The dialogue has a Kaufman-and-Hart crackle, and the story boasts more lotharios, floozies, mobsters, and wised-up dames than an MG-M double feature." New Yorker

Dewey defeats Truman; a novel. Pantheon Bks. 1997 355p o.p.

ISBN 0-679-44425-4 LC 96-26812

"Owosso, Michigan, was Dewey's birthplace, and in the summer and fall of 1948 the townspeople are basking in the national attention that brushes the town. Anne Macmurray, a bookstore clerk and aspiring novelist, is being courted by two men, one a U.A.W. organizer, the other a smug Republican lawyer running for state senator. That romantic rivalry is shaped not only by the political passions of 1948 but also by the skeletons buried (and in one case unburied) in the pasts of other Owossoans. This work is so tightly constructed that it sometimes feels contrived, but Mallon's gift for the telling detail, whether of place or of character, quickly banishes such reservations." New Yorker

Two moons; a novel. Pantheon Bks. 2000 303p o.p.

ISBN 0-375-40025-7 LC 99-34235

This novel is "set in post-Civil War Washington, DC, where 35-year-old war widow Cynthia May lives on her own. Jobs for women are scarce, but Cynthia is a mathematical prodigy, and she finds employment as a 'computer' at the Naval Observatory, inauspiciously located in Foggy Bottom. Here she falls in love with a much younger astronomer, who is already exhibiting symptoms of the dreaded 'miasma,' or malaria. Like the newly discovered Martian moons, Cynthia and her lover orbit around a powerful 'War God,' lecherous Republican party boss Roscoe Conkling, who controls the observatory's budget." Libr J

"Mallon refracts questions of war, woman's rights, and the ordering of the cosmos through the perfect prism of her heroine's mind, adeptly mixing keen social commentary with sheer entertainment." Booklist

Malouf, David, 1934-

Dream stuff; stories. Pantheon Bks. 2000 185p $22

ISBN 0-375-42053-3 LC 99-88859

Includes the following stories: At Schindler's; Closer; Dream stuff; Night training; Sally's story; Jacko's reach; Lone pine; Blacksoil country; Great day

Malouf's stories explore "the racial terrain of Australia, the intricacies of relationships, the lure of the Australian outback, and the contradictions between the outer and in-

Malouf, David, 1934-—*Continued*

ner selves of his characters. The title story, perhaps the strongest in this calmly lyrical and sometimes magical collection concerns a novelist who returns to his native Queensland and confronts his own past and present, discovering that, for better or worse, the past has a hold on him that he cannot escape." Booklist

Harland's half acre. Knopf 1984 230p o.p.
ISBN 0-394-53919-2 LC 84-47680

Frank Harland, an Australian artist, is "a man obsessed by his family's half-mythical past and by its present difficulties. He is inclined, as a result of wandering and poverty, to worry about everybody's difficulties, because, he thinks, 'we were meant to be happy. . . . Suffering's too-easy.' Lonely and always broke despite his growing success, the painter himself becomes something of an obsession with a young lawyer whose prosperous family is the antithesis of the Harlands, and their two stories interweave." Atlantic

This novel "seems a bit too self-conscious in its attempt to create the terms of its own esthetic, too neatly calculated to have the free play of mind of the finest novels. But it is a remarkable book, in which the realist and the dreamer are finally and excitingly fused, both agreed that they have no need of the old world. Henry James rejected America in the 1870's because he felt its culture wasn't rich enough to support the novel. Mr. Malouf has asked the same question about Australia and found a different answer." N Y Times Book Rev

Remembering Babylon. Pantheon Bks. 1993 200p o.p.
LC 93-7888

This novel tells the story of Gemmy Fairley, "an English cabin-boy washed up on the Queensland coast in the 1840s, who is found there by Aboriginals. . . . [Sixteen years later] he is 'found' by some white children. . . . The book tells of the reactions to him of the particular family who take him in, . . . and of those of the school teacher, the minister, and the others he has joined. Amid this, Malouf recalls, in separate chapters, something of the past lives of each of the main characters, in Scotland or England, including that of the white 'native' himself." Times Lit Suppl

"The book is more reflective than polemic. Without excusing the actions of the townsfolk, . . . Malouf shows how difficult original thought is for members of a community that perceives itself as surrounded by danger. The book is a joy to read: richly layered, complex, and dense." Christ Sci Monit

Malraux, André, 1901-1976

Man's fate (La condition humaine); translated by Haakon M. Chevalier. Smith & Hass 1934 360p o.p.

Original French edition, 1933; published in the United Kingdom with title: Storm in Shanghai

"The time is 1927, during the unsuccessful Communist uprising in China. The author focuses on three types of revolutionaries. Ch'en, a Chinese terrorist, believes that Chiang Kai-shek must be killed to start a revolution and is willing to sacrifice himself to bring this about. Kyo, half-French, half-Japanese, is drawn to the revolution because of his belief in human dignity. He finds it difficult to reconcile the idealistic theories of Marx with the political realities of the revolution. Katov, a Russian who has had experience in the revolution in his own country, feels there is strength in the solidarity of his comrades. Though their attempts at revolution fail, each man dies feeling he has given meaning to his life trying to bring change to China." Shapiro. Fic for Youth. 3d edition

Man's hope; translated from the French by Stuart Gilbert and Alastair Macdonald. Random House 1938 511p o.p.

Original French edition, 1937; published in the United Kingdom with title: Days of hope

The story of the first eight months of the Civil War in Spain based on the author's experiences as commander of the Loyalist government's international air force

"Vividly realistic as it is, the book is remarkably free from the senseless dwelling upon physical injuries which often weakens the effect of war novels. M. Malraux has concentrated upon the essential rather than the incidental horrors of war, of civil war in particular." Manchester Guardian

Malraux, Georges André *See* Malraux, André, 1901-1976

Manicka, Rani

The rice mother. Viking 2003 432p $24.95
ISBN 0-670-03192-5 LC 2002-32421

"When 14-year-old Lakshmi marries a widower of 37, she believes that she is leaving her Sri Lankan village for a life of luxury in Malaysia. Instead, she endures hardship and poverty, giving birth to six children in the years before the Japanese invasion of World War II. In this gripping multigenerational saga, the tumultuous history of Malaysia becomes the backdrop for Lakshmi's indomitable spirit. The barbarity of the Japanese, postwar prosperity, the bursting of the Southeast Asian financial bubble, the vice trades of opium, gambling, and sex—all take their toll on Lakshmi's children and grandchildren." Libr J

Mankell, Henning, 1948-

Before the frost; translated by Ebba Segerberg. New Press 2004 375p $24.95
ISBN 1-565-84835-7 LC 2004-55197

Original Swedish edition, 2002

In this "Wallander mystery, the generational torch passes from father Kurt to his equally stubborn daughter, Linda, who recently finished her police training and is anxiously awaiting her first day on the job. But a seemingly random series of events jump-starts her career and enmeshes her and her father, along with Stefan Lindman . . . in a case with global ramifications" Publ Wkly

"Linda has a future in this series; but it takes a seasoned philosopher like Wallander to make sense of the horrors that men do to honor their gods. " N Y Times Book Rev

Dogs of Riga; a Kurt Wallander mystery; translated by Laurie Thompson. Norton 2003 326p $24.95
ISBN 1-56584-787-2 LC 2002-30503

Mankell, Henning, 1948-—*Continued*

Original Swedish edition, 1992

"Set against the chaotic backdrop of eastern Europe after the fall of the Berlin Wall, Mankell's intense, accomplished mystery, the last in his Kurt Wallander series. . . explores one man's struggle to find truth and justice in a society increasingly bereft of either. Here the provincial Swedish detective takes on a probably fruitless task: investigating the murders of two unidentified men washed up on the Swedish coast in an inflatable dinghy." Publ Wkly

Firewall; translated by Ebba Segerberg. New Press (NY) 2002 405p $25.95

ISBN 1-56584-767-9 LC 2002-25543

Original Swedish editon, 1998

A mystery featuring Swedish police inspector Kurt Wallander. A "criminal mastermind is about to press the button and send the global financial network into free fall when his partner is murdered, giving Wallander a window of opportunity to scotch this mischief and let us use our A.T.M.'s again. Although things get pretty tense at the end in Ebba Segerberg's well-paced translation, this a thinking man's thriller bearing the messsage that no infernal machine is a match for a decent man with a sense of good and evil." N Y Times Book Rev

One step behind; translated by Ebba Segerberg. New Press (NY) 2002 408p $24.95

ISBN 1-56584-652-4 LC 2001-34254

Original Swedish edition, 1997

This mystery, featuring chief Inspector Kurt Wallander of the Ystad, Sweden police turns on the "meticulously staged homicide of three friends who costumed themselves as 18th-century bacchants and went into the woods on Midsummer's Eve to party. When a murdered police officer is implicated in the widening investigation, Wallander suspects internal corruption. . . . The sweep and complexity of Mankell's plot are reason enough for tackling this dense book, thoughtfully translated by Ebba Segerberg. But his meditations on surprising subjects like time travel and 'man's relationship to monsters' make him something special." N Y Times Book Rev

The return of the dancing master; translated by Laurie Thompson. New Press 2004 391p $24.95

ISBN 1-56584-860-8

Original Swedish edition, 2000

Swedish policeman Stefan Lindman "faces a host of personal demons, not the least of which is his recent diagnosis of mouth cancer. On leave and unwilling to face up to his illness, he decides to travel to the small village of Sveg, where a retired colleague, Herbert Molin, has been murdered. Helping to investigate the crime, Lindman is shocked to discover that Molin was a lifelong Nazi. Suddenly, Lindman's alternative 'therapy' has landed him in the middle of an international ring of neo-Nazis." Booklist

"With its expansive time frame and meticulous procedural details, the story (as translated by Laurie Thompson) has a density that demands–and rewards–intellectual involvement." N Y Times Book Rev

Mann, Erica *See* Jong, Erica

Mann, Thomas, 1875-1955

The black swan; translated from the German by Willard R. Trask. Knopf 1954 141p o.p.

LC 90-38617

Original German edition, 1953; this is a reissue of the 1954 Knopf edition

Tragic psychological tale of a middle-aged German widow's passion for the young American tutor of her son

In this novelette Mann "returns to the compact dimensions and to the subject matter of Death in Venice (transposed into heterosexual terms)—the infatuation of an aging person for a young one. The current novella—though it is not nearly as memorable a piece of storytelling as the masterpiece of 1913—is a provocative addition to Mann's writings." Atlantic

Buddenbrooks; the decline of a family; translated from the German by John E. Woods. Knopf 1993 648p o.p.

ISBN 0-679-41994-2 LC 92-18990

Original German edition, 1901. First United States edition translated by H. T. Lowe-Potter published 1924 in two volumes

"Mann's first novel, it expressed the ambivalence of his feelings about the value of the life of the artist as opposed to ordinary, bourgeois life. The novel is the saga of the fall of the Buddenbrooks, a family of merchants, from the pinnacle of their material wealth in 1835 to their extinction in 1877." Merriam-Webster's Ency of Lit

Confessions of Felix Krull, confidence man; the early years; translated from the German by Denver Lindley. Knopf 1955 384p o.p.

Originally written as a short story in 1921; this novel was first published 1954 in Germany

"Krull, a charming young man with absolutely no moral awareness, avoids military service and takes a job in a hotel. This begins a series of erotic and criminal escapades that eventually lead the young man to prison, from where he purportedly writes his confessions. Like many of Mann's characters, Krull represents the artist, and his profession indicates the symbolic connection in Mann's mind between the artist and the actor, or charlatan." Reader's Ency. 3d edition

Death in Venice; translated from the German by Kenneth Burke. Knopf 1965 118p o.p.

Original German edition, 1913; this translation first published 1925 as the title novella of a collection

"Gustav von Aschenbach, the hero, is a successful author, proud of the self-discipline with which he has ordered his life and work. On a trip to Venice, however, he becomes aware of mysterious decadent potentialities in himself, and he finally succumbs to a consuming love for a frail but beautiful Polish boy named Tadzio. Though he learns that there is danger of a cholera epidemic in Venice, he finds he cannot leave the city, and eventually dies of the disease. The story is permeated by a rich and varied symbolism with frequent overtones from Greek literature and mythology." Reader's Ency. 4th edition

also in Mann, T. Death in Venice and other tales

also in Mann, T. Stories of three decades

Mann, Thomas, 1875-1955—*Continued*

Death in Venice and other tales; translated from German by Joachim Neugroschel. Viking 1998 366p o.p.

ISBN 0-670-87424-8 LC 98-2803

Contents: The will for happiness; Little Herr Friedemann; Tobias Mindernickel; Little Lizzy; Gladius Dei; Tristan; The starvelings: a study; Tonio Kroger; The wunderkind; Harsh hour; The blood of the Walsungs; Death in Venice

Doctor Faustus; translated from the German by John E. Woods. Knopf 1997 534p o.p.

ISBN 0-375-40054-0 LC 97-2818

A new translation of the novel originally published 1947 in German; first English translation by H. T. Lowe-Parker published 1948

In this novel "the intense and tragic career of the hero Adrian Leverkühn, a composer, is made to parallel the collapse of Germany in World War II. To achieve this end, Mann employs the device of having another character, Serenus Zeitblom, narrate Leverkühn's story from memory, while the war is going on, and intersperse his narrative with remarks about the present situation. In this way, it is implied that it is the same demonic and always potentially destructive energy inherent in Leverkühn's music that is also, on a larger scale, behind the outburst of Nazism. Mann thus suggests that the violent 'Faustian' drive, when it is not diverted into art, or when there is no single artistic genius to harness it into creative process, will be perverted and result in grossly sub-human degradation." Reader's Ency. 4th edition

Joseph and his brothers; translated from the German by H. T. Lowe-Porter; with a new introduction by the author. Knopf 1948 xxi, 1207p $65

ISBN 0-394-43132-4

An omnibus edition of the author's tetralogy based on the Biblical story of Joseph

Contents: The tales of Jacob; Young Joseph; Joseph in Egypt; Joseph the provider

The tales of Jacob (1933; first United States edition 1934 with title: Joseph and his brothers) is mainly the story of Jacob. It describes his long service with Laban, the deception by which Leah was palmed off on Jacob in place of Rachel, the birth of Leah's sons, and of Rachel's death in childbirth

Young Joseph (1934: first United States edition 1935) centers on adolescent Joseph, his father's favorite and the object of his brother's mounting jealousy. After he describes his arrogant dreams and flaunts his beautiful "picture robe," his brothers sell him to an Ishmaelite trader

In Joseph in Egypt (1936: first United States edition 1938 in 2 volumes) Joseph is now owned by Potiphar and eventually becomes the household steward. He rejects the advances by Potiphar's wife who throws him into prison for revenge

Joseph the provider (1943: first United States edition 1944) describes Joseph's imprisonment, rise to power, life in Pharaoh's court, reunion with his brothers and father, settlement in Egypt and death

In these tales Mann has expanded upon "the original story tremendously, but most of the added episodes contribute not so much to the tale itself as to the characters' depth and symbolic significance. In its overall attitude, the 'Joseph' tetralogy is neither ambiguous like 'The Magic Mountain' nor tragic like 'Doktor Faustus,' but unqualifiedly redemptive." Reader's Ency. 4th edition

Joseph in Egypt

In Mann, T. Joseph and his brothers p447-840

Joseph the provider

In Mann, T. Joseph and his brothers p843-1207

The magic mountain; a novel; translated from the German by John E. Woods. Knopf 1995 706p o.p.

ISBN 0-679-44183-2 LC 94-42885

Original German edition, 1924

This novel "tells the story of Hans Castorp, a young German engineer, who goes to visit a cousin in a tuberculosis sanatorium in the mountains of Davos, Switz. Castorp discovers that he has symptoms of the disease and remains at the sanatorium for seven years, until the outbreak of World War I. During this time, he abandons his normal life to submit to the rich seductions of disease, introspection, and death. Through talking with other patients, he gradually becomes aware of and absorbs the predominant political, cultural, and scientific ideas of 20th-century Europe. The sanatorium comes to be the spiritual reflection of the possibilities and dangers of the actual world away from the magic mountain" Merriam-Webster's Ency of Lit

Six early stories; translated from the German with a note by Peter Constantine; edited with an introduction by Burton Pike. Sun & Moon Press 1997 128p o.p.

ISBN 1-55713-298-4

Contents: A vision "Prose sketch"; Fallen; The will to happiness; Death; Avenged, "Study for a novella"; Anecdote

"These newly translated stories give insight into the still-forming mind of the Nobel laureate, revealing his philosophical and literary influences as well as demonstrating the uninhibited experimentation of a young, romantic writer." Publ Wkly

Stories of three decades; translated from the German by H. T. Lowe-Porter. Knopf 1936 567p o.p.

Short stories included are: Little Herr Friedemann; Disillusionment; Dilettante; Tobias Mindernickel; Little Lizzy; Wardrobe; Way to the churchyard; Hungry; Infant prodigy; Gladius Dei; Fiorenza; Gleam; At the prophet's; Weary hour; Blood of the Walsungs; Railway accident; Fight between Jappe and Do Escobar; Felix Krull; Man and his dog; Disorder and early sorrow; Mario and the magician

The novellas are psychological studies. Tonio Kröger is concerned with the struggle between the artist and normal citizen. Tristan's concern deals with music's irrational and frequently destructive powers. Death in Venice is entered separately

The tales of Jacob

In Mann, T. Joseph and his brothers p3-258

Tonio Kröger

In Mann, T. Stories of three decades

Mann, Thomas, 1875-1955—*Continued*

Tristan

In Mann, T. Stories of three decades

Young Joseph

In Mann, T. Joseph and his brothers p261-444

Mansbach, Adam, 1976-

Shackling water. Doubleday 2002 232p o.p.

ISBN 0-385-50205-2 LC 2001-47398

This novel "about an aspiring saxophonist in Harlem . . . introduces us to Latif James-Pearson, an 18-year-old from Boston who moves to New York to hone his chops and, ultimately, to meet his idol, the jazz aristocrat Albert Van Horn. Along the way, Latif faces a series of tests through a relationship with an older white woman, a jazz-club job dealing drugs and eventually an addiction to them; he loses touch with both his music and himself before a tragedy shocks him back to life." N Y Times Book Rev

"This bold, resonant portrait of the artist as a young man isn't flawless, but Mansbach's eloquence and energy are unwavering." Booklist

Mansfield, Katherine, 1888-1923

The garden party and other stories. Knopf 1991 xxxv, 267p o.p.

LC 91-53004

"Everyman's library"

Contents: The tiredness of Rosabel; Frau Brechenmacher attends a wedding; The swing of the pendulum; A birthday; Millie; The woman at the store; Bains Turcs; An indiscreet journey; The little governess; Prelude; Bliss; A married man's story; Carnation; This flower; The man without a temperament; The daughters of the late colonel; Her first ball; The voyage; At the bay; The garden party; Honeymoon

The short stories of Katherine Mansfield. Knopf 1937 688p $22.95

ISBN 0-394-44532-5

"In this comprehensive edition Katherine Mansfield's stories are arranged approximately in chronological order." Introduction

Mansfield, Kathleen Beauchamp *See* Mansfield, Katherine, 1888-1923

Mantel, Hilary

Beyond black. Henry Holt & Co. 2005 365p $26

ISBN 0-00-715775-4 LC 2004-63589

"A John Macrae book"

"A paragon of efficiency, well-schooled in the mundane tasks of an average existence, Colette took the next natural step after finishing secretarial school–marrying a man who would do just fine. After a sobering do-it-yourself divorce, Colette, for the first time, is at a loss as to what to do next. Convinced that she deserves a life-affirming revelation, she strays into the world of psychics and clairvoyants. . . . At a psychic fair in Windsor she sneaks into Alison's show. Alison, beleaguered by spirits since early childhood, lives in a different kind of solitude. She can never escape the dead who speak to her, and the physical pain of their broken bodies–least of all the constance presence of Morris, her low-life spiritual guide." Publisher's note

"This is, I think, a great comic novel. Hilary Mantel's humor, like Flannery O'Connor's, is so far beyond black it becomes a kind of light." N Y Times Book Rev

Mapson, Jo-Ann

Bad Girl Creek; a novel. Simon & Schuster 2001 381p o.p.

ISBN 0-7432-0256-2 LC 2001-27006

"Phoebe DeThomas has lived carefully all her life. Thirty-eight years old and in a wheelchair because of a bad heart, she's always felt dwarfed by her flamboyant aunt Sadie and her successful brother James. Now Sadie has died, bequeathing her a flower farm on California's Central Coast. In order to make a go of it, Phoebe takes in three women as boarder/farmhands. Each of the three is 'homeless,' having recently undergone traumatic life changes: Ness, a black cowgirl with a horse and a secret fear that she has AIDS, has lost her job; Nance, a down-on-her-luck Southern belle, has broken up with ber boyfriend; and Beryl, a former kindergarten aide with a prison record, has been evicted from her apartment. . . . Mapson combines poignancy with the good-natured banter of girlfriends in her tale of women in transition, waiting to be reborn." Publ Wkly

Hank and Chloe; a novel. HarperCollins Pubs. 1993 310p o.p.

LC 92-53377

"Chloe Morgan lives for horses and her dog, Hannah. To earn a slight living and keep bill collectors satisfied, she waits tables at a greasy spoon and teaches horseback riding on the side. Home is a cabin in the backwoods minus electricity or running water. She meets Hank, a college professor, and both find magic where neither expected it." Libr J

"The setting is a small town in Southern California, populated with cowboy types like Wes, the owner of Wes's Feed and Tack, where Chloe pawned her prize saddle; and Hugh Nichols, the owner of the ranch where Chloe's shack stands. . . . First novelist Mapson lines her unsentimental tale of the modern West with real people and an especially strong sense of place." Booklist

Followed by Loving Chloe

Loving Chloe; a novel. HarperCollins Pubs. 1998 347p o.p.

ISBN 0-06-017217-7 LC 97-20578

In this sequel to Hank and Chloe "refined college professor Hank is thrilled when the tough-talking horse-trainer Chloe reenters his life and tells him she is pregnant with his child. Chloe knows that Hanks is a good man, but she cannot fully commit herself to him, having put up her emotional defenses a long time ago, when she was shuttled from one foster home to another as a child. When she goes into labor unexpectedly, local Navajo legend Junior Whitebear delivers her child. Neither Chloe nor Junior is prepared for the intensity of the bond they forge during the delivery, and Chloe is left feeling torn between Hank and Junior." Booklist

"Mapson knows her territory intimately, and she populates it with memorable characters who readily engage

Mapson, Jo-Ann—*Continued*
our emotions. Her dialogue is earthy and funny, her setting evocative, her portrayal of good people facing difficult choices compassionate." N Y Times Book Rev

Marcantel, Pamela

An army of angels; a novel of Joan of Arc. St. Martin's Press 1997 578p o.p.
ISBN 0-312-15030-X LC 96-31791
"In this historical novel, Marcantel resurrects the mysterious Jehanne, the Maid of Orleans, whose devotion to God led her to be burned at the stake for witchcraft before she is 20. Jehanne's visions and voices influenced her at an early age to leave her village and fulfill God's will. Guided to the future King of France, Charles VII, the peasant Jehanne persuades him to give her an army to recapture French lands from Henry VI's England." Libr J
"Rather than portraying Joan as a pious saint, Marcantel characterizes her as a flawed and vulnerable human being often plagued by both doubt and fear. An impassioned chronicle of an unparalleled heroine." Booklist

March, William, 1893-1954

The bad seed. Rinehart 1954 247p o.p.
"Rhoda Penmark at 8 years of age had a mind of her own and a will to match. Aged people doted on her splendid manners, but rogues knew her as one of themselves while older children were afraid of her. Christine, her mother suddenly discovers her daughter's horrible tendencies and also finds out that she is the murderess of two people who stood in her way. Christine resolves to check back and finds that she had been adopted and that the mother she had never known had also been a successful killer. Christine tries to stop the pattern in her daughter, but in the process dies herself." Libr J

Marcom, Micheline Aharonian

The daydreaming boy; Micheline Aharonian Marcom. Riverhead Books 2004 212p $23.95
ISBN 1-573-22264-X LC 2003-55702
"A middle-aged survivor of Turkey's Armenian massacres living in Beirut in the 1960s contemplates his brutal past and loses himself in a series of adulterous trysts that bring him slowly to a realization of the moral compromises he has made. . . . The shadow of impending violence troubles the calm, but it is the grim reality of what has already happened that is most harrowing-the evil that Vahé must confront each day, as much as he might try to make himself more comfortable in the world." Publ Wkly

Margolin, Phillip

After dark. Doubleday 1995 340p o.p.
LC 94-41997
In this novel, lawyer "Tracy Cavenaugh is shaken when she finds Oregon Supreme Court Justice Robert Griffen's clerk, Laura Rizatti, murdered in her office. Tracy thinks that she can put the murder behind her when she goes to work for Matthew Reynolds, a prominent attorney who specializes in death penalty cases—that is, until Justice Griffen also ends up dead a month later." Libr J
"The reversals and revelations are many and diabolically clever. . . . No legal-triller fan, once hooked, will wiggle free of the story line of this hammy but exciting yarn before reaching its utterly surprising, and surprisingly dark, conclusion." Publ Wkly

The burning man. Doubleday 1996 344p o.p.
LC 96-12093
This novel "is set in Eastern Oregon, where a mildly retarded man is charged with the brutal slaying of a young woman. His lawyer, having never tried a capital crime case before, fumbles badly, but a glimmer of native wit gets him back on track. Working the genre with a discipline some popular authors have begun to ignore, Margolin relies on a few crafty stereotypes to keep up the pace and simplify the action. The dialogs in the jailhouse and the interrogation scenes, though, are intense and fierce. The moral zigzags of desperate people are laid out to contrast with the lawyer and his client as they feint and weave to avoid the ultimate penalty." Libr J

The undertaker's widow. Doubleday 1998 312p o.p.
ISBN 0-385-48054-7 LC 97-41143
"Wealthy Portland, OR, businessman Lamar Hoyt Sr. is shot to death in his bed. His wife, Ellen Crease, fires upon and kills the shooter. When the forensic scientist studies the photographs of the crime scene, he sees a discrepancy in the blood spatters, which points to Crease's lying about what happened. Her arraignment and bail hearing is before Richard Quinn, an honest, by-the-book judge who is being blackmailed into ruling against Crease." Libr J
"Margolin gives his material immediacy by making readers privy to Quinn's thinking through every twist and turn of the plot." Booklist

Marías, Javier, 1951-

The man of feeling; translated from the Spanish by Margaret Jull Costa. New Directions 2003 182p $22.95
ISBN 0-8112-1531-8 LC 2002-153935
Original Spanish edition, 1986
"While in Madrid to perform the role of Cassio in Verdi's 'Otello,' a Spanish tenor meets a man whose job is to amuse the neglected wife of a powerful Brussels banker. The paid companion invites the singer on his outings with the woman, setting the stage for an affair. . . . (This). . . would seem to offer little more than banal melodrama. Everything depends, however, on how the plot unfolds. Marias avoids a straightforward delivery in favor of a digressive narrative that moves back and forth in time. . . . This suggestive indirection perfectly suits Marias's preoccupation: the erotic imagination." N Y Times Book Rev

Marillier, Juliet

Foxmask; Juliet Marillier. 1st U.S. ed. TOR Bks. 2004 2003 464p $27.95
ISBN 0-7653-0674-3 LC 2003-71154
"The Norseman Eyvind becomes a Wolfskin a Viking dedicated to Thor and travels to the mystical Orkney Islands, where he meets the Princess Nessa, a seer who be-

Marillier, Juliet—*Continued*

comes his soul mate. As Vikings and Orkney residents work out a peace, a new generation arises to forge strong ties. A question of paternity throws the delicate balance between the two peoples in jeopardy, and some young folk set out on a journey to discover the truth. The author . . . continues her exploration of the fusion of two cultures with strong family ties and great trust in powers beyond the merely human." Libr J

Marinick, Richard, 1951-

Boyos; a novel; Richard Marinick. Kate's Mystery Books 2004 274p $24.95

ISBN 1-932112-32-4 LC 2004-54843

"Set in and around 'Southie,' the South Boston working-class Irish-American enclave . . ., the story focuses on Jack 'Wacko' Curran, a rising young player in the criminal underworld. Local 'boyos' like Curran resent the steady influx of young working professionals, who are gentrifying the area and pricing the old-time residents out. Curran and his coked-out brother, Kevin, work for mob boss Marty Fallon, wholesaling drugs to a network of area dealers. Tired of giving Fallon a cut of every score, Jack dreams of replacing Fallon and figures that the bankroll from the armored-car heist he's planning will put him on his way." Publ Wkly

"The writing is gritty and serious, the action intense, and the characters well drawn and compelling despite their imperfections." Libr J

Marion, Stephen, 1964-

Hollow ground; a novel. Algonquin Bks. 2002 308p $23.95

ISBN 1-56512-323-9 LC 2001-55239

This novel is "set in Alexander City, Tenn.—a place formerly known as Zinctown after the huge mines underneath it, which are beginning to make the ground cave in. Taft, a 14-year-old boy, is finally meeting his father, who skipped town before he was born. . . . Taft's father, Gary, has troubles of his own. He returns to Zinctown and finds his own difficult father dying of cancer; the ghost of his brother, who died before he was born, still haunting him; a woman who still loves him but can't forgive him for deserting her; and a son he doesn't quite know how to relate to." N Y Times Book Rev

"Marion is a poignant writer with a deep sense of compassion for his characters, and he captures the atmosphere of the Southern mining town and its underlying capacity for tragedy." Publ Wkly

Markandaya, Kamala, 1924-2004

A handful of rice; a novel. Crowell 1966 297p o.p.

"A John Day book"

"Ravi, the young man, has run away from his village home [in India] to escape its poverty and the lack of opportunity. In the city he first finds outlet for his ambitions and rebelliousness with a gang of street thieves but then is sucked into the poverty mill when he falls in love with a pretty girl and becomes assistant to her father, a poor tailor with an innate dignity but a long heritage of servility." Booklist

"There are curious echoes of Western proletarian novels here, without the revolutionary hope which relieved their somber gloom. . . . Recommended as a depressing but honest portrayal of a culture with too many people and scarcely the material means to satisfy their barest needs." Libr J

Marks, Laurie J.

Fire logic. TOR Bks. 2002 335p $25.95

ISBN 0-312-87887-7 LC 2001-58352

"A Tom Doherty Associates book"

"The land of Shaftal, occupied by the nasty Sainnites, has just lost its Earth witch ruler and, in doing so, has seemingly lost the magic that the witch held. What follows is bitter guerilla warfare. Into this war comes Zanja na 'Tarwein, speaker for the people of the Ashawala'i, a woman who holds the power of elemental fire. What was not her war suddenly becomes personal when the Sainnites turn on her people and obliterate them in one night's battle. As sole survivor, Zanja becomes a resistance fighter." Publ Wkly

"Marks is an absolute master of fantasy in this book. Her characters are beautifully drawn, showing tremendous emotional depth and strength as they endure the unendurable and strive always to do the right thing." Booklist

Markson, David

Vanishing point; a novel. Shoemaker & Hoard 2004 191p pa $15

ISBN 1-59376-010-8 (pa)

"The premise is that 'The Author' as the narrator refers to himself, is assembling a box of note cards full of information he has gathered over the years with the hope of forging a novel. Life then imitates art as Markson literally accomplishes what his narrator hopes to: he creates a novel out of fragments of ideas and information. Vanishing Point feels a little like a literary Trivial Pursuit, or the associative stream of consciousness produced by a surrealist party game, and it's just as entertaining." Booklist

Marlowe, Hugh, 1929- *See* Higgins, Jack, 1929-

Maron, Margaret

Bootlegger's daughter. Mysterious Press 1992 261p o.p.

LC 91-58021

This mystery takes place in "Cotton Grove, N.C., a close-knit rural community on the outskirts of Raleigh, and introduces savvy Deborah Knott, a lawyer whose singular upbringing as a child of a bootlegging power broker has prepared her well for the county race for district court judge. But just as she begins her campaign . . . Deborah is asked to turn over the dead leaves of an 18-year-old murder case. It seems that the daughter of an old flame can't start her life until she finds out who killed her mother as she watched with uncomprehending infant eyes." N Y Times Book Rev

Fugitive colors. Mysterious Press 1995 260p o.p.

LC 95-1703

This mystery features "Lt. Sigrid Harald of the NYPD. The deaths of a fellow officer and of her artist lover throw Sigrid into decline—until her lover's legacy of

Maron, Margaret—*Continued*
valuable paintings leads to the murder of a greedy art dealer." Libr J

"Maron adeptly establishes a coolly thematic and deceptive link among the deaths as she constructs her affecting mystery out of distinctive blend of art-world politics, past crimes and present grief." Publ Wkly

High country fall; Margaret Maron. Mysterious Press 2004 303p $24

ISBN 0-89296-808-7 LC 2004-1953

Judge Deborah Knott's "engagement to Deputy Sheriff Dwight has stirred a furor in her extended family, so she trades noise at home for the supposed quiet of court in the Blue Ridge Mountains. There . . . she becomes embroiled in a murder case with a wrongfully accused suspect." Libr J

"Deborah's narrative voice, with its engaging tone of amusement at the human foibles she witnesses in her travels, is just the ticket for this dramatic view of the spectacular Blue Ridge Mountains." N Y Times Book Rev

Home fires burning. Mysterious Press 1998 243p $32

ISBN 0-89296-655-6 LC 98-6632

North Carolina Circuit Court Judge Deborah Knott, "who narrates, is at the start of a reelection campaign when a nephew is arrested, with two friends, for desecrating a cemetery. When the same spraypainted graffiti appears at an African American church that's been torched, the young men are suspected of arson. Two more black churches are burned and two bodies uncovered before Deborah fingers the culprit." Publ Wkly

Killer market. Mysterious Press 1997 273p $21.50

ISBN 0-89296-654-8 LC 97-20835

"North Carolina district court judge Deborah Knott unintentionally 'crashes' several manufacturer's receptions at the internationally known Southeastern Furniture Market in High Point, where she becomes involved in murder. Initially befriended by a mysterious and elusive woman with bogus name tags, series protagonist Knott soon runs into an old woman friend from law school as well as a hunky ex-beau now in the furniture business. When Deborah later discovers the man dead, she and police begin investigating." Libr J

Shooting at loons. Mysterious Press 1994 229p o.p.

LC 93-47141

"District Court Judge Deborah Knott, a native North Carolinian, looks forward to filling in for a sick colleague at the Harker's Island courthouse. But on her first fishing trip after arriving on the island, she discovers the body of an old fisherman known to her since childhood. . . . The down-home prose flows well, spiced by Judge Knott's wit, charm, and extended family as well as by references to the local food and drink." Libr J

Slow dollar. Mysterious Press 2002 276p o.p.

ISBN 0-89296-764-1 LC 2002-20098

"It's opening night at Dobbs' Annual Harvest Festival, and Deborah, along with half of Colleton County North Carolina, is intent on riding the Ferris wheel, eating elephant ears, and, finally, throwing quarters at the Dozer game. When Deborah runs out of change, she steps into the interior of the game wagon, where she finds the proprietor dead on the floor, his mouth overflowing with quarters. . . . As always, the mystery takes a backseat to the engaging characters and the charming southern setting." Booklist

Southern discomfort. Mysterious Press 1993 241p o.p.

LC 92-56770

Newly appointed judge Deborah Knott, "threads her way through the intricacies of district court in a small North Carolina town where familial connections abound. Murder rears its ugly head only after shared family stories and relationships establish a stylistic context. Employing her intimate knowledge of the place, Knott discovers who assaulted her teenaged niece and killed a randy building inspector inside an unfinished WomenAid house." Libr J

"Maron's written a thriller that simply oozes southern charm and atmosphere. The clever plot is full of surprises—a good blend of menace, poignancy, and humor. But perhaps Maron's real strength is her refreshing heroine, who doesn't mind admitting she wears a size fourteen dress and who approaches life with humor, determination, and good sense." Booklist

Storm track. Mysterious Press 2000 260p $28

ISBN 0-89296-656-4 LC 99-51761

"The residents of Colleton County, North Carolina, must contend with dual threats: Hurricane Fran, gearing up offshore, and the presence of a nasty murderer in their midst. Lynn Bullock, known as a tramp by all except, perhaps, her husband, is strangled in a local motel, dressed for a tryst, and Deborah's cousin Reid is a top suspect. More bodies turn up as the hurricane arrives to wreak another kind of destruction on the locals." Booklist

"Deborah Knott, the district court judge who presides over this enchanting regional series, guides us through these crises with her customary good sense. . . . Deborah is the voice of sanity and the soul of wit." N Y Times Book Rev

Uncommon clay. Warner Bks. 2001 288p $28

ISBN 0-89296-720-X LC 00-66266

"The famous Nordan family, who live in an area of North Carolina known for its pottery, is being torn apart by a traumatic and bitter divorce. Judge Deborah Knotts . . . oversees distribution of the marital property, but her work is interrupted by a tragic death in the family—reminiscent of a terrible suicide two years earlier." Libr J

This mystery "does more than honor local folk art and the generations of artisans who carry on the regional heritage. It shows us how deeply these homespun crafts are rooted in the collective artistry of individual families—and what a devastating loss it is when these families die out." N Y Times Book Rev

Up jumps the Devil. Mysterious Press 1996 278p o.p.

LC 96-7715

"As the pecan trees of the beautiful North Carolina countryside give way to tract housing, land values are escalating rapidly, and all over Colleton County, longtime neighbors and family members are engaged in acrimonious disputes over whether to sell their family land. In this . . . entry in the Deborah Knott series, the straight-talking, down-to-earth district court judge is

Maron, Margaret—*Continued*
drawn into two murders tied to greed over land-development money." Booklist

"The droll characters and their lilting regional humor seem ever more endearing because we sense their days are numbered." N Y Times Book Rev

Marquand, John P. (John Phillips), 1893-1960

The late George Apley; a novel in the form of a memoir. Little, Brown 1937 354p o.p.

"George Apley, the epitome of the proper Bostonian, has his life reviewed here by another Bostonian, Mr. Willing. The supposed author, also Marquand's creation, is so stuffy himself that the narration has an element of humor that neither man would have been able to recognize. Although Apley was indeed an upright citizen, this narration, however unwittingly, points out the numerous times that he almost fell from grace and the mixed feelings he had when his own children managed to escape from the 'net' of proper Boston society." Shapiro. Fic for Youth. 3d edition

Point of no return. Little, Brown 1949 559p o.p.

This novel describes some decisive days in the life of Charles Gray. At the end of the week he expects to learn if he is to be promoted to the vice-presidency of his New York bank; but in the meantime business takes him to his home town in Massachusetts where he reviews his past life

"Here is the delicate dissection, the evocation of aura, the alert, unfailing eye for the idiosyncrasy which has become an integral part of the individual, which has marked Marquand's best work. . . . His quiet irony plays over this novel constantly, clarifying the quiet, occasionally melancholy passages of the sections which recreate Charles Gray's youth, and sharpening, pointing delicately and clearly the tensions and the desperately followed formulae of the man he has become." Saturday Rev

Márquez, Gabriel García *See* García Márquez, Gabriel, 1928-

Marsh, Jean, 1934-

The House of Eliott. St. Martin's Press 1994 c1993 265p o.p.
LC 94-2671

First published 1993 in the United Kingdom

"The Eliotts are Beatrice and Evangeline, a pair of sisters in 1920s London who discover that their father's death has left them too little to survive on in genteel leisure. Their decision to open a dressmaking salon gives their close relatives apoplexy, but the young women are determined, and they are aided by several charming men who support their enterprise and fall in love with them to boot. There's plenty of period detail in this involving story, particularly regarding the issues of poverty, unemployment, and class discrimination." Booklist

Marsh, Dame Ngaio, 1899-1982

Colour scheme. Little, Brown 1943 314p o.p.

Inspector Roderick Alleyn of Scotland Yard appears two thirds of the way through this tale of mystery and international espionage. "Colonel and Mrs. Claire run a modest spa in northern New Zealand. The inmates are an odd lot, including a down-at-the-heels drunkard, a businessman who is a bounder, a Shakespearean actor, and the actor's secretary. One of the guests is murdered in a boiling mud pool which was originally used for health purposes." New Yorker

Dead water. Little, Brown 1963 244p o.p.

Scotland Yard's Superintendent "Roderick Alleyn finds himself involved unofficially in magic and faith healing when his former French teacher, now a formidable lady of 80, inherits an island off the coast of Cornwall which has, as its chief claim to fame and source of income, a Pixie Well supposed to cure warts, asthma and other ills. . . . Skillful writing, convincing atmosphere, and sharply etched characterization will please Ngaio Marsh fans, but the plot is less complex than some of her others." Publ Wkly

False scent. Little, Brown 1959 273p o.p.

This mystery "takes place in the opulent London home of a famous—and temperamental—actress on her 50th birthday anniversary. The flamboyant people surrounding Mary Bellamy are properly subdued only when the polished Roderick Alleyn of Scotland Yard and his capable assistant, Inspector Fox, enter the scene and uncover the ugly secrets that led to murder." Libr J

Grave mistake. Little, Brown 1978 252p o.p.
LC 78-16910

"When a rich eccentric old lady in a rest home suddenly dies, friends and the police suspect murder. [Inspector] Alleyn's trail leads him to the old lady's daughter, her fiance, his father, a close friend, and a few assorted others including a Scots gardener—named Gardener! When a will turns up leaving all her money to the doctor who runs the rest home, the supposed case of suicide really becomes murder." West Coast Rev Books

Last ditch. Little, Brown 1977 265p o.p.
LC 76-52287

The novel takes place on one of the Channel Islands, to which Ricky, Superintendent Roderick Alleyn's son, "has come during the Easter vacation to write a novel. Here he meets Jasper and Julia Pharamond, friends of his parents, and falls in love with the magnolia-skinned Julia. . . . A riding expedition ends in a fatal accident, attended by suspicious circumstances; at the same time Ricky stumbles, he thinks, across the tracks of a gang of drug smugglers. But Scotland Yard's attention has already been called to the island, and Chief Superintendent Alleyn and Inspector Fox are soon on their way there." Times Lit Suppl

Light thickens. Little, Brown 1982 232p o.p.
LC 82-13085

"A production of *Macbeth*, directed by Peregrine Jay at the Dolphin Theatre, is beset with macabre incidents. During rehearsals, realistic-looking dummy heads turn up in dark corners and on banquet trays, and a rat's head is found in the witch's effects. But the incidents cease, and reviews call the production 'the flawless *Macbeth*'—until the night when the actor playing Macbeth is decapitated during the play. Roderick Alleyn is, of course, in the audience." Libr J

Marsh, Dame Ngaio, 1899-1982—*Continued*

Photo finish. Little, Brown 1980 252p o.p.
LC 80-16697

"A temperamental and stupid diva is pursued by a spiteful 'paparazzo' who specializes in unflattering pictures. Alleyn is seconded by Scotland Yard to go to New Zealand at the request of the singer's friend, a dubious magnate, and is accompanied by Troy, Alleyn's painter-wife. They arrive for the premiere of a bad opera, the work of the singer's latest protégé, a handsome, stupid young man. All the guests are gathered at a lonely lodge, isolated by a storm. The singer is killed, and Alleyn investigates as whiffs of Sicilian vendetta seep out." Libr J

Singing in the shrouds. Little, Brown 1958 272p o.p.

Seeking the killer of a girl delivering flowers to a departing freighter-cruise ship, Inspector Alleyn of Scotland Yard boards the ship as it leaves London. His first problem is to discover whether the murderer is actually on board but there are no clues, though each of his oddly assorted shipmates seems suspect. To solve the mystery, Alleyn sets the stage for the slayer to kill again

When in Rome. Little, Brown 1971 260p o.p.

First published 1970 in the United Kingdom

Set in Italy, "much of the action takes place in an ancient church which reproduces three levels of civilization. . . . The mystery centers on a sinister blackmailing tour entrepreneur who gathers together a motley group of people, some innocent, some with good reason to want him out of the way. Drugs, sex orgies, even more delicate scandals are all grist to his mill and when he meets a very nasty demise the field of suspects is wide open. Not the least of the pleasures here is a charming love affair, and the slightly comic opera encounters between English Inspector Roderick Alleyn and the Rome police." Publ Wkly

Marshall, Catherine, 1914-1983

Christy. McGraw-Hill 1967 496p o.p.

"A spirited young woman leaves the security of her home to become a teacher in Cutter Gap, Kentucky. It is 1912 and the needs of the Appalachian people are great. Christy learns much from the poverty and superstition of the mountain folk. Marshall's Christian faith and ideals are intertwined in the plot, which includes a love story." Shapiro. Fic for Youth. 3d edition

Julie. McGraw-Hill 1984 364p o.p.
LC 84-4448

"Julie Wallace is a fetching, exuberant 18-year-old whose father has given up a post as a minister in Alabama (supposedly due to ill health) and purchased a smalltown newspaper in Pennsylvania. . . . The community and newspaper work give the lively teenager the opportunity to pursue her writing ambitions and also lead to some chaste romantic entanglements. Her father receives renewed faith and self-confidence from his work and from a showdown with the steel magnate." Booklist

"Readers will be moved by the Wallace family's triumphs, through hard work and unstoppable faith, during a critical time in America's history." N Y Times Book Rev

Marshall, Paule, 1929-

Daughters. Atheneum Pubs. 1991 408p o.p.
LC 91-8219

This novel deals with "the culture of blacks in the United States and in the West Indies. The book . . . shifts back and forth between New York City, home of Ursa Beatrice Mackenzie, and the Caribbean island Triunion, Ursa's birthplace and home of her father, a political reformer known simply as the PM, and her American-born mother Estelle. When the story opens, Ursa has just had an abortion and is about to end a stagnant relationship with her long-time boyfriend. She is called to Triunion by Estelle in an attempt to deter the PM from making a deal that could ruin his career." Libr J

This novel "attempts to look at black experience in our hemisphere, to praise what progress has been made and to point to what yet needs to be done. In its willingness to take real stock, to find true answers to complex questions, it is a brave, intelligent and ambitious work." N Y Times Book Rev

The fisher king; a novel. Scribner 2000 222p $23

ISBN 0-684-87283-8 LC 00-28470

"Story of a family in turmoil over the memory of Sonny-Rett Payne, a jazz pianist who fled the racism of New York for Paris in 1949. The action is set in the present, as Sonny's brother, Edgar, now a successful businessman in Brooklyn, organizes a memorial concert for his brother and lures Hattie Carmichael, Sonny's former lover, who lives in Paris with Sonny's grandchild, back to the States for the event. The narrative jumps from the present, as Edgar subtly attempts to gain custody of young Sonny, and the past, as Hattie remembers Sonny-Rett, his music, his wife, and their unconventional life in Paris." Booklist

"Marshall's prose is full of expert dialogue, mellifluous rhythms and sharply drawn portraits of Sonny-Rett's loved ones." N Y Times Book Rev

Praisesong for the widow. Putnam 1983 256p o.p.
LC 82-13215

This novel "tells of a sixtyish widow, Avey Johnson, refined, well-to-do, and complacent. Troubled by strange dreams and symptoms, she cuts short her annual Caribbean cruise and disembarks on a small island. An old man recognizes her as one of the 'people who can't call their nation,' and persuades her to join him and others on their yearly ritual visit to a neighboring island they call home. There, purged of her old self, Avey rediscovers her roots." Libr J

Marshall, Sarah Catherine Wood *See* Marshall, Catherine, 1914-1983

Marsten, Richard, 1926-2005

For works written by this author under other names see Hunter, Evan, 1926-2005; McBain, Ed, 1926-2005

Marston, Edward

The Bawdy basket. St. Martin's Minotaur 2002 262p o.p.

ISBN 0-312-28501-9 LC 2002-2510944

Marston, Edward—*Continued*

An Elizabethan mystery featuring "Nicholas Bracewell, stage manager of Lord Westfield's Men. . . . When a young actor's father is tried, convicted, and hung for a brutal murder he claims he did not commit, his sins are unfortunately visited upon his loyal son. Nicholas agrees to investigate the matter in an effort to clear the unlucky man's name and to restore a promising young thespian to the ranks of his beloved theater company." Booklist

The Devil's apprentice; a novel. St. Martin's Minotaur; distributed by 8 2001 273p o.p.

ISBN 0-312-26574-3 LC 2001-19259

Elizabethan stage manager Nicholas Bracewell "fends off accusations of witchcraft and worse after the troupe performs at a manor house in Essex. A new apprentice taken on there seems to be at the root of the trouble. Lively and entertaining: for fans of Elizabethan historicals." Libr J

The Dragons of Archenfield; a novel. St. Martin's Press 1995 242p o.p.

LC 95-9475

This mystery "set in the time of William the Conqueror, takes soldier Ralph Delchard and lawyer Gervase Bret to disputed territory to settle local claims. They discover, however, that someone—probably a dreaded local lord—has murdered their prime witness." Libr J

An "outstanding medieval mystery brimming with intrigue, suspense, and authentic historical detail." Booklist

The roaring boy; a novel. St. Martin's Press 1995 260p o.p.

LC 95-8568

"Elizabethan stage manager Nicholas Bracewell presents a new kind of play based on a sensational murder case. But the play leads to trouble for his actors, unless he can solve the actual murder." Libr J

"Marston's colorful (and convincing) characterizations shine as Nicholas chases the secrets of the murder in order to save the company. The plot, except for one transparently finagled episode, is expertly wrought, with the suspense building steadily to breathtaking climax and some surprises saved for the very end." Publ Wkly

The stallions of Woodstock. St. Martin's Press 1999 275p o.p.

ISBN 0-312-20021-8 LC 98-50733

First published 1997 in the United Kingdom

In this installment in the author's Domesday series "Gervase Bret and Ralph Delchard, commissioners to King William the Conqueror, are sent to Oxford, England, to settle a land dispute and soon find themselves embroiled in a murder investigation." Publ Wkly

The vagabond clown. St. Martin's Minotaur 2003 292p $24.95

ISBN 0-312-30789-6 LC 2002-191950

"Lord Westfield's Men, the actors' troupe for which Bracewell works as stage manager, are forced to leave their theater after a violent act of sabotage trashes the place. Worse, someone has killed one of Westfield's friends during the melee. Bracewell struggles to save the troupe and its reputation. An outstanding historical." Libr J

The wanton angel; a novel. St. Martin's Press 1999 279p o.p.

ISBN 0-312-20391-8 LC 99-22062

This mystery, set in Elizabethan England, finds Nicholas Bracewell's "acting troupe ejected from its theater at the Queen's Head when one of the actors impregnates the landlord's daughter and is then murdered." N Y Times Book Rev

The wildcats of Exeter; volume VIII of the Doomesday Books. St. Martin's Minotaur 2001 275p il o.p.

ISBN 0-312-25355-9

First published 1998 in the United Kingdom

In this installment tax collectors Gervase Bret and Ralph Delchard travel to Exeter in Devon. "A land dispute, already complicated by many claimants, grows ever more so when the current owner, one Nicolas Picard, meets a grisly death. He's clawed by a wildcat but also has his throat cut. The wildcats of the title also refer to several women wronged by Nicolas, all of whom have claims to his property. Monks peevish and saintly, a jester wise in his foolery, another murder, and some marital mayhem complete the entertaining picture." Booklist

Martel, Yann, 1963-

Life of Pi; a novel. Harcourt 2001 319p $25

ISBN 0-15-100811-6 LC 2001-39737

"Pi Patel, a young man from India, tells how he was shipwrecked and stranded in a lifeboat with a Bengal tiger for 227 days." Booklist

"An impassioned defense of zoos, a death-defying trans-Pacific sea adventure à la 'Kon-Tiki,' and a hilarious shaggy-dog story starring a four-hundred-and-fifty-pound Bengal tiger named Richard Parker: this audacious novel manages to be all of these. . . . This breezily aphoristic, unapologetically twee saga of man and cat is a convincing hands-on, how-to guide for dealing with what Pi calls, with typically understated brio, 'major lifeboat pests.'" New Yorker

Martha, Henry *See* Harris, Mark, 1922-

Martin, George R. R.

A clash of kings. Bantam Bks. 1999 761p (Song of ice and fire) $26.95

ISBN 0-553-10803-4 LC 98-37954

In the second title of the fantasy saga which began with A game of thrones, "a war for succession as king of the realm pits brother against brother in a battle of armies and politics. Caught in the struggle are seven noble families whose fortunes and lives depend on how well they play the game of intrigue, blackmail, kidnapping, treachery, and magic." Libr J

"The novel is notable particularly for the lived-in quality of its world, created through abundant detail that dramatically increases narrative length even as it aids suspension of disbelief; for the comparatively modest role of magic . . . and for its magnificent action-filled climax." Publ Wkly

A game of thrones. Bantam Bks. 1996 694p il o.p.

LC 95-43936

The first volume in A Song of Ice and Fire saga, "combines intrigue, action, romance, and mystery in a family saga. The family is the Starks of Winterfell, a so-

Martin, George R. R.—*Continued*

ciety in crisis due to climatic change that has created decades-long seasons, and a society almost without magic but with human perversity abundant and active. Martin reaches a new plateau in terms of narrative technique, action scenes, and integrating . . . his political views into the story." Booklist

Followed by A clash of kings

Sandkings

In The Best of the Nebulas p547-76

In The Hugo winners p70-132

A song for Lya

In The Hugo winners p483-544

Martin, Malachi

King of kings; a novel. Simon & Schuster 1981 c1980 480p o.p.

LC 80-23950

The author "manipulates almost a surfeit of material—David's endless bloody battles, his perplexing relationship with Adonai in the midst of other gods, his loves and lovers, his friends, his extended family—into a fiery mosaic of a God-haunted man who forged the settlement of Zion." Publ Wkly

"A colorful reworking and elaboration of the biblical story of King David. The great scenes from David's life . . . are played out in heroic terms as Martin paints an epic portrayal that owes more to the cinematic style of Cecil B. DeMille than it does to either the religious or literary elements of the original story." Booklist

Vatican; a novel. Harper & Row 1986 657p o.p.

LC 85-42645

The author "compresses the history of the modern Roman Catholic church into . . . the 40 years since World War II. Its focus is the highly secret inner workings of the Vatican State in Rome, a religious and political bureaucracy that affects not only its members but also individuals and events around the world. The novel opens with the arrival in Rome of Richard Lansing, who at age 24 is the youngest ranking monsignor in the powerful archdiocese of Chicago. We watch as he develops from a politically naive but dedicated religious into a papal emissary and eventually into the highest ranking leader of the Catholic church. . . . This authentic depiction of the world's richest, most powerful religion will stun readers with its revelations and intrigue them with its multitextured plot." Booklist

Windswept House; a Vatican novel. Doubleday 1996 646p o.p.

LC 95-26716

This novel about the Catholic Church in crisis focuses on the "conflict between two American brothers—one a priest, one a lawyer, both heirs to a fortune and to the family manse of Windswept House. . . . [As he develops his plot] . . . Martin's concern is what he sees as the erosion of the Church's moral authority, both from within and without. Here, a Slavic pope who's obviously John Paul II is being maneuvered into approving the Resignation Protocol, which, if enacted, will force him to resign in the name of Church unity. Martin attributes this erosion to a global conspiracy among world powers both East and West, fueled by Satanic influence and by the failure of John Paul XXIII to act upon the Third Prophecy of the Fatima Letter in 1960. The narrative is richly detailed with Church lore." Publ Wkly

Martin, Peter *See* Melville, James, 1931-

Martin, Roy Peter *See* Melville, James, 1931-

Martin, Steve, 1945-

The pleasure of my company; a novella. Hyperion 2003 163p $19.95

ISBN 0-7868-6921-6 LC 2003-49954

This work features "one of the odder yet more charming protagonists in recent fiction, Daniel Pecan Cambridge, a gentle soul suffering from a mild mix of autism and obsessive-compulsive disorder. Daniel, 33, lives in a rundown Santa Monica apartment, his life constricted by an armor of defensive habit. . . his dull days punctuated only by imagined romances and visits by his student social worker, lovely and kind Clarissa. Daniel's ways (a product of child abuse, Martin shows with subtlety) are challenged when Clarissa and her infant son, Teddy, move in to escape an abusive husband. . . . This novella is a delight, embodying a satisfying story arc, a jeweler's eye for detail, intelligent pacing and a clean, sturdy prose style." Publ Wkly

Shopgirl; a novella. Hyperion 2000 130p o.p.

ISBN 0-7868-6658-6 LC 00-38874

The main characters in this novella are Mirabelle Butterfield, "a 28-year-old woman behind the glove counter at the Neiman Marcus department store in Beverly Hills . . . and Ray Porter, the fiftysomething man Mirabelle admits into her solitary life." Time

There is "an impressive gravity about 'Shopgirl.' Its glints of comedy are sharp and dry. . . . The novella has an edge to it, and a deep, unassuageable loneliness." N Y Times Book Rev

Martin, Valerie

Italian fever; a novel. Knopf 1999 259p $22

ISBN 0-375-40542-9 LC 98-31824

"When Lucy Stark's employer falls inelegantly down a well in Tuscany, Lucy must travel there to see that he's given a decent burial. Not surprisingly, within a day she has contracted the kind of gruesome fever that makes you revel in your own health, and she has encountered the kind of Italian lover that makes you book the next flight over. What lingers in the mind, though, is the novel's final touching twist, which slyly dismantles its own satire and casts a long and mysterious shadow over everything that has come before." New Yorker

Mary Reilly. Doubleday 1990 263p o.p.

LC 89-38313

In this retelling of Robert Louis Stevenson's Dr. Jekyll and Mr. Hyde, "Mary Reilly, a loyal, trusted servant in the household of Dr. Jekyll records in her diary the mysterious circumstances which lead to her Master's tragic fate." Libr J

"Whereas the atmosphere of Robert Louis Stevenson's tale was all foggy nights and sinister uncertainties, Mary Reilly weaves a somewhat more ambiguous but equally gripping web of mystery around the same riveting events. In both cases the end product is a fascinating story." Quill Quire

Martin, Valerie—*Continued*

Property. Talese 2003 196p $23.95
ISBN 0-385-50408-X LC 2002-66846
This work "presents itself as a novel about the abuse of power within the loveless marriage between an antebellum plantation owner and his wife, their private suffering amplified by the social context of slavery. Bondage and its invitation to brutality are not unexplored terrain, but embedded within what might be mistaken as a morality play is a more subtle and compelling story—a contest of wills between two women, Manon Gaudet and Sarah, the slave she received from her aunt as a wedding gift." N Y Times Book Rev

Martin, William

Harvard Yard. Warner Bks. 2003 580p map $25.95
ISBN 0-446-53084-0 LC 2003-12329
"When antiquarian bookseller Peter Fallon follows the clues he hopes will lead him to recover a lost Shakespeare play written in the bard's own hand, he himself becomes the target of both underworld thugs and unscrupulous academics. The most compelling action takes place in the past as he traces the utterly fascinating evolution of Harvard University by interweaving it with the intimate history of one of New England's first families. . . . The unexpected twists and turns through history will keep readers guessing and the pages turning." Booklist

Martin, William, 1950-

Annapolis. Warner Bks. 1996 685p o.p.
LC 96-1021
This novel follows the fortunes of two families. "Each generation of Staffords has sent at least one son to sea since the Revolutionary War; the Parrishes, on the wrong side of the war, lost their Annapolis house to the Staffords and are still trying to get it back. Now, a distant cousin seeks to make a documentary film about the Staffords, aided by a black sheep Stafford who has been writing the family history. That history is interspersed with present-day squabbling over the property. But the predominant story is of the naval battles that the Stafford men fought, from skirmishes with pirates in Tripoli to Midway Island to the Tonkin Gulf." Libr J
"A storyteller whose smoothness equals his ambition, Martin has written a panoramic entertainment that brings to vivid life the history of the American struggle to control the high seas." Publ Wkly

Cape Cod. Warner Bks. 1991 652p o.p.
LC 90-50534
In this historical saga the author "follows two intertwined yet bitterly antagonistic families from their Pilgrim origins to the present day." Publ Wkly
"Martin embraces the entire sweep of American history with unflagging relish for authentic detail and private moments. He creates generation after generation of feisty Hilyards and cruel Bigelows, pitting them against one another in religious and political skirmishes and joining them in risky love. They endure hardships and shipwrecks, scandal and imprisonment, shame and anger, and contribute their bit to the making of America." Booklist

Martínez, Nina Marie

¡Caramba!; a tale told in turns of the card. Knopf, distributed by Random House 2004 359p il $24.95
ISBN 0-375-41375-8 LC 2003-56192
This "novel, about the wacky goings-on in small Lava Landing, CA, is written in the form of la loteria, a Mexican version of bingo. Each chapter represents a turn of the cards, in which characters play out their destinies against the backdrop of a dormant volcano. Among them are Javier, a born-again Christian mariachi; his mother, Lulabell, a practicing witch; Lucha, Javier's beloved, who wants to sell her former lover's several kilos of cocaine; and True-Dee, the transvestite beautician. Central to the narrative are Natalie and Consuelo (Nat and Sway), best friends since second grade." Libr J
"At times, ¡Caramba! transcends kitschiness and absurdity to evoke something more authentic. Natalie and Consuelo's relationship, for instance, conveys genuine intimacy, particularly in their unique brand of shorthand-speak." Washington Post Book World

Martini, Steven Paul

The attorney; [by] Steve Martini. Putnam 2000 429p $25.95
ISBN 0-399-14536-2 LC 99-44260
In this suspense novel featuring San Diego attorney Paul Madriani "lottery winner Jonah Hale's drug-addicted daughter demands a big payoff when he won't relinquish the granddaughter she left in his care, then accuses him of sexual abuse when he refuses to deliver. A famed feminist activist helps spirit away mother and daughter and then gets bumped off." Libr J
"Tense courtroom drama, plenty of action, and a deviously twisted plot." Booklist

Compelling evidence; [by] Steve Martini. Putnam 1992 379p o.p.
LC 91-30253
"Ben Potter, successful lawyer and possible U.S. Supreme Court nominee, is found dead in his office—suicide or murder? All of the police evidence points to foul play, and his beautiful young wife, Talia, stands trial for a crime she claims she didn't commit—or did she? Paul Madriani defends Talia, but, in doing so, exposes a part of his own life that he would like to forget." SLJ
"Besides giving us the scoop on ballistics analysis and post-mortem blood distribution, the author answers just about every cynical question you've ever had about the games lawyers play." N Y Times Book Rev

Critical mass; [by] Steve Martini. Putnam 1998 436p o.p.
ISBN 0-399-14362-9 LC 98-24327
"Lawyer Jocelyn 'Joss' Cole sees a big retainer when she's hired by Dean Belden to handle his company's incorporation filings. But after Belden gets a federal subpoena, Joss sees him die in a fiery seaplane explosion. Now she's the only visible link to Belden's company (which was on the receiving end of two decaying nuclear weapons smuggled into the U.S. out of Russia), and that brings her to the attention of arms inspector Gideon van Ry, of the Institute Against Mass Destruction. After the feds determine that the militia has possession of the weapons, Gideon and Joss join the race to try to avert

Martini, Steven Paul—*Continued*
nuclear disaster." Publ Wkly

"A first-rate, post-Cold War espionage thriller that touches on many hot-button themes from today's headlines: distrust of the government, public apathy, high-tech crime, and antigovernment militias." Booklist

The judge; {by} Steve Martini. Putnam 1996 389p o.p.

LC 95-41835

"Judge Armando Acosta has been summarily dismissed from the bench after being arrested on what he maintains is a trumped-up charge of soliciting a prostitute. When the key witness in the case against Acosta is found murdered and all the evidence points to Acosta as the killer, the former judge suddenly finds himself in desperate need of a tough, savvy lawyer to handle his case. An ironic set of circumstances eventually leads him to his longtime enemy Paul Madriani." Booklist

"Legal thrillers don't get much better than this." Publ Wkly

The jury; [by] Steve Martini. Putnam 2001 291p o.p.

ISBN 0-399-14672-5 LC 2001-19834

Madriani, "still struggling to establish his law practice in San Diego, is defending Dr. David Crone, a brilliant genetic researcher accused of killing colleague Kalista Jordan: her strangled and dismembered body was found washed up on a beach. Not only does all the evidence point to Crone, but his lies and deceptions are starting to test the patience of Madriani and his partner, the quick-tempered Harry Hinds. . . .[Martini] takes the moving parts of a standard plot and spins them for maximum effect." Publ Wkly

The list; {by} Steve Martini. Putnam 1997 438p o.p.

LC 96-46410

A novel about "attorney-turned-novelist Abby Chandlis, who stretches the practice of ghost-writing to an extreme and perilous level. Fearful that glamour instead of grammar sells books in today's shallow publishing industry, Chandlis creates Gable Cooper, a strong, handsome, but definitely fictitious alter ego who as 'author' of her new novel should assure its success. Possessed of these qualities, rugged Jack Jermaine seems ideal for the role. However, his spooky past and dangerous tendencies soon cause Abby to regret the entire scheme." Libr J

The author "clearly had a good time writing this fanciful book, in which he manages to incorporate multiple settings, invent gossamer disguises for important publishing personalities and skewer the machinery that produces blockbuster books." Publ Wkly

Prime witness; [by] Steve Martini. Putnam 1993 384p o.p.

LC 93-16908

"When attorney Paul Madriani offers to assist a friend—the county's ailing district attorney, who subsequently dies—in investigating six brutal killings, he becomes entangled in a series of machinations that threaten his career and even his private life." Publ Wkly

"The novel effectively relays the great demands of being a district attorney and also depicts the behind-the-scenes maneuverings of a trial." Booklist

Undue influence; [by] Steve Martini. Putnam 1994 462p o.p.

LC 94-10144

"Recently widowered lawyer Paul Madriani has problems with his sister-in-law Laurel. She is involved in a nasty custody trial, and then she is arrested for the murder of her ex-husband's new wife. After Paul agrees to represent her, he gets sucked into a vipers' tangle involving Laurel, her two children, her ex-husband, a beautiful attorney, a bombing, and mistaken identities." Libr J

"The action builds to a rousing climax through a brilliant series of trial scenes with several surprises. The characters are sharply drawn, the facts of the case are presented simply and the courtroom psychology is laid out vividly." Publ Wkly

Marut, Ret *See* Traven, B.

Mason, Bobbie Ann

Feather crowns. HarperCollins Pubs. 1993 454p o.p.

LC 92-56227

This novel "tells the story of Chrissie Wheeler, a tobacco farmer's wife in Hopewell, Kentucky, who, in 1900, gives birth to America's first recorded quintuplets. Curiosity seekers pass in a steady stream through the Wheeler's small farmhouse. When the babies take ill and die, Chrissie and her husband are persuaded to go on tour, displaying the grotesquely painted bodies of the dead infants to the idly curious." Libr J

"Mason's triumph here is to make her uneducated, bewildered heroine as vivid as the country life she describes." Publ Wkly

In country; a novel. Harper & Row 1985 247p o.p.

LC 85-42579

"Sam, 17, is obsessed with the Vietnam War and the effect it has had on her life—losing a father she never knew and now living with Uncle Emmett, who seems to be suffering from the effects of Agent Orange. In her own forthright way, she tries to sort out why and how Vietnam has altered the lives of the vets of Hopewell, Kentucky. . . . A harshly realistic, well-written look at the Vietnam War as well as the story of a young woman maturing." SLJ

Love life; stories. Harper & Row 1989 241p o.p.

LC 88-45535

Contents: Love life; Midnight magic; Hunktown; Marita; The secret of the Pyramids; Piano fingers; Bumblebees; Big Bertha stories; State champions; Private lies; Coyotes; Airwaves; Sorghum; Memphis; Wish

"Moments of insight emerge in Mason's stories as her Kentuckian characters encounter life's twists and turns. . . . The immediacy of these stories comes not just from Mason's frequent use of the present tense, or her often-criticized references to Wal-Mart and MTV, but, most of all, from her impressive ability to cut to the innermost emotions of a wide range of characters." SLJ

Midnight magic; selected stories of Bobbie Ann Mason; selected & introduced by the author. Ecco Press 1998 301p o.p.

ISBN 0-88001-595-0 LC 97-36369

Mason, Bobbie Ann—*Continued*

Contents: Midnight magic; Bumblebees; The retreat; Love life; Big Bertha stories; Shiloh; Offerings; Drawing names; Coyotes; Residents and transients; Sorghum; Nancy Culpepper; Graveyard day; A new-wave format; Third Monday; Wish; Memphis

This "is a selection of 17 stories drawn from 'Shiloh and Other Stories,' the 1982 debut collection . . . and it's 1989 successor, 'Love life.' The book's characters live in the brave new world of strip malls and franchised food that is the New—or, rather, the New New—South. Most of them are Baptists, and they take the old strictures seriously, even though they're hardly able to live by them." N Y Times Book Rev

Shiloh and other stories; with a foreword by George Ella Lyon. University Press of Ky. 1995 247p $19.95

ISBN 0-8131-1948-0 LC 95-16581

A reissue of the title first published 1982 by Harper & Row

Contents: Shiloh; The rookers; Detroit Skyline, 1949; Offerings; Still life with watermelon; Old things; Drawing names; The climber; Residents and transients; The retreat; The ocean; Graveyard day; Nancy Culpepper; Lying doggo; A new-wave format; Third Monday

"Capturing in vivid detail the emotional frustrations of her characters and the unsettling ambience of her small-town Kentucky settings, Mason portrays the uneasy feelings of people who don't know what they want out of life but who do know that what they have isn't it." Booklist

Zigzagging down a wild trail; stories. Random House 2001 209p $22.95

ISBN 0-679-44924-8 LC 00-66480

Contents: With jazz; Tobrah; Tunica; Thunder snow; Rolling into Atlanta; Three-wheeler; The funeral side; Window lights; Proper gypsies; Night flight; Charger

The author's terrain is "the Kentucky she's famous for writing about, but she has succeeded in making rural America seem exotic, strange, and mysterious, a looking-glass world. This lends a shimmering aura to each expertly rendered, boldly open-ended tale." Booklist

Mason, Daniel

The piano tuner. Knopf 2002 317p $24

ISBN 0-375-41465-7 LC 2002-19069

In this novel, set in 1886, the author "sends piano tuner Edgar Drake deep into Burma. The British War Office, in an attempt to placate one of their key people, has requested the services of Drake to repair a grand piano. Army Sergeant-Major Anthony Carroll has a unique approach to keeping the peace in the southern Shan States—he uses poetry, music, and medicine to establish diplomatic connections with the community and their rulers. . . . Drake is drawn into Carroll's political scheme." Booklist

"Mason proves himself equally adept at scenes of wry humor and moments of rapture; most remarkable, he has written a profound adventure story with an unexpected climax, as the mild piano tuner finally becomes the hero of his own life." New Yorker

Mason, Richard, 1919-1997

The world of Suzie Wong. World Pub. 1957 344p o.p.

The love story of an impecunious English painter and a charming Chinese prostitute. Robert, not understanding Chinese, takes a room in a Hong Kong hotel thinking he has found a cheap boarding house. When it becomes apparent to him that it is a house of prostitution he stays on, partly to paint the girls, and partly because he cannot afford anything better. It is here he meets Suzie

"Though the book may be a little distasteful to some readers it is never sordid or unwholesome. Suzie and the other girls have a high moral code— in their fashion." Libr J

Massey, Sujata

The pearl diver; Sujata Massey. 1st ed. HarperCollins 2004 335p $23.95

ISBN 0-06-621296-0 LC 2003-67614

Japanese American antiques dealer Rei Shimura's "assignment to furnish a new Japanese restaurant in Washington yields wonderful detail about Asian cuisines and the multicultural kitchen workers who prepare them. The narrative dovetails nicely with a moving subplot about a war bride who in her native Japan had been an ama-san, a female shellfish diver, until both stories are swamped by blow-by-blow updates on the heroine's personal life and a smelly red herring about Washington politics. There are still lessons to be learned from the uncluttered and serene lines of Japanese art." N Y Times Book Rev

Massie, Allan, 1938-

Caesar. Carroll & Graf Pubs. 1994 c1993 228p o.p.

LC 94-26430

One of the author's novels set in ancient Rome; previous titles Let the emperor speak (1987) and Tiberius (1993)

First published 1993 in the United Kingdom

"Decimus Junius Brutus, a Roman general and one of Julius Caesar's closest friends, was one of the conspirators who killed Caesar on the Ides of March in 44 B.C. In this fictional memoir written while awaiting his death in Gaul, Brutus (cousin to the better known Marcus Junius Brutus) attempts to justify the murder by recounting Caesar's ever-growing lust for total power and his unbecoming desire to outshine Alexander the Great. Brutus and his friends believe that Caesar's megalomania has led him to betray the Roman Senate and destroy the Republic." Libr J

This work "offers an evocative portrait of ancient Rome as well as a gripping and suspenseful analysis of the most intriguing conspiracy of all time. Superb historical fiction." Booklist

Master's choice [v1]-2: mystery stories by today's top writers and the masters who inspired them; edited by Lawrence Block. Berkley Prime Crime 1999 2v v1 $21.95; pa $5.99; v2 pa $7.50

ISBN 0-425-17031-4 (v1); 0-425-17803-X (v1 pa); 0-425-18225-8 (v2 pa) LC 99-30270

Master's choice [v1]-2: mystery stories by today's top writers and the masters who inspired them—*Continued*

These volumes pair stories chosen as personal favorites by some of the genre's top crime-fiction writers with a story of their own. Among the authors represented are Joe Gores, Sharyn McCrumb, Stuart Kaminsky, Stanley Ellin, and Joyce Carrol Oates

Matheson, Richard, 1926-

Hunted past reason. Forge 2002 335p $24.95

ISBN 0-7653-0271-3 LC 2001-50768

"A Tom Doherty Associates book"

"Two old friends, Bob (a novelist) and Doug (an actor), head off into the woods for a short hiking trip. Bob wants some hands-on experience for a novel he's working on; Doug is an expert in woodsmanship. From the get-go, there is tension between them: Doug seems excessively demanding; Bob reacts a little too sharply to his friend's criticisms of his stamina and abilities. Soon the mood turns dark, transforming the story into a psychological thriller." Booklist

Mathews, Francine

Death in a cold hard light. Bantam Bks. 1998 323p o.p.

LC 97-44253

"While visiting her future in-laws, Nantucket police detective Meredith ('Merry') Folger gets an urgent call from John Folger, her father and Nantucket chief of police. He needs help investigating the apparent drowning of Jay Santorski, a young scalloper. Santorski's death sets off a nor'easter of emotion and crime. . . . Mathews sustains a nail-biting pace to the finale, which takes place in a mansion on a stormy December night. Dialogue crackles, and most of the characters are well rounded." Booklist

Death in a mood indigo. Bantam Bks. 1997 294p o.p.

LC 96-48324

"Detective Meredith Folger of the Nantucket police relishes the thought of solving an eight-year-old murder, especially since the initial missing person's investigation was flubbed by an incompetent. Meredith feels that she 'owes' the dead woman, a prominent female psychiatrist, some kind of resolution, regardless of their impact on her children." Libr J

Mathews, Harry

My life in CIA; a chronicle of 1973. Dalkey Archive Press 2005 203p pa $13.95

ISBN 1-56478-392-8 LC 2004-63478

"Novelist Mathews, an American living in Paris circa 1973, can't convince his French artistic friends he is not a CIA agent, so he resolves to fake the part—it beats soaking up idle time by learning ancient Greek, he thinks. Knowing a spy needs cover, Mathews sets up as 'international travel counsel,' and the audience attending his seminar yields several recruiting prospects. 'Patrick,' also in the consultancy 'business,' develops into Mathews' boon companion to whom he confides his charade. A second prospect from that seminar (a Russian) becomes the plot's vehicle for eliding Mathews from a world of fantasy espionage into something more real, and menacing. Strangers contact him; he accepts a courier mission; Patrick vanishes; the Soviet embassy summons him, as does French counterintelligence, which warns Mathews a Stasi assassin is pursuing him. Evolving in mood from ludicrous to serious, the yarn's inventive literary elements elegantly mesh into a stylish amusement." Booklist

Matthiessen, Peter

Bone by bone. Random House 1999 410p $26.95

ISBN 0-375-50102-9 LC 98-46180

In this final volume in the trilogy about E.J. Watson, "Matthiessen has given us Watson's own story in Watson's own words. . . . That story goes right back to Civil War days in South Carolina, and the terrible childhood E.J. endured at the hands of his drunken, brutal and rascally father and his remote and vindictive mother. Thus were laid the seeds of the later outbursts of violence and rage that so frequently punctuated what should have been a promising life. For Watson, as he portrays himself, is ambitious, hardworking and ever ingenious at figuring ways to make the remote Florida Everglades shores yield riches—a true pioneer spirit." Publ Wkly

Far Tortuga. Random House 1975 408p il o.p.

"Far Tortuga is the name given by West Indian turtle-fishing men to a remote inlet south of Cuba that is not found on modern charts. . . . To hunt the last turtles of the season Capt. Raib Avers sails from Grand Cayman island with a ragged crew in an even more ragged boat, the [Lillias] Eden. . . . The boat tacks about the cays and reefs off the coast of Nicaragua. It is too late to find more than a few turtles. As discord and desperation mount, the crew talks about better days: the folklore of hurricanes and pirate captains, of shipwrecks, ghosts and 'wild niggers' smuggled into Florida. . . . Avers, as a last gamble, strikes out for Far Tortuga." Newsweek

"Almost casually, we have been given a full measure of suspense, adventure, and first-rate descriptive writing; and along with and underneath these things, a group of characters who come fully alive with a complexity and even depth that the usual, traditional story of men at sea never gives us." Choice

Killing Mister Watson. Random House 1990 372p o.p.

LC 89-43424

This historical novel "traces the growth of the legend of Edgar J. Watson, a famed outlaw in the Florida Everglades of a hundred years ago." Voice Lit Suppl

"By the time he was murdered, Watson was one of the most successful sugar-cane farmers between Tampa and Key West. Everyone liked and admired him, but no one trusted him. Proof was always scant but people wound up dead when Watson was around. . . . Matthiessen tells his story through the voice of Watson's family and neighbors in a series of oral histories, diary entries and old newspaper accounts, all of it fiction. By turns droll, rambunctious, foolish and wise, this collective narration mounts into a carefully orchestrated cacophony of contradictory testimony in which suspicion and mistrust are gradually revealed as the base elements of mystery." Newsweek

Followed by Lost Man's River

Matthiessen, Peter—*Continued*

Lost Man's River. Random House 1997 539p o.p.

LC 97-10124

In this sequel to Killing Mister Watson, "Lucius Watson, who has spent most of his life on the move, returns home to try to separate the truths from the myths of his father's killing, forty years earlier. A good part of Mathiessen's sprawling, uneven, novel comes straight from the characters' own mouths, but his ample skills as a naturalist and a journalist are in evidence, too. The Watson story is bound up in the landscape and the bloody history of the region, where gator poaching has given way to gunrunning, and where, nearly a hundred years after Reconstruction, racism is still as firmly rooted and as common as mangroves." New Yorker

Followed by Bone by bone

On the river Styx and other stories. Random House 1989 208p o.p.

LC 86-3206

Six of the stories included in this collection originally appeared in book form in Midnight turning gray, published 1984 in paperback by Ampersand Press

Contents: Sadie; The fifth day; The centerpiece; Late in the season; Travelin man; The wolves of Aguila; Horse latitudes; Midnight turning gray; On the River Styx; Lumumba lives

Matthiessen's "stories delve into brutal facets of humankind and show the often hapless responses of well-intentioned individuals. Bitter scenes of racism are portrayed in several stories, including the title piece, in which a white couple on an innocuous fishing vacation sparks a violent racial backlash." Booklist

Mattison, Alice

The wedding of the two-headed woman. Morrow 2004 275p $23.95

ISBN 0-06-621378-9

"Fifty-something Daisy Andalusia sorts and organizes the clutter of her New Haven, Conn., neighbors for a living, a profession that perfectly complements her affinity for secrets. Married to a man she's not sure she loves, she becomes romantically involved with a client entirely unlike her husband. A tabloid headline she reads while at work, "Two-Headed Woman Weds Two Men," accounts for the title of the book, inspires a community theater production that establishes new and unexpected bonds among its participants and illustrates Daisy's dual role as wife and lover." Publ Wkly

"Mattison's voice is intelligent, spare and without pretense. She lays out Daisy's story in a way that makes it seem as if not much is happening, while quietly weaving in four or five intriguing subplots, including a murder mystery, a rent strike and, toward the end, Sept. 11. All these stories press in on Daisy in some meaningful way, each playing a role in her quest to come to terms with herself." Washington Post

Maturin, Charles Robert, 1782-1824

Melmoth the wanderer; edited with and introduction and notes by Victor Sage. Penguin Books 2000 xxxi, 659p pa $12

ISBN 0-14-044761-x LC 2001-265474

First published 1820 in the United Kingdom

This novel "was in effect the last, and also one of the most effective, of the 'Gothic' school. The tale rushes energetically through every kind of horror and iniquity, and has moments of genuine power. Melmoth, who has sold his soul for the promise of prolonged life, offers relief from suffering to each of the characters, whose terrible stories succeed one another, if they will take over his bargain with the Devil. But Stanton, imprisoned in the cell of a raving lunatic; Moncada in the hands of the Inquisition; Walberg, who sees his children dying of hunger; and many other sufferers, all reject the proposed bargain." Oxford Companion to Engl Lit. 6th edition

Maugham, Somerset *See* Maugham, W. Somerset (William Somerset), 1874-1965

Maugham, W. Somerset (William Somerset), 1874-1965

The best short stories of W. Somerset Maugham; selected, and with an introduction by John Beecroft. Modern Lib. 1957 489p o.p.

Contents: The letter; The verger; The vessel of wrath; The hairless Mexican; Mr. Harrington's washing; Red; Mr. Know-All; The alien corn; The bookbag; The round dozen; The voice of the turtle; The facts of life; Lord Mountdrago; The colonel's lady; The treasure; Rain; P. & O.

Cakes and ale; or, The skeleton in the cupboard. Doubleday, Doran 1930 308p o.p.

This novel, Maugham's "most genial book, is a comedy about the good-natured Rosie Driffield, the wife of a Grand Old Man of Letters; whom most took to be based on Hardy; Alroy Kear, a self-promoting writer, was recognized as Hugh Walpole." Oxford Companion to Engl Lit. 5th edition

Complete short stories. Doubleday 1952 2v o.p.

Contents: v 1: Rain; Fall of Edward Barnard; Mackintosh; Red; Honolulu; The pool; The letter; Before the party; Force of circumstance; The outstation; Yellow streak; P. & O.; Jane Round dozen; Creative impulse; Miss King; Hairless Mexican; Giulia Lazzari; The traitor; His Excellency; Mr. Harrington's washing; Footprints in the jungle; Human element; Virtue; Alien corn; The book-bag; Vessel of wrath; Door of opportunity; Back of beyond; Neil MacAdam

v2: Woman of fifty; Man with the scar; The bum; Closed shop; Official position; Man with a conscience; French Joe; German Harry; Four Dutchmen; End of the flight; Flotsam and Jetsam; Casual affair; Mr. Know-All; Straight flush; Portrait of a gentleman; Raw material; Friend in need; The dream; The taipan; The consul; Mirage; Mabel Masterson; Marriage of convenience; Princess September; In a strange land; Lotus eater; Salvatore; Washtub; Mayhew; Happy man; Point of honour; The mother; Romantic young lady; The poet; Man from Glasgow; Lion's skin, Three fat women of Antibes; Happy couple; Voice of the turtle; Facts of life; Gigolo and gigolette; Appearance and reality; The luncheon; The unconquered; Ant and the grasshopper; Home; The escape; Judgment seat; Sanatorium; Louise; Lord Mountdrago; String of beads; The promise; The verger; Social sense; Colonel's lady; Episode; The kite; The treasure; Winter cruise

Maugham, W. Somerset (William Somerset), 1874-1965—*Continued*

East and West
In Maugham, W. S. Complete short stories

The moon and sixpence. Doran, G.H. 1919 314p o.p.

"Based closely on the life of Paul Gauguin it tells of Charles Strickland, a conventional London stockbroker, who in middle life suddenly decides to desert his wife, family, and business in order to become a painter. He goes to paint in Tahiti, where he takes a native mistress. Eventually Strickland dies of leprosy." Reader's Ency. 4th edition

Of human bondage; introduction by Gore Vidal. Modern Library 1999 xxxix, 611p pa $11.95
ISBN 0-375-75315-X LC 98-46169
First published 1915

This novel's "hero is Philip Carey, a sensitive, talented, club-footed orphan who is brought up by an unsympathetic aunt and uncle. It is a study of his struggle for independence, his intellectual development, and his attempt to become an artist. Philip gets entangled and obsessed by his love affair with Mildred, a waitress. After years of struggle as a medical student, he marries a nice woman, gives up his aspirations, and becomes a country doctor. The first part of the novel is partly autobiographical, and the book is regarded as Maugham's best work." Reader's Ency. 4th edition

The razor's edge. Doubleday 1944 343p o.p.

"The novel is concerned in large part with the search for the meaning of life and with the dichotomy between materialism and spirituality. The main focus of the story is on Larry Darrell, who has returned from service as an aviator in World War I utterly rejecting his prewar values. He is concerned chiefly with discovering the meaning of human existence and eliminating evil in the world. To that end, he spends five years in India seeking—but not finding—answers." Merriam-Webster's Ency of Lit

World over
In Maugham, W. S. Complete short stories

Maugham, William Somerset *See* Maugham, W. Somerset (William Somerset), 1874-1965

Maupassant, Guy de, 1850-1893

The collected stories of Guy de Maupassant. Avenel Bks. 1985 10v in 1 1003p o.p.
LC 84-20316

A reissue of the 1903 edition published by Walter Black, Inc. with title: The complete short stories of Guy de Maupassant

The dark side of Guy de Maupassant; a selection and translation by Arnold Kellett with introduction and notes; foreword by Ramsey Campbell. Carroll & Graf Pubs. 1989 252p o.p.
LC 89-511

Contents: The Horla; The Devil; Two friends; Fear; The hand; Coco; The mannerism; The madwoman; Mohammed-Fripouille; The blind man; At sea; Apparition; Saint-Antoine; The wolf; Terror; The diary of a madman; A vendetta; The smile of Schopenhauer; On the river; He?; Old Milon; The head of hair; The inn; Mother Savage; Was he mad?; The dead girl; Mademoiselle Cocotte; A night in Paris; The case of Louise Roque; The drowned man; Who knows?

Maurois, André, 1885-1967

The collected stories of André Maurois; translated by Adrienne Foulke. Washington Sq. Press 1967 396p o.p.

Contents: Reality transposed; Darling, good evening; Lord of the shadows; Ariane, my sister . . . ; Home port; Myrrhine; Biography; Thanatos Palace Hotel; Friends; Dinner under the chestnut trees; Bodies and souls; The curse of gold; For piano alone; The departure; The fault of M. Balzac; Love in exile; Wednesday's violets; A career; Ten years later; Tidal wave; Transference; Flowers in season; The will; The campaign; The life of man; The Corinthian porch; The Cathedral; The ants; The postcard; Poor Maman; The green belt; The Neuilly Fair; The birth of a master; Black masks; Irene; The letters; The cuckoo; The house

Mawer, Simon, 1948-

The fall; a novel. Little, Brown 2002 370p $24.95
ISBN 0-316-09780-2 LC 2002-73193

"The book takes as its starting point the horrible accident of its title, with James Matthewson, a renowned but now middle-aged mountain climber, tumbling from the face of a Welsh cliff that he should not have been attempting by himself. He dies almost instantly, leaving behind a widow, an estranged best friend and a number of mysteries, among them why he would be climbing such a difficult route without ropes or a helmet. Could the veteran climber have been trying to commit suicide? It's a question for which the bulk of the novel is designed to provide an answer" N Y Times Book Rev

"Intricately weaving time and place, from the bombed-out ruins of World War II London to isolated Alpine mountain peaks, Mawer crafts a sinuously devastating tale of foridden love and faithless betrayal. A haunting and mesmerizing novel from an expert storyteller." Booklist

Maxwell, Robin, 1948-

The Queen's bastard; a novel. Arcade Pub. 1999 436p $24.95
ISBN 1-55970-475-6 LC 98-50502
Sequel to The secret diary of Anne Boleyn

"The reader is asked to believe that Queen Elizabeth I gave birth secretly to a boy, Arthur, son of Robin Dudley, Earl of Leicester, and that loyal servants tricked these parents into thinking their baby was stillborn. To save the queen's honor, Arthur was spirited away and raised by a trusted country gentleman." Libr J

"Arthur's first person narration is cleverly juxtaposed with third-person dramatization of significant events in the queen's life. . . . Maxwell's research examines the biographical gaps in, and documented facts about, the queen's life, making this incredible tale plausible, and the author aptly embellishes her story with rich period details and the epic dramas of the late 16th century." Publ Wkly

Maxwell, Robin, 1948—*Continued*

The secret diary of Anne Boleyn. Arcade Pub. 1997 281p o.p.

ISBN 1-55970-375-X LC 96-49275

This "novel supposes that Anne Boleyn, second wife of King Henry VIII of England, kept a secret diary that was delivered to her daughter, Elizabeth, upon her succession to the throne. Elizabeth was only three when Anne was renounced by Henry, tried for treason, and sentenced to death. Now, despite her queenly schedule, juggling affairs of state and heart, Elizabeth finds time to read her mother's story avidly and learns lessons that will secure her reign." Libr J

"Painting vicious court intrigue, national and international politics and the role of the Reformation, Maxwell brings not only the two queens but all of bloody Tudor England vividly to life." Publ Wkly

Followed by The Queen's bastard

The wild Irish; Robin Maxwell. 1st ed. William Morrow 2003 393p $24.95

ISBN 0-06-009142-8 LC 2003-42184

"When Grace O'Mally, passionate clan chieftain and legendary Irish pirate, visits the court of Elizabeth I to plead for the release of her imprisoned son, the two most extraordinary women of their time find they have much in common. As Grace relates her incredible life and times to Elizabeth, the aging Bess also revisits her own often tragic past. Caught between these two powerful and magnetic females, Elizabeth's favorite courtier and one-time lover, Robert Devereaux, earl of Essex, is inexorably drawn into the tangled web of the Irish rebellion. . . . Superbly crafted, this dynamic tale brings a host of historical characters vividly to life." Booklist

Maxwell, William, 1908-2000

All the days and nights; the collected stories of William Maxwell. Knopf 1995 415p o.p.

LC 94-27509

Contents: Over by the river; The Trojan women; The pilgrimage; The patterns of love; What every boy should know; A game of chess; The French scarecrow; Young Francis Whitehead; A final report; Haller's second home; The gardens of Mont-Saint-Michel; The value of money; The thistles in Sweden; The poor orphan girl; The lily-white boys; Billie Dyer; Love; The man in the moon; With reference to an incident at a bridge; My father's friends; The front and the back parts of the house; The holy terror; What he was like; A love story; The industrious tailor; The country where nobody ever grew old and died; The fisherman who had nobody to go out in his boat with him; The two women friends; The carpenter; The man who had no friends and didn't want any; A fable begotten of an echo of a line of verse by W.B. Yeats; The blue finch of Arabia; The sound of waves; The woman who never drew breath except to complain; The masks; The man who lost his father; The old woman whose house was beside a running stream; The pessimistic fortune-teller; The printing office; The lamplighter; The kingdom where straightforward, logical thinking was admired over every other kind; The old man at the railroad crossing; A mean and spiteful toad; All the days and nights

May, Julian, 1931-

The adversary. Houghton Mifflin 1984 xxxviii, 470p il (Saga of Pliocene exile, v4) o.p.

LC 83-49065

"In this concluding volume of the quartet, King Aiken and the children of the telepathic rebels, exiled from the future Milieu, must fight against Marc Remillard and his allies, the Firvulag. This book will be barely intelligible to those unfamiliar with the rest of the saga—despite May's extensive synopsis—but it should keep the author's regular readers turning pages." Booklist

Intervention, a novel linking the Saga of Pliocene exile with the Galactic Milieu trilogy was published in 1987

Blood Trillium. Bantam Bks. 1992 391p o.p.

LC 92-2888

Second in a fantasy series that started with Black Trillium by Marion Zimmer Bradley, Julian May, and Andre Norton

"The kingdom of Laboruwenda finds itself on the verge of war as a sorcerer thought to be dead returns to reclaim the three talismans of power held by Queen Anigel and her sisters, Kadiya and Haramis." Libr J

"A superior tale, giving life, character and emotion to the three Petals of the Living Trillium as they continue their adventures." Publ Wkly

Followed by Golden Trillium by Andre Norton

Diamond mask; a novel. Knopf 1994 461p o.p.

LC 93-37802

The second book in the Galactic Milieu trilogy is "set in the year 2113 and told through the memoirs of Rogatien Remillard, the story looks back on events that took place half a century earlier, when humanity became part of a vast galactic civilization. Remillard's family, virtually immortal and psychically gifted, has become Earth's most powerful force. On the death of the evil Victor Remillard in 2040, an insane metapsychic creature known as Fury comes into being." Publ Wkly

The author "maintains a personal focus on her luminary characters, opening their private lives to intense scrutiny while at the same time expanding the boundaries of an imaginative future world. Rich in intrigue and vibrating with creative energy, this is a superb addition to sf collections." Libr J

Followed by Magnificat

The golden torc. Houghton Mifflin 1982 xxv, 381p il (Saga of Pliocene exile, v2) o.p.

LC 81-4126

"In this second volume of the saga, May continues the story of the diverse group of time-exiles we met in the first book and shows how they help to bring about the overthrow of the Tanu and the closing of the time gate. . . . May develops her premises seriously and gives her large cast of characters a surprising amount of life." Publ Wkly

Followed by The nonborn king

Jack the bodiless; a novel. Knopf 1992 463p o.p.

LC 91-53176

This is the first volume of the Galactic Milieu trilogy describing events that precipitated the action of the author's Saga of Pliocene exile tetralogy. "As a consortium of five alien races stands ready to accept Earth as a full partner in the Galactic Milieu, the birth of a very special

May, Julian, 1931—*Continued*
child heralds a new stage in human evolution. . . . May combines a compelling vision of humanity's future with the drama and political intrigue surrounding the Remillard family, whose metapsychic powers and personal ambitions shape the destiny of the world." Libr J

Followed by Diamond mask

Magnificat; a novel. Knopf 1996 427p o.p.
LC 95-35088

Concluding volume of the author's Galactic Milieu trilogy. "As human rebellion against the unified mind of the Galactic Milieu intensifies, the psychically powerful Remillard family races against time to find and destroy the murderous Fury. Fascinating characters enhance an intricate and thoughtfully executed plot. [A] satisfying end to a remarkable feat of the imagination." Libr J

The many-colored land. Houghton Mifflin 1981 415p (Saga of Pliocene exile, v1) o.p.

In this first volume of a four part saga "a one-way, fixed-focus time portal to Europe in the Pliocene epoch allows the prehistoric past to become a last frontier and a refuge for misfits fed up with the well-ordered world of the 22nd century. This novel follows the adventures of a group newly arrived in Exile. They are prepared for almost anything but what they actually find, a world ruled by humanoid aliens who can control them with artificially augmented psionic powers. The arrogant, beautiful Tanu are opposed, however, by the ugly, outcast Firvulag. Allied with them the humans may hope to overthrow the Tanu and win the freedom they came for. Deftly combining SF and the Celtic myths of the Tuatha de Danaan, Julian May has made a most enjoyable entertainment that will have readers eagerly turning pages." Publ Wkly

Followed by The golden torc

The nonborn king. Houghton Mifflin 1983 xli, 394p il (Saga of Pliocene exile, v3) o.p.
LC 82-11950

"There is a new balance of power among the 22nd century's voluntary exiles to the Europe of 6-million years ago and the two factions of aliens (Tanu and Firvulag) they found waiting for them there. The humans are no longer slaves, and one of them, a trickster upstart named Aiken Drum, becomes the Tanu king. A new element is introduced in the form of yet another group of (involuntary) exiles, the remnants of the Metapsychic Rebellion of 2083. Beams of mental force clash spectacularly as Aiken seeks their help against Felice, the mad psychic prodigy, and in defending his throne against Tanu traditionalists." Publ Wkly

Followed by The adversary

(jt. auth) Bradley, M. Z. Black Trillium

Mayle, Peter

Anything considered. Knopf 1996 303p $23
ISBN 0-679-44123-9 LC 96-5761

This novel's "protagonist is Bennett, a Brit expatriate on his uppers. Having lost his savings in an investment scam, he is intent on finding the means to reside in Saint-Martin in Provence. He advertises his services: 'Anything considered except marriage'—and is hired by Julian Poe, a stupendously wealthy fellow Brit, who needs help in evading the French income tax. Pretending to be Poe in the latter's Monaco apartment, Bennett becomes involved in the hijacking of a case containing the secret formula for the successful cultivation of the elusive black truffle." Publ Wkly

Mayle has "written an entertaining thriller that moves along apace, but his loyal readers need not worry. Much of his raw material is familiar: wonderful meals decribed in succulent detail; vintage wines, all named to stimulate fantasy; and a rich assortment of French 'characters.'" NY Times Book Rev

Chasing Cézanne. Knopf 1997 295p $23
ISBN 0-679-45511-6 LC 97-71925

"When the photographer Andre Kelly, fresh from a shoot in the south of France, stumbles across a handyman loading a Cézanne onto a plumber's van outside a villa in Cap Ferrat, he uncovers a plot that will nearly cost him his life. It will also lead him to discover true love—but before it does, he must deal with an obnoxious magazine editor, a ruthlessly conniving art trader and a bumbling hit man." N Y Times Book Rev

"The trail to the lost Cézanne becomes a comedy of errors. Along the way, there are vibrant descriptions of Paris, Provence, Cap Ferrat, and of course mouthwatering French meals and wine. Part travelog and part art mystery caper, this . . . is a thoroughly enjoyable romp through the international art world." Libr J

A good year. Knopf 2004 287p $24
ISBN 0-375-40591-7 LC 2003-65674

"On the very day his boss steals his biggest account and maneuvers him out of his job in London's financial district, Max Skinner learns that he's inherited his uncle's vineyard in Provence. Unfortunately, the place is rundown and–worse–the wine it produces is awful. But what about the small plot at the edge of the vineyard that his caretaker badmouths and the private-label 'garage wine' being sold oh-so-discreetly in Bordeaux for $40,000 a case? Then there's the unexpected visit of Californian Christie Roberts, who knows a thing or two about wine herself and may have a valid claim to the estate. Though his plot is predictable, Mayle juggles complications, chicanery, and romance with entertaining and informative tidbits about wine-and his Provence never fails to charm." Libr J

Hotel Pastis; a novel of Provence. Knopf 1993 389p o.p.
LC 93-14641

"Encouraged by a sprightly young Frenchwoman, burned-out advertising executive Simon Shaw buys the local gendarmerie in Luberon, France and turns it into a hotel. Unfortunately, the visitors who crowd the town once the hotel opens include an escaped thief intent on a bank robbery." Libr J

The author "displays his satiric eye for social foibles by skewering advertising execs in England and the U.S.; he is equally adept at evoking typical Provencal villagers. Wickedly sharp and sympathetic at the same time, his characterizations are accurate down to nuances of class differences, voice, accent and vocabulary." Publ Wkly

Maynard, Joyce, 1953-

The usual rules. St. Martin's Press 2003 390p $24.95
ISBN 0-312-24261-1 LC 2002-36754

Maynard, Joyce, 1953-—*Continued*
"The novel is about a thirteen-year-old girl whose mother dies in the World Trade Center on September 11. . . . Not long after that, [her] ne'erdowell biological dad (Peter Pan) shows up and whisks Wendy off with him to California." Women's Rev Books
"Wendy is a real teen and her decisions are correct for her and the young woman she is becoming. This well paced novel looks forward positively rather than backward with anguish, and will reward those who pick it up." SLJ

Mayo, Jim, 1908-1988
For works written by this author under other names see L'Amour, Louis, 1908-1988

Mayor, Archer

The marble mask. Mysterious Press 2000 309p o.p.
ISBN 0-89296-723-4 LC 00-40117
Brattleboro's Joe Gunther has become field commander of the newly formed Vermont Bureau of Investigation. "Designed to be 'a small, elite unit' composed of the cream from Vermont's 68 separate law enforcement agencies, the VBI exists only on paper until the frozen body of a hiker is found on Mt. Mansfield. The 'hiker,' Jean Deschamps of Sherbrooke, Quebec, turns out to be a very unusual homicide victim. . . . Deschamps was head of a notorious crime family in Sherbrooke until his unexplained disappearance in 1947. His reappearance threatens to disrupt a fragile peace between that family, now headed by Deschamps's son, Marcel, and the Sherbrooke Hells Angels. . . . This is a thoroughly entertaining police procedural." Publ Wkly

Occam's razor. Mysterious Press 1999 339p $30
ISBN 0-89296-682-3 LC 99-26221
In this novel Lieutenant Joe Gunther of Brattleboro, Vermont, and his investigators "have to deal with the murder of a man left unconscious on a railroad track, the knifing death of a woman living on the fringes of the law and a series of phone calls that implicate an ambitious politician in both crimes." Publ Wkly
"As a stylist, Mayor is one of those meticulous construction workers who are fascinated by the way things function. He's the boss man on procedures, and he loves to poke around in whatever complicated mechanism is making all the wheels turn." N Y Times Book Rev

The sniper's wife. Mysterious Press 2002 312p $23.95
ISBN 0-89296-767-6 LC 2002-67183
This mystery delves into the troubled past of "Detective Willy Kunkle, of Joe Gunther's Vermont Bureau of Investigation. When Kunkle learns that his ex-wife Mary overdosed on heroin in Manhattan, he hastens there to identify her body. Suspecting murder, he convinces Ward Ogfden, a high-ranking NYPD detective, to reopen the case. In tracing Mary's life in New York, Kunkle revisits his own Manhattan childhood, membership in the NYPD, the trauma of Vietnam and strained relations with his dysfunctional family. When he's arrested during a raid on an illegal club, Joe and detective Sammie Martens, Kunkle's lover, come to New York, and the two country cops prove they're as astute as their city counterparts." Publ Wkly
"Mayor writes a tough story for his tortured protagonist, and the unfamiliar setting brings out a new, edge-of-the-knife side of his incisive descriptive powers." N Y Times Book Rev

Mazor, Julian, 1929-

Friend of mankind and other stories; by Julian Mazor. 1st Paul Dry Books ed. Paul Dry Books 2004 279p $19.95
ISBN 1-589-88016-1 LC 2003-26634
Contents: Gray skies; The Munster final; The Lone Star Kid; Skylark; Friend of mankind; On experience; Storm; Durango; The lost cause; The modern age
The author, "possessed of a classic light touch, is the sort of assured and lucid storyteller readers trust immediately as they sense his acuity and affection for humanity, gravitas and humorous inclination. . . . As Mazor's piquant characters struggle against ambivalence and romantic notions and strive to do the right thing, Mazor subtly reminds readers to cherish life in all its perplexity." Booklist

Mazursky, Paul
(jt. auth) Greenfeld, J. Harry and Tonto

McAuley, Paul J.

White devils; Paul McAuley. 1st ed. TOR Bks. 2004 464p $25.95
ISBN 0-7653-0761-8 LC 2003-57067
"The African continent suffers from plague, civil war, and unchecked genetic experimentation. Sent to investigate a particularly heinous crime in the Congo, Nicholas Hyde and his team come under attack by a group of apelike creatures and find themselves in the middle of a government conspiracy to hide its actions from the common people." Libr J
"Though more complex than necessary, this novel serves as a powerful warning about the sinister possibilities inherent in genetic engineering." Publ Wkly

McBain, Ed, 1926-2005
For works written by this author under other names see Hunter, Evan, 1926-2005

Alice in jeopardy; Ed McBain. Simon & Schuster 2005 292p $25
ISBN 0-7432-6250-6 LC 2004-52478
"Alice Glendenning has been surviving, just barely. When her husband, Eddie, died in a boating accident nearly a year ago, she was left a widow with two very young children and a life insurance policy with a fly-by-night company that has delayed payment because the body was lost at sea. But things can always get worse, much worse. The ransom call comes not long after her two kids don't return home on the bus after school. The instructions are simple: the money from the insurance policy or the kids are dead–plus the standard 'Don't call the cops.' Alice doesn't call the cops, but the baby-sitter does, and soon Alice is mired in a jurisdictional jihad among local, state, and federal law-enforcement agencies of varying levels of competence." Booklist
This is a "skilled performance from a master of the

McBain, Ed, 1926-2005—*Continued*
genre, the pacing and tone just right to keep you tense, curious and amused at each step." Washington Post Book World

The big bad city; a novel of the 87th Precinct. Simon & Schuster 1999 271p o.p.
ISBN 0-684-85512-7 LC 98-40890
"A young woman is murdered in a city park across town from her home. She has no identification except a wedding ring with the inscription IHS. Detetctive Steve Carella of the NYPD's 87th Precinct recognizes the inscription from his Catholic schoolboy days as a Latin monogram for 'Jesus, Savior of Men.' Jane Doe is a nun, Sister Mary Vincent, once known as Kate Cochrane. . . . Meanwhile, the man who killed Carella's father and walked because of an incompetent prosecution, Samson Wilber 'Sonny' Cole, has revenge on his mind." Booklist

Eight black horses; an 87th Precinct novel. Arbor House 1985 250p il o.p.
LC 85-7348
"The Deaf Man, scourge of McBain's famed 87th precinct, returns to plot his biggest coup in this . . . thriller. While Carella, Hawes, Brown, Kling and the other detectives investigate the murder of a woman bank teller, their legendary adversary sends them clues to his operation. . . . By switching the narrative from activities at the precinct to a description of the psychotic's fail-safe plan, the author keeps the tension at white heat from the first word to the shattering conclusion of the drama." Publ Wkly

Fat Ollie's book; a novel of the 87th Precinct. Simon & Schuster 2002 271p $25
ISBN 0-7432-0270-8 LC 2002-75830
This installment features "Det. Oliver Wendell Weeks of the 88th Precinct. Fat Ollie, of the gross appetite and the even grosser ignorance of political correctness. . . . Two major crimes occur at almost the same time: the shooting of Councilman (and possible mayoral candidate) Lester Henderson as he is getting ready for a rally and the theft of the just completed manuscript of Ollie's first novel, Report to the Commissioner. Ollie enlists Carella's help (Henderson lived in the 87th) and pursues both the murderer and the thief." Publ Wkly
"In McBain's howlingly funny sendup, the novel is pure drivel; but Ollie loved it, and darned if we don't like him for that." N Y Times Book Rev

Fiddlers; a novel of the 87th Precinct. Harcourt 2005 259p $25
ISBN 0-15-101216-4 LC 2005-4255
"A blind violinist is shot in the alley behind the restaurant where he works. A sales rep is gunned down in her apartment while cooking dinner. They are both killed with the same gun. Detective Steve Carella and his 87th Precinct team investigate. The case grows more confusing when an elderly priest and an old woman walking her dog are also murdered with the same gun. The killer, a seemingly ordinary man, is on a last fling with a call girl, who doesn't understand the darkness residing within the man she hopes will pull her out of the life. . . . This one will have readers waking in the middle of the night wondering if they, too, have killers inside themselves." Booklist

The frumious Bandersnatch; a novel of the 87th Precinct; Ed McBain. Simon & Schuster 2004 287p $25
ISBN 0-7432-5034-6 LC 2003-57258
"Tamar Valparaiso, a hot young singer on the verge of superstardom, is set to launch her debut CD and video Bandersnatch when she is kidnapped in the middle of a performance for a record industry party and the press. The whole episode is caught on camera, but the masked abductors flee, leaving behind few clues. Steve Carella and Cotton Hawes of the 87th Precinct are called in and are soon joined by a Joint Task Force and FBI agents. Detective Ollie Weeks, resident racist, homophobe, and misogynist, is also back on the scene, this time romancing a fellow officer. McBain displays his usual mastery of the police procedural along with an astute grasp of the music industry, the news media, and publicity, as well as political ramifications within the force." Libr J

Hark!; a novel of the 87th Precinct; Ed McBain. Simon & Schuster 2004 293p il $24.95
ISBN 0-7432-5035-4 LC 2004-49102
"The Deaf Man is not a dead man. The brilliant criminal, double-crossed by his female partner . . . and left for dead, is back to make life miserable for the detectives of the 87th Precinct. The cops' frustration begins with the murder of the Deaf Man's former accomplice, a crime that leads the investigating officers down a dead end. But then come the notes, hand delivered to the precinct by a parade of junkies, prostitutes, and panhandlers, and containing combinations of Shakespearean quotes, encrypted anagrams, and palindromes. The Deaf Man is providing clues to the crime he is going to commit, if only the detectives are clever enough to decipher their meaning." Booklist
"Vintage McBain, complete with pitch-perfect dialogue, subplots that thrust various precinct cops into the spotlight, a pace that encourages the reader to forget about dinner or a good night's rest, and a plot that teases and tantalizes from start to finish." Publ Wkly

Heat; an 87th Precinct novel. Viking 1981 227p o.p.
LC 81-65263
"Jeremiah Newman's death was almost definitely suicide, but certain details—for instance, the air conditioning was off on a 99 degree day—bother Detective Steve Carella. His partner, Bert Kling, has other problems—his wife may be cheating on him and someone's taking shots at him." Libr J

Ice; a major new novel about the world of the 87th Precinct. Arbor House 1983 317p o.p.
LC 82-74061
"A dancer in a hit musical, a cocaine-pushing punk, and a middle-aged diamond merchant have all been 'iced' the same gruesome way, with the same weapon. Searching for the missing links, the cops fan out through a variety of urban enclaves, from the ghetto to the theater district, from high-rent high-rises to 'Ramsey University.'" Newsweek
A "vivid, often brutal, description of life in the ghetto with its subculture of hookers, pushers, addicts, burglars, muggers, rapists and even savage killers. Yet despite this, it is not without its moments of humor, tenderness, compassion and occasional optimism." Best Sellers

McBain, Ed, 1926-2005—*Continued*

Kiss; a novel of the 87th Precinct. Morrow 1991 351p o.p.

LC 91-15908

"Detective Steven Carella must investigate the attempted murder of beautiful Emma Bowles while his father's murderer is tried in the city's courts. Emma's wealthy, handsome stockbroker husband imports a bodyguard for her from Chicago, who stays on the job even after the man who twice tried to kill Emma is found shot *and* hung. Carella and partner Meyer Meyer know something's not right, and doggedly keep investigating. Stoically, Carella also sits in court wondering if his father's killer will be convicted." Booklist

"With its interwoven threads of violence, tenderness and world-weary ruminations on the breakdown of urban life, this is hardboiled mystery in the tradition of Chandler and Hammett. And the ending features the best kind of twist: it's both surprising and satisfying." Publ Wkly

The last dance; a novel of the 87th Precinct. Simon & Schuster 2000 269p il o.p.

ISBN 0-684-85513-5 LC 99-53534

"Detectives Meyer Meyer and Steve Carella are questioning Cynthia Keating, whose father lies lifeless in a nearby bed. Cynthia claims she hasn't touched Andrew Hale since she discovered his body, but the cops suspect she's lying: for one thing, the corpse's feet are blue from postmortem lividity, a sign of death by hanging." Publ Wkly

An "accomplished mix of police procedure, characterization, social commentary and tight plotting that has long distinguished this landmark series." Booklist

Lightning; an 87th Precinct novel. Arbor House 1984 304p o.p.

LC 84-3030

"A grotesque series of crimes confronts the officers of the 87th Precinct. First, two women college track stars are found hanging, lynch-mob style, from the lampposts of brilliantly lit city streets; and then a rapist who harbors wild psycho-sexual/religious hang-ups stalks an ever-increasing number of victims, torturing them through repeated attacks. A key role in catching the maniac is played by gutsy Eileen Burke, an undercover officer in Special Forces whose aggressive work puts her own life in peril. Filled with realistic police procedure, cop humor, and eerie action." Booklist

Lullaby; an 87th Precinct novel. Morrow 1989 350p o.p.

LC 88-13709

"Returning from a party, a couple find their adopted baby and her teenaged sitter murdered. There are so many ramifications, including the later death of the biological mother, that the case seems hopelessly muddled. But Carella and Meyer, outraged by the crime, stick to the wearying routine and finally bring the guilty to book. . . . McBain's staccato dialogue and authentic characters, as always, make . . . [this] a page turner." Publ Wkly

Mischief; a novel of the 87th Precinct. Morrow 1993 346p o.p.

LC 93-10404

"The Deaf Man, nemesis of the beleaguered 87th Precinct, is back, and he's scattering cryptic clues all over town, which only serves to multiply the frustrations of Detective Steve Carella and his coworkers. Not that their usual potpourri of crime doesn't offer its own fair share of frustration: graffiti writers are turning up dead in a series of seemingly random killings; mentally impaired senior citizens are being 'dumped' on local hospitals; and, in a city on the edge of racial violence, a free outdoor concert is expected to attract a quarter-million rap fans. . . . McBain tackles social issues . . . tells a good joke, reveals small details of his regular characters' personalities, and provides subplots that add depth and humanity to all the crime in the foreground." Booklist

The mugger. Armchair Detective Lib. 1990 150p o.p.

LC 90-32352

First published 1956 in paperback

In this 87th Precinct mystery the police "must contend with a plethora of eccentric criminals, including a guy who steals household cats and a mugger who attacks women, then bows debonairly and offers a polite fairwell. . . . McBain fans will instantly recognize the crisp dialogue that the series would soon become famous for: a hypnotic mix of terse truths, perpetual perplexities, and crude coptalk." Booklist

Nocturne. Warner Bks. 1997 291p o.p.

LC 96-42030

In this 87th precinct novel "detectives Carella and Hawes catch the first call on the night shift: the shooting death of a destitute woman who was once a renowned concert pianist. . . . Right away we're hooked, because these cops not only know their procedures, they also value a human life. Before this long, dark night is through, Mr. McBain will make us care abot a 19-year-old hooker who is savagely killed in a gang rape, a pimp and a drug dealer who also die hard and 25 roosters torn up in a cockfight." N Y Times Book Rev

Poison; an 87th Precinct novel. Arbor House 1987 264p o.p.

LC 86-17342

"Detectives Steve Carella and Hal Wallis interrogate beautiful, wealthy Marilyn Hollis when one of her swains dies of poison, possibly a suicide. Marilyn becomes a murder suspect later, as two more men she has been socially and sexually involved with are killed in a development that creates a serious problem for the investigators. Wallis is now the woman's lover, living with her despite Carella's protest. Both detectives continue to track Marilyn's former male companions, looking for a jealous killer. But Wallis, heartsick, begins to believe that Marilyn is guilty. The taut, gripping story closes with a knockout surprise." Publ Wkly

There was a little girl. Warner Bks. 1994 323p o.p.

LC 94-29145

In this Matthew Hope novel "the hero spends most of his time in a semi-coma after being shot outside a bar on the seedy side of Calusa, Fla. . . . Meanwhile, Hope's PI pals Warren Chambers and Toots Kiley, as well as police detective Morris Bloom, try to reconstruct Hope's previous week, probings that are intercut with flashbacks to Hope's own investigation of the years-old suicide of a circus star. What emerges is an intricate, lurid tale of sex, blackmail and murder fueled by greed." Publ Wkly

McBain, Ed, 1926-2005—*Continued*

Three blind mice; a novel. Arcade Pub. 1990 293p o.p.
LC 89-18543

In this Matthew Hope mystery "the Calusa, Fla., lawyer takes on a 'hopeless case,' defending Stephen Leeds, arrested for murder. The victims were three Vietnamese tried but found not guilty of raping Leeds's wife, Jessie. Every bit of evidence ties the crimes to Leeds, who had publicly sworn to avenge his wife's abuse, but Hope believes in his client and works diligently to free him." Publ Wkly

"Mr. McBain's square-jawed dialogue and stout grip on detection procedures give his narrative the muscularity characteristic of the whole Hope series. But the real strength to flex those muscles comes from the perfectly constructed plot." N Y Times Book Rev

Tricks; an 87th Precinct novel. Arbor House 1987 247p o.p.
LC 87-11350

This novel "begins on a Halloween eve, and with the most unlikely of events. Four kids, wearing costumes and garish masks, hold up a series of liquor stores and kill the proprietors before escaping with their plunder. Detectives Brown and Genero make a grisly discovery in a garbage can—a headless torso. A professional magician, Sebastian the Great, puts on a disappearing act that confounds his attractive wife. She appeals to the police for help. Meanwhile, Detective First Class Eileen Burke draws the unenviable assignment of playing a hooker at a notorious bar in hopes of engaging a serial killer who is heavily armed and has a fondness for ladies of the evening." West Coast Rev Books

Vespers; a novel of the 87th Precinct. Morrow 1990 331p o.p.
LC 89-13124

"A priest is killed in his church, which is the scene of a standoff between a drug dealer and his assailants. Meanwhile, four blocks away, devil worshippers hold their own religious meetings. The men of the precinct must find the killer, extract the truth from myriad conflicting accounts, and explore the link with the demonic church." Booklist

Widows; a novel. Morrow 1991 332p o.p.
LC 90-49861

"On the same summer night that a young blond woman, the mistress of a wealthy, older, married man, is stabbed to death, detective Steve Carella's father is killed in his bakery by two thieves. Distracted by grief, Carella, with colleague Arthur Brown, investigates the woman's murder, which is followed by the wealthy man's death and those of his first and second wives." Publ Wkly

(jt. auth) Hunter, E. Candyland

McCabe, Eugene, 1930-

Heaven lies about us; stories; Eugene McCabe. 1st U.S. ed. Bloomsbury 2004 309p $24.95
ISBN 1-582-34427-2 LC 2003-52367

Contents: Heaven lies about us; Truth; Victorian fields; Roma; Music at Annahullion; Cancer; Heritage; Victims; The orphan; The master; The landlord; The mother

"The heaven of Eugene McCabe's title is found in the more rural corners of the Irish border counties, with their centuries-old buildings and calcified layers of piety and tradition. But there isn't much paradise here; McCabe's characters tend to be miserable, improbably eloquent and never, ever dull." N Y Times Book Rev

McCabe, Patrick, 1955-

The butcher boy. Fromm Int. 1993 c1992 215p o.p.
ISBN 0-88064-147-9 LC 93-2831

First published 1992 in the United Kingdom

"Young Francie is a have-not—poor, ignorant, Catholic—in a small Irish town, but he is savvy enough to size up those who do enjoy privilege. His envy is turned up a notch after the deaths of his alcoholic father and emotionally disturbed mother. Francie then engages in increasingly desperate acts, leading to a harrowing depiction of events that are alluded to on the book's first page." Publ Wkly

"'The Butcher Boy' is the side of the murder story never revealed in the newspapers: a map of a murderer's mind, a revelation of a murderer's reason. It is the story of the heritage of madness and loneliness, a stunning picture of the desperation of the unloved." N Y Times Book Rev

Mondo desperado; a serial novel. HarperCollins Pubs. 2000 240p $24
ISBN 0-06-019461-8 LC 99-89331

First published 1999 in the United Kingdom

A novel composed of "short stories, shaggy dog tales and spoofs from the fictitious pen of McCabe's authorial desperado, Phildy Hackball, set in his crazy village of Barntrosna. . . . These 10 intertwined stories mix loony subject matter culled from trashy paperbacks with Hibernian stereotypes and clichés." Publ Wkly

McCaffrey, Anne

Acorna; the unicorn girl; [by] Anne McCaffrey and Margaret Ball. HarperPrism 1997 291p o.p.
LC 97-11099

"Found in a survival pod in space by prospectors, the infant Acorna soon exhibits the ability to analyze deficiencies in plants by taste, purify water and air, and heal. Taken to the planet Kezdet to avoid scientists who want to study her, Acorna discovers barbaric child-labor practices and vows to rescue the children. McCaffrey and Ball have created a magical alien in this fantasy/science fiction story." Libr J

Followed by Acorna's quest

Acorna's people; [by] Anne McCaffrey and Elizabeth Ann Scarborough. HarperPrism 1999 314p o.p.
ISBN 0-06-105094-6 LC 99-12850

In the third title in the series "Acorna is at last among her own. The beautiful healing horn in the center of her forehead and the 'funny' feet and hands that once set her apart now make her one with the telepathic Linyaari who live on as lush agrarian planet where they pursue their peaceful dreams. Acorna's people welcome her with a lavish costume ball-and an already-chosen mate! But Acorna still has much to do before she can enjoy the peaceful home she is offered. The legendary resting place of the lost *Linyaari* ancestors has yet to be found. With the help of the rogue spacetrader Becker and his

McCaffrey, Anne—*Continued*
cat, RK (RoadKill), Acorna must strive to right an unspeakable wrong and defeat an enemy even more cruel than the Khleevi themselves." Publisher's note

Followed by Acorna's world

Acorna's quest; [by] Anne McCaffrey and Margaret Ball. HarperPrism 1998 292p o.p.

ISBN 0-06-105297-3 LC 97-51201

"Acorna has grown into a lovely adolescent humanoid whose physical appearance is reminiscent of the fabled unicorn. Her human protectors plan to help her seek her home world, but she and Calum leave prematurely and follow an unpredictable path on their mission to search the sector of space where her survival pod has launched from. Subsequent events intervene with her quest for home. . . . McCaffrey and Acorna fans will delight in this." Voice Youth Advocates

Acorna's rebels; [by] Anne McCaffrey and Elizabeth Ann Scarborough. Eos 2003 308p $24.95

ISBN 0-380-97899-7 LC 2002-73873

In this sixth title in the series "Acorna continues to hunt for her beloved life-mate, Aari. . . . She travels aboard the starship Condor to the planet Makahomia, which she finds in the grip of a plague killing the sacred temple cats. Acorna fights a desperate reaerguard action against the plague with her horn's healing power, but the mystery clearly lies deeper." Publ Wkly Eos 2003 p. cmp

ISBN 0-380-97899-7 (alk. paper) LC 2002-73873

Acorna's search; [by] Anne McCaffrey and Elizabeth Ann Scarborough. Eos 2001 292p o.p.

ISBN 0-380-97898-9 LC 2001-33562

In this fifth installment in the series "Acorna helps her people, the Linyaari, try to restore their beloved home world, which was literally laid waste by the vicious Khleevi. Aari, the young man so brutally tortured by the Khleevi, is now Acorna's life mate and at work on a survey team trying to locate mountains and rivers in all the rubble." Booklist

Acorna's triumph; [by] Anne McCaffrey and Elizabeth Ann Scarborough. 1st ed. Eos 2004 308p $24.95

ISBN 0-380-97900-4 LC 2003-59622

"The Linyaari home world of Vhiliinyar has been reclaimed, and Acorna, the unicorn-horned girl, has found her life-mate, Aari, who had once suffered at the hands of the Khleevi invaders. However, all is not right, since Aari has changed drastically, and Acorna discovers a new threat of an invasion by the Linyaari's ancient enemies. . . . [The authors] combine their talents in this conclusion to a series about a young woman's growth into maturity and her determined search for her missing people and her vanished mate." Libr J

Acorna's world; [by] Anne McCaffrey and Elizabeth Ann Scarborough. HarperCollins Pubs. 2000 320p o.p.

ISBN 0-06-105095-4 LC 00-28830

In the fourth installment in the series Acorna "finds herself unable to adjust to her native culture because of her upbringing by her human 'uncles' and her involvement in so many space adventures. So she ships out with the salvager Becker; his ship's cat, Roadkill; and Aari, a young man of Acorna's race whose torture at the hands of the vicious, buglike aliens, the Khleevi, has left him hornless and vulnerable." Booklist

All the Weyrs of Pern. Ballantine Bks. 1991 404p (Dragonriders of Pern) o.p.

LC 91-91910

"A Del Rey book"

"The dream of generations of Dragonriders draws within reach as, with the aid of an intelligent computer, the possibility of destroying the devastating phenomenon known as 'Thread' becomes a reality." Libr J

"This is an exciting, full-bodied, richly detailed . . . chapter in the Pern chronicle as the knowledge of the first settlers is united with the wisdom of the descendants. . . . Once again McCaffrey's narrative flows smoothly, maintaining the world and characters she has so lovingly created and setting new challenges for them to meet." Booklist

The chronicles of Pern; first fall. Ballantine Bks. 1993 306p o.p.

LC 93-10079

"A Del Rey book"

Includes the following stories: The survey: P.E.R.N.; The dolphins' bell; The ford of Red Hanrahan; The second weyr; Rescue run

"These five original stories . . . offer a glimpse into the early history of the world of 'thread' and Dragonriders. McCaffrey's unadorned prose allows characters and plot to take center stage." Libr J

The city who fought; [by] Anne McCaffrey, S.M. Stirling. Baen Pub. Enterprises 1993 435p o.p.

ISBN 0-671-72166-6 LC 93-2651

Previous titles in this series published in paperback are: The ship who sang (1969); Partnership (1992); and The ship who searched (1992)

"Space Station SSS-900C, a profitable but out-of-the-way trading and mining center, is attacked by Kolnari, pirates from a planet of sociopathic exiles. While awaiting the arrival of the Central Worlds' Navy, the inhabitants play for time with a major deception planned by Simeon, the shellperson operating the station." Publ Wkly

"Within the fabric of McCaffrey's universe, she and Stirling merge seamlessly, sporting wit, action galore, superior characterization, and plausible hardware." Booklist

Followed by The ship who won (1994)

Crystal line. Ballantine Bks. 1992 294p o.p.

LC 92-53219

"A Del Rey book"

Sequel to Killashandra

In this conclusion of the trilogy, "crystal singer of the Heptite Guild, Killashandra Ree enjoys the benefits of increased longevity and the status of an elite artisan at a terrible price: the slow erosion of her memory. When the Guild faces a crisis that could result in its demise, Killashandra faces a battle to overcome her own fears and learn to trust in someone other than herself." Libr J

Crystal singer. Ballantine Bks. 1982 311p o.p.

LC 82-4009

"A Del Rey book"

In this first volume of a trilogy "Killashandra Ree learns she has failed her final audition despite ten years

McCaffrey, Anne—*Continued*

of all-consuming preparation for a career as a vocal concert soloist. By coincidence that day she meets a vacationing crystal singer, joins him for the remainder of his holiday and becomes acquainted with the side effects and risks of crystal singing. . . . The story ends as she accomplishes a difficult job, cutting and placing black crystal on four remote planets so they may have instant interstellar communication." SLJ

"This is a well-constructed story with a strong-willed and courageous young heroine who finds her niche in the workplace." Voice Youth Advocates

Followed by Killashandra

Dragonflight; volume 1 of "The Dragonriders of Pern". Ballantine Bks. 1978 337p il o.p.
LC 78-16707

"A Del Rey book"

First published 1968 in paperback. Based on two award winning stories entitled: Weyr search and Dragonrider

The planet Pern, originally colonized from Earth but long out of contact with it, has been periodically threatened by the deadly silver Threads which fall from the wandering Red Star. To combat them a life form on the planet was developed into winged, fire-breathing dragons. Humans with a high degree of empathy and telepathic power are needed to train and preserve these creatures. As the story begins, Pern has fallen into decay, the threat of the Red Star has been forgotten, the Dragonriders and dragons are reduced in number and in disrepute, and the evil Lord Fax has begun conquering neighboring holds

Followed by Dragonquest

Dragonquest; volume 2 of "The Dragonriders of Pern". Ballantine Bks. 1979 351p il o.p.
LC 78-19721

"A Del Rey book"

Sequel to Dragonflight

First published 1971 in paperback

The inhabitants of Pern begin to resent the attitudes of the oldtime Dragonriders who were brought forward in time to aid their modern counterparts in defeating the deadly Thread from the Red Star and now feel that their new world owes them a living. The Weyrleader F'lar and his consort Lessa try to mediate between the Dragonriders and the landbound people they had protected, but new forces upset Pern's delicate social structure and threaten to destroy not only the unique privileges of the Dragonriders, but their very reason for existence

Followed by The white dragon

Dragonrider

In The Best of the Nebulas p229-313

Dragon's Kin; [by] Anne McCaffrey [and] Todd McCaffrey. Del Rey/Ballantine Bks. 2003 304p $24.95

ISBN 0-345-46198-3

The action in this Dragonriders of Pern tale "takes place during an unexplored period in the history of Pern, before the coming of the Thread. The watch-whers are already playing a prominent role, however, keeping watch at night at the holds and weyrs and helping in the mines. The protagonists are Kindin and Nuella, young people living in a mining camp. A cave-in wipes out Kindin's father and brothers as well as the old watch-wher, and Kindin moves in with camp Harper. There he learns the skills of being a Harper, including discretion and mediation. Eventually, he and Nuella learn the secret of how watch-whers see in the dark, and about their communication with dragons, which opens a wholly new range of capabilities for the dragon-riders." Booklist

Dragonsdawn. Ballantine Bks. 1988 431p (Dragonriders of Pern) o.p.
LC 88-9307

"A Del Rey book"

Chronologically the first novel in the Dragonriders of Pern series "it tells of the colonizing of the uninhabited planet Pern by a few thousand carefully selected humans, of the colonists' first encounter with the life-threatening spores known as Thread and of the creation (by genetic engineering) of the winged, telepathic, fire-breathing 'dragons' who become the colonists' first line of defense against the periodic falls of Thread." Booklist

Dragonseye. Ballantine Bks. 1997 353p (Dragonriders of Pern) o.p.
LC 96-44206

"A Del Rey book"

In this title, in the Dragonriders of Pern series "the Dragonriders finally get to protect their world from the danger they've been anticipating for 200 years. When signs appear that Thread, the deadly silver strands that devour everything organic, will soon make an appearance, Dragonrider Chalkin's failure to believe in the danger of Threadfall threatens to destroy the entire civilization." Libr J

The author "brings us another diverse cast of responsible, heroic good guys and dragons in a novel that's going to please fans old and new." Publ Wkly

Freedom's landing. Putnam 1995 342p o.p.
LC 94-43820

In this first volume of a series "the Catteni, an alien race of slavers, are settling a habitable but dangerous planet with recalcitrant slaves from a variety of races, including the human; all must learn to cooperate with one another to survive. Among the conscripted colonists is an exiled Catteni noble, Zainal, who is resented by some other colonists because he is a member of the overlord race, and Kristin Bjornsen, a spirited young human who finds herself not only working closely with Zainal but drawn to him romantically." Booklist

"With her customary talent for imaginative storytelling, the author skillfully portrays the environmental and personal challenges faced by the new colonists." Libr J

Followed by Freedom's choice (1997) and Freedom's challenge (1998)

Freedom's ransom. Putnam 2002 288p $23.95

ISBN 0-399-14889-2 LC 2001-56669

"An Ace/Putnam book"

Fourth title in the author's Cattani/Freedom series. "In *Freedom's Challenge* (1998), the colonists on the planet Botany, who were initially dropped there as slaves, freed themselves from the Eosi-dominated Cattani overlords. Now it is time to reestablish contact with Earth and 'ransom' Earth's stolen technological materials, which are in warehouses on the Cattani planet Barevi. Zainal and Kris head an expedition to a decimated and devastated but slowly recovering Earth to trade for items to use in bartering with shifty Barevi merchants." Booklist

McCaffrey, Anne—*Continued*

"The visit to a bleak Manhattan after the Eosian looting is as disturbing, touching and humorous as the trading in the Barevian market." Publ Wkly

The girl who heard dragons. TOR Bks. 1994 352p il o.p.

LC 94-118

"A Tom Doherty Associates book"

Contents: The girl who heard dragons {novelette}; Velvet fields; Euterpe on a fling; Duty calls; A Sleeping Humpty Dumpty Beauty; The Mandalay cure; A flock of geese; The greatest love {novelette}; A quiet one; If Madam likes you; Zulei, Grace, Nimshi, and the damnyankees; Cinderella switch; Habit is an old horse; Lady-in-waiting; The bones do lie

This is a "diverse assortment of 15 short fiction pieces never before gathered in one volume. The heroine of the engaging title story, a new Pern novella and the only Pern tale in the collection, is somewhat akin to Menolly in *Dragonsong* in that she, too, eventually rises above her birthright to follow the destiny that her particular talent dictates. Perhaps the strongest inclusion here is 'The Greatest Love,' also a novella, which predicted in 1977 (when McCaffrey wrote it) the extrauterine fertilization of a human ovum to produce a healthy baby. . . . Other stories focus on everything from spaceship adventure, shifting time-storms, and the unwitting near-destruction of sentient life-forms by human colonists on a distant planet (and the fitting, if gruesome consequences)—to ghosts and romance." Booklist

The girl who heard dragons [novelette]

In McCaffrey, A. The girl who heard dragons p21-64

The greatest love [novelette]

In McCaffrey, A. The girl who heard dragons p169-225

Killashandra. Ballantine Bks. 1985 303p o.p.

LC 85-6193

"A Del Rey book"

In this second volume of the trilogy "crystal singer Killashandra Ree is desperate to get off the crystal-mining planet of Ballybran, so she takes what at first sounds like a routine assignment replacing a shattered crystal in the main Sensory Organ on planet Optheria. While she is there she is also to find out why Optherians never leave the planet. She is kidnapped and marooned on an isolated island, but escapes, only to encounter her handsome kidnapper Lars Dahl, with whom she eventually falls in love." SLJ

"This suspenseful and romantic story exhibits McCaffrey's usual verve in building convincing societies, developing vital characters, and sustaining mood." Booklist

Followed by Crystal line

The Masterharper of Pern. Ballantine Bks. 1998 431p (Dragonriders of Pern) o.p.

ISBN 0-345-38823-2 LC 97-30896

"A Del Rey book"

This installment in the Dragonriders of Pern series "details the life, loves, and heartbreaks of Robinton, Pern's most beloved harper. Readers follow him through a childhood filled with rejection and neglect by his Mastercomposer father, the loss of his wife, the death of his best friend, to his becoming Masterharper of Pern. This is McCaffrey at her best, combining excellent writing with vivid settings and detailed, fully fleshed-out characters." SLJ

Pegasus in space. Ballantine Bks. 2000 373p o.p.

ISBN 0-345-43466-8 LC 99-53225

"A Del Rey book"

"Following *To Ride Pegasus* (1973) and *Pegasus in Flight* (1990), this is a third prequel to the Rowan series. . . . Here, the first space station becomes a reality, and quadriplegic teenager Peter Reidinger, whose telekinetic Talent proved amazing in *Pegasus in Flight*, is the protagonist. Peter tests and hones his ability not only to move his body naturally but also to teleport large objects instantaneously through space. Peter helps other Talents, as such gifted youngsters are called, thwart a mutiny aboard the nearly finished space station." Booklist

The renegades of Pern. Ballantine Bks. 1989 384p il (Dragonriders of Pern) o.p.

LC 89-6694

"A Del Rey book"

This tale "begins during the time of *Dragonquest* and continues beyond the closing of *The White Dragon,* focusing on some of the commoners, and how they cope with the return of the life-consuming Thread. A number of lives intertwine, such as that of the trader boy Jayge Lilcamp, whose family is almost destroyed when his father refuses to believe the first Thread warning." Publ Wkly

The skies of Pern. Ballantine Pub. Group 2001 434p (Dragonriders of Pern) o.p.

ISBN 0-345-43468-4 LC 00-51859

"A Del Rey book"

A Dragonriders of Pern novel. "With the discovery of Aivas, the artificial intelligence hidden for centuries in Pern's southern continent, the residents of the third planet of the sun called Rukbat have learned how to end the threat posed by the periodic fall of Thread from the erratic red star that orbits the planet. Despite the abundance of rediscovered knowledge, new dangers and old fears surface, forcing Dragonriders, Holders, and Craftmasters all to reconsider their purpose and functions in society." Libr J

"As all her Pern novels amply demonstrate, McCaffrey's sexy and cunning dragons carry the day—and the novel—with impeccable, irresistible panache." Publ Wkly

Wehr search

In The Hugo winners p329-87

The white dragon; volume 3 of "The Dragonriders of Pern". Ballantine Bks. 1978 497p il o.p.

LC 77-18913

"A Del Rey book"

Sequel to Dragonquest

"A prologue summarizes the first two volumes of the saga. . . . Young Jaxom and his white dragon Ruth (a male), previously encountered, mature, fight the deadly Threads from the Red Planet, help open the largely unexplored continent and discover in an ancient spaceship a

McCaffrey, Anne—*Continued*

map, key to major changes for Pern. Once all the necessary background is assimilated, it's a rousing adventure and colorful portrayal of a unique and carefully-worked-out culture." Publ Wkly

McCaffrey, Todd J.

(jt. auth) McCaffrey, A. Dragon's Kin

McCaig, Donald

Jacob's ladder; a story of Virginia during the war. Norton 1998 525p o.p.
ISBN 0-393-04629-X LC 97-31165

This historical novel "tells the interlocking story of three families, white and black, masters and slaves. The scion of one slave-owning family, Duncan Gatewood, has an affair with a mulatto slave, Maggie, and when Maggie gives birth to a son, she and the child are sold by Gatewood's angry father. A Gatewood slave, Jesse, is deeply in love with Maggie, and he tries to escape, again and again, to find her and the son he wants to claim for his own. Eventually, he succeeds and enlists in the Union Army and finally confronts his former masters." Libr J

"Delving into letters, diaries and memoirs for period detail, McCaig follows Jesse, Maggie and a large cast of characters through the battlefields, hospitals, prisons and slave wharves of the crumbling Confederacy. Throughout, he binds his narrative with a meticulous respect for authenticity." N Y Times Book Rev

McCall Smith, Alexander, 1948-

In the company of cheerful ladies; Alexander McCall Smith. Pantheon Books 2005 233p $19.95
ISBN 0-375-42271-4 LC 2004-56827

In this installment, "Botswana detective Precious Ramotswe, the traditionally built-and newly married-owner of the No. 1 Ladies' Detective Agency, is saddled with a surfeit of challenging cases and personal crises. There has been an intruder in her home (he managed to escape, but left a telltale pair of trousers in his wake). And the levelheaded sleuth is flustered by an encounter with a man from her past. Meanwhile, Mma Ramotswe's husband, master mechanic Mr. J.L.B. Matekoni, is neck-deep in work after the resignation of one of his apprentices, who has become romantically entangled with a married woman (Mma Ramotswe and assistant detective Grace Makutsi slyly gather the scurrilous details). [The author] renders colorful characters with names that trip off the tongue." Publ Wkly

McCall Smith, R. A. *See* McCall Smith, Alexander, 1948-

McCammon, Robert R.

Boy's life. Pocket Bks. 1991 440p o.p.
LC 91-2813

"In 1964, 12-year-old Cory Mackenson lives with his parents in Zephyr, Alabama. It is a sleepy, comfortable town. Cory is helping with his father's milk route one morning when a car plunges into the lake before their eyes. His father dives in after the car and finds a dead man handcuffed to the steering wheel. Their world no longer seems so innocent: a vicious killer hides among apparently friendly neighbors." Libr J

"McCammon is both a precise and lush writer, and thus the trail Cory takes to deciphering the puzzle the dead man represents quickly firms up into a compelling, even haunting yarn of adult demons being faced and fathomed by the young. This look at life's blacker sides is neither cloying nor jejune." Booklist

Gone south. Pocket Bks. 1992 359p o.p.
LC 92-28062

"Dan, dogged by depression and Agent Orange-induced leukemia, has accidentally killed a man. On the run, he meets Arden, a disfigured woman abandoned at a truck stop. He reluctantly agrees to help her on her journey to the Louisiana swamps where, she believes, the legendary Bright Girl will heal her. Meanwhile, an unlikely pair of bounty hunters is on Dan's trail: Flint began life as a carnival freak, with his Siamese twin's tiny arm and half-formed face protuding from his chest; he is saddled with training Cecil, a self-deprecating and pathetically friendly Elvis impersonator. These four misfits collide and, finally, arrive where the Bright Girl may actually live." Libr J

"The plot flows well and quickly. The extreme characters only point up McCammon's theme: everybody has a hidden deformity and can only become free and happy by facing it. An engrossing read." Booklist

McCann, Colum, 1965-

Dancer; a novel. Metropolitan Bks. 2003 336p $26
ISBN 0-8050-6792-2 LC 2002-71879

"A fictionalized account of the life of Rudolph Nureyev—the Cold War danseur noble lauded as the world's first 'pop star dancer'—as told by those who knew him. Among the narrators are the irrepressible Yulia, the daughter of Nureyev's first ballet teacher, Margot Fonteyn, Rudik's brilliant dance partner; Victor, a gay hustler from the Lower East Side with a penchant for blow; bath houses, and back talk; and others." Libr J

"It's hard to tell what a reader unfamiliar with the outlines of Nureyev's life might make of 'Dancer.' Much, deliberately, is left unsaid. Reduced to words, the dance evaporates—only passion and the personal can make it move again." N Y Times Book Rev

McCarry, Charles

Old boys. Overlook Press 2004 476p $25.95
ISBN 1-58567-545-8 LC 2004-48320

"When Paul Christopher, the enigmatic hero of several earlier McCarry novels, disappears while on a quest for his nonagenarian mother, Lori, his black-sheep cousin, Horace Hubbard, convenes a discreet cadre of over-the-hill spies to find their confrere-and to save the world from Ib'n Awad, an aging Islamic terrorist in possession of 12 nuclear suitcase bombs. In a beguiling twist . . . , all parties also seek a fabled ancient scroll that unmasks Jesus as an agent provocateur, handled by Judas for Roman spymaster Paul. The nonstop peregrinations of this league of extraordinary spooks take them to a score of exotic locales, pitting them against Chechen thugs, Chinese secret police, Nazi doctors, and a case of acute myocardial fibrillation. McCarry's commitment to this fanciful premise is absolute, and the resulting yarn com-

McCarry, Charles—*Continued*
bines the intrepid exploits of John Buchan, the cagey intrigue of Eric Ambler, and the clipped cadences of Dashiell Hammett. Tremendous fun." Booklist

McCarthy, Cormac, 1933-

All the pretty horses. Knopf 1992 301p $27.50
ISBN 0-394-57474-5 LC 91-58560
In the spring of 1950, after the death of his grandfather, sixteen-year-old John Grady Cole "is evicted from the Texas ranch where he grew up. He and another boy Lacey Rawlins, head for Mexico on horseback, riding south until they finally turn up at a vast ranch in mountainous Coahuila, the Hacienda de la Purisima, where they sign on as vaqueros. . . . John Grady's unusual talent for breaking, training and understanding horses becomes crucial to the hacendado Don Hector's ambitious breeding program. For John Grady, La Purisima is a paradise, complete with its Eve, Don Hector's daughter, Alejandra." N Y Times Book Rev
"Though some readers may grow impatient with the wild prairie rhythms of McCarthy's language, others will find his voice completely transporting." Publ Wkly
Followed by The crossing

Blood meridian; or, The evening redness in the West. Random House 1985 337p o.p.
ISBN 0-394-40027-5
"This book is set in the south-west borderland between the United States and Mexico, and follows the experiences of the (unnamed) kid, as he gets involved with a gang of mercenaries called the Glantons, and meets one of the most menacing figures in modern literature, Judge Holden, a huge, pale, manic individual who seems to know every aspect of human culture and to conduct a single-handed and satanic campaign to destroy it all. This is a savage book, full of rape and pillage, with more scalpings described in more detail–the Indians are just as savage as the whites–than (surely) in any other book. It is also beautifully written, a great poetic exploration of nature and the myth of the West." Good Fiction Guide

Cities of the plain. Knopf 1998 291p $27.50
ISBN 0-679-42390-7 LC 98-11583
The final volume of the Border trilogy finds John Grady and Billy Parkam working on a New Mexico cattle ranch in the early 1950s. John Grady "falls in love with an epileptic teenage prostitute across the border in Juarez and vows to rescue her, whatever the cost." Libr J
"McCarthy's language carries a brooding, evolutionary sense of time and labor—in his hands the changing of a tire on an old truck becomes a mythic deed. The weight of history rests on the shoulders of John Grady, too, and he's doomed to learn that 'when things are gone they're gone. They aint comin back.'" New Yorker

No country for old men. Knopf 2005 309p $24.95
ISBN 0-37540-677-8
"Llewelyn Moss, hunting antelope near the Rio Grande, instead finds men shot dead, a load of heroin, and more than $2 million in cash. Packing the money out, he knows, will change everything. But only after two more men are murdered does a victim's burning car lead Sheriff Bell to the carnage out in the desert, and he soon realizes how desperately Moss and his young wife need protection. One party in the failed transaction hires an ex-Special Forces officer to defend his interests against a mesmerizing freelancer, while on either side are men accustomed to spectacular violence and mayhem." Publisher's note
"As devised and refined by James M. Cain, Jim Thompson and their gloomy paperback peers, the crime novel aimed its cheap handgun at the heart of America's most prized beliefs about its destiny: that the loot we've scooped up will belong to us forever and that history allows clean getaways. Cormac McCarthy's 'No Country for Old Men' is as bracing a variation on these noir orthodoxies as any fan of the genre could expect." N Y Times Book Rev

McCarthy, Mary, 1912-1989

Birds of America. Harcourt Brace Jovanovich 1971 344p o.p.
The main character is "Peter Levi, a young American who spends his junior year at the Sorbonne at the time of the bombing of Hanoi and who is much preoccupied with Kant's categorical imperative and the Destruction of Art and the Death of Nature. The Death of Nature, in fact, is the central theme. . . . The final scene, in which Peter develops a near-fatal infection after a swan attack and is visited by Kant in a vision, powerfully resolves the author's theme." Libr J
"Miss McCarthy is astringent and sharp in all the right places, gentle where she should be. What she has written is an honest and appropriate love letter to an essentially decent young American." Publ Wkly

A charmed life. Harcourt Brace & Co. 1955 313p o.p.
"John and Martha Sinnott encounter an amazing assortment of would-be bohemians when, in the hope of gaining a new lease on their marriage, they move to the artistic community of New Leeds. They long for privacy but cocktail parties, drama groups, and Martha's first husband Miles keep breaking in. Even Martha's pregnancy brings unforeseen problems for due to one after-the-party interlude the question of fatherhood broadens to two possibilities: John or Miles. The author is at her brilliant best in this comic tragedy of modern man's dilemma: the fluctuation between belief and unbelief, courage and despair." Booklist

The group. Harcourt Brace & Co. 1963 378p o.p.
The Group is made of "eight Vassar girls of the class of '33 who had lived together during their upperclass years, in the South Tower of Main. We see them first at the wedding of Kay Strong to Harald Petersen a week after Commencement. . . . We see them last at Kay's funeral seven years later." N Y Times Book Rev
"It is perhaps as social history that the novel will chiefly be remembered; but over and above its sensitive observations it has a quality that one has not come to expect from this particular author, and that is compassion." Saturday Rev

The groves of Academe. Harcourt Brace & Co. 1952 302p o.p.
"An intelligent and sophisticated dissection of faculty life at Jocelyn, a small progressive college in Pennsylvania. The impending dismissal of self-styled liberal, Henry

McCarthy, Mary, 1912-1989—*Continued*

Mulcahy, Joycean scholar and instructor in literature, and the spring Poetry Conference are the main incidents in the narrative; but woven around them and even tying them together quite neatly is the probing, satirical and often deadly accurate account of college administration and personalities. A few of America's leading poets seem to appear pseudonymously during the conference." Libr J

McCauley, Stephen

True enough. Simon & Schuster 2001 314p $24
ISBN 0-684-81054-9 LC 00-66177

"Jane Cody, producer of public TV shows of questionable merit in Boston, and Desmond Sullivan, gay New Yorker and biographer of mediocre artists, meet during Desmond's time in Boston as a visiting professor. Jane's new project, a series of televised biographies of the unfamous, may be just the spur he needs to finish his second book about a long-forgotten singer." Booklist

McCauley is "uncannily good at illuminating character through speech. . . . [He] wants nothing more than to entertain us, and if that's become an old-fashioned thing to do, it may be because few writers do it so well." N Y Times Book Rev

McClure, James, 1939-

The steam pig. Harper & Row 1972 c1971 247p o.p.

"A Joan Kahn-Harper novel of suspense"

First published 1971 in the United Kingdom

White Lieutenant Kramer and his Zulu sergeant Zondi investigate the grisly murder of a beautiful white girl in a small South African town

"An absolutely scathing look at contemporary South Africa is provided in [this] . . . novel that is uncanny in its multi-leveled perceptions. It is a grotesquely vivid picture of life under apartheid. But it is also a first-rate mystery with a solution that is a shocker." Saturday Rev

McConchie, Lyn

(jt. auth) Norton, A. Beast Master's ark

McCorkle, Jill, 1958-

Carolina moon; a novel. Algonquin Bks. 1996 260p $18.95
ISBN 1-56512-136-8 LC 96-16115

This novel is "set in the small town of Fulton, North Carolina, and revolves around big-hearted Quee Purdy. Quee is a sixtysomething entrepreneur who has just opened a no-smoking clinic . . . where smokers are loved and pampered right out of their addiction. Her clinic serves as the hub for many charming if wayward folks, including therapist Denny Parks, on the run from a bad marriage and a bad case of nerves, and handyman Tom Lowe, who daily paces off the boundaries of his sunken, underwater property, the sum total of his inheritance from his father." Booklist

"We sense that the author, like a modern-day phrenologist, has her hands on the head of Fulton to study its psychological profile. Seemingly plotless, the novel's final revelation shows how much of a craftswoman McCorkle really is." America

Crash diet; stories. Algonquin Bks. 1992 253p o.p.
LC 91-34313

Contents: Crash diet; Man watcher; Gold mine; First union blues; Departures; Comparison shopping; Migration of the love bugs; Waiting for hard times to end; Words gone bad; Sleeping Beauty, revised; Carnival lights

"Widows, recent divorcées, teenage girls, retired women, and single mothers populate [this collection]. Each woman imparts to McCorkle's fortunate readers a touching, downright bone-tickling account of her individual struggle in the New South." Libr J

Ferris Beach; a novel. Algonquin Bks. 1990 343p o.p.
LC 90-37089

The protagonist and narrator, Katie Burns, tells of growing up in a small town in the South during the 1960s and '70s. "Ferris Beach is where excitement and glamour start—at least that's what Kate thinks as she hears about her cousin Angela who lives there. Kate has had a humdrum, 'normal' childhood; her conservative mother and humorous father have brought her up 'properly,' while Angela has had freedom and romance. But even freedom has its dark side, as Kate finds out." SLJ

"The central metaphor is the place that gives the novel its name—a place associated with ideas of sex, freedom, and broken dreams. . . . Here, Katie will get a powerful dose of reality and suffering rendered so wistfully and obliquely, with multiple forewarnings designed to heighten the sense of foreboding, and a commendable balance of tragedy and mirth, that the full texture of a child's wonder and terror is preserved." Booklist

Final vinyl days and other stories. Algonquin Bks. 1998 212p $18.95
ISBN 1-56512-204-6 LC 97-50540

Contents: Paradise; Last request; Life prerecorded; Final vinyl days; Dysfunction 101; A blinking, spinning, breathtaking world; Your husband is cheating on us; It's a funeral! RSVP; The anatomy of man

"This collection of nine stories is chock full of New South eccentrics, comic moments and perplexing situations. McCorkle's characters grapple with failed romances, temptation and deathbed injunctions. . . . At their funniest and most poignant, McCorkle's stories plunge into her characters' souls and mine the truths about them they themselves can't admit and can't help revealing." Publ Wkly

McCracken, Elizabeth

The giant's house; a romance. Dial Press (NY) 1996 259p o.p.
ISBN 0-385-31433-7 LC 95-52433

"The story begins in a small Cape Cod town in 1950, when a 6-foot-2-inch 11-year-old boy walks up to the 25-year-old librarian's desk, looking for books about magic. James Carlson Sweatt . . . quickly enchants the misanthropic Miss Cort. By the time of his death nine years later, the young giant (now 8 feet 7 inches and 415 pounds) has transformed the heart of the lonely spinster from a tabula rasa into a fully annotated book of love." N Y Times Book Rev

"The reader is mesmerized by this low-key narrative, first lured by Peggy's alternately acerbic and tender

McCracken, Elizabeth—*Continued*

voice, then captivated by James's situation and intrigued by his family, later engulfed by pathos as James's body begins to fail and, finally, amazed by a turn of events that ends the novel with a major surprise. McCracken also invests the narrative with humor, sometimes through Peggy's astringent comments and more often through the use of minor characters who add vivid color and their own distinctive voices." Publ Wkly

Niagara Falls all over again. Dial Press (NY) 2001 308p o.p.

ISBN 0-385-31837-5 LC 2001-28314

This novel chronicles the ups and downs in the relationship between two vaudeville entertainers. It is narrated by an aging Moses Sharensky, who as Mose Sharp was the straight man to his more exuberant partner Rocky Carter

"McCracken understands the ambiguous relationship between comedy and tragedy as well as she understands the relationship between these two funny men. Even a fictional celebrity memoir risks being maudlin, but McCracken knows when to pull back. . . . {She} has a wonderful ear for the way a line or a friendship breaks." Christ Sci Monit

McCrumb, Sharyn

The ballad of Frankie Silver. Dutton 1998 386p o.p.

ISBN 0-525-93969-5 LC 97-24867

A mystery "set in the Appalachians. Sheriff Spencer Arrowood has been summoned to the execution of Fate Harkryder, a man Arrowood put in jail 20 years earlier for the brutal murder of two hikers. While reading over his notes of the case, Arrowood is drawn into researching the story of Frankie Silver, who in 1833 became the first woman to be hung in the state of Tennessee." Libr J

"By working in two time frames and alternating the narrative voice, McCrumb threads both stories into a single pattern, a dense and lovely but very dark design that illustrates the social hypocrisy of the legal system as much as the harshness of mountain justice—then and now." N Y Times Book Rev

Foggy Mountain breakdown and other stories. Ballantine Bks. 1997 326p o.p.

ISBN 0-345-41493-4 LC 97-18787

Contents: Precious jewel; Telling the bees; Love on first bounce; John Knox in paradise; Southern comfort; A snare as old as Solomon; The witness; Not all brides are beautiful; A shade of difference; A wee doch and doris; Remains to be seen; The luncheon; A predatory woman; Happiness is a dead poet; Nine lives to live; Gentle reader; The monster of Glamis; The matchmaker; Old rattler; Among my souvenirs; Typewriter man; Gerda's sense of snow; An autumn migration; Foggy Mountain breakdown

The author "has an uncanny knack for picking up the subtle nuances of dialogue, place, and personality that make her characters and settings sparkle with life. She can perfectly mimic the hillbilly twang of an Appalachian healer or the dulcet, pearshaped tones of an upper-class Briton; she can create the excitement of teenagers in lust, mirror the evil that lurks in a serial killer's heart, or convey the quiet desperation of a woman trapped in a miserable marriage. But most of all, McCrumb can make her readers believe what she writes." Booklist

The hangman's beautiful daughter. Scribner 1992 306p o.p.

LC 91-46057

"Revisiting some of the characters from *If Ever I Return, Pretty Peggy-O* . . . McCrumb weaves Appalachian folklore and death, in natural and unnatural forms, into a story that meanders like a mountain stream through the hills of east Tennessee. . . . Wake County Sheriff Spencer Arrowood asks Laura Bruce, wife of the local Baptist minister, who is now an Army chaplain stationed overseas, to comfort the bereaved at the scene of a bloody murder. Ret. Maj. Paul Underhill, his wife and two of his four children are dead, shot apparently by one of the sons, who took his own life after killing the others. Laura serves as advocate for the surviving children. . . . But when deputy Joe LeDonne discovers that the two have disinterred their father's body from its grave, he wants to know what really happened on the night of the shooting." Publ Wkly

If ever I return, pretty Peggy-O. Scribner 1990 312p o.p.

LC 89-24337

"Two events cause palpitations for the gentle folk of Hamelin, Tennessee. A high school reunion is planned, fanning old jealousies, and Peggy Muryan, a famous 1960s folkie—whose one-time lover and singing partner was reported MIA 20 years before—arrives in town, fixing to stay. Soon threatening letters begin arriving, animals are ritualistically slaughtered, and a local girl bearing a striking similarity to the younger Peggy is pulled from a nearby river. Local policeman Spencer Arrowood must find the killer, deal with the upcoming reunion, and grapple with the volatile collapse of his marriage." Booklist

The author's "strongly individualized characters give serious and intelligent thought to the ghosts raised by the reunion—including the tangible spector of a murderer." N Y Times Book Rev

If I'd killed him when I met him; an Elizabeth MacPherson novel. Ballantine Bks. 1995 277p o.p.

LC 94-23701

"Elizabeth MacPherson, Southern sleuth and forensic anthropologist, investigates a pair of murders for her brother's Virginia law firm." Libr J

"Buoyed by intriguing characters, a wry—sometimes macabre—wit, and lush Virginia atmosphere, McCrumb's mystery spins merrily along on its own momentum, concluding that justice will triumph . . . but in surprising ways." Publ Wkly

MacPherson's lament; an Elizabeth MacPherson mystery. Ballantine Bks. 1992 260p o.p.

LC 92-52661

In this mystery Elizabeth MacPherson's "brother, Bill, a new lawyer, sets up shop in Danville, Va., with Amy Powell (A.P.) Hill, descendant of the southern general known by the same initials. The firm's first few cases aren't auspicious. . . . The pace picks up when the body of a young woman is found in the trunk of A.P.'s client's car and a wealthy businessman from New York wants to buy the house very quickly. Elizabeth, who has

McCrumb, Sharyn—*Continued*

been represented in letters sent from Scotland, finally flies home to help the fledgling attorneys. Interspersed is the tale of Civil War soldier Gabriel Hawks, who with a friend confiscates a part of the Confederate treasury." Publ Wkly

A "witty story that will beguile both mystery buffs and Civil War enthusiasts." Booklist

Missing Susan; an Elizabeth MacPherson mystery. Ballantine Bks. 1991 295p o.p.

LC 91-91887

Elizabeth MacPherson, "an American forensic anthropologist with an interest in historical true-crime cases, takes a busman's holiday: an organized tour of England's most notorious murder sites. Looking forward to a little shoptalk . . . the quick-witted heroine is disappointed to find the obnoxiously eccentric tour guide, Rowan Rover, so guarded and, well, so very nervous about having a chat. Elizabeth attributes Rover's manner to 'a natural shyness on his part,' not knowing that, on an earlier tour of Jack the Ripper's killing ground, the financially strapped guide accepted a murder commission from an American tourist." N Y Times Book Rev

The author "spins the British cozy formula on its ear, slipping in the expected sly one-liner or two and driving her plot so far up a narrative one-way street that only a writer with her nerve and ever-ready wit would have a snowball's chance in hell of pulling the whole tricky caper off." Booklist

The rosewood casket. Dutton 1996 303p o.p.

LC 96-11135

"Old man Stargill is dying, and his four grown sons are called home to the small mountain town where they grew up to say good-bye and carry out their daddy's dying wish: that his 'boys' build him a rosewood casket. But a dying man's wishes aren't the only problems the splintered Stargills are forced to face." Booklist

"Ms. McCrumb spins out the Stargill family secret in the hypnotic tones of a storyteller who knows she has a warming fire at her back and rapt listeners at her feet. Longstanding conflicts and quarrels within this ornery clan give substance to the characters; and some anxiety, if not suspense, is built up when a predatory real estate speculator starts sniffing around the farm. But the author reserves her most persuasive voice for the old stories that she digs out of these ancient hills." N Y Times Book Rev

She walks these hills. Scribner 1994 336p o.p.

LC 94-9458

"In 1779, Katie Wyler, 18, was captured by the Shawnee in North Carolina. The story of her escape and arduous journey home through hundreds of miles of Appalachian wilderness is the topic of ethno-historian Jeremy Cobb's thesis. . . . As Cobb begins to retrace Katie's return journey, 63-year-old convicted murderer Hiram (Harm) Sorley escapes from a nearby prison. Suffering from Korsakoff's syndrome, he has no recent memory. . . . Hamelin, Tenn., police dispatcher Martha Ayers uses the opportunity to convince the sheriff to assign her as a deputy. . . . Deftly building suspense, McCrumb weaves these colorful elements into her satisfying conclusion." Publ Wkly

The songcatcher; a ballad novel. Dutton 2001 321p o.p.

ISBN 0-525-94488-5 LC 00-50831

"McCrumb follows a single ballad through seven generations of the McCourry family, beginning with Malcolm McCourry, kidnapped as a child from the Scottish Isle of Islay in 1751 and brought to the American frontier. The 'songcatcher' is Lark McCourry, a contemporary country-western singer, haunted by her memory of fragments of this ballad from her childhood. Past collides with present when Lark is called home to care for her dying father, from whom she has long been estranged. . . . Investing surprising suspense into Lark's search for the words to the ballad and for the tune of her own life, McCrumb gives the reader intriguing characters, great insight into the landscape and folkways of the South, and rich bits of comedy." Booklist

St. Dale. Kensington 2004 311p $25

ISBN 0-7582-0776-X

"A group of stock car racing fans embarks on a bus tour of Southern speedways—seven states in eight days—as a tribute to legendary NASCAR champion Dale Earnhardt in this meandering road novel modeled after the Canterbury Tales. Harley Claymore, a down-and-out race car driver who yearns to be reinstated, is a tour guide with an encyclopedic knowledge of spectacular races and risk-loving drivers. His 'Where are you folks from?' introduces a diverse group of tour participants: Karen and Shane plan to be married at the first stop, where the bride's Wiccan mother will be waiting, and the groom will try to come to terms with his grief over the death of his hero, Dale, in the 2001 Daytona 500; longtime fan Jim, married 47 years to Arlene, hopes her incipient Alzheimer's won't spoil their enjoyment of the tour; Bill Knight, an Episcopalian priest in smalltown Canterbury, N.H., is chaperone for a dying orphan who was selected for a Last Wish trip; Nebraska resident Ray has proudly plowed his alfalfa field with a giant three (Dale's racing number). Veteran McCrumb provides a lively illustration of the cult of celebrity and offers instructive speculation about the human need for heroes." Publ Wkly

The Windsor knot; an Elizabeth MacPherson mystery. Ballantine Bks. 1990 281p o.p.

LC 90-34168

"Back in Chandler Grove for her nuptials, forensic anthropologist Elizabeth MacPherson finds herself involved in a local police investigation when she is called upon to identify some cremated remains." Booklist

"Elizabeth is less centrally involved in the crime and detection than usual, but this doesn't diminish the appeal of McCrumb's sparkling spoof." Publ Wkly

McCullers, Carson, 1917-1967

The ballad of the sad café [novelette]

In McCullers, C. The ballad of the sad café: the novels and stories of Carson McCullers

In McCullers, C. Collected stories p195-253

In McCullers, C. Complete novels

The ballad of the sad café: the novels and stories of Carson McCullers. Houghton Mifflin 1951 791p o.p.

Contents: This volume contains three novels: The heart is a lonely hunter, The member of the wedding and Reflections in a golden eye; a novelette (the title story) and six short stories

McCullers, Carson, 1917-1967—*Continued*

Clock without hands
In McCullers, C. Complete novels

Collected stories; including The member of the wedding and The ballad of the sad café; introduction by Virginia Spencer Carr. Houghton Mifflin 1987 392p o.p.
LC 87-3944

Contents: Sucker; Court in the west eighties; Poldi; Breath from the sky; The orphanage; Instant of the hour after; Like that; Wunderkind; The aliens; Untitled piece; The jockey; Madame Zilensky and the King of Finland; Correspondence; A tree. A rock. A cloud; Art and Mr. Mahoney; The sojourner; A domestic dilemma; The haunted boy; Who has seen the wind?; The ballad of the sad café; The member of the wedding

"McCullers often wrote about grotesques, people afflicted physically and emotionally. Her themes include loneliness and the mental anguish that stems from love gone awry. Her style is unadorned, quietly rigorous. She's both charming and disquieting—an absorbing challenge to readers of serious fiction." Booklist

Complete novels. Library of America, Distributed to the trade in the United States by Penguin Putnam 2001 827p $35
ISBN 1-931082-03-0 LC 2001-29049

Contents: The heart is a lonely hunter; Reflections in a golden eye; The ballad of the sad café; The member of the wedding; Clock without hands

The heart is a lonely hunter. Modern Lib. 1993 430p $14.95
ISBN 0-679-42474-1 LC 92-51062

A reissue of the title first published 1940 by Houghton Mifflin

"After his friend is committed to a hospital for the insane, John Singer, a deaf mute, finds himself alone. He becomes the pivotal figure in a strange circle of four other lonely individuals: Biff Brannon, the owner of a cafe; Mick Kelly, a young girl; Jake Blount, a radical; and Benedict Copeland, the town's black doctor. Although Singer provides companionship for others, he remains outside the warmth of close relationships." Shapiro. Fic for Youth. 3d edition

also in McCullers, C. The ballad of the sad café: the novels and stories of Carson McCullers p141-498
also in McCullers, C. Complete novels

The member of the wedding. Houghton Mifflin 1946 195p o.p.

"Twelve-year-old Frankie is experiencing a boring summer until news arrives that her older brother will soon be returning to Georgia from his Alaska home in order to marry. Plotting to accompany the newlyweds on their honeymoon occupies much of Frankie's waking hours, while at the same time she is coping with the pressures of puberty and its effects on her body and mind. Particularly revealing are her conversations with her six-year-old cousin and the nurturing black family cook, Bernice." Shapiro. Fic for Youth. 3d edition

also in McCullers, C. The ballad of the sad café: the novels and stories of Carson McCullers p595-791
also in McCullers, C. Collected stories p255-392
also in McCullers, C. Complete novels

Reflections in a golden eye. Houghton Mifflin 1941 182p o.p.

"Set in the 1930s on a Southern army base, the novel concerns the relationships between self-destructive misfits whose lives end in tragedy and murder. The cast of characters includes Captain Penderton, a sado-masochistic, latent homosexual officer; his wife, who is having an affair with Major Langdon; the major's wife, who responds to the trauma of her son's death with self-mutilation; Anacleto, a homosexual servant who is befriended by the major's wife, and an army private who engages in voyeurism." Merriam-Webster's Ency of Lit

also in McCullers, C. The ballad of the sad café: the novels and stories of Carson McCullers p499-567
also in McCullers, C. Complete novels

McCullough, Colleen, 1937-

Caesar; let the dice fly. Morrow 1997 664p il o.p.
ISBN 0-688-09372-8 LC 97-24391

The fifth novel in the Masters of Rome series "opens in 54 B.C., with Caesar civilizing and romanizing the different tribes in Britannia and Gaul. After five years of almost constant warfare, Caesar turns all his political brilliance to defeating Pompey, his former son-in-law, who wants to strip Caesar of his power." Libr J

"Caesar is essentially the same character one recalls from his admittedly self-promoting memoirs—brilliant, ambitious, ruthless and fascinating. The real tragic hero here is Pompey, whose military triumphs are overshadowed by his rival's, whose political fortunes are undermined by Cato and the *boni*, and whose assassination in Alexandria closes this thoroughly Romanized epic novel." N Y Times Book Rev

Caesar's women. Morrow 1996 696p o.p.
ISBN 0-688-09371-X LC 95-34498

The fourth novel in the author's series about the Roman Empire "details Caesar's rise to power from 68-58 B.C. Caesar repeatedly outmaneuvers his enemies, who devise one scheme after another to bring about his political, economic, and social downfall. Eventually he allies himself with Pompey and Crassus to create a formidable triumverate. Despite the book's title, women play minor roles in the novel. Caesar consults his shrewd mother about strategy and depends on her to manage his household. He adores his daughter and misses her dead mother. Nonetheless, he consistently subordinates personal affection to political ambition." Libr J

"With great brio, and ample attention to Roman customs and rites, as well as to the religious, sexual and social institutions of the day, including slavery, McCullough captures the driven, passionate soul of ancient Rome." Publ Wkly

Followed by Caesar

McCullough, Colleen, 1937-—*Continued*

The first man in Rome. Morrow 1990 896p il o.p.

LC 90-37080

The first installment in the Masters of Rome series "outlining the demise of the Roman republic and tracing the origins of the Roman Empire, this volume commences in 110 B.C.E. and revolves around the smoldering political ambitions of two seemingly unsuitable statesmen. Lacking the requisite patrician pedigree, stolid and wealthy Gaius Marius, a brilliant general, acquires respectability by marrying into the irreproachable Julian dynasty. Deprived of his noble birthright by a dissolute and profligate father, the impoverished and curiously amoral Lucius Cornelius Sulla resorts to murder in order to claim an inheritance and purchase his way into the senate. Branded as outsiders, Marius and Sulla forge a formidable alliance, culminating in a succession of unparalled military and political triumphs." Booklist

Followed by The grass crown

Fortune's favorites. Morrow 1993 878p il o.p.

LC 93-534

The third novel in the Ancient Rome series "begins in the year 83 B.C. and runs through 69 B.C., a violent and volatile era that brought the rise and bloody rule of the maniacal, disease-ridden dictator Sulla; the career of the cocky if dense 'Magnus' Pompey; and the youth and education of Julius Caesar." Booklist

"Painstakingly researched, McCullough's Roman saga is like a trip through time. Her characters come to life as do their surroundings. While giving us rollicking good fiction, McCullough has also made clear the bribery and chicanery that made up Roman politics. She has given us clear insight into how Rome found itself changing from a republic to an empire." Libr J

Followed by Caesar's women

The grass crown. Morrow 1991 894p il o.p.

LC 91-17009

In the second novel in the author's series about the Roman Empire "the action hinges on the rivalry between arrogant, paunchy general Marius, eager to fulfill a prophecy and become consul of Rome for a seventh time, and Sulla, a monster who has turned to war-making out of either sexual frustration or boredom. . . . In recreating the Social War between Rome and the rebellious Italian nations (90-88 B.C.), Sulla's crushing of King Mithridates of Pontus and the ensuing bloody Roman civil war, McCullough sustains a keen sense of urgency, framing precarious personal lives against an empire in flux. A quietly magnificent tour de force." Publ Wkly

Followed by Fortune's favorites

An indecent obsession. Harper & Row 1981 317p o.p.

LC 81-47547

This novel is "set in the psychiatric ward of a small military hospital in the South Pacific soon after the end of the Second World War. A novel about duty (the 'indecent obsession'), it has the prescribed mix of best-selling ingredients, romance, sex, violence and paranoia." Oxford Companion to Australian Lit

Morgan's run. Simon & Schuster 2000 604p il o.p.

ISBN 0-684-85329-9 LC 00-41006

A historical saga about Richard Morgan, "a man who falls afoul of villains and suffers the degradation of the 18th-century British penal system. But, as even he admits, he has great luck as a convict. His resourceful cousin, a druggist, fixes him up with survival necessities, and wherever the beautiful, strong, educated Richard goes—overcrowded jails or the hulks of convict transports, suffering the appalling conditions of passage to an unknown continent—he becomes a leader of men. The novel displays fine, informative period details." N Y Times Book Rev

The October horse; a novel about Caesar and Cleopatra. Simon & Schuster 2002 792p $28

ISBN 0-684-85331-0 LC 2002-32753

This sixth and final volume in the Masters of Rome series "traces the last days of the Roman Republic, including the events leading up to the assassination of Julius Caesar and the aftermath of that famous murder. Here, that most renowned of Romans, at the height of his power, and Cleopatra, his illustrious mistress, are at center stage." Booklist

"Though some readers may find the sheer wealth of detail occasionally tedious, the book will find a niche among those who can appreciate the scholarship and research that contributed to recreating Caesar's remarkable career." Libr J

The song of Troy. Orion 2001 c1998 404p maps o.p.

ISBN 0-7528-1705-1 LC 98-215810

First published 1998 in the United Kingdom

"McCullough's version of the 10-year siege of Troy by the armies of Greece unfolds slowly and dramatically, with each chapter narrated by one of the conflict's major players. . . . This vivid portrayal of the people and events of the Trojan War is actually a rewritten version of McCullough's first novel, which was never published." Booklist

The thorn birds. Harper & Row 1977 533p o.p.

"A multigenerational saga of life, love, and death on an Australian sheep ranch." Reader's Ency. 3d edition

"The backdrop to this congested, sensational and often bizarre plot, is the Australian outback, with its dramatic landscapes, vast distances, isolation, bush camaraderie, and natural hazards. The novel aroused lively literary controversy. It was labelled by its critics as a 'potboiler': crudely crafted, sensationally exaggerated, devised to cater to the florid expectations of the mass of undiscriminating readers of modern popular fiction. Its supporters see it as a vigorously-written and racy narrative." Oxford Companion to Australian Lit

McCutchan, Philip, 1920-

Apprentice to the sea. St. Martin's Press 1995 c1994 183p o.p.

LC 94-45091

First published 1994 in the United Kingdom with title: Tom Chatto

This story of life at sea is set in the nineteenth century. "Tom Chatto, 17, fresh from a country vicarage in the West of Ireland, goes to the seaside offices of the Porter Holt Shipping Company and signs aboard a vessel that will carry cargo from Liverpool to South America. He finds among the crew a savage first mate, a remote cap-

McCutchan, Philip, 1920-—*Continued*
tain, and, as a fellow apprentice, a condescending fop." SLJ

"McCutchan effectively and economically limns bustling Liverpool, the daunting mission of beating around the Horn and Victorian England's rigid caste system. Despite its sometimes excessive jargon . . . this spankingly paced novel augurs well for Tom's further voyages." Publ Wkly

Followed by The second mate

Cameron's crossing. St. Martin's Press 1993 171p o.p.
LC 93-24284

"Commander Cameron along with a small crew of enlisted men take passage on the escort carrier HMS *Charger,* which is sailing from Belfast to Norfolk, Virginia, for an overhaul. On passage across the Atlantic HMS *Charger* is beset by a severe North Atlantic storm that not only damages her beyond recovery but reveals the inadequacy of the commanding officer, Captain Mason-Goodson. Cameron takes command in an effort to save both ship and crew from a watery grave." Libr J

"As usual, the stolid, intrepid Cameron soldiers along very ably, while McCutchan's spare prose smartly recreates the lore and real lives of the British navy." Publ Wkly

The last farewell; a novel. St. Martin's Press 1991 308p o.p.
LC 90-49227

"McCutchan weaves a tapestry of stories about the passengers and crew aboard the *Laurentia* as it makes its final voyage from New York to England in 1915. Without a protective escort, Captain Pacey must guide his ship through waters and times more treacherous than he can possibly believe. The U-boat commander has his problems, too, as the action moves from the liner to the submarine to the offices of the British ministers, who, in noncommittal ways, have sentenced the *Laurentia* to its dismal fate. A mesmerizing tale of the sea and the men who pit their lives against nature and politics." Booklist

The new lieutenant. St. Martin's Press 1997 181p o.p.
ISBN 0-312-15604-9 LC 97-10026

First published 1996 in the United Kingdom with title: Tom Chatto, RNR

This "installment of the Tom Chatto military series finds our hero out of the merchant marine and into the Royal Navy Volunteer Reserve in the first year of WWI. Chatto is navigator and third officer (and eventually master) of *Geelong,* an armed decoy battling German U-boats in the Mediterranean, and must face not only hostile submarines but also the personal problems of various shipmates. . . . Though the writing occasionally lapses into generic passages about war disillusionment, readers who have followed Tom Chatto will be interested in the challenges—both epic and personal—posed by The Great War." Publ Wkly

The second mate. St. Martin's Press 1996 c1995 186p o.p.
LC 96-1189

First published 1995 in the United Kingdom with title: Tom Chatto, second mate

"It is now some years after the events of *Apprentice, to the Sea* and Chatto is second mate of a liner on the South American run. After a trouble-plagued voyage, he plays a heroic role in trying to save a derelict sailing ship, with the unexpected help of Patience, the bucko mate from the *Pass of Drumochter. . . . Second Mate* is that rare thing today, a book that could easily have been twice as long without boring the sea-loving reader." Booklist

Followed by The new lieutenant

McDermid, Val

The distant echo. St. Martin's Minotaur 2003 404p $24.95
ISBN 0-312-30199-5 LC 2003-52902

"Winter of 1978, St Andrews University, Scotland. Four drunken young students on their way home from a party stumble upon local barmaid Rosie Duff, who has been raped, stabbed, and left to die. Unable to save her, the men become suspects in the case but are never formally charged. The stigma and shame of the experience follows these men into their adult lives. About 25 years later, two of the four men have been murdered. The remaining two, Alex Gilbery and the Rev. Tom Mackie must identify their friends' killer before they become the next victims of this revenge murder spree." Libr J

"Individually, the characters are sensitively drawn. Collectively, they present the inscrutable face of closed-off communities so terrified of change they would kill for peace." N Y Times Book Rev

A place of execution. St. Martin's Minotaur 2000 403p o.p.
ISBN 0-312-26632-4 LC 00-59145

First published 1999 in the United Kingdom

"When a 13-year-old English schoolgirl goes missing from her Derbyshire village in the winter of 1963, George Bennett, the police inspector in charge of the case, quickly realizes that the secrets of the child's life and possible death are locked in the collective mind of Scardale, an isolated hamlet of inbred families united by their common surnames and their hostility to strangers. Through Bennett's exhaustive efforts, the likely villain is caught and hanged—or so it seems, until the story reaches 35 years into the future for its chilling resolution." N Y Times Book Rev

McDermott, Alice, 1953-

At weddings and wakes. Farrar, Straus & Giroux 1992 213p o.p.
LC 91-42070

Set in Brooklyn during the sixties, this novel "tells the story of an extended Irish-American family observed primarily through the eyes of the children, son and two daughters. Time circles backwards and forwards around a variety of family rituals: holiday meals, vacations at the shore, the wedding of a favorite aunt. The poignant middle-aged romance that develops between the aunt, a former nun, and her suitor, a shy mailman, exacerbates already pronounced family tensions. As they listen to oft-repeated stories about poverty, disease, and early deaths, the children are solemn witnesses to the Irish immigrant experience in America." Libr J

Charming Billy; a novel. Farrar, Straus & Giroux 1998 280p o.p.
ISBN 0-374-12080-3 LC 97-77089

McDermott, Alice, 1953-—*Continued*

This "novel opens at the wake of the debonair Billy Lynch—gifted talker, abandoned suitor, faithful husband, devout Catholic, raging alcoholic. It then ranges back and forth through dozens of family theories and anecdotes to answer the question of what did or didn't make him who he was. At once a love story, a portrait of Irish Catholic Queens, and an ode to an edenic postwar East Hampton, this novel honors the consequences of everyday decisions, both sacred and profane, burnishing them in the retelling to a high shine." New Yorker

Child of my heart. Farrar, Straus & Giroux 2002 242p $23

ISBN 0-374-12123-0 LC 2002-69764

Fifteen-year-old "Theresa's Irish-American 'well-read but undereducated' parents have little money but plenty of foresight; when they see that their only daughter will be beautiful, they move to East Hampton, Long Island, summer playground of New York's richest, in the hopes that Theresa's beauty will eventually win her a wealthy husband." Publ Wkly

This is a "summer idyll in which a cat is hit by a car, a dog is shot, the heroine loses her virginity, and her fairy-like cousin succumbs to a fatal disease and want of parental love. All this loss—of innocence, of dearly loved creatures—and yet, there is not a word of sentimentality or taste of treacle. On the contrary, Child of My Heart is a golden and luminous memory retrieved by a narrator who has achieved a cool and slightly ironic distance from one of those summers in the late fifties or early sixties." Commonweal

That night. Farrar, Straus & Giroux 1987 183p $14.95

ISBN 0-374-27361-8 LC 84-45765

The novel's "narrator reflects on an incident that shattered the serenity and naïveté of her suburban world of the early 1960s, when she was 10 years old. . . . An opening scene of violence played out under a 'bright navy sky' on a soft midsummer night 'when Venus was bright', captures the tone and focus of the novel, which recalls the doomed love affair of teenagers Sheryl and Rick." Publ Wkly

"In spite of its brevity, 'That Night' is a wonderfully unfettered, ample novel, one that celebrates voice, personality and feeling when so much fiction avoids those rewarding characteristics. Ms. McDermott has invested her novel with a strong sense of historical authority, rendering with sure clarity a time and place marked by both a cultural innocence and the premonition of its inevitable loss." N Y Times Book Rev

McDevitt, Jack

Eternity road. HarperPrism 1997 338p o.p.

LC 96-40064

This novel is set a "thousand years or so after a plague-induced collapse of civilization. A hardy band sets out to recover the lost books of the Roadmakers, the builders of what are now the astonishing ruins of that civilization. On the way, the adventurers encounter various exotic societies and mysterious artifacts the Roadmakers left behind, and ultimately, they return with at least part of what they sought. McDevitt redeems the possible overfamiliarity of his quest plot with a large cast of well-handled, original characters." Booklist

Infinity beach. HarperCollins Pubs. 2000 435p $25

ISBN 0-06-105123-3 LC 99-40569

"On the colony world of Greenway, humans still search in vain for evidence of alien intelligence. When Kim Brandywine, fund-raiser for the Seabright Institute's Beacon Project, begins an investigation into the disappearance of her cloned sister Emily, also involved in the search for extraterrestrial life, she opens a door that leads her to her fondest dreams and darkest nightmares." Libr J

McDevitt "has created a future that is technologically sound and filled with hubristic, foolish people who make choices based more on how they will look to history than on what's best for it. Though his aliens are insubstantial . . . the mystery of what happened to Kim's sister and her fellow celestial seekers unfolds as precisely as an origami flower, and will hold readers in thrall." Publ Wkly

Mcdonald, Gregory, 1937-

Carioca Fletch
In Mcdonald, G. The Fletch chronicles

Confess, Fletch
In Mcdonald, G. The Fletch chronicles

Fletch. Bobbs-Merrill 1974 179p o.p.

"A rich young California industrialist, Stanwyck, who is apparently dying of cancer, offers someone he takes to be a beach bum a rich reward if he'll murder him on a particular date. The 'bum' chosen is Fletch, ace journalist, ace philanderer, who accepts the proposition. However, Fletch, who is already investigating the beach drug scene for his newspaper, now investigates Stanwyck—his marital and extramarital life, his relationship with his parents, his obsession with piloting experimental planes. The two strands of the story come together in one deft twist as Fletch . . . both gets the drop on the doublecrossing Stanwyck and uncovers the source of the beach's drugs." Publ Wkly

also in Mcdonald, G. The Fletch chronicles

Fletch and the man who
In Mcdonald, G. The Fletch chronicles

Fletch and the Widow Bradley
In Mcdonald, G. The Fletch chronicles

The Fletch chronicles. Hill & Co. Pubs. 1987-1988 3v o.p.

LC 87-8742

"Rediscovery books"

Contents: one: Fletch won (c1985) entered separately; Fletch, too (c1986) entered separately; Fletch and the Widow Bradley (c1981)

[two]: Fletch (c1974) entered separately; Carioca Fletch (c1984); Confess, Fletch (c1976)

three: Fletch's fortune (c1978); Fletch's moxie (c1982); Fletch and the man who (c1983)

Fletch reflected. Putnam 1994 222p o.p.

LC 94-16640

Fletch's son Jack "heads to the huge Georgia estate of billionaire inventor Chester Radleigh at the request of Shana Steufel, an old, but memorable, one-night stand of

Mcdonald, Gregory, 1937-—*Continued*

Jack's. Shana, who is engaged to one of Radleigh's sons, believes her future father-in-law's life is in danger." Publ Wkly

"The Fletch novels have always offered a unique mix of suspense and cartoonish characterizations. The son of Fletch continues the family tradition." Booklist

Fletch, too. Warner Bks. 1986 249p o.p.
LC 85-41001

In this novel Fletch "finds true love and marries ever-patient Barbara; he finds his long-lost father (who then proceeds to get lost); and he seeks both a murderer and a lost Roman civilization." Booklist

also in Mcdonald, G. The Fletch chronicles

Fletch won. Warner Bks. 1985 265p o.p.
LC 85-40009

"Bucking for meaty assignments as a fledgling newspaper reporter, Fletch seizes the chance to get out of the society pages when Donald Habek is shot dead. Instead of writing his assigned piece on Habek's offer to donate a fortune to the art museum, Fletch sees himself with bylines on the front pages if he can beat Biff Wilson, the crime reporter, in the race to investigate the dead man's background." Publ Wkly

also in Mcdonald, G. The Fletch chronicles

Fletch's fortune
In Mcdonald, G. The Fletch chronicles

Fletch's moxie
In Mcdonald, G. The Fletch chronicles

Son of Fletch. Putnam 1993 236p o.p.
LC 93-684

"Good-natured hero Irwin Maurice ('Fletch') Fletcher discovers he has a heretofore unknown son from a friendly one-night stand 20 years earlier. Somehow son Jack has become involved with a bunch of neo-Nazi thugs fresh out of prison, but Fletch has trouble believing that the fruit of his loins could really be a bad guy at heart. . . . Good pacing, good humor, and good writing make Mcdonald's latest another fan pleaser in a predictable but comfortable series." Booklist

McDonald, Roger, 1941-

Mr. Darwin's shooter. Atlantic Monthly Press 1999 365p o.p.
ISBN 0-87113-733-X LC 98-36819

This novel focuses on the life of a British sailor, Syms Covington. McDonald portrays him as Charles Darwin's aide-de-camp, a man "who, though he's barely mentioned in Darwin's writings, toiled at his side throughout his early career, bagging the vast array of specimens upon which Darwin founded his theory of natural selection." Time

"Mr. MacDonald is a generous, leisurely author who gives the reader a large cast of quirky characters, much peripheral detail, lively action, and a view of nineteenth-century social patterns. Covington, moreover, is no plaster saint, and the Beagle's long voyage offers opportunities for adventure. One need not be pro or anti either Darwin or Genesis to enjoy this well-written tale." Atl Mon

McElroy, Joseph

Actress in the house; a novel. Overlook Press 2003 432p $26.95
ISBN 1-58567-350-1 LC 2002-34555

The plot of this novel turns "literally on the impact of a single glimpsed action—an actor slapping an actress with unfeigned force during a performance of a play—as it registers in the mind of Bill Daley, a man in the audience. The fact of the slap then gathers implication and mystery as Daley returns to the theater after hours and meets the actress, Becca; and finally spirals outward as the two get involved and begin, as any couple might, to ask questions and tell their stories." N Y Times Book Rev

"McElroy's prose, especially his dialogue, is enigmatic and layered with meaning, and the mood he creates is both subtly threatening and achingly wistful. Over a 40-year career, McElroy has been compared to William Gaddis, Don DeLillo, and Thomas Pynchon. This absorbing and unsettling novel, his first in 14 years, may finally bring him the wider recognition he deserves." Booklist

McElroy, Lee, 1926-

For works written by this author under other names see Kelton, Elmer, 1926-

McEwan, Ian

Amsterdam. Doubleday 1999 193p o.p.
ISBN 0-385-49423-8 LC 98-41401

"Two longtime friends meet at the cremation of the woman they shared, beautiful restaurant critic and photographer Molly Lane. Clive Linley, a celebrated composer, and Vernon Halliday, the editor of a financially troubled London tabloid, could never understand Molly's third liaison—with conservative Foreign Secretary Julian Garmony, who is angling to be prime minister, or her marriage to dour but rich publisher George Lane. . . . Immediately afterwards, both Clive and Vernon are enmeshed in a crisis: Clive must finish his commissioned Millennium Symphony so it can premiere in Amsterdam, and Vernon must grapple with the moral issue of publishing photos of Julian Garmony in drag that George has discovered with Molly's effects." Publ Wkly

McEwan "has written a tastily vicious tale in his usual polished prose." Libr J

Atonement; a novel. Doubleday 2002 351p $26
ISBN 0-385-50395-4 LC 2001-44291
First published 2001 in the United Kingdom

The major events of the novel "occur one day in the summer of 1935. Briony Tallis, a precocious 13-year-old with an overactive imagination, witnesses an incident between Cecilia, her older sister, and Robbie Turner, son of the Tallis family's charwoman. . . . It then becomes easy for her to believe that the shadowy figure who assaults her cousin Lola late that night is Robbie. Briony's testimony sends Robbie to prison and, through an early release, into the army on the eve of World War II. Gradually understanding what she has done, Briony seeks atonement first through a career in nursing and then through writing, with the novel itself framed as a literary confession it has taken her a lifetime to write." Libr J

This is a "work of astonishing depth and humanity. . . . The upper-class milieu, the sense of place and time,

McEwan, Ian—*Continued*

are rendered with an exactitude worthy of Elizabeth Bowen. . . . Mr McEwan has achieved the difficult task of combining literary sophistication with moral gravity." Economist

Black dogs. Putnam 1992 xxii, 149p o.p.

LC 92-7418

"The narrator of this taut, questioning tale is an orphan relentlessly drawn to other people's parents. This habit of attraction and need takes full form when Jeremy becomes intrigued with his in-laws. June is spiritual, reclusive, and fatally ill; Bernard is active, pragmatic, and political. They fell in love during the grieving yet determined days following World War II, united by an ardent and idealistic faith in communism and a bold sexual passion. But their bliss was short-lived. The source of the philosophical chasm that quickly opened between them, June's epiphanic confrontation with two black dogs in rural France, is alluded to often but not fully explained until that last chapter." Booklist

This novel is "compassionate without resorting to sentimentality, clever without ever losing its honesty, an undisguised novel of ideas which is also Ian McEwan's most human work." Times Lit Suppl

The child in time. Houghton Mifflin 1987 263p o.p.

ISBN 0-395-42912-9 LC 87-8603

"On a balmy outing to a supermarket with his adored three-year-old daughter, Stephen Lewis, a writer of successful children's books, experiences the unthinkable. His daughter disappears. He searches frantically but can't find his Kate. Finally, despairingly, he must return home, must tell his wife, Julie, the terrible fact." West Coast Rev Books

"Many of the plot turns in the novel may seem improbable and even fanciful, but the feelings expressed by the characters and their sense of time (running up, running down and running out) are, without exception, genuine. . . . [This is an] astonishing book." Time

Enduring love; a novel. Talese 1998 252p o.p.

ISBN 0-385-49112-3 LC 97-23029

First published 1997 in the United Kingdom

As this novel opens, "several men struggle to hold down a hot air balloon that threatens to break free, carrying a small child with it. One by one they let go, until one man is left hanging and is carried off to drop shortly to his death. For [the] narrator, Joe, one of the men struggling to hold down the balloon, this is only the beginning of the nightmare. Another would-be rescuer, a devout Christian [named Jed] who happens to be gay, conceives a passion for Joe and begins stalking him relentlessly, both to convert him and to draw him away from his beloved Clarissa. In the meantime, a mystery grows up around the dead man, a dedicated doctor and family man whose presence in the field that fateful day needs explaining." Libr J

McEwan is a "maestro at creating suspense: the particular, sickening, see-sawing kind that demands a kind of physical courage from the reader to continue reading." New Statesman (1913)

The innocent. Doubleday 1990 270p o.p.

LC 89-25669

"Basing his story on an actual (but little known) incident, McEwan tells of the secret tunnel under the Soviet sector which the British and Americans built in 1954 to gain access to the Russians' communication system. The protagonist, Leonard Marnham, is a 25-year-old, naive, unsophisticated English post office technician who is astonished and alarmed to find himself involved in a top-secret operation. At the same time that he loses his political innocence, Leonard experiences his sexual initiation in a clandestine affair with a German divorcée five years his senior. As his two secret worlds come together, events develop into a gruesome nightmare." Publ Wkly

"There is . . . a point to all this, which is to display the astonishing deeds that human beings can perpetrate and yet retain a measure of innocence. . . . In spite of what has happened, Leonard is able to live with himself. This is far and away Ian McEwan's most mature work." New Statesman Soc

Saturday. Nan A. Talese/Doubleday 2005 289p $26

ISBN 0-385-51180-9

This novel is "set within a single day in February 2003. Henry Perowne is a contented man—a successful neurosurgeon, happily married to a newspaper lawyer, and enjoying good relations with his children. Henry wakes to the comfort of his large home in central London on this, his day off. . . . After an unusual sighting in the early morning sky, he makes his way to his regular squash game with his anaesthetist, trying to avoid the hundreds of thousands marchers filling the streets of London, protesting against the [Iraq] war. A minor accident in his car brings him into a confrontation with a smalltime thug. To Perowne's professional eye, something appears to be profoundly wrong with this young man, who in turn believes the surgeon has humiliated him." Publisher's note

"It's clear that with this volume, Mr. McEwan has not only produced one of the most powerful pieces of post-9/11 fiction yet published, but also fulfilled that very primal mission of the novel: to show how we—a privileged few of us, anyway—live today." NY Times (Late NY Ed)

McFarland, Dennis

A face at the window. Doubleday 1997 309p o.p.

LC 96-31232

In this "ghost story, Cookson Selway flies to England with his wife, who will be sopping up atmosphere for her next mystery. But for Cook the mystery is more immediate; at the hotel, the hypersensitive Cook, who has had odd, out-of-time experiences in the past, hears music no one else hears and then has visitations from a ghostly little girl and her slovenly uncle, who died years ago in a fall from one of the building's window. . . . With the help of Pascal, the French clerk, and an Asian couple who frequent the hotel's dining room, Cook starts investigating his visitors. Soon he is so caught up in them that he leaves reality behind." Libr J

The author "has a most beguiling narrative style: he is sometimes funny and sometimes moving; in descriptions of the hauntings he is so exact that it is easy to suspend disbelief, and in his ulterior purposes he is persuasive. Behind the haunting of Cookson Selway by the ghosts of the hotel and the ghosts of his own past lurks the haunting of the author by the idea of the dysfunctional American family. The whole makes for a thoroughly satisfying novel." N Y Times Book Rev

McFarland, Dennis—*Continued*

The music room. Broadway Bks. 1990 275p o.p.
LC 89-71721

"Marty Lambert, a San Francisco record company executive, is facing an impending divorce when his younger brother Perry, a talented composer, commits suicide in New York. Mystified by his brother's death, Marty goes to New York to seek an explanation, following an elusive trail of clues that leads from his brother's friends to the troubled history of his wealthy Virginia family. In the end he learns as much about himself as Perry, coming to terms with a legacy of alcoholism." Libr J

"In one startling realistic scene after another, with evocative description and a fluid, natural language, 'The Music Room' itself builds to a comprehensive vision, remarkable from its beginning to its surprising, satisfying end." N Y Times Book Rev

School for the blind. Houghton Mifflin 1994 287p o.p.
LC 93-49831

This novel "chronicles the waning years of two elderly siblings, Francis and Muriel Brimm, as they reluctantly come to grips with the past and learn to accept their gradual decline. . . . Walking on the golf course near the Florida town where Muriel has spent her life and to which retired photojournalist Frank has returned, they discover the bones of two students from the nearby school for the blind. The search for the killer's identity forces Frank and Muriel to abandon their own willed 'blindness' and to retrieve memories of their childhood with a mean, alcoholic father and a stern, cold mother." Publ Wkly

"Readers of 'School for the Blind' may find their attention held less by the plot than by everything that supports it. This is an inversion of expectations, but not finally a disappointing one." N Y Times Book Rev

Singing boy; a novel. Holt & Co. 2001 309p $25
ISBN 0-8050-6608-X LC 00-32051

"One night, Malcolm, husband of Sarah and father of eight-year-old Harry, is shot to death in front of his horrified family. . . . We soon realize that Sarah and Harry have no emotional support network. Sarah, unable to resume her work as a chemistry professor at a prestigious Boston university, turns to Malcolm's best friend, Deckard, a black Vietnam vet and recovered drug addict. But for Deckard, Malcolm's murder stirs up not only grief but also painful flashbacks of war and an abusive childhood. As Sarah and Deckard's friendship becomes strained, Harry suffers through nightmares on his own." Libr J

"The language here is always apt, and always in tune with the characters' thoughts. McFarland has a gift for selecting details, so that we see this novel's world with remarkable intimacy." N Y Times Book Rev

McGahern, John, 1934-

By the lake; a novel. Knopf 2002 335p o.p.
ISBN 0-679-41914-4 LC 2001-50258

"The story is an old one: in search of a quieter way of life, Joe and Kate Ruttledge have traded their careers in London for a farm near a small Irish village, where they learn how to raise sheep and are steadily drawn into the lives of their neighbors. There's the Shah, a rich bachelor in search of an heir for his business; John Quinn, a weaselly sexual predator, and a danger to women throughout the county; and Jimmy Joe McKiernan, an I.R.A. leader whose exploits periodically stir up high feeling. McGahern is never sentimental, and the novel's greatest pleasures come from the unflinching probity of his observations." New Yorker

McGarrity, Mark, 1943-2002 *See* Gill, Bartholomew, 1943-2002

McGarrity, Michael

The big gamble; a Kevin Kerney novel. Dutton 2002 272p $23.95
ISBN 0-525-94656-X LC 2002-20755

"When two murder victims turn up after a fire in an abandoned fruit stand on a rural highway, Kerney, now the police chief of Sante Fe, N. Mex., takes a personal interest in the case. One blackened corpse is a John Doe. The other remains belong to a 29-year-old college student, Anna Marie Montoya, who disappeared 11 years before. As it happens, Kerney was involved in the search for the missing Anna Marie. Investigating the John Doe is Kerney's estranged son, Clayton Istee, now a deputy sheriff for the Lincoln County (N. Mex.) police." Publ Wkly

Everyone dies; a Kevin Kerney novel. Dutton 2003 273p $23.95
ISBN 0-525-94761-2 LC 2003-9208

In this installment "an unidentified psycho has his sights set on Kerney, his family, and his soon-to-be-born child. . . . McGarrity contrasts the painstaking investigatory work that leads to identifying a suspect with the personal crisis Kerney and his wife, Sara, face. Uncertain about how a child will affect their relationship, the couple must now contend with a much more immediate threat to their lives." Booklist

"Michael McGarrity is one of those low-key pros who keep the genre honest with realistic crime stories and plain-talking cops who know the procedures." N Y Times Book Rev

The Judas judge; a Kevin Kerney novel. Dutton 2000 274p o.p.
ISBN 0-525-94547-4 LC 99-89181

Kevin Kerney "returns to his childhood home near Tularosa to investigate the murder of six people found at various campgrounds along one stretch of road in southern New Mexico. The trail leads to a retired judge and his disaffected children, all of whom have skeletons aplenty in their dysfunctional closets." Booklist

"McGarrity is no nature writer, and his sketches of dusty desert towns like Alamogordo and Ruidoso are as blunt as his unsentimental character studies. Still, his portrait of the region is a strong one, built on meticulously detailed intelligence gathered, sifted and analyzed for unspoken secrets and lies by the author's own deeply cunning mind." N Y Times Book Rev

Under the color of law; a Kevin Kearney novel. Dutton 2001 272p $23.95
ISBN 0-525-94604-7 LC 00-69406

Kevin Kerney "is settling into his new job as police chief of Santa Fe, N. Mex., and his new subordinates are of two minds whether they should trust him or not. They

McGarrity, Michael—*Continued*

have ample opportunity to observe him in action, because as the book opens, Phyllis Terrell, the estranged wife of an ambassador and ex-military honcho, is found stabbed to death in the kitchen of her hilltop mansion, and Father Joseph Mitchell, an ex-soldier turned priest researching the government's covert operations, turns up dead in the Christian Brothers Residence at the College of Santa Fe." Publ Wkly

McGowan, Heather

Schooling. Doubleday 2001 314p $24.95
ISBN 0-385-50138-2 LC 00-47452

The "story of a young American girl, Catrine Evans, who is bewildered to find herself suddenly installed in an English boarding school after the death of her mother. The book takes in too the innner lives of three men: Catrine's Welsh father, whose old school, Monstead, she now attends, and two Monstead masters, the chemistry instructor and amateur painter, Mr. Gilbert, and the sad, frustrated, literary Mr. Betts." N Y Times Book Rev

"McGowan works in an experimental mode. At once lush and harsh, and inventive in form, the novel reads like an extended sensory exercise. Readers who prefer a straightforward narrative may be bemused, but those willing to accept the challenge will be rewarded with a beautifully written coming-of-age tale." Publ Wkly

McGown, Jill

Murder at the old vicarage. St. Martin's Press 1989 c1988 256p o.p.
LC 88-30603

"A Thomas Dunne book"

First published 1988 in the United Kingdom with title: Redemption

"While snow blankets the small village of Byford, the vicar, George Wheeler, is in a hopeless muddle. . . . He finds himself attracted to a young widow—a fact that has not escaped his wife's notice. In addition, his daughter has moved back to the vicarage in order to escape an abusive husband. When the husband is discovered dead, the three members of the Wheeler family are the prime suspects. What appears to be a simple case of domestic murder to Chief Inspector Lloyd and Sergeant Judy instead becomes a complicated plot to love and revenge." Booklist

"McGown's complex plot is masterful and her sleuths and their predicament are enthralling." Publ Wkly

Picture of innocence. Ballantine Pub. Group 1998 325p o.p.
ISBN 0-449-00250-0 LC 97-45816

"Inspectors Lloyd and Hill study a bizarre case of murder. Someone has finally killed the obnoxious, abusive man who ruined two marriages in his financially motivated quest to produce a male heir." Libr J

This "mystery possesses a wealth of psychological nuance and narrative depth, all the way through to the resolution, a masterpiece of controlled complexity." Publ Wkly

Plots and errors. Ballantine Bks. 1999 375p $22.95
ISBN 0-345-43313-0 LC 99-14226

First published 1998 in the United Kingdom

"When Andy Cope and his wife, Kathy, owners of a struggling detective agency, are found dead in their car . . . Detective Chief Inspector Lloyd rejects the majority opinion that they committed suicide. His theory, that the Copes were murdered, receives serious consideration when their one client, wealthy Mrs. Angela Esterbrook, is shot to death. Why would someone with her sort of money employ an untried agency to carry out an investigation? That's just one of many puzzles that Lloyd and his partner, Judy Hill, confront in a case that defies reason." Publisher's note

The stalking horse. St. Martin's Press 1988 186p o.p.
LC 88-15834

"A Thomas Dunne book"

"Businessman Bill Holt fails to convince anyone that he did not commit the two murders of which he is accused: that of his lifelong friend, Alison Bryant, and of a private detective he never even met, Michael Allsopp, who had been assigned to trail Alison. Holt spends 16 years in prison pondering the link between the crimes and becomes obsessed with discovering the identity of the murderer, belatedly realizing that it had to be one of his acquaintances. When he is paroled, he returns home to the English countryside in quest of the truth and the person who framed him." Publ Wkly

"McGown has constructed a taut, enthralling mystery, borrowing from the hard-boiled and the British procedural styles to write in a way all her own." Booklist

Verdict unsafe. Fawcett Columbine 1997 327p o.p.
LC 97-4949

"In an English Midlands town, Colin Drummond, known as 'the stealth bomber,' is in prison for rape. Forty-year-old Detective Inspector Judy Hill took his confession. Now, after three years in prison, Drummond has been released to be tried again. He harasses Hill with phone calls and threats, and she fears that he will add to his total of four rapes. Judy's lover, Detective Chief Inspector Lloyd . . . is also involved in the case." Libr J

"The pace is methodical and the cast cheerless, but McGown wraps her grim tale in a complex, satisfying solution." Publ Wkly

McGrath, Patrick, 1950-

Asylum. Random House 1997 254p o.p.
ISBN 0-679-45228-1 LC 96-24849

This novel is set in an insane asylum and narrated by Dr. Peter Cleave. It is 1959. "Stella Raphael is a psychiatrist's wife. She is a dissatisfied beauty on the verge of middle age who falls madly in love . . . with Edgar Stark, sculptor, lover, psychopath, killer and inmate of the asylum where her dull husband is the ambitious deputy superintendent. Stella and Edgar embark on a disastrous affair. . . . He escapes from the asylum. And so, a little later, does she." Times Lit Suppl

"It is part of McGrath's bemusing artfulness in Asylum that he can make the reader suffer the fate of all his characters. Everyone in the novel, that is to say, is deranged by their own, and other people's, plausibility. When anyone speaks in Asylum–and McGrath has an extraordinary ear for the hollows in conversation, for the

McGrath, Patrick, 1950-—*Continued*
lurking soliloquies–we seem to see through them in the full knowledge that they never see through themselves." London Rev Books

The grotesque. Poseidon Press 1989 186p o.p.
ISBN 0-671-66509-X LC 89-3486
"The setup is macabre: a distinguished paleontologist is brain-damaged and slowly turning into a vegetable. He cannot speak, but narrates an interior monologue of all he sees and hears: a lot of sexual shenanigans and a particularly grisly murder, all centered around 'Fledge,' the butler, who has ambitions." Publ Wkly
"Part of the fun of reading 'The Grotesque' is recognizing the literary allusions and watching as one after another the subgenres of murder mystery, Gothic horror, social satire, black comedy and stories of the double are invoked and skillfully woven together." N Y Times Book Rev

Martha Peake; a novel of the Revolution. Random House 2000 367p o.p.
ISBN 0-375-50081-2 LC 00-29064
"A Young man named Ambrose is summoned by his dying Uncle William to an ancient pile called Drogo Hall, there to hear the story that the uncle, with the last of his strength, is driven to tell. It is the story of Harry Peake—smuggler, poet, freak, madman, tormented soul—and of his splendid red-haired daughter, Martha, who emigrates to America and becomes an early martyr of the Revolution. But Uncle William is erratic in his delivery and wandering in his mind. . . . So it is Ambrose who by means of sympathy, imagination, intuition, must fashion a coherent account." N Y Times Book Rev
"McGrath is a vivid writer, and his detailed evocations of the atmosphere and settings of its various times and places are among the pleasures of the book." Times Lit Suppl

Spider. Poseidon Press 1990 221p o.p.
ISBN 0-671-66510-3 LC 90-7492
The novel is the "purported journal of Dennis 'Spider' Cleg, a frail, deranged Londoner. . . . After many years away, Spider returns to his old neighborhood in London's East End slums. Ensconced in a small drab room in a grubby boarding house, he keeps a written record in which he reconstructs and grapples with the mysterious events in his childhood that caused his long sojourn in Canada." N Y Times Book Rev
"Despite a less pungent second half, Spider confirms McGrath's mastery of the terrain he's staked out for himself: a twisted place where the most rank, hideous experiences are conveyed in a prose so tight, assured, and essentially self-mocking that he maintains a fine balance between high gothic horror and fussy stylization." Voice Lit Suppl

McGregor, Elizabeth

The ice child. Dutton 2001 372p o.p.
ISBN 0-525-94567-9 LC 00-67703
This novel "centers around three journeys: that of the doomed 1845 Arctic expedition headed by Sir John Franklin; a present-day trek undertaken by a polar bear and her dying cub; and the search, by a journalist named Jo Harper—whose fiancé, a Franklin devotee named Doug Marshall, dies when he is hit by a car—for bone marrow that will save their dying 2-year-old son, Sam." N Y Times Book Rev
"McGregor introduces perhaps one dramatic twist too many, but her novel otherwise artfully mixes historical background, up-to-date medical information about a rare disease, a bit of pop psychologizing and some upbeat lessons about the survival of the human spirit." Publ Wkly

McGuane, Thomas, 1939-

The cadence of grass. Knopf 2002 238p o.p.
ISBN 0-679-44674-5 LC 2001-50623
"Sunny Jim Whitelaw is dead, but he continues to cast a shadow over his family's life. His will requires that his daughter Evelyn patch up her relationship with her no-good husband, Paul—if she doesn't, the ownership and profits of Sunny Jim's Montana bottling plant will be lost." Publ Wkly
"The real engine of the book is not plot . . . but language: McGuane's sentences are like no one else's, crisp and spare, yet some how baroque, and he perpetually balances the picaresque against the sublime." New Yorker

Keep the change. Houghton Mifflin 1989 230p o.p.
ISBN 0-395-48887-7; 0-7710-5517-X
LC 89-30996
"Joe Starling leaves his family's Montana ranch as a teenager, attending Yale and later becoming a successful painter in New York. Now in a state of emotional and spiritual disarray, he returns, hoping to lay claim to the rundown ranch and 'find a restored coordination for his life' in the old values of hard work and closeness to the land. But his romantic notions run aground on the realities of the modern West: He ultimately loses the ranch to his mad Uncle Smitty's scheming and discovers the duplicity of the seemingly innocent Ellen, the ranch owner's daughter he romanced one summer and now longs to return to." Libr J
"Thomas McGuane is the pool shark of our prose. His sentences click with imperious precision. Masse and carom and draw shots follow each other with elan. McGuane puts English on his English so the words swerve with fatal charm. . . . What singles out this novel is the honesty with which McGuane has tested his version of Huck Finn. The final pages have overwhelming authority." Christ Sci Monit

Ninety-two in the shade. Farrar Straus and Giroux 1973 197p o.p.
ISBN 0-374-22259-2 LC 73-76222
This novel concerns Thomas Skelton, who, "having rejected the straight life and become a fishing guide near Key West, Florida, is the victim of an extravagant practical joke designed to drive him out of the guiding business. When Skelton blows up the joker's skiff in retaliation, the joker [Nichol Dance] wanting to establish his 'credence' in his opponent's eyes, promises to kill him should he guide again, Skelton does guide again and the joker kills him." Libr J
Despite "unexpected, complex ironies, the relation of Skelton and Dance is too laconic and abstract to achieve quite the classic fatality McGuane aims for. . . .What keeps [the novel] exciting to read is McGuane's feeling

McGuane, Thomas, 1939-—*Continued*

for the rambunctious oddities, forlorn vulgarity and green beauty of Key West. . . . [This] is, with its faults, a very fine book." Newsweek

Nobody's angel. Random House 1981 227p o.p.
ISBN 0-394-52264-8 LC 81-13885

At 36 melancholy, ex-juvenile delinquent, ex-prep school student, ex-Army captain, Patrick Fitzpatrick "returns to his family's Montana ranch . . . tends his grandfather, a dotty cowpoke, and his loony sister [Mary], and feels exhausted, depleted, bewildered. . . . At a party he meets Claire, a young Oklahoma woman who's beautiful, oil-rich and married. The action moves between Patrick's attempts to keep his family and ranch shipshape and his struggle to . . . woo and conquer Claire." Newsweek

"What stamps this as a McGuane novel are the bizarre episodes he invents for his character and the wit with which he reports them; what is new . . . is a depth of feeling." N Y Times Book Rev

Nothing but blue skies. Houghton Mifflin 1992 349p o.p.
LC 92-23623

"Frank Copenhaver is a mix of modern businessman and old-style rancher. . . . As the novel begins, his wife, Gracie, leaves him, and his domestic upheaval signals a succession of setbacks in his business life. Copenhaver's downward spiral gathers speed as he engages in a series of fleeting sexual liaisons, lands in jail after a bar fight, demolishes the pick-up truck of a fling's jealous cowboy boyfriend, and almost destroys his Montana business empire." Times Lit Suppl

"The author's underlying theme is the unimportance of money by comparison with love, an old point that he makes with novel means and without sentimental sugar." Christ Sci Monit

Panama. Farrar Straus and Giroux 1978 175p o.p.
ISBN 0-374-22942-2 LC 78-12344

"The plot finds drugged-out and washed-up rock star Chet Pomeroy trying to get his act together in wild and wonderful Key West, Florida." Libr J

"Thomas McGuane is the pool shark of our prose. His sentences click with imperious precision. . . . The words swerve with fatal charm." Christ Sci Monit

McHugh, Maureen F.

Nekropolis. Eos 2001 257p o.p.
ISBN 0-380-97457-6 LC 2001-33525

"As a 'jessed' or bonded servant, Hariba possesses a chemically induced sense of loyalty to her master until her growing affection for an artificial construct drives her to an act of desperation and changes her life forever. . . . This luminous tale of forbidden love in a near-future Morocco explores the evolution of human nature in a world where technology has redefined the meaning of the word *human*." Libr J

McInerny, Ralph M., 1929-

The basket case; a Father Dowling mystery; {by} Ralph McInerny. St. Martin's Press 1987 182p o.p.
LC 87-16313

"When Constance Farley Rush leaves her infant son in a basket at Fr. Dowling's church, she means to accuse her ex-husband, Peter Rush, of plotting to kidnap the baby. But . . . someone kills Rush, presenting the priest and his pal, Lt. Keegan of the Fox River, Ill., police, with a knotty case of murder." Publ Wkly

Bishop as pawn; a Father Dowling mystery; [by] Ralph McInerny. Vanguard Press 1978 219p o.p.
LC 78-54978

"Father Dowling's housekeeper's husband returns after a desertion of 15 years, only to be killed. Involved in this odd collection of bits and pieces is a good Catholic girl who wants to marry an irreligous man, leading to a singularly bleak affair, a young undogmatic and fundamentalist priest much disliked by Father Dowling, and an incomprehensible kidnapping of the remarkably smooth bishop." Libr J

Body and soil; an Andrew Broom mystery; {by} Ralph McInerny. Atheneum Pubs. 1989 245p o.p.
LC 88-38209

In this mystery Indiana attorney Andrew Broom, "represents some very unpopular clients, including a strange young man who has confessed to the murder of a local boy. In the midst of that trial, the town's wealthiest couple brawls in public, loudly insists on a divorce, and hires Broom and his partner/nephew as opposing attorneys. Then murder interrupts the proceedings. In a departure from the traditional whodunit, McInerny offers readers front-row seats to observe the villain's activities." Booklist

The book of kills; a mystery set at the University of Notre Dame; [by] Ralph McInerny. St. Martin's Minotaur 2000 275p $23.95
ISBN 0-312-20346-2 LC 00-40257

"A series of pranks, including the kidnapping of the chancellor, has alarmed the Notre Dame administration, and the Knight brothers get the call to investigate. The various shenanigans seem somehow related to the claim by a group of Native Americans that the land on which the famed university stands was stolen from them and should be returned. . . . Another deft and mordantly witty excursion into the rarefied atmosphere of Notre Dame." Publ Wkly

A cardinal offense; [by] Ralph McInerny. St. Martin's Press 1994 372p o.p.
LC 94-3481

"A Father Dowling mystery"

"A man, pursuing an annulment, and his wife, who is opposed, meet separately with Fr. Dowling in St. Hilary's rectory on the same day that the priest receives two surprise tickets to the next Notre Dame-Southern California football game. The husband says his wife was never really a Catholic; she insists that the 30-year marriage and the couple's grown children remain valid. After the man is murdered, Dowling and his cop friend Phil Keegan consider possible suspects." Publ Wkly

McInerny, Ralph M., 1929-*—Continued*

Celt and pepper; [by] Ralph McInerny. St. Martin's Minotaur 2002 210p $22.95

ISBN 0-312-29117-5 LC 2002-69938

"After a young Notre Dame professor/Poet dies unexpectedly, Professor Roger Knight. . . suspects murder. His erudition, coupled with assistance from his brother Philip, a private investigator, ultimately leads to a killer. Solid plotting from a practiced hand." Libr J

Grave undertakings; a Father Dowling mystery; [{by] Ralph McInerny. St. Martin's Minotaur 2000 374p o.p.

ISBN 0-312-20309-8 LC 99-54817

"Mimi O'Toole is hoping for a miracle when she asks Father Dowling in the hospital for absolution for her dying husband, a shooting victim. Vincent O'Toole was known to be an associate of the Pianone crime family, and his funeral draws every notable in the local underworld to St. Hilary's church in Fox River, Ill. The cops don't seem all that anxious to find O'Toole's killer, until someone tries to dig up his grave on Halloween and his casket is later discovered to be empty. In his effort to figure out what happened to O'Toole both before and after death, Father Dowling remains the calm center in a swirl of events." Publ Wkly

Irish coffee; [by] Ralph McInerny. 1st ed. St. Martin's Minotaur 2003 247p $23.95

ISBN 0-312-30901-5 LC 2003-50620

"Everybody likes Fred Neville, who works in Notre Dame's sports information office. Everybody but one person-the person who killed him. A different side of unassuming Fred surfaces when two women arrive at his funeral, each claiming Fred as their fiance. Because South Bend, home of Notre Dame, is always deferential to the university, the locals have no objection when the Knight brothers become unofficial consultants on the case. Phillip Knight is a streetwise PI, and his immensely rotund brother, Roger, is an amateur sleuth and a revered professor of Catholic studies. . . . A fine effort by a deservedly respected genre veteran." Booklist

Irish tenure; a mystery set at the University of Notre Dame; [by] Ralph McInerny. St. Martin's Minotaur 1999 246p o.p.

ISBN 0-312-20345-4 LC 99-16992

"Two young philosophy professors, Amanda Pick and Hans Wiener, are vying for the single tenured spot open in their department. . . . Pick has become the object of obsession of a Chesterton expert on the English faculty, Prof. Sean Pottery. So when her body is found in a lake on campus, Pottery seems like a good suspect. . . . A second murder clouds the issue momentarily, but sleuth Roger Knight, a mountain of a man who holds a chair in Catholic Studies at Notre Dame, uncovers the truth." Publ Wkly

Judas Priest; a Father Dowling mystery; [by] Ralph McInerny. St. Martin's Press 1991 184p o.p.

LC 91-21819

"A seminary friend of Dowling's, former priest Chris Bourke, and his ex-nun wife now promote sexual liberation as televangelists of Enlightened Hedonism (EH). Meeting Dowling one day after Mass, Bourke asks the parish priest to talk about the hard facts of religious life with his daughter, Sonya, who wants to enter the convent. Before Dowling can do that, Sonya is reported kidnapped and then found stabbed to death. . . . Dowling, worldly-wise and armed with ready references to St. Paul and other Church fathers, is at his vintage best." Publ Wkly

Last things; a Father Dowling mystery; [by] Ralph McInerny. St. Martin's Minotaur 2003 307p $24.95

ISBN 0-312-30899-X LC 2003-40641

"Father Dowling first becomes involved with the Bernardo family when Eleanor Wygant asks him to try to persuade her niece, Jessica Bernardo, to stop writing a novel based on the Bernardo family. Eleanor is afraid of the resultant scandal if her long-buried secret is revealed. . . . There is a murder for Father Dowling to solve, of course, but this time McInerny seems more interested in exploring the motivations and entwined family relationships of his characters. There's also plenty of the Catholic minutiae that Father Dowling fans enjoy." Booklist

Prodigal father; a Father Dowling mystery; [by] Ralph McInerny. St. Martin's Minotaur 2002 341p o.p.

ISBN 0-312-29129-9 LC 2001-58865

"When a laicized priest requests a reinstatement to a moribund religious order, the few remaining members of the dwindling Athanasian community initially rejoice. However, when Father Nathaniel begins pressuring the other priests to sell their valuable seminary property, their ranks quickly become divided. After Nathaniel is found with an ax buried in his back, Father Dowling digs for a motive buried deep in the past." Booklist

Requiem for a realtor; a Father Dowling mystery; Ralph McInerny. 1st ed. St. Martin's Minotaur 2004 263p $23.95

ISBN 0-312-32417-0 LC 2004-41858

"Stanley Collins is Fox River's most notorious philandering realtor. His wife, Phyllis, wants to divorce him but is afraid to lose her claim on an impending inheritance. She is stringing along her dentist, love-struck Dave Jameson, who's also a devout Catholic. Jameson is a prominent member of St. Hilary's parish and, as an emissary for Phyllis Collins, asks Father Dowling's advice regarding a divorce and her standing in the church. Circumstances change when Stanley Collins is run down by his own car a couple of blocks from the apartment of a local nightclub torch singer, with whom he is having an affair. Dowling closely watches as the investigation–directed by his closest friend, Phil Keegan, of the Fox River PD–unfolds. . . . McInerny adds a moral catch-22 for Dowling as he struggles to choose between helping solve a murder and betraying the sanctity of a parishioner's confidences." Booklist

Second vespers; a Father Dowling mystery; [by] Ralph McInerny. Vanguard Press 1980 224p o.p.

LC 79-56379

Father Dowling "moves in on the criminals uncovering their various attempts to cheat collectors of O'Rourke memorabilia. Among the characters are two people who have a bookshop located in the old O'Rourke mansion, the local librarian who has a collection of letters, and another who is trying to get his hands on all the available

McInerny, Ralph M., 1929-—*Continued*

O'Rourke papers. When a body is discovered, it throws doubt on the state of the 'estate' and also on the murder of O'Rourke." West Coast Rev Books

Seed of doubt; [by] Ralph McInerny. St. Martin's Press 1993 346p o.p.
LC 93-556

"A Father Dowling mystery"

"The questionable death of a wealthy nonagenarian matriarch, two hitherto unknown portraits by a renowned landscape artist, and a great-granddaughter's search for self form the core of [this] Father Roger Dowling mystery." Booklist

"McInerny delivers a comfy unreality in this genteel whodunit, graced with the trappings of a traditional Catholicism." Publ Wkly

Still life; a novel; [by] Ralph McInerny. Five Star 2000 255p $21.95
ISBN 0-7862-2895-4 LC 00-61724

This mystery features "Captain Egidio Manfredi of the Fort Elbow, Ohio, police force. Manfredi is staring at mandatory retirement when he and his young assistant are ordered to reopen a 30-year-old case involving the disappearance of the poet-wife of a now-retired professor." Booklist

"Clever repartee, hidden alliances both present and past, false claims of guilt, pointed observations on aging, and surprising marriage plans underscore the author's talents." Libr J

Thicker than water; a Father Dowling mystery; [by] Ralph McInerny. Vanguard Press 1981 255p o.p.
LC 81-10432

This "Father Dowling mystery takes off from a couple of petty crimes . . . to a series of bizarre murders. Father Dowling . . . discovers a dead body in a pickup truck parked in front of the rectory. Murders start piling up around the quiet little town." Booklist

McIntosh, K. H.

For works written by this author under other names see Aird, Catherine

McIntyre, Vonda N.

Dreamsnake. Houghton Mifflin 1978 313p o.p.
LC 77-18891

"This is based on McIntyre's Nebula Award-winning novelette, 'Of Mist, and Grass, and Sand,' which is also the first chapter of the book. Snake, the healer, and her three healing serpents attend a young boy ill with a tumor. His fearful parents kill Grass, the dreamsnake, who can ease the dying by removing their pain. Without Grass, Snake is incomplete as a healer, and since the dreamsnakes come from off-world, she cannot get a replacement. To atone for her carelessness in losing Grass, Snake sets off for the city where off-worlders trade, hoping to get more dreamsnakes. She has many heart-stopping adventures, and the reader is engrossed every step of the way." Libr J

Of mist, and grass, and sand
In The Best of the Nebulas p478-93

McKenney, Eileen *See* West, Nathanael, 1903-1940

McKillip, Patricia A., 1948-

Alphabet of thorn; Patricia A. McKillip. 1st ed. Ace Books 2004 314p $22.95
ISBN 0-441-01130-6 LC 2003-62912

"The day that the new queen of Raine is crowned, a translator working in the palace receives a book written in a strange language of thornlike characters. As Nepenthe, the translator, unlocks the language's secret, she learns of a legend from the ancient past that involves her and the queen in an intrigue that threatens the kingdom itself. McKillip . . . creates the atmosphere of a fairy tale with her elegantly lyrical prose and attention to nuance. Her characters are at once intimately personal and larger than life." Libr J

The sorceress and the Cygnet. Ace Bks. 1991 231p o.p.
LC 90-44103

"More than 1000 years ago the Gold King, Dancer, Blind Lady and Warlock fought the Cygnet, lost and were banished. Commoners put their story in the constellations to remember it. Ro Holding has the sign of the Cygnet and rules the other Holds, which have the other signs. But now the Gold King, seeing a way to reestablish the alliance, sets up an elaborate plot to trick Nyx Ro, daughter of the ruling family and a powerful Sorceress, and Corleu, a peasant of the Wayfolk, into releasing the vanquished and helping them find the Heart of the Cygnet." Publ Wkly

This fantasy "features imaginative worldbuilding, strong male and female characters, and an intense (though sometimes esoteric) style." Libr J

Followed by The Cygnet and the firebird (1993)

McKinney-Whetstone, Diane

Blues dancing; a novel. Morrow 1999 307p o.p.
ISBN 0-688-14995-2

"This love story is set in Philadelphia. Verdi is the naive, pampered only child of a prominent Southern preacher who has come north for college, while black student leader Johnson is brash, energetic, and sometimes angry. . . . Caught between the desire for success and the fast life of the streets, Johnson experiments with drugs, ultimately becoming addicted to heroin and getting Verdi addicted as well. Upright, conservative professor Rowe, who believes that it is his duty to guide Verdi in the right direction, falls in love with her and eventually leaves his wife for her. They live together comfortably for 20 years, until Johnson returns and forces Verdi to make a decision that will change her life forever. A captivating read." Libr J

Leaving Cecil Street; a novel; Diane McKinney-Whetstone. 1st ed. Morrow 2004 297p $24.95
ISBN 0-688-16385-8 LC 2003-55845

"Cecil Street is a quiet, tree-lined haven in West Philadelphia, a place where everyone knows everyone else, a place removed from the turmoil and violence of the late 1960s. Yet the residents of Cecil Street have their problems. Joe and Louise's marriage is strained; Johnetta's sexy niece has arrived, ripe for trouble; and teenaged Shay tries to help best friend Neet deal with an unwant-

McKinney-Whetstone, Diane—*Continued*

ed pregnancy. When Neet's abortion goes tragically wrong, everyone on the street must rally around her, while Joe, Louise, and Neet's mother, Alberta, discover how their pasts have now drawn them together. McKinney-Whetstone's portrayal of African American family life is sensitive and compassionate, with characters who love, work, live, and die without veering into soap opera." Libr J

Tempest rising; a novel. Morrow 1998 280p o.p.
LC 97-40942

This "novel is set in Philadephia during the sixties. Three sisters, Bliss, Victoria, and Shern, are raised as privileged middle-class children until tragedy unravels their lives. . . . The death of the family's 'rock' causes the mother to suffer a nervous breakdown, and the girls are removed from her care. The novel focuses on the attention they receive and the relationship that develops between each girl and their caregivers, Mae and Ramona. Mae is a politically connected foster-care provider, but she shows little concern for her own daughter, Ramona. Ramona struggles to accept her role as secondary child-care provider, yet she resents the children and her mother's abuse. Each character is unforgettable." Booklist

McKinzie, Clinton

Crossing the line; Clinton McKinzie. Delacorte Press 2004 373p $23
ISBN 0-385-33637-3 LC 2003-64602

"Antonio Burns is a cop, not a saint. Having earned the scornful nickname "QuickDraw" for a shooting that went very wrong, the Wyoming narcotics agent is fighting for redemption and holding on to his family with all the strength he possesses. His brother, Roberto, is another story. His quicksilver heart, hair-trigger temper, and unquenchable hunger for adrenaline rushes have landed him in prison and make him the right person for an FBI agent with a plan. Agent Mary Chang cool, collected, and always under control wants to take down Jesus Hidalgo, a murderous drug lord who has moved his methamphetamine operation from Mexico to a remote Wyoming canyon. In Roberto, Chang has found someone who can penetrate Hidalgo's heavily guarded crime ranch." Publisher's note

"When the Burns brothers are high up on a rock face or hunting down evil banditos, the pace and intensity shoot skyward. Readers will find themselves hanging on by their fingernails as they wait to see who will fall and who will live to climb again." Publ Wkly

McLaglen, John J., 1938-

For works written by this author under other names see Harvey, John, 1938-

McMahon, Thomas A., 1943-1999

Ira Foxglove. Brook Street Press 2004 169p $21.95
ISBN 0-9724295-3-0 LC 2003-21792

This novel is about "a talented scientist whose . . . heart has been broken physically and spiritually. In an odyssey to repair both Ira ventures on a fantastical journey by blimp to try and recover his fractured family. Along the way he also works on an unorthodox creation of a prosthetic heart." Publisher's note

This is a "darkly genial novella discovered among McMahon's papers a year or so after his death. . . . This may be an early work, set aside for who knows what reason, but it has the same loopy charm and rueful insight as McMahon's previously published fiction." N Y Times Book Rev

Loving Little Egypt; [by] Thomas McMahon. Viking 1987 273p o.p.
ISBN 0-670-81228-5 LC 86-40259

"'Little Egypt' is the name taken by a nearly blind young man, Mourly Vold, who is an unschooled genius in physics. Mourly intuits the principles underlying the nascent long-distance telephone system beginning to link the U.S. in the 1920s. He shares his ability to tap into the telephone circuits with a network of other blind youngsters who soon become known as the 'telephone vandals' and are hunted down by mean, ruthless William Randolph Hearst and brutal, vainglorious Thomas Edison. Counterbalancing these unscrupulous public figures are Alexander Graham Bell, Mourly's benign benefactor, and eccentric physicist Nikola Tesla, who helps Mourly take his revenge on Hearst and his minions." Publ Wkly

"All is resolved in a broadly farcical (though perhaps too hurried) conclusion, with many chuckles along the way and some interesting speculations on the nature of scientific investigation. An intriguing and enjoyable romp." Libr J

McKay's bees. Harper & Row 1979 198p o.p.
ISSN 0-06-0129743
LC 78-20211

"Moving from Massachusetts to Kansas in 1855 with his new wife and a group of German carpenters, Gordon McKay is dead set on making his fortune raising bees–undaunted by Missouri border ruffians newly-minted Darwinism, or the unsettled politics of a country on the brink of civil war." Publisher's note

"McMahon, in such a short novel, should not have been able to bring coherence out of Darwin and Lincoln, bees and machines, East and West, honey and blood. . . . That he manages–that wit, irony, gentleness, passion, and knowledge conspire so successfully–is a wonder of craft." N Y Times (Late NY Ed)

Principles of American nuclear chemistry; a novel. University of Chicago Press 2003 c1970 246p (Phoenix fiction) pa $15
ISBN 0-226-56110-0 LC 2003-48355

First published 1970 by Little, Brown

"What was life like for the scientists working at Los Alamos? Thomas McMahon imagines this life through the wide eyes of young Tim McLaurin, the thirteen-year-old son of an MIT physicist who, inspired by a young woman named Maryann, worked on the project." Publisher's note

"One of the rewarding things about [this] novel . . . is the total absence of any predictable generation-gap bitterness. Beyond lost innocence the book is about a problem that troubles the age–a sense of having pursued wrong priorities too hotly, an awareness of the neglect of life and love that results." Time

McMillan, Rosalyn

Blue collar blues. Warner Bks. 1998 359p $30
ISBN 0-446-52243-0 LC 98-19553

McMillan, Rosalyn—*Continued*

"Thyme Tyler is an African American plant manager for Champion Motors (a hybrid of Ford, GM and Chrysler) who has hit the glass ceiling even though she holds a Ph.D. Khan Davis is a handsomely paid factory worker who faces the threat of layoff and daily struggles for overtime in the plant. The two women maintain a . . . friendship despite their class differences and despite Khan's refusal to forgive Thyme's marriage to a sterotypically lily-white Champion exec." Publ Wkly

McMillan, Terry, 1951-

A day late and a dollar short. Viking 2001 448p o.p.
ISBN 0-670-89676-4 LC 00-46232

Viola Price "and her estranged husband, Cecil, both live in Las Vegas, and their four grown children, while scattered across the country, lead the kind of complicated lives that make Viola sick with worry." N Y Times Book Rev

McMillan "takes a multiperspective view of dysfunctional families with each member of the Price clan giving his or her own version of how screwed up they all are. . . . Their heavy load—incest, substance abuse, poverty, infidelity, death—makes this a soap opera, but it is leavened with a big dollop of sass." Time

Disappearing acts. Viking 1989 384p o.p.
ISBN 0-670-82461-5 LC 88-40412

"Franklin is an on-again off-again construction worker trying to get his life on a firmer foundation. Zora is a music teacher and would-be singer. They meet and start a relationship that initially seems ideal. Soon, however, problems emerge. Franklin's ego has never recovered from his destructive mother's abuse, and the repeated blows the oppressive white society dishes out make him increasingly depressed and hostile. The relationship begins to fall apart. Zora and Franklin have to grow a long way alone before they can come back together." Libr J

"What raises this work above a mere sentimental love story is the finely tuned humor, which McMillan uses effectively to subtly alter the meaning of a scene or to draw the reader into her circle of characters." Booklist

How Stella got her groove back. Viking 1996 368p o.p.
LC 96-15374

"Stella Payne is a successful 42-year-old investment analyst and divorced mother of an 11-year-old son, Quincy. But Stella has begun to feel that her life needs some 'groove.' On the spur of the moment, she plans a trip to Jamaica to relax and escape from her routine. She meets a man, half her age, whose honesty and physical charm challenge her perceptions of what is acceptable and force her to rethink and re-prioritize her image of herself and her life." Booklist

"Readers who have been yearning for a Judith Krantz of the black bourgeoisie—albeit one with a dirty mouth and a more ebullient spirit—will be pleased with this fantasy of sexual fulfillment." Publ Wkly

Waiting to exhale. Viking 1992 409p $22.95
ISBN 0-670-83980-9 LC 91-46564

This novel "tells the stories of four 30ish black women bound together in warm, supportive friendship and in their dwindling hopes of finding Mr. Right. Savannah, Bernadine, Robin and Gloria are successful professionals or self-employed women living in Phoenix. All are independent, upwardly mobile and 'waiting to exhale'—to stop holding their breaths waiting for the proper mate to come along." Publ Wkly

"Terry McMillan's heroines are so well drawn that by the end of the novel, the reader is completely at home with the four of them. They observe men—and contemporary America—with bawdy humor, occasional melancholy and great affection. But the novel is about more than four lives; the bonds among the women are so alive and so appealing they almost seem a character in their own right." N Y Times Book Rev

McMullen, Sean, 1948-

Glass dragons; Sean McMullen. 1st ed. TOR Bks. 2004 495p map $27.95
ISBN 0-7653-0797-9 LC 2003-60677

In this sequel to Voyage of the Shadowmoon (2002), "the honorable vampire Laren, the priestess Terikel, and the voluptuous Lady Velander continue their journey aboard the exploratory ship Shadowmoon. Their search for a doomsday weapon known as the Dragonwall leads them to an encounter with a fugitive bard, a runaway sailor, and a widowed princess. Australian author McMullen depicts a world filled with intrigue and strange magic, where the borders between the living and the dead are thin and where mystical weapons have the power to destroy the world. His sometimes whimsical, always literate style brings a gentle touch of wry humor to a tale of courage and cowardice, love and death, mystery and magic." Libr J

Souls in the great machine. TOR Bks. 1999 448p o.p.
ISBN 0-312-87055-8 LC 99-21934

"A Tom Doherty Associates book"

"In the fortieth century, librarians rule the world. Through a byzantine system of political favor, mathematical expertise, civil service testing, and dueling, the librarians strive for power in the 'mayoralty' of Rochester, the most powerful of several Australian fiefdoms that emerged long ago from a nuclear winter. The highliber is the scheming yet honorable Zarvora. She has ruthlessly assembled scores of mathematicians, who make the Calculor, a bizarre flesh-and-machine supercomputer that Zarvora needs to unify this quasi-medieval world and save it from the impending doom implicit in the Call. . . . Decidedly original, sometimes whimsical, and captivating, this is a genuine tour de force." Booklist

McMurtry, Larry

Anything for Billy. Simon & Schuster 1988 382p o.p.
LC 88-22732

This novel is based on the legend of Billy the Kid (William Bonney), here named Billy Bone. The story is "told by Ben Sippy, a dime novelist from Philadelphia who went west in 1878 in search of the real life he'd made up stories about. There he befriended a likable, bucktoothed 17-year-old who already had a reputation as a killer, and he later wrote a novelette about Billy Bone that gave him his legendary name. . . . The 'real story' is . . . recounted by Sippy in old age." Newsweek

McMurtry, Larry—*Continued*

"McMurtry's prose is as readable as ever, served up in short, episodic chapters that effectively capture time and place, conjure up authentic images of pathetic heroes and villains, and yet pull the reins in on action. The tale's strength lies in Sippy's commanding first-person delivery and the less-than-admirable profile of the title character." Booklist

Boone's Lick; a novel. Simon & Schuster 2000 287p o.p.

ISBN 0-684-86886-5 LC 00-56342

This "novel concerns itself with a trek made by the Cecil clan—the tough-minded matriarch, Mary Margaret; her dissembling brother-in-law, Seth; her children, Shay, G. T., Neva and baby Marcy; and Grandpa Crackenthorpe—from Boone's Lick, Mo., to Fort Phil Kearney, in what would later become the state of Wyoming, shortly after the Civil War." N Y Times Book Rev

"McMurtry's historical novel, told with humor and candor from the perspective of Mary Margaret's oldest son, Shay, is highly recommended for adults and adolescents alike." Libr J

Buffalo girls; a novel. Simon & Schuster 1990 351p o.p.

LC 90-42486

"This is a nostalgic, funny, and sad novel about the Old West when cowboys and Buffalo girls whooped it up. Their behavior was amoral rather than immoral, and they lived by their own special code of behavior. Friendship was often life-saving as well as comforting, and the women of the bawdy houses called their clients 'sweethearts' even if their encounter was only for one night. Jim Ragg and Bartle Bone had become almost a dying breed and Custer, in their opinion, was a stupid old man at Little Big Horn to think that he could fight 3,000 Indians with 200 of his men. Highlights of the book are Bill Cody's (Buffalo Bill's) Wild West show and Calamity Jane's (whose drunkenness was calamitous) letters to a daughter. Fact and fiction are entwined in an enjoyable story that is mythic and memorable." Shapiro. Fic for Youth. 3d edition

By sorrow's river; a novel. Simon & Schuster 2003 347p (Berrybender narratives, Book 3) $26

ISBN 0-7432-3304-2 LC 2003-53892

"In this third volume of McMurtry's Berrybender Narratives, Lord Berrybender and his obnoxious, sniveling brood are, surprisingly, still alive on the dangerous Great Plains of Wyoming and Colorado. The wry story of mountainman adventure and European stupidity, set in the 1830s, is just as wacky and gruesome as its predecessors." Publ Wkly

Cadillac Jack; a novel. Simon & Schuster 1982 395p o.p.

LC 82-5962

"Jack was a rodeo bulldogger before he graduated to roaming America 'in a pearl-colored Cadillac with peach velour interior,' scouting for antiques he can resell to collectors. . . . But now Jack is undergoing a midlife crisis, juggling old wives and new girl friends as he flounders in the amiable venality and lechery of Washington, D.C." Libr J

"The sheer exuberance of McMurtry's imagination makes this book well worth reading." West Coast Rev Books

Comanche moon; a novel. Simon & Schuster 1997 752p o.p.

ISBN 0-684-80754-8 LC 97-29609

This novel "follows Woodrow Call and Augustus McCrae through their years as Texas Rangers as they create legends for themselves fighting the Comanche to open west Texas for settlement." Libr J

"McMurtry has created a sprawling, picaresque novel that, like the history of the West itself, leaves more than a few loose ends. . . . The characters are the novel's strength. McMurtry's rangers are heroic because of their vulnerabilities, not despite them." N Y Times Book Rev

Dead man's walk; a novel. Simon & Schuster 1995 477p o.p.

ISBN 0-684-80753-X LC 95-21011

"We meet Woodrow Call and Gus McCrae when they're novice Texas Rangers not yet 20 years old. They are part of a pack of Rangers bound for new frontiers in the Wild West. Traveling with the team is Mathilda, a heavyset whore who provides both comfort and wisdom. When the group gets word that the town of Santa Fe—full of gold and silver and prosperity—is primed to be captured, they head out for a long, dangerous, and ill-fated journey." Booklist

"If Dead Man's Walk were not a prequel, it would be worth only glancing notice. As things are, it is a satisfactory foothill, with the grand old mountain in view. There are no heroics, though there is plenty of calamity. . . . McMurty has a fine time with youthful damnfoolishness, and so does the reader." Time

The desert rose; a novel. Simon & Schuster 1983 254p o.p.

LC 83-4687

"A topless dancer in a casino, Harmony 'had been said by some to have the best legs in Las Vegas and maybe the best bust too.' But now Harmony is approaching her 39th birthday, and her teenage daughter Pepper has become a contender for those honors. . . . [The] novel charts good-natured Harmony's sudden decline and Pepper's . . . well, peppery rise." Libr J

Duane's depressed; a novel. Simon & Schuster 1999 431p o.p.

ISBN 0-684-85497-X LC 98-45712

In this novel, Duane Moore, rich and bored, surprises a Texas town "by ditching his pickup truck and walking everywhere." Time

"Duane is no intellectual, but he isn't stupid. Abandoning the ordinary ways of making do, he moves to a crude cabin on the prairie and starts trying to figure out where his life stalled. Before long he is seeing a psychiatrist, who has him reading Proust as part of his therapy. Novelistically, some of this seems too, um, made up, but Duane himself is always achingly affecting and real. . . . He is one of McMurtry's greatest characters." Newsweek

The evening star. Simon & Schuster 1992 637p o.p.

LC 92-2596

Sequel to Terms of endearment

Aurora Greenway's "aging boyfriend, the general, has lost some of his zest, and her new lover is the psychoanalyst she's gone to with her troubles. Those troubles include her grandchildren—Tommy, who's in jail for shooting his girlfriend; brilliant Teddy, who met *his* girl-

McMurtry, Larry—*Continued*
friend on a visit to *his* therapist; and pregnant, overweight Melanie, who has picked up yet another hapless boyfriend and is heading for California." Libr J

"The success of a book like this one depends on the tone the author manages to muster up. Mr. McMurtry's is sentimentality laced with comic irony, and it works very well. . . . And if, in the end, Aurora Greenway and her extended and highly dysfunctional family turn out to be more entertaining than genuinely moving, it's reassuring to know that they—and the reader—are in the hands of a real pro." N Y Times Book Rev

Folly and glory. Simon & Schuster 2004 236p (Berrybender narratives, Book 4) $25
ISBN 0-7432-3305-0 LC 2003-64173

"This is the fourth and concluding volume of the Berrybender Narratives. . . . Once again, the heart of the story is the evolving relationship between Tasmin Berrybender and her enigmatic, primitive husband, Jim Snow. Both have changed. Tasmin has learned to cope with the physical demands of a nomadic life and the emotional demands and trauma of motherhood and death. Jim, still capable of savage violence, seems more tender and vulnerable here. As they and their familiar entourage journey eastward from Santa Fe, they encounter various historical personages, including William Clark, Charles Bent, and Davy Crockett. They also endure searing landscapes, cholera, and the constant threat of horrific brutality at the hands of Apaches, Kiowas, Commanches, and slave traders." Booklist

"While McMurtry doesn't stint on frantic action, violence or seemingly round-the-clock gropings, Folly and Glory marks a somber and satisfying end to a long, rambunctious trip." N Y Times Book Rev

Lonesome dove; a novel. Simon & Schuster 1985 843p o.p.
ISBN 0-671-50420-7 LC 85-2192

"Two former Texas Rangers have been running a ramshackle stock operation near the Mexican border with a lot of work and not much success. When they hear rumors of freewheeling opportunities in the newly opened territory, they decide to break camp, pull up stakes, and head north. Their dusty trek is filled with troubles, violence, and unfulfilled yearning." Booklist

"'Lonesome Dove' shows, early on, just about every symptom of American Epic except pretentiousness. McMurtry has laconic Texas talk and leathery, slim-hipped machismo down pat, and he's able to refresh heroic clichés with exact observations about cowboy prudery, ignorance and fear of losing face." Newsweek

Followed by Streets of Laredo (1993) and Dead man's walk (1995)

Loop group. Simon & Schuster 2004 242p $25
ISBN 0-7432-5079-6 LC 2004-52216

"Maggie is divorced, nearing 60, and still gainfully self-employed on the fringes of the Los Angeles movie industry. Following a hysterectomy, she finds herself feeling low and disengaged from her former self and others. This particularly infuriates her three married daughters, who have always been able to count on Maggie's connection to them and her generosity to their families. . . . Maggie teams up with her sexy but aging friend Connie, and they light out on a cross-country trip to Texas. They fling caution to the wind, rail against growing older, and decry the loss of their wild, gallivanting, man-cruising days." Libr J

"Clearly, more sincere praise of the mature woman is overdue. And McMurtry's adulation is more than sincere, it's heated. He doesn't shy away from the pleasures of sexagenarian flesh." N Y Times Book Rev

Sin killer. Simon & Schuster 2002 300p $25
ISBN 0-7432-3302-6 LC 2002-17616

"The first of four tales of the Berrybender family. It's 1832, and Lord and Lady Berrybender—wealthy Brits incongruously venturing into the Wild West—make their way up the Missouri River. . . . Among those in the sizable entourage are 6 of the 14 Berrybender children, including Tasmin, a gutsy, industrious young woman who generally takes charge of the hapless group. . . But Tasmin's independence brings strife, too, especially when she hooks up with frontiersman Jim Snow, an Indian fighter and wanna-be preacher." Booklist

"McMurtry's prose is plain and exact, exhibiting the kind of clarity that appears simple yet is anything but." N Y Times Book Rev

Streets of Laredo; a novel. Simon & Schuster 1993 589p o.p.
LC 93-19279

This sequel to Lonesome Dove "takes place 20 years after the death of Gus McCrae. In this novel, Captain Woodrow Call, McCrae's old partner, tracks a young Mexican train robber, Joe Garza, with the help of a railroad accountant named Brookshire, a Texas deputy named Ted Plunkett and Pea Eye Parker, who is trying to build a family life with his wife Lorena and their children. Across the Texas Panhandle and into northern Mexico, Call pursues his prey." America

"As in some great 19th-century saga, the story has more than its share of improbable coincidences—but these seem only mild contrivances to shape a story packed with action, terror, humor and pathos. *Laredo* is a fitting conclusion to a remarkable feat of reconstruction and sheer storytelling genius." Publ Wkly

Terms of endearment; a novel. Simon & Schuster 1975 410p o.p.

"Houstonian Aurora Greenway, a transplanted New Englander, is a well-to-do widow trying to settle her own life and at the same time to dominate and control the lives of those around her—Emma, her married daughter; Rosie, her long-suffering maid; an array of suitors that includes a retired Patton-style general, an aging yachtsman, a broken-down opera singer, a bank vice president and a truly eccentric Texas millionaire. . . . Aurora alternately delights and infuriates those around her." Libr J

"Suddenly, just when we are enjoying ourselves the most, McMurtry changes his style, and we are plunged into a moving but agonizing realistic account of daughter Emma's death from cancer at 37 and the way in which her family and old friends react. . . . The shift of pace may throw some readers off stride badly. McMurtry certainly remains, however, one of our most exciting novelists." Publ Wkly

Followed by The evening star

McMurtry, Larry—*Continued*

Texasville; a novel. Simon & Schuster 1987 542p o.p.

LC 86-31520

"McMurtry returns to the town of Thalia, Texas, site of the 'The last picture show' (1966). The backwater town of the 1950s has experienced the oil boom and is now enduring the oil glut. Although some of the characters from the previous novel make appearances, McMurtry focuses on oilman Duane Moore—dynamic, yearning, caught up in the maelstrom of times. Duane is struggling with a twelve-million-dollar debt and is further bewildered by the manic behavior of his wife, his children, and other citizens of Thalia, all of whom seem to be reacting to hard times by going slightly berserk." Booklist

"What's funniest, and most lifelike, about McMurtry's . . . book is that his people, having enjoyed a brief but exhilarating run of American abundance (both financial and sexual), don't mind indulging in a little harmless romanticizing of their frontier history, but they're not about to give up what they've got and go back to their arid, windswept beginnings without some kicking and screaming. . . . In its affable, offhand way, McMurtry's novel, which ends with a joke about repetition . . . really is about history, at least as Americans live it." New Yorker

Followed by Duane's depressed

The wandering hill; a novel. Simon & Schuster 2003 302p (Berrybender narratives, Book 2) $26

ISBN 0-7432-3303-4 LC 2002-30595

"In the second installment of 'The Berrybender Narratives,' a tetralogy that opened with Sin Killer, McMurtry continues the saga of the aristocratic Lord Berrybender and his entourage. Having abandoned the luxury steamer on which they traveled up the Missouri River because it was stuck in the ice, the party of 17 family members, servants, and numerous hangers-on waits out the winter at a trading post on the Yellowstone before moving on." Libr J

"The landscape is stunningly beautiful, but the beauty is often disrupted by spasmodic, gruesome violence. Nonetheless, this novel is an engrossing, exciting, and sometimes heart-rending saga of the American West that shows McMurtry at his best." Booklist

Zeke and Ned; a novel; by Larry McMurtry and Diana Ossana. Simon & Schuster 1997 478p o.p.

LC 96-44906

"In the years just after the Civil War, life in the Indian Territory west of Arkansas—Cherokee land since the Trail of Tears—is more than a bit rugged, particularly for the Indians. Guns blaze with minimal provocation. Women are at the mercy of wandering marauders. And when the white man's justice does come, it's usually meted out by thugs from Arkansas, temporarily deputized as Federal marshals. Against this backdrop, a Cherokee named Zeke Proctor accidentally shoots the woman he had planned to bring home as his second wife—a killing that sets in motion a chain of events that destroys several families, nearly leads to war and concludes with a mountaintop standoff between Federal marshals and Zeke's friend and son-in-law, Ned Christie." N Y Times Book Rev

"What gives this well-wrought tale its depth is how McMurtry and Ossana convey the era's various moral shades of gray." Publ Wkly

McNicholl, Damian

A son called Gabriel. CDC Books 2004 343p $22.95

ISBN 1-59315-018-0

"A coming-of-age story set in Northern Ireland during the years 1964-78 . . . . Catholic schoolboy Gabriel Harkin faces formidable obstacles to fitting into his family and community. In the background lurks the threat of religious prejudice; in the foreground is his increasing awareness that he may be homosexual. Subjected to brutal hazing by his more athletic classmates, Gabriel feigns an interest in football and seeks to repress his sexuality. He becomes almost hyperaware of all the characteristics that mark him as different and channels his energy into studying for the exams that will become his ticket out of his insular, increasingly violent hometown. A secret involving his uncle, a conflicted priest, also haunts the family. Perhaps the most poignant aspect of this novel, though, is the way his parents and siblings, although severely limited in their knowledge of how to help him, seek to comfort him in his struggle to conform." Booklist

McPhee, Jenny

No ordinary matter; a novel; Jenny McPhee. Free Press 2004 259p $23

ISBN 0-7432-6072-4 LC 2004-43246

"For more than a decade, thirtysomething sisters Lillian and Veronica have met at a Manhattan Hungarian bakery the first Monday of the month. Stunningly beautiful but ice-cold Lillian is a brilliant neurologist. Her lovely younger sister, warmhearted, insecure Veronica, is a scriptwriter for the wildly popular soap opera Ordinary Matters. Veronica has spent a lifetime worshiping her older sister, who unfailingly swats back at Veronica's overtures. In a series of coincidences that would give Victor Hugo pause, the sisters' already complicated and deeply entwined lives become even more so. A dysfunctional childhood (a dead father and a neglectful mother), a pregnancy, a new lover, a psychiatrist with Tourette's syndrome, several independent private investigations into secret second families, a long-lost brother, and other delicious surprises draw the reader in for the fun." Libr J

McPhee, Martha

Gorgeous lies. Harcourt 2002 326p $31

ISBN 0-15-100613-X LC 2002-7213

Sequel to Bright angel time (1997)

"In 20 years, many things have changed in the lives of the large Furey-Cooper clan. Once the members were widely known as exemplars of a new kind of blended family, living out the utopian visions of patriarch Anton. Now Anton lies virtually helpless, dying slowly with many dreams unrealized and his magnum opus on human sexuality unwritten. The siblings gather at the family farm, linked painfully not only by grief but also by longtime resentments, disappointments, and misunderstandings that fester as Anton's end approaches." Libr J

"As the novel unfolds, Anton's unlikely past is revealed: his Texas childhood, his early stint in a Jesuit seminary and his grand passion for the communal haven of Chardin. His insatiable need for connection—particularly with women—can be repellant (as when he pursues one of his stepdaughters), but it is his infectious zest for life that drives this invigorating of convoluted novel." Publ Wkly

McPherson, Jessamyn West *See* West, Jessamyn, 1902-1984

Mda, Zakes, 1948-

The Madonna of Excelsior. Farrar, Straus and Giroux 2004 258p $23
ISBN 0-374-20008-4 LC 2003-54728
"In 1971, nineteen citizens of Excelsior, a farming community in South Africa's rural Free States, were charged with breaking apartheid's Immorality Act, which forbade sexual relations between blacks and whites on the pretext of avoiding miscegenation. The women were jailed as they awaited trial and their white counterparts were released on bail. In the end, the state withdrew the charges, but the accused women's lives, already complicated, became harder than ever. Mda tells the story of a family at the heart of the scandal." Publisher's note
"The voice that emerges suggests not just a writer who can seduce us through beautiful language and unfailing humor. We also encounter a writer who has the power to shock and frighten us, to astound and anger and unsettle us. The Madonna of Excelsior suggests, in short, that his is a voice for which one should feel not only affection but admiration." N Y Times Book Rev

Means, David

The secret goldfish; stories. Fourth Estate 2004 211p $22.95
ISBN 0-00-716489-0 LC 2004-50617
Contents: Lightning man; Sault Ste. Marie; It counts as seeing; Blown from the bridge; A visit from Jesus; Petrouchka [with omissions]; Elyria man; The project; Hunger; Counterparts; Dustman appearances to date; Carnie; The nest; Michigan death trip; The secret goldfish
"With stunning simplicity, Means offers 15 stirring portraits of tragedy, loss, and love." Esquire

Medlicott, Joan A.

Gardens of Covington; a novel; [by] Joan Medlicott. Thomas Dunne Bks. 2001 326p $23.95
ISBN 0-312-27555-2 LC 2001-19149
Sequel to The ladies of Covington send their love
"Amelia, Grace and Hannah are now happily ensconced in their beautiful old farmhouse in the foothills of North Carolina, but when developers threaten to turn their Eden into a condo haven, Hannah at least is up in arms. Grace and her lover, Bob, are busy preparing to open a tearoom and Amelia's photography talent continues to bloom. She falls for a man she meets in a fender-bender, but the new romance isn't all sweetness and light." Publ Wkly

The ladies of Covington send their love; {by} Joan Medlicott. St. Martin's Press 2000 326p o.p.
ISBN 0-312-25329-X LC 99-89922
"A Thomas Dunne book"
"Grace, Hannah, and Amelia are about as different as any three women can be, but the petty miseries of their dismal retirement boarding house near Philadelphia have forged an iron bond of friendship. When Amelia unexpectedly inherits a dilapidated farmhouse in North Carolina, the women screw up their collective courage and decide to renovate the house." Booklist
"The women grow in self-confidence until one publishes a book, one finds love, and one runs a physically demanding business. The ending is pure fantasy, but readers will enjoy the ride." Libr J

Meek, M. R. D.

If you go down to the woods. Severn House 2001 217p $25.99
ISBN 0-7278-5647-2
"The murder of a young girl puts Newton folk on edge. Lennox Kemp, . . . and pregnant wife Mary become involved despite themselves. A bright, appealing work." Libr J

Mehta, Gita

Raj; a novel. Simon & Schuster 1989 479p o.p.
LC 88-38504
An "historical novel that traces the life of an Indian princess from her birth during the year of Queen Victoria's Diamond Jubilee in 1897 until India wins its independence from the empire in the mid-twentieth century. Princess Jaya treads a path that leads from the ancient traditions of the maharajas—in which the woman was subjugated to the man—through the days in which India was held and exploited as a British possession; she becomes in the end a woman who has achieved her own independence and identity along with her country." Booklist
"Grounded in details of ancient royal tradition and Hindu ritual, Jaya's story counterpoints a vanished way of life against the complex political realities involved in the passing of the Raj and the birth of the modern nations of India and Pakistan." Publ Wkly

A river Sutra. Doubleday 1993 291p o.p.
LC 92-35779
"The narrator has left his high-ranking government job and the bustling life of the city for the tranquility of the country. He manages a rest house along the banks of the sacred Narmada River, devoting quiet hours to contemplation of the river's might, mystery, and beauty. But this seemingly peaceful realm is actually electric with the passion and tragedy of human existence as pilgrims from all walks of life make their way to the holy river. As our innkeeper converses with these troubled travelers, he becomes immersed in their startling stories." Booklist
"This is an idealized India, free of political and religious violence. 'A River Sutra' takes place in a fabled land of the romantic imagination, drawing on timeless literary traditions. Told with skill and sensitivity, Gita Mehta's tales are a delight to read, bringing to Western readers the mystery and drama of a rich cultural heritage." N Y Times Book Rev

Meloy, Maile

Liars and saints; a novel. Scribner 2003 260p $24
ISBN 0-7432-4435-4 LC 2002-30852
"The Santerres, starting with lovely Yvette and uptight Teddy, a World War II marine, are hardly a typical Catholic family. When their eldest daughter gets pregnant in high school, Yvette concocts an elaborate ruse and convinces Teddy that the baby is theirs. Similar secret

Meloy, Maile—*Continued*

begettings, concealed identities, and hidden anguish occur in each subsequent generation as Yvette becomes increasingly religious and Teddy struggles to love his rule-breaking progeny." Booklist

"Meloy's unerring mastery of narrative is remarkable. The disciplined economy and resonant clarity of her prose allow her to present a complex story in swift, lean chapters. The alternating points of view of eight main characters shine with authenticity and illuminate the moral complexities felt by each generation." Publ Wkly

Meltzer, Brad

Dead even. Weisbach Bks. 1998 401p o.p.

ISBN 0-688-15090-X LC 98-5935

New Yorkers "Sara Tate and Jared Lynch are married to each other and to their legal careers: he's a rising star for the defense in a big firm; she's just starting as an assistant district attorney after six months of job seeking. On her first day, Sara hears that a budget cut could put her back on the unemployment lines, so she swipes a burglary case earmarked for a top man in the pecking order. But this is more than a routine burglary, and a powerful villain named Oscar Rafferty wants it to go away. He hires Jared to defend the accused, a sadistic monster called Tony Kozlow, telling him that unless Kozlow walks, Sara dies." Publ Wkly

The author "gives the reader well-rounded characters; demonizing neither prosecution nor defense, he shows both as human beings doing a job." Libr J

The first counsel. Warner Bks. 2001 479p $25.95

ISBN 0-446-52728-9 LC 00-28963

"Michel Young, an idealistic lawyer in the White House counsel's office, is on a date with Nora, the very sexy, intriguing, enigmatic daughter of the president, when they see the chief counsel in a compromising position. Nora's questionable behavior quickly throws them into the middle of a plot that involves blackmail and murder." Booklist

Meltzer "relies on some heavy-handed techniques to generate suspense . . . and the plot has a familiar Hollywood ring to it. But Meltzer's relentless narrative finally digs its hooks in, and even skeptical readers will want to continue through the twists and turns, if only to confirm their own predictions." Publ Wkly

The tenth justice. Morrow 1997 389p o.p.

ISBN 0-688-15089-6 LC 96-44815

"Hotshot young lawyer Ben Addison is on top of the world. Just out of Yale Law School, he's already landed the highly desirable top job of clerk to a Supreme Court justice, experiences instant chemistry with his new co-clerk Lisa, and shares an apartment with three lifelong friends. Then a misplaced trust leads Ben to reveal a confidential court decision, and his world begins to crash. With Ben's career in jeopardy and a blackmailer on his trail, his friends use their job connections at the State Department, a Washington newspaper, and a senator's office to aid Ben and Lisa in a plot to apprehend Ben's blackmailer." Libr J

"Meltzer moves the story along at a crisp pace, spicing the action and legalese with lively banter and intriguing D.C. arcana." Publ Wkly

The zero game; Brad Meltzer. Warner Bks. 2004 460p $25.95

ISBN 0-446-53098-0 LC 2003-15157

"Bored congressional staffer Harris Sandler plays something called the zero game with his coworkers, but it turns deadly when a vote concerning an abandoned gold mine in South Dakota is brought to the floor. Together with a 16-year-old Senate page named Viv Parker, Harris finds himself being chased by a ruthless killer in the halls of the Capitol as well as in the bowels of the mine." Libr J

This thriller is "packed with plenty of backroom D.C. ambience and lots of action." Booklist

Melville, Herman, 1819-1891

Billy Budd, sailor.

Written in 1891 but in a still "unfinished" manuscript stage when Melville died. First publication 1924 in the United Kingdom, as part of the Standard edition of Melville's complete works

"Narrates the hatred of petty officer Claggart by Billy, handsome Spanish sailor. Billy strikes and kills Claggart, and is condemned by Captain Vere even though the latter senses Billy's spiritual innocence." Haydn. Thesaurus of Book Dig

also in Melville, H. The complete shorter fiction

The complete shorter fiction; with an introduction by John Updike. Knopf 1997 478p $20

ISBN 0-375-40068-0

"Everyman's library"

Contents: The piazza; Bartleby, the scrivener; Benito Cereno; The lightning-rod man; The encantadas; or, Enchanted isles; The bell-tower; Fragments from a writing desk; Authentic anecdotes of "Old Zack"; Hawthorne and his mosses; The happy failure; The fiddler; Cock-a-doodle-doo!; Poor man's pudding; Rich man's crumbs; The two temples: Temple second; The paradise of bachelors; The tartarus of maids; Jimmy Rose; The 'gees; I and my chimney; The apple-tree table; Billy Budd, sailor; The two temples: Temple first

The confidence-man: his masquerade; edited, with an introduction and notes by John Bryant. Modern Library 2003 xlix, 331p pa $11.95

ISBN 0-375-75802-X LC 2003-44561

First published 1857

"The scene is a Mississippi River boat, ironically named the 'Fidele.' A plotless satire taking place on April Fool's Day, the book is filled with characters difficult to distinguish from one another; most of them are different manifestations of the confidence man. A sign hanging on the door of the 'Fidele's' barbershop expresses the theme: 'No Trust.' The confidence man, king of a world without principle, succeeds in gulling men by capitalizing on false hopes and offering false pity. At the end of the book, the flickering light hanging above the table where an old man reads the Bible goes out completely." Reader's Ency. 4th edition

Mardi: and a voyager thither

In Melville, H. Typee: a peep at Polynesian life; Omoo: a narrative of adventures in the South Seas; Mardi: and a voyager thither

Melville, Herman, 1819-1891—*Continued*

Moby-Dick; or, The whale; illustrated by Rockwell Kent. Modern Library 1992 xxxv, 822p il $21
ISBN 0-679-60010-8 LC 92-50222
First published 1851
"Moby Dick is a ferocious white whale, who was known to whalers as Mocha Dick. He is pursued in a fury of revenge by Captain Ahab, whose leg he has bitten off; and under Melville's handling the chase takes on a significance beyond mere externals. Moby Dick becomes a symbol of the terrific forces of the natural universe, and Captain Ahab is doomed to disaster, even though Moby Dick is killed at last." Univ Handbook for Readers and Writers
"'Moby-Dick' had some initial critical appreciation, particularly in Britain, but only since the 1920s has it been recognized as a masterpiece, an epic tragedy of tremendous dramatic power and narrative drive." Oxford Companion to Engl Lit. 5th edition

also in Melville, H. Redburn, his first voyage; White-jacket, or, The world in a man-of-war; Moby-Dick, or, The whale

Omoo: a narrative of adventures in the South Seas; edited by Harrison Hayford, Hershel Parker, G. Thomas Tanselle. Northwestern University Press 1999 316p pa $16.95
ISBN 0-8101-1765-7 LC 99-41391
First published 1847 by Harper
"Based on Melville's own experiences in the South Pacific, this episodic novel, in a more comical vein than that of *Typee*, tells of the narrator's participation in a mutiny on a whale ship and his subsequent wanderings in Tahiti with the former doctor of the ship." Merriam-Webster's Ency of Lit

also in Melville, H. Typee: a peep at Polynesian life; Omoo: a narrative of adventures in the South Seas; Mardi: and a voyager thither

Redburn, his first voyage
In Melville, H. Redburn, his first voyage; White-jacket, or, The world in a man-of-war; Moby-Dick, or, The whale

Redburn, his first voyage; White-jacket, or, The world in a man-of-war; Moby-Dick, or, The whale. Literary Classics of the United States, Inc, Distributed to the trade by the Viking Press 1983 1437p $35
ISBN 0-940450-09-7 LC 82-18677
Redburn (1849) is a semiautobiographical novel about a young man's ill-fortuned trip across the Atlantic. White-jacket (1850), another semiautobiographical novel, centers around a young sailor nicknamed for the white jacket that he buys in Peru and wears throughout the novel. It also features an appearance by Jack Chase, a character who appears in several of Melville's works and who is here the first captain of the top, and a vivid description of the floggings and other punishments suffered by the crew for often minor infractions. Moby-Dick is entered separately.

Typee: a peep at Polynesian life. Northwestern Univ. Press 1968 374p il $75
ISBN 0-8101-0161-0
"The Writings of Herman Melville"
First published 1846
"Based on Melville's own experiences, the story tells of the hero and his friend Toby, who jump ship in the Marquesas Islands and wander mistakenly into the valley of Typee, which is inhabited by cannibals. The Typees become their benevolent captors, refusing to allow them to leave. Toby escapes, while the hero, suffering from a leg wound, remains to be nursed by the lovely Fayaway. Tempted to enjoy a somnolent, vegetative existence, the moral American chooses, with regret, to return to civilization." Reader's Ency. 4th edition

also in Melville, H. Typee: a peep at Polynesian life; Omoo: a narrative of adventures in the South Seas; Mardi: and a voyager thither

Typee: a peep at Polynesian life; Omoo: a narrative of adventures in the South Seas; Mardi: and a voyager thither. Library of Am. 1982 1333p $40
ISBN 0-940450-00-3 LC 81-18600
Omnibus edition of the author's first three novels. The first two titles are entered separately. In Mardi, first published 1849, Melville "entertained questions of ethics and metaphysics, politics and culture, sin and guilt, innocence and experience. The complexity of the novel's content, in fact, destroys all pretensions to literary form. Originally a narrative of adventure, 'Mardi' became an allegory of mind." Benet's Reader's Ency of Am Lit

White-jacket: or, The world in a man-of-war
In Melville, H. Redburn, his first voyage; White-jacket, or, The world in a man-of-war; Moby-Dick, or, The whale

Melville, James, 1931-

The chrysanthemum chain. St. Martin's Press 1982 181p o.p.
LC 82-5546
"An English subject living in Japan is murdered and the British consul and the local police want to know why. David Murrow was a distinguished educator but he moved in a rather peculiar, though prominent, circle of friends, which included many political luminaries. There is great concern among them about the case and its possible effect on the out-come of an impending election. . . . Although Melville keeps the action moving in this fast paced novel, he still pays close attention to characterization and background." Best Sellers

A haiku for Hanae. Scribner 1989 195p o.p.
LC 89-10559
"The year is 1968, and the scene is the remote Awaji Island, where a young Mormon missionary (with an eye for the ladies) has been found murdered close to a Shinto shrine. . . . In attempting to solve the case, Otani must link Japanese spirit worship with the large number of sensual, susceptible women who were easy prey for the errant missionary." Booklist

Melville, Jennie
See also Butler, Gwendoline

Melville, Jennie—*Continued*

The morbid kitchen. St. Martin's Press 1996 201p o.p.

LC 96-27985

First published 1995 in the United Kingdom

This "mystery is set in Windsor where, 10 years earlier, a student at an exclusive school was decapitated and two teachers disappeared. The case remains unsolved, the school closed. Now, in order to sell the building, Emily Bailey, sister of the school's late headmistress, must reopen the basement kitchen, sealed after the child's body was found there. She asks series protagonist Chief Superintendent Charmian Daniels . . . to accompany her, and they discover a mummified adult body and a child's head in a cabinet. The case is reopened." Publ Wkly

Mendelson, Cheryl

Morningside Heights; a novel. Random House 2003 326p $24.95

ISBN 0-375-50836-8 LC 2002-31760

The first title of a projected trilogy. The "intersecting lives of a group of Manhattanites living in the staid but rapidly changing Upper West Side neighborhood of Morningside Heights near Columbia University are the focus of this [novel]. . . . Opera singer Charles Braithwaite; his wife, Anne, a pianist; and their three (soon to be four) childen are the novel's ostensible protagonists. The books's real hero, however, is their beloved neighborhood, which they fear they will soon have to leave, unable to afford their cramped apartment." Publ Wkly

"With her motley cast, Mendelson paints an accurate, often comical portrait of the Upper West Side." N Y Times Book Rev

Meredith, George, 1828-1909

The ordeal of Richard Feverel. o.p.

First published 1859

This novel is representative of Meredith's "best work, full of allusion and metaphor, lyrical prose and witty dialogue, with a deep exploration of the psychology of motive and rationalization. The novel's subject is the relationship between a cruelly manipulative father and a son who loves a girl of a lower social class. Both men are self-deluded and proud, and the story's ending is tragic." Merriam-Webster's Ency of Lit

Mérimée, Prosper, 1803-1870

Carmen; translated from the French and illustrated by Edmund H. Garrett, with a memoir of the author by Louise Imogen Guiney. Little, Brown 1896 xxx, 117p il o.p.

Original French edition, 1845

"Georges Bizet's opera *Carmen* is based on the story. As a hot-blooded young corporal in the Spanish cavalry stationed near Seville, Don José is ordered to arrest Carmen, a young, flirtatious Gypsy woman, for assaulting a coworker. Greatly charmed by her, José allows her to escape. He deserts the army, kills two men on Carmen's account, and takes up a life as a robber and smuggler. He is insanely jealous of Carmen, who is unfaithful to him, and when she refuses to change on his behalf, he kills her and surrenders himself to the authorities." Merriam-Webster's Ency of Lit

Mertz, Barbara, 1927-

For works written by this author under other names see Michaels, Barbara, 1927-; Peters, Elizabeth, 1927-

Merullo, Roland, 1953-

In Revere, in those days; a novel. Crown 2002 302p o.p.

ISBN 0-609-61032-5 LC 2002-3678

"In the Italian American enclave outside of Boston known as Revere, MA, Anthony Benedetto experiences the joy and heartbreak of growing up in the late 1960s with a colorful extended family. Raised by his grandparents after his parents' tragic deaths in a plane crash, the sensitive Anthony learns of the immigrant past of his ghettoized (self-imposed and otherwise) forebears, as he and America are propelled full-throttle into the second half of the 20th century. The gifted Merullo. . . .tells Anthony's bittersweet coming-of-age story with crafty narrative and a beautifully vivid description of the time and place." Libr J

Messud, Claire, 1966-

The hunters; two short novels. Harcourt 2001 181p $29

ISBN 0-15-100588-5 LC 00-50571

Contents: A simple tale; The hunters

"These novellas both have displaced protagonists who cannot decide whether to seek a deathlike stillness or to embrace life's mess. In the first, a Toronto cleaning woman finds that the ritualized relationship she enjoys with a long-term employer has provided more continuity than anything else in her life, which has included famine in rural Ukraine, slave labor in Germany, love in a displaced-persons camp, emigration, and a cozy family existence. In widowhood, however, her sense of order is in danger of taking over and annihilating all that is left. Being almost too fastidious to live is also the dilemma of the narrator of the second tale, an American academic in London who loathes the friendly woman who lives downstairs. The tone is Jamesian, but the ending holds a beast in the jungle only for the hapless fellow-tenant." New Yorker

The hunters [novelette]
In Messud, C. The hunters

A simple tale
In Messud, C. The hunters

Mestre-Reed, Ernesto

The second death of Única Aveyano; a novel; Ernesto Mestre-Reed. 1st Vintage Contemporaries ed. Vintage Contemporaries 2004 259p $13

ISBN 1-400-03316-0 (pa) LC 2003-52544

"A Miami nursing home is no place for Unica Aveyano, as she vociferously reminds her daughter-inlaw at every opportunity. Although she is ill with terminal cancer and terribly frail, she cannot bear the thought of spending one more night wandering the halls or sitting by the cracked windows. Miraculously, she finds her way out the door, across a four-lane highway, and into the ocean. When she is rescued by her male nurse, she

Mestre-Reed, Ernesto—*Continued*
gravely tells him that she was led there by a pack of wild angels. Her past is suddenly more alive to her than the present, and she spends hours immersed in memories of her Cuban childhood, her marriage, and her son, a bisexual artist who refused to emigrate with them. She has no time for her mournful husband, who is sick at the thought of being left behind. Mestre-Reed . . . is a lyric novelist of uncommon power, creating a memorable portrait of a woman wracked by longing and memory yet fearlessly embracing her impending death." Booklist

Mewshaw, Michael, 1943-

Shelter from the storm; a novel. Putnam 2003 280p $23.95
ISBN 0-399-14988-0 LC 2002-74640
In this thriller "a feral child from the steppes of Central Asia becomes the bargaining chip in a hostage negotiation. Scarred hero Zack McClintock, a private-sector intelligence agent, travels to ex-Soviet territory in search of his kidnapped son-in-law and finds plenty of people with plenty to hide. . . .This is the sort of intelligent and morally ambitious thriller—like those of Craig Nova or Paul Watkins—that offers a welcome change from typical fare." Libr J

Meyer, Carolyn

Brown eyes blue; a novel. Bridge Works 2003 228p $23.95
ISBN 1-88259-368-5 LC 2002-12674
"Daughter Dorcas' return home is prompted by a call from a friend who tells her about the scandal caused by her mom's latest art exhibit. Instead of the pastoral Amish scenes for which she is know, Lavinia's latest show consists of brilliantly executed, graphic nudes. Dorcas, too, feels reckless and buys an old mansion to convert into an inn, and in the process remakes her own life. Then granddaughter Sasha shows up pregnant and with a lesbian partner." Booklist
"Little do these women guess how much they have in common—shared passions, losses and secrets that lead them to question the choices they have made in their lives. Meyer weaves the story of three generations of women who, with their distinctive voices, will endear themselves to readers." Publ Wkly

Meyer, Deon

Heart of the hunter; translated by K. L. Seegers. Little, Brown 2004 c2003 374p $23.95
ISBN 0-316-93549-2 LC 2003-25683
"Thobela Mpayipheli has settled into a sedate but rewarding life with the woman he loves. He works as a gofer at a South African motorcycle shop and readies his partner's young son for life on a farm-until an ex-boss asks him to perform a dangerous favor. His Xhosa warrior's heart racing, Thobela soon finds himself driving hard toward Nigeria with a hard drive full of secrets the unified government wishes to file away for good." Booklist
"Despite the complexity of its tightly woven plot-skillfully revealed through newspaper articles and intelligence reports-Meyer's U.S. debut moves at a breathtaking pace that will carry readers away. A sympathetic protagonist and the landscape of South Africa add color to the story." Libr J

Meyer, Nicholas

The seven-per-cent solution; being a reprint from the reminiscences of John H. Watson, M.D., as edited by Nicholas Meyer. Dutton 1974 253p o.p.
"In this final memoir, dictated from a nursing home in 1939, Watson [the biographer of the famous detective Sherlock Holmes] confesses that the events he recounted in 'The Final Problem' are a total fabrication. . . . Watson observes that Holmes's agitation over Moriarty's evil doings occurs only when he has been taking cocaine. Fearing that Holmes is destroying himself, Watson tricks him into a trip to Vienna, where he turns him over to Sigmund Freud. . . . Freud cures Holmes of his addiction, and Holmes lingers on to observe that the schizophrenia of one of Freud's patients results from a criminal conspiracy as yet unsuspected by anyone." Newsweek
"In a field replete with pastiche Meyer succeeds because of a superior ear for Conan Doyle's style, a gentle sense of fun, and a talent for plot that few of the imitators have possessed." Libr J

The West End horror; a posthumous memoir of John H. Watson, M.D., as edited by Nicholas Meyer. Dutton 1976 222p o.p.
This novel "is set in London's theatre district in 1895. A much disliked theatre critic has been murdered, and Sherlock Holmes is engaged to find the murderer. His client is another critic of the day whose years of fame are ahead of him: George Bernard Shaw. Inspector Lestrade, Holmes's old foil, is on the scene, but, as always, his efforts are misdirected and before long he has managed to incarcerate an obvious innocent. Clues abound and so too do real but suspicious characters." Best Sellers

Meyers, Kent

The work of wolves; Kent Meyers. 1st ed. Harcourt 2004 416p $24
ISBN 0-15-101057-9 LC 2003-26365
In this novel, set in South Dakota, "several different lives intersect on the edge of the Sioux reservation when a group of mistreated horses is discovered. Carson Fielding, a horse trainer who lives on a farm that has been in his family for several generations, is hired by wealthy landowner Magnus Yarborough to train said horses and teach Rebecca, his young wife, to ride. When Yarborough suspects that the lessons have led to something more, he takes out his anger on Carson through the horses, setting in motion a series of events that draws together Carson; Earl Walks Alone, a Lakota teenager who discovers the half-starved horses in a secluded pen; and Willi, a German exchange student with a troubled past." Libr J
Meyer's "spare dialogue is brilliantly and often comically expressive, and Carson, his taciturn, rational hero, is an original and compelling character. Strong themes of generational responsibility and family history add resonance to this gratifying, very American novel." Publ Wkly

Michael, Judith

Acts of love. Crown 1997 376p o.p.
ISBN 0-517-70324-6

Michael, Judith—*Continued*

In this novel "theater director Lucas Cameron discovers a box of letters left behind by his deceased grandmother, the famous stage actress Constance Bernhardt. The letters were written by her protégée Jessica Fontaine, who disappeared from the stage years before. Even in the midst of his busy world . . . Luke finds himself returning again and again to the letters, recognizing in them a deeply passionate young woman discovering herself and the magic of the theater. Luke begins to realize that he has fallen in love with the woman who wrote them. Finally he can bear it no longer—and tracks down the elusive Jessica Fontaine. But when he travels to her hideaway on Lopez Island off the coast of Washington, nothing is as he expected it." Publisher's note

A certain smile. Crown 1999 301p o.p.
ISBN 0-517-70325-4 LC 98-52333

"Miranda Grant, a 40-year-old widow with two adolescent children, travels from her home in Boulder, Colo., to Beijing. . . . The story focuses on Miranda's relationship with Yuan Li, a successful builder/construction engineer. The son of a Chinese mother and an American soldier, he becomes her soulful guide to China, romance and personal growth. Danger intrudes after Miranda innocently acts as courier for a letter from a former dissident, now in America; the authorities put Miranda and Yuan Li under round-the-clock surveillance." Publ Wkly

Deceptions. Pocket Bks. 1982 472p o.p.
"A Poseidon Press book"

"When twin sisters, who have been mistaken for each other all their lives, are on vacation together in China, they decide on a whim to switch roles for a week, thus beginning a deception that has far-reaching effects. The aristocratic Lady Sabrina, assuming the suburban housewife's duties of her sister Stephanie Anderson, is surprised to find she scarcely misses her former high life, reveling instead in the acceptance and security of being part of a family. Stephanie, leaving her humdrum life behind to assume Sabrina's jet-set life of partying and dealing in antiques, so much enjoys her liberation that she is reluctant to come home. Sabrina has fallen in love with Stephanie's husband; she postpones ending the deception until a freak accident leaves her unsure of her identity at all." Publ Wkly

Followed by A tangled web

Sleeping beauty; a novel. Poseidon Press 1991 539p o.p.
LC 91-31298

"The wealthy, influential Chatham family, founders of a Chicago-based realty empire, present a wholesome image to the outside world. But 30-year-old financial whiz Vince Chatham has raped his 13-year-old niece, Anne, and continues to abuse her sexually. When Anne overcomes her fear and guilt to accuse Vince at a family gathering, she is met with skepticism from her relatives and denial from Vince. After Anne runs away from home, however, Vince is stripped of his position at the corporation; enraged, he vows to destroy the rest of the Chatham clan." Publ Wkly

"Michael does this sort of thing much better than most of the competition: the characters, naturally larger than life, are still believable." Booklist

Michaels, Anne, 1958-

Fugitive pieces. Knopf 1997 294p o.p.
ISBN 0-679-45439-X LC 96-36678
First publishd 1996 in Canada

This "tale revolves around the life of a young Polish Jew, Jakob Beer, who, after witnessing the murder of his parents, is miraculously rescued by Athos, a Greek geologist. A man of heroic intellect and spirituality, Athos risks his life to bring Jakob to Greece only to find that the tide of evil has even reached those hallowed shores. They immigrate to Canada, and their mentor-disciple relationship deepens as each studious year passes." Booklist

Michaels "offers a richly imagined portrait of Jakob's slow progress from reticence to poetic eloquence and of the complex blend of memories, feelings, insights, and experiences that makes him the man he becomes. She even tackles the perpetually troubling question of how so many seemingly ordinary, 'civilized' people could have eagerly committed such monstrous crimes against defenseless children and civilians." Christ Sci Monit

Michaels, Barbara, 1927-

For works written by this author under other names see Peters, Elizabeth, 1927-

The dancing floor. HarperCollins Pubs. 1997 326p o.p.
LC 96-39331

"Frumpy but spunky American tourist Heather Tradescant's vacation in Britain is blighted by her parents' recent death. Hoping to fulfill her late father's dream, she tries to visit the 17th-century garden of Troytan House, home of businessman Frank Karim and his taciturn son, Jordan. Rebuffed, Heather finds a hidden entrance to the estate, but as she wanders through a bramble-thickened maze, she falls at the feet of the Karims enjoying an al fresco breakfast. At first hostile, the Karims soon prove more than hospitable, begging her to stay because they believe she's an horticultural expert. . . . An unlikely object of desire, Heather attracts the men around her through her strong personality, lively wit and huge appetite. She and other well-delineated characters make this tale everything a romance reader can ask for." Publ Wkly

Houses of stone. Simon & Schuster 1993 334p o.p.
LC 93-27926

"Michaels sets her heroine, Professor Karen Holloway, to the task of discovering the provenance of a remnant from an old manuscript. Holloway is convinced that it is a thinly disguised autobiographical novel by an obscure feminist poet whose verses have already helped Holloway carve a niche in the cutthroat business of academia. The professor's archenemies, two fellow literature experts, are equally convinced of the work's value and attempt desperate measures to gain access of the manuscript. Michaels has composed a mystery that is brimming with suspense yet revolves around authorial research rather than money and multiple murders." Booklist

Michaels, Barbara, 1927-—*Continued*

Shattered silk. Atheneum Pubs. 1986 369p o.p.
LC 86-47658

Karen Nevitt "begins a new life in Georgetown after her unhappy marriage crumbles. She plans to open an antique-clothing shop with the encouragement of old and new friends. But a series of seemingly unrelated yet terrifying events begins to unfold, and Karen is caught up in a web of deadly suspense." Libr J

Stitches in time. HarperCollins Pubs. 1995 307p o.p.
LC 95-4286

A "mystery based on a haunted quilt. Rachel Grant is a doctoral student working on her thesis—an investigation of women's garments designed for important rites of passage—when she takes a part-time job at a chic vintage clothing shop run by two women, Kara and her sister-in-law Cheryl. When Cheryl's police officer husband is shot, Rachel is drawn into the family because she moves into Cheryl's home, which is connected to the shop. Meanwhile, the message from the quilt lures Rachel into dangerous misdeeds. The unraveling of the mystery proves fascinating." Booklist

Michaels, Fern

Celebration. Kensington Pub. Corp. 1999 358p o.p.
ISBN 1-57566-402-X LC 98-67474

"When her husband retires and disappears with their savings, Kristine's whole family structure disintegrates as her children express their disgust with her continuing faith in a man they've known for years as a self-centered womanizer. With the help of friends and, eventually, a new love interest, Kristine focuses on work and rebuilds her family's toy business but keeps her new love at arm's length." Booklist

Finders keepers. Kensington Bks. 1998 396p o.p.
ISBN 1-57566-323-6

"Adorable toddler Hannah Larson, only child of poor but decent Grace and Ben, is sitting in her stroller outside a Tennessee gas station when baby-starved Thea and Barnes Roland pull in for a cream soda. Thea snatches the child, Barnes puts pedal to metal and Hannah becomes 'adopted' Jessie, doomed to a life of smothering love and material overabundance in Charleston, S.C., while her birth parents suffer and hope. On her way to NYU . . . Jessie detours through Washington and talks herself into a job as secretary to powerful Texas Senator Angus Kingsley, who has an icy wife, Alexis; a dying mistress, Irene; and a gorgeous son, Tanner. Jessie, of course, marries Tanner, and the trouble really begins." Publ Wkly

Michener, James A., 1907-1997

Alaska. Random House 1988 868p o.p.
LC 87-43232

This novel begins with the prehistory of Alaska before concentrating on the history of the region since the 18th century

"Besides multiple heroes and heroines, there are knaves and opportunists who have depleted Alaska's resources and contributed to the high rates of alcoholism and suicide. One of Michener's favorite words is *noble*, but after mushing through his Arctic saga of persistence and greed, one is not surprised that he uses it mainly to describe grizzly bears, salmon and whales." Time

The bridges at Toko-ri. Random House 1953 146p o.p.

"In this hard-hitting novel of the Korean conflict, Admiral George Tarrant commands the Naval Task Force, whose carrier-based jets are to knock out strategic points throughout Korea. The focal point of the novel is Harry Brubaker, a lawyer who goes reluctantly to war after being called up as a jet pilot. The reader will remember also Beer Barrel, the landing officer who can get the jets back on the carrier's decks, no matter how rough the seas; and Mike Forney, helicopter rescue pilot who gets pilots out of the freezing waters if they are downed." Shapiro. Fic for Youth. 3d edition

Caravans; a novel. Random House 1963 341p o.p.

The story, set in Afghanistan in the year 1946, "focuses on Ellen Jasper, an American bored with her native land, who flees to Afghanistan to become the second wife of a man named Nazrullah. Her parents haven't heard from her in 13 months and Mark Miller, of the U.S. Embassy in that country, is sent to investigate. The search takes Miller into unknown territory. He joins a nomad tribe and experiences a love affair of rare beauty with Mira, daughter of the Great Zulfiqar, chieftain of all the nomadic peoples scattered around Afghanistan. [The novel describes] Ellen's degeneration into a sensualist, [and] the encounter of Miller (a Jew) with an ex-Nazi who tortured Jews." America

Caribbean. Random House 1989 672p o.p.
LC 89-42785

A novel about the "Caribbean islands from the days when the peace-loving Arawak Indians were overpowered by cannibalistic Caribs, to a ship's tour of today's still lush, but troubled, paradise. Sir Francis Drake, pirate Henry Morgan, Horatio Nelson, Haitian General Toussaint L'Ouverture, Fidel Castro march across the pages, and while the pace is sometimes achingly slow, the dialogue stilted and the characterization skimpy, Michener laces the whole with fiery Caribbean drama." Publ Wkly

Centennial. Random House 1974 909p o.p.

"Written to celebrate the United States centennial, the book centers on a fictional town in Colorado. It begins with an examination of the geological formation of the land and a discussion of the first animals to live there. It continues with the arrival of the Indians, the coming of the first settlers, the traders, the search for gold, the building of the railroads, and the start of cattle ranching—virtually all the activities that made this country develop as it did. The conclusion brings us to the social and ecological problems of the 1970s." Shapiro. Fic for Youth. 3d edition

Chesapeake. Random House 1978 865p o.p.
LC 78-2892

"Through the interwoven stories of three families and the Indians, Blacks, and Irish immigrants with whom they interact, Michener chronicles four centuries of life on Maryland's Eastern Shore. . . . Michener elaborates . . . variations on his themes of personal accountability

Michener, James A., 1907-1997—*Continued*
for social change, man's self-expulsion from paradise, and the interrelated ecological network of all things." Libr J

The covenant. Random House 1980 887p o.p.
LC 80-5315

This novel spans 500 years of South African history. Three families mingle "with the outstanding historic figures of their times. They are the Nxumalos, the Van Doorns, and the Saltwoods, representing respectively the African, Afrikaans, and English. . . . Over several hundred years their descendants make contact, and thrive through the contact, only to become adversaries as contact subsequently gives way to conflict. Finally they find themselves irretrievably stuck in the hard concrete of South Africa's racial policies." Christ Sci Monit

Creatures of the kingdom; stories of animals and nature; illustrations by Karen Jacobsen. Random House 1993 281p il o.p.
LC 92-46075

Contents: From the boundless deep; The birth of the Rockies; Diplodocus, the dinosaur; A miracle of evolution; The mastodon; Matriarch, the woolly mammoth; Portrait of Rufous; The beaver; The eagle and the snake; The hyena; Nerka the salmon; Onk-or; The invaders; Jimmy the crab; Lucifer and Hey-You; The Colonel and Genghis Khan

"Gathered in this delightful 'anthology' . . . are sections from Michener's novels that deal with animals and other less animate aspects of the natural world. . . . These selections represent nature writing as its most fluid and involving." Booklist

The drifters; a novel. Random House 1971 751p o.p.

This novel, "narrated by a 60-year-old American financier who roams Europe and Africa in search of good investments, follows six young adults as they travel in search of something else. . . . Each young person has a special set of circumstances with which to contend." NY Times Book Rev

"The Drifters is something of a guidebook loosely dressed up as fiction; a guide to quaint and colorful places, especially on the Iberian peninsula, and to the life-styles of the rebellious young." Saturday Rev

Hawaii. Random House 1959 937p o.p.

A "novel in which the racial origins of Hawaii are traced through several narrative strands that merge in contemporary history. The original Tahitian colonizers welcome the white missionaries who bring in Chinese and Japanese laborers, and all together make up the present-day 'golden' Hawaiian." Wis Libr Bull

"High-domed, long-haired *littérateurs* may argue that Michener's characters are often as paper-thin as the colored image in which Hawaii is held by mainland tourists, but 'Hawaii,' is still a masterful job of research, an absorbing performance of storytelling, and a monumental account of the islands from geologic birth to sociological emergence as the newest, and perhaps the most interesting of the United States." Saturday Rev

Mexico. Random House 1992 625p o.p.
LC 92-50151

In this novel set in Mexico City, "Mexico-born Norman Clay, a journalist for a New York publication, returns to his natal city to report on the bullfights that highlight its annual festival. This year two matadors are joined in a rivalry that could end in death." Libr J

"There are splendid and authentic scenes in the *plaza de toros* that are as dramatic as any written by Ernest Hemingway or Barnaby Conrad, and one chapter, where the bulls' horns are shaved by the father of a torero, is James Michener the storyteller and parabolist at his finest." N Y Times Book Rev

The novel. Random House 1991 446p o.p.
LC 90-53489

"'The novel' is divided into four parts, each told from a different point of view. The first is that of the novelist, Lukas, a plain, clean-living but big-bucks author in his late 60's whose most recent work, 'Stone Walls,' is the final work in the Grenzler Octet, an opus set in the Pennsylvania Dutch country, where he was born and raised. The second voice is that of Yvonne Marmelle, née Shirley Marmelstein, his editor. The third is that of the literary critic Karl Streibert, Lukas's fellow Pennsylvania Dutchman. And the fourth is that of a reader, Jane Garland, grand dame and philanthropist who is also Lukas's friend." N Y Times Book Rev

"To his credit, Michener tries to be fair to both sides of the literary vs. popular fiction debate. The elitist Streibert is presented as an honest, well-intentioned man who genuinely loves literature and worries about the dangers of commercialism. The position Michener seems to be advocating in 'The Novel' is that experimental, elitist fiction and old-fashioned storytelling are both legitimate forms for the novel." Christ Sci Monit

Poland. Random House 1983 556p o.p.
LC 83-4477

"Centering on the fictional village of Bukowo on the Vistula River, the novel's action occurs as a series of vignettes of Polish life from the 1200s to the 1980s. Each chapter tells the story of a different generation of three families of Bukowo—the wealthy magnate counts Lubonski, the minor nobles Bukowski, and peasants Buk." Libr J

"The author's description of the devastating invasions of Poland by Tartars, Germans, Swedes, Turks, Russians and Soviets is historically accurate as well as highly vivid. . . . But the most unforgettable and deeply moving pages of the book are those in which Michener narrates the horrid experiences of the inmates of the Polish concentration camp of Majdanek, where 140,000 Jewish and 220,000 Christian prisoners died. . . . Michener's Poland is an engrossing and fast moving novel by a superb storyteller." America

Recessional. Random House 1994 484p o.p.
LC 94-17414

"Opening with obstetrician Andy Zorn taking a job as manager of one of the nation's poshest retirement and final-care facilities, the novel weaves through the challenges Zorn faces and the experiences of many of the residents of the Palms in Florida. . . . The fine line between euthanasia and the excessive use of mechanical life supports is drawn with poignant scenes of aging and AIDS patients. Despite the dreary subject, this novel is full of life and romance." Booklist

Sayonara. Random House 1954 243p o.p.

The love story of an American Air Corps major and a beautiful Japanese girl. When Major Gruver sets up housekeeping with Hanaogi there is consternation among

Michener, James A., 1907-1997—*Continued*
the Americans, for Gruver is engaged to an American general's daughter. Contrary to the course of Madam Butterfly, in this instance it is the Japanese girl who says Sayonara (farewell) to the American

Space. Random House 1982 622p o.p.
LC 82-40127

This novel "begins at the time of World War II and features characters who eventually find themselves, in one capacity or another, involved with the space program. Some are engineers; some are politicians; some are astronauts." Libr J

"Michener has caught the essence of what motivated and then enfeebled our space program. . . . As usual, Michener has done his homework, this time with affection and excitement as well—his pro-space enthusiasm is the book's driving force, and he has deftly woven an incredible amount of information into the tale." Natl Rev

Tales of the South Pacific. Macmillan 1986 c1947 326p o.p.
LC 86-28450

"Hudson River editions"

A reissue of the title first published 1947

These 18 tales describe "the strain and the boredom, the careful planning and heroic action, the color and beauty of the islands, and all that made up life during the critical days of the war in the Pacific." Wis Libr Bull

Texas. Random House 1985 1096p o.p.
LC 85-8248

This novel covers Texas history from 1527 to the present. "Texas then and now is, in a sense, all here: the Spanish missions; the early settlers; fights with the Comanches and Apaches; the Battle of the Alamo, won by the flamboyant and wily Mexican general Santa Anna . . . Sam Houston's heroic victory at San Jacinto; the birth of the Lone Star Republic—and so on." Publ Wkly

"As a novel, this book is remarkably good. . . . Michener, however, has given us here something even more: a marvelous and sympathetic analysis of historical and social relations." Best Sellers

Miéville, China

Iron council; China Mieville. 1st ed. Del Rey\Ballantine Books 2004 564p $24.95
ISBN 0-345-46402-8 LC 2004-49394

"As the city of New Crobuzon carries on an interminable war against the wizards of Tesh, life becomes more and more repressive for the many humans, near humans, nonhumans, and "the Remade"people subjected to magical body reconstruction as a form of punishment. Cutter, a member of the Caucus, an organization of various factions of rebels, sets off on a journey to locate the legendary Iron Council." Libr J

"In myriad ways, China Miéville's New Crobuzon is an unweeded garden of unearthly delights, and Iron Council a work of both passionate conviction and the highest artistry." Washington Post Book World

Millar, Kenneth *See* Macdonald, Ross, 1915-1983

Miller, Andrew, 1960-

Oxygen. Harcourt 2002 323p $30
ISBN 0-15-100721-7 LC 2001-51459

First published 2001 in the United Kingdom

This novel "tells of Alec Valentine, a translator who leaves his bland life in London to care for his dying mother in the West Country. His golden-boy brother, Larry, is a former tennis champion and now an actor in California whose career and marriage are heading south. When Larry joins his brother in England as their mother lies dying, both of their seemingly failing lives come into focus as their mother's impending death forces them to grapple with their own inadequacies. Interspersed in this family tale is the story of playwright László Lázár, a Hungarian exile living in Paris, whose play Alec is translating." Booklist

"Written in elegant, resonant prose, this book breathes with compassion and honesty, and with the rare quality called hope." Publ Wkly

Miller, Arthur, 1915-2005

Homely girl, a life, and other stories. Viking 1995 115p o.p.
LC 95-14267

These three stories "evoke the pre- and postwar New York City of the author's best-known plays. After being dominated for years by her Communist first husband, the homely girl of the title story finds happiness and fulfillment with a blind musician. In 'Fame,' a newly acclaimed playwright fears he won't be able to write another play. And in 'Fitter's Night,' a cynical Italian metalworker risks his life on a freezing January evening to repair a destroyer headed out to protect a World War II convoy. . . . The ability to sum up in clear, unequivocal prose the essence of an emotion, a situation, a theme—characteristic of Mr. Miller's best writing—makes the reader wish that these stories were longer, and that there were more of them." N Y Times Book Rev

Miller, Henry, 1891-1980

Tropic of Cancer. Grove Press 1961 318p o.p.

First published 1934 in France

"An autobiographical first novel recounting the experiences, sensations, thoughts of Miller, a penniless American in the Paris of the early thirties. It is not so much a novel as an intense journal, written daily about what was happening to him daily . . . as he scrounged for food, devoured books, conversed volubly, and flung himself into numerous beds." New Repub

Miller "uses themes—cadging for food, shelter, and sex; attacks on such bourgeois values as work and marriage; denunciations of traditional art and literature—and imagery—wild, exuberant, often shockingly frank—that together represent a savage, nihilistic (and at times enormously funny) revulsion against a world of stupidity and ugliness." Ency of World Lit in the 20th Century

Followed by Tropic of Capricorn

Tropic of Capricorn. Grove Press 1962 c1961 348p o.p.

First published 1939 in France

"In a form like that of *Tropic of Cancer* the autobiographical account describes the writer's boyhood in Brooklyn, his quest to discover himself by sexual experiences and by other means, and his fury at the faults he finds in many of the values and ways of life in the U.S." Oxford Companion to Am Lit. 6th edition

Miller, Risa

Welcome to Heavenly Heights. St. Martin's Press 2003 230p $23.95
ISBN 0-312-30180-4 LC 2002-31876

This novel follows a group of American Jews who have settled in the West Bank. "Tova struggles with flashes of homesickness and worries about the changes this new life has wrought in her daughter. Nathan and Sandy argue over how to discipline their boisterous and impulsive son, Yossi. Mr. Stanetsky, a Holocaust survivor, carries a dog-eared photograph of his parents and sister with him as he collects rent from his tenants. In the backgrouond, the threat of violence and political upheaval are a constant rumble." Booklist

The author "has peered inside Tova's life to show us the search for joy that lies at the heart of her religious ritual and the beauty of people like her who devote themselves to that search. And then Miller has broken our hearts—with Tova's—byshowing us how horrible it is when the poetic liturgical metaphors of Judaism become the terrible realities of nationalism, when holiness tries to reconcile itself with the inevitable human corruption of statehood." N Y Times Book Rev

Miller, Sue

The distinguished guest. HarperCollins Pubs. 1995 282p o.p.
LC 95-2951

"The guest of the title is a woman who in her seventies wrote a celebrated memoir about being the wife of the radical minister of an integrated church in Chicago, and who eventually split with her husband over issues of black separatism and militancy. Now in her Parkinson's-afflicted eighties, she is visiting her architect son, whose view of his mother is necessarily different from her public image. This novel, as full of rich domestic detail as Miller's previous books, is, like them, a work of consolation informed by a psychotherapeutic perspective—very literal, yet also highly readable." New Yorker

Family pictures; a novel. Harper & Row 1990 389p o.p.
LC 89-46109

This novel chronicles "forty years in the lives of the Eberhardts, a Chicago family. David and Lainey's third child, Randall, is autistic. 'According to the experts of the '50s, the fault is Lainey's for unconsciously rejecting her infant son; David—himself a psychiatrist—agrees with them. A few decades later science will absolve her, but the shock and pain of her husband's betrayal throw a curse on their relationship that is never quite dispelled." Newsweek

"'Family Pictures' is a novel that might have intrigued and startled Woolf—profoundly honest, shapely, ambitious, engrossing, original and true, an important example of a new American tradition that explores what it means, not to light out for the territories but to make a home, live at home and learn what home is." N Y Times Book Rev

For love. HarperCollins Pubs. 1993 301p o.p.
LC 92-54422

"Fortyish freelance writer Lottie leaves her new husband in Chicago to spend part of the summer in Cambridge, Massachusetts, getting the family house ready to sell now that her brother Cameron has placed their alcoholic mother in a nursing home. While she and her son Ryan paint and clean, Lottie examines the concept of love in an article she is writing, studying her own troubled marriage and Cameron's resumption of a love affair with childhood sweetheart Elizabeth. For Elizabeth, who is staying with her mother after leaving her philandering husband, this romance is just a fling. But Cameron's obsessive love for the golden girl of his youth leads to [an accident]." Libr J

Miller "maps emotional terrain carefully, precisely, graphically, with a grit and grace that at first invite the reader's appreciation—and then, before we know it, have us involved." N Y Times Book Rev

The good mother. Harper & Row 1986 310p o.p.
LC 85-45475

In this novel "Anna Dunlap, newly divorced, is shaping a life centered around her three-year-old daughter, Molly. Then Leo Cutter sparks a sexual responsiveness new to Anna . . . Molly and Leo like each other, too, and Anna sees them as a loving family unit—until her ex-husband sues for custody, citing sexual activities that put his child at risk. The love affair is irrevocably changed, as Anna opens her life to a court-appointed psychiatrist and bends the truth to her lawyer's strategy." Libr J

"The fulcrum on which the novel's plot pivots is the allegation by Anna's ex-husband that Anna's lover has molested Molly, and the ensuing custody trial. Miller's treatment of this high point of tension in the novel is dramatic, discreet, compassionate. Each development in the legal process increases the tension. The drama heightens, the suspense builds, character is further developed, and the latitude for choice logically narrowed. Like a final judgment, the custody decision breaks over reader and character alike." Christ Sci Monit

Inventing the Abbotts and other stories. Harper & Row 1987 180p o.p.
LC 86-46089

Contents: Inventing the Abbotts; Tyler and Brina; Appropriate affect; Slides; What Ernest says; Travel; Leaving home; Calling; Expensive gifts; The birds and the bees; The quality of life

"These stories report from a frontier, from the discontented and guilty world of divorce and the single parent, of marriage as a threatened institution, and if the landscape is a bleak and dispiriting one, that is not the author's fault; she is merely giving evidence. As stories they vary—some effective, others less so—but as testimonies of our times they seem highly apposite." NY Times Book Rev

Lost in the forest. Knopf 2005 247p $24.95
ISBN 1-400-04226-7 LC 2004-48963

"Eva, the divorced and happily remarried mother of three, has finally put the disaster of her first marriage behind her and has even become good friends with her ex. Then her second husband is killed in a tragic accident, and the peace Eva has worked so hard to attain is instantly shattered as she succumbs to an overwhelming grief. Her middle child, Daisy, was extremely close to her stepfather and is emotionally paralyzed by the sudden turn of events, unable to process or even speak of her grief. While her older sister, Emily, pretty and popular,

Miller, Sue—*Continued*

is able to reach outside the family for support, and her brother, Theo, is too young to understand what happened, Daisy feels utterly trapped by her own misery and abruptly embarks on an ill-advised affair with a much older, married man." Booklist

"Miller has always been adept at rendering the complexities of family life, the way even well-intentioned, decent people can't walk across a room without wounding at least one person they love. But while some of her plots . . . can be cluttered and occasionally clumsy, Lost in the Forest has a seemingly effortless grace; Miller quickly captures and never loses our attention." N Y Times Book Rev

While I was gone. Knopf 1999 265p o.p.

ISBN 0-375-40112-1 LC 98-14211

In this novel, Joey Becker, a veterinarian married to a minister, "is just beginning to feel dissatisfied with her predictable life when Eli Mayhew, a housemate from her hippie past, moves to town. His presence both reawaken's questions about an old, unsolved murder and kindles in Joey what she has been hungering for: a youthful 'sense of a surprise, that heady feeling of not knowing' what life will bring." Time

"Miller's narrative is a beautifully textured picture of the psychological tug of war between finding integrity as an individual and satisfying the demands of spouse, children and community." Publ Wkly

The world below; a novel. Knopf 2001 275p $25

ISBN 0-375-41094-5 LC 2001-33731

In this novel, two women are "at the center of the narrative: Catherine Hubbard, twice divorced mother of three, the first-person voice of life in the present, and her grandmother, Georgia Rice Holbrooke, the voice of a past time who, after Catherine's discovery of the dead woman's journals, becomes a living presence in her granddaughter's imagination." N Y Times Book Rev

"As Catherine sorts through her grandmother's life, she also sorts through her own: her mother's death, her two marriages, her boyfriends and her children. . . . As readers have come to expect, Miller limns contemporary life in deft, sure strokes, with an unerring ear for the way parents and children talk; no one can parse a modern marriage as well as she can. But in this novel Miller's special gift to readers is her rendering of Georgia's life, particularly the two love stories that mark it." Publ Wkly

Miller, Walter M., 1923-1996

A canticle for Leibowitz; a novel; by Walter M. Miller, Jr. Lippincott 1960 c1959 320p o.p.

"Here is science fiction of the highest literary excellence and thematic intelligence. A monastery founded by the scientist Leibowitz is discovered decades after an atomic war. In the first part of the book a young novice in the monastery is the protagonist; in the second part we see scholars in a new period of enlightenment; and in the final section we observe man's proclivity for repeating mistakes and the apparent inevitability of history's repeating itself." Shapiro. Fic for Youth. 3d edition

The darfsteller

In The Hugo winners p5-71

Millhauser, Steven

An adventure of Don Juan

In Millhauser, S. The king in the tree: three novellas

The king in the tree

In Millhauser, S. The king in the tree: three novellas

The king in the tree: three novellas. Knopf 2003 241p $23

ISBN 0-375-41540-8 LC 2002-72956

"An excitable widow leads the reader on a tour of her house—apparently being offered for sale—in the harrowing 'Revenge'. . . . 'An adventure of Don Juan' finds the famous philanderer, bored with a lifetime of easy conquests, leaving the Continent for a change of scenery on his friend's English estate, where he will experience unrequited desire for the first time. Millhauser retells the tragedy of Tristan and Isolde in the title story. . . . Millhauser's precision, coupled with his brave imagination, makes these stories as smart and fresh as they are grim." Publ Wkly

The knife thrower and other stories. Crown 1998 256p o.p.

ISBN 0-609-60070-2 LC 97-45796

Contents: The knife thrower; A visit; The sisterhood of night; The way out; Flying carpets; The new automaton theater; Clair de Lune; The dream of the consortium; Balloon flight, 1870; Paradise Park; Kaspar Hauser speaks; Beneath the cellars of our town

"In these darkly magical stories, Millhauser turns town squares, backyards, and department stores into strange and luminous realms." New Yorker

Martin Dressler; the tale of an American dreamer. Crown 1996 294p o.p.

ISBN 0-517-70319-X LC 96-683

The author "again examines the American imagination in terms of cosmology. This time, his world-creator is young Martin Dressler, an entrepreneurial wunderkind who starts out at his father's cigar store. What ensues is an expertly woven fable of Victorian Manhattan, as Martin transforms his hunger for 'something else' into a series of colossal hotels. Martin's sights are firmly set on tomorrow, but he's cursed to be forever premodern: the skycraper always seems to lurk around the next turn of the page, but he can envision only period eclecticism. As the new century dawns, Martin's crowning achievement, the Grand Cosmo, begins to look like the ultimate castle in the air, and he ponders—without regret—the consequences of having 'dreamed the wrong dream.'" New Yorker

Revenge

In Millhauser, S. The king in the tree: three novellas

Milligan, J.

Jack Fish; a novel. Soho Press 2005 217p il $23

ISBN 1-569-47382-X LC 2004-48190

This "novel features a man from Atlantis, a spy to be precise, sent into New York to find and assassinate a rogue agent. Along the way, he has to deal with an as-

Milligan, J.—*Continued*

sortment of problems, mostly connected with making the adjustment to breathing air and passing as a Topworlder." Booklist

"Moving from Brooklyn diner to Midtown architecture firm to New Jersey theme park, the novel has the stealthy and web-toed Jack tangling with New York demimondaines and corporate wonks as he dodges a violent gang called the Maltese. The book brims throughout with hyperspecific detail and hipster patois; it's like a Mark Leyner novel, but with a plot, and harpoons." N Y Times Book Rev

Mills, Mark

Amagansett; Mark Mills. Putnam 2004 394p $24.95

ISBN 0-399-15184-2 LC 2004-44394

"In the small town of Amagansett, perched on Long Island's windswept coast, generations have followed the same calling as their forefathers, fishing the dangerous Atlantic waters. Little has changed in the three centuries since white settlers drove the Montaukett Indians from the land. But for Conrad Labarde, a second-generation Basque immigrant recently returned from the Second World War, and his fellow fisherman Rollo Kemp, this stability is shattered when a beautiful New York socialite turns up dead in their nets." Publisher's note

"The novel combines a touching love story, told in flashback, with a nicely detailed procedural starring an unlikely investigative duo: the taciturn Basque and the Amagansett assistant police chief, who hopes to resurrect his career in the wake of scandal. . . . This is a novel to savor, both for its portrait of roughhewn individuals finding selfhood beyond the breakers and for its snapshot of the postwar world not yet locked in the death grip of modernity." Booklist

Min, Anchee, 1957-

Becoming Madame Mao. Houghton Mifflin 2000 337p $25

ISBN 0-618-00407-6 LC 99-58520

A novel about "Jiang Qing, the late wife of Chairman Mao Zedong. . . . In the late 1970s, she went from being one of the most powerful figures in her counry to a convict who would live the rest of her days in prison, reviled by the Chinese people." N Y Times Book Rev

"Min reveals the complexities of love, betrayal, and ambition in this lyrical and thrilling depiction of a once-powerless woman in the jaws of power, giving us an all-too-rare glimpse into the life of a woman within the machine." Ms

Empress Orchid. Hougton Mifflin 2004 336p $24

ISBN 0-618-06887-2 LC 2003-56891

This historical novel portrays the life and times of the nineteenth-century Chinese Empress Dowager Tzu Hsi. In the novel "she is called Orchid by her family and intimates. . . . Min traces Orchid's transformation from a girl determined to maintain some control over her destiny to a young woman wavering in her commitment to a life constructed by empty ritual and burdened by political intrigue." Women's Rev Books

The author "has done a prodigious amount of on-site research to capture the glorious, hopeless last days of the Ching dynasty. . . . Readers will be enthralled by the gorgeously woven cultural tapestry and the psychologically astute portrait of the empress a talented girl from the provinces who married (way) up." Publ Wkly

Mina, Denise

Deception; a novel; Denise Mina. 1st American ed. Little, Brown 2004 c2003 311p $23.95

ISBN 0-316-73592-2 LC 2003-65861

"A 30-year-old forensic psychiatrist newly sacked from Sunnyfields State Mental Hospital, Susan Harriot is convicted of murdering her former patient, serial killer Andrew Gow, in the same manner in which he mutilated his victims. Convinced of her innocence, her husband, Lachlan, searches Susie's secret study for evidence for her appeal." Libr J

"Mina's novel is a smart example of the crime novel as postmodern puzzle, a work that coolly offers to match wits with the unwary reader and is not likely to lose the game." Washington Post Book World

Minot, Susan

Evening. Knopf 1998 264p o.p.

ISBN 0-375-40037-0 LC 98-15437

"Ann Lord's life has been shaped by the men who have married her. As she lies on her deathbed, trying to make some sense of that life, a rediscovered balsam pillow evokes a Maine wedding, in 1954, where she fell in love for the first—and perhaps the last—time. This almost crude conceit produces a narrative of considerable ambition and complexity. . . . For heroine and reader alike, death's painful confusions are tempered by the spirited directness of Ann's younger self, as yet unscathed by time and experience." New Yorker

Folly. Houghton Mifflin 1992 278p o.p.

LC 92-21035

This novel opens in the aftermath of America's entry into the First World War. "Lilian Eliot is the product of Brahmin Boston, whose traditions and socially correct attitudes have been instilled in her. She has been cast in the mold. Yet at times she longs to break free, to be someone different. Lilian sees that her choice of a husband will determine her future, but she finds herself most comfortable with what is familiar and marries accordingly. Later in life she is again faced with the choice—to break free or stay. In making her choice, Lilian finally discovers herself." Libr J

The author's "carefully thought out depiction of Lilian's inner world and of the difficulty of finding an accommodation between desire and reality, silence and self-expression, has a universal resonance." Christ Sci Monit

Lust & other stories. Houghton Mifflin 1989 147p o.p.

LC 89-1677

Contents: Lust; Sparks; Blow; City night; Lunch with Harry; The break-up; The swan in the garden; The feather in the toque; The knot; A thrilling life; Ile Sèche; The man who would not go away

"Men remain emotionally distant and unwilling to commit throughout these 12 short stories, while women

Minot, Susan—*Continued*
attempt to hold back. Alas, love insinuates itself and the man disappears. Minot's writing is sparse and poetic, painfully close to the surface." Libr J

Monkeys. Dutton 1986 159p o.p.
LC 85-30775

Interconnected episodes "trace the fortunes of a large boisterous New England family. Arranged into rough chronological order, the stories dramatize the growing up of the seven Vincent siblings. Their everyday world of family gatherings, teenage parties, and vacations seems frivolous on the surface but is underlaid with tension and ultimately leads to tragedy. The episodic nature of the book leaves a few questions unanswered about the engaging clan, while occasionally some events are reiterated. Yet there is a wonderful sense of slipping into the private, important moments of the Vincents, sharing their fun and their sadness." Booklist

Rapture. Knopf 2002 115p $18
ISBN 0-375-41327-8 LC 2001-38377

"This novella takes place during a single act of oral sex. . . . Benjamin is a handsome and hapless film director with a moneyed and supportive fiancée; Kay is his former production designer, with whom he had a fling on a shoot in Mexico. After three years of agonized liaisons and enforced partings, Benjamin and Kay fall into bed once more, but they seem to bring the rest of their lives along with them, and Minot's saucy conceit evolves into a disconcerting examination of love and war between the sexes." New Yorker

Mirvis, Tova

The outside world; Tova Mirvis. 1st ed. Alfred A. Knopf 2004 283p $24
ISBN 1-400-04161-9 LC 2003-58923

In this novel " 22-year-old Orthodox Tzippy, born and bred in Jewish Brooklyn and insulated from secular society but secretly curious and eager to experience it, is barraged with meddlesome questions and with a slew of seemingly endless carbon-copy dates intended to facilitate her marriage to a reputable yeshiva boy before she turns into a spinster. Meanwhile, not too far away, Naomi and Joel, Modern Orthodox Jews, are straining to knock some sense into their suddenly ultrareligious son, Bryan. . . . When these two formerly separate worlds collide, parents, siblings and spouses must reflect on what their faith means to them and what to do when their beliefs unexpectedly diverge from those of loved ones." Publ Wkly

"Beneath the women's wigs and the men's black fedoras, Mirvis finds reservoirs of belief, doubt, ambition, folly, lust and the rest of the human equation." Washington Post Book World

Mishima, Yukio, 1925-1970

The decay of the angel; translated from the Japanese by Edward G. Seidensticker. Knopf 1974 236p (Sea of fertility) o.p.

Original Japanese edition, 1971

This final novel in the series "treats the themes of purity, beauty, evil and death. . . . [Judge Honda] is now near death, while that spirit of tragic purity which in the earlier stories was respectively incarnate in Kiyoaki, Isao and Ying Chan is found here in Toru, an evil teenaged orphan, Toru is employed, symbolically enough, as a ship watcher when Honda, seeing him as both evil like himself and marked for an early death, adopts him as his son in order to thwart that destiny. Over several years Honda proves no more of a match for Toru than does the bride he chooses for him, but neither man is to escape an eerie doom." Publ Wkly

"The novel concludes with a superbly written scene that casts doubt on the reality of the events described in the four volumes. In the end we discover that the 'sea of fertility' may be as arid as the region of that name on the moon, although it seems to suggest infinite richness." Ency of World Lit in the 20th Century

Runaway horses; translated from the Japanese by Michael Gallagher. Knopf 1973 421p (Sea of fertility) o.p.

Original Japanese edition, 1969

In the second volume of the Sea of fertility cycle "the political and economic upheaval of the 1930's is seen primarily through the eyes of a young zealot intent upon an imperial restoration through assassination of key industrialists and then his own ritual suicide. The secondary strand involves a middle-aged judge whose carefully constructed rational and legalistic life crumbles when exposed to the younger man's idealism." Choice

"Mishima uses the same literary artistry in this novel as in the first but changes the gently romantic tone to one of martial ideology with a weirdly beautiful emphasis on ritual suicide. In the interplay of entanglements between the two novels, each self-contained, the author experiments with the Buddhist doctrine of reincarnation." Booklist

Followed by The Temple of Dawn

The sound of waves; translated by Meredith Weatherby; drawings by Yoshinori Kinoshita. Knopf 1956 182p il o.p.

"Returning to his village after a day on the fishing boats, Shinji, 18 years old, comes upon a beautiful stranger, Hatsue, who is the daughter of the wealthiest man in the village. After several unplanned encounters the two realize that they are in love, but many obstacles must be overcome before they can be married." Shapiro. Fic for Youth. 3d edition

Spring snow; translated from the Japanese by Michael Gallagher. Knopf 1972 389p (Sea of fertility) o.p.

"UNESCO collection of representative works: Japanese series"

Original Japanese edition, 1968

"Kiyoaki Matsugae, a young Japanese, comes from a wealthy family whose attention to the most formal aspects of Japanese life has changed because of their attraction to Western culture. His best friend, Shigekuna Honda, is not so handsome or affluent but is a more serious scholar. The story emphasizes the difference in the character of the two young men as the plot describes the passionate, although ambivalent, love that Kiyoaki feels for the beautiful Satoko. When she concludes that Kiyoaki does not return her love, despite the fact that their affair has been serious and intimate, she allows herself to be betrothed to someone else. As always, what is forbidden becomes more desirable and Kiyoaki tries desperately to regain his loved one. Japanese customs and

Mishima, Yukio, 1925-1970—*Continued*
rituals intervene to bring a tragic ending to this love story." Shapiro. Fic for Youth. 3d edition
Followed by Runaway horses

The Temple of Dawn; translated from the Japanese by E. Dale Saunders and Cecilia Segawa Seigle. Knopf 1973 334p (Sea of fertility) o.p.
Original Japanese edition, 1970
The third volume in the Sea of fertility series is "divided into two parts: the first is set in southeast Asia, where we first see the Thai princess who is the reincarnation of Isao; the second takes place in Japan after World War II, when the old values of society have been corrupted." Ency of World Lit in the 20th Century
Followed by The decay of the angel

The temple of the golden pavilion; translated by Ivan Morris; introduction by Nancy Wilson Ross; drawings by Fumi Komatsu. Knopf 1959 262p il o.p.
"Based on an actual incident in 1950, when a Zen Buddhist acolyte burned down a temple which was a national shrine. Like the real arsonist, the fictional Mizoguchi is ugly and a pathological stutterer, and long before his hostility becomes overt, has developed a compulsion to destroy whatever is morally or physically beautiful. As told by the young acolyte, this is a masterly description of the growth of an obsession and an acute interpretation of the deliberate symbolism underlying Mizoguchi's irrational, perverse behavior." Booklist

Miss Read *See* Read, Miss, 1913-

Mistry, Rohinton, 1952-

Family matters. Knopf 2002 431p o.p.
ISBN 0-375-40373-6
First published 2001 in the United Kingdom
The setting is the "city of Bombay during a 1990s wave of violent religious extremism, and the focus is on and extended Parsi family suffering the long-term consequences of a Juliet and Romeo-like tragedy. Septuagenarian widower Nariman survived the catastrophic love affair, but Parkinson's disease is now eroding his health and autonomy, forcing him to confront his guilt over capitulating to his family's vehement objections to the non-Parsi love of his life and entering into an unhappy arranged marriage with a Parsi widow with two children." Booklist
"Mistry is not just a fiction writer; he's a philosopher who finds meaning—indeed, perhaps a divine plan—in small human interactions. This beautifully paced, elegantly expressed novel is notable for the breadth of its vision as well as its immensely appealing characters and enticing plot." Publ Wkly

Mitcham, Judson

Sabbath Creek; a novel; by Judson Mitcham. University of Georgia Press 2004 169p $22.95
ISBN 0-8203-2577-5 LC 2003-15704
In this novel "14-year-old Lewis Pope is caught in the middle of a dangerous family crisis. While attempting to run away from his abusive father, Lewis and his frightened mother drive aimlessly for days through southern Georgia, unsure where to go or what to do. Their car breaks down in the sleepy backwater of Sabbath Creek, and they end up stranded at a ramshackle hotel owned by a 93-year-old black man named Truman Stroud." Libr J
"Lewis observes everything with the alertness of someone who does not yet take common experiences, such as kissing and drunkenness, for granted; he never resorts to shorthand to convey them, but describes them with a scrupulous fidelity to his own perceptions." N Y Times Book Rev

Mitchard, Jacquelyn

The deep end of the ocean. Viking 1996 434p o.p.
ISBN 0-670-86579-6 LC 95-26234
"When 3-year-old Ben Cappadora disappears from a hotel lobby in Chicago, a presumed kidnap victim, nothing positive ever comes from his loss. The family he leaves behind is ruined. Ben's father, Pat, a kindly restaurateur, develops cardiac problems—the victim of a literal broken heart. His mother, Beth, becomes an emotional zombie. Vincent, the 7-year-old who was watching Ben when he disappeared, grows into a high-I.Q. juvenile delinquent. Baby Kerry has lived in a mournful, hostile house for so long she thinks it's normal." N Y Times Book Rev
"One of the most remarkable things about this rich, moving and altogether stunning first novel is Mitchard's assured command of narrative structure and stylistic resources. Her story about a child's kidnapping and its enduring effects upon his parents, siblings, and extended family is a blockbuster read." Publ Wkly

A theory of relativity. HarperCollins Pubs. 2001 351p $26
ISBN 0-06-621023-2 LC 00-54261
"Keefer Nye, only a year old when her parents die in a car crash near Madison, Wis., is the focal point of a bitter, protracted and precedent-setting custody battle. Keefer's bachelor uncle, 24-year-old science teacher Gordon McKenna, seems the most appropriate custodian for his tiny niece, since he helped his elderly parents care for Keefer while his sister (Keefer's mother, Georgia) battled cancer. Challenging his claim, the affluent Nye grandparents, country-club Floridians, believe that their niece and her husband, born-again Christians, should get custody. Mitchard's nuanced character portrayals are her strong suit; no one is without frailties." Publ Wkly

Twelve times blessed. HarperCollins Pubs. 2003 532p $25.95
ISBN 0-06-621475-0 LC 2002-31781
"True Dickinson has everything: a loving 10-year-old son, Guy; a successsful business; and a cadre of friends who mostly fill the empty places in her life—until she falls for Hank Bannister, a restaurateur 10 years her junior." Booklist
"Mitchard infuses the courtship and domestic life with gentle humor." Publ Wkly

Mitchell, David

Cloud atlas; a novel; David Mitchell. 1st U.S. ed. Random House Trade Paperbacks 2004 509p pa $14.95
ISBN 0-375-50725-6 (pa) LC 2003-69314

Mitchell, David—*Continued*

The author "presents six narratives that evoke an array of genres, from Melvillean high-seas drama to California noir and dystopian fantasy. There is a naïve clerk on a nineteenth-century Polynesian voyage; an aspiring composer who insinuates himself into the home of a syphilitic genius; a journalist investigating a nuclear plant; a publisher with a dangerous bestseller on his hands; and a cloned human being created for slave labor. These five stories are bisected and arranged around a sixth, the oral history of a post-apocalyptic island, which forms the heart of the novel. Only after this do the second halves of the stories fall into place, pulling the novel's themes into focus: the ease with which one group enslaves another, and the constant rewriting of the past by those who control the present. Against such forces, Mitchell's characters reveal a quiet tenacity." New Yorker

Number9dream; a novel. Random House 2002 400p o.p.

ISBN 0-375-50726-4 LC 2001-41910

First published 2001 in the United Kingdom

"Eiji Miyake, the young protagonist, leaves his rural Japanese home and travels to Tokyo to find the father who abandoned him years before. What begins as a fairly straightforward filial quest soon devolves into a kaleidoscopic adventure filled with Japanese mobsters and increasingly baroque futuristic scenarios. What is even more alarming, Eiji does not always maintain a firm grasp on reality. Mitchell's pyrotechnics are never less than interesting." New Yorker

Mitchell, James C., 1942-

Lovers crossing. St. Martin's Minotaur 2003 294p $23.95

ISBN 0-312-31530-9 LC 2003-41350

"Roscoe Brinker, a Tuscon-based private detective and former INS agent, left the service after being shot in the line of duty by, he suspects, a fellow agent. A local business mogul, Mo Crain, hires him to look into the murder of Crain's wife, Sandra, who worked along the border as a nurse helping abandoned and battered children. Sandra seems to have had few enemies, but as Brinker's investigation proceeds, it seems that her death might be linked to a smuggling operation, and to Henry Sanchez, the corrupt INS agent that Brinker believes shot him." Publ Wkly

"The instantly likable Brinker is full of surprises, and the secondary characters who surround him also have great depth." Booklist

Mitchell, Margaret, 1900-1949

Gone with the wind; with a new preface by Pat Conroy and an introduction by James A. Michener. 60th Anniversary ed. Scribner 1996 959p il o.p.

ISBN 0-684-82625-9 LC 95-52609

A reissue of the title first published 1936 by Macmillan

This novel "shows both considerable literary skill and social insight. The heroine, Scarlett O'Hara, is an embodiment of the indomitable spirit of the South. She wants to marry Ashley Wilkes, but he marries Melanie Hamilton instead, and in a pique Scarlett marries Charles Hamilton. Later she marries another man for his money, and then finally marries Rhett Butler, a dashing and outspoken Byronic hero. Around her surges the tumult of the Civil War, the despair of Reconstruction days, and the collapse of the old social order. Scarlett's dogged determination to restore Tara, the family estate, after Sherman destroys Atlanta, attains its goal, but the cost of the realization that she has sacrificed everything else for money and security." Benet's Reader's Ency of Am Lit

Mitchell, Mark

(ed) Penguin book of gay short fiction. See Penguin book of gay short fiction

Mitford, Nancy, 1904-1973

Love in a cold climate

In Mitford, N. The pursuit of love & Love in a cold climate p285-617

The pursuit of love

In Mitford, N. The pursuit of love & Love in a cold climate p[1]-283

The pursuit of love & Love in a cold climate; two novels. Modern Lib. 1994 617p $19.95

ISBN 0-679-60090-6 LC 93-43632

A combined edition of two titles about the Radlett family originally published 1945 and 1949 respectively. Subsequent works about the family and its associates are The blessing (1951) and Don't tell Alfred (1960)

These quasi-autobiographical novels take a satiric look at the various social and amatory trials and triumphs of an eccentric upper-class English family following World War I

Mixon, Laura J.

Burning the ice. TOR Bks. 2002 544p $25.95

ISBN 0-312-86903-7 LC 2002-25368

"A Tom Doherty Associates book"

"The colony of clone family groups laboring to terraform the ice-bound planet Brimstone into a habitable world includes outcast Manda CarliPablo, left alone when her clone sibling died at their birth. A series of suspicious accidents leads her to a pair of discoveries that could mean either the transformation of the colony or its ultimate destruction." Libr J

"While hardly short of action or fascinating scenes of alien contact, the novel's real strength lies in the author's depiction of the future society, with its complex system of degrees of kinship, social obligations and controls, sexual mores and even appropriate pronouns." Publ Wkly

Mizner, David

Political animal; a novel; David Mizner. Soho Press 2004 293p $24

ISBN 1-569-47386-2 LC 2004-11250

"Arnie Schecter ("Shecter the Protector") is running for the New York senate with the help of Director of Communications Ben Bergin. As dedicated as Bergin is to Schecter's liberal causes, he's even more zealous in his pursuit of fellow staffer Calliope Berkowitz. His concern with winning Calli's affection vastly outweighs his zeal for winning the election, and Ben idolizes Calli with a

Mizner, David—*Continued*

sweetly bumbling fervor that exhibits all the angst of a prepubescent youth. Not since Bridget Jones has a character parsed contemporary dating rituals with such a fine degree of anxiety and self-doubt, as Mizner uproariously captures the incipient insanity inherent in both courting and campaigning. An endearing and irreverent love story." Booklist

Moberg, Carl Artur Vilhelm *See* Moberg, Vilhelm, 1898-1973

Moberg, Vilhelm, 1898-1973

The emigrants; a novel; translated from the Swedish by Gustaf Lannestock. Simon & Schuster 1951 366p o.p.

Original Swedish edition, 1949

This is the first volume of a cycle which tells the story of a band of Swedish emigrants to the United States. This volume tells the story in particular of one family, Karl Oskar Nilsson, his wife and children, and his young brother Robert; of their life in Sweden; and of the long, arduous journey across the Atlantic in the summer of 1850

"A novel of peasant life, drawn to the last homely and superstitious detail. It is a story of poverty and heartbreak over which human faith has its will. And it is filled with an earthly humor, the unpredictable flash of human malice and emotion which bring Mr. Moberg's characters sharply into focus." N Y Times Book Rev

Followed by Unto a good land

The last letter home; a novel; translated from the Swedish by Gustaf Lannestock. Simon & Schuster 1961 383p o.p.

Originally published in Sweden 1956 and 1959. Parts 3 and 4 of the author's cycle, the first of which is The emigrants and the second, Unto a good land

"It is solemn, rather slow and quietly moving. Mr. Moberg is at least as much concerned with the thoughts and emotions of his stolid characters as with the historical events of their time." Publ Wkly

Unto a good land; a novel; translated from the Swedish by Gustaf Lannestock. Simon & Schuster 1954 371p o.p.

Sequel to The emigrants

Original Swedish edition, 1952

The book "tells how farmer Karl Oskar Nilsson, his wife and children, and ten other peasants from his own parish in the province of Smaland, sailed in the brig Charlotta in the spring of 1850 to North America, landing ten weeks later at the East River Pier in New York on a sweltering June day and how, by river-boat and steam-wagon, on foot and in an ox-drawn cart, Karl Oskar and his family reach at last the shore of the Minnesota lake where out of the great trees he finds there he hews himself a home." N Y Her Trib Books

Followed by The last letter home

Modesitt, L. E., Jr.

Archform; beauty. TOR Bks. 2002 330p $25.95

ISBN 0-7653-0433-3 LC 2001-59655

"A Tom Doherty Associates book"

"Four hundred years from now, nanotechnology protects the elite and provides clean, safe production for most material needs. But it doesn't eliminate normal human perversity, in either individuals or group relations. When a series of mysterious deaths begins, Modesitt has us see it from the steadily converging viewpoints of a music teacher, a news researcher, a politician (complete with constituents), and an ambitious, ruthless dynastic businessman." Booklist

"Set against a background of biological terrorism, Modesitt's tale explores social issues . . . sure to resonate with many readers. This brilliant novel is as thought provoking as it is entertaining." Publ Wkly

Moggach, Deborah

Tulip fever. Delacorte Press 2000 281p o.p.

ISBN 0-385-33489-3 LC 99-42048

First published 1999 in the United Kingdom

A novel set in 17th-century Amsterdam. "Moggach introduces us to the elderly Cornelis Sandvoort; his beautiful young bride, Sophia, . . . her lover, Jan, who is hired to paint the Sandvoorts' portrait; and Sophia's maid, Maria. As 'Tulip Fever' unfolds, Sophia's tentative romance with Jan gradually becomes so reckless that it is analogous to Amsterdam's obsession with tulips. Made ruthless by love, the couple plan to escape the city. . . . Moggach's book reads like a thriller: it's a novel that ponders what it means to push things too far, and keenly examines what the consequences might be." N Y Times Book Rev

Moloney, Susie

The dwelling; a novel. Atria Bks. 2003 408p $25

ISBN 0-7434-5662-9 LC 2003-276274

In this tale of a haunted house, "Moloney attempts to depict 362 Belisle as a being with a mind of its own, beckoning realtor Glenn Darnley throughout the multiple showings of the house, and claiming or rejecting its inhabitants. The tenants seem quite ordinary until mysterious events begin to occur, each episode terminating at a horrifying moment before Moloney launches into the next inhabitant's story. Newly widowed Glenn's travails connect the sagas of her three buyers, as her thoughts of her dead husband fill the gaps between stories." Publ Wkly

The house "is a character in its own right, but Moloney . . . has thankfully peopled the narrative with other well-developed characters as well, ones with such recognizable strengths and weaknesses that the reader actually cares about their outcomes. The ending is horrible but poignant and exactly fitting." Libr J

Momaday, N. Scott

The ancient child; a novel. Doubleday 1989 313p o.p.

LC 89-31304

"Locke Setman, a highly successful Bay Area painter, fears that he has lost touch with his 'inner child' in the process of making it big. Then, during a brief trip to Oklahoma, he meets a beautiful American Indian woman named Grey who dresses in beaded buckskin, speaks

Momaday, N. Scott—*Continued*
Kiowa and Nanajo like one of the elders, and has elaborate visionary conversations with the ghost of Billy the Kid. Armed with a medicine bundle and a bag of peyote buttons, Grey slowly draws Setman into a magical world of ritual that both revitalizes and transforms him. . . . A fascinating and hypnotically beautiful book that belongs in every collection of Western Americana." Libr J

House made of dawn. Harper & Row 1968 212p o.p.

"Abel, a young American Indian, lives with his grandfather, observing Indian customs, until he is drafted into the army. The story covers the years 1945 to 1952, during which time Abel seems unable to find his place either in the white world, where he is driven to violence, or on the Indian reservation where he was born. The pain of being caught between two cultures is keenly felt and can be comprehended as a problem that has affected other ethnic groups." Shapiro. Fic for Youth. 3d edition

A **moment** on the edge; 100 years of crime stories by women; edited by Elizabeth George. HarperCollins 2004 540p $24.95
ISBN 0-06-058821-7 LC 2003-67608

Contents: A jury of her peers, by Glaspell, S.; The man who knew how, by Sayers, D. L.; I can find my way out, by Marsh, N.; The summer, by Jackson, S.; St. Patrick's Day in the morning, by Armstrong, C.; The purple is everything, by Davis, D. S.; Money to burn, by Allingham, M.; A nice place to stay, by Tyre, N.; Clever and quick, by Brand, C.; Country lovers, by Gordimer, N.; The irony of hate, by Rendell, R.; Sweet baby Jenny, by Harrington, J.; Wild mustard, by Muller, M.; Jemima Shore at the sunny grave, by, Fraser, A.; The case of the Pietro Andromache, by Paretsky, S.; Afraid all the time, by Pickard, N.; The young shall see visions, and the old dream dreams, by Rusch, K. K.; A predatory woman, by McCrumb, S.; Jack be quick, by Paul, B.; Ghost station, by Wheat, C.; New moon and rattlesnakes, by Hornsby, W.; Death of a snowbird, by Jance, J. A.; The river mouth, by Matera, L.; A scandal in winter, by Linscott, G.; Murder-two, by Oates, J. C.; English autumn—American fall, by Walters, M.

"George here collects short mysteries by women, bracketing the 26 entries with two tales about the death of abusive husbands, written more than 80 years apart. Between them springs an entertaining assortment of locked-room murders, theatrical whodunits, white-collar-crime and detective stories, and psychological puzzlers, each headed by revealing author notes." Booklist

Monette, Paul

Afterlife. Crown 1990 278p o.p.
LC 89-48754

In this novel about AIDS "three men whose lovers all died in the same hospital during the same week decide how to live as they await their own illnesses." Booklist

"Despite its comic flourishes, this is a tough, painful book about gay sex and love, pursued in the valley of the shadow of AIDS. And its unrelenting descriptions of the ravages of the disease, along with its sexual details and 'talking dirty,' are surely going to make some readers uncomfortable." N Y Times Book Rev

Monfredo, Miriam Grace

Blackwater spirits. St. Martin's Press 1995 328p o.p.
LC 94-40980

"A Thomas Dunne book"

A "historical mystery featuring Glynis Tryon, librarian in Seneca Falls, N.Y., in the mid-18th century. Glynis and the newly arrived doctor, a young Jewish woman from New York City, overhear a farmer voice fears for his life to Constable Cullen Stuart. Soon the farmer is fatally poisoned, and Cullen enlists Glynis's aid in talking to the farmer's angry widow, who suggests her husband's murder will be followed by others." Publ Wkly

The stalking horse. Berkley Prime Crime 1998 340p o.p.
ISBN 0-425-15783-0 LC 97-21547

This historical mystery is "set just after Lincoln's presidential election. The Southern states are calling for secession and there is talk of war. Bronwyn Llyr, the niece of Seneca Falls, NY, librarian Glynis Tryon, has left school and taken a job as an operative with the Pinkerton Detective Agency. Her first assignment is to accompany a railroad owner to Alabama and learn about possible plans to confiscate the train line. Bronwyn accidentally overhears a conversation about a secret plan called Equus, which she correctly fears is an assassination plot." SLJ

The author "ably mixes real-life figures with her own creations into an engaging brew that combines solid historical research with a fast-moving plot." Publ Wkly

Moning, Karen Marie

The immortal highlander. Delacorte Press 2004 267p $15
ISBN 0-385-33825-2 LC 2004-40764

"For eons Adam Black has aided humanity and meddled in its affairs, much to the chagrin of the queen of the Seelie Court. He has finally pushed her too far and finds himself, a once powerful Fae, invisible and very human. But he is still as resourceful as ever, and finds a way to reach the queen and plea to have his curse lifted with the help of a young lawyer, Gabrielle O'Callaghan, a human born with the ability to see his kind. As old enemies yearn to take advantage of his weakened state, threatening his life and all existence, Adam discovers that Gabrielle threatens a heart he never thought he had." Booklist

Monsarrat, Nicholas, 1910-1979

The cruel sea. Knopf 1951 509p o.p.

"The *Compass Rose* is a British corvette commissioned to convoy duty and to the hunting of German U-boats during World War II. First Mate Lockhart and Skipper Erikson develop a close relationship. When their ship is sunk and few of the crew survive, Lockhart and Erikson team up again on a new ship, undaunted by the experiences visited upon them by the cruel sea." Shapiro. Fic for Youth. 3d edition

Moody, Bill, 1941-

Looking for Chet Baker; an Evan Horne mystery. Walker & Co. 2002 253p $23.95
ISBN 0-8027-3368-9 LC 2001-56772

Moody, Bill, 1941-—*Continued*

In London, jazz pianist and amateur sleuth Evan Horne "meets an old friend, Ace Buffington. An English professor who needs to publish one more book to achieve tenure, Ace wants Horne to help him research real-life jazz great Chet Baker. . . . Horne has no interest in more detective work, but when he gets to Amsterdam, he discovers that Ace has disappeared. Since the police express little interest in finding the missing professor, Horne is obliged to go looking for his buddy himself. Ace's trail parallels that of Chet Baker's last days, so Horne has to learn a lot more about Baker, his legendary talent, his tragic addiction to drugs. Moody does a wonderful job of re-creating the man and his times." Publ Wkly

Moon, Elizabeth

Once a hero. Baen Pub. Enterprises 1997 400p o.p.

ISBN 0-671-87769-0 LC 96-48176

In this novel, "Lt. Esmay Suiza faces a military court hearing following her emergency captaining of a patrol ship during battle after the captain turned out to be a traitor. Tormented by nightmares from repressed memories of sexual assault, Esmay determinedly recaptures her self-esteem and the military's trust." Libr J

"Moon's mastery of contemporary science fiction is evident in every line. The characters spring to life on the page, the intricacies of societies are astutely explored, and the pace never flags." Booklist

The speed of dark. Del Rey Bks. 2002 340p $23.95

ISBN 0-345-44755-7 LC 2002-20771

Set in the near future, this novel "depicts an autistic adult struggling with a momemtous decision. Lou Arrendal functions on a fairly high level: he has a job with a pharmaceutical company and leads a quiet, independent life. . . . When an experimental treatment offers Lou a chance to reverse his autism, he must choose between remaining himself or possibly becoming a different person." Libr J

"Moon is effective at putting the reader inside Lou's mind, and it is both fascinating and painful to see the behavior and qualities of so-called normals through his eyes." Booklist

Moor, Margriet de

Duke of Egypt; a novel; translated from the Dutch by Paul Vincent. Arcade Pub. 2001 245p $24.95

ISBN 1-55970-546-9 LC 2001-45788

Original Dutch edition, 1996

The tale of a "wandering gypsy whose family is torn apart by the cruelty of post-WWII Europe, and who experiments with creating a different life for himself. As the novel begins, it is 1963, and 27-year-old Joseph Andrias's travels with his family caravan are about to be interrupted. On a wet summer day in a bar in Benckelo, in the Twente countryside of eastern Holland, he meets Lucie, a strange, wild redhead, who lives with her father, Gerard, on a horse farm outside town. It is love at first sight for this unlikely pair, who marry and have three children." Publ Wkly

"De Moor's subject is vast, with a hundred dark and lively currents, but her novel is entirely absorbing, and it has the two greatest qualities of all her work: that brave and astute sense of musical form as a way of organizing narrative, and a wonderful sense of passion." N Y Times Book Rev

Moorcock, Michael, 1939-

An alien heat; volume one of a trilogy "The dancers at the end of time". Harper & Row 1973 c1972 158p o.p.

First published 1972 in the United Kingdom

This novel "is set near the end of the world, when Earth is populated by hedonistic immortals who restructure continents and their own bodies at whim. A young man named Jhereck becomes unfashionably obsessed with Mrs. Amelia Underwood, a time traveler from the 19th century, his favorite period. He follows her to London of 1896, where he is tried for murder and hanged, which somehow returns him to the future, sans Amelia but with insights into love and the true human condition. This tale could be called an Art Nouveau morality play or a science fiction comedy of manners. The humor is genuine, the style lush but controlled." Libr J

Followed by The hollow lands

Behold the man

In The Best of the Nebulas p163-202

The dreamthief's daughter; a tale of the albino. Warner Bks. 2001 343p $35

ISBN 0-446-52618-5 LC 00-43836

"In this latest installment in his multivolume saga of the Eternal Champion, Moorcock . . . teams his favorite hero, the melancholy albino swordsman Elric of Melniboné, with Count Ulric von Bek, the last in a line of German noblemen. . . . War is in the offing, and Hitler, having learned that the von Bek family may own both an enchanted sword and the Holy Grail itself, sends SS Major Gaynor von Minct to take possession of these mystical relics so they may be used to further the cause of the Third Reich. Von Bek and Gaynor, however, are merely the current earthly avatars of the Eternal Champion and one of his greatest foes; they are knights fighting in the causes, respectively, of Chaos and Law, in innumerable, gorgeously described, alternate realities." Publ Wkly

The end of all songs; volume three of a trilogy "The dancers at the end of time". Harper & Row 1976 271p o.p.

"Moorcock wraps up his Dancers at the End of Time trilogy with a volume that . . . brings together the two central characters—Jhereck Carnelian, one of the hedonistic immortals who dwell at the End of Time, and Mrs. Amelia Underwood, a reluctant time traveler from Victorian England. Although their reunion is a cause for celebration, the fabric of time has been ruptured, threatening to plunge all into disordered chronological gulfs. Even the inhabitants at the End of Time—an amoral, whimsical, all-but-thoughtless, utterly powerful, and thoroughly likable lot—know concern for the first time in their immortal lives." Booklist

Moorcock, Michael, 1939-—*Continued*

The hollow lands; volume two of a trilogy "The dancers at the end of time". Harper & Row 1974 182p o.p.

In this volume "jaded Jhereck Carnelian is back in his futuristic world after narrowly escaping being hanged in 1896 London while on a time trip with Mrs. Amelia Underwood. He's bored with his life of instant gratification and wants to return to his Victorian lady, but he can't find a working time machine anywhere. Until he falls into a pit full of never-aging children and a robot nurse shoots him back to 1896. Lost in London, he luckily stumbles on Frank Harris and H. G. Wells at the Cafe Royale, and they help reunite him with Amelia." Publ Wkly

Followed by The end of all songs

The skrayling tree; the albino in America. Warner Bks. 2003 330p $24.95

ISBN 0-446-53104-9 LC 2002-27247

"In the sequel to The Dreamthief's Daughter, Oona, protagonist of the earlier book, has married Ulric von Bek, last of his line of Grail Defenders. On vacation in Canada, Ulric is abducted, allegedly to fight a wind demon leading an army bent on destroying a golden city that possesses the Skrayling Tree, a key support of the Multiverse of Moorcock's Eternal Champion yarns. Meanwhile, Oona is in a Native American universe, enlisted by the shaman White Crow to fight pygmies who threaten a golden city. In another universe, Oona's father, Elric, seeking those who forged his black sword, ends up in Vinland's City of Gold, asked to help pygmies there, whose gold has been stolen by an evil giant named . . . White Crow." Booklist

"The tale's power stems largely from the astounding lyricism of the author's prose, the only flaw being the sometimes stilted and overly expository dialogue about the nature of the Multiverse." Publ Wkly

Moore, Brian, 1921-1999

Black robe; a novel. Dutton 1985 246p o.p.

LC 84-21222

"A William Abrahams book"

This is a novel about a French priest in Canada in the 17th century, "Father Laforgue, who must journey from Quebec to a remote village to find out what happened to two other priests. Through snowstorms and along rivers, amid the majestic grandeur of the forests and brushes with sex and death, Laforgue comes to doubt the depth and meaning of his faith." Libr J

"Each culture is seen whole, with intelligence and sympathy, and considering the clichés that prevail about both Indians and priests, that alone makes 'Black Robe' special." N Y Times Book Rev

Cold heaven; a novel. Holt, Rinehart & Winston 1983 265p o.p.

LC 82-18720

"A William Abrahams book"

"Alex and Marie, two Americans on vacation, are pedal-boating in the Baie-des-Anges. Alex dives into the water to swim alongside the little boat. He is hit by an out-of-control motor boat and pronounced dead. But at the hospital, his corpse disappears. Later, returning to their hotel room, Marie finds Alex's wallet, flight tickets and travel checks missing. Throughout, Marie has the feeling that an omnipotent power is controlling her life. She is haunted by a miraculous vision." Libr J

"What begins as an extravagant thriller becomes a metaphysical story of a woman's struggle to regain control of her life. . . . The religious view that Moore expresses here is rarely found in fiction; it has the same kind of freshness that Alaric brought to Rome. 'Cold Heaven's' spell derives from its author's skill at preparing a most meticulously realistic field in which he plants two uncanny seeds—just to see what the effect will be." Newsweek

The color of blood; a novel. Dutton 1987 182p o.p.

LC 87-6695

"A William Abrahams book"

This is the story of Stephen Cardinal Bem, "the Roman Catholic cardinal-primate in an unnamed Soviet-bloc country and the precarious balance he must manage in his renderings to Caesar and to God." Commonweal

The author "invites us to consider the philosophical rather than the personal implications of political action. The thriller format becomes a vehicle to explore . . . the relationship between Church and State, the validity of 'liberation theology', the meaning of 'freedom' and 'responsibility' under a totalitarian régime. . . . Always the consummate craftsman, Moore never allows the tension to slacken." Times Lit Suppl

The emperor of ice-cream; a novel. Viking 1965 250p o.p.

At odds with both his Catholic family and Protestant Belfast, unsuccessful in his college entrance examinations, Gavin Burke considers himself a failure at seventeen. Then with the outbreak of World War II, he joins the Air Raid Precautions, and new encounters change Gavin's relationships with both his family and his girl

"By being very Irish and very individual 'The Emperor of Ice-Cream' succeeds in touching on Everyman's youth. And it does so in a most welcome manner: no sentimentality, much wit and an astringent charm on every page." N Y Times Book Rev

Lies of silence. Doubleday 1990 197p o.p.

LC 90-30681

"Michael Dillon, manager of a hotel in the conflicted area of Ireland, has decided to leave his wife and his country to go to London with the young woman whom he loves. His decision to embark on this new life comes to a shattering stop when he is forced to participate in a terrorist attack by masked men who invade his home. His wife's safety is the leverage used to compel his compliance. The tension is high and the issues faced are moral and political. We are brought close to the danger that is part of everyday life in Northern Ireland." Shapiro. Fic for Youth. 3d edition

The lonely passion of Judith Hearne. Little, Brown 1956 c1955 223p o.p.

"An Atlantic Monthly Press book"

First published 1955 in the United Kingdom with title: Judith Hearne

"Judith Hearne is a middle-aged spinster whose plain looks and loneliness make her depressed and increasingly isolated from any social contact. The other renters in her Belfast boarding house disdain her. Only Mrs. O'Neill,

Moore, Brian, 1921-1999—*Continued*

an old school friend, treats her kindly. When her landlady's brother, Jim Madden, returns from America, he pays some attention to Judith, thinking she has money. Jim's bad character is revealed in many ways, including a sexual attack on a young housemaid, and Judith finds more and more solace in drinking. Her pathetic world falls apart completely when even her religious faith deserts her. This sad novel presents a portrait of despair that is almost unbearable." Shapiro. Fic for Youth. 3d edition

The magician's wife. Dutton 1998 229p o.p.

ISBN 0-525-94400-1 LC 97-34064

"A William Abrahams book"

In this "novel, set in the France and North Africa of 1856, the heroine, Emmeline, is a provincial who is married to the celebrated illusionist Henri Lambert. They are invited to Napoleon III's Compiègne palace, and are eventually introduced to a scheme the Emperor has thought up: Henri is to employ his magician's art to prove to the Bedouins that the colonial French are truly their betters. The story (which ends, literally, with a death-defying trick) is based on a real incident, and Moore has transformed it into superior fiction." New Yorker

The statement. Dutton 1996 250p o.p.

LC 95-43885

"A William Abrahams book"

This "novel dramatizes the narrow escapes and glaring self-deceptions of a 70-year-old Catholic Frenchman, Pierre Brossard, who is being newly pursued for his participation, while a member of the Vichy-affiliated Milici during World War II, in the execution of Jews. Brossard was offically pardoned in 1971 by the French president, but soon afterwards he was condemned internationally for 'crimes against humanity.' He has remained a fugitive ever since, receiving asylum at various sympathetic Catholic monasteries and abbeys in France." Booklist

"'The Statement' is a book to be read in one sitting. A straightforward shocker, a psychological thriller, a chase and travelogue through France, a religio-political conundrum—any way you take it, this is first-class fare." N Y Times Book Rev

Moore, Christopher, 1957-

Fluke; or, I know why the winged whale sings. Morrow 2003 321p $23.95; pa $13.95

ISBN 0-380-97841-5; 0-06-056668-X (pa)

LC 2002-43231

"Nate Quinn spends his time in the waters off Maui researching whales. . . . One day, when photographing the tail of one particular whale to determine its size, Nate spies foot-high letters on the underside spelling out, 'Bite Me.' . . . When Nate finds the group's offices plundered and all of the data either stolen or ruined, the scientists are thrown into the beginning of a bizarre plot complete with . . . scientific explanations, potential alien conspiracies, and well-rounded, hilarious characters." Voice Youth Advocates

Moore, Lorrie

Birds of America. Knopf 1998 291p o.p.

ISBN 0-679-44597-8 LC 98-6144

Contents: Willing; Which is more than I can say about some people; Dance in America; Community life; Agnes of Iowa; Charades; Four calling birds, three French hens; Beautiful grade; What you want to do fine; Real estate; People like that are the only people here: canonical babbling in peed onk; Terrific mother

"These stories chart the intersection of the ridiculous and the tragic. . . . Moore peers into America's loneliest perches, but her delicate touch turns absurdity into a warming vitality." New Yorker

Morales, Adelaida Garcia *See* Garcia Morales, Adelaida

Moran, Thomas

Anja the liar. Riverhead Books 2003 322p $25.95

ISBN 1-573-22260-7 LC 2003-43164

"Walter Fass, a one-armed, ex-Wehrmacht officer, encounters Polish refugee Anja, the 'girl in the empty dress,' behind the wires of a DP camp in Germany. Both are haunted by memories of atrocities and betrayals in which they were complicit during World War II, but they soon agree to strike out together. Resettling on the farm of Walter's Uncle Franz in the Italian border region of Tyrol, they have a daughter and are on the way to establishing normal lives. Then the alluring Mila, a Chetnik who fought beside Walter during Yugoslavia's civil war, appears on their doorstep. She insinuates herself into their lives, becoming Anja's best friend and taking Walter as a lover. But with a hidden agenda, she ensnares them in a web of deception." Libr J

"Moran's subject is the souls, the approximate loves, of an informer, a murderer and a terrorist: as tough a subject as anyone could choose. Since he is a truthful writer as well as an exact and fluent one, there will be no contrived justice for these three, no hero to expose them. In the chaos of postwar Europe, where names and lives are up for grabs, justice isn't often achieved." N Y Times Book Rev

Moravia, Alberto, 1907-1990

Two women; translated from the Italian by Angus Davidson. Farrar, Straus & Giroux 1958 339p o.p.

"The disintegrating effects of war upon the personalities of an Italian mother and her 17-year-old daughter who are evacuated to the country in 1943. Cesira and Rosetta struggle to resist the corruption and dishonor which surround their countrymen but they are defeated by lust and by greed." Publ Wkly

"Through his description of the brutal, dehumanizing forces of war we see Moravia's belief that man is man because he suffers most cogently illustrated. This novel is also probably the most poignant expression of Moravia's view of the human condition." Ency of World Lit in the 20th century

Moreton, Andrew *See* Defoe, Daniel, 1661?-1731

Morgan, Richard K.

Altered carbon. Del Rey Bks. 2003 375p pa $13.95

ISBN 0-345-45768-4 LC 2002-31165

Morgan, Richard K.—*Continued*

First published 2002 in the United Kingdom

"In the 25th century, it's difficult to die a final death. Humans are issued a cortical stack, implanted into their bodies, into which consciousness is 'digitized' and from which—unless the stack is hopelessly damaged—their consciousness can be downloaded ('resleeved') with its memory intact, into a new body. While the Vatican is trying to make resleeving (at least of Catholics) illegal, centuries-old aristocrat Laurens Bancroft brings Takeshi Kovacs (an Envoy, a specially trained soldier used to being resleeved and trained to soak up clues from new environments) to Earth, where Kovacs is resleeved into a cop's body to investigate Bancroft's first mysterious, stack-damaging death." Publ Wkly

A "seamless marriage of hardcore cyberpunk and hard-boiled detective tale." Times (London, England)

Broken angels. Del Rey Bks. 2004 c2003 366p pa $14.95

ISBN 0-345-45771-4 (pa) LC 2003-62515

"In the far future, UN Envoy and special operative Takeshi Kovacs travels to the planet Sanction V to crush a revolution. When he joins a secret team assigned to recover an archaeological find, he becomes involved in a deadly conspiracy that threatens the existence of the human race-and war seems an easy ride in comparison." Libr J

This novel "is clearly the work of a gifted, ambitious storyteller. Morgan's prose is clean and direct, his characters almost uniformly hard-edged, his future convincing, well conceived and decked out with an almost limitless array of technological marvels." Washington Post Book World

Morgan, Robert, 1944-

Gap Creek; a novel. Algonquin Bks. 1999 326p $22.95

ISBN 1-56512-296-8 LC 99-34995

This is the "story of a North Carolina mountain girl who marries at 16 and with her new husband goes to live in Gap Valley, over the border in South Carolina. . . . Julia Harmon has become accustomed to sawing firewood, digging ditches and caring for the livestock on her family's farm while her father dies of consumption. When she marries Hank Richards and begins to keep house for their mean-tempered landlord in Gap Creek, she has no idea of the disasters that await during her first year of marriage." Publ Wkly

"Morgan's come-as-you-are prose brings pleasures of its own. . . . At their finest, his stripped-down and almost primitive sentences burn with the raw, lonesome pathos of Hank Williams's best songs. Even better, there's not a hint of liberal sanctimony in his work; his plain people stubbornly refuse to become archetypes." N Y Times Book Rev

This rock; a novel. Algonquin Bks. 2001 223p $24.95

ISBN 1-56512-303-4 LC 2001-34834

A tale of life in the rural South "set during the years 1921-23. Muir and Moody Powell are locked in a bitter, protracted sibling rivalry. Teenage Muir is ambitious, hardworking, and deeply religious, but he's also frustrated by his own lack of direction. The older Moody, embittered by his father's death and his mother's favoritism of Muir, has taken up with a group of hardbitten moonshiners. When Moody involves Muir in a dangerous liquor run, trying to evade the local sheriff in their Model T on treacherous backroads, Muir decides that it is time to strike out on his own. . . . Morgan writes very simply about hard times and deep faith, and this story will resound with modern readers." Booklist

Moriarty, Laura

The center of everything. Hyperion 2003 291p $22.95; pa $14

ISBN 1-401-30031-6; 0-7868-8845-8 (pa) LC 2002-32898

"Any map clearly shows that Kansas is the center of everything. Ten-year-old Evelyn Bucknow notices it on every map that she sees and truly believes that is where she belongs—in the center. Unfortunately, Evelyn is forced to parent her mother, a flighty, unrealistically romantic woman who is having an affair with her married boss. . . . Fortunately, Evelyn takes the events of her life and her mother's life and learns her lesons, with a few glitches along the way. Young people will find Evelyn appealing and real despite the book's setting in the age of Ronald Reagan and big hair, and they will respond positively to her determination." VOYA

Morrall, Clare

Astonishing splashes of colour; by Clare Morrall. 1st ed. HarperCollins 2004 322p $23.95

ISBN 0-06-073445-0 LC 2004-40895

First published 2003 in the United Kingdom

In this "novel, the first-person narrator, Katherine Wellington, is at the edge of sanity because of a miscarriage three years ago and the presumed death of her mother when she was three. As Katherine searches for a surrogate child and information about her mother, each episode, ironically, increases her sense of loss. When the truth about Katherine's mother is revealed, Morrall has prepared readers for it so well that we are not surprised. Although the situation sounds like a soap opera, Morrall's sympathetic and complex narrator and her artist father and five brothers avoid sentimentality." Booklist

Morrell, David, 1943-

Assumed identity. Warner Bks. 1993 469p o.p.

LC 92-51040

"Undercover agent Brendan Buchanan has spent eight years under 200 assumed identities. He is bereft when his cover is blown on his latest mission. His bosses refuse to give him another role, wanting him to train other agents. Discouraged, he quits the agency when he receives a coded plea for help from Juana Mendez, a past love. With Holly McCoy, a tenacious reporter, he begins to search for Juana. On their way they battle old enemies and former associates." Libr J

"With all the action of a James Bond adventure and just a dash of the melancholy of John le Carré, this is a terrific suspense thriller." Publ Wkly

The brotherhood of the rose; a novel. St. Martin's Press 1984 353p o.p.

LC 83-21324

"Agent-assassins Chris and Saul are orphans who were raised as brothers by enigmatic Eliot, a veteran C.I.A. operative . . . Eliot trained the two to become master

Morrell, David, 1943-—*Continued*

killers, and when he mysteriously turns against them, they band together to destroy him." N Y Times Book Rev

"Though Morrell's tale is thoroughly incredible, its engaging protagonists, whirlwind pace, and heartstopping action scenes make it an adventure of great cinematic appeal." Booklist

The covenant of the flame. Warner Bks. 1991 452p o.p.

LC 90-49445

"Environmental writer Tess Drake is chasing both a story on fatal attacks on polluters around the world and a strange man named Joseph. Aided by NYPD Lt. Craig, Tess discovers that Joseph has been burned to death; in his apartment she and Craig find strange artifacts that point to Albigensian heretics, worshippers of ancient god Mithras. After suggesting that the followers of Mithras and agents of the (still vital) Inquisition remain in lethal combat, Morrell sets the Mithras baddies against Tess." Publ Wkly

Desperate measures. Warner Bks. 1994 408p o.p.

LC 94-279

"Burned-out and grief-stricken after the death of his son, journalist Matthew Pittman is sitting in his bathtub with a loaded revolver pointed at the roof of his mouth when the telephone rings. His suicide interrupted, Mathew is assigned to write an obituary for the dying Jonathan Millgate, an 80-year-old member of a prestigious group that advises U.S. presidents. Soon however, Millgate is kidnapped from his deathbed and killed, and Pittman is accused of the murder. . . . The in-depth characterization, believable and unpredictable plot developments, and psychological depths of this thriller will draw all readers." Libr J

Extreme denial. Warner Bks. 1996 455p o.p.

LC 95-41996

"In Rome, an undercover operation by Brian McKittrick, the spoiled-rotten screw-up son of a CIA legend, ends in a disaster that's offically blamed on the interference of veteran agent Steve Decker. An angry Decker resigns from the Company; 13 months later, he is happily working as a real agent in Santa Fe and falling in love with his beautiful new neighbor, Beth Dwyer. That is, until the night a team of hired killers breaks into his house, wounding Beth and nearly killing him. . . . Questions and loose ends abound but this powerhouse thriller achieves a runaway victory on the basis of sheer storytelling excitement." Publ Wkly

The fifth profession. Warner Bks. 1990 448p o.p.

LC 89-40461

"Hired by wealthy and powerful clients as an executive protector, Savage is assigned to rescue Rachel Stone from her sadistic husband on the Greek island of Mykonos. Joined by Akira, his Japanese counterpart, Savage discovers this case extends far beyond merely protecting and safely delivering a client. Pursued by unknown outside forces, the threesome struggle to stay alive and solve a mystery that spans continents and brings horrifying memories to the surface." SLJ

Morris, Kenneth M.

The deadly trade; [by] Ken Morris. Bancroft Press 2004 373p $25

ISBN 1-890862-35-5 LC 2004-100481

"In San Diego, the police find three abandoned bodies covered with diseased sores. Shortly thereafter, a local biotechnology company's laboratory explodes. Working for a financial firm involved with the biotechnology company, analyst Mack becomes involved in an investigation of the disaster and soon learns that the company scientists were working on a highly toxic disease in cahoots with a terrorist organization. Morris adds a financial twist to the novel's obvious topical relevance. He works hard to make the details clear but doesn't bog the novel down with needless explanation." Libr J

Morris, Mary McGarry

A dangerous woman. Viking 1991 358p o.p.

LC 90-50405

"Martha Horgan, the emotionally disabled protagonist, was gang-raped as a teenager; now, 15 years later, her life is finally flowing smoothly. She has moved away from her cold, domineering aunt and has a job at the cleaners, a room in a boarding house, even a worshipful admirer in Wesley Mount, the town mortician. But someone has been stealing from the till and 'Marthorgan' as her taunters call her, gets canned. Back at her aunt's place she is seduced by the caretaker, a frustrated, manipulative writer, and then must suffer through his affair with her aunt." Libr J

"Morris performs one of the most difficult writing tasks, creating a character crazy enough to be interesting but sane enough to describe her own dilemma." Time

Fiona Range. Viking 2000 418p o.p.

ISBN 0-670-89156-8 LC 99-87724

"Fiona is a love child. Her mother gave birth to her out of wedlock and shortly afterward disappeared. Fiona was brought up alongside three cousins by her aunt and uncle, Arlene and Charles Hollis, leading citizens in their small New England town. . . . When the novel opens, Fiona is running out of patience with her circumstances. Haltingly, she embarks upon a quest: to discover her real family, to find a place where she belongs, to redeem herself. Her progress is often painful." N Y Times Book Rev

"The characters have weirdly varying powers of perception, and that keeps the juggled plots in the air, but it doesn't matter if you guess the gothic family secrets: this author is the literary equivalent of Spanish fly." New Yorker

The lost mother; Mary McGarry Morris. Viking 2005 274p $23.95

ISBN 0-670-03389-8 LC 2004-57170

This novel tells the "story of 12-year-old Thomas and eight-year-old Margaret. . . . Reduced to living in a tent in Vermont during the Depression, the children and their father, Henry Talcott, a butcher who must travel daily seeking work, are barely surviving their abandonment by the children's reluctant mother. The shattered family aches with the desire to bring home beautiful, troubled Irene while Henry crumbles into a 'whipped man... worn down and grim,' and Thomas takes on the role of caretaker. Henry's longtime friend Gladys shows the family

Morris, Mary McGarry—*Continued*

rare kindness, but a longstanding animosity between her crotchety father and Henry makes it impossible for the Talcotts to accept her charity. In typical Morris fashion, the author paints a brutal landscape and authentic characters with delicacy and precision: from the chaotic household of Irene's alcoholic sister to the creepy relationship between a sick boy and his doting mother, who wants to adopt Thomas and Margaret." Publ Wkly

Songs in ordinary time. Viking 1995 740p o.p.
LC 94-44071

A novel set in a small Vermont town during the summer of 1960. "With no support from her alcoholic ex-husband Sam, Marie Fermoyle has struggled for eight years to raise her three children. She is sharp-tongued, bitter, resentful and driven nearly to distraction by unending money worries and her own shame at being a poor divorcée in a staunchly Catholic town. The arrival of mysterious Omar Duvall with his con man's spiel of sudden riches brings Marie hope that she can change her dead-end existence." Publ Wkly

"The novel is frequently perceptive about the bitter pathos bred by the feeling that you've always lived on someone else's leftovers. . . . The novel is also insightful and frightening on the unshakable resilience of family grudges." N Y Times Book Rev

Morris, Scott, 1966-

Waiting for April; a novel; by Scott M. Morris. Algonquin Bks. 2003 340p $24.95
ISBN 1-56512-370-0 LC 2002-38600

"Sanders Royce Collier arrives in the backwater Florida panhandle town of Citrus on Christmas Eve, 1965, to the accompaniment of portentous thunder and lighting . . . . [This novel] is narrated by Sander's teenage son, Roy, who pieces together the history of his father's fateful entanglement with Citrus's Lanier family." Publ Wkly

"Morris is an elegant, self-assured writer. His characters are authetic and overflowing with humanity. A genuinely evocative novel." Booklist

Morris, Willie

Taps; a novel. Houghton Mifflin 2001 340p $26
ISBN 0-618-09859-3 LC 00-68250

"Set in the small Mississippi Delta town of Fisk's Landing in the 1950's, 'Taps' covers a year in the life of 16-year-old Swayze Barksdale, the only son of a widowed mother." Christ Sci Monit

"Over the course of a year, in intervals framed by a dozen graveside ceremonies for men shipped back from Korea to the summer-baked or winter-frozen cemetery outside town, Swayze tells the story of a passing Southern world and his own troubled growing up. . . . Funerals are its talismans and 'Taps' is at it strongest when it describes them." N Y Times Book Rev

Morris, Wright, 1910-1998

Collected stories, 1948-1986. Harper & Row 1986 274p o.p.
LC 86-45334

Contents: The ram in the thicket; The sound tape; The character of the lover; The safe place; The cat in the picture; Since when do they charge admission?; Drrdla; Green grass, blue sky, white house; A fight between a white boy and a black boy in the dusk of a fall afternoon in Omaha, Nebraska; Fiona; Magic; Here is Einbaum; In another country; Real losses, imaginary gains; The cat's meow; The lover and the beloved; The customs of the country; Victrola; Glimpse into another country; Going into exile; To Calabria; Fellow creatures; Wishing you and your loved ones every happiness; Country music; Things that matter; The origin of sadness

"Spanning close to 40 years of Morris's work and ranging in settings throughout the U.S. and in many cities abroad, this collection deals with wartime experiences, race relations in the South and displacement, both cultural and temporal. Through his eyes we glimpse the mysteries of life and the small epiphanies that render them a little more comprehensible." Publ Wkly

Morrison, Toni, 1931-

The bluest eye; with a new afterword by the author. Knopf 1993 215p
LC 93-43124

A reissue of the title first published 1970 by Holt, Rinehart & Winston

"This tragic study of a black adolescent girl's struggle to achieve white ideals of beauty and her consequent descent into madness was acclaimed as an eloquent indictment of some of the more subtle forms of racism in American society. Pecola Breedlove longs to have 'the bluest eye'and thus to be acceptable to her family, schoolmates, and neighbors, all of whom have convinced her that she is ugly." Merriam-Webster's Ency of Lit

Jazz. Knopf 1992 229p $26.95
ISBN 0-679-41167-4 LC 91-58555

This novel "tells the story of Violet and Joe Trace, married for over 20 years, residents of Harlem in 1926. . . . Violet works as an unlicensed hairdresser, doing ladies hair in their own homes, and Joe sells Cleopatra cosmetics door to door. . . . When the novel opens, Joe has shot his 18-year-old lover, Dorcas, and Violet has disfigured the dead girl's body at her funeral in a fit of rage. Joe, who was not caught, is in mourning, crying all day in his darkened apartment, and Violet has taken on the task of finding out whatever she can about Dorcas." Voice Lit Suppl

"As the story unfolds, we come to understand, if not excuse, what happened. The characters themselves cannot excuse their own behavior, which baffles them. Violet is obsessed by the memory of the dead girl whose face she slashed: What was it about her that Joe found so special? She is driven to visit the girl's aunt Alice, who is understandably frightened. . . . Some of the most interesting scenes in the book are the subsequent meetings of these two very different women who come to respect each other, even before they learn to understand each other." Christ Sci Monit

Love. Knopf 2003 201p $23.95
ISBN 0-375-40944-0 LC 2003-52737

"There were days, back in the 1940s and 1950s, when the Cosey Hotel and Resort was the place for blacks to vacation, dance, and dine. Bill Cosey, a charismatic figure greatly attractive to woman, ran the resort. But now Bill is dead, and the story is, as we see, not only a pean to past good times but also a portrait of Bill Cosey's power. . . . Now, in his absence, the women in his life

Morrison, Toni, 1931-—*Continued*

jockey for their own power in the vacuum he left behind; their world now revolves around his will, scribbled many years ago on a dirty menu." Booklist

"Like all of Morrison's best fiction, this is a village novel. Race and racism, ancillary concerns in 'Love' for the most part, throw the small groups she writes about upon one another, steeping their passions. Even when the setting is contemporary, Morrison's books feel old fashioned, set in a world where the perpetual distraction of the media hasn't diluted people's fascination with their neighbors." N Y Times Book Rev

Paradise. Knopf 1998 318p $25
ISBN 0-679-43374-0 LC 97-80913

"In 1950, a core group of nine old families leaves the increasingly corrupted African American community of Haven, Okla., to found in that same state a new, purer community they call Ruby. But in the early 1970s, the outside world begins to intrude on Ruby's isolation, forcing a tragic confrontation. It's about this time, too, that the first of five damaged women finds solace in a decrepit former convent near Ruby. . . . The individual stories of both the women and the townspeople reveal Morrison at her best." Publ Wkly

Song of Solomon. Knopf 1977 337p $27.50
ISBN 0-394-49784-8 LC 77-874

"Chaos marked the world into which Macon (known as Milkman) Dead was born. Each member of his family was haunted by some wild obsession—his father's desire for money, land, and social status, his mother's need for love, his sisters' silence, and his Aunt Pilate's madness. To these was added Macon's desire to unearth the family's buried past. This is a novel of mystery and revelation as it unfolds the lives of four generations of blacks in America." Shapiro. Fic for Youth. 3d edition

Sula. Knopf 1974 c1973 174p $26
ISBN 0-394-48044-9

This "is the story of two black women friends and of their community of Medallion, Ohio. The community has been stunted and turned inward by the racism of the larger society. The rage and disordered lives of the townspeople are seen as a reaction to their stifled hopes. The novel follows the lives of Sula and Nel from childhood to maturity to death." Merriam-Webster's Ency of Lit

Tar baby. Knopf 1981 305p $26.95
ISBN 0-394-42329-1 LC 80-22821

"Retired on the Isle des Chevaliers in the Caribbean, rich Philadelphia businessman Valerian Street and his wife Margaret await the arrival of their estranged son for Christmas; and an already restless household is sharply disrupted when Margaret discovers a primitive black man hiding in her closet. The intruder, called Son, is a fugitive American on the run whose presence alters the lives of the Streets; their devoted black retainers Sydney and Ondine; the Sydney's niece Jade, an educated Paris model with whom Son falls in love." Libr J

"Each of the characters in Toni Morrison's Tar Baby comes with a history, quite a complete history that is given to us in a series of stunning performances." New Repub

Morrow, Bradford, 1951-

Ariel's crossing. Viking 2002 389p $25.95
ISBN 0-670-03095-3 LC 2001-46968

"Morrow uses a woman's search to find her father as a vehicle to explore the dual legacies of Los Alamos and Vietnam in . . . [this] novel in which he revisits a character from *Trinity Fields,* Kip Calder, who becomes the holy grail of a quest by his daughter, Ariel Rankin." Publ Wkly

"As his confused yet noble characters cope with the unexpected, Morrow, evincing an unshakable belief in humanity and life and a love for New Mexico's glorious landscape, dissects the bonds of family and land, ponders questions of integrity and faith, and assesses the toll the nuclear menace exacts from our collective soul." Booklist

Trinity fields. Viking 1995 435p il o.p.
ISBN 0-670-85728-9 LC 94-20125

"Brice McCarthy and Kip Calder are born only hours apart in 1944 in Los Alamos, N.M., where both their fathers are scientists employed by the Manhattan Project to develop the first atomic bomb. Almost inseparable as they're growing up, they drift apart when war takes Kip to Vietnam and propels Brice (who narrates the story) into political activism and a commitment to the woman Kip left behind. Many years later, the friends meet again and Brice . . . finds himself liberated and burdened anew." N Y Times Book Rev

"Though the novel sometimes takes itself too seriously and tries to cover too much ground, it is a largely successful attempt to assess where we have been and where we might be headed, told through the stories of two engaging characters." Christ Century

Morse, Anne Christensen *See* Head, Ann

Mortimer, John Clifford, 1923-

Dunster; [by] John Mortimer. Viking 1992 296p o.p.
LC 92-31451

"Philip Progmire, an Oxford-educated accountant with thespian dreams, has engaged in lifelong skirmishes with journalist Dick Dunster, one of these men whose stock-in-trade is scorn and who disbelieve everything on principle. When Dunster digs up what he believes is the dirt on Philip's employer and friend—a hideous legacy of WW II—Progmire is forced to make some terrible choices among truths, loyalties and responsibilities." Publ Wkly

"What Americans miss by having no tradition of novels that aspire to be both literary and conventional, as 'Dunster' does, is the pleasure of watching an experienced author play with conventional form. . . . This pleasure Mr. Mortimer offers in full measure." N Y Times Book Rev

Felix in the underworld. Viking 1997 246p o.p.
LC 97-16562

This is a novel about a British writer "who suddenly finds himself floundering about in the messy real world. Felix Morsom, once dubbed the Chekhov of Coldsands-on-Sea, is in a bit of rut: his latest novel isn't selling, and his attraction to his publicist has remained drearily unconsummated. Everything changes when a paternity suit arrives in the mail, followed closely by the murder

Mortimer, John Clifford, 1923-—*Continued*
of a man linked to the woman doing the suing." Booklist

"This novel is actually about the characters of literary and legal London, and we soon realize that the point is not just to allow these people to circulate in the pages of narrative but, more importantly, to turn character into caricature. . . . John Mortimer's writing is fluent, gently humorous, and possesses the comic's virtue, tact." Times Lit Suppl

Paradise postponed; [by] John Mortimer. Viking 1986 c1985 373p o.p.
LC 85-40712

First published 1985 in the United Kingdom

"A realistic novel of manners in the grand nineteenth-century British tradition, this sweeping look at postwar England focuses on a group of villagers from the London suburb of Rapstone Fanner. From the upwardly mobile conservative politician through the activist vicar to the jazz-playing country doctor, these characters reflect the comic follies of the modern age as they try to come to grips with an overwhelming sense of expectations unfulfilled." Am Libr

Rumpole à la carte; {by} John Mortimer. Viking 1990 245p o.p.
LC 91-161338

Contents: Rumpole à la carte; Rumpole and the summer of discontent; Rumpole and the right to silence; Rumpole at sea; Rumpole and the quacks; Rumpole for the prosecution

Rumpole and the angel of death; [by] John Mortimer. Viking 1996 260p o.p.
LC 95-41851

Contents: Rumpole and the model prisoner; Rumpole and the way through the woods; Hilda's story; Rumpole and the little boy lost; Rumpole and the rights of man; Rumpole and the angel of death

Rumpole and the golden thread
In Mortimer, J. C. The second Rumpole omnibus p193-442

Rumpole for the defence
In Mortimer, J. C. The second Rumpole omnibus p11-192

Rumpole on trial; [by] John Mortimer. Viking 1992 243p o.p.

Contents: Rumpole and the children of the devil; Rumpole and the eternal triangle; Rumpole and the miscarriage of justice; Rumpole and the family pride; Rumpole and the soothsayer; Rumpole and the reform of Joby Jonson; Rumpole on trial

Rumpole rests his case; [by] John Mortimer. Viking 2002 210p $24.95
ISBN 0-670-03139-9 LC 2002-19046

Contents: Rumpole and the old familiar faces; Rumpole and the rememberance of things past; Rumpole and the asylum seekers; Rumpole and the Camberwell carrot; Rumpole and the actor Laddie; Rumpole and the teenage werewolf; Rumpole rests his case

"With Mortimer's greatly felicitous style and careful plotting, these stories are sheer, absolute reading pleasure." Booklist

Rumpole's last case
In Mortimer, J. C. The second Rumpole omnibus p443-667

Rumpole's return; {by} John Mortimer. Armchair Detective Lib. 1992 c1980 159p o.p.
LC 91-29415

First published 1980 in paperback in the United Kingdom

"After losing in Judge Bullingham's court for the tenth straight time, Rumpole finds the beaches of Florida a welcome change from the dampness of home. Basking in the sun, he comes across an account of the Notting Hill Gate murder in a back copy of *The Times* which sparks a nerve. This is the sort of case he enjoyed. The evidence is stacked against the accused. . . . Rumpole's uncanny assessment of the situation is that the facts are out of synch." Publisher's note

The second Rumpole omnibus; [by] John Mortimer. Viking 1987 667p o.p.

Companion volume to The first Rumpole omnibus (1983)

Contents: Rumpole for the defence (c1981) [variant title: Regina v. Rumpole]; Rumpole and the golden thread (c1983); Rumpole's last case (c1987)

Rumpole for the defence: Rumpole and the confession of guilt; Rumpole and the gentle art of blackmail; Rumpole and the dear departed; Rumpole and the rotten apple; Rumpole and the expert witness; Rumpole and the spirit of Christmas; Rumpole and the boat people

Rumpole and the golden thread: Rumpole and the genuine article; Rumpole and the golden thread; Rumpole and the old boy net; Rumpole and the female of the species; Rumpole and the sporting life; Rumpole and the last resort

Rumpole's last case: Rumpole and the blind tasting; Rumpole and the old, old story; Rumpole and the official secret; Rumpole and the judge's elbow; Rumpole and the bright seraphim; Rumpole and the winter break; Rumpole's last case

The sound of trumpets; {by} John Mortimer. Viking 1999 272p o.p.
ISBN 0-670-87861-8 LC 98-38968

First published 1998 in the United Kingdom

This novel "chronicles the bewildering career of the young Labour candidate Terry Flitton, who madly accepts Titmuss's offer of aid when the local Conservative M.P. is found face down in a swimming pool and the seat Flitton covets becomes vacant." New Yorker

Summer's lease. Viking 1988 288p o.p.

"The advertisement that Molly Pargenter answered made the Tuscany villa to let sound like the ideal place—suspiciously too ideal—for her family to spend its summer vacation. Arriving in Italy with her husband, three daughters, and father, she finds an unusual assortment of locals and English expatriates for neighbors, as well as detailed notes on the proper use of the house left by her absentee landlord, one S. Kettering. Molly's obsession with learning as much as possible about the Kettering household leads her to some ominous conclusions." Libr J

"Mortimer puts in a graceful performance as he untangles a whole bundle of liaisons and portrays a whole array of human emotions with skill and subtlety." Booklist

Mortimer, John Clifford, 1923-—*Continued*

Titmuss regained; [by] John Mortimer. Viking 1990 280p o.p.

ISBN 0-670-82333-3 LC 89-40801

This sequel to Paradise postponed "is the story of how Titmuss . . . attempts to go green. He does so as an expedient to protect his newly acquired country manor, threatened by a new town, and to conserve the votes of the green-welly brigade." Economist

Mortimer's touch remains as light as ever, and the novel is full of beautifully-poised social comedy–but there can be no denying the bitterness with which he views contemporary Britain." New Statesman Soc

Mortman, Doris

The lucky ones. Kensington Bks. 1997 407p o.p.

ISBN 1-57566-204-3 LC 96-80069

"When rising politician Benjamin Knight gets married on a perfect summer day, the four women watching don't realize how prophetic the best man's toast for success is. And over the next 20 years, the women all forge their own ambitious careers: Zoë becomes a foreign affairs analyst, a career choice made in order to get as far from Ben as possible; Celia, Ben's sister-in-law, uses her beauty and talent to build a career in national television; Georgie, Ben's childhood friend, becomes a congresswoman; and Kate, Ben's college classmate, founds a national child protection organization following the murder of her daughter. When a dangerous hostage situation arises overseas in an election year, the current president announces he will not run again. A heated political race erupts, and Ben throws his hat in the ring." Booklist

"In the midst of a well-paced thriller, Mortman takes a bubbly peek into the drawing rooms and back rooms where history is brokered." Publ Wkly

True colors; a novel. Crown 1995 c1994 553p o.p.

LC 94-13068

"The internationally renowned artist Isabelle de Luna, born into the aristocracy of Barcelona, Spain, lost a life of privilege when her mother was brutally raped and murdered. For Isabelle's protection she is sent to New Mexico to live with the Durans, friends of the family who raise her together with their adopted daughter, Nina. As adults, the two young women become successful but lose their bonds of sisterhood." Libr J

"Mortman sets out quite a feast: alluring and sophisticated characters, steamy sex, and a captivating plot involving murder, great wealth and power, international intrigue, art, ambition, and redemption." Booklist

Morton, Brian, 1955-

A window across the river. Harcourt 2003 289p $25

ISBN 0-15-100757-8 LC 2003-5373

"Isaac and Nora—he's a photographer, she's a writer—were once a couple. After a five-year separation, a late-night telephone call draws them together, but their reunion . . . becomes increasingly problematic. Nora is ready to break up with her boyfriend, a professor who wants to become a 'public intellectual.' Isaac, who always believed that he and Nora were destined for one another, is frustrated by the world's indifference to his photography. What's more, he is about to become a character in one of Nora's unnervingly lifelike short stories. Morton is particularly skilled at describing the sharp rattle of artistic failure, and at bringing to life the streets and rooms of New York, where the fates of his lonely and desperate characters unfold." New Yorker

Moses, Kate

Wintering; a novel of Sylvia Plath. St. Martin's Press 2003 292p $23.95

ISBN 0-312-28375-X LC 2002-36753

"A fictionalization of the grueling months following the dissolution of Plath's marriage to Ted Hughes and leading up to her suicide at the age of 30 in 1963. 'Wintering' is beautiful and moving. The narrative voice is a distillation of Plath's diaries, letters and poems; with lyrical dexterity and great economy, Moses portrays a demanding, pitiless woman struggling against the stark fact of her husband's infidelity and her own inner demons." N Y Times Book Rev

Mosher, Howard Frank

The true account; concerning a Vermont gentleman's race to the Pacific against and exploration of the western American continent coincident to the expedition of Captains Meriwether Lewis and William Clark. Houghton Mifflin 2003 337p $24

ISBN 0-618-19721-4 LC 2002-32804

"Private True Teague Kinneson, a Vermont schoolteacher and inventor, writes to Jefferson to recommend himself for the expedition to the Pacific. When Jefferson announces that he's already appointed Captains Meriwether Lewis and William Clark, True, with his teenage nephew, Ticonderoga, in tow, heads West anyway, determined to reach the Pacific first. Ticonderoga narrates their adventures, describing with a straight face the schemes of his daffy uncle." Publ Wkly

"This picaresque tale provides a riotous fictional twist on a revered American legend, irresistibly insane, this novel celebrates the unique brand of homespun humor popularized in the tales of Mark Twain." Booklist

Waiting for Teddy Williams; Howard Frank Mosher. Houghton Mifflin 2004 280p $24

ISBN 0-618-19722-2 LC 2004-42721

"Ethan 'E. A.' Allen is a home-schooled teenage baseball phenom from Kingdom County, Vermont. Raised by his mom, a country-singing hooker, and his grandma, a foulmouthed curmudgeon who has been wheelchair-bound since Bucky Dent's game-winning homer in the 1978 Yankees-Bosox playoff, E. A. is a loner whose best friend is a statue of his namesake, which overlooks Kingdom County's scaled-down version of Fenway Park. Then a stranger named Teddy comes to town, and E. A. has the real-life mentor he needs (and the Red Sox may have a savior). Mosher is a master at combining sweet and sour: his baseball story stirs W. P. Kinsella fantasy with Mark Harris realism, while his view of small-town New England leavens the grit of Annie Proulx or Carolyn Chute with just the right amount of Mosher's own down-to-earth sweetness." Booklist

Mosley, Walter

Always outnumbered, always outgunned. Norton 1997 208p o.p.

ISBN 0-393-04539-0 LC 96-54870

Contents: Crimson shadow; Midnight meeting; The thief; Double standard; Equal opportunity; Marvane Street; Man gone; The wanderer; Lessons; Letter to Theresa; History; Firebug; Black dog; Last rites

"In these interconnected short stories about an aging black man, Socrates Fortlow, living in a makeshift two-room apartment in an abandoned Watts building, Mosley turns on its head the fundamental fantasy of the detective story. . . . These are often difficult stories to read; never sentimental, they are finally, one and all, about pain and how we live with it. Perhaps that's why those brief moments when Socrates eases someone else's pain deliver such a powerful sense of catharsis." Booklist

Bad Boy Brawly Brown. Little, Brown 2002 311p o.p.

ISBN 0-316-07301-6 LC 2002-16232

Los Angeles "teenager Brawly Brown has left home and is running with the radical Urban Revolutionary Party. Easy quickly find the boy, but he is just as quickly caught up in the murder of one of the party's leaders." Booklist

"As Easy persists in his investigation, he is dismissed by black radicals and rousted by racist cops. . . . So he can't really be blamed for spending more time than he should in places like Sam's Hambones soul food diner, engaging in invigorating of often aimless conversations with characters who have little to offer on Brawly's whereabouts but lots to say about whatever is on their minds. Aside from their appealing hero, Mosley's crime novels take their vitality from the racy language and boisterous humanity of his characters, so these neighborhood encounters provide their own joy." N Y Times Book Rev

Black Betty. Norton 1994 255p o.p.

ISBN 0-393-03644-8 LC 94-6839

"Mosley's distinctive black investigator, Easy Rawlins, has moved from Watts to West L.A. with his two adopted children, but trouble still follows him. Hired to locate a sultry female acquaintance from his early days in Houston, Easy searches for her gambler brother and questions her Beverly Hills employer, unwittingly provoking racist police harassment. Meanwhile, friend Raymond ('Mouse') has been released from prison and vows revenge on the snitch who put him there." Libr J

"Mosley gives us a recognizable moment in American history viewed through the eyes of a single black man. This perspective, rare in crime fiction, vivifies not only the black experience but the larger event as well. Here we feel the hot winds that would eventually ignite the Watts riots not as abstract issues in race relations, but as emotions in the hearts of individuals we have come to know and care about." Booklist

Cinnamon kiss. Little Brown 2005 312p $24.95

ISBN 0-316-07302-4 LC 2005-5739

"Easy Rawlins needs some easy money-his daughter is in for some expensive medical treatment-so he agrees to find a missing attorney who seems to be more trouble than he's worth." Libr J

"As ever, Mosley is able to capture the era–hippies, Watts, communes–in brief strokes that provide a brilliant background to Easy's search for solutions to both a convoluted mystery and complex personal problems." Publ Wkly

Devil in a blue dress. Norton 1990 219p $19.95

ISBN 0-393-02854-2 LC 89-25503

In this novel "Ezekiel 'Easy' Rawlins, a young, tough black veteran living in 1948 Los Angeles, only wants respect and enough money to pay his mortgage. When fired from his factory job, however, he undertakes some paid errands for a shady white mobster who wishes to locate a light-haired, blue-eyed beauty. As Easy plumbs his usual hangouts for clues, he relays information to the mobster, runs afoul of the police, meets the mysterious woman, discovers a murder, then investigates in self-defense." Libr J

"Mosley's prose is a little stiff and his plot is far too complicated. But he has a keen eye for period details. . . . And his lowdown humor never deserts him." Newsweek

Fear itself; a mystery. Little, Brown 2003 316p $24.95

ISBN 0-316-59112-2 LC 2003-46092

"Set in 1955 Los Angeles, this . . . thriller finds Fearless and compatriot Paris Minton, the story's narrator, searching for a friend's missing husband. That seemingly simple task rapidly escalates into a case of multiple murders, blackmail, and a quest for a priceless heirloom that makes this Mosley's answer to the Maltese Falcon." Libr J

"It's a tossup which gives more pleasure in Mosley's vibrant views of neighborhood life, the high-stepping, free-talking who bob and weave their way through this convoluted plot, or the colorful local haunts like Henrietta's Gumbo House where they do their shuckin' and jivin'." N Y Times Book Rev

Fearless Jones; a novel. Little, Brown 2001 312p o.p.

ISBN 0-316-59238-2 LC 00-53502

This "mystery is narrated by Paris Minton, a black man who sells used books in nineteen-fifties L.A. Paris's life is perfect—he reads all day without interruption—until a bewitching young woman named Elana Love walks through his door. She's looking for a religious group called the Messenger of the Divine, but the thug who bursts in after her is looking for a bond worth thousands of dollars. Mayhem and seduction ensue, and when Paris's bookstore is burned to the ground, he knows it's time to seek the aid of the incomparable Fearless Jones. The unlikely friendship of these men—Fearless is all fists and testosterone, Paris is a gun-shy truth-seeker—is the source of the novel's humor, and propels the reader through the plot's knottier moments." New Yorker

Gone fishin'; an Easy Rawlins novel. Black Classic Press 1997 244p o.p.

LC 97-124077

This novel marks the first appearance of Mosley's detective-hero, Easy Rawlins. "Written before the other Rawlins novels but never published, it takes Easy and his lethal friend Mouse back to Texas before World War II and their subsequent move to Los Angeles. The 19-year-old Easy . . . knows little of the larger world. His journey to awareness begins with a soul-changing road trip

Mosley, Walter—*Continued*
to the bayous of Pariah, Texas, where Mouse hopes to settle a score with his hated stepfather." Booklist

This is "in some respects, the best of Mosley's novels. . . . It firmly establishes Mosley as a writer whose work transcends the thriller category and qualifies as serious literature." Time

A little yellow dog; an Easy Rawlins mystery. Norton 1996 300p o.p.
ISBN 0-393-03924-2 LC 96-4231

This mystery, set in the early 1960s, finds Easy Rawlins "working in a high school as head custodian for the Board of Education two years after giving up drinking and the 'street life.' When a corpse turns up on school grounds, Easy finds himself reluctantly caught up in the investigation—between the rock and the hard place of the cops and the killers. Mosley writes in the grand tradition of the American hard-boiled private investigator. His dialog is sharp and his characters vivid—the reader can almost feel the mean L.A. streets." Libr J

The man in my basement; a novel. Little, Brown 2004 249p $22.95
ISBN 0-316-57082-6 LC 2003-56317

"Charles Blakey is an unemployed black man, deep in debt, who drinks too much, has few friends, is awkward with women, and lives alone in a large house where the basement is filled with artifacts of his family's rich history. . . . Anniston Bennett, a wealthy white man with mysterious motives, wants to rent Blakey's sizable basement. . . . Bennet wants Blakey to hold him prisoner for 65 days, his way of atoning for 'crimes against humanity'. Blakey is extremely reluctant, but the 'rent' is considerable and his options are dwindling, so he agrees. At first, he's afraid of his voluntary prisoner, but the balance of power begins shifting unpredictably as the two men engage in heated question-and-answer sessions." Booklist

"In this successful and intriguing departure from his usual work, Mr. Mosley creates a substantial subplot about heritage and history. . . . In the end this audacious novel is about facing up to such brutal realities. But it is also about seeking refuge." N Y Times (Late N Y Ed)

A red death. Norton 1991 284p o.p.
ISBN 0-393-02998-0 LC 90-23660

"In this second installment in the series, the calendar has moved ahead to the early 1950s, and the good-natured (and aptly named) Easy is in a pickle. The IRS is after him for hiding income from the apartment buildings he secretly owns; a Red-hating FBI agent strong-arms him into investigating a labor agitator; and the local police suspect him in two murders." Booklist

RL's dream. Norton 1995 267p o.p.
ISBN 0-393-03802-5 LC 95-8695

As this novel opens, "Atwater 'Soupspoon' Wise, an aging bluesman in New York City, is evicted from his apartment. Kiki Waters, a young white woman, takes him in, nursing him back to health and forging the necessary health insurance information to get him treated for cancer. The two form a strange friendship; both are from the South, and both have left behind pasts that demand to be dealt with. Soupspoon knew the legendary Robert 'RL' Johnson in his youth and is haunted by the desire to learn the secret of Johnson's music; Kiki was abused by her father and ran away in her early teens." Libr J

"A mesmerizing and redemptive tale of friendship, love, and forgiveness. . . . [This] is, without doubt, the author's finest achievement to date, a rich literary gumbo with blue-stinged rhythms that make it a joy to read and a book to remember." San Francisco Rev Books

Six easy pieces. Atria Bks. 2003 278p $24
ISBN 0-7434-4252-0

Contents: Smoke; Crimson stain; Silver lining; Gator green; Gray-eyed death; Amber gate

"Mosley is as fine as ever, offering compelling commentary on black-white relations in 1964, writing in a style so simple that it deceives us into thinking wwriting great fiction is as easy as putting one foot in front of the other. It's not, but turning these pages is." Booklist

Walkin' the dog. Little, Brown 1999 260p $35
ISBN 0-316-96620-7 LC 99-16407

Contents: Blue lightning; Promise; Shift, shift, shift; What would you do?; A day in the park; The mugger; That smell; Walkin' the dog; Mookie Kid; Moving on; Rascals in the cane; Rogue

In this "volume of interconnected short stories, Mosley gives his hero, 59-year-old ex-con Socrates Fortlow, a new job, a new home, and a new commitment to ridding his Watts neighborhood of a rogue cop. Overtly political fiction is difficult to pull off, but Mosley makes it work by grounding his issues in the felt life of his characters." Booklist

White butterfly. Norton 1992 272p $19.95
ISBN 0-393-03366-X LC 91-44700

"Black detective Easy Rawlins aids his dangerous-but-loyal friend Mouse, accused of killing several bar girls in 1958 Los Angeles." Libr J

"Standard stuff, to be sure—the makings of your typical made-for-television movie. But what elevates it is the character. It is not just that Rawlins is such an engaging fellow. He is a man who both ages and evolves." N Y Times Book Rev

Mount, Ferdinand, 1939-

The man who rode Ampersand. Carroll & Graf Pubs. 2002 245p $25
ISBN 0-7867-1007-1 LC 2002-67252

First published 1975 in the United Kingdom

This novel is "narrated by Gus Cotton, a midlevel civil servant, and the title character is Gus's father, Harry, a jockey who, after one glorious moment on the back of the great racehorses Ampersand, drifts vaguely through the rest of his life: working as a barman in a rackety London club; falling in love with a Jewish woman of Polish-German ancestry and visiting her in Europe as the Nazis rise to power; fighting in North Africa during World War II; getting a rather disreputable government job recruiting Irish workers for English factories." N Y Times Book Rev

"Mount is so good at conjuring up time and place—here it's pre-Second World War London—that the dust motes make your blink." New Yorker

Mowat, Farley

The Snow Walker. Little, Brown 1975 222p o.p.
"An Atlantic Monthly Press book"

Stories included are: The blinding of André Maloche; Stranger in Taransay; The iron men; Two who were one;

Mowat, Farley—*Continued*

The blood in their veins; The woman and the wolf; The Snow Walker; Walk well, my brother; The white canoe; Dark odyssey of Soosie

The stories range "from the ancient to the overwhelmingly modern. . . . There are tales of starvation, cannibalism out of love, the giving of one body to another with the poignancy of the Eucharist. There are tales so simple and strong you read them again to make sure you haven't been tricked into feeling a story in your stomach for a change." N Y Times Book Rev

Mrazek, Robert J.

Unholy fire; a novel of the Civil War. Thomas Dunne Bks. 2003 299p $24.95
ISBN 0-312-30673-3 LC 2002-32512

"After being critically wounded in a Union battle fiasco, Lieutenant McKitredge is sent to a makeshift hospital on the outskirts of Washington, D. C. to die. Believing he has no chance of survival, well-meaning doctors continually dose him with laudanum. Defying the odds, kit survives, one of the many Civil War heroes to be rewarded with a serious opium addiction. Dispatched to the office of the provost marshal, he is assigned to investigate the cases of thieves, murderers, and deserters. Caught up in a murder case that seems to implicate General Joseph Hooker, he must unravel a perplexing mystery and foil a plot to assassinate the president." Booklist

"Mrazek's portrayal of Civil War battle is stark, graphic, bloody and exciting, and is only exceeded by his memorable description of Washington, D. C. as a Gomorrah on the Potomac." Publ Wkly

Mukherjee, Bharati

Desirable daughters. Theia/Hyperion 2002 310p $24.95
ISBN 0-7868-6598-9 LC 2001-53061

"The youngest of three beautiful sisters in an orthodox Hindu Bengali family, Tara has done the unthinkable: she's left her brilliant husband, a Silicon Valley legend; liberated her artistic son from prep school; and taken up with an ex-biker Buddhist carpenter. Mukherjee's humming power-line sentences carry sparkling commentary on traditional Hindu marriages, caste prejudices, spiritual matters, and the dark side of America's striving Indian immigrant community." Booklist

The holder of the world. Knopf 1993 285p o.p.
LC 93-22066

"Beigh is a contemporary New England woman of Indian heritage, who is in love with technocrat Venn from India. Beigh is obsessed with antiquities. The graduate work she was doing on the subject of the Puritans had led her to the discovery of one of her ancestors, a Hannah Easton, who traveled from her home in New England all the way to India with her trader husband. The author has woven together Hannah's story with Beigh's search for ancient jewels and legends." Libr J

The author is a "wonderful storyteller whose 17th-century Salem and India seem more real than the pale glimpses we have of contemporary America. She is always showing us coincidences and connections." New Statesman (1913)

Jasmine. Grove Weidenfeld 1989 241p o.p.
LC 89-7611

"Jasmine was born in a small Indian village, witnessed her young husband's assassination there, came to the U.S., and now lives with a middle-aged banker in a small Iowa town. Try as she might, Jasmine can't quite shrug off all the traditions and memories of her past, even though she exhibits a formidable resilience in her adjustment to the middle-class heartland. The context of this incomplete transformation is further focused and aggravated by the young Vietnamese boy who is her stepson and whose identity crisis exacerbates Jasmine's own." Booklist

"On the one hand, [this] is a tale of an individual's exile, alienness, transformations, and reckless hopes. On the other, it is an evocation of a country's transformation from pastoral innocence to perversion." Quill Quire

Leave it to me. Knopf 1997 239p o.p.
ISBN 0-679-43427-5 LC 97-5833

"Born in India to an American hippie mother and a Chinese gangster father and then abandoned in an Indian orphanage, [the protagonist] is adopted by an Italian-American family and named Debby DiMartino; twenty-three years later, she graduates from SUNY Albany and sets off on a cross-country road trip to find her Bio-Mom. By the time she arrives in San Francisco . . . and joins up with a group of aging ex-hippies and a psychotic Vietnam vet, it is clear that this kaleidoscopic coming-of-age story is governed not by growing self-awareness but by destiny and karma." New Yorker

The middleman and other stories. Grove Press 1988 197p o.p.
LC 87-35048

Contents: The middleman; A wife's story; Loose ends; Orbiting; Fighting for the rebound; The tenant; Fathering; Jasmine; Danny's girls; Buried lives; The management of grief

The tree bride; Bharati Mukherjee. Theia/Hyperion 2004 293p $23.95
ISBN 1-401-30058-8 LC 2004-42507

"After the firebombing of her San Francisco house and a coincidental meeting during a routine doctor's visit, Calcutta-born Tara Chatterjee is compelled to embark on a most American of journeys, a search for her roots. Her task is to trace the story of her great-great-aunt, Tara Lata, who at the age of five was married to a tree in the Indian village of Mishtigunj. Her search takes her into the heart of her family history." Publisher's note

"The author has fused history, mysticism, treachery and enduring love in a suspenseful story about the lingering effects of past secrets." Publ Wkly

Mulisch, Harry, 1927-

Siegfried; translated by Paul Vincent. Viking 2003 180p $22.95
ISBN 0-670-03253-0 LC 2003-50168

Original Dutch edition, 2001; this translation first published 2002 in the United Kingdom

"A distinguished Dutch author, Rudolf Herter, is in Vienna, having been invited to read form his new masterwork. In a television interview, he . . . {asserts} that it is only through fiction that the uniquely evil figure of Hitler may be truly comprehended. After the reading, he

Mulisch, Harry, 1927-*—Continued*
is approached by an elderly couple, the Falks, who have a story of their own. . . . As domestic servants at Hitler's Bavarian retreat in the waning years of the war, they were witnesses to the jealously guarded birth of Siegfried—the son of Hitler and Eva Braun. For more than fifty years they have kept a secret concerning the child they once raised as their own—and whom they were eventually forced to murder." Publisher's note

"By boldly imagining a Hitler offspring that never was, Harry Mulisch signals his willingness to take real risks in his latest novel in terms of both plot and intellectual aspirations." Washington Post Book World

Müller, Herta, 1953-

The appointment; a novel; translated by Michael Hulse and Philip Boehm. Metropolitan Bks. 2001 214p $23

ISBN 0-8050-6012-X LC 2001-31246

Original German edition, 1997

"The narrator, an unnamed young dress-factory worker of the post-WWII generation, has been summoned for questioning by the secret police; she has been caught sewing notes into men's suits destined for Italy, with the desperate message 'marry me' along with her address. Accused of prostitution in the workplace . . . she loses her job, and her life becomes subject to the whims of Major Albu, who summons her for random interrogation sessions." Publ Wkly

"Muller's writing is dark and sparse, capturing the chilling reality of life in a country in turmoil. It is a gritty novel that will leave one guessing the young woman's fate long after the last page is read." Booklist

Muller, Marcia

Beyond the grave; {by} Marcia Muller and Bill Pronzini. Walker & Co. 1986 236p o.p.

LC 86-7808

"Elena Oliverez, the young director of the Santa Barbara Museum of Mexican Arts, combines her amateur sleuth capabilities with nineteenth-century San Francisco detective John Quincannon's in their search for lost artifacts from one of 'Los ranchos grandes' of Southern California. Quincannon has been dead for many years when Elena discovers by accident, hidden in a marriage coffer she buys for the museum, the first part of his investigative report on his original search for the artifacts. As she follows clues and discovers other parts of the report the mystery heightens in both the past and the present. Quincannon and Elena both encounter murder and deceit on the trail of the artifacts, as well as their own personal problems." Best Sellers

Both ends of the night. Mysterious Press 1997 353p o.p.

LC 97-10129

Sharon McCone "sets out to help a friend and former flying instructor find her missing lover, but soon the friend has been murdered, and a missing-persons case has been transformed into a grudge match. With the help of her own lover and fellow flyer Hy Ripinsky, McCone ventures into the depths of the federal witness protection program, finding first the missing lover and then the killer in the wilds of Minnesota. There's plenty of nicely paced action here, and the flying lore provides effective ballast. Best of all, though, there is McCone at work, both as day-to-day professional detective and as aggrieved friend out for justice." Booklist

The broken promise land. Mysterious Press 1996 388p o.p.

LC 95-52187

San Francisco private eye Sharon McCone investigates "a series of threatening letters sent to her brother-in-law, country singer Ricky Savage. . . Suspects range from higher-ups at the singer's former record label, who resent Savage for starting his own record company, to a former lover, who holds him accountable for alleged promises never kept." Booklist

"Leading Sharon into the rocky psychological terrain of families, Muller gives her meticulously plotted story, with its absorbing picture of the music industry, a commanding emotional authenticity." Publ Wkly

The cavalier in white. St. Martin's Press 1986 207p o.p.

LC 86-3663

This mystery features a "woman detective named Joanna Stark, who is a widow, and ex-security consultant to art galleries and museums, and now lives in the small, wine-country town of Sonoma in northern California. Making a desultory no-go of starting her own art gallery, and feeling bored and restless after the death of her husband, Stark is visited by her ex-partner, who brings news of the theft of a Frans Hals painting, 'The Cavalier in White,' from a San Francisco museum. Stark is lured back into the detecting business and finds that all clues lead to embarrassing and potentially tragic repercussions that will affect people she cares for. Murder further complicates the investigation. A cozy tale in which plot twists well suit the rich atmosphere." Booklist

Cyanide Wells. Mysterious Press 2003 292p map $24.95

ISBN 0-89296-781-1 LC 2002-45516

"Matt Lindstrom leaves the life he has rebuilt in British Columbia to search for his ex-wife, Gwen. After she vanished from their California home, innuendo that he had murdered her ruined him, forcing his relocation. He discovers that she's in a Soledad County town called Cyanide Wells, living with a lesbian lover and an adopted child. When he goes there—For revenge? for solace?—he discovers she has taken off again, this time with the child. He and Carly McGuire, publisher of the county newspaper and Gwen's partner, perform an uneasy dance as they try to bring her back." Booklist

The dangerous hour; Marcia Muller. Mysterious Press 2004 290p $25

ISBN 0-89296-804-4 LC 2003-24625

"The arrest of her newest operative for credit-card theft jeopardizes the apparently rosy future of McCone's Investigations, but Sharon McCone musters the best legal help available. Operative Julia Rafael has overcome a background that includes a juvenile record; however, a recent case she handled for an ambitious Latino city supervisor backfired. Sharon investigates immediately and finds that the supervisor is not all that he appears to be." Libr J

"Muller's plotting isn't quite as tidy as usual . . ., but once again she gives us a solid slice of a San Francisco

Muller, Marcia—*Continued*
community and a protagonist with character. Fans of the sturdy, ongoing series will be especially pleased with the final scene, which opens the way for a new chapter in McCone's personal life." Booklist

Dark star. St. Martin's Press 1989 212p o.p.
LC 89-4114

"Set in San Francisco and the wine country around Sonoma, California, this [work features] . . . intrepid sleuth Joanna Stark. From her house full of valuable paintings a worthless but quite significant one is stolen; what this tells Joanna is that her onetime lover and current enemy, the art dealer and thief Anthony Parducci, is not dead, as she had hoped. Rather, the fascinating but plainly psychotic Parducci is poised to reenter Joanna's life—an event rife with dangerous consequences. . . . Though this isn't her best effort, Muller is a reliable mystery writer who knows all the tricks of the genre." Booklist

Dead midnight. Mysterious Press 2002 289p o.p.
ISBN 0-89296-765-X LC 2002-20097

This mystery has Sharon McCone "gathering evidence for a wrongful-death suit brought by the family of a sensitive young man driven to kill himself by the deplorable working conditions at a trendy online magazine. But events never advance in a straight line in Muller's complicated narratives, and the job that McCone took on because she thought it would help her come to grips with her own brother's suicide turns into a lethal game of industrial sabotage." N Y Times Book Rev

Listen to the silence. Mysterious Press 2000 289p $28
ISBN 0-89296-689-0 LC 99-87734

"When Detective Sharon McCone's father dies suddenly, she is startled to learn that he has requested that she, not her four siblings, go through his personal effects. In a box marked 'Legal Papers,' Sharon discovers a long-secret document that shatters her very identity and threatens to tear her family apart. As she begins to investigate, a Shoshone lawyer who may be the key to the mystery is nearly killed, and Sharon becomes tangled in a land dispute between Native Americans and white developers that involves greed, environmental corruption, racism, and a 40-year-old murder." Libr J

Muller "delivers an emotion-packed tale that adds new depth to her heroine." Publ Wkly

Pennies on a dead woman's eyes; a Sharon McCone mystery. Mysterious Press 1992 297p o.p.
LC 91-58025

Sharon McCone is "repelled by the gruesome details of a 1956 murder case that her San Francisco law firm plans to argue in a mock trial before the city's Historical Tribunal. 'There's too much emotion swirling around' for her liking, and no new evidence to vindicate the woman, recently released from prison, who was convicted of killing her husband's young mistress. Sharon, who acknowledges herself to be 'a demonic researcher,' overcomes her revulsion when she finds some loopholes in the prosecution's case." N Y Times Book Rev

"Muller is perhaps the least showy crime author around. Her protagonist, driven always into dangerous and emotional culs-de-sac, emerges as a pleasing composite of toughness and vulnerability without seeming to be either overstated or overwritten." Booklist

Point deception. Warner Bks. 2001 304p $23.95
ISBN 0-89296-690-4 LC 00-66265

This mystery is "set on the California coast in fictitious Soledad County. . . . Nobody who lives between Point Deception and Cape Perdido will dwell on what happened 13 years earlier, when eight residents of a nouveau-hippie enclave were slaughtered in remote Cascada Canyon. But as the anniversary of the massacre looms, coinciding with the rape and murder of a stranger, the dour townspeople of Signal Port are acting weird enough to galvanize a sheriff's deputy named Rhoda Swift into a quest for 'closure'. Although Swift gets the most talk-time in this well-hammered tale, her spooky neighbors might have brought more penetrating insights to its disquieting theme of collective guilt." N Y Times Book Rev

The shape of dread. Mysterious Press 1989 218p o.p.
LC 89-42606

Sharon McCone "is on the long cold trail of a missing comedian, presumed dead. A young parking valet at the club has been convicted of the 'no-body' crime, and his appeal falls into the sensitive lap of the legal co-op that offers low-paid employment to the spirited McCone." Booklist

"Solid plots, sound procedures and enlightening views of San Francisco's diversified neighborhoods are characteristic of the author's sensible style, which makes up in technical skill what it lacks in esthetics." N Y Times Book Rev

There's something in a Sunday; a Sharon McCone mystery. Mysterious Press 1989 213p o.p.
LC 88-22005

"San Francisco investigator Sharon McCone is hired to watch a man on his day off as he drives from flower garden to flower shop. Then the shirtmaker who has employed her is murdered, the man she follows disappears, a Mission District bum goes into hiding . . . and dark deeds are uncovered at the ranch where the missing man works." Booklist

"This is a provocative work, infused with compassion and sensitivity, that explores the complexities of human relationships and the plight of the homeless." Publ Wkly

Till the butchers cut him down; a Sharon McCone mystery. Mysterious Press 1994 339p o.p.
LC 93-42306

Sharon "McCone has just left the All-Souls Legal Cooperative and opened her own business when an eccentric friend from her UC-Berkeley days, who now specializes in rescuing failing corporations, asks her to find out who is sabotaging his efforts to save a San Francisco shipping firm and threatening his life." Publ Wkly

Trophies and dead things. Mysterious Press 1990 266p o.p.
LC 90-33448

"San Francisco detective Sharon McCone . . . uncovers murderous passions still simmering from the Vietnam anti-war movement when she undertakes an investigation into why a sniper victim changed his will to disinherit his children and leave more than $1 million to four strangers." Publ Wkly

"Like her heroine, Ms. Muller works in a style more admirable for its clarity and efficiency than for boldness or brilliance. Her dense plots are models of construction,

Muller, Marcia—*Continued*
and if her characters lack spark, they are observed in a manner both sensible and rational." N Y Times Book Rev

A walk through the fire. Mysterious Press 1999 293p $23
ISBN 0-89296-688-2 LC 98-51314
In this adventure, "Sharon McCone is seduced by the legends of Hawaii and nearly by one particular Hawaiian. Brought to Kauai initially to investigate 'accidents' on the set of her filmmaker friend's documentary, McCone finds herself dealing with murder, Hawaiian militants, and drug dealers." Libr J

Where echoes live. Mysterious Press 1991 326p o.p.
LC 90-84898
"Private eye Sharon McCone is on the ecological beat, as a renovated gold mine that could lead to environment destruction also leads to several deaths. A good mystery as fresh as today's headlines." Booklist

While other people sleep. Mysterious Press 1998 344p o.p.
ISBN 0-89296-650-5 LC 98-13394
"The renowned Sharon McCone finds life and livelihood threatened by a malicious look-alike. When police detain Sharon for a crime committed by the imposter, anger spurs her to find her double." Libr J
"Muller's straightforward, no-nonsense writing and fully dimensioned characterizations lend credibility and color to her deftly plotted tale." Publ Wkly

A wild and lonely place. Mysterious Press 1995 386p o.p.
LC 94-48255
Sharon McCone's "precious Mission District is looking mean and dirty, and colleagues at her legal collective have turned into greedy bureaucrats. Tossing caution over her shoulder, McCone signs on with a secret security agency to go after the Diplo-bomber, a terrorist who attacks embassies and consulates. The mission takes McCone to a heavily guarded hideaway in the Leeward Islands, where she executes a daring ocean swim in the dead of night to rescue an Arab diplomat's granddaughter from kidnappers." N Y Times Book Rev
"A mellow, engaging and determined Sharon here heads a diverse and intriguing supporting cast." Publ Wkly

Wolf in the shadows. Mysterious Press 1993 356p o.p.
LC 92-50536
"San Francisco private eye Sharon McCone is understandably concerned about the disappearance of her mysterious lover, Hy Ripinsky. When she finds out that he had gone to Mexico to deliver $2 million in ransom, she *really* gets worried." Libr J

Munro, Alice

Friend of my youth; stories. Knopf 1990 273p o.p.
LC 89-43295
Contents: Friend of my youth; Five points; Meneseteung; Hold me fast, don't let me pass; Oranges and apples; Pictures of the ice; Goodness and mercy; Oh, what avails; Differently; Wigtime
"Ms. Munro, who has deepened the channels of realism, is a writer of extraordinarily rich texture; her imagery stuns or wounds and her sentences stick to the rough surfaces of our world." N Y Times Book Rev

Hateship, friendship, courtship, loveship, marriage; stories. Knopf 2001 320p o.p.
ISBN 0-375-41300-6 LC 2001-29870
Contents: Hateship, friendship, courtship, loveship, marriage; Floating bridge; Family furnishings; Comfort; Nettles; Post and beam; What is remembered; Queenie; The bear came over the mountain
"Opulent in their beauty and gem-bright psychology, the extraordinary stories in {this} collection span the spectrum from romance to tales of manners to deep meditations on love and mortality, and all evince Munro's profound understanding of the power of memories and the stories we tell ourselves." Booklist

Lives of girls & women. McGraw-Hill 1971 250p o.p.
"Although the locale is Canada, Del Jordan's story could take place in the United States as well. She lives among hard-working, lower-middle-class people in a family that includes her parents and a brother, Owen. The mother seeks independence from the traditional role of women and even goes 'out on the road,' as her disapproving sisters-in-law term it, to sell encyclopedias. For Del's mother the pursuit of knowledge is an ideal. For Del and her best friend Naomi more interest lies in their maturing and curiosity about sex as a vital part of growing up. There is humor and recognizable adolescent self-questioning. While sexual scenes are explicit, they are also sensitive and real and avoid both vulgarity and titillation. In spite of the experiences that Naomi and Del have, it becomes clear that the paths they will follow will diverge greatly." Shapiro. Fic for Youth. 3d edition

The love of a good woman; stories. Knopf 1998 339p o.p.
ISBN 0-375-40395-7 LC 98-36721
Contents:The love of a good woman; Jakarta; Cortes Island; Save the reaper; The children stay; Rich as stink; Before the change; My mother's dream
"Munro knows her characters intimately, yet she is at peace with the fact that their lives will, and should, retain a fundamental mysterious quality. This paradox, which originates in a knowledge of life, is not often so knowledgeably conveyed in fiction." Yale Rev

The moons of Jupiter; stories. Knopf 1983 c1982 233p o.p.
LC 82-48734
First published 1982 in Canada
Contents: Chaddeleys and Flemings: I Connection; Chaddeleys and Flemings: II The stone in the field; Dulse; The turkey season; Accident; Bardon bus; Prue; Labor Day dinner; Mrs. Cross and Mrs. Kidd; Hard-luck stories; Visitors; The moons of Jupiter
"These stories expose the conundrums of love and mortality. At the least they are engaging, and at their luminous best, reveal precision as the highest wisdom." Saturday Rev

Open secrets; stories. Knopf 1994 293p o.p.
ISBN 0-679-43575-1 LC 94-2099

Munro, Alice—*Continued*

Contents: Carried away; A real life; The Albanian virgin; Open secrets; The Jack Randa Hotel; A wilderness station; Spaceships have landed; Vandals

The author "peoples these exquisite tales with sad, lonely eccentrics leading lives of quiet self-deception. Her heroines are often troubled souls with the unforgiving task of fitting into the rigorously confining community that spawned them. . . . Munro expertly captures the vagaries of history and geography in this satisfying and immensely pleasurable collection." Booklist

Runaway; stories. Knopf 2004 337p $25

ISBN 1-400-04281-X LC 2004-46539

Contents: Runaway; Chance; Soon; Silence; Passion; Trespasses; Tricks; Powers

"Munro's spare style belies the psychological depth of the stories, which feature characters running away from someone or something (often representative of the past) or telling a lie by commission or omission (another form of running away)." Libr J

Selected stories. Knopf 1996 545p $30

ISBN 0-679-44627-3 LC 96-4145

Contents: Walker Brothers cowboy; Dance of the happy shades; Postcard; Images; Something I've been meaning to tell you; The Ottawa Valley; Material; Royal beatings; Wild swans; The beggars maid; Simon's luck; Chaddeleys and Flemings; Dulse; The turkey season; Labor Day dinner; The moons of Jupiter; The progress of love; Lichen; Miles City, Montana; White dump; Fits; Friends of my youth; Meneseteung; Differently; Carried away; The Albanian virgin; A wilderness station; Vandals

"Little gems from one of Canada's best writers, drawn from seven collections." Libr J

Munro, H. H. *See* Saki, 1870-1916

Murakami, Haruki, 1949-

After the earthquake; stories; translated from the Japanese by Jay Rubin. Knopf 2002 181p $22

ISBN 0-375-41390-1 LC 2001-38829

Original Japanese edition, 2000

Contents: UFO in Kushiro; Landscape with flatiron; All god's children can dance; Thailand; Super-frog saves Tokyo; Honey pie

"These six stories, all loosely connected to the disastrous 1995 earthquake in Kobe, are Murakami. . . at his best. The writer, who returned to live in Japan after the Kobe earthquake, measures his country's suffering and finds reassurance in the inevitability that love will surmount tragedy, mustering his casually elegant prose and keen sense of the absurd in the service of healing." Publ Wkly

Kafka on the shore; translated from the Japanese by Philip Gabriel. Knopf 2005 436p $25.95

ISBN 1-400-04366-2 LC 2004-48907

Original Japanese edition, 2002

In this novel, "15-year-old Kafka Tamura runs away from home, both to escape his father's oedipal prophecy and to find his long-lost mother and sister. As Kafka flees, so too does Nakata, an elderly simpleton whose quiet life has been upset by a gruesome murder. . . . What follows is a kind of double odyssey, as Kafka and Nakata are drawn inexorably along their separate but somehow linked paths, groping to understand the roles fate has in store for them." Publ Wkly

"Like his characters' quests, Murakami's expeditions off the worn path of literature can be both rewarding and terrifying. Finishing 'Kafka on the Shore' is like waking from a great dream. Nothing has changed, but everything about the world looks different." Newsweek

South of the border, west of the sun; translated from the Japanese by Philip Gabriel. Knopf 1999 213p o.p.

ISBN 0-375-40251-9 LC 97-49459

"Two only children who were schoolmates and best friends meet again after a 25-year separation. Hajime is now married, the father of two little girls and a successful owner of two jazz clubs. Shimamoto has also changed; she has become a very beautiful woman. She is always immaculately and expensively dressed, but she will not talk about her life or anything that has happened to her. Nevertheless, Hajime believes that he loves her more than life itself; he is convinced that he could leave his family and his business to be with her. After they spend a night together, a night filled with raw passion, she vanishes." Libr J

"The narrative unfolds as an introspective ghost story in which Hajime must exorcise his past in the person of the enigmatic Shimamoto before he can affirm the new direction of his life. The ending, at once tender and hopeful, shows Murakami in a more mellow aspect than his work has exhibited before." Publ Wkly

The wind-up bird chronicle; translated from the Japanese by Jay Rubin. Knopf 1997 610p o.p.

ISBN 0-679-44669-9 LC 97-2813

Original Japanese edition, 1995

"After his wife disappears, unemployed 30-year-old paralegal Toru Okada gets embroiled in a surreal, sprawling drama. . . . As Okada searches for his wife (in an abandoned lot near his home, and in a city park), he encounters characters who are dream-like projections of his own muted fears and desires—among them, a precocious, death-obsessed, 16-year-old neighbor and Okada's brother-in-law, a sinister politician. Peculiar events and strange coincidences abound." Publ Wkly

Murakami's "protagonist is a harmless fellow who merely wants to recover his cat and his wife. The troubles, real and delusional, that he encounters can be seen as extravagant metaphors for every ill from personal isolation to mass murder. The novel is a deliberately confusing, illogical image of a confusing, illogical world. It is not easy reading, but it is never less than absorbing." Atl Mon

Murakami, Ryu, 1952-

In the miso soup; translated by Ralph McCarthy. Kodansha International 2004 180p $22.95

ISBN 4-7700-2957-8

Original Japanese edition, 1997

The novel is "told from the point of view of Xenji, who is twenty years old and self-employed as a tour guide for foreigner wishing to explore Tokyo's sex industry. A few days before New Year's, he is hired by an American, Frank, who Kenji grows to suspect is a serial killer." Am Book Rev

"Beyond one terribly shocking scene, Miso is a

Murakami, Ryu, 1952—*Continued*

thoughtful novel about loneliness, lack of identity and cultural and moral corruption. Through simple yet chilling language, Murakami doesn't condemn his characters. Instead he takes aim at rampant consumerism and the dumbing-down of Japanese and American culture. No one, Murakami seems to say, is completely guilty because we are shaped by the world around us." USA Today

Murasaki Shikibu, b. 978?

The tale of Genji; a novel in six parts; [by] Lady Murasaki; translated from the Japanese by Arthur Waley. Modern Lib. 1960 1135p o.p.

"A Japanese romance of the Heian period (794-1185). . . . This vast chronicle, often considered the world's first novel for its psychological depth, centers on the career of Prince Genji, his progeny, and the women with whom they associate. While delineating the elaborate rituals of courtly life, this work reflects the melancholy beauty of a world in constant flux and the vulnerability of women dependent upon the instability of human affection. Rich in poetry and elaborate wordplay, this work has had tremendous impact on the subsequent literary tradition." Reader's Ency. 4th edition

Murdoch, Iris

An accidental man. Viking 1971 442p o.p.

"The central figure of this novel is one of those accident-prone figures whose . . . misfortune becomes a substitute source of strength. . . . Ever since his brother injured his hand in a childhood incident, the world owes Austin a blank cheque to cover subsequent reverses—which do not fail to arrive. But someone is always sorry for him, always getting him out of trouble even at the price of their own. His self-pity destroys others in accordance with what Miss Murdoch . . . calls 'whatever deep mythological forces control the destinies of men.'" New Statesman (1913)

The bell; a novel. Viking 1958 342p o.p.

"The setting is an Anglican lay community attached to an abbey on one of the great estates of England. . . . The members of this community and its temporary residents are on the whole an odd, and certainly an oddly assorted, bunch. And their high-minded leader is a homosexual who was once involved in a scandal that ended his plans for entering the church. The story concerns itself with the relationships between various members of this hothouse world, with the arrival of a new bell for the abbey and the simultaneous discovery in the lake of the lost fourteenth-century bell about which there is a sinister legend. The climax is an eruption of scandal and disaster." Atlantic

The book and the brotherhood. Viking 1988 c1987 607p o.p.

LC 87-40294

First published 1987 in the United Kingdom

This novel is set in England in the 1980s. "A group of idealistic men and women, who met as students [at Oxford], later formed a society to support one of their number, a brilliant radical named David Crimond, in his efforts to write a major work tackling the big questions of history, politics, philosophy, art, and ethics. As the story opens, the group members, now middle-aged, are having qualms about Crimond and the enterprise they once agreed to fund." Christ Sci Monit

"Despite its excessive length and passages that can seem almost as self-indulgent as the characters they represent, The Book and The Brotherhood demonstrates again and again that Iris Murdoch is among the most gifted descriptive and narrative writers in English—and certainly one of the most consistently entertaining." NY Rev Books

A fairly honourable defeat. Viking 1970 436p o.p.

This is a "treatment of a homosexual menage which, when the chips are down, turns out to be more stable and durable than the happy heterosexual marriage which is subject to the same malicious interference by a cruel manipulator." Publ Wkly

"As is usual with a Murdoch novel, the action in summary seems preposterous. But given her inventiveness, her Gothic imagination, her gift for melodrama and suspense, she creates a world that becomes an effective vehicle for her moral vision." Choice

The good apprentice. Viking 1986 522p o.p.

LC 85-40635

This "novel is organized thematically around sets of opposing characters and structurally around a dramatic string of reversals. Harry Cuno is a monster of will, 'a disappointed spoilt child.' His son Stuart is a monster of will-lessness. Stuart avoids life's complications, while his stepbrother Edward, having precipitated a friend's suicide, is agonizingly caught up in them. Edward seeks absolution from his 'real' father Jesse, a legendary painter and Lear-like figure imprisoned in a decaying 'enchanter's palace' by the sea." Libr J

"The esthetic puzzle is whether the comic story and the spiritual kernel can be held together by Miss Murdoch's archaic stance as an authorial will. And yet no other contemporary British novelist seems to me of her eminence." N Y Times Book Rev

The green knight. Viking 1994 c1993 472p o.p.

LC 93-30618

First published 1993 in the United Kingdom

"Peter Mir, the 'Green Knight' of [this novel's] title, is nearly killed when he intervenes to protect Clement Graffe from being murdered by Graffe's half-brother, Lucas. Mir mysteriously reappears and demands reparation from Lucas, provoking various responses from the two brothers and their circle of friends: Harvey Blacket; Bellamy Jones; the three Anderson sisters, Aleph, Sefton, and Moy; and their mother, Louise." Libr J

"That a cold, dark, evil act should open up a gap through which warmth and light can flood into the world is a paradox characteristic of Iris Murdoch's deeply meditated insight into the nature of the good." London Rev Books

Jackson's dilemma. Viking 1996 249p o.p.

LC 95-39986

First published 1995 in the United Kingdom

"The friends and relatives of Edward Lannion and Marian Fox are gathered at Hatting Hall in readiness for their wedding. On the night before the ceremony is to take place, however, Edward receives word that Marian cannot go through with it. Thus begins a search for the missing Marian that will significantly change the course

Murdoch, Iris—*Continued*

of events. . . . There is a mysterious figure hovering at the periphery, quietly affecting the lives of all the players. In this case, it is a manservant called Jackson, who has insinuated himself into the lives of the main characters and who, while attending to their needs, has made himself indispensable." Libr J

"The peripheries of 'Jackson's Dilemma' are lush with anecdotal material; Murdoch has a way, with her minor or even offstage characters, of suggesting a wealth of motivation, a repletion of interior life." N Y Times Book Rev

The nice and the good. Viking 1968 378p o.p.

The action "begins with a violent death in the chambers of Whitehall faintly suggestive of a Le Carré thriller. . . . At times hilariously funny, slightly shivery (intimations of blackmail, suicide, dabblings in black magic) 'The Nice and the Good' is first and foremost a delightful love story. The friends, relatives, hanger-ons, whose lives revolve around the happily married Octavian and Kate Gray are all seeking after love in their own ways. They find it, too, and sometimes in the most amazing places. The characterizations are superb, the mood that of a happy fairy tale crossed with highly sophisticated sexual comedy." Publ Wkly

Nuns and soldiers. Viking 1981 c1980 505p o.p.
LC 80-16935

First published 1980 in the United Kingdom

This novel explores the tangled lives of recently widowed Gertrude; Tim, a painter; Anne, a former nun; and "Count" Peter who is in love with Gertrude

"The glory of Iris Murdoch at her best—as she almost always is in Nuns and Soldiers—is that she can convey with total respect the awareness, readjusting and hunger, and at the same time 'place' it, with a severe but not savage irony, in a world which hints at quite different forces and priorities." New Statesman (1913)

The philosopher's pupil. Viking 1983 576p o.p.
LC 82-45901

At the heart of this novel are "aging philosopher John Robert Rozanov and his former (and rejected) pupil George McCaffrey. The scene is English spa Ennistone, George's home and Rozanov's birthplace. While the desperately bitter George hopes that Rozanov's unexpected reappearance in Ennistone heralds a reconciliation, it becomes apparent that Rozanov has returned instead to settle the future of his orphaned granddaughter. This he accomplishes, setting in motion a chain of events both farcical and tragic." Libr J

This "collaboration between Murdoch and her imagination is both challenging and irresistible: a combination of gossip and profundity, modern times and ancient edicts." Time

The sea, the sea. Viking 1978 502p o.p.
LC 78-13516

The narrator of this "novel is Charles Arrowby, a former actor and director who has retired from the theater to take up solitary residence in a remote house on a northern coast. His tale begins as a mixture of diary and memoir: alternately he records his first impressions of his new home and reviews his past life as though the better to understand the man he has become. . . . His recollections largely concern a succession of love-affairs with actresses; but before all these, and dwarfing them in its importance to his development, was an unconsummated but passionate childhood relationship with a girl named Hartley, who disappeared abruptly and woundingly from his life before he was twenty and married another man." Times Lit Suppl

Something special; a story; illustrated by Michael McCurdy. Norton 2000 55p $15.95
ISBN 0-393-05007-6 LC 00-40212

First published in Winter's Tale, no.3, 1957

Set in the 1950's this story "concerns one epiphanic evening in the life of Yvonne Geary, a spirited Dublin shopgirl who seeks to flee her oppressive life. Though 24, she still shares a bed with her mother and can only dream of escape on the mail boat to England, the place where 'every Irish person with a soul in them' wants to travel. Even the arrival of a suitor fails to provide release—Sam may be a responsible, doting man, but he is still 'nothing special.' Pressure from her mother persuades Yvonne to go out with him anyway. . . . Murdoch's story can be subtle and heartfelt, most notably as it charts the melancholy, meandering voyage the young couple take toward compromised lives." N Y Times Book Rev

Murkoff, Bruce

Waterborne; a novel. Alfred A. Knopf, Distributed by Random House 2004 397p $25
ISBN 1-400-04038-8 LC 2003-58859

The author "tracks various pilgrims to the Colorado River, where a frenzied workforce is building the Boulder Dam, one of the world's largest. There's Wisconsonite engineer Filius Poe, who led a charmed life until suffering the worst tragedy to befall a young husband and father. Pretty and sweet Lena McCardell, who has fled Oklahoma with her young son after discovering that her husband is a bigamist. And little Lew Beck, a shockingly vicious and violent Jewish outlaw who takes up residence in a black bordello and becomes malevolently obsessed with Lena and Filius." Booklist

"Murkoff's prose style is vigorous and ruggedly American, inflected with a pinch of Bellow and DeLillo, and he's at his best when he applies it to the grandeur of the Western landscape, or scenes of men massed in industrial armies to tame that landscape." Nation

Murphy, Garth

The Indian lover. Simon & Schuster 2002 439p $26
ISBN 0-7432-1943-0 LC 2002-29433

This novel "spans the years 1845 to 1851—the final days of California under the rule of Spain and Mexico—and follows the fortunes of a young Cupa Indian rancher and starry-eyed American pioneer." Publ Wkly

"Rich in characterization . . . this is an exhilarating adventure story that also imparts a full-bodied picture of a long-vanished way of life and a little-known historic conflict." Booklist

Murphy, Margaret, 1959-

Darkness falls; Margaret Murphy. 1st St. Martin's Minotaur ed. St. Martin's Minotaur 2004 c2002 355p $24.95
ISBN 0-312-32851-6 LC 2003-70098

Murphy, Margaret, 1959-—*Continued*

This thriller "opens with a cheerfully frantic domestic scene of Clara Pascal prosecuting counsel, wife, mother, and seemingly typical thirtysomething career-home juggler-trying to get to chambers on time while answering the demands of her daughter, excited and clingy on her ninth birthday. Two chapters later, Counsel Pascal is chained to a wall in a stranger's pitch-dark cellar. She is anything but a passive victim, however, as she uses her formidable argumentation skills to keep herself alive." Booklist

"The critical task, as sleekly presented in the form of a police procedural, is to identify the kidnapper and trace him through his underworld associates. Meanwhile, in alternating chapters written in the skin-chilling style of a thriller, Murphy places the reader in the cellar where Clara has been blindfolded, beaten and shackled to the wall by a man who challenges her to defend her values and plead for her life. The objective is still to identify the stranger and determine his motive. But in Murphy's bold treatment, the victim is made to acknowledge her own intimate acquaintance with evil." N Y Times Book Rev

Murray, John, 1962-

A few short notes on tropical butterflies. HarperCollins Pubs. 2003 274p $24.95

ISBN 0-06-050928-7 LC 2002-68883

Contents: The hill station; All the rivers in the world; A few short notes on tropical butterflies; White flour; Watson and the shark; The carpenter who looked like a boxer; Blue; Acts of wisdom, wisdom of man

"One has to admire Murray's range, his willingness to experiment. In some ways, he can be a very attractive writer—above all, in the understated modesty of his authorial presence." N Y Times Book Rev

Murray, Paul, 1975-

An evening of long goodbyes; a novel; Paul Murray. 1st ed. Random House 2004 c2003 424p $24.95

ISBN 1-400-06116-4 LC 2003-58451

"Addicted to Gene Tierney movies and to the ever-diminishing contents of his wine cellar, 24-year-old indolent aristocrat Charles Hythloday is doing his best to avoid dealing with his crumbling estate. Older sister Bel, a worrier of such herculean proportions that she was convinced their pet dog was suffering from a dizzying array of existential terrors, is doing her best to get her brother to engage with life. After it is discovered that Charles has inadvertently filed a series of foreclosure notices in the junk drawer, he is forced to do the unthinkable-get a job." Booklist

This novel is "probably too long by 100 pages, as though Murray thought he'd only have this one chance to get everything in. But he needn't have worried. As a searing critic of contemporary life, a searching observer of sibling relations, and particularly a comic writer, he's at the beginning of a long, witty career." Christ Sci Monit

Murray, Peter, 1952-

See also Hautman, Pete, 1952-

Musil, Robert, 1880-1942

The man without qualities; translated from the German by Sophie Wilkins. Knopf 1995 2v 1774p o.p.

ISBN 0-394-51052-6 LC 92-37943

"The first two volumes of this monumental work were published in 1930 and 1932; a fragmentary third was published posthumously in 1942, and in 1952 the novel appeared, with additional chapters, in one volume. Apart from providing a brilliant, existential portrait of Ulrich, the scholarly, purposeless 'man without qualities' the book is a vivid depiction of Austrian decadence before the outbreak of World War I. This single remarkable work established Musil as one of the most influential German-language novelists in the first half of the 20th century." Reader's Ency. 4th edition

Muske, Carol, 1945-

See also Muske-Dukes, Carol, 1945-

Muske-Dukes, Carol, 1945-

Life after death; a novel. Random House 2001 275p $23.95

ISBN 0-375-50515-6 LC 00-46893

"Boyd was just a step away from becoming an obstetrician-gynecologist when her career was derailed by two people: the charming, wealthy, and mercurial Russell and a mother of three who died while intern Boyd performed an abortion. Her death is not Boyd's fault, but it prompts her to abandon her career and marry Russell, with whom she has a daughter, Freddy. Her life would be idyllic, except for the regret and the anger. One night Russell so enrages Boyd that she tells him to die, and he does. Boyd goes into shock: more guilt, another ghost." Booklist

The author "has shaped an exquisitely written tale with raw emotional appeal, a deeply humanistic story of death, grief and survival." Publ Wkly

Myles, Symon, 1949-

For works written by this author under other names see Follett, Ken, 1949-

The **Mysterious** West; edited by Tony Hillerman. HarperCollins Pubs. 1994 392p o.p.

LC 94-25842

Includes the following stories: Forbidden things, by M. Muller; New moon and rattlesnakes, by W. Hornsby; Coyote peyote, by C. N. Douglas; Nooses give, by D. Stabenow; Who killed Cock Rogers? by B. Crider; Caring for Uncle Henry, by R. W. Campbell; Death of a snowbird, by J. A. Jance; With flowers in her hair, by M. D. Lake; The lost boys, by W. J. Reynolds; Tule fog, by K. Kijewski; The river mouth, by L. Matera; No better than her father, by L. Grant; Dust Devil, by R. Burns; A woman's place, by D. R. Meredith; Postage due, by S. Dunlap; The beast in the woods, by E. Gorman; Blowout in Little Man Flats, by S. M. Kaminsky; Small town murder, by H. Adams; Bingo, by J. Lutz; Engines, by B. Pronzini

"This stunning collection . . . offers readers some

The Mysterious West—*Continued*
wonderful choices in fiction. Each story is strikingly different in tempo, plot, and setting, yet each is part of and contributes to the diversified world of the mysterious West." SLJ

N

Nabb, Magdalen, 1947-

Some bitter taste. Soho Press 2002 247p $24
ISBN 1-569-47317-X LC 2002-70579
"Marshal Guarnaccia of the Florentine police has at last lined up a case against a man accused of importing and exploiting Albanian prostitutes. But he is distracted when a seemingly paranoid old woman who had complained to him about people entering her apartment winds up murdered. Though not strictly a detective, the marshal begins to reconstruct the life of the victim, an early refugee from the Nazis." Libr J
The author "has Simenon's knack of unlocking the deeper mysteries of ordinary people's pedestrian lives. . . . In Nabb's world, nothing is simple and no life, after all, is ordinary." N Y Times Book Rev

Nabokov, Vladimir Vladimirovich, 1899-1977

Ada; or, Ardor: a family chronicle; [by] Vladimir Nabokov. McGraw-Hill 1969 589p o.p.
"In its prodigious length and with the family tree on its frontispiece the book recalls the great 19th-century novels of the author's native Russia, but *Ada* boldly turns its predecessors on their heads. For his rich, sweeping saga of the Veen-Durmanov clan, Nabokov invented an incestuous pair of 'cousins' (actually siblings, Van and Ada), a hybrid country (Amerussia), a familiar but strange planet (Antiterra), and a dimension of malleable time. The novel follows the lovers from their childhood idylls through impassioned estrangements and reunions to a tenderly shared old age. The work's rich narrative style incorporates untranslated foreign phrases, esoteric data, and countless literary allusions." Merriam-Webster's Ency of Lit

also in Nabokov, V. V. Novels, 1969-1974

Bend sinister
In Nabokov, V. V. Novels and memoirs, 1941-1951

King, queen, knave; a novel; [by] Vladimir Nabokov; translated by Dmitri Nabokov in collaboration with the author. McGraw-Hill 1968 272p o.p.
Original Russian edition, 1928
"The image of a deck of playing cards is used throughout the novel. Franz, an unsophisticated young man, works in the department store of his rich uncle Dreyer. Out of boredom Martha, the uncle's young wife, seduces Franz. The lovers subsequently plot to drown Dreyer and marry each other. Martha changes her mind abruptly when she learns that an invention by Dreyer stands to increase his wealth, but she then dies suddenly from pneumonia. Her husband never discovers his wife's duplicity." Merriam-Webster's Ency of Lit

Lolita; [by] Vladimir Nabokov. Knopf 1992 c1955 335p $19
ISBN 0-679-41043-0 LC 92-52931
"Everyman's library"
First published 1955 in France
"Humbert Humbert is a middle-aged intellectual who has a passion for girls between the ages of nine and fourteen. He falls in love with the twelve-year-old Dolores Haze, whom he calls Lolita. In his plot to seduce her, he marries Dolores's mother, whose accidental death then allows Lolita and Humbert to take off on an odyssey across the U.S. Humbert is surprised when, contrary to his schemes, Lolita seduces him and again when she leaves him for Clare Quilty, whom Humbert later murders. Lolita eventually marries Richard F. Schiller. The book presents a quest for eternal innocence, albeit in satirical terms. . . . It combines parody, fanciful imaginative flights, literary puzzles, and a brilliant satirical overview of American culture." Reader's Ency. 4th edition

also in Nabokov, V. V. Novels, 1955-1962

Look at the harlequins!; [by] Vladimir Nabokov. McGraw-Hill 1974 253p o.p.
In this pseudo-autobiographical novel, the narrator, a Russian émigré novelist and college professor who has lived in London, Paris and the United States, recalls his life, loves (including four marriages) and work in a manner which often parodies Nabokov's own life and writings
This is a book "to enchant Nabokov fans and irritate everybody else. . . . [It] is part roman a clef, part fantasy, a tale of 'wives and books interlaced monogrammatically.' It is full of erudite allusions, Russian words in various stages of translation and absurd mistranslation, puns, anagrams, acronyms. Also opinions. . . . Comic, polished, international, [Nabokov] offers sophisticated entertainment, a concoction of romantic and literary matters." Christ Sci Monit

also in Nabokov, V. V. Novels, 1969-1974

Nabokov's dozen; a collection of thirteen stories; [by] Vladimir Nabokov. Doubleday 1958 214p o.p.
Contents: Spring in Fialta; A forgotten poet; First love; Signs and symbols; The assistant producer; The Aurelian; Cloud, castle, lake; Conversation piece, 1945; "That in Aleppo once . . ."; Time and ebb; Scenes from the life of a double monster; Mademoiselle O; Lance

Novels, 1955-1962. Library of Am. 1996 904p $35
ISBN 1-883011-19-1 LC 96-15256
Contents: Lolita; Pnin; Pale fire; Lolita, a screenplay

Novels, 1969-1974. Library of Am. 1996 824p il $35
ISBN 1-883011-20-5 LC 96-15255
Contents: Ada; Transparent things; Look at the harlequins!
Transparent things (1972) is a novella about a rootless American who murders his wife

Novels and memoirs, 1941-1951; . Literary Classics of the U.S. 1996 710p il (Library of America, 87) $35
ISBN 1-883011-18-3 LC 96-15257

Nabokov, Vladimir Vladimirovich, 1899-1977—*Continued*

Contents: The real life of Sebastian Knight; Bend sinister; Speak, memory: an autobiography revisited

The real life of Sebastian Knight (1941) is about a Russian living in Paris who learns about his half-brother, a famous English novelist, by writing his biography. Bend sinister (1947) is about a professor's attempts to maintain his integrity in a totalitarian state.

Pale fire; a novel; [by] Vladimir Nabokov. Putnam 1962 315p o.p.

This novel is "both pedantry and a satire on pedantry. The core of the novel is a 999-line poem by an American author, John Shade—a sort of Robert Frost—which consists mainly of a rather moving meditation on the tragic end of the poet's daughter. After Shade's death, a foolish scholar named Kinbote—an exile from the mythical country of Zembla and a visiting professor of Zemblan at Wordsmith College, New Wye, Appalachia—edits this work, providing a preface and a detailed corpus of notes. But Kinbote has an 'idée fixe'—the history of his own country—and he believes that Shade's poem is an allegory of this history, with Kinbote himself—fantasized into the deposed King Charles Xavier II—as the hero. The humour—and Nabokov's humour is subtle as well as occasionally brutal—lies in the disparity between the simple truth of the poem and the gross self-exalting hallucinations of its editor." Burgess. 99 Novels

also in Nabokov, V. V. Novels, 1955-1962

Pnin; [by] Vladimir Nabokov. Doubleday 1957 191p o.p.

"Not a novel, not really a collection of short stories, but rather a series of sketches, all of them dealing with Timofey Pnin, professor of Russian in a small American university. Each one finds Pnin valiantly trying to cope with the daily crises of American society—Pnin on the wrong train, Pnin learning to drive, Pnin giving a party, Pnin and the washing machine. They are all gently amusing, affectionate portraits of a Russian expatriate of the old school caught up in the inexplicable complexities of daily life." Libr J

also in Nabokov, V. V. Novels, 1955-1962

The real life of Sebastian Knight

In Nabokov, V. V. Novels and memoirs, 1941-1951

The stories of Vladimir Nabokov. Knopf 1996 {i.e. 1995} 659p o.p.

ISBN 0-394-58615-8 LC 95-23466

For this chronologically-arranged collection, "Nabokov's son Dmitri has assembled the 52 stories published in English before Nabokov died in 1977, and translated another 13 written in Russian between 1920 or '21 and 1924." Newsweek

Contents: The wood-sprite; Russian spoken here; Sounds; Wingstroke; Gods; A matter of chance; The seaport; Revenge; Beneficence; Details of a sunset; The thunderstorm; La Veneziana; Bachmann; The dragon; Christmas; A letter that never reached Russia; The fight; The return of Chorb; A guide to Berlin; A nursery tale; Terror; Razor; The passenger; The doorbell; An affair of honor; The Christmas story; The Potato Elf; The aurelian; A dashing fellow; A bad day; The visit to the museum; A busy man; Terra incognita; The reunion; Lips to lips; Orache; Music; Perfection; The admiralty spire; The Leonardo; In memory of L. I. Shigaev; The circle; A Russian beauty; Breaking the news; Torpid smoke; Recruiting; A slice of life; Spring in Fialta; Cloud, castle, lake; Tyrants destroyed; Lik; Mademoiselle O; Vasiliy Shishkov; Ultima thule; Solus rex; The assistant producer; "That in Aleppo once . . ."; A forgotten poet; Time and ebb; Conversation piece, 1945; Signs and symbols; First love; Scenes from the life of a double monster; The Vane sisters; Lance

Transparent things

In Nabokov, V. V. Novels, 1969-1974

Nagy, Gloria, 1945-

The beauty. Overlook Press 2001 290p $26.95

ISBN 1-58567-149-5 LC 2001-21836

"Sardonic John Duckworth, ex-crime reporter, jumps at the chance to leave New York and start a bed-and-breakfast on Cape Cod with his emotionally fragile sister, Faith. . . . It all starts with their very first guest, the beautiful Jasmine Jones who insinuates herself into the Duckworths' lives by manipulating Faith and seducing John. A psychopath of extraordinary proportions, Jasmine single-handedly engineers the destruction of Faith and John's personal and professional lives. Nagy can be very funny as she lampoons various trendy New York locations and gives her narrator the staccato rhythms of a noir character." Booklist

Naipaul, V. S. (Vidiadhar Surajprasad), 1932-

A bend in the river. Knopf 1979 278p o.p.

LC 78-21591

"Salim, an East African of East Indian descent . . . buys a general store in a large town in the interior of an unnamed African country. A man without any 'home ground' to stand on, Salim builds his business out of the rubble left by one post-independence revolution. He discovers a great deal about his own mundane existence and about that of his circle of bewildered young Africans, bedraggled European ex-patriates, and displaced East Indians, as the town (and the country) lurches toward yet another cataclysmic revolt." Saturday Rev

"This is a beautifully composed book, with an almost Conradian power of description. Aesthetically most satisfying, it is also profoundly depressing. But depression is sometimes a stone on the road to literary exaltation." Burgess. 99 Novels

Guerrillas. Knopf 1975 248p o.p.

The action of this novel "takes place on a troubled Caribbean island, inhabited by Asians, Africans, Americans and British colonials. Corruption and poverty are everywhere. . . . The homes of the well-to-do lie hidden in the hills. The poor are angry, the rich are panicked. . . . At the center of the brewing storm are Peter Roche, a white South African and lapsed revolutionary working for an island business; Jane, his British mistress, in confused search of adventure and challenge; and Jimmy Ahmed, a half-Chinese, half-black politician who has set up an agricultural commune that may be giving shelter to the guerrillas. Roche, cynical and self-absorbed, is employed by his firm to control Jimmy. Jimmy is obsessed with visions of personal glory, rape and mystical manhood. Jane, careless and quixotic, becomes the mistress

Naipaul, V. S. (Vidiadhar Surajprasad), 1932-— *Continued*

of both men." Newsweek

"This is a novel without a villain, and there is not a character for whom the reader does not at some point feel deep sympathy and keen understanding, no matter how villainous or futile he may seem." N Y Times Book Rev

Half a life. Knopf 2001 211p $24
ISBN 0-375-40737-5 LC 2001-33730

"Willie Chandran, the central figure here, is born in India in the 1930s, the son of a bitter mixed caste marriage between a Brahmin and a 'backwards' person, or untouchable. . . . Going to London on a scholarship, Willie mixes in immigrant and bohemian circles, and even publishes a book. . . . Willie meets Ana, a woman of mixed African descent, when she writes him a fan letter about his novel. They become lovers. Willie goes back with Ana to her large outback estate in the 'half and half' world of a Portuguese colony like Mozambique, where he remains for 18 years." Publ Wkly

"In the book's last moments a narrative that has seemed to meander pulls suddenly tight, giving 'Half a Life' an interest that lies beyond its relation to Naipaul's other work. . . . The very fissures in its structure, its change from voice to voice, transform 'Half a Life' into a meditation on the difficulties of building a coherent self." N Y Times Book Rev

A house for Mr. Biswas; with an introduction by Karl Miller. Knopf 1995 xxi, 564p $20
ISBN 0-679-44458-0
"Everyman's library"

A reissue of the title first published 1961 by McGraw-Hill

"Trinidad, West Indies, is the setting for the story of lonely Mr. Mohun Biswas, a Hindu of high caste but low economic status. Throughout the book he longs for independence from his wife's large family and a house of his own. In a portrait that is both funny and compassionate, West Indian life is vividly described, especially the relationships among members of Mr. Biswas's family." Shapiro. Fic for Youth. 3d edition

Magic seeds; V.S. Naipaul. Knopf 2004 280p $25
ISBN 0-375-40736-7 LC 2004-48964

At the beginning of this "novel, Willie is in Berlin with his bossy sister, Sarojini. It is 18 years later. Revolution has uprooted Willie's African existence. Sarojini hooks him up with a guerrilla group in India, and Willie, always ready to be molded to some cause, returns to India. The guerrillas, Willie soon learns, are 'absolute maniacs.' But caught up, as ever, in the energy of others, Willie stays with them for seven years. He then surrenders and is tossed into the relative comfort of jail. When an old London friend (a lawyer named Roger) gets Willie's book of short stories republished, Willie's imprisonment becomes an embarrassment to the authorities. He is now seen as a forerunner of 'postcolonial writing.' He returns to London, where he alternates between making love to Perdita, Roger's wife, and looking for a job." Publ Wkly

The author "has written a calculated polemic. . . . Naipaul is suggesting that our racial and ethnic fate is sealed; we can never escape who we are, and must learn to live with our unchosen identities whether we like them or not. It's not a consoling vision; neither is it despairing. It simply is." N Y Times Book Rev

A way in the world; a novel. Knopf 1994 380p o.p.
ISBN 0-394-56478-2 LC 93-44680

In this autobiographical fiction, Naipaul examines "feelings of rootlessness, the realities of the colonial experience, the impact of cultural displacement, and our need to belong. He does so through a series of linked historical narratives. Among them is an imagined vision of Raleigh's desperate but futile search for El Dorado. We are also introduced to Francisco de Miranda, one of the precursors to Bolivar's revolution. We are witness to the irony inherent in the life of Lebrun, a Trinidadian/Panamanian Communist of the 1930s. And then there is Blair, a former co-worker of the narrator in Trinidad, whose African roots prove no help when he becomes an adviser to an East African despot. These are tales of lost souls desperate to find a place at the table but who never quite succeed, leaving them doomed to remain on the fringes of history." Libr J

Naipaul, Vidiadhar Surajprasad *See* Naipaul, V. S. (Vidiadhar Surajprasad), 1932-

Nance, John J.

Fire flight; John J. Nance. Simon & Schuster 2003 353p map $25
ISBN 0-7432-5050-8 LC 2003-59095

"Fires are raging out of control in Yellowstone National Park, and planes from the aging fleet of water tankers are crashing. Veteran pilot Clark Maxwell has returned from retirement to help out—not only in his official capacity but also as an investigator in light of the recurring crashes. Where have the planes been over the preceding winter instead of having lifesaving maintenance performed on them? Maxwell suspects a major cover-up. Despite a rushed and contrived ending, Nance has crafted an exciting and compelling story." Libr J

The last hostage. Doubleday 1998 373p o.p.
ISBN 0-385-49055-0 LC 97-44861

"Airbridge Airlines pilot Ken Wolfe fakes engine trouble to force a landing; then, having tricked his co-pilot off the plane, he takes off. His plan: to extort a confession from a surprise passenger, U.S. Attorney General nominee Rudolph Bostitch. It seems that, as a Connecticut DA, Bostitch covered up for the man who Wolfe believes tortured and killed his 11-year-old daughter. Wolfe rolls the plane to convince the crew that a hijacker with a bomb shares the cockpit, a Flitephone call alerts the FBI and novice female negotiator Kat Bronsky is put on the case." Publ Wkly

"Nance is a master of suspense, and his fast-moving plot has more twists than a corkscrew." Libr J

Medusa's child. Doubleday 1997 388p o.p.
LC 96-27656

"For his livelihood, pilot and small businessman Scott McKay leases a converted Boeing 727 and ferries cargo across the country, much like a truck driver. On one particular flight, however, he comes to realize that his cargo hold contains a thermonuclear bomb: a modern instrument of destruction dubbed the Medusa device and capa-

Nance, John J.—*Continued*

ble of an incredible act of terrorism—destroying every computer chip within a very wide radius. The effort to incapacitate the bomb before it can detonate is the warp and woof of an exciting plot that offers hours of pure diversion." Booklist

Pandora's clock. Doubleday 1995 357p o.p.
LC 95-8409

"Shortly after Quantum Airlines Flight 66 departs Frankfurt, Germany, for New York, one of the passengers succumbs to an apparent heart attack. It may be, however, that Professor Ernest Helms was exposed to a doomsday virus just before boarding his flight; if so, more than 200 passengers and crew members could be dead within a matter of hours. Word of this imminent disaster leaks to governments and media organizations around the world, of course, and the jumbo jet is refused landing clearance everywhere." Publ Wkly

"A uniquely suspenseful and terrifying story." Booklist

Napolitano, Ann

Within arm's reach; a novel; Ann Napolitano. 1st ed. Shaye Areheart Books 2004 308p $23
ISBN 1-400-05188-6 LC 2003-21525

"An Irish-American family in New Jersey, tied together and split apart by the usual family fare, twists and turns on an unexpected pregnancy. Gracie, the 29-year-old advice columnist for the Bergen Record, is addicted to the flush of first contact and pregnant by the guy she's just broken up with. Her sister, Lila, a third-year medical student, is brittle like their mother, Kelly, and sharp like their grandmother Catherine. Aunts and uncles, siblings and cousins, all have their say as the chapters pass from voice to voice, recounting marriages broken, lost, and blooming. The past isn't past, of course, it never is in families, but Napolitano's clear-eyed narrative allows us to see the ghosts and desires along with the current ties that bind." Booklist

Narayan, R. K., 1906-2001

The grandmother's tale and selected stories. Viking 1994 312p o.p.
LC 94-4581

Contents: The grandmother's tale; Guru; Salt and sawdust; Judge; Emden; An astrologer's day; The blind dog; Second opinion; A horse and two goats; Annamalai; Lawley Road; A breath of Lucifer; Under the banyan tree; Another community; The shelter; Seventh house; Cat within; The edge; Uncle

Set in India these stories "emphasize perceptively drawn characters and situations rather than their colorful foreign backdrops. All the tales display a wry, gentle humor." Publ Wkly

Malgudi days. Viking 1982 246p o.p.
LC 81-52204

Contents: An astrologer's day; The missing mail; The doctor's word; Gateman's gift; The blind dog; Fellow-feeling; The tiger's claw; Iswaran; Such perfection; Father's help; The snake-song; Engine trouble; Forty-five a month; Out of business; Attila; The axe; Lawley Road; Trail of the green blazer; The martyr's corner; Wife's holiday; A shadow; A willing slave; Leela's friend; Mother and son; Naga; Selvi; Second opinion; Cat within; The edge; God and the cobbler; Hungry child; Emden

"This selection distills, magically, Malgudi's vibrancy, its mythological-animistic throb, the large and small corruptions of its citizens—from bureaucrats to back-street people—and the reassuring backdrop of its cyclical rhythms. Distinguished writing; rewarding reading." Booklist

Under the banyan tree and other stories. Viking 1985 193p o.p.
LC 85-3234

"An Elisabeth Sifton book"

Contents: Nitya; House opposite; A horse and two goats; The Roman image; The watchman; A career; Old man of the temple; A hero; Dodu; Another community; Like the sun; Chippy; Uncle's letters; All avoidable talk; A snake in the grass; The evening gift; A breath of Lucifer; Annamalai; The shelter; The mute companions; At the portal; Four rupees; Flavour of coconut; Fruition at forty; Crime and punishment; Half a rupee worth; The antidote; Under the banyan tree

"Narayan's clarity, his mastery of technique, his respect for the spectrum of human predicament, his absence of malice and his freedom from a single philosophy that explains everything away put him in the unique position of being able to turn a teeming cultural life into lucid and enjoyable stories." New Statesman

Nasaw, Jonathan Lewis

Twenty-seven bones; a thriller; Jonathan Nasaw. 1st Atria Books hardcover ed. Atria Books 2004 360p $25
ISBN 0-7434-4653-4 LC 2003-69637

"Former FBI agent E.L. Pender heads to St. Luke, one of the Virgin Islands, to help hunt for a murderer whose modus operandi is to torture his victims, cut off their right hands, and leave them to bleed slowly to death. The authorities, fearful of bad publicity, want to keep the killer's existence quiet. Pender, clearly from the mainland and unaccustomed to the speech patterns and social customs of the island, is at a disadvantage as he tries to familiarize himself with the community and its inhabitants. . . . Although the reader knows who is behind the killings, tension arises from not knowing whether Pender will figure it out in time to save other people while putting himself at grave risk." Libr J

Naslund, Sena Jeter

Ahab's wife; or, The star-gazer; a novel. Morrow 1999 668p $28
ISBN 0-688-17187-7 LC 99-22135

"At age 12, Una escapes her religiously obsessed father in rural Kentucky to live with relatives in a lighthouse off New Bedford, Mass. When she is 16—disguised as a boy—she runs off to sea aboard a whaler, which sinks after being rammed by its quarry. Una and two young men who love her are the only survivors of a group set adrift in an open boat, but the dark secret of their cannibalism will leave its mark. Rescued, Una is wed to one of the young men by the captain of the *Pequod,* handsome, commanding Ahab, who has not as yet met the white whale that will be his destiny. . . . Una's later marriage to Ahab—a passionate and intellectually satisfying relationship—the loss of her mother and

Naslund, Sena Jeter—*Continued*

her newborn son in one night, and her life as a rich woman in Nantucket are further developments in a plot teeming with arresting events and provocative ideas." Publ Wkly

Four spirits; a novel. Morrow 2003 524p $26.95
ISBN 0-06-621238-3 LC 2003-51170

"During the civil rights conflict, Birmingham, Ala. was notorious for the ferocity of its racial bigotry: peaceful demonstrators attacked with fire hoses and dogs by police chief Bull Connor; the Klan-set explosion at a black church that killed four little girls. The four victims are only background figures in Naslund's . . . evocation of the city and the era, but they appear to several characters in the form of spirits who promise the reconciliation to come. The novel is constructed as a series of vignettes that follow a dozen or so characters whose lives finally intersect." Publ Wkly

"Naslund has done something unusually fine—she's written a drifting collective portrait of a city in distress. The characters of 'Four Spirits' are deeply entwined, sometimes without knowing it." N Y Times Book Rev

Nathan, Robert, 1894-1985

Portrait of Jennie. Knopf 1940 c1939 212p o.p.

"Eban Adams, a struggling artist who is unable to sell his art work, meets an unusual child named Jennie in the park and immediately begins to prosper. He knows little about her except that she belongs in the past and that every few months, when their paths cross, she has aged by years. His finest painting is a portrait of her, a token of his love, which ends in predestined tragedy." Shapiro. Fic for Youth. 3d edition

Nathanson, E. M., 1928-

The dirty dozen. Random House 1965 498p o.p.

"Project Amnesty was a plan to drop 12 viciously trained American soldier-prisoners (murderers, rapists, thieves, all doomed to either execution or lengthy prison terms) behind the German lines in France just before D-Day. Their trainer-warden, 30-year-old Captain John Reisman resents the assignment." Book Week

This "is not an ordinary war book. The fight here is not so much against the Wehrmacht as it is against self, society, and 'the system.' . . . If the situation seems impossible, if Reisman seems a superman, no matter, for the insights into good and evil are richly rewarding in this exciting and highly compelling novel." Libr J

Nattel, Lilian

The singing fire; a novel; Lilian Nattel. Scribner 2004 321p $25
ISBN 0-7432-4966-6 LC 2003-57344

A novel about "London's 19th-century Jewish ghetto. The story revolves around Nehama and Emilia, a Polish and a Russian immigrant, respectively, who had fled to London to start life anew. While both indeed remake themselves, facing formidable challenges, they do not necessarily find better lives. Each is accompanied by a spirit-guardian who turns up periodically with sotto voce comments about current problems and solutions. The two characters are linked by Gittel, the daughter born to Emilia but adopted by Nehama. Nattel offers a poignant glimpse into a long-gone world, fraught with danger, hardship, poverty, and the daunting boundaries of class, gender, and geography." Libr J

Naylor, Gloria

Bailey's Café. Harcourt Brace Jovanovich 1992 229p o.p.
LC 91-42089

Bailey's Cafe is the setting in which the book's characters "tell stories from their lives. . . . Bailey's and the nearby boarding house (which some call a bordello) offer respite for those who have been battered in the outside world." Libr J

The author "takes us many keys down, and sometimes back up, in this virtuoso orchestration of survival, suffering, courage and humor, sounding through the stories of these lives." N Y Times Book Rev

Linden Hills. Ticknor & Fields 1985 304p o.p.
LC 84-16222

The author "sketches the development of the community of Linden Hills through its founder, Luther Nedeed, and successive generations of Nedeeds, showing in the decline of the family the corrosive effect of ambition, arrogance and the abuse of power. The residents of Linden Hills are similarly subverted by the accommodations, sacrifices and perversions of soul blacks must endure to live in an affluent community, even, as in this case, an all-black one." Publ Wkly

"Its flaws notwithstanding, the novel's ominous atmosphere and inspired set pieces—such as the minister's drunken fundamentalist sermon before an incredulous Hills congregation—make it a fascinating departure for Miss Naylor, as well as a provocative, iconoclastic novel about a seldom-addressed subject." N Y Times Book Rev

Mama Day. Ticknor & Fields 1988 311p o.p.
LC 87-18157

"Willow Springs is a sparsely populated sea island just off America's southeastern coast whose small black community is dominated by the elderly matriarch, Miranda 'Mama' Day. When Mama Day's greatniece, Cocoa, marries, she returns to Willow Springs with her husband for an extended visit. Once there, strange forces—both natural and supernatural—work to separate the couple." Libr J

"When she is not didactically fostering our spiritual instruction, Gloria Naylor serves another worthy purpose beautifully: she invites us to imagine the lives of complex characters at work and play, and gives us a faithfully rendered community in all its seasons." Ms

The men of Brewster Place. Hyperion 1998 173p o.p.
ISBN 0-7868-6421-4 LC 97-45987

"Ben, a neighborhood janitor (and chorus) resurrected from the previous Brewster Place novel, narrates seven tales of neighborhood men and the women who love them. Their travails feature the familiar ills of the inner city, yet Naylor lends these archetypal situations complexity and depth: Basil yearns to be the kind of father he never had but chooses a path that leads to heartbreak; Eugene's restlessness in his marriage and friendship with a transsexual force him to face a difficult fact about himself; Reverend Moreland T. Woods rehearses his political

Naylor, Gloria—*Continued*
aspirations with maneuvers on his church's board; and C.C. Baker, involved in local drug trafficking, keeps a startling truth from the police." Publ Wkly

The women of Brewster Place. Viking 1982 192p o.p.
LC 81-69969

This "novel is set, as the title indicates, in Brewster Place, a block-long dead-end street of run-down apartment buildings in a northern city. In an interrelated series of vignettes, Naylor focuses on seven black women, residents of Brewster Place. She is concerned with the distance between their dreams and realities, problems and solutions; these women are of different ages, come from different backgrounds, react differently to their blackness and to men, and have different notions of personal accomplishment, but all are burdened by being both black and female. Naylor is not angry; she writes with conviction and beautiful language, but spares the reader any bitterness. Characters are not puppets but exist and function as well-rounded personalities." Booklist

Naylor, Phyllis Reynolds, 1933-

After; Phyllis Reynolds Naylor. Soho Press 2003 371p $25
ISBN 1-569-47354-4 LC 2003-50695

"Naylor's novel about 56-year-old Harry Gill's first year as a widower deals in the minutiae of daily life, focusing on the common but incontrovertibly human emotions surrounding death, marriage and family ties. Harry runs a garden shop in a Washington, D.C., suburb. When his wife dies of ovarian cancer, he grieves, but his grief is tempered with bouts of anger, exasperation and longing for other women. This longing is reciprocated. Neighbors, friends and even colleagues hurl themselves at Harry, who, although likable enough, seems to attract them simply because of his new status as an unattached man." Publ Wkly

"Especially in its early sections, the novel will remind many readers of Anne Tyler, with its slightly off-center characters and its sympathetic but wry and somewhat distanced point of view...After is popular fiction for intelligent readers, something always in short supply and always welcome." Washington Post

Nebula awards; showcase [date]; the year's best sf and fantasy chosen by the Science Fiction and Fantasy Writers of America. Harcourt
ISSN 0741-5567

First volume in this series, edited by Damon Knight, was published by Doubleday in 1965. Editors and publishers vary. Variant titles: Nebula award stories; Nebula winners

Included in this annual collection of award-winning stories and runners-up are essays on the writings and events in science fiction as well as lists of winners of Nebula Hugo awards, sponsored by Science Fiction and Fantasy Writers of America

Neel, Janet, 1940-

To die for. St. Martin's Press 1999 240p o.p.
ISBN 0-312-20598-8 LC 99-18077

A mystery featuring Chief Superintendent John McLeish and his wife Francesca. "The investors in Judith Delves's London cafe, including her co-owner, want to sell, but Judith is obstinately against the transaction. Shortly after her friend and partner, Selina, comes around to her way of thinking, Selina's body is found stuffed into an unused freezer." Publ Wkly

Neely, Barbara

Blanche cleans up. Viking 1998 258p o.p.
ISBN 0-670-87626-7 LC 97-39834

Boston cleaning lady Blanche White "takes over her cousin Charlotte's best friend Inez's job as cook at the home of snobbish, phony Allister Brindle, who aspires to be Massachusetts's next governor. Blanche is good at listening at doors and does not like Brindle's fawning over black leaders no one follows; in fact, she does not like any of the comings and goings at the Brindle residence, especially when they lead to murders." Libr J

"Blanche's caustic comments, streetwise attitude and lusty approach to life cast an illuminating light on both ends of the social spectrum and add sparks to an already sizzling mystery." Publ Wkly

Neilson, Melany, 1958-

Persia Café. St. Martin's Press 2001 276p $23.95
ISBN 0-312-26219-1 LC 00-64477

"A town in Mississippi is rocked to its core in 1961 when a young black man is found murdered, washed up on the river's shore. Fannie Leary, the white owner of the town's only café, discovers the body, but when she brings the sheriff back to the scene, it has disappeared. Fannie struggles to reconcile the expectation that she keep silent with what she feels she owes to Mattie, her black cook and cousin of the murdered boy. The story comes out, the FBI comes to investigate, and the white community whose balance she has disrupted shuns Fannie." Libr J

"Neilson lavishes such attention on the town and its people that she captures something precious: the feel of a culture at a particular time and the ineffable moment a heart changes." Publ Wkly

Nelscott, Kris

Stone cribs; Kris Nelscott. 1st ed. St. Martin's Minotaur 2004 323p $24.95
ISBN 0-312-28784-4 LC 2003-50604

"One year after the assassination of Martin Luther King Jr., Smokey Dalton has moved from Memphis to Chicago with an 11-year-old witness to the shooting. There, he investigates rental housing owned by white girlfriend Laura Hathaway. Adding to the unsettled political climate is the fight for the right to abortion, crystallized by Smokey and Laura's involvement in saving a young black woman, pregnant as the result of rape, from death-by-botched-abortion. Smokey subsequently hunts down the rapist, as well as the clumsy abortionist. . . . Nelscott skillfully recreates a troubled 1960s Chicago, complete with sympathetic protagonists who fight its racial inequalities, widespread ignorance, and political ineptness." Libr J

Neville, Katherine, 1945-

The eight; a novel. Ballantine Bks. 1989 c1988 550p o.p.
LC 87-91363

This "novel is in and of itself a complex conundrum featuring two completely interdependent plots. As the action races back and forth between the era of the French Revolution and contemporary America and Algeria, both the historical and modern characters serve as pawns in an intricately executed game of chess. Players compete to unravel the sinister secret and curse of the mythical Montglane Service, an ornate chess set custom designed for Charlemagne, possessing certain mystical powers and endowed with an almost unlimited capacity for good or evil." Booklist

"Involving Napoleon, Talleyrand, Casanova, Voltaire, Rousseau, Robespierre and Catherine the Great in the quest, Neville has great fun rewriting history and making it all ring true." Publ Wkly

New stories from the South: the year's best [date]; edited by Shannon Ravenel. Algonquin Books of Chapel Hill
ISSN 0879-9073

Annual. First published 1986

An annual collection of short stories culled from a wide variety of magazines. Among the authors represented are Frederick Barthelme, George Singleton, Chris Offutt, Tony Earley, Janice Daugharty, and Elizabeth Spencer

Newman, Sandra, 1965-

The only good thing anyone has ever done. HarperCollins Pubs. 2003 389p $24.95
ISBN 0-06-051498-1 LC 2002-38737

"Chrysalis Moffat, a South American orphan, has grown into a psychologically unstable young woman living alone in the California mansion of her adopted parents, both dead. Her brother, Eddie, 'five foot seven inches of sheer depravity,' returns from a slacker trip around the world towing a fake Buddhist guru named Ralph, and together they open the Tibetan School of Miracles in the run-down mansion, selling enlightenment to spiritually destitute Californians. But this is just the first in a series of clever false fronts presented by this sprawling, globe-trotting novel, which hops from California to Colorado, Cairo to Kathmandu, exploring Chrysalis's and Eddie's messy lives and the source of their rampant dysfunctionality." Publ Wkly

Newman, Sharan

The difficult saint. Forge 1999 352p o.p.
ISBN 0-312-86966-5 LC 99-26644

"A Tom Doherty Associates book"

"When her estranged sister, Agnes, becomes the main suspect in the murder of her bridegroom, Catherine Le Vendeur and her immediate family journey from their home in France to Germany in hopes of proving Agnes's innocence. Set in 1146." SLJ

"If Newman doesn't deliver a particularly suspenseful plot, she compensates with her command of the period and her ability to translate her knowledge into an absorbing and entertaining narrative." Publ Wkly

Strong as death. Forge 1996 384p o.p.
LC 96-1410

"A Tom Doherty Associates book"

A "medieval mystery featuring the indefatigable Catherine Le Vendeur. En route to Santiago de Compostela, Spain, in order to petition for a child at the holy shrine of the apostle Saint James, Catherine and her beloved husband, Edgar, join forces with a curious band of pilgrims. Their fellow wayfarers include four aging knights, a couple of wandering musicians, an imperious gentlewoman, a bitter prostitute, and two zealous monks. As their journey progresses, a series of fatal misfortunes plagues various members of their company, prompting Catherine and Edgar to undertake a quiet investigation." Booklist

"Colorful characters and thoroughly researched culture add up to wonderful historical fiction." Libr J

Nexø, Martin Andersen *See* Andersen Nexø, Martin, 1869-1954

Ng, Fae Myenne, 1956-

Bone. Hyperion 1993 193p o.p.
ISBN 1-56282-944-0 LC 92-6028

The novel concerns "two generations of Chinese Americans in San Francisco's Chinatown. Mah, who has worked hard all her life in garment sweatshops, finally is able to own her baby-clothing store. Her husband, Leon, who used to be a merchant seaman, worked two shifts in ships' laundry rooms to provide for his family. Nevertheless, the family is torn apart after Ona, the middle daughter, jumps from the tallest building in Chinatown. . . . Nina, the youngest daughter, leaves Chinatown for New York City and then Leila, the oldest, marries and moves out to the suburbs. Leon, the 'paper son' to old Leung, fails to keep his promise to take Leung's bones back to China." Libr J

"Ng is a master storyteller. Her gift for observation and language make Bone truly extraordinary." Women's Rev Books

Nicholls, David, 1966-

A question of attraction; David Nicholls. 1st U.S. ed. Villard Books 2004 c2003 338p $23.95; pa $13.95
ISBN 1-400-06181-4; 0-8129-7140-X (pa)
LC 2003-59627

"The year is 1985. Brian Jackson, a working-class kid on full scholarship, has started his first term at university. The usual freshman anxiety over fitting in is compounded by the gap between his own humble origins and the privileged backgrounds of his better-off classmates. Brian also has a dark secret–a long-held, burning ambition (stoked by his late father) to appear on the wildly popular TV quiz show University Challenge–and now, finally, it seems the dream is about to become reality." Publisher's note

The author "has a talent for droll dialogue and a wonderful sense of the ridiculous. He marries the agony of adolescence with ironic humor, producing a union of subtlety and slapstick that's not to be missed." USA Today

Nichols, John Treadwell, 1940-

The Milagro beanfield war; by John Nichols; illus. by Rini Templeton. Holt, Rinehart & Winston 1974 445p o.p.

"Joe Mondragon, a very small time troublemaker in the sleepy Chicano town of Milagro, irrigates a little field he owns in order to grow some beans. He is violating the local water laws but the rich and powerful are afraid to take action for fear of arousing Joe's friends and neighbors. (There's a big-money, Milagro-exploiting land development in the offing; they don't want to make waves.) Actually Joe's neighbors are generally resentful of his troublemaking, or are afraid to support him. But they eventually rally to the cause, having been pushed around too long, and the resulting interaction is touching and hilarious by turns." Publ Wkly

"Nichols has written a bawdy, slangy, modern proletarian novel that is—if finally perhaps excessively sentimental—still a consistently entertaining film scenario while at the same time it manages to make funny-serious sense out of a contemporary situation enduring injustice and imminent violence." Choice

The sterile cuckoo; by John Nichols. McKay, D. 1965 210p o.p.

When the heroine, Pookie Adams "first stumbles on the hero, Jerry Payne, waiting at a cross-country bus stop, he sees only a skinny, scrubby-haired girl, balancing a toothpick on her tongue. Then she bursts into speech and Jerry . . . remains bewitched until the last syllable. Her pursuit of Jerry is launched with . . . determination. . . . When fate places the couple at neighboring Eastern colleges, Jerry succumbs to his first frantic affair. . . . As their romance plunges into its second year, they make a final attempt to slow to a more normal pace, but on a New York weekend, somewhat the worse for an over indulgence in Tiki Puka Pukas, their affair staggers to a close." Publisher's note

Nichols, Leigh, 1945-

For works written by this author under other names see Koontz, Dean R. (Dean Ray), 1945-

Nichols, Peter, 1950-

Voyage to the North Star; a novel. Carroll & Graf Pubs. 1999 342p $24

ISBN 0-7867-0664-3

This novel's "protagonist is Will Boden, a skilled seaman down on his luck in depression-era New York. In a moment of ill judgment, he once abandoned the ship he was captaining, and is now reduced to scraping a living, literally, on the waterfront. Along comes Carl Schenck, a wealthy industrialist who wants to ape his idol, Teddy Roosevelt, as a big game hunter, but fears it's all been done. He hits upon the notion to take the beautiful luxury yacht he has just acquired up into the Arctic to hunt for seal, bear, whatever he can find, and among the motley crew he assembles, including a skipper who is a fake British naval officer, is poor Will." Publ Wkly

"A gripping novel of blood lust, human folly, and desperate hope in the tradition of Melville, Conrad, and Jack London." Libr J

Nicholson, Margaret Beda *See* Yorke, Margaret

Niffenegger, Audrey

The time traveler's wife; a novel; by Audrey Niffenegger. MacAdam\Cage 2003 518p $25

ISBN 1-931561-64-8 LC 2003-10159

"Young lovers often believe themselves crossed by fate or by time, but those in Niffenegger's spirited first novel have more reason than most. Henry suffers from Chrono-Impairment—a quasi-medical condition that catapults him, unwillingly, from one random point in time to another. Clare first meets him in 1977, when she is six and he materializes near her parents' garden as a thirty-six-year-old from 2000; he returns regularly throughout her childhood from different times in their shared future. At last, when Clare is twenty and Henry twenty-eight, they meet in his present, and the relationship begins in earnest. But romance proves even trickier than usual when one person keeps vanishing to distant, and occasionally dangerous, times." New Yorker

Niffenegger "writes with the unflinching yet detached clarity of a war correspondent standing at the sidelines of an unfolding battle. She possesses a historian's eye for contextual detail. This is no romantic idyll." USA Today

Nin, Anaïs, 1903-1977

Children of the albatross

In Nin, A. Cities of the interior p128-238

Cities of the interior; introduction by Sharon Spencer. Swallow Press 1974 xx, 589p o.p.

First one-volume version published 1959 by the author. Although intended as a connected work exploring the lives of women, it was originally published as five separate novelettes. This edition contains the expanded and retitled version of the fifth novelette

In Ladders to fire (1946), which concerns a largely American group of characters in Paris, Lillian's hunger for life and love leave her unsatisfied with her seemingly changeless marriage to Larry. She develops an increasingly possessive relationship with Djuna, whose inner clarity and control, concealed beneath a delicate feminine exterior, offer a comforting contrast to her own emotional turbulence. Lillian's love affair with the painter Jay is complicated by the love-hate relationship which they both establish with Sabina

Children of the albatross (1947) focuses on Djuna, who achieved a sense of liberation through dancing after an unhappy childhood in an orphan asylum. It deals with her youthful love for Michael, who fled to a homosexual lover after his jealousy drove them apart, her relationship with the joyful painter Lawrence and the youth Paul who seeks shelter and love from her after fleeing his parent's stifling home, and the relationships of Jay to her, Lillian and Sabina

In The four-chambered heart (1950), Djuna and the Guatemalan guitarist Rango become lovers and Djuna takes up residence on a houseboat in the Seine. Rango's supposedly invalid wife pretends to accept and even welcome the situation, but her feigning of illness and increasingly apparent insanity nearly wreck Djuna's life

In A spy in the house of love (1954), set in and around New York City, Sabina acts out relationships with her husband and lovers who include the opera singer Philip, the African drummer Mambo, and the painter Jay. She explores who longing for freedom and guilty feelings about the lies her many loves seem to make nec-

Nin, Anaïs, 1903-1977—*Continued*
essay

In Seduction of the Minotaur (1961; an expanded version of the Solar barque), Lillian seeks a liberating escape from her past in a Mexican town. Discovering that she is reenacting old relationships with her new acquaintances, she realizes she can transcend her past only by understanding rather than evading it and that her quest for freedom cannot take place apart from her husband, whose changelessness is a necessary complement to her own mutability

The four-chambered heart
In Nin, A. Cities of the interior p239-358

Ladders to fire
In Nin, A. Cities of the interior p1-127

Seduction of the Minotaur
In Nin, A. Cities of the interior p463-589

A spy in the house of love
In Nin, A. Cities of the interior p360-462

Nine hundred ninety nine. See 999: new stories of horror and suspense

Niven, Larry

The burning city; {by} Larry Niven & Jerry Pournelle. Pocket Bks. 2000 486p o.p.
ISBN 0-671-03660-2 LC 99-57479

"In a world where magic is dying and the gods are slowly becoming myth, Whandall Placehold passes from boyhood to manhood in a city beset by devastating Burnings. To save his family and his home from the ravages of the dying god Yangin-Atep, Whandall leaves his familiar surroundings and embarks on a journey of self-discovery that leads to a greater destiny. Set in the world first described in Niven's classic *The Magic Goes Away*, the latest effort by coauthors Niven and Pournelle blends the grim background of a post-apocalyptic world with the mystic intensity of a vision quest." Libr J

Lucifer's hammer; by Larry Niven & Jerry Pournelle. Playboy Press 1977 494p o.p.
LC 77-8074

"The hammer of the title is an eons-old comet that strikes earth with devastating physical and psychological consequences that are meticulously dramatized in the lives of dozens of major and minor characters. The second and more powerful part details the immense task of rebuilding civilization or preserving what remains of it. The authors excel in their suspenseful and thought-provoking hypothesis about the nature of civilized man and the ethics of survival when the future of their fragile community is at stake." Booklist

The Mote in God's Eye; by Larry Niven & Jerry Pournelle. Simon & Schuster 1974 537p o.p.

"Superior space opera in which Earth's interstellar navy contacts and does battle with an enormously hostile alien race. The scenes of space warfare are well handled, and the alien Moties are fascinating." Anatomy of Wonder 4

Followed by The gripping hand (1993)

Ringworld. Ballantine Bks. 1970 342p pa $6.99
ISBN 0-345-33392-6

"The Ringworld, a world shaped like a wheel so huge that it surrounds a sun, is almost too fantastic to conceive of. With a radius of 90 million miles and a length of 600 million miles, the Ringworld's mystery is compounded by the discovery that it is artificial. What phenomenal intelligence can be behind such a creation? Four unlikely explorers, two humans and two aliens, set out for the Ringworld, bound by mutual distrust and unsure of each other's motives." Shapiro. Fic for Youth. 3d edition

The Ringworld engineers. Holt & Co. 1980

"Twenty-three years after their original journey, Louis Wu and Speaker-to-Animals once more find themselves kidnapped companions of a mad Puppeteer who returns with them to Ringworld to steal a transmutation device. The Puppeteer encounters unexpected obstacles to this goal, however: Louis has become a wirehead addicted to the electric current fed almost constantly to his brain; Speaker-to-Animals is now a kzinti Patriarch and resents his enforced participation in the venture; the Ringworld has developed an unstable orbit and is about to desintegrate into its sun." SLJ

"This is a good example of the kind of novel where the basic idea—the Ringworld itself—is the true 'hero.'" Booklist

Followed by The Ringworld throne

The Ringworld throne. Ballantine Bks. 1996 424p o.p.
LC 95-47882

"A Del Rey book"

The third title in the author's Ringworld series "offers two stories crowded into one. A motley array of hominid inhabitants are seeking to defeat a plague of vampires. Meanwhile, returning hero Louis Wu is battling what effectively is a plague of Protectors . . . whose rivalries threaten Ringworld's existence. The battle against the vampires is the more exciting of the two stories, filled with action, scenes of the Ringworld and explorations of ritualistic interspecies sex. Wu's pursuit of the Protectors displays Niven's deft hand at portraying aliens." Publ Wkly

Ringworld's children; Larry Niven. 1st ed. TOR Bks. 2004 $24.95
ISBN 0-7653-0167-9 LC 2003-26581

In this fourth title in the series, "the Ringworld, an artificially engineered realm resembling a ribbon or ring that is home to over a trillion people of wildly different species, faces threats from outsider ships from the inhabited worlds and its own aging superstructure. Newly restored in mind and body, Louis Wu, a member of the first expedition to Ringworld, joins three individuals of different species to prevent the destruction of Ringworld." Libr J

"Action and clever world building should captivate newcomers to Ringworld, while returners will appreciate picking up loose ends from previous Ringworld volumes." Booklist

Saturn's race; [by] Larry Niven & Steven Barnes. TOR Bks. 2000 317p o.p.
ISBN 0-312-86726-3 LC 00-28646

"A Tom Doherty Associates book"

In this futuristic thriller a council led by Saturn, a virtual creation, "attempts to control population growth by

Niven, Larry—*Continued*

causing a whole generation of sterile women. Japanese American computer expert Chaz Kato is actually the grandfather of the young man who, thanks to massive surgery and medication, he appears to be. With his two lovers, American Lenore Myles and Indonesian Clarise Maibang, he discovers an increasingly bloody trail leading to the contraceptive conspiracy, which finally erupts in global war." Booklist

"Brilliantly weaving high-tech internets, augmentation technologies and social issues into a fast-paced cloak-and-dagger action adventure, this novel effortlessly moves from the depths of the ocean to the heights of VR to create a dazzling, seamless whole." Publ Wkly

Nolan, Christopher, 1965-

The banyan tree; a novel. Arcade Pub. 2000 374p $25.95

ISBN 1-559-70511-6 LC 99-76694

First published 1999 in the United Kingdom

The story "focuses on Minnie, who lives on her deceased husband's farm in the Irish countryside, waiting for her youngest son to return home to take it over. . . . The novel alternates between Minnie's present-day life, as she keeps the farm going with only a dog for company, and her memories of her youth; in particular, of Peter, a gentle, handsome man she first met when he came into her father's store. They married soon afterward, with only their mutual affection to guide them." N Y Times Book Rev

"Nolan, for all the Celtic emoting he accommodates here, remains clear-eyed; and there are no pat solutions or tidy conclusions to this tale that stays true to life while at the same time redeeming it through a love of language and a belief in its ability to forge lasting ties among people and things." Publ Wkly

Noon, Jeff

Vurt. Crown 1995 342p o.p.

LC 94-25544

First published 1993 in the United Kingdom

This novel of the future is set in Manchester "Vurt is a type of virtual reality (but without computers), and a kind of drug. You put a coloured feather in your mouth and you're in a dream-world—or a nightmare. Scribble is searching for [Desdemona,] his kid sister (and lover) who went into a Vurt world with him and never came back. He roams the backstreets with a gang of friends, trying to find a dealer who will supply him with a Curious Yellow feather, so he can go back to the same world to find her." New Statesman Soc

This "fluorescent and phantasmagorical novel . . . isn't quite the equal of Anthony Burgess's A Clockwork Orange, with which it is being compared, but in some ways it comes close. It's good enough in its first 50 or 60 pages of atmosphere setting, all smoke machines and flashing strobes, that the reader blinks, shakes his head and wonders whether Noon can sustain the weirdness." Time

Nooteboom, Cees, 1933-

All souls' day; translated from the Dutch by Susan Massotty. Harcourt 2001 338p $31

ISBN 0-15-100566-4 LC 2001-24310

Original Dutch editions, 1998

In this novel, set in Berlin, "protagonists Arthur and Elik are haunted by personal calamities. Arthur, philosophical and quiet, is a documentary filmmaker attempting to recover from the loss of his wife and child in a plane accident. Elik, impulsive and mysterious, is a graduate student who is still deeply troubled by a traumatic childhood incident." Libr J

"Not the least of the novel's satisfactions is the deftness with which Nooteboom incorporates signposts of Western high culture into his densely observant narrative." New Yorker

Nordan, Lewis

Wolf whistle; a novel. Algonquin Bks. 1993 290p o.p.

ISBN 1-56512-028-0 LC 93-1011

"The wolf whistle of the title comes from Bobo, a black teenager from Chicago visiting in Arrow Catcher, Mississippi. Directed at the wife of the town's most prominent white resident, this whistle soon leads to Bobo's murder. Based on the Emmett Till lynching, . . . [this novel] examines the intertwined fates of blacks and poor whites in the Mississippi delta." Libr J

"Propelled by Nordan's musical prose, much of this narrative soars above the commonplace into the realm of myth." Publ Wkly

Nordhoff, Charles, 1887-1947

Botany Bay; by Charles Nordhoff and James Norman Hall. Little, Brown 1941 374p o.p.

"The story of the Australian penal colony at Botany Bay, and especially of Hugh Tallant, an American, who had been stranded in England, turned highwayman, and was one of the first criminals shipped to Botany Bay, where life was bitterly hard and adventurous." Ont Libr Rev

The Bounty trilogy; by Charles Nordhoff and James Norman Hall; illustrated by N. C. Wyeth. Little, Brown 1982 691p il o.p.

"An Atlantic Monthly Press book"

A reissue of the combined volume first published 1936

Based on actual events stemming from a mutiny on a British war vessel in 1787, "this great trilogy begins with the story of the men who mutinied against the now famous Captain Bligh—'Mutiny on the Bounty.' In 'Men Against the Sea' Bligh and his supporters, set adrift in a small boat, made an incredible journey to safety. 'Pitcairn's Island' is the story of the mutineers who found refuge on a remote Pacific island." Books for you

Men against the sea; by Charles Nordhoff and James Norman Hall. Little, Brown 1934 251p o.p.

Sequel to Mutiny on the Bounty

This volume tells the story of Captain Bligh and the eighteen loyal men, who under his leadership sailed in an open boat thirty-six hundred miles from the Friendly Islands in the South Pacific to the Dutch colony of Timor in the East Indies. The story is told as if by Ledward, the surgeon, but the events, the wind and the weather of the narrative are those recorded in Captain Bligh's log

Followed by Pitcairn's Island

also in Nordhoff, C. and Hall, J. N. The Bounty trilogy

Nordhoff, Charles, 1887-1947—*Continued*

Mutiny on the Bounty; by Charles Nordhoff and James Norman Hall. Little, Brown 1932 396p o.p.
ISBN 0-316-61157-3

This narrative is "based on the famous mutiny that members of the crew of the 'Bounty', a British war vessel, carried out in 1787 against their cruel commander, Captain William Bligh. The authors kept the actual historical characters and background, using as narrator an elderly man, Captain Roger Byam, who had been a midshipman on the 'Bounty.' The story tells how the mate of the ship, Fletcher Christian, and a number of the crew rebel and set Captain Bligh adrift in an open boat with the loyal members of the crew." Reader's Ency. 4th edition

Followed by Men against the sea

also in Nordhoff, C. and Hall, J. N. The Bounty trilogy

Pitcairn's Island; by Charles Nordhoff and James Norman Hall. Little, Brown 1934 333p o.p.

Sequel to Men against the sea

"This final volume [of the trilogy] is the history of those mutineers who, with eighteen Polynesian men and women, reached Pitcairn's Island and there destroyed the 'Bounty.' Unvisited for eighteen years, the community fought over women and possession, and all but one of the men died violent deaths. A blood-curdling story, not for the squeamish reader." Booklist

also in Nordhoff, C. and Hall, J. N. The Bounty trilogy

Norman, Howard

The bird artist. Farrar, Straus & Giroux 1994 289p o.p.
LC 94-70542

"Fabian, son of Alaric and Orkney Vas, has spent his entire life in remote Witless Bay, Newfoundland. Looking back on his life, he decides that he has distinguished himself in only two ways: as a modestly successful artist whose illustrations graced the covers of *Bird Lore* magazine and as the murderer of the local lighthouse keeper, Botho August. The murder was the result of excessive coffee consumption combined with the stress brought on by his parents' plan to force him into an arranged marriage with a cousin he had never seen; this in turn would keep him from his hard-drinking girlfriend." Libr J

This work evokes "a way of life, a distinctive community and a fatalistic view of human behavior. The novel sings with tension and sparkles with antic humor." Publ Wkly

The haunting of L. Farrar, Straus & Giroux 2002 326p $24
ISBN 0-374-16825-3 LC 2001-51120

"In 1926, Peter Duvett meets and sleeps with Kala Murie on her wedding day in Churchill, an isolated village on the shores of the Hudson Bay. Kala's husband is Vienna Linn, the photographer Peter has come to assist. He has traveled from Halifax, escaping painful memories of his mother's suicide—or, as he is convinced, her murder. Soon Peter becomes the repository of the emotions and secrets of Kala and Vienna's hazardous partnership." Publ Wkly

"This is a mesmerizing melodrama rendered magical thanks to lyrical evocations of fog and storm, sexual bliss and fear, a conflation of atmospheric conditions and states of mind that makes of the human heart a realm as treacherous and exquisite as the Arctic." Booklist

The museum guard; a novel. Farrar, Straus & Giroux 1998 310p o.p.
ISBN 0-374-21649-5 LC 98-8413

"An orphan whose parents died in a dirigible crash when he was eight, DeFoe is raised in a Halifax hotel by his incorrigibly alcoholic and amorous Uncle Edward, a guard in the town's art museum. High-school dropout DeFoe becomes a guard there, too, and he goes stoically through his days caring for his perennially derelict and self-destructive uncle. DeFoe also tries to nourish his failing relationship with Imogen Linny, the caretaker at the Jewish cemetery, whose debilitating headaches have increased since she's become obsessed with a painting on loan to the museum." Publ Wkly

The author "fills this enigmatic novel with elements of fable and fairy tale blended with memorable characterizations and subtle narrative probings into the nature of self and the consequences of actions." Libr J

Norris, Benjamin Franklin *See* Norris, Frank, 1870-1902

Norris, Frank, 1870-1902

McTeague; a story of San Francisco; edited with an introduction by Kevin Starr. Penguin Books 1994 xlviii, 442p pa $10.95
ISBN 0-14-018769-3

First published 1899 by Doubleday

"A prime example of the American naturalistic novel, *McTeague* treats the gradual degeneration of a stupid, but initially harmless, giant of a man whose instincts are nearer brute than human. McTeague practices dentistry without a license in a poor section of San Francisco's Polk Street and marries Trina, who has just won $5,000 in a lottery. He soon loses his job and takes to drink. Trina becomes a miser, and McTeague murders her in a fit of rage and steals her money but is tracked down and killed by her cousin." Benet's Reader's Ency of Am Lit

also in Norris, F. Novels and essays

Novels and essays. Library of America 1986 1232p $40
ISBN 0-940450-40-2

Contents: Vandover and the brute; McTeague; The octopus; Essays

Vandover and the brute (1914) depicts the degeneration of a once affable and talented young man after he is afflicted with the psychological condition lycanthropy. McTeague and The octopus are entered separately.

The octopus; a story of California. Doubleday 1901 652p o.p.

First volume of an unfinished trilogy The epic of wheat

"The battle waged between the wheat growers and the railroad men in California is the theme of this novel. Concerned with social injustice, man's inhumanity to man, and the relentlessness of power struggles, Norris is able to combine these themes with a love interest." Shapiro. Fic for Youth. 3d edition

Followed by The pit

Norris, Frank, 1870-1902—*Continued*

also in Norris, F. Novels and essays

The pit; a story of Chicago. Doubleday 1903 o.p.

The second volume of the author's unfinished The epic of wheat trilogy "is a story of manipulations in the Chicago Exchange. Curtis Jadwin, a stock speculator, is so absorbed in making money that he neglects his emotionally starved wife Laura. Into this situation steps Sheldon Corthell, dilettante artist, to console her. Laura loves her husband, and postpones for awhile going away with the aesthete. Meanwhile, Jadwin engages in a struggle with the Crookes gang of speculators. He beats them, but is crushed by fluctuations in wheat production. He and Laura effect a reconciliation." Haydn. Thesaurus of Book Dig

Vandover and the brute

In Norris, F. Novels and essays

North, Andrew *See* Norton, Andre, 1912-2005

North, Anthony *See* Koontz, Dean R. (Dean Ray), 1945-

Norton, Alice Mary *See* Norton, Andre, 1912-2005

Norton, Andre, 1912-2005

Beast Master's ark; [by] Andre Norton and Lyn McConchie. TOR Bks. 2002 318p o.p.

ISBN 0-7653-0041-9 LC 2002-67249

Third volume in the author's Beast Master series begun with the Beast Master (1959) and Lord of Thunder (1962)

"A mysterious killer, referred to as 'Death-which-come-in-the-night' by the planet Arzor's indigenous inhabitants, threatens to eradicate sentient life on the desertlike world. Beast Master Storm Hosteen discovers that the only chance of saving his adopted home lies with a young woman name Tani, who has learned to deny her own Beast Master heritage." Libr J

The elvenbane; an epic high fantasy of the Halfblood chronicles; [by] Andre Norton, Mercedes Lackey. Doherty Assocs. 1991 390p (Halfblood chronicles) o.p.

LC 91-21177

"A TOR book"

"In a world ruled by some of the most brutal and tyrannical elves ever encountered, the most persecuted are the part-human, part-elven halfbloods. After her human mother is cast into the desert, [Shana] the bastard daughter of the powerful Lord Dyran survives and is raised by dragons to seek her destiny as the Elvenbane." Booklist

Followed by Elvenblood

Elvenblood; an epic high fantasy; [by] Andre Norton and Mercedes Lackey. Doherty Assocs. 1995 348p (Halfblood chronicles, bk2) o.p.

LC 95-5797

"A TOR book"

"Following rumors of the existence of a tribe of humans immune to the enslaving magics of the land's elven overlords, halfelven rebel Shana and her dragon companion encounter unexpected complications in their struggle for freedom. The talents of collaborators Norton and Lackey blend seamlessly as they expand the background to their epic fantasy to include an exotic desert culture, which provides a rich contrast to the stifling atmosphere of elven society." Libr J

Golden Trillium. Bantam Bks. 1993 296p (Trillium) o.p.

LC 92-43875

Third in the fantasy series that includes Black Trillium by Marion Zimmer Bradley, Julian May, and Andre Norton, and Blood Trillium by Julian May

"Having aided her sisters in establishing peace in the land of Ruwenda, the warrior-maiden Kadiya journeys through the swamps to return the Three-Orbed Sword to the place of its origin only to find that her fight against evil is not yet done. The grande dame of sf and fantasy returns to a favorite theme—the discovery of an ancient and highly advanced lost civilization—in this heroic adventure." Libr J

Redline the stars; [by] Andre Norton, P.M. Griffin. TOR Bks. 1993 304p o.p.

LC 92-43708

"A Tom Doherty Associates book"

The authors "recreate the flavor of Norton's four *Solar Queen* books . . . while updating some concepts and quite a bit of technology. The crew of the Free Trader vessel *Solar Queen*, flying under Capt. Miceál Jellico, has mixed reactions to new crewmate Rael Cofort, who is plying the space lanes as a jack-of-all-trades despite her position as a physician and status as sister of the successful rival Free Trader, Teague Cofort. Upon arriving at Canuche of Halio, the most advanced planet of the sector, the *Queen's* crew is endangered when Rael picks up the odor of man-eating rodents used in a gruesome gem-stealing scheme." Publ Wkly

(jt. auth) Bradley, M. Z. Black Trillium

The **Norton** book of science fiction; North American science fiction, 1960-1990; edited by Ursula K. Le Guin and Brian Attebery; Karen Joy Fowler, consultant. Norton 1993 869p o.p.

ISBN 0-393-03546-8 LC 93-16130

Damon Knight, Robert Silverberg, Connie Willis and Harlan Ellison are among the authors represented in this anthology of more than 60 stories

A "compilation of intelligent and entertaining sf that belongs in virtually every fiction collection." Booklist

Norway, Nevil Shute *See* Shute, Nevil, 1899-1960

Nothing but you; love stories from The New Yorker; edited by Roger Angell. Random House 1997 471p o.p.

ISBN 0-679-45701-1 LC 96-43079

Contents: The diver, by V. S. Pritchett; A country wedding, by L. Colwin; Blackbird pie, by R. Carver; The nice restaurant, by M. Gaitskill; Goodbye Marcus goodbye Rose, by J. Rhys; How to give the wrong impression, by K. Heiny; Marito in Cittá, by J. Cheever;

Nothing but you—*Continued*
The Jack Randa Hotel, by A. Munro; Hey, Joe, by B. Neihart; Here come the Maples, by J. Updike; Yours, by M. Robison; Roses, rhododendron, by A. Adams; Influenza, by D. Menaker; How old, how young, by J. O'Hara; Eyes of a blue dog, by G. Garcia Márquez; We, by M. Grimm; The dark stage, by D. Plante; Song of Roland, by J. Kincaid; The man in the moon, by W. Maxwell; The Kugelmass episode, by W. Allen; The Cinderella waltz, by A. Beattie; Experiment, by J. Barnes; Scarves, beads, sandals, by M. Gallant; Ten miles west of Venus, by J. Troy; The circle, by V. Nabokov; The Profumo affair, by E. Carroll; Elka and Meir, by I. B. Singer; Sculpture 1, by A. Patrinos; Dating your mom, by I. Frazier; The man with the dog, by R. P. Jhabvala; The plan, by E. O'Brien; Spring fugue, by H. Brodkey; In the gloaming, by A. E. Dark; Attraction, by D. Long; Ocean Avenue, by M. Chabon; Love life, by B. A. Mason; After rain, by W. Trevor; Overnight to many distant cities, by D. Barthelme

Novak, Joseph *See* Kosinski, Jerzy N., 1933-1991

Novakovich, Josip

April Fool's Day; a novel; by Josip Novakovich. HarperCollins Publishers 2004 226p map $23.95
ISBN 0-06-058397-5; 0-06-058398-3
LC 2003-67656

"Politics turn personal for Ivan Dolinar, born April 1, 1948, in Croatia, as the ricocheting course of his life reflects the tumult of his home country. His medical studies are cut short when he's imprisoned after a classmate jokes about assassinating Tito, who-along with Indira Gandhi-visits the labor camp and offers Ivan a Cuban cigar and a longer sentence. Released but barred from medicine, Ivan is drafted into the Yugoslav army just before the Croats organize their own defense force, putting him into an absurd and horrific war with his own countrymen. Finding his captain raping his former classmate Selma, Ivan rescues and later marries her, raising her daughter as his own. But marriage, fatherhood, hypochondria, and adultery fail to bring the peace Ivan finds in life after death." Booklist

"A heartfelt novel about the war-torn Balkans that's actually quite funny. . .and touching." GQ

Nunez, Elizabeth

Grace. Ballantine Bks. 2003 294p $23.95
ISBN 0-345-45533-9 LC 2002-26260

"Trinidad-born Justin Peters seemingly has it all: a beautiful, accomplished wife named Sally; a precocious four-year-old daughter; a fabulous brownstone in the hip Fort Greene section of Brooklyn; and a professorship at a public university. Everything is picture perfect until his mate blindsides him by confessing that she is unhappy and planning to move out, taking their child with her." Libr J

"This is a tender, graceful novel of personal amd material struggle that also explores the power of literature and poetry in everyday life." Booklist

Nye, Robert, 1939-

The late Mr. Shakespeare; a novel. Arcade Pub. 1999 398p $25.95
ISBN 1-55970-469-1 LC 98-50763

First published 1998 in the United Kingdom

The narrator of this novel is Pickleherring, "who at age thirteen was recruited into the theater by Mr. Shakespeare himself. The playwright was in need of a lad to play the little prince in King John. Pickleherring stayed with the company all the way to The Tempest. Now ancient, he is holed up in the attic of a London brothel and writing the life of his adored patron." Atl Mon

"Nye brilliantly weaves together almost all the known facts about Shakespeare, a great many of the spurious anecdotes which have been attached to his life, and a tissue of rare inventions of his own." Times Lit Suppl

O

Oates, Joyce Carol, 1938-

American appetites. Dutton 1989 340p o.p.
LC 88-18904

"A William Abrahams book"

"Ian McCullough, 50 years old, is editor of a prestigious journal and a research fellow. His wife, Glynnis, writes cookbooks. Their marriage is not perfect but far from unfulfilling. Then an incident from the past—Ian loaned money to a friend of Glynnis' for an abortion—resurfaces and provokes a horrible row between husband and wife. Glynnis ends up falling through a pane of glass and being killed." Booklist

"A zippy story about successful lives dramatically altered by one sudden and inexplicable lapse of judgment." Publ Wkly

Because it is bitter, and because it is my heart. Dutton 1990 405p o.p.
LC 89-25965

"A William Abrahams book"

This novel "is set in a small town in western New York from the early 1950s to the early 1960s, and follows the . . . fortunes of two families, one white (the Courtneys) and one black (the Fairchilds). When Jinx Fairchild, at 16, gets in a fight with a white kid who has menaced Iris Courtney, 14, and ends up killing him, the secret they share is . . . both a bond and a barrier between the two." Nation

"At its best, the novel awakens the reader to something like the unexpected new comprehensions of the universe that Iris experiences." N Y Rev Books

Bellefleur. Dutton 1980 558p o.p.
LC 79-28193

"A Henry Robbins book"

"In this Gothic novel, Oates weaves a shimmering tapestry made of odd and contradictory threads: a hermaphroditic birth, a vulture that devours an infant, a dwarf with 'powers,' a vampire, a cannibal, religious mystics and clairvoyants. Such are the Gothic trappings of this epic about the Bellefleurs, an old and powerful American family whose estate is located in the Adirondacks and whose history is an interpretation of American history from pioneer days to the present." Benet's Reader's Ency of Am Lit

Black water. Dutton 1992 154p o.p.
LC 91-40463

"A William Abrahams book"

"A 26-year-old woman drowns when a senator's car goes off a bridge; but the point of view in this . . . nov-

Oates, Joyce Carol, 1938-—*Continued*
el belongs to the victim." N Y Times Book Rev

"Those who remember Chappaquiddick can predict Kelly's ultimate fate, but certainly not the horrors she must have suffered strapped to the seat of a car that would become an aqueous death chamber. Immense courage shines through the tangled streams of her thoughts, memories, and hallucinations. As witnesses to her plight, we can only keep vigil as she drifts in and out of consciousness, waiting for the reprieve that surely must be hers. Oates brilliantly redefines the meanings of guilt and innocence, vengeance and reward in this thought-provoking allegory of our life and times." Libr J

Blonde. Ecco Press 2000 738p o.p.
ISBN 0-06-019607-6

"In a five-part narrative corresponding to the stages of [Marilyn] Monroe's life, Oates renders the squalid circumstances of Norma Jeane's upbringing: the damage inflicted by a psychotic mother and the absence of an unknown (and perpetually yearned for) father, and the desolation of four years in a orphanage and betrayal in a foster home. She reviews the young Monroe's rocky road to stardom, involving sexual favors to studio chiefs who thought her sluttish, untalented and stupid, while they reaped millions from her movies, she conveys the essence of Monroe's three marriages and . . . establishes Monroe's insatiable need for security and love." Publ Wkly

"Joyce Carol Oates takes the boldest path to comprehending 'the riddle, the curse of Monroe' by proceeding directly and frankly to fiction. Her novel 'Blonde' is fat, messy and fierce. It's part Gothic, part kaleidoscopic novel of ideas, part lurid celebrity potboiler, and it is seldom less than engrossing." N Y Times Book Rev

A Bloodsmoor romance. Dutton 1982 615p o.p.
LC 82-2416

The novel "details the bizarre goings-on in a 19th-century inventor's family. One daughter becomes a medium, another an actress and Mark Twain's mistress, a third runs away on her wedding night. Even Octavia, the perfect wife, is secretly subversive. . . . The narrator misunderstands and misinterprets much that happens; the reader, therefore, enters into collusion with the characters who use the period's conventions to subvert prescribed female roles." Libr J

Broke heart blues. Dutton 1999 369p $24.95
ISBN 0-525-94451-6 LC 98-51570

A novel "about bad-boy John Reddy Heart, who, in the little upstate New York town of Willowsville, was tried for murder and sent to a detention center. The murder, John Reddy's flight from justice, and his dramatic capture sent a tidal wave of publicity across not only the community but also the country. After he did his time, John Reddy came back to Willowsville, and because his family left town, he lived by himself while resuming his high school education. But he is now a legend, and his legend casts a shadow over the town for years to come." Booklist

Oates "dramatizes how wanting and memory compete. It's about how lonely, unhappy people mythologize their adolescence. . . . This is not a bashful or subtle book. It doesn't woo you so much as run you down." N Y Times Book Rev

The collector of hearts; new tales of the grotesque. Dutton 1998 321p o.p.
ISBN 0-525-94445-1 LC 98-17508

"A William Abrahams book"

Contents: The sky blue ball; Death mother; The hand-puppet; Schroeder's stepfather; The sepulchre; The hands; Labor Day; The collector of hearts; Demon; Elvis is dead: why are you alive?; Posthumous; The omen; The sons of Angus MacElster; The affliction; Scars; An urban paradox; Unprintable; Intensive; Valentine; Death astride bicycle; The dream-catcher; Fever blisters; The crossing; Shadows of the evening; The temple; The journey

Faithless; tales of transgression. Ecco Press 2001 386p o.p.
ISBN 0-06-018525-2 LC 00-60007

Contents: Au Sable; Ugly; Lover; Summer sweat; Questions; Physical; Gunlove; Faithless; The scarf; What then, my life?; Secret, silent; A Manhattan romance; Murder-two; The vigil; We were worried about you; The stalker; The vampire; Tusk; The high school sweetheart: a mystery; Deathwatch; In Copland

"As the subtitle suggests, the book's preoccupation is sin, but otherwise the stories are richly various. They range from quiet, intimate tales-such as the chilling opening effort, 'Au Sable,' about a man let in on a suicide he cannot prevent—to the satiric fantasia on TV journalism and police brutality that closes the volume." Publ Wkly

The falls; a novel; Joyce Carol Oates. Ecco 2004 481p $26.95
ISBN 0-06-072228-2 LC 2004-43310

"A man climbs over the railings and plunges into Niagara Falls. A newlywed, he has left behind his wife, Ariah Erskine, in the honeymoon suite the morning after their wedding. 'The Widow Bride of the Falls,' as Ariah comes to be known, begins a restless, seven-day vigil in the mist, waiting for his body to be found. At her side throughout, confirmed bachelor and pillar of the community Dirk Burnaby is unexpectedly transfixed by the strange, otherworldly gaze of this plain, strange woman." Publisher's note

"Set around Niagara, the story reflects all the romance, mystery, and terror of that spectacular waterfall. It's a great confluence of tones-grotesque and domestic, tragic and comic. The currents of various styles and points of view blend together in a way that can't possibly work, but does." Christ Sci Monit

Foxfire; confessions of a girl gang. Dutton 1993 328p o.p.
LC 92-43858

"The leader of Foxfire, a flamboyant girl gang, is Legs Sadovsky, a tall, angular blond with enough attitude to turn her upstate New York hometown on its ear. It's 1955 and Legs, Lana, Rita, Goldie, and Maddy, the gentle narrator, are almost 16 and most certainly not sweet. These gals live on the wrong side of the tracks; their parents are deceased or alcoholic, their home lives depressing and loveless. They form Foxfire for the same reason kids always form gangs: for mutual support and protection, to demand respect, and acquire power." Booklist

"Legs Sadovsky is a brilliant creation—wholly heroic, wholly convincing, racing for her tragic consummation impelled by a finer sensibility and a more thoughtful dar-

Oates, Joyce Carol, 1938-—*Continued*
ing than is usually granted to the tragic male outlaws we love and need. . . . 'Foxfire' burns brightly; it is completely assured and occasionally exhilarating." N Y Times Book Rev

A garden of earthly delights. Vanguard Press 1967 440p o.p.

The book describes the early life of Clara Walpole, the daughter of a migrant farm worker; her life after she leaves her father; her romance with a rum-runner; and her marriage to a rich man, whom she convinces is the father of her illegitimate baby. The final part of the novel deals with the childhood and adolescence of Swan, the son

"The book has much to say of society's indifference to the plight of the disadvantaged, and of the shallowness of a way of life based entirely on getting and spending." Libr J

Haunted; tales of the grotesque. Dutton 1994 310p o.p.

LC 93-25223

"A William Abrahams book"

Contents: Haunted; The doll; The bingo master; The white cat; The model [novella]; Extenuating circumstances; Don't you trust me?; The guilty party; The premonition; Phase change; Poor Bibi; Thanksgiving; Blind; The radio astronomer; Accursed inhabitants of the House of Bly; Martyrdom

"All the pieces here have a redeeming literary bent, although some are transparent in their motives. Undoubtedly a master of this form, Oates plies her craft like a skilled seducer, setting the mood and moving in for the conquest night after night after night." Publ Wkly

Heat, and other stories. Dutton 1991 397p o.p.

LC 91-8007

"A William Abrahams book"

Contents: House hunting; The knife; The hair; Shopping; The boyfriend; Passion; Morning; Naked; Heat; The buck; Yarrow; Sundays in summer; Leila Lee; The swimmers; Getting to know all about you; Capital punishment; Hostage; Craps; Death valley; White trash; Twins; The crying baby; Why don't you come live with me it's time; Ladies and gentlemen; Family

I am no one you know; stories. Ecco 2004 290p $24.95

ISBN 0-06-059288-5 LC 2003-61283

Contents: Curly Red; In hiding;I'm not your son, I am no one you know; Abiding and abetting; Fugitive; Me & Wolfie, 1979; The girl with the blackened eye; Cumberland breakdown; Upholstery; Wolf's Head Lake; Happiness; Fire; The instructor; The skull: a love story; The deaths: an elegy; Jorie (& Jamie): a deposition; Mrs. Halifax and Rickie Swann: a ballad; Three girls; The mutants

"Oates is vitally concerned, even obsessed, with the most primal and disturbing encounters between females and males, and her new searing short stories explore the malevolent aspects of human sexuality with unflinching authenticity and a cathartic fascination." Booklist

I lock my door upon myself. Ecco Press 1990 98p o.p.

LC 90-31878

"In turn-of-the-century rural America, willful and elusive Calla, muzzled by an enforced marriage, church, and kin she no longer cares about, chooses a life of inertia and indifference until the arrival of roving black water dowser Tyrell Thompson." Libr J

Is this "all a parable of the artist's position as an observer and interpreter of society? Is it an illustration of how a writer constructs a coherent story out of disjointed events? Either way, it provokes thought." Atlantic

Marriages and infidelities; short stories. Vanguard Press 1972 497p o.p.

Contents: The sacred marriage; Puzzle; Love and death; 29 inventions; Problems of adjustment in survivors of natural/unnatural disasters; By the river; Extraordinary popular delusions; Stalking; Scenes of passion and despair; Plot; The children; Happy onion; Normal love; Stray children; Wednesday's child; Loving, losing, loving a man; Did you ever slip on red blood?; The metamorphosis; Where I lived, and what I lived for; The lady with the pet dog; The spiral; The turn of the screw; The dead; Nightmusic

Marya; a life. Dutton 1986 310p o.p.

LC 85-16283

"A William Abrahams book"

In this novel, which begins in "a mining town near the Erie Canal, eight-year-old Marya Knauer's father is bludgeoned to death. Her mother walks away from Marya and her infant brothers. Raised by her uncle's family, and sexually abused by her cousin, Marya develops a shell: she's quick-witted, sarcastic and . . . friendless because she's so hard, so bright. She discovers that her reputation for brillance serves as 'a sort of glass barrier that would keep other people at a distance.' Driven by work, Marya presses through graduate school, becomes a tenured professor at a college much like Dartmouth, then quits to become a lioness in the New York literary world." Newsweek

"Marya's development and her innermost fears and insecurities are revealed in a very personal, almost autobiographical manner. A major work by an important writer." Libr J

Middle age; a romance. Ecco Press 2001 464p o.p.

ISBN 0-06-620946-3 LC 2001-23062

"Adam Berendt, an eccentric sculptor, goes sailing on the Hudson River one Fourth of July. A nearby boat capsizes, and Adam leaps in to save a drowning child. He gets to her in time, but is struck by a heart attack as he holds her afloat, and dies. Adam's death is the engendering mistake, the accidental firecracker that sets off the rest of the book. In 'Middle Age,' the people affected are those left behind: Adam Berendt's neighbors in Salthill-on-Hudson." N Y Times Book Rev

"So often dark and malicious, Oates is oddly lighthearted in this gawky but mordant novel about people caught in that awkward transitional stage between youth and old age." Christ Sci Monit

Missing mom. Ecco 2005 434p $25.95

ISBN 0-06-081621-X LC 2005-40002

Oates, Joyce Carol, 1938-—*Continued*

"Nicole, 31, is living an extended adolescence, still in rebellion against her parents' suburban middle-class, do-the-right-thing lifestyle. Her father has recently died; her older, domestic diva sister is prone to histrionics. Nicole herself is involved with a married man and does not have a clue how her actions may impact other people. Everything changes in an instant when Nicole's mother, Gwen, dies in a violent assault. After the ensuing investigations and memorials, everyone is surprised when Nicole steps into her mother's shoes and gradually begins to adopt aspects of Gwen's personality. Within this transformative process, hidden details of Gwen's life come to light." Libr J

"Oates's grip on crime, violence and the long-buried is sure, but Missing Mom is actually more disturbing in its relentless, dead-on accretion of small-time, small-town, middle-class details. Oates piles them on with pitiless virtuosity." N Y Times Book Rev

The model
In Oates, J. C. Haunted p99-144

My heart laid bare. Dutton 1998 531p $26.95
ISBN 0-525-94442-7 LC 98-10531
"A William Abrahams book"

"Upstate New York is the setting for this historical yarn, which centers on the dark life of one Abraham Licht. Little is known of this stranger who came to town—the community of Muirkirk in the Chautauqua Valley—in the last decade of the nineteenth century and bought the abandoned property belonging to the Church of the Nazarene. Cult leader? Preacher? What the locals do not know is that he is a devious man who prods his children to follow his dishonest behavior; in the case of one son, this leads to murder." Booklist

It is "impossible to resist the pull of Oates's lush narrative. Abraham Licht is unforgettable. As chief orchestrator of a family's misbehaviors, he becomes the quintessential silver fox, a rogue to remember." Publ Wkly

(ed) The Oxford book of American short stories. See The Oxford book of American short stories

Rape; a love story. Carroll & Graf 2004 154p $16
ISBN 0-7867-1294-5

A novel "about the nearly fatal beating and gang rape of Teena MacGuire on the Fourth of July in the small town of Niagara Falls. Teena and her 12-year-old daughter, Bethel, are walking home from a party when the vicious attack takes place, and Bethel only narrowly escapes her mother's terrible fate. Terrorized but valiant, Bethel identifies their assailants and is determined to testify, but the townspeople close ranks behind the indicted brutes, their sons and brothers, and Teena is assaulted all over again in court. But there is one man on the case who possesses a clear and unshakable sense of justice, and his empathic connection with Bethel is at the heart of this lean and potent tale." Booklist

Solstice. Dutton 1985 243p o.p.
LC 84-18710
"A William Abrahams book"

This novel "concerns recently divorced Monica Jensen, who takes a job teaching at a private boys' school in Pennsylvania. She is determined to throw herself into her work and to do the best she can, but she doesn't reckon on becoming acquainted with the local famous artist, one Shelia Trask, an ironically distant but absorbing personality, a disturbing presence and a dominating force. Their new friendship quickly intensifies, then breaks off, and Monica tries to believe it is for the best, that she's back in full control of her life. That does not last long, though; the friendship blossoms again, and this time their parasitical relationship is finally ruinous." Booklist

"*Solstice* goes well beyond technique; as an investigation of friendship and art it is provocative, relentless and splendid." Publ Wkly

The tattooed girl; a novel. Ecco Press 2003 307p $25.95
ISBN 0-06-053106-1 LC 2002-192736

"When a reclusive, 38-year-old writer hires a near-illiterate young woman as an assistant at his suburban home in Carmel Heights, near Rochester, N. Y., he's unaware that a vehement anti-Semitism seethes beneath her tattoo-branded exterior. Renowned for The Shadows—his great early success, a novel based on his grandparents' experiences in Germany during the Holocaust—Joshua Seigl confuses his friends and sparks the anger of his hypomaniac sister, Jet, when despite their objections he refuses to fire the young woman." Publ Wkly

"Seigl's failure to cut it as a likable man is perhaps unintentional irony. His failure to understand his assistant, on the other hand, is marvelously controlled satire. All the time he is patronizing her she is hating him, yet he just cannot see it. Oates's portrayal of the employer-employee relationship is wonderfully smart and subtle." N Y Times Book Rev

Them; introduction by Greg Johnson; afterword by the author. 2000 Modern Library ed. Modern Lib. 2000 xxiv, 546p $21.95
ISBN 0-679-64025-8 LC 99-54471

A reissue of the title first published 1969 by Vanguard Press

"Violent and explosive in both incident and tone, the work is set in urban Detroit from 1937 to 1967 and chronicles the efforts of the Wendell family to break away from their destructive, crime-ridden background. Critics praised the novel for its detailed social observation and its bitter indictment of American society." Merriam-Webster's Ency of Lit

We were the Mulvaneys. Dutton 1996 454p o.p.
LC 96-17267
"A William Abrahams book"

An upstate New York "family, loving parents and four children, are destroyed when one daughter is raped by a high-school classmate. Wealthy, churchgoing and optimistic in their hubristic heyday, the Mulvaneys are not prepared for the psychological dysfunction that follows the act of violence." Publ Wkly

"Oates has written an uncharacteristically cathartic book with a provocatively happy ending. . . . Oates eloquently employs daily details, cataloguing Corinne's antiques, mapping Patrick's Ithaca jogging route, calculating the number of paint gallons required to spruce up High Point Farm. She is a vivid storyteller, and the occupations, names and places are rich in allusive imagery. . . . Oates is fascinated by the markings of kinship. Particularly impressive is her shaping of siblings' passions, allegiances and resentments." Nation

Oates, Joyce Carol, 1938-—*Continued*

What I lived for. Dutton 1994 608p o.p.
LC 94-549

"A William Abrahams book"

This "novel is set in Union City, a fictional place on the New York shores of Lake Erie, something like Buffalo. It tells the story of Jerome (Corky) Corcoran, a two-bit politician and businessman. Though the book opens with the murder of Corky's father in 1959, the bulk of the action takes place over one long weekend in 1992. A lost weekend, it begins when Corky learns that his lover, Christina Kavanaugh, has been conducting their affair with the permission of her crippled husband, a discovery that shatters Corky's ego and sets him ricocheting all over the city, from one reversal to another, following a zigzag course through layers of social class, racial division, political machination and economic distress." N Y Times Book Rev

Where are you going, where have you been?; selected early stories. Ontario Review Press 1993 522p o.p.
LC 92-44899

Contents: Edge of the world; The fine white mist of winter; First views of the enemy; At the seminary; What death with love should have to do; Upon the sweeping flood; In the region of ice; Where are you going, where have you been?; Unmailed, unwritten letters; Accomplished desires; How I contemplated the world from the Detroit House of Correction and began my life over again; Four summers; Love and death; By the river; Did you ever slip on red blood?; The lady with the pet dog; The turn of the screw; The dead; Concerning the case of Bobby T.; In the warehouse; Small avalanches; The widows; The translation; Bloodstains; Daisy; The molesters; Silkie

Where is here?; stories. Ecco Press 1992 193p o.p.
LC 92-3634

Contents: Lethal; Area man found crucified; Imperial presidency; Bare legs; Turquoise; Biopsy; The date; Angry; The ice pick; The mother; Sweet!; Forgive me!; Transfigured night; Actress; The false mirror; From the life of. . .; The heir; "Shot"; Letter, lover; My madman; Cuckold; The escape; Murder; Insomnia; Love, forever; Old dog; The artist; The wig; The maker of parables; Embrace; Beauty salon; Abandoned; Running; Pain; Where is here?

Will you always love me? and other stories. Dutton 1996 326p o.p.
LC 94-43865

"A William Abrahams book"

Contents: Act of solitude; You petted me, and I followed you home; Good to know you; The revenge of the foot, 1970; Politics; The missing person; Will you always love me?; Life after high school; The goose-girl; American, abroad; The track; The handclasp; The girl who was to die; June birthing; The undesirable table; Is laughter contagious?; The brothers; The lost child; Christmas night 1962; The passion of Rydcie Mather; The vision; Mark of Satan

"Joyce Carol Oates's readers have come to expect from her a sensationalistic terrain of accident, suicide, rape, murder and madness, all of which are well represented in this collection, which includes none of the small, too-precious moments that can vitiate the short story." N Y Times Book Rev

Obradovi´c, Nadežda

(ed) Looking for a rain god: an anthology of contemporary African short stories. See Looking for a rain god: an anthology of contemporary African short stories

O'Brian, Patrick

Blue at the mizzen. Norton 1999 261p il $24
ISBN 0-393-04844-6 LC 99-42043

"With Bonaparte finally through troubling the nations of Europe, Jack Aubrey and Stephen Maturin . . . are on a hydrographic and diplomatic journey to Chile. There Aubrey's crew aboard H.M.S. Surprise lends its support to the Chilean independence movement and the forces of Bernardo O'Higgins." New Yorker

"There is nothing in this century that rivals Patrick O'Brian's achievement in his chosen genre. His novels embrace with loving clarity the full richness of the 18th-century world." N Y Times Book Rev

The commodore. Norton 1995 281p $22.50
ISBN 0-393-03760-6 LC 95-2653

First published 1994 in the United Kingdom

Another "novel in O'Brian's series following Captain (now Commodore) Jack Aubrey and his surgeon friend, Stephen Maturin, through the naval side of the Napoleonic Wars. Although O'Brian is ingenious at devising new adventures, it is the richness of his characters which justifies his readers' continuing enthusiasm. The most arresting moments in this installment come not in battle but in dramas of parenthood and marriage far from the sea. O'Brian acknowledges Jane Austen as one of his inspirations, and she need not be ashamed of the affiliation." New Yorker

The golden ocean; a novel. Day, J. 1957 c1956 316p il o.p.

First published 1956 in the United Kingdom

"This novel is based on the exploits of Commodore George Anson, who set out in 1740 with five men-of-war to circle the globe and returned four years later with one ship and a small but very wealthy crew. The expedition is seen through the eyes of Peter Palafox, a young midshipman who blossoms into an able-bodied seaman. . . . As always, the author's erudition and humor are on display. . . . The attention to period speech and detail is uncompromising, and while the cascades of nautical lore can be dizzying, both aficionados and newcomers will be swept up by the richness of Mr. O'Brian's prodigious imagination." N Y Times Book Rev

The hundred days. Norton 1998 280p $24
ISBN 0-393-04674-5 LC 98-35866

"The title refers to Napoleon's escape from Elba and brief return to power. Capt. Jack Aubrey must stop a Moorish galley, loaded with gold for Napoleon's mercenaries, from making its delivery. . . . We're quickly reacquainted with the two heroes: handsome sea dog Jack Aubrey, by now a national hero, and Dr. Stephen Maturin, Basque-Irish ship's doctor, naturalist, English spy and hopelessly incompetent seaman." Publ Wkly

O'Brian, Patrick—*Continued*

"Battles there are aplenty, and O'Brian matches Forester in the excitement, detail and bloody realism of his reconstructions. But these naval tales are blended into a larger panorama of Georgian society and politics, science, medicine, botany and the whole conspectus of contemporary Enlightenment knowledge about the natural world." N Y Times Book Rev

The unknown shore. Norton 1995 313p $23

ISBN 0-393-03859-9 LC 95-32887

First published 1959 in the United Kingdom

"Based on British Commodore Anson's 1740 circumnavigation of the world . . . this is the story of HMS *Wager,* a ship separated from Anson's squadron while sailing around Cape Horn. The *Wager* is shipwrecked off Patagonia, and the largest part of the narrative details the hardships of the diminishing band of survivors on that inhospitable shore. . . . Though this novel isn't quite as polished or stylish as the author's later work, it's a most honorable ancestor." Publ Wkly

The wine-dark sea. Norton 1993 261p $22.50

ISBN 0-393-03558-1 LC 93-1521

One of a series of novels set during the Napoleonic Wars and featuring Jack Aubrey, a "Royal Navy captain, and his friend Stephen Maturin, who sails with him as ship's surgeon and undercover intelligence agent. . . . On this occasion, duty takes them to the South Pacific. Here, Aubrey is to harry enemy shipping and—the true purpose of the voyage—to land Maturin in Peru to foment the independence movement against Spain." Times Lit Suppl

"The naval actions are bang-on and bang-up—fast, furious and bloody—and the Andean milieu is as vivid as the shipboard scenes." Publ Wkly

The yellow admiral. Norton 1996 261p $24

ISBN 0-393-04044-5 LC 96-24149

"As their careers have advanced and their children have grown, Captain Jack Aubrey and Stephen Maturin have battered Napoleon's ships and thwarted his spies, but here, at last, the Emperor is Elba-bound, and our heroes are left high and dry. Aubrey, ashore at half pay and with scant hope of promotion, prays that peace may not last long—a sentiment doubtless shared by O'Brian's readers. Still, Elba is not St. Helena, so war will surely return, if only for a short finale." New Yorker

O'Brien, Dan, 1947-

The contract surgeon; a novel. Lyons Press 1999 316p $24.95

ISBN 1-55821-932-3 LC 99-35243

This novel is "based on the true story of the unusual friendship between Crazy Horse and Dr. Valentine McGillicuddy, a civilian surgeon contracted to serve with the army during the Indian wars on the Great Plains. McGillicuddy relates the tale as an old man. . . . He faces his greatest moral test when Crazy Horse is bayoneted in the back by a soldier, and McGillicuddy is pressured by the army to keep the famous warrior alive, because his death would spur on the Indians to renewed battle. . . . This powerful story is a thinking man's western, in which action is secondary to O'Brien's nuanced exploration of character and the tragic dimensions of a morally fraught conflict." Publ Wkly

O'Brien, Edna

The country girls

In O'Brien, E. The country girls trilogy and epilogue p3-175

The country girls trilogy and epilogue. Farrar, Straus & Giroux 1986 531p o.p.

LC 85-32113

Omnibus edition of three titles originally published separately in 1960, 1962 and 1964 respectively, with an epilogue added by the author

Contents: The country girls (c1960); The lonely girl (c1962) [variant title: Girl with the green eyes (1964)]; Girls in their married bliss (c1964; first United States edition 1968)

The country girls portrays two friends, Kate and Baba, growing up in Ireland. They are sent to a convent school they despise and they contrive to get expelled and move to Dublin. In The lonely girl, Kate, now 21, becomes involved first with an older married man, then with a filmmaker. Eugene encourages and pampers her, but she is unresponsive. The relationship disintegrates and she moves to London. In Girls in their married bliss, Kate has married Eugene and has a son, but the marriage is destroyed when Eugene's indifference pushes Kate into a love affair. Meanwhile, Baba settles into marriage and financial security with an architect, and pulls through the crisis of a pregnancy brought on by a one-night stand. The Epilogue contains Baba's reflections, twenty years later

"O'Brien's particular appeal is that she can be tender yet merciless, romantic yet grittily sexual. She resides admirably where quality and popular writing intersect." Booklist

Down by the river. Farrar, Straus & Giroux 1997 265p $23

ISBN 0-374-14327-7 LC 96-39251

First published 1996 in the United Kingdom

"Adolescent Mary MacNamara lives in rural Ireland with her mother and father. She finally escapes her father's sexual abusiveness by going away to a convent school, but she must return home shortly thereafter when her mother dies. Mary feels unable to share her predicament with people who might help, although the hope that someone will guess lingers with her. Soon, she finds herself pregnant, but even then, she can't find the voice to speak about the true circumstances of the conception. She runs away, and in the process, her problem escalates to the point where governmental figures get involved." Booklist

"It's not issues that obsess O'Brien, it's people—the feckless girl and her monster of a father. With a devouring eye for detail, right down to the fly trapped in the mother's coffin, she makes their nightmare unforgettably palpable." Newsweek

A fanatic heart; selected stories of Edna O'Brien. Farrar, Straus & Giroux 1984 461p o.p.

LC 84-13762

Contents: The Connor girls; My mother's mother; Tough men; The doll; The bachelor; Savages; Courtship; Ghosts; Sister Imelda; The love object; The mouth of the cave; Irish revel; The rug; Paradise; A scandalous woman; Over; The creature; The house of my dreams; Number 10; Baby blue; The small-town lovers; Christmas ros-

O'Brien, Edna—*Continued*

es; Ways; A rose in the heart of New York; Mrs. Reinhardt; Violets; The call; The plan; The return

"Each story is superbly written and, despite the overall seriousness, graced by humor." Publ Wkly

Girls in their married bliss

In O'Brien, E. The country girls trilogy and epilogue p381-508

House of splendid isolation. Farrar, Straus & Giroux 1994 232p $21

ISBN 0-374-17309-5 LC 93-42602

"The story centers on a tormented encounter between young IRA fugitive/killer McGreevy and his hostage—rich, reclusive, middle-aged Josie O'Meara. Both have been widowed by the protracted 'troubles.' Josie, a former barmaid, who once did a stint as a domestic in Brooklyn, reminisces before and during her 'captivity' on her advantageous but flawed marriage." Publ Wkly

The author "manages to sum up a century of Irish sorrow in this taut, lyrical novel, filled with scenes so vividly rendered they seem captured in a flash of lightning. Not the least of O'Brien's accomplishments is her ability to present both sides of the Irish problem in all their complexity without settling heavily on either side." Libr J

In the forest. Houghton Mifflin 2002 262p $24

ISBN 0-618-19730-3 LC 2001-51883

From an early age, Michen O'Kane "displays spontaneous unsociability, for which he is punished with unremitting cruelty, first by his wife-beating father, then by the villagers of Cloosh, his small Irish village, and then by the Irish juvenile detention system, where he is sodomized and psychologically tortured. O'Kane comes back to Cloosh a ticking bomb, hearing voices in his head. After he sets up a camp in the woods, he sets his sights on a relative stranger in the village, a free spirit named Eily Ryan who, with her son, Maddie, is living a modern, single mother's lifestyle obscurely disapproved of by the conservative villagers. One morning O'Kane kidnaps her and the boy. She's forced to drive O'Kane to his woods, passing through the village in full view of several frightened bystanders, who do nothing to help her. After murdering his two victims, O'Kane kidnaps a priest and repeats the act." Publ Wkly

A novel about "how a community can be collectively paralyzed by fear. The result is a brilliant illumination of human nature." Booklist

Lantern slides; stories. Farrar, Straus & Giroux 1990 223p o.p.

LC 90-33594

Contents: "Oft in the stilly night"; Brother; The widow; Epitaph; What a sky; Storm; Another time; A demon; Dramas; Long distance; A little holiday; Lantern slides

"O'Brien's short stories expand on the anguish and brutality endemic to modern Irish lives, and her characters have more than their own secret problems to brood and moon about. . . . O'Brien mines her home territory to splendid effect with her glinting looks at what the Irish have made of their struggle and what Ireland has made of their unhappy lives." Booklist

The lonely girl

In O'Brien, E. The country girls trilogy and epilogue p179-377

Time and tide. Farrar, Straus & Giroux 1992 325p o.p.

LC 92-3962

"Nell is a devoted young wife, but she is also a rebel against tyranny, be it from husband or parents. Inevitably, her two sons, Paddy and Tristan, become pawns in the lengthy . . . battle that her separation from her husband involves. Nell adores her sons, yet at the same time she is . . . searching for love and adventure. Her restlessness, her dabbling with drugs and bohemia, take her to the brink and back, but not before she has lost house and home." Publisher's note

This novel is O'Brien's "harshest yet most beautiful work. She has a touchy, rich theme: the sexuality of the bond between mothers and sons. . . . O'Brien brings together the earthy and the delicately poetic: she has the soul of Molly Bloom and the skills of Virginia Woolf." Newsweek

Wild Decembers. Houghton Mifflin 2000 259p $24

ISBN 0-618-04567-8 LC 99-56110

First published 1999 in the United Kingdom

This novel is set in "the tiny western Irish village of Cloontha. . . . Michael Bugler has arrived fresh from a sheep farm in Australia to claim the land left to him by a deceased uncle, and the newcomer's presence stirs up the villagers. Especially agitated is Joseph Brennan, whose ancestral farm borders Bugler's property. . . . Relations between the two men skid into a series of affronts, real or perceived, while Breege, Brennan's younger sister, looks on with mounting dread." Time

"The novel is a dirge that keens and lulls by turns. The entrancing rhythms and refrains, the density and chant-like, drumming fragmentation work on the reader like magic. . . . O'Brien combines this lyricism with a masterly storytelling instinct, so that [the novel] reads at once like an intricate poem and a taut, suspenseful page-turner." Commonweal

O'Brien, Tim, 1946-

Going after Cacciato; a novel. Delacorte Press 1978 338p o.p.

LC 77-11723

"Paul Berlin's squad is sent to retrieve Cacciato, a young deserter from the Vietnam War. Fantasy colors the progress of the squad as a dream of peace and the possibility of forsaking war follow them through many adventures. The horror and destruction of war is vividly conveyed and the language is rough, as would be expected. Cacciato becomes a kind of symbol for resisting bureaucratic militarism and an enviable model for Berlin himself." Shapiro. Fic for Youth. 3d edition

In the Lake of the Woods. Houghton Mifflin 1994 306p o.p.

LC 94-5395

The protagonist of this novel "is a politician whose promising career has been destroyed by the revelation of his misconduct in Vietnam. His wife, well aware that Vietnam torments his dreams, had known nothing of the [My Lai] murder and massacre underlying the nightmares. The husband is equally ignorant of her opinions on several important matters. When the two retreat to a cabin in the wilds of Minnesota to recover from the shock of a disastrous election, their partnership ex-

O'Brien, Tim, 1946-—*Continued*

plodes." Atl Mon

"What O'Brien really offers is a portrait of one man and woman at the most critical juncture of their relationship. It's a dark portrait, taking issue with a stock notion of commercial fiction: that after suffering comes redemption. Maybe not. Maybe there's only oblivion. A beautifully written, haunting novel that evokes lives in deep crisis." Booklist

July, July. Houghton Mifflin 2002 322p $26
ISBN 0-618-03969-4 LC 2002-32232

"It's July 2000 and members of the Darton Hall College class of 1969 are gathered, one year behind schedule, for their 30th reunion. Focusing on sharply drawn characters and life's pivotal moments rather than on a strong linear plot, O'Brien follows the ensemble cast (which includes a Vietnam vet, a draft dodger, a minister, a bigamous housewife and a manufacturer of mops) for whom 'the world had whittled itself down to now or never,' as they drink, flirt and reminisce. Interspersed are tales of other Julys, when each character experienced something that changed him forever." Publ Wkly

The things they carried; a work of fiction. Houghton Mifflin 1990 273p o.p.
LC 89-39871

This is a collection of stories about American soldiers in Vietnam. . . . All of the stories "deal with a single platoon, one of whose members is a character named Tim O'Brien." N Y Times Book Rev

"This book may be self-conscious . . . but through its determination to treat these men with dignity and decency it proves immensely affecting." Newsweek

Tomcat in love. Broadway Bks. 1998 347p $26
ISBN 0-7679-0202-5 LC 98-29846

"Thomas H. Chippering, occupying the Rolvaag Chair in Modern American Lexicology at the University of Minnesota, has lost his wife to an oily Tampa tycoon. The loquacious Abe Lincoln look-alike and Vietnam hero can't imagine why, but it may have something to do with her discovery of the Torah-size ledger he keeps for recording the pertinent details (including city of origin) of every woman he dallies with. Vulnerable to 'well-sculpted enrollees' and obsessed with language, betrayal, and revenge, Tom is a baby-boomer Humbert Humbert, unencumbered by gravitas." New Yorker

O'Connell, Carol

Crime school. Putnam 2002 352p o.p.
ISBN 0-399-14928-7 LC 2002-22860

Detective Kathy Mallory, "of the Special Crimes Unit, comes face to face with her past when she and her partner are called to a crime scene in which a call girl has been ritualistically murdered. The call girl, Sparrow, offered Mallory protection when she was a child but later betrayed her. Before Mallory has time to call up her knowledge of Sparrow's past in finding the killer, she and her partner are thrown into a morass of spree killings on the streets of New York. O'Connell's crime-scene investigations techniques ring true, her plotting is breathtaking, and her psychology acute. Searing suspense." Booklist

Judas child. Putnam 1998 340p $24.95
ISBN 0-399-14380-7 LC 97-46504

"When two remarkable fifth-grade girls—Gwen Hubble, the beautiful daughter of the lieutenant governor, and Sadie Green, an imaginative and plucky child obsessed with horror comics and movies—are kidnapped from the St. Ursula's Academy, two adults afflicted by their own tragedies are drawn into the investigation. Forensic psychologist Ali Cray draws stares both for her slit skirts and for a disfiguring facial scar, the result of a secret childhood trauma. Policeman Rouge Kendall is haunted by the memory of his twin sister's murder 15 years earlier. The killer was supposedly caught, but similarities between the old murder and the current case make Cray begin to doubt." Publ Wkly

"O'Connell thoughtfully tackles material that in other hands would be merely sensational. Dark in tone, gripping suspense, and tempered with the hope of redemption, this is highly recommended." Libr J

Killing critics. Putnam 1996 308p o.p.
LC 95-43894

"NYPD detective Kathleen Mallory revisits a 12-year-old double murder case first investigated by her beloved adoptive father. . . . The murder of a second-rate performance artist in mid-performance has many associations to the earlier, grisly and still unsolved homicides, which also touched the art world." Publ Wkly

"As mesmerizing as the murder case is, it's heartless, soulless Mallory herself—computer genius, street fighter, provocative waif, peerless investigator, manipulative beauty—who's absolutely the star of this brilliant thriller." Booklist

Mallory's oracle. Putnam 1994 286p o.p.
LC 94-2234

"The investigation of a series of murders of wealthy, elderly women from the Gramercy Park area intensifies when Louis Markowitz, the head of the NYPD Special Crimes Section, is found dead with the third victim. Kathleen Mallory, his adopted daughter and a policewoman assigned to office duty, is beautiful, intelligent, fiercely independent, and obsessed with finding the killer. Mallory's computer skills supplement the street-survival savvy she learned before her adoption and the 'wall' of clues and case details left by Markowitz." Libr J

The author's "writing is stunning in its luminosity, originality, simplicity, and power. Her plot is ingenious, inventive, and enigmatic, and her characters sparkle with originality and charm." Booklist

The man who cast two shadows. Putnam 1995 278p o.p.
LC 94-43797

This mystery features New York cop Kathleen Mallory. "Taken off suspension to cover the murder of a woman at first identified as Mallory herself, she pits her uncanny intelligence and formidable computer skills against a compulsive and evasive adversary. Moments of wry humor invade the author's incisive prose, tempering an admirable female protagonist sure to gather a following." Libr J

Shell game. Putnam 1999 374p $24.95
ISBN 0-399-14495-1 LC 98-54715

"When an aged magician dies in Central Park during a magic trick gone awry, everyone thinks it's a terrible accident. NYPD detective Kathleen Mallory knows better but can't convince her boss, her partner, her friends, or

O'Connell, Carol—*Continued*
the dead man's fellow magicians, who have gathered for a magic festival in New York. The old magicians draw Mallory into a 50-year-old murder mystery involving the death of a young woman hiding from the Nazis in occupied Paris. . . . The characters are intriguing, and the plot's hairpin twists and turns are dazzling." Libr J

Stone angel. Putnam 1997 341p o.p.
LC 96-44504

Computer whiz and New York cop Kathleen Mallory "leaves the Big Apple to return to her enigmatic Southern beginnings. Seventeen years earlier, in the hamlet of Dayborn, La., the murder of a young woman, Cass Shelley, set off events that transformed her six-year-old daughter, Kathy, into the thief who, four years later, would be rescued from the New York streets by the cop who became her adoptive father. Returning to Dayborn like an avenging angel, Mallory is soon arrested for the murder of a local evangelist near her old house." Publ Wkly

How the author "manages to imbue what's basically a who-was-that-masked-man tall tale of revenge with Molierian elegance is as great a mystery as who killed Mallory's mother nearly two decades ago." New Yorker

O'Connor, Edwin, 1918-1968

All in the family. Little, Brown 1966 434p o.p.

"An Atlantic Monthly Press book"

"The Kinsellas are a wealthy, Irish Massachusetts family, dominated—at first—by the father, who insists that his sons enter politics to clean up a thoroughly corrupt political situation. One son is elected Governor, but political power subtly affects him, ethical problems evoke sharp differences and cause the eventual breakup of the family." Libr J

"The plot though rather melodramatic is outweighed by the felicitous childhood recollections of Jack, the authenticity of dialog, and the skillful establishment of political atmosphere." Booklist

The last hurrah. Little, Brown 1956 427p o.p.

"Typical of the old style political boss Frank Skeffington had kept his power as mayor of a large eastern U.S. city for almost 40 years. During the course of his last campaign . . . he is seen not only as the corrupt grafter ruthless with his enemies but also as a man of infinite charm who truly loved his city." Booklist

"A revealing study of a benevolent dictator at work. More, it is a genuine portrait of all the ebullience and rascality, loyalty and duplicity that enliven the typical Irish-American community." Christ Sci Monit

O'Connor, Flannery

Collected works. Library of Am. 1988 1281p $35

ISBN 0-940450-37-2 LC 87-37829

Contents: Wise blood; A good man is hard to find; The violent bear it away; Everything that rises must converge; Stories and occasional prose; Letters

The complete stories. Farrar, Straus & Giroux 1971 555p o.p.

This collection is "arranged in chronological order from the story she wrote for her master's thesis at the University of Iowa to 'Judgement Day.' . . . The stories here include the original openings and other chapters of her two novels 'Wise Blood' and 'The Violent Bear It Away.'" N Y Times Book Rev

Everything that rises must converge. Farrar, Straus & Giroux 1965 xxxiv, 269p o.p.

Contents: Everything that rises must converge; Greenleaf; A view of the woods; The enduring chill; The comforts of home; The lame shall enter first; Revelation; Parker's back; Judgement Day

also in O'Connor, F. Collected works p481-696

A good man is hard to find and other stories. Harcourt Brace & Co. 1955 251p o.p.

Contents: A good man is hard to find; The river; The life you save may be your own; A stroke of good fortune; A temple of the Holy Ghost; The artificial nigger; A circle in the fire; A late encounter with the enemy; Good country people; The displaced person

also in O'Connor, F. Collected works p133-328

The violent bear it away. Farrar, Straus & Cudahy 1960 243p o.p.

"A macabre tale set in the backwoods of Georgia and presenting the fanatical mission of a boy intent on baptizing a still younger boy." Oxford Companion to Am Lit. 6th edition

also in O'Connor, F. Collected works p329-480

Wise blood. Harcourt Brace & Co. 1952 232p o.p.

This novel "centers on Hazel Motes, a discharged serviceman who abandons his fundamentalist faith to become a preacher of anti-religion in a Tennessee city, establishing the 'Church Without Christ.' Motes is a ludicrous and tragic hero who meets a collection of equally grotesque characters. One of his young followers, Enoch Emery, worships a museum mummy. Hoover Shoats is a competing evangelist who creates the 'Holy Church of Christ Without Christ.' Asa Hawks is an itinerant preacher who pretends to have blinded himself to show his faith in redemption." Merriam-Webster's Ency of Lit

also in O'Connor, F. Collected works p1-132

O'Connor, Frank, 1903-1966

Collected stories; introduction by Richard Ellmann. Knopf 1981 701p o.p.
LC 81-1253

The author "grew up with 'the troubles,' but the Ireland he evokes in these 72 stories . . . is the provincial life of his Cork boyhood." Libr J

O'Connor, Joseph, 1963-

Star of the Sea. Harcourt 2003 386p $25

ISBN 0-15-100908-2 LC 2003-1984

"The Star of the Sea is a leaky old tub sailing from Ireland to New York in the terrible winter of 1847, carrying in its staterooms a reluctantly interwined collection of characters." N Y Times Book Rev

The author "brillantly weaves together an intriguing plot, a cast of memorable characters, and some stunning-

O'Connor, Joseph, 1963-—*Continued*

ly realistic dialog. Universal themes of love, loyalty, vengeance, and violence are explored in the context of a troubled class-ridden society convulsed by the catastropic potato blight." Libr J

O'Connor, Mary Flannery *See* O'Connor, Flannery

O'Connor, Robert, 1959-

Buffalo soldiers. Knopf 1993 323p o.p.
LC 92-54278

"The hero of this novel is Ray Elwood, a soldier stationed at a United States Army base in present-day Germany. Elwood is a battalion clerk, a wily factotum to a buffoonish colonel whose vanity and ineptitude provide Elwood with the opportunity—and the cover—to pursue his real vocations, which are to deal drugs to his fellow G.I.'s, to get high and to survive." N Y Times Book Rev

"O'Connor writes bitter, funny prose and creates bureaucratic snafus of the first order. Alternating scenes of Army idiocy and clinically realistic drug addiction are far more compelling than O'Connor's attempt to attribute his hero's bracing nihilism to his tragic past. Toward its end the book falters, as Elwood flirts with maudlin self-pity. But O'Connor misfires now and then only because he aims high." Publ Wkly

O'Dell, Tawni

Back roads. Viking 1999 338p $24.95
ISBN 0-670-88760-9 LC 99-20649

In this novel, set in a small Pennsylvania coal town, 19-year-old Harley Altmyer is saddled with the "custody of three younger siblings—a responsibility inherited when his mother killed his abusive father and went to prison for life. While he works two dead-end jobs to support his sisters, Harley lusts after a married neighbor, Callie Mercer. When Callie indicates that she's attracted to him, too, the resulting sexual fireworks set off a series of events with tragic consequences." Libr J

"Harley's first-person account of the deterioration of his family and his own slow-motion meltdown is harrowing. O'Dell, a native of western Pennsylvania, renders finely detailed characters and settings in a desperate and failed mining town. This is a riveting first novel of violence, incest, murder, and madness." Booklist

Coal Run; Tawni O'Dell. Viking 2004 354p $24.95
ISBN 0-670-89995-X LC 2003-62645

"After more than 15 years living in Florida, Ivan Zoschenko returns to his home in western Pennsylvania, his arrival coinciding with the release from prison of his highschool alter ego, Reese Raynor. Ivan is not thrilled to return home: he had gladly left behind memories of the explosion at the mine that killed his father and nearly 100 other miners when he was six, and he doesn't look forward to hearing the locals' reaction to the bizarre injury that brought his career as a pro football player to an abrupt end. But here he is, sleeping on his sister's couch and working temporarily as deputy for the sheriff's office. The novel takes place over the course of only one week, yet O'Dell manages to give the story an epic dimension through masterful intercutting of past and present. Reese's pending release drives the plot, and as the day nears, Ivan confronts his own demons and secrets with true-to-life reluctance." Booklist

Odom, Mel, 1950-

The destruction of the books; Mel Odom. 1st ed. Tor 2004 381p $25.95
ISBN 0-7653-0723-5 LC 2003-27368

"Almost 100 years after the events of The Rover (2002), Edgewick Lamplighter is grandmagister at the Vault of All Known Knowledge, a secret repository of books rescued from destruction by the dreaded goblinkin. This time the protagonist is Jugh, another halfling, whom Wick rescued from goblin slavers and made his apprentice. Feeling an outsider on the island, Jugh ships out as a crew member on one of the ships that service and help protect the island. But when he discovers that a book is aboard a goblin ship, he manages with great difficulty and danger to retrieve it and take it back to the island. The book turns out to be designed to open a path for dark forces to invade the island and destroy the library." Booklist

"The narrative moves along at a snappy pace, with much good humor, zest and color." Publ Wkly

O'Donnell, Lillian

Blue death. Putnam 1998 215p $22.95
ISBN 0-399-14367-X LC 97-47589

"The proud mother of an adopted toddler as well as the head of her own homicide division, NYPD Lieutenant Norah Mulcahaney learns how difficult it is to balance home life and work. . . . Just when her live-in sitter suddenly quits, she's confronted with a case that has left some NYPD higher-ups a little nervous. It seems there's been a rash of suicides among police officers. . . . A clever, low-key puzzler, this is a nice break from the usual violent, high-octane police procedural." Booklist

No business being a cop. Putnam 1979 255p o.p.
LC 78-18341

"Detective Norah Mulcahaney has been newly promoted to Detective Sergeant and put in charge of a rash of murders of police women, with the murderer resolved to kill all the female police on the force! One after another they are killed off while Norah hunts exasperatedly for the killer. Finally, she herself becomes a potential victim, thus forcing the killer to reveal himself and his motives." West Coast Rev Books

The other side of the door. Putnam 1987 256p o.p.
LC 87-21013

In this police procedural Norah Mulcahaney "plays a bit part, advising Detective Gary Reissig, her partner from *Ladykiller* (1984), on a muddled case. Reissig tries but fails to protect Alyssa Hanriot from further attacks by a man of unknown identity, who beats her badly in the dark and threatens to kill her." Publ Wkly

Pushover. Putnam 1992 239p o.p.
LC 91-30205

Norah Mulcahaney "is called in to investigate the murder of an aging screen star, only to find, in addition, that the woman's grandson is missing. While sorting through

O'Donnell, Lillian—*Continued*

suspects and evidence for a kidnapping charge, Norah is also asked to assist the New York City transit authority police in finding the 'perp' who pushes young women to their deaths from subway platforms. O'Donnell's snappy style sets the pace here, as Mulcahaney races to solve the mysteries before another death occurs." Booklist

The raggedy man. Putnam 1995 232p o.p.
LC 95-3925

"When NYPD sergeant Ray Dixon nudges PI Gwenn Ramadge into hiring a suspended rookie detective for help in an investigation, the Brooklyn investigator . . . is drawn into a bitter—but for readers, delicious—brew of murder and police corruption." Publ Wkly

Used to kill. Putnam 1993 240p o.p.
LC 92-29821

"Emma Trent, a dance teacher and young widow now married to older executive Douglas Trent, returns home one night to find her husband bludgeoned to death in an apparent burglary. . . . Then Adam McClure, one of Emma's young male students, kills himself after police find the baseball bats he and his friend Paulie Kellen used to commit the murder; Adam leaves a note incriminating Emma, who hires Gwenn to clear her name. . . . The kind-hearted, tough female PI resolves the tale with a neat twist." Publ Wkly

A wreath for the bride. Putnam 1990 239p o.p.
LC 89-10245

"On a honeymoon cruise a new bride falls to her death from the deck of the ship. Previously, a car bomb claimed one of the bridesmaids. Private investigator Gwenn Ramadge has no difficulty believing the girl's husband to be responsible. She once dated the dissipated Lothario. Trouble is, he has an alibi, even if it is an adulterous one, and several days later another new bride dies. . . . Taking her time getting to the dirty deeds, she begins by carefully exploring the characters of the dead girls and their less-than-charming spouses." Booklist

O'Donovan, Michael *See* O'Connor, Frank, 1903-1966

Ōe, Kenzaburō

An echo of heaven; translated by Margaret Mitsutani. Kodansha Am. 1996 204p $25
ISBN 4-7700-1986-6

Original Japanese edition, 1989

"K., the author's double, has been asked to write the story of an acquaintance of his, Marie Kuraki, a woman of great charm and intellect whose life is torn apart after her two disabled sons throw themselves into the sea. . . . Marie goes on a quest for meaning, searching for an alternative to her grim reality. She joins a radical cult that eventually moves to California. When this group dissolves, she hesitantly takes up the offer to become a symbol of fortitude and saintliness in a small Mexican farming village." Publ Wkly

"This profound novel is . . . as concerned with common humanity as with art and ideas. Indeed, it constitutes an argument that art is greatest when it is concerned with the essentially human, with death, suffering, fellowship, and sex—each of which figures prominently in it." Booklist

Nip the buds, shoot the kids; translated and introduced by Paul St. John Mackintosh and Maki Sugiyama. Boyars, M. 1995 189p $22.95
ISBN 0-7145-2997-4 LC 94-40897

Original Japanese edition, 1958

"In the waning days of WW II, a group of Japanese reformschool boys are evacuated to a remote village in a densely wooded valley. The villagers treat the teenagers horribly, making them bury a mountain of animal corpses, locking them into a shed for the night and feeding them raw potatoes. The unnamed narrator—one of the group's leaders—discovers that a plague is ravaging the valley. When a couple of people are infected by the disease, the villagers panic. Believing the boys to be infected, the villagers remove themselves to the other side of the valley and block the only road out of town. At first, the boys can think only of escape, but then . . . they start to make the village their own. . . . But each pleasant turn, every apparently liberating step away from unremitting brutality, serves to make the characters' inevitable future suffering even more painful." Publ Wkly

The pinch runner memorandum; translated by Michiko N. Wilson and Michael K. Wilson. Sharpe, M.E. 1994 251p $59.95
ISBN 1-56324-183-8 LC 93-26114

"An East Gate book"

Original Japanese edition, 1976

"Based on the metaphor of a sandlot baseball pinch runner, the novel centers around the exchange of identities of a father and a son who venture out together to confront the kingpin of the political underworld. Ōe unfolds the adventure through the complex narrative structure of the protagonist's words, which sometimes resonate and sometimes clash with the narrative voice of his ghost-writer, who initiates the tale. These two layers of the text are further enriched by a third voice, that of the idiot son Mori who speaks to his 'switch*ed*-over' father through the conduit of their clasped hands. Simultaneously, the reader is treated to a smorgasbord of satire, black humor, *manga*-like slapstick, Mikhail Bakhtin's grotesque realism, and various socio-political phenomena such as marginalization, factionalism, and terrorism." Introduction

A quiet life; translated from the Japanese by Kunioki Yanagishita with William Wetherall. Grove Press 1996 240p o.p.
LC 96-25795

Original Japanese edition, 1990

"A famous Japanese writer whose first name begins with K takes off with his wife for a year to become writer in residence at 'one of the several campuses of the University of Carolina,' leaving their almost equally famous son, an idiot savant who is a remarkable composer, in the care of their daughter, Ma-chan. It is Ma-chan, a conscientious young woman acutely aware of the responsibility that devolves on her during her parents' absence, who tells the story related in Kenzaburo Oe's novel 'A Quiet Life,' and the translators, Kunioki Yanagishita and William Wetherall, admirably succeed in conveying a certian archness of style that infuses the work with Ma-chan's personality." N Y Times Book Rev

Rouse up, o young men of the new age; {by} Kenzaburo Oe. Grove Press 2002 272p o.p.
ISBN 0-8021-1710-4 LC 2001-51298

Ōe, Kenzaburō—*Continued*

Original Japanese edition, 1983

"A Japanese author, who mirrors this book's author, broods on the life and works of William Blake while writing some episodic fiction that closely resembles this novel. The narrator, who has a disabled son, finds his own life and works transformed by Blake, but his interpretation of Blake also changes as his personal circumstances change; the same is true of his son's hilarious utterances. This elegant work is a mordantly entertaining reflection on the uses of literature and imagination." New Yorker

The silent cry; translated by John Bester. Kodansha Int./USA 1974 274p $25

ISBN 4-7700-0450-8

Original Japanese edition, 1967

"Set in the 1960s, the primary story is about the relationship between two brothers. The elder, Mitsu, is a reclusive scholar; the younger, Takashi, is drawn to political activism. They return to their ancestral village, where Takashi attempts to stage a protest against the nouveau riche Korean who is taking over the village. As the last descendant of an old and honorable family, he considers this a significant gesture. Takashi becomes increasingly violent and eventually murders a young woman. In disgrace he reveals the guilt of his past to Mitsu and commits suicide." Merriam-Webster's Ency of Lit

Somersault; a novel; translated from the Japanese by Philip Gabriel. Grove Press 2003 570p $29.95

ISBN 0-8021-1738-4 LC 2002-29746

Original Japanese edition, 1999

This novel "takes place against the background of a religious cult's terrorist plan (even more drastic than Aum Shinrikyo's 1995 gas attack on the Tokyo subway), which is thwarted when the cult's leaders appear on television to renounce their creed-the 'somersault' of the title. Now, ten years later, the cult's charismatic guru is planning to reestablish his church. . . . Through the believers' motivations for joining the cult, Oe explores the struggle of contemporary Japanese to situate themselves between a traditional culture and the bullet-train pace of the boom years." New Yorker

O'Faoláin, Seán, 1900-1991

The collected stories of Seán O'Faoláin. Little, Brown 1983 1304p il o.p.

LC 83-205346

"An Atlantic Monthly Press book"

Contents: Midsummer night madness and other stories: Midsummer night madness; Lilliput; Fugue; The small lady; The bombshop; The death of Stevey Long; The patriot

A purse of coppers: A broken world; The old master; Sinners; Admiring the scenery; Egotists; Kitty the wren; My son Austin; A born genius; Sullivan's trousers; A meeting; Discord; The confessional; Mother Matilda's book; There's a birdie in the cage

Teresa and other stories: Teresa; The man who invented sin; Unholy living and half dying; The silence of the valley; Innocence; The trout; Shades of the prison house; The end of a good man; Passion; A letter; Vive la France; The woman who married Clark Gable; Lady Lucifer

From the finest stories of Sean O'Faolain: Childybawn; Lovers of the lake; The fur coat; Up the bare stairs; One true friend; Persecution mania; The Judas touch; The end of the record; Lord and master; An enduring friendship

I remember! I remember!: I remember! I remember!; The sugawn chain; A shadow, silent as a cloud; A touch of autumn in the air; The younger generation; Love's young dream; Two of a kind; Angels and ministers of grace; One night in Turin; Miracles don't happen twice; No country for old men

The heat of the sun: In the bosom of the country; Dividends; The heat of the sun; The human thing; One man, one boat, one girl; Charlie's Greek; Billy Billee; Before the daystar; £1000 for Rosebud; A sweet colleen

The talking trees and other stories: The planets of the years; A dead cert; Hymeneal; The talking trees; The time of their lives; Feed my lambs; Our fearful innocence; Brainsy; Thieves; Of sanctity and whiskey; The kitchen

Foreign affairs and other stories: The faithless wife; Something, everything, anything, nothing; An inside outside complex; Murder at Cobbler's Hulk; Foreign affairs; Falling rocks, narrowing road, cul-de-sac stop; How to write a short story; Liberty

Unpublished stories: Marmalade; From Huesca with love and kisses; The wings of the dove—a modern sequel; The unlit lamp; One fair daughter and no more; A present from Clonmacnois

Foreign affairs and other stories
In O'Faoláin, S. The collected stories of Seán O'Faoláin p1061-1226

The heat of the sun
In O'Faoláin, S. The collected stories of Seán O'Faoláin p700-886

I remember! I remember!
In O'Faoláin, S. The collected stories of Seán O'Faoláin p544-699

Midsummer night madness and other stories
In O'Faoláin, S. The collected stories of Seán O'Faoláin p9-162

A purse of coppers
In O'Faoláin, S. The collected stories of Seán O'Faoláin p163-319

The talking trees and other stories
In O'Faoláin, S. The collected stories of Seán O'Faoláin p889-1060

Teresa and other stories
In O'Faoláin, S. The collected stories of Seán O'Faoláin p320-445

Ogilvie, Elisabeth, 1917-

When the music stopped. McGraw-Hill 1989 326p o.p.

LC 88-28636

"Author Eden Winters, finds herself in the midst of local scandal and terrifying deaths. Set in a small town along the Maine coast, the plot turns on the return to town of two aging sisters who had left on the wings of scandal decades earlier. While there are plenty of people

Ogilvie, Elisabeth, 1917-—*Continued*
with reason to despise the returning ladies—who audaciously take up residence in the area's most elegant house—there are just as many people, such as Eden and her family, who are delighted to see them. When the women are found brutally murdered, suspects abound, including a stranger who alternately captures Eden's suspicions and heart. Well-crafted fiction that holds the reader's attention and avoids contrivance." Booklist

O'Hagan, Andrew, 1968-

Personality. Harcourt 2003 311p $25
ISBN 0-15-101000-5 LC 2003-5369
"In a decayed resort town on the Isle of Bute in the nineteen-seventies, an Italo-Scottish family pins its hopes on the youngest member, Maria, who is working on her singing and her hair. At thirteen, she is wisked off to London, where she wins a talent contest on television. By sixteen, she is a famous pop singer. By twenty, she is anorexic and half-mad. (Soon she also has a homicidal admirer stalking her.) The analysis of her thoughts, a miasma of fear and narcissism, is the core of the novel. . . . At the same time, the book is so bustling and rich—we get every old lady and barfly on the island, with their letters, diaries, secrets—that the darkness seems lit from end to end." New Yorker

O'Hara, John, 1905-1970

Appointment in Samarra. Modern Lib. 1994 c1934 xxi, 269p $14.95
ISBN 0-679-60110-4 LC 94-4340
A reissue of the title first published 1934 by Harcourt Brace & Co.
"Julian English is not a bad man, only a very weak one. He is popular with the country-club set, has the right connections with the local bootlegger, and has an attractive wife. He succeeds in offending the man who holds the mortgage on his car dealership and the bootlegger whose girl he pays too much attention to when he has again had too much to drink. When his wife announces her intention to divorce him, Julian feels that there is nothing left for him in life." Shapiro. Fic for Youth. 3d edition
"The novel is written episodically, but achieves integration by its hard-boiled theme of the destructive effects of fast living." Haydn. Thesaurus of Book Dig

Butterfield 8; a novel. Harcourt Brace & Co. 1935 310p o.p.
"A novelization of the sensational lives of the nightclub set involved in an actual New York murder case. Young Gloria Wandrous is found drowned on a beach near New York. The problem is to find the murderer and his motive. The investigation, described in machine-gun reportage, reveals that Gloria had had a good education, but owing to an adolescent sexual experience had become a 'party girl' in the unsavory life of New York speakeasies and luxurious Long Island clubs. Under the sleekness of Park Avenue sophistication, O'Hara reveals New York's hard soullessness." Haydn. Thesaurus of Book Dig

Collected stories of John O'Hara; selected and with an introduction by Frank MacShane. Random House 1984 414p o.p.
LC 84-42661
Contents: The doctor's son; It must have been spring; Over the river and through the woods; Price's always open; Are we leaving tomorrow; Pal Joey; The gentleman in the tan suit; Good-by, Herman; Olive; Do you like it here; Now we know; Free; Too young; Bread alone; Graven image; Common-sense should tell you; Drawing room B; The pretty daughters; The moccasins; Imagine kissing Pete; The girl from California; In the silence; Exactly eight thousand dollars exactly; Winter dance; The flatted saxophone; The friends of Miss Julia; How can I tell you?; Ninety minutes away; Our friend the sea; Can I stay here?; The hardware man; The pig; Zero; Fatimas and kisses; Natica Jackson; We'll have fun

From the terrace; a novel. Random House 1958 897p o.p.
"Alfred Eaton, the younger son of Samuel Eaton, steel magnate of Port Johnson, Pennsylvania, had a tolerably happy childhood until the death of his older brother William, when Alfred was twelve. After the death of his favorite son, Samuel Eaton retreated into an obsessive grief. Alfred's mother, neglected, turned elsewhere for affection and Alfred was left to grow up as best as he could, closer to the servants than to his parents. The rest of his life though rewarded with business success and filled with a variety of amorous adventures, was basically barren and loveless." Booklist
The novel describes "the ways of Social Register families on the Pennsylvania-New York axis—especially in sexual encounters and marriage—in what may be described as morbidly fascinating detail. Indeed the novel's central achievement is surely the impression it conveys of the morality—or amorality, of immorality—of this class." N Y Her Trib Books

Ten North Frederick. Random House 1955 408p o.p.
A character study of one of the 'first citizens' of a Pennsylvania town, Gibbsville. "In the first quarter of a crowded, eventful narrative, Joe Chapin is seen only through the eyes of some of those at [his] funeral. Then [O'Hara] . . . switches back to Joe's parents, who established the home at Ten North Frederick Street, where Joe lived all his life. He tells Joe's story from the beginning, and the stories of those whose lives have touched Joe's at some significant point." N Y Times Book Rev

Okuizumi, Hikaru, 1956-

The stones cry out; translated from the Japanese by James Westerhoven. Harcourt Brace & Co. 1999 138p $20
ISBN 0-15-100365-3 LC 98-14434
Original Japanese edition, 1993
This "novel features Tsuyoshi Manase, the owner of a successful bookstore who is also a husband, the father of two sons, and a self-taught geologist. . . . Troubled by memories of World War II, Manase must deal with an alcoholic wife, an eventual divorce, and the untimely death of his two children." Libr J
"A monstrous tale, *The Stones Cry Out* is written with a lyrical beauty that only underscores the horror

Okuizumi, Hikaru, 1956—*Continued*
Manase's life becomes. As Okuizumi elegantly plays Manase's nightmare out, Manase is compelled to reenact the real atrocities he has tried so desperately to forget." Booklist

Ólafur Jóhann Ólafsson

The journey home; [by] Olaf Olafsson. Pantheon Bks. 2000 296p $24
ISBN 0-375-42061-4 LC 00-39186
Original Icelandic edition, 1999
"Disa leads a serene life in England as the co-owner of a small hotel, where she shares a passion for cooking and nature with her partner, Anthony. When Disa is diagnosed with a fatal illness, she travels back to Iceland, revealing an unsettled past. The daughter of a doctor, she left her small village to be educated in Reykjavik. Disa soon alienated her mother by choosing a career as a chef and falling in love with Jacob, a German Jew. Disa and Jacob share a passionate, bohemian life in the English countryside until he returns to Germany to help his parents escape the Holocaust. Waiting for Jacob, Disa works in the house of an influential family and is swept into painful and startling events." Libr J
"This is not a morose novel, but one lifted by love, friendship and cooking, an art Disa has spent much of her life perfecting at an English country inn. Hers is a hard, unflinching life, and one skillfully revealed in a steady stream of memories that accompanies Disa on a last migration back to her Arctic nest." Time

Olsen, Tillie

Tell me a riddle; a collection. Lippincott 1961 156p o.p.
Contents: I stand here ironing; Hey sailor, what ship; O yes; Tell me a riddle
"In writing which is individualized but not eccentric, experimental but not obscure, Mrs. Olsen has created imagined experience which has the authenticity of autobiography or memoir. With a faultless accuracy, her stories treat the very young, the mature, the dying—poor people without the means to buy or invent lies about their situations—and yet her writing never succumbs to mere naturalism." Commonweal

O'Marie, Carol Anne

Death goes on retreat; [by] Sister Carol Anne O'Marie. Delacorte Press 1995 230p o.p.
LC 95-8458
"When Sister Mary Helen and bosom companion, Sister Eileen, arrive at St. Colette's Sanctuary, they are dismayed to discover that they are actually an entire week early for their scheduled conference. Undaunted, they join the retreat for diocesan priests already in progress. While taking an early morning stroll, Mary Helen uncovers the lifeless remains of a former seminarian." Booklist
"Sister Mary Helen's gentle insights inform this story about age-old prejudices with a quiet wisdom." Publ Wkly

Death of an angel. St. Martin's Press 1997 211p $21.95
ISBN 0-312-15107-1 LC 96-48770
"A Thomas Dunne book"
In this mystery, "a serial rapist and murderer is loose in a wealthy San Francisco neighborhood. When a friend of Sister Mary Helen's becomes the killer's latest victim, the sister decides to get involved in the case. At the same time, readers are drawn into the story of fat Angela Bowers, who works at Sister Mary Helen's college and is being pushed to the breaking point by her abusive, bedridden mother. These two stories come dramatically together in a conclusion that, while not totally unexpected, is still riveting." Booklist

The missing Madonna. Delacorte Press 1988 253p o.p.
LC 88-15349
In this novel "the gregarious Sister Mary Helen investigates the disappearance of an old college chum by enlisting the aid of her San Francisco chapter of OWL's (Older Women's League), a feisty bunch of busybodies who shame and nag the police into doing their duty." NY Times Book Rev

Murder in ordinary time. Delacorte Press 1991 245p o.p.
LC 91-20455
"Sister Mary Helen, the spry, elderly amateur detective . . . finds herself caught up in her third murder investigation. She doesn't even try to hide her interest or her snooping—er . . . sleuthing. After all, the victim could just as easily have been Sister Mary Helen herself because she was on the television news set when gorgeous investigative reporter Christina Kelly bit the poisoned cookie. . . . Sister Mary Helen tracks down the culprit by using both her wiles and ker kitchenside manners. Neatly plotted, entertaining mystery fare." Booklist

O'Nan, Stewart, 1961-

The good wife; Stewart O'Nan. Farrar, Straus and Giroux 2005 312p $24
ISBN 0-374-28139-4 LC 2004-53247
"One night Patty Dickerson wakes up to a phone call from her husband, Tommy, who has been arrested for an unspecified crime. He is soon charged with murder, cannot afford a decent lawyer and is sentenced to 25 years to life. Patty, 27 and pregnant, understands she will now make her living, raise her child and spend her nights alone." N Y Times Book Rev
"From the trial, through the various appeals process, the visits to the prison, the waiting, the hoping, the struggle to make ends meet, and the gradual resilience and self-sufficiency, O'Nan, with seldom a false beat, perceptively and compassionately depicts the bureaucratic insanities of the penal system and the hardships, fears, and frustrations of those left behind." Booklist

The names of the dead. Doubleday 1996 399p o.p.
LC 95-36745
"As an army medic in Vietnam in 1969, Larry Markham had the job of keeping the wounded alive. But first aid never seemed to help, and the men died anyway. Now, 13 years later, Larry has a dead-end job delivering snack cakes in Ithaca, New York. His marriage is on the rocks, his father is showing signs of Alzheimer's disease, and an ex-CIA assassin from his veterans' support group is stalking him. Feelings of stress and helplessness bring

O'Nan, Stewart, 1961-—*Continued*

on flashbacks of the war." Libr J

"O'Nan's language is powerfully restrained; his word pictures of the war and its effect on the men who fought there are fresh and vivid. He rightfully refuses to pander to our desire for easy answers and happy endings." Booklist

The night country; or, The darkness on the edge of town. Farrar, Straus & Giroux 2003 229p $23

ISBN 0-374-22215-0 LC 2002-44765

"The aftermath of a Halloween tragedy haunts a New England town on the one-year anniversary of a typical teen joyride that ended with a car wrapped around a tree. Toe, Marco, and Danielle were instantly killed. Kyle lives on, sort of; a severe brain injury obliterates the rebel in him, the accident leaving him with the mind of a child. Tim, 'the lucky one' in the backseat, his arms around Danielle, survived but now has a death wish. Officer Brooks, the first on the scene, was terribly alterered by the event, and his life in shambles." Booklist

"O'Nan is wonderful at describing teenage ritual, the simultaneous desire for the comforting familiarity of friends and the lust for speed and novelty and excitement that will lift teenagers out of the confines of their suburban town, the routine of school, out of their own restless bodies." N Y Times Book Rev

A prayer for the dying; a novel. Holt & Co. 1999 195p $22

ISBN 0-8050-6147-9 LC 98-39613

"Soon after the Civil War, Jacob Hansen, a Union veteran, is working as pastor, sheriff, and undertaker in the town of Friendship, Wisconsin; while some resist the intensity of his faith, Jacob sees himself as the town's spiritual caretaker. When diphtheria breaks out, he takes increasingly harsh measures to prevent it from spreading, and the consequences of his right-minded actions unfold with accelerating horror." New Yorker

Snow angels. Doubleday 1994 305p o.p.

ISBN 0-385-47574-8 LC 94-12037

This novel follows the disintegration of two households in a small western Pennsylvania town in the dead of winter. One is Arthur Parkinson's. Arthur, small yet wise for his 15 years, is coping with his parents' divorce and the loss of their home. While he picks his way through the emotional land mine his parents have created, Arthur falls in love, learns to drive, and, strangely enough, gets drawn into the wreck of his former babysitter's life. As a child, Arthur adored Annie for her long red hair and joshing indulgences. Now he can't believe the sickening irony of having to be the one person out of dozens of searchers who finds the body of her drowned three-year-old daughter. Arthur's narrative alternates with the sad tale of Annie's busted marriage, the mental breakdown of her estranged husband, and her Booklist

The author "weaves together these seemingly disparate small-town tragedies–one narrated in the first person, the other in the third–with consummate skill, seamlessly shifting the focus among characters he wishes to make the reader care about." Libr J

Wish you were here. Grove Press 2002 517p $25

ISBN 0-8021-1715-5 LC 2001-58638

"Now that her husband, Henry, is dead, Emily Maxwell, the matriarch of the clan, is selling the family retreat near Chautauqua, N.Y. Emily and her sister-in-law, Arlene, drive up together from Pittsburgh for a last summer visit; Emily's son, Ken, and his wife, Lise, come next with their two children; and finally Emily's daughter, Meg, and Meg's son and daughter arrive. For seven days the Maxwells interact, with Emily's disappointment in her children prompting them to assess their lives themselves." Publ Wkly

"O'Nan gets all the details right—the irritations that arise from too much forced intimacy, the clutter and cast-offs that accumulate in a summerhouse that has been in the same family for years, the worn and slightly tacky ambience of an old resort, the tedium of days with nothing important to do." Booklist

A world away. Holt & Co. 1998 338p $23

ISBN 0-8050-5774-9 LC 97-36727

"Set during the Second World War, this bleak but tender novel chronicles a Long Island family's struggle to stay intact. There are James and Anne Langer, whose marriage is failing; Rennie, their enlisted (and missing) son; Dorothy, his pregnant, lonely wife; and Jay, the second, overprotected son, whose nightmares bring the shadowy claustrophobia of war eerily close to home. The plot is familiar, but O'Nan's description of life in the face of daily devastation—both personal and historical—is unfaltering." New Yorker

Ondaatje, Michael, 1943-

Anil's ghost. Knopf 2000 307p $25

ISBN 0-375-41053-8 LC 99-59208

In this novel "Anil Tissera, 33, a forensic anthropologist, returns to the Sri Lanka she left at age 18 as one member of a U.N. team allowed into the country by the government to investigate alleged human rights violations, i.e. death squad murders. Her assigned partner . . . is a Sri Lankan archaeologist named Sarath Diyasena, 49, who is, by virtue of his position, a government employee. Anil immediately wonders whether her co-worker will be helping her or reporting on her. . . . Before long, they turn up a suspiciously fresh skeleton in a government-protected archaeological site." Time

"Anil comes with Western-bred investigative passion: the certainty that facts are there to be unearthed and that truth is to be constructed out of them. Sarath, a polymorphous spirit and the book's most memorable figure, cautions that the real truth of his country is ambiguous and unobtainable. . . . It is Ondaatje's extraordinary achievement to use magic in order to make the blood of his own country real." N Y Times Book Rev

The English patient; a novel. Knopf 1992 307p $25

ISBN 0-679-41678-1 LC 92-53089

"Four diverse people who suffer from the physical and emotional damages of WW II meet in a deserted Tuscan villa. The badly burned English patient will die without revealing his identity, his young nurse will begin to recover her will to live, the maimed thief will watch over her and the Anglo-Indian bomb-defusing specialist will learn to exist in the atomic age." Publ Wkly

"This is a poetic and solemn narrative of the horrible process of war, the discipline, displacement, loss, and

Ondaatje, Michael, 1943-—*Continued*

sudden, desperate love. Ondaatje seems to whisper, even confess each scene to his readers, handling them gingerly like shards of shattered glass." Booklist

In the skin of a lion; a novel. Knopf 1987 243p o.p.

LC 87-45340

The main character in this novel "is Patrick Lewis, who grows up in Canadian logging country and in 1923, at the age of twenty-one, arrives in Toronto 'as if it were land after years at sea'. He becomes one of an army of searchers for Ambrose Small, millionaire personification of 'bare-knuckle capitalism', who has vanished. Lewis's success in the search brings him into contact with Small's lover Clara Dickens and then into a deepening relationship with Clara's intimate friend Alice Gull, an actress and political activist." Times Lit Suppl

Ondaatje is a "beautiful writer. What he writes about most beautifully is *work*. Mr. Ondaatje is passionate about process, the way work, particularly construction of all kinds, is done and how it feels to do it. This is, of course, a rarity in fiction at any time, and one can only be grateful for a man who is not focused on the classroom, the bedroom and the bar." N Y Times Book Rev

O'Neal, Kathleen M.

See also Gear, Kathleen O'Neal

O'Neill, Anthony

The lamplighter; a novel. Scribner 2003 308p $25

ISBN 0-7432-4349-8 LC 2002-36453

"It is 1886. Although the new electric lamp has conquered Paris and London, it has yet to make its way to Edinburgh, whose medieval streets and modern boulevards are still illuminated at dusk by the 'leeries,' the traditional lamplighters. But someone—or something—is also coming out in the evenings, leaving a trail of horribly mutilated bodies: those of a professor, a lighthouse keeper, and a shady businessman. Assigned to the case is acting Chief Inspector Carus Groves." Libr J

O'Neill, Egan, 1921-

For works written by this author under other names see Shannon, Dell, 1921-

O'Neill, Jamie

At swim, two boys; a novel. Scribner 2002 572p $27

ISBN 0-7432-2294-6 LC 2001-57694

First published 2001 in the United Kingdom

This is the "story of two boys—scholarly, reticent James and cocksure, poverty-stricken Doyle—and their tragic involvement in the 1916 Easter Uprising. . . . James and Doyle strike up a friendship at Forty Foot, a local beach, and make plans to swim to Muglins Rock far out in Dublin Bay on Easter Sunday a year hence. As the two draw closer and eventually fall in love, they must contend with disapproval of their relationship from peers and from the church and the jealousy of upper-class Anthony MacMurrough, who has served time in jail for sexual misconduct." Booklist

"In this novel the cause of Ireland and the cause of gay people fuse with a complete lack of apology or embarrassment. . . . O'Neill is not, however, being patly outrageous; the closeness and exactness of his vision prove that." N Y Times Book Rev

Kilbrack; or, Who is Nancy Valentine?; Jamie O'Neill. Scribner trade pa. ed. Scribner 2004 305p pa $14

ISBN 0-7432-5595-X (pa) LC 2003-65911

"O'Leary Montague, a facially scarred amnesiac as the result of a car accident, travels to the Irish village of Kilbrack because it is the setting of his favorite novel, Ill Fares the Land, by Nancy Valentine. The small-town residents prove to be deeply eccentric, with habits ranging from button hoarding to cocaine addiction, so O'Leary, a veritable bundle of nervous tics and obsessions, fits right in. His desire to write a biography of the revered Nancy Valentine leads him to a hapless meeting with reclusive Valentine Brack, a still raffish if aging member of the landed gentry who harbors a terrible secret. O'Neill sends up the rural Irish to a fare-thee-well, devoting paragraph after paragraph to the hidebound villagers' convoluted conversations, so cryptic in tone that they inevitably lead to absurdly comic misunderstandings." Booklist

Orczy, Emmuska, Baroness, 1865-1947

Adventures of the Scarlet Pimpernel. Doubleday, Doran 1929 302p o.p.

Further "exploits of the Scarlet Pimpernel, Sir Percy Blakeney, the daring Englishman, who, with his loyal friends and helpers, rescues aristocrats from the guillotine during the French Revolution. Each chapter records a separate adventure." Cleveland Public Libr

The elusive Pimpernel. Dodd, Mead 1908 344p o.p.

Another chapter in the adventurous life of The Scarlet Pimpernel, that thorn in the side of the terrorists of the French Revolution, and a delivering angel to condemned aristocrats. In an increasingly tense situation, this languid, Englishman deliberately enters the French trap in an attempt to rescue his wife, the beautiful Marguerite Blakeney

The Scarlet Pimpernel.

First published 1905 by Putnam

"An adventure story of the French Revolution. The apparently foppish young Englishman, Sir Percy Blakeney, is found to be the daring Scarlet Pimpernel, rescuer of distressed aristocrats." Reader's Ency. 4th edition

Orwell, George, 1903-1950

Animal farm; with an introduction by Julian Symons. Knopf 1993 xl, 113p $16

ISBN 0-679-42039-8 LC 92-54299

"Everyman's library"

First published 1945 in the United Kingdom; first United States edition 1946

"The animals on Farmer Jones's farm revolt in a move led by the pigs, and drive out the humans. The pigs become the leaders, in spite of the fact that their government was meant to be 'classless.' The other animals soon find that they are suffering varying degrees of slavery. A

Orwell, George, 1903-1950—*Continued*
totalitarian state slowly evolves in which 'all animals are equal but some animals are more equal than others.' This is a biting satire aimed at communism." Shapiro. Fic for Youth. 3d edition

Keep the aspidistra flying. Harcourt Brace & Co. 1956 248p o.p.

First published 1936 in the United Kingdom

"The leading character Gordon Comstock, a writer, rebels against middle-class interest in money and single-minded aspirations for a 'good' job and respectability, symbolized for him by the aspidistra growing tenaciously in every parlor." Booklist

"Not pretty, but powerful, accurate, and fair. This book projects as do few others the desperate expedients and blind rage of the educated moneyless. And Orwell's power is wielded responsibly. Neither the rebels nor the hucksters are romanticized, nor is life—which wins in the end." Chicago Sunday Trib

Nineteen eighty-four.

First published 1949 by Harcourt, Brace

"A dictatorship called Big Brother rules the people in a collectivist society where Winston Smith works in the Ministry of Truth. The Thought Police persuade the people that ignorance is strength and war is peace. Winston becomes involved in a forbidden love affair and joins the underground to resist this mind control." Shapiro. Fic for Youth. 3d edition

O'Shaughnessy, Mary

For works written by this author in collaboration with Pamela O'Shaughnessy see O'Shaughnessy, Perri

O'Shaughnessy, Pamela

For works written by this author in collaboration with Mary O'Shaughnessy see O'Shaughnessy, Perri

O'Shaughnessy, Perri

Acts of malice; a novel. Delacorte Press 1999 387p $23.95

ISBN 0-385-33276-9 LC 98-55253

Lake Tahoe attorney and single mother Nina Reilly's "client in this case is Jim Strong, a local ski bum whose family owns the swanky Paradise resort. Jim stands accused of killing his younger brother Alex, who was stomped to death by someone wearing ski boots whose imprints on Alex's chest match the soles of Jim's footgear. But the suspect claims he's being framed by his adulterous wife, Heidi, who gave a statement to police and has gone into hiding. The case gives Reilly the willies, as disturbing events ensue that cast doubt on her client." Publ Wkly

Breach of promise. Delacorte Press 1998 435p $23.95

ISBN 0-385-31872-3 LC 98-5519

Lake Tahoe's "Nina Reilly, struggling in her legal practice, accepts the impossible-to-win case of Lindy Markov, a woman who wants just desserts after the wealthy man she lived with for 20 years, never legally married, left her for a younger woman." Libr J

"O'Shaughnessy offers up a gripping courtroom drama, throws in pithy ethical and moral dilemmas and some surprising plot twists, and adds plenty of heart-stopping action." Booklist

Invasion of privacy. Delacorte Press 1996 419p o.p.

LC 96-1251

"Tahoe-area attorney Nina Reilly was shot at the end of Motion *to Suppress. As t*he increasingly alarming facts of her latest case pile up, she is haunted by memories of that wounding. No less haunting are certain details of her personal past, which Nina's new client, Terry London, an energetically spiteful documentary filmmaker, seems to know as much about as Nina does. Out of that past and into Tahoe comes Kurt Scott, the father of Nina's son, Bob. Almost immediately, Terry is murdered, Kurt is accused of the crime and Nina must assemble his murder defense. . . . Fans of the genre will luxuriate in this deft, multileveled tale of legal and criminal treachery, whose pleasures include elegant courtroom sleight-of-hand and the eerily wintry backdrop of Lake Tahoe." Publ Wkly

Motion to suppress. Delacorte Press 1995 420p o.p.

LC 95-5615

"When attorney Nina Reilly agrees to represent Tahoe barmaid Misty Patterson in a divorce suit, she gets more than she bargained for. Within days, Misty is accused of the murder of her husband, and Nina, still bruised from the collapse of her own marriage, undertakes the defense." Libr J

"Although the characterizations are a bit uncertain (the luscious Misty is unbelievably prim and proper), the plot is a real puzzler, with twists diabolical enough to take to court." N Y Times Book Rev

Obstruction of justice. Delacorte Press 1997 392p o.p.

LC 96-48585

In this thriller, attorney Nina Reilly is "a witness to the death by lightning of a construction mogul in the Tahoe Mountains. When his father returns from a business trip, he wants Nina to have the body exhumed and autopsied for signs of murder, setting off a family furor. Suddenly, the grave is empty, the bodies of both father and son turn up in a smoldering mountain cabin, and the grandson is charged with murder. Nina is then asked to clear the grandson amid an increasingly complex series of interrelationships involving the D.A., his dead wife, a not-so-grieving widow, and, of course, the gardener. . . . A compelling story with some great courtroom drama and a likable heroine." Libr J

Presumption of death. Delacorte Press 2003 390p $24.95

ISBN 0-385-33645-4 LC 2003-46199

"Nina Reilly, who is taking some time off after her clash with the California State Bar . . . visits old haunts in Carmel Valley with her longtime boyfriend, investigator Paul Von Wagoner, and her dog, Hitchcock. When Willis Whitefeather is accused of murder, it quickly becomes apparent that Nina will have more to contend with than the bothersome case of poison oak she has been nursing." Libr J

"Well-rounded and likable characters set against a richly described backdrop of some of the loveliest country in the world." Publ Wkly

O'Shaughnessy, Perri—*Continued*

Unlucky in law; Perri O'Shaughnessy. Delacorte Press 2004 376p $25

ISBN 0-385-33646-2 LC 2004-47840

In this legal thriller California lawyer Nina Reilly has "moved herself and 14-year-old son Bob from their usual Tahoe turf to the Monterey Peninsula to spend time with her lover, PI Paul van Wagoner. Paul has asked Nina to marry him, offering a big diamond to seal the deal. Nina puts him off while she prepares for a big trial: she's newly employed at Pohlmann, Cunningham, and Turk, and her first case, working with Klaus Pohlmann, is defending 28-year-old Stefan Wyatt, charged with murder and grave robbing. O'Shaughnessy has been accused of sloppy plotting in the past, but not so here." Publ Wkly

Writ of execution. Delacorte Press 2001 403p o.p.

ISBN 0-385-33483-4 LC 2001-28468

"Jessie Potter, trying to dodge an alleged stalker, slides up to a dollar slot machine and tries to look like a regular gambler. Unlike most gamblers, however, she hits the jackpot, winning a prize of more then $7 million. Down-on-his-luck Silicon techie Kenny Leung witnesses the jackpot and is dazzled by the woman and her money. To keep her win discreet, Jessie enlists Kenny's help and hires popular Lake Tahoe attorney Nina Reilly to protect her interests." Booklist

"Readers will relish the myriad plot details and the procedural drama, and enjoy the cast of offbeat characters." Publ Wkly

Ossana, Diana

(jt. auth) McMurtry, L. Zeke and Ned

Oster, Christian

My big apartment; translated and with an introduction by Jordan Stump. University of Neb. Press 2002 155p $55; pa $20

ISBN 0-8032-3567-4; 0-8032-8612-0 (pa) LC 2002-17977

Original French edition published, 1999

"In a nutshell, [this is] the story of a man who loses his keys and finds a life, sort of, maybe. That's all that really happens—well, that and a few laps in a pool and a driving lesson and an episiotomy. The specifics don't much matter anyway. This is simply the course the man, a Parisian called Gavarine, follows, and he has no more control over his fate than the leaf in the stream has over the eddy." N Y Times Book Rev

Otsuka, Julie, 1962-

When the emperor was divine; a novel. Knopf 2002 141p o.p.

ISBN 0-375-41429-0 LC 2002-20814

This novel traces the "fortunes of a Japanese-American family from the spring of 1942—when President Roosevelt's evacuation order came through—to the spring of 1946. In four brief chapters, we follow a mother, daughter and son from their comfortable home in Berkeley through their five months in a temporary @assembly center' (a converted stable at a racetrack south of San Francisco) to an internment camp in Topaz, Utah, where they spend three years." N Y Times Book Rev

Otsuka "demonstrates a breathtaking restraint and delicacy throughout this supple and devastating first novel." Booklist

Otto, Whitney

How to make an American quilt. Villard Bks. 1991 179p $20

ISBN 0-679-40070-2 LC 90-48233

This novel "set in the small central California town of Grasse, chronicles the local quilting circle and its eight members. The stories of these women's lives are framed by a ninth one, that of the narrator, Finn Bennett-Dodd (granddaughter of one of the members), an about-to-be-married eavesdropper who is collecting advice. As she prepares for her own adult life, Finn has a wide array of stories and lessons to sort through." N Y Times Book Rev

"Otto has tremendous insight and compassion, understanding the rareness of a perfect marriage, the anger of thwarted lives, and the vagaries of love and motherhood." Booklist

Øvstedal, Barbara, 1925-

For works written by this author under other names see Laker, Rosalind, 1925-

Owen, John Pickard *See* Butler, Samuel, 1835-1902

The **Oxford** book of American detective stories; edited by Tony Hillerman, Rosemary Herbert. Oxford Univ. Press 1996 686p $35; pa $18.95

ISBN 0-19-508581-7; 0-19-511792-1 (pa) LC 95-4504

This collection includes stories by B. Pronzini, E. A. Poe, E. S. Gardner, E. Queen and M. Muller

The **Oxford** book of American short stories; edited by Joyce Carol Oates. Oxford Univ. Press 1992 768p $40; pa $18.95

ISBN 0-19-507065-8; 0-19-509262-7 (pa) LC 92-1353

"Fifty-six short stories showcase this ever-vital and challenging art form's suppleness and power from Washington Irving's classic, 'Rip Van Winkle,' to the work of Sandra Cisneros. While Oates couldn't resist masterpieces such as Ernest Hemingway's 'A Clean, Well-Lighted Place,' her goal was 'familiar names, unfamiliar titles,' and her intention was to call our attention to works by the likes of Edgar Allan Poe, Harriet Beecher Stowe, Henry James, Kate Chopin, William Carlos Williams, and Saul Bellow that aren't anthologized to death. . . . Her standards of excellence are consistent throughout." Booklist

The **Oxford** book of English ghost stories; chosen by Michael Cox and R. A. Gilbert. Oxford Univ. Press 1987 c1986 504p o.p.

LC 86-8690

The Oxford book of English ghost stories—*Continued*

First published 1986 in the United Kingdom

Arranged chronologically, the forty-two stories gathered here "date from the 1820s . . . to the 1980s. . . . In addition to featuring those writers one would expect to find here—Sheridan Le Fanu, M. R. James, and Walter de la Mare, for example—there is also a bounty of wonderful authors with whom U.S. audiences may not be familiar." Booklist

The **Oxford** book of English love stories; edited by John Sutherland. Oxford Univ. Press 1997 452p $30

ISBN 0-19-214237-2 LC 96-38252

Contents: The adventure of the Black Lady, by A. Behn; The picture, by W. Hazlitt; The trial of love, by M. Shelley; The heart of John Middleton, by E. Gaskell; Dennis Haggarty's wife, by W. M. Thackeray; The Parson's daughter of Oxney Colne, by A. Trollope; To Esther, by A. Ritchie; Enter a dragoon, by T. Hardy; Olive's lover, by C. C. K. Gonner; The wish house, by R. Kipling; Miss Winchelsea's heart, by H. G. Wells; A long-ago affair, by J. Galsworthy; Claribel, by A. Bennett; Episode, by W. S. Maugham; Fifty pounds, by A. E. Coppard; The legacy, by V. Woolf; Samson and Delilah, by D. H. Lawrence; The tunnel, by J. Cary; Something childish but very natural, by K. Mansfield; Love and money, by P. Bentley; Hubert and Minnie, by A. Huxley; A love story, by E. Bowen; Blind love, by V. S. Pritchett; The blue film, by G. Greene; Stone boy with dolphin, by S. Plath; An English unofficial rose, by P. Theroux; The loneliness of the long-distance runner, by S. Maitland; A small spade, by A. Mars-Jones

The **Oxford** book of English short stories; edited by A.S. Byatt. Oxford Univ. Press 1998 xxx, 439p $40; pa $18.95

ISBN 0-19-214238-0; 0-19-288111-6 (pa)
LC 97-44998

In this anthology Byatt "includes necessary masters—Rudyard Kipling, Saki, D. H. Lawrence, and V. S. Pritchett, to name a few. But . . . she draws into the fold the work of several extremely talented writers of which few readers on this side of the Atlantic will have heard. Falling into this category are such writers as Malachi Whitaker, H. E. Bates, Sylvia Townsend Warner, and Charlotte Mew." Booklist

The **Oxford** book of gothic tales; edited by Chris Baldick. Oxford Univ. Press 1992 xxiii, 533p o.p.

LC 91-27290

This chronologically arranged anthology contains thirty-seven stories dating from the 18th to 20th century. Among the authors are Hawthorne, Poe, Stevenson, Hardy, Faulkner, Welty, Borges, Angela Carter and Isabel Allende

The **Oxford** book of Irish short stories; edited by William Trevor. Oxford Univ. Press 1989 567p o.p.

LC 88-28147

"The great Irish writers—from Oliver Goldsmith and Oscar Wilde to James Joyce and Edna O'Brien—are represented in a collection for older advanced readers." Booklist

The **Oxford** book of Jewish stories; edited by Ilan Stavans. Oxford Univ. Press 1998 493p $30

ISBN 0-19-511019-6 LC 98-16631

Contents: The rabbi's son, by Rabbi Nakhman of Bratzlav; The calf, by S. J. Abramovitsh; If not higher . . ., by I. L. Peretz; A Yom Kippur scandal, by Sholem Aleichem; The mother, by I. Svevo; Tug of love, by I. Zangwill; The kiss, by L. Shapiro; America and I, by A. Yezierska; Holy land, by L. Lewisohn; Before the law, by F. Kafka; At night, by D. Bergelson; The fool and the forest demon, by Der Nister; Camacho's wedding feast, by A. Gerchunoff; A whole loaf, by S. Y. Agnon; The street of crocodiles, by B. Schulz; The story of my dovecot, by I. Babel; The Spinoza of Market Street, by I. B. Singer; The sacrifice of the prisoner, by E. Canetti; Prophet in our midst: a story for Passover, by A. M. Klein; In dreams begin responsibilities, by D. Schwartz; Angel Levine, by B. Malamud; Looking for Mr. Green, by S. Bellow; House at the sea, by N. Ginzburg; The hand that fed me, by I. Rosenfeld; The mirror maker, by P. Levi; The key game, by I. Fink; Midrash on happiness, by G. Paley; Letter from his father, by N. Gordimer; Family ties, by C. Lispector; The shawl, by C. Ozick; The true waiting, by E. Wiesel; The Zulu and the Zeide, by D. Jacobson; Criers and kibitzers, kibitzers and criers, by S. Elkin; Playing ball on Hampstead Heath, by M. Richler; Bertha, by A. Applefeld; The conversion of the Jews, by P. Roth; Dogs and books, by D. Kiš; The Yatir evening express, by A. B. Yehoshua; In the name of his name, by A. Muñiz-Huberman; The ballad of the false messiah, by M. Scliar; Nomad and viper, by A. Oz; The conversion, by I. Goldemberg; Useful ceremonies, by F. Prose; Lazar Malkin enters heaven, by S. Stern; The legacy of Raizel Kaidish, by R. Goldstein; Postscript to a dead language, by M. J. Bukiet; Bottles, by A. L. Domecq; Elvis, Axl, and Me, by J. Eidus; Cherries in the icebox, by D. Grossman; Three nightmares, by I. Stavans; Endless visibility, by J. Rosen; The art biz, by A. Goodman

The **Oxford** book of Latin American short stories; edited by Roberto González Echevarria. Oxford Univ. Press 1997 481p o.p.

LC 97-5395

Contents: The slaughter house, by E. Echeverria; He who listens may hear—to his regret: confidence of a confidence, by J. M. Gorriti; Fray Gomez's scorpion, by R. Palma; Where and how the Devil lost his poncho, by R. Palma; Midnight mass, by Machado de Assis; The death of the Empress of China, by R. Dario; Yzur, by L. Lugones; The decapitated chicken, by H. Quiroga; The baby in pink buckram, by J. do Rio; The man who re-

The Oxford book of Latin American short stories—*Continued*
sembled a horse, by R. Arevalo Martinez; The braider, by R. Guiraldes; The man who knew Javanese, by A. H. de Lima Barreto; Peace on high, by R. Gallegos; The Christmas turkey, by M. de Andrade; The Daisy dolls, by F. Hernandez; The photograph, by E. Amorim; The clearing, by L. M. Levinson; The garden of forking paths, by J. L. Borges; Journey back to the source, by A. Carpentier; The tree, by M. L. Bombal; The legend of "El Cadejo", by M. A. Asturias; Encarnacion Mendoza's Christmas eve, by J. Bosch; The third bank of the river, by J. G. Rosa; The image of misfortune, by J. C. Onetti; Tell them not to kill me!, by J. Rulfo; Hahn's pentagon, by O. Lins; The switchman, by J. J. Arreola; The featherless buzzards, by J. R. Ribeyro; Meat, by V. Pinera; Unborn, by A. A. Roa Bastos; The night face up, by J. Cortazar; Cooking lesson, by R. Castellanos; The doll queen, by C. Fuentes; The walk, J. Donoso; Balthazar's marvelous afternoon, by G. Garcia Marquez; The challenge, by M. Vargas Llosa; The crime of the mathematics professor, by C. Lispector; Buried statues, by A. Benitez-Rojo; A woman's back, by J. Balza; The warmth of things, by N. Pinon; The threshold, by C. Peri Rossi; The parade ends, by R. Arenas; When women love men, by R. Ferre; Penelope, by D. Trevisan

The **Oxford** book of modern fairy tales; edited by Alison Lurie. Oxford Univ. Press 1993 455p $30; pa $14.95

ISBN 0-19-214218-6; 0-19-282385-X (pa)
LC 92-28007

This volume is "full of old favorites and some priceless new gems, with a wonderful chronological arrangement that allows readers to absorb information on literary developments and trends, or simply to enjoy the well-told tales. . . . The whole collection is first rate and demonstrates beautifully that modern fairy tales are not just for kids." SLJ

The **Oxford** book of science fiction stories; edited by Tom Shippey. Oxford Univ. Press 1992 xxvi, 587p o.p.

LC 92-9512

Contents: The land ironclads, by H. G. Wells; Finis, by F. L. Pollack; As easy as ABC, by R. Kipling; The metal man, by J. Williamson; A Martian odyssey, by S. G. Weinbaum; Night, by J. W. Campbell; Desertion, by C. D. Simak; The piper's son, by L. Padgett; The monster, by A. E. van Vogt; The second night of summer, by J. H. Schmitz; Second dawn, by A. C. Clarke; Crucifixus etiam, by W. M. Miller; The tunnel under the world, by F. Pohl; Who can replace a man?, by B. Aldiss; Billennium, by J. G. Ballard; The ballad of lost C'mell, by C. Smith; Semley's necklace, by U. K. Le Guin; How beautiful with banners, by J. Blish; A criminal act, by H. Harrison; Problems of creativeness, by T. M. Disch; How the whip came back, by G. Wolfe; Cloak of anarchy, by L. Niven; A thing of beauty, by N. Spinrad; The screwfly solution, by R. Sheldon; The way of cross and dragon, by G. R. R. Martin; Swarm, by B. Sterling; Burning chrome, by W. Gibson; Silicon muse, by H. Schenck; Karl and the ogre, by P. J. McAuley, Piecework, by D. Brin

The **Oxford** book of short stories; chosen by V.S. Pritchett. Oxford Univ. Press 1981 547p $35; pa $16.95

ISBN 0-19-214116-3; 0-19-282113-X (pa)
LC 81-156872

In addition to one of his own short stories, Pritchett has selected 40 others, written in English during the 19th and 20th centuries. Most of the authors are English, Irish or American and include Somerset Maugham, D. H. Lawrence, Faulkner, Twain, and Eudora Welty

The **Oxford** book of spy stories; edited by Michael Cox. Oxford Univ. Press 1996 356p $30

ISBN 0-19-214242-9 LC 95-15519

Includes the following stories: Parker Adderson, philosopher, by A. Bierce; The red carnation, by E. Orczy; The rider in the dawn, by A. T. Quiller-Couch; The Brass Butterfly, by W. Le Queux; Peiffer, by A. E. W. Mason; Mr. Collingrey, MP, by E. Wallace; The lit chamber, by J. Buchan; The reckoning with Otto Schreed, by E. P. Oppenheim; Giulia Lazzari, by W. S. Maugham; Judith, by C. E. Montague; The pigeon man, by V. Williams; Jumbo's wife, by F. O'Connor; Affaire de coeur, by W. E. Johns; Flood on the Goodwins, by A. D. Divine; How Ryan got out of Russia, by E. J. M. D. P. Dunsany; A patriot, by J. Galsworthy; A double double-cross, by P. Cheyney; The army of the shadows, by E. Ambler; Citizen in space, by R. Sheckley; Risico, by I. Fleming; Keep walking, by G. Household; Paper casualty, by L. Deighton; Signal Tresham, by M. Gilbert; Final demand, by J. Wainwright; The rocking-horse spy, by T. Allbeury; The great divide, by W. Haggard; A branch of the service, by G. Greene; Waiting for Mrs. Ryder, by D. Hoch

The **Oxford** book of travel stories; edited by Patricia Craig. Oxford Univ. Press 1996 441p $35

ISBN 0-19-288031-4 LC 96-51543

Contents: The holly-tree, by C. Dickens; The lazy tour of two idle apprentices, by C. Dickens; A ride across Palestine, by A. Trollope; From Miltzow to Lauterbach, by E. Von Arnim; A Journey, by E. Wharton; Human habitation, by E. Bowen; Cruise, by E. Waugh; Travelogue, by R. Lardner; Show Mr. and Mrs. F. to number-, by F. S. Fitzgerald; Local colour, by W. Plomer; Gliding gulls and going people, by W. Sansom; Deliverance, by R. West; A good man is hard to find, by F. O'Connor; Request stop, by D. Jacobson; Big trip to Europe, by J. Kerouac; Brimmer, by J. Cheever; A journey to the seven streams, by B. Kiely; Scholar and gypsy, by A. Desai; The lady from Guatemala, by V. S. Pritchett; Loser wins, by P. Theroux; Death in Jerusalem, by W. Trevor; Siegfried on the Rhine, by S. T. Warner; The faithful, by E. Hardwick; The bridge at Arta, by J. I. M. Stewart; Greyhound people, by A. Adams; The compartment, by R. Carver; A long night at Abu Simbel, by P. Lively; The man who blew away, by B. Bainbridge; Chinese funeral, by J. Gardam; The kyogle line, by D. Malouf; Cuckoo clock, by D. Johnson; Somewhere else, by R. Ingalls; Questions of travel, by E. Bishop

The **Oxford** book of twentieth-century ghost stories; edited by Michael Cox. Oxford Univ. Press 1996 425p o.p.
LC 96-4913

Contents: In the dark, by E. Nesbit; Rooum, by O. Onions; The shadowy third, by E. Glasgow; The diary of Mr. Poynter, by M. R. James; Mrs. Porter and Miss Allen, by H. Walpole; The nature of the evidence, by M. Sinclair; Night-fears, by L. P. Hartley; Bewitched, by E. Wharton; A short trip home, by F. Scott Fitzgerald; Blind man's buff, by H. R. Wakefield; The blackmailers, by A. Blackwood; Yesterday street, by T. Burke; Smoke ghost, by F. Leiber; The cheery soul, by E. Bowen; All but empty, by G. Greene; Three miles up, by E. J. Howard; Close behind him, by J. Wyndham; The quincunx, by W. De la Mare; The tower, by M. Laski; Poor girl, by E. Taylor; I kiss your shadow, by R. Bloch; A woman seldom found, by W. Sansom; The Portobello road, by M. Spark; Ringing the changes, by R. Aickman; On terms, by C. Brooke-Rose; The only story, by W. Trevor; The loves of lady purple, by A. Carter; Revenant as typewriter, by P. Lively; The little dirty girl, by J. Russ; Watching me, watching you, by F. Weldon; The July ghost, by A. S. Byatt; The highboy, by A. Lurie; The meeting house, by J. Gardam

Oz, Amos

Don't call it night; translated from the Hebrew by Nicholas de Lange. Harcourt Brace & Co. 1996 199p o.p.
LC 96-14587

Original Hebrew edition, 1994

This novel is set in Tel Kedar, an Israeli town in the Negev Desert. "The human beings who relate the place to us—speaking alternate chapters through most of the book—are Theo, a sixty-year-old semi-retired planner, and [his lover] Noa, a forty-five-year-old teacher of literature." Times Lit Suppl

"This novel is a piece of sweet but melancholy chamber music—light but not necessarily insubstantial. It belongs to a genre of restful novel that is ruled by an esthetic of peace and a yearning for peace. If one is looking for politics, there is that—clearly, if quietly." N Y Times Book Rev

Fima; translated from the Hebrew by Nicholas de Lange. Harcourt Brace & Co. 1993 322p o.p.
LC 92-44200

"A Helen and Kurt Wolff book"

Original Hebrew edition, 1991

"Efraim 'Fima' Nisan, sometime poet, sometime journalist, full-time dreamer, polemicist, philosopher and receptionist at a Jerusalem gynecological clinic, has made a mess of what was once a promising life. Twice divorced, supported mainly by gifts from his loving father, he bumbles through his days in an absentminded fog interrupted by long interior monologues and obsessive verbal diatribes in which he rails against the corruption of Israeli values." Publ Wkly

"Not only does Mr. Oz strive toward a Chekhovian compassion for his characters, but his novel depends . . . on making us believe in the possibility of last-minute grace. When tragedy strikes, we watch Fima rise to the occasion and begin to tap his own resources of generosity, humility, common sense, and his sense of purpose." N Y Times Book Rev

Panther in the basement; translated from the Hebrew by Nicholas de Lange. Harcourt Brace & Co. 1997 147p $21

ISBN 0-15-100287-8 LC 97-20577

Original Hebrew edition, 1995

"It is Jerusalem in 1947, during the final days of the British mandate in Palestine, and Proffy, a twelve-and-a-quarter-year-old Jewish boy, is leading a double life. In his parents' eyes, Proffy (short for Professor) is a word savant. By his own definition, he is second-in-command of the underground organization F. O. D. (Freedom or Death), for whose noble cause he scatters bent nails and composes war slogans like 'Perfidious Albion, hands off Zion!' Proffy's identity as an eloquent militant is threatened, however, when his compatriots charge him with treason for befriending a British policeman, and he is forced to reevaluate the implications of word 'enemy.'" New Yorker

The same sea; translated from the Hebrew by Nicholas de Lange in collaboration with the author. Harcourt 2001 201p $30

ISBN 0-15-100572-9 LC 2001-24121

Original Hebrew edition, 1999

This novel depicts "the lives of four people brought together by death: Albert, an aging tax lawyer whose wife recently died of ovarian cancer; his son Enrico, who flees to Tibet; Enrico's girlfriend, Dita, a voluptuous screenwriter; and Bettine, a widowed accountant who is drawn into an uncomfortable intimacy with Albert." New Yorker

"Never has the author's writing been more controlled and polished. . . . His depictions of his characters' lives are tableaux vivants, succint and visual." Times Lit Suppl

Ozick, Cynthia

The cannibal galaxy. Knopf 1983 161p o.p.
LC 82-48719

"Joseph Brill, who prefers to be called Principal Brill, teaches a dual curriculum of European scholarship and Judaic literature in his school. An escapee from the Holocaust which killed most of his family, Brill searches for the bright pupils who will add luster to his mediocre school in Middle America. When Hester Lilt enrolls her daughter Beulah, he has great hopes because of the mother's intellect. He fails to perceive the potential spark of genius in the daughter and is thrown into confusion when Beulah achieves fame in her adult years." Shapiro. Fic for Youth. 3d edition

Heir to the glimmering world. Houghton Mifflin 2004 310p $24

ISBN 0-618-47049-2 LC 2004-42723

"In 1933, the Mitwissers, a family of German Jews, arrive in America after a narrow and eccentric escape from Berlin. . . . After landing somewhat haphazardly in New York, they place an ad for help in a local paper. The only applicant for the job is an eighteen-year-old orphan, Rose Meadows, who narrates the story, and who observes the Mitwissers with the dry neutrality of an invisible servant. Her duties are vaguely defined-part nanny,

Ozick, Cynthia—*Continued*

part secretary-and her salary comes intermittently, the family's sole source of income being the whimsy of a troubled benefactor. Ozick portrays this ramshackle household to dazzling effect, as it adjusts to its many states of exile-from a sense of security, from cherished ideas, and from the consolations of each other." New Yorker

"In 1933, the Mitwissers, a family of German Jews, arrive in America after a narrow and eccentric escape from Berlin. . . . After landing somewhat haphazardly in New York, they place an ad for help in a local paper. The only applicant for the job is an eighteen-year-old orphan, Rose Meadows, who narrates the story, and who observes the Mitwissers with the dry neutrality of an invisible servant. Her duties are vaguely defined—part nanny, part secretary—and her salary comes intermittently, the family's sole source of income being the whimsy of a troubled benefactor. Ozick portrays this ramshackle household to dazzling effect, as it adjusts to its many states of exile—from a sense of security, from cherished ideas, and from the consolations of each other." New Yorker

The Messiah of Stockholm; a novel. Knopf 1987 141p $15.95

ISBN 0-394-54701-2 LC 86-46014

"The protagonist, Lars Andemening, a book reviewer for a Stockholm newspaper, is obsessed with Bruno Schulz, a Polish Jewish writer murdered by the Nazis. Lars, an orphan, believes that he is Schulz's son. His dream is to find his father's lost manuscript, 'The Messiah.' When a manuscript bearing that name turns up, Lars's determination to know the truth about its provenance leads him to increasingly dark waters." Christ Sci Monit

This "novel is a complex and fascinating meditation on the nature of writing and the responsibilities of those who choose to create—or judge—tales. Yet on a purely realistic level, it manages to capture the atmosphere of Stockholm and to be, at times, very funny indeed about the daily operations of one of the city's newspapers and Lars's peculiar detachment from everyday work and life." N Y Times Book Rev

The Puttermesser papers. Knopf 1997 235p $23

ISBN 0-679-45476-4 LC 96-39155

This book presents "five previously published episodes from the imagined life of Ruth Puttermesser. . . . The first paper, 'Puttermesser: Her Work History, Her Ancestry, Her Afterlife,' introduces the protagonist, age 34, as a New York Jew who has quit the 'blue-blood Wall Street' law firm where she was going nowhere fast. She is now working in the Department of Receipts and Disbursements of the City of New York, where she is going nowhere even faster." N Y Times Book Rev

"This entertaining fable is a social commentary as well as a comic tour de force, and it bristles with Ozick's formidable intelligence and wit." Publ Wkly

Rosa

In Ozick, C. The shawl

The shawl. Knopf 1989 69p $12.95

ISBN 0-394-57976-3 LC 89-2652

"This volume comprises a five-page short story entitled 'The Shawl' and a novella entitled 'Rosa.' Both first appeared in The New Yorker, the first in 1981, the second in 1984. 'The Shawl' focuses on an . . . incident in a Nazi concentration camp where Rosa Lubin, Polish Jew, has hidden her fifteen-month-old baby, Magda, in a shawl. . . . Rosa's fourteen-year-old niece, Stella, steals the shawl; subsequently, in the search for it, Magda is killed by a camp guard, who flings the baby against an electrified fence. . . . 'Rosa' opens three decades later in Miami, where Rosa, now a fifty-eight-year old, resides in the 'dark hole' of a single room at a hotel for elderly retirees. . . . She is being begrudgingly subsidized by her forty-nine-year-old niece, Stella, who appeared in 'The Shawl.'" Commonweal

"Rosa is brilliantly realized. Her dark night of the soul is lit by flashes of insight about memory, culture, old age, a welcome meditation on the euphemistic inadequacy of the word 'survivor.'" N Y Times Book Rev

P

Packer, Ann

The dive from Clausen's pier; a novel. Knopf 2002 369p pa $14 o.p.

ISBN 0-375-41282-4; 0-375-72713-2 (pa) LC 2001-42522

"A reckless attempt to impress Carrie, Mike's dive off Clausen's Pier rendered him paralyzed. Now Carrie finds herself torn between the loyalty she's expected to feel toward Mike and her need to transform herself. She takes a dive of her own—into adulthood—when she escapes to New York." Booklist

Packer, ZZ, 1973-

Drinking coffee elsewhere. Riverhead Bks. 2003 238p $24.95; pa $14

ISBN 1-57322-234-8; 1-57322-378-6 (pa) LC 2002-73971

"The predominantly African American characters in Packer's first collection of short fiction struggle to maintain their sense of self while they confront unexpected life events." Booklist

Paddock, Jennifer

A secret word; a novel; Jennifer Paddock. Simon & Schuster 2004 206p $13

ISBN 0-7432-4707-8 (pa) LC 2003-57343

This is the "story of three girls from Fort Smith, Ark., linked for life by a high school tragedy. In 1986, tennis and country club pals Sarah and Chandler hitch a ride to lunch from the less privileged Leigh; they're pursued by footballer Trey, who crashes his car and dies. Flash forward to 1990: Chandler and Sarah have gone to college; Leigh stays behind to work at a dry cleaner's. But their paths continue to intersect, and Paddock follows her characters through 15 years as they peel apart and reunite, capturing each of the young women in separate first-person chapters." Publ Wkly

"Filled with many moving and sometimes devastating moments and observations, Paddock's first novel is three coming-of-age stories for the price of one." Booklist

Page, Katherine Hall

The body in the basement. St. Martin's Press 1994 289p o.p.
LC 94-25764

"A Thomas Dunne book"

This Faith Fairchild mystery "centers around the Massachusetts housewife and caterer's next-door neighbor, occasional employee and friend, Pix Miller. Early in the summer on Sanpere Island, Maine, Pix and her daughter check the construction work on the Fairchilds' summer cottage and discover a quilt-wrapped body buried where the foundation will soon be poured. Dead is Mitchell Pierce, an antiques seller and house restorer with a host of enemies on the island. . . . Pix begins asking questions and, although she often calls Faith with progress reports, ends up solving that murder and one that follows. This leisurely tale, with recipes for fish chowder, corn bread and blueberry tart, nicely frames the down-to-earth, eminently likable Pix, who proves an enjoyable stand-in for Faith." Publ Wkly

The body in the Big Apple. Morrow 1999 239p $22
ISBN 0-688-15748-3 LC 99-33511

This prequel to the Faith Fairchild series "catches the amateur sleuth at the start of her career. . . . It's winter in Manhattan and 23-year-old Faith is darting from one holiday party to the next, bearing hearty comfort foods to a chic clientele of East Side socialites and yuppies. . . . At one of these soirees Faith runs into an old school chum, now married to an up-and-coming politician, who confides that she is being blackmailed." N Y Times Book Rev

The body in the bog. Morrow 1996 276p o.p.
LC 96-3468

"Sleuth Faith Fairchild occupies her time in small-town Massachusetts with her husband, Tom, a preacher; their two small children; Have Faith, her catering business; and an occasional murder. When wetlands are converted into a chi-chi housing development, poison pen letters fly, one of the houses burns, and police discover murder. Faith's persistent quest for clues exposes many secrets, but the ultimate confrontation occurs in Have Faith's kitchen. Well-delineated action and characters mix easily with Faith's attendant domesticity." Libr J

The body in the bookcase. Morrow 1998 244p $22
ISBN 0-688-15747-5 LC 98-36708

A mystery featuring Faith Fairchild, "the Aleford, Mass., caterer, wife and mother of two. Faith, like everybody else in town, is appalled when 80-year-old Sarah Winslow is found dead after her house is burglarized. After her own home is broken into, Faith decides to solve the crimes. . . . Page's tale is tightly written, with strong characterizations and delightful descriptions of its New England setting." Publ Wkly

The body in the fjord. Morrow 1997 278p $22
ISBN 0-688-14574-4 LC 97-24377

"Caterer Faith Fairchild's part-time employee, Pix Miller, departs for Norway, where a friend has suddenly disappeared. Eighth in a charming series, complete with food talk, stolen antiques, murder—and recipes." Libr J

The body in the lighthouse; a Faith Fairchild mystery. HarperCollins Pubs. 2003 327p $23.95
ISBN 0-380-97844-X LC 2002-68859

"Intrepid part-time caterer/sleuth Faith Fairchild. . . vacations with her family on an island off the coast of Maine, but they don't get much relaxation. Ill feelings between year-round residents and summer visitors reach a crisis when a developer is found dead near the lighthouse. Faith investigates, with the usual spine-tingling results." Libr J

The body in the vestibule. St. Martin's Press 1992 211p o.p.
LC 92-18455

"A Thomas Dunne book"

This Faith Fairchild mystery is "set in Lyons, France. Faith, four months pregnant, her husband Tom, a minister who is finishing research for his dissertation, and their three-year-old Ben live in a huge fifth-floor apartment. Taking out the garbage one evening, Faith finds the body of a homeless man from the neighborhood in the trash bin. When the police arrive, however, the body is gone and Faith's credibility is in question. At a party she meets Chief Inspector Michel Ravier, who asks about the body and tells her to call if she witnesses anything else unusual. . . . With beautifully detailed descriptions of Lyons added to Faith's intelligent observations, Page . . . continues to hit the mark with this charming series." Publ Wkly

Palahniuk, Chuck

Diary; a novel. Doubleday 2003 260p $24.95
ISBN 0-385-50947-2 LC 2003-43900

This "is the story of a lonely artist named Misty Marie Wilmot and the spooky community of blue-blood islanders she's married into. . . . Her story takes the form of a diary written to her husband, Peter, who lies contorted and comatose in the hospital after a suicide attempt. On Waytansea Island, the Wilmot ancestral home, Misty struggles to take care of their daughter, Tabbi, and Peter's mother, Grace, while making ends meet as a maid at the island hotel." N Y Times Book Rev

"Catchy, jarring prose, cryptic pronouncements and baroque flights of imagination are instantly recognizable, and [the author's] sharp, bizarre meditations on the artistic process make this twisted tale one of his most memorable works to date." Publ Wkly

Lullaby; a novel. Doubleday 2002 260p o.p.
ISBN 0-385-50447-0 LC 2001-52979

"Middle-aged journalist Carl Streator discovers that all children who died of SIDS are read the same poem the night before their deaths. . . Once he discovers that simply reciting the poem in someone's direction is invariably fatal, Streator can't stop murdering. Then he finds out that Helen Hoover Boyle, a real-estate agent who sells the same haunted houses over and over again, knows the secret, too. They set out on a grand literary road trip to destroy all extant copies of the song." Booklist

"This is vintage Palahniuk: weird, creepy, twisted, upsetting, and ultimately a great read for anyone who wants to be scared for pleasure." Libr J

Paley, Grace

The collected stories. Farrar, Straus & Giroux 1994 386p $27.50

ISBN 0-374-12636-4 LC 93-42230

This volume includes stories from three previously published collections

Contents: The little disturbances of man: Goodbye and good luck; A woman, young and old; The pale pink roast; The loudest voice; The contest; An interest in life; An irrevocable diameter; The used-boy raisers; A subject of childhood; In time which made a monkey of us all; The floating truth

Enormous changes at the last minute: Wants; Debts; Distance; Faith in the afternoon; Gloomy tune; Living; Come on, ye sons of art; Faith in a tree; Samuel; The burdened man; Enormous changes at the last minute; Politics; Northeast playground; The little girl; A conversation with my father; The immigrant story; The long-distance runner

Later the same day: Love; Dreamer in a dead language; In the garden; Somewhere else; Lavinia: an old story; Friends; At that time; Anxiety; In this country, but in another language, my aunt refuses to marry the men everyone wants her to; Mother; Ruthy and Edie; A man told me the story of his life; The story hearer; This is a story about my friend George, the toy inventor; Zagrowsky tells; The expensvie moment; Listening

Palliser, Charles

The quincunx. Ballantine Bks. 1990 c1989 788p o.p.

LC 89-91787

"Set in England during the 1820s and '30s, the novel is chiefly narrated by a character who first appears as a young boy named John Mellamphy. He lives with his mother in a small village; he has no knowledge of his father, nor does he realize that Mellamphy is not his real surname. Gradually, he comes to understand that his mother possesses something that a number of other people desperately want. It is the codicil to an old, disputed will concerning the immense Huffam estate. The present holder of that property, Sir Perceval Mompesson, wants to obtain the codicil so he can destroy it." Time

"This is not an ironic parody à la Barth, not an echo of Eco, but a genuine reproduction of a full-bodied 19th-century page-turner of a novel, set in late Regency England, thick with characters of all classes, with plots, counterplots, fore-bodings, reversals and interpolated tales. . . . Mr. Palliser's re-creation of this period is absolutely convincing, his dialogue never jars, his command of details never falters." N Y Times Book Rev

The unburied. Farrar, Straus & Giroux 1999 403p $25

ISBN 0-374-28035-5 LC 99-14740

"On a visit to an old school friend in Thurchester, England, professional historian Courtine looks forward to doing research in the cathedral library and renewing ties; he does not expect to become embroiled in a controversy surrounding a centuries-old mystery, nor does he anticipate being a major witness to a gruesome murder." Libr J

"All the murders are puzzles, and Palliser constructs his plot like a maze and lures his readers into it. The book's ruthless consistency of style and the somewhat bleak view of humankind set it apart from the usual thriller." New Yorker

Palmer, Michael, 1942-

Miracle cure. Bantam Bks. 1998 399p $23.95

ISBN 0-553-10523-X LC 98-4884

A medical thriller revolving around a new drug "called Vasclear, a heart medication being developed at the Boston Heart Institute by Newbury Pharmaceuticals. The FDA is being pressured by a Massachusetts senator (who, it turns out, is secretly taking Vasclear himself) to approve the release of the drug. And Vasclear may be the magic wand that can save the life of Jack 'Coach' Holbrook, whose health is declining after a quintuple bypass. Coach's son, Brian . . . not only faces the ethical dilemma of stealing the drug if he can't place his father as a test patient but also finds evidence of potentially dangerous side effects—evidence that could derail the drug's release to the public." Publ Wkly

Natural causes. Bantam Bks. 1994 389p o.p.

LC 93-26832

"Sarah Baldwin lived in Thailand for several years and acquired both an understanding and a practical knowledge of acupuncture and herbal medicine. Now an obstetric resident at the Medical Center of Boston, she becomes involved with a mysterious disease, a nascent diet-treatment empire, and unmitigated greed. When the wealthy father of one of the disease's victims sues Sarah for malpractice, the story starts moving on several fronts." Booklist

"Palmer uses medical dialog to submerge readers in the race to save other pregnant women still at risk and to combat the greed of treacherous medical killers. Surprises and action make for an excellent read; the climax is both plausible and frightening. The characters are all pleasingly real." Libr J

The patient. Bantam Bks. 2000 324p $24.95

ISBN 0-553-10983-9 LC 99-57838

This medical thriller features "Dr. Jessie Copeland, a neurosurgeon in her 40s with a combined under-graduate degree in biology and mechanical engineering. Now working under egomaniacal chief surgeon Carl Gilbride at a top Boston hospital, Jessie gets to try out ARTIE (Assisted Robotic Tissue Incision and Extraction) on cadavers, while Gilbride coaxes foundations to cough up millions for the revolutionary new procedure. Attracted by the media attention, . . . shadowy terrorist Claude Malloche, known as 'the Mist,' who also has a brain tumor, comes to the hospital for treatment—and winds up holding patients and staff hostage in case the operation fails. It's finally up to Jessie and a rogue CIA agent to keep everyone healthy." Publ Wkly

The society. Bantam Bks. 2004 351p $25

ISBN 0-553-90057-9 LC 2004-303038

This thriller begins "with the murder of several loathsome CEOs of HMOs in Massachusetts. Dr. Will Grant is a talented and caring physician in the Boston area who works long hours and hates the unfair and obstructive practices of the big insurance companies. Patty Moriarity is a rookie state cop whose first big case is investigating the deaths of the health care vultures. After some early research, Patty suspects Will, but soon enough that's all

Palmer, Michael, 1942-—*Continued*

straightened out and they're smooching on the couch. After Will is drugged and collapses during a delicate operation, things get rough: he's kicked out of his hospital for drug abuse and sued. Next he's being tortured, while Patty, shot after attempting to save the boorish chauvinist detective who has taken over her case, lies in a coma. The action is a bit preachy in the beginning, but once Palmer gets all his characters in place, the suspense builds." Publ Wkly

Pamuk, Orhan, 1952-

My name is Red; translated from the Turkish by Erdağ Göknar. Knopf 2001 417p o.p.

ISBN 0-375-40695-6 LC 2001-29866

Original Turkish edition, 1998

"In 16th-century Istanbul master miniaturist and illuminator of books Enishte Effendi is commissioned to illustrate a book celebrating the sultan. Soon he lies dead at the bottom of a well, and how he got there is the crux of this novel. A number of narrators give testimony to what they know about the circumstances surrounding the murder." Libr J

"The Ottoman Istanbul, which Mr. Pahmuk depicts with skill and linguistic energy, is a rich, cruel and claustrophobic world where art leads, through dark alleyways to murder. The novel is also about the conflicts of Turkishness, about . . . a society caught between religious zealotry and an authoritarian state—themes as relevant to Turkey now as they were 400 years ago." Economist

Snow; translated by Maureen Freely. Knopf 2004 426p $26

ISBN 0-375-40697-2

Original Turkish edition, 2002

"Upon returning to his home in secular Turkey, a poet named Ka discovers two things that will change his life: Ipek, the girl he loved as a child, still lives in the city of Kars, and the community has been stunned by a rash of suicides of zealously religious girls who refused to remove their head scarves while in public. With an investigator's eye, Ka seeks out information about the tragedies from all sources, eventually leading to the man at the eye of the storm, Blue, a charismatic Islamite who will not let the message that these girls carried be silenced." Libr J

"Pamuk's sometimes exhaustive conversations and descriptions create a stark picture of a too-little-known part of the world, where politics, religion and even happiness can seem alternately all-consuming and irrelevant. A detached tone and some dogmatic abstractions make for tough reading, but Ka's rediscovery of God and poetry in a desolate place makes the novel's sadness profound and moving." Publ Wkly

Paravisini-Gebert, Lizabeth

(ed) Green cane and juicy flotsam. See Green cane and juicy flotsam

Paretsky, Sara

Bitter medicine. Morrow 1987 321p o.p.

LC 86-33238

"A young Hispanic woman and her premature infant die in a wealthy suburban hospital. Her doctor is found beaten to death the next day. As a favor to Lottie Herschel, her long-time friend and mentor, Chicago private investigator and lawyer V. I. Warshawski agrees to look into the case. Abortion and medical ethics are the backdrop for this powerful and moving novel." Libr J

Blacklist; a V.I. Warshawski novel. Putnam 2003 415p $24.95

ISBN 0-399-15085-4 LC 2003-43157

"A dead reporter, a missing Egyptian boy wanted in connection with terrorist activities, and an elderly woman convinced that an intruder is in her family manse are all elements of Paretsky's . . . novel featuring Chicago private investigator V. I. Warshawski. As V. I. looks into these peoples' lives, she discovers connections among them. She uncovers a story of betrayal and secrets that spans several generations and involves Chicago's wealthiest families, the Red Scare, and the House Un-American Activities Committee hearings of the 1950s. As always, V. I.'s determined pursuit of the truth ensures at least a few heart-stopping moments." Libr J

Blood shot; a novel. Delacorte Press 1988 328p o.p.

LC 88-3861

"Blood Shot takes [the detective-heroine V.I. Warshawski] back to the working-class Chicago neighbourhoods of her youth, where a callous industrialist lurks at the centre of a deadly web of violence and intrigue." Quill Quire

Burn marks. Delacorte Press 1990 340p o.p.

LC 89-23418

This "adventure of Chicago private eye Victoria Iphenigia Warshawski begins with arson and proceeds to homicide as the intrepid V.I. contends with ambitious politicians, a construction-business scam, a corrupt cop and the best intentions of her closest family friends." Publ Wkly

"The 'whydunit' in Ms. Paretsky's books is often embedded in the fabric of problems that confront us all—the poisoned environment, for example, or urban blight. This extra dimension adds an immediacy to 'Burn Marks' that is not found in many private-eye novels." N Y Times Book Rev

Deadlock; a V.I. Warshawski mystery. Dial Press (NY) 1984 252p o.p.

LC 83-14324

In this novel V. I. Warshawski "becomes involved in a case after her cousin, a former ice hockey star now working for a grain company, is killed on the waterfront. The police list the death as an accident. Warshawski starts poking around and kicks over the inevitable can of worms." N Y Times Book Rev

Fire sale. Putnam 2005 402p $25.95

ISBN 0-399-15279-2 LC 2005-47601

This entry draws V. I. Warshawski "back to her South Chicago roots when she reluctantly agrees to coach the girls basketball team at her former high school, which is struggling with poverty, teen pregnancy, a lack of equip-

Paretsky, Sara—*Continued*
ment, and gang influence. The old neighborhood has declined, too, and when a small local factory is sabotaged, V.I. is persuaded to investigate. Meanwhile, she hopes to gain financial support for the basketball team from By-Smart, a megadiscount chain whose founder also grew up in South Chicago. In a series of events that includes an explosion at the local factory, a horrifying murder, and the disappearance of a basketball player, V.I. is drawn into a deadly conflict between By-Smart and South Chicago's residents. Fast-paced and as entertaining." Libr J

Ghost country. Delacorte Press 1998 386p $24.95
ISBN 0-385-29933-8 LC 98-12294
Chicagoans "Harriet and Mara Stonds have been raised in luxuary by their grandfather, famous neurosurgeon Abraham Stonds. Harriet is the apple of her grandfather's eye—tall, blond, successful at everything she does, always the good girl. Mara plays the role of ugly stepsister, at least to her grandfather, who has told her for years that she's lazy, stupid, and ungrateful. But things are about to change for the Stonds family. A drunken opera singer, a softhearted psychotherapist, a group of homeless women, and a mysterious visitor who performs miracles will each play a key role in opening the eyes of Harriet and Mara to a world they've never imagined. This book is rich, astonishing, and affecting." Booklist

Guardian angel. Delacorte Press 1992 370p o.p.
LC 91-24976
While investigating a local manufacturer Chicago private eye V.I. Warshawski uncovers a bond-parking scheme that reaches into her ex-husband's law firm and ties into the bizarre behavior of her neighbors
"The plot serves nicely to bring V.I. into contact with tough, down-and-out types, whom Ms. Paretsky draws extremely well. . . . Bits and pieces of V.I.'s background are worked into the narrative unobtrusively, so that we come to know her as the story progresses, the way we come to know people in real life." N Y Times Book Rev

Hard time; a V.I. Warshawski novel. Delacorte Press 1999 384p $24.95
ISBN 0-385-31363-2 LC 99-22214
When V. I. Warshawski "swerves to avoid a body lying in the middle of the road, she never imagines that her search for the reasons behind the vicious beating death of Nicola Aguinaldo will take her from the upper classes of Chicago society to a long stint behind bars at a private women's prison overrun with sadistic guards and almost equally threatening inmates." Libr J

Indemnity only; a novel. Dial Press (NY) 1982 244p o.p.
LC 81-5452
"Chicago private eye V. I. Warshawski is hired to locate a young woman and instead comes across the body of her boyfriend, a crooked union, and an insurance scam. Thugs beat V. I. up, and another man is murdered. This is all standard hard-boiled detective stuff, except that V. I. is a woman—tough, independent, good looking, and believable. Paretsky has done an excellent job of presenting a real female private eye, without falling into parody." Libr J

Killing orders. Morrow 1985 288p o.p.
LC 84-27270
V. I. Warshawski's "75-year-old aunt, a harridan and religious hypocrite, calls on V.I. for help. There is no love lost between the two, but family is family. The aunt is involved with fake securities found in the safe of the church for which she is the treasurer. Nobody really believes she forged the stock certificates. But who did? V.I. sets out to solve the mystery." N Y Times Book Rev

Total recall; a V.I. Warshawski novel. Delacorte Press 2001 414p o.p.
ISBN 0-385-31366-7 LC 2001-28801
"At a Chicago conference on Jews and Christians, an unassuming man calling himself Paul Radbuka makes some startling assertions. Claiming that a recovered memory therapist has recently helped him to regain memories of a childhood destroyed by the Holocaust, he seeks to find his true family. Before she knows it, private detective V.I. Warshawski is drawn into the turmoil unleashed by these claims and watches helplessly as her dearest friend and mentor, Lotty Hershel, is consumed by a past she wishes to forget." Libr J
This mystery "is written with the stylistic verve and intellectual energy of a writer just coming into her own." N Y Times Book Rev

Tunnel vision. Delacorte Press 1994 432p o.p.
LC 94-6050
Chicago private detective V.I. Warshawski uncovers a "cynical swindle when she tries to help a wretched family she finds living in the basement of her office building. After getting the bum's rush from an advocacy group for the homeless and from feminist friends protecting their own grants, V.I. sticks out her jaw and goes it alone on this dirty, complicated fraud case. Mustn't feel sorry for V.I., though, because her outrage gives her the strength to take on the whole corrupt establishment. This principled private eye intimidates people because she doesn't know the meaning of compromise and won't tolerate moral slackers." N Y Times Book Rev

Windy City blues; V. I. Warshawski stories. Delacorte Press 1995 258p o.p.
LC 95-8302
Contents: Grace notes; The Pietro Andromache; Strung out; At the old swimming hole; The Maltese cat; Settled score; Skin deep; Three-dot po; The Takamoku joseki
"Although V.I.'s just as feisty and tough-talking as ever, she presents a somewhat softer side in this series of stories that gives a nostalgic nod to Vic's friends, family, and past." Booklist

(ed) A Woman's eye. See A Woman's eye

Pargeter, Edith, 1913-1995
For works written by this author under other names see Peters, Ellis, 1913-1995

Parini, Jay

The apprentice lover; a novel. HarperCollins Pubs. 2002 307p $24.95
ISBN 0-06-621071-2 LC 2001-39675
"Derailed by his brother's death in Vietnam, Alex Massolini, Parini's immensely likable, jejune hero, has dropped out of Columbia and secured the position of sec-

Parini, Jay—*Continued*
retary for the renowned Scots writer Rupert Grant, currently ensconced in a villa on Capri with his astute yet longsuffering wife and two lovely and worshipful 'research assistants.' . . . Parini's lucent and sensuous tale nimbly dissects the confluence of ego and art and ponders the unending wounds of war, ultimately affirming the consoling power of literature, however disappointing writers themselves may be. Wittily drawn cameos of W. H. Auden, Graham Greene, and Gore Vidal add to the deep pleasures of this smart, graceful novel." Booklist

Parker, Barbara, 1947-

Blood relations. Dutton 1996 374p o.p.
LC 95-32085

"Prosecutor Sam Hagen is known for being a straight arrow, so he's the perfect choice to investigate a potentially explosive case and dismiss it for lack of evidence. Or so think both his boss, the Miami DA, who has his eye on national office and doesn't want controversy, and the city manager, who's courting the tourist industry. The plaintiff is a young model who claims that several men, including a well-connected local businessman and a football player turned actor, raped her. Hagen believes the girl and, despite political pressure, pursues the case." Publ Wkly

"Stylish writing, glamorous characters, a glitzy setting, and an intricately constructed plot—there's a formula for success in any genre of popular fiction." Booklist

Criminal justice. Dutton 1997 304p o.p.
LC 96-44143

"Dan Galindo was a Boy Scout among the Federal prosecutors in Miami. Because he refused to put a flawed and sleazy witness on the stand, a drug kingpin walked. His virtue was rewarded by the loss of his job, forcing him to take up private legal scut work. Now, defending a beautiful but scary rock musician on a minor criminal charge, Dan finds himself in a web of money launderers, suspected bigtime drug lords, informants and ruthless narcs who may even have murdered to cover their tracks." N Y Times Book Rev

The author "has written a brutal commentary on the Miami music scene, offering unforgettable characters and some hilarious potshots at suburbia." Libr J

Suspicion of betrayal; a novel. Dutton 1999 347p $23.95
ISBN 0-525-94468-0 LC 98-52080

This suspense novel features Miami "attorney Gail Connon, whose love affair with high-powered defense attorney Anthony Quintana is going full-speed ahead. Gail's plate is way too full as she tries to save her struggling solo practice while addressing a custody dispute with her ex over their 10-year-old daughter, Karen. Just when Gail thinks everything's under control, the bottom falls out when Karen starts receiving anonymous death threats." Booklist

Suspicion of deceit. Dutton 1998 358p $23.95
ISBN 0-525-94401-X LC 97-38429

A novel featuring attorneys Gail Connor and Anthony Quintana. "To build business for her new solo practice, Gail takes on the Miami Opera as a client, only to learn of a pending crisis: the rising young bass-baritone scheduled to play Don Giovanni in Mozart's opera sang recently in Castro's Cuba. The singer may be in danger, as may several of Gail's opera contacts who have ties to puzzling aspects of Anthony's past, ties that lead back to Nicaragua in the late 1970s." Booklist

"The narrative triumphs, . . . thanks to Parker's rich mix of tropical politics, edgy romance and secrets from the past." Publ Wkly

Suspicion of guilt. Dutton 1995 388p o.p.
LC 94-24282

"Miami attorney Gail Connor has no idea what's in store for her when she accepts old friend Patrick Norris as a client. The estate of wealthy Althea Tibbett is one prize in a bitter battle between unreformed flower child Patrick, his artistic cousins, and an assortment of charities. Soon, Connor finds deeper and deeper complications, including murder, career criminals, and financial misdeeds of the lowest kind." Libr J

"Parker controls her narrative assuredly—she's at her best with boardroom scenes that crackle with tension—and she unabashedly goes after the big finish. While some of the characterization seems clichéd, it all fits the steamy Miami setting of power and ambition." Publ Wkly

Suspicion of vengeance. Dutton 2001 359p $23.95
ISBN 0-525-94601-2 LC 2001-33521

Gail Connor "is asked to take on the case of an old family friend's grandson, Kenny Ray Clark, who was convicted of the stabbing death of a housewife over a decade earlier, indirectly causing the death of her infant son. Now, after 11 years on death row, his appeals are about to run out. Anthony, Gail's on-again, off-again fiancé, himself a high-powered Florida attorney, warns her of the futility of trying to save Clark. But Gail digs into the records and finds, among other things, a drunk defense attorney, a bogus confession and a witness who would have provided an alibi but was threatened by police." Publ Wkly

Parker, Dorothy, 1893-1967

Here lies; the collected stories of Dorothy Parker. Viking 1939 362p o.p.

Contents: Arrangement in black and white; Sexes; Wonderful old gentleman; Telephone call; Here we are; Lady with a lamp; Too bad; Mr. Durant; Just a little one; Horsie; Clothe the naked; Waltz; Little Curtis; Little hours; Big blonde; From the diary of a New York lady; Soldiers of the republic; Dusk before fireworks; New York to Detroit; Glory in the daytime; Last tea; Sentiment; You were perfectly fine; Custard heart

Parker, Robert B., 1932-

Appaloosa. Putnam 2005 276p $24.95
ISBN 0-399-15277-6 LC 2004-58745

In this western, "deputy Everett Hitch recounts the struggle between lawman Virgil Cole and outlaw rancher Randall Bragg for control of the little town of Appaloosa. Modeled on Wyatt Earp, Cole is the kind of man who never loses a fight, and he comes close to taking down the murderous Bragg with ease, until Bragg's hired guns rescue him by abducting Cole's romantic interest and using her as a hostage. This precipitates a long chase, a struggle with wandering Kiowa, and a gunfight

Parker, Robert B., 1932-—*Continued*
reminiscent of the OK Corral. The story gallops along to a surprise ending, but beneath the trappings of this gunfighter novel, Parker really has something to say about the nature of men and women in the Old West." Libr J

Back story. Putnam 2003 291p $24.95
ISBN 0-399-14977-5 LC 2002-36901
"As the title implies, the story is full of references to the past, starting with an unsolved 1974 robbery in which a young California mother visiting her sister was shot dead when she went to cash some traveler's checks at the old Shawmut Bank in Boston. Spenser takes the case to give the victim's daughter peace of mind, only to discover that he has disturbed a cover-up involving the F.B.I., an organized crime figure and the remnants of a gang of counterculture revolutionaries." N Y Times Book Rev

"The repartee between Spenser and Hawk is fast and funny; the sentiment between Spenser and Susan and the musings about Spenser's code are only occasionally cloying; and there's a scattering of remarkable action scenes including a tense shootout in Harvard Stadium." Publ Wkly

A Catskill eagle; a Spenser novel. Delacorte Press/Seymour Lawrence 1985 311p o.p.
LC 84-28617
After Spenser "receives a plea for help from true love Susan Silverman (who is being restrained by the son of a shadowy armaments manufacturer), Spenser travels from Boston to California to Chicago to Connecticut to Idaho, taking Hawk, his favorite colleague, with him on the rescue quest. All this is mainly an excuse for derring-do and violence. At one point the FBI and CIA contract with Spenser to kill the armaments manufacturer. The plot may be ridiculous, but the dialogue is snappy as usual, and the characters are fascinating." Libr J

Ceremony; a Spenser novel. Delacorte Press/Seymour Lawrence 1982 182p o.p.
LC 81-15106
"Spenser is called upon to rescue a young girl who's fallen into prostitution in Boston's Combat Zone, an urban disaster area and human wasteland of crime and pain. Not the least of April Kyle's problems is that she doesn't want to be rescued. She is as elusive as the ruthless men who exploit her. Spenser has to dig deep. And what he comes up with is knowledge and evidence of a prostitution ring that reaches the top levels of the state government. Spenser blows the whistle, and these fine gentlemen are exposed for what they are." Best Sellers

Chance. Putnam 1996 307p o.p.
LC 95-49950
"A second-echelon hoodlum, Julius Ventura, hires Spenser and his partner/sidekick Hawk to find his daughter's missing husband, a middle-management criminal named Anthony Meeker, who, it turns out, had money-handling responsibilities. Speedily determining that Meeker liked to gamble, Spenser and his lover, psychiatrist Susan Silverman, and Hawk depart for Las Vegas." Publ Wkly

"Parker's stouthearted hero proves that he is still as tough and manly as they come, and more principled than ever in this punchy private-eye caper." N Y Times Book Rev

Cold service; Robert B. Parker. Putnam 2005 305p $24.95
ISBN 0-399-15240-7 LC 2004-56608
"As the tale begins, the heretofore-indestructible Hawk is recovering from a near-death experience: shot in the back while protecting a bookie from the upstart Ukrainian Mob. It's payback time, of course, but not before Hawk nurses himself back to psychic and physical health. Meanwhile, Spenser does a bit of sleuthing on his own, determining that Hawk's assailants are the tip of a Ukrainian iceberg that has stuck its tentacles deep into Boston's underworld. Payback, Hawk style, requires eliminating not just the shooters but also the entire Mob. The action comes in a rush near the end, but the satisfying part here is watching Parker dig deeply into the remarkable friendship between two tough guys constitutionally averse to the whole touchy-feely side of life." Booklist

Crimson joy. Delacorte Press 1988 211p o.p.
LC 87-33043
"When Police Lieutenant Marty Quirk is faced with an insane serial killer, who threatens to ignite all of Boston into a racial bonfire, he turns to Spenser for help. There aren't many clues to point the way, until the killer makes it personal by first going after Spenser and then his lady, psychologist Susan Silverman. Never one to take such an affront lightly, Spenser and his pal Hawk set out to put an end to these brutal murders." West Coast Rev Books

"Parker skillfully weaves Susan's objective theorizing, Spenser's *mot juste* narrative, and the killer's subjective emotions into fascinating psychological interplay." Libr J

Death in paradise. Putnam 2001 294p o.p.
ISBN 0-399-14779-9 LC 2001-31874
Jesse Stone, "erstwhile drunk and now sheriff of small-town Paradise, Mass., tackles two criminal and two personal mysteries here: the murder of a teenage girl found shot dead in a local lake, and the chronic beating of a local wife by her husband; the conundrum of Jesse's attraction to alcohol, and the mess of his love life, shaped by his dependence upon his estranged wife but encompassing a highly sexed affair with a school principal." Publ Wkly

"Given his raw nerves, bursts of violence and unhealthy devotion to his ex-wife, Jesse is still unpredictable and a little scary. Let's trust Parker to keep him on the edge." N Y Times Book Rev

Double Deuce. Putnam 1992 224p o.p.
LC 91-29594
In this novel Spenser "finds himself, at the behest of his pal Hawk, defending the residents of a gang-terrorized Boston housing project known as Double Deuce. The drive-by shooting of a teenage mother and her child brings the duo into a confrontation with gangleader Major Johnson and his posse." Publ Wkly

Double play. Putnam 2004 288p $24.95
ISBN 0-399-15188-5 LC 2004-40029
"In this standalone historical from Parker, it is 1947, and the Brooklyn Dodgers have signed Jackie Robinson at first base. While a young Bobby Parker (that is, the author) avidly follows the national pastime, Joseph Burke, a shell-shocked World War II veteran, is working as a bodyguard in New York City. Emotionally stunted, Joseph lives in a world devoid of feeling-until he becomes Robinson's bodyguard." Libr J

Parker, Robert B., 1932-—*Continued*

"Parker pretty much defies category altogether in this deeply felt and intimately told memory tale, which takes place during the historic baseball season of 1947, when Jackie Robinson broke the color bar in major-league baseball by playing first base for the Brooklyn Dodgers. Fusing this chapter of sports history with a hardboiled gangster plot and haunting recollections of his own Boston boyhood, Parker fashions a hugely entertaining fiction that also serves as a blueprint for the themes that preoccupy him as a writer and the code of values that sustains his work." N Y Times Book Rev

Early autumn; a Spenser novel. Delacorte Press/Seymour Lawrence 1981 212p o.p.
LC 80-17736

"Private detective Spenser is hired to find the teen-age son of a divorced couple. The father's underworld connections make it a dangerous job, but when Spenser realizes the emotionally starved boy is being used as a pawn by his parents, he takes the boy to the Maine woods to build up his self-confidence, then digs up enough dirt on the parents to blackmail them into supporting the boy financially but leaving him alone. Lots of witty writing, some tough-guy action, a little sex, and a layer of philosophy of life give this book something for everyone. And it hangs together quite well if you don't mind the concoction." Libr J

Family honor. Putnam 1999 322p $22.95
ISBN 0-399-14566-4 LC 99-27488

Private detective Sunny Randall "is hired by a powerful family to find their runaway daughter, Millicent, who, it transpires, is hooking and needs rescuing. . . . Millicent, it happens, witnessed a conspiracy to murder arising from her cold, ambitious parents—her father aims to be governor—and the Italian mobsters who control them. The mobsters now want her dead, and Sunny, too, if need be. . . . The high suspense is equaled by the emotional power of Sunny's bonding with the damaged girl. A bravura performance." Publ Wkly

Gunman's rhapsody. Putnam 2001 289p o.p.
ISBN 0-399-14762-4 LC 00-53327

This western details the time Wyatt Earp "and his brothers spend in Tombstone, culminating in the shootout at the O.K. Corral." Publ Wkly

The novel "shows surprising fidelity to most of the known facts without letting them get in the way of a good story. Parker's strengths here, as in his crime novels, are plot and dialogue." N Y Times Book Rev

Hugger mugger. Putnam 2000 307p o.p.
ISBN 0-399-14587-7 LC 99-56105

"Spenser has been hired by Walter Clive, a race horse owner in Lamarr, GA. to work with the local security firm in order to find out who killed three of his horses. Clive is particularly concerned about Hugger Mugger, believed to be the next Secretariat." Libr J

"Culture shock brings out a certain waggishness in Spenser, who is fascinated by the elaborately staged lives of the horsy set and more amused than appalled by the character flaws he uncovers beneath all the polite gentility. Without compromising his expert sleuthing techniques . . . he manages to pick up enough regional skills to communicate with the devious natives in their own idiom—and catch them at their own wicked games." N Y Times Book Rev

Hush money. Putnam 1999 309p $22.95
ISBN 0-399-14458-7 LC 98-37344

In this mystery Boston private eye Spenser "is thrown by the lethal combination of sex (straight, gay, kinky) and politics (racial, sexual, academic) that erupts at a certain university in Cambridge when an African-American professor is implicated in the suicide of a militantly gay graduate student. In a situation that adds to his discomposure, Spenser finds himself being sexually hounded by a woman whom he has just rescued from the similarly unhealthy attentions of a former boyfriend." NY Times Book Rev

Looking for Rachel Wallace; a Spenser novel. Delacorte Press/Seymour Lawrence 1980 219p o.p.
LC 79-20776

Spenser's assignment is "to serve as bodyguard to Rachel Wallace, best-selling writer of books supporting feminism and lesbianism. Spenser and Wallace find the promotional tour truly perilous; Wallace is barred from a speaking enagagement, has a pie thrown at her at an autographing session, and is kidnapped by an ultra-right-wing group." Booklist

Melancholy baby; Robert B. Parker. Putnam 2004 296p $24.95
ISBN 0-399-15218-0 LC 2004-50377

"Boston P.I. Sunny Randall is unhappy to learn that the ex-husband she still loves is getting married to someone else. Her life seemingly a mess, Sunny seeks the help of psychiatrist Susan Silverman. In between sessions that probe her relationship with her insufferable mother and beloved father, Sunny works on the case of Sarah Markham, a distraught 21-year-old woman who wants to track down her biological parents. The only trouble is that the couple who raised her claim she's theirs but refuse to take a DNA test to prove it. Sunny soon learns that Sarah's parents have lied about their past. . . . Parker, as always, leavens his story with sly wit while relying on dialog to advance the plot and develop character." Libr J

Mortal stakes. Houghton Mifflin 1975 172p o.p.
"Midnight novel of suspense"

"Marty Raab is a pitcher for the Boston Red Sox. . . . His whole life, all his interests revolve around baseball. Yet tiny rumors have reached management's ears that Raab is throwing games or shaving runs. To forestall the possibility of a major scandal, Spenser, a private investigator, is called in by management." Best Sellers

Night passage. Putnam 1997 322p $21.95
ISBN 0-399-14304-1 LC 97-6901

"Jesse Stone's career as an LAPD homicide detective is over, as is his marriage, thanks largely to booze. The good news is that Paradise, Massachusetts, needs a police chief. What Stone doesn't know is that city father Hasty Hathaway and acting chief Lou Burke are looking for a pushover to put in charge, and they figure a lush might do nicely. They pick the wrong lush." Booklist

This mystery features "complex, expertly shaded relationships, especially romantic, as Jesse flails and fails at loving both his ex-wife and his new girlfriend. The most powerful romance here, though, is between Parker and the written word." Publ Wkly

Parker, Robert B., 1932-—*Continued*

Pale kings and princes; a Spenser novel. Delacorte Press 1987 256p o.p.

LC 86-29125

"Wheaton, Massachusetts has become the cocaine capital of the Northeast. A young investigative reporter looking for a story is murdered there and his boss hires Boston-based private eye Spenser . . . to find the killer. No one talks; but by his presence and contacts with townspeople Spenser upsets the drug lord and things begin to erupt." Libr J

Paper doll. Putnam 1993 223p o.p.

LC 92-30528

In this novel, Spenser is hired by "Louden Tripp to investigate the murder of his wife. Olivia Tripp was bludgeoned to death, the apparent victim of random street crime. Tripp feels the Boston PD glossed over the case. Spenser . . . decides to check Olivia's background. That thread takes him to Alton, South Carolina." Booklist

"Mr. Parker has trimmed his language and characterizations right down to the knuckle to tell this poignant story about the false fronts that people put up to shield themselves from shame. There's no flab on Spenser, either." N Y Times Book Rev

Pastime. Putnam 1991 223p o.p.

LC 91-8745

Boston PI Spenser "searches for the mother of Paul Giacomin, the young man saved by the burly sleuth 10 years earlier in *Early Autumn*. Spenser, now 'middle class and uptown,' is given to drinking Scotch at the Ritz with Susan Silverman, his self-possessed psychiatrist lover, and talking to their dog as if it were a child. But he still works out at the gym with his black friend Hawk, and can stand up to crime boss Joe Broz while trailing Paul's mother to the hideaway of her gangster boyfriend, who has recently stolen a million dollars from the mob." Publ Wkly

"Spenser's sagas are less tales of ratiocination than fables of exemplary conduct; the occasional violence or dubiety of the hero's actions is redeemed by the justice of his judgment, the righteousness of his character." NY Times Book Rev

Perchance to dream; Robert B. Parker's sequel to Raymond Chandler's The big sleep. Putnam 1991 271p o.p.

LC 90-47004

"Private eye Philip Marlowe spins a yarn of greed, madness and death with the cool-eyed cynicism (and good-guy core) that made him the classic hardboiled dick. The era is post-WWII . . . possibly early '50s . . . the L.A. dream beginning to sour. Psychotic Carmen Sternwood is missing from an expensive sanatorium. After sultry Vivian has enlisted suave gangster Eddie Mars to locate her sister, the family butler, Norris, hires Marlowe for the same purpose." Publ Wkly

"Parker plots with little more scope and linear logic than Chandler ever managed, and he fires off enough smart-ass one-liners to keep most readers happy. It's true, he never ventures near the subterranean emotional depths that Chandler would occasionally explore, but, after all, sequels—even when, they're written by the same person—rarely match the originals." Booklist

Perish twice. Putnam 2000 291p o.p.

ISBN 0-399-14668-7 LC 00-55939

"Mary Lou Goddard is the CEO of Great Strides, a feminist organization dedicated to the advancement of women in all areas of life. She is being stalked; her office was vandalized and threatening messages left on her answering machine. She hires former cop and Boston private investigator Sunny Randall to track down her tormentor. It's not long before Sunny has confronted Lawrence B. Reeves. Soon thereafter, Reeves is found dead; the cops call it suicide, but Sunny says murder." Booklist

"With its smooth blend of mystery, action and psychological probings, this is yet another first-rate, though not innovative, offering from a reliable old master." Publ Wkly

Playmates. Putnam 1989 222p o.p.

LC 88-23824

This mystery has Boston private detective Spenser "investigating rumors of point shaving by members of a nationally ranked college basketball team in the Boston area. Suspicion focuses on the team's star performer, an all-American power forward named Dwayne Woodcock, and soon Spenser in his peculiar way finds himself seeking at once to resolve the mystery and protect the culprit." N Y Times Book Rev

Potshot. Putnam 2001 294p o.p.

ISBN 0-399-14710-1 LC 00-68342

"Spenser takes on the job of clearing out a gang of 'mountain trash' who are intimidating the residents of Potshot, Arizona. Even the supremely resourceful Spenser needs a little help with this one, so he drafts six of his compadres from previous adventures." Booklist

"Rounding up this posse of urban gunslingers—all hard-bitten veterans of previous Spenser novels—was pure inspiration on Parker's part, because another shrewd way of keeping a sleuth in shape over the long haul is to guarantee that he has some fun." N Y Times Book Rev

School days. Putnam 2005 295p $24.95

ISBN 0-399-15323-3 LC 2005-74690

"A wealthy grandmother hires Spenser to clear her 17-year-old grandson of being the coconspirator and co-killer in a school shooting at a private school that has left five students, a teacher, and an administrator dead. The boy's buddy has named him, and he has confessed to the crime. Everyone–police, school officials, the defense lawyer, and the immediate family–has given up on the kid, but Spenser has never seen a slammed door he didn't long to break down. Soon he's questioning everyone in the kid's circle, looking for the chink in that slammed door. Along the way, he rummages through all sorts of closets in the privileged world of the private school, turning up links to the underworld." Booklist

Shrink rap. Putnam 2002 304p $24.95

ISBN 0-399-14930-9 LC 2002-24826

The Sunny Randall novel "has the Boston private eye on a national book tour with a best-selling author who is being stalked by her former husband, an unethical and possibly unhinged psychiatrist. The situation proves ideal for Parker's patented brand of knowing humor, yielding glossary snapshots of dithering book dealers, dollar-driven publishers and awe-struck fans." N Y Times Book Rev

Small vices. Putnam 1997 308p $21.95

ISBN 0-399-14244-4 LC 96-9827

Parker, Robert B., 1932-—*Continued*

"Ellis Alves, a black man with sexual assaults on his record, was convicted easily when two witnesses said they saw him kidnap the victim. Former prosecutor Rita Fiore suspects a frame-up, however, and hires old pal Spenser to investigate, . . . Sure enough, reopening the case pits them against the victim's influential parents, her hostile tennis-star boyfriend and his wealthy family, and the state cop who arrested Alves. Four Boston thugs can't force Spenser off the case, but an imported hit man pours several bullets into him." Publ Wkly

"Mr. Parker has written a powerful piece about the defeat and reclamation of a hero, but I wouldn't say that Spenser's dance with death teaches the old knight to act his age. . . . By virtue of his mythic death and rebirth, he has defied mortality altogether and become like some fertility god who lowers himself into the ground each winter and comes roaring back to life each spring." N Y Times Book Rev

Stardust. Putnam 1990 256p o.p.
LC 90-8140

Private detective "Spenser is hired to guard Jill Joyce, television's top star, while her show is shooting on location near Boston Common." N Y Times Book Rev

"There is no denying the efficient economy with which Stardust proceeds to its surprisingly unforeseeable conclusion. This is first-rate literary candy." Quill Quire

Sudden mischief. Putnam 1998 288p $22.95
ISBN 0-399-14370-X LC 97-40703

Susan Silverman "asks Spenser to investigate the sexual harassment suit that has been filed against her first husband, Brad Sterling. Susan's ambivalence about Brad's predicament doesn't make the case easy for Spenser; nor does the gradually disclosed involvement of the noted Harvard Law School professor whose young wife is one of the plaintiffs." Publ Wkly

"Nothing inhibits Spenser and Hawk, his menacing sidekick, from swapping manly repartee. Parker gives these two bruisers plenty of room for their verbal bobbing and weaving, generously setting up great scenes at the gym, on various stakeouts and in one seriously tough bar in the South End." N Y Times Book Rev

Taming a sea-horse; a Spenser novel. Delacorte Press/Seymour Lawrence 1986 250p o.p.
LC 85-29297

Spenser is "in grave danger on an all but unpaid quest to avenge the deaths of a prostitute he met briefly and a pimp he disliked. He confronts slick mob bosses, two-bit thugs and corrupt financiers, relying on his wits but not fearing to apply a little muscle." Time

Thin air. Putnam 1995 293p o.p.
LC 94-39046

Spenser's "friend and ultradeadly ally, Hawk, is off in Burma, leaving Spenser on his own when longtime pal Frank Belson of Boston Homicide needs help. Belson's beautiful young bride, Lisa St. Claire, has disappeared. When Belson is wounded in an ambush that may be related to Lisa's disappearance, Spenser undertakes the search." Booklist

Trouble in Paradise. Putnam 1998 324p $22.95
ISBN 0-399-14433-1 LC 98-7354

This novel finds Jesse Stone, "the chief of police of modest Paradise, Mass., battling a ruthless gang of thieves even as he jousts with personal demons. Two parallel plotlines tell the story. One follows career criminal James Macklin and his moll, Faye, and their planning and subsequent execution of the heist of all the money and valuables on super-rich Stiles Island, which is connected by bridge to Paradise. Meanwhile, there's Stone, a cool customer who's not afraid to step on wealthy toes but who can't get his love life in order and can barely control his taste for booze. . . . Stone's romantic entanglements, particularly his troubled relationship with his ex-wife, add texture to the novel." Publ Wkly

Valediction; a Spenser novel. Delacorte Press/Seymour Lawrence 1984 228p o.p.
LC 83-15197

"A cultish religious group appears to be laundering money for a drug cartel. Spenser is hired by a dance teacher to find his girlfriend, presumably kept by the cult against her will." Best Sellers

The author "has a lot to say about the damaging effects of love in this novel. Especially about the ways people betray themselves and each other when under the influence." Wilson Libr Bull

Walking shadow. Putnam 1994 270p o.p.
LC 94-5127

Boston PI Spenser "encounters danger, venality and plenty of comic material in this . . . tale spanning the worlds of experimental theater and illegal immigration. While he'd rather be at work renovating the old farmhouse that he and his lover, psychiatrist Susan, have bought in nearby Concord, Spenser agrees to find out who is following the Artistic Director of the Port City Theater Company, on whose board of directors Susan sits." Publ Wkly

The widening gyre; a Spenser novel. Delacorte Press/Seymour Lawrence 1983 183p o.p.
LC 82-22083

"Spenser is security officer for Meade Alexander, running for the U.S. Senate. The candidate has received tapes of his wife Ronnie engaged in sex with an unrecognizable male. The anonymous donor threatens to make the tape public unless Meade drops out of the race. Suspecting mobster Joe Broz, said to have Alexander's opponent in his pocket, the detective follows trails to Broz's college-student son, Gerry. The result is that Spenser gets proof that Gerry is blackmailing Meade and others, as well as dealing in drugs, to make himself 'a man of respect' like his father. The detective knows his life is on the line when he gives the facts to Joe." Publ Wkly

Widow's walk. Putnam 2002 294p o.p.
ISBN 0-399-14845-0 LC 2001-48771

"Attorney Rita Fiore, who's worked with the Boston PI before, hires Spenser to find out if her new client, Mary Smith, . . . indeed shot to death her husband, banker and Mayflower descendant Nathan Smith, as the evidence indicates. . . . The writing is as clean as fresh ice, and from the opening sentence ('I think she's probably guilty,' Rita Fiore said to me), it's clear that readers are in the hands of a vet who knows what he's doing." Publ Wkly

(jt. auth) Chandler, R. Poodle Springs

Parker, T. Jefferson

Black water. Hyperion 2002 338p o.p.
ISBN 0-7868-6804-X LC 2001-51903

"Merci Rayborn, homicide detective for the Orange County, California, sheriff's department, has a crime scene that's a puzzler. And it's going to be very high profile—it's in an upscale enclave of million-dollar estates, and one of the victims is a cop. Gwen Wildcraft is dead, and her husband, Archie, is unconscious with a severe head wound. Wildcraft is a patrol officer with the department, and his gun appears to be the murder weapon. Merci's superiors would prefer a quick call of murder-suicide, but her instincts tell her that's the wrong conclusion. . . . A thoughtful, multilayered tale in which crime is a catalyst rather than the centerpiece." Booklist

The blue hour. Hyperion 1999 359p $23.95
ISBN 0-7868-6288-2 LC 98-43135

This Orange County, California, police procedural pairs "retired expert cop Tim Hess with brash young detective Merci Rayborn. They're an unlikely team fighting a nasty serial killer who abducts wealthy, attractive women, eviscerates them, and then apparently saves their bodies." Libr J

"Solid police work, beefed up with some ingenious devices from Parker's bottomless bag of tricks, makes it all come out right—but not before the wondrously weird characters have taken this lurid plot to its outer limits." N Y Times Book Rev

California girl. Morrow 2004 370p $24.95
ISBN 0-060-56236-6

A mystery set in 1960s Southern California. "The Becker boys (Andy the homicide reporter, Nick the cop, and David the minister; Clay was killed in Vietnam) grew up near the Vonns, a troubled, abusive family burdened with more than its share of tragedy. When 19-year-old beauty queen Janell Vonn, the essence of a California girl, is found beheaded in the abandoned SunBlesst packing house, the Becker brothers begin their separate quests to find her killer, finally bringing him to justice while realizing redemption for themselves. But 40 years after a conviction, it becomes apparent that the Beckers were wrong, very wrong. Drenched in lust, love, betrayal, and unfulfilled promise, California Girl features masterly plotting, smart prose, and memorable characters." Libr J

Cold pursuit. Hyperion 2003 360p $23.95
ISBN 0-7868-6805-8 LC 2002-32940

"The murder of retired San Diego Port Commissioner and local politician Pete Braga falls in the lap of homicide detective Tom McMichael, whose family has a multigenerational feud going with the Bragas. Parker makes the most of a standard mystery device here—murder driven by a motive from the distant past—but the real joy of the novel is its remarably evocative prose, which flows seamlessly from lyrical descriptions of rainy San Diego to crisp, no-nonsense dialogue." Booklist

Laguna heat. St. Martin's Press 1985 342p o.p.
LC 85-10055

"The hero is Tom Shephard, 'the new and sole member of the Laguna Beach Police Homicide Division.' Normally, one man would be all that is needed; there are not many homicides in Laguna Beach. But suddenly a sadistic murderer is loose, burning bodies after mutilating them. Shephard, an experienced cop, gets a lead very fast, is attacked and hurt, finds his home vandalized and goes through other harrowing experiences, many psychological." N Y Times Book Rev

"Parker's narrative is a bit heavy-handed, but his ultimately satisfying novel delivers deep and sensitive characterizations." Booklist

Little Saigon. St. Martin's Press 1988 354p o.p.
LC 88-11586

"Chuck Frye, a surf bum who has recently failed at journalism, business and marriage, lives in the shadow of his war-hero brother Bennett, and their father, a wealthy real-estate tycoon. Bennett's Vietnamese wife is a singer whose protest music has made her a heroine among anticommunists and Asian expatriates. When she is kidnapped during a performance, Chuck joins the search for her, hoping to end his estrangement from the Frye clan. But the more he learns about the crime's motive—politics, gang warfare or revenge are all possibilities—the more intently his family tries to shut him out of the investigation." Publ Wkly

Pacific beat. St. Martin's Press 1991 364p o.p.
LC 90-27411

"John Weir, an ex-sheriff's department employee, and brother-in-law Raymond battle corrupt police, development-at-all-cost advocates, and a known sex offender when they try to find the murderer of John's beloved sister. Splayed against the coastal community of Newport Beach, California, where oldtime residents hope to elect a 'slow-growth' candidate, their investigation reveals ever-deeper layers of deception. This exciting, multidimensional plot should grab even the most demanding mystery reader." Libr J

Red light. Hyperion 2000 326p o.p.
ISBN 0-7868-6600-4 LC 99-47293

A police procedural featuring homicide detective Merci Rayborn. "The murders of two prostitutes 30 years apart provide the framework for this . . . crime melodrama about police corruption and political ambition in Southern California's Orange County." Publ Wkly

"Although Parker handles the current-day investigation with some detachment, he puts a lot of heart into the 30-year-old mystery. Teasing out the truth from tapes, forensic evidence, newspaper clippings and the spotty memories of grizzled police veterans, he vividly reconstructs the turmoil of the Vietnam era." N Y Times Book Rev

Silent Joe. Hyperion 2001 341p o.p.
ISBN 0-7868-6728-0 LC 00-53938

"Joe Trona is a dutiful son, but horrible facial scars have made him an outcast. He lived in an orphanage until he was adopted at five by Will Trona, a powerful politician in Southern California's Orange County. As a hulking teenager and later as a young man, Joe became Will's right-hand man—running errands, extracting revenge on enemies, protecting his flank—all the while living a lonely life because of his disfigurement. One night, Joe drops his guard for a moment, and Will is gunned down. Despite aggressive investigations by the FBI and sheriff's department, Joe seeks his own vengeance." Publ Wkly

"A complex mix of seemingly unconnected plot lines, vivid characterization, and real mystery merge to form a truly satisfying thriller." Libr J

Parker, T. Jefferson—*Continued*

Where serpents lie. Hyperion 1998 432p $23.95
ISBN 0-7868-6287-4 LC 97-2633
A thriller set in "Orange County, California, where cop Terry Naughton, head of Crimes Against Youth, a division he helped create, is fiercely trying to track down a creepy pedophile who calls himself Horridus . . . before he kills one of the young girls that he has kidnapped. It seems that besides child pornography and rape, Horridus is also into snakes—really big, hungry snakes—and there's evidence that he has used these 'pets' to dispose of victims in the past. . . . This taut police procedural mixes high supense with believable characters; it's a real page-turner." Libr J

Parkhurst, Carolyn, 1971-

The dogs of Babel. Little, Brown 2003 264p $21.95
ISBN 0-316-16868-8 LC 2002-43644
"When the book opens, Paul, a linguist who lives in suburban Virginia, has just learned that his wife, Lexy Ransome, has died in their backyard in a mysterious fall from an apple tree. Lorelei is the sole witness to this event, and Paul resolves to make her reveal what hapened. Never mind that she is a dog. He will each her to talk." N Y Times Book Rev
"As Paul slips into ever more desperate behavior, we hear an account of his and Lexy's courtship and marriage—the tender, tentative union of two damaged people. But then Paul contacts a man convicted of operating on dogs to install vocal chords, and what had been a poignant, affecting tale turns truly frightening . . . . Parkhurst delivers a remarkable debut in quiet, authoritative prose." Libr J

Parkinson, Heather, 1974-

Across open ground; a novel. Bloomsbury Pub. 2002 248p $23.95
ISBN 1-58234-243-1 LC 2001-56527
"The book is set in 1917, and news of World War I reaches the Idaho high country like a faint trace of wood smoke. Parkinson weights her story equally between Walter Pascoe, a 17-year-old sheepherder, and the woman he falls in love with—a trapper named Trina Ivy. Their brief summer idyll ends when Walter departs to fight in the trenches of France. Pregnant and penniless, Trina must stay in Idaho and fend for herself." N Y Times Book Rev
"The narrative is often powerful, . . . with a concern for female characters and a tenderness generally absent from more conventional books about this era in the American West." Publ Wkly

Parks, Gordon

The learning tree. Harper & Row 1963 303p o.p.
"At 12 years of age Newt is awakening to the world around him in his small town of Cherokee Flats, Kansas, in the 1920s. There is the impact of a first sexual experience and a first love, and because he is a Negro, special responsibility of behavior when one individual may represent an entire group in the eyes of the community." Shapiro. Fic for Youth. 3d edition

Parks, Suzan-Lori

Getting mother's body; a novel; [by] Suzanne Lori. Random House 2003 257p $23.95
ISBN 1-400-06022-2 LC 2002-31762
"Billy Beede is a girl with troubles. Unmarried, pregnant by a married man, and needing a lot of money fast, Billy decides to travel from Texas to Arizona to retrieve her dead mother's body, hoping to find a small fortune in jewels presumably buried in the grave." Libr J
"Set in the summer of 1963, and recounted in a slow, Southern drawl befitting the mood, the story unravels from a myriad of viewpoints, including the no-good custom coffin salesman who's fathered Billy's unborn baby, the one-legged neighbor in love with Billy, and her deceased mother's feisty lesbian lover." Publ Wkly

Parks, Tim

Destiny. Arcade Pub. 2000 248p $24.95
ISBN 1-559-70517-5 LC 00-130423
First published 1999 in the United Kingdom
"The narrator, Christopher Burton, learns that Marco, his schizophrenic son, has committed suicide by stabbing himself with a screwdriver. His first reaction, however, is not shock or grief; he thinks that now, at last, he can leave his hateful wife. 'Destiny' examines how and why he arrives at this grotesque response." N Y Times Book Rev
"As Burton's stream of consciousness approaches disintegration, he finally admits truths about himself and his behavior in what becomes a deeply affecting portrait of a man in mental anguish." Publ Wkly

Parry, Richard

The winter wolf; Wyatt Earp in Alaska. Forge 1996 380p $24.95
ISBN 0-312-86017-X LC 96-18269
"A Tom Doherty Associates book"
"It's 1897, and the days of the OK Corral are a memory, but notoriety is still a burden for hard-up Wyatt Earp. He and his second wife, Josie, are heading north to Alaska to make their fortune in the gold rush. Circumstances conspire against him, however, and he must settle for law-related jobs. At every turn, he's wary that an old nemesis may be coming up behind him, but the greatest danger zeroing in on Earp is the son he didn't know he had." Booklist
"The inevitable confrontation between father and son packs geniune emotional wallop. Parry, who lives in Alaska, skillfully evokes both era and place." Publ Wkly

Parsons, Julie

Mary, Mary; a novel. Simon & Schuster 1999 c1998 299p $22.50
ISBN 0-684-85324-8 LC 98-33753
First published 1998 in the United Kingdom
In this novel, a "middle-aged widow named Margaret Mitchell returns to her native Ireland from New Zealand to care for her dying mother. Concerned when her 20-year-old daughter, Mary, fails to return from an evening out with friends, Margaret is devastated when the girl's raped and mutilated body is fished out of the river. In her rage and grief, she spurns the compassion of the

Parsons, Julie—*Continued*
homicide detective who loves her and takes her own revenge on the sadistic killer, who has slipped through the courts on a technicality and is now stalking her." N Y Times Book Rev

"Parsons writes short, quickly paced scenes that raise the suspense level in taut increments, and her story is full of genuine surprises and fresh plot twists. While shocking, the novel's conclusion is powerful and convincing." Publ Wkly

Passos, John Dos *See* Dos Passos, John

Pasternak, Boris Leonidovich, 1890-1960

Doctor Zhivago; [by] Boris Pasternak. Pantheon Bks. 1958 558p o.p.

First published 1957 in Italy

"The account of the life of a Russian intellectual, Yurii Zhivago, a doctor and a poet, during the first three decades of the 20th c. A broad epic picture of Russia is developed as the background to Zhivago's family life, his creative ecstasies, his love for Lara (another man's wife), his emotional upheavals, wanderings, and moments of happiness. Though the novel ends with Zhivago's decline and death as a result of what the author saw as the dehumanization of life that prevailed in the postrevolution years, the epilogue is full of expectations of the freedom that is to come." Ency of World Lit in the 20th Century

Patchett, Ann

Bel canto; a novel. HarperCollins Pubs. 2001 318p $25

ISBN 0-06-018873-1 LC 00-53671

"An impoverished South American country hosts a birthday extravaganza for a Japanese industrialist in the hope of securing new foreign investment. The lure? An internationally renowned lyric soprano. Indeed, when Roxane Coss sings, even the ragtag terrorists who are about to flood through the air-conditioning vents and take the guests hostage hold their breath, transported by the beauty of her voice. Patchett's tragicomic novel—a fantasia of guns and Puccini and Red Cross negotiations—invokes the glorious, unreliable promises of art, politics, and love." New Yorker

Paterson, James Hamilton- *See* Hamilton-Paterson, James

Paton, Alan

Ah, but your land is beautiful. Scribner 1982 c1981 271p o.p.

LC 81-13547

First published 1981 in the United Kingdom

This novel on racial unrest in South Africa covers the years 1952 to 1958 "and charts the response of the newly formed Liberal Party to the Suppression of Communism Act, the dispossession of black farmers, the destruction of Sophiatown, the disenfranchisement of Coloured voters, the influence of the Broederbond within the Nationalist Party and the rise to power of their premier, 'Dr. Hendrik'. . . . The parts played by Trevor Huddleston, Patrick Duncan, Geoffrey Clayton, Helen Joseph and . . . other historic figures, living and dead, are interspersed with the imagined destinies of representatives from different sections of the community." New Statesman (1913)

"Alan Paton's considerable practical life in South Africa aside, his place in the literature of social protest has been secured by his steady devotion to the ideal of the empathetic imagination in fiction." N Y Times Book Rev

Cry, the beloved country. Scribner Classics 2003 316p $26

ISBN 0-7432-6195-X

First published 1948 by Scribner

"Reverend Kumalo, a black South African preacher, is called to Johannesburg to rescue his sister. There he learns that his son Absalom has been accused of murdering a young white attorney whose interests and sympathies had been with the natives. Despite this, the attorney's father comes to the aid of the minister to help the natives in their struggle to survive a drought." Shapiro. Fic for Youth. 3d edition

Tales from a troubled land. Scribner 1961 128p o.p.

Contents: Life for a life; Sponono; Ha'penny; The wasteland; The worst thing of his life; The elephant shooter; Debbie go home; Death of a tsotsi; The divided house; A drink in the passage

"Most of the tales are told from the point of view of a compassionate white director of a boy's reformatory; however, one of the most moving concerns a native shepherd who, though innocent, becomes a victim when his employer is robbed." Booklist

Too late the phalarope. Scribner 1953 276p o.p.

"The story is basically that of a well loved white police lieutenant who in his need turns to a native girl. He is betrayed, reported and thus brings shame on himself and his family. The narrator of the story is an aunt who fills in the entire picture of family pride, righteous disdain, unbending adherence to an imposed restriction, and the falsity of many basic customs in parts of South Africa." Libr J

"The book is written with superb simplicity. It is cadenced but unaffected; it will inevitably be called Biblical and yet there is no conscious parodying of scriptual prose. It flows relentlessly to its crisis, and sometimes we cry out at its power. The people are all clear and real, the South African backgrounds are colorfully and deeply etched. The conflicts are diverse but they all contribute to the basic struggle; father and son, races, languages, prejudices." Christ Sci Monit

Paton Walsh, Jill, 1937-

A desert in Bohemia. St. Martin's Press 2000 335p $23.95

ISBN 0-312-26263-9 LC 00-693431

"A young woman named Eliska has just pulled herself out of a pit filled with bodies and run to the local castle to hide; its residents have left in such haste that there is bread still rising in the kitchen and an abandoned baby crying for milk. It is 1945, and the Red Army is booting out the good with the bad. The people we glimpse in this novel's opening chapter—Eliska, two Communist soldiers, a count who is an alleged Nazi collaborator, a neighboring aristocrat, and the baby—are revealed at in-

Paton Walsh, Jill, 1937-—*Continued*

tervals over the following forty years as they cope with exile, repression, impoverishment, and torture. Nearly all of them earn our pained affection—for their frailty and for their kindnesses to each other, across generations and distances and ideologies." New Yorker

(jt. auth) Sayers, D. L. Thrones, dominations

Patterson, Harry, 1929- *See* Higgins, Jack, 1929-

Patterson, Henry, 1929- *See* Higgins, Jack, 1929-

Patterson, James

1st to die; a novel. Little, Brown 2001 424p $32
ISBN 0-316-66600-9 LC 00-61123

"The story opens in San Francisco with the gruesome murder of a bride and groom on their wedding night. Detective Lindsay Boxer is called to the scene, just after learning she is suffering from a rare and potentially life-threatening blood disease. For help with the case, she calls on her best friend, Claire, a medical examiner, and, reluctantly at first, Cindy, a newspaper reporter who is covering the story. . . . Patterson keeps up the suspense until the very last page." Booklist

Along came a spider; a novel. Little, Brown 1993 435p o.p.
LC 92-24581

"Alex Cross, a black Washington, D.C., police detective with a Ph.D. in psychology, and Jezzie Flanagan, a white motorcycling Secret Service agent, become lovers as they work together to apprehend a chilling psychopath who has kidnapped two children from a posh private school. . . . Patterson's storytelling talent is in top form in this grisly escapist yarn." Libr J

The beach house; a novel; by James Patterson and Peter de Jonge. Little, Brown 2002 358p o.p.
ISBN 0-316-96968-0 LC 2001-50474

"Jack Mullen, a law-school student, is devastated when he learns that his beloved younger brother, Peter, has drowned while working as a valet at a ritzy party in the Hamptons. Jack is also suspicious; although Peter's death is ruled a suicide by the local police, Jack can't believe that his brother would go for a swim on a chilly evening when he was supposed to be working. . . . Despite the danger and the unexpected and often unpleasant revelations about his brother along the way, Jack is tenacious, and the novel races along to a somewhat implausible climax. But if Patterson fails to completely convince, he certainly doesn't fail to thrill." Booklist

Cat & mouse; a novel. Little, Brown 1997 399p o.p.
LC 97-20277

Black Washington, D.C. detective/psychologist Alex Cross' "old nemesis, psychopath Gary Soneji, is dead set on killing Alex in the ugliest, most terrifying way he can devise, but first, he's decided to play a game of cat and mouse with his intended victim. In Europe, a sadistic torturer dubbed 'Mr. Smith' is on the loose, and if Soneji is the king of cat and mouse, Mr. Smith is the grand high emperor. Elusive and terrifying, he performs autopsies on his living victims. FBI Agent Thomas Pierce has been assigned to the Smith case, but he's come back to America especially to help Alex track down Soneji." Booklist

"All story lines connect in this thriller, whose driving plot will distract you from thinking about its implausibilities and keep you turning pages to the last." Libr J

Cradle and all; a novel. Little, Brown 2000 325p o.p.
ISBN 0-316-69061-9 LC 99-36037

In this reworking of Patterson's 1980 novel Virgin, "Anne Fitzgerald, ex-nun turned detective, and Justin O'Carroll, priest turned detective, are hired by the Archbishop of Boston to help investigate apparent virgin pregnancies of two otherwise normal teenage girls." Booklist

"While not subtle, this novel tackles issues of faith with admirable gusto." Publ Wkly

Four blind mice; a novel. Little, Brown 2002 387p $27.95
ISBN 0-316-69300-6 LC 2002-67540

"Alex Cross is on the brink of retirement from the Washington Police Force when his best friend, John Sampson, comes to him with an urgent request. Sampson's friend, Sergeant Ellis Cooper, has just been convicted by a military court for the murders of three women. Cooper swears he's innocent, and Sampson believes him." Booklist

"The action leads, as is Patterson's custom, to a firecracker string of climaxes; the finale finds Cross handcuffed and stripped naked in deep woods, about to be killed. Throughout, Patterson expertly balances the conspiratorial action with intriguing developments in Cross's domestic life." Publ Wkly

Hide & seek; a novel. Little, Brown 1996 356p o.p.
LC 95-35928

"Beautiful Maggie Bradford seems to have it all: a successful career as a singer/songwriter, fame, money, and two precious children. However, she killed her first husband in self-defense and now she's in jail awaiting trial for the murder of her second husband, Will Shepherd, a charming, psychotic professional soccer player. At first, Maggie's marriage seems fine, but soon Will begins to act irrationally. The increasing tension comes to a head when Maggie comes to believe that Will has been sexually abusing her daughter, the resulting confrontation ends in Will's death and Maggie's arrest. Climaxing in Maggie's celebrity trial, this page-turner delivers a solid punch, complete with a surprise ending." Libr J

Honeymoon; a novel; by James Patterson and Howard Roughan. Little, Brown and Co 2005 393p $27.95
ISBN 0-316-71062-8 LC 2004-9895

"Nora Sinclair has a gorgeous Connecticut fiance, Connor. She had an equally sexy Boston husband, Jeffrey. But bad things happen to the men Nora gets involved with—her first husband died of a heart attack, and before long Connor meets a similar fate. The FBI is suspicious and sends agent John O'Hara to pose as an insurance investigator who dangles a tantalizing prize in front of Nora: a $1.9 million life-insurance policy on Connor's life, payable to Nora. She is suspicious, but she goes along with John's investigation into Connor's death. John

Patterson, James—*Continued*
isn't able to dig up much on Nora, but he does find himself in an awkward predicament when he realizes he's attracted to her." Booklist

Jack and Jill; a novel. Little, Brown 1996 432p o.p.

LC 96-8037

This novel features "African American psychologist-turned-detective Alex Cross. . . . Alex is troubled when a young child is murdered near the school his son attends and frightened when the murderer strikes again. On the other side of town, away from the scary inner-city D.C. streets, a pair of killers who call themselves Jack and Jill are terrorizing the movers and shakers by murdering a series of high-profile people. . . . A fast-paced, electric story that is utterly believable." Booklist

Kiss the girls; a novel. Little, Brown 1995 451p o.p.

LC 94-14177

"'Casanova' works the East Coast, 'The Gentleman Caller' works the West Coast, and these two serial killers might just be working together. Washed-up Washington, D.C., police detective Alex Cross gets involved when his niece is abducted." Libr J

The lake house; a novel. Little, Brown 2003 376p $26.95

ISBN 0-316-60328-7 LC 2002-36844

Sequel: When the wind blows (1998)

A thriller "about a group of children who have been genetically engineered to fly. . . . Beautiful Max and handsome Ozymandias lead the group of six children who are fighting to stay with Kit and Frannie, the couple that saved them from the School, where they were being held by the scientists who created them. The court returns the children to their biological parents, but only Max knows how much danger they're in. Max is privy to information about Resurrection, another project that is even more daring and groundbreaking than the one that created the children. . . . An unexpected and sweet romance between Max and Oz alleviates the nail-biting suspense somewhat, but as usual, Patterson gets his readers in his grip from page one and doesn't let go until the last page is turned." Booklist

Lifeguard; a novel; by James Patterson and Andrew Gross. 1st ed. Little, Brown and Co 2005 394p $26.95

ISBN 0-316-05785-1 LC 2004-23414

"Ned Kelly grew up on the wrong side of the tracks in Brockton, but he got out, and now his life seems to be falling into place. He's interested in a beautiful woman named Tess and has decided to chance one last heist with four of his childhood friends. Ned's job is simple–all he has to do is set off several house alarms while his friends hit the real target, the mansion of Dennis Stratton, to steal three valuable paintings. But when Ned's friends enter the house and discover the paintings already gone, they realize they've been double-crossed, and before Ned can reach them, all four are murdered. Then Tess is found dead in her hotel room, and, fearing how bad things are looking for him, Ned goes on the lam, hoping to clear his name. . . . He's being pursued by Federal Agent Ellie Shurtleff, an art expert, who becomes an unlikely ally. Packing all the punches readers have come to expect from Patterson's books, this one delivers at every turn." Booklist

London bridges; a novel. Little, Brown and Co 2004 391p $27.95

ISBN 0-316-71059-8 LC 2004-16752

"Terrorists have seized the worlds largest cities. London, Washington, DC, New York, and Frankfurt will be destroyed, unless their demands are met. . . . Heading up the investigation by the FBI, CIA, and Interpol, Alex Cross is stunned when surveillance photos show Geoffrey Shafer, the Weasel, near one of the bombing sites. He senses the presence of the Wolf as well, the most vicious predator he has ever battled." Publisher's note

"The book is a model of economy, delivering a full package of suspense, emotion and characterization in a minimum number of words." Publ Wkly

Pop! goes the weasel; a novel. Little, Brown 1999 423p $26.95

ISBN 0-316-69328-6 LC 99-21473

In this suspense novel Alex Cross "is working on a series of Jane Doe murders in southeast Washington. His hard-nosed boss doesn't want to waste precious resources investigating the deaths of a bunch of 'worthless prostitutes and druggies,' but Cross is convinced the women are the victims of a particularly deadly serial killer. He's right, of course, and he nearly meets his match in Geoffrey Shafer, respectable British Embassy staffer by day, homicidal maniac by night." Booklist

"If Shafer is almost too good to be true—another fictional psychopath with infinite resources—Patterson is shrewd enough to show him making mistakes . . . as he comes apart at the seams. The killer is caught in the middle of the narrative, setting the scene for a bold courtroom drama." Publ Wkly

Roses are red; a novel. Little, Brown 2000 400p o.p.

ISBN 0-316-69325-1 LC 00-28192

In this Alex Cross thriller set in Washington, D.C. a sociopath calling himself "the Mastermind" orchestrates a series of bank robberies, but he "isn't content to relieve the banks of their cash. He also has to torment the bankers by massacring their families when the mood strikes him. Having captured people's attention with these acts of cunning cruelty, the Mastermind pulls off a *coup de théâtre* when he hijacks a tour bus carrying the wives and children of insurance company executives and demands $30 million in ransom." N Y Times Book Rev

Suzanne's diary for Nicholas; a novel. Little, Brown 2001 266p $28

ISBN 0-316-96944-3 LC 00-50707

"The story alternates between diary entries, written by a young wife and mother named Suzanne to her newborn son, Nicholas, and the present, as the diary is read by Kate, who has just been abandoned by her new love—who happens to be Matthew, the young husband in the diary. . . . How Kate, Matthew, and Suzanne connect in the beginning of the novel and what happens by the pretty predictable ending will entertain and please most readers." Libr J

When the wind blows; a novel. Little, Brown 1998 416p $25

ISBN 0-03-166932-4 LC 98-14367

Patterson, James—*Continued*

"Dr. Frannie O'Neill hasn't recovered from her husband's brutal murder only months earlier. When handsome FBI agent Kit Harrison rents a cabin from her, Frannie is almost too grief-stricken to notice. Then one night, as Frannie is driving home, she sees a small girl—flying! She's shocked and intrigued, but when she tells Kit about the child, he's unsurprised. The girl is part of the case he's secretly working on. A group of scientists is determined to create a genetically superior 'superrace' at a secret lab hidden in the Colorado mountains—which Kit is desperately trying to find-and the flying child is one of their successes. But their failures are unbelievably horrifying." Booklist

Patterson, Richard North

Balance of power. Ballantine Bks. 2003 611p $27.95

ISBN 0-345-45017-5 LC 2003-51848

"Gun control and tort reform are the thorny issues tackled in this political drama, with Patterson hero Kerry Kilcannon ensconced in the White House and planning his marriage to former television journalist Lara Costello." Publ Wkly

"This complex novel has a fascinating debate at its heart. To his credit, Patterson has done his research, and though it's clear which side he's on, he does a good job of presenting all the arguments." Booklist

Conviction; a novel; Richard North Patterson. 1st ed. Random House 2005 465p $25.95

ISBN 0-345-45019-1 LC 2004-51175

"Fifteen years ago, brothers Rennell and Payton Price were sentenced to death for the brutal murder of nine-year-old Thuy Sen. Now, as Rennell's scheduled execution approaches, pro bono lawyer Theresa Peralta Page (also seen in Eyes of a Child), along with her attorney husband and attorney stepson, takes his final appeal all the way to the Supreme Court. At the same time, Theresa deals with her troubled teenage daughter and her own guilt. While it is apparent that the author opposes the death penalty, Patterson nevertheless provides compelling evidence for both sides of the argument." Libr J

Dark lady; a novel. Knopf 1999 384p $25.95

ISBN 0-679-45043-2 LC 99-23565

"Stella Marz is the assistant county prosecutor in a struggling Midwestern city. Her boss is running for mayor, and Stella hopes to be elected to his job. First, however, she must investigate the deaths of two prominent men—the project manager for the construction of a new baseball stadium and the city's leading defender of drug cases." Libr J

"Patterson is familiar with the civic shenanigans that can destroy a community, and he draws wisely on the history and geography of Cleveland to portray a city struggling to escape its bondage to organized crime, racial conflict and the entrenched corruption of its elected officials." N Y Times Book Rev

Degree of guilt. Knopf 1993 547p o.p.

LC 92-54446

"TV journalist Mary Carelli shoots and kills famous writer Mark Ransom in his hotel room, claiming that Ransom tried to rape her. The man she asks to defend her is Christopher Paget, with whom she has had a complicated relationship: Paget is the father of Mary's son, who lives with Paget and whom Mary has not seen for eight years. Paget agrees to defend Mary to protect his son." Libr J

"For those not put off by the sudsy plotting and the People magazine cast, the legal machinations are satisfactorily intricate." Time

Eyes of a child. Knopf 1995 593p o.p.

LC 94-28630

"The plot concerns the death of ne'er-do-well Ricardo Arias, who may or may not have committed suicide. Because of the widely publicized custody battle waged with Arias by his ex-wife and her lover, Christopher Paget (hero of *Degree of Guilt*), both are investigated and Paget indicted." Libr J

"Local San Francisco politics and an accusation of child molestation against Paget's teenage son contribute to this complex brew, in which . . . narrative skill and legal know-how take precedence over characterization and credibility." Publ Wkly

The final judgment. Knopf 1995 437p o.p.

LC 95-35083

"San Francisco lawyer Carolyn Masters, featured in *Eyes of a Child* returns as this story's central character, drawn back to her New England home on the eve of her presidential appointment to the Court of Appeals. Her young niece Brett is accused of brutally murdering the boy she loves, and Caroline comes to her defense. Caroline has had no contact with her family in years and now must confront the sister and father who fatally betrayed Caroline's own young love 20 years before." Libr J

"Filled with surprises, 'The Final Judgment' uses a backdrop of courtroom fireworks to tell a tightly wound story of loss and betrayal." N Y Times Book Rev

No safe place. Knopf 1998 497p o.p.

LC 98-14573

"The main character, Kerry Kilcannon, is an Irish Catholic U.S. senator, reminiscent of the Kennedy brothers. Embroiled in a close campaign with the vice president for the Democratic presidential nomination, Kilcannon struggles to maintain his honesty and upright values in a sleazy world where everything depends on image and the proper spin. At the same time, a militant right-to-lifer vows to kill Kilcannon for his pro-choice stance on abortion. Throughout the constant twists and turns of the plot, Patterson builds realistic supporting characters and brings to life the surrealistic world of a presidential campaign." Libr J

Protect and defend; a novel. Knopf 2000 549p il o.p.

ISBN 0-679-45044-0 LC 00-712975

"When the Chief Justice drops dead at the inauguration of Kerry Kilcannon, the charismatic new president appoints federal judge Caroline Masters to the high court and begins assembling a strategy to get her approved by a contentious Congress. Meanwhile, a pregnant teen with a damaged fetus goes to court to challenge her parents, who helped to pass a new parental-consent law that prevents her from having an abortion. The two events become intertwined. . . . Patterson skillfully juggles a large cast of characters and controversies." SLJ

Patterson, Richard North—*Continued*

Silent witness. Knopf 1997 493p o.p.
LC 96-36672

This novel "revolves around a friendship that begins on a high-school football field and is tested half a lifetime later in a Lake City, Ohio, courtroom. Tony Lord, a noted California criminal lawyer, returns to the home of his youth to defend his oldest friend, Sam Robb, against the charge of murdering his 16-year-old mistress. Lord takes the sordid case in part because his own life was nearly shattered when, as a teenager, he was suspected of murdering his own girlfriend." Publ Wkly

"*Silent Witness* is more than a typical legal thriller; it is a story about the growth of two men and how each one deals with and subsequently changes after experiencing the anguish and the introspection that come from being accused of murder." Booklist

Pattison, Eliot

The skull mantra. St. Martin's Minotaur 1999 403p $24.95
ISBN 0-312-20478-7 LC 99-23847

"Sentenced to penal servitude in Tibet, Shan, a disgraced prosecutor, is assigned instead to complete a pro forma investigation of the gruesome murder of a Chinese official. The party line is that dissident Tibetan monks are to blame, but Shan quickly realizes that the truth lies in other directions." Libr J

"Set against a background that is alternately bleak and blazingly beautiful, this is at once a topnotch thriller and a substantive look at Tibet under siege." Publ Wkly

Patton, Frances Gray, 1906-2000

Good morning, Miss Dove; illustrated by Garrett Price. Dodd, Mead 1954 218p o.p.

Miss Dove had taught geography in the same school for thirty-five years; some people in town thought that was too long. Miss Dove was a stern disciplinarian with old-fashioned ideas and ideals, but on the April day when she was stricken in the classroom the whole town came to realize how much Miss Dove had meant in their lives

"Leavened with wit and sound common sense, written with an unerring rightness of touch, the whole book rings with the truth about human nature in its nicer aspects." N Y Her Trib Books

Paul, Barbara, 1925-

For works written by this author under other names see Laker, Rosalind, 1925-

Paul, Jasmine, 1972-

A girl, in parts. Counterpoint 2002 241p $24
ISBN 1-58243-218-X LC 2002-6100

A novel about a "child of nine who lives with her mother, stepfather, and small half-brother in rural West Virginia poverty. Dottie hates her life, but she prefers it to the unknown that awaits her in Washington State, where the family noves. However, she is pleasantly surprised by her new living conditions and social possibilities. . . . She determines to overcome her physical shortcomings to win a spot on the girl's basketball team. In doing so, she wins the respect of the Native American girls on the team." Libr J

"Paul's sure grasp of her narrator's voice and keen observations make both the ordinary and unusual aspects of one childhood shine." Publ Wkly

Paul, Jim, 1950-

Elsewhere in the land of parrots. Harcourt 2003 405p $24
ISBN 0-15-100495-1 LC 2003-7918

When reclusive poet David Huntington "receives an exotic parrot from his father, his preferred life of airless solitude is turned upside down, and in frustration David soon tosses it out his apartment window. Little does he know that through that open window his carefully controlled and spiritless existence has begun its exit as well. David's guilty search for the bird serendipitously leads him into an adventure outside his quiet apartment and all the way to the swamplands of Ecuador, where a young researcher named Fern happens to be studying the same type of parrot in its native habitat." Libr J

"Paul's story successfully weds an odd theme —the ethology of parrots—to the perennial fascinations of human courtship behavior." Publ Wkly

Pawel, Rebecca, 1977-

Death of a nationalist. Soho Press 2003 262p $24
ISBN 1-56947-304-8 LC 2002-26921

"Madrid in 1939 is filled with bomb craters, desecrated churches and nearly abandoned streets, while black markets are just about the only markets with anything to sell. The hatreds and atrocities shared by the Nationalists (supported by the Communists) still simmer and erupt in sporadic violence. The Guardia Civil has the responsibility to maintain authority—and their enthusiasm and ruthlessnesss for enforcing order terrorizes the citizens. The intertwined fates of Sergeant Tejada Alonzo Leon of the Guardia Civil and that of Gonzalo Llorente, a wounded Republican in hiding are handled with unusual skill and subtlety." Publ Wkly

Paxson, Diana L.

(jt. auth) Bradley, M. Z. Priestess of Avalon

Pearce, Mary Emily, 1932-

Apple tree lean down; [by] Mary E. Pearce. St. Martin's Press 1976 494p o.p.

This volume contains Apple tree lean down, Jack Mercybright and The sorrowing wind, originally published separately in the United Kingdom in 1973, 1974 and 1975 respectively

The combined stories provide a chronicle of three "earthy families inhabiting the rural Midlands during the late 18th and early 19th century. Beth Tewke forsakes easy living when she estranges her prosperous grandfather by marrying poor Jesse Izzard. Betony, their eldest child, is sharp and ambitious. In her teens she goes to London to establish a career as a teacher but becomes disillusioned with the hypocrisy and ill-treatment of the poor in the city. . . . Giving up the chances of an advantageous marriage, she devotes herself to the local school and to the care of invalid soldiers quartered nearby, to

Pearce, Mary Emily, 1932-—*Continued*
the general welfare of her community." Publ Wkly

"Many novels have depicted the upper classes of this era; few have delved so deeply into the lives of the common laborers and the lower middle class." Libr J

Followed by The land endures (1978) and Seedtime and harvest (1982)

Apple tree lean down [novel]
In Pearce, M. E. Apple tree lean down

Cast a long shadow; [by] Mary E. Pearce. St. Martin's Press 1983 c1977 246p o.p.
LC 83-2953

First published 1977 in the United Kingdom

"The blissful early years of Richard Lancy and Ellen Wainwright's marriage in the small English village of Dingham are shattered after Richard is accidentally trapped in the cellar of a burned-out mill for 16 days. Richard's horrifying experience distorts his entire life and disrupts his family as well. After throwing his wife and son out of their house (and forcing them to find refuge with the compassionate village blacksmith), the disturbed Richard lurks about as a specter. His haunting presence torments Ellen and John and threatens the new lives they try to forge for themselves in this closed, watchful English village." Booklist

"Old-fashioned story-telling, people one cares about and low-key charm add up to solid reading pleasure." Publ Wkly

Jack Merrybright
In Pearce, M. E. Apple tree lean down p203-332

The sorrowing wind
In Pearce, M. E. Apple tree lean down p333-494

Pearl, Matthew

The Dante Club; a novel. Random House 2003 372p $24.95
ISBN 0-375-50529-6 LC 2002-17886

A literary thriller about a "serial murderer who draws gory inspiration from the torments of Dante's Inferno. . . . The author sets this novel in Boston in 1865, when Henry Wadsworth Longfellow, James Russell Lowell, and Oliver Wendell Holmes were translating Dante into English. As they work through the cantos, the Dante-inspired corpses arrive on cue, and the versifiers must turn detective." New Yorker

Pears, Iain

Death and restoration; a Jonathan Argyll mystery. Scribner 1998 223p $22
ISBN 0-684-81461-7 LC 97-39932

This mystery features "esthete-sleuth, Jonathan Argyll, and his companion, Flavia di Stefano, a senior, investigator for Italy's Art Theft Squad. Most of the legwork falls to Flavia when an icon is stolen from a rundown monastery in Rome and a French dealer is discovered floating in the Tiber. This frees up Jonathan to sprinkle his acidic wit on art experts and thieves like Dan Menzies, . . . who has been engaged by the monastery to apply his savage artistry to its dubious Caravaggio." N Y Times Book Rev

The dream of Scipio. Riverhead Bks. 2002 398p o.p.
ISBN 1-57322-202-X LC 2001-58916

"Juggles three different historical periods, radically different but united by the presence of a siege—the fall of the Roman Empire in the fourth century, the spread of the plague in the fourteenth century, and World War II in the twentieth century. The setting in all three interlocking plots is Provence, and there is a love story at the center of each. The fabric that connects the characters and their stories across centuries is a neoPlatonic essay called 'The Dream of Scipio' written by Manlius Hippomanes at the point when Gaul was about to be overrun by barbarians." Booklist

"Pears builds a multilayered tale of moral choice, love, danger and loss. Like an archaeologist, he uncovers worlds beneath worlds in a few square miles of Provencal earth." N Y Times Book Rev

The immaculate deception. Scribner 2000 221p o.p.
ISBN 0-7432-1257-6 LC 2001-267391

In this Jonathan Argyll "mystery, set in Rome and Tuscany, the police investigator Flavia di Stefano is called in to find a painting that has been stolen by a radical performance artist; meanwhile, her husband, an art historian, is trying to track down the provenance of a beguiling little fifteenth-century Virgin that belongs to Flavia's former boss. Like those classic Nick and Nora whodunits, this book is really a comedy in disguise: the plot twists are finely turned, our heroes flirt harmlessly with danger, and in the end everyone gets what he may not have known he wanted all along." New Yorker

An instance of the fingerpost. Riverhead Bks. 1998 691p $27
ISBN 1-57322-082-5 LC 97-23899

First published 1997 in the United Kingdom

"Robert Boyle, the devout chemist, and John Thurloe, Cromwell's inscrutable spymaster, are among the historical characters who figure in this richly imagined mystery set in Oxford in the sixteen-sixties, after Charles II has been restored to the throne. A Fellow of New College is found dead, and a woman accused of whoring and witchcraft is sentenced to hang for the murder. Three narrators—all unreliable and all self-interested—tell their versions of the story, which unfolds in a turbulent atmosphere of scientific, political, and religious dissent. Not until a fourth, and final, narrator speaks are the mysteries, including the meaning of the book's title, revealed." New Yorker

The last judgment. Scribner 1996 c1993 224p o.p.
LC 95-38120

First published 1993 in the United Kingdom

"Jonathan Argyll, British art dealer, and his amour, Flavia de Stefano, a member of Rome's art-theft squad, have decided to marry after happy months of living together. But first, there's business to tend to. On a buying trip to Paris, Jonathan is asked by a colleague to deliver a valuable painting to a client in Rome. He soon discovers that whoever is interested in this picture seems to wind up dead. . . . A sophisticated, adventurous, and gripping story that is sure to hold wide appeal." Booklist

Pearson, Ridley

The angel maker; a novel. Delacorte Press 1993 341p o.p.
LC 92-36573

In this crime thriller someone is "running around with a scalpel removing a kidney here, a lung there, then selling the organs to desperate patients willing to pay upward of $15,000. This grisly brand of 'harvesting' comes to light in Seattle when victims begin turning up minus a part or two. It's the job of a police psychologist named Daphne Matthews, aided by her piano-playing ex-lover, Lou Boldt, to try to bring the perpetrator of these ghastly crimes to justice." N Y Times Book Rev

"Pearson's engaging forensic detail . . . and brisk prose will have readers racing to the cliffhanger climax." Publ Wkly

The art of deception. Hyperion 2002 451p o.p.
ISBN 0-7868-6724-8 LC 2002-69055

This Lou Boldt-Daphne Matthews suspense novel "finds the Seattle police lieutenant and his forensic psychologist colleague investigating two cases that ultimately become one. Boldt is tracking a serial killer, and Matthews is investigating the death of a woman who was thrown from Seattle's Aurora Bridge. . . . Pearson makes particularly good use of his Seattle setting this time; the legendary Underground (created when the city was rebuilt after its great fire of 1889) has often appeared in mysteries, but Pearson's detail-rich treatment goes well beyond the typical clichés of dark passages and abandoned storefronts. On every level, this series remains one of the mystery genre's great pleasures." Booklist

Beyond recognition. Hyperion 1997 480p o.p.
LC 96-21125

"A rag and a bone are literally all the Seattle PD has to work with after a violent fire consumes a home and its helpless female occupant, a divorced mother. When a second victim dies the same way, detective Lou Boldt and police psychologist Daphne Matthews begin the process of profiling a serial killer who uses rocket fuel to torch women because they resemble his mother. Elsewhere, a young boy named Ben, whose abusive stepfather has all but driven him into the street, has been befriended by a fraudulent 'psychic' named Emily Richland, who hires Ben to scout her clients' vehicles while they're meeting with her. This task leads, . . . to Ben witnessing an exchange of cash for rocket fuel, a sighting that in turn eventually takes the police to their killer." Publ Wkly

"Moving from one punchy scene to the next, this fuse-burning suspense tale is wonderful reading for a wide audience." Libr J

The body of David Hayes; Ridley Pearson. 1st ed. Hyperion 2004 344p $23.95
ISBN 0-7868-6725-6 LC 2003-56575

In this "Detective Lou Boldt thriller, computer whiz David Hayes has embezzled $17 million from the bank where he worked and hidden it within the computer system. Now paroled for the crime, he wants to get the money and be free of all competing parties, including some utterly ruthless Russian Mafia types who will stop at nothing to get the loot. Years before, Hayes had an affair with Boldt's wife—now VP of systems at the bank—and he blackmails her into helping him recover the money. Though dedicated and skilled, Boldt and his team are human and fallible; Boldt must balance his jealousy as a husband with his professionalism as a detective. Pearson's novels are always well written, and he takes special care with richly drawn subordinate characters." Libr J

Chain of evidence. Hyperion 1995 348p o.p.
LC 95-32320

"Police Lieutenant Joe 'Dart' Bartelli is called to one suicide after another of various psychopaths (a vicious child molester, a hard-core pornographer) in the Hartford, Connecticut, area. The deaths seem more like murders to Dart, who was well trained in police investigation by his mentor, former police sergeant Walter Zeller. Dart carefully, plausibly tracks down the killer with the help of former love, Ginny, fellow lieutenant Abby Lang, and various three-dimensional characters who add believably to his painstaking search. Bad guys, burnouts, and screwups—all the characters are well delineated." Libr J

Cut and run. Hyperion 2005 368p $23.95
ISBN 0-7868-6726-4 LC 2004-63844

"Hope Stevens, a technical consultant for the Justice Department, helped indict the deadly Romero white-collar crime family in a million-dollar fraud investigation. For six years, she's been in the witness protection program, waiting to testify. Now, the Romeros have infiltrated the program's participant list, and she's in grave danger. Roland Larson, a U.S. marshal in St. Louis who met Hope just before she was admitted to the program, still pines for her and is determined to find her." Publ Wkly

"Sure, the heroine's Blackberry will chime at precisely the wrong moment, but we know that in the end the killer will be caught, that justice will be served, and that the hero will arrange it so that the little girl gets the dog she wanted. Every so often, the reader gets what he or she wants too: a little comfort food for the mind." N Y Times Book Rev

The first victim. Hyperion 1999 381p $23.95
ISBN 0-7868-6440-0 LC 98-49992

"Inside a shipping container that has washed ashore near Seattle during a storm is heard the 'unmistakable cry of human voices.' From this dramatic opening springs . . . [this] Lou Boldt thriller, in which the Seattle Police Department goes head to head with the INS to bust an immigrant-smuggling ring run by Chinese gangs." Libr J

"Boldt's usual partner, forensic psychologist Daphne Matthews, plays a lesser role this time, but in her place Pearson substitutes television news anchor Stevie McNeal, who mounts her own investigation, thus introducing a meaty subplot involving media excesses. As always, Pearson builds suspense incrementally, brilliantly amassing details until his plot reaches critical mass at just the right moment." Booklist

Middle of nowhere; a novel. Hyperion 2000 375p o.p.
ISBN 0-7868-6563-6 LC 99-51670

"Seattle police lieutenant Boldt and forensic psychologist Matthews must contend not only with a string of robbery assaults—one victim of which is a fellow officer—but also with the effects of a 'blue flu' that has left the department seriously understaffed and riddled with

Pearson, Ridley—*Continued*
internal conflict." Booklist

This thriller "boasts simmering suspense, a plot with a level of detail that comes only from painstaking research, and dynamic chemistry between Boldt and his colleagues and family." Publ Wkly

No witnesses; a novel. Hyperion 1994 365p o.p.
LC 94-11158

"Wealthy food industry mogul Owen Adler receives a series of FAXes demanding that he liquidate his business and commit suicide within a month. The alternative is that consumers of Adler Foods will begin to die. After the deadline passes and two children are hospitalized with a mysterious infection, Adler lets his girlfriend, Seattle forensic psychologist Daphne Matthews, contact detective Lou Boldt. Boldt's empathy for the rising number of victims compels him to put his life at risk as he coordinates an extended investigation while trying to prevent mass panic." Libr J

The Pied Piper. Hyperion 1998 497p $23.95
ISBN 0-7868-6300-5 LC 97-49709

"Recently promoted Seattle Police Lieutenant Boldt and forensic psychologist Matthews attempt to catch the Pied Piper, a kidnapper who snatches infants from their cribs and leaves a toy flute as his calling card. Moving from city to city up the West Coast, the Piper has completely confounded both the FBI and local police." Booklist

Probable cause. St. Martin's Press 1990 275p o.p.
LC 89-24127

"Forensic investigator James Dewitt takes a new job, as a police sergeant in Carmel, California, hoping to put his past behind him—a past that includes his shooting to death the man who murdered his wife and permanently disabled one of his daughters. But after little more than two months, he fears he has a serial killer on his hands, a *trapper*—someone who slyly sets out traps, baits them, and then draws his victims in. The rapid twists and turns in the plot soon establish Dewitt as a suspect, even while his daughters' lives, and his, are in jeopardy. . . . This is fiction for true true-crime buffs, filled with clues, both planted and missed, fancy forensic footwork, and intriguing snares." Booklist

Undercurrents. St. Martin's Press 1988 386p o.p.
LC 88-1014

"A killer is on the loose—a brutal, terrifying murderer who was himself supposed to be dead. Seattle Police Sergeant Lou Boldt, haunted by the deaths of the man he believed to have been the Cross Killer (so called because of the crosses he slashes onto his victims) and of the real criminal's new victims, is in charge of the case and determined to solve it. . . . *Undercurrents* is not for the squeamish; it is grittily detailed and no punches pulled. But Pearson clearly understands what makes a good mystery move, and this one sprints breathlessly along, taking the reader with it to a surprising, and satisfying, conclusion." West Coast Rev Books

Pearson, T. R., 1956-

Blue Ridge. Viking 2000 243p $24.95
ISBN 0-670-89269-6 LC 00-25826

"Ray Tatum is the new sheriff's deputy in sleepy Hogarth, Va., where some hikers discover a human skeleton, its skull bashed in, on the Appalachian Trail. Investigating the case with the help of a brassy female African-American park ranger named Kit Carson, Ray is forced to come to terms with the collapse of his marriage, his somewhat arid life and the nature of the backwoods town he calls home. Meanwhile, Ray's cousin Paul, an actuary in Roanoke, is summoned to Manhattan to identify what may be the remains of a young man named Troy, the son he never really knew." Publ Wkly

"Pearson has never been timid about pushing form to its limits, and his splendid prose is also artifical, stunningly so—high-pitched, evocative, decorative and closer to the human heart than the rictus-grinned pseudo-realism of many modern mysteries." N Y Times Book Rev

Cry me a river; a novel. Holt & Co. 1993 258p o.p.
LC 92-13860

"A police officer is found brutally murdered in a small southern town, his head so disfigured by bullet wounds that he can only be identified by the distinctive smell of his hair tonic. A fellow officer vows to find the killer. Accompanied by a whiskey-addled sidekick who functions as a backwoods Dr. Watson, the investigator assembles clues, interviews suspects, proposes and discards theories, and in the process paints the portrait of an entire community." Libr J

A short history of a small place; a novel. Linden Press/Simon & Schuster 1985 381p o.p.
LC 84-29720

"Narrated by young Louis Benfield [this] is the story of Miss Myra Angelique Pettigrew, sister of the late mayor of a small Southern town, who is elegant and beautiful and has gone quite mad. After many years of seclusion, she finally emerges from her home to jump to her death from the water tower. In the process of telling his tale, Louis offers vignettes about other residents of Neely, N.C., and their strange habits and activities." Publ Wkly

"Pearson handles the interlinked strands of these stories with a truly wonderful offhand comic style that doesn't dismiss the reality of his characters' lives." Booklist

Peck, Robert Newton, 1928-

A day no pigs would die. Knopf 1973 c1972 150p $25; pa $5.50
ISBN 0-394-48235-2; 0-679-85306-5 (pa)

"Rob lives a rigorous life on a Shaker farm in Vermont in the 1920s. Since farm life is earthy, this book is filled with Yankee humor and explicit descriptions of animals mating. A painful incident that involves the slaughter of Rob's beloved pet pig is instrumental in urging him toward adulthood. The death of his father completes the process of his accepting responsibility." Shapiro. Fic for Youth. 3d edition

Pelecanos, George P.

The big blowdown. St. Martin's Press 1996 313p o.p.
LC 95-53148

"Set in Washington, D.C., from the 1930s to the 1950s, Pelecanos's . . . novel traces a group of boyhood friends as they make their way in the richly detailed Greek and Italian neighborhoods of the city. Peter Karras, a Greek, and his friend Joe Recevo, an Italian, grow up together, serve separately in World War II, and reunite for a time after the war as Joe becomes involved in organized crime in the city. Peter cannot stomach the practice of shaking down immigrants for loan vigorish and is brutally cast out by the gangsters, as Joe stands by. The two friends will inevitably cross paths again." Libr J

"Pelecanos lovingly recreates old Washington with small details about soft-drink brands, finned cars and cherished smokes. The ending is a haze of gunsmoke that drifts away to leave a mixed tableau of heroism and futility. With stylistic panache and forceful conviction, Pelecanos delivers a darkly powerful story of the American city." Publ Wkly

Drama city; a novel; [by] George Pelecanos. Little, Brown and Co 2005 291p $24.95
ISBN 0-316-60821-1 LC 2004-16757

"After serving eight years for a drug rap, Lorenzo Brown is trying to live a straight life. Working as a Humane Society officer in Washington, DC, doesn't provide the life of wealth that Lorenzo had enjoyed as part of the drug game, but he's doing okay. His parole officer, Rachel Lopez, is fighting her own battle against a tough past and reckless behavior. A violent act committed by a character from Lorenzo's old life places both Lorenzo and Rachel in jeopardy. Now, Lorenzo must decide whether to risk his second chance at a straight life for a shot at vengeance." Libr J

"There is a fierce inevitability to the way George Pelecanos's new book unfolds. Drama City is unleashed, not simply set in motion. In the tough, imperiled parts of Washington, where his earlier books have been set, Mr. Pelecanos puts the forces of good and evil on a collision course, igniting the kind of suspense that hinges on heartbreak. As this lean, stirring, knife-edged novel escalates, the question is not whether one of its principals will become a casualty. The question is when." N Y Times (Late N Y Ed)

Hard revolution; a novel; [by] George Pelecanos. Little, Brown 2004 376p $24.95
ISBN 0-316-60897-1 LC 2003-54501

This novel "tells the story of two brothers-one a rookie police officer, one a recently returned Vietnam veteran-caught up in the chaos that engulfed D.C. in 1968, when riots followed the assassination of the Reverend Martin Luther King, Jr. Derek Strange is his family's straight arrow, but his older brother Dennis has always had a harder time. Home from the war and in several varieties of trouble, Dennis is in danger of making one bad decision too many. While Derek tries to be there for Dennis, no amount of brotherly love can save Dennis from Alvin Jones, a local drug dealer who draws him into his web." Publisher's note

"Pelecanos's foray into Strange's past does not in the end diminish, but rather adds to, our sense of his complexity and humanity. In narrating Derek's buried crime story, Pelecanos has further tapped into an archetypal vein of family experience in the black community since the 1950's, as drugs, murder and prison cut a swath through three generations of young men." N Y Times Book Rev

Hell to pay; a novel. Little, Brown 2002 344p $24.95
ISBN 0-316-69506-8 LC 2001-38111

This mystery, set in Washington, D.C., features ex-cop detectives Derek Strange and Terry Quinn. "As a black man with plenty of miles behind him, Strange has access to neighborhoods where his Irish partner would be handed his head; but both of them take big chances when they cross Worldwide Wilson, a menacing pimp who breaks in teenage runaways, and then go after the wild street kids who shot the 9-year-old quarterback of the Petworth Panthers, the Pee-Wee team Strange coaches. Pelecanos's style is one of total-shock immersion in the sights, sounds and cultural codes of the dangerous world he roams." N Y Times Book Rev

Right as rain; a novel. Little, Brown 2001 332p o.p.
ISBN 0-316-69526-2 LC 00-34886

This novel is set in Washington D.C. The hero is a "middle-aged black ex-cop named Derek Strange. Shortly after the book begins, Strange is hired by the mother of Chris Wilson, a black policeman who has been killed by a white colleague during a street altercation. The white cop, Terry Quinn, came upon Wilson holding another man at gunpoint. When it looked to Quinn as if Wilson was pointing his weapon at Quinn and his partner, Quinn fired, killing the man. Officially exonerated by his department, Quinn, . . . quit. He sees Strange's investigation as his means of clearing the suspicion that lingers around him." N Y Times Book Rev

"What is perhaps most remarkable about this outstanding novel . . . is the way his plot-rich, extremely violent stories parallel the turbulence of his characters' inner lives. We care about these characters passionately, and we savor their tentative moments of tranquility as we do our own." Booklist

Shame the devil; a novel. Little, Brown 2000 299p $24.95
ISBN 0-316-69523-8 LC 99-29854

This novel picks up the story of Marcus Clay and Dimitri Karras ten years after the events in The sweet forever, with the aging childhood friends "settling into the quiet pleasures of middle age. Then a restaurant robbery goes bad, the entire staff is murdered, the gunman's brother is killed, and Karras' toddler son, crossing the wrong street at the wrong time, is run over by the speeding getaway car. Three years later Karras is adrift, his marriage over, his only solace coming in weekly meetings with the families of the shooting victims. Into this simmering pot Pelecanos stirs the killer, Frank Farrow, returned to Washington and determined to avenge the death of his brother." Booklist

"Pelecanos is one of those dangerous writers who aren't afraid to take risks, so there's a merciless reality to his characters and a cold clarity about the way they talk, think and feel. Whatever their flaws, none of the people in this writer's world are ashamed to tell the truth." N Y Times Book Rev

Pelecanos, George P.—*Continued*

Soul circus; a novel. Little, Brown 2003 341p $24.95

ISBN 0-316-60843-2 LC 2002-16207

"Strange and Quinn once again find themselves struggling to save even one not-yet-lost young soul from the ravages of drugs and violence, but this time their knightly pursuits are undermined by a growing sense of moral ambivalence." Booklist

"Pelecanos is fascinated with the way things work, and he takes apart the gun trade like an urban anthropologist, fitting the pieces into the drug business and the gang culture with an exactness that is breathtaking—and depressing. At the same time, he treats his criminals like human beings, talking their talk, driving their cars, listening to their music, getting into their world with something that can only be called sympathy." N Y Times Book Rev

The sweet forever; a novel. Little, Brown 1998 298p $23.95

ISBN 0-316-69109-7 LC 97-41963

Sequel to King Suckerman (1997)

"Dirty cops, drug money, racism, violence, and sex all mar 1980s Washington, D.C. When a neighborhood drug dealer's collection man crashes and burns in front of Marcus Clay's record store, an opportunist makes off with the guy's sack of cash. The drug dealer and associates will try anything to get the money back, including threatening Clay and employees, one of whom, coke-happy Dimitri Karras . . . knows what happened to the cash." Libr J

"Pelecanos's kickback style works just as well when his characters put down their weapons to watch a ball game or to hit the music clubs on a Friday night. This may be a battleground, but it's also Pelecanos's home ground, and he knows the territory as well as any crime writer alive." N Y Times Book Rev

Followed by Shame the devil

Penguin book of gay short fiction; edited by David Leavitt and Mark Mitchell; introduction by David Leavitt. Viking 1994 655p o.p.

LC 93-1390

Contents: A poem of friendship, by D. H. Lawrence; Arthur Snatchfold, by E. M. Forster; Sally Bowles, by C. Isherwood; Me and the girls, by N. Coward; My father and myself, by J. R. Ackerley; May we borrow your husband? by G. Greene; Hands, by S. Anderson; The teacher of American business English, by J. Kirkup; Falconer, by J. Cheever; The folded leaf, by W. Maxwell; Servants with torches, by D. Windham; Jimmy, by D. Hogan; Torridge, by W. Trevor; Some of these days, by J. Purdy; A glass of blessings, by B. Pym; Reprise, by E. White; Dramas, by E. O'Brien; "Mrs. Tefillin", by L. Kramer; Spunk, by P. Bailey; The times as it knows us, by A. Barnett; The princess from Africa, by D. Plante; Adult art, by A. Gurganus; The Cinderella waltz, by A. Beattie; Good with words, by S. Greco; Nothing to ask for, by D. McFarland; Ignorant armies, by M. Cunningham; Run, mourner, run, by R. Kenan; Six fables, by B. Cooper; Perrin and the fallen angel, by P. Wells; My mother's clothes: the school of beauty and shame, by R. McCann; A place I've never been, by D. Leavitt; Notes towards a performance of Jean Racine's tragedy Athalie, by N. Bartlett; Buried treasure, by G. Glickman; Self-portrait in twenty-three rounds, by D. Wojnarowicz; Jump or dive, by P. Cameron; Gentlemen can wash their hands in the gents', by C. Coe; The dancing lesson, by G. Albarelli; A real doll, by A. M. Homes; The whiz kids, by A. M. Homes

The **Penguin** book of lesbian short stories; edited by Margaret Reynolds. Viking 1994 c1993 429p o.p.

LC 93-34061

First published 1993 in the United Kingdom

Includes the following stories: Martha's lady, by S. O. Jewett; Prince Charming, by R. Vivien; Leves amores, by K. Mansfield; The wise Sappho, by H.D.; Miss Furr and Miss Skeene, by G. Stein; Ladies almanack, by D. Barnes; Miss Ogilvy finds herself, by R. Hall; Nuits blanches, by Colette; Olivia, by D. Strachey; The blank page, by I. Dinesen; Cities of the interior, by A. Nin; I am a woman, by A. Bannon; Les guérillès, by M. Wittig; These our mothers, by N. Brossard; Sweethearts, by J. A. Phillips; Esther's story, by J. Nestle; How to engage in courting rituals 1950s butch-style in the bar, by M. Mushroom; Bread, by R. Brown; His nor hers, by J. Rule; 5½ Charlotte Mews, by A. Livia; Lullaby for my dyke and her car, by S. Maitland; Don't explain, by J. Gomez; A lesbian appetite, by D. Allison; The vampire, by P. Califia; The secret of Sorrerby Rise, by F. Gapper; City of boys, by B. Nugent; Cold-blooded, by M. Atwood; Words for things, by E. Donoghue; The language of the body, by K. Acker; The poetics of sex, by J. Winterson

Penman, Sharon Kay

Cruel as the grave; a medieval mystery. Holt & Co. 1998 242p $22

ISBN 0-8050-5608-4 LC 98-13085

"A Marian Wood book"

"Young Justin de Quincy, bastard son of a highly placed clergyman, toils as a special agent for Eleanor of Aquitaine. The dowager queen is attempting to hold the throne for her beloved son, Richard the Lionheart, held captive by the Holy Roman Emperor, against the machinations of her youngest son, John. A neighbor asks Justin to investigate the death of a young Welsh girl named Melangell." Publ Wkly

"Penman's clear prose and engrossing plot, the skill with which she brings the politics, people, and ambience of medieval England alive, and her engaging characters make this a must-read, must-have mystery." Booklist

Dragon's lair; a medieval mystery; Sharon Kay Penman. G.P. Putnam's Sons 2003 322p $23.95

ISBN 0-399-15077-3 LC 2003-46745

In this mystery, "Justin de Quincy, tries to recover, quite literally, a king's ransom in coffers of precious metals and bales of wool, which are as valuable as gold, that have been stolen in northern Wales. It's 1193, and Queen Eleanor of Aquitaine fervently needs to ransom her eldest son, Richard Lionheart, from the Holy Roman Emperor before King Philippe of France can interfere and her younger son, John, can seize the crown. Justin proceeds into the thickets and wild forests of Wales, where he's deeply mistrusted both as an Englishman and

Penman, Sharon Kay—*Continued*
an outsider. He must penetrate abundant Welsh intrigues and deceptions in order to discover the treasure as well as solve murders and comfort bereaved lovers. Despite a large cast of characters from every social class, Penman keeps them all clearly distinguishable." Publ Wkly

Falls the shadow. Holt & Co. 1988 580p o.p.
LC 87-32255

In this second volume of the trilogy begun with Here be dragons "Penman focuses on the mid-13th-century reign of England's Henry III and stories of those who opposed that inept king. A main detractor is French-born Simon de Montfort, Earl of Leicester, who leads the fight for parliamentary restrictions on the monarch, and later becomes Henry's brother-in-law through marriage to Eleanor, Countess of Pembroke. She emerges as a major figure, as does a distant relative by marriage, Llewelyn ap Gruffydd, who fights for supremacy in Wales." Libr J

Followed by The reckoning

Here be dragons. Holt, Rinehart & Winston 1985 704p o.p.
LC 84-23480

This first title in the author's historical trilogy about 13th century England "is the story of one man, a Welsh prince called Llewelyn the Great, who dares to dream of peace and who will spend a lifetime trying to wrest his country away from feudal England. Standing in his way is King John, who marries his daughter, Joanna, to Llewelyn in hopes of taming the rebellious prince. Penman focuses her novel on the tempestuous emotional and political battles that Joanna is forced to endure as both the daughter and wife of warring kings." Booklist

Followed by Falls the shadow

The queen's man; a medical mystery. Holt & Co. 1996 291p $20
ISBN 0-8050-3885-X LC 96-15027

"A Marian Wood book"

"In the troubled time of King Richard, his mother, Eleanor of Aquitaine, commissions Justin de Quincey, the bastard son of the bishop of Chester, to find the murderer of a goldsmith in her employ. Thus dunked into the dangerous waters of royal conspiracy, Justin defies one treachrous current after another." Libr J

"Penman's authentic period details, larger-than-life characters, and fast-paced plot add up to great reading for both mystery fans and history buffs." Booklist

The reckoning. Holt & Co. 1991 592p o.p.
LC 90-27099

Set in 13th-century Wales and England, this concluding volume in the author's trilogy "continues the saga of three royal families, those of swashbuckling Llewelyn ap Gruffydd, prince of Wales, and his fractious, treasonous brothers; the children of heroic Lord Simon de Montfort . . . and the ruling house of England, now headed by wily Edward I." Publ Wkly

"The action involves religious and political intrigue, battles and plots. The players include well-researched historical personages and fictional characters. As with Penman's other historical novels, this one is both informative and enjoyable. Settings, events, and individuals are well drawn." Libr J

The sunne in splendour. Holt, Rinehart & Winston 1982 936p o.p.
LC 81-20149

"Today most historians agree that England's Richard III has been unjustly maligned. Penman's novel tells of a devoted brother who, as Duke of Gloucester, faithfully served his brother King Edward IV and earned a reputation for personal integrity. Richard's own tragedy begins with the death of Edward, when political circumstances force him to claim the crown for himself and declare his brother's children illegitimate. Did Richard murder the young princes as Tudor chroniclers claim? No, says Penman, and she gives a plausible account as to what might have happened." Libr J

"The novel covers a great deal of ground, tracing the shifting alliances and the battles between the noble houses of York and Lancaster from 1459, when Richard was seven to 1492, seven years after his death on Bosworth Field. . . . A historical novel of the first rank." Publ Wkly

Time and chance. Putnam 2002 515p o.p.
ISBN 0-399-14785-3 LC 2001-48255

"A Marian Wood book"

Sequel to: When Christ and his saints slept

This second volume of the author's medieval trilogy "re-creates the drama, the intrigue, and the passion that distinguished the lives of Henry Plantagenet, Eleanor of Aquitaine, and Thomas Becket. Though the subject has been exhaustively chronicled in both history and literature, this fictionalized account of the trials and tribulations of this prominent trio of historical figures manages to breathe new life into a familiar story." Booklist

When Christ and his saints slept. Holt & Co. 1995 746p il o.p.
LC 94-22593

With this novel, "Penman inaugurates a trilogy focusing on the lives of King Henry II of England and his colorful consort, Eleanor of Aquitaine. This initial volume paints the background of Henry II's reign: the civil war that raged in England for two decades as the result of a dispute between his mother and her cousin over the succession to the throne. From the darkness of this quarrel, which left England completely wrung out, ultimately stepped Henry Plantagenet, whose ascension as Henry II brought the country back into the light." Booklist

The author "showcases her mastery of the historical novel in this long and thoroughly engrossing study of pragmatic politics, idealism, and the role of women during the 12th century. She brings to life a vast array of unforgettable characters, both historical and invented, all of whose loyalties are being constantly tested by the chaos of the times." Libr J

Penzler, Otto, 1942-

(ed) Best American mystery stories [date] See Best American mystery stories [date]

Percy, Walker, 1916-1990

Lancelot. Farrar, Straus & Giroux 1977 257p o.p.

This story is told as a monologue by its protagonist Lancelot Lamar who "discovers himself to be a cuckold. (He confirms his initial suspicions by spying with the

Percy, Walker, 1916-1990—*Continued*
help of a videotape machine.) One night he leaps upon the coupled bodies of wife and lover and attempts to bear-hug them to death. He fails, but he does manage to slit the lover's throat with a Bowie knife. The New Orleans mansion in which this action takes place has a wing . . . built atop a capped natural gas well. Lance . . . uses the residual methane to blow up the mansion. Others perish, but he is thrown clear by the blast, and survives to tell his tale from his madhouse cell." Atlantic

In this novel the author "knowledgeably fingers what he perceives as the rotting fabric of Southern aristocratic life, and describes it with vividness and a kind of affection, even as he starts to shred it." Christ Sci Monit

The last gentleman. Modern Lib. 1997 c1966 442p $18.50
ISBN 0-679-60272-0 LC 97-15381

The hero, 25-year-old Williston Bibb Barrett, "returns to the South without identity, suffering from periodic amnesia and spells of 'déjà vu', with their telescoping of ancestral past and personal present. He hires on as tutor-companion to Jamie, a dying boy, son of 'Poppy' Vaught, a rich Alabama auto dealer, brother of Kitty, the displaced Southern belle Barrett loved at first sight—through his telescope up North in Central Park. . . . What Barrett seeks is some clue as to how to live." Newsweek

"The plot is less important than the delineation of character, the preoccupation with the way people speak and define themselves geographically and historically . . . and the rendering of a composite South." Burgess. 99 Novels

Followed by The second coming

Love in the ruins; the adventures of a bad Catholic at a time near the end of the world. Farrar, Straus & Giroux 1971 403p o.p.

"An extravaganza with a Southern setting is a satire on pseudoprofound novels and a sardonic commentary on the bogging down of religion, culture, and interracial, intergroup and interpersonal relationships in the not-too-distant future. The narrator is one Dr. More, descendant of Sir Thomas More, who believes he has invented a device that will analyze and cure the woes of society." Booklist

"A beautifully comic and humane work, the satirist's projection of a grotesque future world based on the realities of the present and stimulus to thought and evaluation and, hopefully, to improvement. Percy's style shows mastery of language." Choice

The moviegoer. Knopf 1961 241p $26
ISBN 0-394-43703-9

"A philosophical exploration of the problem of personal identity, the story is narrated by Binx Bolling, a successful but alienated businessman. Bolling undertakes a search for meaning in his life, first through an obsession with the movies and later through an affair." Merriam-Webster's Ency of Lit

The second coming. Farrar, Straus & Giroux 1980 359p o.p.
LC 80-12899

In this sequel to The last gentleman, Will Barrett "has become a widowed, middle-aged millionaire. He didn't marry Kitty, who he loved in the earlier book, but a crippled heiress. He has had an unforeseen success as a Wall Street lawyer, fathered a [daughter] . . . and now, retired, suffers undiagnosed fall-downs on the golf course. Released from the amnesia that used to afflict him, he remembers . . . his suicidal father's attempt to kill him before taking his own life. Will meets and falls in love with a schizophrenic girl escaped from an asylum, who speaks in rhymes and is gradually revealed to be Kitty's daughter." Newsweek

"A beautiful . . . exploration of Percy's recurrent theme—an individual man's search for the hand of God in the meaningless muddle of contemporary life." Booklist

The thanatos syndrome. Farrar, Straus & Giroux 1987 372p o.p.
LC 86-29409

This work's central character, Dr. Thomas More, a psychiatrist, last appeared in Love in the Ruins. After having been released from prison (he sold amphetamines to truck drivers), he returns to his Feliciana (Louisiana) practice to find his patients behaving strangely. With the help of his cousin Lucy Lipscomb, an epidemiologist, he discovers that his medical colleagues have been secretly adding heavy sodium to the water supply in an experiment intended to control antisocial behavior. Psychiatric symptoms disappear, but human beings regress to pre-primate stage

"All of Percy's fiction revolves around a central question: can humane, civilized life survive this murderous, mechanized century? . . . But Percy has done more here than simply repeat himself. The theme may be familiar, but the variations decidedly are not. For one thing, this novel embodies Percy's most detailed, explicit attack on contemporary materialism and science. For another, the philosophical warfare has been artfully disguised as a thriller." Time

Perdue, Lewis

Slatewiper. Forge 2003 367p $24.95
ISBN 0-7653-0111-3 LC 2002-45496

"A Tom Doherty Associates book"

"In Tokyo, a particularly violent and deadly plague has broken out. Inexplicably, it seems as if the virus only uses Koreans as its carrier. Enter Lara Blackwood, a genetic engineer recruited to fight this virus that somehow piggybacks itself on people with specific genetic characteristics. Ejected from her own company, Lara sees in this investigation her chance to get herself back in the research game, but she doesn't count on uncovering a genetic weapon of unimaginable power. . . . Perdue unflinchingly treads on Crichton's turf but emerges with a novel that feels fresh and original." Booklist

Perec, Georges, 1936-1982

Life; a user's manual; translated by David Bellos. Godine 1987 581p o.p.
ISBN 0-87923-700-7 LC 87-8782

Original French edition, 1978

The author of this novel set in a Paris apartment house on a single day describes the building's 100 rooms and the life stories of past and present occupants as a painting in progress, the work of one of the tenants

"The inextricable incoherence of things is presumably

Perec, Georges, 1936-1982—*Continued*
the basic theme of the late Georges Perec's work, but this pessimistic view of life is dramatized with inventiveness, audacity, and even humor." Atlantic

A void; translated by Gilbert Adair. HarperCollins Pubs. 1994 285p o.p.
ISBN 0-00-271119-2
Original French edition, 1969
This novel was written and translated without using the letter "e." The plot "concerns (probably) the disappearance of one Anton Vowl (A. Vowl) and the attempts of an irregular group of friends to discover what's what. The Sphinx is consulted, and the white whale, and clues start to glimmer dangerously: there are 26 cartons, but the fifth one is missing." N Y Times Book Rev
"Gilbert Adair has now shown quite brilliantly that a lipogrammatic text in one language can be more than adequately done into another, retaining not only the alphabetical constraint but much of the virtuosity of the original." London Rev Books

Pérez Galdós, Benito, 1843-1920

Doña Perfecta; translated by Mary J. Serrano; introduction by William Dean Howells. Harper & Row 1896 319p o.p.
Original Spanish edition, 1876
"The social problem which engrosses so much of the author's interest, the struggle between scientific and social enlightenment and the tyrannous obscurantism of the church, is here set forth in the domestic conflict of a group of characters and the political strife agitating a provincial town. Dona Perfecta is a devout lady whose daughter is sought by a promising young man, a representative of modernism. A wily priest is her chief ally, and eventually the rival intrigues drag in a host of forces on either side." Baker. Guide to the Best Fic

Torquemada; translated from the Spanish by Frances M. López-Morillas. Columbia Univ. Press 1986 569p o.p.
LC 85-19560
Omnibus edition of the author's Torquemada tetralogy portraying middle-class Madrid society, and focusing on the miserly Francisco de Torquemada from the time he is 50 years old to his deathbed ten years later. The novels were originally published separately in the late nineteenth century
Contents: Torquemada at the stake; Torquemada on the cross; Torquemada in Purgatory; Torquemada and Saint Peter

Torquemada and Saint Peter
In Pérez Galdós, B. Torquemada p405-569

Torquemada at the stake
In Pérez Galdós, B. Torquemada p1-60

Torquemada in Purgatory
In Pérez Galdós, B. Torquemada p221-404

Torquemada on the cross
In Pérez Galdós, B. Torquemada p61-220

Pérez-Reverte, Arturo

Captain Alatriste; translated from the Spanish by Margaret Sayers Peden. Putnam 2005 253p $23.95
ISBN 0-399-15275-X LC 2004-60210
"Captain Alatriste, a veteran of Spain's Flemish wars, deploys his sword for anyone who will pay, which inevitably leads him into some dicey situations; the one detailed here is a commission to assassinate, under the cover of darkness, two Englishmen on a visit to Madrid. At the last moment, Alatriste decides against running them through and spares their lives—which turns out to be fortunate on a diplomatic level, since his intended victims are revealed to be the Prince of Wales and the Duke of Buckingham, in Spain to attempt to arrange a marriage between the prince and the Spanish king's daughter." Booklist
"Equipped with a quick-witted, charismatic hero and much to provoke and goad him, Mr. Pérez-Reverte has the makings of a flamboyantly entertaining series. Captain Alatriste ends with a wicked flourish, an evil laugh and a strong likelihood that the best is yet to come." N Y Times (Late N Y Ed)

The Club Dumas; translated from the Spanish by Sonia Soto. Harcourt Brace & Co. 1996 362p il $23
ISBN 0-15-100182-0 LC 96-11962
Original Spanish edition, 1993
"Corso, a tough-guy bibliophile living in Madrid, is hired by a wealthy client to track down a rare seventeenth-century book on how to summon the Devil. He soon finds himself in noir metafiction in which he's been cast as D'Artagnan and is threatened by characters suspiciously like Richelieu's agents—a menacing man with a scar and a blonde with a fleur-de-lis tattoo. Even a reader armed with a Latin dictionary and a copy of 'The Three Musketeers' cannot anticipate the thrilling twists of this stylish, Escher-like mystery." New Yorker

The fencing master; translated from the Spanish by Margaret Jull Costa. Harcourt Brace & Co. 1999 245p $24
ISBN 0-15-100181-2 LC 98-35536
Original Spanish edition, 1988
This novel is set in the Spain of 1868. "All Madrid, with the exception of Don Jaime, is preoccupied with political plots and rumors of the Queen's abdication. Don Jaime is a fencing master devoted to honor and his art. He is an anachronism, which causes him serious difficulty with murders and stolen documents." Atl Mon
"In lieu of snappy pater, Pérez-Reverte provides artful, intricate conversation. Rather than send his characters on a relentless search, he provides them with an inexorable unfolding of revelation, increasingly ghastly. And instead of the clever puzzle that lies at the heart of many a lesser crime novel, he substitutes a subtle meditation on the deeper mysteries of fate and choice." N Y Times Book Rev

The nautical chart; translated from the Spanish by Margaret Sayers Peden. Harcourt 2001 466p o.p.
ISBN 0-15-100534-6 LC 2001-39446
Original Spanish edition, 2000
"This is the story of a down-and-out sailor ('We could call him Ishmael, but in truth his name is Coy') who

Pérez-Reverte, Arturo—*Continued*

washes up in modern-day Barcelona, where he is recruited to join in the treasure hunt for a cargo of emeralds . . . that went down with a merchant ship that sank off the Spanish coast in 1767." N Y Times Book Rev

"Adept as ever at mixing historical and contemporary material, Perez-Reverte takes his genrebending to another level this time by merging the swashbuckling spirit of the best sea adventures with an introspective, philosophical meditation on the idea of navigation." Booklist

Perlman, Elliot

Seven types of ambiguity. Riverhead Books 2004 628p $27.95

ISBN 0-571-20717-0 LC 2004-45348

This is a novel, "told from seven perspectives, about the effects of the brief abduction of six-year-old Sam Geraghty by Simon Heywood, his mother Anna's ex-boyfriend. Charismatic, unemployed Simon is still obsessed with Anna nine years after their breakup-to the dismay of his present lover, Angelique, a prostitute. Anna's stockbroker husband, Joe, is one of Angelique's regulars, which feeds Simon's flame. When Angelique turns Simon in to the cops, he claims he had permission to pick Sam up; his fate hinges on whether Anna will back up his lie. Most of the perspectives are linked to Simon's shrink, Alex Klima, who writes to Anna and counsels Simon, Angelique and Joe's coworker, Dennis." Publ Wkly

"This is an exciting gamble of a novel, one willing to lose its shirt in its bid to hold you. Be prepared to give it time. Be prepared to skim when you come to a particularly annoying digression. But most of all be prepared to stay with it for the long haul. It's worth it." N Y Times (Late N Y Ed)

Perrotta, Tom, 1961-

Joe College. St. Martin's Press 2000 306p o.p.

ISBN 0-312-26184-5 LC 00-31722

"Danny, a New Jersey working-class boy at Yale, circa 1980, finds himself both enchanted by a schoolmate and dodging calls from a hometown girlfriend. Spring break, and the inevitable crisis, loom." Newsweek

"Perrotta's genius is his ability to depict student culture with dead-on accuracy. His satiric touch is like a light, but killing frost." Christ Sci Monit

Little children; Tom Perrotta. 1st ed. St. Martin's Press 2004 355p $24.95

ISBN 0-312-31571-6 LC 2003-15947

"The eponymous children in this satirical novel are actually adults who, chafing at the burdens of parenthood, try to recreate their unencumbered youth. Sarah, an overeducated young homemaker, likens her tantrum-prone daughter to a 'brooding Russian epileptic' out of Dostoevsky, and pines for lost college days of feminism and bisexuality. While her husband orders used panties online, she has furtive sex with a stay-at-home dad whose repeated failure to pass the bar has earned him the contempt of his gorgeous wife. The humor is sometimes cruel, but Perrotta never betrays the complexity of his characters." New Yorker

Perry, Anne, 1938-

Ashworth Hall. Fawcett Columbine 1997 373p $24

ISBN 0-449-90844-5 LC 96-47716

In this "mystery featuring Scotland Yard Superintendent WIlliam Pitt and his wife, Charlotte, the two leave the mean streets of Victorian London for Charlotte's sister's country home, Ashworth Hall, where a group of Irish Catholic and Protestant politicians are meeting, under the guise of a social weekend, to negotiate the sticky issue of home rule for Ireland. When two mysterious deaths occur, it's clear to Pitt that there is someone at the house party who wants to scuttle the talks and perhaps see Ireland erupt in civil war." Libr J

Pitt is "at home in the country, which gently softens his city-hardened sensibilities. . . . In the end, though, it is his shrewd wife, Charlotte, who cuts to the core of the nationalist issues and reduces them to human scale. This subtle play on sex roles, a constant in this rewarding series, may well be the secret of its profound appeal." NY Times Book Rev

Bedford Square. Fawcett Columbine 1999 330p $24.95

ISBN 0-449-90633-7 LC 98-29854

"Through a campaign of 'whisper, suspicion and innuendo,' someone is slandering men of high position in 1891 London society, and it is up to Thomas Pitt, commander of the Bow Street police station, to scotch these poisonous rumors of dishonorable behavior before reputations are destroyed and lives ruined. Through his discreet investigations, the sympathetic Pitt exposes the subtle cruelty of the anonymous letters that bring disgrace to one man and death to another." N Y Times Book Rev

Belgrave Square. Fawcett Columbine 1992 361p o.p.

LC 91-73144

"While investigating the murder of back-street usurer William Weems, killed when one of his own gold coins is fired from a gun [Inspector Thomas] Pitt learns that the victim had been blackmailing members of London's high social circles." Publ Wkly

The author "paints handsome portraits of . . . [Victorian] aristocratic society and provides luxurious details of the gala balls and garden parties, the fashionable outings at Covent Garden and the Royal Academy of Arts, where they congregate to preen themselves. But it isn't all done for show. The author has the eyes of a hawk for character nuance and her claws out for signs of the criminal injustices rampant among the privileged classes during this gilded historical period." N Y Times Book Rev

Bethlehem Road. St. Martin's Press 1990 309p o.p.

LC 89-78014

"Three Members of Parliament have had their throats slit while crossing the Westminster Bridge. All three voted against female suffrage. As Pitt investigates, his suspicions fall on a vocal and much-wronged suffragette; other unlikely candidates include anarchists and madmen. As usual, Pitt's wife, Charlotte, and her delightful Great Aunt Vespasia play sleuths as well." Libr J

"The author's concern with presenting an unassailable argument for her feminist cause tends to drag the pace and dull the action. But her finely drawn characters

Perry, Anne, 1938-—*Continued*
couldn't be more comfortable within the customs and sensibility of their historical period." N Y Times Book Rev

Bluegate Fields. St. Martin's Press 1984 308p o.p.
LC 84-11769

"Inspector Pitt and his splendid wife, Charlotte, pursue [a] murder investigation that takes them from the squalor of the slums to the hypocrisy of high-society drawing rooms in Victorian London. Pitt is uncomfortable with a case built against a humorless tutor by a zealous young policeman who possesses a potentially obstructive reverence for the upper class. However the witnesses appear irrefutable . . . and Pitt's superior is adamant about not reopening so embarrassing a case—a teenager from a wealthy family was murdered in a bathtub and shoved down a London sewer. Charlotte, impelled by the tutor's wife, launches her own campaign to prove that the wrong man has been arrested." Booklist

A breach of promise. Fawcett Columbine 1998 374p $25
ISBN 0-449-90849-6 LC 98-21212

"Gifted architect Killian Melville begs barrister Sir Oliver Rathbone to defend him in what is certain to be an ugly breach-of-promise suit. Melville claims he never asked lovely young Zillah Lambert, the daughter of his mentor and patron Barton Lambert, to marry him. Unfortunately, the young lady and her mother think otherwise. . . . Days later, Melville is dead, an apparent suicide. Rathbone can't get the unfortunate young man out of his mind and determines to get to the bottom of the case." Booklist

"Aside from the jarring coincidence that sets up the resolution, the story is full of feeling and weighted with intelligent thought about the status of women in mid-Victorian society." N Y Times Book Rev

Brunswick gardens. Fawcett Columbine 1998 389p $25
ISBN 0-449-90845-3 LC 97-38441

In this Victorian mystery, the Rev. Ramsay Parmenter is, "a revered churchman whose faith has been profoundly undermined by the taunting arguments of his Darwinist assistant, Unity Bellwood, a fine scholar but 'a dangerous woman, both foolish and destructive.' When the contentious Unity comes to a violent end in Parmenter's home, Thomas Pitt, the head of London's Bow Street police force, has the unenviable task of determining which of the three resident clergymen did the deed." N Y Times Book Rev

"Perry explores modern themes of feminism, discrimination, and free love within the well-defined strictures of Victorian mores, and her characters emerge as realistic and credible." Libr J

Cain his brother. Fawcett Columbine 1995 390p o.p.
LC 95-8680

Genevieve Stonefield comes to Victorian detective William Monk "for help, believing that her missing husband, the upright Angus Stonefield, has been murdered by his depraved twin brother, Caleb. When Monk finds evidence of Angus's death, he also comes upon a makeshift typhoid hospital staffed by his two friends, Lady Callandra Daviot and Hester Latterly." Publ Wkly

"This one deserves high marks for superb plotting, fine writing, intriguing characters, and outstanding historical detail." Booklist

Cardington Crescent. St. Martin's Press 1987 314p o.p.
LC 86-27942

A Victorian "mystery featuring the stalwart Inspector Thomas Pitt of Scotland Yard and his inquisitive wife, Charlotte. When Charlotte's beloved sister is suspected of poisoning her philandering husband, the Pitts undertake the investigation of the unfortunate victim's seemingly irreproachable, upper-crust family. Amid the luxurious splendor of an elegant town house and the hideous squalor of a London slum, they uncover a scandalous web of depravity and corruption that has inevitably culminated in the murder. A detailed period puzzler suffused with atmosphere, emotion, and suspense." Booklist

A dangerous mourning. Fawcett Columbine 1991 330p o.p.
LC 91-70655

"Murder in an aristocratic London household pits Inspector William Monk . . . against the Victorian sense of propriety, a bootlicking superior officer and a family's fierce determination to protect its reputation. Octavia Haslett, widowed daughter of Sir Basil Moidore, is found stabbed to death in her bedroom dressed only in nightclothes; when Monk proves no outsider could have entered the house that night, the family and servants remain sole suspects. As tension mounts in the household and a handsome and disliked footman becomes a scapegoat, Monk covertly arranges to introduce Hester Latterly, who served with Florence Nightingale in the Crimea and has helped Monk before, as a nurse in the Moidore home." Publ Wkly

Death of a stranger. Ballantine Bks. 2002 337p o.p.
ISBN 0-345-44005-6 LC 2002-66735

This Monk mystery "opens with the murder of a wealthy railroad businessman in a brothel. Outraged by the crime, high society pressures the police into cracking down on prostitution. But a police presence is bad for business, and the pimps take out their frustration on the call girls. These battered women seek medical assistance at a Coldbath Square clinic rum by Monk's wife, Hester. . . . Meanwhile, a mysterious young socialite asks Monk to investigate her fiancé, a partner in a successful railroad company that, she fears, is involved in fraud and corruption." Libr J

Defend and betray. Fawcett Columbine 1992 385p o.p.
LC 92-52665

In Victorian London a "proud nurse and a brilliant lawyer team up with former policeman William Monk to defend a sympathetic upper-class woman who confesses to murdering her much-respected husband in a fit of jealousy." Libr J

"The climactic trial, and its ugly disclosures, are well wrought. . . . Throughout, the plight of the intelligent, educated woman who is not rich—her need for a meaningful independence, her culture's resistance to her fulfillment—is, while not deeply explored, frequently touched upon." N Y Times Book Rev

Perry, Anne, 1938—*Continued*

The face of a stranger. Fawcett Columbine 1990 328p o.p.

LC 90-34169

"William Monk, attached to the police in 1856 London, returns to work with amnesia after otherwise recovering from a nasty accident. Assigned to solve the murder of an aristocrat wounded in the Crimean War, he discovers, while hiding his memory loss from others, that he abhors his own character." Libr J

The author "understands her amnesiac sleuth so intimately that she knows he can rediscover himself only in moments of inspiration along the trail of his quarry. This, and the fact that Monk has more to learn about himself even as the story concludes, are brilliant touches that effectively blend contemporary understanding of character with a Victorian sensibility." N Y Times Book Rev

Farriers' Lane. Fawcett Columbine 1993 374p o.p.

LC 92-54390

"In the wave of anti-Semitic hysteria in 1884 that follows the crucifixion of an English gentleman, a young Jewish actor is hastily tried and executed for the crime. Five years later, a justice of the appeals court is murdered when he attempts to reopen the sensational case. Only a man of discretion, intelligence and integrity—a man like Inspector Thomas Pitt of the Bow Street police division—can solve the devious affair of passion and political intrigue in Victorian London." N Y Times Book Rev

Funeral in blue. Ballantine Bks. 2001 344p o.p.

ISBN 0-345-44001-3 LC 2001-37481

A mystery featuring Hester and William Monk. "In the studio of a London artist, two women have been murdered, one of them the wife of Dr. Kristian Beck, a physician from Vienna with whom Hester's dear friend, Lady Callandra, is secretly in love. When Beck is charged with the murder, Callandra enlists the aid of Hester and William. . . . The author excels at re-creating the ambience of 1860s London streets." Publ Wkly

Half Moon Street. Ballantine Bks. 2000 312p o.p.

ISBN 0-345-43298-3 LC 99-55232

"Superintendent Pitt is summoned to the Thames when police discover the body of a young man dressed in a torn green velvet gown, manacled to a punt, 'in parody of ecstasy and death'. At first it seems the victim is Henri Bonnard, a functionary in the French embassy; eventually, Pitt and dour sidekick Sergeant Tellman identify the body as Delbert Cathcart, a gifted photographer. Was there a connection between Cathcart and lookalike Bonnard?" Publ Wkly

"Perry sinks inspector Pitt knee-deep in the morally suspect world of the theater and the completely subterranean culture of pornography. . . . Cameos from Oscar Wilde and W.B. Yeats add to the sense of artistic turmoil set against middle-class timidity." Booklist

Highgate rise. Fawcett Columbine 1991 330p o.p.

LC 90-85131

"Inspector Thomas Pitt, is appalled by the callousness of an arsonist who torches a physician's town house, burning his wife to death. Pitt's highborn wife, Charlotte, shares his horror when she learns that the dead woman was a quiet crusader on behalf of poor slum tenants. . . . Ms. Perry gives Pitt a breather from his customary gutter research by confining his investigation to the victim's upper-class social circle. Following her own conscience, Charlotte insinuates her way into elegant drawing rooms where the author's satirical wit is free to spread its rather showy skirts." N Y Times Book Rev

The Hyde Park headsman. Fawcett Columbine 1994 392p o.p.

LC 93-22124

Inspector Thomas Pitt "struggles to solve the brutal and confounding murder of Captain the Honorable Oakley Winthrop, R.N., who's been found beheaded in Hyde Park. Pitt suspects the victim knew his killer, but it's only after three more deadly murders take place that enough evidence can be mustered to accuse the real killer." Booklist

No graves as yet; a novel of World War I. Ballantine Bks. 2003 642p $25.95

ISBN 0-345-45652-1 LC 2003-52233

'This is the debut novel in Perry's projected five-book series about a British family during World War I. The family in question includes brothers Matthew and Joseph Reavley and sisters Judith and Hannah, whose parents are killed in a car accident when the book opens. Reavley pere had been on his way to deliver a document that purports to be of national importance. Matthew, a trusted employee in the Intelligence Service, can't quite believe that the document could really threaten Britain's honor. Meanwhile, Joseph, an ordained minister and teacher of classical languages at Cambridge, struggles with the senseless murder of his brilliant protege." Libr J

"Perry's melancholy evocation of the 'eternal afternoon' that would soon turn to night all over England is lovely." N Y Times Book Rev

Paragon Walk. St. Martin's Press 1981 204p o.p.

"A psychopathic killer stalks the fashionable London neighborhood called Paragon Walk—the rapist's atrocities are as incredible, and terrifying to the Paragon Walk aristocrats as a sudden outbreak of the bubonic plague. Inspector Pitt's investigation of one brutal slaying, that of 17-year-old Fanny Nash, leads him to his own family—and himself." Booklist

Pentecost Alley. Fawcett Columbine 1996 405p o.p.

LC 95-43557

"Two years after the short, bloody reign of Jack the Ripper, a wave of terror rips through Whitechapel . . . when a local prostitute is savagely murdered. Thomas Pitt, who heads the Bow Street police command, promises to bring the sadistic killer to justice." N Y Times Book Rev

"Perry has created a superbly plotted, grippingly suspenseful period piece filled with intriguing characters and fascinating descriptions of the manners and customs of Victorian London." Booklist

Perry, Anne, 1938-—*Continued*

Resurrection row. St. Martin's Press 1981 204p o.p.

LC 81-8846

"For no discernible reason, someone digs up the corpses of recently buried citizens and sets them up in public places. With these crimes demanding Pitt's concentration, he also has to investigate the murder of Godolphin Jones—an artist, pornographer and blackmailer. The detective's efforts to gather evidence against Jones's clients, obvious suspects, are fruitless until (as always) his quick-witted wife Charlotte drops a startling hint." Publ Wkly

Seven dials. Ballantine Bks. 2003 345p $25.95

ISBN 0-345-44007-2 LC 2002-35605

"When the Egyptian mistress of a senior cabinet minister is discovered in her garden in the middle of the night, using a wheelbarrow to dispose of the body of a junior diplomat, the apparent crime of passion turns into an international incident. Thomas Pitt. . . chafes at the order from Special Branch to extricate the government official, Saville Ryerson, from the affair; but he sees the gravity of the political situation. . . . Although the focus of the plot tends to drift, the visual panorama is voluptuous to behold." N Y Times Book Rev

The shifting tide. Ballantine Bks. 2004 328p $25.95

ISBN 0-345-44009-9

In 1873, private inquiry agent "William Monk agrees to look into the theft of some African ivory from a ship docked in London." Libr J

"In scenes that could have come out of Dickens's Our Mutual Friend, Monk wanders the teeming streets and ventures into the perilous river traffic, at one point chatting up an old sailor who yearns for the days of an even more exciting era of privateering. As the sailor says, 'River's full o' tales,' and Perry knows how to bring them to life." N Y Times Book Rev

Shoulder the sky. Ballantine Bks. 2004 338p $25.95

ISBN 0-345-45654-8

This sequel to No graves yet "follows the wartime careers of the Reavley siblings. Joseph, serving as a chaplain at the Western Front, strives to build morale among the troops amidst the harsh realities of World War I. He is also determined to find out who murdered Eldon Prentice, an abrasive, arrogant journalist, even though no one else cares. Judith finds meaning in her life by driving ambulances near Ypres and falling in love with the married general she chauffeurs. Back in London, Matthew secretly investigates the identity of the 'Peacemaker,' who would manipulate the British into surrendering. Matthew has a personal stake in stopping him, because the 'Peacemaker' orchestrated the deaths of the Reavley parents." Libr J

"Questions about the morality of war resonate throughout this harrowing novel, which Perry has constructed with hallmark attention to period detail and sense of place. Her vivid evocations of the battlefield . . . are unforgettable." Booklist

The silent cry. Fawcett Columbine 1997 361p $24.95

ISBN 0-449-90848-8 LC 97-16848

In this Victorian mystery "one man is found murdered and another on the edge of death in the notorious London slum called St. Giles. Although it looks as if they may have engaged in a mortal fight, they are in fact father and son from a well-to-do family. Later, links develop between these men and a series of violent rapes of prostitutes. Hester Latterly, nurse and protector of the surviving son, Rhys, counterbalances detective William Monk in their mutual pursuit of the truth." Libr J

"With her grimly detailed descriptions of the match factories, sweatshops, paupers hospitals and tenement 'rookeries' crowded into these slums, Perry brings a rank sense of reality to the wretched living conditions of the working poor." N Y Times Book Rev

The sins of the wolf. Fawcett Columbine 1994 374p o.p.

LC 94-12099

"Nurse Hester Latterly, who served courageously in the Crimean War and has assisted former policeman William Monk in many of his investigations . . . is charged with murdering a patient for personal gain. Hester hires on to accompany aging but lively Mary Farraline by train from Edinburgh to London and to administer the proper dose of heart medication. But Mary dies enroute—and her pearl brooch is discovered in Hester's bag. The dead woman's family, the police and most of Edinburgh are convinced that Hester killed her to obtain the pin. Coming to her aid are former policeman Monk, barrister Oliver Rathbone and Lady Callandra Daviot." Publ Wkly

Slaves of obsession. Ballantine Bks. 2000 344p o.p.

ISBN 0-345-43326-2 LC 00-40375

"William Monk, agent of enquiry, is employed to discover who is blackmailing respectable merchant and arms dealer Daniel Alberton. Monk soon finds himself investigating Alberton's murder, however, and looking for the murderer on the battlefield at Bull Run." Libr J

"Perry's images of the carnage and confusion of battle are relentless in their intensity, unflinching in their truth-telling detail." N Y Times Book Rev

Southampton Row. Ballantine Bks. 2002 326p o.p.

ISBN 0-345-44003-X LC 2001-52664

Thomas Pitt "ventures into the world of spiritualism when, on the eve of a critical parliamentary election, the wife of the Liberal candidate is implicated in the murder of a clairvoyant. As she has done increasingly in recent books, Perry links the crime to a secret political cabal known as the Inner Circle and draws everyone into its machinations. . . . Perry's proto-feminists have the kind of intellectual radiance that eludes their spouses." N Y Times Book Rev

A sudden, fearful death. Fawcett Columbine 1993 383p o.p.

LC 93-214115

Victorian sleuth William Monk is "summoned to investigate the rape of a respectable young woman in her family's backyard. With little legwork or concrete evidence, Monk solves the case summarily. The remainder of the novel concerns the mystery of the fatal strangling of an educated and ambitious nurse who had served with Florence Nightingale in the Crimea." N Y Times Book Rev

Perry, Anne, 1938-—*Continued*

Traitor's gate. Fawcett Columbine 1995 411p o.p.

LC 94-27624

This mystery, set "in turn-of-the-century London, has Inspector Thomas Pitt and his wife, Charlotte, investigating the mysterious death of Thomas' mentor, Sir Arthur Desmond. The death has been ruled a suicide, but Sir Arthur's son is convinced his father was murdered for attempting to expose treason in the Colonial Office." Booklist

"In combination with her meticulous research, Ms. Perry's infallible feeling for the historical moment yields animated political debate over the colonization of Africa, glittering views of Victorian society at play and tantalizing glimpses of a confident, assertive creature known as the 'new woman.'" N Y Times Book Rev

The twisted root. Ballantine Bks. 1999 346p $25

ISBN 0-345-43325-4 LC 99-34689

"A beautiful widow named Miriam Gardiner has disappeared, leaving behind a distraught fiancé and a dead coachman. Monk is called in to find Gardiner and then must uncover the truth when she is charged with murdering the coachman." Libr J

Weighed in the balance. Fawcett Columbine 1996 355p o.p.

LC 96-34824

William Monk "a Victorian-era 'agent of inquiry,' is still haunted by a baffling amnesia, and he feels that his associates—the rigidly proper barrister Sir Oliver Rathbone and the uncompromising and outspoken nurse Hester Latterly—have taken on more than they can handle when Sir Oliver decides to defend Countess Zorah Rostova against a slander charge. The patriotic Zorah has accused Princess Gisela of Felzburg of murdering her husband, Prince Friedrich, heir to the throne, who presumably had died as a result of a fall from a horse. Gisela is suing. " Publ Wkly

"Monk, the dark and brooding hero who infuses this luxuriantly detailed series with its romantic soul, is not immune to the seductive appeal of this aristocratic crowd. . . . But he also comes to understand the human passions behind the political forces that transformed Europe in the mid-1800's." N Y Times Book Rev

The Whitechapel conspiracy. Ballantine Bks. 2001 341p o.p.

ISBN 0-345-43328-9 LC 00-64206

"When Pitt delivers the testimony that condemns a prominent man for murder, he is 'rewarded' by being shuffled off to the Special Branch, which operates in London's risky East End." Libr J

Perry's interpretation of the Jack the Ripper killings is "a beauty, brilliantly presented, ingeniously developed and packed with political implications that reverberate on every level of British society." N Y Times Book Rev

Perry, Thomas

Blood money; a novel. Random House 2000 351p $24.95

ISBN 0-679-45304-0 LC 99-18340

In this Jane Whitefield suspense novel "Bernie 'the Elephant' Lupus, who handled—in his head—the finances of 12 major mob families for 50 years, fakes his own murder and winds up in the hands of Jane, at first out to help only his maid. But soon the three of them, along with an accountant, are involved in a plot to steal over $14 billion of the mob's investments and then donate the funds to charity." Libr J

"Perry's inventive ways of keeping Jane and her charges one step ahead of the mob squad are downright dazzling—all the more so because they pass up coldblooded technology and go for good old human wit and ingenuity." N Y Times Book Rev

The butcher's boy. Scribner 1982 313p o.p.

LC 82-653

"A nameless hit man known as 'the Butcher's Boy' completes two killings, one of a U.S. senator, for Fieldstone Co. But when he tries to collect his $200,000 payoff, he finds that the unknown Mafia figure behind Fieldstone is out to get him and everyone who's had contact with him. Meanwhile Justice Department agent Elizabeth Waring is drawn in to investigate Fieldstone. She comes close to psyching out the true story, but it's the Butcher's Boy who becomes the hero by setting up for the Feds the Mafia chieftain at the heart of the evil doings." Libr J

Dance for the dead. Random House 1996 324p o.p.

LC 95-32716

In this thriller, Native American private agent Jane Whitefield, "appoints herself the guardian angel of Timmy Phillips, a little boy with a big trust fund. The master criminal who had Timmy's foster parents murdered has an ingenious scheme for plundering his inheritance; but, since 'none of this works if the heir is alive,' Jane takes aggressive action to save his life." N Y Times Book Rev

Dead aim; a novel. Random House 2002 366p $24.95

ISBN 1-400-06003-6 LC 2002-68100

"For someone who made millions in real estate and retired when he was 38, Robert Mallon lacks the wit and imagination to figure out how to enjoy his good fortune. Some nascent feelings are awakened in his anesthetized soul when he accepts a sexual favor from Catherine Broward, a young woman he pulls out of the ocean in front of his Santa Barbara beach house when she tries to drown herself. After Catherine turns around and kills herself anyway, the newly energized hero plays detective to determine the circumstances of her life and death." N Y Times Book Rev

Death benefits; a novel. Random House 2001 383p $24.95

ISBN 0-679-45305-9 LC 00-41476

San Francisco insurance data analyst John Walker is "sleepwalking through his young life when the boss assigns him to assist a private detective on an inside job involving Walker's ex-girlfriend, a claims adjuster who disappeared after being implicated in a $12 million scheme to defraud the company. Judicious applications of Perry's knowing wit energize the tutor-pupil dynamics between Walker and Max Stillman, the crafty and somewhat sinister P.I. who calls the shots on this case." N Y Times Book Rev

The face-changers; a novel. Random House 1998 372p $24

ISBN 0-679-45303-2 LC 97-34078

Perry, Thomas—*Continued*

Seneca Indian guide Jane Whitefield "is asked by her surgeon husband to help his old mentor, Dr. Richard Dahlman, who has been accused of murdering his research partner. In her attempts to keep Dahlman out of the hands of the law and far away from the two men who want to kill him, she finds that someone is using her name to make people disappear permanently, and Dahlman has gotten caught in the backlash. . . . The plot is full of heart-stopping suspense, Native American lore, and engaging characters, but the real pull is how Jane will surmount adversity and still keep her honor and ethics intact." Libr J

Metzger's dog. Scribner 1983 314p o.p.
LC 83-9080

"Soldier of fortune Chinese Gordon and his three inept friends steal $1 million in cocaine from a university that was going to use it for experimental purposes. Gordon then inadvertently latches onto secret papers revealing American connivance in Latin America and decides to blackmail the CIA, whereupon the agency sends their top operative to recover the documents." Booklist

"Smoothly styled and humorous, the incredible story line exterminates the bungling creeps and prospers the ne'er-do-wells; but Gordon's cohorts never hurt anyone and they seem to have a great time. No deep characterization, philosophizing, or seriousness, just fast fun for the reader." Libr J

Pursuit; a novel. Random House 2002 370p $24.95
ISBN 0-679-45306-7 LC 2001-40365

The key players in this thriller "are James Varney, a sociopathic hit man whose handiwork has left 13 people dead in a Louisville, Ky., restaurant, and Roy Prescott, the professional manhunter hired to track him down by the father of one of the victims. . . . Although Prescott initiates most of the fiendish maneuvers, he is checkmated at every turn by his opponent's ability to anticipate or recover from each trap. When this brilliant game is finally called, it isn't advanced weaponary or high-tech skills that determine the victor; it's one player's greater insights into the other's twisted mind—a mind very much like his own." N Y Times Book Rev

Shadow woman. Random House 1997 350p $22
ISBN 0-679-45302-4

Native American private agent Jane Whitefield "engineers the 'disappearance' of Peter Hatcher from his old life at Pleasure, Inc., a gambling casino. But the casino's honchos think Peter knows too much about their expansion plans and hire a brutally vicious hit team to find, and assassinate, him." Libr J

"Although the frantic pace allows no time for sightseeing, Perry lingers long enough over Pete's amiable character to make him worth all this excruciating suspense." N Y Times Book Rev

Sleeping dogs. Random House 1992 337p o.p.
LC 91-27137

This novel "brings Charles Ackerman—a.k.a., the Butcher's Boy, a killing-machine-for-hire—out of retirement in England and back to the United States to silence those people he mistakenly thinks have discovered his whereabouts. The story follows Ackerman as he travels coast to coast slaughtering one crime family's head honchos. Perry's book is well written, moves rapidly, and thankfully keeps the gore minimal." Libr J

Vanishing act. Random House 1995 289p o.p.
LC 94-17413

"Jane Whitefield is a Seneca Indian from upstate New York who has set herself up as a one-woman underground railroad to help worthy fugitives disappear. . . . A desperate man like John Felker is right up her alley. A burned-out cop who quit the job to become an accountant, Felker was set up on an embezzlement rap. But he grabbed the dough anyway, and now he has a contract on his head. Drawing on her clan contacts, Jane guides Felker on a trip into oblivion, via a rugged route across the Canadian border. This is all very satisfying and quite scenic—until certain deadly reversals tip off Jane that her operation has been compromised." N Y Times Book Rev

Pesci, David

Amistad; the thunder of freedom. Marlowe & Co. 1997 292p $22.95; pa $12.95
ISBN 1-56924-748-X; 1-56924-703-X (pa)
LC 96-54050

"In August 1839, Singbe-Pleh, a Mende tribesman, led his fellow African captives aboard the Spanish ship Amistad in successful revolt. The Africans took over the ship but could not sail it back to Africa. They were captured and put on trial in Connecticut. . . . The case was politically charged, with proslavery President Van Buren's administration wanting to give the Africans to Spain, abolitionists rallying for their freedom, and former President John Quincy Adams eventually defending them before the Supreme Court. Pesci deftly blends the facts of this fascinating historical episode with story." SLJ

Peshkov, Alekseĭ Maksimovich *See* Gorky, Maksim, 1868-1936

Peshkov, Alexei Maximovich *See* Gorky, Maksim, 1868-1936

Peters, Elizabeth, 1927-

For works written by this author under other names see Michaels, Barbara, 1927-

The ape who guards the balance; an Amelia Peabody mystery. Avon Bks. 1998 376p $24
ISBN 0-380-97657-9 LC 97-44189

"Prospects for the 1907 excavation season in Egypt seem lackluster for the Emersons, since Professor Emerson, Amelia's beloved husband, can't abide the fools who administrate such activities—and makes no secret of that fact. But the family, including their adult son, Ramses, and his foster siblings, Nefret and David, departs for Egypt nevertheless after incidents in London point to the resurfacing of their old nemesis, known as the Master Criminal." Publ Wkly

"Although Peters lets the younger generation handle most of the derring-do in this romantic tale, Amelia remains an irrepressible delight." N Y Times Book Rev

Children of the storm. Morrow 2003 400p $25.95
ISBN 0-06-621476-9 LC 2002-41083

This installment, set in 1919, finds Amelia Peabody "back in Egypt, reunited with her extended brood of family and friends (a helpful preface sorts them all out)

Peters, Elizabeth, 1927-—*Continued*
and anticipating an enriching season at the archaeological dig being excavated by her husband. In some respects, the story follows the formula of the 14 earlier books in this spirited series—precious tomb artifacts go missing and the logical suspect turns up dead, necessitating adventures filled with romance and fraught with peril." N Y Times Book Rev

The deeds of the disturber; an Amelia Peabody mystery. Atheneum Pubs. 1988 289p o.p.
LC 87-33457
"Determined Victorian feminist Peabody refuses to be intimidated by a phenomenon reported at the British Museum, where a *sem* priest is supposedly working a curse in revenge for the desecration of an ancient mummy. The priest's supernatural figure is momentarily glimpsed at the exhibit, before a murderer strikes. Disobeying Emerson, of course, Peabody lays her life on the line and unmasks the decidedly human villain." Publ Wkly

The falcon at the portal; an Amelia Peabody mystery. Avon Twilight 1999 366p $24
ISBN 0-380-97658-7 LC 99-19595
In this novel the "plot elements include stolen and forged artifacts, treacherous defamations of character, a murder, a love affair gone disastrously wrong, and . . . the effect of the rising nationalist movement in 1911 Egypt on Amelia's family." Booklist

The golden one. Morrow 2002 429p o.p.
ISBN 0-380-97885-7 LC 2001-52169
"On arriving in Luxor for a season of archaeological investigation, Amelia {Peabody Emerson} and her family discover that war (it's 1917) has taken its toll on their beloved Egypt. Before too long, the conflict intrudes on their plans and embroils them in an adventure, complete with double agents, Turkish spies, derring-do, and the ever-puzzling Sethos. At the same time, they must reckon with tomb robbers, killers, and antiquities fraud." Booklist

Guardian of the horizon. Morrow 2004 416p $24.95
ISBN 0-06-621471-8 LC 2003-67665
"During 1907-08, an era unaccounted for in previous Amelia Peabody tales, the redoubtable detective must help Prince Tarek of the Lost Oasis keep his throne." Libr J
"Peters' writing works on several levels. She maintains a fast-paced mystery story, her characters are complex, and the fictional cast interacts with historical figures convincingly." Archaeology

He shall thunder in the sky; an Amelia Peabody mystery. Morrow 2000 400p o.p.
ISBN 0-380-97659-5 LC 00-25807
In this episode, set in 1915, Amelia Peabody's family's "annual excavations in Egypt are overshadowed by the specter of world war. An invasion of Egypt by the Turks seems imminent, the climate is ripe for spies, and it isn't long before the Emerson clan is up to its eyebrows in intrigue. Then there's Emerson's discovery of a beautiful gold statue: Has the ardent archvillain Sethos returned with more tricks? Peters works in drama galore, plus the usual shots of wry humor and local color." Booklist

The hippopotamus pool. Warner Bks. 1996 384p o.p.
LC 95-31886
In this mystery set in 19th century Egypt, Amelia Peabody "is celebrating the turn of the century at a New Year's Eve ball at Shepheard's Hotel in Cairo when she and her husband, the sexy Egyptologist Radcliffe Emerson, are approached by a mysterious stranger who hands over a scarab ring that he claims was recovered from the lost tomb of Queen Tetisheri. 'Oh, good Gad!' Emerson explodes. 'Are we to have another of these melodramatic distractions?' Indeed we are—and it's a dandy one too. Such romantic nonsense. Such fun." N Y Times Book Rev

The last camel died at noon. Warner Bks. 1991 352p il o.p.
LC 90-26759
In this mystery archaeologist Amelia Peabody, "her handsome, fearless husband, Radcliffe, and their precocious 11-year-old son, Ramses, are in the Sudan, searching for archeologist Willoughby Forth, who disappeared 14 years earlier with his new wife. Rescued in the desert after every camel in their caravan dies, the Emersons are taken to a lost city where ancient Egyptian customs have been carried into modern times. There, entangled in two half-brothers' battle for the throne, Amelia and family fight for the freedom of the slave class while ferreting out the fate of Forth and his bride." Publ Wkly
"The Emersons are decidedly unstodgy Victorians—feminist, democratic, egalitarian, respectful of other cultures—and charming, witty, entertaining sleuths." Booklist

Legend in green velvet. Dodd, Mead 1976 241p o.p.
"Susan, a U.S. college student, is involved in her first exploration of an archaeological site. Susan's primary interests lie in Scottish history. . . . The plot develops as Susan is sightseeing in her Scottish dreamland. She meets a young Scotsman and together they stumble upon a murder. . . . The couple is pursued by the police and by the real murderers. As they elude the pursuers by hiding in forests and caves, they discover the answers to the reason for the murder frame-up." Best Sellers

Lion in the valley; an Amelia Peabody mystery. Atheneum Pubs. 1986 291p o.p.
LC 85-48126
"The stouthearted Victorian Englishwoman, Amelia Peabody Emerson, and her lusty, irascible husband are back in Egypt (with their precocious eight-year-old son, Ramses in tow). . . . The master criminal whom they thwarted but did not bring to justice in 'The Mummy Case' is once again up to nefarious deeds, which include kidnapping Amelia in order to woo her. Murder, mayhem . . . and a pair of distressed young lovers, not to mention a modicum of archaeological pursuits, round out a decided treat for fans of the indomitable duo—or, perhaps, with Ramses, it is now a trio." Booklist

Lord of the silent. Morrow 2001 404p il o.p.
ISBN 0-380-97884-9
In the fall of 1915, Amelia Peabody "and Emerson continue to dig into the past with gusto, while leaving the more energetic encounters with grave robbers and war-borne villains to their swashbuckling son, Ramses."

Peters, Elizabeth, 1927-—*Continued*

N Y Times Book Rev

"Plenty of strange doings are afoot in the desert, and readers will find all the delicious trappings of a vintage Peters extravaganza—lost tombs, kidnappings, deadly attacks, mummies and sinister villains." Publ Wkly

The mummy case. Congdon & Weed 1985 313p o.p.

LC 84-21500

"Victorian Amelia Peabody with her virile husband Emerson and precocious son Ramses embarks on a . . . archaeological dig in Egypt—but not before the death of a dealer in stolen antiquities. A disappearing mummy case and missing Coptic Papyri are the clues in this slapstick comedy-mystery. The ample archaeological detail is vivid, albeit a bit confusing. The irresistable attraction of this story: the heroine's droll tone and intrepid spirit." Libr J

The murders of Richard III. Dodd, Mead 1974 244p o.p.

This novel is "set in an English country mansion where a weekend meeting is being held by an eccentric group devoted to proving the innocence of King Richard III in the murders of the princes in the Tower of London. Although the weekend's highlight is to be the public unveiling of a document clearing Richard, the group prepares for the momentous occasion by dressing and acting as persons in King Richard's life in a charade that turns to the macabre as a malicious practical joker begins recreating some of the killings attributed to Richard." Booklist

Night train to Memphis. Warner Bks. 1994 353p o.p.

LC 94-3967

Vicky Bliss, "a curator at Munich's National Museum, is asked to go undercover on a cruise down the Nile. Her mission: to spot who among her fellow passengers might be the master criminal about to carry out a major theft of valuable antiquities. Vicky has a sneaking suspicion that the thief the police are after is the mysterious man she knows as John, who's perfectly capable of illegal activities and who's been both her sworn enemy and her sometime lover. When John shows up on the cruise and a crew member is murdered, Vicky begins to fear her suspicions are correct—but she doesn't have enough evidence to rule out the other passengers. This one is vintage Peters at her entertaining best." Booklist

Seeing a large cat. Warner Bks. 1997 386p il o.p.

LC 96-37998

"Amelia Peabody and family begin the 1903 'digging' season in Egypt with the usual anticipation. At least two pleas for help and a mysterious warning about a Valley of the Kings tomb, however, complicate life and lead to the expected dangerous adventure." Libr J

"Amelia's unquenchable *joie de l'aventure* continues to define the exuberant style of these mysteries, but Peters doesn't leave it at that. There are always grand views of Egyptian antiquities in her stories, as well as acidic caricatures of globe-trotting tourists and the endlessly entertaining spectacle of busy professional parents confounded by their own progeny." N Y Times Book Rev

The snake, the crocodile, and the dog. Warner Bks. 1992 340p o.p.

LC 92-54096

In this mystery novel, archaeologist Amelia Peabody Emerson and her husband leave their son Ramses in England to excavate in Egypt. "Amelia anticipates time alone with Emerson, but the Master Criminal devises otherwise: In his quest for directions to the . . . Lost Oasis, he attempts abduction, subterfuge, and espionage." Libr J

Trojan gold; a Vicky Bliss mystery. Atheneum Pubs. 1987 o.p.

LC 86-26486

Art historian Vicky Bliss "receives a photograph of a modern woman dressed in the gold jewelry that Schliemann discovered in his archaeological excavation of Troy. The gold has been missing since the night the Soviet Army marched into Munich in 1945. The usual assortment of male admirers gather round, all trying to outmaneuver Vicky; but she manages to side-step nicely and come out the winner in this scintillating, captivating tale." Libr J

Peters, Ellis, 1913-1995

The benediction of Brother Cadfael. Mysterious Press 1992 348p il maps o.p.

LC 91-50965

A combined edition of A morbid taste for bones and One corpse too many, both entered separately. This volume also includes a description of Cadfael country by Rob Talbot and Robin Whiteman

Brother Cadfael's penance; the twentieth chronicle of Brother Cadfael. Mysterious Press 1994 292p o.p.

LC 94-27140

This Brother Cadfael mystery "has the gentle monk leaving his cloister on a journey that will prove both dangerous and wrenching. In twelfth-century Britain, a rebellion has arisen, with factional fighting between the knights supporting Empress Maud and those swearing allegiance to her cousin Stephen. Philip FitzRobert, a traitor to the empress, has taken 30 hostages, among them a young man named Olivier de Bretagne, who is Cadfael's son from a chance encounter years earlier. Although Cadfael has lost tract of the boy's mother, he's never forgotten his son, and once he finds out that Olivier has been spirited away and imprisoned, nothing . . . can keep him from setting out to find the young man who has never known his true father." Booklist

Dead man's ransom; the ninth chronicle of Brother Cadfael. Morrow 1985 189p o.p.

LC 84-22668

First published 1984 in the United Kingdom

This "novel focuses on the brutality of civil war between England and Wales in the early twelfth century, as the Benedictine monk is pulled into a hostage drama that turns into a politically repercussive murder. A young Welshman is exchanged for the sheriff of Shropshire and taken to Cadfael's abbey, where he falls in love with the sheriff's daughter. The sheriff's subsequent murder leaves rampant speculation that the young lovers are the perpetrators of the crime. Cadfael, as ever, is patient and insightful. A wonderfully atmospheric whodunit." Booklist

Peters, Ellis, 1913-1995—*Continued*

Death to the landlords!. Morrow 1972 221p o.p.

The setting is "southern India, and the landlords are wealthy landholders who are the objectives of a terrorist murder gang. Dominic Felse . . . is at the center of the action, touring with a casual American acquaintance. The two young men meet up again and again with some of the same people as they travel India's Cape Comorin, among them a very intense English girl and a shy Indian nurse. Although the setting seems idyllic and the young people most attractive there is an undercurrent of brutal violence that hits home hard. The deaths are achieved by bombing. . . . Most effective of all is the interesting, perceptive, intuitive portrait of . . . problem-ridden India that emerges." Publ Wkly

Fallen into the pit. Mysterious Press 1994 c1951 324p o.p.

LC 92-50656

First published 1951 in the United Kingdom

"This mystery launched Peters's Inspector Felse series. Set in Britain just after WW II, the main sleuth here is not actually George Felse but his 13-year-old son Dominic. He and his best friend, Pussy Hart, are playing when Dom finds the body of Helmut Schauffler, an ex-P.O.W. who had stayed on after the war in the Comerford area. An autopsy indicates that Schauffler's skull was fractured by blows that were 'precise, neat and of murderous intention.' Helmut, a loathsome blend of cruelty, cowardice and anti-Semitism, is hardly mourned, but his death so rends the village's social fabric that solving the case is imperative. In his first murder investigation, George has difficulty viewing his neighbors as suspects." Publ Wkly

Flight of a witch. Mysterious Press 1991 c1964 232p o.p.

LC 90-84895

First published 1964 in the United Kingdom

This "mystery revolves around the sheer beauty of 18-year-old Annet Beck, whom no one . . . knows very well. The story is told in the third person, primarily from the vantage point of Tom Kenyon, new sixth-form mathematics teacher in a small Shropshire village, who becomes a boarder at Annet's house and, like virtually every other man who comes in contact with her, falls in love with her at first sight. Did Annet indeed have a Rip van Winkle experience at the mysterious Hallowmount, where, it is said, a witch coven used to meet, or was her five-day absence a cover-up for something else? That's what Inspector George Felse would like to know when Annet is identified as being near the scene of a robbery-murder in Birmingham." Booklist

The heretic's apprentice. Mysterious Press 1990 c1989 186p o.p.

LC 89-34989

First published 1989 in the United Kingdom

"Accused of heresy and murder, Elave, a young clerk to a benefactor of the Abbey of Shrewsbury, seeks the aid of the medieval sleuth Brother Cadfael in a puzzling tale of politics, theology, and a priceless illuminated manuscript." Booklist

The hermit of Eyton Forest. Mysterious Press 1988 224p o.p.

LC 87-40398

"A 10-year-old boy in school at the abbey suddenly finds himself Lord of Eaton when his father dies. His grandmother has plans for him; she wants him to marry a neighboring heiress. The abbot refuses to let him go. The grandmother takes steps to get him back. During all this, a mysterious monk living as a hermit and an equally mysterious young man who runs errands for him make their presence strongly felt. A nobleman is murdered, and the sharp eyes of Brother Cadfael notice things that are not apparent to all." N Y Times Book Rev

The holy thief. Mysterious Press 1992 246p o.p.

LC 92-50451

"The Benedictine monks at the Abbey of St. Peter and Paul in Shrewsbury are devastated by the inexplicable disappearance of their holiest and most revered relic, the remains of their patroness and guardian, Saint Winifred. Much to Brother Cadfael's consternation, the theft of the sacred casket could lead to the exposure of his own benign transgression. Years earlier, in compliance with the saint's final wish, he secretly exhumed her bones and buried them in her native Wales. Now Cadfael must recover the reliquary and solve a murder in order to protect himself and to exonerate a young monk accused of the crime." Booklist

"Twelfth-century Shropshire comes vividly alive when peopled with Peter's aristocratic ladies, sturdy lawmen, eager squires and, above all, devout—and devious—monks." Publ Wkly

Monk's-hood; the third chronicle of Brother Cadfael. Morrow 1981 c1980 223p il o.p.

LC 80-26326

First published 1980 in United Kingdom

In this novel Brother "Cadfael investigates the murder by monkshood of Gervase Bonel, a wealthy man who was about to donate his lands to the monastery. Along the way, Cadfael becomes swept up in the monastery's internecine power plays. Peters' language has a full, rich cadence, and her story is wonderfully vivid." Booklist

A morbid taste for bones. Morrow 1978 c1977 191p o.p.

First published 1977 in the United Kingdom

"When the cold and ambitious prior of the Benedictine monastery of Shrewsbury hears about the supposed miraculous powers attached to the bones of a long-dead obscure Welsh saint, he covets them for his abbey. The fact that the local Welsh villagers and their lord love their little saint and want to keep her with them is to be overruled by power and might. Sent to accompany the saint's remains back to Shrewsbury is Brother Cadfael, a most endearing detective. Come late to the cloister, after life as a warrior, he understands fully the needs of the flesh as well as those of the spirit. When two murders occur before the bones can be removed, it is Cadfael who will solve the mystery, sort out two pairs of lovers and in a most ingenious final ploy even make happy little Saint Winifred whose bones are at stake. The medieval background is portrayed very charmingly." Publ Wkly

also in Peters, E. The benediction of Brother Cadfael p3-129

Peters, Ellis, 1913-1995—*Continued*

One corpse too many; a medieval novel of suspense. Morrow 1980 c1979 191p il o.p.
LC 80-176

First published 1979 in the United Kingdom

This novel about monk-detective, Brother Cadfael, "takes us back to the world of 12th-century England as Stephen and Empress Maud are feuding for the throne. The castle at Shrewsbury falls in battle to Stephen, and he orders the mass execution of the 94 dissidents. Cadfael is sent to assure the dead are given a decent Christian burial. He finds one corpse too many—a victim, not of battle or execution, but of willful murder." Book World

also in Peters, E. The benediction of Brother Cadfael p211-348

The pilgrim of hate; the tenth chronicle of Brother Cadfael. Morrow 1985 c1984 190p o.p.
LC 85-62509

First published 1984 in the United Kingdom

"It is A.D. 1141, a year that brings a tide of pilgrims to the Benedictine Abbey at Shrewsbury. The occasion is a joyous one—a celebration in honor of St. Winifred, whose sacred relics were transferred to the abbey from Wales four years earlier. . . . Meanwhile, far away in embattled Winchester, a knight, supporter of the Empress Maud (who is campaigning against Stephen for the throne of England), is mysteriously murdered. But this seemingly disparate event, Cadfael begins to suspect, may be connected to the arrival at the shrine of a pair of pilgrims." Publisher's note

The potter's field; the seventeenth chronicle of Brother Cadfael, of the Benedictine Abbey of Saint Peter and Saint Paul, at Shrewsbury. Mysterious Press 1990 230p o.p.
LC 90-6340

"After the body of a woman is found buried in a Benedictine Abbey field, Brother Cadfael tries to discover the woman's identity and locate the person responsible for her unlawful burial." Booklist

"In place of the pretty romances with which the author often lightens her historically plausible fictions, Ms. Peters provides darker characters and a more somber view of Shrewsbury life. More than the brilliant detection of a crime, the true subject of her wintry tale is human misery, as it extends from the meanest peasant cottage to the grandest manor house." N Y Times Book Rev

Rainbow's end. Morrow 1979 c1978 190p o.p.
LC 79-87538

First published 1978 in the United Kingdom

"An elegant and wealthy antiques dealer has become over night the local 'squire' in the Middlehope valley of the West Country. Despite his beautiful manor house, his attractive wife and his determination to do all the right things, Rainbow antagonizes the locals enough to make one of them toss him out of a church spire. Felse, intelligent, compassionate, perceptive, realizes early on that some rambunctious choir boys have it in for the victim and that his lovely wife has her real interests elsewhere. Pulling it all together involves old manuscripts, a ruined abbey, nighttime boyish pranks and adult sexuality. Very entertaining all the way." Publ Wkly

A rare Benedictine. Mysterious Press 1989 c1988 118p il $19.95
ISBN 0-89296-397-2 LC 89-42603

First published 1988 in the United Kingdom

Contents: A light on the road to Woodstock; The price of light; Eye witness

The author "reveals for the first time how her medieval sleuth, Brother Cadfael, came to his calling at Shrewsbury Abbey. . . . For all his spirituality, mild Brother Cadfael once again impresses us with his practical grasp of the criminal side of human nature." N Y Times Book Rev

The rose rent; the thirteenth chronicle of Brother Cadfael. Morrow 1986 190p o.p.
LC 87-5733

"When Judith Perle, a most generous benefactor of the abbey, vanishes without a trace, Cadfael immediately connects her disappearance with the vicious murder of a pious young monk and the seemingly senseless destruction of a rose bush. An accomplished whodunit meticulously wrought with a wealth of medieval detail." Booklist

Saint Peter's Fair; the fourth chronicle of Brother Cadfael. Morrow 1981 219p il o.p.
LC 81-11020

Brother Cadfael, "who led an adventurous life in the world before becoming a monk, is on the side of young love, honor and truth as he investigates deaths taking place while a local fair is in full swing. A well-respected merchant is found murdered, and his lovely daughter takes it upon herself to keep secrets so she involves two young men, both of whom fancy her. Another death occurs. Peters has an authentic eye and ear for her 12th century way of life and death, and engages our interest all the way." Publ Wkly

The sanctuary sparrow; the seventh chronicle of Brother Cadfael. Morrow 1983 221p o.p.
LC 83-5389

Brother Cadfael "undertakes the problems of young Liliwin, a juggler and acrobat of Shrewsbury who stands accused of pilfering the valuables of one Master Walter Aurifaber, the townships's goldsmith, while Liliwin was amusing Aurifaber and the assembled patrons who were at the wedding feast of Aurifaber's son, Daniel." West Coast Rev Books

The summer of the Danes. Mysterious Press 1991 251p o.p.
LC 91-11621

In this novel Brother Cadfael "must pilgrimage deep into Wales on an errand of Church diplomacy. He is accompanied by young Brother Mark and the passionate Heledd, a young woman fleeing an arranged marriage. The three become pawns in the battle between two Welsh princes and the mercenary Danes whom one prince has hired to help vanquish his brother. There is a murder to be considered when Bledri ap Rhys—who has offended everyone from Heledd's father, Canon Meirion, to countless common soldiers—is found in his bed, stabbed through the heart." Publ Wkly

Peters, Ellis, 1913-1995—*Continued*

The virgin in the ice; the sixth chronicle of Brother Cadfael. Morrow 1983 c1982 220p il o.p.
LC 82-14500

First published 1982 in the United Kingdom

"The setting is England during the winter of 1139, A.D. Brother Cadfael, who has taken a vow against war and arms, finds himself in a country torn by civil war. Brother Elyas, a fellow monk of a nearby town, is sent to deliver two orphans, Ermina and Yves Hugonin, and their chaperone Sister Hilaria, to Laurence d'Angers, the childrens' uncle. During the journey Ermina sees her chance to escape and marry her lover. . . . Brother Elyas is attacked by a brutal band of marauders and left for dead. Brother Cadfael, sent on a medical errand to look after Brother Elyas, takes over his responsibility to bring the three safely to Laurence d'Angers. During his journey, Brother Cadfael discovers a murder and feels morally obliged to solve it." Best Sellers

Peters, Maureen, 1935-

For works written by this author under other names see Black, Veronica, 1935-

Peterson, Paula W.

Women in the grove. Beacon Press 2004 205p $20
ISBN 0-8070-8352-6 LC 2003-14314

Contents: A miracle; Africa; Big brother; The woman in the long green coat; Cherry's ghost; Alfie and grace; The a's and the i's; In the grove; Song of Camille

"Each of the stories in this beautiful collection focuses on a woman living with HIV/AIDS. . . . [Peterson] clearly knows her subject, and she challenges the reader to put an individual face and story on the HIV/AIDS epidemic. Rich with emotion, this book is too good to be categorized as any one genre of fiction but should be celebrated and read widely." Libr J

Petry, Ann Lane

The street; [by] Ann Petry. Houghton Mifflin 1946 435p o.p.

"Set in Long Island, New York, in suburban Connecticut, and in Harlem, *The Street* is the story of intelligent, ambitious Lutie Johnson, who strives to make a better life for herself and her son despite a constant struggle with sexual brutality and racism." Merriam-Webster's Ency of Lit

Phillips, Arthur, 1969-

Prague; a novel. Random House 2002 367p o.p.
ISBN 0-375-50787-6 LC 2001-48975

A novel "about a group of young American (and on Canadian) expatriates living in Budapest in 1990, just after the Communist empire has collapsed." Publ Wkly

"In Phillips's wry and skillful telling, a sexual tryst or the renting of an apartment can become a tragicomic pantomime about East and West. . . . As 'Prague' progresses, each of the five foreigners at the cafe table becomes less and less attractive, and the satiric edge to Phillips's portrayal sharpens into something close to anger: at their solipsism, their savage cynicism, their detachment from their surrounding and from one another." N Y Times Book Rev

Phillips, Caryl

Cambridge; a novel. Houghton Mifflin 1992 c1991 183p o.p.
LC 91-53127

First published 1991 in the United Kingdom

A nineteenth-century "Englishwoman, Emily Cartwright, is despatched by her father, an absentee plantation-owner, to visit his sugar estate in the West Indies. Most of the novel (following a third-person prologue signalling her departure) consists of Emily's journal, in which her impressions of the voyage and plantation life are described. . . . Elements of gothic mystery unfold through her eyes, around the puzzling presence in the Great House of a slave woman, Christiana, who dabbles in *obeah*, and the repeated chastisement of Cambridge, a literate, Christian slave, by the enigmatic overseer, Mr. Brown." Times Lit Suppl

"In 'Cambridge' there is action aplenty—sex, violence, beatings, madness, murder—as, separately and equally, the Englishwoman and the displaced African find their sad endings. Events and ideas matter in this fictional world, but not as much as the humanity, with all its depths and nuances, of the characters. Mr. Phillips's artistry and integrity overwhelm all stereotypes." N Y Times Book Rev

Crossing the river. Knopf 1994 c1993 237p o.p.
LC 93-35933

First published 1993 in the United Kingdom

This novel "begins in 18th-century Africa as three children—Nash, Martha and Travis—are sold into slavery. What follows are 'their' life stories along with excerpts from the logbook of the slave ship's captain. Nash returns to Africa as a Christian missionary in the 1830s. Martha is a former slave whom we meet as she lays dying in Denver, having failed to reach California and find her only child, taken from her years before. Travis is reincarnated as an American GI stationed in England in 1943; his story is . . . told by the British woman he marries." Libr J

"One of the values of fiction is that it can tell the story anew, can go back and include a neglected truth. 'Crossing the River' does this and is therefore a book with an agenda. Mr. Phillips proposes that the diaspora is permanent, and that blacks throughout the world who look to Africa as a benevolent fatherland tell themselves a stunted story. They need not to trace but to put down roots. The message, however, is neither simply nor stridently conveyed." N Y Times Book Rev

Dancing in the dark. Knopf 2005 209p $23.95
ISBN 1-4000-4396-4 LC 2005-44106

"This novel centers on the life of Bert Williams, the black vaudeville performer of the late 19th and early 20th centuries. He and his partner George Walker performed to wild acclaim on New York City and London stages, with Williams often donning blackface." Libr J

"As subjects for historical novels go, Bert Williams is an inspired choice; his strange career exemplified all the ironies and paradoxes that confronted the African-American performers of his time. . . . Dancing in the Dark is riveting when it recreates mores and social conventions our culture has done its best to forget." N Y Times Book Rev

A distant shore. Knopf 2003 277p $23.95
ISBN 1-400-04109-0

Phillips, Caryl—*Continued*

"Two lonely lives intertwine in this . . . novel set in contemporary England. Dorothy has recently moved to a new subdivision in a small village after a forced retirement leaves her desperate for a new life. Solomon, an illegal immigrant escaping a violent past in Africa, is the night watchman at the subdivision. They form a cautious friendship despite the distrust and isolation each is experiencing in new surroundings." Libr J

"This muted, sad novel breaks down the distinction between the placed and the displaced, dissolving our sense of security, if we had one, about safely belonging in the world, dispelling our illusion of being at home. We are all adrift, Phillips says, whether we know it or not: a fact not of race or nationality, but of the human condition." N Y Times Book Rev

The nature of blood. Knopf 1997 212p $23
ISBN 0-679-45470-5 LC 96-49641

"The novel's primary voice belongs to Eva Stern, a young woman who has just been liberated by the English army from a German camp. Through a series of flashbacks and recollections, Eva remembers life with her family, and then her experience in the camp. Phillips intercuts Eva's story with two wildly discontinuous narratives: one a retelling of *Othello* in Othello's own voice; the other an account of the 15th-century persecution of the money-lending Jews of the Italian city Portobuffole, who were accused of murdering a Christian child." Publ Wkly

"Phillips's object in creating a work in which dialogue, description and characterization are of no real significance has been, laudably enough, to protect the universality of his themes." Times Lit Suppl

Phillips, Jayne Anne, 1952-

MotherKind; a novel. Knopf 2000 295p $24
ISBN 0-375-40194-6 LC 99-49256

"Over the course of a year, Kate, a resolutely independent poet and editor, becomes enmeshed in domesticity: she has a baby, acquires two stepchildren, and discovers that her mother is dying of cancer. Kate has always resisted her mother's desire to care for others perfectly, but she's now preoccupied with making crisp French fries, turning down beds, ironing out problems; frequently overwhelmed, she must also rely on nurses and efficient neighbors. Phillips, an abundantly talented writer, never lapses into sentimentality while describing this woman." New Yorker

Phillips, Susan Elizabeth

Ain't she sweet; Susan Elizabeth Phillips. 1st ed. Morrow 2004 383p $24.95
ISBN 0-06-621124-7 LC 2003-59297

"Fifteen years ago, Sugar Beth Carey reigned supreme over the small Mississippi town of Parrish, but now she's returning home a little bit shabby around the edges to claim a valuable painting left to her by her disapproving aunt. Fifteen years ago, Colin Byrne arrived in Parrish from England as a new teacher only to have his career destroyed by a spiteful young Sugar Beth. Fifteen years ago, Sugar Beth had everything Winnie Davis ever wanted, but because Winnie had the one thing Sugar Beth could never have, she turned Winnie's life into a perpetual hell. So now Colin, a bestselling author, and Winnie, Parrish's richest citizen, are determined to exact revenge for Sugar Beth's past sins, but much to their surprise, neither one finds revenge to taste quite as sweet as they expected once they get to know the new Sugar Beth." Booklist

This "light, contemporary, and enjoyable love story is filled with alluring plot lines." Libr J

Pickard, Nancy

The 27 ingredient chili con carne murders. Delacorte Press 1993 296p o.p.
LC 92-17498

The author completes a "story begun by Virginia Rich, a onetime food writer and, at the time of her death in 1984, the author of three . . . culinary mysteries." N Y Times Book Rev

"In her home in New England, the widowed Mrs. Potter receives a call from Ricardo Ortega, manager of her Arizona ranch, who hints at trouble. Alarmed, she flies out to find that Ricardo and his granddaughter have disappeared. As neighboring ranchers and friends conduct a search, Mrs. Potter tries to determine the cause of Ricardo's unease. . . . Suspense with dollops of romance and gossip makes this offering irresistible." Publ Wkly

Blue corn murders; a Eugenia Potter mystery. Delacorte Press 1998 257p $21.95
ISBN 0-385-31224-5 LC 98-11354

In this mystery based on Virginia Rich's notes, Pickard "continues the adventures of 64-year-old Arizona rancher Eugenia Potter, taking her to an archaeological hiking camp in Colorado. There, amid splendid scenery and mystical ancient cities, Eugenia encounters idiosyncratic characters, a camp management under stress, and savage murder. Among the suspects are a spiteful old woman on the camp's board of directors, a pair of selective teachers, and a spacey blonde Indian wannabe. Delightful plot, colorful surroundings, and solid prose makes this a winner." Libr J

Bum steer; a Jenny Cain mystery. Knopf 1990 240p o.p.
LC 89-49198

This novel takes "Jenny Cain, director of the Port Frederick Civic Foundation, to Kansas City, where she hopes to discover why a dying millionaire has willed a vast cattle ranch to her little-known foundation. Thwarted upon arrival by the man's murder, she visits the ranch, fraternizes with two transplanted cowboys, searches out three ex-wives, and takes on a troubled teenager—all in hopes of finding the murderer." Libr J

"Although Jenny gets perkier, her companions more eccentric and their adventures more hair-raising as the hunt goes on, Ms. Pickard maintains her control over the derring-do and delivers an exciting climax." N Y Times Book Rev

But I wouldn't want to die there; a Jenny Cain mystery. Pocket Bks. 1993 243p o.p.
LC 93-15772

"When a colleague . . . in New York is stabbed to death in a street mugging, Jenny does the generous, if unlikely, thing: she moves into her friend's still-warm apartment, temporarily takes over her job and sets out to find her killer." NY Times Book Rev

"Pickard's in fine form here, combining a wonderfully

Pickard, Nancy—*Continued*
acerbic, wickedly humorous commentary on the 'joys' of big-city life with a keep-'em-guessing plot and a smart, sexy, sensible . . . heroine." Booklist

Confession; a Jenny Cain mystery. Pocket Bks. 1994 307p o.p.
LC 93-87794
"One steaming August day, Jenny, recently resigned as director of a foundation, and her police lieutenant husband, Geof Bushfield, are visited at home by angry 17-year-old David Mayer, who announces that he is Geof's illegitimate son by Judy Mayer, a high school classmate of Geof's. The winter before, Judy, an invalid, had been killed by her husband Ron, who then committed suicide. David, foulmouthed and hateful, demands that Geof reopen the case and prove the deaths were murders." Publ Wkly
"Fortunately, Geof and Jenny have a strong sense of humor, a sturdy marriage, plenty of common sense, and enough love to get them through one of the toughest tests they've faced together. Fine reading from an outstanding mystery writer." Booklist

Dead crazy; a Jenny Cain mystery. Pocket Bks. 1988 276p o.p.
LC 88-15324
"As director of a charity foundation in a small Massachusetts town, Jenny runs into community opposition—and two nasty murders—when she tries to purchase an abandoned church for restoration as a recreation center for the mentally disabled." N Y Times Book Rev
"Pickard nicely balances Jenny's wit and likability against her tough-minded, realistic examination of mental illness and its treatment. An outstanding mystery series." Booklist

Generous death. Scribner 1993 c1984 239p o.p.
First published 1984 in paperback
This is the "first Jenny Cain story that Pickard wrote and serves as an introduction to the attractive and vivacious director of the Port Frederick Civic Foundation as well as to other characters who figure prominently in the series. The plot concerns the murders of several wealthy donors to the foundation. If the nasty little poems left with each of the bodies are any indication, Jenny herself may be the next victim." Booklist

Marriage is murder; a Jenny Cain mystery. Dark Harvest 1987 210p o.p.
LC 87-4911
"Three homicides in two weeks: each victim the husband of a battered wife, each family beset by drinking problems, poverty, and too many children to feed. Either the wives are fighting back with a vengeance, or someone is doing their fighting for them. This is Pickard's fourth mystery starring wealthy young philanthropist Jenny Cain and her lover, policeman Geof Bushfield." Booklist
"An energetic array of Jenny's friends and co-workers keep this novel—a fine mix of romance, violence, and sleuthing—moving at a fast clip." Publ Wkly

No body; a Jenny Cain mystery. Scribner 1986 227p o.p.
LC 86-13118
Jenny Cain, "serving as the head of the Port Frederick Civic Foundation, relates events that stun the population in her New England town when a mud slide reveals the disappearance of 133 bodies, supposedly interred during the 19th century in the old cemetery. At the same time, the corpse of Sylvia Davis is found in the casket with John Rudolph just before he's due to be buried in the new cemetery. The next day, Rudolph's widow is murdered, and Jenny sets out to gather evidence on possible killers." Publ Wkly

The truth hurts. Simon & Schuster 2002 328p $24
ISBN 0-7434-1203-6 LC 2002-510452
In this Marie Lightfoot mystery, "the Florida-based true crime writer is working on a book about her parents, civil rights activists in Alabama who disappeared in 1963 when Lightfoot was a toddler. She's suddenly threatened by a mysterious fan, who signs his emails Paulie Barnes and demands that she collaborate with him on a book about her own murder, or he'll start killing her friends, including her lover, Franklin DeWeese." Publ Wkly
"The campaign of terror against Lightfoot, involving psychological torture through devices like e-mail and FedEX, is wickledly well constructed and convincing." Booklist

Twilight; a Jenny Cain mystery. Pocket Bks. 1995 312p o.p.
LC 95-30614
In this mystery Jenny is "juggling the first ever Port Frederick Fall Festival and the request of her friend Nellie Kennedy, who wants help in getting rid of 'God's Highway,' a controversial hiking/bike path. Lately, a series of fatal accidents on the path has caused the town to look at closing it, a move environmentalists, hikers, and bikers vehemently oppose." Booklist
"Jenny's telling observations on love and marriage, family and friendships and small-town politics add texture to this well-wrought puzzle." Publ Wkly

The whole truth. Pocket Bks. 2000 264p $22.95
ISBN 0-671-88795-5 LC 99-46816
A mystery "featuring true-crime writer Marie Lightfoot. Lightfoot's latest project is investigating Raymond Raintree, accused of kidnapping and brutally murdering six-year-old Natalie McCullen. At first the case against Raintree seems straightforward. But when Lightfoot digs into Raintree's past to uncover the full story she discovers that he might be just as much of a victim as McCullen." Libr J
"By alternating chapters from Lightfoot's book about the case with coverage of the trial and the sleuth's search for information, Pickard effectively uses her character's work in progress as a narrative device." Booklist

Pickens, Cathy

Southern fried; Cathy Pickens. 1st ed. St. Martin's Minotaur 2004 277p $23.95
ISBN 0-312-32492-8 LC 2003-58548
"After losing her job in Columbia, attorney Avery Andrews returns home to Dacus, SC, where everybody knows everybody else's business. She soon lands a corporate client, Garnet Mills, which is due for an inspection by government environmental authorities. Not surprisingly, the plant blows up, and vital documents are destroyed. Meanwhile, Avery becomes involved in a 15-year-old missing-persons case. Police have just recovered the body of the woman, a former Garnet employee, and

Pickens, Cathy—*Continued*
are suspicious of her husband, who has just returned to town. Pickens's lively first mystery . . . features tidy plotting rounded out with gossipy humor, colorful characters, and Southern ethos." Libr J

Picoult, Jodi, 1966-

My sister's keeper; a novel. Atria 2004 423p $25

ISBN 0-7434-5452-9 LC 2004-300043

"Thirteen-year-old Anna Fitzgerald walks into the office of lawyer Campbell Alexander and announces she wants to sue her parents for the rights to her own body. Anna was conceived after her older sister, Kate, developed a rare form of leukemia at the age of two, and has donated bone marrow and blood to her sister. Now she has been asked to donate a kidney, and she intends to refuse. Campbell is a jaded young man who nevertheless decides to take her case pro bono. Anna's parents are shocked when they learn of her lawsuit, and her mother, a former civil defense attorney, decides to represent them. Anna refuses to budge on her position despite the fact that she clearly loves her sister and longs for her family's happiness. As the gripping court case builds, the story takes a shocking turn." Booklist

"Picoult's timely and compelling novel will appeal to anyone who has thought about the morality of medical decision making and any parent who must balance the needs of different children." Libr J

Vanishing acts; a novel. Atria Books 2005 418p $25

ISBN 0-7434-5454-5 LC 2004-59454

"Delia Hopkins has led a charmed life. Raised in rural New Hampshire by her widowed father, Andrew, she now has a young daughter, a handsome fiance, and her own search-and-rescue bloodhound, which she uses to find missing persons. But as Delia plans her wedding, she is plagued by flashbacks of a life she can't recall. And then a policeman knocks on her door, revealing a secret that changes the world as she knows it." Publisher's note

"Picoult weaves together plot and characterization in a landscape that is fleshed out in rich, journalistic detail, so that readers will come away with intriguing questions rather than pat answers." Publ Wkly

Piercy, Marge

Braided lives; a novel. Summit Bks. 1982 443p o.p.

LC 81-16695

This novel concerns the lives of two women who were girls during the 1950's. Parents, friends, lovers appear as the story "follows its narrator-heroine, Jill Stuart, now 40 and an established writer who claims that her 'idea of hell is to be young again,' from her 1950's adolescence in working-class Detroit to the university in Ann Arbor, and on to New York. Jill writes, loves, suffers, commits herself to radical politics and reproductive rights, and survives. Throughout, her emotional anchor is her . . . friendship with Donna, her cousin and college roommate." Libr J

"As with most of Piercy's work, this is very political, and a major theme here is abortion—the dire need for safe, legal abortion. But while abortion is the visible theme, what lies beneath it is a rich, complex and thoroughly satisfying examination of life." Publ Wkly

City of darkness, city of light; a novel. Fawcett Columbine 1996 479p o.p.

LC 96-24748

This historical novel is set in Paris during the French Revolution. The narrative is presented from the viewpoints of six historical figures: Danton, Robespierre, Condorcet, Madame Roland (Manon Philipon), Claire Lacombe, an actor, and Pauline Léon, "a Parisian chocolate shop owner who, as a child, witnesses the torture and execution of those who riot for bread, and goes on to become a leader of the radically feminist Revolutionary Republican Women. . . . The narrative begins with key incidents from each character's childhood. The earliest chapter is dated 1765, and the last 1812." Women's Rev Books

"If you love great historical fiction, this rousing, thought-provoking novel should go to the top of your list. . . . Marge Piercy brings the French Revolution to life." Ms

Gone to soldiers; a novel. Summit Bks. 1987 703p o.p.

LC 86-30118

This is an "episodic story of World War II both at home and abroad. The turmoil of these years is shown through the lives of the numerous characters, from the female French Jewish Resistance fighter; to the Jewish factory worker/college student from Detroit and the U.S. ferry pilot, both women taking on men's roles, and the latter not wanting to give them up; to the cryptanalyst in Washington, D.C., escaping from the narrow life of his family; to the 'women's magazine' writer finally able to cover the war." Libr J

"In many male war novels character development is sacrificed; the 'woman's touch' here is excellent. The battlefront is not all blood and guts—there is also the grief of separation from family and the mitigating solace of friendship. On the home front there are race riots as well as ration books, and the heartbreak of shattered families." N Y Times Book Rev

The longings of women; a novel. Fawcett Columbine 1994 455p o.p.

LC 93-34125

"The three heroines are Leila, a middle-aged Boston college professor and writer; her long-suffering and secretly homeless 60-ish housekeeper Mary; and Becky, an ambitious young wife accused of murdering her husband and who is the subject of Leila's new book. All three face problems typical of women ill-used by men and by society." Publ Wkly

"As Piercy draws us into the alarming predicaments of each of these women, she traces the progress of their struggles to earn respect and love with unerring accuracy and discernment. Magnetic from start to finish." Booklist

Small changes. Doubleday 1973 562p o.p.

"A chronicle novel that takes two women through perhaps a decade: Miriam, a sensual intellectual who abandons her complex relationships with two men to marry a third and bear him children; and Beth, who we first see as a mechanic's fragile bride and who over the years evolves into a radical lesbian. Beth finds herself as an

Piercy, Marge—*Continued*
activist while Miriam disintegrates." Libr J

"Avoiding both flights into political rhetoric and deterioration into soap opera, the novel depicts a new reality. If it is flawed, it lies perhaps in oversimplification, in her suggestion that Beth has found a 'solution' with another woman. . . . Nevertheless most of the book rings true." New Repub

Summer people; a novel. Summit Bks. 1989 380p o.p.
LC 89-30007

"After 11 years, the ménage à trois of Dinah Adler and Willie and Susan DeWitt is a strong family unit, accepted in its Cape Cod community. Dinah is a respected composer, devoted to her music, and Willie is a sculptor and carpenter happy with his life (and the envy of the local men). But Susan's growing discontent—with her work as a fabric designer and her role as unofficial gofer and hostess for summer people—ruptures the relationship and leads to tragedy." Libr J

"Piercy eschews sensationalism in portraying her unorthodox trio; her characterizations are solid and believable. Some readers may find the story's pace too deliberate, but those who like to ponder the ways in which character influences fate will welcome this solidly satisfying novel." Publ Wkly

Three women. Morrow 1999 309p $25
ISBN 0-688-17106-0 LC 99-13324

This novel centers on "Suzanne Blume, an idealistic but pragmatic law professor. Approaching 50 and the mother of two grown daughters, Suzanne is enjoying her busy and productive life when, nearly simultaneously, her stroke-weakened mother, Beverly, and her unsettled older daughter, Elena, arrive on her doorstep in need of expensive and time-consuming attention. Until her stroke, Beverly had been an old-style leftist who majored in men and minored in child-rearing. Elena is a lost soul who is still recovering from a violent episode in her teens. Suzanne must also deal with Jake, a man with whom a cozy on-line flirtation has suddenly become an in-the-flesh reality." N Y Times Book Rev

"Piercy keeps the plot humming with issues of motherhood, Judaism, generational tensions, sexuality, and independence. Her pacing is confident, as usual, and she interweaves the three narrative threads with aplomb. Apart from Jake, who remains an elusive sketch, Piercy's insight into her characters' emotional lives is an accurate reflection of intergenerational tensions." Publ Wkly

Vida. Summit Bks. 1979 412p o.p.
LC 79-19298

"Wanted for a 1970 bombing which stemmed from her radical antiwar activism, Vida has been a fugitive and underground revolutionary for nine years. Shifting the narrative back and forth between the present and the years from 1967 to 1974. Piercy traces the evolution of a political movement through Vida's perceptions and her relationships with a small band of fellow adherents." Libr J

This novel "is not 'simply' a novel but a political brief. I have my differences with 'Vida,' but I think they are substantive rather than literary. It is an interesting—and challenging—book. . . . Marge Piercy has written about movement people before but never, I think, as lovingly as here." N Y Times Book Rev

Woman on the edge of time. Knopf 1976 369p o.p.

"A Hispanic-American mother undergoes experimental psychosurgery. She makes psychic contact with the 22nd-century world that has resulted from a feminist revolution whose success may depend on the subversion of the experiments in which she is involved. Outstanding for the elaborate description of the future utopia and the graphic representation of the inhumanity inherent in the way that contemporary people can and do treat one another." Anatomy of Wonder 4

Pilcher, Robin

A risk worth taking; Robin Pilcher. 1st ed. Thomas Dunne Bks. 2004 308p $24.95
ISBN 0-312-27002-X LC 2003-58564

"Dan Porter had it all: the nice house in suburban London, three children, a beautiful wife, and a great job in finance until the dot-com crash and 9/11 changed his outlook about life and making money. Dan lost a good friend in the tragedy, and is now content being a househusband focusing on his family, while his wife, Jackie, pursues her high-level job with a fashion designer, but changes in income have caused strife. His wife and daughters want their old life back, and Jackie perceives Dan and their son, Josh, as loafers because they seem content with less. Recognizing his wife's discontent, Dan takes action after reading an article in a women's magazine about a woman who started a clothing company in a remote area of Scotland and now wants to sell. Dan travels to Scotland with the hope of buying the company and expanding the business, but he finds something much more valuable. Pilcher offers a charming story about life in the new millennium and one man's pursuit of happiness." Booklist

Pilcher, Rosamunde, 1924-

Coming home. St. Martin's Press 1995 728p $25.95
ISBN 0-312-13451-7 LC 95-21656

"A Thomas Dunne book"

"The book's heroine is Judith Dunbar, who is a schoolgirl of 13 when the tale begins in 1935. Sent to boarding school in Cornwall because her parents are posted to Singapore, Judith becomes friends with Loveday Carey-Lewis, who introduces her to a family and an estate, Nancherrow, that is to influence her for the rest of her life. Pilcher does a marvelous job of describing life in England before World War II." Booklist

Flowers in the rain & other stories. St. Martin's Press 1991 277p o.p.
LC 91-18237

"A Thomas Dunne book"

Stories included are: The doll's house; Endings and beginnings; Flowers in the rain; Playing a round with love; Christabel; The blackberry day; The red dress; A girl I used to know; The watershed; Marigold garden; Weekend; A walk in the snow; Cousin Dorothy; Whistle for the wind; Last morning; Skates

"Throughout this collection of stories, Pilcher maintains a pervasive gentility along with an abiding wisdom. Filled with poignant scenes, romantic and bittersweet, these stories, many written earlier in the author's career, will appeal to readers of Pilcher's very successful novels." Booklist

Pilcher, Rosamunde, 1924-—*Continued*

September. St. Martin's Press 1990 536p o.p.
LC 89-70340

"A Thomas Dunne book"

"A lavish coming-out party for the daughter of one of the leading families of a town in the Scottish Highlands brings together characters whose lives change in various ways during the novel's four-month span. The Airds and the Balmerinos of Strathcroy and their friends and relatives in London, Majorca and the States are the focal point of the love affairs, domestic complications, estrangements, reconciliations and other gently momentous events." Publ Wkly

"Character is at the heart of a story, and this fine tale has plenty of that." N Y Times Book Rev

The shell seekers. St. Martin's Press 1987 530p o.p.
LC 87-28345

"A Thomas Dunne book"

"Set in England's Cotswolds, the novel begins with a crisis: the mother has signed herself out of the hospital against doctor's orders and is determined to resume her independent life. This introduces the two daughters and one son who must deal not only with their mother and with each other, but also with the relationships they have established for better or worse in their own lives." Booklist

"It is a measure of this story's strength and success that a reader can be carried for more than 500 pages in total involvement with Penelope, her children, her past and the painting that hangs in her country cottage. 'The Shell Seekers' is a deeply satisfying story, written with love and confidence." N Y Times Book Rev

Voices in summer. St. Martin's Press 1984 215p o.p.
LC 83-22998

"Laura, married to Alec, an older divorcé, feels alienated from the people and events of her husband's past, especially his daughter and longtime friends. A recuperative stay with Alec's aunt and uncle in a lovely Cornwall mansion finally forces these and many other issues into the open." Booklist

The author "evokes the sense of contentment that flows from affection grounded in a comfortable lifestyle, all of which makes for gently entertaining reading." Publ Wkly

Winter solstice. Thomas Dunne Bks. 2000 454p $27.95

ISBN 0-312-24426-6 LC 00-31713

A novel set in "northern Scotland, where five vaguely connected people find themselves together at Christmas in a large Victorian house. . . . Elfrida, a lonely retired actress, befriends Oscar, who is barely surviving the grief of the deaths of his wife and daughter in a car crash. Carrie, bereft after an aborted love affair, takes over the holiday care of her 14-year-old niece, Lucy, who is unwanted by her mother, grandmother, and indifferent father, Sam, in town to take charge of the old woolen mill, is reeling because his wife left him for another man. What lifts this saga above melodrama is the author's skill at creating believable, multifaceted characters." Libr J

Pincherle, Alberto *See* Moravia, Alberto, 1907-1990

Pirandello, Luigi, 1867-1936

The outcast; authorized translation from the Italian by Leo Ongley. Dutton 1925 334p o.p.

Condemned and cast out by husband and father for a crime she has not committed, Marta makes a brave attempt to build life over again. She goes with her mother and sister to a town where she is unknown and there supports them by teaching. After a time happiness comes back to the three. Then the man for whose sake Marta was persecuted comes to their village. He finds Marta lovelier and more desirable than ever. The result is inevitable. The outcry against her breaks forth afresh, and she is forced into the situation she has tried to escape. Too late her chastened husband sues for forgiveness. This drama of Italian life draws to a close in a moving scene of reconciliation

The novel is "significant thematically for its unconventional treatment of adultery and historically for its subtle undermining of the assumptions of naturalism on which it appears to be based." Ency of World Lit in the 20th Century

Short stories; selected, translated and introduced by Frederick May. Oxford Univ. Press 1965 xxxvi, 260p o.p.

"Oxford library of Italian classics"

Contents: The little hut; The cooper's cockerels; A dream of Christmas; Twelve letters; Fear; The best of friends; Bitter waters; The jar; The tragedy of a character; A call to duty; In the abyss; The black kid; Signora Frola and her son-in-law, Signor Ponga; The man with the flower in his mouth; Destruction of the man; Puberty; Cinci; All passion spent; The visit; The tortoise; A day goes by

Pirie, David

The patient's eyes; the dark beginnings of Sherlock Holmes. St. Martin's Minotaur 2002 244p il o.p.

ISBN 0-312-29095-0

"A 'fictional' account of Arthur Conan Doyle's early life that relates how his association with Edinburgh physician Joseph Bell was the inspiration for his Holmes character. Pirie vividly evokes the dark ambience of Victorian England, his prose is elegant, and his gift for mimicking the slightly haughty tone of Doyle's writing is uncanny." Booklist

Plaidy, Jean, 1906-1993

For works written by this author under other names see Carr, Philippa, 1906-1993; Holt, Victoria, 1906-1993

The captive Queen of Scots. Putnam 1970 c1963 410p o.p.

Sequel to Royal road to Fotheringay (1968)

First published 1963 in the United Kingdom

"The story of the last 18 years of Queen Mary's life, during which she was first a prisoner of her Scottish enemies and later, after a dramatic escape and flight to England, the captive of her archenemy, Queen Elizabeth. Treated with at least some respect due a queen, Mary is pictured with her retinue of loyal friends and servants, living in varying degrees of discomfort and confinement

Plaidy, Jean, 1906-1993—*Continued*

as she moved from one castle to another at the whim of Elizabeth. She emerges as a generous, overly trustful, emotional victim, attractive even as she grew older though not wise, who met her tragic fate because she could not cope with the treachery and intrigue of both friends and enemies." Booklist

Murder most royal. Putnam 1972 542p o.p.

First published 1949 in the United Kingdom

"Concentrating on Anne Boleyn and her younger cousin Catherine Howard, the author follows the two from childhood to death on the block, with her usual thoroughness, sentimentality, and overdramatization, sparing the reader few details of torture, violence, intrigue, or thwarted love affairs." Booklist

The pleasures of love; the story of Catherine of Braganza. Putnam 1992 c1991 329p o.p.

LC 91-34593

First published 1991 in the United Kingdom

When Catherine, daughter of King John IV of Portugal, finally married Charles II her "happiness as the new Queen of England was short-lived. The Merry Monarch's notorious affairs amused the public but devastated Catherine, who longed for the love only a husband and children could provide. When it became clear that Catherine was barren, the people verged on rebellion and court intimates intrigued against her, hoping that Charles would divorce his queen, marry one of his mistresses, and beget an heir. But while Charles would never be faithful to Catherine, he loved her and was her fiercest protector. And in the end, their struggle against their enemies only drew the king and queen closer together." Publisher's note

The reluctant queen; the story of Anne of York. Putnam 1991 c1990 299p o.p.

LC 90-48299

First published 1990 in the United Kingdom

"When King Edward IV married for love and his new Queen set out to destroy the Nevilles, disaster followed. Longtime allies suddenly became enemies, enemies became fellow conspirators, and Anne became the bargaining chip in her father's battle to choose the next king and remain the Kingmaker. Refusing to accept the future being forced upon her, Anne married her longtime friend Richard, the king's younger brother, not dreaming one day soon Richard would crown himself. Their marriage thrusts them both back into the political maelstrom that will change their lives forever." Publisher's note

The rose without a thorn. Putnam 1994 c1993 255p o.p.

LC 93-34598

First published 1993 in the United Kingdom

Young Katherine Howard is "given the chance to go to the Royal Court as a lady-in-waiting to the queen, Anne of Cleaves—enabling her to be near her handsome cousin, Thomas Culpepper. But when she catches the eye of the unhappily married king, Henry VIII, she is compelled to abandon her plans for a life with Thomas and eventually agrees to marry the king. Overwhelmed by the change in her fortunes, bewildered and flattered by the adoration of her husband, Katherine settles down to enjoy her life as queen. Such bliss is short-lived as Katherine's promiscuous ways come back to haunt her." Publisher's note

The scarlet cloak. Putnam 1992 c1985 335p o.p.

LC 92-8516

First published 1957 in the United Kingdom under the pseudonym Ellalice Tata

"In the years 1572-1578, when the faith and fanaticism of one man—King Philip II of Spain—trouble the whole of Europe, His Most Catholic Majesty's plans against accused heretics meet with stubborn, angry resistance. Dashing Blasco Carramadino and his devout older brother, Domingo, live in the quiet province of Andalusia, where the king's fanaticism is rarely felt. But soon they will be caught in a web of intrigue, as Philip plots the overthrow of England and its return to the one true faith." Publisher's note

The sixth wife. Putnam 1969 c1953 252p o.p.

First published 1953 in the United Kingdom

Henry VIII chooses Catharine Parr, fiancee of his brother-in-law, to become his sixth wife after he has condemned Catharine Howard to death. This novel tells Catharine Parr's story from the time she becomes queen until her death

"All the figures of history are here: Mary Tudor and Elizabeth, the young frail Edward VI, Lady Jane Grey, the Herberts and the Suffolks and the Seymours, the Tower of London, the torture chambers, the heretics and heretic-baiting—all the persons and the panolpy and the cruelty of the Tudor era—and the story of Catherine Parr appears to be authentic. If this seems to lack the intensity, the roar and gusto that properly belongs to this period in history, it is an entertaining and even absorbing novel." Best Sellers

William's wife. Putnam 1993 276p o.p.

LC 92-32588

In this historical novel about the "struggle for power between Catholic and Protestant, England's heir to the throne, the lovely and bright Princess Mary, is forced to marry William of Orange in order to prevent the kingdom from falling under Catholic rule. Despite Mary's attempts to win her husband's love, the dour, power-hungry William won't even feign affection for her; instead, he continues a blatant affair with Elizabeth Villiers. As the inevitable power struggle ensues between her husband and her father, James II, Mary finds herself torn between marital and filial loyalties. But with the crown of England the ultimate prize, Mary discovers that while she is James's daughter, she is first and foremost William's wife." Publisher's note

Plain, Belva

Blessings. Delacorte Press 1989 340p o.p.

LC 89-1565

"The entanglements of a teenage romance surface more than a decade later to disrupt the life of a successful attorney. Jennie Rakowski finally has her life together. She provides legal counsel for poor, battered women and is on the verge of marrying a charming, widowed corporate attorney with three small children. Suddenly, Jill, the daughter Jennie gave up for adoption 19 years earlier, appears at Jennie's door; even worse, Jill brings along the man who fathered her then disappeared from Jennie's life." Booklist

"The author stretches an awkward subplot concerning mob-connected real estate developers far too thin, but her

Plain, Belva—*Continued*
mixture of romance, suspense, and deeply felt familial conflicts should leave her fans well entertained." Publ Wkly

Crescent City; a novel. Delacorte Press 1984 429p o.p.
LC 84-5045

A novel "set against the backdrop of America's South during the Civil War. At the story's center is Miriam Raphael, a European Jew transplanted as a child to New Orleans, the 'Crescent City' nestled at the mouth of the Mississippi. Both she and her older brother, David, must adjust to what seems a bright, promising new land filled with languid days and lavish feasts. But all too quickly their eyes are opened to the grimmer features of their landscape—the slaves whom David vows to set free and the southern tradition of youthful marriage, which Miriam, herself no better off than a slave, must gracefully endure." Booklist

Evergreen; a novel. Delacorte Press 1978 593p o.p.
LC 77-20778

"The young orphan Anna shows her spunk by leaving Poland to make a way for herself in the turn-of-the-century U.S.A. Opting for domestic service rather than the sweatshops of lower Manhattan, she becomes infatuated with the master's son, Paul Werner. His marriage to another woman puts a damper on Anna's longing, and she settles for poor but loyal Joseph Friedman. Joseph is hard working and has a vision of fulfilling the American Dream. He persuades his wife to borrow some money from the Werners, and Anna finds herself asking Paul for the money. He gladly obliges, but the old flame is fanned into heedless passion and Anna leaves with the money and a secret she will carry with her for the rest of her life." Best Sellers

"This warm and sympathetic family saga gives life and meaning to the commonplace events of unspectacular lives." Publ Wkly

Followed by The golden cup

Fortune; a novel. Delacorte Press 1999 356p $25.95
ISBN 0-385-31692-5 LC 99-17794

At the start of this novel "earnest young Robb MacDaniel leaves his loyal fiancée, Lily, in the small Southern town where they grew up, in order to pursue a law degree, using insurance money from an accident that has killed his parents. In the big city, Robb falls for Ellen, the Wellesley-educated daughter of local legal icon Wilson Grant. Marrying Ellen, Robb firmly steps up the ladder of success, casting off ideals, as he cast off Lily, at each rung. Robb's professional rise and moral descent drive him to increasingly desperate acts, but he doesn't allow his struggles with regret to thwart his ambition." Publ Wkly

The golden cup. Doubleday 1986 399p o.p.
LC 86-8851

Evergreen, "told the story of immigrant Anna Friedman and her love for Paul Werner. Here the focus shifts to Paul's aunt, Hennie DeRivera, from age 18 in 1891 through World War I. As a volunteer, Hennie teaches English at a settlement house where she meets Daniel Roth. Their relationship is frowned upon by her family, but they marry when she becomes pregnant. Her uncertainty over whether Dan would have married her otherwise is aggravated by his roving eye. The grown-up Paul, Hennie's son Fred, and Leah, an orphan she raises, are also featured." Libr J

The author "invests her story with dignity and historical relevance while insightfully depicting the class consciousness of Progressive Era Americans." Publ Wkly

Followed by Tapestry

Harvest. Delacorte Press 1990 409p o.p.
LC 90-34417

This novel continues the "saga of the Werners and their extended clan as they reaffirm their Jewish heritage during the stormy 1960s. Dark, sensitive Iris, daughter of the glowing, russet-haired Anna (by urbane banker Paul Werner—unbeknownst to Iris) is married to wealthy, improvident Dr. Theo Stern, whose European glamour excites other women. Iris's jealousy goads her to play at her own romance with a sinister partner. Her four children are growing up, but rebel Steve balks at his bar mitzvah, already anticipating the anarchist/bomb expert he will be at college, radicalized by cynical professor Tim Powers, whom he doesn't know is his distant cousin. When Paul's wife dies and his mistress leaves to fulfill her mission as a doctor in Israel, Paul hovers protectively over Iris's, troubled family." Publ Wkly

Her father's house. Delacorte Press 2002 342p $25.95
ISBN 0-385-33472-9 LC 2002-23781

"Donald Wolfe, a 25-year-old North Dakota native, comes to New York City in 1968 to practice law; five years later, he meets and falls for the captivating Lillian Morris. Marrying in haste, he repents big time when Lillian reveals herself to be disturbingly erratic. After she becomes pregnant, the two divorce, but when Donald judges his daughter, Bettina, to be neglected, he kidnaps her. Taking to the road, he invents a new past for himself and adopts the name Jim, renaming his daughter Laura. Many years later, the truth is revealed and Jim stands trial for kidnapping." Publ Wkly

Homecoming. Delacorte Press 1997 212p $16.95
ISBN 0-385-31980-0 LC 97-23880

"Determined to unite all the members of her estranged family, Byrne family matriarch Annette invites them for a weekend. Will her two sons, haunted by a divisive court case in which one testified against the other, resume speaking to each other? Will Annette's granddaughter Cynthia let go of her bitterness toward the unfaithful husband she plans to divorce? And will Ellen's interfaith marriage to Mark finally be accepted—by both their families? It takes more than good intentions to bring this divided clan back together in this uplifting little novel." Libr J

Looking back. Delacorte Press 2001 340p $25.95
ISBN 0-385-33471-0 LC 00-65691

A "story about three college roommates—brainy Norma, lovely Amanda, preppy Cecile. . . . When the three women graduate, Amanda, desperate to escape her lower-class background, marries Larry Balsan, Norma's brother, who is in the family real estate business. As Mrs. Balsan, she can shop to her heart's content, but she soon realizes she is not as happy as Cecile, who marries her college sweetheart, or even Norma, who is biding her time until she meets Mr. Right." Publ Wkly

Plain, Belva—*Continued*

Random winds. Delacorte Press 1980 496p o.p.
LC 79-26845

"Three generations of doctors in the Farrell family span the gamut from a dedicated general practitioner in the Adirondack Mountains of New York to a world-renowned but troubled brain surgeon and on to a budding feminist medical student with a career/marriage conflict. This is a dynamic record of domestic tragedies to be endured, bitter arguments to be fought, and agonizing choices to be made as the Farrells sort out lives, loves, and hopes and set forth to challenge medical traditions and forbidden passions." Booklist

The author "knows how to sweep from one dramatic scene to another, often evoking poignancy, and the irony underlying Martin's daughter's romance with Fern's stepson produces a bittersweet ending." Publ Wkly

Tapestry. Delacorte Press 1988 440p o.p.
LC 87-22346

"Paul Werner, the key figure of a powerful New York banking family, is the protagonist in this saga of one man's concerns with the impending doom of World War II and the plight of his German-Jewish relatives and friends. Paul is caught in a passionless, childless marriage, and he struggles for years with the memory and reality of his first love and subsequent affairs of the heart." Libr J

Followed by Harvest

Whispers. Delacorte Press 1993 331p o.p.
LC 92-36572

"The Fergusons seem to have it all. Lynn runs their comfortable home in an affluent Connecticut suburb, her husband Robert is headed for a major position with his corporation and their eldest daughter Emily has been accepted at Yale. But it's a facade. Robert's inexplicable rages lead him to physically abuse Lynn; at times he is cruelly dictatorial with Emily and her troubled younger sister Annie." Publ Wkly

"Plain's purposes in rehearsing this scenario . . . are to illustrate what an abusive relationship is, to inculcate that it can afflict women in even the best strata of society, to sympathetically model getting out of such a situation, and to stress how difficult getting out can be even—perhaps especially—for a good, smart, talented woman. She succeeds admirably and affectingly." Booklist

Plath, Sylvia

The bell jar; with an introduction by Diane Wood Middlebrook. Knopf 1998 xxv, 229p $17
ISBN 0-375-40463-5 LC 98-27309

"Everyman's library"

First published 1963 in the United Kingdom; first United States edition published 1971 by Harper & Row

"Esther Greenwood, having spent what should have been a glorious summer as guest editor for a young woman's magazine, came home from New York, had a nervous breakdown, and tried to commit suicide. Through months of therapy, Esther kept her rationality, if not her sanity. In telling the story of Esther, Plath thinly disguised her own experience with attempted suicide and time spent in an institution. Like Esther, she was rehabilitated and finished college. She went to London, married poet Ted Hughes, had three children and published some poetry and this novel. When she felt the world slipping away from her again, she did commit suicide." Shapiro. Fic for Youth. 3d edition

Poe, Edgar Allan, 1809-1849

The collected tales and poems of Edgar Allan Poe. Modern Lib. 1992 1026p $20
ISBN 0-679-60007-8 LC 92-50231

A reissue of The complete tales and poems of Edgar Allan Poe published 1938

This volume contains short stories, poems, and a sampling of Poe's essays, criticism and journalistic writings

Complete stories and poems of Edgar Allan Poe. Doubleday 1966 819p $21.95
ISBN 0-385-07407-7

This volume contains five sections: Tales of mystery and horror; Humor and satire; Flights and fantasies; The narrative of A. Gordon Pym of Nantucket and The poems

Short stories included are: The murders in the Rue Morgue; The mystery of Marie Rogèt; The black cat; The gold-bug; Ligeia; A descent into the maelstrom; The tell-tale heart; The purloined letter; The assignation; Ms. found in a bottle; William Wilson; Berenice; The fall of the House of Usher; The cask of Amontillado; The pit and the pendulum; A tale of the ragged mountains; The man of the crowd; Morella; "Thou art the man"; The oblong box; The conversation of Eiros and Charmion; Metzengerstein; The masque of the Red Death; The premature burial; The imp of the perverse; The facts in the case of M. Valdemar; Hop-Frog; The system of Doctor Tarr and Professor Fether; The literary life of Thingum Bob, Esq.; How to write a Blackwood article; A predicament; Mystification; Loss of breath; The man that was used up; Diddling; The angel of the odd; Mellonta Tauta; The thousand-and-second tale of Scheherazade; X-ing a paragrab; The business man; A tale of Jerusalem; The sphinx; Why the little Frenchman wears his hand in a sling; Bon-bon; The Duc de l'Omelette; Three Sundays in a week; The devil in the belfry; Lionizing; Some words with a mummy; The spectacles; Four beasts in one; Never bet the devil your head; The balloon-hoax; Mesmeric revelation; Eleanora; The island of the fay; The oval portrait; The domain of Arnheim; Landor's cottage; The power of words; The colloquy of Monos and Una; Von Kempelen and his discovery

The imaginary voyages: The narrative of Arthur Gordon Pym; The unparalleled adventure of one Hans Pfaall; The journal of Julius Rodman. Twayne Pubs. 1981 667p o.p.
LC 81-2915

"Collected writings of Edgar Allan Poe"

Omnibus edition of three titles, the first of which is entered separately under variant form: The narrative of Arthur Gordon Pym of Nantucket, The unparalleled adventure of one Hans Pfaall, first published 1835 describes a voyage to the moon and The journal of Julius Rodman, an unfinished novel first published anonymously in 1840 deals with exploration of the Missouri River Basin

Poe, Edgar Allan, 1809-1849—*Continued*

The journal of Julius Rodman

In Poe, E. A. The imaginary voyages: The narrative of Arthur Gordon Pym; The unparalleled adventure of one Hans Pfaall; The journal of Julius Rodman p508-653

The murders in the Rue Morgue

In Poe, E. A. The purloined letter [and] The murders in the Rue Morgue p1-55

The narrative of Arthur Gordon Pym of Nantucket. Harper 1838 201p o.p.

"A New England boy stows away on a whaler, surviving mutiny, savagery, cannibalism, and wild pursuit. At the end of the story, the hero drifts toward the South Pole in a canoe; before him, out of the mist, rises a great white figure. There is some confusion in detail, because Poe, serializing the story, often did not pick up the loose ends. Based on the factual travels of J. N. Reynolds, whose book Poe had reviewed." Reader's Ency. 4th edition

also in Poe, E. A. The collected tales and poems of Edgar Allan Poe

also in Poe, E. A. Complete stories and poems of Edgar Allan Poe p617-736

also in Poe, E. A. The imaginary voyages: The narrative of Arthur Gordon Pym; The unparalleled adventure of one Hans Pfaall; The journal of Julius Rodman p4-365

The purloined letter [and] The murders in the Rue Morgue; illustrated by Rick Schreiter. Watts 1966 85p il o.p.

These two stories feature Monsieur C. Auguste Dupin. In "The murders in the Rue Morgue," a mother and daughter are the victims of a grisly murder that baffles the police. "The purloined letter" poses the problem of a woman of royal rank who is being blackmailed by a government official on the basis of a compromising letter. The police fail in the search, but Dupin is able to locate the missive

The unparalleled adventure of one Hans Pfaall

In Poe, E. A. The imaginary voyages: The narrative of Arthur Gordon Pym; The unparalleled adventure of one Hans Pfaall; The journal of Julius Rodman p366-506

Poey, Delia

(ed) Iguana dreams. See Iguana dreams

Pohl, Frederik, 1919-

The annals of the Heechee. Ballantine Bks. 1987 388p o.p.

LC 86-26584

"A Del Rey book"

Sequel to Heechee rendezvous

In this episode "the human-Heechee cooperation that first materialized in 'Heechee Rendezvous' has solidified as the two races unite against a common enemy. Once again Robinette Broadhead—alive after death as a machine-stored personality, compliments of Heechee technology—is called upon to face a dangerous challenge. He is the only one able to meet eyeball to eyeball with the deadly Foe, aliens determined to mold the universe to their own needs. . . . The novel is gripping, both in story line and in the colorful depiction of the alien Heechee." Booklist

Beyond the blue event horizon. Ballantine Bks. 1980 327p o.p.

LC 79-21757

"A Del Rey book"

Sequel to Gateway

"Multimillionaire Robinette Broadhead, still mourning the loss of his great love from the first book, backs an expedition to investigate one of the alien Heechee's 'food factories.' Earth is overpopulated, and the ship's resources are desperately needed to prevent mass starvation. The members of the expedition are all from the same family: Lurvey, a veteran space pilot and her engineer husband; Lurvey's money hungry father, and her precocious 14-year-old sister. Despite the tensions which surface during their three and a half year voyage, the family manages to successfully make contact with the factory and its innocent, human occupant. They begin to explore the marvels of the alien technology, but events on Earth and the inhabitants of another Heechee spaceship threatens to end the expedition in disaster." Voice Youth Advocates

Followed by Heechee rendezvous

The boy who would live forever; a novel of Gateway; Frederik Pohl. 1st ed. Tor Books 2004 380p $25.95

ISBN 0-7653-1049-X LC 2004-49579

A title set in the author's Heechee universe. "When recently orphaned Stan Avery inherits enough money to buy a trip to Gateway, the alien Heechee waystation that allows travel to all parts of space, he doesn't realize that his voyage has effectively cut him off forever from the world he left behind. Pohl's first Gateway novel in 15 years (the 1977 original Gateway won the Hugo and Nebula Awards) revitalizes a favorite far-future setting as it tells the tale of a young man's journey to self-realization amid the stars." Libr J

Chernobyl; a novel. Bantam Bks. 1987 355p o.p.

LC 86-47896

The author "re-creates in fiction the massive 1986 Ukrainian nuclear power plant disaster. The book opens during normal days just before the accident; suspense builds, as the reader expects the worst. Characters that would actually have been on the scene are seen being overwhelmed by berserk technology, their lives shattered. The tale is gripping, and the locale well established." Libr J

Gateway. St. Martin's Press 1977 313p o.p.

First volume in the author's Heechee saga

"The novel's protagonist, Robinette Broadhead, suffers from tremendous feelings of guilt: for the death of his parents, for his wealth (a stroke of luck he feels he does not deserve), and for the living death of his girl friend

Pohl, Frederik, 1919-*—Continued*
and fellow crew members. Gateway presents Broadhead's story in chapters that alternately describe his life before the novel opens and record present conversations between Broadhead and his computer psychiatrist, Sigfrid von Shrink. With a sensitive mixture of humor and sympathy, Pohl explores Broadhead's condition and ends with one of the finest affirmations of humanity in any literary work." New Ency of Sci Fic

Followed by Beyond the blue event horizon

Heechee rendezvous; a novel. Ballantine Bks. 1984 311p o.p.
LC 83-15637

"A Del Rey book"

Sequel to Beyond the blue event horizon

In this novel "the elusive, benevolent aliens called Heechee are forced to come out of hiding because the future not only of humankind but of the universe itself is at stake. Compelled by personal reasons, tycoon Robinette Broadhead takes part in another dangerous venture into space, moving inexorably toward his surprising yet fitting destiny." Booklist

Followed by The annals of the Heechee

Homegoing. Ballantine Bks. 1989 279p o.p.
LC 88-7413

"A Del Rey book"

"An alien spaceship lands on Earth for a double purpose: to give the people of Earth the benefit of their advanced technology and to return to them a human rescued in infancy and raised by the kangaroo-like Hakh'hli to be as 'human' as possible—under the circumstances. Pohl's unerring gift for satire delivers a splendidly skewed alien-eye-view of human culture while spinning a touching, slightly quirky story of a young man's coming of age." Libr J

Man Plus. Random House 1976 215p o.p.

"The novel describes the transformation of a human astronaut into a cyborg capable of living on Mars and confronts the question of human dignity: as the central character, Roger Torraway, becomes less 'human,' the people who were once so important to him are unable to cope with what he is, and Roger must also learn to handle the new thing he has become. Moreover, Roger's reflections on his growing inability to control his own life parallel the thoughts of people throughout the country who believe the world has gone out of control. The result is a remarkably readable novel that succeeds in presenting a fully rounded character in an SF setting." New Ency of Sci Fic

Mars Plus; [by] Frederik Pohl, Thomas T. Thomas. Baen Pub. Enterprises 1994 342p $20
ISBN 0-671-87605-8 LC 93-44782

Fifty years after the events in Man Plus, "man is, or seems to be, on Mars to stay, but things have become . . . strange, even compared to the population of cyborgs, half-cyborgs and just plain humans who now occupy the Red Planet. The computer net on which all Martian life depends has long seemed to have 'a mind of its own,' and now that mind seems to be in a very bad mood." Publisher's note

The space merchants; by Frederik Pohl and C. M. Kornbluth. Ballantine Bks. 1953 179p o.p.

"Control of the Venus economy and market is the sought-after plum of mega-advertising agencies. Mitchell Courtenay must persuade colonists to go there, but he is thwarted by the despised conservationists. Sabotage, warfare, and the degradation of the life of a consumer pervade this attack on modern consumer society." Shapiro. Fic for Youth. 3d edition

"Kornbluth later stated that he and Pohl packed into this story everything they hated about advertising, and it came out with Swiftian savagery. One of the first novels by writers with primary roots in the pulps to make an impact in mainstream circles." Anatomy of Wonder 4

Followed by The merchants' war (1984)

The world at the end of time. Ballantine Bks. 1990 393p o.p.
LC 89-18462

"A Del Rey book"

"As vast intelligences play deadly power games using stars for pawns, the fledgling colonists on the planet Home fight to maintain their existence while 'unknown forces' wreak havoc with the laws of physics and the universe. Pohl's sparkling wit attaches itself to macro- and microcosmic themes in a novel which pits a luckless human hero against a childlike being of inordinate power and extraordinary paranoia. Grand in scope, poignant in delivery." Libr J

Popp, Walter, 1913-1977

(jt. auth) Schlink, B. Self's punishment

Porlock, Martin *See* MacDonald, Philip, 1899-1981

Porter, Katherine Anne, 1890-1980

The collected stories of Katherine Anne Porter. Harcourt Brace & World 1965 495p o.p.

Contains three collections of short stories: Flowering Judas, and other stories (1935); The leaning tower, and other stories (1944); Pale horse, pale rider (1939); and four additional short stories: Virgin Violeta; The martyr; The fig tree; and Holiday

"These are perfect examples of the short story and are representative not only of the best American writing but of the best in the world." SLJ

Flowering Judas and other stories. Harcourt Brace Jovanovich 1935 285p o.p.

First published 1930. This edition adds four additional stories

Contents: María Concepción; Magic; Rope; He; Theft; That tree; The jilting of Granny Weatherall; Flowering Judas; The cracked looking-glass; Hacienda

also in Porter, K. A. The collected stories of Katherine Anne Porter p3-170

The leaning tower, and other stories. Harcourt Brace & Co. 1944 246p o.p.

Contents: The source; The witness; The circus; The old order; The last leaf; The grave; The downward path to wisdom; A day's work; The leaning tower

also in Porter, K. A. The collected stories of Katherine Anne Porter p321-495

Porter, Katherine Anne, 1890-1980—*Continued*

Noon wine

In Porter, K. A. The collected stories of Katherine Anne Porter p222-68

In Porter, K. A. Pale horse, pale rider: three short novels

Old mortality

In Porter, K. A. The collected stories of Katherine Anne Porter p173-221

In Porter, K. A. Pale horse, pale rider: three short novels

Pale horse, pale rider [novelette]

In Porter, K. A. The collected stories of Katherine Anne Porter p269-317

In Porter, K. A. Pale horse, pale rider: three short novels

Pale horse, pale rider: three short novels. Modern Library ed. Modern Lib. 1998 205p $18.95

ISBN 0-679-60303-4 LC 98-12008

A reissue of the title first published 1939 by Harcourt, Brace

Contents: Old mortality; Noon wine; Pale horse, pale rider

In the title story "Miranda, a young journalist, is caught in a personal dilemma. She must choose between a career and a commitment to Adam, a soldier on leave during World War I. Porter's simple tale becomes more complex as Miranda's anxieties and fears about war, death, and personal loss are revealed. She hovers close to death during the terrbile flu epidemic of 1918. Miranda survives and the war ends, but it brings her no happiness because the epidemic has claimed Adam as a victim." Shapiro. Fic for Youth. 3d edition

also in Porter, K. A. The collected stories of Katherine Anne Porter p173-317

Ship of fools. Little, Brown 1962 497p o.p.

"An Atlantic Monthly Press book"

"A satire in which the world is likened to a ship whose passengers, fools and deranged people all, are sailing toward eternity. Porter's novel is set in 1931 aboard a German passenger ship returning to Bremerhaven, Germany, from Veracruz, Mexico. The ship carries a microcosm of peoples, including Germans, Americans, Spaniards, Gypsies, and Mexicans, Jews, anti-Semites, political reactionaries, revolutionaries, and neutrals coexist aboard ship, at the same time that jeaolusy, cruelty and duplicity pervade their lives." Merriam-Webster's Ency of Lit

Porter, William Sydney *See* Henry, O., 1862-1910

Portis, Charles

The dog of the South. Knopf 1979 245p o.p.

ISBN 0-394-4506146 LC 78-65780

This novel "features Ray Midge, a bore with few interests and even less ambition whose major pastime is collecting old weapons. But when Ray's wife runs off with her first husband, the hated Guy Dupree, along with Ray's car and credit cards, the jilted husband takes to the road, driving from Arkansas to Honduras to reclaim all that he has lost." Book Magazine

"Simultaneously hilarious and heart breakingly odd. . . you find yourself laughing so hard in sections that tears run down your face." Baltimore Sun

Gringos; a novel. Simon & Schuster 1991 269p o.p.

ISBN 0-671-72457-6 LC 90-42476

This novel "features Jimmy Burns, an idler from Louisiana transplanted to Mexico, where he ekes out a living finding missing persons and doing odd jobs. Equally odd are the other motley expatriates. Ninety-pound Louise Kurle, who's writing a book about benign space dwarfs, suspects her missing husband, Rudy, was abducted by UFOs. Big Dan, a paunchy ex-con guru/white supremacist/kidnapper, poses to his band of deranged hippies as El Mago, the wizard whom the Mayas predict will appear at the end of time. Murder, adventure and Indian lure animate a Mexico aswarm with New Age mystics, kooks, skinheads, graduate students, maverick archeologists and looters of shrines." Publ Wkly

"'Gringos,' by far, is Portis's most inward-turning book, a story of a grownup trying to grow up, to keep it together with some dignity. Watching him pull it off is one of the finest pleasures afforded by any novel in a long time." Newsweek

Masters of Atlantis; a novel; by Charles Portis. Knopf 1985 247p o.p.

ISBN 0-394-54683-0 LC 85-40212

This novel "concerns the establishment of the order of Gnomons, a secret society purporting to teach the hidden knowledge of Atlantis. The action begins in 1917, when soldier Lamar is relieved of $200 by a fast-talking stranger in exchange for the key to Gnomonism. The plot spins dizzily along as sly Sydney Hen and antic Austin Popper are drawn into the society, engineer a farcical schism, and espouse assorted crackpot causes. . . . Those who enjoy deadpan comedy should get a good laugh here." Libr J

Norwood. Simon & Schuster 1966 190p o.p.

LC 66-21822

The hero of this book, Norwood Pratt, "an ex-Marine and would-be Country and Western singing star, covers a good stretch of the American highway on a series of fool's errands (picking up a wife along the way)." Book Week

"An artlessness and simplicity in style and plot skillfully projects Norwood and his problems quite convincingly. For those readers more interested in characterization than action." Libr J

True grit; a novel. Simon & Schuster 1968 215p o.p.

"Mattie Ross, a fourteen-year-old living in Yell County, Arkansas, is determined to get justice when her father is killed by a hired hand. She is joined in her quest by Rooster Cogburn, a U.S. marshal, and by a Texas Ranger. This strange trio faces a series of perilous encounters requiring true grit to confront them." Shapiro. Fic for Youth. 3d edition

Potok, Chaim, 1929-2002

The ark builder
In Potok, C. Old men at midnight

The chosen; a novel. Simon & Schuster 1967 284p o.p.

"Living only five blocks apart in the Williamsburg section of Brooklyn, New York, Danny and Reuven meet as opponents in a softball game. Out of this encounter evolves a strong bond of friendship between a brilliant Hasidic Jew and a scholar who is Orthodox in his religious thinking. During the course of their relationship Reuven becomes the means by which Danny's father, a rabbi, can communicate with his son, who has been reared under a code of silence." Shapiro. Fic for Youth. 2d edition

Followed by The promise

The gift of Asher Lev. Knopf 1990 369p o.p.
LC 89-43401

Sequel to My name is Asher Lev

"Following the death of his beloved uncle, Asher, who is now middle-aged and settled in France, finds he must return with his family to the Brooklyn Hasidic Jewish community from which he has been exiled 20 years. Greeted there with suspicion and anger by many who still insist that his art is anathema to Hasidim—a sentiment that continues to haunt his relationship with his father, a tireless, well-respected ambassador for the religious community's Rebbe—Asher finds himself struggling once again to balance art and faith, this time in a difficult emotional coming-to-terms that involves the future of his five-year-old son, Avrumel." Booklist

My name is Asher Lev. Knopf 1972 369p o.p.

"Young Asher Lev is an obedient son of strict Jewish parents. When his artistic endeavors are discovered, he is sent to a religious leader for consultation because artists are not viewed favorably by the Hasidim. Asher's struggle for fulfillment and his ultimate rejection by his parents are poignantly drawn." Shapiro. Fic for Youth. 3d edition

Followed by The gift of Asher Lev

Old men at midnight. Knopf 2001 273p $23
ISBN 0-375-41071-6 LC 2001-33861

"A collection of three novellas that share a character, Ilana Davita Dinn, and the theme of the effects of war on men's lives. In 'The Ark Builder,' which takes place the summer before she begins college, Ilana begins to teach English to a young boy, Noah, who has survived the Holocaust. . . . In the second story [The war doctor] Ilana is hardly present at all; a former KGB officer leaves her the story of his life in written form. . . . Finally, in 'The Troupe Teacher,' Ilana, now a writer, coaxes a disturbing story out of Benjamin Walter, a professor of warfare. A moving and powerful book." Booklist

The promise. Knopf 1969 358p o.p.

Sequel to The chosen

"Reuven Malter and Danny Saunders, two Jewish friends living in Brooklyn, choose to alter the destinies chosen for them by their fathers. Reuven, studying to be a rabbi, finds his vocation blocked by a challenge to his scholarship and his father's book. Danny, who is studying clinical psychology, risks his career by a decision, based on intuition, that he feels can save a young boy's sanity." Shapiro. Fic for Youth. 3d edition

The troupe teacher
In Potok, C. Old men at midnight

The war doctor
In Potok, C. Old men at midnight

Pottinger, Stanley, 1940-

The fourth procedure. Ballantine Bks. 1995 550p o.p.
LC 94-34282

In this novel "corpses of antiabortionists keep turning up in Washington, D.C., in unlikely spots, but even more unlikely is their condition—all have fresh incisions and a toy doll with a message stuffed inside it. Drawn into this web of murder and mystery is a wide variety of characters whose seemingly random connections turn out to be not so random after all. Each one has a past that sheds light on the current abortion controversy." Libr J

"Pottinger handily proves the adage that politics makes strange bedfellows, adding ironic twists that skewer long-accepted assumptions." Publ Wkly

The last Nazi. St. Martin's Press 2003 324p $24.95
ISBN 0-312-27676-1 LC 2003-53852

"Melissa Gale, a lawyer and agent with an investigative unit of the FBI, is on the trail of the mysterious Adalwolf, a former assistant to Joseph Mengele, who aided in experiments on concentration camp prisoners. For Melissa it's not just a job, it's a personal mission because her grandmother died in a concentration camp. When she and her partner botch the swat team operation, their careers are put in jeopardy, and the elusive Nazi is emboldened to continue with his plot to develop a killer virus." Booklist

"Be prepared to feel horror for a villain who is not only the last Nazi but also one of the most terrifying." Libr J

Pouncey, Peter R., 1937-

Rules for old men waiting; a novel; [by] Peter Pouncey. Random House 2005 210p $21.95
ISBN 1-400-06370-1 LC 2004-54174

This novel "details the last days of historian, war veteran, and proud Scotsman Robert MacIver. Upon the death of his beloved wife, MacIver is at loose ends and in rapidly failing health. Rambling around his large old house on the Cape, he determines that he will meet his fate with dignity. Without a shred of self-pity, he formulates a set of rules to get by, including eating regular meals, keeping warm, and listening to music. He also sets about writing a fairly gripping story set during World War I about a group of conflicted soldiers. This story, in turn, acts as a conduit for his own memories—his experiences in combat, his great love affair with his wife, the death of their son in Vietnam, the rewards of their respective careers as a teacher and a painter." Booklist

"As MacIver's book-within-a-book takes shape, Pouncey reminds us how the smallest choices can make a dramatic difference in the breadth and scope not just of a story but of a life." N Y Times Book Rev

Pournelle, Jerry, 1933-
(jt. auth) Niven, L. The burning city
(jt. auth) Niven, L. Lucifer's hammer
(jt. auth) Niven, L. The Mote in God's Eye

Powell, Anthony, 1905-2000

The acceptance world
In Powell, A. A dance to the music of time

At Lady Molly's
In Powell, A. A dance to the music of time

Books do furnish a room
In Powell, A. A dance to the music of time

A buyer's market
In Powell, A. A dance to the music of time

Casanova's Chinese restaurant
In Powell, A. A dance to the music of time

A dance to the music of time. University of Chicago Press 1995 12v in 4 pa set $72.80
ISBN 0-226-67719-2 LC 94-47228
An omnibus reissue of the twelve titles comprising The Music of time series, which were originally published separately
Contents: [v1] First movement: A question of upbringing (1951); A buyer's market (1952); The acceptance world (1955)
[v2] Second movement: At Lady Molly's (1957); Casanova's Chinese restaurant (1960); The kindly ones (1962)
[v3] Third movement: The valley of bones (1964); The soldier's art (1966); The military philosophers (1968)
[v4] Fourth movement: Books do furnish a room (1971); Temporary kings (1973); Hearing secret harmonies (1975)
"The novels, spanning a period of over fifty years, from the early 1920s, describe the school days, youth, and maturity of the narrator-hero, Nicholas Jenkins, and his upper-class cohorts, especially the egregious Widmerpool. Though primarily satiric in tone, they express an underlying melancholy about life and time reminiscent of Marcel Proust." Reader's Ency. 4th edition

Hearing secret harmonies
In Powell, A. A dance to the music of time

The kindly ones
In Powell, A. A dance to the music of time

The military philosophers
In Powell, A. A dance to the music of time

A question of upbringing
In Powell, A. A dance to the music of time

The soldier's art
In Powell, A. A dance to the music of time

Temporary kings
In Powell, A. A dance to the music of time

The valley of bones
In Powell, A. A dance to the music of time

Powell, Dawn

Angels on toast
In Powell, D. Novels, 1930-1942

Come back to Sorrento
In Powell, D. Novels, 1930-1942

Dance night
In Powell, D. Novels, 1930-1942

The golden spur
In Powell, D. Novels, 1944-1962

The locusts have no king
In Powell, D. Novels, 1944-1962

My home is far away
In Powell, D. Novels, 1944-1962

Novels, 1930-1942. Library of Am. 2001 1068p $35
ISBN 1-931082-01-4 LC 00-54595
Contents: Dance night (1930); Come back to Sorrento (1932); Turn, magic wheel (1936); Angels on toast (1940); A time to be born (1942)
Dance night is about obsessive longing set in a 1920s Ohio factory town. Come back to Sorrento depicts a woman's friendship with a music teacher. Turn, magic wheel is a satirical look at New York's literary world. Angel on toast is a comic treatment of New York businessmen on the make. A time to be born portrays a monstrously egotistical woman just before America's entry into World War II

Novels, 1944-1962. Library of Am. 2001 969p $35
ISBN 1-931082-02-2 LC 00-54596
Contents: My home is far away (1944); The locusts have no king (1948); The wicked pavilion (1954); The golden spur (1962)
My home is far away is the fictionalized memoir of Powell's life in small town Ohio. The locusts have no king is a satirical look at a scholar's brush with celebrity. The wicked pavilion portrays the habitués of a Greenwich Village cafe. The golden spur is a satirical look at the Manhattan art world of the late 1950s

A time to be born
In Powell, D. Novels, 1930-1942

Turn, magic wheel
In Powell, D. Novels, 1930-1942

The wicked pavilion
In Powell, D. Novels, 1944-1962

Powell, Padgett

Edisto; a novel. Farrar, Straus & Giroux 1984 183p o.p.
ISBN 0-374-14651-9 LC 83-25334
"His parents' separation is a difficult problem for 12-year-old Simons. The 'Doctor' (his mother) says he should be a writer. The 'Progenitor' (his father) says he should play baseball. And Taurus (his mother's friend) says the boy has enough on his mind just being 12. Cast between these poles of adult influence, Simons gropes his way into adolescence under the coastal sun of Edisto,

Powell, Padgett—*Continued*
South Carolina." Libr J

This is "distinctly a tour de force. . . . Powell's ear is acute: one of the pleasures of the book is his ability to catch the nuances of Southern speech, whether it is the malicious conversation of the Doctor's academic colleagues at a cocktail party or the genial banter of country Negroes at the fishing pier." N Y Times Book Rev

Edisto revisited; a novel. Holt & Co. 1996 145p o.p.
ISBN 0-8050-4237-7 LC 95-34071

This sequel, set in South Carolina, "begins with Simons [Manigault] having a short but steamy affair with first-cousin Patricia. . . . This proves too much for poor recent college graduate Simons, who escapes for a series of adventures deeper south. He tries his hand at fishing in Corpus Christi, quits, and again flees, this time to visit with Taurus, Simons's alcoholic mother's former lover, who is a game warden in the deepest bayou in Louisiana. All the while he debates accepting the responsibility concomitant with adulthood." Libr J

"'Edisto Revisited' is a puzzling work of high style, a rendering of haplessness that seems to poeticize passivity. While his novel may make you wonder if it has much of what is called meaning, Mr. Powell finally overpowers such doubts with his countless quotable passages, his humor and his seductive evocation of the romance of giving up." N Y Times Book Rev

Powell, Sophie, 1980-

The Mushroom Man. Putnam 2003 196p $23.95
ISBN 0-399-14963-5 LC 2002-21355

At the heart of this novel is a "child's invented fairy tale, set in a Welsh forest, about an amiable hermit who fashions umbrellas from wild mushrooms to protect the local fairy population from the rain. . . . Eleven-year-old Amy—a triplet who lives on a farm in the Welsh countryside with her identical sisters; her older brother, Joseph; and her widowed mother, Beth—is the creator of the tale. One night she tells it to her 6-year-old cousin, Lily, who's so enchanted that she sets out to find the mushroom man and goes missing in the process, thus setting the novel's plot in motion. . . . The Welsh countryside has never seemed so alluring, or the existence of simple magic, despite the nasty disappointments of adult life, so probable." N Y Times Book Rev

Power, Susan, 1961-

The grass dancer. Putnam 1994 300p o.p.
LC 93-47199

"Set on a North Dakota reservation, 'The Grass Dancer' tells the story of Harley Wind Soldier, a young Sioux trying to understand his place among people whose intertwined lives and shared heritage move backward in time in the narrative from the 1980's to the middle of the last century." N Y Times Book Rev

This "is a passionate portrayal of universal human emotions and a vivid account of Native American history and culture." SLJ

Powers, J. F. (James Farl), 1917-1999

Morte d'Urban. Doubleday 1962 336p o.p.

"Father Urban, member of a Catholic order that is financially impoverished, spends his time in two worlds, the religious and the secular. He must try to gain friends and funds for the Clementine order and yet make decisions that may cost him the friendship of his wealthy benefactors, among them eccentric and willful Billy Cosgrove and Mrs. Thwaites. The wide cast of characters within the church and the world outside makes for both a sad and amusing portrait." Shapiro. Fic for Youth. 3d edition

Wheat that springeth green. Knopf 1988 335p o.p.
LC 87-46104

This novel "illuminates the world of the Catholic parish. Set in the turbulent months of the late 1960s, it gently and satirically probes the inner mysteries of a younger and perhaps wiser Catholic Church. Its focus is Father Joe Hackett, a tenacious rebel of the faith in his mid-40s who has tested himself on women and drink in his youth and now seems on the verge of religious suicide." Libr J

"The beauty of Mr. Powers's writing lies in its art's being almost invisible. The craft and balance of the novel's literary achievement are discernible in every sentence, but only on second thought, so thoroughly has the author subordinated form to function." N Y Times Book Rev

Powers, James Farl *See* Powers, J. F. (James Farl), 1917-1999

Powers, John R.

Do black patent-leather shoes really reflect up?; a fictionalized memoir. Regnery Bks. 1975 227p o.p.

Sequel to The last Catholic in America

Powers "reproduces the insulated milieu of the big-city Catholic school where harsh discipline and religious fervor molded students for an alternatively naive and cynical survival. The interludes of sentimentality don't detract as Powers' episodic structure and genuine affection carry the day." Booklist

The last Catholic in America; a fictionalized memoir. Saturday Review Press 1973 228p o.p.

"Eddie Ryan, salesman, pauses during a business trip to visit the haunts of a South Side Chicago neighborhood where, in the 1950's, he spent his youth. The scene triggers . . . memories of his Catholic upbringing in St. Bastion's parish, where sin was clearly defined, and punishment and reward handily dispensed." Libr J

"Bittersweet variations on the familiar U.S. literary theme of growing up Catholic . . . strike funny, trite, sometimes overlong, and inevitably sensitive chords. The nostalgic entertainment, occasionally bordering on the mawkish, rings true with seriocomic overtones and honest dialog." Booklist

Followed by Do black patent-leather shoes really reflect up?

Powers, Richard, 1957-

Galatea 2.2. Farrar, Straus & Giroux 1995 329p o.p.
ISBN 0-374-19948-5 LC 94-44319
In this novel, "protagonist Richard Powers is a humanist-in-residence at the Center for the Study of Advanced Science, where he uses his literary expertise to help Dr. Philip Lentz, a cognitive neurologist, win a bet that he can create a thinking machine capable of passing a comprehensive master's exam in English. As the computer, Helen, learns the fundamentals of language and literature, she develops a sense of her own identity and self-worth. Paralleling Powers' growing attachment to Helen is a reassessment of the year he spent living in Holland writing his novels and the demise of his longtime relationship with a former student." Booklist

"Powers may be the last humanist with a scientific competence, an invaluable thing when the notion that humans may be just another variety of complex system haunts our sense of ourselves. In its strongest moments Galatea 2.2 realizes the possibilities of that position splendidly." Nation

The gold bug variations. Morrow 1991 639p o.p.
ISBN 0-688-09891-6 LC 90-20267
The novel "jumps back and forth between the late '50s, when brilliant scientists Stuart Ressler is involved with an Illinois research team trying to break the mysteries of DNA coding, and the '80s, when librarian Jan O'Deigh and computer programmer Franklin Todd get to know Ressler, now holding an insignificant night job at a massive computer database operation in Brooklyn, N.Y., and try to figure what derailed his promising career." Publ Wkly

"Mr. Powers's page is Velcro. Every allusion possible is compulsory. His novel is a dense, symmetrical symphony in which no note goes unsounded." N Y Times Book Rev

Operation wandering soul; a novel. Morrow 1993 352p o.p.
ISBN 0-688-11548-9 LC 92-43860
"Set in the pediatric ward of a large metropolitan hospital, this novel is äbout the plight of the world's children in a time of cynicism, corruption and easy destruction of life. The only recognizable adults are surgical resident Richard Kraft, desperately weary of trying to patch up the shattered lives and bodies of innocents, and therapist Linda Espera, who tries to instill hope through storytelling and play-acting. The two are deeply involved with a band of patients led by a precociously wise but hopelessly crippled Thai girl and a cynical, commanding boy whose rare disease has withered his body into that of an old man." Publ Wkly

This novel is "filled with glorious examples of both high and low culture. Mr. Powers is a cerebral writer with a deep awareness of the material world. . . . But the culture on which his book draws most heavily is children's culture. The therapist's unconventional treatment for her patients requires her and the surgeon to spin tales about imperiled children throughout history. . . . The prose sprints in and out of these tales with verbal dexterity and great flashes of wit." N Y Times Book Rev

Plowing the dark. Farrar, Straus & Giroux 2000 415p $25
ISBN 0-374-23461-2 LC 99-45084
"In Seattle, a woman painter joins a team of software engineers who are devising a virtual-reality module; at the same time, an American hostage, moldering in a bare cell in Beirut, tries to mentally reconstruct his Stateside existence. Powers's intellectual dexterity is dazzling, especially in the descriptions of virtual-realty programming, and he has plenty to say about the intersections of art, war, commerce, and literature." New Yorker

Prisoner's dilemma. Beech Tree Bks. 1988 348p o.p.
ISBN 0-688-07350-6 LC 87-31824
"The present of the novel is late 1978. Edward Hobson's recurring fainting spells have worsened, and two of his children–Artie, a 25-year-old law student, and Rachel, a 23-year-old actuary–have come home to DeKalb to see him, their mother, and two children still living at home, the just-divorced Lily and high school senior Eddie. During this weekend visit and a Christmas reunion in Chicago, the family tries to decide what to do about Edward's health." New Repub

"Prisoner's Dilemma is a paradigm for the nuclear game, the only door left ajar by Hobbes's enlightened self-preservation, the dictates of right reason. Or, is Artie's last oracular pronouncement on his father's legacy the hard answer: 'What we can't bring about in no way releases us from what we must.' We finish this novel, as we do all grand fiction, ready to figure on. Prisoner's Dilemma is magnificent." Nation

The time of our singing. Farrar, Straus & Giroux 2002 631p $28
ISBN 0-374-27782-6 LC 2002-22397
"The book follows the mixed-race Strom family through much of the 20th century, from 1939—when German-Jewish physicist David Strom meets Delia Daley, a black, classically trained singer from Philadelphia—through the 1990s." Publ Wkly

"Powers's blending of unlikely tones in order to probe the problems of a society that continues to insist, all grays to the contrary, on seeing everything in terms of black and white is, more often than not, a fascinating, stimulating and moving artistic imagining of a harmony that continues to elude us in life." N Y Times Book Rev

Poyer, David

Black storm. St. Martin's Press 2002 292p o.p.
ISBN 0-312-26969-2 LC 2001-58562
In this "Dan Lenson adventure, Poyer injects the special ops ace into the heart of Operation Desert Storm and confrontation with the menace of Iraqi biological warfare. Attached, along with Major Maddox, a female army doctor, to a marine recon team aiming to infiltrate Baghdad and target a suspected bioweapons site, Lenson survives claustrophobic rides in a milk truck's tank, mad SAS men, and capture and torture by the Iraqis. . . . The remarkably vivid portraits he draws of the variety of men and women drawn to serve their country merit high praise, too." Booklist

China Sea. St. Martin's Press 2000 337p il o.p.
ISBN 0-312-20287-3 LC 99-55067

Poyer, David—*Continued*

A naval adventure featuring Lt. Commander Dan Lenson. "It is 1990-91, at the start of the Gulf War. The navy, ready to discard the *U.S.S. Gaddis*, has asked Lenson to ready the ship for a final voyage. Accompanied by a crew of misfits and brigrats, Lenson endures a journey filled with bungling allies, hurricanes, a chronic supply problem, and piracy. The crew is ready to mutiny—the vagueness of his orders and a disgruntled executive officer have undermined Lenson's authority. And to top it all off, Lenson soon realizes that one of his crew is committing murders in every port." Libr J

Lenson and his crew "engage the Chinese in a climactic battle that ranks high among single-ship actions in maritime fiction. Readers who can meet Poyer halfway with knowledge of modern seafaring stand to be especially richly rewarded." Booklist

The circle. St. Martin's Press 1992 432p o.p.
LC 92-2980

The author "gives us an ensign fresh out of Annapolis, assigned to a destroyer in the North Atlantic. His ship is an obsolete bucket of plates and bolts held together by mucilage. The ship is undermanned and has a resentful crew. The executive officer is a sadistic right-wing bully. Ship and crew battle furious storms. They are ordered to join the North Atlantic fleet for exercises, and something terrible occurs that results in a court-martial. The young ensign undergoes a trial by fire." NY Times Book Rev

"The individual events convincingly present the gritty details of life aboard a pre-computer-age destroyer, and Poyer provides a compelling sense of the Cold War Navy's operational dynamics." Publ Wkly

The command; David Poyer. 1st ed. St. Martin's Press 2004 386p map $24.95
ISBN 0-312-31836-7 LC 2003-28058

"After receiving the Congressional Medal of Honor for action in Iraq, Commander Daniel V. Lenson is given new orders: 'Take over as skipper of USS Thomas W. Horn.' His mission: Prepare the Tomahawk-equipped strike destroyer and her crew for the Red Sea, where she'll join an international task force searching for weapons of mass destruction." Publisher's note

A country of our own; a novel of the Civil War at sea. Simon & Schuster 2003 429p $24
ISBN 0-684-87134-3 LC 2003-45435

"Lt. Ker Claiborne has reluctantly relinquished his commission in the U.S. Navy and joined the Confederacy. He's an anomaly—a Virginian who opposes slavery. The plot follows Claiborne throughout the South and then across the Atlantic as captain of a highly successful and feared rebel commerce raider. There are enough spies, plots, battles, storms, and shipwrecks to satisfy any reader." Libr J

Down to a sunless sea; a Tiller Galloway thriller. St. Martin's Press 1996 306p o.p.
LC 96-3120

Ex-Navy SEAL Tiller Galloway's "troubles are unending. He's broke, his boat is destroyed, his partnership is dissolving, and the teenaged son he hasn't seen in years unexpectedly arrives in a stolen car. So when the wife of an old friend, Bud, calls with news of her husband's death and requests Tiller's help selling his cave-diving business, Tiller heads south with son in tow. And once in the murky darkness of Florida's submerged tunnels, Tiller soon discovers the dangers and thrills of cave diving, along with evidence that Bud's drowning was no accident, but part of a conspiracy involving drugs and water rights." Libr J

"The cave-diving scenes are riveting, claustrophobic, terrifying, and beautiful, and Tiller has grown into one of the most spectacularly flawed and failed characters ever to seek redemption in popular fiction." Booklist

Fire on the waters; a novel of the Civil War at sea. Simon & Schuster 2001 445p o.p.
ISBN 0-684-87133-5 LC 2001-20307

This novel "introduces naval officer Elisha Eaker. The pampered son of a successful shipping magnate, Eli enlists to take a stand for his country and against his overbearing father. Commissioned to protect the Union forces at Fort Sumter, Eli and Captain Parker Bucyrus Tresevant, a Southerner torn between allegiances, sail into the danger, intrigue, and indecision necessarily engendered by a nation at war with itself." Booklist

"An interesting character study of a young man's coming of age as well as an accurate historical novel." Libr J

The gulf. St. Martin's Press 1990 xx, 442p o.p.
LC 90-36140

"Dan Lenson, is the executive officer on a frigate in the Persian Gulf, assigned to convoy a succession of oil tankers through perilous waters. Lenson's shipmates include hard-living helicopter pilots, minor crooks, and idealistic young officers. Not far away, a group of divers, naval reservists, must battle the hostility of 'real' sailors as they undertake a dangerous mission of their own. Lenson's physical and mental courage are sorely tried in the climactic scenes, where he battles enemies and the ocean itself." Libr J

Thunder on the mountain. Forge 1999 382p $25.95
ISBN 0-312-86494-9 LC 98-43454

"A Tom Doherty Associates book"

"A fiery accident at a Pennsylvania oil refinery in 1935 inspires the workers at Thunder Oil Company to strike. During a bitterly cold winter in the depths of the Depression, workers are desperate for decent food, better wages, warm housing, and fair treatment from management. When a ruthless professional strikebreaker and a CIO organizer with thinly veiled Communist sympathies join the dispute, the strike escalates to betrayal, sabotage, and murder." Libr J

Poyer's "pitch-perfect dialogue and explosive imagery capture both sides of the bloody battle that gave birth to the unions. This is a stunning period tale in which the oft-forgotten essence of the American dream is visible in every chapter." Publ Wkly

Pramoedya Ananta Toer *See* Toer, Pramoedya Ananta, 1925-

Pratchett, Terry

The color of magic; a novel of Discworld; Terry Pratchett. Harper 2005 224p pa $13.95
ISBN 0-06-085592-4 LC 2005-46289

Pratchett, Terry—*Continued*

First published 1983 by St. Martin's Press with title: The colour of magic

This first book of Discworld features the tourist Twoflower, the wizard Rincewind, and several other unusual characters as they travel together on a flat planet.

The fifth elephant; a novel of Discworld. HarperPrism 2000 321p o.p.

ISBN 0-06-105157-8 LC 99-43960

"When news of a dispute over the dwarven succession reaches the city of Ankh-Morpork, Lord Vetinari dispatches an unlikely group of ambassadors—including a dwarf, a werewolf, a troll, and the intrepid Watch Commander Vines—to address the problem." Libr J

"Pratchett cheerfully takes readers on an exuberant tale of mystery and invention. . . . Along the way, he skewers everything from monarchy to fascism, as well as communism and capitalism, oil wealth and ethnic identities, Russian plays, immigration, condoms and evangelical Christianity—in short, most everything worth talking about." Publ Wkly

Going postal; a novel of Discworld; Terry Pratchett. 1st ed. HarperCollins 2004 377p $24.95

ISBN 0-06-001313-3 LC 2004-47391

"When petty con man Moist von Lipwig is hung for his crimes . . . it appears to be the end. But this is Discworld after all, a world 'a lot like our own but different.' Moist awakes from the shock of his hanging to find that the city's Patrician, Lord Vetinari, has assigned him a government job (a fate worse than death?) restoring the defunct postal system. Of course, there is much more to restore than the flow of letters and packages. Justice as well as communication has been poorly served by a hostile takeover of the 'clacks' a unique messaging system that is part semaphore, part digital, and under the monopoly of the Grand Trunk Company. Before Moist can get very far into the job, he encounters ghosts, the voices of unsent letters, and a ruthless corporate conspiracy. . . . The author's inventiveness seems to know no end, his playful and irreverent use of language is a delight, and there is food for thought in his parody of fantasyland." SLJ

Monstrous regiment; a novel of Discworld. HarperCollins Pubs. 2003 353p $24.95

ISBN 0-06-001315-X LC 2003-50800

"Polly Perks, an exuberantly determined Borogravian barmaid, decides to disguise herself as a man to infiltrate the Tenth Foot Light Infantry (aka the Ins-and-Outs) and find her missing soldier brother, Paul." Publ Wkly

"Pratchett revels in pricking pomp and assurance, but it isn't going too far to say that of late his real subject, like Wilfred Owen's, is the pit of war. Pratchett's approach may be less lyrical, but he can move from farce to sadness in seconds." N Y Times Book Rev

Thief of time; a novel of Discworld. HarperCollins Pubs. 2001 324p o.p.

ISBN 0-06-019956-3 LC 00-65347

"The cast includes Death; Miss Susan, Death's granddaughter; Jeremy Clockson, a clockmaker; Lobsang, a novice monk; and Lu-Tze, a sweeper at the temple of the History Monks. When a mysterious lady asks Jeremy to make a clock that is perfectly timed (even to the last tick), trouble begins—it seems that such a clock would have the power to stop time completely." Publ Wkly

"This is Discworld, an adolescent Oz in which far fewer folks are immortal, but long life doesn't entail decrepitude; magic works; and politics and culture are fluid, far off, and mostly for old guys. Spun out of words and wit, it is as light and curiously tasty as cotton candy." Booklist

Thud!; a novel of Discworld. HarperCollins 2005 384p $24.95

ISBN 0-06-081522-6 LC 2005-46271

"Commander Sam Vines of Ankh-Morpork's City Watch finds a 'perfect day' going downhill quickly. Not only is there a murderer loose in the city but Sam also faces pressure to add a vampire to a police force that already contains trolls and werewolves and an old rivalry that threatens to break out into overt warfare. It's all in a day's work for the City Watch in the latest novel set in the author's hilariously surreal Disc World." Libr J

The truth; a novel of Discworld. HarperCollins Pubs. 2000 324p il o.p.

ISBN 0-380-97895-4 LC 00-31928

"When he stumbles upon the dwarven secret of movable type, young scribe William de Word discovers a new career and starts a newspaper—the first of its kind in the city of Ankh-Morpork. Pratchett's . . . 'Discworld' novel takes on the press and investigative journalism in a hilarious romp that examines the fleeting nature of truth and lies." Libr J

Preston, Douglas

Brimstone; [by] Douglas Preston and Lincoln Child. Warner Bks. 2004 497p $25.95

ISBN 0-446-53143-X LC 2004-1968

A mystery featuring FBI agent Pendergast. "In an exotic mansion, Jeremy Grove's charred remains are discovered in an otherwise locked and barricaded room. The area smells of brimstone, and singed into the floorboard appears to be a cloven hoofprint. According to rumor, Jeremy made a Faustian pact with Satan in his youth. Did the Dark Lord finally demand payment? Pendergast can't resist a mystery, and he incorporates the help of police officers from the authors' previous novels. In addition, a major character appears courtesy of Wilkie Collins's The Woman in White." Libr J

"Erudite, swiftly paced, brimming (occasionally overbrimming) with memorable personae and tense set pieces, this is the perfect thriller." Publ Wkly

The cabinet of curiosities; {by} Douglas Preston and Lincoln Child. Warner Bks. 2002 466p o.p.

ISBN 0-446-53022-0 LC 2001-39580

"Construction of an apartment building in Manhattan is haltred when excavators discover the remains of 36 dismenbered bodies, the apparent victims of a serial killer who operated more than a century ago. Archaeologist Nora Kelly and FBI agent Pendergast (both have appeared in the authors' previous books) team up to track down the identity of the long-dead killer." Booklist

This novel features "fabulous locales, colorful characters, pointed riffs on city and museum politics, cool forensic and paleontological speculation and several gripping set pieces including an extended white-knuckle climax." Publ Wkly

Preston, Douglas—*Continued*

The codex; Douglas Preston. Forge 2004 396p $24.95

ISBN 0-7653-0700-6 LC 2003-49427

"A treasure hunter and tomb raider, Maxwell Broadbent is one of the wealthiest men on the planet owing to his extensive art collection. Dying of cancer, he decides to force his three estranged sons to work together for their inheritance. Leaving them a videotape of his plan, Max takes everything of value and buries himself and the goods somewhere in the world. To claim their inheritance, his sons have to find the tomb. Others are watching and rooting them on so that they can claim the rewards for themselves. One item of significance is a Mayan codex that contains the secret instructions to create medicine from the native jungle plants. This discovery would revolutionize the pharmaceutical industry. Fascinating characters, exotic jungle scenery, and surprising twists make this nonstop thrill ride well worth deciphering." Libr J

Reliquary; [by] Douglas Preston, Lincoln Child. Forge 1997 382p $24.95

ISBN 0-312-86095-1 LC 96-53533

"A Tom Doherty Associates book"

In this sequel to Relic "Margo Green, the curator of the Natural History Museum in New York, rejoins police lieutenant Vincent D'Agosta, FBI agent Pendergast, and famed evolutionist Dr. Frock as they try to solve multiple cases of brutal murders. Their search focuses on the 'mole people' who live deep within the infinite mazes of underground tunnels lying beneath New York City." SLJ

"Although *Reliquary* is a sequel, its exposition carries us easily into the new plot and excites interest in seeing what Preston and Child come up with next, after this yarn's all-loose-ends-tied finale." Booklist

Riptide; [by] Douglas Preston and Lincoln Child. Warner Bks. 1998 417p $25

ISBN 0-446-52336-4 LC 97-23907

"Dr. Malin Hatch is at first reluctant to let the Thalassa Group plunder his Ragged Island, off the coast of Maine, in yet another attempt to reclaim pirate Red Ned Ockham's 17th-century treasure. But its leaders assure him that they have the technology and skill to breach the deadly Water Pit that has claimed the lives of countless treasure hunters. They also have the encrypted diary of the Pit's designer, which, they claim, holds the key to the treasure's reclamation." Libr J

"Machine-gun pacing, startling plot twists and smart use of legend, scientific lore (including cyptanalysis) and the evocative setting carry the day." Publ Wkly

Still life with crows; [by] Douglas Preston and Lincoln Child. Warner Bks. 2003 435p $24.95

ISBN 0-446-53142-1 LC 2002-192401

FBI Agent Pendergast arrives "in tiny Medicine Creek, KS, just in time to investigate a series of gruesome murders. Life in rural Medicine Creek usually revolves around the local turkey-processing plant and growing corn, but all hell breaks loose when a female corpse is found in a clearing in a cornfield, surrounded by a ring of dead crows impaled on arrows." Libr J

Tyrannosaur Canyon. Forge 2005 368p $24.95

ISBN 0-765-31104-6 LC 2005-5171

"A prospector discovers the treasure of his lifetime and takes bullets in the back for his effort. With his dying breath, he gives a journal to innocent bystander Tom Broadbent (the hero of Preston's . . . The Codex) and asks Tom to deliver the information to his daughter. The prospector's killer, of course, wants the ledger, so now Tom and his wife are in mortal danger. Why is the journal so valuable? It contains information leading to the fossilized remains of a complete Tyrannosaurus rex, a scientific discovery worth millions and a lifetime of accolades to the finder. In addition, a mysterious black ops agency wants the skeleton to hide a deadly secret originally discovered on the moon over 30 years ago by the crew of Apollo 17. The truth will shake the foundation of paleontology to its core. Preston's exhilarating and absorbing science-based effort will thrill readers from the first page to the last." Libr J

Preston, Richard

The Cobra event; a novel. Random House 1997 404p $25.95

ISBN 0-679-45714-3 LC 98-106915

"When two completely unrelated people die horrifically in New York City, Alice Austen, a young doctor working for the Centers for Disease Control in Washington, D.C., is called in to investigate. What Austen finds in New York is like nothing she has ever seen; two victims whose symptoms include self-cannibalism and brains that have turned to mush. More victims follow, and soon she realizes that the mystery illness was caused by a manmade virus that spreads as easily as the common cold. Drawing on her findings, a team of government scientists is formed and set up on Governor's Island in the middle of New York Harbor. Their job is to find the person behind the virus and to stop him before he causes a worldwide outbreak." Libr J

"Preston marshals his narrative with sufficient precision to persuade and terrify readers." Publ Wkly

Price, Eugenia

Savannah. Doubleday 1983 595p o.p.

LC 82-45572

The first volume in the author's Savannah quartet; other titles To see your face again (1985); Before darkness falls (1987) and Stranger in Savannah (1989)

This "novel tells the story of a handsome young Yankee, Mark Browning, who finds a secure place for himself in the gracious society of Savannah, Georgia, in the early 19th century. Browning, befriended by a merchant named Robert Mackay, is taken into the man's mercantile firm, and soon finds himself in love with Mackay's virtuous wife. The situation is further complicated by Mark's growing attraction to his first cousin, Caroline Cameron, and his relationship with a blackguard uncle, Osmund Kott, who may or may not be on the edge of true repentance and conversion to Christianity." Publ Wkly

Price, Nancy, 1925-

Sleeping with the enemy. Simon & Schuster 1987 c1986 332p o.p.

LC 86-29778

"Battered women don't usually have the courage of Sara Burney. Desperate and bruised physically and emotionally, she evolves a plan to flee her obsessive hus-

Price, Nancy, 1925-—*Continued*

band. She knows he will come after her and kill her eventually, so that mere flight will offer only temporary reprieve. So she decides to 'get lost.' She assumes a new identity, a new look, and seeks respite and a new life hundreds of miles from their home in Massachusetts. . . . Price has written an absorbing tale and her language has a sensual quality that transports the reader into her panoramas that affect all the senses." West Coast Rev Books

Price, Reynolds, 1933-

Blue Calhoun. Atheneum Pubs. 1992 373p $23

ISBN 0-689-12146-6 LC 91-22877

This novel depicts circumstances in the life of "Blue (short for Bluford) Calhoun, a 65-year-old salesman in a music store in Raleigh. . . . The tale that Blue has to tell takes the form of a lengthy epistle addressed to his teenage granddaughter, who blames him for failing to prevent the suicide of her father. In his attempt to win her understanding and 'mercy,' Blue ranges over the main events in his life since 1956, the year when, at the age of 35, he falls in love with a 16-year-old girl named Luna Absher." N Y Times Book Rev

"Price is in top form here, forcing us to wrestle with Blue even as he wrestles with himself, portraying his anguish in painfully clear, clean prose that captures perfectly the rhythms of the South and of the human heart." Libr J

The collected stories. Atheneum Pubs. 1993 625p $25

ISBN 0-689-12147-4 LC 92-36807

Contents: Full day; The Warrior Princess Ozimba; The enormous door; A told secret; Watching her die; Serious need; The company of the dead; A sign of blood; Rapid eye movements; Twice; Washed feet; Sleeping and waking; Morning places; Michael Egerton; The last news; The anniversary; Invitation; My parents, winter 1926; The knowledge of my mother's coming death; Life for life; Design for a tomb; Endless mountains; Long night; A new stretch of woods; The last of a long correspondence; Deeds of light; Walking lessons; His final mother; This wait; The happiness of others; A dog's death; Scars; Waiting at Dachau; The golden child; Truth and lies; Breath; Toward home; The names and faces of heroes; Nine hours alone; Night and silence; Summer games; A chain of love; Two useful visits; A final account; Uncle Grant; Troubled sleep; Good night; An evening meal; Bess Waters; An early Christmas

"Many of the characters in these magical, quietly revelatory, death-obsessed tales are transformed by chance encounters, in settings that include Price's native south but also range throughout the world." Publ Wkly

The foreseeable future. Atheneum Pubs. 1991 253p $21.95

ISBN 0-689-12110-5 LC 90-45463

Contents: The fare to the moon; The foreseeable future; Back before day

"In his eloquent and distinctive voice, Price reveals in each of these stories how love and memory, loss and redemption, and essential human goodness 'prop' us up and allow us to move forward into an uncertain future." Libr J

The good priest's son. Scribner 2005 278p $26

ISBN 0-7432-5400-7 LC 2004-65383

"On September 11, 2001, Mabry Kincaid—a fiftyish art conservator—is flying home after a much-needed rest in Rome and Paris. Halfway across the Atlantic, his plane is diverted from New York to Nova Scotia. Two days later, when the United States has recovered sufficiently from the attack on the World Trade Center, Mabry discovers that his downtown New York loft is uninhabitable. He flies south to North Carolina instead to visit his aged father. A widowed Episcopalian priest, Tasker Kincaid has been injured in a recent fall and is cared for by live-in Audrey Thornton, an African-American divinity student at Duke University, and her grown son, Marcus, an ambitious painter." Publisher's note

This novel is "thematically rich—indeed, it is rather bowed by its meanings—and features many pleasing Southern voices, along with an impeccable depiction of the region's deep-rooted traditions." N Y Times Book Rev

Kate Vaiden. Atheneum Pubs. 1986 306p o.p.

LC 85-48143

In this novel, Kate Vaiden tells her own story "to justify herself to a son she abandoned as a baby and hasn't seen in 40 years. The decisive event in Kate's life occurred in 1938, when she was 11. Her father inexplicably murdered her mother and killed himself, leaving a letter that Kate doesn't read until many years later. . . . [Kate] is lovingly raised by a taciturn aunt and uncle with a secret sorrow she gradually learns: their homosexual son, Walter, ran off 12 years earlier with another local boy. When Walter comes home on a visit, he befriends Kate, who later runs off to live with him and has a child by his lover." Newsweek

"Mr. Price's successful creation of a female voice may be a tour de force, but it never feels like a showy ventriloquial act. Instead, Kate is a wholly convincing girl and a not improbable woman." N Y Times Book Rev

The promise of rest. Scribner 1995 353p o.p.

LC 94-48086

Conclusion of the author's Mayfield family trilogy begun with The surface of earth (1975) and The source of light (1981). "Wade Mayfield, great-grandson of the woman whose runaway marriage in 1903 set the family's tragic 20th-century history in motion, is dying of AIDS. Long estranged from his parents (his black lover, Wyatt Bondurant, hated them as complicit beneficiaries of the South's racist past), Wade comes home to North Carolina in April 1993, after Wyatt's death. His mother, Ann, has left his father, Hutchins, claiming that her husband has shut her out of his life for years. Meanwhile, Hutchins's lifelong friend and onetime lover, Strawson Stuart, makes his own reproaches about Hutchins's inability to fully accept love. Extended family and friends gather around the dying Wade, grappling with matters as general as America's poisoned racial heritage and as intimate as the Mayfield legacy." Publ Wkly

Roxanna Slade. Scribner 1998 301p $25

ISBN 0-684-83292-5 LC 97-39167

This is the "story of a women's life, told in her own precise and feisty voice. Roxanna Slade has not led what would be considered an outwardly distinguished life, a life she clearly recalls now in her 90s. Certainly not in

Price, Reynolds, 1933-—*Continued*
her dotage, for she is still as alert as ever, Roxanna recounts the contents of her long decades on earth." Booklist

"Many of the virtues that have endeared Price . . . to readers are present in this story of a North Carolina woman and several generations of her family. Price's musically cadenced, nostalgia-washed prose, plangent with portent and loss and vibrant with imagery, is as beguiling as ever. His picture of life in the South a century ago is imbued with candor about customs and attitudes—especially those concerning women and race." Publ Wkly

The tongues of angels. Atheneum Pubs. 1990 192p $17.95
ISBN 0-689-12093-1 LC 89-37427

This novel focuses on "Bridge Boatner, a famous painter who looks back at the summer of 1954, when he was a counselor at a camp in North Carolina; and Raphael Noren, a prematurely wise, otherworldly 14-year-old who was a camper there that summer. . . . [The two] had come to the camp to find a way to cope with the sudden death of a parent. . . . Boatner finds himself as an artist that summer, producing a painting that stands the test of time." Time

"As much prey to mutual irritation as to esteem, they worry and argue their way—the 14-year-old boy and the 21-year-old man—through the 10-week intimacy of the camp, cut of from so-called civilization and therefore free, in terms they hold in common, to aim beyond the commonplace: into myth, art, ritual and pain." N Y Times Book Rev

Price, Richard, 1949-

Clockers. Houghton Mifflin 1992 599p o.p.
LC 91-43318

The author "divides his narrative between two main characters: Strike (a k a Ronald Dunham), the black crew leader of a small-time group of cocaine dealers—the 'clockers' of the title—in the slums of northern New Jersey, and Rocco Klein, an experienced but disillusioned white homicide detective who's about to take early retirement. The stories of Rocco and Strike are pulled together when Strike's by-all-accounts paragon brother, Victor, confesses to an apparently routine drug murder and Rocco, refusing to believe Victor guilty, becomes convinced that he's taking the heat for his brother." N Y Times Book Rev

This is "an incredible course in urban street life, particularly the crack culture." Booklist

Freedomland. Broadway Bks. 1998 546p $25
ISBN 0-7679-0024-3 LC 98-10527

A novel set in an inner-city neighborhood in northern New Jersey. "Through a haze of shock and exhaustion, a young white woman manages to tell a disjointed story of being carjacked by a black man outside the Henry T. Armstrong housing projects; she claims her four-year-old son was asleep in the backseat. Asthmatic black policeman Lorenzo 'Big Daddy' Council catches the case and can sense the political firestorm brewing in the background. . . . As the frantic search for the boy ensues, the media, project residents, a neighboring majority white police district, black activists, and a zealous missing-children's group all converge on the scene, each with their own agendas." Booklist

"Price's characters are, as usual, dead-on, and his eye for unflinchingly capturing humans at their very best—and very worst—is unrivaled." Libr J

Samaritan. Knopf 2003 377p $25
ISBN 0-375-41115-1

"Ray Mitchell, an Emmy-nominated TV writer who returned to teach pro bono at his old high school amid the projects of Dempsy, New Jersey, has had his head bashed in. Nerese Ammons, a cop 10 weeks from retirement, takes the case personally because of a good turn Ray did her when they were children. But Ray, deteriorating in the hospital, doesn't want to tell her who attacked him." Booklist

"'Samaritan' is two books. One belongs to Ray, the other to Nerese, a division emphasized by the use of cuts and jumps. Chapters recounting Ray's return to Dempsy are interspersed with scenes fo Nerese's investigation of the whos and whys of this return. The structure, though obtrusive, does its job, bringing stereoscopic depth to the events." N Y Times Book Rev

Pritchett, V. S. (Victor Sawdon), 1900-1997

Complete collected stories. Random House 1991 c1990 1219p o.p.
LC 90-47478

First published 1990 in the United Kingdom

Contents: Sense of humour; A spring morning; Main road; The evils of Spain; Handsome is as handsome does; The aristocrat; The two brothers; X-ray; The scapegoat; Eleven o'clock; The upright man; Page and monarch; Miss Baker; You make your own life; The sailor; The lion's den; The saint; It may never happen; Pocock passes; The Oedipus complex; The voice; Aunt Gertrude; Many are disappointed; The chestnut tree; The ape; The clerk's tale; The fly in the ointment; The night worker; Double divan; The landlord; Passing the ball; A story of Don Juan; The ladder; The satisfactory; Things as they are; The sniff; The collection; The wheelbarrow; The fall; When my girl comes home; The necklace; Just a little more; The snag; On the scent; Citizen; The key to my heart; Noisy flushes the birds; Noisy in the doghouse; Blind love; The nest builder; A debt of honour; The cage birds; The skeleton; The speech; The liars; Our oldest friend; The honeymoon; The chain-smoker; The last throw; The Camberwell beauty; The diver; Did you invite me?; The rescue; The marvellous girl; The spree; Our wife; The lady from Guatemala; On the edge of the cliff; A family man; The Spanish bed; The wedding; The worshippers; The vice-consul; The accompanist; Tea with Mrs. Bittell; The fig tree; A careless widow; Cocky Olly; A trip to the seaside; Things; A change of policy; The image trade

(ed) The Oxford book of short stories. See The Oxford book of short stories

Pritchett, Victor Sawdon *See* Pritchett, V. S. (Victor Sawdon), 1900-1997

Prize stories: The O. Henry Awards. Anchor Bks. (NY)
ISSN 0079-5453

Prize stories: The O. Henry Awards—*Continued*

First collection, published in 1919 with title: O. Henry Memorial Award prize stories, was edited by Blanche C. Williams

This annual anthology of outstanding short stories by American authors includes contributions by such authors as John Updike, Joyce Carol Oates, Alice Adams, Alice Munro, Louise Erdrich, Andrea Barrett, and T. Coraghessan Boyle

Pronzini, Bill

Bleeders; a "Nameless Detective" novel. Carroll & Graf Pubs. 2002 213p o.p.

ISBN 0-7867-0942-1

"Hired to safeguard a blackmailed husband's final payoff, Nameless is almost killed and his client is murdered. In addition, the money, the husband, the husband's mistress and a vicious killer all go missing. Nameless has patrolled the mean streets of San Francisco for a long time, and nobody knows them better or performs the traditional PI role better." Publ Wkly

Blue lonesome. Walker & Co. 1995 207p o.p.

LC 95-13049

"Two quotes that connect hell, the devil, and loneliness foreshadow the suicide of a woman known as Ms. Lonesome. The often-solitary James Messenger sets out in search of the aloof woman's identity even though he spoke to her only once. He finds himself in Beulah, Nevada, a harsh countryside dominated by embittered people, violent murder, and mulish sensibilities. Pronzini skillfully handles Messenger's quest. He uses jazz to accompany changes in mood, but is not verbose." Libr J

Bones. St. Martin's Press 1985 196p o.p.

LC 85-1708

"The 'Nameless Detective' is hired by Michael Kiskadon to find out why his father, pulp writer Harmon Crane, committed suicide 35 years ago. This proves to be a locked room puzzle. The twisting plot eventually turns up three murders. This is a crisply written mystery with perfect pacing; new clues are cunningly placed so that reader interest is constantly piqued." Libr J

Crazybone; a "nameless detective" novel. Carroll & Graf Pubs. 2000 197p o.p.

ISBN 0-7867-0730-5

Pronzini's nameless detective "lumbers down the San Francisco Peninsula to a private enclave of wooded estates and walled country clubs to find out why a grieving widow has refused a $50,000 insurance settlement for the accidental death of her husband. The look of @raw terror' on the woman's face when he confronts her . . . suggests that she might have something to hide, and the nameless hero does a good job of ferreting out her secret. But the real fun comes from watching the old war horse plod through a hostile social environment, observing the swells at their selfish pursuits and making them regret every condescending sneer they threw in his face." N Y Times Book Rev

Deadfall. St. Martin's Press 1986 212p o.p.

LC 86-3669

In this 'Nameless Detective' novel, the "San Francisco private eye is on a stakeout on a quiet residential street, waiting to repossess a deadbeat's car. He hears a gunshot coming from one of the houses on the street, goes in, and finds a mortally wounded man crawling from room to room. Lawyer Leonard Purcell's dying word is 'deadfall.' Does his death have any connection with the death of his wheeler-dealer brother six months before? No one is better at finding links between tricky homicides than 'Nameless,' and no one is more poetic in relating the details of a case: his crisp language renders a blood-spattered room almost beautiful." Booklist

Hardcase; a "Nameless Detective" mystery. Delacorte Press 1995 215p o.p.

LC 95-5723

This mystery "opens as the California PI, approaching 60, marries his longtime girlfriend, Kerry. After a civil ceremony marked by his nervous clumsiness, Nameless takes on a client who wants him to find her birthparents. Melanie Ann Aldrich has just discovered that she was adopted and is sure there's a reason her adoptive parents, who are deceased, kept this information from her. Nameless fairly quickly identifies the woman's birthparents, but that's just the beginning." Publ Wkly

Illusions; a "Nameless Detective" novel. Carroll & Graf Pubs. 1997 243p o.p.

LC 97-4274

"Shaken by the suicide of his former partner and onetime best friend, a pathetic figure whose life had shrunk to 'drinking, brooding, building his own private gallows day by day,' Nameless throws himself into a job for a Santa Fe businessman who wants to contact his former wife. The woman is easily found; but before the shamus can cash his check, a second suicide delivers another body blow to his code of ethics and deposits another load of guilt on his conscience. . . . The parallel investigations offer prime examples of Pronzini's ace plotting techniques . . . and if you can take the mood swings, Nameless is a good man to walk you through the noir landscape." N Y Times Book Rev

In an evil time. Walker & Co. 2001 266p $23.95

ISBN 0-8027-3353-0 LC 00-49996

"Jack Hollis, a family man and law-abiding citizen, is ready to cross the line. His daughter, Angela, is being stalked by her abusive second husband, David Rakubian, a successful personal-injury lawyer in San Francisco. In fact, it's Rakubian's knowledge of the law's limitations that makes him so dangerous to Angela and her toddler son. Jack has weighed the options and sees Rakubian's death as the only way out for his daughter. . . . [Pronzini] has fashioned a nail-biter out of the issue of domestic abuse and the law's inability to deal with it effectively." Booklist

Nightcrawlers; a nameless detective novel. Forge 2005 301p $24.95

ISBN 0-7653-0931-9 LC 2004-56323

"A Tom Doherty Associates book"

"The 'Nameless' detective is doing his best to settle into semiretirement after making his longtime assistant, Tamara Corbin, a partner in the agency and adding Jake Runyon, a former cop, as a field operative. However, some cases require Nameless' attention. Thugs are roaming the streets of San Francisco's Castro district, attacking gay men. Runyon's son's lover is one of the thug's victims, prompting Runyon and Nameless to investigate.

Pronzini, Bill—*Continued*
Meanwhile Tamara, on a routine surveillance of a credit deadbeat, sees her subject carry something into his house that raises the hair on the back of her neck. The long-running Nameless series continues to evolve. With the novels no longer exclusively first-person narratives by Nameless, parallel plotlines have been introduced from multiple points of view, giving readers a chance to view Nameless as others see him. And, as always, the novels are never just about crime." Booklist

Nothing but the night. Walker & Co. 1999 260p $23.95
ISBN 0-8027-3330-1 LC 98-43720
Until their final, violent "confrontation, Cameron Gallagher and Nick Hendryx pursue their lives on separate trajectories. A prosperous California vintner . . . Cam is tormented by his childhood memory of the night his father killed his mother. A trucker whose sanity took a nose dive when a hit-and-run accident left his young wife in a coma, Nick rides the night with a tattered police sketch of the driver, looking for vengeance. It's a dark and twisty road to the big smashup, but these characters travel well." NY Times Book Rev

Quarry; a "Nameless Detective" mystery. Delacorte Press 1992 216p o.p.
LC 91-15284
In this novel the "Nameless Detective hunts for a methodical, brutal stranger who is pursuing withdrawn Grady Haas, 31, daughter of rancher Arlo Haas, the detective's old friend. Secretive Grady won't tell why she has suddenly left her job as an insurance adjuster specializing in marine claims and returned to the Salinas Valley. Nameless finds that her San Francisco apartment has been thoroughly tossed. All he has to go on are the three claims Grady had been investigating and her ex-boyfriend's savage beating by a stranger seeking Grady's whereabouts." Publ Wkly
"Pronzini can get a shade overwrought . . . but his detective is a welcome journey into yesterday, where a shamus could bend the law and not have to agonize about it for too long afterwards." Booklist

Sentinels; a "Nameless Detective" mystery. Carroll & Graf Pubs. 1996 213p o.p.
LC 96-21602
Nameless "leaves San Francisco to try to find Helen McDowell's missing daughter, Allison, a University of Oregon student who was driving home to visit and bringing with her a surprise. But she and her surprise, a black boyfriend, had car trouble in the tiny town of Creekside, Calif., on the Oregon border. Allison had called her mother, saying they should be on their way next day, but she never arrived." Publ Wkly

Spook; a nameless detective novel. Carroll & Graf Pubs. 2003 233p $25
ISBN 0-7867-1086-1
"The case seems simple enough. Spook, a homeless street person, becomes a fixture at a local business; its employees provide assistance as needed for the obviously mentally disturbed individual. He is murdered in an especially heinous assault. His unofficial 'family' wants San Francisco private investigator 'Nameless' to learn his real identity. Nameless hands the case over to his newly hired field operative, Jake Runyon, a former Seattle cop. . . . A fascinating entry in a series that continues to redefine noir fiction even as it honors its roots." Booklist

Step to the graveyard easy. Walker & Co. 2002 165p $21.95 o.p.
ISBN 0-8027-3375-1 LC 2001-55914
"Matt Cape is 35 and stuck in a rut: when his wife catches him in bed with another woman, he quits his job and takes to the road, leaving his old life (or lack thereof) behind. He heads south, then west, eventually landing in San Francisco, where he is fleeced in a card game by Boone Judson and his sidekick, Tanya. Cape gets his and the other players' money back, along with some mysterious photographs. He returns the money to its owners and follows the cardsharps to Lake Tahoe, where he also tracks down the people in the photos and warns them that they may be in danger." Publ Wkly
"Compelling modern noir with a thought-provoking conclusion." Booklist

A wasteland of strangers. Walker & Co. 1997 257p $22.95
ISBN 0-8027-3301-8 LC 96-50927
"Beneath the surface in the northern California resort community of Pomo swirls a viper's nest of desire, jealousy, loneliness, and crime. When a sexual assault occurs, the obvious suspect is an outsider, John Faith; after all, the sheriff doesn't like Faith's interest in a sexy local widow he fancies himself. Neither does a boozy reporter, who launches a yellow-journalism campaign against the outsider. When the widow is murdered, the town explodes." Booklist
"The story fairly tears along to the jolting climax. Even after everyone has his or her say in the epilogue, readers still don't know John Faith's secrets. But that mystery is more haunting than maddening. Pronzini's . . . story is a gem." Publ Wkly
(jt. auth) Muller, M. Beyond the grave

Prose, Francine, 1947-

Blue angel; a novel. HarperCollins Pubs. 2000 314p $25
ISBN 0-06-019541-X LC 99-40564
This novel "charts the downward spiral of a creative writing professor caught up in a sexual harassment scandal. Ten years ago, Ted Swenson wrote a major novel about growing up with a crazy father who later killed himself. Now Swenson's blocked on a new novel with a contrived plot and hasn't written anything in years. An autobiographical writer in the throes of a mid-life crisis, he feels he's suffocating in his comfortable, boring job at a small New England college, stuck with a predictable wife, a sullen daughter, and a life that offers him nothing to write about. So he becomes entranced by his most talented student, Angela, a girl with numerous facial piercings who can spin a page-burning novel out of her imagination." Libr J
An "ironic gloss on Von Sternberg's tragedy of erotic abasement. . . . Prose's retelling focuses less on the ridiculous and self-destructive behavior of the professor . . . than on the far more laughable (and hazardous) rigidity of the politically correct behavior codes governing his tiny Vermont campus." New Yorker

Prose, Francine, 1947-—*Continued*

A changed man; a novel; Francine Prose. HarperCollins Publishers 2005 421p $24.95

ISBN 0-06-019674-2 LC 2004-47448

A "satire of liberal pieties, the radical right and the fund-raising world. The 'changed man' of the title is Vincent Nolan, a 32-year-old tattooed ex-skinhead who appears one morning in the New York offices of World Brotherhood Watch, a foundation headed by Meyer Maslow, a Holocaust survivor. Vincent declares that he has had a personal conversion (never mind that it was triggered by a heavy dose of Ecstasy) and wants to work with the foundation to 'save guys like me from becoming guys like me.' Meyer takes Vincent on faith—and convinces Bonnie Kalen, the foundation's fundraiser, to put Vincent up in the suburban home she shares with her two sons, Max, 12, and Danny, 16. Prose tears into this unusual premise with the piercing wit that has become her trademark." Publ Wkly

Household saints. St. Martin's Press 1981 227p o.p.

LC 80-29116

"When Joseph Santangelo, the sausagemaker, wins the bride, Catherine, in a pinochle game, he sets in motion a pattern of events laced with ancient Mediterranean customs, superstition and religion that affect the women in his life. In addition to Catherine, there is his mother, a nonstop oracle of doom, and his Americanized daughter who seeks and perhaps finds Jesus in obsessive domesticity. A skillful fabulist, [the author] . . . not only captures the domestic scenes and smells of Little Italy but allows her 'naifs' to unfold in recognizable earthiness and warmth as they confront life's mysteries." Publ Wkly

Hunters and gatherers. Farrar, Straus & Giroux 1995 247p o.p.

LC 95-3569

This novel's "protagonist, Martha, is a relentlessly literal-minded person (she's a fact checker at a chic women's magazine) whose emotional life is a mess, and who takes up, in the wake of a failed romance, with a group of zany women who have allied themselves with a contemporary Goddess cult. Their leader, Isis Moonwagon, is a sweepingly compassionate but accident-prone former academic who sees visions but has to fight hard to keep her often brutally cynical troops in line." Publ Wkly

This is a "delightful satire, . . . irreverent, funny, critical, compassionate. . . . Prose brilliantly captures the absurdities and hypocrisies inherent in such groups. The women obsess about wombs, menstrual periods and the glories of being female. Yet separatism does not remove the worst dynamics between women." Women's Rev Books

Primitive people. Farrar, Straus & Giroux 1992 227p o.p.

LC 91-28692

"Simone is an illegal immigrant from Haiti, working as an au pair for a family in upstate New York. There, she learns about American life from the shallow, self-centered 'primitive people' around her: her employer Rosemary, who is camping out with her withdrawn children in the ancestral home of her estranged husband; Rosemary's brittle and caustic best friend Shelly, an interior decorator; and Shelly's narcissistic, sexually ambiguous boyfriend Kenny, who owns a children's hair salon." Libr J

This "comedy of manners has a serious purpose but it is never earnest and provides a lot of shrewd and malicious fun. . . . The author finds it hard to write a dull sentence. Her gargoyles are sometimes gruesome. They are also witty and she has a perfect ear for the chatter of this particular set of rich Americans." Economist

Proulx, Annie

Accordian crimes; [by] E. Annie Proulx. Scribner 1996 381p o.p.

LC 96-16299

"Following successive owners of an accordion—from its creator, an Italian immigrant, who was lynched in Louisiana in 1891, to some fatherless black children living on the edge of a noxious landfill in 1991—this twelve-car pileup of a book brims with the sort of disasters you read about on the inside pages of the paper." New Yorker

Bad dirt; Wyoming stories 2; Annie Proulx. Scribner 2004 219p $25

ISBN 0-7432-5799-5 LC 2004-56530

Contents: The hellhole; The Indian wars refought; The trickle down effect; What kind of furniture would Jesus pick?; The old badger game; Man crawling out of trees; The contest; The Wamsutter wolf; Summer of the hot tubs; Dump junk; Florida rental

"This poignant and often humorous collection is packed with well-drawn characters that linger in the mind and heart. As expected, the Wyoming landscape is the enduring character in each story, silently wielding its magical and brutal power." Libr J

Close range; Wyoming stories; watercolors by William Matthews. Scribner 1999 283p il $23.50

ISBN 0-684-85221-7 LC 98-56066

Contents: The half-skinned steer; The mud below; 55 miles to the gas pump; The bunchgrass edge of the world; A lonely coast; Job history; Pair of spurs; People in Hell just want a drink of water; The governors of Wyoming; The blood bay; Brokeback Mountain

"Geography, splendid and terrible, is a tutelary deity to the characters in 'Close Range': hardpan ranchers, battered cowpokes and bull riders, bar girls and bar brawlers. Their lives are a futile uphill struggle conducted as a downhill, out-of-control tearaway. Proulx writes of them in a prose that is violent and impacted and mastered just at the point where, having gone all the way to the edge, it is about to go over." N Y Times Book Rev

Postcards; by E. Annie Proulx. Scribner 1992 308p il o.p.

LC 91-25089

"Postcards are the only communication between Loyal Blood and the poor, hardworking farm family he leaves behind in Vermont. The secret Loyal carries with him—the accidental killing of his girlfriend, Billy—is revealed in the first pages, and, thereafter, as he prospects for uranium, traps coyotes, or digs for dinosaur bones, his messages continue to arrive home from across the U.S., long after his father has died and his brother, sister, and mother have moved away." Booklist

"Ms. Proulx's expansion of the concept of postcards is what transforms a rambling tale into a minimalist saga.

Proulx, Annie—*Continued*

. . . Story makes this novel compelling; technique makes it beautiful. What makes 'Postcards' significant is that Ms. Proulx uses both story and technique to make real the history of post-World War II America." N Y Times Book Rev

The shipping news. Scribner 1993 337p o.p.
LC 92-30315

The author tells "the story of a washed-up newspaperman who decides to resettle in the Newfoundland town of his ancestors—bringing with him an elderly aunt and two young daughters." Libr J

The author "blends Newfoundland argot, savage history, impressively diverse characters, fine descriptions of weather and scenery, and comic horseplay without ever lessening the reader's interest in Quoyle's progress from bumbling outsider to capable journalist." Atlantic

That old ace in the hole; a novel. Scribner 2002 361p $26

ISBN 0-684-81307-6 LC 2002-30462

This novel's "hero, Bob Dollar, a decent sort who was abandoned at 8, is sent by his company to Woolybucket, Tex., to scout locations for factory hog farms, but is soon smitten with the high, flat country, the locals and their tales of stubborn ranchers, plagues of locusts and family farms undone by corporate greed." N Y Times Book Rev

Proust, Marcel, 1871-1922

The captive
In Proust, M. The captive [and] The fugitive
In Proust, M. Remembrance of things past p1-422

The captive [and] The fugitive; translated by C.K. Scott Moncrieff & Terence Kilmartin; revised by D.J. Enright. Modern Lib. 1993 957p (In search of lost time, v5) $24.95

ISBN 0-679-42477-6 LC 93-15168

Sequel to Sodom and Gomorrah

Original French edition, 1923

In The captive "Albertine is living in the narrator's Paris home, where he attempts to keep complete watch on her activities. The Verdurins provoke a scandalous rupture between Morel and Charlus. Albertine suddenly flees, just as the narrator is ready to dismiss her. [In the fugitive] the narrator seeks the return of Albertine, but after her death he observes the gradual encroachment of oblivion on grief until, on a trip to Venice, he finds his pain completely cured. Gilberte has become the social-climbing Mlle de Forcheville; she marries Saint-Loup, who is now Morel's lover." Merriam-Webster's Ency of Lit

Followed by Time regained

Cities of the plain [variant title: Sodom and Gomorrah]
In Proust, M. Remembrance of things past p623-1169

The complete short stories of Marcel Proust; compiled and translated by Joachim Neugroschel; foreword by Roger Shattuck. Cooper Sq. Pubs. 2001 201p $25.95

ISBN 0-8154-1136-7 LC 00-65739

Contents: The death of Baldassare Silvande, Viscount of Sylvania; Violante or high society; Fragments of commedia dell'Arte; Social ambitions and musical tastes of Bouvard and Pécuchet; The melancholy summer of Madame de Breyves; Portraits of painters and composers; A young girl's confession; A dinner in high society; Regrets, reveries the color of time; The end of jealousy; Norman things; Memory; Portrait of Madame X.; Before the night; Another memory; The indifferent man

This collection contains Proust's "first literary endeavor, 'Pleasures and Days,' translated into English for the first time in 50 years, along with six additional stories, never before seen in English. . . . Delicately translated by Neugroschel . . . these early musings are priceless, insightful venturing into the mind of a maturing virtuoso." Booklist

The fugitive [variant title: The sweet cheat gone]
In Proust, M. The captive [and] The fugitive
In Proust, M. Remembrance of things past p425-706

The Guermantes way; translated by C.K. Scott Moncrieff and Terence Kilmartin; revised by D.J. Enright. Modern Lib. 1993 834p (In search of lost time, v3) $23.95

ISBN 0-679-60028-0 LC 92-33975

Sequel to Within a budding grove

Original French edition published 1920-1921

"The narrator, whose family have been tenants in the large Guermantes home in Paris, conducts his laborious ascent to the summit of high society, finally attending the duchesse de Guermantes's reception. He also describes Saint-Loup's passion for the actress and prostitute Rachel, and the death of his own beloved grandmother." Reader's Ency. 4th edition

Followed by Sodom and Gomorrah

also in Proust, M. Remembrance of things past p3-620

Remembrance of things past. Random House 1981 3v o.p.
LC 79-5542

Includes the seven volumes, published separately and entered in this catalog. Volume one and two translated by C. K. Scott Moncrieff and Terence Kilmartin; volume three by C. K. Scott Moncrieff, Terence Kilmartin and Andreas Mayor

Contents: v1: Swann's way; Within a budding grove; v2: The Guermantes way; Cities of the plain; v3: The captive; The fugitive (variant title: The sweet cheat gone); Time regained (variant title: The past recaptured)

This "is the first complete English version of Proust's masterpiece, translated from the definitive 1954 Pléiade edition, Terence Kilmartin has checked the Scott Moncrieff translation (which comprised the first 11 volumes of the English language version and was made from the uneven first French edition) against the impeccable Clarac-Ferre Pléiade edition. The 12th volume, Andreas Mayor's 1970 translation of 'Time Regained' was the only English translation based on the Pléiade edition prior to this one and has been incorporated into it with only minor changes." Libr J

Proust, Marcel, 1871-1922—*Continued*

Sodom and Gomorrah; translated by C.K. Scott Moncrieff and Terence Kilmartin; revised by D.J. Enright. Modern Lib. 1993 747p (In search of lost time, v4) $22.95

ISBN 0-679-60029-9 LC 92-27272

Sequel to The Guermantes way

Original French edition published 1921-1922. Variant title: Cities of the plain

"Marcel again meets Swann at a reception given by the Princesse de Guermantes, a cousin of the Duchesse. Swann is now suffering from a deadly ailment. He is an ardent adherent of Alfred Dreyfus. Swann urges Marcel to write to Gilberte, since she speaks of him frequently. But Gilberte, no longer has any enchantment for Marcel; Albertine again holds his affections. She offers herself to him, but distracted by physical attachments for other owmen, he desires her company only at intervals to titillate his jaded senses. Eventually he is drawn closer to her, but now his suspicion that she is a Lesbian causes him jealousy and endless torment." Haydn. Thesaurus of Book Dig

Followed by The captive

Swann's way; translated by C.K. Scott Moncrieff and Terence Kilmartin; revised by D.J. Enright. Modern Lib. 1992 xx, 615p (In search of lost time, v1) $21.95

ISBN 0-679-60005-1 LC 92-25657

Original French edition, 1913

The first volume of the In search of lost time series "describes in an involved parenthetical style, with a multitude of details, the brilliant society in which the author moved. The 'Marcel' of the story is Proust's own counterpart, and it is through his hypersensitive and critical eye that we examine the tastes, feelings, motives and actions of the characters, most of whom can be identified as real people." Enoch Pratt Free Libr

Followed by Within a budding grove

also in Proust, M. Remembrance of things past p3-462

Time regained; translated by Andreas Mayor and Terence Kilmartin; revised by D.J. Enright. Modern Lib. 1993 749p (In search of lost time, v6) $24.95

ISBN 0-679-42476-8 LC 93-3628

Sequel to The fugitive

Original French edition, 1927

In this final volume of the series "World War I accelerates the kaleidoscopic changes in society. The narrator attends a reception of the new princesse de Guermantes, actually the former Mme Verdurin, and finds most of his acquaintances almost unrecognizable. He has enjoyed three 'privileged moments' of memory, and in contemplating them discovers that his vocation is to be the shaping of his experiences into a literary work of art." Reader's Ency. 4th edition

Time regained [variant title: The past recaptured]

also in Proust, M. Remembrance of things past p709-1107

Within a budding grove; translated by C.K. Scott Moncrieff and Terence Kilmartin; revised by D.J. Enright. Modern Lib. 1992 749p (In search of lost time, v2) $24

ISBN 0-679-60006-X LC 92-25656

Sequel to Swann's way

Original French edition, 1918

"As he grows up, Marcel falls in love with Swann's daughter, Gilberte. It is a deep and poetic attachment, but she gradually tires of him; his ardent nature and his attentions begin to irritate her. Out of wounded pride he avoids her, although he continues his friendly relations with the Swanns. Two years later he feels he is thoroughly cured of his hopeless passion, when he becomes involved with Albertine, a beautiful brunette he meets in Balbec. But he eventually discovers that she is interested only in platonic relations with men, and so he suffers another disappointment." Haydn. Thesaurus of Book Dig

Followed by The Guermantes way

also in Proust, M. Remembrance of things past p465-1018

Puig, Manuel

Kiss of the spider woman; translated from the Spanish by Thomas Colchie. Knopf 1979 281p o.p.

LC 78-14307

Original Spanish edition, 1976

"Mostly consisting of dialogue between two men in an Argentine jail cell, the novel traces the development of their unlikely friendship. Molina is a middle-aged homosexual who passes the long hours in prison by acting out scenes from his favorite movies. Valentin is a young socialist revolutionary, who initially berates Molina for his effeminacy and his lack of political conviction. Sharing the hardships of a six-month prison term, the two eventally forge a strong relationship that becomes sexual. In an ironic role reversal at the end of the novel, Molina dies as a result of his involvement in politics while Valentin escapes the pain of torture by retreating into a dream world." Merriam-Webster's Ency of Lit

Purdy, James, 1923-

In a shallow grave. Arbor House 1975 140p o.p.

ISBN 0-87795-124-4 LC 75-30399

"Garnet Montrose is a man severely disfigured in the war, a modern leper, an often drugged prophet of the disintegration of values. Unwilling to hide in a veteran's hospital, Montrose returns to his home in Virginia. Obsessed with a childhood sweetheart, now the widow Georgina Rance, he devises an elaborate system of correspondence to woo her, depending on his 'applicants' to carry letters to the lady. The relationship with these applicants forms the basis of the book. Quintus Pearch is quiet and mysterious, a wraithlike character who reads to Montrose from abstract tomes and rubs his master's feet with cynical adoration. Potter Daventry is a wild young man with twisted values and a go-for-broke attitude. Daventry courts Georgina for Montrose, then for himself. He marries her and is carried away by a freak storm. The implications are biblical in proportion; Purdy utilizes every subtlety and shading of language to enhance the demented howlings of these three lost souls. Purdy's skill consists of taking the familiar and distorting it; the results are often eerie." Independent Publisher

Purdy, James, 1923-—*Continued*

Malcolm. Farrar Straus and Cudahy 1959 215p o.p.

LC 59-14689

This is, "a bizarre, comic novel of the picaresque, presenting the strange experiences of a 15-year-old boy as in his search for his lost father he wanders through a world of depravity. It was dramatized (1965) by Albee." Oxford Companion to Am Lit. 6th edition

The nephew. Farrar Straus and Cudahy 1960 210p o.p.

LC 60-15672

This novel "tells of the revelations following the death in war of the nephew of a doting spinster, a retired schoolteacher, in a small Midwest town, who decides to write a memorial booklet. She thereby learns more than she wants to about him and about life as she discovers he was a homosexual." Oxford Companion to Am Lit. 6th edition

Pushkin, Aleksandr Sergeevich, 1799-1837

Alexander Pushkin: complete prose fiction; translated with an introduction and notes, by Paul Debreczeny; verse passages translated by Walter Arndt. Stanford Univ. Press 1983 545p $60

ISBN 0-8047-1142-9 LC 81-85450

Included in this volume are the following titles: The blackamoor of Peter the Great; A novel in letters; The tales of the late Ivan Petrovich Belkin; A history of the village of Goriukhino; Roslavlev; Dubrovskii; The Queen of Spades; Kirdzhali; Egyptian nights; and the novel: The captain's daughter

Also included are the following unfinished fictional fragments: The guests were arriving at the dacha; In the corner of a small square; A tale of Roman life; We were spending the evening at Princess D's dacha; Maria Schoning

This collection also contains the non-fictional History of Pugachev (which furnishes historical background for The captain's daughter) and Appendices which contain minor fictional fragments and outlines

"The translations are accurate and graceful and well supported by an ample array of footnotes." Libr J

The captain's daughter
In Pushkin, A. S. Alexander Pushkin: complete prose fiction p266-357

Putney, Mary Jo

A kiss of fate. Ballantine Bks. 2004 340p $23.95

ISBN 0-345-44916-9

"Born into a legendary family of mages known as the Guardians, Gwyneth Owens believes that she has little inherited power. She does, however, have a destiny to fulfill. When the Guardian elders seek to forestall a coming disaster by invoking her Guardian oath and asking her to marry Duncan Macrae, Lord Ballister, the most powerful weather mage in the realm, she cannot honorably refuse. Although they are already attracted to each other, Gwyneth can't forget the single kiss from him that sent alarming visions of destruction flaming through her mind—or the sword that he held in his hand. Intelligent, compelling characters that appeal to both heart and mind, a brilliant blending of history and fantasy, and a beautifully unfolding love relationship combine to produce a magical tale." Libr J

Puzo, Mario, 1920-1999

The family; a novel; completed by Carol Gino. ReganBooks 2001 373p il o.p.

ISBN 0-06-039445-5 LC 2001-31876

"In his final novel, 'The Family' Puzo died in 1999, and this book was completed by his companion, the novelist Carol Gino-he has dipped back into 15th-century Italy to tell the tale of the Borgia family, led by Cardinal Rodrigo Borgia, who became Pope Alexander VI." N Y Times Book Rev

"The saga is lush, full of detail, with characters who manage to be larger than life while seeming entirely realistic. The dialogue is slightly ornmented but never clumsy, and the plot is appropriately epic in scope, mixing fact and fiction seamlessly." Booklist

The godfather. Putnam 1969 446p $24.95

ISBN 0-399-10342-2

This novel focuses on "Vito (Don) Corleone, boss of an important New York City Mafia family. Names, places, crimes have been changed, but the Mafia world remains true to fact. Here is Cosa Nostra: the wars of the competing families; their changing 'business enterprises'; their struggle for power and money; their weapons—graft, guns, spies, violence, murder. A wide variety of characters are colorfully drawn. The Don comes though as a person you will remember." Libr J

The last Don. Random House 1996 482p o.p.

LC 96-3401

"The story opens in 1965, with Don Clericuzio, head of the most powerful Mafia family in the country, deciding to make his enterprises legit. He is looking ahead to his grandchildren's lives, wanting them to enjoy his largesse without the danger inherent in life in the criminal underworld. Zoom—we're transported to the present day and involved in how the don's plans for his family's future are playing out. Hollywood and Las Vegas provide venues for one grandson's attempts, at the expense of another grandson, to undermine the master plan." Booklist

"Mr. Puzo wraps up his intricate plot with the same ingenuity he exhibits throughout this satisfying novel." N Y Times Book Rev

Omerta. Random House 2000 316p o.p.

ISBN 0-375-50254-8 LC 00-28082

In this novel, a Mafia don has been killed by "rivals eager to take over their victim's legal banking empire. His . . . offspring, content with their legitimate careers, want to cash out to their father's killers. But a trusted . . . nephew had promised the old don that the banks would always remain in the family." Time

"Despite its familiar subject matter, the novel—which shuttles among Sicily, England and America—is unpredictable and bracing, but its greatest strength is Puzo's voice, ripe with age and wisdom, as attentive to the scent of lemons and oranges in a Sicilian garden as to a good man's sudden, bloody death. This is pulp raised to art." Publ Wkly

Puzo, Mario, 1920-1999—*Continued*

The Sicilian. Linden Press 1984 410p o.p.
LC 84-17087

This novel "follows the wayward career of one handsome, charismatic renegade, Salvatore (Turi) Guilliano, who creates and works at enhancing his romantic hero image. While the peasants of postwar Sicily adore Turi, the Mafia leaders resent his territorial infringements. . . . After seven years of increasing difficulties, Turi can do no more: with the help of the exiled Michael Corleone (son of the Godfather), he attempts to escape to America." Libr J

"Perhaps only an American writer with deep Sicilian roots and passions could have succeeded as Mr. Puzo has in symbolizing a desperate society through the deeds of a desperado, and in revealing how thin is the line that often separates a freedom-fighter from a terrorist." N Y Times Book Rev

Pye, Michael, 1946-

The pieces from Berlin. Knopf 2002 335p $24
ISBN 0-375-41436-3 LC 2002-20524

This novel "examines the shady life of fictional Lucia Muller-Ross, who spirited vanloads of valuable antiques entrusted to her by their Jewish owners out of Berlin and into Switzerland at the end of WWII. Sixty years later, Lucia is the elderly, proud and respected owner of an antiques shop in Zurich, when Sarah Freeman, a Holocaust survivor, spies in the store's window a table she once owned. Sarah's anguished need for emotional restitution sparks a tragic upheaval in Lucia's family." Publ Wkly

"Pye writes well, and this is a mature novel. It must also be said that it is not an easy novel, in its themes or its structure. A lot of assembling and clue-tracking is required to make sense of the narrative. It's a page-turner, but often one is turning the pages backward to find some lost, or tenuous, connection. Yet this hard work seems appropriate, even necessary." N Y Times Book Rev

Pym, Barbara

An academic question. Dutton 1986 182p o.p.
LC 86-4509

Set in an English provincial university, the story is narrated by Caro Grimstone, the bored young wife of an anthropology professor. Caro "finds a cure for her tedium at a local old-people's home, where she reads to the elderly and becomes a party to her husband's purloining of an important manuscript. This little theft sparks a sequence of rivalries both academic and amorous, and the manuscript itself falls victim to a mini student riot." Publisher's note

"Assembled by Pym's literary executor from two separate, discarded drafts, this tale . . . is slightly more acid than Pym's usual work but bears her characteristic wit." Newsweek

Civil to strangers
In Pym, B. Civil to strangers and other writings p7-170

Civil to strangers and other writings. Dutton 1988 c1987 388p o.p.
LC 87-30341

First published 1987 in the United Kingdom

This is a volume of selections from Pym's unpublished writings. It contains a complete novel, Civil to strangers, written in 1936, sections of three others: Gervase and Flora, Home front novel, and So very secret, written between 1937 and 1941, four short stories (So, some tempestuous morn; Goodbye Balkan capital; The Christmas visit; Across a crowded room) and a radio talk

"We are not often given the chance to witness a writer's struggle to find a voice. But this 'last sheaf,' blemishes and all, shows us how very hard Barbara Pym worked for the voice she eventually found." N Y Times Book Rev

Excellent women. Dutton 1978 c1952 256p o.p.
LC 78-19877

First published 1952 in the United Kingdom

"Mildred Lathbury, 30ish, a spinster, a clergyman's daughter, is an excellent woman, one who, with no life of her own to speak of, finds herself somewhat unwillingly a part of the lives of others. Her days are made up of small things—church, flowers, dinner with the bachelor vicar and his sister, brief encounters with neighbors. . . . Pym's singular world is a lonely, bittersweet familiar place. She travels it with rueful wit, views the human landscape with a wise, sharp, compassionate eye." Publ Wkly

A few green leaves. Dutton 1980 250p o.p.
LC 80-18905

This novel is set in an "Oxfordshire village. The cast of characters includes Emma Howick, an anthropologist who records her observations of the behavior of the local inhabitants; Thomas Dagnall, a clergyman more interested in researching past burial customs than in attending to the welfare of his flock; and Miss Lickerish, an elderly eccentric who shares her cottage with hedgehogs." Libr J

"All the people in A Few Green Leaves are completely realistic: the sort of people we meet every day of our lives and never particularly notice. . . . Miss Pym's art endows them with a significance which they could never possess in life." Times Lit Suppl

Jane and Prudence. Dutton 1981 222p o.p.
LC 81-68399

First published 1953 in the United Kingdom

"Jane is the somewhat scatterbrained wife of a country vicar; Prudence, once her student at Oxford, works at a 'vague cultural organization' in London, where she alternately revels in and despairs over her unrequited passion for the rather dreary little man who is her employer. As she goes about doing 'those tasks in the parish that seem within her powers,' Jane knows she really is unsuited to be a clergyman's wife—she somehow never seems to have the right money for the collection plate—but she does love Nicholas. And in her good-hearted, if usually ineffectual, way she tries to look after Prudence too, hoping to supply a suitable man for her younger friend." Libr J

Quartet in autumn. Dutton 1978 c1977 218p o.p.
LC 78-58498

First published 1977 in the United Kingdom

This novel "follows the lives and thoughts of four elderly single people on the verge of retirement, in a society that has no time for them but relegates them to the impersonal care of the Welfare State. Here Pym achieves something of a tour de force, showing, with wit and compassion, how ordinary quirky acts of impulsive kindness and human feeling make the difference between despair and hope." Libr J

Pym, Barbara—*Continued*

The sweet dove died. Dutton 1979 c1978 208p o.p.

LC 78-74024

First published 1978 in the United Kingdom

"Leonora Eyre is single, beautiful, fastidious, slightly affected, more than slightly vain. Approaching 50, she attracts a widowed antique dealer, Humphrey, whom she decides to bypass for his 24-year-old nephew, James. . . . Leonora asks, she thinks, no more than the pleasure of James's company, but [then tries] . . . to eliminate her rivals, first a feckless young woman named Phoebe, then a more formidable foe, an American homosexual who plays power games more openly and ruthlessly than Leonora can." Newsweek

"Pym's extraordinary vision of an ordinary world wherein she details the intricacies of loneliness, the ditherings of hesitating souls, the comedies of errors, sexual and asexual makes this a little masterpiece." Publ Wkly

An unsuitable attachment. Dutton 1982 256p o.p.

LC 82-70741

"The world of which Pym writes is the Anglican parish with its attractive young vicar; his wife, overly devoted to her cat; the unmarried sister-in-law and her garish dress; the veterinarian and his sister; the shy anthropologist. 'An unsuitable attachment' refers to that formed between John, a young, sometime actor, and Ianthe, an older librarian." Libr J

"The bygone mysteries of the Church of England and the lost snobberies of empire return as ghostly and gently comic echoes of themselves in the habits and pretensions of Barbara Pym's people, who, like the good antiques that furnish their rented bed-sitters . . . are no longer quite appropriate to the present day." N Y Times Book Rev

Pynchon, Thomas

The crying of lot 49. Lippincott 1966 183p o.p.

"Oedipa Maas becomes a coexecutor of the estate of her former multi-millionaire lover, Pierce Inverarity. She becomes involved in tracking down the significance of a geometric symbol that appears to have some connection with the existence of an ancient, revolutionary mail service. In this search, she meets a strange assortment of characters, loses her husband, her psychiatrist (named Hilarious!), and her lover. The author aims his arrows at many of those phenomena that have turned people into things. Among his targets are rock 'n' roll (a group called 'The Paranoids'), right-wing extremists, and a strange group called Inamorati Anonymous." Shapiro. Fic for Youth. 3d edition

Gravity's rainbow. Viking 1973 760p o.p.

The antihero of this novel "is Tyrone Slothrop, an American lieutenant stationed in London during the Blitz. . . . The Lieutenant becomes the equipment of PISCES (Psychological Intelligence Schemes for Expediting Surrender) when his bizarre gift is discovered: Slothrop erections anticipate German rocket launchings. . . . In his desperate attempts to avoid being taken over as a pure instrument, Slothrop runs for it, from London to the Riviera to Berlin, pursued by Furles disguised as Baggy-pants comedians." Atlantic

"Fiction allows at last what was forbidden to the original suffering poets and novelists of 1914-18—the utmost in obscene description, the limit of masochistic pornography. If 'Gravity's Rainbow' is often nauseating it is in a good cause. This is the war book to end them all." Burgess. 99 Novels

Mason & Dixon. Holt & Co. 1997 773p $27.50

ISBN 0-8050-3758-6 LC 97-6467

"From historical odds and ends and the Field Journal they left behind, Pynchon re-imagines Mason and Dixon before, during and after the four-plus years, 1763-1767, they took to draw their 244-mile-long line through the American wilderness, dividing the proprietorships of the Penns of Pennsylvania and the Calverts of Maryland, ordaining our North and South. From his omnivorous reading, with his diabolical genius for mimicry, he also re-creates their tumultuous era." Nation

V.; a novel. Lippincott 1963 492p o.p.

This novel is a "parody of the 'Black Humor' techniques it employs. The multiple plots involve the *schlemiel* Benny Profane, a hunter of alligators in New York's sewers, and Herbert Stencil, who becomes obsessed by his pursuit of V., an initial he found in his dead father's notebooks. V.'s various manifestations include a femme fatale, a spy, and a hag who happened to be present at every significant event in Europe from 1890 to World War II." Reader's Ency. 4th edition

Vineland. Little, Brown 1990 385p o.p.

LC 89-13025

"Vineland, a zone of blessed anarchy in northern California, is the last refuge of hippiedom, a culture devasted by the sobriety epidemic, Reaganomics, and the Tube. Here, in an Orwellian 1984, Zoyd Wheeler and his daughter Prairie search for Prairie's long-lost mother, a Sixties radical who ran off with a narc." Libr J

This is "manifestly the work of a man of quick intelligence and quirky invention. Many of its episodes flicker with an appealingly far-flung humor. And Pynchon displays throughout Vineland what might be called an internal loyalty: he keeps the faith with the generally feckless and almost invariably inarticulate misfits he assembles, tracking their looping thoughts and indecisive actions with a patience that seems grounded in affection." N Y Rev Books

Pywell, Sharon L.

What happened to Henry; [by] Sharon Pywell. G.P. Putnam's Sons 2004 292p $19.95

ISBN 0-399-15168-0 LC 2003-62239

The plot of this novel revolves around a "tightly knit family. Henry, Lauren, and Winston Cooper are 10, 7, and 5 in 1960, when their newborn sister dies of SIDS. Henry pulls his younger siblings through their grief while their mother is barely functioning and their father is lost in his work. But four years later, Henry begins to crack, becoming obsessed with a picture of a man near Hiroshima's firestorm. . . . A powerful novel full of surprises, unbreakable sibling bonds, and insightful reflection on the power of love to overcome grief." Booklist

Q

Qashu, Sayed, 1975-

Dancing Arabs; by Sayed Kashua ; translated from the Hebrew by Miriam Shlesinger. Grove Press 2004 227p $24
ISBN 0-8021-4126-9 LC 2003-67765
Original Hebrew edition, 2002
"After solving a quiz-show riddle, the young Palestinian protagonist earns the rare opportunity to study at a Jewish university in Jerusalem. There is hope for him, so we suspect, and for his village and people. In Jerusalem, though, he feels the truth of his father's pessimism ('once an Arab, always an Arab, and you don't stand a chance') and finds and forfeits forbidden love with Naomi. Yet nationalism, optimism, and his family's hope that his intelligence will lead to the first Arab atom bomb fizzle out and leave a headachy and resentful middle-aged man, unhappily married to an Arab wife back in the borderlands." Booklist

Qiu Xiaolong

When red is black; Qiu Xiaolong. Soho Press 2004 309p $25
ISBN 1-569-47369-2 LC 2003-23436
"When Yin Lige, the author of a banned book, is found murdered in her Shanghai apartment, detective Yu Guangming and his boss, Chief Inspector Chen Cao, must solve a case that may have far-reaching political and social implications." Publ Wkly
This mystry "offers a complex and riveting portrait of Shanghai, a city in transition from a proletarian dictatorship to a capitalist playground." Washington Post Book World

Queen, Ellery

The best of Ellery Queen; four decades of stories from The mystery masters; edited by Francis M. Nevins, Jr. and Martin H. Greenberg. Beaufort Bks. 1985 238p o.p.
LC 84-21572
Contents: The glass-domed clock; The bearded lady; The mad tea-party; Man bites dog; Mind over matter; The inner circle; The Dauphin's doll; The three widows; Snowball in July; My queer Dean!; GI story; Miracles do happen; Last man to die; Abraham Lincoln's clue; Wedding anniversary

A fine and private place. World Pub. 1971 214p o.p.
"The 'padrone,' Nino Importuna, heads a huge conglomerate. He catches one of his executives embezzling, and as the price of freedom, demands that he hand over his young daughter as the aging Nino's bride. Of course, this is the perfect setup for murder. First Nino's two brothers, who share in the conglomerate, die, then Nino himself. For the solution, Ellery Queen returns to his (their) original style of detection—a stream of bizarre clues that confuse the detective Queen no end." Publ Wkly

The Roman hat mystery; a problem in deduction. Stokes, F.A. 1929 325p o.p.
"Inspector Richard Queen and his son Ellery tackle a puzzling murder with immense thoroughness and almost fatiguing pertinacity. Though the egregious bonhomie of the Queens and Ellery's pseudo bookishness occasionally irritate, the neatness of the plot involving a missing hat in a theater murder cannot be denied. But the police procedure is not what it would be now, and the criminal's luck in carrying out his complex plan strains the believables." Barzun. Cat of Crime. Rev and enl edition

The tragedy of X
In Queen, E. The XYZ murders p7-216

The tragedy of Y
In Queen, E. The XYZ murders p217-419

The tragedy of Z
In Queen, E. The XYZ murders p421-575

The XYZ murders; three mysteries in one volume complete and unabridged: The tragedy of X; The tragedy of Y; The tragedy of Z. Lippincott 1961 575p o.p.
These books were originally published under the name of Barnaby Ross in 1932, 1932 and 1933 respectively
Drury Lane, retired Shakespearean actor and brilliant connoisseur of crime, helps New York City's District Attorney Bruno and Inspector Thumm solve the mysteries

Quick, Amanda, 1948-

For works written by this author under other names see Krentz, Jayne Ann, 1948-

I thee wed. Bantam Bks. 1999 341p $23.95
ISBN 0-553-10084-X LC 98-37168
"Strong-willed, and with a redhead's combustible temper, paid companion Emma Greyson finds herself embroiled in a dangerous adventure with the dashing Edison Stokes. A wealthy member of Regency England's 'Polite World,' Stokes follows the clue in a dying man's last words to arrive at Ware Castle, where he suspects a dark plot is underway. At the castle he encounters Emma, who stands out among the era's decadent and depraved society as a woman of sharp intelligence. . . . Attractive protagonists, loose bodices, thwarted love and odds overcome prove themselves once again the ingredients for success in this genre." Publ Wkly

Late for the wedding. Bantam Bks. 2003 322p $24.95
ISBN 0-553-80271-2 LC 2002-34254
"The killer, an insider with easy access to the opulent homes of Regency England's elite, has left his calling card, a memento-mori ringa jeweled, coffin-topped band with a white skull inside. He's clever, but not nearly clever enough to fool the fearless team of Lavinia Lake and Tobias March." Booklist
"As this engaging effort demonstrates, Quick has the Regency-murder mystery mix down to a fine science." Publ Wkly

The paid companion. Putnam 2004 418p $24.95
ISBN 0-399-15174-5 LC 2003-62348

Quick, Amanda, 1948-—*Continued*

"Elenora Lodge is in quite a fix. Her stepfather lost her farm and all of her possessions in a mining venture, and her fiance dumps her faster than the proverbial hot potato. But Elenora is practical and pragmatic. So when Arthur Lancaster, earl of St. Merryn, offers her a position as a paid companion, she accepts. St. Merryn is in a bit of a fix himself. His favorite uncle has been murdered, and he's sworn vengeance on the killer, a mad alchemist intent on perfecting the ultimate weapon of mass destruction. Unfortunately, St. Merryn's fiancee has also dumped him, and his renewed status as one of London's most eligible bachelors is interfering with his quest for justice, hence his paying Elenora to pose as his new fiancee. . . . {Quick} mixes humor, suspense, and tantalizing historical detail with all the savory ingredients her fans have come to expect: a feisty, resourceful heroine; a hero with a decidedly dangerous edge; witty repartee; and strongly appealing secondary characters." Booklist

Slightly shady. Bantam Bks. 2001 343p o.p.
ISBN 0-553-80188-0 LC 00-58528

"Londoner Lavinia Lake had made a comfortable home for herself and her niece, running an antique store in Rome. Little did she know, however, that a band of thieves was using her quaint little shop for their illegal purposes. This bit of information was made perfectly clear to Lavinia when one Tobias March barged in and began tearing the antique shop—junk shop, to be more precise—apart, searching for incriminating evidence." Booklist

"Arch humor and the expert removal of bodices are Quick's stock in trade, and the old formula still works splendidly." Publ Wkly

Wicked widow. Bantam Bks. 2000 297p o.p.
ISBN 0-553-10087-4 LC 99-59194

"Regency-era historical romance features Madeline Deveridge, a misunderstood London widow with a reputation for murder, and the strapping Artemis Hunt, a secret owner of the Dream Pavilions, a popular pleasure garden. When one of Madeline's maids is abducted outside the Dream Pavilions, she blackmails Artemis into helping her in the rescue. . . . A delicious combination of adventure and romance, this lively tale keeps the reader enthralled from start to finish." Booklist

Quill, Monica, 1929-

For works written by this author under other names see McInerny, Ralph M., 1929-

Quindlen, Anna

Black and blue. Random House 1998 293p $23
ISBN 0-679-43539-5 LC 97-25208

This novel's "protagonist is Frannie Benedetto, a 37-year-old Brooklyn housewife, mother and nurse who finally finds the courage to escape from her violent husband Bobby, a New York City cop. Under an assumed identity in a tacky central Florida town, Frannie and her 10-year-old son, Robert, attempt to build a new life, but there is a price to pay, and when it comes, it carries the heartstopping logic of inevitability and the irony of fate." Publ Wkly

"Following fault lines of power, dependence, and love, Quindlen takes her heroine to a bereaved country where there are no answers, only choices; in Brooklyn-born Frannie, she has created an utterly believable, flinty character." New Yorker

Blessings; a novel. Random House 2002 226p o.p.
ISBN 0-375-50223-8 LC 2002-24802

"The wealthy and reclusive 80-year-old Lydia Blessing lives in the eponymous 'Blessings,' the country estate to which she was banished by her family after the death of her husband in World War II. Two events conspire to change the remaining years of Lydia's life: she hires Skip Cuddy as a handyman, and a baby is abandoned on her doorstep. Skip, whose friendship with some local lowlifes led to a stint in jail, tries to hide the existence of the baby from his prickly and critical employer, to no avail. Both Skip and Lydia fall in love with the baby, whom they name Faith, and in spite of their misgivings come together as a makeshift family." Libr J

"Quindlen's fine-tuned ear for the class distinctions of speech results in convincing dialogue. Evoking a bygone patrician world, she endows Blessings with an almost magical aura. While it skirts sentimentality by a hairbreadth, the narrative is old-fashioned in a positive way." Publ Wkly

Object lessons. Random House 1991 262p o.p.
LC 90-48656

This novel describes a summer in the life of an Irish American family in suburban New York in the 1960s. The central figure is twelve-year-old Maggie, daughter of Tommy Scanlan and Connie, an Italian American whose father is a cemetery caretaker in the Bronx. Tommy's father John, who made a fortune in religious goods and construction, is dying after a stroke, but still seeks to control the lives of his children and grandchildren, especially Tommy, the rebel

"Quindlen's social antennae are acute: she conveys the fierce ethnic pride that distinguishes Irish and Italian communities, their rivalry and mutual disdain. Her character portrayal is empathetic and beautifully dimensional, not only of Maggie but of her mother, who experiences her own wrenching rite of passage." Publ Wkly

One true thing. Random House 1994 289p o.p.
LC 94-22238

This novel "follows the psychological travails of Ellen Gulden, who against all personal inclinations returns home to care for her dying mother, Kate, and eventually finds herself accused of mercy-killing. Ellen, an intelligent though not particularly warm person, has spent her life earning her professor father's approval. After achieving high school valedictorian and Harvard honors, she aspires to advance her New York career. At her father's insistence, however, she leaves her job and takes on the role of nurse and homemaker. Through long hours as companion to Kate, she discovers the real value of her mother's life." Libr J

"Quindlen's story sustains an emotional momentum, and she addresses difficult issues with compassion." Publ Wkly

Quoirez, Françoise *See* Sagan, Françoise, 1935-2004

R

Raban, Jonathan

Waxwings; a novel. Pantheon Bks. 2003 281p $24

ISBN 0-375-41008-2 LC 2003-42997

"Tom Janeway is a professor of writing, a novelist and a public radio commentator; his wife, Beth, works for GetaShack.Com, a startup providing virtual neighborhood tours for prospective house buyers. They have a four-year-old son named Finn, and they appear content. Behind the happy facade, though, Beth has grown deeply unhappy with her self-absorbed husband. . . . Unfolding in counterpoint to Raban's chronicle of the rather civilized collapse of their marriage is the story of a shady Chinese immigrant called Chick; he survives a horrific journey to America and becomes an off-the-books contractor who bullies Tom into employing him to renovate their gloomy old house after Beth moves out." Publ Wkly

This novel "succeeds as a sharply observed satire of the Internet boom and as a bittersweet meditation the American dream." Libr J

Rabb, Jonathan

The book of Q; a novel. Crown 2001 375p o.p.

ISBN 0-609-60483-X LC 00-47550

"Father Ian Pearse, a researcher at the Vatican Library, stumbles upon an ancient conspiracy that could destroy the Catholic Church. Long thought dead, a dangerous sect called the Manichaeans has resurfaced, and Pearse must decipher an enigmatic prayer if he is to stop their plan. His life in jeopardy, Pearse finds that the closer he gets to the truth, the closer he gets to the Pope himself." Libr J

"A solid, hard-edged tale set in a climate of Catholic intrigue and social controversy." Publ Wkly

Rabinovitch, Sholem *See* Sholem Aleichem, 1859-1916

Rabinowitz, Sholem Yakov *See* Sholem Aleichem, 1859-1916

Rabinowitz, Solomon *See* Sholem Aleichem, 1859-1916

Radcliffe, Ann Ward, 1764-1823

The mysteries of Udolpho; [by] Ann Radcliffe; edited with an introduction and notes by Jacqueline Howard. Penguin Books 2001 xxxix, 653p (Penguin classics) pa $13

ISBN 0-14-043759-2 LC 2001-277143

First published 1794 in the United Kingdom

"The orphaned Emily St Aubert is carried off by her aunt's villanous husband Montoni to a remote castle in the Apennines, where her life, honour, and fortune are threatened and she is surrounded by apparently supernatural terrors. These are later explained as due to human agency and Emily escapes, returns to France and, after further mysteries and misunderstandings, is reuinted with her lover Valancourt." Oxford Companion to Engl Lit. 6th edition

Rae, Hugh C., 1935-

See also Stirling, Jessica

Rampling, Anne *See* Rice, Anne, 1941-

Rand, Ayn, 1905-1982

Anthem. 50th anniversary ed, with a new introduction and appendix by Leonard Peikoff. Dutton 1995 253p $23.95

ISBN 0-525-94015-4 LC 95-9854

First published 1946 by Pamphleteers

"A short novel about a heroic dissenter in a future monolithic and collectivized state." Oxford Companion to Am Lit. 6th edition

Atlas shrugged. Random House 1957 1168p o.p.

"In a technological civilization Rand's characters remain insecure and look to the government for protection. In exchange they sacrifice their creativity and independence. The heroes, a copper tycoon and an inventor, reject this philosophy and fight for the individualist." Shapiro. Fic for Youth. 3d edition

The fountainhead. Macmillan 1943 754p o.p.

First published by Bobbs-Merrill

This novel "celebrates the achievements of an architect (presumably suggested by Frank Lloyd Wright) who is fiercely independent in pursuing his own ideas of design and who is therefore an example of the author's concept of Objectivism, which lauds individualism and 'rational self-interest.'" Oxford Companion to Am Lit. 5th edition

We the living. Random House 1959 433p o.p.

Originally published in 1936 by Macmillan, this edition of Rand's first novel contains a foreword describing the plight of the individual in the Soviet Union since then. It is the story of post-revolutionary Russia, and of a woman torn between two men who love her, one a Communist, the other an aristocrat

Randall, Alice

The wind done gone. Houghton Mifflin 2001 210p $23

ISBN 0-618-10450-X LC 00-46544

The premise of this parodic sequel to Gone with the Wind is "that Scarlett O'Hara was half sister to a slave, the illegitimate daughter of Scarlett's father and her beloved Mammy. Randall's book, which picks up about a month after 'Gone with the Wind' left off, is made up of the . . . diary of this overlooked woman, Cynara. Throughout, Randall lifts characters and plot lines directly from Mitchell's novel, though she tweaks the names." N Y Times Book Rev

"Cynara's voice and character are, in fits and starts, inspired and inspiring. Newly emancipated and literate, she acquires, by virtue of what she calls her 'crazy quilt' education, an arresting fictional presence." Time

Rankin, Ian, 1960-

Black and blue; an Inspector Rebus mystery. St. Martin's Press 1997 394p o.p.

LC 97-25381

Edinburgh police detective John Rebus "has a lot on his plate: an oil-rig worker has been sadistically murdered (or has he?), a television news series has prompted

Rankin, Ian, 1960-—*Continued*
an inquiry into one of Rebus' earlier cases, and—worst of all—a serial killer is on the loose." Booklist

"Rankin has a point to make about the corrosive effects of human wickedness that, if left unchecked, seeps into the bloodstream and poisons the national body—a point well made in his blunt and bruising style." N Y Times Book Rev

The black book; an Inspector Rebus novel. Penzler Bks. 1994 c1993 278p o.p.

LC 94-8929

Frist published 1993 in the United Kingdom

In this mystery novel, Inspector Rebus of Edinburgh "has alienated his girlfriend, his ne'er-do-well brother has deposited himself in Rebus' apartment with every appearance of staying for good, his promising new sergeant has been mugged, and his most unfavorite colleague is again out to discredit Rebus. But Rebus' personal troubles pale when a local butcher is stabbed, and the investigation leads Rebus to conclude that the attack is somehow connected to a years-old unsolved arson-homicide case. . . . Rankin's compelling and original plot is *almost* as intriguing as the gruff, tough, rebellious Rebus, whose rough exterior hides a charming, funny, tenderhearted human being we'd all like to know." Booklist

Dead souls; an Inspector Rebus novel. St. Martin's Minotaur 1999 406p $24.95

ISBN 0-312-20293-8 LC 99-44276

In this novel "Inspector John Rebus, is in another of his black moods. A colleague commits suicide; the teenage son of his high school sweetheart goes missing; a pedophile crawls onto his turf; and a mad-dog killer arrives from America to play a sadistic game of chicken with him. An irreligious man who harbors a perverse streak of spirituality, Rebus blames blind fate (or an uncaring God) for conjoining these seemingly random circumstances into a force field of evil so strong that it sweeps aside his sense of decency and pulls him in." N Y Times Book Rev

The falls; an Inspector Rebus novel. St. Martin's Minotaur 2001 c2000 399p $24.95

ISBN 0-312-20610-0 LC 2001-41946

First published 2000 in the United Kingdom

Inspector Rebus "needs all his interviewing skills to get a handle on Philippa Balfour, a 20-year-old art student at the University of Edinburgh who has gone missing. It's like extracting molars to get information from Philippa's father, mother, boyfriend or friends, who are in turn too controlling, browbeaten, calculating or clueless to be anything but obstructive. The plot opens up when a nasty little doll in a creepy little coffin directs Rebus to an interactive game that Philippa has been playing on the Internet." N Y Times Book Rev

Rankin combines "complicated multiple plot lines with finely drawn characters and fascinating Scottish lore and settings." Libr J

The hanging garden; an Inspector Rebus novel. St. Martin's Press 1998 335p $24.95

ISBN 0-312-19278-9 LC 98-12404

First published 1997 in the United Kingdom

John Rebus, "an Edinburgh detective-inspector and father of a 24-year-old daughter, feels especially protective of a young Serbian woman coerced into prostitution by a local mobster. The woman's inability to communicate adds to the frustration of an unproductive, ongoing police surveillance and the continuation of crimes associated with the mobster. At the same time, Rebus investigates a local ex-Nazi's alleged role in a French war crime." Libr J

A question of blood; an Inspector Rebus novel; Ian Rankin. 1st American ed. Little, Brown and Co 2004 406p $22.95

ISBN 0-316-09564-8 LC 2003-59549

First published 2003 in the United Kingdom

"Rebus finds himself in hot water again, this time literally, with severely scalded hands, the result of either too hot dish or bathwater. After the stalker of a colleague turns up dead-in a fire-suspicion naturally falls on Rebus, who is suspended for the duration of the investigation. Meanwhile, a school shooting reminiscent of the Dunblane massacre in 1996 leaves two students and the assailant dead, with a third wounded. It all seems elementary enough, until Rebus, with time on his bandaged hands, is called in as a consultant." Libr J

"This series's strength starts with Rebus himself, who . . . has emerged as the baddest of the bad boys of modern crime fiction. He is fiftyish, overweight, alcoholic, a chain smoker, surly, short-tempered, divorced, estranged from his family, a loner, a nut about obscure rock-and-roll groups, hostile to all authority and possibly psychotic. Needless to say, women love him—ladies love outlaws—and his police colleagues tolerate him because he's an ace detective." Washington Post Book World

Resurrection men; an Inspector Rebus novel. Little, Brown 2003 436p $23.95

ISBN 0-316-76684-4 LC 2002-16271

"It's the perfect cover. Edinburgh Detective Inspector John Rebus, the maverick's maverick, guilty of throwing a coffee cup at his superior officer, is sent to a remedial 'career counseling' course on being a better team player. But the fix is in; Rebus' real assignment is to investigate four Glasgow renegade coppers also forced to take the course." Booklist

"We are well and truly in Rankin country—a shady world where good and evil are relative terms and truth is an arbitrary concept." N Y Times Book Rev

Set in darkness. St. Martin's Press 2000 415p o.p.

ISBN 0-312-20609-7

"Rebus has been assigned to a bogus task force called the Policing of Parliament Liaison Committee. Things liven up, though, when a body is found inside a bricked-up fireplace in one of the buildings under construction for the new Scottish Parliament. That's a tantalizing enough mystery, but when a top politico is found dead at the construction site, Rebus has something he can sink his teeth into—a decades-old crime whose tentacles touch the present and lead to a new confrontation with Rebus' longtime nemesis, Edinburgh crime boss Big Ger Cafferty. . . . Nobody writes darker than Rankin." Booklist

Rash, Ron

Saints at the river; Ron Rash. Henry Holt 2004 239p $24

ISBN 0-8050-7487-2 LC 2003-67630

Rash, Ron—*Continued*

"When the 12-year-old daughter of a wealthy banker drowns in South Carolina's Tamassee River, her death sets off an emotionally charged battle between the grieving parents, who want to put up a dam to recover her body, and the local environmentalists, who will risk everything to defend the pristine state of their river. . . . The book is rich with nuance, mostly because Rash selects Maggie Glenn as his first-person narrator. A Tamassee native who now works as a news photographer in the state capital, Columbia, Maggie has deep ties to the town, but she's detached from the main fray. As a result, her news angles and her romantic attachments keep shifting. Maggie's rage against her father isn't sufficiently explored to carry the weight it bears in the plot, but Rash compensates for this weakness by creating detailed, highly particular characters." Publ Wkly

Rathbone, Julian, 1935-

The last English king. St. Martin's Press 1999 381p $24.95

ISBN 0-312-24213-1 LC 99-55913

"William the Conqueror defeated King Harold at the Battle of Hastings in 1066, and three years later Walt, one of Harold's personal guards, is wandering continental Europe as a broken man. He encounters Quint, an ex-monk, and together they decide to travel to the Holy Land. On their journey, Walt finally begins to heal by telling his story to Quint." Booklist

"Rathbone takes considerable historical liberties, writing in contemporary vernacular modern prose and painting King Edward as a man more interested in Harold's fetching brother Tostig than in the sister, whom he is slated to marry. However, Rathbone defends his decisions convincingly in an author's note, and his narrative presents an interesting interpretation of a tumultuous period in English history." Publ Wkly

Rattray, Simon, 1920-1995

For works written by this author under other names see Hall, Adam, 1920-1995

Raucher, Herman

Summer of '42. Putnam 1971 251p o.p.

This is a novel "describing with great accuracy what it was like to be a 15-year-old boy just entering the obsessed-with-sex stage of life in the wartime summer of 1942. Hermie and Oscy and Benji are three tough, foul-mouthed but innocent Brooklyn boys spending the summer on Packett Island off the coast of Maine. The central story revolves around Hermie's tender and believable relationship with a war widow who initiates him into sex at the end of the novel." Publ Wkly

"There is hilarity here and vulgarity, warmth and humanity—and so much detail and nostalgia that the work seems almost like a historical novel." Libr J

Ravenel, Shannon

(comp) The Best American short stories of the eighties. See The Best American short stories of the eighties

(ed) New stories from the South: the year's best [date] See New stories from the South: the year's best [date]

Rawlings, Marjorie Kinnan, 1896-1953

Short stories; edited by Rodger L. Tarr. University Press of Fla. 1994 376p $49.95

ISBN 0-8130-1252-X LC 93-30649

Contents: Cracker chidlings; Jacob's ladder; Lord Bill of the Suwannee River; A plumb clare conscience; A crop of beans; Gal young un; Alligators; Benny and the bird dogs; The pardon; Varmints; A mother in Mannville; Cocks must crow; Fish fry and fireworks; The pelican's shadow; The enemy; In the heart; Jessamine Springs; The provider; The shell; Black secret; Miriam's houses; Miss Moffatt steps out; The friendship

Raymond, Jonathan

The half-life; a novel; Jonathan Raymond. Bloomsbury 2004 355p $23.95

ISBN 1-582-34448-5 LC 2003-22602

"In the early nineteenth century, a half-starved band of fur trappers struggles through the Oregon woods. Their young, diffident cook is intimidated by the rougher members of the group. When another young man, fleeing from some vengeful Russians, stumbles into camp, a friendship blossoms. Move ahead to the Reagan era. A teenager is dragged by her mother to live in an Oregon commune. Lonely and resentful while living among slightly absurd, aging counterculturists, she is drawn to the only other young woman in the settlement, and as their bond grows, they work together on a film project. The discovery of a pair of skeletons buried on the commune provides the link between these pairs of friendships. Raymond, in his first novel, seamlessly links the two narratives with elegant and often haunting prose. The characters are finely drawn, and Raymond poses them against a seductively beautiful landscape." Booklist

Rayner, Richard

The cloud sketcher; a novel. HarperCollins Pubs. 2001 435p o.p.

ISBN 0-06-019634-3 LC 00-56695

This novel is "about a young Finn whose early contact with an elevator convinces him to construct buildings so high that they tickle the clouds. Surviving Finland's early brush with the Bolsheviks, he begins his architectural career, but soon the re-emergence of his first sweetheart drives him to New York City, where he meets other architects, gangsters, {and} capitalists." Libr J

The author "vividly captures details of Finnish culture, history and landscape and the developing architectural aesthetic of the age. This is an old-fashioned novel in the best sense: full of incident and passion, presenting a slice of history and relating a gripping story." Publ Wkly

Read, Miss, 1913-

Affairs at Thrush Green; illustrations by J. S. Goodall. Houghton Mifflin 1984 c1983 256p il o.p.

LC 84-6702

First published 1983 in the United Kingdom

"The catastrophic fire that destroyed Thrush Green rectory in *Gossip from Thrush Green*, has caused Charles Henstock and his wife, Dimity, to move into the luxurious, large rectory in Lulling, thus drawing the adventures

Read, Miss, 1913—*Continued*
of the residents of these two towns even closer. . . . Henstock tends to his new duties with gracious vigor despite his own doubts and those expressed by several parishioners." Booklist

At home in Thrush Green; illustrated by J.S. Goodall. Houghton Mifflin 1986 c1985 261p il o.p.
LC 86-20864

First published 1985 in the United Kingdom

The author describes "a year of bustling and visiting at Thrush Green. The creation of eight homes for elderly residents on the site of the old vicarage takes up much of the novel's action, absorbing the interests of the villagers as the recipients must be decided upon and settled in. School life under the stern Miss Watson and the more amiable Miss Fogarty also receives a share of attention. Readers familiar with Thrush Green's inhabitants will be delighted to note the changes in the lives of their favorite characters and will be pleased as always by the book's emphasis on familiar annual patterns." Booklist

Chronicles of Fairacre; comprising: Village school, Village diary and Storm in the village; illustrated by J. S. Goodall. Houghton Mifflin 1977 c1964 534p il o.p.

First published 1964 in the United Kingdom. A combined edition of three titles first published separately in 1956 (1955 in the United Kingdom), 1957, and 1959 (1958 in the United Kingdom) respectively

Village school describes one year in the life of an English schoolmistress in a two-room church-governed school in the rural English village of Fairacre. Through her eyes we see the whole of village life with its fetes, sales, outings, festivals, quarrels and friendships. Village diary continues the account of school and village life. When a retired male school teacher settles in the village, the villagers hope for a romance for their schoolmistress until a wife appears. In Storm in the village, the "storm" is caused by fear that the British Atomic Research Authority is going to take over Harold Miller's "Hundred Acre Field" to make room for a new housing development and that the village school will be closed

Farewell to Fairacre; illustrations by John S. Goodall. Houghton Mifflin 1994 213p il o.p.
LC 94-25628

"With an influx of new students, Miss Read's worries about the future of her beloved school can finally be set aside. In their wake, however, come concerns about the head mistress' own health. Two small strokes spur her decision to retire, and she spends her final months in her usual busy fashion, tending to her students at Fairacre, fending off the surprising attentions of two suitors, and becoming ever more comfortable with thoughts of a new life ahead. Nostalgic without being sentimental, this is a fitting conclusion to a delightful series, recalling old friends and pleasant times in a tranquil English village." Booklist

Friends at Thrush Green; illustrations by John S. Goodall. Houghton Mifflin 1991 c1990 244p il o.p.
LC 91-10857

First published 1990 in the United Kingdom

In this novel "we meet a crazy-quilt collection of delightfully eccentric characters who eagerly await and gossip endlessly about their old friends' return visit. The town's attention is also riveted to the pending sale of the much-loved residence abutting the schoolhouse at Thrush Green, speculation about which gives rise to a cornucopia of interesting tales and rumors surrounding various townspeople. While some readers might deem Miss Read's novel sluggish for its seeming uneventfulness, many others will be drawn to this throwback to an easier, slower-paced life." Booklist

Mrs. Pringle; illustrations by John S. Goodall. Houghton Mifflin 1990 c1989 165p il o.p.
LC 90-4669

First published 1989 in the United Kingdom

This novel focuses on the exploits of Mrs. Pringle, the custodian of the school in the village of Fairacre

Return to Thrush Green; illustrated by J.S. Goodall. Houghton Mifflin 1979 255p il o.p.
LC 79-858

First published 1978 in the United Kingdom

In this chronicle of Thrush Green "Albert Piggott, the sexton, is his usual irascible self despite the efforts of his wandering wife and his loyal daughter. On the other hand, the return of Joan Young's ailing father works out much better than expected. Miss Fogarty handles the school crises capably and finds that some clouds do have silver linings. As flowers bloom and birds do nest, neighbors chat away as usual, and Dotty Harmer cares for her stray animals and offers acorn coffee to friends. Best of all is the village's newest romance, one that takes just about everyone by surprise." Publ Wkly

Storm in the village
In Read, Miss. Chronicles of Fairacre p361-534

Thrush Green; illustrated by J.S. Goodall. Houghton Mifflin 1960 c1959 226p il o.p.

First published 1959 in the United Kingdom

"Confined to the events of May 1, the day when Mrs. Curdle's traveling carnival brings its special magic to Thrush Green, the story tells what takes place in the lives of a small boy, a lonely girl, an elderly doctor and his young assistant, and various other people, including the redoubtable Mrs. Curdle herself." Booklist

Village diary
In Read, Miss. Chronicles of Fairacre p177-360

The village school
In Read, Miss. Chronicles of Fairacre p9-176

Read, Piers Paul, 1941-

Alice in exile. St. Martin's Press 2002 344p $24.95

ISBN 0-312-30398-X

"As striking in her beauty as she is shocking in her behavior, Alice Fry has an uninhibited sexuality that makes her attractive to two very different men. Pregnant with fiance Edward Cobb's child, Alice is abandoned by him when her father becomes embroiled in a sexual scandal that threatens Cobb's political ambition. With no one to turn to and nowhere to go, Alice is rescued by Baron von Rettenberg, a womanizing Russian nobleman who hires

Read, Piers Paul, 1941-—*Continued*

her as his children's governess. . . .To read Read is to be caught up in an epic wonder of passion, scandal, adn international intrigue." Booklist

The professor's daughter. Lippincott 1971 276p o.p.

Henry Rutledge, "the professor is a middle-aged old-line liberal who has dabbled in politics behind the scenes in the Kennedy era. In . . . flashbacks we learn how and why he and his wife have become the kind of people they are, and what has gone wrong with their marriage. The professor's daughter is something else again, desperate, attempting suicide, all but destroyed sexually and every other way by traps she has drifted into without ever understanding what was happening to her. When father and daughter strike up an incongruous but ultimately quite believable alliance with a group of campus radical activists who believe assassination is a valid revolutionary tool, tension mounts to a keen pitch." Publ Wkly

A season in the West. Random House 1989 238p o.p.

LC 88-29682

"Defecting from Czechoslovakia, writer Josef Birek is taken under the wing of Laura Morton, the wife of a wealthy banker, who works part-time as a translator at a foundation for dissident émigrés. Shallow, discontented Laura sees her opportunity: she introduces the naive, idealistic Birek to her friends and literary contacts, invites him to move into her home and eventually begins an affair with the overwhelmed young man. Lionized by London's sophisticated social set, Birek finds himself financially and spiritually enslaved, while Laura becomes obsessed by the liaison." Publ Wkly

"Read engages his audience with biting pictures of British publishing and banking circles, while the romance is played up for all its blazing erotic qualities. Witty commentary on sedate lives moved by unruly passions." Booklist

Reardon, Lisa

Blameless; a novel. Random House 2000 319p o.p.

ISBN 0-375-50405-2 LC 99-55524

Mary Culpepper, the 34-year-old protagonist "drives a school bus in a small Michigan town. . . . After one of the children from her bus route asks Mary to go into his house to check on his ill sister, she discovers that the girl has died. Mary is then forced to wrestle with the burden of testifying against the mother accused of the murder and trying to outwit a phantom she calls the Night Visitor, who invades her sleep with haunting images of the young victim." N Y Times Book Rev

"The small-town life, with a limited group of family and friends, modest entertainments, softball and county fairs, and nowhere to hide, is right on target. Mary is so alive she practically leaps from the pages." Libr J

Reasoner, James

Antietam. Cumberland House 2000 383p $22.95

ISBN 1-58182-084-4 LC 00-22578

This novel focuses on "the Brannon clan of Culpepper County, Virginia. As the hostilities move ever closer and finally threaten the security of the family farm in northern Virginia, each of the six Brannon siblings is faced with an inevitable crisis of either the heart or the conscience. . . . Fraught with passion, tension, and tenderness, this enthralling family saga will appeal to fans of epic well-researched historical fiction." Booklist

Redfern, Elizabeth

Auriel rising; Elizabeth Redfern. G.P. Putnam's Sons 2004 386p $24.95

ISBN 0-399-15105-2 LC 2003-58507

The "setting is London in 1609, and the city is rife with hostility between Catholics and Protestants. Two years after he was involved in the escape of a Catholic prisoner, young Ned Warriner has returned to London to find that he still has many enemies, one of them now married to the love of his life, Kate. Even worse, he has stumbled upon a mysterious letter that appears to contain the secret for making gold but in reality contains the seeds of a plot that reaches to the highest levels of British royalty. With not only personal survival but national security at stake, Ned must decipher the contents while navigating the dangerous relationships between some of the city's most powerful men." Booklist

"Redfern sets a blistering pace and never breaks stride or tone. Resisting the standard static historical tableau, she gives us a troubled city constantly reinventing itself, peopled by souls no less changeable." N Y Times Book Rev

The music of the spheres. Putnam 2001 420p $24.95

ISBN 0-399-14763-2 LC 00-68343

"A tale of murder and intrigue set in 1795 London. Jonathan Absey is a clerk at the Home Office whose job is to search out spies in the war with France. Instead, he spends much of his time trying to discover who murdered his daughter, a red-haired prostitute. In his quest for justice, he enlists the reluctant help of half-brother Alexander. An amateur astronomer, Alexander ingratiates himself with an unusual group of French émigrés who are searching the skies for an elusive new planet they call Selene. Secret agents, murdered prostitutes, and the love of science all combine in an enjoyable if slow-paced story." Libr J

Redfield, James

The celestine prophecy; an adventure. Warner Bks. 1994 246p $19.95

ISBN 0-446-51862-X LC 93-61754

"The saga begins when the unnamed middle-aged male narrator whimsically quits his nondescript life to track down an ancient Peruvian manuscript (pretentiously called the Manuscript) containing nine Insights that supposedly prophesy the modern emergence of New Age spirituality. South of the border, he encounters resistance from the Peruvian government and church authorities, who believe the document will undermine traditional family values. While dodging evil soldiers, paranoid priests and pseudoscientific researchers, our hero sequentially discovers all nine Insights during a series of chance encounters. Redfield has a real talent for page-turning action." Publ Wkly

Followed by The tenth insight (1996)

Reed, Barry, 1927-2002

The choice. Crown 1991 358p o.p.
LC 90-48217

"Frank Galvin is at the peak of his legal career with a blue-chip Boston law firm. As chronicled in *The Verdict* [1980] he has risen to the height of Boston's legal set through a brilliant performance in a highly publicized hospital case. When he is approached by a young and inexperienced attorney with evidence that a highly touted new wonder drug may cause birth defects, he sees it as an opportunity to exert his firm's sense of humanity. However, the firm is the principal legal counsel for the drug's manufacturer. What seems at first to be a simple matter of potential conflict of interest rapidly escalates into an intricate web of intrigue involving both U.S. and British law as well as medical ethics." Libr J

The deception. Crown 1997 372p o.p.
LC 97-163579

"Young tennis star Donna DiTullio is hospitalized after a suicide attempt and treated as a manic-depressive by the renowned Dr. Sexton. After a startling recovery due to treatment with an experimental medication, Donna is scheduled to leave St. Anne's psychiatric center when she falls from a fifth-floor balcony. Severely brain injured, she has little chance for recovery. Attorney Dan Sheridan is brought in by the DiTullio family to sue the doctor, the hospital, and its owner, the Archdiocese of Boston." SLJ

"A thoroughly researched, intriguing tale about both the legal and psychiatric professions." Booklist

The indictment. Crown 1994 370p o.p.
LC 94-8346

This novel concerns "a possible grand jury indictment against a prominent doctor suspected of murdering a young woman. When Boston attorney Dan Sheridan agrees to defend Dr. Christopher Dillard, he pits himself against a DA with an eye on a U.S. Senate seat and a shady Irish kingmaker who wants the entire case buried. Sheridan also becomes an unwitting target of an FBI sting operation against local lawyers suspected of criminal ties, even as he becomes romantically involved with the agent who is working undercover as one of his secretaries." Publ Wkly

"Reed surrounds the mystery plot with an intriguing, behind-the-scenes look at the historically fascinating sociopolitical world of Boston, and he offers plenty of detail on the decision-making, strategy, and processes that go into preparing a criminal case." Booklist

Reed, Ernesto Mestre- *See* Mestre-Reed, Ernesto, 1964-

Reed, Ishmael, 1938-

Japanese by spring. Atheneum Pubs. 1993 225p o.p.
LC 92-36280

A "satiric thrust at university life in America. Ambitious black professor Chappie Puttbutt wants to rise at predominantly white Jack London University, but he gets more than he bargained for when his serene tutor in Japanese—actually leader of a filthy-rich group of Asians—suddenly buys the university and threatens to take over the American West." Libr J

"Borrowing from vivid African-American slang and turning academic jargon inside out, Mr. Reed constructs brilliant verbal fusillades that reduce his targets to their most ridiculous components." N Y Times Book Rev

Reeman, Douglas

A ship must die. Morrow 1979 284p o.p.
LC 79-66009

"In January 1944 Captain Richard Blake, Royal Navy, is preparing to hand over his battle-scarred cruiser 'Andromeda' to the Australian navy. Before he can do so, a German commerce raider appears in the Indian Ocean, and Blake is ordered to destroy him." Libr J

"Reeman gives dimension to his characters and imparts his usual sense of realism in vivid scenes of battle action." Booklist

Reichs, Kathleen J.

Bare bones; [by] Kathy Reichs. Scribner 2003 306p $23.95
ISBN 0-7432-3346-8 LC 2003-40725

"Tempe, a forensic anthropologist, is back home in Charlotte, N.C., anticipating a nice, long vacation from the county medical examiner's office, when a series of unnatural disasters drags her back to the lab. . . . Whether she's examining the pulverized remains of the victims of a suspicious plane crash or reassembling the bones of an illegally slaughtered bear, Tempe is a pro's pro at her job, but also a compassionate woman who isn't afraid to show her outrage at the cruelty done to man and beast for the sake of a dirty dollar." N Y Times Book Rev

Deadly décisions; [by] Kathy Reichs. Scribner 2000 333p $25
ISBN 0-684-85971-8 LC 00-22220

Forensic anthropologist Temperance Brennan "is outraged at the death of a child in a war among bikers vying for the Quebec province drug trade, and she joins the investigation. Tension mounts as she becomes embroiled in the rivalries of outlaw motorcycle gangs, 'the mafia of the new millennium.' The case becomes more complex as another biker is killed and the death and dismemberment of a teenage girl years before in North Carolina are linked to the Quebec biker mayhem." Libr J

"The author doesn't dumb down the scientific stuff, delivering the full textbook version of subjects like hydrocephalus, blood-spatter analysis, ground-penetrating radar devices and the history of outlaw motorcycle clubs in North America." N Y Times Book Rev

Death du jour; {by} Kathy Reichs. Scribner 1999 379p $25
ISBN 0-684-84118-5 LC 98-48763

This mystery opens with forensic anthropologist Temperance Brennan "digging up the body of a nun buried more than a century ago in a convent graveyard in Quebec. While her job is to identify the corpse as a possible saint, Tempe's attention is drawn to the grisly killings of four-month-old twin boys and their parents. At the same time, Tempe's troubled sister Harry comes to Montreal to take a self-help workshop. Investigating these deaths leads Tempe back to the Carolinas, where more bodies are discovered on an island monkey preserve, and clues point to a mysterious cult." Libr J

Reichs, Kathleen J.—*Continued*

"Well presented are Tempe's refreshing compassion in the face of relentless autopsies, her ability to describe a corpse with judiciously graphic detail and her penchant for revealing the art behind the science on such matters as the preservation of a corpse's teeth." Publ Wkly

Déjà dead; [by] Kathleen Reichs. Scribner 1997 411p o.p.

LC 97-2990

"Dr. Tempe Brennan, a trowel-packing forensic anthropologist from North Carolina, works in Montreal's Laboratoire de Médecine Légale examining recovered bodies to help police solve missing-persons cases and murders. It's clear to Tempe that the remains of several women killed and savagely mutilated point to a sadistic serial killer, but she can't convince the police. Determined to prevent more brutal deaths, she sleuths solo, tracking her quarry through Montreal's seedy underworld of hookers, where her anthropologist friend Gabby, doing her own scary research, is being stalked by a creep. . . . Except for imparting an excess of lab information, Reichs, also a forensic anthropologist, drives the pace at a heady clip. A first-class writer, she dazzles readers with sensory imagery that is apt, fresh, and funny." Libr J

Grave secrets. Scribner 2002 317p $25

ISBN 0-684-85973-4 LC 2002-22695

"While in Guatemala to assist in the exhumation of an old mass grave, forensic specialist Temperance Brennan is called upon to determine whether a body found in a septic tank is that of the missing daughter of the Canadian ambassador to Guatemala. The gruesome search, vividly described, leaves even the toughened Tempe aghast." Booklist

Monday mourning; [by] Kathy Reichs. Scribner 2004 305p $25

ISBN 0-7432-3347-6 LC 2004-45263

This Temperance Brennan mystery "finds the forensic anthropologist in Montreal to testify in a murder case. Arriving a day early to prepare, she becomes caught up in a new investigation when three sets of human bones are discovered in the basement of a pizza parlor. Examining the remains, she discovers that the victims were Caucasian and female. Antique buttons found near the bodies lead Homicide Detective Claudel to believe that the remains are over a century old, but Tempe is not so convinced and investigates with the help of her friend Anne, who has come to visit while contemplating her marriage. Readers of the series will be pleased to see the relationship between Tempe and Detective Andrew Ryan develop further." Libr J

Reid, Van

Peter Loon; a novel. Viking 2002 298p $24.95

ISBN 0-670-03052-X LC 2002-512629

This first installment in the author's historical series "chronicles the adventures of Peter Loon, a 17-year-old boy from backwoods Maine whose mother, Rosemund, sends him on an odd quest after the Revolutionary War. When she was a girl, Rosemund had two suitors: Silas Loon and Obed Winslow. She married Silas, but never really loved him, and when he dies in an accident in the 18th century of her marriage, she sends Peter to find Obed." Publ Wkly

"Reid has an excellent sense of dramatic situation, draws shrewd characters, and makes good use of suspense. Writing with power, restraint, and a light comic touch, he keeps a surprise till the last." Libr J

Reisman, Nancy

The first desire. Pantheon Books 2004 310p $24

ISBN 0-375-42308-7 LC 2004-44665

"The catalyst for this narrative about the hidden dramas of a Jewish family living in Buffalo from the late 1920s to 1950 occurs offstage. Rebecca Cohen, wife of jewelry store owner Abe, has died, leaving five adult children. Goldie, the eldest, on whom the responsibility for caring for her siblings has fallen, suddenly disappears without a word. Her departure leaves Sadie Cohen Feldstein, the only married sister, to cope with her tyrannical father and difficult siblings, who live together in the family home." Publ Wkly

"The novel is both lovely and heartbreaking in its vision of family ties at their most inevitable." N Y Times (Late N Y Ed)

Remarque, Erich Maria, 1898-1970

All quiet on the western front; translated from the German by A. W. Wheen. Little, Brown 1929 291p $24.95

ISBN 0-316-73992-8

"Four German youths are pulled abruptly from school to serve at the front as soldiers in World War I. Only Paul survives, and he contemplates the needless violation of the human body by weapons of war. No longer innocent or lighthearted, he is repelled by the slaughter of soldiers and questions the usefulness of war as a means of adjudication. Although the young men in this novel are German, the message is universal in its delineation of the feelings of the common soldier." Shapiro. Fic for Youth. 3d edition

Followed by The road back

Arch of triumph; translated from the German by Walter Sorell and Denver Lindley. Appleton-Century 1945 455p o.p.

"A story of Paris in the period preceding the [Second World] war. The central character is a German doctor who, having escaped from the Nazis, is living illegally in France, subject to deportation if the police discover his presence. Without a passport and identification papers he is not allowed to practice, but in secret performs difficult operations for a well-known society doctor. Other refugees, figures from the underworld, outcasts and derelicts are the characters in a book which pictures a society nearing its doom." Wis Libr Bull

The night in Lisbon; translated by Ralph Manheim. Harcourt, Brace & World 1964 244p o.p.

Original German edition, 1962

"One night in Lisbon in 1942 a German refugee offers passage to the U.S. and his passport to another refugee on condition that he be kept company through the night and that he be permitted to tell his story. The narration reveals the first refugee's flight from Germany in the 1930's, his hazardous return after five years to see his

Remarque, Erich Maria, 1898-1970—*Continued*
wife, his second escape in which his wife joins him, and their subsequent flight from place to place in Europe during which, in spite of dangers, they achieved moments of intense happiness because of their mutual love and understanding." Booklist

The road back; translated from the German by A. W. Wheen. Little, Brown 1931 343p o.p.

Sequel to All quiet on the western front

Containing some of the characters of All quiet on the western front, this story is about a "little group of war-weary, disillusioned German soldiers [who] return to their homes and find that adjustment to peace in a Fatherland which is a rioting, cynical republic is impossible." Cleveland Public Libr

"A profoundly moving, a painfully moving, document. Unlike tragedy, it has no katharsis, but, like a tragedy, it has to be looked at open-eyed, honestly, courageously." Spectator

A time to love and a time to die; translated from the German by Denver Lindley. Harcourt Brace & Co. 1954 378p o.p.

"Ernst, a young German soldier, gets a furlough in the closing days of World War II. He marries Elizabeth, a neighbor girl, who grew up while he was away. Their brief but touching honeymoon helps them to discover love and each other—a time to love. Upon his return from a furlough, Ernst is sent to guard four Russian prisoners. In a generous gesture, he releases them, but one of them, turns on him and kills him—a time to die." Wis Libr Bull

"The whole story is told with great restraint, with little sentimentality for those in misery and with little open rage at those who caused it." Chicago Sunday Trib

Renault, Mary, 1905-1983

The bull from the sea. Pantheon Bks. 1962 343p o.p.

"A sequel to *The King Must Die*, this mythological novel begins with Theseus, King of Athens, returning in triumph from Crete, where he has killed the Minotaur. On a subsequent adventure he captures and falls in love with the warrior princess, Hippolyta. Although married to Phaedra of Crete, Theseus continues his relationship with Hippolyta and both women bear him sons. Tragedy occurs when Phaedra is attracted to and spurned by Hippolyta's youthful son." Shapiro. Fic for Youth. 3d edition

Fire from heaven. Pantheon Bks. 1969 375p o.p.

"This is the story of Alexander the Great from his earliest childhood until the death of his father, Philip of Macedonia. . . . We meet everyone who ever influenced the young Alexander—Aristotle, his teacher; Hephaiston, his friend and lover; Olympias, his strange priestess mother; and scores of others. This was a time of ritual feasts and bacchanalian orgies, of unbashed sexual freedom, of bloody wars and insidious plottings, of pageantry and splendor, myths and mysteries." Publ Wkly

Followed by The Persian boy

Funeral games. Pantheon Bks. 1981 335p o.p.
LC 81-47273

This concludes the story of Alexander the Great that began in Fire from heaven and The Persian boy. "At 32 Alexander is dying in Babylon. The generals, two pregnant wives and a covey of conspirators keep a jackal-like vigil, anticipating the fight for possession of the empire, extending from Europe to India, that will break out when the godlike leader dies. At his death, the murderous power struggle ensues—Alexander's mother and his brain-injured half-brother, Philip, vie with the Regent and other extrafamilial seekers of the throne." Publ Wkly

"Miss Renault's main problem has been to make these monsters and monomaniacs believable, and this, at times with disconcerting insight, she does. . . . It might be argued that Funeral Games lacks a dominant central character. In fact the true center is the empty throne, and it is Alexander himself who, in death as in life, commands the scene absolutely." N Y Rev Books

The king must die. Pantheon Bks. 1958 338p o.p.

"Retold by its hero, the legend of Theseus becomes a logical sequence of adventures that befell a slight, wiry, quick-witted youth impelled to prove his manhood in a semibarbaric society that put a premium on size and brawn. Although, at seventeen, he was already a king and a seasoned warrior, Theseus obeyed his patron god's prompting and voluntarily joined a company of young people conscripted for the bull-dances in Crete, became a renowned bull-leaper, and took advantage of an earthquake to overthrow the Cretan kingdom." Booklist

Followed by The bull from the sea (1962)

The last of the wine. Pantheon Bks. 1956 389p o.p.

"This is a fictionalized account of Athens during the years of the Peloponnesian War told by Alexias, a young Athenian of good family background. We learn the details of daily life within the Greek city state, including the literary, cultural, recreational, and political texture of the time. One very memorable account is that of a wrestling match at the Isthmian Games." Shapiro. Fic for Youth. 3d edition

The Persian boy. Pantheon Bks. 1972 432p o.p.

This sequel to Fire from heaven continues the "story of Alexander the Great, focusing upon his momentous expedition into Asia. This time we observe events through the eyes of Bagoas, a beautiful Persian eunuch who was loved by King Darius and then by Alexander himself. The multiple facets of Renault's art, familiar to a host of admirer's, are once again apparent: a particularly sensitive depiction of boyhood and youth; an astounding grasp of the facts and the spirit of the ancient world; an unerring sense of the dramatic which, along with her superb descriptive powers, brings to life a great historical period." Libr J

Followed by Funeral games

Rendell, Ruth, 1930-

See also Vine, Barbara, 1930-

Adam and Eve and Pinch me; a novel. Crown 2002 356p $25

ISBN 0-609-61025-2 LC 2001-32539

First published 2001 in the United Kingdom

This psychological thriller "concerns the wreckage wrought on a variety of Londoners by a womanizing con man who speaks in rhymes. . . . Araminta 'Minty' Knox, the fragile center of the plot, is a 30-something woman, alone and obsessed with hygiene, who works in

Rendell, Ruth, 1930-—*Continued*
a dry-cleaning shop. All the world is a petri dish for Minty, who sees germs everywhere, which she attacks with Wright's Coal Tar Soap. She is equally tormented by the ghosts she imagines, her domineering 'Auntie' and the man who took her virginity." Publ Wkly

"Part ghost story, part serial-killer hunt, part excoriation of the wicked ways of Westminster and Fleet Street, this tale tightens the noose of suspense through the build-up of vivid domestic and social detail." Booklist

Blood lines; long and short stories. Crown 1996 215p o.p.

LC 96-852

Contents: Blood lines; Lizzie's lover; Burning end; The carer; The man who was the god of love; Expectations; Shreds and slivers; Clothes; Unacceptable levels; In all honesty; The strawberry tree

"In this collection of short stories, Rendell is at her best, using her own quixotic brand of dark humor and an often heartwrenching poignancy to produce 11 minimasterpieces." Booklist

The bridesmaid. Mysterious Press 1989 259p o.p.

LC 88-43471

"Londoner Philip Wardman falls for a beautiful, enigmatic woman he meets at his sister's wedding. Wardman abhors any depiction of violent death, but Senta believes they should each kill someone to prove their love for each other. He fantasizes a murder, while she, an actress and perhaps just a little mad, tells a quite convincing story of murdering one of his enemies. What he discovers about her tale leads to grief and horror." Libr J

"Ms. Rendell is a diabolically subtle writer. For much of this claustrophobic study of mutual obsession, she has us peering into Senta's mind through Philip's eyes, suspiciously analyzing her bizarre statements and mysterious behavior. But, like a cunning old spider, the author has caught two flies in her web; and in the end, Philip proves the more interesting study, with his phobia about violence and his fanaticism for propriety." N Y Times Book Rev

Collected stories. Pantheon Bks. 1988 c1987 536p o.p.

LC 87-35949

First published 1987 in the United Kingdom

The fallen curtain and other stories contains the following stories: The fallen curtain; People don't do such things; A bad heart; You can't be too careful; The double; The venus fly trap; The clinging woman; The vinegar mother; The fall of a coin; Almost human; Divided we stand

Means of evil contains the following stories: Means of evil; Old wives' tales; Ginger and the Kingsmarkham chalk circle; Achilles heel; When the wedding was over

The fever tree and other stories contains the following stories: The fever tree; The dreadful day of judgement; A glowing future; An outside interest; A case of coincidence; Thornapple; May and June; A needle for the devil; Front seat; Paintbox place; The wrong category

The new girl friend and other stories of suspense contains the following stories: The new girl friend; A dark blue perfume; The orchard walls; Hare's house; Bribery and corruption; The whistler; The convolvulus clock; Loopy; Fen Hall; Father's Day; The green road to Quephanda

The crocodile bird. Crown 1993 361p o.p.

LC 93-14734

"After the police question her mother, Eve, about the death of Jonathan Tobias, the owner of Shrove House, 16-year-old Liza runs away with Sean, the young garden hand at the remote English manor. It is to him, over the course of 101 nights, that Liza gradually reveals her strange upbringing, living alone with Eve in the gatehouse of the Tobias estate." Publ Wkly

"A kind of fairy-tale unreality informs this narrative, for all its present-day accoutrements; it is written in careful, straightforward, almost childlike prose; and it keeps you on tenterhooks, once you've surrendered to the atmosphere." Times Lit Suppl

Death notes. Pantheon Bks. 1981 207p o.p.

LC 81-47211

"When the banns are read for aging, world-renowned musician Manual Carmague and a woman many years his junior, it signals the reappearance of Carmague's long-lost daughter, Natalie. Carmague is found drowned before his wedding day and after confiding to his fiancée that he believes 'Natalie' to be an imposter. Obsessed with the desire to solve the mystery, [Chief Inspector] Wexford, 'on holiday in the States,' seeks information concerning Natalie's past and coincidentally provides the reader with a delightfully dry British point of view concerning Americans." Libr J

The face of trespass. Doubleday 1974 184p o.p.

"Published for the Crime Club"

"Gray Lanceton, depressed, impoverished and struggling with a serious writing block, holes up in the 'hovel,' a shabby cottage deep in the English woods. He is in flight from himself and the world. Gradually we learn what has brought him to this pass—a feverish sexual obsession with a willful married woman who is always promising to come away with him forever—if only her tiresome husband can be gotten out of the way." Publ Wkly

The author "conveys the derelict half-dream, half-nightmare life Gray is leading in an Essex hovel far better than a crime-writer need, and through this . . . makes credible the blindness that allows him to be led to total disaster." Times Lit Suppl

The fallen curtain and other stories
In Rendell, R. Collected stories p1-135

The fever tree and other stories
In Rendell, R. Collected stories p265-406

Going wrong. Mysterious Press 1990 260p o.p.

LC 90-40421

"Guy Curran—remarkably handsome, rich, the product of London's underworld, at once ill educated and quite bright—is obsessed with Leonora Chisholm, a childhood sweetheart who has drawn away from him, indeed plans to marry another man, but who oddly and somewhat irresolutely continues to have a rital lunch with Curran every Saturday. Curran repeatedly convinces himself that she is still in love with him but has been turned away by a college roommate, or her mother, stepfather or some other evil figure." N Y Times Book Rev

"Rendell is a master of depicting the long, slow slide into madness, making each tiny step toward the abyss resound with chilling logic." Publ Wkly

Rendell, Ruth, 1930-*—Continued*

Harm done; an Inspector Wexford mystery. Crown 1999 346p $24

ISBN 0-609-60547-X LC 99-20432

Three of the cases Wexford is involved in "have to do with the abuse of women or children. The crimes range from the ridiculous (a petulant university girl and a mentally challenged girl from a low-income housing project are each kidnapped to do housework and returned for ineptitude) to the monstrous (Wexford and his men must protect a child molester who was released from prison while a rich man tortures his wife in the comfort of his spacious home." Publ Wkly

Heartstones; illustrations by George Underwood. Harper & Row 1987 80p il o.p.

LC 86-46098

"The Harper short novel series"

"Adolescent Elvira is in intense spiritual communion with her father; she plans to devote all the rest of her life to him. Elvira's mother is dead, and her sister is outside the orbit that Elvira and her father have created for themselves. This arrangement works fine, as long as it lasts, but trouble arrives in the form of a woman Elvira's father wants to marry. Elvira is determined the marriage will not take place. And, alas, the fiancée dies—violently!" Booklist

"Such is Rendell's mastery of psychological suspense that throughout we remain unsure of the seriousness of Elvira's intentions." Libr J

A judgment in stone. Doubleday 1978 c1977 188p o.p.

LC 77-76961

"Despite our knowing on p.2 who will die, and at whose hand, we are carried along by the powerful suspense of events in one upper-middle-class English family. The sense of impending doom amply takes the place of detective work, of which there is a little in the last three short chapters. The depiction of the 'perfect servant' is masterly and the whole thing a tour de force." Barzun. Cat of Crime. Rev and enl edition

The keys to the street; a novel of suspense. Crown 1996 326p $24

ISBN 0-517-70685-7 LC 96-3114

A novel about the "homeless denizens who haunt Regent's Park in London. Residents of the exclusive neighborhoods abutting the park make a point of not even noticing wretches like Effie and Dill and Pharaoh and Roman. Only Mary Jago, a frail, sensitive young woman who has recently moved into the neighborhood as a housesitter, pays any attention to these street people—until someone starts killing them and impaling their bodies on the spiked railings that surround the park. . . . All the characters are drawn with psychological insight, but it takes a visionary author to see the bonds that connect them all." N Y Times Book Rev

Kissing the gunner's daughter. Mysterious Press 1992 378p o.p.

LC 91-50615

"Chief Inspector Reginald Wexford investigates his first case in four years, conducting us to stately Tancred House, where celebrity writer Davina Flory and her family have been murdered. The only survivor is granddaughter Daisy, who is pointedly contrasted with Wexford's own rebellious daughter." Libr J

This is an "intricate story that hinges on vanity and self-deception, a story in which the most minor and seemingly innocent relationships are charged with meaning and malice." N Y Times Book Rev

Live flesh. Pantheon Bks. 1986 272p o.p.

LC 86-4922

"The main character of [this novel] is a mentally disturbed young man. Driven by an uncontrollable panic, Victor Jenner has committed several rapes. He shoots a promising young police officer in the back, confining David Fleetwood to a wheelchair for the rest of his life. Victor is sent to prison for 14 years. After he is released he befriends David and his girlfriend Clare, with disastrous results." Christ Sci Monit

"The obvious way to write this novel would have been to tell it through the eyes of the crippled policeman; Rendell takes the bolder path of getting inside the mind of Jenner. . . . [This] is a frightening, resonant novel—an extraordinary achievement." New Statesman (1913)

Make death love me. Doubleday 1979 246p o.p.

LC 78-22621

"Alan Groombridge, the manager of a small English village bank, [is] bound to a daily grind. . . . But Groombridge is a romantic; he longs to break away from his non-existence to a real life. Fate, in the form of two teenage bank robbers, gives Groombridge his chance. Rendell splices two stories throughout this thriller: the story of Groombridge's assistant, Joyce, held captive by the bank robbers, and that of Groombridge himself, freed from his old life, but still trapped by a lack of identity." Booklist

Master of the moor. Pantheon Bks. 1982 218p o.p.

LC 82-47871

"On one of his solitary walks on the moor, Stephen Walby finds the body of a young woman, shorn of her blonde hair. A very strange character, Stephen seems a likely suspect in the killing until evidence found with a second body points away from him. But Stephen discovers the killer's lair in an abandoned mine on the moor and feels a kinship with him, eventually killing another blonde woman and disposing of the body in imitation of him." Libr J

Means of evil, five mystery stories

In Rendell, R. Collected stories p137-262

Murder being once done. Doubleday 1972 201p o.p.

"Published for the Crime Club"

Chief Inspector Wexford "recovering from an ailment is staying with his nephew, a highly placed policeman in London. A particularly sordid murder takes place in a cemetery and the nephew is placed in charge of the case. The old man, shrewd and afraid of being in the way, takes a hand in investigating the singularly squalid background of the crime." Libr J

The new girl friend and other stories of suspense

In Rendell, R. Collected stories p409-536

Rendell, Ruth, 1930-—*Continued*

Road rage. Crown 1997 344p o.p.

LC 97-1200

"Taking what he vows will be his last walk in the deep woods that border his Sussex village, Chief Inspector Reginald Wexford contemplates with dread the new superhighway that will soon plow it all under. . . . But whatever sympathy he feels for the militant conservationists who pitch camp in Framhurst Great Wood to protest the highway is lost when a radical splinter group calling itself Sacred Globe kidnaps five innocent people—including Wexford's wife—and threatens to kill them unless the road is stopped." N Y Times Book Rev

A sight for sore eyes. Crown 1999 327p $24

ISBN 0-609-60417-1 LC 98-27654

"Rendell charts a harrowing collision course for two preternaturally beautiful teen-agers: Teddy Brex, an unloved child who grows up to be a sociopath, and Francine Hill, an overprotected child who grows up to be his ideal victim. . . . Reaching back a generation to get more traction for her macabre love story, Rendell takes a ruthless probe to every person (from Teddy's emotionally arrested parents to the faceless stranger who murdered Francine's mother) who had a hand in shaping the psyches of this ill-met pair. Spare and unforgiving, these incisive character studies illuminate the darker corners of Teddy's and Francine's family histories without dimming the originality of their bizarre lives." N Y Times Book Rev

Simisola. Crown 1995 327p o.p.

LC 95-8428

This novel features Chief Inspector Reginald Wexford. A "Nigerian-born doctor in Kingsmarkham, England, reports his daughter, Melanie, as missing. Not long afterward, the body of a young black woman is found. She turns out not to be Melanie . . . and is conjectured rather to be an immigrant female, probably Nigerian, who was forced to work as a slave for one of the well-to-do local families. Another young woman, who may have spoken to the dead girl, is murdered." N Y Times Book Rev

"Rendell's long acquaintance with her characters has not diminished the freshness of her work, nor her consummate storytelling. Rather, in Simisola, she offers a finely tuned moral tale that raises questions as it solves crimes." Times Lit Suppl

A sleeping life. Doubleday 1978 180p o.p.

LC 77-27716

When Chief Inspector Wexford is "called in to investigate the murder of one Rhoda Comfrey he is baffled to be unable to learn anything at all about her private life, friends, or means of supporting herself. His only clue, an expensive leather wallet, leads him up and down blind alleys until a chance remark by his own daughter, whose marriage is in jeopardy, leads him to Webster's International Dictionary and a brilliant deduction about the motive of the murderer." Shapiro. Fic for Youth. 3d edition

Speaker of Mandarin; a new Inspector Wexford mystery. Pantheon Bks. 1983 223p o.p.

LC 83-47745

In this installment Rendell removes "Wexford from his usual context. The first half of the book concerns his vacation in China at the invitation of his nephew, who is attending conferences. The story is well researched and shows a typical guided tour in communist China, with visits to schools, plants, and factories, some of which Wexford skips. A series of strange events occurs, including the death of a Chinese guide during a scenic tour down a river, as well as Wexford's experience of visions or hallucinations. The second half of the book is a typical investigation of a murder that reflects back upon the events overseas." Murphy. Ency of Murder and Mystery

Thirteen steps down; a novel. Crown 2005 c2004 340p $25

ISBN 1-4000-9842-4 LC 2005-750

First published 2004 in the United Kingdom

"Fitness-equipment repairman Mix Cellini lodges in a crumbling London mansion presided over by octogenarian Gwendolen Chawcer. Mix and Gwendolen have little in common except a lack of nurturing as children that has impaired their ability to develop meaningful relationships. The decay of the house mirrors the disintegration of Mix's personality as his obsessions with fame, murder, and beautiful model Nerissa Nash (a fellow lodger) eat his mind like a cancer. The creepiness of the mansion and its occupants is so pronounced that it is, at times, difficult to maintain interest in their fate. However, Rendell . . . veers away from the expected in her characters and in her plot, which saves the novel and makes for riveting reading." Libr J

The tree of hands. Pantheon Bks. 1985 c1984 271p o.p.

LC 84-19002

First published 1984 in the United Kingdom

"Benet, successful author and unwed mother, is visited by her mentally unstable mother, Mopsa. When the baby dies, Mopsa snatches another child to give to Benet. Substitute-baby Jason is the offspring of child abuser, larcenous Carol. The child's putative father is a gigolo intent on defrauding his current patroness. The story explores spectrum of parental feeling against a background of pervasive anxiety and impending doom. This is not a mystery, really, but rather an engrossing psychological thriller." Libr J

An unkindness of ravens; a new Inspector Wexford mystery. Pantheon Bks. 1985 245p o.p.

LC 84-26624

This novel "concerns a missing husband who months later is found murdered. Investigation reveals some unpleasant things about his marital arrangments and sexual preferences. Wexford also has to deal with a society of young women who draw ravens with a woman's face on their arms." N Y Times Book Rev

"Rendell, always with a keen eye toward social observation, offers sharp insights into feminism, pregnancy, and the mother-child relationship, while providing a thought-provoking mystery." Libr J

Resnick, Mike, 1942-

The return of Santiago. TOR Bks. 2003 464p $25.95

ISBN 0-7653-0224-1 LC 2002-75660

Sequel to: Santiago (1986)

"A century after the alleged demise of the legendary Santiago, the greatest outlaw of the Inner Frontier, a petty thief named Danny Briggs stumbles upon a lost col-

Resnick, Mike, 1942-—*Continued*
lection of poems by Black Orpheus, the interstellar bard whose verses immortalized Santiago. Inspired by his discovery, Briggs—now renamed Dante—sets off across the galaxy in search of someone to re-create the legend of Santiago and start a rebellion against the enemies of freedom." Libr J

"An eminently satisfying space western, with just the right mixture of fast-drawing gunmen and talented women to keep the action going." Booklist

Reuland, Rob

Semiautomatic; a novel; Robert Reuland. 1st ed. Random House 2004 242p $24.95
ISBN 0-375-50502-4 LC 2003-46806

"Brooklyn prosecutor Andrew Giobberti has been exiled to the Appeals Bureau for so long he's almost forgotten that putting away murderers is in his DNA. Almost. When he's pulled out of purgatory to rescue a politically sensitive homicide trial prepped by a green, painfully ethical prosecutor, Giobberti's soon ready for his courtroom comeback. But even as he shows his unwilling partner the ropes they'll use to encircle the defendant's neck, disturbing holes start appearing in the case" Booklist

This thriller is "notable not for violence but for subtle characterizations, moral ambiguities and exceptional writing." Washington Post Book World

Reuss, Frederick, 1960-

Henry of Atlantic City. MacMurray & Beck 1999 249p o.p.
ISBN 1-87844-889-7 LC 99-26946

This novel "begins in the modern-day casino town where Henry's father, a chief security officer at Caesar's Palace with mob connections, is on the run for embezzlement. The six-year-old Henry, being a precocious (he has a photographic memory) but lonely child, spends his time poring over The Coptic Gnostic Library and comes to think of himself as living the life of a saint in fifth-century Byzantium. And so the new and old worlds conflate into one seamless whole in young Henry's mind. . . . The rest of the story follows Henry as he winds through several cities, encountering thieves, prostitutes, and priests who baffle and are baffled by him." Booklist

"Reuss's manner—a spare third-person narrative, sticking largely to terms and phrases Henry knows—becomes a courageously concentrated show of authorial control and tonal fidelity." Publ Wkly

Horace afoot. MacMurray & Beck 1997 278p o.p.
ISBN 1-878448-79-X LC 97-21601

In this novel, "Quintus Horatius Flaccus, a man of wealth and mystery, moves to Oblivion, a small midwestern town. Horace, who changed his name from William Blake, is fleeing from the vagaries and dissonance of contemporary life. Horace's idiosyncracies—no car, wandering the town at odd hours, a propensity for turning up in the wrong places at the wrong times and frequently without clothes, his random phone calls to engage Oblivionites in Socratic dialogues on topics such as what is love—do not endear him to the town's residents. Gradually, real life intrudes as Horace becomes friends with a dying librarian, rescues a rape victim, and becomes the target of a malicious adolescent." Booklist

This novel "combines two strands of plot: a sly satire of Midwestern life and a restrained account of how a closed heart comes to be unlocked. . . . combines two strands of plot: a sly satire of Midwestern life and a restrained account of how a closed heart comes to be unlocked." N Y Times Book Rev

The wasties. Pantheon Bks. 2002 229p $23
ISBN 0-375-42071-1 LC 2001-55450

"English professor Michael 'Caruso' Taylor has lost the ability to speak and embarks on a journey of infantilization that progressively strips him of his autonomy—a condition he labels 'the wasties.' He grows entirely dependent on others: his pregnant wife, Gina; his nurse, Theresa; and a host of health-care professionals who attempt to rein in his childish impulses. Taylor communicates via scribbled messages, IBM ThinkPad and hand gestures." Publ Wkly

"This should appeal to sophisticated readers who like darkly humorous, cerebral fiction." Booklist

Reverte, Arturo Pérez- *See* Pérez-Reverte, Arturo

Reynolds, Margaret

(ed) The Penguin book of lesbian short stories. See The Penguin book of lesbian short stories

Reynolds, Marjorie, 1921-1997

The Starlite Drive-in; a novel. Morrow 1997 282p $23
ISBN 0-688-15389-5 LC 97-728

"When developers find a body in a well at the old Starlite Drive-In, Callie Ann Benton knows whose body it is. It takes her back to when she was 12; her father ran the drive-in, and her mother, Teal, had become completely trapped inside her house by agoraphobia. It traps her father, too, forcing him to give up dreams, and his resentment comes out in nasty sniping, continuous putdowns that drain her—until a drifter named Charlie Memphis arrives, falls in love with Teal, and plans to take her and Callie away. This stunning novel is told by 12-year-old Callie, torn between her crush on Memphis, her love for her father, and her resentment of her mother's sexuality and personhood." Libr J

Reynolds, Sheri

A gracious plenty; a novel. Harmony Bks. 1997 205p $21
ISBN 0-609-60225-X LC 97-21544

The narrator "is a deeply troubled woman growing up in a Southern fundamentalist culture. Hideously burned in an accident when she was only 4, Finch Nobles is shunned and persecuted. . . . Worse yet, she becomes the inspirational 'project' of the adult women's Sunday school class. Wishing she were already dead and buried, she dedicates herself to caring for the local cemetery, where she communes with the spirits of the departed." NY Times Book Rev

"Lyricism and the gentle voice of her heroine carry this poignant but redemptive story of an emotionally and physically scarred woman who finds her way out of the land of the dead and into the land of the living." Publ Wkly

Rhodes, Jewell Parker

Voodoo dreams; a novel of Marie Laveau. St. Martin's Press 1993 436p o.p.
LC 93-24283

This novel is about "Marie Laveau, New Orleans' legendary nineteenth-century voodoo queen. Although few biographical facts are known about Marie, Rhodes has parlayed them into a character of vast dimension and feminine power. Like her grandmother and mother before her, Marie is a *voodooienne,* a woman visited and possessed by the African god Damballah, and the third Marie Laveau to suffer the consequences of this terrifying blessing in a world poisoned by the sin of slavery. As Rhodes imagines Marie's strange and painful life, from her protected childhood deep in the bayou to her reign as healer in New Orleans, she evokes all the lust, tumult, and cruelty of that race-obsessed city." Booklist

Rhys, Jean

After leaving Mr. Mackenzie. Knopf 1931 227p o.p.

This "work is a study of the gradual breakdown of a kept woman who is no longer kept. The parting from Mr. Mackenzie marks the downward turning point in Julia's life, a bleak one at best, though one with a few illusions. It is the loss of these that Julia is not able to face. Spiritually isolated and lacking a means of support, Julia attempts to return to her sister and invalid mother. After a devastatingly bleak encounter, the sisters remain as morally and spiritually isolated from each other as their mother, the victim of a stroke, remains from them." Libr J

"The 'feeling of foreboding, of anxiety, as if her heart were being squeezed' that afflicts Julia Martin afflicts the reader so freshly that a catastrophic final crash would come as a relief. Jean Rhys refuses us that. Her special subject is the longevity of fecklessness. We read her with apprehension—fascinated, embarrassed. She is an extraordinary artist." Newsweek

The collected short stories; introduction by Diana Athill. Norton 1987 403p o.p.
LC 88-138678

Contents: Illusion; A spiritualist; From a French prison; In a café; Tout Montparnasse and a lady; Mannequin; In the Luxemburg Gardens; Tea with an artist; Trio; Mixing cocktails; Again the Antilles; Hunger; Discourse of a lady standing a dinner to a down-and-out friend; A night; In the Rue de l'Arrivée; Learning to be a mother; The blue bird; The grey day; The Sidi; At the Villa d'Or; La grosse Fifi; Vienne; Till September Petronella; The day they burned the books; Let them call it jazz; Tigers are better-looking; Outside the machine; The lotus; A solid house; The sound of the river; I spy a stranger; Temps perdi; Pioneers, oh, pioneers; Good-bye Marcus, good-bye Rose; The Bishop's feast; Heat; Fishy waters; Overture and beginners please; Before the deluge; On not shooting sitting birds; Kikimora; Night out 1925; The Chevalier of the Place Blanche; The insect world; Rapunzel, Rapunzel; Who knows what's up in the attic; Sleep it off lady; I used to live here once; Kismet; The whistling bird; Invitation to the dance

Quartet. Simon & Schuster 1929 228p o.p.

First published 1928 in the United Kingdom with title Postures

"The ingredients: an English girl in Paris, married to a Polish adventurer, who is imprisoned for theft and leaves her penniless, a stranger except for casual acquaintances in the foreign colony, to become the guest of an English couple, a man who desires her and can arouse her passion, and his wife, who keeps the girl in the home where she has her always under observation, always at a disadvantage, until she can finally crush her. The attitudes of the three are exposed with pitiless precision—the utter helplessness of the victim, the diabolic ingenuity of the wife, the social cowardice of the husband which makes a peculiarly disgusting setting for his lust. The background of Paris, in its cold hostility, with its tedious round of mechanical pleasures, throws the episode into harsh relief." Bookman (NY)

Wide Sargasso Sea; introduction by Francis Wyndham. Norton 1967 c1966 189p o.p.

First published 1966 in the United Kingdom

This novel, "set in Dominica and Jamaica during the 1830s, presents the life of the mad Mrs. Rochester from 'Jane Eyre,' a Creole heiress here called Antoinette Cosway; in the brief last section she is imprisoned in the attic in Thornfield Hall." Oxford Companion to Engl Lit. 6th edition

Riboud, Barbara Chase- *See* Chase-Riboud, Barbara, 1939-

Rice, Anne, 1941-

Blackwood Farm. Knopf 2002 527p $26.95
ISBN 0-375-41199-2 LC 2003-272519

In this ninth volume in the author's vampire chronicles "fledgling vampire Quinn Blackwood makes a desperate appeal to the older, stronger Lestat to save his loved ones from Goblin, a doppelganger out to destroy them. Since Quinn entered the dark world of the undead, the once caring and protective Goblin has amassed tremendous strength and a ruthlessness that cannot be controlled. Lestat is intrigued but refuses to make a decision until Quinn tells his life story. Slowly, the dark, Gothic settings and eccentric characters that make Rice's fiction so fascinating emerge." Libr J

Blood and gold; or, The story of Marius. Knopf 2001 471p (Vampire chronicles) $26.95
ISBN 0-679-45449-7 LC 2001-94703

This eighth volume of the Vampire chronicles features Marius, a mentor to Lestat, the creator of Armand, and the lover of Pandora. "The intellectual and artistic 'Child of the Millennia' meets ice-age Thorne, another vampire, who's just waking up after a very long sleep and is eager to hear his history. Marius grants Thorne's wish, taking him and the reader on a rollicking vampire adventure through time." Booklist

Blood canticle. Knopf 2003 305p $25.95
ISBN 0-375-41200-X LC 2002-192475

This tenth volume of the Vampire chronicles takes up where "Blackwood Farm ended, the now-doppelganger-free Quinn Blackwood and Lestat save Quinn's true love, the witch Mona Mayfair, from certain death by making her an immortal. In his effort to attain sainthood, Lestat

Rice, Anne, 1941—*Continued*
must deal with a lot of metaphysical angst. The opulent Blackwood estate and its spooky swamps, as well as New Orleans and a Caribbean isle, provide the settings for many elegant costume changes as the exquisite vampiric triumvirate gleefully suck several deserving victims dry and lay waste to dozens of a drug lord's minions." Publ Wkly

The Feast of All Saints. Simon & Schuster 1979 571p o.p.
LC 79-16680

"The world of the Free People of Color (the 'gens de couleur libre') in antebellum New Orleans (the old French city) is the background for this romantic historical novel that brings to life an era and a place. . . . Quadroon Marcel Ste. Maria and his lovely sister Marie, children of a white plantation owner, and the lovely Cecile, his dusky mistress, grow up in the demimonde, housed and supported and educated as gentility by their father, but destined to be separated from his world by virtue of their mixed blood. . . . [The story] pits passion and principle and love against the hard realities of class and color in old New Orleans." Publ Wkly

Interview with the vampire. Reset for anniversary ed. Knopf 1996 340p $27.95; pa $7.99
ISBN 0-394-49821-6; 0-345-33766-2 (pa)
LC 96-232882

First published 1976

"In contemporary New Orleans a young reporter listens as Louis, a vampire, unfolds his tale. His story spans several hundred years . . . of a Faustian search for some meaning to his life-in-death existence, an existence complicated by his relationship to three other vampires. Lestat, the vampire who made him, is hated by Claudia, the five-year-old extraordinarily beautiful child-vampire Louis loves. . . . After Claudia attempts to kill Lestat she and Louis go to Europe in search of other vampires. In Paris they find Armand, Master Vampire, and he and Louis fall in love, remaining together for a time after Claudia's death in a state of meaningless immortality." Libr J

Lasher; a novel. Knopf 1993 577p $30
ISBN 0-679-41295-6 LC 93-12246

"Returning to the Mayfair clan she introduced in *The Witching Hour* Rice offers another vast, transcontinental saga of witchcraft and demonism in the tradition of Gothic melodrama. . . . Embedded in this antique demonism is a contemporary tale of incest and family abuse that achieves resonance. It is maintained through the character of Lasher, both child and man at the same time, who manipulates his victims with his own pain. At their best, Rice's characters rise above the more wooden plot machinations with an ironic and modern complexity." Publ Wkly

Followed by Taltos

Memnoch the Devil. Knopf 1995 353p $25
ISBN 0-679-44101-8 LC 95-77866

The fifth volume of the Vampire chronicles "finds vampire Lestat de Lioncourt being courted by fallen archangel Memnoch, a.k.a. Satan, to be his lieutenant in Hell, but not for the purpose of pursuing evil. Memnoch instead desires Lestat's help in redeeming souls." Libr J

The author "boldly probes the significance of death, belief in the afterlife and other spiritual matters." Publ Wkly

Followed by The vampire Armand

Merrick; a novel. Knopf 2000 307p $26.95
ISBN 0-679-45448-9 LC 99-88556

The seventh volume of the Vampire chronicles. Narrated "by the fledgling David Talbot, the book introduces Merrick, a potent witch with the usual irresistible charms, who aids David in a request involving a desperate Louis—a request that climaxes in disaster and alters Louis profoundly." Libr J

"This volume merges several long-running plots. . . . Merrick must revisit the Guatemalan rainforest, where she traveled as a young girl, to locate a secret treasure trove of ominous ancient runes. Displaying her imaginative talents for atmosphere and suspense, Rice creates a riveting scene that shows Merrick's awesome magic at work." Publ Wkly

The queen of the damned; the third book in the vampire chronicles. Knopf 1988 448p (Vampire chronicles) $27.50
ISBN 0-394-55823-5 LC 88-45311

In this third volume in the Vampire chronicles "the plot revolves around an internecine struggle in vampiredom. On one side is 6000-year-old Akasha, who has concluded that the world would be a safer, more peaceful and equitable place if women ran it. Her plan is to set herself up as the reigning Goddess of Earth; then to kill off all human males except a few breeders, until such time when female values are firmly in place and males can be allowed to flourish again. Her opponents argue that you can't make a peaceful world through violence." Ms

"Don't let the title or the subject matter fool you; this is quality fiction written with care and intelligence. There are no false steps or wasted words in the multilayered plot, and the many characters each have a distinct voice. It's not absolutely necessary to have read the other 'Chronicles' to understand this one, but it would add greatly to the richness of the whole." Libr J

Followed by The tale of the body thief

Servant of the bones. Knopf 1996 387p $26
ISBN 0-679-43301-5 LC 95-49357

This is the story "of Azriel, a young Jewish man in ancient Babylonia who must mystically take on the form of the god Marduk. He is instead transformed into a spirit, destined to travel through time, summoned forth periodically by a Master, for whom he brings wealth and power. At the end of the 20th century, however, Azriel finds that he has developed the power to summon himself and work for good and the love of others." Libr J

The author's "research into science, history and Jewish scholarship will probably leave readers impressed and entertained." Publ Wkly

The tale of the body thief. Knopf 1992 430p $30
ISBN 0-679-40528-3 LC 92-53085

In this fourth novel in the Vampire chronicles Lestat encounters Raglan James, "a mortal con man whose extraordinary psychic powers let him cheat the vampire out of his demonic, enormously powerful body. . . . Lestat, in a male human body, charges about the world with his mortal friend David Talbot, trying to reclaim his vampire

Rice, Anne, 1941—*Continued*

body." Time

"Readers who crave a happy ending, a justice and a moral coherence that transcend the muddle they really live in, may feel [the author] has broken faith with them. After all, isn't that what escapist fiction is supposed to provide? Grown-ups, on the other hand, will be intelligently entertained, and no more disquieted than usual." Newsweek

Followed by Memnoch the Devil

Taltos; lives of the Mayfair witches. Knopf 1994 467p $25

ISBN 0-679-42573-X LC 93-35693

"This third book in the Mayfair Witches series tells the story of Ash, a centuries-old Taltos who resides in New york City. The Taltos grow to a height of seven feet, carry an extra set of chromosomes, and have a superior intelligence that enables them to digest dictionaries and encyclopedias in moments. There is something rotten in the state of the Talamasca, an order of scholars who study the supernatural and keep records of the Mayfair witches. When one such scholar is murdered, Rowan Mayfair, the mother of the two late Taltos in *Lasher*, and husband Michael Curry investigate. . . . Although this novel is a suspenseful and sometimes thought-provoking page-turner, it does not stand on its own; the first two books in the series must be read first." Libr J

The vampire Armand. Knopf 1998 387p (Vampire chronicles) $26.95

ISBN 0-679-45447-0 LC 98-14579

The sixth volume of the Vampire chronicles follows the vampire Armand "from his boyhood in Kiev Rus, a conquered city under the rule of the Mongols, to ancient Constantinople, where he is sold into slavery by vicious Tartars, to the palazzo in Renaissance Venice, where he meets the great vampire Marius, who gives him the gift of the vampire blood and shows him how to be an 'ethical' vampire. . . . As always, Rice paints a fascinating and dazzling historical tapestry, providing a beautifully written and incredibly absorbing tale." Booklist

The vampire Lestat; the second book in the chronicles of the vampires. Knopf 1985 481p $27.50

ISBN 0-394-53443-3 LC 85-40123

In this second volume of the Vampire chronicles Lestat "isn't dead, but has been alive, well, and resting in his New Orleans crypt since 1929. The chance to become the lead singer with a satanic heavy metal rock band is just enough to wrest him from his unquiet grave, however, and Lestat's desires to become a celebrity and to set the world straight on vampires prompt him to recount his life." Booklist

This novel "is ornate and pungently witty. In the classic tradition of Gothic fiction, it teases and tantalizes us into accepting its kaleidoscopic world. Even when they annoy us or tell us more than we want to know, its undead characters are utterly alive. Their adventures and frustrations are funny, frightening and surprising at once." N Y Times Book Rev

Followed by The queen of the damned

Vittorio the vampire; new tales of the vampires. Knopf 1999 292p $19.95

ISBN 0-375-40160-1 LC 98-14209

In this novel, "Vittorio tells of his human life and the dramatic events that led him to join the ranks of the undead. He is 16, living the privileged life of the nobility in Renaissance Italy, when a host of vampires savagely attacks his family. His parents, brother, and sister are ruthlessly murdered, but Vittorio has caught the eye of the beautiful vampiress Ursula and is spared. Eventually, Vittorio has his revenge on the demons who have destroyed his loved ones, but he pays a terrible price." Libr J

The witching hour; a novel. Knopf 1990 965p $29.95

ISBN 0-394-58786-3 LC 90-53103

Rice "tells the story of the prominent and wealthy Mayfair family who, for five centuries, has cavorted with a supernatural entity that has brought them both great bounty as well as abject misery. Neurosurgeon Rowan Mayfair inherits the family fortune, along with the sinister attentions of this entity. When Rowan saves the life of Michael Curry their fates become entwined, and together they seek to understand and destroy the terrible force that holds her family in its power. Helping them in this dangerous task is occult investigator Aaron Lightner. . . . Although a bit long-winded at times, this is still a compelling novel." Libr J

Followed by Lasher

Rice, Luanne

Blue moon. Viking 1993 305p o.p.

LC 92-50732

This novel focuses on "four generations of a Rhode Island resort-town fishing family. The action focuses primarily on the grand-daughters of the family founders (and mainly on the youngest, Cass), who are helping their parents run the family's waterfront restaurant. . . . Dad is thinking of retiring and selling off the waterfront property to developers, Cass's teenage son can't believe how incredibly dense his parents are, and Billy, Cass's husband, is nearly lost at sea." Libr J

"Such a rare combination of realism and romance comes along well, once in a blue moon. You don't have to be a sucker for happy endings to love this book, but it helps." N Y Times Book Rev

Cloud Nine; a novel. Bantam Bks. 1999 323p $19.95

ISBN 0-553-11063-2 LC 98-47796

"Sarah Talbot is the survivor of a very difficult form of cancer. She has once again taken charge of her destiny and reopened her bedding shop, Cloud Nine, when an emotionally wounded young pilot and his daughter come into her life." Libr J

"Rice, a blessedly spare writer, is especially skilled at getting inside the heads of the teen-agers as they watch the adults navigate through years of unfinished business-of-the-heart." N Y Times Book Rev

Dance with me; Luanne Rice. Bantam Books 2004 339p $22.95

ISBN 0-553-80227-5 LC 2003-70886

"Jane Porter is traveling back to her hometown of Twin Rivers, Rhode Island, with a heavy heart. She has stayed away as much as possible for the last 15 years, while her sister, Sylvie, has remained in town and taken care of their ill mother. The girls' mother was once a

Rice, Luanne—*Continued*
proud school principal who raised her brilliant daughters alone after her husband deserted them and then, because of her pride and fear of abandonment, convinced young Jane to give her newborn child up for adoption when the father wanted nothing to do with them. Jane has always regretted that decision and now wants to see her daughter. The opportunity arises when she meets her daughter's uncle, Dylan, who has lost his wife and daughter. Dylan and Jane both have an aura of tragedy about them. He and Jane become involved, and through him she develops a relationship with her daughter, Chloe, without revealing the fact that she is Chloe's birth mother. Once again, Rice captures the wonder of life, warts and all, and puts in a bid for hope." Booklist

Home fires. Bantam Bks. 1995 312p o.p.
LC 94-23911

In this novel,"privileged New Yorker Anne Davis returns to her New England island childhood home after the death of her four-year-old daughter and the breakup of her marriage. Seeking solitude from her sister, who has never left the island, she finds kinship—and love—with a scarred fireman who understands tragedy, having survived it himself. At the same time she reconnects with her teenaged niece, whose high school days are in danger of becoming a haze of alcohol and lust. . . . A strikingly real story of family feelings and grief." Libr J

Safe harbor. Bantam Bks. 2002 337p o.p.
ISBN 0-553-80218-6 LC 2001-49954

A novel set in the seaside town of Black Hall, Connecticut. "Grief-stricken Dana Underhill returns home to care for her two nieces, Quinn and Allie, following the death of her sister, Lily, and Lily's husband, Mike, in a sailing accident. Dana, a professional painter, had intended to whisk her nieces back to France with her, but her plans are put on hold when she realizes that change may not be what's best for Quinn and Allie. Indeed. Quinn, a cigarette-smoking 12-year-old with a chip on her shoulder, is dead set against leaving, particularly since she's determined to uncover the circumstances surrounding her parents' deaths. . . . Dana's childhood acquaintance, oceanographer and Yale professor Sam Trevor, arrives to provide Dana with a shoulder to lean on and to help Quinn find the answers she seeks." Publ Wkly

The secret hour. Bantam Bks. 2003 335p $22.95
ISBN 0-553-80224-0 LC 2002-27985

"Marine biologist Kate Harris travels from Washington, D.C., to Connecticut on a mision of love. She is searching for her missing sister, Willa, who disappeared six months earlier, and whom Kate believes might be a victim of a serial killer whose lawyer is John O'Rourke. . . . As John helps her, pursuing answers to questions that put them both at grave risk, their lives become deeply entwined. Rice's lyrical style reveals the mind of a serial killer and humanizes the dilemma of justice by the book versus justice for victims." Booklist

Summer light. Bantam Bks. 2001 372p o.p.
ISBN 0-553-80122-8 LC 2001-25475

A novel about wedding planner May Taylor and her "daughter, Kylie, a special child who seems to feel things more deeply than others and who sees angels. It's Kylie who brings her mother and Bruins hockey star, Martin Cartier, together. For Martin, its love at first sight, but May is leery of relationships. She finally agrees to marriage, but life is complicated as their careers require that they live alternately in Connecticut, Canada, and Boston. . . . With her gift, Kylie tries to unite the family in the face of tragedy, and the prolific Rice skillfully blends romance with magic." Booklist

Rich, Virginia

The baked bean supper murders. Dutton 1983 267p o.p.
LC 83-70156

"Eugenia Potter arrives at her sometime home in Northcutt Harbor, Me., just in time for the annual baked-bean dinner. She is also just in time to see her dearest friends carried off, first by accident and then by natural causes. She begins to feel uneasy, and when her beloved weimaraner is electrocuted in an accident that saves her own life, she takes another look at the earlier deaths. While Mrs. Potter goes about discovering who is responsible for what she determines to be murder, we get to sample Maine cooking, complete with recipes." Publ Wkly

"Colorful and chatty, with a fleet of diverse, realistic characters, this novel presents the rich tapestry of small-town life." Libr J

The cooking school murders. Dutton 1982 207p o.p.
LC 81-22162

"Harrington, Iowa, has its own 'beautiful people' and 12 of them gather for the first session of a gourmet cooking class. James Redmond, chef 'extraordinaire,' instructs his students in the versatility of a thin, sharp boning knife. The next day, the enrollment is minus three. One lies dead, stabbed with a boning knife. One is an apparent suicide and murderer. One is drowned accidentally. Eugenia Potter, home on a visit, knows the town and suspects that not all is what it seems." Publ Wkly

The Nantucket diet murders. Delacorte Press 1985 276p o.p.
LC 84-21501

"It is the middle of winter in Nantucket, and a group of year-round residents, more or less well-to-do widows who call themselves 'Les Girls,' gather to welcome home an old friend, Eugenia Potter, an erstwhile member of the group who now resides in Arizona and Maine. Their latest subject for talk is the arrival of a charismatic diet doctor, the mysterious Count Tony Ferencz, who has Les Girls all in a flutter and looking better than they have in years. No sooner has Eugenia arrived however, than strange events begin to occur. . . . Eugenia finally manages to find the answers in a dangerous and suspense-filled conclusion. Fans of Nantucket and haute cuisine will find and enjoy both in this somewhat over-long, but well-written book." Publ Wkly

Richards, David Adams, 1950-

The bay of love and sorrows; a novel. Arcade Pub. 2003 307p $24.95
ISBN 1-55970-650-3 LC 2002-38348

"In the early Seventies, Michael Skid, the privileged son of a judge, returns to his hometown on the Oyster River in rural New Brunswick from his postgraduate wanders through India. He takes up with a dangerous crowd, including Everette Hutch, an ex-convict who

Richards, David Adams, 1950-—*Continued*

makes a practice of surreptitiously taping his friends in order to blackmail them later, and his coterie of drug-using associates." Libr J

"Michael is as naive as the other downtrodden individuals Everette has chosen as pawns to carry out his darkly laid plans, and the tragic events that ensue will forever be ingrained in the minds of the townpeople residing in The Bay of Love and Sorrows. Richards' story falls into place with the ease of a domino rally, providing all of the elements for a riveting story." Booklist

Richardson, Samuel, 1689-1761

Clarissa; or, The history of a young lady. o.p.

First published 1749

In this epistolary novel Clarissa Harlowe "has been coldly commanded by her tyrannical family to marry Mr. Solmes, a man she despises. She refuses, even though it pains her to defy her parents. Locked in her room, isolated from family and friends, Clarissa corresponds secretly with Robert Lovelace, a suitor disapproved of by her family; she finally throws herself upon his protection and flees with him. It soon becomes clear to her, however, that Lovelace's sole aim is to seduce her. Her virtue is so great that Lovelace becomes obsessively absorbed in breaking it down." Reader's Ency. 4th edition

Pamela. o.p.

First published 1740-1741

"On the death of Pamela Andrews' mistress, her mistress's son, Mr. B, begins a series of mild stratagems designed to end in Pamela's seduction. These failing, he abducts her and renews his siege in earnest. Pamela spurns his advances, and halfway through the novel Mr. B offers marriage. In the second half of the novel, Pamela wins over those who had disapproved of the misalliance." Merriam-Webster's Ency of Lit

Richler, Mordecai, 1931-2001

Barney's version; a novel, with footnotes and an afterword by Michael Panofsky. Knopf 1997 355p $25

ISBN 0-679-40418-X LC 97-37033

At sixty-seven, Barney Panofsky, "has decided to set the record straight about his Bohemian days in Paris in the 1950s, his circle of famous and infamous acquaintances, his wildly successful career as a television producer, and his three wildly unsuccessful marriages. Mostly, though, he is writing his memoirs to clear his name of the murder of his once-cherished friend, the nearly important writer Bernard 'Boogie' Moscovitch." Quill Quire

"What entertains and affects us in 'Barney's Version' is the headlong, spendthrift passage of a life, redeemed from oblivion in the unbridled telling. The edge of the grave makes a lively point vantage." New Yorker

Solomon Gursky was here; a novel. Knopf 1990 413p o.p.

LC 89-43393

This is a "reworking of Canadian history that chronicles the fortunes of the mythical Gursky family. . . . From patriarch Ephraim, a con man who arrived with a doomed British Arctic exploration team, through his bootlegger grandsons Bernard, Solomon, and Morrie, who parlayed prohibition into a distillery fortune, the Gurskys' penchant for grand and petty larceny is played off against upper-crust-Canadian and English society, torn between greed and anti-Semitism. Moses Berger, Solomon's appropriately alcoholic biographer, assembles the pieces of Gursky history in a hilarious narrative that jumps back and forth from Victorian England to modern Montreal and all points in between." Libr J

Richler is a "ringmaster, making his performers do dazzling backflips without missing a beat. At the same time he is a moralist, recoiling from those who would sentimentalize the Holocaust or make power a sacrament." Time

Richler, Nancy, 1957-

Your mouth is lovely; a novel. Ecco Press 2002 357p $25.95

ISBN 0-06-009677-2 LC 2002-23521

This "novel summons up the lost world of the Russian shtetls around the Pripet marshes in Ukraine, and shows how those communities were first changed and then annihilated by the events that led, ultimately, to the Russian Revolution. At the center of Richler's tale is Miriam Lev, whose mother drowned herself when she was a day old, and who at age six is taken in hand by her father's new wife, Tsila, a harsh, beautiful seamstress who teaches Miriam the alphabet and dreams of another life. After an ill-starred and and painful series of events, Miriam ends up, at nineteen, in Siberia, having shot an officer of the Tsar at point-blank range. Miriam's hegira is told here as a letter to her own daughter, whom she hasn't seen since she gave birth to her, in prison. Richler's work recalls the stories of Isaac Babel, in which the knowable is charged with mystery." New Yorker

Richter, Conrad, 1890-1968

The awakening land. Knopf 1966 3v in 1 o.p.

Contents: The trees; The fields; The town

This trilogy depicts " a pioneer family and settlement's slow evolution from virgin wilderness to an organized community." Reader's Ency. 4th edition

The fields

In Richter, C. The awakening land p169-329

The light in the forest. Knopf 1953 179p o.p.

Companion volume to A country of strangers (1966)

"John Butler is kidnapped at the age of four and raised by Delaware Indians. Eleven years later, under a truce agreement between the Indians and the colonials, he is forcibly returned to his family. Irrevocably divided in his heart, he escapes and goes back to the Indians but is sent away after the failure of an Indian ambush." Shapiro. Fic for Youth. 3d edition

The sea of grass. Knopf 1937 149p o.p.

"Set in New Mexico in the late 19th century, the novel concerns the often violent clashes between the pioneering ranchers, whose cattle range freely through the vast sea of grass, and the farmers, or 'nesters,' who build fences and turn the sod. Against this background is set the triangle of rancher Colonel Jim Brewton, his unstable Eastern wife Lutie, and the ambitious Brice Chamberlain. Richter casts the story in Homeric terms, with the children caught up in the conflicts of their parents." Merriam-Webster's Ency of Lit

Richter, Conrad, 1890-1968—*Continued*

The town
In Richter, C. The awakening land p331-630

The trees
In Richter, C. The awakening land p1-167

Rickards, John

Winter's end; John Rickards. 1st U.S. ed. Thomas Dunne Books 2003 297p $23.95
ISBN 0-312-31097-8 LC 2003-46874
"Sheriff Dale Townsend asks for an old friend's help in interrogating a very slippery and clever murder suspect in small-town Maine. Dale himself found the suspect standing over the victim clutching the alleged murder weapon, but the guy refuses to give his name or answer any questions. When Dale's PI friend Alex Rourke, an ex-FBI agent good at interrogation, appears, he bores a few chinks in the guy's armor. Strangely, the suspect knows about Alex and seemed to expect him. An attention-getting plot, riveting prose, calculated suspense, and tense, human-interest subplotting mark this noteworthy first novel." Libr J

Ricks, Thomas E.

A soldier's duty; a novel. Random House 2000 250p $24.95
ISBN 0-375-50544-X LC 2001-18601
"When a peacekeeping mission in Afghanistan goes tragically wrong, officers led by Gen. B.Z. Ames form a treasonous group called the 'Sons of Liberty' to unravel American foreign policy and further General Ames's position. Army majors Cindy Sherman and Bud Lewis are newly assigned to the Pentagon, where they become involved in both sides of the developing problem." Libr J
"One would have to look far for a novel that touches so deftly on the complexities and challenges of leadership of military organizations at the highest levels." Parameters

Ridgway, Keith

The parts; Keith Ridgway. 1st U.S. ed. Thomas Dunne Books 2004 2003 457p $24.95
ISBN 0-312-32769-2 LC 2004-41874
"On an isolated estate outside of Dublin, Delly Roche, a fabulously wealthy widow, longs for death and an escape from the memory of her infidelity. She is cared for by her enormously obese companion of 20 years, romance novelist Kitty Flood, and by her adopted son, Dr. George Addison-Blake, who may or may not be deranged. Meanwhile, in a seedier section of town, rentboy Koz is being wooed by nervous, kindly producer Barry, who wants to date him but is too shy to say so and also wants him to appear on a new, hard-hitting radio show. The show's host, Joe Kavanaugh, is struggling to right himself after succumbing to a noisy, dissolute midlife crisis. These days, Joe's greatest wish is to befriend his gentle immigrant neighbors, who regard him with a certain amount of horror. In gorgeous, discursive prose, Ridgway brings the six characters together in a convoluted plot fairly brimming with paranoia; explosive, bitter humor; and heartbreak." Booklist

Ridley, John, 1965-

A conversation with the Mann; a novel. Warner Bks. 2002 433p o.p.
ISBN 0-446-52836-6 LC 2001-52605
This "roman a clef is set against the backdrop of 19501960s Hollywood, Rat Pack Las Vegas and the Civil Rights movement, The fictional narrator is a mordant, world-weary Harlem-raised black comic, Jackie Mann, who irreverently recounts a journey from poverty to his symbol of success, an appearance on The Ed Sullivan Show, a path strewn with compromise and degradation. . . . Ridley vividly brings to life noirish panoramas of high-stakes show business, as well as the myriad humiliations endured by a black man trying to win fame in segregated America. The novel is a veritable 'who's who' of well-known showbiz personalities." Publ Wkly

Those who walk in darkness. Warner Bks. 2003 310p $24.95
ISBN 0-446-53093-X LC 2002-193352
This "novel questions the nature of heroism in a near future where cops battle mutated 'metanormals' with telepathy, pyrokinetics, and other superpowers. Officer Soledad O'Roark is a successful 'freak' killer, unquestioning in her belief that they are dangerous and need to be desroyed." Libr J
"For all the bleakness . . . Ridley makes it hard not to pull for Soledad. Readers will find themselves torn between sympathy, empathy, pity and disgust, often on the same page." Publ Wkly

Riggs, Cynthia

Jack in the pulpit; Cynthia Riggs. 1st ed. Thomas Dunne Books\St. Martin's Minotaur 2004 211p $22.95
ISBN 0-312-33011-1 LC 2003-69540
In this "installment in her Victoria Trumbull series, Riggs offers a kind of prequel that explains why Victoria's granddaughter, Elizabeth, first came to live with her 92-year-old grandmother, and how Victoria became a deputy for the West Tisbury police. While the town's old and new ministers-both named Jack-try to forge a positive relationship, West Tisbury's residents are dropping like flies. Four people die within a short time, and all appear to have eaten gifts of food. New police chief Casey O'Neill relies on Victoria, who knows the town and everyone in it, to help her figure out what's going on." Booklist
"A sensitive observer of the scene, Riggs writes with warmth and humor about all-too-human characters with whom readers can readily identify." Publ Wkly

Rikki *See* Ducornet, Rikki

Riley, Judith Merkle

In pursuit of the green lion. Delacorte Press 1990 440p o.p.
LC 90-32498
"This novel continues the story of spunky Margaret [begun in A vision of light] widowed once again and married to acerbic scholar Gregory who rescues her from her former husband's rapacious relatives only to plunge her into the midst of his own family's greedy machina-

Riley, Judith Merkle—*Continued*
tion to control her wealth. The eternal wars of the 14th century beckon, however, and Gregory, now a knight in the Duke of Lancaster's forces in France, is captured. Margaret, accompanied by wise Mother Hilde and alchemist Brother Malachi journeys to the stronghold of the sinister Count of St. Medard, where once again her unusual powers and quick wit overcome the forces of evil." Libr J

"In this non-stop picaresque adventure quips fly as thickly as a barrage of arrows; a steady stream of drunken noblemen, corrupt priests, scheming ladies and truculent ghosts keep the action white-hot." Booklist

The serpent garden. Viking 1996 467p o.p.
LC 95-36067

"Susanna Dallet is determined to support herself after the untimely death of her spouse and turns to the art of miniature portraiture, a profession she learned from her enlightened father. After Susanna becomes enmeshed in the political intrigue of the court of Henry VIII, she is sought after by a heretical religious sect, a minor demon, and a free-spririted archangel, all of whom believe she is the key to their success. Riley . . . creates a stunning period fantasy that combines historical detail with magical realism." Libr J

A vision of light. Delacorte Press 1989 442p o.p.
LC 88-17514

"14th century Englishwoman Margaret of Ashbury heeds a 'voice' commanding her to compose her life story. Her kindly old husband Roger Kendall pays for her to dictate her memoirs to unfrocked Brother Gregory. . . . First married at 14 to a sadistic fur merchant—reputed to be the Devil—who leaves her for dead during the Plague, Margaret survives to become apprenticed to the herbalist Mother Hilde. In trances of divine light Margaret gains the healing gift, and envisions a forged, steel-fingered weapon for the soldierly work of midwifery. But these forceps and Margaret's powers stir the envy of priests and male doctors, and she is forced to clear herself of witchcraft." Publ Wkly

This "is a chronicle rich with the ambience and flavor of the Middle Ages, but it is a 14th-century story told with a 20th-century sensibility." N Y Times Book Rev

Followed by In pursuit of the green lion

Rinaldi, Nicholas

Between two rivers. HarperCollins 2004 448p $24.95

ISBN 0-06-057876-9

This novel "tells the intertwined stories of a dozen or so residents of a posh Manhattan apartment building. . . . At the centre of it is Farro Fescu, Echo Terrace's Romanian concierge. . . . [The residents] include Theo Tattafruge, an Egyptian-born plastic surgeon who specialises in sex-change operations, and Karl Vogel, a former Luftwaffe ace. There is Muhta Saad, a slimy Iraqi spice merchant, and, high up in the penthouse, Harry Falcon, a frozen-foods magnate dying of cancer." Economist

"Though the timeline of Between Two Rivers steers inevitably toward the horrors of 9/11, there is nothing overdetermined or reductive about the stories themselves. Rinaldi . . . indulges his characters in their untidy lives, and readers who do the same will find their patience rewarded." N Y Times Book Rev

Rinehart, Mary Roberts, 1876-1958

The case of Jennie Brice
In Rinehart, M. R. Mary Roberts Rinehart's mystery book p349-442

The circular staircase; with illustrations by Lester Ralph. Bobbs-Merrill 1908 362p il o.p.

Featuring the detective talents of Mr. Jamieson, this novel concerns a maiden aunt and her nephew and niece who take a country house for the summer and are plunged into a series of mysterious crimes

also in Rinehart, M. R. Mary Roberts Rinehart's mystery book p3-178

Haunted lady
In Rinehart, M. R. Miss Pinkerton: adventures of a nurse detective p249-403

The man in lower ten
In Rinehart, M. R. Mary Roberts Rinehart's mystery book p181-345

Mary Roberts Rinehart's mystery book; The circular staircase, The man in lower ten [and] The case of Jennie Brice. Rinehart 1947 442p o.p.

An omnibus volume of the titles first published 1908, 1909, and 1913 respectively

In The man in lower ten "The Washington Flier is wrecked, just after a murder has been commited as a result of a tangle of forgery and blackmail." Barzun. Cat of Crime

The case of Jennie Brice is about a reporter on the lookout for a sensational story who arranges a disappearance, but it turns to murder

Miss Pinkerton [novel]
In Rinehart, M. R. Miss Pinkerton: adventures of a nurse detective p95-245

Miss Pinkerton: adventures of a nurse detective. Rinehart 1959 403p o.p.

Contents: The buckled bag; Locked doors; Miss Pinkerton (1932); Haunted lady (1942)

Two short stories and two novels featuring the exploits of nurse Hilda Adams

Rinehart, Steven

Built in a day; a novel. Doubleday 2003 241p $23.95

ISBN 0-385-49855-1 LC 2003-41968

"Andrew, the antihero of this blackly humorous novel, is still in college in his 30s, has a job as a youth counselor that involves nothing more than hanging out with teens all day and is skilled at manipulating women. When his new wife dies, leaving him in charge of her teenaged sons and 16-year-old foster daughter, he finally has adult responsibility thrust upon him. He responds to his new role by taking his sexually precocious female charge to bed and making starry-eyed plans to marry her while also thinking about seducing her social worker." Publ Wkly

Rinehart, Steven—*Continued*

"The charm of the protagonist, clearly, is not the primary appeal of this novel. The charms of Rinehart's writing, however, more than countervail; though stripped-down and deadpan, his sentences pack a lot of raw, juicy comic power." N Y Times Book Rev

Riordan, Rick

Cold Springs. Bantam Bks. 2003 340p $23.95
ISBN 0-553-80236-4 LC 2003-40365

"Cold Springs is an east Texas wilderness boarding school for troubled teens. Haunted by his own unresolved guilt over his daughter's death from a heroin overdose nine years earlier, ex-teacher Chadwick now makes his living escorting children into this boot camp for losers, giving them a second chance whether they want it or not. When an ex-lover asks him to locate her self-destructive 15-year-old daughter and take her to Cold Springs, Chadwick finds himself involved in a case of blackmail, murder, and financial skullduggery." Libr J

Riordan's "voice is fresh yet sure, with insights so trenchant they nearly provoke tears. And Riordan's characters, even the minor ones, are achingly believable." Booklist

Robards, Karen

Ghost moon. Delacorte Press 2000 313p $24.95
ISBN 0-385-31972-X LC 99-47420

"Summoned home at the request of a dying stepaunt, single mom Olivia Morrison returns to LaAngelle Plantation in the steamy swamps of Louisiana with her eight-year-old daughter, Sara. . . . What she discovers is that her closest cousin, Seth, is also divorced and the father of an eight-year-old daughter, who suffers mightily from spoiled rich-kid syndrome. Meanwhile, alternate chapters detail the stalkings of a serial killer who preys on girls the same age as Sara. . . . As Olivia works toward reconciliation with her stepfamily, she is haunted by dreams of her mother's supposed suicide. She also finds herself romantically drawn to Seth." Booklist

Robards "has crafted a mossy modern gothic drenched in gore. . . . [She] conveys the dusty heat of the Louisiana summer, and has an ear for the nuances of dialogue." Publ Wkly

To trust a stranger. Pocket Bks. 2001 341p o.p.
ISBN 0-671-78653-9 LC 2001-52056

"Julie Carlson, once a poor girl from the wrong side of the tracks but now the beautiful owner of a successful boutique in Charleston, S.C., seems to have it all. As the novel begins, however, a hit man circles her suburban mansion: Julie's rich husband, Sid, has hired thugs to kill her. Unaware of the danger she is in but convinced that Sid is cheating on her, Julie slips out of the house just in time and follows her husband to the red-light district, where she serendipitously—and literally—runs into private detective Mac McQuarry, dressed up in drag to spy on a client's husband. . . . Soon she and Mac are working together to get the goods on Julie's crooked husband." Publ Wkly

Robb, Candace M.

The cross-legged knight; an Owen Archer mystery; [by] Candace Robb. Mysterious Press 2003 321p $23.95
ISBN 0-89296-772-2 LC 2002-27248

"When William of Wykeman, bishop of Winchester, fears reprisal after being blamed for the death of a local knight by his irate family, Owen Archer. . . must protect him. In the meantime, Owen copes with wife Lucie's overwhelming sorrow upon losing the child she was carrying." Libr J

"Once again, Robb provides the reader with an evocative and suspenseful whodunit thoroughly bolstered by a wealth of authentic historical detail." Booklist

A gift of sanctuary; an Owen Archer mystery; [by] Candace Robb. St. Martin's Press 1998 195p $22.95
ISBN 0-312-19266-5 LC 98-41394

In this medieval mystery Owen Archer returns "to his native Wales to inspect the duke's Welsh fortifications and to recruit two companies of archers in anticipation of a threatened French invasion of the British Isles. Joined on his journey by poet and author Geoffrey Chaucer, the two must solve a perplexing murder and investigate a possible case of treason against the crown." Booklist

"Robb deftly interweaves a complex story of love, passion and murder into the troubled and tangled fabric of Welsh history, fashioning a rich and satisfying novel." Publ Wkly

The riddle of St. Leonard's; a medieval mystery. St. Martin's Press 1997 303p o.p.
LC 97-16231

"The plague is taking its toll in 14th-century York, and all the one-eyed former royal spy wants is to weather it without losing any family members. However, Owen is called to detective duty by the master of St. Leonard's Hospital when its pensioners start dying in rapid succession." Publ Wkly

"An evocative historical mystery steeped in authentically gritty period detail." Booklist

Robb, J. D., 1950-

For works written by this author under other names see Roberts, Nora, 1950-

Robbins, David L., 1954-

The last citadel; a novel of the Battle of Kursk. Bantam Bks. 2003 421p $24.95
ISBN 0-553-80177-5 LC 2003-44304

"The battle for the Soviet city of Kursk in July 1943 during World War II involved two million soldiers. Code-named Citadel, it was Hitler's frenzied—and final—attempt to defeat Russia on the eastern front and was the largest buildup of German armed power of the war. Robbins re-creates the battle in this rousing novel: its characters being Hitler; his generals and advisers; Russian, German, and Spanish foot soldiers and tank drivers; fighter pilots (both men and women); partisans; and even elderly men and women digging trenches." Booklist

Robbins, David L., 1954—*Continued*

War of the rats; a novel. Bantam Bks. 1999 392p $23.95

ISBN 0-553-10817-4 LC 98-43918

"Inspired by actual events, this novel is set during the battle of Stalingrad during World War II. The plot centers around two crack snipers, one Russian, one German, who pursue each other to the death in a series of cat-and-mouse maneuvers." Libr J

"The final confrontation takes a while to play out, but once Robbins . . . gets to the heart of the matter, he presents a riveting account of a battle within a battle, and the sniper motif proves an ideal vehicle to analyze the strengths and weaknesses of both sides." Publ Wkly

Robbins, Harold, 1916-1997

Sin city. Forge 2002 383p $25.95

ISBN 0-7653-0001-X LC 2002-69257

"A Tom Doherty Associates book"

"Jack 'Lucky' Riordan is the illegitimate and unwanted son of millionaire Howard Hughes, exiled from Las Vegas to face a hardscrabble existence. The tale begins in the 1960s when an adult Riordan returns to Vegas, seeking his fortune in the gaming industry. His street smarts stand him in good stead as he shrewdly acquires wealth and power." Booklist

"Though questions linger about just how much Robbins contributed to later books published under his name, this posthumous novel moves quickly and is great fun, a roman à clef reminiscent of his early bestselling bildungsroman." Publ Wkly

Robbins, Tom

Fierce invalids home from hot climates. Bantam Bks. 2000 415p o.p.

ISBN 0-553-10775-5 LC 99-51683

"Switters, the protagonist, is an errand boy for the CIA, a secret lover of Broadway show tunes and a pedophile. On assignment in Peru . . . Switters encounters a Kandakandero medicine man who gives him mind-altering drugs and wisdom, but in exchange inflicts a curse: if Switters's feet ever touch the ground, he will be struck dead instantly. So Switters spends the rest of the novel in a wheelchair, although this in no way slows him down. He returns to Seattle, chases after his 16-year-old stepsister and numerous art students, then embarks on a mission to Syria to sell gas masks to Kurds; there, he beds a nun who even so remains a virgin. In true Robbins style, the writing throughout is lush and sexy, containing a great deal of witty social and political commentary." Publ Wkly

Half asleep in frog pajamas. Bantam Bks. 1994 386p o.p.

LC 94-11549

In this novel "Gwen, an endangered stockbroker, is involved with straitlaced Belford and his born-again monkey. When she is attracted to Larry—who has cancer and is currently between trips to Timbuktu—she must choose among the American dream, the Timbuktu alternate, and something else." Libr J

"The yarn has a genuineness, a warmth, a humor, and an incredibly compelling plot, which hold our attention to the end." Booklist

Jitterbug perfume. Bantam Bks. 1984 342p o.p.

LC 84-45233

"Priscilla Partido, a Seattle member of Daughters of the Daily Special (waitresses with college degrees), gets a beet tossed in her window; Madame Devalier and V'lu Jackson, New Orleans purveyors of fine perfume, get a beet too; so do the owners of LeFever Odeurs in Paris. What does it all mean? . . . The real theme here is immortality, in the person of Alobar, a 1000-year-old Nordic imp who sports across the globe (ending up as Einstein's janitor) with the secrets to olfactory wisdom and eternal life and love. Also at large is a Leary-esque philanderer, Wiggs Dannyboy, who as founder of an immortalist sect, the Last Laugh Foundation, accompanies Priscilla on her quest for happiness and the perfect (beet-based) scent. Robbins is still in top form, still mixing the lunatic and the thoughtful—or rather, doing a literary watusi up every page and jitterbugging back down." Publ Wkly

Skinny legs and all. Bantam Bks. 1990 422p il o.p.

LC 89-18309

"A painter's struggle with her art, a restaurant opened as an experiment in brotherhood, the journey of several inanimate objects to Jerusalem, a preacher's scheme to hasten Armageddon, and a performance of a legendary dance: these are the diverse elements around which Robbins has built this wild, controversial novel. Ellen Cherry Charles, one of the 'Daughters of the Daily Special' in *Jitterbug Perfume*, takes center stage. She has married Boomer Petway and moved to New York, hoping to make it as a painter. Instead, she winds up a waitress at the Isaac and Ishmael, a restaurant co-owned by an Arab and a Jew. . . . Few contemporary novelists mix tomfoolery and philosophy so well." Libr J

Still life with Woodpecker. Bantam Bks. 1980 277p o.p.

LC 81-103498

This novel "relates the meeting (at an ecological 'Care Fest') and subsequent love affair between Leigh-Cheri, an all-American princess of a deposed royal line, and Bernard Mickey Wrangle, alias The Woodpecker, an anarchistic bomber and self-styled 'outlaw.' He is captured and imprisoned; she . . . tries to remain close to him by mimicking his experience, living as a recluse in her parents' attic. When he rejects this as a futile gesture, she agrees to marry a fabulously wealthy oil-sheik and, having been introduced by her solitary incarceration with [a] packet of Camels to the mysteries of pyramid-power, demands a new, full-sized pyramid as a wedding gift. The story's climax is her reunion with Bernard in the inner sanctum of this pyramid." Times Lit Suppl

"The author's prose, as spasmodic as his heroine's sex life, is marbled with limping puns heavily splattered with recurrent motifs and a boyish zeal for the scatalogical." SLJ

Villa incognito. Bantam Bks. 2003 241p $27.50

ISBN 0-553-80332-8 LC 2003-40353

"The novel begins with the story of Tanuki, a badgerlike Asian creature with a reputation as a changeling and trickster and a fondness for sake. Also part of the cast is a beautiful young woman who may or may not have Tanuki's blood in her veins. . . and three American MIAs who have chosen to remain in Laos long

Robbins, Tom—*Continued*
after the Vietnam War. Events are set in motion when one of the MIAs, dressed as a priest, is arrested with a cache of heroin taped to his body. In vintage Robbins style, the plot whirls every which way, as the author, writing with unrestrained glee, takes potshots at societal pillars: the military, big business and religions of all ilks. The language is eccentric, electrifying and true to the mark." Publ Wkly

Roberts, Gillian

Adam and evil; an Amanda Pepper mystery. Ballantine Bks. 1999 248p $22.95
ISBN 0-345-42934-6 LC 99-14225
"Philadelphia prep-school teacher Amanda Pepper . . . and her class happen to be in the Free Library during a murder. When one of her students subsequently disappears, police believe that they've identified the culprit. Amanda, of course, disagrees." Libr J
"Although the mystery is somewhat implausible, book lovers will enjoy Roberts' detours into the pricey hobby of book collecting. The story also gives libraries the acclaim they deserve, with many vivid descriptions of the majestic Free Library." Booklist

The bluest blood; an Amanda Pepper mystery. Ballantine Bks. 1998 230p $22
ISBN 0-345-40326-6 LC 97-26868
"Something isn't quite right with Philadelphia bluebloods Neddy and Tea Roederer, benefactors of the Philadelphia Prep School library. Philly Prep teacher and amateur sleuth Amanda Pepper sees the first signs in the Roederers' son's glum manner. Then a more urgent problem appears: the crusade of the Reverend Harvey Spiers' book-burning Moral Ecologists—the same Reverend Spiers whose stepson, Jake, is best friends with the Roederers' son. As Amanda talks with both boys, she realizes there are much deeper problems, and when the crusading Reverend Spiers is murdered, she knows things have spun out of control." Booklist
A "swift and intriguing spin through the sometimes murderous precincts of Philadelphia." Publ Wkly

Claire and present danger. Ballantine Bks. 2003 244p $23.95
ISBN 0-345-45490-1 LC 2002-43654
"Because of disturbing anonymous letters, a rich old lady hires Philadelphia schoolteacher Amanda Pepper. . .to investigate the 'credentials' of her son's evasive fiancee. What Amanda finds may be murder, both past and present." Libr J

Helen hath no fury; an Amanda Pepper mystery. Ballantine Bks. 2000 228p $23
ISBN 0-345-42933-8 LC 00-40360
"Schoolteacher Amanda Pepper seeks the person who killed a member of her book club the day after members discussed a fictional suicide. Amanda's probes, . . . bring her dangerously close to the villain." Libr J
"Roberts skillfully negotiates some rather tricky emotional waters in this . . . addition to a series notable for its smooth mix of traditional mystery conventions with the darker underpinnings of modern crime fiction." Publ Wkly

The mummers' curse; an Amanda Pepper mystery. Ballantine Bks. 1996 231p $21
ISBN 0-345-40323-1 LC 96-3472
"Philadelphia schoolteacher Amanda Pepper . . . witnesses the murder of a clown in the Mummer's Parade. When a fellow teacher (and principal suspect) falsely names Amanda as his alibi, she begins sleuthing. Fascinating plot and wit-filled prose." Libr J

Roberts, Kenneth Lewis, 1885-1957

Arundel; by Kenneth Roberts. Doubleday, Doran 1930 618p o.p.
An historical novel of the Revolutionary period, the setting of which is the garrison house at Arundel in southern Maine. Steven Nason, the hero of the story, goes with his friend Benedict Arnold on a hazardous expedition against Quebec. Young Nason has a very personal interest in the success of the enterprise, since Mary Mallinson, the girl he loves, has been taken by the Indians and is a captive in Quebec. Steven's recollections of the hardship and dangers of the expedition, and its blunders and failure in spite of individual acts of heroism, make up the bulk of the narrative
Followed by Rabble in arms

Lydia Bailey; by Kenneth Roberts. Doubleday 1947 488p o.p.
"A susceptible young Maine lawyer who has fallen in love with the portrait of a girl he believes to be in Haiti reaches the island just as Napoleon's attempt to take over the government sets off the bloody . . . uprising under Toussaint. The hero finds the girl, and from that point the extremely elaborate plot carries them through an encounter with Tobias Lear, the pig-headed evil genius of Jefferson's State Department; spirited engagements against the French; capture by Barbary pirates and slavery in Tripoli; and, finally, the Tripolitan War and its intrigues and political jealousies." New Yorker

Northwest Passage; by Kenneth Roberts. Doubleday, Doran 1937 709p o.p.
"This sprawling novel describes Major Robert Rogers' expedition in 1759 to destroy the Indian town of St. Francis and then his idea of finding an overland route to the Northwest. . . . In preparing his novel, Roberts made extensive research and unearthed documents that historians had believed were lost. The book is one of Roberts' best works." Benet's Reader's Ency of Am Lit

Oliver Wiswell; [by] Kenneth Roberts. Doubleday, Doran 1940 836p o.p.
"The American revolution as seen by Oliver Wiswell, a young American who remained loyal to the English government, and was therefore the victim of fanatics, bent not only on fighting for liberty but also on destroying the liberty of others. Hounded out of his home in Milton, he fled to Boston with his father and a constantly devoted friend. He experienced there the privations of war and observed the tactical stupidities of the English. Then on to Halifax, England, France and finally back to America, where he fought with the Loyalists. The war over, Oliver found again his childhood sweetheart and turned with new hope to Nova Scotia." Booklist

Rabble in arms; a chronicle of Arundel and the Burgoyne invasion; by Kenneth Roberts. Doubleday, Doran 1933 870p o.p.
Sequel to Arundel
The principal villain of this realistic, unromantic tale of the American Revolution is the American Congress, the

Roberts, Kenneth Lewis, 1885-1957—*Continued*
real hero is Benedict Arnold. The story relates the adventures of a group of men from Arundel, Maine, who fight with the American forces in the campaign ending with the battle of Saratoga. Men and events, politics and battles are seen through the eyes of one Peter Merrill, mariner, who tells the story

Followed by The Lively Lady (1931) and Captain Caution (1934)

Roberts, Nora, 1950-

Carolina moon. Putnam 2000 438p o.p.
ISBN 0-399-14592-3 LC 99-47968

This is "the story of Tory Bodeen, a young woman haunted by the murder of her childhood friend years ago. . . . At the mercy of her ruthless father, who routinely beat her, Tory found brief solace with her friend Hope Lavelle. After Hope's unsolved murder, Tory grew up, left home, worked hard, and now financially independent has returned to her birthplace to open a small gift shop and try to put the memories of the past to rest. When another young woman in the town is brutally murdered, Tory realizes her premonition that the killer is still at large is horrifyingly true." Libr J

"There are no saccharine reconciliations here. Even when a few over-the-top sex scenes and hackneyed phrasings slip in, Robert's witty dialogue and moody descriptions soon counteract them. This is romantic drama at its best." Publ Wkly

Midnight Bayou. Putnam 2001 352p o.p.
ISBN 0-399-14824-8 LC 2001-41643

"When wealthy Boston attorney Declan Fitzgerald discovers that Manet Hall, a dilapidated mansion on the bayou just outside New Orleans, is for sale, he leaves his practice and moves in to renovate, restore, and redecorate. Independent and tough, bar owner Lena fascinates him from the minute he lays eyes on her. Believing that he's incapable of romance, he's amazed by how quickly and overwhelmingly he falls head over heels in love with her. But he worries about his own sanity when he experiences fugue states that leave him with memories of events and people who lived in the mansion more than 100 years earlier. . . . Roberts has cleverly crafted an enticing tangle of times and relationship." Booklist

The reef. Putnam 1998 440p $23.95
ISBN 0-399-14441-2 LC 98-21329

"Brainy, well-bred marine archeologist Tate Beaumont and pearl-in-the-rough treasure hunter Matthew Lassiter . . . pursue the treasures of the Caribbean, mining Spanish ships that came to grief hundreds of years ago. They're both after the legendary piece of jewelry known as Angelique's Curse, famed for both the beauty of its flawless ruby and the burden of bad luck that dogged its various owners. Will Tate locate the jewel and use it to found a museum, or will Matthew win out and use it as an instrument of revenge against evil Silas VanDyke, who murdered his father?" Publ Wkly

River's end. Putnam 1999 420p $23.95
ISBN 0-399-14470-6 LC 98-36160

"One summer night in 1979, four-year-old Olivia Tanner finds her doped-up father, Sam, bloodied shears in hand, poised over the dead body of her movie-star mom. Haunted by the image of 'the monster' pursuing her, Olivia is sent to live with her grandparents in the Pacific Northwest, where she is sheltered from her memories by towering Douglas firs. Two decades later, the specter of the 'monster' returns. From prison, her father urges young investigative reporter Noah Brady—son of the police detective who discovered Olivia after the murder—to research the crime." Publ Wkly

The villa. Putnam 2001 421p $25.95
ISBN 0-399-14712-8 LC 00-59159

"Tereza Giambelli is, at age 67, the commanding head of the family winery operations both in Italy and California's Napa Valley. When she and her husband, who owns the MacMillan family winery, decide to merge their operations and restructure the combined venture, all hell breaks loose. Granddaughter Sophia, head of public relations, is forced into working with Tyler MacMillan, who has been in charge of the vineyards, and both have to work together in the other's area of expertise." Booklist

"Roberts has penned a fast-paced, clearly plotted story of jealousy, greed, and family discord set in the heart of the Napa Valley, peopled with characters you care about, and well laced with equal helpings of romance and suspense." Libr J

Robinson, Elisabeth

The true and outstanding adventures of the Hunt sisters; a novel. Little, Brown 2004 327p $23.95
ISBN 0-316-73502-7 LC 2003-47713

"As a Hollywood producer, Olivia has suffered through her share of bad movies, but now her own life rivals the worst box office bomb. She has lost her job at Universal Pictures, is on the verge of being evicted, and has been dumped by her true love when she learns that her sister Maddie has leukemia." Libr J

"Over the course of about 200 letters (and a few e-mails), Robinson succinctly shows the full range of Olivia's emotions and relationships, from the optimism she tries to instill in her shocked family to the admiration she holds for Maddie's spouse. She poignantly portrays the frustration of trying to sustain a relationship while engaged in a consuming profession." USA Today

Robinson, Kim Stanley

Antarctica. Bantam Bks. 1998 511p $24.95
ISBN 0-553-10063-7 LC 97-41701

"Antarctica in the 21st century serves as a site for scientific research, tourism, and industrial exploitation—until a terrorist attack by environmental extremists calls into question humanity's right to invade the earth's last unexplored continent." Libr J

This is "an exhilarating addition to a body of work distinguished by two elements all too rare in modern science fiction: a sense of character and a sense of place. Robinson brings the two together by writing about people who are in love with where they are." N Y Times Book Rev

Blue Mars. Bantam Bks. 1996 609p o.p.
LC 95-46700

In this concluding volume of the trilogy "colonists almost succeed in terraforming Mars. While they fight for independence from Earth and attempt to avert a civil war, they find their new civilization threatened by an ice

Robinson, Kim Stanley—*Continued*

age." Libr J

"Conceptually and stylistically, the Mars trilogy is mature science fiction, a landmark in the history of the genre. It requires close reading and amply rewards the effort." N Y Times Book Rev

Green Mars [novelette]
In Robinson, K. S. The Martians

The Martians. Bantam Bks. 1999 336p $24.95
ISBN 0-553-80117-1 LC 99-13115

Set in the universe of the author's Mars trilogy this volume includes vignettes, essays, fables, poems, and the following short stories: Michel in Antarctica; Exploring Fossil Canyon; Maya and Desmond; Four teleological trails; Coyote makes trouble; Michel in provence; Arthur Sternbach brings the curveball to Mars; Jackie on Zo; Keeping the flame; Big Man in love; Sexual dimorphism; What matters; Sax moments; A Martian romance; Purple Mars

"Also included is 'Green Mars,' a previously published novella about climbing Olympus Mons, the highest mountain in the solar system. . . . Some of the pieces here will be of interest only to those who have already read the trilogy, but the finest of the short fiction stands firmly on its own. As is the norm with Robinson's work, the stories are beautifully written, the characters are well developed and the author's passion for ecology manifests on every page." Publ Wkly

Red Mars. Bantam Bks. 1993 519p il o.p.
LC 92-21607

This novel, the first of a trilogy "concerns the first permanent settlement on Mars, a multinational band of 100 hardy experts, and their mission—to begin making Mars habitable for humans by releasing underground water and oxygen into the atmosphere. Unfortunately, they are divided over whether this is a desirable step in human evolution or an ecological crime." Booklist

"A novel fully inhabited both by detailed technical processes and by people whose careers those processes are; it is also a novel with a complex sense of political reality. . . . This is one of the finest works of American SF because it is one of the few that aspire to the dignity of the genuinely tragic." Times Lit Suppl

Followed by Green Mars

The years of rice and salt. Bantam Bks. 2002 658p o.p.
ISBN 0-553-10920-0 LC 2001-43492

"The premise is that a mutating, hypervirulent strain of the fourteenth-century Black Death has wiped out nearly the entire population of Europe, and Islam has moved into Europe, China into North America, and South Asia holds the balance between them, thanks to high military skills and energy. All three parties compete for Africa." Booklist

"Because this alternate history is set in the same lawful universe as ours, its science must be the same. Because its people have the same basic human needs, their societies resemble ours. However, as events march toward the alternative year of 2002, some of his characters come to believe, despite much evidence to the contrary, that they can change the way they live. The reader is left to ponder whether this is an illusion." N Y Times Book Rev

Robinson, Lynda Suzanne

Murder at the feast of rejoicing; a Lord Meren mystery; [by] Lynda S. Robinson. Walker & Co. 1996 229p $20.95
ISBN 0-8027-3274-7 LC 95-33190

This novel is set in "the sun-seared landscape of the Egyptian Nile in the days of Tutankhamun. One of the young Pharoah's close confidants, Lord Meren, visits his family estate for a brief rest but finds, instead, that his sister has invited a tedious group of friends and relatives for a family celebration. One of these unwelcome guests has the bad taste to be murdered." SLJ

"Good scholarship authenticates the historical setting; imagination provides the sense of danger and romance to make it come alive." N Y Times Book Rev

Murder at the God's gate; a Lord Meren mystery; [by] Lynda S. Robinson. Walker & Co. 1995 236p $19.95
ISBN 0-8027-3198-8 LC 94-28806

"Young King Tutankhamun's chief adviser/agent Lord Meren, known to some as the Falcon, investigates the murder of a priest in a temple dedicated to the teenaged Tut. Robinson . . . surrounds Meren with palace and temple intrigue, authentic details of daily life, and frequent mention of a wide assortment of indigenous animals." Libr J

Robinson, Marilynne

Gilead; Marilynne Robinson. 1st ed. Farrar, Straus and Giroux 2004 247p $23
ISBN 0-374-15389-2 LC 2004-47063

This is an "epistolary autobiography written by the Rev. John Ames to his son in 1956; the father, dying of heart disease, is 77 and the boy is 6. A Congregationalist minister in fictional Gilead, Iowa, Ames is a bachelor until late in life and a loner even then. His grandfather was a gun-toting abolitionist who ran with John Brown. His father was a pacifist. Ames himself is . . . somewhat more equivocal than either. How to act, when to intercede, when to stand back-these are his abiding questions. When the prodigal son of another local minister comes home, Ames discovers that this young man harbors a secret. Ames tries to help, but his good intentions mire him in the same intractable problems of race-America's original sin-that ensnared his grandfather." Newsweek

"Gilead possesses the quiet ineluctable perfection of Flaubert's A Simple Heart as well as the moral and emotional complexity of Robert Frost's deepest poetry. There's nothing flashy in these pages, and yet one regularly pauses to reread sentences, sometimes for their beauty, sometimes for their truth." Washington Post Book World

Robinson, Patrick, 1939-

Kilo class. HarperCollins Pubs. 1998 442p $25
ISBN 0-06-019129-5 LC 97-51172

In this sequel to Nimitz class, "the plot concerns 10 formidable Soviet-built Kilo Class patrol submarines, which can run submerged at speeds up to 17 knots without being detected, travel 6,000 miles before refueling, and fire nuclear-tipped torpedoes. An insolvent Russian military has agreed to sell them to China. With the subs,

Robinson, Patrick, 1939-—*Continued*
China could control the Taiwan Strait, blocking Western trade routes. The Chinese could then attack and conquer Taiwan. The U.S. Navy must stop delivery of the subs without starting World War III." Booklist

Nimitz class. HarperCollins Pubs. 1997 411p il o.p.
LC 96-46872
"The Nimitz Class nuclear aircraft carrier USS *Thomas Jefferson* and its accompanying Carrier Battle Group is secretly attacked and destroyed. At first, the loss of the carrier and its 6000-person crew is deemed an accident, but Lieutenant Commander Bill Baldridge convinces the president that the ship was attacked by a diesel sub with a nuclear-tipped torpedo. The ensuing investigation takes him from Britain's top-flight submarine school to the depths of the Bosporus in pursuit of a rogue Iraqi sub captain and his commandeered Russian submarine." Libr J

"Military fiction fans will admire [the author's] authoritative exploitation of weaponry and tactics, however, and most readers will be engaged, despite some sluggish passages, by his persuasive cautionary tale about the perils of military downsizing at a time when rogue nations are amassing weapons of great and terrible destructiveness." Publ Wkly

Followed by Kilo class

Robinson, Peter, 1950-

Close to home; a novel of suspense. Morrow 2003 389p $24.95
ISBN 0-06-019878-8 LC 2002-71901
"A moody chap on the sunniest of days, Peter Robinson's Yorkshire copper, Inspector Alan Banks, slips into a melancholy funk. . . when he returns to his boyhood home—indeed, to his own narrow bed in his old room in his parents' house—to help with an investigation into the death of a former schoolmate. Graham Marshall was 14 when he disappeared in 1965, and the belated discovery of his skeletal remains brings a rush of painful memories to the middle-aged detective who had been his best friend and the keeper of their secrets." N Y Times Book Rev

Cold is the grave. Morrow 2000 369p o.p.
ISBN 0-380-97808-3 LC 00-37231
Yorkshire's Inspector Alan Banks "devoutly loathes his distant and chilly superior officer, Chief Constable Jimmy Riddle. But when Riddle spots his wayward 16-year-old daughter, Emily, posing nude on a pornographic Web site, Banks, who has a teenage daughter of his own, hasn't the heart to turn down the distraught father's plea to journey down to the fleshpots of London and rescue the girl." N Y Times Book Rev

"Banks discovers the precariousness of Emily's position in her new life and, more disturbingly, the grotesque truth behind a facade of perfect family life. A cunningly constructed plot, enhanced by Robinson's engaging descriptions and insights." Booklist

The first cut; Peter Robinson. 1st ed. Dark Alley 2004 310p $13.95
ISBN 0-06-073535-X (pa) LC 2003-67660
"Recent university graduate Kirsten survives a brutal Jack the Ripper-style attack of which she has no memory. As Kirsten recovers, she becomes fixated on finding the man who nearly killed her. Miles away, Martha has come to the coastal town of Whitby, where she is doing research for a book. Or is she? Carefully surveying her surroundings, Martha grows more obsessed with the object of her trip. The women's stories are told in alternate chapters until the unsettling end. This atmospheric tale of suspense will keep readers wondering what's really going on." Libr J

In a dry season. Avon Bks. 1999 422p $24
ISBN 0-380-97581-5 LC 98-47391
"When a drought dries up a reservoir in the Yorkshire dales and uncovers the ruined village of Hobb's End, Inspector Alan Banks of the North Yorkshire Police is given the punishing assignment of identifying the human skeleton that also emerges from the mud. In a tricky feat of parallel narration, Robinson juxtaposes Banks's attempts to reconstruct the history of Hobb's End with the efforts of a former resident to keep its secrets buried." NY Times Book Rev

Innocent grave; an Inspector Banks mystery. Berkley Prime Crime 1996 346p o.p.
LC 95-38218
This story finds "Inspector Alan Banks attempting to solve the murder of 16-year-old Deborah Harrison, who was found strangled to death in a graveyard. The victim was the daughter of a prominent businessman, who wants the killer apprehended posthaste. A suspect is identified, jailed, and sent to trial, only to be declared innocent." Booklist

"Although the story follows the classical form of a whodunit, the characters have complexity and the issues range broad and deep, raising interesting moral questions about bigotry, class privilege and the terrible crime of being different." N Y Times Book Rev

Playing with fire; Peter Robinson. 1st ed. William Morrow 2004 354p $23.95
ISBN 0-06-019877-X LC 2003-56569
In this installment, DCI Alan Banks and Annie Cabot, "his associate and former lover, investigate an arson fire that destroyed two canal barges and left two charred corpses. Banks and Annie must determine who was the intended victim: Thomas McMahon, a failed artist, or Tina Aspern, a teenaged heroin addict who had fled an abusive stepfather. A second firey death a few days later leads the duo to uncover an art forgery scheme involving the great British painter J.M.W. Turner." Libr J

"Characterization is Robinson's real strength. Virtually every character is etched with care, precision and emotional insight." Publ Wkly

Robinson, Roxana

A perfect stranger; and other stories; Roxana Robinson. Random House 2005 235p $23.95
ISBN 0-375-50918-6 LC 2004-59537
Contents: Family Christmas; The face-lift; Assistance; Choosing sides; At the beach; Blind man; The treatment; Assez; Intersection; Shame; The football game; Pilgrimage; A perfect stranger

Robinson's "finely tuned realism, as well as her settings and characters—New York, its bedroom communi-

Robinson, Roxana—*Continued*
ties, the Eastern seaboard and the comfortable upper-middle-class living there—recall Cheever and Updike. . . . The collection's most affecting stories touch on the chasm between parents and children, husbands and wives. Robinson's ear is wonderful, her graceful prose a real pleasure." Publ Wkly

Sweetwater; a novel. Random House 2003 319p $24.95
ISBN 0-375-50916-X LC 2002-31830
"A widow for two years, 47-year-old Isabel Green marries her ardent suitor, Paul Simmons, hoping that her affection for him will turn into love. During a visit to Sweetwater Lodge, the Simmons family's lakeside compound in the Adirondacks, she meets Paul's cold disapproving parents, Douglas and Charlotte. . . and his bachelor brother, Whit, with whom Paul maintains a vicious sibling rivalry. Fundamental issues soon convince Isabel that her marriage is a dreadful mistake." Publ Wkly
"Robinson writes big solid scenes bubbling with tension, that hold the reader's interest. She has always shown her characters' flaws, and the dark emotions stirred up by divorce and parenthood; here she has reached farther to relate her characteristic predicaments to the larger world outside." N Y Times Book Rev

Robinson, Spider

By any other name
In The Hugo winners p141-97

Callahan's con. TOR Bks. 2003 286p $23.95
ISBN 0-7653-0270-5 LC 2003-40285
"A Tom Doherty Associates book"
"When Jake Stonebender and his wife, Zoey, move to Florida and open up the Place, the latest incarnation of the unusual bar once known as Callahan's Place, he acquires a collection of strange friends, including a talking German shepherd, a merman, and a foul-mouthed parrot. An encounter with the Florida bureaucracy over the homeschooling of his hyperintelligent daughter, Erin, and the intrusion of the local Mafia result in a grand scheme to outwit both intrusions and rescue Jake's missing wife in the process. Robinson's latest entry in his Callahan series features more zaniness, good humor, and bad jokes." Libr J

Stardance [novelette]
In The Hugo winners p327-88

Roger Caras' Treasury of great cat stories. Dutton 1987 495p $19.95
ISBN 0-525-24398-4 LC 86-2200

"A Truman Talley book"
An anthology featuring feline tales by Kipling, Wodehouse, Saki, Gallico, Twain, and others

Roger Caras' Treasury of great dog stories. Dutton 1987 497p $19.95
ISBN 0-525-24399-2 LC 86-6264

"A Truman Talley book"
Among the authors represented in this collection are Turgenev, Narayan, Bradbury, Terhune and O. Henry

Rogers, Jane, 1952-

Mr. Wroe's virgins; Jane Rogers. Overlook Press 1999 276p o.p.
ISBN 0-87951-702-6 LC 99-10232
First published 1992 in the United Kingdom
This novel, "based on historical events and set in Lancashire in 1830, begins when John Wroe, 'prophet' of a Judeo-Christian sect, claims that God has instructed him to comfort himself by taking seven virgins into his home. The story spans the nine months the women spend under Wroe's roof before he is ousted by his congregation following charges of indecency." Booklist
"Rogers's wry account of the Christian Israelite community's abbreviated tenure is alternately narrated by four of the chosen virgins. . . . The virgins' narratives read like four diaries spliced together to create a chronology of events, incidentally providing a forum of conflicting opinions and perspectives." N Y Times Book Rev

Roiphe, Anne Richardson, 1935-

Lovingkindness; a novel; by Anne Roiphe. Summit Bks. 1987 279p o.p.
LC 87-6448
"Annie Johnson, widowed before the birth of her daughter Andrea, is a modern, successful, professional woman. Her relations with Andrea has been marked with alienation on her daughter's part, as she appears to be intent on destroying her life as a drop-out from schools, an abuser of drugs, and a young woman who has already experienced three abortions. Annie Johnson seeks psychiatric help for Andrea with no success. It is not until Andrea, finding herself a visitor in Israel, is taken into a yeshiva community that some change in her behavior comes about. The rigorous, although warm, Jewish orthodox discipline appears to change Andrea into a submissive young woman living a life completely foreign to anything her mother understands. The destruction inherent in some parent-child conflicts is painfully described here." Shapiro. Fic for Youth. 3d edition

Rölvaag, Ole Edvart, 1876-1931

Giants in the earth; a saga of the prairie; by O. E. Rölvaag; translated from the Norwegian. Harper 1927 465p o.p.
This novel "chronicles the struggles of Norwegian immigrant settlers in the Dakota territory in the 1870s. . . . The book's indomitable protagonist, Per Hansa, his wife Beret, their children, and three other Norwegian immigrant families settle at Spring Creek, living in makeshift sod huts. Surviving the winters' fierce blizzards, they see their crops destroyed by locusts in summer. They nonetheless persist; new settlers arrive, and the community grows." Merriam-Webster's Ency of Lit
Followed by Peder Victorious

Peder Victorious; a novel; by O. E. Rölvaag; translated from the Norwegian; English text by Nora O. Solum and the author. Harper 1929 350p o.p.
"Carries on the characters of 'Giants in the earth,' the interest centering in Peder Victorious and Beret, the boy's mother, against the background of a community no longer intensely struggling with the soil, but adapting it-

Rölvaag, Ole Edvart, 1876-1931—*Continued*
self to the ways of the new country, or resisting adaptation as Beret continues to do. The boy Peder, with his changing ideas and his ardent pursuit of girls is a foil for the character of Beret, perhaps the most finely conceived personality in the book." N Y Libr

Followed by Their father's God (1931)

Roosevelt, Elliott, 1910-1990

A first class murder. St. Martin's Press 1991 261p o.p.
LC 90-48994

"An Eleanor Roosevelt mystery"

"When First Lady of mystery Eleanor Roosevelt boards the *Normandie* to return to America, she is pleased to learn that Henry Luce, Charles Lindbergh, Jack Benny, Josephine Baker, and the young John F. Kennedy are among her traveling companions. She is not so pleased when the Russian ambassador, also on board, dies of strychnine poisoning, but she sets about to solve the mystery anyway." Publ Wkly

The Hyde Park murder. St. Martin's Press 1985 231p o.p.
LC 85-1752

"A stock swindle threatens to keep two young lovers apart. Bob Hannah is the son of the indicted financier, and his fiancée's father wants no part of a family marked by scandal. Mrs. Roosevelt's matchmaking for the two sweethearts is further complicated when the elder Hannah dies in what is claimed to be a suicide. Bob Hannah and Eleanor suspect murder." Wilson Libr Bull

"The author's fascinating glimpses into history, into the Roosevelts at home, and into corrupt politics are delivered in a measured and surefooted manner." Booklist

Murder and the First Lady. St. Martin's Press 1984 227p o.p.
LC 83-24659

"This historical mystery is set just before World War II, when international tensions are at a peak. Philip Garber, a lowly bookkeeper and assistant to the chief usher at the White House, is found murdered. Eleanor Roosevelt turns sleuth when it's discovered that Garber was found dead in the room of her British secretary, Pamela Rush-Hodgeborne." Booklist

Murder at midnight; an Eleanor Roosevelt mystery. St. Martin's Press 1997 216p $20.95
ISBN 0-312-15596-4 LC 96-53530

"A Thomas Dunne book"

"Judge Horace Blackwell, friend and adviser to the president, is stabbed to death in his White House suite, and Sara Carter, a black maid, is arrested after finding the body. After promising the girl a fair hearing and gaining the confidence of lead investigator Lawrence Pickering, Eleanor takes an active role. Her doubts about Sara's guilt lead to some disturbing discoveries, not least of which is that the judge appears to have been a sadistic womanizer. . . . Peopled with famous lights of 1933, including Babe Ruth, William Faulkner and Gertrude Stein, Washington, D.C., is bought to life in the mirror of the White House." Publ Wkly

Murder at the palace. St. Martin's Press 1987 232p o.p.
LC 87-27961

"A Thomas Dunne book"

This novel "is set at Buckingham Palace in wartime London. On a visit to British and American troops (including son Elliott), Mrs. Roosevelt greets the king and queen, princesses Margaret and Elizabeth, and Sir Alan Burton. . . . When Burton becomes a suspect in a top-secret and terribly embarrassing murder case, Mrs. Roosevelt comes to his aid." Booklist

Murder in Georgetown; an Eleanor Roosevelt mystery. St. Martin's Press 1999 230p $23.95
ISBN 0-312-24221-2 LC 99-26719

"A Thomas Dunne book"

"Eleanor Roosevelt comes to the rescue of a lovely young woman who is wrongly accused of murder. As the First Lady investigates the circumstances surrounding the crime, readers discover that she has helped to place the accused in a job where she can spy on the President's rivals. Through personal interactions among the Roosevelts, their staff, friends, and business associates, readers are treated to unique insights into the White House in the 1930s." SLJ

Murder in the Blue Room. St. Martin's Press 1990 215p o.p.
LC 89-77677

"A Thomas Dunne book"

"Set in 1942 during Soviet Foreign Minister Molotov's secret visit to FDR, [this] mystery . . . finds the author's mother, Eleanor Roosevelt, solving a double murder and combating racial discrimination in the armed forces. A droll, yet affectionate, portrait that is standard but intriguing fare." Booklist

Murder in the map room; an Eleanor Roosevelt mystery. St. Martin's Press 1998 251p il $21.95
ISBN 0-312-18168-X LC 97-37243

"A Thomas Dunne book"

"When Mrs. Roosevelt discovers a murder in the White House during the state visit of Madame Chiang Kai-shek in 1943, her investigation is hampered by both diplomatic protocol and the fact that the U.S. is deeply involved in a war raging on two fronts. . . . As usual, Elliot Roosevelt's respectfully playful portrayal of his down-to-earth mother as a clever sleuth is enough to keep the pages turning." Booklist

Murder in the Oval Office; an Eleanor Roosevelt mystery. St. Martin's Press 1989 247p o.p.
LC 88-18848

"A Thomas Dunne book"

"Her sense of justice (not to mention her curiosity) sparked by the murder of a Southern Congressman during a White House soiree, the resourceful First Lady shows spunk and wit, and also considerable charm, in her investigation of the locked room puzzle." N Y Times Book Rev

Murder in the Rose Garden. St. Martin's Press 1989 232p o.p.
LC 89-35326

"A Thomas Dunne book"

"During the summer of 1936, popular Washington hostess Vivian Taliafero is strangled in the White House

Roosevelt, Elliott, 1910-1990—*Continued*

Rose Garden. . . . The First Lady helps the Secret Service and the D.C. police gather information about the murdered woman who was, it turns out, an extortionist. . . . Vivian's partner in blackmail, photographer Joe Bob Skaggs, is killed, as is one of their victims, while Mrs. Roosevelt strives to solve the mystery." Publ Wkly

The White House pantry murder; an Eleanor Roosevelt mystery. St. Martin's Press 1987 231p o.p.

LC 86-26249

"A Thomas Dunne book"

"It is December, 1941, and Winston Churchill is a guest at the White House. The body of an unidentified man is found in the White House freezer. When weapons are found in a storm sewer leading to the White House, espionage or an assassination attempt is suspected. Mrs. Roosevelt, ably assisted by Secret Service agent Deconcini and British Lieutenant-Commander Leach, must find the person responsible before something terrible happens." Libr J

Roosevelt, Kermit

In the shadow of the law; Kermit Roosevelt. Farrar, Straus and Giroux 2005 370p $24

ISBN 0-374-26187-3 LC 2004-24222

This novel "goes behind the scenes at Morgan Siler, one of Washington, D.C.'s most powerful K Street law firms, as several lawyers become embroiled in two difficult cases: a pro bono death penalty case in Virginia and a class action suit brought against a Texas chemical corporation after an explosion kills dozens of workers. . . . Though the novel features plenty of satisfying twists and turns, the book transcends the legal thriller genre. Roosevelt . . . offers a fascinating insider's look into the culture of a high-stakes firm, while also presenting a considered meditation on the law itself and its potential to compromise those driven to practice it." Publ Wkly

Roquelaure, A. N. *See* Rice, Anne, 1941-

Rosen, Jonathan

Joy comes in the morning; Jonathan Rosen. 1st ed. Farrar, Straus and Giroux 2004 389p $25

ISBN 0-374-18026-1 LC 2004-1742

"In her work as a hospital volunteer, Deborah Green, a Manhattan rabbi, encounters an ailing Holocaust survivor—recovering from a debilitating stroke and a suicide attempt—and his skeptical son. To complicate matters, she is beautiful and single, while the skeptical son is a shy bachelor; the romance causes crises of faith for both, as they negotiate their divergent attitudes toward their religion. As the story moves from wedding to funeral and back again, and Deborah officiates at the momentous changes in other people's lives, she increasingly finds her own life empty of the things that she has always counselled her congregation to treasure. Served with the merest teaspoon of schmaltz, Rosen's touching novel of Jewish manners thoughtfully addresses the question of whether piety can teach us faith." New Yorker

Rosenberg, Nancy Taylor

Abuse of power. Dutton 1997 326p $23.95

ISBN 0-525-93768-4 LC 96-44141

In this novel, "policewoman Rachel Simmons takes on a corruption-riddled police force. Molested as a child, she is filled with a fiery purpose and uncompromising honesty. These scruples act against her when she witnesses an abuse of police authority and reports it. The duel between Rachel's conscience and her own family's safety forms the basis of the plot line. The novel moves rapidly to a powerful conclusion." Libr J

Buried evidence. Hyperion 2000 359p o.p.

ISBN 0-7868-6619-5 LC 00-35073

Sequel to Mitigating circumstances

"Lily Forrester, formerly of the Ventura DA's office, is now DA in Santa Barbara. Her ex-husband, John Forrester, who has been living with their 18-year-old daughter, Shana, is losing his battle with the bottle and has been arrested for vehicular manslaughter. . . . John blackmails Lily into bailing him out of jail, bartering Lily's secret in an effort to escape prosecution. (Six years before, Shana was brutally raped while Lily was forced to look on, and Lily shot and killed the wrong man in retaliation.) The real rapist has recently been released on parole and is once again stalking the two women." Publ Wkly

First offense. Dutton 1994 338p o.p.

LC 94-550

"Probation officer Ann Carlisle's husband, a highway patrolman, disappeared mysteriously four years ago, and it's been tough for Ann and her 12-year-old son to put their lives back together. A new love interest plus a heavy caseload at work are just beginning to help heal Ann's wounds when she becomes involved in a narcotics trial that will unravel her life all over again." Booklist

"Just when readers will have figured all the angles, savvy Rosenberg unveils the villain and flips the plot into an exciting manhunt, with Ann as bait." Publ Wkly

Interest of justice; a novel. Dutton 1993 368p o.p.

LC 93-13005

"Lara Sanderstone, a California judge, finds her life turned upside down when her house is burglarized, her sister and brother-in-law are brutally murdered, and she's left with a sullen 14-year-old nephew to care for. With the help of police sergeant Ted Rickerson, Lara tries to determine if the crimes were the random work of some sicko or if one of the deadbeats she's sent to prison is out for revenge." Booklist

"Lara Sanderstone is such an intelligent, finely detailed character that even the unlikeliest plot twists work in this absorbing legal thriller." Publ Wkly

Mitigating circumstances. Dutton 1993 362p o.p.

LC 92-23035

In this novel "Lily Forrester, a district attorney in Southern California, is an ambitious woman with a deteriorating marriage. Her life becomes a nightmare when both she and her daughter are brutally attacked. Recognizing their attacker, but unwilling to submit her child to the abuse of the legal system, Forrester moves to deal out justice herself." Libr J

"For all the adrenaline that the author pumps into her story, her writing is far more persuasive when it isn't so feverish—during intimate mother-daughter exchanges, for example, and in the realistically mundane procedures of ordinary, hard-working cops and lawyers." N Y Times Book Rev

Rosenberg, Nancy Taylor—*Continued*

Sullivan's law. Kensington Bks. 2004 314p $24
ISBN 0-7582-0618-6

Carolyn Sullivan is a "probation officer attending night school to become an attorney. Juggling her coursework and her job is hard enough, let alone having to worry about how she'll handle single parenthood with her preteen daughter and college-bound son. Carolyn's pressures only mount when one of her probationary charges, convicted killer and paranoid schizophrenic Daniel Metroix, is arrested for rape. . . . Rosenberg puts it all together here with another thoroughly believable heroine dealing with corruption, greed, deceit, and danger." Booklist

Trial by fire. Dutton 1996 339p o.p.
LC 95-34478

"Stella Cataloni is the Dallas district attorney's top hand. Shortly after winning a highly controversial case, she is accused of murder. And so a nightmare of buried memories, false friends, unknown enemies, love betrayed, and a family in conflict begins." Libr J

"The plot begins to twist from the first and tightens and turns on almost every page. Rosenberg sprinkles her story with plenty of mayhem, the requisite professional jealousy, a little cocaine, and even a romance for her heroine." Booklist

Rosenberg, Robert

This is not civilization. Houghton Mifflin 2004 293p $24
ISBN 0-618-38601-7

"In far-off Kyrgyzstan, Anarbek Tashtanaliev deals with stubborn daughter Nazira even as he tries to maintain the sham that his village's collective is still producing cheese; communism may have fallen, but the government keeps sending stipends. Flash forward to an Apache reservation, where well-meaning but hapless Jeff Hartig has failed in his attempt to establish a teen center, notwithstanding his friendship with Adam Dale, son of a tribal councilman. Jeff ends up as a Peace Corps volunteer in Anarbek's village, then reappears in Istanbul, where he works for the U.S. government processing refugees. For various reasons, Anarbek, Adam, and Nazira all converge on Jeff. And then the brutal 1999 earthquake hits." Libr J

"This is risky comedy that in less deft hands would clunk into condescension, but Rosenberg keeps it aloft with a sweet sense of appreciation. . . . What a generous, bighearted book this is, perceptive enough to catch the goodness in all these well-intentioned people." Christ Sci Monit

Ross, Ann B.

Miss Julia throws a wedding. Viking 2002 308p o.p.
ISBN 0-670-03105-4 LC 2001-56798

"The inimitable Miss Julia pushes an indecisive couple toward matrimong in this Southern comedy-of-manners, . . . which begins with the protagonist frustrated at the inability of her friend, Miss Hazel, to get her beau to propose. But another opportunity surfaces when Sheriff Coleman Bates proposes to his lawyer girlfriend Binkie Enloe. . . . Ross gets a bit carried away with wedding details, but her cheeky style works flawlessly once Miss Julia digs into the romantic intrigue and begins to ply her unique combination of common sense and old-fashioned, smalltown wisdom." Publ Wkly

Ross, Leonard Q. *See* Rosten, Leo, 1908-1997

Ross, Malcolm *See* Ross-Macdonald, Malcolm

Ross-Macdonald, Malcolm

For they shall inherit; a novel; [by] Malcolm Macdonald. St. Martin's Press 1985 c1984 591p o.p.
LC 84-52352

First published 1984 in the United Kingdom with title: In love and war

This "novel is set in 19th century England and centers on a dynamic friendship, cemented in boyhood, between clever, ambitious, working-class Freddy and aristocratic Clive, son of the wealthy industrialist who is Freddy's first employer. The fireworks begin when they fall in love with the same woman and Freddy finds himself the legal father of his friend's child. Thereupon they embark on careers that feature exotic adventures in South Africa, South America, the Middle East and elsewhere, accompanied by Freddy's relentless rise to power and wealth, finally at Clive's expense, and the inextricable social and genetic intertwining of their two families." Publ Wkly

"MacDonald skillfully depicts the English class system and the struggles inherent in it. The characters are multi-faceted and solidly drawn, and the writing is smooth. An absorbing portrayal of human emotion and an individual's will to prevail." Libr J

The rich are with you always. Knopf 1976 483p o.p.

"In this sequel to 'The World From Rough Stones' Macdonald continues the interlocking family dramas of John and Nora Stevenson, born dirt poor, driving hard for money and power in Victorian England, and Walter and Arabella Thornton, aristocratic, unhappy, the Stevensons' opposites in every way. It is Nora and John who dominate this part of the saga in the fierce get-rich-quick era of railroad schemes and bonanzas and bankruptcies." Publ Wkly

Followed by Sons of fortune (1978)

Tamsin Harte. St. Martin's Press 2000 345p il $24.95
ISBN 0-312-20628-3 LC 99-88104

"Set in a Cornish fishing village at the turn of the last century. . . . Tamsin Harte and her mother, Harriet, fall from the upper echelon of society when Tamsin's father dies and his shipping firm goes bankrupt. They open a boarding house to get by. Energetic, enterprising and ambitious, Tamsin discovers that she has a mind suited to business enterprises. (Her secret ambition is to build 'the best hotel in Cornwall.') When it comes to romance, however, she is still bound by tradition." Publ Wkly

The Trevarton inheritance; [by] Malcolm Macdonald. St. Martin's Press 1996 395p $24.95
ISBN 0-312-14748-1 LC 96-20035

Ross-Macdonald, Malcolm—*Continued*

This novel's protagonist, Crissy Moore, "loses both parents and her grandfather within a few days. Determined to keep her orphaned family of six together, she puts herself at the mercy of the grandmother who years ago disowned Crissy's mother. The old woman offers Crissy the position of lady's maid while secretly arranging to break up the family by having all the other children placed in agencies throughout Cornwall. A secondary plot concerns the attempt of Crissy and Jim, the young man she eventually marries, to establish a business photographing tourists at the seaside." Libr J

"Macdonald always maintains a brisk narrative pace, and his sound social commentary adds to the reader's enjoyment." Publ Wkly

The world from rough stones. Knopf 1975 535p il o.p.

"Within a year, in the early 1840s, John Stevenson, with Nora at his side, rises from the ranks of railroad construction laborer to the position of a respected and influential contractor. Nora, the ragged and starving teenage girl who had come to John out of the night, becomes his wife. . . . The minor characters, Walter and Arabella Thornton, are middleclass English who are swept along by the tumultuous Stevensons. Walter driven by his sexual fantasies and urges, and Arabella, the pious and good but frigid wife." Best Sellers

"This saga of England in 1839-40 and the start of a great railroad building dynasty opens fast and never once lets up its pace and drama. Above all, its people are believable human beings, caught up in the tumultuous movement of beginning social change." Publ Wkly

Followed by The rich are with you always

Rossner, Judith, 1935-2005

August. Houghton Mifflin 1983 376p o.p.
LC 83-6191

"'August,' when analysts vacation, is the tale of an analysis, with parallel story-lines for patient and doctor. Teenaged golden girl Dawn Henley has a bizarre background: orphaned as an infant, she was raised by a beloved lesbian aunt and her lover, whose 'divorce' sent Dawn to an analyst. Fortyish Dr. Lulu Shinefeld is twice divorced with a grown daughter from whom she's estranged. So Dawn becomes Dr. Shinefeld's 'analytic daughter.'" Libr J

"Rossner writes about the technical side of analysis and simultaneously shows it at work. In spite of a few awkward passages that tell rather than show how analysis works and an unavoidable lack of completeness resulting from the nature of her topic, Rossner has written a fascinating study of the human mind growing." Best Sellers

Emmeline. Simon & Schuster 1980 331p o.p.
LC 80-15553

The novel concerns Emmeline Mosher who "was 13 years old in 1839 when she was sent from her family's farm in Maine to earn 55 cents a week in the cotton mills of Lowell, Mass. There she was seduced by an overseer, gave birth to a child at the home of an aunt before her fifteenth birthday and returned to her parents without telling them her secret. Her venture into the world had saved her family from destitution. In her 30s, having resigned herself to a single life, she made a happy marriage, which ended in calamity. She lived another 40 years as an outcast. . . . Her story is true, according to [the author]." Newsweek

The author "handles her material so meticulously that she inspires a renewed respect for the complexities of skillful story-telling. Instead of propagandizing, she evinces complete respect for the period and setting of her story." Books of the Times

Looking for Mr. Goodbar. Simon & Schuster 1975 284p o.p.

This novel opens with the police transcript of a murderer's confession. The novel "is based loosely on the actual case of Roseann Quinn, a quiet, rigidly brought-up Catholic schoolteacher, who was wholly unremarkable except that she sought out her sexual partners in New York singles bars. The last of them bashed in her skull on New Year's Day, 1973. The question the author asks as she tours the life of Theresa Dunn, the Roseann Quinn-like character of the book, is 'What's a nice girl like you doing in a place like this?'" N Y Times Book Rev

"The tale is stark, capably told, believable; Rossner's prose is a delight, and her sense of the inner life of her characters, all tortured, is deft and sure. This is a very good novel." Booklist

Perfidia; a novel. Talese 1997 308p o.p.
LC 97-10882

This is the "story of a model high-school student who kills her alcoholic, violently abusive mother in self-defense. . . . When she is five years old, narrator Maddy Stern is taken by her restless, amoral mother, Anita, from Hanover, N.H., where her father is a professor at Dartmouth, to Santa Fe, where Anita wholeheartedly enters into the 1970s drug and sex scene." Publ Wkly

"Rossner reveals a gritty new style, stripped down to the clean bones of feeling. 'Perfidia' is an unsparing close-up of the seductive attachment and growing repulsion of a mother and daughter who mean far too much to each other." N Y Times Book Rev

Rosten, Leo, 1908-1997

Captain Newman, M.D. Harper 1962 c1961 331p o.p.

First published 1961 in the United Kingdom

"Describes life in a hospital at an Air Force base in the Southwest during the war. Captain Newman, chief of the psychiatric ward, is a warm, kindly person, the antithesis of the military man, and it is around him that the story revolves. The action is made up of a series of episodes." Libr J

"A book of great insight, warmth and humor. . . . It is a tremendously impressive piece of verbal tight-rope walking. There are the expected flashes of GI humor, the much-documented war of rank, there are also moments of great tenderness and understanding in this chronicle of that most delicate of explorations, the exploration into the shattered minds that are the common responsibilities of all of us." N Y Her Trib Books

Roth, Henry, 1906-1995

Call it sleep. Ballou, R.O. 1934 599p o.p.

"The years between the sixth and ninth birthdays of a young boy are described in this vivid, sensitive portrayal of a Jewish childhood in the ghettos of Brownsville, and

Roth, Henry, 1906-1995—*Continued*
the Lower East Side in New York. Because David's father is a violent and bitter man, the child always turns to his mother, with whom he is very close. Her love protects him from the terrors of street gangs, poverty, the sexual conflicts between his parents, and his own initiation into sex by a lame girl. A literary technique that distinguishes between the language used by members of this family when they are speaking their native tongue (Yiddish) and when they speak broken English they have learned as immigrants in the United States is an unusual feature in this remarkable book." Shapiro. Fic for Youth. 3d edition

A diving rock on the Hudson. St. Martin's Press 1995 418p (Mercy of a rude stream, v2) o.p.

This second volume of the author's autobiographical cycle "continues the saga of Ira Stigman, teenage son of Orthodox Jewish immigrant parents, as he struggles to find his way in the larger world. Narrated by the now elderly Ira, it effectively evokes both life in 1920s New York and the angst of adolescent existence. In Ira's case, this angst results not only from the growing distance that separates his and his parents' views of the world but from uncontrollable urges that drive him to violate one of society's strongest taboos."

"Simultaneously, we are inside the mind of a troubled adolsecent and that of an aged but still mentally vital man, a man engaged with words, with concepts, obsessively reconsidering the role of the artist and in particular his own responsibility in portraying events truthfully." Booklist

Followed by From bondage

From bondage. St. Martin's Press 1996 397p (Mercy of a rude stream, v3) $25.95

ISBN 0-312-14341-9

This third volume of Roth's autobiographical cycle "continues the story of Ira Stigman, son of East European Jewish immigrant parents and now college aged, as he struggles to find his way in 1920s New York. But, like the previous volumes, it is also the story of Ira the octogenarian writer who, nearing the end of his life, is trying to come to terms with both the forces and the choices that shaped it. Paralleling Roth's own experience, this volume focuses on the beginnings of what was to become a decade-long affair between Ira and NYU professor Edith Welles." Libr J

Followed by Requiem for Harlem

Requiem for Harlem. St. Martin's Press 1997 291p il (Mercy of a rude stream, v4) $24.95

ISBN 0-312-16980-9 LC 97-17824

This concluding volume of Roth's autobiographical cycle picks up the story in 1927. "Still living in the Harlem slums with his parents and young sister, City College senior Ira Stigman is on fire with Milton's poetry and wracked by guilt over his sexual relations with his 16-year-old cousin Stella. Although the reader has known since volume three that Ira's eventual deliverer and muse will be his NYU English instructor (and the mistress of his best friend), Roth delays the inception of this affair until the novel's conclusion and meanwhile dwells on what seem red herrings: Stella's pregnancy scare and her grandfather's apparent discovery of her trysts with Ira." Publ Wkly

"Even as we see the older writer commenting ruefully on all that has come to pass, we see the young artist taking in every detail of the world. . . . And if it is hard to sympathize with either the egocentric youth or the rueful old man, taken together they meld into a living whole. This is Roth's achievement, this double vision of the artist as both young and old man, hungry and regretful, flawed and penitent." N Y Times Book Rev

A star shines over Mt. Morris Park. St. Martin's Press 1994 290p (Mercy of a rude stream, v1) o.p.

LC 93-37270

The first volume of Roth's autobiographical cycle. "Ira Stigman, the protagonist narrates both as a boy, in the past, and in the present, as a philosophical and pain-wracked octogenarian. Young Ira's tale begins in 1914, when he and his parents move from the East Side's cozy Jewish enclave to Harlem, then primarily Irish. This dislocation, which makes Ira despise his Jewishness, coincides with the arrival of his mother's parents and siblings, fresh off the boat from Austria-Hungary. As Ira copes with all these changes, he takes comfort in books. . . . As he navigates the rough course of his impoverished life from ages 8 to 15, he reports on the absurdities and abusiveness of family life, school, and various jobs as well as the shadow of war, the many hues of anti-Semitism and racism, and the shock of sexuality." Booklist

"Mr. Roth remains an admirable craftsman, and the scenes of immigrant life in the second decade of the century are evoked with persuasive concreteness." N Y Times Book Rev

Followed by A diving rock on the Hudson

Roth, Joseph, 1894-1939

The bust of the emperor
In Roth, J. and Hofmann, M. The collected stories of Joseph Roth

The collected stories of Joseph Roth; translated with an introduction by Michael Hofmann. Norton 2002 400p $27.95

ISBN 0-393-04320-7 LC 2001-44747

This collection includes three novellas: The triumph of beauty, The bust of the emperor and The leviathan, and the following short stories: The honors student; Barbara; Career; The place I want to tell you about. . .; Sick people; Rare and ever rarer in this world of empirical fact. . .; The Cartel; April the story of a love affair; The blind mirror; The grand house opposite; Strawberries; This morning, a letter arrived; Youth; Stationmaster Fallmerayer

The triumph of beauty explores the impact of a fickle hypochondriac on her husband. In the bust of the emperor an elderly nobleman continues to perform dutifully even after the state renders his commitment obsolete. The leviathan portrays a coral merchant preoccupied with the mystery of the exotic life forms that provide his livelihood

"Combining a shrewd reportorial eye with a taste for the fantastic and droll, Roth portrays characters living materially and spiritually impoverished lives in isolated Eastern European villages and those left homeless in their own homes in the tumultuous aftermath of World War I." Booklist

Roth, Joseph, 1894-1939—*Continued*

The leviathan

In Roth, J. and Hofmann, M. The collected stories of Joseph Roth

The triumph of beauty

In Roth, J. and Hofmann, M. The collected stories of Joseph Roth

Roth, Philip

American pastoral. Houghton Mifflin 1997 423p o.p.

LC 96-49368

"Swede Levov's life has been charmed from the time he was an all-star athlete at Newark's Weequahic high school. . . . He successfully runs his father's glove factory, refusing to be cowed by the race riots that rock Newark, marries a shiksa beauty-pageant queen, who is smart and ambitious, buys a 100-acre farm in a classy suburb—the epitome of serene, innocent, pastoral existence—and dotes on his daughter, Merry. But when Merry becomes radicalized during the Vietnam War, plants a bomb that kills an innocent man and goes underground for five years, Swede endures a torment that becomes increasingly unbearable as he learns more about Merry's monstrous life." Publ Wkly

"This cultural horror story is deepened by Roth's genius for blending humor, pathos, sympathy and rage. . . . You will search the shelf of contemporary fiction long and hard to find a parental nightmare projected with the emotional force and verbal energy that Roth brings to American Pastoral." Time

The anatomy lesson. Farrar, Straus & Giroux 1983 291p o.p.

LC 83-11645

"Roth's novelist/hero in The Ghost Writer and Zuckerman Unbound, Nathan Zuckerman at 40 can no longer write: he has lost his subject ('as a medium for his books he had ceased to be') and is losing his hair. Severely incapacitated by chronic pain . . . and addicted to painkillers, Zuckerman decides to become a doctor, one who deals not in words but in real 'stuff,' 'the lowest of genres—life itself.' He ends up in a hospital rather than medical school when a disastrously euphoric return to Chicago, scene of his first literary triumph, results in a drug-induced breakdown." Libr J

"A ferocious, heartfelt book. . . . One might venture to say that, like a goodly number of Roth's previous works, 'The Anatomy Lesson' revolves around the paradox of incarnation—the astonishing coexistence in one life of infantilism and intelligence, of selfishness and altruism, of sexual appetite and social conscience—and has the form and manner of a monologue conducted under psychoanalysis." New Yorker

also in Roth, P. Zuckerman bound: a trilogy and epilogue

The breast

In Roth, P. Novels, 1967-1972

The dying animal. Houghton Mifflin 2001 156p $22

ISBN 0-618-13587-1 LC 00-54225

David Kepesh, protagonist of Roth's The breast and The professor of desire, "is now an eminent 70-year-old cultural critic and lecturer at a New York college, recalling a devastating, all-consuming affair he had eight years before with voluptuous 24-years-old Consuela Castillo, a graduate student and daughter of a prosperous Cuban émigré family." Publ Wkly

"Like many works of modern literature, The Dying Animal ends on a note of radical ambiguity and indeterminacy. What is rather unusual about it is the way it challenges the reader at every point to define and defend his own ethical position toward the issues raised by the story. It is a small, disturbing masterpiece." N Y Rev Books

The ghost writer. Farrar, Straus & Giroux 1979 179p o.p.

LC 79-13146

"A brief but intricate tale about a young writer [Nathan Zuckerman] who, when accused of travestying his fellow Jews, seeks counsel from a respected older Jewish author and finds this distinguished figure ambiguously involved with a girl whom the young writer fantasizes to be Anne Frank." Oxford Companion to Am Lit. 6th edition

Followed by Zuckerman unbound

also in Roth, P. Zuckerman bound: a trilogy and epilogue

Goodbye, Columbus

In Roth, P. Novels & stories, 1959-1962

Goodbye, Columbus, and five short stories. Modern Lib. 1995 298p $17.95; pa $13

ISBN 0-679-60159-7; 0-679-74826-1 (pa)

LC 94-44528

A reissue of the title first published 1959 by Houghton Mifflin

"The title story in this collection is about a young Radcliffe girl and a Rutgers boy who learn that there is more to love than exuberance and passion. All of the stories dramatize the dilemma of modern American Jews, torn between two worlds." Publ Wkly

The great American novel. Holt, Rinehart & Winston 1973 382p o.p.

"Sportswriter 'Word' Smith narrates the chaotic history of a forgotten ('suppressed,' he claims) third major league and its bungling nemeses the Ruppert Mundays, a team of neurotic misfit leftovers. In 1943, war has decimated the league; the Mundys are cast out from their stadium (which is needed for wartime priorities) on 'an endless road trip,' to wander the circuit and suffer." Libr J

This novel is "at once a burlesque and an allegory, its telling of the downfall of a great baseball team serving as a satirical parallel to contemporary American political and social events." Oxford Companion to Am Lit. 6th edition

The human stain. Houghton Mifflin 2000 361p $26

ISBN 0-618-05945-8 LC 99-89867

"Coleman Silk, a brilliant classics professor at sleepy Athena College in western Massachusetts, is forced into early retirement by the zealots of political correctness when an African American student accuses him of using the word *spook* as a racial epithet. This groundless claim

Roth, Philip—*Continued*
is supported by the department chair, a French feminist motivated by sexual jealousy. The irony is that Silk, who has always claimed to be Jewish, is in fact African American himself. Not even his wife and children know the truth. . . . Silk asks his neighbor Nathan Zuckerman to write a book about the affair, and *The Human Stain* is Zuckerman's final report, completed after Silk's untimely death." Libr J

"Roth is clearly enjoyed himself. The Human Stain is as fresh, as angry and as bitterly amused as his early fiction. It vibrates with mockery, disapproval, poetry, and a healthy dose of personal vindictiveness that one would be tempted to dismiss as unworthy if it weren't so funny." New Leader

I married a communist. Houghton Mifflin 1998 323p $26
ISBN 0-395-93346-3 LC 98-16797

"Roth's old alter ego, Nathan Zuckerman, narrates the story of Ira Ringold, aka Iron Rinn, a supremely idealistic political radical and celebrated radio star of the 1950s who is blacklisted and brought to ruin when his wife, Eva Frame (a self-hating Jewish actress born Chava Fromkin), writes an expose called *I Married A Communist.* The impetus for Eva's treacherous act is Ira's insistence that she evict her 24-year-old daughter from their house." Publ Wkly

"What Zuckerman/Roth does with this imagined material is constantly mesmerizing. Library shelves groan under the weight of books published about the witch hunts and blacklistings during the Truman and Eisenhower presidencies, but it would be hard to find one among them that presents as nuanced, as humanly complex an account of those years as I Married a Communist." Time

Letting go. Random House 1962 630p $12.50
ISBN 0-394-43305-X

Gabe Wallach is "a young university instructor who is literally unable to let go in his personal relationships. This is true with his father, a well-to-do Jewish dentist who suffers because his wife is dead and his only child lives in Chicago instead of New York; with Martha Reganhart, a divorcée, mother of two small children, a woman Gabe loves enough to make his mistress but not his wife; and with Paul and Libby Herz, a young couple suffering the difficulties arising from a mixed marriage, no money, inability to have children, and a host of other problems real and imagined." Libr J

also in Roth, P. Novels & stories, 1959-1962

My life as a man. Holt, Rinehart & Winston 1974 330p o.p.

The "novel consists of three stories: a long autobiographical narrative told by the novelist Peter Tarnopol, preceded by two of Peter's stories, 'useful fictions' in which elements of his 'true story' are metamorphosed. Peter's alter ego, Nathan Zuckerman, is, like his author, a highly self-conscious intellectual urban Jew, adept at eliciting astonishing sexual performances from teen-age girls, but fatally drawn into a disastrous marriage with an older, damaged woman who is incapable of sexual response." Newsweek

Novels & stories, 1959-1962; Philip Roth. Library of America 2005 913p $35
ISBN 1-931082-79-0 LC 2005-40916

Contents: Goodbye, Columbus; Five short stories; Letting go

Novels, 1967-1972. Library of America 2005 671p $35
ISBN 1-931082-80-4 LC 2005-40917

Contents: When she was good; Portnoy's complaint; Our gang; The breast

When she was good and Portnoy's complaint are entered separately. Our gang (1971) is a satire of the Nixon administration, featuring a president named Trick E. Dixon. The breast (1972) is "a novella about a male professor of literature who suffers a Kafka-like transformation into a gigantic breast." Oxford Companion to Am Lit. 6th edition

Our gang
In Roth, P. Novels, 1967-1972

The plot against America. Houghton Mifflin Co 2004 391p $26
ISBN 0-618-50928-3 LC 2004-47490

"When the renowned aviation hero . . . Charles A. Lindbergh defeated Franklin Roosevelt by a landslide in the 1940 presidential election, fear invaded every Jewish household in America. Not only had Lindbergh, in a nationwide radio address, publicly blamed the Jews for selfishly pushing America toward a pointless war with Nazi Germany, he negotiated a cordial 'understanding' with Adolf Hitler, whose conquest of Europe and virulent antiSemitic policies he appeared to accept with difficulty. . . . [The protagonist Philip Roth] recounts what it was like for his Newark family . . . during the menacing years of the Lindbergh presidency." Publisher's note

"Philip Roth has written a terrific political novel, though in a style his readers might never have predicted. . . . The novel is sinister, vivid, dreamlike, preposterous and, at the same time, creepily plausible." N Y Times Book Rev

Portnoy's complaint. Random House 1969 274p o.p.

"An irreverently funny account of a modern man torn between the repressive, traditional values embodied by his Jewish mother, his passion for WASP women, and his desperate desire to be released from the past to create himself as a human being out of his own nothingness." Reader's Ency. 4th edition

"Roth has the courage to wish to show things as he has experienced them, but the exaggerations of *Portnoy's Complaint* have a shrillness which could be considered unwholesome if the book were not so funny. It is very funny." Burgess. 99 Novels

also in Roth, P. Novels, 1967-1972

The Prague orgy
In Roth, P. Zuckerman bound: a trilogy and epilogue

Sabbath's theater. Houghton Mifflin 1995 451p o.p.
LC 95-914

"Mickey Sabbath is an elderly relic of the diabolical young puppeteer who was once arrested for coaxing a young Columbia student's breast out of her blouse with the sheer effrontery of his insinuating performing fingers. Now, living in obscure poverty in New Hampshire with

Roth, Philip—*Continued*
a wife who's in aggressive recovery from the alcoholism to which he has driven her, he is reviewing his life. . . . He has had a deliriously erotic relationship with Drenka, the concupiscent wife of a local Yugoslavian innkeeper, and her sudden death from cancer quite undoes him." Publ Wkly

"There is plenty of the nasty in this virtuoso performance by our best literary stand-up comic. . . . The verbal play is almost tactile, like slaps, as the narrative moves from third-person comic to first-person perverse confession, but there is a polemical energy that lifts it beyond verbal playfulness; at times the message is painful." N Y Times Book Rev

When she was good. Random House 1967 306p o.p.

This is "a story of a girl obsessed with her own criteria of what a man should be. Set in a Midwestern town the novel is concerned with Lucy Nelson, who disappointed with a feckless father, fights him and scorns her mother for her love of him. Having wreaked havoc in her parents' marriage, she applies the same steely demands to a husband who has been either the seduced or the seducer depending on whose view is accepted. She destroys the marriage and herself in a final abandonment to her compulsion." Booklist

"Roth knows exactly what he's doing. With unerring fidelity, he records the flat surface of provincial American life, the look and feel and sound of it—and then penetrates it to the cesspool of its invisible dynamisms. Beneath the 'good,' and impelling it, he says, lies the horrid." Newsweek

also in Roth, P. Novels, 1967-1972

Zuckerman bound: a trilogy and epilogue. Farrar, Straus & Giroux 1985 784p o.p.

LC 84-23265

An omnibus edition of the author's Zuckerman novels: The ghost writer, Zuckerman unbound and The anatomy lesson, together with a new novella, The Prague orgy

In the Prague orgy "Zuckerman pays a calamitous visit to Czechoslovakia on an Aspern Papers mission to rescue the unpublished manuscript of a great martyred Yiddish writer. The young Zuckerman once spun a feverish fantasy in which he appeased his disapproving Jewish parents by bringing Anne Frank home to Newark as his bride. His heroic Prague quest is no more successful. It ends sardonically, with Zuckerman forced to listen to a cultural commissar extol the great American writer Betty MacDonald." Newsweek

Zuckerman unbound. Farrar, Straus & Giroux 1981 225p o.p.

LC 81-4640

"After three marriages and a respected body of fiction, Nathan Zuckerman has suddenly struck free with the scandalous and subversive success of a book about a Portnoyish complainer called Carnovsky. The promising apprentice of The Ghost Writer who engaged in biographical fantasy, has himself become a creature of public fantasy who cannot cope comfortably even with material success. The consequences range from bizarre comedy (the plague of a ruined quiz show contestant who claims his life has been plagiarized) to the distortion of family relations." Libr J

Followed by The anatomy lesson

also in Roth, P. Zuckerman bound: a trilogy and epilogue

Rothman, Judith, 1935-

For works written by this author under other names see Black, Veronica, 1935-

Roughan, Howard

(jt. auth) Patterson, J. Honeymoon

Roy, Arundhati

The god of small things. Random House 1997 321p o.p.

LC 96-39190

A novel "set in the tiny river town of Ayemenem in Kerala, India. The story revolves around a pair of twins, brother and sister, whose mother has left her violent husband to live with her blind mother and kind, if ineffectual, brother, Chacko. Chacko's ex-wife, an Englishwoman, has returned to Ayemenem after a long absence, bringing along her and Chacko's lovely young daughter. Their arrival not only unsettles the already tenuous balance of the divisive household, it also coincides with political unrest." Booklist

"If the symbolism is a trifle overdone, the lush local color and the incisive characterizations give the narrative power and drama." Publ Wkly

Roza, Luiz Alfredo García- *See* García-Roza, Luiz Alfredo, 1936-

Rozan, S. J.

Winter and night. St. Martin's Minotaur 2002 338p $24.95

ISBN 0-312-24555-6 LC 2001-48659

In this mystery featuring New York PIs Lydia Chin and Bill Smith it is "Smith's turn to tell the story, which here concerns his teenage nephew, Gary Russell, the athlete son of his estranged sister Helen. When Gary is arrested for pickpocketing in Manhattan, the boy asks for his uncle's help. Gary denies running away from his Warrenstown, N. J. home; he was doing something important. Then the boy vanishes, drawing Smith and Chin into a nightmarish case in which a small town's obsession with its high school football team overwhelms standards of justice and morality." Publ Wkly

Ruark, Robert

Uhuru; a novel of Africa today. McGraw-Hill 1962 555p o.p.

This novel "tells of the Kenya of 1960—eight years after the Mau-Mau rebellion—a Kenya where native Africans are heard in the House of Parliament and the UN, where modern-day sophistication is blended with ancient tribal customs to produce a new form of cannibalism, where one nauseating throat-cutting ceremony follows another nauseating betrayal of ethics and morals." Libr J

Ruggero, Ed

The academy; a novel of West Point. Pocket Bks. 1997 448p $24

ISBN 0-671-89169-3 LC 97-26832

Ruggero, Ed—*Continued*

"Wayne Holder, senior cadet at West Point, is at the center of a series of scandals that endanger the very existence of the 200-year-old institution. An instructor's error in judgment leads his wife to unusual efforts to protect his job. A publicity-hungry senator's public hearings threaten major downsizing of the academy, another instructor's extramarital affair is blowing up, Holder's roommate commits suicide, and Wayne himself has misdeeds to conceal." Libr J

Ruggero "has written a fascinating story that mixes hardheaded realism about what it takes to be a soldier with over-the-top flourishes." Publ Wkly

Ruiz, Luis Manuel, 1973-

Only one thing missing; translated from the Spanish by Alfred Mac Adam. Grove Press 2003 308p $24

ISBN 0-8021-1730-9 LC 2002-29723

Original Spanish edition, 2000

"A distraught young woman living in Seville, Spain, Alicia has just lost her husband and only child in a horrible accident. She suffers from terrifying nightmares of wandering through a nameless city whose monuments and inhabitants begin appearing to her during waking moments. Carmen Barroso, the most sought-after psychotherapist in Seville. . . treats her with hynosis and medication but is strangely dismissive of her harrowing dreams. . . . Aided by her brother-in-law, Esteban, who loves her deeply, Alicia comes to realize that she is the victim of a sinister conspiracy with roots in devil worship." Libr J

"As translated by Adam, Ruiz's prose is ornate and word-drunk. Ruiz sometimes falls in love with the sound of his narrator's voice, but it is easy to forgive him." Booklist

Ruiz Zafón, Carlos, 1964-

The shadow of the wind; translated by Lucia Graves. Penguin Press 2004 486p $24.95

ISBN 1-59420-010-6 LC 2003-062376

Original Spanish edition, 2001

"In post-World War II Barcelona, young Daniel is taken by his bookseller father to the Cemetery of Forgotten Books, a massive sanctuary where books are guarded from oblivion. Told to choose one book to protect, he selects The Shadow of the Wind, by Julian Carax. He reads it, loves it, and soon learns it is both very valuable and very much in danger because someone is determinedly burning every copy of every book written by the obscure Carax. . . . Daniel's initiation into the mysteries of adulthood is given the same weight as the mystery of the book-burner. And the setting—Spain under Franco—injects an air of sobriety into some plot elements that might otherwise seem soap operatic. Part detective story, part boy's adventure, part romance, fantasy, and gothic horror, the intricate plot is urged on by extravagant foreshadowing and nail-nibbling tension." Booklist

Rule, Ann

Possession; a novel. Norton 1983 348p o.p.

LC 82-14377

This is a "tale of a psychotic killer stalking a deputy sheriff and his wife as they backpack in the Washington wilderness. The woman, insecure and dependent despite her beauty, and then with her mind unhinged by her husband's death, transfers her allegiance to the stranger, who says he will lead her to safety. Her subsequent rape, the sexual relationship she develops with the rapist, and his lurid fantasies are distasteful, but the parallel story of her husband's partner's search for the pair, his gathering of evidence, and his defense in the murder investigation brought against him exemplifies highly competent crime writing." Libr J

Runyon, Alfred Damon *See* Runyon, Damon, 1884-1946

Runyon, Damon, 1884-1946

Blue plate special

In Runyon, D. Guys and dolls p345-505

Guys and dolls. Lippincott 1950 505p o.p.

An omnibus volume of three titles first published by F.A. Stokes in 1931, 1935 and 1934 respectively and analyzed in Short story index

Contents: Guys and dolls: Bloodhounds of Broadway; Social error; Lily of St. Pierre; Butch minds the baby; Lillian; Romance in the roaring forties; Very honorable guy; Madame La Gimp; Dark Dolores; "Gentlemen, the King!"; Hottest guy in the world; Brain goes home; Blood pressure

Money from home: Earthquake; Bred for battle; Breach of promise; Story goes with it; Sense of humor; Broadway financier; Broadway complex; It comes up mud; Nice price; Pick the winner; Undertaker song; Tobias the terrible

Blue plate special: Hold 'em Yale!; That ever-loving wife of Hymie's; What, no butler?; Brakeman's daughter; Snatching of Bookie Bob; Dream Street Rose; Little Miss Marker; Dancing Dan's Christmas; Old doll's house; Lemon drop kid; Three wise guys; Princess O'Hara; For a pal

Money from home

In Runyon, D. Guys and dolls p167-337

Rusch, Kristine Kathryn

(ed) The Best from Fantasy & Science Fiction: a 45th anniversary anthology. See The Best from Fantasy & Science Fiction: a 45th anniversary anthology

Rush, Norman

Mating. Knopf 1991 480p o.p.

LC 90-25752

The author "relates the tale of an American female anthropologist in Africa, whose thesis research (on fertility) has already gone dead when she falls for a man who is in Africa running a utopian community for unfortunate women." Booklist

"Mr. Rush has created one of the wiser and wittier fictive meditations on the subject of mating. His novel illuminates why we yield when we don't have to. It seeks to illuminate the nature of true intimacy—how to define it, how to know when one has achieved it. And few books evoke so eloquently that state of love at its apogee." N Y Times Book Rev

Mortals; a novel. Knopf 2003 715p $26.95

ISBN 0-679-40622-0 LC 2002-43289

Rush, Norman—*Continued*

This "novel is about middle-class Americans in Botswana, Africa. . . . The protagonist is a minor secret CIA agent in the early 1990s with the region in turmoil as Mandela struggles to come to power across the border. Ray's not quite sure how he landed in his spy job, but he quite likes it. He's sure he's never been involved with anything really bad. What matters to him is his beautiful wife, Iris. After 17 years, he's still totally obsessed with every part of her body, every glance, every funny word. But is she having an affair with Morel, the black American doctor who believes the way to fix broken Africa is to get rid of Christianity? When Ray is sent on a bungled mission and lands up with the brutal apartheid paramilitary, Morel comes to the rescue, and the two bond in a prison cell." Booklist

"The richness of Rush's vision, and its stringent moral clarity, sweep the reader into his brilliantly observed world." Publ Wkly

Rushdie, Salman

East, west; stories. Pantheon Bks. 1995 c1994 214p o.p.

LC 94-28277

First publishd 1994 in the United Kingdom

Contents: Good advice is rarer than rubies; The free radio; The prophet's hair; At the auction of the ruby slippers; Christopher Columbus and Queen Isabella of Spain consummate their relationship (Santa Fé, AD 1492); The harmony of the spheres; Chekov and Zulu; The courter

"Rushdie's brilliant style reinforces his stories' marvelous combination of dignity and poignancy. Though these stories were originally published in such periodicals as the *New Yorker* and the *Atlantic,* the collection will serve for many readers as an introduction to Rushdie's talent in the short story form." Booklist

The ground beneath her feet; a novel. Holt & Co. 1999 575p $26

ISBN 0-8050-5308-5 LC 98-42407

"Ormus Cama, a supernaturally gifted musician, and his beloved, Vina Apsara, a half-Indian woman with a soul-thrilling voice, meet in Bombay in the late '50s, discover rock and roll, and form a band that goes on to become the world's most popular musical act. Narrator Rai Merchant, their lifelong friend, is a world-famous photographer and Vina's 'backdoor man.' Rai tells the story of their great, abiding love . . . which thrives on obstacles. . . . Ultimately, Ormus and Vina reenact the Orpheus myth, not once but twice." Publ Wkly

"Vina and Ormus are icons, not fully formed characters. But that's the point. And Rai . . . is the most moving character Rushdie's ever created." Newsweek

Haroun and the sea of stories. Viking 1990 219p o.p.

LC 90-45496

"This delightful fantasy is filled with adventures, amusing characters with names like Iff and Butt, and villains to fight against and defeat. Rushdie's puns and rhymes will be enjoyed by young and old—the catchy tunes by the younger readers and the political allegory by the adults. Rashid is a professional story-teller whose son, Haroun, delights in hearing them. When Rashid's source of stories seems to have disappeared Haroun faces many dangerous opponents to help his father regain his Gift of Gab." Shapiro. Fic for Youth. 3d edition

Midnight's children; with an introduction by Anita Desai. Knopf 1995 xxxi, 589p $20

ISBN 0-679-44462-9 LC 90-38447

"Everyman's library"

A reissue of the title first published 1980 in the United Kingdom; 1981 in the United States

"The novel is about Shiva and Saleem, two of the 1,001 babies born in the hour following independence at midnight on August 15, 1947. It is notable as much for its portrayal of contemporary politics in India as for the brilliance of its style and insights into human nature and mind." Reader's Ency. 4th edition

The Moor's last sigh. Pantheon Bks. 1996 c1995 435p o.p.

LC 95-24392

First published 1995 in the United Kingdom

"A picaresque recounting of the rise, decline and plunge to extinction of a Portuguese merchant family anciently established in southern India, focusing on the period from 1900 to the present. The hapless narrator, Moraes Zogoiby, . . . has composed these pages during exile and imprisonment in a replica of the Alhambra built and run by a madman (a former protégé of the family) in rural Andalusia. Moraes, nicknamed the Moor, is the last living member of the da Gama-Zogoiby line." N Y Times Book Rev

This is a "marvellously inventive display of verbal dexterity; an exuberant, entertaining, zestful novel which proves, if proof were needed, that Mr Rushdie's spirit remains undiminshed." Economist

The satanic verses. Viking 1989 546p $27.95

ISBN 0-670-82537-9 LC 88-40266

A "panoramic novel which moves with dizzying speed from the streets and film studios of Bombay to multicultural Britain, from Argentina to Mount Everest, as Rushdie questions illusion, reality, and the power of faith and tradition in a world of hijackers, religious pilgrimages and warfare, and celluloid fantasy." Oxford Companion to Engl Lit. 6th edition

Shalimar the clown. Random House 2005 398p $25.95

ISBN 0-679-46335-6 LC 2005-42796

"Los Angeles, 1991. Ambassador Maximilian Ophuls . . . is murdered in broad daylight on his illegitimate daughter India's doorstep, slaughtered by a knife wielded by his Kashmiri Muslim driver, a mysterious figure who calls himself Shalimar the clown. The dead man is a . . . charismatic World War II Resistance hero, a man of formidable intellectual ability, a former US ambassador to India and subsequently America's counter-terrorism chief. The murder looks at first like a political assassination, but turns out to be passionately personal. This is the story of Max Ophuls, his killer and his daughter–and of a fourth character, the woman who links them, whose story finally explains them all." Publisher's note

"Rushdie has written an intensely political novel, infused with recent events, but its emotional scope reaches so far beyond our current crisis and its vision into the vagaries of the heart is so perceptive that one can imagine Shalimar the Clown being read long after this age of sacred terror has faded into history." Washington Post Book World

Rushdie, Salman—*Continued*

Shame. Knopf 1983 319p o.p.

LC 83-48103

"Omar Khayyam Shakil is an improbable hero, lugging his great bulk through the turbulence of modern Pakistan on two very tired feet. He is a reluctant hero as well, preferring sensual delight to the dictates of inexorable fate. But Omar Khayyam is a man of destiny, drawn into the political power struggle between Raza Hyder and Iskander Harappa, and doomed by his love for Sufiya Zinobia, Hyder's retarded daughter." Libr J

"This novel of crossed family destinies in contemporary Pakistan teems with interesting characters, dramatic events, and marvellous verbal inventions. . . . It recreates an exotic but thoroughly believable world that is a delight to experience." Quill Quire

Russell, Mary Doria, 1950-

Children of God; a novel. Villard Bks. 1998 438p $23.95

ISBN 0-679-45635-X LC 97-42160

"Having returned from a disastrous, 21st-century expedition to the planet Rakhat, Jesuit Father Emilio Sandoz, the sole survivor of the mission, faces public rage over the order's part in the war between the gentle Runa and the predatory Jana'ata—fury more than matched by the priest's own self-hatred and religious disillusionment. . . . He is forced to return to Rakhat with a new expedition more interested in profits than prophets. When they discover the planet in turmoil and the Runa precariously in power, the temptation to interfere is more than they can withstand." Publ Wkly

"Russell succeeds in painting an alien culture with remarkably detailed verisimilitude." N Y Times Book Rev

The sparrow. Villard Bks. 1996 408p o.p.

LC 96-11180

This novel about first contact with an extraterrestrial civilization features "Father Emilio Sandoz, a Jesuit linguist whose messianic virtues hide his occasional doubt about his calling. . . . The narrative ping-pongs between the years 2016, when Sandoz begins assembling the team that first detects signs of intelligent extraterrestrial life, and 2060, when a Vatican inquest is convened to coax an explanation from the physically mutilated and emotionally devastated priest." Publ Wkly

"An intriguing venture into the journey of faith by way of science fiction, anthropology and the Society of Jesus. . . . God is the silent character in this story." America

Followed by Children of God

A thread of grace; a novel; Mary Doria Russell. 1st ed. Random House 2005 430p $25.95

ISBN 0-375-50184-3 LC 2004-50942

"As the story opens, the mountainous region of northwest Italy has been relatively untouched by WWII, and even Jews have been safe. When Italy breaks with Germany in 1943 and pulls out of southern France, thousands of Jewish refugees cross the mountains in search of safety. But the German occupation of Italy poses a new threat." Booklist

"This is a morality play that at times uses black humor, and then shifts to solemn reflection or moving portraiture. A Thread of Grace is deft, sensate, ruthless in its moral incisiveness, and affirming in that even in the worst of times, the lamp of humanity cannot be completely extinguished." Hudson Rev

Russo, Richard, 1949-

Empire Falls. Knopf 2001 483p $29.95

ISBN 0-679-43247-7 LC 2001-88568

"Miles Roby is a typical Russo hero: wry, unlucky in love and money; and just a little bit smarter than the people who populate his run-down industrial town. In this case, the town is Empire Falls, Maine, where Miles manages a restaurant that serves as a kind of meeting hall for the novel's large cast of characters. There's David, Miles's recovering-alcoholic brother; Walt, the health-club entrepreneur who has stolen Miles's estranged wife; Tick, Miles's precocious, befuddled teenage daughter; and Francine Whiting, the rich widow who runs everything. Russo is preoccupied with the death of a certain version of the American dream, but his belief in the power of comedy—sometimes low, sometimes high—rescues his work from bathos and elvates it into the realm of literature." New Yorker

Nobody's fool. Random House 1993 549p o.p.

LC 92-56844

"Sixty-year-old Sully is *nobody's fool*, except maybe his own. Out of work (undeclared-income work is what he does, when he can), down to his last few bucks, hampered by an arthritic broken knee, Sully is worried that he's started on a run of bad luck. And he has. The banker son of his octogenarian landlady wants him evicted; Sully's estranged son comes home for Thanksgiving only to have his wife split; Sully's own high-strung ex-wife seems headed for a nervous breakdown; and his longtime lover is blaming him for her daughter's winding up in the hospital with a busted jaw. But Sully's biggest problem is the memory of his own abusive father." Libr J

"A grand read sparkling with witty dialogue and memorable characters, Russo's novel is a rollicking tale of a born loser on a downward slide. An economically depressed upper New York State community is the setting, and its lower-middle-class and blue-collar inhabitants are portrayed with empathy and a shrewd understanding of human nature." Publ Wkly

The risk pool. Random House 1988 479p o.p.

LC 88-42666

"A story on not-so-successful folk in a decaying town in New York as seen through the eyes of Ned Hall, better known as 'Sam's son.' Sam was once an average citizen who grew up, married, and went off to fight in World War II but returned a drifter. Leaving his wife and small son at home, he would haunt the bars and pool halls and hobnob with his cronies. Now and then he'd appear from nowhere to take Ned with him. When Ned's mother, Jenny, trips over the edge, Ned goes to live with Sam in a delapidated loft above the town's one department store and share his father's roguish life." Libr J

"A superbly original, maliciously funny book, peopled by characters that most of us would back away from plenty fast if they ever lurched toward our barstool. It is Mr. Russo's brilliant, deadpan writing that gives their wasted lives and miserable little town such haunting power and insidious charm." N Y Times Book Rev

The straight man. Random House 1997 391p o.p.

LC 96-48578

"Hank Devereaux was voted interim chair of the English department at a Pennsylvania college based on his loudly voiced contempt for bureaucratic procedures.

Russo, Richard, 1949-—*Continued*

Long mired in old grievances and thwarted ambitions, the contentious English faculty figure they can count on Hank to do absolutely nothing, thereby preserving the status quo. They figured wrong. Perpetual wise guy Hank has managed to stir things up on all fronts." Booklist

"The novel's greatest pleasures derive not from any blazing impatience to see what happens next, but from pitch-perfect dialogue, persuasive characterization and a rich progression of scenes, most of them crackling with an impudent, screwball energy reminiscent of Howard Hawks's movies." N Y Times Book Rev

The whore's child; and other stories. Knopf 2002 225p o.p.

ISBN 0-375-41168-2 LC 2002-19023

Contents: The whore's child; Monhegan light; The farther you go; Joy ride; Buoyancy; Poison; The mysteries of Linwood Hart

"Russo's rueful understanding of the twisted skein of human relationships is as sharp as ever, and the dialogue throughout is barbed, pointed and wryly humorous." Publ Wkly

Rutherfurd, Edward

The forest; a novel. Crown 2000 598p il o.p.

ISBN 0-609-60382-5 LC 00-22219

This historical saga focuses on "the New Forest, part of the southern coast of England bounded by the English Channel. Rutherfurd traces the lives of peasants, smugglers, churchmen, woodsmen, and upper-class families from the 11th to the 20th centuries. These assorted men and women take part in the events surrounding the death of King Rufus (William the Conqueror's son), the failure of the Spanish Armada, England's Civil War, and more." Libr J

London. Crown 1997 829p $25.95

ISBN 0-517-59181-2 LC 97-10176

First published 1995 in the United Kingdom

This "fictional history of London is told through the experiences of a group of diverse families who, over the generations, meet, mingle, intermarry, and feud. Beginning with prehistory and continuing to the present, Rutherfurd combines geological details, historical events, real people, and his fictional characters to bring London to life." Libr J

The princes of Ireland; the Dublin saga; Edward Rutherfurd. 1st ed. Doubleday 2004 776p $27.95

ISBN 0-385-50286-9 LC 2003-70005

"Beginning in the tribal, pre-Christian times of the warrior kings at Tara, this first book in a two-part novelized history of Ireland sweeps readers through the early centuries of Druids, chieftains, monks, Vikings, noblemen, merchants, and mercenaries, ending with the disastrous invasion of England that tragically changed the course of Irish history. Through the eyes of the men and women who built the mighty city that became Dublin, the unfolding of a colorful and turbulent history is told with energy and a meticulous attention to historical detail." Libr J

Russka; the novel of Russia. Crown 1991 760p o.p.

LC 90-34457

"Tells the story of a Ukrainian village . . . and some of the families who lived there from A.D. 180 to the 1917 Revolution and, anecdotally, almost to the present." N Y Times Book Rev

The book "does provide a sweeping overview of the land whose very vastness and complexity make it overwhelming and fascinating." Christ Sci Monit

Sarum; the novel of England. Crown 1987 897p o.p.

LC 87-6710

This novel, set in Salisbury, England, aims to trace English history from the last Ice Age to the present through the lives of five fictional families

"Rutherfurd is strong on the explication of trends and the narration of events. But he relies heavily on the repetition of character types. Nevertheless, 'Sarum' is fascinating and will appeal to Anglophiles, history buffs, and fans of epic-style novels." Christ Sci Monit

Ryan, Rachel, 1948-

For works written by this author under other names see Brown, Sandra, 1948-

Ryder, Jonathan *See* Ludlum, Robert, 1927-2001

Ryer, Johnathan *See* Ludlum, Robert, 1927-2001

S

Saavedra, Miguel de Cervantes *See* Cervantes Saavedra, Miguel de, 1547-1616

Sabatini, Rafael, 1875-1950

Captain Blood; his odyssey. Houghton Mifflin 1922 356p o.p.

"Peter Blood was many things in his time—soldier, country doctor, slave, pirate, and finally Governor of Jamaica. Incidentally, he was an Irishman. Round his humorous-heroic figure Mr. Sabatini has written an exciting romance of the Spanish Main, the facts of which he alleges to have been found in the diary and log books of one Jeremiah Pitt, a follower of Monmouth in 1685 and Blood's faithful companion in adventure." Times Lit Suppl

Scaramouche; a romance of the French revolution. Houghton Mifflin 1921 392p o.p.

"The story, primarily of love and adventure, is woven around a hero who devoted himself to furthering the republican cause during the first years of the French Revolution (1788-1792). The title character, successively a lawyer, politician, swordsman, and buffoon, crosses paths repeatedly with his sworn enemy, in the end attaining love and happiness." Lenrow. Reader's Guide to Prose Fic

Followed by Scaramouche, the king-maker (1931)

Saberhagen, Fred, 1930-

Berserker fury. TOR Bks. 1997 383p $23.95
ISBN 0-312-85939-2 LC 97-1157
"A Tom Doherty Associates book"
This adventure "finds the intelligent, deadly Berserker machines infiltrating human colonies to destroy them. The humans have cracked the Berserkers' codes and plan a battle defense. Although it helps to be familiar with the series, this novel can stand alone." Libr J

Berserker's star. TOR Bks. 2003 368p $24.95
ISBN 0-7653-0423-6 LC 2003-41016
"A Tom Doherty Associates book"
"Wanted in parts of the galaxy for his theft of a powerful space cannon, pilot Harry Silver accepts a business proposition from a mysterious woman who claims she wants to rescue her husband from cultists on Maracanda, a pseudo-planet wedged between a black hole and a neutron star. En route, Silver discovers that his passenger's agenda is not quite what it seems and, after making planefall, he finds that Maracanda holds secrets and terrors beyond his worst fears. . . . Witty dialog, clever plot twists, and a likeably roguish protagonist make this a good selection for most sf collections." Libr J

The fifth book of lost swords: Coinspinner's story. Doherty Assocs. 1989 244p o.p.
LC 89-39878
"A TOR book"
"When the legendary sword Woundheale disappears from its resting place in the White Temple of Sarykam, investigations reveal that the Sword of Chance, Coinspinner, is once again loose in the world." Libr J

The first book of lost swords: Woundhealer's story. Doherty Assocs. 1986 281p o.p.
LC 86-50319
"A TOR book"
This book begins a new sequence in the author's fantasy series about mythical swords
"Hoping to find a cure for the mysterious illness that has cursed his son since birth, Prince Mark makes a pilgrimage to the shrine of the legendary sword Woundhealer only to find that his enemies have preceded him." Libr J
A "pleasant adventure that benefits greatly from Saberhagen's narrative gifts as the various strands leapfrog forward, keeping the reader off balance but constantly intrigued." Publ Wkly

The fourth book of lost swords: Farslayer's story. Doherty Assocs. 1989 252p o.p.
LC 89-11638
"A TOR book"
"Two rival families wage a war of attrition and vengeance for possession of 'Farslayer,' one of the 12 Lost Swords made by the gods and imbued with unearthly powers. A grim sense of fatality underlies the deceptive simplicity of the author's style." Libr J

The last book of swords: Shieldbreaker's story. TOR Bks. 1994 255p o.p.
LC 93-43232
"A Tom Doherty Associates book"
In this concluding book of the saga, "battle extends from palace to peasant hut—indeed, all the way to the moon—and is loaded with remnants of premagical technology as well as the secret of why the Old World fell and magic came to rule. Key to the battle against Vikata the Dark King is Prince Mark's second son, Prince Stephen, who turns out to be a formidable wielder of swords. By the time journeys and battles are done, the only one of the twelve swords that survives is Woundhealer, for even the terrifying Shieldbreaker has perished." Booklist

The second book of lost swords: Sightblinder's story. Doherty Assocs. 1987 248p o.p.
LC 87-50477
"A TOR book"
"The present story limits itself to a single locale, the island castle of the wizard Honan-Fu, where Prince Mark is imprisoned in ice alongside the wizard by the usurper called the Ancient One. Mark's friends find themselves the temporary allies of Honan-Fu's traitorous daughter, Ninazu, and of the magician emperor, currently incognito with a traveling show. . . . An entertainment of high order." Publ Wkly

The seventh book of lost swords: Wayfinder's story. TOR Bks. 1992 251p o.p.
LC 92-858
"A Tom Doherty Associates book"
"One of 12 magical swords forged by the Gods, Wayfinder has the power to guide its possessor to whatever the seeker wants. Chance brings Wayfinder to Ben of Purkinje, who uses it to find Woundhealer, the sword with powers to cure the injured wife of Prince Mar of Sarykam. The evil magician Wood also wants the swords; his attack on Ben brings Mark, and even more swords, into the fray. . . . Saberhagen keeps the plot moving, providing a pleasurable light reading experience." Publ Wkly

The sixth book of lost swords: Mindsword's story. TOR Bks. 1990 250p o.p.
LC 90-38899
"A Tom Doherty Associates book"
"Intended as a peace offering from Prince Murat to the Princess Kristin, the Mindsword—one of the legendary weapons used in the war that brought about the death of the gods—plunges two countries into near-war as the well-meaning Murat falls victim to the sword's seductive powers. Saberhagen treads a fine line between fantasy and moral fable in his latest addition to a popular series." Libr J

The third book of lost swords: Stonecutter's story. Doherty Assocs. 1988 247p o.p.
LC 87-51397
"A TOR book"
This novel "deals with the search of Prince al-Farabi and Magistrate Wen Chang for the lost sword Stonecutter. The book's virtues include a cast of well-drawn characters and some vividly realized societies, as well as Saberhagen's usual spare prose and sound narrative technique." Booklist

Sackville-West, V. (Victoria), 1892-1962

All passion spent. Doubleday, Doran 1931 294p o.p.
"When Lady Slane, after the death of her famous husband, shocks her family by going to live by herself in a little house in Hempstead, she is for the first time in her

Sackville-West, V. (Victoria), 1892-1962—*Continued*

eighty-eight years asserting her right to live her own life. The year of quiet reminiscences there is not without exciting moments, for a man who has loved her silently for sixty years renews his friendship, tells her of his love, then suddenly dies, and leaves her his enormous fortune. What she does with this fortune is another instance of her self-assertion. Gentle, charming Lady Slane, her family, and her friends, drawn with wit and skill in this tale of graceful old age, create an impression of subtlety and beauty." Booklist

The Edwardians. Doubleday, Doran 1930 314p o.p.

The setting of this story of Edwardian England is the beautiful old manor-house of Chevron. The characters are grouped around Sebastian, the young heir to the dukedom, and his mother, a famous hostess of the day. Individuals count for less in the novel—a decadent but decorative society. The close of the story, marked by King George's coronation, finds the young duke breaking with the traditions that have bound him, not unwillingly, and starting a new era for himself

"'The Edwardians' is of undoubted excellence from two points of view. First, it is a magnificent portrait of a class and an era. Secondly, it is remarkable for its excellent prose style." Springfield Repub

Sackville-West, Victoria *See* Sackville-West, V. (Victoria), 1892-1962

Safire, William

Freedom. Doubleday 1987 xxl, 1,125p o.p.

LC 86-29254

This novel spans the first twenty months of the Civil War. It covers the period "between Lincoln's suspension of habeas corpus and his signing of the Emancipation Proclamation." Libr J

"The book is a triumph of historical imagination. . . . Safire uses the trained eye of a Washington insider to show us the characters' tentative political and military gropings based on limited information and sketchy precedents. . . . Our scribe tells this monumental and heartbreaking tale in a way one won't soon forget." Christ Sci Monit

Scandalmonger. Simon & Schuster 2000 496p il o.p.

ISBN 0-684-86719-2 LC 99-58831

This historical novel is set in the new American republic during the 1790s. The cast of characters includes Alexander Hamilton, Aaron Burr, Thomas Jefferson, and James Monroe, as well as two journalists. "William Cobbett is a pompous English import who bloviated in his Porcupine's Gazette on behalf of Hamilton and his law-and-order Federalists. His rival in vitriol is James Thomson Callender, wanted for sedition in his native Scotland. He was Jefferson's hit man who, when slighted, . . . spread informed innuendo about his arrangement with slave and lover Sally Hemings." Time

"Since his book is a work of fiction, . . . it cannot easily do what a work of history can—explain the larger social and cultural context for particular events. Nonetheless, Safire has a historian's feel for the period and uses history as fairly and as honestly as one could expect." NY Rev Books

Sagan, Carl, 1934-1996

Contact; a novel. Simon & Schuster 1985 432p o.p.

LC 85-14645

"Ellie Arroway, working with a huge array of radio telescopes in the New Mexico desert, discovers a signal from the star Vega. The message has several levels, one of which contains instructions for building a faster-than-light spacecraft. A debate ensues between scientists and religious leaders as to whether or not such a machine should be built; the scientists win, and finally the long-sought 'contact' is established." Booklist

"A serious blend of science fact and speculation with a fast-paced and well-crafted story . . . suggesting that Sagan is more interested in illustrating human relations and human response than depicting alien creatures. . . . Sagan has provided a novel of ideas, and finds drama in how people interact with them in a situation of challenge and discovery." Christ Sci Monit

Sagan, Françoise, 1935-2004

Bonjour tristesse; translated from the French by Irene Ash. Dutton 1955 128p o.p.

Original French edition, 1954

"The story of a jealous, sophisticated 17-year-old girl whose meddling in her father's impending remarriage leads to tragic consequences, it was written with 'classical' restraint and a tone of cynical disillusionment. The book showed the persistence of traditional form during a period of experimentation in French fiction." Merriam-Webster's Ency of Lit

Sagan, Nick, 1970-

Idlewild. Putnam 2003 275p $23.95

ISBN 0-399-15097-8 LC 2003-43152

"A young man wakes up in what appears to be a pumpkin patch; while he cannot remember his own name, he has the feeling that he has just survived an attempt on his life. He soon discovers that his nom de game is Halloween, that he is one of 10 students in some kind of exclusive school, and that someone is indeed trying to kill him." N Y Times Book Rev

Saint, Dora Jessie *See* Read, Miss, 1913-

Saint, H. F. (Harry F.)

Memoirs of an invisible man. Atheneum Pubs. 1987 396p o.p.

LC 85-48144

"A clash between a scientist and an antinuclear demonstrator at a nuclear energy plant catalyzes an explosion that renders Nick Halloway, a securities analyst, invisible. Realizing that he will become a caged, scrutinized guinea pig if he surrenders to federal intelligence agents, Nick makes a run for his freedom. . . . Nick displays the distinct sensibilities of a fugitive and a Wall Street smart guy as he invisibly fends for himself in the jungles he knows best—the East Side of Manhattan and the trader's desk." Publ Wkly

"The CIA agents, always just one step behind, are deliciously funny Keystone Cops, ridiculous in their attempts to capture a non-entity. This delightful first novel up-

Saint, H. F. (Harry F.)—*Continued*
dates a common childhood fantasy with the excitement of a spy story and a hilarious adult portrayal of life and love under the most peculiar conditions." Libr J

Saint, Harry F. *See* Saint, H. F. (Harry F.)

Saint-Aubin, Horace de *See* Balzac, Honoré de, 1799-1850

Saint-Exupéry, Antoine de, 1900-1944

The little prince; written and illustrated by Antoine de Saint-Exupery; translated from the French by Richard Howard. Harcourt 2000 83p il $18; pa $12

ISBN 0-15-202398-4; 0-15-601219-7 (pa) LC 99-50439

A new translation of the title first published 1943 by Reynal & Hitchcock

"This many-dimensional fable of an airplane pilot who has crashed in the desert is for readers of all ages. The pilot comes upon the little prince soon after the crash. The prince tells of his adventures on different planets and on Earth as he attempts to learn about the universe in order to live peacefully on his own small planet. A spiritual quality enhances the seemingly simple observations of the little prince." Shapiro. Fic for Youth. 3d edition

Night flight; preface by André Gide; translated by Stuart Gilbert. Century 1932 198p o.p.

"In a story that captures the adventures of early aviation, Rivière, chief of the airport at Buenos Aires, supervises the night flights of airmail in South America. He challenges his crew to meet any and all obstacles. When one of his three mail planes crashes over the Andes, he dispatches the European mail plane on schedule anyway." Shapiro. Fic for Youth. 3d edition

Sakamoto, Kerri

One hundred million hearts; Kerri Sakamoto. 1st. U.S. ed. Harcourt 2003 279p $23

ISBN 0-15-101037-4 LC 2003-57064

"Set in Toronto, the novel opens with 32-year-old Miyo narrating the story of her life with her Canadian-born Japanese father, Masao, who singlehandedly raised her. When he suddenly falls ill, Miyo is surprisingly reunited with Setsuko, her father's former live-in girlfriend. Miyo then learns that she has a half-sister, Hana, living in Japan. In the rest of the story, Sakamoto focuses on Miyo's emotional journey to Japan to meet her sister, which also leads to the unraveling of her father's past as a kamikaze pilot." Libr J

"Sakamoto is a gentle storyteller who never forces the point, but rather lets the details slowly surface." Booklist

Saki, 1870-1916

The short stories of Saki; with an introduction by Christopher Morley. Modern Lib. 1983 c1930 $12.95

ISBN 0-394-60428-8 LC 83-5468

First published 1930 by Viking; first Modern Library edition 1951

Contents: Reginald; Reginald on Christmas presents; Reginald on the academy; Reginald at the theatre; Reginald's peace poem; Reginald's choir treat; Reginald on worries; Reginald on house-parties; Reginald at the Carlton; Reginald on besetting sins; Reginald's drama; Reginald on tariffs; Reginald's Christmas revel; Reginald's Rubaiyat; Innocence of Reginald; Reginald in Russia; Reticence of Lady Anne; Lost Sanjak; Sex that doesn't shop; Blood-feud of Toad-water; Young Turkish catastrophe; Judkin of the parcels; Gabriel-Ernest; Saint and the goblin; Soul of Laploshka; Bag; Strategist; Cross currents; Baker's dozen; Mouse; Esmé; Match-maker; Tobermory; Mrs. Packletide's tiger; Stampeding of Lady Bastable; Background; Hermann the Irascible—a story of the great weep; Unrest-cure; Jesting of Arlington Stringham; Sredni Vashtar; Adrian; Chaplet; Quest; Wratislav; Easter egg; Filboid Studge, the story of a mouse that helped; Music on the hill; Story of St. Vespaluus; Way to the dairy; Peace offering; Peace of Mowsle Barton; Talking-out of Tarrington; Hounds of fate; Recessional; Matter of sentiment; Secret sin of Septimus Brope; "Ministers of grace"; Remoulding of Groby Lington; She-wolf; Laura; Boar-pig; Brogue; Hen; Open window; Treasureship; Cobweb; Lull; Unkindest blow; Romancers; Schwartz-Metterklume method; Seventh pullet; Blind spot; Dusk; Touch of realism; Cousin Teresa; Yarkand manner; Byzantine omelette; Feast of Nemesis; Dreamer; Quince tree; Forbidden buzzards; Stake; Clovis on parental responsibilities; Holiday task; Stalled ox; Storyteller; Defensive diamond; Elk; "Down pens"; Nameday; Lumberroom; Fur; Philanthropist and the happy cat; On approval; Toys of peace; Louise; Tea; Disappearance of Crispina Umberleigh; Wolves of Cernogratz; Louis; Guests; Penance; Phantom luncheon; Bread and butter miss; Bertie's Christmas; Forewarned; Interlopers; Quail seed; Canossa; Threat; Excepting Mrs. Pentherby; Mark; Hedgehog; Mappined life; Fate; Bull; Morivera; Shock tactics; Seven cream jugs; Occasional garden; Sheep; Oversight; Hyacinth; Image of the lost soul; Purple of the Balkan kings; Cupboard of the yesterdays; For the duration of the war; Square eggs; Birds on the western front; Gala programme; Infernal parliament; Achievement of the cat; Old town of Pskoff; Clovis on the alleged romance of business; Comments of Moung Ka

Salinger, J. D. (Jerome David), 1919-

The catcher in the rye. Little, Brown 1951 277p $24.95; pa $5.99

ISBN 0-316-76953-3; 0-316-76948-7 (pa)

"The story of adolescent Holden Caulfield who runs away from boarding-school in Pennsylvania to New York where he preserves his innocence despite various attempts to lose it. The colloquial, lively, first-person narration, with its attacks on the 'phoniness' of the adult world and its clinging to family sentiment in the form of Holden's affection for his sister Phoebe, made the novel accessible to and popular with a wide readership, particularly with the young." Oxford Companion to Engl Lit. 5th edition

Franny & Zooey. Little, Brown 1961 201p $24.95; pa $5.99

ISBN 0-316-76954-1; 0-316-76949-5 (pa)

Salinger, J. D. (Jerome David), 1919-—*Continued*

"At 20, Franny Glass is experiencing desperate dissatisfaction with her life and seems to be looking for help via a religious awakening. Her brother Zooey tries to help her out of this depression. He recalls the influence on their growth and development of their appearance as young radio performers on a network program called 'It's a Wise Child.' An older brother, Buddy, is also an important component of the interrelationships in the Glass family." Shapiro. Fic for Youth. 3d edition

Nine stories. Little, Brown 1953 302p $24.95; pa $5.99

ISBN 0-316-76956-8; 0-316-76950-9 (pa)

This collection "introduced various members of the Glass family who would dominate the remainder of Salinger's work. Critical response divided itself between high praise and cult worship. Most of the stories deal with precocious, troubled children, whose religious yearnings—often tilting toward the East—are in vivid contrast to the materialistic and spiritually empty world of their parents. The result was a perfect literary formula for the 1950s." Benet's Reader's Ency of Am Lit

Raise high the roof beam, carpenters, and Seymour: an introduction. Little, Brown 1963 248p $24.95

ISBN 0-316-76957-6

This volume "reprints stories from *The New Yorker* (1955, 1959), in which Buddy Glass tells, first, of his return to New York during the war to attend his brother Seymour's wedding and of Seymour's jilting of the bride and then of their later elopement; and, second, after Seymour's suicide, of Buddy's own brooding, to the point of breakdown, upon Seymour's virtues, human and literary." Oxford Companion to Am Lit. 6th edition

Seymour: an introduction
In Salinger, J. D. Raise high the roof beam, carpenters, and Seymour: an introduction p1

Zooey
In Salinger, J. D. Franny & Zooey

Salinger, Jerome David *See* Salinger, J. D. (Jerome David), 1919-

Sallis, James, 1944-

Cypress Grove. Walker & Co. 2003 255p $24

ISBN 0-8027-3380-8 LC 2002-41480

"Turner ('just Turner'), a former Memphis cop who went to prison for something he'd like to forget, has dropped out of human circulation and buried himself in a cabin in the deep woods. Because Turner's communication skills are rusty, Sallis gives him a constrained narrative voice, the guarded speech of a man so wary of emotion that the very act of speaking seems to leave his throat raw. When the sheriff of this rural backwater asks for his help with a murdered drifter who was found with a wooden stake in his chest, Turner crawls out of hibernation." N Y Times Book Rev

Salter, James

Last night; James Salter. Knopf 2005 132p $20

ISBN 1-4000-4312-3 LC 2004-57793

Contents: Comet; Eyes of the stars; My Lord you; Such fun; Give; Platinum; Palm Court; Bangkok; Arlington; Last night

"All of the stories in 'Last Night' are superb, but the title story is the tautest and most memorable. . . . This story about the consequences of adultery gives new meaning to the phrase 'the morning after.' Despite its shocking plot twist, the story maintains the exacting, calm narrative voice that has distinguished all of Salter's work. His characters may be haunted by death and disappointment, but Salter never judges them, never even pretends to have them neatly pegged. He lets them stay elliptical, in shadow." N Y Times Book Rev

Salvatore, R. A.

Immortalis. Ballantine Bks. 2003 487p il map $26.95

ISBN 0-345-44122-2 LC 2002-33046

"Jilseponie Wyndon is no longer Queen of Ursal. Her newly rediscovered, totally unscrupulous son, Aydrian, has usurped the throne. In alliance with the unscrupulous, perhaps even demon-possessed weretiger and Abellican priest Marcallo De'Unnero, Aydrian sets out to conquer the world, initially without any scruples as to who gets killed in the process. But the alliance begins to fray as De'Unnero realizes that his protégé is more magically potent and ruthless than he is." Booklist

"A satisfying tale of personal responsibility, forgiveness, and redemption, this conclusion to the second 'DemonWars' trilogy features strong, memorable characters and superb plotting and storytelling." Libr J

Salzman, Mark

Lying awake. Knopf 2000 181p $21

ISBN 0-375-40632-8 LC 99-89890

"It's 1997, and Sister John of the Cross, a Carmelite nun in a monastery just outside Los Angeles, seeks treatment for epilepsy, although the remedy threatens to diminish her formidable spiritual powers." Publ Wkly

"Salzman, who doesn't claim to be a believer, handles the religious setting amazingly well. His artistic intuition helps him avoid the sermonizing that might tempt a more religious (or antireligious) writer. He clearly loves his characters." Christ Century

Samjatin, Jewgenij *See* Zamíàtin, Evgeniĭ Ivanovich, 1884-1937

Sanchez, Thomas, 1944-

King Bongo; a novel of Havana. Knopf 2003 309p $25

ISBN 0-679-40696-4 LC 2002-40770

"The title character of Sanchez's latest novel is a Cuban American living in Havana in 1957, just before Castro's revolution. Ethnically and socially, Bongo is a man of two worlds, by day a mild-mannered insurance salesman, by night an acclaimed bongo drum virtuoso. Bongo's sister, a stunning exotic dancer known as the Panther, has not been seen since the night the Tropicana was

Sanchez, Thomas, 1944-—*Continued*

bombed by terrorists. Bongo's desperate search for her takes him to every corner of the decadent city." Libr J

"The byzantine plot is neatly constructed and thoroughly involving but never an end in itself. Sanchez shows us a city and a people on the eve of revolution but filters it all through the emotions of a conflicted hero, sympathetic to the cause but loyal only to himself and those he loves. Havana is both setting and soul in this pulsing bolero of a novel." Booklist

Sand, George, 1804-1876

Lélia; translated, with an introduction by Maria Espinosa. Indiana Univ. Press 1978 xxi, 234p o.p.
LC 77-23639

Original French edition, 1833

"Independent and sensual Lélia has had many lovers. Now repelled by physical passion, which represents the means by which men dominate women, Lélia tells her sister Pulchérie, a courtesan, that neither celibacy nor love affairs satisfy her. Pulchérie suggests that Lélia become a courtesan; she may find fulfillment by giving pleasure to others. Lélia tries to seduce Sténio, a young poet who is in love with her; she cannot continue, however, and sends Pulchérie in her stead. As a result of this betrayal, Sténio falls into utter debauchery, and despite attempts to rescue him, he comes to a tragic end." Merriam-Webster's Ency of Lit

Marianne. Carroll & Graf Pubs. 1988 171p o.p.
LC 88-7308

Original French edition, 1876

"Marianne Chevreuse, the 25-year-old heroine of this romantic tale set in 1825 . . . is independent yet intensely female, and she breaks many conventions of society while living by her own deeply held moral beliefs. Pierre André is an older man who has known her since her childhood. When asked to introduce her to a prospective suitor, he discovers his own love for Marianne. The plot twists and turns until the unsuitable Philippe Gaucher—who is indeed gauche—is sent packing and Pierre and Marianne are betrothed. While very much a period piece, this last scrap of Sand's tremendous oeuvre is a charming bit of entertainment." Publ Wkly

Sandburg, Carl, 1878-1967

Remembrance Rock. Harcourt Brace & Co. 1948 1067p o.p.

"Sandburg's only novel, the work is a massive chronicle that uses historical facts and both historical and fictional characters to depict American history from 1607 to 1945 in a mythic, passionate tribute to the American people." Merriam-Webster's Ency of Lit

Sanders, Dori

Clover; a novel. Algonquin Bks. 1990 183p $17.95
ISBN 0-945575-26-2 LC 89-39072

After her father dies within hours of being married to a white woman, Clover Hill, a ten-year-old black girl, learns with her new stepmother to overcome grief and to adjust to a new place in their rural Black South Carolina community

The author "has staked out an impressive new territory here, replete with peach farmers, textile workers, drunks and crazy people, with the newly middle class as well as the terminally poor. As a specimen of the new realism in regional fiction, 'Clover' is very much the genuine item." N Y Times Book Rev

Sanders, Lawrence, 1920-1998

The first deadly sin. Putnam 1973 566p o.p.

This novel "pits a psychopathic killer loose in New York against a tough, dedicated police officer who is not without his own hangups. Telling his story alternately from the psychopath's point of view and that of the detective, Mr. Sanders draws the two men closer and closer together on an inevitable collision course. Probing the dark side of the killer's mind, his sexual conflicts and involvement with a strange trio of brother, sister and valet who are as kinky as they come, he shows the man's accelerating descent into total madness. Meanwhile, Captain Edward X. Delaney, in whose upper East Side precinct a series of random murders is taking place, accepts an undercover assignment to track down the man responsible." Publ Wkly

The fourth deadly sin. Putnam 1985 380p o.p.
LC 84-24789

"When psychiatrist Dr. Ellerbee is beaten to death with a ball-peen hammer, retired detective Edward X. Delaney agrees to supplement the police investigation. The victim's beautiful wife provides a list of potentially violent patients for Delaney and his team to question." Libr J

"Delaney displays that combination of computerlike efficiency and human touch that make him such an appealing detective. It's a masterly performace, not only chilling, but thought-provoking and often touching." Publ Wkly

Guilty pleasures. Putnam 1998 310p $24.95
ISBN 0-399-14365-3 LC 97-32937

Scandal rocks a wealthy South Florida publishing family as brother and sister "battle for future control of the empire—never guessing that a trusted family friend with a hidden agenda is quietly manipulating them all." Publisher's note

McNally's dilemma. Putnam 1999 309p $24.95
ISBN 0-399-14490-0 LC 99-20988

"McNally is a Palm Beach gumshoe who, with his attorney father, makes up the firm of McNally and Son's Department of Discreet Inquiries. . . . This time, the action begins with a late-night call from wealthy Melva Ashton Manning Williams, who has just blown away her second husband, Geoff Williams, née Wolinsky, after finding him in the arms of another woman. Things quickly shift from murder to blackmail and puzzles within puzzles, all of which Archy sorts out in his usual stylish fashion." Booklist

McNally's gamble. Putnam 1997 307p $24.95
ISBN 0-399-14248-7 LC 96-50369

A "comic whodunit featuring Archy McNally, the foppish but likable head of 'discreet inquiries' at his father's law firm in Palm Beach, Fla. This time Archy's task is to investigate the credentials of a suspicious investment adviser, Frederick Clemens, and his secretary, Felix Katz. . . . Mr. Sanders clearly delights in playing up the bum-

Sanders, Lawrence, 1920-1998—*Continued*
bling, spoof aspects of this detective yarn, especially during its climactic but unavoidably funny denouement." NY Times Book Rev

McNally's luck. Putnam 1992 319p o.p.
LC 92-1394

"Hot on the trail of a stolen cat on behalf of a client of his family's law firm, McNally and Son, Archy enters Palm Beach's seamy nether-world of psychics, charlatans, and thieves. His seemingly innocuous search for the missing cat leads him to the heart of a grisly and intricate plot. As the body count climbs, Archy must resolve the links between several violent local murders and the disappearance of the ill-tempered feline." Publisher's note

McNally's puzzle. Putnam 1996 311p o.p.
LC 95-45703

In this mystery, playboy/sleuth Archy McNally "must dig into the gruesome death of a millionaire parrot-shop owner named Hiram Gottschalk in an attempt to unravel the circumstances of his passing and the tangled mess of the family he leaves behind. . . . The real focus is on Archy's prancing and preening and so-called life of the mind as he tools around south Florida entertaining the millionaire's twin daughters, fencing with his housekeeper and tracking the bizarre activities—parrot smuggling is one, perhaps—of Gottschalk's troubled stepson." N Y Times Book Rev

McNally's secret. Putnam 1992 317p o.p.
LC 91-9803

"Four priceless U.S. airmail stamps issued in 1918 and known as 'inverted Jennies' have been stolen from a wealthy matron's mansion in Palm Beach. . . . McNally's task is to find the thief 'without the barest hint of scandal coming to light.' There are lots of suspects, a couple of deaths, and a fine romance." Booklist

McNally's trial. Putnam 1995 309p o.p.
LC 94-33943

Palm Beach's Archy McNally, "an occasional investigator for his stuffy lawyer father, here agrees to look into the sudden 'uptick' in business that is worrying a pretty exec at the exclusive Whitcomb Funeral Homes. Too many people are dying, observes the woman, and being shipped up north in coffins." Publ Wkly

The novel "boasts a delightful assembly of supporting characters, especially Archy's pal, the totally dissolute, utterly inept would-be detective Binky Watrous. A pleasant diversion." Booklist

The second deadly sin. Putnam 1977 412p o.p.
LC 77-3652

A "police procedural in which Edward X. Delaney, recently retired as Manhattan's chief of detectives, returns by invitation of the department to work on the mystery-murder of a thoroughly unlikable genius, painter Victor Maitland. Delaney, a curious mixture of force and sensitivity, is teamed with a young sergeant, whose drinking has brought him to the edge of dismissal. The two, with an accidentally added starter, Jason T. Jason (black, smart, and very big), by a combination of hard work, intuition, and some luck finally track down the killer." Booklist

The sixth commandment; a novel. Putnam 1979 350p o.p.
LC 78-13158

When the investigator for a philanthropic group arrives in a small upstate New York town to research the application for a grant made by a former Nobel laureate in medicine, "the town's leading citizen, no suspicions are aroused. Yet, a few interviews reveal that the town is shielding some damaging secret about the famous man. When the sleuth penetrates the screen he finds a sordid love affair, but also the shocking revelation that the doctor is using human subjects in his experiments to achieve immortality." Libr J

"This gloomy escapade about a hard-drinking, chain-smoking, world-pitying investigator . . . is brimful of juice and excitement, with some insight and much foolishness—a genuinely riveting diversion." New Yorker

Sullivan's sting. Putnam 1990 348p o.p.
LC 89-70046

This novel "profiles the slimy underbelly of south Florida, where con men posing as financial wizards bilk greedy, unsuspecting investors out of their money (aging widows are a prime mark). The main player here is sexy David Rathbone, a man who apparently could sell igloos to Eskimos. Equally sexy undercover cop Rita Angela Sullivan is on a mission from the SEC to 'sting' Rathbone. She traps her prey, starts to play house, and moves in for the kill—then finds herself falling in love with the guy." Booklist

The tenth commandment; a novel. Putnam 1980 385p o.p.
LC 80-13002

Joshua Bigg, "chief investigator for a New York law firm, gets two tough assignments from his bosses. One is a missing person case: a crotchety professor whose family want an estate settlement. The other is an apparent suicide: an aging textile manufacturer whose merry young widow has suddenly become religiously attracted to a churchless clergyman. Bigg plows his way through mountains of clues, allies himself with a black police detective and unearths evidence to indicate that the suicide was murder and that the missing man is dead." Publ Wkly

The third deadly sin. Putnam 1981 444p o.p.
LC 80-26325

"Sergeant Boone of Manhattan's Homicide Squad persuades former Chief of Detectives Delaney to help find what police fear most, a random killer. The two men . . . begin the slow, almost hopeless, scrupulously painstaking chore of tracking down and piecing together the tiniest clues. The detecting account alternates with vivid, step-by-step descriptions of drab Zoe Kohler, who tarts herself up periodically and ritually murders men she picks up in convention-crowded hotels. In the telling, Sander's characters discuss facets of feminism and crime provocatively, and not at all simplistically, adding to the dimensions of a superior mystery." Publ Wkly

The Timothy files. Putnam 1987 380p o.p.
LC 86-25496

Three novella-length episodes "feature Timothy Cone, 'the Wall Street dick,' who works for an investigative agency. . . . The files deal respectively with a murderous real-estate conglomerate, a fertility clinic devoted to

Sanders, Lawrence, 1920-1998—*Continued*
considerably more than 'original biotechnological research' and an investment house involved in drugs—though only detective work of the highest caliber can discover the seamy details." Publ Wkly

Timothy's game. Putnam 1988 382p o.p.
LC 87-29073

This novel is "set on Wall Street, where clever detective Timothy Cone dresses in Salvation Army chic, chain-smokes Camels, and drinks too much. Cone has a cat named Cleo who eats ham hocks, potato salad, and garlic salami, and a girlfriend named Samantha who sports long, auburn hair. Throw in a foul-mouthed woman who owns a garbage-hauling firm controlled by the mob, an insider-trading leak, murder, and a tong war in Chinatown, and you have the usual brand of Sanders' readable fiction." Booklist

Sandford, John, 1944-

Broken prey. Putnam 2005 390p $26.95
ISBN 0-399-15272-5 LC 2005-42981

Lucas Davenport, a "Minnesota State Bureau of Criminal Apprehension investigator, had lately been doing political fix-it jobs for the governor, but this time he's got a psychopathic serial killer on his hands. . . . The first victim, a young woman, was 'scourged' with a wire whip; number two, a young man, had his penis cut off. Evidence first points to recently released sex offender Charlie Pope. Though Charlie is pretty dumb and the killer is extremely smart, it takes Davenport and his series partner, Detective Sloan, a while to realize they're chasing the wrong guy. Sandford introduces some lighter moments, the most entertaining about Davenport's new iPod and his quest to compile a list of the 100 best rock songs ever recorded, which every cop on the force gives him suggestions for. These moments allow readers to catch their breath amid the otherwise nonstop tension." Publ Wkly

Certain prey. Putnam 1999 339p $24.95
ISBN 0-399-14496-X LC 99-19048

"Trying to avoid facing his empty personal life, enigmatic Minneapolis Deputy Police Chief Lucus Davenport is jolted out of the doldrums by the handiwork of professional hitwoman Clara Rinker, in town to do what she does best. Adding to his problems is glamorous defense attorney Carmel Loan, a clever and intimidating lawyer. When Davenport suspects an alliance between the two women, he soon faces two deadly enemies. Sandford keeps the level of suspense dizzyingly high as he shifts viewpoints between the women and Davenport." Booklist

Chosen prey. Putnam 2001 357p o.p.
ISBN 0-399-14728-4 LC 2001-18594

"Troubled by both city politics and his relationship with his fiancee, Minneapolis Deputy Police Chief Lucas Davenport finds the comfortable routines of a murder investigation as soothing as a worn pair of jeans. The discovery of a young woman's body, missing 18 months, leads to a local pornographic photography ring that posts its handiwork on the Internet." Booklist

Easy prey. Putnam 2000 407p o.p.
ISBN 0-399-14613-X LC 00-23962

"Minnesota-born supermodel Alie'e Maison is back in Minneapolis for a photo shoot. At the raucous wrap party, she turns up dead. Lucas Davenport, the millionaire homicide specialist who often corrals serial killers, is called to the scene." Booklist

"Although Lucas makes his own strong fashion statement . . . his smooth professional moves are the best feature of his style. A shrewd gamester who made his personal fortune designing computer games, he follows sound police procedures and devises one intricate ploy after another to draw out the killers." N Y Times Book Rev

Hidden prey; John Sandford. Putnam 2004 393p $26.95
ISBN 0-399-15180-X LC 2004-44351

"When a Russian man is found murdered on the shores of Lake Superior, Lucas Davenport must join forces with a cop from Moscow to track down the culprit." Libr J

"Readers will be pleased with this relaxed version of the moody Minneapolis investigator. In past novels, the womanizing Davenport would have romanced the good-looking Russian lady, but the new Davenport is content to play the part of friend and protector and go back to his cozy family with an unstained and remarkably contented soul." Publ Wkly

Mind prey. Putnam 1995 323p o.p.
LC 95-3790

"When psychiatrist Andi Manette and her two young daughters are kidnapped, [Davenport] must discover whether it's a ransom snatch, the work of one of Andi's ex-patients or the ruse of someone in her life who might benefit from her death. . . . Readers know the kidnapper is John Mail, a scary ex-patient who's entertained nasty dreams of Andi for years. . . . Sandford expertly ratchets up the suspense from beginning to the brutal finish." Publ Wkly

Mortal prey. Putnam 2002 354p o.p.
ISBN 0-399-14863-9 LC 2002-19051

Assassin Clara Rinker, an old nemesis of Lucas Davenport's "is now back on the prowl, looking for revenge against old enemies from Kansas City who killed her fiancé and shot her in the gut. The bullet spared her life, but not that of her baby. The FBI, knowing she's headed to Missouri, assembles a huge team of shirt-and-tie, laptop-carrying agents, but also taps Davenport to make the trip. . . . Longtime fans should take note that changes are ahead for Davenport. He's marrying his sweetie, Dr. Weather Karkinnen, and they're having a kid. He's also about to leave the city police force, following his boss, Rose Marie Roux, to a job with the state police." Publ Wkly

Naked prey. Putnam 2003 359p $26.95
ISBN 0-399-15043-9 LC 2003-41364

Lucas Davenport "is now Director of Regional Studies in the Minnesota Bureau of Criminal Apprehension, which is a fancy name for the job of investigating difficult crimes as quickly as possible and answering to the governor of the state. Known for his ability to solve the unsolvable, he goes to a remote area of the state to discover why a black man and a white woman were hanged in a groove of trees. . . . Fast paced and full of surprises, this may be Sandford's best novel yet." Libr J

Sandford, John, 1944-—*Continued*

Night prey. Putnam 1994 336p o.p.

LC 94-7564

"Minneapolis deputy police chief Lucas Davenport is on the trail of a serial killer—this time a particularly nasty specimen with a yen for disemboweling his victims. Meagan Connell, an investigator from a state agency, plays the . . . role of Davenport's feisty, determined female assistant. Davenport is also peripherally involved in a case that appears to involve the Seeds, a loosely organized group of white supremacists." Booklist

"Despite its length, *Night Prey* is a tight, fast-moving thriller with appealing good guys and a suitably evil villain. Especially fascinating among the characters is Policewoman Connell." Libr J

Rules of prey. Putnam 1989 316p o.p.

LC 89-4040

"A killer who calls himself the 'maddog' has been murdering Minneapolis women, seemingly without pattern or motive. The crimes are linked only by their brutality and by the slayer's 'signature': at each scene, he leaves a written rule of crime, such as 'Never kill anyone you know,' or, 'Never carry a weapon after it has been used.' Into the case comes Lucas Davenport, a policeman with five kills in the line of duty, a surefire sense of how to handle the thirsty media and strong instincts about the killer's psyche." Publ Wkly

Silent prey. Putnam 1992 320p o.p.

LC 91-43696

"Mad pathologist Bekker's face is battered and broken after his encounter with unorthodox Minneapolis cop Lucas Davenport in *Eyes of Prey*. Now Bekker's on the loose again, having escaped during his trial and landed in New York City. Even more nutso than ever, he's determined to exact revenge on Lucas and to continue his evil experiments, in which he searches the eyes of his victims in the few, pain-creased seconds before death." Booklist

Sudden prey. Putnam 1996 360p o.p.

LC 96-4598

This Lucas Davenport adventure "opens with the Candy LaChaise gang's robbery of a Minnesota credit union. When Candy is ambushed and killed by Davenport and his men, Candy's husband, Dick LaChaise, swears vengeance on the spouses and families of all officers involved. A series of attacks ensue in which spouses are killed at work. With the lives of Davenport's own daughter and his fiancée threatened, he quickly metamorphoses into a hunting machine himself." Libr J

Winter prey. Putnam 1993 336p o.p.

LC 92-42072

"In a rural area of northern Wisconsin, a family of three is savagely wiped out by the Iceman, who then torches their house. In pursuit of a damaging photograph—a snapshot of him in a sexual situation with a local boy—this fiend puts no value on human life. Enter Davenport, the laconic, slightly cynical ex-cop from Minneapolis, who uncovers several disturbing truths before determining the Iceman's identity." Publ Wkly

"Davenport, a cool, cynical man of action, is entirely in his element in this harsh terrain—so bitter that it turns animals against men, so brutal that it turns men into beasts." N Y Times Book Rev

Santmyer, Helen Hooven, 1895-1986

"—and ladies of the club". Ohio State Univ. Press 1982 1344p o.p.

LC 81-22401

"In 1868 in a small town in southwestern Ohio, a group of women form a literary club. Through the personal, political, and social upheavals of the next 64 years the club remains the one constant factor in the lives of these diverse women and their descendants." Libr J

The author's "perceptive saga is steeped not just in the changing political, religious, and social mores of the period covered, but also in the personal joys, sorrows, and scandals that beat the cadence of life in a midwestern town. This novel has an old-fashioned dignity and seriousness that will win some readers and lose others, and although its girth is perhaps its most notable quality, its literary scope and depth of feeling are equally impressive." Booklist

Saramago, José, 1922-

All the names; translated by Margaret Jull Costa. Harcourt 2000 238p $24

ISBN 0-15-100421-8

Original Portuguese edition 1997; this translation first published 1999 in the United Kingdom

"The title refers to the miles of archival records among which the protagonist toils at the Registry of Births, Marriages and Deaths in an unnamed small country whose inhabitants still live by ancient rules of hierarchical social classes. . . . A penurious, reclusive, lonely bachelor, Senhor José has only one secret passion: he collects clippings about famous people and surreptitiously copies their birth certificates, purloining them from the registry at night and returning them stealthily. Purely by accident, the index card of a 36-year-old woman unknown to him becomes entangled in the clippings he steals. Suddenly, he is stricken by a need to learn about this woman's life." Publ Wkly

"Modest, self-mocking, mildly ironic, yet magisterial, Saramago's gentle voice rings with the unmistakable authority of the true artist." Christ Sci Monit

Blindness; a novel; translated from the Portuguese by Giovanni Pontiero. Harcourt Brace & Co. 1998 294p $22

ISBN 0-15-100251-7 LC 98-12009

Original Portuguese edition, 1995; this translation first published 1997 in the United Kingdom

"A man waiting in his car for a red light to turn green is the first of an entire city's population—with one exception—to be blinded by a 'milky sea' of dazzling whiteness. The inexplicably disabled victims grope and stumble their way through nightmarish landscapes—first an asylum where those initially afflicted are quarantined, and then the chaotic, squalid streets to which they return. Saramago's surreal allegory explores the ability of the human spirit to prevail in even the most absurdly unjust of conditions, yet he reinvents this familiar struggle with the stylistic eccentricity of a master." New Yorker

The cave; translated from the Portuguese by Margaret Jull Costa. Harcourt 2002 307p $25

ISBN 0-15-100414-5 LC 2002-2355

Saramago, José, 1922-—*Continued*

Original Portuguese edition, 2000

"Widowed Cipriano Algor is a 64-year-old Portuguese potter who finds his business collapsing when the demand dries up for his elegant, handcrafted wares. His potential fate seems worse than poverty—to move with his daughter, Marta, and his son-in-law, Marcal Gacho, into a huge, arid complex known as 'The Center,' where Gacho works as a security guard. But Algor gets an order from the Center for hundreds of small ceramic figurines, a task that has Marta and Algor hustling to meet the delivery date." Publ Wkly

"As a further warning against the urge to seek safety on common ground—moving to the center, as it were—the writer highlights the menaces of cliche by parodying the worldly-wise narrative interventions of an earlier era. . . . Such deft manipulations in Saramago's style are brilliantly rendered in Margaret Jull Costa's agile English version of his Portuguese." N Y Times Book Rev

The history of the siege of Lisbon; translated from the Portuguese by Giovanni Pontiero. Harcourt Brace & Co. 1997 c1996 314p o.p.
LC 96-46826

Original Portuguese edition 1989; this translation first published 1996 in the United Kingdom

"Raimundo Silva, proofreader for a Portuguese publishing house, violates the fundamental ethic of his profession by adding the word *not* to a sentence in a history textbook, so it reads that in 1147 the king of Portugal reconquered Lisbon from the Saracens with out any help from the Crusaders. Although the change is caught, and an errata slip added to the book, Silva's supervisor, rather than firing him, asks him to write an alternative history based on his emendation of the text." Booklist

"Although the novel's stream-of-consciousness technique, baroque prose and paragraphs that run on for pages may daunt some readers, this hypnotic tale is a great comic romp through history, language and the imagination." Publ Wkly

Saroyan, William, 1908-1981

The human comedy; illustrated by Don Freeman. Harcourt Brace Jovanovich 1989 c1943 242p il $17

ISBN 0-15-142301-6 LC 89-32785

"An HBJ modern classic"

A reissue of the title first published 1944

"Homer, the narrator, identifies himself in this novel as a night messenger for the Postal Telegraph office. He creates a view of family life in the 1940s in a small town in California. His mother, Ma Macauley, presides over the family and takes care of four children after her husband dies. Besides Homer, there is Marcus, the oldest, who is in the army; Bess; and Ulysses, the youngest, who describes the world from his perspective as a solemn four-year-old." Shapiro. Fic for Youth. 3d edition

Sarrantonio, Al

(ed) 999: new stories of horror and suspense. See 999: new stories of horror and suspense

Sarton, May, 1912-1995

Anger; a novel. Norton 1982 223p o.p.
LC 82-7843

"Successful Boston banker Ned Fraser finds himself captivated by an unexpected encounter with mezzo-soprano Anna Lindstrom. He pursues the gifted, determined-to-be-famous performer without success until, at a chance meeting, he wins her—somewhat to the surprise of them both. They marry within a short time, no starry-eyed youngsters, but two mature adults. Both are settled in their emotional patterns: she given to outspoken and tempestuous outbursts of joy and despair, he to internalizing his feelings and maintaining the proper facade. This results in a lack of communication that threatens their marriage until Anna penetrates Ned's reserve. A romantic, yet realistic portrait." Libr J

As we are now; a novel. Norton 1973 133p $10.95

ISBN 0-393-08372-1

This book is "a novel in the form of a diary, written by a retired schoolteacher. Mentally tough but not quite physically able to care for herself, she is deposited by relatives in an old people's home. Subjected to subtle humiliations, petty and almost unthinking cruelties, deprived of all mental stimulus, she fights a tough battle to preserve first her dignity, then her sanity." Christ Sci Monit

"It is a bitter book, more a tract than a novel, and an utterly desolating experience, as it is meant to be. There are complexities that unwind themselves now and then, which preserve the concerns of the novel; but on the whole, the work is a piece of rhetoric, and very good rhetoric, too. . . . For the book satisfies in the way that cold anger can when it is pure, despairing, and written with no aim but the impulse to record the way things are." Saturday Rev/World

Kinds of love; a novel. Norton 1970 464p o.p.

The novel "is set in a small New Hampshire town much visited over the years by summer people. Christina and Cornelius Chapman, elderly and long-standing summer people, have retreated to Williard following Cornelius's partly crippling stroke and have resolved to winter there for the first time. Around them and around their house swirl the events of the story." N Y Times Book Rev

"The touching friendship of two elderly women, the love/hate relationship of the permanent residents and the summer people, and a young girl's discovery of the magic and the pain of love are some of the threads in this quiet tale." Booklist

A reckoning; a novel. Norton 1978 254p o.p.
LC 78-9691

"Laura Spelman, genteel Boston widow, has just learned that she is dying of cancer. Determined to take a candid look at herself as a means of tying up loose ends, she is surprised to find her thoughts turning mostly to women. Confiding in strangers, avoiding her family, Laura speaks of discovering herself as a woman. In particular, she examines her relationships with her domineering mother and with a dearly loved friend, the two people who, she feels, have shaped her life most profoundly. Ironically, as her body becomes increasingly unfamiliar, her old, unexamined passions begin to resolve themselves." Atlantic

Sarton, May, 1912-1995—*Continued*

"Sarton incorporates . . . the issues of mother/daughter relationships, what it is to be a woman (and a man), and the conflict of art and life." Libr J

A small room; a novel. Norton 1961 249p o.p.

"Lucy Winter, professor and seeker of refuge in the kingdom of a progressive [New England] women's college, becomes involved when a top student is caught in a case of plagiarism, and peace dissolves. The faculty must face the guilt of having pushed for intellectual attainment with inadequate knowledge and consideration for emotional factors, i.e. the crime of not teaching 'the whole child.' Each person reacts to crisis differently—sometimes disastrously, but all can meet finally in the small room to evaluate the past and to agree on the college's proposed plan for the future." Libr J

Sarton "presents her cast of faculty types with scrupulous respect. There is no villain among them. . . . The essence of this novel is not so much in the conflict of characters as in the conflict in ideas—and ideas about teaching." N Y Her Trib Books

Sartre, Jean Paul, 1905-1980

The age of reason; translated from the French by Eric Sutton. Knopf 1947 397p (Roads to freedom, 1) o.p.

Original French edition, 1945

First of a series of three novels by the French philosopher, exponent of existentialism. The scene of this novel is Paris in 1938. A fourth title was never completed

"The central character is Mathieu, a professor of philosophy who writes one short story a year. . . . The problem that obsesses Mathieu, that of freedom, how to remain free, is worked out in the story and exemplified in the lives of the characters. . . . Mathieu differs from your ordinary character of fiction in that he is motivated by this abstract ethical ideal to keep his freedom. It is assailed as soon as the novel opens, for he learns that his mistress is pregnant; the action consists largely of his attempts to raise by borrowing—in the end, by stealing—the five thousand francs required to procure an abortion; unnecessarily, as it turns out, for Marcelle decides to marry someone else and have the child." Spectator

Followed by The reprieve

Intimacy, and other stories; translated by Lloyd Alexander. New Directions 1952 c1948 270p o.p.

First published 1948 in a limited edition with title: The wall, and other stories

Contents: The wall; The room; Erostratus; Intimacy; The childhood of a leader

"The most impressive thing about the book, rising from it like a stench, is a disgust for life, a sense of universal defilement. The insistence on the physical in the stories is indistinguishable from an aversion to it." New Repub

Nausea; translated from the French by Lloyd Alexander. New Directions 1949 238p o.p.

Original French edition, 1938

"*Nausea* is written in the form of a diary that narrates the recurring feelings of revulsion that overcome Roquentin, a young historian, as he comes to realize the banality and emptiness of existence. As the attacks of nausea occur more frequently, Roquentin abandons his research and loses his few friends. In an indifferent world, without work, love, or friendship to sustain him, he must discover value and meaning within himself." Merriam-Webster's Ency of Lit

The reprieve; translated from the French by Eric Sutton. Knopf 1947 445p (Roads to freedom, 2) o.p.

Original French edition, 1945

This sequel to The age of reason "confines itself to the eight frenetic days that led to the Munich Pact and the rape of Czechoslovakia. The original characters reappear merging now with many others as a shocked France mobilizes for war. Sartre, the leading exponent of Existentialism manages in this kaleidoscope novel to re-create the confusion, even the odor of the fear that gripped Europe in September, 1938." Libr J

Followed by Troubled sleep

Troubled sleep; translated from the French by Gerald Hopkins. Knopf 1950 421p (Roads to freedom, 3) o.p.

Sequel to The reprieve

Original French edition, 1949; published in the United Kingdom with title: Iron in the soul

"A story of the French people after the fall of Paris in World War II, of many individuals of different walks of life and their reactions to defeat." Publ Wkly

"No other book gives such insight into the anguished feelings of the French as they passed from apathy to consciousness of their dignity as men revolting against fate, accepting their solidarity with other men—wretched, but lucid and free fighters." Saturday Rev

Saul, John

Black lightning. Fawcett Columbine 1995 392p $23

ISBN 0-449-90864-X LC 95-7600

This thriller "begins with serial killer Richard Kraven going to the chair. Just before he does, he has a last word with the reporter who led the cry for his execution, Anne Jeffers. He says he's not guilty and only regrets not getting to watch her die. Just as Kraven's croaking, Jeffers' architect husband, Glen, has a totally unexpected near-fatal heart attack. And then, after two years' hiatus (the time between Kraven's apprehension and execution), murders awfully like the ones Kraven died for start up again." Booklist

Darkness. Bantam Bks. 1991 341p o.p.

LC 90-25842

This is the "tale of a little town in the Florida swamps where a lot of old guys are remarkably youthful and a lot of kids rather soulless. 'Dead in the eyes' is how folks see these children, a new one of whom, Kelly Anderson, has just come to town with her adoptive parents. She hooks up with another teenager, also an adoptee, Michael Sheffield. Together they find out about, and are irresistibly drawn to, a mysterious circle of children controlled by the Dark Man that meets deep in the swamp." Booklist

The homing. Fawcett Columbine 1994 389p $21.50

ISBN 0-449-90863-1 LC 93-50606

Saul, John—*Continued*

"Karen Spellman and her daughters Julie, 16, and Molly, 9, move from L.A. back to the bucolic community in which Karen grew up. For with the girls' father years dead, Karen has remet and decided to marry farmer Russell Owen. Things start going awry right away: at Karen and Russell's home wedding, Molly is stung by a bee, and although it's happened before with no untoward results, this time she nearly dies. More accidents with bees and other insects occur—not least to Julie—and while local entomologist Carl Henderson, who works for the agricultural branch of a huge chemical company, is able to provide seemingly effective antivenins when folks react badly to bites, he also occasionally behaves most peculiarly." Booklist

The author provides "splendidly creepy bug-infested house of horrors and a fitting revenge for the villain." Libr J

The Manhattan Hunt Club. Ballantine Bks. 2001 313p o.p.

ISBN 0-345-43330-0 LC 2001-25956

This thriller "details a nightmarish game in which a conspiracy of New York's wealthy and evil elite hunt human quarry in the city's abandoned subterranean tunnels. One of the hunted is Jeff Converse, a New York City college student who, after being falsely convicted of a brutal crime, is kidnapped as he is being transported from the courthouse and left below the streets in the endless maze of forgotten tunnels that exist beneath the city. Here, in the pitch-dark, with no weapons, food, or water, he is left to try to survive the hunters." Booklist

"The premise of a Manhattan Hunt Club skirts absurdity, as do the villainous members of the club, but Saul scores points about society's treatment of the homeless. The prose is serviceable, the action rough, intense and often distasteful—in other words, this is vintage Saul." Publ Wkly

Midnight voices. Ballantine Bks. 2002 341p o.p.

ISBN 0-345-43331-9 LC 2002-283839

"Mother of two and widow of a murdered Central Park jogger, Caroline Evans thinks she has found the answer to her prayers in her new husband, Anthony Fleming. The family moves into his apartment in the Rockwell, a storied old Upper West Side building. Ryan and Laurie, the children, quickly begin to have nightmares in which they are haunted by menacing voices, while Ryan realizes that he doesn't like his creepy stepfather." Publ Wkly

"This is good, drafty atmospheric horror stuff unafraid to indulge in not-at-all subtle gory bits." Booklist

Nightshade. Ballantine Bks. 2000 308p o.p.

ISBN 0-345-43329-7 LC 00-25918

"The life of high school student Matt Hapgood turns into the stuff of nightmares when his grandmother moves in with his family. She brings with her the terrifying spirit of her dead daughter, Cynthia, the beautiful, beloved, older sister of Matt's mother, Joan, who had been the tormented, abused younger child. All the suffering of those early years is brought into Matt's household from the moment his stepfather is shot to death while they are hunting together. Soon Matt, his mother, and his grandmother have horrifying visions of Cynthia in all her malevolent beauty, and they watch helplessly as she instigates brutal killings." Libr J

The presence. Fawcett Columbine 1997 338p $25

ISBN 0-449-91055-5 LC 97-14756

Anthropologist Katharine Sundquist has recently moved to Hawaii with her teenage son Michael. "Katharine has come to the islands to study anomalies of early human development found in the lava beds of Maui. She is quickly distracted from her work by Michael's suddenly worsening asthma attacks and by the inexplicable disappearance and death of several boys with whom he went on a secret nighttime scuba dive. It's only a matter of time before she discovers that her research and Michael's problems are interrelated through the Serinus Project, a covert scientific experiment funded by her employer for the purpose of investigating the genetic origins of human life. . . . Although he breaks no new ground, Saul distills familiar elements of horror, science fiction and the cyberthriller into a potent brew." Publ Wkly

The right hand of evil. Ballantine Bks. 1999 344p $25

ISBN 0-345-43316-5 LC 98-51980

In this psychological thriller a "family moves into an old house, intending to refurbish it as a hotel, but, soon, both the father and his son begin to act rather oddly. . . . Saul makes Ted, the father, a raving alcoholic who becomes, under the influence of whatever's possessing him, a model dad. In several places, the story seems to be going in one way, until Saul wrenches it in a different direction, keeping his readers on their toes. Although the novel is sometimes drastically overwritten . . . the author clearly succeeds in his primary mission: to give readers a serious case of the willies." Booklist

Second child. Bantam Bks. 1990 341p o.p.

LC 89-77149

Melissa "doesn't fit into the snooty social life of the exclusive East Coast beach community of Secret Cove, and her cruel mother hates her for this failing. The arrival of Melissa's beautiful half-sister, Teri, exacerbates the situation. Melissa escapes her mother's punishments by entering a trance state where her imaginary friend D'Arcy protects her. And who is D'Arcy? Apparently, the ghost of a spurned servant girl who returned an engagement ring still attached to her severed hand. Murderous Teri tries to manipulate Melissa's apparent psychosis, but D'Arcy intercedes. Mother and half-sister are evil incarnate." Booklist

Shadows. Bantam Bks. 1992 390p o.p.

LC 92-1317

"Ten-year-old genius Josh MacCallum is bored, lonely and almost always angry at his older, teasing classmates. After he attempts suicide, his frantic single mother jumps at the chance to enroll him in the Academy, a school for very gifted kids in Northern California. Run by aloof Dr. Engersol and matronly housemother Hildie, the school, which occupies an old mansion, offers Josh a friend in another genius, Amy Carlson. . . . Engersol and Hildie are revealed as nasty and the mad-scientist plot hurtles to a violent conclusion featuring dueling brains connected to a mainframe computer." Publ Wkly

Saulnier, Beth

Ecstasy. Mysterious Press 2003 342p $23.95

ISBN 0-89296-750-1 LC 2002-26519

Saulnier, Beth—*Continued*

In this mystery featuring reporter Alex Bernier "Alex gets saddled with covering the Melting Rock Music Festival, a four-day annual event held in nearby Jaspersburg. . . . The story really begins, however, when one of the kids, and then another, dies of a drug overdose. Alex enlists the aid of her policeman boyfriend to determine if the overdose were truly accidental." Publ Wkly

Savery, Constance

(jt. auth) Brontë, C. Emma

Sayers, Dorothy L. (Dorothy Leigh), 1893-1957

Busman's honeymoon; a love story with detective interruptions. Harper & Row 1986 c1937 381p $17.95

ISBN 0-06-055021-X LC 86-45139

First published 1937 by Harcourt, Brace

"Not near the top of her form, but remarkable as a treatment of the newly wedded and bedded pair of eccentrics, Peter Wimsey and Harriet Vane, with Bunter in the offing and three local characters, chiefly comic. Peter's mother-dowager duchess of Denver-Peter's sister, John Donne, a case of vintage port, and the handling of 'corroded sut' provide plenty of garnishing for an indifferent murder, even if we weren't also given an idea of Lord Peter's sexual tastes and powers under trying circumstances." Barzun. Cat of Crime. Rev and enl edition

Clouds of witnesses. Dial Press (NY) 1927 288p o.p.

Variant title: Clouds of witness

The unpleasant duty of clearing his brother, the Duke of Denver, of a murder charge devolves upon Lord Peter Wimsey. Even when his only sister is involved—the dead man was her unregretted fiancé—Lord Peter does not lose his head

The Dawson pedigree. Dial Press (NY) 1928 c1927 299p o.p.

First published 1927 in the United Kingdom; reissued 1987 by Harper & Row with title: Unnatural death

A chance remark overheard in a restaurant starts a long inquiry and an apparently natural death is proved to have been a murder. But Lord Peter Wimsey, aided by his friends, Parker from Headquarters, and that garrulous and delightful maiden lady, Miss Climpson, has a very difficult time to catch the murderer

The documents in the case; by Dorothy L. Sayers and Robert Eustace. Brewer & Warren 1930 304p o.p.

A reissue of the title first published 1930 by Brewer & Warren

An "account, largely in letter form, of a case of poisoning by synthetic muscarine alkaloid made to look like mushroom poisoning. Evidence of optical activity and what it means beautifully handled, although the authors are said to have made a mistake in their choice of the particular mushroom to which the 'accidental' death should be attributed. Characters outstanding." Barzun. Cat of Crime. Rev and enl edition

The five red herrings; (Suspicious characters). Harper & Row 1958 c1931 306p il o.p.

First published 1931. Variant title: Suspicious characters

Lord Peter Wimsey had always found himself welcome in the proud Scottish village of Kirkcudbright, although the villagers were not ordinarily tolerant of outsiders. But one day the body of an artist was found on the pointed rocks. The artist might have fallen, but there were too many suspicious elements in his death, especially when six suspects had wished him dead. Lord Peter uses all his ingenuity to unravel the tangles of this crime

"A work that grows on rereading and remains in the mind as one of the richest, most colorful of her group studies. The Scottish setting, the artists in the colony, the train-ticket puzzle, and the final chase place this triumph among the four or five chefs d'oeuvre from her hand." Barzun. Cat of Crime. Rev and enl edition

Gaudy Night. Harcourt Brace & Co. 1936 469p o.p.

First published 1935 in the United Kingdom

Harriet's return to Oxford for the Gaudy Dinner is welcomed by poison-pen letters and attempted blackmail. Lord Peter, of course, summons all his skill to detect the blackmailer and win Harriet

"Harriet Vance and the grown-up nephew of Lord Peter help give variety, and the college scene justifies good intellectual talk. The motive is magnificently orated on by the culprit, a scene that in itself is a unique bit of work. And though the don-esses are sometimes hard to keep apart, the architecture is very good." Barzun. Cat of Crime. Rev and enl edition

Hangman's holiday. Harper & Row 1987 c1961 191p $21.95

ISBN 0-06-055033-3 LC 86-45691

A reissue of the title first published 1933 by Harcourt, Brace and analyzed in Short story index

Short stories included are: The image in the mirror; The incredible elopement of Lord Peter Wimsey; The queen's square; The necklace of pearls; The poisoned Dow '08; Sleuths on the scent; Murder in the morning; One too many; Murder at Pentecost; Maher-shalal-hashbaz; The man who knew how; The fountain plays

Have his carcase. Brewer, Warren & Putnam 1932 448p o.p.

Harriet Vane finds a body on the beach and Lord Peter Wimsey has a case to solve. Other ingredients of the mystery are an ivory-handled razor, three hundred pounds in gold coins and a coded message

"A great achievement, despite some critics' carping. The people, the motive, the cipher, and the detection are all topnotch. Here, too, is the first (and definitive) use of hemophilia as a misleading fact. And surely the son, the mother, and her self-deluded gigolo are definitive types." Barzun. Cat of Crime. Rev and enl edition

In the teeth of the evidence and other stories. Harcourt Brace & Co. 1940 311p o.p.

First published 1939 in the United Kingdom

Short stories included are: Absolutely elsewhere: a Lord Peter Wimsey story; Arrow o'er the house; Bitter almonds: a Montague Egg story; Blood sacrifice; My best thriller; Dilemma; Dirt cheap: a Montague Egg story; False weight: a Montague Egg story; In the teeth of

Sayers, Dorothy L. (Dorothy Leigh), 1893-1957—*Continued*

the evidence; Inspiration of Mr. Budd; Leopard lady; The milk-bottles; Nebuchadnezzar; Professor's manuscript: a Montague Egg story; Scrawns; Shot at goal: a Montague Egg story; Suspicion

Lord Peter; a collection of all the Lord Peter Wimsey stories; compiled and with an introduction by James Sandoe; coda by Carolyn Heilburn; codetta by E.C. Bentley. Harper & Row 1972 464p o.p.

Analyzed in Short story index

Contents: The abominable history of the man with copper fingers; The entertaining episode problem of Uncle Meleager's will; The fantastic horror of the cat in the bag; The unprincipled affair of the practical joker; The undignified melodrama of the bone of contention; The vindictive story of the footsteps that ran; The bibulous business of a matter of taste; The learned adventure of the Dragon's Head; The piscatorial farce of the stolen stomach; The unsolved puzzle of the man with no face; The adventurous exploit of the cave of Ali Baba; The image in the mirror; The incredible elopement of Lord Peter Wimsey; The queen's square; The necklace of pearls; In the teeth of the evidence; Absolutely elsewhere; Striding folly; The haunted policeman

Murder must advertise; a detective story. Harcourt Brace & Co. 1933 344p o.p.

Lord Peter Wimsey, less whimsical and more interesting than usual, enters the advertising profession in order to solve the possible murder by catapult of an advertising copywriter

"A superb example of Sayers' ability to set a group of people going. The advertising agency is inimitable, and hence better than the De Momerie crowd that goes with it." Barzun. Cat of Crime. Rev and enl edition

The nine tailors. Harcourt Brace Jovanovich 1989 c1934 397p il $15.95

ISBN 0-15-165897-8 LC 89-38102

"An HBJ modern classic"

A reissue of the title first published 1934

"One New Year's Eve, Lord Peter Wimsey, driving through a snowstorm, goes off the road near Fenchurch, St Paul, and is the chance guest of the rector. A providential visit all around, for Peter, acquainted with the ancient art of bellringing, acts that night as a substitute, but further than that, he finds use for his versatile mind later, upon the shocking discovery of a mutilated corpse in another man's grave. The unusual plot is developed with dexterity and ingenuity." N Y Libr

Strong poison. Brewer & Warren 1930 344p o.p.

Because Harriet Vane's lover died of arsenic poisoning, and because Harriet was writing a book on the subject of poisons, everybody—except Lord Peter Wimsey—was convinced of her guilt. Lord Peter, with the aid of the inimitable Miss Climpson, gets to work on the business of clearing Harriet

Thrones, dominations; [by] Dorothy L. Sayers and Jill Paton Walsh. St. Martin's Press 1998 312p $23.95

ISBN 0-312-18196-5 LC 97-42585

In 1936, Dorothy L. Sayers began a mystery novel featuring Lord Peter Wimsey and Harriet Vane. The "partial manuscript has now been completed . . . according to her outline by Jill Paton Walsh. . . . Sayers's story opens in 1936 at a restaurant in Paris, where Harriet and Peter are enjoying a brief respite between the execution of the murderer he brought to justice in Busman's Honeymoon and the demands of the Wimsey family and social position back home. At the restaurant they are introduced to Laurence and Rosamund Harwell, a rich Englishman and his beautiful young wife, and the lives of the two couples begin to intertwine—and, to take a dangerous turn." Publisher's note

Paton Walsh "has made a valiant and resourceful stab at mimicry. No devotee of Lord Peter and his novelist wife Harriet Vane will want to miss it." New Stateman (Engl)

The unpleasantness at the Bellona Club. Harper & Row 1986 c1928 345p $17.95

ISBN 0-06-055026-0 LC 86-45145

A reissue of the title first published 1928 by Payson & Clarke

Lord Peter Wimsey investigates the murder of an elderly member of a staid men's club

Whose body? Boni & Liveright 1923 278p o.p.

When a nude corpse, wearing a golden pince-nez only, is found in the bathtub of the flat of a timid little architect, and the discovery coincides with the disappearance of a wealthy financier, Sir Reuben Levy, whom the body resembled, Sir Peter's sporting blood is aroused. Together with a friend from Scotland Yard he unofficially, playfully, as it were, conducts a roundabout inquiry under the jealous eye of the bungling official Scotland Yard investigators and finally tracks down the murderer

Saylor, Steven, 1956-

The house of the Vestals; the investigations of Gordianus the Finder. St. Martin's Press 1997 260p $22.95

ISBN 0-312-15444-5 LC 97-7597

Contents: Death wears a mask; The tale of the treasure house; A will is a way; The lemures; Little Caesar and the pirates; The disappearance of the Saturnalia silver; King Bee and honey; The Alexandrian cat; The house of the Vestals

"Saylor serves up a collection of short stories designed to fill in some of the gaps that have piqued the curiosity of devoted fans of his popular Roma Sub Rosa series. Set between the years 80 and 72 B.C., these nine tales document some of the early adventures of Gordianus the Finder. . . . While each brief mystery presented is a gem in and of itself, readers will delight in the informational overview provided by the collection as a whole. As usual, Saylor does a superb job of seamlessly incorporating the tumultuous history of the Roman Republic into the narrative flow." Booklist

The judgment of Caesar; a novel of Ancient Rome; Steven Saylor. 1st ed. St. Martin's Minotaur 2004 290p maps $24.95

ISBN 0-312-27119-0 LC 2003-69548

This "installment, set in Alexandria, once again features Caesar, now maneuvering between the two rivals for the Egyptian throne, Ptolemy and Cleopatra, in an ef-

Saylor, Steven, 1956-—*Continued*

fort to consolidate his own claim to rule Rome. Gordianus's reputation as an honest fact finder, and his familiarity with the centers of power, make him a valuable asset to all three leaders, even as he grapples with a bitter personal loss." Publ Wkly

"Readers will be equally absorbed by the bloody history unfolding (Saylor's description of the beheading of Pompey is both suspenseful and wrenching); by the historical figures depicted (Ptolemy listening to his flute player with the head of Pompey in a clay jar at his feet is a miniature study in royal pathology); and by the mysteries Gordianus must solve to keep his own head. Wonderful reading." Booklist

A mist of prophecies. St. Martin's Press 2002 270p o.p.

ISBN 0-312-27121-2 LC 2001-58901

A mystery set in "Rome during the Civil War. A beautiful young woman, given the street name Cassandra for her habit of delivering prophesies, is found murdered. Gordianus is disturbed that no one claims her body—even though, he reflects, someone cared enough to murder her. Yet, at Cassandra's funeral pyre, seven of the most powerful women in Rome, including the wives of Caesar, Cicero, and Marc Antony, attend. Gordianus sorts out the tangled motives of the women who watched Cassandra burn, believing one of them to be her murderer. Saylor brings a wealth of historical information lightly to bear on a chilling mystery." Booklist

Rubicon; a novel of ancient Rome. St. Martin's Press 1999 276p $23.95

ISBN 0-312-20576-7 LC 99-18090

In this mystery "Gordianus the Finder attempts to solve the murder of Pompey's cousin Numerius. The civilized world of 49 B.C.E. is in turmoil at the onset of the Roman Civil War. Julius Caesar has crossed the Rubicon River into Italy with his hand-picked troops. Pompey, his chief rival for control of Rome, has fled Rome with his followers from the Senate, and all is chaos as the people leave the city. . . . This novel is an excellent blending of mystery and history." Libr J

Scarborough, Elizabeth Ann

(jt. auth) McCaffrey, A. Acorna's people
(jt. auth) McCaffrey, A. Acorna's rebels
(jt. auth) McCaffrey, A. Acorna's search
(jt. auth) McCaffrey, A. Acorna's triumph
(jt. auth) McCaffrey, A. Acorna's world

Schaefer, Jack Warner, 1907-1991

The collected stories of Jack Schaefer; with an introduction by Winfield Townley Scott. Houghton Mifflin 1966 520p o.p.

Contents: Major Burl; Miley Bennett; Emmet Dutrow; Sergeant Houck; Jeremy Rodock; Cooter James; Kittura Remsberg; General Pingley; Elvie Burdette; Josiah Willett; Something lost; Leander Frailey; Jacob; My town; Old Anse; That Mark horse; Ghost town; Takes a real man; Out of the past; Hugo Kertchak, builder; Prudence by name; Harvey Kendall; Cat nipped; Stalemate; Nate Bartlett's store; Salt of the earth; One man's honor; The old man; The coup of Long Lance; Enos Carr; The fifth man; Stubby Pringle's Christmas

"The author's mastery of narrative technique, his excellent character development, and his consistently concise description combine in avoiding the unfortunate aspects of typical 'Western' fiction and melodrama." Libr J

Monte Walsh. Houghton Mifflin 1963 501p o.p.

This novel of the old West follows Monte from runaway boy to trail hand, to topnotch cowhand and bronc buster, to aging saddle bum and encompasses the rise, the peak and the eventual collapse of the open range

"His characters seem real, and, according to the author, the characters and the episodes are based upon historical accounts. This is not just another 'Western.' It is worthy of a place alongside the writing of Will James and Eugene Manlove Rhodes." Libr J

Shane; [by] Jack Schaefer; illustrated by John McCormack. Houghton Mifflin 1954 214p il $18

ISBN 0-395-07090-2

Illustrated edition of the title first published 1949

"Wyoming in 1889 is the scene of conflict between cattlemen and homesteaders when Shane mysteriously disappears. He works hard as a hired hand for the Starrett family, and young Bob Starrett grows to love him, unaware that he is a feared gunfighter escaping his past." Shapiro. Fic for Youth. 3d edition

Schickler, David

Sweet and vicious. Dial Press 2004 242p $23

ISBN 0-385-33568-7 LC 2004-47830

"Sexy and willful, Grace McGlone is saving herself for the right man. When Henry Dante pulls into the small Wisconsin town where she works at the car wash, she instantly knows he's the one. He knows it too. But when Grace discovers Henry has 'The Planets'—a stolen set of famous Spanish diamonds—stashed in the back seat of his truck, she's having none of it. She's 'trying for heaven,' and the ill-gotten jewels must go. And so they do, in a race across the American landscape from Chicago to Yellowstone, pursued by a savage gangster obsessed by the diamonds he thought were his." Publisher's note

"Schickler is a rare find; with straightforward and yet deeply insightful writing, he mixes love, violence, ardor, and humor in this funny and heartbreaking modern-day fable." Booklist

Schine, Cathleen

The love letter. Houghton Mifflin 1995 257p o.p.

LC 95-5202

"One summer morning in her 41st year, Helen MacFarquhar, the divorced owner of an audaciously pink bookstore in an exclusive Connecticut shore town, finds a mysterious letter in her mail. Addressed 'Dear Goat,' and signed 'As Ever, Ram,' it is a love letter of such intensity and passion that she becomes obsessed by its urgently suggestive message. The effect of that letter on Helen's orderly life is the burden of this comedy of manners." Publ Wkly

"As light, and as risky, as a soufflé, The Love Letter indulges an enchanting fantasy, while invoking the powerful interplay of language and love. Literature, Schine suggests, can make booksellers glamorous, can ignite passion in the most unlikely of settings, and can even allow doomed love to live on." N Y Rev Books

Schlink, Bernhard

The reader; translated from the German by Carol Brown Janeway. Pantheon Bks. 1997 218p $20

ISBN 0-679-44279-0 LC 97-1511

Original German edition, 1995

"In post WW II Germany, a teenage boy is seduced by a streetcar conductor twice his age who insists that he read to her before they make love. Years later, when he is a law student, she appears as a defendant on trial for war crimes during the Nazi era. This novel raises provocative questions about guilt and responsibility, as well as the power of literature to heal and bind." Publ Wkly

Self's punishment; [by] Bernhard Schlink and Walter Popp; translated from the German by Rebecca Morrison. Vintage Books 2005 248p pa $14

ISBN 0-375-70907-X LC 2004-57166

This mystery features former Nazi prosecutor turned investigator Gerhard Self. "It's the early 1980s, and Self has been hired by a boyhood friend to smoke out a hacker who's playing havoc with the computers at Rhineland Chemical Works. But after Self springs a trap that gets the troublemaker murdered, he gradually faces the guilt he still carries for his youthful embrace of National Socialism. His simple refusal to let himself off the hook and step back into his old public prosecutor's role after the war doesn't seem like penance enough anymore. . . . Self's unwitting participation in the new crime drives him to pursue the path of justice wherever it may lead. A fascinating exploration of how people often manage to carve out normal lives even after being complicit in terrible acts." Booklist

Schmitz, Ettore *See* Svevo, Italo, 1861-1928

Scholz, Carter

The amount to carry; stories. Picador 2003 208p $23

ISBN 0-312-26901-3 LC 2002-192667

Contents: The eve of the last Apollo; A catastrophe machine; Blumfeld, an elderly bachelor; The menagerie of Babel; A draft of Canto CI; Altamira; Travels; At the shore; The nine billion names of God; Invisible ink; Mengele's Jew; The amount to carry

"In each keenly meta-physical fable Scholz, a connoisseur of the imagination, parses the language of science, literature, art, and music as he ponders the quintessentially human habit of telling stories, a valiant attempt to render sense out of the delirium of existence." Booklist

Radiance. Picador 2002 388p $24

ISBN 0-312-26893-9 LC 2001-56018

"It is the mid-1990s, and the press has just learned that a recent demonstration of a missile interception system was rigged. Leo Highet, the Machiavellian director of a California defense lab, is forced from his position and replaced by his rival Philip Quine, a closet peacenik." Libr J

"Wickedly satiric and eggheaded in its level of scientific detail, 'Radiance' is a serious, engrossing novel." N Y Times Book Rev

Schulberg, Budd

Waterfront; a novel. Random House 1955 320p o.p.

"The prize-winning screen play 'On the waterfront' has been expanded into a novel which differs on several counts from the film. It remains an angry indictment of racketeering in the labor unions along the New Jersey waterfront, but the happy ending of the screen play has been supplanted by a tragic one, in which the hero Terry Malloy is murdered by the henchmen of Johnny Friendly, the labor racketeer, and the terrorism along the waterfront continues. The more leisurely framework of the novel form permits the author to document to the full the abuses in longshoremen's unions, without sacrificing the explosive force of the film." Booklist

What makes Sammy run? Modern Lib. 1941 303p o.p.

"The protagonist, Sammy Glick, is a tough New York youth who works his way into a position of power in the motion-picture industry, where his harshness and crude manners are not out of place." Benet's Reader's Ency of Am Lit

Schupack, Deborah

The boy on the bus; a novel. Free Press 2003 215p $23

ISBN 0-7432-4220-3 LC 2002-32179

"One afternoon, Vermont housewife Meg discovers that the boy on the school bus outside her door is almost, but not quite, her eight-year-old son, Charlie. . . . Meg's panic recalls her aloof, restless husband from his job in Canada and her bratty, rebellious teenage daughter from boarding school, but neither they nor the local sheriff nor the family doctor can verify Charlie's authenticity." Publ Wkly

"Motherhood with all its contradictions has rarely been shown so nakedly. Schupack gives us Meg's view and everyone else's in overlapping layers. . . . From beginning to end in this novel, nothing is ordinary, while at the same time everything is." N Y Times Book Rev

Schwartz, Gil

See also Bing, Stanley

Schwartz, John Burnham

Reservation Road; a novel. Knopf 1998 292p o.p.

LC 98-14580

This novel focuses on "two unhappy Connecticut families linked by one violent moment. The Learners are the victims of tragedy: an ordinary stop at a country gas station turns to horror when their oldest child is killed by a hit-and-run driver in full view of his father, Ethan. As his wife and small daughter suffer through grief, depression, and guilt, Ethan is consumed by his compulsion to find and punish his son's murderer after the police give up. Nearby, . . . Dwight Arno tortures himself with his memories of speeding away from the accident." Libr J

"The story is told in the alternating voices of father, mother and murderer, which overlap and swell to a crescendo in an operatic chorus of pain." Economist

Schwartz, Leslie

Angels Crest; a novel; Leslie Schwartz. 1st ed. Doubleday 2004 303p $23.95
ISBN 0-385-51185-X LC 2003-64635

"Ethan Denton is out for a drive with his three-year-old son, Nate, in the woods of Northern California, when he decides to stop to follow several bucks he spots just off the road. When he returns 15 minutes later, his son is gone, and his own personal hell, as well as that of the small town of Angels Crest, is just beginning. Ethan's alcoholic ex-wife, Cindy, who lost custody of Nate; his former best friend, Glick, who slept with Cindy; Rocksan and Jane, a settled lesbian couple; and Jack, a lonely judge from outside the town are among those who help Ethan search for his son. . . . This beautiful, moving novel works brilliantly as a study of a tragedy and the various characters' reactions to the tragedy itself, as well as how it causes them to reexamine their own lives." Booklist

Schwartz, Lynne Sharon

Disturbances in the field. Harper & Row 1983 371p o.p.
LC 83-47555

"Lydia is a chamber musician . . . Victor is an artist, and their life in Manhattan is at last coming together. Lydia revels in the individual personalities of her four children and of her best women friends from college (Barnard) with whom, as in the old days, she argues philosophy in the most sincere, least highbrow manner possible. But her two youngest children are killed in a bus crash, a tragedy so profound she doesn't know how to react. . . . Then Victor moves out to live with another woman, although neither he nor Lydia can totally divorce themselves from all they have shared together." Publ Wkly

"There are weighty passages and themes here, not for the casual reader. However, the journey from resignation to a grudging reaffirmation of living, of returning to the field, disturbs the reader's own field with its unmistakable ring of truth." Libr J

The fatigue artist; a novel. Scribner 1995 320p il $23
ISBN 0-684-80247-3 LC 94-48009

"Laura, the protagonist narrator, is a Manhattan woman suffering from Chronic Fatigue Syndrome (CFS), the catch-all diagnosis for a patchwork quilt of vague symptoms including weakness, tiredness, malaise, and muscle aches. Laura endures her increasingly debilitating illness while trying to cope with the violent death of her husband, the demands of two lovers, her complicated relationship with her stepchildren, the pressures of social obligations, and the stress of her writing career." New Leader

"Like Laura, Schwartz is a writer's writer, indulging in lavish description, then subverting clichés with succinct turns of phrase. Her dialogue is arrestingly urbane." Women's Rev Books

In the family way; an urban comedy. Morrow 1999 325p $24
ISBN 0-688-17071-4 LC 99-22134

"The story takes place in an apartment building on New York's Upper West Side and centers on Roy, a psychotherapist; his first wife, Bea, a caterer; and their quest to preserve family. Bea's mother is the landlady of the building, and the tenants include Bea's lesbian sister, Bea's Russian lover, the superintendent, and Roy's second and current wife. In an attempt to keep her four children and their father together, Bea convinces Roy and his new wife to reside in her mother's building." Libr J

"A fast-paced, hugely entertaining novel about a group of people unwilling to compromise on their hopes for happiness." Booklist

The writing on the wall; a novel; Lynne Sharon Schwartz. Counterpoint 2005 297p $24
ISBN 1-582-43299-6 LC 2004-24877

Renata, this novel's protagonist, "is a secretive individual-and solitary, until boyfriend Jack comes into her life. On the morning of September 11, 2001, she is walking to work across the Brooklyn Bridge when the World Trade Center is attacked. It becomes clear in the days ahead that Renata cannot keep memories of her buried past-of a twin sister, a betrayal, of family truths too ugly to acknowledge-at bay." Publisher's note

This novel "would have been excellent already without its 9/11 ballast. It is full of intuitive dread, as if Joan Didion had written Play It As It Lays in the same Brooklyn boarding house where Norman Mailer was writing Barbary Shore." Harper's

Schwarz, Christina

All is vanity; a novel. Doubleday 2002 368p $24.95
ISBN 0-385-49972-8 LC 2002-67583

"This novel concerns a Manhattan schoolteacher named Margaret who quits and tries her hand at writing about something . . . far afield: the ennui of a Vietnam vet. . . . [Later] Margaret ditches Vietnam, and secretly bases her novel on her friend Letty's life. Letty's husband has a falshy new job at a museum in California, and the couple's been spending crazy money trying to seem less nouveau and more riche. Margaret encourages Letty to spend without end." Newsweek

"Schwarz's portrait of the talentless, self-absorbed Margaret is surgically accurate. . . . Anyone who has ever tried to write and been blocked will howl with recognition at the indignities that befall the novelist. . . . The novel is both a page turner and a cautionary tale of consumerism run amok." N Y Times Book Rev

Drowning Ruth. Doubleday 2000 338p $23.95
ISBN 0-385-50253-2 LC 00-29523

"In 1919, while serving as a nurse in a Milwaukee hospital for severely wounded soldiers, Amanda Starkey . . . goes home to rest at her parents' farm in rural Wisconsin. . . . The only people living there now are Matilda Neumann, Amanda's younger sister, and Mattie's three-year-old daughter, Ruth. Carl Neumann, the husband and father, is still recovering in France from his wartime injuries. And then, suddenly, Mattie too is dead, having fallen through the ice on a nearby lake and drowned." Time

"The vivid realism of the novel's setting adds depth to an already gripping plot. . . . Schwarz maintains her mystery with an expert hand, arriving at far more than a simple determination of guilt." N Y Times Book Rev

Schwarz-Bart, André, 1928-

The last of the just; translated from the French by Stephen Becker. Atheneum Pubs. 1960 374p o.p.

Original French edition, 1959

This novel "traces the martyrdom of the Jews through thirty-six generations of the Levy family, culminating with the death of Ernie in the Auschwitz concentration camp." Reader's Ency. 4th edition

"The thread that runs through the narration is the ancient Jewish tradition of the Lamed-Vov, according to which the world reposes upon 36 Just Men, who often are not aware themselves of the position they hold. . . . Harrowing as the book is, it is a valuable addition to the titles on the Holocaust, lest we forget how inhumane man can be." Shapiro. Fic for Youth. 3d edition

Scoppettone, Sandra, 1936-

Everything you have is mine. Little, Brown 1991 261p o.p.

LC 90-48889

"Lauren Laurano, a bighearted, wisecracking lesbian who makes her debut here as a Manhattan private eye, brings cunning as well as caring to her investigation of the murder of a young rape victim who might have met her killer by hooking into a dating service on her personal computer." N Y Times Book Rev

Gonna take a homicidal journey. Little, Brown 1998 229p $22.95

ISBN 0-316-77665-3 LC 97-44247

"While helping her life partner and friends renovate a beach place in a small Long Island town, private investigator Lauren Laurano becomes sidetracked by murder. Hired by the old-money cousin of a supposed suicide, Lauren soon detects a pattern that may include the deaths of several women and children. Each suspect she questions withholds crucial information; meanwhile, the idea of a police conspiracy grows. The wide-ranging, all-encompassing case may seem shallow or far-fetched, but Scoppettone's tongue-in-cheek attitude makes the book work." Libr J

My sweet untraceable you. Little, Brown 1994 275p o.p.

LC 93-47426

"NYC lesbian private eye Lauren Laurano agrees to search for the truth about an ex-con's mother who has been presumed dead for 38 years." Libr J

"Scoppettone is a highly entertaining writer with her fingers on current political and commercial pulses. So she ably transmits the modish urban-grit feel of Laurano's encounters with Manhattan's winos, weirdos, and wise guys as she counterpoints the complex case her sleuth is solving with the deterioration from AIDS of the brother of Laurano's lesbian partner of 14 years." Booklist

Scott, Anne

Calpurnia. Knopf 2003 293p $24

ISBN 0-375-41380-4 LC 2002-30096

"Elizabeth Oliver is overseeing the sale of an estate called Calpurnia, a large Philadelphia mansion once owned by Maribel Archibald Davies, painter and self-appointed bohemian. As Elizabeth gathers, organizes, and catalogs the items of the estate, she finds herself drawn into the family's intimate relationships as well as the mysterious circumstances surrounding Maribel's death." Booklist

"Scott sets the book in the 1980's, before online antique auctions and the advent of dot-com billionaires who might have competed fiercely to buy a flashy old pile like Calpurnia. Her central theme, however, the impulse to make and live with art, is timeless." N Y Times Book Rev

Scott, Joanna

Tourmaline; a novel. Little, Brown 2002 279p $23.95

ISBN 0-316-77618-1 LC 2002-67111

"In 1956, extravagant, debt-ridden Murray Murdoch takes his wife and four young sons on a vacation to Elba, where he becomes convinced that he can profit from the island's abundant deposits of semiprecious gems. When the summer comes to an end and Murray still hasn't found the valuable tourmaline that he's looking for, the Murdochs decide to postpone their departure indefinitely. Their idyllic existence is shattered when a mysterious local girl goes missing and the community begins to suspect that the 'investor from the United States' is somehow involved. The story is told by Ollie, the youngest of the four boys, who was five when the family arrived on the island and is 50 now." Publ Wkly

"Book reviewers are fond of calling belletristic novels 'poetic.' 'Tourmaline' isn't poetic because of its pretty writing but because of its sympathetic ordering and reordering of ideas, its philosophical probing." N Y Times Book Rev

Scott, Michael, 1959-

(jt. auth) Llywelyn, M. Silverhand

(jt. auth) Llywelyn, M. Silverlight

Scott, Paul, 1920-1978

The day of the scorpion; a novel. Morrow 1968 483p o.p.

This second volume of the Raj quartet tells the lives of Sarah and Susan Layton, Lady Manners and Parvati; Kasim and his two sons and Captain Merrick, all caught up in the violence and strife that engulfed India when the Congress Party adopted a resolution calling for a nationwide insurrection

The author's "ability in characterization and in realization of the love-hate relationship of Indian and Englishman are again amply demonstrated in a poignant story constantly interest-holding." Booklist

Followed by The towers of silence

also in Scott, P. The Raj quartet

A division of the spoils; a novel. Morrow 1975 597p o.p.

In this concluding volume of The Raj quartet, the end of the British rule in India is viewed primarily through the eyes of Guy Perron, a young historian serving as a sergeant in an army intelligence unit. The novel "spans the pivotal years 1945-1947 just before India and Pakistan gained independence. Central to the plot is Ronald Merrick, wounded, enigmatic colonel of the police whose

Scott, Paul, 1920-1978*—Continued*
interference in the lives of members of the British Raj . . . leads to cruelties as well as to revelations of individual responsibilities." Booklist

"Scott makes nothing simple; thus his work bears a disturbing resemblance to life. He mixes up lovers, friends, enemies, families, servants, strangers, soldiers, businessmen, murders, suicides, illnesses in five or six interrelated stories. . . . And all have one focus: corrupted British morality in India." N Y Times Book Rev

also in Scott, P. The Raj quartet

The jewel in the crown; a novel. Morrow 1966 462p o.p.

This is the first volume of The Raj quartet

"Around a central incident of the rape of a young Englishwoman in an Indian garden in August, 1942, the author has woven a . . . picture of India before independence. The two main threads of plot are the fate of the raped girl and the tragic end of an elderly English school-teacher who is a very brave woman. There are other stories within the story. . . . This is a masterly narrative, a leisurely and skillful depiction of a wide Indian landscape and a large canvas showing people who are made very real. It is also a dissection of Anglo-British animosities." Publ Wkly

Followed by The day of the scorpion

also in Scott, P. The Raj quartet

The Raj quartet. Morrow 1976 4v in 1 o.p.

Contents: The jewel in the crown; The day of the scorpion; The towers of silence; A division of the spoils

Staying on; a novel. Morrow 1977 215p o.p. LC 77-1491

"After India succeeds in obtaining independence from Britain, Tusker and Lucy Smalley, part of the British colonial army, stay on in the country where almost all their married life has been spent. The book describes their relationships with the Indians who, at this point, constitute all of their daily and social contacts. . . . There is humor in the informative portrayals of the relationships between the British and the Indians, and the final scene is as simple and moving a description of loss as has ever been written." Shapiro. Fic for Youth. 3d edition

The towers of silence; a novel. Morrow 1972 c1971 392p o.p.

First published 1971 in the United Kingdom

In the third volume of the Raj quartet "attention focuses on Barbara Batchelor, the retired mission-school teacher, and many, but not all, of the events are seen through her eyes. This time the Manners case and Congress leader Mohammed Ali Kasim are relegated to the background, but the earlier reported activities of Mildred Layton and her daughters, Teddie Bingham, Captain Merrick, and others are repeated." Libr J

"This elegy on the decline and fall of the Indian empire sounds harsh notes, but is moving as well. Mr. Scott has the trick of being sympathetic without ever losing his clear sightedness." Times Lit Suppl

Followed by A division of the spoils

also in Scott, P. The Raj quartet

Scott, Sir Walter, 1771-1832

The bride of Lammermoor; edited by J.H. Alexander. Columbia Univ. Press 1995 398p $44.50

ISBN 0-231-10572-X LC 96-143055

First published 1819

"The most tragic of Scott's romances, on which Donizetti's opera 'Lucia di Lammermoor' is based. The last scion of a ruined family and the daughter of his ancestral enemy in possession of the estates fall in love. For a while there is a glimpse of hope and happiness; but the ambitious mother opposes the match, prophecies and apparitions prognosticate tragedy, and the romance closes in death and sorrow. . . . Caleb Balderstone, the faithful retainer, is one of Scott's humorous creations, whose obstinate care for his unhappy master relieves the overpowering tragedy." Baker. Guide to the Best Fic

Ivanhoe; a romance. Modern Lib. 1997 xxxvii, 535p $16

ISBN 0-679-60263-1 LC 96-48579

First published 1819

"The action occurs in the period following the Norman Conquest. The titular hero is Wilfred, knight of Ivanhoe, the son of Cedric the Saxon, in love with his father's ward Rowena. Cedric, however, wishes her to marry Athelstane, who is descended from the Saxon royal line and may restore the Saxon supremacy. The real heroine is Rebecca the Jewess, daughter of the wealthy Isaac of York, and a person of much more character and charm than the mild Rowena. Richard the Lion-Hearted in the guise of the Black Knight and Robin Hood as Locksley play prominent roles." Reader's Ency. 4th edition

Kenilworth. o.p.

First published 1821

A novel "famous for its portrayal of Queen Elizabeth and her court. The other principal characters are Robert Dudley, the earl of Leicester, who entertains ambitions of becoming king-consort, and his beautiful, unhappy wife, Amy Robsart. She suffers neglect, insult and finally death at his hands." Reader's Ency. 4th edition

Rob Roy; with an introduction by Eric Anderson. Knopf 1995 xliii, 494p $20

ISBN 0-679-44362-2

"Everyman's library"

First published 1817; first Everyman's library edition 1906

"Full of intrigue with political overtones, it is set in northern England just before the Jacobite rebellion of 1715, and it is considered one of the author's masterpieces. Francis Obaldistone, the novel's hero, contends with his jealous, unscrupulous cousin Rashleigh for the hand of the beautiful Diana Vernon. Aided by the Scottish outlaw Rob Roy (based on a historical Jacobite outlaw), Francis succeeds in exposing Rashleigh's villainy." Merriam-Webster's Ency of Lit

Scott, Warwick, 1920-1995

For works written by this author under other names see Hall, Adam, 1920-1995

Scottoline, Lisa

Dead ringer. HarperCollins Pubs. 2003 339p $25.95

ISBN 0-06-051493-0 LC 2002-191931

Scottoline, Lisa—*Continued*

A "legal caper featuring the lady lawyers of series heroine Bennie Rosato's Philadelphia law firm Rosato and Associates. This time out it's Bennie playing the lead role, as she fights to save her financially sinking firm; mother her lovable partners, Mary DiNunzio and Judy Carrier; solve the murder of a valuable client; and battle her evil twin, Alice. . . . Bennie grows on you, and soon enough you're rooting for the home team and laughing at her corny jokes." Publ Wkly

Killer smile; Lisa Scottoline. 1st ed. HarperCollins 2004 358p $25.95

ISBN 0-06-051495-7 LC 2003-67650

In this installment in the "series starring the all-female Philadelphia law firm of Rosato & Associates, young Mary DiNunzio takes center stage. Mary has taken on a pro bono case representing her 'peeps' an Italian American business group (the circolo) working on behalf of the estate of Amadeo Brandolini, who committed suicide while interned during World War II. The estate seeks reparations, and Mary feels drawn to the case, so much so that others fear she's obsessed with it. Under the guise of taking a vacation, Mary visits the site of the internment camp in Montana where Amadeo killed himself and finds herself with still more unanswered questions. Interesting author's notes at the end of this engaging drama disclose Scottoline's own discovery of her grandparents' internment, lending this unusual story a welcome authenticity." Booklist

Legal tender. HarperCollins Pubs. 1996 291p o.p.

LC 96-7165

The protagonist of this legal thriller is Philadelphian Bennie Rosato "a ravishing six-foot blonde, one of two partners in a thriving law firm. In quick order, the foundations of her world come crashing down. Her partner and ex-lover, Mark, turns up murdered shortly after he tells Bennie that he is planning to dissolve the partnership. It's not surprising that she then becomes the cops' prime suspect. When the murder weapon is found in her apartment, Bennie goes underground. Then a drug company CEO is killed, and she is falsely accused of that death, too." Publ Wkly

Mistaken identity. HarperCollins Pubs. 1999 480p $24

ISBN 0-06-018747-6 LC 98-43200

In this legal thriller "maverick lawyer Bennie Rosato must defend a woman claiming not only to have been framed for a murder by the Philadelphia police but also to be Bennie's long-lost identical twin sister. Rosato is shocked when she meets the woman, who turns out to look just like her; and as she unfolds the questionable and mysterious circumstances surrounding the case, Rosato reveals level after level of corruption." Booklist

Scottoline "succeeds in creating a brisk, multilayered thriller that plunges Rosato & Associates into a maelstrom of legal, ethical and familial conundrums, culminating in an intricate, dramatic and intense courtroom finale." Publ Wkly

Moment of truth. HarperCollins Pubs. 2000 358p o.p.

ISBN 0-06-019609-2 LC 99-89325

"Lawyer Jack Newlin faces his most difficult assignment when he has to convince the police to accept his confession to a crime he didn't commit. Coming home to find his wife stabbed to death, Jack assumes the killer is their 16-year-old daughter, a super model who had recently announced her pregnancy. To insure his conviction, he hires novice lawyer Mary Di Nunzio to defend him. Not only does Mary develop a crush on him but she also is determined to prove him innocent." SLJ

"Sharp, funny characters, crafty plot twists, and a flavorful depiction of high- and lower-middle Philadelphia society will keep readers riveted to this tense, often mischievous page-turner." Publ Wkly

Rough justice. HarperCollins Pubs. 1997 344p o.p.

LC 97-5810

"During the biggest snowstorm in the history of Philadelphia, the jury is out. The defense is confident of a verdict of not guilty, but then client Elliot Steere admits to his council that he is a murderer. Marta Richter does not take this revelation happily. In fact, she's so outraged that she wants her client's secret revealed no matter what it does to her career. Steere isn't about to let her blow his chances, and with powerful connections, money, and muscle, he works from his jail cell to silence Marta and her colleagues before the sequestered jury makes a decision." Libr J

"Scottoline deftly balances the varied personalities of the women and manages a large cast, including judge and jury, with precision. She skillfully depicts personal quirks that give her characters dimension." Publ Wkly

Running from the law. HarperCollins Pubs. 1995 232p o.p.

LC 95-24319

"Rita Morrone has a smart way with words and a shifty code of ethics, attributes that give this Philadelphia trial lawyer a jump on the legal competition. . . . [The plot] has Rita defending her fiancé's father, a Federal judge . . . in a sexual harassment suit. When the woman who brought these charges is murdered, Rita conducts her own investigation into the too-perfect Hamilton family." N Y Times Book Rev

The vendetta defense. HarperCollins Pubs. 2001 390p o.p.

ISBN 0-06-018507-4 LC 00-50556

A legal yarn featuring Judy Carrier of Philadelphia's all-female firm of Rosato & Associates. The plot "revolves around Anthony 'Pigeon Tony' Lucia, a lovable septuagenarian who killed his longtime rival, Angelo Coluzzi, who murdered Lucia's wife in their native Italy 60 years ago. Coluzzi, the wealthy, mob-connected owner of a big construction firm, always seems to get the upperhand-until Pigeon Tony breaks his neck during a showdown at the pigeon-racing club where they're both members. Pigeon Tony freely admits he killed Coluzzi, but maintains he was justified because of the longstanding Italian tradition of vendetta; Carrier knows it will be a big stretch to make that argument fly before a 21st-century American jury." Publ Wkly

Searles, John

Boy still missing. Morrow 2001 292p o.p.

ISBN 0-688-17570-8 LC 00-40758

Searles, John—*Continued*

"It is 1971, and one of 15-year-old Dominick Pindle's regular activities is a game of sorts—the game is less funny to his mother—that he calls Find-Father-First. The key is to spot his father's truck and then pull him out of whatever bar he's drinking in. Life has become increasingly difficult for this Massachusetts family; Dominick's father carries on with another woman, his mother becomes involved with a police officer, and a bizarre accidental death leads Dominick—through a series of twisted circumstances—to kidnap a child in Manhattan." N Y Times Book Rev

"Searles builds suspense and excitement with surprising turns of plot weaving back into one another, and while many of the secondary characters lack depth, Dominic Pindle will resonate with readers." Booklist

Sebald, Winfried Georg, 1944-2001

Austerlitz; [by] W.G. Sebald; translated by Anthea Bell. Random House 2001 298p il $25.95

ISBN 0-375-50483-4 LC 2001-19785

"The unnamed narrator met Austerlitz, an architectural historian, in Belgium in the '60s, then lost track of his friend in the '70s. When they accidentally run into each other in 1996, Austerlitz tells the story that occupies the rest of the book—the story of Austerlitz's life. For a long time, Austerlitz did not know his real mother and father were Prague Jews. . . . While exploring the Liverpool Street railroad station in London, Austerlitz experiences a flashback of himself as a four-year-old. Gradually, he tracks his history, from his birth in Prague to a cultivated couple through his flight to England, on the eve of WWII, on a train filled with refugee children." Publ Wkly

"As so often in Sebald's fiction, direct connections are never highlighted in the vast loops and sudden knottings of his rhetoric, but the reader cannot escape the inference that in the long sweep of history the Nazis were not alone, but that an inquirer searching for meaning is." NY Times Book Rev

The emigrants; [by] W.G. Sebald; translated by Michael Hulse. New Directions 1996 237p il $22.95

ISBN 0-8112-1338-2 LC 96-22223

Original German edition, 1995

The four fictional "accounts/reports/reminiscences tell of . . . people who left Germany in the 20th century. Three are about Jews who went to England or Switzerland—either in the 1930s or before WW I—die or commit suicide long after WW II, but who, nonetheless, are victims of the Holocaust. One is about the narrator's non-Jewish great uncle, who went to America at the turn of the century, led an adventuresome life, and died a horrible death in the 1950s." Choice

"A profound and original work . . . . W. G. Sebald has created an end-of-century meditation that explores the most delicate, most painful, most nervously repressed and carefully concealed lesions of the last hundred years. Illuminatingly engaged with the history and literature of the modern era, Mr. Sebald's book gains power through its poetic obsessions with the past." N Y Times Book Rev

Vertigo; [by] W.G. Sebald; translated by Michael Hulse. New Directions 2000 263p il $23.95

ISBN 0-8112-1430-3 LC 99-58955

Original German edition published 1990; this translation first published 1999 in the United Kingdom

"The first-person narrator travels through Europe during the 1980s, spurred on by history's ghosts and his own melancholic yearning for adventure. Having left his base in England to explore Vienna, Venice and Verona, he concludes with a bittersweet pilgrimage to his hometown in southwestern Germany. In four nonlinear chapters, the narrator sustains himself along his journey by establishing parallels with places and personages throughout history." Publ Wkly

"W.G. Sebald is unusual for a literary star. He fuses genres (travelogue, biography, the novel, meditation, myth), confounding the categories most readers are used to. The narrator of 'Vertigo' offers a fair account of Mr. Sebald's intricate methods. . . . This is poetic or philosophical fiction for readers content to follow the path of a remarkable author's thoughts without the guard-rail of an overarching story." Economist

Sebold, Alice

The lovely bones. Little, Brown 2002 328p $21.95

ISBN 0-316-66634-3 LC 2001-50622

Sebold's "heroine, 14-year-old Suzy Salmon, is murdered in the first chapter, on her way home from school. Suzy narrates the story from heaven, viewing the devastating effects of her murder on her family." Booklist

"As pleasant as Susie's heaven is, there's no God there, and certainly no Jesus. This is spirituality for an age that's ecumenical to a fault. But emotionally, it's faultless. Sebold never slips as she follows this family. The risks she walks are enough to give you vertigo." Christ Sci Monit

See, Carolyn

The handyman. Random House 1999 220p $22.95

ISBN 0-375-50155-X LC 98-21098

"Bob Hampton, a future great artist, leads a quintessentially California life as a freelance handyman before he answers his true calling; in the course of a hot Los Angeles summer, he worries about his lack of aesthetic sophistication, comforts lonely housewives in the time-honored way, and rescues a drowning child and an AIDS patient. Despite a confusing start, the novel quickly takes on the brightness of a sun-dazzled swimming pool and makes a case for shadowless living—a state its hero achieves through an unlikely combination of application and hedonism." New Yorker

See, Lisa

Dragon bones; a novel. Random House 2003 348p $24.95

ISBN 0-679-46320-8 LC 2002-24871

"The controversial construction of a massive dam on the Yangzi River is the backdrop for the latest adventures of Liu Hulan, inspector in the Ministry of Public Security in Beijing, and her husband, American lawyer

See, Lisa—*Continued*
David Stark." Publ Wkly

"Hulan and David must overcome their estrangement and work together to solve the crimes. In a land where bribery and corruption are the norm, there are many suspects. The novel flows beautifully, engaging readers in the mystery while gently introducing them to China's rich cultural history." Libr J

Segal, Erich, 1937-

Love story. Harper & Row 1970 131p o.p.

"Oliver is Harvard, rich, a big campus athlete. Jenny is a Radcliffe scholarship student in music from a poor Italian Catholic background. They meet, fall in love, and marry, even though the boy's father wants him to go to law school first. Jenny gives up a chance to study in Paris and works to put her young husband through law school—and they win out to the beginnings of a great life and promising career for him. Then tragedy steps in." Publ Wkly

"A very professionally crafted short first novel. The author makes no great claims of insight for his work. Indeed, the story is all on the surface. But it is funny and sad and generally recommended." Libr J

Followed by Oliver's story (1977)

Seiffert, Rachel

Field study. Pantheon Books 2004 215p $19.95
ISBN 0-375-42259-5 LC 2003-66364

Contents: Field study; Reach; Tentsmuir sands; Dog leg lane; Blue; Architect ; The late spring; The crossing; Frances John Jones; Dimitroff; Second best

In this collection of stories, "all set primarily in Europe, we meet a variety of characters, among them an architect losing his grip on his profession and on reality, a British soldier AWOL in World War II Italy, a teenaged couple struggling with the reality of becoming parents, and an American woman driving her elderly father-in-law to his former street in East Berlin. . . . This is a fine collection from a young writer who displays a modern Europe with its particular social and political issues amid universal human themes." Libr J

Self, Will

Dorian; an imitation. Grove Press 2002 277p $23
ISBN 0-8021-1729-5 LC 2002-29962

"In this retelling of Oscar Wilde's The Picture of Dorian Gray, most of the original's characters are cleverly transmuted into their late-20th-century counterparts: dissolute Henry Wotton, now openly homosexual with a nasty heroin habit; his protege, eager young video artist 'Baz' Hallward; and the title character, the quintessential amoral narcissist. . . . Self uses Wilde's plot to examine post-Stonewall gay life, from its drug-fueled hedonistic excesses to the reckoning of the AIDs epidemic. The novel skewers every layer of British society—street hustlers, members of Parliament and the idle rich." Publ Wkly

Seth, Vikram, 1952-

An equal music. Broadway Bks. 1999 380p $25
ISBN 0-7679-0291-2 LC 99-20421

As violinist Michael Holme "travels through Europe as a member of a quartet, he reminisces about his lost love, Julia McNicholl, a pianist. The former lovers are reunited, but the depth of their love and trust is put to the test when Michael discovers that not only is Julia married and the mother of a young son but that she is also going deaf." Libr J

Seth's "writing is a throwback, freely romantic, wondrously out of date, totally unhedged. His book attempts no cool, contains not a single pose. He can be playful with language, though not distractingly so. . . . The book is also stocked with humor, which appears when it is most needed, as the story grows almost suffocatingly sad." Natl Rev

A suitable boy; a novel. HarperCollins Pubs. 1993 1349p o.p.
LC 92-54744

"Set in the post-colonial India of the 1950s, this sprawling saga involves four families—the Mehras, the Kapoors, the Chatterjis and the Khans—whose domestic crises illuminate the historical and social events of the era. Like an old-fashioned soap opera (or a Bombay talkie), the multi-charactered plot pits mothers against daughters, fathers against sons, Hindus against Muslims and small farmers against greedy landowners facing government-ordered dispossession." Publ Wkly

This novel is, "at its heart an elegy as well as a comedy of manners, about a traditional society in a time of change, and about a leisurely world of graces giving way to a new, more democratic time." Times Lit Suppl

Seton, Anya, d. 1990

Avalon. Houghton Mifflin 1965 440p o.p.

"The romance is a deep lifelong attachment between a wandering French prince, an idealistic, poetic man, and a Cornish girl of peasant and Viking blood. The story opens in a courtly, gentle mood which changes to fury, lust and murderous greed when the scene shifts to the English court, and to adventure and exploration when the girl is captured by her father's people and the Vikings take the center of the stage." Publ Wkly

"Late tenth- and early eleventh-century life in England and in the lands colonized by the Norsemen [i.e. Iceland] is re-created from early Anglo-Saxon chronicles, French manuscripts, and secondary sources. . . . The action and milieu are vivid and though the characterization is not strong the psychological and historical motivations are believable. An honest historical novel for enthusiasts of the genre." Booklist

Dragonwyck. Houghton Mifflin 1944 336p o.p.

An American "Gothic" novel. The time is the 1830's and 1840's; the place, New York City and the great Van Ryn estate, Dragonwyck, on the Hudson. A young farm girl, a distant cousin of the Van Ryn's goes to live at Dragonwyck as governess to the Van Ryns' small daughter. At the death of the child's mother, Miranda becomes the second Mrs. Van Ryn. The story of Miranda's gradual horrified awakening follows

"For all its trappings and devices—and they are good, spine-chilling trappings, handled with considerable skill—the novel manages to have life and substance." NY Her Trib Books

Seton, Anya, d. 1990—*Continued*

Green darkness. Houghton Mifflin 1973 c1972 591p o.p.

First published 1972 in the United Kingdom

"Reincarnation is the theme of [this] . . . novel. A 16th-century Benedictine monk, Stephen Marsdon, falls prey to a consuming passion for alluring Celia de Bohun and forsakes his vows. The tragic end of the lovers, involving murder and suicide, brings, nearly 400 years later, madness and near death to their reincarnations, newlyweds Celia and Richard Marsdon. Fortunately, a Hindu doctor (himself a reincarnated Italian physician in Tudor England who longed for warmer climates) hovers nearby to monitor the proceedings and brings the souls to rest." Libr J

Katherine. Houghton Mifflin 1954 588p o.p.

Historical romance about the life of Katherine Swynford, sister-in-law of Geoffrey Chaucer, and mistress and later wife of John Gaunt

"It is a story that demands no intellectual or emotional effort from the reader. . . . But Miss Seton presents her facts accurately. Her research extends as far as visiting what remains of any of John of Gaunt's 30 castles and her zest for her subject communicates itself to the reader." San Francisco Chron

The Winthrop woman. Houghton Mifflin 1958 586p o.p.

In this biographical novel the author rallies to the defense of a maligned historical figure. "The young widow Elizabeth Winthrop was perhaps the most unwilling Puritan who ever came to New England, for she detested and feared Governor John Winthrop, who was her uncle as well as her father-in-law. A second marriage to Robert Feake, the governor's choice, dragged through years of Robert's increasing insanity; when he deserted her Elizabeth secured a divorce in New Amsterdam, contracted a common-law marriage with virile William Hallet, and found with him a love that was adequate recompense for exile and persecution." Booklist

"The novel is noteworthy for its insights into the Puritan 'Bible Commonwealth.'" Saturday Rev

Settle, Mary Lee

Charley Bland. Farrar, Straus & Giroux 1989 207p il o.p.

ISBN 0-374-12078-1 LC 89-207125

"Having fled the suffocating small-town environment of her West Virginia home and recreated herself as a writer in postwar Paris, the heroine of this condensed, lyric novel returns to discover that having dreams come true is sometimes disastrous. For there she again meets Charley Bland, the golden boy she worshiped as a child, now the town's most eligible–and elusive–bachelor. . . . The affair they begin quickly demolishes everything this woman had made of herself in the years she had been away." Libr J

This novel's "precision and emotional power urge one to listen ferociously for the hidden melodies that reveal the history underneath the social plottings, the story not just of people but of a world." N Y Times Book Rev

The killing ground. Farrar, Straus & Giroux 1982 385p o.p.

LC 82-2477

"In this novel, the last of the Beulah Quintet, Settle describes the various homecomings of Hannah McKarkle, a woman from an affluent West Virginia coal-mining family who has pursued a writing career in New York. In 1960, Hannah returns to find that her brother Johnny has been killed by a man who turns out to be a poor distant relative. The brother's death, the intricate interplay among classes in the closed rural society of West Virginia, and the inevitable pull of one's native home on the heart and soul are central to her subsequent visits in 1978 and 1980." Libr J

O Beulah Land; a novel. Viking 1956 368p o.p.

First published volume of the author's Beulah Quintet, set in rural West Virginia. Chronologically follows Prisons (1973). Subsequent titles in the series: Know nothing (1960); The scapegoat (1980) and The killing ground

Historical novel of the Virginia frontier from 1754 to 1775. "Jonathan Lacey is a strong man, as only a gentleman is strong. And he is a gentleman, by the standards of the Virginia wilderness country in the years preceding the American Revolution. After his service at the Battle of Little Meadows in 1775, Johnny scouts and surveys far into the mountains, and leads a heterogeneous group of early Americans westward with him, to claim and clear his bounty land in the undefended King's Part of the colony, beyond the Proclamation Line. It is on this land, called Beulah by Jeremiah the New Light preacher, that Johnny proves his strength." N Y Times Book Rev

Seymour, Gerald

The heart of danger. HarperCollins Pubs. 1995 358p o.p.

LC 95-4808

"Behind the lines in former Yugoslavia is a mass grave of victims of Serbian atrocities. The grave's excavation elicits a mystery: the body of Dorrie Mowat, a young British woman. What was Dorrie doing there, and why did she die? Britain's Security Service refers her anxious mother to ex-agent Bill Penn to investigate. As Penn draws closer to the truth, he enters the dangerous territory of Serbian warlord Milan Stankovic. Searching for evidence of war crimes, he puts life on the line by going into the war zone to try to bring Stankovic to justice." Libr J

"Using this wheels-within-wheels frame, Seymour constructs a harshly detailed novel about a dirty little war, peopled with a wide variety of deeply etched characters and suffused with a nearly palpable sense of despair and weariness." Publ Wkly

Killing ground. HarperCollins Pubs. 1997 390p o.p.

LC 96-51178

"Twenty-three-year-old Charlotte 'Charlie' Parsons is suffocating. Living at home with her parents in a small village in Cornwall, she sees no future except teaching snotty first-formers in the village primary. But excitement enters her life twice in one day. First, she receives a letter from Giuseppe and Angela Ruggerio, the Italian family Charlie worked for one wonderful summer. Will she come back to Italy and take care of the three Ruggerio children? To Charlie, it's a heaven-sent oppor-

Seymour, Gerald—*Continued*
tunity to escape. Later that day, she's visited by a coldly sinister American DEA agent named Axel Moen, who plans to use Charlie to reel in Mario Ruggerio, brother of Giuseppe and capo of the Sicilian Mafia. . . . A gripping thriller that leads to a shattering climax." Booklist

Shaara, Jeff, 1952-

The glorious cause; a novel of the American Revolution. Ballantine Bks. 2003 638p $26.95
ISBN 0-345-42756-4 LC 2002-34240
Sequel to Rise to rebellion
This novel is "told from the perspectives of various historical players. George Washington is prominent, as are Benjamin Franklin, the under appreciated Nathanial Greene, and, intriguingly, Britain's Lord Cornwallis." Libr J
"This is vivid and compelling historical fiction, but also a primer on leadership and the arts of war and diplomacy. Shaara reaches new heights here, with a narrative that's impossible to put down." Publ Wkly

Gods and generals; [by] Jeff Shaara. Ballantine Bks. 1996 498p $25
ISBN 0-345-40492-0 LC 95-53360
This novel "focuses simultaneously on the lives of four men who played significant roles in the military side of the Civil War in battles leading up to the great one at Gettysburg. The novel follows Stonewall Jackson, Winfield Scott Hancock, Joshua Chamberlain, and Robert E. Lee from 1858 to 1863, giving the reader splendidly detailed witness to how the war drew them into commanding positions. As should be the case with good historical fiction, Shaara, in taking actual figures from the past, rekindles them; he uses the personal experiences of these four men to meaningfully explore the political and military issues of the day." Booklist

Gone for soldiers. Ballantine Bks. 2000 424p il o.p.
ISBN 0-345-42750-5 LC 00-22745
This novel of the Mexican-American War focuses on "then-Captain Robert E. Lee's induction into the mysteries of supreme command. The future rebel is first seen shelling the defenses of Vera Cruz in 1847. After the city falls, Lee bends an attentive ear to the leadership methods of his boss, General Winfield Scott. When not making mental notes of Scott's decision, Lee tends to think about duty, God, and country—but mostly duty." Booklist
"The book is simply wonderful, populated with eminently human heroes who are called upon to perform Herculean tasks in a war muddied beyond redemption by the ambitions of back-home and battlefield politicians." Libr J

The last full measure; [by] Jeff Shaara. Ballantine Bks. 1998 560p maps $25
ISBN 0-345-40491-2 LC 97-49383
This volume follows "the course of the war in Virginia from Lee's retreat from Gettysburg to his surrender at Appomattox Court House. Ulysses S. Grant has come East to assume command of all Federal forces and to confront Lee, and the war they make is marked by such horrendous battles as The Wilderness and Spotsylvania. As characters, Grant and Lee dominate this book. . . . Civil War buffs will find Shaara nodding on some small details, but they generally will be delighted with this book." Libr J

Rise to rebellion. Ballantine Bks. 2001 492p $26.95
ISBN 0-345-42753-X LC 2001-18448
"The first of two projected novels on the American Revolution, Rebellion takes the reader from the Boston Massacre to the signing of the Declaration of Independence." Libr J
"Making excellent use of a you-are-there approach, Shaara focuses on a handful of prominent historical figures, including Benjamin Franklin, George Washington, John and Abigail Adams, and British general Thomas Gage. . . . Shaara's novel gives historical figures flesh-and-blood viability." Booklist

Shaara, Michael, 1929-1988

The killer angels; a novel. Random House 1993 374p il $24
ISBN 0-679-42541-1 LC 92-38365
This is a fictionalized account of four days in July, 1863 at the Battle of Gettysburg. The point of view of the Southern forces is represented by Generals Robert E. Lee and James Longstreet, while Colonel Joshua Chamberlain and General John Buford are the focus for the North
"Shaara's version of private reflections and conversations are based on his reading of documents and letters. Although some of his judgments are not necessarily substantiated by historians, he demonstrates a knowledge of both the battle and the area. The writing is vivid and fast moving." Libr J

Shabtai, Yaakov

Uncle Peretz takes off; short stories; translated from the Hebrew by Dalya Bilu. Overlook Press 2004 239p $24.95
ISBN 1-585-67340-4 LC 2004-58316
Contents: Adoshem; Model; True tenderness; Uncle Shmuel; A marriage proposal; Past continuous; Cordoba; Twilight; The voyage to Mauritius; A private and very awesome leopard; Uncle Peretz takes off; The visit; Departure; The Czech tea service
"At their best, the stories in this collection . . . are masterful, ironically drawn character studies evoking the Israeli frontier spirit under the British mandate while capturing the shift from old world religiosity to new world secularism. Originally published in Hebrew in 1972, the collection is bookended by two linked stories chronicling the deaths of the narrator's grandparents and with them the loss of Jewish traditions." Publ Wkly

Shacochis, Bob

Swimming in the volcano; a novel. Scribner 1993 519p $22
ISBN 0-684-19260-8 LC 92-37116
"In 1976, Mitchell Wilson signs on as an agricultural economist on St. Catherine, a fictional island in the Lesser Antilles. Just as he has settled into a routine and a circle of expatriate and native friends, his life is disrupted by the appearance of his first love, the volatile Johanna.

Shacochis, Bob—*Continued*

Equally unsteady is the island's ruling coalition, which is coming apart under threat from a counterrevolutionary menace fabricated by discontented members." Publ Wkly

"This may sound like a fast-paced thriller, but though there's a mystery to crack at the heart of this richly detailed novel, Shacochis in fact offers a chilling evocation of the misunderstandings that arise between feckless Americans and struggling islanders for whom St. Catherine's is no paradise." Libr J

Shade, Eric, 1970-

Eyesores; stories. University of Ga. Press 2003 205p $24.95

ISBN 0-8203-2432-9 LC 2002-7151

Contents: Eyesores; Blood; The heart hankers; Superfly; A rage forever; Stability; Kaahumanu; A final reunion; Hoops and wires and plugs; The last night of the couonty fair; Souvenirs

A collection of stories set in a small Pennsylvania town. "Windfall, recently bypassed by a freeway, is losing its blue-collar jobs and shuddering toward new life as a destination for golfers. Residents are torn between the desire for and the fear of change. . . . Shade captures perfectly the way in which it's hard to leave your mistakes behind when you're surrounded by people who remember when you made them." Booklist

Shakespeare, Nicholas

Snowleg; Nicholas Shakespeare. 1st U.S. ed. Harcourt 2004 386p $25

ISBN 0-15-101146-X LC 2004-47543

"British student Peter Hithersay learns on his sixteenth birthday that his real father was an East German political prisoner, and his life is never the same. Developing an obsession with all things German, he opts to attend medical school in Hamburg. Lured to Leipzig by a theatrical troupe and his own desire to see the scene of his mother and father's brief tryst, he ends up falling in love with a willful, passionate young woman nicknamed Snowleg. But at a crucial moment in their relationship, he fails her. For the next 20 years, he struggles on all fronts, succumbing to drug addiction and a series of empty affairs. Shakespeare paints an especially chilling picture of the repressed lives of East Germans, one in which a young girl's straightforward declaration of love takes on near-heroic stature. A beautifully written, utterly compelling story of love and politics." Booklist

Shalev, Tseruyah

Husband and wife; [by] Zeruya Shalev; translated from the Hebrew by Dalya Bilu. Grove Press 2002 311p $24

ISBN 0-8021-1718-X LC 2001-58479

"Na'ama is a social worker who heals ailing young mothers and their children, though she is unable to turn an observant eye on the lives of her own husband and child, or herself. When her husband, Udi, a healthy hiking guide who periodically leaves the family for long, solitary jaunts into nature, wakes up one morning unable to move his legs, Na'ama begins an inner monologue, wrestling over whether to take him to a hospital. . . or whether to keep him at home, where she and their nine-year-old daughter Noga can finally have a constant relationship with him." Publ Wkly

Shalev, Zeruya *See* Shalev, Tseruyah

Shames, Laurence

Mangrove squeeze. Hyperion 1998 309p $22.95

ISBN 0-7868-6301-3 LC 97-35880

"The Russian mafia is alive and well in Key West, operating a string of T-shirt shops as a cover for their more nefarious activities. Selling advertising space for the local newspaper, Suki Sperakis meets Lazslo Kalynin, who in a fit of lust reveals too much about the real business he and his Russian cohorts are conducting. Because Suki knows too much Lazslo is ordered to kill her. On the other side of town, Suki has met Aaron Katz, a former New Yorker renovating a guest house while taking care of his aging father. . . . [Shames] has included his signature cast of geriatric zanies and organized-crime types doing what they do best—causing mayhem and hilarity in the seemingly calm, sun-drenched streets of Florida." Libr J

Virgin heat; a novel. Hyperion 1997 274p $21.95

ISBN 0-7868-6203-3 LC 96-26804

"Beautiful Angelina, the slightly strange daughter of a mobster just out of prison, runs away from home to find her true love, the now—Key West bartender who betrayed her father years earlier. Once in town, Angelina hooks up with simpatico gay Michael—also looking for love. Angelina's concerned favorite uncle soon arrives, as does a government agent keeping tabs on the bartender. And Angelina's vengeful father cannot be far behind." Libr J

"The plot of this slapstick caper, a gravity-defying structure of impossible coincidences, has been built for fun, not analysis. But into this raucous hilarity Mr. Shames sneaks some nice observations on fading mobsters." N Y Times Book Rev

Welcome to paradise; a novel. Villard Bks. 1999 220p $22.95

ISBN 0-375-50252-1 LC 98-50785

This "caper novel finds Big Al Marracotta, a low-level mobster, vacationing in Key West while his rival, an equally inept thug, plots to have him bumped off. Stumbling into the fray is a nerdy furniture salesman from New Jersey who happens to have the same 'Big Al' license plate as his mobster namesake. The hitmen naturally confuse their Als, and the chaos begins." Booklist

Shames "is both hilariously funny as well as insightful in his handling of his characters." Libr J

Shamsie, Kamila, 1973-

Kartography. Harcourt 2002 305p $24

ISBN 0-15-101010-2 LC 2003-4989

"Karachi, Pakistan's largest city, is a place under constant siege: ethnic, factional, sectarian and simply random acts of violence are the order of the day. This violence—and the lingering legacy of the civil war of 1971—is the backdrop for the story of Raheen and Karim, a girl and boy raised together in the 1970s and '80s, whose lives are shattered when a family secret is revealed. . . . This is a complex novel, deftly executed and rich in emotional coloratura and wordplay." Publ Wkly

Shan Sa, 1972-

The girl who played go; translated from the French by Adriana Hunter. Knopf 2003 312p $22.95

ISBN 0-4000-4025-6

Original French edition, 2001

"When a young Japanese soldier meets a lovely 16-year-old Chinese girl playing Go in the Square of a Thousand Winds, they form a silent bond, meeting daily to play the game. As a fragmented China battles for her dignity, the 1930 Japanese occupation of Manchuria is in full force. The girl and the soldier are opponents in more than just a game of Go; they are on opposite sides of a deadly war in which their muted love receives a crushing blow." Booklist

"The alternating parallel tales add an extra spark of energy to this swift-moving novel, as Sa portrays tenderness and brutality with equal clarity." Publ Wkly

Shange, Ntozake

Betsey Brown; a novel. St. Martin's Press 1985 207p o.p.

LC 85-2663

The novelist presents "the life of a prosperous black family in St. Louis during 1957, the year of school desegregation. The story focuses on three generations of women, 13-year-old Betsey Brown and her mother and grandmother." Libr J

"Miss Shange is a superb storyteller who keeps her eye on what brings her characters together rather than what separates them: courage and love, innocence and the loss of it, home and homelessness. Miss Shange understands backyards, houses, schools and churches. [This novel] rejoices in—but never sentimentalizes—those places on earth where you are accepted, where you are comfortable with yourself." N Y Times Book Rev

Sassafrass, Cypress & Indigo; a novel. St. Martin's Press 1982 224p o.p.

LC 82-5565

This novel "tells of three sisters from Charleston, South Carolina. Indigo, the youngest, is full of magic and has trouble reconciling her inner worlds and reality. She bridges the gap with her poetry and her violin playing; both reveal an idiosyncratic style. Sassafrass, the oldest, writes and weaves, lives in Los Angeles with a man who seems a sometime thing, and tries to make sense of life, its connections and memories. Cypress is a dancer living in New York: 'when she danced, she was alive; when she danced, she was free.'" Publ Wkly

"Poetry, magical spells, recipes, and choreographs are woven into the narrative providing a vital interplay between the sisters and their creations. The setting of much of the story, Charleston, South Carolina, becomes a place of magic and joy for the reader." Libr J

Shannon, Dell, 1921-

Chaos of crime. Morrow 1985 190p o.p.

LC 84-22624

"A maniac is loose on the streets of Los Angeles, tying prostitutes to their beds, beheading them, disemboweling them, and then surgically dissecting them like laboratory animals. Detective Luis Mendoza and the Los Angeles Police Department are sufficiently stumped in trying to locate this madman who never leaves a clue—until finally the discovery of a rare French wristwatch helps to reveal a seemingly unlikely killer." Booklist

The Manson curse. Morrow 1990 262p o.p.

LC 90-36989

An American reporter based in London visits his novelist friend in Cornwall and becomes curious about the writer's obsession with the occult

Shannon, Doris

See also Giroux, E. X.

Shapiro, Fred R., 1954-

(ed) Trial and error. See Trial and error

Sharpe, Matthew, 1962-

The sleeping father; a novel. Soft Skull Press 2003 291p pa $14

ISBN 1-932360-00-X (pa) LC 2003-13840

"Divorced, depressed Bernard Schwartz is taking Prozac, but the accidental ingestion of another antidepressant lands him in a coma. His adolescent children, the conflicted and caustically witty Chris, and the serious, earnestly spiritual Cathy, must muddle through their father's helplessness in this character-driven tale." Publ Wkly

"Sharpe's arch tone is charmingly at odds with the sprawling, inclusive structure of 'The Sleeping Father.' His raised-eyebrow formality suggests a host surveying unwanted guests, yet he keeps waving more and more characters in the front door. He's a rare find: an ironist who actually seems to like other people." N Y Times Book Rev

Shaw, Irwin, 1913-1984

Beggarman, thief. Delacorte Press 1977 436p o.p.

LC 77-24523

Sequel to Rich man, poor man

"Wayward brother Tom Jordache has been murdered, leaving his son Wesley with a legacy of violence and revenge that is echoed in his nephew Billy, who becomes involved in a terrorist group in Brussels while serving in the U.S. Army. The story does not focus entirely on the second generation—the tangled lives of the older Jordaches are also featured. . . . Scenes from the earlier novel are interwoven allowing the unfamiliar reader to complete enjoyment and understanding." Booklist

Bread upon the waters. Delacorte Press 1981 438p o.p.

LC 81-3106

This novel "concerns the effects of misdirected philanthropy on a middle-class New York family—the Strands. Allen Strand is a history teacher at a public (state) school. His wife Leslie gives piano lessons to bring in extra money. Jimmy, their son, has ambitions to be a rock singer. The elder daughter, Eleanor, is an executive in a large corporation, and the younger daughter, Caroline is a sporty schoolgirl. One night Caroline . . . saves a millionaire called Russell Hazen from attack by a gang of muggers. She takes him home to have a wound dressed and Hazen is swiftly entranced by the warmth

Shaw, Irwin, 1913-1984—*Continued*
and harmony of the Strand family. His gratitude prompts him to set about making their dreams come true." Times Lit Suppl

Evening in Byzantium. Delacorte Press 1973 368p o.p.

The author writes of "a once-famous Hollywood producer, now 48, something of a has-been, who is reliving the past and preparing a final conquest of the future at the Cannes Film Festival. Jesse Craig is in trouble and he knows it. His marriage has been a failure, he is desperately fond of his daughter but cannot help her at a crisis moment in her own life, his attractive mistress is making demands he no longer cares to meet, and a shrewd, tough-minded young woman interviewer has him just where she wants him." Publ Wkly

Rich man, poor man. Delacorte Press 1970 723p o.p.

"A family chronicle which tells the story of the three children of Axel Jordache, a baker in a small town on the Hudson River. Thomas becomes a prizefighter, Rudolph a successful business man, and Gretchen eventually achieves a theatrical career after being seduced by the local mill-owner. . . . This is the dawn-to-dusk, 1940's-to-1970's, success-to-failure, poor-to-rich spectrum." N Y Times Book Rev

"Each member of the clan is doomed in one way or another. They fight, love, live hard and their fortunes are inevitably intertwined. Mr. Shaw has juxtaposed their rise and fall against a panoramic picture of the times. . . . This may not be great literature but it certainly has popular appeal." Publ Wkly

Followed by Beggarman, thief

Short stories: five decades. Delacorte Press 1978 756p o.p.

LC 78-16020

Contents: The eighty-yard run; Borough of cemeteries; Main currents of American thought; Second mortgage; Sailor off the Bremen; Strawberry ice cream soda; Welcome to the city; The girls in their summer dresses; Search through the streets of the city; The monument; I stand by Dempsey; God on Friday night; Return to Kansas City; Triumph of justice; No jury would convict; The lament of Madame Rechevsky; The deputy sheriff; Stop pushing, Rocky; "March, march on down the field"; Free conscience, void of offense; Weep in years to come; The city was in total darkness; Night, birth and opinion; Preach on the dusty roads; Hamlets of the world; Medal from Jerusalem; Walking wounded; Night in Algiers; Gunners' passage; Retreat; Act of faith; The man with one arm; The passion of Lance Corporal Hawkins; The dry rock; Noises in the city; The Indian in depth of night; Material witness; Little Henry Irving; The house of pain; A year to learn the language; The Greek general; The green nude; The climate of insomnia; Goldilocks at graveside; Mixed doubles; A wicked story; Age of reason; Peter Two; The sunny banks of the river Lethe; The man who married a French wife; Voyage out, voyage home; Tip on a dead jockey; The inhabitants of Venus; In the French style; Then we were three; God was here but he left early; Love on a dark street; Small Saturday; Pattern of love; Whispers in bedlam; Where all things wise and fair descend; Full many a flower; Circle of light

The young lions. Random House 1948 689p o.p.

"World War II changes the lives of Christian, ex-Communist and Nazi; Michael, a Broadway stage manager; and Noah, an American Jew married to a Christian woman. We follow their lives during the years 1938 to 1945 as they experience frustrations, hardships, and the dangers of the war. The three fight, and two are killed." Shapiro. Fic for Youth. 3d edition

Sheehan, Aurelie

The anxiety of everyday objects; a novel; Aurelie Sheehan. Penguin Books 2004 278p pa $14

ISBN 0-14-200370-0 (pa) LC 2003-49873

This novel is "set at the law firm of Grecko Mauster Crill, where Winona Bartlett toils as a secretary. She has the potential to be much more and, indeed, aspires to be a filmmaker. Her would-be film, entitled The Anxiety of Everyday Objects, centers on the theme of how people misreading something as simple as a street sign can gain significant insight into their lives. The only one who seems to see Winona's potential (other than Rex, the cute lawyer who has a crush on her) is the firm's new associate, Sandy Spires, who has been hired in conjunction with a case involving the beauty makeover consulting firm Lisa Box. Sandy–beautiful, glamorous, and blind–befriends Winona, treating her to a day at a spa and introducing her to a filmmaker. But as Winona becomes interested in Sandy as a subject for her film, she gradually realizes Sandy may be as manipulative as she is charming. A quirky, introspective novel about a creative woman finding her footing in a very corporate world." Booklist

Sheehan, Edward R. F.

Cardinal Galsworthy; a novel. Viking 1997 493p o.p.

ISBN 0-670-87392-6 LC 97-235

"When we first meet Larry . . . he is 26, living in his hometown of Winnipeg, Manitoba, pleased with his work as a floral designer, and not quite ready to admit that he is in love with his girlfriend, Dorrie. He never gets the chance to freely decide because Dorrie gets pregnant and they get married. His parents send them to England on their honeymoon, and Larry experiences crucial but unhelpful revelations about the nature of love, and more constructively, stumbles upon a passion that becomes his life's work: the design of hedge mazes." Booklist

"Shields extends . . . respect to even the novel's more minor characters, whose appearances, however fleeting, manage to imply whole, complicated, unique and always changing lives." Times Lit Suppl

Shelby, Philip

Days of drums; a novel. Simon & Schuster 1996 318p o.p.

LC 95-31045

"Rookie Secret Service agent Holland Tylo, daughter of the late Senator Beaumont, has a plum assignment in guarding Senator Westbourne during a meeting of Washington moguls at his estate. As she escorts the senator to his guest house for a late night tryst, he's suddenly shot dead, and her career with him. As the investigation pro-

Shelby, Philip—*Continued*
gresses, more bodies fall while a professional assassin stalks Washington. Holland becomes both hunter and hunted as she fights to vindicate herself and sort out the good guys from the bad." Libr J

"Shelby delivers an edge-of-the-seat page-turner with a likable cool-headed heroine." Booklist

Gatekeeper. Simon & Schuster 1998 331p $25
ISBN 0-684-84260-2 LC 97-39934

"Hollis Fremont, a functionary at the American embassy in Paris, is duped by her superior and boyfriend, Paul McGann, into accompanying a man she believes to be a small-fry criminal back to the States for country-club prison incarceration. In fact, the rumpled expat turns out to be 'the Handyman,' a freelance assassin on a mission. At Kennedy Airport the Handyman bolts and disappears, and Hollis falls under the protective wing of Sam Crawford (the Gatekeeper of the title), who is an agent for the mysterious Omega group. While the Handyman stalks his quarry around the Statue of Liberty, Hollis and her 'friends' . . . try to track him down." Publ Wkly

"Well-defined characters, compelling intrigue, and a crisp-paced plot whisk the reader along. And Hollis Fremont is no wimpy damsel in distress." Libr J

Sheldon, Alice Hastings Bradley *See* Tiptree, James, 1916-1987

Sheldon, Raccoona, 1916-1987
See also Tiptree, James, 1916-1987

Sheldon, Sidney, 1917-

Are you afraid of the dark?; by Sidney Sheldon. 1st ed. Morrow 2004 337p $25.95
ISBN 0-06-055934-9 LC 2004-42874

"Four scientists working for the New York-based Kingsley International Group have died or disappeared within 24 hours. Wolfish top boss Tanner Kingsley vows to find the perpetrator; meanwhile, stunning artist Diane Stevens, wife of a just-murdered KIG scientist, and supermodel Kelly Harris, whose husband has likewise been killed, find themselves under attack by mysterious strangers." Publ Wkly

"This novel is short on character development and long on cliched literary techniques, but it is, nevertheless, the best kind of guilty pleasure." Booklist

The doomsday conspiracy. Morrow 1991 412p $22
ISBN 0-688-08489-3 LC 91-12109

"Navy Commander Robert Bellamy is assigned to investigate the crash of a weather balloon in the Swiss Alps. All witnesses to the accident must be found and questioned. However, for Bellamy it is the beginning of a journey of terror into the incomprehensible. From Washington to London, Zurich, Rome, and Paris the story unfolds to reveal Bellamy's past—why the woman he loves most cannot return his love, why his friends become his deadly enemies, and why the world must never learn an incredible secret shielded by an unknown lethal force." Publisher's note

Master of the game. Morrow 1982 495p o.p.
LC 82-60920

"Kate Blackwell, born of a loveless marriage, striving through will, intelligence, and charm to control one of the richest conglomerates in the world, uses her power in wonderfully fiendish ways, which almost result in the destruction of those she loves most. The South African diamond mines provide vivid adventure; when the scene shifts to the United States, we encounter the more political maneuverings of business, but the pace never slackens." Libr J

Rage of angels. Morrow 1980 504p o.p.
LC 80-13328

"Young lawyer Jennifer Parker makes an incredible blunder in her first day as assistant D.A. Fired and in disgrace, she is reduced to serving writs to earn a living. Smart and stubborn, she perseveres, taking on unpromising clients. By inspired strategies of courtroom drama, she wins a few spectacular cases. Soon the world is taking notice, especially the Mafia. Their attractive offers are refused, but one day Parker must ask them for help in a desperate situation. In return, she becomes a Mafia mouthpiece, tempered somewhat by her love affair with the Mafioso." Libr J

Windmills of the gods. Morrow 1987 384p o.p.
LC 86-23593

The heroine of this novel is a "college lecturer from Kansas elevated to the politically volatile position of ambassador to Romania. Mary Ashley is plunged unaware into a cauldron of intrigue. Her surprise appointment, coming after the mysterious death of her husband, is the first stage in a newly elected president's plans to cement East-West relations. Up against Mary and the president are a secret alliance of political extremists and a ruthless international assassin known as Angel." Booklist

"The story speeds along and the epilogue is a chiller." Libr J

Shelley, Mary Wollstonecraft, 1797-1851

Frankenstein; or, The modern Prometheus; with an introduction by Wendy Lesser. Knopf 1992 xxxiii, 231p $15
ISBN 0-679-40999-8 LC 91-53195
"Everyman's library"
First published 1818

"The tale relates the exploits of Frankenstein, an idealistic Genevan student of natural philosophy, who discovers at the university of Ingolstadt the secret of imparting life to inanimate matter. Collecting bones from charnelhouses, he constructs the semblance of a human being and gives it life. The creature, endowed with supernatural strength and size and terrible in appearance, inspires loathing in whoever sees it." Oxford Companion to Engl Lit. 5th edition

Maurice; or, The fisher's cot; a tale; edited with an introduction by Claire Tomalin. Knopf 1998 179p il $20
ISBN 0-375-40473-2 LC 98-88124

The manuscript of this previously unpublished story was discovered in Italy in 1997. It "is the tale of a lost child and opens with a small boy in tears following a coffin. It is set on the coast in Devonshire. . . . It was written in Pisa in 1820, about a year after Mary Shelley

Shelley, Mary Wollstonecraft, 1797-1851—*Continued*
had lost her own child, little William Shelley, to a lethal fever. . . . The child in the story, Maurice, is befriended by a kindly old fisherman and is eventually found by his loving father." N Y Rev Books

Shepard, Sam, 1943-

Great dream of heaven; stories. Knopf 2002 142p $20
ISBN 0-375-40505-4 LC 2002-70054
Contents: The remedy man; Coalinga 1/2 way; Berlin Wall piece; Blinking eye; Betty's cats; The door to women; Foreigners; Living the sign; The company's interest; Concepción; It wasn't Proust; Convulsion; An unfair question; A frightening seizure; Tinnitus; The stout of heart; Great dream of heaven; All the trees are naked
"Each involving story is psychologically loaded, but what lassoes the reader is the tension between Shephard's acuity and tenderness, his high regard for the recklessness of life." Booklist

Shepherd, Michael *See* Ludlum, Robert, 1927-2001

Sher, Ira

Gentlemen of space. Free Press 2003 291p $23
ISBN 0-7432-4218-1 LC 2002-192807
This "novel is told from the perspective of Georgie Finch, whose father, Jerry—a high school science teacher—wins a trip to the moon. Jerry's rise to celebrity status as an astronaut brings a crowd of media and the curious, who suddenly disrupt the lives of Georgie and his mother, Barbara, in the small community of Magnolia Court, Fl. While Jerry is on the moon, Barbara learns that he had an affair with Georgie's babysitter, who is now pregnant." Libr J
"Sher's affection for his characters is clear, and they shine with softly absurd humor . . . and a DeLillo-like nostalgia for Americana and belief. This is a beautiful, eloquent first novel." Booklist

Sherman, Jory

The Baron war. Forge 2002 318p o.p.
ISBN 0-7653-0255-1 LC 2001-54750
"A Tom Doherty Associates book"
"Set in the lawless Texas landscape, this latest installment in Sherman's Baron series . . . reaches a watershed on the eve of the Civil War. Grieving the shameful death of his wife, Caroline, estranged patriarch Martin Baron must mend fences with his son, Anson—the new owner of the family's Box B Ranch—in order to face a deadly threat from a fractious neighbor, Matteo Aguilar. . . . Strong female characters and plenty of romance could help this title bridge the western gender gap." Publ Wkly

Sherrill, Martha

My last movie star; a novel of Hollywood. Random House 2003 349p $23.95
ISBN 0-375-50769-8 LC 2002-69707
"Fed up with her manipulative editor, entertainment journalist Clementine James is packing up to move to her boyfriend's Virginia farm when Flame magazine asks her to write an in-depth profile of captivating actress Allegra Coleman. When their interview ends in a car crash, Clementine awakes to find herself a celebrity. Allegra has vanished, and Clementine was the last person to see her. Allegra's disappearance catapults her into instant superstardom." Booklist
"The novel is as much a celebration of screen legends (buffs will be drawn to Sherrill's filmography) as it is a cautionary tale." N Y Times Book Rev

Sherwood, Frances, 1940-

The book of splendor. Norton 2002 348p $25.95
ISBN 0-393-02138-6 LC 2002-520
"A young, illiterate Jewess of dubious birth, given to fanciful stories, Rochel is able to escape poverty through an arranged marriage to Zev, a widowed tailor. This domestic scene is played out in the shadow of 17th-century imperial Prague alongside oppression and poverty during the reign of Habsburg Emperor Rudolph. . . . The characters include the famous Rabbi Loew, who fashions the man of mud, the Golom of Prague; astromomers Tycho Brahe and Johannes Kepler; the alchemists John Dee and Edward Kelley; and an assortment of spies, lepers, monks, and mountebanks." Libr J
This is a "provocative, gripping novel that's part farce, historical adventure, theological meditation, and bodice-ripping romance. Fans of magic realism will love this." Booklist

Shields, Carol

The republic of love. Viking 1992 366p o.p.
LC 91-16154
"Fay McLeod and Tom Avery are likable souls: kind to their parents, close to friends and co-workers, dedicated to their professions (she's a folklorist, he's a radio talk show host). But thus far both have been unlucky in love. Fay has never married; Tom has married and divorced rather too often. Participating on the periphery of lives of married friends has begun to pall. They finally meet, and it is a *coup de foudre* for both, but Fay is leaving that night for a month of mermaid research in Europe. Even when she returns, their affair is jeopardized by upheavals in others' lives." Libr J
"Not only are Fay and Tom exceptionally likable and capable of arresting insights, their worlds are complete and organic. Secondary characters are respectfully but economically drawn via short monologues, and the city of Winnipeg bustles in the background." Publ Wkly

The stone diaries. Viking 1994 361p il o.p.
LC 93-30239
This "novel provides, glancingly, a panorama of 20th-century life in North America. Written in a diary format, it traces the life of one seemingly unremarkable woman: Daisy Goodwill Flett, who is born in 1905 and lives into the 1990's." N Y Times Book Rev
This book is a "miraculous meeting of intellectual rigour and imaginative flow. On the one hand, it's a sharp-as-tacks investigation into the limits of the autobiographical form; on the other, a novel of effortless pleasure and sensuality. Daisy Goodwill . . . attempts intermittently to tell the story of a life remarkable only in its large tracts of ordinariness." New Statesman (1913)

Shields, Carol—*Continued*

Unless; a novel. Fourth Estate/HarperCollins Pubs. 2002 213p o.p.

ISBN 0-00-714107-6 LC 2002-19923

Reta Winters-loving helpmate "to a doctor, mother of three cheerful daughters, and author of a successful comic novel—has always considered herself happy, even blessed. Then her eldest child, nineteen-year-old Norah, briefly disappears and resurfaces as a panhandling mute on a Toronto street corner, holding up a homemade placard that says 'Goodness.' Shields's ability to use Reta's darkest fears to reveal the order lurking in chaos, without ever losing her light touch . . . is nothing short of astonishing." New Yorker

Shields, David

Dead languages; a novel. Knopf 1989 245p o.p.

LC 88-13444

This "coming-of-age novel, set in California, tells the . . . story of Jeremy Zorn, whose 1960s childhood is centered on one problem: his stuttering. Jeremy's highly literate parents, both journalists, use language to earn their living: 'My family was living in language whereas I was dying in it.' Jeremy's goal is to rid himself of the prison that words have made for him. Many of his cures are amusing (learning Latin, no need to articulate) or sad (love affairs with insensitive and inappropriate girls)." Booklist

"As touching and funny a rendering of adolescence as *The Catcher in the Rye.* Those recently emerged from adolescence will readily see its truth; the well read will delight at Shields's ability with narrative. But *Dead Languages* speaks to everyone who has ever struggled to articulate an emotion and failed to find the words." Libr J

Shigekuni, Julie

Invisible gardens. Thomas Dunne Bks. 2003 240p $23.95

ISBN 0-312-31183-4 LC 2003-41354

"Bittersweet story of a year in the life of Lily Soto, a Japanese American academic and mother of two young children who is married to a pathologist. The family lives in New Mexico, where Lily teaches at a college and her husband works at the morgue. Lily alternates between dutifully fulfilling her obligations as historian, wife, and mother and suffering a midlife crisis, which causes her to wonder about such basic issues as who she is and where she's headed." Libr J

"This is mostly a taut, well-modulated tale. Readers may be a bit baffled by the resolution, but Shigekuni beautifully describes Lily's subtle sense of isolation in her marriage." Publ Wkly

Shikibu, Murasaki *See* Murasaki Shikibu, b. 978?

Shippey, T. A. (Tom A.)

(ed) The Oxford book of science fiction stories. See The Oxford book of science fiction stories

Shirley, John, 1953-

Demons. Ballantine Pub. Group 2002 372p $25

ISBN 0-345-44647-X LC 2001-43478

"A Del Rey book"

This "apocalyptic tale, redolent with the terror of inexplicable carnage, is two novels in one: a first-person account of an initial advent of demons in everyday reality, followed by the story of their later return. Ira, narrator of the first, plays a significant role in the second, and Shirley links the two episodes nearly seamlessly. Ira reports a world gone mad with demonic possession, its people clinging to normality for dear life." Booklist

Shoemaker, Bill, 1931-

Stalking horse. Fawcett Columbine 1994 311p o.p.

LC 93-22125

Ex-jockey Coley Killebrew is enlisted by Raymond Starbuck, "the man who ruined his career to help stop an underworld takeover of one of the nation's great tracks. The assignment takes him to Louisiana's Magnolia Park, where he insinuates himself into a milieu of fast horses, even faster women, and a dangerous array of unsavory characters presided over by corrupt aristocrat Remy Courville." Booklist

"The plot is big, complicated and thoroughbred-fast as Coley's hard-boiled, first-person chapters alternate with a third-person focus on Starbuck. Shoemaker's characters provide the most fun." Publ Wkly

Shoemaker, Willie *See* Shoemaker, Bill, 1931-2003

Sholem Aleichem, 1859-1916

The adventures of Menahem-Mendl; translated from the Yiddish by Tamara Kahana. Putnam 1969 222p o.p.

Original Yiddish edition published 1909 in Russia

This book "consists of an exchange of letters between the hero and his . . . wife Sheineh-Sheindl, whom he has left behind looking after the children in their . . . native town of Kasrilevka while he tries to make his fortune in the big city—first Odessa, then Kiev. Menahem-Mendl is . . . [an] over-optimistic schemer who somehow contrives to make a living out of thin air; at one moment he is a currency speculator . . . then next a dabbler in commodities, after that a would-be broker, a journalist, a matchmaker, an insurance agent." N Y Rev of Books

The adventures of Mottel, the cantor's son; translated by Tamara Kahana; illustrated by Ilya Schor. Abelard-Schuman 1953 342p il o.p.

"The lighthearted humor of young Mottel, the narrator, adds a touch of pathos to the stories of an impoverished Jewish family in a European village, its wanderings in Europe en route to America, and finally its arrival and settlement in the U.S." Booklist

The best of Sholom Aleichem; edited by Irving Howe and Ruth R. Wisse. New Republic Bks. 1979 276p o.p.

Contents: The haunted tailor; A Yom Kippur scandal; Eternal life; Station Baranovich; The pot; The clock that struck thirteen; Home for Passover; On account of a hat; Dreyfus in Kasrilevke; Two anti-semites; A Passover expropriation; If I were Rothschild; Tevye strikes it rich;

Sholem Aleichem, 1859-1916—*Continued*
The bubble bursts; Chava; Get thee out; From Mottel the cantor's son; Bandits; The guest; The Krushniker delegation; One in a million; Once there were four

The further adventures of Menachem-Mendl; New York—Warsaw—Vienna—Yehupetz; translated by Aliza Shevrin. Syracuse Univ. Press 2001 172p $26.95
ISBN 0-8156-0677-X LC 00-55701
"Written in Yiddish in 1913 and only now translated into English, it's a sequel to *The Adventures of Menachem-Mendl*, which was first translated and published in the U.S. in 1969. Loosely based on Aleichem's experience, the story is told in the form of letters between Menachem-Mendl (who now has a job as a writer on a Warsaw newspaper) and his wife, Sheyne-Sheyndl, left behind with the children in a Kasrilevka village, where she faces crushing poverty and persecution." Booklist

The nightingale; or, The Saga of Yosele Solovey the cantor; translated by Aliza Shevrin. Putnam 1985 240p o.p.
LC 85-12073
Originally written in Yiddish and copyrighted 1917
"The cantor's son, Yosele Solovey, has a voice so lovely that he is called 'The Nightingale.' He is a timid lad, living in a small town (shtetl) that is peopled with earthy as well as flighty types. Innocently, he is introduced to nefarious pursuits like gambling and womanizing by a famous cantor who is a wheeler-dealer and whose influence creates havoc in Yosele's life and in the shtetl's, as well." West Coast Rev Books
This "is more than a popular novel; it is a social document, a study of a failed artist and, in its way, an early feminist work." N Y Times Book Rev

Tevye's daughters; translated by Frances Butwin. Crown 1949 302p o.p.
Contents: Bubble bursts; If I were Rothschild; Modern children; Competitors; Another page from The Song of Songs; Hodel; Happiest man in Kodno; Wedding without musicians; What will become of me; Chava; Joys of parenthood; Littlest of kings; Man from Buenos Aires; May God have mercy; Schprintze; The merrymakers; Easy fast; Little pot; Two shalachmones; Tevye goes to Palestine; Gymana-sia; Purim feast; From Passover to Succos; Get thee out; Passover expropriation; The German; Third class
Translated from the Yiddish, many of these stories are "about the seven daughters of Tevye the Dairyman and the life each chooses as she comes of age in Russia during the years preceding the first World War." Publ Wkly

Sholokhov, Mikhail Aleksandrovich, 1905-1984

And quiet flows the Don; [by] Mikhail Sholokhov; translated from the Russian by Stephen Garry. Knopf 1934 755p o.p.
"Set in the Don River basin of southwestern Russia at the end of the czarist period, the novel traces the progress of the Cossack Gregor Melekhov from youthful lover to Red Army soldier and finally to Cossack nationalist. War—in the form of both international conflict and civil revolution—provides the epic backdrop for the narrative and determines its tone of moral ambiguity." Merriam-Webster's Ency of Lit
Followed by The Don flows home to the sea

The Don flows home to the sea; [by] Mikhail Sholokhov; translated from the Russian by Stephen Garry. Knopf 1941 777p o.p.
This translation first published 1940 in the United Kingdom
This sequel to And quiet flows the Don, covers the period following the Revolution of 1917 to the end of the civil war in 1921. The narrative traces the fortunes of a group of Cossacks as they fight alternately with the Reds and the Whites
"It is a tale of misfortunes multiplied, yet a broad and earthy humor and the hearty Cossack gaiety break continuously over the grim surface. At the end the Cossack, with his intense individualism, his passionate love of the land, and his primitive pride, stands revealed." Nation
Followed by Seeds of tomorrow (1959)

Sholom Aleichem *See* Sholem Aleichem, 1859-1916

Shonk, Katherine

The red passport. Farrar, Straus & Giroux 2003 209p $22
ISBN 0-374-24847-8 LC 2003-7680
Contents: The death of Olga Vasilievna; Our American; The young people of Moscow; My mother's garden; Kitchen friends; The conversion; The wooden village of Kizhi; Honey month
In this "collection set primarily in post-Communist Russia, expatriates and natives alike endeavor to make their way in a new social and economic landscape, often sharing an intense desire for whatever the other possesses: money, freedom, love, family. . . . Shonk is at her best examining the lives of Americans whom the natives revere as potential saviors at the same time they dismiss them as frivolous tourists who could never hope to understand life in the former Soviet republic. That tension lends these stories an impressive vitality." Publ Wkly

Shreve, Anita, 1946-

All he ever wanted. Little, Brown 2003 310p $25.95
ISBN 0-316-78226-2 LC 2002-36847
"Escaping from a New Hampshire hotel fire at the turn of the 20th century, Prof. Nicholas Van Tassel catches sight of Etna Bliss and is instantly smitten. She does not reciprocate his feeling, for she has her own unrequited lust, for freedom and independence. That they marry guarantees tragedy. Nicholas tells the story in retrospect, writing feverishly on a train trip in 1933 to his sister's funeral in Florida." Publ Wkly
"Aside from an exchange of letters between his wife and his rival, everything is seen from the point of view of Nicholas, who grows increasingly jealous and pathetic, his motives couched in formal, self-justifying language that almost always sounds like a form of evasion. In the end, he admits, he's telling 'the story of a faintly ridiculous man,' but luckily it's a tale that also flirts with full-scale tragedy as well as the darkest kind of comedy." N Y Times Book Rev

Shreve, Anita, 1946-—*Continued*

Eden Close; a novel. Harcourt Brace Jovanovich 1989 265p $17.95

ISBN 0-15-127582-3 LC 89-34712

"As next-door neighbors, 'best buddies,' and then awkward adolescents, Eden and Andy find solace in each other's company until a tragic event occurs as Andy prepares to leave their small home town and heads off to college. The awful accident drives them apart, but then inadvertently draws them together again some 15 years later. Their relationship is rekindled when Andy returns home to attend his mother's funeral." Libr J

"'Eden Close' is not a novel of suspense but one of sensibility. Its insights are keen, its language measured and haunting. In it, a sense of loss and then of rupture is everywhere." N Y Times Book Rev

Fortune's Rocks; a novel. Little, Brown 2000 453p $24.95

ISBN 0-316-78101-0 LC 99-42665

The protagonist is "15-year-old Olympia Biddeford, the only child of wealthy, cultured, and well-meaning parents. It's summer, and the Biddefords have moved for the season into their New Hampshire seaside cottage. . . . [As the novel begins] Olympia suddenly senses that she is no longer a child. Even her father, who has been home-schooling her, detects something different about his smart and beautiful daughter as he instructs her to read a book of socially conscious essays written by Dr. John Haskell, who, along with his wife and children, will be their dinner guest. Olympia evinces no interest until she and Haskell—41, handsome, and intense—come face-to-face and are shot through with that awful current that signals love-at-first-sight. Their reckless affair precipitates a scandal of immense proportions, resulting in a harrowing separation and pregnancy." Booklist

"The level of suspense never falters, but becomes breathtaking during a custody court battle. . . . The astounding denouement of cascading events will leave no reader unmoved." Publ Wkly

The last time they met; a novel. Little, Brown 2001 313p $28

ISBN 0-316-78114-2 LC 00-53496

In this novel featuring Thomas Janes, first introduced in the author's The weight of water, "we learn the history of Thomas's great love with fellow poet Linda Fallon. The novel is told in reverse time, starting with the present, when Linda and Thomas, now in their fifties, reconnect at a literary festival. The middle section takes place in Africa, where the couple, then age 26, had a disastrous affair that horribly affected a number of loved ones and changed their own lives forever." Libr J

"Romantic regret is Anita Shreve's subject in this instantly captivating novel. . . . Fiction writers could go to school on Shreve's command of scene." Atl Mon

Light on snow; a novel; Anita Shreve. 1st ed. Little, Brown and Co 2004 305p $24.95

ISBN 0-316-78148-7 LC 2004-8907

"After retreating from a family tragedy to a house tucked away in the New Hampshire woods, 12-year-old Nicky and her father are thrust back into the world when one wintry afternoon they discover an abandoned newborn outdoors. How they deal with the reality of the baby's mother, who shows up at their house, and the detective who is hellbent on putting the pieces together is narrated by a now-adult Nicky looking back at her past." Libr J

"The story shifts brilliantly between childlike visions of a simple world and the growing realization of its cruel ambiguities. Aside from a few saccharine moments and a rather pat ending, Shreve does a skilled job of portraying grief, conflict and anger while leaving room for hope, redemption and renewal." Pub Wkly

The pilot's wife; a novel. Little, Brown 1998 293p $23.95

ISBN 0-316-78908-9 LC 97-51647

"Kathryn Lyons has just had the shock of her life. Roused from bed in the middle of the night, she has discovered that her husband, an airline pilot, has been killed in a crash. But Kathryn soon has a lot more to handle. A tape recovered from the plane suggests that husband Jack committed suicide, taking a planeload of people, with him, and the news is leaked to the press. As she scrambles to deal with importuning reporters, oily investigators, and her grieving daughter, Kathryn starts uncovering unsettling little facts." Libr J

"The climax, less dramatic than meditative, may strike some readers as too muted: understatement is one of this novel's strengths. What haunts us is the way Jack's secret life gradually weakens its hold on Kathryn's imagination and ours." Publ Wkly

Resistance; a novel. Little, Brown 1995 222p o.p.

LC 94-39269

"In December 1943, an American fighter plane is downed near a small village in Belgium. The pilot, Lt. Ted Brice, is rescued by a member of the local resistance movement. As he is hidden in the small attic at the home of Claire Daussois, he becomes acutely aware of the danger to himself as well as his hostess and her husband. A bond develops between Claire and Ted during his 20-day stay that changes both of their lives forever." SLJ

The author "adds subtle gray shadings to a familiar morality tale of good and evil, bravery and betrayal. In her vivid story, . . . Ms. Shreve questions the very nature of courage." N Y Times Book Rev

Sea glass; a novel. Little, Brown 2002 378p o.p.

ISBN 0-316-78081-2 LC 2002-20897

"The year is 1929 and Honora Beecher and her husband, Sexton, are just settling into a new marriage and a cottage on the coast of New Hampshire. While Honora fixes up the derelict house and searches for bits of sea glass on the beach, Sexton risks everything they own to buy the house they both love. Along with millions of other Americans, he is blindsided by the stock market crash and finds himself penniless. The only work he can find is in a nearby mill, where a labor conflict is erupting into violence." Publisher's note

"Shreve does not use her characters frivolously. They reveal who they are through their actions, with the author—who writes with admirable economy—rarely having to point a finger or underline the obvious. The true power of her novel comes from the appalling social conditions she describes so vividly, the grim but heroic lives her characters live." N Y Times Book Rev

Shreve, Anita, 1946-—*Continued*

Strange fits of passion; a novel. Harcourt Brace Jovanovich 1991 336p o.p.

LC 90-23874

This novel opens "with oblique hints of a violent event—here a murder committed by a woman in response to domestic abuse—then segues to flashbacks that slowly reveal the circumstances leading up to it. A reporter who wrote a book about the crime shares her notes, presented in alternating versions and voices. Most affecting is the voice of the accused woman, who flees Manhattan with her six-month-old daughter to seek sanctuary in a coastal Maine village where she is protected by the clannish but sympathetic townspeople. She finds temporary solace in an affair with a sensitive lobsterman, but is betrayed to her husband by another man out of jealousy." Publ Wkly

The weight of water. Little, Brown 1997 246p $22.95

ISBN 0-316-78997-6 LC 96-21326

"In 1873, two women living on the Isles of Shoals, a lonely, windswept group of islands off the coast of New Hampshire, were brutally murdered. A third woman survived, cowering in a sea cave until dawn. More than a century later, Jean, a magazine photographer working on a photoessay about the murders, returns to the Isles with her husband, Thomas, and their five-year-old daughter, Billie, aboard a boat skippered by her brother-in-law, Rich, who has brought along his girlfriend, Adaline. As Jean becomes immersed in the details of the 19th-century murders, Thomas and Adaline find themselves drawn together—with potentially ruinous consequences." Publ Wkly

"Deftly moving among almost as many plot lines as there are islands and employing at least two distinct voices, Ms. Shreve unravels themes of adultery, jealousy, crimes of passion, incest, negligence, loss and guilt, and then manages somehow to knit them all together into an engrossing tale." N Y Times Book Rev

Where or when; a novel. Harcourt Brace & Co. 1993 240p o.p.

LC 92-39392

"When 44-year-old real estate insurance salesman Charles Callahan sees a photograph of poet Siăn Richards, he recognizes her as the young woman he met three decades earlier at a Catholic camp for teenagers. Impulsively, he writes Siăn, and sets in motion the love affair they were destined to have. Though both are married and have children, each is unfulfilled, craving true partnership." Publ Wkly

The "two main characters are not presented in isolation, enveloped by a cloud of concupiscence. Instead, they are placed against a richly drawn background that encompasses everything from the grim reality of a deteriorating economy to the thin black dirt of the Richards farm." N Y Times Book Rev

Shreve, Susan Richards

A country of strangers. Simon & Schuster 1989 239p o.p.

LC 88-28735

"Outside of Washington, D.C., in the midst of World War II, Charley Fletcher strives to create a perfect community for himself and his family. He purchases a large rural estate, but, in doing so, has to confront the Bellows, the black tenants who have moved into the empty residence from their shacks on the property. Fletcher's awkward, friendly overtures are met with bewilderment and hostility, though his step-daughter, Kate, finally finds some success when she forms a deep alliance with Prudential Bellows, 13 years old and awaiting the birth of a child." Booklist

This is an "ambitious novel that attempts to create a parable of how racial harmony may be achieved. And, because of their youthful exuberance and quirkiness, Prudential and Kate are finally memorable characters." N Y Times Book Rev

Daughters of the new world. Doubleday 1992 471p o.p.

LC 91-8146

This "novel chronicles the lives of a remarkable family of women. The story begins with passionate Anna, a servant who marries the master's son; scandal drives the couple west. Daughter Amanda grows up with the Chippewe Indians and then, disguising herself as a man, becomes a photographer in France during World War I. Her daughter Sara, Sara's youngest daughter Eleanor, and Eleanor's two young daughters bring the novel into the present." Libr J

"As the novel unfolds and daughters become mothers, mothers grandmothers, grandmothers great-grandmothers, Shreve explores the wonder of personalities and genetics, the astonishing accommodation and resiliency of women, the courage and dignity of true love, and the surge of change that has driven this unlikely century. An enveloping, rewarding, and heroic tale told with great skill and much heart." Booklist

Plum & Jaggers; a novel. Farrar, Straus & Giroux 2000 228p o.p.

ISBN 0-374-23462-0 LC 99-47619

"Sam is the only one of the four McWilliams kids who can remember exactly what happened on the day their parents were killed in the terrorist bombing of a Rome-bound train. Their Scottish-born father and American mother had led the family on a carefree tour of the world, but after the tragedy, the kids–all under seven–are shipped off to their nice but vague grandparents in Grand Rapids. Years later, Sam turns his orphan family unit into a comedy team inspired by the missing parents, whose nicknames for each other were Plum and Jaggers. They are a big hit on late-night television." Booklist

Shreve "writes eloquently, painting a story of tragedy, obsession, love, and loss with a broad brush." Libr J

The visiting physician. Talese 1996 288p o.p.

LC 95-23877

"Twenty-odd years ago, Helen Fielding suffered severe trauma on a visit to her aunt in small-town Ohio when her toddler sister disappeared while in Helen's care. Now a doctor, Helen returns to Meridian as an outbreak of legionella threatens the town's children. One child is dead, another has disappeared, and so has the town doctor. Meridian itself has lost its collective innocence after being the subject of an unscrupulous TV director's documentary on the perfect small town. . . . A well-structured method of revealing the past adds to the story's appeal." Libr J

Shriver, Lionel

We need to talk about Kevin. Counterpoint 2003 400p $25

ISBN 1-58243-267-8 LC 2002-152753

"This is the story, narrated in the form of letters to her estranged husband, of Eva Katchadourian, whose son has committed the most talked-about crime of the decade—a school shooting reminiscent of Columbine." Libr J

"It's a harrowing, psychologically astute, sometimes even darkly humorous novel, with a clear-eyed, hard-won ending and a tough-minded sense of the difficult, often painful human enterprise." Publ Wkly

Shteyngart, Gary

The Russian debutante's handbook. Riverhead Bks. 2002 452p o.p.

ISBN 1-57322-213-5 LC 2001-47676

"Failurchka-Mother's Little Failure-is what Vladimir Girshkin's overweening Russian immigrant mother calls her 25-year-old son at the beginning of this picaresque . . . first novel. Vladimir is stuck in a dead-end job and saddled with girlfriend Challah, 'queen of everything musky and mammal-like.' Then through a series of chance encounters, he is catapulted to the eastern European city of 'Prava' to find himself welcomed into the fold of powerful Mafiosi." Libr J

"Shteyngart's playful, carnivalesque sensibility fits within a Russian satirical-fantastic tradition that stretches from Nikolai Gogol in the 19th century to Mikhail Bulgakov in the Stalin period and Vassily Aksyonov in the Soviet twilight. The sturdy conventions of the traditional novel . . . are blithely disregarded in favor of digressive, madcap inventiveness." N Y Times Book Rev

Shulman, Alix Kates

Memoirs of an ex-prom queen; a novel. Knopf 1972 274p o.p.

"In the third grade, tomboy Sasha realizes that 'there's only one thing worth bothering about: becoming beautiful,' and begins to apply herself to that end. At 15 she has succeeded: she is elected queen of the high school prom and loses her virginity the same evening, an occurrence not at all coincidental, since she measures beauty in terms of sex appeal. By her 25th birthday, she's had 25 lovers. Although she's intelligent (a Columbia Ph.D. candidate) and ambitious, she is unable to escape the trap she has set for herself. Her identity is determined only in terms of her femininity and her relationships with men. Her ideas and ambitions must be sacrificed to theirs, if necessary, and it always seems to 'be' necessary. Her decline from potential philosopher to typical housewife appears completed by the birth of her children, but age and fading looks finally prove to be her salvation." Publ Wkly

Shulman, Max, 1919-1988

The many loves of Dobie Gillis; eleven campus stories. Doubleday 1951 223p o.p.

Contents: Unlucky winner; She shall have music; Love is a fallacy; Sugar bowl; Everybody loves my baby; Love of two chemists; Face is familiar but—; Mock governor; Boy bites man; King's English; You think you got trouble

"Here are 11 short stories dealing with Dobie Gillis, of the crew cut set, and his adventures and misadventures on the Golden Gopher's campus. The stories appeared individually in the Saturday Evening Post, American Magazine and other periodicals. Most of the time Dobie is becoming infatuated or disinfatuated with one fair coed or another, and the woes and worries which these damsels bring with them supply obstacles for the nimble-witted freckled Casanova." San Francisco Chron

Rally round the flag, boys!. Doubleday 1957 278p o.p.

"The setting is a small Connecticut town where three ethnic groups struggle for dominance—the Commuters, the Italians, and the Yankee Natives. The establishment of a Nike base in the town leads to no end of hilarious complications." Libr J

"A bit of lusty fun at the expense of commuters, exurbian manners and mores, teen-age cults, Army red tape, progressive education, and whatever else catches the author's satiric eye." Booklist

Shute, Nevil, 1899-1960

The legacy; a novel. Morrow 1950 308p o.p.

Published in the United Kingdom with title: A town like Alice

A novel about a young British "girl who returns to the Far East to follow up people who had shared her horrible experiences as a Japanese prisoner. In so doing, she finds love and helps to rehabilitate an Australian ghost town." Libr J

On the beach. Morrow 1957 320p o.p.

"A nuclear war annihilates the world's Northern Hemisphere, and as atomic wastes are spreading southward, residents of Australia try to come to grips with their mortality. In spite of the inevitability of death, these people face their end with courage and live from day to day. They even plant trees they may never see mature." Shapiro. Fic for Youth. 3d edition

Siddons, Anne Rivers

Colony; a novel. HarperCollins Pubs. 1992 466p o.p.

LC 91-58357

"Muskrattish Maude Gascoigne, raised in the swamps, discovers the outer world on the fateful night her older brother brings home a Princeton buddy, Bostonian Peter Chambliss, to escort her to the traditional St. Cecilia's coming-out ball in Charleston. Instant and deep, her love for Peter catapults her into the highly structured world of the summering place called 'Retreat.' This saga of three generations of Chamblisses culminates in Maude's desperate struggle to protect and pass the legacy on to her granddaughter before the place is destroyed." Booklist

"Ms. Siddons portrays children paying for the mistakes of their parents, and sees patterns of behavior being passed from one generation to the next. Most of all, she explores the complex, often unpredictable, nature of love. To her credit, these themes are never presented in a heavy-handed fashion; they never interfere with the enjoyment of a well-told story." N Y Times Book Rev

Siddons, Anne Rivers—*Continued*

Downtown; a novel. HarperCollins Pubs. 1994 374p o.p.

LC 94-9202

"Protagonist Maureen 'Smoky' O'Donnell emerges from the Savannah docks to write for Atlanta's award-winning *Downtown* magazine. Mentored by the charismatic editor-in-chief, Smoky gets awards for covering the city's war on poverty. As the novel gains momentum, she dumps wealthy Brad to find adventure with Freedom Summer veteran Lucas—only to lose him to the war in Vietnam." Libr J

"What's intriguing about Siddons is how much she transcends the usual parameters of fluff fiction, both in terms of literary finesse and penetrating intelligence." Booklist

Fault lines; a novel. HarperCollins Pubs. 1995 327p o.p.

LC 95-32157

A novel about three Southern women "who have failed to find internal happiness. Merritt Fowler has spent her entire life in the role of caretaker. After the death of her mother, Merritt provides for her naïve and illustrious sister, Laura, who longs to be an actress. But when Merritt meets Pomeroy (Pom) Fowler, the doctor on a crusade to save the world, Laura exits her life. Soon Merritt finds herself taking care of Pom's two sons; his aging, senile mother; and their daughter, Glynn, who is battling anorexia. When Pom's mother lights all Glynn's clothes on fire, the young woman flees to California to seek solace with her Aunt Laura. Merritt soon follows, and there the three women attempt to rectify their tormented relationships. Siddons keeps readers absorbed until the climactic ending." Libr J

Heartbreak Hotel. Simon & Schuster 1976 252p o.p.

"Maggie Deloach, a Southern beauty of the 50s, seems well on the way to success Dixie-style. Sorority girl, well-born, a leader, she is pinned to Boots Claiborne, scion of an old land-owning Delta family. It would seem that marriage and a happy-ever-after life are ahead of her. But Randolph University exposes her to more that frat parties and frivolity. A professor, a reporter and a student from New Jersey sow the seeds of questions. A visit to Boot's family and an ugly incident there make Maggie's questions more insistent and, for her, unnerving since they not only challenge her carefully planned future, but reveal stirring in the South she had never anticipated." Publ Wkly

Hill towns; a novel. HarperCollins Pubs. 1993 356p o.p.

LC 92-54720

"An American couple reassess their marriage as they travel from the 'hilltowns' of North Carolina to the 'hilltowns' of Italy. While college professor Hays Bennett seemed dashing stateside, wife Cat finds that he suddenly pales in comparison with a sexy painter they meet." Libr J

This novel features the "heady atmospheres of Rome, Venice, and the hill towns of Tuscany. Siddons is keenly attuned to the power of these fabled locales and brilliantly describes them as bewitched and perversely saturated with both beauty and death." Booklist

Homeplace; a novel. Harper & Row 1987 330p o.p.

LC 86-46099

"Micah Winship is a successful journalist living in New York City, a troubled childhood in small-town Georgia far behind her. Her father's illness, however, brings her back to the home she had fled in fury and disgrace 20 years earlier in the wake of a family storm concerning Micah's growing interest in the Civil Rights Movement. Now, in this hot summer visit, the past encroaches on the present, and Micah is drawn back into the family politics and sexual drama of her adolescence." Libr J

"About love and death, greed and passion, the pull of family and the push of self, *Homeplace* is a deeply moving story of a fierce and necessary forgiveness." Publ Wkly

Islands; Anne Rivers Siddons. 1st ed. HarperCollins 2004 374p $24.95

ISBN 0-06-621111-5 LC 2003-51139

"When Charleston protagonist Anny Butler marries Dr. Lewis Aiken, she becomes a member of the 'Scrubs' a longtime group of friends who all have medical connections. For years, they share their free time together at a communal beach house. Then misfortune begins to plague the group, resulting in three deaths. . . . Gaynelle Toomer, a Harley-riding, freckle-faced, enormous-breasted librarian, is hired to do odd jobs for the Scrubs. She and her seven-year-old daughter, Britney, a beauty pageant contestant regular, become constant companions to Anny's frail friend, Camilla. Camilla, the stabilizing force of this group, turns out to be not at all what she appears, making the story's end a shocker." Libr J

King's oak; a novel. Harper & Row 1990 623p o.p.

LC 89-46116

"Moving with her daughter to elite Georgia hunt country, Andy Calhoun is drawn . . . to Tom Dabney, a 'crazy' man passionately committed to the primeval woods where he lives. Finally succumbing to her attraction to Tom, she becomes involved with his efforts to save the woods from the nuclear wastes emanating from the Big Silver nuclear weapons plant." Libr J

The author "does know how to endow a story with undeniable narrative drive." N Y Times Book Rev

Nora, Nora; a novel. HarperCollins Pubs. 2000 263p $25

ISBN 0-06-017613-X LC 00-40996

"In 1961, Nora, an outrageous, exotic, outspoken woman who smokes cigarettes and drives a pink Thunderbird, arrives in the sleepy, segregated town of Lytton, GA. While some residents are ruffled by her 'unsouthern' behavior, the effect Nora has on her adolescent and impressionable cousin Peyton is electric, opening Peyton's senses to the world around her." Libr J

"In addition to her impeccable re-creation of Southern speech and atmosphere, Siddons captures the angst of adolescence with practiced skill." Publ Wkly

Outer banks; a novel. HarperCollins Pubs. 1991 400p o.p.

LC 90-56370

"Kate Abrams hasn't spoken to three of her sorority sisters for 28 years. But now Ginger, the eager rich girl who stole and married Kate's brilliant boyfriend, is host-

Siddons, Anne Rivers—*Continued*

ing a reunion at her home in Nags Head, N.C. And Cecie, the orphan whose wit and cynical reserve attracted Kate, and Fig Newton, the unsightly and bumbling outcast, will both attend. . . . The narrative flows smoothly, journeying seamlessly between places and eras. While the pseudo-thriller ending seems pat, Siddons displays real strength in her subtle characterizations and delineation of emotional nuances." Publ Wkly

Peachtree Road; a novel. Harper & Row 1988 566p o.p.

LC 88-45060

"Sheppard Gibbs Bondurant 3d, the benumbed, reclusive son of an aristocratic Georgia family, narrates the tale, which spans some 40-odd years of life on Peachtree Road, the axis of Atlanta's exclusive Buckhead section. Baroque rituals precisely dictate the pattern of Buckhead's social fabric, and Shep devotes his life to protecting his beloved cousin Lucy from these censorious standards." N Y Times Book Rev

"An ambitious and masterful work with a sharp vision." Booklist

Sweetwater Creek; a novel. HarperCollins 2005 356p $24.95

ISBN 0-06-621335-5 LC 2005-46279

"Twelve-year-old Emily Parmenter helps in the family business of raising hunting spaniels at their Charleston area plantation, Sweetwater Farm. Her only pals are her own dog, Elvis, and her deceased older brother, Buddy (who speaks to her from the grave). But her life is about to change radically with the arrival of rich, sophisticated 20-year-old Lulu Foxworth. During her visit to the plantation, she falls in love with the dogs and Emily's family before moving in. . . . Under Lulu's tutelage, Emily leaves her child's world and enters one for which she's not quite ready. As usual, Siddons never lets you forget where you are–the essence of South Carolina's Low Country is prominently featured and intricately . . . described." Libr J

Sidor, Steven

Skin River; Steven Sidor. 1st St. Martin's Minotaur ed, 1st U.S. ed. St. Martin's Minotaur 2004 241p $23.95

ISBN 0-312-32949-0 LC 2004-46784

"When a psychotic almost kills the single-mother/waitress who lives above his rural Wisconsin tavern, Buddy Bayes goes ballistic. Buddy recently found the severed hand of a different victim, and because of his own former criminal life in Chicago, he feels both attacks may be a message for him. So he secretly returns to the Windy City to see if there's still a contract on him, while back in Wisconsin the serial killer continues to operate with chilling immunity. Deft descriptions, slick prose, and growing tension mark this first novel." Libr J

Siegel, Barry

Actual innocence. Ballantine Bks. 1999 280p $24.95

ISBN 0-345-41309-1 LC 99-31266

California attorney Greg Monarch "is asked to defend his onetime lover, Sarah Trant, who's on Death Row for killing a man. Greg's extremely reluctant to get reinvolved with Sarah, whose emotional instability and bizarre behavior nearly ruined him years ago. But there's something compelling about the case that Greg can't resist. Once he arrives in El Nido, the isolated valley town where the murder occurred, Greg finds a web of corruption blocking his path to the truth." Booklist

"Though some of the plot turns are predictable, Siegel beautifully captures the flavor of scandal in a small community—the knowing looks, the awkward silences, the amateur attempts at coverup. The novel ends, appropriately, not with big-city drama, but with a quiet, small town America nod-nod-wink-wink deal." Publ Wkly

Siegel, James, 1954-

Derailed. Warner Bks. 2003 339p $23.95

ISBN 0-446-53158-8 LC 2002-73572

Charles Schine "writes advertising copy and worries a lot about his stressed-out wife and diabetic daughter. Charles makes his fatal mistake one morning on the 9:05 commuter train from Babylon to Penn Station, when he looks up from his newspaper. . . and makes eye contact with a beautiful stockbroker named Lucinda. One thing leads to another, but their hotel tryst is interrupted by an armed intruder who rapes Lucinda, pistol-whips Charles and proceeds to blackmail them. Desperate, Charles resorts to criminal measures to stop this sadistic torment." N Y Times Book Rev

"With its clean prose, high-velocity plotting and just the right amount of emotional shading darkening its sharply drawn characters, this novel is the bomb." Publ Wkly

Siegel, Lee

Love and other games of chance; a novelty. Viking 2003 418p $27.95

ISBN 0-670-89461-3 LC 2002-29635

This novel is "organized as a game of Snakes and Ladders, with each chapter representing a square on the game board; the reader can choose between a traditional reading, from start to finish, and a playful one, letting the roll of the dice decide. The story follows Isaac Schlossberg, a swindler, circus performer and entertainer. As Schlossberg travels around the world (and across the board), his stunts—from childhood appearances in sideshow acts with his Jewish immigrant parents at the turn of the century to his attempts to beat Sir Edmund Hillary to the top of Mount Everest—are woven together into one exceptionally tall tale." Publ Wkly

Siegel, Sheldon

Final verdict. Putnam 2003 391p $25.95

ISBN 0-399-15042-0 LC 2002-37189

This legal procedural features "law partners Mike Daley and ex-wife Rosie Fernandez working together in their San Francisco firm, Fernandez, Daley and O'Malley. . . . Skid row resident Leon Walker, successfully represented by Michael and Rosie in a murder case 10 years earlier, reappears and seeks legal help once again. Leon is charged with the murder of Tower Grayson, a Silicon Valley venture capitalist found stabbed to

Siegel, Sheldon—*Continued*

death in a Dumpster behind a liquor store. Publ Wkly

"An ending that's full of surprises—both professional and personal—provides the perfect finale to a supremely entertaining legal thriller." Booklist

Sienkiewicz, Henryk, 1846-1916

The deluge; in modern translation by W. S. Kuniczak. Copernicus Soc. of Am. 1991 2v o.p.
LC 91-5047

Original Polish edition, 1886

In this second volume of the trilogy "a mere five years have passed since the knights of the Polish-Lithuanian Commonwealth threw back the Cossack invasion from the East, yet a new and far more dangerous threat appears: Swedish troops are pouring across the Northern border. . . . Central to the story is Andrei Kmita, a young Lithuanian noble whose ruthlessness obscures his military sagacity and bravery, branding him an outlaw. But for the love of the beautiful Olenka, he undertakes to reshape his character in the forge of battle, and in so doing helps save king, country, and church from the heretic invaders." Libr J

Followed by Fire in the steppe

Fire in the steppe; in modern translation by W. S. Kuniczak. Copernicus Soc. of Am.; distributed by Hippocrene Bks. 1992 717p $24.95
ISBN 0-7818-0025-0 LC 92-218600

Original Polish edition, 1887

"The Polish people's struggle against Cossacks, Tartars and Turks in the 1670s prefigures modern Poland's quest for nationhood in this [final] installment of the rousing epic of love, war, adventure and madness. Basia, the gutsy, bright, determind heroine, who chases bandits on horseback, riding a man's saddle, almost steals the show from her Hamlet-like husband, Col. Pan Volodyovski." Publ Wkly

This "is an unabashed, extravagant celebration of romance and patriotism, but with a difference: the novel ends with wrenching scenes of Polish nobility, courage and hope in the face of defeat—showing why Sienkiewicz's trilogy is so beloved in his native country." N Y Times Book Rev

Quo Vadis; a narrative of the time of Nero; translated from the Polish by Jeremiah Curtin. Little, Brown 1896 541p o.p.

A historical novel dealing with the "Rome of Nero and the early Christian martyrs. The Roman noble, Petronius, a worthy representative of the dying paganism, is perhaps the most interesting figure, and the struggle between Christianity and paganism supplies the central plot, but the canvas is large. A succession of characters and episodes and, above all, the richly colorful, decadent life of ancient Rome give the novel its chief interest. The beautiful Christian Lygia is the object of unwelcome attentions from Vinicius, one of the Emperor's guards, and when she refuses to yield to his importunities, she is denounced and thrown to the wild beasts of the arena. She escapes and eventually marries Vinicius, whom Peter and Paul have converted to Christianity." Reader's Ency. 4th edition

With fire and sword; in modern translation by W.S. Kuniczak; foreword by James A. Michener. Copernicus Soc. of Am. 1991 1135p o.p.
LC 91-161

Original Polish edition, 1883

"The first book in a trilogy covering Polish history from 1648 to 1673. The novel's main stage is occupied by the Ukrainian cossacks' rebellion against the Poles. Yan Skshetuski, a Polish lieutenant dispatched to gather information about the rebellion, is taken prisoner by the cossacks. After numerous battles, retreats, and betrayals on both sides, the revolt culminates in the cossacks' siege of the city of Zbaraz." Booklist

This novel "should have taken place in the general literary repertory long ago, alongside the works of the elder Dumas, Walter Scott, Margaret Mitchell." N Y Times Book Rev

Followed by The deluge

Silber, Joan

Ideas of heaven; a ring of stories. W.W. Norton 2004 250p $23.95
ISBN 0-393-05908-1 LC 2003-24324

Contents: My shape; The high road; Gaspara Stampa; Ashes of love; Ideas of heaven; The same ground

"Six elegantly connected stories explore, through first-person narratives, the conflicts and commonalities of love, faith and sex. A minor character in the first story becomes the narrator in the second, and so on, with each story building on its predecessor until they come full circle. . . . Silber uses the device of interwoven narratives beautifully; these lengthy stories can stand alone, but the subtle connections and emotional resonances help create a satisfying structural unity." Publ Wkly

Siler, Jenny

Flashback; Jenny Siler. 1st ed. Holt & Co. 2004 259p $25
ISBN 0-8050-7211-X LC 2003-55254

"'Eve' is found unconscious in a field in Burgundy, France; the shot to the head that put her there destroyed most of her personal memories. The only remnants of her past are a ferry ticket with Arabic letters, physical evidence that she has had a child, and recurring dreams of confused violence. When thugs kill the nuns who have taken Eve in, she is forced to flee France in a desperate attempt to unravel the mystery of her identity. Using the ferry ticket as a lead, Eve travels to North Africa in search of herself, only to find violence, death, and mystery." Libr J

"In Flashback, Siler darkens the lost-identity theme and transfers the action to exotic locations in Morocco, lending a Hitchcock-like sense of disorientation to a story of international espionage that is thick with atmosphere." N Y Times Book Rev

Silko, Leslie, 1948-

Gardens in the dunes; a novel; [by] Leslie Marmon Silko. Simon & Schuster 1999 479p $25
ISBN 0-684-81154-5 LC 98-51987

Set in the 19th century this is the "tale of two sisters, the last remaining members of the ancient Sand Lizard tribe. Sister Salt, so called for her light skin, and her

Silko, Leslie, 1948-—*Continued*

younger sister, Indigo, learn all about the hidden, life-sustaining plants of the desert from Grandma Fleet, who teaches them how to live happily with a minimum of material goods and a wealth of knowledge. Such self-sufficiency is essential if they are to stay free from the misery of reservation life, but even so their liberty is put at risk when they travel to the mean little town of Needles, Arizona, where hundreds of Indians gather to dance in anticipation of the arrival of the Messiah. In the chaotic aftermath of the miraculous visitation, the girls lose their mother and grandmother and then are cruelly separated by the authorities." Booklist

Sillitoe, Alan

The loneliness of the long-distance runner. Knopf 1960 c1959 176p o.p.

First published 1959 in the United Kingdom

Contents: The loneliness of the long-distance runner; Uncle Ernest; Mr. Raynor the schoolteacher; The fishing-boat picture; Noah's ark; On Saturday afternoon; The match; The disgrace of Jim Scarfedale; The decline and fall of Frankie Buller

"This collection of short stories portrays life from the point of view of the English working class. The unnamed narrator in the title story, which is probably the best known in the book, is a roguish young man who has been in trouble with authority all his life. He is told by the head of a Borstal institution where he is an inmate that he can reform himself by training to be a long-distance runner. He enters into training, and during practice runs, his thoughts go back to the circumstances that led to his detention. The climax of the story is in a track meet between his penal institution and a private school. The boy easily outruns his competitors but pulls up at the finish line and refuses to cross it, thus revenging himself against the head of the institution and spoiling the victory of the other school." Shapiro. Fic for Youth. 3d edition

Saturday night and Sunday morning. Knopf 1959 c1958 239p o.p.

First published 1958 in the United Kingdom

This novel's "protagonist, anarchic young Arthur Seaton, lathe operator in a Nottingham bicycle factory, provided a new prototype of the working class Angry Young Man; rebellious, contemptuous towards authority in the form of management, government, the army, and neighbourhood spies, he unleashes his energy on drink and women, with quieter interludes spent fishing in the canal. . . . A landmark in the development of the post-war novel." Oxford Companion to Engl Lit. 6th edition

Silone, Ignazio, 1900-1978

Bread and wine; a new version translated from the Italian by Harvey Fergusson II; with a new preface by the author. Atheneum Pubs. 1962 331p o.p.

First published 1937 in the United States by Harper

"Translated from the edition revised by the author to modify the political concepts of the original." Publ Wkly

"The hero, Pietro Spina, returns to his native Abruzzi after fifteen years of exile to continue his antifascist agitation. As he travels through the country, disguised as a priest, he sees the inroads made upon the Italian character by Mussolini's rule. Finding that the underground movement is in chaos and doubting the validity of his old revolutionary slogans, he eventually flees to avoid certain arrest." Reader's Ency. 4d edition

Followed by The seed beneath the snow (1942)

Silva, Daniel

The marching season; a novel. Random House 1999 418p $25.95

ISBN 0-375-50089-8 LC 98-53464

This "thriller follows Michael Osbourne, a retired C.I.A. officer, as he is forced back into his former trade. His mission: to protect his father-in-law, the newly appointed American Ambassador to London, from assassination at the hands of a rogue Protestant faction opposed to the Good Friday accords for peace in Ireland. Stepping in to support this faction—and to assist in the assassination plot—is the Society for International Development and Cooperation, a shadowy organization of powerful arms dealers, intelligence operatives and crime associations." N Y Times Book Rev

The mark of the assassin; a novel. Villard Bks. 1998 465p $25

ISBN 0-679-45563-9 LC 98-5268

"When an airliner is shot down after taking off from New York's Kennedy Airport, an Islamic terrorist group called the Sword of Gaza is immediately blamed for the crime. But CIA operative Michael Osbourne suspects a different perpetrator, a lone assassin with the code name October who, years earlier, took the life of Osbourne's girlfriend in a London confrontation." Publ Wkly

"With concise, vivid character sketches, Silva weaves a swiftly paced, internationally tangled plot." Libr J

Prince of Fire. Putnam 2005 369p $25.95

ISBN 0-399-15243-1 LC 2004-60066

"Not long after an explosion in Rome destroys the Israeli embassy compound, a file linked to the terrorists behind the bombing surfaces; it contains a remarkably comprehensive account of the career of Gabriel Allon, including the date of his recruitment by the Israeli secret service. Living in Venice and about to embark upon the restoration of a priceless Rubens painting, Gabriel, a talented art restorer and a reluctant spy, must return to Israel and the auspices of the agency bureaucrats. He is assigned the task of identifying the bombers, which eventually results in a face-to-face meeting with Yassar Arafat, the man responsible for the death of Gabriel's child and the maiming of his wife some 10 years earlier. He suspects that Arafat is deeply connected to the Rome bomber, whom Gabriel believes is a third-generation terrorist who has been protected and schooled as a mastermind by Arafat himself. Along with the meticulously detailed plot, Silva . . . provides a clear-eyed chronicle of the endless warfare between the Israelis and the Palestinians." Booklist

The unlikely spy. Villard Bks. 1996 481p o.p.

LC 96-27961

"Alfred Vicary, the hero of Daniel Silva's spy thriller, is a meek, balding historian drafted into British intelligence by his pal Winston Churchill and given the job of keeping one of the most crucial secrets of World War II from falling into Nazi hands: Operation Mulberry, the

Silva, Daniel—*Continued*
Allied plan to build two huge artificial harbors in southern England, then drag them across the Channel after D-Day. Vicary's chief opponent is the beautiful Catherine Blake, a volunteer nurse in a London hospital who is actually a ruthless German agent." N Y Times Book Rev

"The contest of minds and wills between Blake and Vicary—each holding millions of lives and the future of their respective countries at stake—is riveting, intriguing, and suspense-filled." Booklist

Silverberg, Robert

The collected stories of Robert Silverberg. v1: Secret sharers. Bantam Bks. 1992 546p o.p.
LC 92-9958

Contents: Homefaring; Basileus; Dancers in the time-flux; Gate of horn, gate of ivory; Amanda and the alien; Snake and ocean, ocean and snake; Tourist trade; Multiples; Against Babylon; Symbiont; Sailing to Byzantium; Sunrise on Pluto; Hardware; Hannibal's elephants; The pardoner's tale; The iron star; The secret sharer; House of bones; The dead man's eyes; Chip runner; To the promised land; The Asenion solution; A sleep and a forgetting; Enter a soldier. Later: enter another

Downward to the Earth
In Silverberg, R. A Robert Silverberg omnibus

Gilgamesh the king. Arbor House 1984 320p o.p.
LC 84-12434

"Fantasy, myth, and ancient history interweave seamlessly in this powerful retelling of the epic of Gilgamesh, the Sumerian god-king who sought eternal life and found instead the bitter wisdom of mortality. Silverberg extends his mastery of the fantasy genre to the re-creation of the magic and mystery of ancient Sumer, uncovering the deep human truths that lie beneath the legend. Elegantly written." Libr J

The king of dreams. HarperCollins Pubs. 2001 451p $25
ISBN 0-06-105171-3 LC 00-46648

"With the death of Confalume, the Coronal Prestimion prepares to assume the position of Pontifex and retire from the world, turning his duties over to his designated heir, Lord Dekkeret. However, the emergence of an ancient evil to threaten the lands of Majipoor demands desperate measures as Prestimion and Dekkeret risk their destinies for the safety of their realm. . . .The author's graceful style and narrative talent once more creates a world of genuine wonder and adventure." Libr J

The longest way home. Eos 2002 294p $25.95
ISBN 0-380-97858-X LC 2001-55601

"Joseph Master Keilloran, young heir to the great House Keilloran, is visiting relatives 10,000 miles from home when a rebellion of the serflike Folk turns his world—a planet conquered long ago by his ancestors—upside down. Joseph, who has never questioned the wealth and privilege to which he was born, barely escapes with his life. Cut off from all sources of comfort and support, he decides to walk home, across a huge continent he knows almost nothing about." N Y Times Book Rev

"While neither the protagonist of this bildungsroman nor his transformation is remarkable, the land that our young hero journeys through and the exotic creatures that inhabit it testify to the author's rich imagination." Publ Wkly

Lord Valentine's castle. Harper & Row 1980 449p o.p.
LC 79-2658

"Majipoor is an enormous planet inhabited by intelligent beings and ruled by a benevolent lord. . . . The story begins as Valentine, a young amnesiac, wanders into the city of Pidruid in time for a festival celebrating a once-in-a-lifetime visit of another Valentine, Lord Valentine, the supreme ruler of the planet. Early in the book readers know what Valentine is slow to understand; he is the real Lord Valentine and the one in power is an imposter. On a coming-of-age journey to Lord Valentine's Castle, gathering friends, supporters, and ultimately troops en route, Valentine discovers his true identity and gains a better understanding of the people and place he is destined to rule. A good story, inventively told, which abounds with adventure and curious characters." SLJ

Followed by Majipoor chronicles

Majipoor chronicles; a novel. Arbor House 1982 314p il o.p.
LC 81-67589

In this sequel to Lord Valentine's castle, the protagonist is "a bored teenage clerk in the House of Records who risks his job and more by delving into forbidden records of the Registry of Souls. This Registry holds every minute, every experience of billions of inhabitants of Majipoor since it was colonized thousands of years ago. By calling up a record, he is given the opportunity to live episodes from the lives of famous and ordinary people of both sexes." SLJ

"Majipoor is probably the finest creation of Silverberg's powerful imagination and certainly one of the most fully realized worlds in modern sf." Booklist

Followed by Valentine Pontifex

The man in the maze
In Silverberg, R. A Robert Silverberg omnibus

The mountains of Majipoor. Bantam Bks. 1995 225p o.p.
LC 94-28950

Sequel to Valentine Pontifex

"Exiled to Majipoor's forsaken borderlands for an act of youthful folly, Prince Harpirias accepts—with considerable misgivings—a final chance to redeem his past disgrace by accepting a mission to rescue a group of hostages from the hostile barbarians who inhabit the icy mountains at Majipoor's end. . . . Silverberg transforms an otherwise standard coming-of-age story into an allegorical rite of passage." Libr J

Nightwings [novelette]
In The Hugo winners p503-57
In Silverberg, R. Phases of the moon
In Silverberg, R. A Robert Silverberg omnibus

Phases of the moon; stories of six decades. Subterranean Press 2004 625p $40
ISBN 1-931081-99-9

Silverberg, Robert—*Continued*

Contents: Road to nightfall; The Macauley circuit; Sunrise on Mercury; Warm man; To see the invisible man; Flies; Passengers; Nightwings [novelette]; Sundance; Good news from the Vatican; Capricorn games; Born with the dead; Schwartz between the galaxies; The far side of the bell-shaped curve; The Pope of the chimps; Needle in a timestack; Sailing to Byzantium; Enter a soldier. Later: enter another; Hunters in the forest; Death do us part; Beauty in the night; The Millennium Express; With Caesar in the underworld

"One of the great rewards of this generous book is the journey of discovery, watching his growth from stories capably told but still in debt to their pulp antecedents to high-quality fiction that is indubitably Silverberg's own." Publ Wkly

A Robert Silverberg omnibus; The man in the maze; Nightwings; Downward to the Earth. Harper & Row 1981 544p o.p.

LC 80-8232

An omnibus edition of three titles first published separately 1969, 1969, and 1970 respectively

In the novel Nightwings Earth is taken over by aliens; the man in the maze dramatizes aspects of alienation and Downward to the Earth employs religious imagery in a story of repentence and rebirth

All three novels in this collection "feature strong but psychologically wounded male protagonists, descriptions of bizarre beings and far-away worlds and imaginative, if sometimes unrealistic plots. . . . For readers who appreciate swiftly-paced action." Voice Youth Advocates

Roma eterna. Eos 2003 396p $25.95

ISBN 0-380-97859-8 LC 2002-35416

This is "a what-if history of the world, starting from the premise that the Roman Empire never fell. Spaning 1,500 years, the narrative unfolds in a world without Christianity. It seems that the failure of the ancient Hebrews to escape Pharaonic oppression prevented the rise of mystical religious cults in the province of Syria Palaestina, thereby guaranteeing the survival of Roman hegemony down to the beginning of space travel. Silverberg, who has written numerous popular works of history and archaeology, brings his alternate Rome to life by blending invention with a dazzling array of details borrowed from the annals of the real Rome." N Y Times Book Rev

Sorcerers of Majipoor. HarperPrism 1997 462p il o.p.

LC 96-35027

"This prequel to the Majipoor novels explores the conflict in Lord Valentine's Castle and Valentine Pontifex." Libr J

"This novel has more sorcery and court intrigue than action, but it is not slow paced. Moreover, Silverberg uses the length of this yarn to develop both major and minor characters. As for the setting, Majipoor is already so well developed that Silverberg can drop almost any sort of story into it." Booklist

Valentine Pontifex. Arbor House 1983 347p o.p.

LC 83-45526

"A complicated sequel, this follows 'Lord Valentine's Castle' in action and 'The Majipoor Chronicles' in setting. Silverberg now explores Valentine as a maturing politician and statesman seeking a way to communicate with the Metamorph adversaries who are destroying Majipoor with famines." Libr J

Followed by The mountains of Majipoor

(jt. auth) Asimov, I. Nightfall

Simak, Clifford D., 1904-1988

The big front yard

In The Hugo winners p171-226

Simenon, Georges, 1903-1989

Inspector Maigret and the killers; translated from the French by Louise Varèse. Doubleday 1954 187p o.p.

"Published for the Crime Club"

Original French edition, 1952. Variant title: Maigret and the gangsters

"Inspector Lognon, widely known as 'the most dismal man in the Paris police,' is always trying to solve some spectacular case that will land him with Maigret's Crime Squad on the Quai des Orfevres. Lognon's latest exploit involves a drug stakeout during which he sees a car pull up to the curb and a body dumped out on the pavement. By the time Lognon makes his call, another car has pulled up to retrieve the corpse. Maigret joins Lognon in finding the disappearing body, while events become more outlandish and dangerous. The witty pace featuring kidnappings and shootings, is effectively sustained throughout." Booklist

Maigret and the apparition; translated by Eileen Ellenbogen. Harcourt Brace Jovanovich 1976 159p o.p.

"A Helen and Kurt Wolff book"

Original French edition, 1964; published in the United Kingdom with title: Maigret and the ghost

The book "begins with the shooting of a policeman who has been dogged by bad luck all his career. This time, however, as Maigret investigates, he discovers that the badly wounded Lognon was actually on the trail of a major conspiracy involving the art world and French, British, American participants. Also at the heart of the case is an old man's helpless love for a feckless young wife." Publ Wkly

Maigret and the black sheep; translated from the French by Helen Thomson. Harcourt Brace Jovanovich 1976 158p o.p.

"A Helen and Kurt Wolff book"

Original French edition, 1972

"The victim is a retired carton manufacturer who has been shot, without apparent motive, while sitting at home in his favorite armchair. To [Chief Inspector Maigret's] chagrin, he can find no crack or crevice in the utter respectability of the dead man's life. . . . The season is the end of summer. Parisians are drifting back to the city from their vacations, there is a nip in the air. . . . Maigret sips his beer in several cafés, confers with his faithful colleague Lapointe, and ponders the many facts of this . . . case." New Yorker

Simenon, Georges, 1903-1989—*Continued*

Maigret and the burglar's wife; translated by J. Maclaren-Ross. Harcourt Brace Jovanovich 1989 167p o.p.

LC 89-15625

"A Helen and Kurt Wolff book"

Original French edition, 1951

"Inspector Maigret responds to a call for help from a respectable housewife, remembering her as a cheeky hooker called Lofty. Her husband, 'Sad Freddie,' an inept safecracker, has fled their home in Paris after seeing a dead woman in a residence he planned to rob. Assuring the detective that her husband is a simple burglar, incapable of murder, Lofty convinces Maigret and his men to investigate." Publ Wkly

Maigret and the fortune-teller; translated by Geoffrey Sainsbury. Harcourt Brace Jovanovich 1989 140p o.p.

LC 88-16301

"A Helen and Kurt Wolff book"

Original French edition, 1944

Maigret "is forewarned of a murder but fails to prevent it. He tracks down the villain by exercising his famous 'capacity for putting himself in other people's shoes.' In this case, the shoes belong to a woebegone old man, apparently senile, who was found at the scene of the crime. Obviously more terrified of his wife and daughter than he is of the thunderous Maigret, the old man piques the policeman's interest and so leads him to the solution." Booklist

Maigret and the Hotel Majestic; translated from the French by Caroline Hiller. Harcourt Brace Jovanovich 1978 c1977 174p o.p.

LC 77-84398

"A Helen and Kurt Wolff book"

Original French edition, 1942; this translation first published 1977 in the United Kingdom

Maigret faces "the murder of Emilienne Clark, a sophisticated French woman married to a wealthy American. The setting in a Parisian luxury hotel with a dozen possible suspects ranging from a mysterious and elegant guest to an insignificant and humble breakfast cook." Best Sellers

Maigret and the loner; translated from the French by Eileen Ellenbogen. Harcourt Brace Jovanovich 1975 161p o.p.

"A Helen and Kurt Wolff book"

Original French edition, 1971

"In hot summer, Maigret tackles the case of an elderly recluse found murdered in a condemned and abandoned house where he had apparently holed up for some time." Barzun. Cat of Crime. Rev and enl edition

Maigret and the madwoman; translated from the French by Eileen Ellenbogen. Harcourt Brace Jovanovich 1972 176p o.p.

"A Helen and Kurt Wolff book"

Original French edition, 1970

"Maigret exerts himself to make up for his failure to prevent the murder of a nice old lady who had told him of her fears. He goes to Toulon to interview a suspect and generally behaves as a chief superintendent should. Madame Maigret plays a larger part than usual." Barzun. Cat of Crime. Rev and enl edition

Maigret and the Nahour case; translated by Alastair Hamilton. Harcourt Brace Jovanovich 1982 c1967 160p o.p.

LC 82-47661

"A Helen and Kurt Wolff book"

Original French edition, 1967

"When the young woman turned up at the doctor's office for treatment of a bullet wound, the doctor did not know that the young man with her was her lover or that the body of her husband was about to be discovered. As . . . Inspector Maigret probes into the matter, his investigation leads to an intriguing array of characters and to a pack of lies that almost prevents him from getting to the bottom of it all." Publ Wkly

Maigret and the Saturday caller; translated by Tony White. Harcourt Brace Jovanovich 1991 124p o.p.

LC 90-46032

"A Helen and Kurt Wolff book"

Original French edition, 1962

"Maigret is visited by a harelipped man who confesses that he wants to murder his wife and her lover but hasn't yet done so. Needless to say, Maigret cannot dismiss the man's plans as the fantasy of a harmless lunatic and begins to probe around the edges, irritated by the handicaps imposed by the public prosecutor's recent restrictions on police powers." Booklist

Maigret and the spinster; translated from the French by Eileen Ellenbogen. Harcourt Brace Jovanovich 1977 155p o.p.

LC 76-27416

"A Helen and Kurt Wolff book"

Original French edition, 1942

"A pathetic old maid who has been haunting Maigret's office with vague tales of midnight prowlers comes with a real tale of terror, but Maigret neglects to see her. When the woman's elderly, miserly aunt is found murdered, and the spinster turns up strangled in a broom closet at police headquarters, Maigret feels both personal guilt and a supreme challenge. His investigation involves all the other tenants in the building where the two murdered women lived." Publ Wkly

Maigret and the toy village; translated by Eileen Ellenbogen. Harcourt Brace Jovanovich 1979 139p o.p.

LC 79-1843

"A Helen and Kurt Wolff book"

Original French edition, 1944

In this novel "Maigret, the solemn, slow-moving, yet brilliant Chief Superintendent of the Police Judiciare, is entangled in the most exasperating murder case of his career. A man is slain in a new suburban housing development (the 'toy village' of the title). The prime suspect is his housekeeper, a young woman who has the motive for murder (she stands to inherit the old man's money), plenty of opportunities to execute the crime, and a maddening propensity for keeping Maigret at bay." Booklist

Maigret and the wine merchants; translated from the French by Eileen Ellenbogen. Harcourt Brace Jovanovich 1971 187p o.p.

"A Helen and Kurt Wolff book"

Original French edition, 1970

"A wealthy wine merchant [in Paris] is shot down. His

Simenon, Georges, 1903-1989—*Continued*
wife takes the news with complete unsurprise and a shrug of the shoulders. His business associates discuss him as some sort of artifact coolly, unemotionally. His mistresses neither liked nor disliked him. Eventually the murderer comes into Maigret's sight." N Y Times Book Rev

Maigret bides his time; translated by Alastair Hamilton. Harcourt Brace Jovanovich 1985 c1966 165p o.p.

LC 84-25134

"A Helen and Kurt Wolff book"

Original French edition, 1965; this translation first published 1966 in the United Kingdom

This novel "combines a delight in the sensual world with an exploration of the horrors of human cruelty. The plot revolves around the murder of master jewel thief and gang leader Manuel Palmari, a criminal Maigret has known for many years and whose death he half-guiltily mourns. The chief suspect is Palmari's young mistress, though Maigret finds many more suspects and motives crowded into the deceased man's life. Maigret's investigation does not end until a welter of vice has been uncovered—and more murder is committed. Vintage Simenon." Booklist

Maigret goes home; translated by Robert Baldick. Harcourt Brace Jovanovich 1989 139p o.p.

LC 89-2011

"A Helen and Kurt Wolff book"

Original French edition, 1931; this translation first published 1940 in the United Kingdom

"The countess of the estate where Maigret grew up drops dead during early mass on All Souls' Day, shocked to death by a fake newspaper report falsely reporting the suicide of her son. Although the estate had been heavily mortgaged to pay for the son's debts and the countess' young lovers, the inheritance is still not inconsiderable, and, of course, there are at least three likely suspects." Booklist

Maigret in exile; translated by Eileen Ellenbogen. Harcourt Brace Jovanovich 1979 c1978 162p o.p.

LC 78-13771

"A Helen and Kurt Wolff book"

Original French edition, 1942; this translation first published 1978 in the United Kingdom

"Having fallen from grace in his department in Paris, Maigret has been sent to the Northern Provinces for a cooling off period. He is bored and depressed, an outsider in the small fishing villages of the area, until murder rears its ugly head. When an unknown corpse appears in the home of a retired judge, all changes for Maigret, and everyone becomes his friend and wants to help." West Coast Rev Books

Maigret in Holland; translated by Geoffrey Sainsbury. 2nd ed. Harcourt Brace & Co. 1993 165p o.p.

LC 92-30504

"A Helen and Kurt Wolff book"

Original French edition, 1931; first English translation with title Crime in Holland, published 1940 in the collection Maigret abroad

"Although Maigret speaks no Dutch, he is called to Holland to assist a compatriot, Jean Duclos. Unfortunately, Duclos was present when Conrad Popinga, a former captain in the merchant marine, was murdered, and the Dutch police think Duclos, along with Popinga's wife and sister-in-law, a young sailor, and a local farm girl, is a prime suspect. Once the capable but long-suffering Maigret arrives, he methodically reviews the evidence and questions suspects. . . . Readers will marvel at the inspector's brilliant logic." Booklist

Maigret's memoirs; translated from the French by Jean Stewart. Harcourt Brace Jovanovich 1985 c1963 134p o.p.

LC 85-8591

"A Helen and Kurt Wolff book"

Original French edition, 1951; this translation first published 1963 in the United Kingdom

"Inspector Maigret, upset by writer Georges Simenon's 'caricature' of him, decides to correct the world's misconception of his personality and his cases by writing his memoirs. . . . Maigret outlines a few criminal cases, digresses about the Parisian weather, explains his dislike for Simenon, and presents his views on the criminal mind and on life in general in this odd but marvelous 'autobiographical' account." Booklist

Maigret's revolver; translated from the French by Nigel Ryan. Harcourt Brace Jovanovich 1984 c1952 167p o.p.

LC 84-4634

"A Helen and Kurt Wolff book"

Original French edition, 1952; this translation first published 1956 in the United Kingdom

In this novel "the inspector's cherished weapon—a gift from the F.B.I.—is stolen from his home by a young man who snatches it from a mantelpiece while Mme Maigret's back is turned. Supposedly, the young man is waiting to talk to the Inspector when he returned from police headquarters. Thus begins a tangled tale of a psychotic man who commits a gruesome murder and a reluctant trip by Maigret to London in order to track down the young man with the gun." West Coast Rev Books

"Here, Simenon devotes himself almost exclusively to the workings of the intricate plot, rather than (as in so many other Maigrets) to the inner workings of the detective himself." Booklist

Maigret's war of nerves; translated by Geoffrey Sainsbury. Harcourt Brace Jovanovich 1986 c1940 151p o.p.

LC 85-24749

"A Helen and Kurt Wolff book"

Original French edition, 1931; first United States edition published 1940 with title: The patience of Maigret

Maigret is convinced that Heurtin, a condemned prisoner is innocent. The Inspector persuades officials to allow Heurtin to escape hoping that he will lead Maigret to the real killer

Simmons, Dan

Endymion. Bantam Bks. 1996 486p o.p.

LC 95-33191

"The protagonist, a good-hearted soldier named Raul Endymion, sets off on a quest with historic consequences: he must keep from harm a young girl who

Simmons, Dan—*Continued*
holds the key to a rebirth of human civilization. Arrayed against him is the power of the Pax, a militarized Catholic Church that offers its adherents a literal resurrection of the body. It is Mr. Simmons's inspiration to embody the Pax in the person of Father Captain Federico de Soya, a starship commander who pursues Endymion and the young girl from one exotic planet to the next." N Y Times Book Rev

Followed by The rise of Endymion

Ilium. Eos 2003 576p $25.95
ISBN 0-380-97893-8 LC 2002-44791

"Restored to life by the 'gods,' a race of beings who dwell on the heights of Olympos, 20th-century scholar Thomas Hockenberry travels back in time to observe the events of the Trojan War, as chronicled in Homer's epic poem. There, one of the gods recruits him in a secret war against her brother and sister deities. Set in a far future in which the population of true humans is kept strictly regulated by extraplanetary forces and machine intelligences study Proust and Shakespeare as they perform their duties throughout the universe." Libr J

"For answers to the mysteries laid out in 'Ilium'—from the true identity of the Olympian gods to the fate of robots and humans and of the 'little green men' on Mars for whom communication means death—you will have to wait for the promised sequel. For now, matching wits with Simmons and his lively creations should be reward enough." N Y Times Book Rev

Olympos. HarperCollins 2005 690p $25.95
ISBN 0-380-97894-6 LC 2005-40024

In this sequel to Ilium, "posthumans masquerading as the Greek gods and living on Mars travel back and forth through time and alternate universes to interfere in the real Trojan War, employing a resurrected late 20th-century classics professor, Thomas Hockenberry, as their tool. Meanwhile, the last remaining old-style human beings on a far-future Earth must struggle for survival against a variety of hostile forces. Superhuman entities with names like Prospero, Caliban and Ariel lay complex plots, using human beings as game pieces. From the outer solar system, an advanced race of semiorganic Artificial Intelligences, called moravecs, observe Earth and Mars in consternation, trying to make sense of the situation, hoping to shift the balance of power before out-of-control quantum forces destroy everything. This is powerful stuff, rich in both high-tech sense of wonder and literary allusions, but Simmons is in complete control of his material as half a dozen baroque plot lines smoothly converge on a rousing and highly satisfying conclusion." Publ Wkly

The rise of Endymion; a novel. Bantam Bks. 1997 579p o.p.
LC 97-5658

In this concluding volume of the author's series about a far-future interstellar society, "most of the galaxy is populated by born-again Christians and ruled by the Catholic pope. Nonbelievers are persecuted and forced to accept the cruciform parasite, which allows people to be resurrected. The biggest threat to the establishment is Aenea, a young female architectural apprentice who teaches peace and the way to immense knowledge of the heart and mind. Aided by her lover, Raul Endymion, Aenea exposes organized religion as a parasite of the Core—the sentient evolution of the World Wide Web." Libr J

"For vastness of scope, clarity of detail and seriousness of purpose, Simmons's epic narrative is on a par with Isaac Asimov's Foundation series, Frank Herbert's 'Dune' books, Gene Wolfe's multipart 'Book of the New Sun'; and Brian Aldiss's Helliconia trilogy. No one in modern science fiction . . . has dealt more sensitively with the interface between religion and science." N Y Times Book Rev

Simon, Claude, 1913-2005

The trolley; translated from the French by Richard Howard. New Press (NY) 2002 112p o.p.
ISBN 1-56584-734-2 LC 2002-19026

Original French edition, 2001

"The structure of this novelette alternates between the recollections of the narrator during his youth (in particular the trolley that transported him to school every day) and the recounting of his experience in a hospital in old age." Libr J

This "slim but dense new novel is indebted to Proust in everything from its labyrinthine, parentheses-laden sentences to its meditations on memory and painstaking representations of a bygone time." N Y Times Book Rev

Simon, Roger Lichtenberg, 1943-

Director's cut; a Moses Wine novel. Atria Bks. 2003 241p $23
ISBN 0-7434-5802-8

"For some reason, agents interrogate Hollywood private investigator Moses Wine. . .about his possible links to terrorists. Shortly thereafter, Moses signs on (undercover) with a movie crew filming in Prague to investigate the disturbing appearance of symbolic plastic snakes on set and elsewhere. Lo and behold, terrorists kidnap him and the film's lead actress. The incident ends badly for the terrorists but results in Moses directing the film, supposedly about overcoming sins of the Holocaust. A particularly relevant plot, then, filled with action and suspense and set against arresting Czech backdrop." Libr J

Simpson, Dorothy, 1933-

A day for dying; an Inspector Luke Thanet novel. Scribner 1996 279p $21
ISBN 0-684-81568-0 LC 95-45786

First published 1995 in the United Kingdom

"Inspector Luke Thanet and Sergeant Mike Lineham head the investigation into the apparent murder of Max Jeopard, a handsome but manipulative scion of a wealthy family." Libr J

"The pleasure here is watching Thanet meticulously pick his way through 'the complex web of relationships' within a tight circle of family and friends to arrive at an understanding of what would make a person kill for love." N Y Times Book Rev

Dead and gone; an inspector Luke Thanet novel. Scribner 2000 247p o.p.
ISBN 0-684-86336-7 LC 99-39091

First published 1999 in the United Kingdom

"Inspector Thanet is the very model of the paternalistic English detective, offering comfort to the relatives of a

Simpson, Dorothy, 1933-—*Continued*
woman who was pushed down a well to her death, while shrewdly picking apart every detail of their alibis until he lays bare every dirty little secret in this affluent, complacent household. Tactful and discreet, Thanet is also relentless as he guides the investigation backward in time. . . . A perfect puzzle, perfectly solved." N Y Times Book Rev

Dead by morning. Scribner 1989 277p o.p.
LC 89-6270

"Inspector Thanet is faced with a murder at a luxurious English country inn and an overzealous superintendent who is busily reorganizing with all the annoying haste of the newly promoted." Booklist

Dead on arrival. Scribner 1987 c1986 242p o.p.
LC 86-10243

First published 1986 in the United Kingdom

This novel "about the admirable British Inspector Luke Thanet involves the murder of Steven Long, possibly by Harry Carpenter, whose wife and child have died after Steve caused their car to crash. But the detective's methodical habits lead him to question others with reasons to hate the murder victim: his former wife and her new lover and Steve's younger brothers. Only his twin, Geoffrey, has a kind word for the deceased trouble-maker." Publ Wkly

"To fiddle with identical twins in crime fiction is very dangerous, but our author meets the menace head-on and escapes disaster by a daring twist that deserves applause." Barzun. Cat of Crime. Rev and enl edition

Doomed to die. Scribner 1991 245p o.p.
LC 91-4185

"Inspector Thanet's mother-in-law has had a heart attack; Sergeant Lineham's wife is clinically depressed; and Superintendent Draco has just learned that his beloved wife, Angharad, has leukemia. Among the civilian populace of this suddenly blighted Kentish town, a young nanny is stricken with a ruptured appendix, and the woman who takes her place, a tormented artist with an abusive husband and a dying mother, is found murdered." N Y Times Book Rev

"Confirmed clue-sniffers should be ready for a surprise here: both the solution and the sinner are shockers, though eminently fair ones." Booklist

Last seen alive; a Luke Thanet mystery. Scribner 1985 220p o.p.
LC 85-14530

The author "invites us to reflect on the murder by strangling of a lovely woman, widowed, who is spending one night only in a small Kentish village, ostensibly to hear a violin recital. What could possibly account for a killing under such conditions? The congenial pair of Thanet and Lineham uncovers several 'pasts,' 20 years distant, when all parties were teen-agers in school. Dramatic surprises punctuate a piece of detection in which the ratiocination is neither static nor obvious." Barzun. Cat of Crime. Rev and enl edition

No laughing matter. Scribner 1993 262p o.p.
LC 93-19799

Scotland Yard's Inspector Luke Thanet investigates the murder of a "vintner who went through the laboratory window of his prosperous family-owned vineyard in the Kentish countryside." N Y Times Book Rev

"Simpson turns out her usual high-caliber tale and gives the reader more to ponder than a simple mystery. Her shrewd understanding of what makes humans tick results in a story that is both entertaining and thought-provoking." Booklist

Once too often; an Inspector Luke Thanet novel. Scribner 1998 223p o.p.
LC 97-32513

In this Thanet mystery, an "unlikable woman named Jessica Dander, a reporter for a newspaper in Kent, is found lying at the foot of the stairs in her home, her neck broken. Even though the death appears to be an accident, any number of people might have killed her: the husband she humiliated, the lover she annoyed, the teenage admirer she fascinated. With the exception of Thanet, a thoughtful man with a rich emotional history, the characters are well observed without being especially complex." N Y Times Book Rev

Suspicious death; a Luke Thanet mystery. Scribner 1988 247p o.p.
LC 88-22507

"Detective Inspector Luke Thanet, who keeps the peace in the Kent countryside . . . [is] a man of gentle mien, he is inclined to use psychology and tact, rather than showboat heroics, when pursuing his murder inquiries. Here that fastidious demeanor allows the detective to worm his way into the village of Telford Green, where the mistress of the local manor has been done in. It's plod, plod, plod all the way, as Thanet painstakingly dissects the victim's unlovable character and reconstructs her intriguingly complex relationships with the villagers. Like Inspector Thanet, the reader leaves Telford Green footsore but satisfied." N Y Times Book Rev

Wake the dead. Scribner 1992 250p o.p.
LC 92-19962

"Inspector Luke Thanet investigates the murder of Isobel Fairleigh, a rich, ruthless, manipulative old woman who stopped at nothing to further the political career of her son, Hugo. Thanet has to decide who among Isobel's acquaintances and relatives might have hated the old woman enough to smother her while she lay half-conscious following a stroke." Booklist

Simpson, Mona

Anywhere but here. Knopf 1987 c1986 406p o.p.
LC 86-45282

The "novel opens with its two heroines, Adele and her daughter Ann, fleeing their provincial home-town in Wisconsin for a fresh start in California. . . . Adele is both protector and manipulator, encouraging Ann's success as a child star but also displaying her own unrealistic expectations and selfish motives. Ann tolerates her mother's lying and eccentricity, but she longs for a rootedness her mother cannot give her. The . . . flashbacks to stories told by Adele's Wisconsin relatives give us a sense of the home they have left behind, and the disparity between it and their new home." Libr J

"Any single episode could stand on its own, but Simpson keeps piling them on, building with strength and grace." Booklist

Off Keck Road. Knopf 2000 167p o.p.
ISBN 0-375-41010-4 LC 00-40569

Simpson, Mona—*Continued*

"When Bea Maxwell returns to her small home town, in 1964, after college and a stint at a big-city ad agency, she wants to believe that this is not the end of her story—that the chapter including 'the startling redemption' is still to come. But what follows is less a story than a catalogue of fragile moments that never crystallize into actual events. Bea wrestles with the propriety of a woman telephoning a man, flirts awkwardly with a priest, and deflects a sexual advance from her married boss, to her regret. It's not easy to write a novel in which the central tragedy is that nothing happens, but the author uses the cumulative power of small details to convince us that Bea's stalled life is a life worth knowing." New Yorker

Sinclair, April

Ain't gonna be the same fool twice; a novel. Hyperion 1996 324p o.p.

LC 95-33051

In this sequel to Coffee will make you black, "Jean 'Stevie' Stevenson attends college before heading to San Francisco to seek a career in broadcasting. The irrepressible 'Stevie' continues to grapple with her self esteem and sexual orientation in this literary gem." Booklist

Coffee will make you black. Hyperion 1994 239p o.p.

LC 93-13271

This novel's protagonist "is Jean ('Stevie') Stevenson, a spunky 11-year-old when the story begins; a high-school student when it concludes. The setting is Chicago, circa 1965-70. . . . Raised by a strict, if well-meaning, mother and an affectionate, if vague, father, Stevie soon finds herself caught up in one of the many riddles of youth: to be cool or be square. . . . Meanwhile, she is listening to Dr. Martin Luther King and Malcolm X and liberating herself from the confines of her upbringing and her fear of being 'different.'" Booklist

"Sinclair gives a realistic portrayal of personal awakening during a politically tumultuous time." Publ Wkly

I left my back door open; a novel. Hyperion 1999 290p $22.95

ISBN 0-7868-6229-7 LC 98-50784

"Gun-shy after several catastrophic relationships, Chicago deejay Daphne (Dee Dee) Dupree is an outwardly successful African-American woman aching for self-realization. Sassy from the safety of her broadcasting booth, the heavyset 41-year-old jauntily offers her weight as the cause of a recent breakup. . . . In reality, Dee Dee struggles with the shame of being fat and bulimic. She yearns for mature love and the self-confidence she's sure will accompany finding the right man." Publ Wkly

"Many readers will respond to this novel's honesty, to its colloquial humor and to its exacting exploration of Daphne's relationship woes." N Y Times Book Rev

Sinclair, Upton, 1878-1968

The jungle; introduction by Jane Jacobs. Modern Library 2002 xx, 382p pa $9.95

ISBN 0-375-75950-6 LC 2001-44823

First published 1906 by Doubleday, Page

"Jurgis Rudkus, an immigrant from Lithuania, arrives in Chicago with his father, his fiancée, and her family. He is determined to make a life for his bride in the new country. The deplorable conditions in the stockyards and the harrowing experiences of impoverished workers are vividly described by the author." Shapiro. Fic for Youth. 3d edition

Singer, Isaac Bashevis, 1904-1991

Collected stories; A friend of Kafka to Passions. Library of America 2004 856p (Library of America) $35

ISBN 1-931082-62-6 LC 2003-66057

The sixty-five short stories in this volume have appeared in the three books: A friend of Kafka and other stories (1970); A crown of feathers and other stories (1973); Passions and other stories (1975).

Collected stories: Gimpel the fool to The letter writer; [Ilan Stavans is the editor of this volume] Library of America 2004 789p $35

ISBN 1-931082-61-8 LC 2003-66055

The fifty-four short stories in this volume have appeared in the four books: Gimpel the fool & other stories (1955); The Spinoza of Market Street (1966); Short Friday & other stories (1964); and The séance & other stories (1968). Gimpel the fool & other stories is entered separately.

The collected stories of Isaac Bashevis Singer. Farrar, Straus & Giroux 1982 610p o.p.

Collected stories: One night in Brazil to The death of Methuselah. Library of America 2004 899p $35

ISBN 1-931082-63-4 LC 2003-66081

Most of the short stories in this volume have appeared in the six books: Old love (1979); The collected stories of Isaac Bashevis Singer (1982); Image & other stories (1985); Gifts (1985); and The death of Methuselah & other stories (1988). Also included are thirteen uncollected stories at the end of the volume. The collected stories of Isaac Bashevis Singer and The death of Methuselah are entered separately.

A crown of feathers and other stories
In Singer, I. B. Collected stories

The death of Methuselah and other stories. Farrar, Straus & Giroux 1988 244p o.p.

LC 87-21238

Contents: The Jew from Babylon; The house friend; Burial at sea; The recluse; Disguised; The accuser and the accused; The trap; The smuggler; A peephole in the gate; The bitter truth; The impresario; Logarithms; Gifts; Runners to nowhere; The missing line; The hotel; Dazzled; Sabbath in Gehenna; The last gaze; The death of Methuselah

Enemies, a love story. Farrar, Straus & Giroux 1972 280p o.p.

Originally written in Yiddish, 1966

This novel is "about a Polish Jew who, out of gratitude, marries the girl who helped him escape the Nazis after he believes his wife is dead, takes a mistress whom he bigamously weds when she becomes pregnant, and then discovers that his first wife has also escaped from Poland to New York." Oxford Companion to Am Lit. 6th edition

Singer, Isaac Bashevis, 1904-1991—*Continued*

"The book has the surface gaiety, ribaldry and surprise of a medieval fabliau. Yet the New York subways, telephone calls, Bronx Zoo, bus trip to the Adirondacks are solidly, meticulously real. Herman's three women expand into mythic dimension. . . . Whether or not you accept its ending, [this] is a brilliant, unsettling novel." Newsweek

The estate. Farrar, Straus & Giroux 1969 374p o.p.

Sequel to The manor (1967)

This novel covers the last years of the nineteenth century. It explores the lives of a Polish Jewish family who have emerged from the ghettos to seek a new life in a country that is itself struggling to emerge from a feudal past.

"Even in their manner of dying, Singer's characters seem to be literally swept away by storms of passion. Indeed, the only thing that keeps the book from disintegrating into an anthology of melodramatic episodes is Singer's unfaltering stylistic control." N Y Times Book Rev

The family Moskat; translated from the Yiddish by A.H. Gross. Knopf 1950 611p o.p.

"Panoramic in sweep, the novel follows many characters and story lines in depicting Jewish life in Warsaw from 1911 to the late 1930s. Singer examines Hasidism, Orthodoxy, the rise of secularism, the breakdown of 19th-century traditions, assimilation, Marxism, and Zionism." Merriam-Webster's Ency of Lit

A friend of Kafka and other stories
In Singer, I. B. Collected stories

Gimpel the fool and other stories. Farrar, Straus & Giroux 205p o.p.

First published 1955 by Noonday and analyzed in Short story index

Contains the following stories: By the light of memorial candles; Fire; From the diary of one not born; Gentleman from Cracow; Gimpel the fool; Joy; Little shoemakers; The mirror; Old man; The unseen; Wife killer

also in Singer, I. B. Collected stories: Gimpel the fool to The letter writer

The image and other stories
In Singer, I. B. Collected stories: One night in Brazil to The death of Methuselah

An Isaac Bashevis Singer reader. Farrar, Straus & Giroux 1971 560p o.p.

This anthology "contains among works previously published in journals and other collections, 15 short stories, a novel 'The magician of Lublin,' and four episodes not included in the English translation of 'In my father's court.'" Booklist

The magician of Lublin. Farrar, Straus & Giroux 246p o.p.

Originally serialized 1959 in Yiddish newspaper; first published in book form 1960 by Noonday

"The novel is set in late 19th-century Poland. It concerns Yasha Mazur, an itinerant professional conjurer, tightrope walker, and hypnotist. He loves five women, including his barren and pious wife. To support himself, his assorted women, and his future plans to escape to Italy, he attempts a robbery and fails. Yasha has a crisis of conscience and returns to his wife, becoming a recluse. People begin to refer to him as Jacob the Penitent, and they flock to him as if to a holy man." Merriam-Webster's Ency of Lit

also in Singer, I. B. An Isaac Bashevis Singer reader p317-560

Old Love
In Singer, I. B. Collected stories: One night in Brazil to The death of Methuselah

Passions and other stories
In Singer, I. B. Collected stories

The séance & other stories
In Singer, I. B. Collected stories: Gimpel the fool to The letter writer

Shadows on the Hudson; translated by Joseph Sherman. Farrar, Straus & Giroux 1998 548p $28
ISBN 0-374-26186-5 LC 97-18677

Originally serialized 1957-1958 in Yiddish newspaper

A novel "about a postwar circle of emigres who gather for Sabbath dinners in the Upper West Side apartment of the wealthy Boris Makaver. The events are unceasingly tempestuous: Grein, an investor with a passionate streak, runs off to Miami with Anna, Makaver's daughter (both are married); Luria, whom Anna abandoned, begins to have visions of his first wife, Sonia, who died in the camps; Solomon, Makaver's oldest friend, re-establishes contact with his first wife, who left him for a Nazi; and so on. Nothing that happens, however, is so pressing that it cannot be interrupted for fierce argument—about sin, the dead, lost pieties, God's betrayals." New Yorker

Short Friday & other stories
In Singer, I. B. Collected stories: Gimpel the fool to The letter writer

Shosha. Farrar, Straus & Giroux 1978 277p o.p.

Originally serialized 1974 in Yiddish newspaper

"Against the tragic backdrop of war clouds about to break and wash Warsaw into World War II, Singer sets his despairing protagonist, Aaron Greidinger. The young writer, caught between ambitious dreams and a Poland gone mad, between his youthful religion and the passionless cynicism of his present, escapes political confrontations by involving himself with women: a devout Communist; a peasant maid; his friend's wife; a visiting American actress, for whom he writes an unsuccessful play; and his still childlike early love, Shosha. It is Shosha he chooses to marry, an act seemingly devoid of hope but which Aaron sees as penitence for self-betrayal and one which sets a pattern for his deliverance." Booklist

"Why do people write so rarely about how funny Singer can be? Without ever resorting to parody, he has a wonderful gift for having his characters discuss great issues—the meaning of life, good versus evil, the plight of modern man, death and immortality—and making the reader chuckle only when the author wants him to." Newsweek

The Spinoza of Market Street
In Singer, I. B. Collected stories: Gimpel the fool to The letter writer

Singer, Israel Joshua, 1893-1944

The brothers Ashkenazi; [by] I. J. Singer; translated from the Yiddish by Maurice Samuel. Knopf 1936 642p o.p.

"Deals with the rise and decay of the textile city of Lodz, Poland, and with the fortunes of the Polish-Jewish brothers, Max and Jacob Ashkenazi, whose personalities gradually come to dominate the life of the town. . . . What gives the book its significance is not the picture of nineteenth-century Jewish family life, and not the characterizations of the two brothers, but the clear exposition of the class struggle of which Max and Jacob form unconscious parts." New Yorker

Sinisalo, Johanna, 1958-

Troll; a love story; translated from the Finnish by Herbert Lomas. Grove Press 2004 278p pa $12

ISBN 0-8021-4129-3 (pa) LC 2003-69113

Original French edition 2000; this translation first published 2003 in the United Kingdom with title: Not before sundown

"Thirtysomething Angel, on the way home from the bar one winter night, rescues a young troll from a gang of boys. Bleary and hungover the next morning, he thinks perhaps he dreamed the rescue—until he discovers the troll drinking from the toilet. Falling utterly under its spell, he names it, a male, Pessi, and frantically searches for information on its care and feeding. He discovers that trolls emit pheromones with powerful erotic effects on others nearby, which explains why things become bizarre for Angel. Keeping the essentially wild Pessi as a sort of pet eventually leads to disaster and an accidental killing. Angel escapes with Pessi to the forest, where he meets Pessi's older relations." Booklist

"Sinisalo handles all this mythic conflict in an admirably matter-of-fact way; her main innovations have to do with the novel's narrative structure. She has all the players drawn into Angel's dark fairy-tale intrigue relate their part in short first-person snippets, which are then intercut with reference materials, of both online and print vintage, recounting the Finnish history of troll-sightings and the symbolic significance of the forest creatures in the nation's myth and folklore." Washington Post Book World

Sittenfeld, Curtis

Prep; a novel; Curtis Sittenfeld. Random House 2005 406p $21.95

ISBN 1-400-06231-4 LC 2004-46858

"Lee Fiora, a scholarship student at the prestigious Ault School (not Ault Academy, as her parents embarrassingly refer to it), negotiates her days there in a blaze of self-consciousness that is, by turns, hilarious and excruciating: 'I believed then that if you had a good encounter with a person, it was best not to see them again for as long as possible.' And yet she becomes an expert on the rituals that govern the rarefied microenvironment in which she finds herself: the students' fondness for catchphrases like 'therein lies the paradox' and 'LMC' (lower middle class); the taboo against enthusiasm for anything other than sports; the fact that the school always sings 'God be with you till we meet again' at chapel before breaks. In the end, Lee's incisive vision of herself and others is her downfall but also—as this richly textured narrative suggests—her greatest gift." New Yorker

"This readable coming-of-age tale . . . [is] suitable for YA collections if mildly sexually explicit scenes are not objectionable." Libr J

Sjöwall, Maj, 1935-

Cop killer; the story of a crime; [by] Maj Sjöwall and Per Wahlöö; translated from the Swedish by Thomas Teal. Pantheon Bks. 1975 296p o.p.

Original Swedish edition, 1974

"A divorced woman is murdered, has 'disappeared,' but Martin Beck, Chief Detective Inspector, is called in from Stockholm to investigate. Prime suspect is a former convict who lived near the victim, Sigbrit; and her ex-husband, ex-ship captain, may also be guilty. It takes a midnight shoot-out between three cops and two teenagers to help speed the identification of the real killer." Best Sellers

The laughing policeman; [by] Maj Sjöwall and Per Wahlöö; translated from the Swedish by Alan Blair. Pantheon Bks. 1970 211p o.p.

Original Swedish edition, 1968

In this Martin Beck mystery "a Stockholm city bus is found one rainy night with a cargo of bullet-riddled corpses. Nothing unites the passengers that could explain the mass murder, but one of the victims is a young colleague from the homicide division. . . . The gloomy weather of the Swedish winter, the commercialization of Christmas, Vietnam War protests, and the low morale of the much-criticized police leave Beck and his harassed colleagues with not much to laugh about. The atmosphere and ingenious plotting of the novel make it one of the best in the series." Murphy. Ency of Murder and Mystery

The locked room; [by] Maj Sjöwall and Per Wahlöö: translated from the Swedish by Paul Britten Austin. Pantheon Bks. 1973 311p o.p.

Original Swedish edition, 1972

"A man commits suicide or is murdered in a completely locked room [in Stockholm]. He is shot but there is no weapon. Martin Beck rises from his sick bed to handle this situation." Best Sellers

The man on the balcony; the story of a crime; [by] Maj Sjöwall and Per Wahlöö; translated from the Swedish by Alan Blair. Pantheon Bks. 1968 180p o.p.

Original Swedish edition, 1967

"The chief problem is child murder in Stockholm, and it is a macabre race with death when the only clues are disturbing and intangible for Beck and for the 75-man force assigned to help him." Libr J

Murder at the Savoy; [by] Maj Sjöwall and Per Wahlöö; translated from the Swedish by Amy and Ken Knoespel. Pantheon Bks. 1971 216p o.p.

Original Swedish edition, 1970

"In the dining room of the posh Savoy hotel in Malmö, Viktor Palmgren's address is interrupted when a killer guns him down, then escapes through a window. Was the wealthy industrialist murdered for personal rea-

Sjöwall, Maj, 1935—*Continued*

sons—or for political motives related to his arms shipments to Africa? Once again Chief Inspector Martin Beck of Swedish National Police goes into action." Saturday Rev

Skinner, B. F. (Burrhus Frederic), 1904-1990

Walden two. Macmillan 1948 266p o.p.

"Unlike most post-World War II science fiction, which considered social control by psychological conditioning to be a form of hell on Earth, Skinner presented it grandly as utopian. The structure of the story (which, as a story, doesn't amount to much) is a debate between an advocate of human free choice and a champion of behavioral manipulation, which is offered as the answer to all of society's ills." Anatomy of Wonder 4

Skinner, Burrhus Frederic *See* Skinner, B. F. (Burrhus Frederic), 1904-1990

Skvorecky, Josef

When Eve was naked; stories of a life's journey. Farrar, Straus & Giroux 2002 352p $25

ISBN 0-374-14975-5 LC 2002-20652

Contents: Why I lernt how to read; Eve was naked; Why do people have soft noses?; A remarkable chemical phenomenon; How my literary career began; My Uncle Kohn; My teacher, Mr. Katz; Dr. Strass; The cuckoo; Fragments about Rebecca; Feminine mystique; An insoluble problem of genetics; Three bachelors in a fiery furnance; The end of Bull Mácha; Spectator on a February night; Laws of the jungle; Filthy cruel world; Song of forgotten years; Pink champagne; The mysterious events at night; Wayne's hero; According to Poe; Jezebel from Forest Hill; A magic mountain and a willowy wench

"Like memory, the collection is kaleidoscopic, shifting perspectives, hurtling jerkily through time, filtering its narrative through the author's momentary preoccupations. Written over a period of 50 years, the stories read to some extent like a diary, capturing an emotional landscape in lucid detail." N Y Times Book Rev

The **Sleeper** wakes; Harlem Renaissance stories by women; edited and with an introduction by Marcy Knopf; foreword by Nellie Y. McKay. Rutgers Univ. Press 1993 xxxix, 277p o.p.

LC 92-30446

Contents: The sleeper wakes; Double trouble [and] Mary Elizabeth, by J. R. Fauset; Wedding day, by G. Bennett; Free, by G. D. Johnson; Funeral; The typewriter [and] Prologue to a life, by D. West; One boy's story; Drab rambles [and] Nothing new, by M. Bonner; The closing door, by A. W. Grimké; Bathesda of Sinners Run, by M. I. Owens; The foolish and the wise: Sallie Runner is introduced to Socrates and Sanctum 777 N.S.D.C.O.U. meets Cleopatra, by L. A. Pendleton; Cross crossings cautiously [and] Three dogs and a rabbit, by A. S. Coleman; Blue aloes [and] To a wild rose, by O. B. Graham; His great career [and] Summer session, by A. Dunbar-Nelson; Masks [and] Mademoiselle 'Tasie, by E. B. Thompson; John Redding goes to sea [and] The bone of contention, by Z. N. Hurston; Sanctuary; The wrong man [and] Freedom, by N. Larsen

"This anthology rescues short stories written by the women writers of the Harlem Renaissance from archival obscurity. . . . While these writers share some common themes . . . each has her own distinctive voice, and none sacrifices the art of storytelling for polemics. A passionate, dynamic, and invaluable collection." Booklist

Slouka, Mark

God's fool. Knopf 2002 271p $24

ISBN 0-375-40216-0 LC 2001-53975

This novel about Siamese twins Chang and Eng Bunker is narrated by Chang "The story follows the twins across three continents, from a prosperity in Siam marred by the loss of their father and many siblings; to a life of exploitation in Europe; and finally to America, where the brothers eventually ditch Barnum and retire to North Carolina. There the family of Chang and Eng grows to include wives, children and even more loss." Booklist

"Slouka, a gifted stylist, eschews much of the freak-show energy that thrust Chang and Eng onto the stage of world history, in favor of an alluring balance between the elegiac and the ironic." Publ Wkly

Smiley, Jane, 1949-

The age of grief; a novella and stories. Knopf 1987 213p o.p.

LC 87-45120

Contents: The pleasure of her company; Lily; Jeffrey, believe me; Long distance; Dynamite; The age of grief

"These short pieces are about male-female relations—the high points and the pitfalls (more of the latter than the former). Smiley knows her characters inside out and lets the reader in on everything she knows." Booklist

The age of grief [novelette]

In Smiley, J. The age of grief p119-213

Good faith. Knopf 2003 417p $26

ISBN 0-375-41217-4 LC 2002-73096

"Everyone trusts Joe Stratford, the affable Pennsylvania real-estate agent who narrates Smiley's ninth novel—his clients, his bankers, his boss, his boss's sexy married daughter, and even the irascible contractor who builds the most beautiful houses in the country. But when Marcus Burns, a charismatic I.R.S. agent turned developer, comes to town, Joe feels that no one else understands his potential the way Marcus does. With Joe as his partner, Marcus soon seduces half the county into investing in a development venture that he says will make everyone rich. It is hard to imagine a novelist better suited to taking on the S.& L. scandals of the nineteen-eighties than Smiley." New Yorker

The Greenlanders. Knopf 1988 555p o.p.

LC 88-2758

An "historical novel based on the tenth-century settlement of Greenland by Norseman Erik the Red and a band of Norse colonists. After flourishing in Greenland for centuries, the colonists disappeared, leaving behind only their buildings and artifacts." Booklist

"Vivid, even stunning descriptions of the land and customs of these 'lost settlements' are the book's strong points. Characterizations are less successful; many per-

Smiley, Jane, 1949-—*Continued*
sonalities remain wooden throughout the lengthy action. Nevertheless, the exotic subject matter will appeal to historical novel fans." Libr J

Horse heaven. Knopf 2000 561p o.p.
ISBN 0-375-40600-X LC 99-52728

In this novel about thoroughbred horse racing Smiley introduces "new characters in nearly every chapter, from rich and troubled owners to eccentric and troubled trainers; nervous fillies and scampish stallions; a boy with the gift for picking winners; an articulate, horse-crazy 11 year-old girl; a gorgeous store clerk who catches the eye of a wealthy rap star then goes horse-crazy; horse-crazy Irish cousins; an animal communicator who can tune into a horse's stream of consciousness; a kind horse masseur; a calm and creative veterinarian; and a young mother trying valiantly to run her grandfather's stud farm." Booklist

"What's remarkable about Smiley's handling of horses as characters is that she manages to bring it off at all—and more, she does it brilliantly." N Y Times Book Rev

Moo. Knopf 1995 414p o.p.
LC 94-12840

"This metafiction, set in a sprawling Midwestern university known as Moo, concerns an economics professor who's cozy with corrupt Latin-American governments and rapacious corporations, a seven-hundred-pound hog named Earl Butz, many couples in and out of love, and a secretary who quietly runs the whole place. As usual, Smiley knows more than seems likely about everything from equine management and the niceties of butchering to—of course—the nuances of how people feel and behave toward animals of their own species." New Yorker

A thousand acres. Knopf 1991 371p $25
ISBN 0-394-57773-6 LC 91-52720

The author "creates an idyllic world of family farm life in Iowa in 1979: the neat yard, freshly painted house, clean clothes on the line, and fertile, well-tended fields. The owner of these well-managed acres is Larry Cook, who abruptly decides to turn the farm over to his two eldest daughters and their husbands. Ginny and Ty are hard-working farmers who try to placate her ornery father, while sister Rose and hard-drinking Pete try to stand up to him. Dark secrets surface after the property transfer and the family's careful world unravels with a grim inevitability." Libr J

"What makes this novel such a triumph is Smiley's brilliant twist on the Lear story: she tells it not from Larry's point of view but from his eldest daughter's. . . . In the end Smiley does what Shakespeare himself never did: she creates a female heroine who grows through her own anguish until she towers over the hero and conquers him." Newsweek

Smith, Alexander McCall *See* McCall Smith, Alexander, 1948-

Smith, April, 1949-

Good morning, killer. Knopf 2003 356p $24
ISBN 0-375-41240-9 LC 2002-35917

"This kidapping thriller starts off like most kidnapping thrillers, with the abduction of a pampered teenager, 15-year-old Juliana Meyer-Murphy, that has the local cops running around in circles. But we know we're in uncharted territory here when Juliana returns home, raped, battered and deeply traumatized, and Ana Grey, the F.B.I. agent assigned to the case, is so distressed by the girl's condition that she ignores procedures and starts acting on impulse. . . . A risk taker herself, Smith writes in the forceful style of a true literary maverick, someone who has earned the right to break a few rules." N Y Times Book Rev

North of Montana; a novel. Knopf 1994 295p $23
ISBN 0-679-43197-7 LC 94-12311

As this mystery opens, "success-hungry L.A.-based FBI agent Ana Grey is just waiting for the case that will catapault her from the humdrum Bank Robbery Squad into the exalted Kidnapping and Extortion Division. The hoped-for promotion is Ana's first step to her ultimate goal: a plum job as Special Agent in Charge. But department politics, a jealous supervisor, and Ana's abrasive impatience detour her to a case that's a real hot potato. Glamorous movie star Jayne Mason, past her prime but still adored by her fans, claims a local M.D. hooked her on painkillers. She wants his head on a platter courtesy of the FBI, even though the doctor appears to be clean as a whistle." Booklist

This is "an LA novel in the tradition of some of the best writers of detective fiction. . . . There are swift, vivid portraits of scene and characters." Times Lit Suppl

Smith, B. J., 1957- *See* Smith, Brad, 1957-

Smith, Betty, 1896-1972

Joy in the morning. Harper & Row 1963 308p o.p.
LC 62-14560

"When their families find out that Annie McGairy and Carl Brown have married, the two are cut off without a cent. Carl, a law student, takes a full-time job and goes to law school at night. Annie, who had dropped out of school to help her family, longs to be at college. She is given a chance to audit a course in literature because of her abiding interest in it. Her pregnancy, however, increases the pressure on their lives, and only their deep love sees them through their difficulties." Shapiro. Fic for Youth. 3d edition

A tree grows in Brooklyn; a novel. Harper & Row 1943 443p o.p.

"Life in the Williamsburg section of Brooklyn during the early 1900s is rough, but the childhood and youth of Francie Nolan is far from somber. Nurtured by a loving mother, Francie blossoms and reaches out for happiness despite poverty and the alcoholism of a father whose weakness is somewhat compensated for by his lovable disposition." Shapiro. Fic for Youth. 3d edition

Smith, Brad, 1957-

All hat; a novel. Holt & Co. 2003 308p $24
ISBN 0-8050-7217-9 LC 2002-27307

"His attempt to live 'a half-ass normal life' doomed out of the starting gate, ex-con Ray Dokes hatches a plot to swap racehorses before a race. Set in rural Onario and featuring an ensemble cast of delightfully eccentric, even

Smith, Brad, 1957-—*Continued*
downright loopy, characters, this big-hearted caper novel mixes laugh-out-loud-comedy with streaks of country noir that call to mind Daniel Woodrell." Booklist

Smith, Caesar, 1920-1995

For works written by this author under other names see Hall, Adam, 1920-1995

Smith, Diane

Pictures from an expedition. Viking 2002 277p o.p.

ISBN 0-670-03129-1

"Set in the Montana badlands a decade after the Civil War, the novel begins with fossil hunters stumbling upon the remains of possibly the largest dinosaur ever uncovered. Thrown in with a peripatetic crew of scientists and settlers, explorers and exploiters, Eleanor Peterson, a scientific illustrator hired to document their discoveries, recounts those daring days through her remembrances of the circumstances that inspired a series of paintings done by her traveling companion and mentor, Augustus Starwood, an eccentric artist." Booklist

Smith's "precise evocation of the stark western landscape matches her exacting portrayal of scientific debate and the assimilation of new theories." Publ Wkly

Smith, Dodie, 1896-1990

I capture the castle. Little, Brown 1948 343p il o.p.

LC 48-4880

"From its memorable opening line, 'I write this sitting in the kitchen sink', the 17-year-old narrator, Cassandra Mortmain, captivates the reader as she describes a life of penury in a gloomy Gothic castle with her oddball family. Wise beyond her years, romantic and lyrical, yet beadily perceptive . . ., Cassandra is wonderfully engaging and believable." Good Fiction Guide

Smith, Florence Margaret *See* Smith, Stevie, 1902-1971

Smith, Julie, 1944-

82 Desire; a Skip Langdon novel. Ballantine Pub. Group 1998 309p $24

ISBN 0-449-00060-5 LC 98-22259

"Russell Fortier, a prominent businessman, has vanished. His wife asks Langdon, a New Orleans detective, to look into his disappearance. Later, a private detective who was investigating Fortier turns up dead, and one of his employees, a poet and freelance computer expert, wants to know how Fortier's disappearance is connected with the murder. . . . The novel is intricately constructed, and while Smith keeps nothing important unfairly hidden from her readers, she manages to spring some nice little surprises." Booklist

The Axeman's jazz. St. Martin's Press 1991 341p o.p.

LC 91-19064

"A Thomas Dunne book"

In this mystery featuring New Orleans homicide detective Skip Langdon, "the killer, who calls himself the Axeman after an infamous murderer who terrorized New Orleans in the early 1900's, preys on the most vulnerable souls who frequent the city's many 12-step programs. . . . Thwarted by the anonymity given their members by these groups, the murder task force goes undercover at meetings, posing as alcoholics, drug addicts and co-dependents." N Y Times Book Rev

"With an acute ear for New Orleans speech and a sharp eye for the city's social stratification, Smith keeps the reader's heart palpitating to the end of this mystery of unusual depth, which leaves Skip in love, confident she's a good cop and triumphant over social-climbing, tradition-bound parents." Publ Wkly

Crescent city kill; a Skip Langdon novel. Fawcett Columbine 1997 326p $23.50

ISBN 0-449-91000-8 LC 97-22099

"New Orleans police detective Skip Langdon pits her skills against a vigilante group known as The Jury. Skip suspects her old nemesis, the con man and killer Errol Jacomine." Libr J

"The New Orleans ambiance is less pronounced than in most Skip Langdon mysteries, but Smith's colorful characterizations and the showdown with Jacomine make this an excellent addition to the series." Publ Wkly

House of blues; a Skip Langdon novel. Fawcett Columbine 1995 343p o.p.

LC 94-48823

"Arthur Hebert, a prominent restaurateur and domineering patriarch hated by his children, doesn't attend the opening of his restaurant in New Orleans' first casino—because he's been gunned down at home while enjoying his usual Monday evening meal of red beans and rice. Hebert's daughter, his son-in-law and his baby granddaughter have vanished. In the race to find the killer and the missing family, Skip calls on the denizens of the New Orleans underworld. . . . Smith carries off a tricky balancing act, rendering Skip heroic while imbuing her with a credibly textured emotional life. But the real star of this superb effort is New Orleans, which has never seemed more dangerous or alluring." Publ Wkly

Jazz funeral; a Skip Langdon novel. Fawcett Columbine 1993 365p o.p.

LC 92-54997

This mystery featuring New Orleans cop Skip Langdon is "about the murder of a local jazz entrepreneur and the disappearance of his 16-year-old sister. . . . Even though she wears her badge like a piece of jewelry, Skip has the social skills to pump information from her uptown friends, and her amateur detection methods pay off with solid insights into an emotionally bankrupt family. Ms. Smith takes special pains to be gentle with a musically gifted teen-ager who runs away from the horrors of home to join a family band very much like the Neville Brothers. The kid is a bit of a brat, but the portrayal has such integrity that it makes up for Skip's lax procedures." N Y Times Book Rev

The kindness of strangers; a Skip Langdon novel. Fawcett Columbine 1996 338p $21

ISBN 0-449-90937-9 LC 95-52460

Langdon "takes on the Big Easy's corrupt political machine, as three 'pick the best of the worst' candidates line up for the mayoral race. New Orleans voters, tired of years of corruption and scandal, are leaning toward

Smith, Julie, 1944-—*Continued*
Errol Jacomine, a Christian right-winger who appears to have the right stuff. But Skip senses evil lurking behind Jacomine's jovial facade, and she figures to discredit him before he gains control of the city. . . . Smith serves up a gritty, gripping story along with a big helping of action and a pinch of humor." Booklist

Louisiana hotshot. Forge 2001 335p $24.95
ISBN 0-7653-0058-3 LC 2001-18958
"A Tom Doherty Associates book"
A mystery set in New Orleans featuring "Talba Wallis (aka Baroness de Pontalba), the black poet/computer expert and would-be investigator. . . . Answering an unlikely ad with her customary bravado lands her a job as assistant to aging PI Eddie Valentino. The young black female and 65-year-old Italian male have striking similarities that offset their obvious differences. Both are stubborn and strongly attached to, if somewhat alienated from, their families. Throw in a vulnerable young girl, Cassandra, being preyed on by a rap star's hanger-on identified only by the nickname 'Toes,' and you have a story that spans generations, races and lifestyles." Publ Wkly

Mean woman blues. Forge 2003 304p $24.95
ISBN 0-7653-0552-6 LC 2003-40018
"A Tom Doherty Associates book"
"The Formosan termites that infest new Orleans every May haunt police detective Skip Langdon's dreams, an apt image for the gnawing fear that her happiness will collapse. That happiness is based on the fact that her long distance lover, a documentary filmmaker, has moved to New Orleans. Her fear is that her enemy, an evangelical fanatic who aspires to the mind control of Jim Jones, is coming back to kill her, after a disappearance of two years." Booklist

New Orleans beat; a Skip Langdon novel. Fawcett Columbine 1994 359p o.p.
LC 93-46506
New Orleans detective Skip Langdon "investigates the suspicious death of a man who was involved with an electronic bulletin board community." Libr J
"Smith is a skilled writer who can evoke the steamy, mysterious ambience of New Orleans while simultaneously proving that computer jargon can be comprehensible even to the 'computer-challenged.' This is a humorous, suspenseful mystery." Booklist

Smith, Lee, 1944-

The devil's dream. Putnam 1992 315p o.p.
LC 92-1027
The author traces the history of country music "through several generations of the Bailey family of Grassy Springs, Virginia. Starting in 1833 with the marriage of Moses Bailey, a preacher's son who thinks fiddle music is the voice of the Devil laughing, to Kate Malone who comes from a fiddle-playing family, the Baileys are torn between their love of God and their love of music. Plain Baptist hymns and haunting Appalachian ballads shape the lives of the early generations. Grandsons R.C. and Durwood marry Lucie and Tampa, who, as the Grassy Branch Girls, take part in the early 'hillbilly recordings' of the 1920s. Rose Annie and Blackjack Johnny Raines are the 'King and Queen of Country Music' in the Rockabilly 1950s until Rose Annie shoots Johnny after he's cheated on her once too often. Cousin Katie Crocker abandons the bland Nashville sound of the 1960s when she cuts a traditional record with her family at the Opryland Hotel." Libr J
"It is ultimately the writer's sensibility that gives 'The Devil's Dream' its charm and power. If there's weeping to be done, Ms. Smith allows her reader to weep, but she never descends to sentimentality." N Y Times Book Rev

Fair and tender ladies. Putnam 1988 316p o.p.
LC 88-10915
This novel of life in the Appalachians "unfolds through a series of letters written by Ivy Rowe, a Virginia mountain girl. Ivy, born with the century, begins her letter writing when she is about 10 years old; the letters continue for nearly 65 years." N Y Times Book Rev
An "exquisite novel. . . . Through Ivy's curiously spelled and situated letters, we see the growth not only of her own family, but also of wider Appalachia." Christ Sci Monit

Family linen. Putnam 1985 272p o.p.
LC 85-3664
"The Hess clan gather in their hometown of Booker Creek, Virginia, upon the death of their matriarch, Miss Elizabeth. There are some serious skeletons in the family closet—sexual abuse, an illegitimate child, a murder. The family history is recounted in turn by relatives spanning four generations, and their narratives reveal both comical attempts to seek solace and bewilderment at the complexity of their lives." Booklist
"This is a companionable, chatty book populated by people who tell us about themselves in a rambling style and with good humor." N Y Times Book Rev

The last girls; a novel. Algonquin Bks. 2002 384p o.p.
ISBN 1-565-12363-8 LC 2002-18671
"A Shannon Ravenel book"
In this novel, a "group of former coeds, who once traveled down the Mississippi on a raft of their own construction, reunite to make the same trip on a fancy steamboat to scatter the ashes of one departed member. Along the way, we learn the stories of the unmarried Harriet, wealthy romance writer and once-poor West Virginia girl Anna, straying society wife Courtney, and Catherine and husband Russell." Libr J
Smith is "perhaps best known for her nuanced portraits of gritty, often dirt-poor Appalachian women. It's a pleasure to see her directing her talents to a different class of women with a different set of concerns." N Y Times Book Rev

Me and my baby view the eclipse; stories. Putnam 1990 206p o.p.
LC 89-27377
Contents: Bob, a dog; Mom; Life on the moon; Tongues of fire; Dreamers; The interpretation of dreams; Desire on Domino Island; Intensive care; Me and my baby view the eclipse
"Tiny explosions, little surprises, minor epiphanies pepper the lives of Smith's characters. . . . Revelatory writing from a master storyteller." Libr J

Smith, Lee, 1944-—*Continued*

Oral history. Putnam 1983 286p o.p.
LC 82-18081

This "is the tale of the working out of a family curse, the revenge of a red-haired witch spurned by one Almarine Cantrell. Almarine (b.1876), is a subsistence farmer, the owner of all of Hoot Owl Holler in the western corner of Virginia, husband of two women, father of seven, stepfather of one, grandfather of at least five and a regional figure to reckon with. The story is told in a series of voices and includes mountain neighbors and citizens of nearby Tug and Black Rock." Nation

"Smith is excellent at making the separate voices distinctive. . . . Serious fiction readers will be interested in Smith's techniques and will appreciate her decision to utilize this 'oral history' format to best achieve her intentions." Booklist

Saving Grace. Putnam 1995 273p o.p.
LC 94-43904

"Florida Grace is the daughter of Virgil Shepherd, a snake-handling self-appointed preacher who starves and sometimes abandons his many children. Of all these, Gracie is the 'contentious and ornery' one who will not embrace Jesus—though she does, along the way (between the ages of seven and thirty-eight), embrace a half brother, a kindly minister, and middle-class luxury. Grace narrates, in irresistible Southern mountain tones." New Yorker

Smith, Lillian Eugenia, 1897-1966

Strange fruit; a novel; [by] Lillian Smith. Reynal & Hitchcock 1944 371p o.p.

This novel, set in a small town in Georgia, is about the love of an educated black girl for a white man. The reaction to this affair results in murder and a lynching

This is a "regional novel, in the finest sense. As such, it offers a magnificently detailed picture of the small-town South, lashed by an urge for self-destruction as old as time. The author has suggested no cure for that urge: you will find no black messiahs here, no white devils." N Y Times Book Rev

Smith, Martin Cruz

December 6; a novel. Simon & Schuster 2002 339p o.p.
ISBN 0-684-87253-6 LC 2002-29437

This "thriller is set in Tokyo in the last days of 1941, just before the bombing of Pearl Harbor; its central character, the American Harry Niles, grew up in Japan, where his missionary parents were preaching the Word. Harry isn't very holy, however: he owns a night club called the Happy Paris, dabbles in assorted short cons, and spends much of his time with various mistresses. . . . As the rumors of war heat up, Harry finds that he has become too Japanese, and the Japanese suspect him of being a spy. Smith's plot is more than slightly reminiscent of 'Casablanca' and the spectre of the Second World War seems, at this distance, almost quaint, but the characters are so well drawn and the local color so colorful that these quibbles hardly interfere with the novel's pleasures." New Yorker

Gorky Park. Random House 1981 365p o.p.
LC 80-6022

"Chief Investigator Renko of the Moscow police is determined to solve the mystery of the three mutilated bodies in Gorky Park, despite obstruction by other officials. His main help comes from New York police Lt. William Kirwin, in Moscow to find his brother, who turns out to be one of the Gorky Park victims. Renko falls in love with Irina, the major witness in the affair, and is brought with her to New York by agents of both nations to defuse what's become a serious situation." Libr J

The author "has succeeded in rendering very believable, realistic, and gripping portrayals of certain segments of Soviet society and of one man's search for meaning." Christ Sci Monit

Havana Bay; a novel. Random House 1999 329p $25.95
ISBN 0-679-42662-0 LC 99-235977

Arkady Renko "has been summoned to Havana to identify the body of his old comrade, Russian embassy attaché Sergei Sergeevich Pribluda. The Cuban police maintain that Pribluda died of a heart attack while fishing from an inner tube in Havana Bay, but that unlikely scenario has Arkady wondering. Nevertheless, he is too consumed by his wife's recent death to investigate—until the embassy's interpreter comes at him with a knife." Publ Wkly

"His earnest unsentimentality and calm tenaciousness on the hunt are what make Renko one of the most interesting detectives in modern fiction. What a clever stroke for Smith to dispatch him to Havana, where sentimentality and passion are in rare abundance." N Y Times Book Rev

Polar Star. Random House 1989 386p il o.p.
LC 88-43232

This mystery "finds former Moscow investigator Arkady Renko toiling as a second-class seaman on a Russian factory ship, the *Polar Star,* which is part of a joint U.S.-Soviet fishing venture in the Bering Sea. Labeled 'politically unreliable' after the events of *Gorky Park,* Renko has spent years dodging the KGB in Siberia—hence, his ignominious station on the ship's 'slime line,' gutting and chopping fish. Things change when the body of a Russian girl, who worked in the ship's galley, turns up in a fish net. At first unwillingly, Renko becomes swept up in the investigation, which leads to cocaine trafficking, elaborate espionage plots, and a grisly climax on the ice-covered sea." Booklist

"Rich in humor, generous in spirit, endlessly entertaining and deeply serious, 'Polar Star' is not merely the work of our best writer of suspense, but of one of our best writers, period." N Y Times Book Rev

Red Square. Random House 1992 418p o.p.
LC 92-50166

"Just prior to the 1991 attempted coup, [Arkady Renko] finds himself reestablished as an investigator with the Moscow police and struggling to contain a flourishing underworld in the newly democratic Soviet Union. . . . A seemingly straightforward murder investigation leads Arkady first to corruption in high places, then to official censure, and finally to Munich, where he is reunited with Irina, the lover who got him in . . . trouble back in the early 1980s." Booklist

Smith, Martin Cruz—*Continued*

Rose. Random House 1996 364p o.p.
LC 95-37914

Until 1872, Jonathan Blair "was an avid explorer of Africa's Gold Coast, but now he has been exiled by his employer, Bishop Hannay, to the Lancashire mining town of Wigan. Blair's ostensible mission is to find John Rowland, the missing curate who was engaged to Hannay's daughter, but he quickly learns that he'll need all his bush survival skills just to stay alive in Wigan, where no one seems to want the curate found." Publ Wkly

"*Rose* has everthing a compelling novel needs: Blair is a fascinating protagonist, by turns a hero and a boor; other significant characters are complex and as multifaceted as a chunk of coal; the mystery is gripping. But it is the horrific, mesmerizing portrayal of the dark, hellish Wigan, the mines themselves, and the lives of miners that makes this novel much more than a good read." Booklist

Stallion Gate. Random House 1986 321p o.p.
LC 85-24444

"In a New Mexico blizzard, four men cross a barbed-wire fence at Stallion Gate to select the test site for the first atomic weapon. They are Oppenheimer, the physicist; Groves, the general; Fuchs, the spy. The fourth man is Sergeant Joe Peña, a hero, informer, fighter, musician, Indian. Oppenheimer and Groves have hidden Los Alamos on a mesa surrounded by vast Indian reservations. . . . To it come soldiers, roughnecks and scientists, including Anna Weiss, a mathematician and refugee from the Holocaust with whom Joe falls in love." Publisher's note

"Obviously Stallion Gate is not meant to be taken too literally. There is a touch of the folk hero about Peña as he moves across the New Mexican landscape. A conscious stylist, Smith relies strongly on emotional echoes and calibrated suspense." Time

Wolves eat dogs; a novel. Simon & Schuster 2004 337p $25.95

ISBN 0-684-87254-4 LC 2004-52585

Senior Investigator Arkady Renko "must determine whether the defenestration death of a Russian tycoon was suicide or murder. The discovery of radioactive salt in the dead man's apartment leads Renko to the abandoned Ukrainian towns of Chernobyl and Pripyat, still dangerously contaminated 18 years after the world's deadliest nuclear accident. There he finds a ghostly world inhabited by scavengers, elderly villagers, and a small group of Russian militia and scientists. As Renko pursues his investigation, he uncovers a greater crime, the sad legacy of Soviet ineptitude and corruption." Libr J

Smith, Mary-Ann Tirone *See* Tirone Smith, Mary-Ann, 1944-

Smith, Mary-Ann Tirone, 1944-

She's not there; a Poppy Rice novel. Holt & Co. 2003 317p map $25

ISBN 0-8050-7223-3 LC 2002-68592

"FBI agent Poppy Rice is taking some time off with boyfriend Joe at his vacation home on Block Island. . . . Her enforced relaxation falls by the wayside after only a few days when she stumbles across the body of a teenage girl from the island's summer weight-loss camp." Booklist

"The ease with which Poppy gets technical support from Washington and manpower from the Rhode Island mainland is some stretch, but that doesn't take away from her shrewd analysis of the isolationist island mentality or her understanding of teenage behavior." N Y Times Book Rev

Smith, R. A. McCall *See* McCall Smith, Alexander, 1948-

Smith, Robert Kimmel, 1930-

Jane's house. Morrow 1982 344p o.p.
LC 82-2277

"This book is about how one family deals with the loss of a parent. Paul Klein's wife of 18 years, Jane, died suddenly, leaving him to raise their two children, Hilary and Bobby. The first part of the book deals with Paul's slow adjustment to single parenthood, emphasizing the day-to-day problems. Then he meets Ruth, a lively and intelligent advertising woman. They fall in love and marry. The second part of the story is seen mostly through Ruth's eyes, as she tries to gain the children's friendship." Libr J

Smith, Rosamond, 1938-
See also Oates, Joyce Carol, 1938-

Smith, Rosamund *See* Oates, Joyce Carol, 1938-

Smith, Scott B.

A simple plan; a novel. Knopf 1993 335p o.p.
LC 92-42478

"When Hank Mitchell, his obese, feckless brother Jacob and Jacob's smarmy friend Lou accidentally find a wrecked small plane and its dead pilot in the woods near their small Ohio town, they decide not to tell the authorities about the $4.4 million stuffed into a duffel bag. Instead, they agree to hide the money and later divide it among themselves. The 'simple plan' sets in motion a spiral of blackmail, betrayal and multiple murder." Publ Wkly

This novel is so "cunningly imagined that for the most part Mr. Smith drags us willingly through what in less deft hands could be a morally repugnant story." N Y Times Book Rev

Smith, Stevie, 1902-1971

Novel on yellow paper; or, Work it out for yourself. New Directions 1994 252p il (A revived modern classic) pa $10.95

ISBN 0-8112-1239-4 LC 93-49827

First published 1936 in the United Kingdom

This novel is "narrated in the first person by Pompey Casmilus, who lives with her darling Auntie Lion, and is an outpouring of her thoughts and feelings about the world around her–about fear, love, death, marriage, religion, sex, anti-Semitism; about her friends and lovers and her childhood. To list the topics cannot begin to capture the delicious flavour, which is whimsical, poetic, self-deprecatingly (or at times, mercilessly) humorous, and often absurd." Good Fiction Guide

Smith, Wilbur A.

The angels weep; [by] Wilbur Smith. Doubleday 1983 c1982 468p o.p.
LC 82-45885

First published 1982 in the United Kingdom

The the third volume in the saga of the Ballantyne family in Rhodesia. "Part I, which starts in 1895, centers on the complex relations among various Ballantynes—preeminently pioneer settler Zouga, his missionary-doctor sister Robyn and his gold-prospecting son Ralph—and the diamond-hungry, empire-building Cecil Rhodes. But it also covers (from an inside perspective) a bloody and abortive Matabele rebellion and the skulduggery in high places that precipitated the Boer War. Part II, which is set in 1977 and might have been called 'African Revenge,' features the gory transition from Rhodesia to Zimbabwe and the end of the Ballantynes' 'great African adventure.'" Publ Wkly

Followed by The leopard hunts in darkness

Birds of prey; a novel; [by] Wilbur Smith. St. Martin's Press 1997 554p o.p.
LC 97-8192

"In 1667, Sir Francis Courteney commands his ship off the coast of Africa in England's war against the Dutch. He has groomed his son Hal to succeed him as captain. *Birds of Prey* chronicles Hal's swift and bloody passage to manhood after his father's torture and death at the hands of the Dutch. Escaping with the remaining crew, Hal makes his way overland to claim his father's hidden treasure and confront the treacherous English captain who betrayed them." Libr J

"Smith's depiction of the African coast, and of life aboard ship, is vivid and believable. He handles the action sequences well, opting for short, trenchant paragraphs to sustain momentum. . . . Smith knows what his readers want, and once again he delivers the goods." Publ Wkly

Followed by Monsoon

Cry wolf; [by] Wilbur Smith. Douleday 1977 c1976 401p o.p.
LC 76-50791

First published 1976 in the United Kingdom

"British neer-do-well Gareth Swales and a Texas mechanic named Jack Barton settle on an arrangement of self-interests. The year is 1935, the place Tanganyika, their goal, delivering to Ethiopia armed personnel carriers—for a swollen profit, of course. Amid bantering dialogue which reveals Gareth to be a delicious character indeed, the pair plunge northward towards an amorous intrigue and invading Italians." Publ Wkly

Elephant song; [by] Wilbur Smith. Random House 1992 c1991 498p il o.p.
LC 91-53113

First published 1991 in the United Kingdom

"Acclaimed documentary filmmaker and African ecologist Daniel Armstrong vows revenge after a gang of poachers steals a huge cache of South African government-protected ivory, in the process brutally killing Chief Warden Johnny Nzou, Armstrong's childhood friend, and his family. Tracing the smuggling operation to its highest source, Armstrong comes up against a sadistic Chinese diplomat and his profoundly wealthy clan, an unscrupulous entrepreneur expatriate from India, a knighted British tycoon, assorted thugs and a torture-crazed leopard guarding a warehouse." Publ Wkly

Flight of the falcon; [by] Wilbur Smith. Doubleday 1982 c1980 545p o.p.
LC 81-43328

First published 1980 in the United Kingdom

The first of the author's Ballantyne novels. "In 1854 no medical school in England would enroll a woman student. Yet, Robyn Ballantyne masqueraded as a male and obtained her medical degree. With this same determined willfulness Robyn persuades her brother to return to Africa with her to seek their long-lost missionary father. Although each pursues a separate goal, they both find themselves enmeshed in the greed, danger, and human misery of the African slave trade. Robyn's burning hatred of the slavers also leads her to two men, though her heart's choice conflicts with her head's choice." Libr J

Followed by Men of men

Golden fox; [by] Wilbur Smith. Random House 1991 c1990 433p o.p.
LC 90-39062

First published 1990 in the United Kingdom

This novel in the Courtney family series is set in 1969. "Ramón de Santiago y Machado is a fallen Spanish marques working for the KGB and involved with Cuban guerrillas fighting in Africa. He sets his sights on Isabella Courtney, daughter of South African industrialist Shasa Courtney, woos her, and impregnates her, with the hollow promise that he will make things legit as soon as his divorce comes through. It's all a ruse, of course. Ramon's intentions are dastardly, and his superiors abduct the child that is born and blackmail Isabella into helping them sabotage the political and military plans of the white South African government." Booklist

"Smith excels at creating finely drawn characters; descriptive settings in London, Europe, and Africa; and a masterful development of an action-packed thriller that gets better as each new predicament unfolds." SLJ

Hungry as the sea; [by] Wilbur Smith. Doubleday 1980 c1978 395p o.p.
LC 78-22368

First published 1978 in the United Kingdom

"Toppled from his position as chairman of Christy Marine, a worldwide shipping consortium, and losing his wife and son to its new chairman, Nicholas Berg is left with a struggling towing and salvage company." Libr J

"A story of rescue and salvage that keeps the reader prisoner of a narrative told by one who has mastered the arts of pace, description and suspense." Best Sellers

The leopard hunts in darkness; [by] Wilbur Smith. Doubleday 1984 423p o.p.
LC 84-4078

This volume in the author's Ballantyne saga focuses on "best-selling author Craig Mellow [who] decides to return to his native land for several reasons. He knows a poaching ring is operating to destroy the wildlife that is an African treasure; he suspects this ring is protected by someone high in the government of Zimbabwe. He's been hired by the World Bank to investigate these activities along with reports of a pending Russian-supported coup. He wants to see how his homeland has fared since the Ian Smith regime. Most of all, he is seeking his roots—the links with the past that have provided the raw material for his successful writing." Libr J

Smith, Wilbur A.—*Continued*

Men of men; [by] Wilbur Smith. Doubleday 1983 c1981 578p o.p.

LC 82-45566

First published 1981 in the United Kingdom

This second title in the author's series about the Ballantyne family is set in Southern Africa of the late 19th century and examines how the family is drawn into the empire-building schemes of Cecil Rhodes

"The author's intricately plotted, fast-paced novel describes without prejudice the dreams of the men and women, both European and African, to whom [Africa] was home. The reader comes to know each one and feels the pain of the inevitable conflict." Libr J

Followed by The angels weep

Monsoon; [by] Wilbur Smith. St. Martin's Press 1999 613p $26.95

ISBN 0-312-20339-X LC 99-24554

"A Thomas Dunne book"

This sequel to Birds of Prey "finds Sir Hal Courtney and his sons up to their bloody sword arms in piracy, intrigue, treachery and civil war in late 17th and early 18th century East Africa and Arabia. . . . Wealthy English landowner Sir Hal earned his fortune as a sea captain with the East India Company. To protect his overseas investments, he becomes a privateer to combat Arab pirates attacking company ships from bases in Zanzibar and Madagascar. Accompanied by three of his four sons, Sir Hal embarks on a desperate voyage that will bring either glory and treasure or ruin. . . . Clever plot twists and lavish historical detail attend the siblings' adventures." Publ Wkly

Power of the sword; [by] Wilbur Smith. Little, Brown 1986 618p o.p.

LC 86-10279

"The central characters in this robust tale of politics, adventure and romance set in South Africa are stepbrothers Manfred and Shasa, sons of Centaine Courtney (from 'The Burning Shore'), owner of a diamond mine. As representatives, respectively, of the Afrikaner cause and that of the more liberal, English-speaking whites, headed in the early days by Jan Smuts, they are, however, destined to be enemies. . . . What Smith may lack in subtlety, he makes up for in raw vigor." Publ Wkly

Followed by Rage

Rage; by Wilbur Smith. Little, Brown 1987 627p o.p.

LC 87-3078

This novel in the Courtney family saga is set in post-World War II South Africa. "Shasa Courtney is a wealthy United Party minister to the South African Parliament. A moderate of English heritage, he is often opposed to the Nationalist Party's Manfred De La Rey, an Afrikaner. Their mother, the matriarchal Centaine Courtney-Malcomess, is able to mediate their conflicts but not to control Shasa's wife, Tara, who . . . falls in love with the black Moses Gama, an advocate of violent opposition to apartheid." Publ Wkly

"The interlocking stories of these and many others, set against the authentic African historical and cultural background that Smith so effectively provides, produces both a compelling tale and some real insights into South Africa." Libr J

Followed by A time to die

River god; [by] Wilbur Smith. St. Martin's Press 1994 c1993 530p o.p.

LC 93-45249

"A Thomas Dunne book"

First published 1993 in the United Kingdom

This novel, set in Egypt ca.1780 B.C., "tells the story of Taita the eunuch, slave to a noble's daughter. Taita narrates the dramatic events of which he was either witness or participant as his mistress receives the dubious honor of marriage to the pharaoh. The brutality of life in ancient times is everywhere evident in Taita's tale, which involves fatal intrigue at every turn. It's clear Smith knows his subject: his graphic depiction of lust, bloodletting, politics, and, in Taita's case, honor is firmly grounded in rich details that evoke the period." Booklist

Followed by The seventh scroll

The seventh scroll; [by] Wilbur Smith. St. Martin's Press 1995 486p o.p.

LC 95-768

"A Thomas Dunne book"

This sequel to River god "pairs blueblood, devil-may-care Sir Nicholas Quenton-Harper, who recently has lost his wife and children in a tragic accident, and half-English, half-Egyptian archeologist Royan Al-Sima, herself recently bereaved, in a desperate race to unearth Pharaoh Mamose's fabulous treasures. Their rival in this quest is Gotthold von Schiller, an old, crazed, murderous German collector of antiquities whose mistress, a porno actress, dresses up as an ancient Egyptian queen to titillate him. The major clue is the eponymous seventh scroll, key to the tomb's location, written by ancient Egyptian scribe Taita." Publ Wkly

"Smith excels at action sequences, getting his attractive heroes and despicable villains into and out of hugely entertaining predicaments, all the while tossing off vivid descriptions, bits of historical detail, and classic low-key British banter." Booklist

A time to die; [by] Wilbur Smith. Random House 1990 c1989 448p o.p.

LC 89-27360

First published 1989 in the United Kingdom

This novel in the Courtney family saga, focuses on "Sean Courtney, Rhodesian African Rifles officer turned big-game hunter. Leading a safari on his licensed land in Africa, Courtney is lured over the Mozambique border in pursuit of a long-sought elephant trophy, for which his client promises him half a million dollars. Courtney turns into the quarry, however, when a Mozambiquan guerrilla leader kidnaps the client's daughter, Claudia, and forces Courtney into abetting the rebel cause. A few stolen American-made missiles and the devastation of a Soviet-equipped helicopter base later, Courtney and Claudia are fleeing for their lives through the African wilderness." Booklist

Followed by Golden fox

Smith, Zadie

The autograph man; a novel. Random House 2002 347p o.p.

ISBN 0-375-50186-X LC 2002-69705

"Tells the story of a young half-Chinese, half-Jewish autograph trader named Alex-Li Tandem who achieves a trade-specific form of enlightenment by tracking down the reclusive aging actress Kitty Alexander, whose ex-

Smith, Zadie—*Continued*

tremely rare signatures are the envy of collectors everywhere." Libr J

"Smith's pen portraits of the shabby, yobbish autograph trading circle are intermittently funny, but her prose is so busy being clever that the laughter never builds. This is disappointing but, even with its faults, the novel points to a literary talent of a high order." Publ Wkly

On beauty. Penguin Press 2005 445p $25.95
ISBN 1-59420-0637

"The Belsey family is multicultural as well as multinational. Howard is English, teaching art history at liberal Wellington College near Boston. His [African-American] wife, Kiki, is from Florida, and as practical as her husband is intellectual. Although they love each other dearly, Howard's waning career and wandering eye have caused a strain. Their children follow their own paths: Jerome is a Christian; Zora is a socially concerned intellectual; and Levi is trying to be a black man of the streets. When Jerome falls in love with the daughter of Howard's archrival, Monty Kipps, the two families are thrown together in a personal and cultural battle. Although the romance sours, Howard and Monty's rivalry kicks up a notch, while Kiki and Mrs. Kipps develop an unlikely bond." Booklist

"Ms Smith has her shortcomings. The novel's first half is under-edited; surely we do not need to meet every guest at an anniversary party. . . . Nevertheless, the book gathers momentum, and the second half gallops along." Economist

White teeth; a novel. Random House 2000 448p $24.95
ISBN 0-375-50185-1 LC 99-43658

"Hapless Archibald Jones fights alongside Bengali Muslim Samad Iqbal in the English army during WWII, and the two develop an unlikely bond that intensifies when Samad relocates to Archie's native London, Smith traces the trajectory of their friendship through marriage, parenthood and the shared disappointments of poverty and deflated dreams." Publ Wkly

"Hopscotching through several continents and 150 years of history, 'White Teeth' encompasses a teeming family saga, a sly inquiry into race and identity and a tender-hearted satire on religious antagonism and cultural bemusement. . . . Smith holds it all together with a raucous energy and confidence." N Y Times Book Rev

Smollett, Tobias George, 1721-1771

Humphry Clinker. o.p.

In this epistolary novel "the letters are written by Matthew Bramble, his sister Tabitha, their niece, their nephew, and their maid, Winifred Jenkins. Each correspondent has a highly individual style and caricatures himself unwittingly. The titular hero of this comic masterpiece, who plays a lesser role than the Brambles, is a workhouse lad who enters into their service by chance and who later becomes a Methodist preacher. He falls in love with Winifred, and is eventually found to be the natural son of Mr. Bramble. The 'expedition' of the title is a family tour through England and Scotland, during which the correspondents express surprisingly varied reactions to the same events. Of particular note is the picture of Hot Wells (a sobriquet for the city of Bath), a fashionable watering place." Reader's Ency. 4th edition

Sneider, Vern, 1916-1981

The Teahouse of the August Moon. Putnam 1951 282p o.p.

This "novel centers around Captain Fisby, member of a Government Team in Okinawa, his colonel, and Plan B for the welfare of the natives. The plan would have gone according to schedule if Fisby hadn't received a gift of two geishas, and if Miss Higa Jiga and other maiden ladies hadn't felt they must compete on an equitable basis with the geishas. The chicanery of the ladies, and Fisby's coping with the situation make this a wonderfully humorous and satirical story." Libr J

Snow, C. P. (Charles Percy), 1905-1980

The affair. Scribner 1960 374p (Strangers and brothers) o.p.

One of the Strangers and brothers series of eleven novels set in England during the first half of the the 20th century. The series is "a sequence of novels comprising the life story of the narrator Lewis Eliot and alternating between his direct and observed experience." Publisher's note

"A novel set in one of England's important universities, the central situation is the dismissal of a young scientist accused of fraud. A re-opening of his case splits the university wide open, both for moral and for political reasons." Publ Wkly

The conscience of the rich. Scribner 1958 342p (Strangers and brothers) o.p.

"As a result of his friendship with Charles March, Lewis Eliot is taken into the private world of one of England's wealthiest and most influential Jewish families and through his eyes the March drama is slowly unfolded; the close bond between Charles, his father, and his sister, Charles's marriage to a gentle Communist, and the ensuing political scandal which estranges father and son, brother and sister. . . . Set in London during the late 1920's and the 1930's." Booklist

Corridors of power. 1964 403p (Strangers and brothers) o.p.

"The workings of inner power in the British government—with key administrators, politicians, and the wealthy manipulators, male and female—[are] traced in a novel of the period 1955-1958. . . . Since the power in this fictional case is concerned with the use of nuclear arms, the fate of the world can easily hang on the fate of one minister, Roger Quaife." Publ Wkly

"We see the corridors of political power illuminated with a fine and discriminating light." Libr J

Homecoming. Scribner 1956 399p (Strangers and brothers) o.p.

"An introspective, subtly shaded novel which again stars Lewis Eliot. . . . Eliot's unhappy marriage to a neurotic woman, her death, and his affair with and eventual marriage to a woman more worthy of his love comprise the chief incidents in a story that accents not the events themselves but their psychological effect upon the persons involved. Crisp, carefully fashioned prose; for the discriminating." Booklist

Snow, C. P. (Charles Percy), 1905-1980—*Continued*

Last things. Scribner 1970 435p (Strangers and brothers) o.p.

"Student protest, Lewis Eliot's decision on whether or not to enter the Labor government's ministry, his serious eye operation during which a cardiac arrest brings him near to death—these are some of the essential plot elements [of this novel]." Publ Wkly

The light and the dark. Scribner 1961 c1947 406p (Strangers and brothers) o.p.

First published 1947 in the United Kingdom

Cambridge University is the scene of the greater part of this character study of a young Cambridge don. In an attempt to curb his dark moods Roy tries promiscuity, drink, concentration on his studies, and religion. With the out-break of the war he joins the RAF and is killed in action

"A painstaking and readable account of university life seen from high table." Times Lit Suppl

The masters. Macmillan 1951 374p (Strangers and brothers) o.p.

"Lewis Eliot, a Cambridge Fellow, tells about the election of a new Master of his college, and uses the rivalry and jealousy attendant on the election to illuminate the lives and hearts of the candidates and their friends and enemies. The book begins with notice of the impending death of the old Master, Vernon Royce, continues at a leisurely rate as Royce waits to die and finally dies, and ends with the election of the new Master." New Yorker

"For a quiet novel of subtle characterization this one contains a surprising element of suspense." Ont Libr Rev

The new men. Scribner 1954 311p (Strangers and brothers) o.p.

The novel describes a group of nuclear scientists and high government officials working together in England during the war. As usual Lewis Eliot is the narrator

The author "handles a fateful new theme with challenging insight and impressive moral sensitivity. . . . [This is a] novel which searchingly explores the moral dilemmas created by the atom bomb." Atlantic

The sleep of reason. Scribner 1969 c1968 483p (Strangers and brothers) o.p.

The book "brings back Sir Lewis Eliot, now retired, 58, living in London. In the nearby university town of his birth, in the midst of his own personal crises of health and family, the concentric circles of his life—past, present, and future—merge to thrust upon him a new and problematical responsibility, one that he finds revolts, horrifies, and fascinates him. The lesbian niece of an old friend is on trial with her lover for the grisly abduction, torture and murder of an eight-year-old boy. Sir Lewis attends the trial at his friend's request, and the trial, the peak of the book, throws into relief some specific and general problems of our age. The two murderesses are seen as miniscule reincarnations of what went on at Auschwitz. Snow ponders the whys, hows, wherefores of such inhuman behavior, and the roles of the courts, medicine, psychiatry, law, the non-participating onlookers." Publ Wkly

Strangers and brothers. Scribner 1960 309p (Strangers and brothers) o.p.

First published 1940 in the United Kingdom

George Passant, a solicitor in an English provincial town, exerts a crucial influence on his group of young protegés, Lewis Eliot among them. An idealist, courageous and high-principled Passant seems destined for great things yet the story ends in his trial for fraud. The reasons for this are revealed

"Essentially the tragedy of a good man defeated by the mediocrity of his world, the story of George Passant is completed in the novel 'Homecoming.' . . . Like all the novels in the series, 'Strangers and Brothers' is distinguished by virtue of its analysis of motive and character and its anatomization of a world in which a smooth mediocrity is the greatest virtue." Libr J

Time of hope. Macmillan 1950 c1949 416p (Strangers and brothers) o.p.

"Here, as in 'Light and the Dark' (1948) Lewis Eliot is the main character that typifies middle class English life, and as in the earlier work, Mr. Snow shows the impact of spiritual values on individuals. The 1930s are the background here and the years are brilliantly drawn. Moral problems are vivid and the characters are varied in their reactions." Libr J

Snow, Charles Percy *See* Snow, C. P. (Charles Percy), 1905-1980

Snow, Lucy *See* Aubert, Rosemary, 1946-

Snow white, blood red; edited by Ellen Datlow & Terri Windling. Morrow 1992 411p o.p.
LC 92-24899

"An AvoNova book"

Contents: Like a red, red rose, by S. Wade; The moon is drowning while I sleep, by C. de Lint; The frog prince, by G. Wilson; Stalking beans, by N. Kress; Snow-drop, by T. Lee; Little red, by W. Wheeler; I shall do thee mischief in the wood, by K. Koja; The root of the matter, by G. Frost; The princess in the tower, by E. A. Lynn; Persimmon, by H. Jacobs; Little Poucet, by S. R. Tem; The changelings, by M. Tem; The Springfield swans, by C. Stevermer; Troll bridge, by N. Gaiman; A sound, like angels singing, by L. Rysdyk; Puss, by E. M. Friesner; The glass casket, by J. Dann; Knives, by J. Yolen; The snow queen, by P. A. McKillip; Breadcrumbs and stones, by L. Goldstein

"The dark and shadowed aspects of well-known folk stories and fairy tales are explored in updated retellings. . . . Some of these tales are enchanting; some are horrifying; most, like the originals, offer insight into human nature." Publ Wkly

Snyder, Don J.

Night crossing; a novel. Knopf 2001 277p $24
ISBN 0-375-40906-8 LC 00-62008

When Nora Andrews, 42 and pregnant, discovers her husband is having an affair she "boards a plane to Ireland alone, where she promptly witnesses a terrorist bombing. Having seen too much, she is drawn into a British anti-IRA plot and is charged with the safekeeping

Snyder, Don J.—*Continued*
of a wounded British soldier." Booklist

"This competent—albeit derivative and inflammatory—thriller delivers some exciting moments as well as insights into the mind of a woman who slowly realizes her own complicity in the wreck of her marriage." Publ Wkly

Solomita, Stephen

Damaged goods. Scribner 1996 380p o.p.
LC 95-33277

"Jilly Sappone truly is 'damaged goods.' The gunshot that wrecked his brain years before also made him into a vicious killer. Released from prison by family connections, he takes revenge on everyone responsible for his prison term. Beginning with his ex-wife, Ann, Jilly and his brainless psychotic partner, Jackson-Davis, commence a spree of kidnapping and violent murders. Ex-cop Stanley Moodrow is hired, as is detective cum-computer-whiz Ginny Gadd, to track down Jilly." Libr J

"The pace is energetic, and with Ginny at his side to blunt his cynicism, Moodrow seems less morose and more alert than we've seen him in a long time." N Y Times Book Rev

A good day to die. Penzler Bks. 1993 297p o.p.
LC 93-19400

"Roland Means, a chronic maverick in the NYPD, is pulled from cop purgatory—ballistics duty—to go after 'King Thong,' the supposed serial killer responsible for the murder of seven male prostitutes in New York City. Vanessa Bouton, a black cop, hates Means's guts but needs his streetwise methods to help prove her hunch that only one killing was prompted by a motive, which the other six are meant to mask." Publ Wkly

"As Means researches the profiled backgrounds of serial killers, he recognizes his own abused childhood; his search for the killer becomes a search for himself. This multiethnic thriller vividly depicts the gritty streets of the city, the dark and feral forest, and the danger lurking in both." Libr J

Last chance for glory. Penzler Bks. 1994 310p o.p.
LC 93-38616

"Marty Blake, an out-of-work private investigator, is hired to help clear the name of a slightly retarded young man wrongly convicted of murder. To aid in the investigation, Marty contacts Sgt. Bela Kosinski, the original arresting officer, who is now retired from the NYPD and drinking himself to death. As this unlikely pair reinvestigate the murder, they find it easy to prove the young man's innocence, but they also discover a murder cover-up that extends into the highest echelons of the police force and New York City government." Libr J

"Blake and Kosinski initially form an uneasy alliance that inevitably turns to friendship, but it happens easily and believably. It's the old mismatched-partner plot, but seldom has it been handled better." Booklist

Solomon, Nina

Single wife; a novel. Algonquin Bks. 2003 307p $23.95
ISBN 1-56512-382-4 LC 2003-40406

"Most men who leave their wives have the courtesy to (at least) leave a note, but not journalist Laz Brookman. At the start of this. . . novel, he casually leaves his New York apartment one morning and never returns. . . . Anxious to save face and preserve the precarious normality of her life, and certain that he will soon return—mysterious several-day-long disappearing acts not being uncommon with her husband—Grace Brookman secretly begins living two lives, Laz's and her own." Publ Wkly

"Solomon tells a funny and bizarre story that is both hard to believe and hard to put down, with characters who are real, almost tangible. She captures the essence of the struggle for self." Libr J

Solzhenitsyn, Aleksandr, 1918-

August 1914; translated by Harry T. Willets. Farrar, Straus & Giroux 1989 854p (Red wheel/knot) o.p.
LC 88-30966

Original Russian edition published 1971 in France; this is an expanded and newly translated version of the title first published 1972 in the United States

Set at the outbreak of the First World War, this novel, the first in a projected series, explores the responsibility for Russia's defeat in the Battle of Tannenberg

"For at least 20 years Mr. Solzhenitsyn has been working on a vast cycle of novels called 'The Red Wheel,' which he envisages as a panorama of modern Russia, but still more as a corrective to what he regards as the distortions of Russian history by writers contaminated with liberal and radical ideas. . . . The book forms the opening volume of 'The Red Wheel,' which is structured as a series of what the author calls 'knots,' or renderings of crucial historical moments that have determined the course of Russian, perhaps all of modern, history." NY Times Book Rev

Followed by November 1916

Cancer ward; translated from the Russian by Nicholas Bethell and David Burg. Farrar, Straus & Giroux 1969 560p o.p.

"Set mostly in a provincial cancer ward, the novel traces the ways in which a number of moribund patients come to terms with their death, centering on an investigation of the moral and psychological development of the exiled hero, Kostoglotov. This novel, in which the cancer ward has been widely interpreted as symbolizing the Soviet state, was typeset for publication in the Soviet Union but never published there until after Perestroika began." Reader's Ency. 4th edition

The first circle; translated from the Russian by Thomas P. Whitney. Harper & Row 1968 580p o.p.

This novel "depicts life in a *sharashka*, i.e., a prison for educated people who carry on scientific research while serving long terms. Encompassing a span of only three days, this long novel both traces the ineluctable apprehension of Innokenty Artemyevich Vologin, a state counselor in the Ministry of Foreign Affairs, and recreates, in an integrated web of short chapters, the daily routine and moral condition of the highly educated inmates of the *sharashka*. The experiences of the hero, Nerzhin, parallel those of the author, while the character of Lev Rubin, the longtime Party member who maintains

Solzhenitsyn, Aleksandr, 1918-—*Continued*
his faith in the Communist ideal despite the injustices done to him and his fellows, is modeled on Lev Kopelev, a central figure in the civil rights movement of the 1960s and 1970s." Reader's Ency. 4th edition

November 1916; translated by H.T. Willetts. Farrar, Straus & Giroux 1998 1014p (Red wheel/knot) $35
ISBN 0-374-22314-9 LC 98-14263
Original Russian edition, 1993
The narrative takes place between October 27 and November 17, 1916 and chronicles the waning years of World War I and events leading to the Russian Revolution
"When Solzhenitsyn relaxes his didactic labors his tremendous gifts as a novelist shine in his creation of characters and his depiction of war on the front line." New Yorker

One day in the life of Ivan Denisovich; translated from the Russian by H. T. Willets; with an introduction by John Bayley. Knopf 1995 xxvii, 159p $15
ISBN 0-679-44464-5
"Everyman's library"
Original Russian edition, 1962; this is a reissue of the translation published 1991 by Farrar, Straus & Giroux
"Drawing on his own experiences, the author writes of one day, from reveille to lights-out, in the prison existence of Ivan Denisovich Shukhov. Innocent of any crime, he has been convicted of treason and sentenced to ten years in one of Stalin's notorious slave-labor compounds. The protagonist is a simple man trying to survive the brutality of a totalitarian system." Shapiro. Fic for Youth. 3d edition

Somers, Jane *See* Lessing, Doris May, 1919-

Sontag, Susan, 1933-2004

In America; a novel. Farrar, Straus & Giroux 2000 387p $26
ISBN 0-374-17540-3 LC 99-54641
"In 1876, 35-year-old Maryna Zalewska, Poland's brilliant, revered actress, packs up her 14-person entourage, including husband, child, maid, and assorted relatives and admirers, and emigrates to Anaheim, CA, determined to shed her glittering life and disappear into the unglamorous anonymity borne of the radical, hardscrabble work of her commune. After a couple of years, with the failure of the farm looming, Maryna returns to the stage in a dazzling U.S. comeback that rockets her to renewed fame, fortune, and smashing success across the nation and overseas." Libr J
This novel "displays Sontag in a relaxed, pleasure-seeking mode, guiding her characters through a long travelogue in time, specifically the beginnings of the gilded age in the brave new world." Time

The volcano lover; a romance. Farrar, Straus & Giroux 1992 419p il $22
ISBN 0-374-28516-0 LC 92-71738
"The 'volcano lover' of the title is Sir William Hamilton, the British diplomat and antiquary who is best remembered as the complaisant husband of Emma Hamilton, notorious mistress of Admiral Nelson. The book is set for the most part in Naples, where, from 1764 until his recall under a cloud in 1800, Sir William was the British envoy to the court of the egregious Bourbon monarch Ferdinand IV, later to become Ferdinand I, King of the Two Sicilies. . . . The novel is a kind of triptych, divided among Hamilton, his wife and Lord Nelson." N Y Times Book Rev
Sontag's "narrative deftly blends the magnetism of personality and the suspense of event with shrewd commentary and sly mockery as she contrasts the habits of thought in that age with ours and reflects on the meaning of mercy and vengeance, self-invention and praise, love and obsession. In all, a memorable group portrait and a brilliant, fresh improvisation on classically grand themes." Booklist

Sorrentino, Gilbert, 1929-

Blue pastoral. North Point Press 1983 315p
ISBN 0-86547-095-2 LC 82-073720
This novel "involves the adventures of Serge and Helene Gavotte as they drag their pushcart across America in a relentless search for the notes that will constitute the 'Perfect Musical Phrase.'. . . [Part of the book] portrays the evils of city life and combines various sorts of prose and poetry–'erotical interlude,' dramatic eclogue, elegy, idyll." N Y Times Book Rev
Serge's odyssey occasions a brutally hilarious literary explosion in which a world of pop-cultural cliches gets a freewheeling linguistic drubbing. . . . Readers lucky enough to have the taste will enjoy. Libr J

The moon in its flight; stories. 2004 266p pa $16
ISBN 1-56689-152-3 LC 2004-665
Contents: The moon in its flight; Decades; Land of cotton; The dignity of labor; The sea, caught in roses; A beehive arranged on human principles; Pastilles; Allegory of innocence; Sample writing sample; Times without number; Subway; Facts and their manifestations; It's time to call it a day; Life and letters;
"A sort of grim nostalgia pervades his stories, many of the best of which are set in a perfectly evoked mid-20th century New York of shabby cocktail lounges and afternoon papers." N Y Times Book Rev

Southgate, Martha

The fall of Rome; a novel. Scribner 2002 223p $23; pa $12
ISBN 0-684-86500-9; 0-7432-2721-2 (pa)
LC 2001-34225
A "novel about a token black teacher at an élite New England boarding school. Jerome Washington is a classics scholar who, armed with a Harvard education and an accent purged of his Georgia-sharecropper roots, has spent his life trying to defeat racism through sheer decorum. But his hermetic existence is threatened by the arrival of a black student from a Brooklyn ghetto and a white female teacher who fancies herself a champion of the underprivileged." New Yorker
The author "delves deeply into the social and emotional elements that unite and divide us. Issues of race, identity, and integrity are intensely explored through a tragic human triangle." Booklist

Spark, Muriel

The Abbess of Crewe. Viking 1974 116p o.p.

Set in the convent of Crewe in England, this novel traces the efforts of Sister Alexandra to win the elective position of abbess. "The problem is Sister Felicity, who has a following amongst the nuns. But Felicity has committed certain indiscretions, and Alexandra and her supporters are able to discredit her." Christ Sci Monit

"The Abbess of Crewe has the closely woven texture and the structural coherence of good poetry: it is executed with a subtlety and intelligence that safeguard against the tones of complacent moralizing that might very easily have spoiled the articulation of the book's themes." Saturday Rev/World

Aiding and abetting. Doubleday 2000 166p o.p.

ISBN 0-385-50153-6 LC 00-55559

"A tall, whitehaired man walks into the Paris consulting room of Hildegaard Woolf, a psychiatrist from Bavaria. Revealing himself as Lord Lucan, he threatens to unmask Dr. Wolf as Beate Pappenheim, a former student revolutionary. Tired of being poor, she had bilked credulous people by persuading them that the menstrual blood she smeared on herself was a sign of the stigmata." Economist

"The unsettling wit of 'Aiding and Abetting' hits the funny bone as hard it pricks the conscience. . . . It's kiln-dried wit that never cracks, with a smile that dares you to laugh. As always [Spark] is breathtakingly deft with the anxieties of well-bred people, people who know how to dress, where to eat, and how to commit the most heinous cruelty. If satire is your cup of tea, . . . [this is a] perfectly seeped book to be savored." Christ Sci Monit

The bachelors. New Directions 1999 186p pa $12.95

ISBN 0-8112-1424-9 LC 99-30688

First published 1960 in the United Kingdom; first published in the United States 1961 by Lippincott

This "novel follows a group of British bachelors whose cozy little world is shattered when they suddenly find themselves the target of blackmail, fraud, and other bits of nastiness courtesy of one of the lads. Spark is always a great read." Libr J

The ballad of Peckham Rye. Lippincott 1960 160p o.p.

"Young Dougal Douglas, the Devil in contemporary clothing, has quite an impact on an industrial town adjacent to London since, among other things, he is responsible for a groom leaving his bride-to-be at the altar and the nervous breakdown of a veteran employee in one of the local factories." Booklist

"A fresh comic style does not appear every day, and that is what Muriel Spark has developed in this expert fantasy. . . . The wackiness is cumulative, the style dead-pan and blow-by-blow, and above all no overt attempt is ever made to get a laugh." N Y Times Book Rev

also in Spark, M. A Muriel Spark trio p233-386

The comforters

In Spark, M. A Muriel Spark trio p13-228

The driver's seat. Knopf 1970 117p o.p.

Originally published in the New Yorker, this is the story of "Lise, a fascinatingly eccentric, pent-up creature whose vacation in the South of Europe turns into a macabre disaster, one she herself helps to bring about." Choice

"The author's perspective is cosmically cool and fantastic: she knows no more about her protagonist, Lise, than does the reader. . . . She follows this woman, another of her slightly bizarre lunatics, through a day's grotesque project, narrating only its circumstances, leaving all motive, all emotion, all inner plan to be inferred. The result is a long, elusive joke that casts as deep an irony on life's arbitrariness as do the more 'compassionate' ironies of, say, E. M. Forster." Nation

A far cry from Kensington. Houghton Mifflin 1988 189p o.p.

LC 88-5904

"The narrator, Mrs. Hawkins, remembers back to 1954 when she was a young war widow living in furnished rooms in a boarding house in South Kensington, London. Mrs. Hawkins was the unwitting confidante of her fellow boarders and coworkers—she was an editor but lost two jobs because of standing up against a writer she believed was a hack. This same man intruded into her private life as well." Booklist

"Spark balances devastatingly eccentric characters and funny situations with darker elements, even pathos. Her well-constructed novel has no loose ends and few contrived situations." Libr J

The finishing school; Muriel Spark. 1st ed. Doubleday 2004 181p $16.95

ISBN 0-385-51282-1 LC 2004-45533

This novel "takes place in a finishing school in Switzerland run by a young married couple. Theirs is not the old-fashioned type of finishing school, in which young ladies learn deportment; rather, it is one in which both male and female students, after high school and before college, take a wide range of courses about culture and civilization. The husband is blocked in performing what is of primary importance to him: his writing. Contributing to his burden is his great envy of the apparent ease and fluidity with which one of the male students seems to be composing his own novel." Booklist

The author "satirically assails, among other subjects, the culture of spectacle that has grown up around novel writing, particularly novel writing by attractive young people." Atl Mon (1993)

The girls of slender means. Knopf 1963 176p o.p.

"The novel, set primarily in London during World War II, focuses on the inhabitants of a residential club for unmarried women and on the friendship of several of them with a young man named Nicholas Farringdon. When tragedy strikes and 13 of the women are killed, Nicholas realizes that there is no safety anywhere, especially for those on whom fortune had once seemed to smile. This epiphany stimulates his conversion to Roman Catholicism. Years later, he dies in Haiti, where he has gone as a missionary." Merriam-Webster's Ency of Lit

The go-away bird

In Spark, M. The stories of Muriel Spark p221-62

Spark, Muriel—*Continued*

Loitering with intent. Coward, McCann & Geoghegan 1981 217p o.p.

ISBN 0-698-11047-1 LC 80-26049

"Would-be novelist Fleur Talbot works for the snooty, irascible Sir Quentin Oliver at the Autobiographical Association, whose members are all at work on their memoirs. When her employer gets his hands on Fleur's novel-in-progress, mayhem ensues when its scenes begin coming true. Generating hilarious turns of phrase and larger-than-life characters (especially Sir Quentin's batty mother), Sparks's inimitable style make this literary joyride thoroughly appealing." Publ Wkly

The Mandelbaum Gate. Knopf 1965 369p o.p.

"The changing shape of any identity, be it of person or of situation, is the theme of this novel, typified by the Mandelbaum Gate of the title, 'hardly a gate at all, but a piece of street between Jerusalem and Jerusalem' . . . The narrative goes and returns piecemeal between the two parts of the Holy Land, focusing on two English characters–Barbara Vaughan, a spinster, half Jewish by birth and Roman Catholic by conviction, come to Israel to be near her archeologist fiance (and lover) in Jordan and to make a pilgrimage to the Holy sites; and Freddy Hamilton, proper foreign officer, moved by an unexpected impulse to change his personal pattern of responsibility and by kindness to keep Barbara from the danger of being apprehended by Jordan authorities because of her background." Libr J

"The novel deals compellingly with issues of religious and personal identity, and makes the story of its protagonist's quest for the reconciliation of the two cultural and religious traditions to which she belongs as exciting as any thriller." Oxford Companion to 20th-century Lit in Engl

Memento mori. Lippincott 1959 c1958 224p o.p.

"Several elderly London friends receive anonymous telephone calls with a single message: 'Remember you must die.' Each hears and interprets the words differently. Old rivalries and romances still color the friends' relations, and Spark makes clear that their personalities in old age are but a continuation of their earlier lives." Merriam-Webster's Ency of Lit

also in Spark, M. A Muriel Spark trio p393-608

A Muriel Spark trio; The comforters; The ballad of Peckham Rye; Memento mori. Lippincott 1962 608p o.p.

The three complete novels reprinted here were first published 1957, 1960 and 1959 respectively. The comforters is a novel in experimental form. It is a book within a book, in which many of the characters are neurotics or oddities of some sort. The most normal character is Louisa Jepp, aged seventy-eight, whose experiments with smuggling diamonds provide much of the action. The scene is England, and Roman Catholic life is part of the background

Open to the public; new & collected stories. New Directions 1997 376p $24.95

ISBN 0-8112-1367-6 LC 97-20607

Contents: The Portobello Road; The curtain blown by the breeze; The black madonna; Bang-bang you're dead; The Seraph and the Zambesi; The twins; The Playhouse called Remarkable; The pawnbroker's wife; Miss Pinkerton's apocalypse; 'A sad tale's best for winter'; The leaf sweeper; Daisy Overend; You should have seen the mess; Come along, Marjorie; The ormolu clock; The dark glasses; A member of the family; The house of the famous poet; The fathers' daughters; Open to the public; Alice Long's dachshunds; The go-away bird; The first year of my life; The gentile Jewesses; The executor; The fortune-teller; Another pair of hands; The dragon; The girl I left behind me; Going up and coming down; The pearly shadow; Chimes; The thing about police stations; Harper and Wilton; Ladies and gentlemen; Lavishes ghost; The hanging judge

"With 10 tales new to American readers, *Open to the Public* brings Spark's stories up to date with the rest of her prolific output." Publ Wkly

The prime of Miss Jean Brodie. Lippincott 1962 c1961 187p o.p.

First published 1961 in the United Kingdom

"Miss Jean Brodie, teacher at the Marcia Blaine School for Girls in Edinburgh in the 1930s, gathers around herself a group of young girls who are set apart from other students as the Brodie set: Monica Douglas, who will be famous for her mathematical ability; Rose Stanley, who will be famous for her sex appeal; Eunice Gardiner, of great swimming and gymnastic ability; Sandy Stranger, of the small eyes and outstanding vowel sounds; and Mary MacGregor, who is considered a silent lump. Miss Brodie will make these girls the 'crème de la crème,' especially if they will follow her advice to recognize their prime. Her teaching is unorthodox and her relationship with the students most informal, so that they are privy to her affair with the school's music teacher. We get glimpses into the future of these young girls and are made aware that students are capable of treachery as well as teacher-worship." Shapiro. Fic for Youth. 3d edition

Reality and dreams. Houghton Mifflin 1997 160p o.p.

ISBN 0-395-83811-8 LC 96-52913

First published 1996 in the United Kingdom

Ä glimpse of a girl selling hamburgers at a French campground ignites film director Tom Richard's imagination, and around it he builds his latest movie. When the film is still in production, he suffers a serious accident and awakens to find his vision being threatened as others try to take over the story. He also awakens to disruptions in his 'real' life-many of those around him are losing their jobs, his daughters' marriages are in the process of breaking up, and long held resentments/jealousies, both personal and professional, are coming to the surface.¨Libr J

Dame Muriel is as enigmatic in this novel, as distinct, as relentlessly observant of human habits and unguarded moments as she has ever been.¨N Y Times Book Rev

The stories of Muriel Spark. Dutton 1985 314p o.p.

LC 85-10355

Contents: The Portobello Road; The curtain blown by the breeze; The Black Madonna; Bang-bang you're dead; The Seraph and the Zambesi; The twins; The Playhouse called Remarkable; The pawnbroker's wife; Miss Pinkerton's apocalypse; A sad tale's best for winter; The leaf-sweeper; Daisy Overend; You should have seen the mess; Come along, Marjorie; The ormolu clock; The

Spark, Muriel—*Continued*
dark glasses; A member of the family; The house of the famous poet; The father's daughters; Alice Long's dachshunds; The go-away bird; The first year of my life; The Gentile Jewesses; The executor; The fortune-teller; Another pair of hands; The Dragon

Sparks, Nicholas

A bend in the road. Warner Bks. 2001 341p o.p.
ISBN 0-446-52778-5 LC 2001-26419
Deputy sheriff Miles Ryan's "high school sweetheart, Missy, was killed in an unsolved hit and run accident, leaving him to raise their son, Jonah, in New Bern, N.C. [Sarah Andrews'] politically ambitious husband, Michael, dumped her when her ovaries proved inactive, and she fled to New Bern to teach, and love, other people's kids. Miles and Sarah meet at a parent-teacher conference, and the sparks fly. But there's a fly in the ointment as well." Publ Wkly
"Sparks brings a powerful tale of true love to fruition, proving that love stories can be sweet without being cloying." Booklist

The guardian. Warner Bks. 2003 384p $24.95
ISBN 0-446-52779-3 LC 2002-192411
"On Christmas Eve, Julie Barenson, 25 years old and newly widowed, finds an unexpected present—a Great Dane pup that her late husband, Jim, had arranged for her to receive after her died from a brain tumor. . . . Julie's new dog, Singer, turns out to be a better judge of character than she, which is unfortunate because the dog nearly gives away the book's ending when he growls warily at Richard Franklin, the new man in Julie's life." Publ Wkly

Message in a bottle. Warner Bks. 1998 322p $20
ISBN 0-446-52356-9 LC 97-39158
"Boston parenting columnist Theresa Osborne has lost faith in the dream of everlasting love. Three years after divorcing her cheating husband, the single mother is vacationing on Cape Cod when she finds a bottle washed up on the shore. Inside, a message begins: 'My Dearest Catherine, I miss you.' Subsequent publication of the poignant missive in her column turns up two more letters, found by others, from the same mysterious writer, Garrett Blake. Piqued by his epistolary constancy, Theresa follows the trail to North Carolina, where she discovers that Garrett has been mourning his late wife for three years; writing the seaborne messages is his only solace. Theresa also finds that Garrett just might be ready to love again . . . and that she might be the woman for him." Publ Wkly

Nights in Rodanthe. Warner Bks. 2002 212p o.p.
ISBN 0-446-53133-2 LC 2002-66189
"Adrienne Wills is a 45-year-old mother of three whose husband recently abandoned her for a younger woman. When she visits the small coastal town of Rodanthe, North Carolina, seeking a bit of respite from her problems, she meets Paul Flanner, a 54-year-old doctor who has sold his thriving medical practice and come to Rodanthe to escape his own tortured past." Booklist
"Sparks builds a taut, plausible relationship between his protagonists." Publ Wkly

The notebook. Warner Bks. 1996 214p $16.95
ISBN 0-446-52080-2 LC 96-33815
"At 80, Noah Calhoun reads daily from a notebook containing the love story of Noah and Allie. We learn of the teenaged lovers, their 14-year separation and reunion in New Bern, North Carolina, just weeks before Allie is to marry another man. Back in the present, we learn that Noah and Allie did marry and were happy for more than 40 years. Now, they are residents of a nursing home, separated both by rooms and, more profoundly, by Allie's Alzheimer's. Noah's daily reading from the notebook is not to himself; he reads aloud to Allie, hoping that the power of their love story will reach her." Libr J

A walk to remember. Warner Bks. 1999 240p $19.95
ISBN 0-446-52553-7 LC 99-12079
In Beaufort, North Carolina in 1958, 17-year-old high school senior Landon Carter takes Jamie Sullivan, the minister's daughter, to the homecoming dance, stars with her in the Christmas play, and falls in love with her, only to discover her sad secret
The author "is a master at pulling heartstrings and bringing a tear to his readers' eyes. . . . Told in Landon's down-home voice, this bittersweet tale will enthrall Sparks' numerous fans." Booklist

Sparks, Timothy *See* Dickens, Charles, 1812-1870

Spence, Gerry

Half-moon and empty stars; a novel. Scribner 2001 412p $27
ISBN 0-7432-0276-7 LC 00-54738
"A Lisa Drew book"
"No one in Twin Buttes, Wyo., is surprised when 'half-breed' Charlie Redtail is charged with the murder of Ronnie Cotler. After all, when he was only 10, Charlie witnessed Cotler joining with local lawmen to murder his father, Joseph, a jobless, alcoholic Arapahoe. Back then, lawyer Abner Hill had unsuccessfully brought a wrongful-death suit against Joseph's killers, and the futility of seeking justice in the 'white man's court' has seared the boy's soul. . . . Despite occasional shifts into rhetorical hyperdrive, Spence's style is richly evocative." Publ Wkly

Spencer, Elizabeth

Knights and dragons
In Spencer, E. The stories of Elizabeth Spencer p127-218

The light in the piazza
In Spencer, E. The southern woman p258-311

The southern woman; new and selected fiction. Modern Lib. 2001 448p $23.95
ISBN 0-679-64218-8 LC 00-54612
Contents: The little brown girl; The eclipse; First dark; A southern landscape; Ship island; The fishing lake; The adult holiday; Sharon; The finder; The Bufords; A Christian education; Indian summer; The girl who loved horses; The business venture; The white azalea; The visit; The cousins; The light in the piazza (novella); I,

Spencer, Elizabeth—*Continued*
Maureen; Jack of diamonds; The skater; The legacy; The master of shongalo; The runaways; The weekend travelers; First child; Owl

"This collection offers selections from the Mississippi native's earlier short fiction together with several new stories. Best known of the earlier fiction is her stunning novella, *The Light in the Piazza* (1960), the deceptively simple tale of an American mother and daughter in Florence." Libr J

The stories of Elizabeth Spencer; with a foreword by Eudora Welty. Doubleday 1981 429p o.p.
LC 79-6601

The stories included in this collection were written between 1944 and 1977 and were originally published in various periodicals. The novelette Knights & dragons was published separately in 1965 by McGraw-Hill. It concerns an American divorcee living in Rome. Other stories in the collection are: The little brown child; The eclipse; First dark; A southern landscape; Moon rocket; The white azalea; The visit; Ship Island; The fishing lake; The adult holiday; The Pincian gate; The absence; The day before; The Bufords; Judith Kane; Wisteria; A bad cold; Presents; On the Gulf; Sharon; The finder; Instrument of destruction; Go South in the winter; A kiss at the door; A Christian education; Mr. McMillan; I, Maureen; Prelude to a parking lot; Indian summer; The search; Port of embarkation: The girl who loved horses

Spencer, James, 1924-

The pilots. Putnam 2003 268p $23.95
ISBN 0-399-14973-2 LC 2002-73449

"There is a touch of Tales of the South Pacific to the adventures of Steve Larkin, a fighter pilot and the author's stand-in, who bails out of his plummeting aircraft and lands on a grimly hazardous jungle island inhabited by head-hunting, spear-toting savages. They capture and inmprison Steve in a fetid hut, and the situation seems bleak, but after some days of testing his intentions, two nubile young women make it clear he is welcome. . . . Scenes in Australia, where the pilots go for rest, are vivid and poignantly capture the pain of the women there who have lost their men. This is not self-conscious writing, but it successfully balances the beauty of flying with the terrors of life-and-death combat, and is a worthy addition to the literature of WWII." Publ Wkly

Spencer, LaVyrle

Bitter sweet. Putnam 1990 382p o.p.
LC 89-38089

"The untimely death of her husband leaves Maggie Pearson wealthy but emotionally bereft. Two decades after she has left home, Maggie returns to Wisconsin to fortify her spirits and decides to open a bed-and-breakfast despite dire warnings from her tight-lipped mother and the hurt fury of her college-age daughter. Her first love, Eric Severson, is also back in town, running a family-owned charter fishing boat to the great displeasure of his beautiful, ambitious wife." Publ Wkly

"Readers who can accept the plausibility of Maggie's original separation from Eric will enjoy following her journey of self-discovery and reawakening." Booklist

Forgiving. Putnam 1991 382p o.p.
LC 90-42821

"Sarah Merritt arrives in Deadwood, Dakota territory, in 1876 with her father's printing press and two ambitions—to find her sister Addie and to establish a local newspaper. In a town of mining bachelors, Sarah quickly becomes the center of attention in more ways than one, particularly when she knocks heads with marshal Noah Campbell, her soon-to-be romantic interest. Sarah finds Addie working in a local brothel and commences a long struggle to win back her affection and her soul." Publ Wkly

"Bowing to the formulaic demands of historical romance without descending into parody or cliché, Spencer gives us an interesting, titillating story peopled by intriguingly human characters." Booklist

Small town girl. Putnam 1997 364p o.p.
LC 96-24317

"When small-town girl Tess McPhail followed the pull of Nashville's glittering lights, she placed her dreams on becoming a country singer. Eighteen years later, she is a megastar and is caught in a whirlwind of tours, recording sessions, and financial meetings—a whirlwind that crashes to a stop when her sister demands her help in caring for their mother. Angered at her sister's orders, Tess breezes in to town for a month and crashes straight into the past in the form of Kenny Kronek, the boy-next-door 'dork' from high school who has been helping her mother." Booklist

That Camden summer. Putnam 1996 368p o.p.
LC 95-20055

In 1916, divorceé Roberta Jewett, "returns to her provincial hometown of Camden, Maine, in order to build a new life for herself and her three daughters. Braving adversaries such as her lecherous brother-in-law, condemning mother, and a community that considers a divorced woman little better than a prostitute, Roberta Jewett behaves 'scandalously,' securing a job as a country nurse to support her children, learning to drive, and buying a 'Model-T car.' Roberta is embittered by her humiliating marriage to an outrageous philanderer, but not surprisingly she 'finds love' with Gabriel Farley, the gruff yet inwardly sensitive widowered carpenter retained to renovate her home. Although predictable and somewhat belabored, Spencer's latest novel is overall an enjoyable read." Libr J

Spencer, Scott

Endless love. Knopf 1979 417p o.p.
LC 79-2089

"A 17-year-old boy, David Axelrod, forbidden to see his girl friend, Jade Butterfield, for 30 days because their love affair has become too intense, sets fire to the Butterfield house on an impulse. That act changes everyone's life: the Butterfield family is scattered, and David is sent to a mental institution and forbidden ever to contact them. This novel is a record of the subsequent ten years of David's life, and his one goal of being reunited with Jade." Libr J

The author "has achieved something quite remarkable in this unabashedly romantic and often harrowing novel. He has created an adolescent love that is believably endless. . . . Mr. Spencer has an acute grasp of character

Spencer, Scott—*Continued*
and situation. He gives us details that make these often tormented people uncommonly convincing." N Y Times Book Rev

A ship made of paper; a novel. HarperCollins Pubs. 2003 351p $24.95
ISBN 0-06-018534-1 LC 2002-68922
"Daniel Emerson is a New York City lawyer who has returned to his hometown of Leyden, N.Y., a picturesque Hudson Valley village, with his girlfriend Kate, a novelist, and her daughter, Ruby. Kate drinks and obsesses about the O.J. Simpson trial instead of writing fiction. Daniel finds himself falling in love with Iris Davenport, an African-American grad student at the local university. Iris is married to Hampton Welles, an investment adviser. The book records Iris and Daniel's affair from both perspectives and poses the question, is their fleeting happiness really worth so much ruin." Publ Wkly
"The interracial aspect allows Spencer. . .to explore both subtle and overt forms of racism among liberals and conservatives and the heavy burden of living with a consciousness of race and the responsibility of setting an unimpeachable example." Libr J

Spencer-Fleming, Julia

In the bleak midwinter. Thomas Dunne Bks. 2002 308p $23.95
ISBN 0-312-28847-6 LC 2001-51303
A mystery set in the "upstate New York town of Millers Kill. As the new (and first female) priest of St. Alban's Episcopal Church, Clare [Fergusson] faces her first test when an infant is left on the rectory doorstep by an unwed teenage mother who is found frozen to death by the river. More crises follow in this freshly conceived and meticulously plotted whodunit when a police investigation raises suspicions about two parishioners who are frantic to adopt the child, and when Clare's own inquiries within her conservative flock turn up troubling evidence of domestic abuse." N Y Times Book Rev

Spiegelman, Ian, 1974-

Everyone's burning; a novel. Villard Bks. 2003 164p $18.95
ISBN 1-400-06056-7 LC 2002-33191
"A nightmarish tour of the drug-fueled subculture of Queens. Leon Koch, a recent high-school graduate, leads a streamlined existence: his goals are to avoid getting killed by any of the neighborhood psychopaths who might have any grievance (real or imagined) against him and to make sure he has enough cocaine and alcohol to cushion his bleak existence. He bounces from one dead-end job to another and seeks out sadomasochistic relationships with the equally damaged women who make up his world." Booklist
"Spiegelman's characters talk to one another like David Mamet's: in staccato bursts, with verve and irony." N Y Times Book Rev

Spiegelman, Peter

Black maps. Knopf 2003 285p $22.95
ISBN 1-4000-4075-2 LC 2003-273218
This mystery introduces John March, "a Manhattan P.I. who walks the mean streets of Beaver and Broad. As the rebel son in four generations of merchant bankers, who turned his back on the family business to become a cop . . . he's quick enough to grasp the byzantine forensic accounting procedures that fire up this technically accomplished financial mystery." N Y Times Book Rev

Sprott, Duncan

The Ptolemies; Duncan Sprott. Knopf 2004 xxii, 462p maps $25.95
ISBN 1-400-04154-6 LC 2004-5305
"Sprott chronicles the calamitous, ill-fated reign of the first Greek pharaoh of Egypt. . . . The initial chapters chart Ptolemy's ascension from soldier to leader in Egypt, where he becomes a satrap, keeping the body of the late Alexander the Great around as a good luck charm. After consolidating his power, Ptolemy agonizes over the decision to declare himself pharaoh while facing military challenges from a parade of enemies; he also must overcome emotional fallout from his exhausting relationship with his two wives, Berenike and Eurydice. . . . Sprott's scholarship and his command of the material is formidable and impressive, and structurally the novel hangs together despite the author's insistence on documenting much of the historical minutiae of Ptolemy's reign." Publ Wkly

St. Claire, Erin, 1948-
For works written by this author under other names see Brown, Sandra, 1948-

Stabenow, Dana

Blood will tell. Putnam 1996 241p o.p.
LC 95-31816
"Ancestral Alaska is at stake when Kate's grandmother, matriarch of their tribe, drags Kate to an important Federation of Natives meeting. Suspicious deaths threaten development decisions until Kate investigates. Evocative." Libr J

Breakup. Putnam 1997 242p o.p.
LC 96-38195
"The Alaskan spring brings problems and new hope for Kate Shugak. She must investigate a murder near home even as she takes over the role of clan leader from her Aleut grandmother." Libr J
This mystery "offers a tough, insightful heroine; a set of intriguing, slightly eccentric supporting characters; and a healthy dose of Alaskan atmosphere." Booklist

A fine and bitter snow. St. Martin's Minotaur 2002 211p $24.95
ISBN 0-312-20548-1 LC 2002-22863
The "Alaskan P.I. finds herself in the middle of a volatile situation involving proposed drilling for oil in a wildlife preserve. A ranger there is fired for political reasons, and then an important conservationist is poisoned." Libr J
"Rich with details about life in this snowbound culture, the story moves at a steady pace to a classic ending." Publ Wkly

Fire and ice; a Liam Campbell mystery. Dutton 1998 264p $23.95
ISBN 0-525-94438-9 LC 98-14581

Stabenow, Dana—*Continued*

Stabenow "traces the twisting life of Alaska State Trooper Liam Campbell in this series debut. Campbell steps off a plane in the town of Newenham, his new posting, leaving behind him in Anchorage a tattered career, a dead son and a wife in a coma. His first moments in town bring him into close contact with pilot Wy Chouinard, the woman he really loves, and the headless corpse of her flying partner, Bob DeCreft, who was decapitated by the propeller of Wy's plane." Publ Wkly

This mystery "is full of raucous action, complicated characters, evocative scenery, and inventive plot." Libr J

Hunter's moon; a Kate Shugak mystery. Putnam 1999 260p $23.95

ISBN 0-399-14468-4 LC 98-33465

Aleut sleuth Kate Shugak "and her boyfriend sign on here as wilderness guides for the management team of a German software company whose arrogant C.E.O. fancies himself a big-game hunter. . . . His cowed employees would have been better advised to bone up on 'The Most Dangerous Game,' because the first big catch is one moose, a few salmon and two junior executives." NY Times Book Rev

Killing grounds. Putnam 1998 273p $22.95

ISBN 0-399-14356-4 LC 97-23900

"Alaskan private investigator Kate Shugak . . . who practically wallows in the surrounding wild beauty of nature, spars with an abusive, strikebreaking fisherman who later winds up dead. Kate's recently returned lover, enigmatic kin, and eccentric acquaintances make this a delightful read." Libr J

Play with fire. Berkley Prime Crime 1995 282p o.p.

LC 94-34665

Alaskan Kate Shugak "investigates the mysterious disappearance of Daniel Seabolt, son of a local born-again preacher whose Bible-thumping sermons threaten certain hellfire and damnation for those foolish enough to be unredeemed. . . . When Daniel's charred, badly decomposed body is found in the ashes of a recent forest fire, folks figure he was an unlucky victim, but Kate finds plenty of unanswered questions." Booklist

The author "endows her writing with admirable sensory descriptions of flora and fauna, and provides unusual settings for her deceptively simple plot. A fine selection." Libr J

The singing of the dead. St. Martin's Minotaur 2001 254p map $23.95

ISBN 0-312-20957-6 LC 2001-19146

"Anne Gordaoff, candidate for the Alaska state senate, is receiving threatening letters. Though sharp, fiesty Aleutian PI Kate Shugak is still recovering from her last job, she allows herself to be talked into protecting Anne." Libr J

"With well-drawn characters, splendid scenery and an insider's knowledge of Alaskan history and politics, this fine novel ranks as one of Stabenow's best." Publ Wkly

So sure of death; a Liam Campbell mystery. Dutton 1999 275p $23.95

ISBN 0-525-94519-9 LC 99-25121

"Alaska state trooper Liam Campbell begins to investigate the murders of a family on a fishing boat and an archaeologist on a dig. Meanwhile, on a personal level, he entertains two very different visitors: his overbearing, perfectionist father and his great love Wyanet Chouinard. Personal and professional come together when Wyanet helps with the investigations and when the murders appear to be linked to Liam's father." Booklist

Stack, Andy *See* Rule, Ann

Stafford, Jean, 1915-1979

The collected stories of Jean Stafford. Farrar, Straus & Giroux 1969 463p o.p.

Contents: Maggie Meriwether's rich experience; The children's game; The echo and the nemesis; The maiden; A modest proposal; Caveat emptor; Life is no abyss; The hope chest; Polite conversation; A country love story; The bleeding heart; The lippia lawn; The interior castle; The healthiest girl in town; The tea time of stouthearted ladies; The mountain day; The darkening moon; Bad characters; In the zoo; The liberation; A reading problem; A summer day; The philosophy lesson; Children are bored on Sunday; Beatrice Trueblood's story; Between the porch and the altar; I love someone; Cops and robbers; The captain's gift; The end of a career

Standiford, Les

Black Mountain; a novel. Putnam 2000 320p o.p.

ISBN 0-399-14584-2 LC 99-32943

This thriller's protagonist "is Richard Corrigan, a NYC transit cop who takes down a homeless man apparently threatening New York governor Fielding Dawson. In reward, Dawson invites Corrigan to join him and 15 others, including a film crew and pretty USA Magazine reporter Dara Wylie, on a highly publicized foray into the Absaroka. In Wyoming, meanwhile, a pair of hired killers, one man, one woman, are—for reasons revealed only at novel's end—plotting to wipe out the Dawson expedition." Publ Wkly

"Even the most contrived scenes . . . capture the treacherous beauty of the wilderness, defined here in the crisp lines and clear detail of an assured author's strong prose style." N Y Times Book Rev

Bone Key. Putnam 2002 319p o.p.

ISBN 0-399-14874-4 LC 2002-19052

"This time out, Deal travels to Key West to talk over a prospective project. He finds trouble, . . . first in a bar, where the smoky-voiced singer turns out to be the unresolved love of his life. He next finds trouble on the side of the road, where he witnesses cops beating up a black kid. Both chanteuse and youth are tied in with the real-estate developer. Deal finds these ties lead to murder and a 60-year-old secret cache buried in the Keys." Booklist

"The labyrinthine plot, involving a case of rare wine worth $100,000, will delight oenophiles. Thriller buffs in general and readers of South Florida mysteries in particular should find this one well up to Standiford's standard." Publ Wkly

Deal on ice; a novel. HarperCollins Pubs. 1997 239p o.p.

LC 96-8431

Miami sleuth John Deal "sets out to find the murderer of a bookstore-owning friend, who dies holding a religious tract. Deal finds himself struggling against danger-

Standiford, Les—*Continued*
ously ultraconservative preacher James Ray Willis, whose megalithic organization plots to control all area media. A solid crime novel." Libr J

Deal with the dead; a novel. Putnam 2001 302p o.p.
ISBN 0-399-14704-7 LC 00-55938
In this John Deal novel, "the independent building contractor working in South Florida is still marinating in his guilt over how his wife was nearly killed during his last caper and his agony over the splintering apart of their marriage. A blast from Deal's late father's checkered past, in the form of a visit from one of Dad's cronies just after Deal has been awarded a lucrative waterfront project, theatens to annihiliate his carefully pieced together recovery. . . . The action is nonstop, the setting of volatile South Florida from the 1950s to the present is fascinating, and the characterization of a man forced to defend what he loves because of the greed of others is compelling." Booklist

Havana run. Putnam 2003 304p $24.95
ISBN 0-399-15059-5 LC 2002-37021
John Deal "is rebuilding the failed Miami construction firm he inherited from his father, dead by suicide. Soon after moving to Key West to oversee a major construction contract, Deal is approached by Antonio Fuentes, a mysterious businessman, who attempts to hire him to oversee a huge rebuilding project in Havana, slated to begin once Castro has departed the scene. Deal has his suspicions, especially after Fuetes offers a check for a million dollars as a retainer." Publ Wkly
"Standiford does a superb job of setting up his complex plot, using the color-drenched, ever-threatening Havana landscape both to ratchet up the tension and to emphasize the otherworldly nature of this latest and most baffling call from the grave." Booklist

Presidential Deal; a novel. HarperCollins Pubs. 1998 290p $24
ISBN 0-06-018655-0 LC 97-31642
In this episode, Miami builder John Deal "achieves national hero status when he and ex-cop sidekick Vernon Driscoll save a boatload of Cuban refugees from drowning in Biscayne Bay. Modestly protesting the ordinariness of his act, Deal is awarded the Presidential Medal of Valor. As a campaign gimmick, the president moves the presentation ceremony to Miami, and the accidental hero is unwittingly caught in a sinister web of high-level chicanery. . . . For all the baroqueness of the plot, Standiford builds a tight narrative with credibly flawed characters and a powerful sense of place." Publ Wkly

Stark, Richard
For works written by this author under other names see Westlake, Donald E.

Backflash. Mysterious Press 1998 292p $20
ISBN 0-89296-662-9 LC 98-16346
"Master crook and murderer Parker . . . approached by a retired anti-gambling state-bureaucrat-turned-consultant, organizes an attempt to rob a riverboat casino during its trial run on the Hudson River. Despite reservations about the consultant's motivations, Parker gathers a group of heisters, who board the boat, where an undercover newspaper reporter threatens to ruin the plan. No unnecessary words here, just the cool, resourceful Parker, careful plotting, dry humor, and thorough preparation." Libr J

Breakout. Mysterious Press 2002 299p $23.95
ISBN 0-89296-779-X LC 2002-23492
This is an "entry in the Parker series. After a pharmaceutical heist goes south, Stark's strong, silent antihero faces a dose of hard time. While awaiting arraignment in an overcrowded detention center, Parker formulates an escape with the help of two fellow prisoners, a crooked defense attorney, and sometime-partner-in-crime Ed Mackey. A series of breakouts follow, as Parker and company hit pothole after pothole on their crooked road to freedom." Booklist
"Richard Stark (the name that Donald E. Westlake uses when he lets Parker off the leash) writes with ruthless efficiency. His bad guys are polished pros who think hard, move fast and turn on a dime in moments of crisis. And because talk doesn't come cheap, every bit of dialogue counts." N Y Times Book Rev

Comeback. Mysterious Press 1997 292p o.p.
LC 97-7019
In this mystery, master thief Parker "teams up with two men and a woman to steal $400,000 in small bills from a sleazy televangelist's 'Christian Crusade.' The heist goes off perfectly—until one of the crew attempts to eliminate his partners to claim the whole score." Booklist
"The plot for this caper is a cunningly engineered sequence of catastrophes, each one set in motion by some seemingly minor miscalculation that escalates into disaster. Oiling the machinery is the author's biting irony toward characters who talk the big talk about love and trust and loyalty but ditch their Christian values for a hot babe or a cool buck. In a world of warped values, an honest crook like Parker is a true treasure." N Y Times Book Rev

Stavans, Ilan
(ed) The Oxford book of Jewish stories. See The Oxford book of Jewish stories

Stead, Christina, 1902-1983

The man who loved children; with an introduction by Doris Lessing. Knopf 1995 xxxvii, 529p $22
ISBN 0-679-44364-9
"Everyman's library"
A reissue of the title first published 1940 by Simon & Schuster
"Unfolding a harrowing portrait of a disintegrating family, Stead examines the hostility between a husband and wife: Sam Pollit, revealed to be a tyrannical crank far removed from the civilized man he thinks he is, whose claim to love his children lends the ironic title; and Henny, who has become a bitter virago." Merriam-Webster's Ency of Lit

Stearn, Jess
(jt. auth) Caldwell, T. I, Judas

Steel, Danielle

The house on Hope Street. Delacorte Press 2000 231p $19.95

ISBN 0-385-33306-4 LC 00-25688

"Married legal team Liz and Jack Sutherland have a successful family law practice and a house on Hope Street near San Francisco, where they live with their five happy children (one with special needs). Liz and her children's lives are changed forever when Jack is murdered on Christmas Day. In the year following the murder, Liz struggles to come to terms with the loss of her husband, both personally and professionally, and is dealt another devastating blow when her eldest son has a near-fatal accident. Divorced doctor Bill Webster saves her son and becomes close to Liz, much to the chagrin of her daughters, who accuse her of betraying their dead father." Libr J

Johnny Angel. Delacorte Press 2002 181p $19.95

ISBN 0-385-33549-0 LC 2001-37188

"Killed in a car crash after his senior prom, 17-year-old Johnny Peterson is sent back to earth as an angel. His mission: to fix certain troubles left unresolved at the time of his death involving his girlfriend, Becky, her impoverished mother and his dysfunctional family. . . . Steele's heartfelt depiction of the central relationship between Johnny and his mother is touching, and few readers will get through the revelation of Johnny's final gift with dry eyes." Publ Wkly

Journey. Delacorte Press 2000 323p $26.95

ISBN 0-385-31687-9 LC 00-31512

"To the outside world, Washington, D.C., television coanchor Maddy Hunter appears to have an enviable life. . . . Yet Maddy—whose current husband saved her from a physically abusive former spouse—is trapped in another relationship that's as devastating and destructive as her first. Jack doesn't hit Maddy, but he subjects her to mind games, putdowns and constant undermining; it's obvious psychological abuse to observers, though not to Maddy. Using Maddy's participation in a commission on violence against women chaired by the nation's First Lady, Steel explicates the various forms of spousal abuse." Publ Wkly

The kiss. Delacorte Press 2001 347p $26.95

ISBN 0-385-33540-7 LC 00-66009

"Isabelle Forrester is the unhappy wife of a coldhearted and distant Parisian banker. . . . Unable to bear the strain of her lonely, unhappy life, Isabelle strikes up an innocent friendship—conversing mostly by phone or mail—with American Bill Robinson. A Washington power broker, Robinson is also trapped in an unhappy marriage. The pair's relationship intensifies steadily until they finally agree to meet in London for a few passionate days. There they are involved in a serious car accident, which leaves them both in a coma, fighting for their lives." Booklist

Lone eagle. Delacorte Press 2001 396p $26.95

ISBN 0-385-33537-7 LC 00-64381

"From the moment beautiful, enormously poised 17-year-old Bostonian Kate Jamisen meets handsome, much older Joe Allbright just before Pearl Harbor at a debutante party, she's desperately in love. . . . The two try to pretend they can just be friends, but passion flares between them on the eve of war. When Joe returns from Europe, after years in a German prison camp, everyone expects they will marry, but Joe cannot commit and Kate moves on. She goes to New York, marries a college friend and has a son; meanwhile, Joe estabishes an airplane-building empire. Still, they can't forget each other, and when they meet up again, even social mores can't keep them apart." Publ Wkly

No greater love. Delacorte Press 1991 392p $23

ISBN 0-385-29909-5 LC 90-29106

As this novel "opens, the boisterous Winfield family is boarding the ill-fated ocean liner *Titanic* for their return to America from England. Kate Winfield, mistress of the perfect family, nobly stays behind with her beloved husband and thrusts her children into the lifeboats under the care of 20-year-old daughter Edwina. After the disaster, Edwina takes seriously her mother's entreaty to care for her five siblings, who range in age from 2 to 16. For the next 12 years, Edwina, aided by a substantial inheritance, dutifully cares for the kids, even to the point of pursuing her runaway teenage sister back to England (by boat) and wresting her out of the arms of a cad. Steel's tale eventually takes an interesting turn into the early days of Hollywood." Booklist

Sunset in St. Tropez. Delacorte Press 2002 230p $19.95

ISBN 0-385-33546-6 LC 2001-47517

Three pairs of friends in their 50s and 60s decide to vacation together in St. Tropez

"Shortly before the vacation begins, one of the women dies of a heart attack, and the other women are scandalized when her supposedly grieving husband brings along a hot, young movie star in his wife's stead. Another scandal soon unfolds as another husband is revealed to be having an affair with a much younger woman. In addition, the house the group has rented (sight unseen) turns out to be a dump and comes complete with two very strange caretakers, who lend a bit of comic relief to the high drama all around them." Booklist

Steele, Allen M.

Coyote; a novel of interstellar exploration. Ace Bks. 2002 390p $23.95

ISBN 0-441-00974-3 LC 2002-74517

"At first, this novel. . . looks like a fairly conventional tale of high-tech intrigue—in this case, rebels against a right-wing American dictatorship plot to steal the prototype interstellar spaceship built to immortalize the government's ideology by planting a colony of fanatics on another star's planet. However, once the freedom seekers arrive on the new world, Coyote, things get a lot more interesting. Coyote, is habitable but alien, full of flora and fauna that upset the colonists' easy preconceptions." Publ Wkly

"A much-foreshadowed 'surprise' ending is by far the least of the surprises in Steele's bag of tricks. But each page of this novel bears evidence of fresh thought about the opportunities inherent in science fiction to take the familiar and make it new." N Y Times Book Rev

Stefaniak, Mary Helen

The Turk and my mother; a novel; Mary Helen Stefaniak. 1st ed. W.W. Norton 2004 316p $24.95

ISBN 0-393-05924-3 LC 2004-1102

Stefaniak, Mary Helen—*Continued*

This novel explores the "history of a Croatian-American family settled in Milwaukee after World War I. The book's Decameron-esque framework is set from the beginning as George, the first-generation American son of Josef and Agnes, is on his deathbed, surrounded by his adult children. The stories he tells about life in Milwaukee in the 1930s lead to stories-within-stories told by his grandmother Staramajka, the family matriarch, who steals the show. . . . Stefaniak's easy familiarity with the vernacular idioms of the old country and the new, and her zestful, respectful ear for different voices, create a world whose past, present and story-loving afterlife are at once magical and grounded in reality." Publ Wkly

Stegner, Wallace Earle, 1909-1993

All the little live things. Viking 1967 345p o.p.

"When Joseph Allston, 64, and his wife, Ruth, move West to their 'Prospero's island' (rural California, near San Francisco), the retirement days 'drip away like honey off a spoon.' They live quietly without involvement . . . hoping to erase scars caused by the death of their rebellious son. The press of life first intrudes on them when young Jim Peck, a bearded free-thinker, camps on their property. . . . Then a young married couple, Marian and John Caitlin, arrive in the neighborhood, and the Allstons find themselves exposed to a depth of emotional involvement with others they had not wanted to experience ever again." Publ Wkly

"Mr. Stegner's narrative skill and his talent for imaginative recreation is evident throughout the book. His choice of words, the turn of a phrase, evoking a scene, an emotion, or a personality are to be savored. His writing, leisurely as it may appear, can be dramatic and moving." Best Sellers

Followed by The spectator bird

Angle of repose; [by] Wallace Stegner. Doubleday 1971 569p o.p.

This novel "is set mainly in the West in the late 1800's; but the central characters cannot be confined to the West nor to the 19th Century. They have a healing effect on the narrator, their grandson and biographer. . . . The beautiful, talented, charming Susan and her inarticulate engineer husband Oliver Ward rough it in mining camps and desolate, unfinished irrigation project camps. Their lives are hard and their marriage is strained past redemption. Yet their suffering and their strength do redeem." Libr J

The Big Rock Candy Mountain; [by] Wallace Stegner. Duell, Sloan & Pearce 1943 515p o.p.

This novel is set in far western states and Saskatchewan from about 1906 to 1942. The "principal characters are Bo Mason, his wife Elsa, and their two boys. Life is an almost continuous moving day because the next town, county, or state persistently beckons to Bo as the place where he will make his fortune." Libr J

"A well-written study of the footloose family. . . . The life of the household is a misery of continual cruelty and often crushing poverty, alternating with occasional scenes of simple family happiness which stand out beautifully and unforgettably." New Yorker

Collected stories of Wallace Stegner. Random House 1990 525p o.p.

LC 89-37342

Contents: The traveler; Buglesong; Beyond the glass mountain; The berry patch; The women on the wall; Balance his, swing yours; Saw gang; Goin' to town; The view from the balcony; Volcano; Two rivers; Hostage; In the twilight; Butcher bird; The double corner; The colt; The Chink; Chip off the old block; The sweetness of the twisted apples; The blue-winged teal; Pop goes the alley cat; Maiden in a tower; Impasse; The volunteer; A field guide to the western birds; Something spurious from the Mindanao deep; Genesis; The wolfer; Carrion spring; He who spits at the sky; The city of the living

"This retrospective . . . exhibits a mastery of the effortlessly beautiful metaphor, an abiding interest in the American West, and an ability to create quick but complete portraits and concise but fully engrossing narratives." Booklist

Crossing to safety; {by} Wallace Stegner. Random House 1987 277p o.p.

LC 87-20482

"The Langs and the Morgans, young couples who meet when their husbands begin teaching at a Wisconsin university, forge bonds of wonderful, lasting friendship. Charity Lang and Sally Morgan are unlike in personality but see each other through devastating crises because of that friendship. Sid Lang is a frustrated poet whose life is over-directed by his wife; Larry Morgan, much less financially secure than Sid, realizes a slow but successful climb to a position of noted writer. This novel has no violence, explicit sex or ugliness. Instead it is a hymn to solid marriages and loyalty in friendship. The dramatic events are those that occur in the lives of ordinary people." Shapiro. Fic for Youth. 3d edition

The spectator bird; [by] Wallace Stegner. Random House 1976 214p o.p.

Retired literary agent Joseph Allston, who "moved west with his wife Ruth in Stegner's novel 'All the Little Live Things' is still waging his gentle battles with age (he's nearly seventy now), the younger generation, and guilt about his son's accidental death years ago. A post card from Countess Astrid Wredel-Krarup, with whom the Allstons stayed on a trip to [Denmark] in 1954, revives Joe's interest in an old journal which tells an intriguing story about the Countess and adds dimension to Joe's character and the Allston's marriage." Libr J

"Since Mr. Stegner is not one to beat his reader over the head with a moral, the tale can be interpreted in several ways, but regardless of interpretation, it is consistently elegant and entertaining reading." Atlantic

Stein, Gertrude, 1874-1946

Three lives; stories of the good Anna, Melanctha, and the gentle Lena. Grafton Press 1909 279p o.p.

"Written in a clear and masterly style, free from any of its author's later stylistic mannerisms, this book consists of three character studies of women. 'The Good Anna' deals with a kindly but domineering German servingwoman; 'Melanctha' is concerned with an uneducated but sensitive black girl; and 'The Gentle Lena' is about a pathetically feebleminded young German maid." Reader's Ency. 4th edition

Steinbeck, John, 1902-1968

Adam and his sons
In Steinbeck, J. The portable Steinbeck

The affair at 7, rue de M—
In Steinbeck, J. The portable Steinbeck

Breakfast
In Steinbeck, J. The portable Steinbeck

Breakfast and work
In Steinbeck, J. The portable Steinbeck

Cannery Row. Viking 1945 208p o.p.

"In this episodic work Steinbeck returned to the manner of Tortilla Flat (1935) and produced a rambling account of the adventures and misadventures of workers in a California cannery and their friends." Herzberg. Reader's Ency of Am Lit

Followed by Sweet Thursday (1954)

also in Steinbeck, J. Novels, 1942-1952

Choice and responsibility
In Steinbeck, J. The portable Steinbeck

The chrysanthemums
In Steinbeck, J. The portable Steinbeck

Danny
In Steinbeck, J. The portable Steinbeck

East of Eden. Viking 1952 602p o.p.

"The saga of more than half a century in the lives of two American families—the Trasks, a mixture of gentleness and brutality doled out in unequal measure and the Hamiltons, Steinbeck's own forebears, a well adjusted, lovable group who provide a tranquil background for the turbulent careers of the Trasks. The scene is chiefly Salinas, California from the turn of the century through the first World War, and thanks to a great wealth of fascinating detail woven through the plot, we are given a complete and unforgettable picture of country and small town life during the period." Libr J

Steinbeck's "most ambitious post-war novel is . . . a parable of the fall of man, of Cain and Abel, and of human possibility, showing many of the virtues of his best books, but touched with sentimentality, melodrama and intrusive commentary." Penguin Companion to Am Lit

also in Steinbeck, J. Novels, 1942-1952

Flight
In Steinbeck, J. The portable Steinbeck

The flood
In Steinbeck, J. The portable Steinbeck

Frog hunt
In Steinbeck, J. The portable Steinbeck

A future we can't foresee
In Steinbeck, J. The portable Steinbeck

The gift
In Steinbeck, J. The portable Steinbeck

The grapes of wrath. Viking 1939 619p o.p.

"In this moving book, Steinbeck wrote a classic novel of a family's battle with starvation and economic desperation. The story also tells in vivid terms the story of the westward movement and the frontier. The Joads, Steinbeck's central figures, are 'Okies,' farmers moving west from a land of drought and bankruptcy to seek work as migrant fruit-pickers in California. They are beset by the police, participate in strike violence, and are harried by death." Benet's Reader's Ency of Am Lit

The great mountains
In Steinbeck, J. The portable Steinbeck

The harness
In Steinbeck, J. The portable Steinbeck

How Mr. Hogan robbed a bank
In Steinbeck, J. The portable Steinbeck

In dubious battle. Covici-Friede 1936 349p o.p.

"One of the more important books to come out of the proletarian movement. This was Steinbeck's first successful novel. 'In Dubious Battle' deals with a fruit strike in a California valley and the attempts of the radical leaders to organize, lead, and provide for the striking pickers. Perhaps the most important, although not the central, character is Doc Burton, who helps the strikers and is concerned with seeing things as they exist, without labels of good and bad attached. The strike fails, and Jim, one of the two leaders, is senselessly killed." Benet's Reader's Ency of Am Lit

also in Steinbeck, J. Novels and stories, 1932-1937

The last clear definite function of man
In Steinbeck, J. The portable Steinbeck

The leader of the people
In Steinbeck, J. The portable Steinbeck

Life and death
In Steinbeck, J. The portable Steinbeck

The long valley. Viking 1938 304p o.p.

Contents: The chrysanthemums; The white quail; Flight; The snake; Breakfast; The raid; The harness; The vigilante; Johnny Bear; The murder; St. Katy the virgin; The red pony; The leader of the people

This volume "includes the four magnificent 'Red Pony' stories, and could serve as an admirable introduction to Steinbeck, showing his characteristic interests—the tensions of the town and country, of past and present, of labour and ownership, as well as the objectivity of biological observation and a sort of Lawrencean mystic concept of personal power." Penguin Companion to Am Lit

Ma and Tom
In Steinbeck, J. The portable Steinbeck

Migrant people
In Steinbeck, J. The portable Steinbeck

Molly Morgan
In Steinbeck, J. The portable Steinbeck

The moon is down; a novel. Viking 1942 188p o.p.

This novel describes the occupation of a small mining town, presumably in Norway, by an unidentified army, evidently German. The villagers resort to sabotage and completely ignore the invaders whenever possible. In the

Steinbeck, John, 1902-1968—*Continued*
end the courageous village mayor is shot to bring the people to terms. The mayor goes to his death reciting Socrates's dying message, knowing full well that his people will understand his death, and will continue their resistance

also in Steinbeck, J. Novels, 1942-1952

Novels, 1942-1952. Library of America, Distributed to the trade in the United States by Penguin Putnam 2001 983p il $35
ISBN 1-931082-07-3 LC 2001-38119
Contents: The moon is down; Cannery Row; The pearl; East of Eden

Novels and stories, 1932-1937; John Steinbeck. Library of America, Distributed to the trade in the U.S. by Penguin Books USA 1994 909p $35
ISBN 1-88301-101-9 LC 94-2943
Contents: The pastures of heaven; To a god unknown; Tortilla Flat; In dubious battle; Of mice and men
The pastures of heaven (1932) is a linked collection of short stories, all of which deal with the inhabitants of the California farm community of the same name. To a god unknown (1933) tells the story of a California farmer who performs pagan fertility rites to ensure good crops. After a long drought, the farmer commits suicide at his own altar of worship. Tortilla Flat, In dubious battle, and Of mice and men are entered separately.

Of mice and men. Covici-Friede 1937 186p o.p.
"Two uneducated laborers dream of a time when they can share the ownership of a rabbit farm in California. George is a plotter and a schemer, while Lennie is a mentally deficient hulk of a man who has no concept of his physical strength. As a team they are not particularly successful, but their friendship is enduring." Shapiro. Fic for Youth. 3d edition

also in Steinbeck, J. Novels and stories, 1932-1937

also in Steinbeck, J. The portable Steinbeck

The pastures of heaven
In Steinbeck, J. Novels and stories, 1932-1937

Pat Humbert's
In Steinbeck, J. The portable Steinbeck

The pearl; with drawings by José Clemente Orozco. Viking 1947 122p il o.p.
"Kino, a poor pearl-fisher, lives a happy albeit spartan life with his wife and their child. When he finds a magnificent pearl, the Pearl of the World, he is besieged by dishonest pearl merchants and envious neighbors. Even a greedy doctor ties his professional treatment of their baby when it is bitten by a scorpion to the possible acquisition of the pearl. After a series of disasters, Kino throws the pearl away since it has brought him only unhappiness." Shapiro. Fic for Youth. 3d edition

also in Steinbeck, J. Novels, 1942-1952

Pilon
In Steinbeck, J. The portable Steinbeck

The pirate
In Steinbeck, J. The portable Steinbeck

The portable Steinbeck; revised, selected, and introduced by Pascal Covici, Jr. Viking 1971 xlii, 692p o.p.
"Viking portable library"
First published 1943 with title: Steinbeck
This volume contains the complete texts of the short novels Of mice and men and The red pony; selections from the novels The pastures of heaven, Tortilla Flat, In dubious battle, The grapes of wrath, and Cannery Row; four short stories from The long valley; and excerpts from a travel book, Sea of Cortez, and a memorial to a friend, "About Ed Ricketts"
Short stories included are: Flight; The snake; The harness; The chrysanthemums; The affair at 7, rue de M—; How Mr. Hogan robbed a bank
A collection of the author's works, mainly fiction, some complete, some excerpted

The promise
In Steinbeck, J. The portable Steinbeck

The red pony
In Steinbeck, J. The long valley
In Steinbeck, J. The portable Steinbeck

The short reign of Pippin IV; a fabrication; drawings by William Péne du Bois. Viking 1957 188p il o.p.
A satire on French politics. Having run out of governments the French decide to revive the monarchy and settle on Pippin, a quiet amateur astronomer who happens to be a descendant of Charlemagne. Bored with the whole situation Pippin is instrumental in starting a revolution, and finally wanders off home

The snake
In Steinbeck, J. The portable Steinbeck

Sweet Thursday. Viking 1954 273p o.p.
Sequel to Cannery Row
After World War II the "Palace Flophouse passed into new hands, the Bear Flag Café got a new madam named Fauna (nee Flora), and Doc lost his old pleasure in women, liturgical music, and the Western Biological Laboratories. Then Suzy came to Cannery Row . . . [and] egged on by the others, she brought Doc back to his prewar contentment." Booklist

Technology and a technocrat
In Steinbeck, J. The portable Steinbeck

Timshel
In Steinbeck, J. The portable Steinbeck

To a god unknown
In Steinbeck, J. Novels and stories, 1932-1937

Tortilla Flat; illustrated by Ruth Gannett. Covici-Friede 1935 316p o.p.
"This episodic tale concerns the poor but carefree 'paisano' Danny and his friends Pillon, Pablo, Big Joe Portagee, Jesus Maria Corcoran, and the old Pirate, all of whom gather in Danny's house, which Steinbeck tells us 'was not unlike the Round Table.' The novel (accepted after nine publishers had turned it down) contrasts the complexities of modern civilization with the simple life of the 'paisanos.'" Benet's Reader's Ency of Am Lit

Steinbeck, John, 1902-1968—*Continued*
also in Steinbeck, J. Novels and stories, 1932-1937

Tortillas and beans
In Steinbeck, J. The portable Steinbeck

The treasure hunt
In Steinbeck, J. The portable Steinbeck

Tularecito
In Steinbeck, J. The portable Steinbeck

The turtle
In Steinbeck, J. The portable Steinbeck

The wayward bus. Viking 1947 312p o.p.
"A novel in which the passengers on a stranded bus in California become a microcosm of contemporary American frustrations." Camb Guide to Lit in Engl

The winter of our discontent. Viking 1961 311p o.p.
Ethan Allen Hawley, the impoverished heir to an upright New England tradition is the focus of this story. Ethan, under pressure from his restless wife and discontented children who want more of this world's goods than his grocery store job provides, decides to take a holiday from his scrupulous standards to achieve wealth and success. What happens as he compromises with his integrity makes up this story
In this novel Steinbeck "continues his exploration of the moral dilemmas involved in being fully human, this time in contemporary America, where choices between genteel poverty and corrupt comfort press in upon the protagonist with a force and reality that suggest no easy resolution." Ency of World Lit in the 20th Century

Steinbeck, Thomas

Down to a soundless sea. Ballantine Bks. 2002 283p o.p.
ISBN 0-345-45576-2
Includes the novella Sing Fat and the Imperial Duchess of Woo and the following short stories: The night guide; The wool gatherer; Blind luck; An unbecoming grace; The dark watcher; Blighted cargo
Sing Fat and the Imperial Duchess of Woo "about a Chinese immigrant who meets the love of his life while studying medicine with an older Chinese apothecary." Publ Wkly
This "collection draws on folklore, historical research, and tales that Steinbeck (son of John) heard growing up. The stories celebrate the early lore of Monterey County, CA. . . . Set in the dusky past of horse trails, grizzly bears, and small fishing villages and ranging forward to the early 1930s, they portray humble people living in a beautiful but often unforgiving environment." Libr J

Steinhauer, Olen

The Bridge of Sighs. St. Martin's Minotaur 2003 278p $23.95
ISBN 0-312-30245-2 LC 2002-68127
"Set in 1948 in a small, unnamed Eastern European country devastated by WWII and still occupied by Russian troops, [this novel]. . . introduces 22-year-old homicide inspector Emil Brod of the People's Militia. Brod's police academy training has prepared him for neither the rude reception he receives from his homicide comrades nor the difficult and risky asignment handed him as his initiation." Publ Wkly
"This is an intelligent, finely polished debut, loaded with atmospheric detail that effortlessly re-creates the rubble-strewn streets of the postwar period in an Eastern state 'liberated' from German occupation by the Russians." Libr J

Steinke, Rene

Holy skirts. Morrow 2005 360p $24.95
ISBN 0-688-17694-1 LC 2004-52783
This is a "fictionalized account of the true adventures of Baroness Elsa von Freytag-Loringhoven, a poet, artist's model and friend of Marcel Duchamp whose irrepressible life bordered on the fashionably sordid. Fleeing her burgher home in Swinemunde, Germany, at age 19 for the liberation–and poverty–of Berlin circa 1904, Elsa learns early to lie about her past and dress outrageously (often in male clothing), attracting numerous men who provide entrée to high society." Publ Wkly
"Steinke's writing is vivid and wonderful, and she can make even a sorrowful story entertaining because she never allows the character's melancholy to infect the prose. The baroness might have been sad, but not tragic. The heroism of her spirit is expressed in a way that transcends the shroud of misfortune." Hudson Rev

Stemple, Jane H. Yolen *See* Yolen, Jane

Stendhal, 1783-1842

The charterhouse of Parma; translated from the French by Richard Howard; illustrations by Robert Andrew Parker. Modern Lib. 1999 507p il maps $24.95
ISBN 0-679-60245-3 LC 98-36417
Original French edition, 1839. Variant title: The chartreuse of Parma
"The scene is a little Italian Court, whither the young adventurer Fabrice has found his way, and in dramatic importance plays second fiddle to the fascinating Duchess Sanseverina and her jealous lover, the astute minister, Count Mosca. The book opens with a famous narrative of the battle of Waterloo. It is a novel that set a standard of flawless technique, of the lucid unfolding of character and motive, of accurate comprehension of the inherent disorder of life, that has rarely been approached in dramatic narration." Baker. Guide to the Best Fic

The red and the black.
Original French edition, 1830; first United States edition published 1898 by G.H. Richmond
"The author's most celebrated work, it is equally acclaimed for its psychological study of its protagonist—the provincial young romantic Julien Sorel—and as a satiric analysis of the French social order under the Bourbon restoration. Its intensely dramatic plot is purposively romantic in nature, while Stendhal's careful portraiture of Sorel's inner states is the work of a master realist, foreshadowing new developments in the form of the novel." Reader's Ency. 4th edition

Stephens, Eve *See* Anthony, Evelyn, 1928-

Stephenson, Neal

Cryptonomicon. Avon Bks. 1999 918p $27.50
ISBN 0-380-97346-4 LC 99-11685
This novel's "dual plots include a World War II tale of codebreaking, espionage and Nazi gold; and a contemporary tale of a software startup trying to establish a Data Haven on a remote Pacific island." Newsweek

"This fast-paced, genre-transcending novel is full of absorbing action, witty dialogue and well-drawn characters. Amazingly, it is also, even at its tremendous length, only the first volume in what promises to be one of the most extravagant literary creations of the turn of the millennium—and beyond." Publ Wkly

The diamond age; or, Young lady's illustrated primer. Bantam Bks. 1995 455p o.p.
ISBN 0-553-09609-5 LC 94-30486
"A Bantam spectra book"

"In the 22nd century, nation-states have withered away, to be replaced by 'phyles,' groups of people united by self-defined interests. . . . The action in 'The Diamond Age' centers on the neo-victorians, who share an admiration for the social discipline of 19th-century England, and a group of Chinese who are trying to erect a neo-Confucian phyle in the power vacuum left by the collapse of the 'Mao Dynasty.' On his own initiative, a neo-Victorian Equity Lord orders a 'bespoke engineer' named John Percival Hackworth to fashion an interactive primer that will teach young people a genuinely subversive lesson: that only by questioning everything they are taught about their world can they hope to become truly useful members of their phyle. When the primer falls into the hands of Nell, a child of the despised underclass, the repercussions are global." N Y Times Book Rev

"With breathtaking vision and insight, Stephenson establishes himself as not only a major voice in contemporary sf but also a prophet of technology's future." Booklist

Steptoe, Lydia *See* Barnes, Djuna, 1892-1982

Sterling, Bruce

Holy fire; a novel. Viking 1996 326p o.p.
LC 96-15139

"Mia Ziemann so dreaded pain and death that at 93 she'd undergone all the miracles that science could offer to extend her life. In 2095 the world is so medically obsessed and globally hooked into the Net that Mia exists, more than lives, in a sterile environment. After the death of an old lover, she undergoes a radical medical procedure that rejuvenates her and propels her on a quest for the holy fire of love she lacks." Libr J

The author "understands that salvation in a posthuman world can only be a process, not a prize. He has written a book in praise of ambiguity that manages to find consoling moments of joy in the most unlikely places." N Y Times Book Rev

Stern, Steve, 1947-

The angel of forgetfulness; Steve Stern. Viking 2005 403p $24.95
ISBN 0-670-03387-1 LC 2004-57155

Stern "combines three distinct but interlinked narratives. The first tells the story of Nathan Hart, a Jewish immigrant on the Lower East Side circa 1910 who woos young Jewish bohemian Keni by telling her the second narrative—a tale about an angel named Mocky and his half-human son, Nachman, both of them also living on the Lower East Side in self-imposed exile from heaven. The third narrative belongs to Keni's nephew Saul, a morose, lonely young man who embarks on an odyssey through the post-Vietnam sexual and psychedelic revolutions that takes him to a hippie commune and an avant-garde theater troupe before he settles down as a hermetic Jewish-studies scholar." Publ Wkly

The author "has little interest in reworking Yiddish literature's social realist strains, or in excavating the political events that helped shape the world he loves. What he offers instead is a rollicking compendium of myth and historical tidbits, of dybbuks, wonder-working rebbes and clandestine prayer houses where lapsed Talmud students meditate on the holy letters of God's name until they levitate." N Y Times Book Rev

Sterne, Laurence, 1713-1768

The life and opinions of Tristram Shandy, gentleman
In Sterne, L. The life and opinions of Tristram Shandy, gentleman and A sentimental journey through France and Italy p1-689

The life and opinions of Tristram Shandy, gentleman and A sentimental journey through France and Italy. Modern Lib. 1995 832p $19.50
ISBN 0-679-60091-4

A combined edition of two titles first published 1759-67 and 1768 respectively

The life and opinions of Tristram Shandy, gentleman is the "chaotic account by Tristram of his life from the time of his conception to the present. . . . In between are sandwiched his 'opinions,' long-winded and philosophical reflections on everything under the sun, including his novel, and accounts of the lives of 'Yorick'; his father, Walter Shandy; his mother; and his Uncle Toby. . . . The form of the book is in fact the character of Tristram himself, doomed by improbably fantastic fatalities to write a hodgepodge instead of a history." Reader's Ency. 4th edition

A sentimental journey is a "combination of autobiography, fiction, and observations made by Sterne on his own travels, chronicles the journey through France of a charming and sensitive young man named Yorick and his servant LaFleur. (Though the title mentions Italy, the book ends before they reach that country.)" Merriam-Webster's Ency of Lit

A sentimental journey through France and Italy
In Sterne, L. The life and opinions of Tristram Shandy, gentleman and A sentimental journey through France and Italy p691-832

Stevens, David, 1940-
(jt. auth) Haley, A. Mama Flora's family

Stevens, Marcus, 1959-

The curve of the world; a novel. Algonquin Bks. 2002 302p $23.95

ISBN 1-56512-336-0 LC 2001-56530

"Lewis Burke is aboard a plane forced to make an emergency landing in the Congo. Once on the ground, the passengers become the hostages of rebels. Lewis sees an opportunity to escape and plunges into the rain forest. Meanwhile, Lewis' wife, Helen, learns that his plane is down and departs immediately for Kinshasa with their seven-year-old son, blind since birth. The diffident Lewis lurches through the wilderness with no idea of how to survive, while the tenacious Helen defies U.S. diplomats and sets out for the rebel-held interior. Their stories are told in parallel." Booklist

Stevens summons the African "landscape and atmosphere with vividly descriptive detail, and captures the terror of a man reduced to life's essentials." Publ Wkly

Useful girl; a novel; by Marcus Stevens. 1st ed. Algonquin Books of Chapel Hill 2004 306p $24.95

ISBN 1-565-12366-2 LC 2003-70808

"When a construction crew uncovers the remains of a Cheyenne girl, the foreman, anxious about deadlines, orders his men to keep working. Charlie White Bird is not willing to overlook this breach in regulations, and he enlists the foreman's daughter, Erin Douglass, in his quest to rebury the remains in a sacred place. Erin, still grieving the recent death of her mother and unable to draw her reticent father into any meaningful conversation, finds in her passionate relationship with Charlie an outlet for her repressed emotions. In parallel with this contemporary love story, Stevens recreates the life of the young Cheyenne girl and the circumstances that led to her death." Booklist

"The descriptions of late 19th-century battles and living conditions are unsettling in their vivid and authentic detail, riveting even the least historically minded reader, and the account of Erin's plight is clear-eyed and uncompromising. Writing with compassion and grace, Stevens delivers a timeless story of brutality and forgiveness." Publ Wkly

Stevenson, Jane, 1959-

The shadow king. Houghton Mifflin 2003 304p $24

ISBN 0-618-14913-9 LC 2003-47899

This is the second volume of the author's historical trilogy. "Here the protagonist is Balthasar, the son of the queen of Bohemia (sister to Britain's late King Charles I) and the queen's secret husband, Pelagius, a prince of the West African nation of Oyo. Having completed his medical studies in Leiden, Balthasar returns to Zeeland to establish his practice. Circumstances involve him with Aphra Behn, the so-called first feminist writer. Unhappily married to a Dutchman, she is a spy for England; she steals the papers that certify Balthasar's royal birth. A decade later, after the plague has decimated Europe, Balthasar moves to Restoration England, where he marries a servant woman, Sibella. Her family roots are gentry, and her father has willed her property in Barbados, so the newlyweds settle in the Caribbean." Publ Wkly

"Stevenson has immersed herself in the literature of the period, and one can sense the heady zest with which she details Balthasar's medical treatments or spins off a line of dialogue." N Y Times Book Rev

The winter queen. Houghton Mifflin 2002 307p $25

ISBN 0-618-14912-0

First published 2001 in the United Kingdom with title: Astraea

This first volume of a projected trilogy is set during the 17th century "in the chilly capital of Protestant Holland. [Stevenson] rewrites the story of Othello in the love between Pelagius van Overmeer, a dispossessed African prince, and the Winter Queen, the exiled Elizabeth of Bohemia." New Statesman (Engl)

"Without apparent strain, Stevenson extends her reach to Calvinist doctrine, Yoruba divination, 17th-century European politics and the details of daily life in the Low Countries. In her hands, the clandestine love story is inseparable from the political and spiritual preoccupations of the time, making vivd a world no less complex and capricious than our own." N Y Times Book Rev

Stevenson, Robert Louis, 1850-1894

The beach of Falesá

In Stevenson, R. L. The complete short stories p307-71

In Stevenson, R. L. The complete short stories of Robert Louis Stevenson

In Stevenson, R. L. The strange case of Dr. Jekyll and Mr. Hyde, and other famous tales

The complete short stories; edited and introduced by Ian Bell. Centenary ed. Holt & Co. 1994 2v set $50

ISBN 0-8050-3203-7 LC 93-79628

Contents: v1 The Plague-Cellar; When the devil was well; Edifying letters of the Rutherford family; An old song; A lodging for the night; Will o' the Mill; The Sire de Malétroit's door; The Suicide Club: Story of the young man with the cream tarts; Story of the physician and the Saratoga trunk; The adventure of the hansom cabs; The Rajah's diamond: Story of the bandbox; Story of the young man in holy orders; Story of the house with the green blinds; The adventure of Prince Florizel and a detective; Providence and the guitar; The pavilion on the links; The story of a lie [novelette]; Thrawn Janet; The body snatcher; The Merry Men [novelette]

v2 The treasure of Franchard; Diogenes; Zero's tale of the explosive bomb; Markheim; Dr Jekyll and Mr Hyde [novelette]; The misadventures of John Nicholson [novelette]; Olalla; The enchantress; The bottle imp; The beach of Falesá [novelette]; The Isle of Voices; The waif woman; Fables

The complete short stories of Robert Louis Stevenson; with a selection of the best novels; edited and with an introduction by Charles Neider. Viking 1969 xxx, 678p o.p.

Contents: A lodging for the night; Story of the young man with the cream tarts; Story of the physician and the Saratoga trunk; The adventure of the hansom cab; Story of the bandbox; Story of the young man in holy orders; Story of the house with green blinds; The adventure of

Stevenson, Robert Louis, 1850-1894—*Continued*

Prince Florizel and a detective; Providence and the guitar; The Sire de Maletroit's door; Will o' the mill; The story of a lie [novelette]; Thrawn Janet; The merry men [novelette]; The body snatcher; Markheim; Strange case of Dr. Jekyll and Mr. Hyde [novelette]; The bottle imp; The beach of Falesá [novelette]; The isle of voices

The strange case of Dr. Jekyll and Mr. Hyde is entered separately. In The story of a lie (first published 1879 in New Quarterly magazine, 1882 in book form) Dick Naseby, a young Englishman, becomes estranged from his father due to a misunderstanding and from the girl he loves due to his concealment of the true character of her father—an untalented, parasitical but likable painter, whom the girl hasn't seen since childhood and romantically idolizes. The Merry Men (1887) is set on an island off the coast of Scotland. It deals with a man of dour religious temperament who kills the survivor of a shipwreck in a fit of drunken madness and is driven to death by his guilt after another shipwreck. The beach of Falesá (first published 1893 in Island nights' entertainments) concerns a trader on a South Seas island whose marriage to a native woman is promoted by a business rival who knows that she is the object of a native taboo which will pass on to her husband

Dr. Jekyll and Mr. Hyde [variant title: The strange case of Dr. Jekyll and Mr. Hyde]

In Stevenson, R. L. The complete short stories p102-64

The Merry Men

In Stevenson, R. L. The complete short stories p436-77

In Stevenson, R. L. The complete short stories of Robert Louis Stevenson

The misadventures of John Nicholson

In Stevenson, R. L. The complete short stories p165-222

The story of a lie

In Stevenson, R. L. The complete short stories p361-408

In Stevenson, R. L. The complete short stories of Robert Louis Stevenson

The strange case of Dr. Jekyll and Mr. Hyde; with an introduction by Joyce Carol Oates. Vintage Books 1991 97p pa $8.95

ISBN 0-679-73476-7 LC 90-50600

First published 1886. Variant title: Dr. Jekyll and Mr. Hyde

"The work is known for its vivid portrayal of the psychopathology of a 'split personality.' The calm, respectable Dr. Jekyll develops a potion that will allow him to separate his good and evil aspects for scientific study. At first Jekyll has no difficulty abandoning the drug induced persona of the repulsive Mr. Hyde, but as the experiments continue the evil personality wrests control from Jekyll and commits murder. Afraid of being discovered, he takes his life; Hyde's body is found, together with a confession written in Jekyll's hand." Merriam-Webster's Ency of Lit

also in Stevenson, R. L. The complete short stories of Robert Louis Stevenson

also in Stevenson, R. L. The strange case of Dr. Jekyll and Mr. Hyde, and other famous tales p1-69

The strange case of Dr. Jekyll and Mr. Hyde, and other famous tales; with photographs of the author and his environment as well as illustrations from early editions of the stories, together with an introduction by W. M. Hills. Dodd, Mead 1961 339p il o.p.

"Great illustrated classics"

Contents: The strange case of Dr. Jekyll and Mr. Hyde [novelette]; The pavilion on the links; A lodging for the night; Markheim; The Sire de Malétroit's door; The beach of Falesá [novelette]; The suicide club; Story of the young man with the cream tarts; Story of the physician and the Saratoga trunk; The adventures of the hansom cab

The title novelette is entered separately, and the novelette: The beach of Falesá is described under: The complete short stories of Robert Louis Stevenson. The three-part story: The suicide club, which originally appeared in The New Arabian Nights (1882) is a partly satirical fantasy-adventure story about a sinister London club which exploits the nihilistic tendencies of its members, and the mysterious Prince Florizel who opposes it

Stewart, Edward, 1938-1996

Deadly rich. Bantam Bks. 1991 566p o.p.

LC 91-17638

A "thriller about a serial murderer who calls himself 'Society Son of Sam.' His first victim is a wealthy socialite found unpleasantly done in on a dressing room floor of an exclusive department store, and after a few more high society types are similarly dispatched, Lieutenant Vince Cardozo of the NYPD finds himself deeply involved in Yuppie scandal." Libr J

Mortal grace. Doubleday 1994 490p o.p.

LC 94-1280

In this mystery NYPD Lieutenant Vince Cardozo investigates "the brutal murders of several homeless teenagers. The first body is found dismembered and lodged in a Styrofoam carton in a city park. When the pieces of the body are autopsied, a Communion wafer is discovered under the corpse's tongue. More gruesome killings follow, all connected by the wafer clue. . . . Stewart has written a cleverly plotted (if lengthy) story with psychologically complex characters, a provocative, multilayered plot, and a series of perplexing clues that will baffle the most astute armchair detectives." Booklist

Stewart, Fred Mustard, 1932-

Ellis Island; a novel. Delacorte Press 1983 396p o.p.

LC 82-14301

"In 1907 five young immigrants arrive at the legendary Ellis Island, the gateway to the American Dream. There's Jacob Rubenstein, fortunate to escape the pogrom that destroyed his family; Tom Banicek, who fled conscription into the Austro-Hungarian Army; Marco Santorelli, possessed of magnificent looks and driving ambition; and the beautiful O'Donnell sisters, escaping the Irish troubles." Libr J

Stewart, Fred Mustard, 1932-—*Continued*

"Stewart is a wonderful storyteller, and his novel—sentimental and even corny in spots—is nevertheless thoroughly satisfying." Publ Wkly

The glitter and the gold. New Am. Lib. 1989 452p o.p.
LC 89-33620

The "story of the Collingwoods of California—offspring of a German Jewish bourgeoise and a farmer-turned-bank robber, whom we meet at the center of the nineteenth century. Immigrating to California in the wake of the Gold Rush, Emma de Meyer takes over her husband's store after his death and prospers enough to bankroll escaped con Archer Collingwood all the way to the U.S. Senate. The generations roll down to the present day, when Claudia Collingwood is fighting off a rapacious, murderous, Anglo-Chinese businessman who wants the family ranch." Booklist

The magnificent Savages. Delacorte Press 1996 383p o.p.
LC 95-53162

"A Tom Doherty Associates book"

"In the 1850s, the Savage family dominates the New York shipping industry with fast clipper ships that make runs to China. With the patriarch on his deathbed, the oldest brother, Sylvaner, arranges for the murder of his young, illegitimate half-brother, Justin, on Justin's first voyage to China as a cabin boy. Justin manages to survive the attack and so begins a life of adventure. He first falls in with Chinese pirates, eventually marrying the pirate queen, Chang-mei. Then, with the Taiping revolt in full force, Chinese officials send Justin to Europe to learn the art of modern warfare with Giuseppe Garibaldi. All the while, Sylvaner's insane jealousy continues to hound Justin." Libr J

Followed by The young Savages

The naked Savages. Forge 1999 349p $24.95
ISBN 0-312-86790-5 LC 99-24482

"A Tom Doherty Associates book"

Third title in the author's Savage family chronicles. "As the turn of the century approaches, youthful patriarch Johnny Savage joins Teddy Roosevelt's Rough Riders in Cuba. Although he is prepared to die for the glory of his country, Johnny's enthusiasm wanes when he is shot and permanently injured by a disgruntled socialist journalist. Returning to the U.S. minus one leg, he turns his attention to his devoted wife, his spoiled children, and his thriving business. . . . A hugely entertaining family saga steeped in history and set against a glittering international backdrop." Booklist

The Savages in love and war. Forge 2001 304p o.p.
ISBN 0-312-87485-5 LC 2001-33526

"A Tom Doherty Associates book"

Fourth title in the author's Savage family chronicles. "Assuming patriarchal status from a rapidly declining Johnny Savage, young Nick attempts to resuscitate both the moribund Savage fortune and his own ailing love life during the lean Depression years. Finance, however, takes a back seat to intrigue and diplomacy when he becomes ambassador to Germany on the eve of World War II. Meanwhile, sister Brook and her aristocratic French husband join the Resistance, and the Savage cousins attempt to overcome the Japanese threat to their Asian enterprises." Booklist

The young Savages. Forge 1998 303p $23.95
ISBN 0-312-86412-4 LC 97-40423

"A Tom Doherty Associates book"

This second novel in the Savage family chronicles "focuses on Justin Savage's two children. Half-Chinese and half-Caucasian, 27-year-old Julie is shunned by the snobbish New York social world of the 1880s, and so she heads west to begin a new life. Much to Papa's dismay, she marries a disreputable rogue who made his fortune in gambling and bordellos in San Francisco. Julie's younger brother Johnny, a rake dissatisfied with his position at his father's bank, takes off to explore the Dakotas with Teddy Roosevelt. The adventures of the younger generation take them to China, Hong Kong, England, Italy, and France, as they strive to find happiness and fulfillment. . . . Stewart paints a colorful picture of the lives of the rich and famous in late-19th-century America and Britain." Libr J

Followed by The naked Savages

Stewart, Mary, 1916-

Airs above the ground. Mill, M.S. 1965 286p o.p.

Vanessa, a young English veterinarian, "after inadvertently discovering that her husband is not just a traveling salesman but doubles as a secret agent, helps him solve a case involving the Lipizzan horses, a medieval Austrian castle, a circus, a murder, and a narcotics ring." Booklist

The crystal cave. Morrow 1970 521p o.p.

First title in the author's Merlin trilogy. "Presumed to be the offspring of the daughter of the King of Wales and the devil himself, Merlin spends a difficult childhood in the court of the king. He learns much that is mystical under the tutelage of a learned wizard and gains a knowledge of several languages. Escaping to 'Less Britain,' Merlin becomes an important element in the struggle to unite all Britain. The book is rich in descriptions of fifth-century Britain and Brittany, the Druids and their fearful rites, and the superstitions surrounding pagan worship." Shapiro. Fic for Youth. 3d edition

Followed by The hollow hills

also in Stewart, M. Mary Stewart's Merlin trilogy

The Gabriel hounds. Forge 1967 320p o.p.

"This story is freely based on the accounts of the life of the Lady Hester Stanhope." Author's note

"Traveling in the Middle East Christy Mansel runs into her second cousin Charles in Damascus and the pair decide to visit their great aunt, an eccentric recluse who lives in a crumbling palace in Lebanon. Odd even for their aunt's household the situation at the castle arouses the cousins' suspicions, and their investigation turns up a startling secret in the underground passages." Booklist

The hollow hills. Morrow 1973 499p o.p.

This second novel in the author's Merlin trilogy begins with "Merlin's dismissal by Uther, Arthur's father, who has nonetheless promised to deliver the babe, when born, to Merlin's care. The book traces Merlin's travels to the east, during which time he monitors, through his second sight, Arthur's growth in Brittany and in England. Merlin returns to finish Arthur's education, and the book concludes with Arthur being proclaimed king. With this

Stewart, Mary, 1916—*Continued*
Merlin epic Mary Stewart has rightly won an honorable place among the modern writers of Arthurian legend." Tymn. Fantasy Lit

Followed by The last enchantment

also in Stewart, M. Mary Stewart's Merlin trilogy

The ivy tree. Mill, M.S. 1961 320p o.p.

A Canadian girl visiting England is mistaken for a missing and supposedly dead heiress to an estate "by handsome Connor Winslow, a cousin of the runaway, and now manager of Whitescar. Finally convinced that she is Mary Grey, he and his dour sister Lisa persuade her to masquerade as the long-gone Annabel, promising her the opportunity to claim the considerable legacy left to Annabel by her mother on condition that she surrender her share in Whitescar to Connor upon the death of Uncle Matthew. Reluctantly, Mary enters into the scheme, but soon repents but finds herself too deeply involved." Best Sellers

The last enchantment. Morrow 1979 538p o.p.
LC 79-12937

This is the concluding volume of a trilogy about "Merlin the Enchanter, set amidst the turbulent events of fifth-century Britain when Arthur became High King. . . . This novel tells of the early years of Arthur's reign: the battles with the Saxons, building of Camelot, marriages with two successive Guiniveres, and birth of Mordred" Libr J

also in Stewart, M. Mary Stewart's Merlin trilogy

Mary Stewart's Merlin trilogy. Morrow 1980 919p maps $29.95
ISBN 0-688-00347-8 LC 80-21019

An omnibus edition of: The crystal cave, The hollow hills and The last enchantment, first published 1970, 1973 and 1979 respectively

The first novel in this trilogy based on Arthurian legends concerns the difficult childhood and youth of the magician Merlin who grows up as a bastard at the court of the King of Wales where he is believed to be the offspring of the King's daughter and the devil. He gains much knowledge from a learned wizard and escapes to "Less Britain" where he becomes involved in efforts to unite all of Britain. The second novel tells of Merlin's involvement with the childhood of Arthur and Arthur's search for the magical sword, Caliburn. The last novel deals with Merlin's death and Arthur's turbulent reign

The author's "skill in creating colorful characters, suspense, and a brooding atmosphere serves her well in portraying England's Dark Ages, where witches, sorcerers, and tragic kings moved heroically through an enchanted land. Though Arthur's rise to power is the subject, the true star and narrator of the tale is Merlin the magician." Husband. Sequels

The moon-spinners. Mill, M.S. 1963 c1962 303p o.p.

First published 1962 in the United Kingdom

"Nicola Ferris, an English girl on vacation in Crete, decides to walk the last mile over a rough track to the tiny village where she is expected the next day. She walks into a mystery. She stumbles upon a shepherd's hut guarded by a Greek who threatens to kill her if she makes a sound. Inside the hut, she finds a young Englishman seriously wounded and much upset by her intrusion. In her determination to help him, she is drawn into his dangerous situation." Horn Book

My brother Michael. Mill, M.S. 1960 313p o.p.

This suspense story has "a modern Greek setting enriched by classical antiquities and haunted by the shades of Hellenic tragedy. Camilla Haven, the heroine-narrator, is on her way to Delphi when she encounters Simon Lester, an English schoolmaster who has come to investigate the death of his brother Michael, supposedly killed fighting during World War II. A strange letter written just before his death leads Camilla, along with Simon, through a terrifying maze of danger and violence to an amazing discovery on the slopes of Mount Parnassus." Booklist

Nine coaches waiting. Mill, M.S. 1959 c1958 342p o.p.

First published 1958 in the United Kingdom

"Intelligent, spirited Linda Martin comes to Valmy, an isolated château in the French Alps, as English governess to nine-year-old Philippe, the orphaned Comte de Valmy. After several frightening 'accidents' Linda discovers that her pupil is the object of a murder plot which apparently involves his crippled uncle and the latter's handsome son Raoul, with whom she is in love." Booklist

The stormy petrel. Morrow 1991 189p o.p.
LC 91-14509

The title "refers to both a little seabird and a boat piloted by one of the two young men who intrude upon young professor Rose Fenemore's country-cottage holiday on one of the smaller Hebrides. Unfortunately, the Petrel pilot, although he's the handsomer, turns out to be a dicey character. It's the other gent, helming another boat, who's steadier, though plainer." Booklist

"The visitors are jumpy, evasive and mutually antagonistic, and Rose's suspicions are aroused. The mystery of their relationship and real purpose, never menacing, is quickly solved, and takes second place to Stewart's vivid rendering of Moila's lochs, glens and wild birds, especially the graceful stormy petrels who nest there." Publ Wkly

Thunder on the right. Mill, M.S. 1958 c1957 284p o.p.

First published 1957 in the United Kingdom

"Jennifer answers her cousin Gillian's plea to visit a French convent in the Pyrenees where Gillian hopes to become a nun. On her arrival from England, Jennifer discovers that her cousin has supposedly died after a mysterious auto accident. She does some sleuthing and unveils smuggling and murder. All the ingredients for a mystery-love story with authentic background." Libr J

Touch not the cat. Morrow 1976 336p o.p.

A "tale set on a family estate in England. Garbled words of warning uttered by her dying father lead Bryony Ashley into danger as she investigates the intricacies of past and present intrigues within the Ashley family. Bryony's inherited extrasensory abilities add to the suspenseful story." Booklist

The wicked day. Morrow 1983 453p o.p.
LC 83-12091

The author "returns to the Arthurian world she portrayed . . . in her Merlin trilogy. The principal character is Mordred, born of the incestuous liaison between Ar-

Stewart, Mary, 1916-—*Continued*

thur the High King and his half-sister, the evil sorceress and northern queen Morgause. Mordred is summoned to Camelot by the formidable warrior king, along with Morgause and her four legitimate but ungovernable sons, and told of his true parentage. After growing to manhood in Arthur's court . . . Mordred is left in charge of the kingdom, and of Queen Guinevere, while Arthur is off fighting the Romans in Brittany. Reported dead, the king returns to Britain and there ensues the fulfillment of the 'wicked day' that has been prophesied by Merlin." Publ Wkly

Wildfire at midnight. Appleton-Century-Crofts 1956 214p o.p.

Gianetta Brooke comes to the Isle of Skye to forget the husband she has painfully divorced and finds herself in danger as a series of murders takes place

Stirling, Jessica

The island wife. St. Martin's Press 1998 c1997 410p $24.95

ISBN 0-312-19289-4 LC 98-35162

First published 1997 in the United Kingdom

This novel, first of a trilogy, "about a dysfunctional nineteenth-century family living on the rural Scottish island of Mull focuses on two sisters, Innis and Biddy Campbell, one modest, intelligent, and thoughtful; the other seductive, self-centered, and conniving. When both take an interest in Michael Tarrant, a handsome and mysterious shepherd, conflicts arise, and bitter emotions and dark family secrets are exposed." Booklist

"The characters are well drawn, with realistic motivations, and the atmosphere is 'like the island itself, two-faced and moody.' Some of the Scottish words will be unfamiliar to Americans, but this does not detract from the enjoyment." Libr J

Followed by The wind from the hills

Lantern for the dark. St. Martin's Press 1992 377p o.p.

LC 92-3601

"Set in eighteenth-century Scotland, this tale opens with Clare Kelso, an accused murderer, meeting her new legal representative, Cameron Adams. Adams is convinced of Kelso's innocence on the charge of infanticide, but her reluctance to disclose her secrets leaves him powerless to save her from hanging. His persuasive powers must first be tested in the jail cell before he can even begin to work on the judiciary." Booklist

The author "deploys fully realized characters against the background of a greedy and corrupt society operating under a thin veneer of respectability. This richly detailed morality tale features a taut trial scene and a cache of surprising secrets that will keep readers totally involved." Publ Wkly

Followed by Shadows on the shore

The marrying kind. St. Martin's Press 1996 c1995 359p o.p.

LC 96-1191

First published 1995 in the United Kingdom

Set in pre-WWII Glasgow, This sequel to the The penny wedding "coming-of-age novel centers around third-year medical student Alison Burnside as she struggles toward the realization that having it all is impossible. At the same time, all the characters, one way or another, illustrate just how naïve the world was on the eve of Hitler's reign of terror. . . . Exposing her characters to feminism, class conflict and the stormclouds of war, Stirling expertly guides them through the growing pains of the heart into genuine maturity." Publ Wkly

The penny wedding. St. Martin's Press 1995 c1994 394p o.p.

LC 95-1732

First published 1994 in the United Kingdom

"A working-class Scottish family strives to survive personal tragedy and financial devastation during the Great Depression. When her mother unexpectedly dies and her father loses his job, gifted and intelligent 17-year-old Alison Burnside expects to forgo her dreams of obtaining a medical degree in order to help support her struggling family. Before she has a chance to leave school, however, her favorite teacher and her four older brothers intervene on her behalf. . . . A bittersweet portrait of a realistically flawed family banding together out of a sense of love, loyalty, and necessity in a heartfelt effort to overcome poverty and misfortune." Booklist

Followed by The marrying kind

The piper's tune. St. Martin's Press 2002 486p $26.95

ISBN 0-312-28870-0 LC 2001-57854

"Eighteen-year-old Lindsay Franklin gets an unexpected jolt when her shipbuilding magnate grandfather gives her a share of the family business. At the same time, her all-too-charming Irish cousin, the womanizing Forbes McCulloch, comes to Glasgow to learn the family business from the bottom up and sets his sights on marrying Lindsay. The style and design of the cover give the impression that this is a historical romance, but the tale is much more than a formulaic love story. Stirling does a bang-up job of illustrating how character shapes a person's life." Publ Wkly

Shadows on the shore. St. Martin's Press 1994 c1993 346p o.p.

LC 93-42102

First published 1993 in the United Kingdom

In this sequel to Lantern for the dark Clare Kelso Quinn "is now a prosperous salt dealer and a widow with an eight-year-old daughter. Quinn's placid life is altered when Frederick Striker reappears, counting on his charm to once again seduce a docile Clare. It seems he is effective, for she plans to marry him, a move that would place all of her late husband's inheritance into Striker's hands. But Clare is a far stronger, cleverer woman than she once was, and she also wants vengeance." Booklist

"The narrative keeps the reader guessing; flashes of dry wit and humorous characterizations . . . again indicate that Stirling is a deft practitioner of the genre." Publ Wkly

The wind from the hills. St. Martin's Press 1999 442p $25.95

ISBN 0-312-24433-9 LC 99-50171

First published 1998 in the United Kingdom

This novel, the second in the Isle of Mull trilogy begun with The island wife, finds Innis married to Michael Tarrant and Biddy a wealthy widow with few ties to her past

Stirling, Jessica—*Continued*

The workhouse girl. St. Martin's Press 1997 472p o.p.

LC 97-5500

First published 1996 in the United Kingdom

Set in Victorian Scotland, "Stirling's tale follows Cassie Armitage into an unfortunate marriage to the evil, deceitful, and abusive Reverend Robert Montague. Cassie's servant, Nancy Winfield, is the workhouse girl of the book's title. Nancy shares the story's center stage and is as engaging and likable as her wealthy counterpart. But it is Nancy's station in life to carry the weight of an illegitimate child on her very capable and resourceful shoulders. . . . A thoroughly entertaining and satisfying read." Booklist

Stirling, S. M.

(jt. auth) McCaffrey, A. The city who fought

Stoker, Bram, 1847-1912

The Bram Stoker bedside companion; 10 stories by the author of Dracula; edited and with an introduction by Charles Osborne. Taplinger 1973 224p o.p.

Contents: The secret of the growing gold; Dracula's guest; The invisible giant; The Judge's House; The burial of the rats; A star trap; The squaw; Grooken sands; The combeen man (from The snake's pass); The Watter's Mou'

Dracula; edited with an introduction and notes by Maurice Hindle; preface by Christopher Frayling. Penguin Books 2003 xlvii, 454p pa $11

ISBN 0-14-143984-X LC 2003-269578

First published 1897

"Count Dracula, an 'undead' villain from Transylvania, uses his supernatural powers to lure and prey upon innocent victims from whom he gains the blood on which he lives. The novel is written chiefly in the form of journals kept by the principal characters—Jonathan Harker, who contacts the vampire in his Transylvanian castle; Harker's fiancee (later his wife), Mina, adored by the Count; the well-meaning Dr. Seward; and Lucy Westenra, a victim who herself becomes a vampire. The doctor and friends destroy Dracula in the end, but only after they drive a stake through Lucy's heart to save her soul." Merriam-Webster's Ency of Lit

Midnight tales; edited and with an introduction by Peter Haining. Owen, P.; distributed by Dufour Eds. 1990 182p il o.p.

Contents: The dream in the dead house; The spectre of doom; The dualitists; Death in the wings; The Gombeen man; The squaw; A deed of vengeance; The man from Shorrox'; The Red Stockade; Midnight tales; A criminal star; The bridal of death

Stone, Irving, 1903-1989

The agony and the ecstasy; a novel of Michelangelo. Doubleday 1961 664p o.p.

"Michelangelo's career is traced from his promising boyhood apprenticeships to the painter Ghirlandajo and the sculptor Bertoldo thru all the many years of his flowering genius. . . . Florence and Rome are the principal cities which serve as background for the development of the artist's life and work." Chicago Sunday Trib

"Stone's Michelangelo is an idealized version, purged not only of ambisexuality, but of the egotism, faultfinding, harsh irony, and ill temper that we know were characteristic of Michelangelo." Saturday Rev

Love is eternal; a novel about Mary Todd and Abraham Lincoln. Doubleday 1954 468p o.p.

This novel presents a sympathetic portrait of Mary Todd Lincoln. The author absolves her from the shrewishness with which many historians have clothed her and pictures her marriage to Abraham Lincoln as a great love story

"Recommended in spite of the controversial nature of its interpretation of Mary Todd Lincoln." Booklist

Lust for life; a novel of Vincent van Gogh; illustrated with 150 reproductions of Vincent van Gogh's pictures arranged by J. B. Neumann. Twentieth anniversary ed. Doubleday 1954 507p il o.p.

First published 1934 by Longmans, Green and Co.

"Vincent Van Gogh lived a turbulent life but throughout it he was loved and supported by his brother, Theo. Sons of a Dutch Protestant minister, Vincent and Theo were raised rather strictly, but Vincent's love of color and movement led him into the life of an artist. He always felt challenged to fill a blank canvas with light and color. Vincent's search for meaning and fulfillment in his life took him over Europe but only toward the end of his life did he meet other artists who shared his artistic views, and it was not until after his death that his work began to be appreciated." Shapiro. Fic for Youth. 3d edition

The passions of the mind; a novel of Sigmund Freud. Doubleday 1971 808, xxxiip o.p.

In this novel the author "takes Freud from his 26th year, when he was still involved in physiology research and smitten with his wife-to-be (Martha Bernays), through over half-a-century in Vienna. He leaves him as the great man arrives in England, bedevilled by cancer and shattered by the ugly political realities of Hitler." Publ Wkly

Stone, Katherine

Happy endings. Kensington Pub. Corp. 1994 362p o.p.

"Raven Winter is the best entertainment attorney in the business. She is handling the reclusive, best-selling author Holly, who fears that Jason Cole, an Academy Award-winning filmmaker, is going to change the happy ending in the film version of her book. Nick is introduced to this group when Raven distractedly jogs in front of his nursery truck. . . . Most romance readers expect a happy ending, but the pleasure comes in the journey to reach it, and Stone does not disappoint." Libr J

Stone, Robert, 1937-

Bay of souls. Houghton Mifflin 2003 249p $25

ISBN 0-395-96349-4 LC 2002-192171

Stone, Robert, 1937-—*Continued*

"Michael Ahearn is a respected professor of literature at a small college in the upper Midwest, with a lovely wife and 12-yer-old son, but a vague dissatisfaction gnaws at him, exacerbated by a frightening incident while deer hunting and the near-death of his son from exposure. When Michael meets a new professor, the beautiful and electrifying Lara Purcell, he falls under her spell and launches an affair, endangering his marriage and his relationship with his son. At Lara's prompting, Michael travels with her to her Caribbean island home of St. Trinity, a nation rife with political violence, where Lara hopes to repossess the soul she believes has been captured by a voodoo goddess." Publ Wkly

"Unusual (for Stone) in is brevity, this is a highly concentrated work, probably the least violent yet most unnerving of his novels. And the philosophical conflict dramatized in it ends surprisingly, in a way that provokes new questions about what Stone is up to in his writing." N Y Times Book Rev

Damascus Gate. Houghton Mifflin 1998 500p $26

ISBN 0-395-66569-8 LC 97-49615

"Chris Lucas, this novel's protagonist, an American journalist of mixed Catholic and Jewish background, is in Israel 'writing a book on the Jerusalem syndrome'—the phenomenon of religious pilgrims who believe that God has called them there for a special purpose. In his research, he encounters some of the city's . . . seekers, including Sonia Barnes, a nightclub singer and practicing Sufi, Adam De Kuff, a manic-depressive who has been manipulated into believing that he is the Messiah, and the House of the Galilean, a fundamentalist-Christian group plotting with ultra-Orthodox Jews to bomb the Temple Mount." Libr J

Stone "is so comprehending of Israel's convoluted workings and its bifurcated culture—where the Biblical fervor of Jerusalem coexists with the disco fever of Tel Aviv—that he makes other writers on the subject seem like the breeziest of literary tourists." New Yorker

Dog soldiers; a novel. Houghton Mifflin 1974 342p o.p.

This novel "chronicles the nightmarish misadventure of Converse, Marge, and Hicks, who smuggle a bundle of Vietnamese heroin into the U.S. only to be pursued and 'ripped off' by a corrupt narcotic agent." Libr J

"Part melodrama, part morality play, 'Dog Soldiers' offers a vision of a predatory, insensate society from which all moral authority has fled. It is a world in which innocence or vestigial remnants of decent behavior prove fatal to their owners; Hicks . . . is nearly violent enough to survive, but he is done in by his own loyalty to Marge. All of this corruption and vulnerability, this savagery and stoned withdrawal, this combination of passion and cynicism works convincingly, for Stone is a very good storyteller indeed." Newsweek

A flag for sunrise; a novel. Knopf 1981 439p o.p.

ISBN 0-394-40757-1 LC 81-47507

"A dramatic tale with political and philosophic views of a Latin American country undergoing revolution in the post-Vietnam era." Oxford Companion to Am Lit. 6th edition

This book is "at once a high-tension adventure tale, a densely plotted political novel and, at its heart, a meditation on the inavailability of God. Stone writes as if announcements of the death of the novel had not reached him: 'A Flag for Sunrise' shows narrative confidence, crisscrossed motives, a moral sense and sustained inventiveness of an amplitude we have almost given up expecting from fiction." Newsweek

Outerbridge Reach. Ticknor & Fields 1992 409p o.p.

LC 91-34875

This novel concerns Owen Browne, an ex-navy man who has become a successful sailboat salesperson. "Avid for honor and glory, he enters a highly publicized, round-the world, singlehanded sailboat race. As the loneliness and exertion of his voyage tests Browne, so the attention of a shallow filmmaker test Anne, Browne's wife. Both learn truths about themselves and one another which destroy one spouse but which compel the other to further trials of strength and will." Libr J

"Robert Stone's blend of heroic aspiration and mordantly deflationary irony results in something like tragicomedy. . . . But whatever you call it, 'Outerbridge Reach' seems to me a triumph—a beautifully and painstakingly composed piece of literary art." N Y Times Book Rev

Stone, Zachary, 1949-

For works written by this author under other names see Follett, Ken, 1949-

Stories not for the nervous. See Alfred Hitchcock presents: Stories not for the nervous

Stout, Rex, 1886-1975

All aces; A Nero Wolfe omnibus. Viking 1958 442p o.p.

Contents: Some buried Caesar (1939); Too many women (1947); and, Trouble in triplicate (1949) which consists of three short stories: Before I die; Help wanted, male; Instead of evidence

In Some buried Caesar, Nero Wolfe leaves his New York kitchen and orchid conservatory to solve a mystery in an upstate community of wealthy cattle breeders. Too many women has Mr. Wolfe and Archie, his roving reporter disguised as a personnel expert, delving into the conflicts, personalities and activities of an engineering supply company involved in murder

Blood will tell

In Stout, R. Trio for blunt instruments p169-247

The cop-killer

In Stout, R. Kings full of aces p369-420

Death of a doxy; a Nero Wolfe novel. Viking 1966 186p o.p.

The problem of money and the possibility of divided loyalty concerns both Nero Wolfe and Archie as they seek to clear their sometime assistant, Orrie Cather, of a murder charge

"First-rate Stout done at the age of eighty. The tightness of the plot, the wit, and the people are done with sureness and speed, so that the book, though short, gives

Stout, Rex, 1886-1975—*Continued*
one the sense of having lived through a long stretch of tense expectation." Barzun. Cat of Crime. Rev and enl edition

Die like a dog
In Stout, R. Royal flush p431-74

Door to death
In Stout, R. Five of a kind p399-441

The doorbell rang; a Nero Wolfe novel. Viking 1965 186p o.p.
"Nero Wolfe tangles with the FBI, on behalf of a wealthy woman who has sent as gifts to prominent people 10,000 copies of Fred Cook's book criticizing the FBI. . . . She is being shadowed and spied on by the FBI. To the surprise of Wolfe and of Archie Goodwin, they have the good will of the New York Police Department. The New York Police believe that FBI agents have murdered a magazine writer who was doing an article on the FBI. The police are powerless to prove anything or to prosecute. Clever and ingenious, this ranks among the best Rex Stout mysteries." Publ Wkly

Fer-de-lance
In Stout, R. Royal flush p1-180

The final deduction
In Stout, R. Three aces

Five of a kind; the third Nero Wolfe omnibus. Viking 1961 441p o.p.
Contains the complete text of: The rubber band, first published 1936 by Farrar & Rinehart; In the best families, and Three doors to death, both originally published 1950 by Viking. Included in the latter title are these three novelettes: Man alive; Omit flowers; and Door to death

Gambit; a Nero Wolfe novel. Viking 1962 188p o.p.
"Nero Wolfe, with his usual witty, urbane, conversational approach, looks into a case of arsenic poisoning in a Manhattan chess club." Publ Wkly
"There is more detection in this story than in any other of the mulling-and-quizzing sort; here we really see N.W.'s thoughts whirring. Moreover, Archie is in excellent form, and although a chess tournament is a feature, the game itself is not. The great scene is that in which Nero reads and burns the pages of Webster's Dictionary, Third Edition." Barzun. Cat of Crime. Rev and enl edition

Home to roost
In Stout, R. Kings full of aces p325-68

In the best families
In Stout, R. Five of a kind p155-303

Kill now—pay later
In Stout, R. Trio for blunt instruments p1-87

Kings full of aces; a Nero Wolfe omnibus. Viking 1969 472p o.p.
Contains three separately published titles: Too many cooks (1938), Plot it yourself (1959) and Triple jeopardy (1952). The latter contains three novelettes: Home to roost, The cop-killer, and The squirt and the monkey

Man alive
In Stout, R. Five of a kind p307-55

Might as well be dead
In Stout, R. Three aces

Murder by the book
In Stout, R. Royal flush p181-333

Murder is corny
In Stout, R. Trio for blunt instruments p89-167

The next witness
In Stout, R. Royal flush p337-84

Omit flowers
In Stout, R. Five of a kind p356-98

Plot it yourself
In Stout, R. Kings full of aces p189-322

Royal flush; the fourth Nero Wolfe omnibus. Viking 1965 474p o.p.
Contains the complete text of: Fer-de-lance (1934); Murder by the book (1951) and Three witnesses (1956). The latter title includes the three novelettes: The next witness; When a man murders and Die like a dog

The rubber band
In Stout, R. Five of a kind p1-153

Some buried Caesar
In Stout, R. All aces p1-153

The squirt and the monkey
In Stout, R. Kings full of aces p421-72

Three aces; a Nero Wolfe omnibus. Viking 1971 473p o.p.
Contents: Too many clients (1960); Might as well be dead (1956); The final deduction (1961)

Three doors to death
In Stout, R. Five of a kind p307-441

Three witnesses
In Stout, R. Royal flush p335-474

Too many clients
In Stout, R. Three aces

Too many cooks
In Stout, R. Kings full of aces p1-187

Too many women
In Stout, R. All aces p155-302

Trio for blunt instruments; a Nero Wolfe threesome. Viking 1964 247p o.p.
Contents: Kill now—pay later; Murder is corny; Blood will tell
"Three stories featuring Nero Wolfe and Archie Goodwin. They concern the defenestration of a businessman, the murder of a deliveryman, and a bloodstained tie sent to Archie from Greenwich Village." Publ Wkly

Triple jeopardy
In Stout, R. Kings full of aces p325-472

Trouble in triplicate
In Stout, R. All aces p303-442

Stout, Rex, 1886-1975—*Continued*

When a man murders
In Stout, R. Royal flush p385-430

Stowe, Harriet Beecher, 1811-1896

The minister's wooing
In Stowe, H. B. Uncle Tom's cabin: or, Life among the lowly; The minister's wooing; Oldtown folks p521-876

Oldtown folks
In Stowe, H. B. Uncle Tom's cabin: or, Life among the lowly; The minister's wooing; Oldtown folks p877-1468

Uncle Tom's cabin; with an introduction by Alfred Kazin. Knopf 1995 xxix, 494p $20
ISBN 0-679-44365-7
"Everyman's library"
"The book relates the trials, suffering, and human dignity of Uncle Tom, an old slave. Cruelly treated by a Yankee plantation owner, Simon Legree, Tom dies as the result of a beating. Uncle Tom is devoted to Little Eva, the daughter of his white owner, Augustine St. Clare. Other important characters are the mulatto girl Eliza; the impish black child Topsy; Miss Ophelia St. Clare, a New England spinster; and Marks, the slave catcher. The setting is Kentucky and Louisiana." Reader's Ency. 4th edition

also in Stowe, H. B. Uncle Tom's cabin: or, Life among the lowly; The minister's wooing; Oldtown folks p1-519

Uncle Tom's cabin: or, Life among the lowly; The minister's wooing; Oldtown folks. Library of Am. 1982 1477p il $47.50
ISBN 0-940450-01-1 LC 81-18629
Omnibus edition of three titles first published 1852, 1859 and 1869 respectively
In the minister's wooing, a young woman rejects her suitor because he has no religious faith. Oldtown folks concerns the everyday life of a small Massachusetts town

Stowe, Harriet Elizabeth *See* Stowe, Harriet Beecher, 1811-1896

Straight, Susan

The gettin place. Hyperion 1996 488p $22.95
ISBN 0-7868-6086-3 LC 95-50065
"The principal setting is Rio Seco, a fictional California city outside of L.A. The 'gettin place' of the title is a parcel of land along an old canal where the extended Thompson clan has its adobe homes and the family businesses—a garage and towing yard, a rib joint and a small olive orchard. When the bodies of two white women are found burned in a dilapidated car in the lot, and when the body of a man dressed in drag is discovered nearby, the Thompsons become the focus of law enforcement attentions." Publ Wkly
"Against the backdrop of the under-acknowledged race riots of 1920s Tulsa and the contrastingly media-saturated 1992 L.A. riots, Straight realizes the chillingly natural, almost blithe cynicism and violence of teenagers, the profound weight of hard history on the old, and the bewilderment of those in-between. A lyrical and unflinching stunner." Libr J

Highwire moon; a novel. Houghton Mifflin 2001 306p map $24
ISBN 0-618-05614-9 LC 00-53878
"The story of an illegal Mexican immigrant named Serafina, the novel chronicles the 12-year aftermath of an INS raid that separates her from her American daughter. Told in the alternating voices of parent and child, the novel explores numerous worlds: migrant workers are juxtaposed with amphetamine addicts; homeless teens with well-tended foster children; industrial laborers with indigenous farm workers." Libr J
"Susan Straight's Rio Seco is a microcosm of suspicious, segregated America, a place where racism often boils down to fear, ignorance and willful obliviousness." N Y Times Book Rev

I been in sorrow's kitchen and licked out all the pots; a novel. Hyperion 1992 355p o.p.
LC 92-3566
"Self-conscious and restless around people, Marietta is happiest alone in the woods behind her tiny coastal community of old slave cabins in South Carolina. Even though it's the late 1950s, life there has a distinctly antebellum flavor. Her father died before she drew breath, so when her mother dies, Marietta, only 15, takes off on her own to Charleston. Her size and blue-black skin amaze and intimidate people, but she finds work and works hard, ever-watchful and courageous. When she becomes pregnant, she goes home to have her twins, two strapping boys, and finds work on the abandoned plantation that is being restored to attract tourists. In a distressing sort of déjà vu, Marietta finds herself reenacting the lives of her ancestors, an impossible, even dangerous situation as the fight for civil rights ignites across the South." Booklist
"Time and place . . . are evoked with stirring accuracy. But it is Marietta's intricate constitution, and the Gullah rhythms streaming through her mind, that give the novel its special edge and distinction." N Y Times Book Rev
Followed by Blacker than a thousand midnights (1994)

Straub, Peter

The buffalo hunter
In Straub, P. Houses without doors p109-207

Floating dragon. Putnam 1983 515p o.p.
LC 82-15057
"Against the background of a small New England town, this novel examines the consequences of an industrial accident coupled with supernatural evil. . . . DRG, a top-secret and highly dangerous drug, is leaked accidentally into the atmosphere in the community of Hampstead; this coincides with a string of brutal murders, mass suicides of children and the presence of representatives of the town's four founding families. Graham Williams, with his knowledge of the area's history, suspects it is more than coincidence. He uncovers a thirty year pattern of sinister events which have plagued Hampstead since its foundation. As madness and death tighten their grip on the town, Williams and his friends must find a way to defeat the force they've nicknamed Dragon." West Coast Rev Books

Straub, Peter—*Continued*

The author "builds a nasty little edifice of horror out of the standard ingredients of small-town New England Gothic and features a richness of background and incident that any writer would envy." Quill Quire

Ghost story. Coward, McCann & Geoghegan 1979 483p o.p.

LC 78-27120

"Set largely in a snow-bound village in present-day upstate New York, this . . . tale of supernatural menace pits two elderly lawyers, a novelist, and a teenager against a life-form that thrives on one's memories and with time on one's blood." Libr J

"With considerable technical skill, Peter Straub has constructed an extravagant entertainment which, though flawed, achieves in its second half some awesome effects." Newsweek

The Hellfire Club. Random House 1995 462p o.p.

LC 95-21773

"A former nurse in Vietnam, Nora Chancel lives in Westerholm, Connecticut, with her ineffectual husband, Davey. While visiting the local police station to identify the most recent victim of a serial killer, Nora is kidnapped by the accused killer, the satirical villain Dick Dart. Intertwined with the kidnapping plot is an account of the terrifying events that followed the writing of a horror story at the Shorelands writers' colony in 1938. Fighting her own demons from Vietnam, Nora becomes stronger and braver as the story progresses. The climax brings the two stories together, as Dart and Nora visit Shorelands. Horror meets horror in this bizarre, enigmatic tale, which reveals itself in onion-like layers." Libr J

Houses without doors. Dutton 1990 358p o.p.

LC 90-2902

Contents: Blue rose; The juniper tree; A short guide to the city; The buffalo hunter {novella}; Something about a death, something about a fire; Mrs. God {novella}

"'The Buffalo Hunter' fastidiously chronicles the fixations of a 35-year-old who numbs his fear of women by sucking his coffee and cognac from baby bottles. In the ambitious gothic thriller/academic spoof 'Mrs. God,' a fatuous professor is lured to a creepy English mansion crammed with grisly secrets to research the papers of his poet ancestress; dead babies provide a subtheme. . . . In addition to having popular allure, Straub's fictions are playfully postmodern, resonating with insights on genre, craft and process." Publ Wkly

In the night room; a novel; Peter Straub. 1st ed. Random House 2004 330p $21.95

ISBN 1-400-06252-7 LC 2004-51425

In this sequel to Lost boy lost girl, horror novelist Tim Underhill receives "an e-mail sent to him by the spirit of an ancient Byzantine, who explains that the daughter of one of the serial killers in Lost boy lost girl wasn't murdered by her father, as Tim supposed; that the exceedingly strange fan who cornered Tim in his local breakfast hangout is an embodiment of the wronged murderer's spirit; and that, yes, that was an angel Tim saw fly away over Manhattan while he walked home. Meanwhile, over in New Jersey, YA novelist Willy Patrick is about to marry mysterious Mitchell Faber when she comes upon evidence that he is responsible for her husband's violent, gangland-like killing. She flees Faber's estate, pursued by his minions, to New York and into a reading-signing appearance by Tim. There is a catch to this, for Willy's plot is that of the new novel Tim has been writing; that is, a character Tim created has emerged in his reality. As Tim and Willy repair to their hometown, Millhaven, Illinois, to slake the murderer's spirit, his real and her fictive worlds converge toward an ending that promises, like that of Lost boy lost girl, the transcendent redemption of violated souls. Inventive and moving." Booklist

Koko. Dutton 1988 562p o.p.

LC 88-3864

In this first volume of the author's Blue rose trilogy "innocent people are suddenly murdered in Singapore. Each mutilated victim is found with a playing card in his mouth, the mysterious word 'Koko' written on it in blood. Four Vietnam vets who used to do the same thing with some of the enemy they killed during the war, realize the killings are being done by a member of their own platoon and fly to Singapore to stop him." West Coast Rev Books

"The characters are realistic and complex, and the story continues to resonate in the mind long after the final page is turned." Publ Wkly

Lost boy lost girl; a novel. Farrar, Straus & Giroux 2003 281p $24.95

ISBN 1-4000-6092-3 LC 2003-046689

"A woman commits suicide for no apparent reason. A week later, her son—beautiful, troubled fifteen-year-old Mark Underhill—vanishes from the face of the earth. To his uncle, horror novelist Timothy Underhill, Mark's inexplicable absence feels like a second death. After his sister-in-law's funeral, Tim searches his hometown of Millhaven for clues that might help him unravel this mystery of death and disappearance." Publisher's note

"Inquisitive and open-minded as Tim is, he makes it easy for Mr. Straub to move from conventionally hair-raising effects . . . to the more happening teenage world of cyberscares. Strongly visual without resorting to secondhand cinematic imagery, the book is equally well equipped to play both kinds of tricks." N Y Times (Late N Y Ed)

Magic terror; seven tales. Random House 2000 335p o.p.

ISBN 0-375-50393-5 LC 99-53216

Includes the following stories: Ashputtle; Isn't it romantic?; The ghost village; Bunny is good bread; Pork pie hat; Hunger, an introduction; Mr. Clubb and Mr. Cuff

"Straub is not called a master of horror for nothing. In this collection of seven tales, ranging from the story of a grade school teacher with an evil secret to a Vietnam War grunt whose reality is @melting at the edges,' Straub shows that horror comes in numerous forms—many of which are not so much frightening as deeply disturbing." Libr J

Mr. X; a novel. Random House 1999 482p $25.95

ISBN 0-679-40138-5 LC 98-47688

"From childhood, Ned Dunstan has experienced precognitive visions. . . . Summoned home to Edgerton, Ill., by a premonition of his mother's death on the eve of his 35th birthday, Ned finds himself implicated in a tangle

Straub, Peter—*Continued*

of felonies and murders, all of which point to someone strenuously manipulating events to frame him. Digging into local history, he finds reason to believe that the mysterious father he never knew, or possibly a malignant doppelgänger, are pulling the strings. . . . [Straub's] evocative prose, a seamless splice of clipped hard-boiled banter and poetic reflection, contributes to the thick atmosphere of apprehension that makes this one of the most invigorating horror reads of the year." Publ Wkly

Mrs. God
In Straub, P. Houses without doors p223-352

Mystery. Dutton 1990 548p il o.p.
LC 89-7734

Second title in the author's Blue rose trilogy. "When a traffic accident nearly ends his young life, Tom Pasmore experiences all the usual near-death sensations: warm lights at the end of tunnels and friendly faces beckoning him onward. But by cheating death, his life is forever changed. Tom becomes obsessed with murder, with detection, and especially with a recent killing on Mill Walk, the fictional Caribbean island where his family lives. Tom's sleuthing mania is fed by an eccentric neighbor, Lamont von Heilitz, a famous retired detective. . . . The remarkable depth of characterization make apparent the fact that *Mystery* is meant to be much more than a conventional shocker. For the most part, Straub delivers the goods." Booklist

Shadowland. Coward, McCann & Geoghegan 1980 417p o.p.
LC 80-23691

A "modern fairy tale of an aging, amoral magician and his two prep-school apprentices. In fact, the Brothers Grimm are two of the magic-provided characters that Tom Flanagan, the apprentice selected to be the next king of the magicians, meets during a mystifying and ultimately violent summer at a rambling Vermont estate called Shadowland. Others include his true love Rose, who may be a mermaid, and Coleman Collins, the magician, who may have been Rose's lover in Paris during the 1920's. The structure of the novel is somewhat complicated: What happens at Shadowland reflects the terrors and frustrations encountered by Tom and Del, the magician's nephew and longtime heir apparent, at an Arizona prep school the year before. The actual story, though, is pieced together and related 20 years afterward by a classmate of theirs now a writer. This is an ambitious patchwork fantasy of shifting reality." Libr J

The throat. Dutton 1993 689p o.p.
LC 92-36604

In this conclusion to the author's trilogy "the citizens of Millhaven, Ill., thought they had overcome the unsolved serial murders that plagued the town in the 1940s—the killer had scrawled the words 'Blue Rose' near the bodies—but another resident has just fallen prey to a new Blue Rose. The victim's husband, John Ransom, enlists the aid of Tim Underhill, a high school buddy and fellow Vietnam vet who has written a book about the murders. Although Tim thinks of his hometown as 'oddly interchangeable' with Vietnam, he returns to join forces with famed local sleuth Tom Pasmore to solve both the earlier and the later murders. . . . Painted from a darkly colorful palette, Straub's characters inhabit a razor-edged world of unremitting suspense." Publ Wkly

(jt. auth) King, S. Black house

Strauss, Darin

The real McCoy; a novel. Dutton 2002 326p o.p.
ISBN 0-525-94651-9 LC 2002-23545

"It's the end of the nineteenth century, and Kid McCoy—a small-time boxer long past his prime—comes to young Virgil Selby's town. McCoy is beaten so badly that he dies. Virgil drags the dying man to the forest, learns the location of Kid McCoy's next fight, and then—poof—becomes Kid McCoy, Kid, née Virgil, ends up in a Chinese railroad worker community, where he meets Johnny Gold, a first-rate flimflam man with a habit of not finishing his . . . McCoy and Gold team up, and eventually McCoy cons his way to a world boxing title, becoming the toast of New York society." Booklist

The author has "taken the tale of an all-but-forgotten boxer and used it as his jumping-off point to worry questions of identity and the thin, often nonexistent lines between filmflamming and lying and storytelling itself." N Y Times Book Rev

Streeter, Edward, 1891-1976

Father of the bride; illustrated by Gluyas Williams. Simon & Schuster 1999 234p il $23
ISBN 0-684-86354-5 LC 98-55355

A reissue of the title first published 1949

"From the day of her engagement to the end of the wedding day, the bride and her trousseau, her plans and her wedding, the in-laws and the guests, and especially the effect on his home life and his bank account are seen through the eyes of the Father of the Bride." Wis Libr Bull

"To be the father of the bride is to play a painful role as Mr. Stanley Banks discovers when preparations are launched for the big event of his one and only. The very good fun of this warmly human tale is pointed up with touches of pathos." Ont Libr Rev

Strieber, Whitley

The forbidden zone. Dutton 1993 309p o.p.
LC 93-6726

"Not long after physicist Brian Kelly and his pregnant wife hear human screams coming from within a dirt mound, inhabitants of their upstate New York town are attacked by wasp-like fireflies, women transformed into grub-like creatures are dug from the earth and an otherworldly being terrorizes motorists from its Dodge Viper. Brian theorizes that somehow the space-time fabric has been breached, and before long he and a few companions are engaged in a classic battle with an army of ancient demons." Publ Wkly

"The action and danger in this novel are exciting, and while the physics and the explanation for the horrific events are rather muddy, the story works well as a Lovecraft-style tale brought into modern times." Libr J

The last vampire. Pocket Bks. 2001 303p $24.95
ISBN 0-7434-1720-8 LC 2001-21013

Sequel to The hunger (1981)

Miriam Blaylock "plans to attend various conclaves of the Keepers, as vampires refer to themselves. What none

Strieber, Whitley—*Continued*

of them anticipates, however, is that their human prey has discovered their existence and, what is worse, has the means to eradicate them. First in Thailand, then in France, whole lairs are destroyed by a group of vampire slayers led by CIA agent Paul Ward. Only Miriam manages to escape the slaughter. She flees back to her nest in New York City. Paul wants to follow only to be told by his superiors that the President has decided that vampires have human rights, which means that Paul may be guilty of murder." Libr J

"There's much here to admire, not least Strieber's expert modulation of tone and dialogue as POV shifts from Miriam (fluid, refined) to Paul (muscular, slangy)." Publ Wkly

Majestic. Putnam 1989 317p o.p.

LC 89-8495

The author "combines fictitious confessions and military documents with genuine newspaper reports to depict a reputed encounter with alien beings near New Mexico's Roswell Army Air Field in 1947. What appears to be a disabled U.F.O. is discovered, and a paranoid military appoints a man named Will Stone to direct the investigation—and to conceal the incident in an operation code named Majestic. Forty years later, Stone reveals the cover-up to a shocked reporter, Nicholas Duke, who narrates the tale." N Y Times Book Rev

"Strieber has managed to weave two major themes in ufology (crashes and abductions) into an intriguing and unconventional tale that has both the dialogue and flavor of postwar America as well as the surrealistic aura of contemporary fiction." Booklist

Warday; and the journey onward; [by] Whitley Strieber and James W. Kunetka. Holt, Rinehart & Winston 1984 374p o.p.

LC 83-18678

"On Oct. 28, 1988, the Soviet Union launches a surprise attack on the United States. Ten-megaton atomic bombs detonate over Washington, San Antonio and the eastern edge of Queens. Smaller bombs strike the Minuteman and MX missile fields spread out across the northern plains. Washington and San Antonio are 'instantly vaporized.' Manhattan escapes destruction but is abandoned. Five years later, two writers brave the hazards of post-Warday travel to report back to us on how surviving America 'feels and tastes and smells.'" NY Times Book Rev

The Wolfen. Morrow 1978 252p o.p.

LC 78-7482

"Two cops are brutally killed and their guts are devoured by what appears to be a pack of wild animals. The police in charge, a middle-aged slob and a newly fledged woman detective, bicker endlessly through the killings of a blind man, a couple of junkies, and more, while the pack, mutant wolves, kill for food and to keep their secret from being discovered. This is a very specialized form of animal disaster novel, but much more suspenseful and imaginative than most. The windup is total thrill." Libr J

Strindberg, August, 1849-1912

The scapegoat; translated from the Swedish by Arvid Paulson; introduction by Richard B. Vowles. Eriksson 1967 175p o.p.

Original Swedish edition, 1906

"Strindberg's scapegoat is Edward Libotz, a struggling young lawyer who tries to find a life for himself in a bourgeois Swedish mountain village. Haunted by a family background that plagues him wherever he goes, and scorned by people who make his life almost unbearable, he still manages to triumph over stupidity and bigotry and becomes a quiet hero." Libr J

Stroby, Wallace

The barbed-wire kiss. St. Martin's Minotaur 2003 340p $24.95

ISBN 0-312-30034-4 LC 2002-35879

"Ex-cop Harry Rane, recovering from the death of his wife and forced into semi-retirement by a bullet wound, comes to the rescue of his longtime friend Bobby. Bobby has made a big mistake: he has invested money with a partner for a 'one-time' drug buy. The partner has disappeared with the cash, but the supplier, a suspicious character under scrutiny by New Jersey cops, still wants his money." Libr J

"Although the story advances predictably. . . Stroby does wonders with his blue-collar characters, the hard-working fishermen and mechanics and bar waitresses who put their hand to petty crime the way they play the lottery—to try their luck and get a thrill, the way they did when the seashore was a kinder place to live." N Y Times Book Rev

Stross, Charles

Iron sunrise. Ace Bks. 2004 355p $23.95

ISBN 0-441-01159-4

"When the explosion of a G2 star destroys the planet Moscow, the survivors send a counterattack against the suspected attackers, the New Dresden system. When New Dresden denies responsibility, Old Earth agent Rachel Mansour investigates to stave off outright war. Only a teenager named Wednesday knows what's been going on, but she is unaware of her knowledge." Libr J

"Stross skillfully balances suspense and humor throughout, offering readers—especially fans of Iain M. Banks and Ken MacLeod—a fascinating future that seems more than possible." Publ Wkly

Strout, Elizabeth

Amy and Isabelle. Random House 1999 303p $22.95

ISBN 0-375-50134-7 LC 98-19995

"Amy Goodrow, 16, is the shy only child of Isabelle, single mother. Isabelle's shame over the secret of her daughter's illegitimacy and her hunger for respectability keep her painfully isolated from the community of the New England mill town where she has made her home. Even before Amy's relations with her teacher become known, her beauty and her burgeoning sexuality arouse uncomfortable feelings of competitiveness in Isabelle, as well as dread at the prospect of her daughter's flight from Isabelle's carefully constructed nest." Publ Wkly

Strout, Elizabeth—*Continued*

"As the cacophony of disaster grows ever louder in contemporary culture, Strout has written an excellent novel about enduring the banalities of ordinary life." New Yorker

Struther, Jan, 1901-1953

Mrs. Miniver. Harcourt Brace & Co. 1942 298p o.p.

First published 1939 in the United Kingdom; first United States edition published 1940. This 1942 edition adds a story: Mrs. Miniver makes a list

Contents: Mrs. Miniver comes home; New car; Guy Fawkes' day; Eve of the shoot; Christmas shopping; Three stockings; New engagement book; Last day of the holidays; In search of a charwoman; First day of spring; On Hampstead Heath; Country house visit; Mrs. Downce; Married couples; Drive to Scotland; Twelfth of August; At the games; Autumn flit; Gas masks; "Back to normal"; Badger and the echidna; Wild day; New Year's Eve; Choosing a doll; At the dentist's; Pocketful of pebbles; Brambles and apple-trees; Khelim rug; On the river; Left and right; "Doing a mole"; New dimension; London in August; Back from abroad; At the hop-picking; "From needing danger . . ."; Mrs. Miniver makes a list

Stuart, Ian, 1922-1987 *See* MacLean, Alistair, 1922-1987

Stubbs, Harry Clement *See* Clement, Hal, 1922-2003

Stubbs, Jean, 1926-

Family games. St. Martin's Press 1994 294p o.p.

LC 93-44054

The Malpas family assembles for Christmas at their Cornwall farmhouse: "headstrong daughter Blanche, an unwed mother, brings her infant son and temporarily abandons her feud with her father, the brilliant and irascible Anthony; recently separated son Edward, still reeling from his wife's departure, arrives with his two children; and beautiful, dependent daughter Lydia surprises the others by bringing a likable woman friend instead of another one of a parade of 'moneyed and moronic' male beaux. At the close of the Malpases' impromptu Christmas Eve open house, three unexpected visitors appear, Magi-like, at the door. One is Natalie, Anthony's imperious twin sister; another is Katrina, Edward's estranged wife; the third is Daniel Kidd, the father of Blanche's child." Publ Wkly

"The writer appears fully in control of this entertaining romp concerning one very dysfunctional, if provocative, family." Booklist

Like we used to be. St. Martin's Press 1990 c1989 387p o.p.

LC 89-27133

First published 1989 in the United Kingdom

"This is the story of Leila and Zoe Gideon, sisters who are in every way different, yet who love each other and their marvelous British family unreservedly. The story begins with Zoe's wedding and Leila's first love affair in the summer of 1953, and spans the next 15 years. Zoe struggles to create a loving home with her difficult husband, Matthew. Leila, the rebellious sister, makes an independent life for herself as an artist in London. Told alternately by Leila and Zoe, the book has leisurely pace filled with emotional detail. This will appeal to lovers of old-fashioned family novels." Libr J

"Social ferment and family history are vigorously blended in a dramatic style characteristic of a master storyteller." Publ Wkly

Sturgeon, Theodore, 1918-1985

Slow sculpture

In The Best of the Nebulas p403-18

Styron, Alexandra

All the finest girls; a novel. Little, Brown 2001 259p $23.95

ISBN 0-316-89080-4 LC 00-50051

"Addy Abraham is 32, single, childless and dissatisfied with her work restoring paintings for a Manhattan museum. Addy is somewhat estranged from her father (a well-known philosophy professor) and from her mother, who relegated a good deal of Addy's upbringing to a Caribbean nanny named Louise; much of the novel takes place on the island of St. Clair, where Addy has traveled for Louise's funeral." N Y Times Book Rev

Styron "beautifully juxtaposes Addy's past and the present on St. Claire, dealing deftly with a series of ironies. Although some readers may find Addy slow to catch on, Styron's gift is to make the reader feel real grief for her characters and real relief for Addy when she begins to make a peace with herself and her parents." Publ Wkly

Styron, William, 1925-

The confessions of Nat Turner. Modern Lib. 1994 xliv, 428p $18.95; pa $14

ISBN 0-679-60101-5; 0-679-73663-8 (pa)

LC 94-9393

A reissue of the title first published 1967 by Random House

This "account of an actual person and event is based on the brief contemporary pamphlet of the same title presented to a trial court as evidence and published in Virginia a year after the revolt of fellow slaves led by Turner in 1831. Imagining much of Turner's youth and early manhood before the rebellion that he headed at the age of 31, Styron in frequently rhetorical and pseudo-Biblical style has Turner recall his religious faith and his power of preaching to other slaves." Oxford Companion to Am Lit. 5th edition

Lie down in darkness. Bobbs-Merrill 1951 400p o.p.

"Mr. Styron takes a marriage for the framework of his story, the journey of a hearse to the cemetery for his action, and the suicide of a young woman for his impetus, his mood, and his climax. The marriage is that of Milton and Helen Loftis, a Virginia couple, and the hearse, which they follow in separate limousines, carries the remains of their daughter Peyton, who is in death, as she was in life, only a symbol of her parents' mutual hatred,

Styron, William, 1925-—*Continued*
their despair, and their overpowering self-pity." New Yorker

"The book is not bleakly written. On the contrary, it is richly and even (in the best sense) poetically written. . . . If the parts seem to succeed each other with no apparent logic or dialectic, each part is brilliantly made and lovingly accomplished." Atlantic

Set this house on fire. Random House 1960 507p o.p.

"The narrator, Peter Leverett, a government employee returning to the U.S., stops in the little Italian village of Sambuco to see his old schoolmate Mason Flagg. The next morning the satyrical Flagg is found dead at the base of a cliff, a peasant girl has been raped and beaten until she dies, and Cass Kinsolving, a drunken, psychoneurotic American painter and the butt of Flagg's devilish humor, has temporarily disappeared. Though the case is written off as one of murder and suicide, the remainder of the novel probes minutely the past lives of the main characters, focusing through Peter's concern and his desire to know the whole truth. A large part of the action takes place in the Mediterranean village, but the novel is also one of contemporary America and Americans; of a world of conflict, too much wealth, too much sex and commercialism, too prevalent shallowness and lack of values." Libr J

Sophie's choice. Modern Lib. 1998 599p $22; pa $14

ISBN 0-679-60289-5; 0-679-73637-9 (pa)
LC 97-36895

A reissue of the title first published 1979

"Sophie Zawistowska is a Polish Catholic who has somehow survived Auschwitz and resettled in America after the war. Here, in a Jewish boarding house in Flatbush, she meets two men—Nathan Landau, a brilliant but dangerously unstable Jew who becomes her lover; and Stingo, a young Southern writer (and autobiographical simulacrum of Styron himself). The novel traces Stingo's intense involvement with the lovers—their euphoric highs as well as their cataclysmic descents into psychopathy—and his growing fascination with the horror of Sophie's past." Libr J

"It was a daring act for Styron, whose sensibilities are wholly Southern, to venture into the territory of the American Jew, to say nothing of his plunge into European history. The book is powerfully moving." Burgess. 99 Novels

A Tidewater morning: three tales from youth. Random House 1993 142p o.p.

LC 93-3639

"Three long short stories (each previously published in *Esquire*) form a triptych capturing as if in amber a trio of moments in Paul Whitehurst's youth and early manhood. In 'Love Day,' he's a Marine preparing to participate in the assault on Okinawa in the last days of World War II. . . . 'Shadrach' features a younger Paul's reactions (he's 10 that summer) to an ancient black man who returns to the local plantation where he was born in slavery, to die and be buried. . . . The triptych's final panel, 'A Tidewater Morning,' is actually situated chronologically between its predecessors, and it's the most affecting of the three. With a pungency that keenly pierces the reader's heart by use of a blade devoid of sentimentality, Paul recalls his father's disgust with a God that would take in such an excruciating manner the life of his wife, Paul's mother." Booklist

Suarez, Virgil, 1962-

(ed) Iguana dreams. See Iguana dreams

Sukenick, Ronald, 1932-2004

Mosaic man. FC2 1999 261p il pa $14.95

ISBN 1-57366-079-5 (pa) LC 98-53043

This novel traces and creates the story of Sukenick's own life (a sort of autobiography, in documentary novel form) and fashions the story of Jewish identity, particularly in the twentieth century. It reworks other narratives along the way, including the text of Genesis. Booklist

"The present volume, which includes collage-like pages and other devices reviewers tend to call experimental, is basically a meditation on what it means to be Jewish, and a serious writer, in the century of the Holocaust." N Y Times Book Rev

Sullivan, Eleanor

(ed) Fifty years of the best from Ellery Queen's Mystery Magazine. See Fifty years of the best from Ellery Queen's Mystery Magazine

Suri, Manil

The death of Vishnu. Norton 2001 295p $24.95

ISBN 0-393-05042-4 LC 00-58414

"The lives and loves of residents of an apartment house in Bombay unfold as Vishnu, a drunk, lies dying on the steps that serve as his home. As his neighbors argue over the cost of an ambulance, the sick man drifts in and out of consciousness, reflecting on the meaning of his life." Libr J

"Its clever structure allows [this book] to display a manageable cross-section of contemporary Indian life, including class and religious frictions. But Suri . . . has more to offer here than gentle social comedy. During the course of the novel, Vishnu's soul disentangles itself from his earthly remains and begins ascending the apartment house stairs. As this spirit looks back on the life just ending, Suri's novel achieves an eerie and memorable transcendence." Time

Süskind, Patrick

Perfume: the story of a murderer; translated from the German by John E. Woods. Knopf 1986 255p o.p.

LC 86-45419

Original German edition, 1985

Set in eighteenth-century France, Perfume relates the "tale of Jean-Baptiste Grenouille, a person as gifted as he was abominable. Born without a smell of his own but endowed with an extraordinary sense of smell, Grenouille becomes obsessed with procuring the perfect scent that will make him fully human." Libr J

"Those readers who feel they are wasting their time with novels unless they are picking up facts will welcome Süskind's encyclopedic overview of the methods of making perfume. Like the best scents, there is something fundamentally formulaic about this novel, but its effects will linger long after it has been stoppered." Time

Sutcliff, Rosemary, 1920-1992

Sword at sunset. Coward-McCann 1963 495p o.p.

A novel based on historical facts about the legendary Arthur. "The time is the century after the last Roman legions leave Britain, and Arthur is desperately striving to hold Britain against the Saxons, Picts, and other invading savage tribes. [This is] the story of his tragic fate, his good times and bad." Publ Wkly

Sutherland, J. A. *See* Sutherland, John, 1938-

Sutherland, John, 1938-

(ed) The Oxford book of English love stories. See The Oxford book of English love stories

Sutton, David, 1944-

(ed) The Best horror from Fantasy tales. See The Best horror from Fantasy tales

Svevo, Italo, 1861-1928

Zeno's conscience; translated from the Italian by William Weaver with an introduction by Elizabeth Hardwick. Knopf 2001 xlix, 437p $20 o.p.

ISBN 0-375-41330-8 LC 2001-40821

"Everyman's library"

Original Italian edition, 1923; previous English translations had title: The confessions of Zeno

"Confessions of Zeno is disguised as the story of [the author's] life as prepared by a psychoanalyst's patient for his doctor, and it is a masterpiece of sleepy wit and biting irony. Zeno is a foolish fellow. He is lazy, inquisitive, a master of indecision, always planning to give up his pet vices, always trying new careers, always expecting to do great things at something else, salving his conscience after each relapse and failure in the most mischievous, comic and natural ways. There is no describable plot to Zeno's confessions." Outlook

This is "a highly human story and its material is fundamentally as sound as its method. . . . The work of a man who wrote to please himself, it has an individuality and originality you cannot escape noticing, and it has, too, a fine and comprehensive knowledge of its character." N Y Times Book Rev

Swanwick, Michael

Bones of the earth. HarperCollins Pubs. 2002 335p o.p.

ISBN 0-380-97836-9 LC 2001-40196

"Swanwick writes about paleontologists who travel back to the Mesozoic to study dinosaurs firsthand, with a technology supplied by enigmatic aliens. . . . His focus never strays far from the two reluctant collaborators, Griffin and the Old Man, who have transformed paleontology into an experimental science. The air of competence they adopt in their day-to-day operations cannot mask their anxiety over who ultimately are the experimenters and who are the subjects." N Y Times Book Rev

Swarthout, Glendon Fred

Bless the beasts and children; [by] Glendon Swarthout. Doubleday 1970 205p o.p.

"Six rich teenagers, rejected by their parents and avoided by their peers, group together at Box Canyon Summer Boys' Camp. Fragile egos and self-destructive personalities begin to heal under the leadership of Cotton, who gently pokes fun at their soft spots while building up their self-esteem. An effort on the part of the group to stop the wanton slaughter of buffalo provides a high point of suspense." Shapiro. Fic for Youth. 3d edition

The homesman; {by} Glendon Swarthout. Weidenfeld & Nicolson 1988 239p o.p.

LC 88-10102

"After venturing west of the Missouri to stake claims in uncharted territory, a number of settlers find the earth fallow and the desolate, lonely winters unbearable. When four of the wives go mad, the local minister entrusts a prim, strong-willed young schoolmarm, Mary Bee Cuddy, to transport them back to Iowa by covered wagon. With her, virtually against his will, is Briggs, a dishonest, foul-mouthed land-grabber (he steals other peoples' claims) whom Mary Bee saved from a lynching in exchange for his help." Publ Wkly

"Swarthout captures both the adventurous spirit and the sometimes abysmal realities of frontier life." Booklist

The shootist; [by] Glendon Swarthout. Doubleday 1975 186p o.p.

"J. B. Books, last of the West's big-time gunfighters and stoic sufferer of terminal cancer, plays out his death rites. Ensconced in a boarding house in El Paso, Books is approached by a host of exploiters who desire to use his impending death to enhance their own reputations and monetary status; the shootist, however, plans otherwise. He maneuvers his adversaries' self-aggrandizing behavior to his advantage, engineering them to carry out his desire; a quick and respectable death by bullet." Booklist

"This is definitely more than a Western; the characterization is flawless, the plot absorbing and convincing." Libr J

Swerling, Beverly

Shadowbrook; a novel of love and war; Beverly Swerling. Simon & Schuster 2004 490p il $24.95

ISBN 0-7432-2812-X LC 2003-64127

"Covering the years 1754-1760, with the British, French and Indians slaughtering each other for king and empire, Swerling tells of two men who straddle the white and red man's worlds, desperate to preserve the best of each culture, but fearful they will lose everything they love. Quentin Hale is a gentleman turned scout whose family owns a prosperous New York plantation called Shadowbrook. He is white, but also follows the Indian ways of his adopted tribe, the Potawatomi. Cormac Shea is part-Irish and part-Indian, nearly a brother to Hale, but he wants all whites driven from Canada. Together these men find themselves caught up in a bloody war neither wants, but they must fight to save the plantation and create a homeland for the Indians. . . . Surrounding them are colorful historical figures like the young George Washington, the hapless General Braddock and the powerful Ottawa chief, Pontiac." Publ Wkly

Swift, Graham, 1949-

Last orders. Knopf 1996 294p o.p.
LC 96-13726

"On a bleak spring day, four men meet in their favorite pub in a working-class London neighborhood. They are about to begin a pilgrimage to scatter the ashes of a fifth man, Jack Dodds, friend since WWII of three of them, adoptive father to the fourth. By the time they reach the seaside town where Jack's 'last orders' have sent them, the tangled relationship among the men, their wives and their children has obliquely been revealed." Publ Wkly

"The narrative is parceled out among . . . four men, as well as Amy, the widow, Vince's wife, Mandy, and Jack, the dead man. The accent is flat London vernacular, and the tone varies between mordant humor, gentle regret, and deep sorrow. Swift carries off this feat of ventriloquism with admirable skill." N Y Rev Books

Waterland. Poseidon Press 1984 309p il o.p.
ISBN 0-671-49863-0 LC 83-21248

This novel "concerns Tom Crick, an English history teacher in his mid-50s who, as the novel opens, has just been forced to accept early retirement. In response to his students' belief that history is a 'fairy-tale' and only the 'here and now' matters, Crick has abandoned the formal curriculum to tell stories about his childhood in East England's Fens. The headmaster, a physicist, shares the students' opinion of the past, and Crick's 'trying to put himself into history' is the last straw. But Crick won't go–his students are for once interested in his 'crazy yarns' until one day his wife goes mad and steals a baby from a supermarket shopping cart. The prospect of retirement gives Crick the freedom to tell his pupils the lurid story that lies behind his wife's theft." Nation

"The novel exceeds credibility and attenuates our tolerance in exactly the same degree as it creates, through [Swift's] own words, the portrait of a man who is deeply disturbed, and who is vainly attempting to build a structure from these words which will protect him from his childlessness, from his failure to create the future." Times Lit Suppl

Swift, Jonathan, 1667-1745

Gulliver's travels; with an introduction by Pat Rogers. Knopf 1991 xlv, 318p map $20
ISBN 0-679-40545-3 LC 91-53011

"Everyman's library"

First published 1726

"In the account of his four wonder-countries Swift satirizes contemporary manners and morals, art and politics—in fact the whole social scheme—from four different points of view. The huge Brobdingnagians reduce man to his natural insignificance, the little people of Lilliput parody Europe and its petty broils, in Laputa philosophers are ridiculed, and finally all Swift's hatred and contempt find their satisfaction in degrading humanity to a bestial condition." Baker. Guide to the Best Fic

Swift, Margaret *See* Drabble, Margaret, 1939-

Symons, Julian, 1912-1994

Death's darkest face. Viking 1990 272p o.p.
LC 90-50049

Symons "introduces the novel by explaining that what we are about to receive is a manuscript that came into his hands by chance. Symons warns that we should not take every detail at face value. The 'author' of the manuscript is Geoffrey Elder, an actor who died at the end of the seventies. The story he tells tracks back and forth through his life from the thirties to the sixties, in an attempt to get to the bottom of a mystery that has always perplexed him: what really happened to the scurrilous modernist poet Hugo Headley, who disappeared in mysterious circumstances in 1936?" New Statesman Soc

"Mr. Symons could remove all the mystery elements of this story and still have a wonderful novel, but as we near the end, we are happier for the challenge of solving the crime." N Y Times Book Rev

The Kentish manor murders. Viking 1988 191p o.p.
LC 87-40460

"A Viking novel of mystery and suspense"

"The detective in this book is an actor famous for his Sherlock Holmes readings. A reclusive billionaire engages him for a private reading. It seems that the man is a Conan Doyle enthusiast and a collector of Holmesiana. It seems also that an unknown Sherlock Holmes story has just turned up and the actor is asked to be a go-between in a sale to the billionaire. But is he really the billionaire? Or is he an impersonator? Fun and games, in Mr. Symons' best style." N Y Times Book Rev

Playing happy families. Viking 1995 308p o.p.
LC 94-15119

"The adult children of John and Eleanor Midway gather for their parents 30th wedding anniversary. Champagne is poured; good food is served. But a crisis changes the lives of the Midways, or perhaps it renders visible aspects of their lives formerly hidden. Their firebrand daughter Jenny vanishes one afternoon; she is revealed as wild and promiscuous. In grief, John falls into the arms of his secretary, while Eleanor becomes an unlikely restaurant mogul. Eleanor's son Eversley, visiting from America, negotiates the sale of a priceless work of art with the gallery where Jenny worked. That odd coincidence sets Detective Superintendent Hilary Catchpole on a hunt for a killer." Publ Wkly

Something like a love affair. Mysterious Press 1992 199p o.p.
LC 92-5980

"Judith is in bad shape long before she finds out the sordid truth about her husband, a successful architect of perfectionist temperament. Bored to distraction by her doll-like existence in a Sussex suburb . . . she has been writing herself passionate love letters cribbed from historical romances. When that mute cry for attention goes unnoticed, Judith throws herself into an obsessive affair with the loutish youth who has been giving her driving lessons. The next step is murder." N Y Times Book Rev

"Symons' tale is chillingly and compellingly told. Exploring the dark underside of the human spirit, it's story of a desperate woman who can no longer cope." Booklist

T

Tademy, Lalita

Cane River. Warner Bks. 2001 418p il o.p.
ISBN 0-446-53052-2 LC 00-43682
"Five generations and a hundred years in the life of a matriarchal black Louisiana family are encapsulated in this . . . novel that is based in part upon the lives, as preserved in both historical record and oral tradition, of the author's ancestors. . . . Her frank observations about black racism add depth to the tale, and she demonstrates that although the practice of slavery fell most harshly upon blacks, and especially women, it also constricted the lives and choices of white men. Photos of and documents relating to Tademy's ancestors add authenticity to a fascinating story." Publ Wkly

Taibo, Paco Ignacio, 1949-

Returning as shadows; [by] Paco Ignacio Taibo II; translated from the Spanish by Ezra E. Fitz. St. Martin's Press 2003 455p $24.95
ISBN 0-312-30156-1 LC 2002-35388
"As this sequel to The Shadow of a Shadow (1991) begins, it is 1941, and Mexico, a neutral country, is buzzing with crypto-Nazi espionage. The Germans have three aims: to secure coffee beans for a caffeine-addicted Adolf Hitler, to establish a covert submarine base in the Gulf of Mexico and to complete some occult process involving Hitler's former adviser and guru, Eric Jan Hanussen. Hanussen, who has broken with the Nazis, is disguised as an inmate in a Mexico city nuthouse. His roommate, ex-lawyer Alberto Verdugo, rules as a sort of narrating magus over the story." Publ Wkly
"Unlike some other writers who use the thriller genre, [the author] has a novelists's sensibility, the education of a truly literary man and the notebook of a journalist—which means that in his books the world in all its oddity is always bigger, much bigger, than just the plot." N Y Times Book Rev

Tait, Dorothy *See* Fairbairn, Ann, 1901 or 2-1972

Tan, Amy

The bonesetter's daughter. Putnam 2001 353p o.p.
ISBN 0-399-14643-1 LC 00-62673
The novel "is divided into three sections. The first, set in present-day California, introduces us to Ruth Young, a Chinese-American woman whose 10-year relationship with the man she loves is deteriorating for reasons she doesn't understand. . . .The middle section of the novel is the memoir written a few years earlier by Ruth's mother, LuLing, so that her daughter will know the truth about LuLing's life in China. The third section focuses once more on Ruth, and what she will do with the knowledge she has gained." N Y Times Book Rev
"A fine and highly readable novel, The Bonesetter's Daughter is essentially about writing and the act of writing, what fuels it and how it is created. More specifically still, it is about how we, as women creatively express ourselves via language." Women's Rev Books

The hundred secret senses. Putnam 1995 358p o.p.
LC 95-31791
"Nearing divorce from her husband, Simon, Olivia Yee is guided by her elder half-sister, the irrepressible Kwan, into the heart of China. Olivia was five when 18-year-old Kwan first joined her family in the United States, and though always irritated by Kwan's oddities, Olivia was entranced by her eerie dreams of the ghost World of Yin. Only when visiting Kwan's home in Changmian does Olivia realize the dreams are, in Kwan's mind, memories from past lives. . . . Tan tells a mysterious, believable story and delivers Kwan's clipped, immigrant voice and engaging personality with charming clarity." Libr J

The Joy Luck Club. Putnam 1989 288p $24.95
ISBN 0-399-13420-4 LC 88-26492
"Four aging Chinese women who knew life in China before 1949 and now live in San Francisco meet regularly to play mah-jongg and share thoughts about their American-born children. In alternating sections we learn about the cultural differences between the elderly 'aunties' and the younger generation. When one of the older women dies, her daughter is pressed to take her place in the Joy Luck Club. Her feeling of being out of place gradually gives way to an understanding of the need to retain cultural continuity and an appreciation for the strength and endurance of the older women." Shapiro. Fic for Youth. 3d edition

The kitchen god's wife. Putnam 1991 415p o.p.
LC 91-7828
"Pressed to tell her American-born daughter the truth about her life in China, Winnie unburdens herself of old angers and fears, recounting her violient, war-wrenched youth and the barbaric tyranny of her arranged marriage." Am Libr
"Within the peculiar construction of Amy Tan's second novel is a harrowing, compelling and at times bitterly humorous tale in which an entire world unfolds in a Tolstoyan tide of event and detail." N Y Times Book Rev

Saving fish from drowning. Putnam 2005 474p $26.95
ISBN 0-399-15301-2 LC 2005-48724
Ön an ill-fated art expedition into the southern Shan state of Burma, eleven Americans leave their Floating Island Resort for a Christmas-morning tour-and disappear. . . . They find themselves deep in the jungle, where they encounter a tribe awaiting the return of the leader and the mythical book of wisdom that will protect them from the ravages and destruction of the Myanmar military re-Publisher's note
"Amy Tan has created a meta-fable of Orwellian stature, where Americans abroad think they know best, yet follow others blindly; where illusions and assumptions meet self-righteousness and arrogance." Ms.

Tanenbaum, Robert

Act of revenge; a novel; [by] Robert K. Tannenbaum. HarperCollins Pubs. 1999 402p $25
ISBN 0-06-019218-6 LC 98-54268
"Butch Karp, chief assistant New York DA, and his cohorts are trying to figure out the who and why of an important mafioso's murder. Karp's wife, security con-

Tanenbaum, Robert—*Continued*
sultant Marlene Ciampi, is puzzling over a case of her own involving a Mafia wife and is almost killed in the process. Karp's 12-year-old genius daughter, Lucy, a language whiz and as inscrutable as her Chinese friends, turns out to be important to both cases and at serious risk." Booklist

"Tanenbaum has crafted a believably twisted gem of a gangster tale with visceral action and smooth comic relief in a technicolor, Big Apple setting that waxes nostalgic for the 'gentleman' killers of yesteryear." Publ Wkly

Corruption of blood; [by] Robert K. Tanenbaum. Dutton 1995 347p o.p.

LC 95-12803

When Butch Karp "is lured from his unhappy berth in the Manhattan District Attorney's office to assist in the recently reopened Kennedy investigation, he must wade through conspiracy theories, stale evidence and the perennial Washington quagmire. . . . Karp's wife, the formidable Marlene Ciampi . . . joins her husband in the capital. Marlene, reluctant to join the 'wife-of' set, soon takes up an avenue of inquiry seemingly unrelated to the Kennedy conundrum when she sets out to clear the besmirched name of Richard Dobbs, the father of Karp's Congressional sponsor, who died in 1963. As in all good thrillers, everything that rises must converge, and so it is with Marlene's sleuthing and her husband's." N Y Times Book Rev

Falsely accused; [by] Robert K. Tanenbaum. Dutton 1996 304p o.p.

LC 96-17305

A legal thriller featuring married lawyers Butch Karp and Marlene Ciampi. In this episode "Bruce has spent over a year as the well-compensated pit bull litigator for a downtown law firm, and Marlene is getting antsy after a year-plus as a full-time mom. Soon Marlene partners with cop Harry Bello in a PI firm, and Karp sues New York City for former Chief Medical Examiner Murray Selig, fired at the urging of Manhattan DA (and Karp/Ciampi nemesis) Sanford Bloom. Tanenbaum draws together subplots involving political and police corruption, domestic violence, and illegal immigration in an involving tale that also illuminates Karp's and Ciampi's romantic and parental challenges." Booklist

Hoax; a novel; [by] Robert K. Tanenbaum. 1st Atria Books hardcover ed. Atria Books 2004 490p $25.95

ISBN 0-7434-5288-7 LC 2004-47941

A suspense novel featuring New York District Attorney Butch Karp. "The vicious murder of a West Coast rapper sets things in motion, unleashing a white-hot cascade of events that expose violence, greed, and corruption not only at the NYPD and the DA's office but also at the city's Catholic archdiocese. Tanenbaum . . . rentlessly builds suspense and gets ever closer to the hearts and minds of his singular characters." Booklist

Immoral certainty; [by] Robert K. Tanenbaum. Dutton 1991 282p o.p.

LC 90-13841

"The action is set mainly in the wilds of New York City's East Village, where a serial killer who brutalizes children is on the rampage. There's also a messy Mob hit in Little Italy to complicate the lives of no-nonsense D.A. Butch Karp and his colleague and 'occasional main squeeze,' Marlene. Are the cases related? And just how involved is one Felix Tighe, an ambitious yet minor-league criminal with a major-league mother fixation. The novel boasts a wealth of well-developed characters (the principals as well as the minor players); a slew of gallows humor; and a visceral prose style ideally suited to dealing with the sickening brutality of child abuse." Booklist

Irresistible impulse; [by] Robert K. Tanenbaum. Dutton 1997 346p o.p.

LC 97-16331

A legal thriller featuring NYDA Butch Karp and his wife Marlene Ciampi, the head of her own PI firm. "Against the advice of everyone from his boss to his secretary, Karp takes on the prosecution of a high-visibility defendant: a young white man charged with the brutal murders of elderly black women. Meanwhile, Marlene's cases win more publicity than she needs, as well as threats to her safety and that of her family." Booklist

Tanenbaum's "authentic background detail and his likable characters provide irresistible entertainment." Publ Wkly

Reckless endangerment; [by] Robert K. Tanenbaum. Dutton 1998 324p $23.95

ISBN 0-525-94347-1 LC 98-4902

This thriller "pits Deputy DA Karp, his detective cronies Raney and Fulton and his security-expert wife, Marlene, against an amorphous army of Palestinians terrorizing New York." Publ Wkly

"Tanenbaum controls the strands of his complex plot and maintains readers' interest in the growing Karp-Ciampi clan." Booklist

Reversible error; [by] Robert K. Tanenbaum. Dutton 1992 294p o.p.

LC 91-34464

New York "assistant D.A. Butch Karp faces a dilemma. A rogue cop is on the streets, taking out drug dealers, but Karp's investigation is brought to a halt when he is asked to suppress evidence. Sharing center stage with Karp's case is that of the D.A.'s colleague and lover, Marlene, who is on the trail of a rapist who wraps a pair of panty hose around each victim. With some unexpected help, Marlene spots a similarity in the victims. . . . With twin plots sizzling and exploding, the novel takes us inside the psyches of its characters, revealing the crime fighters' dark humor, rigid notions of right and wrong, and righteous anger." Booklist

True justice; [by] Robert K. Tanenbaum. Pocket Bks. 2000 374p il o.p.

ISBN 0-7434-0589-7 LC 00-708721

"Butch Karp, New York's assistant district attorney, and wife Marlene Ciampi, who heads an agency concerned with protecting battered women, find themselves in the middle of a crisis-and at each other's throats-when a newborn is murdered and the public demands that the teenaged mother be held accountable. Then their precocious daughter, Lucy gets involved." Libr J

"Each of the deftly drawn characters wrestles with the moral dilemmas raised by the intertwined plots in a believable way, and readers will close *True Justice's* final page satisfied they've wrestled with those dilemmas a bit themselves." Booklist

Tanizaki, Jun'ichirō, 1886-1965

The Makioka sisters; translated and introduced by Edward G. Seidensticker. Knopf 1993 xxxv,498p $20

ISBN 0-679-943452-0 LC 92-55051

"Everyman's library"

Original Japanese edition, 1949; this translation first published 1957

"The four Makioka sisters represent the upper middle-class Japanese tradition and customs, though their circumstances leave them little substance to support this way of life. Two of the four sisters are unmarried. The elder, Yukiko, is retiring and highly conscious of her place in society. The younger, Taeko, is more susceptible to pernicious influences of a changing society. The conflict of personalities and environmental adjustments provide the motivating center for this novel." Libr J

"The narrative is very quiet, very leisurely. At times it seems interminable, but it is like the pigment used by a Renaissance painter to build up his picture. It is done with utmost skill and results in a dignified masterpiece of great beauty and quality." Chicago Sunday Trib

Tanner, Edward Everett *See* Dennis, Patrick, 1921-1976

Tapply, William G.

Bitch Creek; a novel; by William G. Tapply. Lyon's Press 2004 292p $22.95

ISBN 1-592-28435-3 LC 2004-48954

"Stoney Calhoun works in Kate Balaban's bait/tackle shop in small-town Maine but has gaps in his memory after five years in an institution. When mutual friend and fishing guide Lyle goes missing, Stoney searches, finding the man's 'secret' trout stream and the man himself suspiciously drowned. Lyle's client, meanwhile, has disappeared. Aided by determination, logic, a psychic vision or two, and Kate's love, Stoney discovers that he was the intended target and that he's really an experienced investigator." Libr J

The author "mixes crisp plotting and character development with a subtle sense of time and place." Booklist

Client privilege. Delacorte Press 1990 260p o.p.

LC 89-23729

"Acting on behalf of his client and best friend, Judge Popowski (Pops) [Boston attorney] Coyne meets a TV reporter, Wayne Churchill, who threatens the judge's virtually certain appointment to the federal courts. Implicitly trusting the judge's statement that the newsman has no real grounds for blackmail, Coyne refuses Churchill's demand of $10,000 for his silence. The reporter's murder that same night brings the police to question the attorney, who, standing on client privilege, withholds Pops's name and therefore risks his own arrest as the killer. The circumstances force Coyne to search for the guilty party in order to clear himself." Publ Wkly

Close to the bone. St. Martin's Press 1996 208p o.p.

LC 96-18990

"A Thomas Dunne book"

Boston lawyer Brady Coyne "recommends Paul Cizek, a fishing buddy and a defense attorney with a reputation as a miracle worker, to defend a client's son involved in a fatal DUI rap. Cizek takes and wins the case, but privately explains to Coyne how his victories are eating at him. He detests the people he is defending—the child molester, the Mafia hit man and now an unremorseful alcoholic. When Cizek, depressed and separated from his wife, disappears and his empty boat is found drifting in a storm, the police assume accident or suicide. But Coyne's investigation, undertaken at the behest of Cizek's wife, and accruing dead bodies suggest more sinister possibilities. . . . Tapply treats his characters and his readers with respect." Publ Wkly

Cutter's run; a Brady Coyne novel. St. Martin's Press 1998 274p $23.95

ISBN 0-312-18561-8 LC 98-5331

"Boston lawyer Brady Coyne, in rural Maine for the weekend to visit his 'virtual spouse' Alex, stops and offers Charlotte Gillespie, a middle-aged black woman, a ride. In short order, someone poisons her dog and paints swastikas on her cabin door. Then Charlotte disappears. Brady explores the obvious: wanna-be klansmen and skinheads. Brady eventually realizes it may have been Carlotte's past and not her present—as an unwelcome resident in an unfriendly town—that resulted in her disappearance. Brady also realizes his relationship with Alex may not be as rock solid as he thought. . . . [This] mystery reaffirms Tapply's reputation for sound plotting, sterling dialogue, and poignant glimpses into the heart of a lonely man." Booklist

Dead meat; a Brady Coyne mystery. Scribner 1987 213p o.p.

LC 86-26143

"Heeding the call of one of his eccentric, well-to-do clients, Brady packs rod and reel and journeys to Raven Lake Lodge in the wilds of Maine, where his friend Tiny Wheeler, the lodge's owner, is trying to cope with the disappearance of a guest and a takeover bid by a group of Indian activists, who contend that the lodge is situated on sacred tribal ground. It doesn't take Brady long to realize that the situations are inextricably linked in a web of intrigue that points toward organized crime." Booklist

Dead winter; a Brady Coyne novel. Delacorte Press 1989 230p o.p.

LC 88-13867

"A friend's daughter-in-law has been murdered on board the family yacht and Brady Coyne, the attorney-turned-sleuth, is called in when all fingers point to the victim's husband. This is the first in a trio of murders in which Brady becomes involved. A mysterious bald man is murdered in a nearby town and a young waitress with a brutal husband is slain locally. Yet only Brady sees the connections and starts a search to find out not only who-dun-it, but how these three unrelated murders are connected." West Coast Rev Books

"The plot takes some gothic turns—bastardy, incest, and earlier violent death—but Tapply never neglects his nicely defined characterizations or loses his cool control over narrative tension in this very satisfying caper." Publ Wkly

First light; the first ever Brady Coyne/J.W. Jackson novel; [by] William G. Tapply and Philip R. Craig. Scribner 2002 351p $24

ISBN 0-7432-2208-3 LC 2001-49053

Tapply, William G.—*Continued*

This mystery, set on Martha's Vineyard, features "Boston lawyer Brady Coyne and former cop J.W. Jackson. . . . When tough businessman Jack Bannerman's wife goes missing, he hires private detective Jackson to find her. A parallel missing person's case develops when Coyne, Jackson's buddy, arrives for a fishing derby, only to see his elderly client Sarah Fairchild's private nurse vanish mysteriously in the midst of a nasty dispute over the future of ailing Mrs. Fairchild's sizable beachfront property." Publ Wkly

Muscle memory; a Brady Coyne novel. St. Martin's Press 1999 257p $23.95

ISBN 0-312-20563-5 LC 99-22042

When Boston "lawyer Brady Coyne agrees to handle a divorce case, he opens the door to trouble. His client, in hock to the mob, disappears, and his client's wife is found murdered." Libr J

Tapply "integrates Coyne's personal travails and his professional obligations, marking this novel as a model addition in a mature series: smoothly written, accessible to new readers and solidly plotted." Publ Wkly

Past tense; a Brady Coyne novel. St. Martin's Minotaur 2001 292p o.p.

ISBN 0-312-28442-X LC 2001-41943

"Brady Coyne and girlfriend Evie . . . become prime suspects when a stalker from Evie's past winds up dead outside the couple's rented Cape Cod cottage. Evie's subsequent disappearance sends the Boston attorney into investigative mode." Libr J

Scar tissue. St. Martin's Minotaur 2000 276p $24.95

ISBN 0-312-26679-0 LC 00-40229

Once Boston attorney Brady Coyne's "suspicions are aroused about a tragic road accident that swept two teenagers to their deaths in an icy river, he handles the sleazy business of small-town rot with the commitment and discretion that distinguish him as a sleuth. Tapply's understated style may forever condemn Coyne to a dull love life; but it serves the sordid nature of the story and well suits the hero." N Y Times Book Rev

Tight lines; a Brady Coyne novel. Delacorte Press 1992 277p o.p.

LC 91-31880

Brady Coyne, "a Boston lawyer whose client base is profoundly rich if not famous, is called to the side of Susan Ames, a wealthy widow dying of cancer. Using the pretense of establishing ground rules for the disposition of the historically significant family estate, she asks Brady to find the daughter she hasn't seen in 11 years." Booklist

A void in hearts; a Brady Coyne mystery. Scribner 1988 198p o.p.

LC 88-12203

"A marginally unscrupulous private eye, Les Katz, gets himself killed after blackmailing a client. Brady is called to the sleuth's deathbed but arrives too late, leaving him no choice but to figure out what happened." Booklist

Tarkington, Booth, 1869-1946

Alice Adams; illustrated by Arthur William Brown. Doubleday, Page 1921 434p il o.p.

"A social climber, the title character is ashamed of her unsuccessful family. Hoping to attract a wealthy husband, she lies about her background, but she is found out and is shunned by those whom she sought to attract. At the novel's end, she knows her chances for happiness and a successful marriage are bleak, but she remains unbowed." Merriam-Webster's Ency of Lit

The magnificent Ambersons. Modern Library 1998 268p pa $12.95

ISBN 0-375-75250-1 LC 98-19552

First published 1918 by Doubleday, Page

"The novel traces the growth of the United States through the decline of the once-powerful, socially prominent Amberson family. Their fall is contrasted with the rise of new industrial tycoons and land developers, whose power comes not through family connections but through financial dealings and modern manufacturing." Merriam-Webster's Ency of Lit

Tarr, Judith, 1955-

A fall of princes. Doherty Assocs. 1988 401p (Avaryan rising, v3) o.p.

LC 87-51392

"A TOR book"

In the concluding volume of the trilogy "two princes of mutually hostile lands find themselves thrown together in a battle for survival that forges an unlikely bond between them that could save—or destroy—both their kingdoms." Libr J

"Tarr's background in medieval history sustains her excellent world building, and the intrigue here is abundant and detailed." Booklist

The hall of the mountain king. Doherty Assocs. 1986 278p (Avaryan rising, v1) o.p.

"A TOR book"

"In the kingdom of Ianon, Mirain is heir to the realm of his father, the Sun God. This tale concerns itself primarily with Mirain's successful defense of his claim against the treacheries of his mortal relatives. Occasional lapses in narrative technique only slightly detract from Tarr's characterizations and obvious command of language." Booklist

Followed by The lady of Han-Gilen

Household gods; [by] Judith Tarr & Harry Turtledove. TOR Bks. 1999 508p $27.95

ISBN 0-312-86487-6 LC 99-39241

"A Tom Doherty Associates book"

"After a frustrating day in which her professional work goes unrecognized owing to her gender, lawyer and single-parent Nicole Gunther-Perrin falls asleep in her Los Angeles home and awakens in the second century as a Roman widow in the frontier town of Carnuntum." SLJ

"Drawing on a wealth of fascinating historical material and fleshing it out with snappy dialogue, superb characterizations and a genuinely appealing heroine, Tarr and Turtledove genially prove how much fun it can be to go back to Oz—and even better, that there's no place like home." Publ Wkly

Tarr, Judith, 1955-—*Continued*

The lady of Han-Gilen. Doherty Assocs. 1987 310p il (Avaryan rising, v2) o.p.
LC 87-205780

"A TOR book"

In this second volume of the trilogy, "Elian, the Lady of Han-Gilen, is beautiful, intelligent, stubborn and hot-tempered. Through her own insistence, she is skilled in martial as well as courtly arts, a horsewoman, hawker, linguist, musician, etc. When nobles ask for her hand, she bests them in their special talents and sends them packing. Her search for an equal or better leads her to a choice between handsome, witty High Prince Ziad-Ilarios, heir to the sophisticated Asanion empire, and her childhood companion Mirain, son of a priestess and a god, a barbarian conqueror who is building his own empire." Publ Wkly

Followed by A fall of princes

Lady of horses. Forge 2000 415p $25.95
ISBN 0-312-86114-1 LC 00-27653

"A Tom Doherty Associates book"

This prehistoric epic's "heroine, Sparrow, possesses the gift of divination, but as a girl in a culture that only values males, she is compelled to conceal it. She must also hide her forbidden passion for horses. When she and her sister-in-law, Keen, are discovered with the horse herd, they flee taking the king stallion with them. They end up in a land where females are not stigmatized, and where they are free to worship the Horse Goddess. . . . Tarr blends mythology and fantasy to make an unrecorded era of time vibrant and alive while brilliantly depicting nomadic cultures." Booklist

Pillar of fire. Forge 1995 448p o.p.
LC 95-6315

"A Tom Doherty Associates book"

"This narrative is based on an intriguing premise: What if Moses, patriarch of monotheism, and the Pharaoh Akhenaten, who forbade the Egyptians from worshiping any god save the sun god Aten, were one and the same? After all, Akhenaten's body disappeared after his death, and Moses rose to prominence shortly thereafter. The third-person narration sticks close to the point of view of Nofret, a young Hittite slave girl who serves the Pharaoh's third daughter." Publ Wkly

"Tarr makes of this intriguing speculation an exhilarating ride, powerfully written, through a lost world of chariot races, royalty, revolt, and enduring loyalty that is sure to please many readers." Booklist

Queen of swords. Forge 1997 464p o.p.
LC 96-33220

"A Tom Doherty Associates book"

This historical novel "focuses on the reign of Melisende, the oldest daughter of Baldwin II, King of Jerusalem. She ruled from 1129 to 1153, first as queen to Fulk of Anjou, who succeeded her father, then as regent to her son. When he reached his majority, she refused to relinquish her power until he forced her from the throne. The story is told from the viewpoints of her son and a lady-in-waiting, Richildis, and her family. Richildis came to the Holy Land on the ship with Fulk searching for her brother. She stayed on to serve the queen." Libr J

"A richly textured tapestry steeped in history and fraught with romance, adventure, and intrigue." Booklist

Queen of the Amazons; Judith Tarr. 1st ed. Tor 2004 320p $23.95
ISBN 0-7653-0395-7 LC 2003-61396

"After refusing to kill her newborn daughter, proclaimed 'soulless' by the Seer, Amazon Queen Hyppolyta vows that only her child will succeed her as ruler of her people. With her customary storytelling skill, the author of Lord of the Two Lands portrays the life and times of one of ancient history's most enigmatic and compelling women, reputedly the lover of Alexander the Great and the leader of a fierce army of female warriors. Tarr's elegant style and historical accuracy, along with her ability to construct believable characters, make this tale a strong addition to most libraries and essential for fans of historical fantasy." Libr J

Tarrant, John, 1927-

For works written by this author under other names see Egleton, Clive, 1927-

Tartt, Donna

The little friend. Knopf 2002 555p $26
ISBN 0-679-43938-2 LC 2002-66878

"The death of nine-year-old Robin Cleve Dufresnes, found hanging from a tree in his own backyard in Alexandria, Miss., has never been solved. The crime destroyed his family: it turned his mother into a lethargic recluse; his father left town; and the surviving siblings, Allison and Harriet, are now, 12 years later—it is the early '70s—largely being raised by their black maid and a matriarchy of female relatives. . . . [Harriet] vows to solve the mystery of her brother's death and unmask the killer, whom she decides, without a shred of evidence, is Danny Ratliff, a member of a degenerate, redneck family of hardened criminals." Publ Wkly

Tartt's "book is a ruthlessly precise reckoning of the world as it is—drab, ugly, scary, inconclusive—filtered through the bright colors and impossible demands of childhood perception. It grips you like a fairy tale, but denies you the consoling assurance that it's all just make-believe." N Y Times Book Rev

The secret history. Knopf 1992 523p o.p.
ISBN 0-679-41032-5 LC 92-53053

This novel "is set on a small college campus in Vermont. Dissatisfied with the crass values of their fellow students, a small corps of undergraduates groups itself around a favored professor of classics, who nurtures both their sense of moral elevation and an insularity from conventional college life that ultimately proves fatal. Among Prof. Julian Morrow's followers are Henry Winter, a tall scion of a wealthy St. Louis family, . . . the twins Charles and Camilla Macaulay, both intellectually gifted and eccentric only in their excessive mutual devotion; Francis Abernathy, a dandyish homosexual slowly awakening to his sexuality; and Edmund (Bunny) Corcoran, . . . [who] becomes the group's victim." N Y Times Book Rev

"Tartt records the aftereffects of unpunished crime with great skill." New Repub

Tate, Ellalice, 1906-1993

For works written by this author under other names see Carr, Philippa, 1906-1993; Holt, Victoria, 1906-1993; Plaidy, Jean, 1906-1993

Tawada, Yoko, 1960-

Where Europe begins; translated from the German by Susan Bernofsky; from the Japanese by Yumi Selden; with a preface by Wim Wenders. New Directions 2002 208p $23.95

ISBN 0-8112-1515-6 LC 2002-5196

Contents: The bath; The reflection; Spores; Canned foreign; The talisman; Raisin eyes; Storytellers without soul; Tongue dance; Where Europe begins; A guest

"Tawada's stories shift between the transparent and the opaque, even on the same page; they agitate the mind like songs half remembered or treasure boxes whose keys are locked within." N Y Times Book Rev

Tax, Meredith

Rivington Street. Morrow 1982 431p o.p.

LC 81-22587

"This is the story of Russian immigrant men and women caught up in the social upheavals at the beginning of this century. Set on the Lower East Side of New York, the book concerns strong-willed Hannah Levy, her daughters, Sarah, a social activist, and Ruby, a creative designer of clothes, and their beautiful and romantic friend, Rachel Cohen. It is the women who dominate this book. Their struggle to survive the terrible working conditions and low pay of jobs in the garment industry and the violence that comes when they demand a better life make an absorbing story. Tax has used real incidents—the fire at the Triangle Waist factory, a strike of garment workers, and the jailing of suffragists—to add color and authenticity to the story." Libr J

Followed by Union Square

Union Square. Morrow 1988 437p o.p.

LC 88-9075

This sequel to Rivington Street focuses on a "mostly Russian-born family of socialist workers and confirmed Marxists, forced by pogroms to flee to America's Lower East Side, where their political divisiveness continues. . . . The focus is on Hannah and Moyshe Levy and their daughter Sarah, who has married Marxist apologist Avi Spector. The ideological rift between the Levys and the Spectors widens when, at the onset of the Depression, Moyshe sides with the Bundists while Avi supports the Stalinists. As Sarah campaigns for unions and women's right to decent pay, her sister Ruby, married to Ben Berliner, becomes a force in the fashion industry." Publ Wkly

"The point of Meredith Tax's novels isn't the quality of her prose. She is telling gritty, satisfying stories." NY Times Book Rev

Taylor, Elizabeth, 1912-1975

Mrs. Palfrey at the Claremont. Viking 1971 178p o.p.

A tale about an elderly British widow who takes up residence in one of those shabby, genteel hotels along London's Cromwell Road. She is at a desperate loss for what to do with herself to fill in the time and try to make her fellow lodgers believe she still has some semblance of a personal life. The portraits of the elderly and crotchety residents are drawn with a pen only lightly tipped in acid, and Mrs. Palfrey herself is very human and endearing. She finds her real hope for the future in pretending that a rather callow but not unkind casual acquaintance is really her grandson." Publ Wkly

Taylor, Kamala Purnaiya *See* Markandaya, Kamala, 1924-2004

Taylor, Peter Hillsman, 1917-1994

A summons to Memphis; {by} Peter Taylor. Knopf 1986 209p o.p.

LC 86-45417

"A son, now a grown man, recounts the family's subservience to a strong-willed father. Against a background of Southern manners in Memphis and Nashville, the Carver daughters and sons experience frustration of their hopes to marry and enjoy family lives of their own. The mother, soon after her marriage to George Carver, withdraws from resisting his authority. The daughters never find suitors who suit their father. One brother, escaping to war, is killed and the narrator, Philip, a bachelor still at 49, is summoned home by his sisters to prevent their father, at 81, from remarrying. The seemingly selfless care given by the daughters might stem from self-interest rather than filial devotion." Shapiro. Fic for Youth. 3d edition

Taylor, Robert Lewis

The travels of Jaimie McPheeters. Doubleday 1958 544p o.p.

"Fourteen-year old Jaimie McPheeters, the son of Sardius McPheeters, an unsuccessful, windy-minded doctor who is given to gambling and drink, sets out with his father from their Louisville home in the spring of 1849 for the California gold fields, and in the course of the next three years or so is kidnapped by outlaws; is captured by Indians; witnesses a lot of brutality, including a duel, fires, killings, and some startling Indian cruelty; suffers semi-starvation and degradation; and in the end, after his father's death, becomes part owner of a handsome California ranch, where he settles with his mother, his sisters, and his Indian sweetheart." New Yorker

"The piquant combination of solid historical content, satisfying adventure, good literary style, sophisticated wit and humor will give this book wide appeal." Libr J

Tella, Alfred

(jt. auth) Anthony, P. The willing spirit

Templeton, Edith, 1916-

Gordon. Pantheon Bks. 2001 226p $22

ISBN 0-375-42194-7 LC 2002-70427

First published 1966 in the United Kingdom under the pseudonym Louise Walbrook

"This eerie tale of sexual obsession is narrated by a young woman adrift in London just after the Second World War. She meets a 'frightening, sinister, implacable' psychiatrist who, over all protest, invades her, body and mind, arousing previously unsuspected tastes for submission and humiliation. One part 'Story of O' to two parts Muriel Spark, the book beautifully evokes the tightened belts and loose morals of postwar London." New Yorker

Tennant, Emma, 1937-

Pemberley; or Pride and prejudice continued. St. Martin's Press 1993 184p $18.95

ISBN 0-312-10793-5 LC 94-171082

"It is the Christmas season, and Elizabeth Darcy (Elizabeth Bennet of *Pride and Prejudice*) now the uneasy mistress of the great estate of Pemberley, anticipates the holidays with growing trepidation. Her foolish widowed mother and two of her sisters, flighty Kitty and pedantic Mary, are soon to descend upon the household. Adding to the guest list, as well as the complications, are her husband's formidable aunt, Lady Catherine de Bourgh, and the Wickhams (the cad who eloped with Elizabeth's sister after his unsuccessful attempt to run off with her sister-in-law). Sweet-tempered Jane will also be present, but her imminent confinement is a constant reminder to Elizabeth of her own barrenness." Libr J

The author's "narrative is made uncomfortably compelling by her utter mastery of Austen's style. In its pace and sensibility, the text virtually breathes Jane Austen; the malaise that Ms. Tennant so powerfully exploits is solidly rooted in her model." N Y Times Book Rev

Followed by An unequal marriage

Tepper, Sheri S.

The family tree; [by] Sherri S. Tepper. Avon Bks. 1997 377p $23

ISBN 0-380-97478-9 LC 96-33222

"While investigating the separate murders of three geneticists, police sergeant Dora Henry stumbles upon talking animals from the future who have come 3000 years into their past to prevent the extinction of their species before a plague destroys most humans. Overnight, sentient weeds and trees begin taking over the suburbs and carrying off babies from families with more than two children." Libr J

Tepper "reprises a number of her standard themes in this novel that's at once earnest and whimsical: the evils of sexism, overpopulation and patriarchal religion; the danger of fouling our environmental nest; animal rights; the need to take drastic action to solve our problems. As always, she's highly didactic." Publ Wkly

The fresco. Avon Eos 2000 406p o.p.

ISBN 0-380-97879-2 LC 00-34838

"While hunting for mushrooms in the mountains of New Mexico, Benita Alvarez-Shipton, abused wife of drunkard Bert Shipton, is greeted by Chiddy and Vess of the 'Pistach people,' a race of benevolent, nonhuman aliens intent on assisting Earthlings in resolving some longstanding problems (crime, abuse of women, etc.), so that they may join a confederation of galactic beings. Benita travels to Washington, D. C., and becomes the intermediary between the Pistach and the president. Meanwhile, a separate group of predatory aliens, looking to make humans into a new item in the galactic buffet, joins forces with extremist politicians who want to discredit the president." Booklist

"Tepper's talent for creating believable human and alien characters lends power and credibility to her work and makes her a convincing portrayer of sociologically oriented sf." Libr J

The gate to Women's Country. Doubleday 1988 278p o.p.

LC 88-387

"A Foundation book"

"A feminist fable set somewhere in the Pacific Northwest 300 years after a nuclear holocaust. Men and women now live in separate but adjacent communities. Although the men are organized into military garrisons, the women appear to have the upper hand in government, deciding matters of trade and law and, most important, reproduction. . . . The elaborate society that the author takes such pains to describe is based on a big lie; the story she tells is part of the deception. Some will find this narrative strategy as distasteful as the secret it conceals. But Ms. Tepper is not afraid to ask hard questions, beginning with this: If biology is destiny, how can society hope to control its self-destructive tendencies without controlling biology as well?" N Y Times Book Rev

Grass. Doubleday 1989 426p o.p.

LC 89-30105

"A Foundation book"

In this first volume of a trilogy "diplomats are dispatched to the planet Grass in search of the cure for a deadly disease that is spreading throughout inhabited space. The human settlers, xenophobic and conservative landed gentry, lead an existence tightly structured around the Hunt, a complex and violent ritual involving the use of alien mounts that seem nearly demonic in their malevolence. The presence of a number of not particularly sympathetic religious groups adds complexity to the situation. This is a beautifully written novel with well-developed characters and a number of very interesting aliens." Anatomy of Wonder 4

Followed by Raising the stones

Northshore. Doherty Assocs. 1987 248p (Awakeners, v1) o.p.

LC 86-50961

"A TOR book"

"The World River flows west; to travel east—on water or land—is to risk the wrath of the Awakeners, the feared keepers of the secrets of the dead. Brought together by a miracle, Thrasne, a Boatman with a gift for carving wood and asking questions, and Pamra Don, an Awakener disillusioned by the 'truths' of her religion, challenge the teachings of centuries in an attempt to discover the hidden secrets of their world." Libr J

"The interwoven stories of love and politics, the painstakingly developed characters and customs, all pale beside a world so vividly created that the book seems to be illustrated." Voice Youth Advocates

Followed by Southshore

Raising the stones. Doubleday 1990 453p o.p.

LC 90-30191

"A Foundation book"

In this second volume of the trilogy set in a far away galaxy "a community of good people (who live in peace and harmony under the subtle mind control of an alien intelligence they refer to as 'the God') are threatened by a sect of religious fanatics (whose megalomaniacal creed not only permits the enslavement of unbelievers but 'insists' on it)." N Y Times Book Rev

This is a "complicated, exciting narrative that explores central questions of religion and faith, and of the dangers and usefulness of technology." Women's Rev Books

Followed by Sideshow

Tepper, Sheri S.—*Continued*

Sideshow. Bantam Bks. 1992 467p o.p.
LC 91-40420

In this concluding volume of the trilogy begun with Grass, "a sentient fungus has infested most of the galaxy, reworking the life forms it inhabits to enhance their physical and spiritual comfort. The people of the planet Elsewhere, however, see the fungus's contented hosts as slaves; to preserve free will on Elsewhere, the rulers have imposed absolute cultural relativity within which pleasant and unsavory societies coexist, their integrity rigidly maintained by Enforcers. But powers have arisen to challenge the status quo." Publ Wkly

"Tepper's imaginative vision holds forth and delivers one of her most challenging works." Libr J

Singer from the sea. Avon Eos 1999 426p $24
ISBN 0-380-97480-0 LC 99-10231

"Despite her status as a young noblewoman of the planet Haven, Genevieve rebels against the strict regulations concerning highborn women. Defying her father's wishes, she seeks her own forbidden destiny and discovers the dark secrets that lie at the heart of her world and its forgotten history. Tepper . . . continues to explore the intricacies of human societal structures and the complex connections between humans and their environment, combining stylistic grace with imaginative insight." Libr J

Six moon dance. Avon Eos 1998 454p $23
ISBN 0-380-97479-7 LC 98-11918

"A series of earthquakes and volcanic eruptions, heralding the conjunction of Newholme's six moons, serves as a catalyst for a visit by the artificial intelligence known as the Questioner, an entity with the power to save—or destroy—worlds in crisis. As the planet's ruling priestesses strive to conceal their world's questionable dealings with its 'invisible' race of indigenous creatures, a small group of social outcasts seeks to bring the truth to light, forcing a choice between transformation or annihilation. Tepper combines a treatise on the politics of gender with a transcendent celebration of love and renewal." Libr J

Southshore. Doherty Assocs. 1987 250p (Awakeners, v2) o.p.
LC 86-51487

"A TOR book"

The second volume of the author's science fiction diptych begun with Northshore. "While ex-Awakener Pamra Don—now truly awakened—leads a crusade against the evil done in the name of religion, the Boatman Thrasne embarks on a voyage across the World River to search for a land of safety on the legendary 'Southshore.'" Libr J

The author "continues her gradual, teasing revelations about the planet's history, particularly in the wonderful story of Tharius Don, who became a cleric to get at the books that would answer his youthful questions. As before, this clever, intricately constructed world is appropriately distant and cool." Publ Wkly

The visitor; a novel. Eos 2002 407p o.p.
ISBN 0-380-97905-5 LC 2001-40197

"Dismé Latimer is an orphan, tyrannized by an evil stepmother and stepsister who deprive her of her heritage. Her rigid, corrupt society is ruled by a bureaucracy that keeps its people in line through a systematic and legally sanctioned use of torture, as its leaders pursue the black arts in their quest for power. Dismé secretly possesses a forbidden book, the memoir of her ancestor, Nell Latimer, who was a scientist at the time of The Happening. A thousand years earlier, an asteroid (the 'Visitor') hit Earth, nearly wiping out the human race and causing huge changes in geography and climate." SLJ

"Tepper has created a mesmerizing story full of intriguing characters, resonant images and powerful themes." Publ Wkly

Teran, Boston

The prince of deadly weapons. St. Martin's Minotaur 2002 371p $24.95
ISBN 0-312-27118-2 LC 2002-69839

The serpentine plot "has Rudd—supposedly blinded early on in a subway attack, but even this is left in doubt at the end—investigating the death of the man whose corneas he inherited by infiltrating a gang of smugglers and killers whose nastiness is exceeded only by their ineptitude." Publ Wkly

"This thriller combines a feverish New Journalism writing style with the kind of philosophical ruminations popular in freshman dorms after all the pot has been smoked. . . . For every over-amped paragraph . . . Teran uncorks a passage of startling power and beauty. With a bit more restraint, he might have delivered one of the year's most powerful noir novels." Booklist

Terrell, Whitney

The huntsman. Viking 2001 358p il o.p.
ISBN 0-670-89465-6

"Stan Granger, loner and fisherman, pulls the body of a young white woman from the Missouri River. It's not his first encounter with a waterlogged corpse, but this time it's someone he knows. She was Clarissa Sayers, the strange and wild daughter of a federal judge, and her death was caused not by drowning but by a blow to the head. Suspicion centers on Booker Short, a young black parole violator from Oklahoma with whom she'd been having an affair." Libr J

Terrell provides a "Dreiseresque study of Kansas City in the nineties, in all its complicated manners and minutiae. An unsung corner of the American landscape, the city is the real hero here, as white and black, rich and poor, old and young collide." New Yorker

Tevis, Walter S., 1928-1984

The queen's gambit; [by] Walter Tevis. Random House 1983 243p o.p.
LC 82-15058

This "is the story of an orphan girl who is taught to play chess by the janitor of her orphanage. Beth Harmon has genius; she wins her first tournament when she is 14, becomes American champion at 18 and starts the international circuit. She may well be the second best player in the world. Only the world champion, a Russian . . . is stronger than she, and she is scared to death of him. The climax of the book comes when they meet over the board in a Moscow tournament." N Y Times Book Rev

"Familiarity with chess is not needed in order to enjoy this book though aficionados will delight in its evocation of their esoteric freemasonry." Times Lit Suppl

Texier, Catherine

Victorine. Pantheon Books 2004 324p $24
ISBN 0-375-42124-6 LC 2003-54860
The author "imagines the life of her great-grandmother, who left her husband and two children in a French provincial town in the late 1890's and supposedly ran off to Indochina with a customs officer. The affair might have lasted a year and a half; in 1900, Victorine returned to her husband in France and gave birth to a third child." N Y Times Book Rev
"With lush, vivid description, Texier brings to life both the world around Victorine and the woman herself." Libr J

Tey, Josephine, 1896-1952

Brat Farrar. Macmillan 1950 c1949 219p o.p.
First published 1949 in the United Kingdom
"The scene is an English country home owned by the orphaned Ashby children and managed for them by their aunt, who has made a success of the horses she bred and exhibited. Simon, charming and spoiled, is about to take over as he comes of age, when a well-coached imposter arrives and claims to be the elder brother who had disappeared eight years before, leaving a suicide note." Booklist
also in Tey, J. Three by Tey

The daughter of time. Macmillan 1952 c1951 204p o.p.
First published 1951 in England
"Alan Grant, injured policeman hospitalized and bored, is diverted by a photograph of Richard III, commonly conceded murderer of the princes in the Tower. With the invaluable assistance of a research student, Grant's convalescence becomes a lively pursuit of the truth as shown by records in Richard's time." Libr J
The author "not only reconstructs the probably historical truth, she re-creates the intense dramatic excitement of the scholarly research necessary to unveil it." N Y Times Book Rev
also in Tey, J. Four, five and six by Tey

Four, five and six by Tey. Macmillan 1958 3v in 1 o.p.
"Murder revisited series"
An omnibus edition of three complete Scotland Yard mysteries in which Inspector Alan Grant solves the crimes. Includes The singing sands (1952) and The daughter of time (1951) and A shilling for candles (1936), about a film star whose death by strangulation is the focus of Grant's investigation

The Franchise affair. Macmillan 1948 238p o.p.
"A lawyer in an English country town answers an appeal for help from two women who, having only recently inherited a home, were still outsiders to the townspeople and, being independent, reserved, and unusual, were called witches. When a girl in another town accused them of imprisoning, starving, and beating her in their attic, they were helpless, for the circumstantial evidence seemed indisputable. Good characterization, good writing, and to the lawyer's surprise, an emotional involvement for him." Booklist
also in Tey, J. Three by Tey

The man in the queue. Macmillan 1953 213p o.p.
First published 1929 by Dutton under the pseudonym Gordon Daviot
A man is stabbed to death waiting in the ticket line of a popular London musical, and Inspector Grant of the C.I.D. is assigned to the case
"Every detail of the discovery of first the identity and then the murderer of the knifed man is admirably invented, and the story, at first sight a simple build-up . . . turns out to be a serious inductive exercise." Springfield Repub

Miss Pym disposes. Macmillan 1948 213p o.p.
First published 1946 in the United Kingdom
An English woman psychologist delivers a lecture at a physical training college and decides to stay a little longer. She becomes very friendly with some of the seniors, and eventually finds herself involved in an "accident" which turns out to be a murder
also in Tey, J. Three by Tey

A shilling for candles
In Tey, J. Four, five and six by Tey

The singing sands. Macmillan 1953 c1952 221p o.p.
First published 1952 in the United Kindgom. Variant title: Grant's last case
A cryptic fragment of verse, found near a dead man on a train en route to Scotland is Inspector Grant's only clue to the identity of the man's murderer
also in Tey, J. Four, five and six by Tey

Three by Tey; Miss Pym disposes; The Franchise affair [and] Brat Farrar; with an introduction by James Sandoe. Macmillan 1954 3v in 1 o.p.
"Murder revisited series. A Cock Robin mystery"
An omnibus edition of three titles entered separately

Thackeray, William Makepeace, 1811-1863

The history of Henry Esmond, esquire. o.p.
First published 1852; first United States edition published 1879 by Harper with title: Henry Esmond
"The story, narrated by Esmond, begins in 1691 when he is 12 and ends in 1718. Its complexity of incident is given unity by Esmond and his second cousin Beatrix, who stand out against a background of London society and the political life of the time. Beatrix dominates the book. One of Thackeray's great creations, she is a heroine of a new type, emotionally complex and compelling, but not a pattern of virtue." Merriam-Webster's Ency of Lit
Followed by The Virginians

Vanity fair.
First published 1848
"The book is a densely populated, multi-layered panorama of manners and human frailties. . . . The novel deals mainly with the interwoven fortunes of two women, the wellborn, passive Amelia Sedley and the ambitious, essentially amoral Becky Sharp, the latter perhaps the most memorable character Thackeray created. The adventuress Becky is the character around whom all the men play their parts." Merriam-Webster's Ency of Lit

Thackeray, William Makepeace, 1811-1863— *Continued*

The Virginians. o.p.

First published 1857; first United States edition published 1869 by Fields, Osgood & Co.

"A sequel to 'Henry Esmond', it relates the story of George and Harry Warrington, the twin grandsons of Colonel Henry Esmond. The novel follows the brothers from boyhood in America, through various experiences in England, and finally through the American Revolution, in which George fights on the British side and Harry on the side of his friend George Washington." Reader's Ency. 4th edition

Thayer, James Stewart

Five past midnight; a novel; [by] James Thayer. Simon & Schuster 1997 352p $23

ISBN 0-684-80025-X LC 97-12446

A "thriller about Jack Cray, a lone American commando sent to assassinate Hitler in the waning days of WWII. The only man standing between him and the Fuhrer is Otto Dietrich, Berlin's finest detective, whose brother was implicated in the June 1944 attempt to kill Hitler. Freed from jail specifically for this assignment and kept on a short leash by the Gestapo, Dietrich tracks Cray from Colditz prison to the vividly realized chaos of bomb-ravaged Berlin and the bunker where Hitler has gone to ground. . . . Historical matters aside, the only real lapse in verisimilitude is Cray's super-human resistance to pain." Publ Wkly

Thayer, Nancy, 1943-

An act of love. St. Martin's Press 1997 245p $22.95

ISBN 0-312-15471-2 LC 97-14404

"Owen and Linda McFarland, both novelists, have been married for seven years and reside on a Massachusetts farm with Bruce and Emily, the children from each of their respective first marriages. Their uneventful existence is disrupted, however, when Emily, now a teenager attending the same boarding school as Bruce, attempts suicide. After voluntarily staying on at the psychiatric hospital, Emily whose recent behavioral changes include sudden weight gain and newfound religious devotion, reveals in therapy that the reason behind her despair is that her stepbrother raped her, a charge that Bruce vehemently denies." Publ Wkly

"Thayer's prose is fluid and concise, her characters rich and human, her dialogue easy and believable." Booklist

Belonging. St. Martin's Press 1995 341p o.p.

LC 95-15457

"Joanna Jones is the single and successful star of a television show, *Joanna Jones' Fabulous Homes.* Her romantic involvement with the show's married coproducer, Carter Amberson, suits her just fine until, nearly 40, she discovers that she is pregnant with Carter's twins. Understanding that Carter refuses to divorce his wife and fearing that he might convince her to have an abortion, she takes a leave of absence from her work and escapes to a creaking old house she discovered and bought in Nantucket." Libr J

"The story surely captivates at moments and mostly satisfies. Except for the overattention to material and social superficiality, Thayer's story of a woman's quest for self-identity and self-affirmation does inspire." Booklist

Between husbands and friends; a novel. St. Martin's Press 1999 241p $22.95

ISBN 0-312-20613-5 LC 99-27233

"Narrator Lucy West, 37, is a self-employed mother of two; her husband, Max, edits the local newspaper in Sussex, a Boston suburb. Suave, irreverent Kate Cunningham and her husband, Chip, an attorney, move to Sussex in 1987; Kate and Lucy meet at their children's preschool and become fast friends. Soon the couples summer together on Nantucket, and their lives grow ever more entwined. Thayer's narrative jumps back and forth between the couples' present and their shared past. . . . Readers prepared for the slow pace of Thayer's plot will appreciate her detailed, realistic records of motherhood, child-rearing and domestic routine in Sussex and Nantucket." Publ Wkly

Everlasting. Viking 1991 322p o.p.

LC 90-50462

"Catherine Eliot, at 18, is aimless until she falls into a job in a flower shop and realizes that this is the business she was born for. Though her social register family has cut her off, she uses her own social connections to build her business into a giant. This rejected daughter does all she can to rescue her family from financial and emotional distress. Though her help is neither understood nor appreciated, Catherine eventually finds contentment in herself, her marriage, and her business. An absorbing story and heroine." Libr J

Family secrets. Viking 1993 338p o.p.

LC 92-50746

At the center of this novel is "Diane, driven, successful, and suffering the disillusionment of mid-life crisis. The FBI contacts her in an attempt to locate her recently widowed mother, who they believe possesses top-secret information. At the same time, Julia, her unhappily college-bound daughter who's desperately in love with the boy next door and more desperately in need of breaking away from her mother's expectations, runs off to be married. Meanwhile, Diane's mother, Jean, captures the foregone dream of her youth: traveling through Europe with no itinerary, enjoying only quiet, anonymous days of her very own. Gradually, gently, the lives of these women unfold before us and Jean's mysterious secret is revealed." Booklist

My dearest friend. Scribner 1989 342p o.p.

LC 89-6276

"Divorcée Daphne Miller is the mother of a 16-year-old daughter who takes off abruptly for California to live with a father she has not heard from for 14 years. Deprived of child support payments, Daphne moves into a country shack. Once a college professor like her ex-husband and two married swains, she is now a lowly but plucky department secretary. Flashbacks reveal her best friend's betrayal and its impact on Daphne's marriage, and counterpoint her slow recovery during which Daphne again allows friends to play key roles in her life." Publ Wkly

Thayer, Steve

The weatherman; a novel. Viking 1995 452p $21.95

ISBN 0-670-84958-8 LC 94-20142

"Dixon Bell is a television meteorologist with an eerie gift for reading the weather. Rick Beanblossom is a news producer who hides his disfigured face behind a mask. Andrea Labore is the beautiful cop turned reporter whom they both love. Meanwhile, the Calendar Killer is strangling a woman each season during a significant weather event. When Bell is arrested and accused of the murders, Beanblossom and Labore join forces to prove his innocence. The novel's characters are deeply developed, and the riveting plot is cloaked in descriptive episodes of weather. Additionally, readers will receive a fascinating view of the intense machinations of television news productions." Libr J

Theroux, Alexander, 1939-

Darconville's cat. Doubleday 1981 704p o.p.

"The hero works as English lecturer in an American Southern women's college and falls in love with a student. Marriage is proposed and arranged, but the false hilding falls for another man. Revenge is planned and curses are articulated, but Darconville meets natural death in Venice. This simple tale easily fills 704 pages, for, in the Rabelaisian manner, it is decorated with monstrous catalogues, liturgies, baroque pastiches, diaries–anything, in fact, to prevent the story from moving fast" Burgess. 99 Novels

Theroux, Marcel

The confessions of Mycroft Holmes; a paper chase. Harcourt 2001 216p $23

ISBN 0-15-100647-4 LC 00-49894

"Damien March, an American-born BBC journalist, inherits a house from an eccentric novelist uncle in the States. He soon scraps his job and goes to live on his uncle's dilapidated estate on an island off the coast of Cape Cod. . . . Then Damien lays his hands on a box of his uncle's manuscripts. Included in the box is the start of a whimsical mystery to be solved by Sherlock Holmes's wiser older brother, Mycroft." Publ Wkly

"The story moves forward with a pleasant, unthrillerish pressure. The novel's other great delight is Damien's narration; Theroux extracts full value from his rootless, skeptical, sharp-eyed perspective." N Y Times Book Rev

Theroux, Paul

The collected stories. Viking 1997 660p o.p.

LC 96-52417

Contents: World's end; Zombies; The imperial icehouse; Yard sale; Algebra; The English adventure; After the war; Words are deeds; White lies; Clapham Junction; The odd-job man; Portrait of a lady; The prison diary of Jack Faust; A real Russian ikon; A political romance; Sinning with Annie; A love knot; What have you done to our Leo?; Memories of a curfew; Biographical notes for four American poets; Hayseed; A deed without a name; You make me mad; Dog days; A burial at Surabaya; Polvo; Low tide; Jungle bells; Warm dogs; The consul's file; Dependent wife; White Christmas; Pretend I'm not here; Loser wins; The flower of Malaya; The Autumn dog; Dengué fever; The South Malaysia Pineapple Growers' Association; The butterfly of the laruts; The tennis court; Reggie Woo; Conspirators; The Johore murders; The tiger's suit; Coconut gatherer; The last colonial; Triad; Diplomatic relations; Dear William; Volunteer speaker; Reception; Namesake; An English unofficial rose; Children; Charlie Hogle's earring; The exile; Tomb with a view; The man on the Clapham omnibus; Sex and its substitutes; The honorary Siberian; Gone West; A little flame; Fury; Neighbors; Fighting talk; The Winfield wallpaper; Dancing on the radio; Memo

Doctor DeMarr
In Theroux, P. Half Moon Street

Doctor Slaughter
In Theroux, P. Half Moon Street

Half Moon Street; two short novels. Houghton Mifflin 1984 219p o.p.

LC 84-10495

This work "contains two novellas on a single theme: the terrors of leading a double life. In 'Doctor DeMarr,' the shorter work, a man who believes his twin brother to be dead steps into his brother's life. . . . [In 'Doctor Slaughter,' an] American woman on a study grant in London finds nothing working well for her until she sells her talents to an 'escort service.'" Newsweek

"Theroux endows these two cautionary tales with a palpable sense of danger and a trenchant wit that are both disturbing and enticing." Booklist

Hotel Honolulu. Houghton Mifflin 2001 424p $26

ISBN 0-618-09501-2 LC 00-54125

"The episodic narrative is presided over by two protagonists: the unnamed narrator, a has-been writer who leaves the mainland to manage the seedy Hotel Honolulu, and raucous millionaire Buddy Hamstra, the hotel's owner and former manager, who fired himself to give the narrator his job." Publ Wkly

"The book brims with eccentric characters and their wild, usually morbid tales." Atl Mon

Kowloon Tong. Houghton Mifflin 1997 243p o.p.

LC 96-29717

"Neville 'Bunt' Mullard is a quintessential Englishman: he likes eating at Fatty's Chophouse, going to the races, and having tea and oaties with Mum. Only Bunt was born and bred in Hong Kong, where he now runs a factory that his father established with Mr. Chuck, who has just died and left his shares to the Mullard family. Bunt is trying to ignore the imminent Chinese takeover of Hong Kong, but then Mr. Hung arrives from the mainland, demanding to buy the well-situated factory—and backing up his demands with some ugly tactics." Libr J

The Mosquito Coast; a novel; with woodcuts by David Frampton. Houghton Mifflin 1982 374p o.p.

LC 81-6787

"Allie Fox, a cantankerous Yankee inventor fed up with an America gone soft, pursues his obsession with total self-sufficiency to the wild coast of Honduras, dragging his devoted but uneasy family behind. His aim is to make a 'slightly better job than God' of this poisoned world, as far from cheeseburgers and drive-in churches

Theroux, Paul—*Continued*
as possible. And his ingenious pioneer Eden actually works, until his swelling egomania finally topples it." Libr J

"The physical impact of the style, the exact observation, the occasional intrusion of the hallucinatory make this a remarkable work of art; its philosophical content is profound." Burgess. 99 Novels

My other life. Houghton Mifflin 1996 456p $24.95
ISBN 0-395-82527-X LC 96-16245

This autobiographical novel "tracks its narrator from his days with the Peace Corps in Africa to a teaching job in Singapore, and on to London with his English wife." N Y Times Book Rev

"Mr. Theroux has developed the what-if? fantasy of another life into a novel about exactly that—his own imaginary life as a wandering literary man with a sideline in teaching and a talent for the inadvertent collection of Potiphar's wives. The episodic tale . . . is interesting, sometimes acid, reading all the way." Atl Mon

My secret history. Putnam 1989 511p o.p.
LC 88-32182

"From an early adolescence torn between a call to the priesthood and the call of the flesh, through late-adolescent sexual initiation and a young adult's escapades as a teacher in Africa, to a grown man's crisis in marriage, Theroux recounts the 'secret history' of Andy Parent, a writer suspiciously resembling Theroux himself." Libr J

"'My secret history' is about the permanence of marriage in the face of mistrust and infidelity; it's about the wisdom of women and the foolishness of men; and it's about mature love as the necessary and sometimes successful antidote to youthful selfishness." N Y Times Book Rev

Picture palace; a novel. Houghton Mifflin 1978 359p o.p.
LC 77-18725

"At seventy, Maude Pratt is a world famous photographer. . . . As the book opens, a young man is sifting through her photographs to prepare a retrospective of her work. The images bring up buried memories of her photographic adventures, her incestuous longings for her brother, and the many self-deceptions that marked her life." Saturday Rev

Picture palace "is an elaborate visual conceit, a sublime meditation on seeing and knowing. Confident and commanding, the author displays his narrative gifts which range from the laconic to the lyrical, the telescopic to the microscopic. This is a novel which, like a photograph, one will return to again and again." Christ Sci Monit

Thom, James Alexander

The children of first man. Ballantine Bks. 1994 547p $23
ISBN 0-345-37005-8 LC 93-42240

"Eight centuries ago, Madoc, an illegitimate son of a mediocre Welsh king, may have led ten boatloads of his countrymen across the Atlantic and settled them in the Tennessee and Ohio River valleys. Thom's multigenerational historical novel . . . enlarges the scant evidence for this legend. Madoc's Welsh build a benevolent colony (complete with castles), die by hubris, and repeat their history." Libr J

"There are epic battles among the Welsh and the Native Americans and between the tribes themselves, as well as hurricanes, tornadoes, floods, and diseases; the sex is bawdy and the violence is unrelentingly bloody, but the individual human spirit shines through. . . . A terrifically entertaining novel, particularly in dealing with the advance of white society from the Native American viewpoint." Booklist

Panther in the sky. Ballantine Bks. 1989 655p il o.p.
LC 88-48012

The "portrait of Tecumseh, the renowned Shawnee chief and warrior who established a confederacy of tribes in order to resist U.S. encroachment into the Ohio valley, is suitably suffused with fascinating elements of native American lore, legend, and culture. . . . Action and reflection are juxtaposed in a riveting narrative that animates a remarkable cast of celebrated characters and vivifies recorded events. This respectful version of the life of a heroic and courageous native American represents historical fiction at its finest." Booklist

The red heart. Ballantine Bks. 1997 454p map $25
ISBN 0-345-41719-4 LC 97-18577

A "novel based on the well-known true life story of Frances Slocum. The five-year-old daughter of a Pennsylvania Quaker family, Slocum was kidnapped by Delaware Indians in 1778 and adopted by an Indian woman who raised the child as her own. In Thom's telling of her story, we see Slocum grow into a respected figure among the Miamis, becoming Maconakwa—Little Bear Woman—and raising a family on her own. The events of her life are set against the gradual destruction of Indian life on the early U.S. frontier. . . . Thom's research is exhaustive, his eye for detail impressive." Publ Wkly

Thomas, Chantal, 1945-

Farewell, my queen; a novel; translated by Moishe Black. Braziller 2003 239p $22.50
ISBN 0-8076-1514-5 LC 2003-45192
Original French edition, 2002

"For 11 years, in her post as deputy reader to Marie Antoinette, {Agathe-Sidonie} Laborde's devotion to the vain and moody queen never wavered. Then, as the storming of the Bastille rocked the Bourbon dynasty, Laborde's own life began to unravel. . . . In Moishe Black's excellent translation . . . Versailles is transformed from the seat of power into the last retreat of a disintegrating monarchy. In language both vivid and elegant, the novel also captures the mood of panic that soon had servants and soldiers fleeing their posts, and nobles, clergy and hangers-on looking to save their skins." N Y Times Book Rev

Thomas, Craig, 1942-

Firefox. Holt, Rinehart & Winston 1977 288p o.p.
LC 77-71356

"When intelligence leaks out that the Soviets have developed an incredibly sophisticated warplane code-named Firefox, with a speed of Mach 5, the Western allies, who

Thomas, Craig, 1942-—*Continued*
couldn't match it in years, decide to 'steal' the plane during its first test flight. The CIA and Britain's SIS join forces, and they pick Vietnam vet Mitchell Gant—emotionally unstable, but a superb pilot—to nab Firefox." Publ Wkly

"Suspenseful to the end, the psychological ups and downs are well handled, as are the flight sequences." Booklist

Followed by Firefox down (1983)

Thomas, D. M.

The white hotel. Viking 1981 274p o.p.
LC 80-52004

This novel "tells the story of 'Anna G.,' a fictitious patient of Freud's. Anna, an intelligent and sensitive musician, suffers from recurring pains in her left breast and ovary, with no organic cause. The 'white hotel' is the setting of Anna's vivid sexual fantasies and visions of death. Anna's poetry and journal, as well as Freud's covering letters and his case history of her analysis, are followed by a narrative history of Elisabeth Erdman ('Anna G.')." Libr J

"Repetition, stunningly enacted in imagery that continually circles in on itself, is the method by which Thomas binds us to his prose. The white hotel is the leitmotif. . . . The richness of this book is reminiscent of a painstakingly woven tapestry; one can focus on the details but must be absorbed by the whole." New Repub

Thomas, Dylan, 1914-1953

The collected stories. New Directions 1984 362p o.p.
LC 84-6822

Contents: After the fair; The tree; The true story; The enemies; The dress; The visitor; The vest; The burning baby; The orchards; The end of the river; The lemon; The horse's ha; The school for witches; The mouse and the woman; A prospect of the sea; The holy six; Prologue to an adventure; The map of love; In the direction of the beginning; An adventure from a work in progress

Portrait of the artist as a young dog: The peaches; A visit to grandpa's; Patricia, Edith, and Arnold; The fight; Extraordinary little cough; Just like little dogs; Where Tawe flows; Who do you wish was with us; Old Garbo; One warm Saturday

A fine beginning; Plenty of furniture; Four lost souls; Quite early one morning; A child's Christmas in Wales; Holiday memory; The crumbs of one man's year; Return journey; The followers; A story; Brember; Jarley's; In the garden; Gasper, Melchior, Balthasar

Portrait of the artist as a young dog
In Thomas, D. The collected stories p122-238

Thomas, Elizabeth Marshall, 1931-

The animal wife. Houghton Mifflin 1990 289p o.p.
LC 90-4485

"A Peter Davison book"

This novel "is set in Siberia 20,000 years ago. . . . While out hunting, Kori captures a woman from another tribe whom he names Muskrat. Their evolving relationship and the interactions among the family tribe members as they move from their summer grounds to their winter grounds in the constant search for food form the heart of the novel." Libr J

The author "has created a novel of rare beauty and depth. . . . In Ms. Thomas's spare, evocative prose is much wisdom about men and women and the limits of our understanding of each other." N Y Times Book Rev

Reindeer Moon. Houghton Mifflin 1987 338p o.p.
LC 86-18530

"A Peter Davison book"

"We meet the protagonist, Yanan, as a young girl, living with her family in what is now Siberia. Just a few chapters into the narrative, she dies and becomes a spirit who must serve the members of her lodge by finding food for them, often by taking on the form and behavioral characteristics of animals or birds. The story proceeds in flashback as Yanan relates the memories of her youth." Publ Wkly

"What makes the reader care for this young girl so far removed from us by time and distance is that in telling her story the author conveys sentiments and feelings not remote from our own today." N Y Times Book Rev

Thomas, Michael M.

Black money. Crown 1994 309p o.p.
LC 93-33813

This novel "tracks a criminal scam from its detection in a small California mall through its connections to South American drug cartels, the Mafia, and the highest reaches of the U.S. government. A middle-level federal bureaucrat and the socially well-connected editor of a muckraking magazine join forces to expose an enormously complicated scheme for laundering drug money." Booklist

Thomas "writes a very exciting and almost-too-believable tale of power politics and international crime." Libr J

Hanover Place. Warner Bks. 1990 479p $19.45
ISBN 0-446-51330-X LC 89-40038

"Hanover Place, in 1924, is the site of a moderately successful brokerage house owned by the Warringtons. Thomas' novel charts the triumphs, losses, and peccadilloes of the Warringtons and their kind, also serving up a portrait of the world of high finance, from the rudimentary days of stocks (and the Depression) to the modern age of junk bonds, forced mergers, unfriendly takeovers, and so on. One prominent theme here is anti-Semitism, symbolized by a bright young Jewish clerk who is upgraded into the partners' circle, yet must endure the bigotry of the WASPish men and women who dominate high-level New York society. Later, financial revenge is wrought. A big tale of Americans and their money certain to entertain." Booklist

Thomas, Rosie

All my sins remembered. Bantam Bks. 1992 c1991 548p o.p.
LC 92-8547

First published 1991 in the United Kingdom

This "tale revolves around interviews biographer Elizabeth Ainger records with her grandmother's elderly cou-

Thomas, Rosie—*Continued*

sin, Clio, an accomplished novelist. Once three generations of family history are reconstructed, Elizabeth's project has revealed much more than girlish crushes and failed love affairs. This rousing, thoroughly engaging read moves from Victorian drawing rooms to bohemian Bloomsbury and Nazi Germany, with painful secrets and bittersweet betrayals revealed at every turn." Booklist

Other people's marriages. Morrow 1994 c1993 425p o.p.

LC 93-8885

First published 1993 in the United Kingdom

"Within a few weeks of her arrival in the London suburb of Grafton, a young widow begins an affair with a married man. The affair is soon discovered, however, and it sets off a chain reaction of infidelities through five married couples." N Y Times Book Rev

"Effective, precise details vivify physical settings (various homes are as acutely rendered as the cathedral, the novel's central symbol), and the characters, some unappealing but all understandable, are well drawn." Libr J

Thomas, Ross, 1926-1995

Ah, treachery!. Mysterious Press 1994 274p o.p.

LC 94-15118

"In 1989, army major Edd 'Twodees' Partain took part in an illegal operation in El Salvador that his former comrades now want expunged from the record. Meanwhile, top political fund-raiser Millicent Altford needs to recover $1.2 million in stolen under-the-table contributions. These two scenarios dovetail as Altford engineers to have Partain, who was drummed out of the service for assaulting a superior officer, fired from his job in a Wyoming gun store in order to hire him to 'ride shotgun' as she goes after the loot. . . . Thomas's yarn reaffirms his expertise at the black-humored political thriller." Publ Wkly

The fourth Durango. Mysterious Press 1989 312p o.p.

LC 89-3091

Durango, California is "the ideal hideout for a man with a price on his life. For a fee, the shrewd mayor and her loyal chief of police offer sanctuary to a judge who has just done time on a cooked-up bribery charge. The judge and his son-in-law, a disbarred lawyer, move into 'the only money-losing Holiday Inn west of Beirut' and devise a plan for smoking out the person with the vendetta against the judge. For an even bigger fee, the mayor and her top cop are game to conspire in the scheme—until an extremely ugly man comes to town and starts shooting up the citizenry." N Y Times Book Rev

Voodoo, Ltd. Mysterious Press 1992 282p $19.95

ISBN 0-89296-451-0 LC 91-51185

"Ione Gamble, an actress 'with a face known throughout the world,' is in a real jam. The police think she murdered her former lover, Billy Rice, a dissolute publishing heir and independent movie producer, at his Malibu beach house. Gamble isn't so sure about that, since she was blind drunk at the time. Desperate, she hires Enno Glimm, who will spare no expense in recruiting a discreet hypnotist to probe her alcoholic blackout for the truth without concurrently selling her story to the tabloids. Glimm's company, based in Germany, is a sort of global office-temp agency that fills unusual short-term employment requirements." N Y Times Book Rev

Thomas, Sherree

(ed) Dark matter. See Dark matter

Thomas, Thomas T.

(jt. auth) Pohl, F. Mars Plus

Thomason, Dustin

(jt. auth) Caldwell, I. The rule of four

Thompson, Jean, 1950-

Wide blue yonder; a novel. Simon & Schuster 2002 367p $24

ISBN 0-7432-0512-X LC 2001-34157

"It's summer 1999 in Springfield, IL, and Harvey Sloan's sole interest in life continues to be the Weather Channel. His great-niece, Josie, possessed by a hopeless teenage love, confides in Abe Lincoln. Her divorced mother, Elaine, starts to believe that a good or bad day is indicated by her car's service engine light. Meanwhile, Rolando Gottschalk, armed with a gun and an unknown agenda, seems to be headed to Springfield from Los Angeles, leaving a wake of random destruction. Add Mitch, a gorgeous cop, and Rosa, a Mexican cleaning woman, to the mix and you have a novel with characters both memorable and believable." Libr J

Tilghman, Christopher

Mason's retreat. Random House 1996 290p $22

ISBN 0-679-42712-0 LC 95-4716

The "title refers to an estate on Maryland's Eastern Shore that Edward Mason inherits from a maiden aunt and to which he brings his impoverished family in 1937. Edward, a confirmed Anglophile, has lived in England since 1923, but increasing debts have forced him to leave his small manufacturing firm in the hands of its foreman and return to America. To him it seems provincial and barren, but his wife and eldest son hope to make their home there." Libr J

The author "elegantly evokes both the physical landscape and the hermetic society and inbred culture of the Chesapeake Bay area. . . . In supple and beautifully inflected prose, he makes astute observations about the enduring blight of racism, the fallibility of human nature, the sacrifice of children as hostages to fortune and the inevitability of retribution—all conveyed with an illuminating, unflinching but compassionate eye." Publ Wkly

Timm, Uwe, 1940-

Morenga; translated from the German by Breon Mitchell. New Directions 2003 340p $25.95

ISBN 0-8112-1514-8 LC 2002-15248

Original German edition, 1978

This novel is "an oddly fragmented montage that offers a . . . view of the title figure, a charismatic black South-West African who led the Hottentot and Herero uprising against the Germans after the Boer War. The initial protagonist is a fictional German military veterinarian . . . . The early chapters concern the mysterious fate of a col-

Timm, Uwe, 1940-—*Continued*

league who disappears from [the veterinarian's] unit. From there, Timm turns to the uprising itself, his depiction of Morenga's role broken up by snapshots of secondary characters." Publ Wkly

The "fragmentary approach has great cumulative moral power, making us consider all sides of the story without forgetting that there were victims who deserve some remembrance." N Y Times Book Rev

Tinti, Hannah

Animal crackers; Hannah Tinti. Dial Press 2004 197p $22.95

ISBN 0-385-33743-4 LC 2003-70125

Contents: Animal crackers; Home sweet home; Reasonable terms; Preservation; Slim's last ride; Hit man of the year; Talk turkey; How to revitalize the snake in your life; Gallus, gallus; Bloodworks; Miss Waldron's red colobus

"Tinti boldly parses primal emotions in her stealthy short stories, which, like cats' paws, conceal weapons of great precision. Each tale posits interaction between animals and humans, which, rather than offering cuddly moments, lead to vicious or spooky confrontations. Zoos make perfect theaters for Tinti's creepy and caustic satires. . . . Tinti's fables are dark and wily, grim yet morbidly fascinating exposures of both our animal selves and our uniquely human psychoses." Booklist

Tiptree, James, 1916-1987

The girl who was plugged in
In The Hugo winners p397-434

Houston, Houston, do you read?
In The Best of the Nebulas p420-60
In The Hugo winners p200-56

Tirone Smith, Mary-Ann, 1944-

Love her madly; a novel. Holt & Co. 2002 307p $25

ISBN 0-8050-6648-9 LC 2001-39306

This thriller "introduces Poppy Rice, FBI agent and brassy gal all around, who blusters her way into a capital punishment case obviously inspired by that of real-life convicted killer Karla Faye Tucker, executed a few years ago. Rona Leigh Glueck awaits the execution chamber, 'about to be the first woman put to death by the people of Texas since the Civil War,' but Poppy deduces that Ms. Glueck's wrists were too dainty to have wielded a heavy ax in a double homicide." Publ Wkly

"Smith delivers a smart, irreverent heroine; pitch-perfect Texan dialogue; gasp-worthy plot twists; and quite a bit of substance along with the action. Poppy has some serious and scathing things to say about the death penalty, religion, and Texas politics." Booklist

She smiled sweetly; a Poppy Rice mystery; Mary-Ann Tirone Smith. 1st ed. Holt & Co. 2004 275p $25

ISBN 0-8050-7224-1 LC 2003-55757

FBI agent Poppy Rice "agrees to help a friend's mom find closure in the case of the death of a pregnant woman in her native Ireland during the 1970s, but before you can say 'Erin go bragh,' the body of another pregnant young woman with an Irish link washes up on a beach in Boston Harbor. Police detective and Hindu/Catholic Rocky Patel heads the Beantown investigation of the American victim, and his coolness and wisdom complement Poppy's no-nonsense professionalism." Publ Wkly

Titmarsh, Michael Angelo *See* Thackeray, William Makepeace, 1811-1863

Toer, Pramoedya Ananta, 1925-

All that is gone; translated from the Indonesian by Willem Samuels. 1st ed. Hyperion East 2004 255p $23.95

ISBN 1-401-36663-5 LC 2003-56675

Contents: All that is gone; Inem; In twilight born; Circumcision; Revenge; Independence Day; Acceptance; The rewards of marriage

"A sense of duty is perhaps natural for a writer who spent nearly two decades as a political prisoner under three different regimes. But the striking achievement of these stories is an unshakable innocence of voice and a willingness to leave judgment to the reader. Pramoedya's art is made more of sadness than of anger, and he is particularly adept at narrating from a child's perspective—as when a six-year-old boy sees his best friend, a girl of eight, married off, beaten by her husband, and, after she flees, made a social outcast." New Yorker

The girl from the coast; translated by Willem Samuels. Hyperion 2002 280p $22.95

ISBN 0-7868-6820-1 LC 2002-69063

Original Indonesian edition, 1987

In this "tale of feudal Java, a beautiful young woman from a poor fishing village has the misfortune of catching the eye of a Muslim aristocrat who asks to marry her, but who, after a brief ceremony in which a dagger takes the place of the groom, merely installs her in his bleak residence as a lowly concubine. . . . As Toer unfurls this entrancing, indelible tale based on his grandmother's hard life, he deftly dissects the conventions that enable a brutal few to oppress the suffering many." Booklist

Toews, Miriam, 1964-

A complicated kindness; a novel; Miriam Toews. Counterpoint 2004 246p $23

ISBN 1-582-43321-6 LC 2004-7960

"Sixteen-year-old Nomi Nichol is a Mennonite, which, she wryly observes, 'is the most embarrassing subsect of people to belong to if you're a teenager.' Because Mennonites shun modern ways, Nomi's repressively fundamentalist community on the plains of Manitoba is a tourist attraction for Americans searching 'for a glimpse backwards in time.' Half of Nomi's family, 'the better-looking half' as she puts it, is missing. Her older sister has fled the stifling strictures of their hometown, while her mother has also vanished after having been excommunicated by her own brother, the local minister, whom Nomi dubs 'The Mouth of Darkness.' That leaves the 16-year-old to look after her gentle, bewildered father and to deal with her own loneliness and persistent memories of how her family came undone." Booklist

"Nomi's hunger for life prevents the novel from being

Toews, Miriam, 1964-—*Continued*
as bleak as her situation might suggest; her account of her trials is veined with a dark humor that glints with the glee of payback." N Y Times Book Rev

Tóibín, Colm, 1955-

The blackwater lightship; a novel. Scribner 2000 273p o.p.

ISBN 0-684-87389-3 LC 00-21036

First published 1999 in the United Kingdom

Helen O'Doherty is a school principal living in Dublin, Ireland, whose brother Declan is "dying of AIDS. Declan's wish is to be moved to the home of their acerbic grandmother, Dora, who lives on a cliff overlooking the sea. Guiltstricken to discover that her brother has been ill for years and never confided in her, Helen moves in as well, . . . along with her mother, Lily, and Declan's friends, Larry and Paul." N Y Times Book Rev

"The novel shows us discreetly what a practical, complicated matter dying is, how much logistics and paraphernalia it requires, and its unflinchingly exact style is a kind of respect paid to this. The commonplce and the catastropic lie cheek-by-jowl." London Rev Books

The heather blazing. Viking 1993 245p o.p.

ISBN 0-670-84789-5 LC 92-50350

First published 1992 in the United Kingdom

The novel "explores the rigidly controlled mind and soul of a high court Dublin judge, Eamon Redmond. Toibin . . . [presents the] particulars of Redmond's life: his devotion to the law, his daughter's out-of-wedlock pregnancy, his controversial decision in a case concerning the expulsion of a pregnant high school student, and his wrenching memories of his motherless childhood and his father's debilitation after a stroke." Booklist

"Toibin weaves past and present together in a way designed to extract the maximum resonance from the juxtaposition. One of the book's surprises is its subtle humor, its awareness of small ironies." Voice Lit Suppl

The master. Scribner 2004 338p $25

ISBN 0-7432-5040-0 LC 2003-67376

This novel depicts the writer Henry James during his middle years. "What Toibin has so boldly done—and so brilliantly and successfully—is forge a sympathetic imagining of James' interior life. . . . Even the reader who knows little about Henry James or his work can enjoy this marvelously intelligent and engaging novel, which presents not on a silver platter but in tender, opened hands a beautifully nuanced psychological portrait." Booklist

Tolkien, J. R. R. (John Ronald Reuel), 1892-1973

The book of lost tales; part I-II; edited by Christopher Tolkien. Houghton Mifflin 1984 2v (History of Middle Earth) o.p.

LC 83-12782

Part one first published 1983 in the United Kingdom

Contents: pt. 1 The cottage of lost play; The music of the Ainur; The coming of the Valar and the building of Valinor; The chaining of Melko; The coming of the Elves and the making of Kôr; The theft of Melko and the darkening of Valinor; The flight of the Noldoli; The tale of the Sun and Moon; The hiding of Valinor; Gilfanon's tale: the travail of the Noldoli and the coming of Mankind

pt. II: The tale of Tinúviel; Turambar and the Foalókë; The fall of Gondolin; The Nauglafring; The tale of Eärendel; The history of Eriol; AElfwine of England

"These fascinating stories of fairies and elves battling evil creatures shed considerable light on the evolution of Tolkien's elaborate fictional world." Booklist

The fellowship of the ring; being the first part of The lord of the rings. 2nd ed. Houghton Mifflin 1986 c1965 423p il $21.95

ISBN 0-395-48931-8 LC 88-120282

First published 1954

"Frodo, a home-loving young hobbit, inherits the magic ring which his uncle Bilbo brought back from the adventures described in the juvenile fantasy 'The hobbit'. This sequel, expressly addressed to adults, is the first of a three-part saga that tells of Frodo's valiant journey undertaken to prevent the ring from falling into the hands of the powers of darkness. Elves, dwarfs, hobbits, men, and sundry evil beings, each as real as the other, populate an allegorical tale that shows how power corrupts." Booklist

Followed by The two towers

also in Tolkien, J. R. R. The lord of the rings

The hobbit; or, There and back again; illustrated by Michael Hague. Houghton Mifflin 1984 290p il $29.95

ISBN 0-395-36290-3 LC 84-9023

First published 1937 in the United Kingdom; first United States edition 1938

"This fantasy features the adventures of hobbit Bilbo Baggins, who joins a band of dwarves led by Gandalf the Wizard. Together they seek to recover the stolen treasure that is hidden in Lonely Mountain and guarded by Smaug the Dragon. This book precedes the *Lord of the Rings* trilogy." Shapiro. Fic for Youth. 3d edition

"It must be understood that this is a children's book only in the sense that the first of many readings can be undertaken in the nursery. . . . [The hobbit] will be funniest to its youngest readers, and only years later, at a tenth or twentieth reading, will they begin to realize what deft scholarship and profound reflection have gone to make everything in it so ripe, so friendly, and in its own way so true." Times Lit Suppl

The lord of the rings. 2nd ed. Houghton Mifflin 1986 c1966 3v

The trilogy was first published 1954-55 in the United Kingdom. This revised edition first published 1966 in the United Kingdom

Contents: v1 The fellowship of the ring; v2 The two towers; v3 The return of the king

"This is a tale of imaginary gnomelike creatures who battle against evil. Led by Frodo, the hobbits embark on a journey to prevent a magic ring from falling into the grasp of the powers of darkness. The forces of good succeed in their fight against the Dark Lord of evil, and Frodo and Sam bring the Ring to Mount Doom, where it is destroyed." Shapiro. Fic for Youth. 3d edition

The return of the king; being the third part of The lord of the rings. 2nd ed. Houghton Mifflin 1986 c1965 440p $21.95

ISBN 0-395-48930-X LC 88-195987

Tolkien, J. R. R. (John Ronald Reuel), 1892-1973—*Continued*

First published 1955 in the United Kingdom

In the concluding volume of the trilogy "The dark lord of evil is overthrown, the rightful king comes into his own, and the Age of Men begins." Booklist

also in Tolkien, J. R. R. The lord of the rings

The Silmarillion; edited by Christopher Tolkien. Houghton Mifflin 1977 365p o.p.

LC 77-8025

"Tolkien began writing these introductory legends in 1917 and, sporadically throughout his life, continued adding to them; his son Christopher has edited and compiled the various versions into a single cohesive work. Two brief tales, which outline the origin of the world and describe the gods who create and rule, precede the title story about the Silmarils—three brilliant, jewel-like creatures who are desired and fought over, setting up a clash between good and evil." Booklist

The two towers; being the second part of The lord of the rings. 2nd ed. Houghton Mifflin 1986 c1965 352p $21.95

ISBN 0-395-48933-4 LC 88-195969

First published 1954

"Here the Companions of the Ring, separated, meet Saruman the wizard, cross the Dead Marshes, and prepare for the Great War in which the power of the Ring will be undone." Libr J

Followed by The return of the king

also in Tolkien, J. R. R. The lord of the rings

Tolkien, John Ronald Reuel *See* Tolkien, J. R. R. (John Ronald Reuel), 1892-1973

Tolkin, Michael

Under radar. Atlantic Monthly Press 2002 212p $24

ISBN 0-87113-848-4 LC 2002-16390

"While on vacation in Jamaica with his family, Tom Levy becomes enraged when one of the hotel guests encourages Tom's young daughter to dance in a suggestive manner for the audience at a reggae concert. Convinced that his daughter has been permanently damaged, Tom kills the man and is sentenced to life in prison. There he hears a story that affects him so profoundly that it turns his hair white and puts him in a coma. He awakens years later a radically changed man." Booklist

"This is a book in which every character has a story to tell, none of them immediately comprehensible. Appropriate to a novel that trades so assuredly in spiritual mysteries, 'Under Radar' leaves us like puzzled pilgrims, struggling with the meaning of the cruel fable that has been so enticingly told." N Y Times Book Rev

Tolstaıa, Tat´iana, 1951-

The slynx; [by] Tatyana Tolstaya; translated by Jamey Gambrell. Houghton Mifflin 2003 278p $24

ISBN 0-618-12497-7 LC 2002-27627

Original Russian edition, 2000

In a postapocalyptic Russia, "in a society turned primitive by nuclear holocaust, people hunt mice and tremble at the mention of a mysterious forest creature called the slynx; of course, they are utterly ignorant, as books are banned. . . . Benedikt, scribe to the tyrant who rules this sorry land . . . has yet to read a book, but in the course of the novel he discovers the libraries owned by the Oldeners, those who recall the world before the fateful blast. Not surprisingly, he finds that literature is both liberating and dangerous." Libr J

"It takes some time for a plot to develop, but Tolstaya sketches a vivid picture of life in this permanent winter. . . . In this extended fable, she captures the Russian yearning for culture, even in desperate circumstances. Gambrell ably translates the mix of neologisms and plain speech with which Tolstaya describes this devastated world." Publ Wkly

Tolstaya, Tatyana *See* Tolstaıa, Tat´iana, 1951-

Tolstoy, Leo, graf, 1828-1910

Anna Karenina; edited and introduced by Leonard J. Kent and Nina Berberova. Modern Lib. 1993 xxvii, 927p $22.95

ISBN 0-679-60079-5 LC 93-43634

Written in 1873-1876

This novel "is the story of a tragic, adulterous love. Anna meets and falls in love with Aleksei Vronski, a handsome young officer. She abandons her child and husband in order to be with Vronski. When she thinks Vronski has tired of her, she kills herself by leaping under a train. The idea for the story reputedly came to Tolstoy after he had viewed the body of a young woman who committed a similar suicide. A subplot concerns the contrasting happy marriage of Konstantin Levin and his young wife Kitty. Levin's search for meaning in his life and his love for a natural, simple existence on his estate are reflections of Tolstoy's own moods and thoughts of the time." Reader's Ency. 4th edition

Childhood, Boyhood and Youth; translated from the Russian by C. J. Hogarth. Knopf 1991 314p $17

ISBN 0-679-40578-X LC 91-52984

"Everyman's library"

Originally published separately, 1852, 1854 and 1857 respectively; this edition first published 1912

"An autobiographical trilogy. . . . 'Childhood' was the first of Tolstoy's works to receive wide attention. The descriptions of life on a provincial estate are among the best depictions of nature in Russian literature." Reader's Ency. 4th edition

The Cossacks

In Tolstoy, L., graf. The short novels of Tolstoy

The Cossacks [excerpt]

In Tolstoy, L., graf. The portable Tolstoy p358-434

The death of Iván Ilyitch

In Tolstoy, L., graf. The short novels of Tolstoy

Tolstoy, Leo, graf, 1828-1910—*Continued*

The death of Ivan Ilyitch, and other stories; a new translation from the Russian by Constance Garnett. Dodd, Mead 1927 362p o.p.

Contents: The death of Ivan Ilyitch; Family happiness; Polikushka; Two hussars; The snowstorm; Three deaths

The Devil

In Tolstoy, L., graf. The Kreutzer sonata, The Devil, and other tales

In Tolstoy, L., graf. The short novels of Tolstoy

Divine and human and other stories; new translations by Peter Sekirin. Zondervan 2000 211p $19.99

ISBN 0-310-22367-9 LC 00-20791

Contents: The son of a thief; The repentant sinner; The archangel Gabriel; The prayer; The poor people; A coffeehouse in the city of Surat; Kornei Vasiliev; A grain of rye the size of a chicken egg; The berries; Stones; The big dipper; The power of childhood; Why did it happen?; Divine and human; The requirements of love; Sisters

"These 16 selections from Tolstoy's final eclectic collection of tales titled *The Sunday Reading Stories* represent the Russian novelist's turn away from the troubling human condition in *Anna Karenina* toward a growing preoccupation with moral issues." Publ Wkly

Family happiness

In Tolstoy, L., graf. The Kreutzer sonata, The Devil, and other tales

In Tolstoy, L., graf. The short novels of Tolstoy

Father Sergius

In Tolstoy, L., graf. The Kreutzer sonata, The Devil, and other tales

God sees the truth, but waits

In Tolstoy, L., graf. The portable Tolstoy p475-83

Hadji Murád

In Tolstoy, L., graf. The short novels of Tolstoy

How much land does a man need?

In Tolstoy, L., graf. The portable Tolstoy p506-22

The Kreutzer sonata

In Tolstoy, L., graf. The portable Tolstoy p523-601

The Kreutzer sonata, The Devil, and other tales; translation of Family happiness, by J. D. Duff, and of other stories by Aylmer Maude; with an introduction by Aylmer Maude. Oxford Univ. Press 1957 xxi, 375p o.p.

Contents: Family happiness; The Kreutzer sonata; The Devil; Father Sergius; François; The porcelain doll

Master and man

In Tolstoy, L., graf. The portable Tolstoy p602-52

In Tolstoy, L., graf. The short novels of Tolstoy

Polikúshka

In Tolstoy, L., graf. The short novels of Tolstoy

The portable Tolstoy; selected and with a critical introduction, biographical summary, and bibliography by John Bayley. Viking 1978 888p o.p.

LC 78-6784

This anthology contains the complete text of the play The power of darkness, the novelette The Kreutzer sonata, ten short stories and philosophical, religious, social and critical writings including essays from What is art?

The power of darkness [play]

In Tolstoy, L., graf. The portable Tolstoy p747-825

The raid

In Tolstoy, L., graf. The portable Tolstoy p169-99

Resurrection. o.p.

Original Russian edition, 1899

"The story deals with the spiritual regeneration of a young nobleman, Prince Nekhlyudov. In his earlier years, he seduced a young girl, Katyusha Maslova. She became a prostitute and later became involved with a man she is accused of poisoning. Nekhlyudov, serving on the jury, recognizes her and decides that he is morally guilty for her predicament. He decides to marry her, and when she is convicted he follows her to Siberia to accomplish his aim. Maslova is repelled by his reforming zeal. She marries another prisoner, but is finally convinced of Nekhlyudov's sincerity and accepts his friendship." Reader's Ency. 4th edition

Sevastopol

In Tolstoy, L., graf. The portable Tolstoy p239-93

The short novels of Tolstoy; selected with an introduction by Philip Rahv; translated by Aylmer Maude. Dial Press 1946 xx, 716p o.p.

Contents: Two hussars; Family happiness; The Cossacks; Polikúshka; The death of Iván Ilyitch; The Devil; Master and man; Hadji Murád

Short stories; selected and introduced by Ernest J. Simmons. Modern Lib. 1964-1965 2v o.p.

Contents: v 1: A history of yesterday; The raid; A billiard-markers' notes; The wood-felling; Sevastopol in December 1854; Sevastopol in May 1855; Sevastopol in August 1855; Meeting a Moscow acquaintance in the detachment; The snow storm; Lucerne; Albert; Three deaths; Strider; The porcelain doll

v2: God sees the truth, but waits; A prisoner in the Caucasus; The bearhunt; What men live by; A spark neglected burns the house; Two old men; Where love is, God is; Evil allures, but good endures; Little girls wiser than men; Elias; The story of Iván, the Fool; The repentant sinner; The three hermits; The imp and the crust; How much land does a man need; A grain as big as a hen's egg; The godson; The empty drum; Esarhaddon, King of Assyria; Work, death and sickness; Three questions; The memoirs of a madman; After the ball; Fëdor Kuzmich; Alyósha

Tolstoy, Leo, graf, 1828-1910—*Continued*

Strider
In Tolstoy, L., graf. The portable Tolstoy p435-74

Two Hussars
In Tolstoy, L., graf. The portable Tolstoy p294-357
In Tolstoy, L., graf. The short novels of Tolstoy

War and peace; translated by Constance Garnett. Modern Lib. 1994 1386p $24.95
ISBN 0-679-60084-1 LC 93-38836
Original Russian edition, 1864-1869
"The story covers roughly the years between 1805 and 1820, centering on the invasion of Russia by Napoleon's army in 1812 and the Russian resistance to the invader. Over five hundred characters, all carefully rendered, populate the pages of the novel. Every social level, from Napoleon himself to the peasant Platon Karatayev, is represented. Interwoven with the story of the war are narrations of the lives of several main characters, especially those of Natasha Rostova, Prince Andrey Bolkonsky, and Pierre Bezukhov. These people are shown as they progress from youthful uncertainties and searchings toward a more mature understanding of life." Reader's Ency. 4th edition

What men live by
In Tolstoy, L., graf. The portable Tolstoy p484-505

The wood-felling
In Tolstoy, L., graf. The portable Tolstoy p200-38

Tomasi di Lampedusa, Giuseppe, 1896-1957

The Leopard; [by] Giuseppi di Lampedusa; translated from the Italian by Archibald Colquhoun. Pantheon Bks. 1960 319p o.p.
Original Italian edition, 1958
This historical novel "describes the impact of Garibaldi's invasion of Sicily and the subsequent unification of Italy on an aristocratic Sicilian family who had flourished under the Bourbon kings. The novel's depiction of the failure of the *Risorgimento* created heated political debates when it was first published. However, the controversy subsided and the book was widely recognized as a penetrating psychological study of an age, written in a highly symbolic and richly poetic style." Reader's Ency. 4th edition

Toole, John Kennedy, 1937-1969

A confederacy of dunces; foreword by Walker Percy. Louisiana State Univ. Press 1980 338p $24.95
ISBN 0-8071-0657-7 LC 79-20190
The protagonist of this novel set in New Orleans is Ignatius J. Reilly, "a medievalist whose fortunes take a downward turn when he is nearly arrested for being a 'suspicious character.' Things only get worse when he and his mother (leaving the Night of Joy bar, where they've gone to soothe their nerves after the near-arrest) run their car into a building, and Ignatius is forced to find a job to pay for the damages." Christ Sci Monit
"At the heart of this splendid mock-heroic with its blundering and canniness, its falstaffian excesses and 'Alice in Wonderland' wit, lies a profound sense of solitude. Like everything else in Ignatuis J. Reilly's world, the absence of love is larger than life." Newsweek

Torsvan, Berick Traven *See* Traven, B.

Torsvan, Traven *See* Traven, B.

Tournier, Michel

The four wise men; translated from the French by Ralph Manheim. Doubleday 1982 255p o.p.
ISBN 0-385-17723-2 LC 81-43550
Original French edition, 1980
In the first three sections of this novel "we see the 'traditional' three kings as individuals–Gaspar, Balthasar and Melchior. . . . Then there are two sections about the despotic Herod, a section on the Nativity itself as witnessed and reported by a beast of burden (the ass in the stable that eve), and, finally . . . the story of a fourth regal figure, Taor. He is a naive and benign young Indian prince, who basically is interested in exotic sweets. He misses the Nativity [and] wanders lost in strange lands for years." America
"The tour de force of Mr. Tournier's novel is the invention of a fourth Wise Man, Taor. . . . Almost every episode in Mr. Tournier's novel reduces itself to stunning paradox. . . . 'The Four Wise Men' is a work of extraordinary clarity." N Y Times Book Rev

Friday; translated from the French by Norman Denny. Johns Hopkins University Press 1997 c1969 235p pa $25
ISBN 0-8018-5592-6 LC 96-45295
Original French edition, 1967; this translation first published 1969 by Doubleday
A retelling of the legend of Robinson Crusoe. "Cast away on a tropical island . . . Crusoe sets out to tame it, to remake it in the image of the civilization he has left behind. Alone and against incredible odds, he almost succeeds. Then a mulatto named Friday appears and teaches Robinson that there are, aftere all, better things in life than civilization." Publisher's note
"M. Tournier is a cultivated and disciplined writer, and his Robinson, the son of a Yorkshire draper, is most likable. . . . The castaway has that quaint and peculiarly English stolidity that seems to exist only in the imagination of the French." New Yorker

The ogre; translated from the French by Barbara Bray. Johns Hopkins University Press 1997 c1972 373p pa $19.95
ISBN 0-8018-5590-x LC 96-46778
Original French edition, 1970; this translation first published 1972 by Doubleday and in the United Kingdom by Collins with title: The Erl-king
This novel "traces the life of Abel Tiffauges, a huge French garage mechanic, from his childhood memories . . . to his 1940-4 experience as a prisoner of war, ending up working at a training camp for young boys at Kaltenborn." Good Fiction Guide

Tournier, Michel—*Continued*

A work that "bears patently the marks of greatness. It relentlessly pushes individual idiosyncrasy to–and even beyond–the point of universality. It covers simultaneously the events inside one head and one continent. It uses documentary knowledge–minute and encyclopedic knowledge of photography, history, zoology, anthropometry, weaponry– to illustrate the otherwise undocumentable progress of a human obsession." New Yorker

Townsend, Sue

Adrian Mole; the Cappucino years. Soho Press 2000 c1999 390p o.p.

ISBN 1-56947-204-1 LC 99-87241

First published 1999 in the United Kingdom

"Now in his 'cappucino years,' Adrian is a single father and chef who struggles financially. His personal life continues to be complicated by his dysfunctional family, his still unrequited love for Pandora Braithwaite, and the revelation that he is father to not one but two sons." Libr J

"Adrian is a comic Job in a world gone mad with irony and greed. But his confused heart brims with love and good intentions, and Townsend skewers end-of-the millennium Britain with acumen and glee." Booklist

The Adrian Mole diaries. Grove Press 1986 c1985 342p o.p.

LC 86-226

First published 1985 in the United Kingdom; A combined edition of two titles: The secret diary of Adrian Mole, age 13 $\frac{3}{4}$ (1982); and Growing pains (1984)

"The messy, inconsistent world of adulthood is seen through the eyes of a 14-year-old aspiring intellectual and poet. Adrian Mole begins his diary when spots appear on his face and his parents' marriage dissolves. By the diary's end he has been in love, become helpmate to a feisty 89-year-old, and held his mother's hand during the birth of his sister. Adrian's pithy commentary records the ludicrousness of school and state bureaucracy and the aberrations of the nuclear age." Booklist

Followed by Adrian Mole: the lost years

Adrian Mole: the lost years. Soho Press 1994 309p $22

ISBN 1-56947-014-6 LC 94-11276

"Portions of this text appeared in *The True Confessions of Adrian Albert Mole,* while @Adrian Mole and the Small Amphibians' appeared in *Adrian Mole, From Minor to Major. Adrian Mole, The Wilderness Years* appears in its entirety. All were first published in Great Britain." Verso of title page

"Adrian's latest diaries chronicle his mighty struggle to survive the adolescent and postpubescent years. His outrageous clothes and strong views about everything from the government to unwed mothers can't disguise the angst he suffers: he's still trying to find a niche for his unrecognized genius. . . . Townsend is a satirist of the first order, offering brilliantly witty humor peppered with sobering insights into the troubles and traumas of working-class Brits." Booklist

Growing pains

In Townsend, S. The Adrian Mole diaries

Number 10; Sue Townsend. Soho 2003 277p $24

ISBN 1-569-47349-8 LC 2003-50562

This novel combines "social satire with an odd-couple road trip. The buddy team includes Jack, a policeman who grew up on the edge of squalor but manages to emerge a decent and levelheaded man. The other half is Edward, reared in privilege to take his all-but-predestined place as prime minister. Struck with the realization that he has no idea what life is like for ordinary citizens, Edward sets off, incognito, for a week-long safari into the land of the common folk, with Jack as his escort. Because it's hard for the prime minister to travel unnoticed, he does what any sensible man would do—slips into a wig and high heels and becomes 'Edwina.' The book doesn't lack for skewering observations of the upper and lower classes, but Edward and Jack are both such well-meaning characters, the book comes off ultimately as more affirming than biting." Booklist

The secret diary of Adrian Mole, age 13 $\frac{3}{4}$

In Townsend, S. The Adrian Mole diaries

Tracy, P. J.

Monkeewrench. Putnam 2003 373p $23.95

ISBN 0-399-14978-3 LC 2002-68139

"When people start dying in strange ways in Minneapolis, everyone wonders what the murderer will do next—everyone except the employees of Monkeewrench Software, who are all too aware that their new serial-killer computer game is the model for the crimes. They go to the police with the what, where, and when of the next murders and quickly become suspects themselves." Booklist

"Unlike the conventionally dimwitted cops and hick sheriff's deputies, Grace and her four geek partners in the software company . . . add real flavor to the proceedings with their colorful jargon and quirky personas. These techno-nerds may be freaks—and one of them may even be a killer—but they have style." N Y Times Book Rev

Trafzer, Clifford E.

(ed) Earth song, sky spirit. See Earth song, sky spirit

Traven, B.

The treasure of the Sierra Madre. Knopf 1935 366p o.p.

Original German edition, 1927

This novel analyzes the "psychology of greed in telling of three Americans searching for a lost gold mine in Mexican mountains." Oxford Companion to Am Lit. 6th edition

Traver, Robert, 1903-1991

Anatomy of a murder. St. Martin's Press 1958 437p o.p.

"Not the usual murder mystery but a review by the lawyer for the defense from the time he takes the case of an army lieutenant who admits to having killed the man who raped his wife, until the end of the trial. Much attention is given to establishing the fact of rape. Although the recital is wordy it maintains suspense in showing the legal and personal resources the lawyer calls on to build his defense and the way that rivalry between prosecution and defense shapes the trial." Booklist

Tremain, Rose

The color. Farrar, Straus & Giroux 2003 382p $25

ISBN 0-374-12605-4 LC 2002-192528

This novel, set in the mid-19th century, centers on Joseph and Harriet Blackstone, who have married and emigrated to New Zealand in search of a better life. "Together with Joseph's mother, they attempt to build a farm on the flats outside of Christchurch, but when Joseph finds gold in the creek, he becomes obsessed by 'the color', as the fabulous metal is known. Abandoning both women, he travels by ship to the west coast, where he encounters hundreds of other desperate men and the clamorous, filthy, dehumanizing conditions in which they live. . . . By the time [Harriet] does join him, each of them despises the other, yet the discovery of gold binds them in a new way." Publ Wkly

"As the story gathers momentum, it widens . . . . Tremain's excursions into the minds of her Maori and Chinese characters are written with a blend of sympathy and irony that sabotages our expectations of things exotic and inscrutable." N Y Times Book Rev

Music & silence. Farrar, Straus & Giroux 2000 485p o.p.

ISBN 0-374-19989-2 LC 99-42880

First published 1999 in the United Kingdom

"British lutenist Peter Claire arrives in Copenhagen in 1629 to join the orchestra of King Christian IV. Depressed after a doomed love affair with a soulful Irish countess, Peter finds his melancholy mood mirrored by that of the king, who is beset by both financial and marital crises. That fruitless wars and profligate spending by the Danish nobility have depleted the country's coffers is the king's public woe; privately, his heart is anguished by the behavior of his consort, Kristen Munk, who despises her own children, keeps her spouse from her bed and is carrying on with a German mercenary." Publ Wkly

"So hypnotic are Rose Tremain's seductive paragraphs that we are borne along without effort in a world which is neither fact nor fiction but has the strengths of both, with a uniquely sensitive imagination at work." N Y Rev Books

Sacred country. Atheneum Pubs. 1993 c1992 323p $21

ISBN 0-689-12170-9 LC 92-21457

First published 1992 in the United Kingdom

"At the age of six, Mary Ward, standing with her family in a wintry Suffolk field to observe a two-minute silence in honor of the death of King George VI, comes to the realization that she was meant to be a boy. From this beginning in 1952 until 1980, Tremain tells the evocative tale of Mary's lonely quest to transform herself into Martin. Emotionally abandoned by her parents, Mary finds refuge first with her grandfather, Cord, and later with her schoolteacher, Miss McRae." Libr J

The author "gives us a precisely imagined landscape and a complicated group of characters that we come to care deeply about." N Y Times Book Rev

The way I found her. Farrar, Straus & Giroux 1998 358p $25

ISBN 0-374-28666-3 LC 97-32676

First published 1997 in the United Kingdom

"Thirteen-year-old Lewis Little—dog-lover, chess player, amateur detective—joins his mother on a summer translating job in Paris to see the city and improve his French. But when he meets their glamorous hostess, Valentina Gavrilovich, with her infectious laugh, her cerise lipstick, and her large white breasts, his life is changed forever. And when Valentina vanishes he dedicates himself, like a knight from one of the medieval romances she writes, to rescuing her. Lewis's own narrative of innocence and experience is curiously reminiscent of the nineteen-fifties, and the effect is one of pleasurable nostalgia." New Yorker

Tremaine, Jennie *See* Chesney, Marion

Trenhaile, John

The gates of exquisite view. Dutton 1988 374p o.p.

LC 87-13630

"Saga of English capitalist Simon Young, his Hong Kong enterprise, and the secrets in his supercomputer." Smith. Cloak and Dagger Fic

"Trenhaile craftily weaves a portentous web of political intrigue, masking until the final pages the exact nature of his characters' intentions and loyalties. . . . Neatly paced suspense from a master of the genre." Booklist

Trevanian

The Eiger sanction. Crown 1972 316p o.p.

"American art professor-mountain climber Dr. Jonathan Hemlock moonlights as an assassin in the employ of the Search and Sanction Division of the mythical counter-assassination bureau known as C-11. In his last mission before retirement, he is sent along on a top-flight mountain climbing expedition in Switzerland with orders to liquidate one of three companions known to have killed an unlucky C-11 agent in Montreal. Not knowing the identity of the assassin Hemlock ruthlessly plans to bump off all three." Smith. Cloak and Dagger Fic

Hot night in the city. St. Martin's Press 2000 277p o.p.

ISBN 0-312-24202-6 LC 00-29679

"Thomas Dunne books"

Contents: Hot night in the city; Minutes of a village meeting; Snatch off your cap, kid!; The sacking of Miss Plimsoll; How the animals got their voices; After hours at Rick's; That Fox-of-a-Beñat; Mrs. McGivney's nickel; Sir Gervais in the enchanted forest; Easter story; The engine of fate; The apple tree; Hot night in the city II

"The 13 stories in this collection show Trevanian to be a storyteller as versatile as he is skillful, using a variety of voice, time, and place to leave the reader with a smile, a shake of the head, or a shudder." Libr J

Incident at Twenty Mile. St. Martin's Press 1998 308p $24.95

ISBN 0-312-19233-9 LC 98-19401

"Matthew Dubcheck wanders into the dying silver-mining town of Twenty-Mile, Wyoming, and declares himself the Ringo Kid, after the hero of his favorite dime novels. The romanticized West clashes with the real West when an escaped con comes to town, befriends

Trevanian—*Continued*
Matthew, and the wheels begin to turn toward an inevitably tragic conclusion. The anti-western is also a staple of the genre, and this tragicomic tale takes its place alongside such similar efforts as *True Git* and poet David Waggoner's delightful *Where Is My Wandering Boy Tonight?*" Booklist

Shibumi. Crown 1979 374p o.p.
LC 78-20950

This novel relates the "feats of Hel, the world's highest-paid assassin. Hel guns down political terrorists of the CIA, PLO, and various other organizations, then takes on the superpower of espionage agencies, the Mother Company." Publ Wkly

The summer of Katya. Crown 1983 242p o.p.
LC 83-1790

"The time is 1914 and the story takes place in a small French Basque village. Dr. Jean-Marc Montjean, young and newly graduated from medical school, meets and falls in love with Katya, a beautiful young girl. Their encounter comes by way of an accident that befalls Katya's brother Paul, to whom she is very attached. Jean-Marc becomes involved with their family and begins to pay court to Katya. He is warned that any romantic attachment is out of the question because of her delicate health. A mystery in the background of the family hangs over all their relationships, and in a final meeting there is a shocking climax that leaves the reader stunned." Shapiro. Fic for Youth. 3d edition

Trevor, Elleston, 1920-1995

For works written by this author under other names see Hall, Adam, 1920-1995

Trevor, William, 1928-

A bit on the side. Viking 2004 244p $24.95
ISBN 0-670-91507-6

Contents: Sitting with the dead; Traditions; Justina's priest; An evening out; Graillis's legacy; Solitude; Sacred statues; Rose wept; Big bucks; On the streets; The dancing-master's music; A bit on the side

The author "reveals his native Ireland as a world sandwiched between modernity and its accompanying wealth, secularism and vulgarity, and a past that was more soulful and pious but also more restrictive. . . . Trevor . . . explores the many sources and shadings of regret with his usual delicate but brilliant psychological nuance, brightened occasionally by nostalgia for the lost love that once impelled his characters forward." Publ Wkly

The collected stories. Viking 1992 1261p o.p.
LC 92-54071

Contents: A meeting in middle age; Access to the children; The general's day; Memories of Youghal; The table; A school story; The penthouse apartment; In at the birth; The introspections of J. P. Powers; The day we got drunk on cake; Miss Smith; The Hotel of the Idle Moon; Nice day at school; The original sins of Edward Tripp; The forty-seventh Saturday; The ballroom of romance; A happy family; The grass widows; The Mark-2 wife; An evening with John Joe Dempsey; Kinkies; Going home; A choice of butchers; O fat white woman; Raymond Bamber and Mrs. Fitch; The distant past; In Isfahan; Angels at the Ritz; The death of Peggy Meehan; Mrs. Silly; A complicated nature; Teresa's wedding; Office romances; Mr. McNamara; Afternoon dancing; Last wishes; Mrs. Acland's ghosts; Another Christmas; Broken homes; Matilda's England; Torridge; Death in Jerusalem; Lovers of their time; The raising of Elvira Tremlett; Flights of fancy; Attracta; A dream of butterflies; The bedroom eyes of Mrs. Vansittart; Downstairs at Fitzgerald's; Mulvihill's memorial; Beyond the pale; The blue dress; The teddy-bears' picnic; The time of year; Being stolen from; Mr. Tennyson; Autumn sunshine; Sunday drinks; The Paradise Lounge; Mags; The news from Ireland; On the Zattere; The wedding in the garden; Lunch in winter; The property of Colette Nervi; Running away; Cocktails at Doney's; Her mother's daughter; Bodily secrets; Two more gallants; The smoke trees of San Pietro; Virgins; Music; Events at Drimaghleen; Family sins; A trinity; The third party; Honeymoon in Tramore; The printmaker; In love with Ariadne; A husband's return; Coffee with Oliver; August Saturday; Children of the headmaster; Kathleen's field

Death in summer. Viking 1998 214p $23.95
ISBN 0-670-88202-X LC 98-21569

"A sudden death brings together a rootless, shifty young woman named Pettie and the recently widowed Thaddeus Davenant, who is trying to find a nanny for his baby daughter. With a badly typed letter of reference and threadbare clothing, Pettie is quickly turned away, but not before she has formed an irresistible (if deceived) impression of the life she could share with Thaddeus. Trevor inhabits his characters so fully that they seem present before us, and his exploration of their accidental connections demonstrates, yet again, his ability to imbue the most casual actions with unsettling significance." New Yorker

Felicia's journey. Viking 1995 c1994 212p o.p.
LC 94-32413

First published 1994 in the United Kingdom

"When handsome Johnny Lysaght, home from England to visit his mother, first catches sight of Felicia, she is standing outside Hickey's Hotel in a bridesmaid's dress. When the famously fat and affable Mr. Hilditch first catches sight of her, a few months later, she is pregnant and desperate, asking for directions outside a Midlands factory, with her grandmother's stolen pension money stuffed in her plastic carrier bag. Hilditch can tell at a glance that the Irish girl needs a special friend. . . . The insignificance of Felicia's ever-narrowing life is challenged by our terror that she will lose it." New Yorker

"Trevor is chilling and precise in his evocation of the loss of innocence, loss of heart, while he highlights the dismal features of contemporary society. Felicia's journey proceeds in an inimical atmosphere in which disquiet and corruption are the order of the day." New Statesman Soc

The hill bachelors. Viking 2000 244p o.p.
ISBN 0-670-89373-0 LC 00-32485

Contents: Three people; Of the cloth; Good news; The mourning; A friend in the trade; Low Sunday, 1950; Le visiteur; The Virgin's gift; Death of a professor; Against the odds; The telephone game; The hill bachelors

"All the stories deal with the major disappointments and small rewards that life brings, particularly within the arena of love. No story here is less that a bravura performance." Booklist

Trevor, William, 1928-—*Continued*

(ed) The Oxford book of Irish short stories. See The Oxford book of Irish short stories

The silence in the garden. Viking 1988 204p o.p.

LC 87-40662

"Told in an elliptical, slow-moving narrative is this tale of the Rolleston family, a once vital aristocratic Irish family who peters away into seemingly inexplicable hopelessness. The elder sons remain bachelors. . . . The beautiful daughter withers, as she tosses away one fiancé and, in her mid-30s, chooses a man too old for her and incapable of siring children. As poor relation Sarah discovers at last, this is voluntary self-punishment for a shared act of cruelty that had violent repercussions." Libr J

"While the subject might seem common, Trevor's treatment is a dazzling tour de force of epigrammatic detail and psychological insinuation as the writer reconstructs whole lives through the telling deployment of a single episode. Moreover, there is a tissue of lies, secrets, and deceptions that is gradually revealed in the progress of these people's stories. Trevor captures the contradictions and subtle ironies brilliantly." Booklist

Trial and error; an Oxford anthology of legal stories; edited by Fred R. Shapiro and Jane Garry. Oxford Univ. Press 1997 479p $35

ISBN 0-19-509547-2 LC 97-19789

Contents: The two drovers, by W. Scott; Bleak house, by C. Dickens; Adam Bede, by G. Eliot; Roughing it, by M. Twain; Lady Anna, by A. Trollope; Billy Budd, by H. Melville; Weir of Hermiston, by R. L. Stevenson; The cop and the anthem, by O. Henry; The Forsyte saga, by J. Galsworthy; A Jury of her peers, by S. Glaspell; The witness for the prosecution, by A. Christie; The letter, by W. S. Maugham; The majesty of the law, by F. O'Connor; Shooting an elephant, by G. Orwell; Tomorrow, by W. Faulkner; And/or, by S. A. Brown; Happy event, by N. Gordimer; Greenhouse with cyclamens I, by R. West; The floating opera, by J. Barth; Eli, the fanatic, by P. Roth; To kill a mockingbird, by H. Lee; Mr. Portway's practice, by M. Gilbert; The senior partner's ghosts, by L. Auchincloss; The naked civil servant, by Q. Crisp; The French lieutenant's woman, by J. Fowles; An act of prostitution, by J. A. McPherson; A gentleman's agreement, by E. Jolley; The sorcerer of Bolinas Reef, by C. A. Reich; The good mother, by S. Miller; The bonfire of the vanities, by T. Wolfe; American appetites, by J. C. Oates; A lesson before dying, by E. J. Gaines

"The stories treat the human dimension of the law, focusing on the institutions, legal rules, and legal actors. . . . The wide range of situations, predicaments, and interpretation make this a fascinating compilation." Libr J

Trigiani, Adriana

Big Cherry Holler; a Big Stone Gap novel. Random House 2001 272p o.p.

ISBN 0-375-50617-9 LC 2001-18599

It is "now the late 1980s, and Ave Maria and Jack MacChesney have been married 11 years. They have a ten-year-old daughter, Etta, but lost their younger child, Joe, a few years earlier. This loss and other marital stresses have tested their relationship, but the summer brings on the biggest trial yet. As Jack tries to launch a new construction business in Big Stone Gap, VA, Ave Maria and Etta take off for Italy." Libr J

"Although readers of *Big Stone Gap* are going to find this novel more serious, they should rest assured that most of the old favorite small town characters are still there. Catching an earful, usually unsolicited, of their views and advice on life, marriage, and love is a part of the charm of both the predecessor and this follow-up." Booklist

Big Stone Gap; a novel. Random House 2000 272p o.p.

ISBN 0-375-50403-6 LC 99-43306

This novel is about Ave Maria Mulligan, a "35-year-old pharmacist and self-proclaimed town spinster, who is hankering for a bigger, better world than her own in the Blue Ridge Mountains of Virginia in the late 1970s." N Y Times Book Rev

"One chapter, which is based on a real-life campaign visit from John Warner and his then-wife Elizabeth Taylor is a hoot. And you don't want to miss Ave Maria's friend, the sexy Iva Lou Wade, one of the best fictional librarians to come along in years." Libr J

Milk glass moon; a Big Stone Gap novel. Random House 2002 256p o.p.

ISBN 0-375-50618-7 LC 2002-17945

Final volume in the Big Stone Gap trilogy featuring former spinster and town pharmacist Ave Maria MacChesney. "Learning to reconcile her own personal desires with those of her beloved husband and daughter, a middle-aged Ave Maria 'redreams' her future and explores another life path." Booklist

"The folksy dialogue and unabashed sentimentalism can be cloying, but Ave's astringent insights and critical self-appraisal sharpen the tale." Publ Wkly

Tristram, Claire

After. Farrar, Straus and Giroux 2004 194p $20

ISBN 0-374-10390-9 LC 2003-21585

"A widow who has spent lots of television time talking about her husband's death at the hand of terrorists arranges to meet a married man at a rundown hotel, stepping into a veritable 'film noir.' By taking a Muslim lover on the anniversary of her husband's death, she hopes for catharsis." Publ Wkly

"The writing is stark; the dialogue is simple, short. The story is terrifying and disturbing in its directness. It is so graphic that at times it is difficult to read. What emerges are questions of identity and what we think ourselves capable of. What we're left with is the notion that grief and hate can overtake us, no matter who we think we are." USA Today

Trocheck, Kathy Hogan

See also Andrews, Mary Kay, 1954-

Trollope, Anthony, 1815-1882

Barchester Towers. Knopf 1992 xxxiii, 277p $20

ISBN 0-679-40587-9 LC 91-53197

Trollope, Anthony, 1815-1882—*Continued*

First published 1857. Second of the Chronicles of Barsetshire

"Continues the picture of clerical society with its peculiar humors and foibles. The chief incidents are connected with the appointment of a new bishop, the troubles and disappointments this involves, and the intrigues and jealousies of the clergy: the henpecked bishop, the ambitious archdeacon, and the dean, canons, and others, with their wives. The picture of the eccentric Stanhope family is particularly delicious." Lenrow. Reader's Guide to Prose Fic

Followed by Doctor Thorne

Can you forgive her?; with an introduction by A.O.J. Cockshut. Knopf 1994 xxxiii, 447p $23

ISBN 0-679-43595-6 LC 94-6553

"Everyman's library"

First published 1864-65

This first of the Palliser novels "tells the interwoven stories of two women, Alice Vavasor and Lady Glencora M'Cluskie, who struggle to come to terms with the choices available to them concerning marriage." Merriam-Webster's Ency of Lit

Can you forgive her? [abridged]

In Trollope, A. The Pallisers p11-115

The complete shorter fiction; edited by Julian Thompson. Carroll & Graf Pubs. 1992 959p o.p.

Includes the following stories: Relics of General Chassé, a tale of Antwerp; The courtship of Susan Bell; The O'Conors of Castle Conor, County Mayo; La Mère Bauche; An unprotected female at the pyramids; The chateau of Prince Polignac; Miss Sarah Jack of Spanish Town, Jamaica; John Bull on the Guadalquivir; A ride across Palestine; Mrs. General Talboys; The parson's daughter of Oxney Colne; Returning home; The man who kept his money in a box; Aaron Trow; The House of Heine Brothers in Munich; George Walker at Suez; The mistletoe bough; The journey to Panama; The widow's mite; The two generals; Miss Ophelia Gledd; Malachi's Cove; Father Giles of Ballymoy; The geltle Euphemia; Lotta Schmidt; The adventures of Fred Pickering; The last Austrian who left Venice; The Turkish bath; Mary Gresley; Josephine de Montmorenci; The Panjandrum; The spotted dog; Mrs. Brumby; Christmas day at Kirkby Cottage; Christmas at Thompson Hall; Why Frau Frohmann raised her prices; The telegraph girl; The lady of Launay; Alice Dugdale; Catherine Carmichael; or, Three years running; The two heroines of Plumplington; Not if I know it

Doctor Thorne; with an introduction by N. John Hall. Knopf 1993 xxxi, 319p $20

ISBN 0-679-42304-4 LC 93-1853

"Everyman's library"

First published 1858. Third of the Chronicles of Barsetshire

"A story of quiet country life; and the interest of the book lies in the character studies rather than in the plot. The scene is laid in the west of England about 1854. The heroine, Mary Thorne, is a sweet, modest girl, living with her kind uncle Doctor Thorne, in the village of Greshambury, where Frank Gresham, the young heir of Greshambury Park, falls in love with her." Keller. Reader's Dig of Books

Followed by Framley parsonage

The Duke's children [abridged]

In Trollope, A. The Pallisers p387-437

The Eustace diamonds. Knopf 1992 xxxi, 249p $20

ISBN 0-679-41745-1 LC 92-52910

"Everyman's library"

First published 1872

The third Palliser novel. "The story follows two contrasting women and their courtships. Lizzie Eustace and Lucy Morris are both hampered in their love affairs by their lack of money. Lizzie's trickery and deceit, however, contrast with Lucy's constancy. Trollope was understood to be commenting on the malaise in Victorian England that allowed a character like Lizzie, who marries for money, steals the family diamonds, and behaves despicably throughout, to rise unscathed in society." Merriam-Webster's Ency of Lit

The Eustace diamonds [abridged]

In Trollope, A. The Pallisers p189-264

Framley parsonage; with an introduction by Graham Handley. Knopf 1994 xxxi, 587p $20

ISBN 0-679-43133-0

"Everyman's library"

First published 1861. Fourth of the Chronicles of Barsetshire

"The vicar of Framley, a weak but honest young man, is led astray and into debt by a spendthrift M. P., and finds himself in a false position. The other branch of the story deals with his sister's chequered love affair and marriage to young Lord Lufton. A great crowd of characters are engaged in the social functions, the intrigues and the match making, the general effect of which is comic, though graver interest is never far off, and there are situations of deepest pathos." Baker. Guide to the Best Fic

Followed by The small house at Allington

The last chronicle of Barset; with an introduction by Graham Handley. Knopf 1995 xxix, 983p $24

ISBN 0-679-44366-5 LC 95-75205

"Everyman's library"

First published 1867. Sixth in the Chronicles of Barsetshire

"The ecclesiastical society of 'The Warden,' Mr. Harding, Mrs. Proudie, and the rest make their last appearance. The dominant situation is one of intense anguish. A poor country clergyman, proud, learned, sternly conscientious is accused of a felony, and the pressure of family want makes his guilt seem only too probable." Baker. Guide to the Best Fic

The Pallisers; abridged and introduced by Michael Hardwick. Coward, McCann & Geoghegan 1975 c1974 436p o.p.

One volume abridgment of six "parliamentary novels"

Contents: Can you forgive her; Phineas Finn; The Eustace diamonds; Phineas Redux; The prime minister; The Duke's children

Phineas Finn [abridged]

In Trollope, A. The Pallisers p117-88

Phineas Redux [abridged]

In Trollope, A. The Pallisers p265-323

Trollope, Anthony, 1815-1882—*Continued*

The prime minister. o.p.

First published 1876

"Considered by modern critics to represent the apex of the 'Palliser novels', it is the fifth in the series and sustains two plot lines. One records the clash between the Duke of Omnium, now prime minister of a coalition government, and his high-spirited wife, Lady Glencora, whose drive to become the most brilliant hostess in society causes embarrassment for her husband and eventually contributes to his downfall. The second plot reveals the machinations of Ferdinand Lopez, an ambitious social climber who wins the support of Lady Glencora—but not her husband—for an election campaign. The novel brilliantly dissects the politics of both marriage and government." Merriam-Webster's Ency of Lit

The prime minister [abridged]

In Trollope, A. The Pallisers p325-85

The small house at Allington; with an introduction by A.O.J. Cockshut. Knopf 1997 xxix, 740p $23

ISBN 0-375-40067-2

"Everyman's library"

"Country life, its quiet, its pleasures and troubles, monotony and dullness, and with digressions into boarding-house life in London and into high society. Many old friends appear in the usual concourse of characters, among whom stand out Mr. Crosbie, a snobbish and cowardly trifler. . . . Lily Dale, the jilted maiden, amiable and weak Johnny Eames, and the aristocratic doll, Lady Dumbello; all closely copied from life." Baker. Guide to the Best Fic

Followed by The last chronicle of Barset

Trollope, Joanna

The best of friends. Viking 1998 293p $23.95

ISBN 0-670-87973-8 LC 97-49162

First published 1995 in the United Kingdom

"Whittingbourne is one of those charming English towns where families live happily ever after. Gina and Fergus, Hillary and Laurance have grown up, married, and raised their children in the warmth of amiable friendship. But one day it all unravels as Fergus calmly leaves Gina to share his life with a young man in London, and Laurance nearly chucks it all to move to France with Gina in the heat of passion. Their children are devastated and beset with emerging passions of their own." Libr J

"Trollope's facility at spinning an intricate story is enhanced by light-fingered dialogue, and the lesson she spins in this tale of easy pleasure and its complicated aftermath is both sobering and hopeful." Publ Wkly

Brother and sister; Joanna Trollope. 1st U.S. ed. Bloomsbury 2004 311p $23.95

ISBN 1-582-34400-0 LC 2003-62649

"Born to two different mothers but adopted together and raised as brother and sister, David and Nathalie are fiercely close. Even their spouses acknowledge their unique bond, forged by the belief that they are special—'chosen' by each other, though born to different parents. They aren't much concerned about the circumstances of their births until the girlfriend of David's colleague asks them to contact their birth mothers as part of her thesis research. Their decision to do so profoundly affects their lives and the lives of those close to them. When their mothers, who have gone on to have families, finally acknowledge their youthful indiscretions and meet David and Nathalie as adults, it sets off a ripple effect that nearly destroys all the families involved." Libr J

"Trollope is a pointillist of domestic relationships, and she has built an impressive body of work addressing powerful tensions like those that animate Brother and Sister. With well-placed strokes, she brings to life all of her characters, including the complex lives of the birth mothers. She's especially accomplished in her portrayals of children by turns humorous, frustrating or heartbreaking, but never precious." Washington Post Book World

The choir. Random House 1995 261p o.p.

LC 95-11612

First published 1993 in the United Kingdom

"The all-boy choir at Aldminster Cathedral is blessed with a cheerfully ferocious choirmaster, a magnificent seventeenth-century organ, and a celestial new treble in the earthly guise of eleven-year-old Henry Ashworth. But the choir also costs the diocese more than fifty thousand pounds a year, which the dean thinks might be better spent elsewhere—on new lighting, perhaps—and a delicious cathedral-town battle about tradition and privilege ensues. Almost all the characters in this companionable novel are on speaking terms with God, but His will, while frequently consulted, is variously interpreted." New Yorker

Legacy of love; {by} Joanna Trollope writing as Caroline Harvey. Viking 2000 385p o.p.

ISBN 0-670-89181-9 LC 00-36791

"A novel in three parts featuring three generations of daring Englishwomen from the same family who challenge societal mores to pursue love and passion. Although unexceptional in its writing and plot, the book reveals Harvey's vast knowledge of travel and history, from Victorian England and British-ruled Afghanistan to World War II." Libr J

Marrying the mistress. Viking 2000 293p o.p.

ISBN 0-670-89150-9 LC 99-462175

"When a respectable judge named Guy Stockdale decides to leave his 40-year marriage to take up with his longtime mistress, his grown sons warily prepare to weather the consequences. Simon, his mother's favorite, takes her side, and Alan, Simon's gay brother, assumes his usual posture of good-natured temperance. But neither Guy's mistress, Merrion, nor Laura, his left-behind wife, are conventional types, and neither plays her expected role." N Y Times Book Rev

"None of the themes here . . . are terribly unusual, but Trollope's proven ability to present them intelligently, as moral and emotional tangles faced by thinking, interesting people, satisfyingly combines the universally recognizable and the intellectually engaging." Publ Wkly

The men and the girls. Random House 1993 c1992 248p o.p.

LC 93-18421

First published 1992 in the United Kingdom

Oxford is the setting for a "story of the intimate and suddenly volatile relationships of two former school friends, now past 60 years of age. James lives with Kate (who is thirtysomething), her teenage daughter (nose earring, shorn head, black boots, etc.), and crochety Uncle

Trollope, Joanna—*Continued*

Leonard. Hugh's wife, Julia, also thirtyish, is the mother of young twins. Into the very settled lives of these two households comes Beatrice, an elderly spinster, knocked off her bicycle by James' car." Booklist

"One of the pleasures in good contemporary British fiction like 'The Men and the Girls' is the writing itself—deft, fluid, perceptive and concise. Another is the wonderfully wry humor, particularly when its objects are sacred cows. Like Muriel Spark, Joanna Trollope is hilarious about old people, for instance." N Y Times Book Rev

Next of kin. Viking 2001 289p $23.95

ISBN 0-670-89999-2 LC 2001-17743

This novel begins "with the funeral of Caro Meredith, wife of a dairy farmer in the English Midlands. Caro's death is merely the prelude, however, to a series of shattering events for those she left behind—from husband Robin and daughter Judy, a magazine 'subeditor,' to brother-in-law Joe and his wife, Lyndsay, to Robin's parents, Dilys and Harry. The arrival of Judy's unconventional roommate, Zoe, brings a measure of openness to this emotionally closed family and gives Robin some small amount of the love that he lacked throughout his marriage." Libr J

"In addition to crafting an absorbing narrative, Trollope charms with her depiction of several young children, whose speech and behavior are captured with clarity and endearing fidelity." Publ Wkly

Other people's children. Viking 1999 294p $23.95

ISBN 0-670-88513-4 LC 98-40004

"Falling in love with a man does not mean falling in love with his children: that is the premise of this story of linked and sundered families. Josie's second marriage includes three stepchildren, whose loyalty to their inadequate mother makes them hate Josie for her very competence; Elizabeth's beloved fiancé comes with a son she adores and a grown daughter determined to oust her. Trollope may not aim high, but she aims for the heart, and she hits it." New Yorker

The rector's wife. Random House 1994 287p o.p.

LC 94-20625

First published 1991 in the United Kingdom

The provincial English "rector in *The Rector's Wife*, Peter Bouverie, has spent his life and defined his ministry according to what other people think, and he expects his family to do the same. . . . The turning point comes early in the story, when Peter is passed over for a much hoped-for appointment to the position of archdeacon. When his career hits dead end, it becomes bitterly clear that he has no inner resources or satisfying relationships to fall back on. In his marriage and ministry, Peter has dried up. Anna, too, is on the verge of either drying up or going mad. As her frustration deepens over Peter's disappointment and the estrangement between them, she decides to change her life. She begins to carve out small spaces of independence from the parish by transferring their daughter to a Catholic school, taking a job at a local supermarket and, finally, seeking the love absent in her marriage with the brother of the new archdeacon." Christ Century

A Spanish lover. Random House 1996 c1993 334p o.p.

LC 96-24846

First published 1993 in the United Kingdom

"Lizzie has been rather smug about her thriving marriage, her four children, her successful shop, and her big house, but she becomes unconscionably jealous when Frances, her quiet, devoted twin, finds love with the sexy, supportive, but married—and foreign—Luis. This British author excels at setting up the stuff of female fantasy and, from those worn materials, making something that draws you in and slams you with a thud of emotion so authentic it becomes your own." New Yorker

Trotter, William R.

The sands of pride; a novel of the Civil War. Carroll & Graf Pubs. 2002 754p $28

ISBN 0-7867-1013-6 LC 2002-22697

"Opening on New Year's Eve 1860, almost six months before North Carolina's grudging decision to secede from the Union of May 20, 1861, this sprawling account revolves around the bustling seaport of Wilmington, which serves as the lifeline of the Confederacy, Jefferson Davis; the architect of Fort Fisher, Col. William Lamb; Lafayette Baker, deputy director of the fledgling Secret Service; Gen. Robert E. Lee; Gen. Ambrose Burnside; and the naval commander William Barker Cushing are some of the real-life historic figures that are artfully integrated with an extensive dramatis personae of flamboyant and idiosyncratic fictional character." Publ Wkly

Truman, Margaret, 1924-

Murder at Ford's Theatre. Ballantine Bks. 2002 326p $24.95

ISBN 0-345-44489-2 LC 2002-74748

"When the body of congressional intern Nadia Zarinski turns up outside the stage door of Ford's Theatre, D.C. police detectives Mo Johnson and Rick Klayman, who happens to be a Lincoln buff, are assigned the case. Nadia worked in the office of Senator Bruce Lerner, ex-husband of Clarise Emerson, head of Ford's Theatre and nominee for chair of the National Endowment for the Arts. Once Clarise determines with Klayman's help that her son, Jeremiah, was the last to see Nadia alive, she appeals to former attorney Mackensie 'Mac' Smith to represent him." Publ Wkly

Murder at the Library of Congress. Random House 1999 322p $25

ISBN 0-375-50068-5 LC 99-14953

"Pre-Columbian art expert Annabel Smith has been asked to write an article on a second diary of Columbus' voyage—if such an artifact really exists. Her research takes her into the inner workings of LC and leads to the discovery of illicit payoffs and the solutions to a pair of murders, one old, one new." Booklist

Murder at the National Cathedral. Random House 1990 293p o.p.

LC 89-43433

Sleuth Mackensie Smith "and his lover, Annabel Reed, have just been married. Then the Episcopal priest who performed the service is murdered, and criminal law professor Smith launches his investigation. . . . Links be-

Truman, Margaret, 1924-—*Continued*
tween a world peace organization, federal and international spy networks, scorned lovers, activist priests, and distraught choir boys are . . . interwoven into the plot." Booklist

Murder at the Watergate; a novel. Random House 1998 333p $25
ISBN 0-679-43535-2 LC 98-3725
Vice President Joseph Aprile, "is determined to stake out a position on Mexico different from his president's as he prepares to seek the Oval Office in the next election. Mackensie Smith, law professor at George Washington University and a friend of Aprile's is in an ideal position to help, since he is already scheduled to be in Mexico as a U.N. election observer. When Mackensie accepts a clandestine assignment to meet with a Mexican rebel leader on Aprile's behalf, he is launched into a dangerous and deadly game involving diplomats and assassins, politicians and traitors, aristocrats and rebels." Publ Wkly

Murder in Havana. Random House 2001 322p $24.95
ISBN 0-375-50070-7 LC 2001-19079
Ex-CIA agent Max Pauling "gets talked into a supposedly quick and easy job in Cuba. A German pharmaceutical company is trying to buy into Cuba's remarkably advanced cancer research. Pauling's job is to find proof that the German firm is acting as a front for an American company. In traditional spy novel fashion, just about everything that could go wrong does, and Pauling must use his wits, skills and luck to avoid the pitfalls caused by the dealings and double-dealings of various factions." Publ Wkly

Murder in the White House; a novel. Arbor House 1980 235p o.p.
LC 79-54004
"When Secretary of State Blaine is murdered in the Lincoln Sitting Room of the White House, President Webster orders Special Counsel Fairchild to coordinate efforts to solve the case with the authorities. The lawyer turned detective begins investigating everyone with access to the White House, including Webster, the First Lady and her daughter Lynne." Publ Wkly

Murder on Capitol Hill; a novel. Arbor House 1981 255p o.p.
LC 80-70223
"Lawyer Lydia James agrees to the request of Veronica Caldwell to act as counsel for the senatorial committee investigating the killing of her husband, Senate Majority leader Cale Caldwell. He has been stabbed at a reception honoring him, where his black-sheep son Mark, member of a fanatical cult, is among the 200 or more guests. Mark is arrested for the murder, and also on suspicion of having killed Jimmye, Veronica's niece, years earlier, an unsolved crime. His mother and brother, Cale Jr., sorrowfully agree that Mark is guilty, but Lydia believes the charges are trumped up. She gets herself into dicey situations, chasing clues." Publ Wkly

Trumbo, Dalton, 1905-1976

Johnny got his gun. Lippincott 1939 309p o.p.
"Far more than an antiwar polemic, this compassionate description of the effects of war on one soldier is a poignant tribute to the human instinct to survive. Badly mutilated, blind, and deaf, Johnny fights to communicate with an uncomprehending medical world debating his fate." Shapiro. Fic for Youth. 3d edition

Truong, Monique T. D.

The book of salt; [by] Monique Truong. Houghton Mifflin 2003 261p $24
ISBN 0-618-30400-2 LC 2002-192152
"From a few lines in The Alice B. Toklas Cook Book, Truong reimagines the Vietnamese cook who was hired by the famous residents at 27 Rue de Fleurus. Binh, as he calls himself, is an exile from his homeland, where he was denounced because of a homosexual relationship and banished by his brutal father. After three years at sea, Binh ends up in Paris, where he answers Toklas's ad. . . and enters the household of Gertrude Stein." Publ Wkly
"Truong is tapping some trendy territory here: the postcolonial perspective; the book derived from a minor character in another well-known book. . .; the gay novel; the novel of exile. And Truong's central character, the gay Asian houseboy, is something of a stereotype in itself. But nothing in this distinctive novel feels secondhand." N Y Times Book Rev

Truscott, Lucian K., 1947-

Dress gray; [by] Lucian K. Truscott IV. Doubleday 1979 c1978 489p o.p.
LC 78-1250
A West Point "plebe is found drowned; information, quickly suppressed, indicates he was murdered; a cadet, one Rysam Parker Slaight III, gets wind of the coverup and finds himself in trouble with the coverup authorities, a group of West Point officers and some powerful cronies at the Pentagon." New Yorker
Followed by Full dress gray

Full dress gray; [by] Lucian K. Truscott IV. Morrow 1998 384p $25
ISBN 0-688-15993-1 LC 98-4320
In this sequel to Dress gray, Ry Slaight "returns to West Point 30 years later as its newly appointed superintendent. His daughter Jacey is a company commander in the cadet corps. When one of her plebes dies during dress parade, Jacey sets out to find the cause of her death. Not even a brutal assault by fellow cadets stops her in her quest. The investigation leads to the army's highest circles and uncovers a conspiracy to subvert the cadets' treasured Honor Code. The result is a thoroughly satisfying mystery story with an uncommon setting." Libr J

Heart of war. Dutton 1997 370p o.p.
LC 96-29876
The protagonist of this thriller is "Maj. Kara Guldry, a lawyer and West Point graduate who is assigned to investigate the murder of a Lt. Sheila Worthy. Kara soon discovers that the young woman's lover was none other than General Beckwith, the base commander. After her friend, Lannie Love, another Beckwith mistress, is stabbed in a similar manner, Kara is convinced that Beckwith is the key to the murders." Libr J
"Despite some occasionally breathy prose, Truscott's novel provides a fascinating peek behind the olive drab curtain, blending a solid plot with a piercing critique of hypocrisy, power politics and sexual misconduct in today's armed forces." N Y Times Book Rev

Tryon, Thomas

In the fire of spring. Knopf 1991 609p o.p.
LC 91-414

In this sequel to The wings of the morning "a runaway slave, Rose Mills, is helped to safety by the abolitionist Appleton Talcott and two of his daughters as they return home to Pequot Landing. . . . The Talcotts and the slave-owning Grimes family are still feuding, but it's now 1841, and fuel has been added to the fire. First of all, the Talcotts open a school for young black women, which gives the Grimeses something new to holler about. Second, Appleton's wife, Mabel Talcott, is secretly dying. As she ponders her mortality and worries about her children, her dying wish is granted: daughter Aurora, abroad for years with husband and child, returns home. Mab's heart breaks as she learns of her daughter's travails and of her undying love for the true father of her child—none other than the swashbuckling, lady-killing Sinjin Grimes." Booklist

The other. Knopf 1971 280p o.p.

"Bizarre events occur in and around the once-prosperous Perry family in Connecticut during the 1930s. The men have all died mysteriously and brutally. Niles and Holland, 12-year-old twins, seem to be linked to the ghastly deaths and disasters. A compassionate Russian grandmother plays along with Niles's deception and tries to protect him." Shapiro. Fic for Youth. 3d edition

The wings of the morning. Knopf 1990 567p o.p.
LC 89-39513

"Set in the 1820s and 1830s in the small Connecticut town of Pequot Landing, the novel tells of the feud between the town's two first families—the Talcotts and the Grimeses. The link between the two families is the miller's daughter, Georgie Ross—childhood friend to the rakish Sinjin Grimes and former servant and close friend to the Talcotts. Georgie is a levelheaded, independent heroine and her experiences highlight the conditions of women in that time." Libr J

"Unalloyed pleasure for fans of this genre, Tryon's literate 19th-century soap opera is steeped in the rhythms of Trollope and Scott." Publ Wkly

Followed by In the fire of spring

Tsukiyama, Gail

Dreaming water. St. Martin's Press 2002 288p $23.95
ISBN 0-312-20607-0 LC 2001-58896

"At 38, Hana Murayama is dying of Werner's syndrome, a genetic defect that causes premature aging. Hana is almost totally dependent on her mother, Cata, who at 62 is still recovering from the sudden death of her husband, Max. . . . Over the course of two days, Hana and Cate retrace in memory their lives and Max's. Their scattered and sometimes conflicting expectations are brought into sharp focus when Hana's best friend, Laura, now a successful East Coast lawyer, arrives with her two daughters, Hana's godchildren, allowing Hana and Cate to find a measure of the reconciliation that has eluded them." Publ Wkly

T͡Sypkin, Leonid, 1926-1982

Summer in Baden-Baden; a novel; translated from the Russian by Roger and Angela Keys; introduction by Susan Sontag. New Directions 2001 xxi, 146p $23.95
ISBN 0-8112-1484-2 LC 2001-32658

Originally serialized 1982 in Russian emigré weekly; this translation first published 1987 in the United Kingdom

This novel "opens with the unnamed narrator (Tsypkin) bound once more for Leningrad. . . . A century earlier, in the hot summer of 1867, the Dostoyevskys headed for the writers much coveted roulette tables at a German spa in the same carriage that is now taking the narrator across frosty Russia. Tsypkin's story shifts back and forth in time and crosses the borders of several genres." New Leader

"Tsypkin's stream-of-consciousness prose style is associative, inclusive, allusive, detached and yet humane." N Y Times Book Rev

Turgenev, Ivan Sergeevich, 1818-1883

Fathers and sons; a new translation by Michael R. Katz. Norton 1994 157p $25
ISBN 0-393-03559-X LC 92-40010

Original Russian edition, 1862. Variant title: Fathers and children

This novel "concerns the inevitable conflict between generations and between the values of traditionalists and intellectuals. The physician Bazarov, the novel's protagonist, is the most powerful of Turgenev's creations. He is a nihilist, denying the validity of all laws save those of the natural sciences. Uncouth and forthright in his opinions, he is nonetheless susceptible to love and by that fact doomed to unhappiness. In sociopolitical terms he represents the victory of the revolutionary nongentry intelligentsia over the gentry intelligentsia to which Turgenev belonged." Merriam-Webster's Ency of Lit

First love and other stories; [by] Ivan Turgenev; translated by Isaiah Berlin and Leonard Schapiro; introduced by V.S. Pritcett. Knopf 1994 xxxvii, 253p $17
ISBN 0-679-43594-8 LC 94-6233

"Everyman's library"

Contents: First love; Spring torrents; A fire at sea

Spring torrents [variant title: The torrents of spring]

In Turgenev, I. S. First love and other stories

The torrents of spring; [by] Ivan Turgenev; illustrated by Valentin Popov; translated by Ivy and Tatiana Litvonov. Grove Press 1996 174p il $25
ISBN 0-8021-1594-2 LC 96-14697

Original Russian edition, 1872. Variant title: Spring torrents

This classic Russian novel "is a love story beautifully and simply told: a young Russian nobleman, Dimitry Sanin, falls in love with a pure and sweet girl, Gemma, but through unforeseen circumstances and his own weakness he forsakes her for a sensual woman of the world, Maria Nikolayevna, for whom men are mere playthings of the moment. He does so in spite of being fully aware

Turgenev, Ivan Sergeevich, 1818-1883—*Continued*

that this liaison will bring him nothing but ruin and humiliation. . . . This short novel has no political overtones and deals only with the emotional experiences of the characters." Libr J

Turner, Frederick W., 1937-

1929; [by] Frederick Turner. Counterpoint Bks. 2003 390p $25

ISBN 1-58243-265-1 LC 2002-154007

"A brilliant cornet player with an amazing ear, [Bix Beiderbecke] drank himself to death at the age of 28 with illegal Prohibition liquor. . . . Turner offers a fictional take on Beiderbecke's life, giving readers a . . . picture of what life was like for jazz musicians in the years leading up to the Great Depression." Publ Wkly

"Written in a period-appropriate overheated, romantic prose, and incorporating memorable appearances by Capone, Bing Crosby, Maurice Ravel, Paul Whiteman, and Clara Bow, the book is by turns corny, intoxicating, and ineffably sad, like the 'hot' music it is designed to evoke." New Yorker

Turner, Nancy E., 1953-

These is my words; the diary of Sarah Agnes Prine, 1881-1901. ReganBooks 1998 384p $23

ISBN 0-06-039225-8 LC 97-37622

"Based on the real-life exploits of the author's great-grandmother, this fictionalized diary . . . details one woman's struggles with life and love in frontier Arizona at the end of the last century. When she begins recording her life, Sarah Prine is an intelligent, headstrong 18-year-old capable of holding her own on her family's settlement near Tucson. Her skill with a rifle fends off a constant barrage of Indian attacks and outlaw assaults. it also attracts a handsome Army captain named Jack Elliot. By the time she's 21, Sarah has recorded her loveless marriage to a family friend, the establishment of a profitable ranch, the birth of her first child—and the death of her husband. The love between Jack and Sarah, which dominates the rest of the tale, has begun to blossom." Publ Wkly

"The language is rich and fine, sounding true to its time without being precious." Booklist

Turow, Scott

The burden of proof. Farrar, Straus & Giroux 1990 515p $22.95

ISBN 0-374-11734-9 LC 90-33593

Lawyer Sandy Stern featured in Presumed innocent "returns home to find his wife has committed suicide. Stern is currently involved in the defense of his brother-in-law, Dixon, who is accused of shady doings on the commodities market; also involved are Stern's daughter and her husband." Libr J

"The plotting is clear and clean, spun out with Greek inevitability and the niceties of law and finance are lucidly, smoothly, explained. Stern's complex character is well-drawn . . . and the members of his family are individualized and believable. The Federal judges and prosecutors have unique backgrounds and prejudices. Even the minor characters are given faces and personalities." America

The laws of our fathers. Farrar, Straus & Giroux 1996 533p $26.95

ISBN 0-374-18423-2 LC 96-16104

In this legal thriller, "the wife of a state senator has been killed in a drive-by shooting, and Judge Sonia Klonsky is presiding over the trial of the victim's son, who has been accused of masterminding the murder. Most of the protagonists have crossed paths decades before, when they were campus radicals, and there are some distinctly unconvincing flashbacks to the apocalptic days of '69. Still, as the novel gathers momentum it reveals a complex portrait, in which children are forced to live in the shadow of their parents, and chastened middle-aged idealists must reckon with the enthusiasms and sins of their youth." New Yorker

Ordinary heroes. Farrar, Straus & Giroux 2005 384p $25

ISBN 0-374-18421-6 LC 2005-11824

"Stewart Dubinsky is not especially close to his father, David Dubin. Even their names are different, yet David's death prompts Stewart to try and find out more about this enigmatic man. He uncovers some startling information: that his father was engaged to another woman before his mother, and that he was court-martialed during the Battle of the Bulge. Dubinsky decides to write a family history, starts digging, and uncovers a manuscript his father wrote about his war experiences that is alternately moving and horrifying, vindicating, and vilifying and shines light on a side of his parents that he never knew. While some of the historical facts presented are not 100 percent accurate, the book's emotional wallop more than justifies the literary license and should secure its place in the canon of World War II literature." Libr J

Personal injuries. Farrar, Straus & Giroux 1999 403p $27

ISBN 0-374-28194-7 LC 99-30829

"U.S. Attorney Stan Sennett has set his sights on a powerful group of corrupt judges, vowing to prosecute them at any cost. With the help of the FBI, he devises a set of legal traps designed to produce the evidence he needs to convict. The centerpiece of this subversion is Robbie Feaver, a Kindle County personal injury lawyer nabbed for tax evasion by Sennett. . . . Densely packed and tightly constructed, this tangle of human relationships and legal machinations will have Turow fans burning the midnight oil." SLJ

Pleading guilty. Farrar, Straus & Giroux 1993 386p o.p.

LC 93-70819

This novel is narrated by Mack Mallone, a former policeman and now a partner in the law firm of Gage & Griswell. "The firm's senior partners offered him an ultimatum: find the associate who has been embezzling millions of dollars from the firm's lifeblood client, or it's adios. As Mack searches, he encounters his former partner from the police force, nicknamed Pigeyes, who, because Mack testified against him on charges of pocketing cash during busts, is now a private investigator." Booklist

Turow is "genuinely interested in showing what makes his characters behave the way they do. . . . Pleading Guilty is both an irresistible tale and a dark, moral thriller." Time

Turow, Scott—*Continued*

Presumed innocent. Farrar, Straus & Giroux 1987 431p $30

ISBN 0-374-23713-1 LC 87-368

"Rusty Sabich, the chief deputy prosecuting attorney assigned to investigate the murder of his co-worker and former lover, Carolyn Polhemus, is the narrator who draws us into the world of big-city crime and law enforcement as seen through a lawyer's eyes. Because his boss, Raymond Horgan, the Prosecuting Attorney in this unnamed Midwestern city, is up for re-election, Carolyn's murder has become a political issue, and the heat is on Rusty to bring in the killer as soon as he can." N Y Times Book Rev

This novel contains "high drama and suspense, as scenes in and out of the courtroom crackle with the amazing interactions of complex, fascinating characters. This is a great book." Libr J

Reversible errors. Farrar, Straus & Giroux 2002 433p il $28

ISBN 0-374-28160-2 LC 2002-70891

"In 1991, three people were brutally murdered in a Kindle County diner. Prosecutor Muriel Wynn and detective Larry Starczek ferreted out Rommy Gandolf, who soon confessed to the crime. Ten years later, Rommy is on death row, just weeks away from his execution. Arthur Raven has been appointed as his lawyer, but he can't imagine that anything new will turn up despite Rommy's claims of innocence. Then Erno Erdai steps forward." Booklist

"What Turow has done, in book after book, is to give us page turners that are also pleasing literary artifacts, mysteries that are also investigations into coomplex human emotions." N Y Times Book Rev

Turtledove, Harry

Into the darkness. Doherty Assocs. 1999 540p o.p.

ISBN 0-312-86895-2 LC 98-43610

"A Tom Doherty Associates book"

First title in the author's Alternate world fantasy series. "In the beginning, militarily efficient Algarve occupies the Duchy of Bari . . . and is quickly followed by one of Algarve's traditional foes, Unkerlant. . . . Throughout, World War II buffs will search for further reflections in Turtledove's fantastic mirror, but they will also, like other readers, be quickly caught up in the sheer ingenuity of the tale, in which dragons provide airpower, behemoths (think rhinoceroses the size of elephants) are tanks, magic wands take the place of rifles, and submarine warfare is in the hands of leviathan-riders." Booklist

Rulers of the darkness. TOR Bks. 2002 576p il $27.95

ISBN 0-7653-0036-2 LC 2001-58465

"A Tom Doherty Associates book"

Sequel to : Through the darkness

"The fourth volume of the alternate-history saga Darkness deals with the fourth year of a World War II. . . . Kuusamo's sorcerous Manhattan Project has the potential to generate destructive energy by drawing on the past and the future, which is the same way the Algarvians use the life energy of murdered Kaunians. Meanwhile, more conventional counteroffensives against Algarve are in progress, with Unkerlant and Algarve reaching a gigantic confrontation in a battle recognizable as a re-imagining of the Battle of Kursk. One need not, however, be able to run down all of Turtledove's real-world parallels to appreciate how well he presents the human dilemmas of global warfare." Booklist

(jt. auth) Tarr, J. Household gods

Twain, Mark, 1835-1910

The adventures of Huckleberry Finn. Modern Library 1993 xx, 433p $16.95

ISBN 0-679-42470-9 LC 92-51065

First published 1885. This is a companion volume to: The adventures of Tom Sawyer

This novel "begins with Huck's escape from his drunken, brutal father to the river, where he meets up with Jim, a runaway slave. The story of their journey downstream, with occasional forays into the society along the banks, is an American classic that captures the smells, rhythms, and sounds, the variety of dialects and the human activity of life on the great river. It is also a penetrating social commentary that reveals corruption, moral decay, and intellectual impoverishment through Huck and Jim's encounters with traveling actors and con men, lynch mobs, thieves, and Southern gentility." Reader's Ency. 4th edition

also in Twain, M. Mississippi writings

The adventures of Tom Sawyer; [illustrated by True W. Williams]; foreword and notes by John C. Gerber; text established by Paul Baender. University of California Press 2002 c1982 274p il pa $14.95

ISBN 0-520-23575-4

First published 1876. This is a companion volume to: The adventures of Huckleberry Finn

"Tom, a shrewd and adventurous boy, is at home in the respectable world of his Aunt Polly, as well as in the self-reliant, parentless world of Huck Finn. The two friends, out in the cemetery under a full moon, attempt to cure warts with a dead cat. They accidentally witness a murder, of which Muff Potter is later wrongly accused. Knowing that the true murderer is Injun Joe, the boys are helpless with fear; they decide to run away to Jackson's Island. After a few pleasant days of smoking and swearing, they realize that the townspeople believe them dead. Returning in time to hear their funeral eulogies, they become town heroes. At the trial of Muff Potter, Tom, unable to let an innocent person be condemned, reveals his knowledge. Injun Joe flees. Later Tom and his sweetheart, Becky Thatcher, get lost in the cave in which the murderer is hiding. They escape, and Tom and Huck return to find the treasure Joe has buried." Reader's Ency. 4th edition

also in Twain, M. The adventures of Tom Sawyer, Tom Sawyer abroad, Tom Sawyer, detective p31-236

also in Twain, M. Mississippi writings

The adventures of Tom Sawyer, Tom Sawyer abroad, Tom Sawyer, detective; edited by John C. Gerber, Paul Baender, and Terry Firkins. University of Calif. Press 1980 717p il o.p.

LC 76-47974

A combined edition of three Tom Sawyer titles first published 1876, 1894 and 1896, respectively

Twain, Mark, 1835-1910—*Continued*

The American claimant

In Twain, M. The gilded age and later novels

The complete novels of Mark Twain; edited with an introduction by Charles Neider. Doubleday 1964 2v o.p.

Contents: v1: The gilded age (1873); The adventures of Tom Sawyer (1876); The prince and the pauper (1881); Adventures of Huckleberry Finn (1881)

v2: A Connecticut Yankee in King Arthur's court (1889); The American claimant (1892); Tom Sawyer abroad (1894); Pudd'nhead Wilson (1894); Those extraordinary twins (1894); Personal recollections of Joan of Arc (1896); Tom Sawyer, detective (1896)

The complete short stories of Mark Twain; now collected for the first time; edited with an introduction by Charles Neider. Doubleday 1957 xxiv, 676p o.p.

"The sixty pieces which are here hospitably called short stories illustrate both the weaknesses and the strengths of Mark Twain as a writer of fiction." N Y Times Book Rev

A Connecticut Yankee in King Arthur's court; edited by Bernard L. Stein; with an introd. by Henry Nash Smith. Published for the Iowa Center for Textual Studies by the University of California Press 1979 827p il $75

ISBN 0-520-03621-2 LC 77-91761

First published 1889; published in the United Kingdom with title: Yankee at the court of King Arthur

This satiric novel is a "tale of a commonsensical Yankee who is carried back in time to Britain in the Dark Ages, and it celebrates homespun ingenuity and democratic values in contrast to the superstitious ineptitude of a feudal monarchy." Merriam-Webster's Ency of Lit

also in Twain, M. Historical romances

The gilded age; [by] Mark Twain and C. D. Warner. o.p.

First published 1873

"Mark Twain and Dudley Warner were neighbours at Hartford, Conn., when they collaborated in this portrayal of their times; the bitter account of the Easterners is Warner's; the humorist drew the Westerners, scoffed at Washington and Congress, and created the mighty optimist Colonel Sellers." Baker. Guide to the Best Fic

also in Twain, M. The gilded age and later novels

The gilded age and later novels; .; Mark Twain. Library of America, Distributed to the trade in the United States by Penguin Putnam 2002 1053p (The library of America, 130) $40

ISBN 1-931082-10-3 LC 2001-38053

Contents: The gilded age; The American claimant; Tom Sawyer abroad; Tom Sawyer, detective; No. 44, the mysterious stranger

The gilded age is entered separately. In The American claimant (1892), an English viscount travels to America in search of an heir to his father's earldom. There he meets the primary claimant to the title, an eccentric yet good natured inventor, Colonel Mulberry Sanders. In Tom Sawyer abroad (1994), Tom, Huck Finn, and Jim take a trip via balloon across the Atlantic to the Sahara desert. In Tom Sawyer, detective (1896), Tom and Huck solve a complex murder mystery involving a diamond theft and Tom's Uncle Silas. No. 44, the mysterious stranger (1969) is a different version of the posthumously published The mysterious stranger, based on Twain's final manuscript. This version, set in Eseldorf, Austria in 1490, features "a likable young printer's devil, called only No. 44, who is possessed of satanic powers that allow him to master the craft of printing in a few hours. Singlehandedly he speedily produces a Bible and magically summons up phantasmagoric people to print innumerable copies." Oxford Companion to Am Lit. 6th edition

Historical romances; The prince and the pauper, A Connecticut Yankee in King Arthur's court, Personal recollections of Joan of Arc; [notes by Susan K. Harris] Library of Am. 1994 1029p maps (Library of America, 71) $35

ISBN 0-940450-82-8 LC 93-40246

Contents: The prince and the pauper; A Connecticut Yankee in King Arthur's court; Personal recollections of Joan of Arc

In The prince and the pauper (1882), a prince, Edward VI, switches clothes with Tom Canty, a poor boy who looks exactly like him. When the two are discovered, Edward is mistakenly driven from the castle and forced to endure Tom's harsh, impoverished life while Tom experiences Edward's life as royalty. A Connecticut Yankee in King Arthur's court and Personal recollections of Joan of Arc are entered separately.

The man that corrupted Hadleyburg, and other stories and essays. Harper 1900 364p o.p.

Contents: The man that corrupted Hadleyburg; My début as a literary person; £1,000,000 bank-note; Esquimau maiden's romance; My first lie, and how I got out of it; Belated Russian passport; Two little tales; About play-acting; Diplomatic pay and clothes; Is he living or is he dead?; My boyhood dreams; Austrian Edison keeping school again; Death disk; Double-barreled detective story; Petition to the Queen of England

Mississippi writings. Literary Classics of the United States 1982 1084p $30

ISBN 0-940450-07-0 LC 82-9917

Contents: The adventures of Tom Sawyer; Life on the Mississippi; Adventures of Huckleberry Finn; Pudd'nhead Wilson

The adventures of Tom Sawyer, The adventures of Huckleberry Finn, and Pudd'nhead Wilson are entered separately. Life on the Mississippi (1883) is an autobiographical narrative that focuses on the author's childhood near the river.

Mysterious stranger, and other stories. Harper 1922 324p il o.p.

Contents: Mysterious stranger; Horse's tale; Extract from Captain Stormfield's visit to Heaven; Fable; My platonic sweetheart; Hunting the deceitful turkey; McWilliamses and the burglar alarm

No. 44, The mysterious stranger

In Twain, M. The gilded age and later novels

Twain, Mark, 1835-1910—*Continued*

Personal recollections of Joan of Arc; by the Sieur Louis de Conte (her page and secretary); illustrated by G. B. Cutts. Harper 1926 596p il o.p.

First published 1896

"De Conte, who tells the story in the first person, has been reared in the same village with its subject, has been her daily playmate there, and has followed her fortunes in later life, serving her to the end, his being the friendly hand that she touches last. After her death, he comes to understand her greatness; he calls hers 'the most noble life that was ever born into this world save only One.' Beginning with a scene in her childhood that shows her innate sense of justice, goodness of heart, and unselfishness, the story follows her throughout her stormy career. We have her audiences with the king; her marches with her army; her entry into Orleans; her fighting; her trial; her execution; all simply and naturally and yet vividly told. The historical facts are closely followed." Keller. Reader's Dig of Books

also in Twain, M. Historical romances

The prince and the pauper

In Twain, M. Historical romances

Pudd'nhead Wilson. o.p.

First published 1894 with title: The tragedy of Pudd'nhead Wilson

"David Wilson is called 'Pudd'nhead' by the townspeople, who fail to understand his combination of wisdom and eccentricity. He redeems himself by simultaneously solving a murder mystery and a case of transposed identities. The mystery revolves around two children, a white boy and a mulatto, who are born on the same day. . . . The book is an implicit condemnation of a society that allows slavery. It also includes a series of brilliant epigrams which are distillations of Twain's wit and wisdom." Reader's Ency. 4th edition

also in Twain, M. Mississippi writings

Tom Sawyer abroad

In Twain, M. The adventures of Tom Sawyer, Tom Sawyer abroad, Tom Sawyer, detective p251-341

In Twain, M. The gilded age and later novels

Tom Sawyer, detective

In Twain, M. The adventures of Tom Sawyer, Tom Sawyer abroad, Tom Sawyer, detective p357-415

In Twain, M. The gilded age and later novels

Tweedsmuir, John Buchan, Baron *See* Buchan, John, 1875-1940

Two hundred years of great American short stories. See 200 years of great American short stories

Tyler, Anne, 1941-

The accidental tourist. Knopf 1985 355p o.p.
LC 85-40161

"After 20 years of marriage, Macon and Sarah separate. Thus, a man used to intense order in his life finds his existence thrown into disorder; forced to create a new life for himself, Macon must overcome numerous obstacles—particularly his inability to communicate, to relate to other people's needs and problems." Booklist

"Thanks to her inimitable mix of an extraordinary inventiveness with characters and a profound humanity, Tyler makes this book a joy to read." Wilson Libr Bull

The amateur marriage; a novel. Knopf 2004 306p $24.95

ISBN 1-400-04207-0 LC 2003-59536

This novel presents a portrait of the six-decade marriage of a Baltimore couple, Michael and Pauline Anton. "Although acquaintances like to think of them as a perfect couple, Pauline and Michael are constantly bickering, sulking and fighting at home. . . . [Yet] Pauline and Michael are also tied to each other by their children, by shared adventures and, as the years pass, by bonds of memory and inertia. Caring for aging parents, witnessing the illnesses and travails of friends, adapting to a move to the suburbs—these are all experiences that bind Pauline and Michael to each other, even as their very different temperaments and interests increasingly pull them apart." N Y Times (N Y Late Ed)

"In order to illuminate every facet of the couple's interactions and personalities, the story is told from several points of view: those of Michael and Pauline and two of their three children. Although Tyler's prose occasionally slips into banality, she never falters in creating vivid characters whose weaknesses are both credible and compelling." New Yorker

Back when we were grownups; a novel. Knopf 2001 273p $25

ISBN 0-375-41253-0 LC 2001-88107

"After recovering from the shock of becoming a widow in her mid-twenties, Rebecca 'Beck' Davitch has spent several busy decades occupied with managing both her quirky clan of in-laws and their party-hosting business. . . . At 53, Beck is feeling a little rundown herself. She wonders what became of the serious college student she once was and whether she took the right path when she followed her heart to the altar at 19. Beck thus embarks on a quixotic interior journey." Libr J

This "is as perceptive, as full of gentle comedy and human warmth as any of Ms Tyler's previous novels. She manages her quirky, engagingly named characters (Patch, Biddy, NoNo, Jeep, Zeb) beautifully, spinning a web of family tensions with a wonderful lightness of touch—in this, Ms Tyler is matchless." Economist

Breathing lessons. Knopf 1988 327p o.p.
LC 88-45260

"Maggie and Ira Moran, late middle-aged, travel from their home in Baltimore to a friend's funeral in Pennsylvania. The expedition precipitates an introspective journey into their individual and collective pasts and presents and futures." Booklist

This novel has "irresistibly funny passages you want to read out loud and poignant insights that illuminate the serious business of sharing lives in an unsettling world." Publ Wkly

Celestial navigation. Knopf 1974 273p o.p.

Set in Baltimore, this novel tells of artist Jeremy Pauling's attempts to overcome his comfortable isolation and make contact with others

The author "is especially gifted in the art of freeing her characters and then keeping track of them as they

Tyler, Anne, 1941-—*Continued*
move in their unique and often solitary orbits. . . . She has a way of transcribing their peculiarities with such loving wholeness that when we examine them we keep finding more and more pieces of ourselves." N Y Times Book Rev

The clock winder. Knopf 1972 312p o.p.
"It all starts when Elizabeth Abbott agrees to become Mrs. Emerson's handyman for the summer. Before it's over, one of the Emersons (Timothy) kills himself, another (Andrew) shoots Elizabeth, and Mrs. Emerson has a stroke. The 'handyman' finds herself holding the family together and ultimately stays on to become an Emerson herself by marrying Matthew." Libr J
The author has a "remarkable understanding of the intricacies of family life, a sympathy for odd-ball characters who never become merely southern grotesques . . . but are observed so gently that the term 'neurotic' seems equally inappropriate for them." New Repub

Dinner at the Homesick Restaurant. Knopf 1982 303p o.p.
LC 81-13694
"Pearl Tull, an angry woman who vacillates between excesses of maternal energy and spurts of terrifying rage, has been deserted by her husband and has brought up her three children alone. Cody, the eldest, is handsome, wild, and in a lifelong battle of jealousy with his young brother, the sweet-tempered and patient Ezra. Their sister Jenny tries, through three marriages, to find a stability which was never present in Pearl's home. Ezra also tries to achieve a permanence through his homey Homesick Restaurant in Baltimore, but he is cruelly tricked by his brother and is unable to establish any unity in the family." Shapiro. Fic for Youth. 3d edition

Earthly possessions. Knopf 1977 197p o.p.
LC 76-41222
This "novel concerns Charlotte Emory, a 35-year-old woman who goes to her bank in Clarion, Md., one morning to withdraw enough cash to leave her husband. Instead, she is hustled off as hostage to a bank robber and peripatetic demolition-derby rider named Jake Simms. Simms needs funds to get to Florida and take his girlfriend out of a home for unwed mothers. All that he and Charlotte share, apart from the stolen car they are riding in, is a distrust of 'closed-in spaces'—for him, the prison he has just escaped; for her, a household that includes a gaunt preacher husband, two children, three brothers-in-law and a procession of itinerant sinners, soldiers and salesmen." Newsweek
"The book is contrapuntal, alternating chapters of the present action with chapters of first-person flashback. . . . The dialogue has perfect pitch, the visual detail seems astonishing yet apt." New Repub

Ladder of years. Knopf 1995 325p $24
ISBN 0-679-43941-2 LC 94-38909
This novel's protagonist is forty-year-old Delia Grinstead. "Feeling unappreciated and unnoticed by her husband, a family doctor who took over Delia's father's practice, and increasingly unnecessary in the lives of her nearly grown children, Delia wanders off during a family beach vacation and starts a new life in a small town. She's sad and uncertain about her break with her previous life but oddly determined." Libr J
"'Ladder of Years' feels, indeed, like the story of a woman who thought she could prune her life down to a short story, only to find it blooming, unexpectedly, into an Anne Tyler novel. There can be few more delightful revelations." New Yorker

Morgan's passing. Knopf 1980 311p o.p.
LC 79-20272
"A young girl-wife goes into labor while she and her boy-husband are putting on a puppet-show of Cinderella at a church fair in Baltimore in 1967. Her baby is delivered en route to the hospital by a member of the audience who claims to be a doctor. . . . The fake doctor—who lives in a tumultuous . . . cluttered house with an imperturbable wife, seven daughters, his half-senile mother, and crackpot sister—attaches himself to the young couple and their child, following them, popping up at odd moments. Later, after they have all become friends, this attachment, narrows, focusing upon the young wife, with unsettling consequences for everyone." New Repub

A patchwork planet. Knopf 1998 287p $24
ISBN 0-375-40256-X LC 98-84431
This novel, set in Baltimore, "tells the story of a year in the life of 30-year-old Barnaby Gaitlin who, despite coming from a wealthy family, works as an odd-job man. Barnaby is an ordinary and somewhat bewildered man whose life turns on a chance encounter with a woman who may represent the angel that brings change and gives direction to his life." Libr J
"For some readers, the story may indeed be too quiltlike—cozy and cute. But unlike the patchwork it depicts, it is a wonder of construction: everything fits; it's seamless." New Yorker

Saint maybe. Knopf 1991 337p $22
ISBN 0-679-40361-2 LC 91-52704
This novel tells the story of "Ian Bedloe, who believes himself responsible for the death of his older brother, Danny, killed in a late-night car crash after an angry confrontation with Ian. Danny's wife, grief-stricken and unstable, soon commits suicide, leaving behind three children (two from her previous marriage, to a man who has vanished). Overwhelmed by guilt, Ian takes . . . measures to redeem himself." N Y Times Book Rev
"Tyler's remarkable novel pulls at the heart strings and jogs the memories of forgotten youth. . . . While the majority of YA readers lack enough life experiences to appreciate the pure joy of Tyler's descriptions and thoughts, not to steer them in her direction would be a shame." SLJ

Searching for Caleb. Knopf 1976 c1975 309p o.p.
"The Pecks of Baltimore are wealthy, stand-offish, stolidly self-satisfied. In their suburban enclave . . . four generations have lived quietly together . . . [presided over by the] grandfather, Daniel. Only two have rebelled: Caleb, Daniel's dreamy, cello-playing brother who disappeared without a trace 60 years ago, and Duncan, Daniel's grandson. . . . When Duncan marries his cousin Justine, hitherto an ardent Peck, she begins to discover her own thirst for adventure. . . . And so, when Daniel decides to find his lost brother, Justine is the one who joins him." N Y Times Book Rev
"Anne Tyler's tone is understated, ironic, and elliptical, which suits her characters well. Searching for Caleb rarely gives us heights and depths of emotion or the excite-

Tyler, Anne, 1941—*Continued*
ment of discovery, but it does offer the very welcome old-fashioned virtues of a patient, thoughtful chronicle." Saturday Rev

A slipping-down life. Knopf 1970 214p o.p.
"Evie Decker, unattractive and unpopular, and Drumsticks Casey, an unknown rock musician, are misfits living in a small Southern town. They are drawn together in a union which is more bizarre than romantic. It is a union, however, that seems to fulfill the needs of each and makes for a marriage that is marked by quiet desperation." Shapiro. Fic for Youth. 3d edition

The tin can tree. Knopf 1965 273p o.p.
"Six-year-old Janie Rose Pike was killed in a fall from a tractor, an accident which shook but does not really change the little world in which she lived. Mrs. Pike, left stunned and silent by her daughter's death, is too apathetic to pay attention to her 10-year-old son, Simon. Her grown-up niece, who lives with the family, tries to take care of Simon and at the same time to cope with her own problems. It is Simon himself . . . who finally awakens his mother to the need for life to continue." Libr J

U

Uhnak, Dorothy

Codes of betrayal. St. Martin's Press 1997 293p $23.95
ISBN 0-312-15582-4 LC 97-23598
"Nick O'Hara was raised by his uncle Frank, an Irish cop, but his mother was a Ventura, daughter of an underworld crime boss. Nick follows his uncle into the NYPD, juggling professional life and family ties, until his son is killed in a sour drug deal while hanging out with a Ventura cousin. Then he learns his own father was a victim of the Ventura crime family. Marriage on the skids, Nick turns to gambling, loses big, rips off a drug dealer to pay his debts, and winds up snared by the Feds, who offer a deal: exploit his family connection and help bring down the Venturas." Booklist
"This work effectively portrays one man's agony with life gone wrong and the decline of mobster power as the century ends." Libr J

False witness; a novel. Simon & Schuster 1981 314p o.p.
LC 81-1591
"An ambitious bureau chief for the New York district attorney finds she has a racist, sexist, and political bombshell on her hands when a beautiful black talk-show host is brutally raped and disfigured in a vicious attack. But the attorney also finds that this case can propel her right into the D.A.'s office itself, if she plays her cards right, which may or may not involve prosecuting the man actually responsible for the crime. These career plans, however, raise conflicts in the lawyer's private life as legal aspirations slam up against an increasingly recalcitrant and questioning lover." Booklist
"This is a very tough-minded book. It works in terms of making us believe that this is the way in which this attempted murder might have happened. It works very well." Publ Wkly

The investigation; a novel. Simon & Schuster 1977 344p o.p.
LC 77-7981
Sgt. Joe Peters is "a detective on the Queens County district attorney's squad. He accompanies his partner one morning on a house call involving two missing children. The distraught parents are George and Kitty Keeler. George is 'an obese, balding, sloppy middle-aged man' who owns a bar. Kitty, more than twenty years his junior, is a 'very beautiful kid' who manages a health spa owned by a small-time gangster. The Keeler marriage is shaky, and Kitty accuses George of having taken the boys. But when their bodies are found in a nearby park and Kitty's account of her actions begins to sound suspicious, she is indicted for murder. . . . Out of curiosity and an attraction to Kitty, [Peters] sets out to investigate on his own." Newsweek

Law and order; a novel. Simon & Schuster 1973 512p o.p.
"The scene is New York City from 1937 to the 1970s, the leading characters three generations of Irish-American policemen, their families, the women they love and hate, the friends with whom they are linked in fierce loyalty, the enemies they will ruthlessly destroy no matter how much they have to bend or break the law to do it." Publ Wkly

The Ryer Avenue story. St. Martin's Press 1993 406p o.p.
LC 92-43655
"On a winter's night in 1935, six Bronx children flee from the body of a local drunk and child molester felled by blows from his shovel. Later, the miscreant father of one of the children confesses and is executed for the crime; the children swear never to speak of what they believe really happened. Years pass, and the now-adult survivors are summoned together to confront the event again. Lives, careers, families, and more are in grave jeopardy as one of their own plots revenge." Libr J
The author provides "just enough detail, complexity and old-fashioned storytelling verve to keep the plot purring along." N Y Times Book Rev

Victims; a novel. Simon & Schuster 1986 c1985 316p o.p.
LC 85-26246
"Young nurse Anna Grace is stabbed to death on a street in Queens in full view of scores of apartment dwellers who decide not to get involved. Tough, good-looking NYPD detective Miranda Torres investigates the crime in association with bigshot newspaper columnist Mike Stein, whose only goal is to show the insensitivities of modern society without caring who the criminal is or why poor Anna was his victim. Miranda stays honest in trying to do her job, but finds that the well-spring of corruption in law enforcement is so powerful that it even touches her friends in the highest levels of government." Booklist

The witness. Simon & Schuster 1969 222p o.p.
This novel is about the murder of a young black law student who is active in "civil-liberties demonstrations. A New York cop finds the gun in his hand. The city, especially the black population, cries for revenge. But one person saw the gun shoved into his hand—Christie Opara, a detective. . . . The Mayor and the Chief of De-

Uhnak, Dorothy—*Continued*

tectives toil to avert the consequences of a 'long hot summer.'" Best Sellers

"This is a sober story, told with warmth and understanding, and conveying no little of the sometimes painfully ambiguous role of a woman detective." N Y Times Book Rev

Ullman, Ellen

The bug; a novel. Talese 2003 355p $23.95
ISBN 0-385-50860-3 LC 2002-73289

A "novel about the fate of a programmer, Ethan Levin, who wrestles with an ineradicable bug in the heroic era of computing. It is 1984, and Telligentsia is an information technology startup engaged in creating a database and an interface to access it. . . .The story is narrated by Roberta Walton from the perspective of 2000, remembering her first IT job as a quality-checker for Telligentsia, which she takes after a failed bid for an academic job in linguistics." Publ Wkly

"With her thrilling and intellectually fearless first novel, 'The Bug'—which might have been subtitled 'The Postmodern Prometheus,' after Mary Shelley—Ullman reinvents the story of Frankenstein and his sentient beast as an allegory for the birth of the computer." N Y Times Book Rev

Under African skies; modern African stories; edited and with an introduction by Charles R. Larson. Farrar, Straus & Giroux 1997 315p $25
ISBN 0-374-21178-7 LC 96-48601

Contents: The complete gentleman, by A. Tutuola; The eyes of the statue, by C. Laye; Sarzan, by B. Diop; Black girl, by S. Ousmane; Papa, snake & I, by L. B. Honwana; A meeting in the dark, by Ngugi wa Thiong'o; A handful of dates, by T. Salih; Mrs. Plum, by E. Mphahlele; Tekayo, by G. Ogot; Two sisters, by A. A. Aidoo; Girls at war, by C. Achebe; The prisoner who wore glasses, by B. Head; In the hospital, by S. M. Cordor; The true martyr is me, by R. Philombe; Innocent terror, by T. M. Sallah; Africa kills her sun, by K. Saro-Wiwa; Afrika road, by D. Mattera; Why don't you carve other animals, by Y. Vera; The magician and the girl, by V. Tadjo; A prayer from the living, by B. Okri; Effortless tears, by A. Kanengoni; Give me a chance, by M. Nhlapo; Taken, by S. Chimombo; I'm not talking about that, now, by S. Magona; My father, the Englishman, and I, by N. Farah; A gathering of bald men, by M. Langa

An "impressive collection of short stories from sub-Saharan Africa. Published between 1952 and 1996, some translated from French, Portuguese, and Arabic, these stories share a common outrage against Africa's decay, whether from oppressive colonialism and corruption or the repression of tradition and ignorance. These are not folk tales about great chiefs but heart-rending stories about ordinary people . . . trying to make a life for their families, caught up in the political and spiritual struggle for Africa." Libr J

Underwood, Michael, 1916-

A dangerous business. St. Martin's Press 1991 191p o.p.
LC 90-29880

In this "Rosa Epton mystery, the barrister and her lover, Peter Chen, become involved with Britain's Security Service. Rosa sees former client Eddie Ruding in Amsterdam when he is supposed to be in an English prison after a burglary conviction. Shortly thereafter, an attempt is made on her life and Ruding is found murdered outside a prison, but not the one in which he had been incarcerated." Publ Wkly

Undset, Sigrid, 1882-1949

The bridal wreath
In Undset, S. Kristin Lavransdatter

The cross
In Undset, S. Kristin Lavransdatter

Kristin Lavransdatter; translated from the Norwegian. Knopf 1935 3v in 1 $50
ISBN 0-394-43262-2

Contains three novels originally published separately in Norway in 1920, 1921, and 1922 respectively; first United States publication with titles: The bridal wreath (1923); The mistress of Husaby (1925); The cross (1927)

Although the "action takes place in the fourteenth century, the lives of the characters are marked by almost the same problems depicted in modern novels: passion, adultery, premarital pregnancy, ambition, conflict. Kristin, daughter of Lavrans and Ragnfrid, is betrothed to Simon Andressön but falls in love with Erlend Nikulassön and finally wins her father's approval to marry him. Her father realizes on their wedding night that they are already lovers. The book follows Kristin's life as she tries to manage her estate and as her husband loses his lands and leaves her after a bitter quarrel. After several attempts at reconciliation, Erlend returns, only to be killed in a fight. The six sons of Kristin follow different paths. Two die during the Black Plague, which was so dreadful a scourge in that era. The portrayal of this Norwegian woman is vivid and human." Shapiro. Fic for Youth. 3d edition

The mistress of Husaby
In Undset, S. Kristin Lavransdatter

The **Unforgetting** heart: an anthology of short stories by African American women (1859-1993); edited by Asha Kanwar. Aunt Lute Bks. 1993 xxi, 292p o.p.
ISBN 1-879960-31-1 LC 93-3240

Contents: The two offers, by F. E. W. Harper; Aunt Lindy: a story founded on real life, by V. E. Matthews; Tony's wife, by A. Dunbar; A dash for liberty, by P. E. Hopkins; The octoroon's revenge, by R. D. Todd; After many days: a Christmas story, by F. B. Williams; The preacher at Hill Station, by K. D. C. Tillman; Guests unexpected: a Thanksgiving story, by M. K. Griffin; The judgment of Roxenie, by E. W. Smith; Breaking the color-line, by A. McCary; Mammy: a story, by A. F. Ries; Mary Elizabeth: a story, by J. Fauset; Goldie, by A. W.

The Unforgetting heart: an anthology of short stories by African American women (1859-1993)—*Continued*

Grimké; Isis, by Z. N. Hurston; Sanctuary, by N. Larsen; Doby's gone, by A. Petry; In the laundry room, by A. Childress; Brooklyn, by P. Marshall; The funeral, by A. A. Shockley; A happening in Barbados, by L. M. Meriwether; Mom Luby and the social worker, by K. Hunter; The library, by N. Giovanni; After Saturday night comes Sunday, by S. Sanchez; Nineteen fifty-five, by A. Walker; The lesson, by T. C. Bambara; Kiswana Browne, by G. Naylor; Johnnieruth, by B. Birtha; Fifth Sunday, by R. Dove; The life you live (may not be your own), by J. C. Cooper; Ma'Dear, by T. McMillan; Emerald City: Third & Pike, by C. W. Sherman; Croon, by W. Coleman

Unsworth, Barry, 1930-

After Hannibal. Talese 1997 250p il o.p.
ISBN 0-385-48651-0 LC 96-20856

First published 1996 in the United Kingdom

In this novel "five sets of outsiders invade Umbria by renovating houses along a country track. Trouble is made for them by local peasants and by an exploitative speculating Brit, but the real story is the way their various hopes and intrigues retrace ingrained historical patterns. Recognizing these patterns and, in a sense, presiding over them is an Italian lawyer so shrewd and wizardly that he seems supernatural." New Yorker

Losing Nelson; a novel. Talese 1999 338p $23.95
ISBN 0-385-48652-9 LC 99-28757

"Charles Cleasby, a reclusive amateur historian, is obsessed with Lord Admiral Horatio Nelson, hero of the Battle of Trafalgar. Cleasby is fascinated with every detail of his hero's life: myriad historical anniversaries, details of his personal life, and accounts of famous battles that Cleasby reenacts with ship models in his basement. In short, Cleasby is living vicariously through Nelson's life, his hero's exploits compensating for his mundane existence. To assert his divine image of Nelson, Cleasby is determined to disprove Nelson's involvement in a brutal massacre." Booklist

"Unsworth is in complete control of his material, effortlessly sustaining an almost unbearable level of tension that is suddenly resolved in an unusually effective surprise ending." Libr J

Morality play. Talese 1995 192p o.p.
LC 95-4106

This novel, set in 14th century England, is narrated by "Nicholas Barber, a young monk who has forsaken his calling and joined an itinerant troupe of players that gets caught up in the real-life drama of a small-town murder. The crime presents Barber and his fellows with an opportunity to attract a larger-than-usual audience, and they turn sleuths, weaving the bits of information yielded by their investigation into an improvised play that eventually reveals the surprising, sordid truth. Rich in historical detail, Unsworth's well-told tale explores some timeless moral dilemmas and reads like a modern page-turner." Libr J

Sacred hunger. Doubleday 1992 629p o.p.
LC 91-33237

A novel about the 18th century slave trade. "William Kemp hopes to recoup his losses in cotton speculation by entering the Triangular Trade. As ship's doctor, his nephew Matthew experiences firsthand the horrors of shipboard life, ultimately leading a revolt that lands the crew and remaining slaves on the southeastern coast of Florida. Here they try to establish 'a paradise place'." Libr J

"Deftly utilizing a flood of period detail, Unsworth has written a book whose stately pace, like the scope of its meditations, seems accurately to evoke the age. Tackling here a central perversity of our history—the keeping of slaves in a land where 'all men are created equal'—Unsworth illuminates the barbaric cruelty of slavery, as well as the subtler habits of politics and character that it creates." Publ Wkly

The songs of the kings; a novel. Doubleday 2003 338p $26
ISBN 0-385-50114-5 LC 2002-66845

"A stubborn wind from the northeast ushers in rough times for the House of Atreus, and the Greek ships, en route to Troy, remain trapped in the straits at Aulis. Unsworths' retelling of the story, familiar from Euripides, of the sacrifice of Iphigeneia to appease the gods so that the boats can sail is a bold, modern tale with cynical riffs on the themes of duty and power, truth and fiction. His Greek warriors are schemers and media-savvy self-promoters who are desperate to look good in the sung reports that are their equivalent of the news media—songs that are, we realize, the seeds of the Homeric tradition." New Yorker

Stone virgin. Houghton Mifflin 1986 309p o.p.
ISBN 0-395-35412-9 LC 85-24897

"Simon Raikes is given the task of restoring a 15th-century sculpture of the Madonna on a church in Venice. A frustrated artist himself, Simon is compelled to solve certain mysteries: Who was the sculptor? Why was the work suppressed for two centuries? How did it earn consecration? As he begins to painstakingly shear away corrosion, the statue apparently confronts him with visions and stirs his passions. His search for answers leads to a local sculptor's wife, with whom Simon falls in love, and eventually to a new mystery." Libr J

"The strength of Unsworth's novel doesn't lie simply in its critique of masculine love, courtly and carnal, sacred and profane. For Stone Virgin is also a murder mystery, a reflection on mediaevalism versus Renaissance humanism, creator versus critic and—last but not least–an elegy to Venice, its water and stone." New Statesman

Upadhyay, Samrat

The guru of love. Houghton Mifflin 2003 290p $23
ISBN 0-618-24727-0 LC 2002-32234

Ramchandra, a math teacher in 1990s Kathmandu, Nepal, has "become infatuated with one of his tutees, 15-year-old single mother Malati. Unable to endure his obsession, his wife, Goma, has fled to her parents' home with pubescent Sanu and her younger brother, Rakesh. But nothing—neither infidelity nor her rich parents' scorn for a son-in-law who can barely afford a dilapidated apartment with outdoor plumbing—diminishes Goma's love for Ramchandra." Publ Wkly

Upadhyay, Samrat—*Continued*

The author "excels at depicting the thousand small cuts that afflict a middle-class married man having an affair. . . . The writing is emotionally restrained and doesn't call attention to itself. There are no lyrical bursts of exuberance over the country's beauty or the torments of love. At points the novel is excessively terse; when three words would have sufficed, Upadhyay uses two. In spite of that it is gripping, because you like the characters so much, and wish them well." N Y Times Book Rev

Updike, John

The afterlife and other stories. Knopf 1994 316p $24

ISBN 0-679-43583-2 LC 94-9818

Contents: The afterlife; Wildlife; Brother grasshopper; Conjunction; The journey to the dead; The man who became a soprano; Short Easter; A sandstone farmhouse; The other side of the street; Tristan and Iseult; George and Vivian: Aperto, Chiuso, Bluebeard in Ireland; Farrell's caddie; The rumor; Falling asleep up North; The brown chest; His mother inside him; Baby's first step; Playing with dynamite; The black room; Cruise; Grandparenting

"In these mellow, reflective stories, where parents die and grandchildren are born, Updike's heroes are acutely aware of lost glory yet discover the strength to persevere." Libr J

Bech: a book. Knopf 1970 206p o.p.

Contents: Bech in Russia; Bech in Rumania; The Bulgarian poetess; Bech takes pot luck; Bech panics; Bech swings; Bech enters Heaven

"In seven episodes presented in the guise of lectures with a spurious bibliography, the work reveals the literary and personal life of Henry Bech, a distinguished Jewish author of New York. Revelatory incidents include Bech's travels in the 1960s as a kind of cultural ambassador in Russia and Eastern Europe, his visit as a lecturer to adulatory pupils at a girls' school, his diverse romantic affairs, his difficulties in writing as he ages, and his ultimate enshrinement as a major American author." Oxford Companion to Am Lit. 6th edition

Bech at bay; a quasi-novel. Knopf 1998 240p $23

ISBN 0-375-40368-X LC 98-27868

Contents: Bech in Czech; Bech presides; Bech pleads guilty; Bech noir; Bech and the bounty of Sweden

This book "brings readers amusingly up to date on the life and times of Bech, a neurotic Jewish novelist. Skipping merrily along, the real author describes the imaginary author's trip to Czechoslovakia, his stint as head of a pretentious and marginal writers' group, a period of true weirdness in which he literally murders his critics, his late arrival at fatherhood and his receipt of a Nobel prize." Economist

Bech is back. Knopf 1982 195p o.p.

LC 82-161

Contents: Three illuminations in the life of an American author; Bech third-worlds it; Australia and Canada; The Holy Land; Macbech; Bech wed; White on white

Further episodes in the life of Henry Bech. "The novella-length 'Bech Wed' finds him married to suburban Bea who provides three teenagers, a dog, and a house in Ossining where Bech finally finishes his fourth novel, 'Think Big,' which is hyped and heralded after his 15-year silence: 'The squalid book we all deserve,' said Alfred Kazin in the 'New York Times Book Review.' In the other stories . . . Bech tours Third-World countries; writes his name 28,500 times for a new signed edition of an old novel; is interviewed in Canada and Australia; and visits Israel with his Episcopalian bride. An atmospheric travelogue and funny satire of the literary scene." Libr J

Brazil. Knopf 1994 260p $23

ISBN 0-679-43071-7 LC 93-28632

"Tristão Raposo, a nineteen-year-old black child of the Rio slums, and Isabel Leme, an eighteen-year-old upper-class white girl, meet on Copacabana Beach; their flight into marriage takes them to the farthest reaches of Brazil's wild west. Privation, violence, captivity, and reversals of fortune afflict them; his mother curses them, her father harries them with hirelings, and neither lover is absolutely faithful. Yet Tristão and Isabel hold to the faith that each is the other's fate for life." Publisher's note

This novel, "for all its political incorrectness, seems good-natured and bent on self-parody. . . . If the book's surface is sometimes a little sticky, its allegorical underpinnings are graceful and firm." N Y Times Book Rev

The centaur. Knopf 1963 302p $24.95

ISBN 0-394-41881-6

"Utilizing a contemporay setting in Olinger, Pennsylvania, Updike attempts to retell the myth of Chiron, wisest of the centaurs, a creature who gave up his immortality on behalf of Prometheus. In this modern version, Chiron is a high-school science teacher, George Caldwell, and Prometheus is his 15-year-old son, Peter. The story revolves around three critical days in their lives." Shapiro. Fic for Youth. 3d edition

Gertrude and Claudius. Knopf 2000 212p $23

ISBN 0-375-40908-4 LC 99-57601

"Updike turns to Shakespeare's 'Hamlet,' exploring the origin of Gertrude and Claudius' 'reechy kisses.' When the sixteen-year-old Gertrude is unwillingly betrothed to the elder Hamlet, Horwendil, by her father . . . she quickly falls for his brother, Claudius. The two honorably resist their feelings until they are beset by the anxieties of aging; as it turns out, the murder of Horwendil is an act of emotional (and political) desperation rather than cold calculation. Likewise, Updike's portrayal of Gertrude and Claudius' thwarted affections is not just a deft literary exercise but an affecting—and funny—invocation of the abundant desires of what Hamlet called 'this too too solid flesh." New Yorker

In the beauty of the lilies. Knopf 1996 491p $25.95

ISBN 0-679-44640-0 LC 95-23467

The novel "opens in Paterson, New Jersey, in 1910. 'At the moment Mary Pickford fainted' while making a movie close by, Presbyterian minister Clarence Wilmot loses his faith. That loss precipitates another loss: his job. Since 'now he was free—free to sink,' he turns to selling encyclopedias door to door and to an addictive habit of watching the fabulous new medium, moving pictures. Updike then tells of the following three generations of Clarence's family. . . . Updike's soaring novel

Updike, John—*Continued*
becomes an extended yet taut metaphor for the secularization of religion and the concomitant infatuation with movies as a substitute for religion." Booklist

Licks of love; short stories and a sequel. Knopf 2000 359p $25
ISBN 0-375-41113-5 LC 00-34906
Contents: The women who got away; Lunch hour; New York girl; My father on the verge of disgrace; The cats; Oliver's evolution; Natural color; Licks of love in the heart of the cold war; His oeuvre; How was it, really?; Scenes from the fifties; Metamorphosis; Rabbit remembered
"This book of stories, mostly about old wives and girlfriends recollected in middle-aged tranquillity, also includes a novella—a return to the world of Harry Angstrom, Updike's unlikely alter ego. In 'Rabbit Remembered,' it turns out that Rabbit's untimely demise has not diminished his ability to shake up the lives of those around him. His family may not miss him, exactly, but, like the rest of us, they still can't get over him." New Yorker

Memories of the Ford Administration; a novel. Knopf 1992 371p o.p.
LC 92-52955
Professor Alfred Clayton "has received a request from the Northern New England Association of American Historians for his memories and impressions of the Gerald Ford Administration (1974-77). 'Alf' obliges with his memories of a turbulent period in his personal history, as well as pages of an unpublished book he was writing at the time, on the life of James Buchanan, the fifteenth President of the United States (1857-61)." Publisher's note
"Updike's elegant, yet slangy portrait of the Ford era demonstrates considerable finesse. Even more impressive is his authentic, yet unstilted, evocation of Buchanan's era." Christ Sci Monit

Pigeon feathers, and other stories. Knopf 1962 278p $19.95; pa $12
ISBN 0-394-44056-0; 0-449-91225-6 (pa)
These stories "are filled with gentle humor and irony. Youth, marriage, and family life provide most of the themes." Cincinnati Public Libr

The poorhouse fair. Knopf 1959 c1958 185p o.p.
A reissue with a new introduction of the title first published 1959
This novel concerns the lives of a handful of marvelously eccentric and understandable people in a poorhouse on the undulating plains of central New Jersey. It begins on the morning of the annual Fair, an innovation of Conner, the new and very ambitious prefect. Conner's struggle to institutionalize old age inevitably meets the stiff opposition of those who want to individualize it
"This is a wise book with much to say on individualism and conformity, mechanization and craftsmanship, the 'welfare state' and the 'old days'—and, foremost, on 'death' as it is looked upon by the aged and the young. Updike's old people are memorable." Libr J

Rabbit Angstrom; a tetralogy; with an introduction by author. Knopf 1995 xxxi, 1519p $30
ISBN 0-679-44459-9
Contents: Rabbit, run (1960); Rabbit redux (1971); Rabbit is rich (1981); Rabbit at rest (1990)

Rabbit at rest. Knopf 1990 512p o.p.
LC 90-52953
Sequel to Rabbit is rich
"In John Updike's fourth and final novel about ex-basketball player Harry 'Rabbit' Angstrom, the hero has acquired heart trouble, a Florida condo, and a second grandchild. His son, Nelson, is behaving erratically; his daughter-in-law, Pru, is sending out mixed signals; and his wife, Janice, decides in midlife to become a working girl." Publisher's note
"The being that most illuminates the Rabbit quartet is not finally Harry Angstrom himself but the world through which he moves in his slow downward slide, meticulously recorded by one of our most gifted American realists." N Y Times Book Rev
also in Updike, J. Rabbit Angstrom

Rabbit is rich. Knopf 1981 467p $30
ISBN 0-394-52087-4 LC 81-1287
Sequel to Rabbit redux
"Rabbit and Janice have now inherited a half interest in his late father-in-law's business and, having found a kind of place in society, he is a member of the local country club. He is resigned to good relations with Stavros, and he sees Ruth to determine if a chance acquaintance is their daughter. Rabbit finds that the girl is not his daughter, but he does become involved in paternal problems with his son Nelson, now in college, who has gotten his girl friend pregnant." Oxford Companion to Am Lit. 5th edition
"A superlative comic novel that is also an American romance." Time
Followed by Rabbit at rest
also in Updike, J. Rabbit Angstrom

Rabbit redux. Knopf 1971 406p o.p.
Sequel to Rabbit, run
"Updike profiles Harry (Rabbit) Angstrom, 10 years after his first appearance, as a conservative suburbanite no longer running away from responsibilities but unable to resolve the anxieties that are brought to him from outside. His wife takes a lover and, after decrying Rabbit's lack of will to keep her, leaves their home. Rabbit and his thirteen-year-old son Nelson become involved with Jill Pendleton, a young hippie girl whom Rabbit takes into his house; to him she is a sometimes baffling sexual partner, to Nelson an older sister. Jill's friend Skeeter then arrives, a black man of devastating wit and antic humor who initiates Rabbit to marijuana and encourages him to read black history." Booklist
"There are some structural faults, and moments when characters don't ring true. But I can think of no stronger vindication of the claims of essentially realistic fiction than this extraordinary synthesis of the disparate elements of contemporary experience." N Y Times Book Rev
Followed by Rabbit is rich
also in Updike, J. Rabbit Angstrom

Rabbit remembered
In Updike, J. Licks of love p177-359

Rabbit, run. Knopf 1960 307p o.p.
"Contemporary in setting and tone, and brilliant in its evocation of everyday life in America, the novel is about Harry Angstrom ('Rabbit'), a salesman who, on an im-

Updike, John—*Continued*

pulse, leaves home, his alcoholic wife, Janice, and his child, Nelson, to find freedom. After several escapades and a liaison with an ex-prostitute, he returns to his wife and child and attempts to settle down again. In this novel, Updike conveys the longings and frustrations of family life. Rabbit's malaise is not so much a yearning for freedom as, perhaps, a yearning for guiding spiritual values and meaning. At the end, still dissatisfied and guilt-ridden because of the responsibility he feels for the death of his second child, he begins running again." Reader's Ency. 3d edition

Followed by Rabbit redux

also in Updike, J. Rabbit Angstrom

Roger's version. Knopf 1986 328p o.p.
LC 86-45298

"Divinity professor Roger Lambert is visited by Dale Kohler, an earnest young student who wants a grant to prove the existence of God by computer. The visit disrupts Roger's ordinary existence, bringing him into contact with . . . Verna (his half-sister's daughter), and leading to his wife's affair with Dale." Libr J

This novel "succeeds in spite of its symbolic structure. Its power and charm lie in the terrific appeal it makes to our capacity for intellectual wonderment. It's rather thrilling to watch Updike assimilate the new vocabularies of particle physics and computer technology—and then fuse them with the ancient vocabulary of religious belief." Newsweek

S. Knopf 1988 279p o.p.
LC 87-40496

This novel "concerns Sarah Worth, a latter-day Hester Prynne who has become enamored of a Hindu religious leader called the Arhat. A New Englander, she goes west to join his commune in Arizona, and there mingles with the other sannyasins (pilgrims) in the . . . attempt to subdue ego and achieve moksha (salvation, release from illusion)." Publisher's note

This "is an acid comedy of illusions and delusions told entirely in the words of a woman who is both deceived and deceiver." Atlantic

Seek my face. Knopf 2002 276p $23
ISBN 0-375-41490-8 LC 2002-18442

"The action of the novel, such as it is, takes place over a single early-April day at the house in the Vermont countryside of the septuagenarian Hope Chafetz, an artist in her own right and, more famously, widow of the action painter Zack McCoy and ex-wife of the Pop artist Guy Holloway. Kathryn, an ambitious young journalist, has come up from New York to interview this living repository of the history of postwar American art. Through the course of the long day the two women talk, attended by a tape recorder, that ubiquitous tool of contemporary journalism." N Y Times Book Rev

"Despite its uncomplicated premise, the novel achieves a remarkable depth of characterization and a glowing beauty in its articulation of the artistic sensibility." Booklist

Toward the end of time. Knopf 1997 334p $25
ISBN 0-375-40006-0 LC 97-5167

The protagonist, Ben Turnbull, "is a sixty-six-year-old retired investment counselor living north of Boston in the year 2020. A recent war between the United States and China has thinned the population and brought social chaos. . . . Nevertheless, Ben's life, traced by his journal entries over the course of a year, retains many of its accustomed comforts. . . . Something of a science buff, he finds his personal history caught up in the disjunctions and vagaries of the 'many-worlds' hypothesis derived from the indeterminacy of quantum theory." Publisher's note

"Like Updike, Ben can write elegant sentences. Although his temporal excursions (and Updike's researched inventions) at first seem random, they fit together into a paranoid structure by novel's end. Ben's report from the body front and reflections on his failures . . . are simultaneously sad and comic, often worthy of that old endgamer Beckett." Nation

Trust me; short stories. Knopf 1987 302p o.p.
LC 86-46018

Contents: Trust me; Killing; Still of some use; The city; The lovely troubled daughters of our old crowd; Unstuck; A constellation of events; Deaths of distant friends; Pygmalion; More stately mansions; Learn a trade; The ideal village; One more interview; The other; Slippage; Poker night; Made in heaven; Getting into the set; The wallet; Leaf season; Beautiful husbands; The other woman

Villages. Knopf 2004 321p $25
ISBN 1-400-04290-9 LC 2004-43845

This novel "follows its hero, Owen Mackenzie, from his birth in the semirural Pennsylvania town of Willow to his retirement in the rather geriatric community of Haskells Crossing, Massachusetts. In between these two settlements comes Middle Falls, Connecticut, where Owen, an early computer programmer, founds with a partner, Ed Mervine, the successful firm of E-O Data, which is housed in an old gun factory on the Chunkaunkabaug River. Owen's education is not merely technical but liberal, as the humanity of his three villages, especially that of their female citizens, works to disengage him from his youthful innocence." Publisher's note

"Owen's obsession with women's bodies and blithe ignorance of their inner lives can sometimes read like a tedious parody of Updike's earlier work, without a sense of humor to imply the author is in on the joke. Yet Updike still writes lovely sentences and creates a believable portrait of the American village, concealing dark secrets but providing a limited stability." Publ Wkly

The witches of Eastwick. Knopf 1984 307p o.p.
LC 83-49048

"A novel about three Rhode Island women whose marriages have collapsed and who turn to devil worship and witchcraft." Reader's Ency. 4th edition

"While not a typical Updike narrative, the author's glittering wit, pungent observations, and fabled legerdemain at tabulating mundane particulars reach their peaks in the first half of the novel. Only in the last sections does the reader's attention flag." Booklist

Upfield, Arthur W., 1888-1964

Death of a swagman. Doubleday 1945 221p o.p.
"Published for the Crime Club"

Detective Inspector Bonaparte reopens the investigation of the murder of a swagman in New South Wales two

Upfield, Arthur W., 1888-1964—*Continued*
years later. Using the lore of a half-caste, and gossip gleaned from a stint in the local jail, Bony chases his suspect across the dangerous sands of the lonely outback country. Successive murders and a kidnapping occur before the detective is able to solve the case and reveal its part in a larger pattern of crime

"Bonaparte comes through with a solution that is based on one of the most curious motives you're apt to meet up with in or out of a detective story." New Yorker

Uris, Leon, 1924-2003

Armageddon; a novel of Berlin. Doubleday 1964 632p o.p.

Berlin from the close of World War II to the end of the airlift is the setting of this novel. Sean O'Sullivan, an American captain responsible for the military government of the city of Rombaden, nurses a fierce hatred of the Germans, and is faced with a dilemma when he falls in love with a German girl

The author "provides a broad and moving panorama of the rebuilding of postwar Germany at the time when the Allies and the Russians first came to clash over Berlin and its routes of access." Atlantic

Battle cry. Putnam 1953 505p o.p.

"Taking an average group of American boys from their home environment through the ordeal of boot camp, to the battlefields of Guadalcanal, Tarawa, and Saipan, the author fills in a detailed picture of Marine training and traditions." Booklist

Exodus. Doubleday 1958 626p il o.p.

"Following World War II the British forbade immigration of the Jews to Israel. European Jewish underground groups, aided by Palestinian agent Ari Ben Canaan, made every effort to aid these unfortunate victims of Nazi persecution. The novel provides insight into the heritage of the Jews and understanding of the danger involved in helping them reach a safe haven. It also includes the warm love story of Ari and a gentile nurse, Kitty Fremont, who cared very much for the welfare of the Jewish children caught in this nightmare." Shapiro. Fic for Youth. 3d edition

Mila 18. Doubleday 1961 539p $19.95
ISBN 0-385-02076-7

"Mila 18 was the actual command post of the resistance movement organized by the Warsaw Jews. . . . [This is the story] of the handful of men and women who, knowing they had to die, defied the whole German Army with their homemade weapons, and won the respect of the world." N Y Times Book Rev

"Uris' major talent is that he is a master storyteller. And in 'Mila 18' he uses this talent fully and unhampered, in a straight narrative that generates an almost unbelievable dramatic intensity." San Francisco Chron

QB VII. Doubleday 1970 504p o.p.

This novel is "about the trial of an American novelist in Queen's Bench 7 for libeling a Polish surgeon by contending he performed experimental sterilizations of Jews in a concentration camp." Oxford Companion to Am Lit. 5th edition

"Two thirds of this jumbo novel are concerned with the trial, Kelna versus Cady. The judge allows this and overrules that. Dramatic, impassioned confrontations before the Queen's Bench alternate with contributory scenes: the two principals surrounded by worried families, mistresses and friends, the police pressing their search for missing witnesses, the speculation about who's guilty and who's innocent." N Y Times Book Rev

Redemption; a novel. HarperCollins Pubs. 1995 827p o.p.
LC 95-10834

The focus of this sequel is "the conflict between two of the three dominant families of *Trinity*, the tempestuous Larkins and their staid British counterparts, the Hubbles. . . . Uris begins by tracing the Larkin legacy from patriarch Liam's exile to New Zealand, where he becomes squire of a sheep farm; his brother, Conor, becomes a legendary Irish revolutionary. Another Larkin progeny, Liam's son Rory, is acclaimed as a war hero after fighting with the British at Gallipoli, while Rory's brother Dary takes Catholic clerical vows, only to have a powerful love drive him to question both celibacy and his calling. Uris balances the struggles of the Larkins with the more repressed travails of Caroline Hubble, who battles the efforts of her husband to oppress the Irish after losing a pair of sons in the disastrous British battle against the Turks." Publ Wkly

Trinity. Doubleday 1976 751p il $21.95
ISBN 0-385-03458-X

This novel is set in Ireland between the 1840's and 1916. "The trinity includes the Larkin clan of Ballyutogue, Catholic hill-farmers who have eked out a bare subsistence in County Donegal for generations; the powerful Hubble dynasty, British aristocracy which has dominated the area for three centuries; and the McLeods of Belfast, shipyard workers whose Scottish Presbyterian forebears were planted there by the British to solidify the power of the Crown." Christ Sci Monit

"The story has a kind of relentless power, based on the real tragedy of Ireland, and Uris's achievement is that he has neither cheapened nor trivialized that tragedy." N Y Times Book Rev

Urquhart, Jane, 1949-

Away; a novel. Viking 1994 c1993 356p o.p.
LC 94-178660

The "saga of a family who must leave Ireland for Canada during the potato famine of the 1840's. As a young girl in Ireland, Mary is taken 'away' to the faeries after a young sailor (a faerie-daemon) whom she rescued dies in her arms. Although she does eventually marry, have a family, and start a new life in the Canadian wilderness, Mary still hears the call of her sailor and finally leaves her family to live the rest of her life alone by a lake. Her daughter Eileen, in turn, falls in love with an Irish nationalist whose passion is only for his cause; she spends the rest of her life 'away' in thoughts of him." Libr J

"Urquhart's blending of the spiritual and political sides of the Irish makes an amazing story told in a language that is melodious and laden with complex imagery." Booklist

The underpainter. Viking 1997 340p o.p.
LC 97-225317

This is a "symbolic tale about the life of a famous American artist. Austin spends his summers painting in a small Canadian town, and his winters showing off in

Urquhart, Jane, 1949—*Continued*
New York City, a split-down-the-middle life indicative of his disconnectedness. Turned off to emotion at an early age, Austin is unable to return the love of his muse and model, a graceful and mystically self-sufficient woman, or the generosity of his only true friend, a sensitive man who suffers a broken heart and the horrors of war with valor and compassion." Booklist

"Urquhart writes forcefully; her imagery is vivid, and her evocation of time and place is accomplished and assured. There is an impressive density of character and narrative, and her use of illustrative detail is, at times, striking." Times Lit Suppl

V

Vachss, Andrew H.

Choice of evil; [by] Andrew Vachss. Knopf 1999 305p $23

ISBN 0-375-40647-6 LC 99-61596

"At a gay rally in New York City, Burke's friend Crystal Beth is killed in a drive-by shooting. Burke and his tribe of shadowy, semicriminal associates set out to track down the killer, but their investigation is soon impeded by a retaliatory series of murders perpetrated against known gay bashers. . . . Vachss creates a gunmetal gray, paranoid milieu where few can be trusted, where to be mainstream is to be compromised, and where children and women are always—yes, always—at risk." Booklist

Dead and gone; [by] Andrew Vachss. Knopf 2000 333p o.p.

ISBN 0-375-41121-6 LC 00-40565

"Professional killers ambush Burke late one night, putting a bullet in his head and killing his beloved dog, Pansy. Physically, Vachss's self-professed 'outlaw' is a changed man when he finally sneaks out of the hospital. But he's still the same old Burke on the inside. He wants revenge—but he has no idea who masterminded the attack. Thus begins a months-long odyssey that takes him all over the country." Publ Wkly

"The left-for-dead-but-back-for-revenge plot is an old one, but Vachss manages to give it new life. Burke isn't quite as dark as he's been in the past, finding time to wax poetic on Chicago bluesman Son Seals and to discuss hot cars with other gear heads. But the message is the same: no mercy for the exploiters of children." Booklist

Down here; Andrew Vachss. 1st ed. Knopf 2004 289p $19.95

ISBN 1-400-04173-2 LC 2003-58860

Burke "returns from the 'dead' to help a former colleague arrested for attempting to kill a suspected serial rapist. As Burke begins to pull in old favors and reveal his still-living status to select individuals, he discovers obvious holes in the prosecution's theory. The recent overturning of the alleged rapist's conviction makes all of his victims potential murder suspects." Libr J

"This is yet another carefully crafted descent into a hellish environment in which sexual predators roam virtually unchecked, at least until targeted by Burke. One would think the same revenge plot would get old when recast again and again, but, amazingly, Vachss adds enough subtle differences to keep each novel unique and engaging." Booklist

Down in the zero; a novel; by Andrew Vachss. Knopf 1994 259p o.p.

LC 94-12312

In this mystery Burke is "confronted with young adult suicides and sexual blackmail in an affluent Connecticut suburb. Hired to watch the young son of a former lover, Burke is drawn into a bizarre situation populated by characters almost as strange as his friends. The suicides and the sadomasochistic sex, which are weirdly connected, force Burke to enlist his usual cohorts. Fans will want this crisply written work." Libr J

Footsteps of the hawk; [by] Andrew Vachss. Knopf 1995 237p o.p.

LC 95-17596

"The action begins when Burke is approached by a female police officer, Belinda, who wants him to exonerate her lover, now serving time as a serial killer. Belinda contends that the real killer is still on the loose; her lover is a connected guy who probably deserves to be in prison, but he's no killer. So she says. She also pins the cover-up on Morales, a psycho cop with a desire to send Burke to prison for his role in the violent breakup of a child pornography ring. Burke employs his familiar Fagin's army of street types to discover the real killer and the real motives behind the crime. As always in Vachss' work, New York's underbelly is vividly evoked." Booklist

Hard candy; a novel; by Andrew Vachss. Knopf 1989 241p o.p.

LC 89-45272

In this "novel featuring unlicensed New York private eye Burke, word is out that the ex-con PI has become a gun-for-hire. Besides coping with this crazy rumor, Burke contends with two figures from his youth who suddenly turn up. One of them, Candy, now a mini-skirted call girl fond of whips and leashes, wants Burke to rescue her teenaged daughter from a cult in Brooklyn; the other, Wesley, an Uzi-toting hit man, already has the cult's leader, Train, in his sights. When Burke learns that the cult safehouse is a baby-breeding operation, vigilante-style justice ensues." Publ Wkly

Pain management; [by] Andrew Vachss. Knopf 2001 307p o.p.

ISBN 0-375-41322-7 LC 2001-29868

Burke "resurfaces in Portland, Oregon, after an assassin left him for dead in New York. He's living from hand to mouth when he stumbles into a missing-child case. Burke suspects parental involvement in the disappearance of young teen Rosa, but nothing supports the theory. The trail leads first to Portland's red light district, where he hears about a serial killer whom the cops seem unwilling or unable to catch." Booklist

"Vachss finally lets his secondary characters speak for themselves, as opposed to being wholly defined by Burke's inner growl." Publ Wkly

Sacrifice; a novel; by Andrew Vachss. Knopf 1991 271p o.p.

LC 90-53582

"Super-tough Manhattan maverick PI Burke works both sides of the law to save Luke, an eight-year-old suspect in a series of baby murders." Publ Wkly

Vachss, Andrew H.—*Continued*

"Vachss' clipped, blunt, ocassionally overly melodramatic sentences may, in some way, be ripe for parody (à la Mickey Spillane), but they also convey the frightening impact of the somber, shocking, emotionally deadening hellholes that Burke, breaking every civilized rule, battles gamely through." Booklist

Safe house; [by] Andrew Vachss. Knopf 1998 291p o.p.

LC 97-50557

"At the request of Crystal Beth, operator of a Manhattan safe house, Burke agrees to take the case of a mother being stalked by her estranged husband, the leader of a neo-Nazi cell. As Burke untangles the web that connects the white supremacists to protectors in the federal government, he helps foil a terrorist plot that echoes the real Oklahoma City bombing. As always, Burke's exploits are an occasion to provide updates on Max the Silent, Michelle the transsexual and other veterans of his guerrilla underground—and to offer a quick study of the ways in which the justice system fails victims of crime." Publ Wkly

Two trains running; [by] Andrew Vachss. Pantheon Books 2005 447p $25

ISBN 0-4000-4381-6 LC 2004-60127

"Locke City, a Southern mill town turned tourist mecca, is controlled by the firm but benevolent hand of local crime tsar Royal Beaumont. When the New York mafia arrives, he hires former undercover FBI agent Walker Dett to protect his interests. In short snippets of action and dialog, Vachss . . . creates a broad picture of crime in Locke City, from teenage street gangs to crooked national politicians, with the Ku Klux Klan, militant African Americans, and other factions woven into a shocking climax. A riveting page-turner that marks a definite change of direction from the author's dark Burke thrillers." Libr J

Valin, Jonathan

Extenuating circumstances; a novel. Delacorte Press 1989 234p o.p.

LC 88-29933

"When an upstanding Cincinnati businessman and philanthropist, Ira Lessing, turns up missing, Stoner is hired to find him. Before he can begin to look, though, Lessing's blood-soaked BMW is discovered, followed shortly by his savagely beaten body. It seems that Lessing was heavily into S&M, which brought him into contact with two male prostitutes." Booklist

"The story stands as a 'mainstream' novel as well as a fine mystery." Publ Wkly

Missing; a Harry Stoner novel. Delacorte Press 1995 226p o.p.

LC 94-9532

Cincinnati gumshoe Harry Stoner faces a case "involving AIDS and homosexuality. The local cops are so squeamish about gay culture in America's heartland, they won't even entertain the possibility that the suicide of a woman's bisexual lover might actually have been a murder. Once Stoner digs into the dead man's history, the details of his life and death seem all the sadder for the ugliness of their raw context. But instead of preaching a sermon, Mr. Valin writes as if he were leaning both elbows on the bar and giving it to you straight." N Y Times Book Rev

The music lovers; a Harry Stoner mystery. Delacorte Press 1993 233p o.p.

LC 92-31323

Though Cincinnati PI Harry Stoner "usually works his city's mean streets, this case has its beginnings in a cozier milieu. Mild, middle-aged Leon Tubin is missing some prized and valuable LPs. He's convinced that his fellow stereophile club member and all-around bigot Sherwood Leoffler is responsible and hires Stoner to prove it. . . . Rooting his story in crimes of the past, Valin calls on hard-hitting plotting and plenty of audio lore to yield a powerful conclusion that satisfyingly caps the story's gentler start." Publ Wkly

Van de Wetering, Janwillem, 1931-

The Amsterdam cops; collected stories. Soho Crime 1999 254p $22

ISBN 1-56947-171-1 LC 99-23243

Contents: The deadly egg; Six this, six that; The sergeant's cat; There goes ravelaar; The letter in the peppermint jar; Heron Island; Letter present; Houseful of mussels; Holiday patrol; Sure, blue, and dead, too; Hup three; The machine gun and the mannequin; The bongo bungler

"Written during the past 16 years, the stories feature the Amsterdam Murder Brigade's cynical, jowly Detective-Adjutant Henk Grijpstra and his handsome assistant Detective-Sergeant Rinus de Gier." Publ Wkly

The blond baboon; a novel. Houghton Mifflin 1978 194p o.p.

LC 77-17338

"Elaine Carnet, one-time chanteuse, is found by her daughter at the bottom of the stairs leading to the garden. Elaine, retired from the cabaret world, has run a profitable furniture business for some years now. It is not clear who might wish her dead, if anyone did. But . . . [detectives Grijpstra and de Gier] feel Carnet's daughter and her explanation of the events don't ring true." Publ Wkly

The corpse on the dike. Houghton Mifflin 1976 182p o.p.

Grijpstra and De Gier, "Amsterdam municipal policemen, while staking out a petty criminal, run across the corpse of a sad, well-brought-up young man in a shack on a dike. A sharpshooting lesbian is arrested but the uncertainty of the policemen results in further investigation, which uncovers . . . the entire criminal population of the dike." Libr J

The hollow-eyed angel. Soho Press 1996 282p $22

ISBN 1-56947-056-1 LC 95-26296

"A young gay reserve policeman asks the commissaris, who happens to be going to a conference in New York, to investigate the mysterious death of his uncle in Central Park. Rinus de Gier follows the commissaris, who is now very old and nods off during lectures. Meanwhile, Henk Grijpstra investigates the death of a baron on a golf course as a possible homicide." Murphy. Ency of Murder and Mystery

Van de Wetering, Janwillem, 1931-—*Continued*

Just a corpse at twilight. Soho Press 1994 265p $20

ISBN 1-56947-016-2 LC 94-9499

"Responding to de Gier's trans-Atlantic call for help, Grijpstra leaves the cozy embrace of his mistress, Nellie, for a daunting journey to a small coastal island in Maine where his former partner has gone to seek solitude and wisdom . . . and is being blackmailed for having pushed a local woman, his sometime lover, over a cliff to her death. . . . More than one drug-running operation, a money-making scam of lesser proportion, gratuitous cruelty, venality, a Papuan rite of revenge and intelligent, unpredictable humor wrap up this narrative delight." Publ Wkly

The perfidious parrot. Soho Press 1997 280p $22

ISBN 1-56947-102-9 LC 97-2548

In this novel "Grijpstra and de Gier have retired and started a private detective agency. A sleazy character named Carl Ambagt twists their arms into investigating piracy on the high seas—the theft of a chartered oil tanker in the Caribbean. The case takes them to Key West and The Perfidious Parrot, a lap dancing bar, then on to St. Eustatius. Van de Wetering's ribald streak is getting stronger and stronger, his writing looser and looser; in *The Perfidious Parrot*, he writes like a Dutch Carl Hiaasen." Murphy. Ency of Murder and Mystery

Van Gelder, Gordon

(ed) The Best from fantasy & science fiction: the fiftieth anniversary anthology. See The Best from fantasy & science fiction: the fiftieth anniversary anthology

Van Gulik, Robert *See* Gulik, Robert Hans van, 1910-1967

Van Slyke, Helen, 1919-1979

Public smiles, private tears; [by] Helen Van Slyke with James Elward. Harper & Row 1982 o.p.

LC 81-47794

"Beverly Thyson Richmond is an ambitious career woman in the 1940s and 1950s, a time when most women were homemakers and those with careers were viewed skeptically. Beverly chooses to work in a large department store rather than attend college. With the assistance of her mentor, Beverly develops a retailing career that eventually dominates her life." Libr J

"On her death in 1979 Van Slyke . . . left the uncompleted first half of a novel that has now been completed by Elward, a playwright and author of three pseudonymous novels. The result is an expert combination; one cannot tell where the splice occurs, and the spirit and tone are consistent." Publ Wkly

Van Wormer, Laura, 1955-

Jury duty; a novel. Crown 1996 364p o.p.

LC 95-22002

"Van Wormer centers the action on freshman juror and formerly successful novelist Libby Winslow. . . . Libby is at first intrigued by fellow juror Alex, a renovation contractor. Despite his 'Marlboro Man' looks and pointed attentions, however, there is something off-putting about him, so she eventually finds herself drawn to the unassuming William, an investment banker with a heart of gold. As the trial heats up, so does Libby and William's relationship; similarly, juror Melissa, a recovering alcoholic, begins to come to terms with her attraction to a female advertising client." Publ Wkly

The author "has the New York jury scene down cold, from the clerks to the motel out in Queens where the panel is lodged after its deliberations. She cuts smoothly from courtroom to jury room to extrajudicial evening activities." N Y Times Book Rev

Vance, Jack, 1916-

The last castle

In The Hugo winners p245-305

Vance, John Holbrook *See* Vance, Jack, 1916-

Vanderbes, Jennifer

Easter Island; a novel. Dial Press (NY) 2003 304p $24.95

ISBN 0-385-33673-X LC 2002-31588

This novel "parallels two stories: that of Elsa Pendleton, who travels to Easter Island in 1913 with her much older husband and her mentally impaired sister to study the toppled moai statues, and of Dr. Greer Farraday, who in the 1970s escapes grief after the death of her famed scientist husband, accused of fraud, by studying ancient pollen on the island. Both women have been suppressed by circumstance—Elsa, always her sister's caretaker, has made a bid for security by marrying a colleague of her father after his death, and Greer battles prejudice against women scientists." Libr J

"Vanderbes knows how to craft suspense, and the narratives—while packed with vivid historical and scientific detail—move forward on the strength of her fully realized characters." Publ Wkly

Vanderhaeghe, Guy

The last crossing; Guy Vanderhaeghe. 1st American ed. Alantic Monthly Press 2004 393p $24

ISBN 0-87113-912-X LC 2003-60152

"Centered on three English brothers who venture to the American West—one as a missionary, the two others in pursuit when he disappears—this saga encompasses a wide range of characters through alternating narrative voices. In a panorama of late-nineteenth-century Montana and western Canada, Vanderhaeghe details the lawlessness of the early frontier towns and the desperate ferocity of the dying indigenous tribes. He dwells with particular pathos on the children of white traders and Native American women, who are caught between two cultures. The prose can be overripe, particularly in the opening chapters, and moments of historical exposition are clumsily inserted. However, the sweep of the narrative gradually overcomes these missteps, and as the various searches for revenge or redemption get under way the writing achieves unforced grace and power." New Yorker

Vargas Llosa, Mario, 1936-

Aunt Julia and the scriptwriter; translated by Helen R. Lane. Farrar, Straus & Giroux 1982 374p o.p.

LC 82-5159

Original Spanish edition, 1977

In this novel Vargas Llosa "draws on memories of his youth during the mid-1950s, namely his marriage to an aunt despite strong family opposition, and the action-packed soap operas penned by a mad colleague at a Lima radio station where Vargas Llosa was employed. The work's overriding irony stems from the juxtaposition of the two plot lines, the first based on fact and the second on imaginary events. The end result is a kind of metanovel in which the author sees the objective account of his courtship and marriage gradually assume the characteristics of melodrama." Ency of World Lit in the 20th Century

Captain Pantoja and the Special Service; translated from the Spanish by Gregory Kolovakos and Ronald Christ. Harper & Row 1978 244p o.p.

LC 76-26280

Original Spanish edition, 1973

"Pantoja is a diligent young army officer who is sent to the Peruvian tropics to organize a squadron of prostitutes and thus make life more bearable for lonely soldiers stationed in remote out-posts. Because of his puritanical nature and zealously analytical approach to his assignment, Pantoja elicits the reader's guffaws from the beginning, but ultimately he comes to typify the absurd hero who continues to struggle against overwhelming odds. The theme of absurdity is underscored, moreover, by the hilarious parodies of military procedures, the clashing montage of incompatible episodes, and generous doses of irony and the grotesque." Ency of World Lit in the 20th Century

Death in the Andes; translated by Edith Grossman. Farrar, Straus & Giroux 1996 275p o.p.

LC 95-40883

Original Spanish edition, 1993

"Guerrillas, army officers, environmentalists, a bizarre witch and her equally strange husband, and even a couple of French tourists all have their roles to play as the author fashions a plot centering on the mysterious killing of three men in a remote village. Finding the killer is the framework upon which the author develops a pageant of contemporary Peruvian society." Booklist

This novel "begins with a mystery. . . . It concludes with an enigma: How slender is the boundary between civilization and tenebrous horror? The novel's indecipherable mystery is exquisitely attractive to the clear, transparent country that is a genial reader's mind." Atl Mon

The Feast of the Goat; translated from the Spanish by Edith Grossman. Farrar, Straus & Giroux 2001 404p $25

ISBN 0-374-15476-7 LC 2001-33480

Original Spanish edition, 2000

"This fictional portrait of ruthless Dominican Republic dictator Rafael Trujillo focuses on the end of the old 'goat's' life. . . . Vargas Llosa relates Trujillo's story from the perspective of Urania Cabral, a successful New York lawyer who has spent a lifetime in exile but returns to her homeland when the tyrant is finally murdered. Urania hopes to rid herself of the demons that have possessed her since 1961, when as a teenager she was battered and humiliated by the impotent and vindictive old dictator." Libr J

The notebooks of Don Rigoberto; translated by Edith Grossman. Farrar, Straus & Giroux 1998 259p il $23

ISBN 0-374-22327-0 LC 98-70961

Original Spanish edition, 1997

This novel is set in Lima, Peru. "Don Rigoberto and his beautiful wife, Lucrecia, are separated, driven apart by an obscure sexual encounter between Lucrecia and her stepson, the prepubescent Fonchito, who may or may not be a little devil in disguise. Because he misses her so, Don Rigoberto fills notebooks with his graphic longings, while Fonchito visits Lucrecia in the hope of effecting a reconciliation—and in the meantime discusses frankly his identification with the artist Egon Schiele, whose sexual excesses he details with wide-eyed wonder." Libr J

"Vargas Llosa's complex, gorgeous prose, heroically translated by Edith Grossman, sweeps the reader into a rich confusion of art and fact, fiction and reality, fantasy and deed, where there are no vices and the only virtue is imagination." N Y Times Book Rev

The way to paradise; translated by Natasha Wimmer. Farrar, Straus & Giroux 2003 373p $25

ISBN 0-374-22803-5 LC 2003-56379

This is a dual fictional biography of "early-nineteenth-century French-Peruvian workers' rights activist Flora Tristan and her grandson, famous painter Paul Gauguin. In alternating chapters, the author. . . fashions portraits of these two vibrant individuals as he follows Flora in touring France to carry out her campaign to promote labor organization and equality in marriage, and Paul in awakening to his innate sexuality, to say nothing of tapping into his formidable artistic talent, by abandoning France for the South Pacific." Booklist

"A whiff of the lecture hall is detectable all through this book. (Some passages have more dates than an almanac.) But the juxtaposition of Tristan's and Gauguin's stories is fascinating all the same. In their different ways, both were moralists and proselytizers." N Y Time Book Rev

Varley, John, 1947-

Demon. Putnam 1984 464p o.p.

LC 84-4814

The author "concludes his trilogy about Gaea, the sentient asteroid circling Titan. Cirocco Jones and her allies, including various Titanides and a Terran bodybuilder, struggle to provide the last refuge for fugitives from an Earth devastated by nuclear war." Booklist

The golden globe. Ace Bks. 1998 425p $22.95

ISBN 0-441-00558-6 LC 98-14612

"Galactic actor and con man Sparky Valentine runs afoul of the Charonese Mafia on Pluto and takes on the most important role of his long and illustrious career—that of a desperate survivor. Varley . . . artfully combines a rousing sf adventure with generous doses of Shakespearean lore and theater history, all of which serve as an elaborate backdrop for a moving portrait of a child actor who never quite grew up." Libr J

Varley, John, 1947-—*Continued*

The persistence of vision
In The Best of the Nebulas p495-529
In The Hugo winners p459-507

Red thunder. Ace Bks. 2003 411p $23.95
ISBN 0-441-01015-6 LC 2002-38231
"When a Chinese spacecraft, Heavenly Harmony, threatens to land on Mars a few days before the U.S. shuttle vehicle Ares Seven, washed-up ex-astronaut Travis Broussard, his brilliant but uncoventional cousin, Jubal, and four kids from Florida decide to build their own private spaceship, Red Thunder, and get there first in this riveting SF thriller. . . . With hilarious, well-drawn characters, extraordinary situations presented plausibly, plus exciting action and adventure, this book should do thunderously well." Publ Wkly

Titan; illustrated by Freff. Berkley Pub. Corp. 1979 302p il o.p.
LC 78-23865
The first volume of a trilogy that includes Wizard and Demon
"The heroine finds an artificial world among the satellites of Saturn and becomes an agent of its resident intelligence, the godlike Gaea, before being forced to turn against 'her.' Conscientiously nonsexist action-adventure SF." Anatomy of Wonder. 3d edition
Followed by Wizard

Wizard; illustrated by Freff. Berkley Pub. Corp. 1980 354p il o.p.
LC 79-24871
"In this sequel to . . . 'Titan,' Varley continues his exploration of the sentient, wheel-shaped world called Gaea. Twenty years have passed, and now that Earth is aware of her, Gaea has tried to protect herself by becoming valuable to humanity—offering us 'miracles' based on her immense scientific knowledge. Two supplicants for such boons are the central characters: Chris, a man from Earth, and Robin, a woman from the Coven, an all-female orbital colony. To earn their miracles, Gaea requires them to become heroes. To achieve this, they accompany Rocky and Gaby (heroines of the first book, back in supporting roles) on a dangerous odyssey through Gaea's rebellious regions and learn that Gaea herself is the real enemy." Publ Wkly
Followed by Demon

Vasilikos, Vasiles *See* Vassilikos, Vassilis, 1934-

Vassanji, M. G. (Moyez G.), 1950-

The in-between world of Vikram Lall; M.G. Vassanji. 1st U.S. ed. Knopf 2004 369p $25
ISBN 1-400-04216-X LC 2004-48967
"In this novel set among Kenya's Indian diaspora, two ill-fated loves—Vikram Lall's for a young English girl, his sister's for a young African man—symbolize their family's tenuous social position as neither privileged oppressor nor righteous oppressed. Vikram, now in exile in Canada, recounts Kenya's painful process of decolonization and his own role laundering money for government officials, an activity that he justifies as the survival tactic of one considered 'inherently disloyal' because of his race. . . . The book admirably captures the tenor of the postcolonial period: the predicament of the Asian minority, the corruption that marred Kenya's fledgling independence, and the individual tragedies that were the cost of revolution." New Yorker

Vassilikos, Vassilis, 1934-

The few things I know about Glafkos Thrassakis; translated from the Greek by Karen Emmerich. Seven Stories Press 2002 356p $24.95
ISBN 1-58322-527-7 LC 2002-13866
Original Greek edition, 1978
The author "takes as his territory the lawless borderlands between literature and life. Narrated by an unamed biographer (who keeps reminding the reader how much he looks like his subject), the novel purports to tell the life story of the Greek writer Glafkos Thrassakis, which is in turn the pen name of Lazarus Lazaridis, who bears more than a passing resemblance to Vassilis Vassilikos himself. Biographer and subject, subject and author, fiction and fact: masks and doubles proliferate. The result is a deft and witty reflection on writing as well as a moving portrait of the artist as political exile." N Y Times Book Rev

Vera, Yvonne, 1964-

The stone virgins. Farrar, Straus & Giroux 2003 184p $20
ISBN 0-374-27008-2 LC 2002-25004
"As white rule in Rhodesia ends and the nation of Zimbabwe is born, sisters Thenjiwe and Nonceba can finally look forward to full lives, Thenjiwe finding love in their rural village and Nonceba discovering knowledge in boarding school. But when the new president sends forces to the province of Matabeleand to rid the country of his rivals, the sisters and their village are once again terrorized." Libr J
"Vera's impressionistic writing can make it difficult to grasp the political context and chronology of the war, but it perfectly captures the terrifying chaos of the fighting, as well as the rhythms of provincial African life." Publ Wkly

Verne, Jules, 1828-1905

Around the world in eighty days; translated with an introduction and notes by William Butcher. Oxford University Press 1999 xlv, 247p pa $9.95
ISBN 0-19-283778-8
Original French edition, 1873
"The hero, Phileas Fogg, undertakes his hasty world tour as the result of a bet made at his London club. He and his French valet Passepartout, meet with some fantastic adventures, but these are overcome by the loyal servant and the endlessy inventive Fogg. The feat they perform is incredible for its day; Fogg wins his bet, having circled the world in only eighty days." Reader's Ency. 4th edition

Verne, Jules, 1828-1905—*Continued*

Five weeks in a balloon; or, Journeys and discoveries in Africa, by three Englishmen; compiled in French by J. Verne, from the original notes of Dr. Ferguson, and done into English by W. Lackland. Appleton, D. & Co. 1869 345p o.p.

Original French edition, 1863

A description of five weeks of balloon travel, exploring the heart of Africa, visiting such places as the Cape, Zanzibar, The Nile and Timbuctoo

From the earth to the moon, and Round the moon. o.p.

The two books comprising this volume were first published 1865 and 1872 respectively

These titles provide a "striking example of early hard SF, detailing with great precision the preparations and scientific premises (still mostly correct, apart from the deadly effect of acceleration on the passengers) for a voyage to the moon." New Ency of Sci Fic

A journey to the centre of the earth; introduction by David Brin. Modern Library 2003 195,[8]p pa $8.95

ISBN 0-8129-7009-8 LC 2003-59947

Original French edition, 1864. Variant title: A trip to the center of the earth

"More than half the book is given to the preliminaries before the actual descent begins, the first two chapters relying on a standard point of departure, the discovery of a manuscript giving the location of the caverns in Iceland. The narrative shows Verne's intense care in presenting the latest scientific thought of his age, while the sighting of the plesiosaurus and the giant humanoid shepherding mammoths indicates how well he incorporated lengthy imaginary episodes to flesh out the factual report." Anatomy of Wonder 4

The mysterious island; pictures by N. C. Wyeth. Scribner 1988 c1918 493p il $25.95

ISBN 0-684-18957-7 LC 88-3167

Sequel to Twenty thousand leagues under the sea

Original French edition, 1874; first United States edition published 1883 by J. W. Lovell; this is a reissue of the 1918 edition

A story of adventure in three parts: Dropped from the clouds; Abandoned; and The secret of the island

"Five men and a dog are carried out to sea in a balloon and drop from the clouds on the mysterious island. Their Crusoe-like resourcefulness and adventures are the theme of the book." Toronto Public Libr

Paris in the twentieth century; translated by Richard Howard; introduction by Eugen Weber. Random House 1996 222p il $21

ISBN 0-679-44434-3 LC 95-31750

Written in 1863; original French edition published 1994

Set in the 1960s, "the novel depicts Michel Dufrenoy as a poet and humanities scholar at sea in a crass commercial world that has strong overtones of Soviet realism. He befriends a young musician with whom he works; reconnects with his long-lost uncle, a literature professor; and even falls in love with the professor's granddaughter. But despite the kindnesses of his friends, Michel fails to succeed with the technological culture around him. Notable are the predictions about the subway, electric lights, and electronic music." Libr J

Round the moon

In Verne, J. From the earth to the moon, and Round the moon

Twenty thousand leagues under the sea; translated with an introduction and notes by William Butcher. Oxford University Press 1998 xlviii, 445p pa $10.95

ISBN 0-19-282839-8 LC 97-29726

Original French edition, 1870

"The voyage of the Nautilus permitted Verne to describe the wonders of an undersea world almost totally unknown to the general public of the period. Indebted to literary tradition for his Atlantis, he made his major innovation in having the submarine completely powered by electricity, although the interest in electrical forces goes back to Poe and Shelley. So far as the enigmatic ending is concerned, his readers had to wait for the three-part The Mysterious Island (1874-1875) to learn that Nemo had been the Indian warrior-prince Dakkar, who had been involved in the Sepoy Mutiny of 1857." Anatomy of Wonder 4

Vernon, Olympia

Eden. Grove Press 2003 272p $23

ISBN 0-8021-1728-7 LC 2002-33863

"Fourteen-year-old Maddy Dangerfield is called upon to help her cancer-afflicted aunt Pip live out her last days. Maddy's mother, Faye, can't forgive her sister's betrayal of her with her own husband. Maddy is caught in the vortex of unresolved conflicts among the adults: a stoic, overworked mother who can't make peace with a dying sister; an alcoholic husband addicted to gambling; and a fiery aunt who has lived her life on her own terms. The small black community of Pyke County, Mississippi, is also saturated with unresolved conflicts, seething resentments, and violence. . . .Vernon's writing is lyrical and emotionally powerful." Booklist

Veryan, Patricia, 1923-

The riddle of the reluctant rake. St. Martin's Press 1999 309p $23.95

ISBN 0-312-20474-4 LC 99-36352

Concluding title in the author's Riddle trilogy; previous titles The riddle of Alabaster Royal (1997) and The riddle of the lost lover (1998)

"This book chronicles the unfair accusation and cashiering of distinguished Lt.-Col. Hastings Adair . . . for a crime he did not commit: he's accused of robbing a London maiden of her virtue. Court-martialed, and with his family turned against him, Hasty has only his friends Toby Broderick, Jack Vespa and Paige Manderville to help him find the real perpetrator and thus clear his name before some overzealous citizen or ill-meaning conspirator does him in. . . . Her characters nicely delineated, Veryan sets a sprightly pace for her engaging plot, serving up a sparkling romance and a mystery with a subtle denouement." Publ Wkly

The riddle of the skipwrecked spinster. St. Martin's Press 2001 330p o.p.

ISBN 0-312-26942-0 LC 00-45999

Veryan, Patricia, 1923-—*Continued*

In this novel set in Georgian-era England "two story lines are . . . intertwined. One involves Cordelia Stansbury, who flees the country after her gold-digging mother dupes renowned dandy Gervaise Valerian into agreeing to marry the notoriously homely girl. Fleeing to Egypt, where her father digs up antiquities, Cordelia, is shipwrecked off the Cape of Good Hope and only rescued after she has spent a year in the company of savages, her reputation ruined. The other story line features Piers Cranford, a noble young man who takes on the responsiblity of keeping his family estate afloat, leaving his about-to-be-wed twin brother in the dark about the many burdens he shoulders." Publ Wkly

Vida, Nina

Goodbye, Saigon; a novel. Crown 1994 281p o.p.

LC 94-8384

This novel "depicts the lives of Vietnamese immigrants in the violent, gang-ridden Little Saigon of Westminster, California, in the 1990s. The novel's central character, Ahn, comes to the United States with her extended family as a refugee of the Vietnam War. The devastating events of Ahn's life, from her early years in Vietnam to her arrival and adjustment to American life, are slowly revealed through short flashbacks. . . . The plot revolves around Ahn's business partnership with Jana, a white American woman. Ironically, they have led and continue to lead parallel lives despite their vastly different cultures and upbringings." Libr J

The author "delivers a superb range of minor characters, terrific set pieces . . . moments of glorious high comedy and dialogue filled with wit and wonder." NY Times Book Rev

Vida, Vendela

And now you can go; a novel. Knopf 2003 189p $19.95

ISBN 1-400-04027-2 LC 2002-35688

"An armed man waylays a twenty-one-year-old woman, Ellis, in Riverside Park, seeking a partner in suicide, but she survives. . . . Ellis alternately fends off and submits to the consolations of various men; thinks about the child an infertile couple conceived with her eggs; broods over her father's four-year disapearance and unexplained return; jets off to the Philippines on a volunteer mission; then, back in Manhattan, cuts her hair into a mullet. There's plenty of mordant humor along the way." New Yorker

Vidal, Gore, 1925-

1876; a novel. Modern Lib. 1998 524p $22.95

ISBN 0-679-60294-1 LC 98-21216

A volume in the author's American chronicle series

A reissue of the title first published 1976 by Random House

"As in 'Burr,' Charles Schuyler, hinted-at as the illegitimate son of Aaron Burr, again narrates. Now a respected and popular journalist-historian, Schuyler at 63 has returned, after years abroad, to the U.S. in the company of his widowed daughter, the Princess d'Agrigente, who is in need of a well-connected husband—thereby giving Vidal another occasion to crash society's party as he follows Schuyler on his journalistic assignments through New York, the city of Washington, later to Philadelphia for the Centennial, then Cincinnati for the Republican Convention." Publ Wkly

Burr. Modern Lib. 1998 697p $20

ISBN 0-679-60285-2 LC 97-39825

A volume in the author's American chronicle series

"*Burr* is a novel in the form of a memoir told in part by Burr and in part by the young journalist Charles Schuyler, a fictional creation and Vidal's strongest character." Choice

Creation; a novel. Random House 1981 510p il o.p.

LC 79-5528

"The narrator, old and blind and finishing out his days as Persian ambassador to Pericles' Athens, is recounting his life's experiences, mostly as acquired in the service of Darius the Great and his son Xerxes. . . . In particular, he describes his special missions to India, where, as well as meeting a variety of world princes, he converses with the Buddha, and to what is now China, where he becomes a friend and admirer of Confucius." Publ Wkly

Empire; a novel. Modern Lib. 1998 651p $23.95

ISBN 0-679-60293-3 LC 98-21224

A volume in the author's American chronicle series

A reissue of the title first published 1987 by Random House

"The core of Vidal's story is the inexorable march of one Caroline Sanford, newspaper owner, into the inner circle of the Washington, D.C., power elite." Booklist

"Interesting and well-developed real-life characters abound, including, most memorably, Secretary of State and Lincoln's old friend John Hay. Intermixed with the well-researched backdrop of historical characters and events is Caroline's personal story." Libr J

The golden age; a novel. Doubleday 2000 467p $27.50

ISBN 0-385-50075-0 LC 00-43071

Seventh and final volume in the author's American chronicle series. Set chronologically after Washington, D.C.

"The primary figure around which Vidal spins his . . . story is Caroline Sanford, an actress turned Washington newspaper publisher who is also a friend of Franklin Delano Roosevelt. As Vidal's tale opens, we see political Washington divided over the issue of whether to aid the Allies in their fight against German aggression. His large cast of characters includes both real and fictional politicians, moviemakers, and writers." Booklist

"Vidal is best on the surface. His account of the 1940 conventions is a real romp. He depicts F.D.R. with irreverent skill. . . . It's good to know how badly Wendell Willkie could give a public speech; and there are some wonderful scenes in which Eleanor Roosevelt skillfully manipulates her husband and the bosses of the old Democratic Party." N Y Times Book Rev

Hollywood; a novel of America in the 1920s. Modern Lib. 1999 558p $24.95

ISBN 0-679-60292-5 LC 98-46174

A volume in the author's American chronicle series

A reissue of the title first published 1990 by Random House

Vidal, Gore, 1925-—*Continued*

The main characters, newspaper publishers Blaise and Caroline Stanford, first appeared in Washington, D.C. "Assigned to travel to Hollywood [in 1917] to help pull the infant 'photo play' industry behind the war effort, Caroline discovers that, at the age of 40, she has the looks and potential to become a film star. Sold to a world-wide audience as 'Emma Traxler', she begins to understand that cinema has the power to re-shape the world. . . . [Meanwhile], President Wilson is struggling to win support for his vision of a League of Nations. When he fails, the way is open for the Republican Warren Harding to assume power. The ensuing corruption scandals culminate in the Tea Pot Dome affair." New Statesman Soc

Vidal's "highly polished prose style, in part the fruit of his classical training, is a constant delight." N Y Times Book Rev

Lincoln. Modern Lib. 1993 712p o.p.
LC 92-27273

A reissue of the title first published 1984 by Random House

"In the atmosphere of intrigue that permanently settled over Washington City during the Civil War, the initially unpromising Lincoln, an unlikely hero, rises to greatness; despite almost insurmountable troubles that deteriorate his physical and mental well-being, Lincoln shows his true mastery of crisis leadership, necessary not only to save the Union but to refashion it." Booklist

This novel "is not so much an imaginative reconstruction of an era as an intelligent, lucid and highly informative transcript of it, never less than workmanlike in its blocking out of scenes and often extremely compelling." N Y Times Book Rev

Myra Breckinridge
In Vidal, G. Myra Breckinridge {and} Myron p1-213

Myra Breckinridge {and} Myron. Random House 1986 417p $19.95
ISBN 0-394-55376-4 LC 86-11423

Combined edition of two titles first published 1968 and 1974 respectively

In the first novel, Myra who was once Myron seduces both Rusty Godowsky and his girlfriend Mary-Ann Pringle. The sequel is set in 1973. Myron Breckinridge, the alter ego of the transsexual heroine, is pushed through his television screen and onto the set of a 1948 film "Siren of Babylon" starring Maria Montez. He has difficulty in getting out. Myra periodically takes command of Myron's body. She attempts to save the world from overpopulation by altering the male sex

Myron
In Vidal, G. Myra Breckinridge {and} Myron p217-417

The Smithsonian Institution; a novel. Random House 1998 260p $23
ISBN 0-375-50121-5 LC 97-38615

"On Good Friday, 1939, 13-year-old T. is summoned from his D.C. boarding school to the Mall for a mysterious meeting. It seems the outwardly average (if unusually attractive) young man has scribbled, in the margins of a math test, an equation that may be essential to the upcoming war effort. Cloistered with Oppenheimer, Einstein, Charles Lindbergh, the Founding Fathers and other historical personages who have been kept alive in the Smithsonian's magical exhibits, T. struggles to solve the mysteries of space-time, prevent the coming war (in which he is doomed to die) and hold on to cradle-robbing Frankie Cleveland, the immortal 22-year-old version of Grover's First Lady." Publ Wkly

"Fans of Vidal's comic novels can expect the usual mixture of earthiness and erudition, though on a more restrained level; the novel provides the author with the chance to put words in the mouths of a dozen presidents, noted scientists, and pop culture heroes." Libr J

Washington, D.C.; a novel. Modern Lib. 1999 422p $24.95
ISBN 0-679-60291-7 LC 98-46173

A volume in the author's American chronicle series

Set from the New Deal to the McCarthy years this "political novel features the ambitions of both a senator and his young secretary for the Presidency. The senator loses his chance for the Democratic nomination when Roosevelt decides to run for a third term. The secretary, mapping his course to the top, with the help of a journalist invents a non-happening which makes him a national hero. He then blackmails the senator into withdrawing from the race and wins the senatorial seat for himself." Booklist

Villars, Elizabeth, 1941-

The Normandie affair. Doubleday 1982 319p o.p.
LC 81-43727

This novel is "set aboard an opulent cruise liner, the 'Normandie,' in the days when luxury and sumptuousness were taken for granted. Villars' story covers six days of irrevocable change in the lives of several passengers crossing from New York to France in 1936. At the center of this drama is mysterious Anson Sherwood, a wealthy Bostonian with a passion for and inordinate knowledge of the 'Normandie.' Sherwood turns out to be a dedicated meddler who interferes in the lives of his fellow passengers, involving himself in both romantic entanglements and political intrigues, usually with fortuitous results. Neatly bundling drama and romance, Villars has captured the dichotomous nature of shipboard life." Booklist

Vine, Barbara, 1930-
See also Rendell, Ruth, 1930-

Anna's book; {by} Ruth Rendell writing as Barbara Vine. Harmony Bks. 1993 394p o.p.
LC 92-34309

This "tale of psychological suspense revolves around a woman's discovery that the published memoirs of her deceased grandmother hid evidence of an elderly woman's murder and the disappearance of a little girl." Libr J

"Vine's story is utterly riveting, rich and multifaceted in its complexity. Her characters are wonderfully real and fascinatingly unconventional." Booklist

The blood doctor; a novel. Crown 2002 369p il $25
ISBN 1-400-04504-5 LC 2002-18491

Vine, Barbara, 1930—*Continued*

"Martin Nanther—biographer and member of the House of Lords—discovers some blighted roots on his family tree while researching the life of his great-great-grandfather, Henry, an expert on hemophilia and physician to Queen Victoria. Martin contacts long-lost relatives who help him uncover some puzzling events in Henry's life." Publ Wkly

"The story lacks the usual page-turner suspense of the Rendell/Vine novels but makes up for that with unusually detailed glimpses into Victorian life and the inner workings of the House of Parliament, which American readers will find particularly intriguing." Libr J

The brimstone wedding. Harmony Bks. 1996 330p $24

ISBN 0-517-70339-4 LC 95-30280

In this novel, "two women, divided by age and class, share their deepest secrets in an English nursing home in which one cares for the other. There is a sense of secrecy from the start, as Jenny Warner tells dying Stella Newland about her love affair and Stella shares with Jenny the location of her secret house." Libr J

"Both Jenny and Stella embrace their pain with the sense of fatalism that has always been Ms. Vine's literary hallmark. The wonder is that they can speak their hearts in such clear and distinctive voices and yet retain their interior mystery." N Y Times Book Rev

The chimney sweeper's boy; a novel. Harmony Bks. 1998 344p $24

ISBN 0-609-60287-X LC 98-10567

This novel revolves around the "sudden death of Gerald Candless, a celebrated English novelist who lived on the Devon coast with his wife, Ursula, and two daughters to whom he was conspicuously devoted. When one daughter, Sarah, starts researching her father's early history for the biography she has been asked to write, she discovers that he was living under a false identity for most of his life. As more facts emerge from Sarah's research, they both illuminate and contradict the dark views of Gerald's personality supplied by his bitter wife and the deep, if ambiguous, insights contained in his own novels." N Y Times Book Rev

A dark-adapted eye. Bantam Bks. 1986 264p o.p.

LC 85-48231

"A crime writer decides to reopen the case of Vera Hillyard, hanged for murder 30 years before. Hillyard's family is still shattered by events of the past, and her niece Faith Severn decides to protect the series of secrets that enshrouds the family by doing some investigating of her own. This novel proceeds by dark hints, building to an all-eclipsing climax." Booklist

A fatal inversion. Bantam Bks. 1987 268p o.p.

LC 87-47556

Ecalpemos, "the inversion of the title, is the utopian 'someplace' where Adam (now a computer executive), Rufus (now a prosperous doctor) and a handful of others set up an impromptu commune on a landed estate that Adam unexpectedly inherited in 1976. That experiment ended in disaster. Now, 10 years later, someone has finally dug up some incriminating evidence: human bones in a pet cemetery." Newsweek

In this novel "people are barely able to establish links with each other—love and affection are turned inwards. Therein lies the novel's only weakness: there's little of the compassion so important for a humanist like Rendell. . . . [Her eye is] so focused on gloom that she sees little else. That's no condemnation: crime fiction demands such morbidity." New Statesman (1913)

Gallowglass. Harmony Bks. 1990 272p $19.95

ISBN 0-517-57744-5 LC 89-29026

In this novel the "reader comes to know the perversities of lamebrain Joe and his malicious friend, Sandor, who concoct—Sandor actually drawing up the plans, Joe just following along out of dumb adoration—a scheme to kidnap a wealthy woman. Events transpiring in the woman's household—particularly, her relations with and the backgrounds of the people in her domestic employ—add double and triple layers to the conflict." Booklist

"Miss Vine's most penetrating foray yet into the dark mysteries of the heart's obsessions, this haunting novel examines love in many guises—romantic, parental, idolatrous, possessive, selfless, erotic, platonic and sick. The scope of observation is dazzling; the tone, remarkably nonjudgmental." N Y Times Book Rev

Grasshopper; a novel. Harmony Bks. 2000 392p $25

ISBN 0-609-60789-8 LC 00-38281

This novel focuses on "the lonely life of 19-year-old Clodagh Brown in Maida Vale, a fictional north London suburb. Haunted by tragedy in her young life, she befriends a group of equally damaged and alienated youths. Their nocturnal habit is to climb onto the roof and roam on the tops of buildings, from one to another. It is all a daring adventure, until the motives of the various characters collide." Libr J

"Only a handful of writers, in any genre, can match Barbara Vine for imaginative originality and ingenuity. . . . Grasshopper is about good intentions gone wrong, violence, innocence and an encounter with true evil. . . . To say that a book can open your eyes to a different world is a cliché, but rarely has it been more apt than in describing this novel." New Statesman (Engl)

The house of stairs; {by} Ruth Rendell writing as Barbara Vine. Harmony Bks. 1989 c1988 277p o.p.

LC 88-38303

First published 1988 in the United Kingdom

"Elizabeth Vetch, a writer, recalls her adolescence and young womanhood living with her cousin Cosette in a big, eccentric house in the Notting Hill section of London. Lots of people besides Elizabeth and Cosette lived in the House of Stairs, though; it was nest to many of their friends as well. Cosette is intent on recovering her lost youth, and because of her vulnerability in that direction, two residents conspire against her to gain her money. The consequence is violent death, with Elizabeth losing the one person she truly loved. A complex, eloquent novel—sure to retain Vine's large readership and undoubtedly gain her even more followers." Booklist

King Solomon's carpet. Harmony Bks. 1992 c1991 355p o.p.

LC 91-43668

First published 1991 in the United Kingdom

"Tom, a brain-damaged flutist who plays aviary music in the London Underground, is obsessed with Alice, a vi-

Vine, Barbara, 1930-—*Continued*

olinist obsessed with Axel, whose own obsession is with bombs and death. Along with Jed, who loves no one but his pet hawk, and Jasper, a 9-year-old boy who rides the tops of subway cars and loves the danger, they all live in a rotting old Victorian mansion owned by Jarvis Stringer, who has the most interesting obsession of all: the master study he is compiling on the world's subway systems." N Y Times Book Rev

The author "displays her remarkable ability to spot and dissect the terrifying beneath the ordinary, to imbue a setting with its own, almost palpable terror, and to construct in the process a narrative maze filled with constant, fearful surprise." Booklist

No night is too long. Harmony Bks. 1995 c1994 315p $23

ISBN 0-517-79964-2 LC 94-13064

First published 1994 in the United Kingdom

The narrator of this novel, Tim Cornish, a student of creative writing at an English university, is "filled with remorse. . . . Friendless, indifferent to his future, he lives alone in the rotting old house where he grew up, conjuring up the ghost of [Dr Ivo Steadman], the lover he knocked unconscious and left for dead on a desert island. His only correspondent is a mysterious letter writer who taunts him with true stories of castaways who survived." New Statesman Soc

"This is a novel about the effects of passion in which the mood is as bleak as the cold North Sea; a murder mystery in which the crucial killing is imaginary, and the actual killing arbitrary. . . . Nevertheless—the novel does grip and its scheme is impressive; it is hard to withhold applause from an author so lavishly endowed with the capacity to invent interlocking segments of plot." Times Lit Suppl

Vinge, Joan D., 1948-

Catspaw. Warner Bks. 1988 392p o.p.

LC 88-40082

"Hired by the powerful taMing dynasty to protect its Security Council candidate from assassination, a half-human telepath known as 'Cat' uncovers a larger conspiracy that threatens to destroy the remnants of individual freedom in a world controlled by interstellar corporations. Political intrigue, shifting loyalties, and fully realized characters add uncommon depth to this sequel." Libr J

This book is "essentially an adult sequel to Vinge's young adult novel *Psion* [1987]." Booklist

The Snow Queen. Dial Press (NY) 1980 536p o.p.

LC 79-20555

"A Quantum novel"

"An amalgam of SF and heroic fantasy borrowing the structure of Hans Christian Andersen's famous story, set on a barbarian world exploited by technologically superior outworlders, against the background of a fallen galactic empire." Anatomy of Wonder 4

Followed by World's end

The Summer Queen. Warner Bks. 1991 670p o.p.

LC 90-50521

Sequel to World's end

"As the Summer Star ascends in the skies above the planet Tiamat, marking the end of more than a century of exploitation by the technologically advanced Hegemony, Moon Dawntreader—the Summer Queen appointed to lead her people back to their traditional ways—breaks with ancient custom, choosing instead to prepare to meet the Hegemony's inevitable return on equal terms." Libr J

"Plots and subplots proliferate, and although the prose is sometimes florid and the romance and sex scenes overly sentimental, the book is so full of drama, conflict and tragedy that it justifies its length." Publ Wkly

World's end. Bluejay Bks. 1984 230p o.p.

LC 83-21374

In this novel "BZ Gundhalinu, a police inspector who played a minor role in . . . [The Snow Queen] is the central character. Having left Carbuncle at the time of the Change he has traveled to World's End in search of his two irresponsible older brothers. World's End, a barely habitable frontier planet, is center of a 'Company' mining operation but also contains Fire Lake, an unexplained anomaly that appears to drive those who approach it insane." Voice Youth Advocates

Followed by The Summer Queen

Vinge, Vernor

A deepness in the sky. TOR Bks. 1999 606p o.p.

ISBN 0-312-85683-0 LC 98-43457

"A Tom Doherty Associates book"

Prequel to A fire upon the deep

"Representatives of the Qeng Ho, a galactic trading consortium, and the Emergents, a group of long-isolated humans with strange powers, vie for control of one another and for the opportunity to exploit a planet of intelligent nonhumans, called Spiders, who are just reaching their technological maturity." N Y Times Book Rev

Vinge "is among the very best of the current crop of hard SF writers, producing work that is not only fast-paced and intellectually challenging, but also stylishly written and centered on carefully drawn characters." Publ Wkly

A fire upon the deep. TOR Bks. 1992 391p o.p.

LC 91-39020

"A Tom Doherty Associates book"

"Fleeing a menace of galactic proportions, a spaceship crashes on an unfamiliar world, leaving the survivors—a pair of children—to the not-so-tender mercies of a medieval, lupine race. Responding to the crippled ship's distress signal, a rescue mission races against time to retrieve the children and recover the weapon they need to prevent the universe from being forever changed." Libr J

"Thoughtful space opera at its best, this book delivers everything it promises in terms of galactic scope, audacious concepts and believable characters both human and nonhuman." N Y Times Book Rev

Voelker, John Donaldson *See* Traver, Robert, 1903-1991

Voĭnovich, Vladimir, 1932-

Monumental propaganda; translated by Andrew Bromfield. Knopf 2004 365p $25
ISBN 0-375-41235-2 LC 2003-60476
Original Russian edition, 2000
This novel "centers on Aglaya Stepanovna Revkina, a true believer in Stalin, who finds herself bewildered and beleaguered in the relative openness of the Khrushchev era. She believes her greatest achievement was to have browbeaten her community into building an iron statue of the supreme leader, which she moves into her apartment after his death. And despite the ebb and flow of political ideology in her provincial town, she stubbornly, and at all costs, centers her life on her private icon." Publisher's note
"If Frank Capra had been an acerbic Russian novelist and not a sunny American filmmaker, he might have written novels like Vladimir Voinovich's: funny, antic works that pit the little man against the system, ordinary folks against bureaucratic institutions and corrupt authorities." N Y Times (Late N Y Ed)

Vollmann, William T.

Argall. Viking 2001 746p il (Seven dreams, v3) $40
ISBN 0-670-91030-9 LC 2001-17744
"A novel about the founding of the Virginia colony, this is the third volume in Vollmann's . . . historical 'Seven Dreams' series. . . . The book is divided into two sections, the first focusing mainly on John Smith, the second on Pocahontas. Both parts are told in the voice of the dreamer William the Blind, who for this occasion adopts his own weird version of Elizabethan English." Libr J
"The eponymous Captain Argall edges into the foreground in the second part, succeeding Smith as Jamestown's leading spirit; he has the sinister bearing of some Jacobean theater devil—like Iago, there's menace in his meanings. He kidnaps Pokahuntas and manipulates her assimilation into settler culture. Vollman's ability to write in Smith's English and endow it with a contemporary snap is an extraordinary feat." Publ Wkly

Butterfly stories; a novel. Grove Press 1993 279p il o.p.
ISBN 0-8021-1502-0 LC 93-2489
The protagonist of this novel, "known as 'the butterfly boy' in grade school but now simply called 'the journalist,' travels to Southeast Asia to investigate the prostitution problem, accompanied by a photographer. The latter proves to be an impeccable sex tourist, but the journalist is inept. He forgets to use a condom the very first night and suffers from an ever-worsening barrage of fevers and infections thereafter. Then he falls in love with one of the prostitutes and decides to marry." Libr J
There is "great tenderness in Vollman, and wit, and he seems to know his settings intimately; in Butterfly Stories, one enters a vast, introverted, nearly psychotic mind, and the effect is hypnotic." Booklist

Europe central. Viking 2005 832p il $39.95
ISBN 0-670-03392-8 LC 2004-61170
A novel about the "warring authoritarian cultures of Germany and the USSR in the twentieth century. . . . Vollmann compares and contrasts the moral decisions made by various figures from this period some famous, some infamous, some unknown. Also explored in this book are the fates of artists and poets ranging from Kathe Kollwitz and Anna Akhmatova to Marina Tsvetaeva and Van Cliburn. A series of stories examine the complex and elusive Soviet composer Dmitri Shostakovich and the constant Stalinist assaults upon his work and life." Publisher's note
"What sets 'Europe Central' apart from Vollmann's other large-scale historical productions is its strong narrative lines. The pieces are dated and arranged chronologically to give the book a plot that arcs from prewar political machinations to Germany's surge east to Russia's counteroffensive, and that ends with cold war politics in divided Berlin." N Y Times Book Rev

Fathers and crows. Viking 1992 990p o.p.
ISBN 0-670-84333-4 LC 92-18315
This second title in the author's Seven dreams series "is set in the 17th century as Jesuit priests begin their work of converting the Indians to Christianity. . . . The narrator, William the Blind, urges us to approach his narrative by immersing ourselves in the Stream of Time, which will carry us back to the moment when the French first landed on Canadian soil." N Y Times Book Rev
The language "moves interestingly between contemporary colloquial, Hollywood historical, Middle High Tolkientalk, and a quirky and enjoyable poetry: never less than vigorous and inventive. . . . Despite nudges, the narrative grips." Times Lit Suppl

The ice-shirt. Viking 1990 415p il maps o.p.
ISBN 0-670-83239-1 LC 90-50051
This is "the first of seven planned novels in William T. Vollmann's 'symbolic history' of North America, a . . . fusion of Norse myth and legend dealing with the arrival of the first colonists and their encounters with the native Indian and Inuit peoples. Occasionally interrupted by his own travel observations of Greenland, Iceland and the Canadian subarctic—the book is illustrated by sketches and maps the author made during his researches there–his sources are the Greenlandic and Icelandic sagas, the chronicles of travellers, but also Butler's Erewhon, tourism brochures and conversations." New Statesman Soc
"Without apparent strain, the story interweaves numerous characters, sea voyages, murders and supernatural horrors, digressing with relish. . . . 'The Ice-Shirt' impresses mightily in its scope, its scene-painting and its enciphered social messages." N Y Times Book Rev

The rifles. Viking 1994 411p il maps o.p.
ISBN 0-670-84856-5 LC 93-31577
This is the third installment in the author's Seven Dreams series of novels, a symbolic history of North America. This novel, to be volume six in the completed series, "revolves around the fourth Arctic expedition of British explorer Sir John Franklin. This doomed voyage to find the Northwest Passage took place between 1845 and 1848 and resulted in death from starvation or exposure for each of the more than a hundred men involved. Equally important . . . are the adventures of one Captain Subzero, . . . who in the late 1980s travels to the Canadian Arctic towns of Resolute Bay and Pond Inlet, where he falls in love with an Inuit woman named Reepah and discovers that, although more than 140 years separate them, he and John Franklin are one and the same." Na-

Vollmann, William T.—*Continued*

tion

"What The Rifles demonstrates, and what magnetizes the narrative's scattered contexts is the real and binding continuity between nineteenth and twentieth-century patterns of mind-above all, this terrible insistence on our will to power over the world." Yale Rev

The royal family. Viking 2000 780p $40

ISBN 0-670-89167-3 LC 99-56587

This novel is "the story of Henry Tyler, a private detective nursing a penchant for the seedy side of life and an unrequited infatuation with the wife of his brother, John, a . . . contract attorney. Henry is hired by a crude tycoon named Brady to search the Tenderloin, San Francisco's skid row, for an underworld character called the Queen of the Whores." N Y Times Book Rev

"Vollmann is after large-scale social chronicle; he includes characters from nearly every walk of life, and trains his attentions on processes not often seen by the faint of heart. . . . But this hypperrealistic novelist also aims to present a metaphysics: the two brothers stand for two kinds of human being, the chosen and the outcast. As in all Vollmann's novels, the author's encylopedic ambition sometimes overwhelms the human scale; some supporting characters, though, do stay vivid. Vollmann avoids simply glamorizing the outcasts but remains, deep down, a Blakean romantic: prostitution is for him not only the universal indictment of the human race but also, paradoxically, the only paradise we can actually visit." Publ Wkly

Volpi, Jorge

In search of Klingsor; translated by Kristina Cordero. Scribner 2002 414p $26

ISBN 0-7432-0118-3 LC 2002-17582

Original Spanish edition published 1999 in Mexico

This novel operates "at several levels—as a thriller about a U.S. military officer seeking to ferret out the identity of the scientist who directed Nazi research during WWII, as a scientific search for truth by a physicist who encounters Einstein, Von Neumann, Schrödinger, Neils Bohr and other great minds of the 20th century and as a literary novel about a moral quest to destroy an evil that dates back to ancient German folklore." Publ Wkly

The author "delivers a novel that manages to function as a crackling spy thriller while delivering a thoughtful treatist on the nature of love and deception." Booklist

Voltaire, 1694-1778

Candide; translated by Peter Constantine. Modern Library 2005 119p $19.95

ISBN 0-679-64313-3 LC 2004-55244

Original French edition, 1759

"In this philosophical fantasy, naive Candide sees and suffers such misfortune that he ultimately rejects the philosophy of his tutor Doctor Pangloss, who claims that 'all is for the best in this best of all possible worlds.' Candide and his companions—Pangloss, his beloved Cunegonde, and his servant Cacambo—display an instinct for survival that provides them hope in an otherwise somber setting. When they all retire together to a simple life on a small farm, they discover that the secret of happiness is 'to cultivate one's garden,' a practical philosophy that excludes excessive idealism and nebulous metaphysics." Merriam-Webster's Ency of Lit

also in Voltaire. Candide and other stories
also in Voltaire. Voltaire's Candide, Zadig, and selected stories p3-101

Candide and other stories; translated from the French, with an introduction and notes, by Roger Pearson. Knopf 1992 307p $17

ISBN 0-679-41746-X

"Everyman's library"

Contents: Candide; Micromegas; Zadig; The ingenu; The white bull

Voltaire's Candide, Zadig, and selected stories; translated with an introduction by Donald M. Frame. Candide illustrations by Paul Klee. Indiana Univ. Press 1961 351p il o.p.

Contains 14 satiric tales in addition to Candide (1759) and Zadig (1748)

Contents: Candide; Zadig; Micromegas; The world as it is; Memnon; Bababec and the fakirs; History of Scarmentado's travels; Plato's dream; Account of the sickness, confession, death, and apparition of the Jesuit Berthier; Story of a good Brahman; Jeannot and Colin; An Indian adventure; Ingenuous; The one-eyed porter; Memory's adventure; Court Chesterfield's ears and Chaplain Goudman

Zadig
In Voltaire. Candide and other stories
In Voltaire. Voltaire's Candide, Zadig, and selected stories p102-72

Von Goethe, Johann Wolfgang *See* Goethe, Johann Wolfgang von, 1749-1832

Vonnegut, Kurt, 1922-

Bagombo snuff box: uncollected short fiction. Putnam 1999 295p $24.95; pa $13.95

ISBN 0-399-14505-2; 0-425-17446-8 (pa) LC 99-13665

"The 23 stories in this collection were published in magazines . . . during the Fifties and are collected here for the first time. The topics covered include space travel ('Thanasphere'), which describes the first manned orbit of Earth; finding the American dream ('The package'), about a new home full of the latest accessories; and an attempt to impress an old girlfriend (the title story). . . . Although many of the stories are topically dated, the ironic insights and illumination of character are timeless, and no one does it better than Vonnegut." Libr J

Breakfast of champions; or, Goodbye blue Monday!; by Kurt Vonnegut, Jr; with drawings by the author. Delacorte Press 1973 295p il o.p.

"In this novel Pontiac dealer Dwayne Hoover, science fiction writer Kilgore Trout, artist Rabo Karabekian and others play out a drama that runs the gamut from race tensions and sexual fantasies to pollution, the power 'bad chemicals' can exert over a human being, the sheer insanity of trying to prove you are a human being when you suspect you are just another machine in a machine-mad world." Publ Wkly

"In this novel Vonnegut is . . . clearing his head by throwing out acquired ideas, and also liberating some of

Vonnegut, Kurt, 1922-—*Continued*
the characters from his previous books. . . . This explosive meditation ranks with Vonnegut's best." N Y Times Book Rev

Cat's cradle; by Kurt Vonnegut, Jr. Holt, Rinehart & Winston 1963 233p o.p.

"In this mordant satire on religion, research, government, and human nature, a free-lance writer becomes the catalyst in a chain of events that unearths the secret of ice-nine. This is an element potentially more lethal than that produced by nuclear fission. The search leads to a mythical island, San Lorenzo, where the writer also discovers the leader of a new religion, Bokonon." Shapiro. Fic for Youth. 3d edition

Deadeye Dick. Delacorte Press 1982 240p o.p.
LC 82-13024

"In Midland City, Ohio, the [Waltz] family is isolated and scorned by the community for patriarch Otto's ersatz career as an artist and his strident support for Nazi policies. Their wealth and what's left of their social position is decimated when younger son Rudy (Deadeye Dick) accidently shoots a pregnant woman. Father pleads guilty to the crime, Rudy becomes a night-shift pharmacist, author of the prize-winning but unsuccessful play 'Katmandu' and cook and maid for his useless mother. Brother Felix becomes the president of NBC, and mother dies of radiation emitted from the fireplace of their 'shitbox' home. The entire populace is eventually exterminated . . . by the inadvertent dropping of a neutron bomb." SLJ

Galápagos; a novel. Delacorte Press/Seymour Lawrence 1985 295p o.p.
LC 85-4581

"A group of tourists on a cruise survive the end of the world, settling on a small Galapagos Island and beginning a new evolutionary sequence. The ghostly narrator looks back on things from a perspective one million years later." Anatomy of Wonder 4

God bless you, Mr. Rosewater; or, Pearls before swine; by Kurt Vonnegut, Jr. Holt, Rinehart & Winston 1965 217p o.p.

"With a satirist's eye for the meanness of man, especially his greed, Vonnegut tells the story of Eliot Rosewater, president of the Rosewater Foundation, who uses his position to help all petitioners. Discovering a plot to remove him from authority Rosewater gives all his money to over 50 children he is falsely accused of fathering." Booklist

Hocus pocus. Putnam 1990 302p o.p.
LC 90-34535

This novel is set in an America of the future. The story is told by Eugene Debs Hartke, a West Point graduate and Vietnam veteran, as he awaits trial for complicity in a mass escape from a black prison where he has been teaching inmates to read. It is 2001: "most of the United States has been sold to foreigners, and what is left is broken down and depleted. Black markets, race war, martial law, tuberculosis and AIDS are all somewhere between endemic and epidemic." N Y Times Book Rev

"Vonnegut remains an effectual stylist, combining deadpan irony and *faux naiveté*. As usual, his central narrative winds through a mosaic of aphorisms, verbal tics, digressions, homilies, obscure facts. . . . This compendium of devices and concerns may have hardened into a formula, but it has not yet ceased to be a diverting one." Times Lit Suppl

Jailbird; a novel; by Kurt Vonnegut, Jr. Delacorte Press/Seymour Lawrence 1979 246p o.p.
LC 79-12881

This novel "opens with Walter F. Starbuck, a 64-year-old victim of Watergate, about to be released from a Georgia prison for white-collar workers. Bereft of fortune and family (his wife is dead, his son is ungrateful) Starbuck retreats to the past via flashbacks of World War II, old love affairs, and past occupations. Eventually he regains respectability in the ubiquitous RAMJAC Corporation . . . which owns 19% of America and continues to swallow every major enterprise in its path." Libr J

Player piano; by Kurt Vonnegut, Jr. Scribner 1952 295p o.p.

"Paul Proteus, engineer, leads revolt against machine-computer conformist civilization, only to find that when it succeeds, people wish for the machines again. In order or in chaos, mob psychology is stupid. Modern civilization has hate-love affinity for machines. Incisive satire; a classic modern dystopia." Anatomy of Wonder. 3d edition

The sirens of Titan; by Kurt Vonnegut, Jr. Houghton Mifflin 1961 c1959 319p o.p.

First published 1959 in paperback by Dell

This novel "attacks the concept of causality and the confusion of luck with God's will [and] reveals human history as a trivial incident manipulated by the alien Tralfamadorians to further an equally trivial scheme." New Ency of Sci Fic

Slapstick; or, Lonesome no more! a novel. Delacorte Press/Seymour Lawrence 1976 243p o.p.

In this satirical fantasy, President of the United States Dr. Wilbur Daffodil-11 Swain sits in the ruins of Manhattan's Skycraper National Park writing his memoirs. As deformed children, he and his twin sister were separately regarded as idiots but discovered that together they were super-intelligent and went on to write a best-selling child-rearing manual. As president, Wilbur instituted a program to combat loneliness by forming artificial extended families

"Slapstick is a deceptively short and simple book. Its readability should not distract one from the fact that Vonnegut has found a fictional situation which considers serious human problems." New Repub

Slaughterhouse-five; or, The children's crusade: a duty-dance with death. 25th anniversary ed. Delacorte Press 1994 205p il $22.50; pa $6.99

ISBN 0-385-31208-3; 0-440-18029-5 (pa)
LC 94-171120

A reissue of the title first published 1969

This novel "mixes a fictionalized account of the author's experience of the fire bombing of Dresden with a compensatory fantasy of the planet Tralfamadore, the science-fiction element is progressively dominated by the overall concerns of satire, black humor, and absurdism." Reader's Ency. 3d edition

"A masterpiece, in which Vonnegut penetrated to the heart of the issues developed in his earlier absurdist fabulations. A key work of modern SF." Anatomy of Wonder 4

Vonnegut, Kurt, 1922-—*Continued*

Timequake. Putnam 1997 219p il $23.95
ISBN 0-399-13737-8 LC 97-14508
"The cataclysm of the title—in 2001, time undergoes a tremor, and everyone must relive the nineties—provides an excuse for Vonnegut and his longtime alter ego, Kilgore Trout, to trade rants: on desert camouflage, thirties socialism, the joys of waiting in line at the post office, the traitorousness of Dillinger's Hungarian girlfriend, semicolons. The resulting quilt of snippets is equal parts memoir, literary charm, self-congratulation, humanist sermon, randy geriatric fantasy, and toastmasterly jokefest." New Yorker

Welcome to the monkey house; a collection of short works; by Kurt Vonnegut, Jr. Delacorte Press 1968 298p o.p.
"A Seymour Lawrence book"
Contents: Where I live; Harrison Bergeron; Who am I this time?; Welcome to the monkey house; Long walk to forever; The Foster portfolio; Miss Temptation; All the king's horses; Tom Edison's shaggy dog; New dictionary; Next door; More stately mansions; The Hyannis Port story; D.P.; Report on the Barnhouse Effect; The euphio question; Go back to your precious wife and son; Deer in the works; The lie; Unready to wear; The kid nobody could handle; The manned missiles; EPICAC; Adam; Tomorrow and tomorrow and tomorrow

Vreeland, Susan

Girl in hyacinth blue. MacMurray & Beck 1999 242p $17.50
ISBN 1-87844-890-0 LC 99-27405
This novel "follows the trail of an 'unknown' painting by the Dutch master Vermeer—*The Girl in Hyacinth Blue*—from the time of its creation in seventeenth-century Holland to the present day. In each of the eight independent but chronologically linked chapters, the painting shows up as a prop in the lives of different owners, and in telling the circumstances under which these people acquire or lose the painting, Vreeland gives the readers a sense of the evolution of Dutch social history." Booklist
"Vreeland strikes a pleasing balance between the timeless world of the painting as a work of art and the finite worlds of its possessors and admirers—not to mention the world of its subject and its creator. Intelligent, searching and unusual, the novel is filled with luminous moments; like the painting it describes so well, it has a way of lingering in the reader's mind." N Y Times Book Rev

The passion of Artemesia. Viking 2002 288p o.p.
ISBN 0-670-89449-4 LC 2001-26119
Narrated in the "first-person voice of Italian painter Artemisia Gentileschi (1593-1653), the novel tells the story of Gentileschi's life and career in Renaissance Italy. Publicly humiliated and scorned in Rome after her participation as defendant in a rape trial in which the accused is her painting teacher (and father's friend) Agostino Tassi, Artemisia accepts a hastily arranged marriage at the age of 18 to Pietro Stiatessi, an artist in Florence." Publ Wkly
"Vreeland palpably captures Artemisia's joy as she blends colors and watches her artistic imaginings take shape. . . . Although her final confrontation with her father, artist Orazio Gentileschi, feels forced, the novel brilliantly captures the life of an extraordinary artist." Libr J

W

W. G. Sebald *See* Sebald, Winfried Georg, 1944-2001

Wagner, Bruce

The chrysanthemum palace. Simon & Schuster 2005 210p $23
ISBN 0-7432-4339-0 LC 2004-43059
"On the set of a schlocky TV space opera called 'Starwatch,' three children of wealthy and talented parents struggle to attain success of their own. The narrator, Bertie, is the son of the show's creator, and his current acting job is the nadir in a career of ever-shrinking ambition. His companions are Clea, the pill-popping daughter of a sexy actress who died young, and Thad, who is plagued by a personality disorder and the outsized legend of his father, an award-winning author. Suffering in the shadow of parental fame is a familiar trope of tabloid pathos, and the parents here are predictably malevolent. . . . [Wagner's] ability to eviscerate the absurdities of Hollywood, while occasionally hinting at its basic humanity, remains undiminished." New Yorker

I'll let you go; a novel. Villard Bks. 2002 549p o.p.
ISBN 0-375-50002-2 LC 2001-26729
In this novel "twelve-year-old multimillionaire Tull Trotter, whose family is among the richest in America, struggles with the emotional poverty of his upbringing and longs for his missing father, while Amaryllis Kornfeld, an almost stereotypical homeless waif, aspires to spiritual purity in the wake of her mother's murder. As the children—along with Tull's two cousins—attempt to connect with each other and with their fractured families, they must navigate Wagner's Los Angeles, a city overflowing with eccentric philanthropists and violent madmen." New Yorker

Wahlöö, Maj Sjöwall *See* Sjöwall, Maj, 1935-

Wahlöö, Per, 1926-1975
(jt. auth) Sjöwall, M. Cop killer
(jt. auth) Sjöwall, M. The laughing policeman
(jt. auth) Sjöwall, M. The locked room
(jt. auth) Sjöwall, M. Murder at the Savoy

Wakefield, Dan

Starting over. Delacorte Press/Seymour Lawrence 1973 290p o.p.
"Phil Potter, this book's hero, is 34, a failed actor who has become a successful New York public-relations executive. His four-year marriage to Jessica, a lovely model and closet alcoholic, has ended in divorce, and everyone tells him how lucky he is. Lucky? Being alone, he dis-

Wakefield, Dan—*Continued*
covers, can be as bad as a homicidal marriage. So Potter decides to fashion a new life. He moves to Boston, takes a job teaching 'Communications' at Gilpen Junior College and prescribes sexual encounters with every available New England divorcee and matron as the perfect anodyne to his painful isolation." Newsweek

"A powerful, naturalistic depiction of the agony suffered by a man whose affluence merely conceals an utter absence of value and direction." Libr J

Walbert, Kate

The gardens of Kyoto; a novel. Scribner 2001 288p o.p.
ISBN 0-684-86948-9 LC 2001-18876

"Ellen, the self-effacing narrator, mourns the disappearance of her cousin on Iwo Jima during the Second World War, and tries to decipher a book he has left her about the Kyoto gardens. The beauty of these landscapes lies in their impenetrability: one, made up entirely of shadows, must be viewed at night; another may be seen only through a window whose blind is forever drawn. Similarly, Ellen stands on the fringes of other, more dramatic lives, first befriending a fellow-coed whose affair with a married professor ends in an illegal abortion, then falling in love with a traumatized veteran of the Korean War. In precise, delicate prose, the author renders with equal power the quiet desperation of a girl growing up in nineteen-fifies America . . . and the ethereal." New Yorker

Our kind. Scribner 2004 195p $23
ISBN 0-7432-4559-8 LC 2003-66294

"This novel is narrated collectively by a group of older women who have been friends since they were young. . . . The affluent East Coast suburban protagonists of 'Our Kind' came of age in the late 40's and early 50's." N Y Times Book Rev

"Walbert's characters are caught like insects in amber as they make late-in-life discoveries no school could ever teach. Brittle, funny and poignant, this is a prickly treat." Publ Wkly

Walbrook, Louise *See* Templeton, Edith, 1916-

Walker, Alice, 1944-

By the light of my father's smile; a novel. Random House 1998 222p $22.95
ISBN 0-375-50152-5 LC 98-5464

"Susannah and Magdalena are sisters estranged from each other and their parents since adolescence, after Magdalena is beaten by their father for having sex. As each woman expresses her loneliness and anger—Susannah through sexual exploration, Magdalena through food—they are observed by their father's ghost, who seeks a reconciliation with them that comes only after their deaths." Libr J

"Walker has created a romantic but propagandistic fairy tale that veers disconcertingly from the facile to the heartfelt." Booklist

The color purple. 10th anniversary ed. Harcourt Brace Jovanovich 1992 290p il $24
ISBN 0-15-119154-9 LC 91-47202

A reissue of the title first published 1982

"A feminist novel about an abused and uneducated black woman's struggle for empowerment, the novel was praised for the depth of its female characters and for its eloquent use of black English vernacular." Merriam-Webster's Ency of Lit

Now is the time to open your heart; a novel. Random House 2004 240p $24.95
ISBN 1-400-06173-3 LC 2003-54766

"A well-published author, married many times, [Kate] has lived a life rich with explorations of the natural world and the human soul. Now, at fifty-seven, she leaves her lover, Yolo, to embark on a new excursion, one that begins on the Colorado River, proceeds through the past, and flows, inexorably, into the future. As Yolo begins his own parallel voyage, Kate encounters celibates and lovers, shamans and snakes, memories of family disaster and marital discord, and emerges at a place where nothing remains but love." Publisher's note

"Walker's dreamlike novel incorporates the political and spiritual consciousness and emotional style for which she is known and appreciated." Booklist

Possessing the secret of joy. Harcourt Brace Jovanovich 1992 286p $25
ISBN 0-15-173152-7 LC 92-6883

"Walker details the life of Tashi, a woman who grew up in the Olinka tribe in Africa but spent most of her adult life in the U.S. As a child, when the custom of circumcision is ordinarily carried out among Olinka females, Tashi was spared; later, though, her muddled need to reidentify with her origins causes her to submit to the tribal circumciser's blade. Rather than reknitting her soul to that of her people, the episode and its disastrous consequences alienate her body from sexuality and her mind from reality." Booklist

"The people in Ms. Walker's book are archetypes rather than characters as we have come to expect them in the 20th-century novel, and this is by defiant intention. . . . When the novel is operating genuinely on this archetypal level, it has a mythic strength. Its many voices are not rendered as stream-of-consciousness monologues, nor are they made to belong to distinct individuals. Instead, they are highly stylized, operatic, prophetic—and powerfully poetic." N Y Times Book Rev

The temple of my familiar. Harcourt Brace Jovanovich 1989 416p $19.95
ISBN 0-15-188533-8 LC 88-7995

"Time and place range from precolonial Africa to post-slavery North Carolina to modern-day San Francisco; and the characters themselves change and evolve as their stories are told, their myriad histories revealed. Most often present are Miss Lissie, an old woman with a fascinating host of former lives; her companion, the gentle Mr. Hal; Arveyda, a soul-searching musician; his wife Carlotta, who was born in the South American jungle; Fanny, a young woman who has a tendency to fall in love with spirits; and her husband Suwelo, who tries hard but simply does not understand her." Libr J

This is a "novel only in a loose sense. Rather, it is a mixture of mythic fantasy, revisionary history, exemplary biography and sermon. It is short on narrative tension, long on inspirational message." N Y Times Book Rev

The way forward is with a broken heart. Random House 2000 200p $23.95
ISBN 0-679-45587-6 LC 00-27172

Walker, Alice, 1944-—*Continued*

Includes the following stories: To my young husband; Kindred spirits; Olive oil; Cuddling; Charms; There was a river; Uncle Loaf and Auntie Putt-Putt; Blaze; Growing out; Conscious birth; This is how it happened; The brotherhood of the saved

"In seven beautifully written and astoundingly perceptive short stories—admittedly based in fact, then fictionalized—[Walker] homes in on the problems endemic to interracial romance and offers a near stream-of-consciousness reflection on her own ten-year marriage to a white civil rights attorney." Libr J

You can't keep a good woman down; stories. Harcourt Brace Jovanovich 1981 167p o.p.

LC 80-8761

Contents: Nineteen fifty-five; How did I get away with killing one of the biggest lawyers in the States? It was easy; Elethia; The lover; Petunias; Coming apart Fame; The abortion; Porn; Advancing Luna—and Ida B. Wells; Laurel; A letter of the times; or, Should this sado-masochism be saved; A sudden trip home in the spring; Source

Walker, Dale L.

(ed) Westward. See Westward

Walker, Margaret, 1915-1998

Jubilee. Houghton Mifflin 1966 497p o.p.

"Vyry was a slave and the daughter of a slave. She suffered slavery's tribulations and looked forward to the time of freedom to bring her a home of her own and provide an education for her children. The Civil War and the Reconstruction period brought the possibility of that day of jubilation, but the attainment of her two desires still seemed remote. The author gives a clear picture of the everyday life of slaves, their modes of behavior, and the patterns and rhythms of their speech." Shapiro. Fic for Youth. 3d edition

Walker, Mary Willis

All the dead lie down. Doubleday 1998 308p $22.95

ISBN 0-385-47858-5 LC 97-24131

"Several topics concern magazine writer Molly Cates: the upcoming concealed handgun bill in the Texas legislature, the plight of homeless women in Austin, and her refusal to believe her father's suicide some 28 years earlier. So Molly learns how to shoot, interviews bag ladies, and pursues a new source of material about her father. Literate prose, in-depth characterization, and a cleverly manipulated plot." Libr J

Under the beetle's cellar. Doubleday 1995 311p o.p.

LC 95-10708

Crime reporter Molly Cates confronts "cult leader Samuel Mordecai, whose Austin, Texas, compound is just as bound-for-tragedy as David Koresh's. Mordecai believes the end of the world is imminent, and according to a divine vision he's received, he must sacrifice a group of purified 'lambs of God' who'll serve as his ticket into Heaven. To that end, he's kidnapped a school bus driver and 11 children and kept them hostage in a buried bus for 46 days." Booklist

"If there can be such a thing as a heartwarming suspense thriller, then Mary Willis Walker has written a nifty one. . . . The real drama is played underground, where the heroic bus driver draws on his war experiences in Vietnam and every bit of his strength to comfort the children and prepare them for what may well be the end of their world." N Y Times Book Rev

Wallace, Daniel, 1959-

Big fish; a novel of mythic proportions. Algonquin Bks. 1998 180p o.p.

ISBN 1-56512-217-8 LC 98-26216

"William Bloom's father, Edward, is dying. He dies in fact in four different takes, all of which have William and his mother waiting outside a bedroom door as the family doctor tells them it's time to say their goodbyes. He intersperses the four takes with stories (all filtered through William's mind and voice) about the elusive Edward. . . . In a plainspoken style dotted with transcendent passages, Wallace mixes the mundane and the mythical. His chapters have the transformative quality of fable and fairy tale, and the novel's roomy structure allows the mystery and lyricism of the story to coalesce." Publ Wkly

The Watermelon King. Houghton Mifflin 2003 226p $23

ISBN 0-618-22138-7 LC 2002-75941

"Lucy Rider drives into Ashland, AL, on a hot day in 1982 and unintentionally changes the nature of the quiet little town forever . . . . Known as the Watermelon Capital of the World, Ashland celebrates each watermelon crop with a festival, crowning a watermelon king and orchestrating his performance in a fertility rite for the following year's crop. The fertility ritual leads to Lucy's death and to the gradual decline of the town. Eighteen years later, Thomas Rider drives into Ashland, seeking information about his mother and his own roots, and Ashland again takes a Rider to its collective hearts, again leading to tragedy and loss." Libr J

"This is a unique and spellbinding novel, an unforgettable southern tall tale with extraordinary characters." Booklist

Wallace, David Foster

Infinite jest; a novel. Little, Brown 1996 1079p $29.95

ISBN 0-316-92004-5 LC 95-30619

This novel is "set sometime in the next century, on the grounds of a New England tennis academy and in a rehab clinic. Among other things, the book contains perhaps the most moving and hypnotic writing on the psychology of addiction and recovery to be found in modern fiction. There are obsessive riffs on sports, on drugs, and on the hidden horrors of entertainment: the title of the novel refers to the title of a movie that is said to be so 'terminally compelling' that viewers will watch it passively and repeatedly to the point of death. Comparisons with Pynchon are inevitable, and in this case they are fully justified." New Yorker

Oblivion; stories. Little, Brown 2004 329p $25.95

ISBN 0-316-91981-0

Wallace, David Foster—*Continued*

Contents: Mister Squishy; The soul is not a smithy; Incarnations of burned children; Another pioneer; Good old neon; Philosophy and the mirror of nature; Oblivion; The Suffering Channel

"Unpacking our inner lives with empathy and care, Oblivion showcases the incredibly rich textures and crystalline clarity of Wallace's prose, confirming the singular genius of his expansive imagination and resonating with the complexities of minds in motion." American Book Review

Wallace, Irving, 1916-1990

The man; a novel. Simon & Schuster 1964 766p o.p.

This is the story of a black Senator who becomes the first black President of the United States after the deaths, in rapid succession, of first the Vice President and then both the President and the Speaker of the House

The portrayal of the "President as a man, an able, intelligent, politically moderate man who has never been to the fore but must take responsibility overnight, is excellent. With a huge cast of characters and one crisis after another in the plot, this makes an absorbing story." Publ Wkly

The prize. Simon & Schuster 1962 768p o.p.

This novel is an "inquiry into the private lives of a batch of Nobel Prize winners. . . . The prize winners are . . . a French husband-and-wife team of chemists whose marriage is collapsing, a neurotic American heart surgeon broodingly resentful that he must share the award in medicine with an Italian doctor, a gentle German-born physicist from Atlanta who is being wooed by the Communists of East Germany, and an American novelist who is just coming out of a long alcoholic trance. Wallace . . . assembles them all in Stockholm and embarks them on the frenzied series of public and private events that surround Nobel award weeks in the Swedish capital." NY Her Trib Books

Wallace, Lew, 1827-1905

Ben-Hur; a tale of the Christ. Harper 1880 552p o.p.

This novel "depicts the oppressive Roman occupation of ancient Palestine and the origins of Christianity. The Jew Judah Ben-Hur is wrongly accused by his former friend, the Roman Messala, of attempting to kill a Roman official. He is sent to be a slave and his mother and sister are imprisoned. Years later he returns, wins a chariot race against Messala, and is reunited with his now leprous mother and sister. Mother and daughter are cured on the day of the Crucifixion, and the family is converted to Christianity." Merriam-Webster's Ency of Lit

Wallace, Marilyn

(ed) The Best of Sisters in crime. See The Best of Sisters in crime

Wallach, Janet, 1942-

Seraglio. Talese 2003 316p $24.95

ISBN 0-385-49046-1 LC 2002-28698

Based on fact, "this book traces the life of Aimée du Buc de Rivery . . . who was kidnapped at age 13 en route to her home in Martinique. Her pirate captors take her to the Turkish sultan, who enslaves her in the seraglio . . . . There, Aimée befriends Tulip, the black eunuch responsible for her welfare. Tulip recounts Aimée's reluctant initiation into the harem as Nakshidil, her dramatic development from slave girl to woman of pleasure, and her incredible transformation into the valide sultan (mother of the sultan) . . . assisting him in his controversial attempt to westernize 19th-century Turkey." Libr J

"It is to Wallach's credit that at no point does her story seem preposterous. The intrigue and drama of the palace are balanced by capable, authoritative prose and admirable restraint, resulting in a novel at once serious and enchanting." Publ Wkly

Wallant, Edward Lewis, 1926-1962

The pawnbroker; [by] Edward L. Wallant. Harcourt, Brace & World 1961 279p o.p.

"Sol Nazerman is a survivor of the Holocaust. In the past he had been a university teacher in Poland; now he runs a pawnshop in Harlem in which Murillio, a ruthless racketeer, has a financial interest. Into Nazerman's shop come people who are sad, sick, or criminal. He also meets Marilyn Birchfield, a friendly social worker who tries to get past the frozen outward indifference of the pawnbroker. In flashbacks that describe the horror and torture suffered by Nazerman and his family, the reader begins to understand his withdrawal from humanity. The relationship between him and his young, ambitious, and confused assistant, Jesus Ortiz, provides the novel's shattering climax." Shapiro. Fic for Youth. 3d edition

Waller, Robert James, 1939-

The bridges of Madison County. Warner Bks. 1992 171p il o.p.

LC 91-50416

"This is the story of four days that change forever the lives of two lonely people. Robert Kincaid is a roving photographer for *National Geographic* and Francesca Johnson is a housewife whose marriage suffers from a lack of romance. Francesca's family is out of town when Kincaid arrives on the scene, and the pair are instantly attracted. They soon become lovers, and Kincaid asks Francesca to run away with him, but she refuses. Francesca stays loyal to her family, and memories of Kincaid are all that remain." Libr J

"An erotic, bittersweet tale of lingering memories and forsaken possibilities." Publ Wkly

Walsh, Helen, 1977-

Brass. Canongate 2004 296p pa $14

ISBN 1-8419-5484-5 (pa) LC 2005-415744

In this novel set in Liverpool, "nineteen-year-old university student Millie O'Reilley has not taken the news of the impending nuptials of her best mate, 28-year-old Jamie Keeley, very well. Drinking and drugging her way through the evenings, she usually ends up trolling the seedy section of town in search of female prostitutes (the 'brass' of the title). Jamie is growing increasingly impatient with and worried by Millie's behavior and is at a

Walsh, Helen, 1977—*Continued*

loss to explain their relationship to his dim-witted, social-climbing fiancee. What sets this first novel apart within a burgeoning subgenre is Walsh's lyrical prose. Her evocative phrasing both contains and stands in direct contrast to incredibly graphic scenes of depravity, and the result is both disturbing and compelling." Booklist

Walsh, Jill Paton *See* Paton Walsh, Jill, 1937-

Walsh, Pearl S. *See* Buck, Pearl S. (Pearl Sydenstricker), 1892-1973

Waltari, Mika, 1908-1979

The Egyptian; a novel; translated by Naomi Walford. Putnam 1949 503p o.p.

This is the first volume of the author's trilogy which includes the Etruscan and The Roman

Original Finnish edition, 1945

"The novel is set in Egypt during the 18th dynasty when Akhnaton, who ruled from 1353 to 1336 BC, established a new monotheistic cult. Narrated by its protagonist, a physician named Sinuhe who is in contact with both rich and poor, the novel describes the daily life, religion, and politics of the era. His travels take him as far away as Syria and Crete. A confidante of pharaohs, he eventually lives in permanent exile." Merriam-Webster's Ency of Lit

The Etruscan; translated by Lily Leino. Putnam 1956 381p o.p.

This is the second volume of the author's trilogy, the first and third being The Egyptian and The Roman

Original Finnish edition, 1955

Set in the ancient Mediterranean world, this novel recounts "the life story of a wealthy Etruscan who, after a great many fantastic adventures, dies in the year 500 B.C. believing himself to be immortal. . . . Its plot [is filled] with narrow escapes, blighted love affairs and supernatural events." Publ Wkly

"'The Etruscan' is truly a remarkable novel, whether viewed as sheer adventure, or as mysticism with occult meaning." N Y Her Trib Books

The Roman; The memoirs of Minutus Launsus Manilianus, who has won the Insignia of a Triumph, who has the rank of consul, who is chairman of the Priests' Collegium of the god Vespasian and a member of the Roman Senate; English version by Joan Tate. Putnam 1966 637p o.p.

This is the final volume of the trilogy, the first being The Egyptian, and the second, The Etruscan

Original Finnish edition, 1964

The story is set in the first century A.D. during the reigns of Claudius and Nero. Minutus is born in Antioch, comes to Rome at the age of fifteen, visits Jerusalem and Britain with the army, and wins honors and power and has several love affairs. He becomes intimate with Nero and helps him persecute the Christians

"Though Minutus is somewhat wooden, his adventures are astonishing. Waltari shuttles his hero around the empire, from Britain to Ephesus, in order to describe the growing decadence of Rome, the rise of Christianity, and the existence of other religions. Waltari's sense of humor and irony points up his pageant of Roman life." Publ Wkly

Walters, Minette

The breaker. Putnam 1999 351p $23.95

ISBN 0-399-14492-7 LC 98-51836

As this psychological thriller opens "the corpse of an attractive and pregnant woman is discovered washed ashore on the rocky Dorset coast in England. She has been drugged and sexually assaulted, her fingers deliberately broken, her body lashed to a dinghy to ensure her slow and painful death. What resident of the seaside village could be capable of such an atrocious crime?" Libr J

"Walters limits the suspects to two men with sufficient reason (and appropriate perversions) to have wanted the victim dead—the husband she betrayed and the lover she betrayed him with. Instead of making it easier to identify the killer, the narrow field only intensifies the challenge by demanding closer analysis." N Y Times Book Rev

The dark room. Putnam 1995 381p o.p.

LC 95-10616

In this novel, "Jinx Kingsley, daughter of millionaire Adam Kingsley, wakes up in a hospital. Not only is she suffering from amnesia, but she is swathed in bandages after an unsuccesful suicide attempt—her second in as many weeks—in apparent reaction to the news that her fiancé Leo has jilted her and disappeared with Jinx's best friend, Meg. Then Meg's and Leo's . . . bodies are discovered, and Jinx becomes the number-one murder suspect." Booklist

"Motivation is at the heart of The Dark Room. Like all the best detective fiction it challenges readers to work out how a particular character would act faced with specific circumstances. . . . The quest for truth is punctuated by touches of humanity that lift this novel way above others of its genre." New Statesman Soc

The echo. Putnam 1997 338p o.p.

LC 96-37485

"The discovery of a homeless man's body in the garage of a banker's wife leads her—and a journalist interested in the homeless—to find out more about the man. They also reinvestigate the disappearance, years ago, of the banker and a sizable sum of cash. . . . Well-crafted psychological suspense from a master." Libr J

The sculptress. St. Martin's Press 1993 308p o.p.

LC 93-21527

"Roz Leigh, an author embittered by the tragic death of a child and a split from her husband, agrees to write the story of Olive Martin, a grossly fat, untidy woman serving a long prison sentence for the particularly grisly murder of her mother and sister. Visiting Olive in jail, Roz finds herself drawn to the woman, and despite the fact that 'the sculptress' readily confessed to the crime, she begins to find odd discrepancies in the evidence against her." Publ Wkly

"Walters mesmerizes her readers with a sleek, exciting tale whose slick veneer disguises a sinister, menacing evil." Booklist

The shape of snakes. Putnam 2001 384p $24.95

ISBN 0-399-14733-0 LC 00-65319

The novel's protagonist "was traumatized in 1978 by the violent death of a London neighbor who suffered from Tourette's syndrome. 'I could never decide whether 'Mad Annie' was murdered because she was mad or be-

Walters, Minette—*Continued*
cause she was black,' she says. But the cruel nature of the woman's death and the torments she endured from prejudiced neighbors have haunted Mrs. Ranelagh for 20 years. And now it is time for the reckoning. Although the narrator obviously has a hidden agenda, the master manipulator here is Walters, whose commanding control over her inflammatory material—and her readers—distracts the eye from potential murder suspects and directs the mind to the everyday acts of casual inhumanity that are the real issue." N Y Times Book Rev

Wambaugh, Joseph

The black marble. Delacorte Press 1978 354p o.p.

LC 77-14262

"Veteran Los Angeles detective Valnikov is on the bottle and subject to nightmares now that his wife has left him and his close colleague has died. His reluctant partner Natalie thinks he's gone crazy and plans to report his behavior. However, when a top-flight dog handler named Philo, under pressure from loan sharks, 'dognaps' a prize schnauzer from a seemingly wealthy (actually quite poor) Pasadena society woman, Valnikov and Natalie get drawn into the case—and toward each other." Publ Wkly

"The unusual plot is laced with facetiousness that culminates as the bumbling dognapper—a lascivious old trainer who gets stoned at a dog show and comments acridly on the whole ordeal—and the police detective meet for a showdown, locked in a dog cage. A novel of surprises without the grimness of his earlier work." Booklist

The blue knight. Little, Brown 1972 338p o.p.

"An Atlantic Monthly Press book"

A novel about "Bumper Morgan, a fat Irish cop at 50, dyspeptic, lusty, tough, egotistic, with only two days to go before his planned retirement from the Los Angeles police department." Libr J

"The caricature is deliberate; the author means to endow a stereotype with complexity and sentiment. Bumper has his own street ethics. . . . The book tends to be a bit ostentatious in such honesties, as if they established Bumper's credibility. In the end, Wambaugh sentimentalizes Bumper as a sort of repellently lovable super-cop who, whenever he is not strongarming 'pukepots,' is bantering in Yiddish, Spanish or Arabic with the ethnics on the beat." Time

The Delta Star. Morrow 1983 276p o.p.

LC 82-21638

"A Perigord Press book"

The plot of this police novel concerns "a scam to divert the Nobel Prize in Chemistry from one professor to another less deserving. It involves two murders, the Russians, sexual blackmail, the chemistry faculty at Caltech and a . . . police detective." Newsweek

"Perhaps better than any other contemporary writer, Wambaugh is able to convey just what it is that makes cops different from the rest of us and, more important, why. In this latest novel . . . the reader meets an array of Wambaugh's finest, from Rumpled Ronald, who is merely trying to stay alive to collect his pension, to the Bad Czech, who helps solve a double murder all because of a chopstick in his shoe." Libr J

Finnegan's week. Morrow 1993 348p o.p.

LC 93-24890

"The owner of a waste-hauling firm shaves costs by mislabeling drums of highly toxic pesticide and dumping them illegally. When two deaths result, Fin Finnegan teams up with civilian and Navy investigators to solve the series of related crimes." SLJ

"There is a boyish excessiveness to Mr. Wambaugh's writing that produces an odd synergy with his carefully constructed plots and his colorful characters." N Y Times Book Rev

Floaters. Bantam Bks. 1996 293p o.p.

LC 95-26625

In this novel, "two clumsy conspirators try to fix the America's Cup race. A hot number named Blaze Duvall does the grunt work of seducing a dumb sailor into sabotaging the Black Magic, the formidable New Zealand contender. Blaze stands to make a buck from this scheme, but it is really a crime of passion devised by Ambrose Lutterworth, the keeper of the cup, who can't bear to give up his beloved charge. As a spy, the flame-haired Blaze is a bit conspicuous, catching the eye of Fortney and Leeds, a couple of calloused veterans with the harbor police unit that cruises Mission Bay in San Diego." N Y Times Book Rev

The Glitter Dome. Morrow 1981 299p o.p.

"A Perigord Press book"

"Two very human detectives, Martin Welborn and Aloysius Mackey, specialized in converting obvious homicides (unsolved) into official suicides (solved). Their current assignment is the murder of Nigel St. Clair, the president of a film company. For allies, the duo depends upon Weasel and Ferret, a wry team of Narcs." Publ Wkly

"Wambaugh utilizes a brash and earthy style to maximum effect, sketching a grimy, unglamorous landscape of rough action, tough language, and gruesome detail. Artful characterization and occasional humor enliven the whole, and prevent the problems associated with police work (alcoholism, divorce, suicide) from becoming overly depressing." Libr J

The new centurions. Little, Brown 1971 c1970 376p o.p.

"An Atlantic Monthly Press book"

The author "shows us the excitement, danger and sordidness found in the daily work of three young Los Angeles policemen. From the police academy to the first foot patrol, from the first patrol-car duty to the first promotion, Wambaugh follows his three main characters in their professional and personal lives, and shows us that police work, like the ministry, medicine or the military, is a profession demanding 24-hour dedication, determination, discipline and often a frustrating acceptance of defeat." Natl Rev

"As a novel the book has lapses, it wears its exposition on its sleeve—necessarily, perhaps, in view of what it's trying to do—and the three protagonists, though very different in type, are perhaps not sufficiently different in sensibility. . . . But never mind that. What he knows Wambaugh tells truly, perceptively, and well." Book World

Ward, Liza

Outside valentine. Holt & Co. 2004 301p $23

ISBN 0-8050-7598-4

Ward, Liza—*Continued*

"Crosscutting between the late 1950s and the year 1991, and told in a trio of voices, the novel tracks the murderous acts of Charles Starkweather and his 14-year-old girlfriend, Caril Ann Fugate, and their impact on Lowell Bowman, who was orphaned by their rampage." Booklist

"A gifted writer, Ward uses simple imagery to chilling effect. A dog with a broken neck hiding under the bed after its owner has been murdered and a dead schoolgirl with her skirt pulled up—Starkweather says he just wanted to look—are as vivid as anything filmmakers have fashioned from the same raw material." Washington Post Book World

Ward, Mary Jane, 1905-

The snake pit. Random House 1946 278p o.p.

Related in the first person, this tells of the experiences undergone by the patient, Virginia Cunningham, in a state mental hospital. It follows the course of her insanity from her commitment to her final release. It also takes the reader through mental hospital routine in all its reality

"Chronicled so quietly and unemphatically, the horrors of asylum life become infinitely more poignant than they appear in the hands of grimmer writers who are out to shock. Obviously an incomplete picture, but an extraordinarily moving one." New Yorker

Warner, Charles Dudley, 1829-1900

(jt. auth) Twain, M. The gilded age

Warren, Robert Penn, 1905-1989

All the king's men. Harcourt Brace Jovanovich 1990 c1946 531p $19

ISBN 0-15-104772-3 LC 90-36181

"An HBJ modern classic"

First published 1946

"In the South during the 1920s a young journalist, Jack Burden, becomes involved in the drive for political power by soon-to-be governor Willie Stark. The journey is a rocky, disillusioning one, and involves exploitation, deceit, and violence. When asked by Stark to uncover a scandal in the past of Judge Irwin, Jack must weigh the many consequences of such action." Shapiro. Fic for Youth. 3d edition

Band of angels. Random House 1955 375p o.p.

"A lush, full-bodied Civil War story about a Kentucky plantation owner's daughter sold into slavery whose fight becomes an inquiry into the nature of freedom and the quest for individual identity." Oxford Companion to Am Lit. 6th edition

A place to come to; a novel. Random House 1977 401p o.p.

LC 76-50129

"Jediah Tewksbury, a poor white from rural Alabama, grows into the complex, 60-year-old classic scholar who looks back and constructs his life, and this novel. The structure of both is determined by the deaths of people crucial to that growth: primarily his father; then his mentor Stahlmann; a Nazi officer, a classical scholar too, whom he murders; his wife, of cancer; the first husband of his mistress, which haunts his affair; and lastly his mother, which brings him home to the novel's title. Nashville, Chicago, and Europe are important places, too, and it all moves to the subtle variations of Time—in it, through it, outside of it, always measured by it. . . . An altogether masterful performance." Libr J

World enough and time; a romantic novel. Random House 1950 512p o.p.

"The murder in Kentucky of Col. Solomon P. Sharp by Jeroboam O. Beauchamp, whose trial was the sensation of 1826, has been a popular theme for novelists ever since. Warren's version in this novel is based on *The Confession*, which Beauchamp published in 1826. Warren introduced many variations, however, and his quotations from documents are his own inventions." Benet's Reader's Ency of Am Lit

Washington, Alex *See* Harris, Mark, 1922-

Waters, Mary Yukari

The laws of evening; stories. Scribner 2003 177p $23

ISBN 0-7432-4332-3 LC 2002-29429

Contents: Seed; Since my house burned down; Shibusa; Aftermath; Kami; Rationing; The laws of evening; Egg-face; The way love works; Circling the hondo; Mirror studies

"Like the spare and prescribed movements of a Japanese tea ceremony, the stories in The laws of evening. . . present a deceptively smooth and elegant surface. Underneath this unruffled exterior, however, the smallest nuances convey real depth of feeling." N Y Times Book Rev

Watkins, Paul, 1964-

Calm at sunset, calm at dawn. Houghton Mifflin 1989 275p o.p.

ISBN 0-395-50959-9 LC 89-32471

This novel is an "account, in the first person, of a young man's first summer spent crewing on an offshore trawler. . . . Pfeiffer, though the son of a fisherman himself, is pushed by his parents towards college and a less dangerous career. When he is suspended from university after a fight over a stolen camera, he takes to fishing, and thus prompts a confrontation with his troubled father." Times Lit Suppl

The book "carries conviction as an account of what fishermen are like, on shore and off, and what the practice of fishing amounts to. The plain, clear prose is . . . instructive in the way that Orwell is when he writes about his lower depths." London Rev Books

The forger. Picador 2000 322p $25

ISBN 0-312-26593-X LC 00-33631

"Shortly before WWII, David Halifax, a young American painter, receives a mysterious scholarship to study in Paris with the eccentric genius Alexander Pankratov. Halifax supplements his scholarship income by selling his sketches through a charming and unscrupulous art dealer, Guillaume Fleury. When war is declared, the three are enlisted by the French government in an elaborate scheme to prevent classic works of art from falling into German hands." Publ Wkly

Watkins, Paul, 1964-—*Continued*

"Watkins is an extremely facile writer. His novels are thrilling, fast-paced, intricately plotted and extraordinarily atmospheric. Cerebral in the manner of Graham Greene, . . . Watkins, like Greene, can create a wartime sensibility in which every footfall on the stairs has you holding your breath in anticipation. In 'The Forger', he has created a shifting—and shifty—cast of characters whose loyalties and alliances keep changing as the events of the war advance." N Y Times Book Rev

In the blue light of African dreams. Houghton Mifflin 1990 310p o.p.
ISBN 0-395-55136-6 LC 90-35174
This novel, "set in 1926 and 1927, falls into two sections. In the first, Charlie Halifax, a First World War veteran and an ace pilot, is hunting Arabs and avoiding renegade Germans in their pay over the Moroccan Sahara. In the second, Charlie joins with Ivan, his mechanic, in an attempt to win the Orteig prize, to be awarded for the first nonstop flight across the Atlantic between New York and Paris." Times Lit Suppl

Night over day over night. Knopf 1988 293p o.p.
ISBN 0-394-57047-2 LC 87-46102
"This first novel is the story of a 17-year-old who joins the Waffen SS in the summer of 1944. It follows him through the rigors of boot camp and into the horrors of combat. His unit is one of those spearheading the desperate Ardennes offensive (the Battle of the Bulge)." Libr J
"Daring and remarkably assured. . . Watkins proceeds in communicating not only invisible hunts of the blood, noise, and horror of the battlefield, but also the consequences the conditions of violence can have on young unformed minds." N Y Times (Late N Y Ed)

The promise of light. Random House 1993 271p o.p.
ISBN 0-679-41974-8 LC 92-17865
In this novel "set in the 1920s, Ben Sheridan journeys from America to Ireland, from detachment to involvement, from ignorance to knowledge. He is ready to settle into a secure banking job after college, but his expectation of a predictable middle-class future is interrupted by a family crisis requiring him to make what he expects to be a relatively short and simple voyage to the Irish village his father left when Ben was born. Unfortunately, his arrival coincides with the start of IRA hostilities, making it safer for him to lie about his business–the first misstep leading into a quicksand of deceit." Libr J

Watson, Brad

The heaven of Mercury. Norton 2002 333p $23.95
ISBN 0-393-04757-1
In this "southern gothic tale, Finus Bates, an 89-year-old radio announcer, reflects on his thwarted love affair with Birdie Wells. As a child, Finus falls in love with the winsome Birdie when he spies her executing a naked cartwheel. Despite their mutual attraction, Birdie and Finus end up betrothed to others: Birdie to the lecherous son of one of the town's wealthiest families, and Finus to Birdie's best friend, a severe woman with unexpected reservoirs of strength. As Watson traces the lovers' sad histories, he flips to the present day, when Finus investigates the decades-old poisoning of Birdie's husband." Booklist
"Watson lays bare the lives and most intimate secrets of the richest and poorest families in Mercury, MS. The characters' racism may offend some readers, but it is an essential element of that particular time and place." Libr J

Watson, Larry

Orchard; a novel. Random House 2003 241p $24.95
ISBN 0-375-50723-X LC 2002-35654
The author "introduces us to Henry and Sonya House, a couple who have drifted apart after the death of their 4-year-old son. They own an apple orchard that has been in Henry's family for generations. . . . One day . . . Sonja is approached by Ned Weaver, a local artist with a reputation for sleeping with his models, who asks her to pose for him. She agrees . . . Weaver becomes obsessed with Sonja, and Henry . . . becomes increasingly jealous until he confronts Weaver." N Y Times Book Rev
Watson's novel is "an uncompromising, perfectly calibrated double portrait of two couples in rural Wisconsin in the 1950s. . . . Sentences and chapters unfurl with a sense of inevitability, and the narrative possesses an uncommon integrity." Publ Wkly

Watt, Donley

Reynolds; a novel. Texas Christian Univ. Press 2002 191p $24.50
ISBN 0-87565-256-5 LC 2001-53140
This novel "revolves around the misadventures of 46-year-old Ray Reynolds Jr., a bright but underachieving liquor store owner from tiny Clear Lake Creek, who finds himself living in a trailer while trying to rekindle life's spark. Female trouble is high on Reynold's list of issues, starting with his troubled relationship with Joy, a spunky young waitress who wants someone more serious than her bar-hopping partner. . . . But his immediate concern is his brother Perry, a disaffected schoolteacher who has begun stockpiling weapons with a band of his seedy buddies and getting himself in trouble for teaching his strange survivalist doctrine to his students. . . . Watt is a lively narrator from the Lewis Nordan school who creates a spirited crew of oddball characters and defty uses the smalltown Texas setting to play up their various idiosyncrasies." Publ Wkly

Waugh, Evelyn, 1903-1966

Brideshead revisited; with an introduction by Frank Kermode. Knopf 1993 xxxvii, 315p $17
ISBN 0-679-42300-1 LC 93-1854
"Everyman's library"
A reissue of the title first published 1945 by Little, Brown
"The novel, which takes the form of an extended flashback, is narrated by Charles Ryder, an army officer billeted at the eponymous country house, owned by an aristocratic Roman Catholic family headed by Lord and Lady Marchmain. Charles had visited Brideshead with Sebastian Flyte, the Marchmains' younger son, when

Waugh, Evelyn, 1903-1966—*Continued*
both were Oxford undergraduates. In the course of the narrative Ryder conveys his fascination with the family, all of whom are eccentric or unhappy in some way." Oxford Companion to 20th Cent Lit in Engl

The complete stories of Evelyn Waugh. Little, Brown 1999 535p $29.95
ISBN 0-316-92546-2 LC 99-20837
Contents: The balance; A house of gentlefolks; The manager of "The Kremlin"; Love in the slump; Too much tolerance; Excursion in reality; Incident in Azania; Bella Fleace gave a party; Cruise; The man who liked Dickens; Out of depth; By special request; Period piece; On guard; Mr. Loveday's little outing; Winner takes all; An Englishman's home; The sympathetic passenger; My father's house; Lucy Simmonds; Charles Ryder's schooldays; Scott-King's modern Europe; Tactical exercise; Compassion; Love among the ruins; Basil Seal rides again; The curse of the horse race; Fidon's confetion; Multa Pecunia; Fragment of a novel; Essay; The house: an anti-climax; Portrait of young man with career; Antony, who sought things that were lost; Edward of unique achievement; Fragments: they dine with the past; Conspiracy to murder; Unacademic exercise: a nature story; The national game
"These 39 stories span Waugh's writing career, and to a one they demonstrate his trademark wit and sophistication." Booklist

Decline and fall. Doubleday, Doran 1929 c1928 293p o.p.
First published 1928 in the United Kingdom
This novel "recounts the chequered career of Paul Pennyfeather, sent down from Scone College, Oxford, for 'indecent behaviour', as the innocent victim of a drunken orgy. Thus forced to abandon a career in the church, he becomes a schoolmaster at Llanabba Castle, where he encounters headmaster Fagan and his daughters, the dubious, bigamous, and reappearing Captain Grimes, and young Beste-Chetwynde, whose glamorous mother Margot carries him off to the dangerous delight of high society. They are about to be married when Paul is arrested at the Ritz and subsequently imprisoned for Margot's activities in the white slave trade." Oxford Companion to Engl Lit. 6th edition

The end of the battle. Little, Brown 1962 c1961 319p o.p.
Sequel to Officers and gentlemen
First published 1961 in the United Kingdom with title: Unconditional surrender
In this final volume of the trilogy "Guy volunteers for service in Italy with the military government, and he eventually goes to Yugoslavia as a liaison officer with the Partisans. Virginia gives birth to a son (not Guy's) and is killed in an air raid. At the end of the book Guy has again asserted himself, in the rescue of a group of Jewish refugees, and realizes what kind of man he used to be: one who believed that his private honour would be satisfied by war. In an Epilogue we learn that he has remarried and surrounded himself with a family." Camb Guide to Lit in Engl

The loved one; an Anglo-American tragedy. Little, Brown 1948 164p o.p.
"Depicting romance in a mortuary could be gruesome but the author succeeds both in poking satirical fun at the maudlin pretentiousness of the funeral industry and in delighting the reader with a hilarious love story." Shapiro. Fic for Youth. 3d edition

Men at arms. Little, Brown 1952 o.p.
This is the first volume of the trilogy that includes Officers and gentlemen and The end of the battle
This novel "introduces 35-year-old divorced Catholic Guy Crouchback, who after much effort succeeds in enlisting in the Royal Corps of Halberdiers just after the outbreak of the Second World War. Much of the plot revolves around his eccentric fellow officer Apthorpe, an old Africa hand who suffers repeatedly from 'Bechuana tummy', is deeply devoted to his 'thunder box' (or chemical closet), and dies in West Africa at the end of the novel of some unspecified tropical disease, aggravated by Guy's thoughtful gift of a bottle of whisky. Other characters include Guy's ex-wife, the beautiful socialite Virginia Troy, her second (but not her final) husband, Tommy Blackhouse, and the ferocious one-eyed Brigadier Ritchie-Hook, who involves Guy in a near-disastrous escapade." Oxford Companion to Engl Lit. 6th edition
Followed by Officers and gentlemen

Officers and gentlemen. Little, Brown 1955 339p o.p.
Sequel to Men at arms
This novel "continues Waugh's semi-satiric, semi-emotional portrayal of civilian and military life with an account of Guy's training on the Hebridean island of Mugg with a commando unit, and of the exploits of ex-hairdresser Trimmer, now Captain McTavish, which include an affair with Virginia and the blowing up of a French railway; the action moves to Alexandria, then to the withdrawal from Crete, with all but four of 'Hookforce' taken prisoner." Oxford Companion to Engl Lit. 6th edition
Followed by The end of the battle

Vile bodies. Little, Brown 1930 321p o.p.
"Set in England between the wars, the novel examines the frenetic but empty lives of the Bright Young Things, young people who indulge in constant party-going, heavy drinking, and promiscuous sex. At the novel's end, the realities of the world intrude, with Adam Fenwick-Symes, the protagonist, serving on a battlefield at the onset of another world war." Merriam-Webster's Ency of Lit

Weaver, Michael, 1929-

Deceptions. Warner Bks. 1995 454p o.p.
LC 94-17382
"The story concerns two boys who grew up in the Mob's shadow. One is now an artist, the other a hit man. When the hit man fails to kill one victim (because of true love, we learn), powerful forces of vengeance are unleashed. The artist, challenged to rat on his childhood buddy, draws upon murderous resources." Libr J
"Enhanced by strong, sinewy writing, numerous plot twists and a potent melding of sex and violence, this expertly wrought novel proves that Weaver knows what most thriller fans want—and can deliver it in spades." Publ Wkly

Webb, James H.

A sense of honor. Prentice-Hall 1981 308p o.p.
LC 80-25852

"Plebe life at Annapolis in 1968 proceeds as normal while the specter of Vietnam haunts the routine of midshipmen and the careers of recent graduates. Traditional military ways begin to yield to changing times and altered perceptions; on a personal level this conflict is captured in the relationship between a fourth-year student and a plebe who questions the rigid code of honor and unblinking acceptance of the hazing ritual." Booklist

"In this powerful novel, Webb . . . a graduate of the Academy, pulls the reader right into the caldron of Annapolis for a vivid picture of heroes and martinets living according to their various interpretations of 'honor'; and he illuminates the mystique that makes men voluntarily stay in such a meat grinder." Publ Wkly

Weber, Katharine

The little women. Farrar, Straus & Giroux 2003 240p $22
ISBN 0-374-18959-5 LC 2003-44062

In a story narrated by 16-year-old Joanna, the modern-day Little Women of the title "grow up in New York City in cozy upper-middle-class bliss, their perfect family the envy of all. But their smug contentment is shattered when they discover their mother's affair; their father's blasé reaction is almost worse. In protest, Joanna and Amy move in with Meg and her roommate, Teddy Bell, at their off-campus apartment near Yale University. . . . Comments from Meg and Amy pepper the text, contesting the structure of Joanna's story and arguing with her about her perspective and her version of reality." Publ Wkly

"In places, the readers' and author's notes do cause the pace to drag. But fortunately, the story of three teenage girls making a go of living in a New Haven apartment with a cute male roommate is lively, interesting and funny enough to carry one over the sluggish bits. . . . Novels with spurious critical apparatus don't often wear it lightly, but Weber's use of the form is both easy and playful." N Y Times Book Rev

The Music Lesson. Crown 1999 178p o.p.
LC 98-9346

"Patricia Dolan is a fortysomething art history librarian at the Frick Museum in New York when she's accosted by a dangerously charming young Irish cousin. Swept up in a gust of passion, she moves with him to a remote Irish village. Exploiting her knowledge, cousin Michael and his IRA splinter group steal a priceless Vermeer, *The Music Lesson*, for which they hope to extract a ransom from the British monarchy." Libr J

This "mystery is as intricate as an acrostic. A trio of clues—the motives of the narrator, who is a woman recovering from the accidental death of her child; the paintings of Vermeer, and the ideals of Irish nationalism—yield, by the book's close, an almost perfect, if chilling, answer." New Yorker

Weidman, Jerome, 1913-1998

I can get it for you wholesale. Simon & Schuster 1937 370p o.p.

"This novel, a realistic satire, tells the story of an ambitious and unscrupulous young Jew named Harry Bogen, who begins as a shipping clerk in the New York garment center and rapidly becomes a successful dress manufacturer with money to burn. In this process he double-crosses every friend he has, except the chorus girl whose sex appeal is his stimulus. A few compunctions, raised by associations with his mother and a childhood sweetheart, he stifles with a little vague discomfort. His only standard is to be smarter than the other fellow." Saturday Rev

Weiner, Jennifer, 1970-

Little earthquakes; Jennifer Weiner. Atria Bks. 2004 417p $26
ISBN 0-7434-7009-5

This is the "story of four women in Philadelphia who bond over pregnancy and motherhood. Becky, Kelly, and Ayinde meet in yoga class, and the three become friends when Ayinde's water breaks one day after class and they take her to the hospital. Becky is a chef with an adoring husband and an annoying mother-in-law; Kelly is frustrated when her husband loses his job and drags his feet looking for another; Ayinde's husband is a famous basketball player whom she suspects of infidelity. What brings the women together is their love for their newborns. The fourth woman, Lia, watches the group from afar; she's an actress who walked out on her husband after a devastating tragedy. Weiner seamlessly and gracefully weaves the four women's stories together." Booklist

Weinstein, Debra, 1961-

Apprentice to the flower poet Z. Random House 2004 242p $23.95
ISBN 1-400-06155-5

A novel about New York's academic poetry scene. "Z. writes sexy if vapid poems about flowers and love and is hell bent on protecting her turf, pleasing her politically well placed lover, avoiding her actor-writer husband, showcasing her Harvard-bound daughter, and taking full advantage of Annabelle, her initially enthralled, soon disillusioned assistant. An undergraduate steeped in Emily Dickinson, entangled in a weird affair, in debt to her therapist, and eager to learn from the master, Annabelle finds herself doing Z.'s housework, running dubious errands, and, in effect, writing Z.'s poems." Booklist

"What's sharpest about Weinstein's well-metered wit is the way she sinks down into this elite subculture. The whole shameful business has been presatirzed for decades, but Weinstein, a published poet herself, knows where all the bodies are buried." Christ Sci Monit

Weis, Margaret, 1948-

Guardians of the lost; [by] Margaret Weis and Tracy Hickman. HarperCollins Pubs. 2001 592p o.p.
ISBN 0-06-105179-9 LC 2001-40770

Weis, Margaret, 1948-—*Continued*

Sequel to Well of darkness

"The second volume of the Sovereign Stone opens some two centuries after *Well of Darkness* ended. Prince Dagnarus—immortal, thanks to his mastery of Void magic—strives to keep the various races from uniting their portions of the Sovereign Stone, and the human knight, Gustav, sacrifices his life to pass the human portion on." Booklist

In this sequel the authors "again demonstrate their uncanny ability to create meticulously detailed imaginary worlds peopled with complex and vital characters." Libr J

Mistress of dragons. TOR Bks. 2003 381p $25.95

ISBN 0-7653-0468-6 LC 2003-42618

"A Tom Doherty Associates book"

When the Amazonian order of priestesses, who have kept dragons from interfering with humans, is violated by men, a wild and magical conflict ensues, revealing a secret lineage and dark truth about the Parliament of Dragons

"Full of intrigue, magic, and violence, this first book of Dragonvald—a projected trilogy chronicling the battle to preserve the uneasy relationship between dragons and humans—launches the project powerfully. Weis has brilliantly conceived a world viable for both dragons and humans." Booklist

Well of darkness; [by] Margaret Weis and Tracy Hickman. HarperCollins Pubs. 2000 450p pa $7.99 o.p.

ISBN 0-06-105180-2; 0-06-102057-5 (pa) LC 00-41710

"Chosen to serve as the whipping boy of the young Prince Dagnarus, Gareth becomes his master's friend and confidant as they grow to manhood and become embroiled in the affairs of the land. Tempted by dark powers, Gareth seeks to assist the prince in his search for love and glory, unaware of the greater paths each must follow to fulfill his destiny." Libr J

The authors "raise a fairly standard plot far above mediocrity with ingenious world-building touches. . . . Moreover, they render Gareth and Dagnarus' friendship convincingly; the characters' motives are plausible and fully developed, and both retain human appeal." Booklist

Followed by Guardians of the lost

Welch, James, 1940-2003

The heartsong of Charging Elk; a novel. Doubleday 2000 440p $24.95

ISBN 0-385-49674-5 LC 99-58875

"As a young Oglala Sioux, Charging Elk saw the massacre of General Custer's forces at Little Big Horn. . . . Now in his early 20s and on a tour of Europe as part of Buffalo Bill Cody's 'Wild West show' in the 1890s, Charging Elk has become stranded in Marseille, France." Christ Sci Monit

The author "estranges our vision. We have no choice but to feel, as we look through Charging Elk's eyes, what it is like to live in a no man's land forever." N Y Times Book Rev

The Indian lawyer. Norton 1990 349p o.p.

LC 90-6894

"Sylvester Yellow Calf, the hero of this novel, has fought his way, despite the odds, to a top post in a prestigious Montana law firm and now is being wooed as a candidate for Congress by political power brokers. Sylvester, ex-basketball star and Stanford Law School graduate, recognizes that such a move could put him in a position to help his fellow Native Americans and at the same time to work for the preservation of the environment. While his responsibilities are all too clear to him, Yellow Calf hesitates, and, as he ponders his decision, he is drawn by a convict into a web that nearly strangles him." Choice

"The novel contains good, fast-paced action with succinct insight into our ordinary dilemmas." Nation

Welcome, John, 1914-

(ed) The Dick Francis treasury of great racing stories. See The Dick Francis treasury of great racing stories

Weldon, Fay

Big girls don't cry. Atlantic Monthly Press 1998 345p $24

ISBN 0-87113-720-8 LC 98-35702

First published 1997 in the United Kingdom with title: Big women

This novel looks back "at the early days of feminism as experienced by four Londoners. In 1971 Layla, Zoe and Alice gather in Stephie's living room to engage in consciousness-raising while, in an upstairs bedroom, Stephie's husband, Hamish, deprograms a convert. The women, discover this sexual betrayal just as Zoe's abusive husband, Bull, arrives to save her soul from women's lib. Provoked by these outrages, the remaining three decide to establish Medusa, a publishing house devoted to women's works." Publ Wkly

"Just when Weldon's wit starts to sound like fingernails on a blackboard, she relents and reminds us that even in comedy, she's dead serious. . . . It's tempting to find the zany conclusion unsatisfying because it leaves no answers, but that's the privilege of smart satire." Christ Sci Monit

A hard time to be a father. St. Martin's Press 1999 242p $23.95

ISBN 1-58234-011-0

Contents: What the papers say; The ghost of potlatch past; Once in love in Oslo; GUP—or falling in love in Helsinki; Come on, everyone!; Percentage trust; Inside the whale—or, I don't know but I've been told; Move out: move on; New Year's Day; Inspector remorse; My mother said; A libation of blood; Pyroclastic flow; Spirits fly south; Stasi; A great antipodean scandal; New advances; Noisy into the night; A hard time to be a father

Weldon "is at her wry, risk-taking best in this broad collection of 19 stories. . . . In her signature style, Weldon peoples many of these pieces with women who wreak catastrophe in ways that thrill the misanthropic reader." Publ Wkly

Weldon, Fay—*Continued*

The life and loves of a she-devil. Pantheon Bks. 1984 c1983 241p o.p.

LC 84-7070

First published 1983 in the United Kingdom

"A fable about female power and powerlessness, telling the story of Ruth, an ugly woman married to a philandering man, who transforms herself by sheer strength of will into the image of her hated rival." Oxford Companion to 20th-Century Lit in Engl

Rhode Island blues. Atlantic Monthly Press 2000 325p $24

ISBN 0-87113-775-5 LC 00-38576

"Felicity Moore is an attractive, sexually active octogenarian grandmother who has decided to move into the Golden Bowl Complex for Creative Retirement. . . . Felicity's granddaughter, Sophia King, is a 34-year-old British film editor. . . . When Sophia comes to New England to help Felicity settle into the Golden Bowl, she learns that her grandmother had another daughter whom she gave up for adoption more than a half century earlier. While Sophia returns to London in search of her long-lost aunt, Felicity falls in love with a compulsive gambler and together they outsmart the evil and sadistic Nurse Dawn." Publ Wkly

"Weldon employs a merciless form of satire here; she also takes on favorite themes: love and the war between the sexes. But 'Rhode Island Blues'—is about more than that. Just how much more, in fact, is staggering. Here's a short list of topics covered: rape, adoption, prostitution, murder, romance between the elderly, compulsive gambling, family bonds, madness Hollywood, immigration and sadomasochism." N Y Time Book Rev

Wicked women; stories. Atlantic Monthly Press 1997 309p $23

ISBN 0-87113-681-3 LC 96-37499

Contents: End of the line; Run and ask daddy if he has any more money; In the Great War (II); Not even a blood relation; Wasted lives; Love amongst the artists; Leda and the swan; Tale of Timothy Bagshott; Valediction; Through a dustbin darkly; A good sound marriage; Web central; Pains; A question of timing; Red on black; Knock-knock; Santa Claus's new clothes; Baked Alaska; The pardoner; Heat haze

These stories offer "intricate moments in the lives of defeated lovers, insecure cuckolds, perplexed offspring, daring widow/ers, keen children, and underdogs who overcome the oppression of love. Weldon brings together all facets of the relationship race with a unique mastery, using sharp and cultivated prose." Libr J

Worst fears; a novel. Atlantic Monthly Press 1996 200p o.p.

LC 95-52367

The protagonist of this novel is "Alexandra Ludd, a successful stage actress who is performing in Ibsen's *A Doll's House* when her husband, Ned, a theater critic, dies in their country house. Alexandra takes a leave of absence from the London production, only to find that her friends in the country all seem to be engaged in some kind of cover-up regarding the circumstances of Ned's death. It gradually becomes clear to Alexandra that her husband lived a very different and more promiscuous life than she'd ever suspected." Publ Wkly

Fay Weldon is the "quintessential anti-romance novelist and always will be. But she's filed down a few sharp edges in 'Worst Fears,' and that makes it one of her best novels yet." N Y Times Book Rev

Wellesley, Charles *See* Brontë, Charlotte, 1816-1855

Wells, H. G. (Herbert George), 1866-1946

The complete short stories of H. G. Wells. St. Martin's Press 1987 c1927 1038p $19.95

ISBN 0-312-15855-6 LC 87-27478

First published 1927 in the United Kingdom with title: The short stories of H. G. Wells

A collection of 62 short stories and the complete work: The time machine, first published 1895

"A fat, heavy volume packed with humour, strangeness, horror and imaginative stimulus." Daily Telegraph

The first men in the moon
In Wells, H. G. Seven famous novels

The food of the gods
In Wells, H. G. Seven famous novels

In the days of the comet
In Wells, H. G. Seven famous novels

The invisible man. Penguin 2005 xxiv, 161p pa $6

ISBN 0-14-143998-X

First published 1897

"The story concerns the life and death of a scientist named Griffin who has gone mad. Having learned how to make himself invisible, Griffin begins to use his invisibility for nefarious purposes, including murder. When he is finally killed, his body becomes visible again." Merriam-Webster's Ency of Lit

also in Wells, H. G. Seven famous novels

The island of Doctor Moreau. o.p.

First published 1896

This is "an evolutionary fantasy about a shipwrecked naturalist who becomes involved in an experiment to 'humanize' animals by surgery." Oxford Companion to Engl Lit. 6th edition

also in Wells, H. G. Seven famous novels

The island of Dr. Moreau
In Wells, H. G. Seven famous novels

Seven famous novels; with a preface by the author. Knopf 1934 860p o.p.

Contents: The time machine (1895); The island of Dr. Moreau (1896); The invisible man (1897); The war of the worlds (1898); The first men in the moon (1901); The food of the gods (1904); In the days of the comet (1906)

The time machine. Penguin 2005 xxviii, 104p pa $9

ISBN 0-14-143997-1

First published 1895

"Wells advanced his social and political ideas in this narrative of a nameless Time Traveller who is hurtled into the year 802,701 by his elaborate ivory, crystal, and brass contraption. The world he finds is peopled by two

Wells, H. G. (Herbert George), 1866-1946— *Continued*

races: the decadent Eloi, fluttery and useless, are dependent for food, clothing, and shelter on the simian subterranean Morlocks, who prey on them. The two races—whose names are borrowed from the Biblical Eli and Moloch—symbolize Wells's vision of the eventual result of unchecked capitalism: a neurasthenic upper class that would eventually be devoured by a proletariat driven to the depths." Merriam-Webster's Ency of Lit

also in Wells, H. G. The complete short stories of H. G. Wells

also in Wells, H. G. Seven famous novels

Tono-Bungay; edited by Patrick Parrinder; with an introduction and notes by Edward Mendelson. Penguin 2005 xxxiii, 414p pa $14

ISBN 0-14-144111-9

First published 1908

"The narrator is George Ponderevo, son of the housekeeper on a large estate, who is apprenticed to his uncle, Edward Ponderevo, a small-town druggist. His fantastic uncle soon moves to London and makes a fortune from his quack medicine Tono-Bungay. George helps his uncle, ironically observes his rise in the world, and uses some of his money to set himself up as an airplane designer. George resembles H. G. Wells himself—the son of a housekeeper, apprenticed to a druggist, a socialist, and a man with a vision of progress through properly used science." Reader's Ency. 4th edition

The war of the worlds; illustrated by Edward Gorey. New York Review Books [2005] c1960 251p il $16.95

ISBN 1-59017-158-6 LC 2005-3693

First published 1898

"The inhabitants of Mars, a loathsome though highly organized race, invade England, and by their command of superior weapons subdue and prey on the people." Baker. Guide to the Best Fic

In this novel the author "introduced the 'Alien' being into the role which became a cliché—a monstrous invader of Earth, a competitor in a cosmic struggle for existence. Though the Martians were a ruthless and terrible enemy, HGW was careful to point out that Man had driven many animal species to extinction, and that human invaders of Tasmania had behaved no less callously in exterminating their cousins." Sci Fic Ency

also in Wells, H. G. Seven famous novels

Wells, Herbert George *See* Wells, H. G. (Herbert George), 1866-1946

Wells, Ken

Meely LaBauve; a novel. Random House 2000 244p o.p.

ISBN 0-375-50311-0 LC 99-36281

A novel set in the Louisiana bayou. "Emile LaBauve, who goes by the nickname Meely, is a dirt-poor and barely educated 15-year-old whose mother is dead and whose father, an alligator hunter, always seems to be in trouble with the law. A small boy of indeterminate race . . . Meely suffers the taunts of the schoolhouse bully, Junior Guidry, who is also the nephew of an equally hateful but far more dangerous local cop, known simply as Uncle. What propels this book, however, isn't plot but language. . . . It's not only funny but infused with Well's deep love of Cajun patois" N Y Times Book Rev

Welsh, Irvine

Porno. Norton 2002 483p $24.95

ISBN 0-393-05723-2 LC 2002-26362

Sequel to: Trainspotting (1994)

"Things are looking up for Simon David Williamson ('Sick Boy'), who has inherited a pub in his native Edinburgh. He's also ready to break into the movies, specifically that branch identified as the 'adult entertainment industry'. . . . The big issue is whether Simon will meet the psychotic Begbie, to whom he mails unsolicited gay porn in jail." Libr J

This novel "signals, if not a return to form, then at least a return to enthusiastic formlessness—to something like the raw, jagged energy of old." N Y Times Book Rev

Welsh, Louise

The cutting room. Canongate 2002 294p $24

ISBN 1-8419-5280-X LC 2002-437974

"Gay auctioneer Rilke agrees to pack up and sell off an enormous quantity of high-quality goods in an inordinately short amount of time, no questions asked. . . . While clearing out the attic, he discovers a horrfying packet of snuff pornography. Depite his own proclivities for promiscuous, anonymous sex, he is haunted by the woman portrayed in the photographs and determined to discover whether the events depicted actually happened." Booklist

"A remarkable first novel. Like all the best exponents of the genre, Louise Welsh sets up her template and then manipulates it, using the glamour of crime to examine more humdrum kinds of suffering and loss. She piles on atmosphere to produce a Glasgow that is predictably dark and yet still plausible." N Y Times Book Rev

Welty, Eudora, 1909-2001

The bride of Innisfallen and other stories

In Welty, E. The collected stories of Eudora Welty

The collected stories of Eudora Welty. Harcourt Brace Jovanovich 1980 622p $35; pa $16

ISBN 0-15-118994-3; 0-15-618921-6 (pa) LC 80-7947

This volume contains four previously published collections: A curtain of green, and other stories; The wide net, and other stories; The golden apples and The bride of the Innisfallen, and other stories. Also included in this volume are two uncollected pieces: Where is the voice coming from? and The demonstrators

Complete novels. Library of Am. 1998 1009p $35

ISBN 1-883011-54-X LC 97-46702

Contents: The robber bridegroom; Delta wedding; The Ponder heart; Losing battles; The optimist's daughter

A curtain of green

In Welty, E. The collected stories of Eudora Welty p1-149

Welty, Eudora, 1909-2001—*Continued*

Delta wedding; a novel. Harcourt Brace & Co. 1946 247p o.p.

A "portrait of a Southern plantation family in 1923. Set in the context of the wedding of one of the daughters, the novel explores the relationships among members of the Fairchild family, most of whom have been sheltered from any contact with the world outside the Mississippi Delta. Although they quarrel among themselves, they also unite against any threats to the family's status, honoring the belief in the family as a sacred and unchanging entity." Merriam-Webster's Ency of Lit

also in Welty, E. Complete novels

The golden apples. Harcourt Brace & Co. 1949 244p o.p.

Contents: Shower of gold; June recital; Sir Rabbit; Moon Lake; Whole wide world knows; Music from Spain; The wanderers

also in Welty, E. The collected stories of Eudora Welty

Losing battles. Random House 1970 436p il o.p.

"At a large family gathering in Banner, Mississippi, the Renfro and Beecham families have assembled to celebrate Granny's ninetieth birthday. They are also celebrating Jack Renfro's return from the prison farm. As one might expect, the day is made up of reminiscences and recountings of earlier events, so that the novel actually spans many years. One of the key figures is Gloria, an orphan. She is frequently teased about being the daughter of another orphan, Rachel Sojourner, and of one of the Beecham boys who died in World War I. Gloria, who had married Jack just prior to his imprisonment, feels that they must get away from the clan, all of whom seem proud of their ignorance in spite of Miss Julia Mortimer's lifelong struggle to teach them something. It was a losing battle, probably even for Gloria." Shapiro. Fic for Youth. 3d edition

also in Welty, E. Complete novels

The optimist's daughter. Random House 1972 180p o.p.

"This novel is considered the high point of Welty's lengthy career. The strong character study examines 45-year-old Laurel McKelva Hand, who returns from Chicago to Mississippi, where her father is dying. She is forced to consider her complex and ambiguous emotions about her powerful and dynamic father, the impact of this relationship on her life, and her puzzlement at his late marriage to a coarse and shallow woman who is Laurel's own age." Shapiro. Fic for Youth. 3d edition

also in Welty, E. Complete novels

The Ponder heart; drawings by Joe Krush. Harcourt Brace & Co. 1954 156p il o.p.

"Cast as a monologue, [this comic novella] is rich with colloquial speech and descriptive imagery. The narrator of the story is Miss Edna Earle Ponder, one of the last living members of a once-prominent family, who manages the Beulah Hotel in Clay, Miss. She tells a traveling salesman the history of her family and fellow townsfolk." Merriam-Webster's Ency of Lit

also in Welty, E. Complete novels

The robber bridegroom; designed and illustrated by Barry Moser. Harcourt Brace Jovanovich 1987 c1942 134p il $19.95

ISBN 0-15-178318-7 LC 87-21195

A reissue of the title first published 1942 by Doubleday

"A novelette combining fairy tale and ballad form, telling of the wooing of Rosamond, the daughter of a Mississippi planter, by a bandit chief." Oxford Companion to Am Lit. 6th edition

"Miss Welty uses the magic of metaphor and simile like a lyric poet, and writes with a limpid purity, and exquisite sense of descriptive coloring that gives a warm glow of beauty to a fantastic, and unfortunately sometimes tiresome story." Springfield Repub

also in Welty, E. Complete novels

The wide net and other stories

In Welty, E. The collected stories of Eudora Welty

Wener, Louise

The perfect play; Louise Wener. 1st U.S. ed. Morrow 2003 342p $24.95

ISBN 0-06-058547-1 LC 2004-42618

"Thirty-two-year-old Londoner Audrey Ungar is bright, great with numbers, and neurotic, terrified of unpredictability. When she was a girl, her gambler father disappeared and her mother died, leaving her especially afraid of abandonment. Drifting, she keeps her grounded, seemingly perfect boyfriend at arm's length until a chance poker lesson with Big Louie, a fat, agoraphobic Yank gambling genius, proves she's her father's daughter. She quickly becomes obsessed with the game and finds it leading her toward knowledge of her father and herself-and, ultimately, to play a high-stakes game in Las Vegas." Booklist

A "highly entertaining story of Audrey's search for her deserting dad, her torrid affair with gambling and her friendship with Big Louie, an agoraphobic card master. Abandonment issues have never been so funny." USA Today

Wenner, Kate, 1947-

Dancing with Einstein; a novel; Kate Wenner. Scribner 2004 223p $24

ISBN 0-7432-5164-4 LC 2003-65681

"Marea Hoffman, now approaching 30, arrives in New York after years of backpacking around the world. She quickly locates an apartment in Greenwich Village, gets a night job in an organic bakery, and sets to work on unpacking the emotional baggage of her childhood. The daughter of a Princeton physicist, Marea harbors affectionate memories of her surrogate 'grandpa,' Albert Einstein. But her father's work on the hydrogen bomb alienated him from both the pacifist Einstein and Marea's mother, who was raised Quaker. Marea's parents were on the verge of divorce when her father died in a car accident. Determined to deal with her father's death, Marea signs on with four therapists: a Freudian analyst, a New Age Jungian, a feminist, and one, found by chance, without any evident personal agenda." Libr J

"Despite the occasional awkward piece of dialogue, Marea's tortured path to peace, stillness and purpose rings true." Publ Wkly

Werfel, Franz

The forty days of Musa Dagh. Viking 1934 824p o.p.

Original German edition, 1933; published in the United Kingdom with title: The forty days

"Gabriel Bagradian returns to his ancestral village in Syria, where he learns that the Turks are disarming the Armenians and sending them into exile. Gabriel plans the resistance to the Turks and directs the fortification of the mountain Musa Dagh. The Turks are successfully repulsed a number of times but at great cost in lives to the Armenians on the mountain. On the fortieth day the remnant of the Armenian force is rescued by the French." Shapiro. Fic for Youth. 3d edition

The song of Bernadette; translated by Ludwig Lewisohn. Viking 1942 575p o.p.

Original German edition, 1941

A slightly fictionalized version of "the life of Saint Bernadette of Lourdes. While it is not exactly a religious work, it is truly reverent in its approach to the inscrutable, the unfathomable, the divine. There is an engrossing picture of emperor, bishops, priests, nuns, merchants and artisans. A living pageant of the second Empire in France." Ont Libr Rev

Wesley, Mary

Part of the furniture. Viking 1997 c1996 256p o.p.

LC 96-46226

This novel is set in World War II England. "Seventeen-year-old Juno Marlowe has always worshiped the rich young cousins who live next door, but they treat her as though she were 'part of the furniture.' After losing her virginity to them during a rough, crude night of sex, she sees them off at the train station and is caught in an air raid. Taking refuge with an astute stranger, she promises to deliver a letter to his family. And so she ends up living on the estate of widower Robert Copplestone, where she is treated with care and kindness. Forty years Juno's senior, Robert is mortified when he realizes that he is in love with her, but Juno soon forgets her childish fixation on the cousins and talks Robert into marrying her." Booklist

"Wesley's skill with character development and her subtle, amusing dissection of that paramount British preoccupation, family background and breeding, endow this novel with the charm of a comedy of manners and the enduring appeal of a satisfying love story." Publ Wkly

West, Bing *See* West, Francis J., 1940-

West, Dorothy, 1907-1998

The wedding. Doubleday 1995 240p o.p.

LC 94-27285

This novel is "set on Martha's Vineyard during the 1950s and focuses on the black bourgeois community known as the Oval. Dr. Clark Coles and his wife, Corrine, highly respected Ovalites, are preparing for the wedding of their youngest daughter, Shelby, who, much to their consternation, is marrying a white jazz musician. Lute McNeil, a compulsive womanizer who has recently made a fortune in the furniture business, is determined to stop Shelby's wedding; he is confident that he can convince Shelby to marry him, which would bring him the social acceptance he has always craved." Booklist

"Through the ancestral histories of the Coles family, West . . . subtly reveals the ways in which color can burden and codify behavior. The author makes her points with a delicate hand, maneuvering with confidence and ease through a sometimes incendiary subject." Publ Wkly

West, F. J. *See* West, Francis J., 1940-

West, Francis J., 1940-

The Pepperdogs; a novel; [by] Bing West. Simon & Schuster 2003 369p $25

ISBN 0-7432-3589-4 LC 2002-40860

"Capt. Mark Lang commands the 'Pepperdogs,' an elite four-man Marine reconnassiance team that must rescue an officer who has been wounded and kidnapped by a band of brutal and murderous Serbs. As the 'Dogs' make their grueling trek through the rugged Balkan terrain, the action is fast-paced . . . . The emerging technology of close-in and small-unit warfare that West describes is almost as fascinating as the chase. . . . On a different level, there is political action as the incident becomes public via the Internet, and both sides argue just who are the war criminals." Libr J

West, Jessamyn, 1902-1984

Collected stories of Jessamyn West. Harcourt Brace Jovanovich 1986 480p o.p.

LC 86-12031

Contents: Probably Shakespeare; A time of learning; The mysteries of life in an orderly manner; Love, death, and the ladies' drill team; Homecoming; The battle of the suits; Tom Wolfe's my name; Learn to say good-bye; A little collar for the monkey; Public-address system; Foot-shaped shoes; Horace Chooney, M.D.; The linden trees; Breach of promise; The singing lesson; The Calla Lilly Cleaners & Dyers; The wake; Grand opening; Aloha, farewell to thee; Reverdy; Up a tree; There ought to be a judge; Gallup Poll; Alive and real; I'll ask him to come sooner; Hunting for hoot owls; Crimson Ramblers of the world, farewell; Night piece for Julia; Live life deeply; Mother's Day; The heavy stone; 99.6; The day of the hawk; Like visitant of air; The condemned librarian; Child of the century; Flow gently, sweet aspirin; The second (or perhaps third) time round

Cress Delahanty; drawings by Joe Krush. Harcourt Brace & Co. 1953 311p il o.p.

"In story-sketches that reveal with touching humor an adolescent's real problems from her 12th to her 16th year, likable Cress grows up on a California ranch, making her mark at school, exploring the strange ways of 'boys,' and being always loved and cherished by her often bewildered parents." Bookmark

"Anyone who knows adolescence, and especially that of young girls, will love this book. It is beautifully written, with the most extraordinary insight and delicacy." Commonweal

West, Jessamyn, 1902-1984—*Continued*

Except for me and thee; a companion to The friendly persuasion. Harcourt, Brace & World 1969 309p o.p.

"Episodes in the Birdwell family chronicle which round out their story as related in 'The friendly persuasion'. Jess's courting of Eliza, their migration from Ohio to southern Indiana, the building of the new home, and growth of the children to maturity supply material for a low-keyed nostalgic narrative interrupted occasionally by excitement and sorrow, as when Jess becomes a conductor on the Underground Railway and Quaker principles are abandoned by the younger generation during the Civil War and Reconstruction." Booklist

This book "has all the warmth, the sturdy affection, and the quiet humor of its predecessor. . . . In part the charm of the novel owes to the vibrant authenticity of its characters; in great part it is due to the practiced ease and resilience of style." Saturday Rev

The friendly persuasion. Harcourt Brace & Co. 1945 214p o.p.

"The Birdwell family of Indiana led a quiet life until the Civil War came into their lives. They were Quakers and tried to live according to the teachings of William Penn. Jess Birdwell, a nurseryman, loved a fast horse as well as his trees and the people he knew. Eliza, his wife, was a Quaker minister and a gentle, albeit strict, soul. When the war reached Indiana, Josh, the oldest son, was torn between his Quaker upbringing and his belief in the rightness of the Union cause; Mattie was at that difficult age between childhood and womanhood; and Little Jess, the youngest, ran into trouble with Eliza's geese. This is a wonderful family chronicle, with the laughter, tears, and tenderness that can be found in many families." Shapiro. Fic for Youth. 3d edition

The massacre at Fall Creek. Harcourt Brace Jovanovich 1975 373p o.p.

"Fictional treatment of the historic slaughter of nine Indians (mostly women and children) by white settlers on the Indiana frontier in 1824 and the trial for murder which resulted in the killers' deaths by hanging. An eminently readable book. Lovers of American history will find the circumstances well researched; the long-ago time and its people vividly brought to life with terse and witty dialogue and much authentic detail of frontier domesticity. The sub-plots are West's own. These involve a preacher of the old-time religion; his red-haired tomboy daughter, avidly pursued and finally won; lone hunters and their near-savage ways . . . and Indians, whose attitudes and philosophies are presented with sympathy." Choice

West, Mary Jessamyn *See* West, Jessamyn, 1902-1984

West, Morris L., 1916-1999

The clowns of God; [by] Morris West. St. Martin's Press 1990 c1981 370p $19.95

ISBN 0-312-04459-3 LC 89-70344

A reissue of the title first published 1981 by Morrow

This novel takes place in the last decade of the 20th century. As the story opens, "Jean Marie Barette, lately Pope, has been forced into abdication because the cardinals don't know how else to cope with his apocalyptic vision of the approaching end of the world and the second coming of Jesus Christ. What follows [concerns his efforts] . . . to find a way to proclaim his vision without sending his cherished world into a tailspin of chaos and hysteria." Christ Sci Monit

"The fugitive ex-pope posits all the fearful questions about life that have perplexed us since Hiroshima. West's ultimate answers will disturb some and be dismissed by others, but no one will be left unmoved. The sheer power of his prose and his keen understanding of human nature make this novel a stunning accomplishment." Libr J

Followed by Lazarus

The devil's advocate. Morrow 1959 319p o.p.

In this novel "the plot concerns a British Monsignor who investigates the petition for canonization of a man who died before a partisan firing squad in Calabria during World War II. As the investigation progresses, he learns a great deal about the man, his family, the village in which he lived and, especially, about himself." Publ Wkly

"The characters all are firmly, brightly established. The writing, without fanciness or flourish, goes along with a fine, steady drive. There are no profound insights, no remarkable illuminations. But there is an engrossing story, expertly told, about a set of fascinating people whose lives are viewed as meaningful." Chicago Sunday Trib

Lazarus; [by] Morris West. St. Martin's Press 1990 293p o.p.

LC 89-77919

Concluding volume of the author's Vatican trilogy. "Pope Leo XIV faces death from heart disease as the novel opens and is targeted for assassination by a fundamentalist group, but he realizes a need for tolerance and begins to undo the very policies that have made him a reactionary." Smith. Cloak and Dagger Fic

"A tense and exciting thriller, Lazarus also explores world crises and theological politics quite as fascinating to non-Catholics as to Catholics. . . . While the book can be read as a complement to the other two novels, it stands alone as a superb, absorbing novel." Libr J

Masterclass; [by] Morris West. St. Martin's Press 1991 330p o.p.

LC 90-28090

Max Mather "served as the paleographer (manuscript archivist) for a well-known Italian family. But when he comes into possession of two Raphael originals, Max becomes incredibly wily, both about the effect his discovery will have on the international art world and about his prospects for cashing in. Big-time collectors, dealers, and auctioneers are drawn into Mather's game, with the players flitting easily from New York to Zurich to Florence to Amsterdam and back again. Amid all the artsy oneupmanship, West gives us a subplot involving the murder of a Manhattan painter whose brilliance extended from her way with palette and brush to kinky, omnivorous sex. Solid plotting and interesting characters make this flashy novel of intrigue fully enjoyable." Booklist

The shoes of the fisherman; a novel. Morrow 1963 374p o.p.

In this first title in the author's Vatican trilogy, "a humble Ukrainian pope finds himself the central negotiator in an attempt to prevent the United States and the So-

West, Morris L., 1916-1999—*Continued*

viet Union from starting World War III. During the negotiations, the pope must confront the Russian who once tortured him. The work, a popular and critical success, demonstrates West's concern with modern man's inability to communicate with his brother." McCormick and Fletcher. Spy Fic

Followed by The clowns of God

Vanishing point; [by] Morris West. HarperCollins Pubs. 1996 261p o.p.

LC 96-7102

"Carl Strassberger is the only son of a prominent New York financier. Carl has forsaken corporate life and gone off to France to paint. His brother-in-law, groomed to take over the family business in lieu of Carl, disappears. Carl is asked by his father to put his artistic life on hold and search for the missing man. In tracking down his brother-in-law, Carl must assume a new identity and roam the international underground." Booklist

"The suspense occasionally wanders into melodrama, but West compensates with a series of empathetic characterizations that present Carl's artistic view of the world, as well as with an astute analysis of the dysfunctional family dynamic that contributed to Larry's disappearance." Publ Wkly

West, Nathanael, 1903-1940

The complete works of Nathanael West. Farrar, Straus & Cuhady 1957 421p o.p.

"Included here are 'The Dream Life of Balso Snell' 1931, a surrealist sexual nightmare in prose, 'Miss Lonelyhearts,' 1933, a biting satire on modern man and his aspirations, 'A Cool Million,' 1934, melodramatic satire on the American dream of success, and 'The Day of the Locust,' 1939, a bitter tale of Hollywood and its hangers-on." Libr J

A cool million

In West, N. The complete works of Nathanael West p143-256

The day of the locust

In West, N. The complete works of Nathanael West p259-421

In West, N. Miss Lonelyhearts & The day of the locust

The dream life of Balso Snell

In West, N. The complete works of Nathanael West p3-62

Miss Lonelyhearts. Liveright 1933 213p o.p.

"The story of a man who writes an 'advice to the lovelorn' column, the theme of the book is the loneliness of the individual in modern society. The hero tries to live the role of omniscient counselor he has assumed for the paper, but his attempts to reach out to suffering humanity are twisted by circumstances, and he is finally murdered by a man he has tried to help." Reader's Ency. 4th edition

also in West, N. The complete works of Nathanael West p65-140

also in West, N. Miss Lonelyhearts & The day of the locust

Miss Lonelyhearts & The day of the locust. Modern Lib. 1998 289p $15.50

ISBN 0-679-60278-X LC 97-39828

Combined edition of two titles first published 1933 and 1939 respectively. The day of the locust is about Hollywood and the misfits who flock to it in search of the American dream

West, Owen. *See* Koontz, Dean R. (Dean Ray), 1945-

West, Paul, 1930-

Cheops; a cupboard for the sun. New Directions 2002 261p il $25.95

ISBN 0-8112-1519-9 LC 2002-10474

This novel "examines the legacy of the Egyptian leader who built the great pyramids. . . . [It] begins with the once-powerful Cheops fighting a series of grave illnesses. Decadent palace intrigue ensues as various relatives and factions try to capitalize on his impending death. The proceedings are wryly narrated by Osiris, the god of the underworld, who provides observations and commentary on the imminent downfall of the great leader. . . . The novel turns hallucinatory and downright bizarre in the final section as West imagines a link between the music of 19th-century composer Frederic Delius and the burial plans of Cheops. The historical detail is impeccable." Publ Wkly

The dry Danube; a Hitler forgery. New Directions 2000 152p $21.95

ISBN 0-8112-1432-X LC 99-88020

"This novella takes place just before the Great War and is told in the voice of the failed Austrian painter Hitler. Its inspired narrative is stylishly solipsistic, like the paragraphless monolog novels of Austrian writer Thomas Bernhard (whose influence West acknowledges in an afterword). The narrator talks obsessively and bitterly about his two artist heroes, Treischnitt and Kolberhoff, who stubbornly refuse to recognize his brilliance and cooperate as mentors. The awful knowledge of what is to come later for Hitler (and for Europe) keeps the meandering narration from losing its tension. In a surprisingly enjoyable short work, West has found a voice that speaks with fluent authority to magnify a rarely examined historical moment before the Third Reich terrors." Libr J

A fifth of November. New Directions 2001 362p $25.95

ISBN 0-8112-1467-2 LC 00-66840

"Guy, or 'Guido,' Fawkes was captured in a cellar beneath the Parliament building in 1605, where he had stored barrels of gunpowder in order to blow up the next session of Parliament. Robert Cecil, King James's powerful spymaster, a crippled, Machiavellian figure, had Fawkes tortured into confessing the details of a conspiracy, mounted by certain 'recusants' outcast English Catholics. West's central figure is Father Henry Garnet, the fugitive head of the Jesuits in England. . . . Anne Vaux, a devout, feisty Catholic noblewoman, is Garnet's protector. She has Little John Owen, a 'lame and stunted' carpenter, devise 'priestholes' in her houses to hide priests from Protestant vigilantes. West's story is like one of Owen's trompe l'oeil concealments: full of misdirections." Publ Wkly

West, Paul, 1930—*Continued*

This novel "documents in detail the last few months in the life of a Jesuit priest, a victim of the king's vengeful hunt for Fawkes's accomplices, but the novel's message resonates through the immigrant ghettos of European capitals, along the redrawn borders of the former Yugoslavia and, most of all, in the modern Middle East. For West's compelling tale is about religious intolerance and our enduring proclivity for cruelty." Washington Post Book World

Lord Byron's doctor; a novel. Doubleday 1989 277p o.p.

ISBN 0-385-26129-2 LC 89-7735

"Lord Byron's doctor was John Polidori, whom he hired as a traveling companion on his trip to the Continent in 1816. West's novel recreates the diary that Polidori had been commissioned to keep but that never saw print." Libr J

"Through Polidori, West compiles a lurid case history on the cruelty of genius. Shelley may have been 'polite to God and pious towards women,' but Byron was arrogant about both. His disdain toward lesser literary figures was godlike, and his venery demonic. . . . Romanticism and egoism normally go hand in hand. Here they are passionately entwined. Rocking and rolling in Byron's carriage, sailing through storms, discussing the uses of opium or exchanging ghost stories at the Villa Diodati, the group is principally concerned with who will be favored by the muse." Time

Love's mansion. Random House 1992 339p o.p.

ISBN 0-394-58734-0 LC 92-6804

"Set in England, the story moves from the late Victorian era to mid-century, telling the story of two lovers, Harry and Hilly, whose lives are irrevocably changed by World War I. Tantalizingly, the novel's point of view is that of the couple's son, who must look back in time, guessing at motives, imagining dialog, intuiting emotions." Libr J

"As Mr. West has made vividly clear, we have much to learn from the Moxons and their changing world. It is perhaps unfashionable to write about the pain and transformations that characterize the love of a long-married couple, but Mr. West is concerned with something much more personal than literary fashion. At times the astounding 'diligence of human memory' takes off in his book and produces passages that are close to poetry, almost always when his style is at its least extended and inclusive." N Y Times Book Rev

O.K; the corral, the Earps, and Doc Holliday: a novel. Scribner 2000 302p $24

ISBN 0-684-84865-1 LC 99-89924

"On his way from Georgia to the healthier climate of Colorado, consumptive dentist Dr. John Henry Holliday visits Dallas, East Las Vegas and Dodge, gradually abandoning dentistry as he discovers his prowess as a gunfighter and his Keatsian obsession with death. Along the way, he saves the life of Wyatt Earp, marshal and gunman. The two become fast friends and eventually land in Tombstone, Ariz., where they take part in the almost mythical 1881 gunfight between the Clanton Gang and the Earp family at the O.K. Corral." Publ Wkly

West "cares more about character and color than action, and his prose can at times be ponderous. But although some details, like those of Doc's ravaging consumption, require a strong stomach, they serve to depict Holliday as a moving and complex character." N Y Times Book Rev

Sporting with Amaryllis. Overlook Press 1996 158p $19.95

ISBN 0-87951-666-6 LC 96-22766

"In this novel, West presents a fictive portrait of the poet John Milton as a brilliant, virginal, and very curious 17-year-old. On holiday from Cambridge, Milton is picked up on a bustling London street by a dark-skinned [woman] . . . who turns out to be his muse. Obsessed with Virgil, he calls her Amaryllis . . . and embarks on a magical journey that lasts a day but shapes a lifetime." Booklist

"Readers who accept unreservedly Milton's solemn, extravagant sense of his destiny are not likely to be amused by West's conception of how muse Amaryllis worked over youth Milton. West makes the muse anything but 'thankless.' But one doesn't have to swallow a word of West's flamboyant writing to find it piquant. It's pleasanter and more comfortable, certainly, to imagine Milton exuberantly enjoying, and benefiting from, fleshly indulgence than to endure seeing him cruelly cartooned as a bigoted thug and assassin." American Scholar

The tent of orange mist; a novel. Scribner 1995 263p $22

ISBN 0-684-80031-4 LC 95-9077

This novel is set in Nanking during the Japanese invasion of the 1930s. "A 16-year-old girl, Scald Ibis, repeatedly violated by invaders and unaware that her mother has been defiled and her brother beheaded, is forced into prostitution to keep her scholar-father alive." Libr J

"West fills the narrative with fascinating contrasts, matching China against Japan and each against the West, the military against the aristocracy, courtliness against ribaldness, academic abstractions against empirical chaos. Through meticulous prose and stylistic daring, he cultivates subtle cultural insights while making his wrenching, affecting tale credible on both historical and psychological levels." Publ Wkly

The women of Whitechapel and Jack the Ripper. Random House 1991 420p o.p.

ISBN 0-394-58733-2 LC 90-9046

"Painter Walter Sickert, fascinated by the dark side of life in Victorian London, introduces Princess Alexandra's son to the prostitute/models at Cleveland Street. An unwanted pregnancy follows, word of which the royal family desperately attempts to suppress, inadvertently setting off a chain of events which lead to [murder]." Libr J

"The late Victorian period, with all its charm and filth and wretchedness, is delivered up in dazzling set pieces–from frolics with a bathing machine at Yarmouth to a plague of flies descending on London–that never interfere with the story's grimly steady momentum. Mr. West's lyrical, clever prose, now and then too ostentatiously paraded in his previous novels, remains under shrewd control here." N Y Times Book Rev

West, Dame Rebecca, 1892-1983

The birds fall down. Viking 1966 435p o.p.
LC 67-10214

In this novel Count Diakonov, an exiled aristocrat, and Chubinov, an informant and revolutionary, are the central characters. Their long dialogue explores the mystique of pre-Revolutionary Russia and provides a philosophical basis for a complex story of intrigue and treason.

Cousin Rosamund; with an afterword by Victoria Glendinning. Viking 1986 c1985 294p o.p.
LC 85-40780

First published 1985 in the United Kingdom

Last book of the author's trilogy about the Aubrey family, begun with The fountain overflows (1956) and This real night (1985). In this novel "Rose, Mary, and Rosamund come to maturity. . . . It is a maturity that Rose and Mary do not entirely choose for themselves, one they are forced into when Rosamund marries a man of dubious morals and unfathomable vulgarity—a man they can only despise. No longer guided by Rosamund's radiance, Mary and Rose must find their own light. Unable to look beyond the magic circle of their childhood, they retreat to an inn on the Thames, where, with Mr. Morpurgo, Queenie, and Nancy—friends they have known all their lives—they find a haven of security." Publisher's note

In this novel "West's signature talents are again displayed: meticulous rendering of period details, evocation of the spirit of an age through outspoken views on its music, art, fashion, politics and social mores." Publ Wkly

Sunflower; with an afterword by Victoria Glendinning. Viking 1987 c1986 276p o.p.
LC 86-40262

First published 1986 in the United Kingdom

"Sunflower is Sybil Fassendyll, a beautiful, 30 year old actress at the peak of her career. For the past ten years, she has been the mistress of the brilliant but moody and domineering Lord Essington. When she meets American millionaire politician Francis Pitt in London, she soon leaves Essington and becomes involved with Pitt to the point of obsession. Though outwardly a powerfully public woman, Sunflower secretly yearns for marriage and family, home and security." Publisher's note

This "tantalizingly unfinished novel . . . though incomplete, is a finished work of art in its emotional intensity, its analytical force, and its intricately wrought design of tiny, jewel-like details reflecting and amplifying the flash of its major themes." Christ Sci Monit

West, V. Sackville- *See* Sackville-West, V. (Victoria), 1892-1962

Westerfeld, Scott

The risen empire. TOR Bks. 2003 304p $24.95
ISBN 0-7653-0555-0 LC 2002-42952

"A Tom Doherty Associates book"

"In an interstellar empire of 80 human worlds, ruled by an emperor who lets selected humans cheat death, tensions between most humans and the resurrected elite, aka the Risen, are increasing. The Rix, a cult of cyborgs who worship compound AI minds, hunger to liberate the empire's worlds from mere human control. When a Rix raiding party captures the emperor's sister, Capt. Laurent Zai of the Imperial Navy must save her." Publ Wkly

"Westerfeld's speculations about the rise and fall of civilizations are appealingly quirky . . . and his action scenes have a breathless realism that does not gloss over the bloody nature of combat. Perhaps most important, his moral calculus never lapses into Q.E.D. As the narrative jumps from intimate glimpses of the Empire to the Rix Cult and back again, we grow less and less clear about whom we are rooting for." N Y Times Book Rev

Westheimer, David, 1917-2005

Von Ryan's Express. Doubleday 1964 327p o.p.

"Colonel Joseph Ryan is shot down over Italy and is sent to a prisoner-of-war camp, where he imposes military discipline upon the other prisoners. After Italy's surrender, when the prisoners are put on a train for Germany, Ryan plans a daring takeover of the train and gets the men to Switzerland." Shapiro. Fic for Youth. 2d edition

Followed by Von Ryan's return (1980)

Westlake, Donald E.

For works written by this author under other names see Stark, Richard

After I'm gone
In Westlake, D. E. Levine p151-82

The ax. Mysterious Press 1997 273p o.p.
LC 96-52068

This novel "takes a familiar plight—Burke Devore, a middle-level executive at a paper company, has been downsized out of what he had imagined was a secure lifetime job—and gives it a terrifying twist. Not content quietly to abandon his decently prosperous existence, Devore searches out the ideal job at the ideal company and then identifies a half-dozen unemployed potential rivals for the spot and sets out to murder them one by one." Publ Wkly

"As novels go, 'The Ax' is pretty much flawless, with a surprise ending that will unplug your expectations. Burke Devore is American Man at the millennium—as emblematic of his time as George F. Babbitt and Holden Caulfield and Capt. John Yossarian were of theirs. Westlake has written a remarkable book. If you can't relate to it, be thankful." N Y Times Book Rev

Baby, would I lie?; a romance of the Ozarks. Mysterious Press 1994 291p o.p.
LC 93-40485

This comic mystery, featuring characters from the author's Trust me on this, "is set in 'the new Nashville': Branson, Missouri. Singer Ray Jones is accused of one murder and then of a second. Out on bail, he continues to entertain in this theater. Meanwhile, an army of troops from the sleazy tabloid *Weekly Galaxy* descends to bug offices, lie, infiltrate, and do anything else necessary to get some sort of story on the upcoming trial. Also arriving are reporters Sara and Jack, lovers and representatives of a trendy New York magazine called *Trend: The Magazine for the Way We Live This Instant.* The action is jet-fast, and the satiric commentary on country western stars and fans is wonderfully wicked." Libr J

Bad news; by Donald Westlake. Mysterious Press 2001 342p $30
ISBN 0-89296-717-X LC 00-45592

Westlake, Donald E.—*Continued*

In this comic caper "Andy Kelp, Tiny Bulcher and the Murches (Stan and Mom) join Dortmunder in horning in on another crew's scam—cheating two Native American tribes out of one-third of the take from a lucrative Indian casino in upstate New York. Fitzroy Guilderpost, mastermind of the con . . . has enlisted Little Feather Redcorn, a Las Vegas card dealer and showgirl, to pose as the last living member of an extinct tribe with a claim to the casino." Publ Wkly

"Westlake has a genius for comic strategy, and the complications he devises when the casino operators initiate a counterplot to discredit Little Feather have a lunatic brilliance worthy of Abbott and Costello. But Westlake is also a card with characters, and he flashes that talent to terrific effect here." N Y Times Book Rev

Bank shot. Simon & Schuster 1972 224p o.p.

In this novel "criminal mastermind Dortmunder . . . plans to rob a Long Island suburban bank by stealing the whole bank—a mobile trailer home being used temporarily while the new bank building is under construction. Dortmunder's cohorts include Victor, a former FBI agent ousted because he thought the FBI ought to have a secret hand-shake; Herman X, a black militant lock expert; and a female cab driver who wears a neck brace while trying to collect a phoney insurance claim." Booklist

It is Westlake's "triumph that whereas on one hand the reader knows he simply can't take the characters and situations seriously, those characters are so deftly drawn that they are eminently believable." N Y Times Book Rev

The best-friend murder
In Westlake, D. E. Levine p3-31

Come back, come back
In Westlake, D. E. Levine p35-59

Cops and robbers. Evans & Co. 1972 286p o.p.

"Two New York City policemen plot to steal two million dollars. Unable to pull off a heist that large on their own, they offer their services to the Mafia." Chicago. Public Libr

Westlake's "strongest qualities remain his wild but seamless plotting and his tape-recorder ears, but this time his characterizations are more dimensional and compassionate. . . . The exciting ending is a jewel of complexity." Libr J

The death of a bum
In Westlake, D. E. Levine p121-50

Don't ask. Mysterious Press 1993 327p $18.95
ISBN 0-89296-469-3 LC 92-53721

In this novel John Dormunder "and his cohorts agree to steal a religious relic, the femur of a thirteenth-century saint, that is a bone of contention between two fledgling Eastern European countries. Possession of the bone will lead to a seat in the United Nations." Booklist

"If the plot is of no great concern, it is the effortlessness, wit, and sheer good-heartedness of the telling that make 'Don't Ask' such a consistent delight." N Y Times Book Rev

Drowned hopes. Mysterious Press 1990 422p o.p.
LC 89-35859

In this "comedy-mystery, ex-con John Dortmunder and his benevolent criminal cohorts are continuously frustrated in their attempts to recover $700,000 in stolen money from a 50-foot-deep reservoir in upper New York State." Booklist

The feel of the trigger
In Westlake, D. E. Levine p61-87

Good behavior. Mysterious Press 1985 244p o.p.
LC 85-43178

"John Archibald Dortmunder runs across several Manhattan rooftops after trying to pull a break-in. He ends up on the roof of a building in a newly trendy but unsettled neighborhood, then falls through a skylight into a covey of cloistered nuns, who see the thief as an answer to their prayers." Booklist

The author "manages to create characters who are a curious mixture of stereotypes and archetypes. If he is a master of the comic crime caper, and he is, he also does what the best comic writers throughout history have done—make a comment on society." N Y Times Book Rev

The hook. Mysterious Press 2000 280p $30
ISBN 0-89296-588-6 LC 99-36273

"Frustrated by what he sees as outrageous monetary demands from his ex-wife, successful author Bryce Proctorr hires an old acquaintance, Wayne Prentice, to kill her. In a variation on the murder-for-hire theme, Proctorr offers Prentice, also a struggling author, both money and the opportunity to publish under his name. While the arrangement seems ideal for both parties, it soon becomes evident that such is not the case." Libr J

"Westlake salts the stew with lots of fascinating publishing shoptalk, and his portrayal of the psychological unraveling of a writer is made all the more chilling by the quiet realism of its presentation. A fine thriller." Booklist

The hot rock. Simon & Schuster 1970 249p o.p.

"The hot rock is the Balambo Emerald, part of an African exhibit at the New York Coliseum, owned by Akinzi, and coveted by the breakaway state of Talabwo. Major Iko of Talabwo selects John Dortmunder as the mastermind for the heist. But lifting the stone from the Coliseum is only the first caper for Dortmunder's carefully chosen crew." Libr J

This novel "comes awesomely close to the ultimate in comic, big-caper novels; it's . . . filled with mocking style and action and imagination." N Y Times Book Rev

Levine. Mysterious Press 1984 182p o.p.
LC 83-63034

"Six novellas featuring Abe Levine, the 53-year-old Brooklyn detective with the irregular heartbeat. . . . In 'The Best-Friend Murder,' Levine and his partner, Jack Crawley, contend with a college youth who insists he poisoned his best friend, although his motive seems spurious. In 'Come Back, Come Back,' the problem is a successful businessman who looks down from the ledge of a tall building and threatens to jump to his death. . . . 'The Sound of Murder' concerns a ten-year-old girl who could have been the inspiration for 'The Bad Seed,' 'The Death of a Bum' is a psychological piece that Westlake

Westlake, Donald E.—*Continued*
had some difficulty in selling. The final story, 'After I'm Gone,' is a pure action piece that somehow doesn't seem to fit the mold of the other Levine stories, but its interest never flags." West Coast Rev Books

Money for nothing. Mysterious Press 2003 294p $24.95
ISBN 0-89296-787-0 LC 2002-35888
"New York advertising executive Josh Redmont finds himself in the middle of an espionage drama, cast as the hero but utterly unprepared for the role. Seven years earlier, Redmont began receiving $1,000 checks, issued by 'United States Agent'; after trying unsuccessfully to track down the source of the checks, Redmont began depositing them and has been doing so ever since. His 'found money,' however, comes with very big strings, as Josh learns when he is approached by an unassuming-looking man who announces, 'I am from United States Agent. You are now active.'" Booklist
"Although Westlake has written funnier books and his characters could use more dimension, 'Money for Nothing' has all of his trademarks: an ample supply of silliness and suspense wrapped up in a wacky plot." N Y Times Book Rev

Put a lid on it. Mysterious Press 2002 247p $23.95
ISBN 0-89296-718-8 LC 2001-51435
Francis Meehan "is in federal prison for hijacking a mail truck he thought contained computer chips. A presidential reelection official offers him a pardon with a Watergate-type scheme: Meehan must steal a video that, if made public, may prevent the president's reelection." Publ Wkly
This is a "crime caper that also gets some nice digs in as political satire. . . . Although Meehan isn't quite as ingenious a thief as some of Westlake's other criminal protagonists, he's a born philosopher." N Y Times Book Rev

The road to ruin. Mysterious Press 2004 342p $25
ISBN 0-89296-801-X LC 2003-65007
In this Dortmunder caper the "conspicuous target of larcenous intent is one Monroe Hall, the broadly drawn, babyish CEO and chief perpetrator of an Enron-like financial debacle, which has made him a pariah to friends and potential employees but still rich in funds and enemies. When a disgruntled former chauffeur hires Dortmunder and his crew to steal Hall's classic-car collection for the insurance, together with all the swag they can haul, our clumsy confederation of bandits decides to sidestep the estate's elaborate security system by hiring themselves on as staff, with rumpled second-story man Dortmunder in the unlikely role of butler." Booklist
"Ingenuity fuels the plot, but what puts the match to the comedy is the moral outrage of the furiously funny characters." N Y Times Book Rev

Smoke. Mysterious Press 1995 454p o.p.
LC 94-48254
"Freddie Noon is a sharp, likable burglar whose mistake is to break into the offices of two doctors doing so-called research for the Tobacco Institute. Catching him, they make him a human guinea pig for one of their formulas, and—meet disappearing Freddie. Naturally, his life as a burglar gets much easier, but his girlfriend, Peg, isn't too comfortable with an invisible lover." Publ Wkly
"Though Mr. Westlake is a virtuoso plotter, the point of his books, here as ever, is to be found in the interstices. Wicked one-liners and testy miniature monologues about whatever happens to be on the author's mind are scattered generously throughout. The implications of invisibility are played for laughs with near-arrogant skill." N Y Times Book Rev

The sound of murder
In Westlake, D. E. Levine p89-120

The spy in the ointment. Random House 1966 200p o.p.
Pacifist Gene Raxford is mistakenly invited to a meeting of a terrorist group run by his girlfriend's Communist brother. The FBI persuades Gene to infiltrate the group, leading the pacifist gunman into danger and wild adventures

Thieves' dozen. Mysterious Press 2004 183p pa $12.95
ISBN 0-446-69302-2 (pa) LC 2003-70612
Contents: Ask a silly question; Horse laugh; Too many crooks; A midsummer's daydream; The Dortmunder workout; Party animal; Give till it hurts; Jumble sale; Now what; Art and craft; Fugue for felons
A collection of Dortmunder stories. "The swift succession of heists, getaways, scrapes, and screwups gathered in Thieves' Dozen epitomizes the venal joys of the comic caper. . . . The short-story form is well suited to Westlake's sly shenanigans, and he even finds room for snippets of the Runyonesque repartee that gives this inspired nonsense just the right touch of absurd panache." Booklist

Trust me on this. Mysterious Press 1988 293p o.p.
LC 87-22098
"As a young and comely reporter is driving down that highway on route to reporting for her new job at the 'Weekly [Galaxy]' she finds a bloody corpse hanging half-out of a Buick Riviera. When she is assigned to her new editor, a driven personality, as are all who are employed at this paper, she tells him about the corpse on the road thinking he will assign her to the story. But this kind of story is not what interests that kind of paper—the corpse is probably a nobody, the car he was in was surely a nothing. But Sara Joslyn is haunted by what she saw even though she hasn't the time or freedom to look into the matter further." West Coast Rev Books
"In between stories about space battles, 100-year-old twins, dead country music stars and bizarre medical happenings, Mr. Westlake has sandwiched a nice romance and a fairish murder mystery." N Y Times Book Rev

Watch your back. Mysterious Press 2005 310p $24.95
ISBN 0-89296-802-8 LC 2004-61064
"Arnie Albright, a fence so obnoxious his family intervened and sent him to Club Med in hopes he'd become more likable, has returned from the resort minimally improved, but having met the man of his dreams Preston Fareweather, a millionaire who's as comically distasteful as Arnie and who, more importantly, plans to be away from his art-filled New York penthouse indefinitely, on the run from hordes of furious ex-wives. Albright calls

Westlake, Donald E.—*Continued*
in Dortmunder and his pals to take advantage of Fareweather's absence. . . . Events unfold in a delicious sequence, and every step is complemented by great writing." Publ Wkly

What's the worst that could happen? Mysterious Press 1996 373p o.p.

LC 96-12770

"In the midst of burglarizing a Long Island mansion, Dortmunder is caught by billionaire Fairbanks, who claims to the police that Dortmunder's lucky ring (given to Dortmunder by his girlfriend, May) actually belongs to him. Unluckily for Fairbanks, he has robbed the wrong man. Determined to get the ring back, Dortmunder enlists his old cronies in pursuing Fairbanks from Washington's notorious Watergate . . . to a glitzy Las Vegas casino where Dortmunder exacts a satisfying vengeance." Libr J

"Although the gang's dirty tricks are wonderfully ingenious, the characters deliver the real razzle-dazzle. A grandiose guy like Max is cut to order for Mr. Westlake's droll comic style, which reflects a kind of gleeful horror at the schlocky esthetics of the rich and the morally damned." N Y Times Book Rev

Why me? Viking 1983 191p o.p.

LC 82-10921

"Unlucky burgler John A. Dortmunder has made the biggest haul of his life—and he doesn't want it. An enormous ruby ring called the Byzantine Fire has been stolen en route from the United States to Turkey and hidden in the little jewelry store Dortmunder robs. Every cop in New York City, the FBI, several foreign intelligence agencies, a terrorist group or two, and (because they're tired of being hassled by the police) the city's entire criminal population are all after the ring and poor Dortmunder. Westlake's comic talents are well used here." Libr J

Westmacott, Mary, 1890-1976
See also Christie, Agatha, 1890-1976

Westward; a fictional history of the American West: 28 original stories celebrating the 50th anniversary of the Western Writers of America; edited by Dale L. Walker. Forge 2003 432p $25.95
ISBN 0-7653-0451-1 LC 2002-45481

"A Tom Doherty Assiates book"

Contents: First horse, by Coldsmith, D.; Encounter on Horse-Killed Creek, by Gulick, B.; York's story, by Walker, D. L.; Melodies the song dogs sing, by Blevins, W.; Gabe and the doctor, by House, R. C.; A man alone, by Breen, J. V.; Jonas Crag, by Jakes, J.; Inquest in Zion, by Blum, I. B.; Dead Man's Hollow, by Reasoner, J.; The hundred day men, by Black M.;Leaving Paradise, by Carroll, L.; Miss Libbie tells all, by Salzer, S. K.; How I happened to put on the blue, by Carney, O.; The stand, by Braun, M.; The square reporter, by Wheeler, R. S.; Betrayal, by Sandifer, L.; Thirty rangers, by Smith, C.; The whispering, by Graebner, J. E.; The fevers, by Eckhardt, C. F.; I killed King Fisher, by Froh, R.; Noah, by Mehok, E. L.; The big die-up, by Smith, T. D.; Do the dark dance, by Knight, A. W.; Letters to the stove, by Long, E.; East breeze, by Aadland, D.; Big Tim Magoon and the wild west, by Estleman, L. D.; The true facts about the death of Wes Hardin, by Crider, B.

"The collection reveals both the vitality and the diversity of the western genre as well as the enduring appeal of the short story." Booklist

Wetering, Janwillem van de *See* Van de Wetering, Janwillem, 1931-

Wharton, Edith, 1862-1937

The age of innocence. D. Appleton & Co. 1920 364p o.p.

New York City in the 1870s "was a place of tight social stratification with rituals for everything from romance to etiquette at the opera. The young attorney Newland Archer was engaged to lovely, socially acceptable May Welland. He faced the power of family and social mores when he became attracted to May's bohemian cousin, Ellen." Shapiro. Fic for Youth. 3d edition

also in Wharton, E. New York novels p689-958

also in Wharton, E. Novels

A backward glance
In Wharton, E. Novellas and other writings

The buccaneers; a novel; by Edith Wharton; completed by Marion Mainwaring. Viking 1993 406p o.p.

LC 93-13901

"When Wharton died in 1937, she left unfinished a novel about fresh young Americans in class-bound England that *Time* declared would have been her masterpiece. Now Wharton scholar Mainwaring has polished up the rough draft and interpolated a few passages. . . . When the St. George girls and their friend Lizzy Elmsworth aren't accepted in New York society because their bloodlines just don't go back far enough, no matter how rich they are, the St. George governess recommends that they go to England." Libr J

"Ms. Mainwaring has produced a commendably brave pastiche. Throughout the added sections, she turns shadowy walk-ons into full-blown protagonists, twists half-started subplots into integral parts of the story, concocts symbolic names as shamelessly heavy-handed as those of her model, and injects descriptions with a venom that would have made Wharton smile. This new 'Buccaneers' may not be the novel Wharton herself would have written, but it is certainly a lively, engaging piece of fiction." N Y Times Book Rev

Certain people
In Wharton, E. The collected short stories of Edith Wharton

The children. Scribner 282p $25
ISBN 0-684-18453-2

First published 1928 by D. Appleton & Co.

Standing at the rail of the liner, Martin Boyne surveyed his fellow-passengers in the act of coming aboard. 'Not a soul I shall want to speak to—as usual!' was his comment. Then he saw Judy Wheater carrying a fat, rosy baby up the gang plank and he changed his mind. Judy

Wharton, Edith, 1862-1937—*Continued*
was only sixteen, but there was nothing inexperienced in the way she herded her troupe of brothers and sisters and 'steps' over to Europe while her father and mother played at divorce and remarriage. For a whole summer, Martin, old bachelor that he was, joined forces with Judy in her gallant attempt to keep her flock together

The collected short stories of Edith Wharton; edited and with an introduction by R. W. B. Lewis. Scribner 1968 2v o.p.

Contains ten collections of stories: The greater inclination (1899); Crucial instances (1901); The descent of man (1904); The hermit and the wild woman (1908); Tales of men and ghosts (1910); Xingu (1916); Here and beyond (1926); Certain people (1930); Human nature (1933); The world over (1936). Also included are thirteen miscellaneous stories, two dramatic sketches and some articles about the short story and ghost stories

Contents for the short stories included in the volumes are as follows:

The greater inclination: The muse's tragedy; A journey; The pelican; Souls belated: A coward; A cup of cold water; The portrait

Crucial instances: The Duchess at prayer; The angel at the grave; The recovery; The Rembrandt; The moving finger; The confessional

The descent of man: The descent of man; The mission of Jane; The other two; The quicksand; The dilettante; The reckoning; Expiation; The lady's maid's bell; A Venetian night's entertainment

The hermit and the wild woman: The hermit and the wild woman; The last asset; In trust; The pretext; The verdict; The potboiler; The best man

Tales of men and ghosts: The bolted door; His father's son; The Daunt Diana; The debt; Full circle; The legend; The eyes; The blond beast; Afterward; The letters

Xingu: Xingu; Coming home; Autres temps . . .; Kerfol; The long run; The triumph of night; The choice

Here and beyond: Miss Mary Pask; The young gentlemen; Bewitched; The seed of the faith; The temperate zone; Velvet ear pads

Certain people: Atrophy; A bottle of Perrier; After Holbein; Dieu d'amour; The refugees; Mr. Jones

Human nature: Her son; The day of the funeral; A glimpse; Joy in the house; Diagnosis

The world over: Charm incorporated; Pomegranate seed; Permanent wave; Confession: Roman fever; The looking glass; Duration

Miscellaneous short stories: Mrs. Manstey's views; The fullness of life; That good may come; The lamp of phyche; April showers; Friends; The line of least resistance; The letter; The House of the Dead Hand; The introducers; Les metteurs en scène; Writing a war story; All Souls'

Collected stories, 1891-1910; [Maureen Howard selected the contents and wrote the notes for this volume] Library of Am. 2001 928p $35
ISBN 1-88301-193-0 LC 00-57596

Contents: Mrs. Manstey's view; The fulness of life; The lamp of psyche; The valley of childish things, and other emblems; The muse's tragedy; A journey; The pelican; Souls belated; The twilight of the God; A cup of cold water; The touchstone; The Duchess at prayer; The angel at the grave; The recovery; The Rembrandt; The moving finger; Sanctuary; The descent of man; The mission of Jane; The other two; The reckoning; Expiation; The lady's maid's bell; The house of the dead hand; The introducers; The hermit and the wild woman; The last asset; The pretext; The pot-boiler; The best man; His father's son; The daunt Diana; The debt; Full circle; The legend; The eyes

Collected stories, 1911-1937; edited by Maureen Howard. Library of Am. 2001 848p $35
ISBN 1-88301-194-9 LC 00-57595

Contents: Xingu; Coming home; Autres temps . . .; Kerfol; The long run; The triumph of night; Bunner sisters; Writing a war story; The Marne [novelette]; Miss Mary Pask; The young gentlemen; Bewitched; The seed of the faith; Velvet ear-pads; Atrophy; A bottle of Perrier; After Holbein; Mr. Jones; Her son; The day of the funeral; A glimpse; Joy in the house; Charm incorporated; Pomegranate seed; Confession; Roman fever; The looking-glass; Duration; All souls'

Crucial instances
In Wharton, E. The collected short stories of Edith Wharton

The custom of the country. Scribner 594p $55
ISBN 0-684-14655-X
"Hudson River editions"
First published 1913

"The story of Undine Spragg, a young woman with social aspirations who convinces her nouveau riche parents to leave the Midwest and settle in New York. There she captures and marries a young man from New York's high society. This and each subsequent relationship she engineers prove unsatisfactory, chiefly because of her greed and great ambition." Merriam-Webster's Ency of Lit

also in Wharton, E. New York novels p325-688
also in Wharton, E. Novels

The descent of man
In Wharton, E. The collected short stories of Edith Wharton

Ethan Frome. Scribner 1911 195p o.p.

This is "an ironic tragedy of love, frustration, jealousy, and sacrifice. The scene is a New England village, where Ethan barely makes a living out of a stony farm and is at odds with his wife Zeena (short for Zenobia), a whining hypochondriac. Mattie, a cousin of Zeena's comes to live with them, and love develops between her and Ethan. They try to end their impossible lives by steering a bobsled into a tree; instead ending up crippled and tied for the rest of their unhappy time on earth to Zeena and the barren farm. Zeena, however, is transformed into a devoted nurse and Mattie becomes the nagging invalid." Benet's Reader's Ency of Am Lit

also in Wharton, E. Novellas and other writings

False dawn
In Wharton, E. Novellas and other writings

The greater inclination
In Wharton, E. The collected short stories of Edith Wharton

Wharton, Edith, 1862-1937—*Continued*

Here and beyond

In Wharton, E. The collected short stories of Edith Wharton

The hermit and the wild woman

In Wharton, E. The collected short stories of Edith Wharton

The house of mirth. Scribner 329p $50

ISBN 0-684-14658-4

"Hudson River editions"

First published 1905

"The story concerns the tragic fate of the beautiful and well-connected but penniless Lily Bart, who at age 29 lacks a husband to secure her position in society. Maneuvering to correct this situation, she encounters both Simon Rosedale, a rich man outside her class, and Lawrence Selden, who is personally appealing and socially acceptable but not wealthy. She becomes indebted to an unscrupulous man, has her reputation sullied by a promiscuous acquaintance, and slides into genteel poverty. Unable or unwilling to ally herself with either Rosedale or Selden, she finally despairs and takes an overdose of pills." Merriam-Webster's Ency of Lit

also in Wharton, E. New York novels p1-324

also in Wharton, E. Novels

Human nature

In Wharton, E. The collected short stories of Edith Wharton

Madame de Treymes

In Wharton, E. Novellas and other writings

The Marne

In Wharton, E. Collected stories, 1911-1937

The mother's recompense

In Wharton, E. Novellas and other writings

New Year's Day

In Wharton, E. Novellas and other writings

New York novels; foreword by Louis Auchincloss. Modern Lib. 1998 xxi, 958p $27.95

ISBN 0-679-60302-6 LC 98-5465

Contents: The house of mirth (1905); The custom of the country (1913); The age of innocence (1920)

Novellas and other writings. Library of Am. 1990 1137p il $45

ISBN 0-940450-53-4 LC 89-62930

Contents: Madame de Treymes; Ethan Frome; Summer; Old New York; The mother's recompense; A backward glance

In Madame de Treymes (1907), an American woman living in Paris tries to break her engagement with a local aristocrat. Ethan Frome is entered separately. Summer (1917) tells the story of Charity Royall, an adopted New England girl in a poor village who falls in love with a young architect from the city. Old New York (1924) is a collection of four novellas, each set in four different decades: False dawn, The old maid, The spark, and New Year's Day. In The mother's recompense (1925), a promiscuous mother moves in with her daughter only to discover her daughter's fiancee was once one of her own lovers. A backward glance (1934) is the author's autobiography.

Novels; Edith Wharton. Library of America, Distributed in the U.S. and Canada by Viking 1985 1328p $40

ISBN 0-940450-31-3 LC 85-191816

Contents: The house of mirth; The reef; The custom of the country; The age of innocence

The house of mirth, The custom of the country, and the age of innocence are entered separately. In the reef (1912), the "action is confined almost exclusively to a chateau in France and the issue narrowed to a psychological struggle in the mind of the heroine, Anna Leath, who discovers that the man she has agreed to marry has had an affair with the young woman who is about to marry her stepson." Ref Guide to Am Lit. 2d edition

The old maid

In Wharton, E. Novellas and other writings

Old New York

In Wharton, E. Novellas and other writings

The reef

In Wharton, E. Novels

Sanctuary

In Wharton, E. Collected stories, 1891-1910

The selected short stories of Edith Wharton; introduced and edited by R.W.B. Lewis. Scribner 1991 xxi, 390p $24.95

ISBN 0-684-19304-3 LC 91-11433

A "collection of 21 of the author's best stories. Lewis' excellent introduction explains Wharton's appeal and provides a brief overview of her life and prolific literary output." Booklist

The spark

In Wharton, E. Novellas and other writings

The stories of Edith Wharton; selected and introduced by Anita Brookner. Carroll & Graf Pubs. 1990 2v o.p.

Contents: v1 The pelican; The other two; The mission of Jane; The reckoning; The last asset; The letters; Autres temps . . . ; The long run; After Holbein; Atrophy; Pomegranate seed; Her son; Charm incorporated; All Souls'

v2 The lamp of psyche; A journey; The line of least resistance; The moving finger; Expiation; *Les metteurs en scéne*; Full circle; The daunt Diana; Afterward; The bolted door; The temperate zone; Diagnosis; The day of the funeral; Confession

Summer

In Wharton, E. Novellas and other writings

Tales of men and ghosts

In Wharton, E. The collected short stories of Edith Wharton

The touchstone

In Wharton, E. Collected stories, 1891-1910

The world over

In Wharton, E. The collected short stories of Edith Wharton

Xingu

In Wharton, E. The collected short stories of Edith Wharton

Wharton, William

Birdy. Knopf 1979 c1978 309p o.p.
LC 77-28023

"At the close of World War II, in the mental ward of a veteran's hospital, there is a patient whose behavior quite baffles the psychiatrists. The patient's only childhood friend, another soldier who has a severe facial wound, is transferred to the hospital in the hope he may be of help. The friend instantly recognizes that the patient is behaving exactly like a bird. (The keeping of birds had always been an obsession of the patient throughout his adolescence.)" Choice

"Only the most rigorous imagination can make a story of this sort work for a reader who is generally indifferent to birds. Wharton has just such an imagination." Newsweek

Dad; a novel. Knopf 1981 449p o.p.
LC 80-2725

"Jack Tremont is a fifty-two year old American artist who lives in Paris. He is called home to care for his parents, both of whom have recently become ill. His nineteen year old son shows up also, since his grandparent's home is so convenient to the California State University that he has just left. We meet father and son after they leave California and begin a cross country drive. We move back and forth from past to present, comparing and contrasting the perceptions, concerns, and needs of three generations in one family. Each chapter presents a different character's point of view." Best Sellers

"It's an old story, this man-in-the-middle business, but fresh in Wharton's telling because he lets experience—lunch, a crisis, baseball on TV—accumulate as naturally and surely as aging itself." Saturday Rev

Wheeler, Harvey, 1918-2004
(jt. auth) Burdick, E. Fail-safe

Wheeler, Richard S.

Downriver; a Barnaby Skye novel. Forge 2001 304p $25.95
ISBN 0-312-87845-1 LC 2001-40481
"A Tom Doherty Associates book"

A title in the author's "Barnaby Skye series, chronicling the adventures of mountain man Skye and his Crow Indian wife, Victoria. . . . In 1838, Skye and Victoria are on their way from the Rocky Mountains to St. Louis so Skye can compete for a wilderness job as a post trader with the powerful and ruthless American Fur Company. The journey will cover 1,500 miles by land and river and is fraught with peril and treachery. . . . Wheeler is a master of character and plot, and this novel showcases his talents at their peak." Publ Wkly

Eclipse. Forge 2002 380p $27.95
ISBN 0-312-87846-X LC 2001-58978
"A Tom Doherty Associates book"

After returning home to a hero's welcome in 1806 "Meriwether Lewis floundered as the governor of the Louisiana Territory, Beset by financial and political difficulties, a depressed and despondent Lewis apparently either committed suicide or was murdered in the Tennessee backwoods in 1809. Wheeler ponders that puzzle, constructing a chilling scenario in which a delusional, syphilis-wracked Lewis feels duty bound to end his fife rather than bring shame upon his name, his family, and his beloved Corps of Discovery. A riveting re-creation of the tragic final years of an American legend." Booklist

The fields of Eden. Forge 2001 383p $25.95
ISBN 0-312-87309-3 LC 2001-18948
"A Tom Doherty Associates book"

The author "follows the adventures of nine people struggling to survive in the wilds of rugged Oregon Territory in the 1840s. . . . The backdrop is the unstoppable flood of American immigrants into Oregon, onto rich land controlled by the Hudson's Bay Company. Turmoil and uncertainty reign as British, American and Canadian settlers compete bitterly for resources, land, business opportunity and political power. . . . Wheeler is adept at portraying characters facing personal crises, revealing just how fragile and resilient people can be." Publ Wkly

Sierra; a novel of the California gold rush. Forge 1996 380p o.p.
LC 96-8305
"A Tom Doherty Associates book"

"Ulysses McQueen leaves his wife on the family farm in Iowa to seek his fortune in the California gold rush just as Steven Jarvis is mustered out of the army in booming Monterey. After a grueling cross-country trek, McQueen sets about grubbing in the dust near Sutter's Mill, while Jarvis turns to the mercantile trade. McQueen pines for his wife but postpones writing her until his fortune is assured, while Jarvis becomes a workaholic after he is denied the love of his life. Their paths cross in the frenzy of gold fever." Libr J

The author "re-creates the American frontier in fascinating detail, populates it with engaging characters, and, in the process, manages to personalize the great period of western expansion." Booklist

Whetstone, Diane McKinney- *See* McKinney-Whetstone, Diane

Whitaker, Rodney *See* Trevanian

Whitby, Sharon, 1935-
For works written by this author under other names see Black, Veronica, 1935-

White, Bailey

Quite a year for plums; a novel. Knopf 1998 220p $22
ISBN 0-679-44531-5 LC 97-41124

"The women in town are worried about Roger, the peanut virologist. Hilma and Meade discuss him at their weekly readings. Eula frets over his welfare—not to mention his appetite. And everyone else just seems to be content with giving opinions on his budding romance with the strange bird artist, Della. . . . [The author] will make the reader care about this nurturing gaggle of women and other community members in a small, sleepy town in southern Georgia." Libr J

White, Edmund, 1940-

The beautiful room is empty. Knopf 1988 227p o.p.

LC 87-40495

In this sequel to A boy's own story, the author "follows our nameless hero from his final year at prep school in the mid-1950s through his cruisy but self-deprecating college years to the 'turning point' in his life—the famous Stonewall uprising of 1969 in which the clients of a New York gay bar stood up to the policemen trying to close it down. What emerges is the picture of a young man desperately struggling to come to terms with himself, a struggle that is a universal even if the context for every individual is different. Artfully constructed, this work clearly transcends its 'gay' theme." Libr J

Followed by The farewell symphony

A boy's own story. Dutton 1982 217p o.p.

LC 82-9536

In this first volume of an autobiographical trilogy, a nameless narrator reminisces about his homosexual childhood and his conflicting emotions in coming of age during the 1950s. At fifteen years of age, the boy hopes that "he is just passing through a homosexual 'stage.' At prep school he goes to a . . . psychiatrist who pops pills and talks of his own problems—and with no help from this man he begins slowly to see the real dimensions of his own life." Newsweek

This first-person novel is "written with the flourish of a master stylist. . . . It is an endearing portrait of a child's longing to be charming, popular, powerful, and loved, and of his struggles with adults . . . [told with] sensitivity and elegance." Harpers

Followed by The beautiful room is empty (1988) and The farewell symphony (1997)

(ed) The Faber book of gay short fiction. See The Faber book of gay short fiction

The farewell symphony; a novel. Knopf 1997 413p $25

ISBN 0-679-43477-1 LC 97-73825

In this final volume of the author's autobiographical trilogy, "an unnamed narrator reminisces about furtive encounters, literary salons, and the deaths that conclude enduring friendships. He proceeds in roughly chronological fashion from his life in the early 1970s as an aspiring but unpublished writer to life in Europe in the 1990s." Libr J

"White is an 'archeologist of gossip,' and he explicitly chronicles the pre-AIDS heyday he enjoyed, but he coyly leaves aside his stated subject, the death from AIDS of his partner. This perverse tactic works: after the cacophony of voices White has raised fades into the silence of death, the absence of the man who mattered most to him becomes overwhelmingly poignant." New Yorker

The married man; a love story. Knopf 2000 321p $25

ISBN 0-375-40005-2 LC 99-53980

This is the "tale of Austin Smith, an expatriated scion of decayed Southern gentry, who lives on Ile Saint Louis, in Paris. Austin, an expert on 18th-century French furniture, is HIV positive but healthy when he becomes the lover of Julien, a married architect more than 20 years Austin's junior who is in the process of divorcing his wife." Publ Wkly

"A shrewd social observer with a great gift for dialogue, White composes quicksilver scenes bright with wit, then sets aside comedy-of-manners for the luster of tragedy." Booklist

White, Kate

A body to die for. Warner Bks. 2003 294p $23.95

ISBN 0-446-53148-0 LC 2003-41081

"Depressed by her nonexistent love life, Bailey, a freelance true-crime writer for 'Gloss' magazine, leaves Manhattan for some R&R at the Cedar Inn and Spa in Warren, Mass., owned and run by an old friend of her mother's. Her first night there, however, she stumbles on the corpse of one of the inn's female therapists—wrapped in silver Mylar paper. [The therapist's] murder, on top of the accidental death of a male client some months earlier, could spell doom for the inn, unless Bailey can get to the bottom of things." Publ Wkly

"Once again, White's background as editor-in-chief of 'Cosmopolitan' shines through in her snappy dialog, tight plotting, and insider humor. . . . A breezy beach read for mystery fans." Libr J

White, Patrick, 1912-1990

The eye of the storm. Viking 1974 c1973 608p o.p.

First published 1973 in the United Kingdom

"Elizabeth Hunter, once a brilliant socialite and a rich, sensual, materialistic woman, now into her eighties, is dying in her Sydney mansion, perceived as a house-shrine by the nurses and servants who devotedly revolve around her. Mrs. Hunter's crucial experience, during the eye of a cyclone, of harmony between her inner, essential self and the outer void has determined the rest of her life, especially the act of dying. Flawed as she is, her strength and intense authenticity of being is communicated in varying degrees to her servants, her lawyer and to her two inauthentic children, the Princess de Lascabanes and Sir Basil Hunter. The comic brilliance of White's conception of Sir Basil, the weary actor for whom life and acting are perpetually fused, is one of the novel's highlights." Oxford Companion to Australian Lit

The vivisector. Viking 1970 567p o.p.

In this novel "White treats a difficult and complex subject, the act of creation and its costs as realized from within the artist's consciousness. Hurtle Duffield, the artist-protagonist, is the vivisector who cuts up living experiences and relationships for the purposes of his art. But Hurtle also comprehends art as an avenue to a realization of the Divine Vivisector, God, and both the successive women in his life and his paintings represent stages in his quest for a perception of pure being. The quest culminates in his final attempt, disrupted by his last stroke, to paint God. As a background to Hurtle's experiences, described with uncompromising honesty, is White's most comprehensive and intimately realized picture of the changing Australian social milieu." Oxford Companion to Australian Lit

White, Phyllis Dorothy James *See* James, P. D.

White, Robin A.

Typhoon; [by] Robin White. Putnam 2003 388p il map $24.95

ISBN 0-399-14935-X LC 2002-31835

"'Baikal', the last of Russia's giant Typhoon-class submarines . . . . is supposed to be off to the scrap yard at American expense, but corrupt Russian admirals have illegally sold her to China. When the American sub 'Portland' is ordered to [prevent delivery], its aggressive captain, James Vann, becomes obsessed with destroying the 'Baikal', commanded by his old nemesis, Alexander Markov. At the same time, the presence of Lt. Rose Scavullo, the first woman to serve on a U.S. submarine, is a major and divisive distraction . . . . As the ships duel in the Arctic Ocean, war threatens to break out between the United States and China." Libr J

"The international cat-and-mouse game becomes a contest between American technology and Russian cunning. The setting and stirring pace will remind readers of Clancy's 'The Hunt for Red October'. Though the exhaustive technical details may stymie some readers, enthusiasts of naval warfare will delight in them." Publ Wkly

White, Stephen Walsh

The best revenge; [by] Stephen White. Delacorte Press 2003 353p $24.95

ISBN 0-385-33619-5 LC 2002-67593

FBI agent Kelda James's "latest triumph is the discovery of DNA evidence that ostendibly exonerates death-row inmate Tome Clone, convicted of murdering his girlfriend 13 years prior. Curiosity leads Kelda to pick up the released prisoner herself, and the two ot them . . . develop a curious closeness. Kelda recommends esteemed Boulder psychotherapist Dr. Alan Gregory (star of numerous White novels) . . . to Tom to help sort out potential outside-life issues, but this only serves to make matters even stranger, for client confidentiality bars Alan from discussing the two with each other or with his best buddy, a local detective. Not everyone is convinced the DNA evidence proves Tom's innocence, and some other evil force looms in an effort to exact revenge." Booklist

Missing persons; [by] Stephen White. Dutton 2005 391p $25.95

ISBN 0-525-94859-7 LC 2004-27172

"Eight years to the day after JonBenet Ramsey was murdered, her childhood friend and neighbor, Mallory, winds up missing. At first, her disappearance seems unconnected to the disappearance of Diane, one of Boulder (Colorado) psychologist Alan Gregory's colleagues, or the apparent murder of Diane's friend Hannah. But nothing is coincidental in a White murder mystery, and once again, he expertly places the good doctor in the middle of one doozy of a whodunit." Booklist

White, T. H. (Terence Hanbury), 1906-1964

The book of Merlyn; the unpublished conclusion to The once and future king; prologue by Sylvia Townsend Warner; illustrated by Trevor Stubley. University of Tex. Press 1977 xx, 137p il o.p.

LC 77-3454

Sequel to The once and future king

"White, who believed that the central theme of Malory's 'Morte d'Arthur' was to find an antidote to war, pursues that theme here, going to the animals for his answer. Old and defeated King Arthur is led by magician Merlyn into a badger's sett where a group of animals are discussing people. It's Merlyn, however, who becomes chief orator. Publ Wkly

"Writing during World War II, White vented his feelings about the futility of war with a fierceness that sometimes overwhelms the intriguing mixture of fantasy, humor, and rationality which pervaded the tetralogy." Booklist

The candle in the wind

In White, T. H. The once and future king p545-677

The ill-made knight

In White, T. H. The once and future king p325-544

The once and future king. Putnam 1958 677p $25.95

ISBN 0-399-10597-2 LC 58-10760

An omnibus edition of four novels; The sword in the stone (1939), The witch in the wood (1939, now called The Queen of Air and Darkness) and The ill-made knight (1940). A number of alterations have been made in the earlier books. Previously unpublished, The candle in the wind "deals with the plotting of Mordred and his kinsmen of the house of Orkney, and their undying enmity to King Arthur." Times Lit Suppl

"White's contemporary retelling of Malory's Le Mor*te d'Arthur is b*oth romantic and exciting." Shapiro. Fic for Youth. 3d edition

The Queen of Air and Darkness

In White, T. H. The once and future king

The sword in the stone; with decorations by the author and end papers by Robert Lawson. Putnam 1939

First published 1938 in the United Kingdom

An "account of everyday life in a great medieval manor, with two boys, Kay and Wart (who turns out to be King Arthur) learning the code of being a gentleman, busy with hawking, jousting, sword play, and hunting. The whole trend of the story is how the boy Wart was made worthy to become a king." Ont Libr Rev

"Delightful, fantastic, satirical nonsense, for the reader with a background of Arthurian legend." Wis Libr Bull

Followed by The witch in the wood

also in White, T. H. The once and future king p1-213

The witch in the wood; with decorations by the author. Putnam 1939 269p il o.p.

Sequel to The sword in the stone

The boy, Wart, is now a mature King Arthur fighting against other kings for recognition. Merlin and other characters reappear in the fantasy but it is mainly the story of Queen Morguase (the witch in the wood) and her four sons. Set in the Land of Lothian and Orkney

Followed by The ill-made knight (1940)

also in White, T. H. The once and future king

White, Terence Hanbury *See* White, T. H. (Terence Hanbury), 1906-1964

Whitehead, Colson, 1969-

The intuitionist; a novel. Anchor Bks. (NY) 1999 255p $19.95

ISBN 0-385-49299-5 LC 98-6756

This "novel follows the travails of the redoubtable Lila Mae Watson, the first black woman Elevator Inspector in a nameless city very much like New York. Caught between the political machinations of the two factions of the Elevator Guild (the Intuitionists, like Lila, inspect the elevators by a sort of sympathetic insight, whereas the Empiricists actually examine the cables and helical springs), Lila Mae finds herself in the midst of a murky underground war for control over the kingdom of Vertical Transport. Whitehead's prose is graceful and often lyrical and his elevator underworld is a complex, lovingly realized creation." New Yorker

John Henry Days; a novel. Doubleday 2001 389p $24.95

ISBN 0-385-49819-5 LC 00-43143

This is a "character study surrounding the legend of folk hero John Henry. A John Henry festival in a small West Virginia town draws a diverse crowd, including J. Sutter, a freelance writer going from one event to another in search of free food and paid expenses; and Pamela Street, a restless woman grieving for her father. Both are forced to reevaluate their lives, brought together by bonds of race and history." Libr J

"Whitehead relishes slashing through the mindlessness of the age in a voice so intelligent and an idiom so imaginative that it can lift a reader right out of his chair. But he is not remorseless. He likes these people and respects their longings. They have no moral compass, but he has, so we can laugh at them but still grieve for the loss of so much possiblility." N Y Times Book Rev

Whitney, Phyllis A., 1903-

Amethyst dreams. Crown 1997 276p $25

ISBN 0-517-70759-4 LC 97-5000

"When Hallie Knight receives a summons to Topsail Island by the grandfather of her college roommate, she immediately responds. Knowing that Susan has disappeared without a trace piques her curiosity, but she's also glad of the opportunity to escape the pain caused by her husband's infidelity. She never expects to become the catalyst for unraveling the strange fate of her friend or find the courage to reexamine her own life." Booklist

"What matters here are the characters' wonderfully wrought temperaments—no sinners, no saints, but ultimately lots of forgiveness—and the subtle, little glimpses of fear that keep readers looking for answers right up to the satisfying conclusion." Libr J

Columbella. Doubleday 1966 306p o.p.

A mystery-romance set in St. Thomas, Virgin Islands. A young teacher, Jessica Abbott, is hired to tutor the 14-year-old daughter of a wealthy family. She is both drawn to and repelled by the girl's father. But when the mother, a spoiled willful woman, who engages in reckless affairs with young men, is murdered and suspicion falls on the husband, Jessica becomes convinced of the latter's innocence and sets out to discover the real murderer

Domino. Doubleday 1979 351p o.p.

LC 79-7331

"Domino is a ghost town, an abandoned silver mine camp in the Colorado Rockies that holds the secret to young Laurie Morgan's psychic wound. During the 20 years since she left her grandmother's mansion, she has endured nightmarish recollections of a peripheral role in her father's shooting. Now Laurie is summoned to the bedside of that imperious old woman, who needs the assistance of a blood relative if the Morgan territory is to resist the overtures of opportunist land developers." Publ Wkly

The golden unicorn. Doubleday 1976 279p o.p.

"After losing her adoptive parents, [journalist] Courtney Marsh becomes determined to find her natural mother and father. Clues lead to East Hampton, the home of the Rhodes family. They are an exasperating lot, prone to violent outbursts and guilty secrets. Courtney's investigative skills uncover the secret of her birth and involve her in a family scandal that almost causes her death." Libr J

Poinciana. Doubleday 1980 345p o.p.

LC 80-949

"Poinciana is the exquisite Palm Beach estate to which young and naive Sharon comes as chatelaine. Married at a vulnerable period in her life to Ross Logan, 60-year-old robber baron, she becomes another of his possessions, a beautiful object like the netsuke collection in his museum-home. There are counterforces in ex-wives, a senile mother, a scheming daughter and Logan's death before Sharon develops her own resources." Publ Wkly

The singing stones. Doubleday 1990 507p o.p.

LC 89-37137

Lynn McLeod "is an ombudsman for terminally ill children who is suddenly summoned to assist the daughter of her first husband. But the child is not physically ill. She is haunted by the near-fatal accident that crippled her father and the threatening presence of her wicked stepmother (whom everyone believes to be the epitome of quiet kindness). Lynn enters the complicated family situation with great reluctance, bewitched by the spiritualist philosophies of one character yet driven by her own sympathy for a child in distress. A terrific work of romantic suspense in a contemporary setting." Booklist

Spindrift. Doubleday 1975 301p o.p.

This novel is set in Newport, Rhode Island. "Christy Moreland, having recovered from a breakdown after the apparent suicide of her father, newspaperman Adam Keene, arrives at 'Spindrift,' her domineering mother-in-law's estate. Theo [her mother-in-law] is set on keeping young Peter, son of Christy and her passive husband, Joel. Christy is equally determined to get the boy back and to prove her father was murdered. She suspects Theo and others in the lush company, except strong, personable Bruce Perry. With her marriage failing, Christy turns to Bruce who she hopes will help her and with whom she feels she's falling in love." Publ Wkly

Window on the square. Appleton-Century-Crofts 1962 313p o.p.

"When Meegan Kincaid is summoned to the Washington Square home of rich Mr. Brandon Reid, she discovers that the Reids are not looking for a seamstress but want her to see what she can do with Jeremy, a difficult,

Whitney, Phyllis A., 1903—*Continued*

moody boy of nine. Meegan senses the unhappiness that pervades the house and slowly discovers some of the reasons for it. Jeremy is supposed to have willfully shot his father and, after a surprisingly short interval, his mother had married the dead husband's brother. Further to complicate matters, Meegan falls in love with Brandon Reid and makes an implacable enemy of Mrs. Reid's old servant." SLJ

Woman without a past. Doubleday 1991 302p o.p.

LC 90-3860

Molly Hunt "is a budding young star in the world of suspense fiction, yet her psyche is still wounded from the sudden, violent death of her husband. A chance meeting in her publisher's office is the incident that sweeps Molly physically into the Old South ambience of Charleston, South Carolina, and emotionally onto a trail that leads to the discovery of the truth about her parentage and her place within the Mountfort family." Booklist

The author "combines a dynamic, likable heroine with eccentric characters, romantic entanglements, family ghosts and a charming setting." Publ Wkly

Whyte, Jack

The eagles' brood. Forge 1997 412p $25.95

ISBN 0-312-85289-4 LC 97-14295

"A Tom Doherty Associates book"

This third installment in the Camulod Chronicles "takes the story from Caius Merlyn Britannicus' childhood through the conception of Arthur. As a highborn heir of Roman colonists, it is Merlyn's responsibility to protect Camulod and spread Roman civilization. At first he is aided by his cousin, Uther Pendragon, whom he idealizes, but then he starts receiving inklings that Uther may be harboring dark secrets. When love enters Merlyn's life in the form of Cassandra, it signals the end of the cousins' close relationship and starts a series of events that threaten to destroy the colony." Booklist

The author uses "rich period details—early British military tactics, religious philosophies and technologies—to bring the era and its people to vibrant life." Publ Wkly

The singing sword. Forge 1996 383p o.p.

LC 96-19966

"A Tom Doherty Associates book"

"As the novel progresses, and the Roman Empire continues to decay, the colony of Camulod flourishes. But the lives of the colony's main characters, Gaius Publius Varrus—ironsmith, innovator and soldier—and his brother-in-law, former Roman Senator Caius Britannicus, are not trouble-free, especially when their most bitter enemy, Claudius Seneca, reappears. . . . Whyte provides rich detail about the forging of superior weaponry, the breeding of horses, the training of cavalrymen, the growth of a lawmaking body within the community and the origins of the Round Table." Publ Wkly

Followed by The eagles' brood

Wibberley, Leonard, 1915-1983

The mouse that roared. Little, Brown 1955 279p o.p.

LC 54-8294

"The 'Tiny Twenty' overtake the major powers of the world after plotting a bold maneuver to steal the atomic secrets of the United States. Centuries of industrialization and sophistication separate the tiny European nation from the enraged larger countries, who must acquiesce to the will of the former. Underneath this lighthearted tale is a serious warning about the dangers of nuclear power." (Shapiro. Fic for Youth. 3d edition)

Wideman, John Edgar

The cattle killing. Houghton Mifflin 1996 212p o.p.

LC 96-19305

Set in Philadelphia, this novel "begins inside the head of a black novelist who processes images of the city as it is now and as it was when he was growing up. . . . [He] dreams his way back to 1793. A plague is sweeping through the City of Brotherly Love, giving its white citizens feverish delusions that the pestilence is the sinister work of the blacks in their midst, who are themselves immune. Bearing witness to this madness is a young itinerant minister of mixed racial origins who . . . freed his mother from slavery. He wanders about, working at odd jobs, preaching the Gospel. His faith, however sturdy, cannot protect him from the perils of a landscape agitated by disease and race hate." Nation

"Wideman hauntingly evokes the tragic consequences of racial prejudice. Brimming with mysteries and shadowy secrets, the narrative winds elliptically among the stories of blacks whose attempts to rise above bigotry and lead free lives come to heartbreaking conclusions." Publ Wkly

God's gym; John Edgar Wideman. Houghton Mifflin 2005 175p $23

ISBN 0-618-51525-9 LC 2004-54071

Contents: Weight; Hunters; Sharing; The silence of Thelonious Monk; Are dreams faster than the speed of light; Who invented the jump shot; What we cannot speak about we must pass over in silence; Fanon; Who weeps when one of us goes down blues; Sightings

The author "offers ten stories that range widely from family and basketball to illness and death. In addition, race is an important element. . . . Wideman's stories are feasts of language offering up new metaphors and original imagery. He often uses a dreamlike, stream-of-consciousness style, wandering seemingly far from the original story but eventually resolving back to the starting elements. Each story is a gem that grows more brilliant with rereading." Libr J

Philadelphia fire; a novel. Holt & Co. 1990 199p o.p.

LC 90-30590

This novel "is, as the title reflects, centered on the 1985 destruction of the Philadelphia headquarters of an organization called MOVE. The narrator is a black American who has removed himself from his homeland and taken refuge from the cares of life on an easygoing island in the Aegean. Nevertheless, when news of the MOVE incident reaches him, he becomes obsessed with

Wideman, John Edgar—*Continued*
its meaning—to him personally, to black Americans in general." Booklist

"Wideman is best when he is most personal. . . . By turns brilliant and murky, seamless and ragged, Philadelphia Fire is on to something big. Wideman's vision of racism in the U.S. suggests nothing less than a genetic disorder present at the birth of the nation." Time

The stories of John Edgar Wideman. Pantheon Bks. 1992 432p o.p.
LC 91-50839

Contents: All stories are true; Casa Grande; Backseat; Loon man; Everybody knew Bubba Riff; Signs; What he saw; A voice foretold; Newborn thrown in trash and dies; Welcome; Doc's story; The Statue of Liberty; Valaida; Hostages; Surfiction; Rock River; When it's time to go; Concert; Presents; The tambourine lady; Little Brother; Fever; Damballah; Daddy Garbage; Lizabeth: the caterpillar story; Hazel; The Chinaman; The watermelon story; The songs of Reba Love Jackson; Across the wide Missouri; Rashad; Tommy; Solitary; The beginning of Homewood

"The 25 stories pulled together here demonstrate [the author's] eloquence in picturing various elements in the constant friction between black and white societies in the U.S. Family and place are, thus, two prominent themes. He writes lushly, beautifully, yet loudly as well; his voice is deep, rich, booming." Booklist

Two cities. Houghton Mifflin 1998 242p $24
ISBN 0-395-85730-9 LC 98-22915

"Kassima, her husband and sons dead, meets Robert Jones in her native Pittsburgh, sleeps with him, and spends much of the rest of the book doing her best to avoid him: this is a cautious love story. The narrative's anchor is Kassima's elderly tenant, who wanders about Pittsburgh and Philadelphia with a camera, making the invisible visible. Wideman, similarly, is a writer who shows you things you would never have seen without him; his prose at once bears the weight of a brutal, complex legacy and exults in a sort of weightlessness." New Yorker

Wiesel, Elie, 1928-

The accident
In Wiesel, E. Night, Dawn, The accident: three tales p205-318

A beggar in Jerusalem; a novel; translated from the French by Lily Edelman and the author. Random House 1970 211p o.p.

Original French edition, 1969

"This novel consists of the stories of the characters who have gathered at the Wailing Wall in Jerusalem. A 'beggar' named David loiters and waits, in the aftermath of the Six-Day War, in the company of . . . [a] crew of 'beggars.' . . . He is waiting—or passively searching—for his friend Katriel, who has died in the fighting, and for Katriel's widow, Malka. At the same time the 'beggar' is certainly no beggar; his name may not be David. . . . The war is not only the Six-Day War—it is every action in which the Jews have been threatened with destruction. And Katriel may not be dead at all." Book World

"Reading Elie Wiesel is not an easy experience. It is certainly by no means an act of escape, the traditional function of literary entertainment. His works touch all of one's fibers. . . . After we have listened to what Wiesel has to say, other literature seems meaningless." Saturday Rev

Dawn; translated from the French by Frances Frenaye. Hill & Wang 1961 89p o.p.

Original French edition, 1960

"Elisha, a young Jewish terrorist fighting for the creation of Israel in the 1940s, is faced with an agonizing moral dilemma. He is to be the executioner of a British officer in reprisal for the hanging of a captured terrorist. A survivor of the concentration camps and a victim all of his life, Elisha considers whether he is any different from his oppressors if he can execute a helpless prisoner in cold blood." Shapiro. Fic for Youth. 3d edition

also in Wiesel, E. Night, Dawn, The accident: three tales p121-204

The forgotten; translated by Stephen Becker. Summit Bks. 1992 237p o.p.
LC 91-46826

Original French edition, 1989

Holocaust "survivor Elhanan Rosenbaum, now living in New York and a distinguished professor with a psychiatric practice, is tragically losing his prodigious memory. While he can still remember, he creates a 'backup' by bequeathing to his son, Malkiel, his stories of the martyred death of his father in his Carpathian village (for whom his son is named); his teenage stint in the army and his return to a ghetto empty of Jews; his adventures in the underground partisan movement; and his love of Talia, the extraordinary woman who rescued him and who died giving birth to his only son." Libr J

"Mr. Wiesel is a writer of contention and his characters, even when affectionate, speak with a bitter music. The most loving—and the saddest—of these sounds occur in the dark duets between father and son, especially as Elhanan admits to Malkiel that he 'cannot recall the essential thing that I want so much to pass on to you.' Elhanan's faith, his temptation to faith . . is as stunning as the loss he confronts." N Y Times Book Rev

The Golem; the story of a legend; as told by Elie Wiesel and illustrated by Mark Podwal; translated by Anne Borchardt. Summit Bks. 1983 105p il o.p.
LC 83-9304

"The Golem exists only to save his people, the Jews of sixteenth century Prague in this case, from the heinous, antisemitic acts of the gentile population. Mute, made of clay, and given life through the faith of Rabbi Yehuda Loew, the Golem goes about Prague in secret, uncovering the trumped up charges of the gentiles against individual members of the local community. Eventually, at the behest of the Rabbi, the Golem leaves. The narrator asks for his return, knowing the Golem's work is not done." Best Sellers

"This fable is eloquently presented through the combination of Wiesel's facile storytelling skills and Mark Podwal's evocative line drawings." Booklist

The judges; a novel; translated from the French by Geoffrey Strachan. Knopf 2002 209p $24
ISBN 0-375-40909-2 LC 2002-25462

Wiesel, Elie, 1928-—*Continued*

Original French edition, 1999

"A plane bound from New York to Israel is forced to land in a snowstorm in Connecticut, and five passengers are taken to the house of a local man who has the delusion that he is a judge in a capital case. As the guests respond to the judge's more and more personal and insinuating questions, their characters are revealed." Publ Wkly

As the characters "talk about themselves and remember crucial turning points in their lives. Wiesel weaves in Jewish history and mysticism with the characters' personal memories, and he raises the big existential questions about life and death and memory and guilt and forgiveness, with lots of metaphors about scapegoat, fellow traveler, messenger, etc." Booklist

Night
In Wiesel, E. Night, Dawn, The accident: three tales

Night, Dawn, The accident: three tales. Hill & Wang 1972 318p pa $14
ISBN 0-374-52140-9 (pa)

In Dawn, Elisha, a young Jewish terrorist fighting for the creation of Israel in the 1940s is faced with an agonizing moral dilemma. He is to be the executioner of a British officer in reprisal for the hanging of a captured terrorist. A survivor of the concentration camps and a victim all of his life, Elisha considers whether he is any different from his oppressors if he can execute a helpless prisoner in cold blood. Night is a memoir. The accident concerns a survivor of Auschwitz who, recovering from a near-fatal accident, questions the meaning of man's existence and purpose, and death

The oath; translated from the French by Marion Wiesel. Random House 1973 283p o.p.

"Azriel meets a young man attempting to commit suicide. Azriel tries to take the man's mind off his plight by interesting him in a story. It is the story of Kolvillag, where all Jews (but one) were killed on the merest pretext by those whose excuse was the charge of Christ-killers. All of the Jews, however, had taken an oath (of the title) never to tell how they suffered—a kind of weapon of silence against their persecutors. Azriel is now faced with breaking that vow to help save the would-be suicide's life. He tells the tale." America

A "powerful novel, interwoven with threads of Hasidic tales, cabalistic mysticism, Talmudic sayings, and pietistic folklore." Libr J

The testament; a novel; translated from the French by Marion Wiesel. Summit Bks. 1981 346p o.p.
LC 80-27251

Original French edition, 1980

"In modern-day Israel, awaiting his mother's arrival on a plane filled with Russian immigrants, [Grisha] reflects on his childhood and youth and rereads the 'testament of Paltiel Kossover,' a confession/autobiography written by his father in prison shortly before his execution in 1947. The manuscript (which was smuggled out by a stenographer) reveals an idealist dedicated to perfecting humanity, an innocent victim of the machinations of the Soviet regime." Libr J

"In none of Wiesel's earlier novels are the characters so earthy, so real, so finely chiseled, as in this one. Women advance more fully to center stage and play more dominant roles. . . . The almost photographic realism of the narrative gives it a cumulative power that is overwhelming." Christ Century

Twilight; translated from the French by Marion Wiesel. Summit Bks. 1988 217p o.p.
LC 88-2634

Original French edition, 1987

"Raphael is a professor on sabbatical studying at an exclusive upstate New York asylum (the Mountain Clinic, which caters to patients whose 'schizophrenia is linked to Ancient History, to Biblical times'). Wiesel's portraits of these descendants of Adam (one actually believes himself to be Adam) bring a dark humor to this otherwise somber story. Raphael studies not only the patients and staff, but also his own past, reliving the effect of the Holocaust on his family, his own escape, and the loss of his savior, Pedro. . . . Raphael's guilt at having survived has begun to smother him, yet it is his struggle that prompts him to ask such probing questions about God, life, and death." Booklist

"Despite the Holocaust and its atrocities, so specially devised to destroy human life and dignity, we experience in Mr. Wiesel's novel how good the family is, how good people are. Utterly without sentimentality, he gives us a small but real measure of what the world's loss has been." N Y Times Book Rev

Wiesel, Eliezer *See* Wiesel, Elie, 1928-

Wiggen, Henry W. *See* Harris, Mark, 1922-

Wiggins, Marianne

Evidence of things unseen; a novel. Simon & Schuster 2003 383p $25
ISBN 0-684-86969-1 LC 2003-45611

"Born in Kitty Hawk, where the Wright brothers first rose towards the sun, Ray Foster, or 'Fos', . . . is fascinated by radiance. A portrait photographer who deals with the dynamics of light, Fos . . . keeps a lump of phosphorous glowing in a fish tank by his bedside. . . . After signing on as an official photographer for the Tennessee Valley Authority–hence becoming complicit in kicking countless farmers off their ancestral lands to make way for hydroelectric dams–Fos assumes a similar recordkeeping role at the Oak Ridge Laboratory in Tennessee, one of three research sites for the Manhattan project." Economist

"Wiggins fits her lyrical prose to a distinctly rural, Southern cadence, easily blending the vernacular with luminous imagery, adding bits of poetry, passages explaining scientific phenomena, interpolations about the Scopes trial and even references to Moby-Dick, which serves as a leitmotif." Publ Wkly

John Dollar. Harper & Row 1989 214p o.p.
LC 88-45538

"Just after World War I, Charlotte Lewes, a 25-year-old schoolteacher raised on Kipling, is sent to Rangoon to instill British values in the children of English colonists. During a festive sailing expedition, a tidal wave strands her and seaman John Dollar on an island with eight schoolgirls." Libr J

Wiggins, Marianne—*Continued*

"Writing with an impressive degree of control and sophistication, Marianne Wiggins investigates the ghastly processes which crush the marooned children. . . . The phenomenon that particularly fascinates Wiggins in the spiritual disintegration she depicts as the consequence of this spectacle is the growth of a parodic religion." London Rev Books

Wiggs, Susan

The ocean between us. Mira 2004 382p $19.95
ISBN 0-7783-2035-9 LC 2004-557716

"Steve Bennett is a perfect navy officer with a perfect navy family, and he's confident that his world is just the way it should be. But his son wants to be an artist instead of attending the U.S. Naval Academy, and his stalwart and capable wife of 20 years, Grace, is tired of being the perfect navy wife. She wants her own home, and she wants her own career. She's feeling altogether unsettled, but nothing is more unsettling than the secret her husband has hidden from her their entire marriage. Nothing, that is, until the accident on the carrier. Wiggs has done an excellent job of depicting what lies beneath the surfaces of relationships—assumptions, misunderstandings, and expectations." Booklist

Wignall, Kevin

For the dogs. 2004 209p $22
ISBN 0-7432-4756-6 LC 2004-45386

"Stephen Lucas, a recently retired, emotionally stunted hit man, emerges from his Swiss hideaway as a favor to old friend Londoner Mark Hatto, who hires Lucas to surreptitiously guard his daughter, bright, extroverted Ella, while she's vacationing in Italy with her boyfriend. After Ella's entire family is murdered, Lucas foils several serious attempts on Ella's life, and the two of them form an odd, almost familial relationship. The boyfriend soon drops out of the picture as the hit man reluctantly helps Ella exact revenge on those who killed her family. There's plenty of action, but it's the twisting, turning, complicated relationship between Ella and Lucas that forms the core of this compelling novel." Publ Wkly

Wilcken, Hugo, 1964-

The execution; a novel. HarperCollins Pubs. 2002 213p $23.95
ISBN 0-06-018823-5 LC 2001-42410

"Matthew Bourne's life is changed the day he is asked to identify the body of a dead colleague's wife. That cataclysmic event transforms him from a good-looking man with a loving partner, a sweet daughter, plenty of friends, and a good job that supports a cause he believes in to a haggard, hopeless shadow who loses his grip on life." Booklist

"Wilcken can be forgiven for resolving knotty plot problems with a well-timed coincidence here and there; his book is an exciting, nervy thriller that fulfills the demands of the genre while resonating on deeper frequencies." N Y Times Book Rev

Wilcox, Collin

Dead center. Holt & Co. 1992 262p o.p.
LC 91-31076

In this Frank Hastings mystery "a series of powerful and wealthy men are shot to death on the street, the weapon the .22 favored by professional hitmen. The cops finally connect the victims as rather nasty members of the ultra-exclusive Rabelais Club. . . . Old scandals (a hooker's death covered up, a notorious high-stakes poker circle), heavy political and media pressure and glimpses (for us) of the killer's mind-set lead up to Hastings's harrowing, climactic confrontation with the murderer." Publ Wkly

A death before dying. Holt & Co. 1989 231p o.p.
LC 89-11213

"Sex as a near-death experience, performed in front of a video camera for the viewing pleasure of her lover, may provide Meredith Powell with a silver Mercedes and a Nob Hill condo, but it also has her afraid for her life. After confiding her fears to a childhood pal, San Francisco cop Frank Hastings, Meredith turns up dead, strangled and abandoned in the nighttime cold of Golden Gate Park." Booklist

Wilcox "creates suspense through a tightly knit narrative format that confines the novel's action to an 18-day span and flashes short scenes before the reader much like a film montage. This is a smooth performance by a real professional." Publ Wkly

Except for the bones. Doherty Assocs. 1991 282p o.p.
LC 91-21579

"A TOR book"

"Detective Alan Bernhardt looks into the suspicious death of a New York real estate tycoon's latest girlfriend—a death secretly witnessed by the man's estranged stepdaughter in Cape Cod." Libr J

"Wilcox delivers a taut, suspenseful mystery with credible dialogue and good local color." Publ Wkly

Find her a grave. Forge 1993 288p o.p.
LC 93-26557

"A Tom Doherty Associates book"

"Alan Bernhardt is a San Francisco stage director who moonlights as a private eye. He's hired to help the illegitimate daughter of a late Mafia chieftain collect her inheritance, which is buried by the headstone of her mother's grave." Booklist

The author "gradually establishes an authentic mobster milieu, offering the required mix of brutality and honor." Publ Wkly

Full circle. Forge 1994 352p o.p.
LC 94-32703

"A Tom Doherty Associates book"

In Bernhardt's Edge (1988) San Francisco sleuth Alan Bernhardt "saved the life of art expert Betty Giles, who, along with her boyfriend, was blackmailing aged millionaire Raymond DuBois, owner of several pieces of stolen art. Now the FBI is putting heat on Bernhardt to reveal Betty's whereabouts, while DuBois, who would like to preserve his reputation by returning the purloined pieces to their rightful owners, hires Bernhardt to do so." Publ Wkly

Wilcox, Collin—*Continued*

"This is cleverly plotted and populated with a half-dozen self-serving, potentially lethal characters. A truly engrossing read." Booklist

Hire a hangman. Holt & Co. 1991 248p o.p.
LC 90-40317

"Within the first 12 hours after three slugs ruin the arrogant features of ace surgeon Brice Hanchett, the list of suspects is long enough to stretch all the way up the steep hills from Fisherman's Wharf to the swank Russian Hill abode where the shooting occurred. San Francisco cop Frank Hastings scrapes away the surface glamour—the Jaguars and the wood-panelled interiors—and quickly gets to the dirt. . . . Wilcox gets compared with Hammett a lot—and deservedly so. He mines the noir angles of the city with the same restless eye, and his skin-tight plots make the same sudden jumps from the gutter to the high hills and back again." Booklist

Switchback. Holt & Co. 1993 256p o.p.
LC 93-18197

San Francisco's Lt. Frank Hastings "pursues the murderer of a beautiful but selfish young woman who revelled in controlling others. Hastings questions both Haight-Ashbury acquaintances and Nob Hill lovers; meanwhile, constant erotic tension flows from the mutual attraction between Hastings (who lives with divorcée Ann) and bunco squad cop Janet. Wilcox's practiced hand lends a deft descriptive touch, whether to setting, plot or character: add this to the better police procedurals list." Libr J

Wilcox, James, 1949-

Heavenly days; a novel. Viking 2003 199p $23.95
ISBN 0-670-03247-6 LC 2003-50164

A novel set in the small Louisiana town of Tula Springs. "Lou Jones, moving through her fifties at too rapid a pace, is unhappy: her husband lost his job and moved out of their $300,000 'Cajun cabin' and is now living in his parents' house. Plus, Lou, who minds everyone's business except her own, has a doctorate in music but makes more money working as the receptionist for a fundamentalist health club than she could ever earn at the state college. Wilcox adds in some dizzying subplots involving Lou's oldest friend, a scandal at the college, a group of militant lesbians, and marital infidelity." Booklist

Wilde, Oscar, 1854-1900

The picture of Dorian Gray. Modern Library 1992 254p $16.95
ISBN 0-679-60001-9 LC 92-11593

First published 1891 in the United Kingdom; first United States edition published 1895 by G. Munro's Sons

"An archetypal tale of a young man who purchases eternal youth at the expense of his soul, the novel was a romantic exposition of Wilde's Aestheticism. Dorian Gray is a wealthy Englishman who gradually sinks into a life of dissipation and crime. Despite his unhealthy behavior, his physical appearance remains youthful and unmarked by dissolution. Instead, a portrait of himself catalogues every evil deed by turning his once handsome features into a hideous mask." Merriam-Webster's Ency of Lit

Wilder, Elly *See* Roberts, Nora, 1950-

Wilder, Thornton, 1897-1975

The bridge of San Luis Rey; illustrated by Amy Drevenstedt. Boni, A. C. 1967 c1927 235p il o.p.

First published 1927

"On Friday, July 20, 1714, high in the Andes of Peru, the famous bridge of San Luis Rey collapsed, killing the five people who were crossing it. A priest who was witness to the event decided that the tragedy provided the chance to prove the wisdom of God in that instance, and thereafter spent years investigating the lives of the people who had been killed." Shapiro. Fic for Youth. 3d edition

The eighth day. Harper & Row 1967 435p o.p.

"A chronicle of two early 20th-century Midwestern families and their involvement in a murder case raising serious questions about human nature." Oxford Companion to Am Lit. 6th edition

The ides of March. Harper 1948 246p o.p.

This novel offers "divergent views of Caesar's last months seen through letters and documents." Oxford Companion to Am Lit. 6th edition

Theophilus North. Harper & Row 1973 374p o.p.

"A Cass Canfield book"

"In the summer of 1926, a 30-year-old teacher named Theophilus North comes to Newport, R.I., to tutor the children of the fashionably rich and to read out loud. . . . In Newport he discovers nine separate cities differing in age and social class. In these stories of which this novel is composed, North marches through them all—careers and cities—healing the sick, repairing marriages, rescuing a damsel from injustice, restoring life and health to the old and frail, and freedom to the confined." Newsweek

Wilhelm, Kate

And the angels sing; stories. St. Martin's Press 1992 260p o.p.
LC 91-39003

Contents: The look alike; O homo; O femina; O tempora; The chosen; On the road to Honeyville; The great doors of silence; The day of the sharks; The loiterer; The scream; Strangeness, charm and spin; The dragon seed; Forever yours, Anna; And the angels sing

"Positioned on the border between fantasy and mainstream fiction, these 12 stories provide pleasure and provoke thought by undermining the reader's expectations at every turn." N Y Times Book Rev

The best defense. St. Martin's Press 1994 342p o.p.
LC 94-2039

In this legal thriller Barbara Holloway "defends Paula Kennerman, a battered wife accused of killing her daughter and burning down the safe house in which they had been sheltered. . . . The Holloways' crack team of private investigators assures that important clues are devel-

Wilhelm, Kate—*Continued*
oped in time to use as evidence as Barbara skillfully conducts the defense in a suspenseful trial. The ambitious plot-subplot net threads together abortion rights, antifeminist backlash, and the inequities of legal aid for rich and poor." Libr J

The dark door. St. Martin's Press 1988 248p o.p.

LC 88-14777

"A private investigator follows the trail of a serial arsonist only to find himself allied with his prey in an effort to destroy an unearthly device that spreads insanity in its wake." Libr J

"Wilhelm is in top form as the thriller plot races along while characters teeter over an abyss of insanity and loss." Publ Wkly

Death qualified; a mystery of chaos. St. Martin's Press 1991 438p o.p.

LC 90-27504

"Nell Kendricks is charged with murdering her estranged husband, Lucas, who disappeared years ago while working on a top-secret experiment attempting to use chaos theory to change the observer's perception of the universe. Now it appears that Lucas had spent the intervening years drugged and amnesiac, a handyman at the university where the studies had taken place. Attorney Barbara Holloway, who is 'death qualified' (i.e., legally permitted to act in capital cases), agrees to defend Nell, despite having left the profession, disillusioned by its practices." Publ Wkly

"It is difficult to describe the novel's many dimensions, ranging from tense courtroom scenes to the almost fantastic descriptions of the scientific study. Most astonishing is the author's ability to peel off one layer after another, revealing new ways of looking at the same facts." Libr J

The deepest water. St. Martin's Minotaur 2000 279p $23.95

ISBN 0-312-26143-8 LC 00-31724

"Abby Connors is mourning the death of her father, bestselling novelist Jud Vickers, at the age of 48. Jud was a womanizing former ne'er-do-well who had recently found success, only to be murdered at his remote lakefront cabin. The local police baffled, Abby soon finds herself doing her own sleuthing, much to the dismay of her husband, Brice, a financial planner who was always jealous of Jud's primary place in Abby's heart. As Abby investigates further, she discovers secrets in Jud's past as well as an unfinished novel." Publ Wkly

Wilhelm's "characters are well drawn, the setting is real, and the pace keeps the reader raptly involved to the last page." Libr J

Defense for the devil. St. Martin's Press 1999 389p $24.95

ISBN 0-312-19854-X LC 98-44576

"Mitch Arno is a spouse abuser, small-time thug, and general ne'er-do-well. When he trashes wife Maggie's cozy Oregon B&B after his latest 'job,' she kicks him out, and he heads for his brother's house. Meanwhile, Maggie turns to attorneys Barbara Holloway and her father, Frank, to get a restraining order against Mitch and file for damages. Then Mitch turns up dead, and brother Ray is arrested for murder. Maggie persuades Barbara to defend Ray, placing her and her father in the middle of a deadly web of deception and greed." Libr J

"The nuances of courtroom procedure are compellingly presented, . . . including a sophisticated look at the complex psychology of a jury." Publ Wkly

Desperate measures. St. Martin's Minotaur 2001 387p o.p.

ISBN 0-312-27663-X

Barbara Holloway's "latest client is a brilliant young man named Alex Feldman, who has been left hideously deformed by a birth defect. He is accused of killing his next-door neighbor, Gus Marchand, a tyrannical religious Zealot who saw Alex's deformity as the mark of the devil. There is little evidence against him, but Marchand has created such hostility and fear toward Alex in their small, rural community that it seems likely he will be convicted on the basis of his appearance alone. . . . Readers are given all the necessary facts and Alex is an excellent character. Wilhelm does a good job of conveying his anguish and isolation." Publ Wkly

The good children. St. Martin's Press 1998 246p $22.95

ISBN 0-312-17914-6 LC 97-37101

"The McNairs' move into a home of their own near Portland, Oregon, seems too good to be true. All the kids have rooms of their own and the promise from their father of no more transfers. But their idyll is soon shattered; father Will is killed in an industrial accident. Though left relatively financially secure, the family is not the same. Mother Lee can't cope and becomes increasingly reclusive. The four kids must manage the house, their mother, and themselves. Then, one day, they come home to find her dead on the patio. Fearful of being separated, the kids construct a complex scheme to keep their home intact." Libr J

"Brilliantly plotted, lyrically written, alluring and magical, mesmerizing, terrifying, and heartbreakingly funny, Wilhelm's story is a wrenching masterpiece about love, loyalty, and lies that will lodge itself in readers' psyches long after they've finished the last, stunning chapter." Booklist

The Hamlet trap. St. Martin's Press 1987 234p o.p.

LC 87-16368

"Ashland, Oregon, home of the Oregon Shakespearean Festival, provides the setting for this [mystery]. . . . The action centers on the fictional Harley Theatre, a repertory group coexisting in Ashland with the more famous Shakespeare company. When a new director arrives on the scene and selects a controversial winner in a new-playwright's contest, trouble brews. Soon corpses dot the tranquil southern Oregon community, and the niece of the theater's owner is about to be indicted for murder. To the rescue comes an engaging pair of sleuths—ex-cop Charlie Meiklejohn and his psychologist wife Constance Leidl." Booklist

This "is a psychological mystery, and a classic murder puzzle as well. Constance and Charlie are a loving couple and skillful detectives; good company for one another and for the reader." Wilson Libr Bull

Wilhelm, Kate—*Continued*

Juniper time; a novel. Harper & Row 1979 280p o.p.
LC 78-2247

"The world of the near future is on the brink of war because of worldwide drought and depression, and a message that may be from aliens offers the only hope. . . . Cluny has devoted his life to reviving the space station project which had been killed by the depression. Jean blamed the station for her father's death and made linguistics her career. But destiny reunites these former childhood friends when Cluny asks Jean's help in authenticating an apparently alien scroll found in orbit near the station, and Jean decides to take responsibility for shaping history with her conclusions. This is a SF novel of rare depth." Publ Wkly

Justice for some. St. Martin's Press 1993 260p o.p.
LC 93-15046

"Heading for a family gathering at her father's home/water garden business in rural California, widowed Sarah Drexler anticipates a respite from her work as an Oregon state judge. Instead she finds her deductive skills challenged and the lives of those dearest to her threatened. Joining the tense family dinner is Fran Donatio, a woman whose presence Sarah's father Ralph does not explain. The next morning, after Ralph's body is pulled from a lily pond, police Lt. Arthur Fernandez arrives with questions on another matter. . . . This tale . . . offers a bonus in Fernandez who, running his own, equally intelligent investigation in the background, provides a welcome change from the expected solitary-sleuth plot structure." Publ Wkly

Malice prepense. St. Martin's Press 1996 412p o.p.
LC 96-1190

"Attorney Barbara Holloway is hired to defend a 28-year-old brain-injured man who is accused of murdering an Oregon Congressman. With only a pile of rocks found at the murder scene tying the young man to the crime, Holloway skillfully clears him, but her client's father then becomes the prime suspect. Her defense of the now-accused father is much more complex." Libr J

"As Wilhelm spins her riveting tale, she not only makes the legal system comprehensible and compelling but also makes her readers care about her characters, particularly the efficient yet vulnerable Barbara." Publ Wkly

No defense. St. Martin's Press 2000 376p $24.95
ISBN 0-312-20953-3 LC 99-56355

In this legal thriller Oregon attorney Barbara Holloway defends "Lara Jessup, a young widow accused of murdering her much older husband, Vinny, a man with a large insurance policy, a terminal case of cancer, and some very powerful enemies. Jessup's alibi begins to evaporate when her adolescent son contradicts her story, and Holloway is left with no way to defend her except to expose those powerful enemies. . . . Although there is nothing particularly original or surprising here, this well-written novel skillfully captures small-town life in a rural western community with all its benefits and drawbacks." Booklist

Sweet, sweet poison. St. Martin's Press 1990 262p o.p.
LC 89-77847

The first victim in this "mystery is a watchdog named Sadie, owned by Al and Sylvie Zukal, two likable, spectacularly vulgar *kvetches* from the Bronx who invested some recent lottery winnings in a rural estate in Spender's Ferry, N.Y. After the Zukals' young friend David dies, the well-oiled, older detective team of Charlie Meiklejohn and Constance Leidl . . . begins to question the conclusions of the local sheriff, who labels these and additional inventive killings—by poison, drugs, bees and gas—accident or suicide." Publ Wkly

Wilhelm "offers studied prose, an almost too heavy dose of local color, and tightly knit plotting in a novel that isn't like most mysteries. Here, hidden fantasies emerge from the subtext, and narrative detours that would lose most crime writers are handled adroitly." Booklist

Welcome, chaos. Houghton Mifflin 1983 285p o.p.
LC 83-6181

An expanded version of the author's novella The winter beach, published 1981 in the collection Listen, listen

"A serum that immunizes against all disease and stops aging is kept secret by a group of scientists because many people cannot survive the initial administration. Their hopes of increasing its success rate and overcoming the sterility that is its main side effect are dashed when the world comes to the brink of nuclear war because the Soviet government apparently has the secret, and they must decide whether to make public what they know. A gripping account of individuals wrestling with a novel moral dilemma; excellent characterization." Anatomy of Wonder 4

Where late the sweet birds sang. Harper & Row 1976 251p o.p.

"Pollution and pestilence are the consequences of a war that destroys most of the earth and its inhabitants. The elder Sumners have created a scientific research center whose goal is to perfect a technique for cloning since, among the other results of the world disaster, men and women have become sterile. The younger Sumners are victimized by these clones, who perpetuate the form of humans but have no humaneness or humanity." Shapiro. Fic for Youth. 3d edition

Willard, Tom

Buffalo soldiers. Forge 1996 331p $22.95
ISBN 0-312-86041-2 LC 95-53295

"A Tom Doherty Associates book"

"Held captive by the Kiowa and then bartered to a white buffalo hunter, Augustus Sharps is freed in 1869 by troopers of the all-black Tenth U.S. Cavalry, in which he enlists. First in a series chronicling African American contributions to U.S. military history, Willard's . . . well-researched novel traces Augustus's soldiering from Fort Wallace, Kansas, until his retirement to an Arizona ranch." Libr J

Williams, Darren, 1967-

Angel Rock. Knopf 2002 303p $23
ISBN 0-375-41451-7 LC 2002-69369

Williams, Darren, 1967-—*Continued*

"A week after Tom Ferry and his four-year-old half-brother, Flynn Gunn, get lost in Angel Rock, a town in the harsh Australian outback, only Tom returns, with no recollection of what happened. Around the same time, Gibson, a Sydney detective with a drinking problem, is called to investigate the suicide of Darcy Steele, a young girl from Angel Rock who reminds him of his sister, also a suicide." Libr J

"Williams deliberately keeps his prose and action low-key in the early going, relying on details of both scene and character to add tension as he brings his outstanding ensemble to life in a unique and compelling setting. The shocking ending packs a major wallop, establishing Williams as a writer with a formidable array of skills, including the ability to twist both his plots and the genre in some startling, unexpected directions." Publ Wkly

Williams, Joy, 1944-

Honored guest; stories; Joy Williams. 1st ed. Knopf 2004 213p

ISBN 0-679-44647-8 LC 2004-44199

Contents: Honored guest; Congress; Marabou; The visiting privilege; Substance; Anodyne; The other week; Claro; Charity; ACK; Hammer; Fortune

"The troubled characters in Williams' latest short stories, set in locales as diverse as Maine and Mexico, don't have the wherewithal to do anything but brood, with the exception of a forensic anthropologist who solves the mysteries of scattered bones, hair, and teeth, a feat not unlike the one Williams pulls off in these canny and dissecting tales of fractured lives." Booklist

Williams, Linda Verlee *See* Grant, Linda

Williams, Tennessee, 1911-1983

Collected stories; with an introduction by Gore Vidal. New Directions 1985 xxv, 574p o.p.

LC 85-10642

Contents: The angel in the alcove; Chronicle of a demise; Completed; Desire and the black masseur; Field of blue children; "Grand"; Happy August the Tenth; The important thing; The inventory at Fontana Bella; The killer chicken and the closet queen; The kingdom of earth; The knightly quest; The malediction; Mama's old stucco house; Man bring this up road; The mattress by the tomato patch; Miss Coynte of Greene; The mysteries of the Joy Rio; The night of the Iguana; One arm; Oriflamme; The poet; Portrait of a girl in glass; Resemblance between a violin case and a coffin; Sabbatha and solitude; Three players of a summer game; Two on a party; The vengence of Nitocris; The vine; The yellow bird; A lady's beaded bag; Something by Tolstoi; Big Black; A Mississippi idyll; The accent of a coming foot; Twenty-seven wagons full of cotton; Sand; Ten minute stop; Gift of an apple; In memory of an aristocrat; The dark room; The interval; Tent worms; Something about him; Rubio y Morena; The coming of something to Widow Holly; Hard candy; A recluse and his guest; Das Wasser ist Kalt; Mother Yaws

The Roman spring of Mrs. Stone. New Directions 1950 148p o.p.

A wealthy widowed American ex-actress is the heroine of this short novel. At fifty Mrs. Stone is losing her beauty, her stage career is ended, and she finds herself just 'drifting' through an aimless existence in Rome. When an unscrupulous countess introduces a handsome young gigolo to Mrs. Stone it is the beginning of the end

"There are many superb moments, scenes which move with a dramatist's ease. There is a hard candor about Mrs. Stone, about all people who fail at real living and attempt a life of fantasy and fail at that, leaving them vulnerable to annihilation. . . . This different version of Mr. Williams' repeated theme has resulted in a sharp, witty and moving novel." Chicago Sunday Trib

Williams, Thomas Lanier *See* Williams, Tennessee, 1911-1983

Williamson, Penelope

Heart of the west; a novel. Simon & Schuster 1995 591p o.p.

LC 94-33487

"A tale of the settling of the West told from a woman's perspective—three women actually. Clementine Kennicutt is a proper Bostonian lady until she literally bumps into Gus McQueen and elopes with him to Montana. Hannah Yorke is the town prostitute who becomes a prosperous landowner, though she is forever marked by her past. And Erlan Woo is a young Chinese picture bride whose heart remains in China. These three seemingly mismatched characters become fast friends." SLJ

"Williamson gives these characters convincing voices . . . and demonstrates how women could bond and find new identities on the frontier. Williamson tells her story with brio, if a little too much florid prose." Publ Wkly

The outsider. Simon & Schuster 1996 464p o.p.

LC 96-7291

"Rachel Yoder is a young widow with a son trying to survive on a Montana sheep farm in the 1880s. She still grieves for her husband, murdered by the local cattleman's association, but her faith carries her through. As a member of a religious community called the Plain people, she believes that one must not question God's workings. Her beliefs are about to be challenged when a wounded gunfighter named Johnny Cain stumbles onto the Yoder cabin in the midst of a severe snowstorm." Booklist

"This is rich, wonderful reading sure to please any fan of good old-fashioned storytelling." Libr J

Willis, Connie

Doomsday book. Bantam Bks. 1992 445p o.p.

ISBN 0-553-08131-4 LC 91-42819

"Kivrin, a student of medieval history, is sent back in time to 14th-century Oxfordshire to do some hands-on study. Meanwhile, in the near-future present day of the book, an old disease comes back to smite Oxford. In the resultant chaos, no one realises that because of a slip-up, Kivrin has arrived bang in the middle of the Black Death." New Statesman Soc

"As much as I enjoyed [Willis's] story, . . . the time travel device is given no justification, and none of the paradoxical implications of time travel are explored. Doomsday Book is a historical novel with tenuous SF connections. . . . Warts and all, though, this is a cracking good story, and that is the bottom line criterion for any novel, SF or other." New Scientist

Willis, Connie—*Continued*

Passage. Bantam Bks. 2001 594p o.p.
ISBN 0-553-11124-8 LC 00-68052

This novel "concerns the scientific study of near death experiences (NDEs). . . . Psychologist Joanna Lander, an NDE specialist, joins neurologist Richard Wright in a research project employing a psychoactive drug to simulate NDEs. When most of the volunteer subjects drop out, Joanna agrees to go under and finds herself aboard the *Titanic*. She returns time after time to the ill-fated ship and becomes increasingly obsessed with the experience and why it seems so real and familiar. . . . With memorable characters, believable science, and convincing hospital ambiance, an initially slow-moving yarn turns into a page-turner whose explosive climax will rock readers back on their heels." Booklist

To say nothing of the dog; or, How we found the bishop's bird stump at last. Bantam Bks. 1998 434p o.p.
LC 97-16002

"Rich dowager Lady Schrapnell has invaded Oxford University's time travel research project in 2057, promising to endow it if they help her rebuild Coventry Cathedral, destroyed by a Nazi air raid in 1940. . . . Time traveler Ned Henry is suffering from advanced time lag and has been sent, he thinks, for rest and relaxation to 1888, where he connects with time traveler Verity Kindle and discovers that he is actually there to correct an incongruity created when Verity inadvertently brought something forward from the past." Booklist

"No one mixes scientific mumbo jumbo and comedy of manners with more panache than Willis." N Y Times Book Rev

Willis, Mary
See also Walker, Mary Willis

Wilson, A. N. (Andrew Norman), 1950-

The vicar of sorrows. Norton 1994 c1993 391p o.p.
LC 93-11538

First published 1993 in the United Kingdom

"The longtime vicar of Ditcham, Francis Kreer, has a nervous breakdown after the death of his mother, who, without explanation, has left half of his rightful inheritance to her former lover, whom Francis has never met. In a rapid descent into despair, Francis falls in love with a beautiful young vagabond, devastating his dimwitted wife and adolescent daughter. What's more, a sexually frustrated member of his congregation accuses Francis of poking her lasciviously with a broom, among other prurient offenses." N Y Times Book Rev

"Mr. Wilson is a brilliantly mordant observer of human types, of which this book offers a merciless catalogue." Natl Rev

Wilson, Andrew Norman *See* Wilson, A. N. (Andrew Norman), 1950-

Wilson, F. Paul (Francis Paul)

Deep as the marrow. Forge 1997 352p $24.95
ISBN 0-312-86264-4 LC 96-30502

"A Tom Doherty Associates book"

"When President Thomas Winston announces a plan to attack the drug problem by making drugs legal, he's met first with public outrage, then with an assassination plot involving his boyhood friend and personal physician, Dr. John VanDuyne. In a plan masterminded by a Colombian drug lord, six-year-old Katie VanDuyne is kidnapped to persuade her father to give the president an antibiotic that will destroy his bone marrow. The kidnapping goes awry early on, because of the doctor's ethics and a kidnapper's attachment to Katie, but Wilson spins out the action to the last pages, making some persuasive arguments for drug legalization along the way." Libr J

The haunted air; a Repairman Jack novel. Forge 2002 415p $24.95
ISBN 0-312-87868-0 LC 2002-72059

"A Tom Doherty Associates book"

This Repairman Jack novel "teams the righteous urban mercenary with his strangest bedfellows yet: a pair of sham spirit mediums who openly operate their occult con game out of a brownstone in Queens. . . . Jack takes the case of brothers Lyle and Charlie Kenton, who've been threatened by other Big Apple pseudo-psychics for horning in on the lucrative seance scene. No sooner has Jack begun . . . than real ghosts begin popping up along with a secret cult of ritual child murderers. . . . Above all, the novel enhances the enigma of Jack, a hero who commands respect despite his curmudgeonly disdain for contemporary culture, his morally ambiguous work-for-hire ethic and his unsettling appeal to the vigilante in every reader." Publ Wkly

Implant. Forge 1995 348p $23.95
ISBN 0-312-89034-6 LC 95-21886

"A Tom Doherty Associates book"

"Dr. Gina Panzella has returned to Washington, D.C., to practice, hoping to join the legislative process and influence the future of medicine. Her boss, Dr. Duncan Lathram, has similar aspirations, but his aims are less benign. . . . When Gina notices that Lathram's patients keep having violent accidents, she thinks it is only coincidental, but it isn't. Gradually, her reluctant investigation into the accidents jeopardizes her relationship with her lover, an FBI agent, as well as her life. This suspenseful medical thriller has complex, likable characters and an intriguing background, and it raises important questions by pitting self-serving bureaucrats against unethical physicians." Libr J

Legacies. Forge 1998 381p $24.95
ISBN 0-312-86414-0 LC 98-14322

"A Tom Doherty Associates book"

"Jack, a fix-it man who specializes in solving people's problems (and who, as far as the authorities are concerned, doesn't even exist), does a favor for a friend—he recovers some toys stolen from a hospital—and winds up helping a woman solve a deadly mystery from her past. Repairman Jack is a strong man whose moments of compassion don't seem forced, an enigma without being annoyingly mysterious." Booklist

Wilson, Francis Paul *See* Wilson, F. Paul (Francis Paul)

Wilson, John Anthony Burgess *See* Burgess, Anthony, 1917-1993

Wilson, Jonathan, 1950-

A Palestine affair. Pantheon Bks. 2003 257p $23

ISBN 0-375-42209-9 LC 2002-35499

"It is 1924 and the Zionist movement is beginning to gain momentum. Tensions run high between Jews and Palestinians and between Zionist and Orthodox Jews, and none of the groups quite trust the British, who have a mandate to rule the area. To this intrigue Wilson . . . has added . . . murder and gun-running—as well as the introspective themes of a middle-aged artist whose career and marriage are on the down slope, his wife's own search for an identity, and her lover's coming to terms with his." Booklist

"Wilson has devised a story that tautens the sinuous strands of this period into a lethal knot. The strengths of his novel are the tension and pace of its plot, and its ability to suggest the falling barometer of a storm that will break fully only after another quarter century." N Y Times Book Rev

Wilson, Robert, 1957-

The blind man of Seville. Harcourt 2003 434p $26

ISBN 0-15-100835-3 LC 2002-68495

"Javier Falcón, chief homicide detective in Seville, has a ghastly murder to solve, one that inexplicably strikes into the depths of his being. When two similar murders follow, Falcón finds himself facing a midlife crisis as he penetrates his own past to find connections between the victims and his recently deceased father, a famous painter who lived a life of hidden depravity." Libr J

"Wilson . . . is able to hold reader interest at an almost unbearable pitch of excitement throughout this shocker with exquisite plot pacing and intriguing character revelations." Booklist

Wilson, Robert Charles, 1953-

Blind Lake. TOR Bks. 2003 399p $24.95

ISBN 0-7653-0262-4 LC 2003-47345

"A Tom Doherty Associates book"

"When the research facility at Blind Lake, MN, is placed under military blockade and quarantine, the scientists and workers . . . can only connect their enforced isolation with their research on a newly discovered form of alien life on a distant planet. Journalist Chris Carmody, trapped in Blind Lake, finds his life transformed by his chance encounter with researcher Marguerite Hauser and her troubled daughter, Tessa, a young girl whose unusual mind may hold the key to unraveling the alien mystery." Libr J

"No one knows better than Wilson how to manipulate the language of science to suggest the essential unknowability of the universe. . . . The drama at Blind Like gradually expands to encompass humans and aliens in entirely unforeseen ways." N Y Times Book Rev

Wilson, Sloan, 1920-

The man in the gray flannel suit. Simon & Schuster 1955 304p o.p.

The man of the title is the ordinary, upper middle class New York business employee, who at five o'clock heads for his home, wife, and children in Connecticut. Thomas Rath is his name in this book. Tom joins a large corporation, does an honest job, and is evidently headed for bigger money. As an undercurrent to his daily life Tom remembers his war service, the girl he met in Rome, and his illegitimate son

"Thoughtful, searching novel. . . . Sloan Wilson manages to hold the reader's interest and at the same time to solve Rath's problems without distorting his character." N Y Her Trib Books

Wiltse, David

Blown away. Putnam 1996 343p o.p.

LC 96-2387

In this novel, "Karl Atlee, alias Jason Cole, unleashes a series of bombings. . . . After blowing up Cornell University's suicide bridge and killing a student, the madman with a mission bombs the Roosevelt Island tram, the Triborough Bridge, and the Holland Tunnel, taking many more innocent lives. Special Agents John Becker and Pegeen Haddad have been assigned to stop Atlee." Libr J

"Wiltse illuminates a broad spectrum of heroism and villainy with a colorful, often humorous cast of characters that makes agent Becker seem drab by comparison. These engaging folk will hold readers in thrall through a fastpaced, cleverly plotted tale that features plenty of action, on the street and off, and that will leave readers just as the title says." Publ Wkly

Bone deep. Putnam 1995 340p o.p.

LC 95-11089

This suspense novel features FBI agent John Becker. Connecticut's "rain-swollen Saugatuck River floats a bone into a local backyard, prompting the attention of the vacationing Becker and his old friend 'Tee' Terhune, the town's police chief. . . . After marks on the bone reveal that the body it belongs to was cut in pieces before burial, an upriver search turns up a charnel house of companion bones in the loose soil of a Christmas tree farm. A prime suspect arises when Tee gets anonymous tips that one of his officers, the loathsome McNeil, who likes to sleep with high-school girls, is involved in the killings." Publ Wkly

Heartland; a novel. St. Martin's Press 2001 291p o.p.

ISBN 0-312-26957-9 LC 00-45966

"Agent Billy Tree, who investigated the homes of crackpots as part of pre-event security for the Secret Service, has returned to his hometown of Falls City, Nebraska, to recover from physical injuries and his deep shame after his partner was killed on a house search. Billy wants nothing more than to hole up at his sister's home, watching the road and replaying the scene where he failed his partner. But the plight of his old girlfriend and her son, victims of harrowing psychological abuse from the ex-husband, forces Billy to rejoin life. . . . The book's climactic scene, delivers a wrenching psychological portrait along with blood pressure-raising suspense." Booklist

Windling, Terri, 1957-

(ed) Snow white, blood red. See Snow white, blood red

(ed) The Year's best fantasy and horror. See The Year's best fantasy and horror

Winegardner, Mark, 1961-

The Godfather returns. Random House 2004 430p $26.95

ISBN 1-400-06101-6 LC 2004-51380

This is a sequel to Mario Puzo's 1969 novel. "It is 1955. Michael Corleone has won a bloody victory in the war among New York's crime families. Now he wants to consolidate his power, save his marriage, and take his family into legitimate businesses. To do so, he must confront his most dangerous adversary yet, Nick Geraci, a former boxer who worked his way through law school as a Corleone street enforcer, and who is every bit as deadly and cunning as Michael. Their personal cold war will run from 1955 to 1962, exerting immense influence on the lives of America's most powerful criminals and their loved ones." Publisher's note

"This is a phenomenally entertaining, psychologically rich saga that spans the entire Godfather years imagined in novel and film by Mario Puzo (the latter via his screenplays), filling in the blanks, fleshing out the characters, focusing primarily on the time (mid 1950s-early '60s) between when Puzo's landmark novel ended and the film Godfather II begins." Publ Wkly

Winspear, Jacqueline, 1955-

Birds of a feather; a novel. Soho Press 2004 311p $25

ISBN 1-569-47368-4 LC 2003-25732

"A Maisie Dobbs novel"

P.I. Maisie Dobbs "has been hired to find the missing daughter of a wealthy London magnate. As Maisie and her Cockney assistant, Billy Beale, try to track Charlotte Waite down, they discover that three of her old friends have been murdered-poisoned and then bayoneted." Libr J

"The period touches, from clothing to manners, are not only elegantly presented but unostentatious." Booklist

Maisie Dobbs; a novel. Soho Press 2003 294p $24

ISBN 1-56947-330-7 LC 2002-44656

In this novel "set in WWI-era England, humble housemaid Maisie Dobbs climbs . . . up Britain's social ladder, becoming in turn a university student, a wartime nurse and ultimately a private investigator. . . . Her first sleuthing case, which begins as a simple marital infidelity investigation, leads to a trail of war-wounded soldiers lured to a remote convalescent home in Kent from which no one seems to emerge alive." Publ Wkly

"For a clever and resourceful young woman who has just set herself up in business as a private investigator, Maisie seems a bit too sober and much too sad. Romantic readers sensing a story-within-a-story won't be disappointed. But first, they must prepare to be astonished at the sensitivity and wisdom with which Maisie resolves her first professional assignment." N Y Times Book Rev

Pardonable lies; a Maisie Dobbs novel. Henry Holt 2005 342p $23

ISBN 0-8050-7897-5 LC 2005-46388

In this installment, "British psychologist and investigator Maisie Dobbs, who attended university after serving as a nurse in France during World War I, tackles a trio of cases that ranges from the unsettling to the surreal. There's 13-year-old Avril Jarvis, accused of first-degree murder. And Sir Cecil Lawton, QC, who is attempting to honor his late wife's request to determine if their fighter-pilot son is living or dead. And Maisie's rich, trendy friend, Priscilla, desperate for details about her brother, who was killed in the Great War. Maisie pursues clues with the help of her Cockney assistant, Billy, and wisdom imparted by her elegant, if enigmatic, mentor, Maurice. . . . A trip to France reveals a startling connection between the cases but proves traumatic for the former nurse still haunted by her experiences tending to wounded soldiers during the war." Booklist

Winston, Lolly

Good grief. Warner Books 2004 344p $18

ISBN 0-446-53304-1 LC 2003-15207

After thirty-six-year-old Sophie Stanton's husband Ethan dies of cancer, she leaves her job with a technology company in Silicon Valley and winds up in Oregon where she reinvents herself as a baker and finds a new love interest

"Throughout this heartbreaking, gorgeous look at loss, Winston imbues her heroine and her narrative with the kind of grace, bitter humor and rapier-sharp realness that will dig deep into a reader's heart and refuse to let go. Sophie is wounded terribly, but she's also funny, fresh and utterly believable." Publ Wkly

Winterson, Jeanette, 1959-

Sexing the cherry. Atlantic Monthly Press 1990 167p o.p.

ISBN 0-87113-350-4 LC 90-30682

This is a novel "about a prodigious giantess and her explorer son in 17th-century London. Jordan fetches the first pineapple to the court of Charles II, while his mother, The Dog Woman, wreaks vengeance upon Puritans in a brothel. The plague; the flying princesses who defy laws of the courts and gravity; Jordan's travels to the floating city and the botanical wonders of the New World–the tale . . . [involves both] history and fantasy. The two characters eventually merge into the grievously polluted life of modern London." Libr J

"Winterson, whose work is full of profound truths disguised as simple statements, is at her epigrammatic best on the subject of romantic love." Quill Quire

Winthrop, Elizabeth

Island justice. Morrow 1998 356p $25

ISBN 0-688-15920-6 LC 97-36566

A novel about "secret and not-so-secret lives on a small New England island. There's Maggie Hammond, thirtysomething international furniture surveyor, drawn back to the island to sell the house she's inherited from her godmother; Anna Craven, a woman stifled by her overbearing, emotionally abusive husband; Erin Craven, grappling with adolescence; and Sam Matera, local naturalist and science teacher whose love complicates Maggie's decision." Libr J

"Along with the satisfying plot . . . readers are also provided with a good deal of information about the flora and fauna of coastal New England and the delicate balance of its human society. 'Island Justice' is the kind of book that used to be called a 'good read'—and sometimes there's nothing better." N Y Times Book Rev

Winton, Tim

Cloudstreet. Graywolf Press 1992 426p o.p.
ISBN 1-555-97158-X LC 91-42208

"From 1944 to 1964, the Pickles and Lamb families share a large house in a suburb of Perth, on the wrong side of the tracks. The Pickles own the house and are slothful, he a gambler with long streaks of bad luck, she often drunk and adulterous. The tenant Lambs are hard-working. After the latter open a successful grocery on the first floor of the house, the families' lives become intertwined, and home and hearth become an anchor. World War II, Australian politics, the Cuban missile crisis, and Kennedy's assassination take a backseat to their trials and final joy." Libr J

"The writing is sometimes overripe, but that only adds to its charm, and Winton balances the ballast with his wonderful silences, those mesmeric moments listening to the house breathe or the terrible pauses before bad luck strikes. In Cloudstreet, the strange becomes quotidian, and the daily grind coexists with giddy, unfettered insight. Tim Winton has created a narrative both epic and mundane, ethereal and earthy, with characters who are lovable, funny, and full of holes." Voice Lit Suppl

Dirt music; a novel. Scribner 2002 411p $26
ISBN 0-7432-2802-2 LC 2002-17583

First published 2001 in Australia

"At 40, Georgie Jutland, former nurse, inveterate risk-taker, incipient alcoholic and lifelong rebel against her prominent family, has moved in with widowed lobster fisherman Jim Buckridge, "the uncrowned prince" of the western seaside community of White Point. Although Georgie devotes herself to Jim's two young sons, their relationship is uneasy and somehow empty. When she's drawn to shamateur (fish poacher) Luther Fox, who breaks the law to keep his mind from tragic memories, the lives of all three begin to unravel." Publ Wkly

"As well as offering nuanced portraits of three very different characters, [this] is a cracking page-turner which deftly splices together separate narrative threads without ever losing its headlong momentum. . . . Mr Winton comes from Western Australia, a vast state of exceptional natural beauty. . . . He brilliantly conjures its hostile desert spaces and its magnificent coastline. His characters, like the landscape they inhabit, are by turns callous and poetic, vulgar and seductive." Economist

Wishingrad, Jay

(ed) Legal fictions. See Legal fictions

Witt, Martha

Broken as things are; a novel; Martha Witt. 1st ed. Henry Holt 2004 293p $23
ISBN 0-8050-7595-X LC 2003-57003

Fourteen-year-old "Morgan-Lee and her handsome, 'unwell' 15-year-old brother, Ginx, are as emotionally close as twins. They have a secret language—a nonsensical patois that Ginx created—and share a running story about a brother and sister who are given permission to love each other forever and ever. Their mother is an overdelicate flower who's taken to her bed rather than face her son's problems; their father is kind but incapable of taking control; and their younger sister, Dana, has all but abandoned the family, moving into her aunt and uncle's house next door. Everything is proceeding as well as can be expected . . . until Morgan-Lee falls in love with her childhood friend, Billy. Neither sibling is prepared for the inevitable as Morgan-Lee's adolescence strains the family bonds and pitches the household into full-blown crisis." Publ Wkly

"Witt's image-laden prose navigates the obvious territory between sanity and craziness but also beautifully evokes that time in childhood when boundaries between fantasy and reality are not yet clear." Libr J

Wodehouse, P. G. (Pelham Grenville), 1881-1975

The code of the Woosters. Doubleday, Doran 1938 298p o.p.

"It was only the fact that Jeeves belonged to an exclusive club of gentlemen's personal gentlemen, where all the secrets in the lives of employers were filed for reference, that saved Bertie Wooster when the disappearance of an eighteenth-century silver cows-creamer threatened to land him in jail. Two rival collectors who coveted the piece of silver, and two pairs of bickering lovers, made Bertie's life a burden until Jeeves unearthed evidence that was a weapon." Booklist

How right you are, Jeeves. Simon & Schuster 1960 183p o.p.

"Foolishly accepting his Aunt Dahlia's invitation to a house party at her country place while the indispensable Jeeves is off on vacation, Bertie Wooster gets himself embroiled as usual. His entanglements, involving a former headmaster, an old school chum, an American heiress, and a masquerading psychiatrist, among others, have become positively labyrinthine before Jeeves rushes to the rescue." Booklist

The inimitable Jeeves. Autograph ed. British Bk. Centre 1956 192p o.p.

First published 1923 in the United Kingdom

The resourceful valet again takes command of a typical Wodehouse situation

Jeeves and the tie that binds. Simon & Schuster 1971 189p o.p.

"Bertie Wooster's reputation as a kleptomaniac, developed in previous adventures, appears confirmed as he seeks to aid an old pal who is standing for Parliament in Market Snodsbury. Aunt Dahlia, the good aunt, is there, and so is Bertie's former fiancée, Madeline Bassett, who thinks that 'the stars are God's daisy chain and that every time a fairy blows it's wee nose a baby is born.' A loutish lord and a renegade valet play the heavies." Newsweek

Tales from the Drones Club. International Polygonics 1991 352p o.p.
LC 91-8386

First published 1982 in the United Kingdom

Contents: Fate; Tried in the furnace; Trouble down at Tudsleigh; The amazing hat mystery; Goodbye to all cats; The luck of the Stiffhams; Noblesse oblige; Uncle Fred flits by; The masked troubadour; All's well with Bingo; Bingo and the Peke crisis; The editor regrets; Sonny boy; The shadow passes; Bramley is so bracing; The fat of the land; The word in season; Leave it to Algy; Oofy, Freddie and the beef trust; Bingo bans the bomb; Stylish stouts

Wodehouse, P. G. (Pelham Grenville), 1881-1975—*Continued*

A Wodehouse bestiary; edited and with a preface by D.R. Bensen; foreword by Howard Phipps, Jr. Ticknor & Fields 1985 329p o.p.

LC 85-7999

Contents: Unpleasantness at Bludleigh Court; Sir Roderick comes to lunch; Something squishy; Pig-Hoo-o-o-o-ey; Comrade Bingo; Monkey business; Jeeves and the impending doom; Open house; Ukridge's dog college; The story of Webster; The go-getter; Jeeves and the old school chum; Uncle Fred flits by; The mixer

"An anthology of tales featuring animals of all sorts wreaking havoc in the lives of Bertie Wooster, the indomitable Jeeves, Mr. Muliner's various relations, and other familiar characters from the madcap Wodehousian world. The numerous mishaps, involving snakes, pigs, gorillas, swans, dogs, and cats, prove as amusing as ever." Booklist

The world of Jeeves. Harper & Row 1988 c1967 654p o.p.

LC 88-45072

First published 1967 in the United Kingdom

Contents: Jeeves takes charge; Jeeves in the springtime; Scoring off Jeeves; Sir Roderick comes to lunch; Aunt Agatha takes the count; The artistic career of Corky; Jeeves and Chump Cyril; Jeeves and the unbidden guest; Jeeves and the hard-boiled egg; The aunt and the sluggard; Comrade Bingo; The great sermon handicap; The purity of the turf; The metropolitan touch; The delayed exit of Claude and Eustace; Bingo and the little woman; The rummy affair of Old Biffy; Without the option; Fixing it for Freddie; Clustering round young Bingo; Jeeves and the impending doom; The inferiority complex of Old Sippy; Jeeves and the Yule-tide spirit; Jeeves and the song of songs; Episode of the dog Mcintosh; The spot of art; Jeeves and the kid Clementina; The love that purifies; Jeeves and the old school chum; Indian summer of an uncle; The ordeal of young Tuppy; Bertie changes his mind; Jeeves makes an omelette; Jeeves and the greasy bird

Wodehouse, Pelham Grenville *See* Wodehouse, P. G. (Pelham Grenville), 1881-1975

Woiwode, Larry

Indian affairs; a novel. Atheneum Pubs. 1992 290p o.p.

LC 91-30540

Sequel to What I'm going to do, I think

This novel set in Michigan is, "in part, an anatomy of a marriage strained by the death of a baby and racial differences: Chris is a native American and Ellen a white Christian Scientist. They have returned to their home turf to stay in Ellen's grandparents' cabin so Chris can work on his dissertation about the Michigan poet Roethke in peace and quiet, but they get very little of either. . . . Both Chris and Ellen fall into depression. Chris is suffering an identity crisis over the conflict between his native American heritage and his academic pursuits, while Ellen decides to write about her grief over being childless." Booklist

"'Indian Affairs' is an intelligent, psychologically harrowing book." N Y Times Book Rev

What I'm going to do, I think; [by] L. Woiwode. Farrar, Straus & Giroux 1969 309p o.p.

"Ellen is beautiful and frightened; Chris is bright, nervous, alienated, and on the make. They meet at a campus party, have an on-again, off-again relationship that culminates after three years in Ellen's pregnancy and their decision to marry. Most of the story takes place during their honeymoon, during which they discover that their need to love each other is just not strong enough to forge the blissful union that they, in an uncompromising young way, have envisaged." Publ Wkly

Woiwode "has written a touching, sometimes deeply moving novel about youth growing up to the pain of loss, the puzzle of love, and the sense of despair lying near the surface of modern consciousness." N Y Times Book Rev

Followed by Indian affairs

Wolcott, James

The catsitters; a novel. HarperCollins Pubs. 2001 314p $25

ISBN 0-06-019414-6 LC 00-50635

"Johnny Downs is a New York bartender who longs to be a successful actor. Dumped by his girlfriend for reasons that he can't quite grasp, Johnny licks his wounds and takes solace from Darlene Ryder, a straight-talking graduate student whose interest in Johnny is romantic without being sexual: Darlene becomes a kind of relationship coach, offering him counsel in matters of the heart." New Yorker

"This novel has so many hilarious twists and turns that it keeps even the most jaded romance reader turning the pages. Wolcott expertly blends his careening plot with wit, sarcasm, and insight." Libr J

Wolfe, Gene, 1931-

Caldé of the long sun. TOR Bks. 1994 381p (Book of the long sun, bk3) o.p.

LC 94-12915

"A Tom Doherty Associates book"

Sequel to Nightside the long sun (1993) and Lake of the long sun (1994)

The long sun volumes are "set on a vast spaceship known as the Whorl. The inhabitants, having forgotten their origins, think that the Whorl is the universe. Their lives are governed by a religion that deifies the creators of the spaceship, who have immortalized themselves as programs within the Whorl's main computer. In the first two volumes of the series, a young priest of this religion, Patera Silk, learns the truth about the Whorl, but he also has a vision of a god known as the Outsider who seems to transcend the Whorl itself. In the third volume, Silk and his allies confront the corrupt government of the city of Viron; drawn into the battle are some of the gods themselves." N Y Times Book Rev

"The author continues to prove himself one of the genre's most literate writers and luminescent thinkers." Libr J

Followed by Exodus from the long sun

Castleview. Doherty Assocs. 1990 278p o.p.

LC 89-25712

"A TOR book"

"The inhabitants of the small town of Castleview, in a 'forgotten and countrified corner of upstate Illinois,' have

Wolfe, Gene, 1931-—*Continued*
grown accustomed to glimpsing a 'mirage' that resembles a medieval castle suspended in air. With the arrival in town of Will E. Shields, who has just bought a local automobile dealership, mysteries multiply like goose bumps. The town's hospital and funeral home fill with the victims of peculiar accidents, unsavory strangers knock on doors or peer through windows or suddenly appear on rainy highways riding horses with too many legs—and you just know Castleview is in for a major crisis." N Y Times Book Rev

Wolfe's "deceptively simple prose masks a wealth of complexity." Libr J

The Citadel of the Autarch. Timescape Bks. 1983 317p (Book of the new Sun, v4) o.p.
LC 82-5964

In this concluding volume of the tetralogy "Severian, the exiled torturer . . . attains the destiny hinted at since the first book and becomes the Autarch, 'who in one body is a thousand,' ruler of the Commonwealth and potential saviour of a dying Earth waiting for its reddened sun to go out." Publ Wkly

"Wolfe plays with the language like a master wordsmith, yet never loses control of the multi-layered story he's weaving. His style is paradoxically both baroque and simple—the lush beauty of the words never renders the tale impenetrable." Best Sellers

The claw of the conciliator. Timescape Bks. 1981 303p (Book of the new Sun, v2) o.p.
LC 80-20569

In this second volume of the series "Severian, a journeyman torturer, struggles to return the magical Claw of the Conciliator to its guardians. His quest is delayed when men under the leadership of the bandit Vodalus capture him to prevent the execution of a comrade. Severian and his companion Jonas win their freedom by agreeing to carry a message to an agent of Vodalus' at the Castle Absolute, seat of power for the ruling Autarch. Severian has no intention of carrying the promise through, in spite of his admiration for Vodalus. His intention to find his lover and continue his personal quest suffers a temporary setback at the hands of Castle guards." West Coast Rev Books

Followed by The sword of the Lictor

Exodus from the long sun. TOR Bks. 1996 384p (Book of the long sun, bk4) $23.95
ISBN 0-312-85585-0 LC 96-24518

"A Tom Doherty Associates book"

This final installment of the Book of the long sun series is set on "a starship whose inhabitants have forgotten they are on a journey. The starship, which they call the Whorl, is their entire universe, and its legendary creators are gods who speak to them from time to time through Sacred Windows. . . . The central character . . . is Patera Silk, a modest priest who learns the truth about the Whorl and must prepare his people for the necessary flight from the familiar to the unknown." N Y Times Book Rev

"Wolfe's command of language, his empathy with and understanding of his characters, and his narrative mastery are all brilliantly evident as his long, hypnotically compelling saga ends." Booklist

Innocents aboard; new fantasy stories. TOR Bks. 2004 304p $25.95
ISBN 0-7653-0790-1 LC 2003-71143

Contents: The tree is my hat; The old woman whose rolling pin is the sun; The friendship light; Slow children at play; Under hill; The Monday man; The waif; The legend of XI Cygnus; The sailor who sailed after the sun; How the bishop sailed to Inniskeen; Houston, 1943; A fish story; Wolfer; The eleventh city; The night chough; The wrapper; A traveler in desert lands; The walking sticks; Queen; Pocketsful of diamonds; Copperhead; The lost pilgrim

Wolfe "tells wondrously imaginative tales that weave reality with dream and fit so comfortably, or with intentional discomfort, within the psyche that they surely must have dwelt there all along with the other great fables and folk tales, lore and legends that are part of our collective cultural unconscious. The 22 short works of horror and fantasy . . . collected here are further proof that Wolfe ranks with the finest writers of this or any other day." Publ Wkly

The shadow of the torturer. Simon & Schuster 1980 303p (Book of the new Sun, v1) o.p.
LC 79-22371

"A TOR book"

A novel about "the experiences of Severian, a young man apprenticed to a legally sanctioned guild of torturers. . . . When Severian breaks the rules of the guild by allowing a 'client' to commit suicide, he is sent from his strange home, the only place he has known, on a journey through an inhospitable and dangerous world." Libr J

"The book combines elements of fantasy and sf, and the slow pacing is balanced by the excellent characterization and the richly detailed, thoroughly compelling future world." Booklist

Followed by The claw of the conciliator

The sword of the Lictor. Timescape Bks. 1981 302p (Book of the new Sun, v3) o.p.
LC 81-9427

In this third volume of the series "Severian, the torturer demoted to executioner, has reached Thrax, city of his exile, only to find that he can no longer do his work. He lets a prisoner escape rather than kill her (his original crime was to offer a prisoner the escape of death) and flees to the mountains. He meets the Alzabo, a terrifying creature in whom those eaten seem to live on, adopts a son and loses him, fights a revivified tyrant of the past and wins, helps the people of the floating islands, meets aliens and learns something of their true nature. The magical jewel called the Claw of the Conciliator is smashed, but Severian finds its essential heart, which is indeed a claw." Publ Wkly

Followed by The Citadel of the Autarch

The Urth of the new sun. Doherty Assocs. 1987 372p o.p.
LC 87-50478

"A TOR book"

This sequel to the four-volume Book of the new Sun continues "the story of Severian, a one-time torturers' apprentice who becomes Autarch and then leaves Urth to find the 'new sun' that alone can rejuvenate an exhausted humanity." N Y Times Book Rev

For all its obvious unity, the book also has a strongly

Wolfe, Gene, 1931-—*Continued*
picaresque quality, with many episodes and characters developed as lovingly and skillfully as Wolfe can manage—which is very well indeed." Booklist

Wolfe, Thomas, 1900-1938

The complete short stories of Thomas Wolfe; edited by Francis E. Skipp; foreword by James Dickey. Scribner 1987 xxix, 621p o.p.
LC 86-13782
"All 58 of Wolfe's short stories . . . have been edited by Skipp in a way that represents what Wolfe himself may have wanted his audience to read." Booklist

Look homeward, angel; a story of the buried life; with an introduction by Maxwell E. Perkins. Scribner 563p $45; pa $14
ISBN 0-684-15158-8; 0-684-80443-3 (pa)
First published 1929
This novel, autobiographical in character, "describes the childhood and youth of Eugene Gant in the town of Altamont, state of Catawba (said to be Asheville, North Carolina). As Gant grows up, he becomes aware of the relations among his family, meets the eccentric people of the town, goes to college, discovers literature and ideas, has his first love affairs, and at last sets out alone on a mystic and romantic 'pilgrimage.'" Reader's Ency. 4th edition
Followed by Of time and the river (1935)

O lost; a story of the buried life; text established by Arlyn and Matthew J. Bruccoli. Centenary ed. University of S.C. Press 2000 xli, 694p il $34.95
ISBN 1-57003-369-2 LC 00-9503
"The reinsertion of expurgated material puts the marrow back in the novel's bones, making for a richer reading experience." Libr J

Of time and the river; a legend of man's hunger in his youth. Scribner 912p $35
ISBN 0-684-14739-4
First published 1935
In this sequel to Look homeward, angel, "Eugene Gant, the hero, spends two years as a graduate student at Harvard, returns home for the dramatic death of his father, and teaches literature in New York City at the 'School for Utility Culture' (New York University). Eventually he tours France, returning home financially and emotionally exhausted." Reader's Ency. 4th edition

The web and the rock. Harper 1939 695p o.p.
This "is an autobiographical account of a successful young writer from North Carolina living in New York City in the early 20th century. The main character, George Webber, bears many similarities to Eugene Gant, the soul-searching protagonist of Wolfe's earlier novels." Merriam-Webster's Ency of Lit
"Wolfe's large scheme has the scope, massive detail and sense of space and time of an epic structure, but also the redundancy of its cyclic conception. The interest lies with the accurate dialogues, realistic descriptions and passages of poetic rhetoric sometimes of considerable power." Penguin Companion to Am Lit
Followed by You can't go home again

You can't go home again. Harper 1940 743p o.p.
This sequel to The web and the rock "deals with George's life after his return to the U.S.: his continued unsatisfactory romance; his success in writing novels reminiscent of Wolfe's own; his kindly relation and later dissatisfaction with an internationally famous but disillusioned novelist and with his editor, who fatalistically accepts the sickness of civilization; his unsuccessful attempt to return to the roots of his hometown, whose morality has become shoddy during the prosperous decade of the '20s; and his horrid discovery of the destruction of the Germany he had once loved." Oxford Companion to Am Lit. 6th edition

Wolfe, Tom

The bonfire of the vanities. Farrar, Straus & Giroux 1987 659p $25
ISBN 0-374-11534-6 LC 87-17691
"The novel relates the fall of Sherman McCoy, an investment banker making a million a year who seems blind to everything except appearances, sex and money. He lives in the middle of New York City without knowing New York City. He seems barely to know his decorative wife, his decorative daughter or his libidinous mistress, to say nothing of himself. He's all surface is Sherman, and when he blunders off the expressway into the welfare jungle of the South Bronx in his $48,000 Mercedes, into the biggest trouble of his heretofore charmed life, he is without reserves of experience, imagination or moral awareness with which to guide himself." N Y Times Book Rev
"Erupting from the first line with noise, color, tension and immediacy, this immensely entertaining novel accurately mirrors a system that has broken down: from the social code of basic good manners to the fair practices of the law." Publ Wkly

I am Charlotte Simmons. Farrar, Straus and Giroux 2004 676p $28.95
ISBN 0-374-28158-0 LC 2004-47131
"Dupont University–the Olympian halls of learning housing the cream of America's youth, the roseate Gothic spires and manicured lawns suffused with tradition . . . Or so it appears to beautiful, brilliant Charlotte Simmons, a sheltered freshman from North Carolina. But Charlotte soon learns, to her mounting dismay, that for the uppercrust coeds of Dupont, sex, Cool, and kegs trump academic achievement every time. As Charlotte encounters Dupont's privileged elite . . . she gains a new, revelatory sense of her own power, that of her difference and of her very innocence, but little does she realize that she will act as a catalyst in all of their lives." Publisher's note
"Tom Wolfe can make words dance and sing and perform circus tricks, he can make the reader sigh with pleasure before his arias of coloratura description, he can do just about anything in these pages with words, including exaggerate, distort and rant." Washington Post Book World

A man in full; a novel. Farrar, Straus & Giroux 1998 742p $28.95
ISBN 0-374-27032-5 LC 98-29842

Wolfe, Tom—*Continued*

"Set in Atlanta, the plot primarily follows 'Cap'm' Charlie Croaker, an aging ol' boy alpha male real estate tycoon who's a Georgia cracker through and through and a bull in the China closet of life. Croaker's empire begins crumbling when he defaults on a $500-million loan and is besieged by the bank's pit bull repo squad. Add in an OJ-esque college football star accused of raping a white debutante, the mayor and a preacher who try to defend him, and a philosophical convict, all of whom are on a crash course with each other." Libr J

"Among all the animal appetites that are slaked or comically thwarted during the novel there appears one new to Wolfe's fiction. For all their affluence, or their pained lack of same, his chief characters hunger for a code of conduct or a framework of beliefs that will make sense of their lives right now, a blink before the millennium. At its heart, A Man in Full is a cliff-hanging morality tale." Time

Wolff, Maritta M., 1918-2002

Sudden rain; [by] Maritta Wolff. Scribner 2005 434p $26

ISBN 0-7432-5482-1 LC 2004-52149

"Written in the prefeminist early 1970s, this novel features an Alice Adams like cast of well-heeled West Coast characters. The men go off to work, have casual affairs, and come home for cocktail hour expecting their pampered wives to tolerate their indiscretions and look after their homes and children without complaint. The leisurely plot deals with four interconnected couples whose relationships undergo dramatic changes as a Santa Ana wind blows through town. During a four-day weekend of drinking, smoking, and conversation, a long-estranged father and daughter come together, an aerospace engineer resolves to end his fractious marriage and marry his longtime mistress, and a newly divorced young couple attempt a reconciliation. When Wolff . . . died in 2002, her husband found this manuscript in their refrigerator, and it thaws out like a well-preserved artifact." Libr J

Wolff, Tobias, 1945-

Old school; a novel. Knopf 2003 195p $22

ISBN 0-375-40146-6 LC 2003-52930

"It is 1960, and the narrator is beginning his final year at a private school of strong literary traditions. Aspiring writers edit the literary journal and compete to win private audiences with visiting luminaries of letters. This year, the guests are to be Robert Frost, Ayn Rand, and Ernest Hemingway. The narrator is a scholarship student, and though his school prides itself on class blindness, his classmates are well versed in spotting the subtle indicators of economic background. Longing to fit in, he dissembles, cultivating an 'easy disregard' by which he hopes to imply his own privilege. But this doubleness leads him toward an unexpected decision with far-reaching consequences for his future." Booklist

"A fine offering, manly in spirit and style . . . Wolff displays exceptional skill in capturing the small sights and sensations that evoke the whole rarefied world he's taking us back to." Atl Mon (1993)

Wolitzer, Hilma

Hearts. Farrar, Straus & Giroux 1980 342p o.p.

LC 80-18556

"Widowed at 26 after six weeks of marriage, Linda Reismann finds herself pregnant and saddled with her husband's 13-year-old daughter, whom she hardly knows. Robin, a perpetually sullen and hostile child who already looks like a woman, is her stepmother's natural antagonist. . . . Taking only what she can stow in the trunk of her car, Linda drives Robin west from New Jersey. She has three items on her agenda: an abortion, the surrender of Robin to her grandfather in Iowa, and her own new life in California. . . . Robin has her own agenda: to find and take revenge on her mother, who ran out on her when she was 5." Newsweek

"This is a comedy about the heart-wrenching process of growth; it is written with great skill and no condescension. Few readers will fail to be moved." New Repub

Tunnel of love. HarperCollins Pubs. 1994 376p o.p.

LC 93-51064

"Michael di Capua books"

"Linda Reismann is a 24-year-old widow, saddled with an unborn child and teenage Robin, the daughter of her former husband. She travels from Newark to Los Angeles looking for a new start. An aging liquor-store owner hires her, proposes marriage, then is shot by a robber. A Latino dance instructor helps her get work at an upscale aerobic salon, but he turns out to be married. Cynthia Sterling, a wealthy soap-opera producer, hires her as a personal trainer; she supplies incredible medical care and moral support in the aftermath of a terrible car accident (caused by Robin), then files suit for custody of Linda's baby, calling her an unfit mother." Booklist

"The reader is shocked at first by the similarities between this novel and an earlier one, 'Hearts.' . . . In fiction, however, as in nature, God resides in the details. Besides which, while Robin is almost a butterfly in parts of 'Hearts,' here she has advanced backward to become a great fat caterpillar, a gorgeous carbuncle on a solid and good-hearted novel." N Y Times Book Rev

Wolitzer, Meg, 1959-

Surrender, Dorothy; a novel. Scribner 1999 224p $22

ISBN 0-684-84844-9 LC 98-47007

In this novel "three Wesleyan alums—Peter, Maddy, and Adam—react to the sudden death of a beautiful and beloved fourth, Sara. The four had planned to share an August beach house rental. Now, Adam's lover, Shawn, takes her place, the only one not part of the decade-long hermetically sealed group until Sara's death brings them her distraught mother Natalie." Libr J

"Buried within this affecting novel is the troubling question of whether close friendships and close family ties can keep a person from finding romantic intimacy. Wolitzer's Sara didn't live long enough to explore that possibility; perhaps her survivors will be luckier." N Y Times Book Rev

The wife; a novel. Scribner 2003 219p $23

ISBN 0-684-86940-3 LC 2002-36660

Wolitzer, Meg, 1959-—*Continued*

"Joan Castleman is en route to Finland to watch her husband, the renowned author Joe Castleman, win the Helsinki Prize when she decides to leave him. What follows is Joan's fascinating recollection of their marriage, his career, and her fading dreams. Telling her story in alternating segments, she starts in the 1950s with the beginning of the couple's professor-student relationship and continues through to the present, their 40 years of marriage stacking up unspoken regrets." Libr J

"Wolitzer's crisp pacing and dry wit carry us headlong into a devastating message about the price of love and fame." Publ Wkly

Wolven, Scott, 1965-

Controlled burn; stories of prison, crime, and men. Scribner 2005 212p $22

ISBN 0-7432-6011-2 LC 2004-58310

Contents: Taciturnity; Outside work detail; El Rey; Crank; Ball lightning reported; Controlled burn; Tigers; The high iron; The rooming house; Atomic supernova; The copper kings; Underdogs; Vigilance

"Wolven's not as romantic or sympathetic as Hemingway, but it's hard to think that Papa wouldn't appreciate his artistry and imagination." Publ Wkly

A **Woman's** eye; edited by Sara Paretsky. Delacorte Press 1991 448p o.p.

LC 90-28102

Stories included are: Lucky dip, by L. Cody; Murder without a text, by A. Cross; The puppet, by D. S. Davis; Death and diamonds, by S. Dunlap; Getting to know you, by A. Fraser; Full circle, by S. Grafton; Her good name, by C. G. Hart; That summer at Quichiquois, by D. B. Hughes; Discards, by F. Kellerman; Deborah's judgement, by M. Maron; Benny's space, by M. Muller; Where are you, Monica?, by M. A. Oliver; Settled score, by S. Paretsky; The scar, by N. Pickard; A man's home, by S. Singer; Looking for Thelma, by G. Slovo; A match made in hell, by J. Smith; The cutting edge, by M. Wallace; Ghost station, by C. Wheat; Theft of the poet, by B. Wilson; Kill the man for me, by M. Wings

Wood, Barbara, 1947-

The dreaming; a novel of Australia. Random House 1991 453p o.p.

LC 90-52883

"After her parents tragic deaths in 1871, Joanna Drury leaves her native India for Australia, to unlock the secret past that haunted her mother, Lady Emily, and led to her mysterious, sudden death at age 40. In Melbourne, Joanna meets dashing and sensitive frontiersman Hugh Westbrook, and together they build Hugh's sheep station into a thriving enterprise, all the while looking for the source of the 'curse' on Joanna's family that took hold in an ancient time the aborigines call 'the dreaming.' . . . Wood's soft-edged prose, likable characters, and period details are always a big hit with her many fans." Booklist

Green City in the sun. Random House 1988 699p o.p.

LC 87-26527

This "saga takes readers into colorful turn-of-the-century Nairobi, the capital of Kenya and the 'Green City' of the book's title. The story opens in the present, with Dr. Deborah Treverton's return to her native Kenya at the behest of a dying African medicine woman whose curse on the Treverton family caused Deborah to leave Africa 15 years earlier. Now 33, Deborah has come back to learn the truth of her ancestry and to find the man she once planned to marry. Through flash-backs, we learn how Deborah's family came to live in East Africa; about her Aunt Grace's establishment of a medical mission in Kenya 68 years earlier; and about her father's sexual indiscretions and the resultant possibility that Deborah might be part black as well as the half-sister of her former lover." Booklist

"The author has obviously done extensive research into the history of Africa. The cultures, lifestyles and differing ideologies are portrayed with stark reality and a feeling of immediacy." West Coast Rev Books

Perfect Harmony; a novel. Little, Brown 1998 429p $23.95

ISBN 0-316-81653-1 LC 97-37623

"Charlotte Lee is the head of Harmony, a major player in the international herbal-medicine industry. Charlotte has taken the ancient Chinese remedies once concocted in her grandmother's kitchen and turned them into a multimillion-dollar business. But now three people have died after taking Harmony products, and when Charlotte receives a series of threatening e-mail messages, it's clear someone is out to ruin the company. Enter Jonathan Sutherland former FBI agent, computer whiz, and—coincidentally—the man Charlotte has loved since she was a teenager." Booklist

Soul flame. Random House 1987 372p o.p.

LC 86-3893

"Selene, abandoned at birth in order to save her life and raised by a 'healer-woman,' follows her adoptive mother's craft and adds to it through run-ins with other healers throughout the first-century Roman world. Her other tutor is Andreas, a cynical, handsome Greek surgeon with whom she falls in love only to be separated from him and sent on years of travels." Booklist

The author "enriches this dramatic, unpredictable narrative with intriguing material about history, spirituality and the medical practices of antiquity." Publ Wkly

Vital signs. Doubleday 1985 326p o.p.

LC 84-13639

"Three women share an apartment and their dreams in medical school in the late 1960s, each of them driven: Sondra by her suspected black ancestry, Ruth by the father she could never please, Mickey by the birthmark that scarred her psyche more than her face. Each has professional success and personal heartache in the 18-year span of the novel, Sondra working at a medical mission in Kenya, Ruth with a fertility clinic and a large family to juggle, and Mickey, her own scar eradicated, as a plastic surgeon to the rich and famous." Libr J

"Wood's expert knowledge of medicine and her deft interplay of plot and character make this a richly textured and quite credible story that is delightfully unpredictable from the first page through the last." Booklist

Wood, James

The book against God. Farrar, Straus & Giroux 2003 257p $23

ISBN 0-374-11538-9 LC 2002-42600

"Tom Bunting begins his narrative with a survey of his miserable bed-sit in London. He is in exile from the wonderful flat in Islington he used to share with his wife, Jane . . . who earned the rent from her work as a pianist. Penniless and hopelessly given to lying, Tom has also been neglecting his dissertation to scribble little impious aperçus in various notebooks. This he rather grandly calls his 'Book against God'—a sort of anti-Pensées. The book—and in a sense his whole wretched life—is a muffled rebellion against his father, a charming, learned, blissfully married vicar in North England." Publ Wkly

"Much of the novel follows a vaguely allegorical schema designed to force the characters and all that they ostentatiously symbolize (faith, doubt, art, etc.) into a culminating conflict. Among the many reasons you don't necessarily mind havinge your arm twisted in this way is the fact that, first, Wood writes like a dream, and second, the novel is often wildly funny." N Y Times Book Rev

Woodrell, Daniel

The death of sweet mister; a novel. Putnam 2001 196p $23.95

ISBN 0-399-14751-9 LC 00-45972

"A Marian Wood book"

Set in the Missouri hill country, this novel "presents one eventful summer in the life of Shug, a friendless, overweight 13-year-old living with his mother in the caretaker's cottage at the local cemetery. Glenda flirts incessantly, even with her son, who is becoming increasingly aware of her charms. Glenda's husband, Red (who may or may not be Shug's father), comes and goes, bringing money occasionally and strife a lot more often. . . . Shug's efforts to protect his mother from Red, from other admirers, and from her own rash decisions come to a head one hot summer night." Libr J

"Woodrell's merciless realism is shot through with humor and rural wisdom; his work may not be to everyone's taste, but his bleak world is rendered with consummate artistry." Publ Wkly

Give us a kiss; a country noir. Holt & Co. 1996 237p o.p.

ISBN 0-8050-2298-8 LC 95-23458

A "novel set in the Missouri Ozarks, this is the . . . tale of tough-guy midlist novelist Doyle Redmond's transformation into the writer he only dreamed of being. Escaping from trendy California in his estranged wife's Volvo, Doyle reconnects with his roughneck heritage: gun-crazy grandpa and older brother, . . . marijuana farms, and a 50-year-old blood feud with the infamous Dolly clan." Libr J

The author creates a "vanishing South with an accuracy and understanding beyond any genre writer's capability. . . . If one is tempted to hear echoes of William Faulkner, Erskine Caldwell or Andrew Lytle in such themes, no matter. Mr. Woodrell isn't imitating any of them. He's only drawing from the same well they did, but with a different take, a different voice, a sharper sense of irony and satire." N Y Times Book Rev

Woods, Sara

The lie direct. St. Martin's Press 1983 191p o.p.

LC 83-2982

London barrister/detective "Maitland agrees to defend John Ryder, on trial for treason, in spite of the overwhelming evidence against him. Dr. Boris Gollnow defects from Russia and identifies Ryder as the man who has been selling secrets to the Soviets. Winifred Paull, who claims Ryder has married her in a bigamous ceremony, confirms the identification and so do others. Only the accused's legal wife, Carol, and Antony believe in him. Maitland . . . turns detective and searches for proof of perjury by the witnesses for the prosecution. When Winifred is murdered and Carol is charged with that crime, the lawyer's problems magnify." Publ Wkly

Naked villainy. St. Martin's Press 1987 269p o.p.

LC 86-27925

This case featuring barrister-sleuth Antony Maitland, "begins with one of Maitland's friends telling him about cosmetics king Georges Letendre, who, while visiting her sister in London, found a photograph of her naked on an altar at the climactic moment of a Black Mass. Letendre is subsequently murdered, and Maitland is asked to defend the chief suspect, the dead man's son. Maitland delves deeply into the occult and financial chicanery before putting together a brilliant Old Bailey performance." Booklist

Woods, Stuart

Chiefs. Norton 1981 427p o.p.

LC 80-27350

"Set in the small town of Delano, Ga., the novel tells of three Delano police chiefs—a farmer, a sadistic racist and a black—who must deal with the same case: the disappearances and murders of a number of white, teenaged boys over the course of 40 years. The mystery—readers will discern the killer's identity quite early—is played against the South in transition as local politics acquire national prominence when the son of the first chief becomes a candidate for governor and is eyed by the JFK White House as a potential running mate in the reelection campaign." Publ Wkly

Choke; a novel. HarperCollins Pubs. 1995 280p o.p.

LC 95-37300

Chuck Chandler "teaches tennis at an exclusive club in Key West and meets his 'match' in gorgeous Claire Carras and her much older, wealthy husband, Harry. Chuck boats, wines, and dines with the Carrases, beds Claire, then finds himself accused of Harry's apparent murder. . . . Enter Tommy Sculley, formerly with the New York Police Department, now augmenting his pension working for the Key West police. Tommy is streetwise and intelligent, and he won't quit until he finds the truth." Libr J

"Mr. Woods knows how to keep the narrative pace in overdrive, and the twists of the plot, if not always surprising, are satisfactorily developed." N Y Times Book Rev

Cold paradise. Putnam 2001 326p o.p.

ISBN 0-399-14736-5 LC 00-45974

Woods, Stuart—*Continued*

When millionaire Thad Shames asks Stone Barrington "to go to Palm Beach to track down a mysterious woman he met at a party, Barrington sees the mission as little more than a wild goose chase. . . . To his surprise, it doesn't take long to find the woman, but it's an even bigger shock to him to discover that she is Allison Manning, now calling herself Liz, whom he helped when she was accused of killing her husband. . . . That husband is still very much alive, and Liz wants to pay him to leave her alone with some of the money from the insurance scam they pulled off together." Booklist

Dead eyes. HarperCollins Pubs. 1994 303p o.p.
LC 93-14221

"Young Hollywood actress Chris Callaway is poised at the brink of stardom when her world collapses. Shortly after she begins receiving disquieting letters signed 'Admirer,' she is nearly blinded in a fall at the construction site of her new Malibu home. As Admirer becomes a menacing stalker, sending gifts and a gruesome photo and calling on the phone, Chris is stoutly guarded by her best friend and confidant, hairdresser Danny Devere. Also on duty is Beverly Hills police detective and stalker expert Jon Larsen. . . . Woods's style is lean and staccato, if unsubtle, and he's a pro at turning up the suspense." Publ Wkly

Dead in the water; a novel. HarperCollins Pubs. 1997 325p o.p.
LC 97-14255

"City Attorney Stone Barrington is on the small island of St. Marks off the coast of Antigua for vacation. His live-in girlfriend is unable to join him. Since he is at loose ends, he attends the coroner's inquest into the death of Paul Manning, a famous mystery writer who was sailing across the Atlantic when, according to his wife, he died. She is arrested for murder because the island prosecutor has political ambitions of being the next prime minister, and a good murder case is just what he needs. Manning was heavily insured, and within a day or so, $15 million is paid to his estate and then transferred to a Cayman Island account. Barrington takes on Allison Manning's defense with the help of a local barrister." Libr J

"This is a cleverly plotted, witty crime caper with a dash of sex, a likably roughish hero, and a surprising twist at the finish." Booklist

Dirt; a novel. HarperCollins Pubs. 1996 272p o.p.
LC 96-199910

In this novel, "Stone Barrington, a retired police detective turned lawyer/investigator, aids Amanda Dart, a famous gossip columnist, who receives a FAX that threatens to expose her. The FAX, entitled 'Dirt,' is sent not only to Amanda but to much of New York society. Although Amanda makes a living destroying other people's lives, she carefully guards her own reputation. Barrington is brought in to discover the author of 'Dirt,' which exposes the lives of other unscrupulous characters as well." Libr J

"Dripping with name-dropping, haute couture and pricey playthings, and spiced with hormonal aerobics as Stone trolls the siren-infested waters of upscale Manhattan, the narrative rockets toward an abrupt but absolutely stunning denouement." Publ Wkly

Dirty work. Putnam 2003 322p $25.95
ISBN 0-399-14982-1 LC 2002-32975

"Suave cop-turned-lawyer Stone Barrington is asked to hire someone to take photos of Lawrence Fortescue, the husband of a wealthy socialite, with a woman who is presumably his mistress. Stone hires the nephew of an old friend, who proves to be grossly incompetent when he falls through the skylight onto the man he's supposed to be photographing. Fortescu ends up dead, the supposed mistress disappears, and the photographer is charged with manslaughter. As Stone digs deeper, he discovers that Fortescue wasn't killed by the photographer's fall, but by an injection of poison. Enter Carpenter, aka Felicity Devonshire, Stone's contact in British intelligence. Carpenter suspects the woman involved with Fortescue is actually . . . a trained assassin with a grudge." Booklist

Grass roots; a novel. Simon & Schuster 1989 459p o.p.
LC 89-32198

"After years as chief of staff for a venerable Georgia senator, Will Lee decides to run for the seat himself when a stroke cripples his mentor. Standing in his way are an ambitious governor in the Democratic primary and, possibly, a far-right fundamentalist in the general election. In addition, Will must interrupt his campaign to serve as the defense lawyer in a controversial race-murder trial, while elsewhere, a dedicated ex-cop pursues the head of a Klan-like vigilante group that's been carrying out gangland-style killings." Publ Wkly

"A consummate storyteller, Woods . . . demonstrates his narrative ability by intertwining contemporary southern politics and the murder trial into a most satisfying tale." Libr J

Heat. HarperCollins Pubs. 1994 346p o.p.
LC 94-4175

"Unjustly imprisoned, bereft of wife and daughter, ex-DEA agent Jesse Warden is offered a daring gamble: if he can infiltrate and destroy a heavily armed religious cult, he can win his freedom." Libr J

"Despite a few momentary lapses into banal predictability, Woods has concocted a high-octane story filled with nail-biting suspense and enough unusual twists to keep even experienced puzzle-solvers guessing." Booklist

Imperfect strangers. HarperCollins Pubs. 1995 269p o.p.
LC 94-34506

"Woods' 'imperfect' strangers meet on an airplane. Sandy Kinsolving is an attractive, well-dressed man of means. He's flying from London to New York because his father-in-law, who's bankrolled his lucrative wine-selling business, has just had a stroke. Sandy and his wife are far from close, and he's concerned that his father-in-law's death will have unpleasant financial consequences. His seatmate, Peter Martindale, also a well-dressed man of means, is a gallery owner based in San Francisco. It seems that he and his wife are also on the outs, and he, too, stands to lose his livelihood. . . . Peter proposes that they murder each other's wives. The trick here is to complicate matters, and Woods succeeds admirably." Booklist

L.A. dead. Putnam 2000 338p o.p.
ISBN 0-399-14664-4 LC 00-28059

Woods, Stuart—*Continued*

This Stone Barrington thriller "finds the lawyer/sleuth from New York back in Los Angeles on a murder case. . . . His ex-lover, Arrington Calder, stands accused of murdering her husband, movie star and renowned man-about-town Vance Calder, found dead of a gunshot wound in the couple's Bel Air mansion. Upon hearing the news, Barrington, in Italy for his imminent wedding to the lovely but unpredictable Dolce Bianchi, rushes to L.A. to take over Arrington's defense." Publ Wkly

L.A. Times; a novel. HarperCollins Pubs. 1993 329p o.p.

LC 92-54724

"Vincente Michaele Callabrese works as a shakedown artist for the mob in New York City's Little Italy, but moviegoing is his passion. Early in the story, he changes his name to Michael Vincent and makes a break for L.A., where with the help of powerful studio head Leo Goldman he fulfills his dream of becoming a big-time producer. Vincent's *cosa nostra* connections keep in touch, particularly old pal Tommy Provenzano whose rise to power in New York parallels Vincent's in Hollywood. Eventually, Vincent's desire to bring a gentle turn-of-the-century novel to the screen leads him to employ the sorts of techniques and friends that served him in his mafia days." Publ Wkly

New York dead. HarperCollins Pubs. 1991 303p o.p.

LC 90-56374

A mystery "set in Manhattan's Upper East Side, the stomping ground of Stone Barrington, a well-bred but unpretentious detective. . . . Late one evening, as Stone trudges home from Elaine's Restaurant, popular TV newscaster Sasha Nijinsky plummets 12 stories from her terrace and lands on a heap of dirt 20 yards away from him—remarkably, still alive. Stone fails to apprehend the person who flees Sasha's penthouse and, after the ambulance carrying her collides with a fire truck, Sasha herself disappears. Despite the fact that no corpse is in evidence, the baffled NYPD eagerly pins a murder rap on Sasha's distraught lesbian lover. Stone refuses to accept his colleagues' pat solution." Publ Wkly

Orchid Beach. HarperCollins Pubs. 1998 325p $25

ISBN 0-06-019181-3 LC 98-23628

"Army Sergeant Holly Barker has just lost a sexual-harassment case against Colonel Bruno, her former boss. . . . Fortunately, her father, a soon-to-retire master sergeant, knows Chet Marley, the chief of police in Orchid Beach, Florida. Chet is looking for a new deputy chief. It sounds good to Holly, so she packs her gear and sets off for Florida. But when she arrives, she steps into big trouble. The night before, Chet Marley and his best friend were murdered. Shocked at such brutality in peaceful-looking Orchid Beach, Holly sets out to find the killer, only to run into an elaborate conspiracy plot." Booklist

"The story gets extra bite from Holly's intriguing relationship with an inherited canine named Daisy, the clairvoyant Doberman that belonged to her mentor." Publ Wkly

Palindrome. Harper & Row 1991 344p o.p.

LC 90-55587

"When Liz Barwick is beaten nearly to death by her steroid-crazed husband, Baker Ramsey, a star NFL running back, she quickly divorces him, takes a large cash settlement and disappears from public view. Liz, whose book of sports photographs has just been released, takes advantage of her publisher's offer to live in his cottage on an isolated private island off the Georgia coast. But when Ramsey goes on a murderous rampage, Liz's lawyer and publisher and his wife are among his victims. Meanwhile other events are unfolding on Cumberland Island, where Liz becomes involved with the Drummond family." Publ Wkly

Reckless abandon; Stuart Woods. G.P. Putnam's Sons 2004 289p $25.95

ISBN 0-399-15151-6 LC 2003-64799

This thriller features cop-turned-lawyer Stone Barrington and Holly Barker, chief of the Orchid Beach, Florida, police department. "Holly's come to New York hot on the trail of Trini Rodriguez, a bad guy she thought she'd stabbed to death in an earlier adventure. He's currently wanted for (among other things) blowing up a dozen people by hiding bombs in the caskets of two of his earlier victims and detonating them at the funeral. But finding him won't be so simple: he's been placed in the FBI Witness Protection Program and is working with the Feds and the CIA to catch an Arab terrorist group trying to employ the Mafia in a money-laundering scheme. Shortly after Holly takes up residence in Stone's guest room, the two of them are hip deep in the dangerous case and likewise each other. . . . Cross-pollinating all these characters from various books makes for some heavyhanded background exposition at times, but readers with no previous experience will still enjoy this amusing, full-throttle sex and crime romp." Publ Wkly

The run. HarperCollins Pubs. 2000 356p o.p.

ISBN 0-06-019187-2

Sequel to Grass roots (1989)

"Will and Kate Lee, now a Washington power couple, decide to go for broke in their service to the country. Will, a popular senator from Georgia, jumps into the race for the presidency, while Kate, a deputy director at the CIA, cheers him on. . . . The candidate's liberal leanings are anathema to a right-wing militia group from Idaho, whose leader, Zeke Tennant, tracks Will from one campaign stop to another with a duffel bag full of weapons. In a final showdown, Tennant makes one last assassination attempt." Publ Wkly

"A clever, well-constructed story of political ambition and behind-the-scenes skulduggery." Booklist

Santa Fe rules. HarperCollins Pubs. 1992 303p o.p.

LC 91-58476

"You're a rich, successful Hollywood producer who awakens the morning before Thanksgiving in your Santa Fe home with no memory of the previous night. Ignoring your dog's attempts to get you to visit the guest wing of the house, you leave and fly your private plane to Los Angeles. But you never get there: a breakdown forces you to spend the holiday isolated in a small airport town. When you finally see the newspaper the next day, you read that the bodies of your wife, your business partner and a third man—assumed to be you—have been found

Woods, Stuart—*Continued*
in the guest room of the Santa Fe residence. . . . Wolf Willett decides to stay 'dead' for a while and finish work on his new film, then hires a top defense attorney and turns himself in." Publ Wkly

The short forever. Putnam 2002 321p $24.95
ISBN 0-399-14868-X LC 2001-48725
Mogul John Bartholomew hires Stone Barrington "to fly to London and persuade his niece, Erica, to leave her cocaine-smuggling boyfriend, Lance Cabot, and to make sure Lance winds up in jail. Dapper Stone charms Erica, who offers to set him up with her sister, Monica, and then introduces him to Lance. With help from two British investigators, Stone learns John Bartholomew is not who he seems." Publ Wkly
"Filling his story with enough twists and turns to dizzy even the most seasoned reader, Woods keeps the tension high until the last page." Booklist

Swimming to Catalina; a novel. HarperCollins Pubs. 1998 311p o.p.
LC 97-51173
Former NYPD cop turned lawyer Stone "Barrington's former girlfriend Arrington has married Barrington's friend Vance Calder, Hollywood's hottest actor. Three months into the marriage, Arrington's been kidnapped, and Vance calls Barrington to beg for his help. Barrington comes to L.A. only to find a hornet's nest. . . . Despite the fact that this book is definitely politically incorrect and Barrington has apparently never heard of safe sex, it's a highly entertaining read that's chock-full of slam-bang action, fast cars, beautiful women, fine wine, and tart, tongue-in-cheek humor." Booklist

Two-dollar bill. G.P. Putnam's Sons 2005 298p $25.95
ISBN 0-399-15251-2 LC 2004-60068
Stone Barrington "becomes involved with a loud-talking Texan improbably named Billy Bob Barnstormer. It isn't long before Stone regrets ever being introduced to Billy Bob, especially when he leaves a dead body in Stone's guest room. But that is only the beginning of a tale that finds Stone, along with his best friend, Dino Bacchetti, following a twisted trail as they attempt to capture Billy Bob, who, it turns out, is much more dangerous than Stone could ever have imagined. Narrator Roberts slips comfortably into his performance, bringing a nice, down-to-earth quality to his portrayal of Stone." Publ Wkly

Under the lake. Simon & Schuster 1987 301p o.p.
LC 86-31632
"Years ago, in a deceptively quiet Southern town, a wealthy industrialist arranged for the construction of a man-made lake. . . . Now, though, things are stirring in Sutherland's lake; and with the arrival of two strangers, much that has been hidden from the light of day will be revealed. These out-of-towners are John Howell, whose career as an investigative journalist has degenerated so badly that he has accepted a job as a ghost-writer for a fried-chicken mogul, and Heather ('Scotty') MacDonald, an enthusiastic young reporter who has arrived undercover to investigate reports of police corruption." West Coast Rev Books
"Woods' straightforward recounting of the couple's eerie discoveries and dangerous exploits results in a gripping, plausible mystery/ghost story that concludes with suitably ironic twists." Booklist

Worst fears realized. HarperCollins Pubs. 1999 332p $25
ISBN 0-06-019182-1 LC 98-52924
In this Stone Barrington adventure, "the Manhattan lawyer turned investigator faces an indictment for the murder of a woman he's just met. When other brutal murders quickly pile up—all women connected to him or his best friend, Dino Bacchetti of the 19th Precinct—Stone knows that one of a cop's worst fears has been realized: a con with a grudge is bent on vengeance. While trying to save the lives of the women he cares about, Stone struggles to track down the killer and head off a DA who's out to get him for murder." Libr J

Woolf, Virginia, 1882-1941

Between the acts. Harcourt Brace & Co. 1941 219p o.p.
This novel "describes a pageant on English history, written and directed by Miss La Trobe, and its effects on the people who watch it. Most of the audience misunderstand it in various ways; a clergyman reduces its vision to a sermon. But, for a moment, Woolf implies art, has imposed order on the chaos of human life" Reader's Ency. 4th edition

The complete shorter fiction of Virginia Woolf; edited by Susan Dick. Harcourt Brace Jovanovich 1985 313p o.p.
Contents: Phyllis and Rosamond; The mysterious case of Miss V.; The journal of Mistress Joan Martyn; Memoirs of a novelist; The mark on the wall; Kew Gardens; The evening party; Solid objects; Sympathy; An unwritten novel; A haunted house; A society; Monday or Tuesday; The string quartet; Blue & green; A woman's college from outside; In the orchard: Mrs. Dalloway in Bond Street; Nurse Lugton's curtain; The widow and the parrot: a true story; The new dress; Happiness; Ancestors; The introduction; Together and apart; The man who loved his kind; A simple melody; A summing up; Moments of being: 'Slater's pins have no points'; The lady in the looking-glass: a reflection; The fascination of the pool; Three pictures; Scenes from the life of a British naval officer; Miss Pryme; Ode written partly in prose on seeing the name of Cutbush above a butcher's shop in Pentonville; Portraits; Uncle Vanya; The Duchess and the jeweller; The shooting party; Lappin and Lapinova; The searchlight; Gipsy, the mongrel; The legacy; The symbol; The watering place
"Woolf's 46 short stories demonstrate her fondness for experimenting with narrative forms and voices. Arranged chronologically, the pieces range from tales with traditional plot lines to denser interior monologues, and enable the reader to appreciate Woolf's development as a writer of fiction." Publ Wkly

Jacob's room. Harcourt Brace & Co. 1923 303p o.p.
First published 1922 in the United Kingdom
"The life story, character, and friends of Jacob Flanders are presented in a series of separate scenes and moments. The story of this sensitive, promising young man carries him from his childhood, through college at Cam-

Woolf, Virginia, 1882-1941—*Continued*
bridge, love affairs in London, and travels in Greece, to his death in the war. At the end, instead of describing his death, Virginia Woolf describes his empty room." Reader's Ency. 4th edition

Mrs. Dalloway. Knopf 1993 xxviii, 219p $16
ISBN 0-679-42042-8 LC 92-54300
"Everyman's library"
A reissue of the title first published 1925 by Harcourt Brace & Co.
"In this stream-of-consciousness novel all action takes place on a single day. By probing the thoughts and memories of various characters, the author has encompassed several people's lives. Clarissa has a party planned for the evening and is thinking of her daughter's involvement with a religious fanatic. Also in her thoughts are old friends like Sally Seton, who drops by at the party, and Clarissa's former lover, Peter Walsh, who is drawn to Sally, much to Clarissa's chagrin. When a noted psychiatrist arrives late at the party because one of his patients, Septimus Smith, has committed suicide, Clarissa is affected, not because she knew the victim, but because suicide is tantamount to wastefulness." Shapiro. Fic for Youth. 3d edition

Orlando; a biography. Harcourt Brace & Co. 1928 333p il o.p.
"Orlando begins as a young Elizabethan nobleman and ends, three hundred years later, as a contemporary young woman, based on the author's friend Victoria Sackville-West. The novel contains a great deal of literary history and brilliant, ironic insights into the social history of the ages through which Orlando lives. Orlando starts life as a male poet and ends as an equally intense and able woman poet, in order to emphasize the author's belief that women are intellectually men's equals." Reader's Ency. 4th edition

To the lighthouse. Harcourt Brace & Co. 1927 310p $17; pa $9
ISBN 0-15-190737-4; 0-15-690739-9 (pa)
Arranged in three sections, the first "called 'The window,' describes a day during Mr. and Mrs. Ramsay's house party at their country home by the sea. Mr. Ramsay is a distinguished scholar . . . whose mind works rationally, heroically and rather icily. . . . The Ramsays have arranged to take a boat out to the lighthouse, the next morning, and their little son James is bitterly disappointed when a change in weather makes it impossible. The second section, called 'Time passes' describes the seasons and the house, unused and decaying, in the years after Mrs. Ramsay's death. In the third section, the 'Lighthouse,' Mr. Ramsay and his friends are back at the house. He takes the postponed trip to the lighthouse with his now 16-year-old son, who is at last able to communicate silently with him and forgive him for being different from his mother." Reader's Ency. 4th edition

The voyage out. Modern Library ed. Modern Lib. 2000 xliv, 473p $17.95
ISBN 0-679-64028-2 LC 99-54259
First published 1915 in the United Kingdom; first United States edition 1920 by Harcourt Brace & Co.
"The story concerns a young woman of 24, Rachel Vinrace, an innocent, 'unlicked' girl who voyages to South America on board her father's ship, the *Euphrosyne*. Accompanying her are her aunt, Helen Ambrose, and uncle Ridley, together with an assortment of English characters whose social interaction is delicately observed. In South America Rachel meets a young Englishman, Terence Hewet, an aspiring writer working on his first novel. . . . He and Rachel fall in love and become engaged, determined to establish their future marriage on a new basis of equality. However, during an expedition Rachel contracts an unspecified disease and is confined to her bed with a fever. After a fortnight's illness she dies." Camb Guide to Lit in Engl

The waves. Harcourt Brace & Co. 1931 297p o.p.
"Highly original, unconventional, and poetic, it describes the characters, lives, and relationships of six persons living in England. The book is composed of interior monologues, spoken by the six characters in rotation, and of interludes describing the ascent and descent of the sun, the rise and fall of the waves, and the passing of the seasons. These natural cycles symbolize the progress of time, which carries the individual from birth to death." Reader's Ency. 4th edition

The years. Harcourt Brace & Co. 1937 435p o.p.
This novel "traces the history of a family, opening in 1880 as the children of Colonel and Mrs. Pargiter, living together in a large Victorian London house (later described by one of them as 'Hell') wait for their mother's death and the freedom it will bring; it takes them through several carefully dated and documented sections to the 'Present Day' of 1936, and a large family reunion, where two generations gather." Oxford Companion to Engl Lit. 6th edition

Wouk, Herman, 1915-

The Caine mutiny; a novel of World War II. Doubleday 1951 494p o.p.
"The old American mine sweeper 'Caine' patrols the Pacific during World War II. The action shifts from the bridge of the ship to the wardroom and from scenes of petty tyranny on the part of the skipper to incidents of fierce action and heroism on the part of the men. Ensign Willie Keith is assigned to the ship and leads a mutiny against paranoid Captain Queeg, who is eventually brought to trial in a scene that poses the difficulty of weighing evidence to prove that the takeover by the men was justifiable." Shapiro. Fic for Youth. 3d edition

A hole in Texas. Little, Brown 2004 278p $25
ISBN 0-316-52590-1
"Unassuming NASA physicist Guy Carpenter, who abandoned his hunt for a particle called the Higgs Boson, is suddenly in the limelight when the Chinese claim they've made the discovery." Libr J
"The plot is busy but secondary to Carpenter's banter and romantic escapades. Occasionally corny but also playful, thoughtful and passionate." Publ Wkly

Marjorie Morningstar. Doubleday 1955 565p o.p.
"The story of a middle-class Jewish girl who temporarily rejects her upbringing in her infatuation with the world of show business." Reader's Ency. 4th edition

Wouk, Herman, 1915-—*Continued*

War and remembrance; a novel. Little, Brown 1978 1042p o.p.

LC 78-17746

Sequel to The winds of war

This book "covers the events of 1941-1945. particularly as experienced by the fictional Henry family, Captain Victor ('Pug') Henry, continuing his remarkable naval career which brings him into contact with President Roosevelt and other historical luminaries, ends up an admiral. His marriage to Rhoda, however, finally comes undone for good and their oldest son, Warren, is killed at Midway. Byron, the Henrys' other son, eventually commands a submarine in the Pacific, but his Jewish wife, Natalie, their infant son, and her famous uncle, Aaron Jastow, are irresistibly sucked into the clutches of the Nazis." Libr J

Wouk's "work is a journey of extraordinary emotional riches. Quantity in time becomes quality, movement becomes scope, and history becomes human yearning." NY Times Book Rev

The winds of war; a novel. Little, Brown 1971 885p o.p.

"On the broadest of tapestries, Wouk weaves the effect of the preparation and the actual outbreak of World War II upon the family of Commander 'Pug' Henry. The affairs of the Henry family became intertwined with those of others, in such varying scenes as Washington, Berlin, Rome, London, and Moscow. . . . Despite the novel's breadth, the development of Henry's character as the middle-class military leader America needed in the 1940's is surprisingly credible." Choice

Followed by War and remembrance (1978)

Youngblood Hawke; a novel. Doubleday 1962 783p o.p.

A "story about an aspiring novelist named Arthur Youngblood Hawke. Hawke hails from the small coal-mining town of Hovey, Kentucky. From the age of 11, he has dreamed of the time when he will make his mark as a literary great. Upon leaving the Seabees, Hawke hikes to New York City with a completed war novel ready for market. The book is accepted by a successful publishing firm, and thus Artie Hawke's literary career pushes off to a fast start. It also marks the beginning of a lengthy passionate love affair with a wealthy mother of four children; a series of involved legal entanglements as a result of Hawke's obsession with money; and an unfulfilled romance with a pretty and intelligent young girl who edits Hawke's novels." Libr J

Wray, John, 1971-

Canaan's tongue. Alfred A. Knopf 2005 341p $25

ISBN 1-400-04086-8 LC 2004-64902

"Loosely based on the story of pre-Civil War slave stealer John Murrell, a.k.a. 'The Redeemer,' and his 'Mystic Clan' gang, this novel centers on the relationship between gang member Virgil Ball and charismatic leader Thaddeus Morelle. Ball, the son of a Kansas preacher, is simultaneously captivated and repelled by the criminal Morelle. Though he quickly becomes part of the gang's inner circle, he finds himself deeply conflicted about his involvement, a tension that will eventually lead to a violent act of expiation. Yet, in the end, even murder will not free him from the sway of a power older and deeper than Morelle. Wray has crafted an ambitious and strongly allegorical tale about the ability of belief to structure reality." Libr J

Wren, P. C. (Percival Christopher), 1885-1941

Beau Geste. Lippincott 1927 579p o.p.

"A foreign-legion column comes upon a desert fortress manned entirely by dead men. One of the corpses, a sergeant, has apparently been bayoneted by one of his own men. A flashback unravels the mystery of the three English Geste brothers. They confess to jewel theft and enlist in the French Foreign Legion, which sends them to North Africa, where they encounter the tyrannical sergeant." Shapiro. Fic for Youth. 3d edition

Wren, Percival Christopher *See* Wren, P. C. (Percival Christopher), 1885-1941

Wright, Austin McGiffert, 1922-

After Gregory; by Austin Wright. Baskerville Pubs. 1994 292p $20

ISBN 1-880909-12-X LC 94-18861

"Peter Gregory is an English teacher at an Ohio high school who tries to drown himself after two events: an incident with a female student in which he's accused of statutory rape; and an auto accident in which he swerves into the wrong lane while inebriated and kills an entire family. But Gregory's survival instincts get the better of him and, after crawling out of the river, he decides to hitchhike across the country to New York and assume a new identity. While on the road, he encounters Machiavellian billionaire Jack Rome, who gives him a huge sum of money with the condition that he forfeit the cash if he attempts to go back and put his sordid past in order. Wright's . . . ruminations about the modern tendency to shed the past at a moment's notice and become instantly mobile strike a vital chord, and he offers a story with enough twists and turns to keep the reader turning pages." Publ Wkly

Disciples; [by] Austin Wright. Baskerville Pubs. 1997 302p $22

ISBN 1-88090-955-3 LC 97-6134

This novel "begins when a woman's baby is kidnapped by her estranged husband, a near-sociopathic follower of a reclusive man whose disciples call him God Himself. Enlisted in the precarious negotiations to return the child are the woman's father, a retired academic, and one of his admirers, a young black assistant professor." N Y Times Book Rev

"The blinding self-righteousness of these characters sometimes creates terror reminiscent of Edgar Allan Poe's gothic stories. 'Disciples' presents an extraordinary delineation of the causes and functions of fanatical devotion, but it also jolts us from the easy assumption that such tendencies are restricted to the alien world of fanatical groups." Christ Sci Monit (Eastern Ed)

Telling time; a novel; by Austin Wright. Baskerville Pubs. 1995 264p o.p.

ISBN 1-880909-36-7 LC 95-32562

Wright, Austin McGiffert, 1922-—*Continued*

"Former college president and little-published paleontologist Thomas Westerly has a stroke, but not before trying to intervene in a hostage crisis near his retirement home on an island off the coast of Massachusetts. As his extended family gathers to bid farewell and attend the upcoming funeral, Wright's . . . ensemble piece begins to take shape. Thomas's hit-and-run accident, in which he killed a jogger; the sexual pressuring of his fiance, who became his wife; and nebulous reasons for involvement with the island's hostage-taker skew his descendants' opinions and seduce them into looking for additional scandals in Thomas's life. Gradually, life in the Westerly family unfolds as a litany of sexual initiations, resentments, and neuroses, held together by both the patriarch's generous spirit and his blemishes. Told by many voices, the various stories are changing, pathetic, and even hilarious, in a wonderfully multiple portrait of personal history and family relations." Libr J

Tony and Susan; a novel; by Austin Wright. Baskerville Pubs. 1993 334p o.p.
ISBN 1-88090-901-4 LC 92-74825

"At Edward Sheffield's request, Susan Morrow reads [the manuscript of] his first novel, Nocturnal Animals, in which an impulsive change of plan delivers Tony Hastings and his family into the hands of strangers who terrorize them. Passages from Sheffield's novel alternate between Susan's memories of Sheffield (her ex-husband), to details of her current marriage, to her speculations about the writer's and the reader's obligations." Libr J

"To author Wright's credit, Susan and her mental meanderings become as complicated, frightening, and compelling as 'Nocturnal Animals'. And when she worries that Edward cannot possibly end his novel in a totally satisfactory way, the reader wonders the same about both novels: definitely not a problem. 'Tony and Susan' is quite cleverly conceived and executed, a rarity, and it spins in the mind long after the last page is turned." Booklist

Wright, Eric, 1929-

Death in the old country; an Inspector Charlie Salter mystery. Scribner 1985 175p o.p.
LC 85-2395

"Wright mixes appropriate amounts of decent curiosity and quiet authority in the character of Insp. Charlie Salter, when the Canadian policeman and his wife vacation in an English village and encounter murder. While Annie takes in the tourist sites, Salter acts as visiting consultant to the local police. The banter between officials of the two countries adds entertainment to a well-executed plot." Barzun. Cat of Crime. Rev and enl edition

The last hand. Thomas Dunne Bks. 2002 231p o.p.
ISBN 0-312-28330-X LC 2001-51295

Toronto's Charlie Salter "has reached 60, the limit for Canadian police to retire from active service, but he's lost none of his smarts as he looks into the murder of a prominent lawyer found stabbed to death in his apartment, which a woman, who neighbors say dressed like a prostitute, was seen to leave." Publ Wkly

"As usual, Salter has an insight that proves the unraveling of the unconventional case. The real action, however, is internal, as Salter faces down his own fears. A sensitive end to a marvelous series." Booklist

A question of murder. Scribner 1988 200p o.p.
LC 88-11380

Inspector Charlie Salter of the Toronto police "investigates a bombing that occurred within yards of the path of a visiting English princess. Was it a terrorist attempt, a drug-related killing, or a by-product of the friction between street peddlers and the now-upscale shops of Yorkville? Salter sorts it all out in this well-paced and admirably plotted novel. A surefire hit with Salter fans and an excellent recommendation for procedural buffs." Booklist

Wright, Jack R. *See* Harris, Mark, 1922-

Wright, John C.

The golden age; a romance of the far future. TOR Bks. 2002 336p o.p.
ISBN 0-312-84870-6 LC 2001-58468

"A Tom Doherty Associates book"

In this future novel, the first of a projected two-volume saga, Phaethon Radamanthus, the 3,000 year-old scion of one of Earth's most powerful families begins a search for his lost memories

The author "chooses simple pulp-fiction plots to drive us through the technological complexities of Phaethon's world. The hero's quest to regain his lost memories, learn his true identity and reach the stars is undeniably compelling. As a result, having to wait for the next volume is frustrating. Wright's ornate and conceptually dense prose will not be to everyone's taste but, for those willing to be challenged, this is a rare and mind-blowing treat." Publ Wkly

Wright, Richard, 1908-1960

Eight men. World Pub. 1961 250p o.p.

Contents: The man who was almost a man; The man who lived underground; Big black good man; The man who saw the flood; Man, God ain't like that . . .; The man who killed a shadow; The man who went to Chicago

Lawd today!
In Wright, R. Works

Native son. Harper & Brothers 1940 359p o.p.

"Bigger Thomas is black. He is driven by anger, hate, and frustration, which are born out of the poverty that has dominated his life. When he gets a job with the Daltons, a white family, he is confused by their behavior and misinterprets their patronizing friendship. Tragedy follows when he accidentally kills Mary Dalton and escalates when Bigger murders his black girlfriend, Bessie." Shapiro. Fic for Youth. 3d edition

also in Wright, R. Works

The outsider. Harper & Row 1953 440p o.p.

"Cross Damon, a black man who works in the Chicago post office, is caught in a subway accident but escapes without serious injury, though because of a mistaken identity his death is announced. He decides to take advantage of this error to start life anew and thus free himself of his entanglements with women and debts. He goes to New York to live under an assumed name and before long becomes enmeshed in the Communist party.

Wright, Richard, 1908-1960—*Continued*

By it he is used as a murderer, until he is himself killed by a Party member." Oxford Companion to Am Lit. 6th edition

also in Wright, R. Works

Uncle Tom's children; five long stories. Harper & Row 1938 xxx, 384p o.p.

The stories in this collection deal with conflicts between whites and blacks in the South

also in Wright, R. Works

Works. Library of Am. 1991 2v ea $35

ISBN 0-940450-66-6 (v1); 0-940450-67-4 (v2) LC 91-60540

Contents: v1 Early works; v2 Later works

This set contains the complete novels Native son; The outsider (1953); and Lawd today! (1963); the story collection Uncle Tom's children; and the memoir Black boy

Wright, Ronald

Henderson's spear; a novel. Holt & Co. 2002 334p $25

ISBN 0-8050-6996-8 LC 2001-39633

"A John Macrae book"

"Canadian filmmaker Liv Wyvern travels to the South Seas in search of the father she hasn't seen in more than three decades. His fighter jet went down during the Korean War, but she has reason to believe he might have survived and taken refuge in the Marquesas. Liv is jailed in Tahiti on trumped-up murder charges and spends her time writing letters to the daughter she gave up for adoption; a daughter she's never seen. Liv also passes time reading the diary of a Victorian ancestor, Frank Henderson, whose Royal Navy voyages brought him to the South Seas." Booklist

"Romantic but unsentimental, this is a beautifully constructed story with fascinating characters and authentic details that play off one another in surprising and often shocking ways. The thematic homage to Melville is punctuated with other literary allusions that enrich and deepen an already thoroughly engrossing tale of the South Pacific." Publ Wkly

Wright, Stephen, 1946-

Going native; a novel. Farrar, Straus & Giroux 1994 305p o.p.

ISBN 0-374-16490-8 LC 93-10944

This novel explores the "psyches of various distressed characters. The first belongs to an unhappy Chicago-area suburbanite whose husband, Wylie, an average-looking guy with an enigmatic and elusive temperament, disappears one evening while they're entertaining their friends Gerri and Tom H'anna. End of first chapter. Next, Wright thrusts us into the manic realm of Wylie's slovenly crack-head neighbors, who alternate bouts of rough sex with chaotic outings in a beat-up Ford Galaxy. This car reappears in the following chapter when its driver picks up a hitchhiker, who, incidentally, has just stabbed a trucker to death. When the driver introduces himself as Tom Hanna, we realize we've picked up Wylie's trail. He's heading West, and his trip is a grim one." Booklist

"'Going Native' is less a portrait of a potential psychopath than a panoramic dive into a world in which the protagonist blurs to become just one more figure in the landscape. Stephen Wright's America is a paranoiac's, and a satirist's, dream come true." N Y Times Book Rev

M31, a family romance. Harmony Bks. 1988 214p o.p.

ISBN 0-517-56869-1 LC 88-900

"Living on the fringes of sanity, wife Dot and husband Dash make their living lecturing on UFOs. The children outdo their parents in weirdness. One daughter is slowly starving her baby by feeding him nothing but diet beverages. Another daughter, hyperactive and emotionally disturbed, has been denied treatment by her father, who believes that her behavior holds the key to communicating with beings from beyond. The drunken son murders a visitor, hiding the body out back so he can study the process of decomposition. This multifaceted story is told in machine gun prose, generously laced with streams of consciousness." Libr J

Meditations in green. Scribner 1983 342p o.p.

ISBN 0-684-18010-3 LC 83-11666

This is a novel about the Vietnam War. "Stationed with the 1069th Intelligence Unit, James Griffin believed he could keep himself detached from the war, viewing it almost as a movie, but instead the war became more real and he became less so until his former life and persona seemed only a fantasy. Back home, he attempts to find some sense of himself again-as he learns how to meditate like a plant, is befriended by a part-time social worker, and tries to deal with a psychotic friend who is seeking revenge on his sergeant." Libr J

"The narrative works several time frames and points of view into a mesmerizing mosaic of men in combat. . . . The absence of feasible political and military goals turns these soldiers in on themselves, and they take out their frustrations on each other rather than an intangible enemy. Exactly how and why this happens is made graphically clear in this superb [novel]." Quill Quire

Wurts, Janny

(jt. auth) Feist, R. E. Mistress of the empire

Y

Yan Ni *See* Shan Sa, 1972-

Yancey, Richard

A burning in Homeland. Simon & Schuster 2003 341p $25

ISBN 0-7432-3013-2 LC 2002-70833

"In the summer of 1960 the small town of Homeland, FL, waits for the return of Halley Martin, who served 20 years for a brutal, public murder. Illiterate, teenaged Halley worshiped beautiful Mavis and killed to avenge her honor; she's now the wife of Pastor Ned Jeffries, once Halley's prison chaplain. Seven-year-old Shiny Parker is an uneasy witness to the unfolding events. His family has recently taken in Mavis and her precocious ten-year-old daughter, Sharon-Rose, after the pastor was badly burned in the fire that destroyed their home. The past and the present are revealed through Halley's, Mavis's, and Shiny's narratives and letters." Libr J

Yancey, Richard—*Continued*

"Like most melodramas, 'A Burning in Homeland' must balance two competing goals: it seeks to reassure readers with a familiar story and at the same time catch them off guard by pricking at their fears. Richard Yancey's novel is contemporary enough to name those fears—male violence and female sexuality— and old-fashioned enough to include plenty of iconic scenes." N Y Times Book Rev

Yarbro, Chelsea Quinn, 1942-

Blood roses; a novel of Saint-Germain. TOR Bks. 1998 382p $24.95

ISBN 0-312-86529-5 LC 98-23671

"A Tom Doherty Associates book"

"As an exiled foreigner living in the village of Orgon in the midst of 14th-century France, the 3000-year-old vampire Saint-Germain . . . has enough trouble at the best of times convincing the locals that his unusual habits and interests are no threat. . . . Yet even the purest motives aren't enough to withstand the suspicion of the church when Saint-Germain uses his medical skills to heal the Vidame Saint Joachim of a wound no other healer has been able to diagnose. When the church accuses Saint-Germain of helping to spread the plague, the vampire is forced to flee as his lands and goods are seized." Publ Wkly

Yarbro "balances description, action, and romance excellently, producing a briskly paced, highly readable historical fantasy and the only recent series installment that is a good starting point for entering the St. Germain saga." Booklist

Come twilight; a novel of Saint-Germain. TOR Bks. 2000 479p il o.p.

ISBN 0-312-87330-1 LC 00-31710

"A Tom Doherty Associates book"

"While traveling through Spain in the seventh century, Saint-Germain, against his better judgment, saves the life of the mortally wounded Csimenae through a mingling of their blood. Despite his efforts to instruct her in the necessity of unobtrusive coexistence with humans, the haughty, impetuous Csimenae intimidates her countrymen into worshiping her and her son, Aulutis, eventually driving her vampire mentor away. Over the next 500 years, Saint-Germain's travels bring him into contact several times with Csimenae, who engenders a personal vampire army that preys on both unwary pilgrims and invading Moors. . . . Though the incessant details of daily life in the Dark Ages can grow wearisome, they are offset by Saint-Germain's poignant moments of soul-searching over his rare, regrettable moment of fallibility." Publ Wkly

Communion blood; a novel of Saint-Germain. TOR Bks. 1999 477p $26.95

ISBN 0-312-86793-X LC 99-38760

"A Tom Doherty Associates book"

The vampire Count "Saint-Germain is in late-seventeenth-century Italy after the true death of his beloved Olivia Clemens. Trying to settle her affairs as she would have wished, he has to fight fraudulent efforts to settle her estate on an imposter instead of on her faithful servant. Meanwhile, he inevitably runs afoul of the church, this time in the person of a cardinal who is scheming to increase the power of the Papal States and, on the side, abusing his sister. All this makes for quite lively reading in its own right, but the romance's real strength . . . lies in the meticulously researched and vividly written depiction of a long-ago and largely long-forgotten time and place." Booklist

Night blooming. Aspect 2002 429p map $24.95

ISBN 0-446-52981-8 LC 2002-16876

"Yarbro's vampire hero Saint-Germain continues his wanderings through history, this time in the late eighth century. The great French king Karl-lo-Magne summons Saint-Germain, here known as Hiernom Rakoczy, to his court. On the way, Rakoczy and his entourage meet Gynethe Mehaut, a young albino afflicted with a stigmata and awaiting news of her fate at a convent. . . . Volunteering to accompany [Gynethe] to the papal court in Rome, Rakoczy soon finds himself haunting his old haunts and falling in love with his charge. But Gynethe . . . is in great danger from those who feel threatened by her, and all Rakoczy's efforts may not be enough to save her." Booklist

"Richly rewarding for longtime readers, the novel also provides a good entry point for new recruits with its subtly supplied back story." Publ Wkly

Writ in blood; a novel of Saint-Germain. TOR Bks. 1997 543p $26.95

ISBN 0-312-86318-7 LC 97-161

"A Tom Doherty Associates book"

The immortal vampire Count Ragoczy Saint-Germain "has been in many places throughout his long unlife and has usually held an influential station owing to his terrific wealth, intelligence, and diplomatic skills. The setting for this book is Europe between the years 1910 and 1912. War seems imminent, but Russian Czar Nicholas II has a plan that could bring peace. He asks Saint-Germain to visit his uncle Edward VII of Great Britain and his cousin Kaiser Wilhelm of Germany to propose an agreement that would reduce arms production. Saint-Germain agrees." Libr J

The author "creates compelling individuals whose passions seem all the more poignant for the war about to engulf them. Although he too seems helplessly borne on the tide of history, Saint-Germain emerges from this robust romantic tale as a powerful figure of conscience." Publ Wkly

Yarbrough, Steve, 1956-

Prisoners of war; a novel; Steve Yarbrough. 1st ed. Knopf 2004 287p $23

ISBN 0-375-41478-9 LC 2003-40071

"In 1943, Dan Timms awaits being drafted away from the memory of his father's recent suicide, the guilt and sorrow of his mother, and the protection of his enterprising uncle, for whom he and a young black man called L.C. drive a 'rolling store' through the Delta, its plantations now worked by German soldiers whose fighting days are over. As they would seem to be for Dan's friend Marty Stark, returned mysteriously from the front and reassigned to guard men he had been trained to kill. But for L.C., a danger more immediate than the one looming overseas is the society into which he was born." Publisher's note

"Yarbrough writes with quiet compassion about Loring's black population, its reluctance to fight for a country that has so consistently betrayed its democratic

Yarbrough, Steve, 1956-—*Continued*
promise. To this combustible setting will come a peculiar prisoner, one with an 'angry purple stain, either a birthmark or a rash,' who speaks broken English and haunts one of the Loring natives assigned to guard him. It is the fate of this mysterious captive that once again forces the people of Loring to confront what it means to be American, and all the unexpected and often unwarranted sacrifices that identity might comprise." N Y Times Book Rev

Yates, Richard, 1926-1992

The collected stories of Richard Yates; introduction by Richard Russo. Holt & Co. 2001 xx, 472p o.p.

ISBN 0-8050-6693-4 LC 00-61400

Contents: Doctor Jack-o'-lantern; The best of everything; Jody rolled the bones; No pain whatsoever; A glutton for punishment; A wrestler with sharks; Fun with a stranger; The B.A.R. Man; A really good jazz piano; Out with the old; Builders; Oh, Joseph, I'm so tired; A natural girl; Trying out for the race; Liars in love; A compassionate leave; Regards at home; Saying goodbye to Sally; The canal; A clinical romance; Bells in the morning; Evening on the Cote d'Azur; Thieves; A private possession; The comptroller and the wild wind; A last fling, like; A convalescent ego

"Bitterness, loneliness and lack of fulfillment are the central themes of this grim posthumous collection." Publ Wkly

Ye Zhaoyan, 1957-

Nanjing 1937; a love story; translated with an introduction by Michael Berry. Columbia Univ. Press 2002 355p $24.95

ISBN 0-231-12754-5 LC 2002-24156

Original Chinese edition, 2001

This novel is "an unlikely love story set against the grim and chaotic backdrop of the infamous Rape of Nanjing in 1937. When inveterate playboy and indifferent professor Ding Wenyu falls unexpectedly in love, the object of his affection is, unfortunately, the bride at the wedding he is attending. Although he ardently and imprudently pursues Ren Yuyuan, a woman 20 years his junior, she ignores his attentions until her husband, a fighter pilot in the Chinese air force, is reportedly killed in action. As the Japanese invasion progresses and Nanjing is threatened, Wenyu and Yuyuan embark upon a love affair destined to end in tragedy." Booklist

"Ye paints a rich tableau of prewar Chinese politics and social mores. The contrast between the advance of the Japanese and Ding's slow seduction of Ren is both poignant and . . . ironic." Publ Wkly

The **Year's** best fantasy. See The Year's best fantasy and horror

The **Year's** best fantasy and horror; 1st-18th annual collections; edited by Ellen Datlow and Terri Windling. St. Martin's Press 1988-2005 18v

First two annual compilations published with title: The Year's best fantasy

Each annual collection includes short stories, poems, and essays. The nonfiction sections cover such topics as trends in fantasy and horror publishing; fantasy and horror films, television and comics; nonprint media; and obituaries. Over the years contributors of stories have included Charles De Lint, Steve Rasnic Tem, Garry Kilworth, Angela Carter, Karel Capek, Isabel Allende, Stephen King, Jane Yolen, Thomas Ligotti and Clive Barker

Year's best science fiction; 1st-22nd annual collections; edited by Gardner Dozois. St. Martin's Press 1984-2005

First three annual collections published by Bluejay Books

Each annual collection contains stories, a summation of developments in the field, and a list of honorable mentions. Over the years contributors have included Michael Swanwick, Maureen F. McHugh, Charles Sheffield, Cory Doctorow, Kage Baker, Brian Stableford, Gene Wolfe, Nancy Kress, Gregory Benford, and Stephen Baxter

Yglesias, Rafael

Dr. Neruda's cure for evil. Warner Bks. 1996 694p o.p.

LC 95-46461

"Psychiatrist Rafael Neruda submits to the reader his testimony about the treatment of a patient, a young man whom Dr. Neruda thought was cured but who ended up killing his wife and commiting suicide. But before relating this case history, Dr. Neruda offers a detailed explanation of his own traumatic upbringing. . . . From the haunting of his own soul by childhood incest and from his encounters with this young patient who obviously had *not* been cured, Dr. Neruda formulates a concept he calls the evil disorder. Yglesias' vast knowledge of psychotherapy is made not simply accessible but irresistable as he brings the subject down to human scale, configuring complex but credible characters who are both intelligent and troubled." Booklist

Yolen, Jane

Briar Rose. Doherty Assocs. 1992 190p pa $6.99

ISBN 0-312-85135-9; 0-7653-4230-8 (pa)

LC 92-25456

"A TOR book"

"Yolen takes the story of Briar Rose (commonly known as Sleeping Beauty) and links it to the Holocaust. . . . Rebecca Berlin, a young woman who has grown up hearing her grandmother Gemma tell an unusual and frightening version of the Sleeping Beauty legend, realizes when Gemma dies that the fairy tale offers one of the very few clues she has to her grandmother's past. . . . By interpolating Gemma's vivid and imaginative story into the larger narrative, Yolen has created an engrossing novel." Publ Wkly

Yorke, Margaret

Act of violence. St. Martin's Press 1998 282p $22.95
ISBN 0-312-18522-7 LC 98-16546
First published 1997 in the United Kingdom
In this mystery, "a small English village shudders after a murderous rampage by two school-boys, but a manipulative local therapist seems unperturbed." Libr J
"The tension leading to the young toughs' arrest is taut, and the identity of the murderess-turned-counselor kept cleverly obscured until the very end." Publ Wkly

Almost the truth. Mysterious Press 1995 c1994 278p o.p.
LC 94-36601
First published 1994 in the United Kingdom
"Hannah's rape during the course of a burglary shatters her family's happiness, but she makes matters worse by blaming her father. Her father, in turn, seeks a singular and surprising revenge on the rapist, released after a very short prison term." Libr J
"Without sacrificing entertainment to message, this absorbing, utterly unsentimental narrative reminds us that behind crime-related headlines live real people whose futures are marked by the crimes' effects." Publ Wkly

Criminal damage. Mysterious Press 1992 248p o.p.
LC 91-51182
"Mrs. Newton, a widow, enjoys a quiet and determinedly tidy life in the picturesque English village of Middle Bardolph, but storms are brewing that seem likely to unsettle it. Geoffrey, her boring and not very pleasant son, thinks his mother should underwrite the larger home his ambitious wife demands. Temperamental daughter Jennifer is increasingly obsessed with her former lover and his new fiancée and seems bent on disrupting their lives. . . . Yorke . . . mixes this deftly drawn, untrustworthy cast with robbery, violence and a hidden past, keeping readers guessing about what will be done and who will do it." Publ Wkly

False pretences. St. Martin's Press 1999 310p $23.95
ISBN 0-312-19975-9 LC 98-51198
First published 1998 in the United Kingdom
This psychological thriller, set in a small English village, traces "the local secrets exposed by a stranger and the aftermath when her true identity is discovered. Captivating and full-bodied." Libr J

Intimate kill. St. Martin's Press 1985 215p o.p.
LC 85-1754
"Stephen Dawes, convicted of killing his wife 10 years previously, has just been released from prison and is seeking his ex-mistress and their daughter. In his search, he finds out that his lover doesn't want to be found and that the circumstances surrounding his wife's death have extended unresolved into the present. As always, Yorke brilliantly builds suspense and presents, in exquisite detail, insightful views of complex people. This thriller gets better with every page." Booklist

The price of guilt. St. Martin's Press 2000 297p $24.95
ISBN 0-312-25332-X LC 99-88102
First published 1999 in the United Kingdom
"Louise Widdows's mentally abusive husband disappears the same night she suffers injuries in a hit-and-run accident. About the same time, Louise learns she has inherited a cottage, so she moves, hoping to start anew and perhaps locate the son she gave up for adoption 30-odd years earlier." Libr J
"Yorke is a master at making the reader care about meek and lonely middle-aged women. While the latter part of the novel largely fills in the motivations of minor characters in flashback, Colin's fate remains up in the air until the very end—and is as ironic as Louise's, if more just." Publ Wkly

A question of belief. Mysterious Press 1997 282p o.p.
LC 97-20833
First published 1996 in the United Kingdom
In this novel of psychological suspense, an English "department store executive is falsely accused of sexual harassment by a vindictive customer. After losing both his job and the trust of his family, the poor chump fakes his suicide and tramps off to a little village where nobody knows of his shame. Here his fate intersects with that of another outcast, an illiterate teenager who has been shabbily manipulated by a militant animal rights activist with a hidden agenda. Several other folks come out of the woods to play, and although their convergences are strictly contrived, their characters are sharply defined in this fatalistic tale of modern morality in tatters." N Y Times Book Rev

A small deceit. Viking 1991 200p o.p.
LC 91-50147
"A dullish, obsessive-compulsive judge and his timid, unassuming wife become the objects of a newly released rapist's harassment; however, the rapist's continuing life of mail fraud, opportunism, and violence toward women causes the judge and his wife to examine their relationship." Libr J
"Only a writer with Margaret Yorke's smooth cunning and deceptively simplistic narrative technique could whip a taut climax and a cathartic emotional release out of this disciplined, metronomic tale. She isn't showy, or graphic, or gothic. She just instinctively knows her British characters." Booklist

Yoshimoto, Banana, 1964-

Asleep; translated from the Japanese by Michael Emmerich. Grove Press 2000 177p o.p.
ISBN 0-8021-1669-8 LC 99-88699
Contents: Night and night's travelers; Love songs; Asleep
This volume consists "of three novellas, each telling a somewhat mystical tale of haunted slumber. In the first story, a woman mourning a dead lover finds herself sleepwalking; in the next, a woman involved in a relationship with a man, whose wife is in a coma, realizes that she is unable to remain awake; and in the third, a woman finds her dreams inhabited by a dead woman, her former rival in a love triangle. The stories flow easily and quietly from one to the next, and while they have a lyrical, almost poetic, quality, they remain gripping, dramatic, intense, and real." Booklist

Asleep [a novella]
In Yoshimoto, B. Asleep p105-77

Yoshimoto, Banana, 1964-—*Continued*

Goodbye Tsugumi; a novel; translated from the Japanese by Michael Emmerich. Grove Press 2002 186p $23
ISBN 0-8021-1638-8 LC 2001-58460
Original Japanese edition, 1999
"Maria Shirakawa is a thoughtful young woman thrown by family circumstance (her parents never married; with her mother, she is waiting for her father's divorce from his current wife) into growing up with her cousin, Tsugumi Yamamoto, in her aunt and uncle's small inn. Tsugumi, who is chronically ill, possesses a mischievous charm that both maddens and amuses her family. . . . Tsugumi's tenuous health seems to free her from the behavioral norms that govern Maria and Tsugumi's long-suffering older sister, Yoko, allowing her to curse, flirt with boys, concoct elaborate pranks and shock adults in a way Maria resents, envies and admires." Publ Wkly

Kitchen; translated from the Japanese by Megan Backus. Grove Press 1993 152p o.p.
LC 92-12871
Original Japanese edition, 1987
The volume comprises two works of fiction, the title novella and a short story. "Both 'Kitchen' and 'Moonlight Shadow,' each narrated by young women, are about loss. In the longer story, Mikage, the female narrator, moves into the house of Yuichi and his mother/father [a transexual] after the death of her grandmother; in the second, the girl has lost a boyfriend in a car crash, and is granted a vision of her beloved by a mysterious lady on a bridge." Times Lit Suppl
"In supple, precise prose Yoshimoto conveys her protagonists' emotional states by according them unusual sensitivity to the natural world; they share an enhanced vision that makes things shine with luminous clarity or emanate the gloom of mortality." Publ Wkly

Kitchen [novella]
In Yoshimoto, B. Kitchen

Love songs
In Yoshimoto, B. Asleep p67-103

Night and night's travelers
In Yoshimoto, B. Asleep p1-65

Youmans, Marly

Catherwood. Farrar, Straus & Giroux 1996 165p o.p.
ISBN 0-374-11972-4 LC 95-51246
This novel "begins in 1676 with Catherwood and her new husband on a ship bound to the New World. Settling near Albany, New York, Catherwood helps establish her new home in the wilderness, and things go well until she and her baby daughter Elizabeth get lost in the woods." Libr J
"Ms. Youmans's language is trenchant, graceful and, in places, sumptuously archaic, filled with a richness that provides more than just period color. Her prodigious powers of description render with acuity both small moments and large: the sea crossing, a childbirth, snowfall, the slitting of a fawn's throat, the 'rammish' stench of a trapper. Ms. Youmans has written a subtle, intelligent novel." N Y Times Book Rev

The wolf pit. Farrar, Straus & Giroux 2001 342p $24
ISBN 0-374-29195-0 LC 2001-42278
This Civil War novel focuses on "Robin, a young Confederate soldier, and Agate, a mulatto slave girl. In his . . . double tale, each of the characters suffers untold miseries. Robin's are endured in the heat of battle and the horrors of prison camp. while Agate must bear the indignities of slavery. . . The novel's many dramatic and traumatic events will keep the reader breathless, while the haunting, lyrical language and the fierce intelligence behind it reminds us we are reading a writer and storyteller of the first order." Publ Wkly

Young, Carrie

The wedding dress; stories from the Dakota Plains. University of Iowa Press 1992 126p $16.95
ISBN 0-87745-386-1 LC 92-6522
Contents: The wedding dress; Bank night; The skaters; The nights of Ragna Rundhaug; The sins of the fathers; Blue horses; Twilight and June
"Set in the Dakota Plains of the 1930s, [these stories] map the emotional lives and day-to-day struggles of the Norwegian American settlers of that harsh land. Rural in subject matter, yet warm, compassionate, and timeless in theme, Young's stories capture the slow unfolding of the seasons: seasons of marrying, childbearing, romance, unrequited love, and unexpected turns of fate and the human heart." Libr J

Yourcenar, Marguerite

Memoirs of Hadrian; translated from the French by Grace Frick in collaboration with the author. Farrar, Straus and Young 1954 313p o.p.
Original French edition, 1951
"The memoirs portray the emperor on the eve of his death and describe his reflections as he gazes out upon the city that seemed to him indestructible and that he now fears will fall. As with most of her work, the book is a minutely researched reconstruction of actual events in the distant past through which she develops penetrating and fully credible portraits of the people she describes." Reader's Ency. 4th edition

Z

Zabytko, Irene

When Luba leaves home; a profile in stories. Algonquin Bks. 2003 230p $22.95
ISBN 1-56512-332-8 LC 2002-38525
"A Shannon Ravenel book"
Contents: Steve's bar; My black valiant; The celebirty; Saint Sonya; The last boat; Obligation; Pani Ryhotska in love; Lavender soap; The prodigal son enters heaven; John Mars, All-American
"Occasionally awkward, but often shining with quiet grace, these 10 interconnected stories by Zabytko. . . follow the childhood-to-young-adulthood trajectory of Luba Vovkovych, who lives with her Ukrainian immigrant parents in Chicago in the 1900s." Publ Wkly

Zafón, Carlos Ruiz *See* Ruiz Zafón, Carlos, 1964-

Zafris, Nancy

Lucky strike. Unbridled Books 2005 336p $23.95

ISBN 1-932961-04-6 LC 2005-113

"It's 1954, and widowed Jean Waterman has brought her two children west, hoping that the desert air will soothe the weak lungs of her son, Charlie, and that the desert's soil will yield treasures of uranium. She meets Harry, an ex-Mormon traveling salesman who deals in Geiger counters and other prospecting paraphernalia; Jo Dawson, the girlish wife of a good-for-nothing lout determined to spend his last pennies in a quest for uranium; Miss Dazzle, the people person proprietress of the Stagecoach Oasis motel and a host of colorful folk. In the lonely Utah desert, the wanderers form an unlikely family. . . . In this lovely book, Zafris finds power in the slow, mute strangeness of everyday anxiety, the blossoming of hope in a barren desert and the terrible irony of what uranium means to those who seek it." Publ Wkly

Zahn, Timothy

The last command. Bantam Bks. 1993 407p (Star wars, v3) o.p.

LC 92-43876

In this concluding volume of the Star wars trilogy "Thrawn mounts a final siege against the Republic. While Han and Chewbacca struggle to form a wary alliance of smugglers in a last-ditch attack against the Empire, Leia keeps the Alliance together and prepares for the birth of her Jedi twins. But the Empire has too many ships and too many clones to combat. The Republic's only hope lies in sending a small force, led by Luke, into the very stronghold that houses Thrawn's terrible cloning machines." Publisher's note

Zamíàtin, Evgeniĭ Ivanovich, 1884-1937

We; [by] Yevgeny Zamyatin; translated by Mirra Ginsburg. Viking 1972 204p o.p.

First translation published 1924

"The ultimate dystopian novel, presenting a vision of the United States: a society whose suppression of individuality in the cause of order proceeds to the logical limit of eliminating the imagination. Its origin, and the fact that it circulated surreptitiously in Russia as a samizdat publication, encourages a reading that construes it as an attack on Soviet communism, but it actually refers to a much more fundamental tendency in human nature towards conformity and autmatism. Not published in Russia until 1988." Anatomy of Wonder. 5th edition

Zamyatin, Yevgeny Ivanovich *See* Zamíàtin, Evgeniĭ Ivanovich, 1884-1937

Zaroulis, N. L.

Call the darkness light; [by] Nancy Zaroulis. Doubleday 1979 560p o.p.

LC 78-74714

"Orphaned at an early age, Sabra enters the household of a cotton mill manager, but is turned away, unfairly, as a bad influence on one of his daughters. She marries, but is deserted by her husband; goes to work in the mill, but is dismissed for associating with an agitator. The nadir of her fortunes finds her living with the despised immigrant Irish and soliciting in the streets to keep herself and her child alive." Publ Wkly

"Nancy Zaroulis has given a comprehensive account of industrialization and immigration in the early nineteenth century and the ideologies characterizing the period. Her detailed examination of various aspects and social strata of the age is impressive." Best Sellers

The last waltz; [by] Nancy Zaroulis. Doubleday 1984 398p o.p.

LC 81-43547

This novel is "set in Boston around the end of the nineteenth century. The story centers around Isabel January and Marian Childs. Isabel is the pampered darling of the Januarys whose wealth had come from decades of Boston merchant shipping. They take in Marian as a very young woman. Her family has culture, but very little money. Yet her mother pushes her into a position as companion of sorts to various members of the January family. After inheriting January money from a potty old uncle, Marian takes her place in Boston society, and it is she who tells this story." Best Sellers

Massachusetts; a novel; by Nancy Zaroulis. Fawcett Columbine 1991 709p il o.p.

LC 90-82332

The author "tells the story of a single family, the Revells, and through them the history of Massachusetts from the arrival of the *Mayflower* to the present. A Revell or a relative is present at the first Thanksgiving, the Salem witch trials, and the Boston tea party. Revells are shown helping to start the China trade, founding the American factory system and the Boston Symphony, agitating for abolitionism, women's suffrage, or to save Sacco and Vanzetti." Libr J

"Using well-researched background material that takes Bay State history through the 1960s, Zaroulis weaves a fictional tapestry rich with details of real and imaginary characters." Publ Wkly

Zelazny, Roger

Blood of Amber. Arbor House 1986 215p o.p.

LC 86-3530

"A Del Rey book"

Sequel to Trumps of doom

In this seventh installment in the author's Amber fantasy series "the sorcerer Merlin of Amber—aka Merle Corey of San Francisco—learns the identities of two would-be assassins but makes a truce with one to pursue the greater, more dangerous power beyond them. Once again, the limited plot is enlivened by Zelazny's irony, his bravura sequences . . . and his laconic sense of the incongruous." Publ Wkly

Followed by Sign of chaos

The courts of chaos. Doubleday 1978 183p o.p.

LC 78-3263

Sequel to The hand of Oberon

This fifth title in the author's "Amber fantasy series answers many of the questions central to previous installments; the nature of the magical kingdom of Amber and the tangents it sometimes forms with the real world; the mystery behind the disappearance of Oberon the King—which forms the plot of the stories—and the machinations of Corwin, Prince of Amber, and his siblings, who thrive on intrigue." Booklist

Followed by Trumps of doom

Zelazny, Roger—*Continued*

Donnerjack; [by] Roger Zelazny, Jane Lindskold. Avon Bks. 1997 503p $24
ISBN 0-380-97326-X LC 96-48705
"One hundred years ago, the World Net crashed, creating a separate virtual-reality universe complete with its own gods, its own civilizations, its own magic. Virtù can be accessed for recreation or business from our own world, Verité, through virtual bodies. Non of the self-aware programs of Virtù can visit Verité, however, and the more powerful of them deeply resent it. John D'Arcy Donnerjack, instrumental in creating Virtù and among the foremost explorers of its wonders, has fallen in love with an artificial intelligence named Ayradyss. When she dies, Donnerjack follows her to Death's realm and demands her back." Publ Wkly
"The late Zelazny's last novel, completed by Lindskold, is one of his largest and most ambitious. . . . All the mythic resonances we have come to expect from Zelazny are here in abundance." Booklist

The doors of his face, the lamps of his mouth
In The Best of the Nebulas p35-61

The guns of Avalon. Doubleday 1972 180p (Amber) o.p.
Sequel to Nine princes in Amber
In this second volume of the author's Amber series Corwin "again walks the shadow worlds in search of his stolen birthright and encounters dreaded forces of evil conjured up by his own terrible curse." Booklist
Followed by Sign of the unicorn

The hand of Oberon. Doubleday 1976 181p o.p.
"The fourth title in Zelazny's epic fantasy of the world called Amber picks up in mid-dialogue form the conclusion of the previous novel 'Sign of the Unicorn.'" Booklist
"Oberon, the royal leader of the land of Amber, is unexpectedly missing, and his large family of sons and daughters is engaged in searching for him, or else trying to keep him missing." Publ Wkly
Followed by The courts of chaos

He who shapes
In The Best of the Nebulas p73-141

Home is the hangman
In The Hugo winners p5-67

Knight of shadows. Morrow 1989 251p (Amber) o.p.
LC 89-34658
Sequel to Sign of chaos
"The ninth book in Zelazny's Amber sagas. . . . Merlin, son of Corwin, escapes at the last minute from the Citadel of the FourWorlds. He is immediately plunged into intrigue and adventure. By book's end, it is apparent that his travels are not yet complete. Zelazny's pacing and the ingenious games he plays with magic continue to be rewarding." Booklist
Followed by Prince of chaos

Lord Demon; [by] Roger Zelazny and Jane Lindskold. Avon Bks. 1999 276p $23
ISBN 0-380-97333-2 LC 99-20950
"Exiled from their homeland after losing their ancient war against the gods, the demons find a refuge on Earth, striving to maintain an alliance with the human race. When an enemy murders his human servant, Kai Wren, once known as Lord Demon, embarks on a crusade of vengeance, despite the possibility that his actions might shatter the tentative arrangements between mortals and demonkind. Filled with offbeat humor and sparkling images, Zelazny's final novel—completed by his friend and biographer Lindskold—provides a last glimpse into the font of creativity and brash imagination that made Zelazny one of sf's most memorable writers." Libr J

Lord of light. Doubleday 1967 257p o.p.
This novel "describes a planet colonized by refugees from India who are tyrannized by a few of their fellow citizens who have assumed the guise and powers of the Hindu gods. Instead of easing his readers into the strange setting and unfamiliar mythology, Zelazny began the story in the middle, centuries after the initial landing; that the reader can absorb—and care to absorb—the complexities of the plot and setting is a tribute to the author's storytelling ability." New Ency of Sci Fic

Nine princes in Amber. Doubleday 1970 188p o.p.
This tale, the first in the author's Amber series, is a fantasy and adventure story about Corwin, who, following an attack of amnesia, realizes that he is one of nine princes in the kingdom of Amber. Each one of the nine princes and four princesses wants the throne, and war breaks out between the brothers
Followed by The guns of Avalon

Prince of chaos. Morrow 1991 225p (Amber) o.p.
LC 91-17296
Sequel to Knight of shadows
The tenth book in the Amber sagas "takes Merlin Corey to the actual Courts of Chaos, which have figured as offstage presences in the series beginning with *Trumps of Doom.* We now see the Courts from the inside, and a certain amount of the mystery about Corey's world and future is dispelled, although not without the usual quota of intrigues and dangers. The finer nuances of the series are becoming a little hard to appreciate without having followed it from the beginning. The vivid imagination and high command of language, however, can still be enjoyed on a volume-by-volume basis." Booklist

Sign of chaos. Arbor House 1987 214p (Amber) o.p.
LC 87-14509
Sequel to Blood of Amber
In the eighth volume of the author's Amber fantasy series "Merlin Corey follows a confused trail to the Keep of Four Worlds, where he learns the secret of the involvement of the Courts of Chaos in all the intrigues and wars to which he is heir." Booklist
Followed by Knight of shadows

Sign of the unicorn. Doubleday 1975 186p (Amber) o.p.
Sequel to The guns of Avalon
"Third in a series of science fiction-fantasy adventures featuring Corwin, Prince of Amber. . . . Court intrigue is rampant among the surviving princes and princesses of Amber, all of whom weave in and out of Shadow, a

Zelazny, Roger—*Continued*

multi-dimensional world they can manipulate, and unite to rescue a brother imprisoned by evil beings threatening the kingdom. This, though action packed, does not advance the fortunes of Corwin to any extent but does fill in background." Booklist

Followed by The hand of Oberon

Trumps of doom. Arbor House 1985 183p o.p.
LC 84-299

Sequel to The courts of chaos

"A new sequence [in the Amber fantasy series] begins in this sixth volume centering on Corwin's son Merlin, a sorcerer who has followed the father he barely knew from their powerful realm of Amber to an Earth that is one of Amber's many shadowy alternate worlds. Attempts on Merlin's life force him to return to Amber, where he becomes embroiled once more in family quarrels and finally confronts the man who has been stalking him. This fast-paced, colorful tale is enriched by Zelazny's literary analogs of his alternate worlds as he flips from one frame of reference to another (tarot, computers, lawyerly logic) and from one voice to another (hard-boiled detective, classical allusions, high fantasy)." Publ Wkly

Followed by Blood of Amber

Zimler, Richard

The last kabbalist of Lisbon. Overlook Press 1998 318p $24.95
ISBN 0-87951-834-0 LC 97-46184

"A young manuscript illuminator, fruitseller and secretly practicing Jew and kabbalist searches for the murderer of his uncle in this . . . [novel] set during the horrific 1506 Lisbon Inquisition. Outwardly Christian converts, Berekiah Zarco and his family practice Judaism clandestinely and study the Kabbalah, the mystical Jewish philosophy that sees God's presence in all things. Tragedy strikes when Berekiah discovers the naked, bloody bodies of his Kabbalist Uncle Abraham and a young girl, their throats slit, in a secret prayer cellar." Publ Wkly

This novel "first published in Portuguese, vividly recreates the world of ancient Lisbon, presenting Berekiah's mysticism in graceful, albeit occasionally florid, prose. Zimler's portrait of the city (and the New Christians' uneasy place within it) enriches his many-layered narrative, in which a suitably complex cast of characters plays a dangerous game with fate." N Y Times Book Rev

Zola, Émile, 1840-1902

Germinal. o.p.

Original French edition, 1885, one of the Rougon-Macquart series

"A study of life in the mines. . . . Étienne Lanier, a socialist, is forced to work in the mines. Low wages and fines cause a strike, of which Lanier is one of the leaders. He counsels moderation; but hunger drives the miners to desperation, and force is met by force. Several are killed, Lanier is deported, and the miners fall back into their old slavery." Keller. Reader's Dig of Books

Nana. o.p.

Original French edition, 1880, one of the Rougon-Macquart series

"The title character grows up in the slums of Paris. She has a brief career as an untalented actress before finding success as a courtesan. Although vulgar and ignorant, she has a destructive sexuality that attracts many rich and powerful men. Cruelly contemptuous of her lovers' emotions, Nana wastes their fortunes, driving many of them to ruin and even suicide." Merriam-Webster's Ency of Lit

Three faces of love; especially translated for this volume by Roland Gant. Vanguard Press 1969 c1968 151p o.p.

These three early Zola stories explore different kinds of love. In For One Night of Love "Zola tells of a dullard whose passion leads to suicide through his having been accessory in the murder of his rival, killed by the girl, a marquise. 'Round Trip' is a lyric of youthful sensuality triumphing over middle-aged insensitivity. In 'Winkles for M. Chabre' Zola deals with a triangle (aging husband, young wife, young man); the husband has been told to expect a child if he follows a diet of shellfish; he gets the child, unaware that it is not because of winkles. Slight things, these stories, but welcome additions to the austere works usually associated with Zola." Libr J

Zuber, Isabel

Salt. Picador 2002 352p o.p.
ISBN 0-312-28133-1 LC 2001-54892

The author depicts "one woman's life in the American South at the turn of the 20th century. . . . Central to her portrait are the relationships between Anna Maud Stockton Bayley, her adulterous, twice-married husband, John, and their offspring. Forced into marriage after John seduces her, Anna makes the best of it, sewing, gardening and keeping house in the small town of Faith, N.C. Still, she dreams of music, singing, travel and love. But single-minded John, who is avid to increase his land, children and stock, is less interested in his young wife's desires than his own personal gain." Publ Wkly

"Zuber gets the historical details right, and her characters' emotions (especially Anna's—romantic, tender and full of quiet desperation) are handled just as deftly." N Y Times Book Rev

TITLE AND SUBJECT INDEX

This index to the books listed in part 1 includes title and subject entries, arranged in one alphabet. Full information for each book is given in part 1 under the main entry, which is usually the author.

Title entries. Novels are listed under title. Analytical entries are made for novels published in omnibus editions and for novelettes. Such entries carry *In* or *also in* designations and usually include the page numbers in the book where the item is to be found.

Subject entries. Subject headings are printed in capital letters. The listing of a work under a subject indicates that a major portion of the work is about that subject. Under genre headings, such as SCIENCE FICTION or PHILOSOPHICAL NOVELS, works of that genre are listed. Under the heading DETECTIVES a list of individual fictional detectives makes reference to the authors of the detective novels in which they appear. Subdivisions under headings are given first by chronological period, then by topic, and then by place name.

A

ACCIDENTS—*Continued*
Coover, R. The origin of the Brunists
Delinsky, B. The summer I dared
Evans, N. The horse whisperer
Hannah, K. Angel falls
Mawer, S. The fall
Oates, J. C. American appetites
Packer, A. The dive from Clausen's pier
Proulx, A. Postcards
Roy, A. The god of small things
Spark, M. Reality and dreams
Steel, D. The house on Hope Street
Trollope, J. The men and the girls
Vonnegut, K. Deadeye Dick
ACCIDENTS, INDUSTRIAL *See* Industrial accidents
Accordian crimes. Proulx, A.
According to Queeney. Bainbridge, B.
ACCORDIONISTS
Proulx, A. Accordian crimes
ACCOUNTANTS
Coover, R. The Universal Baseball Association, Inc., J. Henry Waugh, Prop.
Mortimer, J. C. Dunster
ACCULTURATION
See also Americanization; Race relations
Momaday, N. S. House made of dawn
The **accusers**. Davis, L.
ACHILLES (GREEK MYTHOLOGY)
Cook, E. Achilles
Achilles. Cook, E.
Acorna. McCaffrey, A.
Acorna's people. McCaffrey, A.
Acorna's quest. McCaffrey, A.
Acorna's rebels. McCaffrey, A.
Acorna's search. McCaffrey, A.
Acorna's triumph. McCaffrey, A.
Acorna's world. McCaffrey, A.
Across open ground. Parkinson, H.
Across the river and into the trees. Hemingway, E.
Act of betrayal. Buchanan, E.
An **act** of love. Thayer, N.
Act of revenge. Tanenbaum, R.
Act of violence. Yorke, M.
Active service. Crane, S.
In Crane, S. The complete novels of Stephen Crane p429-592
ACTORS
See also Motion picture actors and actresses; Strolling players; Theater life
Baldwin, J. Tell me how long the train's been gone
Banville, J. Eclipse
Bernhard, T. Woodcutters
Bram, C. Lives of the circus animals
Burgess, A. A dead man in Deptford
Carroll, J. Fault lines
Davies, R. World of wonders
Denker, H. This child is mine
Diehl, W. 27
Irving, J. A son of the circus
Irving, J. Until I find you
Isaacs, S. Almost paradise
Kaplow, R. Me and Orson Welles
Korda, M. Curtain
L'Engle, M. Certain women
L'Engle, M. A live coal in the sea
Leonard, E. Get Shorty
Lessing, D. M. Love, again
Matheson, R. Hunted past reason
Miller, W. M. The darfsteller
Nye, R. The late Mr. Shakespeare
Varley, J. The golden globe
Wagner, B. The chrysanthemum palace
West, N. The day of the locust
Westlake, D. E. Money for nothing
Wolcott, J. The catsitters
Actress in the house. McElroy, J.
ACTRESSES
See also Motion picture actors and actresses; Strolling players; Theater life
Alcott, L. M. Behind a mask [novelette]
Baldwin, J. Tell me how long the train's been gone
Blatty, W. P. The exorcist
Bradford, B. T. The triumph of Katie Byrne
Bradford, B. T. Voice of the heart
Clark, M. H. Weep no more, my lady
Colette. Chance acquaintances
Dart, I. R. Show business kills
Didion, J. Play it as it lays
Dunne, J. G. Playland
Fuentes, C. Diana, the goddess who hunts alone
Goudge, E. Such devoted sisters
Grøndahl, J. C. Lucca
Harris, E. L. Not a day goes by
Holland, C. Lily Nevada
Iyer, P. Abandon
Kennedy, W. Quinn's book
Koeppen, W. A sad affair
Korda, M. Curtain
Leonard, E. LaBrava
Lord, B. B. The middle heart
McElroy, J. Actress in the house
Michael, J. Acts of love
Oates, J. C. Blonde
Pilcher, R. Winter solstice
Sontag, S. In America
Steel, D. Sunset in St. Tropez
Tey, J. A shilling for candles
Thomas, R. Voodoo, Ltd
Weldon, F. Worst fears
West, N. The day of the locust
West, Dame R. Sunflower
Williams, T. The Roman spring of Mrs. Stone
Acts of faith. Caputo, P.
Acts of love. Michael, J.
Acts of malice. O'Shaughnessy, P.
The **actual**. Bellow, S.
Actual innocence. Siegel, B.
Ada. Nabokov, V. V.
also in Nabokov, V. V. Novels, 1969-1974
Adam and Eve and Pinch me. Rendell, R.
Adam and evil. Roberts, G.
Adam and his sons. Steinbeck, J.
In Steinbeck, J. The portable Steinbeck
Adam Bede. Eliot, G.
ADAMS, JOHN, 1735-1826
About
Shaara, J. Rise to rebellion
ADAMS, JOHN QUINCY, 1767-1848
About
Pesci, D. Amistad
Addie Pray. Brown, J. D.
ADELAIDE (AUSTRALIA) *See* Australia—Adelaide
ADIRONDACK MOUNTAINS (N.Y.)
Doctorow, E. L. Loon Lake
Robinson, R. Sweetwater
Admiral Hornblower in the West Indies. Forester, C. S.
ADOLESCENCE
See also Boys; Girls; Youth
Abraham, P. The romance reader
Adam, C. Love and country
Banks, R. Rule of the bone
Bass, C. Maiden voyage
Bassani, G. The garden of the Finzi-Continis
Betts, D. Souls raised from the dead
Bowen, E. The death of the heart
Braff, J. The unthinkable thoughts of Jacob Green
Brown, L. Fay
Brown, L. Joe
Burns, O. A. Cold Sassy tree
Capote, T. Other voices, other rooms
Coe, J. The Rotters' Club
Cohen, L. H. Heart, you bully, you punk
Colette. Claudine at school
Colette. Gigi
Colette. The tender shoot
DeLillo, D. Ratner's star
Doctorow, E. L. Billy Bathgate
Doig, I. English Creek
Durham, D. A. Gabriel's story
Earley, T. Jim the boy
Estleman, L. D. Sudden country
Eugenides, J. Middlesex
Eugenides, J. The virgin suicides

ADVENTURE—*Continued*
Clavell, J. Shogun
Clavell, J. Tai-Pan
Clavell, J. Whirlwind
Cody, L. Rift
Conrad, J. The Nigger of the Narcissus
Conrad, J. Nostromo
Cooper, J. F. The Deerslayer
Cooper, J. F. The last of the Mohicans
Cooper, J. F. The Leatherstocking tales
Cooper, J. F. The Pathfinder
Cooper, J. F. The prairie
Cornwell, B. The archer's tale
Cornwell, B. Sharpe's battle
Cornwell, B. Sharpe's company
Cornwell, B. Sharpe's devil
Cornwell, B. Sharpe's eagle
Cornwell, B. Sharpe's enemy
Cornwell, B. Sharpe's fortress
Cornwell, B. Sharpe's gold
Cornwell, B. Sharpe's havoc
Cornwell, B. Sharpe's honour
Cornwell, B. Sharpe's prey: Richard Sharpe and the Expedition to Copenhagen, 1807
Cornwell, B. Sharpe's regiment
Cornwell, B. Sharpe's sword
Cornwell, B. Sharpe's Trafalgar
Cornwell, B. Sharpe's Waterloo
Costain, T. B. The black rose
Crichton, M. Sphere
Cussler, C. Atlantis found
Cussler, C. Black wind
Cussler, C. Dragon
Cussler, C. Fire ice
Cussler, C. Inca gold
Cussler, C. Lost city
Cussler, C. Sahara
Cussler, C. Treasure
Cussler, C. Valhalla rising
Cussler, C. White death
Darnton, J. Neanderthal
Dickey, J. Deliverance
Doyle, Sir A. C. The lost world
Du Maurier, Dame D. Jamaica Inn
Dumas, A. The Count of Monte Cristo
Dumas, A. The three musketeers
Dunnett, D. Caprice and Rondo
Dunnett, D. Checkmate
Dunnett, D. Gemini
Dunnett, D. Pawn in frankincense
Dunnett, D. Scales of gold
Dunnett, D. To lie with lions
Dunnett, D. The unicorn hunt
Eco, U. Baudolino
Elegant, R. S. Manchu
Estleman, L. D. Billy Gashade
Fesperman, D. The warlord's son
Finney, P. Gloriana's torch
Forester, C. S. Admiral Hornblower in the West Indies
Forester, C. S. The African Queen
Forester, C. S. Beat to quarters
Forester, C. S. Commodore Hornblower
Forester, C. S. Flying colours
Forester, C. S. Hornblower and the Atropos
Forester, C. S. Hornblower and the Hotspur
Forester, C. S. Hornblower during the crisis, and two stories: Hornblower's temptation and The last encounter
Forester, C. S. The last nine days of the Bismarck
Forester, C. S. Lieutenant Hornblower
Forester, C. S. Lord Hornblower
Forester, C. S. Ship of the line
Forester, C. S. To the Indies
Forsyth, F. The day of the jackal
Forsyth, F. The whispering wind
Gatewood, R. The sound of the trees
Gear, K. O. People of the masks
Gear, K. O. People of the mist
Gear, K. O. People of the silence
Gilman, D. The amazing Mrs. Pollifax
Gilman, D. Caravan
Gilman, D. The elusive Mrs. Pollifax
Gilman, D. Mrs. Pollifax and the Hong Kong Buddha
Gilman, D. Mrs. Pollifax on safari
Gilman, D. A palm for Mrs. Pollifax
Gilman, D. The unexpected Mrs. Pollifax
Graham, W. The twisted sword
Greene, G. Our man in Havana
Greene, G. Travels with my aunt
Grimes, M. Biting the moon
Grisham, J. The testament
Haggard, H. R. King Solomon's mines
Haggard, H. R. She
Harrison, H. King and emperor
Harrison, H. One king's way
Harrison, H. The Stainless Steel Rat joins the circus
Harrison, H. The Stainless Steel Rat sings the blues
Hesse, H. Narcissus and Goldmund
Higgins, J. Flight of eagles
Higgins, J. Storm warning
Hilton, J. Lost horizon
Hoffman, A. The probable future
Holland, C. The angel and the sword
Holland, C. The firedrake
Holland, C. Jerusalem
Hope, A. The prisoner of Zenda
Horgan, P. A distant trumpet
Hughes, R. A. W. A high wind in Jamaica
Innes, H. The wreck of the Mary Deare
Jakes, J. American dreams
Jakes, J. California gold
Jennings, G. Raptor
Johnston, T. C. Cry of the hawk
Johnston, T. C. Dance on the wind
Johnston, T. C. Death rattle
Johnston, T. C. Dream catcher
Johnston, T. C. Wind walker
Johnston, T. C. Winter rain
Jones, D. C. This savage race
Kay, G. G. The last light of the sun
Kaye, M. M. Trade wind
Kelton, E. The way of the coyote
Keneally, T. To Asmara
Lackey, M. Firebird
Lambdin, D. King's captain
L'Amour, L. Last of the breed
L'Amour, L. May there be a road
L'Amour, L. Off the Mangrove Coast
L'Amour, L. The walking drum
Leonard, E. Cuba libre
Llywelyn, M. Druids
Llywelyn, M. The last prince of Ireland
Llywelyn, M. Pride of lions
Llywelyn, M. Red Branch
London, J. The Sea-Wolf
Ludlum, R. The Bourne identity
Ludlum, R. The Bourne supremacy
Ludlum, R. The Bourne ultimatum
Lustbader, E. V. Floating city
Lustbader, E. V. Second skin
Lustbader, E. V. White Ninja
MacInnes, H. Above suspicion
MacInnes, H. The Venetian affair
MacLean, A. Force 10 from Navarone
MacLean, A. The guns of Navarone
MacLean, A. Ice Station Zebra
MacLean, A. Night without end
MacLean, A. When eight bells toll
Martel, Y. Life of Pi
Martin, W. Cape Cod
McCammon, R. R. Gone south
McCutchan, P. Apprentice to the sea
McCutchan, P. Cameron's crossing
McCutchan, P. The last farewell
McCutchan, P. The new lieutenant
McCutchan, P. The second mate
McDevitt, J. Eternity road
McDonald, R. Mr. Darwin's shooter
McMurtry, L. Comanche moon
McMurtry, L. Dead man's walk
McMurtry, L. Lonesome dove
McMurtry, L. Streets of Laredo
Michener, J. A. Alaska
Michener, J. A. Caravans
Michener, J. A. Caribbean
Michener, J. A. The drifters
Michener, J. A. Hawaii
Morrell, D. Assumed identity
Murphy, G. The Indian lover

AFRICA—20th century—*Continued*
Cook, R. Chromosome 6
Cussler, C. Sahara
Greene, G. A burnt-out case
Lessing, D. M. The golden notebook
Lessing, D. M. The sweetest dream
Naipaul, V. S. A bend in the river
Smith, W. A. Elephant song

Native peoples

See also Ibo (African people); Zulus (African people)
Bellow, S. Henderson the rain king
Hulme, K. The nun's story
Ruark, R. Uhuru
Smith, W. A. Men of men
Timm, U. Morenga

Politics

See Politics—Africa

Race relations

Gordimer, N. A guest of honor

AFRICA, CENTRAL *See* Central Africa
AFRICA, EAST *See* East Africa
AFRICA, GERMAN EAST *See* East Africa
AFRICA, SOUTH *See* South Africa
AFRICA, SOUTHERN *See* Southern Africa
AFRICA, WEST *See* West Africa

AFRICAN AMERICAN SERVANTS
Epstein, L. San Remo Drive
Watson, B. The heaven of Mercury

AFRICAN AMERICAN SOLDIERS
Carter, V. O. Such sweet thunder
Katzenbach, J. Hart's war

AFRICAN AMERICAN WOMEN
Cooper, J. C. The future has a past

AFRICAN AMERICANS
See also African American servants; African American soldiers; African American women; Blacks; Mulattoes; Slavery
Ansa, T. M. You know better
Baldwin, J. Early novels and stories
Baldwin, J. Going to meet the man
Baldwin, J. Just above my head
Bambara, T. C. Gorilla, my love
Barrett, W. E. The lilies of the field
Bohjalian, C. A. The buffalo soldier
Busch, F. The night inspector
Callahan, J. F. Flying home and other stories
Calling the wind
Campbell, B. M. Brothers and sisters
Campbell, B. M. Singing in the comeback choir
Campbell, B. M. What you owe me
Campbell, B. M. Your blues ain't like mine
Card, O. S. Magic street
Carter, S. L. The emperor of Ocean Park
Chesnutt, C. W. Stories, novels, & essay
Cleage, P. Babylon sisters
Cooper, J. C. The wake of the wind
Crafts, H. The bondswomans narrative
Dexter, P. Train
Doctorow, E. L. Ragtime
Dodd, S. M. Ethiopia
Doig, I. Prairie nocturne
Dove, R. Through the ivory gate
Dry, R. Leaving
Due, T. My soul to keep
Durham, D. A. Gabriel's story
Durham, D. A. A walk through darkness
Estleman, L. D. Black powder, white smoke
Fairbairn, A. Five smooth stones
Faulkner, W. The reivers
Gaines, E. J. The autobiography of Miss Jane Pittman
Gibbons, K. On the occasion of my last afternoon
Gurganus, A. Saint monster
Haley, A. Mama Flora's family
Harris, E. L. And this too shall pass
Harris, E. L. If this world were mine
Harris, E. L. Not a day goes by
Harris, M. Bang the drum slowly
Haynes, D. The full Matilda
Himes, C. The collected stories of Chester Himes
Hughes, L. Laughing to keep from crying
Hughes, L. Not without laughter
Hughes, L. Short stories of Langston Hughes
Hughes, L. Simple speaks his mind
Hughes, L. Simple stakes a claim
Hughes, L. Simple takes a wife
Hughes, L. Simple's Uncle Sam
Hurston, Z. N. The complete stories
Hurston, Z. N. Jonah's gourd vine
Hurston, Z. N. Moses, man of the mountain
Hurston, Z. N. Novels and stories
Hurston, Z. N. Their eyes were watching God
Joe, Y. My fine lady
Jones, E. P. The known world
Kidd, S. M. The secret life of bees
Lee, H. To kill a mockingbird
Lewis, W. H. I got somebody in Staunton
Mansbach, A. Shackling water
Marshall, P. Daughters
Marshall, P. Praisesong for the widow
Martin, V. Property
McCullers, C. Clock without hands
McCullers, C. The member of the wedding
McMillan, T. A day late and a dollar short
McMillan, T. How Stella got her groove back
McMillan, T. Waiting to exhale
Mitcham, J. Sabbath Creek
Morrison, T. Jazz
Morrison, T. Love
Morrison, T. Song of Solomon
Morrison, T. Tar baby
Mosley, W. The man in my basement
Mosley, W. RL's dream
Naylor, G. Bailey's Café
Naylor, G. Linden Hills
Naylor, G. Mama Day
Naylor, G. The men of Brewster Place
Naylor, G. The women of Brewster Place
Parks, G. The learning tree
Parks, S.-L. Getting mother's body
Petry, A. L. The street
Phillips, C. Crossing the river
Phillips, C. Dancing in the dark
Powers, R. The time of our singing
Price, R. The good priest's son
Price, R. Clockers
Reed, I. Japanese by spring
Roth, P. The human stain
Rush, N. Mortals
Sanders, D. Clover
Shange, N. Sassafrass, Cypress & Indigo
Sinclair, A. Ain't gonna be the same fool twice
The Sleeper wakes
Smith, L. E. Strange fruit
Southgate, M. The fall of Rome
Spencer, S. A ship made of paper
Stowe, H. B. Uncle Tom's cabin
Styron, W. The confessions of Nat Turner
The Unforgetting heart: an anthology of short stories by African American women (1859-1993)
Unsworth, B. Sacred hunger
Vernon, O. Eden
Walker, A. By the light of my father's smile
Walker, A. Possessing the secret of joy
Walker, A. The temple of my familiar
Walker, A. The way forward is with a broken heart
Walker, A. You can't keep a good woman down
Walker, M. Jubilee
Wallace, I. The man
Whitehead, C. The intuitionist
Whitehead, C. John Henry Days
Wideman, J. E. God's gym
Wideman, J. E. Philadelphia fire
Wideman, J. E. The stories of John Edgar Wideman
Willard, T. Buffalo soldiers
Wolfe, T. A man in full
Wright, R. Eight men
Wright, R. Native son
Wright, R. The outsider
Wright, R. Uncle Tom's children
Wright, R. Works
Youmans, M. The wolf pit

Agatha Raisin and the wizard of Evesham. Beaton, M. C.
The **age** of discretion. Beauvoir, S. d.
In Beauvoir, S. d. The woman destroyed p9-85
The **age** of grief. Smiley, J.
The **age** of grief [novelette] Smiley, J.
In Smiley, J. The age of grief p119-213
The **age** of innocence. Wharton, E.
also in Wharton, E. New York novels p689-958
also in Wharton, E. Novels
Age of iron. Coetzee, J. M.
The **age** of miracles. Gilchrist, E.
The **age** of reason. Sartre, J. P.
AGED *See* Old age
The **agent**. Higgins, G. V.
AGENTS, SECRET *See* Spies

AGING
Gerritsen, T. Life support

AGNOSTICISM
Joyce, J. A portrait of the artist as a young man
The **agony** and the ecstasy. Stone, I.

AGORAPHOBIA
Reynolds, M. The Starlite Drive-in
The **Aguero** sisters. García, C.
Ah, but your land is beautiful. Paton, A.
Ah, sweet mystery of life. Dahl, R.
Ah, treachery! Thomas, R.
Ahab's wife; or, The star-gazer. Naslund, S. J.
Aiding and abetting. Spark, M.

AIDS (DISEASE)
Barker, C. Sacrament
Bellow, S. Ravelstein
Burke, S. Safelight
Cleage, P. What looks like crazy on an ordinary day—
Cunningham, M. The hours
Gaitskill, M. Veronica
Hoffman, A. At risk
Monette, P. Afterlife
Peterson, P. W. Women in the grove
Price, R. The promise of rest
Self, W. Dorian
Tóibín, C. The blackwater lightship
Vollmann, W. T. Butterfly stories
White, E. The married man
Ain't gonna be the same fool twice. Sinclair, A.
Ain't she sweet. Phillips, S. E.
Air Battle Force. Brown, D.
AIR CRASHES *See* Airplane accidents

AIR MAIL SERVICE
Saint-Exupéry, A. d. Night flight

AIR PILOTS
Bates, H. E. Fair stood the wind for France
Brown, D. Air Battle Force
Brown, D. Chains of command
Brown, D. Shadows of steel
Brown, D. Warrior class
Brown, D. Wings of fire
Coonts, S. Final flight
Coonts, S. Flight of the Intruder
Coonts, S. Fortunes of war
Coonts, S. The Intruders
Coonts, S. The minotaur
Francis, D. Rat race
Gann, E. K. The high and the mighty
Griffin, W. E. B. The aviators
Griffin, W. E. B. By order of the President
Heller, J. Catch-22
Higgins, J. Flight of eagles
Jakes, J. American dreams
L'Amour, L. Last of the breed
Michener, J. A. The bridges at Toko-ri
Michener, J. A. Sayonara
Nance, J. J. Fire flight
Nance, J. J. The last hostage
Nance, J. J. Medusa's child
Rice, L. Cloud Nine
Saint-Exupéry, A. d. The little prince
Saint-Exupéry, A. d. Night flight
Shreve, A. The pilot's wife
Shreve, A. Resistance
Spencer, J. The pilots
Steel, D. Lone eagle
Thomas, C. Firefox
Watkins, P. In the blue light of African dreams

AIR TRAVEL
Follett, K. Night over water
Gann, E. K. The high and the mighty
AIR WARFARE *See* Military aeronautics; World War, 1939-1945—Aerial operations

AIRCRAFT CARRIERS
Michener, J. A. The bridges at Toko-ri
Airframe. Crichton, M.

AIRLINES
See also Airports

Flight attendants

See Flight attendants
AIRMEN *See* Air pilots

AIRPLANE ACCIDENTS
Crichton, M. Airframe
Koontz, D. R. Sole survivor
AIRPLANE CARRIERS *See* Aircraft carriers

AIRPLANES
See also Transport planes
Follett, K. Night over water
Nance, J. J. Pandora's clock
Thomas, C. Firefox

Accidents

See Airplane accidents

Pilots

See Air pilots
Airport. Hailey, A.

AIRPORTS
Glendinning, V. Flight
Hailey, A. Airport
Airs above the ground. Stewart, M.

AKHENATON, KING OF EGYPT, FL. CA. 1388-1358 B.C.

About

Tarr, J. Pillar of fire

ALABAMA
Battle, L. The Florabama Ladies' Auxiliary & Sewing Circle
Capote, T. A Christmas memory
Childress, M. Crazy in Alabama
Cook, T. H. Breakheart Hill
Flagg, F. Fried green tomatoes at the Whistle-Stop Cafe
Franklin, T. Hell at the breech
Kincaid, N. Verbena
Lee, H. To kill a mockingbird
McCammon, R. R. Boy's life
Wallace, D. The Watermelon King

Birmingham

Naslund, S. J. Four spirits

Mobile

Kerley, J. The hundredth man

Montgomery

Brown, R. M. Southern discomfort

ALAMO (SAN ANTONIO, TEX.)

Siege, 1836

Harrigan, S. The gates of the Alamo
Alas, Babylon. Frank, P.

ALASKA
Boyle, T. C. Drop City
Brand, M. Chinook
Kantner, S. Ordinary wolves
Kesey, K. Sailor song
Michener, J. A. Alaska

Frontier and pioneer life

See Frontier and pioneer life—Alaska

Anchorage

Harrison, K. The seal wife
Alaska. Michener, J. A.

TITLE AND SUBJECT INDEX

ALLEGORIES—*Continued*
Beagle, P. S. The unicorn sonata
Bradley, M. Z. The firebrand
Brooks, T. The sword of Shannara
Bunyan, J. The pilgrim's progress
Caldwell, T. Ceremony of the innocent
Calvino, I. Mr. Palomar
Camus, A. The fall
Cheever, J. Oh, what a paradise it seems
Coetzee, J. M. Life & times of Michael K.
De Lint, C. Trader
Drabble, M. The witch of Exmoor
Elkin, S. Stanley Elkin's The magic kingdom
Ellison, H. The deathbird
Faulkner, W. A fable
Flanagan, R. Gould's book of fish
García Márquez, G. The autumn of the patriarch
García Márquez, G. One hundred years of solitude
Gardner, J. Grendel
Gardner, J. The sunlight dialogues
Golding, W. Darkness visible
Golding, W. The inheritors
Golding, W. Lord of the Flies
Golding, W. The scorpion god: three short novels
Grass, G. Cat and mouse
Grass, G. The flounder
Hansen, E. F. Tales of protection
Hesse, H. Narcissus and Goldmund
Hesse, H. Siddhartha
Hoban, R. Riddley Walker
Hoban, R. Turtle diary
Hrabal, B. Too loud a solitude
Irving, J. A prayer for Owen Meany
Kadare, I. Spring flowers, spring frost
Kafka, F. The castle
Kafka, F. The trial
King, S. The stand
Krüger, M. The cello player
Le Guin, U. K. The beginning place
Lessing, D. M. Shikasta
Lewis, C. S. Out of the silent planet
Lewis, C. S. Perelandra
Lewis, C. S. That hideous strength
Lewis, C. S. Till we have faces
Maḥfūẓ, N. Children of the alley
Malamud, B. Dubin's lives
Malamud, B. The natural
Martin, V. Mary Reilly
Melville, H. Mardi: and a voyager thither
Murdoch, I. The green knight
Oates, J. C. Black water
O'Connor, F. The violent bear it away
Ōe, K. Nip the buds, shoot the kids
Orwell, G. Animal farm
Ozick, C. The Messiah of Stockholm
Percy, W. Lancelot
Porter, K. A. Ship of fools
Powers, R. Operation wandering soul
Robbins, T. Jitterbug perfume
Robbins, T. Still life with Woodpecker
Rushdie, S. Haroun and the sea of stories
Rushdie, S. Midnight's children
Rushdie, S. Shame
Saint-Exupéry, A. d. The little prince
Saramago, J. All the names
Saramago, J. Blindness
Saramago, J. The cave
Silko, L. Gardens in the dunes
Stevenson, R. L. The strange case of Dr. Jekyll and Mr. Hyde
Tepper, S. S. The visitor
Theroux, P. The Mosquito Coast
Tolkien, J. R. R. The fellowship of the ring
Tolkien, J. R. R. The hobbit
Tolkien, J. R. R. The lord of the rings
Tolkien, J. R. R. The return of the king
Tolkien, J. R. R. The Silmarillion
Tolkien, J. R. R. The two towers
Updike, J. Brazil
Updike, J. The witches of Eastwick
Whitehead, C. The intuitionist
Wiggins, M. John Dollar
Wilde, O. The picture of Dorian Gray

Alley Kat blues. Kijewski, K.
Almayer's folly. Conrad, J.
In Conrad, J. Tales of the East and West p1-128
Almost. Benedict, E.
Almost paradise. Isaacs, S.
Almost perfect. Adams, A.
An **almost** perfect moment. Kirshenbaum, B.
Almost the truth. Yorke, M.
Aloft. Lee, C.-R.
Alone. Gardner, L.
Along came a spider. Patterson, J.
Alphabet of thorn. McKillip, P. A.

ALPS
Johnson, D. L'affaire
Mann, T. The magic mountain
Mawer, S. The fall

The **altar** of the body. Brenna, D.
Altered carbon. Morgan, R. K.
Altered states. Brookner, A.
Altered states. Chayefsky, P.

ALUMNI, COLLEGE *See* College alumni

Alva & Irva. Carey, E.
Alvin Journeyman. Card, O. S.
Always a body to trade. Constantine, K. C.
Always outnumbered, always outgunned. Mosley, W.

ALZHEIMER'S DISEASE
Cumyn, A. Losing it
Gutcheon, B. R. Five fortunes
Hays, T. The pleasure was mine
Sparks, N. The notebook

Amagansett. Mills, M.
The **amateur** marriage. Tyler, A.

AMATEUR THEATRICALS
House, T. The beginning of calamities

The **amazing** adventures of Kavalier and Clay. Chabon, M.
The **amazing** Mrs. Pollifax. Gilman, D.

AMAZON RIVER VALLEY
Cussler, C. Inca gold
Hamilton-Paterson, J. Gerontius
Walker, A. Now is the time to open your heart

AMBASSADORS *See* Diplomatic life

The **ambassadors**. James, H.

Amber [series]
Zelazny, R. Blood of Amber
Zelazny, R. The courts of chaos
Zelazny, R. The hand of Oberon
Zelazny, R. Nine princes in Amber
Zelazny, R. Trumps of doom

AMBITION
See also Self-made men
Archer, J. As the crow flies
Archer, J. First among equals
Archer, J. The fourth estate
Archer, J. Kane & Abel
Archer, J. The prodigal daughter
Auchincloss, L. Her infinite variety
Bradford, B. T. Hold the dream
Bradford, B. T. A woman of substance
Caldwell, T. Captains and kings
Carter, S. L. The emperor of Ocean Park
Cookson, C. The obsession
Crichton, R. The Camerons
Daley, R. Wall of brass
Delderfield, R. F. God is an Englishman
Dexter, P. The paperboy
Dunne, D. The two Mrs. Grenvilles
Fuentes, C. The death of Artemio Cruz
Greeley, A. M. Thy brother's wife
Jakes, J. California gold
Laker, R. Banners of silk
Marsh, J. The House of Eliott
Millhauser, S. Martin Dressler
Plain, B. Fortune
Rand, A. The fountainhead
Ridley, J. A conversation with the Mann
Ross-Macdonald, M. The rich are with you always
Ross-Macdonald, M. Tamsin Harte
Ross-Macdonald, M. The world from rough stones
Schulberg, B. What makes Sammy run?
Stendhal. The red and the black
Trollope, A. The Eustace diamonds

TITLE AND SUBJECT INDEX

AMERICANS—France—*Continued*
Daley, R. The innocents within
Daley, R. Nowhere to run
Highsmith, P. The talented Mr. Ripley
James, H. The ambassadors
James, H. The American
James, H. Madame de Mauves
Johnson, D. Le divorce
Johnson, D. L'affaire
Johnson, D. Le mariage
Krantz, J. Mistral's daughter
Marshall, P. The fisher king
Mathews, H. My life in CIA
Miller, H. Tropic of Cancer
Nin, A. Children of the albatross
Nin, A. The four-chambered heart
Nin, A. Ladders to fire
Shaw, I. Evening in Byzantium
Steel, D. Sunset in St. Tropez
Truong, M. T. D. The book of salt
Watkins, P. The forger
Welch, J. The heartsong of Charging Elk
Wharton, E. Madame de Treymes
White, E. The married man

Germany

Barnes, D. Nightwood
Berger, T. Crazy in Berlin
Buckley, W. F. Nuremberg
Carroll, J. Secret father
Deaver, J. Garden of beasts
Ford, R. The student conductor
Isaacs, S. Shining through
Just, W. S. The weather in Berlin
Kanon, J. The good German
O'Connor, R. Buffalo soldiers
Thayer, J. S. Five past midnight
Uris, L. Armageddon
Vonnegut, K. Slaughterhouse-five

Guatemala

Henley, P. Hummingbird house

Honduras

Theroux, P. The Mosquito Coast

Hong Kong

Coonts, S. Hong Kong

Hungary

Phillips, A. Prague

India

Bacon, C. There is room for you
Bromfield, L. The rains came
Mukherjee, B. The holder of the world

Ireland

Binchy, M. Firefly summer
Binchy, M. Tara Road
Donleavy, J. P. The ginger man
Gordon, M. Pearl
Labiner, N. Miniatures
Lordan, B. But come ye back
Watkins, P. The promise of light
Weber, K. The Music Lesson

Islands of the Pacific

Melville, H. Omoo: a narrative of adventures in the South Seas
Spencer, J. The pilots

Israel

Leonard, E. The hunted
Miller, R. Welcome to Heavenly Heights
Stone, R. Damascus Gate
Uris, L. Exodus

Italy

Greeley, A. M. Irish stew!
Grisham, J. The broker
Hawthorne, N. The marble faun
Hayter, S. Bandit queen boogie
Hemingway, E. Across the river and into the trees
Hemingway, E. A farewell to arms
Howells, W. D. A foregone conclusion
Howells, W. D. Indian summer
James, H. The Aspern papers
James, H. Daisy Miller
James, H. Roderick Hudson
Leonard, E. Pronto
Lieberman, H. H. The girl with Botticelli eyes
Martin, M. Vatican
Martin, V. Italian fever
Rabb, J. The book of Q
Scott, J. Tourmaline
Siddons, A. R. Hill towns
Spencer, E. Knights and dragons
Spencer, E. The light in the piazza
Styron, W. Set this house on fire
Williams, T. The Roman spring of Mrs. Stone

Jamaica

Tolkin, M. Under radar

Japan

Bird, S. The Yokota Officers Club
Dickey, J. To the white sea
Lee, D. Country of origin
Murakami, R. In the miso soup
Smith, M. C. December 6

Marquesas Islands

Melville, H. Typee: a peep at Polynesian life

Mexico

Doerr, H. Consider this, señora
Doerr, H. Stones for Ibarra
Fuentes, C. Apollo and the whores
Fuentes, C. Diana, the goddess who hunts alone
Fuentes, C. The old gringo
Hambly, B. Days of the dead
Hansen, R. Atticus
Johansen, I. And then you die—
Michener, J. A. Mexico
Morrell, D. Assumed identity
Nin, A. Seduction of the Minotaur
Portis, C. Gringos
Traven, B. The treasure of the Sierra Madre

Middle East

Bromell, H. Little America

North Africa

Bowles, P. Let it come down
Bowles, P. The sheltering sky

Okinawa

Sneider, V. The Teahouse of the August Moon

Peru

Lynn, A. Now you see it

Portugal

L'Engle, M. The love letters

Romania

Wiesel, E. The forgotten

Russia

Buckley, W. F. Last call for Blackford Oakes
D'Amato, B. White male infant
DeMille, N. The charm school
Freemantle, B. The button man
Harris, R. Archangel
L'Amour, L. Last of the breed
Shonk, K. The red passport

Rwanda

Leonard, E. Pagan babies

Scotland

Peters, E. Legend in green velvet

Serbia

West, F. J. The Pepperdogs

Sicily

Hersey, J. A bell for Adano

Singapore

Clavell, J. King Rat

Southeast Asia

Lederer, W. J. The ugly American

TITLE AND SUBJECT INDEX

ANGLO-SAXONS
Gardner, J. Grendel
Rathbone, J. The last English king
Sutcliff, R. Sword at sunset
The **angry** tide. Graham, W.
Anil's ghost. Ondaatje, M.
ANIMAL ABUSE *See* Animal welfare
Animal crackers. Tinti, H.
Animal dreams. Kingsolver, B.
Animal farm. Orwell, G.
ANIMAL WELFARE
Coetzee, J. M. Disgrace
Pelecanos, G. P. Drama city
Yorke, M. A question of belief
The **animal** wife. Thomas, E. M.
ANIMALS
See also names of individual animals
Burnford, S. Bel Ria
Burnford, S. The incredible journey
Goethe, J. W. v. Novella
Grimes, M. Biting the moon
Irving, J. Setting free the bears
Michener, J. A. Creatures of the kingdom
Orwell, G. Animal farm
Wells, H. G. The island of Doctor Moreau
White, T. H. The book of Merlyn
Wodehouse, P. G. A Wodehouse bestiary

Treatment

See Animal welfare
Anja the liar. Moran, T.
ANN ARBOR (MICH.) *See* Michigan—Ann Arbor
Anna Karenina. Tolstoy, L., graf
The **annals** of the Heechee. Pohl, F.
ANNAPOLIS (MD.) *See* Maryland—Annapolis
Annapolis. Martin, W.
Anna's book. Vine, B.
ANNE, OF AUSTRIA, 1601-1666 *See* Anne, Queen, consort of Louis XIII, King of France, 1601-1666
ANNE, QUEEN, CONSORT OF LOUIS XIII, KING OF FRANCE, 1601-1666

About

Anthony, E. The Cardinal and the Queen
Dumas, A. Twenty years after
ANNE, QUEEN, CONSORT OF RICHARD III, KING OF ENGLAND, 1456-1485

About

Plaidy, J. The reluctant queen
ANNE BOLEYN, QUEEN, CONSORT OF HENRY VIII, KING OF ENGLAND, 1507-1536

About

Anthony, E. Anne Boleyn
Maxwell, R. The secret diary of Anne Boleyn
Plaidy, J. Murder most royal
Anne Boleyn. Anthony, E.
Annie Dunne. Barry, S.
Annie John. Kincaid, J.
The **anniversary** and other stories. Auchincloss, L.
The **Anodyne** Necklace. Grimes, M.
ANOREXIA NERVOSA
Levenkron, S. The best little girl in the world
O'Hagan, A. Personality
Another country. Baldwin, J.
also in Baldwin, J. Early novels and stories
Another world. Barker, P.
Another you. Beattie, A.
ANSON, GEORGE ANSON, BARON, 1697-1762

About

O'Brian, P. The golden ocean
Answer as a man. Caldwell, T.
Answered prayers. Capote, T.
ANTARCTIC REGIONS
See also Arctic regions
Bainbridge, B. The birthday boys
Cussler, C. Shock wave
Robinson, K. S. Antarctica
Antarctica. Robinson, K. S.
The **antelope** wife. Erdrich, L.
Anthem. Rand, A.
Anthony Adverse. Allen, H.
ANTHROPOLOGISTS
Calisher, H. Sunday Jews
Gear, W. M. Dark inheritance
Gear, W. M. Raising Abel
Jackson, S. The haunting of Hill House
Johnson, A. Parasites like us
Lively, P. Spiderweb
Ondaatje, M. Anil's ghost
Pym, B. An academic question
Pym, B. A few green leaves
Pym, B. An unsuitable attachment
Vanderbes, J. Easter Island
ANTIETAM, BATTLE OF, 1862
Reasoner, J. Antietam
Antietam. Reasoner, J.
ANTIGUA AND BARBUDA
Kincaid, J. Annie John
Kincaid, J. Mr. Potter
ANTIQUE DEALERS
See also Art dealers
Gash, J. The Vatican rip
McMurtry, L. Cadillac Jack
Pym, B. The sweet dove died
Welsh, L. The cutting room
ANTIQUES
Neville, K. The eight
Pye, M. The pieces from Berlin
ANTIQUITIES
See also Archeology
ANTISEMITISM
See also Holocaust, Jewish (1933-1945); Jews—Persecutions
Appelfeld, A. The conversion
Appelfeld, A. Katerina
Bassani, G. The garden of the Finzi-Continis
Baxter, C. Saul and Patsy
Begley, L. Schmidt delivered
Bellow, S. The victim
Busch, F. A handbook for spies
Follett, K. A dangerous fortune
Greenberg, J. I never promised you a rose garden
Hamill, P. Snow in August
Hobson, L. K. Z. Gentleman's agreement
Isaacs, S. Red, white and blue
Lipman, E. The Inn at Lake Devine
Malamud, B. The fixer
Oates, J. C. The tattooed girl
Pears, I. The dream of Scipio
Richler, M. Solomon Gursky was here
Roth, P. The plot against America
Schwarz-Bart, A. The last of the just
Thomas, M. M. Hanover Place
ANTOINETTE, JOS'EPHE JEANNE MARIE *See* Marie Antoinette, Queen, consort of Louis XVI, King of France, 1755-1793
ANTONIUS, MARCUS, CA. 83-30 B.C.

About

George, M. The memoirs of Cleopatra
Antrax. Brooks, T.
ANTS
Byatt, A. S. Morpho Eugenia
The **Anubis** slayings. Doherty, P. C.
Anvil of stars. Bear, G.
The **anvil** of the world. Baker, K.
ANXIETY *See* Fear
The **anxiety** of everyday objects. Sheehan, A.
Any human heart. Boyd, W.
Anything considered. Mayle, P.
Anything for Billy. McMurtry, L.
Anything goes. Bell, M. S.
Anything you say can and will be used against you. Drummond, L. L.
Anywhere but here. Simpson, M.
APACHE INDIANS
Fergus, J. The wild girl: the notebooks of Ned Giles, 1932
Gipson, F. B. Savage Sam
Littell, R. Walking back the cat
Rosenberg, R. This is not civilization

ARGENTINA—*Continued*

Buenos Aires

Cortázar, J. Hopscotch
Puig, M. Kiss of the spider woman
Saint-Exupéry, A. d. Night flight

ARGENTINE REPUBLIC *See* Argentina

ARGENTINES

Europe

Blasco Ibáñez, V. The four horsemen of the Apocalypse

France

Cortázar, J. Hopscotch

ARGENTINIANS *See* Argentines

Ariel's crossing. Morrow, B.

ARISTOCRACY

See also Courts and courtiers; Society novels
Roth, J. The bust of the emperor

England

Barnard, R. Corpse in a gilded cage
Colegate, I. The shooting party
Cookson, C. The glass virgin
Eden, D. The Salamanca drum
Hardwick, M. The Duchess of Duke Street
Heyer, G. Lady of quality
James, H. An international episode
James, H. Lady Barberina
Plaidy, J. The rose without a thorn
Riley, J. M. The serpent garden
Sackville-West, V. The Edwardians
Thackeray, W. M. The history of Henry Esmond, esquire
Wodehouse, P. G. The code of the Woosters
Wodehouse, P. G. Tales from the Drones Club

France

Dickens, C. A tale of two cities
Du Maurier, Dame D. The scapegoat
Haasse, H. S. In a dark wood wandering
James, H. The American
Laker, R. To dance with kings
Orczy, E., Baroness. Adventures of the Scarlet Pimpernel
Orczy, E., Baroness. The elusive Pimpernel
Orczy, E., Baroness. The Scarlet Pimpernel
Proust, M. The Guermantes way
Proust, M. Sodom and Gomorrah
Riley, J. M. The serpent garden
Stendhal. The red and the black

Italy

Bassani, G. The garden of the Finzi-Continis
Stendhal. The charterhouse of Parma

Japan

Mishima, Y. Spring snow

Poland

Bernstein, M. A. Conspirators

Russia

West, Dame R. The birds fall down

Sicily

Tomasi di Lampedusa, G. The Leopard

ARIZONA

See also Tonto Basin (Ariz.)
Abrahams, P. Their wildest dreams
Rosenberg, R. This is not civilization

19th century

Henry, W. Mackenna's gold
Horgan, P. A distant trumpet
Silko, L. Gardens in the dunes
Turner, N. E. These is my words

20th century

Jance, J. A. Kiss of the bees
Kingsolver, B. Animal dreams
Kingsolver, B. The bean trees
Kingsolver, B. Pigs in heaven
Mapson, J.-A. Loving Chloe

Frontier and pioneer life

See Frontier and pioneer life—Arizona

Phoenix

McMillan, T. Waiting to exhale

Tucson

Cullin, M. Undersurface
Kingsolver, B. Pigs in heaven

The **Arizona** clan. Grey, Z.

The **ark** builder. Potok, C.
In Potok, C. Old men at midnight

ARKANSAS

Harington, D. Ekaterina
Harington, D. With
Paddock, J. A secret word

19th century

Jones, D. C. Elkhorn Tavern
Jones, D. C. The search for Temperance Moon
Jones, D. C. This savage race

20th century

Grisham, J. A painted house
Hunter, S. Black light

Farm life

See Farm life—Arkansas

Frontier and pioneer life

See Frontier and pioneer life—Arkansas

Hot Springs

Hunter, S. Hot Springs

ARMADA, 1588

Finney, P. Gloriana's torch

Armadillo. Boyd, W.

Armageddon. Uris, L.

ARMAMENTS

See also Munitions

ARMED FORCES

United States

See United States—Armed forces

ARMENIAN GENOCIDE, 1915-1923 *See* Armenian massacres, 1915-1923

ARMENIAN MASSACRES, 1915-1923

Werfel, F. The forty days of Musa Dagh

ARMENIANS

Marcom, M. A. The daydreaming boy

Syria

Werfel, F. The forty days of Musa Dagh

ARMIES

See also Great Britain. Army

ARMS AND ARMOR

See also Munitions

Arms and the women. Hill, R.

ARMY AIR FORCES (U.S.) *See* United States. Army Air Forces

ARMY HOSPITALS *See* Hospitals and sanatoriums

An **army** of angels. Marcantel, P.

ARMY OFFICERS *See* Germany—Army—Officers; Peru—Army—Officers; Poland—Army—Officers; Russia—Army—Officers

ARNOLD, BENEDICT, 1741-1801

About

Roberts, K. L. Arundel
Roberts, K. L. Rabble in arms

Around the time of Clemente Colling. Hernández, F.
In Hernández, F. and Allen, E. Lands of memory

Around the world in eighty days. Verne, J.

Arrest Sitting Bull. Jones, D. C.

Arrowsmith. Lewis, S.
also in Lewis, S. Arrowsmith; Elmer Gantry; Dodsworth

Arrowsmith; Elmer Gantry; Dodsworth. Lewis, S.

ARSON

Ackroyd, P. The Clerkenwell tales
Chazin, S. Flashover
Emerson, E. W. Pyro
Emerson, E. W. Vertical burn
Hautman, P. Doohickey

Asleep [a novella] Yoshimoto, B.
In Yoshimoto, B. Asleep p105-77
The **Aspern** papers. James, H.
In James, H. Complete stories, 1884-1891
In James, H. The complete tales of Henry James
In James, H. The Henry James reader p165-254
In James, H. Short novels of Henry James p257-354
The **asphalt** jungle. Burnett, W. R.

ASSASSINATION
Anthony, E. The Janus imperative
Archer, J. The eleventh commandment
Bernstein, M. A. Conspirators
Bromell, H. Little America
Brown, D. Wings of fire
Buckley, W. F. Last call for Blackford Oakes
Buckley, W. F. Mongoose, R.I.P
Carr, P. The black swan
Clancy, T. Red rabbit
Coonts, S. Under siege
Costello, M. Big if
Deaver, J. Garden of beasts
Egleton, C. Hostile intent
Ellroy, J. The cold six thousand
Follett, K. The man from St. Petersburg
Folsom, A. R. The day after tomorrow
Folsom, A. R. Day of confession
Forsyth, F. The day of the jackal
Forsyth, F. The dogs of war
Friedman, B. J. A father's kisses
Griffin, W. E. B. Blood and honor
Griffin, W. E. B. Secret honor
Grisham, J. The pelican brief
Higgins, J. The eagle has flown
Higgins, J. Edge of danger
Higgins, J. Eye of the storm
Higgins, J. Touch the devil
Higgins, J. The White House connection
Hunter, S. Havana
Hunter, S. Time to hunt
Ludlum, R. The apocalypse watch
Ludlum, R. The scorpio illusion
Lustbader, E. V. Dark homecoming
Milligan, J. Jack Fish
Mishima, Y. Runaway horses
Morrell, D. The brotherhood of the rose
Perry, T. The butcher's boy
Perry, T. Sleeping dogs
Shelby, P. Days of drums
Shelby, P. Gatekeeper
Silva, D. The marching season
Thayer, J. S. Five past midnight
Trevanian. The Eiger sanction
Trevanian. Shibumi
Westlake, D. E. Money for nothing
Woods, S. Dirty work
Woods, S. The run
The **assassination** of Jesse James by the coward Robert Ford. Hansen, R.
ASSASSINATIONS SELECT COMMITTEE *See* United States. Congress. House. Select Committee on Assassinations
Assault with intent. Kienzle, W. X.
The **assistant**. Malamud, B.
also in Malamud, B. A Malamud reader p75-305
Assumed identity. Morrell, D.
Asta's book. See Vine, B. Anna's book
Asteroid wars [series]
Bova, B. The precipice

ASTEROIDS
Pohl, F. Beyond the blue event horizon
Pohl, F. Gateway
Pohl, F. Heechee rendezvous
Astonishing splashes of colour. Morrall, C.
Astraea. See Stevenson, J. The winter queen

ASTROLOGERS
Goldstein, L. The alchemist's door

ASTRONAUTS
Gerritsen, T. Gravity
Michener, J. A. Space
Sher, I. Gentlemen of space
Tiptree, J. Houston, Houston, do you read?

ASTRONOMERS
Greer, A. S. The path of minor planets
Hazzard, S. The transit of Venus
Mallon, T. Two moons
Redfern, E. The music of the spheres

ASTROPHYSICISTS
Bova, B. Jupiter
Asylum. McGrath, P.
At Bertram's Hotel. Christie, A.
At end of day. Higgins, G. V.
At home in Thrush Green. Read, Miss
At Lady Molly's. Powell, A.
In Powell, A. A dance to the music of time
At risk. Hoffman, A.
At swim, two boys. O'Neill, J.
At the Jim Bridger. Carlson, R.
At the mountains of madness, and other novels. Lovecraft, H. P.
At the sign of the Cat and Racket. Balzac, H. d.
In Balzac, H. d. The short novels of Balzac
At weddings and wakes. McDermott, A.

ATATÜRK, KEMAL, 1881-1938
About
De Bernieres, L. Birds without wings

ATHEISM
Ackroyd, P. The Clerkenwell tales
Wood, J. The book against God
Athena. Banville, J.
ATHENS (GREECE) *See* Greece—Athens

ATHLETES
Abrahams, P. The fan
Coldsmith, D. The long journey home
Lupica, M. Wild pitch
Patterson, J. Hide & seek
ATLANTA (GA.) *See* Georgia—Atlanta
ATLANTIC CITY (N.J.) *See* New Jersey—Atlantic City
ATLANTIC OCEAN
World War, 1939-1945
See World War, 1939-1945—Atlantic Ocean

ATLANTIS
Cussler, C. Atlantis found
Milligan, J. Jack Fish
Atlantis found. Cussler, C.
Atlas shrugged. Rand, A.

ATOMIC BOMB
Bock, D. The ash garden
Burdick, E. Fail-safe
Clancy, T. The sum of all fears
Collins, L. The fifth horseman
Cussler, C. Dragon
Follett, K. Triple
Golding, W. Lord of the Flies
Griffin, W. E. B. The last heroes
Griffin, W. E. B. The secret warriors
Griffin, W. E. B. The soldier spies
Kanon, J. Los Alamos
Krauss, N. Man walks into a room
McMahon, T. A. Principles of American nuclear chemistry
Smith, M. C. Stallion Gate
Snow, C. P. The new men
Strieber, W. Warday
Vonnegut, K. Cat's cradle
Wenner, K. Dancing with Einstein
Wibberley, L. The mouse that roared
Wiggins, M. Evidence of things unseen
ATOMIC ENERGY *See* Nuclear energy
ATOMIC SUBMARINES *See* Nuclear submarines
ATOMIC WARFARE *See* Nuclear warfare

ATONEMENT
Greene, G. Brighton rock
Haynes, M. Chalktown
Howatch, S. The heartbreaker
Atonement. McEwan, I.

ATROCITIES
See also Holocaust, Jewish (1933-1945); Jews—Persecutions; Massacres; Torture; World War, 1939-1945—Atrocities

AUSTRIAN SOLDIERS *See* Soldiers—Austria

AUSTRIANS

England

Goudge, E. The heart of the family

Yugoslavia

Handke, P. Repetition

The **author** of "Beltraffio". James, H.
In James, H. Complete stories, 1874-1884
In James, H. The complete tales of Henry James
In James, H. The Henry James reader

AUTHORITARIANISM *See* Totalitarianism

AUTHORS

See also Art critics; Authorship; Dramatists; Poets; Women authors names of individual authors, dramatists, poets, etc.

Abrahams, P. Their wildest dreams
Ames, J. Wake up, sir!
Amis, M. The information
Auster, P. The book of illusions
Auster, P. Leviathan
Auster, P. Oracle night
Ballard, J. G. The kindness of women
Banville, J. Ghosts
Barth, J. Coming soon!!!
Barth, J. The last voyage of somebody the sailor
Barth, J. The Tidewater tales
Baxter, C. The feast of love
Bellow, S. Humboldt's gift
Bellow, S. Ravelstein
Bellow, S. What kind of day did you have?
Berger, T. Being invisible
Block, L. Small town
Boswell, R. Century's son
Boyd, W. Any human heart
Boyle, T. C. East is East
Bradbury, M. To the Hermitage
Bradbury, R. Green shadows, white whale
Brockmeier, K. The truth about Celia
Brown, S. Charade
Bryan, M. The afterword
Bulgakov, M. A. The master and Margarita
Burgess, A. Earthly powers
Byatt, A. S. Babel Tower
Byatt, A. S. The biographer's tale
Cameron, P. The city of your final destination
Capote, T. Answered prayers
Carey, P. Jack Maggs
Chabon, M. Wonder boys
Chalmers, R. Who's who in hell
Clark, M. H. The Anastasia syndrome
Coe, J. The closed circle
Coetzee, J. M. The master of Petersburg
Colette. Claudine married
Conroy, P. Beach music
Cook, T. H. Evidence of blood
Cook, T. H. Instruments of night
Davies, R. What's bred in the bone
Dixon, S. Frog
Dixon, S. Gould
Dixon, S. Old friends
Doctorow, E. L. Lives of the poets [novelette]
Dodd, S. M. Ethiopia
Drabble, M. The gates of ivory
Dunne, J. G. Playland
Dunne, J. G. The red, white, and blue
Dunning, J. Two o'clock, eastern wartime
Durrell, L. Balthazar
Durrell, L. Clea
Ellis, B. E. Lunar Park
Endō, S. Scandal
Estleman, L. D. Sudden country
Fast, H. Citizen Tom Paine
Foer, J. S. Everything is illuminated
Fowles, J. Daniel Martin
Freeling, N. One more river
Fuentes, C. Diana, the goddess who hunts alone
Furst, A. Blood of victory
Gaddis, W. A frolic of his own
Geary, J. M. Spiral
Gide, A. The counterfeiters (Les faux-monnayeurs)
Godwin, G. The good husband
Godwin, G. Mr. Bedford
Golding, W. The paper men
Greene, G. The end of the affair
Greene, G. The honorary consul
Grimes, M. Foul matter
Groom, W. Such a pretty, pretty girl
Hamilton-Paterson, J. Loving monsters
Hammett, D. Tulip
Handke, P. My year in the no-man's-bay
Harrison, J. I forgot to go to Spain
Hassler, J. Rookery blues
Heller, J. Good as Gold
Heller, J. Portrait of an artist, as an old man
Helprin, M. Ellis Island
Hemingway, E. True at first light
Hofmann, G. Lichtenberg and the little flower girl
Hofmann, G. Luck
Hosseini, K. The kite runner
Irving, J. The world according to Garp
James, H. The Aspern papers
James, H. The author of "Beltraffio"
Jance, J. A. Kiss of the bees
Johnston, W. Human amusements
Keillor, G. Love me
Keneally, T. The tyrant's novel
Kinder, C. Honeymooners
King, S. Bag of bones
King, S. The dark half
King, S. Desperation
King, S. Misery
King, S. Salem's Lot
Kotzwinkle, W. The bear went over the mountain
Krauss, N. The history of love
Kundera, M. Slowness
Labiner, N. Miniatures
Leavitt, D. The body of Jonah Boyd
Leavitt, D. Martin Bauman
Leavitt, D. While England sleeps
Lelchuk, A. Ziff
Lodge, D. Therapy
Lodge, D. Thinks—
London, J. Martin Eden
Lopez, B. H. Resistance
Mailer, N. Tough guys don't dance
Malamud, B. Dubin's lives
Malamud, B. The tenants
Mann, T. Death in Venice
Markson, D. Vanishing point
Matheson, R. Hunted past reason
Mathews, H. My life in CIA
Maugham, W. S. Cakes and ale
McCauley, S. True enough
McEwan, I. The child in time
Michener, J. A. The novel
Miller, A. Oxygen
Mortimer, J. C. Felix in the underworld
Mulisch, H. Siegfried
Murdoch, I. The book and the brotherhood
Nabokov, V. V. Look at the harlequins!
Nabokov, V. V. The real life of Sebastian Knight
Naipaul, V. S. Half a life
Naipaul, V. S. Magic seeds
Naipaul, V. S. A way in the world
Oates, J. C. The tattooed girl
Ōe, K. A quiet life
Ōe, K. Rouse up, o young men of the new age
O'Neill, J. Kilbrack; or, Who is Nancy Valentine?
Parini, J. The apprentice lover
Pearl, M. The Dante Club
Pouncey, P. R. Rules for old men waiting
Powell, A. Books do furnish a room
Powers, R. Galatea 2.2
Price, R. Samaritan
Prose, F. Blue angel
Read, P. P. A season in the West
Richler, M. Barney's version
Roberts, N. River's end
Roth, H. From bondage
Roth, H. Requiem for Harlem
Roth, P. The anatomy lesson
Roth, P. The ghost writer
Roth, P. My life as a man
Roth, P. Zuckerman bound: a trilogy and epilogue
Roth, P. Zuckerman unbound
Schwarz, C. All is vanity

TITLE AND SUBJECT INDEX

AUTOBIOGRAPHICAL STORIES—*Continued*
Vassilikos, V. The few things I know about Glafkos Thrassakis
Vonnegut, K. Slaughterhouse-five
Vonnegut, K. Timequake
Ward, M. J. The snake pit
West, Dame R. Sunflower
White, E. The farewell symphony
Wolfe, T. Look homeward, angel
Wolfe, T. O lost
Wolfe, T. Of time and the river
Wolfe, T. The web and the rock
The **autobiography** of Miss Jane Pittman. Gaines, E. J.
Autobiography of my mother. Kincaid, J.
The **autograph** man. Smith, Z.
AUTOMATA *See* Robots
AUTOMATION
Vonnegut, K. Player piano
AUTOMOBILE ACCIDENTS *See* Traffic accidents
AUTOMOBILE DRIVERS
See also Chauffeurs; Hit-and-run drivers
AUTOMOBILE INDUSTRY
Estleman, L. D. Thunder City
Jakes, J. American dreams
McMillan, R. Blue collar blues
AUTOMOBILE RACES
Jakes, J. American dreams
AUTOMOBILES
Estleman, L. D. Edsel
Hawke, E. Ash Wednesday
King, S. Christine
King, S. From a Buick 8
Accidents
See Traffic accidents
Touring
Barthelme, F. Painted desert
Gifford, B. Wild at heart
Gifford, B. Wyoming
McMurtry, L. Cadillac Jack
McMurtry, L. Loop group
The **autumn** of the patriarch. García Márquez, G.
Avalon. Lawhead, S.
Avalon. Seton, A.
AVANT GARDE STORIES *See* Experimental stories
AVARICE
See also Misers
Amidon, S. Human capital
Archer, J. The fourth estate
Atwood, M. The blind assassin
Barbash, T. The last good chance
Bunn, T. D. The great divide
Caputo, P. Acts of faith
Cleage, P. Babylon sisters
Coughlin, W. J. The heart of justice
Dickens, C. Our mutual friend
Fast, H. Greenwich
Follett, K. A dangerous fortune
Frayn, M. Headlong
Frey, S. W. The legacy
Goddard, R. Beyond recall
Gregory, P. Earthly joys
Grisham, J. The partner
Hammond, G. The hitch
Harris, J. Coastliners
Hiaasen, C. Stormy weather
Hospital, J. T. Oyster
Jakes, J. Charleston
Jen, G. Typical American
Johansen, I. And then you die—
Lanchester, J. Fragrant Harbor
Le Carré, J. Single & Single
Lopez, B. H. Resistance
Maḥfūẓ, N. Children of the alley
McCarthy, C. No country for old men
Meyers, K. The work of wolves
Norman, H. The haunting of L
Palmer, M. Miracle cure
Palmer, M. Natural causes
Pérez Galdós, B. Torquemada
Phillips, A. Prague
Richler, M. Solomon Gursky was here
Robbins, T. Half asleep in frog pajamas
Roberts, N. The villa
Smith, S. B. A simple plan
Thomas, M. M. Black money
Tremain, R. The color
Unsworth, B. Sacred hunger
Wolfe, T. A man in full
Avaryan rising [series]
Tarr, J. A fall of princes
Tarr, J. The hall of the mountain king
Tarr, J. The lady of Han-Gilen
Avenger. Forsyth, F.
AVIATION *See* Aeronautics
AVIATORS *See* Air pilots
The **aviators**. Griffin, W. E. B.
Awake. Graver, E.
Awakeners [series]
Tepper, S. S. Northshore
Tepper, S. S. Southshore
The **awakening** land. Richter, C.
Away. Urquhart, J.
The **ax**. Westlake, D. E.
The **Axeman's** jazz. Smith, J.
AZORES
Alison, J. Natives and exotics
Aztec. Jennings, G.
Aztec blood. Jennings, G.
AZTECS
Falconer, C. Feathered serpent
Fuentes, C. The two shores
Jennings, G. Aztec
Jennings, G. Aztec blood

B

"B" is for burglar. Grafton, S.
Babbitt. Lewis, S.
also in Lewis, S. Main Street & Babbitt
Babel Tower. Byatt, A. S.
Babel's children. Barker, C.
In Barker, C. In the flesh
Babi Yar. Anatoli, A.
BABI YAR MASSACRE, 1941
Anatoli, A. Babi Yar
Baby, would I lie? Westlake, D. E.
Babylon revisited, and other stories. Fitzgerald, F. S.
BACHELORS *See* Single men
The **bachelors**. Spark, M.
The **Bachman** books: four early novels by Stephen King. King, S.
Back roads. O'Dell, T.
Back story. Parker, R. B.
Back when we were grownups. Tyler, A.
Backflash. Stark, R.
A **backward** glance. Wharton, E.
In Wharton, E. Novellas and other writings
Bad boy. Goldsmith, O.
Bad Boy Brawly Brown. Mosley, W.
Bad company. Higgins, J.
The **bad** detective. Keating, H. R. F.
Bad dirt. Proulx, A.
Bad Girl Creek. Mapson, J.-A.
Bad love. Kellerman, J.
Bad men. Connolly, J.
Bad news. Westlake, D. E.
The **bad** place. Koontz, D. R.
Bad publicity. Frank, J.
The **bad** samaritan. Barnard, R.
The **bad** seed. March, W.
Badenheim 1939. Appelfeld, A.
Badge of honor [series]
Griffin, W. E. B. The investigators
Griffin, W. E. B. The murderers
Badger boy. Kelton, E.
Badlands. Bowen, P.

TITLE AND SUBJECT INDEX

BATTLES
See also names of individual battles
Caputo, P. Horn of Africa
Cornwell, B. The archer's tale
Cornwell, B. Battle flag
Cornwell, B. The bloody ground
Cornwell, B. Copperhead
Cornwell, B. Enemy of God
Cornwell, B. Excalibur
Cornwell, B. Rebel
Cornwell, B. Sharpe's company
Cornwell, B. Sharpe's devil
Cornwell, B. Sharpe's eagle
Cornwell, B. Sharpe's enemy
Cornwell, B. Sharpe's honour
Cornwell, B. Sharpe's regiment
Cornwell, B. Sharpe's sword
Cornwell, B. Sharpe's Trafalgar
Cornwell, B. Sharpe's Waterloo
Cornwell, B. The winter king
Coyle, H. W. Look away
Coyle, H. W. Until the end
Del Vecchio, J. M. The 13th valley
Griffin, W. E. B. Line of fire
Holland, C. Jerusalem
Jennings, G. Raptor
Kuniczak, W. S. The thousand hour day
Llywelyn, M. Druids
Llywelyn, M. The last prince of Ireland
Mallinson, A. A close run thing
Marcantel, P. An army of angels
McCutchan, P. The new lieutenant
Sienkiewicz, H. The deluge
Sienkiewicz, H. Fire in the steppe
Sienkiewicz, H. With fire and sword
Tolstoy, L., graf. War and peace

BATTLESHIPS *See* Warships

BATZ-CASTELMORE, CHARLES, COMTE D'ARTAGNAN
See Artagnan, Charles de Batz-Castelmore, comte d', 1613?-1673

Baudolino. Eco, U.

BAUM, L. FRANK (LYMAN FRANK), 1856-1919
Parodies, imitations, etc.
D'Amato, B. Hard road
Maguire, G. Son of a witch

BAUM, LYMAN FRANK *See* Baum, L. Frank, 1856-1919

BAVARIA (GERMANY) *See* Germany—Bavaria

The **Bawdy** basket. Marston, E.
The **Bay** of Angels. Brookner, A.
The **bay** of love and sorrows. Richards, D. A.
Bay of souls. Stone, R.
Be cool. Leonard, E.
Be my knife. Grossman, D.
The **beach** house. Patterson, J.
Beach music. Conroy, P.
The **beach** of Falesá. Stevenson, R. L.
In Stevenson, R. L. The complete short stories p307-71
In Stevenson, R. L. The complete short stories of Robert Louis Stevenson
In Stevenson, R. L. The strange case of Dr. Jekyll and Mr. Hyde, and other famous tales
The **bean** trees. Kingsolver, B.
The **Beans** of Egypt, Maine. Chute, C.
The **bear** and the dragon. Clancy, T.
The **Bear** Flag. Holland, C.

BEAR FLAG REVOLT, 1846
Holland, C. The Bear Flag

The **bear** went over the mountain. Kotzwinkle, W.

BEARE, DONAL CAM O'SULLIVAN *See* O'Sullivan Beare, Donal Cam, 1560-1618

Bearing an hourglass. Anthony, P.
The **bearkeeper's** daughter. Bradshaw, G.

BEARS
Jenkins, W. F. Exploration team
King, S. The girl who loved Tom Gordon
Kotzwinkle, W. The bear went over the mountain

The **beast** God forgot to invent. Harrison, J.
The **beast** God forgot to invent [novelette] Harrison, J.
In Harrison, J. The beast God forgot to invent
The **beast** in the jungle. James, H.
In James, H. Complete stories, 1898-1910
In James, H. The complete tales of Henry James
In James, H. The Henry James reader p357-400
Beast Master's ark. Norton, A.

BEAT GENERATION *See* Bohemianism

Beat to quarters. Forester, C. S.

BEATNIKS *See* Bohemianism

Beau Geste. Wren, P. C.
The **beautiful** and damned. Fitzgerald, F. S.
also in Fitzgerald, F. S. Novels and stories, 1920-1922 p435-795
A **beautiful** death. Haymon, S. T.
Beautiful girl. Adams, A.
The **beautiful** room is empty. White, E.
The **beauty**. Nagy, G.

BEAUTY SHOPS
Brown, R. M. Loose lips

Because it is bitter, and because it is my heart. Oates, J. C.
Because the night. Ellroy, J.
In Ellroy, J. L.A. noir p207-425
Bech: a book. Updike, J.
Bech at bay. Updike, J.
Bech is back. Updike, J.

BECKET, THOMAS À *See* Thomas, à Becket, Saint, Archbishop of Canterbury, 1118?-1170

Becoming Madame Mao. Min, A.
Bed & breakfast. Battle, L.
A **bed** in heaven. Loo, T. d.
Bedford Square. Perry, A.

BEDOUINS
Moore, B. The magician's wife

Bee season. Goldberg, M.
The **beekeeper's** apprentice. King, L. R.

BEER INDUSTRY
Canin, E. Carry me across the water

BEES
Anderson-Dargatz, G. A recipe for bees
Bergen, D. See the child
Jackson, M. Five boys
McMahon, T. A. McKay's bees

The **Beet** Queen. Erdrich, L.
Before and after. Brown, R.
Before I say goodbye. Clark, M. H.
Before the frost. Mankell, H.
Before women had wings. Fowler, C. M.
A **beggar** in Jerusalem. Wiesel, E.
Beggarman, thief. Shaw, I.
Beggars & choosers. Kress, N.
Beggars in Spain. Kress, N.
Beggars ride. Kress, N.
The **beginning** of calamities. House, T.
The **beginning** place. Le Guin, U. K.

BEHAVIOR MODIFICATION
See also Brainwashing
Cussler, C. Deep six
Koontz, D. R. Night chills

Behind a mask [novelette] Alcott, L. M.
In Alcott, L. M. Behind a mask: the unknown thrillers of Louisa May Alcott p1-104
Behind a mask: the unknown thrillers of Louisa May Alcott. Alcott, L. M.
Behindlings. Barker, N.

BEHN, APHRA, 1640-1689
About
Stevenson, J. The shadow king

Behold the man. Moorcock, M.
In The Best of the Nebulas p163-202

BEIDERBECKE, BIX, 1903-1931
About
Turner, F. W. 1929

BEIJING (CHINA) *See* China—Beijing

Being a green mother. Anthony, P.
Being dead. Crace, J.
Being invisible. Berger, T.
Being there. Kosinski, J. N.

BEIRUT (LEBANON) *See* Lebanon—Beirut

Bel canto. Patchett, A.
Bel Ria. Burnford, S.

TITLE AND SUBJECT INDEX

Blood Junction. Carver, C.
Blood lines. Harrod-Eagles, C.
Blood lines. Rendell, R.
Blood lure. Barr, N.
Blood meridian. McCarthy, C.
Blood money. Egleton, C.
Blood money. Perry, T.
Blood mud. Constantine, K. C.
Blood music. Bear, G.
In Bear, G. The collected stories of Greg Bear
Blood of Amber. Zelazny, R.
Blood of victory. Furst, A.
Blood on the moon. Ellroy, J.
In Ellroy, J. L.A. noir p1-206
Blood on the wood. Linscott, G.
The **blood** oranges. Hawkes, J.
Blood rain. Dibdin, M.
Blood relations. Parker, B.
Blood roses. Yarbro, C. Q.
Blood shot. Paretsky, S.
Blood sympathy. Hill, R.
Blood Trillium. May, J.
Blood type. Greenleaf, S.
Blood will tell. Stabenow, D.
Blood will tell. Stout, R.
In Stout, R. Trio for blunt instruments p169-247
Blood will tell. See Christie, A. Mrs. McGinty's dead
Blood work. Connelly, M.
Bloodchild and other stories. Butler, O. E.
Bloodhounds. Lovesey, P.
The **bloodied** ivy. Goldsborough, R.
Bloodlines. Burke, J.
A **Bloodsmoor** romance. Oates, J. C.
Bloodstream. Gerritsen, T.
The **bloody** ground. Cornwell, B.
The **bloody** moonlight. Brown, F.
In Brown, F. Hunter and hunted
Bloody season. Estleman, L. D.
Blow fly. Cornwell, P. D.
Blown away. Wiltse, D.
Blue Adept. Anthony, P.
The **blue** afternoon. Boyd, W.
Blue angel. Prose, F.
Blue at the mizzen. O'Brian, P.
Blue Calhoun. Price, R.
Blue collar blues. McMillan, R.
Blue corn murders. Pickard, N.
Blue death. O'Donnell, L.
Blue Deer thaw. Harrison, J.
Blue diary. Hoffman, A.
The **blue** flower. Fitzgerald, P.
The **blue** hour. Parker, T. J.
The **blue** knight. Wambaugh, J.
Blue lonesome. Pronzini, B.
Blue Mars. Robinson, K. S.
Blue moon. Rice, L.
Blue pastoral. Sorrentino, G.
Blue plate special. Runyon, D.
In Runyon, D. Guys and dolls p345-505
Blue Ridge. Pearson, T. R.

BLUE RIDGE MOUNTAINS
Hamner, E. The homecoming
Hamner, E. Spencer's Mountain
Blue shoe. Lamott, A.
Bluebeard's egg and other stories. Atwood, M.
Bluegate Fields. Perry, A.
Blues dancing. McKinney-Whetstone, D.
The **bluest** blood. Roberts, G.
The **bluest** eye. Morrison, T.
BOARDERS *See* Boarding houses

BOARDING HOUSES
Balzac, H. d. Père Goriot (Old Goriot)
Bausch, R. Rebel powers
Egolf, T. Skirt and the fiddle
Naylor, G. Bailey's Café
Ross-Macdonald, M. Tamsin Harte
Spark, M. A far cry from Kensington
Tyler, A. Celestial navigation
BOARDING SCHOOLS *See* School life
The **boat**. Buchheim, L.-G.

BOATS AND BOATING
See also Sailing vessels; Tugboats
Barth, J. The Tidewater tales
Bob the gambler. Barthelme, F.
Bodily harm. Atwood, M.
Body. Crews, H.
The **body**. King, S.
In King, S. Different seasons p299-451
Body & soul. Conroy, F.
Body and soil. McInerny, R. M.
The **body** artist. DeLillo, D.
Body count. Kienzle, W. X.
Body double. Gerritsen, T.
The **body** in the basement. Page, K. H.
A **body** in the bath house. Davis, L.
The **body** in the Big Apple. Page, K. H.
The **body** in the bog. Page, K. H.
The **body** in the bookcase. Page, K. H.
The **body** in the fjord. Page, K. H.
The **body** in the library. Christie, A.
The **body** in the lighthouse. Page, K. H.
The **body** in the vestibule. Page, K. H.
The **body** of David Hayes. Pearson, R.
The **body** of Jonah Boyd. Leavitt, D.
The **body** on the beach. Brett, S.
A **body** to die for. White, K.
BODYBUILDING *See* Weight lifting

BODYGUARDS
Parker, R. B. Double play
BOERS *See* Afrikaners

BOHEMIANISM
Kerouac, J. The Dharma bums
Kerouac, J. On the road
Maugham, W. S. Of human bondage
McCarthy, M. A charmed life
Powell, A. Casanova's Chinese restaurant
Powell, A. Hearing secret harmonies

BOHEMIANS

United States
See Czechs—United States
BOLEYN, ANNE *See* Anne Boleyn, Queen, consort of Henry VIII, King of England, 1507-1536

BOLÍVAR, SIMÓN, 1783-1830
About
García Márquez, G. The general and his labyrinth
BOLSHEVISM *See* Communism
Bolt. Francis, D.
Bomb grade. Freemantle, B.
BOMBAY (INDIA) *See* India—Bombay
Bomber's law. Higgins, G. V.
BOMBING MISSIONS *See* World War, 1939-1945—Aerial operations

BOMBS
See also Atomic bomb
Crais, R. Demolition angel
Grisham, J. The chamber
Knox, E. Billie's kiss
Lutz, J. Final seconds
Nance, J. J. Medusa's child
Snyder, D. J. Night crossing
Wiltse, D. Blown away
Bon voyage. Coward, N.
In Coward, N. The collected stories of Noël Coward p562-630

BONANNO, JOSEPH, 1905-2002
About
Latour, J. The Havana World Series
BONAPARTE, NAPOLEON *See* Napoleon I, Emperor of the French, 1769-1821
The **bondswomans** narrative. Crafts, H.
Bone. Ng, F. M.
Bone by bone. Matthiessen, P.
The **bone** collector. Deaver, J.
Bone deep. Wiltse, D.
Bone harvest. Logue, M.
Bone Key. Standiford, L.
The **bone** of contention. Hurston, Z. N.
In Hurston, Z. N. Novels and stories p968-78
The **bone** people. Hulme, K.

BOYS—*Continued*
Chong, K. Baroque-a-nova
Clark, M. H. Silent night
Coe, J. The Rotters' Club
Conroy, P. The lords of discipline
Deane, S. Reading in the dark
Dickens, C. David Copperfield
Dickens, C. Dombey and Son
Dickens, C. Oliver Twist
Doyle, R. Paddy Clarke, ha ha ha
Earley, T. Jim the boy
Edgerton, C. Where trouble sleeps
Emmons, C. His mother's son
Faulkner, W. The reivers
Flagg, F. Standing in the rainbow
Foer, J. S. Extremely loud and incredibly close
Frayn, M. Spies
French, A. Billy
Gifford, B. Wyoming
Gipson, F. B. Old Yeller
Gipson, F. B. Savage Sam
Golding, W. Lord of the Flies
Grisham, J. The client
Grisham, J. A painted house
Haddon, M. The curious incident of the dog in the night-time
Hamill, P. Snow in August
Hilton, J. Good-bye Mr. Chips
Hofmann, G. Luck
Hornby, N. About a boy
House, T. The beginning of calamities
Hughes, L. Not without laughter
Jackson, M. Five boys
Johnson, W. The devil you know
Johnston, W. Human amusements
Kantner, S. Ordinary wolves
Kay, T. The runaway
Keillor, G. Lake Wobegon summer 1956
King, D. The ha-ha
King, S. Apt pupil
King, S. The body
King, T. Truth & Bright Water
Knowles, J. Peace breaks out
Knowles, J. A separate peace
Kosinski, J. N. The painted bird
Kotzwinkle, W. E.T.
Lansdale, J. R. The bottoms
Lansdale, J. R. A fine dark line
Lethem, J. The fortress of solitude
Lychack, W. The wasp eater
Marion, S. Hollow ground
Marshall, P. The fisher king
Martel, Y. Life of Pi
McCabe, P. The butcher boy
McNicholl, D. A son called Gabriel
Merullo, R. In Revere, in those days
Meyers, K. The work of wolves
Mitcham, J. Sabbath Creek
Morris, W. Taps
Mosher, H. F. Waiting for Teddy Williams
Murakami, H. Kafka on the shore
Ōe, K. Nip the buds, shoot the kids
O'Nan, S. A world away
O'Neill, J. At swim, two boys
Oz, A. Panther in the basement
Parker, R. B. Double play
Powell, P. Edisto
Powers, J. R. The last Catholic in America
Price, R. The tongues of angels
Purdy, J. Malcolm
Raucher, H. Summer of '42
Reuss, F. Henry of Atlantic City
Richter, C. The light in the forest
Roth, H. Call it sleep
Roth, H. A star shines over Mt. Morris Park
Ruiz Zafón, C. The shadow of the wind
Saroyan, W. The human comedy
Saul, J. Shadows
Scott, J. Tourmaline
Searles, J. Boy still missing
Shelley, M. W. Maurice
Southgate, M. The fall of Rome
Steinbeck, J. The red pony
Swarthout, G. F. Bless the beasts and children
Tilghman, C. Mason's retreat
Townsend, S. The Adrian Mole diaries
Tremain, R. The way I found her
Trollope, J. The choir
Twain, M. The adventures of Huckleberry Finn
Twain, M. The adventures of Tom Sawyer
Vargas Llosa, M. The notebooks of Don Rigoberto
Wells, K. Meely LaBauve
White, E. A boy's own story
Williams, D. Angel Rock
Wolff, T. Old school
Woodrell, D. The death of sweet mister
Woolf, V. Jacob's room
Zafris, N. Lucky strike

The **boys** from Brazil. Levin, I.
Boy's life. McCammon, R. R.
A **boy's** own story. White, E.
BOZ *See* Dickens, Charles, 1812-1870
Bradbury stories. Bradbury, R.

BRAHE, TYCHO, 1546-1601

About

Sherwood, F. The book of splendor

Braided lives. Piercy, M.

BRAIN
Darnton, J. Mind catcher
Krauss, N. Man walks into a room

Brain. Cook, R.

BRAINWASHING
Higgins, J. Day of judgment
Koontz, D. R. Sole survivor
Koontz, D. R. Strangers

The **Bram** Stoker bedside companion. Stoker, B.
Brass. Walsh, H.
Brat Farrar. Tey, J.
also in Tey, J. Three by Tey
Brave new world. Huxley, A.

BRAZIL

20th century

Amado, J. Dona Flor and her two husbands
Amado, J. Gabriela, clove and cinnamon
Grisham, J. The testament
Hatoum, M. The brothers
Levin, I. The boys from Brazil
Updike, J. Brazil

Frontier and pioneer life

See Frontier and pioneer life—Brazil

Politics

See Politics—Brazil

Bahia

Amado, J. Dona Flor and her two husbands
Amado, J. Gabriela, clove and cinnamon
Amado, J. Showdown

Brazil. Updike, J.
Brazzaville Beach. Boyd, W.
Breach of duty. Jance, J. A.
Breach of promise. O'Shaughnessy, P.
A **breach** of promise. Perry, A.
Bread and wine. Silone, I.
Bread upon the waters. Shaw, I.
Break in. Francis, D.
The **breaker**. Walters, M.
Breakfast. Steinbeck, J.
In Steinbeck, J. The portable Steinbeck
Breakfast and work. Steinbeck, J.
In Steinbeck, J. The portable Steinbeck
Breakfast at Tiffany's. Capote, T.
In Capote, T. Breakfast at Tiffany's: a short novel and three stories
Breakfast at Tiffany's: a short novel and three stories. Capote, T.
Breakfast of champions. Vonnegut, K.
Breakheart Hill. Cook, T. H.
Breakheart Pass. MacLean, A.
Breaking news. MacNeil, R.
Breaking the tongue. Loh, V.
Breaking up is hard to do. Gorman, E.
Breakout. Stark, R.
Breakup. Stabenow, D.
The **breast**. Roth, P.
In Roth, P. Novels, 1967-1972

TITLE AND SUBJECT INDEX

BRITISH—India—*Continued*
Kaye, M. M. Shadow of the moon
Scott, P. The day of the scorpion
Scott, P. A division of the spoils
Scott, P. The jewel in the crown
Scott, P. The Raj quartet
Scott, P. Staying on
Scott, P. The towers of silence

Ireland

Davis-Goff, A. This cold country
Llywelyn, M. 1921
Uris, L. Redemption
Uris, L. Trinity

Israel

Spark, M. The Mandelbaum Gate

Italy

Craig, A. Love in idleness
Forster, E. M. A room with a view
Gash, J. The Vatican rip
Godden, R. The battle of the Villa Fiorita
Godden, R. Pippa passes
Hamilton-Paterson, J. Loving monsters
Mortimer, J. C. Summer's lease
Parks, T. Destiny
Powell, A. Temporary kings
Scott, J. Tourmaline
Seymour, G. Killing ground
West, M. L. The devil's advocate
Wignall, K. For the dogs

Japan

Clavell, J. Gai-Jin
Clavell, J. Shogun
Hazzard, S. The great fire

Kenya

Wood, B. Green City in the sun

Lebanon

Stewart, M. The Gabriel hounds

Malaysia

Carey, P. My life as a fake

Mexico

Lowry, M. Under the volcano

Norway

Francis, D. Slayride

Palestine

Oz, A. Panther in the basement
Wiesel, E. Dawn
Wilson, J. A Palestine affair

Panama

Le Carré, J. The tailor of Panama

Polynesia

Wright, R. Henderson's spear

Russia

Bradbury, M. To the Hermitage
Egleton, C. A killing in Moscow
Francis, D. Trial run
Freemantle, B. Dead men living
Read, P. P. Alice in exile

South Africa

Francis, D. Smokescreen
Harries, A. Manly pursuits
Lessing, D. M. Children of violence
Michener, J. A. The covenant
Spark, M. The go-away bird

Spain

Hemingway, E. The sun also rises

Switzerland

Brookner, A. Hotel du Lac
Pye, M. The pieces from Berlin

Tahiti

Maugham, W. S. The moon and sixpence

Turkey

Holt, V. Secret for a nightingale

Uganda

Hill, R. Dream of darkness

United States

Bristow, G. Celia Garth
Dibdin, M. Thanksgiving
Dickens, C. Martin Chuzzlewit
Elkin, S. Stanley Elkin's The magic kingdom
Faulks, S. On Green Dolphin Street
Fraser, G. M. Flashman & the angel of the Lord
Gregory, P. Virgin earth
Iyer, P. Abandon
James, H. An international episode
Lasdun, J. The horned man
Lemann, N. Malaise
L'Engle, M. The other side of the sun
Lodge, D. Paradise news
McMurtry, L. By sorrow's river
McMurtry, L. Folly and glory
McMurtry, L. Sin killer
McMurtry, L. The wandering hill
Pynchon, T. Mason & Dixon
Raban, J. Waxwings
Theroux, M. The confessions of Mycroft Holmes
Vanderhaeghe, G. The last crossing
Vollmann, W. T. Argall
Waugh, E. The loved one
Wener, L. The perfect play

Vietnam

Greene, G. The quiet American

West Africa

Forester, C. S. The African Queen
Greene, G. The heart of the matter

West Indies

Naipaul, V. S. Guerrillas
Phillips, C. Cambridge

Yugoslavia

MacLean, A. Force 10 from Navarone

Zaire

Edric, R. The book of the heathen

BRITISH ANTARCTIC ("TERRA NOVA") EXPEDITION (1910-1913)
Bainbridge, B. The birthday boys

BRITISH ARISTOCRACY *See* Aristocracy—England

BRITISH COLUMBIA *See* Canada—British Columbia

BRITISH SOLDIERS *See* Soldiers—Great Britain

BRITISH WEST INDIES *See* West Indies

BRITTANY (FRANCE) *See* France—Brittany

Broke heart blues. Oates, J. C.

Broken angels. Morgan, R. K.

Broken as things are. Witt, M.

Broken for you. Kallos, S.

Broken prey. Sandford, J.

The **broken** promise land. Muller, M.

The **broker**. Grisham, J.

BRONTË, EMILY, 1818-1848

Manuscripts

Barnard, R. The case of the missing Brontë

BRONX (NEW YORK, N.Y.) *See* New York (N.Y.)—Bronx

BROOKLYN (NEW YORK, N.Y.) *See* New York (N.Y.)—Brooklyn

BROTHELS *See* Prostitution

Brother and sister. Trollope, J.

Brother Cadfael's penance. Peters, E.

Brother Wind. Harrison, S.

The **brotherhood** of the rose. Morrell, D.

Brotherhood of the tomb. Easterman, D.

Brotherhood of war [series]
Griffin, W. E. B. The aviators
Griffin, W. E. B. The new breed
Griffin, W. E. B. Special ops

Brotherly love. Dexter, P.

BROTHERS
See also Brothers and sisters; Half-brothers; Stepbrothers; Twins

BUCHAREST (ROMANIA) *See* Romania—Bucharest
Bucket nut. Cody, L.
Bucking the sun. Doig, I.
BUDAPEST (HUNGARY) *See* Hungary—Budapest
Buddenbrooks. Mann, T.
BUDDHA, GAUTAMA *See* Gautama Buddha
Buddha Da. Donovan, A.
BUDDHISM
See also Zen Buddhism
Burdett, J. Bangkok 8
Burdett, J. Bangkok Tattoo
Donovan, A. Buddha Da
Endō, S. Deep river
Hesse, H. Siddhartha
Mishima, Y. The Temple of Dawn
Mishima, Y. The temple of the golden pavilion
Pattison, E. The skull mantra
Zelazny, R. Lord of light
Buddy Cooper finds a way. Connelly, N. O.
BUENOS AIRES (ARGENTINA) *See* Argentina—Buenos Aires
BUFFALO, AMERICAN *See* Bison
BUFFALO (N.Y.) *See* New York (State)—Buffalo
BUFFALO BILL, 1846-1917
About
McMurtry, L. Buffalo girls
BUFFALO BILL'S WILD WEST COMPANY
Welch, J. The heartsong of Charging Elk
Buffalo girls. McMurtry, L.
The **buffalo** hunter. Straub, P.
In Straub, P. Houses without doors p109-207
The **buffalo** soldier. Bohjalian, C. A.
Buffalo soldiers. O'Connor, R.
Buffalo soldiers. Willard, T.
The **bug**. Ullman, E.
BUILDING
Follett, K. Pillars of the earth
Hodgins, E. Mr. Blandings builds his dream house
The **building** of Jalna. De la Roche, M.
Built in a day. Rinehart, S.
BULGARIA
Sofia
Gilman, D. The elusive Mrs. Pollifax
The **bull** from the sea. Renault, M.
BULL RUN, 1ST BATTLE, 1861
Cornwell, B. Rebel
Bullet Park. Cheever, J.
BULLFIGHTERS AND BULLFIGHTING
Blasco Ibáñez, V. Blood and sand
Hemingway, E. The sun also rises
Michener, J. A. Mexico
BULLFIGHTING *See* Bullfighters and bullfighting
Bum steer. Pickard, N.
BUNKER, CHANG, 1811-1874
About
Slouka, M. God's fool
BUNKER, ENG, 1811-1874
About
Slouka, M. God's fool
Bunker 13. Bahal, A.
BUONAROTTI, MICHELANGELO *See* Michelangelo Buonarroti, 1475-1564
BUONARROTI, MICHEL ANGELO *See* Michelangelo Buonarroti, 1475-1564
Burden of desire. MacNeil, R.
The **burden** of proof. Turow, S.
BUREAUCRACY
See also Civil service
Bulgakov, M. A. The master and Margarita
Frayn, M. A landing on the sun
Whitehead, C. The intuitionist
Burger's daughter. Gordimer, N.
The **burglar** in the closet. Block, L.
The **burglar** in the library. Block, L.
The **burglar** in the rye. Block, L.
The **burglar** on the prowl. Block, L.
The **burglar** who liked to quote Kipling. Block, L.
The **burglar** who painted like Mondrian. Block, L.
The **burglar** who studied Spinoza. Block, L.
The **burglar** who traded Ted Williams. Block, L.
BURGLARS *See* Thieves
BURIAL *See* Funeral rites and ceremonies
Buried alive. See Dostoyevsky, F. The house of the dead
Buried evidence. Rosenberg, N. T.
BURIED TREASURE
Conrad, J. Nostromo
Cussler, C. Inca gold
Cussler, C. Treasure
DeMille, N. Plum Island
Forester, C. S. Hornblower and the Atropos
Preston, D. Riptide
BURMA
Block, L. Tanner on ice
Ghosh, A. The glass palace
Mason, D. The piano tuner
Tan, A. Saving fish from drowning
Burn. Lutz, J.
Burn marks. Paretsky, S.
BURNES, SIR ALEXANDER, 1805-1841
About
Hensher, P. The Mulberry empire
Burning angel. Burke, J. L.
The **burning** bride. Lawrence, M. K.
The **burning** city. Niven, L.
The **burning** house. Beattie, A.
A **burning** in Homeland. Yancey, R.
The **burning** man. Margolin, P.
Burning Marguerite. Inness-Brown, E.
Burning the ice. Mixon, L. J.
Burning your boats. Carter, A.
A **burnt-out** case. Greene, G.
BURR, AARON, 1756-1836
About
Vidal, G. Burr
Burr. Vidal, G.
The **burying** field. Abel, K.
BURYING GROUNDS *See* Cemeteries
BUSES
Steinbeck, J. The wayward bus
Accidents
See Traffic accidents
BUSINESS
See also Advertising; Department stores; Merchants
Birmingham, S. The Auerbach will
Birmingham, S. The LeBaron secret
Gaddis, W. J R
Heffernan, W. The Dinosaur Club
Howells, W. D. The rise of Silas Lapham
Norris, F. The pit
O'Hara, J. From the terrace
Tarkington, B. The magnificent Ambersons
Theroux, P. Kowloon Tong
Vonnegut, K. Jailbird
Wilson, S. The man in the gray flannel suit
Unscrupulous methods
Archer, J. The fourth estate
Baldacci, D. Total control
Bellow, S. More die of heartbreak
Bernhardt, W. Silent justice
Birmingham, S. Carriage trade
Brown, S. White hot
Browne, G. A. Hot Siberian
Bunn, T. D. The great divide
Cannell, S. J. The Viking funeral
Clavell, J. Noble house
Coughlin, W. J. The heart of justice
Crichton, M. Airframe
Crichton, M. Disclosure
Crichton, M. Rising sun
Dunne, D. An inconvenient woman
Estleman, L. D. Edsel
Estleman, L. D. Thunder City
Frey, S. W. The inner sanctum
Goddard, R. Into the blue
Hailey, A. Strong medicine
Ignatius, D. A firing offense
Le Carré, J. The constant gardener

C

CALAMITY JANE, 1852-1903

About

McMurtry, L. Buffalo girls

CALCUTTA (INDIA) *See* India—Calcutta

Caldé of the long sun. Wolfe, G.

Calder pride. Dailey, J.

CALGARY (ALTA.) *See* Canada—Calgary

Calico Palace. Bristow, G.

CALIFORNIA

Allende, I. Zorro
Bear, G. Dead lines
Butler, O. E. Parable of the sower
Butler, O. E. Parable of the talents
Gibson, W. All tomorrow's parties
Gibson, W. Virtual light
Jakes, J. California gold
Koontz, D. R. The taking
Koontz, D. R. Velocity
Miller, S. Lost in the forest
Parker, T. J. California girl
Schwartz, L. Angels Crest
Steinbeck, J. The pastures of heaven

19th century

Bristow, G. Jubilee Trail
De Blasis, C. The proud breed
Fowler, K. J. Sister Noon
Holland, C. The Bear Flag
Holland, C. An ordinary woman
L'Amour, L. The Californios
L'Amour, L. The lonesome gods
Murphy, G. The Indian lover
Stewart, F. M. The glitter and the gold

1846-1900

Allende, I. Daughter of fortune
Baker, K. Mendoza in Hollywood
Bristow, G. Calico Palace
Holland, C. Lily Nevada
Holland, C. Pacific Street
Holland, C. Railroad schemes
Norris, F. The octopus
Steinbeck, J. East of Eden
Wheeler, R. S. Sierra

20th century

Boyle, T. C. Drop City
Boyle, T. C. Riven Rock
Brown, D. The tin man
Caputo, P. Equation for evil
Crais, R. Hostage
Cunningham, M. The hours
Dart, I. R. The Stork Club
Del Vecchio, J. M. Carry me home
Delinsky, B. Coast road
Erickson, S. The sea came in at midnight
Fast, H. The immigrant's daughter
Fast, H. Second generation
Ferrigno, R. Heartbreaker
Ferrigno, R. The Horse Latitudes
Follett, K. The hammer of Eden
Goudge, E. One last dance
Goudge, E. Stranger in paradise
Gould, J. Time to say goodbye
Groom, W. Such a pretty, pretty girl
Gutcheon, B. R. Saying grace
Kinder, C. Honeymooners
Koontz, D. R. False memory
Koontz, D. R. Fear nothing
Koontz, D. R. Intensity
Koontz, D. R. Seize the night
Koontz, D. R. Sole survivor
Lee, C. Y. The flower drum song
Lemann, N. Malaise
Leonard, E. Mr. Majestyk
Mapson, J.-A. Bad Girl Creek
Mapson, J.-A. Hank and Chloe
Martini, S. P. The judge
Muller, M. Cyanide Wells
Otsuka, J. When the emperor was divine
Otto, W. How to make an American quilt
Parker, T. J. Little Saigon
Parker, T. J. Silent Joe
Pronzini, B. In an evil time
Pronzini, B. Nothing but the night
Pronzini, B. A wasteland of strangers
Pynchon, T. The crying of lot 49
Pynchon, T. Vineland
Roberts, N. The villa
Rosenberg, N. T. Abuse of power
Rosenberg, N. T. Interest of justice
Rosenberg, N. T. Mitigating circumstances
Saroyan, W. The human comedy
Saul, J. The homing
Siddons, A. R. Fault lines
Siegel, B. Actual innocence
Steel, D. The house on Hope Street
Stegner, W. E. All the little live things
Steinbeck, J. East of Eden
Steinbeck, J. The grapes of wrath
Steinbeck, J. In dubious battle
Steinbeck, J. The long valley
Steinbeck, J. Of mice and men
Steinbeck, J. The wayward bus
Stewart, F. M. The glitter and the gold
Straight, S. The gettin place
Straight, S. Highwire moon
Teran, B. The prince of deadly weapons
Thomas, R. The fourth Durango
Tsukiyama, G. Dreaming water
Ullman, E. The bug
West, J. Cress Delahanty
Woods, S. Dead eyes

Farm life

See Farm life—California

Frontier and pioneer life

See Frontier and pioneer life—California

Gold discoveries

See California—1846-1900

Beverly Hills

Dexter, P. Train
Martin, S. Shopgirl
Wagner, B. I'll let you go

Carmel

O'Shaughnessy, P. Presumption of death

Hollywood

Adler, E. All or nothing
Barker, C. Coldheart Canyon
Bradbury, R. A graveyard for lunatics
Cannell, S. J. Hollywood tough
Dart, I. R. Show business kills
Didion, J. Play it as it lays
Dunne, D. An inconvenient woman
Dunne, J. G. Playland
Epstein, L. San Remo Drive
Fitzgerald, F. S. The last tycoon
Goudge, E. Such devoted sisters
Harrison, J. Westward ho
Jakes, J. American dreams
Knode, H. The ticket out
Koontz, D. R. The face
Korda, M. Curtain
Lankford, T. Earthquake weather
Leonard, E. Be cool
Leonard, E. Get Shorty
Puzo, M. The last Don
Schulberg, B. What makes Sammy run?
Sherrill, M. My last movie star
Steel, D. No greater love
Stone, K. Happy endings
Vidal, G. Hollywood
Vidal, G. Myra Breckinridge {and} Myron
Wagner, B. The chrysanthemum palace
Wambaugh, J. The Glitter Dome
Waugh, E. The loved one
West, N. The day of the locust
Woods, S. L.A. Times

Los Angeles

Abu-Jaber, D. Crescent
Allende, I. The infinite plan
Boyle, T. C. The tortilla curtain
Brin, D. Kiln people
Campbell, B. M. 72 hour hold

CARPENTERS
Eliot, G. Adam Bede
Carriage trade. Birmingham, S.
Carrie. King, S.
CARRIERS, AIRCRAFT *See* Aircraft carriers
Carry me across the water. Canin, E.
Carry me home. Del Vecchio, J. M.
CARS (AUTOMOBILES) *See* Automobiles
CARTER, HOWARD, 1874-1939
About
Holland, C. Valley of the Kings
CARTOGRAPHERS
Humphreys, H. Afterimage
CARTOONISTS
Ha Jin. In the pond
Casanova's Chinese restaurant. Powell, A.
In Powell, A. A dance to the music of time
The **case** book of Sherlock Holmes. Doyle, Sir A. C.
In Doyle, Sir A. C. The complete Sherlock Holmes
The **case** has altered. Grimes, M.
Case histories. Atkinson, K.
The **case** of Jennie Brice. Rinehart, M. R.
In Rinehart, M. R. Mary Roberts Rinehart's mystery book p349-442
A **case** of need. Crichton, M.
The **case** of the missing Brontë. Barnard, R.
The **case** of the postponed murder. Gardner, E. S.
The **case** of the sulky girl. Gardner, E. S.
Cashelmara. Howatch, S.
Casino Royale. Fleming, I.
Cass Timberlane. Lewis, S.
CASSANDRA (GREEK MYTHOLOGY)
Bradley, M. Z. The firebrand
Cast a long shadow. Pearce, M. E.
Cast of shadows. Guilfoile, K.
Cast the first stone. See Himes, C. Yesterday will make you cry
CASTE
India
Roy, A. The god of small things
CASTELMORE, CHARLES BATZ-, COMTE D'ARTAGNAN *See* Artagnan, Charles de Batz-Castelmore, comte d', 1613?-1673
The **castle**. Kafka, F.
Castle Rackrent. Edgeworth, M.
CASTLES
Holt, V. Bride of Pendorric
Stewart, M. Nine coaches waiting
Castleview. Wolfe, G.
CASTRATI *See* Eunuchs
CASTRO, FIDEL, 1926-
About
Hunter, S. Havana
Cat & mouse. Patterson, J.
Cat and mouse. Grass, G.
also in Grass, G. The Danzig trilogy
Cat chaser. Leonard, E.
Cat in a midnight choir. Douglas, C. N.
Cat in a neon nightmare. Douglas, C. N.
Cat on the scent. Brown, R. M.
The **cat** who ate Danish modern. Braun, L. J.
The **cat** who blew the whistle. Braun, L. J.
The **cat** who brought down the house. Braun, L. J.
The **cat** who came to breakfast. Braun, L. J.
The **cat** who lived high. Braun, L. J.
The **cat** who robbed a bank. Braun, L. J.
The **cat** who said cheese. Braun, L. J.
The **cat** who sang for the birds. Braun, L. J.
The **cat** who saw stars. Braun, L. J.
The **cat** who smelled a rat. Braun, L. J.
The **cat** who sniffed glue. Braun, L. J.
The **cat** who tailed a thief. Braun, L. J.
The **cat** who went underground. Braun, L. J.
CATASTROPHES *See* Disasters
Catch-22. Heller, J.
Catch as cat can. Brown, R. M.
The **catcher** in the rye. Salinger, J. D.

CATERERS AND CATERING
Binchy, M. Scarlet Feather
Haynes, D. The full Matilda
CATHARINE HOWARD, QUEEN, CONSORT OF HENRY VIII, KING OF ENGLAND, D. 1542
About
Plaidy, J. Murder most royal
Plaidy, J. The rose without a thorn
CATHARINE PARR, QUEEN, CONSORT OF HENRY VIII, KING OF ENGLAND, 1512-1548
About
Plaidy, J. The sixth wife
Cathedral. Carver, R.
CATHEDRAL LIFE
Dickens, C. The mystery of Edwin Drood
Hugo, V. The hunchback of Notre Dame
L'Engle, M. A severed wasp
Palliser, C. The unburied
Trollope, A. Barchester Towers
Trollope, J. The choir
CATHEDRAL TOWNS
See also Cathedral life
CATHEDRALS
Dickens, C. The mystery of Edwin Drood
Follett, K. Pillars of the earth
L'Engle, M. A severed wasp
CATHERINE, OF BRAGANZA, QUEEN, CONSORT OF CHARLES II, KING OF ENGLAND, 1638-1705
About
Plaidy, J. The pleasures of love
CATHERINE HOWARD *See* Catharine Howard, Queen, consort of Henry VIII, King of England, d. 1542
CATHERINE PARR *See* Catharine Parr, Queen, consort of Henry VIII, King of England, 1512-1548
Catherwood. Youmans, M.
CATHOLIC BISHOPS
Cather, W. Death comes for the archbishop
Cather, W. Shadows on the rock
CATHOLIC CHURCH *See* Catholic faith
CATHOLIC CLERGY *See* Catholic priests
CATHOLIC FAITH
See also Cardinals; Catholic bishops; Catholic priests; Convent life; Inquisition; Monasticism and religious orders
Alexie, S. Reservation blues
Barrett, W. E. The lilies of the field
Böll, H. The clown
Butler, R. O. They whisper
Caldwell, T. Answer as a man
Carroll, J. The city below
Carroll, J. Prince of peace
Cather, W. Death comes for the archbishop
Cather, W. Shadows on the rock
Clark, M. H. Silent night
Cronin, A. J. A pocketful of rye
Cronin, A. J. A song of sixpence
Deane, S. Reading in the dark
Dunne, J. G. The red, white, and blue
Eco, U. The name of the rose
Endō, S. Deep river
Endō, S. The samurai
Erdrich, L. The last report on the miracles at Little No Horse
Girzone, J. F. The shepherd
Godden, R. In this house of Brede
Gordon, M. The company of women
Gordon, M. Final payments
Gordon, M. Pearl
Grass, G. Cat and mouse
Greeley, A. M. Ascent into hell
Greeley, A. M. The cardinal virtues
Greeley, A. M. Lord of the dance
Greeley, A. M. Thy brother's wife
Greeley, A. M. White smoke
Greeley, A. M. Younger than springtime
Greene, G. Brighton rock
Greene, G. The end of the affair
Greene, G. The heart of the matter
Greene, G. Monsignor Quixote
Greene, G. The power and the glory

CHINA—19th century—*Continued*
Min, A. Empress Orchid
Stewart, F. M. The magnificent Savages

War of 1840-1842

Clavell, J. Tai-Pan

20th century

Gao Xingjian. Soul mountain
García, C. Monkey hunting
Li, P.-h. Farewell to my concubine
Lord, B. B. The middle heart
Tan, A. The Joy Luck Club
Ye Zhaoyan. Nanjing 1937

1900-1949

Bosse, M. J. Fire in heaven
Bosse, M. J. The warlord
Brady, J. Warning of war
Buck, P. S. Dragon seed
Buck, P. S. East wind: west wind
Buck, P. S. The good earth
Buck, P. S. A house divided
Buck, P. S. Pavilion of women
Buck, P. S. Sons
Cronin, A. J. The keys of the kingdom
Elegant, R. S. Dynasty
Han, S. Till morning comes
Hersey, J. A single pebble
Lin Yutang. Moment in Peking
Lord, B. B. Spring Moon
Malraux, A. Man's fate (La condition humaine)
Shan Sa. The girl who played go
Tan, A. The kitchen god's wife
West, P. The tent of orange mist

1949-

Elegant, R. S. Dynasty
Gao Xingjian. Buying a fishing rod for my grandfather
Ha Jin. The bridegroom
Ha Jin. The crazed
Ha Jin. In the pond
Ha Jin. Waiting
Han, S. Till morning comes
Min, A. Becoming Madame Mao
Tan, A. The bonesetter's daughter
Tan, A. The hundred secret senses

Communism

See Communism—China

Courts and courtiers

See Courts and courtiers—China

Farm life

See Farm life—China

Kings and rulers

Buck, P. S. Imperial woman

Peasant life

See Peasant life—China

Politics

See Politics—China

Prisoners and prisons

See Prisoners and prisons—China

Beijing

Michael, J. A certain smile

Guangzhou

Clavell, J. Tai-Pan

Hong Kong

See Hong Kong

Peking

See China—Beijing

Shanghai

Ballard, J. G. Empire of the Sun
Harrison, K. The binding chair
Ishiguro, K. When we were orphans
Malraux, A. Man's fate (La condition humaine)

Tibet

Alai. Red poppies
Hilton, J. Lost horizon
Pattison, E. The skull mantra

CHINA. ARMY *See* China. People's Liberation Army

CHINA. PEOPLE'S LIBERATION ARMY
Bosse, M. J. The warlord

China boy. Lee, G.
China Sea. Poyer, D.
China white. Maas, P.

CHINATOWN (NEW YORK, N.Y.) *See* New York (N.Y.)—Chinatown

CHINESE

Cuba

García, C. Monkey hunting

Hawaii

Michener, J. A. Hawaii

New Zealand

Tremain, R. The color

Singapore

Loh, V. Breaking the tongue

United States

Allende, I. Daughter of fortune
Buck, P. S. A house divided
Fast, H. The immigrants
Fowler, K. J. Sarah Canary
Lee, C. Y. The flower drum song
Raban, J. Waxwings
Steinbeck, J. Cannery Row
Williamson, P. Heart of the west

CHINESE AMERICANS
Friedman, P. Grand jury
Jen, G. The love wife
Jen, G. Mona in the promised land
Jen, G. Typical American
Jen, G. Who's Irish?
Lee, G. China boy
Lee, G. Honor & duty
Ng, F. M. Bone
Tan, A. The bonesetter's daughter
Tan, A. The hundred secret senses
Tan, A. The Joy Luck Club
Tan, A. The kitchen god's wife
Wood, B. Perfect Harmony

The **Chinese** bell murders. Gulik, R. H. v.

CHINESE PEOPLE'S LIBERATION ARMY *See* China. People's Liberation Army

CHINESE SOLDIERS *See* Soldiers—China

Chinook. Brand, M.

CHIPPEWA INDIANS
Erdrich, L. The antelope wife
Erdrich, L. The bingo palace
Erdrich, L. Four souls
Erdrich, L. The last report on the miracles at Little No Horse
Erdrich, L. Love medicine
Erdrich, L. The painted drum
Erdrich, L. Tracks

The **Chisholms**. Hunter, E.

CHIVALRY
See also Knights and knighthood; Middle Ages
Cervantes Saavedra, M. d. Don Quixote de la Mancha
Doyle, Sir A. C. The White Company
Twain, M. A Connecticut Yankee in King Arthur's court
White, T. H. The once and future king

Chocolat. Harris, J.
The **choice**. Reed, B.
Choice and responsibility. Steinbeck, J.
In Steinbeck, J. The portable Steinbeck
Choice of evil. Vachss, A. H.
The **choir**. Trollope, J.

CHOIRS (MUSIC)
Trollope, J. The choir

Choke. Woods, S.

CHOLERA
Holman, S. The dress lodger

The **chosen**. Potok, C.
Chosen prey. Sandford, J.

TITLE AND SUBJECT INDEX

The **city** who fought. McCaffrey, A.
CIVIL RIGHTS DEMONSTRATIONS *See* African Americans—Civil rights
CIVIL SERVICE
Dickens, C. Little Dorrit
Frayn, M. A landing on the sun
Greene, G. The heart of the matter
Snow, C. P. Homecoming
Civil to strangers. Pym, B.
In Pym, B. Civil to strangers and other writings p7-170
Civil to strangers and other writings. Pym, B.
CIVIL WAR
England
See England—17th century
Spain
See Spain—Civil War, 1936-1939
United States
See United States—Civil War, 1861-1865
Civil wars. Brown, R.
CIVILIZATION AND TECHNOLOGY *See* Technology and civilization
CIXI *See* Tz'u-hsi, Empress dowager of China, 1835-1908
Claire and present danger. Roberts, G.
CLAIRVOYANCE
Ansa, T. M. The hand I fan with
Conrad, J. Secret agent
García, C. Dreaming in Cuban
Hoffman, A. The probable future
McCrumb, S. The hangman's beautiful daughter
The **Clan** of the Cave Bear. Auel, J. M.
CLANS
See also Tribes
Clara. Galloway, J.
The **clarinet** polka. Maillard, K.
Clarissa. Richardson, S.
Clarissa Harlowe. See Richardson, S. Clarissa
CLARK, WILLIAM, 1770-1838
About
Hall, B. I should be extremely happy in your company
A **clash** of kings. Martin, G. R. R.
CLASS DISTINCTION
See also Middle classes; Social classes
Bainbridge, B. Every man for himself
Brown, R. M. Southern discomfort
Cambor, K. In sunlight, in a beautiful garden
Carey, P. Jack Maggs
Chevalier, T. Girl with a pearl earring
Cookson, C. The glass virgin
Cookson, C. The upstart
Crane, S. Active service
Crane, S. The third violet
Dreiser, T. An American tragedy
Dunne, D. People like us
Forster, E. M. A room with a view
Greene, G. The tenth man
Grisham, J. A painted house
Hijuelos, O. Empress of the splendid season
Ishiguro, K. The remains of the day
James, H. The American
Leavitt, D. While England sleeps
Paddock, J. A secret word
Quindlen, A. Blessings
Rice, A. The Feast of All Saints
Richler, M. Solomon Gursky was here
Siddons, A. R. Colony
Stirling, J. The marrying kind
Tarkington, B. Alice Adams
Wharton, E. The buccaneers
Wolff, T. Old school
Yancey, R. A burning in Homeland
Class reunion. Jaffe, R.
CLASS STRUGGLE
Crichton, R. The Camerons
Singer, I. J. The brothers Ashkenazi
The **classic** Philip José Farmer, 1952-1964—1964-1973. Farmer, P. J.
Classics of the macabre, Daphne du Maurier's. Du Maurier, Dame D.
Claudine and Annie. Colette
In Colette. The complete Claudine p516-632
Claudine at school. Colette
In Colette. The complete Claudine p1-206
In Colette. Six novels p1-234
Claudine in Paris. Colette
In Colette. The complete Claudine p209-364
Claudine married. Colette
In Colette. The complete Claudine p367-510
CLAUDIUS, EMPEROR OF ROME, 10 B.C.-54
About
Graves, R. Claudius, the god and his wife Messalina
Graves, R. I, Claudius
Claudius, the god and his wife Messalina. Graves, R.
The **claw** of the conciliator. Wolfe, G.
Clea. Durrell, L.
also in Durrell, L. The Alexandria quartet: Justine; Balthazar; Mountolive [and] Clea p653-884
CLEANING WOMEN
See also Charwomen; Maids (Servants)
Hijuelos, O. Empress of the splendid season
Messud, C. A simple tale
Clear and present danger. Clancy, T.
Clear light of day. Desai, A.
CLEOPATRA, QUEEN OF EGYPT, D. 30 B.C.
About
Essex, K. Kleopatra
Essex, K. Pharaoh
George, M. The memoirs of Cleopatra
Cleopatra's sister. Lively, P.
CLERGY
See also Evangelists; Rabbis; Women clergy
Baldwin, J. Go tell it on the mountain
Brooks, G. March
Clark, M. Plain heathen mischief
Daley, R. The innocents within
Doctorow, E. L. City of God
Field, R. All this, and heaven too
Gaines, E. J. In my father's house
Guterson, D. Our Lady of the Forest
Hawthorne, N. The scarlet letter
Heinlein, R. A. Job: a comedy of justice
Hurston, Z. N. Jonah's gourd vine
Lehrer, J. The special prisoner
Lewis, S. Elmer Gantry
MacDonald, J. D. One more Sunday
Miller, S. While I was gone
Price, R. The good priest's son
Robinson, M. Gilead
Smith, M. C. Rose
Stirling, J. The workhouse girl
Wideman, J. E. The cattle killing
Wood, J. The book against God
Yancey, R. A burning in Homeland
CLERGY, ANGLICAN AND EPISCOPAL *See* Anglican and Episcopal clergy
CLERGY, CATHOLIC *See* Catholic priests
CLERGY, ITINERANT *See* Itinerant clergy
The **Clerkenwell** tales. Ackroyd, P.
CLERKS
See also Civil service
Camus, A. The stranger
Kafka, F. The trial
Pym, B. Quartet in autumn
The **client**. Grisham, J.
Client privilege. Tapply, W. G.
The **clinic**. Kellerman, J.
CLIPPER SHIPS *See* Sailing vessels
The **cloak** and the staff. Dickson, G. R.
In The Hugo winners p209-43
The **clock** winder. Tyler, A.
Clock without hands. McCullers, C.
In McCullers, C. Complete novels
Clockers. Price, R.
CLOCKS AND WATCHES
Kurzweil, A. The grand complication
A **clockwork** orange. Burgess, A.
CLONES *See* Asexual reproduction
Clonk clonk. Golding, W.
In Golding, W. The scorpion god: three short novels p63-114

The **collected** stories of Katherine Anne Porter. Porter, K. A.
The **collected** stories of Louis Auchincloss. Auchincloss, L.
The **collected** stories of Mavis Gallant. Gallant, M.
The **collected** stories of Max Brand. Brand, M.
The **collected** stories of Noël Coward. Coward, N.
The **collected** stories of Philip K. Dick. Dick, P. K.
The **collected** stories of Richard Yates. Yates, R.
The **collected** stories of Robert Silverberg. Silverberg, R.
The **collected** stories of Seán O'Faoláin. O'Faoláin, S.
Collected stories of Wallace Stegner. Stegner, W. E.
Collected stories of William Faulkner. Faulkner, W.
Collected stories: One night in Brazil to The death of Methuselah. Singer, I. B.
Collected tales. De la Mare, W.
The **collected** tales and poems of Edgar Allan Poe. Poe, E. A.
The **collected** tales of E. M. Forster. Forster, E. M.
The **collected** tales of Nikolai Gogol. Gogol', N. V.
Collected works. O'Connor, F.

COLLECTIVE SETTLEMENTS

Boyle, T. C. Drop City
Gardam, J. Faith Fox
McPhee, M. Gorgeous lies
Raymond, J. The half-life

California

Sontag, S. In America

United States

Follett, K. The hammer of Eden
Piercy, M. Small changes
Updike, J. S
Varley, J. The persistence of vision

The **collector**. Fowles, J.
The **collector** of hearts. Oates, J. C.

COLLECTORS AND COLLECTING

Chatwin, B. Utz
Hornby, N. High fidelity
Smith, Z. The autograph man

COLLEGE ALUMNI

Jaffe, R. Class reunion

COLLEGE LIFE

See also College students; School life; Students; Teachers
Barth, J. Giles goat-boy

Canada

Davies, R. The lyre of Orpheus
Davies, R. The rebel angels

England

Amis, K. Lucky Jim
Bragg, M. Crossing the lines
Lewis, C. S. That hideous strength
Lodge, D. Nice work
Lodge, D. Thinks—
Pym, B. An academic question
Snow, C. P. The masters
Snow, C. P. The sleep of reason

France

McCarthy, M. Birds of America

Ireland

Binchy, M. Circle of friends

Italy

Du Maurier, Dame D. The flight of the falcon

Scotland

Atkinson, K. Emotionally weird

United States

Abrahams, P. Crying wolf
Barth, J. The end of the road
Corman, A. Prized possessions
Fitzgerald, F. S. This side of paradise
Galbraith, J. K. A tenured professor
Godwin, G. The good husband
Hassler, J. The dean's list
Hassler, J. Rookery blues
Hynes, J. The lecturer's tale
Jaffe, R. Class reunion
Lasdun, J. The horned man
Leebron, F. G. In the middle of all this
McCarthy, M. The groves of Academe
Nabokov, V. V. Pnin
Nichols, J. T. The sterile cuckoo
O'Brien, T. Tomcat in love
Perrotta, T. Joe College
Powers, R. Galatea 2.2
Prose, F. Blue angel
Reed, I. Japanese by spring
Roth, P. Letting go
Russo, R. The straight man
Salinger, J. D. Franny & Zooey
Sarton, M. A small room
Shulman, M. The many loves of Dobie Gillis
Sinclair, A. Ain't gonna be the same fool twice
Smiley, J. Moo
Smith, B. Joy in the morning
Tartt, D. The secret history
Theroux, A. Darconville's cat
Updike, J. Memories of the Ford Administration
Wolfe, T. Of time and the river

COLLEGE STUDENTS

See also College life
Barthelme, F. Elroy Nights
Caldwell, I. The rule of four
Cooley, M. The archivist
Nicholls, D. A question of attraction
Roth, H. Requiem for Harlem
Vida, V. And now you can go
Weber, K. The little women
Weinstein, D. Apprentice to the flower poet Z
Wolfe, T. I am Charlotte Simmons
Wood, J. The book against God

COLLEGE TEACHERS *See* Teachers

The **colloquy** of the dogs. Cervantes Saavedra, M. d.
In Cervantes Saavedra, M. d. Three exemplary novels p125-217

COLOMBIA

Daley, R. A faint cold fear
García Márquez, G. The general and his labyrinth
Grippando, J. A king's ransom

Rural life

García Márquez, G. Chronicle of a death foretold
García Márquez, G. Collected novellas
García Márquez, G. In evil hour
García Márquez, G. Leaf storm, and other stories
García Márquez, G. No one writes to the colonel, and other stories
García Márquez, G. One hundred years of solitude

COLOMBO, CRISTOFORO *See* Columbus, Christopher

Colonel Chabert. Balzac, H. d.
In Balzac, H. d. The short novels of Balzac

COLONIAL UNITED STATES *See* United States—To 1776

COLONIALISM *See* Imperialism

COLONIES

Great Britain

See Great Britain—Colonies

COLONIES, ARTIST *See* Artist colonies

Colony. Siddons, A. R.
The **colony** of unrequited dreams. Johnston, W.
The **color**. Tremain, R.
The **color** of blood. Moore, B.
The **color** of magic. Pratchett, T.
The **color** of night. Lindsey, D. L.
The **color** purple. Walker, A.

COLORADO

Haruf, K. Eventide
Michener, J. A. Centennial
White, S. W. Missing persons

19th century

Dallas, S. The diary of Mattie Spenser
Edgerton, C. Redeye
Gear, K. O. Thin moon and cold mist

20th century

Borland, H. When the legends die
Cather, W. The song of the lark
Greenberg, J. No reck'ning made
Grey, Z. The vanishing American
Haruf, K. Plainsong

The **complete** short stories of Ambrose Bierce. Bierce, A.
The **complete** short stories of Guy de Maupassant. See Maupassant, G. d. The collected stories of Guy de Maupassant
The **complete** short stories of H. G. Wells. Wells, H. G.
The **complete** short stories of Jack London. London, J.
The **complete** short stories of Marcel Proust. Proust, M.
The **complete** short stories of Mark Twain. Twain, M.
Complete short stories of Nathaniel Hawthorne. Hawthorne, N.
The **complete** short stories of Robert Louis Stevenson. Stevenson, R. L.
The **complete** short stories of Thomas Wolfe. Wolfe, T.
The **complete** shorter fiction. Melville, H.
The **complete** shorter fiction. Trollope, A.
The **complete** shorter fiction of Virginia Woolf. Woolf, V.
The **complete** stories. Asimov, I.
The **complete** stories. Hurston, Z. N.
The **complete** stories. Kafka, F.
The **complete** stories. Malamud, B.
The **complete** stories. O'Connor, F.
Complete stories, 1864-1874. James, H.
Complete stories, 1874-1884. James, H.
Complete stories, 1884-1891. James, H.
Complete stories, 1892-1898. James, H.
Complete stories, 1898-1910. James, H.
Complete stories and poems of Edgar Allan Poe. Poe, E. A.
Complete stories of Erskine Caldwell. Caldwell, E.
The **complete** stories of Evelyn Waugh. Waugh, E.
The **complete** stories of Truman Capote. Capote, T.
The **complete** tales and poems of Edgar Allan Poe. See Poe, E. A. The collected tales and poems of Edgar Allan Poe
The **complete** tales of Henry James. James, H.
The **complete** tales of Washington Irving. Irving, W.
The **complete** twenty thousand leagues under the sea. See Verne, J. Twenty thousand leagues under the sea
The **complete** Western stories of Elmore Leonard. Leonard, E.
The **complete** works of Isaac Babel. Babel′, I.
The **complete** works of Nathanael West. West, N.
The **complete** works of O. Henry. Henry, O.
A **complicated** kindness. Toews, M.
Compliments of a fiend. Brown, F.
In Brown, F. Hunter and hunted

COMPOSERS

Conroy, F. Body & soul
Frame, R. The lantern bearers
Galloway, J. Clara
Grumbach, D. Chamber music
Hesse, H. Gertrude
Hijuelos, O. A simple Habana melody: from when the world was good
Krüger, M. The cello player
Mann, T. Doctor Faustus
McEwan, I. Amsterdam
Ōe, K. A quiet life
Piercy, M. Summer people

Compromising positions. Isaacs, S.
Compulsion. Ablow, K. R.
Compulsion. Levin, M.

COMPULSORY MILITARY SERVICE *See* Draft

COMPUTER HACKERS

Gibson, W. Neuromancer

COMPUTER PROGRAMMING *See* Programming (Computers)

COMPUTER SIMULATION *See* Virtual reality

COMPUTERS

See also Programming (Computers)
Anderson, P. Goat song
Brunner, J. Stand on Zanzibar
Card, O. S. The call of earth
Card, O. S. Earthborn
Card, O. S. Earthfall
Card, O. S. The memory of earth
Card, O. S. The ships of earth
Costello, M. Big if
Coupland, D. Microserfs
Crichton, M. Disclosure
Crichton, M. The terminal man
Crumey, A. Mr. Mee
Danvers, D. The fourth world
Darnton, J. Mind catcher
Francis, D. Twice shy
Heinlein, R. A. The moon is a harsh mistress
Iles, G. The footprints of God
Iles, G. Mortal fear
Kunzru, H. Transmission
Lustbader, E. V. Second skin
Lustbader, E. V. White Ninja
Nance, J. J. Medusa's child
Powers, R. The gold bug variations
Saul, J. Shadows
Stephenson, N. Cryptonomicon
Thomas, M. M. Black money
Trenhaile, J. The gates of exquisite view
Ullman, E. The bug
Updike, J. Roger's version
Updike, J. Villages
Wilhelm, K. Death qualified
Wood, B. Perfect Harmony

Comrade Charlie. Freemantle, B.
The **con** man's daughter. Dee, E.

CON MEN *See* Swindlers and swindling

Conan Doyle's tales of medical humanism and values: Round the red lamp. Doyle, Sir A. C.

CONCENTRATION CAMPS

See also Political prisoners; World War, 1939-1945—Prisoners and prisons
Albahari, D. Götz and Meyer
Daley, R. The innocents within
De Hartog, J. The lamb's war
Iles, G. Black cross
Otsuka, J. When the emperor was divine
Styron, W. Sophie's choice

The **concrete** blonde. Connelly, M.
The **condor** passes. Grau, S. A.

CONDUCT OF LIFE *See* Ethics

CONDUCTORS (MUSIC)

Ford, R. The student conductor

A **confederacy** of dunces. Toole, J. K.

CONFEDERATE AGENTS *See* Spies

CONFEDERATE STATES OF AMERICA

Kantor, M. Andersonville

CONFEDERATE STATES OF AMERICA. ARMY

Brown, R. M. High hearts
Burke, J. L. White doves at morning
Cornwell, B. Copperhead
Cornwell, B. Rebel
Jones, D. C. Elkhorn Tavern
Keneally, T. Confederates
Shaara, J. Gods and generals
Shaara, J. The last full measure
Youmans, M. The wolf pit

Confederates. Keneally, T.
Confess, Fletch. Mcdonald, G.
In Mcdonald, G. The Fletch chronicles

CONFESSION

Banville, J. The book of evidence

Confession. Pickard, N.
Confessional. Higgins, J.
Confessions of Felix Krull, confidence man. Mann, T.
The **confessions** of Mycroft Holmes. Theroux, M.
The **confessions** of Nat Turner. Styron, W.
The **confessions** of Zeno. See Svevo, I. Zeno's conscience
The **confidence-man:** his masquerade. Melville, H.
The **confidential** agent. Greene, G.
In Greene, G. 3: This gun for hire, The confidential agent, The ministry of fear
Confinement. Brown, C.

CONFLICT OF GENERATIONS

Berger, T. Vital parts
Cunningham, M. Flesh and blood
Jen, G. Mona in the promised land
Lee, C. Y. The flower drum song
Lurie, A. The war between the Tates
Meloy, M. Liars and saints
Napolitano, A. Within arm's reach
Read, P. P. The professor's daughter
Snow, C. P. The sleep of reason
Stegner, W. E. All the little live things
Thayer, N. Family secrets
Trollope, J. The men and the girls
Turgenev, I. S. Fathers and sons
Tyler, A. A slipping-down life

COURTS AND COURTIERS—England—*Continued*
Gregory, P. Earthly joys
Holt, V. My enemy the Queen
Lewis, H. W. I am Mary Tudor
Maxwell, R. The Queen's bastard
Maxwell, R. The secret diary of Anne Boleyn
Penman, S. K. Falls the shadow
Penman, S. K. Here be dragons
Penman, S. K. The reckoning
Penman, S. K. The sunne in splendour
Penman, S. K. Time and chance
Penman, S. K. When Christ and his saints slept
Plaidy, J. The captive Queen of Scots
Plaidy, J. Murder most royal
Plaidy, J. The pleasures of love
Plaidy, J. The reluctant queen
Plaidy, J. The rose without a thorn
Plaidy, J. The sixth wife
Plaidy, J. William's wife
Riley, J. M. The serpent garden
Seton, A. Katherine

France

Anthony, E. The Cardinal and the Queen
Bradshaw, G. The wolf hunt
Davis, K. Versailles
Dumas, A. The iron mask [variant title: The man in the iron mask]
Dumas, A. The three musketeers
Haasse, H. S. In a dark wood wandering
Laker, R. To dance with kings
Riley, J. M. The serpent garden
Thomas, C. Farewell, my queen

Italy

Sontag, S. The volcano lover
Stendhal. The charterhouse of Parma
Tomasi di Lampedusa, G. The Leopard

Japan

Mishima, Y. Spring snow
Murasaki Shikibu. The tale of Genji

Scotland

Dunnett, D. Gemini

Turkey

Wallach, J. Seraglio

COURTS-MARTIAL
Blake, M. Marching to Valhalla
DeMille, N. Word of honor
Jones, D. C. The court-martial of George Armstrong Custer
Nordhoff, C. Mutiny on the Bounty
Poyer, D. The circle

The **courts** of chaos. Zelazny, R.
The **courts** of love. Gilchrist, E.

COURTSHIP
Burns, O. A. Leaving Cold Sassy
Colette. Claudine in Paris
Colette. Gigi
Colwin, L. Happy all the time
James, H. Daisy Miller
James, H. Washington Square
Purdy, J. In a shallow grave
Stowe, H. B. The minister's wooing

Cousin Bette. Balzac, H. d.
Cousin Kate. Heyer, G.
Cousin Pons. Balzac, H. d.
Cousin Rosamund. West, Dame R.

COUSINS
Balzac, H. d. Cousin Bette
Barry, S. Annie Dunne
Brenna, D. The altar of the body
Capote, T. A Christmas memory
Chabon, M. The amazing adventures of Kavalier and Clay
Colwin, L. Happy all the time
Dew, R. F. The evidence against her
Du Maurier, Dame D. My cousin Rachel
Faulkner, W. The mansion
Howard, M. The Magdalene
Jakes, J. American dreams
James, H. The Europeans
King, T. Truth & Bright Water
McCorkle, J. Ferris Beach
McDermott, A. Child of my heart
Mitford, N. Love in a cold climate
Mitford, N. The pursuit of love
Morris, M. M. Fiona Range
Pearson, T. R. Blue Ridge
Robards, K. Ghost moon
Seton, A. Dragonwyck
Siddons, A. R. Nora, Nora
Siddons, A. R. Peachtree Road
Stewart, M. The Gabriel hounds
Thomas, R. All my sins remembered
Walbert, K. The gardens of Kyoto
Weber, K. The Music Lesson
Yoshimoto, B. Goodbye Tsugumi
Yoshimoto, B. Night and night's travelers

The **covenant**. Michener, J. A.
The **covenant** of the flame. Morrell, D.

COVINGTON, SYMS, 1813-1861

About

McDonald, R. Mr. Darwin's shooter

COWARDICE
Conrad, J. Lord Jim
Crane, S. The red badge of courage
Fleming, T. J. Time and tide

COWBOYS
Clark, W. V. T. The Ox-bow incident
Durham, D. A. Gabriel's story
Eagle, K. The last true cowboy
Estleman, L. D. Bloody season
Evans, N. The horse whisperer
Houston, P. Cowboys are my weakness
McCarthy, C. All the pretty horses
Schaefer, J. W. Monte Walsh

Cowboys are my weakness. Houston, P.
COWHANDS *See* Cowboys
COWS *See* Cattle
Coyote. Barnes, L.
Coyote. Steele, A. M.
Coyote summer. Gear, W. M.
Coyote waits. Hillerman, T.

COYOTES
Kingsolver, B. Prodigal summer

Crabwalk. Grass, G.

CRACK (DRUG)
Carcaterra, L. Apaches

Cradle and all. Patterson, J.
The **cradle** will fall. Clark, M. H.
Cranford. Gaskell, E. C.
Crash diet. McCorkle, J.
The **crazed**. Ha Jin
Crazy for you. Crusie, J.

CRAZY HORSE, SIOUX CHIEF, CA. 1842-1877

About

Blevins, W. Stone song
Johnston, T. C. Turn the stars upside down
O'Brien, D. The contract surgeon

Crazy in Alabama. Childress, M.
Crazy in Berlin. Berger, T.
Crazybone. Pronzini, B.

CREATION (LITERARY, ARTISTIC, ETC.)
See also Authorship
Ishiguro, K. The unconsoled

Creation. Vidal, G.
Creatures of the kingdom. Michener, J. A.
CREDIBILITY *See* Truthfulness and falsehood
A **creek** called Wounded Knee. Jones, D. C.
Creek Mary's blood. Brown, D. A.

CREOLES
Hambly, B. Days of the dead
Hambly, B. Dead water
Hambly, B. A free man of color
Hambly, B. Graveyard dust
Hambly, B. Sold down the river
Hambly, B. Die upon a kiss
Hambly, B. Wet grave
Tademy, L. Cane River

Crescent. Abu-Jaber, D.
Crescent City. Plain, B.

CRIME AND CRIMINALS—*Continued*
Patterson, J. Along came a spider
Patterson, J. Lifeguard
Pearson, R. Cut and run
Pelecanos, G. P. The big blowdown
Pelecanos, G. P. Drama city
Pelecanos, G. P. Shame the devil
Pelecanos, G. P. The sweet forever
Perry, T. Blood money
Perry, T. Dance for the dead
Perry, T. Metzger's dog
Perry, T. Vanishing act
Price, R. Clockers
Price, R. Freedomland
Puzo, M. The godfather
Puzo, M. The last Don
Puzo, M. Omerta
Reed, B. The indictment
Rendell, R. Going wrong
Rendell, R. A judgment in stone
Rendell, R. Make death love me
Rosenberg, N. T. Abuse of power
Rosenberg, N. T. First offense
Rosenberg, N. T. Mitigating circumstances
Sanders, L. Sullivan's sting
Shames, L. Mangrove squeeze
Shames, L. Virgin heat
Shames, L. Welcome to paradise
Sheldon, S. Rage of angels
Sidor, S. Skin River
Stark, R. Backflash
Stark, R. Breakout
Stark, R. Comeback
Tanenbaum, R. Act of revenge
Tanenbaum, R. Corruption of blood
Tanenbaum, R. Immoral certainty
Tanenbaum, R. Reversible error
Thomas, M. M. Black money
Thomas, R. Voodoo, Ltd
Tolstoy, L., graf. Resurrection
Uhnak, D. Victims
Vachss, A. H. Two trains running
Vine, B. A dark-adapted eye
Vine, B. Grasshopper
Wambaugh, J. The blue knight
Wambaugh, J. The Delta Star
Wambaugh, J. Finnegan's week
Wambaugh, J. The Glitter Dome
Wambaugh, J. The new centurions
Weaver, M. Deceptions
Welsh, I. Porno
Westlake, D. E. Bad news
Westlake, D. E. Bank shot
Westlake, D. E. Cops and robbers
Westlake, D. E. Don't ask
Westlake, D. E. Drowned hopes
Westlake, D. E. Good behavior
Westlake, D. E. The hot rock
Westlake, D. E. Put a lid on it
Westlake, D. E. The road to ruin
Westlake, D. E. Thieves' dozen
Westlake, D. E. Watch your back
Westlake, D. E. What's the worst that could happen?
Westlake, D. E. Why me?
Wiltse, D. Blown away
Winegardner, M. The Godfather returns
Woods, S. Grass roots
Woods, S. Reckless abandon
Woods, S. Two-dollar bill
Crime and Mr. Campion. Allingham, M.
Crime and punishment. Dostoyevsky, F.
Crime from the mind of a woman. See A moment on the edge
Crime in Holland. See Simenon, G. Maigret in Holland
CRIME PASSIONEL *See* Crimes of passion
Crime school. O'Connell, C.
Crime stories and other writings. Hammett, D.
CRIMEAN WAR, 1853-1856
Bainbridge, B. Master Georgie
CRIMES OF PASSION
See also Murder stories
Tolstoy, L., graf. The Kreutzer sonata
Yancey, R. A burning in Homeland
Criminal damage. Yorke, M.
Criminal intent. Bernhardt, W.
Criminal justice. Parker, B.
CRIMINALLY INSANE *See* Insane, Criminal and dangerous
CRIMINALS *See* Crime and criminals
Criminals. Livesey, M.
Crimson joy. Parker, R. B.
The **crimson** petal and the white. Faber, M.
Critical injuries. Barfoot, J.
Critical mass. Martini, S. P.
CRO-MAGNON MAN *See* Prehistoric man
CROATIA
Novakovich, J. April Fool's Day
Seymour, G. The heart of danger
CROATIAN AMERICANS
Stefaniak, M. H. The Turk and my mother
CROATS
Australia
Coetzee, J. M. Slow man
The **crocodile** bird. Rendell, R.
The **cross**. Undset, S.
In Undset, S. Kristin Lavransdatter
The **cross-legged** knight. Robb, C. M.
Crossing the line. McKinzie, C.
Crossing the lines. Bragg, M.
Crossing the river. Phillips, C.
Crossing to safety. Stegner, W. E.
The **Crossley** baby. Carey, J.
Crow Lake. Lawson, M.
The **crown** of Columbus. Dorris, M.
A **crown** of feathers and other stories. Singer, I. B.
In Singer, I. B. Collected stories
Crucial instances. Wharton, E.
In Wharton, E. The collected short stories of Edith Wharton
Cruel as the grave. Penman, S. K.
Cruel justice. Bernhardt, W.
The **cruel** sea. Monsarrat, N.
CRUELTY
See also Atrocities; Violence
Banks, R. Continental drift
Conroy, P. The lords of discipline
Hough, R. The stowaway
Kantor, M. Andersonville
Kosinski, J. N. The painted bird
Ōe, K. Nip the buds, shoot the kids
West, P. Lord Byron's doctor
CRUELTY TO CHILDREN *See* Child abuse
Crumbtown. Connelly, J.
Crusader's cross. Burke, J. L.
CRUSADES
See also Knights and knighthood
Connell, E. S. Deus lo volt!
Eco, U. Baudolino
Holland, C. Jerusalem
The **crush**. Brown, S.
A **cry** from the dark. Barnard, R.
A **cry** in the night. Clark, M. H.
Cry me a river. Pearson, T. R.
Cry of the hawk. Johnston, T. C.
Cry of the wind. Harrison, S.
Cry, the beloved country. Paton, A.
Cry wolf. Smith, W. A.
The **crying** of lot 49. Pynchon, T.
Crying wolf. Abrahams, P.
CRYONICS
Berger, T. Vital parts
CRYPTOGRAPHY
Brown, D. The Da Vinci code
Harris, R. Enigma
Stephenson, N. Cryptonomicon
Cryptonomicon. Stephenson, N.
The **crystal** cave. Stewart, M.
also in Stewart, M. Mary Stewart's Merlin trilogy
The **crystal** city. Card, O. S.
The **crystal** frontier. Fuentes, C.
Crystal line. McCaffrey, A.
Crystal singer. McCaffrey, A.
CUBA
Alvarez, J. In the name of Salomé

CYSTIC FIBROSIS
Thayer, N. Between husbands and friends
CZECH AMERICANS
Chabon, M. The amazing adventures of Kavalier and Clay
CZECH REFUGEES
Read, P. P. A season in the West
CZECH REPUBLIC
See also Czechoslovakia
Prague
Chatwin, B. Utz
Goldstein, L. The alchemist's door
Klíma, I. No saints or angels
Kundera, M. Ignorance
Roth, P. The Prague orgy
Sherwood, F. The book of splendor
CZECHOSLOVAKIA
See also Czech Republic
Demetz, H. The house on Prague Street
Hrabal, B. I served the King of England
Hrabal, B. Too loud a solitude
Kundera, M. The book of laughter and forgetting
Kundera, M. The joke
Kundera, M. Laughable loves
Kundera, M. The unbearable lightness of being
CZECHS
England
Read, P. P. A season in the West
United States
Cather, W. My Antonia
Cather, W. O pioneers!
Kafka, F. Amerika

D

"D" is for deadbeat. Grafton, S.
DA GAMA, VASCO *See* Gama, Vasco da, 1469-1524
DA VINCI, LEONARDO *See* Leonardo, da Vinci, 1452-1519
The **Da** Vinci code. Brown, D.
Dad. Wharton, W.
Daddy's little girl. Clark, M. H.
The **Dain** curse. Hammett, D.
In Hammett, D. Complete novels
The **Daisy** Ducks. Boyer, R.
Daisy Miller. James, H.
also in James, H. Complete stories, 1874-1884
also in James, H. The complete tales of Henry James
also in James, H. The Henry James reader p403-61
also in James, H. Short novels of Henry James p1-58
DAKOTA INDIANS
Brown, D. A. Killdeer Mountain
Harrison, J. The road home
Hill, R. B. Hanta yo
Jones, D. C. Arrest Sitting Bull
Power, S. The grass dancer
DALLAS (TEX.) *See* Texas—Dallas
Damage. Hart, J.
Damaged goods. Solomita, S.
Damascus Gate. Stone, R.
The **damnation** game. Barker, C.
DAMS
Cambor, K. In sunlight, in a beautiful garden
Doig, I. Bucking the sun
Wiggins, M. Evidence of things unseen
Dan Leno and the Limehouse Golem. See Ackroyd, P. The trial of Elizabeth Cree
A **dance** at the slaughterhouse. Block, L.
Dance for the dead. Perry, T.
Dance hall of the dead. Hillerman, T.
also in Hillerman, T. The Joe Leaphorn mysteries
Dance night. Powell, D.
In Powell, D. Novels, 1930-1942
Dance on the wind. Johnston, T. C.
A **dance** to the music of time. Powell, A.
Dance with me. Rice, L.
Dancer. McCann, C.
DANCERS
Brown, C. The hatbox baby
Durrell, L. Justine
Godden, R. Thursday's children
Hamilton, J. The short history of a prince
Hiaasen, C. Strip tease
Lutz, J. Dancing with the dead
McMurtry, L. The desert rose
Nin, A. Children of the albatross
Robinson, S. Stardance [novelette]
Dancers at the end of time [series]
Moorcock, M. An alien heat
Moorcock, M. The end of all songs
Moorcock, M. The hollow lands
Dancers in mourning. Allingham, M.
In Allingham, M. Crime and Mr. Campion p363-575
Dancing after hours. Dubus, A.
Dancing Arabs. Qashu, S.
Dancing at the Rascal Fair. Doig, I.
The **dancing** floor. Michaels, B.
Dancing girls and other stories. Atwood, M.
Dancing in the dark. Kaminsky, S. M.
Dancing in the dark. Phillips, C.
Dancing with Einstein. Wenner, K.
Dancing with the dead. Lutz, J.
Dandelion wine. Bradbury, R.
DANES
See also Vikings
England
Høeg, P. The woman and the ape
The **danger**. Francis, D.
A **dangerous** business. Underwood, M.
A **dangerous** fortune. Follett, K.
The **dangerous** hour. Muller, M.
A **dangerous** mourning. Perry, A.
Dangerous visions. Entered in Part I under title
A **dangerous** woman. Morris, M. M.
Dangling man. Bellow, S.
also in Bellow, S. Novels, 1944-1953
Daniel Martin. Fowles, J.
Danny. Steinbeck, J.
In Steinbeck, J. The portable Steinbeck
DANTE ALIGHIERI, 1265-1321
About
Pearl, M. The Dante Club
The **Dante** Club. Pearl, M.
The **Dante** game. Langton, J.
DANZIG (POLAND) *See* Poland—Gdansk
The **Danzig** trilogy. Grass, G.
Daphne du Maurier's classics of the macabre. Du Maurier, Dame D.
Darconville's cat. Theroux, A.
The **darfsteller**. Miller, W. M.
In The Hugo winners p5-71
The **dark**. Entered in Part I under title
A **dark-adapted** eye. Vine, B.
DARK AGES *See* Europe—392-814; Middle Ages
A **dark** coffin. Butler, G.
The **dark** design. Farmer, P. J.
The **dark** door. Wilhelm, K.
The **dark** half. King, S.
Dark homecoming. Lustbader, E. V.
Dark horse. Hoag, T.
Dark inheritance. Gear, W. M.
Dark justice. Bernhardt, W.
Dark lady. Patterson, R. N.
Dark matter. Entered in Part I under title
Dark matter. Kerr, P.
The **dark** path. Hunt, W. H.
Dark rivers of the heart. Koontz, D. R.
The **dark** room. Walters, M.
Dark Rosaleen. Brand, M.
In Brand, M. Max Brand's best western stories
The **dark** side of Guy de Maupassant. Maupassant, G. d.
Dark star. Muller, M.
The **dark** tower and other stories. Lewis, C. S.
Dark voyage. Furst, A.
The **dark** wind. Hillerman, T.
also in Hillerman, T. The Jim Chee mysteries
A **darker** place. King, L. R.

The **dearly** departed. Lipman, E.
DEATH
See also Bereavement; Dead; Deathbed scenes
Agee, J. A death in the family
Anthony, P. On a pale horse
Auster, P. Timbuktu
Banks, R. The sweet hereafter
Barker, C. Sacrament
Bellow, S. The dean's December
Bellow, S. Ravelstein
Bellows, N. On this day
Berg, E. The art of mending
Betts, D. Souls raised from the dead
Bialosky, J. House under snow
Bohjalian, C. A. The buffalo soldier
Bohjalian, C. A. Midwives
Brautigan, R. An unfortunate woman
Cather, W. Lucy Gayheart
Coetzee, J. M. Age of iron
Crace, J. Being dead
Craven, M. I heard the owl call my name
Davies, R. The cunning man
DeLillo, D. White noise
Dexter, P. Brotherly love
Duncan, G. Death of an ordinary man
Fowler, C. M. Remembering Blue
Gatewood, R. The sound of the trees
Glass, J. Three Junes
Godwin, G. The good husband
Hart, J. Damage
Hoffman, A. At risk
Inness-Brown, E. Burning Marguerite
Johnson, S. The sailmaker's daughter
Jönsson, R. My life as a dog
Kawabata, Y. The sound of the mountain
Keneally, T. River town
King, S. The body
King, S. The long walk
Klein, R. The moth diaries
Lively, P. Moon tiger
Lively, P. Passing on
Mann, T. Death in Venice
Mason, B. A. Feather crowns
Maynard, J. The usual rules
McCrumb, S. The rosewood casket
McDermott, A. At weddings and wakes
McFarland, D. School for the blind
Monette, P. Afterlife
Morgan, R. K. Altered carbon
Morrison, T. Love
Muske-Dukes, C. Life after death
Oates, J. C. Middle age
Ōe, K. An echo of heaven
Okuizumi, H. The stones cry out
O'Nan, S. A prayer for the dying
Price, R. The promise of rest
Rice, L. Home fires
Rice, L. Safe harbor
Roth, P. Sabbath's theater
Roy, A. The god of small things
Sarton, M. A reckoning
Schwartz, J. B. Reservation Road
Schwartz, L. S. The fatigue artist
Searles, J. Boy still missing
Settle, M. L. The killing ground
Spark, M. Memento mori
Steel, D. Johnny Angel
Suri, M. The death of Vishnu
Swift, G. Last orders
Tóibín, C. The blackwater lightship
Tolstoy, L., graf. Master and man
Trevor, W. Death in summer
Trollope, J. Next of kin
Tyler, A. Saint maybe
Tyler, A. The tin can tree
Varley, J. The persistence of vision
Wallace, D. Big fish
Wilhelm, K. The good children
Wolitzer, M. Surrender, Dorothy
Yoshimoto, B. Asleep [a novella]
Yoshimoto, B. Kitchen
Death and restoration. Pears, I.
Death and taxes. Dunlap, S.
Death and the chaste apprentice. Barnard, R.
Death and the lover. See Hesse, H. Narcissus and Goldmund
A **death** at St. Anselm's. Holland, I.
A **death** before dying. Wilcox, C.
Death benefits. Perry, T.
Death by accident. Crider, B.
Death by jury. Lutz, J.
Death by sheer torture. Barnard, R.
Death by the light of the moon. Hess, J.
Death comes for the archbishop. Cather, W.
also in Cather, W. Willa Cather, later novels
Death dream. Bova, B.
Death du jour. Reichs, K. J.
A **death** for a dancer. Giroux, E. X.
Death for a dietitian. Giroux, E. X.
A **death** for a dodo. Giroux, E. X.
Death goes on retreat. O'Marie, C. A.
Death in a cold hard light. Mathews, F.
Death in a mood indigo. Mathews, F.
Death in a tenured position. Cross, A.
Death in Berlin. Kaye, M. M.
Death in disguise. Graham, C.
Death in Dublin. Gill, B.
Death in holy orders. James, P. D.
Death in Kashmir. Kaye, M. M.
Death in lacquer red. Dams, J. M.
Death in paradise. Hart, C. G.
Death in paradise. Parker, R. B.
Death in summer. Trevor, W.
Death in the Andes. Vargas Llosa, M.
"A **death** in the desert". Cather, W.
In Cather, W. Early novels and stories
A **death** in the family. Agee, J.
also in Agee, J. Let us now praise famous men; A death in the family, and shorter fiction
Death in the old country. Wright, E.
Death in Venice. Mann, T.
also in Mann, T. Death in Venice and other tales
also in Mann, T. Stories of three decades
Death in Venice and other tales. Mann, T.
Death is now my neighbor. Dexter, C.
Death lives next door. Butler, G.
Death notes. Rendell, R.
The **death** of a bum. Westlake, D. E.
In Westlake, D. E. Levine p121-50
Death of a celebrity. Beaton, M. C.
Death of a dentist. Beaton, M. C.
Death of a doxy. Stout, R.
Death of a dustman. Beaton, M. C.
Death of a ghost. Allingham, M.
In Allingham, M. Crime and Mr. Campion p7-175
Death of a hero. Haymon, S. T.
Death of a hussy. Beaton, M. C.
The **death** of a Joyce scholar. Gill, B.
Death of a literary widow. Barnard, R.
Death of a macho man. Beaton, M. C.
Death of a nag. Beaton, M. C.
Death of a nationalist. Pawel, R.
Death of a poison pen. Beaton, M. C.
Death of a Russian priest. Kaminsky, S. M.
Death of a salesperson, and other untimely exits. Barnard, R.
Death of a stranger. Perry, A.
Death of a swagman. Upfield, A. W.
Death of a village. Beaton, M. C.
Death of an addict. Beaton, M. C.
Death of an angel. O'Marie, C. A.
Death of an expert witness. James, P. D.
The **death** of an Irish lover. Gill, B.
The **death** of an Irish sea wolf. Gill, B.
The **death** of an Irish tinker. Gill, B.
Death of an ordinary man. Duncan, G.
The **death** of Artemio Cruz. Fuentes, C.
The **death** of Iván Ilyitch. Tolstoy, L., graf
In Tolstoy, L., graf. The short novels of Tolstoy
The **death** of Ivan Ilyitch, and other stories. Tolstoy, L., graf
The **death** of love. Gill, B.
The **death** of Methuselah and other stories. Singer, I. B.
The **death** of sweet mister. Woodrell, D.
The **death** of the heart. Bowen, E.
The **death** of Vishnu. Suri, M.
Death on a cold, wild river. Gill, B.
Death on the Downs. Brett, S.
Death on the Nile. Christie, A.
Death penalty. Coughlin, W. J.

DEPARTMENT STORES
Archer, J. As the crow flies
Birmingham, S. Carriage trade
Bradford, B. T. Hold the dream
Bradford, B. T. A woman of substance
Davies, V. Miracle on 34th Street
Martin, S. Shopgirl
DEPRESSION, 1929 *See* Business depression, 1929
DEPRESSIONS, BUSINESS *See* Business depression, 1929
Derailed. Siegel, J.
DERBYSHIRE (ENGLAND) *See* England—Derbyshire
DERELICTS
Innes, H. The wreck of the Mary Deare
The **descent** of man. Wharton, E.
In Wharton, E. The collected short stories of Edith Wharton
The **desert** crop. Cookson, C.
A **desert** in Bohemia. Paton Walsh, J.
The **desert** rose. McMurtry, L.
The **deserter**. Langton, J.
DESERTION, MILITARY *See* Military desertion
DESERTION AND NONSUPPORT
Gaines, E. J. In my father's house
DESERTS
See also Sahara
Caputo, P. Horn of Africa
Herbert, F. Children of Dune
Silko, L. Gardens in the dunes
Zafris, N. Lucky strike
Desirable daughters. Mukherjee, B.
Desperate measures. Morrell, D.
Desperate measures. Wilhelm, K.
Desperation. King, S.
DESTINY *See* Fate and fatalism
Destiny. Parks, T.
Destiny: child of the sky. Haydon, E.
Destroyer. Cherryh, C. J.
DESTRUCTION OF EARTH *See* Earth, Destruction of
The **destruction** of the books. Odom, M.
DESTRUCTION OF THE JEWS *See* Holocaust, Jewish (1933-1945)
Detective. Hailey, A.
DETECTIVE AND MYSTERY STORIES *See* Mystery and detective stories
The **detective** wore silk drawers. Lovesey, P.
DETECTIVES
Adams, Doc. See stories by Boyer, R.
Adams, Hilda. See stories by Rinehart, M. R.
Aldington, Claire. See stories by Holland, I.
Alleyn, Superintendent Roderick. See stories by Marsh, Dame N.
Archer, Lew. See stories by Macdonald, R.
Archer, Owen. See stories by Robb, C. M.
Argyll, Jonathan. See stories by Pears, I.
Arnold, Jessie. See stories by Henry, S.
Baley, Elijah. See stories by Asimov, I.
Balzic, Mario. See stories by Constantine, K. C.
Banks, Chief Inspector Alan. See stories by Robinson, P.
Barnaby, Chief Inspector. See stories by Graham, C.
Battle, Superintendent. See stories by Christie, A.
Bayles, China. See stories by Albert, S. W.
Bear, Goldy. See stories by Davidson, D. M.
Bearpaw, Molly. See stories by Hager, J.
Beaumont, J. P. See stories by Jance, J. A.
Beaumont, Ned. See stories by Hammett, D.
Beck, Inspector Martin. See stories by Sjöwall, M.
Beresford, Tommy. See stories by Christie, A.
Bernhardt, Alan. See stories by Wilcox, C.
Bernier, Alex. See stories by Saulnier, B.
Bittersohn, Max. See stories by MacLeod, C.
Bliss, Vicky. See stories by Peters, E.
Bolitar, Myron. See stories by Coben, H.
Bonaparte, Inspector Napoleon. See stories by Upfield, A. W.
Bond, James. See stories by Fleming, I.
Bond, James. See stories by Gardner, J. E.
Bosch, Harry. See stories by Connelly, M.
Bracewell, Nicholas. See stories by Marston, E.
Bradshaw, Charlie. See stories by Dobyns, S.
Brady, Joanna. See stories by Jance, J. A.
Brandstetter, Dave. See stories by Hansen, J.
Bray, Nell. See stories by Linscott, G.
Brennan, Temperance. See stories by Reichs, K. J.
Brinker, Roscoe. See stories by Mitchell, J. C.
Broom, Andrew. See stories by McInerny, R. M.
Brown, Father. See stories by Chesterton, G. K.
Brunetti, Guido. See stories by Leon, D.
Burke. See stories by Vachss, A. H.
Burns, Antonio. See stories by McKinzie, C.
Burtonall, Clare. See stories by Gash, J.
Cadfael, Brother. See stories by Peters, E.
Cain, Jenny. See stories by Pickard, N.
Calhoun, Stoney. See stories by Tapply, W. G.
Campbell, Liam. See stories by Stabenow, D.
Campion, Albert. See stories by Allingham, M.
Cardinal, John. See stories by Blunt, G.
Cardozo, Lieutenant Vincent. See stories by Stewart, E.
Carella, Lieutenant Steve. See stories by McBain, E.
Carlucci, Rugs. See stories by Constantine, K. C.
Carlyle, Carlotta. See stories by Barnes, L.
Carver, Fred. See stories by Lutz, J.
Castang, Henri. See stories by Freeling, N.
Cates, Molly. See stories by Walker, M. W.
Charles, Nick. See stories by Hammett, D.
Charles, Nora. See stories by Hammett, D.
Chee, Jim. See stories by Hillerman, T.
Chen, Inspector. See stories by Qiu Xiaolong
Clement, Jules. See stories by Harrison, J.
Coffin, John. See stories by Butler, G.
Cole, Elvis. See stories by Crais, R.
Colorado, Kat. See stories by Kijewski, K.
Cone, Timothy. See stories by Sanders, L.
Continental Op. See stories by Hammett, D.
Cooperman, Benny. See stories by Engel, H.
Corbett, Hugh. See stories by Doherty, P. C.
Corning, Ken. See stories by Gardner, E. S.
Costa, Nic. See stories by Hewson, D.
Coyne, Brady. See stories by Tapply, W. G.
Cribb, Detective-Sergeant. See stories by Lovesey, P.
Crow, Inspector Angus. See stories by Gardner, J. E.
Cuddy, John Francis. See stories by Healy, J. F.
Cunningham, John. See stories by Hammond, G.
Dalgliesh, Commander Adam. See stories by James, P. D.
Dalton, Smokey. See stories by Nelscott, K.
Dalziel, Inspector. See stories by Hill, R.
Daniels, Chief Superintendent Charmian. See stories by Melville, J.
Darling, Annie. See stories by Hart, C. G.
Darling, Max. See stories by Hart, C. G.
Davenport, Lucas. See stories by Sandford, J.
De Gier, Sergeant Rinus. See stories by Van de Wetering, J.
De Quincy, Justin. See stories by Penman, S. K.
Deal, John. See stories by Standiford, L.
Decker, Peter. See stories by Kellerman, F.
Dee, Judge. See stories by Gulik, R. H. v.
Delafield, Kate. See stories by Forrest, K. V.
Delaney, Chief Edward X. See stories by Sanders, L.
Delaware, Alex. See stories by Kellerman, J.
Delchard, Ralph. See stories by Marston, E.
Demarkian, Gregor. See stories by Haddam, J.
Devlin, Paul. See stories by Heffernan, W.
Diamond, Peter. See stories by Lovesey, P.
Dobbs, Maisie. See stories by Winspear, J.
Dowling, Father. See stories by McInerny, R. M.
Du Pré, Gabriel. See stories by Bowen, P.
Dupin, C. Auguste. See stories by Poe, E. A.
Edward VII, King of Great Britain. See stories by Lovesey, P.
Elizabeth I, Queen of England. See stories by Harper, K.
Epton, Rosa. See stories by Underwood, M.
Fairchild, Faith. See stories by Page, K. H.
Fairweather, Doran. See stories by Hardwick, M.
Falco, Marcus Didius. See stories by Davis, L.
Fandorin, Erast. See stories by Akunin, B.
Fansler, Kate. See stories by Cross, A.
Felse, Dominic. See stories by Peters, E.
Felse, Superintendent George. See stories by Peters, E.
Fielding, Kit. See stories by Francis, D.
Flannery, Jimmy. See stories by Campbell, R. W.
Fletch. See stories by Mcdonald, G.
Flynn, Terry. See stories by Granger, B.
Folger, Meredith. See stories by Mathews, F.
Fonesca, Lew. See stories by Kaminsky, S. M.
Forsythe, Robert. See stories by Giroux, E. X.
Friedman, Kinky. See stories by Friedman, K.

DETECTIVES—*Continued*
Sayler, Catherine. See stories by Grant, L.
Scarpetta, Kay. See stories by Cornwell, P. D.
Schulz, Goldy. See stories by Davidson, D. M.
Scudder, Matthew. See stories by Block, L.
Seddon, Carole. See stories by Brett, S.
Self, Gerhard. See stories by Schlink, B.
Sewell, Hitchcock. See stories by Cockey, T.
Shandy, Peter. See stories by MacLeod, C.
Shimura, Rei. See stories by Massey, S.
Shore, Jemima. See stories by Fraser, A.
Shugak, Kate. See stories by Stabenow, D.
Sixsmith, Joe. See stories by Hill, R.
Slider, Inspector Bill. See stories by Harrod-Eagles, C.
Sloan, Inspector. See stories by Aird, C.
Small, Rabbi David. See stories by Kemelman, H.
Smith, Bill. See stories by Rozan, S. J.
Smith, Jill. See stories by Dunlap, S.
Smith, Mac. See stories by Truman, M.
Smith, Truman. See stories by Crider, B.
Spade, Sam. See stories by Hammett, D.
Spenser. See stories by Parker, R. B.
Stark, Joanna. See stories by Muller, M.
Stone, Jesse. See stories by Parker, R. B.
Stoner, Harry. See stories by Valin, J.
Strange, Derek. See stories by Pelecanos, G. P.
Sughrue, C. W. See stories by Crumley, J.
Tanner, John Marshall. See stories by Greenleaf, S.
Taylor, Jack. See stories by Bruen, K.
Thanet, Detective Inspector Luke. See stories by Simpson, D.
Thatcher, John Putnam. See stories by Lathen, E.
Thorn. See stories by Hall, J. W.
Tibbs, Virgil. See stories by Ball, J. D.
Trethowan, Superintendent Perry. See stories by Barnard, R.
Trumbull, Victoria. See stories by Riggs, C.
Tryon, Glynis. See stories by Monfredo, M. G.
Van der Valk, Inspector. See stories by Freeling, N.
Walker, Amos. See stories by Estleman, L. D.
Wallander, Chief Inspector Kurt. See stories by Mankell, H.
Wallander, Kurt. See stories by Mankell, H.
Warshawski, V. I. See stories by Paretsky, S.
Watkins, Claire. See stories by Logue, M.
Weaver, Benjamin. See stories by Liss, D.
Weggins, Bailey. See stories by White, K.
West, Helen. See stories by Fyfield, F.
Wexford, Chief Inspector. See stories by Rendell, R.
Whistler. See stories by Campbell, R. W.
White, Blanche. See stories by Neely, B.
Wimsey, Lord Peter. See stories by Sayers, D. L.
Wine, Moses. See stories by Simon, R. L.
Wolfe, Nero. See stories by Goldsborough, R.
Wolfe, Nero. See stories by Stout, R.
Wycliffe, Superintendent. See stories by Burley, W. J.
Wylie, Eva. See stories by Cody, L.
Zen, Aurelio. See stories by Dibdin, M.
Zondi, Detective Sergeant Mickey. See stories by McClure, J.

DETECTIVES, PRIVATE
Adler, E. All or nothing
Atkinson, K. Case histories
Brin, D. Kiln people
Gores, J. Cons, scams & grifts
Gores, J. Contract null & void
Hill, R. Blood sympathy
Ishiguro, K. When we were orphans
Kaminsky, S. M. Vengeance
Koontz, D. R. The bad place
Lethem, J. Motherless Brooklyn
McPhee, J. No ordinary matter
Patterson, J. Cradle and all
Pelecanos, G. P. Right as rain
Pronzini, B. Bleeders
Pronzini, B. Bones
Pronzini, B. Crazybone
Pronzini, B. Deadfall
Pronzini, B. Hardcase
Pronzini, B. Illusions
Pronzini, B. Nightcrawlers
Pronzini, B. Quarry
Pronzini, B. Sentinels
Pronzini, B. Spook
Rickards, J. Winter's end
Robards, K. To trust a stranger
Seymour, G. The heart of danger
Smith, J. Louisiana hotshot
Straub, P. The throat
Vollmann, W. T. The royal family

DETROIT (MICH.) *See* Michigan—Detroit

Deus lo volt! Connell, E. S.

DEVEREAUX, ROBERT
About
Maxwell, R. The wild Irish

Devices and desires. James, P. D.

DEVIL
Benét, S. V. The Devil and Daniel Webster
Bulgakov, M. A. The master and Margarita
Rice, A. Memnoch the Devil
Spark, M. The ballad of Peckham Rye
Twain, M. No. 44, The mysterious stranger

The **Devil**. Tolstoy, L., graf
In Tolstoy, L., graf. The Kreutzer sonata, The Devil, and other tales
In Tolstoy, L., graf. The short novels of Tolstoy

The **Devil** and Daniel Webster. Benét, S. V.
Devil in a blue dress. Mosley, W.
The **devil** knows you're dead. Block, L.
The **devil** tree. Kosinski, J. N.

DEVIL WORSHIP *See* Satanism

The **devil** you know. Johnson, W.
The **devils**. See Dostoyevsky, F. The possessed
The **devil's** advocate. West, M. L.
The **devil's** alternative. Forsyth, F.
The **Devil's** apprentice. Marston, E.
The **devil's** blind spot. Kluge, A.
Devil's claw. Jance, J. A.
The **devil's** dream. Smith, L.
The **devil's** hunt. Doherty, P. C.
The **devil's** larder. Crace, J.
The **devil's** teardrop. Deaver, J.
Devil's Valley. Brink, A. P.
Devil's waltz. Kellerman, J.

DEVON (ENGLAND) *See* England—Devon

The **dew** breaker. Danticat, E.

DEWEY, THOMAS E. (THOMAS EDMUND), 1902-1971
About
Mallon, T. Dewey defeats Truman

Dewey decimated. Goodrum, C. A.
Dewey defeats Truman. Mallon, T.

DEWI, ST *See* David, King of Israel

DHARMA
Kerouac, J. The Dharma bums

The **Dharma** bums. Kerouac, J.
The **diagnosis**. Lightman, A. P.

DIALOGUE *See* Conversation

Dialogues of the dead; or, Paronomania! Hill, R.
The **diamond** age. Stephenson, N.
Diamond dust. Lovesey, P.
Diamond mask. May, J.

DIAMOND MINES AND MINING
Cussler, C. Shock wave
Davies, L. Wilderness of mirrors
Sheldon, S. Master of the game
Smith, W. A. Men of men

Diamond solitaire. Lovesey, P.

DIAMONDS
See also Diamond mines and mining
Browne, G. A. Hot Siberian
Gross, J. The books of Rachel
Haggard, H. R. King Solomon's mines
Spark, M. The comforters
Trollope, A. The Eustace diamonds

Diana, the goddess who hunts alone. Fuentes, C.

DIARIES (STORIES ABOUT)
Cooley, M. The archivist
Higgins, J. Bad company
MacNeil, R. Burden of desire
Maxwell, R. The secret diary of Anne Boleyn
Miller, S. The world below
Wright, R. Henderson's spear

DIARIES (STORIES IN DIARY FORM)
See also Letters (Stories in letter form)
Beauvoir, S. d. The woman destroyed [novelette]
Bellow, S. Dangling man

A **diving** rock on the Hudson. Roth, H.
Divining women. Gibbons, K.
A **division** of the spoils. Scott, P.
also in Scott, P. The Raj quartet
DIVORCE
See also Desertion and nonsupport; Divorced persons; Marriage problems
Banks, R. Affliction
Bellow, S. What kind of day did you have?
Byatt, A. S. Babel Tower
Colette. Julie de Carneilhan
Corman, A. Kramer versus Kramer
Delinsky, B. A woman's place
Donleavy, J. P. The lady who liked clean rest rooms
Drabble, M. The needle's eye
Galsworthy, J. In chancery
Galsworthy, J. Over the river
Godden, R. The battle of the Villa Fiorita
Howells, W. D. A modern instance
Isaacs, S. Close relations
Johnson, D. Le divorce
King, T. Survivor
Michaels, B. Shattered silk
Miller, S. The distinguished guest
Miller, S. The good mother
O'Nan, S. Snow angels
Trollope, J. Other people's children
Tyler, A. The amateur marriage
Wakefield, D. Starting over
Wharton, E. The custom of the country
Le **divorce**. Johnson, D.
DIVORCED PERSONS
Abrahams, P. The fan
Abrahams, P. Their wildest dreams
Adam, C. Love and country
Allende, I. The infinite plan
Barthelme, F. The brothers
Bausch, R. Rebel powers
Beattie, A. Picturing Will
Berg, E. Open house
Betts, D. Souls raised from the dead
Chadwick, C. It's all right now
Connelly, N. O. Buddy Cooper finds a way
Delinsky, B. Coast road
Erdrich, L. Tales of burning love
Ford, R. Independence Day
Gordon, M. Immaculate man
Grenville, K. The idea of perfection
Grøndahl, J. C. Lucca
Hart, J. The reconstructionist
Hiaasen, C. Strip tease
Hoffman, A. Second nature
Hoffman, A. Seventh heaven
Hoffman, A. Turtle Moon
Lamb, W. I know this much is true
Lamott, A. Blue shoe
Leithauser, B. A few corrections
Mantel, H. Beyond black
McMillan, T. How Stella got her groove back
Miller, S. Lost in the forest
Miller, S. The world below
Morris, M. M. Songs in ordinary time
Muller, M. Cyanide Wells
O'Brien, E. Time and tide
O'Brien, T. Tomcat in love
Plain, B. Her father's house
Rosenberg, N. T. Buried evidence
Schwartz, L. Angels Crest
Schwartz, L. S. In the family way
Shields, C. The republic of love
Smiley, J. Good faith
Sparks, N. Nights in Rodanthe
Spencer, E. Knights and dragons
Spencer, L. That Camden summer
Tyler, A. A patchwork planet
Watt, D. Reynolds
Woods, S. Palindrome
DIVORCÉES *See* Divorced persons
DIVORCÉS *See* Divorced persons
Dixie City jam. Burke, J. L.
DIXON, JEREMIAH, 1733-1779
About
Pynchon, T. Mason & Dixon

The **djinn** in the nightingale's eye. Byatt, A. S.
In Byatt, A. S. The djinn in the nightingale's eye: five fairy stories
The **djinn** in the nightingale's eye: five fairy stories. Byatt, A. S.
Do androids dream of electric sheep? Dick, P. K.
Do black patent-leather shoes really reflect up? Powers, J. R.
Do Lord remember me. Lester, J.
DOCK HANDS *See* Longshore workers
Doctor Criminale. Bradbury, M.
Doctor DeMarr. Theroux, P.
In Theroux, P. Half Moon Street
Doctor Faustus. Mann, T.
Doctor Grimshawe's secret. Hawthorne, N.
Doctor No. Fleming, I.
Doctor Slaughter. Theroux, P.
In Theroux, P. Half Moon Street
Doctor Thorne. Trollope, A.
Doctor Zhivago. Pasternak, B. L.
Doctored evidence. Leon, D.
DOCTORS *See* Physicians; Surgeons; Women physicians
The **doctor's** house. Beattie, A.
DOCUMENTS *See* Manuscripts
The **documents** in the case. Sayers, D. L.
Dodsworth. Lewis, S.
also in Lewis, S. Arrowsmith; Elmer Gantry; Dodsworth
The **dog** of the South. Portis, C.
DOG SLED RACING *See* Sled dog racing
Dog soldiers. Stone, R.
The **dog** who bit a policeman. Kaminsky, S. M.
Dog years. Grass, G.
also in Grass, G. The Danzig trilogy
DOGS
Agnon, S. Y. Only yesterday
Auster, P. Timbuktu
Brown, L. The rabbit factory
Burnford, S. Bel Ria
Burnford, S. The incredible journey
Carroll, J. The wooden sea
Edgerton, C. Redeye
Ellison, H. A boy and his dog
Faber, M. The hundred and ninety-nine steps
Gipson, F. B. Old Yeller
Gipson, F. B. Savage Sam
Guterson, D. East of the mountains
Haddon, M. The curious incident of the dog in the night-time
King, S. Cujo
Koontz, D. R. Watchers
London, J. The call of the wild
London, J. White Fang
London, J. White Fang, and other stories
Parkhurst, C. The dogs of Babel
Roger Caras' Treasury of great dog stories
Siddons, A. R. Sweetwater Creek
Sparks, N. The guardian
Wambaugh, J. The black marble
The **dogs** of Babel. Parkhurst, C.
Dogs of Riga. Mankell, H.
The **dogs** of war. Forsyth, F.
Doing wrong. Keating, H. R. F.
Dolley. Brown, R. M.
The **dollmaker**. Arnow, H. L. S.
Dolly. Brookner, A.
Dolores Claiborne. King, S.
Dombey and Son. Dickens, C.
DOMESTIC RELATIONS *See* Family life
DOMINICA
Kincaid, J. Autobiography of my mother
DOMINICAN AMERICANS
Alvarez, J. How the García girls lost their accents
Alvarez, J. In the name of Salomé
Alvarez, J. Yo!
Díaz, J. Drown
DOMINICAN REPUBLIC
Alvarez, J. In the name of Salomé
Alvarez, J. In the time of the butterflies
Danticat, E. The farming of bones
Vargas Llosa, M. The Feast of the Goat
Domino. King, R.
Domino. Whitney, P. A.

E

EAST INDIANS—United States—*Continued*
Mukherjee, B. Desirable daughters
Mukherjee, B. The holder of the world
Mukherjee, B. Jasmine
Mukherjee, B. The tree bride
East into Upper East. Jhabvala, R. P.
East is East. Boyle, T. C.
East is east. Lathen, E.
East of Eden. Steinbeck, J.
also in Steinbeck, J. Novels, 1942-1952
East of the mountains. Guterson, D.
EAST SIDE, LOWER (NEW YORK, N.Y.) *See* New York (N.Y.)—Lower East Side
East Side story. Auchincloss, L.
EAST TIMOR (INDONESIA)
Lee, M. The canal house
East, west. Rushdie, S.
East wind: west wind. Buck, P. S.
EASTER ISLAND
Vanderbes, J. Easter Island
Easter Island. Vanderbes, J.
EASTER REBELLION, 1916 *See* Ireland—Sinn Fein Rebellion, 1916
EASTERN EUROPE
Kostova, E. The historian
Mewshaw, M. Shelter from the storm
Moore, B. The color of blood
Communism
See Communism—Eastern Europe
Easy meat. Harvey, J.
Easy prey. Sandford, J.
Eater. Benford, G.
ECCENTRICS AND ECCENTRICITIES
Barker, N. Behindlings
Boyle, T. C. East is East
Boyle, T. C. Road to Wellville
Brenna, D. The altar of the body
Cadwalladr, C. The family tree
Carey, E. Alva & Irva
Childress, M. Crazy in Alabama
Clark, N. The Hills at home
Connelly, N. O. Buddy Cooper finds a way
Coover, R. The origin of the Brunists
Crews, H. Body
Crews, H. A feast of snakes
Crews, H. Scar lover
Dallas, S. The Persian Pickle Club
Davis-Goff, A. This cold country
Dennis, P. Auntie Mame
Drabble, M. The witch of Exmoor
Dufresne, J. Deep in the shade of paradise
Edgerton, C. Killer diller
Edgerton, C. Where trouble sleeps
Erdrich, L. The Beet Queen
Erickson, S. The sea came in at midnight
Fitzgerald, P. The gate of angels
Gardam, J. Faith Fox
Gardner, J. October light
Goldberg, M. Bee season
Hansen, E. F. Tales of protection
Hansen, R. Isn't it romantic?
Harington, D. Ekaterina
Hiaasen, C. Stormy weather
Holman, S. The mammoth cheese
Howatch, S. The wonder-worker
Irving, J. A son of the circus
Irving, J. A widow for one year
Jackson, M. Five boys
Johnston, W. Human amusements
Kallos, S. Broken for you
Kay, T. Shadow song
Kurzweil, A. The grand complication
Labiner, N. Miniatures
Lansdale, J. R. Sunset and sawdust
Leonard, E. Maximum Bob
Lindgren, T. Hash
Martin, S. The pleasure of my company
Martínez, N. M. ¡Caramba!
McCabe, P. Mondo desperado
McCorkle, J. Carolina moon
McCrumb, S. St. Dale
McGahern, J. By the lake
McMahon, T. A. Ira Foxglove
McMurtry, L. By sorrow's river
McMurtry, L. Folly and glory
McMurtry, L. Loop group
McMurtry, L. Sin killer
McMurtry, L. The wandering hill
Mitford, N. Love in a cold climate
Mitford, N. The pursuit of love
Morrall, C. Astonishing splashes of colour
Mosher, H. F. The true account
Mount, F. The man who rode Ampersand
Murakami, H. The wind-up bird chronicle
Murray, P. An evening of long goodbyes
Novakovich, J. April Fool's Day
O'Neill, J. Kilbrack; or, Who is Nancy Valentine?
Ozick, C. Heir to the glimmering world
Pearson, T. R. A short history of a small place
Portis, C. The dog of the South
Portis, C. Gringos
Portis, C. Masters of Atlantis
Portis, C. Norwood
Reuss, F. Horace afoot
Robbins, T. Villa incognito
Smith, D. Pictures from an expedition
Smith, D. I capture the castle
Spark, M. A far cry from Kensington
Spark, M. Loitering with intent
Steinke, R. Holy skirts
Theroux, P. Hotel Honolulu
Toole, J. K. A confederacy of dunces
Townsend, S. Number 10
Tyler, A. Back when we were grownups
Tyler, A. Morgan's passing
Unsworth, B. Losing Nelson
Vine, B. King Solomon's carpet
Watt, D. Reynolds
Wilcox, J. Heavenly days
Wright, S. M31, a family romance
Zafris, N. Lucky strike
The **echo**. Walters, M.
Echo burning. Child, L.
An **echo** of heaven. Ōe, K.
Echoes. Binchy, M.
Eclipse. Banville, J.
Eclipse. Wheeler, R. S.
ECOLOGY
Ballard, J. G. Rushing to paradise
Llywelyn, M. The elementals
Michener, J. A. Chesapeake
Robinson, K. S. Antarctica
ECONOMISTS
Galbraith, J. K. A tenured professor
Ecstasy. Saulnier, B.
The **ecstatic**. LaValle, V. D.
ECUADOR
See also Galapagos Islands
Paul, J. Elsewhere in the land of parrots
Eden. Lem, S.
Eden. Vernon, O.
Eden Close. Shreve, A.
Edge of danger. Higgins, J.
The **edge** of town. Garlock, D.
EDINBURGH (SCOTLAND) *See* Scotland—Edinburgh
EDISON, THOMAS A. (THOMAS ALVA), 1847-1931
About
McMahon, T. A. Loving Little Egypt
Edisto. Powell, P.
Edisto revisited. Powell, P.
EDITORS
See also Journalists; Women editors
Akst, D. The Webster chronicle
Beattie, A. The doctor's house
Bushnell, C. Lipstick jungle
James, H. The Aspern papers
Siddons, A. R. Downtown
Edsel. Estleman, L. D.
EDUCATION
See also Books and reading; Teachers
Dickens, C. Hard times

TITLE AND SUBJECT INDEX

ENGLAND—20th century—*Continued*
Barker, P. Another world
Barker, P. Border crossing
Benson, E. F. Make way for Lucia
Binchy, M. Silver wedding
Bradford, B. T. Hold the dream
Bradford, B. T. A woman of substance
Bragg, M. Crossing the lines
Bragg, M. A son of war
Burgess, A. The pianoplayers
Cadwalladr, C. The family tree
Campbell, R. The Count of Eleven
Campbell, R. The last voice they hear
Campbell, R. The long lost
Campbell, R. Nazareth Hill
Campbell, R. The one safe place
Campbell, R. Silent children
Colegate, I. The shooting party
Cookson, C. The year of the virgins
Delderfield, R. F. Give us this day
Delderfield, R. F. The green gauntlet
Delderfield, R. F. A horseman riding by
Drabble, M. A natural curiosity
Drabble, M. The radiant way
Drabble, M. The realms of gold
Drabble, M. The witch of Exmoor
Dunmore, H. A spell of winter
Dunmore, H. With your crooked heart
Eden, D. The American heiress
Eden, D. The Salamanca drum
Ford, F. M. The last post
Forster, E. M. Maurice
Forster, E. M. A room with a view
Fowles, J. The collector
Francis, D. Forfeit
Francis, D. High stakes
Francis, D. Twice shy
Frayn, M. Headlong
Frayn, M. A landing on the sun
Fyfield, F. Undercurrents
Galsworthy, J. End of the chapter
Gardam, J. Faith Fox
Gardam, J. The flight of the maidens
Gaskin, C. The charmed circle
Goddard, R. Into the blue
Godden, R. In this house of Brede
Graham, W. Stephanie
Hart, J. Damage
Hart, J. Sin
Howatch, S. Absolute truths
Howatch, S. Glamorous powers
Howatch, S. Glittering images
Howatch, S. Mystical paths
Howatch, S. Scandalous risks
Howatch, S. Ultimate prizes
Howatch, S. The wonder-worker
Humphreys, H. The lost garden
James, P. D. Innocent blood
Judd, A. Legacy
Kunzru, H. The impressionist
Lawton, J. Old flames
Leslie, J. A. C. The ghost and Mrs. Muir
Lessing, D. M. The fifth child
Lively, P. Heat wave
Lively, P. Moon tiger
Lively, P. Passing on
Lodge, D. Nice work
Lodge, D. Therapy
Lodge, D. Thinks—
McEwan, I. Enduring love
McGowan, H. Schooling
McGrath, P. Asylum
McGrath, P. The grotesque
Michaels, B. The dancing floor
Miller, A. Oxygen
Mitford, N. Love in a cold climate
Mitford, N. The pursuit of love
Mortimer, J. C. Dunster
Mortimer, J. C. Paradise postponed
Mortimer, J. C. The sound of trumpets
Mortimer, J. C. Titmuss regained
Murdoch, I. The book and the brotherhood
Murdoch, I. Jackson's dilemma
Nicholls, D. A question of attraction
Pearce, M. E. Apple tree lean down [omnibus volume]
Perry, A. No graves as yet
Powell, A. Books do furnish a room
Powell, A. A dance to the music of time
Powell, A. Hearing secret harmonies
Powell, A. The soldier's art
Pym, B. Quartet in autumn
Rendell, R. The crocodile bird
Robinson, P. The first cut
Self, W. Dorian
Seton, A. Green darkness
Sillitoe, A. The loneliness of the long-distance runner
Sillitoe, A. Saturday night and Sunday morning
Smith, S. Novel on yellow paper
Snow, C. P. Corridors of power
Snow, C. P. Last things
Snow, C. P. The new men
Snow, C. P. Time of hope
Spark, M. The comforters
Spark, M. Memento mori
Stubbs, J. Like we used to be
Swift, G. Last orders
Swift, G. Waterland
Thomas, R. Other people's marriages
Townsend, S. Adrian Mole
Townsend, S. The Adrian Mole diaries
Townsend, S. Adrian Mole: the lost years
Tremain, R. Sacred country
Trevor, W. Felicia's journey
Trollope, J. The best of friends
Trollope, J. The choir
Trollope, J. Other people's children
Trollope, J. A Spanish lover
Uris, L. QB VII
Vine, B. The brimstone wedding
Walters, M. The sculptress
Waugh, E. Brideshead revisited
Waugh, E. Decline and fall
Weldon, F. Worst fears
Wells, H. G. Tono-Bungay
Wesley, M. Part of the furniture
West, Dame R. Sunflower
Wilson, A. N. The vicar of sorrows
Wodehouse, P. G. The code of the Woosters
Wodehouse, P. G. The inimitable Jeeves
Wodehouse, P. G. Jeeves and the tie that binds
Wodehouse, P. G. Tales from the Drones Club
Woolf, V. Jacob's room
Woolf, V. The years
Yorke, M. Almost the truth
Yorke, M. A question of belief

Aristocracy

See Aristocracy—England

Civil War

See England—17th century

Coal mines and mining

See Coal mines and mining—England

College life

See College life—England

Communism

See Communism—England

Courts and courtiers

See Courts and courtiers—England

Farm life

See Farm life—England

Politics

See Politics—England

Prisoners and prisons

See Prisoners and prisons—England

Race relations

Walters, M. The shape of snakes

Rural life

Atkinson, K. Human croquet
Austen, J. Emma
Austen, J. Mansfield Park

ENGLAND—*Continued*

London

Ackroyd, P. The Clerkenwell tales
Brookner, A. The rules of engagement
Chadwick, C. It's all right now
Coe, J. The closed circle
Gardam, J. The queen of the tambourine
Hand, E. Mortal love
Hoban, R. Her name was Lola
Hornby, N. High fidelity
Hornby, N. A long way down
Howatch, S. The heartbreaker
Lebrecht, N. The song of names
Livesey, M. Banishing Verona
McEwan, I. Saturday
Rendell, R. Thirteen steps down
Rutherfurd, E. London
Spark, M. The bachelors
Spark, M. Loitering with intent
Winterson, J. Sexing the cherry

London—16th century

Kellerman, F. The quality of mercy

London—17th century

Kerr, P. Dark matter
Redfern, E. Auriel rising
Stevenson, J. The shadow king

London—Plague, 1665

Defoe, D. A journal of the plague year

London—18th century

Alexander, B. Smuggler's moon
Bainbridge, B. According to Queeney
Bosse, M. J. The vast memory of love
Dickens, C. A tale of two cities
Donoghue, E. Slammerkin
Follett, K. A place called freedom
King, R. Domino
Redfern, E. The music of the spheres
Richardson, S. Clarissa
Roberts, K. L. Northwest Passage

London—19th century

Ackroyd, P. The trial of Elizabeth Cree
Austen, J. Sense and sensibility
Carey, P. Jack Maggs
Crichton, M. The great train robbery
Dickens, C. Little Dorrit
Dickens, C. Martin Chuzzlewit
Dickens, C. Oliver Twist
Dickens, C. Our mutual friend
Faber, M. The crimson petal and the white
Galsworthy, J. The Indian summer of a Forsyte
Galsworthy, J. The man of property
Gardner, J. E. The return of Moriarty
Gardner, J. E. The revenge of Moriarty
Griesemer, J. Signal & noise
Heyer, G. The grand Sophy
Hill, T. The love of stones
Jakeman, J. In the Kingdom of mists
James, H. The golden bowl
Martin, V. Mary Reilly
Moorcock, M. An alien heat
Moorcock, M. The hollow lands
Nattel, L. The singing fire
Palliser, C. The quincunx
Quick, A. Slightly shady
Quick, A. Wicked widow
Smith, Z. White teeth
Stevenson, R. L. The strange case of Dr. Jekyll and Mr. Hyde
Trollope, A. Phineas Finn [abridged]
West, P. The women of Whitechapel and Jack the Ripper
Wilde, O. The picture of Dorian Gray

London—20th century

Ali, M. Brick lane
Amis, K. The Russian girl
Amis, M. The information
Amis, M. London fields
Archer, J. First among equals
Barnard, R. A murder in Mayfair
Barnard, R. Out of the blackout
Barnes, J. Love, etc.
Bawden, N. Family money
Beckett, S. Murphy
Binchy, M. Light a penny candle
Bowen, E. The death of the heart
Bowen, E. The heat of the day
Boyd, W. Armadillo
Brookner, A. Altered states
Brookner, A. The Bay of Angels
Brookner, A. Dolly
Brookner, A. Falling slowly
Brookner, A. Family and friends
Brookner, A. A private view
Brookner, A. Undue influence
Byatt, A. S. Babel Tower
Byatt, A. S. Possession
Byatt, A. S. A whistling woman
Carter, A. Wise children
Cary, J. The horse's mouth
Chalmers, R. Who's who in hell
Clark, M. H. The Anastasia syndrome
Cronin, A. J. The citadel
Dark, A. E. Think of England
Davies, L. Wilderness of mirrors
Deighton, L. SS-GB: Nazi-occupied Britain 1941
Donleavy, J. P. The ginger man
Drabble, M. The gates of ivory
Drabble, M. The middle ground
Drabble, M. The needle's eye
Fielding, H. Bridget Jones: the edge of reason
Fielding, H. Bridget Jones's diary
Follett, K. The man from St. Petersburg
Follett, K. Paper money
Ford, F. M. A man could stand up
Frayn, M. Spies
French, N. Beneath the skin
Fyfield, F. Blind date
Gallico, P. Mrs. 'Arris goes to Paris
Galsworthy, J. End of the chapter
Galsworthy, J. A modern comedy
Galsworthy, J. To let
Godden, R. An episode of sparrows
Godden, R. Thursday's children
Godwin, G. Mr. Bedford
Gordon, M. Living at home
Graham, W. The walking stick
Greene, G. The end of the affair
Greene, G. The human factor
Greene, G. The ministry of fear
Hambly, B. Those who hunt the night
Hardwick, M. The Duchess of Duke Street
Hilton, J. Random harvest
Hoban, R. Turtle diary
Høeg, P. The woman and the ape
Hornby, N. About a boy
Hornby, N. How to be good
Howatch, S. The high flyer
Huxley, A. Point counter point
Keyes, M. Last Chance Saloon
Korda, M. Curtain
Le Carré, J. The looking glass war
Leavitt, D. While England sleeps
Leebron, F. G. In the middle of all this
Lessing, D. M. Ben, in the world
Lessing, D. M. The four-gated city
Lessing, D. M. The good terrorist
Lessing, D. M. Love, again
Lessing, D. M. The real thing
Lessing, D. M. The sweetest dream
Lively, P. City of the mind
Livesey, M. The missing world
Llewellyn, R. None but the lonely heart
Lovesey, P. On the edge
Lurie, A. Foreign affairs
Marsh, J. The House of Eliott
Maugham, W. S. Of human bondage
Mawer, S. The fall
McEwan, I. Amsterdam
McGrath, P. Spider
Moorcock, M. The end of all songs
Mortimer, J. C. Felix in the underworld
Mount, F. The man who rode Ampersand
Murdoch, I. An accidental man
Murdoch, I. A fairly honourable defeat

EPILEPTICS—*Continued*
Dostoyevsky, F. The idiot
Salzman, M. Lying awake
EPISCOPAL CLERGY *See* Anglican and Episcopal clergy
An **episode** of sparrows. Godden, R.

EPISODIC NOVELS

Munro, A. Lives of girls & women
Oates, J. C. Bellefleur
EPLF *See* Eritrean People's Liberation Front
An **equal** music. Seth, V.
Equation for evil. Caputo, P.

ERITREA (ETHIOPIA)

Keneally, T. To Asmara
ERITREAN PEOPLE'S LIBERATION FRONT
Keneally, T. To Asmara
The **Erl-king**. See Tournier, M. The ogre
EROTICISM *See* Sex

ESCAPED CONVICTS

Baldacci, D. The simple truth
Bausch, R. The Gypsy Man
Deaver, J. A maiden's grave
Hunter, S. Dirty white boys
McCrumb, S. She walks these hills

ESCAPES

Bates, H. E. Fair stood the wind for France
Dumas, A. The Count of Monte Cristo
Forester, C. S. Flying colours
Forester, C. S. Hornblower and the Atropos
Hersey, J. The wall
Higgins, J. The Valhalla exchange
King, S. Rita Hayworth and Shawshank redemption
Stark, R. Breakout
Westheimer, D. Von Ryan's Express
The **Escher** twist. Langton, J.
ESKIMOS *See* Aleuts; Inuit
ESP *See* Extrasensory perception
ESPIONAGE *See* International intrigue; Spies
ESSEX (ENGLAND) *See* England—Essex
The **estate**. Singer, I. B.
ESTATES *See* Houses
The **eternal** husband. Dostoyevsky, F.
In Dostoyevsky, F. The short novels of Dostoevsky p343-473
The **eternal** moment. See Forster, E. M. The collected tales of E. M. Forster
Eternity road. McDevitt, J.
Ethan Frome. Wharton, E.
also in Wharton, E. Novellas and other writings

ETHICS

See also Conscience; Medical ethics; Political ethics; Sin; Truthfulness and falsehood; Utilitarianism
Barbash, T. The last good chance
Buffa, D. W. The defense
Caputo, P. Horn of Africa
Coughlin, W. J. Death penalty
Coughlin, W. J. Shadow of a doubt
Dexter, P. The paperboy
Gordimer, N. The house gun
Plain, B. Fortune
Reed, B. The choice
Reuland, R. Semiautomatic
Shreve, A. Strange fits of passion
Snow, C. P. The affair
Snow, C. P. The new men
Steinbeck, J. The winter of our discontent
Wharton, E. Sanctuary

ETHIOPIA

Cody, L. Rift
Keneally, T. To Asmara
Smith, W. A. Cry wolf

Politics

See Politics—Ethiopia
Ethiopia. Dodd, S. M.
In Dodd, S. M. O careless love

ETHNOLOGISTS

Lovecraft, H. P. The mound

ETRURIANS *See* Etruscans
The **Etruscan**. Waltari, M.

ETRUSCANS

Waltari, M. The Etruscan
Eucalyptus. Bail, M.
Eugénie Grandet. Balzac, H. d.

EUNUCHS

King, R. Domino
Smith, W. A. River god

EURASIANS

Bosse, M. J. Fire in heaven
Stewart, F. M. The young Savages

EUROPE

See also Central Europe; Eastern Europe
Bradbury, M. Doctor Criminale

To 476

Llywelyn, M. The horse goddess

392-814

Jennings, G. Raptor
Yarbro, C. Q. Night blooming

11th century

Holland, C. The firedrake

12th century

Eco, U. Baudolino
L'Amour, L. The walking drum

15th century

Dunnett, D. Caprice and Rondo
Dunnett, D. Niccolò rising
Dunnett, D. Race of scorpions
Dunnett, D. Scales of gold
Dunnett, D. The spring of the ram
Dunnett, D. To lie with lions
Dunnett, D. The unicorn hunt

16th century

Dunnett, D. Checkmate

17th century

Maalouf, A. Balthasar's odyssey

18th century

Allen, H. Anthony Adverse

19th century

Cornwell, B. Sharpe's battle
Cornwell, B. Sharpe's company
Cornwell, B. Sharpe's eagle
Cornwell, B. Sharpe's enemy
Cornwell, B. Sharpe's gold
Cornwell, B. Sharpe's honour
Cornwell, B. Sharpe's regiment
James, H. The portrait of a lady

20th century

Archer, J. A matter of honor
Freeling, N. One more river
Greene, G. Orient Express
Ishiguro, K. The unconsoled
Moor, M. d. Duke of Egypt
Pynchon, T. Gravity's rainbow
Sartre, J. P. The reprieve
Tournier, M. The ogre
West, Dame R. The birds fall down
Wiesel, E. The oath
Yarbro, C. Q. Writ in blood

Politics

See Politics—Europe
EUROPE, CENTRAL *See* Central Europe
EUROPE, EASTERN *See* Eastern Europe
Europe central. Vollmann, W. T.

EUROPEANS

Africa

Forsyth, F. The dogs of war

China

Elegant, R. S. Mandarin

EXPERIMENTAL STORIES—*Continued*
Erickson, S. The sea came in at midnight
Foer, J. S. Extremely loud and incredibly close
Gaddis, W. Agapé agape
Gaddis, W. A frolic of his own
Gaddis, W. J R
Gaddis, W. The recognitions
García Márquez, G. The autumn of the patriarch
Grass, G. My century
Gray, A. Poor things
Handke, P. The left-handed woman
Harington, D. Ekaterina
Hernández, F. Lands of memory [novelette]
Hoban, R. Her name was Lola
Howard, M. Natural history
Joyce, J. Finnegans wake
Joyce, J. Ulysses
Kesey, K. Sailor song
Markson, D. Vanishing point
Mitchell, D. Cloud atlas
Naipaul, V. S. A way in the world
Ōe, K. The pinch runner memorandum
Oz, A. The same sea
Perec, G. Life
Perec, G. A void
Pérez-Reverte, A. The Club Dumas
Powers, R. The gold bug variations
Pynchon, T. Gravity's rainbow
Saramago, J. The history of the siege of Lisbon
Sebald, W. G. The emigrants
Silko, L. Gardens in the dunes
Sinisalo, J. Troll
Sorrentino, G. Blue pastoral
Sukenick, R. Mosaic man
T͡Sypkin, L. Summer in Baden-Baden
Vollmann, W. T. The ice-shirt
Walker, A. The temple of my familiar
Wallace, D. F. Infinite jest
Wideman, J. E. The cattle killing
Wideman, J. E. Philadelphia fire
Wright, R. Lawd today!

EXPERIMENTS, SCIENTIFIC *See* Scientific experiments
Exploration team. Jenkins, W. F.
In The Hugo winners p95-142

EXPLORERS
Bainbridge, B. The birthday boys
Barrett, A. The voyage of the Narwhal
Boyle, T. C. Water music
Forester, C. S. To the Indies
Gilman, C. P. Herland
Gilman, C. P. Moving the mountain
Gilman, C. P. With her in Ourland
Glancy, D. Stone heart
Hall, B. I should be extremely happy in your company
Johnston, W. The navigator of New York
McDonald, R. Mr. Darwin's shooter
Mosher, H. F. The true account
Poe, E. A. The journal of Julius Rodman
Thom, J. A. The children of first man
Verne, J. Five weeks in a balloon
Vollmann, W. T. Argall
Vollmann, W. T. The rifles
Wheeler, R. S. Eclipse

Extenuating circumstances. Valin, J.
EXTERMINATION, JEWISH *See* Holocaust, Jewish (1933-1945)

EXTINCT CITIES
See also Pompeii (Ancient city)
Whitney, P. A. Domino

Extinction. Bernhard, T.

EXTORTION
Abrahams, P. Crying wolf
Colette. Julie de Carneilhan
Dickens, C. Our mutual friend
Ferrigno, R. The Horse Latitudes
Gardner, J. E. License renewed
Godey, J. The taking of Pelham one two three
Leonard, E. Freaky Deaky
Leonard, E. LaBrava
Lindsey, D. L. The rules of silence
Siegel, J. Derailed
Wambaugh, J. The black marble
Weber, K. The Music Lesson

EXTRASENSORY PERCEPTION
See also Clairvoyance; Telepathy
Anderson, P. The Saturn game
Bradley, M. Z. The house between the worlds
Greeley, A. M. Irish cream
Greeley, A. M. Irish stew!
King, S. The dead zone
King, S. The shining
Koontz, D. R. The bad place
Le Guin, U. K. The left hand of darkness
Lessing, D. M. The four-gated city
Lustbader, E. V. Black Blade
Roberts, N. Carolina moon
Stewart, M. Touch not the cat
Wilson, R. C. Blind Lake
Woods, S. Under the lake

Extreme denial. Morrell, D.
Extremely loud and incredibly close. Foer, J. S.
The **eye** in the door. Barker, P.
Eye of the abyss. Browne, M.
Eye of the needle. Follett, K.
Eye of the storm. Higgins, J.
The **eye** of the storm. White, P.
Eyes of a child. Patterson, R. N.
Eyesores. Shade, E.
EYEWITNESSES *See* Witnesses
The **Eyre** affair. Fforde, J. Leonard, E.

F

"F" is for fugitive. Grafton, S.
The **Faber** book of gay short fiction. Entered in Part I under title
A **fable**. Faulkner, W.
also in Faulkner, W. Novels, 1942-1954 p665-1072

FABLES
See also Allegories
Chandra, V. Red earth and pouring rain
Ozick, C. The Puttermesser papers
Rushdie, S. Haroun and the sea of stories
Sinisalo, J. Troll
Tan, A. Saving fish from drowning
Tolkin, M. Under radar

The **fabulous** clipjoint. Brown, F.
In Brown, F. Hunter and hunted
The **fabulous** riverboat. Farmer, P. J.
Fabulous small Jews. Epstein, J.

FACE

Abnormalities and deformities
Busch, F. The night inspector
Kellogg, M. Tell me that you love me, Junie Moon

The **face**. Koontz, D. R.
A **face** at the window. McFarland, D.
The **face-changers**. Perry, T.
The **face** of a stranger. Perry, A.
The **face** of deception. Johansen, I.
The **face** of trespass. Rendell, R.
The **face** on the wall. Langton, J.

FACTORIES
See also Clothing industry; Labor and laboring classes
Lodge, D. Nice work
Theroux, P. Kowloon Tong
Zaroulis, N. L. Call the darkness light

FACULTY (EDUCATION) *See* Teachers
Fahrenheit 451. Bradbury, R.
Fahrenheit 451 [novelette] Bradbury, R.
In Bradbury, R. Fahrenheit 451 p19-150
The **Fahrenheit** twins. Faber, M.
In Faber, M. The courage consort
Fail-safe. Burdick, E.

FAILURE
DeMarinis, R. Sky full of sand
Lipsyte, S. Home land
Scott, J. Tourmaline
Wheeler, R. S. Eclipse

A **faint** cold fear. Daley, R.
Fair and tender ladies. Smith, L.
Fair land, fair land. Guthrie, A. B.

FAMILY CHRONICLES—*Continued*
Du Maurier, Dame D. Hungry Hill
Dunne, D. A season in purgatory
Dunnett, D. Niccolò rising
Dunnett, D. Race of scorpions
Dunnett, D. The spring of the ram
Eden, D. The Salamanca drum
Edgeworth, M. Castle Rackrent
Elegant, R. S. Dynasty
Elegant, R. S. Mandarin
Erdrich, L. The antelope wife
Esterházy, P. Celestial harmonies
Eve, N. The family orchard
Fast, H. The immigrants
Fast, H. The immigrant's daughter
Fast, H. The legacy
Fast, H. Second generation
Faulkner, W. Flags in the dust
Faulkner, W. Sartoris
Ferber, E. Show boat
Follett, K. A dangerous fortune
Fredriksson, M. Hanna's daughters
Galsworthy, J. End of the chapter
Galsworthy, J. The Forsyte saga
Galsworthy, J. The man of property
Galsworthy, J. A modern comedy
García, C. The Aguero sisters
García, C. Dreaming in Cuban
García, C. Monkey hunting
García Márquez, G. One hundred years of solitude
Gaskin, C. The charmed circle
Gibbons, K. Charms for the easy life
Graham, W. The angry tide
Graham, W. Bella Poldark
Graham, W. The four swans
Graham, W. The loving cup
Graham, W. The miller's dance
Graham, W. The stranger from the sea
Graham, W. The twisted sword
Grau, S. A. The condor passes
Grau, S. A. The keepers of the house
Greeley, A. M. Lord of the dance
Gross, J. The books of Rachel
Haley, A. Mama Flora's family
Halter, M. The book of Abraham
Harrison, J. The road home
Hawthorne, N. The House of the Seven Gables
Haynes, D. The full Matilda
Hegi, U. The vision of Emma Blau
Hijuelos, O. The fourteen sisters of Emilio Montez O'Brien
Hill, R. B. Hanta yo
Høeg, P. The history of Danish dreams
Howard, M. Natural history
Howatch, S. Cashelmara
Howatch, S. Penmarric
Howatch, S. The wheel of fortune
Hunter, E. The Chisholms
Isaacs, S. Almost paradise
Isaacs, S. Red, white and blue
Jakes, J. American dreams
Jakes, J. Charleston
Jakes, J. Heaven and hell
Jakes, J. Homeland
Jakes, J. Love and war
Jakes, J. North and South
Jennings, G. Aztec
Jhabvala, R. P. Shards of memory
Kennedy, W. Very old bones
Kesey, K. Sometimes a great notion
Krantz, J. Mistral's daughter
Laker, R. To dance with kings
L'Amour, L. The Sacketts: beginnings of a dynasty
Laskas, G. M. The midwife's tale
Lawrence, D. H. The rainbow
L'Engle, M. Certain women
Lessing, D. M. The sweetest dream
Lofts, N. The haunting of Gad's Hall
Lord, B. B. Spring Moon
Maḥfūẓ, N. Palace of desire
Maḥfūẓ, N. Palace walk
Maḥfūẓ, N. Sugar Street
Manicka, R. The rice mother
Mann, T. Buddenbrooks
Marquand, J. P. The late George Apley
Martin, W. Annapolis
Martin, W. Cape Cod
McCrumb, S. The songcatcher
McCullough, C. The thorn birds
Michener, J. A. Chesapeake
Michener, J. A. Mexico
Michener, J. A. Poland
Miller, S. Family pictures
Morrison, T. Song of Solomon
Mukherjee, B. The tree bride
Nabokov, V. V. Ada
Naylor, G. Linden Hills
Ng, F. M. Bone
Oates, J. C. Bellefleur
Pearce, M. E. Apple tree lean down [omnibus volume]
Piercy, M. Three women
Pilcher, R. September
Pilcher, R. The shell seekers
Plain, B. Evergreen
Plain, B. The golden cup
Plain, B. Harvest
Plain, B. Random winds
Plain, B. Tapestry
Powers, R. The time of our singing
Price, E. Savannah
Puzo, M. The family
Richler, M. Solomon Gursky was here
Ross-Macdonald, M. For they shall inherit
Ross-Macdonald, M. The rich are with you always
Ross-Macdonald, M. The world from rough stones
Rushdie, S. The Moor's last sigh
Rushdie, S. Shame
Rutherfurd, E. Russka
Rutherfurd, E. Sarum
Scott, Sir W. The bride of Lammermoor
Seth, V. A suitable boy
Shange, N. Betsey Brown
Shaw, I. Beggarman, thief
Shaw, I. Rich man, poor man
Sheldon, S. Master of the game
Shreve, S. R. Daughters of the new world
Siddons, A. R. Colony
Simpson, M. Anywhere but here
Singer, I. B. The family Moskat
Smith, L. The devil's dream
Smith, L. Family linen
Smith, L. Oral history
Smith, W. A. The angels weep
Smith, Z. White teeth
Stegner, W. E. Angle of repose
Steinbeck, J. East of Eden
Stewart, F. M. The glitter and the gold
Stewart, F. M. The naked Savages
Stewart, F. M. The Savages in love and war
Tademy, L. Cane River
Tarkington, B. The magnificent Ambersons
Thackeray, W. M. The Virginians
Thomas, M. M. Hanover Place
Trollope, J. Legacy of love
Tryon, T. In the fire of spring
Tryon, T. The wings of the morning
Tyler, A. Dinner at the Homesick Restaurant
Tyler, A. Searching for Caleb
Uhnak, D. Law and order
Undset, S. Kristin Lavransdatter
Updike, J. In the beauty of the lilies
Uris, L. Trinity
Urquhart, J. Away
Welty, E. Losing battles
West, D. The wedding
Winton, T. Cloudstreet
Wood, B. Green City in the sun
Woolf, V. The years
Zaroulis, N. L. Massachusetts

FAMILY CURSES
Caldwell, T. Captains and kings
Hawthorne, N. The House of the Seven Gables
Holt, V. Bride of Pendorric
Smith, L. Oral history
Wood, B. The dreaming

Family games. Stubbs, J.
Family happiness. Colwin, L.

FAMILY LIFE—*Continued*
Holman, S. The mammoth cheese
Hood, A. Places to stay the night
Hooper, K. Finding Laura
Howard, M. The Magdalene
Howatch, S. Sins of the fathers
Hughes, L. Not without laughter
Hustvedt, S. What I loved
Irving, J. The Hotel New Hampshire
Irving, J. The world according to Garp
Jen, G. The love wife
Jewett, S. O. The country of the pointed firs
Johnson, D. Le divorce
Johnston, W. Human amusements
Jones, D. C. Elkhorn Tavern
Jones, D. C. This savage race
Kafka, F. Metamorphosis
Kaufman, S. Diary of a mad housewife
King, S. Pet sematary
Kingsolver, B. The poisonwood Bible
Klíma, I. No saints or angels
Lamb, W. I know this much is true
Lawrence, D. H. The white peacock
Le, T. D. T. The gangster we are all looking for
Leavitt, D. The lost language of cranes
Lee, C. Y. The flower drum song
Lee, C.-R. Aloft
Lee, G. Honor & duty
L'Engle, M. A live coal in the sea
L'Engle, M. The other side of the sun
Lessing, D. M. The four-gated city
Lightman, A. P. The diagnosis
Lin Yutang. Moment in Peking
Llewellyn, R. How green was my valley
MacDonald, A.-M. The way the crow flies
Maine, D. The preservationist
Marshall, C. Julie
Marshall, P. The fisher king
Mason, B. A. Feather crowns
Mason, B. A. In country
McCabe, P. The butcher boy
McCorkle, J. Ferris Beach
McCrumb, S. The rosewood casket
McCullers, C. The member of the wedding
McCullough, C. The thorn birds
McDermott, A. At weddings and wakes
McDermott, A. Charming Billy
McEwan, I. Saturday
McFarland, D. The music room
McGuane, T. The cadence of grass
McMillan, T. A day late and a dollar short
McMurtry, L. Boone's Lick
McNicholl, D. A son called Gabriel
McPhee, M. Gorgeous lies
Meloy, M. Liars and saints
Meredith, G. The ordeal of Richard Feverel
Merullo, R. In Revere, in those days
Michael, J. Sleeping beauty
Miller, R. Welcome to Heavenly Heights
Miller, S. The world below
Minot, S. Folly
Minot, S. Monkeys
Mistry, R. Family matters
Mitchard, J. The deep end of the ocean
Mitford, N. Love in a cold climate
Mitford, N. The pursuit of love
Moberg, V. The emigrants
Moberg, V. The last letter home
Moberg, V. Unto a good land
Morris, M. M. Songs in ordinary time
Morrison, T. Song of Solomon
Mortimer, J. C. Paradise postponed
Mortimer, J. C. Summer's lease
Murdoch, I. A fairly honourable defeat
Naipaul, V. S. A house for Mr. Biswas
Napolitano, A. Within arm's reach
Oates, J. C. A Bloodsmoor romance
Oates, J. C. The falls
Oates, J. C. Them
Oates, J. C. We were the Mulvaneys
O'Connor, E. All in the family
Ōe, K. A quiet life
O'Hara, J. Ten North Frederick
O'Nan, S. Snow angels
O'Nan, S. Wish you were here
O'Nan, S. A world away
Otsuka, J. When the emperor was divine
Parks, S.-L. Getting mother's body
Paton, A. Too late the phalarope
Paul, J. A girl, in parts
Peck, R. N. A day no pigs would die
Picoult, J. My sister's keeper
Pilcher, R. Voices in summer
Plain, B. Evergreen
Plain, B. Harvest
Plain, B. Homecoming
Plain, B. Tapestry
Plain, B. Whispers
Potok, C. My name is Asher Lev
Powers, R. Prisoner's dilemma
Price, R. The promise of rest
Prose, F. Household saints
Proulx, A. Postcards
Pywell, S. L. What happened to Henry
Quindlen, A. Blessings
Quindlen, A. Object lessons
Reasoner, J. Antietam
Reisman, N. The first desire
Reynolds, M. The Starlite Drive-in
Rice, L. Blue moon
Rice, L. Home fires
Richter, C. The awakening land
Roberts, N. The villa
Rölvaag, O. E. Giants in the earth
Rölvaag, O. E. Peder Victorious
Rossner, J. Emmeline
Roth, H. Call it sleep
Roth, H. A star shines over Mt. Morris Park
Roy, A. The god of small things
Russo, R. Nobody's fool
Salinger, J. D. Franny & Zooey
Salinger, J. D. Raise high the roof beam, carpenters, and Seymour: an introduction
Sanders, L. Guilty pleasures
Saroyan, W. The human comedy
Schwartz, J. B. Reservation Road
Schwartz, L. S. Disturbances in the field
Schwartz, L. S. In the family way
Scott, J. Tourmaline
Searles, J. Boy still missing
Sebold, A. The lovely bones
Settle, M. L. Charley Bland
Sharpe, M. The sleeping father
Shaw, I. Bread upon the waters
Shields, D. Dead languages
Shreve, A. The weight of water
Siddons, A. R. Peachtree Road
Siddons, A. R. Sweetwater Creek
Sinclair, A. Coffee will make you black
Singer, I. B. The estate
Singer, I. B. The family Moskat
Smiley, J. A thousand acres
Smith, B. A tree grows in Brooklyn
Smith, D. I capture the castle
Smith, R. K. Jane's house
Smith, Z. On beauty
Snow, C. P. The conscience of the rich
Snow, C. P. Last things
Snow, C. P. Time of hope
Spencer, S. Endless love
Stead, C. The man who loved children
Stefaniak, M. H. The Turk and my mother
Stegner, W. E. The Big Rock Candy Mountain
Steinbeck, J. The grapes of wrath
Stirling, J. The penny wedding
Straight, S. The gettin place
Struther, J. Mrs. Miniver
Stubbs, J. Family games
Stubbs, J. Like we used to be
Styron, A. All the finest girls
Styron, W. Lie down in darkness
Tanizaki, J. The Makioka sisters
Tarkington, B. Alice Adams
Tartt, D. The little friend
Taylor, P. H. A summons to Memphis
Thayer, N. An act of love
Thompson, J. Wide blue yonder
Tilghman, C. Mason's retreat

FANTASIES—*Continued*
Brooks, T. Morgawr
Brooks, T. Running with the demon
Brooks, T. The scions of Shannara
Brooks, T. The sword of Shannara
Brooks, T. The talismans of Shannara
Brooks, T. The wishsong of Shannara
Brooks, T. Wizard at large
Bujold, L. M. The hallowed hunt
Byatt, A. S. The djinn in the nightingale's eye
Byatt, A. S. The djinn in the nightingale's eye: five fairy stories
Calvino, I. Baron in the trees
Calvino, I. Invisible cities
Capote, T. The grass harp
Card, O. S. Alvin Journeyman
Card, O. S. The crystal city
Card, O. S. Enchantment
Card, O. S. Heartfire
Card, O. S. Magic street
Card, O. S. Prentice Alvin
Card, O. S. Red prophet
Card, O. S. Seventh son
Carey, E. Alva & Irva
Carroll, J. The wooden sea
Carter, A. Nights at the circus
Chayefsky, P. Altered states
Cherryh, C. J. Cloud's rider
Cherryh, C. J. The collected short fiction of C.J. Cherryh
Cherryh, C. J. Fortress of dragons
Cherryh, C. J. Rider at the gate
Coover, R. Briar Rose
Coover, R. Pinocchio in Venice
Craig, A. Love in idleness
Dark matter
Davies, R. Murther & walking spirits
Davies, V. Miracle on 34th Street
De Lint, C. Memory and dream
De Lint, C. Someplace to be flying
De Lint, C. Trader
Dickens, C. The cricket on the hearth
Dickinson, C. A shortcut in time
Dickson, G. R. The dragon and the djinn
Dickson, G. R. The dragon at war
Dickson, G. R. The dragon in Lyonesse
Dickson, G. R. The dragon knight
Dickson, G. R. The dragon on the border
Dickson, G. R. The dragon, the Earl, and the troll
Donaldson, S. R. The Illearth war
Donaldson, S. R. Lord Foul's bane
Donaldson, S. R. The One Tree
Donaldson, S. R. The power that preserves
Donaldson, S. R. Reave the Just and other tales
Donaldson, S. R. The runes of the earth
Donaldson, S. R. White gold wielder
Donaldson, S. R. The woman who loved pigs
Donaldson, S. R. The wounded Land
Eddings, D. Belgarath the sorcerer
Eddings, D. Guardians of the west
Eddings, D. Polgara the sorceress
Ellison, H. Adrift just off the Islets of Langerhans: latitude 38° 54′ N, longitude 77° 00′ 13″ W
Estrin, M. Insect dreams
Everett, P. L. American desert
Faber, M. The Fahrenheit twins
Feist, R. E. Mistress of the empire
Feist, R. E. Rage of a demon king
Feist, R. E. Rise of a merchant prince
Feist, R. E. Shadow of a dark queen
Feist, R. E. Shards of a broken crown
Fforde, J. The Eyre affair
Fforde, J. Thursday Next in Lost in a good book
Fforde, J. Thursday Next in Something rotten
Fforde, J. Thursday Next in The well of lost plots
Foster, A. D. Kingdoms of light
Foster, A. D. A triumph of souls
Gaiman, N. Anansi boys
Gaiman, N. Stardust
Gilman, C. P. Herland
Gilman, C. P. Moving the mountain
Gilman, C. P. With her in Ourland
Golding, W. The scorpion god
Goldstein, L. The alchemist's door
Grass, G. The flounder
Haggard, H. R. She
Hamill, P. Forever
Hand, E. Mortal love
Harington, D. With
Haydon, E. Destiny: child of the sky
Haydon, E. Prophecy
Haydon, E. Requiem for the sun
Helprin, M. Winter's tale
Hesse, H. The fairy tales of Hermann Hesse
Hesse, H. The glass bead game (Magister Ludi)
Hilton, J. Lost horizon
Hoban, R. Turtle diary
Hobb, R. The mad ship
Hobb, R. Ship of magic
Hudson, W. H. Green mansions
Jones, D. W. A sudden wild magic
Kafka, F. Amerika
Kay, G. G. The last light of the sun
King, S. The stand
Knox, E. Daylight
Kurtz, K. The harrowing of Gwynedd
Kurtz, K. King Kelson's bride
Kurtz, K. The quest for Saint Camber
Kurtz, K. St. Patrick's gargoyle
Kurtz, K. The temple and the stone
Kurtz, K. Two crowns for America
Lackey, M. The fairy godmother
Lackey, M. Firebird
Lackey, M. Joust
Lackey, M. The serpent's shadow
Lackey, M. Winds of fate
Lackey, M. Winds of fury
Larsen, J. Silk road
Lawhead, S. Avalon
Le Guin, U. K. The beginning place
Le Guin, U. K. Changing planes
Le Guin, U. K. Orsinian tales
Le Guin, U. K. The other wind
Lee, T. White as snow
Leiber, F. Gonna roll the bones
Leslie, J. A. C. The ghost and Mrs. Muir
Levin, I. The Stepford wives
Lewis, C. S. Out of the silent planet
Lewis, C. S. Perelandra
Lewis, C. S. That hideous strength
Llywelyn, M. The elementals
Llywelyn, M. Red Branch
Llywelyn, M. Silverhand
Llywelyn, M. Silverlight
Lustbader, E. V. Mistress of the pearl
Maguire, G. Son of a witch
Marillier, J. Foxmask
Marks, L. J. Fire logic
Martin, G. R. R. A clash of kings
Martin, G. R. R. A game of thrones
May, J. The adversary
May, J. Blood Trillium
May, J. The golden torc
May, J. The many-colored land
May, J. The nonborn king
McCaffrey, A. Acorna
McCaffrey, A. Acorna's people
McCaffrey, A. Acorna's quest
McCaffrey, A. Acorna's rebels
McCaffrey, A. Acorna's search
McCaffrey, A. Acorna's triumph
McCaffrey, A. Acorna's world
McCaffrey, A. All the Weyrs of Pern
McCaffrey, A. The chronicles of Pern
McCaffrey, A. Crystal line
McCaffrey, A. Crystal singer
McCaffrey, A. Dragonflight
McCaffrey, A. Dragonquest
McCaffrey, A. Dragonrider
McCaffrey, A. Dragon's Kin
McCaffrey, A. Dragonsdawn
McCaffrey, A. Dragonseye
McCaffrey, A. The girl who heard dragons [novelette]
McCaffrey, A. Killashandra
McCaffrey, A. The Masterharper of Pern
McCaffrey, A. Pegasus in space
McCaffrey, A. The renegades of Pern
McCaffrey, A. The skies of Pern
McCaffrey, A. The white dragon

FARM LIFE—*Continued*

Illinois

Ferber, E. So Big

Iowa

Smiley, J. A thousand acres
Waller, R. J. The bridges of Madison County

Ireland

Barry, S. Annie Dunne
Hardie, K. A winter marriage
Nolan, C. The banyan tree
O'Brien, E. Wild Decembers

Kentucky

Mason, B. A. Feather crowns

Minnesota

Clark, M. H. A cry in the night

Missouri

Garlock, D. The edge of town

Nebraska

Cather, W. O pioneers!

New England

Wharton, E. Ethan Frome

New Hampshire

Benét, S. V. The Devil and Daniel Webster

North Carolina

Frazier, C. Cold Mountain

Norway

Undset, S. Kristin Lavransdatter

South Africa

Lessing, D. M. The grass is singing

South Dakota

Rölvaag, O. E. Giants in the earth
Rölvaag, O. E. Peder Victorious

Southern States

Kingsolver, B. Prodigal summer

Sweden

Moberg, V. The emigrants

Tennessee

McCrumb, S. The rosewood casket

Texas

Proulx, A. That old ace in the hole

Vermont

Gardner, J. October light
Peck, R. N. A day no pigs would die
Proulx, A. Postcards

Virginia

Shreve, S. R. A country of strangers

Wales

Chatwin, B. On the Black Hill
Llewellyn, R. Green, green, my valley now

Western States

Stegner, W. E. The Big Rock Candy Mountain

Wisconsin

Hamilton, J. A map of the world
Schwarz, C. Drowning Ruth
Watson, L. Orchard

FARM TENANCY *See* Tenant farming
FARMERS *See* Farm life
The **farming** of bones. Danticat, E.
Farriers' Lane. Perry, A.
Farslayer's story. See Saberhagen, F. The fourth book of lost swords: Farslayer's story

FASCISM

See also Communism; Dictators; National socialism; Totalitarianism
Roth, P. The plot against America

Italy

Bassani, G. The garden of the Finzi-Continis
Silone, I. Bread and wine

United States

Lewis, S. It can't happen here

The **fashion** in shrouds. Allingham, M.
In Allingham, M. Three cases for Mr. Campion p9-255

FASHION INDUSTRY AND TRADE

Bushnell, C. Lipstick jungle
Laker, R. Banners of silk
Marsh, J. The House of Eliott

FASHION MODELS

Brown, S. French Silk
Gaitskill, M. Veronica
MacNeil, R. The voyage
Rendell, R. Thirteen steps down

Fat Ollie's book. McBain, E.
Fat Tuesday. Brown, S.
A **fatal** attachment. Barnard, R.
A **fatal** glass of beer. Kaminsky, S. M.
A **fatal** inversion. Vine, B.
A **fatal** vineyard season. Craig, P. R.

FATE AND FATALISM

Anthony, P. With a tangled skein
García Márquez, G. Chronicle of a death foretold
Ōe, K. The silent cry
Wilder, T. The bridge of San Luis Rey

Father Abraham. Faulkner, W.
Father and son. Maas, P.
Father Brown mystery stories. Chesterton, G. K.
The **Father** Brown omnibus. Chesterton, G. K.
Father Melancholy's daughter. Godwin, G.
Father of the bride. Streeter, E.
Father Sergius. Tolstoy, L., graf
In Tolstoy, L., graf. The Kreutzer sonata, The Devil, and other tales
Fatherland. Harris, R.

FATHERS

See also Fathers and daughters; Fathers and sons; Fathers-in-law; Stepfathers
Banks, R. Affliction
Dickens, C. Hard times
Esterházy, P. Celestial harmonies
Morris, M. M. The lost mother

Fathers and children. See Turgenev, I. S. Fathers and sons
Fathers and crows. Vollmann, W. T.

FATHERS AND DAUGHTERS

See also Fathers and sons; Parent and child
Atwood, M. Surfacing
Bail, M. Eucalyptus
Balzac, H. d. Eugénie Grandet
Balzac, H. d. Père Goriot (Old Goriot)
Banville, J. Eclipse
Begley, L. Schmidt delivered
Bellow, S. Mr. Sammler's planet
Betts, D. Souls raised from the dead
Boyd, W. The blue afternoon
Brockmeier, K. The truth about Celia
Brown, J. D. Addie Pray
Burgess, A. The pianoplayers
Campbell, R. Nazareth Hill
Campbell, R. Pact of the fathers
Carr, P. The black swan
Clark, M. H. I'll be seeing you
Coben, H. No second chance
Coetzee, J. M. Disgrace
Cohen, L. H. Heart, you bully, you punk
Conrad, J. Almayer's folly
Cookson, C. The Maltese Angel
Cookson, C. The upstart
Coulter, C. Impulse
Dailey, J. Calder pride
Danticat, E. The dew breaker
De Bernières, L. Corelli's mandolin
Dee, E. The con man's daughter
Delinsky, B. Coast road
Delinsky, B. Flirting with Pete
Deutermann, P. T. Darkside
Dickens, C. Dombey and Son
Didion, J. The last thing he wanted
Dixon, S. Interstate
Doig, I. Ride with me, Mariah Montana
Donovan, A. Buddha Da

FATHERS AND SONS—*Continued*
Russo, R. Nobody's fool
Russo, R. The risk pool
Saul, J. The right hand of evil
Schwartz, J. B. Reservation Road
Segal, E. Love story
Sher, I. Gentlemen of space
Smith, W. A. Birds of prey
Smith, W. A. Monsoon
Snow, C. P. The conscience of the rich
Snow, C. P. The sleep of reason
Stevenson, R. L. The misadventures of John Nicholson
Stewart, M. The wicked day
Stone, R. Bay of souls
Straub, P. Mr. X
Taylor, R. L. The travels of Jaimie McPheeters
Townsend, S. Adrian Mole
Turow, S. Ordinary heroes
Updike, J. The centaur
Vanderhaeghe, G. The last crossing
Vargas Llosa, M. The notebooks of Don Rigoberto
Wallace, D. Big fish
Watkins, P. Calm at sunset, calm at dawn
Watkins, P. The promise of light
Wells, K. Meely LaBauve
Wharton, W. Dad
Wiesel, E. The forgotten
Wilson, R. The blind man of Seville
Wood, J. The book against God
Wright, R. Henderson's spear

Fathers and sons. Turgenev, I. S.

FATHERS-IN-LAW
Mewshaw, M. Shelter from the storm
Plain, B. Looking back

A **father's** kisses. Friedman, B. J.
The **fatigue** artist. Schwartz, L. S.
The **Faulkner** reader. Faulkner, W.
Fault lines. Carroll, J.
Fault lines. Siddons, A. R.

FAUST LEGEND
Mann, T. Doctor Faustus

Fay. Brown, L.

FBI *See* United States. Federal Bureau of Investigation

FEAR
Bausch, R. The Gypsy Man
Du Maurier, Dame D. Rebecca
French, N. Land of the living
Heller, J. Something happened
King, S. The girl who loved Tom Gordon
Koontz, D. R. False memory

Fear itself. Mosley, W.
Fear nothing. Koontz, D. R.
Fear of flying. Jong, E.
Fear of frying. Churchill, J.
Fearless Jones. Mosley, W.
The **Feast** of All Saints. Rice, A.
The **feast** of love. Baxter, C.
A **feast** of snakes. Crews, H.
The **Feast** of the Goat. Vargas Llosa, M.
Feather crowns. Mason, B. A.
Feathered serpent. Falconer, C.
The **feats** and adventures of Raoul de Bragelonne. See Dumas, A. The iron mask [variant title: The man in the iron mask]

FEDERAL BUREAU OF INVESTIGATION (U.S.) *See* United States. Federal Bureau of Investigation

The **feel** of the trigger. Westlake, D. E.
In Westlake, D. E. Levine p61-87
Felicia's journey. Trevor, W.
Felix in the underworld. Mortimer, J. C.
Felix Krull. See Mann, T. Confessions of Felix Krull, confidence man

FELL, MARGARET *See* Fox, Margaret Askew Fell, 1614-1702

The **fellowship** of the ring. Tolkien, J. R. R.
also in Tolkien, J. R. R. The lord of the rings

FEMINISM
Alvarez, J. In the name of Salomé
Atwood, M. The robber bride
Ballard, J. G. Rushing to paradise
Bass, C. Maiden voyage
Battle, L. Storyville
Boyle, T. C. Riven Rock
Brink, A. P. Imaginings of sand
Franklin, M. The end of my career
Franklin, M. My brilliant career
French, M. My summer with George
French, M. Our father
French, M. The women's room
Gilman, C. P. Herland
Gilman, C. P. Moving the mountain
Gilman, C. P. With her in Ourland
Irving, J. The world according to Garp
Isaacs, S. Close relations
James, H. The Bostonians
Jong, E. Fear of flying
Lessing, D. M. The golden notebook
Lessing, D. M. The sweetest dream
Martínez, N. M. ¡Caramba!
Naslund, S. J. Ahab's wife; or, The star-gazer
Paretsky, S. Ghost country
Piercy, M. Braided lives
Piercy, M. City of darkness, city of light
Piercy, M. Small changes
Piercy, M. Three women
Prose, F. Hunters and gatherers
Roiphe, A. R. Lovingkindness
Rush, N. Mating
Tarr, J. Queen of swords
Tepper, S. S. The fresco
Tepper, S. S. The gate to Women's Country
Tepper, S. S. Singer from the sea
Tepper, S. S. Six moon dance
Walker, A. Possessing the secret of joy
Weldon, F. Big girls don't cry

FENCING
Pérez-Reverte, A. The fencing master

The **fencing** master. Pérez-Reverte, A.
Fer-de-lance. Stout, R.
In Stout, R. Royal flush p1-180

FERRARA (ITALY) *See* Italy—Ferrara

Ferris Beach. McCorkle, J.
The **ferryman** will be there. Aubert, R.

FERTILIZATION IN VITRO
McCaffrey, A. The greatest love [novelette]

FESTIVALS
Crews, H. A feast of snakes
Du Maurier, Dame D. The flight of the falcon

Fête fatale. Barnard, R.

FETUS
See also Pregnancy

FEUDALISM
Clavell, J. Gai-Jin
Clavell, J. Shogun

FEUDS
Graham, W. The black moon
Swerling, B. Shadowbrook
Tryon, T. In the fire of spring
Tryon, T. The wings of the morning
Woodrell, D. Give us a kiss

The **fever** tree and other stories. Rendell, R.
In Rendell, R. Collected stories p265-406
A **few** corrections. Leithauser, B.
A **few** dying words. Gosling, P.
A **few** green leaves. Pym, B.
A **few** short notes on tropical butterflies. Murray, J.
The **few** things I know about Glafkos Thrassakis. Vassilikos, V.
Fiasco. Lem, S.
Ficciones. Borges, J. L.

FIDDLERS *See* Violinists

Fiddlers. McBain, E.
Fidelity. Berry, W.

FIELD, HENRIETTE
About
Field, R. All this, and heaven too

Field of thirteen. Francis, D.
Field study. Seiffert, R.

FIELDING, HENRY, 1707-1754
About
Bosse, M. J. The vast memory of love

A **flag** for sunrise. Stone, R.
Flags in the dust. Faulkner, W.
FLAMENCO DANCERS *See* Dancers
FLANDERS (BELGIUM) *See* Belgium—Flanders
Flanders sky. Freeling, N.
FLANNIGAN, KATHERINE MARY O'FALLON
About
Freedman, B. Mrs. Mike
Flappers and philosophers. Fitzgerald, F. S.
In Fitzgerald, F. S. Novels and stories, 1920-1922 p249-433
Flashback. Barr, N.
Flashback. Siler, J.
Flashman. Fraser, G. M.
Flashman & the angel of the Lord. Fraser, G. M.
Flashman and the mountain of light. Fraser, G. M.
Flashman and the tiger. Fraser, G. M.
Flashover. Chazin, S.
Flashpoint. Barnes, L.
FLAUBERT, GUSTAVE, 1821-1880
About
Barnes, J. Flaubert's parrot
Flaubert's parrot. Barnes, J.
Flavia and her artists. Cather, W.
In Cather, W. Early novels and stories
FLEMING, IAN, 1908-1964
Parodies, imitations, etc.
Gardner, J. E. Cold fall
Gardner, J. E. License renewed
Flesh and blood. Cunningham, M.
Flesh and blood. Harvey, J.
Flesh and bones. Levine, P.
Flesh wounds. Greenleaf, S.
Fletch. Mcdonald, G.
also in Mcdonald, G. The Fletch chronicles
Fletch and the man who. Mcdonald, G.
In Mcdonald, G. The Fletch chronicles
Fletch and the Widow Bradley. Mcdonald, G.
In Mcdonald, G. The Fletch chronicles
The **Fletch** chronicles. Mcdonald, G.
Fletch reflected. Mcdonald, G.
Fletch, too. Mcdonald, G.
also in Mcdonald, G. The Fletch chronicles
Fletch won. Mcdonald, G.
also in Mcdonald, G. The Fletch chronicles
Fletch's fortune. Mcdonald, G.
In Mcdonald, G. The Fletch chronicles
Fletch's moxie. Mcdonald, G.
In Mcdonald, G. The Fletch chronicles
FLIERS *See* Air pilots
Flight. Burke, J.
Flight. Glendinning, V.
Flight. Steinbeck, J.
In Steinbeck, J. The portable Steinbeck
FLIGHT ATTENDANTS
Leonard, E. Rum punch
Flight lessons. Gaffney, P.
Flight of a witch. Peters, E.
Flight of eagles. Higgins, J.
The **flight** of the falcon. Du Maurier, Dame D.
Flight of the falcon. Smith, W. A.
Flight of the Intruder. Coonts, S.
The **flight** of the maidens. Gardam, J.
Flight of the Old Dog. Brown, D.
Flights of angels. Gilchrist, E.
Flirting with Pete. Delinsky, B.
Floaters. Wambaugh, J.
The **floating** book. Lovric, M.
Floating city. Lustbader, E. V.
Floating dragon. Straub, P.
The **floating** opera. Barth, J.
The **flood**. Steinbeck, J.
In Steinbeck, J. The portable Steinbeck
Flood tide. Cussler, C.
Floodgate. MacLean, A.
FLOODS
See also Disasters
Cambor, K. In sunlight, in a beautiful garden
Faulkner, W. If I forget thee, Jerusalem
Hassler, J. The Staggerford flood
Marshall, C. Julie
The **Florabama** Ladies' Auxiliary & Sewing Circle. Battle, L.
FLORENCE (ITALY) *See* Italy—Florence
FLORIDA
Frank, P. Alas, Babylon
Haldeman, J. W. The coming
Hiaasen, C. Skinny dip
McBain, E. Alice in jeopardy
Morris, S. Waiting for April
Sher, I. Gentlemen of space
Yancey, R. A burning in Homeland
18th century
Unsworth, B. Sacred hunger
19th century
Matthiessen, P. Bone by bone
Matthiessen, P. Killing Mister Watson
20th century
Banks, R. Continental drift
Crews, H. Scar lover
Dexter, P. The paperboy
Fowler, C. M. Before women had wings
Fowler, C. M. Remembering Blue
Hiaasen, C. Basket case
Hiaasen, C. Lucky you
Hiaasen, C. Native tongue
Hiaasen, C. Sick puppy
Hiaasen, C. Skin tight
Hiaasen, C. Stormy weather
Hiaasen, C. Strip tease
Hoffman, A. Turtle Moon
Irving, C. Final argument
Leonard, E. Cat chaser
Leonard, E. LaBrava
Leonard, E. Maximum Bob
Leonard, E. Riding the rap
Leonard, E. Rum punch
Leonard, E. Stick
Lustbader, E. V. Dark homecoming
Matthiessen, P. Lost Man's River
McFarland, D. School for the blind
Michener, J. A. Recessional
Poyer, D. Down to a sunless sea
Quindlen, A. Black and blue
Rawlings, M. K. Short stories
Sanders, L. Guilty pleasures
Sanders, L. Sullivan's sting
Saul, J. Darkness
Updike, J. Rabbit at rest
Woods, S. Orchid Beach
Key West
Hemingway, E. To have and have not
Hersey, J. Key West tales
Lurie, A. The last resort
McGuane, T. Ninety-two in the shade
McGuane, T. Panama
Robinson, S. Callahan's con
Shames, L. Mangrove squeeze
Shames, L. Virgin heat
Shames, L. Welcome to paradise
Woods, S. Choke
Miami
Bell, C. The Perez family
Buchanan, E. Pulse
Cook, R. Terminal
Elkin, S. Mrs. Ted Bliss
Grippando, J. The informant
Hailey, A. Detective
Hall, J. W. Rough draft
Hoffman, J. Retribution
Leonard, E. LaBrava
Leonard, E. Pronto
Lindsay, J. P. Darkly dreaming Dexter
Parker, B. Blood relations
Parker, B. Criminal justice
Parker, B. Suspicion of betrayal
Parker, B. Suspicion of deceit
Parker, B. Suspicion of guilt
Parker, B. Suspicion of vengeance
Palm Beach
Fielding, J. Missing pieces
Hoag, T. Dark horse
Whitney, P. A. Poinciana

Four spirits. Naslund, S. J.
The **four** swans. Graham, W.
Four to score. Evanovich, J.
Four ways to forgiveness. Le Guin, U. K.
The **four** wise men. Tournier, M.
The **fourteen** sisters of Emilio Montez O'Brien. Hijuelos, O.
The **fourth** book of lost swords: Farslayer's story. Saberhagen, F.
The **fourth** deadly sin. Sanders, L.
The **fourth** Durango. Thomas, R.
The **fourth** estate. Archer, J.
The **fourth** hand. Irving, J.

FOURTH OF JULY

Lockridge, R. Raintree County
Lurie, A. Only children

The **fourth** procedure. Pottinger, S.
The **fourth** protocol. Forsyth, F.
The **fourth** world. Danvers, D.

FOX, GEORGE, 1624-1691

About

De Hartog, J. The peaceable kingdom

FOX, MARGARET ASKEW FELL, 1614-1702

About

De Hartog, J. The peaceable kingdom

FOX HUNTING

Brown, R. M. Outfoxed

Foxfire. Oates, J. C.
Foxmask. Marillier, J.
Fractal mode. Anthony, P.
Fragrant Harbor. Lanchester, J.
Framley parsonage. Trollope, A.

FRANCE

14th century

Cornwell, B. Vagabond
Pears, I. The dream of Scipio
Yarbro, C. Q. Blood roses

15th century

Chevalier, T. The lady and the unicorn
Haasse, H. S. In a dark wood wandering
Marcantel, P. An army of angels
Twain, M. Personal recollections of Joan of Arc

16th century

Plaidy, J. The scarlet cloak
Riley, J. M. The serpent garden

17th century

Anthony, E. The Cardinal and the Queen
Dumas, A. The iron mask [variant title: The man in the iron mask]
Dumas, A. The three musketeers
Dumas, A. Twenty years after
Laker, R. To dance with kings

18th century

Davis, K. Versailles
Dickens, C. A tale of two cities
Doherty, P. C. The masked man
Dumas, A. The Queen's necklace
Koen, K. Through a glass darkly
Kundera, M. Slowness
Laker, R. To dance with kings
Sterne, L. A sentimental journey through France and Italy
Süskind, P. Perfume: the story of a murderer

1789-1799

Dickens, C. A tale of two cities
Forester, C. S. Lord Hornblower
Orczy, E., Baroness. Adventures of the Scarlet Pimpernel
Orczy, E., Baroness. The elusive Pimpernel
Orczy, E., Baroness. The Scarlet Pimpernel
Piercy, M. City of darkness, city of light
Sabatini, R. Scaramouche
Thomas, C. Farewell, my queen

1799-1815

Forester, C. S. Lord Hornblower

19th century

Colette. Claudine at school
Flaubert, G. Sentimental education
Hugo, V. Les misérables
Moore, B. The magician's wife
Sand, G. Lélia
Sand, G. Marianne

1815-1848

Field, R. All this, and heaven too
Stendhal. The red and the black

1848-1870

Werfel, F. The song of Bernadette

1870-1940

Céline, L.-F. Journey to the end of the night
Faulkner, W. A fable
Ford, F. M. No more parades

20th century

Brookner, A. Incidents in the Rue Laugier
Cocteau, J. The impostor
Colette. The complete Claudine
Colette. Music-hall sidelights
Furst, A. Kingdom of shadows
Glendinning, V. Flight
Handke, P. My year in the no-man's-bay
Harris, J. Chocolat
Hemingway, E. The garden of Eden
Kundera, M. Identity
Kundera, M. Slowness
Mayle, P. Chasing Cézanne
Moore, B. The statement
Proust, M. The captive
Proust, M. The captive [and] The fugitive
Proust, M. The fugitive [variant title: The sweet cheat gone]
Proust, M. The Guermantes way
Proust, M. Remembrance of things past
Proust, M. Sodom and Gomorrah
Proust, M. Time regained [variant title: The past recaptured]
Sartre, J. P. The reprieve

1940-1945

Bates, H. E. Fair stood the wind for France
Daley, R. The innocents within
Faulks, S. Charlotte Gray
Follett, K. Jackdaws
Francis, C. Night sky
Furst, A. Red gold
Greene, G. The tenth man
Hijuelos, O. A simple Habana melody: from when the world was good
Pears, I. The dream of Scipio
Sartre, J. P. Troubled sleep

Aristocracy

See Aristocracy—France

Army

Tolstoy, L., graf. War and peace

Army—Foreign Legion

Wren, P. C. Beau Geste

Army—Officers

Conrad, J. The duel

Coal mines and mining

See Coal mines and mining—France

College life

See College life—France

Courts and courtiers

See Courts and courtiers—France

German occupation, 1940-1945

See France—1940-1945

Kings and rulers

Steinbeck, J. The short reign of Pippin IV

Politics

See Politics—France

Prisoners and prisons

See Prisoners and prisons—France

Rural life

Balzac, H. d. The country doctor

FRENCH—*Continued*

Indochina

Texier, C. Victorine

Ireland

Flanagan, T. The year of the French

Russia

Bradbury, M. To the Hermitage
Makine, A. Dreams of my Russian summers

Thailand

Houellebecq, M. Platform

United States

Cather, W. Death comes for the archbishop
Field, R. All this, and heaven too
Hansen, R. Isn't it romantic?

FRENCH AND INDIAN WAR, 1755-1763 *See* United States—French and Indian War, 1755-1763
The **French** lieutenant's woman. Fowles, J.
FRENCH REVOLUTION *See* France—1789-1799
FRENCH RIVIERA *See* Riviera (France and Italy)
French Silk. Brown, S.
FRENCH SOLDIERS *See* Soldiers—France
Frenchman's Creek. Du Maurier, Dame D.
The **fresco**. Tepper, S. S.
FREUD, SIGMUND, 1856-1939

About

Meyer, N. The seven-per-cent solution
Stone, I. The passions of the mind
Thomas, D. M. The white hotel

FREYTAG-LORINGHOVEN, ELSA VON, BARONESS, 1874-1927

About

Steinke, R. Holy skirts

Friday. Heinlein, R. A.
Friday. Tournier, M.
Friday the rabbi slept late. Kemelman, H.
Fried green tomatoes at the Whistle-Stop Cafe. Flagg, F.
A **friend** of Kafka and other stories. Singer, I. B.
In Singer, I. B. Collected stories
Friend of mankind and other stories. Mazor, J.
Friend of my youth. Munro, A.
A **friend** of the earth. Boyle, T. C.
The **friend** of the family. Dostoyevsky, F.
In Dostoyevsky, F. The short novels of Dostoevsky p617-811
The **friendly** persuasion. West, J.
FRIENDS *See* Friendship
FRIENDS, SOCIETY OF *See* Society of Friends
Friends at Thrush Green. Read, Miss
The **friends** of Eddie Coyle. Higgins, G. V.
FRIENDSHIP

See also Love

Adler, E. Fortune is a woman
Amidon, S. The new city
Atwood, M. The robber bride
Balzac, H. d. Cousin Pons
Barnes, J. Love, etc.
Beattie, A. My life, starring Dara Falcon
Bellow, S. Ravelstein
Berger, T. Best friends
Bernhard, T. Walking
Binchy, M. Circle of friends
Binchy, M. Light a penny candle
Binchy, M. Scarlet Feather
Bradford, B. T. Voice of the heart
Brookner, A. Brief lives
Buckley, W. F. Elvis in the morning
Canin, E. For kings and planets
Cantor, J. Great Neck
Carroll, J. Prince of peace
Clements, M. Midsummer
Coe, J. The Rotters' Club
Colwin, L. A big storm knocked it over
Dallas, S. The Persian Pickle Club
Dart, I. R. Show business kills
Dixon, S. Old friends
Doig, I. Dancing at the Rascal Fair
Erdrich, L. The Beet Queen
Evans, N. The smoke jumper
Frayn, M. Spies
Gaitskill, M. Veronica
Gardam, J. The flight of the maidens
Gilchrist, E. Nora Jane and company
Goddard, R. Into the blue
Goldsmith, O. Bad boy
Gordon, M. Final payments
Gowdy, B. The romantic
Grumbach, D. The book of knowledge
Gutcheon, B. R. Five fortunes
Hammond, D. C. Going to bend
Harris, E. L. If this world were mine
Hassler, J. The Staggerford flood
Herlihy, J. L. Midnight cowboy
Highsmith, P. The boy who followed Ripley
Hirshberg, G. The Snowman's children
Hosseini, K. The kite runner
Jaffe, R. The room-mating season
Jakes, J. North and South
Kafka, K. Miranda's vines
Kay, T. Shadow song
Keyes, M. Last Chance Saloon
King, D. The ha-ha
King, S. Dreamcatcher
King, S. Hearts in Atlantis
Klein, R. The moth diaries
Knowles, J. Indian summer
Knowles, J. A separate peace
Lebrecht, N. The song of names
Lehane, D. Mystic river
L'Engle, M. A severed wasp
Lethem, J. The fortress of solitude
Li, P.-h. Farewell to my concubine
Longyear, B. B. Enemy mine
Lord, B. B. The middle heart
Mapson, J.-A. Bad Girl Creek
Matheson, R. Hunted past reason
Mawer, S. The fall
McCracken, E. Niagara Falls all over again
McDermid, V. The distant echo
McEwan, I. Amsterdam
McMillan, T. Waiting to exhale
Medlicott, J. A. The ladies of Covington send their love
Monette, P. Afterlife
Morrison, T. Sula
Morrow, B. Trinity fields
Mortimer, J. C. Dunster
Mosley, W. RL's dream
Murdoch, I. The book and the brotherhood
Murdoch, I. Jackson's dilemma
Oates, J. C. Solstice
O'Brien, T. July, July
O'Neill, J. At swim, two boys
Paddock, J. A secret word
Pelecanos, G. P. The big blowdown
Phillips, C. A distant shore
Pilcher, R. Coming home
Pilcher, R. Winter solstice
Plain, B. Looking back
Potok, C. The promise
Powell, A. A question of upbringing
Powell, D. Come back to Sorrento
Price, R. The tongues of angels
Pym, B. Jane and Prudence
Raymond, J. The half-life
Ross-Macdonald, M. For they shall inherit
Schwarz, C. All is vanity
Shamsie, K. Kartography
Siddons, A. R. Islands
Siddons, A. R. Outer banks
Steel, D. Sunset in St. Tropez
Stegner, W. E. Crossing to safety
Steinbeck, J. Of mice and men
Steinbeck, J. Tortilla Flat
Swift, G. Last orders
Taylor, E. Mrs. Palfrey at the Claremont
Thayer, N. Between husbands and friends
Trollope, J. The best of friends
Trollope, J. The men and the girls
Walbert, K. Our kind
Weaver, M. Deceptions
Weiner, J. Little earthquakes
Wharton, W. Birdy
Wiggins, M. Evidence of things unseen

FRUIT PICKERS *See* Migrant labor
The **frumious** Bandersnatch. McBain, E.
FUGATE, CARIL ANN
About
Ward, L. Outside valentine
The **fugitive** [variant title: The sweet cheat gone] Proust, M.
In Proust, M. The captive [and] The fugitive
In Proust, M. Remembrance of things past p425-706
Fugitive colors. Maron, M.
Fugitive pieces. Michaels, A.

FUGITIVE SLAVES
Crafts, H. The bondswomans narrative
Durham, D. A. A walk through darkness
Tryon, T. In the fire of spring
Twain, M. The adventures of Huckleberry Finn

FUGITIVES
See also Escaped convicts; Fugitive slaves; Manhunts; Outlaws
Ablow, K. R. Compulsion
Coben, H. Gone for good
Deaver, J. A maiden's grave
Draper, R. Hadrian's walls
Moore, B. The statement
Piercy, M. Vida
Riordan, R. Cold Springs
Saint, H. F. Memoirs of an invisible man
Saul, J. The Manhattan Hunt Club
Smith, A. Good morning, killer
Spark, M. Aiding and abetting
Wray, J. Canaan's tongue
Fugitives' fire. Brand, M.
Full circle. Wilcox, C.
Full dress gray. Truscott, L. K.
The **full** Matilda. Haynes, D.
Funeral games. Renault, M.
Funeral in Berlin. Deighton, L.
Funeral in blue. Perry, A.

FUNERAL RITES AND CEREMONIES
Agee, J. A death in the family
Duncan, G. Death of an ordinary man
Faulkner, W. As I lay dying
Lipman, E. The dearly departed
Styron, A. All the finest girls
Styron, W. Lie down in darkness
Tyler, A. Breathing lessons
Waugh, E. The loved one
Welty, E. Losing battles
Welty, E. The optimist's daughter

FUR TRADE
Guthrie, A. B. The big sky
The **further** adventures of Menachem-Mendl. Sholem Aleichem

FUTURE
See also Science fiction
Amis, M. London fields
Anderson, P. Genesis
Anderson, P. Goat song
Anderson, P. Harvest of stars
Anderson, P. Harvest the fire
Anderson, P. Orion shall rise
Anderson, P. The stars are also fire
Asimov, I. The caves of steel
Asimov, I. Forward the Foundation
Asimov, I. Foundation
Asimov, I. Foundation and earth
Asimov, I. Foundation and empire
Asimov, I. Foundation's edge
Asimov, I. The naked sun
Asimov, I. Prelude to Foundation
Asimov, I. Robots and empire
Asimov, I. The robots of dawn
Asimov, I. Second Foundation
Atwood, M. The handmaid's tale
Atwood, M. Oryx and Crake
Auster, P. In the country of last things
Ballard, J. G. Super-Cannes
Banks, I. Look to windward
Barnes, J. The merchants of souls
Barnes, J. England, England
Barry, M. Jennifer Government
Bear, G. Anvil of stars
Bear, G. Dead lines
Bear, G. The forge of God
Bear, G. Foundation and chaos
Benford, G. Foundation's fear
Benford, G. Timescape
Benson, A. The plague tales
Bova, B. Saturn
Boyle, T. C. A friend of the earth
Brin, D. Earth
Brin, D. Foundation's triumph
Brin, D. Kiln people
Brin, D. The postman
Brown, D. Chains of command
Brown, D. Flight of the Old Dog
Brown, D. Night of the hawk
Brunner, J. Stand on Zanzibar
Burgess, A. A clockwork orange
Butler, O. E. Parable of the sower
Butler, O. E. Parable of the talents
Carr, C. Killing time
Cherryh, C. J. Destroyer
Cherryh, C. J. Foreigner
Cherryh, C. J. Inheritor
Cherryh, C. J. Invader
Cherryh, C. J. Precursor
Clancy, T. Debt of honor
Clancy, T. Red Storm rising
Clancy, T. The sum of all fears
Clarke, A. C. Beyond the fall of night
Coyle, H. W. Bright star
Cunningham, M. Specimen days
Cussler, C. Shock wave
Danvers, D. The fourth world
Delany, S. R. Stars in my pocket like grains of sand
Delany, S. R. Time considered as a helix of semi-precious stones
Doctorow, C. Down and out in the Magic Kindgom
Donaldson, S. R. This day all gods die: the gap into ruin
Ellison, H. A boy and his dog
Eskridge, K. Solitaire
Farmer, P. J. Dayworld
Farmer, P. J. Dayworld breakup
Farmer, P. J. Riders of the purple wage
Foster, A. D. The mocking program
Foster, A. D. Phylogenesis
Gear, W. M. Raising Abel
Gibson, W. All tomorrow's parties
Gibson, W. Neuromancer
Gibson, W. Virtual light
Goonan, K. A. Crescent city rhapsody
Goonan, K. A. Light music
Grippando, J. The abduction
Guilfoile, K. Cast of shadows
Haldeman, J. W. The coming
Haldeman, J. W. Forever free
Haldeman, J. W. Forever peace
Haldeman, J. W. The forever war
Harlan, T. House of reeds
Harrison, P. Storming Intrepid
Heinlein, R. A. Friday
Heinlein, R. A. The moon is a harsh mistress
Helprin, M. Winter's tale
Herbert, F. Children of Dune
Herbert, F. Dune
Herbert, F. Dune messiah
Herbert, F. God Emperor of Dune
Herbert, F. Heretics of Dune
Hesse, H. The glass bead game (Magister Ludi)
Hoban, R. Riddley Walker
Hoffman, E. The secret
Huxley, A. Brave new world
Katzenbach, J. State of mind
Kerr, K. Snare
Kesey, K. Sailor song
King, S. The long walk
King, S. The running man
Knebel, F. Seven days in May
Koontz, D. R. Night chills
Lawhead, S. Avalon
Lessing, D. M. The memoirs of a survivor
Lessing, D. M. Shikasta
McAuley, P. J. White devils
McDevitt, J. Eternity road
McDevitt, J. Infinity beach
McHugh, M. F. Nekropolis

GERMANY—Army—*Continued*
Solzhenitsyn, A. August 1914

Army—Officers

Kirst, H. H. The return of Gunner Asch

Communism

See Communism—Germany

Navy

Buchheim, L.-G. The boat

World War, 1939-1945

See World War, 1939-1945—Germany

Bavaria

MacLean, A. Where eagles dare

Berlin

Barnes, D. Nightwood
Berger, T. Crazy in Berlin
Carroll, J. Secret father
Deaver, J. Garden of beasts
Deighton, L. Berlin game
Deighton, L. Charity
Deighton, L. Funeral in Berlin
Deighton, L. London match
Grass, G. Too far afield
Isherwood, C. The Berlin stories
Just, W. S. The weather in Berlin
Kanon, J. The good German
Kaye, M. M. Death in Berlin
Koeppen, W. A sad affair
McEwan, I. The innocent
Nabokov, V. V. King, queen, knave
Nooteboom, C. All souls' day
Pye, M. The pieces from Berlin
Uris, L. Armageddon

Bonn

Böll, H. The clown
Le Carré, J. A small town in Germany

Cologne

Böll, H. The silent angel
Gross, C. Scholarium

Dresden

Vonnegut, K. Slaughterhouse-five

Düsseldorf

Mann, T. The black swan

Nuremberg

Buckley, W. F. Nuremberg
Germinal. Zola, É.
GERMS *See* Microorganisms
Gerontius. Hamilton-Paterson, J.
GERONTOLOGISTS *See* Physicians
Gertrude. Hesse, H.
Gertrude and Claudius. Updike, J.
GESTAPO *See* National socialism
A **gesture** life. Lee, C.-R.
Get Shorty. Leonard, E.
The **gettin** place. Straight, S.
Getting it right. Buckley, W. F.
Getting mother's body. Parks, S.-L.
GETTYSBURG, BATTLE OF, 1863
Gingrich, N. Gettysburg
Shaara, M. The killer angels
Gettysburg. Gingrich, N.
GHETTOS *See* Jews—Segregation
The **ghost** and Mrs. Muir. Leslie, J. A. C.
Ghost country. Paretsky, S.
Ghost moon. Robards, K.
A **ghost** of a chance. Crider, B.
The **ghost** road. Barker, P.
GHOST STORIES
See also Gothic romances; Horror stories; Supernatural phenomena
Alcott, L. M. The abbott's ghost
Amis, K. The Green Man
Ansay, A. M. Midnight champagne
Barker, C. In the flesh [novelette]
Beagle, P. S. A fine and private place
Bear, G. Dead lines
Berg, E. Range of motion
Byatt, A. S. The conjugial angel
Card, O. S. Homebody
Card, O. S. Treasure box
Coulter, C. The heiress bride
The dark
Davies, R. Murther & walking spirits
DeLillo, D. The body artist
Dickens, C. A Christmas carol
Dickens, C. The complete ghost stories of Charles Dickens
Ellis, B. E. Lunar Park
Famous ghost stories
Gutcheon, B. R. More than you know
Hansen, E. F. Tales of protection
Harington, D. Ekaterina
Harwood, J. The ghost writer
Hooper, K. Haunting Rachel
Jackson, S. The haunting of Hill House
James, H. The turn of the screw
Kallos, S. Broken for you
King, S. Bag of bones
Leslie, J. A. C. The ghost and Mrs. Muir
The Literary ghost
Livesey, M. Eva moves the furniture
Lofts, N. Gad's Hall
Lofts, N. The haunting of Gad's Hall
Lovecraft, H. P. The mound
Lurie, A. Women and ghosts
McFarland, D. A face at the window
Moloney, S. The dwelling
O'Nan, S. The night country
The Oxford book of English ghost stories
The Oxford book of twentieth-century ghost stories
Saul, J. Second child
Steel, D. Johnny Angel
Straub, P. Ghost story
Straub, P. Mrs. God
Tan, A. The hundred secret senses
Woods, S. Under the lake
Ghost story. Straub, P.
Ghost town. Coover, R.
GHOST TOWNS *See* Extinct cities
The **ghost** walker. Coel, M.
The **ghost** writer. Harwood, J.
The **ghost** writer. Roth, P.
also in Roth, P. Zuckerman bound: a trilogy and epilogue
GHOSTS *See* Ghost stories
Ghosts. Banville, J.
The **ghostway**. Hillerman, T.
also in Hillerman, T. The Jim Chee mysteries
Giant. Ferber, E.
GIANTS
McCracken, E. The giant's house
Swift, J. Gulliver's travels
Wells, H. G. The food of the gods
The **giant's** house. McCracken, E.
Giants in the earth. Rölvaag, O. E.
The **gift**. Steinbeck, J.
In Steinbeck, J. The portable Steinbeck
The **gift** of Asher Lev. Potok, C.
A **gift** of sanctuary. Robb, C. M.
The **gift** of stones. Crace, J.
GIFTED CHILDREN
Gaddis, W. J R
Potok, C. My name is Asher Lev
Gigi. Colette
In Colette. Gigi. Julie de Carneilhan. Chance acquaintances p9-74
In Colette. Six novels p649-97
Gigi. Julie de Carneilhan. Chance acquaintances. Colette
The **gilded** age. Twain, M.
also in Twain, M. The gilded age and later novels
The **gilded** age and later novels. Twain, M.
The **gilded** six-bits. Hurston, Z. N.
In Hurston, Z. N. Novels and stories p985-96
Gilead. Robinson, M.
Giles goat-boy. Barth, J.
Gilgamesh the king. Silverberg, R.
GILLIGAN'S ISLAND (TELEVISION PROGRAM)
Carson, T. Gilligan's wake

GRANDMOTHERS—*Continued*
Cisneros, S. Caramelo
Colette. Gigi
De la Roche, M. Jalna
Desai, A. Fire on the mountain
García Márquez, G. The incredible and sad tale of innocent Eréndira and her heartless grandmother
Jhabvala, R. P. Heat and dust
L'Engle, M. A live coal in the sea
Makine, A. Dreams of my Russian summers
Miller, S. The world below
Read, Miss. Thrush Green
Ross-Macdonald, M. The Trevarton inheritance
Tóibín, C. The blackwater lightship
Tryon, T. The other
Weldon, F. Rhode Island blues
Whitney, P. A. Domino
Yolen, J. Briar Rose
The **grandmother's** tale and selected stories. Narayan, R. K.

GRANDPARENTS
Gardam, J. Faith Fox
Merullo, R. In Revere, in those days
Mitchard, J. A theory of relativity

GRANDSONS
Bergen, D. See the child
Hays, T. The pleasure was mine

GRANT, ULYSSES S. (ULYSSES SIMPSON), 1822-1885

About

Byrd, M. Grant
Gingrich, N. Grant comes east
Shaara, J. The last full measure
Grant. Byrd, M.
Grant comes east. Gingrich, N.
Grant's last case. See Tey, J. The singing sands
The **grapes** of wrath. Steinbeck, J.
Grass. Tepper, S. S.
The **grass** crown. McCullough, C.
The **grass** dancer. Power, S.
The **grass** harp. Capote, T.
The **grass** is singing. Lessing, D. M.
Grass roots. Woods, S.
Grasshopper. Vine, B.
Grave mistake. Marsh, Dame N.
Grave music. Harrod-Eagles, C.

GRAVE ROBBERS
Holman, S. The dress lodger
Grave secrets. Reichs, K. J.
Grave undertakings. McInerny, R. M.
Gravedigger. Hansen, J.
Graveyard dust. Hambly, B.
A **graveyard** for lunatics. Bradbury, R.
The **graveyard** game. Baker, K.
The **graveyard** position. Barnard, R.
GRAVEYARDS *See* Cemeteries
Gravity. Gerritsen, T.
Gravity's rainbow. Pynchon, T.
The **great** American novel. Roth, P.
The **great** and secret show. Barker, C.
GREAT AUNTS *See* Aunts

GREAT BRITAIN
See also England; Northern Ireland; Scotland; Wales
Block, L. The collected mystery stories
McCullough, C. The song of Troy

Armed forces

See also Great Britain. Army

Colonies

Clavell, J. Tai-Pan

GREAT BRITAIN. ARMY
Cornwell, B. Redcoat
Cornwell, B. Sharpe's battle
Cornwell, B. Sharpe's fortress
Cornwell, B. Sharpe's prey: Richard Sharpe and the Expedition to Copenhagen, 1807
Cornwell, B. Sharpe's Trafalgar
Kaye, M. M. The far pavilions
Kaye, M. M. Shadow of the moon
Llewellyn, R. None but the lonely heart
Waugh, E. Men at arms
Waugh, E. Officers and gentlemen

Officers

Boulle, P. The bridge over the River Kwai
Cornwell, B. Sharpe's company
Cornwell, B. Sharpe's eagle
Cornwell, B. Sharpe's enemy
Cornwell, B. Sharpe's gold
Cornwell, B. Sharpe's honour
Cornwell, B. Sharpe's regiment
Cornwell, B. Sharpe's sword
Forester, C. S. Hornblower and the Atropos
Forester, C. S. Ship of the line
Mallinson, A. A close run thing
Waugh, E. The end of the battle
GREAT BRITAIN. NAVY *See* Great Britain. Royal Navy

GREAT BRITAIN. PARLIAMENT
Archer, J. First among equals

GREAT BRITAIN. ROYAL NAVY
Forester, C. S. Admiral Hornblower in the West Indies
Forester, C. S. Beat to quarters
Forester, C. S. Flying colours
Forester, C. S. Mr. Midshipman Hornblower
Lambdin, D. King's captain
McCutchan, P. The new lieutenant
Monsarrat, N. The cruel sea
O'Brian, P. The hundred days
O'Brian, P. The unknown shore
O'Brian, P. The yellow admiral
Unsworth, B. Losing Nelson

Officers

Forester, C. S. Hornblower and the Hotspur
Forester, C. S. Hornblower during the crisis, and two stories: Hornblower's temptation and The last encounter
Forester, C. S. Lieutenant Hornblower
McCutchan, P. Cameron's crossing
O'Brian, P. Blue at the mizzen
O'Brian, P. The commodore
O'Brian, P. The wine-dark sea
Reeman, D. A ship must die
GREAT BRITAIN. WOMEN'S LAND ARMY *See* Women's Land Army (Great Britain)
A **great** deliverance. George, E.
The **great** divide. Bunn, T. D.
Great dream of heaven. Shepard, S.
Great expectations. Dickens, C.
The **great** fire. Hazzard, S.
The **great** Gatsby. Fitzgerald, F. S.
also in Fitzgerald, F. S. The Fitzgerald reader p105-238

GREAT-GRANDMOTHERS
Baldacci, D. Wish you well
Great lion of God. Caldwell, T.
The **great** mountains. Steinbeck, J.
In Steinbeck, J. The portable Steinbeck
Great Neck. Cantor, J.
Great racing stories. See The Dick Francis treasury of great racing stories
Great short works of Joseph Conrad. Conrad, J.
Great stories of the American West. Entered in Part I under title
The **great** train robbery. Crichton, M.
The **greater** inclination. Wharton, E.
In Wharton, E. The collected short stories of Edith Wharton
The **greatest** evil. Kienzle, W. X.
The **greatest** love [novelette] McCaffrey, A.
In McCaffrey, A. The girl who heard dragons p169-225

GRECO-TURKISH WAR, 1921-1922
Karnezis, P. The maze

GREECE
See also Cephalonia Island (Greece); Lesbos Island (Greece)
Bova, B. Orion and the conqueror
Bradley, M. Z. The firebrand
Cook, E. Achilles
Crane, S. Active service
Doherty, P. C. The godless man
Doherty, P. C. The house of death
Jong, E. Sappho's leap
Renault, M. The bull from the sea
Renault, M. Fire from heaven
Renault, M. Funeral games
Renault, M. The king must die
Renault, M. The last of the wine
Unsworth, B. The songs of the kings

GUILT—*Continued*
McEwan, I. Atonement
McEwan, I. The innocent
Miller, S. Family pictures
Moran, T. Anja the liar
Morrison, T. Jazz
Muske-Dukes, C. Life after death
Nordan, L. Wolf whistle
O'Dell, T. Coal Run
Ōe, K. An echo of heaven
Ōe, K. The silent cry
Rossner, J. Looking for Mr. Goodbar
Schlink, B. The reader
Schwartz, J. B. Reservation Road
Schwarz, C. Drowning Ruth
Shakespeare, N. Snowleg
Shreve, A. The weight of water
Smith, S. B. A simple plan
Styron, W. Sophie's choice
Trevor, W. The silence in the garden
Tyler, A. Saint maybe
Uhnak, D. The Ryer Avenue story
Vine, B. A fatal inversion
Wiesel, E. Twilight
Wright, A. M. After Gregory
Guilt. Lescroart, J. T.
Guilty as sin. Hoag, T.
Guilty pleasures. Sanders, L.

GUITARISTS
Bell, M. S. Anything goes
The **gulf**. Poyer, D.

GULF STREAM
Hemingway, E. The old man and the sea
GULF WAR, 1991 *See* Persian Gulf War, 1991
Gulliver's travels. Swift, J.
GUNBOATS *See* Warships
Gunman's rhapsody. Parker, R. B.
Gunner Asch goes to war. See Kirst, H. H. Forward, Gunner Asch!
GUNS *See* Firearms
The **guns** of Avalon. Zelazny, R.
The **guns** of Navarone. MacLean, A.
The **guru** of love. Upadhyay, S.
Guys and dolls. Runyon, D.
Gwen Bristow's Plantation trilogy. Bristow, G.

GYPSIES
Gores, J. Cons, scams & grifts
Hugo, V. The hunchback of Notre Dame
King, S. Thinner
Mérimée, P. Carmen
Moor, M. d. Duke of Egypt
The **Gypsy** Man. Bausch, R.
The **Gyrth** chalice mystery. Allingham, M.
In Allingham, M. Three cases for Mr. Campion p421-604

H

"H" is for homicide. Grafton, S.
H.P. Lovecraft. Lovecraft, H. P.
The **ha-ha**. King, D.
Had a good time. Butler, R. O.
Hadji Murád. Tolstoy, L., graf
In Tolstoy, L., graf. The short novels of Tolstoy

HADRIAN, EMPEROR OF ROME, 76-138
About
Yourcenar, M. Memoirs of Hadrian
Hadrian's walls. Draper, R.
A **haiku** for Hanae. Melville, J.
HAIRDRESSERS *See* Beauty shops

HAITI
Danticat, E. The dew breaker

Revolution, 1791-1804
Bell, M. S. All souls' rising
Bell, M. S. Master of the crossroads
Bell, M. S. The stone that the builder refused
Roberts, K. L. Lydia Bailey

20th century
Danticat, E. Krik? Krak!
Greene, G. The comedians

Port-au-Prince
Greene, G. The comedians

HAITIAN REFUGEES
Banks, R. Continental drift

HAITIANS

Dominican Republic
Danticat, E. The farming of bones

United States
Danticat, E. The dew breaker
Prose, F. Primitive people
Half a heart. Brown, R.
Half a life. Naipaul, V. S.
Half asleep in frog pajamas. Robbins, T.
The **half** brother. Christensen, L. S.

HALF-BROTHERS
Christensen, L. S. The half brother
Kesey, K. Sometimes a great notion
Murdoch, I. The good apprentice
Smith, W. A. Power of the sword
Smith, W. A. Rage
Stewart, F. M. The magnificent Savages
HALF-CASTES *See* Mixed bloods
The **half-life**. Raymond, J.
Half-moon and empty stars. Spence, G.
Half Moon Street. Perry, A.
Half Moon Street. Theroux, P.

HALF-SISTERS
Dailey, J. Heiress
Fielding, J. Missing pieces
García, C. The Aguero sisters
HALIFAX (N.S.) *See* Canada—Halifax
The **hall** of the mountain king. Tarr, J.

HALLET, ELIZABETH FONES WINTHROP FEAKE, B. 1610
About
Seton, A. The Winthrop woman
The **hallowed** hunt. Bujold, L. M.

HALLUCINATIONS AND ILLUSIONS
See also Personality disorders

HAMILTON, LADY EMMA, 1761?-1815
About
Sontag, S. The volcano lover

HAMILTON, SIR WILLIAM, 1730-1803
About
Sontag, S. The volcano lover
The **Hamilton** case. De Kretser, M.
The **hamlet**. Faulkner, W.
also in Faulkner, W. Novels, 1936-1940 p727-1075
also in Faulkner, W. Snopes p1-349
The **Hamlet** trap. Wilhelm, K.
Hammer and the cross [series]
Harrison, H. King and emperor
Harrison, H. One king's way
The **hammer** of Eden. Follett, K.
The **hammer** of God. Clarke, A. C.
Hammerfall. Cherryh, C. J.
Hammerheads. Brown, D.
HAMPSHIRE (ENGLAND) *See* England—Hampshire

HAND
Irving, J. The fourth hand
The **hand** I fan with. Ansa, T. M.
The **hand** of Oberon. Zelazny, R.

HAND-TO-HAND FIGHTING
See also Wrestling
A **handbook** for spies. Busch, F.
In Busch, F. Don't tell anyone
A **handful** of rice. Markandaya, K.
The **handmaid's** tale. Atwood, M.
Hands of a stranger. Daley, R.
Handsome Harry, or, The gangster's true confessions. Blake, J. C.
The **handsome** road. Bristow, G.
In Bristow, G. Gwen Bristow's Plantation trilogy p263-530

The **heart** of the matter. Greene, G.
Heart of the West. Henry, O.
In Henry, O. The complete works of O. Henry p109-266
Heart of the west. Williamson, P.
Heart of war. Truscott, L. K.
Heart, you bully, you punk. Cohen, L. H.
Heartbreak Hotel. Siddons, A. R.
Heartbreaker. Ferrigno, R.
The **heartbreaker**. Howatch, S.
Heartburn. Ephron, N.
Heartfire. Card, O. S.
Heartland. Wiltse, D.
Hearts. Wolitzer, H.
Hearts and bones. Lawrence, M. K.
Hearts in Atlantis. King, S.
The **heart's** wild surf. See Johnson, S. The sailmaker's daughter
The **heartsong** of Charging Elk. Welch, J.
Heartstones. Rendell, R.
Heartwood. Burke, J. L.
Heat. McBain, E.
Heat. Woods, S.
Heat and dust. Jhabvala, R. P.
Heat, and other stories. Oates, J. C.
The **heat** of the day. Bowen, E.
The **heat** of the sun. O'Faoláin, S.
In O'Faoláin, S. The collected stories of Seán O'Faoláin p700-886
Heat wave. Lively, P.
The **heather** blazing. Tóibín, C.

HEAVEN
Heinlein, R. A. Job: a comedy of justice
Sebold, A. The lovely bones
Heaven and hell. Jakes, J.
Heaven lies about us. McCabe, E.
The **heaven** of Mercury. Watson, B.
Heavenly days. Wilcox, J.
Heaven's edge. Gunesekera, R.
Heaven's prisoners. Burke, J. L.
Heaven's reach. Brin, D.
HEBRIDES (SCOTLAND)
See also Skye (Scotland)
Stewart, M. The stormy petrel
Woolf, V. To the lighthouse

HEDONISM
Colette. Claudine married
Kazantzakis, N. Zorba the Greek
Kundera, M. Slowness
See, C. The handyman
Hedwig and Berti. Arkin, F.
Heechee rendezvous. Pohl, F.
Heir apparent. Coscarelli, K.
Heir to the glimmering world. Ozick, C.
Heiress. Dailey, J.
The **heiress** bride. Coulter, C.
HEIRESSES *See* Inheritance and succession; Wealth
HEIRS *See* Inheritance and succession; Wealth
Helen hath no fury. Roberts, G.
HELENA, SAINT, CA. 255-329
About
Bradley, M. Z. Priestess of Avalon
Hell at the breech. Franklin, T.
Hell to pay. Pelecanos, G. P.
The **Hellfire** Club. Straub, P.
Helliconia spring. Aldiss, B. W.
Helliconia summer. Aldiss, B. W.
Helliconia winter. Aldiss, B. W.
Hello, darkness. Brown, S.
Hello to the cannibals. Bausch, R.
Help the poor struggler. Grimes, M.
HEMINGS, HARRIET, 1801-1876
About
Chase-Riboud, B. The President's daughter
HEMINGS, SALLY, 1773-1835
About
Chase-Riboud, B. Sally Hemings
The **Hemingway** reader. Hemingway, E.
Henderson the rain king. Bellow, S.
also in Bellow, S. The portable Saul Bellow
Henderson's spear. Wright, R.
HENRIQUEZ, CAMILA SALOMÉ UREÑA- *See* Ureña-Henriquez, Camila Salomé, 1894-1973
HENRÍQUEZ, SALOMÉ UREÑA DE *See* Ureña de Henríquez, Salomé, 1850-1897
HENRY II, KING OF ENGLAND, 1133-1189
About
Penman, S. K. Time and chance
Penman, S. K. When Christ and his saints slept
HENRY III, KING OF ENGLAND, 1207-1272
About
Penman, S. K. Falls the shadow
HENRY VIII, KING OF ENGLAND, 1491-1547
About
Anthony, E. Anne Boleyn
Lewis, H. W. I am Mary Tudor
Maxwell, R. The secret diary of Anne Boleyn
Plaidy, J. Murder most royal
Plaidy, J. The rose without a thorn
Plaidy, J. The sixth wife
Henry Esmond. See Thackeray, W. M. The history of Henry Esmond, esquire
The **Henry** James reader. James, H.
Henry of Atlantic City. Reuss, F.
Her father's house. Plain, B.
Her infinite variety. Auchincloss, L.
Her mother's daughter. French, M.
Her name was Lola. Hoban, R.
HERBERT, HENRY HOWARD MOLYNEUX *See* Carnarvon, Henry Howard Molyneux Herbert, 4th Earl of, 1831-1890
HERCEGOVINA *See* Bosnia and Hercegovina
Hercule Poirot's casebook. Christie, A.
Here and beyond. Wharton, E.
In Wharton, E. The collected short stories of Edith Wharton
Here be dragons. Penman, S. K.
Here lies. Parker, D.
Here on Earth. Hoffman, A.
The **heretic's** apprentice. Peters, E.
Heretics of Dune. Herbert, F.
Herland. Gilman, C. P.
also in Gilman, C. P. The Charlotte Perkins Gilman reader
also in Gilman, C. P. Charlotte Perkins Gilman's Utopian novels p150-269

HERMAPHRODITISM
Eugenides, J. Middlesex
Jennings, G. Raptor
The **hermit** and the wild woman. Wharton, E.
In Wharton, E. The collected short stories of Edith Wharton
The **hermit** of Eyton Forest. Peters, E.
The **hermit's** story. Bass, R.
HEROES
See also Heroism

HEROIN
Robbins, T. Villa incognito
HEROISM
See also Courage
Brown, D. A. Killdeer Mountain
Keneally, T. Flying hero class
HERTFORDSHIRE (ENGLAND) *See* England—Hertfordshire
Herzog. Bellow, S.
He's one, too. Gurganus, A.
In Gurganus, A. The practical heart
HICKOCK, MARTHA JANE CANARY *See* Calamity Jane, 1852-1903
HICKOK, JAMES BUTLER *See* Hickok, Wild Bill, 1837-1876
HICKOK, WILD BILL, 1837-1876
About
Dexter, P. Deadwood
Hidden prey. Sandford, J.
Hide & seek. Patterson, J.
Hideaway. Koontz, D. R.
The **high** and the mighty. Gann, E. K.
High country. Barr, N.
High country fall. Maron, M.
High crimes. Finder, J.
High fall. Dunlap, S.
High fidelity. Hornby, N.
High five. Evanovich, J.
The **high** flyer. Howatch, S.
High hearts. Brown, R. M.
HIGH SCHOOLS *See* School life
High stakes. Francis, D.
A **high** wind in Jamaica. Hughes, R. A. W.

HOLOCAUST, JEWISH (1933-1945)
See also Jews—Persecutions
Albahari, D. Götz and Meyer
Amis, M. Time's arrow
Appelfeld, A. Badenheim 1939
Bellow, S. The Bellarosa connection
Busch, F. A memory of war
Cooley, M. The archivist
Delbanco, N. What remains
Demetz, H. The house on Prague Street
Fast, H. The bridge builder's story
Harris, R. Fatherland
Hersey, J. The wall
Iles, G. Black cross
Keneally, T. Schindler's list
Korda, M. Worldly goods
Lebrecht, N. The song of names
Ozick, C. The Messiah of Stockholm
Ozick, C. Rosa
Ozick, C. The shawl
Russell, M. D. A thread of grace
Sebald, W. G. Austerlitz
Sebald, W. G. The emigrants
Uris, L. Mila 18
Wiesel, E. The forgotten
Wiesel, E. Twilight
Yolen, J. Briar Rose

HOLOCAUST SURVIVORS
Bailey, P. Uncle Rudolf
Bellow, S. Mr. Sammler's planet
Campbell, B. M. What you owe me
Chatwin, B. Utz
Conroy, P. Beach music
Demetz, H. The house on Prague Street
Easterman, D. The final judgement
Fast, H. The bridge builder's story
Krauss, N. The history of love
Messud, C. A simple tale
Michaels, A. Fugitive pieces
Ozick, C. The shawl
Phillips, C. The nature of blood
Potok, C. The ark builder
Prose, F. A changed man
Pye, M. The pieces from Berlin
Rosen, J. Joy comes in the morning
Singer, I. B. Shadows on the Hudson
Wallant, E. L. The pawnbroker
Wiesel, E. The accident
Wiesel, E. The forgotten
Wiesel, E. Twilight

HOLY COAT
Douglas, L. C. The robe

Holy fire. Sterling, B.
HOLY GRAIL *See* Grail
Holy skirts. Steinke, R.
The **holy** thief. Peters, E.

HOLY WEEK
Faulkner, W. A fable

Home fires. Rice, L.
Home fires burning. Maron, M.
Home is the hangman. Zelazny, R.
In The Hugo winners p5-67
Home land. Lipsyte, S.
Home to roost. Stout, R.
In Stout, R. Kings full of aces p325-68
Homebody. Card, O. S.
The **homecoming**. Hamner, E.
Homecoming. Plain, B.
Homecoming. Snow, C. P.
Homecoming [series]
Card, O. S. The call of earth
Card, O. S. Earthborn
Card, O. S. Earthfall
Card, O. S. The memory of earth
Card, O. S. The ships of earth

HOMECOMINGS
Faulkner, W. Soldiers' pay
Fowles, J. Daniel Martin
Settle, M. L. The killing ground

Homegoing. Pohl, F.
Homeland. Jakes, J.

HOMELESS PERSONS
Auster, P. In the country of last things
Auster, P. Timbuktu
Coetzee, J. M. Age of iron
Grisham, J. The street lawyer
Hendrie, L. Remember me
Kennedy, W. Ironweed
Lessing, D. M. Ben, in the world
Piercy, M. The longings of women
Rendell, R. The keys to the street
Saul, J. The Manhattan Hunt Club
Wagner, B. I'll let you go
Walters, M. The echo

Homely girl, a life, and other stories. Miller, A.
Homeplace. Siddons, A. R.

HOMER
Parodies, imitations, etc.
Simmons, D. Ilium
Simmons, D. Olympos

HOMES *See* Houses
HOMES FOR THE ELDERLY *See* Old age homes
The **homesman**. Swarthout, G. F.

HOMESTEADING
See also Frontier and pioneer life
Aldrich, B. S. A lantern in her hand
Doig, I. Dancing at the Rascal Fair
Stegner, W. E. The Big Rock Candy Mountain

The **homing**. Saul, J.

HOMOSEXUALITY
See also Bisexuality; Lesbianism
Bainbridge, B. Master Georgie
Baldwin, J. Just above my head
Baldwin, J. Tell me how long the train's been gone
Banville, J. The untouchable
Barker, C. Sacrament
Barker, P. The eye in the door
Bellow, S. Ravelstein
Bram, C. Lives of the circus animals
Burgess, A. A dead man in Deptford
Burgess, A. Earthly powers
Capote, T. Answered prayers
Cullin, M. Undersurface
Cunningham, M. Flesh and blood
Dart, I. R. The Stork Club
Dickinson, P. Some deaths before dying
Doenges, J. God of gods
Durrell, L. Clea
The Faber book of gay short fiction
Forster, E. M. Maurice
Frame, R. The lantern bearers
Geary, J. M. Spiral
Gide, A. The counterfeiters (Les faux-monnayeurs)
Gide, A. The immoralist
Glass, J. Three Junes
Gregory, P. Earthly joys
Grumbach, D. The book of knowledge
Grumbach, D. Chamber music
Gurganus, A. He's one, too
Gurganus, A. Preservation news
Hamilton, J. The short history of a prince
Hamilton-Paterson, J. Loving monsters
Harris, E. L. And this too shall pass
Himes, C. Yesterday will make you cry
Hobson, L. K. Z. Consenting adult
House, T. The beginning of calamities
James, H. The pupil
Keyes, M. Last Chance Saloon
Leavitt, D. The lost language of cranes
Leavitt, D. Martin Bauman
Leavitt, D. While England sleeps
Lessing, D. M. The good terrorist
Mann, T. Death in Venice
McCauley, S. True enough
McEwan, I. Enduring love
McNicholl, D. A son called Gabriel
Monette, P. Afterlife
Murdoch, I. The bell
Murdoch, I. A fairly honourable defeat
O'Neill, J. At swim, two boys
Penguin book of gay short fiction
Price, R. Kate Vaiden
Price, R. The promise of rest
Puig, M. Kiss of the spider woman

HORROR STORIES—*Continued*
Rice, A. The vampire Lestat
Rice, A. Vittorio the vampire
Rice, A. The witching hour
Saul, J. Darkness
Saul, J. The homing
Saul, J. Midnight voices
Saul, J. Nightshade
Saul, J. The presence
Saul, J. Second child
Saul, J. Shadows
Shelley, M. W. Frankenstein; or, The modern Prometheus
Stevenson, R. L. The strange case of Dr. Jekyll and Mr. Hyde
Stoker, B. The Bram Stoker bedside companion
Stoker, B. Dracula
Stoker, B. Midnight tales
Straub, P. The buffalo hunter
Straub, P. Floating dragon
Straub, P. Ghost story
Straub, P. The Hellfire Club
Straub, P. In the night room
Straub, P. Lost boy lost girl
Straub, P. Magic terror
Straub, P. Mr. X
Straub, P. Shadowland
Strieber, W. The forbidden zone
Strieber, W. The last vampire
Strieber, W. The Wolfen
Tryon, T. The other
Woods, S. Under the lake
The Year's best fantasy and horror

HORSE BREEDING

De Blasis, C. A season for Swans

HORSE FARMS

Hoag, T. Dark horse

The **horse** goddess. Llywelyn, M.
Horse heaven. Smiley, J.
The **Horse** Latitudes. Ferrigno, R.

HORSE RACING

See also Jockeys
The Dick Francis treasury of great racing stories
Francis, D. 10 lb. penalty
Francis, D. Bolt
Francis, D. Bonecrack
Francis, D. Break in
Francis, D. Come to grief
Francis, D. The danger
Francis, D. Driving force
Francis, D. Field of thirteen
Francis, D. For kicks
Francis, D. Forfeit
Francis, D. High stakes
Francis, D. Hot money
Francis, D. Longshot
Francis, D. Nerve
Francis, D. Rat race
Francis, D. Risk
Francis, D. Slayride
Francis, D. Smokescreen
Francis, D. To the hilt
Francis, D. Twice shy
Francis, D. Whip hand
Francis, D. Wild horses
Mount, F. The man who rode Ampersand
Shoemaker, B. Stalking horse
Smiley, J. Horse heaven
Smith, B. All hat

HORSE TRADING

Faulkner, W. Father Abraham

The **horse** whisperer. Evans, N.
The **Horse** You Came In On. Grimes, M.
A **horseman** riding by. Delderfield, R. F.

HORSEMANSHIP

Kosinski, J. N. Passion play

HORSES

See also Lippizaner horses
Brand, M. Dark Rosaleen
Cherryh, C. J. Cloud's rider
Cherryh, C. J. Rider at the gate
Evans, N. The horse whisperer
Francis, D. Banker
Francis, D. Flying finish
Francis, D. Knockdown
Hawkes, J. Sweet William
McCarthy, C. All the pretty horses
Meyers, K. The work of wolves
Steinbeck, J. The red pony
Tarr, J. Lady of horses

The **horse's** mouth. Cary, J.

HOSPITALS AND SANATORIUMS

Barker, P. The eye in the door
Barker, P. The ghost road
Barker, P. Regeneration
Clark, M. H. The cradle will fall
Cook, R. Brain
Cook, R. Coma
Cook, R. Contagion
Cook, R. Godplayer
Cook, R. Terminal
Crichton, M. A case of need
Crichton, M. The terminal man
Cronin, A. J. A pocketful of rye
Douglas, L. C. Magnificent obsession
Gerritsen, T. Harvest
Gerritsen, T. Life support
Greene, G. A burnt-out case
Hemingway, E. A farewell to arms
Hooker, R. MASH
Hulme, K. The nun's story
Jackson, C. The lost weekend
Jones, J. Whistle
Kesey, K. One flew over the cuckoo's nest
Mann, T. The magic mountain
McCullough, C. An indecent obsession
Palmer, M. Natural causes
Powers, R. Operation wandering soul
Rosten, L. Captain Newman, M.D.
Sanders, L. The sixth commandment
Simon, C. The trolley
Solzhenitsyn, A. Cancer ward
Wharton, W. Birdy
Willis, C. Passage
Wood, B. Soul flame

Hostage. Crais, R.

HOSTAGES

Clark, M. H. Silent night
Crais, R. Hostage
Deaver, J. A maiden's grave
Greene, G. The tenth man
Grisham, J. The street lawyer
King, S. Misery
Lively, P. Cleopatra's sister
O'Brien, E. House of splendid isolation
Palmer, M. The patient
Patchett, A. Bel canto
Patterson, J. Roses are red
Powers, R. Plowing the dark
Rule, A. Possession
Tyler, A. Earthly possessions
Wiesel, E. Dawn
Wiesel, E. The judges

Hostile intent. Egleton, C.
Hot. Lutz, J.
The **hot** kid. Leonard, E.
Hot money. Francis, D.
Hot night in the city. Trevanian
The **hot** rock. Westlake, D. E.
Hot Siberian. Browne, G. A.
Hot six. Evanovich, J.
Hot Springs. Hunter, S.
Hotel. Hailey, A.
Hotel du Lac. Brookner, A.
Hotel Honolulu. Theroux, P.
The **Hotel** New Hampshire. Irving, J.
Hotel Paradise. Grimes, M.
Hotel Pastis. Mayle, P.

HOTELS, TAVERNS, ETC.

Amado, J. Gabriela, clove and cinnamon
Amis, K. The Green Man
Brookner, A. Hotel du Lac
Caldwell, T. Answer as a man
Conrad, J. Victory

HUMOR—*Continued*

Adams, D. So long, and thanks for all the fish
Alvarez, J. How the García girls lost their accents
Alvarez, J. Yo!
Ames, J. Wake up, sir!
Amis, K. Lucky Jim
Ansay, A. M. Midnight champagne
Balzac, H. d. Droll stories
Bell, C. The Perez family
Bellow, S. Henderson the rain king
Bellow, S. Mr. Sammler's planet
Berger, T. Little Big Man
Berger, T. Reinhart's women
Berger, T. The return of Little Big Man
Berger, T. Sneaky people
Boyle, T. C. Water music
Bradford, R. Red sky at morning
Braff, J. The unthinkable thoughts of Jacob Green
Breslin, J. The gang that couldn't shoot straight
Brown, R. M. Loose lips
Brown, R. M. Six of one
Capote, T. The grass harp
Carter, A. Wise children
Cary, J. The horse's mouth
Chappell, H. A whole world of trouble
Cheever, J. The Wapshot chronicle
Cheever, J. The Wapshot scandal
Cline, R. What to keep
Crichton, R. The secret of Santa Vittoria
Davies, V. Miracle on 34th Street
Dawson, C. The mother-in-law diaries
Dennis, P. Auntie Mame
Dezenhall, E. Money wanders
Dickens, C. The posthumous papers of the Pickwick Club
Donovan, A. Buddha Da
Edgerton, C. Where trouble sleeps
Ephron, N. Heartburn
Faulkner, W. The reivers
Fielding, H. Bridget Jones: the edge of reason
Fielding, H. Bridget Jones's diary
Flagg, F. Fried green tomatoes at the Whistle-Stop Cafe
Flagg, F. Standing in the rainbow
Flagg, F. Welcome to the world, baby girl!
Fraser, G. M. Flashman
Fraser, G. M. Flashman & the angel of the Lord
Fraser, G. M. Flashman and the mountain of light
Fraser, G. M. Flashman and the tiger
Fraser, G. M. Royal Flash
Frayn, M. Headlong
Friedman, B. J. A father's kisses
Gilchrist, E. The cabal [novelette]
Goodman, A. Paradise park
Greene, G. Monsignor Quixote
Greene, G. Travels with my aunt
Hašek, J. The good soldier Svejk
Hautman, P. Doohickey
Heffernan, W. The Dinosaur Club
Heller, J. Catch-22
Helprin, M. Ellis Island
Hemingway, E. The torrents of spring
Hiaasen, C. Lucky you
Hiaasen, C. Skinny dip
Hodgins, E. Mr. Blandings builds his dream house
Hooker, R. MASH
Hornby, N. How to be good
Hughes, L. Simple speaks his mind
Hughes, L. Simple stakes a claim
Hughes, L. Simple takes a wife
Hughes, L. Simple's Uncle Sam
Irving, J. The Hotel New Hampshire
Irving, J. The water-method man
Kafka, F. Amerika
Karbo, K. Motherhood made a man out of me
Keillor, G. Lake Wobegon days
Keillor, G. Lake Wobegon summer 1956
Keillor, G. WLT
Kingsolver, B. The bean trees
Kotzwinkle, W. The bear went over the mountain
Kundera, M. The book of laughter and forgetting
Lardner, R. You know me, Al
Leslie, J. A. C. The ghost and Mrs. Muir
Levi, P. The monkey's wrench
Lipman, E. The Inn at Lake Devine
Lipman, E. The ladies' man
Lipsyte, S. Home land
Lupica, M. Wild pitch
Lurie, A. Only children
Martin, S. The pleasure of my company
McCabe, P. Mondo desperado
McMurtry, L. Cadillac Jack
McMurtry, L. Duane's depressed
McMurtry, L. The evening star
McMurtry, L. Terms of endearment
McMurtry, L. Texasville
Milligan, J. Jack Fish
Murdoch, I. The nice and the good
Murray, P. An evening of long goodbyes
Nabokov, V. V. Pnin
Pearson, T. R. A short history of a small place
Portis, C. The dog of the South
Portis, C. Gringos
Portis, C. Masters of Atlantis
Portis, C. Norwood
Portis, C. True grit
Powell, D. Angels on toast
Pratchett, T. The fifth elephant
Pratchett, T. The truth
Pym, B. Jane and Prudence
Rinehart, S. Built in a day
Ross, A. B. Miss Julia throws a wedding
Roth, P. My life as a man
Roth, P. Portnoy's complaint
Roth, P. Sabbath's theater
Runyon, D. Guys and dolls
Rushdie, S. Midnight's children
Rushdie, S. Shame
Saint, H. F. Memoirs of an invisible man
Schine, C. The love letter
Shames, L. Mangrove squeeze
Shames, L. Virgin heat
Shames, L. Welcome to paradise
Sholem Aleichem. The adventures of Menahem-Mendl
Sholem Aleichem. The adventures of Mottel, the cantor's son
Sholem Aleichem. The further adventures of Menachem-Mendl
Shulman, M. The many loves of Dobie Gillis
Shulman, M. Rally round the flag, boys!
Smith, S. Novel on yellow paper
Smollett, T. G. Humphry Clinker
Sneider, V. The Teahouse of the August Moon
Spark, M. The comforters
Spark, M. The prime of Miss Jean Brodie
Steinbeck, J. Cannery Row
Steinbeck, J. Sweet Thursday
Stevenson, R. L. The misadventures of John Nicholson
Streeter, E. Father of the bride
Struther, J. Mrs. Miniver
Svevo, I. Zeno's conscience
Swarthout, G. F. Bless the beasts and children
Taylor, R. L. The travels of Jaimie McPheeters
Toole, J. K. A confederacy of dunces
Townsend, S. Adrian Mole
Townsend, S. The Adrian Mole diaries
Townsend, S. Adrian Mole: the lost years
Trollope, A. The Duke's children [abridged]
Twain, M. The adventures of Huckleberry Finn
Twain, M. The adventures of Tom Sawyer
Wallace, D. Big fish
Waugh, E. Decline and fall
Waugh, E. The loved one
Waugh, E. Men at arms
Waugh, E. Officers and gentlemen
Welty, E. The Ponder heart
West, J. Cress Delahanty
West, J. Except for me and thee
West, J. The friendly persuasion
Westlake, D. E. Bad news
Westlake, D. E. Bank shot
Westlake, D. E. Don't ask
Westlake, D. E. Drowned hopes
Westlake, D. E. Good behavior
Westlake, D. E. The hot rock
Westlake, D. E. Money for nothing
Westlake, D. E. Put a lid on it
Westlake, D. E. The road to ruin
Westlake, D. E. Smoke
Westlake, D. E. The spy in the ointment
Westlake, D. E. Thieves' dozen

I

I wish I had a red dress. Cleage, P.

IBO (AFRICAN PEOPLE)

Achebe, C. Things fall apart

Ice. McBain, E.

ICE AGE *See* Prehistoric times

The **ice** child. McGregor, E.

ICE HOCKEY *See* Hockey

The **Ice** Maiden. Buchanan, E.

The **ice** queen. Hoffman, A.

The **ice-shirt**. Vollmann, W. T.

Ice Station Zebra. MacLean, A.

Iced. Clark, C. H.

ICELAND

10th century

Seton, A. Avalon

20th century

Ólafur Jóhann Ólafsson. The journey home

Reykjavik

Hallgrímur Helgason. 101 Reykjavik

ICELANDERS

England

Ólafur Jóhann Ólafsson. The journey home

Icy clutches. Elkins, A. J.

IDAHO

Adam, C. Love and country
Parkinson, H. Across open ground
Woods, S. Heat

The **idea** of perfection. Grenville, K.

Ideas of heaven. Silber, J.

IDENTITY *See* Personality

Identity. Kundera, M.

The **ides** of March. Wilder, T.

The **idiot**. Dostoyevsky, F.

Idlewild. Sagan, N.

If Beale Street could talk. Baldwin, J.

If ever I return, pretty Peggy-O. McCrumb, S.

If I forget thee, Jerusalem. Faulkner, W.
In Faulkner, W. Novels, 1936-1940 p493-726

If I'd killed him when I met him. McCrumb, S.

If not now, when? Levi, P.

If on a winter's night a traveler. Calvino, I.

If this world were mine. Harris, E. L.

If you go down to the woods. Meek, M. R. D.

IGBO (AFRICAN PEOPLE) *See* Ibo (African people)

Ignorance. Kundera, M.

Iguana dreams. Entered in Part I under title

IKHNATON *See* Akhenaton, King of Egypt, fl. ca. 1388-1358 B.C.

Ilium. Simmons, D.

I'll be seeing you. Clark, M. H.

I'll let you go. Wagner, B.

The **ill-made** knight. White, T. H.
In White, T. H. The once and future king p325-544

Ill met in Lankhmar. Leiber, F.
In The Hugo winners p55-115

Ill wind. Barr, N.

The **Illearth** war. Donaldson, S. R.

ILLEGAL ALIENS *See* Undocumented aliens

ILLEGITIMACY

See also Unmarried mothers

Allen, H. Anthony Adverse
Allison, D. Bastard out of Carolina
Archer, J. Kane & Abel
Bradshaw, G. The bearkeeper's daughter
Brown, C. Confinement
Brown, R. Half a heart
Burke, J. L. Cimarron rose
Carter, A. Wise children
Cheever, J. Bullet Park
Dailey, J. Calder pride
Dickens, C. Bleak House
Dreiser, T. Jennie Gerhardt
Dunnett, D. Pawn in frankincense
Eden, D. The American heiress
Faulkner, W. The sound and the fury
Fielding, H. The history of Tom Jones, a foundling
Findley, T. The piano man's daughter
Gaines, E. J. In my father's house
Gardner, J. Nickel mountain
Hawthorne, N. The scarlet letter
Henley, P. In the river sweet
Higgins, J. The president's daughter
Howatch, S. Penmarric
Jennings, G. Aztec blood
Kennedy, W. Very old bones
Krantz, J. Mistral's daughter
Kunzru, H. The impressionist
L'Engle, M. A live coal in the sea
Lofts, N. Gad's Hall
Maxwell, R. The Queen's bastard
Oates, J. C. A garden of earthly delights
Plain, B. Blessings
Rossner, J. Emmeline
Stewart, F. M. The magnificent Savages
Stirling, J. The workhouse girl
Strout, E. Amy and Isabelle
Stubbs, J. Family games
Tryon, T. In the fire of spring
Updike, J. Rabbit remembered
Vine, B. Anna's book

ILLINOIS

Dickinson, C. A shortcut in time
Hoffman, E. The secret
Powers, R. Prisoner's dilemma

19th century

Dickens, C. Martin Chuzzlewit
Diehl, W. Reign in hell

20th century

Bradbury, R. Dandelion wine
Straub, P. Mr. X
Straub, P. The throat
Thompson, J. Wide blue yonder
Wilder, T. The eighth day

Farm life

See Farm life—Illinois

Chicago

Algren, N. The man with the golden arm
Bellow, S. The actual
Bellow, S. The adventures of Augie March
Bellow, S. Dangling man
Bellow, S. The dean's December
Bellow, S. Humboldt's gift
Bellow, S. Ravelstein
Bellow, S. What kind of day did you have?
Birmingham, S. The Auerbach will
Brown, C. The hatbox baby
Campbell, B. M. Your blues ain't like mine
Cisneros, S. Caramelo
Cisneros, S. The house on Mango Street
D'Amato, B. Good cop, bad cop
Diehl, W. Primal fear
Diehl, W. Show of evil
Doenges, J. God of gods
Dreiser, T. Jennie Gerhardt
Dreiser, T. Sister Carrie
Dybek, S. I sailed with Magellan
Ellis, D. Life sentence
Farrell, J. T. Studs Lonigan
Fielding, J. Tell me no secrets
Greeley, A. M. Ascent into hell
Greeley, A. M. Irish cream
Greeley, A. M. Irish lace
Greeley, A. M. Irish stew!
Greeley, A. M. Lord of the dance
Greeley, A. M. Second spring
Greeley, A. M. September song
Greeley, A. M. Thy brother's wife
Greeley, A. M. Younger than springtime
Guilfoile, K. Cast of shadows
Hailey, A. Airport
Hamilton, J. Disobedience
Harris, E. L. And this too shall pass
Hemon, A. Nowhere man
Jakes, J. Homeland
Just, W. S. An unfinished season
Miller, S. The distinguished guest

IMPERSONATIONS
See also Impostors; Mistaken identity
Alcott, L. M. Behind a mask [novelette]
Allende, I. Daughter of fortune
Brown, D. A. Killdeer Mountain
Brown, R. M. High hearts
Cooper, J. F. The red rover
DeMille, N. The charm school
Dickens, C. Our mutual friend
Dickens, C. A tale of two cities
Du Maurier, Dame D. The scapegoat
Dumas, A. The Queen's necklace
Dyja, T. Meet John Trow
Eden, D. The American heiress
Erdrich, L. The last report on the miracles at Little No Horse
Greene, G. The tenth man
Helprin, M. Ellis Island
Higgins, J. Night of the fox
Holland, C. The angel and the sword
Hope, A. The prisoner of Zenda
Leonard, E. Pagan babies
Michael, J. Deceptions
Stewart, M. The ivy tree
Tey, J. Brat Farrar
Townsend, S. Number 10
Twain, M. The American claimant
Twain, M. The prince and the pauper
Twain, M. Pudd'nhead Wilson
Yorke, M. False pretences
Implant. Wilson, F. P.
The **importance** of a piece of paper. Baca, J. S.
The **impostor**. Cocteau, J.
IMPOSTORS
See also Impersonations
James, H. The Aspern papers
Kunzru, H. The impressionist
Makine, A. Music of a life
Mathews, H. My life in CIA
Strauss, D. The real McCoy
The **impressionist**. Kunzru, H.
IMPROBABLE STORIES
See also Fantasies
Impulse. Coulter, C.
In a dark wood wandering. Haasse, H. S.
In a dry season. Robinson, P.
In a heartbeat. Adler, E.
In a shallow grave. Purdy, J.
In America. Sontag, S.
In an evil time. Pronzini, B.
The **in-between** world of Vikram Lall. Vassanji, M. G.
In chancery. Galsworthy, J.
In Galsworthy, J. The Forsyte saga p363-639
In country. Mason, B. A.
In danger's path. Griffin, W. E. B.
In dubious battle. Steinbeck, J.
also in Steinbeck, J. Novels and stories, 1932-1937
In evil hour. García Márquez, G.
In La-La Land we trust. Campbell, R. W.
In love and war. See Ross-Macdonald, M. For they shall inherit
In my father's house. Gaines, E. J.
In our time. Hemingway, E.
Die **in** plain sight. Lowell, E.
In pursuit of the green lion. Riley, J. M.
In pursuit of the proper sinner. George, E.
In Revere, in those days. Merullo, R.
In search of Klingsor. Volpi, J.
In search of lost time [series]
Proust, M. The captive [and] The fugitive
Proust, M. The Guermantes way
Proust, M. Sodom and Gomorrah
Proust, M. Swann's way
Proust, M. Time regained [variant title: The past recaptured]

Proust, M. Within a budding grove
In sunlight, in a beautiful garden. Cambor, K.
In the beauty of the lilies. Updike, J.
In the best families. Stout, R.
In Stout, R. Five of a kind p155-303
In the bleak midwinter. Spencer-Fleming, J.
In the blue light of African dreams. Watkins, P.
In the cage. James, H.
In James, H. Complete stories, 1892-1898
In James, H. The complete tales of Henry James
In James, H. What Maisie knew, In the cage, The pupil
In the company of cheerful ladies. McCall Smith, A.
In the country of last things. Auster, P.
In the days of the comet. Wells, H. G.
In Wells, H. G. Seven famous novels
In the electric mist with Confederate dead. Burke, J. L.
In the family way. Schwartz, L. S.
In the fire of spring. Tryon, T.
In the flesh. Barker, C.
In the flesh [novelette] Barker, C.
In Barker, C. In the flesh
In the forest. O'Brien, E.
In the garden of Iden. Baker, K.
In the heat of the night. Ball, J. D.
In the hills of Monterey. Brand, M.
In the Kingdom of mists. Jakeman, J.
In the Lake of the Woods. O'Brien, T.
In the middle of all this. Leebron, F. G.
In the miso soup. Murakami, R.
In the moon of red ponies. Burke, J. L.
In the name of Salomé. Alvarez, J.
In the night season. Bausch, R.
In the pond. Ha Jin
In the presence of enemies. Coughlin, W. J.
In the presence of the enemy. George, E.
In the river sweet. Henley, P.
In the shadow of the law. Roosevelt, K.
In the skin of a lion. Ondaatje, M.
In the teeth of the evidence and other stories. Sayers, D. L.
In the time of the butterflies. Alvarez, J.
In this house of Brede. Godden, R.
In this mountain. Karon, J.
In this sign. Greenberg, J.
Inadmissable evidence. Friedman, P.
Inca gold. Cussler, C.
Incarnations of immortality [series]
Anthony, P. And eternity
Anthony, P. Bearing an hourglass
Anthony, P. Being a green mother
Anthony, P. For love of evil
Anthony, P. On a pale horse
Anthony, P. Wielding a red sword
Anthony, P. With a tangled skein
INCAS
Cussler, C. Inca gold
INCEST
Butler, R. O. The deep green sea
Chute, C. The Beans of Egypt, Maine
Dunmore, H. A spell of winter
Eugenides, J. Middlesex
French, M. Our father
Grumbach, D. The book of knowledge
Hatoum, M. The brothers
King, S. Gerald's game
Korda, M. Curtain
Lewis, M. G. The monk
Loo, T. d. A bed in heaven
Michael, J. Sleeping beauty
Noon, J. Vurt
O'Brien, E. Down by the river
O'Dell, T. Back roads
Rice, A. Lasher
Rossner, J. Emmeline
Roth, H. A diving rock on the Hudson
Shreve, A. The weight of water
Stirling, J. The island wife
Theroux, P. Picture palace
Yglesias, R. Dr. Neruda's cure for evil
Incident at Twenty Mile. Trevanian
Incidents in the Rue Laugier. Brookner, A.
An **inconvenient** woman. Dunne, D.
The **incredible** and sad tale of innocent Eréndira and her heartless grandmother. García Márquez, G.
In García Márquez, G. Collected stories p262-311
In García Márquez, G. Innocent Eréndira, and other stories p1-59
The **incredible** journey. Burnford, S.
The **incredulity** of Father Brown. Chesterton, G. K.
In Chesterton, G. K. The Father Brown omnibus p433-630
An **indecent** obsession. McCullough, C.
Indecision. Kunkel, B.
Indemnity only. Paretsky, S.

INDIANS OF NORTH AMERICA—*Continued*
Perry, T. Blood money
Perry, T. Dance for the dead
Perry, T. The face-changers
Perry, T. Shadow woman
Perry, T. Vanishing act
Roberts, K. L. Northwest Passage
Silko, L. Gardens in the dunes
Smith, M. C. Stallion Gate
Spence, G. Half-moon and empty stars
Stevens, M. Useful girl
Welch, J. The Indian lawyer
West, J. The massacre at Fall Creek
Westlake, D. E. Bad news
Woiwode, L. Indian affairs

Captivities

Berger, T. Little Big Man
Giles, J. H. Hannah Fowler
Larsen, D. The white
McCrumb, S. She walks these hills
Richter, C. The light in the forest
Thom, J. A. The red heart

Reservations

King, T. Truth & Bright Water
Rosenberg, R. This is not civilization

Wars

See also United States—French and Indian War, 1755-1763
Blake, M. Marching to Valhalla
Chiaventone, F. J. Moon of bitter cold
Combs, H. The scout
Cooper, J. F. The Deerslayer
Cooper, J. F. The last of the Mohicans
Cooper, J. F. The Pathfinder
Cooper, J. F. The prairie
Edmonds, W. D. Drums along the Mohawk
Johnston, T. C. Turn the stars upside down
O'Brien, D. The contract surgeon

California

L'Amour, L. The Californios

Canada

King, T. Truth & Bright Water
Vollmann, W. T. Fathers and crows

Montana

Dorris, M. A yellow raft in blue water

New Mexico

Cather, W. Death comes for the archbishop

North Dakota

Erdrich, L. The bingo palace
Erdrich, L. The last report on the miracles at Little No Horse
Erdrich, L. Love medicine
Erdrich, L. Tracks
Power, S. The grass dancer

Southwestern States

Jance, J. A. Kiss of the bees

Virginia

Vollmann, W. T. Argall

Washington (State)

Alexie, S. Indian killer
Alexie, S. Reservation blues

INDIANS OF SOUTH AMERICA

Hudson, W. H. Green mansions

The **indictment**. Reed, B.
Indigo slam. Crais, R.

INDIVIDUALISM

Knowles, J. Indian summer
Orwell, G. Nineteen eighty-four
Pasternak, B. L. Doctor Zhivago
Rand, A. Anthem
Rand, A. Atlas shrugged
Rand, A. The fountainhead

INDOCHINA

See also Vietnam

INDOCTRINATION, FORCED *See* Brainwashing

INDONESIA

Toer, P. A. The girl from the coast

The **indulgent** husband. See Colette. Claudine married

INDUSTRIAL ACCIDENTS

Cussler, C. Sahara
DeLillo, D. White noise

INDUSTRIAL CONDITIONS

Dickens, C. Hard times
Singer, I. J. The brothers Ashkenazi
Zaroulis, N. L. Call the darkness light

INDUSTRIALISTS *See* Capitalists and financiers

INDUSTRIALIZATION *See* Industrial conditions

INFANTICIDE

Appelfeld, A. Katerina
James, H. The author of "Beltraffio"
Korelitz, J. H. The Sabbathday River
Stirling, J. Lantern for the dark
Tanenbaum, R. True justice

INFANTS

Brown, C. The hatbox baby
Carey, J. The Crossley baby

Infinite jest. Wallace, D. F.
The **infinite** plan. Allende, I.
Infinity beach. McDevitt, J.
Infinity's shore. Brin, D.
The **informant**. Grippando, J.
The **information**. Amis, M.

INFORMERS

See also Treason
Moran, T. Anja the liar

The **inheritance**. Alcott, L. M.

INHERITANCE AND SUCCESSION

See also Wills
Alcott, L. M. The mysterious key and what it opened
Cheever, J. The Wapshot chronicle
Cookson, C. The obsession
Coscarelli, K. Heir apparent
Coughlin, W. J. In the presence of enemies
Dailey, J. Heiress
Delinsky, B. Flirting with Pete
Dickens, C. Bleak House
Dickens, C. Great expectations
Dickens, C. Our mutual friend
Francis, D. Straight
Fuentes, C. Sons of the Conquistador
Gould, J. The best is yet to come
Grisham, J. The testament
Gross, J. The books of Rachel
Hautman, P. Doohickey
Hawthorne, N. Doctor Grimshawe's secret
Holt, V. Kirkland Revels
James, H. Washington Square
James, H. The wings of the dove
Johnson, D. L'affaire
Korda, M. The fortune
Martin, W. Annapolis
McGuane, T. The cadence of grass
Miller, S. The world below
Morrison, T. Love
Palliser, C. The quincunx
Parker, B. Suspicion of guilt
Perry, T. Dance for the dead
Preston, D. The codex
Renault, M. Funeral games
Scott, A. Calpurnia
Stewart, M. The ivy tree
Stirling, J. The piper's tune
Thackeray, W. M. The history of Henry Esmond, esquire
Thayer, N. Everlasting
Theroux, M. The confessions of Mycroft Holmes
Twain, M. The American claimant
Wharton, E. Sanctuary
White, P. The eye of the storm
Woods, S. Imperfect strangers

Inheritor. Cherryh, C. J.
The **inheritors**. Golding, W.
The **inhuman** condition. Barker, C.
The **inimitable** Jeeves. Wodehouse, P. G.
The **inland** sea. See Cooper, J. F. The Pathfinder

TITLE AND SUBJECT INDEX

INTERNATIONAL INTRIGUE—*Continued*
Coonts, S. The minotaur
Coonts, S. The red horseman
Coyle, H. W. Bright star
Cussler, C. Cyclops
Cussler, C. Deep six
Cussler, C. Dragon
Cussler, C. Fire ice
Cussler, C. Raise the Titanic!
Cussler, C. Sahara
Cussler, C. Treasure
Davies, L. Wilderness of mirrors
Deighton, L. Berlin game
Deighton, L. Charity
Deighton, L. Faith
Deighton, L. Funeral in Berlin
Deighton, L. Game, set & match
Deighton, L. Hope
Deighton, L. The Ipcress file
Deighton, L. London match
Deighton, L. Mexico set
Deighton, L. Spy hook
Deighton, L. Spy line
Deighton, L. Spy sinker
Deighton, L. XPD
Didion, J. The last thing he wanted
Durrell, L. Mountolive
Egleton, C. Blood money
Egleton, C. Hostile intent
Egleton, C. Warning shot
Finder, J. The Moscow Club
Fleming, I. Casino Royale
Fleming, I. Doctor No
Fleming, I. From Russia, with love
Fleming, I. Goldfinger
Fleming, I. The man with the golden gun
Fleming, I. On Her Majesty's Secret Service
Fleming, I. You only live twice
Follett, K. Code to zero
Follett, K. Lie down with lions
Follett, K. Triple
Folsom, A. R. The day after tomorrow
Forsyth, F. The day of the jackal
Forsyth, F. The deceiver
Forsyth, F. The devil's alternative
Forsyth, F. The dogs of war
Forsyth, F. The fist of God
Forsyth, F. The fourth protocol
Francis, C. Wolf winter
Fraser, G. M. Royal Flash
Freemantle, B. Bomb grade
Freemantle, B. Charlie's apprentice
Freemantle, B. Comrade Charlie
Gardner, J. E. License renewed
Gilman, D. The amazing Mrs. Pollifax
Gilman, D. The elusive Mrs. Pollifax
Gilman, D. Mrs. Pollifax and the Hong Kong Buddha
Gilman, D. Mrs. Pollifax on safari
Gilman, D. A palm for Mrs. Pollifax
Gilman, D. The unexpected Mrs. Pollifax
Goldman, W. Marathon man
Grady, J. Six days of the condor
Greene, G. 3: This gun for hire, The confidential agent, The ministry of fear
Greene, G. The captain and the enemy
Greene, G. The ministry of fear
Greene, G. Our man in Havana
Greene, G. The quiet American
Greene, G. Travels with my aunt
Grisham, J. The broker
Hall, A. The Quiller memorandum
Hall, A. Quiller Salamander
Hall, A. Quiller solitaire
Harris, R. Fatherland
Harris, T. Black Sunday
Harrison, P. Storming Intrepid
Higgins, J. Day of judgment
Higgins, J. The eagle has flown
Higgins, J. The eagle has landed
Higgins, J. Edge of danger
Higgins, J. Eye of the storm
Higgins, J. The president's daughter
Higgins, J. Touch the devil
Hillhouse, R. Rift zone
Hunter, S. Havana
Ignatius, D. A firing offense
Le Carré, J. Absolute friends
Le Carré, J. The honourable schoolboy
Le Carré, J. The little drummer girl
Le Carré, J. The looking glass war
Le Carré, J. The night manager
Le Carré, J. Our game
Le Carré, J. A perfect spy
Le Carré, J. The quest for Karla
Le Carré, J. The Russia house
Le Carré, J. The secret pilgrim
Le Carré, J. Single & Single
Le Carré, J. A small town in Germany
Le Carré, J. Smiley's people
Le Carré, J. The spy who came in from the cold
Le Carré, J. The tailor of Panama
Le Carré, J. Tinker, tailor, soldier, spy
Littell, R. The company
Ludlum, R. The Aquitaine progression
Ludlum, R. The Bourne identity
Ludlum, R. The Bourne supremacy
Ludlum, R. The Bourne ultimatum
Ludlum, R. The Gemini contenders
Ludlum, R. The Holcroft covenant
Ludlum, R. The Matarese Circle
Ludlum, R. The Parsifal mosaic
Ludlum, R. The Rhinemann exchange
Ludlum, R. The Scarlatti inheritance
Ludlum, R. The scorpio illusion
Lustbader, E. V. Floating city
Lustbader, E. V. Jian
Lustbader, E. V. Shan
MacInnes, H. Prelude to terror
MacInnes, H. Ride a pale horse
MacInnes, H. The Venetian affair
MacLean, A. Ice Station Zebra
MacLean, A. Where eagles dare
Mailer, N. Harlot's ghost
Martini, S. P. Critical mass
Morrell, D. The brotherhood of the rose
Morrell, D. The fifth profession
Neville, K. The eight
The Oxford book of spy stories
Robinson, P. Kilo class
Robinson, P. Nimitz class
Sheldon, S. Windmills of the gods
Siler, J. Flashback
Silva, D. The marching season
Smith, W. A. The leopard hunts in darkness
Thomas, C. Firefox
Trenhaile, J. The gates of exquisite view
Westlake, D. E. Money for nothing
White, R. A. Typhoon

INTERNATIONAL MARRIAGES
Bosse, M. J. Fire in heaven
Drabble, M. The needle's eye
Gordimer, N. The pickup
James, H. The golden bowl
James, H. Lady Barberina
James, H. Madame de Mauves
James, H. The siege of London
Stevenson, R. L. The beach of Falesá

INTERNET (COMPUTER NETWORK)
West, F. J. The Pepperdogs

INTERPLANETARY COMMUNICATION *See* Interstellar communication

INTERPLANETARY TRAVEL *See* Interplanetary voyages

INTERPLANETARY VISITORS
See also Martians
Anderson, P. The longest voyage
Anthony, P. Chaos mode
Anthony, P. DoOon mode
Anthony, P. Fractal mode
Anthony, P. Virtual mode
Bear, G. Anvil of stars
Bear, G. The forge of God
Benford, G. Eater
Buckley, C. T. Little green men
Clarke, A. C. Rama II
Clarke, A. C. Rendezvous with Rama
Dickson, G. R. The cloak and the staff

IRELAND—*Continued*

French invasion, 1798

Flanagan, T. The year of the French

19th century

Du Maurier, Dame D. Hungry Hill
Flanagan, T. The tenants of time
Howatch, S. Cashelmara
Mallinson, A. A close run thing
O'Connor, J. Star of the Sea
Uris, L. Trinity

20th century

Banville, J. The book of evidence
Binchy, M. Circle of friends
Binchy, M. The copper beech
Binchy, M. Firefly summer
Binchy, M. The glass lake
Binchy, M. Light a penny candle
Binchy, M. The return journey
Bradbury, R. Green shadows, white whale
Doyle, R. A star called Henry
Flanagan, T. The end of the hunt
Higgins, J. Confessional
Higgins, J. Drink with the Devil
Joyce, J. Dubliners
Joyce, J. Finnegans wake
Joyce, J. Ulysses
Llywelyn, M. 1921
Llywelyn, M. 1949
McCabe, P. Mondo desperado
O'Brien, E. House of splendid isolation
O'Brien, E. Lantern slides
O'Connor, F. Collected stories
Parsons, J. Mary, Mary
Powell, A. The valley of bones
Tóibín, C. The blackwater lightship
Uris, L. Redemption
Uris, L. Trinity
Weber, K. The Music Lesson

Sinn Fein Rebellion, 1916

Llywelyn, M. 1916
O'Neill, J. At swim, two boys

College life

See College life—Ireland

Farm life

See Farm life—Ireland

Peasant life

See Peasant life—Ireland

Politics

See Politics—Ireland

Rural life

Barry, S. Annie Dunne
Binchy, M. Echoes
Davis-Goff, A. This cold country
Hardie, K. A winter marriage
McCabe, E. Heaven lies about us
McCabe, P. The butcher boy
McGahern, J. By the lake
Nolan, C. The banyan tree
O'Brien, E. The country girls
O'Brien, E. Down by the river
O'Brien, E. In the forest
O'Brien, E. Wild Decembers
O'Neill, J. Kilbrack; or, Who is Nancy Valentine?
Watkins, P. The promise of light

Cork (County)

Trevor, W. The silence in the garden

Donegal (County)

Greeley, A. M. Irish cream

Dublin

Banville, J. Athena
Beckett, S. Murphy
Binchy, M. Evening class
Binchy, M. The lilac bus: stories
Binchy, M. Quentins
Binchy, M. Scarlet Feather
Binchy, M. Tara Road
Donleavy, J. P. The ginger man
Doyle, R. Paddy Clarke, ha ha ha
Doyle, R. The woman who walked into doors
Flanagan, T. The end of the hunt
Joyce, J. Dubliners
Joyce, J. Finnegans wake
Joyce, J. A portrait of the artist as a young man
Joyce, J. Ulysses
Llywelyn, M. 1916
Murdoch, I. Something special
Murray, P. An evening of long goodbyes
O'Brien, E. The lonely girl
O'Neill, J. At swim, two boys
Ridgway, K. The parts
Tóibín, C. The heather blazing

Galway

Labiner, N. Miniatures
Lordan, B. But come ye back

Mayo

Flanagan, T. The year of the French

IRISH

Australia

Keneally, T. River town
McCullough, C. The thorn birds

Canada

Urquhart, J. Away

Egypt

Durrell, L. Balthazar
Durrell, L. Justine

England

Beckett, S. Murphy
Keyes, M. Last Chance Saloon
O'Brien, E. Time and tide
Trevor, W. Felicia's journey
Trollope, A. Phineas Finn [abridged]
Trollope, A. Phineas Redux [abridged]

Italy

Binchy, M. Evening class

Mexico

Lawrence, D. H. The plumed serpent (Quetzalcoatl)

New Zealand

Uris, L. Redemption

United States

Baker, K. Paradise Alley
Binchy, M. Tara Road
Breslin, J. Table money
Caldwell, T. Answer as a man
Caldwell, T. Captains and kings
Dreiser, T. Jennie Gerhardt
Farrell, J. T. Studs Lonigan
Higgins, G. V. The patriot game
Howard, M. The Magdalene
L'Amour, L. The Californios
McDermott, A. At weddings and wakes
O'Connor, E. All in the family
O'Connor, E. The last hurrah
Uhnak, D. Law and order

IRISH AMERICANS

Cabbage and bones
Carroll, J. The city below
Dorris, M. Cloud chamber
Dunne, D. A season in purgatory
Greeley, A. M. Irish cream
Greeley, A. M. Irish lace
Greeley, A. M. Irish stew!
Greeley, A. M. Second spring
Greeley, A. M. September song
Greeley, A. M. Younger than springtime
Hamill, P. Snow in August
Hijuelos, O. The fourteen sisters of Emilio Montez O'Brien
Howard, M. Natural history
Kelly, T. Empire rising
McDermott, A. Charming Billy

ITALIANS—*Continued*

United States

Breslin, J. The gang that couldn't shoot straight
Fast, H. The immigrants
Malamud, B. The assistant
Puzo, M. The godfather
Waller, R. J. The bridges of Madison County

ITALY

See also Capri; Pompeii (Ancient city); Sardinia (Italy); Sicily

Eco, U. The mysterious flame of Queen Loana

14th century

Eco, U. The name of the rose

15th century

Dunant, S. The birth of Venus
Eliot, G. Romola
Puzo, M. The family
Rice, A. Vittorio the vampire
Stone, I. The agony and the ecstasy

16th century

Stone, I. The agony and the ecstasy

17th century

Vreeland, S. The passion of Artemesia
Yarbro, C. Q. Communion blood

18th century

Stendhal. The charterhouse of Parma

19th century

Calvino, I. Baron in the trees
Hawthorne, N. The marble faun
James, H. Daisy Miller
Tomasi di Lampedusa, G. The Leopard

20th century

Bassani, G. The garden of the Finzi-Continis
Godden, R. The battle of the Villa Fiorita
Godden, R. Pippa passes
Heller, J. Catch-22
Helprin, M. A soldier of the great war
Hemingway, E. Across the river and into the trees
Leonard, E. Pronto
Lieberman, H. H. The girl with Botticelli eyes
Martin, V. Italian fever
Seymour, G. Killing ground
Siddons, A. R. Hill towns
Silone, I. Bread and wine
Unsworth, B. After Hannibal

Aristocracy

See Aristocracy—Italy

College life

See College life—Italy

Courts and courtiers

See Courts and courtiers—Italy

Fascism

See Fascism—Italy

Peasant life

See Peasant life—Italy

Politics

See Politics—Italy

Rural life

Crichton, R. The secret of Santa Vittoria
Du Maurier, Dame D. The flight of the falcon
Styron, W. Set this house on fire

World War, 1939-1945

See World War, 1939-1945—Italy

Calabria

West, M. L. The devil's advocate

Elba

Scott, J. Tourmaline

Ferrara

Bassani, G. The garden of the Finzi-Continis

Florence

Du Maurier, Dame D. My cousin Rachel
Dunant, S. The birth of Venus
Eliot, G. Romola
Forster, E. M. A room with a view
Howells, W. D. Indian summer
Stone, I. The agony and the ecstasy

Milan

Eco, U. Foucault's pendulum
Greeley, A. M. Irish stew!
King, R. Domino

Naples

Sontag, S. The volcano lover

Parma

Stendhal. The charterhouse of Parma

Rome

Hawthorne, N. The marble faun
Rabb, J. The book of Q
Silverberg, R. Nightwings [novelette]
Stone, I. The agony and the ecstasy

Rome—15th century

Hansen, E. F. Tales of protection

Rome—19th century

James, H. Roderick Hudson

Rome—20th century

Gash, J. The Vatican rip
Martin, M. Vatican
West, M. L. The shoes of the fisherman
Williams, T. The Roman spring of Mrs. Stone

Turin

Gordon, M. The rest of life

Tuscany

Ammaniti, N. I'm not scared
Craig, A. Love in idleness
Ondaatje, M. The English patient

Venice

Alison, J. The marriage of the sea
Godden, R. Pippa passes
Hemingway, E. Across the river and into the trees
Hewson, D. Lucifer's shadow
Howells, W. D. A foregone conclusion
James, H. The Aspern papers
Lovric, M. The floating book
MacInnes, H. The Venetian affair
Mann, T. Death in Venice
Phillips, C. The nature of blood
Powell, A. Temporary kings
Unsworth, B. Stone virgin
Wharton, E. The children

ITHACA (N.Y.) *See* New York (State)—Ithaca

ITINERANT CLERGY

Eliot, G. Adam Bede
Reid, V. Peter Loon

It's all right now. Chadwick, C.
Ivanhoe. Scott, Sir W.
The **ivy** tree. Stewart, M.

J

"J" is for judgment. Grafton, S.
J R. Gaddis, W.
Jack and Jill. Patterson, J.
Jack Fish. Milligan, J.
Jack in the pulpit. Riggs, C.
Jack Maggs. Carey, P.
Jack Merrybright. Pearce, M. E.
In Pearce, M. E. Apple tree lean down p203-332
Jack the bodiless. May, J.

JACK THE RIPPER

About

West, P. The women of Whitechapel and Jack the Ripper

Jackdaws. Follett, K.

JAZZ MUSIC—*Continued*
Joe, Y. My fine lady
Marshall, P. The fisher king
Turner, F. W. 1929

JEALOUSY
Amis, M. The information
Balzac, H. d. Cousin Bette
Cather, W. Sapphira and the slave girl
Chevalier, T. Girl with a pearl earring
D'Amato, B. Good cop, bad cop
Eliot, G. Middlemarch
Goudge, E. Such devoted sisters
Hart, J. Sin
Hatoum, M. The brothers
Hawkes, J. The blood oranges
Klein, R. The moth diaries
Lebrecht, N. The song of names
Mann, T. Young Joseph
Norman, H. The haunting of L
Oates, J. C. The falls
Pirandello, L. The outcast
Proust, M. The captive
Proust, M. The fugitive [variant title: The sweet cheat gone]
Rendell, R. Going wrong
Roberts, N. The villa
Shreve, A. The weight of water
Spark, M. The finishing school
Stewart, F. M. The magnificent Savages
Tolstoy, L., graf. The Kreutzer sonata
Watson, L. Orchard

JEANNE D'ARC, SAINT *See* Joan, of Arc, Saint, 1412-1431
Jeeves and the tie that binds. Wodehouse, P. G.
JEFFERSON, THOMAS, 1743-1826

About

Chase-Riboud, B. The President's daughter
Chase-Riboud, B. Sally Hemings
Erickson, S. Arc d'X

Jemima Shore at the sunny grave and other stories. Fraser, A.
JEMISON, MARY, 1743-1833

About

Larsen, D. The white

Jennie Gerhardt. Dreiser, T.
also in Dreiser, T. Sister Carrie; Jennie Gerhardt; Twelve men

Jennifer Government. Barry, M.

JERUSALEM
Bulgakov, M. A. The master and Margarita
Eve, N. The family orchard
Grossman, D. Be my knife
Grossman, D. Someone to run with
Holland, C. Jerusalem
Oz, A. Fima
Oz, A. Panther in the basement
Qashu, S. Dancing Arabs
Spark, M. The Mandelbaum Gate
Stone, R. Damascus Gate
Tarr, J. Queen of swords
Wiesel, E. A beggar in Jerusalem

Jerusalem. Holland, C.
Jerusalem Inn. Grimes, M.

JESUITS
Blatty, W. P. The exorcist
Eco, U. The island of the day before
Higgins, J. Day of judgment
Russell, M. D. Children of God
Russell, M. D. The sparrow
Vollmann, W. T. Fathers and crows
West, P. A fifth of November

JESUS BARABBAS *See* Barabbas (Biblical figure)
JESUS CHRIST

About

Asch, S. Mary
Asch, S. The Nazarene
Bulgakov, M. A. The master and Margarita
Caldwell, T. I, Judas
Crace, J. Quarantine
Douglas, L. C. The Big Fisherman
Douglas, L. C. The robe
Kazantzakis, N. The last temptation of Christ
Mailer, N. The Gospel according to the Son
Wallace, L. Ben-Hur

Crucifixion

Moorcock, M. Behold the man

Nativity

Tournier, M. The four wise men

The **jewel** in the crown. Scott, P.
also in Scott, P. The Raj quartet

JEWEL ROBBERIES *See* Robbery
The **jewel** that was ours. Dexter, C.

JEWELRY
See also Diamonds; Emeralds; Necklaces; Pearls; Rings; Rubies
Bellow, S. A theft
Hill, T. The love of stones
Parks, S.-L. Getting mother's body
Tolkien, J. R. R. The Silmarillion
Trollope, A. The Eustace diamonds

JEWISH-ARAB RELATIONS
Girzone, J. F. Joshua in the Holy Land
Harris, T. Black Sunday
Wilson, J. A Palestine affair

JEWISH-BLACK RELATIONS *See* African Americans—Relations with Jews
JEWISH HOLOCAUST (1933-1945) *See* Holocaust, Jewish (1933-1945)

JEWISH REFUGEES
See also Holocaust survivors
Arkin, F. Hedwig and Berti
Bellow, S. Mr. Sammler's planet
De Hartog, J. Star of Peace
Delbanco, N. What remains
Sebald, W. G. The emigrants
Uris, L. Exodus
Wiesel, E. The accident

JEWISH SECTS *See* Pharisees

JEWISH WOMEN
Nattel, L. The singing fire
Ozick, C. The Puttermesser papers
Sherwood, F. The book of splendor

JEWS
See also Antisemitism; Hasidism; Israelis; Jewish-Arab relations; Jewish women; Judaism; World War, 1939-1945—Jews
Albahari, D. Götz and Meyer
Asch, S. Moses
Bailey, P. Uncle Rudolf
Bellow, S. The Bellarosa connection
Bezmozgis, D. Natasha and other stories
Diamant, A. The red tent
Easterman, D. The final judgement
Englander, N. For the relief of unbearable urges
Eve, N. The family orchard
Goodman, A. Paradise park
Gross, J. The books of Rachel
Halkin, H. Tevye the dairyman and The railroad stories
Halter, M. The book of Abraham
Isaacs, S. Red, white and blue
Korelitz, J. H. The Sabbathday River
Michaels, A. Fugitive pieces
The Oxford book of Jewish stories
Oz, A. Fima
Oz, A. Panther in the basement
Ozick, C. The shawl
Pears, I. The dream of Scipio
Potok, C. Old men at midnight
Rice, A. Servant of the bones
Sebald, W. G. The emigrants
Sholem Aleichem. The best of Sholom Aleichem
Singer, I. B. The collected stories of Isaac Bashevis Singer
Singer, I. B. The death of Methuselah and other stories
Spark, M. The Mandelbaum Gate
Sukenick, R. Mosaic man
Wiesel, E. A beggar in Jerusalem
Wiesel, E. The forgotten
Wiesel, E. Night, Dawn, The accident: three tales

Persecutions

See also Holocaust, Jewish (1933-1945)
Anatoli, A. Babi Yar
Appelfeld, A. Badenheim 1939
Appelfeld, A. Katerina

JEWS—*Continued*

Rome

Asch, S. The Apostle

Russia

Anatoli, A. Babi Yar
Babel´, I. Red cavalry
Courter, G. The midwife
Malamud, B. The fixer
Potok, C. The war doctor
Richler, N. Your mouth is lovely
Sholem Aleichem. The adventures of Menahem-Mendl
Sholem Aleichem. The further adventures of Menachem-Mendl
Sholem Aleichem. The nightingale
Sholem Aleichem. Tevye's daughters
Wiesel, E. The testament

United States

Arkin, F. Hedwig and Berti
Beagle, P. S. A fine and private place
Bellow, S. The adventures of Augie March
Bellow, S. Herzog
Bellow, S. Mr. Sammler's planet
Bellow, S. Ravelstein
Birmingham, S. The Auerbach will
Canin, E. Carry me across the water
Delbanco, N. What remains
Doctorow, E. L. The book of Daniel
Doctorow, E. L. Ragtime
Ephron, N. Heartburn
Epstein, J. Fabulous small Jews
Fast, H. The immigrants
Fast, H. The outsider
Goldberg, M. Bee season
Heller, J. Good as Gold
Hobson, L. K. Z. Gentleman's agreement
Lipman, E. The Inn at Lake Devine
Malamud, B. Dubin's lives
Ozick, C. The cannibal galaxy
Plain, B. Crescent City
Plain, B. Evergreen
Plain, B. Harvest
Plain, B. Tapestry
Powers, R. The time of our singing
Roth, P. The anatomy lesson
Roth, P. The ghost writer
Roth, P. Goodbye, Columbus
Roth, P. Goodbye, Columbus, and five short stories
Roth, P. I married a communist
Roth, P. Letting go
Roth, P. My life as a man
Roth, P. Novels & stories, 1959-1962
Roth, P. The plot against America
Roth, P. Portnoy's complaint
Roth, P. Zuckerman bound: a trilogy and epilogue
Roth, P. Zuckerman unbound
Shaw, I. The young lions
Siegel, L. Love and other games of chance
Styron, W. Sophie's choice

Jian. Lustbader, E. V.

JIANG QING, 1914-1991

About

Min, A. Becoming Madame Mao

The **Jim** Chee mysteries. Hillerman, T.
Jim the boy. Earley, T.
Jitterbug. Estleman, L. D.
Jitterbug perfume. Robbins, T.

JOAN, OF ARC, SAINT, 1412-1431

About

Marcantel, P. An army of angels
Twain, M. Personal recollections of Joan of Arc

Job: a comedy of justice. Heinlein, R. A.

JOCKEYS

Francis, D. Bolt
Francis, D. Bonecrack
Francis, D. Break in
Francis, D. Come to grief
Francis, D. Flying finish
Francis, D. Hot money
Francis, D. Nerve
Francis, D. Rat race
Francis, D. Risk
Francis, D. Slayride
Francis, D. Straight
Francis, D. Whip hand
Mount, F. The man who rode Ampersand
Smith, B. All hat

Joe. Brown, L.
Joe College. Perrotta, T.
The **Joe** Leaphorn mysteries. Hillerman, T.

JOHANNESBURG (SOUTH AFRICA) *See* South Africa—Johannesburg

JOHN, KING OF ENGLAND, 1167-1216

About

Penman, S. K. Here be dragons

JOHN, OF GAUNT, DUKE OF LANCASTER, 1340-1399

About

Seton, A. Katherine

JOHN BROWN'S RAID, HARPERS FERRY, W.VA., 1859
See Harpers Ferry (W.Va.)—John Brown's raid, 1859

John Dollar. Wiggins, M.
John Henry Days. Whitehead, C.

JOHN PAUL II, POPE, 1920-2005

About

Clancy, T. Red rabbit

John Redding goes to sea. Hurston, Z. N.
In Hurston, Z. N. Novels and stories p925-39
Johnny Angel. Steel, D.
Johnny got his gun. Trumbo, D.

JOHNSON, SAMUEL, 1709-1784

About

Bainbridge, B. According to Queeney

JOHNSTOWN (PA.) *See* Pennsylvania—Johnstown

The **joke**. Kundera, M.
Jolie Blon's Bounce. Burke, J. L.
Jonah's gourd vine. Hurston, Z. N.
In Hurston, Z. N. Novels and stories p1-171
Jonathan Strange & Mr. Norrell. Clarke, S.

JONES, JOHN PAUL, 1747-1792

About

Cooper, J. F. The pilot

JORDAN

Spark, M. The Mandelbaum Gate

Jo's boys. Alcott, L. M.
In Alcott, L. M. Little women; Little men; Jo's boys

JOSEPH (BIBLICAL FIGURE)

About

Mann, T. Joseph and his brothers [omnibus edition]

Joseph and his brothers. [omnibus edition] Mann, T.
Joseph and his brothers (Tales of Jacob). See Mann, T. The tales of Jacob
Joseph Andrews. Fielding, H.
Joseph in Egypt. Mann, T.
In Mann, T. Joseph and his brothers p447-840
Joseph the provider. Mann, T.
In Mann, T. Joseph and his brothers p843-1207
Joshua and the children. Girzone, J. F.
Joshua and the city. Girzone, J. F.
Joshua in the Holy Land. Girzone, J. F.
Joshua, the homecoming. Girzone, J. F.
The **journal** of Julius Rodman. Poe, E. A.
In Poe, E. A. The imaginary voyages: The narrative of Arthur Gordon Pym; The unparalleled adventure of one Hans Pfaall; The journal of Julius Rodman p508-653
A **journal** of the plague year. Defoe, D.

JOURNALISM

Westlake, D. E. Trust me on this

JOURNALISTS

See also Women journalists

Allende, I. Of love and shadows
Anthony, E. The Janus imperative
Bahal, A. Bunker 13
Barbash, T. The last good chance
Barker, P. Double vision
Böll, H. The lost honor of Katharina Blum
Brink, A. P. Devil's Valley
Brown, D. A. Killdeer Mountain
Buckley, C. T. Little green men
Buckley, C. T. No way to treat a First Lady
Busch, F. The night inspector
Byrd, M. Grant
Camus, A. The plague

L

The **late** George Apley. Marquand, J. P.
The **late** Mr. Shakespeare. Nye, R.
Later novels and other writings. Chandler, R.
Later short stories, 1888-1903. Chekhov, A. P.
The **lathe** of heaven. Le Guin, U. K.

LATIN AMERICA

Allende, I. Eva Luna
Allende, I. Of love and shadows
García Márquez, G. Love in the time of cholera
García Márquez, G. Of love and other demons
Naipaul, V. S. A way in the world
The Oxford book of Latin American short stories

Politics

See Politics—Latin America

LATIN AMERICANS

Europe

García Márquez, G. Strange pilgrims

LATINOS (U.S.) *See* Hispanic Americans
Laughable loves. Kundera, M.
Laughing Boy. La Farge, O.
The **laughing** policeman. Sjöwall, M.
Laughing to keep from crying. Hughes, L.

LAVEAU, MARIE, 1794-1881

About

Rhodes, J. P. Voodoo dreams

Lavender lies. Albert, S. W.

LAW AND LAWYERS

See also Judges; Trials; Women lawyers

Amidon, S. The new city
Auchincloss, L. Honorable men
Auchincloss, L. The realist
Baldacci, D. Absolute power
Baldacci, D. The simple truth
Baldacci, D. Wish you well
Banks, R. The sweet hereafter
Begley, L. Schmidt delivered
Bernhardt, W. Criminal intent
Bernhardt, W. Cruel justice
Bernhardt, W. Dark justice
Bernhardt, W. Murder one
Bernhardt, W. Silent justice
Brandon, J. Local rules
Brandon, J. Rules of evidence
Brookner, A. Altered states
Brown, S. The alibi
Brown, S. Fat Tuesday
Buckley, C. T. No way to treat a First Lady
Buffa, D. W. The defense
Buffa, D. W. The judgment
Buffa, D. W. The prosecution
Bunn, T. D. The great divide
Burke, J. L. Bitterroot
Burke, J. L. Cimarron rose
Burke, J. L. Heartwood
Burke, J. L. In the moon of red ponies
Busch, F. Closing arguments
Camus, A. The fall
Carroll, J. Memorial bridge
Carter, S. L. The emperor of Ocean Park
Clark, M. H. Remember me
Connell, E. S. Mr. Bridge
Connell, E. S. Mrs. Bridge
Connelly, M. The Lincoln lawyer
Coughlin, W. J. Death penalty
Coughlin, W. J. In the presence of enemies
Coughlin, W. J. Shadow of a doubt
Cozzens, J. G. By love possessed
Crichton, M. Disclosure
Davies, R. The manticore
De Kretser, M. The Hamilton case
DeMille, N. The Gold Coast
Denker, H. This child is mine
Dickens, C. Bleak House
Dickens, C. The posthumous papers of the Pickwick Club
Diehl, W. Primal fear
Diehl, W. Reign in hell
Diehl, W. Show of evil
Drabble, M. The needle's eye
Dunne, J. G. Nothing lost
Dunne, J. G. The red, white, and blue
Ellis, D. Life sentence
Folsom, A. R. Day of confession
Forsyth, F. Avenger
Friedman, P. Grand jury
Friedman, P. Inadmissable evidence
Friedman, P. Reasonable doubt
Gaddis, W. A frolic of his own
Gordimer, N. The house gun
Gordon, N. The company you keep
Greene, G. The tenth man
Grippando, J. Hear no evil
Grippando, J. A king's ransom
Grisham, J. The chamber
Grisham, J. The client
Grisham, J. The firm
Grisham, J. The last juror
Grisham, J. The partner
Grisham, J. The pelican brief
Grisham, J. The rainmaker
Grisham, J. The runaway jury
Grisham, J. The street lawyer
Grisham, J. The summons
Grisham, J. The testament
Grisham, J. A time to kill
Higgins, G. V. The agent
Higgins, G. V. Defending Billy Ryan
Higgins, G. V. The Mandeville talent
Hoag, T. Guilty as sin
Hoffman, J. Retribution
Humphreys, J. The fireman's fair
Irving, C. Final argument
Isaacs, S. Shining through
Katzenbach, J. Hart's war
Kaufman, S. Diary of a mad housewife
Kennedy, D. The big picture
King, S. Thinner
Le Carré, J. Single & Single
Lee, H. To kill a mockingbird
Legal briefs
Legal fictions
Lescroart, J. T. The 13th juror
Lescroart, J. T. A certain justice
Lescroart, J. T. The first law
Lescroart, J. T. Guilt
Lescroart, J. T. Hard evidence
Lescroart, J. T. The hearing
Lescroart, J. T. The mercy rule
Lescroart, J. T. Nothing but the truth
Lescroart, J. T. The oath
Lescroart, J. T. The second chair
Ludlum, R. The Aquitaine progression
Maas, P. China white
Margolin, P. After dark
Margolin, P. The burning man
Martin, M. Windswept House
Martini, S. P. The attorney
Martini, S. P. Compelling evidence
Martini, S. P. The judge
Martini, S. P. The jury
Martini, S. P. Prime witness
Martini, S. P. Undue influence
McCullers, C. Clock without hands
McElroy, J. Actress in the house
Meltzer, B. Dead even
Meltzer, B. The first counsel
Meltzer, B. The tenth justice
Miller, S. The good mother
Mishima, Y. The decay of the angel
Mishima, Y. Runaway horses
Mishima, Y. The Temple of Dawn
Mortimer, J. C. Rumpole à la carte
Mortimer, J. C. Rumpole and the angel of death
Mortimer, J. C. Rumpole on trial
Mortimer, J. C. Rumpole rests his case
Mortimer, J. C. Rumpole's return
Mortimer, J. C. The second Rumpole omnibus
Palmer, M. Natural causes
Parker, B. Blood relations
Parker, B. Criminal justice
Parker, B. Suspicion of betrayal
Parker, B. Suspicion of deceit
Parker, B. Suspicion of vengeance
Patterson, R. N. Balance of power
Patterson, R. N. Conviction
Patterson, R. N. Dark lady

LENO, DAN, 1861-1904
About
Ackroyd, P. The trial of Elizabeth Cree
LEONARDO, DA VINCI, 1452-1519
About
Brown, D. The Da Vinci code
The **Leopard**. Tomasi di Lampedusa, G.
The **leopard** hunts in darkness. Smith, W. A.
LEOPOLD, NATHAN FREUNDENTHAL, 1904 OR 5-1971
About
Levin, M. Compulsion
LEPROSY
Greene, G. A burnt-out case
LESBIANISM
See also Homosexuality
Alvarez, J. In the name of Salomé
Anshaw, C. Lucky in the corner
Barnes, D. Nightwood
Berger, T. Reinhart's women
Colette. Claudine married
Grumbach, D. The book of knowledge
Grumbach, D. Chamber music
Hall, R. The well of loneliness
Hallgrímur Helgason. 101 Reykjavik
Henley, P. In the river sweet
Humphreys, H. Afterimage
Hunter, E. Lizzie
Lurie, A. The last resort
Meyer, C. Brown eyes blue
Muller, M. Cyanide Wells
Naylor, G. The women of Brewster Place
Nin, A. Ladders to fire
Parks, S.-L. Getting mother's body
The Penguin book of lesbian short stories
Piercy, M. Small changes
Ridgway, K. The parts
Schwartz, L. Angels Crest
Schwartz, L. S. In the family way
Sinclair, A. Ain't gonna be the same fool twice
Snow, C. P. The sleep of reason
Truong, M. T. D. The book of salt
Vine, B. The house of stairs
Walsh, H. Brass
LESBOS ISLAND (GREECE)
Jong, E. Sappho's leap
A **lesson** before dying. Gaines, E. J.
Let it come down. Bowles, P.
In Bowles, P. The sheltering sky; Let it come down; The spider's house
Let me call you sweetheart. Clark, M. H.
Let us now praise famous men; A death in the family, and shorter fiction. Agee, J.
A **lethal** involvement. Egleton, C.
Letter from home. Hart, C. G.
A **letter** of Mary. King, L. R.
The **letter** of the law. Green, T.
LETTERS (STORIES ABOUT)
Bainbridge, B. According to Queeney
Bellow, S. Herzog
Campbell, R. The Count of Eleven
Coetzee, J. M. Age of iron
French, N. Beneath the skin
Kundera, M. Identity
Labiner, N. Miniatures
L'Engle, M. The love letters
Michael, J. Acts of love
Purdy, J. In a shallow grave
Schine, C. The love letter
Sparks, N. Message in a bottle
Wharton, E. The touchstone
LETTERS (STORIES IN LETTER FORM)
Berg, E. The pull of the moon
Davies, R. Fifth business
Gardam, J. The queen of the tambourine
Goethe, J. W. v. The sorrows of young Werther
Grass, G. Dog years
Grossman, D. Be my knife
Hailey, E. F. A woman of independent means
Kingsolver, B. The poisonwood Bible
Lardner, R. You know me, Al
Murdoch, I. An accidental man
Poe, E. A. The unparalleled adventure of one Hans Pfaall
Price, R. Blue Calhoun
Richardson, S. Clarissa
Richardson, S. Pamela
Richler, N. Your mouth is lovely
Robinson, E. The true and outstanding adventures of the Hunt sisters
Robinson, M. Gilead
Sholem Aleichem. The adventures of Menahem-Mendl
Sholem Aleichem. The further adventures of Menachem-Mendl
Shriver, L. We need to talk about Kevin
Smith, L. Fair and tender ladies
Smollett, T. G. Humphry Clinker
Updike, J. S
Walker, A. The color purple
Letters from the underworld. See Dostoyevsky, F. Notes from underground
Letting go. Roth, P.
also in Roth, P. Novels & stories, 1959-1962
LEUKEMIA
Doerr, H. Stones for Ibarra
Picoult, J. My sister's keeper
Robinson, E. The true and outstanding adventures of the Hunt sisters
Segal, E. Love story
Leviathan. Auster, P.
The **leviathan**. Roth, J.
In Roth, J. and Hofmann, M. The collected stories of Joseph Roth
Levine. Westlake, D. E.
Lew Archer, private investigator. See Macdonald, R. Ross Macdonald's Lew Archer, private investigator
LEWIS, MERIWETHER, 1774-1809
About
Hall, B. I should be extremely happy in your company
Wheeler, R. S. Eclipse
LEWIS AND CLARK EXPEDITION (1804-1806)
Glancy, D. Stone heart
Hall, B. I should be extremely happy in your company
Wheeler, R. S. Eclipse
LEXINGTON, BATTLE OF, 1775
Fast, H. April morning
LEXINGTON (MASS.) *See* Massachusetts—Lexington
Liar. Burke, J.
Liars and saints. Meloy, M.
LIBEL
Galsworthy, J. The silver spoon
LIBERIA
Banks, R. The darling
LIBERTY
Asimov, I. The Bicentennial Man
Coetzee, J. M. Life & times of Michael K.
Erickson, S. Arc d'X
Sartre, J. P. The age of reason
Liberty falling. Barr, N.
Liberty Square. Forrest, K. V.
Libra. DeLillo, D.
LIBRARIANS
Brink, A. P. The rights of desire
Cambor, K. In sunlight, in a beautiful garden
Cooley, M. The archivist
Hoffman, A. The ice queen
Krentz, J. A. Smoke in mirrors
Kurzweil, A. The grand complication
McCracken, E. The giant's house
Pym, B. An unsuitable attachment
Schwartz, L. S. The writing on the wall
The **library** policeman. King, S.
In King, S. Four past midnight p401-604
LIBYA
Brown, D. Wings of fire
LIBYANS
United States
DeMille, N. The lion's game
License renewed. Gardner, J. E.

Lion in the valley. Peters, E.
The **lion's** game. DeMille, N.
LIPPIZANER HORSES
Stewart, M. Airs above the ground
Lipstick jungle. Bushnell, C.
LIQUOR INDUSTRY *See* Liquor traffic
LIQUOR TRAFFIC
See also Moonshiners
Estleman, L. D. Whiskey River
Francis, D. Proof
LISBON (PORTUGAL) *See* Portugal—Lisbon
The **list**. Martini, S. P.
The **list** of Adrian Messenger. MacDonald, P.
Listen to the silence. Muller, M.
Listening woman. Hillerman, T.
also in Hillerman, T. The Joe Leaphorn mysteries
The **Literary** ghost. Entered in Part I under title
LITERARY LIFE
See also Authors
Amis, M. The information
Bainbridge, B. According to Queeney
Balzac, H. d. Lost illusions
Barnes, D. Nightwood
Bolaño, R. By night in Chile
Boyle, T. C. East is East
Bradbury, M. Doctor Criminale
Byatt, A. S. Possession
Chabon, M. Wonder boys
Harington, D. Ekaterina
Keillor, G. Love me
Lelchuk, A. Ziff
Martin, V. Italian fever
Michener, J. A. The novel
Parini, J. The apprentice lover
Powell, D. Turn, magic wheel
Wolitzer, M. The wife
LITHUANIA
Brown, D. Night of the hawk
LITHUANIANS
United States
Sinclair, U. The jungle
Little America. Bromell, H.
Little Big Man. Berger, T.
Little black book of stories. Byatt, A. S.
Little children. Perrotta, T.
The **little** dog laughed. Hansen, J.
Little Dorrit. Dickens, C.
The **little** drummer girl. Le Carré, J.
Little earthquakes. Weiner, J.
The **little** friend. Tartt, D.
Little green men. Buckley, C. T.
Little men. Alcott, L. M.
In Alcott, L. M. Little women; Little men; Jo's boys
The **little** prince. Saint-Exupéry, A. d.
Little Saigon. Parker, T. J.
The **little** sister. Chandler, R.
In Chandler, R. Later novels and other writings
Little women. Alcott, L. M.
In Alcott, L. M. Little women; Little men; Jo's boys
The **little** women. Weber, K.
Little women; Little men; Jo's boys. Alcott, L. M.
A **little** yellow dog. Mosley, W.
A **live** coal in the sea. L'Engle, M.
Live flesh. Rendell, R.
LIVERPOOL (ENGLAND) *See* England—Liverpool
Lives of girls & women. Munro, A.
Lives of the circus animals. Bram, C.
Lives of the poets. Doctorow, E. L.
Lives of the poets [novelette] Doctorow, E. L.
In Doctorow, E. L. Lives of the poets p81-145
LIVIA, EMPRESS, CONSORT OF AUGUSTUS, EMPEROR OF ROME, 58? B.C.-29
About
Graves, R. I, Claudius
Living at home. Gordon, M.
In Gordon, M. The rest of life: three novellas
Lizzie. Hunter, E.
LLEWELYN AP IORWERTH, D. 1240
About
Penman, S. K. Here be dragons
LLYWELYN AP GRUFFYDD, D. 1282
About
Penman, S. K. The reckoning
LOANS
See also Moneylenders
Local anaesthetic. Grass, G.
Local girls. Hoffman, A.
Local rules. Brandon, J.
The **locked** room. Sjöwall, M.
Locked rooms. King, L. R.
The **locusts** have no king. Powell, D.
In Powell, D. Novels, 1944-1962
LODZ (POLAND) *See* Poland—Lodz
LOEB, RICHARD A., 1905 OR 6-1936
About
Levin, M. Compulsion
LOGGERS
Guterson, D. Our Lady of the Forest
Loitering with intent. Spark, M.
Lolita. Nabokov, V. V.
also in Nabokov, V. V. Novels, 1955-1962
LONDON (ENGLAND) *See* England—London
LONDON (ENGLAND). TOWER *See* Tower of London (England)
London. Rutherfurd, E.
London bridges. Patterson, J.
London fields. Amis, M.
London match. Deighton, L.
also in Deighton, L. Game, set & match
London observed. See Lessing, D. M. The real thing
LONDON ZOOLOGICAL GARDENS
Hoban, R. Turtle diary
Lone eagle. Steel, D.
LONELINESS
Bowen, E. The death of the heart
Brookner, A. The Bay of Angels
Brookner, A. Falling slowly
Brookner, A. Fraud
Brookner, A. Making things better
Brookner, A. A private view
Brookner, A. The rules of engagement
Brookner, A. Undue influence
Chadwick, C. It's all right now
Coupland, D. Eleanor Rigby
Greenberg, J. Rites of passage
Grimes, M. When the mousetrap closes
Harrison, K. The seal wife
Heller, Z. What was she thinking?
Hoban, R. Turtle diary
Martin, S. Shopgirl
Moore, B. The lonely passion of Judith Hearne
Nolan, C. The banyan tree
Pym, B. Excellent women
Pym, B. Quartet in autumn
Pym, B. The sweet dove died
Rossner, J. Looking for Mr. Goodbar
Taylor, E. Mrs. Palfrey at the Claremont
Tyler, A. The accidental tourist
West, N. Miss Lonelyhearts
The **loneliness** of the long-distance runner. Sillitoe, A.
The **lonely** girl. O'Brien, E.
In O'Brien, E. The country girls trilogy and epilogue p179-377
The **lonely** passion of Judith Hearne. Moore, B.
The **lonely** silver rain. MacDonald, J. D.
Lonesome dove. McMurtry, L.
The **lonesome** gods. L'Amour, L.
Long after midnight. Johansen, I.
The **long** dark tea-time of the soul. Adams, D.
A **long** finish. Dibdin, M.
The **long** goodbye. Chandler, R.
also in Chandler, R. Later novels and other writings
LONG ISLAND (N.Y.)
Begley, L. Schmidt delivered
Benchley, P. Jaws
DeMille, N. The Gold Coast
DeMille, N. Plum Island
Fitzgerald, F. S. The Great Gatsby
Hoffman, A. Seventh heaven
House, T. The beginning of calamities

LOUISIANA—New Orleans—*Continued*
Ferber, E. Saratoga trunk
Grau, S. A. The condor passes
Hailey, A. Hotel
Hambly, B. Dead water
Hambly, B. A free man of color
Hambly, B. Graveyard dust
Hambly, B. Sold down the river
Hambly, B. Die upon a kiss
Hambly, B. Wet grave
Harris, T. Black Sunday
Inness-Brown, E. Burning Marguerite
Percy, W. Lancelot
Percy, W. The moviegoer
Plain, B. Crescent City
Rhodes, J. P. Voodoo dreams
Rice, A. The Feast of All Saints
Roberts, N. Midnight Bayou
Toole, J. K. A confederacy of dunces
Warren, R. P. Band of angels
Louisiana hotshot. Smith, J.

LOVE
Helprin, M. A soldier of the great war
Sarton, M. Kinds of love
Love. Morrison, T.

LOVE AFFAIRS
See also Courtship; Love stories; Lovers; Marriage problems
Abrahams, P. A perfect crime
Adam, C. Love and country
Adams, A. After the war
Adams, A. Almost perfect
Adler, E. Now or never
Alison, J. The marriage of the sea
Alvarez, J. How the García girls lost their accents
Amis, K. The Russian girl
Anthony, E. The Cardinal and the Queen
Anthony, E. The tamarind seed
Appelfeld, A. The conversion
Atwood, M. The blind assassin
Atwood, M. Life before man
Baldwin, J. Another country
Bank, M. The girls' guide to hunting and fishing
Barthelme, F. The brothers
Barthelme, F. Elroy Nights
Beattie, A. Another you
Beattie, A. Love always
Beattie, A. My life, starring Dara Falcon
Begley, L. Schmidt delivered
Bellow, S. What kind of day did you have?
Berger, T. Best friends
Berger, T. Reinhart's women
Betts, D. Souls raised from the dead
Blake, J. C. Under the skin
Blanchard, K. The deed
Bowen, E. The heat of the day
Boyd, W. The blue afternoon
Bradford, B. T. Voice of the heart
Brookner, A. Falling slowly
Brown, R. M. Southern discomfort
Brown, S. French Silk
Busch, F. A handbook for spies
Busch, F. A memory of war
Bushnell, C. Lipstick jungle
Butler, R. O. The deep green sea
Byatt, A. S. A whistling woman
Casey, J. Spartina
Cather, W. Lucy Gayheart
Chase-Riboud, B. Sally Hemings
Cheever, J. Oh, what a paradise it seems
Coe, J. The closed circle
Coetzee, J. M. The master of Petersburg
Colette. Chéri
Colette. The last of Chéri
Colwin, L. Family happiness
Condon, R. Prizzi's family
Condon, R. Prizzi's honor
Cook, T. H. The Chatham School affair
Doig, I. Prairie nocturne
Dostoyevsky, F. The gambler
Dunmore, H. With your crooked heart
Dunne, D. An inconvenient woman
Dunne, J. G. Playland
Eco, U. The mysterious flame of Queen Loana
Endō, S. The girl I left behind
Faulkner, W. If I forget thee, Jerusalem
Faulks, S. Birdsong
Faulks, S. On Green Dolphin Street
Fielding, H. The history of Tom Jones, a foundling
Fielding, J. Missing pieces
Findley, T. The piano man's daughter
Follett, K. The man from St. Petersburg
French, M. The bleeding heart
French, M. The women's room
Fuentes, C. Diana, the goddess who hunts alone
Gordimer, N. The conservationist
Gordimer, N. A guest of honor
Gordimer, N. My son's story
Gordon, M. The company of women
Gordon, M. Final payments
Gordon, M. Immaculate man
Gordon, M. Living at home
Graham, W. Stephanie
Graver, E. Awake
Greene, G. The end of the affair
Greer, A. S. The path of minor planets
Griesemer, J. Signal & noise
Groom, W. Such a pretty, pretty girl
Grossman, D. Be my knife
Ha Jin. Waiting
Hamilton, J. Disobedience
Hart, J. Sin
Hazzard, S. The transit of Venus
Heller, Z. What was she thinking?
Hemingway, E. The garden of Eden
Henley, P. In the river sweet
Higgins, G. V. Swan boats at four
Hooper, C. A child's book of true crime
Howatch, S. Mystical paths
Howatch, S. Penmarric
Howatch, S. Scandalous risks
Howatch, S. Ultimate prizes
Huddle, D. La Tour dreams of the wolf girl
Hunter, E. Privileged conversation
Irving, J. A widow for one year
Isaacs, S. Close relations
James, H. The ambassadors
James, H. In the cage
James, H. What Maisie knew
Jen, G. Typical American
Jhabvala, R. P. Heat and dust
Johnson, D. L'affaire
Jones, J. From here to eternity
Kawabata, Y. Snow country
Kawabata, Y. Thousand cranes
Kempadoo, O. Tide running
Keneally, T. A family madness
Keyes, M. Last Chance Saloon
Keyes, M. The other side of the story
Kim, S. The interpreter
King, T. Survivor
Korda, M. Curtain
Korda, M. The immortals
Krantz, J. Mistral's daughter
Krüger, M. The cello player
Kundera, M. Immortality
Kundera, M. The unbearable lightness of being
Leavitt, D. While England sleeps
Lee, M. The canal house
Lefcourt, P. Eleven Karens
L'Engle, M. A live coal in the sea
Leonard, E. Cat chaser
Lescroart, J. T. Guilt
Lipman, E. The dearly departed
Lively, P. The photograph
Lively, P. The road to Lichfield
Lively, P. Spiderweb
Llywelyn, M. 1949
Lodge, D. Thinks—
Lurie, A. Foreign affairs
Lurie, A. The last resort
MacNeil, R. The voyage
Malamud, B. Dubin's lives
Marías, J. The man of feeling
Martin, V. Italian fever
Martini, S. P. Compelling evidence
Mattison, A. The wedding of the two-headed woman

LOVE STORIES—*Continued*

Bellow, S. The actual
Berg, E. Never change
Berry, W. Jayber Crow
Biguenet, J. Oyster
Binchy, M. Echoes
Binchy, M. Evening class
Binchy, M. The glass lake
Böll, H. The silent angel
Bonner, C. Lily
Bonner, C. Looking after Lily
Bradford, B. T. A sudden change of heart
Bradford, B. T. Where you belong
Bradley, M. Z. The forest house
Bradshaw, G. The wolf hunt
Bragg, M. Crossing the lines
Brand, M. Dust across the range
Brink, A. P. The rights of desire
Bristow, G. Calico Palace
Brontë, A. The tenant of Wildfell Hall
Brontë, C. Jane Eyre
Brontë, C. The professor
Brontë, C. Villette
Brontë, E. Wuthering Heights
Brookner, A. Altered states
Brookner, A. Brief lives
Brown, C. Confinement
Brown, C. The hatbox baby
Brown, C. Lamb in love
Brown, R. M. Riding shotgun
Brown, S. Charade
Brown, S. Chill factor
Burke, S. Safelight
Byatt, A. S. The biographer's tale
Byatt, A. S. Possession
Cameron, P. The city of your final destination
Carey, P. Oscar & Lucinda
Chalmers, R. Who's who in hell
Chevalier, T. The lady and the unicorn
Cleage, P. I wish I had a red dress
Cohen, L. H. Heart, you bully, you punk
Colette. The kepi
Colwin, L. Happy all the time
Conley, R. J. Mountain windsong
Cook, T. H. Breakheart Hill
Cookson, C. A house divided
Cookson, C. The Maltese Angel
Cookson, C. The obsession
Cookson, C. The upstart
Cookson, C. The year of the virgins
Coulter, C. The heiress bride
Coward, N. Bon voyage
Crane, S. Active service
Crane, S. The third violet
Crowley, J. The translator
Crusie, J. Bet me
Crusie, J. Crazy for you
Crusie, J. Faking it
Dailey, J. Calder pride
Daley, R. The innocents within
De Bernières, L. Corelli's mandolin
De Blasis, C. The proud breed
De Blasis, C. Swan's chance
Dee, J. Palladio
Del Vecchio, J. M. For the sake of all living things
Delinsky, B. Coast road
Delinsky, B. Lake news
Delinsky, B. The summer I dared
DeMille, N. Spencerville
Denker, H. Mrs. Washington and Horowitz, too
Dew, R. F. The evidence against her
Dickens, C. Barnaby Rudge
Dickens, C. Great expectations
Docx, E. The calligrapher
Dodd, S. M. Ethiopia
Doig, I. Dancing at the Rascal Fair
Dorris, M. The crown of Columbus
Dostoyevsky, F. Poor people
Drabble, M. The realms of gold
Du Maurier, Dame D. Frenchman's Creek
Dunn, S. The big love
Durham, M. The man who loved Cat Dancing
Eagle, K. The last true cowboy
Eden, D. The American heiress
Erdrich, L. The bingo palace
Erdrich, L. Tales of burning love
Esquivel, L. Like water for chocolate
Evans, N. The horse whisperer
Evans, N. The loop
Evans, N. The smoke jumper
Fast, H. The bridge builder's story
Fast, H. The immigrants
Fast, H. Redemption
Faulks, S. Charlotte Gray
Feather, J. The widow's kiss
Finney, J. Time and again
Fitzgerald, P. The blue flower
Fitzgerald, P. The gate of angels
Fleming, T. J. When this cruel war is over
Follett, K. Lie down with lions
Follett, K. A place called freedom
Ford, R. The student conductor
Fowler, C. M. Remembering Blue
Fowles, J. Daniel Martin
Fowles, J. The French lieutenant's woman
Frazier, C. Cold Mountain
Freda, J. The patience of rivers
French, M. My summer with George
Gaffney, P. Circle of three
Gaffney, P. Flight lessons
Gage, E. Pandora's box
García Márquez, G. Love in the time of cholera
García Márquez, G. Of love and other demons
Garlock, D. The edge of town
Gifford, B. Wild at heart
Gilman, D. Caravan
Glendinning, V. Flight
Godden, R. Pippa passes
Goethe, J. W. v. The sorrows of young Werther
Golden, A. Memoirs of a geisha
Goldsmith, O. Bad boy
Goudge, E. Garden of lies
Goudge, E. Stranger in paradise
Goudge, E. Such devoted sisters
Goudge, E. Trail of secrets
Goudge, E. Green Dolphin Street
Gould, J. The best is yet to come
Gould, J. A moment in time
Gould, J. Time to say goodbye
Gowdy, B. The romantic
Graham, W. The black moon
Graham, W. The miller's dance
Grass, G. The call of the toad
Greeley, A. M. Irish lace
Greeley, A. M. Younger than springtime
Greenberg, J. Of such small differences
Grenville, K. The idea of perfection
Grøndahl, J. C. Lucca
Gunesekera, R. Heaven's edge
Gutcheon, B. R. More than you know
Hannah, K. Angel falls
Hannah, K. On Mystic lake
Hansen, R. Isn't it romantic?
Harris, E. L. And this too shall pass
Harrison, K. The seal wife
Hassler, J. The dean's list
Hassler, J. Rookery blues
Hawke, E. Ash Wednesday
Hawthorne, N. Fanshawe
Hay, E. A student of weather
Hazzard, S. The great fire
Hearon, S. Ella in bloom
Helprin, M. Ellis Island
Hemingway, E. A farewell to arms
Henley, P. Hummingbird house
Hewson, D. Lucifer's shadow
Heyer, G. The grand Sophy
Hilton, J. Random harvest
Hoban, R. Her name was Lola
Høeg, P. The woman and the ape
Hoffman, A. Here on Earth
Hoffman, A. The ice queen
Hoffman, A. Turtle Moon
Hofmann, G. Lichtenberg and the little flower girl
Holt, V. The black opal
Holt, V. The India fan
Holt, V. Secret for a nightingale
Hornby, N. High fidelity

LOVE STORIES—*Continued*
Shreve, A. Eden Close
Shreve, A. Resistance
Siddons, A. R. Colony
Siddons, A. R. King's oak
Sienkiewicz, H. The deluge
Smith, M. C. Rose
Smith, W. A. Golden fox
Sparks, N. A bend in the road
Sparks, N. The guardian
Sparks, N. Message in a bottle
Sparks, N. Nights in Rodanthe
Sparks, N. The notebook
Sparks, N. A walk to remember
Spencer, E. The light in the piazza
Spencer, L. Bitter sweet
Spencer, L. Forgiving
Spencer, L. Small town girl
Spencer, L. That Camden summer
Spencer, S. Endless love
Steel, D. The house on Hope Street
Steel, D. Journey
Steel, D. The kiss
Steel, D. Lone eagle
Steel, D. No greater love
Stevens, M. Useful girl
Stevenson, J. The winter queen
Stevenson, R. L. The story of a lie
Stewart, M. The stormy petrel
Stirling, J. The marrying kind
Stirling, J. The penny wedding
Stone, K. Happy endings
Styron, W. Sophie's choice
Thayer, N. Family secrets
Theroux, A. Darconville's cat
Thomas, R. All my sins remembered
Tremain, R. Music & silence
Trevanian. The summer of Katya
Tryon, T. The wings of the morning
Turgenev, I. S. First love and other stories
Turgenev, I. S. Spring torrents [variant title: The torrents of spring]
Turgenev, I. S. The torrents of spring
Turner, N. E. These is my words
Unsworth, B. Stone virgin
Updike, J. Brazil
Uris, L. Redemption
Urquhart, J. Away
Vargas Llosa, M. Aunt Julia and the scriptwriter
Veryan, P. The riddle of the reluctant rake
Veryan, P. The riddle of the skipwrecked spinster
Villars, E. The Normandie affair
Vine, B. The brimstone wedding
Waller, R. J. The bridges of Madison County
Watson, B. The heaven of Mercury
Wesley, M. Part of the furniture
West, J. The massacre at Fall Creek
Wharton, E. Summer
Wharton, E. The touchstone
Wideman, J. E. Two cities
Williamson, P. Heart of the west
Williamson, P. The outsider
Winthrop, E. Island justice
Wood, B. Perfect Harmony
Wood, B. Soul flame
Wood, B. Vital signs
Love story. Segal, E.
The **love** wife. Jen, G.
The **loved** one. Waugh, E.
LOVELACE, ADA KING, COUNTESS OF, 1815-1852
About
Crowley, J. Lord Byron's novel
The **lovely** bones. Sebold, A.

LOVERS
Howard, M. Children with matches
Kundera, M. Identity
Piercy, M. Summer people
Lovers crossing. Mitchell, J. C.
Love's mansion. West, P.
Loves music, loves to dance. Clark, M. H.
Loving Chloe. Mapson, J.-A.
The **loving** cup. Graham, W.
Loving Little Egypt. McMahon, T. A.
Loving monsters. Hamilton-Paterson, J.
Lovingkindness. Roiphe, A. R.
LOWELL (MASS.) *See* Massachusetts—Lowell
LOWER EAST SIDE (NEW YORK, N.Y.) *See* New York (N.Y.)—Lower East Side
LOYALISTS, AMERICAN *See* American loyalists
LUCAN, RICHARD JOHN BINGHAM, EARL OF, 1934-
About
Spark, M. Aiding and abetting
Lucca. Grøndahl, J. C.
Lucia in London. Benson, E. F.
In Benson, E. F. Make way for Lucia p179-358
LUCIANO, LUCKY, 1897-1962
About
Higgins, J. Luciano's luck
Luciano's luck. Higgins, J.
Lucia's progress. See Benson, E. F. The worshipful Lucia
Lucifer's hammer. Niven, L.
Lucifer's shadow. Hewson, D.
Luck. Hofmann, G.
The **Luck** of Roaring Camp, and other tales. Harte, B.
Lucky girls. Freudenberger, N.
Lucky in the corner. Anshaw, C.
Lucky Jim. Amis, K.
The **lucky** ones. Mortman, D.
Lucky strike. Zafris, N.
Lucky you. Hiaasen, C.
Lucy. Kincaid, J.
Lucy Gayheart. Cather, W.
In Cather, W. Willa Cather, later novels
LUKE, SAINT
About
Caldwell, T. Dear and glorious physician
Lullaby. McBain, E.
Lullaby. Palahniuk, C.
LUMBER INDUSTRY
See also Loggers
Bernhardt, W. Dark justice
Kesey, K. Sometimes a great notion
LUMBERJACKS *See* Loggers
LUMBERMEN *See* Loggers
Lunar Park. Ellis, B. E.
Lust & other stories. Minot, S.
Lust for life. Stone, I.
Lydia Bailey. Roberts, K. L.
Lying awake. Salzman, M.
Lying in wait. Jance, J. A.
LYNCHING
Clark, W. V. T. The Ox-bow incident
Lansdale, J. R. The bottoms
Lescroart, J. T. A certain justice
Nordan, L. Wolf whistle
Smith, L. E. Strange fruit
The **lyre** of Orpheus. Davies, R.

M

"M" is for malice. Grafton, S.
M31, a family romance. Wright, S.
Ma and Tom. Steinbeck, J.
In Steinbeck, J. The portable Steinbeck
MACABRE STORIES *See* Horror stories
MACEDONIA
Bova, B. Orion and the conqueror
MACGREGOR, ROBERT *See* Rob Roy, 1671-1734
The **MacGuffin**. Elkin, S.
MACHINERY AND CIVILIZATION *See* Technology and civilization
Mackenna's gold. Henry, W.
MacPherson's lament. McCrumb, S.
The **mad** dog: stories. Böll, H.
Mad dogs & Scotsmen. Hammond, G.
The **mad** ship. Hobb, R.
Madame Bovary. Flaubert, G.
Madame de Mauves. James, H.
In James, H. Complete stories, 1864-1874
In James, H. The complete tales of Henry James

MARRIAGE—*Continued*
James, H. The wings of the dove
Karon, J. Out to Canaan
Kinder, C. Honeymooners
Koen, K. Through a glass darkly
Leebron, F. G. In the middle of all this
Lordan, B. But come ye back
McEwan, I. Black dogs
Meloy, M. Liars and saints
Meltzer, B. Dead even
Minot, S. Folly
Moor, M. d. Duke of Egypt
Moore, B. The magician's wife
Oates, J. C. The falls
O'Nan, S. The good wife
Pouncey, P. R. Rules for old men waiting
Price, R. Roxanna Slade
Pym, B. An academic question
Pym, B. Civil to strangers
Rice, L. Blue moon
Sarton, M. Anger
Seth, V. A suitable boy
Shreve, A. All he ever wanted
Shreve, A. Sea glass
Siddons, A. R. Hill towns
Stegner, W. E. Crossing to safety
Stegner, W. E. The spectator bird
Stirling, J. The piper's tune
Stone, R. Outerbridge Reach
Thayer, N. Between husbands and friends
Thayer, N. Family secrets
Theroux, P. My secret history
Thomas, E. M. The animal wife
Toer, P. A. The girl from the coast
Trollope, J. The men and the girls
Trollope, J. Next of kin
Tyler, A. The amateur marriage
Tyler, A. Breathing lessons
Vidal, G. 1876
Weiner, J. Little earthquakes
West, P. Love's mansion
West, Dame R. Cousin Rosamund
Wharton, E. The buccaneers
Wolff, M. M. Sudden rain
Wood, B. The dreaming
Wright, A. M. Tony and Susan

MARRIAGE, CHILDLESS *See* Childless marriage
MARRIAGE, INTERFAITH *See* Interfaith marriage
MARRIAGE, INTERRACIAL *See* Interracial marriage

MARRIAGE BROKERS
Pym, B. Jane and Prudence

MARRIAGE COUNSELING *See* Marriage problems
Marriage is murder. Pickard, N.
The **marriage** of Phaedra. Cather, W.
In Cather, W. Early novels and stories
The **marriage** of the sea. Alison, J.

MARRIAGE PROBLEMS
See also Divorce; Family life; Interfaith marriage; Love affairs
Abrahams, P. A perfect crime
Adams, A. After the war
Akst, D. The Webster chronicle
Allison, D. Bastard out of Carolina
Amado, J. Dona Flor and her two husbands
Amis, K. The Russian girl
Anderson, S. Poor white
Anderson-Dargatz, G. A recipe for bees
Atwood, M. Life before man
Auchincloss, L. Honorable men
Auchincloss, L. The stoic
Banville, J. Eclipse
Barnes, J. Love, etc.
Barth, J. The end of the road
Barthelme, F. The brothers
Barthelme, F. Elroy Nights
Basch, R. The passion of Reverend Nash
Bausch, R. Hello to the cannibals
Bausch, R. Violence
Beattie, A. Another you
Beattie, A. Chilly scenes of winter
Beattie, A. Falling in place
Beattie, A. My life, starring Dara Falcon
Beauvoir, S. d. The age of discretion
Beauvoir, S. d. The mandarins
Beauvoir, S. d. The monologue
Bellow, S. Herzog
Berg, E. The pull of the moon
Bergen, D. See the child
Berger, T. Best friends
Berger, T. Sneaky people
Berger, T. Vital parts
Berne, S. A perfect arrangement
Binchy, M. Tara Road
Bohjalian, C. A. The buffalo soldier
Boswell, R. Century's son
Bowles, P. The sheltering sky
Boyd, W. Brazzaville Beach
Bradford, B. T. Hold the dream
Bradford, B. T. A sudden change of heart
Breslin, J. Table money
Brontë, A. The tenant of Wildfell Hall
Brookner, A. Altered states
Brown, R. M. High hearts
Brown, R. Civil wars
Brown, R. Tender mercies
Buck, P. S. Pavilion of women
Bushnell, C. Lipstick jungle
Butler, R. O. They whisper
Cain, J. M. Mildred Pierce
Cain, J. M. The postman always rings twice
Campbell, B. M. Singing in the comeback choir
Carroll, J. Prince of peace
Casey, J. Spartina
Cather, W. A lost lady
Coe, J. The closed circle
Colette. Chance acquaintances
Colette. Claudine and Annie
Colette. The last of Chéri
Colwin, L. Family happiness
Cookson, C. The upstart
Coulter, C. Rosehaven
Cronin, A. J. The citadel
Cumyn, A. Losing it
Cunningham, M. The hours
Daley, R. Hands of a stranger
Dallas, S. The diary of Mattie Spenser
Dark, A. E. Think of England
Dawson, C. The mother-in-law diaries
De la Roche, M. Jalna
DeMille, N. The Gold Coast
Dickens, C. Hard times
Donleavy, J. P. The ginger man
Donovan, A. Buddha Da
Drabble, M. The needle's eye
Drabble, M. The realms of gold
Dreiser, T. Sister Carrie
Du Maurier, Dame D. The house on the strand
Durrell, L. Justine
Durrell, L. Mountolive
Eliot, G. Middlemarch
Elkin, S. The MacGuffin
Emmons, C. His mother's son
Ephron, N. Heartburn
Erdrich, L. Four souls
Erdrich, L. Tales of burning love
Fast, H. The immigrants
Fast, H. The outsider
Ferber, E. Giant
Fielding, J. See Jane run
Fitzgerald, F. S. The beautiful and damned
Fitzgerald, F. S. The Great Gatsby
Flaubert, G. Madame Bovary
Ford, F. M. No more parades
Fox, P. A servant's tale
French, M. The women's room
Fromm, P. As cool as I am
Galsworthy, J. The Forsyte saga
Galsworthy, J. The man of property
Galsworthy, J. Swan song
Galsworthy, J. The white monkey
García Márquez, G. Chronicle of a death foretold
Gardner, J. Mickelsson's ghost
Gibbons, K. Divining women
Gifford, B. Wyoming
Godden, R. The battle of the Villa Fiorita
Godwin, G. Evensong

MARRIAGE PROBLEMS—*Continued*
Smiley, J. The age of grief [novelette]
Smith, B. Joy in the morning
Smith, W. A. Hungry as the sea
Snow, C. P. Homecoming
Snyder, D. J. Night crossing
Solomon, N. Single wife
Sontag, S. The volcano lover
Spark, M. The finishing school
Spark, M. Reality and dreams
Spencer, S. A ship made of paper
Stead, C. The man who loved children
Steel, D. Journey
Steel, D. The kiss
Stegner, W. E. Angle of repose
Stirling, J. The workhouse girl
Stone, R. Bay of souls
Stubbs, J. Family games
Stubbs, J. Like we used to be
Styron, W. Lie down in darkness
Symons, J. Something like a love affair
Tanizaki, J. The Makioka sisters
Tax, M. Union Square
Thayer, N. My dearest friend
Thomas, R. Other people's marriages
Tilghman, C. Mason's retreat
Tolstoy, L., graf. Anna Karenina
Tolstoy, L., graf. The Kreutzer sonata
Tremain, R. The color
Trigiani, A. Big Cherry Holler
Trollope, A. The prime minister
Trollope, J. The best of friends
Trollope, J. Marrying the mistress
Trollope, J. The rector's wife
Trollope, J. A Spanish lover
Tyler, A. The accidental tourist
Tyler, A. The amateur marriage
Tyler, A. Earthly possessions
Tyler, A. Ladder of years
Tyler, A. Morgan's passing
Upadhyay, S. The guru of love
Updike, J. Rabbit redux
Updike, J. Rabbit, run
Vargas Llosa, M. The notebooks of Don Rigoberto
Vine, B. The chimney sweeper's boy
Waller, R. J. The bridges of Madison County
Watson, B. The heaven of Mercury
Watson, L. Orchard
Weber, K. The little women
Weldon, F. The life and loves of a she-devil
Wharton, E. The custom of the country
Wharton, E. Ethan Frome
Wharton, E. Madame de Treymes
Whitney, P. A. Amethyst dreams
Whitney, P. A. Poinciana
Whitney, P. A. Spindrift
Wiggs, S. The ocean between us
Wilhelm, K. The deepest water
Wilson, A. N. The vicar of sorrows
Wilson, J. A Palestine affair
Woiwode, L. Indian affairs
Woiwode, L. What I'm going to do, I think
Wolitzer, M. The wife
Wood, B. Vital signs
Woods, S. Imperfect strangers
Ye Zhaoyan. Nanjing 1937
Zuber, I. Salt

Marriages and infidelities. Oates, J. C.
The **married** man. White, E.
The **marrying** kind. Stirling, J.
Marrying off mother and other stories. Durrell, G. M.
Marrying the mistress. Trollope, J.

MARS (PLANET)
Barnes, J. The sky so big and black
Bova, B. Mars
Bova, B. Return to Mars
Bradbury, R. The Martian chronicles
Lewis, C. S. Out of the silent planet
Pohl, F. Man Plus
Pohl, F. Mars Plus
Robinson, K. S. Blue Mars
Robinson, K. S. Green Mars [novelette]
Robinson, K. S. The Martians
Robinson, K. S. Red Mars
Simmons, D. Ilium
Simmons, D. Olympos

Mars. Bova, B.
Mars Plus. Pohl, F.
Martha Peake. McGrath, P.
Martha Quest. Lessing, D. M.
In Lessing, D. M. Children of violence

MARTHA'S VINEYARD (MASS.)
Carter, S. L. The emperor of Ocean Park
Hoffman, A. Illumination night
West, D. The wedding

MARTIAL ARTS
Donohue, J. J. Sensei

The **Martian** chronicles. Bradbury, R.

MARTIANS
See also Interplanetary visitors; Mars (Planet)
Heinlein, R. A. Stranger in a strange land

The **Martians**. Robinson, K. S.
Martin Bauman. Leavitt, D.
Martin Chuzzlewit. Dickens, C.
Martin Dressler. Millhauser, S.
Martin Eden. London, J.

MARY I, QUEEN OF ENGLAND, 1516-1558
About
Harper, K. The Poyson garden
Lewis, H. W. I am Mary Tudor

MARY II, QUEEN OF GREAT BRITAIN, 1662-1694
About
Plaidy, J. William's wife

MARY, BLESSED VIRGIN, SAINT
About
Asch, S. Mary
Guterson, D. Our Lady of the Forest
Kirshenbaum, B. An almost perfect moment

MARY, QUEEN OF SCOTS, 1542-1587
About
George, M. Mary Queen of Scotland and the Isles
Plaidy, J. The captive Queen of Scots

Mary. Asch, S.
Mary, Mary. Parsons, J.
Mary Queen of Scotland and the Isles. George, M.
Mary Reilly. Martin, V.
Mary Roberts Rinehart's mystery book. Rinehart, M. R.
Mary Stewart's Merlin trilogy. Stewart, M.
MARY TUDOR *See* Mary I, Queen of England, 1516-1558
Marya. Oates, J. C.

MARYLAND
See also Chesapeake Bay (Md. and Va.)
Chappell, H. A whole world of trouble
Gaffney, P. Flight lessons
Michener, J. A. Chesapeake

17th century
Barth, J. The sot-weed factor

19th century
De Blasis, C. A season for Swans
De Blasis, C. Swan's chance

20th century
Amidon, S. The new city
Brown, R. M. Loose lips
Tilghman, C. Mason's retreat
Tyler, A. Searching for Caleb

Annapolis
Deutermann, P. T. Darkside
Martin, W. Annapolis

Baltimore
Auster, P. Timbuktu
Bell, M. S. Ten Indians
Tyler, A. The amateur marriage
Tyler, A. Back when we were grownups
Tyler, A. Celestial navigation
Tyler, A. The clock winder
Tyler, A. Dinner at the Homesick Restaurant
Tyler, A. Ladder of years
Tyler, A. Morgan's passing
Tyler, A. A patchwork planet
Tyler, A. Saint maybe

MILITARY AERONAUTICS—*Continued*
Coonts, S. Final flight
Coonts, S. Flight of the Intruder
Coonts, S. Fortunes of war
Coonts, S. The Intruders
Coonts, S. The minotaur
Heller, J. Catch-22
Malraux, A. Man's hope
Thomas, C. Firefox

MILITARY DESERTION
Frazier, C. Cold Mountain
Hemingway, E. A farewell to arms
O'Brien, T. Going after Cacciato

MILITARY EDUCATION
Conroy, P. The lords of discipline
Webb, J. H. A sense of honor

MILITARY HISTORY
See also Great Britain. Army

The **military** philosophers. Powell, A.
In Powell, A. A dance to the music of time

MILITARY SCHOOLS *See* Military education

MILITARY SERVICE, COMPULSORY *See* Draft

MILITARY TRAINING CAMPS
McCullers, C. Reflections in a golden eye

MILITIA MOVEMENTS
Burke, J. L. Bitterroot
Diehl, W. Reign in hell
Isaacs, S. Red, white and blue
Martini, S. P. Critical mass

Milk and honey. Kellerman, F.
Milk glass moon. Trigiani, A.
The **mill** on the Floss. Eliot, G.

MILLERS
Pearce, M. E. Cast a long shadow

The **miller's** dance. Graham, W.

MILLIONAIRES
See also Capitalists and financiers; Wealth
Bellow, S. Henderson the rain king
Binchy, M. Firefly summer
Fowles, J. The magus
Knowles, J. Indian summer
Korda, M. Worldly goods
Lemann, N. Malaise
Leonard, E. Split images
Vonnegut, K. God bless you, Mr. Rosewater

MILTON, JOHN, 1608-1674

About

West, P. Sporting with Amaryllis

Mind/reader. Freemantle, B.

MIND AND BODY
Darnton, J. Mind catcher
Lightman, A. P. The diagnosis

Mind catcher. Darnton, J.

MIND CONTROL *See* Brainwashing

Mind prey. Sandford, J.

MIND READING *See* Telepathy

Mindsword's story. See Saberhagen, F. The sixth book of lost swords: Mindsword's story

MINERS *See* Coal mines and mining; Copper mines and mining; Diamond mines and mining; Gold mines and mining; Mines and mining

MINES AND MINING
See also Coal mines and mining; Copper mines and mining; Diamond mines and mining; Gold mines and mining
Burke, J. L. Bitterroot
Stegner, W. E. Angle of repose

Miniatures. Labiner, N.

MINING TOWNS
Marion, S. Hollow ground

MINISTERS *See* Clergy

The **minister's** wooing. Stowe, H. B.
In Stowe, H. B. Uncle Tom's cabin: or, Life among the lowly; The minister's wooing; Oldtown folks p521-876

The **ministry** of fear. Greene, G.
also in Greene, G. 3: This gun for hire, The confidential agent, The ministry of fear

MINNEAPOLIS (MINN.) *See* Minnesota—Minneapolis

MINNESOTA
Hassler, J. The Staggerford flood
Johnson, W. The devil you know
Powers, J. F. Morte d'Urban

19th century

Moberg, V. The last letter home
Moberg, V. Unto a good land

20th century

Brenna, D. The altar of the body
Hassler, J. The dean's list
Hassler, J. Rookery blues
Hoag, T. Guilty as sin
Hoag, T. Night sins
Keillor, G. Lake Wobegon days
Keillor, G. Lake Wobegon summer 1956
Keillor, G. WLT
Lewis, S. Cass Timberlane
Lewis, S. Main Street [novelette]
Lewis, S. Main Street, the story of Carol Kennicott
Muske-Dukes, C. Life after death
O'Brien, T. In the Lake of the Woods
O'Brien, T. July, July
O'Brien, T. Tomcat in love

Farm life

See Farm life—Minnesota

Frontier and pioneer life

See Frontier and pioneer life—Minnesota

Minneapolis

Hoag, T. Dust to dust
Thayer, S. The weatherman
Tracy, P. J. Monkeewrench

St. Paul

Keillor, G. Love me

MINOR PLANETS *See* Asteroids

The **minority** report. Dick, P. K.
The **minotaur**. Coonts, S.
Mint julep murder. Hart, C. G.

MIRABEL FAMILY

About

Alvarez, J. In the time of the butterflies

Miracle cure. Palmer, M.
Miracle on 34th Street. Davies, V.

MIRACLES
Bozai, Á. To err is divine
Paretsky, S. Ghost country
Werfel, F. The song of Bernadette

MIRANDA, FRANCISCO DE, 1750-1816

About

Naipaul, V. S. A way in the world

Miranda's vines. Kafka, K.
The **mirror** crack'd. Christie, A.
The **mirror** crack'd from side to side. See Christie, A. The mirror crack'd
Mirror dance. Bujold, L. M.
The **misadventures** of John Nicholson. Stevenson, R. L.
In Stevenson, R. L. The complete short stories p165-222

MISCEGENATION
See also Interracial marriage
Brown, R. M. Southern discomfort
Chase-Riboud, B. The President's daughter
Chase-Riboud, B. Sally Hemings
Paton, A. Too late the phalarope
Randall, A. The wind done gone
Tademy, L. Cane River

Mischief. McBain, E.
Mischief in Maggody. Hess, J.
Les **misérables**. Hugo, V.

MISERS
Balzac, H. d. Eugénie Grandet
Dickens, C. A Christmas carol
Eliot, G. Silas Marner

Misery. King, S.
Misery loves Maggody. Hess, J.
Miss Julia throws a wedding. Ross, A. B.

MISSISSIPPI—Jackson—*Continued*
Gilchrist, E. The cabal [novelette]
MISSISSIPPI RIVER
Ferber, E. Show boat
Smith, L. The last girls
Twain, M. The adventures of Huckleberry Finn
Twain, M. The adventures of Tom Sawyer
Twain, M. Mississippi writings
Welty, E. The robber bridegroom
Mississippi writings. Twain, M.
MISSOURI
Twain, M. The adventures of Tom Sawyer
Twain, M. Pudd'nhead Wilson
Woodrell, D. Give us a kiss
19th century
Jiles, P. Enemy women
20th century
Flagg, F. Standing in the rainbow
Flagg, F. Welcome to the world, baby girl!
Garlock, D. The edge of town
Spencer, L. Small town girl
Woodrell, D. The death of sweet mister
Farm life
See Farm life—Missouri
Kansas City
Connell, E. S. Mr. Bridge
Connell, E. S. Mrs. Bridge
Terrell, W. The huntsman
Saint Louis
Shange, N. Betsey Brown
MISSOURI RIVER
McMurtry, L. Sin killer
Poe, E. A. The journal of Julius Rodman
Wheeler, R. S. Downriver
A **mist** of prophecies. Saylor, S.
MISTAKEN IDENTITY
See also Impersonations
Collins, W. The woman in white
Delany, S. R. Time considered as a helix of semi-precious stones
Henry, A. Learning to fly
Stewart, M. The ivy tree
Mistaken identity. Scottoline, L.
Mister Roberts. Heggen, T.
Mistral's daughter. Krantz, J.
The **mistress** of Alderley. Barnard, R.
Mistress of dragons. Weis, M.
The **mistress** of Husaby. Undset, S.
In Undset, S. Kristin Lavransdatter
Mistress of Mellyn. Holt, V.
Mistress of the empire. Feist, R. E.
Mistress of the pearl. Lustbader, E. V.
MISTRESSES
Barnard, R. The mistress of Alderley
Cameron, P. The city of your final destination
Faber, M. The crimson petal and the white
Gould, J. The best is yet to come
King, R. Domino
Leavitt, D. The body of Jonah Boyd
Martin, V. Property
Trollope, J. Marrying the mistress
The **mists** of Avalon. Bradley, M. Z.
MITCHELL, MARGARET, 1900-1949
Parodies, imitations, etc.
Randall, A. The wind done gone
Mitigating circumstances. Rosenberg, N. T.
Mitsou. Colette
In Colette. Six novels p339-410
MIXED BLOODS
See also Eurasians; Mulattoes
Erdrich, L. The antelope wife
Erdrich, L. The Beet Queen
Humphreys, J. Nowhere else on earth
Jennings, G. Aztec blood
Powers, R. The time of our singing
MOBILE (ALA.) *See* Alabama—Mobile
Moby-Dick; or, The whale. Melville, H.
also in Melville, H. Redburn, his first voyage; White-jacket, or, The world in a man-of-war; Moby-Dick, or, The whale
The **mocking** program. Foster, A. D.
The **model**. Oates, J. C.
In Oates, J. C. Haunted p99-144
MODELS, ARTISTS' *See* Artists' models
MODELS, FASHION *See* Fashion models
A **modern** comedy. Galsworthy, J.
A **modern** instance. Howells, W. D.
In Howells, W. D. Novels, 1875-1886
MOHAMMEDANISM *See* Islam
MOHAMMEDANS *See* Muslims
MOHAWK VALLEY (N.Y.)
Edmonds, W. D. Drums along the Mohawk
MOHEGAN INDIANS
Cooper, J. F. The last of the Mohicans
MOHICAN INDIANS *See* Mohegan Indians
MOLINA, RAFAEL LEÓNIDAS TRUJILLO *See* Trujillo Molina, Rafael Leónidas, 1891-1961
Moll Flanders. Defoe, D.
Molloy. Beckett, S.
In Beckett, S. Molloy, Malone dies, The unnamable
Molloy, Malone dies, The unnamable. Beckett, S.
Molly Morgan. Steinbeck, J.
In Steinbeck, J. The portable Steinbeck
Moment in Peking. Lin Yutang
A **moment** in time. Gould, J.
Moment of truth. Scottoline, L.
A **moment** on the edge. Entered in Part I under title
The **moment** she was gone. Hunter, E.
Mona in the promised land. Jen, G.
MONACO
Mayle, P. Anything considered
MONASTERIES *See* Monasticism and religious orders
MONASTICISM AND RELIGIOUS ORDERS
See also Abbeys; Convent life; Jesuits; Monks
Gulik, R. H. v. The haunted monastery
Miller, W. M. A canticle for Leibowitz
Monday mourning. Reichs, K. J.
Monday the rabbi took off. Kemelman, H.
Mondo desperado. McCabe, P.
MONET, CLAUDE, 1840-1926
About
Jakeman, J. In the Kingdom of mists
MONEY
See also Finance
Amidon, S. Human capital
Grippando, J. Found money
Grisham, J. The summons
Thomas, M. M. Black money
Money for nothing. Westlake, D. E.
Money from home. Runyon, D.
In Runyon, D. Guys and dolls p167-337
Money wanders. Dezenhall, E.
MONEYLENDERS
See also Pawnbrokers
Dickens, C. Nicholas Nickleby
Pérez Galdós, B. Torquemada
MONGOLS
Costain, T. B. The black rose
Mongoose, R.I.P. Buckley, W. F.
The **monk**. Lewis, M. G.
Monkeewrench. Tracy, P. J.
Monkey hunting. García, C.
Monkey planet. See Boulle, P. Planet of the Apes
Monkey wrench. Cody, L.
MONKEYS
Chandra, V. Red earth and pouring rain
Monkeys. Minot, S.
The **monkey's** wrench. Levi, P.
MONKS
See also Monasticism and religious orders
Eco, U. The name of the rose
Hesse, H. Narcissus and Goldmund
Kadare, I. The three-arched bridge

MOSES (BIBLICAL FIGURE)
About
Asch, S. Moses
Tarr, J. Pillar of fire
Moses. Asch, S.
Moses, man of the mountain. Hurston, Z. N.
In Hurston, Z. N. Novels and stories p335-595
The **Mosquito** Coast. Theroux, P.
Mosses from an old manse. Hawthorne, N.
In Hawthorne, N. Tales and sketches, including Twice-told tales, Mosses from an old manse, and The snow-image; A wonder book for girls and boys; Tanglewood tales for girls and boys, being a second Wonder book
Mostly harmless. Adams, D.
The **Mote** in God's Eye. Niven, L.
The **moth** diaries. Klein, R.
Mother Aegypt and other stories. Baker, K.
A **mother** and two daughters. Godwin, G.
Mother earth, father sky. Harrison, S.
The **mother-in-law** diaries. Dawson, C.
Mother of kings. Anderson, P.
Mother of pearl. Haynes, M.
MOTHERHOOD *See* Mothers
Motherhood made a man out of me. Karbo, K.
MotherKind. Phillips, J. A.
Motherless Brooklyn. Lethem, J.
MOTHERS
See also Mothers and daughters; Mothers and sons; Mothers-in-law; Stepmothers
Arnow, H. L. S. The dollmaker
Bawden, N. Family money
Colwin, L. A big storm knocked it over
Colwin, L. Goodbye without leaving
Eden, D. The Salamanca drum
Goudge, E. Thorns of truth
Kincaid, N. Verbena
Moses, K. Wintering
Oates, J. C. Them
Pilcher, R. The shell seekers
Sheldon, S. Master of the game
Smith, L. Family linen
Steel, D. The house on Hope Street
Weiner, J. Little earthquakes
MOTHERS AND DAUGHTERS
See also Parent and child
Abrahams, P. Their wildest dreams
Adams, A. Caroline's daughters
Alther, L. Kinflicks
Alvarez, J. In the name of Salomé
Ansa, T. M. You know better
Anshaw, C. Lucky in the corner
Atkinson, K. Emotionally weird
Bacon, C. There is room for you
Badami, A. R. Tamarind woman
Bainbridge, B. According to Queeney
Baldacci, D. The winner
Battle, L. Bed & breakfast
Battle, L. Southern women
Bausch, R. The Gypsy Man
Belfer, L. City of light
Berg, E. Range of motion
Berg, E. What we keep
Bialosky, J. House under snow
Binchy, M. The glass lake
Blatty, W. P. The exorcist
Bohjalian, C. A. Midwives
Bosse, M. J. Fire in heaven
Bradford, B. T. Power of a woman
Bradford, B. T. A sudden change of heart
Bradford, B. T. Where you belong
Brenna, D. The altar of the body
Brookner, A. The Bay of Angels
Brookner, A. Fraud
Brookner, A. Incidents in the Rue Laugier
Brown, R. Half a heart
Cain, J. M. Mildred Pierce
Campbell, B. M. 72 hour hold
Campbell, B. M. What you owe me
Carr, P. Daughters of England
Cleage, P. Babylon sisters
Cline, R. What to keep
Coetzee, J. M. Age of iron
Cookson, C. The black velvet gown
Delinsky, B. For my daughters
Didion, J. A book of common prayer
Doerr, H. Consider this, señora
Dorris, M. A yellow raft in blue water
Dunmore, H. With your crooked heart
Erdrich, L. The painted drum
Evans, N. The horse whisperer
Fitch, J. White oleander
Flagg, F. Welcome to the world, baby girl!
Fowler, C. M. Before women had wings
Fredriksson, M. Hanna's daughters
French, M. Her mother's daughter
Gaffney, P. Circle of three
García, C. Dreaming in Cuban
Gibbons, K. Charms for the easy life
Gibbons, K. Sights unseen
Godwin, G. A mother and two daughters
Gordon, M. Pearl
Goudge, E. Garden of lies
Goudge, E. Stranger in paradise
Goudge, E. Such devoted sisters
Goudge, E. Trail of secrets
Griesemer, J. Signal & noise
Gutcheon, B. R. Five fortunes
Gutcheon, B. R. Saying grace
Harris, J. Chocolat
Harris, J. Five quarters of the orange
Hearon, S. Ella in bloom
Hemans, D. River woman
Henley, P. In the river sweet
Hoffman, A. Here on Earth
Hoffman, A. The probable future
Hoffman, E. The secret
Jakes, J. Savannah; or, A gift for Mr. Lincoln
James, P. D. Innocent blood
Johnson, S. The sailmaker's daughter
Joyce, G. The limits of enchantment
Karbo, K. Motherhood made a man out of me
Keyes, M. The other side of the story
Kidd, S. M. The mermaid chair
Kincaid, J. Annie John
Kincaid, J. Autobiography of my mother
Kingsolver, B. Pigs in heaven
Kirshenbaum, B. An almost perfect moment
Krantz, J. Mistral's daughter
Lamott, A. Blue shoe
Laskas, G. M. The midwife's tale
Leroy, M. Postcards from Berlin
Lively, P. Heat wave
Lively, P. Passing on
Manicka, R. The rice mother
Marshall, P. Daughters
Maxwell, R. The secret diary of Anne Boleyn
McMurtry, L. Buffalo girls
McMurtry, L. The desert rose
McMurtry, L. Terms of endearment
Meyer, C. Brown eyes blue
Miller, S. The good mother
Moravia, A. Two women
Mukherjee, B. Leave it to me
Oates, J. C. Marya
Oates, J. C. Missing mom
Oates, J. C. Rape
Ozick, C. Rosa
Parsons, J. Mary, Mary
Phillips, J. A. MotherKind
Piercy, M. Three women
Plain, B. Blessings
Powell, S. The Mushroom Man
Quindlen, A. Object lessons
Quindlen, A. One true thing
Rendell, R. The crocodile bird
Rhys, J. After leaving Mr. Mackenzie
Rice, L. Dance with me
Rice, L. Home fires
Rice, L. Summer light
Richler, N. Your mouth is lovely
Robards, K. Ghost moon
Roiphe, A. R. Lovingkindness
Rosenberg, N. T. Buried evidence
Rosenberg, N. T. Mitigating circumstances
Ross-Macdonald, M. Tamsin Harte
Rossner, J. Perfidia
Schwarz, C. Drowning Ruth

MOTION PICTURES—*Continued*
Kalfus, K. The commissariat of enlightenment
Kesey, K. Sailor song
Knode, H. The ticket out
Lankford, T. Earthquake weather
Leonard, E. Get Shorty
Oates, J. C. Blonde
Percy, W. The moviegoer
Raymond, J. The half-life
Schulberg, B. What makes Sammy run?
Shaw, I. Evening in Byzantium
Sheehan, A. The anxiety of everyday objects
Updike, J. In the beauty of the lilies
Vidal, G. Hollywood
Vidal, G. Myra Breckinridge {and} Myron
West, N. The day of the locust
Motion to suppress. O'Shaughnessy, P.
MOTOR BUSES *See* Buses
Motor City blue. Estleman, L. D.
Motown. Estleman, L. D.
The **mound**. Lovecraft, H. P.
In Lovecraft, H. P. The horror in the museum, and other revisions p96-163
MOUND BUILDERS
Gear, K. O. People of the lakes
Gear, K. O. People of the lightning
Gear, W. M. People of the river
Gear, W. M. People of the sea
MOUNTAIN CLIMBING *See* Mountaineering
MOUNTAIN LIFE
House, S. A parchment of leaves
Woodrell, D. Give us a kiss

Southern States

Arnow, H. L. S. The dollmaker
Bausch, R. The Gypsy Man
Caldwell, E. God's little acre
Hamner, E. The homecoming
Hamner, E. Spencer's Mountain
Marshall, C. Christy
Morgan, R. This rock
Smith, L. Fair and tender ladies
Smith, L. Oral history
Mountain man. Fisher, V.
Mountain time. Doig, I.
Mountain windsong. Conley, R. J.
MOUNTAINEERING
Mawer, S. The fall
Robinson, K. S. Green Mars [novelette]
Trevanian. The Eiger sanction
MOUNTAINS
See also Adirondack Mountains (N.Y.); Andes; Appalachian Mountains; Catskill Mountains (N.Y.); Himalaya Mountains; Sierra Madre Mountains (Mexico); Volcanoes
The **mountains** of Majipoor. Silverberg, R.
Mountolive. Durrell, L.
also in Durrell, L. The Alexandria quartet: Justine; Balthazar; Mountolive [and] Clea p391-652
Mourn not your dead. Crombie, D.
MOURNING *See* Bereavement
MOURNING CUSTOMS *See* Funeral rites and ceremonies
The **mouse** that roared. Wibberley, L.
The **mousetrap**. See Christie, A. Three blind mice
The **moviegoer**. Percy, W.
MOVING (HOUSEHOLD GOODS)
Paul, J. A girl, in parts
MOVING PICTURE INDUSTRY *See* Motion pictures
MOVING PICTURES *See* Motion pictures
The **moving** target. Macdonald, R.
In Macdonald, R. Archer in Hollywood p3-169
Moving the mountain. Gilman, C. P.
In Gilman, C. P. The Charlotte Perkins Gilman reader
In Gilman, C. P. Charlotte Perkins Gilman's Utopian novels p37-149
Mr. & Mrs. Bo Jo Jones. Head, A.
Mr. Bedford. Godwin, G.
In Godwin, G. Mr. Bedford and the muses p1-104
Mr. Bedford and the muses. Godwin, G.
Mr. Blandings builds his dream house. Hodgins, E.
Mr. Bridge. Connell, E. S.
Mr. Darwin's shooter. McDonald, R.
Mr. Majestyk. Leonard, E.
In Leonard, E. Elmore Leonard's Dutch treat: 3 novels
Mr. Mee. Crumey, A.
Mr. Midshipman Hornblower. Forester, C. S.
Mr. Norris changes trains. See Isherwood, C. The last of Mr. Norris
Mr. Palomar. Calvino, I.
Mr. Paradise. Leonard, E.
Mr. Parker Pyne, detective. Christie, A.
Mr. Potter. Kincaid, J.
Mr. Sammler's planet. Bellow, S.
Mr. Wroe's virgins. Rogers, J.
Mr. X. Straub, P.
Mrs. 'Arris goes to Paris. Gallico, P.
Mrs. Bridge. Connell, E. S.
Mrs. Dalloway. Woolf, V.
Mrs. de Winter. Hill, S.
Mrs. God. Straub, P.
In Straub, P. Houses without doors p223-352
Mrs. Kimble. Haigh, J.
Mrs. McGinty's dead. Christie, A.
Mrs. Mike. Freedman, B.
Mrs. Miniver. Struther, J.
Mrs. Palfrey at the Claremont. Taylor, E.
Mrs. Pargeter's package. Brett, S.
Mrs. Pargeter's plot. Brett, S.
Mrs. Pargeter's point of honour. Brett, S.
Mrs. Pargeter's pound of flesh. Brett, S.
Mrs. Parkington. Bromfield, L.
Mrs. Pollifax and the Golden Triangle. Gilman, D.
Mrs. Pollifax and the Hong Kong Buddha. Gilman, D.
Mrs. Pollifax and the whirling dervish. Gilman, D.
Mrs. Pollifax, innocent tourist. Gilman, D.
Mrs. Pollifax on safari. Gilman, D.
Mrs. Pollifax pursued. Gilman, D.
Mrs. Pringle. Read, Miss
Mrs. Ted Bliss. Elkin, S.
Mrs. Washington and Horowitz, too. Denker, H.
The **mugger**. McBain, E.
MULATTOES
Brown, R. Half a heart
Cather, W. Sapphira and the slave girl
Chase-Riboud, B. The President's daughter
McCaig, D. Jacob's ladder
Mda, Z. The Madonna of Excelsior
Rice, A. The Feast of All Saints
Walker, M. Jubilee
Warren, R. P. Band of angels
Youmans, M. The wolf pit
The **Mulberry** empire. Hensher, P.
MULTIPLE PERSONALITY
See also Dual personality; Personality disorders
Clark, M. H. All around the town
MULTIPLE SCLEROSIS
Coupland, D. Eleanor Rigby
Price, R. The good priest's son
A **multitude** of sins. Ford, R.
The **mummers'** curse. Roberts, G.
The **mummy** case. Peters, E.
MUNITIONS
Coulter, C. Impulse
Smith, W. A. Cry wolf
Murder and the First Lady. Roosevelt, E.
Murder at Ford's Theatre. Truman, M.
Murder at midnight. Roosevelt, E.
Murder at Monticello. Langton, J.
Murder at Monticello; or, Old sins. Brown, R. M.
Murder at the cat show. Babson, M.
Murder at the feast of rejoicing. Robinson, L. S.
Murder at the Gardner. Langton, J.
Murder at the God's gate. Robinson, L. S.
Murder at the Library of Congress. Truman, M.
Murder at the National Cathedral. Truman, M.
Murder at the old vicarage. McGown, J.
Murder at the palace. Roosevelt, E.
Murder at the Savoy. Sjöwall, M.
The **murder** at the vicarage. Christie, A.
Murder at the Watergate. Truman, M.
Murder being once done. Rendell, R.
The **murder** book. Kellerman, J.

MURDER STORIES—*Continued*
Ellis, D. Life sentence
Ellroy, J. The black dahlia
Ellroy, J. Blood on the moon
Estleman, L. D. Edsel
Estleman, L. D. Jitterbug
Faber, M. The hundred and ninety-nine steps
Fairstein, L. The bone vault
Fairstein, L. Cold hit
Fairstein, L. Entombed
Fairstein, L. Final jeopardy
Fairstein, L. Likely to die
Fast, H. Greenwich
Fast, H. Redemption
Faulkner, W. Requiem for a nun
Faulkner, W. Sanctuary
Feather, J. The widow's kiss
Ferrigno, R. The Horse Latitudes
Field, R. All this, and heaven too
Fielding, J. Don't cry now
Finder, J. Company man
Folsom, A. R. The day after tomorrow
Foster, A. D. The mocking program
Freemantle, B. The button man
French, A. Billy
French, N. Beneath the skin
Friedman, P. Inadmissable evidence
Friedman, P. Reasonable doubt
Fyfield, F. Undercurrents
Gaines, E. J. The gathering of old men
García Márquez, G. Chronicle of a death foretold
García Márquez, G. The incredible and sad tale of innocent Eréndira and her heartless grandmother
Gear, K. O. The summoning God
Gear, W. M. Raising Abel
Geary, J. M. Spiral
Gerritsen, T. The apprentice
Gerritsen, T. Body double
Gerritsen, T. The sinner
Goddard, R. Beyond recall
Goddard, R. Into the blue
Gordimer, N. The house gun
Goudge, E. One last dance
Graham, W. Stephanie
Greene, G. Brighton rock
Griffin, W. E. B. Final justice
Griffin, W. E. B. The murderers
Grimes, M. Foul matter
Grippando, J. Hear no evil
Grippando, J. The informant
Grisham, J. A painted house
Grisham, J. A time to kill
Gross, C. Scholarium
Gruber, M. Valley of bones
Guest, J. Killing time in St. Cloud
Guest, J. The tarnished eye
Guilfoile, K. Cast of shadows
Guterson, D. Snow falling on cedars
Haddon, M. The curious incident of the dog in the night-time
Hambly, B. A free man of color
Hambly, B. Graveyard dust
Harris, R. Fatherland
Harris, T. Red Dragon
Harris, T. The silence of the lambs
Harrison, C. The Havana room
Harstad, D. Code sixty-one
Hart, C. G. Letter from home
Hewson, D. Lucifer's shadow
Heyer, G. Penhallow
Hiaasen, C. Basket case
Higgins, G. V. The agent
Higgins, G. V. The Mandeville talent
Highsmith, P. Ripley under ground
Highsmith, P. Ripley's game
Hill, R. Dream of darkness
Hirshberg, G. The Snowman's children
Hoag, T. Dust to dust
Hoag, T. Kill the messenger
Høeg, P. Smilla's sense of snow
Hoffman, A. Blue diary
Hoffman, A. The probable future
Hoffman, A. The river king
Hoffman, A. Turtle Moon
Hoffman, J. Retribution
Hoffman, W. Wild thorn
Holden, C. The jazz bird
Holt, V. The black opal
Holt, V. The Judas kiss
Hooper, K. Finding Laura
Hunter, E. Candyland
Hunter, E. Lizzie
Hunter, S. Dirty white boys
Iles, G. Mortal fear
Isaacs, S. After all these years
Isaacs, S. Lily White
Jakeman, J. In the Kingdom of mists
Johansen, I. And then you die—
Johansen, I. Blind alley
Johansen, I. The face of deception
Johansen, I. The killing game
Kanon, J. Los Alamos
Kasischke, L. The life before her eyes
Katzenbach, J. Hart's war
Katzenbach, J. Just cause
Katzenbach, J. State of mind
Kay, T. The runaway
Kaye, M. M. Death in Berlin
Kelman, J. Summer of storms
Kennedy, D. The big picture
Kim, S. The interpreter
King, S. Dolores Claiborne
King, S. Misery
King, S. Rage
Knode, H. The ticket out
Koontz, D. R. From the corner of his eye
Koontz, D. R. Intensity
Koontz, D. R. Velocity
Lankford, T. Earthquake weather
Lansdale, J. R. The bottoms
Lansdale, J. R. A fine dark line
Lansdale, J. R. Sunset and sawdust
Lawrence, M. K. The burning bride
Lawrence, M. K. Hearts and bones
Le Carré, J. The constant gardener
Lehane, D. Mystic river
Leonard, E. Split images
Lescroart, J. T. The 13th juror
Lescroart, J. T. The first law
Lescroart, J. T. Guilt
Lescroart, J. T. Hard evidence
Lescroart, J. T. The hearing
Lescroart, J. T. The mercy rule
Lescroart, J. T. Nothing but the truth
Lescroart, J. T. The oath
Lescroart, J. T. The second chair
Letts, B. Shoot the moon
Levin, I. A kiss before dying
Lewis, J. The king is dead
Lindsey, D. L. An absence of light
Lindsey, D. L. The color of night
Lovesey, P. On the edge
Lowell, E. Die in plain sight
Ludlum, R. The Sigma protocol
Lustbader, E. V. Black Blade
Lustbader, E. V. Floating city
Lutz, J. Dancing with the dead
Lutz, J. Final seconds
MacLean, A. Night without end
Mailer, N. The executioner's song
Mailer, N. Tough guys don't dance
March, W. The bad seed
Margolin, P. After dark
Margolin, P. The burning man
Margolin, P. The undertaker's widow
Martini, S. P. The attorney
Martini, S. P. The judge
Martini, S. P. Prime witness
Martini, S. P. Undue influence
Matthiessen, P. Bone by bone
Matthiessen, P. Killing Mister Watson
Matthiessen, P. Lost Man's River
McCabe, P. The butcher boy
McCammon, R. R. Boy's life
McCorkle, J. Carolina moon
McCrumb, S. The hangman's beautiful daughter
McCrumb, S. If ever I return, pretty Peggy-O
McDermid, V. The distant echo
McEwan, I. The innocent

MURDER STORIES—*Continued*
Traver, R. Anatomy of a murder
Truscott, L. K. Heart of war
Turow, S. The laws of our fathers
Turow, S. Reversible errors
Uhnak, D. The Ryer Avenue story
Uhnak, D. Victims
Unsworth, B. Morality play
Unsworth, B. Stone virgin
Vine, B. Anna's book
Vine, B. No night is too long
Walters, M. The breaker
Walters, M. The dark room
Walters, M. The sculptress
Walters, M. The shape of snakes
Wambaugh, J. Floaters
Ward, L. Outside valentine
Warren, R. P. World enough and time
Welsh, L. The cutting room
Welty, E. The Ponder heart
West, M. L. Masterclass
West, P. The women of Whitechapel and Jack the Ripper
Westlake, D. E. The hook
Whitney, P. A. Columbella
Whitney, P. A. Domino
Whitney, P. A. The singing stones
Wilhelm, K. Death qualified
Wilhelm, K. The deepest water
Wilhelm, K. Defense for the devil
Wilhelm, K. Desperate measures
Wilhelm, K. Malice prepense
Wilhelm, K. No defense
Wilson, F. P. Implant
Wilson, R. The blind man of Seville
Wiltse, D. Bone deep
Woods, S. Chiefs
Woods, S. Choke
Woods, S. Dead in the water
Woods, S. Dirt
Woods, S. Grass roots
Woods, S. Imperfect strangers
Woods, S. L.A. dead
Woods, S. Orchid Beach
Woods, S. Palindrome
Woods, S. Santa Fe rules
Woods, S. Worst fears realized
Wright, A. M. Disciples
Wright, R. Henderson's spear
Yancey, R. A burning in Homeland
Zimler, R. The last kabbalist of Lisbon

Murder takes a break. Crider, B.

MURDER TRIALS *See* Trials

Murder unprompted. Brett, S.

Murder walks the plank. Hart, C. G.

Murder with mirrors. Christie, A.

MURDERERS
See also Murder stories
Baldacci, D. The winner
Barker, P. Border crossing
Brown, S. Charade
Brown, S. Chill factor
Campbell, R. Silent children
Clark, M. H. Nighttime is my time
De Blasis, C. A season for Swans
Deaver, J. The devil's teardrop
Dexter, P. The paperboy
Fielding, J. Missing pieces
Fitch, J. White oleander
Freemantle, B. Mind/reader
Fyfield, F. Blind date
Gerritsen, T. The surgeon
Grisham, J. The last juror
Hailey, A. Detective
Harris, T. Hannibal
Irving, J. A son of the circus
Jance, J. A. Kiss of the bees
Katzenbach, J. The madman's tale
Kerley, J. The hundredth man
King, S. Black house
Lehane, D. Shutter Island
Lindsay, J. P. Darkly dreaming Dexter
McCrumb, S. The ballad of Frankie Silver
Mina, D. Deception
Murakami, R. In the miso soup
O'Brien, E. In the forest
O'Connell, C. Judas child
Parker, T. J. The blue hour
Parker, T. J. Where serpents lie
Piercy, M. The longings of women
Richler, N. Your mouth is lovely
Scottoline, L. Rough justice
Spark, M. Aiding and abetting
Trevor, W. Felicia's journey
Westlake, D. E. The ax

The **murderers**. Griffin, W. E. B.

Murder@maggody.com. Hess, J.

The **murders** in the Rue Morgue. Poe, E. A.
In Poe, E. A. The purloined letter [and] The murders in the Rue Morgue p1-55

The **murders** of Richard III. Peters, E.

A **Muriel** Spark trio. Spark, M.

Murphy. Beckett, S.

Murther & walking spirits. Davies, R.

Muscle memory. Tapply, W. G.

Muse of art. Anthony, P.

The **museum** guard. Norman, H.

MUSEUM OF NATURAL HISTORY (NEW YORK, N.Y.)
See American Museum of Natural History

The **Mushroom** Man. Powell, S.

MUSIC
Mann, T. Tristan
Powers, R. The time of our singing

Music & silence. Tremain, R.

MUSIC HALL ENTERTAINERS *See* Entertainers

Music-hall sidelights. Colette
In Colette. Six novels p237-337

MUSIC HALLS (VARIETY THEATERS, CABARETS, ETC.)
See also Vaudeville

The **Music** Lesson. Weber, K.

The **music** lovers. Valin, J.

Music of a life. Makine, A.

The **music** of the spheres. Redfern, E.

The **music** room. McFarland, D.

MUSIC TEACHERS
Doig, I. Prairie nocturne
Hernández, F. Around the time of Clemente Colling
Powell, D. Come back to Sorrento

MUSICIANS
See also Accordionists; Conductors (Music); Drummers; Flutists; Guitarists; Pianists; Saxophonists; Trumpet players; Violinists
Baldwin, J. Another country
Baldwin, J. Just above my head
Balzac, H. d. Cousin Pons
Cather, W. Lucy Gayheart
Davies, R. The lyre of Orpheus
Edgerton, C. Killer diller
Flagg, F. Standing in the rainbow
Hassler, J. Rookery blues
Hesse, H. Gertrude
Hewson, D. Lucifer's shadow
Hijuelos, O. The Mambo Kings play songs of love
Hornby, N. High fidelity
L'Engle, M. A severed wasp
L'Engle, M. The small rain
McGuane, T. Panama
Mendelson, C. Morningside Heights
Mosley, W. RL's dream
Sarton, M. Anger
Seth, V. An equal music
Smith, L. The devil's dream
Tremain, R. Music & silence
Turner, F. W. 1929
Tyler, A. Searching for Caleb
Tyler, A. A slipping-down life
West, Dame R. Cousin Rosamund

MUSLIMS
See also Islam
Caputo, P. Acts of faith
De Bernieres, L. Birds without wings
Pamuk, O. My name is Red
Seth, V. A suitable boy
Tristram, C. After

MUSTAFA KEMAL *See* Atatürk, Kemal, 1881-1938

MYSTERY AND DETECTIVE STORIES—Egypt—*Continued*
Peters, E. Night train to Memphis
Peters, E. Seeing a large cat
Peters, E. The snake, the crocodile, and the dog
Robinson, L. S. Murder at the feast of rejoicing
Robinson, L. S. Murder at the God's gate

England

Aird, C. After effects
Allingham, M. Crime and Mr. Campion
Allingham, M. Three cases for Mr. Campion
Atherton, N. Aunt Dimity, detective
Atherton, N. Aunt Dimity digs in
Atkinson, K. Case histories
Aubert, R. The ferryman will be there
Babson, M. Canapes for the kitties
Babson, M. The company of cats
Babson, M. Murder at the cat show
Bannister, J. No birds sing
Bannister, J. True witness
Barnard, R. The bad samaritan
Barnard, R. The bones in the attic
Barnard, R. The case of the missing Brontë
Barnard, R. The corpse at the Haworth Tandoori
Barnard, R. Corpse in a gilded cage
Barnard, R. Death and the chaste apprentice
Barnard, R. Death by sheer torture
Barnard, R. Death of a literary widow
Barnard, R. Death of a salesperson, and other untimely exits
Barnard, R. A fatal attachment
Barnard, R. Fête fatale
Barnard, R. The graveyard position
Barnard, R. A hovering of vultures
Barnard, R. The masters of the house
Barnard, R. No place of safety
Barnard, R. Out of the blackout
Barnard, R. A scandal in Belgravia
Barnard, R. The skeleton in the grass
Barnard, R. Unholy dying
Beaton, M. C. Agatha Raisin and the day the floods came
Beaton, M. C. Agatha Raisin and the fairies of Fryfam
Beaton, M. C. Agatha Raisin and the quiche of death
Beaton, M. C. Agatha Raisin and the witch of Wyckhadden
Beaton, M. C. Agatha Raisin and the wizard of Evesham
Beaton, M. C. Death of a celebrity
Brett, S. The body on the beach
Brett, S. Dead room farce
Brett, S. The dead side of the mike
Brett, S. Death on the Downs
Brett, S. Mrs. Pargeter's plot
Brett, S. Mrs. Pargeter's point of honour
Brett, S. Mrs. Pargeter's pound of flesh
Brett, S. Murder in the museum
Brett, S. Murder unprompted
Brett, S. A reconstructed corpse
Brett, S. The torso in the town
Brett, S. What bloody man is that?
Buckley, F. To shield the Queen
Burley, W. J. Wycliffe and the quiet virgin
Burley, W. J. Wycliffe and the redhead
Butler, G. Coffin knows the answer
Butler, G. A dark coffin
Butler, G. Death lives next door
Butler, G. A double Coffin
Cannell, D. Bridesmaids revisited
Cannell, D. God save the Queen!
Cannell, D. How to murder your mother-in-law
Cannell, D. The spring cleaning murders
Cannell, D. The thin woman
Cannell, D. The trouble with Harriet
Cannell, D. The widows club
Chabon, M. The final solution
Charles, K. A dead man out of mind
Chesney, M. Snobbery with violence
Chesterton, G. K. Father Brown mystery stories
Chesterton, G. K. The Father Brown omnibus
Chesterton, G. K. The innocence of Father Brown
Christie, A. The A.B.C. murders
Christie, A. And then there were none
Christie, A. At Bertram's Hotel
Christie, A. The body in the library
Christie, A. By the pricking of my thumbs
Christie, A. Curtain
Christie, A. Endless night
Christie, A. Evil under the sun
Christie, A. The harlequin tea set and other stories
Christie, A. Hercule Poirot's casebook
Christie, A. The Hollow
Christie, A. The mirror crack'd
Christie, A. Miss Marple: the complete short stories
Christie, A. Mr. Parker Pyne, detective
Christie, A. Mrs. McGinty's dead
Christie, A. The murder at the vicarage
Christie, A. A murder is announced
Christie, A. The murder of Roger Ackroyd
Christie, A. Murder with mirrors
Christie, A. The mysterious affair at Styles
Christie, A. The mystery of the blue train
Christie, A. N or M!
Christie, A. The pale horse
Christie, A. A pocket full of rye
Christie, A. Sad cypress
Christie, A. The secret of chimneys
Christie, A. Sleeping murder
Christie, A. Thirteen at dinner
Christie, A. Three blind mice and other stories
Christie, A. Towards zero
Christie, A. The witness for the prosecution and other stories
Cody, L. Bucket nut
Cody, L. Head case
Cody, L. Monkey wrench
Collins, W. The moonstone
Collins, W. The woman in white
Conrad, J. Secret agent
Cornwell, B. Gallows thief
Crombie, D. And justice there is none
Crombie, D. Kissed a sad goodbye
Crombie, D. Mourn not your dead
Cullin, M. A slight trick of the mind
Davis, L. A body in the bath house
Dean, S. F. X. It can't be my grave
Dexter, C. The daughters of Cain
Dexter, C. Death is now my neighbor
Dexter, C. The jewel that was ours
Dexter, C. Morse's greatest mystery and other stories
Dexter, C. The remorseful day
Dexter, C. The secret of annexe 3
Dexter, C. The way through the woods
Dexter, C. The wench is dead
Dickens, C. Bleak House
Dickens, C. The mystery of Edwin Drood
Dickinson, P. Skeleton-in-waiting
Dickinson, P. The yellow room conspiracy
Doherty, P. C. The demon archer
Doherty, P. C. The devil's hunt
Doherty, P. C. A tournament of murders
Doyle, Sir A. C. Adventures of Sherlock Holmes
Doyle, Sir A. C. The complete Sherlock Holmes
Doyle, Sir A. C. Famous tales of Sherlock Holmes
Doyle, Sir A. C. The hound of the Baskervilles
Doyle, Sir A. C. The return of Sherlock Holmes
Doyle, Sir A. C. The sign of four
Doyle, Sir A. C. The valley of fear
Ferrars, E. X. Blood flies upward
Ferrars, E. X. Thy brother death
Francis, D. 10 lb. penalty
Francis, D. Banker
Francis, D. Bolt
Francis, D. Break in
Francis, D. Come to grief
Francis, D. The danger
Francis, D. Driving force
Francis, D. Field of thirteen
Francis, D. Hot money
Francis, D. Longshot
Francis, D. Nerve
Francis, D. Proof
Francis, D. Rat race
Francis, D. Risk
Francis, D. Shattered
Francis, D. Straight
Francis, D. To the hilt
Francis, D. Whip hand
Francis, D. Wild horses
Fraser, A. The cavalier case
Fraser, A. Cool repentance
Fraser, A. Jemima Shore at the sunny grave and other stories
Fraser, A. Oxford blood

MYSTERY AND DETECTIVE STORIES—England—*Continued*

Perry, A. Weighed in the balance
Perry, A. The Whitechapel conspiracy
Peters, E. The deeds of the disturber
Peters, E. The last camel died at noon
Peters, E. The benediction of Brother Cadfael
Peters, E. Brother Cadfael's penance
Peters, E. Dead man's ransom
Peters, E. Fallen into the pit
Peters, E. Flight of a witch
Peters, E. The heretic's apprentice
Peters, E. The hermit of Eyton Forest
Peters, E. The holy thief
Peters, E. Monk's-hood
Peters, E. A morbid taste for bones
Peters, E. One corpse too many
Peters, E. The pilgrim of hate
Peters, E. The potter's field
Peters, E. Rainbow's end
Peters, E. A rare Benedictine
Peters, E. The rose rent
Peters, E. Saint Peter's Fair
Peters, E. The sanctuary sparrow
Peters, E. The summer of the Danes
Peters, E. The virgin in the ice
Pickard, N. Bum steer
Pirie, D. The patient's eyes
Rendell, R. Collected stories
Rendell, R. Death notes
Rendell, R. Harm done
Rendell, R. Kissing the gunner's daughter
Rendell, R. Master of the moor
Rendell, R. Murder being once done
Rendell, R. Road rage
Rendell, R. Simisola
Rendell, R. A sleeping life
Rendell, R. Speaker of Mandarin
Rendell, R. An unkindness of ravens
Robb, C. M. The riddle of St. Leonard's
Robinson, P. Close to home
Robinson, P. Cold is the grave
Robinson, P. In a dry season
Robinson, P. Innocent grave
Robinson, P. Playing with fire
Sayers, D. L. Busman's honeymoon
Sayers, D. L. Clouds of witnesses
Sayers, D. L. The Dawson pedigree
Sayers, D. L. The documents in the case
Sayers, D. L. Gaudy Night
Sayers, D. L. Have his carcase
Sayers, D. L. Lord Peter
Sayers, D. L. Murder must advertise
Sayers, D. L. The nine tailors
Sayers, D. L. Strong poison
Sayers, D. L. Thrones, dominations
Sayers, D. L. The unpleasantness at the Bellona Club
Sayers, D. L. Whose body?
Simpson, D. A day for dying
Simpson, D. Dead and gone
Simpson, D. Dead by morning
Simpson, D. Dead on arrival
Simpson, D. Doomed to die
Simpson, D. Last seen alive
Simpson, D. No laughing matter
Simpson, D. Once too often
Simpson, D. Suspicious death
Simpson, D. Wake the dead
Symons, J. Death's darkest face
Symons, J. The Kentish manor murders
Symons, J. Playing happy families
Tey, J. Brat Farrar
Tey, J. The daughter of time
Tey, J. Four, five and six by Tey
Tey, J. The Franchise affair
Tey, J. The man in the queue
Tey, J. The singing sands
Tey, J. Three by Tey
Underwood, M. A dangerous business
Winspear, J. Birds of a feather
Winspear, J. Maisie Dobbs
Winspear, J. Pardonable lies
Woods, S. The lie direct
Woods, S. Naked villainy
Wright, E. Death in the old country
Yorke, M. Act of violence
Yorke, M. Criminal damage
Yorke, M. Intimate kill
Yorke, M. A small deceit

France

Black, C. Murder in the Sentier
Bond, M. Monsieur Pamplemousse
Bond, M. Monsieur Pamplemousse rests his case
Doherty, P. C. The masked man
Elkins, A. J. Skeleton dance
Freeling, N. A dwarf kingdom
Freeling, N. Flanders sky
Newman, S. The difficult saint
Newman, S. Strong as death
Page, K. H. The body in the vestibule
Poe, E. A. The purloined letter [and] The murders in the Rue Morgue
Simenon, G. Inspector Maigret and the killers
Simenon, G. Maigret and the apparition
Simenon, G. Maigret and the black sheep
Simenon, G. Maigret and the burglar's wife
Simenon, G. Maigret and the fortune-teller
Simenon, G. Maigret and the Hotel Majestic
Simenon, G. Maigret and the loner
Simenon, G. Maigret and the madwoman
Simenon, G. Maigret and the Nahour case
Simenon, G. Maigret and the Saturday caller
Simenon, G. Maigret and the spinster
Simenon, G. Maigret and the toy village
Simenon, G. Maigret and the wine merchants
Simenon, G. Maigret bides his time
Simenon, G. Maigret goes home
Simenon, G. Maigret in exile
Simenon, G. Maigret's memoirs
Simenon, G. Maigret's revolver
Simenon, G. Maigret's war of nerves

Germany

Kaye, M. M. Death in Berlin
Peters, E. Trojan gold
Schlink, B. Self's punishment

Greece

Doherty, P. C. The gates of hell
Doherty, P. C. The house of death

Guatemala

Reichs, K. J. Grave secrets

Guernsey (Channel Islands)

Gash, J. The rich and the profane

India

Kaye, M. M. Death in Kashmir
Keating, H. R. F. Bribery, corruption also
Keating, H. R. F. Cheating death
Keating, H. R. F. Doing wrong
Keating, H. R. F. Inspector Ghote trusts the heart
King, L. R. The game
Peters, E. Death to the landlords!

Ireland

Bruen, K. The guards
Bruen, K. The killing of the tinkers
Gill, B. Death in Dublin
Gill, B. The death of an Irish lover
Gill, B. The death of an Irish sea wolf
Gill, B. The death of an Irish tinker
Gill, B. The death of love
Gill, B. Death on a cold, wild river
Haymon, S. T. A beautiful death

Israel

Kemelman, H. Monday the rabbi took off
Kemelman, H. One fine day the rabbi bought a cross

Italy

Camilleri, A. The snack thief
Davis, L. Venus in copper
Dibdin, M. And then you die
Dibdin, M. Blood rain
Dibdin, M. Così fan tutti
Dibdin, M. Dead Lagoon
Dibdin, M. A long finish

MYSTERY AND DETECTIVE STORIES—United States—*Continued*

Block, L. The burglar who painted like Mondrian
Block, L. The burglar who studied Spinoza
Block, L. The burglar who traded Ted Williams
Block, L. The collected mystery stories
Block, L. A dance at the slaughterhouse
Block, L. The devil knows you're dead
Block, L. Eight million ways to die
Block, L. Even the wicked
Block, L. Everybody dies
Block, L. Hope to die
Block, L. Like a lamb to slaughter
Block, L. A long line of dead men
Block, L. Out on the cutting edge
Block, L. The sins of the fathers
Block, L. Some days you get the bear
Block, L. Sometimes they bite
Block, L. A ticket to the boneyard
Block, L. A walk among the tombstones
Block, L. When the sacred ginmill closes
Bowen, P. Badlands
Box, C. J. Savage run
Box, C. J. Winterkill
Boyer, R. The Daisy Ducks
Bradbury, R. A graveyard for lunatics
Braun, L. J. The cat who ate Danish modern
Braun, L. J. The cat who blew the whistle
Braun, L. J. The cat who brought down the house
Braun, L. J. The cat who came to breakfast
Braun, L. J. The cat who lived high
Braun, L. J. The cat who robbed a bank
Braun, L. J. The cat who said cheese
Braun, L. J. The cat who sang for the birds
Braun, L. J. The cat who saw stars
Braun, L. J. The cat who smelled a rat
Braun, L. J. The cat who sniffed glue
Braun, L. J. The cat who tailed a thief
Braun, L. J. The cat who went underground
Brown, F. The bloody moonlight
Brown, F. Compliments of a fiend
Brown, F. Dead ringer
Brown, F. The fabulous clipjoint
Brown, F. Hunter and hunted
Brown, R. M. Cat on the scent
Brown, R. M. Catch as cat can
Brown, R. M. Murder at Monticello; or, Old sins
Brown, R. M. Murder on the prowl
Brown, R. M. Murder, she meowed
Brown, R. M. Pay dirt; or, Adventures at Ash Lawn
Brown, R. M. Rest in pieces
Brown, R. M. Whisker of evil
Brown, R. M. Wish you were here
Brown, S. Hello, darkness
Buchanan, E. Act of betrayal
Buchanan, E. Cold case squad
Buchanan, E. Contents under pressure
Buchanan, E. Garden of evil
Buchanan, E. The Ice Maiden
Buchanan, E. Margin of error
Buchanan, E. Miami, it's murder
Buchanan, E. Suitable for framing
Buchanan, E. You only die twice
Burke, J. L. Black cherry blues
Burke, J. L. Burning angel
Burke, J. L. Cadillac jukebox
Burke, J. L. Crusader's cross
Burke, J. L. Dixie City jam
Burke, J. L. Heaven's prisoners
Burke, J. L. In the electric mist with Confederate dead
Burke, J. L. Jolie Blon's Bounce
Burke, J. L. Last car to Elysian Fields
Burke, J. L. A morning for flamingos
Burke, J. L. The neon rain
Burke, J. L. Purple cane road
Burke, J. L. A stained white radiance
Burke, J. L. Sunset limited
Burke, J. Bloodlines
Burke, J. Bones
Burke, J. Flight
Burke, J. Hocus
Burke, J. Liar
Burke, J. Remember me, Irene
Burnett, W. R. The asphalt jungle
Campbell, R. W. In La-La Land we trust
Campbell, R. W. Pigeon pie
Carr, C. The alienist
Carr, C. The angel of darkness
Caunitz, W. J. Chains of command
Caunitz, W. J. One Police Plaza
Caunitz, W. J. Suspects
Chandler, R. The big sleep
Chandler, R. The high window
Chandler, R. The lady in the lake
Chandler, R. Later novels and other writings
Chandler, R. The little sister
Chandler, R. The long goodbye
Chandler, R. Playback
Chandler, R. Poodle Springs
Chandler, R. Raymond Chandler
Chandler, R. Stories and early novels
Child, L. Echo burning
Child, L. The enemy
Child, L. One shot
Child, L. Persuader
Child, L. Without fail
Churchill, J. Fear of frying
Churchill, J. A groom with a view
Churchill, J. The merchant of menace
Clark, C. H. Snagged
Clark, C. H. Twanged
Clark, M. H. All through the night
Clark, M. H. Deck the halls
Clark, M. H. The lottery winner
Clark, M. H. My gal Sunday
Clark, M. H. Weep no more, my lady
Clark, M. H. While my pretty one sleeps
Coben, H. Darkest fear
Coben, H. One false move
Cockey, T. Hearse case scenario
Cockey, T. Murder in the hearse degree
Coel, M. The dream stalker
Coel, M. The ghost walker
Collins, M. A. Angel in black
Collins, M. A. Chicago confidential
Connelly, M. Angels flight
Connelly, M. The black ice
Connelly, M. Blood work
Connelly, M. City of bones
Connelly, M. The closers
Connelly, M. The concrete blonde
Connelly, M. A darkness more than night
Connelly, M. Lost light
Connelly, M. The narrows
Connelly, M. Trunk music
Constantine, K. C. Always a body to trade
Constantine, K. C. Blood mud
Constantine, K. C. Brushback
Constantine, K. C. Family values
Constantine, K. C. Grievance
Constantine, K. C. The man who liked slow tomatoes
Constantine, K. C. The man who liked to look at himself
Constantine, K. C. Saving room for dessert
Cornwell, P. D. Blow fly
Cornwell, P. D. Postmortem
Craig, P. R. A deadly Vineyard holiday
Craig, P. R. A fatal vineyard season
Craig, P. R. A shoot on Martha's Vineyard
Craig, P. R. Vineyard enigma
Craig, P. R. A vineyard killing
Crais, R. The forgotten man
Crais, R. Indigo slam
Crais, R. L.A. requiem
Crais, R. The last detective
Crais, R. Sunset express
Crider, B. Death by accident
Crider, B. A ghost of a chance
Crider, B. Murder is an art
Crider, B. Murder takes a break
Crider, B. The prairie chicken kill
Cross, A. The collected stories of Amanda Cross
Cross, A. Death in a tenured position
Cross, A. Honest doubt
Cross, A. An imperfect spy
Cross, A. The James Joyce murder
Cross, A. The players come again
Cross, A. The puzzled heart
Cross, A. Sweet death, kind death

MYSTERY AND DETECTIVE STORIES—United States—*Continued*

Hess, J. Madness in Maggody
Hess, J. Maggody and the moonbeams
Hess, J. Mischief in Maggody
Hess, J. Misery loves Maggody
Hess, J. Murder@maggody.com
Hess, J. Out on a limb
Hiaasen, C. Skin tight
Hillerman, T. The blessing way
Hillerman, T. Coyote waits
Hillerman, T. Dance hall of the dead
Hillerman, T. The dark wind
Hillerman, T. The fallen man
Hillerman, T. The first eagle
Hillerman, T. The ghostway
Hillerman, T. Hunting badger
Hillerman, T. The Jim Chee mysteries
Hillerman, T. The Joe Leaphorn mysteries
Hillerman, T. Listening woman
Hillerman, T. People of Darkness
Hillerman, T. Sacred clowns
Hillerman, T. The sinister pig
Hillerman, T. Skinwalkers
Hillerman, T. Talking God
Hillerman, T. A thief of time
Hillerman, T. The wailing wind
Himes, C. Cotton comes to Harlem
Holland, I. A death at St. Anselm's
Hornsby, W. A hardlight
Hunter, E. The moment she was gone
Isaacs, S. Compromising positions
Isaacs, S. Magic hour
Jackson, J. A. No man's dog
James, P. D. Death in holy orders
James, P. D. Death of an expert witness
Jance, J. A. Birds of prey
Jance, J. A. Breach of duty
Jance, J. A. Dead to rights
Jance, J. A. Devil's claw
Jance, J. A. Lying in wait
Jance, J. A. Skeleton canyon
Jones, D. C. The search for Temperance Moon
Kaminsky, S. M. The big silence
Kaminsky, S. M. Dancing in the dark
Kaminsky, S. M. A fatal glass of beer
Kaminsky, S. M. Lieberman's choice
Kaminsky, S. M. Lieberman's day
Kaminsky, S. M. Lieberman's folly
Kaminsky, S. M. Lieberman's thief
Kaminsky, S. M. Not quite kosher
Kaminsky, S. M. Retribution
Kaminsky, S. M. The Rockford files: Devil on my doorstep
Kaminsky, S. M. The Rockford files: the green bottle
Kaminsky, S. M. To catch a spy
Kaminsky, S. M. Tomorrow is another day
Kaminsky, S. M. Vengeance
Kellerman, F. Day of atonement
Kellerman, F. The forgotten
Kellerman, F. Grievous sin
Kellerman, F. Jupiter's bones
Kellerman, F. Justice
Kellerman, F. Milk and honey
Kellerman, F. Moon music
Kellerman, F. Prayers for the dead
Kellerman, F. Sanctuary
Kellerman, F. Serpent's tooth
Kellerman, F. Stone kiss
Kellerman, F. Street dreams
Kellerman, J. Bad love
Kellerman, J. Billy Straight
Kellerman, J. The clinic
Kellerman, J. Devil's waltz
Kellerman, J. Dr. Death
Kellerman, J. Monster
Kellerman, J. The murder book
Kellerman, J. Over the edge
Kellerman, J. Private eyes
Kellerman, J. Self-defense
Kellerman, J. Silent partner
Kellerman, J. Survival of the fittest
Kellerman, J. Therapy
Kellerman, J. Time bomb
Kellerman, J. The web
Kellerman, J. When the bough breaks
Kemelman, H. The day the rabbi resigned
Kemelman, H. Friday the rabbi slept late
Kemelman, H. Saturday the rabbi went hungry
Kemelman, H. Sunday the rabbi stayed home
Kemelman, H. Thursday the rabbi walked out
Kemelman, H. Wednesday the rabbi got wet
Kienzle, W. X. Assault with intent
Kienzle, W. X. Body count
Kienzle, W. X. Chameleon
Kienzle, W. X. Death wears a red hat
Kienzle, W. X. The gathering
Kienzle, W. X. The greatest evil
Kienzle, W. X. The man who loved God
Kienzle, W. X. No greater love
Kienzle, W. X. The rosary murders
Kijewski, K. Alley Kat blues
Kijewski, K. Copy Kat
Kijewski, K. Honky tonk Kat
Kijewski, K. Kat scratch fever
Kijewski, K. Kat's cradle
Kijewski, K. Stray Kat waltz
Kijewski, K. Wild Kat
King, L. R. Locked rooms
Koontz, D. R. Dragon tears
Koryta, M. Tonight I said goodbye
Kozak, H. J. Dating dead men
La Plante, L. Cold blood
Langton, J. The deserter
Langton, J. Divine inspiration
Langton, J. Emily Dickinson is dead
Langton, J. The Escher twist
Langton, J. The face on the wall
Langton, J. God in Concord
Langton, J. Murder at Monticello
Langton, J. Murder at the Gardner
Langton, J. Natural enemy
Langton, J. The shortest day
Lathen, E. Brewing up a storm
Lathen, E. Going for the gold
Lathen, E. Right on the money
Lathen, E. Something in the air
Lathen, E. A stitch in time
Lehane, D. Gone, baby, gone
Lehane, D. Prayers for rain
Lehane, D. Sacred
Leonard, E. When the women come out to dance, and other stories
Lethem, J. Motherless Brooklyn
Levine, P. Flesh and bones
Lewin, M. Z. And baby will fall
Logue, M. Bone harvest
Lutz, J. Burn
Lutz, J. Death by jury
Lutz, J. Hot
Lutz, J. Lightning
Lutz, J. Oops!
MacDonald, J. D. Cinnamon skin
MacDonald, J. D. A deadly shade of gold
MacDonald, J. D. The deep blue good-by
MacDonald, J. D. The dreadful lemon sky
MacDonald, J. D. The empty copper sea
MacDonald, J. D. Free fall in crimson
MacDonald, J. D. The green ripper
MacDonald, J. D. The lonely silver rain
MacDonald, J. D. The long lavender look
MacDonald, J. D. Nightmare in pink
MacDonald, J. D. One fearful yellow eye
MacDonald, J. D. A purple place for dying
MacDonald, J. D. The scarlet ruse
MacDonald, J. D. The turquoise lament
Macdonald, R. Archer in Hollywood
Macdonald, R. Archer in jeopardy
Macdonald, R. The far side of the dollar
Macdonald, R. The Galton case
Macdonald, R. The goodbye look
Macdonald, R. Ross Macdonald's Lew Archer, private investigator
Macdonald, R. Sleeping beauty
Macdonald, R. The underground man
MacLeod, C. The corpse in Oozak's Pond
MacLeod, C. Exit the milkman
MacLeod, C. The Gladstone bag
MacLeod, C. Rest you merry

MYSTERY AND DETECTIVE STORIES—United States—*Continued*

Parker, R. B. Shrink rap
Parker, R. B. Small vices
Parker, R. B. Stardust
Parker, R. B. Sudden mischief
Parker, R. B. Taming a sea-horse
Parker, R. B. Thin air
Parker, R. B. Trouble in Paradise
Parker, R. B. Valediction
Parker, R. B. Walking shadow
Parker, R. B. The widening gyre
Parker, R. B. Widow's walk
Parker, T. J. Laguna heat
Parker, T. J. Pacific beat
Pearson, R. Probable cause
Pelecanos, G. P. Hard revolution
Pelecanos, G. P. Hell to pay
Pelecanos, G. P. Soul circus
Perry, T. The butcher's boy
Perry, T. Death benefits
Perry, T. Sleeping dogs
Pickard, N. The 27 ingredient chili con carne murders
Pickard, N. Blue corn murders
Pickard, N. But I wouldn't want to die there
Pickard, N. Confession
Pickard, N. Dead crazy
Pickard, N. Generous death
Pickard, N. Marriage is murder
Pickard, N. No body
Pickard, N. The truth hurts
Pickard, N. Twilight
Pickard, N. The whole truth
Pickens, C. Southern fried
Pronzini, B. Bleeders
Pronzini, B. Blue lonesome
Pronzini, B. Bones
Pronzini, B. Crazybone
Pronzini, B. Deadfall
Pronzini, B. Hardcase
Pronzini, B. Illusions
Pronzini, B. Nightcrawlers
Pronzini, B. Quarry
Pronzini, B. Sentinels
Pronzini, B. Spook
Queen, E. A fine and private place
Queen, E. The Roman hat mystery
Reichs, K. J. Bare bones
Rich, V. The baked bean supper murders
Rich, V. The cooking school murders
Rich, V. The Nantucket diet murders
Riggs, C. Jack in the pulpit
Rinehart, M. R. The circular staircase
Rinehart, M. R. Mary Roberts Rinehart's mystery book
Rinehart, M. R. Miss Pinkerton: adventures of a nurse detective
Robb, C. M. The cross-legged knight
Roberts, G. Adam and evil
Roberts, G. The bluest blood
Roberts, G. Claire and present danger
Roberts, G. Helen hath no fury
Roberts, G. The mummers' curse
Roosevelt, E. A first class murder
Roosevelt, E. The Hyde Park murder
Roosevelt, E. Murder and the First Lady
Roosevelt, E. Murder at midnight
Roosevelt, E. Murder at the palace
Roosevelt, E. Murder in Georgetown
Roosevelt, E. Murder in the Blue Room
Roosevelt, E. Murder in the map room
Roosevelt, E. Murder in the Oval Office
Roosevelt, E. Murder in the Rose Garden
Roosevelt, E. The White House pantry murder
Rozan, S. J. Winter and night
Sallis, J. Cypress Grove
Sanders, L. The fourth deadly sin
Sanders, L. McNally's dilemma
Sanders, L. McNally's gamble
Sanders, L. McNally's luck
Sanders, L. McNally's puzzle
Sanders, L. McNally's secret
Sanders, L. McNally's trial
Sanders, L. The Timothy files
Sanders, L. Timothy's game
Sandford, J. Broken prey
Sandford, J. Certain prey
Sandford, J. Chosen prey
Sandford, J. Easy prey
Sandford, J. Hidden prey
Sandford, J. Mind prey
Sandford, J. Mortal prey
Sandford, J. Naked prey
Sandford, J. Night prey
Sandford, J. Rules of prey
Sandford, J. Silent prey
Sandford, J. Sudden prey
Sandford, J. Winter prey
Saulnier, B. Ecstasy
Scoppettone, S. Everything you have is mine
Scoppettone, S. Gonna take a homicidal journey
Scoppettone, S. My sweet untraceable you
Shannon, D. Chaos of crime
Shoemaker, B. Stalking horse
Simon, R. L. Director's cut
Smith, A. North of Montana
Smith, J. 82 Desire
Smith, J. The Axeman's jazz
Smith, J. Crescent city kill
Smith, J. House of blues
Smith, J. Jazz funeral
Smith, J. The kindness of strangers
Smith, J. Louisiana hotshot
Smith, J. Mean woman blues
Smith, J. New Orleans beat
Solomita, S. Damaged goods
Solomita, S. A good day to die
Solomita, S. Last chance for glory
Spencer-Fleming, J. In the bleak midwinter
Spiegelman, P. Black maps
Stabenow, D. Blood will tell
Stabenow, D. Breakup
Stabenow, D. A fine and bitter snow
Stabenow, D. Fire and ice
Stabenow, D. Hunter's moon
Stabenow, D. Killing grounds
Stabenow, D. Play with fire
Stabenow, D. The singing of the dead
Stabenow, D. So sure of death
Standiford, L. Bone Key
Standiford, L. Deal on ice
Standiford, L. Deal with the dead
Standiford, L. Presidential Deal
Stewart, E. Deadly rich
Stewart, E. Mortal grace
Stout, R. All aces
Stout, R. Death of a doxy
Stout, R. The doorbell rang
Stout, R. Five of a kind
Stout, R. Gambit
Stout, R. Kings full of aces
Stout, R. Royal flush
Stout, R. Three aces
Stout, R. Trio for blunt instruments
Stroby, W. The barbed-wire kiss
Tapply, W. G. Bitch Creek
Tapply, W. G. Client privilege
Tapply, W. G. Close to the bone
Tapply, W. G. Cutter's run
Tapply, W. G. Dead meat
Tapply, W. G. Dead winter
Tapply, W. G. First light
Tapply, W. G. Muscle memory
Tapply, W. G. Past tense
Tapply, W. G. Scar tissue
Tapply, W. G. Tight lines
Tapply, W. G. A void in hearts
Truman, M. Murder at Ford's Theatre
Truman, M. Murder at the Library of Congress
Truman, M. Murder at the National Cathedral
Truman, M. Murder at the Watergate
Truman, M. Murder in the White House
Truman, M. Murder on Capitol Hill
Truscott, L. K. Dress gray
Truscott, L. K. Full dress gray
Turow, S. Pleading guilty
Twain, M. Tom Sawyer, detective
Uhnak, D. The investigation
Uhnak, D. The witness

NATIONAL SOCIALISM—*Continued*
Hijuelos, O. A simple Habana melody: from when the world was good
Iles, G. Black cross
Keneally, T. Schindler's list
King, S. Apt pupil
Korda, M. Worldly goods
Ludlum, R. The apocalypse watch
Ludlum, R. The Holcroft covenant
Ludlum, R. The Scarlatti inheritance
MacInnes, H. Above suspicion
Moore, B. The statement
Pottinger, S. The last Nazi
Schlink, B. The reader
Shaw, I. The young lions
Taibo, P. I. Returning as shadows
Thayer, J. S. Five past midnight
Tournier, M. The ogre
Uris, L. Mila 18
Vollmann, W. T. Europe central
Volpi, J. In search of Klingsor

NATIONALISM
Grass, G. The call of the toad
Werfel, F. The forty days of Musa Dagh

Native son. Wright, R.
also in Wright, R. Works
Native tongue. Hiaasen, C.
Natives and exotics. Alison, J.
The **natural**. Malamud, B.
Natural causes. Palmer, M.
A **natural** curiosity. Drabble, M.
Natural enemy. Langton, J.
Natural history. Howard, M.

NATURALISTS
See also Paleontologists
Anderson, A. Darwin's wink
Barrett, A. The voyage of the Narwhal
García, C. The Aguero sisters
Gregory, P. Virgin earth
Hudson, W. H. Green mansions
Lurie, A. The last resort
Wells, H. G. The island of Doctor Moreau

NATURE
Alison, J. Natives and exotics
Goethe, J. W. v. Novella
Kantner, S. Ordinary wolves
McCarthy, M. Birds of America
Steinbeck, J. To a god unknown
Thomas, E. M. Reindeer Moon

NATURE CONSERVATION
Cheever, J. Oh, what a paradise it seems

The **nature** of blood. Phillips, C.
Nausea. Sartre, J. P.
The **nautical** chart. Pérez-Reverte, A.
NAVAHO INDIANS *See* Navajo Indians

NAVAJO INDIANS
Hillerman, T. The blessing way
Hillerman, T. Coyote waits
Hillerman, T. Dance hall of the dead
Hillerman, T. The dark wind
Hillerman, T. The fallen man
Hillerman, T. The first eagle
Hillerman, T. The ghostway
Hillerman, T. Hunting badger
Hillerman, T. The Jim Chee mysteries
Hillerman, T. The Joe Leaphorn mysteries
Hillerman, T. Listening woman
Hillerman, T. People of Darkness
Hillerman, T. Sacred clowns
Hillerman, T. Skinwalkers
Hillerman, T. Talking God
Hillerman, T. A thief of time
Hillerman, T. The wailing wind
La Farge, O. Laughing Boy
Mapson, J.-A. Loving Chloe

NAVAL BATTLES
See also United States—Revolution, 1775-1783—Naval operations; United States—Civil War, 1861-1865—Naval operations; Sea stories; World War, 1914-1918—Naval operations; World War, 1939-1945—Naval operations
Forester, C. S. Beat to quarters
Forester, C. S. Commodore Hornblower
Forester, C. S. Hornblower and the Atropos
Forester, C. S. The last nine days of the Bismarck
Forester, C. S. Ship of the line
Martin, W. Annapolis
McCutchan, P. Cameron's crossing
White, R. A. Typhoon

NAVAL OBSERVATORY (U.S.) *See* United States Naval Observatory
The **navigator** of New York. Johnston, W.
The **Nazarene**. Asch, S.
Nazareth Hill. Campbell, R.
NAZIS *See* National socialism
NAZISM *See* National socialism
NDEBELE (AFRICAN PEOPLE) *See* Matabele (African people)
Neanderthal. Darnton, J.

NEANDERTHAL RACE
See also Prehistoric man
Golding, W. The inheritors

NEAR-DEATH EXPERIENCES
Willis, C. Passage

NEAR EAST *See* Middle East

NEBRASKA
Hansen, R. Isn't it romantic?
Ward, L. Outside valentine

19th century

Aldrich, B. S. A lantern in her hand
Cather, W. My Antonia
Cather, W. O pioneers!

20th century

Cather, W. A lost lady
Harrison, J. The road home
Wiltse, D. Heartland

Farm life

See Farm life—Nebraska

Frontier and pioneer life

See Frontier and pioneer life—Nebraska

Nebula awards. Entered in Part I under title

NECKLACES
Dumas, A. The Queen's necklace

Necrochip. See Harrod-Eagles, C. Death to go
Needful things. King, S.
The **needle's** eye. Drabble, M.

NEEDLEWORK
Hendrie, L. Remember me

NEGROES *See* African Americans

NEIGHBORS
Baxter, C. The feast of love
Berger, T. Neighbors
Brookner, A. A private view
Cheever, J. Bullet Park
Gowdy, B. The romantic
Hamilton, J. A map of the world
Hoffman, A. Illumination night
Lively, P. Spiderweb
McKinney-Whetstone, D. Leaving Cecil Street
Mendelson, C. Morningside Heights
Messud, C. The hunters [novelette]
Miller, S. For love
Parker, T. J. California girl
Shreve, A. Eden Close
Unsworth, B. After Hannibal

Neighbors. Berger, T.
Nekropolis. McHugh, M. F.

NELSON, HORATIO NELSON, VISCOUNT, 1758-1805

About

Sontag, S. The volcano lover
Unsworth, B. Losing Nelson

NELSON, WILLIE

About

Friedman, K. Roadkill

Nemesis. Asimov, I.

NEW JERSEY—20th century—*Continued*
Roth, P. American pastoral
Updike, J. The poorhouse fair

Atlantic City

Dezenhall, E. Money wanders
Leonard, E. Glitz
Reuss, F. Henry of Atlantic City

Newark

Roth, P. The human stain
Roth, P. I married a communist
Roth, P. The plot against America

Trenton

DeVido, B. Every time I talk to Liston
The **new** lieutenant. McCutchan, P.
The **new** men. Snow, C. P.
NEW MEXICO
Bradford, R. Red sky at morning
Cather, W. Death comes for the archbishop
Cather, W. The professor's house
Estleman, L. D. City of widows
Gear, K. O. The summoning God
Hendrie, L. Remember me
McCarthy, C. Cities of the plain
Morrow, B. Ariel's crossing
Nichols, J. T. The Milagro beanfield war
Schaefer, J. W. Monte Walsh
Shigekuni, J. Invisible gardens
Strieber, W. Majestic

Los Alamos

Kanon, J. Los Alamos
McMahon, T. A. Principles of American nuclear chemistry
Morrow, B. Trinity fields
Smith, M. C. Stallion Gate

Santa Fe

Morrell, D. Extreme denial
Mortman, D. True colors
Rossner, J. Perfidia
Woods, S. Santa Fe rules
NEW ORLEANS (LA.) *See* Louisiana—New Orleans
New Orleans beat. Smith, J.
A **new** song. Karon, J.
NEW SOUTH WALES (AUSTRALIA) *See* Australia—New South Wales
NEW SOUTHWEST *See* Southwestern States
New stories from the South: the year's best [date] Entered in Part I under title
New Year's Day. Wharton, E.
In Wharton, E. Novellas and other writings
NEW YORK (N.Y.)
Cook, R. Marker
Cunningham, M. Specimen days
Foer, J. S. Extremely loud and incredibly close
Hamill, P. Forever
Kaplow, R. Me and Orson Welles
Tanenbaum, R. Hoax

19th century

Baker, K. Paradise Alley
Bromfield, L. Mrs. Parkington
Busch, F. The night inspector
Carr, C. The alienist
Carr, C. The angel of darkness
Crane, S. Maggie: a girl of the streets (a story of New York)
Crane, S. Maggie: a girl of the streets [novelette]
Doctorow, E. L. The waterworks
Field, R. All this, and heaven too
Finney, J. Time and again
Millhauser, S. Martin Dressler
Vidal, G. 1876
Wharton, E. The age of innocence
Wharton, E. The buccaneers
Wharton, E. Old New York
Whitney, P. A. Window on the square

20th century

Adler, E. In a heartbeat
Auchincloss, L. The book class
Auchincloss, L. Her infinite variety
Auchincloss, L. Honorable men
Auchincloss, L. The stoic
Baker, D. Young man with a horn
Baker, K. Dreamland
Baldwin, J. Another country
Beattie, A. Falling in place
Bellow, S. Mr. Sammler's planet
Birmingham, S. The Auerbach will
Bradford, B. T. The triumph of Katie Byrne
Bradford, B. T. Where you belong
Bromfield, L. Mrs. Parkington
Browne, G. A. West 47th
Caldwell, T. Ceremony of the innocent
Canin, E. For kings and planets
Carcaterra, L. Apaches
Carcaterra, L. Gangster
Chabon, M. The amazing adventures of Kavalier and Clay
Clark, M. H. Before I say goodbye
Clark, M. H. A stranger is watching
Colwin, L. A big storm knocked it over
Colwin, L. Family happiness
Condon, R. Prizzi's family
Condon, R. Prizzi's glory
Condon, R. Prizzi's honor
Condon, R. Prizzi's money
Conroy, F. Body & soul
Conroy, P. The prince of tides
Cook, R. Brain
Cook, R. Contagion
Daley, R. Man with a gun
Daley, R. Wall of brass
Davies, V. Miracle on 34th Street
Denker, H. Mrs. Washington and Horowitz, too
Doctorow, E. L. City of God
Dos Passos, J. Manhattan transfer
Dreiser, T. Sister Carrie
Fairstein, L. Cold hit
Fairstein, L. Final jeopardy
Fairstein, L. Likely to die
Fast, H. Redemption
Faulks, S. On Green Dolphin Street
Fitzgerald, F. S. The Great Gatsby
Fitzgerald, F. S. May Day
Fox, P. A servant's tale
Frey, S. W. The vulture fund
Girzone, J. F. Joshua and the city
Godey, J. The taking of Pelham one two three
Goudge, E. Garden of lies
Goudge, E. Trail of secrets
Grant, M. Officer down
Heller, J. Closing time
Helprin, M. Winter's tale
Hijuelos, O. Empress of the splendid season
Hobson, L. K. Z. Gentleman's agreement
Howatch, S. Sins of the fathers
Hunter, E. The blackboard jungle
Hunter, E. Candyland
Hustvedt, S. What I loved
Isaacs, S. Shining through
Jackson, C. The lost weekend
Jen, G. Typical American
Kelly, T. Empire rising
Kelman, J. Summer of storms
Leavitt, D. The lost language of cranes
Leavitt, D. Martin Bauman
Lieberman, H. H. The girl with Botticelli eyes
Malamud, B. The tenants
Miller, H. Tropic of Capricorn
Nathan, R. Portrait of Jennie
Nin, A. A spy in the house of love
O'Hara, J. Butterfield 8
Ozick, C. The Puttermesser papers
Piercy, M. Braided lives
Plain, B. Her father's house
Plath, S. The bell jar
Powell, D. Angels on toast
Powell, D. The locusts have no king
Powell, D. Turn, magic wheel
Preston, D. Reliquary
Preston, R. The Cobra event
Rand, A. The fountainhead
Rayner, R. The cloud sketcher
Rossner, J. August
Roth, H. A diving rock on the Hudson

NEW YORK (N.Y.)—Manhattan—*Continued*
Levin, I. Rosemary's baby
Lynn, A. Now you see it
Malamud, B. The tenants
Mallon, T. Bandbox
McElroy, J. Actress in the house
McPhee, J. No ordinary matter
Meltzer, B. Dead even
Mendelson, C. Morningside Heights
Morton, B. A window across the river
O'Hara, J. Butterfield 8
Packer, A. The dive from Clausen's pier
Pearson, T. R. Blue Ridge
Percy, W. The last gentleman
Preston, D. The cabinet of curiosities
Price, R. The good priest's son
Prose, F. Household saints
Rinaldi, N. Between two rivers
Robinson, R. Sweetwater
Robinson, S. By any other name
Rosen, J. Joy comes in the morning
Sanders, L. The tenth commandment
Saul, J. The Manhattan Hunt Club
Saul, J. Midnight voices
Schulberg, B. Waterfront
Schwartz, L. S. Disturbances in the field
Schwartz, L. S. In the family way
Schwarz, C. All is vanity
Singer, I. B. Shadows on the Hudson
Solomon, N. Single wife
Strieber, W. The Wolfen
Vida, V. And now you can go
Weber, K. The little women
Westlake, D. E. Cops and robbers
Woods, S. Dirt
Woods, S. Two-dollar bill
Wouk, H. Marjorie Morningstar

Queens

Breslin, J. Table money
Isaacs, S. Close relations
LaValle, V. D. The ecstatic
McDermott, A. Charming Billy
Spiegelman, I. Everyone's burning

NEW YORK (STATE)
See also Adirondack Mountains (N.Y.); Long Island (N.Y.); Mohawk Valley (N.Y.)
Oates, J. C. The falls
Oates, J. C. Missing mom

17th century

Youmans, M. Catherwood

18th century

Cooper, J. F. The Deerslayer
Cooper, J. F. The last of the Mohicans
Cooper, J. F. The Pathfinder
Cooper, J. F. The spy

19th century

Crane, S. The monster
Seton, A. Dragonwyck

20th century

Abraham, P. The romance reader
Banks, R. Rule of the bone
Banks, R. The sweet hereafter
Barbash, T. The last good chance
Busch, F. Closing arguments
Busch, F. A handbook for spies
Card, O. S. Treasure box
Cheever, J. Bullet Park
Clements, M. Midsummer
Cook, T. H. Instruments of night
Dreiser, T. An American tragedy
Freda, J. The patience of rivers
Gardner, J. Nickel mountain
Godwin, G. The finishing school
Gould, J. A moment in time
Hansen, R. Mariette in ecstasy
Lee, C.-R. A gesture life
Lurie, A. Only children
Malamud, B. Dubin's lives
Oates, J. C. Because it is bitter, and because it is my heart
Oates, J. C. Broke heart blues
Oates, J. C. Foxfire
Oates, J. C. I lock my door upon myself
Oates, J. C. Middle age
Oates, J. C. My heart laid bare
Oates, J. C. We were the Mulvaneys
Oates, J. C. What I lived for
O'Connell, C. Judas child
O'Nan, S. Wish you were here
Perry, T. Dance for the dead
Perry, T. The face-changers
Perry, T. Shadow woman
Perry, T. Vanishing act
Plain, B. Homecoming
Prose, F. Primitive people
Puzo, M. The godfather
Quindlen, A. Object lessons
Rice, L. Cloud Nine
Russo, R. Nobody's fool
Russo, R. The risk pool
Shreve, A. Eden Close
Spencer, S. A ship made of paper
Straub, P. Ghost story
Strieber, W. The forbidden zone
Westlake, D. E. Drowned hopes
Winegardner, M. The Godfather returns

21st century

Oates, J. C. The tattooed girl
Shriver, L. We need to talk about Kevin

Frontier and pioneer life

See Frontier and pioneer life—New York (State)

Politics

See Politics—New York (State)

Albany

Kennedy, W. Ironweed
Kennedy, W. Quinn's book
Kennedy, W. Roscoe
Kennedy, W. Very old bones

Batavia

Gardner, J. The sunlight dialogues

Buffalo

Belfer, L. City of light
Reisman, N. The first desire

Cooperstown

Cooper, J. F. The pioneers

Corinth

Lurie, A. The war between the Tates

Ithaca

O'Nan, S. The names of the dead

New York City

See New York (N.Y.)

Niagara Falls

Belfer, L. City of light
Oates, J. C. The falls
Oates, J. C. Rape

Saratoga Springs

Ferber, E. Saratoga trunk

Westchester County

Boyle, T. C. World's end
Donleavy, J. P. The lady who liked clean rest rooms
Green, G. D. The juror
Jen, G. Mona in the promised land

New York dead. Woods, S.
New York novels. Wharton, E.
NEW YORKER (PERIODICAL)
Keillor, G. Love me

NEW ZEALAND
Tremain, R. The color

19th century

Goudge, E. Green Dolphin Street

20th century

Hulme, K. The bone people

No witnesses. Pearson, R.
NOAH (BIBLICAL FIGURE)
About
Maine, D. The preservationist
NOBEL PRIZES
Wallace, I. The prize
NOBILITY *See* Aristocracy
Noble house. Clavell, J.
Nobody's angel. McGuane, T.
Nobody's fool. Russo, R.
Nocturne. McBain, E.
Noise. Clement, H.
The **nonborn** king. May, J.
None but the lonely heart. Llewellyn, R.
None to accompany me. Gordimer, N.
Noon wine. Porter, K. A.
In Porter, K. A. The collected stories of Katherine Anne Porter p222-68
In Porter, K. A. Pale horse, pale rider: three short novels
Nora Jane and company. Gilchrist, E.
In Gilchrist, E. The courts of love
Nora, Nora. Siddons, A. R.
NORMANDIE (STEAMSHIP)
Villars, E. The Normandie affair
The **Normandie** affair. Villars, E.
NORMANDY (FRANCE) *See* France—Normandy
NORTH AFRICA
See also Sahara
North and South. Jakes, J.
NORTH CAROLINA
Adams, S. K. My old true love
Brown, S. Chill factor
Dierbeck, L. One pill makes you smaller
Gibbons, K. Divining women
Gurganus, A. The oldest living Confederate widow tells all
Hickam, H. H. The keeper's son
Huyler, F. The laws of invisible things
Inman, R. Captain Saturday
McCrumb, S. The songcatcher
Patterson, J. Four blind mice
Price, R. The good priest's son
Sparks, N. The guardian
18th century
Gabaldon, D. A breath of snow and ashes
19th century
Crafts, H. The bondswomans narrative
Humphreys, J. Nowhere else on earth
Slouka, M. God's fool
Trotter, W. R. The sands of pride
20th century
Adams, A. After the war
Adams, A. A southern exposure
Betts, D. Souls raised from the dead
Bunn, T. D. The great divide
Card, O. S. Lost boys
Earley, T. Jim the boy
Edgerton, C. Killer diller
Edgerton, C. Walking across Egypt
Edgerton, C. Where trouble sleeps
Gibbons, K. Charms for the easy life
Gibbons, K. Sights unseen
Godwin, G. Evensong
Godwin, G. A mother and two daughters
Godwin, G. A Southern family
Gurganus, A. Blessed assurance: a moral tale
Gurganus, A. He's one, too
Gurganus, A. A hog loves its life: something about my grandfather
Gurganus, A. The practical heart [novelette]
Gurganus, A. Preservation news
Gurganus, A. Saint monster
McCorkle, J. Carolina moon
Medlicott, J. A. Gardens of Covington
Medlicott, J. A. The ladies of Covington send their love
Pearson, T. R. A short history of a small place
Percy, W. The second coming
Price, R. Blue Calhoun
Price, R. Kate Vaiden
Price, R. The promise of rest
Price, R. Roxanna Slade
Price, R. The tongues of angels
Ross, A. B. Miss Julia throws a wedding
Sparks, N. A bend in the road
Sparks, N. Nights in Rodanthe
Sparks, N. The notebook
Sparks, N. A walk to remember
Tyler, A. A slipping-down life
Tyler, A. The tin can tree
Wolfe, T. The web and the rock
Zuber, I. Salt
Farm life
See Farm life—North Carolina
NORTH DAKOTA
Erdrich, L. The Master Butchers Singing Club
19th century
Jones, D. C. Arrest Sitting Bull
20th century
Erdrich, L. The Beet Queen
Erdrich, L. The bingo palace
Erdrich, L. The last report on the miracles at Little No Horse
Erdrich, L. Tales of burning love
Erdrich, L. Tracks
Power, S. The grass dancer
Frontier and pioneer life
See Frontier and pioneer life—North Dakota
North of Montana. Smith, A.
North of nowhere, south of loss. Hospital, J. T.
Northanger Abbey. Austen, J.
also in Austen, J. The complete novels of Jane Austen
NORTHERN IRELAND
Deane, S. Reading in the dark
Llywelyn, M. 1972
Maas, P. Father and son
McNicholl, D. A son called Gabriel
Snyder, D. J. Night crossing
Politics
See Politics—Northern Ireland
Belfast
Moore, B. The emperor of ice-cream
Moore, B. Lies of silence
Moore, B. The lonely passion of Judith Hearne
NORTHERN RHODESIA *See* Zambia
NORTHMEN *See* Vikings
Northshore. Tepper, S. S.
NORTHUMBERLAND (ENGLAND) *See* England—Northumberland
NORTHWEST, OLD *See* Old Northwest
NORTHWEST, PACIFIC *See* Pacific Northwest
Northwest Passage. Roberts, K. L.
NORTHWEST TERRITORIES *See* Canada—Northwest Territories
The **Norton** book of science fiction. Entered in Part I under title
NORWAY
Hansen, E. F. Tales of protection
To 1397
Anderson, P. Mother of kings
Undset, S. Kristin Lavransdatter
20th century
Francis, C. Wolf winter
Farm life
See Farm life—Norway
Rural life
Undset, S. Kristin Lavransdatter
NORWEGIAN AMERICANS
Young, C. The wedding dress
NORWEGIANS
See also Vikings
United States
Rölvaag, O. E. Giants in the earth

NOVELETTES—*Continued*
Hemingway, E. The Hemingway reader
Hemingway, E. The torrents of spring
Hernández, F. Around the time of Clemente Colling
Hernández, F. Lands of memory [novelette]
Hilton, J. Good-bye Mr. Chips
Howard, M. Big as life
Howard, M. Children with matches
Howard, M. The Magdalene
Hrabal, B. Too loud a solitude
The Hugo winners
James, H. The Aspern papers
James, H. Complete stories, 1864-1874
James, H. Complete stories, 1874-1884
James, H. Complete stories, 1884-1891
James, H. Complete stories, 1892-1898
James, H. Complete stories, 1898-1910
James, H. The complete tales of Henry James
James, H. The Henry James reader
James, H. Short novels of Henry James
James, H. What Maisie knew, In the cage, The pupil
Kafka, F. Metamorphosis
Kawabata, Y. Snow country, and Thousand cranes
Kawabata, Y. Thousand cranes
King, S. Different seasons
King, S. Four past midnight
Kundera, M. Slowness
L'Amour, L. Monument Rock [novelette]
L'Amour, L. Rustler roundup
Le Guin, U. K. Four ways to forgiveness
Lessing, D. M. The fifth child
Lessing, D. M. The other woman
Levin, I. The Stepford wives
London, J. The call of the wild
Loo, T. d. A bed in heaven
Lovecraft, H. P. The mound
Makine, A. Music of a life
Mann, T. The black swan
Mann, T. Death in Venice
Mann, T. Tonio Kröger
Mann, T. Tristan
Martin, S. The pleasure of my company
Martin, S. Shopgirl
McCaffrey, A. The girl who heard dragons [novelette]
McCaffrey, A. The greatest love [novelette]
McCullers, C. The ballad of the sad café [novelette]
McEwan, I. Black dogs
Melville, H. Billy Budd, sailor
Mérimée, P. Carmen
Messud, C. The hunters
Messud, C. A simple tale
Millhauser, S. An adventure of Don Juan
Millhauser, S. The king in the tree
Millhauser, S. The king in the tree: three novellas
Millhauser, S. Revenge
Minot, S. Monkeys
Minot, S. Rapture
Nabokov, V. V. Transparent things
Nebula awards
Nin, A. Cities of the interior
Oates, J. C. Black water
Oates, J. C. I lock my door upon myself
Oates, J. C. The model
Oates, J. C. Rape
Oster, C. My big apartment
Otsuka, J. When the emperor was divine
Oz, A. Panther in the basement
Ozick, C. The Messiah of Stockholm
Ozick, C. Rosa
Poe, E. A. The imaginary voyages: The narrative of Arthur Gordon Pym; The unparalleled adventure of one Hans Pfaall; The journal of Julius Rodman
Poe, E. A. The narrative of Arthur Gordon Pym of Nantucket
Porter, K. A. Noon wine
Porter, K. A. Old mortality
Porter, K. A. Pale horse, pale rider [novelette]
Porter, K. A. Pale horse, pale rider: three short novels
Potok, C. The ark builder
Potok, C. Old men at midnight
Potok, C. The troupe teacher
Potok, C. The war doctor
Pym, B. Civil to strangers
Rand, A. Anthem
Rendell, R. Heartstones
Robinson, K. S. Green Mars [novelette]
Roth, J. The bust of the emperor
Roth, J. The leviathan
Roth, J. The triumph of beauty
Roth, P. The dying animal
Roth, P. The Prague orgy
Sagan, F. Bonjour tristesse
Salinger, J. D. Franny & Zooey
Salinger, J. D. Raise high the roof beam, carpenters, and Seymour: an introduction
Sand, G. Marianne
Segal, E. Love story
Silverberg, R. Phases of the moon
Simenon, G. Maigret and the fortune-teller
Simenon, G. Maigret and the Saturday caller
Simenon, G. Maigret goes home
Simon, C. The trolley
Smiley, J. The age of grief [novelette]
Spark, M. The Abbess of Crewe
Spark, M. The driver's seat
Spark, M. The go-away bird
Spencer, E. Knights and dragons
Spencer, E. The light in the piazza
Steinbeck, J. Of mice and men
Steinbeck, J. The pearl
Steinbeck, J. The red pony
Stevenson, R. L. The beach of Falesá
Stevenson, R. L. The merry men
Stevenson, R. L. The misadventures of John Nicholson
Stevenson, R. L. The story of a lie
Stevenson, R. L. The strange case of Dr. Jekyll and Mr. Hyde
Stout, R. The cop-killer
Stout, R. Die like a dog
Stout, R. Door to death
Stout, R. Home to roost
Stout, R. Man alive
Stout, R. The next witness
Stout, R. Omit flowers
Stout, R. The squirt and the monkey
Stout, R. When a man murders
Straub, P. The buffalo hunter
Straub, P. Mrs. God
Theroux, P. Half Moon Street
Tolstoy, L., graf. The Kreutzer sonata
Tolstoy, L., graf. Master and man
Tolstoy, L., graf. The short novels of Tolstoy
T͡Sypkin, L. Summer in Baden-Baden
Turgenev, I. S. First love and other stories
Updike, J. Rabbit remembered
Welty, E. The Ponder heart
West, N. The dream life of Balso Snell
West, P. The dry Danube
Westlake, D. E. Levine
Wiesel, E. Dawn
Wiesel, E. Night, Dawn, The accident: three tales
Williams, T. The Roman spring of Mrs. Stone
Yoshimoto, B. Asleep
Yoshimoto, B. Kitchen [novella]
Yoshimoto, B. Love songs
Yoshimoto, B. Night and night's travelers

NOVELISTS *See* Authors
Novella. Goethe, J. W. v.
In Goethe, J. W. v. The sorrows of young Werther, and Novella p169-201
NOVELLAS *See* Novelettes
Novellas and other writings. Wharton, E.
NOVELS, UNFINISHED *See* Unfinished novels
Novels. Wharton, E.
Novels & stories. London, J.
Novels, 1875-1886. Howells, W. D.
Novels, 1920-1925. Dos Passos, J.
Novels, 1930-1935. Faulkner, W.
Novels, 1930-1942. Powell, D.
Novels, 1936-1940. Faulkner, W.
Novels, 1942-1952. Steinbeck, J.
Novels, 1942-1954. Faulkner, W.
Novels, 1944-1953. Bellow, S.
Novels, 1944-1962. Powell, D.
Novels, 1955-1962. Nabokov, V. V.
Novels, 1957-1962. Faulkner, W.
Novels, 1969-1974. Nabokov, V. V.
Novels and essays. Norris, F.
Novels and stories. Hurston, Z. N.

O

Of such small differences. Greenberg, J.
Of time and the river. Wolfe, T.
Off Keck Road. Simpson, M.
Off the chart. Hall, J. W.
Off the Mangrove Coast. L'Amour, L.
Office of innocence. Keneally, T.

OFFICE WORKERS

Hynes, J. Kings of infinite space
Moon, E. The speed of dark

Officer down. Grant, M.
Officers and gentlemen. Waugh, E.
The **officers'** wives. Fleming, T. J.

OGLALA INDIANS

Blevins, W. Stone song
Chiaventone, F. J. Moon of bitter cold
Johnston, T. C. Turn the stars upside down
O'Brien, D. The contract surgeon
Welch, J. The heartsong of Charging Elk

The **ogre**. Tournier, M.
Oh, what a paradise it seems. Cheever, J.

OHIO

Santmyer, H. H. "—and ladies of the club"

18th century

Richter, C. The awakening land

19th century

Anderson, S. Poor white
Anderson, S. Tar: a midwest childhood
Anderson, S. Winesburg, Ohio
Richter, C. The awakening land

20th century

Bialosky, J. House under snow
Crusie, J. Crazy for you
DeMille, N. Spencerville
Dew, R. F. The evidence against her
Dove, R. Through the ivory gate
King, S. The regulators
Kitchen, J. The house on Eccles Road
Morrison, T. The bluest eye
Morrison, T. Sula
Patterson, R. N. Silent witness
Powell, D. Come back to Sorrento
Powell, D. Dance night
Powell, D. My home is far away
Shreve, S. R. The visiting physician
Smith, S. B. A simple plan
Vonnegut, K. Deadeye Dick

Frontier and pioneer life

See Frontier and pioneer life—Ohio

Cincinnati

Holden, C. The jazz bird

Columbus

Crusie, J. Faking it

OHIO RIVER VALLEY

Settle, M. L. O Beulah Land

Frontier and pioneer life

See Frontier and pioneer life—Ohio River Valley

OIL INDUSTRY *See* Petroleum industry
OIL WELLS *See* Petroleum industry
OJIBWA INDIANS *See* Chippewa Indians
OKINAWA (JAPAN) *See* Japan—Okinawa

OKLAHOMA

Blanchard, A. The breathtaker
Hart, C. G. Letter from home
Letts, B. Shoot the moon

19th century

Ferber, E. Cimarron

20th century

Hunter, S. Dirty white boys
Morrison, T. Paradise

Frontier and pioneer life

See Frontier and pioneer life—Oklahoma

Politics

See Politics—Oklahoma

Tulsa

Bernhardt, W. Criminal intent
Bernhardt, W. Cruel justice
Bernhardt, W. Murder one
Bernhardt, W. Silent justice
Straight, S. The gettin place

OLD AGE

See also Aging
Amis, K. The old devils
Barnard, R. A cry from the dark
Bawden, N. Family money
Bradford, B. T. Hold the dream
Bromfield, L. Mrs. Parkington
Brookner, A. Fraud
Brookner, A. Making things better
Calisher, H. Sunday Jews
Cary, J. The horse's mouth
Cheever, J. Oh, what a paradise it seems
Coetzee, J. M. Age of iron
Conrad, J. The end of the tether
Cooper, J. F. The prairie
Denker, H. Mrs. Washington and Horowitz, too
Dickinson, P. Some deaths before dying
Dixon, S. Old friends
Edgerton, C. Walking across Egypt
Elkin, S. Mrs. Ted Bliss
Fast, H. Redemption
Galsworthy, J. The Indian summer of a Forsyte
Galsworthy, J. Swan song
García Márquez, G. No one writes to the colonel
Gardner, J. October light
Gordon, M. Final payments
Greenfeld, J. Harry and Tonto
Gurganus, A. The oldest living Confederate widow tells all
Hassler, J. The Staggerford flood
Hemingway, E. The old man and the sea
Hilton, J. Good-bye Mr. Chips
Kawabata, Y. The sound of the mountain
King, S. Insomnia
Krauss, N. The history of love
Lindgren, T. Hash
Malamud, B. Dubin's lives
McFarland, D. School for the blind
McMurtry, L. The evening star
Medlicott, J. A. Gardens of Covington
Medlicott, J. A. The ladies of Covington send their love
Messud, C. A simple tale
Mestre-Reed, E. The second death of Única Aveyano
Michener, J. A. Recessional
Miller, S. The distinguished guest
Mistry, R. Family matters
Mosley, W. RL's dream
Pouncey, P. R. Rules for old men waiting
Price, R. The good priest's son
Purdy, J. The nephew
Quindlen, A. Blessings
Roth, P. Sabbath's theater
Sackville-West, V. All passion spent
Sarton, M. As we are now
Sarton, M. Kinds of love
Scott, A. Calpurnia
Scott, P. Staying on
Simon, C. The trolley
Spark, M. Memento mori
Sparks, N. The notebook
Stegner, W. E. The spectator bird
Taylor, E. Mrs. Palfrey at the Claremont
Trollope, J. The men and the girls
Tyler, A. A patchwork planet
Updike, J. The poorhouse fair
Updike, J. Seek my face
Weldon, F. Rhode Island blues
Wharton, W. Dad
White, P. The eye of the storm
Wiesel, E. The forgotten

OLD AGE HOMES

See also Nursing homes; Retirement communities
Sarton, M. As we are now
Updike, J. The poorhouse fair

Old boys. McCarry, C.
The **Old** Contemptibles. Grimes, M.

OREGON—*Continued*

Portland

Buffa, D. W. The defense
Buffa, D. W. The judgment
Buffa, D. W. The prosecution

ORIENT AND OCCIDENT *See* East and West
Orient Express. Greene, G.
The **origin** of the Brunists. Coover, R.
Original sin. James, P. D.
Orion among the stars. Bova, B.
Orion and the conqueror. Bova, B.
Orion in the dying time. Bova, B.
Orion shall rise. Anderson, P.

ORISKANY, BATTLE OF, 1777

Edmonds, W. D. Drums along the Mohawk

Orlando. Woolf, V.

ORLÉANS, CHARLES D' *See* Charles, d'Orléans, 1394-1465

ORNITHOLOGISTS

Brown, J. G. Audubon's watch

An **ornithologist's** guide to life. Hood, A.

ORPHANS

Alcott, L. M. The inheritance
Alexander, B. Smuggler's moon
Allende, I. Eva Luna
Berry, W. Jayber Crow
Brontë, C. Emma
Brontë, C. Jane Eyre
Brontë, E. Wuthering Heights
Brown, J. D. Addie Pray
Brown, R. Civil wars
Capote, T. The grass harp
Cronin, A. J. A song of sixpence
D'Amato, B. White male infant
Dickens, C. Great expectations
Dickens, C. The old curiosity shop
Dickens, C. Oliver Twist
Doctorow, E. L. The book of Daniel
Høeg, P. Borderliners
Holland, C. Railroad schemes
Holt, V. The black opal
Holt, V. The Judas kiss
Inness-Brown, E. Burning Marguerite
Irving, J. The cider house rules
Johnston, W. The navigator of New York
Lawson, M. Crow Lake
Mitchard, J. A theory of relativity
Mukherjee, B. Leave it to me
Newman, S. The only good thing anyone has ever done
Nin, A. Children of the albatross
Norman, H. The museum guard
Ozick, C. Heir to the glimmering world
Ozick, C. The Messiah of Stockholm
Ross-Macdonald, M. The Trevarton inheritance
Sholem Aleichem. The adventures of Mottel, the cantor's son
Shreve, S. R. Plum & Jaggers
Tevis, W. S. The queen's gambit
Wallace, D. The Watermelon King
Ward, L. Outside valentine
Wilhelm, K. The good children
Wood, B. The dreaming

Orsinian tales. Le Guin, U. K.
The **O'Ruddy**. Crane, S.
In Crane, S. The complete novels of Stephen Crane p593-790
Oryx and Crake. Atwood, M.
Oscar & Lucinda. Carey, P.

OSS *See* United States. Office of Strategic Services

O'SULLIVAN BEARE, DONAL CAM, 1560-1618

About

Llywelyn, M. The last prince of Ireland

O'Sullivan's march. See Llywelyn, M. The last prince of Ireland

OSWALD, LEE HARVEY, 1939-1963

About

DeLillo, D. Libra

The **other**. Tryon, T.
Other people's children. Trollope, J.
Other people's marriages. Thomas, R.
The **other** side of silence. Brink, A. P.
The **other** side of the door. O'Donnell, L.
The **other** side of the story. Keyes, M.
The **other** side of the sun. L'Engle, M.
Other voices, other rooms. Capote, T.
The **other** wind. Le Guin, U. K.
The **other** woman. Lessing, D. M.
In Lessing, D. M. Stories p157-211
Our father. French, M.
Our game. Le Carré, J.
Our gang. Roth, P.
In Roth, P. Novels, 1967-1972
Our kind. Walbert, K.
Our Lady of the Forest. Guterson, D.
Our man in Havana. Greene, G.
Our mutual friend. Dickens, C.
Out of India. Jhabvala, R. P.
Out of Phaze. Anthony, P.
Out of sight. Leonard, E.
Out of the blackout. Barnard, R.
Out of the silent planet. Lewis, C. S.
Out on a limb. Hess, J.
Out on the cutting edge. Block, L.
Out to Canaan. Karon, J.
Outbreak. Cook, R.
The **outcast**. Pirandello, L.
Outcasts. Brand, M.
In Brand, M. Max Brand's best western stories

OUTDOOR LIFE

See also Country life; Wilderness survival

Outer banks. Siddons, A. R.

OUTER SPACE

See also Space flight

Communication

See Interstellar communication

Outerbridge Reach. Stone, R.
Outfoxed. Brown, R. M.

OUTLAWS

See also Brigands and robbers

Bonner, C. Lily
Bonner, C. Looking after Lily
Carey, P. True history of the Kelly gang
Estleman, L. D. Billy Gashade
Estleman, L. D. Black powder, white smoke
Estleman, L. D. City of widows
Estleman, L. D. White desert
Grey, Z. Last of the Duanes
Hansen, R. The assassination of Jesse James by the coward Robert Ford
Henry, W. Mackenna's gold
Humphreys, J. Nowhere else on earth
Jones, D. C. The search for Temperance Moon
L'Amour, L. The outlaws of Mesquite
McMurtry, L. Anything for Billy
McMurtry, L. Streets of Laredo
Murkoff, B. Waterborne
Resnick, M. The return of Santiago
Williamson, P. The outsider

The **outlaws** of Mesquite. L'Amour, L.
Outside valentine. Ward, L.
The **outside** world. Mirvis, T.
The **outsider**. Fast, H.
The **outsider**. Williamson, P.
The **outsider**. Wright, R.
also in Wright, R. Works
Over the edge. Kellerman, J.
Over the river. Galsworthy, J.
In Galsworthy, J. End of the chapter p593-897
The **overcoat,** and other tales of good and evil. Gogol´, N. V.

OVERLAND JOURNEYS

Bristow, G. Jubilee Trail
Holland, C. An ordinary woman
Hunter, E. The Chisholms
Wolitzer, H. Hearts

OVERLAND JOURNEYS TO THE PACIFIC

Guthrie, A. B. The way West
Mosher, H. F. The true account
Taylor, R. L. The travels of Jaimie McPheeters
Vanderhaeghe, G. The last crossing

The **Ox-bow** incident. Clark, W. V. T.

OXFORD (ENGLAND) *See* England—Oxford

Oxford blood. Fraser, A.

The **Oxford** book of American detective stories. Entered in Part I under title

P

PALESTINE—*Continued*

20th century

Oz, A. Panther in the basement
Uris, L. Exodus
Wiesel, E. Dawn
Wilson, J. A Palestine affair
A **Palestine** affair. Wilson, J.
PALESTINIAN ARABS
See also Jewish-Arab relations
Keneally, T. Flying hero class
Qashu, S. Dancing Arabs
Palindrome. Woods, S.
Palladio. Dee, J.
The **Pallisers**. Trollope, A.
PALM BEACH (FLA.) *See* Florida—Palm Beach
A **palm** for Mrs. Pollifax. Gilman, D.
Pamela. Richardson, S.
PANAMA
Galbraith, D. The rising sun
Le Carré, J. The tailor of Panama
Panama. McGuane, T.
Pandora's box. Gage, E.
Pandora's clock. Nance, J. J.
Pandora's star. Hamilton, P. F.
Panther in the basement. Oz, A.
Panther in the sky. Thom, J. A.
PAPACY *See* Catholic faith; Popes
Paper doll. Parker, R. B.
The **paper** men. Golding, W.
Paper money. Follett, K.
The **paperboy**. Dexter, P.
PAPERS *See* Manuscripts
Parable of the sower. Butler, O. E.
Parable of the talents. Butler, O. E.
PARABLES
See also Allegories
Appelfeld, A. The conversion
Brink, A. P. Devil's Valley
Butler, O. E. Parable of the sower
Butler, O. E. Parable of the talents
Crace, J. The gift of stones
Fitzgerald, P. The gate of angels
Girzone, J. F. Joshua and the children
Girzone, J. F. Joshua and the city
Girzone, J. F. Joshua in the Holy Land
Girzone, J. F. Joshua, the homecoming
Girzone, J. F. The shepherd
Goethe, J. W. v. Novella
Grass, G. Dog years
Han, S. The enchantress
Hemingway, E. The old man and the sea
Hrabal, B. I served the King of England
Kadare, I. The three-arched bridge
Kosinski, J. N. Being there
Kotzwinkle, W. The bear went over the mountain
Le Guin, U. K. The telling
Llywelyn, M. The elementals
Oates, J. C. I lock my door upon myself
Paretsky, S. Ghost country
Roth, J. The bust of the emperor
Spark, M. The Abbess of Crewe
Steinbeck, J. East of Eden
Steinbeck, J. The pearl
Tremain, R. The way I found her
Vonnegut, K. Deadeye Dick
Vonnegut, K. Galápagos
Weldon, F. The life and loves of a she-devil
Wright, A. M. After Gregory
Parade's end. Ford, F. M.
Paradise. Morrison, T.
Paradise Alley. Baker, K.
Paradise news. Lodge, D.
Paradise park. Goodman, A.
Paradise postponed. Mortimer, J. C.
Paragon Walk. Perry, A.
PARALYSIS
See also Paraplegics
Barfoot, J. Critical injuries
Kafka, K. Miranda's vines
PARANOIA
Campbell, R. Pact of the fathers
Gibson, W. Pattern recognition
Koontz, D. R. False memory
Koontz, D. R. Sole survivor
Pynchon, T. Vineland
Wright, S. Going native
PARAPLEGICS
Kellogg, M. Tell me that you love me, Junie Moon
Parasites like us. Johnson, A.
A **parchment** of leaves. House, S.
Pardonable lies. Winspear, J.
PARENT AND CHILD
See also Conflict of generations; Fathers and daughters; Fathers and sons; Mothers and daughters; Mothers and sons
Bambara, T. C. Those bones are not my child
Banks, R. Affliction
Beattie, A. Picturing Will
Berne, S. A perfect arrangement
Bragg, M. Crossing the lines
Brookner, A. Family and friends
Brown, R. Before and after
Card, O. S. Lost boys
Carroll, J. Fault lines
Chaon, D. You remind me of me
Clark, M. H. Remember me
Clements, M. Midsummer
Cumyn, A. Losing it
Dart, I. R. The Stork Club
Denker, H. This child is mine
Dixon, S. Gould
Doctorow, E. L. The book of Daniel
Dorrestein, R. Without mercy
Duncan, G. Death of an ordinary man
Fromm, P. As cool as I am
García, C. The Aguero sisters
Gilchrist, E. Nora Jane and company
Godden, R. The battle of the Villa Fiorita
Gordimer, N. The house gun
Greene, G. The captain and the enemy
Haddon, M. The curious incident of the dog in the night-time
Hearon, S. Footprints
Hustvedt, S. What I loved
Ishiguro, K. When we were orphans
James, H. What Maisie knew
Krauss, N. The history of love
Lamott, A. Blue shoe
L'Engle, M. A live coal in the sea
Lessing, D. M. The fifth child
Levenkron, S. The best little girl in the world
Lurie, A. Only children
Lurie, A. The war between the Tates
McDermott, A. Child of my heart
McEwan, I. The child in time
Meloy, M. Liars and saints
Michaels, F. Finders keepers
Miller, S. Family pictures
Miller, S. Lost in the forest
Mirvis, T. The outside world
Mistry, R. Family matters
Nolan, C. The banyan tree
Oates, J. C. Middle age
Parks, T. Destiny
Perrotta, T. Little children
Powell, P. Edisto
Price, R. Blue Calhoun
Price, R. Roxanna Slade
Rash, R. Saints at the river
Rice, L. Cloud Nine
Schwartz, L. Angels Crest
Sharpe, M. The sleeping father
Spencer, S. A ship made of paper
Straight, S. I been in sorrow's kitchen and licked out all the pots
Tarkington, B. Alice Adams
Thayer, N. Between husbands and friends
Tilghman, C. Mason's retreat
Trollope, J. The best of friends
Trollope, J. Other people's children
Turow, S. The laws of our fathers
Tyler, A. The clock winder
Tyler, A. Dinner at the Homesick Restaurant
Wagner, B. The chrysanthemum palace
Weber, K. The little women

PHILOSOPHICAL NOVELS—*Continued*
Hansen, R. Mariette in ecstasy
Harrar, G. The spinning man
Hazzard, S. The great fire
Heinrich, W. The king's evil
Helprin, M. A soldier of the great war
Hoban, R. Riddley Walker
Høeg, P. Borderliners
Høeg, P. The woman and the ape
Hulme, K. The bone people
Hustvedt, S. What I loved
Ishiguro, K. Never let me go
Johnson, C. R. Middle passage
Kadare, I. The Successor
Koeppen, W. The hothouse
Kundera, M. Identity
Kundera, M. Ignorance
Kundera, M. Immortality
Kundera, M. Slowness
Kundera, M. The unbearable lightness of being
Kurzweil, A. The grand complication
Le Guin, U. K. The dispossessed
Lehrer, J. The special prisoner
Lem, S. Solaris
Lessing, D. M. Mara and Dann
Lewis, C. S. Out of the silent planet
Lewis, C. S. Perelandra
Lewis, C. S. That hideous strength
Lightman, A. P. The diagnosis
Lightman, A. P. Einstein's dreams
Lively, P. City of the mind
Lodge, D. Thinks—
Maḥfūẓ, N. Children of the alley
Maḥfūẓ, N. Palace of desire
Maḥfūẓ, N. Sugar Street
Malouf, D. Harland's half acre
Malouf, D. Remembering Babylon
Mann, T. The magic mountain
Marías, J. The man of feeling
Maugham, W. S. The razor's edge
McCarthy, C. All the pretty horses
McCarthy, C. Cities of the plain
McCarthy, M. Birds of America
McEwan, I. Atonement
McEwan, I. Black dogs
Melville, H. Mardi: and a voyager thither
Michaels, A. Fugitive pieces
Mishima, Y. The temple of the golden pavilion
Mitchell, D. Cloud atlas
Moore, B. Black robe
Moore, B. The statement
Mosley, W. The man in my basement
Mulisch, H. Siegfried
Murakami, H. The wind-up bird chronicle
Murdoch, I. The book and the brotherhood
Murdoch, I. The good apprentice
Murdoch, I. The green knight
Murdoch, I. Jackson's dilemma
Murdoch, I. The philosopher's pupil
Naylor, G. Linden Hills
Nooteboom, C. All souls' day
Norman, H. The museum guard
Ōe, K. An echo of heaven
Ōe, K. Nip the buds, shoot the kids
Ondaatje, M. Anil's ghost
Ondaatje, M. The English patient
Ozick, C. The cannibal galaxy
Pamuk, O. My name is Red
Percy, W. The last gentleman
Percy, W. The moviegoer
Percy, W. The second coming
Percy, W. The thanatos syndrome
Pérez-Reverte, A. The nautical chart
Phillips, C. Cambridge
Powers, R. The gold bug variations
Powers, R. Operation wandering soul
Powers, R. Plowing the dark
Powers, R. Prisoner's dilemma
Powers, R. The time of our singing
Pywell, S. L. What happened to Henry
Reuss, F. Henry of Atlantic City
Reuss, F. Horace afoot
Robbins, T. Skinny legs and all
Russell, M. D. Children of God
Russell, M. D. The sparrow
Saint-Exupéry, A. d. The little prince
Saramago, J. All the names
Saramago, J. The cave
Saramago, J. The history of the siege of Lisbon
Sartre, J. P. Nausea
Scott, J. Tourmaline
Sebald, W. G. Austerlitz
Sebald, W. G. The emigrants
Sebald, W. G. Vertigo
Sheehan, E. R. F. Cardinal Galsworthy
Shields, C. Unless
Simon, C. The trolley
Singer, I. B. Shadows on the Hudson
Spark, M. Aiding and abetting
Stone, R. Bay of souls
Stone, R. Outerbridge Reach
Suri, M. The death of Vishnu
Tournier, M. Friday
Tournier, M. The ogre
Updike, J. Roger's version
Vidal, G. Creation
Voltaire. Zadig
Vonnegut, K. Galápagos
Whitehead, C. The intuitionist
Wiesel, E. The forgotten
Wiesel, E. The judges
Wiesel, E. Twilight
Zimler, R. The last kabbalist of Lisbon

Phineas Finn [abridged] Trollope, A.
In Trollope, A. The Pallisers p117-88

Phineas Redux [abridged] Trollope, A.
In Trollope, A. The Pallisers p265-323

PHOENIX (ARIZ.) *See* Arizona—Phoenix

Photo finish. Marsh, Dame N.

The **photograph**. Lively, P.

PHOTOGRAPHERS
See also Women photographers
Barker, C. Sacrament
Beattie, A. Picturing Will
Coetzee, J. M. Slow man
Colegate, I. Winter journey
Fergus, J. The wild girl: the notebooks of Ned Giles, 1932
Greeley, A. M. Second spring
Greeley, A. M. Younger than springtime
Jakes, J. Homeland
Kennedy, D. The big picture
Llywelyn, M. 1972
Mayle, P. Chasing Cézanne
McFarland, D. School for the blind
Morton, B. A window across the river
Norman, H. The haunting of L
Rushdie, S. The ground beneath her feet
Theroux, P. Picture palace
Vollmann, W. T. Butterfly stories
Waller, R. J. The bridges of Madison County
Wideman, J. E. Two cities
Wiggins, M. Evidence of things unseen

PHOTOGRAPHS
Dickinson, P. Some deaths before dying
Lively, P. The photograph

Phylogenesis. Foster, A. D.

PHYSICALLY HANDICAPPED
See also Blind; Deaf; Hunchbacks; Paraplegics; Physically handicapped children; Quadriplegics
Brown, R. Tender mercies
Dunn, K. Geek love
Evans, N. The horse whisperer
Graham, W. The walking stick
Greenberg, J. Of such small differences
Laskowski, T. Every good boy does fine
Mapson, J.-A. Bad Girl Creek
Maugham, W. S. Of human bondage
McCracken, E. The giant's house
McCullers, C. The ballad of the sad café [novelette]
Purdy, J. In a shallow grave
Rendell, R. Live flesh
Reynolds, S. A gracious plenty
Stewart, M. Nine coaches waiting
Trumbo, D. Johnny got his gun

PHYSICALLY HANDICAPPED CHILDREN
Graver, E. Awake

POLICE

Amis, M. Night train
Berger, T. Suspects
Cook, T. H. The interrogation
Daley, R. A faint cold fear
Daley, R. Nowhere to run
King, S. Rose Madder
Leonard, E. Out of sight
Rendell, R. Live flesh

Alabama

Kerley, J. The hundredth man

Arkansas

Hunter, S. Pale horse coming

Atlanta (Ga.)

Johansen, I. Blind alley

Bangkok (Thailand)

Burdett, J. Bangkok 8
Burdett, J. Bangkok Tattoo

Baton Rouge (La.)

Drummond, L. L. Anything you say can and will be used against you

Boston (Mass.)

Adler, E. Now or never
Gerritsen, T. The apprentice
Gerritsen, T. Body double
Gerritsen, T. The sinner
Gerritsen, T. The surgeon
Higgins, G. V. Bomber's law
Lehane, D. Mystic river
Palmer, M. The society

California

Caputo, P. Equation for evil
Crais, R. Hostage
Foster, A. D. The mocking program
Koontz, D. R. Dragon tears
Muller, M. Point deception
Parker, T. J. Black water
Parker, T. J. The blue hour
Parker, T. J. California girl
Parker, T. J. Red light
Parker, T. J. Where serpents lie
Rosenberg, N. T. Abuse of power
Rosenberg, N. T. Interest of justice
Wambaugh, J. Finnegan's week
Woods, S. Dead eyes

Chicago (Ill.)

D'Amato, B. Good cop, bad cop
Harris, E. L. And this too shall pass

Connecticut

Pearson, R. Chain of evidence

Detroit (Mich.)

Estleman, L. D. Jitterbug
Leonard, E. Freaky Deaky
Leonard, E. Mr. Paradise
Leonard, E. Split images

Eastern Europe

Steinhauer, O. The Bridge of Sighs

England

See also Police—London (England)
Keating, H. R. F. The bad detective
McDermid, V. A place of execution

Florida

Hoffman, A. Turtle Moon
Leonard, E. Maximum Bob
Leonard, E. Rum punch
Woods, S. Choke
Woods, S. Orchid Beach
Woods, S. Reckless abandon

Georgia

Woods, S. Chiefs

Hollywood (Calif.)

See Police—Los Angeles (Calif.)

Houston (Tex.)

Lindsey, D. L. An absence of light

Indiana

Collins, M. Lost souls

Iowa

Harstad, D. Code sixty-one

Ireland

Parsons, J. Mary, Mary

Las Vegas (Nev.)

Ellroy, J. The cold six thousand

London (England)

Deighton, L. SS-GB: Nazi-occupied Britain 1941
Forsyth, F. The day of the jackal
Fyfield, F. Blind date
Gilbert, M. The killing of Katie Steelstock

Los Angeles (Calif.)

Cannell, S. J. Hollywood tough
Cannell, S. J. Riding the snake
Cannell, S. J. Vertical coffin
Cannell, S. J. The Viking funeral
Crais, R. Demolition angel
Crichton, M. Rising sun
Dexter, P. Train
Dunne, J. G. True confessions
Ellroy, J. Because the night
Ellroy, J. The black dahlia
Ellroy, J. Blood on the moon
Ellroy, J. L.A. confidential
Ellroy, J. L.A. noir
Ellroy, J. Suicide hill
Ellroy, J. White jazz
Hoag, T. Kill the messenger
Knode, H. The ticket out
Ridley, J. Those who walk in darkness
Shannon, D. Chaos of crime
Wambaugh, J. The black marble
Wambaugh, J. The blue knight
Wambaugh, J. The Delta Star
Wambaugh, J. The Glitter Dome
Wambaugh, J. The new centurions

Maine

Connolly, J. Bad men
King, T. Survivor

Massachusetts

See also Police—Boston (Mass.)
Gardner, L. Alone
Hoffman, A. The river king

Miami (Fla.)

Gruber, M. Valley of bones
Hailey, A. Detective
Hoffman, J. Retribution
Leonard, E. Glitz

Michigan

Finder, J. Company man

Minnesota

Hoag, T. Dust to dust
Hoag, T. Night sins
Tracy, P. J. Monkeewrench

Mississippi

Brown, L. Fay

Nevada

King, S. Desperation

New Jersey

Price, R. Clockers
Price, R. Freedomland
Price, R. Samaritan

New Orleans (La.)

Abel, K. The burying field
Abel, K. Cold steel rain
Brown, S. Fat Tuesday
Burke, J. L. The neon rain

POLITICS—*Continued*

Canada

Johnston, W. The colony of unrequited dreams
MacNeil, R. The voyage

Central America

Didion, J. A book of common prayer
Stone, R. A flag for sunrise

Chile

Allende, I. The house of the spirits

China

Bosse, M. J. The warlord
Buck, P. S. Imperial woman
Ha Jin. In the pond
Li, P.-h. Farewell to my concubine
Min, A. Becoming Madame Mao

Egypt

Durrell, L. Mountolive

England

Anthony, E. Anne Boleyn
Archer, J. First among equals
Barnard, R. A murder in Mayfair
Coe, J. The closed circle
Delderfield, R. F. A horseman riding by
Drabble, M. The radiant way
Goddard, R. Into the blue
Hart, J. Damage
Maxwell, R. The secret diary of Anne Boleyn
McEwan, I. Amsterdam
Mortimer, J. C. The sound of trumpets
Mortimer, J. C. Titmuss regained
Penman, S. K. Time and chance
Penman, S. K. When Christ and his saints slept
Snow, C. P. Corridors of power
Thackeray, W. M. The history of Henry Esmond, esquire
Trollope, A. The Eustace diamonds
Trollope, A. Phineas Finn [abridged]
Trollope, A. The prime minister

Ethiopia

Keneally, T. To Asmara

Europe

Dunnett, D. Niccolò rising
Dunnett, D. Race of scorpions
Dunnett, D. The spring of the ram
Fraser, G. M. Royal Flash
Sartre, J. P. The reprieve

France

Beauvoir, S. d. The mandarins
Steinbeck, J. The short reign of Pippin IV

Guatemala

Henley, P. Hummingbird house

Hawaii

Michener, J. A. Hawaii

India

Mehta, G. Raj
Rushdie, S. Shalimar the clown
Scott, P. A division of the spoils

Ireland

Carr, P. The black swan
Flanagan, T. The end of the hunt
Uris, L. Redemption
Uris, L. Trinity

Italy

Silone, I. Bread and wine
Tomasi di Lampedusa, G. The Leopard

Kentucky

Warren, R. P. World enough and time

Latin America

Allende, I. Eva Luna
Allende, I. Of love and shadows
García Márquez, G. The autumn of the patriarch

Massachusetts

Martin, W. Cape Cod

Middle Western States

Patterson, R. N. Dark lady

New York (State)

Isaacs, S. Close relations
Kennedy, W. Roscoe
Oates, J. C. What I lived for

Northern Ireland

Moore, B. Lies of silence

Oklahoma

Ferber, E. Cimarron

Rome

Massie, A. Caesar
McCullough, C. Caesar
McCullough, C. Caesar's women
McCullough, C. The first man in Rome
McCullough, C. Fortune's favorites
McCullough, C. The grass crown
Waltari, M. The Roman

Russia

Koestler, A. Darkness at noon
Pasternak, B. L. Doctor Zhivago

South Africa

Brink, A. P. Imaginings of sand
Gordimer, N. Burger's daughter
Gordimer, N. My son's story
Gordimer, N. None to accompany me
Gordimer, N. A sport of nature
Paton, A. Ah, but your land is beautiful
Smith, W. A. Rage

South America

Conrad, J. Nostromo

Southern States

Warren, R. P. All the king's men
Woods, S. Grass roots

Texas

Michener, J. A. Texas

United States

Lewis, S. It can't happen here
Mallon, T. Dewey defeats Truman
Roth, P. Our gang
Sandburg, C. Remembrance Rock
Vidal, G. Hollywood

United States—To 1900

Adams, H. Democracy
Brown, R. M. Dolley
Byrd, M. Grant
Jakes, J. Heaven and hell
Jakes, J. Love and war
Lockridge, R. Raintree County
Safire, W. Scandalmonger
Stone, I. Love is eternal
Twain, M. The gilded age
Vidal, G. 1876
Vidal, G. Burr
Vidal, G. Empire
Vidal, G. Lincoln

United States—1900-

Baldacci, D. Saving Faith
Buckley, W. F. Getting it right
Buckley, W. F. The Redhunter
Caldwell, T. Captains and kings
Carroll, J. The city below
Clancy, T. Executive orders
Clark, M. H. Stillwatch
Cussler, C. Deep six
Doctorow, E. L. The book of Daniel
Drury, A. Advise and consent
Dunne, D. A season in purgatory
Dunne, J. G. Nothing lost
Ellis, D. Life sentence
Ellroy, J. American tabloid
Frank, J. Bad publicity
Frey, S. W. The inner sanctum
Gordon, N. The company you keep

POVERTY—*Continued*
Hardy, T. Jude the obscure
Hijuelos, O. Empress of the splendid season
Hugo, V. Les misérables
Hurston, Z. N. Seraph on the Suwanee
Laskas, G. M. The midwife's tale
Lawson, M. Crow Lake
Maḥfūẓ, N. Children of the alley
Maḥfūẓ, N. Midaq Alley
Malouf, D. Harland's half acre
Markandaya, K. A handful of rice
Morgan, R. Gap Creek
Morris, M. M. The lost mother
Morris, M. M. Songs in ordinary time
Morrison, T. The bluest eye
Morrison, T. Sula
Norris, F. McTeague
Oates, J. C. A garden of earthly delights
Oates, J. C. Them
Parks, S.-L. Getting mother's body
Paul, J. A girl, in parts
Sinclair, U. The jungle
Smith, Z. White teeth
Stirling, J. The penny wedding
Straight, S. I been in sorrow's kitchen and licked out all the pots
Vernon, O. Eden
Welty, E. Losing battles
Woodrell, D. The death of sweet mister
Wright, R. Native son

POWER (SOCIAL SCIENCES)
See also Political ethics
Alai. Red poppies
Archer, J. First among equals
Burgess, A. Earthly powers
Carter, S. L. The emperor of Ocean Park
Clavell, J. Gai-Jin
Clavell, J. Shogun
Heinlein, R. A. Citizen of the galaxy
Holland, C. Pillar of the Sky
Howatch, S. Sins of the fathers
Martin, M. Vatican
Min, A. Becoming Madame Mao
Puzo, M. The family
Rand, A. Atlas shrugged
Sheldon, S. Master of the game
Spark, M. The Abbess of Crewe
Thomas, M. M. Hanover Place
Vargas Llosa, M. The Feast of the Goat
Vidal, G. Empire

The **power** and the glory. Greene, G.
Power of a woman. Bradford, B. T.
The **power** of darkness [play] Tolstoy, L., graf
In Tolstoy, L., graf. The portable Tolstoy p747-825
Power of the sword. Smith, W. A.
The **power** that preserves. Donaldson, S. R.
The **Poyson** garden. Harper, K.
The **practical** heart. Gurganus, A.
The **practical** heart [novelette] Gurganus, A.
In Gurganus, A. The practical heart
Practical magic. Hoffman, A.

PRAGMATISM
See also Utilitarianism

PRAGUE (CZECH REPUBLIC) *See* Czech Republic—Prague
Prague. Phillips, A.
The **Prague** orgy. Roth, P.
In Roth, P. Zuckerman bound: a trilogy and epilogue
The **prairie**. Cooper, J. F.
also in Cooper, J. F. The Leatherstocking tales p879-1317
The **prairie** chicken kill. Crider, B.

PRAIRIE LIFE
Aldrich, B. S. A lantern in her hand
Cather, W. My Antonia
Cather, W. O pioneers!

Prairie nocturne. Doig, I.
Praisesong for the widow. Marshall, P.
A **prayer** for Owen Meany. Irving, J.
A **prayer** for the dying. O'Nan, S.
Prayers for rain. Lehane, D.
Prayers for the dead. Kellerman, F.
The **precipice**. Bova, B.
PRECOGNITIONS *See* Premonitions
Precursor. Cherryh, C. J.

PREDESTINATION
Irving, J. A prayer for Owen Meany
Wilder, T. The bridge of San Luis Rey

PREDICTIONS *See* Prophecies

PREGNANCY
See also Abortion
Barth, J. The Tidewater tales
Berne, S. A perfect arrangement
Brown, L. Fay
Campbell, B. M. Singing in the comeback choir
Hallgrímur Helgason. 101 Reykjavik
Hannah, K. On Mystic lake
Haruf, K. Plainsong
Hawke, E. Ash Wednesday
Hood, A. Ruby
McPhee, J. No ordinary matter
Napolitano, A. Within arm's reach
O'Brien, E. Down by the river
Parks, S.-L. Getting mother's body
Patterson, J. Cradle and all
Pottinger, S. The last Nazi
Read, P. P. Alice in exile
Schwartz, L. S. In the family way
Snyder, D. J. Night crossing
Weiner, J. Little earthquakes

PREHISTORIC ANIMALS *See* Fossils

PREHISTORIC MAN
See also Prehistoric times
Auel, J. M. The Clan of the Cave Bear
Auel, J. M. The Mammoth Hunters
Auel, J. M. The plains of passage
Auel, J. M. The shelters of stone
Auel, J. M. The Valley of Horses
Cornwell, B. Stonehenge, 2000 B.C.
Darnton, J. Neanderthal
Gear, K. O. People of the lakes
Gear, K. O. People of the lightning
Gear, K. O. People of the owl
Gear, W. M. People of the river
Gear, W. M. People of the sea
Golding, W. The inheritors
Harrison, S. Brother Wind
Harrison, S. Call down the stars
Harrison, S. Cry of the wind
Harrison, S. Mother earth, father sky
Harrison, S. My sister the moon
Harrison, S. Song of the river
Holland, C. Pillar of the Sky
Tarr, J. Lady of horses
Thomas, E. M. The animal wife
Thomas, E. M. Reindeer Moon

PREHISTORIC TIMES
See also Megalithic monuments; Stone Age
Auel, J. M. The Clan of the Cave Bear
Auel, J. M. The Mammoth Hunters
Auel, J. M. The plains of passage
Auel, J. M. The shelters of stone
Auel, J. M. The Valley of Horses
Bakker, R. T. Raptor Red
Crace, J. The gift of stones
Golding, W. Clonk clonk
Holland, C. Pillar of the Sky
Thomas, E. M. The animal wife
Thomas, E. M. Reindeer Moon

PREJUDICES
See also Antisemitism; Race relations
Bambara, T. C. Those bones are not my child
Brown, R. Civil wars
Brown, S. The witness
Coldsmith, D. The long journey home
Dexter, P. Paris Trout
Girzone, J. F. Joshua and the children
Grau, S. A. The keepers of the house
Grisham, J. A painted house
Guterson, D. Snow falling on cedars
Katzenbach, J. Hart's war
Keneally, T. River town
Lee, D. Country of origin
Matthiessen, P. Lost Man's River
Morrison, T. Tar baby
Pérez Galdós, B. Doña Perfecta

PRISONERS AND PRISONS—*Continued*
France
Dumas, A. The Count of Monte Cristo
Jamaica
Tolkin, M. Under radar
Russia
See also Prisoners and prisons—Siberia (Russia)
Solzhenitsyn, A. The first circle
Siberia (Russia)
Dostoyevsky, F. The house of the dead
Solzhenitsyn, A. One day in the life of Ivan Denisovich
United States
Bausch, R. The Gypsy Man
Goldsmith, O. Pen pals
Hunter, S. Pale horse coming
Siegel, J. Derailed
Turow, S. Reversible errors
Prisoner's dilemma. Powers, R.
PRISONERS OF WAR
See also Concentration camps; World War, 1939-1945—Prisoners and prisons
Clancy, T. Without remorse
Ha Jin. War trash
Kantor, M. Andersonville
Novakovich, J. April Fool's Day
Shute, N. The legacy
Vonnegut, K. Slaughterhouse-five
Prisoners of war. Yarbrough, S.
PRISONS *See* Prisoners and prisons
PRIVATE DETECTIVES *See* Detectives, Private
PRIVATE EYE STORIES *See* Detectives, Private; Mystery and detective stories
Private eyes. Kellerman, J.
PRIVATE SCHOOLS *See* School life
A **private** view. Brookner, A.
Privileged conversation. Hunter, E.
The **prize**. Wallace, I.
Prize stories: The O. Henry Awards. Entered in Part I under title
Prized possessions. Corman, A.
Prizzi's family. Condon, R.
Prizzi's glory. Condon, R.
Prizzi's honor. Condon, R.
Prizzi's money. Condon, R.
Probability moon. Kress, N.
Probability sun. Kress, N.
Probable cause. Pearson, R.
The **probable** future. Hoffman, A.
PROBATION OFFICERS
Leonard, E. Maximum Bob
Pelecanos, G. P. Drama city
Rosenberg, N. T. First offense
Rosenberg, N. T. Sullivan's law
PROBLEM CHILDREN *See* Emotionally disturbed children
PROCTOR, EZEKIEL, 1831-1907
About
McMurtry, L. Zeke and Ned
The **prodigal** daughter. Archer, J.
Prodigal father. McInerny, R. M.
Prodigal summer. Kingsolver, B.
The **professor**. Brontë, C.
PROFESSORS *See* Teachers
The **professor's** daughter. Read, P. P.
The **professor's** house. Cather, W.
In Cather, W. Willa Cather, later novels
PROGRAMMING (COMPUTERS)
Tracy, P. J. Monkeewrench
Ullman, E. The bug
PROLETARIAN NOVELS
Nichols, J. T. The Milagro beanfield war
Steinbeck, J. The grapes of wrath
Steinbeck, J. In dubious battle
Zola, É. Germinal
The **Prometheus** deception. Ludlum, R.
The **promise**. Potok, C.
The **promise**. Steinbeck, J.
In Steinbeck, J. The portable Steinbeck
The **promise** of light. Watkins, P.
The **promise** of rest. Price, R.
Pronto. Leonard, E.
Proof. Francis, D.
PROPAGANDA
Kalfus, K. The commissariat of enlightenment
A **proper** marriage. Lessing, D. M.
In Lessing, D. M. Children of violence
PROPERTY
See also Real estate
Property. Martin, V.
PROPHECIES
Ackroyd, P. The Clerkenwell tales
Bradley, M. Z. The firebrand
Dunnett, D. Checkmate
Prophecy. Haydon, E.
The **prophet**. Asch, S.
Prose and poetry. Crane, S.
The **prosecution**. Buffa, D. W.
PROSPECTORS
Zafris, N. Lucky strike
PROSTITUTES
See also Comfort women; Courtesans
Brown, L. The rabbit factory
Burgess, A. The pianoplayers
Busch, F. The night inspector
Clancy, T. Without remorse
Crane, S. Maggie: a girl of the streets (a story of New York)
Crane, S. Maggie: a girl of the streets [novelette]
Defoe, D. Moll Flanders
Faber, M. The crimson petal and the white
Faulkner, W. Sanctuary
Fuentes, C. Apollo and the whores
Hambly, B. Wet grave
Holman, S. The dress lodger
Howatch, S. The heartbreaker
Jones, D. C. The search for Temperance Moon
Lent, J. Lost nation
Lessing, D. M. Ben, in the world
Maḥfūẓ, N. Midaq Alley
Mason, R. The world of Suzie Wong
McCarthy, C. Cities of the plain
McMurtry, L. Buffalo girls
McMurtry, L. Dead man's walk
O'Hara, J. Butterfield 8
Parker, T. J. Red light
Perlman, E. Seven types of ambiguity
Redfern, E. The music of the spheres
Spencer, L. Forgiving
Vollmann, W. T. Butterfly stories
Williamson, P. Heart of the west
PROSTITUTION
See also Prostitutes
Battle, L. Storyville
Burdett, J. Bangkok 8
Burdett, J. Bangkok Tattoo
Donoghue, E. Slammerkin
Gruber, M. Valley of bones
Harrison, K. The binding chair
Martini, S. P. Compelling evidence
Theroux, P. Doctor Slaughter
Vargas Llosa, M. Captain Pantoja and the Special Service
Vollmann, W. T. The royal family
West, P. The tent of orange mist
Protect and defend. Patterson, R. N.
PROTESTANT REFORMATION *See* Reformation
The **proud** breed. De Blasis, C.
PROVENCE (FRANCE) *See* France—Provence
PROVINCETOWN (MASS.) *See* Massachusetts—Provincetown
PSYCHE (GODDESS)
Lewis, C. S. Till we have faces
PSYCHIATRISTS
See also Mentally ill—Care and treatment; Psychoanalysts; Women psychiatrists
Ablow, K. R. Compulsion
Barker, P. Border crossing
Barker, P. The eye in the door
Barker, P. The ghost road
Barker, P. Regeneration

PSYCHOLOGICAL NOVELS—*Continued*
Fowler, C. M. Before women had wings
Fowles, J. The collector
Freeling, N. One more river
Freemantle, B. Mind/reader
French, N. Beneath the skin
French, N. Land of the living
Fyfield, F. Blind date
Fyfield, F. Undercurrents
Gaddis, W. Agapé agape
Gaitskill, M. Veronica
Gann, E. K. The high and the mighty
García Márquez, G. Chronicle of a death foretold
García Márquez, G. The general and his labyrinth
Gardam, J. The queen of the tambourine
Gibbons, K. Sights unseen
Gide, A. The counterfeiters (Les faux-monnayeurs)
Gide, A. The immoralist
Glendinning, V. Flight
Godden, R. Black Narcissus
Godwin, G. The finishing school
Golding, W. Darkness visible
Gordimer, N. The house gun
Gordimer, N. None to accompany me
Gordimer, N. The pickup
Graham, W. The walking stick
Grass, G. The tin drum
Green, G. D. The juror
Greene, G. Brighton rock
Greene, G. The end of the affair
Greer, A. S. The path of minor planets
Grippando, J. The informant
Grumbach, D. Chamber music
Guterson, D. Our Lady of the Forest
Hamilton, J. Disobedience
Hamilton, J. A map of the world
Hamilton-Paterson, J. Gerontius
Handke, P. The left-handed woman
Handke, P. Repetition
Hansen, R. Mariette in ecstasy
Hardie, K. A winter marriage
Hardy, T. Jude the obscure
Hardy, T. The return of the native
Harrar, G. The spinning man
Harrison, K. The seal wife
Hart, J. The reconstructionist
Hart, J. Sin
Haruf, K. Eventide
Haruf, K. Plainsong
Haskell, J. American purgatorio
Hatoum, M. The brothers
Hawkes, J. Second skin
Hawthorne, N. The marble faun
Hay, E. A student of weather
Hazzard, S. The great fire
Heinrich, W. The king's evil
Heller, J. Something happened
Heller, Z. What was she thinking?
Hesse, H. Demian
Hill, R. Dream of darkness
Himes, C. Yesterday will make you cry
Hirshberg, G. The Snowman's children
Hoban, R. Angelica's Grotto
Høeg, P. Borderliners
Hoffman, A. Blue diary
Hoffman, A. The ice queen
Hoffman, A. Illumination night
Hoffman, E. The secret
Hofmann, G. Luck
Hornby, N. A long way down
Hospital, J. T. Due preparations for the plague
Hospital, J. T. Oyster
Howatch, S. Glamorous powers
Howatch, S. The heartbreaker
Howatch, S. The high flyer
Huddle, D. La Tour dreams of the wolf girl
Hughes, R. A. W. A high wind in Jamaica
Humphreys, J. The fireman's fair
Hunter, E. Candyland
Hunter, E. The moment she was gone
Hunter, E. Privileged conversation
Hustvedt, S. What I loved
Inness-Brown, E. Burning Marguerite
Ishiguro, K. Never let me go
Ishiguro, K. The remains of the day
Ishiguro, K. The unconsoled
Jackson, C. The lost weekend
James, H. The Aspern papers
James, H. Roderick Hudson
James, H. Washington Square
James, H. The wings of the dove
Johansen, I. Final target
Jong, E. Fear of flying
Joyce, J. A portrait of the artist as a young man
Judd, A. Legacy
Just, W. S. The weather in Berlin
Kasischke, L. The life before her eyes
Kelman, J. Summer of storms
Keneally, T. River town
Kincaid, J. Lucy
King, D. The ha-ha
King, L. R. A darker place
King, S. Dolores Claiborne
King, S. Gerald's game
King, S. Rose Madder
King, T. Survivor
Kingsolver, B. Animal dreams
Kingsolver, B. The poisonwood Bible
Kitchen, J. The house on Eccles Road
Koeppen, W. The hothouse
Koeppen, W. A sad affair
Koontz, D. R. False memory
Kosinski, J. N. The devil tree
Krauss, N. The history of love
Krauss, N. Man walks into a room
Lamb, W. I know this much is true
Lasdun, J. The horned man
Laskowski, T. Every good boy does fine
LaValle, V. D. The ecstatic
Lawrence, D. H. The rainbow
Lawrence, D. H. Sons and lovers
Lawrence, D. H. Women in love
Le, T. D. T. The gangster we are all looking for
Lee, C.-R. A gesture life
Lee, M. The canal house
Lehrer, J. The special prisoner
Leithauser, B. A few corrections
L'Engle, M. A live coal in the sea
Leroy, M. Postcards from Berlin
Lessing, D. M. Ben, in the world
Lessing, D. M. The fifth child
Lessing, D. M. The grass is singing
Levin, M. Compulsion
Lewis, J. The king is dead
Lightman, A. P. Reunion
Ligon, S. Safe in heaven dead
Lively, P. City of the mind
Lively, P. Cleopatra's sister
Lively, P. Moon tiger
Lively, P. Passing on
Lively, P. The photograph
Livesey, M. Banishing Verona
Livesey, M. Criminals
Livesey, M. Eva moves the furniture
Livesey, M. The missing world
Loo, T. d. A bed in heaven
Lutz, J. Dancing with the dead
Lynn, A. Now you see it
MacNeil, R. The voyage
Malraux, A. Man's fate (La condition humaine)
Mann, T. Death in Venice
Mann, T. Tonio Kröger
Mann, T. Tristan
March, W. The bad seed
Marcom, M. A. The daydreaming boy
Marías, J. The man of feeling
Martin, S. The pleasure of my company
Maugham, W. S. Of human bondage
McCabe, P. The butcher boy
McCullers, C. The heart is a lonely hunter
McCullers, C. The member of the wedding
McDermid, V. A place of execution
McDermott, A. Charming Billy
McElroy, J. Actress in the house
McEwan, I. Atonement
McEwan, I. The child in time
McEwan, I. Enduring love
McEwan, I. The innocent

PSYCHOLOGICAL NOVELS—*Continued*
Theroux, M. The confessions of Mycroft Holmes
Thomas, D. M. The white hotel
Tóibín, C. The master
Tolkin, M. Under radar
Tolstoy, L., graf. Anna Karenina
Tolstoy, L., graf. The Kreutzer sonata, The Devil, and other tales
Tournier, M. The ogre
Tremain, R. Sacred country
Tremain, R. The way I found her
Trevanian. The summer of Katya
Trevor, W. Death in summer
Trevor, W. The silence in the garden
Tristram, C. After
Trollope, J. Brother and sister
Tryon, T. The other
Turow, S. The burden of proof
Turow, S. Presumed innocent
Tyler, A. Breathing lessons
Tyler, A. Celestial navigation
Tyler, A. Dinner at the Homesick Restaurant
Tyler, A. Ladder of years
Ullman, E. The bug
Unsworth, B. Losing Nelson
Urquhart, J. The underpainter
Vanderbes, J. Easter Island
Vine, B. Anna's book
Vine, B. The blood doctor
Vine, B. The chimney sweeper's boy
Vine, B. A dark-adapted eye
Vine, B. A fatal inversion
Vine, B. Gallowglass
Vine, B. Grasshopper
Vine, B. The house of stairs
Vine, B. King Solomon's carpet
Vine, B. No night is too long
Wallace, D. F. Infinite jest
Walsh, H. Brass
Walters, M. The breaker
Walters, M. The dark room
Walters, M. The echo
Walters, M. The sculptress
Walters, M. The shape of snakes
Wenner, K. Dancing with Einstein
West, P. The dry Danube
West, P. O.K
West, P. The tent of orange mist
Westlake, D. E. The ax
Westlake, D. E. The hook
Wharton, E. Ethan Frome
Wharton, E. The reef
Whitney, P. A. The singing stones
Wiesel, E. The accident
Wiesel, E. Dawn
Wiesel, E. The testament
Wilcken, H. The execution
Wilhelm, K. Death qualified
Wilhelm, K. The good children
Wilson, R. The blind man of Seville
Wiltse, D. Heartland
Winton, T. Dirt music
Woiwode, L. Indian affairs
Wolfe, T. Look homeward, angel
Wolfe, T. O lost
Wolfe, T. The web and the rock
Wolfe, T. You can't go home again
Wolitzer, M. Surrender, Dorothy
Woolf, V. Between the acts
Woolf, V. Jacob's room
Woolf, V. Mrs. Dalloway
Woolf, V. To the lighthouse
Woolf, V. The voyage out
Woolf, V. The waves
Woolf, V. The years
Wright, A. M. After Gregory
Wright, A. M. Tony and Susan
Yglesias, R. Dr. Neruda's cure for evil
Yorke, M. Almost the truth
Yorke, M. False pretences
Yorke, M. The price of guilt
Yorke, M. A question of belief

PSYCHOLOGISTS

Bell, M. S. Ten Indians
Busch, F. A memory of war
Carr, C. The alienist
Carr, C. The angel of darkness
Carr, C. Killing time
Dart, I. R. The Stork Club
Dobyns, S. Boy in the water
Ferrigno, R. The Horse Latitudes
Gruber, M. Valley of bones
Katzenbach, J. State of mind
O'Connell, C. Judas child
White, S. W. The best revenge
White, S. W. Missing persons
Willis, C. Passage

PSYCHOLOGY, PHYSIOLOGICAL *See* Physiological psychology

PSYCHOPATHS *See* Insane, Criminal and dangerous; Personality disorders

PSYCHOTHERAPISTS *See* Psychotherapy

PSYCHOTHERAPY

Duisberg, K. W. The good patient
Fast, H. The bridge builder's story
Lamb, W. I know this much is true
Paretsky, S. Ghost country
Ruiz, L. M. Only one thing missing
Spark, M. Aiding and abetting

The **Ptolemies**. Sprott, D.

PTOLEMY I SOTER, KING OF EGYPT, 367 OR 6-283 OR 2 B.C.

About

Sprott, D. The Ptolemies

PUBLIC HOUSING

Read, Miss. Storm in the village

PUBLIC RELATIONS

Dezenhall, E. Money wanders

PUBLIC SCHOOLS *See* School life

Public smiles, private tears. Van Slyke, H.

PUBLIC UTILITIES

See also Electricity

PUBLISHERS AND PUBLISHING

See also Newspapers; Periodicals
Archer, J. The fourth estate
Bank, M. The girls' guide to hunting and fishing
Beattie, A. Love always
Colwin, L. A big storm knocked it over
Du Maurier, Dame D. The house on the strand
Eco, U. Foucault's pendulum
Grimes, M. Foul matter
Heller, J. Best enemies
Ignatius, D. The Sun King
Kotzwinkle, W. The bear went over the mountain
Lemann, N. Malaise
Martini, S. P. The list
Michener, J. A. The novel
Powell, A. Books do furnish a room
Sanders, L. Guilty pleasures
Saramago, J. The history of the siege of Lisbon
Spark, M. A far cry from Kensington
Vidal, G. Empire
Vidal, G. The golden age
Vidal, G. Washington, D.C.
Weldon, F. Big girls don't cry
Wouk, H. Youngblood Hawke

PUBS *See* Hotels, taverns, etc.

Pudd'nhead Wilson. Twain, M.
also in Twain, M. Mississippi writings

PUEBLO INDIANS

Gear, K. O. People of the silence
Gear, K. O. The summoning God

PUGILISM *See* Boxing

The **pull** of the moon. Berg, E.

Pulse. Buchanan, E.

PUMPING IRON *See* Weight lifting

PUNS

Farmer, P. J. Riders of the purple wage

The **pupil**. James, H.
In James, H. Complete stories, 1884-1891
In James, H. The complete tales of Henry James
In James, H. Short novels of Henry James p355-405

Q

R

RACE RELATIONS—*Continued*

Hawaii

See Hawaii—Race relations

India

See India—Race relations

South Africa

See South Africa—Race relations

United States

See United States—Race relations

RACEHORSES *See* Horses

RACIAL INTERMARRIAGE *See* Interracial marriage

RACING

See also Automobile races; Horse racing

McCrumb, S. St. Dale

RACISM *See* Antisemitism; Prejudices; Race relations

RACKETEERS *See* Crime and criminals; Gangsters; Mafia

RACKETS *See* Gambling

RADCLIFFE COLLEGE

Adams, A. Superior women

Radiance. Scholz, C.

The **radiant** way. Drabble, M.

RADIATION

Physiological effect

Shute, N. On the beach
Wiggins, M. Evidence of things unseen

RADICALISM *See* Radicals and radicalism

RADICALS AND RADICALISM

See also Anarchism and anarchists

Banks, R. The darling
Cantor, J. Great Neck
Fuentes, C. Diana, the goddess who hunts alone
Gordon, N. The company you keep
Leonard, E. Freaky Deaky
Lessing, D. M. The good terrorist
Lessing, D. M. The sweetest dream
Piercy, M. Vida
Plain, B. Harvest
Read, P. P. The professor's daughter
Turow, S. The laws of our fathers

RADIO

Dunning, J. Two o'clock, eastern wartime
Keillor, G. WLT
Ridgway, K. The parts
Vargas Llosa, M. Aunt Julia and the scriptwriter

RADIO BROADCASTING

Brown, S. Hello, darkness
Shields, C. The republic of love
Sinclair, A. I left my back door open

RADIO PROGRAMS

Elkin, S. The Dick Gibson show

RADIOACTIVITY

See also Uranium

A **rag,** a bone, and a hank of hair. Gash, J.

Rage. King, S.
In King, S. The Bachman books: four early novels by Stephen King

Rage. Smith, W. A.

Rage of a demon king. Feist, R. E.

Rage of angels. Sheldon, S.

The **raggedy** man. O'Donnell, L.

Ragtime. Doctorow, E. L.

The **raid**. Tolstoy, L., graf
In Tolstoy, L., graf. The portable Tolstoy p169-99

Railroad schemes. Holland, C.

The **railroad** stories. See Halkin, H. Tevye the dairyman and The railroad stories

RAILROADS

See also Subways

Cather, W. A lost lady
Ferber, E. Saratoga trunk
Norris, F. The octopus
Rand, A. Atlas shrugged
Ross-Macdonald, M. The rich are with you always
Ross-Macdonald, M. The world from rough stones

Travel

Greene, G. Orient Express
West, Dame R. The birds fall down

RAIN FORESTS

Stevens, M. The curve of the world

The **rainbow**. Lawrence, D. H.

Rainbow Six. Clancy, T.

Rainbow's end. Grimes, M.

Rainbow's end. Peters, E.

The **rainmaker**. Grisham, J.

The **rains** came. Bromfield, L.

Raintree County. Lockridge, R.

Raise high the roof beam, carpenters, and Seymour: an introduction. Salinger, J. D.

Raise the Titanic! Cussler, C.

Raising Abel. Gear, W. M.

Raising the stones. Tepper, S. S.

Raj. Mehta, G.

The **Raj** quartet. Scott, P.

RALEGH, WALTER *See* Raleigh, Sir Walter, 1552?-1618

RALEIGH, SIR WALTER, 1552?-1618

About

Naipaul, V. S. A way in the world

Rally round the flag, boys! Shulman, M.

Rama II. Clarke, A. C.

Rama revealed. Clarke, A. C.

RAMESES II, KING OF EGYPT *See* Ramses II, King of Egypt

RAMSES II, KING OF EGYPT

About

Gedge, P. House of illusions
Gedge, P. Lady of the reeds

RANCH LIFE

See also Cowboys

Adam, C. Love and country
Brand, M. Dust across the range
Dailey, J. Calder pride
Davis, C. Winter range
De Blasis, C. The proud breed
Doig, I. English Creek
Eagle, K. The last true cowboy
Evans, N. The loop
Ferber, E. Giant
Grey, Z. Woman of the frontier
Guthrie, A. B. Arfive
Guthrie, A. B. These thousand hills
L'Amour, L. The Californios
Latham, A. Code of the West
McCarthy, C. All the pretty horses
McCarthy, C. Cities of the plain
McCullough, C. The thorn birds
McGuane, T. Keep the change
McGuane, T. Nobody's angel
Meyers, K. The work of wolves
Richter, C. The sea of grass
Schaefer, J. W. Monte Walsh
Schaefer, J. W. Shane
Sherman, J. The Baron war
Steinbeck, J. Of mice and men
Steinbeck, J. The red pony
Turner, N. E. These is my words
Williamson, P. The outsider

Random harvest. Hilton, J.

Random winds. Plain, B.

Range of motion. Berg, E.

RAPE

Barnard, R. A cry from the dark
Brink, A. P. The other side of silence
Coetzee, J. M. Disgrace
Cookson, C. The Maltese Angel
Corman, A. Prized possessions
Daley, R. Hands of a stranger
Davis, A. Wonder when you'll miss me
Fielding, J. Tell me no secrets
French, M. Our father
Garlock, D. The edge of town
Gerritsen, T. The surgeon
Grisham, J. A time to kill
Kay, T. The runaway
Lawrence, M. K. Hearts and bones
Lewis, M. G. The monk

REFORMERS
See also Abolitionists
REFUGEES
See also Exiles
Bellow, S. The Bellarosa connection
Brookner, A. Family and friends
Kosinski, J. N. The painted bird
Le, T. D. T. The gangster we are all looking for
Ozick, C. Heir to the glimmering world
REFUGEES, AUSTRIAN *See* Austrian refugees
REFUGEES, CUBAN *See* Cuban refugees
REFUGEES, CZECH *See* Czech refugees
REFUGEES, GERMAN *See* German refugees
REFUGEES, HAITIAN *See* Haitian refugees
REFUGEES, JEWISH *See* Jewish refugees
REFUGEES, RUSSIAN *See* Russian refugees
REFUGEES, VIETNAMESE *See* Vietnamese refugees
REGENCY ENGLAND *See* England—19th century
Regeneration. Barker, P.
Regina v. Rumpole. See Mortimer, J. C. Rumpole for the defence
The **regulators**. King, S.
Reign in hell. Diehl, W.
REINCARNATION
Anthony, P. Isle of woman
Anthony, P. Shame of man
Bradley, M. Z. Lady of Avalon
Chandra, V. Red earth and pouring rain
Ellison, H. The deathbird
Hooper, K. Finding Laura
Mailer, N. Ancient evenings
Mishima, Y. The decay of the angel
Seton, A. Green darkness
Zelazny, R. Lord of light
Reindeer Moon. Thomas, E. M.
Reinhart in love. Berger, T.
Reinhart's women. Berger, T.
The **reivers**. Faulkner, W.
also in Faulkner, W. Novels, 1957-1962 p722-971
REJUVENATION
Haggard, H. R. She
RELATIVES *See* Family life
RELATIVITY (PHYSICS)
See also Space and time
RELIGION
See also Agnosticism; Biblical stories; Buddhism; Catholic faith; Christianity; Clergy; Conversion; Faith; God; Judaism; Mormons and Mormonism; Paganism
Ackroyd, P. The Clerkenwell tales
Agee, J. The morning watch
Asimov, I. Nightfall
Baker, K. In the garden of Iden
Baldwin, J. Go tell it on the mountain
Bozai, Á. To err is divine
Bryan, M. The afterword
Bunyan, J. The pilgrim's progress
Butler, O. E. Parable of the talents
Doctorow, E. L. City of God
Donaldson, S. R. Penance
Dostoyevsky, F. The brothers Karamazov
Dunn, S. The big love
Eliot, G. Romola
Fowler, C. M. Before women had wings
Golding, W. The scorpion god
Goodman, A. Paradise park
Greene, G. A burnt-out case
Hansen, R. Mariette in ecstasy
Harrison, H. One king's way
Heinlein, R. A. Job: a comedy of justice
Herbert, F. God Emperor of Dune
Herbert, F. Heretics of Dune
Howatch, S. The high flyer
Iles, G. The footprints of God
Irving, J. A prayer for Owen Meany
Kafka, F. The castle
King, S. Desperation
Leonard, E. Touch
Lewis, S. Elmer Gantry
MacDonald, J. D. One more Sunday
Maḥfūẓ, N. Children of the alley
Marshall, C. Christy
Marshall, C. Julie
Martin, G. R. R. A song for Lya
Mason, B. A. Feather crowns
Mishima, Y. The temple of the golden pavilion
Murdoch, I. The bell
Murdoch, I. The green knight
O'Connor, F. Wise blood
Ōe, K. An echo of heaven
Pérez Galdós, B. Doña Perfecta
Robbins, T. Skinny legs and all
Salinger, J. D. Franny & Zooey
Spark, M. The Mandelbaum Gate
Stone, R. Damascus Gate
Stowe, H. B. The minister's wooing
Tepper, S. S. Northshore
Tepper, S. S. Southshore
Tolkin, M. Under radar
Updike, J. In the beauty of the lilies
Updike, J. S
Vidal, G. Creation
West, M. L. The devil's advocate
Wood, J. The book against God
RELIGION, PRIMITIVE *See* Religion
RELIGIOUS LIFE *See* Convent life; Monasticism and religious orders
Reliquary. Preston, D.
The **reluctant** queen. Plaidy, J.
The **remains** of the day. Ishiguro, K.
REMARRIAGE
Barfoot, J. Critical injuries
Hardie, K. A winter marriage
Mitchard, J. Twelve times blessed
Robinson, R. Sweetwater
Trollope, J. Marrying the mistress
Trollope, J. Other people's children
The **Rembrandt** panel. Banks, O. T.
Remember me. Clark, M. H.
Remember me. Hendrie, L.
Remember me, Irene. Burke, J.
Remembering Babylon. Malouf, D.
Remembering Blue. Fowler, C. M.
Remembrance of things past. Proust, M.
Remembrance Rock. Sandburg, C.
The **remorseful** day. Dexter, C.
REMUS, GEORGE, 1876-1952
About
Holden, C. The jazz bird
RENAISSANCE
See also Italy—15th century; Italy—16th century
Rendezvous with Rama. Clarke, A. C.
The **renegades** of Pern. McCaffrey, A.
REPENTANCE
See also Sin
Repetition. Handke, P.
REPORTERS *See* Journalists
The **reprieve**. Sartre, J. P.
REPRODUCTION, ASEXUAL *See* Asexual reproduction
The **republic** of love. Shields, C.
Requiem for a nun. Faulkner, W.
also in Faulkner, W. Novels, 1942-1954 p471-664
Requiem for a realtor. McInerny, R. M.
Requiem for Harlem. Roth, H.
Requiem for the sun. Haydon, E.
RESCUE OPERATIONS *See* Search and rescue operations
RESCUES
Brown, D. Night of the hawk
RESEARCH
Michener, J. A. Space
Reservation blues. Alexie, S.
Reservation Road. Schwartz, J. B.
Resistance. Lopez, B. H.
Resistance. Shreve, A.
RESISTANCE MOVEMENTS (WORLD WAR, 1939-1945)
See World War, 1939-1945—Underground movements
RESISTANCE TO GOVERNMENT
Alvarez, J. In the time of the butterflies
Westerfeld, S. The risen empire

ROGUES AND VAGABONDS—*Continued*
Brown, J. D. Addie Pray
Colette. The tender shoot
Doctorow, E. L. Loon Lake
Kerouac, J. The Dharma bums
Kerouac, J. On the road
Mann, T. Confessions of Felix Krull, confidence man
Oates, J. C. My heart laid bare
Siegel, L. Love and other games of chance
Steinbeck, J. Cannery Row
Steinbeck, J. Sweet Thursday
Steinbeck, J. Tortilla Flat
Rolling stones. Henry, O.
In Henry, O. The complete works of O. Henry p941-1060
Roma eterna. Silverberg, R.
The **Roman**. Waltari, M.
ROMAN CATHOLIC CHURCH *See* Catholic faith
ROMAN CATHOLIC RELIGION *See* Catholic faith
ROMAN EMPIRE *See* Rome
The **Roman** hat mystery. Queen, E.
ROMAN SOLDIERS *See* Soldiers—Rome
The **Roman** spring of Mrs. Stone. Williams, T.
The **romance** of Monte Beni. See Hawthorne, N. The marble faun
The **romance** reader. Abraham, P.
ROMANCES (GOTHIC) *See* Gothic romances
ROMANCES (LOVE STORIES) *See* Love affairs; Love stories

ROMANIA
Furst, A. Blood of victory
Wiesel, E. The forgotten

Bucharest
Bellow, S. The dean's December
The **romantic**. Gowdy, B.

ROME
Silverberg, R. Roma eterna

510-30 B.C.
Davis, L. The accusers
Davis, L. A dying light in Corduba
Davis, L. Three hands in the fountain
Davis, L. Time to depart
Fuentes, C. The two Numantias
Massie, A. Caesar
McCullough, C. Caesar
McCullough, C. Caesar's women
McCullough, C. The first man in Rome
McCullough, C. Fortune's favorites
McCullough, C. The grass crown
McCullough, C. The October horse
Saylor, S. The house of the Vestals
Saylor, S. The judgment of Caesar
Saylor, S. A mist of prophecies
Saylor, S. Rubicon
Wilder, T. The ides of March

30 B.C.-476 A.D.
Asch, S. The Nazarene
Borchardt, A. The silver wolf
Caldwell, T. Dear and glorious physician
Costain, T. B. The silver chalice
Davis, L. One virgin too many
Douglas, L. C. The robe
Graves, R. Claudius, the god and his wife Messalina
Graves, R. I, Claudius
Harris, R. Pompeii
Lytton, E. B. L., Baron. The last days of Pompeii
Pears, I. The dream of Scipio
Sienkiewicz, H. Quo Vadis
Tarr, J. Household gods
Wallace, L. Ben-Hur
Waltari, M. The Roman
Wood, B. Soul flame
Yourcenar, M. Memoirs of Hadrian

476-1420
Yarbro, C. Q. Night blooming

Kings and rulers
Golding, W. Envoy extraordinary

Politics
See Politics—Rome

ROME (ITALY) *See* Italy—Rome
Romola. Eliot, G.
Rookery blues. Hassler, J.
The **room-mating** season. Jaffe, R.
A **room** with a view. Forster, E. M.
also in Forster, E. M. A room with a view and Howards End
A **room** with a view and Howards End. Forster, E. M.
ROOMING HOUSES *See* Boarding houses

ROOMMATES
Jaffe, R. The room-mating season

ROOSTERS
García Márquez, G. No one writes to the colonel
Rosa. Ozick, C.
In Ozick, C. The shawl
The **rosary** murders. Kienzle, W. X.
Roscoe. Kennedy, W.

ROSE, BILLY, 1899-1966

About
Bellow, S. The Bellarosa connection
Rose. Smith, M. C.
Rose Madder. King, S.
The **rose** rent. Peters, E.
The **rose** without a thorn. Plaidy, J.
Rosehaven. Coulter, C.
Rosemary remembered. Albert, S. W.
Rosemary's baby. Levin, I.
Roses are red. Patterson, J.
The **rosewood** casket. McCrumb, S.
Ross Macdonald's Lew Archer, private investigator. Macdonald, R.
Rostnikov's vacation. Kaminsky, S. M.
The **Rotters'** Club. Coe, J.
Rough cider. Lovesey, P.
Rough draft. Hall, J. W.
Rough justice. Scottoline, L.
Round the moon. Verne, J.
In Verne, J. From the earth to the moon, and Round the moon
Round the red lamp. Doyle, Sir A. C.
In Doyle, Sir A. C. Conan Doyle's tales of medical humanism and values: Round the red lamp p15-302
Rouse up, o young men of the new age. Ōe, K.
Roxanna Slade. Price, R.

ROYAL CANADIAN MOUNTED POLICE
Freedman, B. Mrs. Mike
The **royal** family. Vollmann, W. T.
Royal Flash. Fraser, G. M.
Royal flush. Stout, R.
The **royal** physicians visit. Enquist, P. O.
The **rubber** band. Stout, R.
In Stout, R. Five of a kind p1-153
Rubicon. Saylor, S.

RUBIES
Roberts, N. The reef
Westlake, D. E. Why me?
Ruby. Hood, A.

RUDOLF II, HOLY ROMAN EMPEROR, 1552-1612

About
Sherwood, F. The book of splendor
Rueful death. Albert, S. W.
The **rule** of four. Caldwell, I.
Rule of the bone. Banks, R.
Rulers of the darkness. Turtledove, H.
Rules for old men waiting. Pouncey, P. R.
The **rules** of engagement. Brookner, A.
Rules of evidence. Brandon, J.
Rules of prey. Sandford, J.
The **rules** of silence. Lindsey, D. L.
Rum punch. Leonard, E.
RUMANIA *See* Romania
Rumble, young man, rumble. Cavell, B.
Rumpole à la carte. Mortimer, J. C.
Rumpole and the angel of death. Mortimer, J. C.
Rumpole and the golden thread. Mortimer, J. C.
In Mortimer, J. C. The second Rumpole omnibus p193-442
Rumpole for the defence. Mortimer, J. C.
In Mortimer, J. C. The second Rumpole omnibus p11-192
Rumpole on trial. Mortimer, J. C.
Rumpole rests his case. Mortimer, J. C.

RUSSIAN SECRET POLICE *See* Police—Russia
RUSSIAN SOLDIERS *See* Soldiers—Russia
RUSSIANS

Australia

Keneally, T. A family madness

Canada

Messud, C. A simple tale

England

Amis, K. The Russian girl
Follett, K. The man from St. Petersburg
Judd, A. Legacy
Lawton, J. Old flames

Germany

Turgenev, I. S. Spring torrents [variant title: The torrents of spring]
Turgenev, I. S. The torrents of spring
Uris, L. Armageddon

United States

Crowley, J. The translator
Harington, D. Ekaterina
Nabokov, V. V. Pnin
Shames, L. Mangrove squeeze

Russka. Rutherfurd, E.
Rustler roundup. L'Amour, L.
In L'Amour, L. End of the drive p93-239
Ryan's rules. See Leonard, E. Swag
The **Ryer** Avenue story. Uhnak, D.

S

S. Updike, J.
SAAVEDRA, MIGUEL DE CERVANTES *See* Cervantes Saavedra, Miguel de, 1547-1616
Sabbath Creek. Mitcham, J.
The **Sabbathday** River. Korelitz, J. H.
Sabbath's theater. Roth, P.

SABOTAGE

Follett, K. Night over water
MacLean, A. Force 10 from Navarone
MacLean, A. The guns of Navarone
Vonnegut, K. Player piano

SABOTEURS *See* Sabotage
SACAGAWEA, B. 1786

About

Glancy, D. Stone heart
Hall, B. I should be extremely happy in your company

SACAJAWEA *See* Sacagawea, b. 1786
Sackett. L'Amour, L.
In L'Amour, L. The Sacketts: beginnings of a dynasty
The **Sacketts:** beginnings of a dynasty. L'Amour, L.
Sacrament. Barker, C.
Sacred. Lehane, D.
Sacred clowns. Hillerman, T.
Sacred country. Tremain, R.
Sacred hunger. Unsworth, B.
Sacrifice. Vachss, A. H.
A **sad** affair. Koeppen, W.
Sad cypress. Christie, A.

SADISM

See also Cruelty
Snow, C. P. The sleep of reason
Templeton, E. Gordon

SAFARIS *See* Hunting—Africa
Safe harbor. Rice, L.
Safe house. Vachss, A. H.
Safe in heaven dead. Ligon, S.
Safelight. Burke, S.
Saga of Pliocene exile [series]
May, J. The adversary
May, J. The golden torc
May, J. The many-colored land
May, J. The nonborn king

SAHARA

Bowles, P. The sheltering sky
Cussler, C. Sahara
Gilman, D. Caravan

Sahara. Cussler, C.
SAIGON (VIETNAM) *See* Vietnam—Ho Chi Minh City

SAILING VESSELS

Eidson, B. One bad thing
Higgins, J. Storm warning
Stone, R. Outerbridge Reach

The **sailmaker's** daughter. Johnson, S.
Sailor song. Kesey, K.
SAILORS *See* Seamen

SAINT HELENA

Hansen, B. The monsters of St. Helena

SAINT LOUIS (MO.) *See* Missouri—Saint Louis
Saint maybe. Tyler, A.
Saint monster. Gurganus, A.
In Gurganus, A. The practical heart
SAINT PAUL *See* Paul, the Apostle, Saint
Saint Peter's Fair. Peters, E.
SAINT PETERSBURG (RUSSIA) *See* Russia—St. Petersburg

SAINT THOMAS (VIRGIN ISLANDS OF THE U.S.)

Whitney, P. A. Columbella

SAINTS

West, M. L. The devil's advocate

Saints at the river. Rash, R.
SAKYAMUNI *See* Gautama Buddha

SALAMANCA, BATTLE OF, 1812

Cornwell, B. Sharpe's sword

The **Salamanca** drum. Eden, D.

SALAZAR, ANTONIO DE OLIVEIRA, 1889-1970

About

Antunes, A. L. The inquisitors' manual

SALEM (MASS.) *See* Massachusetts—Salem
Salem's Lot. King, S.

SALES PERSONNEL AND SELLING

Berger, T. Sneaky people
Flagg, F. Standing in the rainbow
Gurganus, A. Blessed assurance: a moral tale
Gurganus, A. Saint monster
Kafka, F. Metamorphosis
Updike, J. Rabbit is rich
Vonnegut, K. Breakfast of champions

SALESMEN AND SALESMENSHIP *See* Sales personnel and selling
Sally Hemings. Chase-Riboud, B.
Salt. Zuber, I.
The **salt** eaters. Bambara, T. C.
A **salty** piece of land. Buffett, J.

SALVAGE

Cussler, C. Dragon
Cussler, C. Inca gold
Cussler, C. Raise the Titanic!
Cussler, C. Treasure
Innes, H. The wreck of the Mary Deare

SALVATION

See also Atonement

Samaritan. Price, R.
The **same** sea. Oz, A.

SAMURAI

Clavell, J. Gai-Jin
Clavell, J. Shogun
Endō, S. The samurai
Mishima, Y. Runaway horses

The **samurai**. Endō, S.
SAN ANTONIO (TEX.) *See* Texas—San Antonio
SAN FRANCISCO (CALIF.) *See* California—San Francisco
San Remo Drive. Epstein, L.
SANATORIUMS *See* Hospitals and sanatoriums
Sanctuary. Faulkner, W.
also in Faulkner, W. Novels, 1930-1935
Sanctuary. Kellerman, F.
Sanctuary. Wharton, E.
In Wharton, E. Collected stories, 1891-1910
The **sanctuary** sparrow. Peters, E.
Sand castles. Freeling, N.

SATIRE—*Continued*

Fraser, G. M. Flashman & the angel of the Lord
Fraser, G. M. Flashman and the mountain of light
Fraser, G. M. Flashman and the tiger
Fraser, G. M. Royal Flash
Frayn, M. A landing on the sun
Gaddis, W. A frolic of his own
Gaddis, W. J R
Gaddis, W. The recognitions
Galbraith, J. K. A tenured professor
García Márquez, G. In evil hour
García Márquez, G. One hundred years of solitude
Gardam, J. Faith Fox
Gilman, C. P. Herland
Gilman, C. P. Moving the mountain
Gilman, C. P. With her in Ourland
Gogol′, N. V. Dead souls
Golding, W. The inheritors
Golding, W. The scorpion god: three short novels
Grass, G. The call of the toad
Grass, G. Dog years
Grass, G. Local anaesthetic
Grass, G. The tin drum
Gray, A. Poor things
Greene, G. Our man in Havana
Greenfeld, J. Harry and Tonto
Grimes, M. Foul matter
Ha Jin. In the pond
Haldeman, J. W. The coming
Harington, D. Ekaterina
Hašek, J. The good soldier Svejk
Heinlein, R. A. Job: a comedy of justice
Heinlein, R. A. The moon is a harsh mistress
Heinlein, R. A. Stranger in a strange land
Heller, J. Closing time
Heller, J. Good as Gold
Hemingway, E. The torrents of spring
Hesse, H. The glass bead game (Magister Ludi)
Hiaasen, C. Native tongue
Hiaasen, C. Sick puppy
Hiaasen, C. Stormy weather
Hiaasen, C. Strip tease
Hodgins, E. Mr. Blandings builds his dream house
Høeg, P. The history of Danish dreams
Høeg, P. The woman and the ape
Holman, S. The mammoth cheese
Hornby, N. About a boy
Hrabal, B. I served the King of England
Hughes, R. A. W. A high wind in Jamaica
Huxley, A. Brave new world
Huxley, A. Point counter point
Hynes, J. Kings of infinite space
Hynes, J. The lecturer's tale
Inman, R. Captain Saturday
Irving, J. A prayer for Owen Meany
Irving, J. The world according to Garp
Isaacs, S. After all these years
Isaacs, S. Close relations
Ishiguro, K. The remains of the day
James, H. The Bostonians
Jen, G. Mona in the promised land
Johnson, A. Parasites like us
Johnson, D. L'affaire
Kadare, I. Spring flowers, spring frost
Kafka, F. Amerika
Kalfus, K. The commissariat of enlightenment
Kaufman, B. Up the down staircase
Keillor, G. Love me
King, S. The running man
King, T. Truth & Bright Water
Kirn, W. Mission to America
Kirst, H. H. Forward, Gunner Asch!
Kirst, H. H. The return of Gunner Asch
Kirst, H. H. The revolt of Gunner Asch
Klein, J. Primary colors
Klein, J. The running mate
Kosinski, J. N. Being there
Kotzwinkle, W. The bear went over the mountain
Krauss, N. The history of love
Kunkel, B. Indecision
Lasdun, J. The horned man
Le Carré, J. The tailor of Panama
Leavitt, D. Martin Bauman
Lehrer, J. The last debate
Lehrer, J. Purple dots
Lelchuk, A. Ziff
Lem, S. Memoirs of a space traveler
Lewis, C. S. That hideous strength
Lewis, S. Babbitt
Lewis, S. Cass Timberlane
Lewis, S. Dodsworth
Lewis, S. Elmer Gantry
Lewis, S. It can't happen here
Lewis, S. Main Street [novelette]
Lewis, S. Main Street, the story of Carol Kennicott
Lodge, D. Nice work
Lodge, D. Paradise news
Lodge, D. Therapy
Lurie, A. The war between the Tates
Maguire, G. Son of a witch
Mantel, H. Beyond black
Marquand, J. P. The late George Apley
Marquand, J. P. Point of no return
Martin, V. Italian fever
Martini, S. P. The list
Maugham, W. S. Cakes and ale
Mayle, P. Hotel Pastis
McCarthy, M. Birds of America
McCarthy, M. A charmed life
McCarthy, M. The group
McCarthy, M. The groves of Academe
McEwan, I. Amsterdam
McGrath, P. The grotesque
McMahon, T. A. Loving Little Egypt
Melville, H. The confidence-man: his masquerade
Mitford, N. Love in a cold climate
Mitford, N. The pursuit of love
Mortimer, J. C. Felix in the underworld
Mortimer, J. C. Paradise postponed
Mortimer, J. C. The sound of trumpets
Mortimer, J. C. Titmuss regained
Murakami, H. The wind-up bird chronicle
Murdoch, I. The book and the brotherhood
Murdoch, I. A fairly honourable defeat
Nabokov, V. V. Lolita
Nabokov, V. V. Pale fire
Nabokov, V. V. Pnin
Naipaul, V. S. A house for Mr. Biswas
Ōe, K. The pinch runner memorandum
O'Neill, J. Kilbrack; or, Who is Nancy Valentine?
Orwell, G. Animal farm
Orwell, G. Keep the aspidistra flying
Orwell, G. Nineteen eighty-four
Palahniuk, C. Lullaby
Pearson, T. R. Cry me a river
Percy, W. Love in the ruins
Perrotta, T. Joe College
Perrotta, T. Little children
Phillips, A. Prague
Pohl, F. Homegoing
Pohl, F. The space merchants
Portis, C. Gringos
Powell, A. A dance to the music of time
Powell, D. The golden spur
Powell, D. The locusts have no king
Powell, D. Turn, magic wheel
Powell, D. The wicked pavilion
Powers, J. F. Morte d'Urban
Powers, J. F. Wheat that springeth green
Prose, F. Blue angel
Prose, F. A changed man
Prose, F. Household saints
Prose, F. Hunters and gatherers
Prose, F. Primitive people
Pym, B. An academic question
Pym, B. Civil to strangers
Pynchon, T. The crying of lot 49
Pynchon, T. V.
Pynchon, T. Vineland
Raban, J. Waxwings
Read, P. P. A season in the West
Reed, I. Japanese by spring
Reuss, F. Horace afoot
Richler, M. Barney's version
Richler, M. Solomon Gursky was here
Robbins, T. Fierce invalids home from hot climates
Robbins, T. Half asleep in frog pajamas
Robbins, T. Jitterbug perfume

Schmidt delivered. Begley, L.
Scholarium. Gross, C.
SCHOLARS
See also Intellectuals
Amis, K. The Russian girl
Bellow, S. Herzog
Bellow, S. More die of heartbreak
Bulgakov, M. A. The master and Margarita
Byatt, A. S. The biographer's tale
Cather, W. The professor's house
Crumey, A. Mr. Mee
Davies, R. The rebel angels
Dorris, M. The crown of Columbus
Eco, U. Foucault's pendulum
Frayn, M. Headlong
Gross, C. Scholarium
Hawthorne, N. Fanshawe
Hesse, H. The glass bead game (Magister Ludi)
Hill, R. The Stranger House
Hofmann, G. Lichtenberg and the little flower girl
Langton, J. Emily Dickinson is dead
Messud, C. The hunters [novelette]
Michaels, B. Houses of stone
Powell, D. The locusts have no king
Powers, R. Galatea 2.2
Snow, C. P. The light and the dark
Updike, J. Roger's version
Warren, R. P. A place to come to
White, E. The married man
School days. Parker, R. B.
School for the blind. McFarland, D.
SCHOOL LIFE
Agee, J. The morning watch
Spark, M. The finishing school

Arizona

Straub, P. Shadowland

Belgium

Brontë, C. The professor
Brontë, C. Villette

Denmark

Høeg, P. Borderliners

England

Brontë, C. Emma
Delderfield, R. F. To serve them all my days
Dickens, C. David Copperfield
Dickens, C. Nicholas Nickleby
Hilton, J. Good-bye Mr. Chips
Ishiguro, K. Never let me go
McGowan, H. Schooling
Read, Miss. Chronicles of Fairacre
Swift, G. Waterland

Europe

L'Engle, M. The small rain

France

Colette. Claudine at school
Flaubert, G. Sentimental education

Germany

Grass, G. Local anaesthetic

Ireland

O'Brien, E. The country girls

Scotland

Spark, M. The prime of Miss Jean Brodie

United States

Alcott, L. M. Jo's boys
Alcott, L. M. Little men
Auchincloss, L. The Rector of Justin
Conroy, P. The lords of discipline
Cook, T. H. The Chatham School affair
Dobyns, S. Boy in the water
Gutcheon, B. R. Saying grace
Hoffman, A. The river king
Hunter, E. The blackboard jungle
Kaufman, B. Up the down staircase
Klein, R. The moth diaries
Knowles, J. Peace breaks out
Knowles, J. A separate peace
Patton, F. G. Good morning, Miss Dove
Powers, J. R. Do black patent-leather shoes really reflect up?
Powers, J. R. The last Catholic in America
Saul, J. Shadows
Sinclair, A. Coffee will make you black
Sittenfeld, C. Prep
Southgate, M. The fall of Rome
Sparks, N. A walk to remember
Wolff, T. Old school

SCHOOL SUPERINTENDENTS AND PRINCIPALS
Auchincloss, L. The Rector of Justin
Belfer, L. City of light
Dobyns, S. Boy in the water
Godwin, G. Evensong
Gutcheon, B. R. Saying grace
Guthrie, A. B. Arfive
Ozick, C. The cannibal galaxy
SCHOOL TEACHERS *See* Teachers
Schooling. McGowan, H.
SCHOOLS *See* School life
SCHULZ, BRUNO, 1892-1942

About

Ozick, C. The Messiah of Stockholm
SCHUMANN, CLARA, 1819-1896

About

Galloway, J. Clara
SCHUMANN, ROBERT, 1810-1856

About

Galloway, J. Clara
SCIENCE FICTION
See also End of the world; Extrasensory perception; Fantasies; Future; Interplanetary visitors; Interplanetary voyages; Interplanetary wars; Life on other planets; Robots; Space colonies; Space flight; Space ships; Time travel
Adams, D. Dirk Gently's holistic detective agency
Adams, D. The Hitchhiker's Guide to the Galaxy
Adams, D. Life, the universe, and everything
Adams, D. The long dark tea-time of the soul
Adams, D. Mostly harmless
Adams, D. The restaurant at the end of the universe
Adams, D. So long, and thanks for all the fish
Aldiss, B. W. Helliconia spring
Aldiss, B. W. Helliconia summer
Aldiss, B. W. Helliconia winter
Anderson, P. Genesis
Anderson, P. Going for infinity
Anderson, P. Harvest of stars
Anderson, P. Harvest the fire
Anderson, P. Operation Chaos
Anderson, P. Operation Luna
Anderson, P. Orion shall rise
Anderson, P. The stars are also fire
Anthony, P. Blue Adept
Anthony, P. Chaos mode
Anthony, P. DoOon mode
Anthony, P. Fractal mode
Anthony, P. Hope of earth
Anthony, P. Isle of woman
Anthony, P. Juxtaposition
Anthony, P. Muse of art
Anthony, P. Out of Phaze
Anthony, P. Phaze doubt
Anthony, P. Robot Adept
Anthony, P. Shame of man
Anthony, P. Split infinity
Anthony, P. Unicorn point
Anthony, P. Virtual mode
Asher, N. L. The skinner
Asimov, I. The best science fiction of Isaac Asimov
Asimov, I. The caves of steel
Asimov, I. The complete robot
Asimov, I. The complete stories
Asimov, I. Fantastic voyage
Asimov, I. Forward the Foundation
Asimov, I. Foundation
Asimov, I. Foundation and earth
Asimov, I. Foundation and empire
Asimov, I. Foundation's edge
Asimov, I. The gods themselves
Asimov, I. I, robot
Asimov, I. The naked sun

SCIENCE FICTION—*Continued*
Heinlein, R. A. The moon is a harsh mistress
Heinlein, R. A. The puppet masters
Heinlein, R. A. Stranger in a strange land
Herbert, B. Dune: House Atreides
Herbert, B. Dune: House Corrino
Herbert, B. Dune: House Harkonnen
Herbert, B. Dune: The Butlerian jihad
Herbert, F. Chapterhouse: Dune
Herbert, F. Children of Dune
Herbert, F. Dune
Herbert, F. Dune messiah
Herbert, F. God Emperor of Dune
Herbert, F. Heretics of Dune
Høeg, P. The woman and the ape
The Hugo winners
Ishiguro, K. Never let me go
Jenkins, W. F. Exploration team
Kerr, K. Snare
Keyes, D. Flowers for Algernon
Knight, D. F. The best of Damon Knight
Koontz, D. R. Strangers
Kotzwinkle, W. E.T.
Kress, N. Beggars & choosers
Kress, N. Beggars in Spain
Kress, N. Beggars ride
Kress, N. Probability moon
Kress, N. Probability sun
Le Guin, U. K. Betrayals
Le Guin, U. K. The birthday of the world and other stories
Le Guin, U. K. City of illusions
Le Guin, U. K. The dispossessed
Le Guin, U. K. A fisherman of the inland sea
Le Guin, U. K. Forgiveness day
Le Guin, U. K. Four ways to forgiveness
Le Guin, U. K. The lathe of heaven
Le Guin, U. K. The left hand of darkness
Le Guin, U. K. A man of the people
Le Guin, U. K. The telling
Le Guin, U. K. A woman's liberation
Leiber, F. The Wanderer
Lem, S. Eden
Lem, S. Fiasco
Lem, S. His Master's Voice
Lem, S. Memoirs of a space traveler
Lem, S. Solaris
Lessing, D. M. Mara and Dann
Lessing, D. M. Shikasta
Levi, P. The sixth day, and other tales
Lewis, C. S. Out of the silent planet
Lewis, C. S. Perelandra
London, J. The star rover
May, J. The adversary
May, J. Diamond mask
May, J. The golden torc
May, J. Jack the bodiless
May, J. Magnificat
May, J. The many-colored land
May, J. The nonborn king
McAuley, P. J. White devils
McCaffrey, A. Acorna
McCaffrey, A. Acorna's people
McCaffrey, A. Acorna's quest
McCaffrey, A. Acorna's rebels
McCaffrey, A. Acorna's search
McCaffrey, A. Acorna's triumph
McCaffrey, A. Acorna's world
McCaffrey, A. All the Weyrs of Pern
McCaffrey, A. The city who fought
McCaffrey, A. Dragonflight
McCaffrey, A. Dragonquest
McCaffrey, A. Dragon's Kin
McCaffrey, A. Dragonsdawn
McCaffrey, A. Dragonseye
McCaffrey, A. Freedom's landing
McCaffrey, A. Freedom's ransom
McCaffrey, A. The greatest love [novelette]
McCaffrey, A. The Masterharper of Pern
McCaffrey, A. The renegades of Pern
McCaffrey, A. The skies of Pern
McCaffrey, A. The white dragon
McHugh, M. F. Nekropolis
McIntyre, V. N. Dreamsnake
McMullen, S. Souls in the great machine
Miéville, C. Iron council
Miller, W. M. A canticle for Leibowitz
Modesitt, L. E., Jr. Archform
Moon, E. Once a hero
Moorcock, M. An alien heat
Moorcock, M. Behold the man
Moorcock, M. The end of all songs
Moorcock, M. The hollow lands
Morgan, R. K. Altered carbon
Morgan, R. K. Broken angels
Nebula awards
Niven, L. Lucifer's hammer
Niven, L. The Mote in God's Eye
Niven, L. Ringworld
Niven, L. The Ringworld engineers
Niven, L. The Ringworld throne
Niven, L. Ringworld's children
Niven, L. Saturn's race
Norton, A. Beast Master's ark
Norton, A. Redline the stars
The Norton book of science fiction
The Oxford book of science fiction stories
Patterson, J. The lake house
Patterson, J. When the wind blows
Pohl, F. The annals of the Heechee
Pohl, F. Beyond the blue event horizon
Pohl, F. The boy who would live forever
Pohl, F. Gateway
Pohl, F. Heechee rendezvous
Pohl, F. Homegoing
Pohl, F. Man Plus
Pohl, F. Mars Plus
Pohl, F. The space merchants
Pohl, F. The world at the end of time
Resnick, M. The return of Santiago
Ridley, J. Those who walk in darkness
Robinson, K. S. Antarctica
Robinson, K. S. Blue Mars
Robinson, K. S. Green Mars [novelette]
Robinson, K. S. The Martians
Robinson, K. S. Red Mars
Robinson, S. Callahan's con
Russell, M. D. Children of God
Russell, M. D. The sparrow
Saberhagen, F. Berserker fury
Saberhagen, F. Berserker's star
Sagan, C. Contact
Sagan, N. Idlewild
Saul, J. The presence
Shelley, M. W. Frankenstein; or, The modern Prometheus
Silverberg, R. The collected stories of Robert Silverberg
Silverberg, R. The king of dreams
Silverberg, R. The longest way home
Silverberg, R. Lord Valentine's castle
Silverberg, R. Majipoor chronicles
Silverberg, R. The mountains of Majipoor
Silverberg, R. Phases of the moon
Silverberg, R. A Robert Silverberg omnibus
Silverberg, R. Roma eterna
Silverberg, R. Sorcerers of Majipoor
Silverberg, R. Valentine Pontifex
Simmons, D. Endymion
Simmons, D. Ilium
Simmons, D. Olympos
Simmons, D. The rise of Endymion
Steele, A. M. Coyote
Stephenson, N. The diamond age
Sterling, B. Holy fire
Stross, C. Iron sunrise
Swanwick, M. Bones of the earth
Tepper, S. S. The family tree
Tepper, S. S. The fresco
Tepper, S. S. Grass
Tepper, S. S. Northshore
Tepper, S. S. Raising the stones
Tepper, S. S. Sideshow
Tepper, S. S. Singer from the sea
Tepper, S. S. Six moon dance
Tepper, S. S. Southshore
Tepper, S. S. The visitor
Tolstaia, T. The slynx
Updike, J. Toward the end of time
Varley, J. Demon
Varley, J. The golden globe

SCOTS

England

Spark, M. The ballad of Peckham Rye

France

Faulks, S. Charlotte Gray

Panama

Galbraith, D. The rising sun

United States

Doig, I. Dancing at the Rascal Fair
Glass, J. Three Junes
Pouncey, P. R. Rules for old men waiting

SCOTT, ROBERT FALCON, 1868-1912

About

Bainbridge, B. The birthday boys

SCOTT, WINFIELD, 1786-1866

About

Shaara, J. Gone for soldiers

The **scout**. Combs, H.

SCOUTS AND SCOUTING

Berger, T. Little Big Man
Combs, H. The scout
Cooper, J. F. The Deerslayer
Cooper, J. F. The last of the Mohicans
Cooper, J. F. The Leatherstocking tales
Forsyth, F. The whispering wind

SCRIPTWRITERS *See* Authors

SCULPTORS

Barker, P. Double vision
Hawthorne, N. The marble faun
Hesse, H. Narcissus and Goldmund
James, H. Roderick Hudson
Piercy, M. Summer people
Stone, I. The agony and the ecstasy
Unsworth, B. Stone virgin

The **sculptor's** funeral. Cather, W.
In Cather, W. Early novels and stories

The **sculptress**. Walters, M.

SCULPTURE

See also Statues; Wood carving

SCYTHIANS

Llywelyn, M. The horse goddess

SEA *See* Ocean

The **sea**. Banville, J.

The **sea** came in at midnight. Erickson, S.

SEA CAPTAINS *See* Seamen; Shipmasters

Sea glass. Shreve, A.

Sea of fertility [series]
Mishima, Y. The decay of the angel
Mishima, Y. Runaway horses
Mishima, Y. Spring snow
Mishima, Y. The Temple of Dawn

The **sea** of grass. Richter, C.

SEA STORIES

See also Seamen; Whaling names of wars with the subdivision Naval operations

Beach, E. L. Run silent, run deep
Buchheim, L.-G. The boat
Caputo, P. The voyage
Conrad, J. The end of the tether
Conrad, J. Lord Jim
Conrad, J. The Nigger of the Narcissus
Conrad, J. Tales of land and sea
Conrad, J. Typhoon
Conrad, J. Youth
Cooper, J. F. The pilot
Cooper, J. F. The red rover
Cooper, J. F. Sea tales: The pilot, The red rover
De Hartog, J. The captain
Eidson, B. One bad thing
Fleming, T. J. Time and tide
Forester, C. S. Admiral Hornblower in the West Indies
Forester, C. S. Beat to quarters
Forester, C. S. Commodore Hornblower
Forester, C. S. Flying colours
Forester, C. S. Hornblower and the Atropos
Forester, C. S. Hornblower and the Hotspur
Forester, C. S. Hornblower during the crisis, and two stories: Hornblower's temptation and The last encounter
Forester, C. S. The last nine days of the Bismarck
Forester, C. S. Lieutenant Hornblower
Forester, C. S. Lord Hornblower
Forester, C. S. Mr. Midshipman Hornblower
Forester, C. S. Ship of the line
Heggen, T. Mister Roberts
Higgins, J. Storm warning
Hough, R. The stowaway
Innes, H. The wreck of the Mary Deare
Lambdin, D. King's captain
London, J. The Sea-Wolf
MacLean, A. When eight bells toll
Martel, Y. Life of Pi
Martin, W. Annapolis
Matthiessen, P. Far Tortuga
McCutchan, P. Apprentice to the sea
McCutchan, P. Cameron's crossing
McCutchan, P. The last farewell
McCutchan, P. The new lieutenant
McCutchan, P. The second mate
Melville, H. Billy Budd, sailor
Melville, H. Moby-Dick; or, The whale
Melville, H. Omoo: a narrative of adventures in the South Seas
Melville, H. Redburn, his first voyage
Melville, H. Redburn, his first voyage; White-jacket, or, The world in a man-of-war; Moby-Dick, or, The whale
Melville, H. White-jacket: or, The world in a man-of-war
Monsarrat, N. The cruel sea
Nordhoff, C. The Bounty trilogy
Nordhoff, C. Men against the sea
Nordhoff, C. Mutiny on the Bounty
Nordhoff, C. Pitcairn's Island
O'Brian, P. Blue at the mizzen
O'Brian, P. The commodore
O'Brian, P. The golden ocean
O'Brian, P. The hundred days
O'Brian, P. The unknown shore
O'Brian, P. The wine-dark sea
O'Brian, P. The yellow admiral
Pérez-Reverte, A. The nautical chart
Poe, E. A. The narrative of Arthur Gordon Pym of Nantucket
Poyer, D. Black storm
Poyer, D. China Sea
Poyer, D. The circle
Poyer, D. The command
Poyer, D. The gulf
Reeman, D. A ship must die
Sabatini, R. Captain Blood
Smith, W. A. Birds of prey
Smith, W. A. Hungry as the sea
Smith, W. A. Monsoon
Stewart, F. M. The magnificent Savages
Stone, R. Outerbridge Reach
Unsworth, B. Sacred hunger
Verne, J. The mysterious island
Verne, J. Twenty thousand leagues under the sea
Watkins, P. Calm at sunset, calm at dawn

Sea tales: The pilot, The red rover. Cooper, J. F.

The **sea,** the sea. Murdoch, I.

The **Sea-Wolf**. London, J.
also in London, J. Novels & stories

The **seal** wife. Harrison, K.

SEAMEN

See also Midshipmen; Sea stories; Shipmasters; Vikings

Beach, E. L. Run silent, run deep
Conrad, J. The Nigger of the Narcissus
Cooper, J. F. The pilot
Forester, C. S. Ship of the line
Heggen, T. Mister Roberts
Hough, R. The stowaway
Innes, H. The wreck of the Mary Deare
Lambdin, D. King's captain
London, J. The Sea-Wolf
Matthiessen, P. Far Tortuga
McCutchan, P. Apprentice to the sea
McCutchan, P. Cameron's crossing
McCutchan, P. The last farewell
McCutchan, P. The new lieutenant
McCutchan, P. The second mate
Melville, H. Billy Budd, sailor
Melville, H. Moby-Dick; or, The whale

SECRET SERVICE—*Continued*
MacLean, A. When eight bells toll
Morrell, D. The brotherhood of the rose
Redfern, E. The music of the spheres
Shelby, P. Days of drums
Shelby, P. Gatekeeper
Silva, D. The unlikely spy
Smith, W. A. Golden fox
Snyder, D. J. Night crossing
Stewart, M. Airs above the ground
Wiltse, D. Heartland
SECRET SERVICE (U.S.) *See* United States. Secret Service
SECRET SOCIETIES
See also Freemasons
Ludlum, R. The Matarese Circle
Neville, K. The eight
Portis, C. Masters of Atlantis
The **secret** warriors. Griffin, W. E. B.
Secret window, secret garden. King, S.
In King, S. Four past midnight p247-399
A **secret** word. Paddock, J.
SECRETARIES
Bing, S. You look nice today
Leavitt, D. The body of Jonah Boyd
Sheehan, A. The anxiety of everyday objects
Vida, N. Goodbye, Saigon
The **secrets** of Jin-Shei. Alexander, A.
The **secrets** of the Princess de Cadignan. Balzac, H. d.
In Balzac, H. d. The short novels of Balzac
SECTS
Rogers, J. Mr. Wroe's virgins
SEDUCTION
Colette. Mitsou
Dierbeck, L. One pill makes you smaller
Endō, S. The girl I left behind
Fraser, G. M. Flashman
Fraser, G. M. Royal Flash
Kundera, M. Slowness
Mawer, S. The fall
Nabokov, V. V. Lolita
Tolstoy, L., graf. Resurrection
Seduction of the Minotaur. Nin, A.
In Nin, A. Cities of the interior p463-589
See Jane run. Fielding, J.
See no evil. Bland, E. T.
See the child. Bergen, D.
Seed of doubt. McInerny, R. M.
Seeing a large cat. Peters, E.
Seek my face. Updike, J.
SEGREGATION *See* Race relations
Seize the day. Bellow, S.
Seize the day [novelette] Bellow, S.
In Bellow, S. The portable Saul Bellow
In Bellow, S. Seize the day
Seize the night. Koontz, D. R.
Seizure. Cook, R.
SELECT COMMITTEE ON ASSASSINATIONS *See* United States. Congress. House. Select Committee on Assassinations
Selected short stories. Gorky, M.
The **selected** short stories of Edith Wharton. Wharton, E.
Selected short stories of Franz Kafka. Kafka, F.
Selected stories. Munro, A.
The **selected** stories of Mavis Gallant. See Gallant, M. The collected stories of Mavis Gallant
The **selected** stories of Patricia Highsmith. Highsmith, P.
Selected stories of Roald Dahl. Dahl, R.
SELF-DEFENSE *See* Martial arts
Self-defense. Kellerman, J.
SELF-MADE MEN
See also Success
Caldwell, T. Captains and kings
Grau, S. A. The condor passes
James, H. The American
Weidman, J. I can get it for you wholesale
West, N. A cool million
SELF-SACRIFICE
Dickens, C. A tale of two cities
French, M. Her mother's daughter
Tolstoy, L., graf. Resurrection
Wolitzer, M. The wife
SELFISHNESS
Balzac, H. d. Père Goriot (Old Goriot)
Self's punishment. Schlink, B.
SELIM III, SULTAN OF TURKEY, 1761-1808
About
Wallach, J. Seraglio
Semiautomatic. Reuland, R.
SENATE (U.S.) *See* United States. Congress. Senate
SENECA INDIANS
Larsen, D. The white
Sense and sensibility. Austen, J.
also in Austen, J. The complete novels of Jane Austen
A **sense** of honor. Webb, J. H.
A **sense** of reality. Greene, G.
In Greene, G. Collected stories p164-323
Sensei. Donohue, J. J.
Sentimental education. Flaubert, G.
A **sentimental** journey through France and Italy. Sterne, L.
In Sterne, L. The life and opinions of Tristram Shandy, gentleman and A sentimental journey through France and Italy p691-832
Sentinels. Pronzini, B.
A **separate** peace. Knowles, J.
SEPOY REBELLION *See* India—British occupation, 1765-1947
September. Pilcher, R.
SEPTEMBER 11 TERRORIST ATTACKS, 2001
Foer, J. S. Extremely loud and incredibly close
Maynard, J. The usual rules
Price, R. The good priest's son
Schwartz, L. S. The writing on the wall
September song. Greeley, A. M.
Seraglio. Wallach, J.
Seraph on the Suwanee. Hurston, Z. N.
In Hurston, Z. N. Novels and stories p597-920
SERBIA
See also Kosovo (Serbia)
Novakovich, J. April Fool's Day
SERGEANTS *See* Soldiers
The **serpent** garden. Riley, J. M.
Serpent war saga [series]
Feist, R. E. Rage of a demon king
Feist, R. E. Rise of a merchant prince
Feist, R. E. Shadow of a dark queen
Feist, R. E. Shards of a broken crown
The **serpent's** shadow. Lackey, M.
Serpent's tooth. Kellerman, F.
Servant of the bones. Rice, A.
SERVANTS
See also African American servants types of household employees
Amado, J. Gabriela, clove and cinnamon
Böll, H. The lost honor of Katharina Blum
Bosse, M. J. The vast memory of love
Brooks, G. Year of wonders
Cookson, C. The black velvet gown
Dickens, C. The posthumous papers of the Pickwick Club
Faulkner, W. Requiem for a nun
Faulkner, W. The sound and the fury
Gordimer, N. July's people
Greene, G. A burnt-out case
Hemingway, E. The torrents of spring
Murdoch, I. Jackson's dilemma
Pushkin, A. S. The captain's daughter
Scott, Sir W. The bride of Lammermoor
Thomas, C. Farewell, my queen
Verne, J. Around the world in eighty days
Servants of the map. Barrett, A.
A **servant's** tale. Fox, P.
Set in darkness. Rankin, I.
Set this house on fire. Styron, W.
Setting free the bears. Irving, J.
In Irving, J. 3 by Irving p1-284
Sevastopol. Tolstoy, L., graf
In Tolstoy, L., graf. The portable Tolstoy p239-93
Seven days in May. Knebel, F.
Seven dials. Perry, A.
Seven dreams [series]
Vollmann, W. T. Argall

SHORT STORIES—*Continued*
Bowles, P. Collected stories, 1939-1976
Bowles, P. The delicate prey and other stories
Bowles, P. A hundred camels in the courtyard
Bowles, P. Midnight mass
Bowles, P. The stories of Paul Bowles
Bowles, P. Things gone and things still here
Boyle, K. Fifty stories
Boyle, T. C. After the plague
Boyle, T. C. T.C. Boyle stories
Bradbury, R. Bradbury stories
Bradbury, R. Fahrenheit 451
Bradbury, R. The golden apples of the sun
Bradbury, R. I sing the Body Electric! stories
Bradbury, R. The illustrated man
Bradbury, R. The Martian chronicles
Bradbury, R. Quicker than the eye
Bradbury, R. The stories of Ray Bradbury
Bradley, M. Z. The best of Marion Zimmer Bradley
Brand, M. The collected stories of Max Brand
Brand, M. Max Brand's best western stories
Buck, P. S. East and West
Busch, F. The children in the woods
Butler, O. E. Bloodchild and other stories
Butler, R. O. Had a good time
Byatt, A. S. The djinn in the nightingale's eye: five fairy stories
Byatt, A. S. Elementals
Byatt, A. S. Little black book of stories
Byatt, A. S. The Matisse stories
Cabbage and bones
Caldwell, E. Complete stories of Erskine Caldwell
Calisher, H. The collected stories of Hortense Calisher
Callahan, J. F. Flying home and other stories
Calling the wind
Calvino, I. Under the jaguar sun
Camus, A. Exile and the kingdom
Canin, E. The palace thief
Capote, T. Breakfast at Tiffany's: a short novel and three stories
Capote, T. The complete stories of Truman Capote
Capote, T. A tree of night, and other stories
Card, O. S. Maps in a mirror
Carlson, R. At the Jim Bridger
Carter, A. Burning your boats
Carver, R. Cathedral
Carver, R. What we talk about when we talk about love
Carver, R. Where I'm calling from
Cather, W. Willa Cather's collected short fiction, 1892-1912
Cavell, B. Rumble, young man, rumble
A Century of great Western stories
Chandler, R. Raymond Chandler
Chandler, R. Stories and early novels
Chaon, D. Among the missing
Cheever, J. The stories of John Cheever
Cheever, J. Thirteen uncollected stories
Chekhov, A. P. Early short stories, 1883-1888
Chekhov, A. P. Later short stories, 1888-1903
Chekhov, A. P. Longer stories from the last decade
Cherryh, C. J. The collected short fiction of C.J. Cherryh
Chesnutt, C. W. Stories, novels, & essay
Chesterton, G. K. Father Brown mystery stories
Chesterton, G. K. The Father Brown omnibus
Chesterton, G. K. The innocence of Father Brown
Chopin, K. Complete novels and stories
Christie, A. The harlequin tea set and other stories
Christie, A. Hercule Poirot's casebook
Christie, A. Miss Marple: the complete short stories
Christie, A. Mr. Parker Pyne, detective
Christie, A. Three blind mice and other stories
Christie, A. The witness for the prosecution and other stories
Cisneros, S. Woman Hollering Creek and other stories
Clark, M. H. The Anastasia syndrome and other stories
Clark, M. H. The lottery winner
Clark, M. H. My gal Sunday
Clarke, A. C. The collected stories of Arthur C. Clarke
Colette. The collected stories of Colette
Conrad, J. Great short works of Joseph Conrad
Conrad, J. The portable Conrad
Conrad, J. Tales of land and sea
Conrad, J. Tales of the East and West
Cook, K. L. Last call
Cooper, J. C. The future has a past
Coward, N. The collected stories of Noël Coward
Cozarinsky, E. The bride from Odessa
Crane, S. The complete short stories & sketches of Stephen Crane
Crane, S. The portable Stephen Crane
Crane, S. Prose and poetry
Crane, S. The red badge of courage and other stories
Cross, A. The collected stories of Amanda Cross
Dahl, R. Ah, sweet mystery of life
Dahl, R. Selected stories of Roald Dahl
Dangerous visions
Dann, J. Jubilee
Danticat, E. Krik? Krak!
The dark
Dark matter
Day, C. The circus in winter
De la Mare, W. Collected tales
DeMarinis, R. Borrowed hearts
DeRosso, H. A. Riders of the shadowlands
Dexter, C. Morse's greatest mystery and other stories
Díaz, J. Drown
The Dick Francis treasury of great racing stories
Dickens, C. Christmas stories
Dickens, C. Christmas tales
Dickens, C. The complete ghost stories of Charles Dickens
Dickens, C. Sketches by Boz
Dinesen, I. Last tales
Dinesen, I. Seven Gothic tales
Dinesen, I. Shadows on the grass
Dinesen, I. Winter's tales
Dinosaurs [story collection]
Dixon, S. The stories of Stephen Dixon
Doctorow, E. L. Lives of the poets
Doctorow, E. L. Sweet land stories
Dodd, S. M. O careless love
Doenges, J. What she left me: stories and a novella
Doerr, H. The tiger in the grass
Donaldson, S. R. Reave the Just and other tales
Dorris, M. Working men
Dostoyevsky, F. The best short stories of Dostoevsky
Doyle, Sir A. C. Adventures of Sherlock Holmes
Doyle, Sir A. C. The best science fiction of Arthur Conan Doyle
Doyle, Sir A. C. The complete Sherlock Holmes
Doyle, Sir A. C. Conan Doyle's tales of medical humanism and values: Round the red lamp
Doyle, Sir A. C. Famous tales of Sherlock Holmes
Doyle, Sir A. C. The return of Sherlock Holmes
Doyle, Sir A. C. Tales of terror and mystery
Doyle, Sir A. C. Uncollected stories
Drake, D. Grimmer than hell
Drummond, L. L. Anything you say can and will be used against you
Du Maurier, Dame D. Daphne du Maurier's classics of the macabre
Du Maurier, Dame D. Don't look now
Dubus, A. Dancing after hours
Dumas, A. Short stories
Durrell, G. M. Marrying off mother and other stories
Dybek, S. I sailed with Magellan
Earth song, sky spirit
Effinger, G. A. George Alec Effinger live! from planet Earth
Endō, S. The final martyrs
Engel, M. P. Strangers and sojourners
Englander, N. For the relief of unbearable urges
Epstein, J. Fabulous small Jews
Estleman, L. D. General murders
The Faber book of gay short fiction
Famous ghost stories
Farmer, P. J. The classic Philip José Farmer, 1952-1964—1964-1973
Faulkner, W. Collected stories of William Faulkner
Faulkner, W. The Faulkner reader
Faulkner, W. Go down, Moses
Faulkner, W. Uncollected stories of William Faulkner
Faulkner, W. The unvanquished
Fifty years of the best from Ellery Queen's Mystery Magazine
Fitzgerald, F. S. Babylon revisited, and other stories
Fitzgerald, F. S. The Basil and Josephine stories
Fitzgerald, F. S. The Fitzgerald reader
Fitzgerald, F. S. Flappers and philosophers
Fitzgerald, F. S. The short stories of F. Scott Fitzgerald
Fitzgerald, F. S. Six tales of the jazz age, and other stories
Fitzgerald, F. S. The stories of F. Scott Fitzgerald
Fitzgerald, F. S. Tales of the jazz age

SHORT STORIES—*Continued*
Lethem, J. Men and cartoons
Leung, B. World famous love acts
Levi, P. The sixth day, and other tales
Lewis, C. S. The dark tower and other stories
Lewis, W. H. I got somebody in Staunton
The Literary ghost
Lively, P. Pack of cards and other stories
London, J. The complete short stories of Jack London
London, J. Novels & stories
London, J. Short stories of Jack London
London, J. South Sea tales
London, J. Stories of Hawaii
London, J. White Fang, and other stories
Looking for a rain god: an anthology of contemporary African short stories
Lovecraft, H. P. At the mountains of madness, and other novels
Lovecraft, H. P. The Dunwich horror, and others
Lovecraft, H. P. H.P. Lovecraft
Lovecraft, H. P. The horror in the museum, and other revisions
Lovecraft, H. P. Tales of H.P. Lovecraft
Lurie, A. Women and ghosts
Macdonald, R. Ross Macdonald's Lew Archer, private investigator
MacLeod, A. Island
Malamud, B. The complete stories
Malamud, B. A Malamud reader
Malouf, D. Dream stuff
Mann, T. Death in Venice and other tales
Mann, T. Six early stories
Mann, T. Stories of three decades
Mansfield, K. The garden party and other stories
Mansfield, K. The short stories of Katherine Mansfield
Mason, B. A. Love life
Mason, B. A. Midnight magic
Mason, B. A. Shiloh and other stories
Mason, B. A. Zigzagging down a wild trail
Master's choice [v1]-2: mystery stories by today's top writers and the masters who inspired them
Matthiessen, P. On the river Styx and other stories
Maugham, W. S. The best short stories of W. Somerset Maugham
Maugham, W. S. Complete short stories
Maupassant, G. d. The collected stories of Guy de Maupassant
Maupassant, G. d. The dark side of Guy de Maupassant
Maurois, A. The collected stories of André Maurois
Maxwell, W. All the days and nights
Mazor, J. Friend of mankind and other stories
McCabe, E. Heaven lies about us
McCaffrey, A. The chronicles of Pern
McCaffrey, A. The girl who heard dragons
McCorkle, J. Crash diet
McCorkle, J. Final vinyl days and other stories
McCrumb, S. Foggy Mountain breakdown and other stories
McCullers, C. The ballad of the sad café: the novels and stories of Carson McCullers
McCullers, C. Collected stories
Means, D. The secret goldfish
Melville, H. The complete shorter fiction
Michener, J. A. Creatures of the kingdom
Michener, J. A. Tales of the South Pacific
Miller, A. Homely girl, a life, and other stories
Miller, S. Inventing the Abbotts and other stories
Millhauser, S. The king in the tree: three novellas
Millhauser, S. The knife thrower and other stories
Minot, S. Lust & other stories
A moment on the edge
Moore, L. Birds of America
Morris, W. Collected stories, 1948-1986
Mortimer, J. C. Rumpole à la carte
Mortimer, J. C. Rumpole and the angel of death
Mortimer, J. C. Rumpole on trial
Mortimer, J. C. Rumpole rests his case
Mortimer, J. C. The second Rumpole omnibus
Mosley, W. Always outnumbered, always outgunned
Mosley, W. Six easy pieces
Mosley, W. Walkin' the dog
Mowat, F. The Snow Walker
Mukherjee, B. The middleman and other stories
Munro, A. Friend of my youth
Munro, A. Hateship, friendship, courtship, loveship, marriage
Munro, A. The love of a good woman
Munro, A. The moons of Jupiter
Munro, A. Open secrets
Munro, A. Runaway
Munro, A. Selected stories
Murray, J. A few short notes on tropical butterflies
The Mysterious West
Nabokov, V. V. Nabokov's dozen
Nabokov, V. V. The stories of Vladimir Nabokov
Narayan, R. K. The grandmother's tale and selected stories
Narayan, R. K. Malgudi days
Narayan, R. K. Under the banyan tree and other stories
Nebula awards
New stories from the South: the year's best [date]
The Norton book of science fiction
Nothing but you
Oates, J. C. The collector of hearts
Oates, J. C. Faithless
Oates, J. C. Haunted
Oates, J. C. Heat, and other stories
Oates, J. C. I am no one you know
Oates, J. C. Marriages and infidelities
Oates, J. C. Where are you going, where have you been?
Oates, J. C. Where is here?
Oates, J. C. Will you always love me? and other stories
O'Brien, E. A fanatic heart
O'Brien, E. Lantern slides
O'Brien, T. The things they carried
O'Connor, F. Collected works
O'Connor, F. The complete stories
O'Connor, F. Everything that rises must converge
O'Connor, F. A good man is hard to find and other stories
O'Connor, F. Collected stories
O'Faoláin, S. The collected stories of Seán O'Faoláin
O'Hara, J. Collected stories of John O'Hara
Olsen, T. Tell me a riddle
The Oxford book of American detective stories
The Oxford book of American short stories
The Oxford book of English ghost stories
The Oxford book of English love stories
The Oxford book of English short stories
The Oxford book of gothic tales
The Oxford book of Irish short stories
The Oxford book of Jewish stories
The Oxford book of Latin American short stories
The Oxford book of modern fairy tales
The Oxford book of science fiction stories
The Oxford book of short stories
The Oxford book of spy stories
The Oxford book of travel stories
The Oxford book of twentieth-century ghost stories
Packer, Z. Drinking coffee elsewhere
Paley, G. The collected stories
Paretsky, S. Windy City blues
Parker, D. Here lies
Paton, A. Tales from a troubled land
Penguin book of gay short fiction
The Penguin book of lesbian short stories
Peters, E. A rare Benedictine
Peterson, P. W. Women in the grove
Pilcher, R. Flowers in the rain & other stories
Pirandello, L. Short stories
Poe, E. A. Complete stories and poems of Edgar Allan Poe
Porter, K. A. The collected stories of Katherine Anne Porter
Porter, K. A. Flowering Judas and other stories
Porter, K. A. The leaning tower, and other stories
Price, R. The collected stories
Price, R. The foreseeable future
Pritchett, V. S. Complete collected stories
Prize stories: The O. Henry Awards
Proulx, A. Bad dirt
Proulx, A. Close range
Proust, M. The complete short stories of Marcel Proust
Pushkin, A. S. Alexander Pushkin: complete prose fiction
Pym, B. Civil to strangers and other writings
Queen, E. The best of Ellery Queen
Rawlings, M. K. Short stories
Rendell, R. Blood lines
Rendell, R. Collected stories
Rhys, J. The collected short stories
Robinson, K. S. The Martians
Robinson, R. A perfect stranger
Roger Caras' Treasury of great cat stories
Roger Caras' Treasury of great dog stories
Roth, J. The collected stories of Joseph Roth

SHOSHONI INDIANS
Glancy, D. Stone heart
Hall, B. I should be extremely happy in your company
Shoulder the sky. Perry, A.
Show boat. Ferber, E.
Show business kills. Dart, I. R.
Show of evil. Diehl, W.
Showdown. Amado, J.
A **shower** of silver. Brand, M.
In Brand, M. Stolen gold: a western trio
Shrink rap. Parker, R. B.
Shutter Island. Lehane, D.

SIAMESE TWINS
McCammon, R. R. Gone south
Slouka, M. God's fool

SIBERIA (RUSSIA)
Dostoyevsky, F. The house of the dead
Freemantle, B. Dead men living
L'Amour, L. Last of the breed
Pasternak, B. L. Doctor Zhivago
Richler, N. Your mouth is lovely

Prisoners and prisons
See Prisoners and prisons—Siberia (Russia)
The **Sicilian**. Puzo, M.

SICILY
Hersey, J. A bell for Adano
Higgins, J. Luciano's luck
Pirandello, L. The outcast
Puzo, M. The Sicilian
Tomasi di Lampedusa, G. The Leopard

Aristocracy
See Aristocracy—Sicily

Peasant life
See Peasant life—Sicily

SICK CHILDREN
Leroy, M. Postcards from Berlin
McIntyre, V. N. Of mist, and grass, and sand
Zafris, N. Lucky strike
Sick puppy. Hiaasen, C.

SICKERT, WALTER, 1860-1942
About
West, P. The women of Whitechapel and Jack the Ripper
SIDDHĀRTHA *See* Gautama Buddha
Siddhartha. Hesse, H.
Sideshow. Tepper, S. S.
SIEGE OF BADAJOZ *See* Peninsular War, 1807-1814
The **siege** of London. James, H.
In James, H. Complete stories, 1874-1884
In James, H. The complete tales of Henry James
Siegfried. Mulisch, H.
Sierra. Wheeler, R. S.

SIERRA MADRE MOUNTAINS (MEXICO)
Traven, B. The treasure of the Sierra Madre
A **sight** for sore eyes. Rendell, R.
Sightblinder's story. See Saberhagen, F. The second book of lost swords: Sightblinder's story
Sights unseen. Gibbons, K.
Sightseeing. Lapcharoensap, R.
The **Sigma** protocol. Ludlum, R.
Sign of chaos. Zelazny, R.
The **sign** of four. Doyle, Sir A. C.
also in Doyle, Sir A. C. The complete Sherlock Holmes
also in Doyle, Sir A. C. Famous tales of Sherlock Holmes p187-311
The **sign** of the book. Dunning, J.
Sign of the unicorn. Zelazny, R.
Signal & noise. Griesemer, J.
Silas Marner. Eliot, G.
Silence. Endō, S.
The **silence** in the garden. Trevor, W.
The **silence** of the lambs. Harris, T.
The **silence** of the rain. García-Roza, L. A.
The **silent** angel. Böll, H.
Silent children. Campbell, R.
The **silent** cry. Ōe, K.
The **silent** cry. Perry, A.
Silent Joe. Parker, T. J.
Silent justice. Bernhardt, W.
Silent night. Clark, M. H.
Silent partner. Kellerman, J.
Silent prey. Sandford, J.
Silent thunder. Estleman, L. D.
Silent witness. Patterson, R. N.
Silk road. Larsen, J.
The **Silmarillion**. Tolkien, J. R. R.
The **silver** chalice. Costain, T. B.
The **Silver** Ghost. MacLeod, C.

SILVER MINES AND MINING
Conrad, J. Nostromo
Trevanian. Incident at Twenty Mile
The **silver** spoon. Galsworthy, J.
In Galsworthy, J. A modern comedy
Silver wedding. Binchy, M.
The **silver** wolf. Borchardt, A.
Silverhand. Llywelyn, M.
Silverlight. Llywelyn, M.
Simisola. Rendell, R.
A **simple** Habana melody: from when the world was good. Hijuelos, O.
A **simple** plan. Smith, S. B.
Simple speaks his mind. Hughes, L.
Simple stakes a claim. Hughes, L.
Simple takes a wife. Hughes, L.
A **simple** tale. Messud, C.
In Messud, C. The hunters
The **simple** truth. Baldacci, D.
Simple's Uncle Sam. Hughes, L.

SIN
Greene, G. Brighton rock
Sin. Hart, J.
Sin city. Robbins, H.
Sin killer. McMurtry, L.

SINGAPORE
Boulle, P. The bridge over the River Kwai
Clavell, J. King Rat
Loh, V. Breaking the tongue
Singer from the sea. Tepper, S. S.

SINGERS
Bailey, P. Uncle Rudolf
Cather, W. The song of the lark
Childress, M. Tender
Doig, I. Prairie nocturne
Erdrich, L. The Master Butchers Singing Club
Faber, M. The courage consort [novelette]
Grossman, D. Someone to run with
Hammond, G. The hitch
Hesse, H. Gertrude
Hijuelos, O. A simple Habana melody: from when the world was good
Jackson, S. Caught up in the rapture
Joe, Y. My fine lady
King, R. Domino
Li, P.-h. Farewell to my concubine
Marías, J. The man of feeling
McCrumb, S. If ever I return, pretty Peggy-O
McCrumb, S. The songcatcher
O'Hagan, A. Personality
Patchett, A. Bel canto
Patterson, J. Hide & seek
Powers, R. The time of our singing
Pynchon, T. The crying of lot 49
Rushdie, S. The ground beneath her feet
Sarton, M. Anger
Smith, L. The devil's dream
Spencer, L. Small town girl
Thomas, D. M. The white hotel
Tyler, A. A slipping-down life
Singing boy. McFarland, D.
The **singing** fire. Nattel, L.
Singing in the comeback choir. Campbell, B. M.
Singing in the shrouds. Marsh, Dame N.
The **singing** of the dead. Stabenow, D.
The **singing** sands. Tey, J.
also in Tey, J. Four, five and six by Tey
The **singing** stones. Whitney, P. A.
The **singing** sword. Whyte, J.
Singing the sadness. Hill, R.
Single & Single. Le Carré, J.

SISTERS—*Continued*
Gould, J. Time to say goodbye
Hansen, R. Mariette in ecstasy
Hart, J. Sin
Hay, E. A student of weather
Hazzard, S. The transit of Venus
Hearon, S. Ella in bloom
Hijuelos, O. The fourteen sisters of Emilio Montez O'Brien
Hoffman, A. Practical magic
Jackson, S. We have always lived in a castle
Kelman, J. Summer of storms
Lawrence, D. H. Women in love
Lin Yutang. Moment in Peking
Lipman, E. The ladies' man
Lively, P. The photograph
Marsh, J. The House of Eliott
McKinney-Whetstone, D. Tempest rising
McPhee, J. No ordinary matter
Michael, J. Deceptions
Mortman, D. True colors
Mukherjee, B. Desirable daughters
Ng, F. M. Bone
Oates, J. C. A Bloodsmoor romance
Picoult, J. My sister's keeper
Powell, S. The Mushroom Man
Rhys, J. After leaving Mr. Mackenzie
Rice, L. Home fires
Rice, L. Safe harbor
Rice, L. The secret hour
Robinson, E. The true and outstanding adventures of the Hunt sisters
Sakamoto, K. One hundred million hearts
Shange, N. Sassafrass, Cypress & Indigo
Siddons, A. R. Fault lines
Silko, L. Gardens in the dunes
Smiley, J. A thousand acres
Spencer, L. Forgiving
Stirling, J. The island wife
Stirling, J. The wind from the hills
Stubbs, J. Like we used to be
Tan, A. The hundred secret senses
Tanizaki, J. The Makioka sisters
Trollope, J. A Spanish lover
Vanderbes, J. Easter Island
Vera, Y. The stone virgins
Walker, A. By the light of my father's smile
Walker, A. The color purple
Weber, K. The little women
West, Dame R. Cousin Rosamund

SISTERS AND BROTHERS *See* Brothers and sisters

SISTERS-IN-LAW
Colette. Claudine and Annie
Kingsolver, B. Prodigal summer

SITTING BULL, DAKOTA CHIEF, 1831-1890
About
Jones, D. C. Arrest Sitting Bull

SIX-DAY WAR *See* Israel-Arab War, 1967
Six days of the condor. Grady, J.
Six early stories. Mann, T.
Six easy pieces. Mosley, W.
Six moon dance. Tepper, S. S.
Six novels. Colette
Six of one. Brown, R. M.
Six tales of the jazz age, and other stories. Fitzgerald, F. S.
Sixes and sevens. Henry, O.
In Henry, O. The complete works of O. Henry p811-940
The **sixth** book of lost swords: Mindsword's story. Saberhagen, F.
The **sixth** commandment. Sanders, L.
The **sixth** day, and other tales. Levi, P.
The **sixth** wife. Plaidy, J.
Sixty stories. Barthelme, D.
Skeleton canyon. Jance, J. A.
Skeleton crew. King, S.
Skeleton dance. Elkins, A. J.
The **skeleton** in the grass. Barnard, R.
Skeleton-in-waiting. Dickinson, P.
Sketches by Boz. Dickens, C.
The **skies** of Pern. McCaffrey, A.
Skin River. Sidor, S.
Skin tight. Hiaasen, C.

SKINHEADS
Prose, F. A changed man
The **skinner**. Asher, N. L.
Skinny dip. Hiaasen, C.
Skinny legs and all. Robbins, T.
Skinwalkers. Hillerman, T.
Skirt and the fiddle. Egolf, T.
The **skrayling** tree. Moorcock, M.
Skulduggery. Hart, C. G.
The **skull** beneath the skin. James, P. D.
The **skull** mantra. Pattison, E.
Sky coyote. Baker, K.
Sky full of sand. DeMarinis, R.
The **sky** so big and black. Barnes, J.

SKYE (SCOTLAND)
Stewart, M. Wildfire at midnight
Slammerkin. Donoghue, E.
Slapstick. Vonnegut, K.
Slatewiper. Perdue, L.
Slaughter. Kelton, E.
Slaughterhouse-five. Vonnegut, K.

SLAVE TRADE
Johnson, C. R. Middle passage
Kaye, M. M. Trade wind
Phillips, C. Crossing the river
Smith, W. A. Flight of the falcon
Unsworth, B. Sacred hunger
Wray, J. Canaan's tongue

SLAVERY
See also Abolitionists; African Americans; Fugitive slaves; Slave trade; Underground railroad
Bell, M. S. All souls' rising
Bell, M. S. Master of the crossroads
Bell, M. S. The stone that the builder refused
Brink, A. P. A chain of voices
Brooks, G. March
Burke, J. L. White doves at morning
Butler, O. E. Kindred
Caputo, P. Acts of faith
Cather, W. Sapphira and the slave girl
Chase-Riboud, B. The President's daughter
Chase-Riboud, B. Sally Hemings
Condé, M. I, Tituba, black witch of Salem
Crafts, H. The bondswomans narrative
De Hartog, J. The peculiar people
Durham, D. A. A walk through darkness
Gaines, E. J. The autobiography of Miss Jane Pittman
García, C. Monkey hunting
Gibbons, K. On the occasion of my last afternoon
Hambly, B. Sold down the river
Hansen, B. The monsters of St. Helena
Heidish, M. A woman called Moses
Heinlein, R. A. Citizen of the galaxy
Jakes, J. Charleston
Jones, E. P. The known world
L'Engle, M. The other side of the sun
Martin, V. Property
McCaig, D. Jacob's ladder
Pesci, D. Amistad
Phillips, C. Cambridge
Phillips, C. Crossing the river
Plain, B. Crescent City
Rhodes, J. P. Voodoo dreams
Smith, W. A. River god
Stowe, H. B. Uncle Tom's cabin
Styron, W. The confessions of Nat Turner
Tademy, L. Cane River
Twain, M. Pudd'nhead Wilson
Vance, J. The last castle
Walker, M. Jubilee
Wallach, J. Seraglio
Warren, R. P. Band of angels
Youmans, M. The wolf pit

SLAVES *See* Slavery
Slaves of obsession. Perry, A.
The **slayers** of Seth. Doherty, P. C.
Slayride. Francis, D.

SLED DOG RACING
Henry, S. Murder on the Iditarod Trail

SLEEP
Kress, N. Beggars & choosers

SMALL TOWN LIFE—*Continued*
McCrumb, S. She walks these hills
McCullers, C. Clock without hands
McCullers, C. The heart is a lonely hunter
McMurtry, L. Duane's depressed
McMurtry, L. Texasville
Medlicott, J. A. Gardens of Covington
Medlicott, J. A. The ladies of Covington send their love
Miller, S. While I was gone
Miller, S. The world below
Morris, M. M. A dangerous woman
Morris, M. M. Fiona Range
Morris, M. M. Songs in ordinary time
Morris, W. Taps
Mosher, H. F. Waiting for Teddy Williams
Naylor, G. Mama Day
Nichols, J. T. The Milagro beanfield war
Nordan, L. Wolf whistle
Oates, J. C. Broke heart blues
Oates, J. C. Missing mom
Oates, J. C. Rape
O'Dell, T. Back roads
O'Dell, T. Coal Run
O'Hara, J. Ten North Frederick
O'Nan, S. Snow angels
Otto, W. How to make an American quilt
Parks, G. The learning tree
Patton, F. G. Good morning, Miss Dove
Pearson, T. R. Blue Ridge
Pearson, T. R. Cry me a river
Pearson, T. R. A short history of a small place
Phillips, S. E. Ain't she sweet
Plain, B. Her father's house
Powell, D. Come back to Sorrento
Powell, D. Dance night
Powell, D. My home is far away
Poyer, D. Thunder on the mountain
Price, R. Roxanna Slade
Pronzini, B. A wasteland of strangers
Purdy, J. The nephew
Rash, R. Saints at the river
Reardon, L. Blameless
Reuss, F. Horace afoot
Reynolds, S. A gracious plenty
Richards, D. A. The bay of love and sorrows
Rinehart, S. Built in a day
Roth, P. When she was good
Russo, R. Empire Falls
Russo, R. Nobody's fool
Russo, R. The risk pool
Santmyer, H. H. "—and ladies of the club"
Saroyan, W. The human comedy
Sarton, M. Kinds of love
Schupack, D. The boy on the bus
Schwartz, J. B. Reservation Road
Settle, M. L. Charley Bland
Sholem Aleichem. The nightingale
Shreve, A. Strange fits of passion
Shreve, S. R. The visiting physician
Siddons, A. R. Nora, Nora
Siegel, B. Actual innocence
Simpson, M. Off Keck Road
Smith, L. Family linen
Sparks, N. A bend in the road
Spencer, L. Bitter sweet
Spencer, L. That Camden summer
Spencer, S. A ship made of paper
Steinbeck, J. East of Eden
Stowe, H. B. Oldtown folks
Straub, P. The throat
Strout, E. Amy and Isabelle
Tarkington, B. Alice Adams
Thomas, R. The fourth Durango
Trigiani, A. Big Cherry Holler
Trigiani, A. Big Stone Gap
Trigiani, A. Milk glass moon
Tryon, T. In the fire of spring
Tryon, T. The wings of the morning
Twain, M. Pudd'nhead Wilson
Updike, J. Villages
Wallace, D. The Watermelon King
Watson, B. The heaven of Mercury
Watt, D. Reynolds
Welty, E. The golden apples
Welty, E. Losing battles
Welty, E. The optimist's daughter
White, B. Quite a year for plums
Wilcox, J. Heavenly days
Williams, D. Angel Rock
Wiltse, D. Heartland
Winthrop, E. Island justice
Wolfe, T. Look homeward, angel
Wolfe, T. O lost
Woods, S. Chiefs
Yancey, R. A burning in Homeland
Yarbrough, S. Prisoners of war
Zuber, I. Salt

Small vices. Parker, R. B.

SMALLWOOD, JOSEPH R., 1900-1991
About
Johnston, W. The colony of unrequited dreams

A **smile** on the face of the tiger. Estleman, L. D.
Smiley's people. Le Carré, J.
also in Le Carré, J. The quest for Karla p679-952
Smilla's sense of snow. Høeg, P.

SMITH, JOHN, 1580-1631
About
Vollmann, W. T. Argall

SMITHSONIAN INSTITUTION
Vidal, G. The Smithsonian Institution

The **Smithsonian** Institution. Vidal, G.
Smoke. Westlake, D. E.
Smoke in mirrors. Krentz, J. A.
The **smoke** jumper. Evans, N.
Smokescreen. Francis, D.

SMOKING
Gutcheon, B. R. Five fortunes

SMUGGLERS *See* Smuggling
Smuggler's moon. Alexander, B.

SMUGGLING
Alexander, B. Smuggler's moon
Cussler, C. Flood tide
Cussler, C. Inca gold
Du Maurier, Dame D. Jamaica Inn
Eidson, B. One bad thing
Hemingway, E. To have and have not
Maas, P. Father and son
Spark, M. The comforters
Stone, R. Dog soldiers

The **snack** thief. Camilleri, A.
Snagged. Clark, C. H.
The **snake**. Steinbeck, J.
In Steinbeck, J. The portable Steinbeck
The **snake** pit. Ward, M. J.
The **snake** tattoo. Barnes, L.
The **snake,** the crocodile, and the dog. Peters, E.
Snakepit. Isegawa, M.

SNAKES
McIntyre, V. N. Of mist, and grass, and sand
Parker, T. J. Where serpents lie

Snapshot. Barnes, L.
Snare. Kerr, K.
Sneaky people. Berger, T.
The **sniper's** wife. Mayor, A.
Snobbery with violence. Chesney, M.
Snopes. Faulkner, W.
Snow. Pamuk, O.
Snow angels. O'Nan, S.
Snow country. Kawabata, Y.
In Kawabata, Y. Snow country, and Thousand cranes p1-175
Snow country, and Thousand cranes. Kawabata, Y.
Snow falling on cedars. Guterson, D.
The **snow** goose. Gallico, P.
The **snow-image**. Hawthorne, N.
In Hawthorne, N. Tales and sketches, including Twice-told tales, Mosses from an old manse, and The snow-image; A wonder book for girls and boys; Tanglewood tales for girls and boys, being a second Wonder book
Snow in August. Hamill, P.
The **Snow** Queen. Vinge, J. D.
SNOW STORMS *See* Storms
The **Snow** Walker. Mowat, F.
Snow white, blood red. Entered in Part I under title
Snowleg. Shakespeare, N.

SOLDIERS—*Continued*

France

Balzac, H. d. The country doctor
Colette. The kepi
Faulkner, W. A fable
Flanagan, T. The year of the French

Germany

Böll, H. The silent angel
Böll, H. A soldier's legacy
Crichton, R. The secret of Santa Vittoria
Higgins, J. The eagle has landed
Kirst, H. H. Forward, Gunner Asch!
Kirst, H. H. The return of Gunner Asch
Kirst, H. H. The revolt of Gunner Asch
Remarque, E. M. All quiet on the western front
Remarque, E. M. A time to love and a time to die
Robbins, D. L. War of the rats
Shaw, I. The young lions
Solzhenitsyn, A. August 1914
Watkins, P. Night over day over night

Great Britain

Barker, P. The eye in the door
Barker, P. The ghost road
Barker, P. Regeneration
Boulle, P. The bridge over the River Kwai
Cornwell, B. Sharpe's battle
Cornwell, B. Sharpe's company
Cornwell, B. Sharpe's eagle
Cornwell, B. Sharpe's enemy
Cornwell, B. Sharpe's fortress
Cornwell, B. Sharpe's gold
Cornwell, B. Sharpe's havoc
Cornwell, B. Sharpe's honour
Cornwell, B. Sharpe's prey: Richard Sharpe and the Expedition to Copenhagen, 1807
Cornwell, B. Sharpe's regiment
Cornwell, B. Sharpe's sword
Cornwell, B. Sharpe's Trafalgar
Cornwell, B. Sharpe's Waterloo
Ford, F. M. A man could stand up
Ford, F. M. No more parades
Llewellyn, R. None but the lonely heart
MacLean, A. Force 10 from Navarone
MacLean, A. The guns of Navarone
Mallinson, A. A close run thing
Ondaatje, M. The English patient
Scott, P. A division of the spoils
Waugh, E. Men at arms
Waugh, E. Officers and gentlemen

Japan

Shan Sa. The girl who played go

Rome

Bradley, M. Z. The forest house
Douglas, L. C. The robe
Llywelyn, M. Druids

Russia

See also Cossacks
Robbins, D. L. War of the rats
Solzhenitsyn, A. August 1914
Tolstoy, L., graf. War and peace

United States

See also African American soldiers
Bristow, G. Celia Garth
Brown, R. M. High hearts
Clavell, J. King Rat
Coyle, H. W. Until the end
Crane, S. The red badge of courage
Daley, R. The innocents within
Del Vecchio, J. M. The 13th valley
Del Vecchio, J. M. For the sake of all living things
Dos Passos, J. Three soldiers
Fleming, T. J. Dreams of glory
Griffin, W. E. B. The aviators
Griffin, W. E. B. The new breed
Griffin, W. E. B. Special ops
Hawke, E. Ash Wednesday
Hersey, J. A bell for Adano
Higgins, J. Night of the fox
Hooker, R. MASH
Horgan, P. A distant trumpet
Jones, D. C. Elkhorn Tavern
Jones, J. From here to eternity
Jones, J. The thin red line
Jones, J. Whistle
Mailer, N. The naked and the dead
Nathanson, E. M. The dirty dozen
O'Brien, T. Going after Cacciato
O'Nan, S. A world away
Purdy, J. The nephew
Ricks, T. E. A soldier's duty
Shaara, J. Gone for soldiers
Shaw, I. The young lions
Shulman, M. Rally round the flag, boys!
Willard, T. Buffalo soldiers
Wright, S. Meditations in green

Vietnam

Bao Ninh. The sorrow of war

SOLDIERS, BLACK *See* African American soldiers
The **soldier's** art. Powell, A.
In Powell, A. A dance to the music of time
A **soldier's** duty. Ricks, T. E.
A **soldier's** legacy. Böll, H.
In Böll, H. The stories of Heinrich Böll p316-81

SOLDIERS OF FORTUNE

Caputo, P. Horn of Africa
Elegant, R. S. Manchu
Forsyth, F. The dogs of war
Smith, W. A. Cry wolf

Soldiers' pay. Faulkner, W.
The **soldier's** return. Bragg, M.
Sole survivor. Koontz, D. R.
SOLICITORS *See* Law and lawyers
Solitaire. Eskridge, K.
Solomon Gursky was here. Richler, M.

SOLOMON ISLANDS

See also World War, 1939-1945—Solomon Islands
London, J. South Sea tales

Solstice. Oates, J. C.

SOMALIA

Farah, N. Links

Some bitter taste. Nabb, M.
Some buried Caesar. Stout, R.
In Stout, R. All aces p1-153
Some days you get the bear. Block, L.
In Block, L. The collected mystery stories p443-568
Some deaths before dying. Dickinson, P.
Some do not. Ford, F. M.
In Ford, F. M. Parade's end
Somebody else's music. Haddam, J.
Someone to run with. Grossman, D.
Someone to watch over me. Bausch, R.
Someplace to be flying. De Lint, C.
Somersault. Ōe, K.
SOMERSET (ENGLAND) *See* England—Somerset
Something borrowed, something black. Estleman, L. D.
Something happened. Heller, J.
Something in the air. Lathen, E.
Something like a love affair. Symons, J.
Something rising (light and swift). Kimmel, H.
Something special. Murdoch, I.
Something wicked this way comes. Bradbury, R.
Sometimes a great notion. Kesey, K.
Sometimes I dream in Italian. Ciresi, R.
Sometimes they bite. Block, L.
In Block, L. The collected mystery stories p43-175
A **son** called Gabriel. McNicholl, D.
Son of a witch. Maguire, G.
Son of Fletch. Mcdonald, G.
A **son** of the circus. Irving, J.
A **son** of war. Bragg, M.
A **song** for Lya. Martin, G. R. R.
In The Hugo winners p483-544
The **song** of Bernadette. Werfel, F.
Song of ice and fire [series]
Martin, G. R. R. A game of thrones
The **song** of names. Lebrecht, N.
A **song** of sixpence. Cronin, A. J.
Song of Solomon. Morrison, T.
The **song** of the lark. Cather, W.
also in Cather, W. Early novels and stories p291-706

SOUTH CAROLINA—Charleston—*Continued*
Brown, S. The alibi
Conroy, P. The lords of discipline
Jakes, J. Charleston
Robards, K. To trust a stranger
Shange, N. Sassafrass, Cypress & Indigo
Siddons, A. R. Islands

SOUTH CHINA SEA
Greer, A. S. The path of minor planets
Poyer, D. China Sea

SOUTH DAKOTA
Meyers, K. The work of wolves

19th century
Jones, D. C. A creek called Wounded Knee
Rölvaag, O. E. Giants in the earth
Rölvaag, O. E. Peder Victorious

Farm life
See Farm life—South Dakota

Frontier and pioneer life
See Frontier and pioneer life—South Dakota

South of the border, west of the sun. Murakami, H.
SOUTH SEA ISLANDS *See* Islands of the Pacific
South Sea tales. London, J.

SOUTHAMPTON INSURRECTION, 1831
Styron, W. The confessions of Nat Turner

Southampton Row. Perry, A.

SOUTHEAST ASIA
Browne, G. A. 18mm blues
Landers, S. Coswell's guide to Tambralinga
Lederer, W. J. The ugly American
Straub, P. Koko
Vollmann, W. T. Butterfly stories

SOUTHERN AFRICA
Smith, W. A. The leopard hunts in darkness
Smith, W. A. Men of men

Southern cross. Greenleaf, S.
Southern discomfort. Brown, R. M.
Southern discomfort. Maron, M.
A **southern** exposure. Adams, A.
A **Southern** family. Godwin, G.
Southern fried. Pickens, C.
Southern ghost. Hart, C. G.
SOUTHERN RHODESIA *See* Zimbabwe

SOUTHERN STATES
See also Old Southwest; Reconstruction names of individual states
Barker, C. Galilee
Bell, M. S. Anything goes
Faulkner, W. As I lay dying
Faulkner, W. Light in August
Ferber, E. Show boat
Gay, W. I hate to see that evening sun go down
Lester, J. Do Lord remember me
O'Connor, F. Everything that rises must converge
O'Connor, F. A good man is hard to find and other stories
Powell, P. Edisto revisited
Smith, L. The devil's dream
Smith, L. Oral history
Walker, A. The color purple

19th century
Brown, R. M. High hearts
Gibbons, K. On the occasion of my last afternoon
Mitchell, M. Gone with the wind
Price, E. Savannah
Walker, M. Jubilee

20th century
Adams, A. A southern exposure
Allison, D. Bastard out of Carolina
Bambara, T. C. The salt eaters
Brown, J. D. Addie Pray
Brown, L. Joe
Brown, R. M. Southern discomfort
Burns, O. A. Leaving Cold Sassy
Capote, T. The grass harp
Childress, M. Crazy in Alabama
Conroy, P. The prince of tides
Crews, H. Body
Crews, H. Scar lover
Dexter, P. Paris Trout
Dickey, J. Deliverance
Edgerton, C. Where trouble sleeps
Faulkner, W. Pylon
Flagg, F. Coming attractions
Flagg, F. Fried green tomatoes at the Whistle-Stop Cafe
Gaines, E. J. The gathering of old men
Gibbons, K. Charms for the easy life
Gibbons, K. Ellen Foster
Gibbons, K. A virtuous woman
Gifford, B. Wild at heart
Gilchrist, E. The cabal and other stories
Godwin, G. A Southern family
Grau, S. A. The keepers of the house
Hurston, Z. N. Seraph on the Suwanee
Lee, H. To kill a mockingbird
McCorkle, J. Crash diet
McCorkle, J. Ferris Beach
McCorkle, J. Final vinyl days and other stories
McCullers, C. Clock without hands
McCullers, C. The heart is a lonely hunter
McCullers, C. Reflections in a golden eye
Pearson, T. R. A short history of a small place
Percy, W. The last gentleman
Percy, W. Love in the ruins
Plain, B. Fortune
Price, R. Roxanna Slade
Reynolds, S. A gracious plenty
Siddons, A. R. Heartbreak Hotel
Siddons, A. R. Homeplace
Siddons, A. R. Outer banks
Siddons, A. R. Peachtree Road
Smith, L. Me and my baby view the eclipse
Smith, L. Saving Grace
Spencer, E. The southern woman
Tyler, A. Earthly possessions
Warren, R. P. A place to come to
White, B. Quite a year for plums
Woods, S. Chiefs

Farm life
See Farm life—Southern States

Frontier and pioneer life
See Frontier and pioneer life—Southern States

Mountain life
See Mountain life—Southern States

Politics
See Politics—Southern States

Social life and customs
Welty, E. Complete novels

The **southern** woman. Spencer, E.
Southern women. Battle, L.
Southshore. Tepper, S. S.
SOUTHWEST, NEW *See* Southwestern States
SOUTHWEST, OLD *See* Old Southwest

SOUTHWESTERN STATES
See also Santa Fe Trail
Barrett, W. E. The lilies of the field
Barthelme, F. Painted desert
Horgan, P. A distant trumpet

Frontier and pioneer life
See Frontier and pioneer life—Southwestern States

SOVIET UNION *See* Russia
Space. Michener, J. A.

SPACE AND TIME
See also Time travel
Benford, G. Timescape
Heinlein, R. A. Job: a comedy of justice

SPACE COLONIES
Anderson, P. The sharing of flesh
Bova, B. The precipice
Clement, H. Noise
Heinlein, R. A. The moon is a harsh mistress
Jenkins, W. F. Exploration team
Le Guin, U. K. The word for world is forest

SPIES—*Continued*
Brown, D. Shadows of steel
Buchan, J. The thirty-nine steps
Buckley, W. F. Last call for Blackford Oakes
Buckley, W. F. Mongoose, R.I.P
Buckley, W. F. Spytime
Carr, P. Voices in a haunted room
Clancy, T. The Cardinal of the Kremlin
Clancy, T. Debt of honor
Clancy, T. The hunt for Red October
Clavell, J. Noble house
Coonts, S. The minotaur
Cooper, J. F. The spy
Cornwell, B. Sharpe's havoc
Cornwell, B. Sharpe's regiment
Cornwell, B. Sharpe's sword
Cussler, C. Deep six
Cussler, C. Raise the Titanic!
Davies, R. What's bred in the bone
Deaver, J. Garden of beasts
Deighton, L. Berlin game
Deighton, L. Charity
Deighton, L. City of gold
Deighton, L. Faith
Deighton, L. Funeral in Berlin
Deighton, L. Game, set & match
Deighton, L. Hope
Deighton, L. The Ipcress file
Deighton, L. London match
Deighton, L. Mexico set
Deighton, L. Spy hook
Deighton, L. Spy line
Deighton, L. Spy sinker
Deighton, L. SS-GB: Nazi-occupied Britain 1941
Deighton, L. XPD
DeMille, N. The charm school
Diehl, W. 27
Doctorow, E. L. The book of Daniel
Dunning, J. Two o'clock, eastern wartime
Egleton, C. Blood money
Egleton, C. A double deception
Egleton, C. The honey trap
Egleton, C. Hostile intent
Egleton, C. A killing in Moscow
Egleton, C. A lethal involvement
Egleton, C. Warning shot
Finder, J. The Moscow Club
Finney, P. Gloriana's torch
Fleming, I. Casino Royale
Fleming, I. Doctor No
Fleming, I. From Russia, with love
Fleming, I. Goldfinger
Fleming, I. The man with the golden gun
Fleming, I. On Her Majesty's Secret Service
Fleming, I. You only live twice
Fleming, T. J. Dreams of glory
Follett, K. Code to zero
Follett, K. Eye of the needle
Follett, K. Hornet flight
Follett, K. The key to Rebecca
Follett, K. Lie down with lions
Forsyth, F. The deceiver
Forsyth, F. The devil's alternative
Forsyth, F. The fist of God
Francis, C. Wolf winter
Freemantle, B. Bomb grade
Freemantle, B. Charlie's apprentice
Freemantle, B. Comrade Charlie
Freemantle, B. Dead men living
Furst, A. Dark voyage
Gardner, J. E. Cold fall
Gardner, J. E. License renewed
Gilman, D. The amazing Mrs. Pollifax
Gilman, D. The elusive Mrs. Pollifax
Gilman, D. Mrs. Pollifax and the Hong Kong Buddha
Gilman, D. Mrs. Pollifax on safari
Gilman, D. A palm for Mrs. Pollifax
Gilman, D. The unexpected Mrs. Pollifax
Goldman, W. Marathon man
Grady, J. Six days of the condor
Greene, G. 3: This gun for hire, The confidential agent, The ministry of fear
Greene, G. The human factor
Greene, G. The ministry of fear
Greene, G. Our man in Havana
Hall, A. Quiller Balalaika
Hall, A. The Quiller memorandum
Hall, A. Quiller Salamander
Hall, A. Quiller solitaire
Higgins, J. The eagle has flown
Higgins, J. The eagle has landed
Isaacs, S. Shining through
Jakes, J. On secret service
Judd, A. Legacy
Kaye, M. M. Death in Kashmir
Keneally, T. Confederates
Koontz, D. R. Watchers
Le Carré, J. Absolute friends
Le Carré, J. The honourable schoolboy
Le Carré, J. The little drummer girl
Le Carré, J. The looking glass war
Le Carré, J. The night manager
Le Carré, J. Our game
Le Carré, J. A perfect spy
Le Carré, J. The quest for Karla
Le Carré, J. The Russia house
Le Carré, J. The secret pilgrim
Le Carré, J. A small town in Germany
Le Carré, J. Smiley's people
Le Carré, J. The spy who came in from the cold
Le Carré, J. The tailor of Panama
Le Carré, J. Tinker, tailor, soldier, spy
Lindsey, D. L. The color of night
Littell, R. The company
Littell, R. Walking back the cat
Ludlum, R. The Bourne identity
Ludlum, R. The Bourne supremacy
Ludlum, R. The Bourne ultimatum
Ludlum, R. The Parsifal mosaic
Lustbader, E. V. Jian
Lustbader, E. V. Shan
MacInnes, H. Prelude to terror
MacInnes, H. Ride a pale horse
MacLean, A. Ice Station Zebra
MacLean, A. Where eagles dare
Mailer, N. Harlot's ghost
Mathews, H. My life in CIA
McCarry, C. Old boys
McEwan, I. The innocent
Morrell, D. Assumed identity
Morrell, D. The brotherhood of the rose
Ondaatje, M. The English patient
The Oxford book of spy stories
Silva, D. The unlikely spy
Smith, M. C. Stallion Gate
Taibo, P. I. Returning as shadows
Trenhaile, J. The gates of exquisite view
Trevanian. The Eiger sanction
West, Dame R. The birds fall down
Westlake, D. E. The spy in the ointment

Spies. Frayn, M.
Spindrift. Whitney, P. A.
The **spinning** man. Harrar, G.
The **Spinoza** of Market Street. Singer, I. B.
In Singer, I. B. Collected stories: Gimpel the fool to The letter writer

SPINSTERS *See* Single women

Spiral. Geary, J. M.
Spiral. Healy, J. F.
The **spirit** caller. Hager, J.

SPIRITUALISM
Byatt, A. S. The conjugial angel
Griesemer, J. Signal & noise
Howatch, S. The high flyer
Jackson, S. The haunting of Hill House
Mantel, H. Beyond black
Paretsky, S. Ghost country
Spark, M. The bachelors
Vargas Llosa, M. Death in the Andes

A **splash** of red. Fraser, A.
Split images. Leonard, E.
Split infinity. Anthony, P.

SPLIT PERSONALITY *See* Dual personality

The **spoils** of Poynton. James, H.

SPOKANE INDIANS
Alexie, S. Reservation blues

Stolen gold: a western trio. Brand, M.

STONE AGE

Golding, W. Clonk clonk
Harrison, S. Brother Wind
Harrison, S. Call down the stars
Harrison, S. Cry of the wind
Harrison, S. Mother earth, father sky
Harrison, S. My sister the moon
Harrison, S. Song of the river
Thomas, E. M. The animal wife

Stone angel. O'Connell, C.
Stone cribs. Nelscott, K.
The **stone** diaries. Shields, C.
Stone heart. Glancy, D.
Stone kiss. Kellerman, F.
The **stone** monkey. Deaver, J.
Stone song. Blevins, W.
The **stone** that the builder refused. Bell, M. S.
Stone virgin. Unsworth, B.
The **stone** virgins. Vera, Y.
Stonecutter's story. See Saberhagen, F. The third book of lost swords: Stonecutter's story

STONEHENGE (ENGLAND)

Cornwell, B. Stonehenge, 2000 B.C.
Holland, C. Pillar of the Sky

Stonehenge, 2000 B.C. Cornwell, B.
The **stones** cry out. Okuizumi, H.
Stones for Ibarra. Doerr, H.
Stories. Lessing, D. M.
STORIES ABOUT DIARIES *See* Diaries (Stories about)
STORIES ABOUT LETTERS *See* Letters (Stories about)
Stories and early novels. Chandler, R.
STORIES IN DIARY FORM *See* Diaries (Stories in diary form)
Stories not for the nervous. See Alfred Hitchcock presents: Stories not for the nervous
Stories, novels, & essay. Chesnutt, C. W.
The **stories** of Alice Adams. Adams, A.
The **stories** of Edith Wharton. Wharton, E.
The **stories** of Elizabeth Spencer. Spencer, E.
The **stories** of Eva Luna. Allende, I.
The **stories** of F. Scott Fitzgerald. Fitzgerald, F. S.
Stories of five decades. Hesse, H.
Stories of Hawaii. London, J.
The **stories** of Heinrich Böll. Böll, H.
The **stories** of John Cheever. Cheever, J.
The **stories** of John Edgar Wideman. Wideman, J. E.
The **stories** of Muriel Spark. Spark, M.
The **stories** of Paul Bowles. Bowles, P.
The **stories** of Ray Bradbury. Bradbury, R.
The **stories** of Richard Bausch. Bausch, R.
The **stories** of Stephen Dixon. Dixon, S.
STORIES OF THE FUTURE *See* Future
Stories of three decades. Mann, T.
The **stories** of Vladimir Nabokov. Nabokov, V. V.

STORIES WITHIN A NOVEL

Atwood, M. The blind assassin
Atwood, M. Lady Oracle
Barnes, J. A history of the world in 10½ chapters
Barth, J. The Tidewater tales
Baxter, C. The feast of love
Boyd, W. The blue afternoon
Byatt, A. S. Babel Tower
Carey, P. Jack Maggs
Conley, R. J. Mountain windsong
Erdrich, L. Tales of burning love
Fowles, J. The magus
Gardner, J. October light
Hammett, D. Tulip
Hansen, E. F. Tales of protection
Harwood, J. The ghost writer
King, S. The breathing method
King, S. Misery
Pouncey, P. R. Rules for old men waiting
Rice, A. Servant of the bones
Rinaldi, N. Between two rivers
Roth, P. The ghost writer
Tan, A. The Joy Luck Club
Vargas Llosa, M. Aunt Julia and the scriptwriter
Vidal, G. Burr
Wallace, D. Big fish
Waller, R. J. The bridges of Madison County
Wiesel, E. The testament
Wright, A. M. Tony and Susan

The **Stork** Club. Dart, I. R.
Storm in Shanghai. See Malraux, A. Man's fate (La condition humaine)
Storm in the village. Read, Miss
In Read, Miss. Chronicles of Fairacre p361-534
Storm track. Maron, M.
Storm warning. Higgins, J.
Storming heaven. Brown, D.
Storming Intrepid. Harrison, P.

STORMS

See also Hurricanes; Tornadoes
Ansay, A. M. Midnight champagne
Brand, M. Dust across the range
Brown, S. Chill factor
Caputo, P. The voyage
Erdrich, L. Tales of burning love
Hailey, A. Airport
Sparks, N. Nights in Rodanthe

The **stormy** petrel. Stewart, M.
Stormy weather. Hiaasen, C.
Story in Harlem slang. Hurston, Z. N.
In Hurston, Z. N. Novels and stories p1001-10
The **story** of a lie. Stevenson, R. L.
In Stevenson, R. L. The complete short stories p361-408
In Stevenson, R. L. The complete short stories of Robert Louis Stevenson

STORYTELLING

Atkinson, K. Emotionally weird
Barth, J. The last voyage of somebody the sailor
Brink, A. P. Imaginings of sand
Chandra, V. Red earth and pouring rain
Coetzee, J. M. Elizabeth Costello
Crace, J. The gift of stones
Erdrich, L. Tracks
Gurganus, A. The oldest living Confederate widow tells all
Harrison, S. Call down the stars
Holthe, T. U. When the elephants dance
Mehta, G. A river Sutra
Naylor, G. Bailey's Café
Potok, C. Old men at midnight
Powers, R. Operation wandering soul
Rushdie, S. Haroun and the sea of stories
Stefaniak, M. H. The Turk and my mother
Tolkin, M. Under radar

Storyville. Battle, L.

STOUT, REX, 1886-1975

Parodies, imitations, etc.

Goldsborough, R. The bloodied ivy
Goldsborough, R. The missing chapter

The **stowaway**. Hough, R.

STOWAWAYS

Hough, R. The stowaway

Straight. Francis, D.
The **straight** man. Russo, R.
The **strange** case of Dr. Jekyll and Mr. Hyde. Stevenson, R. L.
also in Stevenson, R. L. The complete short stories of Robert Louis Stevenson
also in Stevenson, R. L. The strange case of Dr. Jekyll and Mr. Hyde, and other famous tales p1-69
The **strange** case of Dr. Jekyll and Mr. Hyde, and other famous tales. Stevenson, R. L.
Strange fits of passion. Shreve, A.
Strange fruit. Smith, L. E.
The **strange** mutiny of Gunner Asch. See Kirst, H. H. The revolt of Gunner Asch
Strange pilgrims. García Márquez, G.
The **stranger**. Camus, A.
The **stranger** from the sea. Graham, W.
The **Stranger** House. Hill, R.
Stranger in a strange land. Heinlein, R. A.
Stranger in paradise. Goudge, E.
A **stranger** is watching. Clark, M. H.
Strangers. Koontz, D. R.
Strangers and brothers. Snow, C. P.
Strangers and brothers [series]
Snow, C. P. The affair
Snow, C. P. The conscience of the rich
Snow, C. P. Corridors of power
Snow, C. P. Homecoming

SUCCESS—*Continued*
Gage, E. Pandora's box
Goudge, E. Such devoted sisters
Haynes, D. The full Matilda
James, H. The American
Johnston, W. Human amusements
Lee, C.-R. Aloft
Marsh, J. The House of Eliott
Millhauser, S. Martin Dressler
O'Hara, J. Ten North Frederick
Thayer, N. Everlasting
West, N. A cool million
SUCCESSION *See* Inheritance and succession
The **Successor**. Kadare, I.
Such a pretty, pretty girl. Groom, W.
Such devoted sisters. Goudge, E.
Such sweet thunder. Carter, V. O.

SUDAN
Caputo, P. Acts of faith
A **sudden** change of heart. Bradford, B. T.
Sudden country. Estleman, L. D.
A **sudden,** fearful death. Perry, A.

SUDDEN INFANT DEATH SYNDROME
Palahniuk, C. Lullaby
Sudden mischief. Parker, R. B.
Sudden prey. Sandford, J.
Sudden rain. Wolff, M. M.
A **sudden** wild magic. Jones, D. W.

SUFFERING
See also Good and evil
The **sufferings** of young Werther. See Goethe, J. W. v. The sorrows of young Werther
SUFFOLK (ENGLAND) *See* England—Suffolk

SUFISM
Iyer, P. Abandon
Sugar Street. Maḥfūẓ, N.
Sugartown. Estleman, L. D.

SUICIDE
Amis, M. Night train
Bambara, T. C. The salt eaters
Barth, J. The floating opera
Bernhard, T. Amras
Bernhard, T. Playing Watten
Bernhard, T. Woodcutters
Boswell, R. Century's son
Brautigan, R. An unfortunate woman
Caldwell, T. Ceremony of the innocent
Chong, K. Baroque-a-nova
Cook, T. H. The Chatham School affair
Cooley, M. The archivist
DeLillo, D. The body artist
Didion, J. Play it as it lays
Due, T. The good house
Eugenides, J. The virgin suicides
Flaubert, G. Madame Bovary
Ford, F. M. The good soldier
Gordon, M. The rest of life
Guterson, D. East of the mountains
Hawkes, J. Second skin
Hoffman, A. The river king
Hornby, N. A long way down
Koontz, D. R. Sole survivor
Labiner, N. Miniatures
McFarland, D. The music room
Mishima, Y. Runaway horses
Oates, J. C. The falls
Oates, J. C. What I lived for
Ōe, K. An echo of heaven
Ōe, K. The silent cry
Palahniuk, C. Diary
Pamuk, O. Snow
Parks, T. Destiny
Percy, W. The second coming
Perry, T. Dead aim
Plath, S. The bell jar
Roth, P. When she was good
Saul, J. Shadows
Styron, W. Lie down in darkness
Thayer, N. An act of love
Turow, S. The burden of proof
Tyler, A. The clock winder
Wheeler, R. S. Eclipse
Williams, D. Angel Rock
Suicide hill. Ellroy, J.
In Ellroy, J. L.A. noir p427-644
A **suitable** boy. Seth, V.
Suitable for framing. Buchanan, E.
A **suitable** vengeance. George, E.
Sula. Morrison, T.

SULLA, LUCIUS CORNELIUS
About
McCullough, C. The first man in Rome
McCullough, C. Fortune's favorites
McCullough, C. The grass crown
Sullivan's law. Rosenberg, N. T.
Sullivan's sting. Sanders, L.
The **sum** of all fears. Clancy, T.

SUMERIANS
Silverberg, R. Gilgamesh the king

SUMMER
Bradbury, R. Dandelion wine
Clements, M. Midsummer
Summer. Wharton, E.
In Wharton, E. Novellas and other writings

SUMMER CAMPS
Price, R. The tongues of angels
Swarthout, G. F. Bless the beasts and children
The **summer** I dared. Delinsky, B.
Summer in Baden-Baden. T͡Sypkin, L.
Summer light. Rice, L.
Summer of '42. Raucher, H.
The **summer** of Katya. Trevanian
Summer of storms. Kelman, J.
The **summer** of the Danes. Peters, E.
Summer people. Piercy, M.
The **Summer** Queen. Vinge, J. D.

SUMMER RESORTS
Appelfeld, A. Badenheim 1939
Benchley, P. Jaws
Craig, A. Love in idleness
Kay, T. Shadow song
Morrison, T. Love
O'Nan, S. Wish you were here
Raucher, H. Summer of '42
Siddons, A. R. Colony
SUMMER VACATIONS *See* Vacations
Summer's lease. Mortimer, J. C.
The **summoning** God. Gear, K. O.
The **summons**. Grisham, J.
A **summons** to Memphis. Taylor, P. H.
The **sun** also rises. Hemingway, E.
also in Hemingway, E. The Hemingway reader p89-289
The **sun** dog. King, S.
In King, S. Four past midnight p605-763
The **Sun** King. Ignatius, D.
Sunday Jews. Calisher, H.
Sunday the rabbi stayed home. Kemelman, H.
The **sundowners**. Cleary, J.
Sunflower. West, Dame R.
The **sunlight** dialogues. Gardner, J.
The **sunne** in splendour. Penman, S. K.
Sunset and sawdust. Lansdale, J. R.
Sunset express. Crais, R.
Sunset in St. Tropez. Steel, D.
Sunset limited. Burke, J. L.

SUPER BOWL GAME (FOOTBALL)
Harris, T. Black Sunday
Super-Cannes. Ballard, J. G.
Superior women. Adams, A.

SUPERNATURAL PHENOMENA
See also Demoniac possession; Ghost stories; Horror stories
Allende, I. The house of the spirits
Amis, K. The Green Man
Ansa, T. M. The hand I fan with
Ansa, T. M. You know better
Barker, C. The forbidden
Barker, C. Galilee
Borchardt, A. The silver wolf

SUSPENSE NOVELS—*Continued*
Baldacci, D. The winner
Barnard, R. The mistress of Alderley
Barnard, R. A murder in Mayfair
Bausch, R. In the night season
Bear, G. Dead lines
Berberian, V. The cyclist
Bernhardt, W. Criminal intent
Bernhardt, W. Murder one
Bernhardt, W. Silent justice
Blanchard, K. The deed
Block, L. Hit list
Block, L. Small town
Block, L. Tanner on ice
Bond, L. Day of wrath
Bova, B. Death dream
Bradford, B. T. The triumph of Katie Byrne
Brandon, J. Rules of evidence
Brown, D. Air Battle Force
Brown, D. Chains of command
Brown, D. Flight of the Old Dog
Brown, D. Hammerheads
Brown, D. Night of the hawk
Brown, D. Shadows of steel
Brown, D. Storming heaven
Brown, D. The tin man
Brown, D. Warrior class
Brown, D. Wings of fire
Brown, D. The Da Vinci code
Brown, S. The alibi
Brown, S. Charade
Brown, S. Chill factor
Brown, S. The crush
Brown, S. Exclusive
Brown, S. Fat Tuesday
Brown, S. Hello, darkness
Brown, S. The switch
Brown, S. White hot
Brown, S. The witness
Browne, G. A. 18mm blues
Browne, G. A. 19 Purchase Street
Browne, G. A. Hot Siberian
Browne, G. A. West 47th
Browne, M. Eye of the abyss
Buchanan, E. Pulse
Buckley, W. F. Last call for Blackford Oakes
Buckley, W. F. Spytime
Buffa, D. W. The defense
Buffa, D. W. The judgment
Burke, J. L. Bitterroot
Burke, J. L. Cimarron rose
Burke, J. L. Heartwood
Burke, J. L. In the moon of red ponies
Byatt, A. S. Possession
Caldwell, I. The rule of four
Campbell, R. The last voice they hear
Campbell, R. The one safe place
Campbell, R. Pact of the fathers
Campbell, R. Silent children
Cannell, S. J. Riding the snake
Cannell, S. J. The Viking funeral
Caputo, P. Equation for evil
Carr, C. The alienist
Carr, C. The angel of darkness
Carroll, J. The wooden sea
Carter, S. L. The emperor of Ocean Park
Carver, C. Blood Junction
Chazin, S. Flashover
Clancy, T. The bear and the dragon
Clancy, T. The Cardinal of the Kremlin
Clancy, T. Clear and present danger
Clancy, T. Debt of honor
Clancy, T. Executive orders
Clancy, T. The hunt for Red October
Clancy, T. Patriot games
Clancy, T. Rainbow Six
Clancy, T. Red rabbit
Clancy, T. Red Storm rising
Clancy, T. The sum of all fears
Clancy, T. The teeth of the tiger
Clancy, T. Without remorse
Clark, M. H. All around the town
Clark, M. H. Before I say goodbye
Clark, M. H. The cradle will fall
Clark, M. H. A cry in the night
Clark, M. H. Daddy's little girl
Clark, M. H. I'll be seeing you
Clark, M. H. Let me call you sweetheart
Clark, M. H. Loves music, loves to dance
Clark, M. H. Moonlight becomes you
Clark, M. H. Nighttime is my time
Clark, M. H. No place like home
Clark, M. H. On the street where you live
Clark, M. H. Pretend you don't see her
Clark, M. H. Remember me
Clark, M. H. The second time around
Clark, M. H. Silent night
Clark, M. H. Stillwatch
Clark, M. H. A stranger is watching
Clark, M. H. We'll meet again
Clark, M. H. Where are the children?
Clark, M. H. You belong to me
Coben, H. Gone for good
Coben, H. The innocent
Coben, H. Just one look
Coben, H. No second chance
Cody, L. Rift
Collins, L. The fifth horseman
Collins, M. The resurrectionists
Connelly, M. Chasing the dime
Connelly, M. Void moon
Connolly, J. Bad men
Cook, R. Acceptable risk
Cook, R. Chromosome 6
Cook, R. Contagion
Cook, R. Marker
Cook, R. Mortal fear
Cook, R. Mutation
Cook, R. Outbreak
Cook, R. Seizure
Cook, R. Terminal
Cook, R. Toxin
Cook, R. Vector
Cook, R. Vital signs
Cook, T. H. Evidence of blood
Cook, T. H. Instruments of night
Cook, T. H. Places in the dark
Coonts, S. America
Coonts, S. Cuba
Coonts, S. Final flight
Coonts, S. Fortunes of war
Coonts, S. Hong Kong
Coonts, S. The Intruders
Coonts, S. The minotaur
Coonts, S. The red horseman
Coonts, S. Under siege
Coscarelli, K. Heir apparent
Costello, M. Big if
Coulter, C. Impulse
Coulter, C. The maze
Coulter, C. The target
Crais, R. Demolition angel
Crais, R. Hostage
Crichton, M. Airframe
Crichton, M. A case of need
Crichton, M. Disclosure
Crichton, M. Prey
Crichton, M. Rising sun
Cussler, C. Atlantis found
Cussler, C. Black wind
Cussler, C. Cyclops
Cussler, C. Deep six
Cussler, C. Dragon
Cussler, C. Fire ice
Cussler, C. Flood tide
Cussler, C. Inca gold
Cussler, C. Lost city
Cussler, C. Raise the Titanic!
Cussler, C. Sahara
Cussler, C. Shock wave
Cussler, C. Treasure
Cussler, C. Valhalla rising
Cussler, C. White death
Daley, R. Nowhere to run
D'Amato, B. Good cop, bad cop
D'Amato, B. White male infant
Darnton, J. The experiment
Darnton, J. Neanderthal

SUSPENSE NOVELS—*Continued*
Hambly, B. A free man of color
Hambly, B. Graveyard dust
Hambly, B. Sold down the river
Hambly, B. Die upon a kiss
Hambly, B. Wet grave
Hardie, K. A winter marriage
Harrar, G. The spinning man
Harris, R. Archangel
Harris, R. Enigma
Harris, R. Fatherland
Harris, R. Pompeii
Harris, T. Black Sunday
Harris, T. Hannibal
Harris, T. Red Dragon
Harris, T. The silence of the lambs
Harrison, C. Afterburn
Harrison, C. The Havana room
Harrison, P. Storming Intrepid
Henry, A. Learning to fly
Hewson, D. Lucifer's shadow
Hiaasen, C. Lucky you
Higgins, J. Bad company
Higgins, J. Cold Harbour
Higgins, J. Confessional
Higgins, J. Day of judgment
Higgins, J. Day of reckoning
Higgins, J. Drink with the Devil
Higgins, J. Edge of danger
Higgins, J. Eye of the storm
Higgins, J. Luciano's luck
Higgins, J. Midnight runner
Higgins, J. Night of the fox
Higgins, J. The president's daughter
Higgins, J. Touch the devil
Higgins, J. The White House connection
Highsmith, P. The boy who followed Ripley
Highsmith, P. Ripley under ground
Highsmith, P. Ripley's game
Highsmith, P. The talented Mr. Ripley
Highsmith, P. The talented Mr. Ripley; Ripley under ground; Ripley's game
Hill, R. Dream of darkness
Hill, R. The Stranger House
Hill, S. Mrs. de Winter
Hillhouse, R. Rift zone
Hirshberg, G. The Snowman's children
Hoag, T. Dark horse
Hoag, T. Dust to dust
Hoag, T. Guilty as sin
Hoag, T. Kill the messenger
Hoag, T. Night sins
Høeg, P. Smilla's sense of snow
Hoffman, J. Retribution
Hooper, K. Finding Laura
Hooper, K. Haunting Rachel
Hospital, J. T. Due preparations for the plague
Howatch, S. The high flyer
Hunter, E. Privileged conversation
Hunter, S. Black light
Hunter, S. Dirty white boys
Hunter, S. Havana
Hunter, S. Time to hunt
Huyler, F. The laws of invisible things
Ignatius, D. A firing offense
Iles, G. Black cross
Iles, G. The footprints of God
Iles, G. Mortal fear
Irving, C. Final argument
Jance, J. A. Kiss of the bees
Johansen, I. And then you die—
Johansen, I. Blind alley
Johansen, I. The face of deception
Johansen, I. Final target
Johansen, I. The killing game
Johansen, I. Long after midnight
Johansen, I. The ugly duckling
Johnson, W. The devil you know
Judd, A. Legacy
Kanon, J. The good German
Kanon, J. Los Alamos
Katzenbach, J. The analyst
Katzenbach, J. Just cause
Katzenbach, J. The madman's tale
Katzenbach, J. State of mind
Kellerman, F. The quality of mercy
Kelman, J. Summer of storms
Kerley, J. The hundredth man
King, L. R. A darker place
King, L. R. Keeping watch
King, S. The dead zone
King, S. Dolores Claiborne
King, S. Dreamcatcher
King, S. Gerald's game
King, S. Insomnia
King, S. Misery
King, S. Rose Madder
Knebel, F. Seven days in May
Knox, E. Daylight
Koontz, D. R. The bad place
Koontz, D. R. By the light of the moon
Koontz, D. R. Dark rivers of the heart
Koontz, D. R. The face
Koontz, D. R. False memory
Koontz, D. R. Fear nothing
Koontz, D. R. From the corner of his eye
Koontz, D. R. Intensity
Koontz, D. R. Lightning
Koontz, D. R. Seize the night
Koontz, D. R. Sole survivor
Koontz, D. R. The taking
Koontz, D. R. Velocity
Krentz, J. A. Lost and found
Krentz, J. A. Smoke in mirrors
Krist, G. Chaos theory
Lawton, J. Old flames
Le Carré, J. The constant gardener
Le Carré, J. The honourable schoolboy
Le Carré, J. The little drummer girl
Le Carré, J. The night manager
Le Carré, J. A perfect spy
Le Carré, J. The quest for Karla
Le Carré, J. The Russia house
Le Carré, J. Smiley's people
Le Carré, J. The spy who came in from the cold
Le Carré, J. Tinker, tailor, soldier, spy
Lehane, D. Shutter Island
Leonard, E. Bandits
Leonard, E. Cat chaser
Leonard, E. Freaky Deaky
Leonard, E. Glitz
Leonard, E. The hunted
Leonard, E. Killshot
Leonard, E. LaBrava
Leonard, E. Mr. Paradise
Leonard, E. Split images
Leonard, E. Stick
Leonard, E. Touch
Leroy, M. Postcards from Berlin
Lescroart, J. T. A certain justice
Lescroart, J. T. The first law
Lescroart, J. T. Guilt
Lescroart, J. T. Hard evidence
Lescroart, J. T. The hearing
Lescroart, J. T. The mercy rule
Lescroart, J. T. Nothing but the truth
Lescroart, J. T. The oath
Lescroart, J. T. The second chair
Levin, I. The boys from Brazil
Lieberman, H. H. The girl with Botticelli eyes
Lindsey, D. L. An absence of light
Lindsey, D. L. The color of night
Lindsey, D. L. The rules of silence
Littell, R. Walking back the cat
Long, J. The reckoning
Lovesey, P. On the edge
Lowell, E. Die in plain sight
Ludlum, R. The apocalypse watch
Ludlum, R. The Aquitaine progression
Ludlum, R. The Bourne identity
Ludlum, R. The Bourne supremacy
Ludlum, R. The Bourne ultimatum
Ludlum, R. The Gemini contenders
Ludlum, R. The Holcroft covenant
Ludlum, R. The Janson directive
Ludlum, R. The Matarese Circle
Ludlum, R. The Matlock paper
Ludlum, R. The Parsifal mosaic

SUSPENSE NOVELS—*Continued*

Reichs, K. J. Déjà dead
Rendell, R. The bridesmaid
Rendell, R. Heartstones
Rendell, R. A judgment in stone
Rendell, R. The keys to the street
Rendell, R. Live flesh
Rendell, R. Make death love me
Rendell, R. Master of the moor
Rendell, R. A sight for sore eyes
Rendell, R. Thirteen steps down
Reuland, R. Semiautomatic
Rice, L. The secret hour
Ridley, J. Those who walk in darkness
Riordan, R. Cold Springs
Robards, K. Ghost moon
Robards, K. To trust a stranger
Robbins, D. L. War of the rats
Robbins, H. Sin city
Roberts, N. Carolina moon
Roberts, N. Midnight Bayou
Roberts, N. The reef
Roberts, N. River's end
Roberts, N. The villa
Robinson, P. Kilo class
Robinson, P. Nimitz class
Robinson, P. The first cut
Rosenberg, N. T. Buried evidence
Rosenberg, N. T. First offense
Rosenberg, N. T. Interest of justice
Rosenberg, N. T. Sullivan's law
Ruiz, L. M. Only one thing missing
Ruiz Zafón, C. The shadow of the wind
Sanchez, T. King Bongo
Sanders, L. The first deadly sin
Sanders, L. Guilty pleasures
Sanders, L. The second deadly sin
Sanders, L. The sixth commandment
Sanders, L. Sullivan's sting
Sanders, L. The tenth commandment
Sanders, L. The third deadly sin
Saul, J. Black lightning
Saul, J. The Manhattan Hunt Club
Saul, J. Nightshade
Saul, J. The presence
Saul, J. Shadows
Schickler, D. Sweet and vicious
Scottoline, L. Legal tender
Scottoline, L. Mistaken identity
Scottoline, L. Moment of truth
Scottoline, L. Rough justice
Scottoline, L. Running from the law
Seymour, G. Killing ground
Shannon, D. The Manson curse
Shelby, P. Days of drums
Shelby, P. Gatekeeper
Sheldon, S. Are you afraid of the dark?
Sheldon, S. The doomsday conspiracy
Shreve, A. Resistance
Shreve, A. The weight of water
Sidor, S. Skin River
Siegel, B. Actual innocence
Siegel, J. Derailed
Siegel, S. Final verdict
Siler, J. Flashback
Silva, D. The marching season
Silva, D. The mark of the assassin
Silva, D. Prince of Fire
Silva, D. The unlikely spy
Smith, A. Good morning, killer
Smith, M. C. December 6
Smith, M.-A. T. She's not there
Smith, S. B. A simple plan
Smith, W. A. Elephant song
Smith, W. A. Golden fox
Smith, W. A. The seventh scroll
Snyder, D. J. Night crossing
Sparks, N. A bend in the road
Sparks, N. The guardian
Standiford, L. Black Mountain
Stark, R. Breakout
Steinhauer, O. The Bridge of Sighs
Stephenson, N. Cryptonomicon
Stevens, M. The curve of the world
Stewart, M. Airs above the ground
Stewart, M. The moon-spinners
Stewart, M. My brother Michael
Stewart, M. The stormy petrel
Stone, R. Damascus Gate
Straub, P. Koko
Straub, P. The throat
Strieber, W. Majestic
Taibo, P. I. Returning as shadows
Tanenbaum, R. Act of revenge
Tanenbaum, R. Corruption of blood
Tanenbaum, R. Falsely accused
Tanenbaum, R. Hoax
Tanenbaum, R. Irresistible impulse
Tanenbaum, R. Reckless endangerment
Tanenbaum, R. True justice
Tartt, D. The secret history
Teran, B. The prince of deadly weapons
Thayer, J. S. Five past midnight
Thomas, C. Firefox
Thomas, M. M. Black money
Thomas, R. Ah, treachery!
Thomas, R. The fourth Durango
Tirone Smith, M.-A. Love her madly
Tirone Smith, M.-A. She smiled sweetly
Tracy, P. J. Monkeewrench
Trenhaile, J. The gates of exquisite view
Trevanian. The Eiger sanction
Trevor, W. Felicia's journey
Truscott, L. K. Heart of war
Turow, S. The laws of our fathers
Turow, S. Personal injuries
Turow, S. Reversible errors
Uhnak, D. Codes of betrayal
Ullman, E. The bug
Vargas Llosa, M. Death in the Andes
Vine, B. Gallowglass
Vine, B. Grasshopper
Vine, B. King Solomon's carpet
Vine, B. No night is too long
Volpi, J. In search of Klingsor
Walker, M. W. Under the beetle's cellar
Wallace, I. The man
Walters, M. The breaker
Walters, M. The dark room
Walters, M. The echo
Walters, M. The sculptress
Walters, M. The shape of snakes
Watkins, P. The forger
Weaver, M. Deceptions
West, M. L. The clowns of God
West, M. L. Masterclass
West, M. L. Vanishing point
Westlake, D. E. Money for nothing
White, S. W. The best revenge
White, S. W. Missing persons
Whitney, P. A. Amethyst dreams
Whitney, P. A. Columbella
Whitney, P. A. Domino
Whitney, P. A. The singing stones
Whitney, P. A. Spindrift
Whitney, P. A. Woman without a past
Wilcken, H. The execution
Wilhelm, K. The best defense
Wilhelm, K. The deepest water
Wilhelm, K. Defense for the devil
Wilhelm, K. Desperate measures
Wilhelm, K. Malice prepense
Wilhelm, K. No defense
Wilson, F. P. Deep as the marrow
Wilson, F. P. Implant
Wilson, J. A Palestine affair
Wilson, R. The blind man of Seville
Wiltse, D. Blown away
Wiltse, D. Bone deep
Wiltse, D. Heartland
Wood, B. Perfect Harmony
Woods, S. Choke
Woods, S. Cold paradise
Woods, S. Dead eyes
Woods, S. Dead in the water
Woods, S. Dirt
Woods, S. Dirty work
Woods, S. Grass roots

SYMBOLISM—*Continued*
Mann, T. The black swan
Mann, T. Death in Venice
Mann, T. The magic mountain
Melville, H. Billy Budd, sailor
Melville, H. Mardi: and a voyager thither
Melville, H. Moby-Dick; or, The whale
Momaday, N. S. The ancient child
Murakami, H. The wind-up bird chronicle
Murdoch, I. Nuns and soldiers
Nabokov, V. V. Ada
Nabokov, V. V. Pale fire
O'Brien, T. In the Lake of the Woods
Ōe, K. An echo of heaven
Ōe, K. The pinch runner memorandum
Ōe, K. The silent cry
Okuizumi, H. The stones cry out
Percy, W. Lancelot
Poe, E. A. The narrative of Arthur Gordon Pym of Nantucket
Porter, K. A. Ship of fools
Powers, R. Operation wandering soul
Pynchon, T. V.
Roth, P. The breast
Roy, A. The god of small things
Rushdie, S. The ground beneath her feet
Rushdie, S. The satanic verses
Sheehan, E. R. F. Cardinal Galsworthy
Silverberg, R. Downward to the Earth
Tan, A. The bonesetter's daughter
Theroux, P. The Mosquito Coast
Thomas, D. M. The white hotel
Updike, J. Roger's version
Urquhart, J. The underpainter
Walbert, K. The gardens of Kyoto
Wiesel, E. A beggar in Jerusalem
Woiwode, L. Indian affairs
Woiwode, L. What I'm going to do, I think
Woolf, V. Between the acts
Woolf, V. The waves

SYMPATHY
See also Empathy

SYRIA
Caldwell, T. Dear and glorious physician
Werfel, F. The forty days of Musa Dagh

SYRIANS

Brazil

Amado, J. Gabriela, clove and cinnamon

T

T.C. Boyle stories. Boyle, T. C.
TA CH'ING DYNASTY *See* Manchus
Table money. Breslin, J.
TABOO *See* Superstition
TADZHIKISTAN *See* Tajikistan

TAE KWON DO
Bell, M. S. Ten Indians

TAHITI
Maugham, W. S. The moon and sixpence
Melville, H. Omoo: a narrative of adventures in the South Seas

TAHOE, LAKE (CALIF. AND NEV.) *See* Lake Tahoe (Calif. and Nev.)
Tai-Pan. Clavell, J.
The **tailor** of Panama. Le Carré, J.

TAILORS
Markandaya, K. A handful of rice

TAIPING REBELLION, 1850-1864
Elegant, R. S. Mandarin
Stewart, F. M. The magnificent Savages

TAIWAN
White, R. A. Typhoon

TAJIKISTAN
Darnton, J. Neanderthal

The **taking**. Koontz, D. R.
The **taking** of Pelham one two three. Godey, J.
TALAVERA CAMPAIGN, 1809 *See* Peninsular War, 1807-1814
The **tale** of Genji. Murasaki Shikibu
The **tale** of the body thief. Rice, A.
A **tale** of two cities. Dickens, C.
The **talented** Mr. Ripley. Highsmith, P.
In Highsmith, P. The talented Mr. Ripley; Ripley under ground; Ripley's game
The **talented** Mr. Ripley; Ripley under ground; Ripley's game. Highsmith, P.
Tales and sketches, including Twice-told tales, Mosses from an old manse, and The snow-image; A wonder book for girls and boys; Tanglewood tales for girls and boys, being a second Wonder book. Hawthorne, N.
Tales from a troubled land. Paton, A.
Tales from the Drones Club. Wodehouse, P. G.
Tales from Watership Down. Adams, R.
Tales of burning love. Erdrich, L.
Tales of good and evil. See Gogol′, N. V. The overcoat, and other tales of good and evil
Tales of H.P. Lovecraft. Lovecraft, H. P.
The **tales** of Jacob. Mann, T.
In Mann, T. Joseph and his brothers p3-258
Tales of land and sea. Conrad, J.
Tales of men and ghosts. Wharton, E.
In Wharton, E. The collected short stories of Edith Wharton
Tales of protection. Hansen, E. F.
Tales of terror and mystery. Doyle, Sir A. C.
Tales of the East and West. Conrad, J.
Tales of the jazz age. Fitzgerald, F. S.
In Fitzgerald, F. S. Novels and stories, 1920-1922 p797-1054
Tales of the night. Høeg, P.
Tales of the South Pacific. Michener, J. A.

TALIBAN (AFGHANISTAN)
Brown, D. Air Battle Force
Hosseini, K. The kite runner

The **talismans** of Shannara. Brooks, T.
Talking God. Hillerman, T.
The **talking** trees and other stories. O'Faoláin, S.
In O'Faoláin, S. The collected stories of Seán O'Faoláin p889-1060
Tallgrass. Coldsmith, D.
Taltos. Rice, A.
The **tamarind** seed. Anthony, E.
Tamarind woman. Badami, A. R.
Taming a sea-horse. Parker, R. B.
Tamsin Harte. Ross-Macdonald, M.
TANGIER (MOROCCO) *See* Morocco—Tangier
The **tangle** box. Brooks, T.

TANNENBERG, BATTLE OF, 1914
Solzhenitsyn, A. August 1914

Tanner on ice. Block, L.
Tapestry. Plain, B.
Taps. Morris, W.
Tar: a midwest childhood. Anderson, S.
Tar baby. Morrison, T.
Tara Road. Binchy, M.
The **target**. Coulter, C.
The **tarnished** eye. Guest, J.
The **tartan** sell. Gash, J.

TASMANIA (AUSTRALIA)
Hooper, C. A child's book of true crime

A **taste** for death. James, P. D.
The **tattooed** girl. Oates, J. C.
TAVERNS *See* Hotels, taverns, etc.

TEACHERS
See also Students; Tutors
Abe, K. The woman in the dunes
Albahari, D. Götz and Meyer
Amis, K. Lucky Jim
Barth, J. The end of the road
Barthelme, F. The brothers
Barthelme, F. Elroy Nights
Battle, L. The Florabama Ladies' Auxiliary & Sewing Circle
Baxter, C. Saul and Patsy
Beattie, A. Another you
Bellow, S. The dean's December
Bellow, S. Ravelstein

TELEPATHY—*Continued*
Vinge, J. D. Catspaw

TELEPHONE
McMahon, T. A. Loving Little Egypt

TELEVISION
Crichton, M. Airframe
Green, G. The last angry man
Irving, J. The fourth hand
Johnston, W. Human amusements
King, S. The running man
Kosinski, J. N. Being there
Lodge, D. Therapy
MacNeil, R. Breaking news
Robinson, S. Stardance [novelette]
Thayer, N. Belonging
Thayer, S. The weatherman
Wagner, B. The chrysanthemum palace

TELEVISION PRODUCERS AND DIRECTORS
Clark, M. H. Stillwatch
McCauley, S. True enough

TELEVISION PROGRAMS
Brown, S. Charade
Connelly, J. Crumbtown
McPhee, J. No ordinary matter
Nicholls, D. A question of attraction

Tell me a riddle. Olsen, T.
Tell me how long the train's been gone. Baldwin, J.
Tell me no secrets. Fielding, J.
Tell me that you love me, Junie Moon. Kellogg, M.
Tell no tales. Bland, E. T.
The **telling**. Le Guin, U. K.
Telling time. Wright, A. M.
Tempest rising. McKinney-Whetstone, D.

TEMPLARS
Holland, C. Jerusalem
Kurtz, K. The temple and the stone

The **temple** and the stone. Kurtz, K.
The **Temple** of Dawn. Mishima, Y.
The **temple** of my familiar. Walker, A.
The **temple** of the golden pavilion. Mishima, Y.
Temporary kings. Powell, A.
In Powell, A. A dance to the music of time
Temporary shelter. Gordon, M.
Ten Indians. Bell, M. S.
Ten lb. penalty. See Francis, D. 10 lb. penalty
Ten little Indians. Alexie, S.
Ten little niggers. See Christie, A. And then there were none
Ten North Frederick. O'Hara, J.

TENANT FARMING
Delderfield, R. F. A horseman riding by
Faulkner, W. The mansion

The **tenant** of Wildfell Hall. Brontë, A.
The **tenants**. Malamud, B.
The **tenants** of time. Flanagan, T.
Tender. Childress, M.
Tender mercies. Brown, R.
The **tender** shoot. Colette
In Colette. The collected stories of Colette p421-48

TENEPAL, MALINALLI *See* Marina, ca. 1505-ca. 1530

TENNESSEE
Agee, J. The morning watch
Brown, L. The rabbit factory
Lewis, J. The king is dead
McCrumb, S. The ballad of Frankie Silver
Wiggins, M. Evidence of things unseen

20th century

Alther, L. Kinflicks
Marion, S. Hollow ground
McCrumb, S. The hangman's beautiful daughter
McCrumb, S. If ever I return, pretty Peggy-O
McCrumb, S. The rosewood casket
McCrumb, S. She walks these hills
O'Connor, F. The violent bear it away
O'Connor, F. Wise blood

Farm life

See Farm life—Tennessee

Knoxville

Agee, J. A death in the family

Memphis

Faulkner, W. The reivers
Faulkner, W. Sanctuary
Grisham, J. The firm
Taylor, P. H. A summons to Memphis

TENNIS
Wallace, D. F. Infinite jest
Woods, S. Choke

The **tent** of orange mist. West, P.
The **tenth** commandment. Sanders, L.
The **tenth** justice. Meltzer, B.
The **tenth** man. Greene, G.
A **tenured** professor. Galbraith, J. K.
Teresa and other stories. O'Faoláin, S.
In O'Faoláin, S. The collected stories of Seán O'Faoláin p320-445
Terminal. Cook, R.

TERMINAL ILLNESS
Berg, E. Never change
Christensen, K. The Epicure's lament
Gaddis, W. Agapé agape
Gould, J. Time to say goodbye
Hood, A. Places to stay the night
L'Engle, M. Certain women
McPhee, M. Gorgeous lies
Miller, A. Oxygen
Minot, S. Evening
Ólafur Jóhann Ólafsson. The journey home
Tóibín, C. The blackwater lightship
Tsukiyama, G. Dreaming water

The **terminal** man. Crichton, M.
Terms of endearment. McMurtry, L.

TERRORISM
See also Violence
Adams, L. Harbor
Berberian, V. The cyclist
Bond, L. Day of wrath
Brown, D. Storming heaven
Brown, D. The tin man
Carr, P. The black swan
Clancy, T. Patriot games
Clancy, T. Rainbow Six
Clancy, T. Red Storm rising
Clancy, T. The sum of all fears
Clancy, T. The teeth of the tiger
Collins, L. The fifth horseman
Cook, R. Vector
Coonts, S. America
Coonts, S. Final flight
Coonts, S. The red horseman
Coyle, H. W. Bright star
DeMille, N. The lion's game
Egleton, C. The honey trap
Egleton, C. Warning shot
Estleman, L. D. Kill zone
Finder, J. The zero hour
Forsyth, F. The devil's alternative
Grant, M. Officer down
Greeley, A. M. Irish lace
Greene, G. The comedians
Griffin, W. E. B. By order of the President
Griffin, W. E. B. The investigators
Harris, T. Black Sunday
Higgins, J. Confessional
Higgins, J. Drink with the Devil
Higgins, J. Edge of danger
Higgins, J. Eye of the storm
Higgins, J. Midnight runner
Higgins, J. Touch the devil
Higgins, J. The White House connection
Houellebecq, M. Platform
Johansen, I. And then you die—
Keneally, T. Flying hero class
Le Carré, J. The little drummer girl
Lessing, D. M. The good terrorist
Ludlum, R. The Bourne ultimatum
Ludlum, R. The Janson directive
Ludlum, R. The Matarese Circle
Ludlum, R. The Prometheus deception

TOLSTOY, LEO, GRAF, 1828-1910
About
Kalfus, K. The commissariat of enlightenment
Tom Chatto. See McCutchan, P. Apprentice to the sea
Tom Chatto, RNR. See McCutchan, P. The new lieutenant
Tom Chatto, second mate. See McCutchan, P. The second mate
Tom Jones. See Fielding, H. The history of Tom Jones, a foundling
Tom Sawyer abroad. Twain, M.
In Twain, M. The adventures of Tom Sawyer, Tom Sawyer abroad, Tom Sawyer, detective p251-341
In Twain, M. The gilded age and later novels
Tom Sawyer, detective. Twain, M.
In Twain, M. The adventures of Tom Sawyer, Tom Sawyer abroad, Tom Sawyer, detective p357-415
In Twain, M. The gilded age and later novels
Tomcat in love. O'Brien, T.
Tomorrow is another day. Kaminsky, S. M.
The **tongues** of angels. Price, R.
Tonight I said goodbye. Koryta, M.
Tonio Kröger. Mann, T.
In Mann, T. Stories of three decades
Tono-Bungay. Wells, H. G.

TONTO BASIN (ARIZ.)
Grey, Z. The Arizona clan
The **Tonto** woman and other western stories. Leonard, E.
Tony and Susan. Wright, A. M.
Too far afield. Grass, G.
Too late the phalarope. Paton, A.
Too loud a solitude. Hrabal, B.
Too many clients. Stout, R.
In Stout, R. Three aces
Too many cooks. Stout, R.
In Stout, R. Kings full of aces p1-187
Too many women. Stout, R.
In Stout, R. All aces p155-302

TORIES, AMERICAN *See* American loyalists

TORNADOES
Blanchard, A. The breathtaker
TORONTO (ONT.) *See* Canada—Toronto
Torquemada. Pérez Galdós, B.
Torquemada and Saint Peter. Pérez Galdós, B.
In Pérez Galdós, B. Torquemada p405-569
Torquemada at the stake. Pérez Galdós, B.
In Pérez Galdós, B. Torquemada p1-60
Torquemada in Purgatory. Pérez Galdós, B.
In Pérez Galdós, B. Torquemada p221-404
Torquemada on the cross. Pérez Galdós, B.
In Pérez Galdós, B. Torquemada p61-220
The **torrents** of spring. Hemingway, E.
also in Hemingway, E. The Hemingway reader p25-86
The **torrents** of spring. Turgenev, I. S.

TORRES CORTEZ, HERNÁN
About
Fuentes, C. Sons of the Conquistador
Fuentes, C. The two shores
The **torso** in the town. Brett, S.
The **tortilla** curtain. Boyle, T. C.
Tortilla Flat. Steinbeck, J.
also in Steinbeck, J. Novels and stories, 1932-1937
Tortillas and beans. Steinbeck, J.
In Steinbeck, J. The portable Steinbeck

TORTURE
Danticat, E. The dew breaker
Lehrer, J. The special prisoner
Total control. Baldacci, D.
Total recall. Paretsky, S.

TOTALITARIANISM
See also Communism; Dictators; Fascism; National socialism
Alvarez, J. In the time of the butterflies
Antunes, A. L. The inquisitors' manual
Bellow, S. The dean's December
Bolaño, R. By night in Chile
Chatwin, B. Utz
Danticat, E. The dew breaker
Del Vecchio, J. M. For the sake of all living things
Farah, N. Links
Hrabal, B. I served the King of England
Isegawa, M. Snakepit
Kadare, I. The Successor
Keneally, T. The tyrant's novel
Khadra, Y. The swallows of Kabul
Koestler, A. Darkness at noon
Kundera, M. The joke
Müller, H. The appointment
Nabokov, V. V. Bend sinister
Orwell, G. Animal farm
Orwell, G. Nineteen eighty-four
Saramago, J. The cave
Steele, A. M. Coyote
Vollmann, W. T. Europe central
Zamíàtin, E. I. We
Touch. Leonard, E.
Touch not the cat. Stewart, M.
Touch the devil. Higgins, J.
Touched by the dead. See Barnard, R. A murder in Mayfair
The **touchstone**. Wharton, E.
In Wharton, E. Collected stories, 1891-1910
Tough guys don't dance. Mailer, N.
The **toughest** Indian in the world. Alexie, S.
La **Tour** dreams of the wolf girl. Huddle, D.

TOURIST TRADE
Bowles, P. Up above the world
Gilman, D. Mrs. Pollifax on safari
Harris, J. Coastliners
Houellebecq, M. Platform
Lodge, D. Paradise news
Tan, A. Saving fish from drowning
TOURISTS *See* Tourist trade
Tourmaline. Scott, J.
A **tournament** of murders. Doherty, P. C.

TOUSSAINT LOUVERTURE, 1743?-1803
About
Bell, M. S. All souls' rising
Bell, M. S. Master of the crossroads
Bell, M. S. The stone that the builder refused
Toward the end of time. Updike, J.
Towards zero. Christie, A.

TOWER OF LONDON (ENGLAND)
Kerr, P. Dark matter
The **towers** of silence. Scott, P.
also in Scott, P. The Raj quartet
The **town**. Faulkner, W.
also in Faulkner, W. Novels, 1957-1962 p1-326
also in Faulkner, W. Snopes p351-671
The **town**. Richter, C.
In Richter, C. The awakening land p331-630
A **town** like Alice. See Shute, N. The legacy
Toxin. Cook, R.
Tracks. Erdrich, L.
Trade wind. Kaye, M. M.
Trader. De Lint, C.

TRADERS
Stevenson, R. L. The beach of Falesá

TRADESCANT, JOHN, 1608-1662
About
Gregory, P. Virgin earth

TRADESCANT, JOHN, D. 1637?
About
Gregory, P. Earthly joys

TRAFFIC ACCIDENTS
See also Hit-and-run drivers
Agee, J. A death in the family
Baldacci, D. Wish you well
Banks, R. The sweet hereafter
Cookson, C. The year of the virgins
Delinsky, B. Coast road
Elkin, S. The MacGuffin
Grøndahl, J. C. Lucca
Henry, A. Learning to fly
King, T. Survivor
Livesey, M. The missing world
McEwan, I. Saturday
Mitchard, J. A theory of relativity
Oates, J. C. Black water
O'Nan, S. The night country
Sherrill, M. My last movie star
Steel, D. The kiss
Wiesel, E. The accident
Wright, A. M. After Gregory

TRIALS—*Continued*
Friedman, P. Inadmissable evidence
Friedman, P. Reasonable doubt
Galsworthy, J. Maid in waiting
Galsworthy, J. Over the river
Galsworthy, J. The silver spoon
Green, G. D. The juror
Green, T. The letter of the law
Grippando, J. Hear no evil
Grisham, J. The partner
Grisham, J. The rainmaker
Grisham, J. The runaway jury
Grisham, J. A time to kill
Guterson, D. Snow falling on cedars
Hamilton, J. A map of the world
Higgins, G. V. Defending Billy Ryan
Hoag, T. Guilty as sin
Holden, C. The jazz bird
Hunter, E. Lizzie
Irving, C. Final argument
Jones, D. C. The court-martial of George Armstrong Custer
Katkov, N. Blood & orchids
Katzenbach, J. Hart's war
Koestler, A. Darkness at noon
Korelitz, J. H. The Sabbathday River
Lawrence, M. K. Hearts and bones
Lehrer, J. The special prisoner
Lescroart, J. T. The 13th juror
Lescroart, J. T. The hearing
Lescroart, J. T. The mercy rule
Levin, M. Compulsion
Margolin, P. After dark
Margolin, P. The burning man
Martini, S. P. Compelling evidence
Martini, S. P. The judge
Martini, S. P. The jury
Martini, S. P. Prime witness
Martini, S. P. Undue influence
Meltzer, B. Dead even
Miller, S. The good mother
Oates, J. C. American appetites
O'Shaughnessy, P. Acts of malice
O'Shaughnessy, P. Breach of promise
O'Shaughnessy, P. Invasion of privacy
O'Shaughnessy, P. Motion to suppress
O'Shaughnessy, P. Obstruction of justice
O'Shaughnessy, P. Writ of execution
Parker, B. Blood relations
Parker, B. Suspicion of guilt
Patterson, J. Hide & seek
Patterson, R. N. Degree of guilt
Patterson, R. N. Eyes of a child
Patterson, R. N. The final judgment
Patterson, R. N. Silent witness
Pesci, D. Amistad
Picoult, J. My sister's keeper
Plain, B. Her father's house
Reardon, L. Blameless
Reed, B. The choice
Reed, B. The deception
Reuland, R. Semiautomatic
Rosenberg, N. T. Trial by fire
Scottoline, L. Mistaken identity
Scottoline, L. Rough justice
Scottoline, L. Running from the law
Scottoline, L. The vendetta defense
Siegel, S. Final verdict
Snow, C. P. The sleep of reason
Spence, G. Half-moon and empty stars
Stirling, J. Lantern for the dark
Traver, R. Anatomy of a murder
Turow, S. The laws of our fathers
Turow, S. Presumed innocent
Uris, L. QB VII
Van Wormer, L. Jury duty
Warren, R. P. World enough and time
Welty, E. The Ponder heart
West, J. The massacre at Fall Creek
Wilhelm, K. The best defense
Wilhelm, K. Death qualified
Wilhelm, K. Defense for the devil
Wilhelm, K. Desperate measures
Wilhelm, K. Malice prepense
Wilhelm, K. No defense
Woods, S. Dead in the water
Woods, S. Grass roots

TRIBES

Darnton, J. Neanderthal

Tricks. McBain, E.
The **trimmed** lamp. Henry, O.
In Henry, O. The complete works of O. Henry p1365-1483

TRINIDAD AND TOBAGO

Kempadoo, O. Tide running
Naipaul, V. S. A house for Mr. Biswas
Naipaul, V. S. A way in the world

Trinity. Uris, L.
Trinity fields. Morrow, B.
Trio for blunt instruments. Stout, R.
A **trip** to the center of the earth. See Verne, J. A journey to the centre of the earth
Triple. Follett, K.
Triple jeopardy. Stout, R.
In Stout, R. Kings full of aces p325-472

TRIPLETS

Powell, S. The Mushroom Man

Tripoint. Cherryh, C. J.
TRIPOLITAN WAR, 1801-1805 *See* United States—Tripolitan War, 1801-1805

TRISTAN, FLORA, 1803-1844

About

Vargas Llosa, M. The way to paradise

TRISTAN (LEGENDARY CHARACTER)

Millhauser, S. The king in the tree

Tristan. Mann, T.
In Mann, T. Stories of three decades

TRISTAN Y MOSCOZO, FLORE CÉLESTINE THÉRÈSE HENRIETTE *See* Tristan, Flora, 1803-1844

Tristram Shandy. See Sterne, L. The life and opinions of Tristram Shandy, gentleman
The **triumph** of beauty. Roth, J.
In Roth, J. and Hofmann, M. The collected stories of Joseph Roth
The **triumph** of Katie Byrne. Bradford, B. T.
A **triumph** of souls. Foster, A. D.
Trojan gold. Peters, E.

TROJAN WAR

Bradley, M. Z. The firebrand
McCullough, C. The song of Troy
Simmons, D. Ilium
Simmons, D. Olympos
Unsworth, B. The songs of the kings

Troll. Sinisalo, J.
The **troll** garden. Cather, W.
In Cather, W. Early novels and stories
In Cather, W. Willa Cather's collected short fiction, 1892-1912
The **trolley**. Simon, C.
Trophies and dead things. Muller, M.
Tropic of Cancer. Miller, H.
Tropic of Capricorn. Miller, H.
Trouble for Lucia. Benson, E. F.
In Benson, E. F. Make way for Lucia p941-1119
Trouble in Paradise. Parker, R. B.
Trouble in triplicate. Stout, R.
In Stout, R. All aces p303-442
A **trouble** of fools. Barnes, L.
The **trouble** with Harriet. Cannell, D.
Troubled sleep. Sartre, J. P.
The **troupe** teacher. Potok, C.
In Potok, C. Old men at midnight

TROY (ANCIENT CITY)

See also Trojan War

TRUCKS

Accidents

See Traffic accidents

The **true** account. Mosher, H. F.
The **true** and outstanding adventures of the Hunt sisters. Robinson, E.
True at first light. Hemingway, E.
True believers. Haddam, J.
True colors. Mortman, D.
True confessions. Dunne, J. G.

UNITED STATES—Civil War, 1861-1865—*Continued*
Jakes, J. On secret service
Jakes, J. Savannah; or, A gift for Mr. Lincoln
Jiles, P. Enemy women
Johnston, T. C. Cry of the hawk
Jones, D. C. Elkhorn Tavern
Kantor, M. Andersonville
Keneally, T. Confederates
McCaig, D. Jacob's ladder
Mitchell, M. Gone with the wind
Mrazek, R. J. Unholy fire
Plain, B. Crescent City
Poyer, D. Fire on the waters
Reasoner, J. Antietam
Safire, W. Freedom
Shaara, J. Gods and generals
Shaara, J. The last full measure
Shaara, M. The killer angels
Trotter, W. R. The sands of pride
Vidal, G. Lincoln
Warren, R. P. Band of angels
Wray, J. Canaan's tongue
Youmans, M. The wolf pit

Civil War, 1861-1865—Naval operations

Poyer, D. A country of our own

1865-1898

Ferber, E. Saratoga trunk
Jakes, J. Heaven and hell
Twain, M. The gilded age
Wharton, E. The age of innocence

20th century

Allende, I. The infinite plan
Berger, T. Sneaky people
Buckley, W. F. Elvis in the morning
Buckley, W. F. Getting it right
Carroll, J. Memorial bridge
Carroll, J. Prince of peace
Carson, T. Gilligan's wake
Céline, L.-F. Journey to the end of the night
DeLillo, D. Libra
DeLillo, D. Underworld
Didion, J. Play it as it lays
Doctorow, E. L. Loon Lake
Doctorow, E. L. Ragtime
Dos Passos, J. The 42nd parallel
Dos Passos, J. 1919
Dos Passos, J. U.S.A.
Dunne, J. G. The red, white, and blue
Ellroy, J. American tabloid
Ellroy, J. The cold six thousand
Fast, H. The legacy
Fitzgerald, F. S. The beautiful and damned
Franzen, J. The corrections
Gaddis, W. A frolic of his own
Gordon, N. The company you keep
Greeley, A. M. September song
Greenberg, J. In this sign
Grumbach, D. The book of knowledge
Heller, J. Something happened
Jakes, J. American dreams
Johnson, C. R. Dreamer
Kerouac, J. The Dharma bums
Kerouac, J. On the road
King, S. Hearts in Atlantis
Klein, J. Primary colors
Kosinski, J. N. Being there
Lewis, S. Babbitt
Mailer, N. Harlot's ghost
McMahon, T. A. Loving Little Egypt
Morrow, B. Trinity fields
Nabokov, V. V. Lolita
Piercy, M. Vida
Proulx, A. Accordian crimes
Proulx, A. Postcards
Roth, P. The great American novel
Shaw, I. Beggarman, thief
Shaw, I. Rich man, poor man
Stewart, F. M. Ellis Island
Stewart, F. M. The naked Savages
Stewart, F. M. The Savages in love and war
Turner, F. W. 1929
Updike, J. In the beauty of the lilies
Updike, J. Memories of the Ford Administration
Vidal, G. The golden age
Vidal, G. Washington, D.C.
Vonnegut, K. Jailbird
Wiggins, M. Evidence of things unseen
Wouk, H. War and remembrance
Wouk, H. The winds of war
Wright, S. Going native

Armed forces

Knebel, F. Seven days in May

College life

See College life—United States

Communism

See Communism—United States

Defenses

Cussler, C. Raise the Titanic!

Fascism

See Fascism—United States

Politics

See Politics—United States

Presidents

See Presidents—United States

Prisoners and prisons

See Prisoners and prisons—United States

Race relations

Alexie, S. Indian killer
Amidon, S. The new city
Baldwin, J. Another country
Baldwin, J. If Beale Street could talk
Bambara, T. C. The salt eaters
Bambara, T. C. Those bones are not my child
Banks, R. Continental drift
Bell, M. S. Ten Indians
Brandon, J. Rules of evidence
Brown, R. M. Southern discomfort
Brown, R. Civil wars
Brown, R. Half a heart
Brown, S. The witness
Campbell, B. M. Brothers and sisters
Campbell, B. M. What you owe me
Campbell, B. M. Your blues ain't like mine
Caputo, P. Equation for evil
Carroll, J. The city below
Chesnutt, C. W. Stories, novels, & essay
Childress, M. Crazy in Alabama
Cooper, J. C. The wake of the wind
Dexter, P. Paris Trout
Doctorow, E. L. Ragtime
Doig, I. Prairie nocturne
Dry, R. Leaving
Dunne, J. G. Nothing lost
Ellison, R. Invisible man
Epstein, L. San Remo Drive
Estleman, L. D. King of the corner
Estleman, L. D. Motown
Fairbairn, A. Five smooth stones
Faulkner, W. Intruder in the dust
Faulkner, W. Light in August
Fowler, K. J. Sarah Canary
French, A. Billy
Gaines, E. J. The gathering of old men
Gaines, E. J. A lesson before dying
Gibbons, K. Divining women
Grau, S. A. The keepers of the house
Grey, Z. The vanishing American
Grisham, J. The chamber
Grisham, J. A painted house
Grisham, J. A time to kill
Gurganus, A. Blessed assurance: a moral tale
Haley, A. Mama Flora's family
Hambly, B. A free man of color
Haynes, M. Mother of pearl
Hughes, L. Not without laughter
Hughes, L. Simple speaks his mind
Hughes, L. Simple stakes a claim
Hughes, L. Simple takes a wife
Hughes, L. Simple's Uncle Sam

UNITED STATES. FEDERAL BUREAU OF INVESTIGATION—*Continued*
Carroll, J. Memorial bridge
Coben, H. The innocent
Coulter, C. The maze
Coulter, C. The target
D'Amato, B. White male infant
Deaver, J. The devil's teardrop
Deaver, J. A maiden's grave
DeMille, N. The lion's game
Finder, J. The zero hour
Follett, K. The hammer of Eden
Griffin, W. E. B. The investigators
Grippando, J. The informant
Grisham, J. The firm
Hall, J. W. Rough draft
Higgins, G. V. At end of day
Isaacs, S. Red, white and blue
Johnson, C. R. Dreamer
King, L. R. A darker place
Maas, P. Father and son
Nance, J. J. The last hostage
Patterson, J. Honeymoon
Patterson, J. Lifeguard
Patterson, J. When the wind blows
Pottinger, S. The last Nazi
Preston, D. Brimstone
Preston, D. The cabinet of curiosities
Preston, D. Reliquary
Preston, D. Still life with crows
Reed, B. The indictment
Smith, A. Good morning, killer
Smith, A. North of Montana
Smith, M.-A. T. She's not there
Tirone Smith, M.-A. Love her madly
Tirone Smith, M.-A. She smiled sweetly
Turow, S. Personal injuries
White, S. W. The best revenge
Wiltse, D. Blown away
Wiltse, D. Bone deep

UNITED STATES. MARINE CORPS
Brady, J. Warning of war
Griffin, W. E. B. Blood and honor
Griffin, W. E. B. Close combat
Griffin, W. E. B. Counterattack
Griffin, W. E. B. Honor bound
Griffin, W. E. B. In danger's path
Griffin, W. E. B. Line of fire
Griffin, W. E. B. Under fire
Uris, L. Battle cry
Webb, J. H. A sense of honor
West, F. J. The Pepperdogs

UNITED STATES. NATIONAL AERONAUTICS AND SPACE ADMINISTRATION
Michener, J. A. Space

UNITED STATES. NATIONAL GUARD
Brown, D. Storming heaven

UNITED STATES. NATIONAL SECURITY COUNCIL
Clancy, T. Clear and present danger

UNITED STATES. NAVAL ACADEMY *See* United States Naval Academy

UNITED STATES. NAVY
Deutermann, P. T. Sweepers
Fleming, T. J. Time and tide
Grippando, J. Hear no evil
Heggen, T. Mister Roberts
Martin, W. Annapolis
Melville, H. White-jacket: or, The world in a man-of-war
Michener, J. A. The bridges at Toko-ri
Poyer, D. Black storm
Poyer, D. China Sea
Poyer, D. The circle
Poyer, D. The command
Poyer, D. A country of our own
Poyer, D. Fire on the waters
Poyer, D. The gulf
Robinson, P. Kilo class
Wambaugh, J. Finnegan's week
Wiggs, S. The ocean between us
Wouk, H. The Caine mutiny

Officers
Katkov, N. Blood & orchids
White, R. A. Typhoon
Wouk, H. War and remembrance

UNITED STATES. OFFICE OF STRATEGIC SERVICES
Griffin, W. E. B. The last heroes
Griffin, W. E. B. The secret warriors
Griffin, W. E. B. The soldier spies

UNITED STATES. PEACE CORPS *See* Peace Corps (U.S.)

UNITED STATES. SECRET SERVICE
Costello, M. Big if
Shelby, P. Days of drums

UNITED STATES. SUPREME COURT
Baldacci, D. The simple truth
Meltzer, B. The tenth justice
Patterson, R. N. Protect and defend

UNITED STATES MILITARY ACADEMY
Lee, G. Honor & duty
Ruggero, E. The academy
Truscott, L. K. Dress gray
Truscott, L. K. Full dress gray

UNITED STATES NAVAL ACADEMY
Deutermann, P. T. Darkside
Webb, J. H. A sense of honor

UNITED STATES NAVAL OBSERVATORY
Mallon, T. Two moons

The **Universal** Baseball Association, Inc., J. Henry Waugh, Prop. Coover, R.

UNIVERSITY LIFE *See* College life

UNIVERSITY OF CAMBRIDGE
Snow, C. P. The affair
Snow, C. P. The light and the dark
Snow, C. P. The masters

UNIVERSITY OF NOTRE DAME
McInerny, R. M. The book of kills
McInerny, R. M. Celt and pepper
McInerny, R. M. Irish coffee
McInerny, R. M. Irish tenure

UNIVERSITY OF OXFORD
Sayers, D. L. Gaudy Night

UNIVERSITY STUDENTS *See* College life

An **unkindness** of ravens. Rendell, R.
The **unknown** shore. O'Brian, P.
Unless. Shields, C.
The **unlikely** spy. Silva, D.
Unlucky in law. O'Shaughnessy, P.

UNMARRIED COUPLES
Chalmers, R. Who's who in hell
Hawke, E. Ash Wednesday
Mapson, J.-A. Loving Chloe
McMillan, T. Disappearing acts
Spencer, S. A ship made of paper
Walker, A. Now is the time to open your heart

UNMARRIED MOTHERS
Erdrich, L. The bingo palace
Francis, C. Night sky
Gordon, M. The company of women
Holman, S. The dress lodger
Hood, A. Ruby
Llywelyn, M. 1949
Richler, N. Your mouth is lovely
Sheldon, S. Rage of angels
Shreve, A. Fortune's Rocks
Straight, S. I been in sorrow's kitchen and licked out all the pots
Thayer, N. Belonging
Upadhyay, S. The guru of love

The **unnamable**. Beckett, S.
In Beckett, S. Molloy, Malone dies, The unnamable
Unnatural death. See Sayers, D. L. The Dawson pedigree
The **unparalleled** adventure of one Hans Pfaall. Poe, E. A.
In Poe, E. A. The imaginary voyages: The narrative of Arthur Gordon Pym; The unparalleled adventure of one Hans Pfaall; The journal of Julius Rodman p366-506
The **unpleasantness** at the Bellona Club. Sayers, D. L.
An **unsuitable** attachment. Pym, B.
An **unsuitable** job for a woman. James, P. D.
The **unthinkable** thoughts of Jacob Green. Braff, J.
Until I find you. Irving, J.
Until the end. Coyle, H. W.
Unto a good land. Moberg, V.
The **untouchable**. Banville, J.

V

VATICAN—*Continued*
West, M. L. Lazarus
Vatican. Martin, M.
The **Vatican** rip. Gash, J.
VAUDEVILLE
McCracken, E. Niagara Falls all over again
The **vault**. Lovesey, P.
Vector. Cook, R.
Velocity. Koontz, D. R.
VENDETTA *See* Revenge
The **vendetta** defense. Scottoline, L.
The **Venetian** affair. MacInnes, H.
VENGEANCE *See* Revenge
Vengeance. Kaminsky, S. M.
VENICE (ITALY) *See* Italy—Venice
VENUS (PLANET)
Bova, B. Venus
Lewis, C. S. Perelandra
Pohl, F. The space merchants
Zelazny, R. The doors of his face, the lamps of his mouth
Venus. Bova, B.
Venus in copper. Davis, L.
Verbena. Kincaid, N.
Verdict unsafe. McGown, J.
VERMEER, JOHANNES, 1632-1675
About
Chevalier, T. Girl with a pearl earring
Vreeland, S. Girl in hyacinth blue
VERMEER VAN DELFT, JAN *See* Vermeer, Johannes, 1632-1675
VERMONT
Morris, M. M. The lost mother
Mosher, H. F. Waiting for Teddy Williams
Schupack, D. The boy on the bus
Tartt, D. The secret history
Updike, J. Seek my face
20th century
Beattie, A. Love always
Bohjalian, C. A. The buffalo soldier
Bohjalian, C. A. Midwives
Gardner, J. October light
Lipman, E. The Inn at Lake Devine
Mayor, A. Occam's razor
Miller, S. The world below
Morris, M. M. A dangerous woman
Morris, M. M. Songs in ordinary time
Peck, R. N. A day no pigs would die
Prose, F. Blue angel
Proulx, A. Postcards
Straub, P. Shadowland
Farm life
See Farm life—Vermont
VERMOUTH *See* Wine and wine making
Veronica. Gaitskill, M.
VERSAILLES (FRANCE) *See* France—Versailles
Versailles. Davis, K.
Vertical burn. Emerson, E. W.
Vertical coffin. Cannell, S. J.
Vertigo. Sebald, W. G.
Very old bones. Kennedy, W.
Vespers. McBain, E.
The **veteran**. Forsyth, F.
VETERANS
Purdy, J. In a shallow grave
VETERANS (AMERICAN CIVIL WAR, 1861-1865)
Bahr, H. The year of Jubilo
Busch, F. The night inspector
Byrd, M. Grant
Cambor, K. In sunlight, in a beautiful garden
O'Nan, S. A prayer for the dying
Smith, D. Pictures from an expedition
VETERANS (KOREAN WAR, 1950-1953)
Percy, W. The moviegoer
Walbert, K. The gardens of Kyoto
VETERANS (PERSIAN GULF WAR, 1991)
Littell, R. Walking back the cat
VETERANS (SOUTH AFRICAN WAR, 1899-1902)
Delderfield, R. F. A horseman riding by
VETERANS (VIETNAMESE WAR, 1961-1975)
Bausch, R. Rebel powers
Busch, F. Closing arguments
Butler, R. O. The deep green sea
Butler, R. O. They whisper
Clancy, T. Without remorse
Del Vecchio, J. M. Carry me home
Deutermann, P. T. Sweepers
Forsyth, F. Avenger
Green, N. The angel of Montague Street
Harris, T. Black Sunday
Harrison, C. Afterburn
Heinemann, L. Paco's story
Hoffman, W. Wild thorn
Hunter, S. Time to hunt
King, D. The ha-ha
King, L. R. Keeping watch
King, S. Hearts in Atlantis
Maillard, K. The clarinet polka
Mason, B. A. In country
McCammon, R. R. Gone south
McFarland, D. Singing boy
Morris, M. M. Fiona Range
Morrow, B. Ariel's crossing
O'Brien, T. In the Lake of the Woods
O'Nan, S. The names of the dead
Stone, R. Dog soldiers
Straub, P. Koko
Straub, P. The throat
Thayer, S. The weatherman
Thomas, R. Ah, treachery!
Vonnegut, K. Hocus pocus
Walker, M. W. Under the beetle's cellar
Webb, J. H. A sense of honor
VETERANS (WORLD WAR, 1914-1918)
Barker, P. Another world
Erdrich, L. The Master Butchers Singing Club
Faulkner, W. Soldiers' pay
Ford, F. M. The last post
Garlock, D. The edge of town
Parkinson, H. Across open ground
Remarque, E. M. The road back
Watkins, P. In the blue light of African dreams
Wiggins, M. Evidence of things unseen
VETERANS (WORLD WAR, 1939-1945)
Algren, N. The man with the golden arm
Battle, L. War brides
Böll, H. The silent angel
Bragg, M. Crossing the lines
Bragg, M. The soldier's return
Bragg, M. A son of war
Burnard, B. A good house
Canin, E. Carry me across the water
Cookson, C. A house divided
Dickinson, P. Some deaths before dying
Fast, H. The bridge builder's story
Fast, H. The outsider
Greeley, A. M. Younger than springtime
Guterson, D. Snow falling on cedars
Hawkes, J. Second skin
Hazzard, S. The great fire
Heller, J. Closing time
Hunter, S. Hot Springs
Jones, J. Whistle
Knowles, J. Indian summer
Knowles, J. Peace breaks out
Lee, C.-R. A gesture life
Lehrer, J. The special prisoner
McEwan, I. Atonement
Okuizumi, H. The stones cry out
Pouncey, P. R. Rules for old men waiting
Steel, D. Lone eagle
Turow, S. Ordinary heroes
Wharton, W. Birdy
Wilson, S. The man in the gray flannel suit
VETERANS DAY
Ford, F. M. A man could stand up

TITLE AND SUBJECT INDEX

VIOLENCE—*Continued*
Llywelyn, M. 1916
Llywelyn, M. 1972
Lustbader, E. V. Black Blade
Matthiessen, P. Bone by bone
Matthiessen, P. Lost Man's River
McCarthy, C. Blood meridian
McCarthy, C. No country for old men
McGuane, T. Ninety-two in the shade
Miller, R. Welcome to Heavenly Heights
Naslund, S. J. Four spirits
Oates, J. C. The tattooed girl
O'Dell, T. Back roads
Patterson, J. Hide & seek
Pawel, R. Death of a nationalist
Pelecanos, G. P. The big blowdown
Pelecanos, G. P. Drama city
Pelecanos, G. P. Shame the devil
Pelecanos, G. P. The sweet forever
Phillips, C. Cambridge
Poyer, D. Thunder on the mountain
Price, R. Samaritan
Richards, D. A. The bay of love and sorrows
Rushdie, S. Shalimar the clown
Shamsie, K. Kartography
Shriver, L. We need to talk about Kevin
Spiegelman, I. Everyone's burning
Straight, S. The gettin place
Tristram, C. After
Vachss, A. H. Two trains running
Vargas Llosa, M. Death in the Andes
Vera, Y. The stone virgins
Vernon, O. Eden
Vida, N. Goodbye, Saigon
Vine, B. A fatal inversion
Vine, B. King Solomon's carpet
Walker, A. Possessing the secret of joy
Wiltse, D. Heartland
Woods, S. L.A. Times
Wright, S. Going native
Violence. Bausch, R.
The **violent** bear it away. O'Connor, F.
also in O'Connor, F. Collected works p329-480

VIOLINISTS
Egolf, T. Skirt and the fiddle
Lebrecht, N. The song of names
Virgin earth. Gregory, P.
Virgin heat. Shames, L.
The **virgin** in the ice. Peters, E.

VIRGIN ISLANDS OF THE UNITED STATES
See also Saint Thomas (Virgin Islands of the U.S.)
Nasaw, J. L. Twenty-seven bones

VIRGIN MARY *See* Mary, Blessed Virgin, Saint
The **virgin** suicides. Eugenides, J.

VIRGINIA
See also Chesapeake Bay (Md. and Va.)
Brown, R. M. Riding shotgun
Holman, S. The mammoth cheese

To 1800

Gregory, P. Virgin earth
L'Amour, L. To the far blue mountains
Thackeray, W. M. The Virginians
Vollmann, W. T. Argall

18th century

Follett, K. A place called freedom
Settle, M. L. O Beulah Land

19th century

Brown, R. M. High hearts
Cather, W. Sapphira and the slave girl
Cornwell, B. Copperhead
Cornwell, B. Rebel
Jones, E. P. The known world
McCaig, D. Jacob's ladder
Reasoner, J. Antietam
Styron, W. The confessions of Nat Turner
Youmans, M. The wolf pit

20th century

Baldacci, D. Wish you well
Bausch, R. In the night season
Bausch, R. The Gypsy Man
Dee, J. Palladio
Deutermann, P. T. Sweepers
Gaffney, P. Circle of three
Godwin, G. Father Melancholy's daughter
Hamner, E. The homecoming
Hamner, E. Spencer's Mountain
Michaels, B. Stitches in time
Pearson, T. R. Blue Ridge
Pearson, T. R. Cry me a river
Shreve, S. R. A country of strangers
Smith, L. Fair and tender ladies
Smith, L. Family linen
Smith, L. Oral history
Styron, W. Lie down in darkness
Theroux, A. Darconville's cat
Trigiani, A. Big Cherry Holler
Trigiani, A. Big Stone Gap
Trigiani, A. Milk glass moon

Farm life

See Farm life—Virginia

Frontier and pioneer life

See Frontier and pioneer life—Virginia

Charlottesville

Brown, R. M. Outfoxed
The **Virginians**. Thackeray, W. M.

VIRGINITY
Rogers, J. Mr. Wroe's virgins
Virtual light. Gibson, W.
Virtual mode. Anthony, P.

VIRTUAL REALITY
Bova, B. Death dream
Eskridge, K. Solitaire
Gibson, W. All tomorrow's parties
Gibson, W. Virtual light
Niven, L. Saturn's race
Noon, J. Vurt
Powers, R. Plowing the dark
Sagan, N. Idlewild
Zelazny, R. Donnerjack
A **virtuous** woman. Gibbons, K.

VIRUSES
Bear, G. Darwin's radio
DeMille, N. Plum Island
Koontz, D. R. Seize the night
Nance, J. J. Pandora's clock
Pottinger, S. The last Nazi
Preston, R. The Cobra event
The **vision** of Emma Blau. Hegi, U.
A **vision** of light. Riley, J. M.

VISIONS
See also Dreams
The **visiting** physician. Shreve, S. R.
The **visitor**. Tepper, S. S.
VISITORS FROM OUTER SPACE *See* Interplanetary visitors
Vital parts. Berger, T.
Vital signs. Cook, R.
Vital signs. Wood, B.
VITICULTURE *See* Wine and wine making
VITORIA CAMPAIGN, 1813 *See* Peninsular War, 1807-1814
Vittorio the vampire. Rice, A.
VIVISECTION *See* Medicine—Research
The **vivisector**. White, P.
The **voice** of the city. Henry, O.
In Henry, O. The complete works of O. Henry p1253-1364
Voice of the heart. Bradford, B. T.
Voices in a haunted room. Carr, P.
Voices in summer. Pilcher, R.
A **void**. Perec, G.
A **void** in hearts. Tapply, W. G.
Void moon. Connelly, M.
The **volcano** lover. Sontag, S.

VOLCANOES
Harris, R. Pompeii
Lytton, E. B. L., Baron. The last days of Pompeii
Verne, J. A journey to the centre of the earth
Voltaire's Candide, Zadig, and selected stories. Voltaire

W

WAR—*Continued*
Forsyth, F. Avenger
Haldeman, J. W. Forever peace
Harrison, H. West of Eden
Karnezis, P. The maze
Khadra, Y. The swallows of Kabul
Lee, M. The canal house
Lopez, B. H. Resistance
Moravia, A. Two women
Potok, C. Old men at midnight
Potok, C. The troupe teacher
Seymour, G. The heart of danger
Sienkiewicz, H. The deluge
Sienkiewicz, H. Fire in the steppe
Tolkien, J. R. R. The Silmarillion
Turtledove, H. Into the darkness
Turtledove, H. Rulers of the darkness
West, F. J. The Pepperdogs
White, T. H. The book of Merlyn
Ye Zhaoyan. Nanjing 1937
War and peace. Tolstoy, L., graf
War and remembrance. Wouk, H.
The **war** between the Tates. Lurie, A.
War brides. Battle, L.
WAR CORRESPONDENTS *See* Journalists
WAR CRIME TRIALS
Buckley, W. F. Nuremberg
DeMille, N. Word of honor
Schlink, B. The reader
WAR CRIMINALS
Forsyth, F. The Odessa file
King, S. Apt pupil
Levin, I. The boys from Brazil
Moore, B. The statement
Mortimer, J. C. Dunster
Ondaatje, M. Anil's ghost
Seymour, G. The heart of danger
Uris, L. QB VII
The **war** doctor. Potok, C.
In Potok, C. Old men at midnight
WAR OF 1812 *See* United States—War of 1812
War of the Gods. Anderson, P.
War of the rats. Robbins, D. L.
WAR OF THE ROSES *See* England—15th century
The **war** of the worlds. Wells, H. G.
also in Wells, H. G. Seven famous novels
War trash. Ha Jin
Warday. Strieber, W.
WARLOCKS *See* Witchcraft
The **warlord**. Bosse, M. J.
Warlord chronicles [series]
Cornwell, B. Enemy of God
Cornwell, B. Excalibur
Cornwell, B. The winter king
The **warlord's** son. Fesperman, D.
Warning of war. Brady, J.
Warning shot. Egleton, C.
Warrior class. Brown, D.
WARSAW (POLAND) *See* Poland—Warsaw
WARSHIPS
See also Nuclear submarines
Fleming, T. J. Time and tide
Reeman, D. A ship must die
WARWICKSHIRE (ENGLAND) *See* England—Warwickshire
WASHINGTON, GEORGE, 1732-1799
About
Fleming, T. J. Dreams of glory
Shaara, J. The glorious cause
WASHINGTON (D.C.)
Pelecanos, G. P. Drama city
Roosevelt, K. In the shadow of the law
Vidal, G. The Smithsonian Institution
19th century
Adams, H. Democracy
Brown, R. M. Dolley
Byrd, M. Grant
Jakes, J. On secret service
Mallon, T. Two moons
Mrazek, R. J. Unholy fire
Vidal, G. 1876
Vidal, G. Empire
Vidal, G. Lincoln
20th century
Baldacci, D. Absolute power
Baldacci, D. Saving Faith
Baldacci, D. The simple truth
Brown, S. Exclusive
Buckley, C. T. Little green men
Buckley, C. T. No way to treat a First Lady
Carter, S. L. The emperor of Ocean Park
Clark, M. H. Stillwatch
Coonts, S. Under siege
Deaver, J. The devil's teardrop
Drury, A. Advise and consent
Faulks, S. On Green Dolphin Street
Frank, J. Bad publicity
Grisham, J. The pelican brief
Haynes, D. The full Matilda
Heller, J. Good as Gold
Ignatius, D. The Sun King
Krist, G. Chaos theory
Lehrer, J. The last debate
Lehrer, J. Purple dots
McMurtry, L. Cadillac Jack
Meltzer, B. The first counsel
Meltzer, B. The tenth justice
Meltzer, B. The zero game
Michaels, B. Shattered silk
Patterson, J. Along came a spider
Patterson, J. Cat & mouse
Patterson, J. Jack and Jill
Patterson, J. Kiss the girls
Patterson, J. Pop! goes the weasel
Patterson, J. Roses are red
Patterson, R. N. Balance of power
Pelecanos, G. P. The big blowdown
Pelecanos, G. P. Right as rain
Pelecanos, G. P. Shame the devil
Pelecanos, G. P. The sweet forever
Pottinger, S. The fourth procedure
Shelby, P. Days of drums
Stead, C. The man who loved children
Steel, D. Journey
Tanenbaum, R. Corruption of blood
Vidal, G. The golden age
Vidal, G. Hollywood
Vidal, G. Washington, D.C.
Wilson, F. P. Deep as the marrow
Wilson, F. P. Implant
Georgetown
Blatty, W. P. The exorcist
WASHINGTON (STATE)
Guterson, D. Our Lady of the Forest
Paul, J. A girl, in parts
20th century
Alexie, S. Reservation blues
Bernhardt, W. Dark justice
Guterson, D. East of the mountains
Guterson, D. Snow falling on cedars
Hannah, K. Angel falls
Hannah, K. On Mystic lake
Roberts, N. River's end
Seattle
Alexie, S. Indian killer
Coupland, D. Microserfs
Doig, I. Mountain time
Emerson, E. W. Pyro
Emerson, E. W. Vertical burn
Goldsmith, O. Bad boy
Kallos, S. Broken for you
Martini, S. P. The list
Pearson, R. The angel maker
Pearson, R. The art of deception
Pearson, R. Beyond recognition
Pearson, R. The body of David Hayes
Pearson, R. The first victim
Pearson, R. Middle of nowhere
Pearson, R. No witnesses
Pearson, R. The Pied Piper

WEDDINGS
Ansay, A. M. Midnight champagne
Cookson, C. The year of the virgins
Johnson, D. Le mariage
Karon, J. A common life
McCullers, C. The member of the wedding
Ross, A. B. Miss Julia throws a wedding
Streeter, E. Father of the bride
Welty, E. Delta wedding
West, D. The wedding
Wednesday the rabbi got wet. Kemelman, H.
Weep no more, my lady. Clark, M. H.
Wehr search. McCaffrey, A.
In The Hugo winners p329-87
Weighed in the balance. Perry, A.

WEIGHT LIFTING
Brenna, D. The altar of the body
Crews, H. Body
The **weight** of water. Shreve, A.
Welcome, chaos. Wilhelm, K.
Welcome to Hard Times. Doctorow, E. L.
Welcome to Heavenly Heights. Miller, R.
Welcome to paradise. Shames, L.
Welcome to the monkey house. Vonnegut, K.
Welcome to the world, baby girl! Flagg, F.
We'll meet again. Clark, M. H.
Well of darkness. Weis, M.
The **well** of loneliness. Hall, R.
The **well** of lost plots. See Fforde, J. Thursday Next in The well of lost plots
Well-schooled in murder. George, E.

WELLES, ORSON, 1915-1985
About
Kaplow, R. Me and Orson Welles

WELSH
North America
Thom, J. A. The children of first man
The **wench** is dead. Dexter, C.

WEREWOLVES
Anderson, P. Operation Chaos
Anderson, P. Operation Luna
Borchardt, A. The silver wolf
Strieber, W. The Wolfen

WERNER'S SYNDROME
Tsukiyama, G. Dreaming water
WERWOLVES *See* Werewolves
Wessex tales. Hardy, T.
WEST (U.S.) *See* Western States
West 47th. Browne, G. A.

WEST AFRICA
See also Niger River
Boyle, T. C. Water music
Céline, L.-F. Journey to the end of the night
Forsyth, F. The dogs of war
Greene, G. The heart of the matter
The **West** End horror. Meyer, N.

WEST INDIAN AMERICANS
Marshall, P. The fisher king

WEST INDIANS
England
Walters, M. The shape of snakes
United States
Condé, M. I, Tituba, black witch of Salem
Kincaid, J. Lucy

WEST INDIES
See also Trinidad and Tobago
Atwood, M. Bodily harm
Forester, C. S. Admiral Hornblower in the West Indies
Fox, P. A servant's tale
Marshall, P. Praisesong for the widow
Morrison, T. Tar baby
Naipaul, V. S. Guerrillas
Rhys, J. Wide Sargasso Sea
Shacochis, B. Swimming in the volcano
Politics
See Politics—West Indies

WEST INDIES REGION *See* Caribbean region
West of Eden. Harrison, H.
West of the Pecos. Grey, Z.
WEST POINT (MILITARY ACADEMY) *See* United States Military Academy

WEST VIRGINIA
Hoffman, W. Wild thorn
Maillard, K. The clarinet polka
Paul, J. A girl, in parts
Settle, M. L. Charley Bland
Settle, M. L. The killing ground
Whitehead, C. John Henry Days
WESTCHESTER COUNTY (N.Y.) *See* New York (State)—Westchester County

WESTERN STATES
Blake, M. Marching to Valhalla
Dexter, P. Deadwood
Doctorow, E. L. Welcome to Hard Times
Fisher, V. Mountain man
Gatewood, R. The sound of the trees
Grimes, M. Biting the moon
Guthrie, A. B. The big sky
Jones, D. C. Arrest Sitting Bull
Jones, D. C. A creek called Wounded Knee
McMurtry, L. Buffalo girls
McMurtry, L. Comanche moon
McMurtry, L. Dead man's walk
McMurtry, L. Lonesome dove
McMurtry, L. Streets of Laredo
Michener, J. A. Centennial
Momaday, N. S. The ancient child
Murkoff, B. Waterborne
The Mysterious West
Spencer, L. Forgiving
Swarthout, G. F. The homesman
Willard, T. Buffalo soldiers
Farm life
See Farm life—Western States
Frontier and pioneer life
See Frontier and pioneer life—Western States

WESTERN STORIES
See also Adventure; Cowboys; Frontier and pioneer life—Western States; Ranch life; Western States
American West: twenty new stories from the Western Writers of America
Berger, T. Little Big Man
Berger, T. The return of Little Big Man
Bonner, C. Lily
Bonner, C. Looking after Lily
Brand, M. Beyond the outposts
Brand, M. Chinook
Brand, M. Dark Rosaleen
Brand, M. Fugitives' fire
Brand, M. The gentle desperado
Brand, M. In the hills of Monterey
Brand, M. Max Brand's best western stories
Brand, M. The Stingaree
Brand, M. Stolen gold: a western trio
Brand, M. The survival of Juan Oro
Brown, D. A. The way to Bright Star
Byrd, M. Shooting the sun
A Century of great Western stories
Chiaventone, F. J. Moon of bitter cold
Clark, W. V. T. The Ox-bow incident
Coldsmith, D. Raven Mocker
Coldsmith, D. Tallgrass
Combs, H. Brules
Combs, H. The scout
Coover, R. Ghost town
DeRosso, H. A. Riders of the shadowlands
Doctorow, E. L. Welcome to Hard Times
Durham, M. The man who loved Cat Dancing
Eagle, K. The last true cowboy
Edgerton, C. Redeye
Estleman, L. D. Billy Gashade
Estleman, L. D. Black powder, white smoke
Estleman, L. D. Bloody season
Estleman, L. D. City of widows
Estleman, L. D. Journey of the dead
Estleman, L. D. The master executioner

The **winter** king. Cornwell, B.
A **winter** marriage. Hardie, K.
The **winter** of our discontent. Steinbeck, J.
Winter prey. Sandford, J.
WINTER QUEEN *See* Elizabeth, Queen, consort of Frederick V, King of Bohemia, 1596-1662
The **winter** queen. Stevenson, J.
Winter rain. Johnston, T. C.
Winter range. Davis, C.
Winter solstice. Pilcher, R.
The **winter** wolf. Parry, R.
Wintering. Moses, K.
Winterkill. Box, C. J.
Winter's end. Rickards, J.
Winter's tale. Helprin, M.
Winter's tales. Dinesen, I.
WINTHROP, ELIZABETH FONES *See* Hallet, Elizabeth Fones Winthrop Feake, b. 1610
The **Winthrop** woman. Seton, A.

WISCONSIN

King, S. Black house
Packer, A. The dive from Clausen's pier
Sidor, S. Skin River
Watson, L. Orchard

19th century

O'Nan, S. A prayer for the dying

20th century

Ansay, A. M. Midnight champagne
Ansay, A. M. River angel
Hamilton, J. A map of the world
Hamilton, J. The short history of a prince
Simpson, M. Off Keck Road
Spencer, L. Bitter sweet

Farm life

See Farm life—Wisconsin

The **wisdom** of Father Brown. Chesterton, G. K.
In Chesterton, G. K. The Father Brown omnibus p227-431
Wise blood. O'Connor, F.
also in O'Connor, F. Collected works p1-132
Wise children. Carter, A.
The **wise** woman. Gregory, P.
Wish you well. Baldacci, D.
Wish you were here. Brown, R. M.
Wish you were here. O'Nan, S.

WISHES

Byatt, A. S. The djinn in the nightingale's eye

The **wishsong** of Shannara. Brooks, T.
WIT *See* Humor
The **witch** in the wood. White, T. H.
also in White, T. H. The once and future king
The **witch** of Exmoor. Drabble, M.

WITCHCRAFT

See also Demoniac possession; Exorcism; Voodooism

Anderson, P. Operation Chaos
Anderson, P. Operation Luna
Barker, C. The Madonna
Brooks, T. The Elfstones of Shannara
Brooks, T. The sword of Shannara
Card, O. S. Treasure box
Condé, M. I, Tituba, black witch of Salem
Gregory, P. The wise woman
Hoffman, A. Practical magic
Jones, D. W. A sudden wild magic
King, S. Thinner
Levin, I. Rosemary's baby
Lustbader, E. V. White Ninja
Rice, A. Lasher
Rice, A. Merrick
Rice, A. Taltos
Rice, A. The witching hour
Updike, J. The witches of Eastwick

WITCHES *See* Witchcraft
The **witches** of Eastwick. Updike, J.
The **witchfinder**. Estleman, L. D.
The **witching** hour. Rice, A.
With. Harington, D.
With a tangled skein. Anthony, P.
With fire and sword. Sienkiewicz, H.
With her in Ourland. Gilman, C. P.
also in Gilman, C. P. The Charlotte Perkins Gilman reader
also in Gilman, C. P. Charlotte Perkins Gilman's Utopian novels p270-387
With your crooked heart. Dunmore, H.
The **withdrawing** room. MacLeod, C.
Within a budding grove. Proust, M.
also in Proust, M. Remembrance of things past p465-1018
Within arm's reach. Napolitano, A.
Without fail. Child, L.
Without mercy. Dorrestein, R.
Without remorse. Clancy, T.
The **witness**. Brown, S.
The **witness**. Uhnak, D.
The **witness** for the prosecution and other stories. Christie, A.

WITNESSES

Clark, M. H. Pretend you don't see her
Clark, M. H. You belong to me
Leonard, E. Killshot
Pearson, R. Cut and run

WITTGENSTEIN, PAUL, 1907-

About

Bernhard, T. Wittgenstein's nephew

Wittgenstein's nephew. Bernhard, T.
Wizard. Varley, J.
Wizard at large. Brooks, T.
WIZARDS *See* Magicians
WLT. Keillor, G.
A **Wodehouse** bestiary. Wodehouse, P. G.
WOJTYŁA, KAROL *See* John Paul II, Pope, 1920-2005
The **wolf** hunt. Bradshaw, G.
Wolf in the shadows. Muller, M.
The **wolf** pit. Youmans, M.
Wolf whistle. Nordan, L.
Wolf winter. Francis, C.
The **Wolfen**. Strieber, W.

WOLVES

Bradshaw, G. The wolf hunt
Evans, N. The loop

Wolves eat dogs. Smith, M. C.
The **woman** and the ape. Høeg, P.
A **woman** called Moses. Heidish, M.
The **woman** destroyed. Beauvoir, S. d.
The **woman** destroyed [novelette] Beauvoir, S. d.
In Beauvoir, S. d. The woman destroyed p121-254
Woman Hollering Creek and other stories. Cisneros, S.
The **woman** in the dunes. Abe, K.
The **woman** in white. Collins, W.
A **woman** of independent means. Hailey, E. F.
A **woman** of substance. Bradford, B. T.
Woman of the frontier. Grey, Z.
Woman of the inner sea. Keneally, T.
Woman on the edge of time. Piercy, M.
The **woman** who loved pigs. Donaldson, S. R.
In Donaldson, S. R. Reave the Just and other tales p205-55
The **woman** who walked into doors. Doyle, R.
Woman without a past. Whitney, P. A.
A **Woman's** eye. Entered in Part I under title
A **woman's** liberation. Le Guin, U. K.
In Le Guin, U. K. Four ways to forgiveness p145-208
A **woman's** place. Delinsky, B.

WOMEN

See also African American women; Jewish women; Single women

Adams, A. Caroline's daughters
Adams, A. Superior women
Adler, E. Fortune is a woman
Ali, M. Brick lane
Allende, I. Daughter of fortune
Alther, L. Kinflicks
Auchincloss, L. The book class
Bambara, T. C. The salt eaters
Beauvoir, S. d. The woman destroyed
Bellow, S. A theft
Bowen, E. Eva Trout
Bradley, M. Z. The firebrand
Brookner, A. Brief lives
Brown, L. Fay
Brown, R. M. Six of one
Brown, S. Charade
Cather, W. Lucy Gayheart

WOMEN—Psychology—*Continued*
Hearon, S. Footprints
Høeg, P. Smilla's sense of snow
Hoffman, E. The secret
Hood, A. Places to stay the night
Howard, M. Children with matches
Howatch, S. The high flyer
Inness-Brown, E. Burning Marguerite
Isaacs, S. Lily White
Kallos, S. Broken for you
Kasischke, L. The life before her eyes
Kelman, J. Summer of storms
Kidd, S. M. The mermaid chair
Kincaid, J. Autobiography of my mother
Kincaid, J. Lucy
King, S. Dolores Claiborne
King, S. Gerald's game
King, S. Rose Madder
King, T. Survivor
Kingsolver, B. Animal dreams
Kitchen, J. The house on Eccles Road
Klíma, I. No saints or angels
Kundera, M. Identity
Lamott, A. Blue shoe
Lemann, N. Malaise
Lessing, D. M. The good terrorist
Lessing, D. M. Love, again
Lipman, E. The pursuit of Alice Thrift
Lively, P. The road to Lichfield
Lively, P. Spiderweb
Livesey, M. Criminals
Livesey, M. Eva moves the furniture
Mapson, J.-A. Loving Chloe
Martin, V. Italian fever
Mason, B. A. Feather crowns
Mattison, A. The wedding of the two-headed woman
Michael, J. Sleeping beauty
Michaels, F. Celebration
Miller, S. For love
Miller, S. While I was gone
Miller, S. The world below
Minot, S. Evening
Morrall, C. Astonishing splashes of colour
Morris, M. M. A dangerous woman
Mukherjee, B. Leave it to me
Muske-Dukes, C. Life after death
Oates, J. C. Blonde
Oates, J. C. The falls
Oates, J. C. I lock my door upon myself
O'Brien, E. House of splendid isolation
O'Brien, E. Time and tide
Ōe, K. An echo of heaven
Ólafur Jóhann Ólafsson. The journey home
O'Nan, S. The good wife
Packer, A. The dive from Clausen's pier
Patterson, J. Hide & seek
Phillips, C. Cambridge
Phillips, C. A distant shore
Phillips, J. A. MotherKind
Price, R. Roxanna Slade
Quindlen, A. Black and blue
Quindlen, A. One true thing
Reardon, L. Blameless
Reynolds, S. A gracious plenty
Rice, L. Home fires
Robinson, R. Sweetwater
Rosen, J. Joy comes in the morning
Rosenberg, N. T. Abuse of power
Rush, N. Mating
Schwartz, L. S. Disturbances in the field
Schwartz, L. S. The writing on the wall
Shields, C. Unless
Shigekuni, J. Invisible gardens
Shreve, A. The pilot's wife
Shreve, A. Strange fits of passion
Siddons, A. R. Fault lines
Simpson, M. Off Keck Road
Snyder, D. J. Night crossing
Solomon, N. Single wife
Spencer, E. Knights and dragons
Stirling, J. Shadows on the shore
Styron, A. All the finest girls
Symons, J. Something like a love affair
Tennant, E. Pemberley
Texier, C. Victorine
Thayer, N. Belonging
Trevor, W. Felicia's journey
Tyler, A. Back when we were grownups
Tyler, A. Ladder of years
Updike, J. Seek my face
Vanderbes, J. Easter Island
Walker, A. Now is the time to open your heart
Waller, R. J. The bridges of Madison County
Weber, K. The Music Lesson
Weldon, F. Worst fears
Wenner, K. Dancing with Einstein
West, P. The tent of orange mist
Winton, T. Dirt music
Wolitzer, M. The wife
Wright, A. M. Tony and Susan
Yoshimoto, B. Asleep [a novella]
Zafris, N. Lucky strike

Relation to other women

Atwood, M. The robber bride
Battle, L. The Florabama Ladies' Auxiliary & Sewing Circle
Beattie, A. My life, starring Dara Falcon
Berg, E. Range of motion
Binchy, M. Circle of friends
Binchy, M. Light a penny candle
Binchy, M. Tara Road
Bradford, B. T. A sudden change of heart
Bradford, B. T. Three weeks in Paris
Brookner, A. Fraud
Brookner, A. The rules of engagement
Cleage, P. I wish I had a red dress
Dart, I. R. Show business kills
Dawson, C. The mother-in-law diaries
Gaitskill, M. Veronica
Golden, A. Memoirs of a geisha
Goldsmith, O. Pen pals
Goldsmith, O. Young wives
Gutcheon, B. R. Five fortunes
Heller, J. Best enemies
Heller, Z. What was she thinking?
Hood, A. Ruby
Jaffe, R. The room-mating season
Kafka, K. Miranda's vines
Keyes, M. Last Chance Saloon
Kingsolver, B. The bean trees
Koontz, D. R. One door away from heaven
Korelitz, J. H. The Sabbathday River
Mantel, H. Beyond black
Mapson, J.-A. Bad Girl Creek
Martínez, N. M. ¡Caramba!
McMillan, R. Blue collar blues
McMillan, T. Waiting to exhale
McMurtry, L. Loop group
Medlicott, J. A. Gardens of Covington
Medlicott, J. A. The ladies of Covington send their love
Oates, J. C. Solstice
Piercy, M. Braided lives
Plain, B. Looking back
Prose, F. Hunters and gatherers
Pym, B. Jane and Prudence
Schwarz, C. All is vanity
Siddons, A. R. Outer banks
Smith, L. The last girls
Thayer, N. Between husbands and friends
Updike, J. The witches of Eastwick
Vida, N. Goodbye, Saigon
Vine, B. The house of stairs
Weiner, J. Little earthquakes
Weldon, F. Big girls don't cry
Wood, B. Vital signs
Yoshimoto, B. Love songs

Social conditions

See also Feminism
Alvarez, J. In the time of the butterflies
Atwood, M. Alias Grace
Atwood, M. The handmaid's tale
Atwood, M. Life before man
Badami, A. R. Tamarind woman
Banks, R. Continental drift
Battle, L. Southern women
Battle, L. Storyville
Battle, L. War brides
Bausch, R. Hello to the cannibals

WOMEN EDITORS
Carey, P. My life as a fake
Evans, N. The horse whisperer
Spark, M. A far cry from Kensington
WOMEN IN BUSINESS *See* Businesswomen
Women in love. Lawrence, D. H.

WOMEN IN POLITICS
Archer, J. The prodigal daughter
Clark, M. H. Before I say goodbye
Didion, J. A book of common prayer
Ferber, E. Cimarron
Grippando, J. The abduction
Gutcheon, B. R. Five fortunes
Mortman, D. The lucky ones
Women in the grove. Peterson, P. W.

WOMEN JOURNALISTS
Adams, A. Almost perfect
Adler, E. Now or never
Atwood, M. Bodily harm
Brown, S. Exclusive
Carver, C. Blood Junction
Clark, M. H. Daddy's little girl
Clark, M. H. I'll be seeing you
Clark, M. H. The second time around
Coulter, C. Impulse
Crichton, M. Airframe
Daley, R. A faint cold fear
D'Amato, B. White male infant
Didion, J. The last thing he wanted
Drabble, M. The middle ground
Goldsmith, O. Bad boy
Groom, W. Such a pretty, pretty girl
Hart, C. G. Letter from home
Isaacs, S. Red, white and blue
Johnston, W. The colony of unrequited dreams
Lively, P. Cleopatra's sister
MacInnes, H. Ride a pale horse
Morrell, D. Assumed identity
Mortman, D. The lucky ones
Patterson, J. 1st to die
Patterson, R. N. Degree of guilt
Pottinger, S. The fourth procedure
Price, R. Freedomland
Saul, J. Black lightning
Siddons, A. R. Downtown
Sparks, N. Message in a bottle
Steel, D. Journey
Thomas, M. M. Black money
Updike, J. Seek my face
Villars, E. The Normandie affair
Walker, M. W. Under the beetle's cellar
Walters, M. The sculptress
Woods, S. Dirt

WOMEN LAWYERS
Baldacci, D. Total control
Berne, S. A perfect arrangement
Brown, S. The witness
Clark, M. H. The cradle will fall
Clark, M. H. Let me call you sweetheart
Clark, M. H. On the street where you live
Crichton, M. Disclosure
Fairstein, L. Cold hit
Fairstein, L. Final jeopardy
Fairstein, L. Likely to die
Fielding, J. Tell me no secrets
Finder, J. High crimes
Gordimer, N. None to accompany me
Green, T. The letter of the law
Harris, E. L. And this too shall pass
Howatch, S. The high flyer
Isaacs, S. Lily White
Martini, S. P. Critical mass
Martini, S. P. The list
Meltzer, B. Dead even
Michael, J. Sleeping beauty
Murphy, M. Darkness falls
O'Shaughnessy, P. Acts of malice
O'Shaughnessy, P. Breach of promise
O'Shaughnessy, P. Invasion of privacy
O'Shaughnessy, P. Motion to suppress
O'Shaughnessy, P. Obstruction of justice
O'Shaughnessy, P. Presumption of death
O'Shaughnessy, P. Unlucky in law
O'Shaughnessy, P. Writ of execution
Parker, B. Suspicion of guilt
Patterson, R. N. The final judgment
Piercy, M. Three women
Pottinger, S. The fourth procedure
Pottinger, S. The last Nazi
Rosenberg, N. T. Buried evidence
Rosenberg, N. T. Interest of justice
Rosenberg, N. T. Mitigating circumstances
Rosenberg, N. T. Trial by fire
Scottoline, L. Legal tender
Scottoline, L. Mistaken identity
Scottoline, L. Rough justice
Scottoline, L. Running from the law
Scottoline, L. The vendetta defense
Sheldon, S. Rage of angels
Steel, D. The house on Hope Street
Stone, K. Happy endings
Truscott, L. K. Heart of war
Uhnak, D. False witness
Wilhelm, K. The best defense
Wilhelm, K. Death qualified
Wilhelm, K. Defense for the devil
Wilhelm, K. Desperate measures
Wilhelm, K. Malice prepense
Wilhelm, K. No defense
The **women** of Brewster Place. Naylor, G.
The **women** of Whitechapel and Jack the Ripper. West, P.

WOMEN PAINTERS
Updike, J. Seek my face

WOMEN PHOTOGRAPHERS
Allende, I. Portrait in sepia
Bradford, B. T. Where you belong
Byrd, M. Shooting the sun
Clark, M. H. Moonlight becomes you
Gage, E. Pandora's box
Humphreys, H. Afterimage
Johansen, I. And then you die—
Kelman, J. Summer of storms
Rash, R. Saints at the river
Shreve, A. The weight of water
Trollope, J. Next of kin
Woods, S. Palindrome

WOMEN PHYSICIANS
Brown, S. The crush
Cook, R. Outbreak
Cook, R. Vital signs
Emmons, C. His mother's son
Gerritsen, T. Bloodstream
Gerritsen, T. Gravity
Gerritsen, T. Harvest
Gerritsen, T. Life support
Gerritsen, T. The surgeon
Gordon, M. Living at home
Hornby, N. How to be good
Lee, M. The canal house
Lessing, D. M. The sweetest dream
Lipman, E. The pursuit of Alice Thrift
Muske-Dukes, C. Life after death
Palmer, M. Natural causes
Palmer, M. The patient
Preston, R. The Cobra event
Shreve, S. R. The visiting physician
Smith, W. A. Flight of the falcon
Wilson, F. P. Implant
Wood, B. Soul flame
Wood, B. Vital signs

WOMEN POETS
Alvarez, J. In the name of Salomé
Amis, K. The Russian girl
Conroy, P. The prince of tides
Dark, A. E. Think of England
Fitch, J. White oleander
Gilchrist, E. The cabal [novelette]
Jong, E. Sappho's leap
Michaels, B. Houses of stone
Phillips, J. A. MotherKind
Shreve, A. Where or when
Steinke, R. Holy skirts

WORLD WAR, 1939-1945—*Continued*

Collaborationists

Shreve, A. Resistance

Jews

See also Holocaust, Jewish (1933-1945)
De Hartog, J. Star of Peace
Keneally, T. Schindler's list
Levi, P. If not now, when?
Remarque, E. M. The night in Lisbon

Naval operations

De Hartog, J. The captain
Fleming, T. J. Time and tide
Furst, A. Dark voyage
Heggen, T. Mister Roberts
Hickam, H. H. The keeper's son
McCutchan, P. Cameron's crossing
Reeman, D. A ship must die

Naval operations—Submarine

Beach, E. L. Run silent, run deep
Buchheim, L.-G. The boat

Prisoners and prisons

See also Concentration camps
Ballard, J. G. Empire of the Sun
Boulle, P. The bridge over the River Kwai
Clavell, J. King Rat
Higgins, J. The Valhalla exchange
Katzenbach, J. Hart's war
Keneally, T. Schindler's list
Lehrer, J. The special prisoner
Nathanson, E. M. The dirty dozen
Vonnegut, K. Slaughterhouse-five
Westheimer, D. Von Ryan's Express
Yarbrough, S. Prisoners of war

Secret service

Follett, K. Eye of the needle
Follett, K. Jackdaws
Follett, K. The key to Rebecca
Griffin, W. E. B. Secret honor
Higgins, J. Cold Harbour
Iles, G. Black cross
Ludlum, R. The Rhinemann exchange

Underground movements

Daley, R. The innocents within
Faulks, S. Charlotte Gray
Follett, K. Hornet flight
Follett, K. Jackdaws
Francis, C. Night sky
Furst, A. Blood of victory
Furst, A. Red gold
Shreve, A. Resistance
Uris, L. Mila 18

Argentina

Griffin, W. E. B. Blood and honor
Griffin, W. E. B. Honor bound
Griffin, W. E. B. Secret honor

Atlantic Ocean

Monsarrat, N. The cruel sea

Australia

Keneally, T. Office of innocence
McCullough, C. An indecent obsession

Belgium

Hulme, K. The nun's story
Shreve, A. Resistance

Canada

Norman, H. The museum guard

China

Brady, J. Warning of war
Buck, P. S. Dragon seed

Czechoslovakia

Demetz, H. The house on Prague Street

Denmark

Follett, K. Hornet flight

Egypt

Deighton, L. City of gold
Maḥfūẓ, N. Sugar Street

England

Barnard, R. Out of the blackout
Bowen, E. The heat of the day
Deighton, L. SS-GB: Nazi-occupied Britain 1941
Follett, K. Eye of the needle
Follett, K. Hornet flight
Frayn, M. Spies
Gallico, P. The snow goose
Gaskin, C. The charmed circle
Greene, G. The end of the affair
Greene, G. The ministry of fear
Harris, R. Enigma
Higgins, J. Cold Harbour
Higgins, J. The eagle has landed
Humphreys, H. The lost garden
Jackson, M. Five boys
Lebrecht, N. The song of names
McEwan, I. Atonement
Pilcher, R. Coming home
Silva, D. The unlikely spy
Snow, C. P. Homecoming
Spark, M. The girls of slender means
Trollope, J. Legacy of love
Wesley, M. Part of the furniture

Europe

Moran, T. Anja the liar
Mount, F. The man who rode Ampersand
Shaw, I. The young lions

France

Bates, H. E. Fair stood the wind for France
Carter, V. O. Such sweet thunder
Daley, R. The innocents within
Faulks, S. Charlotte Gray
Francis, C. Night sky
Furst, A. Kingdom of shadows
Furst, A. Red gold
Greene, G. The tenth man
Harris, J. Five quarters of the orange
Pears, I. The dream of Scipio
Remarque, E. M. Arch of triumph
Sartre, J. P. Troubled sleep
Watkins, P. The forger

Germany

Böll, H. Group portrait with lady
Böll, H. The silent angel
Böll, H. A soldier's legacy
Grass, G. Crabwalk
Grass, G. Dog years
Iles, G. Black cross
Isaacs, S. Shining through
Kirst, H. H. Forward, Gunner Asch!
Kirst, H. H. The return of Gunner Asch
Kirst, H. H. The revolt of Gunner Asch
MacLean, A. Where eagles dare
Pye, M. The pieces from Berlin
Remarque, E. M. A time to love and a time to die
Thayer, J. S. Five past midnight

Greece

De Bernières, L. Corelli's mandolin

Hungary

Furst, A. Kingdom of shadows
Korda, M. Worldly goods

Indian Ocean

Reeman, D. A ship must die

Ireland

Davis-Goff, A. This cold country
Moore, B. The emperor of ice-cream

Italy

Crichton, R. The secret of Santa Vittoria
Moravia, A. Two women
Ondaatje, M. The English patient
Russell, M. D. A thread of grace

Japan

Dickey, J. To the white sea

X

Y

The **yellow** admiral. O'Brian, P.
A **yellow** raft in blue water. Dorris, M.
The **yellow** room conspiracy. Dickinson, P.

YELLOWSTONE NATIONAL PARK

Nance, J. J. Fire flight

Yesterday will make you cry. Himes, C.
Yo!. Alvarez, J.
The **Yokota** Officers Club. Bird, S.
Yon ill wind. Anthony, P.
YORKSHIRE (ENGLAND) *See* England—Yorkshire
You are not a stranger here. Haslett, A.
You belong to me. Clark, M. H.
You can't go home again. Wolfe, T.
You can't keep a good woman down. Walker, A.
You know better. Ansa, T. M.
You know me, Al. Lardner, R.
In Lardner, R. Ring around the bases
You look nice today. Bing, S.
You only die twice. Buchanan, E.
You only live twice. Fleming, I.
You remind me of me. Chaon, D.
Young Joseph. Mann, T.
In Mann, T. Joseph and his brothers p261-444
The **young** lions. Shaw, I.
Young Lonigan. Farrell, J. T.
In Farrell, J. T. Studs Lonigan
Young man with a horn. Baker, D.
The **young** manhood of Studs Lonigan. Farrell, J. T.
In Farrell, J. T. Studs Lonigan
The **young** Savages. Stewart, F. M.
Young wives. Goldsmith, O.
Youngblood Hawke. Wouk, H.
Younger than springtime. Greeley, A. M.
Your blues ain't like mine. Campbell, B. M.
Your mouth is lovely. Richler, N.

YOUTH

See also Adolescence; Boys; Girls; Students

Barfoot, J. Critical injuries
Bradford, R. Red sky at morning
Chong, K. Baroque-a-nova
Colette. Chéri
Conrad, J. Youth
Cook, T. H. Breakheart Hill
Cronin, A. J. A song of sixpence
Fitzgerald, F. S. The beautiful and damned
Fitzgerald, F. S. This side of paradise
Freda, J. The patience of rivers
Galsworthy, J. The white monkey
Gardam, J. The flight of the maidens
Godden, R. Pippa passes
Guest, J. Ordinary people
Head, A. Mr. & Mrs. Bo Jo Jones
Hesse, H. Demian
Krist, G. Chaos theory
Malamud, B. Dubin's lives
McCarthy, M. Birds of America
Michener, J. A. The drifters
Mishima, Y. The sound of waves
Nichols, J. T. The sterile cuckoo
Salinger, J. D. The catcher in the rye
Siddons, A. R. Heartbreak Hotel
Sillitoe, A. Saturday night and Sunday morning
Smith, B. Joy in the morning
Sparks, N. A walk to remember
Spencer, S. Endless love
Stirling, J. The marrying kind
Stirling, J. The penny wedding
Tarkington, B. Alice Adams
Townsend, S. Adrian Mole: the lost years
Turgenev, I. S. Fathers and sons
Tyler, A. A slipping-down life
Updike, J. Brazil
Weber, K. The little women
Wolfe, T. Of time and the river
Wolfe, T. The web and the rock
Woolf, V. Jacob's room

Youth. Conrad, J.
In Conrad, J. The complete short fiction of Joseph Conrad p151-80
In Conrad, J. Great short works of Joseph Conrad p143-71
In Conrad, J. The portable Conrad
In Conrad, J. Tales of land and sea p7-32

YUGOSLAVIA

See also Bosnia and Hercegovina; Croatia; Serbia

20th century

MacLean, A. Force 10 from Navarone

1945-

Handke, P. Repetition
Seymour, G. The heart of danger

Belgrade

Albahari, D. Götz and Meyer

Sarajevo

See Bosnia and Hercegovina—Sarajevo

YUKON TERRITORY *See* Canada—Yukon Territory

Z

Zadig. Voltaire
In Voltaire. Candide and other stories
In Voltaire. Voltaire's Candide, Zadig, and selected stories p102-72

ZAIRE

Edric, R. The book of the heathen
Griffin, W. E. B. The new breed
Griffin, W. E. B. Special ops
Hulme, K. The nun's story
Kingsolver, B. The poisonwood Bible
Stevens, M. The curve of the world

ZAMBIA

Gilman, D. Mrs. Pollifax on safari

ZANZIBAR

Kaye, M. M. Trade wind

The **zebra-striped** hearse. Macdonald, R.
In Macdonald, R. Archer in jeopardy
Zeke and Ned. McMurtry, L.

ZEN BUDDHISM

Kerouac, J. The Dharma bums

Zeno's conscience. Svevo, I.
Zero eight fifteen v1. See Kirst, H. H. The revolt of Gunner Asch
Zero eight fifteen, v2. See Kirst, H. H. Forward, Gunner Asch!
Zero eight fifteen v3. See Kirst, H. H. The return of Gunner Asch
The **zero** game. Meltzer, B.
The **zero** hour. Finder, J.
Ziff. Lelchuk, A.
Zigzagging down a wild trail. Mason, B. A.

ZIMBABWE

Smith, W. A. The angels weep
Smith, W. A. The leopard hunts in darkness
Vera, Y. The stone virgins

Politics

See Politics—Zimbabwe

ZIONISM

Agnon, S. Y. Only yesterday
Iles, G. Black cross
Phillips, C. The nature of blood
Uris, L. Exodus
Wilson, J. A Palestine affair

Zombie lover. Anthony, P.

ZOMBIES

Hynes, J. Kings of infinite space

Zooey. Salinger, J. D.
In Salinger, J. D. Franny & Zooey
ZOOLOGICAL GARDENS *See* Zoos

ZOOLOGISTS

Lawson, M. Crow Lake

ZOOS

Irving, J. Setting free the bears
Martel, Y. Life of Pi

Zorba the Greek. Kazantzakis, N.
Zorro. Allende, I.